THE OXFORD COMPACT THESAURUS

THE OXFORD

Compact
Thesaurus

Laurence Urdang

OXFORD

Oxford University Press, Great Clarendon Street, Oxford OX2 6DP

Oxford New York

Athens Auckland Bangkok Bogota Bombay Buenos Aires
Calcutta Cape Town Dar es Salaam Delhi Florence Hong Kong
Istanbul Karachi Kuala Lumpur Madras Madrid Melbourne
Mexico City Nairobi Paris Singapore Taipei Tokyo Toronto Warsaw

and associated companies in
Berlin Ibadan

Oxford is a trade mark of Oxford University Press

First published 1991 as The Oxford Thesaurus
This edition first published 1997

British Library Cataloguing in Publication Data
Data available

ISBN 0-19-860120-4

10 9 8 7 6 5 4 3 2

Typeset in Arial and Swift by Latimer Trend Ltd., Plymouth
Printed in Great Britain
by Clays plc, Bungay, Suffolk

Foreword

The biggest problem with a book of this length and complexity is that one's competence and uniformity of judgement improve in the course of its preparation, gaining adequacy in the task only as the deadline for delivery of the manuscript draws nigh. Of course, given all the time in the world one would never complete any project, for each revision would yield not only greater experience but, theoretically, the temptation to achieve perfection, clearly unattainable.

The idea of publishing the *Oxford Thesaurus*, on which this *Compact* edition is based, was first broached to me in 1986. The book was originally to have been some 300,000 words in length; for various reasons, it was subsequently agreed to increase its size, and the book you are holding contains approximately 650,000 words. Although Janet Whitcut and Sue Lloyd read the entire text and checked it for conformity to British idiom, the ultimate responsibility for the *Thesaurus* rests with me, not only for errors of omission and commission but for any benefits that I hope might be derived from its use.

LAURENCE URDANG

Introduction

In its narrowest sense, a synonym is a word or phrase that is perfectly substitutable in a context for another word or phrase. People who study language professionally agree that there is no such thing as an ideal synonym, for it is virtually impossible to find two words or phrases that are identical in denotation (meaning), connotation, frequency, familiarity, and appropriateness. Indeed, linguists have long noted the *economy of language*, which suggests that no language permits a perfect fit, in all respects, between any two words or phrases. Many examples of overlapping can be cited; the more obvious ones in English are those that reflect a duplication arising from Germanic and Romance sources, like *motherly* and *maternal*, *farming* and *agriculture*, *teach* and *instruct*. In such pairs the native English form is often the one with an earthier, warmer connotation. In some instances, where a new coinage or a loan-word has been adopted inadvertently duplicating an existing term, creating 'true' synonyms, the two will quickly diverge, not necessarily in meaning but in usage, application, connotation, level, or all of these. For example, scientists some years ago expressed dissatisfaction with the term *tidal wave*, for the phenomenon was not caused by tides but, usually, by submarine seismic activity. The word *tsunami* was borrowed from Japanese in an attempt to describe the phenomenon more accurately, but it was later pointed out that *tsunami* means 'tidal wave' in Japanese. Today, the terms exist side by side in English, the older expression still in common use, the newer more frequent in the scientific and technical literature.

Any synonym book must be seen as a compromise that relies on the sensitivity of its users to the idiomatic nuances of the language. In its best applications, it serves to remind users of words, similar in meaning, that might not spring readily to mind, and to offer lists of words and phrases that are alternatives to and compromises for those that might otherwise be overused and therefore redundant, repetitious, and boring. The *Oxford Compact Thesaurus* goes a step further by offering example sentences to illustrate the uses of the headwords and their alternatives in natural, idiomatic contexts. In addition, by marking those synonyms that also appear as main entries in the book, the *Compact Thesaurus* offers an effective, useful networking feature that unifies the language covered into an integrated whole.

1. Selection of headwords

Two criteria have been employed: first, headwords have been selected because of their frequency in the language, on the assumption that synonyms are more likely to be sought for the words that are most used; second, some headwords of lower frequency have been included because it would otherwise be impossible to find a suitable place to group together what are perceived as useful sets of synonyms with their attendant illustrative sentences. Obvious listings have been omitted on the grounds that users of the *Compact Thesaurus* can easily find synonyms for say, *abdication* by making nouns out of the verbs listed under *abdicate*. This deliberate attempt to avoid duplication is mitigated in the case of very common words. For the convenience of the user, both *shy* and *bashful* are main entries, as are *method*, *manner*, and *mode*, which, though much the same in some respects, differ in detail and application. In this book, however, *mitigate* is a main entry but not *mitigation*, *mistake* and *mistaken* are main entries but not *mistakenly*, etc. Where it is determined that such derivations are neither automatic nor semantically obvious, separate listings have been provided.

2. Illustrative sentences

On the principle that a word is known by the company it keeps, one or more sentences showing the main entry word in context are provided for each sense discrimination. These have been carefully selected to demonstrate the use of the main entry in a context likely to be encountered in familiar written or spoken ordinary English. (See also **7. Substitutability**, below.)

3. Synonym lists

Each main entry is followed by one or more sense groupings, each illustrated by one or more sentences. An effort has been made to group the synonyms semantically as well as syntactically and idiomatically: that is, each synonym listed within a given set should prove to be more or less substitutable for the main entry in the illustrative sentence.

In some instances, idiomatic congruity may, unavoidably, become strained; where it is felt to be stretched too far—though still properly listed among its accompanying synonyms—a semicolon has been inserted to separate sub-groups of synonyms, and, in many cases, additional illustrative sentences have been provided. Such sub-groupings have been confined largely to distinctions between literal uses and figures of speech, between transitive and intransitive verbs, and between synonyms that differ in more subtle aspectual characteristics of meaning or syntax. (See also **7. Substitutability**, below.)

Not all senses of all words are covered for either or both of the following reasons: the sense, though it exists, is relatively rare in ordinary discourse and writing; there are no reasonable synonyms for it. Thus, this sense of *mercy*,

> an affecting or moving of the mind in any way; a
> mental state brought about by any influence; an
> emotion or feeling; *Mercy is an affection of the mind.*

is not covered for the first reason, as it is a literary and somewhat archaic usage. The same can be said for the sense,

> a bodily state due to any influence.

and for other senses listed in the largest dictionaries but rarely encountered except in literary contexts. Even in such contexts it would be unusual to need a synonym for this word and others like it.

4. Cross-references

Where cross-references between main listings appear in the *Compact Thesaurus*, they are simple and straightforward:

> **superior** *adj.* . . . . **3** See **supercilious**, above.
> —*n.* **4** See **supervisor**, below.

Additionally, a number of cross-references occur within entries, between variant forms of an expression. At the end for *take*, for example, as one can say either *take* or *take it* in the sense of 'understand' etc., the option is shown in the following way:

> **take** *v.* . . . . **19** °understand, °gather, °interpret,
> °perceive, apprehend, °deduce, conclude, °infer,
> °judge, deem, °assume, °suppose, °imagine, °see:
> *I take him to be a fool. I take it from your expression*
> *that you've had bad news.* . . . . **33 take it**:
> **a** °withstand *or* °tolerate *or* °survive punishment
> *or* abuse, °survive: *The Marines are extremely tough*
> *and can take it.* **b** See **19**, above.

In a few entries, the form 'See also' is used.

A unique feature of the *Compact Thesaurus* is the cross-referencing from synonyms to entries. In this system, a degree sign (°) preceding a synonym indicates that this word also appears as a main entry at which the reader may find futher useful synonyms. Thus, users seeking a different aspect or nuance of meaning of a synonym so marked are at once alerted to the fact that it has its own main entry and can look it up directly:

> **locale** *n.* °site, °location, °spot, °place, °setting, venue, °neighbourhood, °situation, locality: *We moved the locale of the film to Spain.*

The degree sign may also appear in front of a plural noun which occurs as a headword in its singular form:

> **pretence** *n.* **1** °show, °display, °pretension, °ostentation, °airs ...
>
> ...
>
> **air** *n.* ... **5 airs**: °pretension, °pretence, °show, affectedness ...

5. Labels

A. All words and phrases that are recognized as being typical of a particular variety of English, whether geographical or stylistic, are labelled. The labels used are those commonly encountered in ordinary dictionaries:

Colloq Colloquial; informal; used in everyday conversation and writing, especially in the popular press and in dramatic dialogue; sometimes avoided where more formal language is felt to be appropriate, as in business correspondence, scholarly works, technical reports, documents, etc.

Slang Belonging to the most informal register and characteristic of spoken English; often originating in the cult language of a particular socio-cultural group. Not sufficiently elevated to be used in most writing (aside from dialogue), although often found in the popular press and frequently heard on popular radio and television programmes.

Taboo Not used in polite society, usually because of the risk of offending sexual, religious, or cultural sensibilities; occasionally encountered on late-night television and radio; often occurring in graffiti and in dialogue in novels, plays, and films.

Archaic Describing an obsolete word or phrase (like *tickety-boo*, *lounge lizard*) that is used deliberately to invoke the feeling of a bygone time.

Old-fashioned Used of a synonym (like *comfit*) that is no longer current but might occasionally be encountered among older speakers and in older writing.

Technical Used of a somewhat specialized word that is not commonly encountered in ordinary, everyday English, like *defalcator*, which appears as a synonym under *swindler*.

Literary Describes a word, like *euchre* 'cheat', that is not usually met with in everyday language, even of the formal genre, but may be found in poetry and other literary works.

Brit, US, Australian, Canadian, New Zealand Marks a word or phrase that occurs mainly in the designated variety.

The meanings of other labels are self-evident.

B. All labels can occur in combination. Usage labels always take precedence over regional labels. For example,

> **pushover** *n.* **1** °sure thing, *Colloq* °piece of
> cake, child's play, °snap, °picnic, walk-over, *US*
> °breeze, *Slang* cinch, *Brit* doddle, *US* lead-pipe
> cinch.

Here, 'sure thing' is standard universal English. All words and phrases following *Colloq* up to the *Slang* label are colloquial: 'piece of cake, . . . walkover' are universal colloquial English, 'breeze' is US colloquial. All synonyms following the *Slang* label are slang; 'cinch' is universal English slang, 'doddle' is confined to British slang, and 'lead-pipe cinch' is confined to American slang.

> **talented** *adj.* . . . *Colloq* ace, crack, top-notch, *Brit*
> wizard, whizzo, *US* crackerjack.

In this entry, all synonyms shown are colloquial, 'ace, crack, top-notch' being universal English, 'wizard, whizzo' British, and 'crackerjack' US.

It must be emphasized that such labels are to some extent impressionistic and are based in the *Compact Thesaurus* on a consensus of several sources: that is, there is no implication that 'breeze' is never used in the sense of 'pushover' except in the US, nor should such an inference be made.

C. Comments regarding what might be viewed as 'correct' in contrast to 'incorrect' usage are generally avoided. For example, the non-standard use of *between* in contexts referring to more than two of anything or of *among* in contexts involving fewer than three goes unmarked. However, if the usage question is confined to what can easily be represented in a 'lexical' environment, then suitable treatment is accorded it; thus 'now' and 'at present' are labelled *Non-Standard* under *presently*. To take another example, 'different to', in the typically British usage *His house is different to mine*, is rarely encountered in American English; in American English, purists condemn 'different than', as in *His house is different than mine*, which is increasingly heard in British English; purists on both sides of the Atlantic prefer 'different from'. Such matters are best left to usage books and to usage notes in dictionaries and are not treated in the *Compact Thesaurus*.

D. Main entry words and sub-entries are not labelled, only the synonyms. Thus, under *beat* appears the idiomatic expression, *beat it*, which is not labelled:

> **8 beat it**: °depart, °leave, abscond, °run off *or*
> away, *Slang US* °take it on the lam, lam out of
> here, *US* hit the road: *You'd better beat it before the*
> *cops come.*

The idiom is not labelled because it is assumed that the user has looked it up to find a substitute for it, hence needs no information about it other than a listing of its alternatives (which are labelled, when appropriate) and an illustrative example. Should users need more detailed information about a given word or phrase, they should resort to a dictionary, the proper repository for such information.

A rare exception to the above rule occurs where a headword has one meaning in British English and quite a different meaning in another regional variety. Thus:

> **subway** *n.* **1** *In US*: underground (°railway),
> tube: *She takes the subway to work.* **2** *In Britain:*
> tunnel, underpass: *Use the subway to cross the road*
> *in safety.*

Here, the two regional labels do not apply to the synonyms (since, for example, 'tunnel' has the same meaning in both British and US English) but to the two definitions of the headword.

E. Synonyms bearing any kind of label appear at the end of the set in which they are listed, except in the case described immediately above.

6. Spelling and other variants

The spellings shown throughout are those preferred by most modern British writers. British variant spellings are shown; if they are variants of the main entry word, they appear as the first word in the set(s) of synonyms following:

> **mousy** *adj.* **1** mousey, . . .
> **movable** *adj.* moveable, . . .

Such variants are also shown when they appear within an entry:

> **movable** *adj.* . . . transferable *or* transferrable, . . .

Common American spelling variants (*humor, traveler, unraveled*) are not shown, but less common ones are listed for convenience. Where both forms are variants in American spelling, they are described by '*or US also*':

> . . . accoutrements *or US also* accouterments, . . .
> . . . phoney *or US also* phony, . . .

This should be understood to mean 'the normal British spelling is *accoutrements* (or *phoney*); this form, together with *accouterments* (or *phony*), occurs in American English'.

7. Substitutability

A. The purpose of a synonym book is to provide the user with a collection of words that are as close as possible in meaning to a designated word. The *Oxford Compact Thesaurus* tries to go a step further by providing examples that not only illustrate the main entry word in a natural contextual environment but also allow the user to substitute as many of the synonyms as possible into the framework of the context. For example:

> **porous** *adj.* spongy, spongelike, permeable, pervious, penetrable: *The rainwater runs through the porous rock and collects in the pools below.*

It is possible to substitute for *porous* in the sample sentence any of the words given as synonyms without any adjustment of the grammar or phrasing of the example. That is not to suggest that the synonyms are identical: 'permeable' and 'pervious' belong to a different register from that of 'spongy, spongelike', being more common in technical usage. Some might argue that 'penetrable' is not synonymous with the other listed words; but it is the function of this book to provide synonyms for the main entries, not for the other synonyms that might be listed. No claim is made—nor could it be made—that synonyms are identical, either to one another or to another word, merely that they fall well within the criteria of what, for practical purposes, is viewed as synonymy in the language.

It is certainly true that substituting for *porous* any of the five listed synonyms will yield five standard English sentences.

B. Some judgement is required of the user in determining the syntax and idiomaticity with which a given word or expression can be substituted in an illustrative context: words are rarely as readily interchangeable in a context as might be components in a chemical or mathematical formula. Moreover, while such formulae are reflective of science, language offers its users the virtually infinite variety available only in art, with each individual speaker of any language being presented with the opportunity to become an artist.

In the following example, nearly all terms can be substituted for *adjoining* in the first illustrative sentence; to create idiomatic parallels to the second sentence, the parenthetical prepositions must be used:

> **adjoining** *adj.* °neighbouring, contiguous (to), adjacent (to), abutting, bordering, next (to): *We have bought the adjoining land and will build our new house there. The land adjoining the supermarket is for sale.*

Interpreting this, the following are all idiomatic: *adjoining land, neighbouring land, contiguous land, adjacent land, abutting land,* and *bordering land.* But if the context requires the adjective to come after *land* (with a following noun), then the parenthetical words must be added to yield constructions that are idiomatic, like *land adjoining the supermarket, land neighbouring the supermarket, land contiguous to the supermarket, land adjacent to the supermarket, land abutting the supermarket, land bordering the supermarket,* and *land next to the supermarket.*

As this is intended as a synonym book and not a work on English collocations, the treatment of idiomaticity cannot be taken further.

C. There are other reasons why direct substitutability is not always possible within a single semantic concept. The following extract demonstrates this:

> **possess** *v.* . . . **3** °dominate, °control, °govern, °consume, take °control of, preoccupy, °obsess; °charm, °captivate, °enchant, cast a °spell on *or* over, °bewitch, enthral: *What possessed her to think that I could help? He behaves as if he is possessed by the devil.*

Here, two aspects of the same sense have been divided by a semicolon, with the synonyms preceding the semicolon illustrated by the first contextual example and those following it by the second. While it may be argued that in this instance the synonyms following the semicolon, with their illustrative sentence, might better have been listed in a separately numbered set, the close semantic association of the two groups would thereby have been lost.

D. Sometimes, where the sub-sense is familiar enough not to require its own example yet needs to be set off from the other synonyms because of a subtle or aspectual semantic distinction, a semicolon is inserted among the synonyms and only one example is provided:

> **practice** *n.* . . . **2** °exercise, °discipline, °drill, practising, °repetition, °rehearsal, training, °preparation, workout, warm-up; °application, °study: *She needs more practice on the beginner's slope before going down the main piste.*

The idiomatic usage of this sense of 'study' and 'application' is sufficiently familiar not to require a separate example.

On the other hand, a second example is needed for the next sense of *practice*:

> . . . **3** °pursuit, °exercise, °work, °profession, °career, °vocation, °conduct; °business, °office: *He genuinely enjoys the practice of law. I heard of a veterinary practice for sale in Yorkshire.*

It would be difficult—perhaps impossible—to defend such fine distinctions in every instance: indeed, as a comparison of the different lengths of the entries in any dictionary will quickly reveal, language does not provide the same levels of sense discrimination for all words. The metaphorical focus and diversity of a language provide for polysemy in some semantico-cultural spheres but not in others. The classic observation often cited to demonstrate this linkage is that of the Inuit language that has a large number of distinguishing words for types of snow or of the African language that has an extensive vocabulary to describe the kinship among its speakers. On the grounds that the lexicon of a language is moulded by speakers who, quite naturally, use it to talk (and write) about things that are important to them, one might be tempted to draw conclusions about the voracity of English-speakers by reflecting that the entry for *take* has about twice as many definitions in most dictionaries as that for *give*.

E. Often, the semicolon may be used to separate transitive uses of a verb from intransitive:

> **preach** v. . . . **2** moralize, sermonize, °advise,
> °counsel, admonish, °reprimand, °lecture,
> °harangue, pontificate; °urge, inculcate,
> °advocate: *Mother used to preach to us about being*
> *charitable. Father preached restraint in all things.*

Because of the behaviour of verbs in English, different synonyms may be required depending on what the object of the verb is and, often, whether the object is a word or phrase or a clause:

> **predict** v. foretell, °prophesy, °forecast, °foresee,
> augur, °prognosticate, forewarn, presage, vati-
> cinate; portend, °foreshadow, foretoken, fore-
> bode; °intimate, °hint, °suggest: *My mother*
> *predicted that there would be moments like this. If*
> *only I could predict the winner of the 2.30!*

F. Wherever possible, the proper prepositional or adverbial particle normally accompanying a verb in a certain sense has been supplied, though it must be emphasized that the one offered is the most frequently used and not, necessarily, the only one acceptable in standard usage. Particles used with some words may vary considerably, owing not only to dialect variation but also to whether the verb is used actively or passively as well as to which nuance of meaning, sometimes far too subtle to be dealt with adequately in a book of this kind, is to be expressed. The following entry illustrates the full treatment that can be accorded to words that occur in a wide variety of grammatical environments:

> **persevere** v. Often, **persevere in** or **with** or
> **at**: °persist, °resolve, °decide, °endure,
> °continue, °carry on or through, °keep at or on
> or up, be °steadfast or °staunch or °constant,
> °keep going, stand °fast or °firm, °see through,
> be or °remain °determined or resolved or
> °resolute or °stalwart or °purposeful or uncom-
> promising, be °tenacious or °persistent or
> °constant or °pertinacious or assiduous or sedu-
> lous, be °tireless or °untiring or indefatigable,
> show °determination or °pluck or °grit, be
> plucky, be °patient or °diligent or °stubborn or
> °inflexible or adamant or °obstinate or obdurate,
> show or exhibit or demonstrate °patience or
> diligence or stubbornness or inflexibility or
> °obstinacy or obduracy, °remain dogged,
> °pursue doggedly, be intransigent or intractable,
> °cling to, °stick to, °support, stop at nothing,
> °sustain, *Colloq* °stick with, °stick (it) out: *We*
> *must persevere if we are to win. I shall persevere in*
> *my loyalty.*

G. In some adjective senses, a split might occur between attributive and predicative uses, though in most such cases, where the syntax is open, only one, usually common, illustration is given. For example, *alone* is used only predicatively or post-positively, not attributively; that is, one cannot say **An alone woman ...* In this particular case, the normal attributive form would be *lone*, but *lone* is not listed as a synonym for *alone* because they are not mutually substitutable. It is acknowledged that the detailed description of the special syntactic ways in which certain words (like *alone, agog, galore*) behave lies outside the province of this book.

Although similar cautions must be observed and adjustments made throughout, it is hoped that the illustrative sentences will provide a substantial basis for the user to identify idiomatic contexts and to discriminate senses that are not always carefully distinguished in dictionaries.

A

abandon v. **1** °give up *or* over, °yield, °surrender, °leave, °cede, let °go, °deliver (up), °turn over, °relinquish: *I can see no reason why we should abandon the house to thieves and vandals.* **2** °depart from, °leave, °desert, °quit, °go away from: *The order was given to abandon ship.* **3** °desert, °forsake, °jilt, °walk out on: *He even abandoned his fiancée.* **4** °give up, °renounce; °discontinue, °forgo, °drop, desist, abstain from: *She abandoned cigarettes and whisky after the doctor's warning.*
—*n.* **5** recklessness, intemperance, wantonness, lack of restraint, unrestraint: *He behaved with wild abandon after he received the inheritance.*

abandoned adj. **1** °left °alone, °forlorn, forsaken, °deserted, neglected; rejected, shunned, °cast off *or* aside, jilted, dropped, °outcast: *An abandoned infant was found on the church steps. Totally alone, she felt abandoned by her friends.* **2** °bad, °immoral, amoral, °wicked, °sinful, °evil, °corrupt, unprincipled, unrestrained, °uninhibited, °reprobate; °loose, °wanton, debauched, °wild, °dissolute, dissipated, °profligate; depraved, °lewd, °lascivious, flagitious: *His abandoned behaviour soon landed him in jail.*

abbreviate v. **1** °shorten, compress, °contract, truncate, °trim, °reduce, °curtail: *We abbreviated some of the longer words to save space.* **2** °shorten, °cut, condense, °abridge, °abstract, °digest, epitomize, summarize, *US* synopsize: *The school presented an abbreviated version of* A Midsummer Night's Dream.

abbreviated adj. skimpy, °brief, revealing: *The dancers' abbreviated costumes shocked some members of the audience.*

abbreviation n. initialism; acronym; shortening, contraction: *UK is one kind of abbreviation, or initialism; NATO, which is pronounced as a word, is another, usually called an acronym.*

abdicate v. °give up, °renounce, disclaim, °waive, disown, °surrender, °yield, °relinquish, °abandon, °resign, °quit: *He abdicated all responsibility for care of the children. She abdicated the throne to marry a commoner.*

abduct v. °kidnap, °carry off, °make away *or* off with, °seize, *Slang US* °snatch, °grab: *The child that was abducted is safe.*

abet v. **1** °encourage, °urge, instigate, °incite, °provoke, egg on, °prod, goad; °aid, °help, °assist: *The jury found that his wife had abetted him in the murder.* **2** countenance, °approve (of), °support, °endorse, °second, °sanction, condone; °further, °advance, °promote, °uphold: *By failing to inform on the terrorists, the neighbours abetted the bombing.*

abeyance n. **in abeyance**: °pending, abeyant, °reserved, in °reserve, shelved, pushed *or* shoved *or* shunted aside, postponed, °put off, suspended, *US* tabled; temporarily °inactive, °dormant, °latent; *Colloq* in a holding °pattern, on the back burner; *Slang* on °hold, in the deep-freeze, on the shelf, on ice, hanging °fire: *Legal proceedings were held in abeyance so that talks could take place to reach an out-of-court settlement.*

abhor v. °hate, °loathe, °detest, abominate, execrate; regard *or* view with °horror *or* dread *or* °fright *or* repugnance *or* °loathing *or* °disgust, °shudder at, °recoil *or* °shrink from; be *or* stand aghast at: *He said that he abhorred any violation of human rights.*

abhorrent adj. °hateful, detestable, abhorred, °abominable, °contemptible, odious, °loathsome, horrid, heinous, execrable, °repugnant; °repulsive, °repellent, °revolting, °offensive, °disgusting, horrifying, °obnoxious: *The idea of war was totally abhorrent to her.*

abide v. **1** °stand, °endure, °suffer, °submit to, °bear, °put up with, °accept, °tolerate, °brook: *How can you abide the company of such a fool?* **2** °live, °stay, reside, °dwell, °sojourn: *Local people believe that the rain god abides in these mountains.* **3** °remain, °stay, °continue, °tarry; °linger, °rest: *He'll abide in my care till he can walk again.* **4 abide by**: °consent to, °agree to, °comply with, °observe, °acknowledge, °obey, °follow, °submit to, °conform to, °keep to, °remain °true to, °stand °firm by, adhere to, °hold to: *You must abide by the rules of the club if you become a member.*

abiding adj. °lasting, °permanent, °constant, °steadfast, °everlasting, unending, °eternal, °enduring, °indestructible; unchanging, °fast, hard and fast, °fixed, °firm, immutable, °changeless: *Her abiding love is a solace to him.*

ability n. **1** adeptness, °aptitude, °facility, °faculty, °capacity, °power, °knack, °proficiency, *Colloq* know-how: *I have perceived your ability to manipulate situations to your own advantage.* **2** °talent, °skill, cleverness, °capacity, °wit, °gift, °genius, °capability: *He has such extraordinary ability it is difficult to see why he doesn't accomplish more.* **3 abilities**: °faculty, faculties, °talent(s), °gift(s), °skill(s): *Her abilities have made her one of the finest cellists of our time.*

ablaze adj. **1** aflame, afire, °burning, on °fire, alight, blazing: *By the time the firemen arrived, the roof was ablaze.* **2** lit up, alight, brilliantly *or* brightly lit, sparkling, gleaming, aglow, °bright, °brilliant, °luminous, illuminated, °radiant: *The ballroom was ablaze with the light from thousands of candles.*

able adj. **1** °capable, °qualified, °competent, °proficient: *I feel quite able to take care of myself, thank you. He is an able tennis player.* **2** °talented, °clever, skilled, °masterful, masterly; °adept, °skilful, °gifted, °superior, °expert, °accomplished: *There is no doubt that Wellington was a very able general.*

abnormal adj. **1** °deviant, deviating, °irregular, °unusual, unconventional, aberrant, *Psych jargon* °exceptional: *The wing of a bat is an abnormal structure.* **2** °peculiar, °unusual, °odd, °strange, °queer, freakish, °unnatural, °extraordinary, °weird, °eccentric, °bizarre, anomalous, aberrant, °perverse, °deviant, °irregular, *Colloq* °offbeat, *Slang* oddball, °kinky, °weirdo: *They certainly make the contestants on that TV show do some very abnormal things.*

abnormality n. **1** irregularity, unconformity, unusualness, °singularity, °eccentricity, unconventionality, uncommonness, deviation, aberration, idiosyncrasy: *The desire in a man to wear women's clothing is viewed as an abnormality.* **2** distortion, anomaly, malformation, deformity: *The child was born with an abnormality of the right foot.*

abode n. °residence, °dwelling, dwelling-place, °house, °home, °domicile, habitation, quarters, °lodging, °accommodation, *Military* billet; *Colloq Brit* digs, diggings: *He was described as being of no fixed abode.*

abolish v. °eliminate, °end, put an °end to, °terminate, °destroy, annihilate, annul, °void, make °void, °demolish, do away with, nullify, °repeal, °cancel, °obliterate, liquidate, °stamp out, °quash, °extinguish, °erase, °delete, expunge; eradicate, extirpate, deracinate, °uproot: *The best way to abolish folly is to spread wisdom. Prohibition in the US was abolished in 1933.*

abolition n. elimination, °end, °termination, annulment, nullification, repudiation, °cancellation; °destruction, annihilation: *1837 marks the abolition of the slave trade in the British Empire.*

abominable adj. **1** °offensive, °repugnant, °repulsive, °vile, °monstrous, °loathsome, odious, execrable, detestable, °despicable, °base, °disgusting, °nauseous, nauseating, °foul, °abhorrent, horrid, °deplorable: *He was accused of crimes too abominable to detail in open court.* **2** °terrible, unpleasant, °disagreeable; °awful, °distasteful, in °bad taste, °horrible, frightful, *Colloq Brit* °beastly: *No one wants to go out in this abominable weather. The décor in this hotel is simply abominable.*

aboriginal n. °native, indigene, autochthon; *Colloq Australian* Abo, *Offensive Australian* aborigine, *Slang Australian contemptuous* boong: *Many aboriginals are not assimilated to modern life.*

abound v. **1** °prevail, °thrive, °flourish: *Disease abounds among the undernourished peoples of Africa.* **2 abound in**: be crowded or °packed or jammed with, be °abundant or °rich in, °proliferate (in or with): *The ship abounds in conveniences.* **3 abound with**: °teem or °swarm or °throng with, be filled or infested with, overflow with: *The ship abounds with rats.*

about adv. **1** °round, around, °close by, °nearby, on every side: *Gather about, for I have something to tell you.* **2** °approximately, around, °nearly, °roughly, more or less, °almost, °close to or upon; give or take: *In 1685 London had been, for about half a century, the most populous capital in Europe. Light travels at about 186,000 miles a second.* **3** to and fro, up and down, back and forth, here and there, hither and yon, °far and wide, hither and thither: *He wandered about aimlessly for several days.* **4** here and there, °far and wide, hither and yon, hither and thither, °helter-skelter: *My papers were scattered about as if a tornado had struck.* **5** around, °prevalent, in the air: *There is a lot of flu about this year.* **6** °approximately, °nearly, °close to, not far from, °almost, °just about, °around: *It is about time you telephoned your mother.*
—prep. **7** °around, °surrounding, encircling: *There is a railing about the monument.* **8** °round, around, all °round, °everywhere, in all directions, all over: *Please look about the room for my hat.* **9** °near, °nearby, adjacent to, °beside, alongside, °close by, nigh: *There were a lot of trees about the garden.* **10** °at hand, *Colloq* on: *I am sorry, but I haven't my cheque-book about me.* **11** °touching, °concerning, connected with, involving, in or with °reference to, in or with °regard to, °regarding, in the °matter of, with °respect to, respecting, °relative to, relating to, apropos, *Formal* anent: *He wrote a book about the Spanish Armada.*

about-turn n. °reversal, °reverse, °turn-about, turn-round, U-turn, volte-face, *US* about-face: *There has been a complete about-turn in the policy concerning immigration.*

above adv. **1** °overhead, on °high, °aloft, in the °sky or heavens: *Far above, the clouds scudded swiftly by.* **2** upstairs: *They lived on the ground floor and the landlady lived above.*
—prep. **3** on, on (the) °top of, upon, °over, atop: *The plume of smoke remained fixed above the volcano. He hasn't got a roof above his head for the night.* **4** °over, more than, °exceeding, in °excess of, beyond, greater than, °surpassing: *The operations are controlled by gears, of which there are above fifty in number.* **5** insusceptible to, °unaffected by, out of reach of, not susceptible or vulnerable or exposed to, °superior to: *The judge is above bribery or other influence.* **6 above all**: before or beyond everything, °first of all, °chiefly, °primarily, in the °first place, °mainly, essentially, at °bottom: *Above all, serve God and country before you serve yourself.*

above-board adv. **1** °openly, candidly, °freely, publicly, frankly, straightforwardly, plainly, for all to see, out in the °open, in the °open: *Donald has always dealt completely above-board with everyone.*
—adj. **2** °open, °candid, °frank, °straight, °direct, °honourable, straightforward, °forthright, guileless, undeceiving, °artless, °ingenuous, undeceptive, undeceitful, °straight from the °shoulder; °honest, °genuine: *The company's dealings have always been above-board.*

abridge v. °shorten, °reduce, condense, °cut, °abbreviate, °cut back, °trim, °curtail, °pare down, °contract, compress, °digest, summarize, epitomize, °abstract, *US* synopsize: *We abridged the original edition of 1000 pages to 480 pages.*

abridgement n. **1** shortening, reduction, °abbreviation, condensation, contraction, truncation, trimming: *The abridgement took ten years.* **2** curtailment: *We protested against the abridgement of our right to picket.* **3** °digest, condensation, °epitome, compendium, °concise edition or version, °cut edition or version; °synopsis, °abstract, °summary, °précis, °outline, résumé: *The one-volume abridgement of the dictionary is easier to use.*

abroad adv. **1** °overseas, in °foreign lands or parts: *We were abroad on assignment for a few years.* **2** broadly, °widely, at °large, near and °far, °far and wide, °everywhere, extensively, publicly: *Don't spread rumours abroad.* **3** °outside, out of doors, away, out and about: *There are few people abroad this early in the morning.*

abrupt adj. **1** °sudden, °hasty, °quick, °precipitate, °snappy; unexpected, unannounced, unplanned, °unforeseen, unanticipated: *The general's abrupt departure has been linked with the disappearance of a great deal of money.* **2** °precipitous, °steep, °sheer, °sudden:

From the ridge there is an abrupt drop of 1000 metres into the valley. **3** °curt, °short, °brusque, °blunt, °bluff, °gruff, uncivil, °rude, °discourteous, °impolite, unceremonious, °snappish: My bank manager gave me an abrupt reply when I asked for an increased overdraft.

absence n. **1** non-attendance, non-presence, non-appearance, truancy: This is Jason's third absence from class in a week. She runs the place in my absence. **2** °lack, °want, deficiency, non-existence; insufficiency, scantiness, paucity, °scarcity, °dearth: In the absence of new evidence, the matter must remain undecided.

absent adj. **1** away, °out, °off, °elsewhere, not °present, missing, gone: Twenty people attended, but Harold was conspicuously absent. **2** missing, lacking, °wanting, °deficient: All warmth is absent from her singing.
—v. **3 absent (oneself) from**: keep or stay away from; °withdraw or °retire from: He absented himself from the court during his father's trial for murder. Absent thee from felicity awhile.

absent-minded adj. °preoccupied, °inattentive, unattentive, °absorbed, unmindful, °absent, °off, °withdrawn, unheeding, °heedless, unheedful, °inadvertent; distracted, abstracted, day-dreaming, in a brown study, in the clouds, °unaware, °oblivious, in a °trance, distrait(e), mooning, (°far) away (somewhere), star-gazing, wool-gathering: The absent-minded professor delivered his lecture to an empty lecture hall.

absolute adj. **1** °perfect, °complete, °total, finished, °thorough, through-and-through, consummate, °flawless, °faultless, unadulterated, °pure, unmixed, unalloyed, °undiluted; °rank: Alan behaved like an absolute gentleman. **2** °complete, °outright, °downright, °genuine, °real, °pure, °out-and-out, °transparent, °unmitigated, °categorical, °unqualified, unconditional, utter, °veritable, unconditioned: Peace is an absolute requirement for prosperity. **3** unrestricted, unrestrained, unconstrained, °unlimited, °unmitigated, °arbitrary, °despotic, °dictatorial, °totalitarian, °supreme, almighty, autocratic, °tyrannical: The days of absolute monarchy are numbered. **4** °positive, °certain, °sure, unambiguous, °unquestionable, °authoritative, verifiable, uncompromised: Few intelligent people would claim absolute knowledge of anything.

absolutely adv. **1** unqualifiedly, unconditionally, unreservedly, unexceptionally, unequivocally, unquestionably, °positively, °definitely, °really, genuinely, decidedly, °surely, °truly, certainly, categorically: She is absolutely the best dancer I have ever seen. I absolutely refuse to go. **2** °totally, °utterly, °completely, °entirely, fully, °quite, °altogether, °wholly: It is absolutely necessary that you undergo surgery.
—interj. **3** certainly, assuredly, °positively, °definitely, of °course, °naturally, indubitably, yes, to be °sure: 'Are you sure you want to go?' 'Absolutely!'

absorbed adj. engrossed, °lost, wrapped up, occupied, °engaged, immersed, buried, °preoccupied, concentrating, °rapt: He was absorbed in his reading.

absorbing adj. engrossing, °engaging, °riveting, captivating, fascinating, °spellbinding, gripping: Maria was watching an absorbing thriller on television.

abstract adj. **1** °theoretical, unapplied, notional, ideational, conceptual, metaphysical, unpractical, °intellectual: It is difficult to capture abstract ideas on paper. **2** non-representational, °symbolic, non-realistic: Museums began buying abstract art in the 1930s.
—n. **3** °summary, °epitome, °synopsis, °essence, °digest, condensation, °survey, conspectus, °extract; °outline, °précis, résumé: By reading the abstracts, you can determine which articles merit reading in full.
—v. **4** epitomize, °abbreviate, °digest, summarize, condense, °shorten, °abridge, °cut, °cut down, US synopsize: The service abstracts articles that appear in scientific journals.

absurd adj. **1** °ridiculous, °silly, °nonsensical, °senseless, °outlandish, °preposterous, °farcical, °mad, °stupid, °foolish, idiotic, imbecilic or imbecile, moronic, °childish; laughable, °ludicrous, risible, °inane, Colloq °crazy, nutty, nuts, Chiefly Brit °daft: The notion that the moon is made of green cheese is absurd. **2** asinine, °senseless, illogical, irrational, unreasoned, °unreasonable, °incongruous, °paradoxical, °unsound, °meaningless: Today, most people view it absurd to believe that the earth is flat.

absurdity n. **1** °folly, silliness, ridiculousness, foolishness, ludicrousness, °nonsense, senselessness, meaninglessness, illogicality, irrationality, unreasonableness, incongruity, °stupidity, Colloq craziness, nuttiness, Chiefly Brit daftness: Many comics rely on absurdity rather than cleverness for humour. **2** °paradox, self-contradiction, °error, °fallacy: No one can abide the man's pretentiousness and other absurdities.

abundance n. overflow, °superfluity, over-abundance, superabundance, °excess, °surplus, oversupply, °glut, °satiety, over-sufficiency; °plenty, plenteousness, plentifulness, plenitude, copiousness, °profusion, Formal nimiety: The days when there was an abundance of fresh drinking-water have come to an end.

abundant adj. **1** °plentiful, overflowing, °ample, copious, over-sufficient, superabundant, plenteous, °profuse, °inexhaustible, °replete, °bountiful, bounteous: The abundant rainfall fills the reservoirs every day. **2** abounding (in), °full (of), °rich (in), °luxuriant, °lavish: We know a stream that is abundant in trout. The abundant vegetation of the rain forest is an ecological wonder.

abuse v. **1** °misuse, misemploy, °pervert, misapply, °exploit: The officer abused his authority in ordering the forced march at midnight. **2** maltreat, ill-use, °injure, °wrong, °hurt, °mistreat, °manhandle, °ill-treat; °damage: I cannot stand by and watch that drunk abuse his wife and family. **3** malign, revile, censure, °upbraid, assail, objurgate, °lambaste, °berate, °rebuke, °scold, reproach, °disparage, traduce, defame, °insult, °swear at, °curse (at), calumniate, °slander, °libel, decry, deprecate, °vilify, °rail against: In the report the director was abused in the most virulent terms.
—n. **4** °misuse, misusage, misemployment, °perversion, misapplication, misappropriation, Rhetoric catachresis: Beware of imitating his abuse of the language. **5** addiction, dependence: They are being treated for drug abuse at the local clinic. **6** maltreatment, illtreatment, °ill °use, °fault: It seemed perfectly natural that he should

defend abuses by which he profited. **7** °self-abuse, self-pollution, masturbation, °violation, defilement; corruption: *The schoolmasters consistently lectured the boys against any abuse of themselves.* **8** revilement, reviling, execration, vituperation, malediction, imprecation, tongue-lashing, calumny, calumniation, vilification, obloquy, scurrility, invective, maligning, upbraiding, berating, objurgation, scolding; billingsgate: *The two parties, after exchanging a good deal of abuse, came to blows.*

abused *adj.* **1** misused: *Permission to use the office copying machine has become an abused privilege.* **2** maltreated, ill-treated, mistreated, °hurt: *It was explained that he had been an abused child.*

abusive *adj.* **1** insulting, °scurrilous, °vituperative, calumnious, calumniatory, offensive, °slanderous, libellous, defamatory, censorious, opprobrious, disparaging, deprecatory, depreciatory, °derogatory, °derisory, derisive, reviling, vilifying, °reproachful; °profane; °rude, °filthy, °dirty, °foul, °vulgar, obscene, smutty, °vile, thersitical: *The Crown refuses to tolerate abusive satire directed at the king. If I hear another word of abusive language out of you, I'll wash out your mouth with soap!* **2** °perverted, misapplied, °improper, °wrong, °incorrect; exploitive, exploitative, exploitatory; °brutal, °cruel, °injurious, °hurtful, °harmful, °destructive: *Despite the abusive treatment of wives, married women commanded much respect.* **3** °corrupt, °venal, °dishonest, °crooked: *The politicians exercised abusive power over the townspeople.*

abysmal *adj.* **1** °awful, appalling, °dreadful, °terrible, °profound: *The government of Nero presented a spectacle of abysmal degradation.* **2** abyssal, °bottomless, °profound, unfathomable, unfathomed: *The abysmal depths have been plumbed in the diving bell.*

abyss *n.* °deep, abysm, °bottomless °gulf, yawning chasm, gaping °void, unfathomable °cavity, impenetrable °depth(s): *The path led straight down into the abyss. In the scandal the MP was plunged into the abyss of disgrace.*

academic *adj.* **1** scholastic, collegiate; °scholarly, °learned, °lettered, erudite: *Green's academic background qualifies him for the professorship. The university began publishing academic journals in the 19th century.* **2** °theoretical, °hypothetical, conjectural, °speculative, °abstract; ivory-tower, °visionary, °idealistic; °impractical, °unrealistic, unpractical: *The car doesn't run, so the question of miles per gallon is purely academic.*

accent *n.* **1** °emphasis, °stress, °force, °prominence, accentuation; °intensity, inflection; °cadence, °beat: *The accent is on the second syllable in 'reward'.* **2** diacritic, diacritical °mark, °mark, accent °mark: *There is an acute accent on the 'e' in 'cliché'.* **3** °pronunciation, articulation, °intonation, °speech °pattern, inflection: *Even after forty years in the country, he still speaks English with an Italian accent.* —*v.* **4** accentuate, °emphasize, °stress, give °prominence to, °mark, underline, underscore, °distinguish, highlight, °set off *or* °apart: *In her speech, the psychologist accented the 'id' in 'idiot'. Why must he always accent the negative aspect of everything?*

accept *v.* **1** °receive, °take, °allow, °permit: *Sorry, but we cannot accept any more applications.* **2** accede (to), °agree (to), assent (to), °consent (to), °acknowledge, °admit, °allow, °recognize: *We accept your request for a hearing.* **3** °assume, °undertake, °take on *or* up, °agree to °bear: *I'll accept the responsibility for replying.* **4** °reconcile oneself to, °suffer, °undergo, °experience, °stand, °withstand, °stomach, °endure, °bear, °resign oneself to, °brook, °allow, °tolerate, °take: *I think I have accepted enough criticism for one day.*

acceptable *adj.* **1** °satisfactory, °adequate, °tolerable, all °right, °sufficient, admissible, °passable, *Colloq* °OK, okay: *The bread and meat were acceptable, but the beer was awful.* **2** °agreeable, °pleasing, °welcome, °satisfying, °delightful, °pleasant, °pleasing: *Most people find her compliments quite acceptable.*

accessible *adj.* approachable, °open, °available, obtainable, reachable, °ready, at °hand, *Colloq* get-at-able: *The president is always accessible to those seeking help. The mechanism is accessible if the cover is removed.*

accessory *n.* **1** °extra, °addition, adjunct, °attachment, component, °frill, *Slang* bells and whistles, doodah, *US and Canadian* doodad: *My food processor has more accessories than I could ever need.* **2** accessary, °accomplice, helper, °assistant, confederate, °colleague, abettor, °aide, collaborator, co-conspirator, conspirator, fellow-criminal, °associate *or* °partner in crime: *Although he did not rob the bank, he drove the getaway car, which legally makes him an accessory before the fact. A seller of stolen goods is an accessory after the fact.* —*adj.* **3** °extra, °subordinate, °auxiliary, additional, ancillary, supplemental, °supplementary, °secondary, adventitious, *Formal* adscititious: *For no apparent reason, the salamander grew an accessory limb near its hind leg.*

accident *n.* **1** °mishap, °misfortune, mischance, misadventure, °blunder, °mistake; °casualty, °disaster, °catastrophe, °calamity: *A high percentage of the road accidents were caused by drunken drivers.* **2** °chance, °fortune, °luck, fortuity, °fluke; serendipity: *I came across the gold ring by accident, when cleaning out a disused cupboard.* **3** °non-essential, °accessory *or* accessary, °extra, °addition: *Melancholy is an almost inseparable accident of old age.*

accidental *adj.* °chance, fortuitous, °lucky, unlucky, serendipitous; undesigned, °unpremeditated, uncalculated, unintended, unintentional, unwitting, °inadvertent; unexpected, unplanned, °unforeseen, unanticipated, adventitious; °casual, °random: *Our meeting was entirely accidental.*

accommodate *v.* **1** °fit, °suit, °adapt, °adjust, °modify; customize: *I shall do my best to accommodate the equipment to your needs.* **2** harmonize, make consistent, °reconcile, °adapt: *It is uncertain whether his version of the incident can be accommodated to ours.* **3** °equip, °supply, °provide, °furnish: *Can you accommodate me with five pounds till tomorrow?* **4** °put up, °house, °lodge, °shelter, °quarter, *Military* billet: *The innkeeper is unable to accommodate us tonight.* **5** °suit, °oblige, convenience, °serve: *I was willing to accommodate you by selling your old car.*

accommodating adj. **1** °obliging, cooperative, °helpful, °hospitable; °considerate, conciliatory, °easy to deal with, pliant, °yielding, compliant, °polite, °friendly, complaisant, °kind, °kindly: *The lady at the complaints desk in the store was most accommodating.* **2** °pliable, °accessible, corruptible, subornable, get-at-able; bribable: *If you want to get off scot-free, we'll have to find an accommodating judge.*

accommodation n. **1** °adaptation, °adjustment, modification, °change, °alteration, conformation, conformity: *Her skilful accommodation to her boss's demands kept the peace in the office.* **2** °settlement, °treaty, compromise: *Negotiations were now opened for an accommodation between the belligerents.* **3** convenience, °favour: *Would you take the mail to the post office as an accommodation to me?* **4** °lodging(s), °room(s), °quarters, °shelter, °housing; °facility, premises, *Brit* digs, *US* accommodations: *We were able to arrange for accommodation at the hotel. Have you seen our new office accommodation?* **5** °loan, (financial) °assistance or °aid; °grant, grant-in-aid: *The man was able to obtain an accommodation from his brother-in-law.*

accompany v. **1** convoy, °escort, chaperon or chaperone, °go (along) with; °attend; usher, °squire: *Allow me to accompany you to your taxi.* **2** °go (along) with, °come with, be associated with, °belong with, °go together with, be linked with: *The roast was accompanied by a bottle of claret.*

accomplice n. °accessory or accessary, °partner in crime, confederate, °ally, °associate, °colleague, °fellow, °henchman, collaborator, conspirator, co-conspirator, abettor, °assistant, fellow-criminal, *Colloq US* °cohort: *The police arrested the safe-cracker and three accomplices within hours of the robbery.*

accomplish v. °fulfil, °perform, °achieve, °carry out, °execute, °carry off, do, °complete, °carry through, °finish, °effect, bring to an °end, conclude, °wind up, °end; attain, °reach, °gain; *Colloq* °bring off, °knock off, °polish off, *Slang* °pull off, *US* °swing, °hack, °cut: *I don't know how she accomplished it, but she sailed around the world single-handed. Has he accomplished his goal yet?*

accomplished adj. consummate, °perfect, °expert, °adept, °skilful, °proficient, °practised, °gifted, °talented, skilled, °professional: *Did you know that she is also an accomplished flautist?*

accomplishment n. **1** °fulfilment, °consummation, °completion, °realization, attainment, °achievement, conclusion, culmination: *After the accomplishment of the task they were all taken out to celebrate.* **2** coup, °feat, °exploit, °triumph, tour de force: *Among her many accomplishments was climbing Mount Everest.* **3** °skill, skilfulness, °talent, °gift, °ability: *Playing the violin is another of his accomplishments.*

accord v. **1** °agree, harmonize, concur, be at °one, °correspond, be in °harmony, be °consistent, °go (together), °coincide, °conform: *His principles and practices do not accord with one another.* —n. **2** °agreement, unanimity, concord, °reconciliation, °harmony, °mutual °understanding, conformity, accordance, °rapport, concert: *The countries are in accord on a beneficial trade balance.* **3** °agreement, °treaty, °pact, °contract: *The accords will be signed at the summit meeting in May.* **4** °agreement, °harmony, congruence; correspondence: *The colours of the curtains are in perfect accord with those of the carpet.*

accordingly adv. **1** °hence, °therefore, °consequently, °thus, in consequence whereof, (and) so: *Smoking was forbidden; accordingly, we put out our cigars.* **2** suitably, in conformity, in compliance; conformably, °appropriately, compliantly: *Dinner-jackets were required, and the men dressed accordingly.*

according to adv.phr. **1** on the °authority of, °consistent with, in conformity or °agreement with, as said or believed or maintained etc. °by: *We are going to play this game according to Hoyle. According to his lawyer, he should never have been acquitted.* **2** conformable to, °consistent with, in conformity with, commensurate with: *The queen greeted them in order, according to rank.*

account v. **1 account for**: °explain, give a °reason for, give or render a °reckoning for, °answer for, °justify, °reckon for: *The treasurer has been able to account for every penny of expense. His desire to conceal his background accounts for his secrecy.* —n. **2** °calculation, accounting, °reckoning, computation, (°financial) °statement; enumeration: *The accounts show that the company has ample funds in reserve. Williams hasn't submitted his expense account for the trip.* **3** °interest, °profit, °advantage, °benefit, °favour; °sake: *Nigel turned his convalescence to good account by writing a best seller. Don't read the book on my account.* **4** °explanation, °statement, °description, °report, °recital, °narrative, °history, °chronicle: *The defendant gave a credible account of his whereabouts at the time of the crime.* **5** °consideration, °use, °worth, °importance, consequence, °note, value, °merit, °standing, °significance, °estimation, °esteem: *The committee decided that length of service is of some account in determining retirement pensions.* **6** °story, °narration, °narrative, °report, °tale, °relation, °description: *Alice's account of the rabbit wearing a waistcoat is unbelievable.* **7 take into account** or **take account of**: °notice, take °note of, °consider, take into °consideration, °allow for: *In passing sentence, the judge took into account the child's poverty and the fact that it was Christmas time.*

accountability n. answerability, °responsibility, °liability, culpability, accountableness: *In a democracy, there can be no reducing the accountability of the government to the citizens.*

accountable adj. answerable, °responsible, °liable, °obliged, obligated: *I am accountable to no man, but the greatest man in England is accountable to me.*

accumulate v. °collect, °gather, °amass, °mass, °pile or °heap up, aggregate, cumulate; °assemble, °store, °stock, °hoard, stockpile, °put or °lay away: *Overnight, the snow accumulated in six-foot drifts about the house. Ill fares the land, to hast'ning ills a prey,/Where wealth accumulates, and men decay.*

accumulation n. **1** collecting, amassing, °gathering, piling or heaping up, aggregation: *One effect of the strike was the accumulation of rubbish in the streets.* **2** °growth, °increase, build-up: *The accumulation of wealth has never proved a valid purpose in life.* **3** °heap, °pile, °mass, °collection,

°hoard, °store, stockpile, °stock, aggregation; assemblage: *Our gardener made sure that there was an ample accumulation of compost.*

accuracy *n.* exactness, correctness, *Loosely* °precision, preciseness: *The translation from the Greek has been accomplished with great accuracy. Rifling the inside of the barrel of a firearm increases its accuracy.*

accurate *adj.* **1** °exact, °correct, error-free, °precise: *She gave an accurate description of the events. There is a nice distinction between 'accurate' and 'precise'.* **2** °careful, °meticulous, °nice, with an eye to *or* for °detail, °scrupulous, °conscientious: *Marvin is a very accurate typist.* **3** unerring, on °target, *Colloq* on the °mark, spot on (°target): *This rifle is accurate if you allow for the wind.*

accusation *n.* °charge, °allegation, indictment, °charge, citation, arraignment, °complaint; °imputation, incrimination, denunciation, impeachment: *The politician denied the accusation of having accepted a bribe.*

accuse *v.* **1** accuse (of *or* with): °blame, censure, °hold responsible (for), °charge (with), °denounce (for), point the °finger (at), cite, call to °account: *She accused the Knave of Hearts of lying.* **2** accuse (of *or* with): °charge, °indict, °impeach, arraign, °incriminate; °attribute, °impute: *The prisoner is accused of assault, criminal damage, and disorderly conduct.*

accustom *v.* °familiarize, °acquaint, habituate, °train, °season; acclimatize *or* acclimate: *Start off by wearing your contact lenses for an hour at a time in order to accustom your eyes to them. She soon accustomed herself to the new surroundings.*

accustomed *adj.* **1** °customary, °habitual, °usual, °traditional, °normal, °regular, °set, °routine, °ordinary, °familiar, wonted, °common, habituated: *The old man took his accustomed place near the fire.* **2** °used: *I've grown accustomed to her face.*

ache *v.* **1** °pain, °hurt, °smart, throb, °pound; °sting: *My jaw has been aching since that tooth was extracted.* **2** °yearn, °long, °hunger, °hanker, pine; crave: *A hostage for a year, he was aching to see his wife and children.* —*n.* **3** °pain, °pang, throbbing, pounding, smarting, soreness: *I have had this ache in my back, Doctor, and I can't stand up straight.* **4** °pang, °pain; °distress; °longing: *There's been an ache in my heart, my darling, ever since you went away.*

achieve *v.* **1** °accomplish, °carry out, °execute, °succeed in, °complete, °fulfil, °bring off *or* about; °realize, °effect: *When the fund reaches its goal, we shall have achieved our purpose.* **2** °accomplish, attain, °reach, °gain, °get, °acquire, °win, °obtain: *She achieved her ends by cheating and conniving.*

achievement *n.* **1** attainment, °accomplishment, °acquisition, acquirement: *As he was still in his thirties, the achievement of great fame still lay ahead for him.* **2** °accomplishment, attainment, °feat, °deed, °exploit, °victory: *The winning of the Nobel prize was her greatest achievement.* **3** °fulfilment, °realization, °accomplishment, attainment, °completion: *What virtue lies more in achievement than in the desire for it?*

acknowledge *v.* **1** °admit, °confess, °allow, °concede, own, °recognize, °accept, accede,

acquiesce; own up to: *We acknowledge that we might have been mistaken. She finally acknowledged my presence by looking up.* **2** °answer, °reply to, °respond to, °react to: *She couldn't possibly acknowledge personally every letter she receives.*

acknowledgement *n.* **1** acknowledging, confessing, admitting, owning, °admission, confession, avowal, affirmation: *His acknowledgement of his involvement in the crime saved the police a great deal of time.* **2** °approval, acceptance, °recognition, °allowance: *By acknowledgement of the parliament, the king was the commander of the army and navy.* **3** °reply, °response, °answer, °recognition: *Our acknowledgement will be in tomorrow's post.*

acme *n.* °peak, apex, °top, °summit, °pinnacle, °zenith; °climax, culmination: *Roger has reached the acme of perfection as a diamond-cutter.*

acquaint *v.* acquaint with: °familiarize with, °inform of *or* about, make °aware of, apprise of, °advise of: *The management requires employees to acquaint themselves with the safety rules.*

acquaintance *n.* **1** °familiarity, °knowledge, acquaintanceship, °understanding, awareness; °experience: *His acquaintance with the works of Coleridge is sparse at best.* **2** °associate, °fellow, °colleague: *She's not a friend of mine, only an acquaintance.*

acquainted *adj.* **1** known to each other *or* one another, °familiar with each other *or* one another, on speaking terms: *I have known Rory for years, but his wife and I are not acquainted.* **2** acquainted with: °familiar with, known to, °aware of, °informed of, °knowledgeable of, conversant with: *I have studied trigonometry, but I am not acquainted with calculus.*

acquire *v.* °get, °obtain, °gain, °win, °earn, °procure, °secure, °come by *or* into; °receive, come into °possession of; °buy, °purchase: *He acquired great wealth by marrying rich old dying widows.*

acquisition *n.* **1** obtaining, getting, acquiring, acquirement, °gain, procurement: *The acquisition of property entails many obligations.* **2** °possession(s), °property, °purchase; °object: *This first edition is a recent acquisition.*

act *n.* **1** °deed, °action, °undertaking, °operation, °step, °move, °feat, °exploit; °accomplishment, °achievement: *The first act of the new commission was to ban smoking in public places.* **2** °performance, °show, °bit, skit, °stand, °routine, °turn, sketch, *Colloq* °thing, *Slang US* shtick: *Stand-up comedians do their acts in nightclubs.* **3** °performance, °pretence, °posture, °stance, feigning, °front, °fake, °dissimulation, °show, °deception, °hoax, °affectation: *She didn't mean what she said—it was just an act.* **4** °bill, law, °decree, edict, statute, °order, ordinance, °command, mandate, °resolution, °measure, enactment: *Are the opening hours of public houses in England regulated by act of Parliament?* —*v.* **5** °behave (oneself), °carry on, deport oneself, comport oneself, °conduct oneself: *I don't know how she'll act when we're in public.* **6** °perform, °play, do: *She is acting in the West End.* **7** °portray, °represent, impersonate, act out, °personify, take *or* °play the °part *or* °role of, personate: *Reginald acts the fool whenever he has had too much to drink.* **8** feign, °pretend, °counterfeit, °fake, dissemble, °make believe, °sham, simulate,

°dissimulate, °posture: *You may think him sincere, but I know he is just acting.* **9** take °effect, °work, °operate, °function, °perform: *This drug will act only if taken with meals.*

action *n.* **1** °activity, °performance, °movement, °motion, °energy, liveliness, vim, °vigour, °spirit, °vitality, °enterprise, °initiative: *Being a man of action, he hates just sitting and reading.* **2** °influence, °effect, °power, °force, °strength: *The action of the moon's gravitational pull causes tides on earth.* **3** °deed, °act, °undertaking, °exertion, °exercise: *The very action of breathing caused me pain.* **4** °remedy, °proceeding, °process: *If they don't stop beating their dog we shall take action against them.* **5** fighting, °combat: *We saw action in the Far East.* **6** °fight, °battle, °engagement, °encounter, °clash, °fray, sortie, °skirmish, affray: *How many men were lost in last night's action?* **7** °effect, effectiveness, °activity, °function, °performance, functioning, °reaction: *What is the action of steroids on the lymph system?* **8 actions**: °behaviour, °conduct, deportment, demeanour, °ways, °manner, manners: *She must be held responsible for her actions.*

activate *v.* °move, actuate, °set in °motion, get started, °energize, get or °set °going, °start, °initiate, °switch or °turn on, trigger; °motivate, °rouse, °arouse, °prompt, °stimulate, °stir, °mobilize, °animate, impel, galvanize, *Colloq US* light a fire under: *The sensor in the pavement activates the traffic signal. Her enthusiasm activated him to go into business for himself.*

active *adj.* **1** °strenuous, °vigorous, °full, °dynamic, °physical; °energetic, °lively, °busy, °brisk, bustling, occupied, on the °move, *Colloq* on the °go, °running: *She is healthier for having led a very active life. He always seems to be active.* **2** acting, °effective, °efficacious, °effectual, working, functioning, °operative, °potent, °influential; °powerful: *The active ingredient in her medicine is an antihistamine.* **3** °energetic, °lively, hyperactive, °animated, spry, °nimble, °quick, °agile, °sprightly: *There is no keeping up with an active child.*

activity *n.* **1** °action, °movement, °motion, °vigour, vim, °energy, liveliness, bustle: *Last week there wasn't much activity in the stock market.* **2** °pursuit, °occupation, °vocation, °work, °function, °operation, °job, °labour, °endeavour, °enterprise, °project, °undertaking, °venture, °interest: *What sort of business activity are you engaged in?*

actual *adj.* **1** existing, existent, °real, °genuine, factual, °true, °authentic, verified, verifiable, °true to °life, °manifest, realized, °realistic, *Colloq* °solid: *The actual cost of the project turned out to be double the estimate.* **2** °present, °current, existent, °real, °genuine, °physical, °tangible: *No telescope has detected any actual volcanic eruption on the moon.*

actually *adv.* °really, in °reality, in °fact, in actuality, in point of °fact, in °truth, °absolutely, as a matter of °fact, °indeed, °truly, °literally: *The interest rates actually charged by banks may vary from those quoted publicly.*

acute *adj.* **1** °sharp, °pointed, °narrow: *The two roads meet at an acute angle.* **2** °severe, °intense, °critical, °crucial, °dangerous, °grave, °serious: *This is the ward for patients with acute illnesses.* **3** °sharp, °cutting, °intense, °severe, °violent, °penetrating, °exquisite, °excruciating, °fierce,

shooting, stabbing, °piercing, °sudden: *The onset of the disease is marked by acute pains in the abdomen.* **4** °keen, °sharp, °sensitive: *The bloodhound is known for its acute sense of smell.* **5** °keen, sharp-witted, °shrewd, °clever, °ingenious, °astute, °sharp, canny, °incisive, discerning, °perceptive, perspicacious, °intelligent, °penetrating, insightful, percipient, °wise, °sensitive, °discriminating; °alert, °aware, on the qui vive: *Such a circumstance could not be lost upon so acute an observer.*

adapt *v.* **1** °suit, °fit, °make °suitable, °qualify: *The structure of the outer ear is adapted to collect and concentrate the vibrations.* **2** °alter, °modify, °change, remodel, °tailor, reshape, °shape, °fashion; °adjust, °accommodate, °accustom, acclimatize or acclimate, habituate: *He adapted the play from an old French comedy. The whale adapts itself to great changes in pressure when it dives thousands of feet.*

adaptable *adj.* °flexible, °pliable, pliant, compliant, accommodative, °tractable, malleable, ductile, °versatile; alterable, °changeable: *Men, in general, are not as adaptable as women.*

adaptation *n.* **1** °fitting, suiting, modifying, adjusting, conversion: *In 1831 electricity was ripe for adaptation to practical purposes.* **2** modification, °change, °adjustment, °accommodation, reworking, customization, °alteration: *She was responsible for the adaptation of her short story to a television play.*

add *v.* **1** °join, °unite, °combine, annex: *5 + 3 denotes that 3 is to be added to 5.* **2** °total, °sum, °sum up, °combine, °count up, °reckon, *Brit* °tot (up), *US* tote (up): *The computer can add all those figures in a few seconds.* **3** °continue, °go on: *'And I won't take no for an answer', she added.* **4 add to**: °increase, °enlarge, °amplify, augment, °supplement: *His articles have added greatly to his reputation as a financial analyst.*

addict *n.* **1** (°habitual) °user, *Slang* junkie, dope-fiend, doper, °head, pot-head, acid-head, pill popper, tripper, *Chiefly US* hophead: *His contributions helped set up the halfway houses for addicts.* **2** °devotee, aficionado, °fan, °admirer, °follower, adherent, °supporter, °enthusiast, *Colloq* buff, °hound, °fiend, groupie, *Slang* °freak, °bug, nut, teeny-bopper: *She became a rock 'n' roll addict in the '60s.*

addition *n.* **1** adding, joining, putting together, uniting, combining: *The addition of this paragraph is uncalled for.* **2** totalling, adding up, summing-up, summation, counting up, °reckoning, totting up: *You have made an error in addition.* **3** addendum, appendix, appendage, °supplement, °increment, augmentation, °extension: *This addition contributes nothing to the manuscript.* **4** °extension, ell, *Brit* annexe, *US* annex, wing: *We used our lottery winnings to pay for an addition to the house.* —*prep.* **5 in addition to**: as well as, °besides, beyond, over and above: *In addition to books, the shop sold greetings cards.* —*adv.phr.* **6 in addition**: °moreover, furthermore, additionally, °besides, withal, to °boot, in or into the °bargain, too, also, as well: *We were compelled to exercise every morning and in addition we went for a ten-mile run each Saturday.*

address *n.* **1** °speech, °talk, discourse, °oration, °lecture; °sermon: *The Prime Minister's address to*

the nation was broadcast last night. **2** °location, °whereabouts: She couldn't write to me because she didn't have my address.
—v. **3** °speak or °talk to; °deliver or °give a °speech to; °lecture: After the coup, the general addressed the crowd in the square. **4** °greet, °hail, accost, °approach: She was addressing strangers in the street to ask their views on women's rights. **5 address oneself to**: °devote or °direct or °apply oneself to: After the holidays, I again addressed myself to studying for examinations.

adept adj. **1** °versed, °proficient, skilled, well-skilled, °expert, °accomplished, °skilful, adroit, °dexterous or dextrous, °able, °masterful, masterly, °polished: She is an adept pianist, and her husband is adept at carpentry.
—n. **2** °expert, °master, °specialist, authority, Colloq dab hand, old hand: He is an adept at anything that one does with one's hands.

adequate adj. **1** °sufficient, °enough, °ample; °satisfactory, °fitting, °equal, °suitable: Is there language adequate to describe my feelings? **2** °passable, °fair, °fair to middling, middling, °average, °tolerable, (°barely) °acceptable, (°barely) °satisfactory, all °right, °competent, not (at all) °bad, so so, Colloq °OK or okay, up to snuff, not that or too °bad, no °great shakes: The music was good, the band only adequate. **3** °equal, °suitable, suited, °fitted up, °proper, °qualified, °competent, °good °enough: Johnson was unsure that he was adequate to the task at hand.

adjoining adj. °neighbouring, contiguous (to), adjacent (to), abutting, bordering, next (to): We have bought the adjoining land and will build our new house there. The land adjoining the supermarket is for sale.

adjust v. **1** °set °right, °arrange, °settle, harmonize, °reconcile, °resolve, set or °put to °rights; arbitrate, mediate; redress, °rectify, °correct, °patch up: The labour and management teams have not been able to adjust their differences. **2** °change, °alter, °modify, °regulate, °set: After he adjusted the pendulum, the clock kept good time. **3** °adapt (to), °accommodate (oneself) (to), °accustom (oneself) (to); get °used (to), acclimatize or acclimate (to), °reconcile (oneself) (to): If she travels a distance east or west, it takes her a few days to adjust to the local time. Army life was very different, but I was able to adjust quickly. **4** °put in °order, °arrange, rearrange, °close or °fasten or zip or button (up): She adjusted the children's coats and did up their shoes.

adjustment n. **1** adjusting, altering, °alteration, °setting, regulating, °regulation, setting or putting °right or aright or to rights, correcting, °correction, calibrating, calibration; tuning: The adjustment of the clocks is my responsibility. **2** °arrangement, °balance, coordination, °order, alignment, °harmony, harmonization: The inspector requires everything to be in perfect adjustment.

administer v. **1** administrate, °manage, °control, °run, °direct, °conduct, superintend, °supervise, °oversee: The president said that she had administered the department well during her year as its head. **2** °execute, °carry on, °carry out; °apply, °implement, °prosecute: It is the responsibility of the police to administer the law, not to make it. **3** °dispense, °supply, °furnish, °give

(out), °provide (with), °mete out, °distribute, °deliver, °deal, °hand out: Doctors sometimes administer drugs that have side effects.

administration n. **1** °management, °direction, °conduct, supervision, °oversight, superintendence, °regulation, °charge: Lord Hampden was given administration of her affairs till she came of age. **2** °authority, °management, US °government: The current administration is in favour of a better health programme. **3** dispensation, administering, supplying, furnishing, °provision, °delivery, °distribution, °application: The judge is charged with the administration of justice.

admirable adj. wonderful, awe-inspiring, °excellent, °estimable, °splendid, °marvellous, °superior, °first-rate, first-class, of the first °water, °great, °fine, Colloq top-drawer, ripsnorting, A-1, Brit smashing, °magic: His performance in Harper's new play is admirable.

admiration n. °wonder, awe; °delight, °pleasure; °esteem, °regard, °appreciation, °respect: She is lost in admiration of her mother's latest painting. Randolph was presented with a gold medal as a token of his colleagues' admiration.

admire v. **1** °wonder or °marvel (at), °delight in: Typically, he most admires people who are wealthy. **2** °esteem, °regard or °respect highly, °look up to, °revere, °idolize, °venerate, °worship: The queen is one of the most admired people in the country.

admirer n. **1** °devotee, aficionado, °fan, °supporter, °enthusiast, adherent, °follower, Slang groupie: Rock stars always seem to be accompanied by a retinue of admirers. **2** beau, °suitor; °lover, °sweetheart, °darling: Scarlett was always surrounded by many admirers.

admission n. **1** access, °admittance, entrée, °entry: The special card gives me admission to the rare book room of the library. **2** °reception, acceptance, °appointment, °institution, induction, °installation, investiture: The committee has at last approved the admission of women into the society. **3** acknowledging, °acknowledgement, allowing, °allowance, admitting, °admittance, conceding, concession: The court refuses to consider the admission of testimony taken under duress. **4** °acknowledgement, confession, concession, °profession, °declaration, disclosure, affirmation, divulgence or divulgement, °revelation: The police were able to extract an admission of guilt from the suspect. **5** ticket, (°entry or °entrance) °fee, °tariff: Admission is free for senior citizens.

admit v. **1** °let in, °allow to °enter, °take or °allow in; °accept, °receive: I opened the window to admit some air. The harbour is too small to admit even one more ship. **2** °allow, °permit, °grant, °brook, °tolerate: The governor will admit no delay in the execution of the sentence, and the prisoner will be hanged at dawn. **3** °accept, °concede, acquiesce, °allow, °grant, °recognize, take °cognizance of: Descartes' principle admitted nothing but what his own consciousness obliged him to admit. **4** °confess, own, °concede, divulge, °reveal, °acknowledge, °declare: She readily admitted to having incited the riot.

admittance n. °leave or °permission to °enter, °entry, entering, °entrance, access, entrée: Admittance to the club is restricted to members.

adolescent n. **1** °teenager, °youth, °juvenile, °minor, °stripling, youngster, US teen, Colloq kid; Slang teeny-bopper: A group of adolescents volunteered to work at the home for the elderly. —adj. **2** teenaged, °young, youthful, maturing, pubescent; °immature, °puerile, °juvenile: Adolescent growth is often dramatic, a gain of two inches in height being not unusual.

adopt v. **1** °take (in), °accept, °take or °accept as one's own: Carol and her husband have adopted two children. **2** °take, °take up or on or over, °embrace, espouse; arrogate, °appropriate: All Hugh's ideas are adopted from others—he's never had one of his own.

adorable adj. °lovable, °beloved, loved, °darling, °sweet, °dear; °delightful, appealing, °attractive, charming, captivating, °fetching: To look at him now, it is hard to imagine what an adorable child he once was.

adore v. **1** °esteem, °honour, °respect, °admire; °idolize, °dote on: An entire generation adored the Beatles. **2** °worship, °venerate, °reverence, °revere, °exalt; °hallow: O! Come let us adore him—Christ, the Lord! **3** °love, be in °love with, °cherish, °fancy, °revere, adulate, Colloq have a crush on, carry the or a torch for: Katie just adores the captain of the football team at school.

adult adj. **1** °mature, grown (up), full-grown, matured, of °age: Now that you are adult, you come into a large inheritance. —n. **2** grown-up: Tiger cubs are cute, but the adults are very dangerous.

adulterate v. °falsify, °corrupt, °alloy, °debase, °water (down), °weaken, °dilute, bastardize, °contaminate, °pollute, °taint, Colloq °doctor; Slang US °cut: Adulterated rape seed oil was found to have caused the deaths of more than 600 people.

advance v. **1** °move or °put or °push or °go forward(s); °approach: Man has advanced the frontier of physical science. The battalion advanced towards the fort with guns blazing. **2** °further, °promote, °forward, °help, °aid, °abet, °assist, °benefit, °improve; °contribute to: The terrorists' dynamiting of the school has done nothing to advance their cause. **3** °go or °move forward, °move (°onward), °go on, °proceed, °get °ahead: As people advance in life, they acquire what is better than admiration—judgement. **4** °hasten, accelerate, °speed: We have advanced the date of our departure from December to October. **5** °move up, °promote: In less than a year, Mrs Leland has been advanced from supervisor to manager of the production department. **6** prepay, °lend: Could you advance me some money till next pay-day? —n. **7** °progress, °development, forward °movement; °improvement, betterment; °headway: Who has done more for the advance of knowledge? **8** °rise, °increase, °appreciation: Any advance in prices at this time would reduce our sales. **9** prepayment, °deposit; °loan: I cannot understand why George is always asking for an advance on his allowance. **10 in advance**: **a** beforehand, °ahead (of °time), °before: You will have to make reservations well in advance. **b** °before, in °front (of), °ahead (of), beyond: The colonel rode in advance of the cavalry.

advantage n. **1** °superiority, °upper hand, dominance, °edge, head °start; °sway; Colloq US and New Zealand °drop: After a year, the advantage was with the Royalists. His height gives him an advantage at basketball. **2** °gain, °profit, °benefit, °interest; °asset, betterment, °improvement, advancement; °use, °usefulness, utility, °help, °service: I have information that will be of advantage to her. **3 to advantage**: °better, (more) °favourably, advantageously: The dress sets off her figure to advantage.

advantageous adj. °profitable, °worthwhile, °gainful, °opportune, °beneficial, °favourable, °useful, valuable: The minister signed an advantageous treaty of commerce with Russia.

adventure n. **1** °exploit, escapade, °danger, °peril; °affair, °undertaking, °feat, °deed; °experience, °incident, °event, °occurrence, °happening, °episode: We shared many wartime adventures. **2** °speculation, °hazard, °chance, °risk, °venture, °enterprise: I lost a fortune in some of his financial adventures. —v. **3** °venture, °hazard, °risk, imperil, °endanger, °jeopardize, °threaten: Would you adventure your pension money in such a scheme? **4** °dare, °wager, °bet, °gamble, °stake, °try one's luck, Brit °punt: She adventured a whole week's salary on the pools.

adventurer n. **1** adventuress, °soldier of fortune, swashbuckler, °hero, °heroine, °daredevil; °mercenary: Errol Flynn often played the role of the adventurer. **2** adventuress, °cheat, °swindler, charlatan, trickster, °rogue, °scoundrel, knave; cad, bounder, °philanderer, fortune-hunter, opportunist: That adventurer is just after Nelson's money.

adventurous adj. °daring, °rash, °brash, °reckless, devil-may-care, °bold, °foolhardy, °hazardous, °risky, °daredevil, °venturesome, adventuresome, temerarious, °audacious, °bold, °intrepid, °brave, °courageous: She was adventurous enough to sail round the world single-handed.

adversary n. **1** foe, °enemy, °opponent, °antagonist, °competitor, °rival: Before beginning to fight, each adversary sized up the other. —adj. **2** °opposed, °hostile, antagonistic, competitive: Why does she always take the adversary position in every argument?

advertisement n. **1** °notice, handbill, blurb, broadside, °bill, °circular, °brochure, °poster, placard, classified, commercial, °spot (°announcement), US car-card, Colloq ad, °plug, Brit advert: The company has placed advertisements in all major media. **2** advertising, °promotion; publicity; °propaganda, ballyhoo, hoop-la, Colloq hype, beating the drum, US puffery: Advertisement on TV may be very effective, but it is very expensive.

advice n. **1** °counsel, °guidance, °recommendation, °suggestion, °opinion, °view; °warning, admonition, Technical parænesis: His solicitor's advice is to say nothing. **2** °information, °news, °intelligence, °notice, notification; communication: Advice has reached the police that a shipment of arms will leave Dover tonight.

advisable adj. recommendable, °expedient, °prudent, °practical, °sensible, °sound, °seemly, °judicious, °wise, °intelligent, °smart, °proper, °politic: It would be advisable for you to keep out of sight for a few days.

advise v. **1** °counsel, °guide, °recommend, °suggest, commend; °caution, admonish, °warn; °urge, °encourage: I advised him to be careful driving at night in that area. **2** °tell, °announce (to), °inform, apprise, °register,

°make known (to), °intimate (to), °notify: *We advised her of our disapproval. The police have advised the defendants of their rights.*

adviser *n.* °counsellor, mentor, °guide, cicerone, °counsel, °consultant, confidant(e): *The chairman always consults his advisers before making a decision.*

advisory *adj.* **1** consultive, consultative, counselling, hortatory, monitory, admonitory, *Technical* paraenetic(al): *Our firm has been engaged in an advisory capacity on the privatization of the utility companies.*
—*n.* **2** °bulletin, °notice, °warning, admonition, °prediction: *The Weather Office has issued a storm advisory for the weekend.*

advocate *v.* **1** °support, °champion, °back, °endorse, °uphold, °recommend, °stand behind, °second, °favour, °speak *or* °plead *or* °argue for *or* in °favour of: *Don't you advocate the policies of the Party?*
—*n.* **2** °supporter, °champion, °backer, upholder, °second, exponent, °proponent, °patron, defender, apologist: *She is an enthusiastic advocate of free speech.* **3** °lawyer, °counsel, intercessor; *Brit* barrister, °solicitor, *US* attorney, counselor-at-law: *The advocate for the opposition is not in court.*

aesthete *n.* connoisseur, art-lover, lover of °beauty, aesthetician *or* esthetician, *US* tastemaker: *It was the aesthetes who set the standard for the art purchased by the museum.*

aesthetic *adj.* **1** artistic, °tasteful, °beautiful; in good, excellent, etc. °taste: *Daphne always does such aesthetic flower arrangements.*
2 °sensitive, artistic, °refined, °discriminating, °cultivated: *These paintings might be realistic, but they are an aesthetic disaster.*

affair *n.* **1** °matter, °topic, °issue; °business, °concern, °interest, °undertaking, °activity: *These are affairs of state and require the approval of a minister.* **2** °concern, °business, *Slang US* beeswax: *Who wiped the fingerprints off the weapon is none of your affair.* **3** °event, °business, °occurrence, °happening, °proceeding, °incident, °operation: *Last night's farewell party was truly a dull affair.* **4** Also, **affaire**: °love affair, amour, °romance, °intrigue, °fling, °liaison, °relationship, *affaire d'amour, affaire de cœur: Lady Constance is having an affair with the gamekeeper.*

affect¹ *v.* **1** °attack, °act upon, °lay °hold of, °strike: *Arthritis has affected his hands and he can no longer play the piano.* **2** °move, °stir, °impress, °touch, °strike; °perturb, °upset, °trouble, °agitate: *The sportsman was not affected by all the taunts and jeers.* **3** °influence, °sway, °change, °transform, °modify, °alter: *Her sudden fame has affected her view of herself.*

affect² *v.* **1** °assume, °adopt, °put on, °pretend (to), feign, °sham, °fake, °counterfeit: *Charles affects a knowledge of high finance.* **2** °choose, °select; °use, °wear, °adopt: *He affected a striped blazer and a boater which he wore at a jaunty angle.*

affectation *n.* **1** affectedness, pretentiousness, artificiality, insincerity, posturing: *She behaves with so much affectation that I never can be sure of her real feelings.* **2** °pretence, simulation, °false °display, °show, °front, °pose, °pretension, façade; °act, °airs: *Some people's charitable concern for others is mere affectation. Using a long cigarette-holder is one of her many affectations.*

affected *adj.* **1** °unnatural, °artificial, °specious, °stilted, °stiff, °studied, °awkward, non-natural, contrived, °mannered: *Dryden found Shakespeare's style stiff and affected.* **2** °pretended, simulated, °hollow, °assumed, feigned, °fake, faked, °false, °counterfeit, °insincere, °spurious, °sham, °bogus, *Colloq* °phoney *or US also* phony: *The heir's affected grief concealed his secret exultation.* **3** °pretentious, °pompous, high-sounding, °mincing, niminy-piminy, *Colloq* la-di-da *or* lah-di-dah *or* la-de-da: *Oliver's affected airs were enough to make his classmates detest him.* **4** attacked, seized, afflicted, °stricken, gripped, touched; °diseased, laid hold of: *Her affected lungs never quite recovered.* **5** afflicted, moved, touched, stirred, distressed, troubled, °upset, °hurt; influenced, swayed, impressed, struck, played *or* worked *or* acted upon: *Many affected theatre-goers enjoyed her performances.*

affection *n.* goodwill, (°high) °regard, °liking, fondness, °attachment, loving °attachment, tenderness, °warmth, °love: *The affection she felt towards her stepchildren was returned many times over.*

affectionate *adj.* °fond, loving, °tender, caring, °devoted, doting, °warm: *She gave her mother an affectionate embrace and boarded the train.*

affiliated *adj.* associated; °attached, connected, combined, °united, joined: *For our members' convenience, the club is now affiliated with one that serves meals.*

affinity *n.* **1** °relationship, °kinship, closeness, °alliance, °connection *or Brit* connexion; °sympathy, °rapport: *He felt an affinity with other redheaded people.* **2** friendliness, fondness, °liking, °leaning, °bent, °inclination, °taste, °partiality, attractiveness, °attraction: *I have an affinity for the sea.*

afflict *v.* °affect, °bother, °distress, °oppress, °trouble, °torment: *Last winter's intense cold afflicted everyone, but those in the north especially.*

affliction *n.* **1** °hardship, °misery, °misfortune, °distress, °ordeal, °trial, tribulation, adversity, °suffering, °woe, °pain, °grief, °torment, wretchedness: *Moses saw the affliction of his people in Egypt.* **2** °curse, °disease, °calamity, °catastrophe, °disaster, °plague, °scourge, tribulation, °trouble: *He often observed that greed was the affliction of the middle class.*

afford *v.* **1** have the °means, be °able *or* °rich °enough, °manage, °bear the °expense, °pay, °provide: *We cannot afford to send the children to better schools.* **2** °give, °spare, °give up, °contribute, °donate; °sacrifice: *The loss of a single day's work was more than I could afford.* **3** °yield, °give, °supply, °produce, °provide, °furnish, °grant, °offer; °give forth: *May kind heaven afford him everlasting rest. The poems afford no explanation.*

afoul *adv.* **afoul of**: entangled with, in °trouble with, in °conflict with, at °odds with: *Barbara fell afoul of the new tax regulations.*

afraid *adj.* **1** °fearful, frightened, °scared, intimidated, apprehensive, lily-livered, white-livered, terrified, °panic-stricken, °faint-hearted, weak-kneed, °timid, timorous, °nervous, °anxious, jittery, on °edge, edgy, °jumpy; °cowardly, pusillanimous, craven, *Colloq* yellow: *Don't be afraid, the dog won't bite you.*

2 °sorry, °unhappy, °regretful, °apologetic, rueful: *I'm afraid I cannot help you find a cheap flat in London.*

age *n.* **1** lifetime, duration, °length of °existence; life-span: *The age of a stag is judged chiefly by its antlers. She was sixteen years of age.* **2** °maturity, °discretion; °majority, adulthood, seniority: *When he comes of age he will inherit millions.* **3** °period, °stage, °time: *Among these people, both boys and girls undergo rites of passage at the age of puberty. He is a man of middle age.* **4** °long °time, aeon or *esp. US* eon; years: *I haven't seen you for an age! The noise went on for ages.* **5** °era, epoch, °period, °time: *The 18th century was known as the Augustan Age in England.*
—*v.* **6** °grow °old(er), °mature, °ripen: *O, Matilda, I age too fast for my years! You must first age the whisky in the barrel, then bottle it.*

aged *adj.* °old, °elderly, superannuated, °ancient, age-old, °grey, °venerable: *The three aged women crouched in their chairs, each with her own memories.*

agency *n.* °means, °medium, instrumentality; intervention, intercession, °action, inter-mediation; °operation, °mechanism, °force, °power, °activity, working(s), °energy: *Pollen is carried from flower to flower by the agency of certain insects.*

agent *n.* **1** °representative, °intermediary, °go-between, °proxy, emissary, °delegate, spokesman, spokeswoman, spokesperson, °deputy, °substitute, surrogate, °advocate, leg-ate, °envoy, °factor: *Our agent in Tokyo will look after the matter for you.* **2** °factor, °agency, °cause, °means, °force, °instrument, °power, °vehicle, °ingredient: *The active agent in this cleaner is ammonia.*

aggravate *v.* **1** °worsen, °intensify, exacerbate, °heighten, °magnify, °increase; °inflame: *They introduce new problems and aggravate the old ones.* **2** °exasperate, °frustrate; °anger, incense, °infuriate; °provoke, °irritate, nettle, rile, vex, °annoy, °harass, hector, °bother; embitter, °rankle, *Colloq* peeve, needle, °get on one's °nerves; *Slang Brit* give (someone) aggro: *Threats only serve to aggravate people.*

aggression *n.* **1** aggressiveness, °hostility, bel-ligerence, combativeness, *Slang Brit* aggro: *The mere crossing of the river is an act of aggression.* **2** °attack, °assault, onslaught, °invasion, encroachment: *The conflict had become a war of aggression.*

aggressive *adj.* **1** combative, °warlike, °martial, °belligerent, bellicose, °pugnacious, °quarrelsome, disputatious, litigious; °hostile, unfriendly: *The Germanic tribes were known to the Romans as aggressive and hardened warriors.* **2** °forward, °assertive, °forceful, °bold, *Colloq* °pushy: *Dennis's aggressive nature may yet make him a good salesman.*

aggressor *n.* °assailant, attacker, instigator, ini-tiator, provoker; °belligerent: *You will find that the Nazis were the aggressors in Poland in 1939.*

agile *adj.* **1** °nimble, quick, °brisk, °swift, °active, °lively, lithe, limber, spry, °sprightly: *Sofia is an agile dancer.* **2** °keen, °sharp, °alert, °dexterous or dextrous, °resourceful, °acute: *With his agile mind Richard was able to solve the problems in no time at all.*

agitate *v.* **1** °excite, °arouse, °rouse, °move, °perturb, °stir up, disquiet, °fluster, °ruffle, °rattle, disconcert, °discomfit, unsettle, °upset, °rock, °unnerve, °shake (up), *Colloq* dis-combobulate: *Rachel was agitated to learn of the bank's threat to foreclose on the mortgage.* **2** °push, °press, °campaign; °promote: *The miners have been agitating for better safety measures.* **3** °stir (up), churn, °disturb, °shake, roil: *The calm lake was agitated by the motor boats.*

agitated *adj.* moved, stirred (up), shaken (up), rattled, °disturbed, °upset, °nervous, per-turbed, jittery, °jumpy, uneasy, °ill at ease, fidgety, disquieted, discomfited, ruffled, flustered, °unsettled, unnerved, wrought up, discomposed, °disconcerted, aroused, roused, °excited, *Colloq* discombobulated: *The sheriff was in a very agitated state about the mob forming outside the jail.*

agitation *n.* **1** shaking, °disturbance, churning, °stirring, turbulence: *The agitation made the solu-tion become cloudy.* **2** °excitement, arousal, rabble-rousing, °provocation, °stirring up, °incitement, °ferment, stimulation, over-stimulation, commotion: *The organized agitation of the crowds continued for weeks after the coup.*

agitator *n.* activist, °rabble-rouser, incendiary, agent provocateur, insurrectionist, °troublemaker, demagogue, firebrand: *The oppos-ition party hires professional agitators to incite the people to riot.*

agog *adj.* °eager, avid, °keen, °enthusiastic, °expectant, °impatient, °breathless: *The children were all agog waiting for Santa Claus to come.*

agonizing *adj.* °painful, distressful, distressing, °harrowing, torturous, racking, °excruciating, tortured, tormented: *We went through an agon-izing reappraisal of our policy on immigration.*

agony *n.* °anguish, °trouble, °distress, °suffering, °misery, wretchedness, °pain, °pangs, °woe, °torment, throes, torture, °affliction: *For two days his parents experienced the agony of not knowing whether he was dead or alive.*

agree *v.* **1** concur, °conform, come or °go together, °coincide, °correspond, harmonize, °reconcile; °accord, °tally, *Colloq* jibe: *At last my cheque-book agrees with my bank state-ment!* **2** Often, **agree to**: °consent to, °favour, acquiesce in or to, °approve of, accede to, assent to: *They finally agreed to our offer. We agreed terms with respect to the contract.* **3** °concede, °grant, °consent, °admit, °approve, °allow, °accept, con-cur; accede (to), acquiesce (in or to), assent (to), see eye to eye: *The committee agreed that she should be given time to comply with the request. I objected and they agreed with me.* **4 agree with**: °suit: *The climate in England agrees with me, strange to say.*

agreeable *adj.* **1** °pleasing, °pleasant, enjoy-able, °pleasurable, °favourable, °delightful, °satisfying, °satisfactory, °good, °nice, °acceptable; to one's °liking or °taste: *He found the Caribbean an agreeable place for a holiday.* **2** in °favour, approving, °willing, consenting, acqui-escent, complying, compliant, in °agreement or °accord, concurring, amenable, °sympathetic, well-disposed; °accommodating, accom-modative: *If Anne's agreeable, we can leave tomorrow.*

agreement *n.* **1** °understanding, covenant, °treaty, °pact, °accord, °compact, °settlement, concordat; °contract, °bargain, *Colloq* °deal: *They drew up a ten-year agreement to be signed at the* summit in Geneva. **2** concord, °harmony, compatibility, °unity, concurrence, unanimity: *Agreement in error is far worse than division for the sake of truth.*

ahead adv. **1** at the or in °front, in °advance, in the °lead or vanguard, up ahead, °before, to the fore: *The general rode ahead.* **2** °winning: *At half time, our team was ahead by two points.* **3** °onward(s), forward(s), on: *Please move ahead if you can.*

aid v. **1** °help, °support, °assist, °facilitate, °back, °abet, °uphold, °promote; succour, °relieve, °subsidize: *The invasion was aided by Richard's subjects. He salved his conscience by aiding a local charity.*
—n. **2** °help, °support, °assistance, °backing, °relief, °benefit, °service, succour, °comfort: *He was convicted of giving aid to the enemy in time of war.* **3** funding, °subsidy, subvention; grant-money, °grant, grant-in-aid, °scholarship: *He could never have gone to university without aid from the endowment.*

aide n. aide-de-camp, °assistant, helper, coadjutor; good or strong right arm, right hand, right-hand man; °colleague, °partner, °ally, °comrade, comrade-in-arms, US cohort, Colloq man Friday, girl Friday, US gal Friday: *The general's aides are always at his side.*

ail v. **1** °trouble, °afflict, °affect, °bother, °distress, °upset, °worry, make °ill or °sick, °pain, °hurt: *I cannot imagine what ails him, and the doctor can find nothing wrong.* **2** °suffer, be or feel °ill or °poorly or unwell or °indisposed, US be °sick: *Granny has been ailing lately.*

ailment n. °illness, sickness, °affliction, °disease, °disorder, indisposition, malady; °disability, °infirmity; malaise, queasiness: *Granny's ailment has been diagnosed as influenza.*

aim v. **1** °direct, °point, °focus, °train, °level: *The guns of the fort are aimed at the narrow pass.* **2 aim at**: °focus on, have designs on, °aspire to, °plan for or on, set one's °sights on, °seek, °strive for, °try for, °wish, °want: *Edward aimed at absolute dominion over that kingdom.* **3** °seek, °intend, °plan: *I aim to retire at fifty, if not before.*
—n. **4** °direction, pointing, °focus, focusing or focussing, sighting: *His aim is so bad that he can't hit the side of a barn with a shotgun.* **5** °purpose, °goal, °ambition, °desire, °aspiration, °object, °end, °objective, °target, °intent, °intention, °plan: *It was never her aim in life to be rich. The aim of the book is set forth in the Foreword.*

aimless adj. **1** °purposeless, °pointless, °frivolous: *After receiving the inheritance she led an aimless life of ease and luxury.* **2** undirected, °erratic, °chance, °haphazard, °random, vagrant, wayward; °wanton: *We were annoyed by the tourists' aimless meandering round the village.*

air n. **1** °atmosphere, ambience or ambiance, °aura, °climate, °feeling, °sense, °mood, °quality: *This restaurant has a delightful air about it.* **2** °breeze, zephyr, °current, °draught; °breath, °puff, °wind: *Light airs sprang up from the south.* **3** °manner, °style, °appearance, °aura, °feeling, °bearing, °quality, °flavour: *Louis has a lugubrious air about him.* **4** °melody, °tune, °song, music: *She was humming airs from some Italian opera.* **5 airs**: °pretension, °pretence,

°show, affectedness; haughtiness, hauteur, °arrogance, °superiority, superciliousness: *He puts on such airs since he got his knighthood.*
—v. **6** ventilate, °freshen, °refresh, aerate: *The chambermaid is airing the room, so you can't go in now.* **7** °show off, °parade, °display, °exhibit; °publish, °broadcast, °circulate, °publicize, make °public or known, °reveal, °expose, °disclose, divulge, °tell, °express, °declare: *Once again Andrew is airing his views on modern art.*

akin adj. Usually, **akin to**: °related (to), allied or connected or °affiliated (to or with), associated (with), germane (to), °like, °alike, °similar (to): *Desultoriness is akin to indolence. Their decision not to show the film smacks of something akin to censorship.*

alarm n. **1** °warning, °alert, danger- or distress-signal; tocsin, bell, gong, °siren, whistle, horn: *At the approach of the storm, the lookouts gave the alarm. The alarm is set to wake me at four o'clock.* **2** °fear, °fright, apprehension, °dismay, trepidation, °terror, °dread, °anxiety, °excitement, °panic, consternation, °distress, nervousness, uneasiness, °discomfort: *He viewed with alarm the arrest of his next-door neighbours.*
—v. **3** °frighten, °scare, °daunt, °startle, °terrify, °panic; °unnerve, °dismay, °disturb, °upset: *She was alarmed at the news of the car crash. Don't be alarmed—such delays are quite normal.*

alcohol n. spirits, °liquor, the °bottle, the cup that cheers, demon rum, John Barleycorn, Colloq °booze, hard stuff, °juice, °moonshine, fire-water, Slang rot-gut, US and Canadian hooch: *Alcohol and driving do not mix.*

alcoholic adj. **1** °intoxicating, inebriating: *His doctor has forbidden him any alcoholic beverage.*
—n. **2** drunkard, °drunk, dipsomaniac, sot, toper, drinker, winebibber, serious or problem drinker, tippler, Colloq barfly, °soak, Slang boozer, alchy or alkie or alky, dipso, stew, rummy, US and Canadian °lush, booze-hound, wino: *The community runs a centre for rehabilitating alcoholics.*

alert adj. **1** °awake, °wide °awake, watchful, °vigilant, °attentive, heedful, °wary, °cautious, on the qui vive, °aware, on guard, on the °lookout, °observant, Colloq on the ball, on one's °toes: *The sentinels must remain alert throughout the night. Kenneth is alert to the perils of smoking cigarettes.* **2** °active, °nimble, °lively, °agile, °quick, spry, °sprightly, °vivacious: *He is an alert and joyous old soul.*
—n. **3** °lookout: *She is always on the alert for new ways of saving money.* **4** °alarm, °warning, °signal, °siren: *Sound the air-raid alert!*
—v. **5** °warn, °caution, °advise, °alarm, forewarn, °signal, °notify: *We must alert him to the fact that the man is a vicious killer.*

alibi n. **1** °excuse, °explanation: *Your alibi places you very close to the scene of the crime.*
—v. **2** °excuse, °explain: *Caught red-handed, she couldn't alibi her way out of it.*

alien adj. **1** °foreign, °strange, °exotic, °outlandish, °unfamiliar: *The customs of the country were alien to me.*
—n. **2** °foreigner, °stranger, outlander, °outsider, non-native, °immigrant, °newcomer: *Aliens are required to register during January.*

alienate v. Usually, **alienate from**: disabuse (of or from), wean away (from), °detach (from), °distance (from): *Gradually the villagers were alienated from their old animistic beliefs.*

alike *adj.* **1** °similar, °akin, resembling *or* °like one another, °akin to *or* °similar to one another, showing *or* exhibiting a °resemblance: *They began to think all religions were alike.*
—*adv.* **2** in °like manner, in the °same manner *or* way, similarly, equally, uniformly, identically: *She believes that all people should be treated alike.*

alive *adj.* **1** living, °live, breathing, among the living, in the land of the living: *My great-grandfather is still alive, in spite of years of defying medical advice.* **2 alive to:** °sensitive *or* °alert to, °aware *or* °conscious of, cognizant of: *She is alive to every slight nuance in the poem.* **3** °alert, °active, °lively, °vivacious, quick, °spirited, °animated, °brisk, spry, °sprightly, °vigorous, °energetic: *Look alive, my lads, and hoist away!* **4** astir, teeming, swarming, thronging, crowded, °packed, buzzing, crawling, jumping, bustling, humming, *Colloq* °lousy: *In a few minutes the water around the corpse was alive with deadly piranha.*

allegation *n.* °charge, °accusation, °complaint; °assertion, avowal, asseveration, °claim, °declaration, °statement, deposition: *I resent the allegation that I never do the washing up.*

allege *v.* °declare, aver, °state, assert, °charge, affirm, avow, asseverate, depose, °say: *The guard alleged that he had caught the boy climbing in a basement window.*

alleged *adj.* described, designated; claimed, avowed, stated; purported, °so-called, suspected, °supposed, °assumed, presumed; °hypothetical, conjectural: *The press reported that the alleged assailant had confessed. He is awaiting trial for his alleged involvement in the bombing.*

alliance *n.* **1** °union, confederation, °combination, °federation, °pact, °league, °association, coalition, affiliation, °connection, °bond; °unity, °affinity: *The alliance between the two empires has been faithfully maintained.* **2** °marriage, °affinity: *The alliance between the two families was welded by the children born of it.*

allot *v.* °distribute, apportion, allocate, earmark, °assign, °parcel *or* °dole out, °deal (out), °divide, °share (out), °dispense: *The millionaire allotted an equal share of his fortune to each of his children.*

allotment *n.* **1** °share, apportionment, °ration, °portion, °quota, °allowance, °measure: *Each prisoner was given a daily allotment of four ounces of black bread and a cup of water.* **2** garden °plot, °kitchen garden, °patch, °tract, °plot, *Brit* market garden, *US* truck garden: *If I don't answer the phone, it's because I am digging my allotment.*

allow *v.* **1** °acknowledge, °admit, °grant, °concede, own: *He allowed that he had not been completely truthful about his movements that night.* **2** °agree to, °concede, °cede to, °admit, °permit, °authorize, °entertain, °consent to: *The judge said that he would allow a plea of 'guilty with an explanation'.* **3** °permit, °let, °suffer: *Please allow the children to select their own friends.* **4** °tolerate, °stand (for), °brook, °sanction, countenance, °permit, °consider, °put up with: *The headmaster refuses to allow such goings-on at his school.* **5** °give, °let (someone) have, °appropriate, °grant, budget, earmark, °assign, allocate, °approve: *The company allowed him $100 a day for expenses.* **6** °make °allowance *or* concession for, °set °apart *or* aside, put aside, take into °account *or* °consideration; °add; °deduct:

You must allow at least an extra hour for the traffic during rush hour. The shipper allows ten kilos for the weight of the container.

allowance *n.* **1** °permission, toleration, °tolerance, sufferance, °admission, concession, °sanction; allowing, permitting, tolerating, °suffering, sanctioning, brooking, countenancing: *There were many causes of difference between them, the chief being the allowance of slavery in the south.* **2** °payment, recompense, °remuneration, reimbursement, °remittance: *Allowance will be made for all reasonable expenses.* **3** °stipend, °dole, pin *or* pocket °money, °quota, °ration; °pension, annuity, allocation: *Bill gets a liberal weekly allowance for expenses.* **4** °deduction, °discount, reduction, °rebate; °credit; tret; tare: *You must make allowance for the weight of the crate.* **5** °excuse(s), concession, °consideration: *Allowance must be made for his poor eyesight.*

alloy *n.* **1** °mixture, °mix, °combination, °compound, composite, °blend, °amalgam, admixture; aggregate: *Brass is an alloy of copper and zinc.*
—*v.* **2** °contaminate, °pollute, °adulterate, °debase, °diminish, °impair, °vitiate: *Their external prosperity was not alloyed by troubles from within.* **3** °change, °modify, °temper, °alter, °moderate, allay: *Gentle persons might by their true patience alloy the hardness of the common crowd.*

ally *n.* **1** °comrade, confederate, collaborator, coadjutor; °accessory, °accomplice; °associate, °partner, °friend: *I had hoped to have you as an ally in my proposal for reorganization. The Allies finally defeated the Nazi war machine in 1945.*
—*v.* **2** °league, °combine, °unite, °join (up), °team (up), °side, °band together, °associate, affiliate, °collaborate, confederate: *In their attempt at a take-over of our company, the raiders have allied themselves with two banks. We shall ally the Romans to us and conquer the territory.*

almost *adv.* °nearly, °about, °approximately, °practically, °virtually, wellnigh, bordering on, on the °brink of, verging on, on the °verge of, little short of; not °quite, all but; °barely, °scarcely, °hardly; *Colloq* damn °near: *We are almost ready to go. You almost broke the window!*

aloft *adv.* °above, °overhead, (up) in the °air, in °flight, up (above); on °high; heavenwards, skyward: *The plane was overloaded, but we finally made it aloft. Five women held the banner aloft.*

alone *adj.* **1** °unaccompanied, unescorted, °solitary, by oneself, tout(e) seul(e), °solo, unattended, unassisted; °abandoned, °desolate, °deserted: *I am alone in the world. Leave me alone.* **2** unequalled, °unparalleled, °unique, °singular, unexcelled, unsurpassed, without °equal, °peerless, °matchless: *As a poet, Don stands alone.*
—*adv.* **3** solitarily, by oneself, °solo: *I'll walk alone.* **4** °only, solely, exclusively, °simply, °just, °merely: *You alone can help me.*

aloof *adv.* **1** °apart, away, at a °distance, °separate; at arm's °length: *We invited Martha to join us but she preferred to remain aloof.*
—*adj.* **2** °private, °reticent, °reserved, °withdrawn, °haughty, °supercilious, °standoffish, °formal, unsociable, °unsocial; °distant, °remote: *Deirdre is quite an aloof sort of person—not what you would call a 'mixer'.* **3** °standoffish, °distant, °remote, °cool, °chilly,

unresponsive, unfriendly, antisocial,
°unapproachable; °unsympathetic, apathetic,
°indifferent, undemonstrative: *Roger keeps himself aloof from the needs of those less fortunate than
he is.*

alter *v.* °change, °revise, °modify, °vary,
°transform; °adjust, °adapt, °convert, remodel:
*After the attack, we altered our opinion of the rebels.
The dress fits better since being altered.*

alteration *n.* °change, modification, °revision,
°transformation; °adjustment, °adaptation,
conversion, remodelling: *We found places where
alterations had been made in the original document.
My new suit needs alteration to fit properly.*

alternate *v.* **1** °rotate, °exchange, °change,
interchange, take turns, go or take, etc. in
°turn, *US* °change off, interexchange: *To help
out, we could alternate our days off.* **2** °succeed,
be in °succession or rotation: *The wallpaper had
alternating stripes of pink, grey, and maroon.*
—*adj.* **3** in rotation, °successive; every other,
every °second: *The embankment revealed alternate
layers of clay and gravel. The nurse visited our district
on alternate days.* **4** °alternative, °second, other:
The alternate selection contains only milk chocolate.
—*n.* **5** °variant, °alternative, °(second) °choice,
US and Canadian °substitute, °deputy, °stand-in,
backup, °understudy; pinch-hitter, *Baseball* designated hitter: *I prefer the alternate to the featured
model. My alternate takes over if I am ill.*

alternation *n.* rotation, °succession; °exchange,
interchange: *In a temperate climate there is the
advantage of the alternation of the seasons.*

alternative *adj.* **1** °alternate, °variant,
(an)other, °different, additional; °substitute, surrogate: *Alternative models are available.*
—*n.* **2** °alternate, °variant, °choice, °option,
°selection; °possibility; °substitute, surrogate:
*The alternative was to remain at home and do nothing.
You leave me no alternative. 'Esthetic' is an American
spelling alternative.*

altogether *adv.* °entirely, °utterly, °completely,
°wholly, °totally, fully, in all respects,
°absolutely, °perfectly, °quite; all in all, in all: *I
don't altogether agree with you. Altogether, you may
be right.*

altruism *n.* selflessness, self-sacrifice, unselfishness, °philanthropy, generosity, °charity, charitableness, humanitarianism, humaneness,
°benevolence, °humanity, public-spiritedness:
*Nick does things for others out of altruism, expecting
nothing in return.*

always *adv.* **1** at all times, again and again, on
all occasions, every or each °time, each and
every °time, without °exception, unexceptionally; °often, °many times, °usually: *He
that indulges hope will always be disappointed. I have
always made coffee this way and see no reason for
changing.* **2** for ever, continually, °ever, perpetually; unceasingly, unendingly, eternally,
evermore, °ever after, everlastingly, till the end
of °time, in °perpetuity: *You are a fool, Mike, and
you will always be a fool.* **3** in any °case, as a last
resort: *You could always refuse to pay.*

amalgam *n.* °mixture, °blend, °combination,
°alloy, °mix, composite, admixture,
°amalgamation; °compound: *The population was
an amalgam of original settlers and new immigrants.*

amalgamate *v.* °blend, °combine, °unite, °mix,
°join, consolidate, °compound, °integrate,
°merge: *The four sentences of the original are amalgamated into two.*

amalgamation *n.* °blend, fusion,
°combination, °mixture, mingling, admixture,
composite, °compound, blending, joining, con-
solidating, consolidation, compounding, commingling, fusing, coalescing, coalescence,
°union, uniting, unification, integration,
°merger, °association, °composition: *The directors
voted for an amalgamation of the two companies
that would benefit both.*

amass *v.* °accumulate, °mass, °pile or °heap or
°rack up, °collect, °gather (together),
°assemble, aggregate, cumulate, °stock or °store
up, °hoard, °set aside: *How many points have you
amassed? Owing to the bountiful harvest, the farmers
amassed huge amounts of grain.*

amateur *n.* **1** layman, non-professional, tiro or
tyro; dabbler, °dilettante, bungler; *Colloq US*
bush-leaguer: *When it comes to repairing cars, I'm
a mere amateur.*
—*adj.* **2** °lay, non-professional, untrained;
°unpaid; °dilettante, amateurish,
°unprofessional, unskilled, inexpert, unskilful,
°clumsy, °mediocre, °inferior, °crude, bungling,
second-rate; *Colloq US* bush-league: *The amateur
theatre group's performance received excellent
reviews. These paintings are strictly amateur and
totally without merit.*

amaze *v.* °astound, °astonish, °surprise, awe,
°stun, °stagger, °take aback, °floor, °dumbfound
or dumfound, confound, °nonplus, stupefy,
Colloq flabbergast, °dazzle: *Annie Oakley amazed
audiences with her fancy shooting. I was amazed that
she still cared for me.*

amazement *n.* °astonishment, °surprise, awe,
°wonder, stupefaction: *He stared at her in amazement, sure that he had misunderstood what she was
saying.*

amazing *adj.* astonishing, astounding, surprising, wonderful, °remarkable,
°extraordinary, °marvellous, °fabulous,
°stunning, °dazzling, staggering, °awesome:
*The Cossacks put on an amazing display of horse-
manship.*

ambassador *n.* °envoy, °delegate, legate, emissary, °minister, plenipotentiary, diplomat;
°agent, °deputy, °representative, (papal) nuncio,
°messenger: *The ambassador must present his credentials to the queen.*

ambiguity *n.* **1** equivocalness, equivocacy,
amphibology or amphiboly; vagueness, indistinctness, uncertainty, indefiniteness, imprecision, inconclusiveness: *Ambiguity of language
must be avoided in legal documents.* **2** equivocation,
double-talk, double-speak, equivoque; °pun,
double entendre, amphibologism: *The minister's
speech was full of ambiguities.*

ambiguous *adj.* **1** °equivocal, amphibological,
amphibolic or amphibolous; misleading: *If one
says 'Taylor saw Tyler drunk', which one was drunk
is ambiguous.* **2** °doubtful, dubious,
°questionable, °obscure, °indistinct, unclear,
°indefinite, indeterminate, °uncertain,
undefined, °inconclusive, uncertain, °vague,
°misty, foggy; °cryptic, Delphic, enigmatic(al),
oracular, °mysterious, °puzzling; confusable:
*The soothsayer's prophecies were sufficiently ambigu-
ous to allow for several conflicting interpretations.*

3 °unreliable, undependable: *How can the doctor decide on a correct diagnosis when the symptoms are ambiguous?*

ambition *n.* **1** °hunger, °thirst, craving, °appetite, arrivisme: *John's relentless ambition may yet be his undoing.* **2** °drive, °enterprise, °energy, °initiative, °vigour, °enthusiasm, zeal, avidity, *Colloq* get-up-and-go: *The company is seeking young men of ambition. You'll never get anywhere, Stewart, since you are totally lacking in ambition.* **3** °goal, °object, °aim, °aspiration, °hope, °desire, °dream, °objective, °wish, °purpose: *It is Olivia's ambition to marry someone with a title.*

ambitious *adj.* **1** aspiring, °hopeful; °enthusiastic: *My son, I am just as ambitious for you as you are for yourself.* **2** °energetic, °enterprising, °vigorous, zealous, °enthusiastic, °eager: *We prefer ambitious young people to those who are seeking a sinecure.* **3** °greedy, °avaricious, overzealous, over-ambitious, *Colloq* °pushy, yuppy: *Howard is a trifle too ambitious, expecting to be department head after only one year.*

ambush *n.* **1** °trap, ambuscade or *Archaic* ambuscado: *The company set up an ambush near the crossroads.* —*v.* **2** lie in wait, °trap, °waylay, ensnare, entrap, °lurk, ambuscade, °intercept, *Colloq* lay in wait, *US* bushwhack: *The guerrillas were ready to ambush the soldiers.*

amend *v.* **1** °reform, change for the better, °improve, °better, ameliorate: *The prisoner believes he could amend his ways if given the chance.* **2** °correct, emend, emendate, °rectify, set to °rights, °repair, °fix, °revise: *Take whatever time you need to amend the text.*

amendment *n.* **1** °correction, emendation, reformation, °change, °alteration, rectification, °repair, °reform, °improvement, amelioration, betterment, enhancement: *The committee approved the amendment of the constitution by the addition of the suggested paragraphs.* **2** °attachment, °addition, addendum; clause, paragraph; °alteration: *A two-thirds majority in the Congress is needed to pass the amendment.*

amends *n.* **make amends**: °compensate, °pay, °repay, make reparation or °restitution, recompense, redress, °remedy, °requite: *How can I make amends for the way I've treated you?*

amiable *adj.* °friendly, well-disposed, °kindly, °kind, °amicable, °agreeable, congenial, °genial, °warm, winsome, °winning, affable, °pleasant, °obliging, °tractable, approachable, °benign, °good-natured, good-hearted, kind-hearted; °affectionate: *Melissa is well named for her sweet and amiable disposition.*

amicable *adj.* °friendly, °amiable, congenial, °harmonious, °brotherly, kind-hearted; °warm, °courteous, °cordial, °polite, °civil, °pleasant; °peaceful, °peaceable: *Our countries have always enjoyed the most amicable relations.*

amid *prep.* mid, in or into the °middle or °midst or °centre of, amongst, °among, surrounded by, in the °thick of, *Literary* amidst: *She is sitting in her cottage, Amid the flowers of May. Without further ado, she plunged amid the waves.*

amiss *adj.* **1** °wrong, at °fault, awry, out of °order, °faulty, °defective, °improper, °untoward; astray, °erroneous, fallacious, °confused, °incorrect, °off: *Something is amiss with the ignition. If I am amiss in my thinking, let me know.* —*adv.* **2** °wrong, awry, °badly, °poorly, imperfectly; inopportunely, unfavourably, unpropitiously: *Everything possible has already gone amiss with the rocket launch.* **3** wrongly, improperly, °badly; incorrectly, inappropriately: *A word of advice might not come amiss here.* **4** **take** or **think (it) amiss**: °mistake, °misinterpret, °misunderstand, take °offence (at): *I trust that you will not take amiss what I intended as constructive criticism.*

among *prep.* **1** amongst, °amid, amidst, mid, in the °midst or °middle or °centre of, surrounded by: *Please take a seat among the people over there. We lay down among the flowers.* **2** amongst, to each or all (of): *The examination booklets were passed out among the students.*

amount *v.* **1 amount to**: **a** °add up to, °total, aggregate, °come (up) to: *Waiter, what does my bill amount to, please?* **b** °become, °develop into: *That son of his will never amount to much.* —*n.* **2** °quantity, °volume, °mass, °expanse, °bulk, °supply, °lot; °number; °magnitude: *What amount of water is needed to fill the container? She eats a huge amount of chocolates every day.* **3** (°sum) °total, aggregate, °extent, °entirety: *What is the amount of the invoice without the tax?*

ample *adj.* **1** °broad, °wide, °spacious, °extensive, °expansive, °great: *Her ample bosom heaved with sobs.* **2** wide-ranging, °extensive, °broad: *In one ample swoop they snatched up all the land.* **3** °abundant, °extensive, °fruitful: *The event proved a very ample subject for history.* **4** °abundant, °full, °complete, °plentiful, copious, °generous, °substantial; °sufficient, °adequate, °enough: *He had stored ample provision of food for the winter.* **5** °liberal, unsparing, unstinted, unstinting, °generous, °substantial, °large, °lavish: *Steve's contributions have always been ample, especially at Christmas time.* **6** copious, °full, °broad, °detailed, °extensive, extended, °thorough: *The subject deserves more ample treatment.*

amplify *v.* **1** broaden, °widen, °extend, °increase, °expand (on), °enlarge (on), expatiate on, °detail; °add to, augment, °supplement: *Let no man comfort him But amplify his grief with bitter words.* **2** °exaggerate, °overstate, °magnify, °stretch: *The reports have amplified the number of horsemen slain in the encounter.* **3** °enlarge (on), °elaborate (on), °stretch, °lengthen, °detail, °embellish, embroider: *He amplifies every point in microscopic detail.*

amply *adv.* **1** °widely, broadly, extensively, greatly, expansively: *This fabric stretches amply enough to fit over the couch.* **2** to a °great °extent, °largely, fully, abundantly: *My confidence in her was amply recompensed by her success.* **3** abundantly, fully, copiously: *The prophecy was amply fulfilled.* **4** fully, °well, liberally, unstintingly, generously, °richly, °substantially, lavishly; sufficiently: *He has been amply paid for his work.*

amulet *n.* °charm, °talisman, good-luck piece; °fetish: *Whenever the man rubbed the silver amulet, his number would win.*

amuse *v.* **1** °divert, °entertain, °please, °beguile, °interest, °occupy: *Perhaps the crossword puzzle will* *amuse her while she is waiting.* **2** make °laugh, °delight, °cheer, *Colloq* °tickle: *That form of rowdy slapstick doesn't amuse me.*

amusement *n.* **1** °entertainment, °diversion, °recreation, °pleasure, °relaxation, °distraction, °enjoyment, °fun, °sport, °joke, °lark, beguilement: *The boys in my class used to pull the wings off flies for amusement. They spent their afternoons in the amusement arcade.* **2** °entertainment, °diversion, divertissement, °recreation, °distraction, °pastime; °game, °sport: *During the festival there are concerts, plays, and other amusements.*

anachronism *n.* misdate, misdating, mis-application; antedate, antedating, pro-chronism; postdate, postdating, parachronism: *The poster showing Cleopatra smoking a cigarette is an anachronism—a prochronism, to be specific.*

analyse *v.* **1** °take °apart or to pieces, °separate, dissect, °break down, anatomize: *If we analyse these statistics for England and Wales, we find no pattern. The scientists are analysing the internal constitution of a glacier.* **2** °examine, °investigate, °study, °scrutinize, °interpret; assess, °evaluate, critique, °criticize, °review; °estimate, assay, °test: *We must first explicitly define and analyse the nature of the sample we found.*

analysis *n.* **1** °examination, °investigation, °study, °scrutiny, enquiry or °inquiry, dissection, assay, °breakdown, °division: *The analysis has shown the presence of arsenic in her soup.* **2** °interpretation, °opinion, °judgement, °criticism, critique; °review: *She disagrees with our analysis of the poem.*

ancestor *n.* forebear, forefather; °forerunner, °precursor, antecedent, *Formal* °progenitor, primogenitor: *His ancestors were transported to Australia in a prison ship, and he's proud of it. The eohippus, only a foot high, was the ancestor of the horse.*

anchor *n.* **1** mooring: *The ship rode at anchor in the harbour.* **2** °stability, °security, °mainstay, °support, stabilizer, holdfast, sheet anchor: *Marie is an anchor to windward for George, who tends to be a bit irresponsible.* —*v.* **3** °attach, affix, °secure, °moor, °fix, °fasten; °pin, rivet, °glue: *You must anchor the foundation before adding the walls. She remained anchored to the spot, refusing to move.*

ancient *adj.* **1** °old, °bygone, °past, °former, earlier, *Literary* olden: *In ancient times there were very few books.* **2** °old, °antique, antediluvian, °primitive, °prehistoric, primeval or *Brit also* primaeval, primordial, Noachian, *Literary* Ogygian: *In those ancient days man had only just come down from the trees.* **3** °old, °old-fashioned, archaic, °time-worn, °aged, ageing, °obsolescent, °antiquated, °elderly, °venerable, °grey, hoary, superannuated, °obsolete, fossil, fossilized: *We were accosted by an ancient crone at the mouth of the cave.*

anger *n.* **1** °rage, wrath, ire, °fury, pique, spleen, choler; °antagonism, irritation, vexation, °indignation, °displeasure, °annoyance, irritability, °resentment, °outrage: *Her anger got the better of her, so she simply punched him.* —*v.* **2** °enrage, °infuriate, °madden, pique, incense, °raise one's hackles, make one's blood °boil, rile, °gall; °annoy, °irritate, vex, nettle, °displease, °exasperate, °provoke: *Father was so angered by the insult that he refused to pay.*

angle[1] *n.* **1** °slant, °oblique, corner, °edge, intersection; °bend, cusp, °point, apex, °projection: *The two walls meet at an angle.* **2** °slant, point of °view, °aspect, °viewpoint, °standpoint, °approach, °position, °side, °perspective: *The managing editor told me he's looking for a new angle on the kidnapping story.*

angle[2] *v.* **angle for**: fish for; °look for, °seek, be after, °try for, °hunt for: *On holiday we went angling for perch. Fran is angling for compliments on her new dress.*

angry *adj.* **1** enraged, °furious, irate, °resentful, ireful, wrathful, piqued, incensed, infuriated, fuming; irritated, °irritable, annoyed, vexed, irascible, provoked, °indignant, exasperated, splenetic, *Literary* wroth, *Colloq* livid, °hot under the collar, on the warpath, (all) steamed up, up in arms, °mad, *Slang* browned off, *Brit* cheesed off: *Father was angry with me for letting the cat out.* **2** °inflamed, irritated, °sore, smarting: *He has an angry lesion where the fetters rubbed against his ankles.*

anguish *n.* **1** °suffering, °pain, °agony, °torment, torture, °misery: *She endured the anguish of toothache rather than go to the dentist.* **2** °suffering, °grief, °distress, °woe, °anxiety: *He underwent terrible anguish in the waiting-room till the surgeon arrived.* —*v.* **3** °disturb, °upset, °distress, °afflict, °trouble; °torment, torture: *The anguished cries of prisoners could be heard.*

animal *n.* **1** °creature, being, mammal, °organism: *Scientists are unlikely to employ the popular division of all things into animal, vegetable, or mineral.* **2** °beast, °brute, °savage, °monster: *Think of the poor girl married to that animal!* —*adj.* **3** zoological, zooid, animalistic: *The sponge is a member of the animal kingdom.* **4** °physical, fleshly, °sensual, °gross, °coarse, °unrefined, uncultured, uncultivated, °rude, °carnal, °crude, bestial, beastlike, subhuman: *His animal appetites occasionally got the better of him.*

animate *v.* **1** °activate, °enliven, invigorate, °stimulate, inspirit, °excite, °stir, °vitalize, °spark, vivify, revitalize, breathe °life into, innervate: *A little enthusiasm would have animated their dull relationship.* **2** °inspire, inspirit, °stimulate, actuate, °move, °motivate, °incite, °rouse, °arouse, °excite, °fire (up), °encourage, °energize, °vitalize, °spur (on or onwards): *He spent the few minutes before the battle in animating his soldiers.* —*adj.* **3** °lively, °spirited, °vivacious, °animated, quick: *A courser more animate of eye, Of form more faultless never had been seen.* **4** °alive, °moving, breathing, *Archaic* quick: *Although they move, plants are not considered to be animate.*

animated *adj.* **1** °lively, °quick, °spirited, °active, °vivacious, °energetic, °vigorous, °excited, °ebullient, °enthusiastic, °dynamic, vibrant, °ardent, enlivened, °passionate, °impassioned, °fervent: *In the corner, Terence was engaged in an animated conversation with Mary.* **2** °mechanical, automated, °lifelike, °moving: *Each Christmas, the shop has an animated window display.*

animation *n.* **1** °spirit, spiritedness, °vitality, °dash, élan, °zest, °fervour, °verve, liveliness, °fire, °ardour, ardency, exhilaration, °intensity, °energy, °pep, °dynamism, °enthusiasm, °excitement, °vigour, vivacity: *Johnson was in high* *spirits, talking with great animation.* **2** enlivenment, liveliness, energizing, invigoration, enlivening, innervation: *The scout leader was credited with the animation of the youths in his care.*

animosity *n.* °hostility, °antagonism, antipathy, °ill will, malevolence, enmity, hatred, animus, °loathing, detestation, °contempt; °bad blood, malice, °bitterness, acrimony, °resentment, °rancour: *The animosity he felt for his brother soon disappeared.*

announce *v.* **1** °proclaim, make °public, °make known, °set *or* °put forth, °put out, °publish, advertise, °publicize, promulgate, °broadcast, herald; °circulate; °tell, °reveal, °disclose, divulge, °declare, °propound: *The appointment of a new prime minister has been announced.* **2** °intimate, °suggest, °hint at, °signal: *The sight of a top hat announced Gordon's presence in the club.* **3** °declare, °tell, °state, aver, assert, asseverate; °notify; °confirm: *The president announced that he was resigning because of the scandal.* **4** foretell, betoken, augur, portend, presage, °harbinger, herald; °signal; °precede: *The sighting of the first crocus announces spring.*

announcement *n.* **1** °declaration, °pronouncement, °proclamation, °statement: *Ladies and gentlemen, I wish to make an announcement.* **2** notification, °notice, °word: *We received an announcement of the wedding but no invitation.* **3** commercial, °advertisement, advert, ad, °spot: *The window was filled with announcements of houses for sale.* **4** °report, °bulletin, communiqué, disclosure: *An announcement has just been received from the fire-fighters at the scene.*

announcer *n.* presenter, °master of ceremonies, °master of the revels, MC, emcee, °reporter, anchorman, anchorwoman, °anchor; newsreader, newscaster, sportscaster, weatherman, weathergirl: *The announcer didn't get my name right.*

annoy *v.* **1** °irritate, °bother, °irk, vex, nettle, °get on (someone's) °nerves, °exasperate, °provoke, incense, rile, °madden, *Colloq* °get at: *The anonymous telephone calls were beginning to annoy us.* **2** °pester, °harass, harry, badger, °nag, °plague, °molest, bedevil, *Colloq* °bug, needle, hassle, *Slang* °get up someone's nose: *Stop annoying me with your persistent requests for money.*

annoyance *n.* **1** irritation, °bother, vexation, exasperation, pique, aggravation, *Colloq* botheration: *Must I put up with the annoyance of that constant bickering?* **2** °nuisance, °pest, irritant, °bore, *Colloq* °pain, °pain in the neck *or* arse *or* US ass: *He's such an annoyance, I wish he'd leave.*

answer *n.* **1** °reply, °response; rejoinder, °retort, riposte, *Colloq* comeback: *The boy's answer is unprintable.* **2** *Law* defence, counter-statement, °plea, °explanation; *Technical* °declaration, replication, rejoinder, surrejoinder, rebutter *or* °rebuttal, surrebutter *or* surrebuttal: *Her answer to the charge was 'Not Guilty'.* **3** °solution, °explanation: *Ten points were taken off because I had the wrong answer to question three.* —*v.* **4** °reply, °respond; °retort, rejoin, riposte: *When I ask you a question, I expect you to answer.* **5** °satisfy, °fulfil, °suffice for, °meet, °suit, °serve, °fit, °fill, °conform to, correlate with: *The bequest answered my needs for the moment.* **6 answer back**: °talk back (to): *How dare you answer your father back!* **7 answer for**: **a** be °accountable *or* °responsible *or* answerable for, be to °blame

for; take *or* undertake responsibility for; °sponsor, °support, °guarantee: *I answer alone to Allah for my motives. So shall my righteousness answer for me.* **b** make °amends for, °atone for, °suffer the consequences of: *Caesar was ambitious and he answered for it with his life.* **c** take *or* accept the blame for: *Andy shouldn't have to answer for his brother's shortcomings.*

antagonism *n.* **1** °opposition, °animosity, enmity, °rancour, °hostility, antipathy: *It is difficult to understand your antagonism towards classical music.* **2** °conflict, °rivalry, °discord, °dissension, °friction, °strife; contention: *Giving jobs only to personal friends has engendered antagonism.*

antagonist *n.* °adversary, °opponent, °enemy, foe; contender, °competitor, °competition, °opposition: *The antagonists prepared to fight.*

anticipate *v.* **1** °forestall, °intercept, °preclude, obviate, °prevent; nullify: *She anticipated her opponent's manoeuvre by moving the queen's bishop one square.* **2** foretell, °forecast, °predict, °prophesy, foretaste, °foresee: *He anticipated that flying would be a future mode of locomotion.* **3** °expect, °look forward to, °prepare for; °count *or* °reckon on: *We eagerly anticipated the arrival of Uncle Robert.*

anticipation *n.* **1** °expectation, expectancy, °hope: *In anticipation of the arrival of Father Christmas, we hung up our stockings.* **2** foreknowledge, precognition; °intuition, presentiment, °feeling; °foreboding, apprehension: *His anticipation of the solar eclipse by a week established him as the foremost scientist of his day.*

antidote *n.* antitoxin, antiserum, antivenin; counteractant, counterirritant; °cure, °remedy, °specific; medication, °medicine, °drug, medicament, *Technical* alexipharmic: *The old prospector says that the best antidote against snakebite is whisky.*

antiquated *adj.* °old, °old-fashioned, outmoded, °passé, out of °date, dated, archaic, °obsolescent, °antique, °obsolete, °quaint, °ancient, antediluvian, medieval *or* mediaeval, °primitive; °extinct; *Colloq* °old hat: *Antiquated laws list penalties for practising witchcraft.*

antique *adj.* **1** °old, °old-fashioned; °antiquated, outmoded, °passé, out of °date, °obsolete: *She wore the antique clothing she had found in the trunk.* —*n.* **2** collectable *or* collectible, collector's °item, bibelot, objet d'art, objet de vertu, °object *or* article of virtu, heirloom, curio, °rarity: *His hobby is collecting antiques.*

anxiety *n.* **1** °solicitude, °concern, uneasiness, disquiet, nervousness, °worry, °dread, angst, apprehension, °foreboding: *Philip began to feel genuine anxiety over Tanya's safety.* **2** °appetite, °hunger, °thirst, °desire, °eagerness, °longing, °ache, °concern: *It is every person's anxiety to obtain for himself the inestimable pearl of genuine knowledge.*

anxious *adj.* **1** troubled, uneasy, disquieted, °uncertain, apprehensive; °solicitous, °concerned, °worried, distressed, °disturbed, °nervous, °tense, °fretful, on °edge, °restless, edgy, perturbed, °upset; °wary, °cautious, °careful, watchful: *She has been terribly anxious about the diagnosis. We were anxious for her safety.* **2** °desirous, °eager, °keen, °enthusiastic, °ardent, °agog, avid, yearning, °longing, aching, °impatient: *I was anxious to visit the Pitti Palace once again.*

apart adv. **1** aside, to one side, by oneself, at a °distance, °separate, °separately: *He stood apart when the awards were given out.* **2** °separately, distinctly, °individually, °singly, °alone, independently: *The provisions of the bill should be seen together as a whole, not viewed apart.* **3** to or into pieces, asunder: *At the touch of the button, the building blew apart.* **4 apart from**: °except for, excepting, °separately from, aside from, °besides, but for, not including, excluding, not counting: *Apart from the immediate family, no one knows of your indiscretions.*

aperture n. °opening, °space, °gap, cleft, °chink, °crevice, °crack, fissure, °hole, chasm: *As much water ran through as the aperture could accommodate.*

apologetic adj. °regretful, °sorry, contrite, °remorseful, °penitent, rueful, °repentant, conscience-stricken: *The lad was most apologetic for having broken the window.*

apologize v. **1** beg or ask pardon, °express °regret(s), feel °sorry or °regretful or °remorse(ful): *You needn't apologize for sneezing.* **2** make or give °excuses or °explanation(s), °defend, °justify, °vindicate, espouse: *You don't have to apologize for her.*

appal v. °dismay, °shock, °discomfit, °unnerve, °intimidate, °terrify, °frighten, °scare, °horrify, °alarm, °startle, °daunt: *The council were appalled to discover that the police superintendent was accepting bribes.*

apparatus n. °equipment, requisites, °tool, °instrument, utensil, °device, °implement, °machine, machinery, °gear, °paraphernalia, °tackle, °outfit; appliance, *Colloq* °contraption, gadgetry, °gadget: *The apparatus needed for the experiment is here.*

apparel n. clothing, attire, °clothes, °dress, raiment, °garments, *Colloq* °gear, rags, glad °rags, duds, *Slang US* threads: *The police found various items of apparel strewn about the flat.*

apparent adj. **1** °evident, °plain, °clear, °obvious, °patent, unmistakable; °conspicuous, °marked, °manifest, °visible, °discernible: *It was apparent to all of us that she would become a successful opera singer.* **2** appearing, °seeming, °illusory, ostensible, °superficial, °outward: *In an apparent show of strength, he ordered his forces to attack the capital.*

apparently adv. **1** °evidently, plainly, °clearly, °obviously, patently, °manifestly: *There is apparently no cure in sight for the disease.* **2** °seemingly, °ostensibly, superficially, °outwardly: *In stop-action photography, the bullet apparently hangs in mid-air.*

appeal v. **1** entreat, supplicate, °solicit, °plead, °petition, °apply, °sue; °beseech, °beg, implore, °pray: *She appealed to the king to release her son from the dungeon.* **2** °attract, be °attractive to, allure, °please; invite, °tempt, °beguile, °fascinate, °interest: *He seems to appeal to older women.*
—n. **3** °application, °suit; entreaty, °call, °request, °supplication, solicitation, °petition, °plea; °prayer: *Her appeal to the court has been dismissed. I don't know if God heard our appeal.* **4** °attraction, °lure, allurement, °charm, °fascination: *It is not hard to see why his type would have some appeal.*

appear v. **1** come forth, become °visible or °manifest, put in an °appearance, °materialize,

°surface, °emerge, °rise, °arise, °come up, °enter (into) the picture, °show oneself, °turn up, °arrive, °come, *Colloq* crop or °show up; *Slang* °show: *Suddenly, a vision appeared before me. His wife appeared after an absence of ten years.* **2** °perform, °act, °play, take the role or part of: *She has appeared as Roxanne in dozens of productions of Cyrano de Bergerac.* **3** °occur, °happen, °come up, be included, °figure, °arrive: *That four-letter word does not appear in written form till the 20th century.* **4** °seem, be °clear or °evident or °plain or °manifest; °look: *It appears that the money was taken while the manager was at lunch.* **5** be published, °come out, become °available: *The next issue will appear in March.*

appearance n. **1** °arrival, advent; °presence; °publication: *I was awaiting the appearance of the book in the shops.* **2** °aspect, °look(s), °form; mien, °air, demeanour; °bearing, °manner: *The doorman would not let him in because of his shabby appearance.* **3** °display, °show: *Their fine horses with their rich trappings made a splendid appearance.* **4** °semblance, °show, °hint, °suggestion; °illusion: *She gave no appearance of wanting to go.*

appetite n. **1** °desire, °inclination, proclivity, °tendency, °disposition, °bent, °preference, °liking, predilection, °zest, fondness, °love, zeal; °enthusiasm; °taste, °relish; *Formal* appetency, appetence: *I have never lost my appetite for chocolate. They tried to suppress their bodily appetites, such as hunger and lust.* **2** craving, °hunger, °thirst, °desire, keenness, hankering, yearning, °longing, °passion, °demand, *Formal* edacity: *She developed an insatiable appetite for reading.*

applaud v. **1** °approve, °express °approval, °clap, °cheer, give (someone) a °hand, *Colloq* °root (for): *The audience applauded when the villain was caught.* **2** °express °approval of, °praise, °laud, °hail, commend: *Susan's parents applauded her decision to apply for university.*

applause n. clapping, acclamation, acclaim, éclat; cheering, °cheers; °approval, commendation, approbation, °praise, °kudos, plaudit(s): *At the curtain there was applause from the audience.*

applicable adj. °fit, °suitable, suited, °appropriate, °proper, apropos, °fitting, °befitting, °pertinent, apt, germane, °right, °seemly, °relevant, apposite: *Are the laws of the mainland applicable to the islands?*

application n. **1** °use, °employment, utilization, °practice, °operation: *The committee wants to see a sterner application of the law with respect to mail-order offers.* **2** relevancy, °relevance, °reference, pertinence, germaneness, appositeness; °bearing: *The application of the regulation to present circumstances is somewhat vague.* **3** °attention; diligence, industriousness, °effort, °perseverance, °persistence, assiduity, °devotion, °dedication, commitment, attentiveness, *Colloq* stick-to-it-iveness; °industry: *Her application to her studies leaves little time for recreation. Without application, you will never develop much skill at the piano.* **4** °request, solicitation; °appeal, °petition, °claim: *Gavin made six job applications. The board will consider your application.*

apply v. **1** °fasten, °fix, affix, °stick, °cement, °glue: *The signs were applied to the window with a special substance.* **2** °administer, °rub in or on, embrocate: *The doctor said to apply this ointment* *before retiring.* **3** °appropriate, °assign, °allot, °credit; °use, utilize, °employ, put to °use: *He had many skills, but failed to apply them in his daily work. The money raised for food was illegally applied to paying the administrators.* **4** °bear, have °bearing; be °relevant, °refer, °pertain, appertain, °relate, °suit: *I am not sure that the law applies to this situation.* **5** °devote, °dedicate, °commit, °focus, °concentrate, pay °attention, °address; do, °attend, °tend, *Colloq* °buckle down (to): *He stubbornly applies himself to the task at hand.* **6** °seek, °go after; °register, °bid, °try out, °put in; audition, °interview, make °application: *Are you qualified to apply for a job as a nanny?* **7** °petition, °solicit; °appeal, °request: *Geraldine applied to the court for compensation.*

appoint *v.* **1** °fix, °set, °settle, °determine, ordain, °authorize, °establish, °destine, °arrange, °assign, °allot, °prescribe, °decree: *The time appointed for the execution has been delayed.* **2** °name, °designate, °nominate, °elect; °assign, °delegate, commission, deputize; °select, °choose: *I was delighted to have been appointed as chairman.* **3** °equip, °fit out, °furnish, °decorate: *They live comfortably in a well-appointed home in the suburbs.*

appointment *n.* **1** °meeting, °date, rendezvous, °engagement; assignation, tryst: *You are again late for your appointment.* **2** nomination, °election; °assignment, designation; °selection, °choice: *We fully approve of his appointment as chairman.* **3** °job, °position, °post, °situation, °office, °place, °assignment, *Colloq* berth, °slot: *He got the appointment as manager.*

appreciate *v.* **1** value, find °worthwhile or valuable; °esteem, °cherish, °enjoy, °admire, °rate or °regard °highly, °prize, °treasure, °respect: *I appreciate all you have done for me. Delia's contribution is not really appreciated.* **2** °increase or °rise or °gain in value or °worth: *The property in this area has been appreciating at a rate of about ten per cent a year.* **3** °understand, °comprehend, °recognize, °perceive, °know, be °aware or cognizant or °conscious of: *Do you appreciate the implications of the new tax law?*

appreciation *n.* **1** °gratitude, thankfulness, gratefulness, thanks; °acknowledgement; °obligation: *She is trying to think of an appropriate way to express her appreciation for all he has done.* **2** °increase, °rise, °advance, °growth, enhancement, °gain; aggrandizement: *The appreciation in the value of the shares made me very wealthy on paper—till the stock-market crash.* **3** °understanding, comprehension, °perception, °recognition, °knowledge, awareness; °realization, °enjoyment; °admiration: *It's fortunate that Richard's appreciation of the finer things in life is supported by his income.*

apprentice *n.* **1** °novice, tiro or tyro, °learner, starter, beginner, °greenhorn, *Colloq US* rookie: *Lever served as an apprentice in the soap factory.* —*v.* **2** indenture, °contract, °bind: *Cartwright was apprenticed to a carpenter before becoming a journeyman cabinet-maker.*

approach *v.* **1** °near, °advance, °draw or °come °near or nearer or °close or closer, *Formal* °come nigh: *Claude approached the table. As night approached, the sky darkened. With approaching manhood, you must take on more responsibilities.* **2** °approximate, °nearly equal, °come °close to, °compare with: *The total is beginning to approach*

your estimate. **3** °make advances or overtures to, °proposition, °propose to, °sound out, make (a) °proposal to, °solicit, *Colloq* °chat up: *Theo makes mincemeat of any man who tries to approach his daughter.* —*n.* **4 approaches**: advances, overtures, proposals, propositions: *Michelle had no intention of discouraging Pierre's approaches.* **5** access, °passage, °way, °path, °course; °entry: *The approach to the house was overgrown with brambles.* **6** °advance, °movement: *Our approach to the gates was being watched very carefully.* **7** °method, °procedure, modus operandi, °way, °technique, °style, °manner, °attitude, *Slang US* MO (= 'modus operandi'): *Our approach in dealing with the problem is different.*

appropriate *adj.* **1** °suitable, apt, °fitting, °fit, °proper, °right, °meet, °becoming, °befitting, °seemly, suited, apropos, °correct, germane, °pertinent, °happy, felicitous: *Will a dinner-jacket be appropriate attire? She has written a poem appropriate to the occasion.* —*v.* **2** °take, °take over, °seize, expropriate, arrogate, annex, impound; commandeer; °steal, °pilfer, filch, usurp, °make away or off with, *Colloq* °pinch, °lift, *Brit* °nick, *US* °boost: *The police appropriated the paintings. Somebody has appropriated my chair.* **3** °set aside or °apart, °devote, °assign, earmark, °allot, apportion: *Most of the money has been appropriated for back taxes.*

appropriately *adv.* fittingly, suitably, °properly, correctly, aptly, rightly, becomingly, meetly: *She came down appropriately dressed for dinner.*

approval *n.* °sanction, approbation, °blessing, °consent, °agreement, concurrence; °endorsement, acceptance, imprimatur, affirmation, éclat, confirmation, mandate, authorization; °licence, °leave, °permission, rubber °stamp, *Colloq* °OK, okay, °go-ahead, green light: *I don't think that the plan will meet with the committee's approval. We gave our approval to proceed.*

approve *v.* **1** Often, **approve of**: °allow, countenance, condone, °permit, °sanction, °authorize, °endorse, put one's imprimatur on, °agree (to), °accept, assent (to), °go along with, *Colloq* °OK or okay, give the green light or °go-ahead or one's °blessing (to), rubber-stamp: *The headmistress would never approve your leaving the building during classes.* **2** °confirm, affirm, °support, °ratify, °uphold, °subscribe to, °second, give the °stamp of °approval to; °favour, commend, °recommend: *Sheila Jones's appointment to the commission has been approved unanimously.* **3 approve of**: °sanction, consider °fair or °good or °right, °accept, °favour, °respect, be °partial to, °like, have °regard for, have a °preference for, °tolerate, °reconcile oneself to: *I always had the feeling that her father didn't quite approve of me.*

approximate *adj.* **1** °rough, °inexact, °loose, °imprecise, estimated, *Colloq* guestimated, ballpark: *The figures are only approximate, not exact.* —*v.* **2** °near, °approach, come °close to, °verge on: *Your estimates approximate those of the budget committee.* **3** °resemble, °approach, look or °seem °like; simulate: *The laboratory tests on rats approximate the way the virus behaves in humans.*

approximately *adv.* approaching; °nearly, °almost, °close to, °about, around, give or take,

°roughly, °generally: *I haven't seen Sally for approx-imately three weeks. There are approximately fifty people in the audience.*

aptitude *n.* **1** °fitness, suitability, appro-priateness, °relevance, applicability, suit-ableness, aptness: *One need only look at an albatross in the air to appreciate its aptitude for flight.* **2** °tendency, propensity, °disposition, predi-lection, °bent, proclivity; °talent, °gift, °ability, °capability, °facility, °faculty, °flair: *Helen dis-plays a natural aptitude for the violin.* **3** °intelligence, quick-wittedness, °intellect; °capacity, aptness: *The aptitude of that new student sets her apart from the others in the class.*

arbitrary *adj.* **1** °capricious, varying, °erratic, °uncertain, °inconsistent, °doubtful, un-predictable, °whimsical, irrational, °chance, °random, °subjective, unreasoned, *Colloq* chancy, iffy: *The choices are entirely arbitrary, totally at the whim of the council and not based on research or knowledge.* **2** °absolute, °tyrannical, °despotic, °authoritarian, magisterial, °summary, °peremptory, autocratic, °dogmatic, imperious, uncompromising, °inconsiderate, high-handed, °dictatorial, *Rare* thetic(al): *The conduct of the archbishop appears to have been arbitrary and harsh.*

arch *adj.* **1** °chief, °principal, °prime, °primary, °pre-eminent, °foremost, °first, greatest, con-summate, °major: *Moriarty was Holmes's arch-enemy.* **2** °clever, cunning, °crafty, roguish, °tricky, °shrewd, °artful, °sly, °designing: *Brendan loves to play his arch pranks on unsus-pecting friends.* **3** waggish, saucy, °mischievous, prankish: *I could tell from the lad's arch expression that he had thrown the snowball.*

ardent *adj.* °eager, °intense, zealous, °keen, °fervent, fervid, °passionate, avid, °fierce, °impassioned, °hot, °warm, °enthusiastic: *Diane was carrying on ardent love affairs with at least three men.*

ardour *n.* °eagerness, °desire, zeal, fervency, °burning °desire, keenness, °fervour, °passion, °heat, °warmth; °enthusiasm: *Bernadette has sup-ported the cause with great ardour.*

arduous *adj.* **1** °laborious, °difficult, °hard, °tough, °strenuous, onerous, °burdensome, back-breaking, *Formal* operose; °painful, tiring, °exhausting, wearisome, fatiguing, taxing, gruelling, °trying, °formidable: *The Sherpas were well equipped for the arduous climb. What an arduous task it is to read the proofs of a dictionary!* **2** °energetic, °strenuous, °vigorous: *Montrose made arduous efforts to reconstruct his army.*

area *n.* **1** °space, °room: *Is there enough floor area here for the carpet?* **2** °extent, °limit, compass, °size, °square footage, acreage: *The area of my greenhouse is thirty square feet.* **3** °space, °field, °region, °tract, °territory, °district, °zone, °stretch; °section, °quarter, °precinct, arron-dissement, °neighbourhood, locality, bailiwick, *US* °block: *An area was set aside for a garden. There has been a lot of crime in that area lately.* **4** °scope, °range, °extent, °breadth, compass, °section: *His studies cover only one area of Scottish history.* **5** court, courtyard, °enclosure, close, yard; °square, °ground, arena, °field, parade-ground, °parade: *The soldiers drill in the area behind the barracks.*

argue *v.* **1** °dispute, °debate, °disagree, °bicker, wrangle, °quarrel, squabble, °spar, °fight, remonstrate, altercate, *Colloq* chiefly *Brit* °row,

°scrap: *The couple next door are continually arguing with each other at the tops of their voices.* **2** °discuss, °reason, °debate, wrangle: *He would argue by the hour, but never for arguing's sake.* **3** make a °case, °talk, °plead, °debate, contend: *I cannot tell whether she's arguing for or against the proposition.* **4** °prove, evince, °indicate, °denote, °demonstrate, °show, establish, °suggest, °signify, betoken: *The increase in street crime argues that the police are not visible enough.* **5** °say, assert, °hold, °maintain, °reason, °claim, con-tend: *The defendant argued that he had never met the witness.* **6 argue into** or **out of**: °persuade or dissuade, °talk out of or into, °prevail (up)on; °convince: *I argued him out of sailing to Bermuda alone. She succeeded in arguing me into going to the tea dance.*

argument *n.* **1** °debate, °dispute, °disagreement, °quarrel, °controversy, polemic, wrangle, squabble, °tiff, spat, altercation; °conflict, °fight, °fracas, affray, °fray, Donny-brook, °feud, *Colloq* °row, falling-out, °scrap, barney: *The argument was about who had invented the wheel. The argument spilt out into the street.* **2** °point, °position, (line of) °reasoning, °logic, °plea, °claim, pleading, °assertion, contention, °case; °defence: *His argument has merit. Arthur's argument falls apart when he brings in the phlogiston theory.*

argumentative *adj.* °quarrelsome, dis-putatious, °belligerent, combative, con-tentious, litigious, °disagreeable, °testy: *Evelyn is irritable and argumentative.*

arise *v.* **1** °rise, °get up, °stand up, °get to one's feet, °wake up, °get out of bed, °awake: *We arose when Lady Spencer entered the room. I have arisen before dawn all my life.* **2** °rise, °go up, °come up, ascend, °climb; °mount: *The full moon arose in the eastern sky.* **3** °come up, be brought up, be mentioned, *Colloq* crop up: *The subject never would have arisen if the waiter hadn't spilt the wine on me.* **4** °spring up, °begin, °start (up), °originate, °come up, *Colloq* crop up: *A very unpleasant situation has arisen regarding the missing funds.*

aroma *n.* **1** °smell, °odour, °fragrance, °scent, °perfume, °savour, °bouquet; redolence: *Don't you just love to be awakened by the aroma of fresh coffee?* **2** °smell, °odour, °character, °aura, °atmosphere, °flavour, °hint, °suggestion: *There is an aroma of dishonesty about them that I can't quite identify.*

aromatic *adj.* °fragrant, °spicy, perfumed, °savoury, °pungent: *A most agreeable scent came from a bowl of aromatic herbs.*

around *adv.* **1** °about, °approximately, °nearly, °almost, °roughly; *circa*: *There were around a dozen of us in the place.* **2** °about, °everywhere, in every °direction, on all sides, all over, °throughout: *By this time the rebels were all around and we couldn't move.* **3** °round, °about, for every-one or all, *US also* °'round: *I don't think we have enough food to go around.* **4** °round, °about, all about, °everywhere, here and there, hither and thither, hither and yon, °far and wide: *The tinker travelled around selling his wares and repairing pots.* —*prep.* **5** °round, °about, °surrounding, encom-passing, enveloping, encircling, on all sides of, in all directions from, enclosing: *The fields around* the castle were cultivated by tenant farmers. **6** °about, °approximately, °roughly; circa: He was born around the turn of the century.

arouse v. **1** °awaken, °raise (up), °wake up, waken, °rouse, °revive, °stir (up): I was aroused by the noise and reached for my pistol. **2** °excite, °stir up, °stimulate, °awaken, °summon up, °spark, Colloq °turn on: My suspicions were aroused because she was carrying my umbrella. **3** °provoke, °encourage, °quicken, °foster, °call forth, °stir up, °kindle, °foment: The song aroused feelings of patriotism among the recruits.

arrange v. **1** °order, °dispose, array, °organize, °sort (out), systematize, °group, °set up, °rank, °line up, align, °form, °position: The teachers arranged the children according to height. The flowers were arranged in a vase so as to conceal the listening device. **2** °settle, °plan, °set (up), °organize, orchestrate, °manipulate, choreograph; predetermine, °decide, °prepare, °determine, prearrange, °devise, °bring about, contrive; °fix it: Everything has been arranged—you won't have to lift a finger. For a small fee I can arrange for you to win the first prize. **3** orchestrate, °score, °adapt: Flemburgh has arranged music for some of the best-known modern composers.

arrangement n. **1** °order, °disposition, grouping, °organization, array, °display, °structure, structuring, ordering, alignment, line-up, Colloq °set-up: Don't you care for the arrangement of the furniture, Milady? **2** °structure, °combination, construction, contrivance, °affair, °set-up: An arrangement of bricks served as a hearth. **3** °settlement, °agreement, terms, °plan, °contract, covenant, °compact: The arrangement called for Bosworth to get ten per cent of the gross profits. **4** orchestration, °score, instrumentation, °adaptation, °interpretation, °version: I prefer Fats Waller's arrangement of 'Sugar Blues'. **5 arrangements**: preparations, plans; °groundwork, planning: Arrangements have been made for the limousine to pick you up at five.

arrest v. **1** °stop, °halt, °check, °stall, °forestall, detain, °delay, °hinder, °restrain, °obstruct, °prevent, °block, °interrupt: The progress of the train has been arrested. **2** catch, °capture, °seize, apprehend, °take, °take in, °take into °custody, detain, Colloq °nab, °pinch, collar, bust, °run in, Brit °nick: Foxworthy was arrested crossing the border. **3** °slow, °retard, °stop: I'm afraid that we have here a case of arrested mental development. —n. **4** °seizure, °capture, apprehension, °detention, °restraint, Colloq bust, US collar: The police have made six arrests. **5** °stop, stoppage, °check, cessation: The doctor said it was a case of cardiac arrest. **6 under arrest**: in °custody, under °legal °restraint, in the hands of the law, imprisoned, arrested: You are under arrest for the murder of one Hugh Brown, and anything you say may be used in evidence against you.

arresting adj. °striking, °shocking, °remarkable, °impressive, electrifying, °stunning, °extraordinary, surprising, °dazzling: It is indeed an experience to be in the presence of such an arresting beauty.

arrival n. **1** coming, advent, °appearance: We have been awaiting your arrival for weeks. **2** °newcomer; °immigrant; °traveller, °passenger; °tourist; Australian °migrant, new °chum: The arrivals on flight 422 were questioned about a bearded passenger on the plane.

arrive v. **1** °come, make one's °appearance, °appear, °turn up, Colloq °show up; Slang °hit (town), °blow in: She arrived only two minutes before the plane was to take off. **2** °succeed, °prosper, °get °ahead (in the world), °reach the °top, Colloq °make it, °make the °grade, °get somewhere, °get there: Yuppies believe that once they own a Mercedes, they've arrived. **3 arrive at**: °come or °get to, °reach; attain: I think that Crumley has arrived at the stage in his career where he merits a promotion.

arrogance n. self-assertion, °impertinence, insolence, °presumption, °nerve, °effrontery, °gall, presumptuousness, self-importance, °conceit, egotism, hauteur, haughtiness, loftiness, °pride, hubris, pompousness, pomposity, °pretension, pretentiousness, °bluster, °snobbery, snobbishness, Colloq snottiness, Slang Brit °side: He has the arrogance to assume that I wish to see him again.

arrogant adj. **1** °presumptuous, assuming, self-assertive, °conceited, °egotistical, °pompous, °superior, °brazen, bumptious, cavalier: It would be most arrogant of me to take for myself the glory that rightfully belongs to the whole team. **2** °haughty, °overbearing, imperious, high-handed, overweening, °disdainful, °contemptuous, °scornful, °snobbish, °supercilious, °lofty, swaggering, Brit toffee-nosed; Colloq uppity, on one's °high horse, °high and °mighty, snotty: Since her husband was made a company director, she's become unbearably arrogant.

art n. **1** °skill, skilfulness, °ingenuity, °aptitude, °talent, artistry, craftsmanship; °knowledge, °expertise; °craft, °technique, adroitness, °dexterity, Colloq know-how: Little art is required to plant turnips. **2** artistry, artisticness; °taste, tastefulness: High art differs from low art in possessing an excess of beauty in addition to its truth. **3** °craft, °technique, °business, °profession, °skill: The fishermen can't employ their art with much success in so troubled a sea. **4** °knack, °aptitude, °faculty, °technique, mastery; °dexterity, adroitness: Conversation may be esteemed a gift, not an art. You have acquired the art of insulting people without their realizing it. **5** °trickery, craftiness, cunning, wiliness, slyness, guile, °deceit, duplicity, artfulness, cleverness, astuteness: You have to admire the art with which she wraps him round her little finger. **6 arts**: °wiles, °schemes, °stratagems, °artifices, °subterfuges, °tricks; °manoeuvres: She was expert in the arts which ladies sometimes condescend to employ for captivation.

artful adj. **1** °scheming, °wily, °sly, cunning, °foxy, °tricky, °crafty, °deceitful, underhand or underhanded, double-dealing, guileful, °disingenuous: That artful fellow managed to sell me a completely useless gadget. **2** °ingenious, °clever, °astute, °shrewd, °dexterous: She has practised her artful deceptions so long that nobody believes anything she says.

artifice n. **1** °skill, cunning, °trickery, °craft, craftiness, artfulness, guile, duplicity, °deception, °chicanery, underhandedness, shrewdness, slyness, wiliness, trickiness: He used artifice to get control of the firm. **2** °stratagem, °device, °manoeuvre, °trick, contrivance, °wile, °ruse, °subterfuge, °expedient, Colloq °dodge: They were deluded by artifices to cheat them out of their money.

artificial *adj.* **1** °unnatural, °synthetic, man-made, manufactured, simulated, °imitation, °plastic: *The museum has a strange collection of artificial teeth on display.* **2** made-up, concocted, °bogus, °fake, °sham, °false, °counterfeit, *Colloq* °phoney *or US also* phony: *The figures used in the sample survey are entirely artificial.* **3** °affected, °unnatural, °forced, °pretended, high-sounding, feigned, °assumed, contrived, °factitious; meretricious, °insincere, °sham, faked, *Colloq* °phoney *or US also* phony: *I tell you that Alan's concern for you is entirely artificial.*

artless *adj.* **1** °innocent, °sincere, guileless, °ingenuous, °true, °natural, °open, unartificial, °genuine, °simple, °direct, °candid, °frank, °honest, straightforward, °above-board, uncomplicated, undevious, undeceptive, *Colloq* upfront, on the °level, on the up and up: *Imitation is a kind of artless flattery.* **2** unpretentious, unassuming, °unaffected, °natural, °simple, °naïve, °unsophisticated, °plain, °ordinary, °humble: *The remarks were those of an artless young man who meant nothing sinister.* **3** unskilled, untalented, unskilful, unpractised, °inexperienced, inexpert, °primitive, unproficient, °incompetent, °inept, °clumsy, °crude, °awkward, bungling: *Clogs must be the most artless footwear ever made.*

ashamed *adj.* °embarrassed, abashed, humiliated, chagrined, mortified, blushing, °shamefaced, °sheepish, red-faced: *I was ashamed to have to admit that it was I who had written the nasty letter.*

ask *v.* **1** °question, interrogate, °query, °quiz; °inquire *or* °enquire (of): *Let's ask the policeman for information. Just ask directions of any passer-by. I merely asked if you were going my way.* **2** °demand, °require, °expect, °request: *Doing his laundry is a lot to ask.* **3** °beg, °apply (to), °appeal (to), °seek (from), °solicit (from), °petition, °plead (to), °beg, °beseech, °pray, entreat, implore: *In the streets, thousands of beggars ask passers-by for alms.* **4** invite, °bid, °summon: *Nellie asked me to dinner.* **5 ask after** *or* **about**: °inquire *or* °enquire after *or* about: *My sister asked after you—wanted to know how you were getting along.* **6 ask for**: **a** invite, °attract, °encourage, °provoke: *You're asking for trouble if you walk alone through that neighbourhood after dark.* **b** °request, °seek: *We asked for more time to finish the project.*

aspect *n.* **1** °viewpoint, point of °view, °position, °standpoint, °side: *Looked at from a different aspect, the problem did not seem insurmountable after all.* **2** complexion, °light, °angle, °interpretation, mien, °face: *His conviction for robbery put a different aspect on hiring him as a security guard.* **3** °exposure, °prospect, °outlook, °orientation: *The western aspect of the room made it sunny in the afternoons.* **4** °side, °feature, °attribute, °characteristic, °quality, °detail, °angle, facet, °manifestation, °element, °circumstance: *There are many aspects of Buddhism that you do not understand.*

aspersion *n.* °slander, °libel, false insinuation, calumny, °imputation, °allegation, detraction, °slur, obloquy, defamation, disparagement: *He resented my casting aspersions on the legitimacy of his birth.*

aspiration *n.* °desire, °longing, yearning, craving, hankering, °wish, °dream, °hope; °ambition, °aim, °goal, °objective, °purpose, °intention, °plan, °scheme, °plot: *It was his lifelong aspiration to marry someone with money.*

aspire *v.* **aspire to**: °desire, °hope, °long, °wish, °aim, °yearn; °dream of: *I'd never aspire to anything higher. He still aspired to being a full professor.*

assailant *n.* attacker, assaulter, mugger: *My assailant threatened me with a knife.*

assault *n.* **1** °attack, onslaught, °onset, °charge, °offensive, blitzkrieg, blitz, °strike, °raid, incursion, sortie; °aggression, °invasion: *At dawn we launched the assault on the fort.* **2** beating, battering, °hold-up, mugging; °rape, °violation, molestation; *Law* battery: *The defendant is accused of assault.*
—*v.* **3** °attack, assail, °set *or* °fall upon, °pounce upon, °storm, °beset, °charge, °rush, °lay into: *The elderly couple were assaulted near their home.* **4** °rape, °violate, °molest: *Three women were assaulted in that neighbourhood last night.* **5** °beat (up), °batter, °bruise, °harm, °hit, °strike, °punch, smite: *She complained that her husband continually assaulted the children.*

assemble *v.* **1** convene, °gather, °call *or* °bring *or* °get together, convoke, °summon, °muster, marshal, °rally, levy, °round up, °collect, congregate, forgather *or* foregather; °meet: *The forces were assembled along the waterfront. A small crowd assembled at the airport.* **2** °accumulate, °gather, °amass, °collect, °bring *or* °group *or* °lump together, °compile, °unite, °join *or* °draw together: *The paintings were assembled from many sources.* **3** °construct, °put together, °erect, °set up, °fit *or* °join *or* °piece together, °connect, °fabricate, °manufacture, °make: *The sculpture was assembled from so-called objets trouvés, or 'found' objects.*

assembly *n.* **1** °gathering, °group, °meeting, assemblage, °body, °circle, °company, congregation, °flock, °crowd, °throng, multitude, °host; horde: *A huge assembly of well-wishers greeted the candidate.* **2** convocation, °council, °convention, congress, °association, conclave; °diet, synod: *The assembly voted to re-elect the incumbent officers.* **3** construction, putting together, erection, °connection, °setting up, °set-up, °fitting *or* joining *or* piecing together, °fabrication; °manufacture, making: *Assembly of the bicycle can be completed in an hour.*

assertion *n.* **1** °statement, °declaration, affirmation, contention, asseveration, averment, avowal, °pronouncement; *Law* affidavit, deposition: *He made the assertion that he had never seen the defendant before.* **2** insistence, °proclamation, °representation, affirmation, confirmation: *The kings exercised their jurisdiction in the assertion of their regal power.*

assertive *adj.* declaratory, affirmative, asseverative; °definite, °certain, °sure, °positive, °firm, °emphatic, °bold, °aggressive, °confident, °insistent; °dogmatic, doctrinaire, °domineering, °opinionated, °peremptory, *Colloq* °bossy, °pushy: *Harold won't obey unless his mother adopts an assertive tone with him.*

asset *n.* **1** Also, **assets**: °property, resources, possessions, holdings, °effects, °capital, °means, valuables, °money, °wealth: *We have to pay a tax on the company's assets. Her only liquid asset was some shares in the Suez Canal Company.* **2** °talent, °strength, °advantage, °resource, °benefit: *His main asset is that he speaks fluent Japanese.*

assign v. **1** °allot, allocate, apportion, consign, °appropriate, °distribute, °give (out), °grant: *A water ration was assigned to each person.* **2** °fix, °set (apart *or* aside), °settle (on), °determine, °appoint, °authorize, °designate, ordain, °prescribe, °specify: *Have they really assigned Thursday as the day of worship? Please sit in the seats assigned to you.* **3** °appoint, °designate, °order; °name, °delegate, °nominate, °attach; °choose, °select; *Brit* °second: *The men have been assigned to their posts. I assigned David to look after the champagne.* **4** °attribute, ascribe, accredit, °put down; °refer: *To which century did the curator assign this vase?*

assignment n. **1** °allotment, allocation, apportionment, giving (out), °distribution: *Assignment of posts in the Cabinet is the responsibility of the Prime Minister.* **2** °task, °obligation, °responsibility, chore, °duty, °position, °post, °charge, °job, °mission, commission; °lesson, homework: *Every agent is expected to carry out his assignment. The school assignment for tomorrow is an essay on Alexander Pope.* **3** °appointment, designation, naming, nomination: *The assignment of Neil Mackay to the post was a stroke of genius.* **4** designation, °specification, ascription: *In ancient medicine, the assignment of the functions of the organs was often wrong.*

assist v. **1** °aid, °help, °second, °support: *He could walk only if assisted by the nurse.* **2** °further, °promote, °abet, °support, °benefit, °facilitate: *The rumours will not assist his election.* **3** °help, succour, °serve, °work for *or* with; °relieve: *She has always assisted the poor.*

assistance n. °help, °aid, °support, succour, °backing, °reinforcement, °relief, °benefit: *Can you get up without my assistance? The scholarship fund offered financial assistance.*

assistant n. **1** helper, helpmate *or* helpmeet, °aid, °aide; aide-de-camp, °second: *These systems make use of rhymes as assistants to the memory.* **2** °deputy, °subordinate, °subsidiary, °auxiliary; underling: *He is now the assistant to the sales manager.*

associate v. **1 associate (with): a** °ally with, °link, °join *or* °unite (with), °combine *or* confederate (with), °connect (with), conjoin (with): *In the 1930s Abe was associated with Dutch and Louis in Murder, Incorporated. I always associate him with fast cars and hard drinking.* **b** °see, be seen with, °socialize *or* fraternize (with), °mix *or* °mingle (with), °go (out) with, consort with, have to do with, *Colloq* °hang out with, *Brit* °pal with *or* about, °pal up (with), *US* °pal around (with): *Mother told me not to associate with boys who use that kind of language.* —n. **2** °colleague, °partner; °fellow, fellow-worker: *I'd like you to meet my associate, Ian Lindsay.* **3** confederate, °ally, collaborator; °accomplice, °accessory: *He and his associates have been sent to prison for conspiracy.* **4** °comrade, °companion, °friend, °mate, buddy; confidant(e): *We have been close associates for many years.* —adj. **5** °subsidiary, °secondary: *She is an associate professor at an American university.* **6** allied, affiliate, °affiliated, associated; °accessory: *Publication is under the direction of an associate company.*

association n. **1** °society, °organization, confederation, confederacy, °federation, °league,

°union, °alliance, guild, coalition, °group; °syndicate, °combine, consortium, cooperative: *The society later became known as the British Association for the Advancement of Science.* **2** °connection, °link, affiliation, °relationship, °bond, °tie, linkage, linking, pairing, joining, conjunction, bonding: *The association between princes and frogs is probably lost on anyone so literal-minded.* **3** °fellowship, intimacy, °friendship, camaraderie, comradeship, °relationship: *There has been a long-standing association between Peter and Wendy.*

assortment n. **1** °group, °class, °category, °batch, °set, °lot, classification, grouping: *Which assortment contains only plain chocolates?* **2** °collection, °pot-pourri, °mixture, mélange, array, agglomeration, conglomeration, °medley, farrago, °variety, °miscellany, °jumble, salmagundi, gallimaufry, °mishmash, *Colloq* mixed bag: *That hat looks like something from the assortment at a jumble sale. A bizarre assortment of people attended the meeting.*

assume v. **1** °accept, °adopt, °take, °use, °employ; arrogate, °appropriate, °take over *or* up, °undertake: *Who will assume the leadership of the party?* **2** °take on (oneself), °take upon (oneself), °put *or* °try on, don, °adopt; °acquire: *Whenever she delivered the information, she assumed the disguise of an old man. That trivial dispute has assumed gargantuan proportions.* **3** °presume, °suppose, °believe, °fancy, °expect, °think, °presuppose, °take, °take for granted, °surmise, *Chiefly US* °guess: *When I saw the knife in his hand, I assumed the chef was going to slice a lemon. The king assumed he had the cooperation of Parliament.* **4** °pretend to, feign, °sham, °counterfeit, simulate, °affect, °fake: *Though she cared deeply, she assumed a devil-may-care attitude.*

assumed adj. **1** appropriated, °taken, usurped, expropriated, pre-empted, seized: *He functions in his assumed capacity as a judge.* **2** °pretended, °put on, °sham, °false, feigned, °affected, °counterfeit, simulated, °spurious, °bogus, °fake; pseudonymous, made-up, *Colloq* °phoney *or US also* phony: *She morosely stared at the floor in assumed contrition. He wrote poetry under an assumed name.* **3** °taken, °taken for granted, presumed, °supposed, accepted, expected, presupposed; °hypothetical, °theoretical, suppositional: *The payment depends materially on the assumed rate of interest.*

assurance n. **1** °promise, °pledge, °guarantee *or* guaranty, °warranty, commitment, °bond, surety; °word, °word of honour, °oath, °vow: *You have the bank's assurance that the money will be on deposit.* **2** °insurance, °indemnity: *His life assurance is barely enough to cover the costs of his funeral.* **3** °certainty, °confidence, °trust, °faith, reassurance, surety, assuredness, certitude; °security: *There is no assurance that Herr Kleister will get the job done.* **4** audacity, °impudence, °presumption, boldness, brazenness, °nerve, °effrontery, insolence, *Colloq* °brass, °gall, cheek, chutzpah: *With an air of assurance they quote authors they have never read.* **5** °self-confidence, self-reliance, °confidence, steadiness, intrepidity, self-possession, °poise, aplomb, coolness, °control, °self-control, °resolve, *Colloq* °gumption, guts, gutsiness: *He has the assurance of one born to command.*

assure v. **1** °secure, stabilize, °settle, °establish, °confirm, °certify, °warrant, °guarantee, °ensure, be °confident of, make or be °sure or °certain: *Force, fear, and the multitude of his guard do less to assure the estate of a prince than the good will of his subjects.* **2** °encourage, inspirit, °reassure, hearten: *Your humanity assures us and gives us strength.* **3** °convince, °persuade, °reassure, make (someone) °certain; °ensure: *What can I do to assure you of my love?* **4** assert, °state, asseverate, °promise: *I assure you that we shall do everything possible to find your dog.*

astonish *v.* °amaze, °surprise, °shock, °astound, °stun, °stagger, °dumbfound or dumfound, °bowl over, °floor, stupefy, °daze, Colloq flabbergast: *She astonished the audience with her gymnastic skill. I was astonished when told my wife had given birth to quintuplets.*

astonishment *n.* °amazement, °surprise, °shock, stupefaction, °wonder, wonderment: *I'll never forget that look of astonishment on his face when he learned he had won.*

astound *v.* °surprise, °shock, °astonish, °stun, °stagger, °dumbfound or dumfound, °bowl over, °floor, stupefy, °bewilder, °overwhelm, Colloq flabbergast: *We were astounded to learn that he had survived all those years on a desert island. The Great MacTavish performs astounding feats of magic and levitation!*

astute *adj.* **1** °shrewd, °subtle, °clever, °ingenious, adroit, °wily, cunning, °calculating, canny, °crafty, °artful, °arch, °sly, °foxy, guileful, underhand, underhanded; Rare astucious: *He had the reputation of being an astute businessman.* **2** °sharp, °keen, °perceptive, °observant, °alert, °quick, °quick-witted, °sage, sagacious, °wise, °intelligent, insightful, perspicacious, discerning, °knowledgeable: *That was a very astute comment, Smedley.*

atmosphere *n.* **1** °air, °heaven(s), °sky, aerosphere: *It is gravity that prevents the earth's atmosphere from drifting off into outer space.* **2** °air, ambience or ambiance, °environment, °climate, °mood, °feeling, °feel, °spirit, °tone: *There's such a friendly atmosphere in the bar of the Golden Cockerel. The atmosphere became very chilly when she told him she was marrying someone else.*

atone *v.* expiate, make °amends, °pay, °repay, °answer, °compensate; redress, °remedy, propitiate, °redeem: *Nothing can atone for her betrayal of him to the enemy. He has atoned for his sins many times over.*

atonement *n.* °amends, propitiation, reparation, repayment, compensation, °payment, °restitution, recompense, expiation, °penance, °satisfaction: *He sent her flowers in atonement, together with a note apologizing profusely for his actions.*

atrocious *adj.* **1** °cruel, °wicked, iniquitous, °villainous, °fiendish, execrable, appalling, °abominable, °monstrous, °inhuman, °savage, barbaric, °brutal, barbarous, heinous, °dreadful, °flagrant, flagitious, °gruesome, °grisly, °ruthless, °ghastly, unspeakable, horrifying, °horrible, °awful, °infamous, °infernal, °satanic, hellish: *They will never forget the atrocious crimes that took place during the war.* **2** °awful, °terrible, °bad, °rotten, horrid, appalling, °frightful, horrendous, Colloq °lousy: *That's the most atrocious book it has ever been my misfortune to review. Priscilla has atrocious taste.*

atrocity *n.* **1** °enormity, wickedness, flagitiousness, iniquity, °infamy, cruelty, heinousness, °horror, °evil, inhumanity, °barbarity, savagery: *The atrocity of the 'Final Solution' was a well-kept secret during the war.* **2** °evil, °outrage, °crime, villainy, °offence: *She could not listen when the prosecutor read a list of the atrocities perpetrated at the camp.*

attach *v.* **1** °fasten, °join, °connect, °secure, °fix, affix; °tack or °hook or °tie or °stick on, °pin, rivet, °cement, °glue, °bond, solder, °weld, braze; °unite; Nautical °bend: *The tag is still attached to your dress. Attach this to the wall. How do I attach the sail to the spar?* **2** °connect, °associate, °assign, affiliate, °enlist, °join, °add, subjoin, Brit °second: *Her brother-in-law has been attached to my regiment.* **3** endear, °attract: *I won't say that we were in love, but I was very closely attached to her.* **4** °fix, affix, °pin, °apply, ascribe, °assign, °attribute, °put, °place: *Why do you attach so much importance to what Dora says?* **5** adhere, °cleave, °stick: *Many legends have attached themselves to Charlemagne.* **6** °seize, °lay °hold of, °confiscate, °appropriate: *If he cannot meet the mortgage payments the bank will attach his house.*

attached *adj.* **1** connected, joined, Brit seconded: *She has been attached to the Foreign Office for many years.* **2** °united, fastened, °fixed: *The knob attached to the outside of the door might come off.* **3** Often, **attached to**: °devoted (to), °partial (to), °fond (of): *I feel closely attached to her. I became attached to the painting and did not wish to sell it.* **4** °spoken for, married, unavailable, °engaged, betrothed: *I would have asked Suzanne out, but I gather she's attached.*

attachment *n.* **1** °fastening; °connection, °tie, °link; °bond: *The attachment of this fitting is too flimsy. William cannot understand how an attachment could have been formed between his wife and his brother.* **2** attaching, °fastening, linking, joining, affixing, fixing, °connection: *The mode of attachment to the wall is not immediately apparent.* **3** °affection, °regard, fidelity, faithfulness, °devotion, °liking, fondness, °affinity, friendliness, °loyalty, °admiration, tenderness, °partiality, °friendship, °love: *We still feel a deep attachment, despite the divorce.* **4** adjunct, °addition, °accessory, °device, appliance, °extra, accoutrement or US also accouterment, appendage, °part; °ornament, °decoration; Colloq °gadget: *With this attachment, the film is advanced automatically. Attachments are available at extra cost.*

attack *v.* **1** assail, °assault, °fall or °set or °pounce upon; °charge, °rush, °raid, °strike (at), °storm; °engage (in battle), °fight; Colloq °mug, °jump: *They were attacked on their way home by a gang of boys. Helicopter gunships were sent out to attack the bunker.* **2** °criticize, censure, °berate; °abuse, revile, inveigh against, °denounce, °condemn, malign, denigrate, decry, °disparage, deprecate, °vilify: *His article attacked the minister for his views on housing.* **3** °begin, °start; °approach, °undertake: *We attacked the meal with gusto.* **4** °affect, °seize; infect: *Rheumatism attacks young and old alike.* **5** °waste, °devour, °destroy, °eat; °erode, corrode, °decompose, °dissolve: *Termites have attacked the beams of the house. Watch how the acid attacks the areas on the plate that have not been protected.*
—*n.* **6** °assault, °onset, °offensive, onslaught, incursion, °raid, °strike, °inroad, °invasion: *The*

enemy responded to our attack with a smokescreen. After capturing the pawn, Karpov launched an attack on the queen. **7** °criticism, censure; °abuse, denunciation, revilement, denigration, decrial, disparagement, deprecation, vilification: *The quarterly's attack is totally uncalled for.* **8** °seizure, °spell, °spasm, °paroxysm; °fit, °bout: *Preston has had another attack of gout. How do you stop an attack of hiccups?* **9** °destruction, wasting; °erosion, corrosion: *Noting the attack on the planks by shipworm, the surveyor declared the vessel unseaworthy. Aluminium will not withstand the attack of the salt air in this area.*

attempt *v.* **1** °try, °essay, °undertake, °take on, °venture; °endeavour, °strive, *Colloq* have *or* take a crack at, °try on, have a °go *or* °shot at: *It is too stormy to attempt the crossing tonight. Is she going to attempt to dive off the cliff tomorrow?* —*n.* **2** °endeavour, °try, °essay; °effort, °undertaking, °bid, *Colloq* °crack, °go, °shot: *The weather cleared sufficiently for another attempt at the summit. He made a feeble attempt to wave.* **3** °attack, °assault: *An abortive attempt was made on the life of the vice-president tonight.*

attend *v.* **1** be °present (at), °go to, be at, °appear (at), °put in an appearance (at), °turn up (at), °haunt, °frequent; °sit in (on), *US and Canadian* audit: *Are you attending the concert? She attends Miss Fiennes's elocution class.* **2** °turn to, pay °attention to, °serve, °tend to, take °care of, °deal with, °handle, °heed, °fulfil: *I shall attend to your request as soon as possible, Madam.* **3** Also, **attend to**: °watch over, °wait on *or* upon, °care for, take °care of, °minister to, °occupy oneself with, °look after, °look out for, °devote oneself to: *Mrs Atterbury attends the patients in the cancer ward on weekdays. The clergyman has his own flock to attend to.* **4** °escort, °accompany, °conduct, convoy, °squire, usher, °wait upon, °follow; chaperon *or* chaperone: *The actress arrived, attended by her entourage of toadies.* **5** °be associated with, °accompany, °result in *or* from, give °rise to: *A departure in the midst of the battle would be attended by great peril, Milord.*

attendance *n.* **1** °presence, °appearance, being: *Your attendance at chapel is required.* **2** audience, °crowd, °assembly, assemblage, °gathering, °turnout, °gate, °house: *The attendance at the fête was greater than we expected.* **3 in attendance**: waiting upon, attending, serving: *The king always has at least four people in attendance.*

attendant *adj.* **1** waiting upon, accompanying, following; resultant, resulting, °related, consequent, concomitant, depending, °accessory: *The circumstances attendant on your acceptance of the post are immaterial.* —*n.* **2** °escort, °servant, °menial, helper, usher *or* usherette, chaperon *or* chaperone; °aide, °subordinate, underling, °assistant; °follower, *Derogatory* lackey, °flunkey, °slave; *Colloq US* °cohort: *He dismissed his attendants and entered the church alone.*

attention *n.* **1** °heed, °regard, °notice; concentration: *Please give your attention to the teacher. Pay attention! Don't let your attention wander.* **2** publicity, °notice, °distinction, acclaim, °prominence, *réclame*, °notoriety; limelight: *She seems to have been getting a lot of attention lately.*

attentive *adj.* **1** heedful, °observant, °awake, °alert, °intent, watchful, concentrating, assiduous; °mindful, °considerate: *James is very attentive*

in class. You really must be more attentive to the needs of others. **2** °polite, °courteous, courtly, °gallant, °gracious, °accommodating, °considerate, °thoughtful, °solicitous, civil, °respectful, deferential: *He is always very attentive to the ladies.*

attest *v.* bear °witness (to), °bear out, °swear (to), °vow, °testify, °certify, °vouchsafe, °declare, assert, asseverate, aver, affirm, °confirm, °verify, °substantiate, °vouch for, *Law* depose, depose and °say, depone: *I attest to the fact that they left the restaurant together. The merits of château-bottled Bordeaux are attested by most epicures.*

attitude *n.* **1** °posture, °position, °disposition, °stance, °bearing, °carriage, °aspect, demeanour: *The attitude of the figures in the sculpture was one of supplication.* **2** °posture, °position, °disposition, °opinion, °feeling, °view, point of °view, °viewpoint, °approach, °leaning, °thought, °inclination, °bent, °tendency, °orientation: *What is your attitude towards the situation in South Africa?*

attract *v.* °draw, invite; °entice, °lure, allure, °appeal to, °charm, °captivate, °fascinate, *Colloq* °pull: *Our attention was attracted by a slight noise in the cupboard. Melissa attracts men the way flowers attract bees.*

attraction *n.* **1** °draw, °appeal; °magnetism; gravitation, *Colloq* °pull: *David confided to Joan that he felt a strong attraction to her. There is an attraction between the north and south poles of these magnets.* **2** °draw, °lure, °enticement, attractant, °inducement; °show, °entertainment, °presentation, performance, *Colloq* °come-on, crowd-puller, crowd-pleaser: *The presence of the movie stars has been a powerful attraction. The producer has planned to repeat the attraction every evening.*

attractive *adj.* attracting, °drawing, pulling, captivating, °taking, °fetching, appealing, luring, °inviting, enticing, °seductive, °engaging, charming, °interesting, °pleasing, °winning, alluring, good-looking, °pretty, °handsome: *The person I'd like to meet needn't be beautiful or stunning—attractive will do nicely.*

attribute *n.* **1** °quality, °character, °characteristic, °property, °feature, °trait, °virtue: *It is surprising how soon historical personages become invested with romantic attributes.* —*v.* **2** ascribe, °impute, °assign, °put down to, °trace to, °charge, °credit: *The shrivelled arm of Richard the Third was attributed to witchcraft. To what do you attribute your interest in birds?*

attribution *n.* °assignment, ascription, °credit: *The curator disagreed with the expert's attribution of the painting to Canaletto.*

audacious *adj.* **1** °daring, °bold, °confident, °intrepid, °brave, °courageous, °adventurous, °venturesome, °reckless, °rash, °foolhardy, °daredevil, devil-may-care, °fearless, doughty, mettlesome: *The troop launched an audacious daylight attack. Cranshaw made an audacious bid for the chairmanship.* **2** °presumptuous, °shameless, °bold, °impudent, °pert, saucy, °defiant, °impertinent, °insolent, °brazen, °unabashed, °rude, °disrespectful, °cheeky, °forward: *Charlotte was so audacious as to assume that she could win.*

aura n. °air, °atmosphere, °feeling, ambience or ambiance, °spirit, °character, °quality, °odour, °aroma, emanation: *There is an aura of elegance about the woman that impresses everyone she meets.*

auspices n. aegis, sponsorship, °authority, °protection, °support, °backing, supervision, °guidance, °patronage, °sanction, °approval, °control, °influence: *The competition is under the auspices of the astronomical society.*

authentic adj. °genuine, °real, °actual, bona fide, °factual, °accurate, °true, °legitimate, °authoritative, °reliable, °veritable, °trustworthy, °faithful, °undisputed: *This is an authentic Chippendale chair.*

authenticate v. °verify, validate, °certify, °substantiate, °endorse, °vouch for, °confirm, corroborate: *You will have to go to the consul to have your passport authenticated.*

author n. °creator, originator, inventor, °father, °founder, framer, initiator, maker, °prime mover, architect, °designer; °writer, novelist, littérateur: *Adolfo was the author of the plot to kill the governor.*

authoritarian adj. °dictatorial, imperious, °totalitarian, autocratic, °arbitrary, °absolute, °dogmatic, °domineering, °strict, °severe, unyielding, °tyrannical, °despotic, Colloq °bossy: *Why do people ever elect an authoritarian government?*

authoritative adj. **1** °official, valid, °authentic, documented, certified, validated, °legitimate, sanctioned; conclusive: *The second edition is usually considered the authoritative one.* **2** °scholarly, °learned, °authentic, valid, °sound, °veritable, verifiable, °accurate, °factual, °faithful, dependable, °reliable, °trustworthy, °true, °truthful: *There is no more authoritative source than Professor Fitzhugh on early Egyptian history.*

authority n. **1** °power, °jurisdiction, °dominion, °right, °control, °prerogative, authorization; hegemony: *Who gave you the authority to tell me what to do? By the authority vested in me, I now pronounce you man and wife.* **2** °word, °testimony, °evidence, Colloq °say-so: *Do not accept anything solely on the authority of the Herald.* **3** °expert, °specialist, °scholar, °sage, °judge, arbiter: *Gardner is an authority on Scottish history.* **4 authorities**: °government, °establishment, officials, officialdom, °powers that be, °police: *The authorities lowered the speed limit.*

authorize v. empower, commission; °sanction, °approve, countenance, °permit, give °leave, °allow, °license, °entitle, °consent or °subscribe to, °endorse, Colloq °OK or okay, give the green light or °go-ahead to: *Who authorized you to speak for all of us?*

automatic adj. **1** self-acting, self-governing, self-regulating, °mechanical, °robot, automated: *Many modern cars are equipped with an automatic choke.* **2** °mechanical, °involuntary, °unconscious, °instinctive or instinctual, °natural, °spontaneous, °impulsive, conditioned, reflex, robot-like, Slang knee-jerk: *Flinching is an automatic reaction to a threatening gesture.* **3** °unavoidable, °inevitable, inescapable, ineluctable: *It is automatic for the tax inspector to suspect people of hiding something.*

auxiliary adj. **1** °helping, assisting, °supportive, aiding, abetting; °helpful, °accessory, °supplementary: *In a well-balanced mind, imagination and understanding are auxiliary to each other.* **2** °subordinate, additional, °subsidiary, °secondary, ancillary, °extra, °reserve; °accessory: *Larger sailing vessels have an auxiliary motor in case the wind fails.* —n. **3** °help, °assistance, °aid, °support, °accessory: *Knowing another language is a useful auxiliary in the study of your own.* **4** helper, °assistant, °aide, alter ego, °supporter, Colloq man Friday, girl Friday: *Let me introduce Pat, my auxiliary, who will help you if I am not available.*

available adj. at or to °hand, at one's disposal, °accessible, °handy, °present, °ready, (readily) obtainable, °convenient, °nearby, °close by, within °reach, on °tap, at one's fingertips or elbow: *Running water is available. If you need me for anything, I am available.*

avant-garde adj. innovative, advanced, °progressive, °experimental, °original, °new, ground-breaking, pioneering, precedent-setting; °revolutionary, °extreme, extremist, Colloq far-out, °way-out: *We disapprove of your avant-garde notions of teaching. Some modern art, avant-garde not very long ago, seems quite conventional today.*

avarice n. °greed, acquisitiveness, cupidity, craving, covetousness, °desire, greediness, °rapacity, selfishness; stinginess, meanness, miserliness, parsimony, tight-fistedness, close-fistedness, niggardliness, penuriousness: *The classic tale of avarice is that of King Midas, whose touch turned everything to gold.*

avaricious adj. °greedy, acquisitive, °grasping, covetous, °mercenary, °selfish; penny-pinching, stingy, °miserly, °mean, parsimonious, tight-fisted, close-fisted, niggardly, °penurious, °tight: *She fell into the clutches of an avaricious lawyer.*

average n. **1** °mean, °norm, °usual, °standard: *The Bell Inn is certainly far above average in accommodation, food quality, and service.* **2 on average**: in the °main, °generally, normally, °usually, °ordinarily, typically, customarily, as a °rule, for the most °part: *On average, I go abroad twice a year on business.* —adj. **3** °normal, common, °usual, °customary, °general, °typical, °ordinary, °regular: *On an average day, the museum has about 2,000 visitors.* **4** °mediocre, middling, run-of-the-mill, commonplace, °common, °ordinary, °undistinguished, unexceptional, Colloq so so: *Boris is only an average violinist, but he's a virtuoso on the harmonica.*

averse adj. °disinclined, unwilling, °reluctant, °resistant, °loath, °opposed, anti, antipathetic, ill-disposed, °indisposed: *He does not appear to be averse to your suggestion: in fact, he seems quite keen on it.*

aversion n. **1** °dislike, abhorrence, repugnance, antipathy, °antagonism, °animosity, °hostility, °loathing, hatred, odium, °horror; disinclination, unwillingness, °reluctance, °distaste: *Does Anne have an aversion to people who smoke? Your aversion to the theatre might be explained as agoraphobia.* **2** °dislike, hatred, °hate, °loathing: *Turnips are a particular aversion of mine.*

avoid v. °shun, °keep (away) from, keep off, leave °alone, keep or °steer clear of, °refrain from, °dodge, circumvent, °sidestep, °elude, °escape, °evade: *The doctor suggested that I avoid chocolate. Why does Bennie avoid looking me straight in the eye?*

awake v. **1** °wake (up), awaken, °get up, °rouse or bestir oneself: *When I awoke, she was standing over me with a pistol.* **2** awaken, °animate, °arouse, °rouse, °stimulate, °revive, °incite, °excite, °activate, °alert, °stir up, °fan, °kindle, ignite, °fire: *Marches awaken my sense of patriotism.* **3 awake to**: awaken to, °wake up to, °realize, °understand, become °aware *or* °conscious of: *I finally awoke to the fact that my tax return was overdue.*
—*adj.* **4** up, aroused, roused, wide awake, up and about, °alert, on the °alert, on the qui vive, watchful, on °guard, °attentive, °conscious; heedful, °alive: *I'm always awake a few minutes before the alarm goes off.*

awaken v. See awake, 1, 2, above.

award v. **1** °grant, °give, °confer, °bestow, °present, °accord, °furnish, endow with; °assign, apportion: *Her dog was awarded the blue ribbon in the club show.*
—*n.* **2** °prize, °trophy, °reward: *The award for the tidiest boats has been won by the Bristol Yacht Club.* **3** °grant, bestowal, °presentation, °endowment, awarding: *Before the award of the prizes, we listened to speeches. Profits were up last year despite a large pay award.*

aware adj. **1** °informed, apprised, °knowledgeable, °knowing, posted, in the °know, °enlightened, au fait, au courant, cognizant, Slang °hip, hep, °wise: *She is well aware of the consequences.* **2** °sensitive, °sensible, °conscious: *I became aware that someone was watching us.*

awesome adj. awe-inspiring, °awful, °imposing, °amazing, wonderful, breathtaking, °marvellous, wondrous, °moving, °stirring, affecting, °overwhelming, °formidable, daunting, °dreadful, °fearsome, °fearful, °frightening, horrifying, °terrifying, °terrible; °unbelievable,

°incredible; alarming, °shocking, °stunning, stupefying, astounding, astonishing: *The eruption of Vesuvius in AD 67 must have been a truly awesome spectacle.*

awful adj. **1** °bad, °terrible, °inferior, °base, °abominable, °rotten, °horrible, horrid; °tasteless, °unsightly, °ugly, °hideous, °grotesque, Slang °lousy, Brit naff, Chiefly US hellacious: *That is an awful piece of sculpture. I feel awful this morning.* **2** °frightful, °shocking, execrable, unpleasant, °grotesque, °nasty, °ghastly, °gruesome, horrendous, horrifying, horrific, °horrible, unspeakable: *That was an awful thing to do.*

awfully adv. °very (much), °badly, °terribly, °extremely, greatly, remarkably, in the worst way, dreadfully, extraordinarily, °exceedingly, excessively, °really, °fearfully, inordinately; incomparably: *I get awfully tired running in the marathon. I'm awfully sorry I'm late. Doreen is an awfully good horsewoman.*

awkward adj. **1** °clumsy, ungainly, °left-handed, ham-handed, ham-fisted, blundering, bungling, maladroit, uncoordinated, undexterous, inexpert, gauche, unhandy, °inept, oafish, unskilled, unskilful, Colloq all °thumbs, butter-fingered, Brit cack-handed: *In his awkward attempt at putting the watch back together, Sam left out a few parts.* **2** °ungraceful, ungainly, inelegant, °wooden, gawky: *The ballerina made an awkward, flat-footed pirouette and stumbled off stage.* **3** °embarrassed, °shamefaced, uncomfortable, °ill at ease, uneasy, out of °place, discomfited, °confused: *He felt awkward being the only boy in the class. Terry made an awkward excuse and left the room.* **4** °dangerous, °hazardous, °risky, °precarious, °perilous: *Be careful, there's an awkward step here.* **5** °difficult, °touchy, °sensitive, °embarrassing, °delicate, unpleasant, uncomfortable, °ticklish, °tricky, °trying, °troublesome, Colloq °sticky: *He's got himself into a very awkward situation indeed.*

B

babble v. **1** °prattle, twaddle, °jabber, gibber, °chatter, °blab, blabber, °gurgle, burble, gabble, *Colloq* °blab, blabber, °gab, ya(c)k, natter, witter, *Brit* rabbit: *The silly fellow kept babbling away, but no one was listening. Madelaine is still too young to talk and just babbles to herself.* **2** divulge, °tell, °disclose, °repeat, °reveal, °tattle, °gossip, °blurt (out), *Colloq* °blab: *Don't tell Nigel about the affair—he'll babble it all over town.*
—n. **3** °gibberish, °nonsense, twaddle, °prattle, °chatter(ing), gibber, °jabber, jibber-jabber, °drivel, °rubbish, *bavardage;* °murmur, hubbub: *Ella's conversation about the financial market is just so much babble.*

baby n. **1** infant, neonate, newborn, babe, babe in arms, °child, toddler, °tot: *The baby is just beginning to teethe.*
—v. **2** cosset, °coddle, °pamper, mollycoddle, °indulge, °spoil, °pet: *He turned out that way because he was babied till he was ten. I know you like to be babied when you're ill.*

back v. **1** °invest in, wager or °bet on: *She backed a 35-to-2 long shot in the Derby, and she won.* **2** Also, **back up: a** °support, °uphold, °stand behind, °promote, °encourage, °help, °second, °side with, °endorse, °aid, °abet, °assist; °sponsor, °subsidize, °underwrite, subvene, °finance, *Slang US and Canadian* bankroll: *Your mother and I will back you if you want to start a business.* **b** °reverse, go or move in °reverse, °go or move °backwards: *He backed into the driveway.* **3 back down (from)** or **off (from)** or **away (from)** or **out (of)** or **up**: °withdraw (from), °retreat (from), °abandon, °retire (from), backtrack (from), °shy away (from), °recoil (from), °turn tail (from): *When Percy stood up to him, the bully backed down. The investment sounded risky, so I backed off. Philippa backed out of singing the leading role. Back up and give me room!*
—n. **4** backside, °rear, *Technical* dorsum: *She stood with her back towards me.* **5 at the back of** or **at someone's back**: behind, following, pursuing, chasing, *US* in back of: *Here come the hounds at the back of the fox. You were at my back in the queue a minute ago.* **6 behind the back of** or **behind someone's back**: surreptitiously, °secretly, clandestinely, privately, furtively, sneakily, slyly; treacherously, traitorously, perfidiously, deceitfully, insidiously: *Graham is always telling tales about you behind your back.* **7 break the back of: a** °overcome, °master: *Now that he's broken the back of that problem he can get on with his work.* **b** *US* crush, °ruin, bankrupt, °destroy, °defeat, vanquish, *Colloq* °break: *The government has tried on many occasions to break the back of the Mafia operation.* **8 on (someone's) back**: *US* weighing (down) on or upon (someone), burdening (someone), lodged with (someone), resting with (someone): *The responsibility for the decision is on your back.* **9 turn one's back on** or **upon**: °abandon, °forsake, °ignore, °disregard, °repudiate, °reject, °cast off, disown, °deny: *He turned his back on her when she needed him most.* **10 with one's back to** or **against the wall**: hard pressed, struggling (against °odds), without hope, with little or no hope,

°helpless, in dire straits, in (serious) °trouble: *After the stock-market crash, some brokers found themselves with their backs to the wall.*
—adj. **11** °rear; °service, servants': *Both back tyres are flat. Please use the back staircase from now on.* **12** *US and Australian and New Zealand* °outlying, °remote, °isolated, °distant; °undeveloped, °primitive, °raw, °rough, °uncivilized: *They raised three boys in the back country, and all of them became doctors.* **13** in arrears, °overdue, past °due, °late; behindhand: *The tax inspector has advised me that I owe thousands in back taxes.*
—adv. **14** to or toward(s) the °rear, rearward(s), °backward(s); away: *We beat back the enemy in severe hand-to-hand fighting. I accepted his offer at once, lest he should draw back. Get back from the edge!* **15** in °return or repayment or °requital or retaliation; again: *I'll pay you back when I have the money. She gave him back as good as he had given.* **16** ago, in °time(s) °past: *Two generations back, his was the finest house in the town.* **17** behind, behindhand, in arrears, °overdue: *We are a week back in the rent.* **18 go back on**: °renege, °fail; °deny, disavow, °break, °repudiate: *He has gone back on his promise to send the payment on the first of every month.*

backbone n. **1** °spine, spinal column: *He's much better since the surgery on his backbone.* **2** °mainstay, °chief or °main °support, °buttress, °pillar: *Sheila has been the backbone of the society, but she has now moved away.* **3** resoluteness, sturdiness, firmness, °determination, °strength (of °character), mettle, purposefulness, °resolution, °courage, °fortitude, °resolve, °will, will-power, °stability, °stamina, staying °power, °grit: *Has she the backbone to run the company alone?*

backer n. **1** °supporter, °advocate, promoter, °sponsor, °patron: *She has always been an enthusiastic backer of adult education.* **2** investor, °benefactor or benefactress, °supporter, underwriter, *Colloq* angel: *The play's backers have made huge profits.* **3** bettor, *Brit* °punter: *His backers are offering odds of 10 to 1.*

background n. **1** °history, °experience, qualifications, credentials, grounding, training; °breeding, °upbringing, °family; curriculum vitae, *Colloq* CV: *His background suits him admirably for the post of ambassador.* **2** °distance, offing, °horizon, °obscurity: *I like the way the coastline disappears into the background towards the edge of the painting.* **3 in the background**: °inconspicuous, °unnoticed, °unobtrusive, behind the scenes, out of the limelight or °spotlight, unseen, out of the °public eye, backstage: *Edward prefers to remain in the background, letting his dealer bid at the auctions.*

backing n. **1** °support, °help, °aid, °assistance, succour; °approval, °endorsement, °patronage, sponsorship: *He knows that he can rely on the backing of his local party.* **2** investment, °money, funds, funding, °subsidy, °grant; sponsorship: *How can you launch the company without backing?*

backlash n. °reaction, °repercussion, °recoil, counteraction, °rebound, °kickback, backfire;

°boomerang: *There was a strong backlash in the USA against giving minorities preferred instead of equal job opportunities.*

backward *adj.* **1** °bashful, °shy, °reticent, diffident, °retiring, °coy, °timid, unwilling, °loath, chary, °reluctant, °averse: *She took him to be a bit backward when he didn't respond to her smile.* **2** °slow, dim-witted, °dull, °stupid, slow-witted, °dumb, °feeble-minded, *Colloq Brit* gormless, °dim: *Some of the more backward students will need extra help.* **3** °slow, °late, behindhand, retarded: *Millie seemed a bit backward in learning to walk.* **4** rearward; to the °rear, behind; to the °past: *She gave him a backward glance. He went on through life with never a backward look.* **5** retrograde, retrogressive, °reverse, regressive: *The ancients were unable to account for the apparently backward motion of the planets.*
—*adv.* **6** °backwards: *Walk backward to the door with your hands up.*

backwards *adv.* **1** rearwards *or* rearward, in °reverse, regressively, retrogressively, °backward; withershins *or* widdershins, *Brit* anti-clockwise, *US* counter-clockwise: *The general, who refused to acknowledge defeat, explained that his troops were 'advancing backwards'. Do the clocks run backwards in Australia, Daddy?* **2** in °reverse; °back to °front: *She can even ride sitting backwards on a galloping horse. I think you're wearing your pullover backwards.*

bad *adj.* **1** °poor, °wretched, °inferior, °defective, °awful, °worthless, °miserable, egregious, execrable, substandard, °unsatisfactory, °disappointing, °inadequate, non-standard, *Colloq* °lousy, °rotten, crummy, *Slang Brit* grotty, naff: *Sometimes they would send him a letter, but he was a bad correspondent. We went to see a rather bad play the other night.* **2** °corrupt, polluted, vitiated, debased, °base, °vile, °foul, °rotten, miasmic, noxious, mephitic, °unhealthy, °poisonous, °injurious, °dangerous, °harmful, °hurtful, pernicious, deleterious, °ruinous: *It wasn't healthy to be so near the bad air of the sewer.* **3** °evil, °ill, °immoral, °wicked, °vicious, °vile, °sinful, depraved, °awful, °villainous, °corrupt, amoral, °criminal, °wrong, unspeakable: *The man was thoroughly bad and deserved everything he got.* **4** unpleasant, °offensive, °disagreeable, °inclement, °severe, °awful, unfavourable, adverse, *Colloq* °lousy, °rotten: *Surely you're not going sailing in this bad weather?!* **5** unfavourable, unlucky, unpropitious, °unfortunate, °inauspicious, troubled, °grim, distressing, discouraging, unpleasant: *Agreeing to do that job might yet turn out to have been a bad decision.* **6** °off, tainted, spoilt *or* spoiled, °mouldy, °stale, °rotten, decayed, putrefied, °putrid, contaminated: *The fridge isn't working and all the food has gone bad. She ate a bad egg and felt ill the next day.* **7** irascible, ill-tempered, grouchy, °irritable, °nasty, °peevish, °cross, crotchety, crabby, °cranky, curmudgeonly: *Don't go near the boss—he's been in a bad mood all day.* **8** °sorry, °regretful, °apologetic, contrite, rueful, °sad, conscience-stricken, °remorseful, °upset: *She felt bad about having invited me.* **9** °sad, depressed, °unhappy, °dejected, °downhearted, disconsolate, °melancholy; °inconsolable: *I feel bad about you losing your purse.* **10** °naughty, ill-behaved, misbehaving, °disobedient, °unruly, °wild; °mischievous: *Ronnie isn't a bad boy, he's*

just bored. **11** distressing, °severe, °grave, °serious, °terrible, °awful, °painful: *He was laid up with a bad case of the mumps.*

badly *adv.* **1** °poorly, defectively, insufficiently, inadequately, unsatisfactorily, carelessly, ineptly, shoddily, deficiently: *We lived in a badly furnished flat in the East End.* **2** unfortunately, unluckily, unsuccessfully, unfavourably, °poorly: *These are an improvement on the former rules, which worked badly.* **3** incorrectly, faultily, defectively, °poorly, improperly, inaccurately, erroneously, unacceptably; ineptly, inartistically, amateurishly, °awfully: *He speaks English badly. He sings badly.* **4** immorally, wickedly, viciously, mischievously, naughtily, shamefully, improperly, villainously: *The school has had its share of badly behaved pupils.* **5** °dangerously, °severely, gravely, critically, grievously, °seriously: *Her father was badly wounded in the war.* **6** unkindly, cruelly, harshly, °severely, wretchedly, dreadfully, improperly, atrociously, horribly, unspeakably: *The prisoners were treated so badly that few survived.* **7** unfavourably, damagingly, critically: *Even her friends spoke badly of her.* **8** °very much, °greatly, °seriously: *Peter is badly in need of extra money.* **9** distressfully, emotionally, °hard: *He took the news badly.*

bag *n.* **1** °sack, shopping bag, reticule, string bag, *Chiefly Brit* carrier bag, *Scots or dialect* °poke, °pocket: *They have helpers at the supermarket who will carry your bags to your car for you.* **2** baggage, °luggage, valise, satchel, °grip, °suitcase, overnight bag, carry-on °luggage *or* bag, Gladstone bag, carpet-bag, portmanteau, toilet kit *or* °case, sponge bag; briefcase, attaché °case, dispatch- *or* despatch-case: *Boarding in London I flew to Buenos Aires while my bag went to Seoul.* **3** °purse, handbag, °evening bag, °wallet, *Highland dress* sporran: *She reached into her bag and felt the gun that the Commander had given her.* **4** crone, °hag, °beast, ogress, gorgon, nightmare, °witch, harridan, *Archaic* beldam, *Slang* °old bat, dog, °monster, *US* two-bagger: *Derek has been romancing some old bag for her money.* **5** °occupation, °hobby, avocation, °business, °vocation, °department, °concern, °affair, *Colloq* °lookout, °worry, *Slang* °thing: *Peter's bag at the moment is learning to play the violin.*
—*v.* **6** catch, °trap, ensnare, °snare, entrap, °capture, °land; °kill, °shoot: *We bagged six pheasants and two partridges this morning.*

balance *v.* **1** °weigh, °estimate, °ponder, °consider, °deliberate, assess, °compare, °evaluate: *We need to balance the advantages and the disadvantages.* **2** °steady, °poise; °equalize, stabilize, °level, °match, °even out *or* up: *The see-saw will balance better if both of you get on the other end.* **3** °compensate (for), °make up for, counterbalance, °offset, °match, °equal; counterpoise: *The column of mercury in the barometer balances the atmospheric pressure on the surface of the bowl. The total of expenses seems to balance the total of income.*
—*n.* **4** °scale(s), steelyard: *According to the balance, the package weighs two pounds.* **5** °control, °command, °authority, °weight, °preponderance: *Britain held the balance of power during those decades.* **6** equilibrium, °stability, steadiness, °footing; equiponderance; °equality, °harmony: *The acrobat almost lost his balance on the high wire. It is important to maintain a balance between presentation and content.*

7 °remainder, °residue, °rest; °excess, °surplus, °difference: *You take these and I'll follow with the balance. My bank balance is down to zero.*

ban v. **1** °prohibit, °forbid, °outlaw, proscribe, interdict, °bar, disallow, debar: *They have banned smoking in all public places.* —n. **2** °prohibition, °taboo, proscription, interdiction, interdict; °embargo, °boycott: *They have put a ban on the sale of alcoholic beverages. The ban against importing firearms is strictly enforced.*

banal adj. trite, hackneyed, stereotyped, clichéd, stereotypical, commonplace, °old hat, °stock, °common, °everyday, °ordinary, °pedestrian, °humdrum, °tired, unoriginal, unimaginative, platitudinous; trivial, °petty, jejune, *Slang* corny: *The book was blasted as banal and boring. The plot of boy-meets-girl, though banal, still brings in the audiences.*

band¹ n. **1** °strip, ribbon, °belt, bandeau, fillet, °tie; °stripe, °line, °border: *He wears a cloth band round his head to keep the sweat out of his eyes. There is a decorative band at the top of each page.* —v. **2** °line, °stripe, °border: *The column is banded at intervals with bas-reliefs depicting scenes from the emperor's life.* **3** °tie, °keep, °bind: *Only those papers that are banded together should be sent off.*

band² n. **1** °company, troop, °platoon, °corps, °group, °body, °gang, horde, °party, °pack, °bunch: *They were set upon by a band of robbers in the forest.* **2** °group, °ensemble, °combination, orchestra, *Colloq* combo: *A jazz band plays at the Civic Centre every Tuesday evening.* —v. **3 band together:** °unite, confederate, °gather *or* °join *or* °league together, °team up, affiliate, °merge, federate: *We must band together if we expect to accomplish anything.*

banish v. **1** °exile, expatriate, deport, extradite, °transport, °eject, oust, °expel, rusticate, °drive out *or* away, °dismiss, excommunicate, °outlaw, °ostracize: *After ten years in prison, the thief was released and banished from the kingdom.* **2** °drive (out *or* away), °expel, °cast out, °dismiss, °reject: *He tried to banish suspicion from his mind.*

banner n. **1** °standard, °flag, °pennant, ensign, burgee, gonfalon, pennon, °streamer, banderole; °symbol: *The flag of the United States is called the star-spangled banner. He is seeking election under the banner of the Tories.* —adj. **2** °leading, °foremost, °momentous, °memorable, °notable, °important, °noteworthy: *The firm had a banner year, with profits up 25 per cent.*

banquet n. **1** °feast, °sumptuous repast *or* °meal, °ceremonial dinner, °lavish dinner: *At the end of the banquet, the guest of honour rose to make a few remarks.* —v. **2** °feast, °indulge, wine and °dine, °regale, °carouse: *The winners of the trophy banqueted night after night on champagne and caviare.*

banter n. °raillery, badinage, persiflage, pleasantry, jesting, joking, °repartee; chaffing, teasing, °chaff; *Colloq* kidding, ribbing: *Despite the good-natured banter between them, Ray knew that Stephen really detested him.*

bar n. **1** °rod, °shaft, °pole, °stick, °stake: *A heavy iron bar is used to tamp the dynamite into place in the hole.* **2** °strip, °stripe, °band, °belt; °streak, °line: *The company trade mark is a narrow red bar around the barrel of every ball-point pen.* **3** °barrier, °obstacle, °obstruction, barricade, °hindrance, °block, °deterrent, °impediment; °ban,

°embargo: *A steel bar was across the entrance. Her pride proved a bar to her success. There is a bar against importing spirits.* **4** sand bar, °shallow, shoal, bank, sandbank: *Because the keel is too deep, the sloop will be unable to cross the bar till high tide.* **5** °tribunal, court, courtroom, lawcourt, bench: *The former mayor was found guilty of corruption at the bar of public opinion.* **6** bar-room, saloon, public house, °café, °lounge, cocktail °lounge, tavern, taproom, canteen, *Brit* °local, wine bar; *Colloq* °pub; *Slang* boozer, gin-mill: *I was at the bar on my third beer when she walked in.* **7** °counter: *We had a quick lunch at the sandwich bar.* —v. **8** °fasten, °close up, °secure, °shut up; °lock, °lock up, padlock: *We tried to get in through the window, but they had barred it.* **9** °block, °obstruct, °stop, °stay, °hinder, °keep (out), °shut out, °exclude, °prevent, °forbid, °prohibit, °set aside; °forestall, °impede, °hamper, °retard, balk, barricade; °ban, °embargo: *After his behaviour, he was barred from the club for a year. A huge man in an ill-fitting dinner-jacket barred my way. The regulations bar the import of firearms.* —prep. **10** °except (for), excepting, excluding, °barring, °outside (of), °save for, aside from, but: *It's all over now bar the shouting.*

barbarian n. **1** °savage, °brute: *The barbarians wore animal skins.* **2** °boor, lowbrow, lout, oaf, °clod, churl, °philistine, ignoramus, yahoo; hooligan, vandal, ruffian, °tough, *Slang Brit* yob, yobbo, skinhead: *Those barbarians ought to be denied admittance to the games.* —adj. **3** °uncivilized, °uncultivated, uncultured, °philistine, °savage; barbarous, barbaric, °coarse, °vulgar, uncouth, °rude; °boorish, loutish, oafish, °crude, °rough, insensitive, churlish, uncivil: *One sees a great deal of barbarian behaviour every day.*

barbarity n. cruelty, inhumanity, ruthlessness, savagery, brutishness, barbarousness, heartlessness, viciousness, cold-bloodedness, bloodthirstiness: *The barbarity of this mass murderer cannot be overstated.*

bare adj. **1** unclothed, °naked, °nude, °stark °naked, unclad, exposed, uncovered, hatless, unshod, undressed, *Brit* starkers; *Colloq* in the altogether, in one's birthday suit, in the buff; *Slang US* bare-ass: *He stood completely bare in the middle of the room.* **2** unconcealed, °undisguised, °open, revealed, °literal, bald, °manifest, °out-and-out, °overt, uncovered, straightforward, °direct, °unvarnished, unembellished, °cold, °hard, °plain, °unadorned, °basic, °simple: *The bare facts point to him as the culprit.* **3** unfurnished, undecorated, °vacant, stripped, °empty: *The landlord entered and found a bare flat—the tenants had done a moonlight flit.* **4** denuded, stripped, leafless, defoliated, shorn, °barren; bared: *After the storm the trees were entirely bare of foliage. The hurricane began blowing in earnest, and the little ketch was driving forward under bare poles.* **5** °plain, °mere, °simple, °minimal, °essential, °absolute, °basic; °meagre, scant, °scanty: *For years we scraped by with only the bare necessities of life.* —v. **6** °expose, °lay bare, uncover, °reveal, °open; undress, °unveil: *The torrential rain had washed away the soil, baring the clay and rock beneath. He tore off his shirt, baring his hairy chest.* **7** °disclose, °reveal, °lay bare, uncover, divulge, °unfold, °tell, °expose, unmask, bring to °light: *Because of* *the way he had treated her, she decided to bare his secrets to the police. Benson bares his soul in his book.* **8** °strip, °divest, denude; defoliate: *The autumn winds bared all the trees in the arboretum.*

barefaced *adj.* **1** unconcealed, °open, °undisguised, °blatant, °manifest, °unmitigated, °outright, °downright, °out-and-out, °sheer, unalloyed, °undiluted: *His proposal is a barefaced attempt to gain control of the committee.* **2** °audacious, °impudent, °shameless, °insolent, °impertinent, °immodest, °bold, arrant, °unabashed, °forward, °brazen, °brassy, saucy, °pert, unblushing, *Colloq* °cheeky: *She said that he was a barefaced liar and that she would have nothing more to do with him.*

barely *adv.* °scarcely, °only, °just, not °quite, °hardly, only °just, no more than: *I barely had my coat off when she said she'd forgotten to shop for dinner.*

bargain *n.* **1** °agreement, °contract, °understanding, °arrangement, covenant, °pact, °compact, °settlement, °transaction, °deal: *We made a bargain—I would provide the materials and he would do the work.* **2** good °deal, *Colloq* give-away, *US* °steal: *If you paid only $100 for this painting, you got a real bargain.*
—*v.* **3** °negotiate, °trade, °haggle, barter, °dicker, chaffer: *We bargained far into the night, and finally came to an agreement after eight hours of discussion.* **4 bargain for**: °expect, °count on, °anticipate, °foresee, take into °account, °allow for, be °prepared for: *Even though the storm had been predicted, it was windier than we had bargained for.*

barren *adj.* **1** °sterile, childless, °infertile: *We won't have any calf from this barren cow.* **2** unproductive, °sterile, °bare, °infertile; °fruitless, °dry, unfruitful, °unprofitable, °poor: *The land was exceedingly stony and barren. The fifteenth century was the most barren period in the history of English literature.*

barrier *n.* **1** °bar, °fence, railing, °wall; ditch, ha-ha: *A barrier was erected at each end of the street. This barrier will keep the dingoes from killing the sheep.* **2** °obstacle, °bar, °obstruction, °block, °impediment, °hindrance: *Neither race, nor creed, nor colour shall be a barrier to success.* **3** °boundary, boundary line, °limit, °frontier: *No mountain barrier lay between France and Flanders.*

barring *prep.* excluding, °exclusive of, °bar, omitting, leaving out, excepting, °except (for), °save for, aside from, °besides, but: *Barring another stock market crash, your money is safe. Nobody else, barring the author, knew the truth of the matter.*

base¹ *n.* **1** °bottom, foot, °support, °stand, °pedestal: *The base of the statue cracked and the whole thing fell down. Have you been able to find a teak base for the new lamp?* **2** °groundwork, °background, °fundamental °principle, °principle, °foundation, underpinning; infrastructure, °basis: *Henry's charter was at once welcomed as a base for the needed reforms.* **3** °root, °theme, °radical, °stem, °core: *In the word interdigitation the base is* -digit-. **4** °home, °station, °camp, starting-point, °point of departure, °post, °centre: *Using the Sherpa village as a base of operations, we set up smaller camps as we began to climb the mountain.*
—*v.* **5** °establish, °found, °secure, °build, °ground, °anchor, °fix, hinge, °form; °derive, °draw: *We are basing all our hopes on his ability to*

do a deal. **6** °establish, headquarter, °post, °station, °position, °place: *The company is based in Guernsey.*

base² *adj.* **1** °low, undignified, °cowardly, °selfish, °mean, °despicable, °contemptible, °filthy, °evil: *He must have had some base motive in revealing to her what Martha had said.* **2** degraded, °degrading, °menial, °inferior, °mean, °unworthy, °lowly, °low, °grovelling, °servile, slavish, subservient, °downtrodden, abject, °miserable, °wretched, °sordid, undignified, ignoble, °dishonourable, °disreputable, °vile, °scurrilous, °wicked, *Colloq* infra dig: *Foolish sinners will submit to the basest servitude, and be attendants of swine.* **3** °mean, °cheap, °sorry, °common, °poor, °shabby, °shoddy: *He cast off his base attire, revealing a splendid suit of armour like burnished gold.* **4** °sordid, °offensive, °lewd, °lascivious, °obscene, °profane, °rude, ribald, °unseemly, °vulgar, °coarse, °dirty, °indecent, °evil-minded, °filthy, °pornographic: *The entertainment in that theatre caters to the basest appetites.* **5** °poor, °shoddy, °cheap, °fake, pinchbeck, °inferior, °counterfeit, °fraudulent, debased, forged, °spurious, °worthless, °bad: *Her jewels look valuable but are, in fact, made of base materials.* **6** °wicked, °evil, °wretched, °corrupt, °shameful, currish, °loathsome, °scurvy, °insufferable, °villainous: *They were labelled as base infidels and treated with contempt and cruelty.*

bashful *adj.* **1** °shy, °retiring, °embarrassed, °meek, abashed, °shamefaced, °sheepish, °timid, diffident, self-effacing, unconfident; °ill at ease, uneasy, uncomfortable, °nervous, °self-conscious, °awkward, °confused, *Colloq* in a tizzy, *US and Canadian* discombobulated: *Henry is so bashful in the presence of women that he blushes merely talking to them.* **2** °modest, °coy, unassuming, unostentatious, demure, °reserved, restrained, *Rare* verecund: *When we first met, she was a bashful young girl of fifteen who had no notion of her own beauty.*

basic *adj.* °fundamental, °essential, °key, °elementary, underlying, °prime, °primary, °root; °principal, °central, °focal, °vital: *He enrolled for a basic course in Sanskrit. We must reconsider the basic facts.*

basis *n.* **1** °foundation, °base, °bottom, °heart, °footing, °principle, underpinning; infrastructure: *The three R's form the basis of elementary education. Do you think our society still rests on the basis of the family?* **2** °essence, main °ingredient or constituent, °point of departure: *The basis of the discussion is that the hospitals are understaffed.*

batch *n.* **1** °quantity, °lot; °amount, °volume: *Mother baked a huge batch of bread.* **2** °set, °group, °number, °quantity, °assortment, °bunch, °pack, °collection: *Please sort this batch of cards into alphabetical order.*

batter *v.* **1** °beat, °hit, °strike, clout, °belabour, °pound, pummel *or* pommel, °pelt, bash, smite, thrash, *Colloq* wallop, clobber: *He was battered till he was black and blue.* **2** °bombard, °attack, °assault: *Battering by the cannons finally breached the wall of the fort.* **3** maltreat, °mistreat, °ill-treat, °abuse; maul, °bruise, °harm, °mangle, disfigure: *The police report an increase in complaints about battered wives and children.*

battle *n.* **1** °fight, °conflict, °combat, °action, °encounter, °clash, °engagement, °struggle, Donnybrook, °fray, *Law* affray; °brawl, °fracas,

mêlée or melee; °contest; duel, hand-to-hand °encounter: *You won the battle, but you lost the war. And now, the battle between the world champion and the challenger!* **2** °argument, °dispute, altercation, °quarrel, °war; °contest, °competition; °struggle, °fight, °crusade, °campaign: *The battle spilt out of the restaurant and into the street. We are not yet winning the battle against AIDS.*
—v. **3** Usually, **battle against**: °fight, contend or °struggle or °fight with or °strive against, °combat: *We must battle against ignorance at every opportunity.*

bauble n. °gewgaw, trinket, °ornament, °trifle, °toy, bagatelle, knick-knack, °plaything, kickshaw: *Wear your diamonds to the ball, my dear, not those cheap baubles.*

bawdy adj. °lewd, °obscene, °taboo, °vulgar, °dirty, smutty, °filthy, °coarse, °earthy, °gross, scatological, °rude, °lascivious, salacious, indelicate, °indecent, indecorous, °broad, °crude, ribald, °risqué, °suggestive, Rabelaisian, °uninhibited, unrestrained, °lusty, *Literary* lubricious or lubricous: *Afterwards, each of us had to recite a bawdy limerick.*

bawl v. **1** °shout, °bellow, vociferate, °roar, °yell, trumpet, thunder, *Colloq* holler: *Fishwives bawled out their wares continuously, creating a deafening din.* **2** °cry, wail, °weep, °keen, squall, blubber, whimper; yelp, *Colloq* yammer: *Stop that bawling or I'll really give you something to cry about!* **3 bawl out**: °scold, °reprimand, °upbraid: *My father bawled me out because I stayed out past midnight.*

beach n. **1** shore, lakeshore, bank, seashore, seaside, lido, strand, °coast, °margin, *Formal* littoral: *The children wanted to go to the beach and build sandcastles.*
—v. **2** °ground, run aground, strand; °careen: *Despite the heavy surf, we finally beached the boat safely.*

beacon n. °signal, °sign, °fire, °light, bonfire, °flare, signal fire, Very °light, °rocket; lighthouse, pharos: *Beacons blazed at the tops of the hills to spread the news of the victory. The drunkard's nose shone like a beacon.*

beam n. **1** °timber, scantling, girder, rafter; °bar, °brace, °plank, °board, stud, trestle: *Are you sure that these beams will support the weight of the upper storeys?* **2** °ray, °gleam, °shaft; pencil: *I could just make out his face in the beam of the electric torch.*
—v. **3** °radiate, °shine; °smile radiantly: *The door opened and the firelight beamed forth onto the snowdrifts. 'I'm so happy to meet you at last', she beamed.*

beamy adj. °broad, °wide, broad in the beam; °big, °heavy, °chubby, chunky, °fat, °obese: *She's quite a beamy boat, with accommodation for eight below. A beamy gentleman sat on my homburg, squashing it flat.*

bear v. **1** °carry, °transport, convey, °move, °take, *Colloq* tote: *She was borne round the stadium on the shoulders of her team-mates.* **2** °carry, °support, sustain, °shoulder, °hold up, °uphold; °suffer, °undergo, °experience, °endure: *Looking after her invalid mother while working is a heavy burden to bear.* **3** °merit, be °worthy of, °warrant; °provoke, invite: *Gordon's suggestion bears looking into.* **4** °stand, °abide, °tolerate, °brook, °survive, °endure, °stand up to; °reconcile oneself to, °admit of, *Colloq* °put up with: *How can you bear such boring people? His actions will not bear examination. I cannot bear to*

see you unhappy. **5** °have, °carry, °show, °exhibit, °display, °sustain: *The getaway car bore German licence plates. The knight bore the scars of many battles. She bears her grandmother's name.* **6** °produce, °yield, °develop, °breed, °generate, engender; °give °birth to, °spawn, °bring forth: *Our apple tree did not bear any fruit this year. She bore thirteen children and still had time to write books.* **7** °entertain, °harbour, °wish: *He bore her no ill will, despite her accusations.* **8 bear on** or **upon**: °relate or have °relevance or be °relevant to or °pertain to, °touch on or upon, °affect, °concern, °have a °bearing on or upon, °influence: *I don't quite see how your illness bears on which school James attends.* **9 bear out**: °confirm, °support, corroborate, °substantiate, °uphold, back up: *The evidence bears out what I said.* **10 bear up**: **a** °survive, °hold out, °stand up, °hold up, °withstand: *Can Alex bear up under the strain of keeping two jobs?* **b** °support, °cheer, °encourage: *What hope have you to bear you up?* **11 bear with**: °put up with, be °patient with, make °allowance(s) for: *Please bear with me, I'm sure you'll think it was worth waiting when you see the finished result.*

bearable adj. °tolerable, °supportable, endurable, °acceptable, °manageable: *The heat last summer was made bearable only by frequent dips in the swimming-pool.*

bearing n. **1** °carriage, deportment, °manner, °behaviour, °conduct, °aspect, demeanour, °posture, °stance, °air, °attitude, mien, °presence: *Lewis's noble bearing makes him noticeable, even in a crowd.* **2** sustaining, supporting, °endurance, °enduring: *Thomas Jefferson considered the government of England totally without morality and insolent beyond bearing.* **3** °aspect, °relation, °reference, °relationship, correlation, pertinence, °relevance, °connection, relevancy, applicability, °application, germaneness, °significance: *The legal bearing of the case will become obvious in court. It is unclear exactly what bearing your remarks have on the situation.* **4** Often, **bearings**: °direction, °orientation, (relative) °position: *The bearing of the lighthouse is now 180°. Which way is north?—I have lost my bearings entirely.*

beast n. **1** °animal, °creature, being: *He loves all the beasts of the field, of the sea, and of the air.* **2** °brute, °savage, °animal, °monster: *I've seen that beast hitting his wife in public.*

beastly adj. **1** °uncivilized, uncultivated, uncivil, °rude, °crude, °boorish, °unrefined, °coarse; °cruel, °inhuman, °savage, barbaric, barbarous, bestial, °brutal: *Priscilla treats Cyril in a beastly way.* **2** °abominable, intolerable, °offensive, unpleasant, °awful, °terrible, °ghastly, horrid, °disagreeable, °horrible, °hateful, execrable; °foul, °vile, °nasty, °rotten, °dirty, °filthy: *If this beastly weather keeps up, the plane may be delayed.*

beat v. **1** °strike, °pound, bash, smite, °batter, pummel or pommel, °belabour, °pelt, clout, thrash, give (someone) a °thrashing or beating, drub, °manhandle, thump, whack, cane, °scourge, °whip, bludgeon, °club, cudgel, fustigate; °whip, °flog, lash, *Colloq* clobber, wallop, give (someone) a once-over: *At first he refused to tell them, but then they beat it out of him.* **2** °defeat, °best, worst, °win (out) over, vanquish, °trounce, °rout, °outdo, °subdue, °overcome, °overwhelm, °pre-empt; °surpass, °conquer, °crush, °master,

US °beat out: *Can they beat Manchester United for the cup? He first beat the Danes, then the Russians.* **3** throb, °pulsate, palpitate, °pound, thump: *I could feel my heart beating against my ribs.* **4** *Nautical* tack: *Close-hauled, the sloop was beating to windward against the howling gale.* **5** hammer, °forge, °shape, °form, °fashion, °make, °mould: *They shall beat their swords into ploughshares.* **6** °mix, °whip, °stir, °blend: *Beat two eggs, then add the flour and sugar.* **7** tread, °wear, °trample: *The hunters beat a path through the forest.* **8 beat it**: °depart, °leave, abscond, °run off *or* away, *Slang US* °take it on the lam, lam out of here, *US* hit the road: *You'd better beat it before the cops come.* **9 beat off**: °drive off *or* away, °rout: *We beat off our attackers, who fled into the forest.*
—*n.* **10** °stroke, °blow: *The signal was to be three beats of a tin cup on the pipes.* **11** °rhythm, °tempo, °measure; °pulse, throb, °stress, pulsation: *In boogie-woogie the beat is eight to the bar.* **12** °course, °round, °tour, °route, °circuit, °run, °path; °area, bailiwick: *In the old days, it was the bobby on the beat who prevented a lot of crime. As a reporter, my beat is the financial news.*
—*adj.* **13** °dead beat, °exhausted, °spent, drained, °worn out, °weary, bone-tired, °fatigued, fagged: *I was really beat after completing the marathon.*

beautiful *adj.* **1** °attractive, charming, °comely, °lovely, good-looking, °fair, °pretty, alluring, appealing, °handsome, °radiant, °gorgeous, *Formal* pulchritudinous, *Scots* °bonny; *Colloq* smashing: *She's not only intelligent, she's beautiful. She entered on the arm of some beautiful youth.* **2** °excellent, °first-rate, unequalled, °skilful, °admirable, °magnificent, °well done; °superb, spectacular, °splendid, °marvellous, wonderful, °incomparable, °superior, °elegant, °exquisite, °pleasant, °pleasing, °delightful, *Colloq* smashing: *The garage did a beautiful job in tuning the engine. Armand's arranged a beautiful wedding reception for us.*

beautifully *adv.* **1** attractively, chicly, fashionably, delightfully, charmingly, splendidly, magnificently, *Colloq* smashingly: *The princess was beautifully dressed in a rose satin ball-gown.* **2** admirably, superbly, excellently, wonderfully, marvellously, splendidly, spectacularly, magnificently, *Colloq* smashingly: *Emily played her solo beautifully.*

beautify *v.* adorn, °embellish, °decorate, °ornament, titivate, °elaborate, garnish, deck (out), bedeck: *The old façade was removed and the building beautified by refacing it with white marble.*

beauty *n.* **1** loveliness, attractiveness, handsomeness, pulchritude: *The beauty of the actress took my breath away.* **2** belle, *Colloq* looker, °knockout, °dream, dreamboat, stunner: *She was one of the great beauties of her day.* **3** °attraction, °strength, °advantage, °asset: *The beauty of the plan lies in its simplicity.*

beckon *v.* °signal, °gesture, °motion; °summon, °bid, °call: *The manager beckoned to me and I went over to see what he wanted.*

become *v.* **1** °turn *or* °change *or* °transform into: *The princess kissed the prince, who immediately became a frog.* **2** °grow *or* °develop *or* evolve into; °mature *or* °ripen into: *It's hard to believe that this dull caterpillar will eventually become a splendid butterfly.* **3** °enhance, °suit, °fit, befit, be °proper

or °appropriate for, °behove *or US* behoove: *Moonlight becomes you, It goes with your hair.* **4** °grace, adorn: *Walter was a man who became the dignity of his function as a commissionaire.* **5 become of**: come of, °happen to: *What will become of you if you don't go to school?*

becoming *adj.* enhancing, beautifying, °seemly; °attractive, °comely, °fetching, °chic, °stylish, °fashionable, °tasteful; °appropriate, °fitting, °fit, °meet, °befitting, °proper, °suitable: *Your new hairdo is most becoming, Frances.*

bedlam *n.* °pandemonium, °uproar, hubbub, commotion, °confusion, °tumult, turmoil, °furore *or US* furor, °chaos; madhouse: *The chancellor's announcement created instant bedlam in the Commons.*

bedraggled *adj.* soiled, °dirty, °muddy, muddied, °untidy, stained, dishevelled, scruffy, messy; °wet, °sloppy, °soaking *or* sopping *or* wringing °wet, soaked, drenched, *Colloq* gungy, *US* grungy: *We took the two bedraggled waifs in out of the pouring rain.*

befitting *adj.* °fitting, °becoming, °due, °suitable *or* suited (to), °appropriate (to), apropos, °proper (to), °seemly (for): *He really ought to behave in a manner befitting his position as chairman. This must be done with a befitting sense of awe.*

before *adv.* **1** °previously, earlier, already, beforehand; °formerly, in the °past; °once: *I have told you before, don't count your chickens.* **2** °ahead, in °advance, in °front, in the forefront, °first, in the vanguard, *Colloq* up °front: *He walked on before, as he knew the way.* **3** °ahead, in the °future, to °come: *Before lie the prospects of surrendering or dying.*
—*prep.* **4** °ahead of, in °advance of, in °front of, forward of: *The king indicated that the page should go before him.* **5** in °front of; in the °presence of: *The entire valley was spread out before me.* **6** °preceding, °previous *or* anterior to, °prior to; on the °eve of: *Before my departure I have to kiss Annie goodbye.* **7** in °preference to, °rather than, sooner than, more °willingly than: *They said they would die before yielding.*
—*conj.* **8** °previous to *or* °preceding the °time when: *This was a nice place before the day-trippers arrived.*

beg *v.* **1** entreat, °beseech, °plead (with), crave, implore, importune, °wheedle, °cajole, supplicate (with), °pray; °ask for, °request: *She begged me to stay.* **2** °solicit, sponge, *Colloq* cadge, °scrounge, *US* panhandle: *When he was an alcoholic, he used to beg drinks off everyone.*

beggar *n.* **1** mendicant, °supplicant, suppliant, alms-man, sponger, °tramp, vagrant, °pauper, *Colloq* cadger, scrounger, *US* panhandler: *We were approached by beggars on every street corner.* **2** °fellow, °man, °person, *Colloq* °chap, °guy, bloke: *I feel sorry for the poor beggar who lost his wallet at the station.*
—*v.* **3** impoverish; °want, °challenge, °defy, baffle: *The misery of those people beggars description.*

begin *v.* **1** °start (out *or* off *or* in *or* on), °initiate, °enter on *or* upon, °set out *or* about, °set out on *or* upon, *Rather formal* °commence: *We began the journey full of enthusiasm.* **2** °start (off), °inaugurate, °originate, °open, °launch, °create, °establish, °found, °set up; °go into: *We began the company five years ago.* **3** °arise, °start,

°originate, *Rather formal* °commence: *The greatness of the Prussian monarchy begins with Frederick II. The paragraph begins in the middle of the page.*

beginning *n.* **1** °start, commencement, °outset, °onset, inception, °dawn, dawning, °birth, genesis, °origin, °creation, day one; origination, °source, well-spring: *There are several competing theories about the beginning of life on earth. The beginning of the idea can be traced to Galileo.* **2** °opening, °start, inception, commencement: *I have plenty of energy at the beginning of the day. The book is good at the beginning, but then it gets boring.*

begrudge *v.* **1** °resent, °envy, °grudge: *She doesn't begrudge him his success.* **2** give (be)grudgingly or unwillingly or reluctantly, °deny, °refuse: *He begrudges her the slightest consideration.*

beguile *v.* **1** delude, °deceive, °cheat, °swindle, °dupe, °fool, °mislead, °hoodwink, bamboozle, °take in: *She was easily beguiled by his solicitude.* **2** °defraud (of), °deprive (of), °cheat (out of or into), °swindle (out of): *Let no man beguile you of your reward.* **3** °charm, °divert, °amuse, °distract, °fascinate, engross, °engage, allure: *I always meet the most beguiling people at Daphne's parties.*

behalf *n.* **on** or *US* **in behalf of**, or **on** or *US* **in one's behalf**: °for, as a °representative of, in °place of, °instead of, in the °name of, on the °part of; in the °interest of, for the °benefit or °advantage of: *The lawyer is acting on behalf of the heirs.*

behave *v.* °act, °react, °function, °operate, °perform, °work, °conduct or deport or comport or °bear (oneself); °act obediently, °act °properly, be °good: *The boy behaved with great insolence. I wish the children would behave themselves.*

behaviour *n.* °conduct, demeanour, deportment, °bearing, °manners, comportment; °action(s): *His behaviour in the presence of the royal couple was abominable.*

behead *v.* decapitate, guillotine, *Archaic* decollate: *Criminals and enemies of the state were formerly beheaded.*

behold *v.* °see, °look at, °regard, °set or °lay eyes on, descry, °notice, °note, espy, °perceive, discern, °remark, °view: *As we emerged from the gorge, we beheld the mountain looming above us.*

beholden *adj.* °obliged, obligated, °indebted, °grateful, in °debt, under (an) °obligation: *She said that she was beholden to him for everything he had done.*

behove *v.* behoove; be required of, be incumbent on, be proper of, be fitting of or for, befit; be advisable for, be worthwhile for, be expeditious for or of, be advantageous to or for, be useful to or for, be beneficial to or for: *It behoves you to be respectful to the chairman of the board.*

belabour *v.* thrash, °beat, pummel or pommel, buffet, °pelt, °lambaste: *We tried to stop the drover from belabouring the poor horse with a whip.*

belated *adj.* °late; behind °time, behindhand, out of °date; delayed, detained: *I forgot your birthday, so here's a belated gift.*

belief *n.* **1** °trust, dependence, °reliance, °confidence, °faith, °security, °assurance: *He retains his belief in the divine right of kings.* **2** acceptance, credence; assent: *His statements are unworthy of belief.* **3** °tenet, °view, °idea, °sentiment, °conviction, °doctrine, dogma,

°principle(s), axiom, °maxim, °creed, °opinion, °persuasion: *The belief that there is no God is as definite a creed as the belief in one God or in many gods.* **4** °intuition, °judgement: *It is her belief that nuclear energy will eventually prove economical.*

believe *v.* **1** °accept, put °faith or credence in or into, find credible, find creditable; °allow, °think, °hold, °maintain, °feel; °take it, °suppose, °assume: *He still believes that the moon is made of green cheese.* **2 believe in**: °trust to or in, °rely upon or on, have °faith or °confidence in, put one's °trust in, be convinced of, °swear by, °credit; have the courage of one's convictions: *Do you believe everything you read in the papers? The chairman believes in your ability to carry out the plan.* **3 make believe**: °pretend, °suppose, °imagine, °fancy, conjecture, °assume: *I used to make believe I was a great detective.*

belittle *v.* °diminish, °minimize, °disparage, °slight, decry, °detract from, °depreciate, °trivialize, deprecate, °degrade, denigrate, °downgrade, de-emphasize, °discredit, °criticize, derogate; °reduce, °mitigate, lessen, undervalue, °underestimate, underrate, °minimize, *Colloq* °play down, pooh-pooh: *He belittles the efforts of others but accomplishes nothing himself.*

belligerent *adj.* **1** warring; °warlike, °militant, warmongering, hawkish, jingoistic, bellicose, °martial: *The belligerent nations have agreed to discuss an accord.* **2** °quarrelsome, °pugnacious, contentious, disputatious, °truculent, °aggressive, °hostile, combative, antagonistic, bellicose: *I cannot see why you have to take such a belligerent attitude towards the chairman.*
—*n.* **3** warring party, °antagonist, °contestant; warmonger, hawk, jingoist, °militant: *Our country has refused to sell arms to the belligerents in the conflict.*

bellow *v.* **1** °roar; °yell, °shout, °blare, trumpet, °howl, *Colloq* holler: *Father was bellowing that he couldn't find his pipe. The public-address system bellowed out my name.*
—*n.* **2** °roar; °yell, °shout, *Colloq* holler: *The bull gave a bellow and charged.*

belong *v.* **1** be a °member (of), be °affiliated or associated or connected (with), be °attached or °bound (to), be a °part (of): *Does he belong to the Green party? He didn't want to belong while his wife was a member.* **2** have a (°proper) °place (in), be °proper (to): *Do you ever get the feeling that you don't belong here?* **3 belong to**: be owned by, be the °property or °possession of: *That coat belongs to me.*

belonging *n.* °association, °connection, °alliance, °relationship, °affinity, °relation: *She says the Church gives her a strong sense of belonging.*

belongings *n.* (personal) °property, °effects, °possessions, °goods, °things, chattels: *He returned home to find all his belongings in the street.*

beloved *adj.* **1** loved, cherished, adored, °dear, dearest, °darling, °precious, treasured; admired, worshipped, revered, esteemed, idolized, respected; valued, prized: *He denied nothing to his beloved children. She was their beloved queen.*
—*n.* **2** °sweetheart, °darling, dearest, °love; °lover, °paramour, inamorata or inamorato, *Colloq* °flame: *He wrote poems to his beloved.*

below *adv.* **1** °lower down, °further down, farther down: *Please see the explanation given below. The department head could no longer resist the pressures from below.* **2** °beneath, underneath,

°under; downstairs, *Nautical* below-decks, *Brit* below-stairs: *Can you hear someone walking about below? They put the captain in irons below.* **3** on °earth, here, in this °world, under the sun: *Man wants but little here below.* —*prep.* **4** °under, underneath, °beneath: *Below the sea live creatures we have never even seen. Barely discernible below his nose was a tiny moustache. Sign your name below 'Yours truly'.* **5** less *or* °lower *or* cheaper than: *The sale price is below cost.* **6** deeper *or* °further *or* farther down than: *The current is strongest about six feet below the surface.* **7** °under, °beneath, underneath: *Her bright eyes peered at him from below the wide hat.* **8** °lower *or* less than, °under: *The temperature was 20 degrees below zero.* **9** °inferior *or* °subordinate to, °lower than: *He gives orders to the servants below him.* **10** °inferior *or* °secondary to, °under, °beneath, °lower than: *In exports, the USA and UK are below Japan.* **11** °beneath, °unworthy of, unbefitting, not °worth: *Mugging old ladies is below contempt.*

belt *n.* **1** sash; *Literary* girdle, cestus, cincture, °zone: *At her belt she wore a dagger in a golden scabbard.* **2** °zone, °band, °strip, °circuit, °perimeter; °area, °swath, °tract, °region, °district: *The planners ensured that each city would be surrounded by a green belt.* —*v.* **3** °strike, °hit, °punch; °beat, thrash: *When he insulted her, I simply belted him.* **4 belt out**: °sing *or* °perform stridently *or* loudly; °put over *or* across: *Sophie Tucker was there, belting out 'One of These Days'.*

bemoan *v.* °lament, °mourn *or* °grieve *or* °weep *or* °moan for: *She bitterly bemoaned the loss of her sole companion, her canary.*

bemuse *v.* **1** °confuse, °muddle, °mix up, addle, befuddle, °perplex, °bewilder, °puzzle, *Colloq US and Canadian* discombobulate: *The actors were thoroughly bemused by the sudden appearance of a horse on stage.* **2** stupefy, benumb, °numb, °paralyse: *I found him, completely bemused, with the empty bottle beside him.*

bend *n.* **1** curve, °turn, turning, corner; °bow, °angle, crook, °hook, curvature, flexure: *Go left at the bend in the road. If you put a bend in a wire hanger, you can fish out the obstruction.* —*v.* **2** °arch, °bow, curve, crook: *Soak the branch in water and it will bend easily. Stop bending my arm—it hurts!* **3** °bow; curtsy *or* curtsey; °kowtow, salaam; °kneel, genuflect: *The cannibal bent down before a pile of skulls.* **4** °incline, °channel, °focus, °direct, °steer, °set; °fix: *He bent his attention on more important matters. She bent her steps towards the cemetery.* **5** °submit, °bow, °yield, give °way, be pliant *or* subservient *or* °tractable: *The cabinet bends to the will of the prime minister.* **6** °incline, °turn, °deflect: *As you can see, the ray is bent by the lens.*

bender *Colloq n.* °drunk, °spree, °revel, carousal, °carouse, bacchanal; *Slang* binge, °jag, *US* toot: *He goes off on a bender whenever his wife leaves him.*

beneath *adv.* **1** °low *or* °lower down, °below, °under, underneath: *Please sign beneath if you agree the terms.* **2** °below, underneath, °under; °underground: *The flowers are above the ground, the roots beneath.* —*prep.* **3** °under, underneath, °below: *Beneath that gruff exterior of his beats a heart of gold.*

4 °below, °unworthy of, unbefitting, undeserving of, not (even) meriting, °lower than: *Your behaviour is beneath criticism.*

benefactor *n.* °patron, °supporter, °sponsor, °donor, °philanthropist; °backer, investor, *Colloq* angel: *Our benefactor has made a donation that will enable the mission to carry on its work.*

beneficial *adj.* **1** °advantageous, °serviceable, °useful, °profitable, °helpful, °supportive, °favourable, °constructive, °good: *No measures could have been more beneficial to the kingdom.* **2** healthful, °healthy, salutary, salubrious; °efficacious, °effective: *A certain amount of sunshine is quite beneficial.*

benefit *n.* **1** °advantage, °profit, °good, °sake, °gain, °aid, °help, °service: *It would be to their benefit to call off the strike.* **2** Often, **benefits**: °perquisite(s), emolument(s), °allowance(s), °extra(s), °fringe benefit(s), *Colloq* °perk(s): *We offer one of the best schemes in the industry for employee benefits.* —*v.* **3** °improve, °aid, °help, °better, °promote, °further, °advance, °forward: *Enrolling on a management course could benefit your chances for advancement.* **4** °profit, °gain: *No one has ever personally benefited a penny from these contributions.*

benevolence *n.* **1** °charity, °kindness, kindliness, °humanity, humanitarianism, beneficence, charitableness, goodness, °altruism, °good will, unselfishness, °philanthropy, generosity, magnanimity: *The poor people in the village used to rely on his benevolence.* **2** °gift, °grant, contribution, °donation, beneficence: *The victims of the famine were recipients of the benevolence of the British people.*

benevolent *adj.* °charitable, well-disposed, °gracious, °good, °kind, °kindly, humane, °humanitarian, well-wishing, °thoughtful, °considerate, °sympathetic, caring, kind-hearted, warm-hearted, compassionate, °benign, benignant; °liberal, °generous, magnanimous, open-handed; °beneficial, °helpful, salutary: *That hypocrite has cast himself in the role of a benevolent despot.*

benighted *adj.* unenlightened, °naïve, °uninformed, °ignorant: *That poor, benighted fool believes that the doctors can cure him.*

benign *adj.* **1** °kindly, °gracious, °good, °kind, kind-hearted, °benevolent, benignant, °warm, warm-hearted, °cordial, °genial, congenial, °tender, tender-hearted, compassionate, °sympathetic, °soft-hearted: *It was Grandad's benign goodwill that kept us together in those hard times.* **2** °bland, °gentle, °mild, °warm: *A benign smile lit the headmaster's face as he announced the awards for scholastic achievement.* **3** °kind, °favourable, °fortunate; salutary, salubrious, °mild, congenial, °propitious: *She recovered rapidly in that most benign climate.* **4** non-fatal, non-malignant, nonvirulent, curable, °harmless: *Fortunately, the biopsy showed that the tumour was benign.*

bent *adj.* **1** curved, deflected, bowed, °crooked, distorted: *He complained to the waiter just because the fork was bent.* **2** °strange, °weird, °peculiar, twisted, °deviant, warped, °wry, awry, °corrupt, corrupted; °perverted, °perverse, °abnormal: *You'd be bent, too, if you'd been in prison for fifteen years.* **3** °dishonest, °crooked, °illegal: *That share deal sounds a bit bent to me: I'll pass.*

4 °determined, °intent, °set, resolved, °resolute, °decided: *Garvey is bent on running in the marathon, despite his sprained ankle.*
—*n.* **5** °turn, °inclination, °direction, °disposition, predisposition, °tendency, °bias, °leaning, proclivity, propensity, °partiality, °prejudice; °ability, °aptitude, °talent, °gift: *She wished to follow the bent of her own taste. He has a natural bent for music.*

bequeath *v.* °leave, °make over, °will, °pass on, °hand down *or* on, °transmit, *Law* °devise: *Aunt Margaret has bequeathed her collection of music boxes to the museum.*

bequest *n.* legacy, °inheritance: *A huge bequest was received by the hospital.*

berate *v.* °scold, chide, °rate, °upbraid, revile, °abuse, °rail at, excoriate, °castigate, objurgate; °harangue: *In the square an ancient virago was berating a butcher.*

bereave *v.* °deprive; °strip, °rob, °dispossess: *The accident bereaved him of his child.*

berserk *adj.* amok, °mad, °violent, °wild, crazed, frenzied, °maniacal: *He went berserk, destroying tables and chairs.*

beseech *v.* supplicate, entreat, implore, °plead (with), °beg, importune, obsecrate: *The prisoners beseeched the king to have mercy on them.*

beset *v.* encompass, °surround, °besiege; assail, °attack, °harass, harry, hector, °bother, °afflict, °trouble: *She was beset by all the problems involved in having a job and a family.*

beside *prep.* **1** alongside, °near, next to, with, °close to, hard by, °nearby, °by: *A handsome young man walked up and sat down beside her.* **2** away from, °wide of, °apart from, unconnected with, °off: *The fact that I owe you money is entirely beside the point.* **3 beside oneself**: out of one's °mind *or* wits, at the end of one's tether, °overwrought, °agitated, °upset, °crazy, °mad: *She was beside herself with grief when she heard the news.*

besides *adv.* **1** in °addition, additionally, also; °further, furthermore, °moreover, as °well, too; to °boot, on top of everything else, into the °bargain: *Maria is our choice for the post and, besides, she's the only qualified person available. On their anniversary he gave her a diamond ring and a sapphire brooch besides.*
—*prep.* **2** over and above, above and beyond, in °addition to, additionally to, as °well as; aside from, °barring, excepting, °except for, excluding, °exclusive of, not counting *or* including, beyond, °apart from, other than: *St Paul became acquainted with many Christians besides his converts.*

besiege *v.* **1** °lay °siege to, beleaguer: *For ten years Troy was besieged by the Greeks.* **2** blockade, °block, °block off *or* up, hem in, °cut off; °surround, °crowd round: *The strikers have besieged the factory gates, not allowing anyone in or out.* **3** importune, °sue, °petition, assail, pressurize *or US* °pressure, °press, °overwhelm, inundate: *The Home Office has been besieged by requests for leniency in your case.*

best *adj.* **1** °superlative, unexcelled, finest, °pre-eminent, °first, °superb, unsurpassed, °superior, °excellent, °paramount, °first-rate, *Colloq* A-1, A-one: *Henry VIII was the best rider, the best lance, and the best archer in England.* **2** kindest, most beneficent, nicest: *Which*

of your brothers is the best to you? **3** °foremost, choicest, °pre-eminent, most °suitable, most °appropriate, most °qualified, most °talented, most °desirable, most °outstanding: *We want the best person to fill the job.* **4** largest, most, greatest: *She had travelled the best part of the way by ship.* **5** richest, wealthiest; first-class, °upper crust, °upper-class: *He associates only with those he considers to be the best people.*
—*n.* **6** finest; °first: *The best is yet to come.* **7** °finery, best °clothes, *Colloq* best bib and tucker: *He was all decked out in his Sunday best.* **8** greatest *or* °maximum effort: *He did his best but it wasn't enough to win.*
—*adv.* **9** most excellently, to the fullest extent, in the most °suitable way, most adroitly, most skilfully, most superbly, most artistically: *All the children performed well, but Alice performed best.* **10** with greatest satisfaction, most successfully: *He who laughs last laughs best.*
—*v.* **11** °win (out) over, °conquer, °beat, °surpass, °overpower, get the °better of, °subdue, °defeat, worst, vanquish, trounce, °rout, °crush, °master, °outdo, °overwhelm, °overcome, °outwit: *He was bested in three falls out of four.*

bestow *v.* °confer; °give, °award, °present, °donate, °grant: *The country has bestowed its highest honours on her.*

bet *n.* **1** wager, °stake, °risk, °venture, *Brit* °punt, *Colloq Brit* °flutter: *He could not afford more than a small bet.*
—*v.* **2** wager, °stake, °gamble, °risk, °hazard, °play, °lay, °put, °chance, °venture, *Brit* °punt: *Every week he bet a small amount on the lottery.*

betray *v.* **1** be *or* prove °false *or* °disloyal to, °sell out, break °faith with, °let down, °fail, °inform on, *Colloq* °sell down the river, *Slang Brit* °shop: *He betrayed her to the enemy.* **2** °reveal, °disclose, divulge, °impart, °tell; °expose, °lay bare: *She betrayed their hide-out to the police. He betrayed an unsuspected streak of cowardice.* **3** lead astray, °mislead, misguide, °deceive, °dupe, °fool, °hoodwink: *He has been betrayed by his own arrogance.*

betrayal *n.* **1** treachery, treason, disloyalty, °perfidy, °traitorousness, faithlessness, bad faith, breach of °faith: *His delivery of the country into the hands of an invader was an outright act of betrayal.* **2** °revelation, divulging, disclosure, divulgence: *People should not be led into betrayals of their secret opinions.*

better[1] *adj.* **1** °superior: *You're a better man than I am, Gunga Din. Can you suggest a better investment than the Channel Tunnel? I know of no better invention than the wheel.* **2** more; greater, larger, bigger: *I waited for her the better part of two hours.* **3** wiser, safer, °well-advised, more °intelligent: *It would be better to wait till tomorrow to tell her.* **4** healthier, haler, heartier, less °ill *or US* °sick, improved; cured, recovered: *You will feel better after you have eaten something.*
—*adv.* **5** preferably, °best; more wisely, more advisedly, more safely: *We had better go before the trouble starts.* **6 better off: a** improved, happier, °well-advised: *You'd be better off attending a technical college.* **b** wealthier, richer: *She is better off than any of us.* **7 think better of**: reconsider, °think twice, °change one's °mind: *He was going to fight but thought better of it.*

—*n.* **8** °advantage, mastery, °superiority, °control: *Don't let the obstacle course get the better of you.* **9 betters**: superiors: *That young imp should learn how to address his elders and betters!*
—*v.* **10** °improve, ameliorate, °advance, °raise, elevate: *It was impossible in those days for labourers to better their condition.* **11** °surpass, °excel, °outdo, °outstrip, °beat, °improve: *She bettered her record in the 100-metre hurdles by two-tenths of a second.*

better² *n.* gambler, speculator, wagerer, gamester, *Brit* °punter, *US* bettor, *Colloq* crap-shooter, °sport: *The betters were gathered round the craps table.*

bewail *v.* °lament, °mourn, °bemoan, °moan *or* °mourn over, °shed tears *or* whimper over, °weep *or* °cry *or* °keen over, beat one's breast over: *Instead of bewailing his condition, why doesn't he do something about it?*

beware *v.* °take °heed, be °careful, be °wary, be °cautious, be on one's °guard, °exercise °caution, °mind, °watch out, °look out, take °care: *There are shoals nearby, so beware. Beware the ides of March!*

bewilder *v.* °confuse, confound, °perplex, °puzzle, °mystify, befuddle, baffle, °bemuse: *I was bewildered by differential calculus.*

bewitch *v.* °enchant, °entrance, spellbind, °charm, °fascinate, °beguile, cast a °spell on *or* over, °captivate, °enrapture: *She easily bewitches men with her sultry good looks and her husky, low voice.*

bias *n.* **1** °prejudice, °partiality; °inclination, °leaning, °bent, °disposition, propensity, °tendency, predilection, predisposition, proclivity: *She shows a marked bias in favour of the Irish.* **2** °angle, °slant, diagonal: *Cut the fabric on the bias.* **3** °influence, impulse, °weight: *If he is under any bias, it is on the side of fairness.*
—*v.* **4** °influence, °affect unduly *or* unfairly, °sway, °incline, °prejudice, °colour, °taint, predispose: *Artists are seldom good critics of art because they have been biased.*

biased *adj.* °prejudiced, °partial; warped, distorted, °jaundiced: *I don't want to listen to your biased opinions about women's rights.*

bicker *v.* °dispute, °quarrel, wrangle, °argue, squabble, °tiff, *Colloq* spat: *The couple next door are always bickering about trifling matters.*

bid *v.* **1** °offer, make an °offer (for), °tender, proffer: *We bid $500 for the painting.* **2** *Archaic or literary* ask, °pray, °press, entreat, °beg, °request, °suggest, invite: *She bade me leave her to mourn alone.* **3** *Formal* command, °demand, °order, °tell, enjoin, °dictate: *Please bid him enter. Custom bade him blow his horn.*

bidding *n.* **1** °invitation, summons: *We attended the ceremony at the bidding of the vice-chancellor.* **2** °command, °order, °dictate, °direction, °instruction, °demand: *The letter was sent to all theatre directors at the bidding of the Arts Minister.*

big *adj.* **1** °large, °great, °grand; °huge, °enormous, °immense, °gigantic, °giant, tremendous, °colossal, Brobdingnagian, °jumbo, *Colloq Brit* socking *or* whacking big *or* °great, *US* humongous: *We live in a big house in the country.* **2** °ample, °hefty, °huge, °bulky, °fat, °obese; °large, °hulking, beefy, °burly, °brawny, strapping, gargantuan, elephantine, °enormous, °gigantic, °immense, °monstrous: *The sumo wrestler was one of the biggest men I'd ever seen.* **3** °tall, grown, °mature, grown-up, °large: *Christopher is certainly big for his age.* **4** °important, °significant, °outstanding, °weighty, consequential, °major, °grave, °momentous, °notable, °noteworthy, °telling: *Changing careers can be one of the biggest decisions of your life.* **5** °important, °prominent, °illustrious, °noteworthy, °notable, °renowned, °eminent, °distinguished, esteemed: *Mr Johnson is a big man in our town.* **6** °generous, magnanimous, °charitable, °unselfish, giving: *It was very big of her to take on the support of the orphanage.* **7** °popular, °famous, °well-known, °successful: *That band is very big with the kids these days.* **8** °capital, °large, °upper case, majuscule: *Always spell London with a big L.*
—*adv.* **9** pompously, boastfully, conceitedly, arrogantly, pretentiously: *Alfred talks big at home, but he's very modest when he's with his friends.* **10** successfully, °well, oustandingly, effectively: *I think your speech went over big with those opposed to the new budget.*

bigoted *adj.* °prejudiced, °intolerant, °biased, °jaundiced, °one-sided, °partial: *The judge was bigoted against Blacks, which accounts for the unfair decision.*

bigotry *n.* °prejudice, °intolerance, °bias, °partiality: *No government that practises bigotry can survive long.*

bigwig *n.* **1** °boss, kingpin, °king, °queen, nabob, VIP, *Colloq* °big shot, °big gun, °big cheese, °big wheel, hotshot, °chief, °brass hat, *US* (°chief) honcho, Mr Big: *The bigwig sits here, at the head of the table.* **2 bigwigs**: brass, brass hats: *Don't let the bigwigs find out what we've done.*

bilious *adj.* ill-tempered, bad-tempered, ill-natured, °peevish, °testy, °cross, °petulant, tetchy, choleric, dyspeptic, °angry, wrathful: *The director was absolutely bilious when he heard we had lost the account.*

bill¹ *n.* **1** invoice, °account; °tally, °reckoning, tabulation, *US (restaurant)* °check, *Colloq US* °tab: *Have you paid the telephone bill?* **2** *US and Canadian* note, banknote, paper °money, *Colloq* folding °money: *The robbers took only small bills, which they could spend easily.*
—*v.* **3** invoice, °charge: *I haven't got my cheque-book with me, please could you bill me.*

bill² *n.* beak, neb, nib, pecker; jaws: *One of the birds had a fish in its bill.*

bind *v.* **1** °tie, °fasten, °secure, make °fast, °tie up: *The thieves bound him hand and foot.* **2** constrain; °hold, °oblige, °obligate: *The contract we signed is equally binding on both parties. The union is bound by an agreement that expires in a month.* **3** gird, °encircle, wreathe, °wrap, °cover, °swathe, bandage: *They were binding his wounded head.* **4** °cement, °stick, cause to adhere; °attach, °connect: *Ordinary glue will bind these pieces together.*
—*n.* **5** *in the US*: dilemma, °predicament, °tight °spot, °difficulty, °situation, *Colloq* pickle, °fix, °jam: *I'm in a real bind because I've invited two girls to the party.* **6** *in Britain*: annoyance, irritant, °bother, °bore, °trial, °ordeal, irritation, vexation, *Colloq* °pain (in the neck or arse): *It was a bit of a bind having to wait three hours at the airport.*

birth *n.* **1** childbirth, °delivery, *Technical* parturition, *Old-fashioned* confinement: *Nicole is expecting the birth of her first baby in early April.*

2 °origin, °creation, °emergence, °beginning, °start, origination: *I believe we may be present at the birth of a powerful idea.* **3** nativity, °origin, °extraction; °parentage, °line, °lineage, ancestry, descent, °family, blood: *She is Scottish by birth. Hortense is of noble birth.*

bisexual *adj.* **1** hermaphrodite *or* hermaphroditic(al), androgynous: *Many of these microscopic animals are bisexual and self-fertilizing.* **2** *Colloq* AC/DC, swinging both ways, *Facetious* ambisextrous: *He was known to have had bisexual relationships.*
—*n.* **3** androgyne, hermaphrodite: *Statistics showed that more women than previously believed were bisexuals.*

bit *n.* **1** °morsel, °piece, °scrap, °fragment, °shred, °particle, °grain, °crumb: *We didn't have a bit of food in the house.* **2** °jot, tittle, whit, scintilla, °trace, °touch, °hint, °suggestion, °suspicion, °particle, iota, °speck, atom: *There's not the slightest bit of evidence to link her with the crime.* **3** °moment, °minute, °second, °flash, *Colloq* two shakes (of a lamb's tail): *I'll be with you in a little bit.* **4** °piece, °share, °equity, °segment, °portion, °part, fraction: *He owns a little bit of the business.*

bitch *n.* **1** °shrew, °nag, termagant, virago, harpy, °fury, spitfire, °scold: *That greedy bitch has the house, and now she's suing me for half my income.* **2** whore, °prostitute, bawd, harlot, call-girl, trollop, strumpet, trull, drab, °tart, floozie *or* floozy *or* floosie, streetwalker, *Colloq* bimbo, pro, *US* hooker, °tramp, hustler: *He roamed the street every night, ending up with some bitch he found in a bar.*
—*v.* **3** °complain, °object, °protest, grumble, *Colloq* °gripe: *Oh, stop your bitching and get on with it!* **4** °bungle, °botch, °ruin, °spoil: *They bitched the job by using too little paint.*

bite *v.* **1** °nip; °chew, °gnaw: *That dog of yours bit a piece out of my ankle.* **2** °sting: *She was bitten by a mosquito.*
—*n.* **3** °mouthful, °morsel, °scrap, °bit, °piece, °taste; °snack, *Slang* nosh: *The survivors hadn't had a bite of food for three days. Come round for a bite on Sunday evening before the concert.* **4** °sting: *These mosquito bites itch horribly.*

biting *adj.* °severe, °harsh, °cutting, °piercing, °penetrating, °keen, °sharp, °bitter; °cold, °wintry, °freezing: *The biting wind went right through his thin coat.*

bitter *adj.* **1** °harsh, acerbic, acrid, °sharp, °caustic, mordant: *I added some cream to the sauce to try and make it taste less bitter.* **2** unappetizing, °distasteful, °unsavoury, unpleasant, hard (to °swallow *or* °take), irritating, °obnoxious, °disagreeable, °nasty, °painful, °unwelcome, °unpalatable: *The demand for additional tax payments was a bitter pill.* **3** °miserable, °grievous, dispiriting, distressing, °cruel, distressful: *Dismissal after all those years in the firm was a bitter experience.* **4** °resentful, °embittered, °rancorous; °hateful: *Andrew felt bitter at not being selected as chairman.* **5** stinging, °cutting, °biting, °harsh, °reproachful, °vicious, acrimonious, °virulent; °cruel, °unkind, unpleasant, °nasty: *His bitter denunciation of other candidates lost him the campaign.* **6** °sharp, °keen, °cutting, °severe, °biting, °cold, °wintry, °freezing: *A bitter gale lashed at the rigging.*

bitterness *n.* **1** harshness, acerbity, acrimony, acrimoniousness, spleen, *Literary* °gall and wormwood: *The bitterness of his opponent's attack was totally uncalled for.* **2** °animosity, hatred, °resentment; °hostility, °antagonism: *She felt bitterness in her heart over the way she had been treated.*

bizarre *adj.* **1** °eccentric, °unusual, unconventional, °extravagant, °whimsical, °strange, °odd, °curious, °peculiar, °queer, °offbeat, °fantastic, °weird, °incongruous, °deviant, °erratic, *Slang* °kinky: *The police thought his behaviour somewhat bizarre and invited him down to the station for questioning.* **2** °grotesque, °irregular, °nonconformist, nonconforming, °outlandish, °outré, °quaint, °fantastic, unconventional: *His house is a bizarre mixture of baroque and modern design.*

blab *v.* °broadcast, °tattle, °babble, °betray, °reveal, °disclose, divulge, °expose: *Don't tell Frieda—she'll blab your secrets all over town.*

blabbermouth *n.* tell-tale, babbler, chatterer, °gossip, *Colloq* °blab, tattle-tale, big-mouth: *Oscar is such a blabbermouth that you can't tell him anything you don't want everyone to know.*

black *adj.* **1** jet, jet-black, coal-black, inky, sooty, swart, °swarthy, raven, ebony, °dusky, *Literary* ebon, hyacinthine: *Her hair was as black as coal.* **2** Negro, Negroid, dark-skinned, *often offensive* coloured: *Most of the Black races originated near or south of the equator.* **3** °dark, °pitch-black, jet-black, coal-black, Stygian; starless, moonless: *He bundled his coat round himself and walked into the black night.* **4** °dark, °sombre, °dusky, °gloomy, °menacing, glowering, louring *or* lowering, °threatening, °funereal: *The sky became black with storm clouds.* **5** °malignant, baleful, baneful, °deadly, deathly, °sinister, °dismal, °hateful, °disastrous: *It was a black day when he came into my life.* **6** °bad, °foul, iniquitous, °wicked, °evil, diabolic(al), °infernal, hellish, °atrocious, °awful, malicious, °abominable, °outrageous, °vicious, °villainous, flagitious, °vile, °disgraceful, °unscrupulous, °unconscionable, unprincipled, blackguardly, knavish, °perfidious, insidious, nefarious, dastardly, treacherous, unspeakable, °shameful, °scurvy, °criminal, felonious: *You have told the blackest lies about me.* **7** °angry, wrathful, °furious, frowning, bad-tempered, sulky, °resentful, clouded, °threatening, glowering: *She gave him a black look and he withered in abject fear.*
—*v.* **8** °boycott, °embargo, blacklist, °ban, interdict: *Because of the dispute over plumbers' wages, the other building-trades unions had blacked every manufacturer in the business.*

blacken *v.* **1** darken, smudge, begrime: *The chimney sweep's face was blackened with soot.* **2** °slander, °libel, asperse, cast aspersions on, traduce, °smear, °sully, °soil, besmirch, °taint, °tarnish, defame, revile, malign, °vilify, °discredit, denigrate: *His article has blackened my reputation.*

blackleg *n.* scab, strikebreaker: *During the strike, the plant was operated by blacklegs.*

blackmail *n.* **1** extortion, °ransom, °tribute, *US* °graft: *Even if you pay the blackmail, that is no guarantee that he won't demand more later.*
—*v.* **2** °extort money from; °force, coerce, compel, °make: *They had discovered his indiscretions and were blackmailing him. He blackmailed her into signing the alimony settlement.*

blade n. **1** °knife, cutting °edge: Don't hold the knife by the blade. **2** Literary sword, rapier, sabre, °dagger, poniard, stiletto, cutlass, bayonet, °knife, penknife, jackknife: She plunged the blade in up to the hilt. **3** leaf, °leaflet, frond, °shoot: The blades of grass were flattened where he had walked. **4** Rather old-fashioned playboy, ladies' °man, man about town, fop, °dandy: He was quite a gay blade in his youth.

blame v. **1** find °fault with, censure, °criticize, °fault; °accuse, °charge, °indict, °condemn, °point to, °point (the finger) at, °rebuke, °reprimand, recriminate, reproach, °scold, reprehend, °reprove: Don't blame me if you can't get to school on time. **2** hold °responsible, fix (the) °responsibility upon or on, put or place or lay (the) blame on, lay at someone's door, °denounce, °incriminate: Why blame Carol for the mess? —n. **3** censure, °criticism, °reproof, °rebuke, °recrimination, °disapproval, disapprobation, reproach, objurgation, condemnation, reprehension: The cyclist put the blame for the accident on me. **4** culpability, °responsibility; °guilt, Slang °rap: Why should you take the blame for something that Donald did?

blameless adj. °faultless, guiltless, °innocent, °irreproachable, unimpeachable: Hugh has led a blameless life.

bland adj. **1** °gentle, °soothing, °smooth, °mild, °suave, urbane, °cool, unruffled, °calm, composed, unemotional, °nonchalant, insouciant: His reaction to the news of the invasion was bland indifference. **2** insipid, °boring, °dull, uninteresting, ennuyant, °tasteless, Colloq US °plain vanilla; Slang US blah: The play is a bland mixture of clichés embedded in a tired plot.

blank adj. **1** °empty, °plain, °bare: I stared at the blank paper, unable to write even my name. **2** unornamented, °unadorned, undecorated, °void: Whenever Irena sees a blank wall she feels compelled to hang a painting on it. **3** °vacant, °empty: The actor's mind went completely blank—he had forgotten his lines. **4** °passive, °impassive, expressionless, emotionless, vacuous, °mindless, unexpressive: He gave us a blank look when asked about the missing rare stamps. **5** °disconcerted, discomfited, nonplussed, °confused, °helpless, resourceless, perplexed, dazed, bewildered: The two old men looked at each other with blank and horror-stricken faces. **6** unrelieved, °stark, °sheer, utter, °pure, unmixed, °absolute, °unqualified: Jack faced the blank prospect of solitary confinement. —n. **7** °space; °line, °box: Please fill in the blanks on the form. **8** °nothing, °zero, °nil; °void, °emptiness: I asked her when the baby was coming, but I drew a blank.

blare v. **1** °blast, °bellow, trumpet, °ring, °boom, °thunder, °roar, bray; °resound, °echo, reverberate, resonate: Everyone in the neighbourhood can hear your hi-fi blaring. —n. **2** °blast, °bellow, °ring, °roar, °boom, °noise, °sound, clamour: The games began with a blare of trumpets.

blasé adj. **1** bored, °jaded, °weary, unimpressed, ennuyé: Her blasé attitude does little to endear her at job interviews. **2** °indifferent, °cool, °superior, °supercilious, °sophisticated, °unmoved, °nonchalant, emotionless, °phlegmatic, apathetic, pococurante, °carefree, light-hearted, insouciant: His blasé behaviour hides his basic feelings of insecurity.

blaspheme v. **1** °curse, °swear, imprecate, execrate, °profane, °damn: They were denounced for blaspheming against God. **2** °abuse, malign, calumniate, defame, °disparage, revile, °put down, decry, deprecate, °depreciate, °belittle: The ungrateful wretches blaspheme the charitable soul who would help them.

blasphemous adj. °profane, °impious, °irreverent, °disrespectful, °sacrilegious, irreligious, °sinful, °wicked, °evil, iniquitous: He was excommunicated for his blasphemous writings.

blast n. **1** °blow, °gust, °wind, °gale: The door opened and a blast of icy air made us shiver. **2** °blare, °sound, °noise, °racket, °din, °bellow, °roar; °boom: At the trumpet-blast thousands of Goths descended screaming on the camp. **3** °explosion, °burst, °eruption, °discharge; detonation: A blast of dynamite levelled all the houses in the vicinity. **4** **(at** or **in) full blast**: fully, at full tilt, at the °maximum, °completely, °thoroughly, °entirely, maximally, Slang with no holds barred, US to the max: The factory was going full blast before the strike. —v. **5** °blow up, °explode, dynamite, °demolish, °destroy, °ruin, °waste, lay °waste, °shatter, °devastate: The pillbox was blasted out of existence by our guns. **6** defame, °discredit, °denounce, °criticize, °attack; °ruin, °destroy: The candidate has been blasted by the press. **7** °curse, °damn: The minister continued to blast the proposal till the legislature dropped it.

blatant adj. **1** °obvious, °flagrant, palpable, °obtrusive, arrant, °shameless, unashamed, °brazen, °overt, °glaring: Those hooligans have shown a blatant disregard for the law. **2** °noisy, clamorous, °loud, bellowing, °strident, vociferous, °rowdy, °boisterous, °obstreperous, °uproarious: The blatant radical faction insists on making itself heard.

blaze n. **1** °flame, °fire, °holocaust, inferno, conflagration: The fuel barrels exploded, feeding the blaze. **2** °outburst, °eruption, flare-up: Her speech fanned the Lower House into a blaze of resentment. **3** °light, brightness, °brilliance, brilliancy, °glow: The blaze of lamps lit up the whole square. —v. **4** °burn, °flare up, °flame: In a few minutes the logs were blazing merrily. **5 blaze away (at)**: °fire, °shoot, open fire, °blast; °bombard, °shell: The enemy appeared, and we just blazed away at them.

bleach v. **1** whiten, °lighten, °fade, blanch, blench, Technical etiolate: My jeans are all bleached by the sun. —n. **2** whitener, chlorine: Add a little bleach to the laundry.

bleak adj. **1** cheerless, °dreary, depressing, °dismal, °gloomy, °sombre, °melancholy, °sad, °unhappy, °mournful: 1940 was one of the bleakest periods in British history. **2** °cold, °chilly, °raw, °bitter: The days were getting shorter, and the bleak winter was setting in. **3** °barren, °bare, exposed, windswept, °desolate: How depressing the bleak landscape of the Russian steppes can be in winter!

blemish v. **1** °deface, °mar, °scar, °impair, disfigure: They did nothing to blemish the beauty of the landscape. **2** °tarnish, °stain, °sully, °spoil, °mar, °flaw, °harm, °damage, °scar, °injure, °bruise, besmirch: She has blemished my reputation by spreading those stories about me.

—n. **3** disfigurement, °scar, °mark, °impairment, °stain, °smear, °blot; °defect, °flaw, °error, °fault, °imperfection, erratum: *Her complexion was entirely without blemish.*

blend *v.* **1** °mix, °mingle, °combine, meld, commingle, intermingle: *The Latakia is blended with the Virginia to produce a fine smoking tobacco.* **2** °shade, °grade, gradate, °graduate, °merge, coalesce, °fuse, °unite: *Note how the pink sky and the tinted clouds blend in this Turner painting.* *—n.* **3** °mixture, °mix, °combination, mingling, meld, commingling, intermingling: *His humour is a fine blend of the sardonic with slapstick.*

bless *v.* **1** consecrate, °hallow, °sanctify; °extol, °glorify, °praise, °revere, °adore: *God bless this ship and all who sail in her. Bless the Lord.* **2** °give, make °happy or °fortunate, endow, °favour, °furnish, °provide, °supply, grace: *She is blessed with one of the most beautiful soprano voices that I have ever heard.*

blessing *n.* **1** benediction, °prayer, consecration: *Each spring the vicar officiated at the blessing of the fleet.* **2** °boon, °favour, °advantage, good °fortune, °godsend, °luck, °profit, °gain, °help, °asset, °gift, °bounty: *Hot, sunny days are a blessing for wine growers.*

blight *n.* **1** °affliction, °disease, °plague, infestation, °pestilence, °scourge: *The crops were visited with a blight that lasted seven years.* **2** °misfortune, °curse, °trouble, °woe, °calamity: *Genius may suffer an untimely blight.* *—v.* **3** °afflict, °infest, °plague, °scourge; wither, °mar, °taint, °blast: *Central Africa has been blighted by famine after famine.*

blind *adj.* **1** sightless, eyeless, unsighted, purblind, stone-blind: *He has been blind from birth.* **2** imperceptive, °slow, insensitive, °thick, °dense, °obtuse, °stupid, weak-minded, dull-witted, slow-witted, dim-witted, *Colloq Brit* gormless: *How blind some parents are! There's another case of the blind leading the blind.* **3** °indiscriminate, undiscriminating, °heedless, °reckless, °rash, °impetuous, °inconsiderate, unreasoning, °mindless, °senseless, °thoughtless, °unthinking, irrational, delusional: *He did her bidding with the blind obedience of a dog.* **4 blind to:** °unaware or °unconscious of, impervious or °insensible to, °unaffected or untouched or °unmoved by: *The critics were blind to her merits as a novelist till many years had passed.* *—v.* **5** °deceive, blindfold, blinker; bamboozle, °hoodwink, °fool: *Wolsey could not blind himself to the true condition of the church. How jealousy blinds people!* **6** °conceal, °hide, °eclipse, °overshadow; °dazzle, blindfold: *The bright lights of the city blinded our view of the airport runway. Her beauty blinded him to her greed.* *—n.* **7** °shade, curtain, °screen, °cover, shutter(s), awning: *The sun is too bright—please draw the blind.* **8** °pretence, °pretext, °front, °cover, smokescreen, °stratagem, °subterfuge, °ruse, °trick, °deception, *Colloq* °dodge; *Slang* scam: *The plumbing service is merely a blind for getting into houses to rob them.*

blindly *adv.* recklessly, heedlessly, deludedly, indiscriminately, rashly, impetuously, irrationally, thoughtlessly, mindlessly, senselessly, unthinkingly: *Despite his parents' warnings, he went blindly on, till one day he was arrested.*

blink *v.* **1** wink, °flicker, *Technical* nictitate: *She blinked in the strong light.* **2** °twinkle, °flicker, °gleam, glimmer, °shimmer, °flash, °sparkle, scintillate, coruscate: *A billion stars blinked in the wintry sky.* **3** °flinch, wince, °shrink, quail, blench, °recoil, °start, °move: *She didn't even blink when she had the injection.* **4 blink at:** wink at, °ignore, °overlook, °disregard: *That inspector has been known to blink at health violations.* *—n.* **5** wink, °flicker: *He switched the cards in the blink of an eye.* **6 on the blink:** out of order, °broken, in °disrepair, not working or operating, not operational, *Slang US* out of whack, on the fritz: *The fridge is on the blink again.*

bliss *n.* °happiness, blitheness, gladness, °joy, blessedness, °delight, felicity, °glee, °enjoyment, °pleasure, joyousness, °cheer, exhilaration, °gaiety, blissfulness, °rapture, °ecstasy: *The bliss of our honeymoon has remained with us throughout our marriage.*

blithe *adj.* **1** blissful, °happy, °cheerful, joyous, °merry, light-hearted, well-pleased, °delighted, °gay, °joyful, °elated, jubilant: *His spirit was blithe and his heart unquenchable.* **2** happy-go-lucky, insouciant, °heedless, °carefree, unconcerned, °blasé, °casual, °detached, °indifferent, uncaring, °careless: *She goes through life with a blithe disregard for the feelings of others.*

bloated *adj.* °swollen, distended, fully, puffy; puffed up, °overgrown, °inflated, °pompous: *He felt bloated after the enormous banquet. That bloated, conceited, self-important petty official had the gall to refuse me a visa.*

blob *n.* °gob, gobbet, globule, °drop, droplet, °bit, gout, °lump, °dab, *Colloq* glob, *Chiefly US and Canadian* smidgen or smidgin: *There's a blob of jelly on your tie.*

block *n.* **1** °piece, chunk, hunk, °lump, °slab; °stump; °brick, cube: *The figure is carved out of a solid block of stone.* **2** °bar, °obstacle, °obstruction, °hindrance, °stumbling-block, °deterrent, °impediment, °barrier: *Her arrival should be no block to your leaving.* *—v.* **3** °obstruct, °close off, barricade; °bar, °shut off; °hinder, °hamper, balk, °impede, °prevent: *Entry to the playing field was blocked by the police.* **4 block out: a** °rough out, °design, °outline, sketch, °lay out, °plan: *The colonel blocked out a strategy for our escape.* **b** °mask, °screen, °blank (out), °erase, °eliminate, °exclude, °blot out, °deny: *She has blocked out that part of her life from her mind.* **5 block (up):** °stuff (up), congest, °clog, *Colloq Brit* bung up: *My nose is all blocked up because of this awful cold.*

bloodshed *n.* °slaughter, °carnage, butchery, °killing, °murder, blood-letting, °violence; genocide: *Let's settle this peaceably and avoid bloodshed.*

bloodsucker *n.* leech, extortionist, extortioner, blackmailer; °parasite, barnacle, *Colloq* sponge, freeloader, °scrounge, scrounger; *Slang US* moocher: *He's nothing but a bloodsucker, always demanding more and more money.*

bloodthirsty *adj.* °murderous, °homicidal, °savage, feral, °cruel, °ruthless, pitiless, °vicious, °brutal, °sadistic, °ferocious, °fierce, *Formal* °sanguinary, *Literary* °fell: *Bloodthirsty pirates had slaughtered the whole crew.*

blot *n.* **1** °stain, °spot, °mark, smudge, blotch, °blemish, disfigurement, °smear, smirch, °scar,

Colloq splodge or *US* also splotch: *An ink blot covered the date of the document. There are a few blots on his record from his time in the army.*
—*v.* **2** °stain, °spot, °spatter, smudge, °mark, °blur: *You have blotted these pages where you wrote with a fountain-pen.* **3 blot one's copybook:** °err, °destroy or °ruin or °mar or °spoil one's °reputation, commit an °indiscretion, °transgress, °sin: *She's certainly blotted her copybook by having an affair with that subaltern.* **4 blot out: a** °obscure, °conceal, °cover (up), °hide, °eclipse, °dim: *The clouds blotted out the sun for a few minutes.* **b** °obliterate, °destroy, °erase, °demolish, efface, annihilate, °delete, °rub or °wipe out: *He subconsciously blotted out all memory of the accident.*

blow[1] *v.* **1** °breathe, °puff, °exhale; °expel: *If the crystals turn green when you blow into the tube, it means that you've had too much to drink. Blow some air into the balloon.* **2** °waft, °puff, whistle, whine, °blast: *An icy wind blew through the cracks in the windows.* **3** *Colloq* bungle, °botch, make a °mess of, muff, mismanage, *Colloq* °screw up, °mess up, °fluff, °bugger up, *Taboo* fuck up: *It was my last chance to win and I blew it.* **4** *Colloq* spend, °lavish, squander, °waste, °throw out or away: *She blew hundreds on that dress and now she won't wear it.* **5** short-circuit, °burn out: *All the fuses blew when I turned on the electric heater.* **6 blow hot and cold:** vacillate, °hesitate, dither, *Colloq* °shilly-shally: *The sales manager has been blowing hot and cold over my proposal for a month now.* **7 blow out: a** °extinguish: *I blew out all the candles in one breath. The match blew out in the wind.* **b** °explode, °burst: *One of my tyres blew out on the way over here.* **c** short-circuit, °burn out: *The lights blew out during the storm.* **8 blow up: a** become °furious or °angry or enraged, °flare up, lose one's °temper, *Slang* blow one's top or *US* also °stack, °flip one's lid: *She nearly blew up when I said I was going to the pub.* **b** °explode, °burst, °shatter, *Colloq* bust; detonate, dynamite, °destroy, °blast: *The bridge blew up with a roar. Demolition experts will blow up the dam.* **c** °enlarge, °inflate, embroider, °magnify, °expand, °exaggerate, °overstate: *The tabloid press has blown up the story out of all proportion.* **d** °enlarge, °magnify, °amplify, °expand, °increase: *Can you blow up just this corner of the photograph?* **e** °inflate; distend, °swell: *We were busy blowing up balloons for the party.*
—*n.* **9** °gale, °storm, °tempest, °whirlwind, tornado, cyclone, °hurricane, typhoon, northeaster, nor'easter: *We can expect a big blow tonight—winds of gale force, they say.*

blow[2] *n.* **1** °stroke, °punch, clout, whack, °hit, °knock, thump, thwack, *Colloq* wallop: *He was felled by a blow to the chin in the fourth round.* **2** °shock, °surprise, °bombshell, °jolt, °bolt from the blue, °revelation: *It came as a blow to learn that she was leaving in a month.*

blue *adj.* **1** depressed, low-spirited, dispirited, °sad, °dismal, down, down in the °mouth, °gloomy, °unhappy, °glum, downcast, crestfallen, chap-fallen, °dejected, °melancholy, °despondent, °downhearted, morose: *I've been feeling blue since Kathleen left me.* **2** °obscene, °vulgar, °indecent, titillating, °pornographic, °dirty, °filthy, °lewd, smutty, °risqué, °bawdy, °sexy, X, X-rated, 18, *US* XXX; indelicate,

°suggestive, off colour, °erotic, °coarse, °offensive, °improper: *There's a place nearby that shows blue movies.*

bluff[1] *v.* **1** °deceive, °hoodwink, °dupe, °mislead, delude, °trick, cozen, °fool, *Colloq* bamboozle: *I bluffed him into believing that I held four aces.* **2** °pretend, feign, °bluster, °fool, *Colloq* kid; *Slang* bullshit: *She became frightened, unaware that I was only bluffing.*
—*n.* **3** °bombast, °bravado, boasting, bragging, °bluster, °show, puffery; °deception, °blind; *Literary* rodomontade, gasconade; *Colloq* °hot air: *Roger's ranting is all bluff—he's really very timid.*

bluff[2] *adj.* **1** blustering, °gruff, °rough, °abrupt, °blunt, °curt, °short, °crude: *Fred's bluff manner puts many people off.* **2** °frank, °open, °hearty, straightforward, °plain, plain-spoken, °outspoken, affable, approachable, °good-natured, °friendly: *That comment is typical of his bluff honesty.*
—*n.* **3** °cliff, escarpment, °precipice, scarp, headland, promontory, palisades: *As you sail down the lower Hudson river, the tall bluffs form a natural wall along the western bank.*

blunder *v.* **1** °stumble, °flounder: *I had somehow blundered into a meeting of the local crime syndicate. She blundered upon the truth when she saw them together.*
—*n.* **2** °mistake, °error, gaffe, faux pas, °slip, slip-up, °howler, *Colloq* boo-boo, screw-up, °fluff, boner, *US* goof, goof-up: *I made a stupid blunder in telling him about the plans.*

blunt *adj.* **1** °dull, °worn: *This knife is too blunt to cut bread.* **2** °abrupt, °curt, rough-spoken, plain-spoken, °short, °direct, °candid, °frank, unceremonious, undiplomatic, °inconsiderate, °thoughtless, °brusque, °outspoken, °bluff, °brash, indelicate, °rude, uncivil, °ungracious, °discourteous, °impolite; straightforward, °straight, uncomplicated, uncompromising: *Ralph may be blunt, but at least you know exactly where you stand with him.*
—*v.* **3** °dull, take the edge off: *You've blunted the scissors cutting that cardboard.* **4** °soften, °mitigate, mollify, soothe; efface, °dim, °obscure, °blur, °weaken: *Mother's love is an absorbing delight, blunting all other sensibilities.*

blur *n.* **1** indistinctness, dimness, haziness, cloudiness, fogginess: *We were unable to pick out the star from the blur of the Galaxy.* **2** °fog, haze, *Brit* fuzz: *Without my spectacles, everything is a blur.*
—*v.* **3** °dim, befog, °obscure, bedim; efface: *My vision was momentarily blurred, and I didn't see the oncoming car.* **4** °obscure, °hide, °conceal, °veil, °mask; °weaken: *The Honourable Gentleman has blurred the distinction between the unemployed and the unemployable.*

blurt *v.* Usually, **blurt out:** °burst out with, utter, °reveal, °disclose, °give away, divulge, *Colloq* °blab: *She blurted out the name of her accomplice.*

blush *v.* be or act °ashamed, redden, °flush, °colour: *He blushed when asked if he still loved Belinda.*

bluster *v.* **1** °storm, °rage, °harangue: *It won't do any good to bluster on about the postal service.* **2** °swagger, °strut, °talk °big, °boast, °brag, °blow one's own horn or trumpet, °show off, crow: *He's always blustering about his conquests.*
—*n.* **3** swaggering, storming, raging, °raving, haranguing, °tumult; °hot °air, puffery,

°bravado, grandiloquence, *Literary* rodomontade: *He's all bluster and will do nothing despite his threats.*

board *n.* **1** °plank, scantling, °timber: *We nailed the last board in place and the house was finished.* **2** table, gaming-table, game table *or* °surface: *I have the chessmen, have you brought the board?* **3** °food, meals, °provisions: *I am moving to the country, where room and board are cheaper.* **4** °council, °committee, directors, directorship, °management, °cabinet, panel, trustees, °advisers: *That issue will be discussed at the meeting of the board.* **5 on board**: aboard, on: *Young children are not allowed on board the boat.*
—*v.* **6** °go aboard, °ship aboard; °enter, °embark on: *We all boarded the ship but it didn't leave for an hour.* **7** °feed; °eat, take meals; °accommodate, °lodge, °house, billet, °quarter; °lodge, °stay, °live, °room; *Colloq* °put up: *Mrs O'Brien already boards three gentlemen at her house, but she has agreed to let me board there too.*

boast *n.* **1** °brag, bragging: *They did not make good their boasts of being the fastest in the competition.*
—*v.* **2** °brag, vaunt, crow, °show off, *Colloq US* °blow *or* toot one's (own) horn *or* trumpet; *Slang* °lay it on thick, °talk big: *He boasted that he was the best poker player in the casino.*

boastful *adj.* °ostentatious, °show-off, bragging, vainglorious, °egotistical, °vain, °conceited: *She's boastful about her wealth, but it was all left to her by her mother.*

boat *n.* °vessel, °craft, skiff, small °craft, motor °boat, speedboat, knockabout, runabout, yacht, motor yacht, sailing-yacht, *Brit* rowing-boat, sailing-boat, *US* row-boat, sailboat, *Colloq* °ship: *I bought a 30-foot boat at this year's show. They went off on a slow boat to China.*

bode *v.* portend, °promise, augur, betoken, forebode, presage; °foreshadow: *The weather bodes well for the picnic.*

body *n.* **1** °corpse, °cadaver, remains, carcass, *Slang* °stiff: *A body has been dragged up from the lake.* **2** °trunk, torso: *They found the body, but the arms, legs, and head were missing.* **3** °main °part *or* °portion, °hull, fuselage: *The body of the plane remained intact, though the wings and superstructure broke away.* **4** °substance, essentials, °main °part, °essence, °heart, °centre, °core: *The body of the book is all right, but the index needs work.* **5** °majority, °bulk, °main °part *or* °portion, °mass(es): *Under Henry VIII the main body of the people were prosperous.* **6** °association, °league, °band, °corps, confederation, °fraternity, °society; °committee, °council; °group, assemblage, °assembly, congress, °company: *It is not within the power of this body to do more than vote on the proposal.* **7** richness, °substance, firmness, consistency, solidity, thickness, density, fullness, viscosity: *This wine has excellent body. Add a little cornflour to give the sauce more body.*

bog *n.* **1** °swamp, fen, °marsh, quagmire: *The peat bogs have yielded interesting fossils.* **2 bog down**: °impede, °slow, °hamper, °encumber, °stymie, °stick, °handicap, °clog, °check, °set back, °hold back: *Traffic is bogged down owing to roadworks.*

bogus *adj.* °counterfeit, °spurious, °fake, °false, °fraudulent, °sham, °imitation, °fictitious,

Colloq °phoney *or US also* phony: *The police reported that a gang was trying to pass bogus money to unsuspecting shop-keepers in the area.*

Bohemian *adj.* °nonconformist, unconforming, unconventional, °unorthodox, °casual, °free and easy: *In the '60s she became a flower person and adopted a Bohemian way of life.*

boil[1] *v.* **1** °bubble, °seethe; °simmer, °stew, steam: *A pot of soup was boiling on the kitchen stove.* **2** °seethe, °fume, sizzle, °smoulder, °chafe, fulminate, °ferment, sputter, splutter, °bluster: *When she learned what he had been saying about her, she boiled with furious indignation.*

boil[2] *n.* abscess, carbuncle, pustule, *Technical* furuncle: *The doctor said the boil had to be lanced at once.*

boisterous *adj.* °rowdy, clamorous, °rough, °noisy, °lively, °exuberant, °unruly, °wild, °undisciplined, °tempestuous, °stormy, turbulent, *Colloq* rambunctious: *The boys were sent outside because of their boisterous behaviour.*

bold *adj.* **1** °courageous, °brave, plucky, °confident, stout-hearted, lion-hearted, °daring, °enterprising, °audacious, °fearless, unafraid, °intrepid, °resolute, °dauntless, undaunted, valiant, °stout, valorous, °stalwart, °adventurous, °venturesome; °reckless, °foolhardy, incautious, °daredevil, °rash: *It would take a bold man to enter the ring with the champion.* **2** °audacious, °presumptuous, °forward, °immodest, °brazen, °impudent, temerarious, °impertinent, °shameless: *It was very bold of you to speak your mind to the boss.* **3** °pronounced, °outstanding, °striking, °vigorous, °clear, °strong, °vivid, °distinct, °conspicuous: *He wrote down their demands in a good, bold hand.*

bolster *v.* °support, °prop (up), °brace, shore up, °buttress, °uphold, back (up), °reinforce, °aid, °help, °assist, °further, °advance: *The miners cited a lack of safety measures to bolster their arguments.*

bolt *n.* **1** arrow, dart, °projectile, °missile, *Historical* °quarrel: *He had only three bolts remaining for the crossbow.* **2** °pin, °bar, °rod, °catch; latch: *We hoped that the bolt would prevent their opening the door.* **3** machine °screw: *Bolts can be tightened or removed, unlike rivets.* **4** °roll, °length: *We sell only full bolts of fabric.* **5** lightning °flash, thunderbolt, *Formal* fulguration: *One bolt travelled down the television aerial and blew out the set.* **6 bolt from** *or* **out of the blue**: °surprise, °shock, °bombshell, °bomb, °blow, °revelation, eye-opener, *Colloq* shocker: *The news of her resignation came like a bolt from the blue.* **7 shoot one's bolt**: °exhaust *or* °use up one's resources, *Slang* °burn out, *US* poop out: *He was fast early in the marathon, but he'd shot his bolt long before the finishing line.*
—*v.* **8** °spring, dart, °shoot off, take °flight, °run (away *or* off), °rush (off *or* away), °break away, °flee, decamp, abscond, °escape, °fly, °dash (off *or* away), *Colloq* skedaddle, scram, *Brit* scarper, do a bunk, do a moonlight °flit, *US* take a (run-out) °powder: *The youths bolted as soon as they saw the police. The couple in room 315 bolted without paying their bill.* **9** °gulp (down), °swallow whole: *When the bell rang, she bolted her breakfast and ran out of the back door.* **10** °fasten, °lock, latch, °secure: *Make sure you bolt your door at night and don't let anyone in.* **11** °fix, °attach, °fasten, °connect, °make °fast to: *The motor must be securely bolted to the workbench.*

—*adv.* **12 bolt upright**: °erect, °straight, rigidly, stiffly: *When her name was called, Penny sat bolt upright in her chair.*

bomb *n.* **1** °bombshell, °shell, °explosive: *One of the bombs blew up the school.*
—*v.* **2** °bombard, °shell, °batter, °blow up: *Last night the railway station was bombed.*

bombard *v.* **1** °batter, °bomb, °shell: *The artillery continued to bombard the enemy with everything in their arsenal.* **2** assail, °attack, °assault, °set upon; °besiege: *The Prime Minister was bombarded with requests to amend the law.*

bombast *n.* °pretentious language, flatulence, °bluster, °show, grandiloquence, magniloquence, °hot air, °bravado, °boast, boasting, *Literary* gasconade, rodomontade; *Colloq* puffery: *The speaker continued to bore the audience with his pompous bombast.*

bombastic *adj.* high-flown, °extravagant, °pompous, °grandiose, grandiloquent, magniloquent, °inflated, fustian, flatulent, turgid, *Literary* euphuistic: *The Minister made a bombastic speech full of emotive appeals, but his actual arguments were unconvincing.*

bombshell *n.* °surprise, °shock, eye-opener, °bomb, °blow, °revelation, °bolt from *or* out of the blue, *Colloq* shocker: *Then came the bombshell—she and Tony had been married the week before.*

bona fide *adj.* °genuine, °authentic, attested, °real, °veritable, °legitimate, °true, valid; in °good faith, °sincere, °honest: *The jeweller affirmed that it was a bona fide ruby. I don't believe her reasons are bona fide.*

bond *n.* **1** °tie(s), shackles, chains, fetters, manacles, °handcuffs, °trammels, thongs, °cord(s), °rope(s); °restraint(s), constraint(s), °check(s), °control(s), °rein(s): *The council is hampered by the bonds of the old regulations.* **2** covenant, °pact, °contract, °agreement, °engagement, °compact, °treaty: *To unite the party a bond of confederacy was formed.* **3** °connection, °link, linkage, °union, °tie, °relationship: *The main bond between us was a shared love of the theatre. The bond between the veneer and the board should hold with a little more glue.*
—*v.* **4** °cement, °bind, °hold together, °stick, cohere: *They use mortar to bond the bricks together.*

bondage *n.* °slavery, °servitude, °subjection, subjugation, enslavement, serfdom, thraldom; vassalage, villeinage: *The poor souls were kept in bondage for most of their lives, forced to row in the galleys till they died.*

bonny *adj.* °beautiful, °comely, °attractive, °pretty, °lovely: *She's grown into quite a bonny lass.*

bonus *n.* °reward, °largesse, hand-out, °perquisite, °extra, °honorarium, °tip, gratuity, °remuneration, compensation, *Colloq* °perk: *Employees often receive a Christmas bonus.*

book *n.* **1** °volume, tome, °work, °publication; hard-cover, soft-cover, paperback: *Our personal library contains more than 5000 books.* **2** libretto, words, lyrics: *Richard Rodgers wrote the music and Oscar Hammerstein the book for several hit shows.* **3** °rules, °laws, °regulations: *He always insists that we go by the book.*
—*v.* **4** °engage, °reserve; earmark, ticket; °order, °register, °enrol, °list, °enlist, log, °record, °post: *Please phone the restaurant and book a table for four for seven-thirty.*

bookkeeper *n.* clerk; accountant, *Brit* chartered accountant, CA, cashier; *US* CPA, certified public accountant: *The office was haunted by the melancholy ghosts of departed bookkeepers.*

bookworm *n.* bibliophile, book-lover, inveterate *or* °ardent reader, *Formal* bibliophage: *Fiona is such a bookworm, she hardly does anything but read.*

boom *v.* **1** °sound, °resound, resonate, °blast, rumble, °thunder, °roar, bang, °explode: *We heard the cannons booming in the distance.* **2** °prosper, °thrive, °flourish, °progress, °grow, °increase, burgeon *or* bourgeon: *Business is booming in every sector.*
—*n.* **3** °blast, rumble, °explosion: *There was a resounding boom and the car went up in flames.* **4** °prosperity, profitability; °growth, °increase, burgeoning *or* bourgeoning: *In this business it is either boom or bust.*

boomerang *v.* °rebound, °recoil, backfire, °miscarry, redound: *His plan boomeranged.*

boon *n.* °gift, °favour, °award, °reward, gratuity, °present; °blessing, °benefit, °advantage: *The mobile library service is a great boon to the elderly in the area.*

boor *n.* **1** °rustic, °peasant, yokel, (°country) bumpkin, °provincial, backwoodsman, *US* hayseed, hill-billy, Juke, Kallikak, *Slang* hick: *The boor is blind to the beauties of nature.* **2** °barbarian, yahoo, oaf, °clod, clodhopper, °philistine, °clown, Grobian; hoyden, *Colloq* lummox, *Slang* galoot, °slob, *US* goop, slobbovian: *The guests behaved like boors, throwing their food at each other.*

boorish *adj.* °rustic, °barbarian, °rude, °crude, °ill-mannered, uncultured, °coarse, clownish, uncouth, loutish, oafish, gawky, °vulgar, ill-bred: *How can you even think of inviting such a boorish fellow?*

boost *n.* **1** °lift, shove *or* °push up *or* upward(s), *Colloq* °leg up; °rise, °raise: *If you give me a boost up, I can reach the window ledge.* **2** °encouragement, °help, °aid, °assistance, °support: *With a boost from your constituency, Trevor should win the vote.* **3** °increase, °rise, *US* °raise, hike: *He was given a slight boost in salary as an incentive to stay.*
—*v.* **4** °lift, shove *or* °push up *or* upward(s), °raise: *He boosted her over the fence. The second stage is intended to boost the rocket beyond the atmosphere.* **5** °encourage, °promote, °help, °aid, °support, °assist, °improve: *A talk from the manager before the game helped to boost the players' morale.* **6** °increase, °raise: *Her salary was boosted twice in one year.*

boot *n.* **1 to boot**: in °addition, into the °bargain, °besides, °moreover, as °well, also, too, additionally: *He's stingy and cruel—and ugly to boot.* **2** shoe, riding-boot, bootee: *I need a new pair of boots for my walking holiday.*
—*v.* **3** °eject, °expel, shove, °propel, °push, *Colloq* °kick: *The landlord booted three rowdies out of the pub.* **4** *Literary* profit, avail, °help, be in °aid of: *What boots it to complain?*

booth *n.* **1** °stall, °stand: *Our company has taken three booths at the book fair.* **2** °compartment, cubicle, °box, kiosk: *We walked across the road to a telephone booth and phoned a garage.*

bootless *adj.* °pointless, unavailing, °vain, °purposeless, °useless, °futile, °worthless, unproductive, °ineffective, °inefficacious,

°fruitless, °unprofitable, profitless, unremunerative, unrewarding, °wasteful, time-wasting, Sisyphean: *It's a bootless task trying to persuade him of the importance of a good education.*

booty *n.* °plunder, °gain, °spoil(s), contraband, takings, °loot, *Slang* swag, boodle, (hot) °goods, °take: *The pirates fought over the booty seized from the Spanish galleon.*

booze *n.* **1** °drink, (°hard) °liquor, °spirit(s), °whisk(e)y, °alcohol, *US* demon rum, John Barleycorn, mountain dew, white lightning, white mule; *Slang* rot-gut, poison, fire-water, mother's ruin, *US and Canadian* sauce, juice, hooch, red-eye: *I ordered plenty of booze for the party.* —*v.* **2** °drink, tipple; *Humorous* bibulate; *Slang* hit the °bottle, *US* hit the sauce: *He has a terrible hangover after boozing all night.*

border *n.* **1** °edge, °margin, hem, binding, trimming, °trim, edging, °periphery, purfle, purfling: *The border of the tablecloth is beautifully embroidered with flowers.* **2** Usually, **borders**: °limit(s), °bound(s), confines: *Sometimes Tony exceeds the borders of good taste.* **3** °boundary, °frontier: *You won't be able to cross the border without a passport.* **4** °frame, frieze, moulding; dado, wainscot *or* wainscoting *or* wainscotting: *The border of the fresco is in Greek fretwork design.* **5** borderline, °edge, °verge, °brink: *She is just on the border of becoming a born-again Christian.* **6** bed, flowerbed, herbaceous °border: *Hollyhocks are growing in the border.* —*v.* **7** °edge, °trim, °bind, °fringe, purfle: *The hem of the skirt is bordered with lace.* **8** °resemble (closely), °approach (closely), °verge upon *or* on: *Isabel's attempts at playing the tuba border on the ludicrous.* **9** °lie alongside, adjoin, abut (on *or* upon), °verge upon *or* on, °touch, be adjacent to: *The territory of the Gauls bordered the western lands of the Germans.*

bore[1] *n.* **1** °hole, drill-hole, borehole: *A bore of six inches was carried to a depth of 2086 feet.* —*v.* **2** °pierce, °perforate, °drill, °penetrate, °puncture, °tap, °punch, °stab, °prick; °sink, °tunnel, °dig (out), °gouge (out); °hollow out: *Bore a hole through this sheet metal. The oil rig is boring through solid rock.*

bore[2] *n.* **1** °annoyance, °nuisance: *Reggie is such a bore—always talking about himself.* —*v.* **2** °weary, °wear out, °tire, °exhaust, °jade: *The programme so bored me that I fell asleep.*

boredom *n.* dullness, dreariness, ennui, °tedium, monotony: *I have to look forward to the boredom of an evening of chamber music.*

boring *adj.* °dull, °monotonous, °tedious, °humdrum, °tiresome, °dreary, °flat, °dead, uninteresting, unexciting, ennuyant, °stale, °tired, °dry, dry-as-dust, arid; tiring, wearying, wearisome, °exhausting, soporific; °repetitious, °wordy, prolix, unending, long-drawn-out: *Felicity's boring old stories put me to sleep.*

borrow *v.* °take, °appropriate, °draw, °adopt, °refer to, °obtain, *Colloq* sponge, cadge, touch (someone) for, *US* °bum; *Slang* mooch: *Has Fred borrowed my lawnmower again?*

Borstal *n.* °youth °custody °centre, approved °school, *Now chiefly US* °reform °school, reformatory: *He was too young to go to prison, so he was sent to a Borstal.*

bosom *n.* **1** °breast, °chest, bust; *Slang* boobs, knockers, tits, titties, pair, jugs, *Brit* Bristols: *The sex goddess's lack of talent was more than compensated for by her ample bosom.* **2** °midst, °interior, °heart, °core, °centre: *She was welcomed into the bosom of the family as if she had been their own child.* **3** °soul, °heart, °heart of hearts, °bowels, blood, *Colloq* °gut: *I know he loves me, I can feel it in my bosom.* —*adj.* **4** °close, °intimate, °dear, °beloved, cherished, °boon, °special, °confidential: *We were once bosom companions.*

bosomy *adj.* big-busted, busty, well-endowed: *This tabloid always has a bosomy model on page 3.*

boss *n.* **1** °chief, °supervisor, °head, administrator, °manager, °foreman, °superintendent, °overseer; °employer, °director, °proprietor, °owner, *Brit* managing director, *US* president, *Dialect* himself, *Colloq* supremo, *Brit* governor, gov., gaffer, *US* °super, °leader, kingpin, °big cheese, the °man, *Slang* honcho, °head *or* °chief honcho, Mr Big, prex *or* prexy: *If you have to leave early, check with the boss. The company boss was interviewed on television last night.* —*v.* **2** °supervise, °head, °manage, °run, °oversee, °overlook, °direct, °control, superintend, °command, take °charge, be in °charge: *Clive has been here only a year and he's already bossing a department.* **3** domineer, °push *or* shove around *or* about, °dominate, °order about, °lord it over: *That slave-driver had better stop bossing me about or I'll quit!*

bossy *adj.* °overbearing, °domineering, °dictatorial, °tyrannical, °despotic, imperious, lordly: *Her boyfriend is awfully bossy—and they're not even married yet.*

botch *v.* °bungle, mismanage, °spoil, *Colloq* °screw *or* louse up, °blow, °mess up, °muck up, make a °mess *or* °hash *or* °muddle of; *Slang* bollocks *or* ballocks *or* *US* bollix up: *Give Gordon an assignment and he's sure to botch it.*

bother *v.* **1** °annoy, °pester, °worry, °irritate, °trouble, hector, °harass, °hound, dog, °nag, °plague, needle, *Colloq* hassle; *Slang US* °nudge: *I wish they'd stop bothering me about paying the telephone bill.* **2** °trouble (about), °fuss (at), make a °fuss (about), °concern oneself (with), °burden: *Too few people are interested in bothering about the welfare of others.* **3** °confuse, °bewilder, °perplex, °perturb, °upset, disconcert, °discomfit: *She was increasingly bothered by her inability to understand the local language.* —*n.* **4** °trouble, °inconvenience: *Those pets must be a lot of bother.* **5** °worry, °annoyance, vexation, °nuisance, irritation, °trouble, °effort, °disturbance, °upset, *Slang* hassle: *Painting the lattice will be more bother than it's worth.* **6** dither, °flutter, *Colloq* tizzy, °pet, °stew, °lather, °sweat: *She seems to have worked herself into quite a bother about something quite insignificant.* **7** °pest, irritant, °nag, °nuisance, *Colloq* °pain, °pain in the neck *or Brit* taboo arse *or US* taboo ass; *Slang US* °nudge: *Mother is such a bother, always asking if I wear my galoshes when it rains.* **8** °disturbance, to-do, ado, commotion, °fuss, °trouble, °disorder, °stir, hubbub: *We ran into a bit of bother at the pub last night.*

bottle *n.* **1** flask, container; decanter: *The milkman left two bottles of milk.* **2** °courage, °nerve, manliness, manfulness, °grit, °backbone, °gumption, mettle, °pluck, Dutch °courage, *Slang* guts; *Colloq* °spunk, starch, *US* moxie: *He was going to tell her off but lost his bottle at the last* *minute.* **3 the bottle**: °alcohol, °alcoholic °drink, °spirit(s), °liquor, °booze, sauce: *He's back on the bottle after only two weeks of being on the wagon.* —*v.* **4 bottle up: a** °contain, °restrain, °hold back, °control, °suppress, °repress, °hold *or* keep in °check, °stifle: *All the emotions, bottled up for so long, burst upon him at once, and he wept pitiably.* **b** °trap, °cut off, hem in, °box in: *With the help of the posse, we can bottle up the gang in the canyon.*

bottom *n.* **1** °seat, °buttocks, °rear, behind, °rear end, backside, *derrière*, rump, °posterior, hindquarters, breech, fundament, gluteus maximus, *Colloq Brit* °bum, *US* hinie, can, duff, tush *or* tushy *or* tushie, tokus *or* tochis *or* tuchis, keister *or* keester, butt, *Taboo slang Brit* arse, *US* ass: *He just sits there on his bottom, never doing a bit of work.* **2** °base, foot, °foundation, °groundwork, substructure, °footing, underpinning, fundament: *A ditch was dug along the bottom of the wall.* **3** °basis, °foundation, °source, °origin, °cause, °heart, °nub: *We have to get to the bottom of the problem.* **4** depths, Davy Jones's locker; bed: *The ship sank to the bottom of the sea.* **5 at bottom**: basically, fundamentally, in the °final *or* °last analysis, °really, in °reality, °truly, in °truth, essentially: *Despite her behaviour at the party, at bottom she is very reserved.* **6 Bottoms up!** Prosit!, To your (very good) health!, Cheers!, Here's to —!, Skol!: *Here's to the whole team—Bottoms up!*

bottomless *adj.* unfathomed, unfathomable, abyssal, °abysmal, °inexhaustible, °unlimited, °immeasurable, unplumbable: *The bottomless ignorance of the man is incredible.*

bounce *n.* **1** °bound, °leap, °hop, °recoil, ricochet, °rebound: *The ball took a bad bounce and the infielder missed it.* **2** °vitality, °energy, °verve, °zest, vivacity, liveliness, °animation, °dynamism, °life, *Colloq* °pep, zip, °go, get-up-and-go: *Betty has so much bounce, she is a bit tiring to have around.* —*v.* **3** °bound, °rebound, °hop; °recoil, ricochet: *The ball bounced over the wall and into the river.*

bound[1] *n.* **1** Usually, **bounds**: °boundary, boundary line, °limit(s), °extent, °border(s), confines: *Please try to keep the dogs within the bounds of the estate. Carl's plan is beyond the bounds of common sense.* —*v.* **2** °limit, °restrict, confine, delimit, °define, circumscribe: *The river bounds the property on the east.*

bound[2] *n.* **1** °leap, °jump, vault, °spring; °bounce, °hop: *With a great bound, the dog was upon me.* **2 by leaps and bounds**: See leap, 7, below. —*v.* **3** °leap, °jump, °hop, °spring, vault, gambol, °caper, romp, °frolic, °bounce, *Colloq* galumph: *The wolfhound came bounding towards me across the meadow.*

bound[3] *adj.* **1** tied, °fast, °fixed, fastened, confined, secured: *We were bound hand and foot and left in the cave.* **2** °obliged, obligated, required, constrained, °forced, compelled: *In the circumstances, Philippa was bound to do as she was told.* **3** °determined, resolved: *Otto is bound to go to the party if Antonia is going.* **4** °likely, °certain, °sure, °destined, predestined, °fated, °doomed: *He is bound to get the sack if he goes on turning up late.* **5** °destined, scheduled, booked; headed, directed: *We were bound for Cardiff.*

boundary *n.* °border(s), °limit(s), °frontier(s); °bound(s), confines, °perimeter: *If you cross that boundary, you will be safely in Switzerland.*

boundless *adj.* °limitless, unbounded, °unlimited; illimitable, °vast, °endless, unending, °infinite, °immense, °enormous, °immeasurable, incalculable, measureless, unrestricted, unchecked, °inexhaustible, unstoppable, unbridled, °uncontrolled, *Literary* vasty: *How can you keep up with a teenager's boundless energy?*

bountiful *adj.* **1** °generous, beneficent, munificent, °liberal, unsparing, unstinting, °charitable, eleemosynary, magnanimous, *Literary* bounteous: *We are grateful to Sir Roger, our most bountiful patron, for endowing this library.* **2** °ample, °abundant, plenteous, °plentiful, copious, °rich, *Literary* bounteous: *Until the Stock Exchange débâcle, these shares paid bountiful dividends.*

bounty *n.* **1** generosity, liberality, munificence, charitableness, °philanthropy, °charity, unselfishness, beneficence, goodness: *The poor used to be dependent on the bounty of the local gentry.* **2** °gift, °present, °largesse, °grant, °subsidy, °endowment, subvention: *People should be given work and not live off the bounty of the state.* **3** °reward, °award, °premium, °bonus, gratuity: *In America they paid a bounty of $50 for every dead wolf.*

bouquet *n.* **1** nosegay, posy, °bunch, °arrangement, °spray: *I sent her a bouquet of spring flowers for her birthday.* **2** °aroma, °scent, °odour, °fragrance, °perfume: *This '83 burgundy certainly has a fine bouquet.* **3** °compliment(s), °praise, commendation: *Mrs Campbell received many bouquets for her performances.*

bourgeois *adj.* **1** middle-class, °conventional, °philistine, capitalistic, propertied; °materialistic, °greedy, money-grubbing, money-hungry: *The yuppies constitute the modern bourgeois element in society.* **2** working-class, proletarian, °plebeian: *In his bourgeois mind he had only his labour to offer.*

bout *n.* **1** °turn, °round, °time, °occasion, °spell, °period, °session: *He's just got over a bout of pneumonia.* **2** °chance, °spree, °stint, °opportunity, innings: *We had long planned this bout of shopping.* **3** °contest, °match, boxing-match, prizefight, °meet, set-to, °struggle, °encounter, °engagement; duel: *A bout has been arranged between the heavyweight champion of the world and a challenger from Puerto Rico.*

bow *n.* **1** °nod; curtsy *or* curtsey, salaam, °kowtow, genuflection, °prostration, °obeisance: *We all bowed respectfully before the emperor.* —*v.* **2** °defer, °yield, °submit, °give in, °bend, °bow down, °capitulate: *I bow to your greater knowledge of the subject.* **3** °bend, °incline, °lower: *The servants bowed their heads when the master entered.* **4** °weigh down, °crush, °overload, °bend down, °burden: *Michael was bowed down by the responsibilities of his new family.* **5** °nod, curtsy *or* curtsey, salaam, °kowtow, genuflect, °prostrate oneself, °make °obeisance: *The natives bowed as the king passed by.*

bowels *n.* °interior, insides, depths; °heart, °centre, °core, intestines, viscera, vitals, belly,

°gut, *Colloq* innards, guts: *We descended the shaft into the very bowels of the earth. She hates me, I can feel it in my bowels.*

bowl[1] *v.* °move, trundle, °wheel, °roll, °spin: *We saw him in his car, bowling along at about 40.*

bowl[2] *n.* dish; basin, °pan: *She brought me a bowl of cereal.*

box[1] *n.* **1** °case, °receptacle, crate, carton, container, °casket, coffer, caddy, °chest: *She keeps her valuables in a small tortoise-shell box on the dressing-table.* —*v.* **2** crate, encase, °package: *The candles are boxed in dozens.* **3 box in** or **up**: °trap, confine, °bottle up, hem in, °enclose, °surround; °pin down: *They have the horses boxed in and are now driving them into the corral.*

box[2] *v.* **1** °fight, °engage in fisticuffs, °spar, °battle: *When he was in the army, he boxed for his regiment.* **2** °strike, buffet, °punch, °hit, *Colloq* slug, sock, whack, thwack, clout, °belt, thump, °lambaste, whomp: *Every time she heard him swear, she'd box his ears.* —*n.* **3** °blow, buffet, °punch, °hit, °strike, *Colloq* slug, sock, whack, thwack, clout, °belt, thump, whomp: *How would you like a box on the ear, you young rascal!*

boy *n.* **1** °lad, °youth, °young °man, °stripling, youngster, schoolboy, °fellow, urchin, brat, *Colloq* kid, °guy, small fry, little shaver: *There were two girls and five boys in my family.* **2** °servant, house-servant, °attendant; lackey, °slave, *Archaic* knave, varlet, °rogue, °wretch, caitiff: *Here! Boy! Bring me another gin and tonic.* **3 old boy**: *Brit* (public) schoolmate; °friend, °chum, °pal, *Archaic* old bean, old egg, old crumpet, dear boy; crony: *I say, old boy, care for a rubber of bridge? Carruthers wouldn't be where he is now if it weren't for the old-boy network.*

boycott *v.* **1** blacklist, °embargo; °avoid, °refuse, °shun, °reject, eschew, °pass over or by: *They are boycotting Fern's Dairy because it won't hire women. The US government is still boycotting cigars from Havana.* —*n.* **2** °embargo, blacklist, blacklisting, °ban: *A boycott of their products soon forced them to change their policies.*

boyish *adj.* **1** °young, youthful, °juvenile, °adolescent: *She liked his boyish good looks.* **2** °childish, °puerile, °juvenile, °immature: *Don't be too hard on them—it was just a boyish prank.*

brace *n.* **1** °bracket, stiffener, °reinforcement, reinforcer, °support, °buttress, °prop, °stay, °strut, truss: *Two steel braces had been installed to steady the columns.* **2** °drill: *He bored three holes in the wood with his brace and auger.* **3** °clasp, °clamp, °buckle, fastener, °clip, holdfast, °catch, coupler, coupling: *Another brace will be needed here to strengthen the handle.* **4** °pair; °couple, °span, °team (of two): *A brace of duelling pistols was sold at auction last week for $20,000. Her carriage was drawn by a brace of palominos.* —*v.* **5** °steady, °reinforce, °support, °strengthen, °prop or shore up: *Iron bars are used to brace the arches.* **6 brace oneself**: °steady or gird or °prepare oneself; °hold or °hang on: *I braced myself against the likelihood that she would refuse.*

bracing *adj.* °invigorating, °tonic, °stimulating, °refreshing, °exhilarating, fortifying, restorative: *I cannot live in the tropics and need the more bracing climate of the north.*

bracket *n.* **1** °support, corbel, °console: *The mantelpiece rests on a pair of stone brackets.* **2** shelf: *Her collection of glass paperweights was arrayed on a bracket in the sitting-room.* **3** °category, °class, °set, °group, grouping, classification, °division, °level; °order, °grade, °rank: *He comes from an altogether different bracket of society.* —*v.* **4** classify, °rank, °group; °unite, °combine, °join, °link: *I wish you wouldn't bracket her with me—our politics are as different as day and night.*

brag *v.* °boast, crow, trumpet, vaunt, °strut, °swagger, °show off, *Colloq* °talk °big, °blow or toot one's own horn or trumpet, °go on about: *He's always bragging about what he did in the war.*

braggart *n.* boaster, bragger, braggadocio, windbag, peacock, °show-off, Scaramouch or Scaramouche, *Slang* big-mouth, loud-mouth, gasbag: *That braggart William Smith talks about himself incessantly.*

braid *n.* **1** °plait: *Katrina wore her blonde hair in a tightly coiled braid on top of her head.* **2** trimming, embroidery, soutache, °lace, fillet, °band, ribbon: *The edges are decorated with narrow braid containing gold thread.* —*v.* **3** plait, intertwine, interlace, °weave, °twist: *At school we learned how to braid leather laces into a belt.*

brain *n.* **1** brains, °intelligence, °intellect, °understanding, °sense, °thought, °imagination, °capacity, perspicacity, perceptiveness, °perception, percipience; °wisdom, sagacity, °wit, discernment, acumen; °knowledge, cognition: *Although she's not yet ten, she has the brain to become a great mathematician.* **2** °genius, °mastermind, °intellectual; °leader, planner: *Many people regard Einstein as the greatest brain of the 20th century. Ivor was clearly the brains of the operation.*

brake *n.* **1** °curb, °check, °restraint, °restriction, constraint, °control, °rein: *The central bank applied a brake to the upward trend of the dollar by buying Deutschmarks.* —*v.* **2** °slow, °slow up or down, °put on or °apply the brakes, °reduce °speed, decelerate, slacken, °hold up: *He braked before the bad curve. She braked the car going down the steep hill.*

branch *n.* **1** °offshoot, arm; limb, bough, °stem, °shoot, °twig, sprig: *The branches of this tree need trimming.* **2** °department, °section, subsection, °division, subdivision, °office, °part, °ramification; affiliate, °subsidiary; spin-off: *What branch of medicine are you going to specialize in? The company maintains branches in New York and Melbourne.* —*v.* **3** ramify, °divide, subdivide, °diverge; °diversify: *This road branches off in three directions. The company will branch out into electronics this year.*

brand *n.* **1** °kind, °make, °type, °sort, °variety; brand °name, °manufacturer, maker, °trade °name, °trade °mark, °label, °mark, marque, *Chiefly US and Canadian* °name brand: *Which brand of toothpaste do you prefer? Our advertising agency is conducting a survey of brand loyalty.* —*v.* **2** °mark, °stamp, °identify, °tag, °label, trade-mark: *We sell only branded merchandise in our shops.* **3** °label, °characterize, °stigmatize, °discredit, °disgrace: *Because his actions at the front were misinterpreted, Corporal Williams was branded as a coward.*

brand-new *adj.* °new, °unused, °fresh, firsthand, °mint, virgin: *We bought a brand-new car last week.*

brash *adj.* **1** °hasty, °rash, °impetuous, °precipitate, °impulsive, headlong, °reckless: *He may be a brash young man, but I think he's going places.* **2** °impudent, °rude, °impertinent, °disrespectful, °insolent, °forward, °audacious, °brassy, °brazen, °bold, °tactless, undiplomatic, °presumptuous, *Colloq* °cheeky, °fresh: *Her brash behaviour has already landed her in trouble with the headmistress.*

brass *n.* °effrontery, °gall, °nerve, temerity, °impudence, insolence, rudeness, *Colloq* cheek, °nerve: *He had the brass to turn down a knighthood.*

brassy *adj.* **1** °impudent, °forward, °insolent, saucy, °brash, °rude, °brazen, °shameless; °coarse, °flashy, florid, °flamboyant; *Colloq* °cheeky, °fresh: *Our landlady was a big brassy blonde.* **2** °harsh, °strident, °tinny, °grating, dissonant, °shrill, °loud: *She has just the right kind of brassy voice for belting out songs like, 'There's No Business Like Show Business'.*

bravado *n.* boldness, °bluster, boasting, braggadocio, °swagger, °front, self-assurance, *Literary* rodomontade, gasconade; °arrogance, pretentiousness, *Colloq* °machismo, *Slang Brit* °side: *With an attempt at bravado, the union leader refused to meet the management representatives.*

brave *adj.* **1** °fearless, °intrepid, °bold, °courageous, °daring, °gallant, °stout, stout-hearted, valiant, valorous, °stalwart, plucky, °staunch, undaunted, °dauntless, unafraid, unfearing, °indomitable, °heroic, *Colloq* °macho, *Slang* gutsy: *Despite her misgivings about her proposal, she put on a brave face in the boardroom. He was brave to face the enemy alone.* **2** °fine, °handsome, °grand, °splendid, °showy, colourful, spectacular, °smart: *The colonel made a brave appearance in full Highland regalia.* —*v.* **3** °challenge, °defy, °dare; °brazen (out), °face, confront, °encounter, °meet: *We had to brave the elements in the open boat. I had to brave my father at breakfast.*

bravery *n.* °daring, °courage, valour, heroism, °fortitude, fearlessness, intrepidity, intrepidness, °pluck, °determination, staunchness, firmness, resoluteness, °resolution, indomitability, stalwartness, *Colloq* °machismo: *One has to admire the bravery of a woman who supported suffrage in the early 1900s.*

brawl *n.* **1** °fight, mêlée *or* melee, °battle, °battle royal, Donnybrook, °fray, wrangle, °dispute, °disorder, brannigan, °fracas, °row, °quarrel, squabble, *Colloq* punch-up, free-for-all, °scrap, ruckus: *The police had to be brought in to break up the brawl.* —*v.* **2** °fight, wrangle; °row, °quarrel, squabble, *Colloq* °scrap: *The two brothers always seem to be brawling.*

brawn *n.* muscle(s), °strength, robustness, brawniness, °might, °power, *Colloq* huskiness: *It must take a lot of brawn to lift those weights.*

brawny *adj.* °muscular, °strong, °tough, °robust, °mighty, °powerful, °burly, strapping, beefy, °hefty, °bulky, *Colloq* °husky: *That brawny fellow tossing the caber is my brother.*

brazen *adj.* °brassy, °shameless, °barefaced, °brash, outspoken, °forward, °immodest, unashamed, °audacious, °candid, °open, °unabashed, brazen-faced; °rude, °impudent, °impertinent, °insolent, saucy, *Colloq* °cheeky, °fresh, *US* sassy: *That's the last time I'll let that brazen hussy near my husband!*

breach *n.* **1** °break, °violation, infraction, disobedience, non-observance, °infringement, contravention: *Their failure to comply with paragraph 3 is a clear breach of our contract.* **2** °break, °rift, °gulf, °split, break-up, °separation, °rupture, severance, °schism, alienation, estrangement: *There seems to be no way to heal the breach between them.* **3** °gap, fissure, °crack, °split, °hole, °opening; chasm: *Their cannon opened a breach in the castle wall.* —*v.* **4** °rupture; °break through, invade: *The sea has breached the dyke. Someone breached the security measures set up for the missile design.*

breadth *n.* **1** °width, wideness, broadness, °beam, °span, °spread, thickness: *The breadth of the cloth is 54in.* **2** °extent, °magnitude, °degree, °amount, °scope, °expanse, °range, °area, °depth, °detail: *I like the breadth of coverage of the six o'clock news.* **3** liberality, largeness, catholicity, latitude: *Great breadth of vision was exhibited in the conference papers.*

break *v.* **1** break °apart *or* up *or* asunder, °fracture, °rupture, break into bits, °come apart, °shatter, °shiver, °crack, °crash, °splinter, °fragment, °split, °burst, °explode, *Colloq* bust: *The ball flew over the fence and broke my neighbour's window. She fell and broke her wrist.* **2** °reveal, °announce, °disclose, divulge, °tell, make °public: *Break the news to him gently.* **3** °relax, °ease up, °improve, ameliorate, °change for the better: *When will this spell of wet weather break?* **4** °demolish, smash, °destroy, °crush, °ruin, °defeat, °foil, °frustrate: *The power of the dictator was finally broken.* **5** °ruin, bankrupt: *He's the man that broke the bank at Monte Carlo.* **6** °weary, °exhaust, °wear out, °weaken, debilitate: *Twenty years in the chain-gang had broken him completely.* **7** °crush, °overcome; cow, °cripple, °demoralize, °weaken, °undermine, °discourage: *The divorce has broken her spirit.* **8** break in, °tame, °discipline, °train, °condition: *I used to break horses for a living.* **9** °violate, °transgress, °disobey, contravene, °defy, °infringe, fail to observe, °ignore, °disregard, °flout: *If you break the law, you'll regret it. They broke the contract.* **10** break off, °discontinue, °interrupt, °sever, °cut off; °give up, °suspend, °disrupt: *We broke relations with Spain after the incident. It is very difficult to break a habit of a lifetime. The narrative breaks at this point, to be taken up later.* **11** break up, °divide, °disperse, °scatter: *The rain is over and the clouds are breaking.* **12** break °loose *or* away *or* forth, °separate from, break out (of), °escape (from), °depart (from): *The ship broke from its moorings during the storm.* **13** break forth, °burst forth; °emerge *or* °come out °suddenly: *The storm broke in all its fury. After a little while, the sun broke through.* **14** demote, *Colloq* bust: *He was broken from sergeant to private.* **15 break away**: °leave, °depart, °separate (oneself): *A small group broke away from the established church to worship as they saw fit.* **16 break down: a** °demolish, °destroy: *All right, men, let's break down that wall.* **b** °decompose, break up; °analyse: *The carbon dioxide molecules and water are broken down by photosynthesis.* **c** °collapse, give °way, °disintegrate, be crushed, be prostrated: *His health has broken down completely.* **17 break**

ground: °initiate, °begin, °commence, °found, °set up, °establish, °inaugurate, be innovative, innovate, *Colloq* break the ice, take the °plunge, °start the ball rolling: *Laser printers have broken new ground in the area of computer printout.* **18 break in: a** °interrupt, interpose, interject, °burst in, °intrude, °intervene, °interfere, °disturb: *If the results of the election become known, we shall break in to keep you informed.* **b** °train, °educate, °prepare; °accustom, °condition, habituate, °wear: *We'll break you in for a week or two on the new machine. Wear your new boots for an hour each day to break them in.* **c** °rob, burgle, burglarize, break and °enter: *Someone broke in and stole my video recorder last night.* **19 break off: a** °discontinue, °stop, °cease, °end: *Sally broke off in mid sentence. After the Fashoda Incident, Britain broke off relations with France.* **b** °disengage; °sever, °detach, °break: *A large branch broke off from the tree and crashed down, narrowly missing me.* **20 break out: a** °escape; °emerge, °appear: *She broke out of prison in 1985 and hasn't been seen since.* **b** °erupt, °come out in, break out in *or* into: *He breaks out in a rash from eating strawberries. A war could break out any minute.* **21 break the ice**: See 17, above. **22 break through**: °penetrate, °force *or* °get through: *Wit, like beauty, can break through the most unpromising disguise.* **23 break up**: See also 11, 16 b, above. **a** disband, disperse; disintegrate: *Heraclius succeeded in breaking up the Persian power.* **b** °fracture, °fragment, comminute: *In the spring, the ice on the river breaks up.* **c** See 24 a, below. **24 break with: a** break up (with), °separate from, °leave, °depart from: *The leader broke with the party and established a new organization. Sally has broken up with Michael.* **b** °renounce, °repudiate, disavow: *They have broken entirely with the traditions we valued so highly.* —*n.* **25** °fracture, °split, °separation, °rupture, °breach, °rift, °schism: *There was a break in a gas pipe. Disagreement over the fishing grounds has resulted in a break in relations.* **26** °gap, °opening, °hole; °crack, °slit: *You can escape through a break in the wall near the bridge.* **27** °interruption, discontinuity, discontinuation, hesitation, °suspension, hiatus, °gap, lacuna, unevenness, irregularity: *There was a five-minute break in transmission from the ship.* **28** °rest, °respite, °rest °period, coffee-break, tea break, °intermission, °interlude, °lull, °pause, playtime, *US* °recess, *Colloq* breather: *We take a break at ten o'clock.* **29** °chance, stroke of luck, °opportunity, °opening: *All he needs is a break to get started.*

breakdown *n.* **1** °collapse, °downfall, °failure, foundering; °destruction, °ruin: *There was a breakdown of our computer system. The arbitrators blamed a breakdown of communication between union and management.* **2** (°mental) °collapse, °nervous breakdown, *Colloq* crack-up: *She had a bad breakdown after her daughter was killed.* **3** °analysis, °run-down, detailing, °review; decomposition, °itemization, classification, dissection, distillation, fractionation: *I want a breakdown of these figures by noon. The chemical breakdown of the substance indicated the presence of arsenic.*

breakneck *adj.* °reckless, °dangerous, °daredevil; °excessive, °careless, headlong, °rash, *Colloq* hell for leather: *The car came round the corner at breakneck speed on two wheels.*

breast *n.* **1** °chest, °bosom, bust; teat, *Technical* mamma, *Slang* boob, knocker, tit, titty: *He clasped the child to his breast. On some beaches in Europe, women bare their breasts when sunbathing.* **2** °soul, °core, °heart, °heart of hearts: *I feel in my breast it is the right thing to do.*

breath *n.* **1** °gust, zephyr, °breeze, °puff, whiff, °stirring, °stir: *There wasn't a breath of air in the tent.* **2** °hint, °suggestion, °indication, °touch, °murmur, °whisper, soupçon: *She never allowed the breath of scandal to affect her behaviour.* **3 take one's breath away**: °astound, °astonish, °surprise, °amaze, °dazzle, °startle, °shock, °stagger: *The sheer beauty of the waterfall takes your breath away.*

breathe *v.* **1** °live, °exist: *She believes that there never breathed a wiser man than her father.* **2** °inhale and °exhale, respire, suspire: *He was breathing regularly.* **3** °exhale, °expel, °puff, °blow: *The banner depicts a dragon breathing fire.* **4** °whisper, °murmur, °hint (at), °suggest, °tell, °speak, °say: *She told me not to breathe a word of it to anybody.*

breathless *adj.* **1** panting, out of °breath, winded, gasping, °exhausted, °spent, °worn out, °tired out, *Colloq Brit* puffed: *We were breathless after carrying the piano up two flights of stairs.* **2** surprised, amazed, astonished, astounded, awestruck, staggered: *The news of Penny's having given birth to twins left me breathless.* **3** °eager, °agog, °feverish, in °suspense: *We were all breathless with anticipation as the compère opened the envelope.*

breed *n.* **1** °kind, °sort, °type, °variety, species; °race, °lineage, °stock, °family, °strain: *What breed of dog won at Crufts this year?* —*v.* **2** °produce, °generate, °bring forth, °create, engender, °hatch, beget, give °rise to, °develop, °cause: *The cheese is so old it's breeding maggots. Familiarity breeds contempt.* **3** °raise, °rear, °cultivate, °propagate: *Charollais cattle are widely bred in Europe today.* **4** °arise, °originate, °appear; °develop, °grow, °increase, multiply: *The sergeant allowed discontent and jealousy to breed within his platoon.*

breeding *n.* **1** rearing, bringing-up, raising, cultivation, °development, propagation: *The breeding of sheepdogs has been Tom's hobby for years.* **2** (good) °upbringing, (good) °manners, °civility, politeness, politesse, gentility, (good) °behaviour: *You can tell from the way she treats people that she has breeding.*

breeze *n.* **1** °breath, °puff, zephyr, °wind, °draught, °gust, *Nautical* cat's-paw: *A breeze sprang up from the north, and the little boat moved forward.* **2** °easy or °simple °job or °task, °nothing, *Colloq* °snap, *Slang* cinch, *US* lead-pipe cinch: *It ought to be a breeze to find someone at that salary.*

breezy *adj.* **1** airy, °fresh, °windy, draughty, °brisk, gusty: *The afternoon was breezy and warm, ideal for walking.* **2** °casual, °carefree, light-hearted, °cheerful, cheery, airy, °lively, °spirited, blithesome, °buoyant: *The chairman's breezy opening of the annual meeting made everyone feel comfortable.*

brevity *n.* shortness, briefness, conciseness, concision, terseness, succinctness, pithiness, compactness, laconicism *or* laconism, °economy: *Brevity is the soul of wit.*

brew *v.* **1** °ferment, cook, °boil; infuse: *Our beer is brewed using the best hops.* **2** concoct, °devise,

°plan, *Colloq* cook up; contrive, °prepare, °bring about, °cause, °produce, °hatch: *They are brewing up a plot to unseat the financial director.* **3** °start, °go on, °hatch, °begin, °form; °stew, °simmer, *Colloq* cook: *A storm is brewing.*
—*n.* **4** beer, ale, stout; tea; beverage, °drink; concoction, °mixture: *She served me some strange brew in which I could detect cinnamon and nutmeg.*

bribe *n.* **1** °graft, °inducement, *Colloq* °kickback, *Chiefly US* payola, *US* plugola: *Some judges were offered bribes for reducing the sentences of convicted felons.*
—*v.* **2** °pay or °buy off, °buy; °corrupt, suborn, *Colloq* °fix; *Slang* °oil, grease (someone's) palm, *Brit* nobble: *The guards were bribed to look the other way during the prison break.*

bric-à-brac *n.* bric-a-brac, °curiosities, knick-knacks, collectables or collectibles, trinkets, °gewgaws, gimcracks; bibelots, curios, objets d'art, objets de vertu: *On Saturday she went to an antiques fair and bought still more bric-à-brac to clutter up the house.*

brick *n.* **1** °block, cube, chunk, hunk, °slab; stone: *I bought a brick of ice-cream to serve for pudding. A university is not just bricks and mortar.* **2** °pal, °comrade, °friend, *Colloq* °chum, *US and Canadian* buddy: *You're a real brick to watch the children for me till I get back.*

bridal *adj.* °nuptial, °wedding; conjugal, connubial, °marriage: *The bridal gown was white, with lace appliqués.*

bridge *n.* **1** °span: *We could build a bridge over the river here.* **2** °link, connexion or °connection, °tie, °bond: *She regarded teaching as a bridge between her studies and a post in school administration.*
—*v.* **3** °span, °cross (over), °go or °pass over, °traverse: *The viaduct bridges the swamp.* **4** °connect, °link, °unite, °join, °tie: *The gap between rich and poor is not easily bridged.*

bridle *n.* **1** °restraint, °curb, °check, °control: *Man has need of a bridle on his passions.*
—*v.* **2** °curb, °check, °restrain, °hold in, °control: *You must learn to bridle your temper.* **3** °bristle, draw oneself up, be or become °indignant, take °offence or °umbrage or affront (at), be affronted or offended (by): *She bridled at the suggestion that she was responsible for Keith's departure.*

brief *adj.* **1** °short, °momentary, °little, °fleeting; °short-lived, transitory, °transient, evanescent, °passing, °temporary, ephemeral, °fugitive: *The lights went back on after a brief interval. His glory was brief.* **2** °short, °concise, °succinct, to the °point; condensed, shortened, °cut, curtailed, °abbreviated, compressed, abridged, °thumbnail, compendious: *The chairman made a few brief remarks. Here is a brief description of what happened.* **3** °curt, °abrupt, °terse, °short, °blunt, °brusque: *You mustn't be so brief with little children.*
—*n.* **4** °summary, °outline, °digest, °précis, résumé, compendium, °abstract, condensation, °abridgement °synopsis, °extract: *This is merely a brief; the full document will follow.* **5 in brief** °briefly, concisely, in °sum, in °summary, to °sum up, succinctly, in a °word: *He is a cutthroat, too—in brief, the greatest scoundrel living.*
—*v.* **6** °advise, °inform, °fill in, °coach, °instruct, °enlighten; °explain, °run through or down: *Howard will brief you on the details.*

briefly *adv.* **1** concisely, tersely, succinctly, in a °word, in °short; bluntly, curtly, in a nutshell, in a °few words, to °sum up: *Briefly, the plan is a complete non-starter.* **2** momentarily, for a °few moments or seconds or minutes, fleetingly, hurriedly, °hastily, °quickly: *I stopped briefly at the post office on my way home.*

bright *adj.* **1** °light, shining, gleaming, °radiant, °brilliant, resplendent, glittering, flashing, *Formal* refulgent, effulgent, fulgent, fulgid, fulgorous; alight, aglow, beaming, °dazzling, °glowing, °luminous, lambent, °incandescent, °ablaze with: *We arrived on a bright, sunny day. The water was bright with phosphorescence.* **2** °clear, cloudless, °fair, unclouded: *It certainly is a bright night—you can see every star.* **3** °shiny, °polished, °lustrous, °glossy, sparkling: *I want that brass so bright I can see my face in it.* **4** °hopeful, °optimistic, °favourable, °propitious, auspicious, °promising, °rosy: *Glenys's job prospects are not very bright.* **5** °brilliant, °vivid, °intense, fluorescent, *US trade mark* Day-Glo: *But you said you wanted the room bright orange, Madam.* **6** °intelligent, °clever, °quick-witted, °witty, °brilliant, keen-minded, sharp-witted, °gifted, °astute, °ingenious, °alert, °smart; °precocious; *Colloq* brainy, on the ball: *No one can deny that Alison is a bright young woman.* **7** °illustrious, °glorious, °splendid, °magnificent, °distinguished, °outstanding: *Today has been one of the brightest days in the history of Britain.* **8** °cheerful, °gay, °happy, °exuberant, °lively, °animated, °vivacious, °spirited: *It is a pleasure to see so many bright faces in the audience.*

brighten *v.* **1** °illuminate, °enliven, °lighten, °cheer up, °liven up, *Colloq* °perk up: *Replacing those heavy draperies with thinner curtains ought to brighten the room.* **2** °shine, °polish, burnish: *The silver could use a bit of brightening up.*

brilliance *n.* **1** brightness, °radiance, °lustre, °splendour, magnificence, °sparkle, °dazzle, °glitter, effulgence, °light: *The brilliance of the opening night rivalled that of Hollywood.* **2** °intelligence, °wit, °intellect, keenness, sharpness, acuteness, °genius, °talent, sagacity; precocity: *Her brilliance shows in her books.*

brilliant *adj.* **1** °bright, shining, °lustrous, °radiant, resplendent, °dazzling, °luminous; °incandescent, glittering, sparkling, °scintillating, coruscating, °twinkling, *Formal* effulgent: *At the show I saw the most brilliant display of diamonds.* **2** °splendid, °magnificent, °superb, °beautiful, °distinguished, °striking, °glorious, °remarkable, °exceptional, °outstanding: *The audience rose for a standing ovation after the brilliant last movement of the concerto.* **3** °illustrious, °famous, °noted, °celebrated, °eminent, °prominent, °renowned, °accomplished: *Paul is one of the country's most brilliant chemists.* **4** °intelligent, °clever, °gifted, °bright, °talented, °smart, °expert, °masterful, °accomplished, °ingenious, °imaginative, °creative; °quick-witted, sharp-witted, keen-witted, °enlightened; °resourceful, discerning, °able, °competent: *Goddard's brilliant mind understood principles of practical rocket flight.*

brim *n.* **1** °edge, °margin, lip, °rim; °brink: *I filled the cup to the brim.*
—*v.* **2** be °full or filled, overflow: *His cup was brimming with steaming mulled wine. They are brimming over with confidence as they approach the race.*

bring v. **1** °carry, °bear, °fetch, °get, °take; °deliver: *Don't forget to bring some wine home for dinner tonight.* **2** °lead, °conduct, convey; °escort, invite, °accompany: *The road brought me to your house. You can bring anyone you like to the party.* **3** °draw, °attract, °lure, allure: *What brings you to London?* **4** °carry, °bear, convey; °report: *She brought word of the uprising.* **5** bring on, bring about, °occasion, give °rise to, be the °source or °cause of, °create, cause, engender, °produce; °contribute to: *The thought of his mother brought tears to his eyes.* **6** °institute, °advance; invoke: *She is bringing charges against him for slander.* **7 bring about**: °occasion, °cause, bring on, °accomplish, °effect, °achieve, °produce: *The government has brought about changes in the health service.* **8 bring down**: **a** °overthrow, depose, oust, unseat, dethrone, °overturn, °topple: *A military faction has brought down the government.* **b** °reduce, lessen, °diminish, °cut (back or down): *The chancellor promised to bring down taxes in the next budget.* **9 bring forth**: **a** °bear, °give °birth to, °produce; °yield: *The kangaroo brings forth young less than an inch in size.* **b** °set forth, bring out or in or up, °introduce, °present, °produce, °put out, °submit, °offer, °advance: *Mr Hanson has brought forth a new sales plan.* **10 bring in**: **a** °earn, °yield, °produce, °realize, °fetch, °return, °sell for: *Advertising brings in more revenue than subscriptions.* **b** See **15**, below. **11 bring off**: °succeed (in), °achieve, °accomplish, do, °carry out or off, °perform, °pull off; *Colloq* °put over: *Do you really think she'll be able to bring off her masquerade?* **12 bring on**: **a** °produce, °put on, °introduce, bring in: *When the children in the audience began to get restless, they brought on the clowns.* **b** °induce, °produce, °occasion, bring about: *Eating strawberries brought on a rash.* **13 bring out**: **a** °display, °feature, °focus on, °illuminate, °set off, °make noticeable or °conspicuous, °emphasize, °develop: *The colour of the dress brings out the blue of your eyes.* **b** °publish, °issue, °release, make known or °public, °produce; °put on, °stage: *They've brought out a new edition of Dickens's works.* **14 bring round** or **around**: **a** °revive, resuscitate, bring to; °restore: *The smelling salts brought her round when she fainted.* **b** °persuade, °win over, °convince, °influence: *Can he be brought round to our way of thinking?* **15 bring up**: **a** °rear, °raise, °care for, °look after, nurture, °breed; °educate, °teach, °train, °tutor: *She has brought up six children on her own.* **b** °introduce, °broach, bring in, °raise, °pen (up), °set forth, °mention, °touch on, °talk about, °discuss; reintroduce, °recall: *Why bring up irrelevant matters like his age?* **c** °raise, elevate: *So far, they have brought up only three survivors from the mine.* **d** °vomit, °throw up, regurgitate, disgorge: *He woke up feeling sick and brought up most of the previous night's meal.*

brink n. **1** °edge, °brim, °rim, °margin, lip, °border: *He lost his footing and almost went over the brink into the gorge.* **2** °verge, °point: *He was on the brink of telling them everything, but suddenly remembered his promise.*

brisk adj. **1** °active, °lively, °busy, °vigorous: *The poachers are doing a brisk trade in rhinoceros horn.* **2** quick, °animated, °sprightly, spry, °energetic, °spirited: *Patrick was a brisk lad, fresh from Oxford.* **3** °strong, °steady, °fresh, °refreshing, °bracing, °invigorating, °stimulating, °crisp, °biting, °bracing, °keen, nippy, °chill, °chilly, °cool, °cold: *A brisk breeze had started up from the north, chilling us through.* **4** °energetic, vibrant, °invigorating, °stimulating: *After a brisk massage, Mariette felt completely revitalized.*

bristle n. **1** °hair, whisker, barb, °prickle, °thorn, quill, *Technical* seta: *Shaving brushes are often made from badger bristles.* —v. **2** °prickle, °rise, °stand up, *Formal* horripilate: *He could feel the hair on the back of his neck bristle.* **3** °seethe, °become °angry or infuriated or °furious or maddened, °boil, °flare up, see red, °bridle: *He bristled with enraged frustration.* **4** °teem, °crawl, be °thick, °swarm, be °alive: *The sea urchin was bristling with sharp spines.*

brittle adj. **1** °fragile, frangible, breakable; friable: *My fingernails become brittle in the cold and break easily.* **2** °frail, °weak, °delicate, °sensitive, °fragile, °insecure: *She might seem strong, but she has a very brittle nature and is easily upset.*

broach v. °introduce, °raise, °open (up), °suggest, °mention, °hint at, °touch on or upon, °bring up or in, °talk about, °advance: *I didn't dare broach the subject of money.*

broad adj. **1** °wide, °expansive, °large, °extensive, °spread out, °ample, °spacious: *The broad highway stretched out for miles before them. Cattle graze in the broad pastures.* **2** °bright, °plain, °open, °full; unshaded: *He had the nerve to kiss me in broad daylight, in front of everyone!* **3** °plain, °clear, °obvious, °emphatic, °explicit, °pronounced, °direct, unconcealed, °undisguised, unsubtle, °evident: *His wink gave a broad hint of what he really had in mind.* **4** °main, °general, generalized, °rough, unspecific, non-specific, °approximate, °sweeping: *Without the details, here is a broad outline of what happened.* **5** plain-spoken, °outspoken, °forthright, °direct, unreserved, °frank, °candid, unrestrained: *When he reached the witness box, he repeated the accusation in broad terms.* **6** °inclusive, °general, °widely applicable, °extensive, wide-ranging, °comprehensive, wholesale; °vague, °imprecise, °indefinite, unfocused, non-specific, unspecified: *We have broad support for these policies. She formulated a broad rule to fit all imaginable cases.* **7** °liberal, °tolerant, °catholic, ecumenical, latitudinarian: *The term 'Broad Church' is said to have been coined by A. H. Clough. The judge feels that he must give the broadest possible interpretation of the law.* **8** °dirty, °blue, °coarse, °rude, °indecent, °vulgar, °improper, indelicate, off colour, °loose, °gross, °obscene, °lewd, °lascivious, °filthy, °pornographic; inelegant, °unrefined, unladylike, ungentlemanly, titillating: *Peter was in the corner telling some of his broad jokes.* —n. **9** °woman, °girl, *Slang* dame, cookie or cooky, skirt, bimbo, bird, chick, °number, doll, piece (of baggage): *We picked up a couple of broads at the dance hall last night.*

broadcast v. **1** °air, °transmit, relay; °radio; televise, telecast: *The programme will be broadcast tonight.* **2** °announce, advertise, °publish, °proclaim; disseminate: *It may be a bad idea to broadcast your plans in advance.* **3** °sow, °scatter, °seed: *The farmer broadcasts this seed instead of planting it.* —n. **4** °programme, °show; °transmission, telecast: *I heard the broadcast on my car radio.*

brochure n. °pamphlet, booklet; catalogue; folder, °leaflet; °tract: *The brochure advertising the company's products will be ready tomorrow.*

broil v. grill, barbecue: *I think hamburgers taste better broiled than fried.*

broke adj. penniless, °indigent, down-and-out, poverty-stricken, °penurious, °impoverished, °insolvent, °destitute, °poor, °needy, bankrupt, ruined, *Colloq* on one's beam-ends, on one's uppers, strapped, °flat or °dead or stony-broke, °hard up, °short, up against it, *US* °flat, on the skids; *Slang Brit* skint: *I was broke after paying the rent—I didn't even have money for food.*

broken adj. **1** fragmented, shattered, shivered, splintered, ruptured, cracked, °split, smashed, pulverized, disintegrated, destroyed, demolished: *A broken Ming vase cannot be worth much.* **2** fractured: *With a broken leg, she certainly won't be competing in the slalom.* **3** enfeebled, weakened, crushed, defeated, beaten, ruined; dispirited, °dejected, discouraged, demoralized, °subdued, debilitated, *Colloq* licked: *Rosa's running away with a sailor left Hugh a broken man.* **4** tamed, trained, disciplined, °obedient, docile, domesticated, °subdued; conditioned: *What use is a horse that isn't broken?* **5** violated, transgressed, disobeyed, contravened, defied, flouted, disregarded, ignored, infringed: *The rules of this club are broken too often: we'll have to tighten things up.* **6** interrupted, °disturbed, discontinuous, °disjointed, °disconnected, fragmented, °fragmentary, °intermittent, °erratic, °sporadic: *I couldn't stop worrying about the operation and had a terrible night of broken sleep.* **7** Also, **broken-down:** out of °order or commission, not working or functioning, in °disrepair, *Slang* on the °blink, out of kilter, kaput, *US* on the fritz, out of whack: *My watch is broken. Why waste money repairing that broken-down car of yours?*

broken-hearted adj. heartbroken, depressed, °downhearted, °dejected, devastated, crushed, overwhelmed, heartsick, downcast, °upset; °forlorn, °sorrowful, disconsolate, °inconsolable, grief-stricken, °miserable, °wretched, °melancholy, heavy-hearted, °sad, °doleful, dolorous, woeful, °woebegone, °gloomy, morose, °glum, cheerless, *Colloq* down: *She was broken-hearted when her puppy was lost.*

broker n. stockbroker; °agent, °dealer, middleman, °intermediary, °go-between, *Brit* stockjobber: *I have phoned my broker to tell him to sell all my shares.*

brooch n. clasp, °pin; °fastening: *She was wearing the cameo brooch I had given to her mother.*

brood n. **1** °young, °offspring, °progeny; children, °family: *A mallard was tending her brood among the rushes.* —v. **2** °incubate, °hatch, °set, °sit, °cover: *The old hen was brooding three eggs.* **3** Also, **brood on** or **over:** °ponder (on or over), °meditate (on or over), °contemplate, ruminate (on or over), °muse (on or over): *He just sits there brooding over the subject of his next novel.* **4** mope, °sulk, °pout, pine, eat one's heart out, °fret, °worry, agonize, °despair: *Don't just brood over the problem, do something about solving it!*

brook¹ n. °stream, rivulet, °run, runnel, rill, *US and Canadian and Australian and New Zealand*

°creek; *No. Eng. dialect* beck, gill or ghyll; *Scots* burn: *The river is fed by numerous brooks from every part of the country.*

brook² v. °endure, °tolerate, °stand, °abide, °put up with, °suffer, °allow: *She runs the business in her own way and brooks no interference from anyone.*

broth n. °stock, bouillon, consommé; soup; decoction: *We tossed food scraps into the large, simmering pot to make a broth.*

brothel n. bordello, whore-house, °house of °ill fame or °ill repute, bawdy-house, bagnio; seraglio, harem, *Obsolete* °stew, *Colloq US* sporting °house, *Slang Brit* knocking-shop, *US* cat-house: *On their first night in Paris, they visited a brothel.*

brother n. sibling; °relation, °relative, °kin, kinsman; °fellow, fellow-man, fellow-clansman, fellow-citizen, fellow-countryman, fellow-creature; °associate, °colleague, confrère, °companion, *Colloq* °pal, °chum, *Brit and Australian* °mate, *US* °buddy: *Some day, perhaps all men will regard each other as brothers.*

brotherhood n. **1** brotherliness, °fellowship, °companionship, °alliance, °friendship, comradeship, camaraderie, °kinship: *We should all live together in harmony and brotherhood.* **2** °fraternity, guild, °society, °association, °order, °league, °union, °organization, °club, community, °circle, °set, °clique: *The tribes fused into a united and enthusiastic brotherhood.*

brotherly adj. °fraternal, °kind, °affectionate, °cordial, °friendly, °amicable, °amiable, °neighbourly, °loyal, °devoted: *The boys grew up together and maintained a brotherly relationship throughout their lives.*

browbeat v. °bully, °intimidate, °threaten, badger, °dominate, cow, °frighten, °discourage, °tyrannize, hector, °harass, keep after, °nag, *Colloq* hassle: *The foreman constantly browbeat anyone who wasn't one of his drinking cronies.*

browse v. °look over or through, °skim (through), °scan, °thumb or °flip or flick through: *I was browsing through some recent acquisitions at the second-hand bookshop.*

bruise n. **1** °injury, °hurt, contusion, °bump, °welt, °scrape, abrasion, °scratch, °wound, black-and-blue °mark, blotch, °blemish, °mark, °spot, discoloration, °damage, *Technical* ecchymosis: *I got this bruise from walking into the corner of the table. The price is lower if the fruit has a few bruises.* —v. **2** °injure, contuse, °hurt, °scrape, °harm, °wound, °damage: *I bruised my knee when I fell down. Being arrested certainly bruised his self-esteem.*

bruiser n. prizefighter, boxer, fighter; °tough, ruffian, bodyguard, °thug, °hoodlum, bouncer, *Colloq* hooligan, °tough °guy, toughie, *Brit* °minder, *US* roughneck, hood, gorilla, plug-ugly, torpedo, enforcer: *The heavyweight contender is really a big bruiser. Mr Big strode in with two of his bruisers.*

brunt n. (full) °force, °burden, onus, °weight, °impact; °shock, °stress, °violence, onslaught: *As the head of the department was on holiday, I had to take the full brunt of the customers' complaints.*

brush¹ n. **1** brushwood, shrubs, undergrowth, branches, °scrub, °brush, bracken, brambles, underbrush, underwood: *It took us three days to clear the brush from around the house.* **2** °thicket,

°brake, copse, grove, boscage: *The fox disappeared into the brush, which was too dense for the dogs to follow.*

brush² *n.* **1** hairbrush, toothbrush, clothes-brush, shoe-brush, nail-brush, paint-brush; broom, dust-broom, besom, *US* °whisk broom: *This brush is too harsh and may damage your teeth.* **2** See brush-off. **3** °encounter, °engagement, °skirmish, *Colloq Brit* °spot of °bother: *Mark has had several brushes with the law.* —*v.* **4** °scrub, °clean; °groom, curry; °sweep, °whisk, °gather: *Brush your teeth twice a day. I brushed down the mare before saddling her. Brush the crumbs off the table.* **5** graze, °touch: *He deliberately tried to brush against her in the corridor.* **6 brush aside** or **away**: °disregard, °dismiss, °put aside, shrug off: *Brushing aside the members' objections, he tried to force the committee's acceptance of the new rules.* **7 brush off**: °dismiss, °ignore, °rebuff, °send off or away or packing: *He asked her out, but she brushed him off.* **8 brush up (on)**: °review, restudy, °go over, °refresh, °study, *Archaic* con: *You should brush up on your geometry before taking trigonometry.*

brush-off *n.* °dismissal, °rebuff, °rejection, snub, *Colloq* cold °shoulder, °put-down, °slap in the face, the (old) heave-ho; *Chiefly US and Canadian* walking papers: *Tanya has given Theo the brush-off—said she never wants to see him again.*

brusque *adj.* °blunt, °rude, °overbearing, °impolite, uncivil, °discourteous, °ungracious, °ill-mannered, unmannerly; churlish, °gruff, °abrupt, °short, °curt, °sharp, °terse, °brash, °bluff: *I could tell that the interviewer had already decided against me by her brusque attitude.*

brutal *adj.* **1** °inhuman, °savage, °cruel, pitiless, °harsh, °severe, barbaric, barbarous, °beastly, bestial, °sadistic, °murderous; inhumane, °heartless, hard-hearted, °unkind, °fierce, stony-hearted, insensitive, unfeeling, °cold-blooded, °unsympathetic, °remorseless, °ruthless, °ferocious, °atrocious, Draconian or Draconic, *Literary* °fell: *Few survived the brutal treatment in the concentration camps.* **2** °rude, °ill-mannered, °coarse, °unrefined, °boorish, ill-bred, °rustic, crass, uncouth, uncultured, uncultivated, °rough, °crude: *His brutal behaviour made him unfit to represent the Crown.*

brute *adj.* **1** brutish, °dull, unfeeling, °senseless, °blind, unintelligent, °unthinking, °thoughtless, °mindless, unreasoning, irrational, °instinctive, °physical, °material; insensate, °unconscious: *He was able to lift the safe without help, by sheer brute strength.* —*n.* **2** °animal, °beast, °savage: *He wrote that man was the middle link between angels and brutes. George behaved like an absolute brute to her.*

bubble *n.* **1** blister, air pocket, globule, droplet: *This painted surface is full of air bubbles.* **2 bubbles**: °froth, °foam, suds, °lather, spume; effervescence, carbonation, °fizz: *The cider is full of bubbles.* —*v.* **3** °foam, °froth, °boil, °seethe, °fizz: *A pot of soup was bubbling on the stove.*

bubbly *adj.* **1** °effervescent, foamy, frothy, fizzy, sparkling: *I could see that the surface was all bubbly.* **2** °effervescent, °merry, °ebullient, bouncy, °animated, °vivacious, °cheerful, cheery, °lively, °excited: *Janet is known for her bubbly personality.*

—*n.* **3** champagne, sparkling wine, sparkling burgundy, Asti spumante, *Colloq Brit* champers: *Let's open a bottle of bubbly and celebrate.*

bucket *n.* pail, scuttle: *Keep this bucket of coal near the hearth.*

buckle *n.* **1** °clasp, fastener, °clip, °fastening, °hook, °catch: *The buckle broke on my belt and my trousers fell down.* —*v.* **2** °collapse, °cave in, °crumple, °bend, °warp, °distort, °twist, °bulge: *The support gave way and the entire wall buckled.*

bug *n.* **1** insect, beetle, larva, grub, caterpillar, butterfly, mosquito, °fly, spider, *Colloq Brit* creepy-crawly, *US* no-see-em: *There's a bug on your collar.* **2** °microbe, °germ, virus; °disease, °affliction, °illness, sickness, °ailment, °disorder, malady, infection; °condition, °complaint, °infirmity, indisposition: *She's caught some kind of bug and won't be in for a few days.* **3** °obsession, °craze, °fad, °mania, °rage: *Almost everyone in those days succumbed to the hula hoop bug.* **4** °enthusiast, faddist, °fan, °fanatic; hobbyist: *She's turned into a fruit machine bug.* **5** listening °device; microphone, transmitter, electronic eavesdropper, °tap: *They planted a bug in the ambassador's telephone.* **6** °fault, °error, °mistake, °failing, °shortcoming, *Colloq* hang-up, glitch: *There's a bug in the program that's preventing the list from being sorted. They can't market the device till they've ironed out all the bugs.* —*v.* **7** °annoy, °irritate, °pester, °irk, °harass, °bother: *I wish Mum'd stop bugging me about my homework.* **8** °tap, °spy on: *They bugged her phone and recorded all her conversations.*

bugger *n.* **1** buggerer, sodomite. **2** chap, °fellow, °man; °boy, °lad, °child, °tot; *Slang chiefly Brit* geezer, *US* °jerk; *Colloq* guy, *Brit* bloke, °fool, idiot: *He's a cute little bugger, isn't he? Who's that silly-looking bugger with Christina?* —*v.* **3** Also, **bugger up**: °ruin, °destroy, °botch, °bungle, °wreck; make a °mess of, *Colloq* °mess or °screw up, *Brit* bollocks or ballocks up, balls up, make a balls-up of, cock up, *US* ball up, bollix up; *Taboo* fuck up: *He's buggered the recording, so we'll have to start again at the beginning. Why does she bugger up everything I try to do?*
4 bugger about or **around**: **a** °fool about, °waste time, °dawdle, *Colloq US* lallygag or lollygag; *Taboo* fuck about or around: *He buggers about the house all the time instead of looking for a job. Don't bugger about with my hi-fi.* **b** °cause complications for, °create difficulties for: *She pretends to be helping me, but she's just buggering me about.* **5 bugger off**: °go away, °depart, °leave, °clear off or out, *Colloq* make tracks, skedaddle, °beat it, *Slang* piss off; *Taboo* fuck off: *Oh, bugger off and leave me alone!*

build *v.* **1** °construct, °erect, °raise, °set up, °assemble: *I hope to build my own house in another year or so.* **2** °found, °establish, °base: *The theory is built on the principle that light travels at 186,000 miles per second.* **3** °develop: *She built the company in about five years.* **4** Also, **build up**: °intensify; °increase, °develop, °enlarge, °strengthen: *The distant hum of voices gradually built to a mighty roar.* —*n.* **5** °physique, °figure, °body, °shape, *Slang* bod: *He has a good build from working out at the gym.*

building *n.* edifice, °structure, construction, erection: *The building where I work is air-conditioned.*

bulge n. 1 °lump, °hump, protuberance, °bump, °swelling, °bulge, °projection: *This wallet is making a bulge in my jacket.*
—v. 2 °protrude, °stick out, °swell (out): *His stomach bulges out over his belt.*

bulk n. 1 °volume, °magnitude, °mass, enlargement, largeness, °size: *The sausage-makers add bread just for bulk.* 2 °majority: *The bulk of the people voted for the proposal.*

bulky adj. °large, °voluminous, °unwieldy, °awkward, ungainly, cumbersome, *Brit* chunky: *The package, though quite bulky, didn't cost much to post.*

bulletin n. °message, °notice, communication, °announcement, communiqué, dispatch or despatch, °report, °account, °flash, °news item, newsflash: *And now, here's a bulletin from the centre court at Wimbledon.*

bully n. 1 persecutor, intimidator, °tyrant: *That bully Roderick is always beating up the younger boys.*
—v. 2 °persecute, °intimidate, °tyrannize, °torment, °browbeat, °daunt, awe, cow, terrorize; hector, °harass, °push around: *Roderick even bullied his best friend into parting with his allowance.*
—adj. 3 *Old-fashioned* jolly, °worthy, °admirable: *Ah, there you are, my bully boy!*
—interj. 4 Usually, **Bully for (someone)!** Bravo!, Great!, Fantastic!, Fabulous!, Marvellous!, Spectacular!; So what?, What of it?; *US* Peachy!, Dandy!, Neat-oh!; *Old-fashioned* Fantabulous!: *'David's won the snooker competition again.' 'Bully for him!'*

bulwark n. 1 °defence or *US* defense, °safeguard, redoubt, bastion, buffer, °barrier, °rampart, fortification: *A strong defence is the best bulwark against aggression from outside.*
—v. 2 °defend, °protect, °shelter: *Marnie's indifference to others bulwarks her against any feelings of contrition.*

bum n. 1 °buttocks, °posterior, hindquarters, fundament, behind, rump, °bottom, *derrière*, °rear °end, backside, °seat, °rear, *Colloq US* fanny, can, hinie, tush or tushy or tushie, tokus or tochis or tuchis, keister or keester, *Taboo slang Brit* arse, *US* ass: *Why don't you get off your fat bum and go out and get a job?!* 2 °tramp, panhandler, °beggar, vagrant, °loafer, °drifter, °vagabond, hobo, °derelict, gypsy; *Brit* caird, °tinker, °traveller; *US* (shopping-) bag lady: *Along the Bowery the doorways and pavements are strewn with bums.*
—adj. 3 °improper, unjustified, °false, trumped up, °untrue, fabricated, made-up, °bogus: *That auto theft charge was a bum rap, but he still served 18 months.* 4 °bad, °awful, unfair, °dishonest, °poor, °rotten, *Slang* °lousy, crummy: *I still think you got a bum deal on that toaster.*
—v. 5 °borrow, °beg, sponge, *Colloq* °scrounge, cadge, °touch, put the °touch on, *US* mooch, °hit, °hit up: *Can I bum a cigarette from you?*

bump n. 1 °blow, °collision, °thud, °hit, °knock, buffet, clunk, whack: *That bump on the head seems to have affected him.* 2 °lump, protuberance, °welt, °swelling, tumescence, °knob, °bulge: *How did you get that bump on your forehead?*
—v. 3 °knock (against), °strike, °hit, °collide (with), °run into, °ram; smash, °crash, *Colloq* wallop: *I bumped into the car in front as I was parking.* 4 **bump into**: °meet, °encounter, °run into or across, °come across, °stumble over: *I bumped into Philippa at the hairdresser's.* 5 **bump off**: °murder, °kill, °put away, assassinate, do away with, °execute, liquidate, dispatch or despatch, *Slang* take for a °ride, °destroy, °eliminate, °rub out, °wipe out, do in, *US* °waste, ice: *They bumped off Wimpy, boss; he was pulled out of the river wearing concrete overshoes.*

bumpy adj. °lumpy, °rough, uneven, °irregular, knobby, knobbly, °pitted; potholed, bouncy, jarring, jerky, rutted: *The skin on his forehead is a bit bumpy. This is the bumpiest road in the town.*

bunch n. 1 °bundle, °cluster, °batch, °clump; °bouquet, nosegay, posy, °spray: *That's a nice-looking bunch of grapes. Mr Herbert arrived with a bunch of flowers for me.* 2 °crowd, °knot, °collection, °group, °lot, °gathering, °cluster, °clutch, °batch, °assortment, °mass: *A bunch of people stood outside the courtroom, awaiting news of the verdict.*
—v. 3 °sort, °class, classify, °categorize, assort, °group together, °bracket: *It would be a mistake to bunch all different kinds of liberals into the same category.* 4 **bunch up**: °gather; smock; °collect, °crowd, °group, °cluster: *The fabric is all bunched up at the bottom. Don't let the people bunch up in front of the exits.*

bundle n. 1 °bunch, °collection, °package, °parcel, °packet, °pack; bale, sheaf; *Archaic* fardel: *I have to leave this bundle at the laundry today. Bring this bundle of hay for the horse.*
—v. 2 °gather (together), °tie up (together), °collect, °pack, °package: *He bundled up all his belongings.* 3 **bundle off** or **out**: dispatch or despatch, °pack off, °hustle or °hurry off or away, °send away or off; decamp, °scurry off or away, *Colloq Brit* do a moonlight °flit: *We bundled Aunt Mary off home as soon as the storm subsided. That couple have bundled out of room 429.*

bungle v. °spoil, °botch, mismanage, °stumble, bumble, *Golf* foozle, *Colloq* °foul or °screw or louse up, °blow, °mess or °muck up, make a °mess or °hash or °muddle of, muff, *Slang Brit* °bugger, *US* snafu, *Taboo* fuck up: *Smith has bungled the job again; we'll have to replace him.*

buoy n. 1 (navigational or channel) °mark or marker, °float; nun (-buoy), can (-buoy), bell buoy, gong (-buoy), °siren, °signal, mooring-buoy, spar-buoy, lollipop: *Returning to port, always leave the red buoys to starboard.*
—v. 2 Often, **buoy up**: °lift, °raise, elevate, °support, hearten, °sustain, °keep up: *We sang songs to buoy up our spirits while the rescuers dug their way towards us.*

buoyant adj. 1 afloat, floating, floatable: *The wood was water-logged and no longer buoyant.* 2 °light, resilient, °lively, °vivacious, °bright, °cheerful, °carefree, °blithe, °animated, °jaunty, bouncy, °ebullient, light-hearted, *Colloq* peppy: *One had to admire his buoyant optimism, even under adverse conditions.*

burden n. 1 °load, °weight, gravamen; °strain, °pressure, °trouble, onus, millstone, °cross, albatross: *The old man put down his burden. The burden of the evidence is against them. His feeling of guilt over her death in the crash was a terrible burden to bear.*
—v. 2 °load, °weigh down, saddle with, °encumber; °tax, °oppress: *The mules were heavily burdened with a month's supply of food. Don't burden me with your problems.*

burdensome *adj.* onerous, cumbersome, °oppressive, °weighty, °troublesome, wearisome, bothersome, distressing, worrying, worrisome, vexatious, °irksome: *A tax on food is burdensome for those on a low income.*

bureau *n.* **1** *Brit* (writing-)desk, *US* °chest of drawers, °chest, dresser, chifferobe, chiffonier: *Simon has a beautiful antique bureau in his office. One of my cuff-links rolled under the bureau.* **2** °office, °agency, °department, °division, °section, subdivision, subsection, desk: *I sent the form to the bureau a month ago, but I still don't have my visa.*

bureaucracy *n.* officialdom, officialism, °government, red tape, °administration, authorities: *The bureaucracy survives because the officials rely on graft for their income.*

burglar *n.* housebreaker, °thief, °robber; sneak-thief, cat °burglar, *US* second-story or second-storey man: *The burglars, remarkably, didn't take the most valuable paintings.*

burial *n.* interment, °funeral, entombment, obsequies, sepulture: *His six ex-wives attended the burial.*

burlesque *n.* **1** °caricature, °lampoon, spoof, °parody, °satire, °mockery, travesty, *Colloq* °take-off; (grotesque) °imitation, vulgarization, °exaggeration: *In the mid-19th century, burlesques drove pantomimes off the stage.* **2** *US* striptease, °strip °show, nudie or girlie °show: *The old comedians insist that burlesque acts were an art form, but the audience went just for the girls.*
—*v.* **3** °satirize, °take off, °lampoon, spoof, °parody, °caricature, travesty: *Cervantes burlesqued the old romances in Don Quixote.*
—*adj.* **4** °satirical, derisive, mock-heroic, mock-pathetic: *She sang a burlesque opera based on Hamlet, called 'Omelette'.*

burly *adj.* °stout, °sturdy, corpulent, °large, °big, °hefty, °stocky, thickset, °brawny, chunky, °heavy, beefy, °muscular, °strong, strapping, °rugged, °tough, *Colloq* °husky: *Two rather burly gentlemen were called in to help me out of the place.*

burn *v.* **1** °blaze, °flame, °flare, °smoulder: *A fire was burning on the hearth.* **2** ignite, set on °fire, °fire, °light, °kindle, incinerate, *Slang* torch: *He burnt the incriminating papers in the fireplace.* **3** °desire, °yearn, °wish, °long, °itch: *He wrote 'Darling, I am burning to be with you tonight'.* **4** °waste, °throw or °fritter away, squander: *Don't worry about Norman, he has money to burn.* **5** overcook, °blacken, char, °singe: *If you're not careful, you'll burn the toast again.*

burning *adj.* **1** °flaming, blazing, °fiery; °ablaze, aflame, afire, on °fire: *When we arrived, the entire building was burning.* **2** vehement, °ardent, °excited, °passionate, °fervent, fervid, °intense, °fiery, °enthusiastic: *She had a burning desire to join that illustrious company.* **3** raging, °violent, parching: *His burning fever had finally subsided a little.* **4** °hot, blazing, °scorching, seething, °withering: *She was married on a burning hot day in July.*

burrow *n.* **1** °excavation, °hole, warren, °tunnel: *The rabbit retreated to its burrow under the hedge.*
—*v.* **2** °dig, delve, °tunnel, °bore, °excavate: *The larvae burrow into the wood where the birds can hear them moving about.*

burst *v.* °break (asunder), °rupture, °shatter, °explode, °blow up; °puncture; *Slang* bust: *If it keeps raining the dam will burst and the valley will be flooded.*

bury *n.* **1** inter, inhume, lay to rest: *They buried her next to her husband as she had requested.* **2** °abandon, °forget, consign to °oblivion, eradicate, extirpate: *The residents buried their differences and united to repel the town planners.* **3** °submerge (oneself), °exile (oneself), °plunge, °become engrossed or °absorbed: *She buried herself in her book.* **4** °conceal, °obscure, °hide, °cover up: *The real story was by now completely buried beneath the mass of legend.* **5** °overwhelm, °overcome, inundate: *I'm so buried in work I can't take a holiday.*

business *n.* **1** °duty, °function, °occupation, °calling, °vocation, °trade, °profession, °work, °province, °area, °subject, °topic, °concern, °affair, °responsibility, °role, °charge, °obligation: *Her business is supplying models for fashion shows. Mind your own business and don't be such a Nosy Parker.* **2** °matter, °job, °task, °subject, °question, °problem, °issue, °point, °affair: *Gentlemen, let us call the meeting to order and attend to the business at hand.* **3** dealing, °transaction; °trade, °commerce, °traffic: *We've never done any business with that company.* **4** °concern, °establishment, °organization, °company, °firm, °house, °enterprise; corporation, partnership, proprietorship: *Rodney wants to sell the business and retire to Spain.*

busy *adj.* **1** occupied, °engaged, employed, °involved: *I can't talk to you now, I'm busy.* **2** working, °industrious, °active, °diligent; bustling, °hectic, °lively, hustling, °energetic: *Are you very busy at the office these days? The diamond district is certainly a busy place.* **3** °ornate, °elaborate, °detailed, °complicated, complex, (over-)decorated, °intricate, baroque, rococo: *Some of the late Victorian architecture is far too busy for my taste.*
—*v.* **4** °occupy, °involve, °employ, °divert, absorb, engross: *She has busied herself with charity work to get her mind off the tragedy.*

busybody *n.* °pry, °snoop(er), °peep(er), °gossip, meddler, Paul Pry, *Colloq* Nosy Parker, *Slang US* buttinsky: *If he so much as sees us talking together, that busybody will probably cook up some sex scandal.*

butcher *n.* **1** °murderer, slaughterer, °killer, ripper, °cutthroat, executioner, annihilator: *That cold-blooded butcher dismembered his victims after strangling them.* **2** destroyer, bungler, muddler: *Look what that butcher of a tailor has done to my suit!*
—*v.* **3** °slaughter, °massacre, °murder, °cut or °hack or hew to pieces, dismember, disembowel, °exterminate, annihilate, °kill, liquidate: *The entire crew was butchered by the islanders.* **4** °botch, °bungle, °foul up, *Colloq* °mess up, make a °mess or °hash of; *Slang* louse up, °screw up, *Brit* bollocks or ballocks up, *US* bollix up; *Taboo* fuck up: *He butchered the restoration of my antique cabinet.*

butt[1] *n.* °target, °end, °object, °prey, °victim, °dupe; gull, *Colloq* pigeon, °sucker; *Brit* Aunt Sally, *Slang US and Canadian* patsy: *He was always the butt of their jokes.*

butt[2] *v.* **1** abut, °join, °meet: *This wall butts up against my garage.* **2 butt in** or **into**: °interfere,

°intrude, °interrupt, *Colloq US* kibitz; °meddle: *Please let me finish a sentence without butting in. Don't butt into my affairs.*

buttocks *n.* °bottom, behind, *derrière*, °seat, °rear, °rear °end, backside, °posterior, hindquarters, fundament, *Colloq Brit* °bum, *US* hinie, can, duff, tush *or* tushy *or* tushie, tokus *or* tochis *or* tuchis, keister *or* keester, butt, °tail, prat; *Slang* cheeks, *Taboo slang Brit* arse, *US* ass: *A person with large buttocks should not wear tight shorts.*

buttonhole *v.* **1** corner, detain, accost, importune, °waylay: *A reporter buttonholed one of the senators for details of the new tax bill.* —*n.* **2** corsage, *US* boutonniere *or* boutonnière: *He wore a rose for a buttonhole.*

buttress *v.* °sustain, °support, °strengthen, °prop (up), °brace, °reinforce, shore up: *Huge beams were needed to buttress the walls after the bombing.*

buxom *adj.* **1** °hearty, °healthy, °vigorous, °lusty, °attractive, °comely, °plump, *Colloq* °hefty: *Sylvia was a buxom serving-wench at the Bugle Horn.* **2** busty, °bosomy, chesty, well-endowed, big-busted: *The centrefolds in this magazine usually show quite buxom women.*

buy *v.* **1** °purchase; °acquire, °obtain, °get, °procure, °gain, °come by, °secure: *Where did you buy that hat?* **2** °accept, °allow, °take, °believe, °swallow, °go for: *Did you buy his story about having his car stolen?* **3** °bribe, suborn, °pay off, °buy off, °corrupt: *That customs man must have been bought or he wouldn't have let the package through.* —*n.* **4** °purchase, °acquisition: *We made a bad buy at the last auction.* **5** Also, **good buy**: °bargain, *Colloq US and Canadian* °steal: *If you paid only $2,000, that was a real buy.*

buyer *n.* °customer, consumer, °client, purchaser: *Is it likely that you will find many buyers of Basque dictionaries in this country?*

buzz *n.* **1** °hum, °murmur, drone: *I lay and listened to the buzz of the bees.* **2** °stir, °ferment, °talk, °undercurrent: *A ringing could be heard*

above the buzz of conversation.* **3** phone °call, °ring: *I think I'll give him a buzz to see if our appointment is still on.* **4** °thrill, feeling of °excitement, °sensation, stimulation, °kick, *Colloq* °high: *I got quite a pleasant buzz from that drink.* —*v.* **5** °hum, °murmur, drone: *The flies were buzzing around the dead squirrel.* **6** °fly down on, zoom on to: *The pilot was grounded for a month for buzzing the airfield.* **7** °telephone, °ring (up), °call (up), phone; °summon, °signal, buzz *or* °ring for: *She said she'd buzz me if she needed anything.*

by *prep.* **1** °near, °beside, next to, °close to, alongside: *I park my car by my house.* **2** via, by °way of, °through; °past: *I go home by High Wycombe.* **3** by °means of, on: *I often travel by train.* **4** °before, not later than, sooner than: *I have to leave by Monday.* **5** during, at: *We travel only by night.* —*adv.* **6** Often, **close by**: °near, °nearby, at °hand, °close, °about, around, *Literary* nigh: *When she is close by I get a tingling sensation.* **7** °past, °nearby: *When he walked by I nearly died.* **8** away, aside: *We put by a little for a rainy day.*

bygone *adj.* °past, °former, olden; of °old, of yore: *In bygone times, the fashion was for high-button shoes.*

bypass *v.* **1** °avoid, °evade, circumvent, °sidestep, skirt, °go *or* °get °round, °detour; °ignore, *Slang* give the go-by: *I shall bypass many problems if I take that route.* —*n.* **2** °detour, alternative (°way, °route, etc.), alternate °way *or* °route: *Take the bypass and avoid the town traffic.*

bystander *n.* °spectator, °onlooker, °observer, °witness, non-participant, passer-by, °eyewitness: *He has always claimed he was an innocent bystander, but I'm not so sure.*

byword *n.* °proverb, °proverbial saying, °parable, °maxim, adage, °motto, °slogan, apophthegm *or* apothegm, aphorism, catchword, catch-phrase: *My byword has always been, Honesty is the best policy.*

C

cab n. °taxi, taxi-cab, *Obsolete* (horse-drawn) hackney, hansom (cab); *Old-fashioned US* °hack: *A cab picked me up and dropped me at the hotel.*

cabal n. **1** °intrigue, °plot, °conspiracy, °scheme: *The cabal against Washington found supporters exclusively in the north.* **2** °junta *or* junto, °clique, °set, coterie, °faction, °band, °league; °unit, °party, caucus, °club; °ring, °gang: *A cabal of artists was formed.*
—v. **3** °intrigue, °plot, conspire, connive, machinate: *The barons began to sow dissension and to cabal against his succession.*

cabaret n. **1** nightclub, °club, nightspot: *The ever-popular entertainer Mimi opened at the Golden Palm cabaret last night.* **2** floor °show, °show, °entertainment, °amusement: *The dinner was poor, but the cabaret was marvellous.*

cabin n. **1** °hut, °shack, °cottage, °cot, shanty; bungalow, °lodge, chalet; *Scots* bothy: *The old trapper lives in a cabin in the forest. You are welcome to come skiing with us and stay in our cabin.* **2** stateroom, °compartment, berth: *We had a cabin on the starboard side.*

cabinet n. **1** cupboard, °bureau, chifferobe, commode, chiffonier, °chest (of drawers), chest-on-chest, tallboy, *US* highboy, lowboy: *The aspirin is in the medicine cabinet. Our china cabinet is, unfortunately, not a genuine Chippendale.* **2** °council, °ministry, °committee, °advisers, senate: *At the age of thirty, he became the youngest member of the cabinet.*

cable n. **1** wire, °line, °rope, hawser, °chain, mooring, strand, °guy: *The cable broke and we were set adrift.* **2** °telegram, wire, cablegram, radiogram, *US* Mailgram: *Send a cable to Jones about the meeting.*
—v. **3** telegraph, wire; °radio: *Cable Jones to come at once.*

cache n. **1** hiding-place, °hole, vault, repository: *There was a small cache concealed by the panelling in the library.* **2** °store, °hoard, °supply, °reserve, °nest egg, stockpile, *Colloq US and Canadian* stash: *The wise hunter keeps a cache of supplies buried along his route.*
—v. **3** °hide, °store, °conceal, squirrel away, °secrete, °bury, *Colloq* stash (away): *I cached the money in a biscuit tin.*

cachet n. **1** °stamp, °feature, distinguishing °mark, °identification: *The cachet of good taste is simplicity of design.* **2** °distinction, °prominence, °importance, °prestige, °dignity: *Her new job doesn't pay much, but it has a certain cachet.*

cadaver n. °corpse, (°dead) °body, remains, *Slang* °stiff: *The medical students and doctors once paid to have cadavers exhumed for anatomical study.*

cadence n. °measure, °beat, °rhythm, °tempo, °accent, °pulse, metre, lilt, °swing: *The snare drum marked the cadence for the marching band.*

café n. coffee-house, coffee °bar, coffee-shop, bistro, °snack °bar, brasserie; tearoom, lunch-room, restaurant, eating-house, canteen; cafeteria, *US* diner, *Colloq* eatery; *Slang Brit* caff, *US* greasy spoon: *We stopped at a café for refreshment.*

cage n. **1** crate, °enclosure, °pen, °pound, coop, hutch: *He keeps rooks in a cage.*
—v. **2** Also, **cage** *or* **in**: confine, °enclose, °pen, impound, °shut up *or* in, coop (up), °imprison; °restrict, °restrain, hem in: *They keep the kitten caged like a wild animal. I don't like to stay caged up in my office all day.*

cajole v. °wheedle, °coax, °beguile, °jolly (along), °cosy along, °seduce, inveigle, °persuade, *Colloq* soft-soap, butter (up), °stroke, sweet-talk: *Robert's wife always has to cajole him to go and visit her mother.*

cajolery n. wheedling, coaxing, blandishment, beguilement, jollying, °persuasion, seduction, inveigling, inveiglement, *Colloq* soft soap, buttering-up, °sweet talk: *She uses cajolery rather than threats to get what she wants.*

cake n. **1** pastry, bun, *Brit* gateau: *Right now, I should like to have a glass of milk and a piece of chocolate cake.* **2** °piece, chunk, °bar, °block, cube, °lump, °loaf, °slab: *Barbara gave me a cake of fancy perfumed soap for my birthday.*
—v. **3** °harden, °solidify, °thicken, congeal, °dry, °coagulate, encrust, consolidate: *You can see where the paint has caked.*

calamitous adj. distressful, dire, °tragic, °disastrous, °destructive, °awful, °devastating, °fatal, °deadly, pernicious, cataclysmic, catastrophic, °ruinous, °dreadful, °terrible: *They seemed unaware of the calamitous consequences of what they were doing to the environment.*

calamity n. **1** °disaster, °destruction, °ruin, °catastrophe, cataclysm, devastation, °tragedy, misadventure, mischance, °mishap: *Calamity befell the town when it was engulfed in a landslide.* **2** °distress, °affliction, °trouble, °hardship, °misery, °tragedy, °misfortune, adversity, °reverse, °ruin, ruination, °desolation, wretchedness: *So full is the world of calamity that every source of pleasure is polluted.*

calculate v. °compute, °reckon, °add up, assess, °evaluate, °count, °figure (out), °estimate, °gauge, °determine, ascertain, °work out: *Bradley was able to calculate the velocity of light. They calculated where the sun would come up at the equinox and built their temple accordingly.*

calculated adj. **1** arranged, designed, planned, °prepared, adjusted, adapted, °fit, °fitted, intended, suited: *The coach was calculated to carry six regular passengers.* **2** °deliberate, °purposeful, °intentional, °premeditated, planned: *The so-called accident was really a calculated attempt to kill me.*

calculating adj. °shrewd, conniving, °crafty, °sly, °scheming, °designing, Machiavellian, manipulative, canny, contriving: *She is a calculating woman, who knows what she wants and manoeuvres people to help her get it.*

calculation n. **1** computation, °reckoning, counting, °estimation, figuring, determining: *We needn't number them one by one, for the total can be arrived at by calculation.* **2** °answer, °product, °result, °figure, °count, °estimate, °amount: *This calculation is wrong, so please do it again.* **3** °estimate, °forecast, °expectation,

°prediction, deliberation; circumspection, cautiousness, wariness, °caution, °prudence, °forethought, °discretion: *His attack was not the inspiration of courage but the result of calculation.*

calculator *n.* computer, adding °machine; abacus: *According to my calculator, the answer should be 7.1592.*

calendar *n.* **1** °appointment book, °schedule, slate, *Brit* °diary, *US* date-book, *US law* docket: *I have next week's lunch date in my calendar.* **2** almanac, °chronology, °chronicle, annal(s): *The ecclesiastical calendar lists today as St David's Day.*

calibrate *v.* °adjust, °graduate; °standardize: *This balance has been dropped on the floor, and you'll have to calibrate it again.*

calibre *n.* **1** diameter, °size, °bore, °gauge: *You need a .38 calibre bullet to fit a .38 calibre pistol.* **2** °merit, °ability, °talent, °capability, competence, °capacity, °quality, °strength, stature: *They should be playing against a team of their own calibre.* **3** °degree, °measure, °stamp, °quality: *I doubt that you will find anyone of equal calibre to Julia in artistic sensibility.*

call *v.* **1** °shout, °cry (out), °hail, °yell, °roar, °bellow, call out, *Colloq* holler: *I heard someone calling my name.* **2** °name, °designate, °denote, denominate, °term, °style, °nickname, °label, °title, °entitle, °tag, °identify, dub, °christen, baptize: *My real name is Angus, but they call me Scotty. A person from Glasgow is called a Glaswegian.* **3** call up, °telephone, phone, °ring (up), dial, *Colloq* °buzz: *As it's her birthday, I must call my mother in Australia. Don't call us, we'll call you.* **4** °summon, invite, °assemble, convoke, convene, °bid, °gather, °collect, °muster, °rally: *From the minaret, the muezzin was calling the faithful to prayer. Many are called but few are chosen.* **5** °visit, °attend; call in; call on: *My great aunt Frederica came to call last Sunday.* **6** °awake, °awaken, °wake up, °rouse, *Colloq Brit* °knock up: *Please call me at six.* **7 call down: a** °appeal to, invoke, °petition, °request, entreat, supplicate: *He called down the wrath of God on the Philistines.* **b** °reprimand, °chastise, °castigate, °upbraid, °scold, °reprove, °rebuke: *He was called down for having left the house after curfew.* **8 call for:** °demand, °request, °ask for, °order, °require, °claim: *The people in room 429 have called for clean towels. The problem calls for your urgent attention.* **b** °pick up, °fetch, °come for, °get, °accompany, *Colloq* °collect: *I'll call for you at seven o'clock.* **9 call forth:** °summon, invoke, °draw on or upon, °evoke; °elicit, °inspire: *Susan called forth all her courage and faced her accusers. He failed to call forth much enthusiasm in his listeners.* **10 call on or upon: a** °request of, entreat, °ask, °appeal; apostrophize: *The teacher called on me today to recite Hamlet's soliloquy.* **b** supplicate, apostrophize, °appeal to: *He called on Æolus, god of the winds, for a fair breeze to carry his ship home.* **c** °visit: *The vicar called on us when we first moved in.* **11 call off:** °cancel; °discontinue; °postpone: *The picnic has been called off because of rain.* **12 call up: a** °summon, °enlist, °recruit, conscript, *US* °draft: *Father was called up as soon as war was declared.* **b** call, °telephone, phone, °ring (up): *Call me up sometime.*

—*n.* **13** °shout, °cry, °yell, °whoop, *Colloq* holler: *I'll be out in the garden, so give me a call if you*

want me. **14** summons, °invitation, °bidding, °notice, notification, °order, °request, °demand, °command; °telephone call, phone call, *Brit* °ring; *Colloq* tinkle: *She received a call to report at once for duty.* **15** °reason, justification, °cause, °need, °occasion, °right, °excuse; °requirement: *You have no call to be abusive, regardless of what you think about him.* **16 on call:** °ready, on °duty, °standing by, on °stand-by, awaiting orders: *They had to remain on call from midnight till eight o'clock.* **17 within call:** within earshot or hearing or (easy) °reach: *Please stay within call in case I need you.*

calling *n.* °vocation, °occupation, °profession, °business, °trade, °employment, °work, °line, °job, métier, °pursuit, °career, °area, °province, (°area of) °expertise, *Brit* °speciality or *US* specialty, *Colloq* °racket: *He found his calling as a veterinary surgeon very satisfying.*

callous *adj.* hardened, °thick-skinned, unfeeling, uncaring, °insensible, insensitive, °hard, hard-hearted, °tough, hardbitten, °cold, °cold-hearted, °heartless, °indifferent, °unsympathetic, apathetic, *Colloq* hard-boiled, hard-nosed: *It was callous of Gerry to go off to the snooker club right after the funeral.*

callow *adj.* °inexperienced, °immature, °juvenile, °naïve, °green, guileless, °unsophisticated, °innocent, °raw, °unfledged, °untried, *Colloq* (still) °wet behind the ears: *It was a mistake to let a callow youth take out the boat alone.*

calm *n.* **1** °quiet, stillness, tranquillity, °serenity, °hush, °peace, peacefulness: *A storm raged outside, but in the harbour was a breathless calm.* **2** calmness, composure, placidity, placidness, °peace, °repose, °sang-froid, coolness, °self-control, equanimity, self-possession: *The calm exhibited by the passengers during the hijacking was admirable.* —*adj.* **3** °quiet, °still, °tranquil, °serene, °peaceful, balmy, halcyon, °mild, undisturbed, unagitated, placid, pacific; motionless, °smooth, °even; windless: *The sea is never calm in the same sense as a mountain lake.* **4** composed, °cool, cool-headed, self-controlled, °impassive, °dispassionate, °unmoved, unruffled, °serene, °tranquil, °sedate, °staid, °stoical, *Colloq* together: *She remained calm while the others panicked.* —*v.* **5** Also, **calm down**: °quiet, °quieten, °still, soothe, °hush, °lull, pacify; mollify, appease, placate, become or make °quiet or pacified or less °agitated, *Colloq* °cool off or down: *The arbitrator did his best to calm the two litigants by suggesting a compromise. After everyone had calmed down, the speaker continued.*

camouflage *n.* **1** °disguise, concealment, cover-up, °cover, °guise, °cloak, °mask, °screen, °blind, (false) °front, °show, façade, °pretence, °trickery, °deception; °protective colouring or coloration, *Technical* apatetic or aposematic or °cryptic colouring or coloration: *Camouflage prevented the enemy from seeing our tanks.* —*v.* **2** °disguise, °cloak, °mask, °cover (up), °hide, °conceal, °screen, °veil; °misrepresent, °falsify: *We camouflaged our movements by fastening twigs and leaves to our helmets.*

camp¹ *n.* **1** camping-ground, camp-ground, bivouac, encampment, camp-site; °settlement; camping-site, *Brit* caravan °site: *The name 'Chester' derives from Latin* castrum, *meaning 'camp', for the*

city was originally the site of a Roman camp. Is there a camp where we can stay overnight? **2** °faction, °set, coterie, °clique, °group, °party, °body: *On this issue, the politicians are divided into two camps.*
—*v.* **3** encamp, °pitch camp, tent: *Our family likes to go camping in the mountains during the summer.* **4** °lodge, bivouac, °settle: *The platoon camped by the river.* **5 camp out:** *Slang* crash: *Mind if I camp out in your pad tonight?*

camp[2] *adj.* **1** °outré, °outrageous, exaggerated, °artless, °affected, inartistic, °extravagant, °artificial, Dadaistic, °theatrical, °mannered, °flamboyant, °showy, °ostentatious, °effeminate, *Colloq* campy: *Some of the kitsch produced in the 1930s was the epitome of camp. His manner is a bit too camp for my taste.*
—*v.* **2** °exaggerate, °show off, °strut, °flaunt, °flounce, °prance, °posture, *Colloq* ham: *Clarence just loves to camp it up whenever there are women around.*

campaign *n.* **1** °operation(s), °manoeuvre(s), °crusade, °action; °drive, °offensive, °push, °effort; °struggle: *Napoleon's Russian campaign ended in disaster. Our next sales campaign will be aimed at teenagers.* **2** °competition, °contest, °rivalry, °race: *Presidential campaigns last for more than a year.*
—*v.* **3** °run, °electioneer, °compete, *Brit* °stand; *US and Canadian* °stump; *Colloq* throw or toss one's hat in the ring: *Next week the Labour candidate will campaign in Yorkshire.*

cancel *v.* **1** °void, annul, invalidate, nullify, °quash; °revoke, rescind, °redeem, °repeal, °abolish, °retract, °withdraw, °recall, °repudiate, abrogate, countermand, °deny: *The bonds have been cancelled and are worthless. She cancelled the incorrect cheque.* **2** °delete, °obliterate, °cross or °strike or °blot out, dele, °rub out, °erase, expunge, efface, eradicate, °quash, deracinate; °eliminate, do away with: *I was forced to cancel the chapter of my book that dealt with M.I.5 activities.* **3** Sometimes, **cancel out:** °neutralize, nullify, counterbalance, countervail, °compensate (for), °make up for, °offset, °counteract: *His later kindnesses cancel his previous injustices.*

cancellation *n.* **1** cancelling, annulment, nullification, rescinding, voiding, rescission, revocation, °abolition, abandonment, withdrawal, abrogation; °repeal: *We found a hotel room in the end because of a late cancellation.* **2** invalidation, revocation, °abolition, discontinuance, °termination, °suppression: *If you fail to pay the premium, the policy is subject to cancellation.* **3** elimination, °abolition; stoppage, cessation: *Owing to the storm, some trains are subject to cancellation.*

candid *adj.* **1** °frank, °open, °plain, °sincere, °ingenuous, °straight, straightforward, °truthful, °forthright, °direct, unequivocal, plain-spoken, plain-speaking, °outspoken, °honest, °artless, °blunt, guileless, open-hearted, °above-board, undeceitful, undeceiving, undeliberative, uncalculating, uncalculated, °unpremeditated, uncontrived, *Colloq* upfront: *Henry offered a very candid account of his feelings. Let us be candid and speak our minds.* **2** °just, °impartial, °objective, °fair, °equitable, unbiased, °unprejudiced, even-handed; unbigoted: *The speaker expressed a candid view of all of the proposals.* **3** unposed, °informal, impromptu: *Here is a candid photo of the two of us in Rome.*

candidate *n.* aspirant, seeker, office-seeker, °runner, °nominee; applicant, entrant; °prospect, °possibility: *There are quite a few candidates for the post.*

candour *n.* **1** openness, frankness, ingenuousness, °simplicity, °naïvety, outspokenness, unreservedness, forthrightness, °honesty, °sincerity, directness, straightforwardness, unequivocalness: *I admire her candour, but the truth sometimes hurts.* **2** impartiality, fairness, °justice, °objectivity, open-mindedness: *In criticism candour is as rare as bigotry is frequent.*

candy *n.* °sweet(s), bon-bon(s), sweetmeat(s), confectionery: *Eating candy can be bad for your teeth.*

cannibal *n.* anthropophagite, man-eater: *They were said to have been captured by cannibals living in remote regions.*

cant *n.* **1** °hypocrisy, insincerity, °sham, °pretence, humbug, sanctimony, sanctimoniousness, lip-service, affectedness, °pretension: *He wasn't really enthusiastic—all that talk was just cant.* **2** °jargon, °shop, shop-talk, argot, °vernacular, slang, °dialect, patois, Creole, pidgin, °gobbledegook or gobbledygook, *Colloq* °lingo: *The criminals use a cant not understood by those outside their fraternity.*

cantankerous *adj.* ill-natured, °quarrelsome, °perverse, °cross, choleric, cross-grained, crabby, curmudgeonly, crusty, grumpy, °surly, irascible, °snappish, bad-tempered, ill-tempered, bearish, °bilious, °peevish, °testy, °irritable, °touchy, °disagreeable, tetchy, °contrary, *Colloq* crotchety, grouchy, *US* °cranky: *Simon used to be so friendly, but he's become a cantankerous old codger.*

canvass *v.* **1** °solicit, °electioneer, °campaign, °poll, *US and Canadian* °stump: *The candidates will be canvassing in farming areas next week.* **2** °survey, °poll, °study, °analyse, °examine, °investigate, °interview, °question: *The statisticians are not satisfied that enough women were canvassed to provide an accurate sample.*
—*n.* **3** solicitation, °campaign: *The party's canvass of rural areas for new supporters was not very successful.* **4** °survey, °study, °investigation, °poll, °examination, °tally: *A canvass of editors shows they have a conservative view of the language.*

canyon *n.* °gorge, °ravine, °gully or gulley, °pass, defile, *Brit dialect* gill or ghyll, *US and Canadian* coulée, gulch; *US* °gap, arroyo: *The canyon created by the river is more than a thousand feet deep.*

cap *n.* **1** hat, °head covering: *The plumber took off his cap and scratched his head.* **2** lid, °top, °cover: *Screw the cap on tight.* **3 cap in hand:** humbly, meekly, servilely, submissively, subserviently, docilely, respectfully: *He went cap in hand to ask for a pay rise.*
—*v.* **4** °surpass, °outdo, °outstrip, °better, °beat, °exceed, °top, °excel: *Betty capped her earlier triumphs by winning the semifinals.* **5** °cover, °protect: *As it's begun to rain, you'd best cap the camera lens.*

capability *n.* °ability, °power, °potential, °capacity, °means, °faculty, wherewithal; °talent, °proficiency, °aptitude, adeptness, °skill, competence: *Deirdre has the capability to be first in her form.*

capable *adj.* **1** °able, °competent, °efficient, °proficient, °qualified, °talented, °gifted, skilled, °skilful, °accomplished, apt, °adept, °clever, °effective, °effectual; °expert, masterly,

°masterful: *Halliwell is quite capable of speaking for himself. He is a capable violinist, but scarcely a virtuoso.* **2 capable of**: °disposed to, °inclined to, predisposed to: *Though violent, he is not capable of murder.*

capacity *n.* **1** °volume, °content, °size, dimensions; °room, °space: *What is the capacity of this bottle in litres? The car is of sufficient capacity to hold only four adults.* **2** °potential, °ability, °capability, competence, °intelligence, °wit, °brain(s), °talent, °aptitude, acumen, °understanding, °sense, °judgement, perspicacity, perceptiveness, °perception, mother °wit, °intellect, °genius, °skill, °gift, °faculty, °power, *Colloq chiefly US* right °stuff, the goods: *They don't yet have the capacity to absorb advanced theory.* **3** °position, °condition, °character, °place, °post, °role, °job, °office, °duty, °responsibility, °province, °sphere, °function; *Law* competency, °qualification: *She has every right to sign cheques in her capacity as director.*

cape¹ *n.* headland, promontory, peninsula, neck, °point, *Archaic* ness: *We sailed round the cape and made for the harbour.*

cape² *n.* °mantle, shawl, °stole, °cloak: *His black cape reached to the floor.*

caper *n.* **1** °skip, °leap, °spring, °frolic, °hop, gambol, °frisk, curvet, gambado: *He can dance, though he does not cut capers.* **2** escapade, °stunt, °mischief, °prank, °high jinks, *US* °crime, burglary, °robbery, *Colloq* shenanigan, dido, °lark, *Slang US and Canadian* °job: *The capers we used to get up to after lights-out in the dormitory!* —*v.* **3** °skip, °hop, °frolic, °leap, °jump, °frisk, romp, gambol, °prance, °cavort, curvet: *She capered about like a lamb in a meadow.*

capital *n.* **1** °head, °top, °crown, °cap: *The column was surmounted by a finely carved capital.* **2** °seat (of °government): *Winnipeg is the capital of Manitoba.* **3** °money, assets, funds, °finance(s), °cash, wherewithal; °wealth, °means, °property, resources, savings, °principal: *My capital is invested in land at the moment.* **4** majuscule, °upper case, large °letter, °initial, *Colloq* °cap: *The chapter titles should be set in capitals.* —*adj.* **5** °chief, °main, °major, °important, °cardinal, °central, °principal, °prime, °primary, °paramount, °pre-eminent, °foremost, °leading: *Our capital responsibility is to ensure the passengers' safety.* **6** first-class, °first-rate, °excellent, °superior, °matchless, °peerless, °choice, °select, °outstanding, °fine, °superb, °splendid, °marvellous, °extraordinary, *Colloq* smashing, °great, °super, *Brit* brill, *Old-fashioned* topping, top-hole, °ripping, ripsnorting: *Eating out tonight was a capital idea.*

capitulate *v.* **1** °surrender, °yield, °give up, °submit, °succumb: *Want of provisions quickly obliged the fortress to capitulate.* **2** acquiesce, °concede, °relent, °give in, °yield: *He begged so piteously that the king finally capitulated and allowed him to live.*

capricious *adj.* °whimsical, °erratic, °flighty, °fickle, mercurial, unsteady, °variable, °unstable, wayward, unpredictable, undependable, °changeable, °impulsive, crotchety, quirky, °unreliable, °inconstant, °fanciful, °wanton: *His decisions are capricious and not based*

on sound judgement. *The weather in March is capricious: as Mark Twain said, if you don't like it, just wait five minutes.*

capsize *v.* °upset, °overturn, °turn turtle *or* upside down, °tip (over), keel over, invert: *When the wind capsized the boat, we lost all our gear overboard.*

captivate *v.* enthral *or US* enthrall, °enslave, °fascinate, °hypnotize, °entrance, °beguile, °charm, enamour, °enchant, °bewitch, °enrapture, °dazzle, infatuate, °attract, allure, °seduce, °win: *Her beauty captivated film-goers everywhere.*

captive *n.* **1** °prisoner, °convict, °hostage, detainee, internee; °slave, bondman *or* bondsman, bondservant: *The captives were kept in a wretched hole.* —*adj.* **2** imprisoned, incarcerated, confined, caged, locked up, under lock and key: *Captive animals lose their free spirit.*

captivity *n.* confinement, °imprisonment, internment, °detention, °custody, incarceration, °restraint; °bondage, °slavery, thraldom *or US* thralldom, enslavement, °servitude; *Archaic* durance: *Some wild creatures do not survive in captivity. Entire populations of conquered territories were taken into captivity in ancient times.*

capture *n.* **1** °seizure, °taking, °catching, °arrest, apprehension, *Slang* °pinch, collar: *They celebrated the capture of the Spanish galleon. The State has offered a reward for the capture of the bank robbers.* —*v.* **2** °seize, °take, °catch, °lay *or* °take °hold of, °grab, apprehend, °arrest, *Slang* °pinch, collar, °nab, *Brit* °nick: *Eventually, they captured the thief on the roof.*

car *n.* **1** (motor) °vehicle, motor car, automobile, passenger car, *Old-fashioned or slang* motor; *Chiefly US* auto; *Colloq* jalopy, heap, pile, crate, °machine, buggy, °transport; *Slang* wheels: *Borrow a car and drive down for the weekend.* **2** (railway) °carriage: *The body was found in a sleeping car of the Orient Express.*

card *n.* **1** playing-card, *Slang* pasteboard: *The winning card was the ten of diamonds.* **2** calling-card, visiting-card, *carte de visite*, °business card: *Visitors used to leave their cards on the silver tray at the front door.* **3** greetings card, Christmas card, birthday card, anniversary card, condolence card, Easter card, New Year card: *I sent Jacquelyn a card for her birthday last year.* **4** postcard, *US* postal card: *Drop me a card when you get there, just so I'll know you're all right.* **5** °index card, °file card: *The names and addresses of our members, formerly held on cards, are now stored in the computer.* **6** membership card; °press card; °union card: *I showed my card at the door and they let me in without any problem.* **7** dance-card: *She told me that her dance-card was full—and was likely to be for the next ten years.* **8** *US* car-card, window-card, show-card: *At the cost of a card on the New York buses, we'd never get our money back.* **9** °credit card; bank card: *You may pay by card or cheque. They won't accept your cheque without a card.* **10** °identity *or* °identification card, I.D. (card): *The police asked to see my card.* **11** °joker, prankster, practical °joker, °wag, humorist, °comedian, comedienne, °funny man *or* woman: *That Oscar—he's quite a card, isn't he?* **12 on** *or esp US* **in the cards**: °destined, °fated, slated, in the offing; °likely, °probable, °possible, °liable: *I doubt that a change of government is on the cards for some time to come.* **13 play one's cards right, well, badly, etc.**: °act, °behave, take °action; °plan, use °strategy: *If Francis plays his cards right, he may be made head of department when Mark leaves.* **14 put** *or* **lay one's cards on the table** *or* **show one's cards**: act °openly, °reveal all, be °forthright, be °direct, be °open, be °honest, be °unsecretive, °Colloq come °clean: *I'm going to put my cards on the table, and let you know all my plans.*

cardinal *adj.* °important, °chief, °key, °special, °main, °central, °principal, °prime, °primary, °essential, °necessary, °fundamental; °supreme, °paramount, highest, °first, °foremost, °leading, °pre-eminent: *The cardinal virtues are justice, prudence, temperance, and fortitude, to which some writers add faith, hope, and charity.*

care *n.* **1** °anxiety, °worry, °trouble, °anguish, disquiet, °distress, °grief, °sorrow, dolour, °sadness, °suffering, °misery, °woe, tribulation: *His haggard look reflected a life of care.* **2** °concern, °regard, °vigilance, mindfulness, °heed, °solicitude; heedfulness, °attention, pains, carefulness, meticulousness, punctiliousness; °caution, circumspection: *The essence of public-spiritedness is care for the common good. He looks after his moustache and beard with great care. Open with care.* **3** °responsibility, °charge, °protection, guardianship, °custody, keeping, °safe keeping; °control, °direction, supervision: *The child has been released into our care.* **4 take care of**: °look after, °attend to, be °responsible for, take °charge of, take °responsibility for; °tend, °nurse: *You should take care of your money. Does she have enough experience to take care of someone who is ill?* —*v.* **5** be °concerned, °trouble oneself, feel °interest, °worry, °fret, °trouble, °mind: *Do you care whether Arnold gets the job he wants? I don't care who you are, you can't come in here!* **6 care for**: **a** °look after, °tend, °attend (to), °watch over, °protect, take care of, °provide for; °nurse: *He cared for his ailing parents for about twenty years.* **b** °like, °fancy, be attracted to, be °fond of, °love, be °keen on, be enamoured of: *Jennifer admitted last night how much she cares for David.*

careen *v.* °heel over, keel over; *US loosely* °career, °sway, °tip, °pitch, veer, °swerve, °lurch: *We hauled out the boat, careened her, and proceeded to caulk her seams.*

career *n.* **1** °employment, °occupation, °calling, °vocation, °pursuit, (life's) °work, °job, °business, livelihood; °profession, °trade, °craft, métier: *She has made a career out of helping others. He is undecided whether to pursue a career in accountancy.* —*v.* **2** °speed, °race, °rush, °dash, °fly, °tear, °hurtle, °bolt, °shoot, *Colloq* zoom: *A bicycle came careering around the corner and knocked him down.*

carefree *adj.* °nonchalant, °easy, °easygoing, insouciant, light-hearted, °blithe, happy-go-lucky, °breezy, airy; °blasé, °indifferent, unconcerned, unworried, trouble-free, worry-free, contented, °happy: *Till he graduated from university, he had lived an entirely carefree life.*

careful *adj.* **1** °cautious, °wary, circumspect, chary, °prudent, watchful, °aware, °alert, °vigilant: *These days one cannot be too careful about*

walking in the city at night. **2** °meticulous, °painstaking, °attentive, punctilious, (well-) organized, °systematic, °precise, °fastidious, °thorough, °scrupulous, °conscientious, °particular, °finicky, finical, °fussy: *The police conducted a careful search for weapons.*

careless *adj.* **1** unconcerned, untroubled, unworried, °casual, °indifferent, °heedless, °thoughtless, °inconsiderate, uncaring, devil-may-care, °irresponsible, °cursory, °lackadaisical, °perfunctory: *No one could approve of the careless way he treats his family.* **2** °inattentive, negligent, °thoughtless, °absent-minded, neglectful, °remiss; unobservant, °unthinking, °imprudent, unmindful, incautious, °unwary, °reckless, slapdash, °rash: *Many of the errors come from being careless.* **3** °inaccurate, °imprecise, °inexact, °incorrect, °wrong, error-ridden, °erroneous, *Colloq* °sloppy: *You won't get a good mark for such a careless paper.* **4** unstudied, °ingenuous, °artless, °casual, °nonchalant: *I dislike his careless way of dressing, but it does show some style.*

caress *n.* **1** °pat, °stroke, fondling, blandishment; °cuddle, °embrace, °hug; nuzzle, °kiss: *He submitted willingly to her caresses.* —*v.* **2** °touch, °pat, °pet, °fondle, °stroke; °cuddle, °embrace, °hug; nuzzle, °kiss: *The kitten approached warily and Isabella caressed it.*

cargo *n.* shipment, consignment, shipload, truckload, wagon-load *or* waggon-load, °load, trainload, *US* carload; °freight, goods, °merchandise: *The cargo of rifles was delivered to the warehouse. The ship was lost with all its cargo.*

caricature *n.* **1** cartoon, °parody, °burlesque, °lampoon, °satire, pasquinade, *Colloq* °take-off, spoof, *Brit* send-up: *The cartoon in the newspaper showed a caricature of the Prime Minister.* —*v.* **2** °parody, °satirize, °lampoon, °burlesque, °ridicule, °mock, °distort, *Colloq* °take off, *Brit* °send up: *Hogarth caricatured Churchill in the form of a bear.*

carnage *n.* °slaughter, butchery, °massacre, blood bath, °holocaust, °killing, *Shoah, Churban or Hurban*: *The battle was fought with much carnage on both sides.*

carnal *adj.* fleshly, °sensual, °animal, bodily, °lustful, °voluptuous, libidinous, °lecherous, concupiscent, °sexual, °erotic, °lascivious, licentious, °lewd, °prurient: *She is intent on satisfying her carnal desires.*

carouse *v.* **1** make °merry, °revel, *Colloq* °party, pub-crawl, make whoopee, go on a °bender *or* tear *or* binge *or* toot, °paint the town red, binge, °booze: *After the cup final, we all caroused till the wee hours.* —*n.* **2** °revel, °spree, °fling, wassail, carousal, °drunk, bacchanal, *Colloq* binge, °bender, °booze, boozer, *Brit* knees-up, *US* °tear, toot: *They go on a carouse on Burns Night every year, then need a day to sleep it off.*

carp *v.* find °fault, °criticize, °cavil, °complain, °nag, °pick at, °pick on, °bully, bullyrag *or* ballyrag, *Colloq* °knock, °pick holes (in), °gripe, *Brit* whinge: *She said that she would leave him if he kept on carping at her about her cooking.*

carriage *n.* **1** (°railway) °coach, *US* °car: *We moved our belongings into the next carriage.* **2** °bearing, mien, °air, °manner, deportment, °conduct, demeanour, °attitude,

°posture, °stance, °presence, °behaviour, comportment: *His upright carriage immediately identified him as a military man.* **3** °freight, freightage, transportation, cartage, shipping; postage: *Carriage is free within mainland Britain.*

carrier *n.* **1** bearer, °porter; transporter, drayman, shipper, haulier *or US* hauler; carter: *The company we use as a carrier is expensive.* **2** transmitter, *Immunology* vector, *US* Typhoid Mary: *She couldn't have caught the disease directly, only through some carrier.*

carry *v.* **1** °transport, convey, °bear, °lug, °drag, °cart, °move, *Colloq* tote, *Slang US* schlep: *He shouldn't carry such heavy packages at his age.* **2** °conduct, convey, °lead, °take, °transport, °transfer, °transmit: *This cable carries the power to the town.* **3** °drive, impel, °conduct, convey, °take, °move: *He travelled aimlessly, wherever the wind carried his ship.* **4** °support, °maintain, °finance: *I had a wife and four children and was unable to carry my brother's family as well.* **5** °bear, °hold up, °uphold, °maintain: *Despite her troubles, she carried her head high.* **6** °win, °take, °sweep, °capture, °gain, °secure: *She carried the election easily.* **7** °stock, °sell, °offer; °display: *We don't carry purple shoes in this shop, Madam.* **8** °broadcast, disseminate, °offer, °release; °communicate, °present, °read, °report, °announce; °give: *The news is carried on this station every night at nine.* **9 carry away**: °transport, °excite, °enrapture, °delight: *He was quite carried away by her attentions.* **10 carry off**: **a** °win, °gain, °capture, °secure: *She managed to carry off the first prize for the third year running.* **b** abscond with, °kidnap, °take, purloin, *Colloq Brit* °pinch, °nick: *I'm afraid that some of your chickens have been carried off by a fox.* **c** °accomplish, °perform, °effect, do, °succeed, °handle *or* °manage successfully, °bring off, °carry out: *We carried off the raid without loss of a single man.* **d** °kill, be *or* °cause the °death of, °cause to °die: *He was carried off by yellow fever in his eightieth year.* **11 carry on**: **a** °continue, °proceed, °go on, °persist, °keep on *or* at, °persevere: *Don't stop—just carry on with what you were doing.* **b** °manage, °conduct, °operate: *Despite the fire, we are carrying on our business as usual.* **c** °misbehave, *Colloq* °act up, °fool around, *Brit* °play up: *The children are carrying on so, I can't get any work done.* **12 carry out** *or* **through**: °perform, °effect, °implement, °complete, °execute, °accomplish, °continue, conclude: *Henry is carrying out his father's wishes according to the terms of his will.*

cart *n.* **1** handcart, pushcart, trolley, barrow, wagon *or Brit also* waggon: *You'll need a cart to carry all these things to the car.* —*v.* **2** °carry, convey, °move, °lug, °drag, tote, °transport, °bring, °haul, *Colloq US* schlep: *Why do you cart that heavy bag everywhere you go?*

carte blanche *n.* °licence, °permission, °sanction, free rein, °authority, °discretion: *She was given carte blanche to spend the money any way she wished.*

carve *v.* **1** hew, °cut, sculpt, °sculpture, °shape, °chisel, °model, °fashion, °engrave, incise, °grave, °whittle, °chip: *The bust is carved out of solid marble.* **2** Often, **carve up** *or* **out**: °divide (up), °cut (up), subdivide, apportion, °parcel out, °allot, °partition: *The gang-leaders carved up the territory, and the killings stopped for a while.*

case[1] *n.* **1** °instance, °example, °event, °occurrence; °happening, °occasion, °circumstance, °state, °situation: *In a recent case a farmer was attacked by a man-eating tiger. Holmes is investigating a case of a missing necklace.* **2** °action, °suit, lawsuit, °dispute; °cause: *I lost my case.* **3** °patient, °invalid, °victim: *Four new cases were admitted to the hospital yesterday.* **4** °specimen, °instance, °example: *Howard is an odd case, isn't he?* **5 in any case**: in any °event, come what may, at all events, anyhow, anyway: *In any case, your decision won't affect me.* **6 in case**: **a** lest, for °fear that: *He was worried in case his wife found out where he had been.* **b** if, in the °event that, if it happens *or* proves *or* turns out that, if it should °happen *or* °prove *or* °turn out that: *In case you were thinking of leaving, remember that we have your car keys.* **7 in case of**: in the °event of; for °fear of: *In case of fire, you must use the staircase. We insured the house in case of fire.* **8 the case**: the °fact, the actuality, the °truth, the °reality, what °really happened *or* took °place: *She said he was drunk, but that's not the case.*

case[2] *n.* **1** °box, container, carton, crate; °chest, holder, °receptacle; °trunk, °suitcase, °casket: *Please order two cases of paper for the copying machine. The cosmetics came in a fitted case lined in velvet.* **2** covering, °cover, °protection, casing, envelope, °wrapper: *The engraving was on the inside of the watch-case. The book came in a case of fine calfskin.* —*v.* **3** encase, °box, crate, °pack, °package, containerize: *The computer arrived, completely cased in rigid foam.*

cash *n.* **1** °money, currency, bills, notes, banknotes, °change, hard cash *or* °money, specie, °coin of the realm, legal °tender, *Slang* moolah, dough, bread, °loot, spondulicks *or* spondulix, *Brit* lolly, °ready, °readies, *US* scratch, gelt, mazuma: *The shop accepts only cash, no charge cards.* —*v.* **2** Also, **cash in**: °change, °sell, liquidate, °exchange; °realize: *She cashed some bonds to pay off the overdraft.*

casket *n.* **1** °chest, °box, container, °case, coffer, °receptacle: *She keeps her jewels in a leather casket on the dressing-table.* **2** °coffin; sarcophagus: *After the funeral, the pallbearers carried the casket from the church.*

cast *n.* **1** °throw, °toss, °pitch, °shy, °lob, °thrust, chuck: *In his next cast, the bowler lightly struck the jack.* **2** dramatis personae, actors and actresses, °players, °performers, troupe, °company: *We invited the cast to a party after the show.* **3** °form, °shape, °mould, °formation, formulation, °arrangement: *She can appreciate the turn of the phrase, the happy cast and flow of the sentence.* **4** °model, casting, °mould; °stamp; °type: *The Ming vase was copied from a cast. There are not many men of the cast of Crocker.* **5** °twist, °turn, irregularity, °warp; squint: *The mare had a cast in her gallop. The pirate had a cast in his left eye.* **6** °turn, °inclination, °bent, °hint, °touch; tinge, °tint, colouring: *He has a melancholy cast of mind.* —*v.* **7** °throw, °toss, °pitch, °fling, °sling, °hurl, °dash, °send, *Colloq* chuck, °shy: *She tore off the gold necklace and cast it into the lake.* **8** °assign, °delegate, °appoint, °designate, °name, °nominate, °choose, °pick, °select: *He has cast me as the villain in his little drama.* **9** °form,

°mould, °found: *The king's death-mask, cast in plaster, was on the floor of the tomb.* **10 cast about for**: °search for, °look for, °seek: *He was casting about for an excuse to avoid going to the Fordyces' for dinner.* **11 cast aside**: °reject, °discard, cast or °throw away *or* out, get °rid of: *The expensive toys had been cast aside and the children were playing with the boxes and wrappings.* **12 cast away**: °maroon, shipwreck: *Jim O'Shea was cast away upon an Indian isle.* **13 cast off**: °throw off, °shed, doff: *One's upbringing cannot be cast off like an old overcoat.* **14 cast out**: °expel, °drive out, °throw out, °evict, °eject, oust, °exile, °remove, cast aside: *She was cast out of the house by her mother, who had married a biker.*

castaway *n.* °reject, cast-off, °outcast, pariah, °exile: *She always looked after the moral well-being of the castaways of society.*

caste *n.* (social) °class, °rank, °order, °level, °stratum, °standing, °position, °station, °status, °estate: *The women of her caste practised suttee.*

castigate *v.* °chastise, °punish, °correct, °penalize, °discipline, °rebuke, °reprimand, read (someone) the riot act, keelhaul, °chasten, °criticize, *Colloq* tell off, °dress down, *Chiefly Brit* tick off, *Brit* carpet, haul over the coals, *US and Canadian* °chew out, rake over the coals, put or call on *or* on to the carpet: *They were castigated in the press for their extravagant lifestyle.*

castle *n.* **1** fortress, °stronghold, citadel: *The king moved to Windsor Castle during the winter.* **2** mansion, °palace, manor-house, °hall, château: *Mr Mooney lives alone in his castle and has nothing to do with his neighbours.*

casual *adj.* **1** °accidental, °chance, °random, fortuitous, unexpected, °unforeseen, °unpremeditated, unplanned, unforeseeable, unpredictable, serendipitous: *It was only a casual remark, but it was taken very seriously. We interviewed casual passers-by.* **2** °uncertain, unsure, °haphazard, °occasional, °random, °irregular, unsystematic, °sporadic, °erratic: *The budget includes provision for both certain and casual revenues.* **3** °indifferent, °nonchalant, °offhand, insouciant, apathetic, °cool, unconcerned, uninterested, pococurante, °dispassionate, °blasé, °relaxed, °lackadaisical: *He may seem casual, but he is genuinely concerned about the patients.* **4** °informal; lounge: *Dinner dress is not required: you may come in casual clothes.* **5** °offhand, happy-go-lucky, °natural, °easy, °easygoing, devil-may-care, unconcerned, °relaxed, *dégagé*, unconstrained: *Phil is quite casual about losing money at roulette.*

casualty *n.* **1** °disaster, °catastrophe, °calamity, °accident, mischance, misadventure, °mishap: *The company insures against casualties at sea.* **2 a** victim, fatality, *Colloq* statistic: *I'm afraid that Jeff was a casualty of last year's cut in personnel. She was only one of thousands of casualties of the earthquake.* **b** Usually, **casualties**: *Chiefly military* wounded, injured, missing, missing in °action, °dead, °fatalities, *US* MIA(s), body count: *The casualties were mounting.*

catastrophe *n.* **1** °disaster, °calamity, cataclysm: *The eruption of Vesuvius was one of the major catastrophes in recorded history.* **2** °misfortune, bad °luck, °shock, °blow, °tragedy, °disaster;

°mishap, mischance, misadventure, °accident, °fiasco, °failure: *Cook reported a catastrophe with the layer cake.*

catch *v.* **1** °capture, °seize, apprehend, °take or °get (°hold of), °grab, °grip, °grasp, °take °captive, °hold, °arrest, °take °prisoner, *Colloq* °nab, °pinch, collar, *Brit* °nick: *The police caught him when he returned to the scene of the crime.* **2** °trap, ensnare, entrap, °snare, °net, °bag, °hook, °round up, corral: *We caught three trout this morning. I caught all the horses that had broken through the fence.* **3** take, °get on *or* on to, °board: *You can catch the London train at Aylesbury.* **4** °surprise, °discover, °find: *They fired him after catching him with his hand in the till.* **5** be seized *or* °taken °hold of by *or* with, °come down with, be afflicted by *or* with, °contract, °get, °suffer from: *You'll catch a cold if you don't wear a hat.* **6** °strike, °hit, °deliver, °fetch, °box: *She caught him a great blow on the ear and he went down.* **7** °tangle, become entangled *or* stuck *or* trapped *or* hooked: *His foot caught in the stirrup when he fell, and he was dragged along.* **8** °restrain, °stop, °check, °curb: *She caught herself before telling the police where the thief was hiding.* **9** °intercept, °grab, °seize, °snatch: *He caught the ball before it touched the ground.* **10** °understand, °see, °comprehend, °grasp, apprehend, °fathom, °perceive, discern, °follow, °take in, °gather, *Colloq* °figure out, °get, catch on (to), get the °drift (of), *Brit* °twig: *I didn't quite catch what you said—please can you repeat it?* **11** °captivate, °charm, °bewitch, °enchant, °fascinate, °seduce, °attract, °entice, allure: *She knows how to use her charms to catch a man.* **12** °attract, °draw: *A very slight movement caught my eye.* **13 catch on: a** °understand, °grasp, °see (through), °comprehend, °get (it), *Brit* °twig: *I didn't catch on to what she planned to do it till it was too late. The joke's on you and you still don't catch on, do you?* **b** °take °hold, °succeed, become °popular *or* °fashionable: *Do you think the hula hoop will catch on again?* **14 catch up: a** absorb, °involve, enthral, °immerse: *He was completely caught up in the plot of the new novel.* **b** °reach, °overtake, °overhaul: *I finally caught up with her as she neared the house.*
—*n.* **15** °capture, °take, °bag, °prize, °trophy: *The catch of the day was a 20-pound pike.* **16** °acquisition; °conquest: *She was considered quite a catch.* **17** °clasp, °hook, °pin, °clip, °fastening, fastener: *The catch on the necklace opened and pearls spilt all over the floor.* **18** °trick, °disadvantage, °hitch, °snag, °fly in the ointment, catch-22, °trap, °problem, drawback, *Colloq US* hooker: *The first book is free, but the catch is that you have to buy four more at the regular price.*

catching *adj.* **1** contagious, °infectious, transmissible, transmittable, communicable: *The doctor said that what I have is not catching.* **2** °attractive, captivating, fascinating, °enchanting, bewitching, entrancing, °winning, enticing, alluring, °fetching: *The strange object in the shop window was most catching to the eye of a passer-by.*

categorical *adj.* °direct, °explicit, °express, unconditional, °firm, °positive, unreserved, unrestricted, °absolute, °outright, °downright, unequivocal, unambiguous, °specific;

°emphatic, °unqualified, °authoritative, °dogmatic, *Technical* apodeictic *or* apodictic: *His denial was clear and categorical.*

categorize v. classify, °class, °sort, °organize, assort, °rank, °order, °section, departmentalize, °group, °arrange: *Should plankton be categorized under zoology or botany?*

category n. °class, classification, °type, °sort, °kind, °variety, °group, grouping, listing, °rank, ranking, °list, °grade, °department, °division, °section, sector, °area, °sphere: °head, heading: *Into which category would you put the partially disabled?*

cater v. **1** °provision, victual; purvey, °provide: *We cater exclusively for housebound gourmets.* **2 cater for** *or* **to:** °indulge, °humour, °serve, dance °attendance on, °pamper, °baby, °coddle, °minister to, °spoil, mollycoddle, cosset, °pander to: *She caters for him night and day. Our music group caters for all levels of ability.*

catholic adj. °universal, °general, °inclusive, all-inclusive, °broad, °wide, °comprehensive, widespread, all-embracing, eclectic, °liberal: *Her musical tastes are catholic—they range from Bach to Berry (Chuck, that is).*

cattle n. livestock, °stock, beef; cows, bulls, bullocks, steers, bovines, oxen: *He spent 20 years as a cowboy, herding cattle in Texas.*

cause n. **1** °origin, °occasion, °source, °root, genesis, °agent, °prime mover, well-spring: *The cause of the train crash is not yet known.* **2** originator, °creator, °producer, °agent, °agency: *His indecision was the cause of many of our problems.* **3** °ground *or* °grounds, justification, °reason, °basis, °call, °motive: *You have no cause to be dissatisfied.* **4** °case, °matter, °issue, °concern; °movement, °undertaking; °ideal, °belief: *We appealed the miners' cause to the high court.* —v. **5** °make, °induce: *What causes hot air to rise?* **6** °effect, °bring on *or* about, give °rise to, °result in, °produce, °create, °precipitate, °occasion, °lead to, °induce, °generate, °provoke, °promote; engender; °motivate, compel: *Overeating causes indigestion.*

caustic adj. **1** °burning, corrosive, °destructive, mordant, astringent: *Sulphuric acid is the caustic agent that eats away the metal.* **2** °sarcastic, °biting, acrimonious, °sharp, °bitter, °sardonic, °cutting, °trenchant, °critical, °scathing, acid, °harsh, °pungent, °virulent: *His caustic remarks do not earn him many friends.*

caution n. **1** °warning, admonition, admonishment, caveat, monition, °advice, °counsel, °injunction: *A word of caution is needed before you go ahead.* **2** wariness, °prudence, °care, °vigilance, °forethought, °heed, watchfulness, alertness, circumspection, °discretion: *Drivers should exercise extra caution in bad weather.* —v. **3** °warn, admonish, forewarn, °tip (off); °advise, °counsel: *Some employees had to be cautioned about arriving on time.*

cautious adj. °wary, heedful, °careful, °prudent, circumspect, watchful, °vigilant, °alert, °discreet, °guarded: *They were very cautious about letting their children go out on their own.*

cave n. **1** cavern, grotto, °hollow, °hole, °cavity, den: *In the cave were prehistoric wall paintings.* —v. **2 cave in: a** °collapse, °break down, give °way, °subside, °fall in *or* inwards: *The earthquake*

caused the walls of the house to cave in. **b** °yield, °submit, give °way; °surrender; *Colloq* °buckle, knuckle under: *After eight hours of questioning, he caved in and told them everything.*

cavil n. **1** °quibble, °complaint: *There is a minor cavil at the wording of the statutes.* —v. **2** °carp, °quibble, split hairs, °complain, find °fault, censure, °criticize, °dispute, °object, demur, *Colloq* nit-pick: *They cavilled at a mere misspelling.*

cavity n. °pit, °hole, °hollow, °opening, crater, °gap; °space: *The limestone is marked with a pattern of cavities. Vowel sounds resonate in the oral cavity.*

cavort v. curvet, °prance, °caper, °frisk, °bound, gambol, romp, °skip, °leap, °jump, °dance: *Stop cavorting about and settle down.*

cease v. **1** °stop, °end, °finish, °leave off, °terminate, °halt, °discontinue, desist (from), °break off (from), °refrain (from): *Will that noise never cease?* —n. **2 without cease:** ceaselessly, endlessly, unendingly, incessantly, interminably, continuously, continually, constantly, ad infinitum, infinitely, perpetually, for ever, eternally, everlastingly, °non-stop, unremittingly: *Sisyphus was condemned to roll his burden uphill without cease.*

cede v. °yield, give °way, °give up, °grant, °give, °surrender, °deliver up, °turn *or* °make *or* °hand over, convey, °transfer, °relinquish, °abandon, °renounce, °abdicate: *Let private concerns always cede to the common good. The territory was ceded to our government in 1792.*

celebrant n. officiant, °official; °priest: *The celebrant at High Mass was the archbishop.*

celebrate v. **1** °hold, °perform, solemnize, ritualize, °observe, °keep, °honour, °officiate at; °sanctify, °hallow, consecrate, °dedicate: *The archbishop himself celebrated holy communion.* **2** °rejoice (in *or* at), °memorialize; have a °party, °revel, make °merry, wassail, *Colloq* °party, °paint the town red, whoop it up: *The entire town celebrated the opening of the bridge with a huge party.* **3** °extol, °praise, °exalt, °glorify, °laud, °eulogize, °honour; lionize: *She was widely celebrated for her achievements.* **4** °publicize, advertise, °broadcast: *The stones themselves would find a Voice, To celebrate his Praise.*

celebrated adj. °famous, °renowned, °well-known, famed, °prominent, °noted, °eminent, °noteworthy, °distinguished, °illustrious, acclaimed: *Their son became a celebrated brain surgeon.*

celebration n. **1** °observance, °observation, °performance, solemnization, hallowing, sanctification, memorialization, commemoration: *The celebration of the Eucharist was delayed because the vicar had been called to a sickbed.* **2** praising, extolling, honouring: *The ceremony was a celebration of their achievements in space exploration.* **3** °party, °fête, *or* fete, °gala, °festivities, °frolic, °revelry, merrymaking: *The New Year's celebration is planned at Jill's house this year.*

celebrity n. **1** °renown, °fame, repute, °reputation, °prominence, eminence, °distinction, °prestige, famousness, °popularity, notability, stardom; °notoriety: *Dr Johnson was not enriched in proportion to his celebrity.* **2** °notable, °dignitary, °star, luminary, °toast of the town, °personage, °name, °personality, superstar: *The hotel lobby was packed with celebrities from show business.*

celestial *adj.* **1** °heavenly, °divine, °spiritual, °godly, paradisiac(al) *or* paradisaic, °sublime, empyrean, Elysian, ethereal, °immortal, °supernatural: *They worshipped Jupiter and other celestial beings.* **2** astronomical, astral: *We studied celestial navigation and how to use a sextant.*

celibacy *n.* **1** bachelorhood, spinsterhood, singleness: *People who say they enjoy celibacy may simply have not met the right partner.* **2** °chastity, virginity, continence, (self-)°restraint, abstinence, °purity: *They have to take a vow of celibacy before entering the priesthood.*

celibate *adj.* **1** °unmarried, °single, unwed: *Both brother and sister remained celibate all their lives.* **2** abstinent, abstemious, continent, ascetic; virgin(al), °pure, °chaste, unsullied, undefiled, °virtuous, °immaculate: *He led the celibate life of a monk for twenty years.* —*n.* **3** bachelor, spinster: *She belonged to an order of female celibates.*

cell *n.* °chamber, °room, apartment, cubicle; °stall: *As a friar, he lived in a small, plain cell for most of his life.*

cellar *n.* basement, vault: *She led me down to the cellar to show me her wine collection.*

cement *n.* **1** mortar, °bond, °glue, gum, paste, solder; adhesive: *You'll need a special kind of cement to stick metal to glass.* —*v.* **2** °stick, °glue, paste, solder, °weld, braze, °bond; °join, °bind, °combine, °unite; cohere, °hold, °cling, adhere: *First cement the tiles to the wall. The ashes and cinders cement readily into a compact mass.*

central *adj.* **1** °middle, medial, median; inner, °inside: *The central reservation between the carriageways will be planted with bushes.* **2** °main, °principal, °important, °chief, °key, °leading, °dominant, °prime, °primary, °pre-eminent, °cardinal, °significant, °essential: *Odysseus is the central figure of the poem.*

centre *n.* **1** °middle, °core, °heart; °nucleus, °focal °point, °hub, °pivot, nave; mid-point: *He stood in the centre of the road. We journeyed to the centre of the earth. The tower is at the centre of the market square. The amount to be paid was at the centre of the controversy. Mark the centre of the line.* —*v.* **2** °focus, °converge, °meet, °concentrate, °cluster: *The business of the meeting centred on the nomination of a chairperson. All my hopes were centred on getting the job as supervisor.*

ceremonial *adj.* **1** °ritual, celebratory, commemorative: *We followed the ceremonial procession.* **2** °formal, °solemn, °stately, °dignified; °ceremonious, august: *The ceremonial robes of his office were white. The ceremonial rites of passage involve many participants.* —*n.* **3** °rite, °ritual, °formality, °ceremony, °service, °observance: *These are the ceremonials prescribed in the Anglican service.*

ceremonious *adj.* **1** °ceremonial, °formal, °dignified, °solemn, *Colloq* °stuffy, °stiff, starchy: *There are many ceremonious procedures involved in a coronation.* **2** courtly, °courteous, °polite, °civil, °correct, °proper, °conventional, punctilious, °careful: *He entered the room and made a ceremonious bow.*

ceremony *n.* **1** °rite, °observance, °solemnity, °service, °ceremonial, °ritual, °formality, °function; obsequies: *I had to attend my grandmother's funeral ceremony and was absent from school.* **2** motions, °formalities *or* °formality, °conventions *or* °convention, niceties, °proprieties, °form, °protocol; lip-service, appearances, pro formas, °etiquette, °decorum: *Going through the ceremony is all they want—they don't care what you believe. Please sign even if only for ceremony's sake.*

certain *adj.* **1** °determined, °set, °fixed, °predetermined, °decided, settled, °firm, °stable, °invariable, established, °standard, °constant, unchanging, °steady, unfluctuating, non-fluctuating, °traditional: *He agreed to pay a certain yearly rent. She met him there every day at a certain time.* **2** °sure, unerring, °definite, dependable, °trustworthy, unfailing, °infallible, °reliable, assured, guaranteed: *How do you know that the dividend is certain?* **3** °sure, °inevitable, inescapable, °destined, predestined, ineluctable, inexorable, °unavoidable, °definite, °firm; unchanging, changeless, °infallible, °permanent, *Colloq* on the cards, a °sure thing, *US* in the cards: *It is not always certain that justice will triumph. Nothing is certain but death and taxes.* **4** indubitable, °indisputable, °undisputed, undoubted, °sure, °doubtless, unequivocal, incontestable, undeniable, °incontrovertible, °absolute, irrefutable, °unquestionable, unquestioned, unarguable, valid: *It is certain only that we exist, according to Descartes.* **5** °confident; assured, °sure, °positive, °definite: *I am certain that she did not steal the money.* **6** °specific, °particular, °definite; unnamed, unspecified, non-specified, non-specific: *He gave us certain information which we now have reason to doubt.*

certainty *n.* **1** °fact, actuality, °reality, °truth, *Colloq* °sure thing: *I would not advise you to neglect a certainty for something doubtful.* **2** °assurance, self-assurance, definiteness, °confidence, °conviction, °faith, authoritativeness, positiveness, certitude: *The certainty with which he played the card showed he expected it to be a winner.* **3 for a certainty**: assuredly, °definitely, certainly, °surely, °positively; °undoubtedly, indubitably, without (a) °doubt, undeniably, unquestionably, °absolutely, *Colloq* for °sure: *I know for a certainty that I cannot fly.*

certify *v.* **1** °confirm, °attest (to), °verify, °testify (to), affirm, aver, asseverate, corroborate, °substantiate, °endorse, °guarantee, °warrant; °swear (to), °bear °witness (to), °vouchsafe, °vouch (for): *I will certify the accuracy of the report. She certified that she was the owner of the car.* **2** °declare, classify, °establish, °confirm: *The magistrate certified the man insane.*

chafe *v.* **1** °rub, °warm (up), °heat (up): *I took the chill off my hands by chafing them a bit.* **2** °rub, abrade, °fret, °gall, °irritate, make °sore: *The skin is very tender where it was chafed.* **3** °fume, °rage, °seethe; °ruffle, vex, °fret, °irritate: *I chafed in impotent rage and exasperation at the ridiculous regulations. To chafe and vex me is a part of her nature.* —*n.* **4** °sore, abrasion, °bruise, soreness, irritation: *The saddle caused a chafe on the inside of my thigh.*

chaff n. 1 °banter, °raillery, °ridicule, badinage, joking, teasing, twitting, *Colloq* kidding, ragging, *Chiefly US and Canadian* joshing: *After the speech, he had to put up with a lot of good-natured chaff from the audience.*
—v. 2 °banter, °tease, °twit, °rail at, *Colloq* kid, °rag, *Chiefly US and Canadian* josh: *When he was in the navy, his family chaffed him for having a girl in every port.*

chain n. 1 °string, series, °combination; °sequence, °succession, °train, °course, °set, concatenation: *He owns a chain of bookshops. Interruption of the food chain can cause serious ecological consequences. A curious chain of circumstances led me to a small hotel at Torquay in February.* 2 °restraint, °check, °trammel, °control, confinement, fetter, °bond, °manacle, °shackle, gyve: *The family finally threw off the chains of poverty.*
—v. 3 °shackle, °secure, °fasten, °bind, gyve; confine, fetter, °restrain, °restrict, °tie, °limit: *Prometheus was chained to a rock as punishment for having brought fire to man. Marguerite felt chained after twenty years of marriage.*

chair n. 1 °seat, armchair, stool, bench, easy chair, rocking-chair: *He offered me a chair so I sat down.* 2 throne, bench, °position, cathedra, °authority; professorship, directorship: *Sue has been offered a chair on the board.* 3 chairperson, chairman, chairwoman, presiding °officer, °leader, °moderator: *The chair ruled on the matter after due consideration.*
—v. 4 °preside, °lead, °govern, °moderate, °run, °direct, °manage, °oversee: *Katherine will chair the meetings during the absence of the president.*

challenge v. 1 °question, °dispute, °defy, °object to, take °exception to, °contest, °doubt, call into °doubt, call into °question, impugn: *I challenge the validity of your accusation.* 2 invite, °dare, °summon, °call out, °provoke: *The duke was challenged to a duel.* 3 °brave, °dare, confront, °defy, °contest: *We could challenge criticism with an easy confidence.*
—n. 4 °question, °dispute, °doubt: *His opinions are open to challenge.* 5 °invitation, °dare, summons, °provocation, confrontation, defiance; °ultimatum: *An older opponent might not have issued such a challenge.* 6 °problem, °demand, stimulation, °trial, °test: *Are you sure that Mr Wilson will be able to meet the challenge of the new position?*

chamber n. 1 °assembly, °body, legislature, judicature, °house, congress, judiciary, senate, °diet; consortium: *She is entitled to sit in the Upper Chamber.* 2 meeting-hall, °reception °room, °assembly °room: *The council chamber was packed with people.* 3 °compartment, °niche, °nook, °cavity: *We hid the gold in a small chamber in the cave.* 4 °room, apartment; bedroom, bedchamber: *On the first floor are the magnificent royal chambers.*

champion n. 1 °victor, °winner, conqueror, title-holder, prizewinner, titleist: *She is the women's singles champion for the fourth year in a row.* 2 defender, °guardian, °protector, °hero, °supporter, °backer, °protagonist, °advocate: *He acquired a reputation as champion of the low-paid.* 3 fighter, combatant, °hero, warrior, campaigner, °veteran: *A stouter champion never handled a sword. The boar is often regarded as the champion among beasts.*
—v. 4 °defend, °protect, °guard; °support, °back, °stand up for, °fight for, °maintain, °sustain,
°uphold; espouse, °forward, °promote, °advocate: *He has always championed the cause of the underdog.*

chance n. 1 °fortune, °luck, °fate: *We met, as chance would have it, at the supermarket. Life is but a game of chance for those who cannot control their destiny.* 2 °opportunity, °time, °turn; °occasion: *You have had your chance to return the money, now it is too late.* 3 Also, **chances**: °likelihood, °probability, °prospect, °odds, °certainty, predictability; conceivability, °possibility: *Chances are that he'll be late. The chance of winning the lottery is pretty remote.* 4 Also, **chances**: °risk, °speculation, °gamble: *You are taking a chance going out there without a weapon. I'll take my chances.* 5 **by chance**: **a** accidentally, unintentionally, inadvertently: *By chance the witness saw him talking to the suspect.* **b** °perhaps, °maybe, °possibly, conceivably: *Have you by chance a match?*
—adj. 6 °casual, °incidental, °accidental, unintentional, °inadvertent; unplanned, °unpremeditated, unexpected, °unforeseen; unlooked-for: *The affair began with a chance meeting at a pub.*
—v. 7 °happen; °occur, come to °pass, take °place, °come about; befall, betide: *We chanced to see him jogging in the park. It chanced that a passer-by called the police.* 8 °risk, °hazard; imperil, °endanger, °jeopardize, °stake, °bet, wager: *Few would chance severe penalties or jail by lying on a tax return. Don't chance everything you've worked for!*

change n. 1 °substitution, replacement, °exchange, interchange, °switch: *You have five minutes for a change of costume. This sunny weather is certainly a change for the better.* 2 °variation, °difference, °switch, °variety, °novelty: *We prefer to live where there is a change of the seasons, not in the tropics.* 3 °variation, °alteration, change-over, °mutation, °shift, modulation, modification, °transformation, metamorphosis, °revolution: *I can't believe the change that has come over Betty since the divorce.* 4 °coin(s), coppers, °silver; (hard) °cash: *I need some change for the coffee machine.*
—v. 5 °exchange, interchange, °switch, °trade, °replace (with), °substitute, *Colloq* swap or swop: *I won't be a minute, I just want to change my shoes. I'd like to change this shirt for a larger size.* 6 °modify, °alter, °modulate; mutate, °transform, metamorphose: *Antoinette has changed since her marriage. I never thought anyone would be able to make her change her mind.* 7 °fluctuate, °shift, °vary; vacillate: *The temperature often changes very rapidly here.* 8 **change to** or **into**: °turn into, °become, °transform, mutate, transmute, °convert, metamorphose: *The alchemists tried to change base metal into gold. Every winter changes into spring—sooner or later.*

changeable adj. 1 °variable, mutable, °protean, °inconstant, °unstable, °unsettled, shifting, °uncertain, °irregular, uneven, unpredictable, labile, °capricious, °erratic, °fickle, °unreliable, undependable, mercurial, °volatile: *The weather has been changeable for the past week.* 2 alterable, modifiable, transformable, convertible: *Their meeting-places were changeable and known only to them.*

changeless adj. 1 unchanging, unvaried, °eternal, °permanent, °fixed, °stable; unchangeable, immutable, unalterable,

°inevitable, °uniform: *We studied photographs of the changeless Martian landscape. The fundamental truths of the Gospel are changeless.* **2** °abiding, °permanent, °constant, °perpetual, °everlasting, °steadfast, unvarying, unchanging: *Nothing could alter my changeless love for you.*

channel *n.* **1** watercourse, canal, waterway, ditch, aqueduct, sluice, trench, trough, gutter, moat; river-bed, stream-bed: *The engineers dug a channel to drain the swamp.* **2** °strait, narrows, neck: *The English Channel connects the North Sea with the Atlantic Ocean.* **3** °furrow, °groove, flute: *The channels cut into this column are not straight.* **4** °course, °means, °way, °approach, avenue, °medium, °path, artery, conduit: *We have to open a new channel of communication with the terrorists.*
—*v.* **5** °direct, convey, °pass, °guide, °lead, °conduct: *Their grievances are being channelled through the information officer.*

chant *n.* **1** °song, psalm, hymn, canticle, plainsong, plainchant, mantra, paean, dirge, monody, descant, carol; singsong: *The war chant of the natives, echoing over the water, struck fear into their enemies.*
—*v.* **2** °sing, intone, descant, carol: *The choir chanted the verses of a lugubrious threnody.*

chaos *n.* formlessness, °disorder, °confusion; °pandemonium, °bedlam, turmoil, °tumult; entropy: *The universe arose out of chaos. If you want to see chaos, look in any teenager's bedroom. There was chaos as the bank closed its doors and ceased trading.*

chaotic *adj.* **1** formless, °shapeless, °incoherent, disordered, °disorderly, disorganized, unorganized, unsystematic, unsystematized, unmethodical, °haphazard, °irregular, °helter-skelter, °confused, °topsy-turvy, jumbled, higgledy-piggledy, *Brit* shambolic: *The present solar system is thought to have condensed from a chaotic mass of nebulous matter. The rules may seem chaotic at first sight.* **2** °tumultuous, °noisy, clamorous, °uproarious, °wild, °riotous, frenzied, °hectic, turbulent, unstuck: *The press conference became chaotic when the president announced his resignation.*

chap *n.* °fellow, °lad, °man, °boy, *Colloq* °guy, geezer, °customer, gink, *Brit* bloke, *Australian* cove, *US* buddy, gazabo or gazebo; *Old-fashioned Brit* (old) egg, (old) bean, (old) crumpet, (old) °boy; *Slang US* bozo: *I went with some of the chaps from the club.*

character *n.* **1** °brand, °stamp, °mark, °symbol, monogram, insigne, badge, °emblem, °sign, °seal, °label; °letter, °number, °figure, °type, °sort, °arbitrary, °peculiar, rune, hieroglyphic *or* hieroglyph: *They used to brand the character of a horse on the forehead of their slaves. We shall need to obtain a set of Cyrillic characters if we are going to print Russian texts.* **2** °characteristic, °quality, °distinction, °trait, °feature, °mark; °sort, °kind, °type, °nature, °description, °attribute; idiosyncrasy, °peculiarity: *He now tried to give the war the character of a crusade. It is the character of some people to be curious.* **3** °morality, °honesty, °integrity, respectability, °rectitude, °honour, °courage, goodness: *Everyone agrees that she is a person of outstanding character.* **4** °person, °personage, °personality, °individual: *Cobbett had more sagacity and foresight than any other public character of his time.* **5** °role, °part,

°personality, characterization, dramatis °persona: *He played the character of Caesar.* **6** °eccentric, °card, *Colloq* oddball, nut, nutter, loony, bat, °weirdo, nutcase, screwball, crackpot, fruit cake, *Australian and old-fashioned Brit* cove: *She was regarded as quite a character because of her many strange habits.* **7** °role, °position, °status, °capacity: *He assumes the character of a Dutch uncle when he speaks to me.* **8 in character**: °fitting, °proper, °suitable, in keeping, °typical, °normal, expected, °characteristic: *It is completely in character for Len to criticize everything he encounters.* **9 out of character**: untypical, atypical, uncharacteristic, °abnormal, unexpected, unfitting: *It would be out of character for Janet to refuse help to someone in need.*

characteristic *adj.* **1** °typical, °representative; °emblematic, °symbolic, °distinctive, idiosyncratic, °symptomatic: *How characteristic it is of them to refuse to go to the dance! These subjects are characteristic of the early Impressionists.*
—*n.* **2** °mark, °trait, °attribute, °feature, °quality, °property, °peculiarity, idiosyncrasy, °character, earmark: *It is a characteristic of bees to swarm.*

characterize *v.* delineate, °describe, °portray, depict, °represent, °define, °brand, °label, °mark, °note, °identify: *She has consistently characterized him as a buffoon. 'Virago' is the term that would best characterize Felicity.*

charade *n.* travesty, °absurdity, °mockery, farce, °parody: *He has made a charade of what could have been a serious relationship.*

charge *n.* **1** °load, °burden, °weight, onus, °impediment; °care, °concern, °obligation: *She feared that she would become a charge on her children.* **2** °price, °fee, °cost: *What is the charge for admission?* **3** °debt, debit, °expense, assessment, °liability: *Any charge against the estate of the deceased will be paid in full.* **4** °care, °custody, °protection, guardianship, wardship, supervision, °jurisdiction, °control, °responsibility, °safe keeping: *We left the children in the charge of Nanny and Nanny in charge of the children.* **5** °order, mandate, °injunction, °precept, °command, °dictate, °direction, °instruction, °demand, exhortation: *The judge's charge to the jury was to ignore the evidence given by the caretaker.* **6** °accusation, °imputation, indictment, °allegation: *The charge is murder. The police decided to drop the charges against him.* **7** °attack, °onset, °action, °assault, sally, °raid, foray, sortie: *At the signal the cavalry began their charge.*
—*v.* **8** °fill, imbue, °load, °instil, pervade, °permeate, °saturate, °suffuse: *The air was highly charged with a stench from the kitchen.* **9** °burden, °entrust, commission, °assign; °afflict, °tax: *He was charged with the supervision of all the military schools.* **10** °command, °order, °bid, enjoin, exhort, °urge, °require, °instruct, °direct: *I charge you not to speak of this matter to anyone.* **11** °blame, censure, °accuse, °indict, cite, °name; °allege, assert: *She charged him with being a hypocrite. He has been charged with assault. It is charged that she was present at the commission of the crime.* **12** °bill, invoice, assess, debit: *Please charge these items to my account. Do not charge me for merchandise not shipped.* **13** °ask, °demand, °claim, °require, °expect: *How much do they charge*

for asparagus at the supermarket? **14** °attack, °assault, °storm, assail, do °battle (with): *Four thousand horsemen stood ready to charge the enemy.*

charitable *adj.* **1** °generous, °liberal, °bountiful, munificent, °unselfish, open-handed, magnanimous, °philanthropic, public-spirited, unsparing, eleemosynary: *Despite her income, Irena has always been most charitable when it comes to worthwhile causes.* **2** well-disposed, °kindly, °kind, beneficent, °benevolent, well-wishing, °lenient, °tolerant, °forgiving, °indulgent, °understanding, compassionate, humane, °sympathetic, °considerate, well-meaning, °good: *They took a charitable view of the matter and decided not to press charges.*

charity *n.* **1** generosity, alms-giving, munificence, liberality, open-handedness, magnanimity, beneficence, °philanthropy, unselfishness, °humanity, humanitarianism, good will: *Your charity towards this hospital has been unequalled by any other donor, Sir Keith.* **2** leniency, big-heartedness, large-heartedness, °benevolence, magnanimity, °indulgence, considerateness, °consideration, compassion, °understanding, °sympathy, kind-heartedness: *We are all urged to show charity towards those who wrong us.* **3** alms, °donation, contribution, °largesse, *Colloq Brit* °dole, *US* °welfare, °relief: *I want the opportunity to work, not the government's charity.*

charm *n.* **1** °amulet, °talisman, °fetish, rabbit's foot, good-luck piece: *She wears a charm to ward off evil spirits.* **2** attractiveness, °appeal, °fascination, allure, °magnetism, desirability, °elegance, urbanity, °sophistication, sophisticatedness, suavity, grace, °refinement, cultivatedness, cultivation, °culture, °polish: °magic, °enchantment, °spell, °sorcery: *To Diderot we go not for charm of style but for a store of fertile ideas. To get ahead Colin relies more on his charm than on his ability.* **3 charms:** °beauty, attractiveness, pulchritude, prettiness, handsomeness, °appeal, allure, °magnetism, °pull, °draw: *For all her charms, I would not trust her one inch.* **4 like a charm:** successfully, °perfectly, miraculously, marvellously, extraordinarily, especially °well: *His appeal to their egos worked like a charm.*

—*v.* **5** °influence, °control, °subdue, °bind, put a °spell on, °bewitch, °enchant, °seduce, °hypnotize, mesmerize, enthral *or US* enthrall, °captivate, °delight, °fascinate, *Literary* °enrapture: *He charmed them with some tale and they gave him their money.* **6** °overcome, °subdue, °calm, soothe, allay, assuage, °hypnotize, mesmerize: *Music is said to have qualities capable of charming savages.*

charmed *adj.* **1** bewitched, spellbound, °enchanted, magical: *Apollonius considered the use of charmed rings essential to quackery.* **2** fortified, protected: *He must lead a charmed life to have survived all those battles.* **3** °pleased, °delighted, °enchanted, °happy: *I am charmed to meet you at last, Madam President.*

charmer *n.* enchanter, enchantress, °sorcerer, sorceress, °magician; vamp, °siren, Circe, Cleopatra, Lorelei, °temptress, °seductress; °seducer, Romeo, Valentino, Don Juan, Lothario, Casanova, lady-killer, ladies' man; °flatterer, °smooth talker, *Colloq* (big-time) °operator, con artist *or* man, *Old-fashioned* smoothie, wolf: *Charlotte has run off with some charmer she met at a party.*

chart *n.* **1** sea-chart, map: *According to the chart, we are fifty miles west of the Lizard.* **2** map, °table, tabulation, graph, diagram; blueprint: *A weather chart appears on page 23. Here is a chart of the highest-yielding unit trusts. She drew up a genealogical chart of the descendants of Queen Victoria.*
—*v.* **3** °plot, °plan, map (out), °design: *He charted a course of action for the company. Have you charted the shortest route between Gibraltar and Cyprus?*

charter *n.* **1** °document, °contract, °compact, °agreement, covenant: *This year we again commemorate the signing of the United Nations charter.* **2** °permit, °permission, °licence *or US* °license, °authority, franchise, °right, °privilege, concession: *He was given an exclusive charter to export furs in 1679.* **3** °lease, °contract: *We have the yacht under charter for the summer.*
—*v.* **4** °license, °authorize, °document, commission, °approve, °certify, franchise, °qualify; °recognize: *He is a chartered accountant, she a chartered surveyor.* **5** °let, °lease, °rent, °hire, °engage, °contract: *I chartered the sloop for three weeks.*

chase *n.* **1** hunting, °hunt, °pursuit: *Police dogs entered the chase and the prisoner was finally caught.* **2** °run after, °follow, °pursue, °track, °go (out) after; court, woo: *The police were chasing a man down the street. Stop chasing women and settle down.* **3 chase away, off, out,** *etc.*: °rout, put to °flight, °hound; °drive away, °off, °out, *etc.*: *I chased the cat away from the birdcage.* ·

chaste *adj.* **1** °pure, virginal, virgin, °celibate, abstinent, continent, °virtuous, undefiled, stainless, unstained, unsullied, unblemished, °decent, °clean, °good, °wholesome, °moral: *Only a knight who was wholly chaste would find the Grail.* **2** °subdued, °severe, restrained, °unadorned, austere, unembellished, °simple, °pure, undecorated, °clean: *In some respects, modern architecture emulates the chaste style of the ancient Egyptians.*

chasten *v.* **1** °discipline, °correct, °chastise, °punish, °castigate: *He used every means to chasten the unruly and disobedient.* **2** °moderate, °temper, °subdue, °curb, °restrain, °repress, °tame, °suppress: *I am not as sanguine as I was—time and experience have chastened me.*

chastise *v.* °punish, °beat, thrash, °belabour, °spank, °whip, °flog, °scourge, birch, cane; °discipline, °chasten, °correct, censure, °berate, °scold: *Pupils are not being chastised as in the old days.*

chastity *n.* °purity, continence, virginity, maidenhood, maidenhead, °virtue, °celibacy, abstinence, abstention, abstemiousness, °restraint, self-restraint, forbearance: *She was a nun and had taken a vow of chastity.*

chat *n.* **1** °conversation, colloquy, °talk, small °talk, °gossip, °palaver, chit-chat, °tête-à-tête, heart-to-heart, *Colloq* °gab, *Chiefly Brit* chin-wag, confab, *Brit* witter, natter, *US and Canadian* °rap, gabfest, bull °session: *We'd get together for a chat every now and then.*
—*v.* **2** °converse, °gossip, °talk, chit-chat, *Colloq* °gab, °chew the fat *or* the rag, jaw, *Brit* witter, natter; *Slang US and Canadian* °rap, bullshit: *We were just chatting when I smelt something burning.* **3** *Brit* **chat up:** flirt *or* dally with, °persuade, °induce, °prevail (up)on, °tempt, °lure, °entice, inveigle, °seduce, °proposition: *Rick chats up every girl he meets.*

chatter v. **1** °prattle, gabble, °jabber, prate, °patter, gibber, cackle, jibber-jabber, Brit chaffer, Colloq °gab, jaw, Brit natter, witter, rabbit on or away, °waffle: *He just kept chattering on about nothing.* **2** clatter, °rattle: *It was so cold my teeth were chattering.*
—n. **3** °prattle, prate, °patter, °gossip, cackle, jabbering, chattering: *I don't want to hear any more chatter in the library.*

cheap adj. **1** °inexpensive, low-priced, bargain-priced, low-cost, sale-priced, cut-price, °reasonable; °economy, budget(-priced): *He was chewing on a cheap cigar. Everything used to be a lot cheaper when I was younger.* **2** °economical; reduced: *Eggs are cheaper by the dozen.* **3** °shoddy, °base, °shabby, °tawdry, °sleazy, tatty, °seedy; °inferior, low-grade, °poor, second-rate, trashy, °worthless, Brit twopenny or tuppenny; Colloq °tacky, Brit tinpot, Slang US two-bit, °lousy, chintzy: *Those cheap pictures ruin the look of the place.* **4** stingy, °miserly, °penurious, niggardly, penny-pinching, cheese-paring, °frugal, °tight, tight-fisted, Scrooge-like, skinflinty: *That cheap brother of yours wouldn't give even a penny to a beggar.*
—adv. **5** inexpensively, cheaply, for a °song, Brit for twopence or tuppence: *You can buy those cheap from any street vendor.* **6** cheaply, °easily, reasonably, for a °song, Brit for twopence or tuppence: *She has sold cheap that which she holds most dear.*
—n. **7 on the cheap**: inexpensively, reasonably, cheaply, at or below °cost, for a °song, Brit for twopence or tuppence; Slang for peanuts: *We buy these watches on the cheap and sell them to tourists.*

cheat n. **1** °swindler, deceiver, °impostor, °fraud, faker, °fake, trickster, confidence man, con man, °operator, charlatan, mountebank, °rogue, shark, Colloq °phoney or US also phony, US snake-oil artist: *It is amazing how many cheats are out there waiting to take advantage of you.*
—v. **2** °swindle, °deceive, bilk, °trick, °take, °fleece, °defraud, euchre, °hoax, °hoodwink, Colloq con, °take in, rook, flimflam, finagle, diddle, °fiddle, move the goalposts, bamboozle, take for a °ride; Slang °rip off: *His own solicitor cheated him out of his inheritance. If you paid ten pounds for that painting, you were cheated.*

check v. **1** °stop, °arrest, °stay, °halt, °obstruct, °block, °limit; °retard, °slow, °brake, °curb, °hinder, °hamper, °impede, °thwart: *They are trying to check the spread of the disease in West Africa.* **2** °restrain, °control, °repress, °stay, °inhibit, °contain, °curb, °restrict: *The animal population is checked only by availability of food.* **3** °authenticate, °verify, °confirm, °substantiate, validate, corroborate, check into, check out, check up on: *Please check his story to make sure he's not lying.* **4** °enquire about or after or into, check into, check (up) on, °examine, °investigate, °inspect, make sure of, °verify, °monitor, °test, °study, °scrutinize: *You'd best check the temperature in the kiln.* **5** °correspond, °coincide, °agree, jibe, °tally, °conform, check out, °fit, °mesh; °compare: *His alibi doesn't check with the witness's statement.* **6 check in**: °arrive, °report: *We check in for work at 0800.* **7 check in** or **into**: °register, °sign in or on, °enrol, log in: *We checked into the hotel.* **8 check into**: °investigate, check out, check up on, °verify, check: *The detective checked into the backgrounds*

of all applicants. **9 check off**: tick (off), °mark, check: *Check off the names in red.* **10 check out**: **a** °depart, °leave; °go: *He checked out of the hotel and took a taxi to the airport.* **b** °investigate, °research, °explore, °enquire into, °look into or at or over, °scrutinize, °examine, °inspect, °probe, °survey, check up on, check, check into, check over: *You had best check out her references before hiring her.* **c** °pass, °pass °muster or °scrutiny, meet °approval, be verified, check: *According to our records, his story checks out.* **d** Slang cash in one's checks or chips, kick the bucket, croak: *Sam checked out last week—heart attack, I think.* **11 check over** or **out**: °review, °verify, °authenticate, check: *Please check over my figures before I submit them to the accountant.* **12 check up (on)**: **a** °investigate, do °research, °probe, °explore, check: *I don't know her name, but I'll check up and let you know.* **b** °determine, °discover, °find out, °look into, check: *I want you to check up on where they eat lunch.*
—n. **13** °stop, stopping, °cease, surcease, hesitation, cessation, stoppage, °interruption, °break, °pause, balk or baulk, discontinuity, discontinuation, discontinuance, °suspension: *The visitors continued to arrive without check, far into the night.* **14** °restraint, °repression, °inhibition, limitation, °curb, °restriction, °control, constraint, °hindrance, °obstruction, °impediment, damper: *He keeps a good check on the foreman. This tax will serve as a check against free trade.* **15** °control, °test, inspection, °examination, °scrutiny, verification, substantiation, authentication, confirmation, validation, corroboration: *We do a thorough check on the quality of every product.* **16** US tick, °mark, °dash, X: *Place a check in the box alongside your choice.* **17** °token, °receipt, counterfoil, °stub; voucher, chit, certificate: *Don't lose your baggage check.* **18** °chip, °counter: *Let's cash in our checks and go home.* **19** Chiefly US bill, °tab, °charge(s): *In the USA, people generally add 15 per cent to the check for a tip.*

cheeky adj. °impudent, °impertinent, °insolent, °audacious, °disrespectful, °rude, uncivil, °forward, °brazen, °pert, saucy: *That cheeky little brat told me to get lost!*

cheer n. **1** °disposition, °frame of mind, °spirit: *They were of good cheer, considering their predicament.* **2** cheerfulness, gladness, °mirth, °joy, °gaiety, blitheness, °happiness, buoyancy, light-heartedness, merrymaking: *There wasn't much cheer at the pub when we learnt of what had befallen poor Grover.* **3** °comfort, °solace, °encouragement, consolation: *She brought in a little breath of cheer from the outside world.* **4** °shout, °cry, hurrah, rah, huzzah, hurray or hooray: *Three cheers for Penelope!*
—v. **5** °comfort, °console, °solace, °encourage, inspirit, °warm, Colloq buck up: *Your friendly note cheered me considerably.* **6** °gladden, °enliven, cheer up, hearten, °buoy up, °brighten, elate, uplift, °lift up: *Let thy heart cheer thee in the days of thy youth.* **7** °applaud, °shout, hurrah, °clap, °yell; Colloq Brit and Australian and New Zealand barrack for: *The crowd cheered for five minutes when Mr Flews stood to speak.*

cheerful adj. **1** joyous, °glad, gladsome, blithesome, °blithe, °happy, cheery, of good °cheer, °joyful, °jolly, °exuberant, jubilant, °gleeful, °gay, light-hearted, °merry: *I am pleased to see that Agatha is so cheerful. Why do you cry at weddings,*

which are supposed to be such cheerful occasions?
2 cheering, gladdening, animating, °bright,
enlivening, cheery, °gay, °buoyant,
°invigorating: She has redecorated the bedroom in
more cheerful colours.

chequered adj. **1** chequer-board, checked;
°patchwork; plaid, tartan: You cannot use a
chequered tablecloth for a formal dinner.
2 °variegated, diversified, alternating, °variable,
good and bad, varying, fluctuating, up and
down; °uncertain: David Williams had a rather
chequered career in the army.

cherish v. **1** °treasure, hold or keep °dear,
°prize: I know that she cherishes every moment you
were together. **2** °foster, °tend, °cultivate,
°preserve, °sustain, nurture, °nourish, °nurse,
cosset: For their sweetness gillyflowers are cherished
in gardens. We cherish little Edward and probably spoil
him a bit too much.

chest n. **1** °box, coffer, °trunk, strongbox,
caddy, °casket, °case: It took four men to carry
the chest outside, where we could open it. Martha kept
her jewels in a small chest on the dresser. **2** °breast;
thorax: The wrestler was pounding his chest and
shouting 'I am the greatest!'

chew v. **1** masticate, °grind, °munch; °bite,
°gnaw: Make sure to chew each mouthful thoroughly.
The puppy chewed up my slipper. **2 chew the fat**
or **rag**: °gossip, °palaver, °chat, °converse, °talk,
Slang US and Canadian bullshit: We sat round the
fire and chewed the fat all evening. **3 chew out**:
°scold, °rebuke, °reprimand: The sergeant chewed
out the recruit because his boots were dirty. **4 chew
over**: °think about or on or over, °consider,
°review, °ponder, ruminate on, °meditate on
or over: I'll chew over your proposal and let you
know.

chic adj. **1** °stylish, °fashionable, à la °mode,
modish, °smart, °tasteful, °elegant;
°sophisticated; Colloq °trendy: Susanna was
always a chic dresser.
—n. **2** °style, °fashion, °good °taste, tastefulness,
°elegance, stylishness, modishness: There is an air
of chic about him that repels many men but attracts
many women.

chicanery n. °trickery, sophistry, °deception,
quibbling, sharp practice, cheating, deviousness, duplicity, pettifoggery, double-dealing,
°artifice, skulduggery: They lost the case because
of the chicanery of their lawyers.

chief n. **1** °head, °leader, °principal, °superior,
°supervisor, °superintendent, °manager,
°overseer, captain, °master, ringleader, chieftain, Dialect himself, Colloq °boss, bossman, Brit
governor, gov., supremo, US °man, kingpin,
(°head or °chief) honcho, number one, numero
uno, headman, °big White Chief, °big Chief,
Great White Father, °big Daddy, °super; Slang
°big cheese, Brit gaffer, Chiefly US Mr Big: You'd
best ask the chief for permission to fly to Rome.
—adj. **2** °head, °leading, ranking, °superior,
°supreme, °foremost, °premier, °first, greatest,
°outstanding: Terry is your chief competition for the
singles trophy. **3** °principal, most °important,
°essential, °key, °paramount, (°first and)
°foremost, °primary, °prime, °main: The chief
reason I came was to see you. Here is a list of the
chief crimes committed in the area last year.

chiefly adv. °mainly, in °particular, °especially,
°particularly, above all, most of all,
°pre-eminently, °principally, °primarily, mostly,

predominantly, °largely, by and °large, on the
°whole, in the °main, °generally, in °general,
°usually, as a °rule: Inflation affected chiefly the price
of food. The Anatomy of Melancholy consists chiefly
of quotations.

child n. **1** °offspring, °descendant, son or daughter, °little one, youngster, Formal °progeny,
°issue, Colloq kid, nipper, Slang Brit sprog: How
many children do you have? **2** foetus, newborn,
neonate, infant, °baby, babe, toddler, °boy or
°girl, °lad or °lass, °stripling, youngster, °youth,
°juvenile, °adolescent, °teenager, °young man
or woman, °young gentleman or lady, Chiefly
Scots laddie or lassie: No children were born in the
village for five years. These miscreants are mere
children, who should not be punished as adults.

childhood n. °infancy, babyhood, boyhood or
girlhood, °youth, °puberty, minority, adolescence, teens: During her childhood the family
moved to Kent. She spent most of her childhood
dreaming about travelling to the moon.

childish adj. °childlike, °juvenile, °puerile,
°infantile, babyish; °immature,
°inexperienced, °naïve, °undeveloped, underdeveloped, retarded; °silly, US sophomoric: They
thought his reaction to their criticism was childish
and petulant.

childlike adj. youthful, °young, °innocent, trustful, °ingenuous, °unsophisticated, °naïve,
°trusting, credulous, °open, undissembling,
unassuming, guileless, °artless: There is a childlike simplicity to some primitive paintings.

chill n. **1** coldness, °cold, coolness, sharpness,
°nip: We put on our jackets to ward off the chill of
the evening. **2** °cold, flu, influenza, (la or the)
grippe, ague, Technical coryza, Colloq (the)
sniffles, sneezles and wheezles: Take off those wet
clothes before you catch a chill. **3** coolness, iciness,
frigidity, aloofness; unfriendliness, °hostility:
Mrs Marlow felt the chill in the stare of her husband's
ex-wife.
—adj. **4** °cold, °cool, numbing, chilling, °chilly,
°raw, °penetrating, °icy, °frigid, °wintry, frosty,
arctic, °polar, glacial: A chill easterly wind made
me shiver. **5** shivering, chilled (through), °numb,
numbed, numbing, benumbed: She kissed me with
a lip more chill than stone. **6** °cold, °cold-blooded,
°aloof, °indifferent, insensitive, unemotional,
°unsympathetic; °chilly: The prison commandant
viewed the corpses with chill detachment.
—v. **7** °cool, °freeze, °refrigerate, ice: The fruit
tastes better if it has been chilled. **8** °dampen,
dispirit, °depress, deject, dishearten, °distress:
The news of mother's illness chilled us all.

chilly adj. **1** °cool, coldish, °cold, °frigid, nippy,
frosty, °icy, °crisp, °chill: The weather has been
quite chilly for May. **2** °chill, °unenthusiastic,
unresponsive, unreceptive, frosty, unwelcoming, °crisp, °cool, °cold, unfriendly, °hostile;
°distant, °aloof: The suggestion that the charity
fair be held in her garden met with a chilly response
from Lady Griffiths.

chime n. **1** bell, set of bells, carillon, °ring,
°peal: Our church has a full chime of eight
bells. **2** ringing, °peal, chiming, tolling, tintinnabulation, clanging, ding-dong, °striking;
tinkle, °jingle, °jangle: We could hear the chimes
of Big Ben from our hotel room.
—v. **3** °ring, °peal, °toll, °sound, tintinnabulate,
clang, °strike: The clock chimed on the hour.
4 °mark, °denote, °indicate, °announce: The

carillon chimed the hour at noon. **5 chime in:**
a °join in, °blend, harmonize: *When singing this round, chime in at the third bar.* **b** °interrupt, intercede, °intrude, °interfere, °break in, *Colloq* °chip in; *Slang* °butt in: *I was about to speak when he chimed in with some silly remark.*

chink *n.* fissure, °rift, °crack, °crevice, °gap, °opening, cleft, °slit, °aperture, °cranny: *We could see daylight through a chink in the fence.*

chip *n.* **1** °fragment, °piece, shard *or* sherd, °splinter, °flake, °sliver, °scrap, °morsel, °bit: *A chip of slate rattled down off the roof.* **2** °counter, marker, °token; °plaque, *US* °check: *He put his chip on number 14.*
—*v.* **3** °chisel, °whittle, hew: *He chipped away at the stone till it fitted perfectly into the hole.*
4 chip in: a °contribute; °participate: *All the neighbours chipped in to pay for the street decorations.* **b** °interrupt, °break in, °intrude, °interfere, intercede, interpose, *Colloq* °chime in: *Clive chipped in with his usual silly comment.*

chirp *v.* **1** tweet, °peep, °twitter, chirrup, warble, trill, cheep, chitter, chirr, °pipe: *I was awakened by the birds, chirping away in the forest.*
—*n.* **2** tweet, °peep, °twitter, chirrup, warble, trill, cheep, chitter, chirr: *The canary gave two chirps and jumped onto its perch.*

chisel *v.* **1** °carve, °cut, °pare, °groove, °shape, °engrave, °grave: *He was chiselling the figure of an eagle out of the board.* **2** °cheat, °defraud, °swindle, bilk, °trick, °fool, °dupe, gull, *Colloq* bamboozle: *The gamblers chiselled him out of a week's wages.*

chivalrous *adj.* courtly, °gracious, °courteous, °polite, °gallant, °noble, knightly, gentlemanly, °considerate, °kind, °charitable, magnanimous: *It was quite chivalrous of you to drive me home.*

chivalry *n.* knight-errantry; °honour, °bravery, °courage, °courtesy, politeness, courtliness, gallantry, °nobility, virtuousness, righteousness, justness, fairness, impartiality, equitableness: *All the noble sentiments blended together constitute chivalry.*

choice *n.* **1** °selection, °election, °preference, choosing, °pick, acceptance: *I don't care for his choice of language.* **2** °option, realm of possibilities; °alternative, °voice, °determination: *She was given no choice in selecting her husband.* **3** °pick, °élite, °flower, °best, °select, cream, crème de la crème: *The king's guard is made up from the choice of the kingdom.*
—*adj.* **4** °select, °exquisite, °special, °superior, °prime, high-quality, °excellent, °pre-eminent, °best, °prize, °first-rate, °exceptional, preferred, °desirable, °ideal, °rare, *Colloq Brit* plummy: *She has the choicest wines in her cellar.* **5** selected, °select, hand-picked, well-chosen, °fit, °appropriate, °fitting: *The eulogy was disposed of in a few choice words.*

choke *v.* **1** suffocate, asphyxiate, °smother, °stifle, strangle, throttle, garrotte *or* garrote *or* garotte, burke: *He choked his elderly victims, then stole their money.* **2** °stop, °fill (up), °block (up), °obstruct, congest, °clog, dam (up), constrict: *The channel is completely choked with weeds.* **3** Also, **choke off:** °smother, °suppress, °stifle, °prohibit, °frustrate, °deny, obviate, °cut off, °stop, put a °stop to; dissuade, °discourage: *His policies choked off any chance for innovation.* **4 choke**

back *or* **down:** °suppress, °repress, °stifle, °restrain: *He choked back the tears when he saw the gravestone.*

choose *v.* °select, °elect, °pick (out), °determine, °judge; °decide, °prefer, opt, °settle upon *or* on: *She had the right to choose the course that seemed the best to her. Given the options, I chose to stay.*

choosy *adj.* °selective, °discriminating, discerning, °fastidious, °finicky *or* finical, °particular, °fussy, °demanding, °exacting, °difficult, °hard to please, *Colloq* picky: *If you weren't so choosy, you wouldn't have to pay so much.*

chop *v.* **1** Also, **chop away** *or* **off:** °cut, °hack, hew, °lop, crop, °cleave, °sever: *Chop away that underbrush. I tried to chop off the end. Don't chop down that tree!* **2** Also, **chop up:** mince; dice, cube; °hash: *Chop up the parsley very fine before adding it to the sauce.*
—*n.* **3** °cut, °blow, °stroke: *With a quick chop of the axe, the branch was severed.*

christen *v.* **1** baptize, anoint: *They are going to christen the baby next week.* **2** °name, °call, dub: *The child was christened Madelaine. The highest peak in Wales is christened Snowdon.*

chronic *adj.* **1** long-lasting, long-standing, °lingering, inveterate, °persistent, continuing, °lasting, long-lived: *The doctor said that the condition, for which there is no cure, is chronic.* **2** inveterate, °persistent, dyed in the wool, confirmed, °habitual, hardened: *Abby is a chronic liar.*

chronicle *n.* **1** °record, °history, °diary, °chronology, °account, °narrative, °description, °report, °register, annal(s), archive: *She has written a chronicle of the events leading up to the War of Jenkins' Ear.*
—*v.* **2** °record, °register, °list, °enter, archive, °document, °describe; °tell, °recount, °narrate, °report, °relate, retail: *In the Iliad Homer chronicled the legends of the Trojan War.*

chronology *n.* °account, °record, °calendar, almanac, °journal, log; °sequence: *Describe the chronology of events preceding your discovery of the body.*

chubby *adj.* podgy *or US* pudgy; stumpy, stubby, chunky, tubby, °plump, °dumpy, thickset, heavy-set, °heavy, °ample, overweight: *She was a bit chubby when a teenager but became a professional model when she was 21.*

chuckle *v.* **1** °laugh, chortle, crow, snigger, °giggle, °titter: *Robin always chuckled when the subject of embezzlement came up.*
—*n.* **2** chuckling, °laugh, chortle, crowing, °giggle; °laughter, snigger, sniggering: *It was hard to resist a chuckle when we saw the looks on their faces.*

chum *n.* **1** °friend, °comrade, °companion; confidant(e), °familiar; °fellow, °colleague, *Colloq* °pal, sidekick, *Chiefly Brit and Australian and New Zealand* °mate, *Chiefly US and Canadian* buddy: *I invited a chum of mine for the weekend.*
—*v.* **2** Often, **chum around:** °associate, *Colloq* °pal (around): *Yes, we used to chum around together in the army.* **3 chum up with:** °ally (oneself) with, be °friendly with, °go with, °associate with, *Colloq* °pal (up *or* about *or* around) with, *US* °team up with: *Lionel chummed up with Ashley to go swimming.*

chummy *adj.* °friendly, °sociable, °intimate, °close, °thick, *Colloq* pally, *US* palsy-walsy, buddy-buddy: *You were very chummy with Peter once, weren't you?*

chute n. 1 °waterfall, °rapid: *The canoe skimmed down the chute with lightning speed.* 2 °slide, °shaft, °channel, °ramp, runway, trough, °incline: *The parcels come down this chute and you have to sort them by postcode.*

circle n. 1 disc *or chiefly US* disk, °ring, hoop, °loop, °band, °wheel, annulus, ringlet; cordon: *Using a compass, he carefully drew a circle. We formed a circle around the speaker.* 2 °set, coterie, °clique, °class, °division, °group, °crowd; °society, °fellowship, °fraternity, °company: *John and I don't move in the same circles.*
—v. 3 °encircle, circumambulate, °go °round *or* around, °tour; circumnavigate: *For exercise, I circle the lake in the park every morning.* 4 °encircle, °surround, gird, °enclose, circumscribe: *Twenty small diamonds circle each star sapphire.*

circuit n. 1 compass, circumference, °perimeter, °periphery, °girth, °border, °boundary, °edge, °limit, ambit, °margin, °outline, confine(s), °bound, °pale: *The circuit of the area amounts to 72 miles.* 2 °round, °tour, ambit, °circle, °orbit, °course, °lap: *The rider completed the circuit of the ranch, mending the fence as he went.*

circular adj. 1 °round, disc-shaped *or chiefly US* disk-shaped, disc-like *or chiefly US* disk-like, discoid; ring-shaped, ring-like, annular: *Notice the circular pattern of growth of this ivy.* 2 °roundabout, °indirect, circuitous, °tortuous, twisting, twisted, anfractuous; periphrastic, circumlocutory; °devious: *We had to take a circular route because the road was closed. Why can't she say what she means instead of being so circular?* 3 illogical, °inconsistent, °redundant, fallacious, irrational, *Formal* °sophistic *or* sophistical: *To say that you exist because you think and that you think because you exist is an example of circular reasoning.*

circulate v. 1 °move *or* °go about *or* °round *or* around, °orbit, °flow, °course, °run, °circle: *The blood circulates from the heart through the arteries and veins and back to the heart.* 2 °spread, °distribute, disseminate, °issue, °publish, °air, °announce, °proclaim, make known, °noise °abroad, bruit about, °report, °broadcast, °reveal, divulge, advertise, °publicize, promulgate, °put about, °bring *or* °put out, °pass out *or* °round *or* around: *He has been circulating the story that his ex-wife cheated on her income tax.* 3 °spread, °go round *or* around, be bruited about, °come out: *A rumour has been circulating about your behaviour at the office party.*

circulation n. 1 °circuit, °course, °orbit, °flow, flowing, °motion: *It was Harvey who discovered the circulation of the blood.* 2 °spread, spreading, dissemination, °transmission, °passage, °distribution, diffusion, °publication, °advertisement, °announcement, issuance, issuing, °pronouncement, °proclamation, promulgation, °broadcast, broadcasting: *The state has again forbidden the free circulation of information.*

circumstance n. 1 Often, **circumstances**: °situation, °condition(s), °state (of affairs); °status, °station, resources, °income, finances: *In the circumstances, all leave is cancelled. Each person will be helped according to the individual circumstance.* 2 °event, °incident, °episode, °occurrence, °affair, °happening, °occasion: *Any unforeseen circumstance could set off a shooting war.*

circumstantial adj. 1 °indirect, °presumptive, evidential *or* evidentiary, interpretive, deduced, presumed, presumable, implicative, implied, inferred, inferential: *Some circumstantial evidence is very strong, as when you find a gun in the suspect's house.* 2 °accidental, °incidental, hearsay, °indirect, unimportant, adventitious, °provisional, °secondary, unessential, °non-essential, fortuitous, °chance, °extraneous: *Such circumstantial trivia have no bearing on the case.* 3 °detailed, °particular, °precise, °explicit, °specific: *We cannot believe that he invented so circumstantial a narrative.*

citizen n. 1 voter; °native; householder, °resident, °inhabitant, °denizen, dweller, freeman; *Brit* patrial, ratepayer; *US* taxpayer: *All citizens are entitled to certain rights.* 2 city-dweller, town-dweller, townsman, townswoman, villager, burgess, oppidan: *She considers herself a citizen of Oxford.*

city n. °metropolis, °municipality, borough, burgh; conurbation, megalopolis; *Brit* urban °district; °see, diocese, bishopric; *New Zealand* urban °area; *Colloq* °town, *US* burg, big apple: *We gave up our flat in the city and moved to the country.*

civil adj. 1 civilian, non-military, °lay, laic, laical, °secular: *There is a distinction between civil law and canon law.* 2 °domestic, °internal; °public: *The economic conditions have led to civil strife.* 3 °polite, °courteous, °respectful, well-mannered, °proper, civilized, °cordial, °formal, courtly, urbane, °polished, °refined: *They are civil enough, but I always have the feeling they really despise tourists.*

civility n. °courtesy, politeness, °respect, comity, urbanity, amiability, °consideration, courteousness, cordiality, °propriety, °tact, °diplomacy, politesse, °protocol: *Despite his rude behaviour at her dinner-party, she treats him with great civility.*

civilization n. 1 °culture, °refinement, cultivation, enlightenment, °edification, °sophistication, °polish: *The Romans brought civilization to many peoples who had been quite barbarous.* 2 °culture, mores, °custom(s): *He has studied Egyptian civilization all his life.*

civilize v. 1 °enlighten, °refine, °polish, edify, °educate, acculturate: *Civilized people do not behave in such a boorish way.* 2 °tame, domesticate; broaden, elevate, acculturate: *The claim that they civilized the Aborigines means only that they forced them to conform to the White man's notion of civilization.*

claim n. 1 °demand, °assertion, °request, °requisition, °petition, °application; °requirement: *As far as the land is concerned, his claim has been denied.* 2 °right(s), °call, °title: *What possible claim could the Miss Dashwoods have on his generosity?*
—v. 3 °demand, °seek, °ask *or* °call (for), °exact, °insist (on *or* upon), °require, °command, be entitled to: *She has every right to claim a share in the estate.* 4 °declare, assert, °allege, °state, °put *or* °set forth, affirm, contend, °maintain: *These measurements lack the degree of accuracy claimed for them. She claims that she was the first person to ring the police.*

clammy adj. 1 °moist, °sticky, gummy, °pasty, viscous, °slimy: *In the swamp the police found a clammy pistol that they believe to be the* *weapon.* **2** °moist, °damp, °humid, °close, °muggy, °wet, °misty, foggy: *It was the kind of clammy summer's day when your shirt sticks to your back.*

clamp *n.* **1** °clasp, °vice, °brace, °clip, fastener: *Use a clamp to hold the pieces together till the glue dries.*
—*v.* **2** °fasten (together), °clip (together), °bracket, make °fast, °clasp: *You should clamp the planks together and plane the edges of both.*

clan *n.* **1** °tribe, °family, °dynasty, °line, °house: *There had been a feud of long standing between the two clans, which culminated in the massacre of Glencoe.* **2** °fraternity, °brotherhood, °party, °set, °clique, coterie, °circle, °crowd, °group, °fellowship, °society, °faction, °family, °tribe, °band, °ring, °gang: *He regards social scientists as a clan quite separate from other scientists.*

clap *v.* **1** °applaud; °cheer, acclaim: *Everyone clapped when the boxer climbed into the ring.* **2** °slap, °strike, °pat: *He clapped me on the shoulder in the friendliest way.* **3** °put, °place, °slap, °fling, °toss, cast, *Colloq* °stick: *He had no sooner set foot in the town when he was clapped in jail.* **4** °impose, °lay, °apply: *The magistrate clapped a severe fine on me for speeding.* —*n.* **5** °crack, °slap, °report, °crash, bang, °snap: *There was a loud clap of thunder, making the house shake.*

clapper *n.* °tongue: *We attached a rope to the clapper of the bell.*

clarify *v.* **1** elucidate, make °clear, °simplify, make °plain, °clear up, °explain, shed *or* throw °light on *or* upon, °illuminate, explicate: *She offered to clarify any points about which we had questions.* **2** °clear, °purify, °clean: *The trout should be lightly basted with clarified butter.*

clarity *n.* **1** clearness, transparency, limpidity, pellucidity: *The clarity of the sea in the tropics is owing to a lack of plankton.* **2** lucidity, °definition, definiteness, distinctness; comprehensibility, understandability, intelligibility, unam-biguousness: *One cannot argue with the clarity of her explanation of Hegelianism.*

clash *n.* **1** °crash, clang, clank, clangour: *The concerto ends with a clash of cymbals.* **2** °collision, smash, (°hostile) °encounter, °conflict, °engagement, °fight, °battle, °disagreement, °difference, °argument, °dispute, altercation, °quarrel, squabble: *He has witnessed many a clash between the prime minister and parliament.* —*v.* **3** °conflict, °fight, °battle, °disagree, °differ, °argue, °dispute, °quarrel, squabble, °feud, wrangle, °cross swords: *My brother and I always clash on the question of who should pay our father's hospital bills.* **4** °conflict, disharmonize, °jar, be at °odds *or* out of keeping: *The pink of the blouse and the fuchsia of the skirt clash badly.*

clasp *n.* **1** fastener, °fastening, °hook, catch, °clip, °pin, °brooch: *The ends were fastened together with a diamond clasp.* **2** °embrace, °hug, °hold, °grasp, °grip: *He held her tight in his clasp.* —*v.* **3** °fasten, °secure, °close, °hold, °hook, °clip, °pin, °clamp: *The robe was clasped by an emerald pin.* **4** °hold, °embrace, take °hold of, °hug, °enclose, °envelop: *The beggar clasped my hand, his eyes seeking mine in piteous supplication.* **5** °grab, °grasp, °seize, °clutch, °grip: *They clasped hands in friendship.*

class *n.* **1** °rank, °grade, °level, °order, °stratum; °caste, °lineage, °birth, °pedigree, °stock, °extraction, descent: *He was born in the 1940s into a family of the middle class.* **2** °category, °division, classification, °group, °genre, °league, °realm, °domain; °kind, °sort, °type: *As a dancer, she is in a class by herself.* **3** °excellence, °merit, °refinement, °elegance, °prestige, °importance, °taste, discernment, °distinction, °bearing, °presence, savoir faire, savoir vivre, °breeding: *He may be a good drinking companion, but he has no class whatsoever.* **4** year, °form, *US* °grade: *We were in the same class at school.* —*v.* **5** classify, °group, °arrange, assort, °type, °categorize, °rank, °grade, °rate, °order: *They are classed as self-employed for these purposes.*

classic *adj.* **1** °standard, °leading, °outstanding, prototypic(al), °definitive, °model, °ideal, archetypal, paradigmatic: *His military career is a classic example of what family connections can achieve.* **2** °legendary, °immortal, °enduring, °deathless, ageless, °timeless, undying, °venerable, °time-honoured; °outstanding, °first-rate, °superior, °excellent, °noteworthy, °notable, °exemplary: *By the time she was ten, she had read most of the classic works of English literature. He collects classic cars.* —*n.* **3** °paragon, °epitome, °outstanding example, exemplar, °model, paradigm, °prototype: *When it comes to comedians, Ronnie is a classic.* **4** °masterpiece, master-work: *The Rolls-Royce Silver Ghost is regarded as a classic by collectors.*

classical *adj.* **1** °standard, °model, °exemplary, °traditional, established, °influential, °authoritative, °serious, °weighty: *Classical authors are those who are regarded as being of good credit and authority in the schools. Montaigne is the earliest classical writer in the French language.* **2** Greek, Latin, Roman: *Architectural styles of the 18th century harked back to Classical designs.*

claw *n.* **1** °talon, °nail: *The cat had scratched her badly with its claws.* —*v.* **2** °scratch, °tear, °scrape, °rake, °slash: *She clawed at his face to break his grip on her throat.* **3** °grapple, °grab, °catch, °scrape, scrabble: *He tried to climb up the embankment, clawing at the steep wall.*

clean *adj.* **1** °pure, undefiled, unsullied, unmixed, unadulterated, uncontaminated, unpolluted, uninfected, °unspoiled *or* unspoilt, °sanitary, disinfected; antiseptic, decon-taminated, purified, °sterile: *The laboratory reports that our well water is absolutely clean. You must use a clean bandage.* **2** unsoiled, untainted, unstained; unsullied; cleansed, cleanly, (freshly) laundered *or* washed, scrubbed; °spotless, °immaculate: *She puts on clean underwear every day in case she's involved in an accident.* **3** clean-cut, °neat, °simple, °definite, uncomplicated, °smooth, °even, °straight, °trim, °tidy: *The edges of the fracture are clean and will mend quickly.* **4** °innocent, °blameless, °inoffensive, °respectable; °decent, °chaste, °pure, °honourable, °good, undefiled, °virtuous, °moral: *The suspect was completely clean—he was out of town at the time of the robbery.* **5** non-radioactive: *They say they've produced a clean bomb, but I don't believe it.* **6** °unarmed, weaponless: *Frisk that suspect and make sure he's clean.* —*adv.* **7** °completely, °entirely, °thoroughly, fully, °totally, °wholly, °altogether, °quite, °utterly, °absolutely: *Geoff's clean out of his mind*

if he believes that. *With one blow he cut the orange clean through.* **8 come clean:** °confess, °acknowledge, make a clean breast, °admit, °make a °revelation, °reveal, *Colloq* own up, °spill the beans; *US dialect* fess up; *Slang* °sing: *In the end he saw that he was trapped and decided to come clean.*
—*v.* **9** °cleanse, °wash, lave, (take a) °shower, sponge, mop, °scrub, °scour, °sweep, dust, vacuum, °polish, °launder, dry-clean, *Brit* hoover; °tidy, °neaten, do up, °straighten up *or* out, unclutter; *Brit* bath; *US and Canadian* bathe: *When we cleaned the urn, we could read the inscription. I have told Richard a thousand times to clean his room.* **10 clean out: a** °exhaust, deplete: *The gambler cleaned her out of every penny she had in the world.* **b** °empty, leave °bare, °clear out, °evacuate: *We must clean out the larder before it can be painted.* **11 clean up: a** clean, °cleanse, °wash, (take a) °shower, *Brit* bath; *US* take a bath, bathe, °wash up: *Clean up, please, dinner is almost ready. It took us a week to clean up the stables.* **b** °purge, °purify, °disinfect, depollute, decontaminate, °clear, sanitize: *The council has led the way towards cleaning up the wetlands of chemical waste.*

cleanse *v.* **1** °clean, absterge, deterge, °wash, °scour, °scrub: *You need a scrubbing brush to cleanse the tub.* **2** °purify, depurate; °purge, °wash away, expiate: *Each prayer repeated has a certain value in cleansing away sin.*

clear *adj.* **1** unclouded, cloudless, °sunny, °fair, sunlit, °fine: *On a clear day, you can see the lighthouse several miles away.* **2** °transparent, limpid, crystalline; translucent, uncloudy, unclouded, pellucid: *The water was clear enough to see the bottom.* **3** °bright, °lustrous, shining, °shiny, sparkling, *Formal* nitid: *We painted the bathroom a lovely clear blue.* **4** °bright, °fresh, unblemished, unscarred: *She has a lovely clear complexion.* **5** °distinct, °sharp, well-defined, °definite; °legible, °readable; °acute, °vivid: *The notes were written in a large clear hand.* **6** understandable, °intelligible, perspicuous, lucid, comprehensible, apprehensible, °discernible, °plain, °obvious, unambiguous, unequivocal, °explicit, °definite, unmistakable, °indisputable, °undisputed, °unquestionable, °incontrovertible: *He has made himself very clear on that point.* **7** °distinct, unclouded, unconfused, °explicit, °plain, °definite, clear-cut, palpable: *I have a clear recollection of her words.* **8** °evident, °plain, °obvious, °patent, °manifest, °apparent: *It became clear that someone was trying to compromise her.* **9** °perceptive, °acute, °sensitive, perspicacious, discerning, °keen: *It was only his clear vision of the situation that saved us all.* **10** °certain, °sure, convinced, °confident, °positive, °determined, °definite, assured: *I am not clear that the subject was a good one.* **11** °pure, unwavering, well-defined, °distinct, clarion, bell-like: *We heard father's clear voice calling from below.* **12** °pure, guileless, °unsophisticated, °innocent, °blameless, °faultless; not °guilty: *I still cannot look her in the eye with a clear conscience.* **13** unencumbered, °free, °net: *In our first year we made a clear profit of 25 per cent.* **14** °unlimited, °unqualified, unquestioned, °unquestionable, °absolute, °complete, °entire; °pure, °sheer, °perfect: *You must allow three clear days for the ascent.* **15** disengaged, disentangled, unentangled, °free,

freed, °rid, °quit, °loose, unencumbered, released: *When the line is clear of any obstruction, hoist sail and let's be off.* **16** °open, unencumbered, °free, unblocked, unobstructed, °unimpeded, °direct: *There is a clear view of the park from here.*
—*adv.* **17** brightly, effulgently, radiantly, luminously, lambently: *The stars were shining clear in the night sky.* **18** distinctly, °clearly, starkly, perceptibly, discernibly, understandably, prominently: *When you see the reef, sing out loud and clear.* **19** °completely, °utterly, °entirely, cleanly, °clean, °wholly, °totally: *The thief got clear away in the confusion.*
—*v.* **20** °clarify, °cleanse, °clean, °purify: *The chemical soon cleared the water of all sediment.* **21** exonerate, absolve, acquit; °excuse, °forgive: *He has been cleared of all charges and released.* **22** Also, **clear up:** °explain, elucidate, explicate, °clarify, make °plain *or* clear, disambiguate: *We should be able to clear up the mystery by this evening.* **23** Also, **clear up:** become °fair *or* cloudless *or* °sunny: *I hope the weather clears in time for the game.* **24** °open (up), °free; unblock, unclog, unstop; disencumber, dislodge: *We were able to clear a path through the jungle. He cleared his throat and began to speak.* **25** °empty: *Clear the land of trees before farming it.* **26** Also, **clear away** *or* **out:** °remove, °eliminate, °take; °cut away *or* down: *Clear those branches from the paths.* **27** disburden, unburden, °purge, °free, °rid: *He has cleared his conscience of any responsibility in the matter.* **28** °leap *or* °jump over, vault: *She cleared the fence easily.* **29** Also, **clear up:** °settle, °discharge, °pay, °square, °defray, °satisfy: *The company has cleared all its debts.* **30 clear off** *or* **out:** °leave, °depart, decamp, °go *or* °run off, °get out, °withdraw, *Slang* °beat it, scram, *Taboo Brit* sod off, *Chiefly Australian* °shoot through, *US and Canadian* take a (run-out) °powder: *I told them to clear off and stop bothering me.* **31 clear up: a** °eliminate, °remove, °settle; °clarify: *I hope we can clear up any misunderstanding between us.* **b** °tidy (up), °neaten (up), put *or* set in °order, clear: *I'll clear up after dinner.*
—*n.* **32 in the clear:** °innocent, not guilty; exonerated, forgiven, absolved; unburdened, disburdened, unencumbered, °free: *The other chap confessed, leaving me in the clear.*

clearance *n.* **1** °space, °gap, °hole, °interval, °separation, °room, °margin, °leeway, °allowance: *You must allow a clearance of 2 millimetres.* **2** °approval, °endorsement, authorization, °consent; °licence, °leave, °permission: *He cannot get security clearance with his prison record.*

clearly *adv.* **1** distinctly; starkly, plainly: *With spectacles, I can see everything more clearly.* **2** °evidently, °apparently, °manifestly, °obviously, certainly, °definitely, °positively, unequivocally, unquestionably, incontestably, without °doubt, °undoubtedly, indubitably, demonstrably, °absolutely, °utterly: *His statement is clearly untrue.* **3** audibly, distinctly, understandably: *I wish she would speak more clearly.*

cleave *v.* °split, °divide, °cut, °cut *or* °chop *or* hew in two *or* asunder, bisect, halve, °separate, °slit, rive: *With a mighty blow the log was cleaved cleanly in two.*

clergyman *n.* **1** ecclesiastic, churchman, cleric, reverend, °divine, man of the °cloth, °holy man, °priest, °minister, chaplain, °father, rabbi,

°pastor, parson, rector, vicar, dean, canon, presbyter, prebendary or prebend, deacon, sexton, sacristan, guru, ayatollah, imam: *In his black frock coat he looked like a clergyman.* **2** °monk, friar, °brother, monastic, °religious: *A clergyman was responsible for his religious education.* **3** °preacher, gospeller, evangelist, revivalist, °missionary, sermonizer: *She was moved by the clergyman's sermon.*

clerical *adj.* **1** ecclesiastical, churchly, °pastoral, sacerdotal, °priestly, hieratic, rabbinical, ministerial, monastic, apostolic, prelatic, papal, pontifical, episcopal, canonical: *He was wearing his clerical vestments.* **2** white-collar, °office, °professional, secretarial, stenographic, accounting, bookkeeping: *He runs the shop and his wife has the clerical responsibilities.*

clever *adj.* **1** skilled, °talented, °skilful, adroit, °dexterous, °gifted, °agile, °quick-witted, °intelligent, °perceptive, discerning, °sharp, sharp-witted, °adept, °able, *Colloq* brainy: *She was very clever at mathematics.* **2** °shrewd, cunning, guileful, canny, °artful, °crafty, °sly, °wily, °foxy: *It was a clever move to sound out the chairman before the meeting.* **3** °intelligent, °wise, °sage, sagacious; °ingenious, °original, °resourceful, Daedalian, inventive, °creative, °smart, °imaginative: *It was very clever of her to memorize the record-book for the competition.* **4** deft, adroit, nimble-fingered, °dexterous, °handy, °skilful: *The old woman is clever with her hands.*

cliché *n.* stereotype, bromide, trite saying, old °saw or °maxim, °truism, platitude, commonplace, banality, *Colloq* chestnut: *The report was full of clichés and convinced no one.*

client *n.* °customer, °patron, shopper; °patient: *She opened a law practice and already has a number of clients.*

clientele *n.* °clients, °patrons, °customers; °custom, °business, °trade, °patronage, following: *What sort of clientele do you expect to attract?*

cliff *n.* °precipice, °bluff, escarpment, scarp, °crag, rock-face, cuesta, °scar or Scots scaur: *The commandos are trained to scale a 100-foot cliff.*

climate *n.* **1** °weather, *Literary* clime: *We are retiring to the Maldives because we like a sunny climate.* **2** °atmosphere, ambience or ambiance, °air; °feeling, °mood, °aura, °milieu, °feel: *In the present climate of opinion, we'd best delay introducing the bill.*

climax *n.* **1** culmination, °height, °acme, apex, °summit, °zenith, apogee, °peak, °high °point, °maximum, °supreme moment: *The war reached its climax at the battle of Arbela.* **2** turning-point, °crisis, crossroads: *The climax of the play occurs in the third act.* **3** orgasm: *She told her psychiatrist that she had never reached a climax with her husband.* —*v.* **4** culminate, °peak, °crest, come to a °head: *The week's events climaxed with the presentation of the gold medal.*

climb *v.* **1** Also, **climb up**: °mount, ascend, °go up, °scale, °shin (up), clamber up, *US* shinny (up): *In one of the games we had to climb a greased pole. Two Japanese teams have climbed Mount Everest.* **2** °creep, °trail, °twine; °grow: *The ivy has climbed all over the garden wall.* **3** °rise, °arise, ascend, °go up, °mount; °advance: *Watch the smoke climb into the sky.* **4 climb along**: °creep, °edge, clamber, °crawl, inch: *The cat burglar climbed along the ledge till he reached the window.*

5 climb down: **a** °descend, °go down: *We shall need a rope to climb down from here.* **b** Usually, **climb down from**: °retreat (from), °withdraw (from), back away (from), °give up, °abandon, °renounce: *He has climbed down from his earlier position regarding women in the priesthood.* —*n.* **6** °grade, °incline, °route, °pitch; ascent; descent: *It was a steep climb to Camp Four.*

clinch *v.* **1** °secure, °settle, °confirm, °determine, conclude, °dispose of, °complete, °wind up, °finalize, *Colloq* °sew up: *He clinched the argument by resigning.* —*n.* **2** °close quarters, °hug, °clasp, °embrace; °cuddle: *The boxers went into a clinch to regain their breath.*

clincher *n.* finishing °touch, °pay-off, punch-line, coup de grâce, °final or crowning °blow: *The point about saving costs proved to be a clincher, and we were given the go-ahead.*

cling *v.* **1** °stick, adhere, °attach, °fasten, °fix: *The detectives found that one of the victim's hairs had clung to the suspect's lapel.* **2** °favour, be or °remain °devoted or °attached to, °embrace, °hang on to, °retain, °keep, °cherish: *He still clung to his old-fashioned notions of honour.* **3 cling together** or **to one another**: °embrace, °hug, °cleave to one another, °clasp one another, °clutch one another, °hold (°fast) to one another, °grasp one another: *The children clung together in the darkness.*

clip¹ *v.* **1** °clasp, °fasten, °fix, °attach, °hold, °clinch; °staple: *Please clip these papers together.* —*n.* **2** °clasp, fastener: *That clip isn't strong enough to hold all these papers.*

clip² *v.* **1** °trim (off), °lop (off), °cut (off), crop, bob, °snip: *The barber clipped my hair short. Roger has clipped two seconds off the record.* **2** °shorten, °reduce, °abbreviate, °diminish, °cut (°short): *The film was clipped by fifteen minutes for television. In her rapid-fire way of speaking, she clipped each word.* **3** °strike, °hit, °punch, smack, °box, cuff, whack, *Colloq* wallop, clout; *Slang* sock: *He was clipped on the jaw and knocked out.* **4** °cheat, °swindle, bilk, overcharge, *Slang* rook: *They clipped him out of a week's wages. She was clipped for a ten per cent 'service fee'.* —*n.* **5** °segment, °interval, °section, °part, °portion, °extract, °cutting, °excerpt, °bit, snippet, °scrap, °fragment: *We were shown a film clip of the cheese-making process.* **6** °blow, cuff, °punch, °hit, °strike, smack, whack, °box, *Colloq* wallop, clout; *Slang* sock: *She gave him a clip at the side of the head and he went down.* **7** °pace, °rate, °speed: *I was riding along at a good clip when my horse shied and I was thrown off.*

clique *n.* °set, coterie, °crowd, °circle, °group: *There was the usual clique from the Sales Department standing round the bar.*

cloak *n.* **1** °mantle, °cape, °robe, °wrap, poncho; °coat, overcoat: *She pulled her cloak around her in the chill night air.* **2** °mantle, concealment, °cover, °screen, °shroud, °veil: *He stole away under the cloak of darkness.* —*v.* **3** °conceal, °hide, °mask, °screen, °veil, °shroud, °cover up; °disguise: *All of the spies' activities were cloaked in secrecy.*

clod *n.* **1** °lump, °mass, °gob, °wad, hunk, chunk; °piece of sod or °turf; *Colloq* glob: *A clod of earth was stuck between the spikes of my golf shoes.* **2** idiot, °fool, °dolt, blockhead, simpleton, dunce, °dope, oaf, Neanderthal, lout, ass, °boor, °clown, ninny, ninny-hammer, bumpkin, clodhopper, *Slang* vegetable, *US and Canadian* °jerk: *He felt a bit of a clod standing there with no idea which way to go.*

clog v. °hamper, °encumber, °impede; °obstruct, °choke (up), °block, congest, °jam: *The road was clogged with returning holiday-makers. A piece of orange peel had clogged the sink drain.*

close v. **1** °shut, close up, °seal; close off, °lock, padlock, °secure, °fasten: *I closed my eyes. Please close the door behind you.* **2** make °inaccessible, °shut, *Chiefly US* place off limits: *The Bodleian Library will be closed for a week.* **3** conclude, °end, °finish, °complete, bring to a close or an °end, °terminate, °climax, *Colloq* °wind up: *A brilliant flourish closes the first movement of the symphony.* **4** conclude, °sign, °seal, °make, °settle, °clinch, °agree, °arrange, °work out, °establish: *Union and management closed a deal, and the strike was called off.* **5** Also, **close down**: °discontinue, °terminate, °stop, °suspend, °shut down, go out of business, °cease operations, close (up), *Colloq* °wind up, °shut up shop, put up the shutters: *Competition from the supermarket forced the greengrocer to close down.* **6** Also, **close off**: °seal, make °inaccessible, °shut (off), °obstruct, obturate: *This wing of the museum has been closed off temporarily.* **7 close one's eyes to**: °ignore, °overlook, °disregard: *You have always closed your eyes to his faults.* **8 close up**: **a** close (down), °shut (up), °lock up: *It's time to close up for the night.* **b** close, °come or °draw or °bring together, °unite, °join; °connect: *We closed up ranks and stood at attention.*
—adj. **9** °near; adjacent, proximate, proximal: *He claims to have had a close encounter with an extraterrestrial. There certainly is a close resemblance between Kathy and her daughter.* **10** closed, °shut (up), °fixed, °fast, °secure, °tight: *The hostages spent a month in close confinement.* **11** °dense, °compact, °tight, °cramped, compressed, °tiny, minuscule, °minute: *I could hardly read the close writing on the matchbox.* **12** °stuffy, °musty, °stale, fusty, confining, °oppressive, airless, unventilated, confined, stifling, suffocating: *They locked me in a room that was so close I could hardly breathe.* **13** °nearly °equal or °even, close-matched, neck and neck, °tight: *It was a close race, but Flanagan won by a hair.* **14** °careful, assiduous, °precise, °detailed, concentrated, °strict, rigorous, °minute, searching, °attentive, °alert, °intent, °intense, °thorough, °painstaking: *Close analysis has revealed that the handwriting is that of a left-handed adult.* **15** °attached, °intimate, °devoted, °familiar, inseparable, close-knit, °solid, °confidential; °fast; *Colloq* °thick, °thick as thieves, pally, *US and Canadian* palsy-walsy, buddy-buddy: *They are a very close family. She and her father are very close.* **16** °private, °privy, °secret, °guarded, closely °guarded, °confidential: *Although it should have been a close secret, the press managed to get hold of it.* **17** °secretive, °reticent, °taciturn, °reserved, close-mouthed, °tight-lipped, °silent: *She is very close about the whereabouts of her husband.* **18** stingy, °mean, °miserly, niggardly, tight-fisted, close-fisted, parsimonious, °penurious, penny-pinching, cheese-paring, Scrooge-like, skinflinty, *Colloq* near, *Brit* mingy: *He's so close he charges his own mother rent.* **19** °secluded, concealed, °shut up or away, °hidden: *The fugitives decided to lie close till nightfall.*
—adv. **20** °near, in the °neighbourhood (of), not °far (from), adjacent (to); alongside; at °hand, °nearby, close by: *The murder took place close to my house. I'm frightened, so please stay close by.* **21 close to** or **on** or **onto**: °nearly, °almost, °about, °practically, °approximately, nigh unto, approaching: *For close to two thousand years the site lay untouched.*
—n. **22** °end, °termination, conclusion, °finish, °completion, cessation; culmination: *By the close of trading, share prices had risen again.*

cloth n. **1** °fabric, °material, textile, *Chiefly Brit* °stuff: *The curtains are made of cloth, not plastic.* **2 the cloth**: the clergy, the (°religious) °ministry, the priesthood: *He is a man of the cloth.*

clothe v. **1** °dress, attire, garb, °apparel, °outfit, °fit out or up, accoutre or *US also* accouter, *Brit* °kit out or up, *Colloq* tog up or out: *He earns barely enough to clothe and feed his family.* **2** endow, °invest, caparison, endue: *They tried to clothe their transactions with the raiment of honesty.*

clothes n.pl. clothing, °apparel, attire, °wear, °dress, °garments, raiment, °wardrobe, °outfit, °ensemble, vestment(s), *Old-fashioned* duds, *Colloq* togs, °gear, °get-up, *Slang* glad °rags, *Brit* clobber; *Slang US* (set of) threads: *Put on some old clothes and make yourself comfortable.*

clown n. **1** jester, °fool, °zany, °comic, °comedian, comedienne, funny man or woman: *Of all the performers at the circus, I like the clowns best.* **2** buffoon, °boor, °rustic, yahoo, oaf, lout, °clod, °dolt, bumpkin, clodhopper, °provincial, °peasant, yokel, *Colloq* lummox; *Slang chiefly US* °jerk; *Old-fashioned* galoot or galloot; *Slang chiefly US and Canadian* hick: *That's the kind of language we expect to hear only from the most ignorant clowns.*
—v. **3** Often, **clown around** or **about**: °fool (around), play the °fool, horse around or about, °caper, cut a °caper or capers, engage in °high jinks or hijinks, *US* cut up, cut didos: *Stop clowning around with that hose and help water the garden.*

club n. **1** cudgel, bat, bludgeon, mace, billy, truncheon, baton, °staff, °stick; cosh, *Chiefly US and Canadian* blackjack: *The blow from the club required six stitches.* **2** °association, °society, °organization, °fraternity, sorority, °fellowship, °brotherhood, sisterhood, °federation, °union, guild, °lodge, °alliance, °league, °order, consortium, °company: *Our sailing club holds an annual race.* **3** clubhouse: *The society's club is near Pall Mall.* **4** nightclub, °cabaret, *Colloq* nightspot: *After the theatre, we stopped at Oscar's club for a nightcap.*
—v. **5** °beat, cudgel, bludgeon, bat, °belabour; °lambaste, baste, thrash, trounce: *The guerrillas caught the traitor and clubbed him to death.* **6** Often, **club together**: °band or °join or °league (together), °team (up), °join forces, °combine, °ally, °associate, confederate, °cooperate: *We clubbed together to purchase the antique clock.*

clue n. **1** °hint, °suspicion, °trace, intimation, °suggestion, °inkling, °indication, °pointer, °lead, °tip, tip-off, °evidence, °information, °advice; °key, °answer, °indicator: *There is no clue pointing to anyone in particular. Any clue to the solution of the mystery disappeared in the fire.*
—v. **2 clue someone in** or *Brit also* **up**: °hint, °suggest, °imply, °intimate, °inform, °advise, °indicate: *She clued us in as to who might have sent the letter.*

clump n. **1** °lump, °mass, °clod, chunk, hunk, °wad, °gob, Colloq glob: As the soup cooled, clumps of fat formed on its surface. **2** °bunch, °cluster; °thicket, copse; wood, Chiefly Brit spinney: The deer disappeared into a clump of trees. That clump will provide good cover for us.
—v. **3** °lump, °mass, °heap, °collect, °gather, °bunch, °pile: She wore her hair clumped on top her head.

clumsy adj. °awkward, ungainly, °unwieldy, °ungraceful, gawky, maladroit, unhandy, unskilful, °inept, bungling, bumbling, cloddish, ox-like, bovine, uncoordinated, lubberly, oafish; gauche, Colloq butter-fingered, ham-fisted, ham-handed, cack-handed: He made a clumsy attempt to put the key in the lock. She gave a clumsy excuse for being in the bank after hours.

cluster n. **1** °collection, °bunch, °clutch, tuft, °bundle: Notice that cluster of flowers near the top of the plant. **2** °collection, °bunch, °group, °knot, °body, °band, °company, °gathering, °crowd, °assembly, congregation, °throng, °flock, assemblage, °swarm: A cluster of well-wishers stood talking with the minister.
—v. **3** °collect, °bunch, °group, °band, °gather, °crowd, congregate, °throng, °assemble, °accumulate, °mass, aggregate: A number of people clustered round the new sculpture. Why do these flowers cluster at this tree?

clutch v. **1** °seize, °snatch, °grab, °grasp, °take or °lay °hold of; °hold; US °snag: She clutched feebly at the rope before losing her grip and plunging into the abyss below. He clutched the child to his bosom.
—n. **2 clutches: a** °grasp, °hold; °embrace: We watched as the gazelle deftly eluded the cheetah's clutches. **b** °influence, °control, °power, °domination, dominance, °possession: He fell into the clutches of the Triads.

clutter n. **1** °mess, °litter, °jumble; °mishmash, olla podrida, °confusion, °hash, gallimaufry, °hotchpotch or US also hodgepodge, °muddle, farrago, °medley: I must insist that you clear up the clutter in your room at once. That philosophy is a clutter of competing ideas. **2** °confusion, °tangle, °chaos, disarray: The town was a clutter of narrow, crooked, dark, and dirty lanes.
—v. **3** Often, **clutter up**: °mess up, °litter, °strew, make a °shambles of: Please don't clutter up my desk with newspaper cuttings.

coach n. **1** °carriage, bus, omnibus, motor °coach: The sightseeing coach broke down near Exeter. **2** °tutor, trainer, °instructor, °teacher, mentor, Brit crammer: Her voice coach says she's not yet ready for grand opera.
—v. **3** °tutor, °train, °instruct, °guide, °direct, °drill, °prepare, °prompt, °school, °exercise, Brit °cram: Her lawyers have coached her in what to say in court.

coagulate v. congeal, gel, °jell, clot, curdle, °set: The white of the egg had coagulated, but the yolk was still runny.

coarse adj. **1** °rough, uneven, °scratchy, °prickly, bristly; °crude, rough-hewn, unfinished, °unrefined: He has a three-day coarse growth of beard. The surface on the furniture is still too coarse. **2** °rude, °boorish, loutish, °crude, °ill-mannered, unpolished, °rough, uncouth, °impolite, uncivil, °unrefined: Nigel's behaviour is coarse, and he spits when he talks. **3** °rude, °indecent, °improper, indelicate, °obscene, °lewd, °vulgar, °gross, smutty, °dirty, °filthy, °foul, °offensive, °lascivious, ribald, °bawdy; foul-mouthed: Don't use that kind of coarse language with me. **4** °inferior, low-quality, second-rate, °shoddy, °tawdry, trashy; kitschy: That shop stocks only the coarsest merchandise.

coast n. **1** seaside, seashore, shore, °sea-coast, strand, °beach, littoral, coastline, seaboard: Be careful of rocks if you sail near the coast.
—v. **2** °glide, °skim, °slide, °sail: The children coasted down the hill on the toboggan.

coat n. **1** overcoat, greatcoat; jacket, anorak, parka, Brit cagoule, Colloq Brit cag: Put on your coat, it's cold out. **2** coating, layer, covering, overlay; °film: Two coats of paint ought to be enough. There was a coat of dust on everything.
—v. **3** °cover, °paint, °spread: We coated the floor with three layers of varnish.

coax v. °persuade, °urge, °wheedle, °cajole, °beguile, °charm, inveigle, °jolly, °manipulate: She coaxed me into spending a weekend with her at Blackpool.

cocky adj. °overconfident, °arrogant, °haughty, °conceited, °self-important, °egotistical, °proud, °vain, prideful, cocksure, saucy, °cheeky, °brash: Since she won the beauty contest, Claire has been entirely too cocky.

coddle v. °pamper, °baby, cosset, mollycoddle, °indulge, °humour, °spoil, Brit cocker: Give him a cold bath and don't coddle him so much.

code n. **1** law(s), °regulation(s), °rule(s), jurisprudence, jus canonicum 'canon law', jus civile 'civil law', jus divinum 'divine law', jus gentium 'universal law', jus naturale 'natural law', corpus juris, pandect, lex non scripta 'common law, unwritten law', lex scripta 'statute law': In the present code there is no statute that forbids keeping a pet gnu. **2** °cipher or cypher, cryptogram: Our agents send all their messages in code. **3** °system, °practice(s), °convention(s), °standard(s), criterion (criteria), °principle(s), °rule(s), °maxim(s), °custom(s), °pattern(s), °structure, °tradition(s), °organization, °protocol, orthodoxy: Our code of behaviour is completely foreign to the islanders.
—v. **4** encode, encipher or encypher, encrypt: It took an hour to code the information.

coffin n. °casket, °pall, (pine) °box; sarcophagus: The coffin was slowly lowered into the grave.

cog n. **1** tooth, gear-tooth, sprocket, ratchet: Stripping the gears means breaking the cogs off them. **2** underling, °pawn, °subordinate, nonentity, °zero, cipher or cypher, °nothing, °nobody, °small fry: He's only a small cog in the organization—we're after the big wheel himself.

cognizance n. °knowledge, awareness, °perception, °notice, consciousness, mindfulness: They ran the gambling den with the full cognizance of the police.

coherent adj. **1** °consistent, °orderly, organized, well-organized, °logical, °rational, °reasonable, well-ordered: The MP set forth a coherent argument against an excise tax. **2** understandable, °sensible, comprehensible, °intelligible, articulate, lucid, °clear: He was so frightened and hysterical that he was unable to tell a coherent story.

cohort n. **1** troop, °squad, squadron, °platoon, brigade, °unit, cadre, wing, legion, °detachment, contingent: Ten select Roman cohorts *were sent against the Mitanni.* **2** °company, °band, °group, °faction, °set, °body, °corps: *She was a member of a small cohort of suffragettes.* **3** °companion, confederate, °accomplice, °associate, °fellow, °comrade, °friend, confrevre: *Gerald then arrived with a few of his cohorts.*

coil *v.* **1** °wind, °twist, °snake, °wrap, enwrap, °spiral, *Nautical* °fake *or* °flake (down): *The rope is coiled round a capstan.*
—*n.* **2** winding(s), °circle(s), °loop, whorl, °spiral, helix, °twist: *His foot caught in the coil of rope and he was carried overboard.*

coin *n.* **1** specie, °money, currency; °change, °cash, °silver: *I have only a few coins in my pocket. As he had no notes he had to pay in coin.*
—*v.* **2** °mint, °stamp: *The US government has stopped coining silver dollars.* **3** °invent, °create, °conceive, °originate, °start, °make up, °fabricate, °frame, concoct, °think *or* °dream up: *James Joyce coined the word 'quark'.* **4 coin it in** *or US only* **coin money**: °earn *or* make °money, become °wealthy, °enrich oneself, *Colloq* °rake it in: *Those rock stars really coin it in from their record sales.*

coincide *v.* °fall *or* °come *or* °go together, °line up, co-occur, °correspond, synchronize, °match, °tally, °agree, (be in) °accord, °equal, jibe: *This year, Easter and Passover coincide. The southern boundary coincides with the Thames.*

coincidence *n.* **1** co-occurrence, simultaneity, correspondence, concurrence, consistency, contemporaneity, synchronism, synchrony, coextension, coevality, coinstantaneity: *The coincidence of twelve by the clock with noon by the sundial is exact only four times in the year.* **2** congruence, °matching, jibing, °agreement, concord, °accord, °harmony, accordance, conformity, congruity, consonance, concomitance: *Fortunately there was a coincidence of views on the main issues.* **3** °chance °occurrence, °fluke, °chance, °accident, °luck, fortuity, fortuitousness, *US and Canadian* happenstance: *By sheer coincidence, I met my next-door neighbour on the train from Glasgow.*

coincidental *adj.* °chance, °lucky *or* unlucky, fortuitous, °accidental, unexpected, unpredicted, unpredictable, °unforeseen: *It was entirely coincidental that we were on the same train.*

cold *adj.* **1** chill, °chilly, frosty, °icy, °keen, nippy, °freezing, °frigid, ice-cold, stone-cold, °bitter, bitter cold, °raw, °biting, biting-cold, numbing, gelid; °wintry, hibernal, brumal; arctic, glacial, °polar, hyperborean *or* hyperboreal, Siberian: *It was so cold that the canal had completely frozen over.* **2** °chilly, chilled; unheated, heatless: *The room is cold; we'd better put the heating on.* **3** °indifferent, apathetic, °chilly, chilling, °cool, °icy, °dispassionate, °unsympathetic, °aloof, unresponsive, spiritless, °frigid, unfriendly, uncordial, °lukewarm; °cold-blooded, insensitive, uncaring, unemotional, undemonstrative, °reserved, °unmoved, °callous, °remote, °distant, standoffish, °unapproachable, stony-hearted, emotionless, unfeeling, °cold-hearted: *My ideas received rather a cold reception. Because she had offended him, she was quite cold to her.* **4** depressing, cheerless, chilling, °gloomy, dispiriting, deadening, disheartening, °bleak, °dismal, discouraging: *The*

sweat stood out on his brow in cold apprehension. **5** unmoving, °stale, trite, stereotyped; °dead: *The coldest word was once a glowing new metaphor.* **6** °weak, °faint, °stale, °old, °dead: *The trail of the tiger had grown cold.* **7** °unprepared, unready: *She hadn't studied and went into the exam cold.* **8** Often, **getting cold**: °far, °distant, °remote, off the °track: *As I searched for the weapon, I felt I was getting cold the further I went from the kitchen.*
—*n.* **9** coldness, frigidity, iciness: *Last winter, the cold killed off many of our shrubs.* **10** head *or* chest *or* common cold, influenza, ague, (la *or* the) grippe, *Technical* coryza, gravedo, *Colloq* sniffles, the flu, °bug, sneezles and wheezles: *I caught a cold waiting for you in the rain.*
—*adv.* **11** °completely, °thoroughly, °entirely, °absolutely, unhesitatingly, °promptly, °immediately, unreservedly, abruptly: *His application to join the police was turned down cold.*

cold-blooded *adj.* **1** *Technical* poikilothermic *or* poikilothermal: *Reptiles are cold-blooded.* **2** unexcited, unemotional, °cool, unimpassioned, unfeeling, °callous, °thick-skinned, insensitive, °heartless, uncaring, °stony, °steely, stony-hearted, °cold-hearted, imperturbable, °unmoved, °indifferent, unresponsive, °unsympathetic, apathetic, °dispassionate: *The murder appeared to be the act of a cold-blooded killer.* **3** °cruel, °brutal, °savage, °inhuman, barbarous, °vicious, barbaric, °merciless, pitiless, °ruthless: *They were victims of a cold-blooded policy of repatriation.*

cold-hearted *adj.* insensitive, °unsympathetic, apathetic, °indifferent, unfeeling, uncaring, °callous, °thick-skinned, °cold, °cool, °frigid, hard-hearted, °heartless, °unkind, °thoughtless, unthoughtful, uncharitable, °ruthless, pitiless, °unmerciful, °cruel, °merciless, °mean: *Putting that kitten out on a snowy night is the most cold-hearted thing you ever did.*

collaborate *v.* °cooperate, °join (forces), °work together, °team up: *We collaborated in writing both the lyrics and music.*

collapse *v.* **1** °fall (down *or* in *or* °apart), °crumple, °cave in, deflate, °crumble, °tumble down, °break down, °go: *When he opened the valve, the balloon collapsed. Hundreds of buildings collapsed in the earthquake.* **2** °fail, (come to an) °end, °fall through, peter out, °disintegrate, °dissolve, °fall flat, °founder, come to nothing *or* naught *or* nought, °break up *or* down, °decline, °diminish, °disappear, °evaporate, go up in smoke, go bankrupt, °go under, *Brit* go to the °wall, *Colloq* °fizzle out: *After the imprisonment of their leader, the entire movement collapsed. Owing to the recession, many businesses collapsed.* **3** °pass out, °faint, °drop, *Colloq* keel over; *Old-fashioned or literary* swoon: *He collapsed on-stage and they took him to his dressing-room.* **4** °break down (mentally), have a (nervous) °breakdown, go to °pieces, °come *or* °fall apart, *Colloq* °crack up, *US also* °crack: *She finally collapsed from overwork and is now in a sanatorium.*
—*n.* **5** cave-in, °breakdown: *The collapse of the house was attributed to termites.* **6** °failure, °downfall, °ruin; disappearance, disintegration, °dissolution, bankruptcy: *Will he be able to survive the collapse of his financial empire?* **7** (°mental)

°breakdown, °prostration, *Colloq* crack-up: *He suffered a mental collapse when his family was killed in a car crash.*

colleague *n.* team-mate, fellow-worker, co-worker; °associate, °comrade, °ally, confrevre, °mate, consociate, *Chiefly Brit and Australian* °mate, *US* buddy: *I have asked some of my colleagues from the office to join us for dinner.*

collect *v.* **1** °gather (together), °get *or* °bring *or* °come together, °amass, °accumulate, °assemble, °compile, °pile up, °heap up, °rack up; convene, congregate, °converge, °rally, °meet: *A crowd had collected outside the mayor's home. They were collecting evidence for their case.* **2** °summon (up), °draw (up), °muster, °gather (up), °concentrate: *She collected all her courage to ask for an increase in salary.*

collected *adj.* °calm, °serene, controlled, °cool, °sedate, composed, °nonchalant, °poised, unruffled, unperturbed, at °ease, °comfortable, °tranquil, unexcited; imperturbable: °confident: *Considering what she's just gone through, Tanya seems quite collected.*

collection *n.* **1** collecting, °gathering, solicitation, garnering, gleaning, °accumulation, amassment, aggregation, *Colloq Brit* whip-round: *The collection of donations in this neighbourhood is going well.* **2** °accumulation, °hoard, °store, assemblage, omnium gatherum; anthology, chrestomathy: *Would you like to come up to see my collection of etchings? They have published some very interesting collections.*

collector *n.* gatherer, accumulator; connoisseur, art-lover: *The rent collector is coming tomorrow. We are collectors of paintings by unknown artists.*

collide *v.* **1** °crash, °strike *or* °dash together: *The cars collided at the bridge.* **2 collide with**: °crash into, smash into, °run into, °bump into, smack into: *The car collided with the bus at the crossing.*

collision *n.* smash-up, smash, °crash, °wreck, °pile-up, *Colloq Brit* prang; *US* crack-up: *There has been a major collision on the Tring road.*

colossal *adj.* **1** °huge, °vast, °enormous, °gigantic, °giant, mammoth, °massive, gargantuan, Cyclopean, Brobdingnagian, °immense, °monumental, titanic, Herculean, elephantine, °jumbo: *Mystery surrounds the exact methods used in moving the colossal stones used in the pyramids.* **2** spectacular, stupendous, wonderful, awe-inspiring, staggering, °extraordinary, °incredible, °overwhelming, °unbelievable: *The old Hollywood extravaganzas were described by press agents as 'colossal'. I think you have made a colossal mistake in failing to hire Cynthia.*

colour *n.* **1** °hue, °tint, tincture, °shade, °tone, °cast, tinge, pigmentation; pigment, dye: *The colours of the curtains don't match the wall.* **2 colours**: **a** °flag, ensign, °standard, °pennant, °banner, burgee: *The sloop hoisted the British colours.* **b** °device, badge, °emblem, insigne *or pl* insignia, °symbol(s), °identification; °identity, °appearance, °face; loyalties: *The investigators found he'd been operating under false colours. She has shown her true colours at last.*
—*v.* **3** °tint, dye, °stain, °paint, crayon, tincture, tinge; pigment: *These sections will stand out better if you colour them red.* **4** °influence, °affect, °distort, °falsify, °taint, °warp, °twist, °slant, °pervert, °bias: *Jealousy colours his opinion of his*

supervisor. **5** °blush, redden, °flush: *After their affair, she visibly coloured whenever they met.* **6** °falsify, °distort, °misrepresent, °disguise, °mask, °conceal: *He feigns confusion when he wishes to colour his true feelings.*

colourless *adj.* **1** °pale, pallid, blanched, °white; °wan, ashen, sallow, waxen, °sickly, washed out: *You could see from his colourless complexion that he had not been outside for months.* **2** °dull, °drab, uninteresting, vacuous, °vapid, °lifeless, °boring, °tedious, spiritless, °dry, dry-as-dust, °dreary, characterless, insipid, °bland, namby-pamby, °lacklustre, uninspiring, uninspired: *She has led a colourless life. Few people have so colourless a personality as he.*

combat *n.* **1** °fight, °encounter, °engagement, duel, °battle, °conflict, °war, warfare; °skirmish: *The two men were locked in single combat.* **2** °struggle, °contest, °strife, °controversy, °dispute, °quarrel, °disagreement, altercation, °vendetta, °feud: *There was endless combat between father and son.* **3** °opposition, °difference, confrontation: *The combat between good and evil can never end.* **4** °action, fighting, °battle, °war: *He was in combat on three occasions. Have you seen any combat?*
—*v.* **5** °fight, (do) °battle, °war, °clash, contend, duel, joust, °wrestle, come to blows, °spar, °grapple (with): *The soldiers are combating hand to hand in the trenches.* **6** °fight, °struggle *or* °strive against, °contest, °oppose, °defy, enter the lists against, °withstand: *There was broad support for measures to combat crime and pollution.*

combination *n.* **1** °union, conjunction, °mixture, °mix, grouping, °set, array: *They always serve the same combination of foods.* **2** °association, °alliance, coalition, °union, °federation, confederation, °combine, syndication, °syndicate, consortium, °trust, bloc, cartel, °party, °society, °organization, °league, °cabal, °conspiracy, °clique; claque: *When they get together they form an unbeatable combination.* **3** °mixture, °amalgam, °compound, compounding, °mix, °alloy, conglomerate, conglomeration, aggregate, aggregation, °amalgamation, °blend, emulsion, °suspension, colloid °solution, °composition, *Technical* parasynthesis, parathesis; mosaic, °patchwork: *From a combination of ingredients the witch made a slimy love potion. A combination of every colour of the rainbow covered the walls.*

combine *v.* **1** °unite, °unify, °join, °connect, °relate, °link, conjoin, °band, °ally, °associate, °integrate, °merge, °pool: *Combine forces, and we'll win.* **2** °blend, °mix, °amalgamate, °mingle, consolidate, °compound, °incorporate, °put together: *Combine the water, butter, and salt in a saucepan.* **3** °blend, °fuse, synthesize, °bind, °bond, °compound, °unite, coalesce, °come together, commingle, °mingle: *When heated, the silver combines with the chlorine.*

come *v.* **1** °approach, °advance, (draw) °near, °move, *Archaic or literary* draw nigh: *The car came towards us. She has come to me for comforting words. Winter is coming.* **2** °arrive, °appear, make *or* put in an appearance, *Colloq* °blow in, °report (in), °turn *or* °show up, °check in, °sign in, clock on *or* in, °roll in: *Winter has come. When Cora comes, we'll ask her.* **3** °enter: *Come into the light, where I can see you.* **4 come about**:
a °occur, °happen, take °place, come up; befall,

Loosely °transpire: *I cannot imagine how this state of affairs came about.* **b** *Nautical* tack, °go about: *After the marker, come about and hoist the spinnaker.* **5 come across**: **a** °find, °discover, °encounter, °meet (up *or* up with), °run across *or* into, °happen *or* °chance upon *or* on, °hit *or* °light on *or* upon, °stumble upon *or* on, *Colloq* °bump into: *I came across some information about Charles.* **b** °pay (up), °settle; °yield, °give up, °submit: *Frank owes me money but refuses to come across.* **c** be communicated *or* understandable, °penetrate, °sink in: *I am not sure that my points came across.* **6 come along**: °fare, do, °progress, °move along: *How is William coming along at his new school?* **7 come apart**: °disintegrate, °crumble, °fall *or* fly to °pieces, °separate, °break (°apart *or* up *or* down): *The carburettor came apart in my hands.* **8 come at**: °attack, °assault, °charge, °rush (at), °fly at, °descend upon *or* on, *Colloq* °go *or* °make for: *She came at me waving her umbrella.* **9 come by**: **a** °acquire, °obtain, °get, °procure, °find, °take *or* °get °possession of, °get *or* °lay °hold of, °get *or* °lay *or* °put (one's) hands *or* US *also* °fingers on; be given: *The tax inspector wondered how she came by such valuable property.* **b** °win, °earn, attain; be awarded: *I came by that trophy fair and square.* **10 come clean**: See clean, 8, above. **11 come down on** *or* **upon**: °pounce on *or* upon, °rebuke, °criticize, revile, °reprimand, °bear down on, °blame: *Mother really came down on us when she discovered who had taken the pie.* **12 come down with**: °succumb to, °contract, °catch, be °stricken *or* afflicted with, °acquire: *He's come down with pneumonia.* **13 come in**: **a** °win, °succeed; *Colloq* °finish (in the money): *My horse came in.* **b** be, °prove, °turn out *or* °prove to be: *Knowing someone on the council can come in handy.* **c** °finish, °end up, °arrive: *Donald came in first in the backstroke.* **d** °enter: *Don't come in, I'm dressing.* **14 come off**: **a** °occur, °happen, come to °pass, take °place, *Loosely* °transpire: *I doubt that the performance will ever come off.* **b** °emerge, °result as: *We came off the winners in Saturday's game.* **15 come out**: **a** be revealed, become °public *or* known *or* common knowledge, °get about *or* around, °get *or* °leak out, °emerge: *The story has come out that he tried to bribe the inspector.* **b** be published *or* issued *or* produced *or* distributed, be shown, be in °print, °première *or* °premiere: *The new edition of the dictionary has just come out.* **c** °end, conclude, °turn out, °terminate, °finish: *How did the chess match come out?* **16 come over**: **a** °go over, °communicate, come across, be communicated, °succeed, be received: *How did my speech come over?* **b** °affect, °influence, °possess: *I can't imagine what's come over Louis.* **c** °visit, °drop *or* °stop by *or* in: *Quentin and his wife came over for dinner last night.* **17 come through**: **a** °recover (from), °recuperate (from), get °well *or* °better: *He came through his operation with flying colours.* **b** conclude *or* °end (up) *or* °finish *or* °wind up successfully *or* satisfactorily, °succeed, °arrive, not °fail *or* °disappoint: *I knew he'd come through.* **18 come to**: **a** °amount to, °add up to, °total, aggregate: *My bill came to more than I had with me.* **b** regain *or* °recover consciousness, °awake(n), °revive, °wake up, come (a)round: *When I came to, I was on the floor with a terrific headache.* **c** °regard, °concern, °relate to,

be a °question of, °involve, be °relevant to, be °involved: *When it comes to real ale, Mario is the expert.* **19 come up**: **a** °arise, °surface, °present itself, be brought up, be broached, come about, °turn up, °rise, *Colloq* crop up: *The question of religion never came up.* **b** °grow, °thrive, °appear: *None of my tulips came up this year.* **c** °rise, °arise: *The moon came up just as the sun was setting.*

comedian *n.* comedienne, humorist, °comic, °wit, °wag, jokesmith; °clown, buffoon, °funny man *or* woman, funster, jester, °fool, °zany, °merry andrew: *The new comedian at the variety show is very funny.*

comely *adj.* good-looking, °pretty, °bonny, °lovely, °fair, °beautiful, °handsome, °attractive, appealing, °wholesome, winsome, °buxom: *She is a comely woman who has had no shortage of suitors.*

come-on *n.* °lure, °attraction, °enticement, °inducement, °temptation, bait; loss-leader: *The free glassware is a come-on to buy a tankful of petrol.*

comfort *v.* **1** °console, °solace, soothe, assuage, °reassure, °relieve, hearten, °cheer, °gladden: *It might comfort you to know that Roderick has recovered completely. He comforted her when the pain became unbearable.* —*n.* **2** consolation, °solace, °relief, °cheer: *I derived some comfort from knowing that my attacker had been caught.* **3** °ease, °luxury, °security, °abundance, °plenty, opulence: *Cordelia lived out her days in comfort after inheriting a fortune from her aunt.*

comfortable *adj.* **1** at °ease, °easy, °tranquil, °serene, °relaxed, contented, untroubled, undisturbed: *After the operation, the nurses did everything they could to make me comfortable.* **2** °well off, °carefree, insouciant, contented, satisfied; self-satisfied, complacent, °smug: *They don't have a lot of money, but they're comfortable enough.* **3** °likeable, °easy, congenial, °amiable, °cordial, °warm, °pleasant, °agreeable, enjoyable, relaxing: *Daphne is a very comfortable sort of person to be with.* **4** °suitable, °acceptable, °adequate, °satisfactory, °reasonable: *The radio was on very loud, so I turned down the volume to a more comfortable level.*

comic *adj.* **1** °funny, droll, comical, °humorous, °hilarious, side-splitting, mirthful, jocose, jocular, °witty, waggish, °clever, facetious, amusing: *Barry's comic routines have made him a popular performer for years.* —*n.* **2** See **comedian**, above.

command *v.* **1** °order, °direct, °bid, enjoin, °charge, °request, °require, °demand, °instruct; °say, °prescribe, °decree: *What the Queen commands must be done.* **2** °control, °dominate, °have *or* °maintain *or* °wield °authority *or* °control *or* °sway *or* °influence over, °hold °sway over; °lead, °rule, °govern, have under one's °thumb, call the tune; °head (up): *Whoever commands the sea commands the town. He commanded a battalion during the war.* **3** °master, °draw upon *or* on, °control, °summon: *The work required all the skill the sculptor could command.* **4** °attract, °earn; °exact, compel, °demand: *Gunga Din's bravery commanded the respect of the entire regiment.* **5** °dominate, °control, °overlook, °look down on; °have, °enjoy, °possess: *The tower commands a view of the entire valley.* —*n.* **6** °order, °direction, behest, mandate, °charge, °bidding, °instruction: *Your wish is my* *command.* **7** °control, °authority, °power, °sovereignty, °dominion, °regulation, °direction, °management, °government, °oversight, °leadership, °charge, °sway, stewardship, °jurisdiction: *The unit is under the command of the colonel.* **8** mastery, °control, (thorough) °grasp *or* °knowledge: *He has a good command of three languages.*

commemorate *v.* °memorialize, °remember, °celebrate, °observe, °dedicate, consecrate, solemnize, °sanctify, °hallow, °reverence, °revere, °honour, °venerate, pay °tribute *or* °homage to, °salute; °immortalize: *We are here to commemorate deeds of valour and the men who performed them.*

commence *v.* **1** °begin, °enter upon, °start, °initiate, °launch, °embark on *or* upon: *Tomorrow morning, we commence the ascent of Mont Blanc.* **2** °begin, °start, °open: *The ceremonies are about to commence.* **3** °begin, °start, °initiate, °launch, °inaugurate, °establish: *We commenced operations at this plant last year.*

comment *n.* **1** °remark, °reference, animadversion, °note, annotation, °criticism, °exposition, °explanation, °expansion, elucidation, clarification, footnote: *The author's comments on his sources appear in the appendix.* **2** commentary, °opinion, °remark, °view, °observation, °reaction: *The judge's comments are not for publication.* —*v.* **3** °remark, °observe, opine, °say: *He commented that he knew nothing about the minister's private life.* **4 comment on** *or* **about**: °discuss, °talk about, °remark on; °reveal, °expose: *She declined to comment on what had happened the previous night.*

commerce *n.* °trade, °business, mercantilism, marketing, merchandising, °traffic, trafficking: *All commerce consists in the exchange of commodities of equal value. My husband is in commerce.*

commit *v.* **1** °entrust, consign, °transfer, °assign, °delegate, hand over, °deliver, °give; °allot, °pledge, allocate: *They committed the goods to traders with strong distribution facilities.* **2** °sentence, °send (away), confine, °shut up, intern, °put away, °imprison, incarcerate: *The judge committed her to prison. You can be committed for such behaviour.* **3** °perpetrate, do, °perform, °carry out: *They committed murder for money.* **4 commit oneself**: °pledge, °promise, covenant, °agree, °assure, °swear, give one's °word, °vow, °vouchsafe, °engage, °undertake, °guarantee, °bind oneself: *He committed himself to buying the company after seeing the books.*

committee *n.* °council, °board, °cabinet, panel, °body, commission: *They have set up a committee to oversee park planning.*

common *adj.* **1** °ordinary, °everyday, commonplace, °prosaic, °usual, °familiar, °customary, °prevalent, °frequent, run-of-the-mill, °general, °normal, °standard, °conventional, °regular, °routine, °stock, °average, °proverbial, °plain, °simple, garden-variety, common or garden, workaday, °undistinguished, unexceptional: *Intermarriage is a common occurrence among the members of the sect. We planted a common variety of carrot.* **2** °mutual, °reciprocal, °joint, shared: *Our common heritage must be protected.* **3** low-class, °ordinary, °plain, °simple, °plebeian, °bourgeois, proletarian, run-of-the-mill,

°vulgar, °unrefined: *Kings avoid dealing with the common people.* **4** °inferior, low-grade, °mean, °cheap, °base: *He was smoking a cigar of the commonest type.* **5** °public, °general, community, communal, collective, non-private, °universal; °well-known: *The contents of the library are the common property of everyone. Their romance is common knowledge in the village.* **6** trite, °stale, hackneyed, °worn out, °banal, °tired, overused, stereotyped, clichéd, stereotypical: *The term 'yuppie' has become too common to have much impact any longer.*

communicate *v.* **1** make known, °impart, °confer, °transmit, °transfer, °hand on *or* down, °share, °pass on *or* along, °send on, °spread; °tell, divulge, °disclose, °reveal, °announce, promulgate, proffer, °tender, °offer, convey, °deliver, °present, °give, °yield, °supply: *Moral qualities are sometimes thought to be communicated by descent. I communicated to them the information that I had about the missiles.* **2** Also, **communicate with**: be in communication (with), °converse (with), °talk (with), °chat (with); °correspond (with); °associate (with), be in °contact *or* °touch (with), °reach: *Donald and I haven't communicated in years. Instead of communicating with him by telephone, she did so via personal notices in the newspaper.* **3** °get *or* °put across, make understandable; °get through to, °reach, be of one °mind, be in °tune, °relate, be in *or* en °rapport, make oneself understood, *Slang* be *or* vibrate on the same frequency *or* wavelength: *He has difficulty in communicating his ideas to his students. We might talk, but are we communicating?*

compact *adj.* **1** °packed, compacted, closely-knit, condensed, concentrated, consolidated, compressed; °dense, °solid, °firm, °thick: *The sesame seeds are mixed with honey and pressed into a compact block.* **2** °tight, °small, °snug, °little: *The table folds up into a compact unit for storage.* **3** condensed, °terse, laconic, °close, pithy, °succinct, °concise, °brief, compendious, °epigrammatic, aphoristic: *The information is given in a compact form with many abbreviations and symbols.*

companion *n.* **1** °fellow, °associate, °comrade, °colleague, confrère, *Colloq chiefly Brit and Australian* °mate, *US and Canadian* buddy: *For ten years they had been constant companions.* **2** °vade-mecum, °manual, handbook, °guide, °reference °book, enchiridion: *They publish a pocket companion listing the month's events.* **3** °escort, chaperon(e), °attendant, *in Spain, Portugal* duenna: *Aunt Dinah is too old to be alone, so we have engaged a companion for her.*

companionship *n.* °fellowship, camaraderie, comradeship, °company, °society, amity, °friendship, °fraternity: *I often enjoy the companionship of an older person.*

company *n.* **1** °companionship, °society, °fellowship; °attendance, °presence; associates, friends, companions, °comrades: *It was a stormy night, and I was only too glad to have his company. A man is known by the company he keeps.* **2** assemblage, °party, °band, °group, retinue, entourage, °suite, °train, coterie, °ensemble, troop, followers, following, °flock; °circle, °assembly, °gathering, °convention, °body, °crowd, °throng, *Theatre* troupe, °cast, °players, actors and actresses, °performers: *The king arrived with* his company at the gate of the city. *The speaker addressed the assembled company. The company leaves today for a month on the road.* **3** °guest(s); °visitor(s), caller(s): *Are you having company for dinner tonight?* **4** °firm, °business, °house, °concern, °institution, °establishment, °enterprise; proprietorship, partnership, corporation, *Brit* public limited company, plc, *Australian and New Zealand and South African* proprietary limited company, Pty: *The company was founded in 1867.*

compare *v.* **1** °liken, °associate, make (an) analogy (with), °refer, analogize: *How can you compare your collection to mine?* **2 compare with**: °resemble, be *or* °look °like, be on a °par with, be in a °class *or* the same °class with, °correspond, °match, °parallel, °approach, °approximate, °bear *or* °merit °comparison (with); °rival, °compete with *or* against, be a °match for: *Your paintings compare well with Picasso's. The new recordings don't begin to compare with the old ones.* **3** °contrast, °measure against, °weigh, juxtapose, °set °side by °side, °relate, correlate: *We need to compare the results of the two surveys.*

comparison *n.* **1** contrasting, °contrast, juxtaposing, juxtaposition, balancing, °balance, weighing: *His comparison of the candidates is prejudiced.* **2** °match, similarity, °resemblance, °likeness, comparability, °relation, °relationship, commensurability, °kinship, °point of °agreement *or* correspondence: *There is no comparison between a racing car and a family car.*

compartment *n.* °division, °section, °partition, °part, °space, °chamber, bay, alcove, °cell, pigeon-hole, locker, cubby-hole, °niche, cubicle, °slot: *Each specimen is in its own separate compartment.*

compensate *v.* **1** recompense, °make up (for), make °restitution *or* reparation, °offset, °make good, indemnify, °repay, °reimburse, redress, °requite; expiate, °atone, make °amends (for): *The company compensated us for the loss of the car. Arriving at school early today, Gerard, does not compensate for having been late yesterday.* **2** °balance, counterpoise, counterbalance, °equalize, °neutralize, °even (up), °square, °offset: *Deduct six ounces to compensate for the weight of the container.* **3** °pay, remunerate, °reward, °repay, recompense: *Two pounds does not compensate me adequately for an hour's work.*

compensatory *adj.* compensative, remunerative, restitutive *or* restitutory, expiatory, reparative *or* reparatory, piacular: *His huge donation to the church was a compensatory offering for his past sins.*

compete *v.* contend, °vie, °struggle, °strive, °conflict, joust, °fence; °fight, °battle, °clash, °collide: *They are competing to see who will become chairman of the company. These two designs compete with one another for the viewer's attention.*

competent *adj.* **1** °adequate, °suitable, °sufficient, °satisfactory, °acceptable, all °right, *Colloq* °OK *or* okay: *Colquhon will make a competent bureau chief.* **2** °qualified, °fit, °capable, °proficient, °able, °prepared: *Do you really think that fellow Johnson competent to write a dictionary?*

competition *n.* **1** °rivalry, contention, striving, °struggle: *The competition for newspaper circulation becomes keener every day.* **2** °contest, °match, °meet, °game, °tournament, °event; championship: *We entered the competition as underdogs.* **3** See **competitor**, below.

competitor *n.* °rival, °opponent, °competition, °opposition, °adversary; °antagonist, °contestant, contender: *Our main competitor has just announced a new product.*

compile *v.* °collect, °put together, °gather, °accumulate, °assemble, °amass, collate, °organize, °order, systematize; anthologize, °compose: *He has compiled a large butterfly collection. Every year she compiles a volume of the best stories.*

complain *v.* grumble, °moan, °groan, wail, grouse, °carp (at), whimper, °cry, °lament, °bemoan, *Colloq* °gripe, °squawk, grouch, *Brit* whinge, *Slang* °bitch, beef, *US* kick: *What are you complaining about now?*

complaint *n.* grumble, °grievance, grouse, *Colloq* °gripe, squawk, *Slang* beef, *US* kick: *I have no complaints about my treatment while I was in hospital.*

complement *v.* **1** °completion, °perfection, confirmation, finishing °touch, °consummation: *The grand tour was considered the necessary complement of an English education in the 18th century.* **2** °crew, °team, °company, °band, °outfit; °quota, °allowance, quorum: *The regiment's full complement was attained by selecting from among the recruits.*
—*v.* **3** °complete, °perfect, °round out *or* off, °set off, °top off; °flesh out: *The setting was complemented by a huge floral arrangement. His argument was complemented by evidence from rare documents.* **4** °supplement, °enhance, °add to: *These are facts that complement but do not contradict her story.*

complete *adj.* **1** °entire, °whole, °intact, uncut, unbroken, °undivided, °unabridged, °full, undiminished, unabated, unreduced: *The complete works of Dickens are available in paperback. They performed the complete opera, a six-hour marathon.* **2** finished, ended, concluded, °over, done, °accomplished, terminated; settled, executed, performed: *The company's figures are not yet complete. When will your building plan be complete?* **3** °entire, °total, °thorough, °absolute, utter, °unqualified, unmixed, unalloyed, °pure, °unmitigated, °rank: *I attribute the disaster to a complete breakdown of communication, together with the complete incompetence of the site manager.* **4** °perfect, consummate, °exemplary, °ideal, °model, °superior, °superlative, °superb, °faultless, °flawless: *Her dissertation is a work of complete scholarship.*
—*v.* **5** conclude, °finish, °end, °bring to an °end, °accomplish, °achieve, do, *Colloq* °wrap up; °finalize: *He stopped after completing ten circuits of the track. Have you completed the prospectus?* **6** °round out, °round off, °perfect; °crown, culminate: *The unit was completed by the addition of five platoons. A golden cupola completed the top of the dome.*

completely *adv.* **1** °entirely, fully, °quite, °wholly, °totally, °altogether, in toto, °thoroughly, °perfectly, °exactly, °precisely, down to the ground, from °start to °finish, from °beginning to °end, from A to Z, from the word °go, in °full; lock, stock, and barrel; °hook, line, and sinker; heart and soul; °root and branch; en masse: *The currency does not completely* represent the wealth of the country. **2** unqualifiedly, unconditionally, °thoroughly, °utterly, °totally, °absolutely, °quite, °altogether, unreservedly: *He's completely mad if he thinks that thing will fly.* **3** °clearly, °expressly, explicitly, unambiguously, °entirely, fully, °totally, °wholly, altogether, unequivocally, °truly, categorically, flatly: *I am completely in agreement with your policy.*

completion *n.* **1** conclusion, °end, °close, °termination, °fulfilment, culmination, °realization, °accomplishment, °finish: *The completion of the building phase is scheduled for next July.* **2** finishing, finalization, wind-up, finishing-off, completing: *The completion of the house is scheduled for next October.*

complexity *n.* **1** °complication, convolution: *We are finding it difficult to understand the complexities of the agreement.* **2** intricacy, involvement, complicatedness; inscrutability: *The complexity of her theory makes it difficult to interpret.*

complicate *v.* **1** °mix up, °entangle, °snarl, °tangle, confound, °muddle, °confuse: *You only complicate matters by bringing up the question of religion in a discussion of money.* **2** °make °complicated *or* complex, make °involved *or* °intricate, make a °shambles *or* °mess *or* °muddle of, °mess up, *Colloq* °screw up: *The phenomena of tides and currents greatly complicate coastwise navigation.*

complicated *adj.* **1** °involved, °intricate, complex, °compound, °elaborate; °ornate, Byzantine, Daedalian, tangled, knotty, °confused, °labyrinthine: *In birds the eye is a more complicated organ than in our own species. His plan is too complicated to understand.*

complication *n.* **1** °complexity, involvement, intricacy, convolution: *The complications of the diagram make it almost impossible to understand.* **2** °difficulty, °problem, °predicament, °dilemma, °obstacle, °obstruction, °snag, °drawback: *Asking for more money might create complications.*

compliment *n.* **1** °praise, °homage, commendation, °honour, °tribute, °flattery, °bouquet, °favour: *The greatest compliment given to my work has been its success.* **2** Usually, **compliments**: °respects, °regards, good *or* best wishes, felicitations, salutations, °greetings: *I stopped by to pay my compliments to your mother.* —*v.* **3** °honour, °praise, pay °homage *or* °tribute to, commend, °laud, °congratulate, felicitate; °flatter: *She came backstage to compliment me on my performance.*

complimentary *adj.* **1** °laudatory, commendatory, encomiastic, panegyrical, eulogistic, congratulatory, °flattering: *The duke was most complimentary about my sculpture.* **2** °free, gratis, on the °house: *The shoehorn is complimentary when you buy a pair of shoes.*

comply *v.* °agree, °obey, °conform, °consent, acquiesce, concur, °submit, °yield, accede; °accord: *They require your signature and I hope you'll comply.*

compose *v.* **1** constitute, °form, °make (up), be a constituent *or* °ingredient *or* component *or* °element of, be a °part of: *Clouds are composed of countless particles of water.* **2** °write, °create, °imagine, °think up, °originate, °frame, °formulate, °make (up), °author, °devise; contrive; °set to music, °arrange: *He composed the poem while travelling on the Flying Scotsman. That*

symphony was composed in 1873. **3 be composed of**: consist of *or* in, comprise, be formed *or* made (up) of, be constituted of: *The new government is composed of a coalition of three parties.* **4 compose oneself**: °calm (down), °quiet *or* °quieten (down), pacify, °control oneself, get °control of *or* over oneself: *They stopped crying and composed themselves.*

composition *n.* **1** °theme, °essay, article, °paper, °story: *The teacher required each of us to write a thousand-word composition every week.* **2** °combination, °make-up, °structure, °form, °assembly, °set-up, °organization, layout, °arrangement, configuration, shaping; °balance, °harmony, °proportion, °placement, placing, construction: *Notice the composition of the various elements in this painting.* **3** °combination, aggregate, °mixture, °compound, compounding, °mix, formulation, °formula, composite, °amalgam, °alloy, mélange, °medley: *The medication was a composition of several odd ingredients.* **4** °creation, origination, formulation, fashioning: *The composition of the opera was begun in 1837.* **5** °make-up, constitution: *What goes into the composition of brass?*

compound *v.* **1** °put together, °combine, °mix, concoct, °compose, °make (up), °formulate, °blend: *They compound curry powder from different spices.* **2** °blend, °merge, coalesce, °combine, °unite, °fuse °come *or* °go together: *Sometimes two words compound to form one, as in 'ingrown', 'outgrow', and 'uptake'.* **3** °aggravate, °intensify, exacerbate, °heighten, augment, °add to, °worsen, °increase; °enhance, multiply: *Demanding your money back now will only compound the problem.* —*adj.* **4** °intricate, complex, °involved, °complicated; composite, multiple, multiform, multifaceted, *Technical* parasynthetic, parathetic: *The compound eye of the fly / Lets it see far better than I. A compound sentence is composed of two or more clauses joined by one or more coordinating conjunctions, express or understood.* —*n.* **5** composite, °blend, °synthesis, °combination, consolidation, *Technical* parasynthesis, parathesis; °mixture, °amalgam, °alloy, merging, °merger, °mix: *Table salt is a compound of the metallic element sodium and the gaseous element chlorine. 'Slithy' is a compound of 'slimy' and 'writhe'.*

comprehend *v.* °understand, °see, °grasp, °conceive, °take in, apprehend, °realize, °fathom, °perceive, discern, absorb, assimilate, °appreciate: *Do you comprehend how serious the matter has become?*

comprehensive *adj.* °inclusive, encompassing, °thorough, °extensive, °full, °exhaustive, °complete, °sweeping, °wide, °broad, °encyclopedic *or* encyclopaedic: *We hope to give comprehensive coverage to all aspects of the subject in our new book.*

compulsive *adj.* compelling, °obsessive, coercive, °urgent, °forceful, °overwhelming, constrained: *She is such a compulsive workaholic that she double-checks everything done by her staff.*

compunction *n.* **1** °remorse, contrition, °regret, uneasiness of °mind, °pang *or* pricking of °conscience, self-reproach: *He has no compunction about hurting your feelings.* **2** hesitation,

°reluctance, °reserve, disinclination, °qualm, °misgiving, unwillingness, °fear: *She has no compunction about speaking her mind.*

compute v. °calculate, °reckon, °figure (out), °work out, °determine, ascertain, °estimate: *My accountant computed my income tax for this year and told me that I was entitled to a refund.*

comrade n. °colleague, °associate, °friend, °companion, crony, confrère, *Colloq* °pal, °chum, *Chiefly Brit and Australian* °mate, *Australian* cobber, *US* buddy: *None of my comrades from the old regiment attended the reunion this year.*

conceal v. **1** °hide, °secrete, °bury, °cover, °disguise, °camouflage: *Packets of a white powdery substance were concealed inside each doll.* **2** °keep °secret or °hidden, °keep °quiet about, °disguise, not °reveal; dissemble: *He concealed his true identity even from his wife.*

concede v. **1** °admit, °allow, °grant, °acknowledge, °confess, own (up or to or up to), °accept: *I conceded that I had no business in the bank after closing.* **2** °grant, °yield, °surrender, °cede, °give up, °submit, °resign, °relinquish, °abandon, °waive: *In chess, upon the loss of a queen, many players will concede. She has conceded any right to the estate of her uncle.*

conceit n. **1** °vanity, °pride, egotism, °self-esteem, self-admiration, self-love, narcissism, vainglory, *amour propre*; °arrogance: *His conceit is matched only by his incompetence.* **2** °fancy, whim, caprice: *Some have a conceit their drink tastes better / In an outlandish cup than on their own.* **3** elaborate figure (of speech), °affectation, strained or far-fetched °metaphor: *A conceit would be calling the waves 'nodding hearse-plumes'.*

conceited adj. °vain, °egotistical, self-centred, egocentric, self-admiring, narcissistic, prideful, °proud, °arrogant, self-involved, °self-important, self-satisfied, °smug, complacent, vainglorious, °snobbish, *Colloq* stuck-up; *Slang* snotty: *That conceited ass really thinks the world of himself.*

conceive v. **1** °have, °bear, beget, sire, °father, give °birth to; become °pregnant (with): *After the twins, they conceived three boys.* **2** °formulate, °devise, °plan, contrive, °create, °plot, °hatch, °develop, evolve, °fabricate, °think or °make up, °form, °frame, °design: *He conceived a scheme for swindling that poor woman out of her life savings.* **3** °think (up), °imagine, °speculate (on), °perceive, °see, °understand, °realize, °comprehend, °envision, °envisage, conjure up, °dream up, hypothesize, postulate, °posit, °suggest, °suppose: *I cannot conceive of any reason why she shouldn't be allowed to take part.*

concentrate v. **1** °focus, °direct, °centre, centralize, °converge, consolidate: *The council concentrated its efforts on refurbishing the schools.* **2** condense, °reduce, distil, °intensify, °refine, °strengthen: *The sap of the sugar maple is concentrated by boiling.* **3** °gather, °collect, congregate, °draw or °bring together, °crowd, °cluster, °group: *Much of the population is concentrated around the large cities.* **4** °think, °focus one's thoughts or °attention, °apply oneself: *I cannot concentrate with the radio on.*

conception n. **1** °birth, °beginning, genesis, inception, commencement, °emergence, °start, inauguration, °initiation, °launch, launching, °origin, origination, °formation, formulation,

introduction: *We were excited to be in at the conception of the scheme.* **2** °idea, °notion, °inkling, °clue, concept; *idée reçu;* °understanding, °knowledge, °appreciation, comprehension: *He has no conception of what is involved in maintaining a yacht.* **3** °design, °plan, °scheme, °proposal, °outline: *Transporting a building from another site instead of constructing one was a bold conception.*

concern v. **1** °refer or °relate to, have °relation or °reference to, be about, °pertain or appertain to, be °pertinent or °relevant to, °regard, °apply to, be connected or °involved with, °bear on, be germane to, °involve, °touch (on): *The matter concerns your inheritance, Cosgrove.* **2** °affect, °have (a) °bearing or (an) °influence on, °involve, °touch; °interest, be of °importance or °interest to: *This war concerns us all.* **3** °worry, °trouble, °disturb, °bother, °perturb, unsettle, °upset, °distress: *He doesn't let anything concern him.* —n. **4** °business, °affair, °problem; °responsibility, °duty, °charge, °task, involvement, *Colloq* °thing; *Slang* bag, shtick: *What she does is no concern of yours. The safety of the passengers is his concern.* **5** °interest, °regard, °consideration, °care, °thought, awareness, °attention: *You should show more concern for those less fortunate than you.* **6** °anxiety, °worry, °solicitude, apprehension, °distress, apprehensiveness, uneasiness, malaise, disquiet, disquietude: *It's only a cold, and no cause for concern.* **7** °business, °firm, °company, °house, °establishment, °enterprise, °organization: *The business is being sold as a going concern.* **8** °matter, °affair, °issue: *The preservation of wildlife is an international concern.*

concerned adj. **1** °involved, °responsible, °interested, °active; caring, °solicitous: *The best governments are run by a concerned citizenry.* **2** troubled, vexed, °anxious, °worried, distressed, uneasy, perturbed, bothered, °upset, °disturbed: *They were not at all concerned about the state of my health.*

concerning prep. °about, °regarding, °relative or relating to, referring to, with or in °reference to, as regards, in or with °regard to, with an °eye to, with °respect to, respecting, apropos (of), as to or for, in the °matter of, on the °subject of, re, *Formal* anent: *Concerning your recent application, please phone this office.*

concise adj. °brief, °terse, laconic, °compact, °direct, °succinct, °epigrammatic, cogent, pithy, compendious, °summary, °trenchant, compressed, condensed, °short; shortened, abridged, curtailed, °abbreviated: *He gave a concise summary of the findings. This is a concise edition of the dictionary.*

concrete adj. °real, °actual, °literal, °realistic, °authentic, valid, °genuine, bona fide, °reliable; °specific, °particular, °definite, °definitive, clear-cut, °material, °physical, °tangible, °substantial: *Have you any concrete evidence for the existence of UFOs?*

condemn v. **1** censure, °blame, °criticize, remonstrate with or against, °denounce, °disparage, reproach, °rebuke, °reprove, °scold, °reprimand, °upbraid: *The council was condemned for failing to provide adequate health care.* **2** °convict, °find °guilty; °sentence, °doom: *The judge condemned them to twenty years' imprisonment.* **3 condemned**: °doomed, damned, °destined, °fated, ordained, fore-ordained; consigned: *He has been condemned to wander forever.*

condescend *v.* °stoop, °deign, °lower *or* °humble *or* demean oneself, come down off one's high horse: *She wouldn't condescend to talk to the stable-boy directly.*

condescending *adj.* patronizing, belittling, °disdainful, °contemptuous, °pompous, °overbearing, high-handed, imperious, °snobbish, °haughty, *Colloq* snooty, *Brit* toffee-nosed; *Slang* snotty: *He thinks he's better than everyone, and I can't stand his condescending manner.*

condition *n.* **1** °state; °circumstance(s), °shape: *What condition is the house in? My bank account is in a poor condition.* **2** °stipulation, °proviso, °demand, °requirement, °term, °qualification, contingency, requisite, °prerequisite: *The terrorists have announced their conditions for releasing the hostages.* **3** working °order, °fitness, °shape, °form, fettle; °health: *He's in good condition, but his car isn't.* **4 conditions**: circumstances; °quarters; °environment: *The ship's crew live in very crowded conditions.*
—*v.* **5** °ready, get *or* make °ready, °prepare, °equip, °outfit, °fit (out *or* up), °adapt, °modify: *The mechanics are conditioning the plane for high-altitude flights.* **6** °train, °educate, °teach; brainwash; °influence, °mould, °persuade: *The children were conditioned to avoid talking to strangers.* **7** °accustom, inure, °adapt, acclimate, acclimatize:.*At this training base, we condition the commandos to all kinds of hardships.*

conduct *n.* **1** °behaviour, actions, demeanour, manners, deportment, comportment, °attitude: *Such conduct will not be tolerated in this school.* **2** °guidance, °direction, °management, supervision, °leadership, °administration, °government, °running, handling, °control, °command, °regulation, operation: *Had the conduct of the war been left up to him, we should have lost.*
—*v.* **3** °guide, °direct, °supervise, °manage, °carry on, °run, °control, °administer, °regulate, °operate: *They conduct a remarkably successful business.* **4** °lead, °guide, °escort, °show (in *or* out), usher: *We were conducted through the gallery by the curator herself.* **5** °channel, °carry, °transmit, convey; °direct: *Electrical power is conducted by the cable.* **6 conduct oneself**: °behave, °act, demean, deport, comport, acquit: *For a six-year-old, he conducted himself very well.*

confer *v.* **1** °converse, °consult, °deliberate, °talk (over), °discuss, °take °counsel: *I shall have to confer with my colleagues on that matter.* **2** *When transitive:*°confer on, °give, °grant, °present, °award; °bestow (on): *The prizes will be conferred after the dinner. He was bewildered by the honours conferred on him.*

conference *n.* °meeting, °convention, symposium, congress, seminar, forum, colloquium; °discussion, °talk, colloquy, *US* bull °session: *In 1988, the conference was held in Budapest.*

confess *v.* °disclose, °acknowledge, °admit, own (up *or* to *or* up to), °declare, avow, make a °clean breast (of); °reveal, divulge, °confirm, °concede, affirm, aver, °testify; disbosom oneself, *Colloq* come °clean: *She confessed her part in the swindle. Confronted with the evidence, he confessed.*

confidence *n.* **1** °trust, °reliance, °faith; °belief: *Your parents have a great deal of confidence in you.* **2** °assurance, °self-confidence, self-assurance, °self-reliance, °poise, aplomb, coolness; °conviction, certitude, boldness, °courage, °nerve: *We admire the confidence she shows in her daring plan.* **3 in confidence**: in °secrecy, in °privacy, privately, confidentially, intimately, *Colloq* on the q.t. *or* Q.T.: *I am telling you this in confidence.*

confident *adj.* **1** °secure, °sure, °certain, assured, °positive, convinced: *I feel confident that we shall get the contract.* **2** °self-confident, self-assured, °self-possessed, reliant, self-reliant, °dauntless, °bold, °cool, cocksure, °fearless, °courageous, *Colloq* °cocky: *He strode into the room with a confident air.*

confidential *adj.* °private, °secret, °intimate; classified; *Colloq* hush-hush: *These confidential papers must never be out of your possession.*

confirm *v.* **1** °ratify, °sanction, °authorize, °endorse, °support, °sustain, °approve, °uphold, back up, validate, °verify, °recognize; °authenticate, accredit: *By-laws shall not take effect unless confirmed by the local authority.* **2** °establish, °settle, affirm, °ensure, °clinch, °substantiate, °guarantee, °bind, °seal: *The king thereby confirmed his control over the islands.* **3** °strengthen, °encourage, °fortify, °reinforce, corroborate, °substantiate, °buttress, °prove: *Later events confirmed his opinion.*

confiscate *v.* °appropriate, °seize, impound, sequester, sequestrate, expropriate, °take (away), commandeer: *The police confiscated my car to use as evidence.*

conflict *n.* **1** °fight, °battle, °combat, °engagement, °struggle, °war, °fray, °fracas, affray, °brawl, Donnybrook: *Gurkha troops entered the conflict.* **2** °dispute, °argument, °controversy, wrangle, contention, °disagreement, altercation, °feud, °quarrel, °row, squabble, °tiff, *Colloq* spat: *The counsellor was unable to resolve the conflict between the sisters regarding the will.* **3** °clash, °antagonism, °difference, °opposition, °disagreement, °variance, °discord: *There is a basic conflict between the interests of labour and of management.*
—*v.* **4** °clash, °disagree, °differ, be °incompatible *or* at °odds *or* at °variance, be in °opposition (to): *The plans conflict on only one point.*

conform *v.* **1** °comply (with), °follow, °observe, °obey, °respect, °abide by, °adapt *or* °adjust (to): *We agree to conform to the rules of the club.* **2** °accord (with), °agree (with), concur (with), °coincide (with), °correspond (with), harmonize (with), °square (with), °match, °tally (with), °fit (in with), be °consistent (with), be in °accord *or* in accordance (with): *Their behaviour did not conform with what is expected in such circles. The two plans do not conform.*

confuse *v.* **1** disconcert, °perplex, °puzzle, °bewilder, °mystify, baffle, °bemuse, befuddle, °discomfit, confound, °fluster, °flummox, °upset, disorient, °embarrass, abash, °shame, °dismay, *Colloq* °rattle, °throw, *Chiefly US* discombobulate, *US and Canadian* buffalo: *She was completely confused by his offer to help.* **2** °disorder, confound, disorganize, °throw into disarray, °muddle, °mix up, °snarl (up), ensnarl, °tangle (up), °entangle, °botch, *Colloq* °mess up, make a °mess of, °screw up, *Brit* make a balls-up of,

US ball up: *He has done more to confuse the situation than to clear it up.* **3** °mix up, confound, °muddle, °jumble, °snarl (up), ensnarl; °blur: *The identities of the children were confused at birth.*

confused *adj.* **1** °mixed up, jumbled, disordered, disorganized, °disorderly, muddled, muddle-headed, snarled (up), messy, baffling, confusing, mystifying, °puzzling, °perplexing; °contradictory, °ambiguous, misleading, °inconsistent, °mixed up, botched (up), *Colloq* higgledy-piggledy: *The accountants have provided a confused set of figures.* **2** bewildered, perplexed, puzzled, baffled, (be)fuddled, mystified, disoriented, discomposed, at °sea, flummoxed, dazed, muddled, bemused, °mixed up, nonplussed, °disconcerted, abashed, °put off, °put out, °disturbed, flustered, °ill at ease, °upset, at sixes and sevens, at a loss, *Rare* metagrobolized, *Colloq* screwed-up, muzzy, out of it, not with it, *Chiefly US* discombobulated, fouled up; *Slang* (all) balled up, *Brit* (all) bollocksed *or* ballocksed (up), *US* (all) bollixed (up), *US and Canadian* snafu: *I have never seen anyone so confused about a simple question of astrophysics.* **3** jumbled, °mixed up, muddled, °disorderly, confusing, messy, disorganized, °topsy-turvy; °miscellaneous, motley, *Brit* shambolic: *The books lay in a confused heap on the floor.*

confusion *n.* **1** °disorder, °mix-up, °mess, °jumble, °muddle, disarray, disarrangement, °chaos, °shambles: *The files are in complete confusion.* **2** °tumult, commotion, °disorder, turmoil, °pandemonium, °bedlam, °chaos: *Untold confusion resulted from sounding the alarm.* **3** °mix-up, confounding; °ambiguity, ambiguousness, °misunderstanding, contradiction, inconsistency: *There is often some confusion between the name of a thing and the thing itself.* **4** mixing, combining, mixing up, intermingling: *The removal firm is responsible for the confusion of your books with mine.* **5** °assortment, °mixture, °pot-pourri, gallimaufry, °hotchpotch *or US and Canadian also* hodgepodge: *A confusion of products lines the shelves.* **6** °embarrassment, discomfiture, mortification, abashment, shamefacedness, chagrin: *He felt terrible confusion when confronted with the evidence.*

congested *adj.* (over)crowded, blocked (up), jammed, crammed, plugged, stopped *or* stuffed (up), choked: *The police are trying to deal with traffic at congested intersections.*

congratulate *v.* felicitate, °compliment: *Her friends congratulated her on winning the award.*

congratulations *interjection.* Felicitations!, Best wishes!, Well done!, Many happy returns!, *Colloq* Nice going!, Good show!: *Heartiest congratulations! You've come in first!*

connect *v.* **1** °join *or* °link *or* °tie (together), °unite: *An old road connects the two towns.* **2** °associate, affiliate, °link, °relate, °league, °tie (in): *The police connected him with the break-in. The institute is connected with a pharmaceuticals company.* **3** °fasten, °bind, °unite, °tie, °link, °join, °attach, °couple, °put together, °secure, °fit, °fix, affix, °stick, °anchor, °lock; rivet, °weld, braze, solder, °screw, °nail, stitch, °sew, °pin, °hook, °staple, °tack, °glue, °cement, °fuse, °seal, °buckle, strap, °bolt, °lash, °chain, °moor: *Connect the parts to the frame.*

connection *n.* **1** uniting, joining, linking, connecting, coupling; °union, °bond, °joint, °link: *The US constitution forbids a formal connection between Church and State. The connection between the fittings has broken.* **2** °link, °tie, (inter)-relation(ship), interplay, °bearing, °reference, °relevance, appropriateness, correlation, °tie-in; coherence, consistency, °association: *Your answer had no connection with the question.* **3** Often, **connections**: °contact, °ally, °acquaintance, °friend (at court); °influence, *Colloq* °pull; *Slang US* drag: *With their connections, they can get away with anything.* **4 connections**: relatives, relations, °family, °kin, kith and °kin: *They have connections in Australia.*

conquer *v.* **1** °overcome, vanquish, °beat, °defeat, °subdue, °crush, °subjugate: *The Moors conquered most of Spain.* **2** °capture, °seize, °win, °gain, °acquire, °obtain; °occupy, annex, °overrun: *They conquered the territory by force of arms.* **3** °overcome, °triumph *or* °prevail over, °beat, surmount, °master, °win out (over): *He has finally conquered the habit of biting his fingernails.*

conquest *n.* **1** vanquishment, subjugation, °defeat, °domination, °subjection: *Hernando Cortés is famous for his conquest of Mexico.* **2** °victory, °triumph, mastery, °win: *He is credited with the conquest of a number of diseases by means of this drug.*

conscience *n.* °morality, morals, °judgement, fairness, sense of right and wrong, ethics, °honour, °standards, °principles, °scruples: *In such matters, your conscience must be your guide.*

conscientious *adj.* **1** °scrupulous, °principled, °fair, °moral, °ethical, °strict, °righteous, right-minded, upstanding, °upright, °honourable, °just, °responsible, high-minded; incorruptible: *Fetherby is a conscientious arbitrator.* **2** °cautious, °careful, °scrupulous, °exacting, °meticulous, punctilious, °painstaking, °diligent, °particular, rigorous, °thorough: *A conscientious effort was made to restore the painting to its original condition.* **3** °prudent, °discreet, °politic, °careful, circumspect, heedful, °attentive, °serious: *Fred is conscientious about keeping secrets.*

conscious *adj.* **1** °aware, °awake, °alert: *I was conscious of an eerie presence. The victim of the attack is now conscious.* **2** °deliberate, °intentional, purposive, °purposeful, °wilful, °studied: *Lydia has been making a conscious effort to be friendlier to me.*

consent *v.* **1** °agree, °comply, concur, accede, acquiesce, °concede, °yield, °submit, °cede, °conform, °give in: *He asked for payment in advance and I consented.* **2 consent to**: °permit, °allow, °agree to, °give in to, °approve, °authorize: *Richard's parents consented to his going on the outing.* —*n.* **3** °approval, assent, °permission, °sanction, authorization, imprimatur, °seal of °approval, *Colloq* °OK, okay, go-ahead: *Have Richard's parents given their consent?* **4** °agreement, acceptance, acquiescence, compliance, °approval, concurrence: *Taxes cannot be raised without the consent of Parliament.*

consequently *adv.* so, °therefore, as a °result *or* consequence, °accordingly, ergo, °hence, °thus: *He was found guilty and, consequently, sentenced to death.*

conservation *n.* °preservation, °protection, °safe keeping, °maintenance, °upkeep,

°management, safeguarding; husbandry, °economy: *The conservation of natural resources must be a priority.*

conservative *adj.* **1** °reactionary, °right, right-wing, rightist, Tory: *In his conservative view, no change is ever for the better.* **2** °cautious, °careful, °prudent, °moderate, °temperate, middle-of-the-road, °sober, °stable; unprogressive, °orthodox, °traditional, conformist, °hidebound, °conventional, °standard, fundamentalist, true-blue, dyed in the wool: *The conservative approach would be to study the problem before making a change. The conservative members voted against electing certain members to the club.* —*n.* **3** °reactionary, rightist, right-winger, Tory, fundamentalist; °moderate, middle-of-the-roader: *He's a conservative and favours a classical education.*

conserve *v.* **1** °keep, °preserve, °hold on to, °save, °spare, °reserve: *Conserve your energy for later, when we get near the top.* **2** °preserve, °maintain, °keep up, take °care of: *These buildings should be conserved for later generations.*

consider *v.* **1** °think about *or* over, take into *or* under consideration, °deliberate (over *or* about), °contemplate (on *or* over), °weigh, °ponder, °mull over, cogitate on, °meditate (on *or* upon *or* over), °reflect (on *or* upon), ruminate (on *or* over), °chew over, °study, °examine: *The council will consider your proposal.* **2** °heed, °mark, take into °account *or* consideration, °reckon with, bear in °mind, °note, °observe, make °allowance for; °esteem, °respect, have °regard for: *Consider your mother's feelings in the matter.* **3** °regard, °look upon; °judge, deem, °take to be, °think, °believe, °gauge, °rate, °estimate, °reckon: *Consider yourself under arrest. I don't consider Simon the best person for the job.*

considerable *adj.* **1** sizeable, °substantial, °large, °big, °great; appreciable, °respectable, °noticeable, largish, biggish, °goodly, °decent, °fair, *Colloq* °tidy: *A considerable crowd were gathered outside.* **2** °important, °worthy, of consequence, of °distinction, °distinguished, °illustrious, °noteworthy, °notable, °remarkable, °estimable, °influential, °respectable: *Some of the most considerable citizens were banished.*

considerate *adj.* °thoughtful, °kind, °kindly, kind-hearted, good-hearted, °helpful, °friendly, °neighbourly, °gracious, °obliging, °accommodating, °charitable, °generous, °unselfish; °sympathetic, compassionate, °sensitive; °attentive; °solicitous: *It was very considerate of you to offer your car.*

consideration *n.* **1** °regard, °concern, attentiveness, °solicitude, thoughtfulness, compassion, °kindness, kindliness, kindheartedness, considerateness, °respect, caring, °care: *Out of consideration for your father, you should complete your studies.* **2** °reward, compensation, °remuneration, °fee, °payment, recompense, emolument, °tip, gratuity, *pourboire,* baksheesh *or* backsheesh; °honorarium: *The boy will look after your luggage for a small consideration, madam.* **3** °thought, deliberation, °reflection, contemplation, rumination, cogitation, °study, °examination: *After some consideration, we have decided that we will finance the project.*

considering *prep.* in °view of, in (the) °light of, bearing in °mind, making °allowance for, taking into consideration *or* °account, looking at, all in all, all things *or* everything considered, inasmuch as, insomuch as: *Considering your background, I doubt that you are qualified.*

consistent *adj.* **1** agreeing, in °agreement, in °harmony, in keeping, °harmonious, in concordance, conforming, in conformance, accordant, compatible, in °accord *or* accordance, consonant: *Her story is not consistent with the facts.* **2** dependable, °regular, °predictable, undeviating, °steady, °steadfast, unchanging, °uniform, unswerving, °constant: *His behaviour, even under pressure, has been quite consistent.*

consistently *adv.* **1** steadily, constantly, regularly, uniformly, °daily, day by day: *Her piano technique is improving consistently.* **2** dependably, unswervingly, staunchly, devotedly, °firmly, resolutely, faithfully, uniformly, unfailingly: *The courts have consistently upheld her claim to custody of the children.*

console *v.* °comfort, soothe, °calm, assuage, °solace, °cheer (up): *Ivan made an effort to console the grieving widow.*

conspicuous *adj.* **1** °obvious, °clear, °evident, °plain, palpable, °perceptible, °patent, °prominent, °apparent, clear-cut, °unquestionable, incontestable, °incontrovertible: *The sultan played a conspicuous role in the kidnapping of the envoy.* **2** °obvious, unmistakable, °prominent, °outstanding, °noticeable, °impressive, °vivid, °obtrusive; °striking, °showy, °garish, °gaudy, °loud, °tawdry, °blatant, °lurid, °vulgar, °flashy, ostentatious: *The silhouette of the castle was conspicuous against the sky. Fingal was again conspicuous, this time in a green wig and bowler.* **3** °notable, °noteworthy, °exceptional, °outstanding, °eminent, °unusual, °marked, °extraordinary, °remarkable, °distinguished, °impressive, °awesome, awe-inspiring, °glorious: *The medal is awarded for conspicuous bravery.*

conspiracy *n.* °plot, °scheme, °stratagem, °intrigue, collusion, °cabal, connivance, foul play, °dirty work: *He suspected them of a conspiracy to defraud their clients.*

constable *n.* policeman, policewoman, (°police) °officer, *US* patrolman, *Colloq* cop, copper, *Brit* bobby; *Slang* flatfoot, fuzz: *A constable was standing on the corner, and we asked him the way.*

constant *adj.* **1** °resolute, °immovable, °steadfast, °firm, dependable, unshakeable *or* unshakable, °determined, unswerving, undeviating, persevering, unwearying, unwearied, °untiring, indefatigable, °tireless, unflagging, unwavering, unfailing, unfaltering, °persistent; °loyal, °true, tried and °true, °devoted, °staunch, trusty, °faithful: *He was her constant companion during her troubles.* **2** incessant, unceasing, ceaseless, °perpetual, °persistent, uninterrupted, °steady, °regular, °invariable, unremitting, unvarying, °relentless, unrelenting, °continuous, °continual; unending, °endless, never-ending, °non-stop, °perennial, °eternal, °everlasting, *Literary* sempiternal: *The constant pain almost made me cry out. Their constant bickering is getting on my nerves.* **3** unchanging, unchanged,

°invariable, unvarying, °fixed, °uniform, unalterable, immutable, °changeless, °persistent: *The numbers might change, but the ratio is constant.*

construct v. 1 °build, °erect, °make, °put together, °frame, °set up, °put up, °assemble: *We constructed a summer-house in the garden.* 2 °fabricate, °devise, °create, °forge, °invent, °formulate, °compose, °shape, °set up, °fashion: *He has constructed a complex argument to support his theory.*

constructive adj. 1 °helpful, °useful, °practicable, °advantageous, °practical, °productive, °beneficial, °positive: *She provided much constructive advice on how to design the factory.* 2 °virtual, inferential, °implicit, inferred, derived, deduced: *As it turned out, the shareholders were the constructive victims of the fraud.*

consult v. 1 Often, **consult with**: °confer (with), °discuss (with), °deliberate (with), °talk over (with), °inquire or °enquire of, °seek °advice from, °ask (of), °question, interrogate, take °counsel (with or of): *I shall have to consult a doctor about my headaches. You should consult with your lawyer.* 2 °refer to, °look up, °seek °information from: *If in doubt, consult the dictionary.*

consultant n. 1 °physician, °doctor, °specialist, °expert: *You ought to get the opinion of another consultant.* 2 °adviser or advisor, °expert, °counsellor or US counselor: *Our financial consultant tells us how to handle the company funds.*

consume v. 1 °devour, °eat (up), °gulp (down), °swallow, °drink (up), °put away, gobble (up); °digest: *When those teenagers come home, they consume everything in sight.* 2 °use up, °exhaust, deplete, °drain, °expend, °diminish, °reduce: *The new car has consumed all our savings.* 3 °waste, °occupy, squander, °fritter away, °dissipate, absorb, °lose, °throw away, °lavish, Slang °blow: *Too much of your time has already been consumed by that problem.* 4 °destroy, °ruin, (lay) °waste, °demolish, °wreck, °gut, °raze, Slang US and Canadian total: *Fire consumed the entire house.* 5 °overcome, °overwhelm, °devastate, °destroy, annihilate, °ravage, (lay) °waste, °wear out, °ruin, °eat up, °devour, do in; preoccupy, °obsess: *He is consumed by jealousy.*

consummation n. 1 °completion, °accomplishment, °fulfilment, °finish, °end, °realization, attainment, °achievement, °success; completing, accomplishing, fulfilling, finishing, ending, realizing, attaining, achieving: *Owning a Rolls Royce was the consummation of her dreams.* 2 °acme, °perfection, °peak, culmination, finishing °touch, conclusion, °grand finale, °climax: *The Nobel prize was the consummation of an arduous life of research.*

contact n. 1 °junction, conjunction, °connection: *If the wires make contact, the fuse will blow.* 2 °acquaintance, °friend, °connection, Colloq US in: *I have a contact on the board of directors.* 3 °touch, communication, °association: *Are you still in contact with Georgina?* —v. 4 get in °touch with, °communicate with, °reach, speak °hold of; phone, °ring (up), °telephone, °speak to or with, °write to, °correspond with: *Try to contact the manager at his home.*

contain v. 1 °hold, °have in it; °bear, °carry: *The capsule contained a deadly poison.* 2 °hold, have the °capacity for, °accommodate, °admit, °carry; °seat: *This bottle contains no more than a*

quart. *The theatre can contain 200.* 3 °restrain, °restrict, confine, °repress, °control, °hold back or in, °curb, °bridle, keep under control, °suppress, °check, °stifle: *He could hardly contain himself when he learnt he had passed the examination.*

contaminate v. defile, °sully, °pollute, °corrupt, °rot, °stain, °soil, °taint, infect, °poison, °foul, °spoil, befoul; °debase, °adulterate, °vitiate: *The river has been contaminated by effluent from a nearby factory.*

contemplate v. 1 °look or °gaze at or on or upon, °behold, °view, °survey, °observe, °regard, °eye; °scan, °scrutinize, °inspect: *I contemplated the scene of the Grand Canal from my hotel room.* 2 ruminate (over), °ponder (on or over), °deliberate (over), °muse (on or over), °meditate or °reflect (on), °think (about or over), °mull over, cogitate (over), °turn over in one's mind, °brood on or over, °chew on or over, °consider, °study, °examine: *She was contemplating the events of the past night. Give me a moment to contemplate.* 3 °plan, °intend, °think of or about, °consider, °entertain the idea or notion of: *After we broke up, I contemplated emigrating to Australia.*

contemporary adj. 1 of the °time, contemporaneous, coeval, coexistent, concurrent, concomitant, °parallel, synchronous, synchronic, °coincidental, coetaneous: *We examined some of the documents contemporary with his reign.* 2 °modern, °current, present-day, °new, up to °date, °stylish, °fashionable, modish, à la °mode, °latest, in; °novel, newfangled, Colloq °trendy: *She always keeps up with contemporary fads in dress and make-up. I find much of the contemporary metal-and-glass architecture rather boring.*

contempt n. °loathing, abhorrence, hatred, odium, °hate; °scorn, disdain, contumely, °disgust: *She has nothing but contempt for cowards.*

contemptible adj. °despicable, °loathsome, detestable, °scurvy, °low, °mean, °base, °inferior, currish, °wretched, °vile, abject, ignominious, °unworthy, °shabby, °shameful: *It was contemptible of you to give away my secret.*

contemptuous adj. °scornful, °disdainful, sneering, derisive, insulting, contumelious, °insolent: *The maestro was contemptuous of my piano-playing.*

content[1] n. 1 °capacity, °volume, °size, °measure: *The content of the barrel is exactly 55 gallons.* 2 Usually, **contents**: ingredients, components, constituents; °load: *The bottle broke and its contents spilt on the floor.* 3 °substance, subject-matter; °significance, purport, °import, °essence, °text, °theme, °topic, °thesis: *The book is amusing but its content is quite trivial.*

content[2] n. 1 °pleasure, °satisfaction, °gratification, °happiness, contentment, contentedness, felicity, °delight: *He kept on singing to his heart's content.* 2 °ease, °comfort, tranquillity, °serenity, °peace, peacefulness, contentedness: *I have a feeling of such content merely being with you.* —adj. 3 °pleased, satisfied, °happy, °delighted, contented, gratified, °glad, °cheerful; °comfortable, fulfilled: *I was quite content to be home once more.* —v. 4 °satisfy, °please, °gratify, soothe, °cheer, °gladden, °delight: *It contented him to be near her.*

contest n. 1 °competition, °match, °tournament, championship, tourney, °meet, °game, °rivalry, °trial: The contest was won by a woman from Shropshire. 2 °strife, °controversy, °dispute, contention, °debate, altercation, °argument, velitation; °conflict, °struggle, °fight, °battle, °combat, °war: The contest is between those for and those against capital punishment.
—v. 3 contend, °argue, °dispute, °debate; °challenge, (call into) °question, °oppose, °counter, confute, °object to, refute: David has decided to contest his father's will.

contestant n. contender, °competitor, °opponent, °rival, °adversary, entrant, °player, °participant: The winner is the contestant from Chearsley.

context n. °structure, framework, °environment, °situation, °circumstance(s); ambience or ambiance, °surround, °surroundings, °frame (of °reference), °setting, °background: It is often hard to understand something taken out of its context.

continual adj. °constant, incessant, °perpetual, °non-stop, °persistent, uninterrupted, °regular, °steady, unbroken, unceasing, ceaseless, °eternal, unremitting, interminable, °endless, unending; Loosely °continuous: She has this continual ringing in her ears.

continue v. 1 °carry on, °proceed (with), °keep up or on or at, °go on (with), °pursue, °persist (in), °persevere (in): Please continue whatever it was you were doing. 2 °endure, °last, °go on, °persist, be prolonged: How long will the curfew continue? 3 °maintain, °keep (on), °prolong, °perpetuate, °carry on (with), °persist in or with, °sustain, °extend: My mother continued her career throughout my childhood. 4 °resume, °pick up, °take up, °carry on (with): Allow me to continue my story and don't interrupt again. 5 °proceed, °go (on), °extend: The road continues for about a mile, ending at the sea.

continuous adj. 1 connected, unbroken, uninterrupted: The wall is continuous except for one gate. 2 incessant, °persistent, °perpetual, °non-stop, unceasing, ceaseless, °constant, unremitting, interminable, °endless, unending; Loosely °continual: A continuous stream of refugees passed through the camp.

contract n. 1 °agreement, °understanding, °deal, °bargain, °arrangement, °pact, commitment, °obligation, °compact: We have just signed a contract to supply office equipment to a new electronics company.
—v. 2 °engage, °agree, °promise, covenant, °undertake: Our company contracted to maintain the roads in this area. 3 °catch, °acquire, °get, °come down with, °develop, °become infected with, Brit °go down with: Eunice contracted diphtheria. 4 °diminish, °shrink, °draw together, °roll (oneself), °narrow, °squeeze, constrict, compress, condense, °decrease, °reduce: When disturbed, the animal contracts itself into a ball. 5 °wrinkle, °knit, crease, corrugate, °pucker: His brow contracted into a frown.

contradict v. 1 °deny, gainsay, °dispute, controvert, °argue against; °oppose: He is very opinionated, and doesn't like to be contradicted. 2 contravene, belie, refute, disallow,

°forbid, disaffirm, °counter, abrogate, nullify, annul, °reverse, °counteract: The evidence yields nothing that contradicts my argument.

contradictory adj. °inconsistent, °paradoxical, °incongruous, conflicting, °incompatible, discrepant; °ambiguous, ambivalent: The witnesses' descriptions of the robbers are contradictory.

contraption n. contrivance, °device, °gadget, °mechanism, °apparatus, Colloq widget, thingumabob or thingamabob, thingumajig or thingamajig, thingummy, whatsit, doodah, thingy, US gizmo or gismo, Rube Goldberg (°invention), whatchamacallit, Colloq Brit gubbins: People began to build all sorts of contraptions that they hoped might fly.

contrary adj. 1 °opposite, °opposing, °opposed, °different, °contradictory, conflicting, antagonistic: Set aside enough time to hear the contrary side of the argument. 2 antagonistic, °perverse, contrarious, °hostile, unfriendly, inimical, cross-grained, refractory, contumacious, °self-willed, °argumentative, unaccommodating, antipathetic, Literary froward: He can disagree, but why must he be so contrary? 3 adverse, unfavourable, °inauspicious, unlucky, °unfortunate, unpropitious, °untoward, °inopportune, °bad, °foul: We ran into contrary winds and were delayed.
—n. 4 °opposite, °reverse: Her present position is the direct contrary of the one she took yesterday.
—adv. 5 perversely, oppositely, contrariwise, contrarily, in °opposition to: The rat in the maze acted contrary to the expected pattern.

contrast v. 1 juxtapose, °oppose, °compare, °distinguish, °differentiate, °discriminate, °set or °place against; °set off: Contrast life in the 18th century with life today. 2 °conflict, °differ or °diverge or °deviate (from): The two styles contrast sharply. Australian speech contrasts with that of Canada in many respects.
—n. 3 °comparison, °difference, °distinction, °disparity, °dissimilarity: The author emphasizes the contrasts between the two economic policies.

contribute v. 1 °give, °furnish, °donate, °bestow, °grant, °present, °provide, °supply: He contributed three paintings by Longchamp to the museum. They contributed generously to the restoration fund. 2 **contribute to**: °add to, °promote, °advance, °help, °aid, °support, °forward, have a hand in, play a °part or °role in: They believe that poor parental supervision contributes to juvenile delinquency.

control v. 1 °command, °dominate, °direct, °steer, °pilot, hold °sway over, °rule, °exercise °power or °authority over, °govern, °manage, °lead, °conduct, be in control (of), call the tune, °guide, °oversee, °supervise: Does she really control the future of the company? 2 °check, °hold back or in °check, °curb, °repress, °contain: Try to control yourself. 3 °suppress, °put down, °master, °subdue, °restrain, °curb, °manage: They were totally unable to control the unruly teenagers.
—n. 4 °command, °direction, °power, °authority, °leadership, °management, °guidance, supervision, °oversight, °charge; °sway, °rule, °jurisdiction: Turn control of the mission over to Mrs Beale. The court is under the control of the State. 5 °restraint, °check, °curb, mastery, °command, dominance, °domination: You must get better control over your emotions. 6 °knob,

button, dial, °handle, lever, °switch; °device, °mechanism: *This control opens the door to the safe.*

controversial *adj.* **1** °debatable, °disputable, °questionable, °moot, °doubtful, °unsettled: *Who will run the department is a controversial matter.* **2** polemical, dialectic, litigious, °factious: *She has studied the controversial writings of the 19th-century feminists.* **3** disputatious, °argumentative, contentious; °provocative: *Race relations have remained a controversial issue for centuries.*

controversy *n.* **1** °dispute, °debate, contention, °argument, argumentation, disputation, wrangling, confrontation, questioning, °disagreement: *The inquest went ahead without controversy.* **2** °argument, °dispute, °disagreement, °quarrel; squabble, °tiff, *Colloq* spat: *Controversy still rages over the theory of natural selection.*

convalesce *v.* °recover, °improve, get °better, °recuperate: *The doctor said I needed only a week to convalesce after the operation.*

convenient *n.* **1** °suitable, commodious, °useful, °helpful, °handy, °serviceable, °expedient, °opportune, °advantageous: *The bus is quite convenient for getting to and from the airport.* **2** °handy, °nearby, within (easy) °reach, at one's fingertips, close at °hand, °available, °accessible; (at the) °ready: *There's a convenient post office round the corner.*

convention *n.* **1** °assembly, °meeting, °gathering, congregation, congress, °conference, symposium, °council, conclave, °diet, synod, seminar: *The annual convention of cat fanciers will take place in June.* **2** °rule, °practice, °custom, °tradition, °usage, °formality, conventionalism: *According to convention, this year's vice-president becomes president next year.*

conventional *adj.* °customary, °habitual, °usual, °normal, °regular, °standard, °orthodox, °traditional, established, °ordinary, °everyday, °common, commonplace, °accustomed, received, agreed; °reactionary, °old-fashioned, °stodgy, °stuffy, °old hat: *Conventional methods of teaching mathematics are being criticized.*

converge *v.* °come *or* °go together, °meet, °join, °unite, °merge, °coincide; °blend: *The roads converge in the valley.*

conversation *n.* °discussion, °talk, °chat, °dialogue, colloquy, °parley; chit-chat, °gossip, discourse, °palaver, *Colloq chiefly Brit* chin-wag: *The conversation about the situation in the Middle East ended abruptly. I want action, not conversation.*

conversationalist *n.* deipnosophist: *It was a pleasure to have dinner with an intelligent conversationalist for a change.*

converse *v.* °discuss, °talk, °speak, °chat, °parley, discourse, °gossip, °chatter: *The men were conversing about her over dinner.*

convert *v.* **1** °change, °modify, °alter, °transform, transmute, mutate, transfigure, transmogrify, remodel, remake, metamorphose: *We converted our rowing-boat into a sailing dinghy.* **2** proselytize, °switch, °change (over): *To avoid the horrors of the Inquisition, many Spanish Jews converted to Catholicism.*

—*n.* **3** proselyte; neophyte, catechumen, °disciple: *Converts are often the most passionate believers.*

convict *v.* **1** find *or* prove °guilty: *She was convicted of theft.*
—*n.* **2** °prisoner, °captive, *Slang* con, jailbird *or Brit also* gaolbird, *Brit* lag: *The rioting convicts burnt down two prison buildings.*

conviction *n.* **1** °proof of °guilt: *After his conviction, he was sentenced to life imprisonment.* **2** °belief, °opinion, °view, °persuasion, °position: *It is her conviction that the painting is by Titian.* **3** °certainty, sureness, positiveness, °confidence, °assurance, certitude: *He doesn't have the courage to back up his convictions.*

convince *v.* °win over, °talk into, °persuade, °bring (a)round, °sway: *I have at last convinced them of the need for more resources.*

cool *adj.* **1** °chilly, °chill, chilling, cooling, unheated; chilled, °cold, °refreshing, °fresh: *It's rather cool outside today. I'd prefer some cool lemonade.* **2** °calm, °serene, °collected, °level-headed, °quiet, unexcited, unemotional, undisturbed, unexcitable, unruffled, unflappable, cool-headed, °relaxed, controlled, under °control, °self-possessed, self-controlled, unperturbed, °phlegmatic, composed, imperturbable: *He remains cool even in a crisis.* **3** °dispassionate, °cold, °cold-blooded, emotionless, °deliberate, °cold-hearted, °calculated, °wilful, °premeditated, °purposeful, purposive: *It was clearly the cool act of a professional criminal.* **4** uninvolved, °distant, °remote, °aloof, °detached, removed, uninterested, unconcerned, °unsympathetic, apathetic, °cold, °cold-hearted, °cold-blooded: *How can you be so cool where human lives are concerned?* **5** °lukewarm, °distant, uncordial, unfriendly, unsociable, °unapproachable, °standoffish, °forbidding, unwelcoming, °cold, °frigid: *After the affair, she was distinctly cool towards him.* **6** °bold, °audacious, °brazen, °overconfident, °presumptuous, °shameless, °unabashed, °impertinent, °impudent, °insolent: *I cannot account for the cool way he insulted his host.*
—*n.* **7** coolness, °chill, chilliness, *Colloq* coolth: *I shall have a sherry to ward off the cool of the evening.* **8** aplomb, °poise, sedateness, °control, °self-control, composure, °sang-froid: *He really lost his cool when she told him he was a lousy driver.*
—*v.* **9** °chill, °refrigerate, ice: *Cool the pudding before serving.* **10** °diminish, °reduce, lessen, abate, °moderate: *Her interest quickly cooled when she discovered he was married.*

cooperate *v.* **1** °collaborate, °work together, °join, °unite, interact, °team up, °join forces, °act jointly *or* in concert: *If we cooperate, the work will be done in half the time.* **2** °participate, °contribute, lend a °hand, °help, °assist: *You must learn to cooperate and not just sit there.*

cooperation *n.* **1** collaboration, teamwork, interaction, synergism *or* synergy: *Only through cooperation will we be able to achieve success.* **2** °support, °help, °aid, °assistance, °patronage, °backing, advocacy, °favour, °helping °hand, °friendship, °blessing, sponsorship, °auspices, backup: *We needed the cooperation of people like you to mount the exhibition.*

coordinate *v.* **1** °organize, classify, °order, °arrange, systemize, systematize, codify,

°categorize, °group, °match (up), °dispose, °rate, °rank, °grade: *Coordinate the information before preparing the report.* **2** harmonize, correlate, °unify, °mesh, synchronize, °integrate, *Colloq* °pull together: *We must coordinate our efforts for the best results.*
—*adj.* **3** °equivalent, °parallel, °correspondent, complementary, correlative, °equal, °reciprocal, coordinating, coordinative, *Technical* paratactic: *The two systems are coordinate and operate in parallel.*

cope *v.* **1** °manage, °get along *or* by, °make do, °survive, subsist, °come through: *Even with seven children to care for, she copes very well.* **2 cope with**: be a °match for, °withstand, contend with *or* against, °handle, °deal with, °dispose of: *I cannot cope with all the work I have been given to do.*

copy *n.* **1** °reproduction, °replica, °facsimile, °likeness, °imitation, °double, °twin, duplication, °duplicate, °transcript, replication, carbon (°copy), photocopy, °print: *She found a copy of the lost manuscript.* **2** °example, °sample, °specimen: *How many copies of the book have been sold?* **3** °text, °writing: *The copy is ready; we are waiting for the illustrations.*
—*v.* **4** °reproduce, °duplicate, replicate, °transcribe: *Don't copy others' work—they might be wrong.* **5** °imitate, °mimic, impersonate, emulate, ape, °parrot, °echo: *Ted copies the rock stars in every possible detail of their dress and behaviour.*

cord *n.* °string, °line, °twine; °rope: *Tie the cord around the parcel twice.*

cordial *adj.* °friendly, °warm, affable, °amiable, °kindly, °genial, °gracious, welcoming, °pleasant, °good-natured, °nice; °courteous, °polite: *After a cordial greeting at the door, the guests were served champagne.*

core *n.* **1** °centre, °heart, °middle, °nucleus, °inside(s): *Remove the core of the apple first.* **2** °essence, marrow, °heart, °pith, °gist, °quintessence, °sum and substance: *The core of the problem is her refusal to consider any alternative.*
—*v.* **3** °pit, °seed: *The pie might have tasted better if you'd cored the apples first.*

corps *n.* °body of men *or* women, troop, cadre, °unit, °detachment, °cohort, °division, battalion, brigade, °platoon, °squad, column, squadron: *We delivered supplies to the medical corps.*

corpse *n.* °body, remains, °cadaver, *Slang* °stiff; of an animal carcass: *The corpses were buried in a mass grave.*

correct *v.* **1** °right, set *or* put °right, °amend, redress, °rectify, °remedy, °repair, °fix; °cure: *A good mechanic will be able to correct the faults in the engine.* **2** °scold, admonish, °rebuke, °reprimand, °berate, chide, °reprove; censure, °blame: *You mustn't correct people for their bad manners.* **3** °punish, °chastise, °chasten, °discipline, °castigate: *The boys were corrected for swearing at the teacher.* **4** °reverse, °offset, °counteract, counterbalance, °neutralize, nullify, °make up for, annul, °cancel; °adjust, °change, °modify: *Adding this fertilizer should correct the acid content of the soil.* **5** °mark, °grade: *The exam papers haven't yet been corrected.*
—*adj.* **6** °proper, °decorous, °decent, °appropriate, °suitable, °fit, °right, °meet, °fitting, °befitting, apt, *de rigueur, comme il faut, Old-fashioned Brit* tickety-boo: *I have found her behaviour correct at all times.* **7** °conventional,

established, °set, °standard, °normal, °orthodox, approved, in °order, *de rigueur, comme il faut,* °usual, natural, °customary, °traditional, done, °right, *Old-fashioned Brit* tickety-boo: *Sending flowers to the funeral parlour would be the correct thing to do.* **8** °accurate, °right, °precise, °exact, °factual, valid, °true, °proper, °fitting, apt, °suitable, °appropriate; °faultless, °perfect, unimpeachable: *Joanna gave the correct answer.*

correction *n.* **1** °improvement, emendation, rectification, redress, °remedy, reparation, °amendment; corrigendum: *With these corrections, the work will be vastly better.* **2** °punishment, castigation, chastisement: *He resented her continual correction of him for trivial things.*

correspond *v.* **1** °agree, °conform, °tally, °comply, °accord, harmonize, be congruous, °match, °coincide: *The results of the surveys correspond.* **2** °write, °communicate, be in °touch *or* °contact: *We have been corresponding for years.*

correspondent *n.* newspaperman, newspaperwoman, pressman, presswoman, °journalist, °reporter, stringer, newsman, newsperson: *Here is a report from our correspondent in Sydney.*

corridor *n.* °hall, hallway, °passage, passageway: *We met in the corridor outside my room.*

corrupt *adj.* **1** °dishonest, untrustworthy, °dishonourable, underhand(ed), °venal, *Colloq* °crooked: *He got off by bribing a corrupt judge.* **2** debased, depraved, °perverted, subverted, °evil, °wicked, °degenerate, degraded: *The inhabitants practised a corrupt form of Christianity.*
—*v.* **3** °debase, °pervert, °subvert, °degrade, deprave, °warp: *A funds manager could easily be corrupted by all that money.* **4** °adulterate, °contaminate, °pollute, °taint, defile, infect, °spoil, °poison: *Drainage from the site has corrupted the purity of the water.* **5** °bribe, suborn, °buy (off): *He thought he knew a juror who might be corrupted.*

cost *n.* **1** °price, °outlay, °payment, °charge, °expense, °expenditure, °rate, °tariff: *The gold strap will double the cost of the watch. If the cost increases, the selling price must go up.*
—*v.* **2** °sell for, °get, °fetch, °bring in, *Colloq* set (someone) back: *This would cost twice as much in London.*

costume *n.* °dress, clothing, attire, °clothes, garb, °apparel, raiment, °garments, °outfit, vestment, livery, °uniform, °kit, *Colloq* °gear, togs, °get-up; *Slang* °rags, *US* threads: *What kind of costume is Celia wearing to the fancy-dress ball?*

cosy *adj.* **1** °comfortable, °snug, °warm, °restful, °secure, relaxing, °easy, *US* cozy, *Colloq* comfy: *They bought a cosy little rose-covered cottage in the Cotswolds.* **2** °convenient, °expedient, self-serving, underhand(ed): *He has a cosy arrangement with the planning board.*

cot *n.* bed, crib; cradle, bunk: *The baby is asleep in his cot.*

cottage *n.* °hut, °shack, °cabin, bungalow, shanty, *Literary* °cot; *US and Canadian* °lodge, chalet: *She's going to stay at our cottage for a week.*

couch *n.* **1** sofa, settee, settle, divan, love-seat, chaise (longue); day-bed; °tête-à-tête, vis-à-vis, siamoise; *US* Davenport: *Come and sit by me on the couch.*

—v. **2** embed, °frame, °style, °express, °phrase: *Her warning was couched in friendly words.*

council *n.* **1** °assembly, °meeting, conclave, °conference, synod, consistory, °convention, congress, congregation, °gathering, convocation, *US* caucus: *The council voted to ban nuclear arms.* **2** °board, °ministry, directors, °cabinet, panel, °committee, °body, directorate, directory, caucus: *She was elected to the council last year.*

counsel *n.* **1** °advice, °judgement, °direction, °opinion, °guidance, °instruction, °recommendation, exhortation, *Technical* paræ-nesis: *Your counsel has always been wise in the past.* **2** consultation, °discussion, deliberation, °consideration: *We took counsel with the cabinet on the matter.* **3** °adviser or advisor, °guide, °counsellor; °lawyer, *Brit* barrister; *US* attorney: *My counsel suggests we settle out of court.*
—v. **4** °advise, °recommend to, °suggest to, °instruct; °guide: *I have counselled her to pursue the matter.*

counsellor *n.* °adviser or advisor, °counsel, °lawyer, *Brit* counsellor-at-law, barrister, *US* counselor, counselor-at-law, attorney: *We have retained Vestley and Stock as our counsellors.*

count *v.* **1** count up or off, °enumerate, °number, °calculate, °add up, °total, °reckon, °compute, °tally, °figure up, quantify, *Colloq* °figure out: *Maddie counted the number of pencils in the box.* **2** °include, °consider, °regard, deem, °judge, °look on or upon: *You can count me among those who favour the idea.* **3 count on or upon:** °rely on or upon, °depend on or upon, be °sure of, °trust, bank on, be °confident of, *Chiefly Brit or US dialect* °reckon on or upon, *Chiefly US* °figure on or upon: *I knew I could count on Moira to do the right thing.*

counter *n.* **1** °token, disc, °chip, °piece, marker: *She placed three counters on the number 14.* **2** °table, °bar: *We do not serve beer at this counter.*

counteract *v.* counterbalance, °neutralize, °correct, annul, nullify, °cancel, °oppose, °mitigate: *The coffee counteracted the effect of the sleeping-pill.*

counterfeit *adj.* **1** forged, °fake, °fraudulent, °imitation, °bogus, °spurious, *Colloq* °phoney or US also phony: *The bank reported the counterfeit money to the police.* **2** make-believe, °sham, °pretended, °pretend, feigned, °insincere, °fake, faked, °false, °artificial, meretricious, pseudo, °factitious, °synthetic, °unreal, simulated: *You were warned about his counterfeit sincerity.*
—n. **3** °fake, °imitation, °forgery, °reproduction, *Colloq* °phoney or US also phony: *This is the original deed, that one is a counterfeit.*
—v. **4** °forge, °copy, °reproduce, °falsify, °imitate; *Slang* hang paper: *He made a living counterfeiting passports.* **5** feign, °pretend, simulate, °put on, °fake: *The suspects have shown signs of wealth that are difficult to counterfeit.*

counterfeiter *n.* *Slang* paper-hanger: *The counterfeiter, who forged only five-pound notes, was arrested today.*

country *n.* **1** °nation, °state, °power; °territory, °realm: *How many countries belong to the British Commonwealth?* **2** (°native) °land, homeland, °fatherland, motherland, mother country: *I would gladly fight for my country.* **3** countryside,

°rural area or surroundings, provinces, hinterlands; mountains, woods, wilderness, outback, *Colloq* sticks, *US* boondocks, boonies: *We are spending our holiday in the country.*

couple *n.* **1** °pair, duo, twosome; °brace, °span, yoke, °team: *They certainly make a nice couple.* **2 a couple of:** a °few, °several, a °handful (of), one or two, three or four: *I'll be with you in a couple of minutes.*
—v. **3** °join, °link, yoke, °combine, °unite, °match up, °connect: *The two carriages are easily coupled together.*

courage *n.* °bravery, valour, boldness, intrepidity, gallantry, dauntlessness, °daring, fearlessness, heroism, °nerve, *Colloq* °grit, guts, °pluck, °spunk, *US* moxie, sand, *Slang Brit* °bottle: *She had the courage to face the two of them alone.*

courageous *adj.* °brave, valiant, valorous, °bold, °intrepid, °gallant, °dauntless, °daring, °fearless, °heroic, *Colloq* plucky: *The soldiers were very courageous and fought against tremendous odds.*

course *n.* **1** °path, °way, °orbit, °route, °run, °track, ambit, °line, °circuit, °passage: *We continued on our course. The sun pursued its fiery course across the heavens.* **2** °movement, °progress, °headway, °advance, °progression; °speed: *The driver slackens his course at the curves.* **3** °procedure, °process, °performance, °routine, °conduct, °order, °practice, dispatch or despatch, °execution: *In the course of her duties, she handles a great deal of money.* **4** °direction, °tack: *If we stay on this course we'll run aground.* **5** °class, °lecture, seminar, °programme: *You should sign up for a course in English grammar.* **6 of course:** °naturally, °surely, certainly, °positively, °obviously, °definitely, assuredly, by all °means; °undoubtedly, indubitably, without (a) °doubt, no °doubt, *Colloq US* °sure: *Of course I'll go to the theatre with you!*

courteous *adj.* °polite, well-mannered, well-behaved, gentlemanly, °ladylike, °well-bred, °polished, urbane, civilized, °respectful, °civil, courtly, °proper, °decorous, °tactful, °considerate, °diplomatic: *He might have been rude to you, but he was always quite courteous to me.*

courtesy *n.* politeness, °elegance, courtliness, politesse, courteousness, °respect, respectfulness, °good manners, °formality, °civility, °ceremony: *I much appreciated the courtesy with which they treated me.*

cover *v.* **1** °protect, °shelter, °shield, °screen, °guard, °defend, °command: *The guns covered the approaches to the town.* **2** Also, **cover up or over:** °conceal, °hide, °bury, °mask, °shroud, °obscure; dissemble; °enclose, °envelop: *I was unable to cover my embarrassment. Her face was covered by the hood of the cloak.* **3** overlie, °spread over, overspread, °lie on, layer, °coat, blanket: *Oil covers the surface of the lake.* **4** °wrap, swaddle: *Mother covered us with warm blankets.* **5** °dress, °clothe, garb, attire, °robe, sheathe: *She was covered in silk from neck to ankle.* **6** °extend or °stretch over, °occupy, engulf, inundate, °submerge: *A lake has covered the original site of Abu Simbel.* **7** °include, °comprehend, °provide for, comprise, °extend over, °contain, °embody, °incorporate, °account for, take into °account, °take in, °deal with: *This report covers our activities* *over the past year.* **8** °act, take °responsibility or °charge, °stand or °sit in, °substitute, °take over, °run things, °double: *Go and get some coffee—I'll cover for you.* **9** °traverse, °complete, °pass or °travel over, °travel, °cross: *With frequent stops, we could not cover more than 50 miles a day.* **10** °compensate for, °defray, be °enough or °sufficient for, °counter, °offset, counterbalance, °make up for, insure or °protect against: *The policy covers losses of up to a million.* —*n.* **11** lid, °top, °cap, covering: *I can't find the cover for this pot.* **12** binding, boards, °wrapper, dust-jacket, jacket: *You can't tell a book by its cover.* **13** Often, **covers**: blanket, quilt, eiderdown, duvet, bedclothes, bedding, (bed) °linen; coverlet, counterpane; *US* comforter: *I crept into bed and pulled the covers over my head.* **14** °shelter, °protection, concealment, hiding-place, hide-out, °retreat, °refuge; °hide, *US and Canadian* blind; *Colloq Brit* hidey-hole: *We tried to find some sort of cover till the sun went down.* **15** °cloak, °screen, °disguise, concealment, °pretence, °front, °camouflage, smokescreen, cover-up, °mask, covering: *His bluster and bullying were only a cover for his cowardice.*

coward *n.* poltroon, craven, dastard, °sissy or cissy, °baby, mouse, °milksop; Scaramouch or Scaramouche; *Colloq* chicken, *Slang* yellow-belly; *US and Canadian* milquetoast: *He's such a coward that he's afraid of his own shadow.*

cowardice *n.* cowardliness, chicken-heartedness, faint-heartedness, timidity, timorousness, pusillanimity: *Owing to the cowardice of the lieutenant, the troop surrendered without a shot being fired.*

cowardly *adj.* °timid, °fearful, frightened, °afraid, °scared, °faint-hearted, timorous, chicken-hearted, chicken-livered, lily-livered, white-livered, craven, namby-pamby, dastardly, pusillanimous, vitelline, *Slang* yellow, yellow-bellied: *The cowardly rascals ran from the battle.*

coy *adj.* °shy, °modest, diffident, demure, °timid, °bashful, °self-conscious, °sheepish, timorous, unassuming, unpretentious; °reserved, self-effacing, °retiring, °evasive, °reluctant, °recalcitrant: *She was so coy she would disappear whenever we had guests.*

crack *n.* **1** °break, °fracture, °chink, °crevice, °rift, °gap, °flaw, °split, fissure, °slit, cleft, check, °rupture, °breach: *The crack in the dam was caused by an earthquake.* **2** °snap, °report, bang, °clap, °shot: *I ducked when I heard the crack of the rifle.* **3** °moment, °instant, °time, °second: *She gets up at the crack of dawn.* —*v.* **4** °snap: *He cracks the whip and the horses start up.* **5** °break, °fracture, °rupture; °shiver, °shatter, smash: *He fell backwards on the pavement and cracked his skull.* **6** fissure, craze, crackle, *US* alligator: *The heat of the sun caused the paint to crack.*

craft *n.* **1** °skill, °ability, artisanship, handiwork, °ingenuity, skilfulness, °art, °talent, °dexterity, cleverness, mastery, expertness, °expertise, °flair, genius, *Colloq* know-how: *Considerable craft is required to make that kind of jewellery.* **2** °deceit, guile, cunning, °fraud, °trickery, wiliness, foxiness, artfulness, craftiness, duplicity: *He exhibits that crooked wisdom called craft.* **3** °trade, °occupation, °calling, °vocation, métier; °profession: *He was a member*

of one of the medieval craft guilds. **4** °vessel, °ship, °boat; hovercraft; aircraft, aeroplane, °plane; spaceship, spacecraft, °rocket: *One day there will be at least as many craft in space as there now are in the air.* —*v.* **5** °make, °fashion, °fabricate: *She crafted the figures out of solid wood.*

crafty *adj.* °artful, cunning, °clever, °shrewd, °foxy, canny, °wily, °sly, °scheming, °calculating, °designing, plotting, °tricky, °sneaky, °deceitful, °shifty, °dodgy, guileful, insidious, double-dealing, °two-faced, duplicitous, treacherous: *That crafty beggar has made off with my life's savings.*

crag *n.* °cliff, °bluff, tor, °peak, °rock, escarpment, scarp, °precipice, *US* palisade: *Soaring above us was a huge crag that we still had to climb.*

cram *v.* **1** °pack, °stuff, overstuff, overcrowd, °jam, °fill: *The car was crammed to the top with suitcases.* **2** °study, burn the midnight oil, *Literary* lucubrate, *Colloq* °grind, *Brit* swot: *Bob can't go out because he's cramming for an exam.*

cramped *adj.* °tight, crowded, incommodious, uncomfortable, °close: *The tiny cabin was too cramped to hold all of us at once.*

crank *n.* **1** °eccentric, °character, °oddity, *Colloq* nut; *Slang Brit* nutter, nutcase: *Pay no attention to Jason, he's just a crank.* **2** monomaniac, °zealot, °fanatic: *The restaurant is patronized mainly by health-food cranks.*

cranky *adj.* **1** °eccentric, °odd, °weird, °strange, °queer, °peculiar, quirky, °capricious, °whimsical: *He's a cranky old bird who hardly goes out at all.* **2** °testy, grouchy, crabby, °short-tempered, °surly, irascible, °waspish, churlish, °gruff, curmudgeonly, °cantankerous, choleric, °snappish, °petulant, °peevish, contentious, °querulous, °irritable, splenetic, *Colloq* crotchety: *He's always cranky before breakfast.*

cranny *n.* °chink, °crevice, °crack, fissure, check, °fracture, °break, °furrow, °split, cleft: *Flowers grew from the crannies in the ancient wall.*

crash *v.* **1** °fall, °topple: *The vase crashed onto the stone floor.* **2** °force, °drive, °run, smash: *He crashed the car into a wall.* **3** bang, °boom, °explode: *The thunder crashed all around us.* —*n.* **4** °boom, bang, smash, °explosion, °blast: *We heard a great crash as the building collapsed.* **5** °disaster, °collapse, °failure: *The stock-market crash has had a devastating effect.*

crawl *v.* **1** °creep, worm, °wriggle, wiggle, °squirm; °edge: *A spider is crawling on your collar.* **2** inch, °creep, °drag: *For a solid hour the cars just crawled along at a snail's pace.* **3** cower, °cringe, grovel, toady, fawn: *Don't worry, he'll soon come crawling, begging you to take him back.* **4** °teem, °abound, °swarm, be °overrun or swamped: *The scene of the crime crawled with police.*

craze *n.* °fad, °fashion, °trend, °enthusiasm, °rage, °mania, °thing, °obsession; last word, dernier cri: *The craze for printed T-shirts goes on and on.*

crazy *adj.* **1** °mad, °insane, demented, °deranged, °unbalanced, unhinged, lunatic, non compos mentis, °daft, certifiable, °mental, touched (in the head), out of one's °mind or °head, °mad as a March hare or hatter, maddened, crazed, *Colloq* barmy or balmy, cuckoo, cracked, crackers, crack-brained, dotty, daffy, dippy, gaga, goofy, crackpot, loony, off one's rocker, have a screw loose, screwy, batty, bats, bats in the belfry, *Brit* barmy (in the crumpet), potty, bonkers, round the bend *or* °twist, off one's chump, doolally, *US* off one's trolley, out of one's gourd, screwball, nuts, nutty (as a fruit cake); *Slang* bananas, *US* out to lunch, meshuga, flaky, flaked-out, (plumb) loco: *His wife thinks he's crazy to want to walk around the world.* **2** °silly, °absurd, °foolish, °nonsensical, °inane, °ridiculous, °preposterous, laughable, risible, °ludicrous, asinine, °stupid, moronic, imbecile *or* imbecilic, idiotic, °feeble-minded, °hare-brained, *Colloq* crackpot: *Someone came up with a crazy idea of a square tennis ball to slow down the game.* **3** °impractical, °impracticable, unworkable, °unsound, °pointless, °imprudent, °rash, °reckless, ill-considered: *Columbus' plan to sail round the world was thought to be crazy at the time.* **4** °enthusiastic, °eager, avid, zealous, °keen, °excited: *I'm really crazy about windsurfing.* **5** °infatuated, °keen on *or* about, °wild, °mad, *Colloq* dotty, *US* nuts, nutty; *Slang US* ape: *Marjorie, I'm absolutely crazy about you.*

create v. **1** °make, °produce, °form, °bring into being, °originate, °conceive; sire, °father: *The question remains whether God created Man or vice versa.* **2** engender, beget, °spawn, °generate, °invent, °imagine, °think up, °frame, °forge, °fashion, °fabricate, °manufacture, °develop, °design, contrive, °devise, °produce, °dream up, °initiate: *Here is where they create many of the most successful television advertisements.*

creation n. **1** °beginning, °origin, °birth, °start, inception, genesis, making, °formation: *The creation of the lake began with the damming of the stream.* **2** °world, the °universe, the cosmos: *He was the most wicked man in the history of all creation.*

creative adj. °imaginative, inventive, originative, artistic, °original, °ingenious, °resourceful: *A truly creative artist seldom lacks for inspiration.*

creator n. **1** originator, °author, initiator, °founder, °father, inventor, architect, °designer, framer, maker, °prime mover: *The creator of this painting must have been a genius.* **2** God, Supreme Being, the Deity: *Some day you will have to answer to your Creator for your sins.*

creature n. **1** being, °organism, °entity, living °thing: *The hound had the saddest face I have ever seen on any creature.* **2 creature comforts**: (°physical *or* bodily *or* °material *or* mundane *or* °superficial *or* non-spiritual) luxuries: *He has the money to enjoy all the creature comforts.*

credit n. **1** °belief, °faith, °trust, credence: *I don't give much credit to what they say.* **2** creditation, °acknowledgement *or* acknowledgment, °attribution, ascription: *Credit for inventing the telegraph goes to Guglielmo Marconi.* **3** °trust, °confidence, faithfulness, reliability, trustworthiness, °honesty, °probity, dependability; solvency: *Her credit rating at the bank is excellent.* **4** °honour, commendation, °praise, °tribute, acclaim, °esteem, °recognition, °merit: *The team's victory in the finals has brought credit to the school.*
—v. **5** °believe, °trust, hold °accountable, put *or* place one's °faith *or* °confidence in, have °faith *or* °confidence in, °rely on, °accept, °depend on *or* upon: *If you credit the Bible, the*

world was created in six days. **6** ascribe, °acknowledge, °attribute, °assign; °impute: *The goal was credited to Barnes.*

creed n. °tenet, dogma, °doctrine, credo, teaching, principles, °belief, set of °beliefs: *She adheres to the creed of the Golden Rule.*

creek n. **1** *in Britain*: inlet, bay, cove, °harbour: *Overnight we moored in a little creek, sheltered from the sea.* **2** *in the US and Canada*: stream, streamlet, °brook, rivulet, rill, runnel, °run, °burn: *We used to fish in the creek behind the house.*

creep v. **1** °crawl, °slither, inch, °squirm, °wriggle, wiggle: *A tiny lizard was creeping up the wall.* **2** °crawl, °drag: *The hours creep by slowly when you have nothing to do.* **3** °steal, °sneak; °slink, skulk, tiptoe, *Colloq* °pussyfoot: *The thief must have crept in through the kitchen window. Someone is creeping about out there in the dark.*

crescent n. **1** demi-lune, semi-lune, lune, lunette: *The moon's crescent hung low in the western sky.*
—adj. **2** crescent-shaped, demi-lune, semi-lune, biconcave, concavo-concave: *For chopping, the chef uses a crescent blade that just fits into a curved wooden bowl.*

crest n. **1** °top, °summit, °pinnacle, °peak, °head, °ridge: *The surfers rode in on the crest of a wave.* **2** °seal, °device, °figure, badge, °emblem, insigne, °symbol, °design: *The school crest shows an inkpot and a scroll.*
—v. **3** °top, °crown, surmount, °cap: *The ancient walls were crested with ivy.* **4** culminate, °reach, °top, *US* °top out: *The flood-waters crested at nine feet.*

crevasse n. °gorge, chasm, °abyss, °ravine, fissure, °crack, °furrow: *One of the climbers fell into a crevasse in the glacier.*

crevice n. °crack, fissure, °chink, cleft, °cranny, °groove, °furrow, °break, °split, °rift: *Water ran down the crevices in the rocks.*

crew n. °group, °company, °band, troupe, °party, °gang, °team, °corps, °body: *We shall need a crew of twenty for tomorrow's job.*

crime n. °offence, °violation, °misdeed, °wrong; felony, misdemeanour; lawlessness: *The number of crimes of violence is increasing.*

criminal adj. **1** °illegal, °unlawful, °illicit, °lawless, °dishonest, *Colloq* °crooked: *Arson is a criminal act. We have to weed out the criminal element.* **2** °wicked, °evil, °bad, °wrong, °corrupt, °vile, °black, °immoral, amoral, °sinful, °villainous, iniquitous, flagitious, depraved; °disgraceful, reprehensible: *The way they treat their children is absolutely criminal.*
—n. **3** °felon, °convict, lawbreaker, °outlaw, °culprit, °offender, °miscreant, malefactor, wrongdoer, °villain, °scoundrel, knave, blackguard; °gangster, Mafioso, desperado, °racketeer, °hoodlum, °thug, hooligan, °tough, ruffian, °terrorist, *Colloq* roughneck, °bad °guy, °black hat, °bad hat, baddie *or* baddy, crook; *Slang* hood, *US* mobster: *He was arrested for consorting with known criminals.*

cringe v. **1** cower, wince, °flinch, quail, °recoil, blench, °tremble, °quiver, °quake *or* °shake in one's boots *or* shoes, °shrink: *That dirty little coward cringed even when they called his name.* **2** °defer, °kowtow, grovel, °crawl, fawn, boot-lick, *US* apple-polish; *Slang* °kiss someone's arse *or US and Canadian* ass, *Taboo slang* brown-nose: *The man cringed before the magistrate, his eyes downcast, tugging his forelock.*

cripple *n.* **1** amputee, paralytic: *He has been a cripple since the accident.* —*v.* **2** disable, °lame, °incapacitate, °handicap, °maim; °impair, °damage, °weaken, debilitate, emasculate, °enervate: *She was crippled when a child. The dictator's power was crippled by the revolt.*

crippled *adj.* **1** °disabled, °lame, handicapped, incapacitated; weakened, °weak, debilitated: *He takes care of his crippled mother. The crippled party platform succumbed to attack from the far left.* **2** damaged, immobilized, inoperative: *The crew stayed with the crippled vessel.*

crisis *n.* **1** turning-point, °critical time *or* °moment: *She has passed the crisis and will be better tomorrow.* **2** °disaster, °emergency, °calamity, °catastrophe, °danger: *The storm has created a crisis and the residents are being evacuated.*

crisp *adj.* **1** °brittle, crunchy, friable, breakable, crumbly, frangible: *Keep the biscuits crisp in this special jar.* **2** curly, crispy, crinkly, frizzy, frizzled: *His hair is brown and crisp, just like his father's.* **3** *US* chip: *I'll bet you can't eat just one potato crisp.*

critical *adj.* **1** carping, °fault-finding, censorious, disparaging, depreciatory *or* depreciative, depreciating, deprecatory *or* deprecative, deprecating, judgemental: *The article was highly critical of the council.* **2** °crucial, °important, °essential, °basic, °key, decisive, °pivotal, °vital, °momentous: *The meeting at the bank will be critical for us.* **3** °grave, °serious, °dangerous, °uncertain, °perilous, °severe, touch-and-go, °ticklish, °sensitive, °touchy, *Colloq* °parlous: *His illness has reached the critical stage.*

criticism *n.* **1** °judgement, °evaluation, appraisal, °analysis, assessment, °estimation, valuation: *Their criticism was generally favourable.* **2** censure, °disapproval, condemnation, disparagement: *I was very upset by her criticism of my behaviour.* **3** critique, °review, commentary: *My sister writes the theatre criticisms for the local paper.*

criticize *v.* **1** °judge, °evaluate, value, assess, appraise, °estimate; °discuss, °analyse: *He criticizes books for the quarterly.* **2** censure, find °fault (with), °carp (at), °cavil (at), °condemn, °attack, °denounce, °disapprove (of), °put down, impugn, °blast, °lambaste, *Colloq* °pan, °knock, *Brit* slate: *His book was criticized because of its poor scholarship. Why must he constantly criticize, even when there's nothing wrong?*

crooked *adj.* **1** °criminal, °dishonest, °illegal, °unlawful, °illicit, °wrong, °perverse, *Slang Brit* °bent: *Selling a stolen painting is crooked.* **2** °bent, bowed, askew, awry, °deformed, distorted, contorted, °lopsided, twisted, °misshapen, °disfigured, warped, °gnarled: *Because of the constant west wind, the trees are all crooked.*

cross *n.* **1** crucifix, rood: *In ancient times, it was common to execute certain criminals by nailing them to a cross.* **2** °hybrid, cross-breed, °mongrel; °blend, °combination: *This fruit is a cross between a plum and a pear.* —*v.* **3 cross off** *or* **out**: °strike out, °erase, °cancel, °rub out, °delete, °wipe out: *After that remark, I'm crossing you off my list.* **4** °meet,

intersect, °join: *The roads cross further on.* **5** °cross over, °go across, °pass over, °span, °traverse: *The bridge crosses the river here.* —*adj.* **6** °peevish, irritated, annoyed, piqued, °irritable, °testy, °snappish, irascible, °surly, choleric, splenetic, grouchy, huffish *or* huffy, pettish, °cranky, grumpy, °touchy, °moody, fractious, vexed, curmudgeonly, °petulant, °waspish, °querulous, °cantankerous, crusty, °short-tempered, on a short fuse, *Colloq* crotchety, *Slang Brit* shirty: *He's cross because he has a headache.* **7** annoyed, irritated, °angry, irate, °furious: *I was very cross that you took the car without permission.*

crouch *v.* °bend (down), squat (down), hunker down, °stoop (down): *If you crouch down, no one will see you in the bushes.*

crowd *n.* **1** °throng, multitude, horde, °swarm, °mass, °press, °flood, °mob, °flock, °pack: *A huge crowd descended on the village square.* **2** °company, °set, °circle, °lot, °bunch, °group, coterie, °clique, claque, °faction: *She doesn't associate with our crowd any longer.* —*v.* **3** °throng, °swarm, °herd, °pour, °pile, °press, °cluster, °gather, °get together, °flood, °flock, °assemble, congregate: *People crowded into the stadium.* **4** °push, °press, °drive, shove, °thrust, °force, °load, °pack, °cram, °jam, corral: *The police crowded the hooligans into vans.* **5** compress, °squeeze, °pack, °jam, °cram, °collect, °stuff: *We were so crowded in the cabin we could hardly breathe.*

crown *n.* **1** coronet, diadem, wreath, fillet, circlet, tiara: *The princess wore a golden crown set with jewels.* **2** °sovereignty, °rule, °dominion, °authority, °government, °realm, rulership, °jurisdiction: *They discovered many lands and annexed them to the Crown.* **3** °monarch, ruler, °sovereign, potentate; °king, °queen, emperor, empress, His *or* Her Majesty, His *or* Her Highness: *The Crown has very little real power these days.* —*v.* **4** enthrone, *Colloq US* coronate: *He was crowned on the death of his father.* **5** °cap, °top, surmount, culminate, °climax, consummate, °fulfil, °reward: *All her years of practising the violin were finally crowned with success.*

crucial *adj.* °critical, decisive, °pivotal, °vital, °momentous, °major, °important, °essential: *It is crucial that you press the right button.*

crude *adj.* **1** °unrefined, °raw, °natural, °original, unprocessed: *Those are the prices of crude oil, not the petrol used in cars.* **2** °rough, unpolished, °rudimentary, °immature, °undeveloped, °primitive, °unrefined, unfinished: *At this stage, she has only a crude idea of the design.* **3** °rough, °coarse, °rude, °unrefined, uncouth, crass, °gross, °rustic, uncivil: *Don't you despise his crude manners?* **4** °blunt, °brusque, °unsophisticated, °inconsiderate, °tasteless, indelicate, °offensive, °improper, °vulgar: *How crude of him to ask her how long since her husband had 'croaked'!*

cruel *adj.* **1** °merciless, pitiless, hard-hearted, °harsh, stony-hearted, °heartless, unsparing, °callous, °beastly, °cold-blooded, °ruthless, °unkind, °hard: *It was cruel of you to refuse to help.* **2** °ferocious, °inhuman, barbaric, barbarous, °brutal, °savage, °bloodthirsty, °vicious, °sadistic, °fiendish, diabolic(al), hellish, °atrocious, Neronian *or* Neronic *or* Neroic: *His captors subjected him to the cruellest tortures.*

cruise v. **1** °sail, °coast, °travel, °journey, voyage; yacht: *We cruise in the Caribbean during the winter.* —n. **2** °sail, voyage, °journey, °boat *or* yachting °trip: *I took a three-day cruise around the Isle of Wight.*

crumb n. °fragment, °morsel, °bite, °scrap, °particle, °shred, snippet, °sliver, °bit, °speck, scintilla, mote, molecule, atom: *There isn't a crumb of food in the house.*

crumble v. °disintegrate, °fragment, break apart, °break up, °shiver, °come to pieces: *Acid rain has caused the stone façade to crumble. In the face of the attack, his resolve crumbled.*

crumple v. °wrinkle, °crush, crease, °rumple, °mangle, crinkle: *Your jacket is all crumpled.*

crunch v. **1** °chew, °bite, °crush, °grind, °munch: *He crunched the nuts between his teeth.* —n. **2** moment of truth, °decision °time, °crisis, °critical °moment, °showdown, crux, °juncture: *You can count on me when it comes to the crunch.*

crusade n. **1** °campaign, °expedition, °holy °war; jihad *or* jehad: *He joined the crusade against the Saracens.* —v. **2** °campaign, °war, °battle; °take up a °cause, °lobby, °fight: *She is crusading for equal rights for women.*

crush n. **1** °break, smash, °crunch, °pulverize, °shiver, °splinter, °pound, °grind: *The vandals crushed the statue to bits with hammers.* **2** °crumple, °wrinkle, crease, crinkle, °rumple, °mangle: *The shirts came back crushed from the laundry.* **3** squash, °pulp, mash, °squeeze, compress, °press: *The machine crushes the oranges and extracts the juice.* **4** °overcome, °defeat, °conquer, vanquish, °beat, thrash; °subdue, °put down, °quash, °quell, °overwhelm, °squelch, °suppress, °repress: *The title-holder crushed the challenger. The junta crushed the uprising without bloodshed.* **5** abash, °embarrass, °shame, °mortify, °depress, °devastate, °humiliate, °disgrace: *She was really crushed when he refused to see her.* —n. **6** °press, °pressure, °crowd: *When the fire alarm sounded, I was almost caught in the crush of the people trying to escape.*

cry v. **1** °weep, °sob, wail, °keen, °bawl, °shed tears: *Paul cried when they took his mother away.* **2** whimper, °snivel, pule, mewl, whine, °moan, °groan, °fret, *Colloq* turn on the waterworks, *Brit* grizzle: *Don't cry over spilt milk.* **3 cry out for**: °demand, °need, °call for, °beg for, °plead for: *Her hair is so untidy it cries out for trimming. Wanton murder cries out for vengeance.* —n. **4** °scream, °shriek, wail, °howl, yowl: *I heard the mournful cries of those being tortured.* **5** °shout, °whoop, °yell, °howl: *Uttering blood-curdling cries, the rebels attacked.* **6** °call, °sound, °note: *The noise was the cry of the lesser grebe to its mate.* **7** °war cry, battle-cry, °slogan, watchword: 'Down with the king!' was the cry used to rally the rabble.* **8 a far cry**: a long °way, °quite a °distance, °remote, °distant, not, not °quite, °very °different (from): *This report is a far cry from what I had expected.*

crypt n. °tomb, vault, mausoleum, °sepulchre, °grave, catacomb; °cellar, basement: *He is buried in the crypt of St Paul's.*

cryptic adj. **1** °secret, °occult, °mystical, °hidden, esoteric, mystic, cabbalistic: *The sarcophagus was covered with cryptic symbols.* **2** °obscure, °mysterious, unclear, °nebulous, °vague, inscrutable, °recondite, arcane, enigmatic, °puzzling: *I cannot make head or tail of her cryptic remarks.*

cuddle v. **1** °snuggle up (to), °nestle *or* °huddle (against): *She cuddled the baby closer to her.* **2** °caress, °embrace, °fondle, °hug, °pet, bill and coo, make °love (to), *Colloq* neck, smooch, *Australian and New Zealand* smoodge *or* smooge, *Slang US* °make out (with), watch the submarine races: *The couple were cuddling in the back seat.* —n. **3** °hug, °embrace, °snuggle: *Give us a cuddle, Janie.*

cue n. **1** °prompt, °hint, °reminder, °signal, °sign: *Give her the cue to start singing.* —v. **2** °signal, °prompt, °remind: *She was cueing me to begin, but I'd lost my voice.*

culprit n. **1** accused, °prisoner: *How does the culprit plead?* **2** °offender, °criminal, malefactor, wrongdoer: *They caught the culprit red-handed.*

cultivate v. **1** °till, °plough, °farm, °work: *These lands have been cultivated since time immemorial.* **2** °grow, °raise, °tend, °produce: *What crops can be cultivated in this climate?* **3** °develop, °promote, °further, °encourage, °foster, °advance: *She's been cultivating a friendship with her boss.* **4** woo, make advances to, ingratiate oneself with, court, pay court to, curry °favour with, *Colloq* °work on, *Slang* suck up to, butter up, *US* shine up to; *Taboo slang* brown-nose: *He is cultivating Trevor only because he wants something from him.*

cultivated adj. °sophisticated, cultured, °educated, °refined, °elegant, soigné(e), civilized, °polished, aristocratic, urbane, °suave, cosmopolitan: *She prefers to go out with cultivated older men.*

culture n. **1** cultivation, °refinement, °sophistication, urbanity, suavity, °elegance, (good) °breeding, °background, erudition, °education, enlightenment, °learning, °taste, °discrimination, savoir faire, savoir vivre, discernment: *She is a lady of considerable culture as well as beauty.* **2** °civilization, mores, °customs, lifestyle, °way of °life, (sense of) values: *In their culture, women make the important decisions.*

curb n. **1** °check, °restraint, °control: *You should put a curb on your tongue.* —v. **2** °check, °restrain, °bridle, °control, °contain, °repress, °subdue, °suppress: *Try to curb your exuberance.*

cure n. **1** course of °treatment, °therapy, °remedy, medication, medicament, °medicine, °drug, °prescription; cure-all, nostrum, panacea: *The doctor said there was no cure for her illness.* —v. **2** °heal, °mend, °restore to °health *or* working °order, °remedy, °rectify, °correct, °repair, °fix: *What can't be cured must be endured.* **3** smoke, pickle, °dry, °salt, °preserve, corn, marinate: *That cured ox tongue is simply delicious!*

curiosity n. **1** inquisitiveness, °interest: *His insatiable curiosity next led him to study astronomy.* **2** snooping, prying, peeping, intrusiveness, meddlesomeness, °interference, *Colloq* nosiness, Nosy Parkerism: *Curiosity killed the cat.* **3** curio, °oddity, °rarity, conversation piece, objet de virtu *or* vertu, objet d'art, found °object; bric-à-brac *or* bric-a-brac, knick-knack, °bauble, trinket, °gewgaw: *The shop sells curiosities, like goblets made from ostrich eggs. In those days, every house had a curiosity cabinet.*

curious *adj.* **1** °inquisitive, inquiring, °interested: *I am curious to know what you were doing in there all night.* **2** snooping, prying, °intrusive, meddlesome, interfering, *Colloq* °nosy: *Our neighbours are entirely too curious about our activities.* **3** °odd, °peculiar, °eccentric, °strange, °outré, °queer, °unusual, °outrageous, °offbeat, °weird, °bizarre, unconventional, freakish, °exotic, °singular, out of the °ordinary, °extraordinary, °erratic, pixilated, °quaint, °outlandish, °grotesque, aberrant, °abnormal, °irregular, °deviant, °deviate, *Colloq* °kinky, nuts, nutty; *Slang Brit* barmy: *How do you explain Frieda's curious behaviour?*

current *adj.* **1** °contemporary, °ongoing, °present, contemporaneous, °simultaneous, coeval: *The current issue of the magazine came out last week.* **2** °prevalent, °prevailing, °common, °popular, accepted, known, widespread, reported, in °circulation, going °round *or* around, bruited about, °widely known, in the °air, present-day: *The current theories reject those of a decade ago.* **3** °fashionable, °stylish, à la °mode, modish, in °vogue, °latest, up to °date, *Colloq* °trendy: *The current trend is towards shorter skirts.* **4** *US* up to date, in the °know, °informed, advised, in °touch, °aware, posted, *au courant, au fait,* on the qui vive: *The* Financial Journal *keeps me current on stock prices.*
—*n.* **5** °stream, °flow, °undercurrent: *The canoe was caught in the current and carried away.* **6** °course, °progress, °tendency, °tenor, °drift, °trend, °inclination, mainstream: *The current of public opinion is turning in favour of policies that are more environmentally responsible.*

curse *n.* **1** malediction, imprecation, denunciation, damnation, execration, °oath: *He heaped curses on all those who opposed him.* **2** °evil, bane, °misfortune, °affliction, °torment, °harm, °scourge, cross to °bear: *The curse of our generation is that so few of us deeply believe anything.* **3** °profanity, °oath, blasphemy, obscenity, bad °language, °dirty °word, swear-word, curse-word: *A stream of curses issued from the bathroom when Joe cut himself shaving.*
—*v.* **4** °damn, execrate, °blast, °denounce, anathematize, excommunicate: *He was cursed by the priests and forbidden ever to enter a temple again.* **5** °swear at, °blaspheme at: *The muleteer was cursing his team.* **6** °burden, saddle, °weigh down, °handicap: *She was cursed with bad eyesight and had to wear thick glasses.*

cursory *adj.* °superficial, °hasty, °hurried, °passing, quick, slapdash, °perfunctory, °rapid, °summary: *She gave the note a cursory glance and threw it away.*

curt *adj.* °abrupt, °short, °terse, °brief, laconic, °concise, °blunt, °gruff, °harsh, °brusque, unceremonious, °snappish, crusty, °rude: *His answer was a curt 'No', without any explanation.*

curtail *v.* °shorten, °abbreviate, °cut °short, °abridge, °diminish, °reduce, °cut, °cut back, °cut down: *Both our working week and our salaries were curtailed.*

cushion *n.* **1** pillow, °bolster, °pad: *The women of the harem sat on cushions on the floor.*
—*v.* **2** °soften, absorb, °mitigate, °reduce, buffer, °insulate, mollify, lessen: *They offered me a month's paid holiday to help cushion the blow of being transferred.*

custody *n.* **1** °care, custodianship, °safe keeping, °protection, °charge, guardianship, keeping: *She was granted custody of the children.* **2** °imprisonment, °detention, incarceration, confinement: *The police took three troublemakers into custody.*

custom *n.* **1** °practice, °habit, °usage, °fashion, °way, wont, °tradition, °routine, °convention, °form: *According to custom, the warriors of the tribe paint their bodies.* **2 customs:** °toll, °duty, impost, °tax, excise, levy, °dues, °tariff: *He was assigned to collect customs and port duties.* **3** °patronage, °support, °business, °trade: *The new butcher needs as much custom as possible.*
—*adv.* **4** °specially, °especially, °expressly, exclusively, °particularly; to °order: *All her clothes are custom-made.*

customary *adj.* **1** °usual, °normal, °conventional, °routine, °everyday, °common, commonplace, °ordinary: *Is it customary for them to eat lunch on the premises?* **2** °accustomed, °habitual, °regular, °traditional, wonted: *I took the customary way home.*

customer *n.* **1** °client, °patron, °buyer, purchaser; consumer: *Mrs Morris is one of our regular customers.* **2** °chap, °fellow, °character, °person, °guy, *Colloq Brit* bloke: *She would never go out with an ugly customer like that.*

cut *v.* **1** °gash, °slash, °slit; °open: *I cut my finger on the glass.* **2** °slice, °cut off, °carve: *Please cut me a thick piece of steak.* **3** Often, **cut up:** °hurt, °wound, °pain, °upset, °grieve, °distress, aggrieve, °slight, °insult, °offend, affront: *I was really all cut up by her nasty remarks.* **4** °trim, °snip, °lop, °clip, crop, °shorten, shear, °chop off; °mow; °dock: *The barber has cut too much off the sides.* **5** °abbreviate, °shorten, crop, condense, °abridge, °edit, cut back, °reduce, cut down; epitomize, °abstract, °digest, summarize, °curtail: *Cut this script to make it fit into the allotted time.* **6** °dilute, °thin, °water (down), °weaken; °degrade, °adulterate: *They cut the rum with water to make grog.* **7** °avoid, °fail to °attend, eschew: *Cynthia cut classes three days this week.* **8** °lower, °reduce, lessen, cut back (on), cut down (on), °slash, °diminish, °decrease, retrench (on), °curtail: *We shall have to cut expenses if the company is to survive.* **9** conclude, °settle, °agree: *Once the deal was cut, there was no going back on it.* **10** °prepare, °draw, °write, °sign: *We'll have accounting cut your cheque and send it at once.* **11 cut back: a** See 5, above. **b** See 8, above. **12** Often, **cut dead:** snub, °slight, °spurn, °shun, °ignore, give the cold °shoulder (to): *Cornelia had the gall to cut Jason dead at his own party.* **13 cut down: a** °fell, °chop *or* hew down: *Don't cut down that tree!* **b** °kill, cut off, °murder, assassinate: *He was cut down in his prime.* **14 cut in:** °interrupt, °intrude, °interfere, *Colloq* °butt in: *Please don't cut in on our conversation.* **15 cut off: a** °cleave, °sever, °chop *or* °lop *or* °hack off: *Cut the branch off near the trunk.* **b** °intercept, °interrupt, °discontinue, °end, °stop, °terminate, °break off: *There was a click and our phone conversation was cut off.* **c** °separate, °sever, °split, estrange: *He's been cut off from the family for years.* **d** disinherit, disown,

°reject: *She was cut off with a shilling.*
16 cut out: **a** °delete, °remove, excise, °strike
or °cross out, °edit out, °omit, cut, °kill, *Technical*
dele: *The publishers made me cut out parts of the
book that they were advised might be
libellous.* **b** °extract, excise, °remove, resect: *My
appendix was cut out years ago.* **c** °stop, °cease,
desist (from), °quit: *Whenever it rains the engine
cuts out. Cut out the clowning around.* **d** °suit,
°equip, °fit: *I don't think Cyril's cut out to be a
lumberjack.* **e** °plan, °prepare, °ready, °organize,
°destine: *He certainly has his work cut out for
him!* **17 cut up**: **a** °chop (up), dice, cube,
mince, cut, °divide (up), °carve (up): *Cut the celery
up very small.* **b** °misbehave: *The football supporters began to cut up rough.* **18 cut up rough**:
get °angry, lose one's °temper, °show
°resentment: *The driver began to cut up rough
when I refused to pay.*
—*n.* **19** °gash, °slash, °incision, °nick, °wound:
I got a nasty cut from that razor. **20** °share,
°portion, °percentage, °piece, dividend, commission: *Blatchley gets a cut on every car we
sell.* **21** reduction, cut-back, curtailment,
°decrease: *The government's cuts in spending affect
us all.* **22** deletion, excision, °omission: *The
author refuses to approve the cuts in the script.*
23 affront, °insult, °offence, °slight, snub, °dig,
jibe, °slap in the face, cold °shoulder:
*The unkindest cut was the accusation of
cheating.* **24** °engraving, °plate: *This cut is too
badly worn for use now.* **25** artwork, °picture,
°illustration, °plate, °drawing, line cut, line
°engraving, half-tone: *The book has 300 cuts and
only 20 pages of text.*
—*adj.* **26** separated, °detached, severed: *I prefer
cut flowers to a plant.* **27** abridged, °abbreviated,
cut-down, shortened, edited, curtailed: *The
magazine published a cut version of the
novel.* **28** reduced, diminished, lowered, discounted: *This shop sells everything at cut prices.*
29 cut and dried: **a** clear-cut, settled,
arranged, °decided, °predetermined, prearranged: *Unfortunately, the solution to this problem is not cut and dried.* **b** °stale, unoriginal,
trite, hackneyed, °old; °dull; °boring: *His suggestions for improvement are always cut and dried.*
c manufactured, °automatic, unchanging,
unchanged: *Mr Mackay will again present his old
cut and dried plan.*

cute *adj.* **1** °pretty, °attractive, °adorable,
°dainty, °lovely, °beautiful, *Colloq US* cunning:
*There were a lot of cute children at the beauty
competition.* **2** °clever, °shrewd, °ingenious,
adroit, °crafty, cunning: *It was very cute of him to
suggest his brother for the job.*

cutthroat *n.* **1** °murderer, °pirate, °killer, °thug,
hatchet man, gunman, assassin, *Slang US* gunsel, torpedo, hit man: *Those streets are frequented
by thieves and cutthroats.*
—*adj.* **2** °merciless, °ruthless, °unmerciful,
unprincipled, °relentless, pitiless, °brutal,
°cold-blooded, °cold-hearted: *Her cutthroat tactics
call for dismissing all executives.* **3** °murderous,
°homicidal, °lethal, °deadly, barbaric, °fierce,
°cruel, barbarous, °savage, °inhuman, °brutal,
brutish, °violent, °ferocious, °bloodthirsty,
°sanguinary, bloody, feral, °vicious, °truculent:
*He was once a member of a gang of cutthroat hood-
lums.*

cutting *adj.* **1** °severe, °biting, °chill, °cold, °icy,
°frigid, °freezing, °raw, °piercing, °penetrating:
*A cutting wind seemed to go right through
me.* **2** °sarcastic, °sardonic, °bitter, °scornful,
sneering, acid, °scathing, acerb(ic), wounding,
°stern, °harsh, °caustic, mordant, acrimonious,
°contemptuous; malevolent, malicious, invidious, °vicious, °venomous: *Her cutting remarks
completely devastated me.*
—*n.* **3** scion, °slip, clipping: *Mrs Galloway allowed
me to take a cutting from her rose bush.*

cycle *n.* **1** °round, rotation, °circle, °course;
series, °sequence, °run, °succession, °pattern: *We
must learn to break the continuous cycles of war and
peace.*
—*v.* **2** °recur, °return, °rotate, recycle, °circle:
*The water from the fountain is cycled back to the
reservoir.*

D

dab v. **1** daub, °pat, °tap, tamp, °touch: *Dab a little more paint into the crevices.*
—n. **2** °touch, °drop, °trace, °bit, mite, °hint, °suggestion, °pinch, °dash, °spot, tinge, *Colloq* dollop, smidgen *or* smidgin: *Add just a dab of mustard to the sauce.* **3** daub, °poke, °pat, °tap, °touch: *Wipe it away with a dab of a damp cloth.*

dabble v. **1** °dip, °splash, °spatter, sprinkle, bespatter, besprinkle, bedabble: *I sat on the rock, dabbling my toes in the pool.* **2 dabble in** *or* **with** *or* **at**: °tinker, °trifle (with), °potter *or* US putter, dally, *Colloq* °fool (around *or* about *or* with *or* about with): *She's not seriously interested in music—she just dabbles in it.*

dab hand n.phr. past °master, °expert, °master, °adept, °authority, wizard, *Colloq* ace: *Oscar is a dab hand at wood-carving.*

daft adj. **1** °foolish, °silly, °giddy, °senseless, °absurd, °ridiculous, °stupid, °nonsensical, fatuous, fatuitous, imbecile *or* imbecilic, idiotic, moronic, °obtuse, cretinous, boneheaded, fat-headed, dim-witted, witless, asinine, attocerebral, weak-minded, simple-minded, brainless, °feeble-minded, feather-brained, rattle-brained, °hare-brained, slow-witted, °halfwitted, fat-witted, addle-pated, addle-brained, *Brit* gormless; *Colloq* °dumb, dopey *or* dopy, daffy; *Slang* cock-eyed, US cockamamie *or* cockamamy, running on 'Empty': *He has the daft idea that he will be appointed managing director.* **2** See **crazy**, **1**, above. **3 daft about**: °mad about, °infatuated with, besotted by *or* with, °sweet on, *Colloq* nuts about, °crazy about: *Those two are daft about each other.*

dagger n. °knife, poniard, skean, °short sword, stiletto, dirk, °blade, kris, bowie °knife, bayonet: *It was his dagger that was sticking out of the man's back.*

daily adj. **1** °diurnal, circadian, °everyday, quotidian: *The daily papers reported nothing about the fire.* **2** °ordinary, °common, commonplace, °everyday, °routine, °regular: *Her trip to the market has become a daily occurrence.*
—adv. **3** constantly, °always, habitually, day after day, regularly, every day, continually, continuously: *The trains run daily between here and London.*

dainty adj. **1** °delicate, °graceful, °fine, °elegant, °exquisite, °neat: *The value lies in this dainty border painted round the edge of the cup.* **2** °fastidious, °sensitive, °squeamish, °finicky *or* finical, over-nice, overrefined, °genteel, °mincing: *He seems somewhat dainty in his choice of words.* **3** °choice, °delicious, delectable, °tasty, appetizing, palatable, toothsome: *They were given a few dainty morsels to nibble while waiting.*
—n. **4** °delicacy, sweetmeat, °treat, comfit, °titbit *or* US tidbit, °morsel: *A plate of dainties was placed beside the bed each night.*

damage n. **1** °harm, °injury, °hurt, °impairment, mutilation, °destruction, devastation: *Fortunately, there was little damage from the storm.* **2** °expense, °price, °cost, °bill, invoice, US °check: *At the restaurant, the damage came to £50.* **3 damages**: compensation, reparation, °indemnity: *We won the suit and were awarded damages of £10,000 for defamation of character.*
—v. **4** °harm, °hurt, °injure; °wound; °mutilate, disfigure, °mar, °deface; °wreck, °ruin, °spoil, °impair: *Although the car was badly damaged, the passengers escaped unharmed. Will this news damage your chances of a promotion?*

damn v. **1** °condemn, °criticize, find °fault with, °berate, °castigate, °upbraid, °attack, °blast, °reprimand, °reprove, remonstrate, °denounce; °blame: *Some would damn him for saving the murderer from drowning, others would damn him if he didn't.* **2** °doom, °condemn, °sentence: *Sisyphus was damned for all eternity to roll a heavy stone up a hill.* **3** °curse (at), °swear (at), execrate: *I damned the day I first set foot in that house.*
—n. **4** °jot *or* tittle, brass farthing, *Slang* hoot, two hoots (in hell), *Slang* tinker's damn *or* cuss: *His opinion isn't worth a damn.* **5 give a damn**: °care, °mind, be °concerned, °worry, *Slang* give a hoot: *Why should he give a damn if the critics panned his play?*

damnable adj. °awful, °terrible, °horrible, horrid, °atrocious, °abominable, °dreadful, °hideous, execrable, accursed, cursed, detestable, °hateful, °abhorrent, °despicable, °loathsome, °wicked, °sinful, °offensive, heinous, pernicious, °infernal, malicious, malevolent, °outrageous, °foul, °rotten, °base, °vile, odious: *He has been telling the most damnable lies about her since they broke up.*

damp adj. **1** °clammy, °moist, wettish; °humid, dank, °misty, dewy, °steamy, °muggy: *Wipe off the table with a damp cloth. Nothing dries out in this damp weather.*
—n. **2** moistness, moisture, dampness, clamminess, humidity: *The mould on the walls is the result of the damp.*

dampen v. **1** °damp, moisten, sprinkle, bedew: *Dampen the clothes before ironing them.* **2** °stifle, °deaden, °damp, °check, °chill, °cool, °restrain, °retard, lessen, °diminish, °reduce, °suppress, abate, °moderate, allay, °subdue, °temper, °dull, °discourage: *His constant chattering on about himself dampened her ardour.*

dance v. **1** °cavort, gambol, °caper, °skip, °leap, romp, trip the light fantastic (toe), US cut a rug, sashay, *Colloq* bop, hoof it: *We danced for joy when we heard the news. Would you care to dance?*
—n. **2** ball, social, dancing °party, thé dansant, US tea dance, °promenade, *Colloq* shindig *or* shindy, hop, bop, US and Canadian prom: *I have invited her to the dance on Saturday evening.*

dandy n. **1** fop, coxcomb, (°gay) °blade, beau, °gallant, lady-killer, ladies' °man, °rake, *Colloq* °swell, clothes-horse, *Brit* toff, blood, US °dude: *He was a great dandy, and spent hours dressing every day.*
—adj. **2** °fine, °splendid, °first-rate, °great, °marvellous, °neat, spectacular: *Penny's father bought her a dandy new car.*

danger n. **1** °peril, °risk, °threat, °hazard, °jeopardy: *The danger of an avalanche is too great* *to go skiing.* **2 in danger of**: °likely (to be), °liable (to be): *If you drink and drive, you are in danger of causing a road accident.*

dangerous *adj.* **1** °risky, °perilous, °hazardous, unsafe, °precarious, °rickety, *Colloq* chancy, iffy: *Rock-climbing is very dangerous.* **2** °threatening, °menacing, °harmful, treacherous: *He is a dangerous criminal, wanted for murder.*

dangerously *adv.* **1** perilously, hazardously, unsafely, precariously, recklessly: *He's a mountain-climber who likes to live dangerously.* **2** ominously, alarmingly: *She is standing dangerously close to the edge.*

dangle *v.* **1** °hang (down), °droop, °depend, °swing, °sway: *The rope dangled from the top of the flag-pole.* **2** °flaunt, brandish, °wave, °flourish: *Competitors often dangle big salary increases in front of those who agree to leave our company.* **3** °wait, *Slang* cool one's heels: *They have kept me dangling for weeks for their decision.*

dapper *adj.* °neat, °spruce, °smart, °trim, well-dressed, °well turned out, °stylish, °fashionable, °elegant, °chic, °dressy; *Colloq* got up *or* dressed to the nines, dressed to kill, °swanky *or* swank, ritzy; *Slang* snazzy, °nifty, spiffy, °sharp, °swell, classy: *Tony looks very dapper in his new Savile Row suit.*

dapple *adj.* **1** spotted, dotted, °mottled, °speckled, °flecked, dappled; brindled; pied, piebald, skewbald, °paint, flea-bitten, *US* pinto: *Take the chestnut mare—I'll ride the dapple grey.* —*v.* **2** °spot, °dot, mottle, speckle, bespeckle, stipple: *Dapple paint on the wall with a sponge to get a mottled effect.*

dare *v.* **1** °challenge, °defy, °provoke; throw down the gauntlet: *She dared me to jump, so I jumped.* **2** °risk, °hazard, °gamble, °venture, °face, make °bold, be so °bold as: *I would never dare to talk to my father that way.* —*n.* **3** °challenge, °provocation, °taunt; °ultimatum: *She took the dare and swam across the lake.*

daredevil *n.* **1** exhibitionist, °showman, °stunt man, °stunt woman; °adventurer, soldier of fortune, *Colloq* °show-off: *William finally got a job as a daredevil in the circus.* —*adj.* **2** °reckless, °rash, death-defying, °impulsive, °daring, °dashing, °impetuous, incautious, °imprudent, °wild, °foolhardy, madcap, devil-may-care; °audacious, °bold, °brave, °fearless, °gallant, °courageous, °intrepid: *Do you consider ski-jumping a sport or an example of daredevil madness?*

daring *n.* **1** °courage, boldness, °bravery, valour, intrepidity, fearlessness, °grit, °pluck, °spirit, mettle, adventurousness, derring-do, *Colloq* guts, °spunk, °nerve; *Slang Brit* °bottle: *Diving from a cliff into the sea takes a lot of daring.* —*adj.* **2** °bold, °audacious, °courageous, °brave, valorous, °intrepid, °fearless, unafraid, plucky, mettlesome, °adventurous, °venturesome, °hardy; °rash, °reckless, *Colloq* gutsy, *US* nervy: *In the 19th century, a few daring explorers penetrated the jungles of Africa.*

dark *adj.* **1** °unlit, unlighted, unilluminated, ill-lighted, ill-lit, °sunless; °black, Stygian, pitch-dark, inky, jet-black: *We cowered in a recess in the dark cave.* **2** °dim, °murky, tenebrous, °shady, °shadowy: *I could scarcely see ahead of me in the dark forest.* **3** °gloomy, °dismal, °dreary, °dull, °drab, subfuscous, subfusc, °bleak, cheerless, °mournful, °dour, °pessimistic, °sombre, °doleful, °joyless, °grim, °sad, °melancholy, °sorrowful: *Why do you always look at the dark side of things?* **4** °evil, °wicked, °vile, °base, °foul, iniquitous, nefarious, black-hearted, °villainous, °sinister, °satanic, °devilish, hellish: *Nostradamus predicted that dark forces would overrun the world.* **5** °murky, °overcast, cloudy, °threatening, °black, °dusky, louring *or* lowering; foggy, °misty; *US* glowering: *Another dark day on the moor and I thought I'd go mad.* **6** °mysterious, °deep, °profound, °incomprehensible, enigmatic, °puzzling, impenetrable, unfathomable, abstruse, °recondite, arcane, °obscure: *She took her dark secret to the grave.* **7** °hidden, concealed, °secret, °occult, mystic(al), °cryptic: *The true reason for his leaving was always kept dark in the family.* **8** brunette; °black, °swarthy, brown; (sun) tanned, *Old-fashioned* swart: *One is fair with dark hair, the other has dark skin.* **9** °ignorant, unenlightened, °benighted: *Our culture passed through a dark phase before the Renaissance.* —*n.* **10** °night, night-time, nightfall: *We waited till dark to make good our escape.* **11** darkness, blackness, °gloom, gloominess, murk, murkiness: *At fifty, isn't he a bit old to be afraid of the dark?* **12** °obscurity, °ignorance: *She was always kept in the dark about his true identity.*

darling *n.* **1** °sweetheart, °beloved, °love, °dear, dearest, true-love: *She insists on buying all her darling's clothes.* **2** °pet, °favourite, apple of one's eye, *Brit* blue-eyed boy *or* girl; *US* fair-haired boy *or* girl: *Frank might have been the black sheep of the family, but he was always his mother's darling.* —*adj.* **3** °beloved, loved, cherished, adored, °dear, °precious, treasured: *He travelled everywhere with his darling niece.* **4** °pleasing, °fetching, °attractive, °adorable, °enchanting, °lovely, alluring, °engaging, bewitching, charming: *Josephine was wearing a darling frock she'd just bought at the Corner Boutique.*

dash *v.* **1** °crash, smash, °shatter, °break, °shiver, °fragment, °split; °destroy, °ruin, °spoil, °frustrate, °obliterate: *The mirror was dashed to smithereens when it fell. The ship didn't see our raft, and our hopes of rescue were dashed.* **2** °hurl, °toss, °throw, °fling, °cast, °pitch, *Colloq* chuck: *We drank a toast, then dashed our glasses into the fireplace.* **3** °rush, °run, dart, °spring, °bolt, °bound, °race, sprint; °hasten, °fly, °hurry, °speed: *I'll have to dash to catch my train.* **4 dash off**: scribble: *I've just dashed off a note to mother.* —*n.* **5** dart, °bolt, °rush, °run, °spurt, °spring, °bound, sprint: *He made a dash for the door but it was too late.* **6** °flourish, élan, °flair, liveliness, °style, °panache, °spirit, brio, °verve, °zest, °spice; °ardour, °fervour, °vigour, °energy: *She is known for her beauty as well as her dash and courage.* **7** °bit, °pinch, soupçon, °hint, °suggestion, °touch, °trace, tinge, °taste, °drop, °piece, *Colloq* smidgen *or* smidgin, *US* tad: *Add a dash of nutmeg at the end.*

dashing *adj.* **1** °spirited, °lively, °impetuous, °energetic, °vigorous, °dynamic, °animated, *Colloq* peppy: *She is now going out with a dashing young fellow from the City.* **2** °fashionable, °stylish, °chic, à la °mode, modish, °smart, °elegant, °dapper, *Colloq Brit* °swish: *That's a* dashing coat, Felicia. **3** °flamboyant, °showy, °ostentatious, °pretentious: *George Hutton was a bit too dashing for her taste.*

data *n.* facts, °information, statistics, °figures, °details, °matter, observations, °material(s); °text; °evidence: *We shall process the data on the computer and print out the results.*

date *n.* **1** °time, year, °season, °period, °day; °age, °era, epoch, °stage, °phase: *These artefacts are from an earlier date than was first supposed.* **2** °appointment, °meeting, °engagement, rendezvous, assignation, tryst; °fixture: *She already has a date for Saturday night.* **3** °escort, °companion, °friend, boyfriend, girlfriend, °girl, °woman, °boy, °man, swain, beau, °lover, *Colloq* steady: *Bob is Sally's date for the dance.* **4 out of date**: °old-fashioned, °old, °ancient, archaic, °antiquated, dated, °passé, outmoded, °obsolete, °obsolescent, *Colloq* °old hat: *This timetable is out of date. Why do you wear those out of date clothes?* **5 up to date**: °modern, °latest, °current, °contemporary, à la °mode, °fashionable, *Colloq* °trendy: *Her taste in music is quite up to date. Use this up-to-date edition of the encyclopedia.*
—*v.* **6** show one's °age, make °obsolete *or* °obsolescent *or* °old-fashioned: *That pompadour hair-do really dates her.* **7** °entertain, °escort, °go out (with), °go steady (with): *Does Michael still date Patsy? Those two are still dating.*

daunt *v.* °intimidate, cow, °discourage, dishearten, dispirit, °unnerve, °shake, °upset, disconcert, °discomfit, °put off, awe, °overawe, °appal, °alarm, °threaten, °frighten, °terrify, °scare, terrorize: *He was daunted by the prospect of facing the entire council.*

dauntless *adj.* °fearless, undaunted, unafraid, unflinching, °stalwart, °brave, °courageous, °bold, °audacious, °intrepid, valorous, °daring, °gallant, °heroic, °venturesome, plucky, stout-hearted, valiant: *Dauntless, the knight rode into the thick of the fray.*

dawdle *v.* °linger, loiter, °straggle, °delay, °procrastinate, dally, °lounge, laze, °idle, °lag, °lie about, °waste °time, *Colloq* dilly-dally, °shilly-shally: *We have to catch the next train, so stop dawdling.*

dawn *n.* **1** daybreak, sunrise, break of °day, °crack of dawn, °first °light, dawning, cock crow, *Literary* aurora, day-spring, *US* sun-up: *We shall attack the castle at dawn.* **2** dawning, °beginning, commencement, °start, °birth, awakening, inception, genesis, °outset, °onset, °origin, °appearance, °arrival, advent, °emergence, inauguration, °rise, °first °occurrence: *The dawn of western civilization has been placed in Anatolia.*
—*v.* **3** °gleam, °break, °brighten, °lighten: *The day dawned on the deserted beach.* **4** °begin, °originate, °commence, °arise, °appear, °emerge, °start, °arrive, °develop, °unfold: *The day of the computer had not yet dawned when I was a child.* **5 dawn on** *or* **upon**: °occur to, °come to °mind, become °apparent *or* °evident to: *It slowly dawned on me that he had been lying all along.*

day *n.* **1** daytime, °daylight, broad °daylight, °light of day: *Sunrise quickly turned night into day.* **2** °time, hour, °age, °period, °era, epoch, °date, °prime, heyday; lifetime: *Her day will come. In his day, there was no telephone.*

day-dream *n.* **1** °reverie, wool-gathering, °fantasy, °fancy, °dream, musing, °castle in the air *or* in Spain, pipedream: *The realities of life have cured me of many day-dreams.*
—*v.* **2** °fantasize, °imagine, °fancy, °envisage, °envision, °dream: *She still day-dreams that a knight in shining armour will come and carry her away.*

daylight *n.* **1** sunlight, °sun, sunshine, °light: *Coming from the cave, we were blinded by the daylight.* **2** °open, broad daylight, °light of day, full °view, full °knowledge, °clarity: *We must bring his treachery out into the daylight.*

daze *v.* **1** °stun, stupefy, °blind, °dazzle, bedazzle, °shock, °stagger, °startle, °astonish, °astound, °amaze, °surprise, °overcome, °overpower, °dumbfound, benumb, °paralyse, *Colloq* °bowl over, °floor, flabbergast; *Slang* blow one's mind: *She was dazed to learn her husband was still alive.* **2** befuddle, °confuse, °bemuse, °bewilder, °puzzle, °mystify, baffle, °perplex, °nonplus, °blind: *He was dazed by the difficulty of the examination.*
—*n.* **3** °confusion, °flurry, °spin, whirl: *The entire week was a continuous daze of cocktail parties and dinner parties.* **4 in a daze**: stupefied, in a °trance, bewildered, °confused, perplexed, disoriented, °dizzy, dazzled, bedazzled, °overcome, overpowered, nonplussed, befuddled, flustered; startled, surprised, shocked, stunned, astonished, astounded, amazed, staggered; bemused, baffled, puzzled, mystified, *Colloq* flabbergasted, bowled over, floored: *Arthur was in a daze to find himself the centre of attention.*

dazzle *v.* **1** °impress, °bewitch, °enchant, °charm, °beguile, °intrigue, °captivate, °fascinate, spellbind, °entrance, °hypnotize, mesmerize: *Every man in the room was dazzled by Mrs d'Arcy's brilliant wit and good looks.* **2** See daze, 1, above.
—*n.* **3** °brilliance, °splendour, magnificence, °sparkle, °glitter, *Slang* razzle-dazzle, razzmatazz: *Many actors are lured to New York by the dazzle of Broadway.*

dazzling *adj.* °bright, °brilliant, resplendent, blinding, bedazzling, °radiant, °splendid, °magnificent, °glorious, sparkling, °scintillating; °stunning, °overwhelming, °overpowering, stupefying, dizzying; °gorgeous; *Colloq* splendiferous, mind-boggling: *In the chest was a dazzling collection of the finest jewels.*

dead *adj.* **1** deceased, °defunct, °extinct, gone, departed, °late, °lifeless, no more, *Colloq* done for, *Slang Brit* gone for a burton: *Both his parents are dead, and his only brother lives in Australia. Lycidas is dead, dead ere his prime.* **2** insensate, °insensible, °numb, paralysed, benumbed, unfeeling: *After the accident, my left thumb was completely dead.* **3** °insensible, °unconscious, °out, dead to the world, deathlike, deathly: *At the news of her son, she fell in a dead faint.* **4** insensitive, unemotional, unfeeling, emotionless, apathetic, °lukewarm, °cool, °cold, °frigid, unresponsive, °unsympathetic, °indifferent, unconcerned, uninterested; °numb, °wooden, °callous, hardened, impervious, inured, °inert: *He has always been dead to others' problems.* **5** °out, smothered, extinguished: *The fire is dead.* **6** °inanimate, °lifeless, °inert, inorganic: *Dead stones speak volumes to the geologist.* **7** °extinct, °obsolete, perished, °past, outmoded,

°disused, expired, °passé: *Latin is a dead language.* **8** °barren, unfruitful, °infertile, unproductive: *That area off the coast is dead as far as fishing goes.* **9** °tired (out), °exhausted, °worn out, °fatigued, °spent, collapsing, in a °state of °collapse, *Slang* bushed, °beat, *Brit* knackered, *US and Canadian* pooped: *We were completely dead after the hike into town.* **10** °dull, lustreless, °flat, °neutral, °vapid, °empty, °bland, °colourless, °grey, beige, °dun: *The walls of the prison were painted a dead white.* **11** °stagnant, motionless, °still, °standing, °static, °inert, unmoving, °inactive, °quiet, °calm: *There were small pools of dead water covered with a green slime. Without a breath of air stirring, the boat was dead in the water.* **12** °boring, °dull, °tedious, °tiresome, °monotonous, °prosaic, uninteresting, run-of-the-mill, °ordinary, commonplace, °dry, insipid, °bland, °flat, two-dimensional, °lifeless, °stiff, °rigid, °stony: *The play was bad, the performance dead.* **13** °dull, muffled, deadened, anechoic, unresounding, non-resonant: *One room in the laboratory was built to be dead to all sound.* **14** °complete, °entire, °total, °absolute, °downright, °thorough, through and through, utter, all-out, °out-and-out, °unqualified, un-relieved, unbroken, °categorical, °outright: *My investment in the anti-gravity pill has so far been a dead loss.* **15** °profound, °deep: *I fell into a dead sleep.* **16** °sudden, °abrupt, °complete, °full: *The train came to a dead stop.* **17** °certain, °sure, unerring, °exact, °precise, °accurate, crack: *According to the records, Calamity Jane was a dead shot.*
—*adv.* **18** °completely, °entirely, °absolutely, °totally, °utterly, °thoroughly, unconditionally, unqualifiedly: *You are dead right about Pontefract.* **19** °completely, °entirely, °absolutely, °totally; °abruptly, °suddenly: *He stopped dead in his tracks and stared at me.* **20** °directly, °exactly, °precisely: *An enormous maelstrom lay dead ahead of the fragile craft.*
—*n.* **21** °depth(s), °extreme, °midst, °middle: *She used to visit his room in the dead of night.*

deaden *v.* **1** °numb, benumb, °paralyse, anaes-thetize, desensitize, °dull; °damp: *This injection will deaden your hand and you'll feel no pain.* **2** °weaken, °moderate, soothe, °mitigate, assuage, °reduce, lessen, °diminish, alleviate, °cushion, °soften, mollify, °blunt, °dull: *He took to drink to deaden the shock of losing his only son.*

deadlock *n.* **1** °standstill, °impasse, °stalemate, stand-off, °draw, stoppage, *Colloq US* Mexican stand-off: *Union and management negotiators have reached a deadlock on the pension issue.*
—*v.* **2** bring or come to a °standstill or °impasse, °stall, °stop, °halt: *The Congress is likely to deadlock on the question of expanding national health benefits.*

deadly *adj.* **1** °lethal, °fatal; °dangerous, per-nicious, °poisonous, noxious, toxic; baleful, °harmful, nocuous: *This drug is deadly if taken in large doses.* **2** °mortal, °implacable, °ruthless, °savage: *They were deadly enemies long after the war was over.* **3** °murderous, °homicidal, °bloodthirsty, °brutal, °vicious, °ferocious, bar-barous, barbaric, °savage, °inhuman, °cold-blooded, °heartless, °ruthless, pitiless, °merciless: *Two deadly killers have escaped from Dartmoor prison.* **4** deathly, deathlike, °pale, pallid, °ghostly, cadaverous, °ghastly, °wan, °white, livid, ashen: *He turned a deadly hue, as if*

he had seen a ghost. **5** °boring, °excruciating, °dull, °tiresome, °tedious, °dreary, °humdrum, °lacklustre, wearying, wearisome: *It was a deadly play put on by deadly actors.* **6** °exact, °precise, °accurate, °true, unerring, unfailing: *Each arrow hit the bull's-eye with deadly accuracy.*

deaf *adj.* **1** hard of hearing, stone-deaf: *Sean is slightly deaf in his left ear.* **2** unhearing, unheed-ful, °heedless, °insensible, insensitive, imper-vious, °indifferent, °oblivious, unresponsive, °unmoved, unconcerned, unyielding: *The judge was deaf to all appeals for clemency.*

deal *v.* **1** °distribute, °dole out, °give out, °parcel out, °mete out, °allot, apportion, °administer, °dispense: *Deal thirteen cards to each of the four players. She dealt out her own brand of justice to criminals.* **2** °buy and °sell, °handle, °stock, do °business, °trade, °traffic: *This shop deals only in the most expensive linens.* **3** °behave, °act, °conduct oneself: *Simon has never dealt openly, so you mustn't trust him.* **4 deal with:** °treat, °handle, take °care of, have to do with, °attend to, °see to, °reckon with, °grapple with, °act on; °practise, °administer, °engage in: *I shall deal with the matter tomorrow.*
—*n.* **5** °transaction, °arrangement, °negotiation, °agreement, °contract, °bargain, °understanding: *The deal to sell the textbook division is off.* **6** Often, **great deal**: (°large or °great) °amount, °lot, (°large or °huge) °quantity; extent: *There's been a great deal of crime in that neighbourhood.*

dealer *n.* °trader, businessman, businesswoman, °merchant, °tradesman, retailer, shopkeeper, vendor, merchandiser; wholesaler, jobber, dis-tributor, stockist, supplier; °broker, °agent, sales-man, *US* storekeeper: *He has been a dealer in precious gems for years.*

dealings *n.pl.* °business, °commerce, °exchange, °trade, °traffic, °transactions, °negotiations; °relations, relationships, °affairs: *All his business dealings are reviewed by his solicitor.*

dear *adj.* **1** °beloved, loved, adored, °darling, °precious, cherished, prized, valued, treasured, °favoured, °favourite, °pet, esteemed, admired, venerated, honoured: *He was my nearest and dearest friend.* **2** °expensive, costly, high-priced, °highly priced, *Colloq* °pricey or pricy: *Tomatoes are much too dear at this time of the year.*
—*n.* **3** °darling, °sweetheart, °beloved, °love, true-love, °sweet, honey, °precious, °pet, °favourite, °treasure, *Colloq* sweetie, sweetie-pie, *Slang* °baby: *My dear, I hope we'll be together always.*
—*adv.* **4** °dearly; at great °cost or °expense, at a high or excessive °price: *That little error will cost you dear, my friend.*

dearly *adv.* **1** greatly, °very much, °indeed, °sincerely: *I should dearly like to go, but I can-not.* **2** affectionately, °fondly, lovingly, tenderly: *He loves his mother very dearly.* **3** expensively, °dear, at °great °cost or °expense, at a °high or °excessive °price, punitively: *The victory at Thal-amos was dearly bought.*

dearth *n.* °scarcity, °want, °need, °lack, defi-ciency, sparseness or sparsity, scantiness, insuf-ficiency, inadequacy, °shortage, paucity, exiguity, °poverty, exiguousness; °absence: *There is a dearth of major roles for black actors.*

death *n.* **1** demise, decease, °passing, °dying, °end: *She was overcome with grief at the news of* his *death*. **2** °end, °termination, cessation, °expiration, expiry: *Nobody mourned the death of the bill in the lower house*. **3** °end, °finish, °termination; extinction, °destruction, extermination, annihilation, eradication, obliteration, extirpation, liquidation, °ruin, °downfall, °undoing: *The invasion marked the death of the Roman Empire*.

deathless *adj.* °eternal, °everlasting, °immortal, undying, imperishable, °permanent, unending, °timeless, never-ending: *In his opinion, his novel was another example of his deathless prose*.

debase *v.* **1** °lower, °degrade, devalue, °depreciate, °depress, demote, deprecate, °belittle, °diminish, °reduce, disparage: *Words which denote fine qualities are in time debased*. **2** °adulterate, °contaminate, °taint, °pollute, °corrupt, °mar, °spoil, °impair, °vitiate, abase, defile, bastardize; °poison: *To increase profits, the manufacturer has debased the traditional formula*.

debatable *adj.* °controversial, arguable, °questionable, °doubtful, dubious, °problematic *or* problematical, °disputable, open *or* subject to °dispute *or* °doubt *or* °question, in °dispute *or* °doubt *or* °question, °moot, polemic *or* polemical, unsure, °uncertain, °unsettled, undecided: *Whether he is the best person for the job is debatable*.

debate *n.* **1** °discussion, °argument, °dispute, altercation, °controversy, wrangle, contention, polemic; argumentation: *I refuse to take sides in the debate over social services*. **2** deliberation, °consideration, (careful) °thought, °reflection, cogitation, meditation, contemplation: *Payment of reparations to the victims of the disaster is a matter for debate*.
—*v.* **3** °argue, wrangle, °dispute, °contest, contend; °discuss, °moot, °question: *We debated only the most important issues*. **4** °deliberate, °consider, °reflect (on), °mull over, °ponder (over), °weigh, ruminate (over), °meditate (on *or* over), °think (over *or* on), °think through: *I have often debated in my own mind the question of capital punishment*.

debonair *adj.* **1** °suave, soigné(e), °elegant, urbane, °refined, °dapper, °genteel, °well-bred, °courteous, °civil, mannerly, °gracious, °polite, affable, °obliging, °pleasant, *Colloq* °smooth: *Despite his vicious temper, he was most debonair in company*. **2** °carefree, insouciant, °gay, °nonchalant, light-hearted, °dashing, charming, °cheerful, °buoyant, °jaunty, °sprightly: *Being handsome and debonair, he was much sought after by hostesses*.

debt *n.* **1** °obligation; °due, indebtedness, °liability, °responsibility, °accountability, °encumbrance: *He owes a debt of gratitude to his wife for her moral support. The company takes care of all debts promptly.* **2 in debt**: under °obligation, owing, °accountable, °beholden, °indebted, °responsible, answerable for, °liable, encumbered, in arrears, °straitened, in dire straits, in (financial) °difficulty *or* °difficulties, in the red, *Colloq US and Canadian* in hock: *I shall always be in debt to you for your help. The London branch is in debt for ten million pounds.*

début *n.* **1** °première *or* premiere, introduction, °initiation, inauguration, °launch *or* launching, coming out: *The young soprano's début at La Scala was a triumph.*

—*v.* **2** °launch, °come out, °enter, °appear: *His plan is to début with a zither accompaniment.*

decadent *adj.* **1** declining, decaying, deteriorating, debased, degenerating, falling off, on the °wane, °withering, degenerative: *The decadent literature of the period was a reflection of the decline in moral standards.* **2** °corrupt, °dissolute, °immoral, debauched, dissipated, °self-indulgent, °degenerate: *His decadent behaviour brought him to the attention of the police.*

decay *v.* **1 a** °decline, °wane, °ebb, °dwindle, °diminish, °decrease: *The magnetic field rapidly decays when the power is removed.* **b** °decline, °waste away, atrophy, °weaken, wither, °degenerate, °deteriorate, °disintegrate; °crumble: *Her great beauty decayed quickly.* **2** °rot, °decompose, moulder, °putrefy, °spoil; °turn, go °bad, °go off: *The flesh has decayed and only a skeleton remains.*
—*n.* **3** °decline, weakening, °failing, fading, deterioration, decadence, degeneration, wasting, atrophy, dilapidation, disintegration, °collapse; °downfall: *The buildings were in an advanced state of decay.* **4** °rot, rotting, decomposition, °mould, putrefaction, mortification: *The decay has weakened the timbers supporting the bridge.*

deceit *n.* **1** °deception, deceitfulness, °fraud, fraudulence, cheating, °trickery, °chicanery *or* chicane, °dissimulation, dishonesty, misrepresentation, double-dealing, duplicity, °hypocrisy, treachery, underhandedness, guile, °craft, slyness, craftiness, cunning, knavery, funny business, *Colloq* °hanky-panky, monkey business: *Inside traders on the Stock Exchange profit enormously from deceit.* **2** °trick, °subterfuge, °stratagem, ploy, °ruse, °manoeuvre, °artifice, °wile, °hoax, °swindle, °double-cross, misrepresentation, °pretence, °sham, contrivance, °shift, confidence °trick, subreption, gloze, *Brit dialect or colloq US* flam; *Colloq* flimflam; *Slang* scam, con, con °trick, con °game: *She was sick of all his lies and deceits.*

deceitful *adj.* °dishonest, underhand(ed), untrustworthy, misleading, °crooked, °insincere, °false, °fraudulent, °counterfeit, °disingenuous, °lying, mendacious, untruthful; °wily, °crafty, °sly, cunning, °scheming, guileful, °artful, °sneaky, double-dealing, °two-faced, °hypocritical, duplicitous, *Colloq* °phoney *or US also* phony: *It was deceitful of you to pretend you loved her when all you wanted was her money.*

deceive *v.* °mislead, delude, °impose on *or* upon, °fool, °hoax, °trick, °cheat, °swindle, °betray, °double-cross, °lead on, °lead up *or* down the garden °path, °lead astray, pull the wool over (someone's) eyes, inveigle, °cajole, *Archaic* cozen; *Colloq* con, bamboozle, °take in, take for a °ride, two-time, move the goalposts; *Slang US* °take: *He deceived even his friends and family into believing he had been a war hero.*

decent *adj.* **1** °becoming, °suitable, °appropriate, °proper, °seemly, °fitting: *Despite the life she led, the woman should have a decent burial.* **2** °seemly, °decorous, °tasteful, °dignified, mannerly, °nice, °clean, °respectable, °polite, °modest, °presentable, °acceptable: *Hereafter, you will use only decent language when speaking to me!* **3** °adequate, °acceptable, °passable, °fair,

°competent, °mediocre, middling, °fair to middling, °moderate, °respectable, not °bad, °ordinary, so so, not °outstanding, unimpressive, °average, neither here nor there, all °right, °reasonable, °tolerable, °satisfactory, °good enough, *Colloq* °OK or okay: *Sales in the first quarter were decent but hardly outstanding.* **4** °courteous, °proper, °right, °fair, °honest, °honourable, °friendly, °considerate, °gracious, °nice, °thoughtful, °obliging, °kind, °generous, accommodating: *You can count on David to do the decent thing.* **5** °chaste, °pure, °virtuous, °modest, °well-bred, °decorous, °well brought up, °nice, °respectable: *Caroline is a decent girl, but no great brain or beauty.*

deception *n.* **1** duplicity, °deceit, °intrigue, °hypocrisy, °fraud, cheating, °trickery, °chicanery *or* chicane, °dissimulation, double-dealing, °subterfuge, sophistry, treachery, knavery, tergiversation; see also **deceit 1**, above: *He practised deception even in his family relationships.* **2** °trick, °ruse, °artifice, °stratagem, °subterfuge, °manoeuvre, °wile, imposture, °hoax, °sham, °pretence; see also **deceit 2**, above: *He tried every deception in the book to separate her from her money.*

deceptive *adj.* **1** misleading, °false, °illusory, deceiving, °unreliable: *He has the look of an athlete, but appearances can be deceptive.* **2** °fraudulent, °deceitful, dishonest, untruthful, °fake, °false, °shifty, fallacious, °specious, °spurious, °bogus, °counterfeit, pseudo, sophistical; °tricky, °dodgy, °evasive, °elusive, °slippery, *Colloq* °phoney *or US also* phony: *The bank is being deceptive about its credit rating.*

decide *v.* **1** °determine, °settle, °resolve, conclude, take *or* reach *or* come to a °decision *or* conclusion, make up one's °mind, arbitrate, °judge, adjudicate, referee, °umpire: *She decided that you were right. They decided the case in my favour.* **2 decide on** *or* **upon**: °fix *or* °fasten *or* °settle on *or* upon, °choose, °select, °pick (out), °elect, opt (for), °commit oneself (to): *I have decided on a British-made car.*

decided *adj.* **1** °definite, °pronounced, °marked, unmistakable, unambiguous, unequivocal, °certain, °sure, °absolute, °obvious, °clear, °evident, °unquestionable, unquestioned, °indisputable, °undisputed, undeniable, irrefutable, incontestable, °unqualified, unconditional, °incontrovertible, °solid: *The party was a decided success.* **2** °fixed, °firm, °resolute, °determined, adamant, °stony, °unhesitating, decisive, °definite, unfaltering, °assertive, asseverative, unswerving, unwavering: *They are decided in their approval of her plan.*

decipher *v.* **1** decode, decrypt; unravel, unscramble, disentangle, °translate, °work out, °explain, °solve, *Colloq* °figure out: *It was Champollion who deciphered the Rosetta Stone.* **2** °read, °interpret, °make out, *Colloq* °figure out: *I can't decipher Theresa's handwriting or what she's trying to say.*

decision *n.* **1** °settlement, °determination, °resolution, settling, resolving, arbitration: *The decision is the umpire's responsibility.* **2** °judgement, conclusion, °resolution, verdict, °sentence, ruling, °finding, °decree, °settlement, °outcome: *According to the decision, the victims will receive*

compensatory damages. **3** °determination, firmness, decidedness, °resolve, decisiveness, conclusiveness, steadfastness, °purpose, purposefulness: *She asserted her position with decision.*

declaration *n.* **1** °statement, °assertion, attestation, deposition, asseveration, affirmation, avowal, °announcement, °proclamation, °pronouncement, °profession: *Henrietta desperately wanted to believe Henry's declaration of love.* **2** °proclamation, °announcement, °pronouncement, promulgation, pronunciamento, edict, ukase, manifesto, °notice: *The colonists issued a declaration of independence.*

declare *v.* **1** assert, °say, °offer, °submit, affirm, °state, aver, asseverate, avow, avouch, °profess, °protest, °swear, °claim, °proclaim; °confirm, °certify, °ratify: *I solemnly declare that the testimony I am to give is true, so help me God.* **2** °announce, °make known, °pronounce, °decree, °rule, °proclaim, herald, promulgate, °publish, °broadcast, trumpet (forth): *Robert has declared his intention to make Marianne his wife.*

decline *v.* **1** °refuse, °turn down, °deny, °reject, demur, °forgo, °veto, °avoid, abstain from: *She declined help with the packages. Roger was offered a professorship at the university but he declined.* **2** °diminish, lessen, °decrease, °wane, °flag, °go down, °fall *or* °taper off, °subside, °ebb, abate, °dwindle, °shrink, °fade, *Colloq* peter out, °run out of steam, *US* °run out of gas: *Demand for hula hoops declined.* **3** °slope *or* °slant (downwards), °descend, °drop *or* °fall off, °dip, °sink: *The meadow declines towards the river.* **4** °deteriorate, °degenerate, °worsen, °fail: *My health has declined over the last year.* **5** °go *or* °drop down, °settle, °dip, °sink, °set: *The sun was declining as I went home.*
—*n.* **6** diminution, °decrease, lessening, °ebb, downturn, fall-off, reduction, abatement, °slump, descent: *There has been a steady decline in the value of the pound.* **7** degeneration, deterioration, °loss, diminution, weakening, debility, °weakness, worsening, °decay, °failing: *We noted a decline in the physical condition of those living nearby.* **8** declivity, (°downward) °slope *or* °slant, descent, °downgrade, °incline: *The path led down a steep decline towards the pond.*

decompose *v.* **1** °disintegrate, °separate, °fall *or* °come °apart, °break up *or* down, take °apart, dissect, anatomize, atomize, °resolve, decompound, °analyse: *By absorption the scientists decomposed the green light into yellow and blue.* **2** °rot, °disintegrate, °decay, moulder, °putrefy; °spoil, °go off *or* °bad, °turn °sour: *The meat will decompose if it is left outside the fridge.*

decorate *v.* **1** °embellish, adorn, °ornament, garnish, embroider, °elaborate, bedeck, deck (out), °trim, °dress (up), °spruce *or* smarten up, °beautify, *Literary* caparison, *Colloq Brit* °tart up: *We decorated the pub for the Christmas holidays.* **2** *Brit* paint, wallpaper, redecorate, furbish, °refurbish, °renovate, °fix up, °restore: *All the bedrooms have been decorated.*

decoration *n.* **1** garnish, °trim, trimming, adornment, °embellishment, °ornament, ornamentation, garnishment: *There's a bit too much decoration on the cake.* **2** medal, laurel, °award, badge, colours, °order, ribbon, °star, garter: *Captain Harder won many decorations in the war.*

decorous *adj.* °becoming, °dignified, °decent, °correct, mannerly, °seemly, °refined, °elegant, °polite, well-behaved, °genteel, demure, °polished, gentlemanly, °ladylike: *Your behaviour was less than decorous at last night's party.*

decorum *n.* 1 °etiquette, °proper °behaviour, °propriety, °good °form, mannerliness, politeness, °dignity, gentility, °good °manners, respectability, courtliness, deportment: *The decorum of the meeting was disturbed by rabble-rousers.* 2 correctness, °propriety, °protocol, punctilio, conformity: *Please observe proper decorum when visiting the embassy.*

decoy *n.* 1 bait, °lure, °trap, °attraction, °enticement, °inducement, stool-pigeon: *The hunters set out their decoys and waited for the ducks.* —*v.* 2 °lure, entrap, °entice, °attract, °induce, °seduce, bait, °trick, °tempt, ensnare, inveigle, allure: *He was decoyed into a dark alley and robbed.*

decrease *v.* 1 °diminish, °reduce, °decline, lessen, °lower, abate, °fall off, °shrink, °shrivel (up), °contract, °dwindle, °ebb, °subside, °wane, °taper off, de-escalate, slacken, °let up, °ease (off *or* up), °curtail, °cut (down *or* back), *Colloq* °run out of steam, *US* °run out of gas: *Demand for tickets to rock concerts has decreased over the years. The number of applicants for work is decreasing.* —*n.* 2 diminution, reduction, °decline, lessening, lowering, abatement, falling off, shrinking, shrivelling, contraction, decrement, dwindling, °ebb, subsidence, tapering off, °wane, de-escalation, slackening, easing (off *or* up), curtailment, °cut, cut-back: *There has been no noticeable decrease in the price of houses in the south-east. Have you noticed the decrease in arrests for dangerous driving?*

decree *n.* 1 °order, mandate, directive, ordinance, edict, law, statute, °regulation, enactment, °act, ruling, dictum, °dictate, °injunction, °sanction, manifesto, °proclamation, promulgation, °determination, °decision, °judgement, rescript, °prescription, pronunciamento, firman, ukase, *Rom Cath Ch* decretal: *The star chamber issued a decree restricting the freedom of the press.* —*v.* 2 °order, °command, °direct, °rule, mandate, ordain, °dictate, °charge, enjoin, °proclaim, °pronounce, °prescribe, °decide, °determine, adjudge, *Scots law* decern: *The council has decreed that no spirits can be sold on Sundays.*

decrepit *adj.* 1 °feeble, enfeebled, °weak, weakened, °frail, °infirm, wasted, °worn out, unfit, debilitated, enervated, °disabled, incapacitated, °crippled, °doddering; out of °shape, in °bad °shape; °aged, °old, °elderly, °ancient, superannuated, senescent, °senile, *Colloq* gaga: *The old man was so decrepit he was unable to lift the cup to his lips.* 2 °dilapidated, deteriorated, crumbling, decayed, decaying, withered, wasted, °antiquated, °tumbledown, broken-down, °rickety, °unstable, °shaky, °ramshackle, °derelict, creaking, creaky, °run-down: *The barn was so decrepit we had to tear it down.*

decrepitude *n.* 1 feebleness, °weakness, °infirmity, debilitation, enervation, incapacity, °old °age, superannuation, senescence, °senility, caducity, dotage: *Her decrepitude was so extreme that she could neither walk nor understand what was said to her.* 2 dilapidation, deterioration, °decay, °ruin: *The house is in an advanced state of decrepitude.*

dedicate *v.* 1 °devote, consecrate, °give (up *or* over), °yield, °offer, °surrender, °commit, °pledge, °assign: *She dedicated her life to helping the poor.* 2 consecrate, °bless, °sanctify, °hallow: *There stands the temple dedicated to Apollo.* 3 inscribe; °address, °assign: *This book has been dedicated to you.*

dedication *n.* 1 °devotion, °assignment, °pledge, commitment, allegiance, adherence, faithfulness, fidelity, °loyalty, devotedness, wholeheartedness, single-mindedness, fixedness, fealty: *I admire Rudolph's dedication to duty.* 2 inscription, °address; °message: *The dedication reads, 'To my mother and father'.* 3 consecration, sanctification, hallowing: *The ceremony for the dedication of the youth centre will be held tomorrow.*

deduce *v.* conclude, °infer, °understand, °gather, °assume, °presume, °derive, °draw, °work out, °divine, glean, °take it, °suppose, °surmise, °suspect, *Slang Brit* suss out: *From the tone of his letter she deduced that he was going to change his mind.*

deduct *v.* °subtract, °take away *or* out *or* off, °take from, °remove, °withdraw, *Colloq* °knock off: *Deduct six from ten and you're left with four.*

deduction *n.* 1 subtraction, diminution, °decrease, reduction, withdrawal, °removal, abstraction: *After deductions for expenses, you'll be left with nothing.* 2 conclusion, °inference, °finding, °reasoning, °result: *After considering the evidence, my deduction is that the butler didn't do it.*

deed *n.* 1 °act, °action; °performance: *Their deeds did not match their promises.* 2 °exploit, °feat, °achievement, °accomplishment: *We are here to honour her for her many deeds, both on and off the tennis court.* 3 °title(-deed), °document, °instrument, indenture, °contract, °agreement: *The bank holds the title-deed until the mortgage is paid off.*

deep *adj.* 1 °extensive, °bottomless, abyssal, unfathomable, °profound; °wide, °broad, yawning, chasmal *or* chasmic: *All our supplies were lost in a deep crevasse in the glacier.* 2 °profound, arcane, °recondite, °difficult, abstruse, °obscure, esoteric, °incomprehensible, beyond *or* °past comprehension, impenetrable, unfathomable, inscrutable, °mysterious, mystic(al), °occult, °weighty, °serious, *Colloq* °heavy: *Religious philosophy is too deep a subject to discuss at breakfast.* 3 °wise, °learned, °sage, sagacious, °astute, perspicacious, °profound, discerning, °acute, °intense, °penetrating, °knowledgeable, °knowing: *Margaret is one of the deepest thinkers on the subject.* 4 °rapt, °absorbed, engrossed, occupied, °preoccupied, °intent, °intense, °involved, °engaged, immersed, °lost, *Colloq* into: *Don't disturb him when he's deep in thought.* 5 °devious, cunning, °shrewd, °crafty, canny, °clever, °knowing, °scheming, °artful, °designing: *He thinks there is a deep plot against him.* 6 °profound, °intense, °sincere, °serious, °heartfelt, °earnest, °ardent, °fervent, °poignant, deep-rooted: *I know of your deep concern for her.* 7 °low, °resonant, booming, resounding, sonorous, rumbling: *The deep sound of thunder rolled across the valley.* 8 °rich, °dark, °intense, °strong: *The sky was a deep blue.* —*n.* 9 **the deep**: the °ocean, the °main, the °sea, the waters, the high °seas, the briny (deep), the °wave(s), Davy Jones's locker, Neptune's or Poseidon's kingdom or domain: *It was midnight on the waters and a storm was on the deep.* —*adv.* **10** °deeply, °far down, °profoundly, intensely, earnestly, heavily: *We drank deep of the cooling liquid.*

deepen *v.* **1** °dig out, °burrow, °sink, dredge, °excavate, °scoop (out): *We'll have to deepen the hole to support the flag-pole.* **2** °intensify, °increase, °concentrate, °strengthen, °expand, °magnify: *The programme reflects a deepening interest in education.*

deeply *adv.* **1** °deep, (far) °downwards or inwards, °way down, °deep down: *The glacier was deeply fissured. She swam to the surface and inhaled deeply.* **2** °profoundly, intensely, strongly, powerfully, °very much, acutely, keenly, gravely, greatly, to a °great °extent, °extremely, °thoroughly, °completely, °entirely, °seriously, °severely, irrevocably, unreservedly; passionately, heavily, emotionally: *She is deeply involved with a man from Kent. They were deeply committed to the labour movement.*

deface *v.* °mar, disfigure, °spoil, °ruin, deform, °blemish, °damage, °mutilate, °harm, °impair, °injure, °destroy: *Nothing should be allowed to deface the beauty of these buildings.*

default *n.* **1** °failure, °fault, °defect, °neglect, °negligence, dereliction, °lapse, °oversight, non-performance, non-fulfilment, inaction: *We won the case because of their default on the contract. The other contestant failed to appear, so Gordon won the match by default.* **2** non-payment, delinquency: *Default in the rent may result in eviction.* —*v.* **3** °fail, °neglect, °dishonour, °lapse, fall °short, come (up) °short: *He has defaulted on a car payment.*

defeat *v.* **1** °overcome, °conquer, vanquish, be °victorious over, get the °better of, °beat, °subdue, °overwhelm, °overpower, °prevail over, °triumph over, °bring down, worst, thrash, °rout, °repulse, °overthrow, trounce, °whip, °crush, °destroy, do in, °best: *The champion defeated the contender in a ten-round match.* **2** °thwart, °frustrate, °disappoint, °check, balk, °stop, °terminate, °end, °finish, °foil: *He never let his handicap defeat his hopes of winning.* —*n.* **3** °conquest, °overthrow, beating, °repulse, trouncing, °rout, vanquishment: *The defeat of our team must be charged to lack of training.* **4** frustration, °undoing, °failure, °miscarriage, °set-back; Waterloo: *The stock market crash spelled the defeat of the company's plan for a share issue.*

defecate *v.* °void (excrement), °move the °bowels, excrete, °eliminate, °evacuate (the °bowels), have a (°bowel) °movement or bm, °open the °bowels, °relieve oneself, *Babytalk* do number two, *Euphemistic* °go to the men's or ladies' (room), °go to the °toilet or bathroom or °lavatory, °excuse (oneself), wash (one's) hands, °go to the powder-room; *Mincing* °go to the little boys' or girls' room; *Colloq Brit* °spend a penny, *Colloq Brit* °go to the loo, °pass a °motion, *Taboo slang* (take a) crap or shit: *The first symptoms of bowel disease are problems when defecating.*

defect *n.* **1** °shortcoming, deficiency, °lack, °want, inadequacy, insufficiency, shortfall, °failure, °weakness, °frailty, °weak point, °imperfection, irregularity, °liability: *See the doctor about that hearing defect.* **2** °blemish, °imperfection, °failing, °weakness, °flaw, °fault, °mark, °stain, irregularity, °mistake, °error: *The products should be inspected for defects before shipping.* —*v.* **3** °desert, °change sides or loyalties, °turn °traitor, °go over; °escape: *Ropovich tried to defect, but the Albanians sent him back.*

defective *adj.* **1** °imperfect, °faulty, °flawed, °deficient, °broken, out of °order, impaired, marred, *Colloq* on the °blink, *US* on the fritz: *The brakes on his car were defective.* **2** retarded, °simple, °feeble-minded, (mentally) °deficient or °incompetent, °backward, subnormal, *Brit education* ESN ('educationally subnormal'), *US education* °exceptional: *Found to be defective, he could not stand trial.*

defector *n.* °deserter, apostate, °turncoat, °traitor, °renegade, *Colloq* rat: *Some political defectors were suspected of being spies.*

defence *n.* **1** °shelter, °protection, °cover, °guard, °safeguard, °shield: *There is no defence against certain illnesses.* **2** fortification, armour, barricade, °screen, °bulwark, °rampart: *Shore defences were set up, including barbed wire entanglements and concrete pillboxes.* **3** °excuse, apology, °reason, apologia, °explanation; justification, vindication, °argument, °plea, advocacy, °support: *His defence for decreasing welfare payments was inadequate. She spoke in defence of nationalizing industry.*

defenceless *adj.* unprotected, exposed, °vulnerable, °unguarded; °helpless, °weak, °powerless, °impotent: *Would you take advantage of a poor, defenceless creature?*

defend *v.* **1** °protect, °watch over, °guard, °safeguard, °keep (safe), °shelter, °shield, °screen, °preserve; °fight for: *We must defend our civil rights.* **2** °fortify, arm, °secure; °fend or °ward off, parry: *Can you defend your position from attack?* **3** °plead for, °speak or °stand up for, °stick up for, go to bat for, °support, °uphold, °stand by, °champion, °stand with or behind or beside, °argue on or for or in °behalf of, hold a °brief for, espouse: *The lawyers defended her right to free speech.*

defer[1] *v.* °put off, °postpone, °delay, °shelve, °lay or °put aside, adjourn, *US* °table; *Colloq Brit* kick into touch: *The judge has deferred his decision.*

defer[2] *v.* Often, **defer to**: °give in (to), °give ground or °way (to), °yield (to), °submit (to), °bow (to), °capitulate (to), °cede (to), accede (to), acquiesce (to); °comply (with), °agree (to): *I'll defer to your decision in the matter.*

deference *n.* **1** °respect, °regard, politeness, °civility, °courtesy, °consideration, °esteem: *They treated him with deference owing to his age.* **2** °obeisance, °submission, acquiescence, °obedience, compliance: *Considering her accomplishments, she is paid little deference.*

defiant *adj.* challenging, °bold, °brazen, °audacious, °daring; °rebellious, °disobedient, °stubborn, °recalcitrant, °obstinate, refractory, unyielding, °insubordinate, °mutinous, °unruly, °self-willed, °aggressive, headstrong, contumacious, °pugnacious, °hostile, °belligerent, antagonistic, *Slang* gutsy, spunky: *His defiant attitude towards authority often gets him into trouble.*

deficient *adj.* **1** °wanting, lacking, °defective, °incomplete, unfinished, °short, °insufficient,

°inadequate, °sketchy, skimpy, °scarce: *Some foods are deficient in vitamins.* **2** °faulty, impaired, °flawed, °imperfect, °incomplete, °defective, °inferior, °unsatisfactory: *Many have a deficient knowledge of their legal rights.*

deficit *n.* °loss, deficiency, shortfall, °shortage, °default: *At the end of the year there was a considerable deficit.*

define *v.* **1** °determine, °establish, °fix, demarcate, °mark off *or* out, delimit, °limit, °lay *or* °set down, circumscribe, °specify, °identify, delineate, °describe: *You must first define the subjects to be covered.* **2** °describe, °explain, °interpret, °spell out, °detail, °clarify, delineate, °expand on, expatiate on *or* upon; °characterize, °state, °name: *No one dictionary defines all the words of a language. Please define exactly what you want me to do.*

definite *adj.* **1** °specific, °particular, °exact, °pronounced, °explicit, °express, °precise: *She came here with a definite purpose.* **2** °sure, °positive, °certain, assured, °fixed, settled, confirmed: *Then we have a definite appointment for two o'clock?* **3** °clear, °plain, well-defined, unambiguous, unequivocal, °distinct, clear-cut, °obvious: *The plans for revision are definite.*

definitely *adv.* °positively, °absolutely, °surely, to be °sure, assuredly, certainly, indubitably, °undoubtedly, categorically, unequivocally, unquestionably, decidedly, °finally, once and for all; plainly, °clearly, °obviously, patently: *Then you're definitely not going to the dance with Waldo? That was definitely the worst movie of the year.*

definition *n.* **1** delineation, delimitation, demarcation, outlining; acutance, °resolution, distinctness, °clarity, sharpness, °focus, °precision: *The definition at the edge of the photograph is fuzzy.* **2** °description, °explanation, explication, clarification, °statement (of °meaning), °sense, °meaning: *How many definitions are there for the word 'good'?*

definitive *adj.* **1** decisive, °final, conclusive, °ultimate: *My definitive answer will be given tomorrow.* **2** °thorough, through and through, °exhaustive, °ultimate, consummate, °complete, °authoritative, °reliable: *She has written the definitive work on the axolotl.* **3** clarifying, unambiguous, °categorical, °absolute, °unqualified, °accurate, °exact, °precise: *We expect a definitive statement from the union regarding their claims.*

deflect *v.* avert, °turn away *or* aside, °deviate, °change, °swerve, °switch, °divert, °shy, veer, °sidetrack; °fend off: *The trajectory of a bullet is deflected by gravity. By deflecting a bit to their left, they managed to regain their original course.*

deformed *adj.* **1** °misshapen, malformed, distorted, twisted, °grotesque, °gnarled, °crooked, contorted, awry, warped, °bent: *This tree is deformed because of the constant wind.* **2** °disfigured, °crippled, °lame, °misshapen; °abnormal: *He was born with a deformed foot.* **3** distorted, warped, °bent, °perverted, twisted, °grotesque; °abnormal: *The deformed personalities of his patients are the subject of my book.*

defraud *v.* °cheat, °swindle, °trick, °beguile, cozen, °dupe, delude, °fool, bilk, °fleece, °victimize, °take in, °deceive, humbug, °hoodwink, flimflam, *Colloq* do, diddle, con, slip one over on, °put (something) over on, pull

a fast one on, fast-talk, °rope in, *US* °take; *Slang* take for a °ride, gyp, °rob, °rip off, rook; *Dialect* flam: *Shareholders are defrauded by insider trading schemes.*

defray *v.* °pay, °settle, °meet, °discharge, liquidate, °clear, °cover, °reimburse, *Colloq* pick up the °bill *or* °tab *or US* °check (for), foot the °bill (for): *The company defrays the cost of all travelling expenses.*

defunct *adj.* **1** °dead, deceased, °extinct: *The dinosaurs have been defunct for millions of years.* **2** inoperative, °inapplicable, °unused, unusable, °invalid, expired, °obsolete, °passé, °dead, °non-existent, outmoded, °out: *Although still on the books, that law is defunct.*

defy *v.* **1** °challenge, °dare, °face, confront, °brave, °stand up to, °flout, °thumb one's nose at, *Colloq Brit* cock a snook at: *The defendant defied the prosecutor to prove the allegations.* **2** °frustrate, °thwart, baffle, °resist, °withstand, °repel, °disobey, °repulse: *Her feats of legerdemain defy the imagination. Copeley has invented a device that defies the law of gravity.*

degenerate *adj.* **1** debased, degraded, °corrupt, corrupted, vitiated, °decadent, depraved, °reprobate, °dissolute, ignoble, °base, °low, °inferior, °vile: *He was a degenerate descendant of a once noble lineage. Ben sank into the depths of a degenerate existence after Penelope left him.*
—*v.* **2** °decline, °deteriorate, °decay, °sink, °worsen; backslide, regress, retrogress, °weaken, go to the dogs, go to °rack and °ruin, *Colloq* go to pot: *He felt that art had degenerated since the days of Rembrandt.*
—*n.* **3** °reprobate, debauchee, °wastrel, °profligate, °rake, rakehell, °roué; °pervert, °deviate: *The detective said that only a degenerate could have committed such a crime.*

degradation *n.* **1** degeneracy, degeneration, deterioration, corruptness, corruption, vitiation, baseness, depravity, turpitude: *History records the moral degradation of a whole society.* **2** disrepute, °discredit, °shame, °humiliation, ignominy, °dishonour, °disgrace, abasement, debasement: *He had to face the degradation of an accusation of child molestation.*

degrade *v.* **1** °downgrade, demote, °break, *Military* cashier, *Ecclesiastical* unfrock, *Law* disbar; depose, unseat; disfranchise *or* disenfranchise; *Military* drum out (of the corps), *Chiefly naval* disrate; *US military* bust: *They degraded him from captain to lieutenant.* **2** °disgrace, °dishonour, °humble, °shame, °discredit, °debase, demean, abase; °humiliate, °mortify, °belittle, deprecate, °depreciate, cheapen, °reduce, °lower: *He has been degraded to mopping the floor.* **3** °dilute, °adulterate, °weaken, °thin, °water (down), °alloy: *Cologne is, essentially, degraded perfume.*

degrading *adj.* demeaning, humiliating, °shameful, shaming, debasing, lowering, discreditable: *Why should you deem selling a degrading occupation?*

degree *n.* **1** °grade, °level, °stage, °class, °caste, °rank, °order, °scale, °standing, °status, °station, °position, °situation, °estate, °condition: *He is entertaining a lady of high degree.* **2** °measure, °magnitude, °extent, °limit, °point; lengths, °step: *All our needs, desires, and goals are biologically determined to some degree.* **3 by degrees**: little by little, °bit by bit, °step by step, inch by inch, inchmeal, °gradually, slowly, (almost) imperceptibly: *By degrees, her health has improved.* **4 to a degree: a** °rather, °somewhat, °quite: *She is to a degree a better dancer than he.* **b** °substantially, considerably, °highly, decidedly, °exceedingly, to a °considerable °extent: *She must be stupid to a degree if she believes in levitation.*

deign v. °condescend, °stoop, °vouchsafe, °concede; °yield, °agree: *Lord Worthington deigned to say good morning to us.*

deity n. °god, goddess, Supreme Being, °creator, demiurge: *Deities in various religions are represented as men, women, or animals.*

dejected adj. downcast, °downhearted, depressed, dispirited, discouraged, °despondent, °low, chap-fallen, crest-fallen, °melancholy, °sad, °unhappy, °gloomy, °glum, °miserable, °blue, low-spirited, in °low spirits, °forlorn, °woebegone, disconsolate, °sorrowful, morose, °heartbroken, heavy-hearted, in the doldrums, *Colloq* down in the dumps, down in the °mouth: *She was bound to feel dejected when she couldn't find a job.*

delay v. **1** °postpone, °put off *or* aside, °defer, temporize, °suspend, °shelve, °put on °hold, °hold in °abeyance, put *or* °keep in a holding pattern, pigeon-hole, put on ice, put in *or* into the deep-freeze, *Colloq* put on the back burner, *Brit* kick into touch, *US* °hold off *or* up (on), °table: *We shall delay our decision till next month.* **2** °hold up *or* back, detain, °impede, °hinder, °retard, °keep, °bog down, °set back, °slow (up *or* down); °stop, °arrest, °halt, °check; °obstruct: *Delivery of the mail has been delayed by the strike. We were delayed by traffic.* **3** loiter, °procrastinate, °hesitate, °poke *or* °drag (along), °tarry, °wait, °lag (behind), °dawdle, °hang back, °stall, °linger, dally, mark time, °potter *or US* putter; vacillate; *Colloq* dilly-dally, °shilly-shally, °drag one's feet: *Stop delaying and get to work.*
—n. **4** °postponement, deferral, deferment, °wait, °hold-up; °set-back: *There will be a ten-day delay in paying the rent.* **5** °lull, °interlude, hiatus, °interruption, °gap, °interval, lacuna, °stop, stoppage, °wait, waiting, °hold-up, °suspension: *After an hour's delay, service was resumed.* **6** tarrying, loitering, dawdling, *Colloq* dilly-dallying, shilly-shallying: *There should be no further delay in shipping the order.*

delectation n. °delight, °enjoyment, °amusement, °entertainment, °diversion, °pleasure, °satisfaction: *For your delectation, Le Moulin Rouge presents La Goulue!*

delegate n. **1** °envoy, °agent, legate, °representative, °ambassador, plenipotentiary, °minister, emissary, commissioner, (papal) nuncio, (papal) internuncio, spokesperson, spokesman, spokeswoman, °go-between: *They kowtowed to the delegate from His Imperial Highness.*
—v. **2** depute, commission, °appoint, °designate, °assign, °name, °nominate, accredit, °authorize, empower, mandate: *The president delegated Ambassador Foxley to represent him at the meeting.* **3** °assign, °give, °hand over *or* on, °pass over *or* on, depute, °transfer, °entrust, °relegate, *Colloq* °pass the buck for, *US* buck: *She has delegated the responsibility to one of the directors.*

delete v. °erase, °cancel, °rub *or* °cross out *or* off, °remove, °blot out, expunge, efface,

°eliminate, °obliterate, °wipe out, eradicate, °strike out, °cut *or* °edit (out), *Publishing* blue-pencil; *Printing* dele: *Delete the old address and insert the new one.*

deliberate adj. **1** °intentional, planned, °studied, °wilful, intended, °premeditated, °calculated, °conscious, prearranged, °purposeful, °preconceived, considered; °cold-blooded: *The insult was deliberate, not a slip.* **2** °slow, °methodical, °careful, °unhurried, paced, °measured, °regular, °even, °steady, °sure, °unhesitating, unfaltering, °confident: *He moved across the room with a deliberate step and tore the medals from the general's tunic.* **3** °careful, °prudent, °cautious, °painstaking, °discreet, considered, °considerate, °thoughtful, well-thought-out, °thorough, °methodical, °systematic, °fastidious, °orderly, punctilious, °dispassionate, °cool, composed, °collected, °calm, °serene, unruffled: *A deliberate speaker, he chose his words with care.*
—v. **4** °consider, °ponder, °think (about *or* over), °weigh, °debate, °meditate (on *or* over), °reflect (on *or* over), cogitate (on *or* over), °study: *I shall need a few days to deliberate on that question.*

deliberately adv. intentionally, on °purpose, purposely, wilfully *or US* willfully, consciously, wittingly, °calculatedly, calculatingly, knowingly, pointedly, resolutely, of one's (own) free °will, on one's own, with one's eyes (wide) open: *She did that deliberately, not by accident.*

delicacy n. **1** fineness, exquisiteness, gracefulness, °beauty, lightness, daintiness: *Notice the delicacy of the tracery in the rose window.* **2** fragility, fragileness, °frailty, frailness, °weakness, °infirmity, feebleness, tenderness; susceptibility: *Because of the delicacy of his constitution, even a cold might be fatal.* **3** °sensitivity, °difficulty, ticklishness, °finesse, nicety, °sensibility: *The delicacy of the situation demands the utmost diplomacy.* **4** °luxury, sweetmeat, °dainty, °titbit *or US* tidbit, °savoury: *The table was laden with delicacies from all over the world.*

delicate adj. **1** °fragile, breakable, °frail, °tender, frangible, °dainty; perishable, °flimsy: *This filament is extremely delicate, so be careful.* **2** °fine, °exquisite, °dainty, °graceful, °elegant, °subtle: *A delicate border of lace sets off the collar.* **3** °feeble, °weak, °sickly, °frail, debilitated, weakened, enfeebled, °unhealthy: *Her condition is too delicate for her to be moved.* **4** °critical, °ticklish, °sensitive, °dangerous, °tricky, °precarious, °touchy, *Slang* °hairy; *Colloq* °sticky: *Rescuing the survivors of the avalanche was a delicate operation.* **5** °dainty, °squeamish, °queasy, °fastidious, °prudish, Victorian, °finicky, finical, °refined, °discriminating, discerning, °sensitive, puristic, °proper, °coy, °modest, demure: *In those days ladies were thought to be too delicate to mention such matters.* **6** °gradual, °subtle, °nice, °precise, muted, °soft, °faint, °subdued: *The delicate shading at the horizon is characteristic of this artist.*

delicious adj. **1** delectable, °luscious, ambrosial, °savoury, mouth-watering, toothsome; °choice, flavourful, °tasty, appetizing, palatable, *Colloq* scrumptious; *Slang* °yummy: *Larry's fried chicken is quite delicious.* **2** enjoyable, °delightful, °pleasurable, °pleasing, °pleasant, °choice, °enchanting, fascinating; °agreeable, charming, °engaging; amusing, °entertaining: *I heard the most delicious bit of gossip about the Browns.*

delight v. **1** °please, °gratify, °satisfy, °gladden, °cheer, °tickle, °amuse, °entertain, °divert, °excite, °thrill, °captivate, °entrance, °fascinate: *We were delighted to hear the Mighty Allen Art Players once again.* **2 delight in** °enjoy, °appreciate, °like, °relish (in), °savour, °revel in, °glory in; °love, °adore; *Colloq* get a kick from or out of; *Slang* °get off on: *She delights in any kind of jazz.*
—n. **3** °pleasure, °gratification, °joy, °satisfaction, °enjoyment, °delectation; °bliss, °ecstasy, °rapture: *She takes great delight in playing practical jokes on her guests. In his dreams he visited the garden of earthly delights.*

delighted adj. °pleased, °happy, °charmed, thrilled, °enchanted, enchanté(e): *I am delighted to meet you. 'Miss Smith, meet Mr Brown.' 'Delighted!'*

delightful adj. **1** °pleasing, °agreeable, °pleasurable, enjoyable, °joyful, °pleasant, °lovely, amusing, °entertaining, diverting, °exciting, °thrilling: *We spent a delightful evening together.* **2** °attractive, congenial, °winning, winsome, charming, °engaging, °exciting; captivating, °ravishing, fascinating, °enchanting: *Georgina is one of the most delightful people I have met in a long time.*

delinquent n. **1** malefactor, (young or youthful) °offender, wrongdoer, lawbreaker, °culprit, °criminal, °miscreant; hooligan, ruffian, roughneck: *The police rounded up six juvenile delinquents and charged them with rowdyism.*
—adj. **2** neglectful, negligent, °derelict, °remiss, °failing, defaulting: *I have been delinquent in my obligations to my mother.* **3** °overdue, °past °due, in arrears, °late, °unpaid: *All these delinquent accounts should be collected as soon as possible.*

delirious adj. **1** °wild, °hysterical, distracted, °incoherent, °rambling, irrational, °raving, ranting, frenzied, °frantic, °disturbed, demented, °deranged, unhinged, °mad, °insane, °crazy, lunatic: *He is still delirious and doesn't know what he's saying.* **2** °wild, °excited, crazed, thrilled, °ecstatic: *She was delirious with joy that Ken was coming home.*

deliver v. **1** °carry, °bring, convey, °distribute, °give or °hand out; purvey, °take °round; °cart, °transport: *Only in a few places in the world do they still deliver milk to the door.* **2** °hand over, °give, °surrender, °cede, °yield, °make over, °relinquish, °give up or over, °commit, °transfer, °turn over, °resign: *We were forced to deliver our children to the enemy as hostages.* **3** set °free, °liberate, enfranchise, °extricate, °release, °save, °rescue; °emancipate, manumit, °redeem; disencumber, disburden, °ransom: *They were delivered from certain death by the arrival of the helicopter. Modern appliances have delivered millions of women from the drudgery of housework.* **4** °give, °present, utter, °read, °broadcast; °proclaim, °announce, °declare, °set forth, °communicate, °make known, °express, °publish, °hand over, °hand out, promulgate, °pronounce, °enunciate: *He has to deliver a speech tonight. The police delivered an ultimatum to the terrorists.* **5** °give, °administer, °inflict, °deal, °direct, °send, °launch, °impart, °throw; °cast, °hurl, °shoot, discharge, °fire: *He delivered a blow on the chin that knocked me out. The ball was delivered with enormous speed.* **6** °bring forth, °bear, °give °birth to, °bring into the °world: *In the next three years, she delivered three more*

girls. **7** °produce, °perform, put one's money where one's mouth is: *Roger had better deliver, or we shall have to take drastic measures.*

delivery n. **1** °distribution, delivering, deliverance, conveyance, transportation, °transport: *The strikers have caused delivery of newspapers to stop.* **2** °liberation, °release, deliverance, emancipation: *His delivery from poverty was still a few years away.* **3** childbirth, parturition; confinement: *Many women find that their second child is an easier delivery.* **4** °presentation, °performance; utterance, enunciation, articulation, °pronunciation, °expression, °execution: *He is an accomplished orator, with a spellbinding delivery.*

delusion n. **1** °deception, °trick, °stratagem, °artifice, °ruse, °pretence: *It was a snare and a delusion to represent the painting as genuine.* **2** °false or °mistaken °impression, °fallacy, °illusion, °mistake, °error, °misconception, misbelief, °hallucination: *He suffers under the delusion that he is a great pianist.*

demand v. **1** °require, °order, °bid, °call (for); °insist, °command: *I demand that you retract that remark! She demanded to know where he was going.* **2** °claim, °ask (for), °require, °insist on; °exact: *They had paid for tickets and demanded entrance.* **3** °require, °call for, °need, °want, necessitate, °cry out for: *This superb dish demands an excellent claret.* **4** °ask (for), °inquire or °enquire, °request; °requisition: *We demanded help from the police.*
—n. **5** °request, °bid, behest, °requisition, °order, insistence; °outcry: *Our demand for service went unheeded.* **6** °want, °need, °requirement, °desire; °market (°demand), marketability; consumer or °customer acceptance: *The demand for our products is low at the moment.* **7 in demand**: wanted, needed, requested, coveted, °popular, sought after, desired, °desirable, *Brit* in °request, *US* on °request: *Bright graduates are always in demand.* **8 on demand**: on °call, on °request, on °presentation, when requested or required; at °once, °immediately, without °delay: *These notes are payable on demand.*

demanding adj. **1** °difficult, °hard, exigent, °tough, °exacting, °trying, taxing: *Edwards is a demanding boss. Diamond cutting is demanding work.* **2** °insistent, clamorous, °urgent, °nagging, °persistent: *Your demanding fans want another encore.*

democratic adj. egalitarian, classless; republican, °representative, °popular, self-governing, autonomous: *The colonists voted for a democratic form of government.*

demolish v. **1** °tear or °pull down, dismantle, °reduce to °ruin(s), smash, °pull to °pieces, °knock down, °raze, °topple, °destroy, °level: *This building will have to be demolished to make room for the new shopping mall.* **2** °destroy, °end, bring to an °end, make an °end of, put an °end to, °devastate, °terminate, annihilate, °overturn, °overthrow, °crush, °defeat, refute, °disprove, °dispose of, °suppress, °squelch, °quash: *With just one phrase he demolished their entire argument.*

demon n. **1** °devil, °evil °spirit, °fiend, cacodemon; °monster, ghoul, °ogre, harpy, vampire: *Medieval demons are generally depicted as having* *horns, hoofs, and tails.* **2** °fanatic, °fiend, °enthusiast, °addict, *Colloq* °freak: *He's a real speed demon when he gets onto the motorway.*

demonstrable *adj.* provable, confirmable, attestable, verifiable; °evident, °self-evident, °obvious, undeniable, °apparent, °manifest, °indisputable, °unquestionable, °positive, °certain, conclusive: *The judge showed a demonstrable bias against my client.*

demonstrate *v.* **1** °show, °prove, make °evident, °establish, evince, °evidence, °exhibit, °manifest: *The increase in arrests demonstrates the efficiency of the police.* **2** °display, °explain, °expose, °describe, °present; °illustrate: *The salesman demonstrated the new camera for us.* **3** °picket, °march, °parade, °rally, °protest: *More than 5000 people demonstrated against the fraudulent election.*

demonstration *n.* **1** °proof, °evidence, °testimony, confirmation, verification, substantiation; °manifestation, °exhibition, °display, °illustration, °indication: *I have seen sufficient demonstration of her ineptitude.* **2** °presentation, °display, °show, °explanation, °description, clarification, elucidation, °exposition, *Colloq* demo: *The student gave an excellent demonstration of how a computer works.* **3** picketing, °march, °parade, °protest, °rally, sit-in, *Colloq Brit* demo: *There have been numerous demonstrations against the government's policies.*

demonstrative *adj.* **1** °open, unrestrained, unconstrained, unreserved, °expansive, °effusive, °emotional, °warm, °tender, °affectionate, loving: *Pat is quite demonstrative, often causing me to blush.* **2** illustrative, indicative, °representative, probative, evidential; provable, °evident: *Her point was proved by several demonstrative arguments. The hostility of these few is demonstrative of what to expect of the entire group.*

demoralize *v.* **1** dispirit, °daunt, dishearten, °discourage, °defeat; °weaken, °cripple, °enervate, devitalize, °depress, °subdue, °crush: *The party's crushing defeat in the election thoroughly demoralized its supporters.* **2** °corrupt, °pervert, deprave, °vitiate, °debase, debauch: *The committee consider him a demoralizing influence and insist he should resign.* **3** °bewilder, °discomfit, °unnerve, °shake (up), °confuse, °fluster, disconcert, °perturb, °disturb, °upset, *Colloq* °rattle: *The demonstrators were completely demoralized when arrested for loitering.*

denial *n.* **1** contradiction, negation, repudiation, refutation, disavowal, disclaimer, disaffirmation: *Her denials notwithstanding, she was found guilty.* **2** retraction, recantation, renunciation, withdrawal: *The arbitrary denial of civil rights to some is unconscionable.* **3** °refusal, °rejection, negation; °veto: *The boy's persistent denial of authority went into his record.*

denizen *n.* °inhabitant, dweller, °occupant, frequenter, °resident; °citizen: *The depths of the seas harbour some strange denizens. Carl is a denizen of The Bottle and Glass.*

denomination *n.* **1** °sect, °persuasion, °school, church, °order: *He is a member of the Mormon denomination.* **2** °sort, °kind, °type, °nature, °variety, °unit, °size, value; °grade, °class, genus, species, °order, classification: *The kidnappers demanded the ransom money in used notes of small denomination.* **3** designation, appellation,

°name, °identification, °style, °title, °tag, °term; designating, naming, identifying, styling, classifying, titling, entitling, tagging, terming, denominating: *The denomination of people by race, creed, colour, or sex is discriminatory.*

denote *v.* **1** °indicate, °specify, °designate, °distinguish, °signify, °mark, °note: *Hypothetical linguistic forms are denoted by an asterisk.* **2** °mean, °name, °symbolize, °represent, betoken: *The word mother denotes 'female parent', but its connotations are far more extensive.*

denounce *v.* **1** °accuse, °brand, °stigmatize, °charge, °blame, °incriminate, °implicate, °complain about: *He has been denounced for the blackguard he is.* **2** °betray, °inform against, °report, °reveal: *He denounced his own son to the authorities.* **3** °criticize, °condemn, decry, denunciate, °attack, assail, censure, impugn, declaim *or* °rail (against), °vituperate, revile, °vilify, inveigh against; °ridicule, (hold up to) °shame, pillory, (heap) °scorn (upon), cast a °slur on: *The playwright was denounced as a neo-Nazi.*

dense *adj.* **1** °compact, °thick, compressed, condensed, °close, °solid, °heavy, impenetrable: *The fox escaped into a dense thicket.* **2** crowded, °packed, °tight, impenetrable, impassable: *There was a dense crowd blocking the exit.* **3** °stupid, °slow, slow-witted, thickheaded, °dull, thick-witted, °obtuse, °stolid, °dim, dim-witted, °foolish, *Colloq* °thick, °dumb: *He may be a gifted artist but he is dense when it comes to money matters.*

deny *v.* **1** °contradict, gainsay, refute, controvert, disaffirm, disclaim, confute, negate, °dispute: *She denies ever having met the defendant.* **2** °reject, °refuse, °withhold, °forbid, °turn down, °decline, disallow; °recall, °revoke, °recant: *He asserts that his right to counsel was denied.* **3** disavow, °repudiate, °renounce, disown, forswear, disclaim: *The witch-doctor demanded sacrifices, saying that the angry gods would not be denied.*

depart *v.* **1** °go, °go away *or* out *or* from *or* off, °leave, °quit, °retire (from), °retreat (from), °withdraw (from), °exit (from), °set out *or* forth *or* off, decamp, abscond, °fly, cut and °run, °skip (out), °run off *or* away *or* out, take to the road, take one's °leave, °check out, °disappear, vanish, °evaporate, *Jocular* toddle off, *Imperative* Begone!, *Colloq* °beat it, scram, shove off, make oneself scarce, *Brit* scarper, *US* hit the road, be out of (someplace), *Slang* °split, *Imperative* get lost, *US* cut (on) out, vamoose, take a (run-out) °powder, lam (on) out, take it on the lam, *Brit* do a moonlight °flit, *Usually imperative* °bugger off, °buzz off, *Taboo, imperative* fuck off: *Our bags are packed and we depart at noon.* **2** Often, **depart from**: °deviate (from), °change, °diverge (from), °turn (aside *or* away) (from), °differ (from), °vary (from), °break away (from), °leave, °abandon, °stray (from), veer (from): *She refused to depart from established practices.*

department *n.* **1** °division, subdivision, °branch, °office, °bureau, °section, °segment, °unit, °part: *Some departments are in another building.* **2** °responsibility, °concern, °worry, °sphere, bailiwick, °jurisdiction, °domain, °control, °area *or* °sphere of °influence *or* °activity: *He was only responsible for the launch of the missiles—where they came down was not his department.*

depend v. **1 depend (on** or **upon):** be contingent or dependent or conditional on, °turn on, hinge on, °pivot on, °hang on, be °subject to, °rest on, be influenced or °determined or conditioned by: *The plans for our picnic depend on the weather.* **2 depend on** or **upon:** °trust (in), °rely on, °count on, °reckon on, bank on, be °sure of, put one's °faith or °trust in: *I knew we could depend on you, Giles, to do the right thing.*

deplorable adj. **1** °lamentable, °regrettable, °sad, woeful, °grievous, °wretched, °miserable, °unfortunate, °awful, distressing, °disturbing, troubling, upsetting, °grave, °serious, °oppressive, °difficult, °desperate, °hopeless, °tragic, °disastrous: *Orphaned at six, he had a deplorable childhood.* **2** °shameful, °disgraceful, °scandalous, °disreputable, °awful, °bad, appalling, °dreadful, °abominable, execrable, °terrible, reprehensible: *What did you think of Annie's deplorable behaviour at last week's dance? That's a deplorable painting.*

deposit v. **1** °place, °leave, °set or °put or °lay (down), °drop, *Colloq US* plunk down: *You are requested to deposit litter in the bin.* **2** °entrust, °leave, °lodge, consign, °keep, °place, °put; °store, °save, °set aside, bank, °lay or °put away, *Brit* °pay in, *Colloq* stash away: *Each morning she deposits the children at the day nursery and goes to work. He deposits money every week in a pension fund.*
—n. **3** down °payment, part or partial °payment, °advance °payment: *A small deposit will hold your purchase until you are ready to pay for it in full.* **4** °precipitate, °sediment, °silt, alluvium, °dregs, lees, °accumulation, deposition: *There is a dark deposit at the bottom of the coffee-pot.*

depreciate v. **1** devalue, devaluate, °decrease, °diminish, lessen, °reduce, °lower, °depress, cheapen, °mark down: *The abundant harvest has depreciated the price of commodities.* **2** °disparage, °diminish, °deride, decry, underrate, undervalue, °underestimate, °minimize, °belittle, °slight, derogate, deprecate, °discredit, denigrate, °run down, vilipend, *Colloq* °play down, *US* °talk down: *When he depreciates another's work he adds nothing to the value of his own.*

depredation n. °plunder, plundering, °pillage, pillaging, despoliation, despoiling, ravaging, sacking, laying °waste, devastation, °destruction; ransacking, °robbery, looting; °ravages: *The depredation caused by ten years of war is unimaginable.*

depress v. **1** deject, dispirit, °oppress, °sadden, °grieve, °cast down, dishearten, °discourage, °dampen, °cast a °gloom or °pall over, °burden, °weigh down: *He's very depressed right now because he failed to get a promotion.* **2** °weaken, °dull, debilitate, °enervate, °sap; °depreciate, cheapen, devalue, devaluate; °diminish, °lower, °bring down, °reduce: *The news about a new oil field depressed the market today.* **3** °press (down), °push (down) (on), °lower: *If the pressure gets too high, just depress this lever.*

depression n. **1** °indentation, dent, dimple, °impression, °pit, °hollow, °recess, °cavity, concavity, °dip: *When the box fell, its corner left a small depression in the top of the metal cabinet.* **2** dejection, °despair, °gloom, downheartedness, °sadness, °melancholy, discouragement, despondency, gloominess, glumness, the blues, unhappiness; *Colloq* the dumps: *A general feeling of depression*

came over us at the doctor's words. **3** °recession, °slump, (°economic) °decline, downturn, *US and Canadian* bust: *The analysts are unable to predict accurately either booms or depressions.*

deprive v. °withhold, °deny, °refuse; °withdraw, °remove, °strip, °dispossess, °take away, expropriate, °divest; mulct: *They deprived him of the right to have visitors.*

deprived adj. °needy, in °want, in °need, °impoverished, °badly off, °destitute, °poor, poverty-stricken, *Euphemistic* underprivileged, disadvantaged: *As a deprived family, they are entitled to a number of benefits.*

depth n. **1** deepness, °extent, °measure, °profundity, profoundness: *The depth of the cavern was at least three miles.* **2** °profundity, profoundness, abstruseness, °obscurity, reconditeness, °complexity, intricacy: *There is great depth of meaning in many proverbs.* **3** °profundity, °wisdom, sagacity, sageness, °understanding, °perception, astuteness, perspicacity, perspicaciousness, °insight, °intuition, acumen, °penetration: *One would scarcely characterize Mickey Mouse as possessed of great depth.* **4** °intensity, °profundity, °strength; vividness, °brilliance, brilliancy, brightness, richness: *It is hard for me to express the depth of my feeling for you. The depth of colour is much better in this picture.* **5 depths:** °deep(s), °abyss, abysm, chasm, °bowels of the earth, (°bottomless) °pit, nethermost reaches or regions, nadir: *As we descended into the depths the temperature increased. She is in the depths of despair and needs your moral support.* **6 in depth:** °thoroughly, comprehensively, in °detail, °profoundly, °deeply, extensively, intensively, concentratedly, probingly: *The specialists have looked into the problem in depth and have no answer yet.*

deputy n. °substitute, replacement, surrogate, °stand-in, °reserve, °proxy; °agent, °operative, °representative, °go-between, °intermediary, spokesperson, spokesman, spokeswoman, °delegate, °ambassador, °minister, emissary, °envoy, legate, (papal) nuncio; *Chiefly US* °alternate: *She excused herself from the meeting, leaving her deputy in charge.*

deranged adj. °mad, °insane, demented, lunatic, unhinged, °unbalanced, °berserk, °crazy, crazed, °psychotic, irrational, *non compos mentis*, out of one's °mind or senses or °head, not all there, of °unsound °mind, crack-brained, °mad as a hatter or March hare, off the rails, *Colloq* touched, dotty, °daft, cracked, bats, cuckoo, *Brit* potty, *US* have nobody home (upstairs), out to lunch, off-the-wall; *Slang* bonkers, dippy, barmy or balmy, batty, screwy, loony, nuts, nutty, wacky, bananas, off one's rocker, off one's trolley, °mental, missing a few marbles, not having all one's marbles, kooky, with a screw loose, *Chiefly Brit* off one's chump, *Chiefly US* (plumb) loco, meshuga: *Police said that the killer was completely deranged and should be approached with caution.*

derelict adj. **1** °deserted, °abandoned, forsaken, neglected; ruined, °dilapidated, °run-down, °tumbledown: *The council has a scheme for the renovation of derelict buildings in the inner city.* **2** negligent, °remiss, neglectful, °delinquent, dilatory, °careless, °heedless, °lax,

°slack, °irresponsible, °slipshod, slovenly, *Colloq* °sloppy: *He was accused of having been derelict in his duty.*
—*n.* **3** vagrant, °tramp, °outcast, pariah, °loafer, °wastrel, °good-for-nothing, ne'er-do-well, malingerer, °vagabond, °slacker, down-and-out, *US and Canadian* hobo, *Colloq US* °bum: *Because of alcohol, he ended up as a derelict.*

deride *v.* °mock, °ridicule, °scoff (at), °jeer (at), °laugh (at), make °fun *or* °sport (of), °tease, °taunt, °twit, °poke °fun (at), make a laughing-stock (of), °sneer (at), °scorn, °flout, disdain, pooh-pooh, °belittle, °diminish, °disparage, °laugh off, *Brit* °rally, *Colloq* °knock, *Brit* take the mickey *or* micky out of: *His classmates had always derided his attempts at getting anywhere with the girls.*

derision *n.* °ridicule, °mockery, °raillery, °laughter, °sarcasm, scoffing, °contempt, °scorn, contumely, °disrespect; °satire, °lampoon, pasquinade, °burlesque, °caricature, travesty: *Her suggestion was greeted with derision.*

derisory *adj.* mocking, ridiculing, °scornful, derisive, °disdainful, °contemptuous, taunting, insulting, contumelious, jeering; °sardonic, °sarcastic, ironic(al), °satirical: *He felt crushed by their derisory laughter.*

derivation *n.* °origin, descent, °extraction, °source, °beginning, °foundation, ancestry, genealogy, etymology, °root: *The derivations of many words are unknown.*

derivative *adj.* **1** derived, borrowed, procured, obtained, acquired; unoriginal, °second-hand, copied, imitative, plagiarized, plagiaristic: *He created nothing of his own—all his compositions were highly derivative.*
—*n.* **2** °derivation, °offshoot, °development, spin-off, by-product: *French, Italian, and other Romance languages are derivatives from Latin.*

derive *v.* **1** °draw, °extract, °get, °obtain, °acquire, °procure, °receive, °secure, °gain, °elicit, °deduce, educe, °infer, °gather, °collect, °harvest, glean, cull, winnow: *I derive no pleasure from punishing you. I derived from her remark that she didn't like the play.* **2 derive from**: °arise from *or* out of, °originate in *or* with *or* from, °emerge from *or* out of, °come (forth) from *or* out of, °arrive from, °issue from, °proceed from, °develop from, °spring from, °flow from, °emanate from, °stem from, be traceable *or* traced to: *The word delicate derives from Latin. All our knowledge is derived from experience.*

derogatory *adj.* depreciatory, depreciating, depreciative, disparaging, abasing, debasing, lowering, denigrating, belittling, diminishing, demeaning, detracting, deflating, minimizing, °mitigating; uncomplimentary, °offensive, insulting: *The family took a somewhat derogatory attitude towards commerce. He said something derogatory about my wife, so I punched him.*

descend *v.* **1** °come *or* °go down, °move down, °climb down, °get down: *The sun was setting as he descended from the mountain.* **2** °decline, °incline (°downwards), °slope, °slant, °dip, °drop, °fall, °plunge, °plummet: *Beyond the curve, the road descends suddenly for a mile.* **3** °stoop, °condescend, °sink, °lower oneself: *If you start shouting, you're just descending to Basil's level.* **4 descend on**: °attack, °assault, invade,

°pounce on *or* upon, °swoop down on *or* upon: *Fighter planes descended in droves and destroyed the base entirely.*

descendant *n.* °offspring, °progeny, °issue, °heir, °posterity, °family; °child, son, daughter, grandchild, scion; °offshoot: *They claim to be descendants of Tsar Nicholas.*

describe *v.* **1** °tell (of), °recount, °relate, give an °account (of), °narrate, °recite, °report, °chronicle; retail: *He described his adventures in Rio.* **2** °detail, °define, °explain, °specify, delineate: *Please describe exactly where you found the body.* **3** °characterize, °portray, °paint, depict, °identify, °label, °style; °represent: *I would describe her as careless rather than uncaring.* **4** °trace, °mark out, °outline, °traverse, °draw: *The trail of the comet described a perfect arc in the black sky.*

description *n.* **1** portrayal, characterization, depiction, (°thumbnail) sketch, °portrait: *Her description of her boss was far from flattering.* **2** °account, °narrative, °story, °report, °representation, °statement, °definition; °explanation, commentary; °chronicle, °history, °record, °narration; °memoir: *I want your detailed description of what led up to the argument.* **3** °sort, °kind, °nature, °character, °type, °variety, °brand, °breed, species, °category, genus, ilk, °genre, °class; °stripe, kidney, feather: *Carstairs is a roué of the worst description.*

desecrate *v.* °profane, defile, °blaspheme (against), °dishonour, °degrade, °debase, befoul, °contaminate, °pollute, °corrupt, °violate, °pervert, °vitiate: *Vandals desecrated the temple of Minerva.*

desert[1] *n.* **1** °waste, wilderness, wasteland, dust bowl: *The nearest oasis was fifty miles away across the desert.*
—*adj.* **2** °barren, °desolate, °uninhabited, unpeopled, °lonely, °deserted; arid, °bare, °vacant, °empty, °wild, uncultivated: *I was marooned on a desert island.*
—*v.* **3** °forsake, °leave, °abandon; °jilt, °throw over; °maroon, strand, °leave to twist (slowly) in the wind; *Colloq* °run *or* °walk out on, °leave flat *or* in the °lurch, leave high and dry: *His courage deserted him when he saw the child's eyes. He has deserted his wife for some floozie.* **4** abscond, °quit, °run away (from), °defect, °abandon; *Military slang* go over the hill: *He deserted and will be court-martialled.*

desert[2] *n.* Often, **deserts**: °payment, recompense, °requital, compensation, °due, °right; °retribution, °justice, *Slang* comeuppance, what's coming to one: *She'll get her just deserts one of these days.*

deserted *adj.* °abandoned, °desolate, forsaken, neglected, °uninhabited, unpeopled, °vacant, vacated, unfrequented, unvisited, unoccupied, °empty; stranded, rejected, God-forsaken, °isolated, °solitary, °lonely, friendless: *At that hour the streets are completely deserted.*

deserter *n.* °runaway, °fugitive, escapee, absconder, °defector, °renegade, °outlaw; °traitor, °turncoat, *Colloq* rat: *Deserters are shot when caught.*

deserve *v.* °merit, °earn, be entitled to, be °worthy of, °rate, °warrant, °justify: *You ought to be nicer to him—he really doesn't deserve such unkind treatment.*

deserved *adj.* merited, earned, °just, °rightful, °suitable, °fitting, °fit, °appropriate, °proper, °right, °fair, °equitable, °meet, warranted, condign: *Carla was never given her deserved credit for catching the thief.*

deserving *adj.* °meritorious, °worthy, merited, commendable, °laudable, °praiseworthy, creditable, °estimable: *Perhaps you should leave your money to a deserving charity.*

design *v.* **1** °plan, °draw up, °think of, °conceive of, °contemplate, °devise, °lay out, visualize, °envisage, °envision, sketch (out), °pattern, °set up: *The building was originally designed as the centre-piece for a whole new development.* **2** °plan, sketch (out), delineate, °outline, °draft, °work or map or °block out, °lay out, °devise, °invent, contrive, °create, °conceive, °originate, °think up, °develop, °organize, °frame, °shape, °mould, °forge, °make, °construct, °form, °fashion: *John Smithers has designed a new sales strategy for the company.* **3** sketch, °draft, °lay out, °draw; °form, °devise: *Who designed the company's new logo?* **4** °intend, °mean, °plan, °purpose, °destine: °scheme, °plot: *The building was originally designed to be a school. The book was designed for children.*
—*n.* **5** °plan, °scheme, °conception, °study, °project, °proposal, °undertaking, °enterprise; blueprint, °pattern, °chart, diagram, layout, map, °drawing, °draft, sketch, °model, °prototype: *The grand design for rebuilding the city was not approved.* **6** °form, °shape, configuration, °pattern, °style, °motif, °format, layout, °make-up, delineation, °arrangement, °organization, °composition, °structure, construction: *I don't much care for her new design of my monogram.* **7** °aim, °purpose, °intention, °objective; °object, °goal, °point, °target, °intent: *My design had been to go at once to London.* **8 designs**: °plot, °intrigue, °stratagem, °cabal, °conspiracy, conniving, manipulation, connivance, °evil °intent or °intentions: *His designs against me have borne bitter fruit.*

designate *v.* **1** °indicate, °specify, pinpoint, particularize, delineate, °point out, °identify, °state, °set forth, °write or °put down, °name: *You should designate your heirs in your will.* **2** °appoint, °nominate, °name, °identify, denominate, °select, °pick, °choose, °elect, °assign, °appropriate, °delegate, depute: *She has not yet designated her successor.* **3** °mean, °stand for, °symbolize, °denote, °represent: *The Greek letter pi designates the ratio of the circumference of a circle to its diameter.* **4** °call, °name, °style, °term, °label, °christen, dub, °nickname, °entitle: *Elvis was publicly designated 'The King of Rock 'n' Roll'.*

designer *n.* **1** °creator, originator, architect, artificer, °author, deviser, inventor; (°interior) decorator, artist; draughtsman: *Raymond Loewy was a designer of locomotives and fountain pens. Lady Mendl was the best-known interior designer of the 1920s.* **2** intriguer, schemer, conniver, plotter, conspirator: *He is a cunning designer who has wormed his way into favour with the management.*

designing *adj.* °scheming, plotting, conniving, conspiring, intriguing, °calculating, °wily, °tricky, cunning, °sly, underhand(ed), °crafty, °artful, °shrewd, Machiavellian, guileful, °deceitful, double-dealing, °devious, treacherous, *Colloq* °crooked: *The prince has fallen prey to designing courtiers.*

desirable *adj.* **1** sought-after, wanted, coveted, longed-for, looked-for, desired: *Few things are more desirable than security in old age.* **2** °attractive, °pleasant, °pleasing, °agreeable, °winning, winsome, captivating, °seductive, alluring, °fetching: *Their daughter had grown up into a most desirable young lady.* **3** °good, °goodly, °excellent, °choice, °fine, °superior, °superb, *Colloq Brit* plummy: *The company has produced some very desirable motor cars.* **4** °profitable, °worthwhile, °beneficial, °advantageous, valuable, °worthy, °estimable, commendable, °admirable: *Lady Chelm's plan possesses many desirable attributes.*

desire *v.* **1** crave, °want, °fancy, covet, °wish for, °hope for, °long or °yearn for, pine or °sigh for, °hanker after, have an °eye or °taste for, °hunger or °thirst for or after, °die for, have one's heart set on, give one's eye-teeth for, *Colloq* have a yen for, *Slang US* have the hots for: *I desire nothing but your happiness. He desired her more than anything else in the world.* **2** °ask for, °request, °order, demand, °solicit, importune, °summon, °require: *Do you desire anything further, sir?*
—*n.* **3** °longing, craving, yearning, hankering, °hunger, °thirst, °appetite; °passion, °lust, libido, lustfulness, concupiscence, lecherousness, lechery, lasciviousness, salaciousness, prurience, *Slang* °hot pants, *US* the hots; *Colloq* yen: *He felt desire rising in him like a fever.* **4** °wish, °request, °urge, °requirement, °order, °requisition, °demand, desideratum; °appeal, entreaty, °petition: *He fulfils her every desire.*

desirous *adj.* wishful, desiring, °longing, yearning, °hopeful, hoping: *I was desirous to learn more about his whereabouts.*

desolate *adj.* **1** °solitary, °lonely, °isolated, °deserted, °forlorn, forsaken, friendless, °alone, °abandoned, neglected; °desert, °uninhabited, °empty, unfrequented, °bare, °barren, °bleak, °remote: *He felt desolate after his wife's death. Tristan da Cunha is a group of four desolate islands in the Atlantic.* **2** laid °waste, ruined, devastated, ravaged, destroyed: *The explosion left the surrounding countryside desolate.* **3** °dreary, °dismal, °wretched, °joyless, cheerless, comfortless, °miserable, °unhappy, down, disconsolate, °sad, °melancholy, °sorrowful, °forlorn, °mournful, °woebegone, °gloomy, °broken-hearted, heavy-hearted, °inconsolable, °dejected, downcast, °downhearted, dispirited, low-spirited, depressed, °melancholy, spiritless, °despondent, distressed, discouraged, °hopeless: *He has brought some happiness into her desolate existence.*
—*v.* **4** depopulate: *The country was desolated by famine.* **5** °destroy, °devastate, °ruin, lay °waste, despoil, °ravage, °demolish, °obliterate, annihilate, °raze, °gut: *Invaders desolated the countryside.* **6** °dismay, dishearten, °depress, °daunt, dispirit, °sadden, deject, °discourage: *He was either buoyed up by renewed hope or desolated by despair.*

desolation *n.* **1** °destruction, °ruin, devastation, °waste, spoliation, despoliation, °sack, °depredation, extirpation, obliteration, ravagement, barrenness, °havoc, °chaos: *We had to shape a new life from the desolation left by the war.* **2** °grief, °sorrow, dreariness, °despair, °gloom, °distress, °melancholy, °sadness,

°misery, °woe, °anguish, wretchedness, dolour, dolefulness, unhappiness: *She felt the desolation of loneliness after her husband's death.*

despair *n.* **1** hopelessness, °desperation, discouragement, disheartenment, despondency, dejection, °depression, °gloom, gloominess, °misery, °melancholy, wretchedness, °distress, miserableness, °anguish; °resignation: *The despair of the prisoners was evident in their ravaged faces.*
—*v.* **2** °give up *or* lose °hope; °surrender, °quit: *We despaired of ever seeing our children again.*

desperate *adj.* **1** °reckless, °foolhardy, °rash, °impetuous, °frantic, frenzied, °panic-stricken: *Desperate measures are required in such a desperate situation.* **2** °careless, °hasty, devil-may-care, °wild, °mad, frenetic, °furious: *They made a last desperate attack on the fort.* **3** °anxious (for), craving, °hungry (for), °thirsty (for), needful (of), °desirous (of), covetous (of), °eager (for), °longing *or* yearning (for), wishing (for), hoping (for), aching (for), pining (for): *She is desperate for attention.* **4** °urgent, °pressing, compelling, °serious, °grave, °acute, °critical, °crucial, °great: *There is a desperate need for medicines at the disaster site.* **5** °precarious, °perilous, life-threatening, °hazardous, °dangerous, °tenuous, °hopeless, beyond hope *or* help: *Avalanches are making the climbers' situation even more desperate.* **6** at one's wits' °end, °forlorn, despairing, °despondent, °wretched, at the °end of one's tether, °frantic: *With no one to turn to for help, he was truly desperate.*

desperation *n.* **1** recklessness, impetuosity, rashness, foolhardiness, imprudence, heedlessness: *Penniless and half-starved, he was driven to desperation and stole a loaf of bread.* **2** °despair, °anxiety, °anguish, anxiousness, despondency, °depression, dejection, discouragement, defeatism, pessimism, hopelessness, °distress, °misery, °melancholy, wretchedness, °gloom, °sorrow: *In a final act of desperation, he attempted suicide.*

despicable *adj.* °contemptible, below *or* beneath *or* beyond °contempt *or* °scorn *or* disdain, °mean, detestable, °base, °low, °scurvy, °vile, °sordid, °wretched, °miserable, ignoble, ignominious, °shabby; °shameful, °shameless, reprehensible: *He is a thoroughly despicable person and you should have nothing more to do with him.*

despise *v.* disdain, °scorn, °look down on *or* upon, be °contemptuous of, °sneer at, °spurn, contemn; °hate, °loathe, °detest, °abhor: *She despised her servants and treated them badly. He despised anyone who had not been to university.*

despite *prep.* in °spite of, °notwithstanding, undeterred by, °regardless of, in the °face *or* teeth of, in defiance of, without °considering, without °thought *or* °consideration *or* °regard for, ignoring: *We went sailing despite the fact that gales had been forecast.*

despondent *adj.* °dejected, °sad, °sorrowful, °unhappy, °melancholy, °blue, depressed, down, downcast, °downhearted, °low, morose, °miserable, disheartened, discouraged, dispirited, low-spirited, down in the °mouth, *Colloq* down in the dumps: *He's been despondent since she went away.*

despot *n.* °absolute ruler, °dictator, °tyrant, °oppressor, autocrat: *History has painted Ivan the Terrible as one of the cruellest despots of all time.*

despotic *adj.* °dictatorial, °tyrannical, °oppressive, °authoritarian, imperious, °domineering, °totalitarian, °absolute, autocratic, °arbitrary: *The country was under the despotic rule of a callous tyrant.*

despotism *n.* autocracy, monocracy, autarchy, totalitarianism, absolutism, dictatorship, °tyranny, °oppression, °suppression, °repression: *She denounced the new laws as another instance of the brutal despotism of the regime.*

dessert *n.* °sweet, *Brit* pudding, *Colloq Brit* pud, afters: *For dessert, I had ice-cream and she had a fruit tart.*

destination *n.* journey's °end, terminus, °stop, stopping-place; °goal, °end, °objective, °target: *Our destination is Bristol.*

destine *v.* **1** °fate, predetermine, predestine, ordain, foreordain, preordain; °doom: *His only ambition was to be a successful farmer, but the gods destined him for greater things.* **2** °design, °intend, °mean, °devote, °assign, °appoint, °designate, °purpose, °mark, earmark, °set aside: *He beheld the chariot destined to carry him heavenwards.*

destined *adj.* **1** meant, intended, designed, °predetermined, foreordained, predestined, °fated; °doomed, written; *US* in *or* on the cards: *His destined end was to be shot while escaping. Oliver was destined to fail at everything he tried. It was destined that the boy would become king.* **2** °certain, °sure, °bound, ineluctable, °unavoidable, °inevitable, inescapable: *Being devoured by monsters is the destined demise of all who dare to enter there.*

destiny *n.* °fate, °doom, °fortune, °lot, kismet, karma: *It is my destiny to be ignored when living and forgotten when dead.*

destitute *adj.* **1** in °want, °impoverished, poverty-stricken, °poor, °indigent, down and out, °needy, on one's uppers, °badly off, penniless, °penurious, impecunious, °insolvent, bankrupt, *Colloq* °hard up, °broke, *US* on skid row: *Why distribute food to destitute families only at Christmas?* **2** Usually, **destitute of**: bereft of, °deficient in, °deprived of, devoid of, lacking (in), °wanting (in), in °need, needful (of), without: *The landscape was entirely destitute of trees.*

destroy *v.* **1** °demolish, °tear *or* °pull down, °raze, °wipe out, °ravage, °wreck, smash, °ruin, °break up *or* down, annihilate, °crush, eradicate, extirpate, °exterminate, °devastate, commit °mayhem, lay °waste, vandalize, *Slang US* °trash: *The invading hordes destroyed everything, leaving desolation in their wake. The storm destroyed fifty houses.* **2** °ruin, do away with, °end, make an °end of, bring to an °end, bring *or* put an °end to, °terminate, °finish, °kill: *Realizing what he had done, he destroyed himself. The trial destroyed his career.* **3** °counteract, °neutralize, nullify, annul, °cancel (out), °reverse; °stop, °interfere with: *Caught embezzling, Martin destroyed everything he had worked for. Sunspot activity destroyed radio transmission this week.* **4** °disprove, refute, confute, °deny, °contradict, negate, °overturn, °overthrow, °ruin, °spoil, °undermine, °weaken, enfeeble, devitalize, °exhaust, disable, °cripple: *By pointing out just one flaw, she destroyed his entire argument.*

destruction *n.* **1** demolition, razing, wrecking, °ruin, ruining, ruination, breaking up *or* down, °mayhem, °havoc, annihilation, devastation, tearing or knocking down, laying °waste, ravagement; rack and °ruin, Colloq wiping out: The destruction of the city took place in 1942. **2** °slaughter, annihilation, °killing, eradication, °murder, extermination, °holocaust, liquidation, °massacre, extinction, genocide, assassination, slaying, putting to °death, putting an °end to, making an °end of, doing away with, putting away, Colloq doing in, wiping out; Slang US rubbing out, rub-out: They were bent on the destruction of an entire people. **3** °undoing, °end, °ruin, ruination, °downfall, °termination, breakup, °breakdown, °collapse: The imprisonment of the bosses spelt the destruction of the entire crime network.

destructive adj. **1** °harmful, °injurious, baneful, pernicious, °dangerous, °hurtful, toxic, °poisonous, °virulent, noxious, °bad, °malignant, baleful, °unwholesome, damaging, °detrimental, deleterious, °devastating; °deadly, °fatal, °lethal, °fell, °killing, internecine: The spray keeps away insects but is destructive of the plant life. **2** °negative, adverse, °opposing, °opposed, °contrary, °contradictory, antithetical, conflicting, unfavourable, condemnatory, °derogatory, disparaging, disapproving, °critical: The playwrights feared and disliked him because of his destructive criticism.

desultory adj. shifting, °devious, unsteady, °irregular, wavering, °inconstant, °fitful, °spasmodic, unmethodical, °disconnected, unsystematic, °disorderly, disordered, unorganized, disorganized, °inconsistent, °random, °haphazard, °chaotic, °erratic, °shifty: He made no more than a desultory effort to stop smoking. The countries engaged in intermittent, desultory warfare for decades.

detach v. °separate, uncouple, °part, disjoin, °disengage, disunite, °disconnect, disentangle, °free, unfasten, °undo, °cut off, °remove: She carefully detached the printer lead from the back of the computer.

detached adj. **1** °disconnected, °unattached, °separate(d), °free, °isolated, disentangled, unfastened, removed, °cut off, divided, disjoined: He suffered from a detached retina. Their new house is detached. **2** °disinterested, °aloof, uninvolved, unemotional, °dispassionate, dégagé(e), °reserved, °impersonal, °impartial, °neutral, °objective, unbiased, °unprejudiced: She seemed rather detached and did not get involved in the discussion.

detachment n. **1** separating, unfastening, disconnecting, detaching, disengaging; °separation, disconnection, disengagement: Most young birds cannot survive a prolonged period of detachment from their parents. **2** aloofness, unconcern, °indifference, coolness, inattention, insouciance: He viewed the carnage of the battle with regal detachment. **3** See detail, 3, below.

detail n. **1** °particular, °element, °factor, °point, °fact, °specific, technicality, component, °item, °feature; °aspect, °respect, °count: He gave us a general idea of the plan but not a single detail. **2** details: °particulars, minutiae, niceties, °fine °points, specifics, technicalities: Must we go into all the details of his dismissal? **3** °detachment, °squad, °party, cadre, °duty, °fatigue, °group: The sergeant appointed a detail to police the area. **4 in detail**: specifically,

°particularly, °thoroughly, in °depth, °item by °item, °point by °point, exhaustively, comprehensively, °inside out, °perfectly: We examined the report in detail.
—v. **5** °specify, °spell out, °itemize, delineate, catalogue, °list, °tabulate, °enumerate, particularize, °recount, cite (chapter and verse): She detailed every little move I was to make. **6** °assign, °appoint, °charge, °delegate, °name, °specify, °send: We have been detailed to act as your bodyguard during your visit.

detailed adj. **1** itemized, °exhaustive, °comprehensive, °thorough, °full, °complete, °inclusive, particularized, °precise, °exact, °minute, blow-by-blow, °circumstantial: He kept a detailed report of everything that happened on D-Day. **2** °intricate, complex, °complicated, °elaborate, °ornate: Note the detailed scrollwork on this screen.

detect v. **1** uncover, °find (out), °discover, °locate, °learn of, ascertain, °determine, °dig up, °unearth: The pathologist detected the presence of prussic acid in the victim's bloodstream. **2** °perceive, °note, °notice, °identify, °spot, °observe, °sense, °read, °scent, °smell, discern, °feel, catch, °find: Did I detect a tone of sarcasm in your reply, young man?

detective n. investigator, private investigator, CID man, policeman, °constable, Colloq private eye, °sleuth, Sherlock, °snoop, snooper, Brit tec, US P.I., dick, hawkshaw; Slang cop, copper, US and Canadian gumshoe, peeper: Detectives have at last solved the case of the missing weapon.

detention n. °custody, confinement, °imprisonment, °captivity, internment, incarceration, °restraint, Archaic or literary durance: The culprit was kept in detention for a week.

deter v. dissuade, °discourage, °inhibit, °intimidate, °daunt, °frighten off or from or away, °scare off or from; °prevent, °stop, °obstruct, °check, °hinder, °impede: I was deterred from entering by three large dogs. Regular spraying of plants helps to deter aphid infestation.

detergent n. **1** cleaner, cleanser, soap (powder or flakes or liquid); surfactant, surface-active agent, detersive: You put too much detergent into the washing machine and it overflowed.
—adj. **2** cleaning, cleansing, washing, purifying, detersive: The detergent effect is reduced if too much soap is used.

deteriorate v. **1** °worsen, °decline, °degenerate, °degrade, °spoil, get worse, °depreciate, °slip, °slide, Colloq °go to pot, °go to the dogs, °go downhill: We have watched their relationship deteriorate over the years. **2** °decay, °decline, °disintegrate, °fall apart, °decompose, °crumble, °erode: The building slowly deteriorated and is now uninhabitable.

determination n. **1** resoluteness, °resolution, firmness, °resolve, steadfastness, °tenacity, °perseverance, °fortitude, doggedness, °persistence, constancy, single-mindedness, °will(-power), Colloq °grit, guts: The idea is a good one, if only she has the determination to see it through. **2** °settlement, °resolution, resolving, °decision, °solution, °judgement, verdict, °outcome, °result, °upshot, conclusion, °end, °termination: None of us could live in peace till the determination of the border dispute. **3** fixing, settling, ascertainment, ascertaining, delimitation, °definition: *The determination of our position is critical in setting our course.*

determine v. **1** °settle, °decide, °clinch, arbitrate, °judge, adjudge, conclude, °terminate, °end: *The ambiguity must be determined one way or the other.* **2** ascertain, °find out, °discover, conclude, °infer, °draw, °learn, °detect; °verify: *From the evidence, they determined the identity of the intruder.* **3** °decide, °choose, °select, °resolve, make up one's °mind, °settle on or upon, °fix on or upon: *You alone can determine which candidate you want to vote for.* **4** °affect, °influence, °act on, °shape, °condition, °govern, °regulate, °dictate: *There were many factors determining my choice.*

determined adj. **1** °decided, °resolute, resolved, °purposeful, dogged, strong-willed, °strong-minded, °single-minded, °tenacious, °intent, °firm, unflinching, unwavering, °fixed, °constant, °persistent, persevering, °steady, unfaltering, °unhesitating, unyielding, °stubborn, °obstinate, adamant: *He was determined not to go. We made a determined effort to locate the wreck.* **2** °fixed, determinate, °definite, °exact, °precise, °distinct, °predetermined, ascertained, identified: *They worked to a previously determined plan. They agreed to pay a percentage of the determined price.*

deterrent n. °hindrance, °impediment, discouragement, disincentive, dissuasion, °check, °hitch, °obstacle, °obstruction, °stumbling-block; °catch, °snag, °rub, °fly in the ointment, °bar, °drawback: *Some experts hold that the death penalty is no deterrent to murder. The only deterrent to your plan is that we are likely to be caught.*

detest v. °despise, °loathe, °hate, °abhor, execrate, abominate: *They served turnips, which I detest, and sat me next to Ida, whom I also detest.*

detour n. **1** °diversion, deviation, circuitous °route or °way, °roundabout °way, °bypass: *The detour took us five miles out of our way.* —v. **2** °deviate, °turn (away) from, °divert, °bypass: *I detoured from the main road and took a short cut.*

detract v. **detract from**: °diminish, °reduce, °take away from, °subtract from, lessen, °depreciate, °disparage: *Once you are in the public eye, your slightest fault detracts from your reputation.*

detriment n. °disadvantage, °drawback, °liability; °damage, °harm, °ill, °impairment, °injury, °hurt, °loss: *He has a tendency to support lost causes, to his own detriment. Seeds survive without detriment where their plants would perish.*

detrimental adj. disadvantageous, °harmful, °injurious, °hurtful, damaging, deleterious, °destructive, °prejudicial, adverse, unfavourable, inimical, pernicious: *I know nothing detrimental about either one of them.*

devastate v. **1** lay °waste, °ravage, °destroy, °waste, °sack, °raze, °ruin, °desolate, °spoil, °wreck, °demolish, °level, °flatten, °gut, °obliterate: *The island was completely devastated by the tidal wave that followed the typhoon.* **2** disconcert, confound, °discomfit, take aback, °nonplus, °shatter, °overwhelm, abash, °shock; °humiliate, °mortify, °embarrass, chagrin, *Colloq* °floor, *US* discombobulate: *She was devastated by the news of Bertie's expulsion from college.*

devastating adj. **1** °keen, °incisive, mordant, °penetrating, °trenchant, °telling; °sardonic, °sarcastic, °bitter, acid, °caustic, °savage, °satirical, °virulent, vitriolic: *Because of his bland manner, his devastating wit often caught people by surprise.* **2** °ravishing, captivating, °enthralling, °stunning, °overpowering, bewitching, °spellbinding; spectacular: *Kathy was wearing a devastating black silk dress.*

develop v. **1** °bring out or forth, °advance, °expand (on or upon), broaden, °enlarge (on or upon), °amplify, evolve, expatiate (on or upon), °elaborate (on or upon), °reveal, lay °open, °expose, °unfold, °disclose, °bare, (°cause to) °grow, °realize the °potential (of); °cultivate, °improve, °promote, °exploit, °strengthen: *The plot is fine, but the characters need to be developed more fully. It is the aim of the school to develop the students' natural abilities.* **2** (make) °grow, °mature, °ripen, °age, °expand: °flower, blossom, bloom, °increase: *You can't develop that idea without financial backing. These shrubs will be fully developed next year.* **3** °exhibit, °display, °show, °demonstrate, °manifest: *She has recently developed an interest in cooking.* **4** °emerge, °arise, °appear, °come out, °come to °light, evolve, °originate, °begin, °commence, °happen, °occur, °come about; °come forth, °result: *A serious fault has developed in the rocket's fuel line. His natural talent for music developed when he joined the school band.*

development n. **1** °occurrence, °happening, °event, °incident, °circumstance, °situation, °condition, °phenomenon: *William Nye will report new developments from the scene.* **2** °evolution, °growth, evolvement, maturation, unfolding, maturing, °maturity, °increase, °expansion, enlargement, °increment; °advance, advancement, °progress; °improvement: *She has studied the region's economic development.*

deviant adj. **1** deviating, °divergent, °different, °abnormal, °strange, uncommon, °unusual, °odd, °peculiar, °curious, aberrant, °eccentric, idiosyncratic, °deviate, °queer, quirky, °weird, °bizarre, °offbeat, °singular, *Slang* °kinky, freaky, *Chiefly Brit* °bent: *They have been observing his deviant behaviour for some time.* **2** See homosexual, 2, below. —n. **3** See homosexual, 1, below.

deviate v. **1** °turn aside or away, °swerve, veer, °wander, °stray, °drift, digress, °diverge; °divert: *He has chosen a path that deviates from the straight and narrow.* —adj., n. **2** See deviant, 1, 3, above.

device n. **1** contrivance, °mechanism, °machine, machinery, °implement, utensil, °apparatus, °instrument, appliance, °tool, °gadget, °gimmick, *Colloq* °contraption, widget, thingumajig or thingamajig, *Brit* gubbins: *She has patented a device for peeling hard-boiled eggs.* **2** °stratagem, °scheme, °trick, °artifice, °ruse, °plot, ploy, gambit, °strategy, °manoeuvre, °machination; machinery, °apparatus, °mechanism, contrivance, °gimmick, °tool, weapon: *They resorted to a variety of devices in order to achieve their ends. That lawyer used every device he could think of to separate Cornelia from her inheritance.* **3** °design, °emblem, °figure, (heraldic) °bearing, insigne, cadency °mark, °mark of cadency, °hallmark, trade °mark, °symbol, badge, coat of arms, °seal, °crest, colophon, logotype, logo, monogram, °charge, °cognizance, signet; °motto, °slogan, °legend: *The family silver bore their device, a lion rampant.* **4 devices**: °pleasure, °disposition, °will, °inclination, °fancy, °desire, whim: *Left to his own devices, he'll survive very well indeed.*

devil *n.* **1** Satan, Lucifer, Mephistopheles, Beelzebub, Asmodeus, Abaddon, Apollyon, Belial, Lord of the Flies, prince of darkness, °spirit of °evil, °evil °spirit, cacodemon, °evil one, °wicked one, archfiend, Fiend, deuce, *Scots* Clootie; *Colloq* Old Harry, (Old) Nick, *US* (Old) Scratch: *In medieval times the devil was given horns, a tail, and cloven hooves.* **2** °brute, °fiend, °demon, °beast, °ogre, °monster, °rogue, °scoundrel, °rake, knave, rakehell, °villain, ghoul, hell-hound, vampire, °barbarian; °witch, hell-cat, °shrew, termagant, vixen, virago, ogress, harpy, °hag, Xanthippe *or* Xantippe, crone: *If you hit me again I'll phone the police, you devil!* **3** °fellow, °person, °chap, °wretch, bloke, °guy, °beggar, °unfortunate, *Colloq* °bugger, *Brit* sod: *The poor devil lost an arm at Gallipoli.* **4** °imp, scamp, °rascal, fox, slyboots, °sly dog, rapscallion, confidence man, trickster, *Colloq* °operator, smoothie, °smooth *or* °slick °operator, con man, con artist: *The little devil has stolen our hearts. The devil wormed his way into our confidence and then made off with our money.* **5 like the devil**: °exceedingly, °extremely, excessively, violently, speedily, confoundedly, deucedly: *The car was going like the devil when it hit the tree. She fought like the devil to protect the house.* **6 — the devil**: in heaven's name, the dickens, in the °world, on God's green earth, in °hell: *What the devil do you think you are doing? Who the devil is she? Where the devil have you put my trousers?*

devilish *adj.* °diabolic(al), °satanic, Mephistophelian, °fiendish, demonic, cacodemonic, demoniac(al), °infernal, hellish, °villainous, °sinister, °wicked, °evil, iniquitous, °sinful, flagitious, heinous, malign, malevolent, °malignant, °cruel, maleficent; impish, °mischievous, prankish, °naughty, °crazy, madcap: *He has come up with a devilish plan for stealing the secret formula.*

devilry *n.* **1** deviltry, °mischief, mischievousness, roguery, naughtiness, rascality, roguishness, diablerie, archness, knavery, knavishness: *His latest bit of devilry is hiding father's bedroom slippers.* **2** deviltry, devilishness, wickedness, °evil, fiendishness, diablerie, cruelty, malice, malevolence, viciousness, perversity, iniquity, hellishness, villainy: *That traitor is up to some devilry.*

devious *adj.* **1** °deceitful, underhand(ed), °insincere, °deceptive, misleading, subreptitious, °sneaky, °furtive, °surreptitious, °secretive, double-dealing, treacherous, °dishonest, °shifty, °smooth, °slick, °slippery, °scheming, plotting, °designing, °foxy, vulpine, °wily, °sly, °crafty, °tricky, *Colloq* °crooked: *The plot to poison the queen was the product of a devious mind.* **2** °indirect, °roundabout, zigzag, °evasive, circuitous, °crooked, °rambling, °serpentine, °tortuous, sinuous, anfractuous: *That is about the most devious bit of reasoning I have ever heard!*

devise *v.* **1** concoct, °make up, °conceive, °scheme, contrive, °dream up, °design, °draft, °frame, °form, °formulate, °plan, °arrange,

°work out, °think up, °originate, °invent, °create, *Colloq* cook up: *He devised a method for making sandals out of leather scraps.* **2** °bequeath, °will, convey, °hand down, °give, °assign, °dispose of, °transfer, °bestow: *I devise to my nephew, Ian Ferguson, my property in Yorkshire.*

devote *v.* **1** °apply, °appropriate, °assign, °allot, °commit, allocate, °set aside *or* °apart, °put away *or* aside, °dedicate, consecrate: *Each of the chapels was devoted to a separate sect.* **2** °apply, °pledge, °dedicate, °commit, °give up: *She has devoted her life to helping others.*

devoted *adj.* °faithful, °true, dedicated, committed, °devout, °loyal, loving, doting, °staunch, °tender, °steadfast, °constant; °ardent, caring, °fond, °earnest, zealous, °enthusiastic: *Your brother was my most devoted friend throughout his life.*

devotee *n.* °fan, aficionado, adherent, votary, °enthusiast, °addict, *Colloq* buff, °fiend, *US* hound; *Slang* °bug, nut, °freak, *US* head, junkie, groupie: *The band was followed about on tour by scores of screaming devotees of rock music.*

devotion *n.* **1** devotedness, devoutness, °reverence; earnestness, religiousness, °piety, religiosity, pietism, godliness, holiness, spirituality, °sanctity; °worship, °prayer, °observance, °ritual: *The sect was noted for its devotion to martyrs and their relics. It is gratifying to see such devotion amongst the younger members of the congregation. They interrupted the holy man at his devotions.* **2** °dedication, consecration, °attachment, °loyalty, devotedness: *His devotion to duty will be remembered by his fellow soldiers.* **3** zeal, °ardour, °fervour, ardency, °intensity, °fanaticism, °eagerness, °enthusiasm, earnestness, °readiness, willingness; °love, °passion, infatuation, fondness, °affection, °attachment, adherence, °loyalty, allegiance: *They would dedicate themselves with slavish devotion to some brutal master.*

devour *v.* **1** wolf (down), °gulp (down), °bolt, °swallow (up), °gorge, gobble (up), gormandize, °cram, °stuff, °eat (up) greedily, *Archaic* gluttonize; *Colloq Brit* pig, *US and Canadian* pig out (on): *He was so hungry when he came in that he devoured two whole pies and a plate of chips.* **2** °consume, °waste, °destroy, °wipe out, °ravage, annihilate, °demolish, °ruin, wreak °havoc (up)on, °devastate, °obliterate, eradicate: *A quarter of Europe was already devoured by the plague.* **3** °relish, °revel in, absorb, be °absorbed by; engulf, °consume, °drink in, °eat up, °swallow up, °take in; °swamp, °overcome, °overwhelm: *He eagerly devoured all of Dickens's novels. The sea devoured its victims silently.*

devout *adj.* **1** °devoted, °pious, °religious, reverent, worshipful, °faithful, dedicated, °staunch, churchgoing; °holy, °godly, °saintly, °pure: *When I last saw him, he had become a devout Christian.* **2** devotional, reverential, °religious, °solemn: *Through devout prayer one might see the kingdom of heaven.* **3** °earnest, °sincere, °genuine, °hearty, °heartfelt, °devoted, °ardent, zealous: *You have my devout best wishes for your happiness.*

dexterity *n.* **1** °touch, nimbleness, adroitness, deftness, °facility, °knack, °skill, °proficiency; sleight of hand: *Much fine rug-weaving is done by little children because of the dexterity of their small fingers.* **2** cleverness, °ingenuity, ingeniousness,

°tact, astuteness, keenness, sharpness, shrewdness, cunning, guile, canniness, artfulness: *I
admire his dexterity in arguing the case in court.
He exercised great dexterity in eluding capture.*

dexterous *adj.* **1** dextrous, deft, lithe, °nimble,
°supple, °agile, °quick, °skilful: *He was a dexterous archer.* **2** °clever, °ingenious, °astute,
°keen, °sharp, °shrewd, cunning, guileful,
canny, °artful, °crafty, °slick: *She was devout in
religion, decorous in conduct, and dexterous in business. He was the most dexterous of our political
leaders.*

diabolic *adj.* **1** diabolical, °devilish, °satanic,
Mephistophelian, demonic, demoniac(al),
°fiendish, hellish, °infernal: *His interest in the
supernatural included participation in diabolic rituals of the most repulsive kind.* **2** diabolical, °cruel,
°wicked, iniquitous, °evil, °fiendish, appalling,
°dreadful, °inhuman, °atrocious, execrable,
°abominable, °awful, °terrible, °damnable,
accursed, horrid, °horrible, °hideous,
°monstrous, odious, °vile, °base, °corrupt, °foul,
depraved, flagitious, heinous, malicious, malevolent, malign, maleficent, °sinister, °sinful,
°impious, °bad: *The prisoners suffered the most
diabolic treatment.*

diagnose *v.* °identify, °name, °determine,
°recognize, °distinguish, pinpoint, °interpret;
°analyse: *The doctor diagnosed the symptoms as those
of rheumatoid arthritis.*

dialect *n.* °speech (pattern), phraseology, °idiom,
°accent, °pronunciation, patois, °vernacular;
°jargon, °cant, slang, argot, °language, °tongue,
Creole, pidgin; brogue, burr, *Colloq* °lingo: *Some
of the regional dialects are hard to understand.*

dialogue *n.* **1** duologue, °conversation,
°discussion, °conference, °talk, °chat, colloquy,
communication: *I wrote down that dialogue—it was
hilarious!* **2** °parley, °conference, °meeting,
°huddle, °tête-à-tête, colloquy, *Colloq US and
Canadian* °rap session: *A meaningful dialogue
between labour and management could easily settle
the question.*

diary *n.* °appointment book, date-book,
°calendar, °engagement book; °journal,
°chronicle, log, °record, annal(s): *According to my
diary, the date we dined was the 1st.*

dicey *n.* °risky, °tricky, °dangerous, °difficult,
°ticklish, unpredictable, °uncertain, unsure,
°doubtful, *Colloq* iffy, chancy, °hairy: *Asking for
another pay rise could be pretty dicey, Daniel.*

dicker *v.* **1** °bargain, °trade, barter, °deal,
°haggle, °negotiate: *If I dicker with him, he may
drop his price.*
—*n.* **2** °bargain, °deal, °haggle, °negotiation: *We
had a bit of a dicker but finally settled on a figure.*

dicky *adj.* dickey, °shaky, °unreliable, unsteady,
°unsound, °faulty, *Colloq* °dodgy: *The engine
sounds a bit dicky to me—you'd better have it
seen to.*

dictate *v.* **1** °say, °prescribe, ordain, °decree,
°demand, °command, °lay down (the law),
°order, °direct, °pronounce, °impose: *It is our
leader who dictates what we may say and do.*
—*n.* **2** °decree, °demand, °command, °order,
°direction, °instruction, °charge,
°pronouncement, edict, fiat, ukase, mandate,
caveat, °injunction, °requirement, °bidding,
behest: *Each must act in accord with the dictates of
his conscience.*

dictator *n.* autocrat, °absolute ruler *or*
°monarch, °despot, overlord, °oppressor, tsar
or czar, °tyrant, Fuehrer *or* Führer: *Among monarchs, Henry VIII certainly could have been characterized as a dictator.*

dictatorial *adj.* **1** °absolute, °arbitrary,
°totalitarian, °authoritarian, autocratic,
all-powerful, omnipotent, °unlimited: *The
peoples of some countries often confer dictatorial
powers on their leaders.* **2** °despotic, °tyrannical,
°authoritarian, iron-handed, °domineering,
imperious, °overbearing, *Colloq* °bossy: *The dictatorial way she runs the department makes those
who work there miserable.*

diction *n.* **1** °language, °wording, (°verbal *or*
°writing) °style, °expression, °usage, expressiveness, °terminology, °word choice, vocabulary,
phraseology, phrasing, °rhetoric: *Please go over
my paper and correct the diction.* **2** articulation,
°pronunciation, enunciation, °delivery, elocution, °oratory, °presentation, °speech,
°intonation, inflection: *That course in public
speaking improved Brian's diction enormously.*

dictionary *n.* lexicon, °glossary, wordbook;
°thesaurus: *My dictionary gives the pronunciation,
etymology, and meanings of hundreds of thousands
of words.*

die *v.* **1** lose one's life, lay down one's life,
°perish, °expire, decease, °suffer °death,
Euphemistic °depart, give up the ghost, be no
more, (go to) meet one's Maker, °breathe one's
last, go to the °happy hunting-grounds, go to
one's reward, go to one's °final *or* °last resting-
place, go west, pay the debt of nature, pay one's
debt to nature, °pass through the pearly gates,
°pass away *or* on, join the majority, go the way
of all flesh; *Slang* pop off, bite the dust, kick
the bucket, croak, *Brit* snuff it, go for a burton,
pop one's clogs, *US* turn up one's toes, cash in
one's chips *or* checks: *He died of tuberculosis, a
rare affliction these days.* **2** Often, **die down** *or*
out *or* **away**: °dwindle, lessen, °diminish,
°decrease, °ebb, °decline, °wane, °subside,
wither (away), °wilt, °melt (away), °dissolve,
peter out, °fail, °weaken, °deteriorate,
°disintegrate, °degenerate, °fade (away), °droop,
moulder, °sink, vanish, °disappear: *We lost the
race because the breeze died down. After the third try,
her enthusiasm died. The sound of the flute died away
among its echoes.* **3** °expire, °end, °stop, °cease:
Your secret will die with me. **4** Usually, **die off** *or*
out: become °extinct, °perish: *By about 200
million years ago, all the dinosaurs had died
out.* **5** °long, pine, °yearn, crave, °hanker,
°want, °desire, °hunger, °ache: *He said he was
dying to meet a real movie star.*

diet[1] *n.* **1** °fare, °food, °nourishment, nutriment,
°sustenance, °subsistence, victuals, intake, aliment: *A well-balanced diet is very important.*
2 regimen, °regime: *She is on a diet of bread and
water.*
—*v.* **3** °fast, abstain; °slim; °reduce: *I am dieting
to lose weight.*

diet[2] *n.* °council, congress, °parliament, senate,
legislature, °house, °chamber, °assembly: *In
Japan, the legislature is called a diet.*

differ *v.* **1** °diverge, °deviate, be °separate *or*
°distinct, be °dissimilar *or* °different, °contrast;
°depart: *Even the leaves of the same tree differ from
one another. These substances differ in their magnetic
properties.* **2** °disagree, °conflict, °contradict, be

°contradictory, °vary, be at °variance, take °issue, °part company, °fall out, °quarrel, °argue: *Opinions differ as to the best way to bring up children. She differed with me on many subjects.*

difference *n.* **1** °distinction, °dissimilarity, °discrepancy, unlikeness, °disagreement, inconsistency, °diversity, °variation, imbalance; °inequality, dissimilitude, incongruity, °contrast, contradistinction, contrariety: *Difference of opinion can be constructive in a business partnership. Being colour-blind, he cannot tell the difference between red and green.* **2** Often, **differences**: °dispute, °quarrel, °argument, °disagreement, °dissension, °conflict: *We were able to settle our differences amicably.* **3** °change, °alteration, metamorphosis, reformation, °transformation, conversion, °adjustment, modification: *Since her operation, the difference in Philippa is surprising.* **4** idiosyncrasy, °peculiarity, °characteristic, °character, °nature: *There are important differences between socialism and communism.* **5** °rest, °remainder, °leftovers, °balance: *After each had taken his share, the difference was 12, which we divided equally among the four of us.*

different *adj.* **1** °unlike, unalike, °dissimilar, conflicting; °contrary, °discrete, contrastive, contrasting, disparate, °divergent, °diverse, °distinct, °opposite, °separate, distinguishable; another or other: *We both enjoy boating but in different ways. When modelling, she assumes a different pose every few seconds.* **2** °unique, °unusual, °peculiar, °odd, °singular, °particular, °distinctive, °personal, °extraordinary, °special, °remarkable, °bizarre, °rare, °weird, °strange, unconventional, °original, out of the °ordinary; °new, °novel, °exceptional, °unheard-of: *And now, for something completely different, we present a juggling trick cyclist.* **3** assorted, °manifold, multifarious, numerous, °abundant, °sundry, °various, °varied, °divers, °many, °several: *Different kinds of breakfast cereal are now available.*

differentiate *v.* **1** °distinguish, °discriminate, contradistinguish, °separate, °contrast, °oppose, °set off or °apart, °tell apart: *They must learn how to differentiate one species from another.* **2** °modify, specialize, °change, °alter, °transform, transmute, °convert, °adapt, °adjust: *All organisms possess the power to differentiate special organs to meet special needs.*

difficult *adj.* **1** °hard, °arduous, °toilsome, °strenuous, °tough, °laborious, °burdensome, onerous, °demanding: *He found it difficult to work the longer hours. The first birth is sometimes difficult.* **2** °puzzling, °perplexing, baffling, enigmatic(al), °profound, abstruse, °obscure, °recondite, complex; °thorny, °intricate, °sensitive, knotty, °problematic(al), °ticklish, scabrous: *Some of the questions in the exam were very difficult. The analyst raised a lot of difficult issues which I had to confront.* **3** intractable, °recalcitrant, obstructive, °stubborn, unmanageable, °obstinate, °contrary, unaccommodating, refractory, unyielding, uncompromising; °naughty, ill-behaved; *Colloq Brit* bloody-minded: *Tessa has three difficult teenagers in the house these days.* **4** troubled, troubling, °tough, °burdensome, onerous, °demanding, °trying, °hard, °grim, °dark, unfavourable, straitening: *We have been through some difficult times together.* **5** °fussy, °particular, °demanding,

°finicky, finical, °fastidious, °critical, °troublesome, *difficile*, °awkward, *Colloq* nit-picking: *I'll go wherever you like; I don't want to be difficult about it. Sharon can be a very difficult person to be with.*

difficulty *n.* **1** °strain, °hardship, arduousness, laboriousness, formidableness, tribulation, painfulness: *Despite much difficulty she succeeded.* **2** °hardship, °obstacle, °problem, °distress, °pitfall, °dilemma, °predicament, °snag, °hindrance; Gordian °knot: *He has encountered difficulties during his career.* **3** Often, **difficulties**: °embarrassment, °plight, °predicament, °mess, °strait(s), °trouble, °scrape, *Colloq* hot water, °jam, pickle, °fix; hot potato: *She always seems to be in financial difficulties.*

diffuse *adj.* **1** °spread (out or about or around), scattered, dispersed, widespread; °sparse, °meagre, °thin (on the ground): *A few diffuse clouds could be seen on the horizon.* **2** °wordy, verbose, prolix, long-winded, loquacious, °discursive, digressive, °rambling, circumlocutory, °meandering, °roundabout, circuitous, periphrastic, ambagious, diffusive, pleonastic: *The style of the book is very diffuse, being extravagantly uneconomic of expression.* —*v.* **3** °spread, °circulate, °distribute, °dispense, °disperse; dispel, °scatter, °broadcast, °sow, disseminate; °dissipate: *The colour rapidly diffused, turning the liquid crimson. She has successfully diffused her ideas of female equality throughout the community.*

dig *v.* **1** °excavate, °burrow, °gouge, °scoop, °hollow out; °tunnel: *He dug a hole in which to set the post.* **2** °nudge, °thrust, °stab, °jab, °plunge, °force, °prod, °poke: *I dug my spurs into my horse and rode off. He kept digging me in the ribs with his finger.* **3** °appreciate, °enjoy, °like, °understand: *They really dig the jazz of the big-band era.* **4** °notice, °note, °look at, °regard: *Hey, man, dig that crazy gear!* **5 dig into**: °probe (into), delve into, °go °deeply into, °explore, °look into, °research, °study: *We dug into many books of forgotten lore to find the words of the magic spell.* **6 dig out** or **up**: °unearth, disinter, exhume, °bring up, °find, °obtain, °extract, ferret out, winkle out, °discover, bring to °light, °expose, dredge up, °extricate, °come up with, *Australian* fossick: *I dug out an old-book on witchcraft. She has dug up some interesting information about your friend Glover.* —*n.* **7** °thrust, °poke, °jab, °stab, °nudge: *She playfully gave him a dig in the ribs.* **8** °insult, insinuation, °gibe, °slur, °taunt, °jeer; *Colloq* °slap (in the face), °wisecrack, °crack, *US* low °blow: *Referring to him as a Dartmoor graduate was a nasty dig.*

digest *v.* **1** assimilate: *She has trouble digesting milk.* **2** °bear, °stand, °endure, °survive, assimilate, °accept, °tolerate, °brook, °swallow, °stomach: *The attack was too much for even him to digest.* **3** °comprehend, assimilate, °understand, °take in, °consider, °grasp, °study, °ponder, °meditate (on or over), °reflect on, °think over, °weigh: *I need a little time to digest the new regulations.* **4** °abbreviate, °cut, condense, °abridge, compress, epitomize, summarize, °reduce, °shorten: *Her assistant had digested the report into four pages by noon.*

—*n.* **5** condensation, °abridgement, °abstract, °précis, résumé, °synopsis, °summary, conspectus, °abbreviation: *I never did read the original novel, only a digest.*

dignified *adj.* °stately, °noble, °majestic, °formal, °solemn, °serious, °sober, °grave, °distinguished, °honourable, *distingué*, °elegant, august, °sedate, °reserved; °regal, courtly, lordly, °lofty, °exalted, °grand: *Despite the abuse, he maintained a dignified demeanour.*

dignify *v.* °distinguish, ennoble, elevate, °raise, °exalt, °glorify, upraise, °lift, uplift, °enhance, °improve, °better, upgrade: *The critic wrote that he wouldn't deign to dignify the book by calling it a novel.*

dignitary *n.* °personage, °official, °notable, °worthy, magnate, °power, higher-up; °celebrity, lion, luminary, °star, superstar, *Colloq* VIP, °bigwig, °big shot, °big wheel, °big °name, °big gun, hotshot, hot stuff, °big noise, °big White Chief, °big Chief, °big Daddy, *Brit* Lord or Lady Muck, high-muck-a-muck, *Slang* °big cheese, *Chiefly US* Mr Big, biggie, °fat cat: *Anyone with a lot of money is treated today as a dignitary.*

dignity *n.* **1** °nobility, majesty, °gravity, gravitas, °solemnity, courtliness, °distinction, stateliness, °formality, °grandeur, eminence; hauteur, loftiness: *She entered and walked with dignity to the throne.* **2** °worth, worthiness, °nobility, nobleness, °excellence, °honour, honourableness, respectability, respectableness, °standing, °importance, greatness, °glory, °station, °status, °rank, °level, °position: *The real dignity of a man lies not in what he has but in what he is.* **3** °self-respect, self-regard, *amour propre*, °self-confidence, °self-esteem, °pride, self-importance: *It was beneath her dignity to speak directly to a footman.*

digression *n.* **1** aside, departure, deviation, °detour, obiter dictum, parenthesis, apostrophe, excursus: *His numerous digressions made it difficult to focus on the main points of the speech.* **2** digressing, deviating, divergence, °going off at a tangent, °rambling, °meandering, straying, wandering, deviation: *Digression from the main theme of his speech only diluted his argument.*

dilapidated *adj.* ruined, broken-down, in ruins, gone to rack and °ruin, wrecked, destroyed, falling °apart, °decrepit, °derelict, battered, °tumbledown, °run-down, °ramshackle, crumbling, decayed, decaying, °rickety, °shaky, °shabby, *Brit* raddled: *We shall have to fix up that dilapidated barn if we expect to use it.*

dilemma *n.* °predicament, °quandary, double °bind, catch-22, °impasse, °deadlock, °stalemate; °plight, °difficulty, °trouble; °stymie, snooker; *Colloq* °bind, °box, °fix, °jam, °spot, pickle, °squeeze: *He was faced with the dilemma of killing the injured animal or allowing it to die in agony.*

dilettante *n.* dabbler, trifler, °aesthete, °amateur: *You know art like a curator; I am a mere dilettante.*

diligent *adj.* persevering, °persistent, °industrious, assiduous, sedulous, °intent, °steady, °steadfast, focused, concentrated, °earnest, °attentive, °conscientious, hard-working, indefatigable, °tireless, °constant, °painstaking, °careful, °thorough, °scrupulous, °meticulous, punctilious: *Only through diligent application was she able to get through law school.*

dilute *v.* °water (down), °thin (down *or* out), °cut, °weaken, °doctor, °adulterate; °mitigate, lessen, °diminish, °decrease: *For the table, wine was often diluted with water. He dilutes his argument by citing irrelevancies.*

dim *adj.* **1** °obscure, obscured, °vague, °faint, °weak, weakened, °pale, °imperceptible, °fuzzy, °indistinct, ill-defined, indiscernible, undefined, °indistinguishable, foggy, clouded, cloudy, °nebulous, blurred, blurry, unclear, °dull, °hazy, °misty, °dark, °shadowy, °murky, tenebrous, °gloomy, °sombre, °dusky, crepuscular: *Her beauty made The bright world dim. We could barely see in the dim light of the cave.* **2** °stupid, °obtuse, doltish, °dull, dull-witted, °foolish, slow-witted, dim-witted, °dense, *Colloq* °thick, °dumb: *Anyone who can't understand that is really quite dim.* —*v.* **3** °obscure, °dull, becloud: *His natural feelings of compassion had been dimmed by neglect.* **4** darken, bedim, °shroud, °shade: *Twilight dims the sky above. The stage-lights dimmed and the curtain fell.*

diminish *v.* **1** °decrease, °decline, abate, lessen, °reduce, °lower, °shrink, °curtail, °contract, °lop, crop, °dock, °clip, °prune, °cut, truncate, °cut down, °abbreviate, °shorten, °abridge, compress, condense, °pare (down), °scale down, °boil down: *As the height increases, the pressure diminishes. The need for police patrols was diminished when we hired security guards.* **2** °belittle, °disparage, °degrade, °downgrade, °discredit, °detract (from), °vitiate, °debase, deprecate, demean, derogate, °depreciate, vilipend, devalue, cheapen, °put down, °dismiss, °humiliate, °reject: *His abuse by the authorities did not diminish him in her eyes.* **3** °wane, °fade, °dwindle, °ebb, °die out or away, peter out, °recede, °subside; slacken, °let up, °wind down, °slow (down), °ease (off), *Colloq* °run out of steam: *Soaking in the hot water, I felt the tensions of mind and body gradually diminishing. The campaign finally diminished to a negligible effort.*

diminutive *adj.* °small, °tiny, °little, °miniature, °petite, °minute, minuscule, mini, °compact, °undersized, °pocket, pocket-sized, pygmy, °elfin, Lilliputian, midget, °wee, microscopic; micro, infinitesimal; *US* vest-pocket, vest-pocket-sized, *Colloq* teeny, teeny-weeny *or* teensy-weensy: *The bride and groom appeared with their diminutive page-boys and bridesmaids behind them.*

din *n.* **1** °noise, clamour, °uproar, shouting, screaming, yelling, babel, clangour, clatter, commotion, °racket, °row, hullabaloo, hubbub, hurly-burly, °rumpus, hollering, °blare, blaring, bray, braying, °bellow, bellowing, °roar, °blast, roaring, °pandemonium, °tumult: *We couldn't hear the speech above the din of the crowd.* —*v.* **2** °instil, drum, hammer: *The names and dates of the British monarchs were dinned into me in childhood.*

dine *v.* °eat, °banquet, °feast, sup, break bread, breakfast, lunch, have a °bite *or* °snack, nibble, *Colloq* °feed, *Slang* nosh: *We'll dine at 8.00, so don't be late.*

dingy *adj.* °dark, °dull, °gloomy, °dim, °lacklustre, faded, discoloured, °dusky, °drab, °dreary, °dismal, cheerless, depressing,

°shadowy, tenebrous, smoky, sooty, grey-brown, smudgy, grimy, °dirty, soiled: *He was a dingy man, in dingy clothes, who lived in a dingy house.*

dip v. **1** °immerse, °plunge, °duck, dunk, douse, bathe, °submerge: *He dipped each dish into the soapy water.* **2** °decline, °go down, °fall, °descend, °sag, °sink, °subside, °slump: *The road dips after the next curve. The price of shares has dipped again.* **3 dip in** or **into**: °dabble in, °play at; °skim, °scan: *I haven't had time to read it, but I dipped into it here and there.*
—n. **4** swim, °plunge; immersion; *Brit* bathe: *We are going for a dip in the pool before dinner.* **5** lowering, °sinking, °depression, °drop, °slump, °decline: *This dip in the price of oil means nothing.*

diplomacy n. **1** °tact, tactfulness, adroitness, °discretion: *She was able to get rid of that rude boor with her customary diplomacy.* **2** statecraft, statesmanship, °negotiation; °intrigue, Machiavellianism, °machination, manoeuvring or maneuvering: *Cardinal Richelieu is considered the founder of modern diplomacy.*

diplomatic adj. °tactful, °discreet, °prudent, °wise, °sensitive, °politic, °courteous, °polite, discerning, °perceptive, perspicacious, °thoughtful: *How diplomatic it was of you to have invited Frances's husband!*

direct v. **1** °manage, °handle, °run, °administer, °govern, °regulate, °control, °operate, superintend, °supervise, °command, °head up, °rule; *Colloq* °call the shots: *She directs the company with an iron hand.* **2** °guide, °lead, °conduct, °pilot, °steer, °show or °point (the °way), be at the °helm; °advise, °counsel, °instruct, °mastermind; usher, °escort: *He has directed the company for 40 years, through good times and bad. Can you direct me to the post office?* **3** °rule, °command, °order, °require, °bid, °tell, °instruct, °charge, °dictate, enjoin; °appoint, ordain: *He directed that the attack be launched at dawn.* **4** °aim, °focus, °level, °point, °train; °turn: *That bullet was directed at my heart. Direct your attention to the front of the room.* **5** °send, °address, °post, °mail: *Please direct the letter to my home.*
—adj. **6** °straight, unswerving, shortest, undeviating, through: *We turned off the direct road to take in the view.* **7** uninterrupted, unreflected, unrefracted, without °interference, unobstructed: *She cannot remain in direct sunlight for very long.* **8** unbroken, lineal: *He claims to be a direct descendant of Oliver Cromwell's.* **9** straightforward, °unmitigated, °outright, °matter-of-fact, °categorical, °plain, °clear, unambiguous, unmistakable, to the °point, without or with no beating about the bush, °unqualified, unequivocal, °point-blank, °explicit, °express: *I expect a direct answer to my direct question. Have you direct evidence of his guilt? That was a gross insult and a direct lie!* **10** straightforward, °frank, °candid, °outspoken, plain-spoken, °honest, °blunt, °open, °uninhibited, unreserved, °forthright, °sincere, unequivocal; undiplomatic, °tactless: *She is very direct in commenting about people she dislikes.*

direction n. **1** directing, aiming, pointing, guiding, °guidance, conducting, °conduct, instructing, °instruction, managing, °management, administering, °administration, governing, °government, supervising, supervision, operating, °operation, °running, °leadership, directorship, directorate, °control, captaincy, handling, manipulation, °regulation, °rule, °charge: *The Freedom Party's direction of the country has led to many reforms.* **2** Often, **directions**: °instruction(s), °information; °bearing, °road, °way, °route, avenue, °course: *To assemble the appliance, follow the directions printed in the leaflet. Can you give me directions to the nearest filling-station?*

directly adv. **1** °straight, in a beeline, unswervingly, undeviatingly, as the crow flies: *This road should take me directly to the beach.* **2** °immediately, at °once, °straight away, °right away, °quickly, °promptly, without °delay, speedily, instantly, *Colloq US and Canadian* momentarily: *She called and I went directly.* **3** °soon, later (on), anon, °presently, in a (little) while, °shortly: *The doctor will be here directly.* **4** °exactly, °precisely, °just; °completely, °entirely: *My garage is directly opposite. The cricket pitch is directly at the centre of the park.*
—conj. **5** as °soon as, when: *The police arrested him directly he entered the building.*

director n. **1** °executive, administrator, °official, °principal; chairman, chairperson, chairwoman, president, vice-president; governor; °head, °chief, °boss, °manager, °superintendent, °supervisor, °overseer, °foreman, headman, *Colloq* kingpin, number one, numero uno, Mr Big, the man; *Slang* °top dog, °top banana, *Brit* gaffer, *US* °big cheese, °head or °chief honcho: *The sale of the company was announced at the meeting of the board of directors.* **2** °guide, °leader; steersman, helmsman, °pilot, °skipper, commander, commandant, captain; cicerone; maestro, concert-master, conductor; impresario: *We were lucky to have a director who really knew what he was doing.*

dirt n. **1** °soil, °mud, °muck, °mire, °grime, slime, °sludge, °ooze, slop; dust, soot; excrement, ordure; °filth, °waste, °refuse, trash, °garbage, °rubbish, offal, °junk, dross, sweepings; leavings, °scrap, orts; *Slang Brit* gunge, *US* grunge: *This vacuum cleaner is guaranteed to pick up any kind of dirt.* **2** °soil, °earth, loam, °ground, clay: *Hydroponics is the technique of farming without dirt, using only liquid nutrients.* **3** indecency, obscenity, smut, °pornography, foulness, corruption, °filth, vileness: *Customs confiscated much of the dirt before it could enter the country.* **4** °gossip, °scandal, °talk, °rumour, °inside information, *Colloq* °low-down, °dope, *Slang US* scuttlebutt: *I got the dirt from David about what really happened at the party.*

dirty adj. **1** °foul, unclean, befouled, soiled, begrimed, sooty, grimy, °filthy, mucky, besmeared, besmirched, polluted, squalid, sullied, stained, spotted, smudged, slovenly, °unwashed, °bedraggled, slatternly, °untidy, *Slang Brit* gungy, *US* grungy: *If you think his shirt was dirty, you should have seen his body!* **2** smutty, °indecent, °obscene, ribald, off colour, °prurient, °risqué, salacious, °lewd, °lascivious, °pornographic, °coarse, licentious, °rude, °blue, scabrous: *His parents were shocked to hear him telling dirty jokes.* **3** unfair, °unscrupulous, unsporting, °dishonest, °mean, underhand(ed), unsportsmanlike, °dishonourable, °deceitful, °corrupt, treacherous, °perfidious, °villainous,

°disloyal; malicious, malevolent, °rotten, °filthy: *It was a dirty trick of Sue's to tell the teacher.* **4** °bad, °foul, °nasty, °stormy, rainy, °windy, blowy, blowing, squally, °sloppy: *We're in for some dirty weather, Mr Christian, so you'd best reduce sail.* **5** °bitter, °resentful, °angry, °furious, wrathful, smouldering: *She gave me a dirty look when I said anything about her sister.* **6** °sordid, °base, °mean, °despicable, °contemptible, ignoble, °scurvy, °low, °low-down, ignominious, °vile, °nasty, °infamous: *That villain has done his dirty work and now we must all suffer. He's nothing but a dirty coward!*
—*v.* **7** °stain, °sully, befoul, °soil, begrime, besmirch, °pollute, °muddy, °smear, defile; °blacken, °tarnish: *She refused to so much as dirty her hands to help us. Are you afraid it will dirty your reputation to be seen with me?*

disability *n.* **1** °handicap, °impairment, °defect, °infirmity, disablement: *James is unable to play tennis owing to his disability.* **2** °inability, incapacity, unfitness, °impotence, powerlessness, helplessness: *The teacher helped her to overcome her disability.*

disabled *adj.* incapacitated, °crippled, °lame; damaged, ruined, impaired, harmed, non-functioning, inoperative, *Slang Brit* scuppered: *Disabled ex-servicemen ought to receive compensation. No parts could be found for the disabled machines.*

disadvantage *n.* **1** deprivation, °set-back, °drawback, °liability, °handicap, °defect, °flaw, °shortcoming, °weakness, °weak spot, °fault: *Being colour-blind has not been a disadvantage in his kind of work.* **2** °detriment, °harm, °loss, °injury, °damage; °prejudice, °disservice: *Failure to send in a tax return will be to your distinct disadvantage.*

disagree *v.* **1** °differ, dissent, °diverge: *She disagrees with most of my ideas. I said the painting was by Hockney, but he disagreed.* **2** °conflict, °dispute, °quarrel, °argue, contend, °contest, °bicker, °fight, °fall out, squabble, wrangle, °debate: *Those who agree on major principles often disagree about trifles, and vice versa.*

disagreeable *adj.* **1** unpleasant, unpleasing, °offensive, °distasteful, °repugnant, °obnoxious, °repellent, °repulsive, objectionable, °revolting, odious: *He found the heat and humidity in the tropics most disagreeable.* **2** °offensive, noxious, °unsavoury, °unpalatable, nauseating, °nauseous, °nasty, sickening, °disgusting, °revolting, °repellent, °abominable, objectionable: *A disagreeable odour arose from the beggar on the doorstep.* **3** bad-tempered, ill-tempered, disobliging, uncooperative, unfriendly, uncivil, °abrupt, °blunt, °curt, °brusque, °short, uncouth, °impolite, bad-mannered, °ill-mannered, °discourteous, °rude, °testy, grouchy, splenetic, °cross, ill-humoured, °peevish, morose, sulky, °sullen: *Brian became quite disagreeable, and now I see him no again.*

disagreement *n.* **1** °difference, °discrepancy, °discord, discordance, discordancy, °dissimilarity, disaccord, °diversity, incongruity, nonconformity, incompatibility: *Can you resolve the disagreement between the results of these experiments?* **2** dissent, °opposition, °conflict, contradiction, °difference, °disparity: *The problem arises from a basic disagreement in their*

principles. **3** °quarrel, °strife, °argument, °dispute, velitation, altercation, °controversy, contention, °dissension, °debate, °clash, *Colloq US* rhubarb: *Their mother had to settle the disagreement between the brothers.*

disappear *v.* **1** vanish, °evaporate, vaporize, °fade (away *or* out), evanesce, *Poetic* evanish: *After granting my wish, the genie disappeared, laughing diabolically.* **2** °die (out *or* off), become °extinct, °cease (to exist), °perish (without a trace): *The dinosaurs, though enormously successful as a species, suddenly disappeared from the earth.*

disappoint *v.* **1** °let down, °fail, dissatisfy: *Miss Sheila disappointed her public by refusing to sing.* **2** °mislead, °deceive, disenchant, *Colloq* °stand up: *She disappointed me by saying she would be there and then not arriving.* **3** °undo, °frustrate, °foil, °thwart, balk, °defeat: *How can I answer you truthfully without disappointing your expectations?*

disappointed *adj.* **1** frustrated, unsatisfied, °dissatisfied, disillusioned, °disenchanted, discouraged, °downhearted, disheartened, downcast, saddened, °unhappy, °dejected, °discontented, °let down: *There will be a lot of disappointed children at Christmas this year.* **2** foiled, thwarted, balked, defeated, °undone, failed, °let down: *Though she campaigned energetically, Theodora was among the disappointed candidates.*

disappointing *adj.* discouraging, dissatisfying, °unsatisfactory, unsatisfying, °disconcerting; °poor, second-rate, °sorry, °inadequate, °insufficient, °inferior, °pathetic, °sad: *The former champion turned in a disappointing performance yesterday evening.*

disappointment *n.* **1** frustration, non-fulfilment, unfulfilment, unsatisfaction, °dissatisfaction, °set-back, °failure, °let-down, °defeat, °blow, °fiasco, °calamity, °disaster, °fizzle, *Brit* damp squib, *Colloq* washout: *Recently he has had one disappointment after another.* **2** dejection, °depression, discouragement, disenchantment, °distress, °regret, mortification, chagrin: *I cannot tell you the disappointment your father and I felt when you failed to get into university.*

disapproval *n.* disapprobation, condemnation, censure, °criticism, °reproof, reproach, °objection, °exception, °disfavour, °displeasure, °dissatisfaction: *The council voiced their disapproval of holding a carnival in the village square.*

disapprove *v.* °condemn, °criticize, censure, °object to, decry, °denounce, °put *or* °run down, deplore, deprecate, °belittle, °look down on, °frown on *or* upon, *Colloq* °knock, °look down one's nose at, tut-tut: *I don't care if you disapprove of my marrying Eustace. The monopolies commission has disapproved the merger.*

disarm *v.* **1** unarm; demilitarize, demobilize, °disband, deactivate: *After the war, most—but not all—European countries disarmed.* **2** °win over, put *or* set at °ease, mollify, appease, placate, pacify, °reconcile, conciliate, propitiate, °charm: *I was completely disarmed by her friendly disposition. Many people found his naïvety disarming.*

disaster *n.* °catastrophe, °calamity, cataclysm, °tragedy, °misfortune, débâcle, °accident, °mishap, °blow, act of God, adversity, °trouble, °reverse: *The flooding of the river was as much of a disaster as the earlier drought.*

disastrous adj. **1** °calamitous, catastrophic, catalysmic, °tragic, °destructive, °ruinous, °devastating, appalling, °harrowing, °awful, °terrible, dire, horrendous, °horrible, horrifying, °dreadful, °fatal: *There has been a disastrous earthquake which killed thousands.* **2** °awful, °terrible, unlucky, °unfortunate, °detrimental, °grievous, °harmful: *The postal strike has had disastrous effects on the mail-order business.*

disband v. °disperse, disorganize, °scatter, °break up, °dissolve, demobilize, deactivate, °retire: *After the war, the special spy force was disbanded.*

discard v. **1** get °rid of, °dispense with, °dispose of, °throw away or out, °toss out or away, °abandon, jettison, °scrap, *Colloq* °trash, °dump, *Slang* ditch: *We discarded boxes of old photographs when we moved house.*
—n. **2** °reject, cast-off: *I felt like a discard from the lonely hearts club.*

discernible adj. **1** °perceptible, °visible, seeable, perceivable, °apparent, °clear, °observable, °plain, detectable; °conspicuous, °noticeable: *A small sailing-boat was discernible on the horizon.* **2** distinguishable, recognizable, identifiable, °distinct: *To me there is a discernible difference between puce and burgundy.*

discharge v. **1** °release, °let out, °dismiss, let go, °send away; °pardon, exonerate, °liberate, (set) °free, acquit, °let off, absolve: *She was discharged from hospital yesterday. He was discharged from police custody last week.* **2** °expel, oust, °dismiss, cashier, °eject, give °notice, *Colloq* °sack, give (someone) the °sack, °fire, °kick out: *He was discharged from his job yesterday.* **3** °shoot, °fire (off); °set or °let off, detonate, °explode: *It is illegal to discharge a firearm or other explosive device in this area.* **4** °emit, °send out or forth, °pour out or forth, °gush; disembogue; °ooze, °leak, exude; excrete, °void: *The sore in his leg continued to discharge pus. We can ill afford to discharge those effluents into the sea.* **5** °carry out, °perform, °fulfil, °accomplish, do, °execute: *He faithfully discharges the duties of his office.* **6** °pay, °settle, liquidate, °clear, °honour, °meet, °square (up): *Before going off on holiday, we discharged all our financial obligations.* **7** °unload, offload, disburden, °empty: *After discharging its cargo, the vessel rode high in the water.*
—n. **8** °release, °dismissal: *What is the date of his discharge from the clinic?* **9** °expulsion, ouster, °dismissal, °ejection, °notice, *Colloq* the axe, the °sack, the boot, *Chiefly US and Canadian* walking papers, *Slang US and Canadian* the bounce, the gate: *Her discharge from the firm was rather ignominious.* **10** shooting, firing (off), °report, °shot; salvo, fusillade, °volley; detonation, °explosion, °burst: *The discharge of a pistol could not be heard at that distance. I heard the discharge from the guns of the firing squad in the courtyard below. The discharge of the bomb maimed three children.* **11** emission, °release, °void, voiding, excretion, excreting, emptying, °flow; °ooze, oozing, pus, suppuration, °secretion, seepage: *The discharge of blood from the wound continued.* **12** °performance, °fulfilment, °accomplishment, °execution, °observance, °achievement: *The discharge of my family responsibilities will have to await my return from the front.* **13** °payment, °settlement, liquidation,

squaring (up), °clearance: *The bank expects full discharge of all debts before they lend any money.* **14** unloading, disburdening, offloading, emptying: *The customer will pay in full after the discharge of his cargo.*

disciple n. **1** °apprentice, °pupil, °student, proselyte, °learner, °scholar: *Pietro Zampollini was a disciple of the great artist Ravelli.* **2** °follower, adherent, °devotee, °admirer, votary; °partisan, °fan, aficionado: *She is a disciple of Louis Armstrong's.*

disciplinarian n. taskmaster, taskmistress, martinet, drill-sergeant; °tyrant, °despot, °dictator: *The headmaster at Briarcliffe was a stern disciplinarian who regularly used to beat us.*

discipline n. **1** training, drilling, regimen, °exercise, °practice, °drill, inculcation, indoctrination, °instruction, °schooling: *Strict discipline is good for young people, according to my father.* **2** °punishment, °penalty, chastisement, castigation, °correction: *The discipline meted out to senior students was very harsh.* **3** °order, °routine, (°proper) °behaviour, °decorum: *The sergeant is there to maintain discipline among the recruits.* **4** °direction, °rule, °regulation, °government, °control, °subjection, °restriction, °check, °curb, °restraint: *There was far too much discipline during my childhood, both at school and at home.* **5** °subject, °course, °branch of knowledge, °area, °field, °speciality or chiefly US and Canadian specialty: *Latin is a discipline which is fast disappearing from our schools.*
—v. **6** °train, °break in, °condition, °drill, °exercise, °instruct, °coach, °teach, °school, °indoctrinate, inculcate; edify, °enlighten, °inform: *The aim of his education is to discipline him to respond to orders.* **7** °check, °curb, °restrain, °bridle, °control, °govern, °direct, °run, °supervise, °manage, °regulate, hold or keep in °check, US ride herd on: *You have to discipline those children or they will always misbehave.* **8** °punish, °chastise, °castigate, °correct, °penalize, °reprove, °criticize, °reprimand, °rebuke: *Discipline that boy or he will just do it again.*

disclose v. **1** °reveal, °impart, divulge, °betray, °release, °tell, °blurt out, °blab, °leak, let °slip, °report, °inform, *Colloq* °spill the beans, °blow the gaff, *Slang* squeal, snitch, squeak, rat, peach, US fink: *To get a shorter sentence, he disclosed all to the police.* **2** °bare, °reveal, °expose, uncover, °show, °unveil: *When the pie was opened, twenty-four blackbirds were disclosed.*

discomfit v. **1** °embarrass, abash, disconcert, °disturb, °confuse, make uneasy or uncomfortable, discompose, °fluster, °ruffle, confound, °perturb, °upset, °worry, unsettle, °unnerve, *Colloq* °rattle, US faze, discombobulate: *Being short, she was discomfited by references to her height.* **2** °frustrate, °foil, °thwart, baffle, °check, °defeat, trump, °outdo, °outwit, °overcome: *Discomfited by her violent reaction, her attacker fled.*

discomfort n. **1** uneasiness, °hardship, °difficulty, °trouble, °care, °worry, °distress, vexation: *She hasn't known the discomfort of being the wife of a miner.* **2** °ache, °pain, °twinge, soreness, irritation; °bother, °inconvenience, °nuisance: *Some discomfort persisted in my legs long after the accident.*

disconcerted adj. discomposed, discomfited, ruffled, uneasy, °put out or off, uncomfortable,

°queasy, flustered, °agitated, °upset, shaken, °unsettled, perturbed, °confused, bewildered, perplexed, baffled, puzzled, US thrown off, Colloq rattled, US fazed, discombobulated; Slang (all) shook (up): They were really disconcerted by the arrival of the police.

disconcerting adj. °awkward, discomfiting, off-putting, upsetting, unnerving, °unsettling, °disturbing, confusing, confounding, bewildering, °perplexing, baffling, °puzzling: I found his persistence quite disconcerting.

disconnect v. °separate, disjoin, disunite, uncouple, °detach, unhook, °undo, °disengage, unhitch; °cut or °break off; °cut or °pull °apart, °part, °divide, °sever: They disconnected the engine after pushing the carriages onto a siding. Disconnect the power before changing the light-bulb.

disconnected adj. **1** unconnected, °separate, °apart, °unattached; °split, separated: A totally disconnected thought suddenly occurred to me. **2** °incoherent, irrational, °confused, illogical, garbled, °disjointed, °rambling, mixed-up, unintelligible, uncoordinated, °random: He lost the debate because his argument was disconnected and lacked cogency.

discontent n. °displeasure, unhappiness, °dissatisfaction, discontentment, °distaste, uneasiness; malaise: He felt discontent at being barred from the club.

discontented adj. displeased, °dissatisfied, °discontent, annoyed, vexed, °fretful, irritated, °testy, piqued, °petulant, °disgruntled, exasperated, Colloq fed up, Slang browned off, pissed off, Brit cheesed or brassed off: The umpire's decision made many fans quite discontented.

discontinue v. °cease, °break off, °give up, °stop, °terminate, put an °end to, °quit, °leave off, °drop; °interrupt, °suspend: Please discontinue newspaper delivery until further notice.

discord n. °strife, °dissension, °disagreement, °conflict, disharmony, contention, disunity, discordance, °division, incompatibility: The seeds of discord between the families were sown generations before.

discordant adj. **1** °contrary, disagreeing, °divergent, °opposite, °opposed, adverse, °contradictory, °incompatible, differing, °different, conflicting, at °odds, °incongruous, in °conflict, in °disagreement, at °variance, °dissimilar: The testimony of the fossils is discordant with the evidence in the legend. **2** inharmonious, dissonant, jarring, cacophonous, unmelodious, unmusical, °harsh, °strident, jangling, °grating: He struck some discordant notes on his zither.

discount v. **1** °reduce, °mark down, °deduct, °lower, take or knock off: As I was buying a dozen, he discounted the price by ten per cent. **2** °diminish, lessen, °minimize, °detract from: One must discount what she says when she's angry. **3** °disregard, °omit, °ignore, °pass or °gloss over, °overlook, °brush off, °dismiss: Those statistics are old and can be discounted.
—n. **4** reduction, mark-down, °deduction, °rebate, °allowance: The shop overstocked the item and is offering it at a big discount.

discourage v. **1** dispirit, dishearten, °daunt, unman, °dismay, cow, °intimidate, awe, °overawe, °unnerve: We were discouraged by the arrival of more enemy troops. **2** °deter, °put off, dissuade, advise or hint against, °talk out of,

°divert from; °oppose, °disapprove (of), Colloq throw cold water on: They discouraged me from applying again. **3** °prevent, °inhibit, °hinder, °stop, °slow, °suppress, obviate: This paint is supposed to discourage corrosion.

discourteous adj. uncivil, °impolite, °rude, unmannerly, °ill-mannered, bad-mannered, °disrespectful, misbehaved, °boorish, °abrupt, °curt, °brusque, °short, ungentlemanly, unladylike, °insolent, °impertinent, °ungracious: He had been discourteous and would not be invited again.

discover v. **1** °find (out), °learn, °perceive, °unearth, uncover, bring to °light, °turn or °dig up, smoke or °search out, °root or ferret out; °determine, ascertain, °track down, °identify; °locate: He discovered the ninth moon of Saturn. We discovered why the tyre had gone flat. **2** °see, °spot, catch °sight or a glimpse of, lay eyes on, °behold, °view, °encounter, °meet (with); °notice, espy, descry, °detect, discern: He discovered Madagascar lying right on their course. **3** °originate, °conceive (of), °devise, contrive, °invent, °make up, °design, °pioneer; °come or °chance or °stumble upon: She discovered a method for tin-plating gold.

discovery n. **1** °finding, °recognition, uncovering, determining, ascertaining, unearthing; origination, °invention, °conception, °idea; °development: Who is credited with the discovery of Christmas Island? That year marks the discovery of a vaccine against smallpox. **2** °exploration, disclosure, detection, °revelation: He's off on a voyage of discovery.

discredit v. **1** °detract, °disparage, defame, °dishonour, °disgrace, °degrade, bring into °disfavour or disrepute, deprecate, demean, °lower, devalue, °depreciate, devaluate, °belittle, °diminish, °reduce; °slur, °slander, °vilify, calumniate, °sully, °smear, °blacken, °taint, °tarnish, besmirch, smirch, °stigmatize, asperse, malign, °libel: Both of them were thoroughly discredited by the scandal. **2** disbelieve, °deny, °dispute, °doubt, °question, raise °doubts about, °distrust, °mistrust, give no credit or credence to: As he's a known liar, you can discredit whatever he tells you. **3** °disprove, °reject, refute, invalidate; °mock, °ridicule: The phlogiston theory is generally discredited by most modern chemists.
—n. **4** °dishonour, °degradation, °disfavour, disrepute, °ill repute, °disgrace, ignominy, °infamy, odium, °stigma, °shame, °smear, °slur, °scandal, obloquy, opprobrium, °humiliation: Her performance has brought discredit to all female saxophonists. **5** °damage, °harm, °reflection, °slur, °aspersion, °slander, defamation, °blot, °brand, °tarnish, °blemish, °taint: The discredit to her reputation is irreparable. **6** °doubt, °scepticism, dubiousness, doubtfulness, °qualm, °scruple, °question, incredulity, °suspicion, °distrust, °mistrust: The new evidence throws discredit on the validity of the previous testimony.

discreet adj. °careful, °cautious, °prudent, °judicious, °considerate, °guarded, °tactful, °diplomatic, circumspect, °wary, chary, heedful, watchful: She has always been very discreet in her business dealings with me.

discrepancy *n.* °gap, °disparity, lacuna, °difference, °dissimilarity, deviation, divergence, °disagreement, incongruity, incompatibility, inconsistency, variance; °conflict, discordance, contrariety: *There is a great discrepancy between what he says and what he means.*

discrete *adj.* °separate, °distinct, °individual, °disconnected, °unattached, discontinuous: *These items must be treated as discrete entities and not taken together.*

discretion *n.* **1** °tact, °diplomacy, °prudence, °care, discernment, °sound °judgement, circumspection, sagacity, common °sense, good °sense, °wisdom, °discrimination: *You can rely on my discretion not to reveal the club's secrets.* **2** °choice, °option, °judgement, °preference, °pleasure, °disposition, °volition; °wish, °will, °liking, °inclination: *Buyers may subscribe to insurance cover at their own discretion.*

discriminate *v.* **1** °distinguish, °separate, °differentiate, discern, draw a °distinction, °tell the °difference: *He cannot discriminate between good art and bad.* **2** °favour, °disfavour, °segregate, show °favour *or* °prejudice *or* °bias for *or* against, be °intolerant: *It is illegal here to discriminate against people on the basis of race, creed, or colour.*

discriminating *adj.* discerning, °perceptive, °critical, °keen, °fastidious, °selective, °particular, °fussy, °refined, °cultivated: *From the wine you chose, I see you are a lady of discriminating tastes.*

discrimination *n.* **1** °bigotry, °prejudice, °bias, °intolerance, °favouritism, one-sidedness, unfairness, inequity: *In Nazi Germany discrimination was practised against everyone except the Nazis.* **2** °taste, °perception, perceptiveness, discernment, °refinement, acumen, °insight, °penetration, keenness, °judgement, °sensitivity; connoisseurship, aestheticism: *He exercises excellent discrimination in his choice of paintings.*

discursive *adj.* wandering, °meandering, digressing, digressive, °rambling, circuitous, °roundabout, °diffuse, long-winded, verbose, °wordy, prolix, °windy: *Frobisher was again boring everyone with his discursive description of life in an igloo.*

discuss *v.* °converse about, °talk over *or* about, °chat about, °deliberate (over), °review, °examine, °consult on; °debate, °argue, thrash out: *We discussed the problem but came to no conclusion.*

discussion *n.* °conversation, °talk, °chat, °dialogue, colloquy, °exchange, deliberation, °examination, °scrutiny, °analysis, °review; confabulation, °conference, powwow; °debate, °argument; *Colloq chiefly Brit* chin-wag, *US and Canadian* bull °session: *The subject of your dismissal came up for discussion yesterday.*

disdainful *adj.* °contemptuous, °scornful, contumelious, derisive, sneering, °superior, °supercilious, °pompous, °proud, prideful, °arrogant, °haughty, °snobbish, lordly, °regal; jeering, mocking, °insolent, insulting, *Colloq* °hoity-toity, high and mighty, stuck-up, highfalutin *or* hifalutin; *Slang* snotty: *She was most disdainful of our efforts to enter the cosmetics market.*

disease *n.* **1** sickness, °affliction, °ailment, malady, °illness, infection, °complaint, °disorder, °condition, °infirmity, °disability, *Archaic* murrain, *Colloq* °bug: *The colonel contracted the disease while in Malaysia.* **2** °blight, cancer, virus, °plague; contagion: *Panic spread through the Exchange like an infectious disease.*

diseased *adj.* °unhealthy, unwell, °ill, °sick, ailing, °unsound, °infirm, out of sorts, abed, infected, contaminated; afflicted, °abnormal: *We must care for the diseased patients before those with broken bones.*

disembark *v.* °land, alight, go *or* put ashore, °get *or* °step off *or* out, °leave; debark, detrain, deplane: *Tomorrow we disembark at Tunis.*

disembodied *adj.* incorporeal, bodiless; °intangible, °immaterial, °insubstantial *or* unsubstantial, impalpable, °unreal; °spiritual, °ghostly, °spectral, °phantom, wraithlike: *She wafted before his eyes, a disembodied spirit.*

disenchanted *adj.* disillusioned, disabused, undeceived, °disappointed; °blasé, °indifferent, °jaundiced, °sour(ed), cynical: *I'm afraid she's now thoroughly disenchanted with her job.*

disengage *v.* °loose, °loosen, unloose, °detach, unfasten, °release, °disconnect, disjoin, °undo, disunite, °divide, °cleave (from), °separate, uncouple, °part, disinvolve, °extricate, °get out (of), °get away (from), °cut °loose, °throw off, °shake (off), get °rid of, °break (with *or* from), °break (up) (with); unbuckle, unhitch, unclasp, unlatch, unbolt, unlock, unleash, unfetter, unchain, unlace, unhook, unbind, untie; (set) °free, °liberate, disentangle: *She was holding on to me so tenaciously that I could hardly disengage myself.*

disfavour *n.* **1** °disapproval, °dislike, °displeasure, disapprobation, unhappiness: *Katerina regards your decision with disfavour.* **2** disesteem, °discredit, °dishonour, °disgrace, disrepute: *After last night's events, we are really in disfavour with the management.* —*v.* **3** °disapprove (of), °dislike, discountenance, °frown on *or* upon: *We strongly disfavour the merger.*

disfigured *adj.* marred, damaged, scarred, defaced, mutilated, injured, impaired, blemished, disfeatured, °deformed, distorted, spoilt *or* spoiled, ruined: *Plastic surgery has repaired her disfigured face.*

disgrace *n.* **1** ignominy, °shame, °humiliation, °embarrassment, °degradation, debasement, °dishonour, °discredit, °disfavour, disrepute, vitiation, °infamy; disesteem, °contempt, odium, obloquy, opprobrium: *His conduct has brought disgrace on his family.* **2** °blemish, °harm, °aspersion, °blot, °scandal, °slur, °stigma, vilification, smirch, °smear, °stain, °taint, °black mark: *The way she has been treated by the company is a disgrace.* —*v.* **3** °shame, °humiliate, °embarrass, °mortify: *He has been disgraced by his son's cowardice.* **4** °degrade, °debase, °dishonour, °discredit, °disfavour, °vitiate, defame, °disparage, °scandalize, °slur, °stain, °taint, °stigmatize, °sully, besmirch, smirch, °tarnish, °smear, asperse, °vilify, °blacken, drag through the mud, reflect (adversely) on: *Once again his actions have disgraced the family name.*

disgraceful *adj.* **1** °shameful, humiliating, °embarrassing, °dishonourable, °disreputable, °infamous, ignominious, °degrading, debasing, degraded, debased, °base, °low, °vile, °corrupt, °bad, °wrong, °sinful, °evil, °mean, °despicable, °contemptible, opprobrious: *He was forced to submit to the most disgraceful punishment.* **2** °shameless, °outrageous, °notorious, °shocking, °scandalous, °improper, °unseemly, °unworthy; °indecent, °rude, °flagrant, °lewd, °lascivious, °delinquent, objectionable: *Your drunken behaviour at the party last night was a disgraceful performance.*

disgruntled *adj.* displeased, °dissatisfied, irritated, peeved, vexed, °cross, exasperated, annoyed, °unhappy, °disappointed, °discontented, °put out; malcontent, °discontent, °testy, °cranky, °peevish, grouchy, grumpy, °moody, °sullen, sulky, ill-humoured, bad-tempered, ill-tempered, *Colloq* fed up, *Slang* browned off, *Brit* cheesed off: *He was disgruntled at the thought of having to go shopping in the pouring rain.*

disguise *v.* **1** °camouflage, °cover up, °conceal, °hide, °mask: *The van was disguised as a hay wagon.* **2** °misrepresent, °falsify, °counterfeit, °fake, °deceive: *They have disguised the true profits to avoid paying taxes.* —*n.* **3** °guise, °identity, cover-up, °camouflage, °appearance, °semblance, °form, °outfit, °costume: *She appeared in the disguise of a policewoman.* **4** °pretence, °deception, °dissimulation, façade, °semblance, *Colloq* °front: *Disguise is seldom resorted to by spies these days.*

disgust *v.* **1** °sicken, °offend, °nauseate, °repel, °revolt, °put off, °outrage, °appal, *Slang* °gross out: *His patronizing attitude disgusts those who work for him.* —*n.* **2** °revulsion, nausea, sickness, repugnance, fulsomeness, °outrage, °distaste, °aversion: *One look at the food filled me with disgust.* **3** °loathing, °contempt, hatred, abhorrence, odium, animus, °animosity, enmity, °antagonism, antipathy, °dislike: *Some feel disgust at the thought of eating insects.*

disgusted *adj.* °nauseated, sickened, °nauseous, °queasy; offended, outraged, *Colloq* fed up (with), °sick (of), °sick and °tired (of); *Slang US* grossed out: *Disgusted customers complain about delays in service.*

disgusting *adj.* nauseating, sickening, °offensive, °outrageous, sick-making, fulsome, °repulsive, °revolting, °repugnant, off-putting, °repellent, °obnoxious, °loathsome, °gross, °vile, °foul, °nasty; unappetizing, °unsavoury, objectionable, °distasteful: *Spitting in public is now considered a disgusting way to behave.*

dishonest *adj.* untrustworthy, underhand(ed), °dishonourable, °fraudulent, °fake, °counterfeit, deceiving, °deceptive, unfair, double-dealing, thieving, thievish, knavish, cheating, deceitful, °lying, untruthful, mendacious, treacherous, °perfidious, °corrupt, °unscrupulous, unprincipled; °two-faced, °hypocritical; *Colloq* °crooked, °shady; *Chiefly Brit slang* °bent: *He was so dishonest he stole from his mother's purse.*

dishonour *v.* **1** °insult, °abuse, affront, °outrage, °slight, °offend, °injure: *His slaughter of the prisoners has dishonoured our flag.* **2** °disgrace, °degrade, °shame, °debase, °humiliate, °mortify, abase, °vitiate, °humble: *We were all dishonoured by our colleague's defection.* **3** defile,

°violate, °ravish, °rape, °seduce, deflower, debauch: *The general learned that his wife had been dishonoured by one of his adjutants.* —*n.* **4** disesteem, °disrespect, irreverence, °slight, °indignity, ignominy, °disgrace, °shame, disrepute, °discredit, °insult, °offence, affront, loss of °face, depreciation, belittlement, disparagement, detraction, derogation, obloquy: *You cannot retreat without dishonour.* **5** °aspersion, defamation, °libel, °slander, °blot, °slur, °smear, smirch, °black mark, °blemish, denigration: *His actions have brought us dishonour.*

dishonourable *adj.* **1** °disgraceful, °degrading, inglorious, ignominious, °shameful, shaming, °base, debased: *After the court martial, he received a dishonourable discharge.* **2** unprincipled, °shameless, °corrupt, °unscrupulous, untrustworthy, treacherous, °traitorous, °perfidious, °dishonest, °hypocritical, °two-faced, duplicitous, °disreputable, discreditable, °base, °despicable; °disloyal, unfaithful, °faithless: *A double agent is considered dishonourable by both governments.* **3** °improper, °unseemly, °unbecoming, °unworthy, °outrageous, objectionable, reprehensible, °flagrant, °bad, °evil, °vile, °low, °mean, °contemptible, below or beneath criticism, °foul, heinous, °dirty, °filthy: *Informing on your classmates is the most dishonourable thing you can do.*

disillusion *v.* disabuse, °disappoint, disenchant, break the spell, °enlighten, set straight, disentrance, disenthral, undeceive: *When I saw her without make-up, I was thoroughly disillusioned.*

disinclined *adj.* °averse, °indisposed, °reluctant, unwilling, °loath, °opposed, unwilling; °hesitant: *I was disinclined to try skydiving.*

disinfect *v.* °clean, °cleanse, °purify, °purge, sanitize, °fumigate, decontaminate, °sterilize: *The bedding will have to be disinfected before it can be used.*

disinfectant *n.* germicide, antiseptic, sterilizer, bactericide, sanitizer, fumigant, decontaminant, decontaminator, purifier, cleaner, cleanser: *Most disinfectants are poisonous.*

disingenuous *adj.* °clever, °artful, °crafty, °sly, on the qui vive, cunning, insidious, °foxy, °wily, °slick, °smooth; °insincere, °false, dishonest, °tricky, °devious, °deceitful, underhand(ed), guileful, °shifty; double-dealing, °two-faced, duplicitous, °hypocritical, °scheming, plotting, °calculating, °designing, contriving: *It is disingenuous to ask for advice when what you want is assistance.*

disintegrate *v.* °break up *or* °apart, °shatter, °come *or* °fall °apart, come *or* go *or* °fall to °pieces, °crumble; °decompose, °rot, °decay, moulder: *The fossil disintegrated in my hands.*

disinterested *n.* unbiased, °impartial, °unprejudiced, altruistic, °objective, °fair, °neutral, open-minded, °equitable, °just, °dispassionate, °detached, even-handed, °impersonal, uninvolved: *The judge is supposed to be a disinterested party.*

disjointed *adj.* **1** disjoined, °separate(d), °disconnected, unconnected, dismembered, disunited, divided, °split (up): *The disjointed parts of the building were kept in a warehouse.* **2** ununified, °loose, °incoherent, °confused, °aimless, directionless, °rambling, muddled, jumbled, °mixed up, °fitful, discontinuous, disorganized, unorganized, °disorderly: *His speech was disjointed—total gibberish.*

dislike v. **1** be °averse to, °mind, °turn from, °disfavour, disesteem, be °put or turned off by; °hate, °loathe, °scorn, °despise, contemn, °detest, abominate, execrate: *I no longer dislike spinach.*
—n. **2** °aversion, °displeasure, °distaste, °disfavour, disesteem, disrelish, disaffection, disinclination; °loathing, hatred, animus, °animosity, antipathy, detestation, °contempt, execration, °ill will; °disgust, repugnance; °hostility, °antagonism: *I took an instant dislike to the fellow. She feels an intense dislike for her father.*

disloyal adj. unfaithful, °faithless, °untrue, °false, untrustworthy, recreant; treasonable or treasonous, treacherous, °traitorous, unpatriotic, °subversive, °perfidious, °deceitful; °renegade, apostate, °heretical: *It would be disloyal of you not to vote along party lines.*

dismal adj. depressing, °gloomy, cheerless, °melancholy, °sombre, °dreary, °sad, °bleak, °funereal, lugubrious, °forlorn, morose, °solemn, °dark, °grim, °wretched, °woebegone, woeful, °black, °blue, °joyless, °doleful, dolorous, °unhappy, °miserable, lowering; °pessimistic: *She was alone, alone on the dismal moor. The prospects for the company looked very dismal.*

dismay v. **1** °alarm, °frighten, °scare, °terrify, °appal, °panic, °horrify, °petrify, °intimidate, cow, disconcert, °unnerve: *We were dismayed when the motor-cycle gang came to the house.* **2** unsettle, discompose, °upset, °discourage, °take aback, °startle, °shock, °put off, dishearten: *I was dismayed to hear she was still married to Grimsby.*
—n. **3** consternation, °alarm, °anxiety, °agitation, °terror, °panic, °horror, °shock, °fright, °fear, trepidation, apprehension, °dread, awe: *The thought of the children alone in the boat filled me with dismay.*

dismiss v. **1** °discharge, oust, °release, give °notice (to), °let °go, °lay off, °throw out, °toss out, °remove, *Chiefly military* cashier, *Old-fashioned military* drum out, *Brit politics* deselect, *Colloq* °fire, °send packing, °kick out, *Brit* °sack, give (someone) the °sack, °boot (out), turn off, *US* give (someone) his or her walking papers, give (someone) a pink slip, can; *Slang* give (someone) the (old) heave-ho: *Gabney has been dismissed without notice.* **2** °reject, °set aside, °repudiate, °spurn, °discount, °disregard, °lay aside, °put out of one's mind, think no more of, °write off, °banish, have or be done with, °scorn, °discard, °ignore, shrug off; °belittle, °diminish, pooh-pooh: *She dismissed the story as just so much gossip.* **3** °disperse, °release, °disband, °send away: *After returning from the mission, the commando unit was dismissed.*

dismissal n. **1** °discharge, °expulsion, °notice, *Colloq* firing, bounce, marching orders, *Chiefly US and Canadian* walking papers, *Brit* °sack, sacking, one's cards, *US* pink slip; *Slang* the (old) heave-ho, *Brit* the boot: *Cholmondley got his dismissal yesterday.* **2** °cancellation, adjournment, °discharge, °end, °release; congé: *The judge ordered dismissal of the charge of murder.*

disobedient adj. **1** °insubordinate, °unruly, °naughty, °mischievous, °bad, ill-behaved, °badly behaved, °obstreperous, unmanageable,

refractory, fractious, °ungovernable, uncomplying, unsubmissive, wayward, non-compliant, incompliant, intractable, °defiant; °delinquent, °derelict, disregardful, °remiss, undutiful: *Disobedient children will be kept in after school.* **2** °contrary, °perverse, °wilful, headstrong, °stubborn, °recalcitrant, obdurate, °obstinate, contumacious, wayward, cross-grained, °opposed, °mutinous, °rebellious, °revolting, anarchic(al), *Colloq* pigheaded: *We cannot tolerate disobedient recruits.*

disobey v. °defy, °break, contravene, °flout, °disregard, °ignore, °resist, °oppose, °violate, °transgress, °overstep, go counter to, °fly in the face of, °infringe, °thumb one's nose at, °snap one's fingers at, *Brit* cock a snook at; °mutiny, °rebel, °revolt, °strike: *You cannot play because you disobeyed the rules. If anyone disobeys, throw him in irons.*

disorder n. **1** disarray, °confusion, °chaos, disorderliness, disorganization, untidiness, °mess, °muddle, °jumble, °hash, °mishmash, °tangle, °hotchpotch or *US and Canadian also* hodgepodge, derangement, °shambles, °clutter: *After the party, the place was in terrible disorder.* **2** °tumult, °riot, °disturbance, °pandemonium, °upheaval, °ferment, °fuss, °unrest, °uproar, hubbub, hullabaloo, commotion, clamour, turbulence, turmoil, °violence, °bedlam, free-for-all, °rumpus, brouhaha, °fracas, affray, °fray, °brawl, Donnybrook, scuffle, °fight, mêlée or melee, battle royal, °battle, civil disorder, °breach of the peace, *Colloq Brit* kerfuffle or carfuffle or kurfuffle, *Slang Brit* bovver: *The army had to be called out to quell the disorder.* **3** °ailment, °illness, sickness, °affliction, malady, °affection, °complaint, °disease: *The doctors diagnosed it as a liver disorder.*
—v. **4** °upset, disarrange, °muddle, °confuse, confound, unsettle, disorganize, discompose, °shake up, °disturb, °mix (up), befuddle, °jumble, °scramble, °tangle, °snarl: *You obscure the sense when you disorder the words.*

disorderly adj. **1** °confused, °chaotic, scrambled, muddled, disordered, °irregular, °untidy, messy, messed-up, disarranged, disorganized, unorganized, jumbled, cluttered, °haphazard, in disarray, °pell-mell, °helter-skelter, *Colloq* °topsy-turvy, higgledy-piggledy: *The books lay about in disorderly array.* **2** °unruly, °uncontrolled, °undisciplined, ungoverned, °disobedient, °mutinous, °rebellious, °lawless, °obstreperous, refractory, turbulent, °violent, °tumultuous, unrestrained, °boisterous, °noisy, °rowdy, °wild; unmanageable, °ungovernable, uncontrollable, intractable: *He was charged with being drunk and disorderly.*

disorientated n. °confused, bewildered, °lost, adrift, (all) at °sea, °mixed up, °uncertain, unsure, °insecure, disoriented, *Colloq* out of it, in a °fog, *Brit* off (the) beam, *US* off the beam: *I left by another door and was completely disorientated for a moment.*

disparage v. **1** °belittle, °diminish, °depreciate, devalue or devaluate, cheapen, °talk down, °discredit, °dishonour, decry, demean, °criticize, denigrate, deprecate, derogate, underrate, undervalue, °downgrade, °reduce, °minimize: *She keeps making remarks that disparage her husband.* **2** °run down, °slander, °libel, defame, traduce, malign, backbite, °vilify, °insult, °stab in the back, *US* back-stab; *Colloq* poor mouth; *Slang US and Canadian* bad-mouth: *A loving person never disparages others.*

disparity *n.* °difference, °discrepancy, °gap, °inequality, unevenness, imbalance, °dissimilarity, °contrast, imparity, inconsistency, incongruity: *Our interests differ owing to the disparity in our ages.*

dispassionate *adj.* **1** °cool, °calm, composed, °self-possessed, unemotional, unexcited, unexcitable, unflappable, °level-headed, °sober, self-controlled, even-tempered, unruffled, °unmoved, °tranquil, °equable, placid, °peaceful, °serene: *You can count on Henry for a dispassionate treatment of the subject.* **2** °fair, °impartial, °neutral, °disinterested, °detached, °equitable, even-handed, unbiased, °just, °objective, °unprejudiced, open-minded, °candid, °frank, °open: *The judge is known to be completely dispassionate in his decisions.*

dispatch *v.* **1** °send off *or* away *or* out, °send on one's way: *We dispatched a messenger with the parcel.* **2** °send, °mail, °post, °transmit, °forward, °ship, °express, °remit, convey, *Chiefly US and Canadian* °freight: *Please dispatch this letter as quickly as possible.* **3** °kill, °murder, slay, °dispose of, put to °death, °execute, do away with, do in, assassinate, liquidate, °finish (off), put an °end to, °put away (for good), *Slang* °polish off, °bump off, °eliminate, gun down, °silence, °get, °erase, °rub out, °knock off, °bury, *US* ice, °hit, take for a °ride, °waste, °zap: *The gang soon dispatched all their rivals.* **4** °hasten, °hurry, °speed up, accelerate, get done, °accomplish, °get through, conclude, °finish off, °complete, °execute, do: *The task was dispatched in just two days.*
—*n.* **5** °haste, °speed, promptness, quickness, °expedition, expeditiousness, celerity, alacrity, swiftness, °hurry, °rapidity: *She concluded the interview with dispatch and sent me away.* **6** communiqué, °report, °bulletin, °story, °news (°item), communication, °message, °piece: *document, instruction, missive: Here is a dispatch from our correspondent on Pitcairn Island.* **7** °execution, °killing, °murder, disposal, assassination, dispatching, slaying: *The dispatch of the consul left us without a representative.*

dispensable *adj.* °disposable, °non-essential, unessential, inessential, °unnecessary, unneeded, °expendable, °superfluous, °needless, °useless: *He said that a dishwasher was a luxury and entirely dispensable.*

dispense *v.* **1** °distribute, °give out, °hand *or* °pass out, °furnish, °supply, °provide, °give away, °deal (out), °dole out, °parcel out, disburse, °mete out, °share (out), °issue, apportion, allocate, °allot, °assign, *Colloq* dish out: *The Red Cross dispensed medicines to the stricken villagers.* **2** °administer, °conduct, °direct, °operate, superintend, °supervise, °carry out, °execute, °discharge, °apply, °implement, °enforce: *It is the governor who dispenses justice in these islands.* **3 dispense with: a** do without, °forgo, °give up, eschew, °relinquish, °refuse, °waive, forswear, abstain (from), °renounce, °reject: *Can we dispense with the jokes and get to work?* **b** do away with, get °rid of, °eliminate, °dispose of, °abolish, °manage *or* do without, °remove, °cancel, °ignore, render °unnecessary *or* °superfluous: *Building on solid rock will dispense with the need for a foundation.*

disperse *v.* **1** °spread (out), °scatter, °broadcast, °distribute, °circulate, °diffuse, disseminate: *The practice is now widely dispersed throughout Asia.* **2** °disband, °spread out, °scatter, °dissipate, °break up; °disappear, vanish; dispel, °dismiss, °rout, °send off *or* away: *The crowd dispersed quietly.*

displace *v.* **1** °move, °transfer, °shift, relocate, dislocate, misplace, °disturb, disarrange, °disorder, unsettle: *The entire population of the village was displaced when the dam was built.* **2** °expel, unseat, °eject, °evict, °exile, °banish, depose, °remove, oust, °dismiss, °discharge, cashier, *Colloq* °fire, °kick *or* °throw out, *Brit* °sack: *The voters displaced the corrupt council.* **3** take the place of, °supplant, °replace, °supersede, °succeed: *Watching television has displaced reading in many modern homes.*

display *v.* **1** °show, °exhibit, °air, °put *or* °set forth, make °visible, °expose, evince, °manifest, °demonstrate, °betray, °reveal, °unveil, °disclose; advertise, °publicize: *Her paintings are being displayed at the gallery today.* **2** unfurl, °unfold, °spread *or* °stretch *or* °open out, °present: *The ship suddenly displayed the Jolly Roger.* **3** °show off, °flaunt, °parade, °flourish, vaunt, *Colloq* flash: *He goes on those quiz programmes only to display his knowledge.*
—*n.* **4** °show, °exhibition, °exhibit, °presentation, array; °demonstration; °exposition, °manifestation, °revelation: *We visited a display of weapons at the armoury. I have seldom seen such a display of ignorance.* **5** °ostentation, °spectacle, °flourish, °show, °parade, °ceremony, °pageantry, °pageant, °splendour, array, panoply, magnificence, °grandeur, °pomp, °splash, éclat, élan, °dash: *The display put on for Queen Victoria's jubilee was truly lavish.*

displease *v.* °offend, °put out, dissatisfy, °upset, °provoke, °exasperate, °worry, °trouble, vex, °annoy, °irritate, pique, °irk, nettle, peeve, °chafe, rile, °ruffle, °anger, °infuriate, °frustrate, get (someone's) goat, *Colloq* miff; *Slang US* °bug: *Having to listen to rock 'n' roll on your damned hi-fi is what displeases me most.*

displeasure *n.* **1** °dissatisfaction, °disapproval, °disfavour, discontentment, °distaste, °dislike, discountenance: *Your parents view your giving up college with displeasure and disappointment.* **2** °annoyance, irritation, vexation, chagrin, °indignation, dudgeon, ire, °anger, exasperation: *He incurred the king's displeasure and was banished from the land.*

disposable *adj.* **1** discardable, throw-away, non-returnable, °paper, °plastic, biodegradable: *The new product is packaged in a disposable container.* **2** °available, °liquid, spendable, usable, °expendable, obtainable: *Her disposable assets include valuable government bonds.*

dispose *v.* **1** °place, °arrange, °move, °adjust, °order, array, °organize, °set up, °situate, °group, °distribute, °put: *She is planning how to dispose the furniture in the room.* **2** °incline, °influence, °persuade, °induce, °bend, °tempt, °move, °motivate, °lead, °prompt, °urge: *Her actions disposed me to cut her out of my will.* **3 dispose of: a** °deal with, °settle, °decide, °determine, conclude, °finish (with): *I hope we can dispose of these matters quickly.* **b** °throw away *or* out, °discard, get °rid of, jettison, °scrap, *Colloq*

°dump, °junk, US °trash: *Dispose of the remains of the broken chair.* **c** °distribute, °give out, °deal out, °give (away), °dispense, apportion, °parcel out, °allot, °part with, °transfer, °make over, °bestow, °sell: *My grandfather disposed of his wealth before he died.* **d** do away with, °finish off, °put away, °demolish, °destroy, °consume, °devour, °eat, *Slang* °kill (off), °knock off, °polish off: *She could dispose of four hamburgers at one sitting. The boys disposed of Louie because he knew too much.*

disposed *adj.* °likely, °inclined, apt, °liable, °given, tending *or* °leaning °towards, °prone, °subject, of a °mind to, minded, °willing, °ready, predisposed: *She was still awake when he got home and seemed disposed to talk.*

disposition *n.* **1** °character, °temper, °attitude, temperament, °nature, °personality, °bent, °frame of mind, °humour, °make-up, °spirit: *Alan's son David has a cheerful disposition.* **2** °arrangement, °organization, °placement, disposal, ordering, grouping, °set, placing: *I don't care much for the disposition of the furniture.* **3** °transfer, transference, dispensation, disposal, °assignment, °settlement, °determination, bestowal, parcelling out, °distribution: *The disposition of father's assets is not your affair.* **4** °determination, °choice, disposal, °power, °command, °control, °management, °discretion, °decision, °regulation: *Distribution of favours is at the disposition of the crown.*

dispossess *v.* °evict, °expel, oust, °eject, °turn *or* °drive out, dislodge, *Colloq* °kick *or* °throw out, *Brit* °boot out, *US* bounce: *The landlord dispossessed them for non-payment of rent.*

disproportion *n.* °inequality, unevenness, °disparity, imbalance, asymmetry, irregularity, lopsidedness, °dissimilarity, inconsistency, incongruity: *Now that we're older, there isn't such a disproportion in our ages.*

disproportionate *adj.* °unbalanced, out of proportion, asymmetrical, °irregular, °lopsided, °dissimilar, °inconsistent, incommensurate, °incongruous; unfair, unequal, uneven, disparate: *The windows are disproportionate to the size of the house. The contractor was paid a disproportionate amount for his work.*

disprove *v.* refute, confute, invalidate, °contradict, negate, °rebut, °discredit, controvert, °puncture, °demolish, °destroy, *Colloq* shoot *or* poke full of holes: *Modern science has disproved the phlogiston theory.*

disputable *n.* °debatable, °moot, °doubtful, °uncertain, dubious, °questionable, undecided, °unsettled, °controversial; arguable: *His claim to ownership of the property is disputable.*

dispute *v.* **1** °argue with *or* against, °question, °debate, °challenge, impugn, gainsay, °deny, °oppose, °fight (against), °object to, take °exception to, °disagree with, °contest, confute, °quarrel with, °doubt, °raise doubts about, dissent (from): *The council dispute his right to build a hotel on that land.* **2** °argue (about), °debate, °discuss, °quarrel about, wrangle over, °differ (on *or* about): *A bill of rights has occasionally been disputed in Parliament.* —*n.* **3** °argument, °debate, °disagreement, °difference (of opinion), °controversy, polemic, °conflict, °quarrel, wrangle, clash; °discussion; *Colloq Brit* argy-bargy *or* argie-bargie *or* argle-bargle: *There is a dispute about the runner's eligibility for the race.* **4** °conflict, °disturbance,

°fight, altercation, °row, °disagreement, °brawl, Donnybrook, °feud, °rumpus, °fracas; °strife, °discord; °tiff, velitation, *US* spat: *Four people have been injured in the dispute.*

disqualify *v.* declare °ineligible *or* °unqualified, °turn down *or* away, °reject, °exclude, °bar, debar, °rule out: *He was disqualified from voting because of his age.*

disregard *v.* **1** °ignore, °overlook, pay little *or* no °heed *or* °attention to, take little *or* no °notice *or* °account of, °dismiss from one's mind *or* thoughts, turn a blind eye *or* deaf ear to, °brush aside, °pass up, wink *or* °blink at, make °light of, let °go by, °gloss over, *Rare* pretermit: *I shall disregard those insulting remarks.* **2** snub, °slight, turn up one's nose at, °disparage, °despise, contemn, disdain, °scorn, (give the) cold °shoulder (to), °cut; underrate, °underestimate, take little *or* no °account of, undervalue, °minimize, °dismiss, °sneeze at, *Slang* °brush off, give the go-by: *Visitors often disregard the cultural attractions of Las Vegas.* —*n.* **3** °disrespect, °contempt, °indifference, inattention, non-observance, °neglect, heedlessness, *Rare* pretermission; disdain, low °regard, disesteem: *Some drive with a profound disregard for the law.*

disrepair *n.* °decay, °ruin, °collapse, dilapidation, deterioration, ruination: *The house is in a terrible state of disrepair.*

disreputable *adj.* **1** °low, °base, abject, °contemptuous, unrespectable, disrespectable, untrustworthy, discreditable, °dishonourable, °disgraceful, reprehensible, °shameful, °despicable, ignominious, °bad, °wicked, heinous, °vicious, iniquitous, °vile, opprobrious, °scandalous, louche, °questionable, dubious, *Colloq* °shady: *She keeps disreputable company.* **2** dishevelled, °unkempt, slovenly, °untidy, °shabby, disordered, messy, °dirty, °bedraggled, scruffy, °seedy, °threadbare, °tattered, *Brit* down at °heel, raddled, *US* down at the °heel(s), *Colloq* °sloppy, *Slang Brit* grotty: *That disreputable beggar is your brother?*

disrespect *n.* rudeness, impoliteness, discourtesy, °incivility, unmannerliness, irreverence, °impudence, °impertinence, insolence, indecorum, *Colloq* cheek: *I meant no disrespect by keeping my hat on, ma'am.*

disrespectful *adj.* °impolite, °rude, °discourteous, uncivil, unmannerly, °ill-mannered, bad-mannered, °irreverent, °impudent, °insolent, indecorous, °pert, saucy, °forward, *Colloq* °fresh, °cheeky: *Sara is sometimes disrespectful to her elders.*

disrobe *v.* undress, °strip, °bare oneself: *She disrobed and put on a swimsuit.*

disrupt *v.* **1** °disorder, °upset, disorganize, °disturb, unsettle, °shake up, disconcert, °agitate: *You've disrupted my plan completely.* **2** °interrupt, °break in *or* into, °interfere (with): *They disrupted the meeting with their loud outbursts.*

dissatisfaction *n.* **1** °discontent, discontentment, unhappiness, °displeasure, non-fulfilment, °disappointment, frustration, °discomfort, uneasiness, disquiet, malaise: *I was left with a feeling of dissatisfaction at the end of the play.* **2** °annoyance, irritation, °dismay, °displeasure: *Complaints concerning dissatisfaction with the food plagued the hospital administrators.*

dissatisfied *adj.* °discontented, displeased, °disappointed, unsatisfied, °discontent, °disgruntled, °unhappy, unfulfilled, ungratified, frustrated: *We return the full purchase price to any dissatisfied customer.*

dissension *n.* °disagreement, dissent, °discord, contention, °strife, °conflict, discordance, °friction: *The issue has sown dissension among the members.*

disservice *n.* °harm, °damage, °injury, °wrong, unkindness, °bad °turn, °disfavour, °injustice: *It was a disservice to tell my boss about my expense account.*

dissident *n.* **1** dissenter, °nonconformist, pro- tester *or* protestor, heretic, °rebel, apostate, recusant; °revolutionary: *Many dissidents were released and allowed to leave the country.* —*adj.* **2** disagreeing, °nonconformist, non- conforming, dissenting, dissentient, apostate, non-compliant, heterodox, °discordant, con- flicting, contentious: *The couple spent ten years in Siberia for promoting their dissident philosophy.*

dissimilar *adj.* °different, °unlike, unalike, °distinct, °separate, contrasting, °diverse, °unrelated, heterogeneous: *The styles are entirely dissimilar.*

dissimilarity *n.* °difference, dissimilitude, unlikeness, °disparity; °discrepancy: *The dis- similarities between art deco and art nouveau are too numerous to mention.*

dissimulate *v.* °pretend, dissemble, feign, °disguise, °camouflage, °cover up, °conceal, °deceive, °misrepresent, °fake, °counterfeit: *She's dissimulating her real attitude towards the wealthy.*

dissimulation *n.* °deception, mis- representation, dissembling, °deceit, °hypocrisy, °sham, °pretence, duplicity, double-dealing: *There can be no dissimulation between honest people.*

dissipate *v.* **1** °scatter, °spread (out), °disperse, be dispelled, °diffuse; disseminate, °sow, °distribute; °break up: *The crowd had dissipated by noon.* **2** °spread thin, °evaporate, vanish, °disappear, vaporize, peter out, °diminish: *By the time we were ready to go, the clouds had dissi- pated.* **3** squander, °waste, °fritter away, °throw away, °burn up, °use up, °exhaust, °run through: *By the time he was twenty, he had dissipated a huge fortune.* **4** °revel, °carouse, °party, sow one's wild oats, burn the candle at both ends, roister, make °merry, debauch, go on a °spree: *Before their marriage, he was seen dissipating in the fleshpots of Europe.*

dissipation *n.* **1** squandering, °waste, waste- fulness, °profligacy, °abandon, abandonment, self-indulgence, self-gratification, over-indulgence, intemperance, hedonism, °fast *or* °high living, *dolce vita*, voluptuousness, sensualism, sybaritism, dissoluteness, °dissolution, °excess(es), wantonness, debauch- ery, carousing, °prodigality, recklessness, °extravagance, rakishness: *Owing to my dissi- pation, I had become an alcoholic vagrant.* **2** disappearance, dispersion, dispersal, dif- fusion, °scattering, vanishing: *The dissipation of the tear-gas was rapid in the strong breeze.* **3** °distraction, °amusement, °diversion, °entertainment: *Reading, once a dissipation, had become an obsession.*

dissociate *v.* °separate, °cut off, °sever, dis- associate, disjoin, °disconnect, °abstract,

°disengage, °detach, °isolate, °distance, °break off (from), °break up (with), °divorce, °set °apart, °segregate: *I have carefully dissociated myself from any political party.*

dissolute *adj.* dissipated, debauched, °abandoned, °corrupt, degenerate, °rakish, °profligate, °wanton, rakehell, intemperate, °incontinent, °loose, licentious, over-indulgent, carousing, °self-indulgent, hedonistic, pleasure-bound, °immoral, amoral, libidinous, unrestrained, depraved: *He has paid dearly for his dissolute life.*

dissolution *n.* **1** disintegration, °separation, breakup, °breakdown, breaking up, breaking down, °collapse, °undoing: *Much ill will attended the dissolution of our marriage.* **2** °destruction, decomposition, °decay, °ruin, °overthrow, dis- solving, disbandment, °dismissal, dispersal, disorganization, discontinuation; adjournment, ending, °end, °termination, conclusion, °finish: *A vote of no confidence led to the dissolution of Parliament.*

dissolve *v.* **1** °melt (away), liquefy, °disperse, °disintegrate, °diffuse, °decompose, °thaw (out), °fuse, deliquesce, °sublime; vanish, °disappear, °fade (away), °diminish, °decline, peter out: *Dissolve one tablet in water. The sugar dissolved in the tea.* **2** °collapse, °break into, °melt into: *She dissolved into tears whenever he shouted at her.* **3** °break up, °disperse, °dismiss, °terminate, °finish, conclude, adjourn, °recess, °disband, °wind up; liquidate: *We took a vote and dissolved the meeting.*

distance *n.* **1** remoteness, °space, °gap, °interval, mileage, footage, °stretch: *What is the distance from here to your house?* **2** aloofness, °detachment, °reserve, coolness, haughtiness, hauteur, stiffness, rigidity: *He maintains a dis- tance between himself and the servants.* —*v.* **3** °separate, °detach, °dissociate, dis- associate: *She distanced herself from her students.*

distant *adj.* **1** °far, far-off, °remote, °far-away, long-way-off; removed: *The creature said he had come from a distant star.* **2** away, °off: *The ship is ten miles distant.* **3** °aloof, °detached, °reserved, °cool, °cold, °haughty, °standoffish, °unapproachable, °inaccessible, °withdrawn, °reticent, °ceremonious, °formal, °stiff, °rigid, °frigid, unfriendly: *You find him warm, but I think him very distant.*

distaste *n.* **1** °dislike, °disfavour, antipathy, disrelish, disinclination; °dissatisfaction, °displeasure, discontentment: *You know of my distaste for cocktail parties.* **2** °aversion, °revulsion, °disgust, nausea, abhorrence, °loathing, repugnance, °horror: *She has a distinct distaste for avocado pears.*

distasteful *adj.* °disgusting, °revolting, sick-making, nauseating, °nauseous, °repugnant, °repulsive, °loathsome, fulsome, °nasty, °disagreeable, °foul, off-putting, °unpalatable, °obnoxious, objectionable, °offensive, unpleas- ing, unpleasant, displeasing: *I found their children's table manners quite distasteful.*

distinct *adj.* **1** °clear, °perceptible, °plain, understandable, °vivid, °definite, well-defined, °precise, °exact, unmistakable, °noticeable, recognizable, °obvious, °patent, °marked, °manifest, °evident, °apparent, °explicit, un- ambiguous, clear-cut, palpable, unequivocal, lucid, °sharp, pellucid, limpid, °transparent:

There is a distinct outline of a figure on the Turin shroud. **2** °separate, °detached, °discrete, °different, °dissimilar, distinguishable, °distinguished; °individual, sui generis, °unique, °special, °singular; °peculiar, °unusual, uncommon, contrasting: *The government of Puerto Rico is distinct from that of the US. He has been charged with three distinct offences.*

distinction *n.* **1** differentiation, °discrimination, °difference, °contrast, °separation, °division, dividing °line; distinctiveness: *Any distinction between them is difficult to discern.* **2** °honour, °credit, °prominence, eminence, °pre-eminence, °superiority, uniqueness, greatness, °excellence, °quality, °merit, °worth, value, °prestige, °note, °importance, °significance, consequence, °renown, °fame, repute, °reputation, °celebrity, °glory, °account: *We all know her as a scholar of distinction.*

distinctive *adj.* distinguishing, °characteristic, °unique, °singular, °distinct, °individual, °typical, idiosyncratic, °peculiar: *She has developed a distinctive style of her own.*

distinguish *v.* **1** °differentiate, °discriminate, °tell the °difference, °tell °apart, °determine, °judge, °decide, °tell who's who or what's what: *He is still unable to distinguish between his own twin daughters.* **2** classify, °categorize, °characterize, individualize, °mark, °identify, °define, °designate, °denote, °indicate, °separate, °single out, °set °apart; °grade, °group: *The male is distinguished by his brighter colouring.* **3** °sense, °make out, °perceive, discern, °pick out, °recognize, °identify, °detect, °notice; °see, espy, descry; °hear; °smell; °taste; °feel: *I could distinguish two people in the dark.* **4** call °attention to, °identify, °mark, °set °apart, °separate, °segregate, °indicate, particularize: *She distinguished herself by her great beauty and her awful voice.*

distinguished *adj.* **1** °celebrated, °famous, °illustrious, °noted, °renowned, °notable, °noteworthy, °pre-eminent, °eminent, °prominent, honoured, respected, °honourable: *Churchill was one of the most distinguished men of his day.* **2** °dignified, °noble, °grand, °stately, distingué, °royal, °regal, aristocratic: *What is he doing in this distinguished gathering?*

distort *v.* **1** °twist, °warp, deform, misshape, contort, gnarl, °bend, disfigure, °wrench: *The car was completely distorted in the crash.* **2** °twist, °warp, °slant, °tamper with, °colour, varnish, torture, °pervert, °misrepresent, °fabricate, °falsify, misstate, °alter, °change, °bend, °garble, °violate: *She distorted the facts if she said it was Bill who had a gun.*

distract *v.* **1** °divert, °deflect, °sidetrack, °turn aside, °draw away: *Sorry, I was distracted for a moment—where were we?* **2** °divert, °amuse, °entertain, °gratify, °delight, °occupy, °interest, absorb, engross: *We found the belly-dancers quite distracting.* **3** °bewilder, °confuse, confound, °perplex, °puzzle, discompose, befuddle, °mystify, disconcert, °fluster, °rattle, °bemuse, °daze, °disturb, °agitate, °trouble, °bother: *I am distracted with doubts about whether to phone the police.*

distraction *n.* **1** bewilderment, befuddlement, °disorder, °disturbance, °upset, °confusion, °agitation: *The princess loves you to*

distraction. **2** °diversion, °entertainment, °amusement: *I was never really interested in him, he was merely a temporary distraction.*

distraught *adj.* distracted, °agitated, troubled, °disturbed, °upset, perturbed, wrought or worked up, °excited, °frantic, at (one's) wits' end, °overwrought, frenetic, °nervous, frenzied, °feverish, °wild, °hysterical, °delirious, irrational, °crazy, °mad, °insane, °berserk, running (ning) amok or amuck: *He is distraught with grief.*

distress *n.* **1** °anguish, °anxiety, °affliction, angst, °grief, °misery, °torment, °ache, °pain, °suffering, °agony, torture, °woe, woefulness, wretchedness; unhappiness, °sorrow, °sadness, °depression, heartache, °desolation: *It is impossible to imagine the distress of a bereaved parent.* **2** °calamity, °trouble, adversity, °catastrophe, °tragedy, °misfortune, °difficulty, °hardship, straits, °trial, °disaster: *Has he no sympathy for the distresses that have beset his people?* —*v.* **3** °bother, °disturb, °perturb, °upset, °trouble, °worry, harrow, harry, vex, °harass, °plague, °oppress, °grieve, °torment, torture, °afflict: *The thought of Miss Camberley as a hostage distressed us all.*

distribute *v.* **1** °deal or °dole out, °parcel out, °give (out), °mete out, °dispense, apportion, °allot, °share (out), °partition, °divide up, °assign, °issue, °circulate, °pass out, °pass °round or around, °hand out, °deliver, convey, *Colloq* dish or spoon out: *Emergency rations were distributed to the flood victims.* **2** °disperse, °scatter, °strew, °spread (°round or around or about), °diffuse, disseminate: *Mammals are uniformly distributed over the globe.* **3** °sort, classify, °class, °categorize, assort, °arrange, °group, °file, °order: *Distribute the packages according to their size.*

distribution *n.* **1** apportionment, °allotment, allocation, °assignment, parcelling out, sharing; deployment: *She supervised the distribution of the prizes.* **2** issuance, °circulation, dissemination, giving (out), dispersal, dispensation; deployment: *The distribution of food parcels is being handled by charities.* **3** °arrangement, °disposition, grouping, classification, °disposition, °order, ordering, °division, cataloguing, codification; deployment: *What is the distribution of scientists among the population?*

district *n.* °territory, °region, °section, sector, °division, °partition, °part, °precinct, locality, °area, °locale, °department, °province, community, °quarter, °neighbourhood, °ward: *We need a new hospital in our district.*

distrust *v.* **1** °mistrust, °doubt, °question, be °sceptical of, be circumspect or °cautious about, °suspect, be °suspicious or °wary of, °discredit, disbelieve, *Colloq* smell a rat; *Colloq* be °leery of: *I distrusted her motives from the very beginning.* —*n.* **2** °mistrust, °doubt, doubtfulness, uncertainty, °misgiving(s), °scepticism, °suspicion, disbelief, incredulity, incredulousness, hesitation, °caution, wariness, °qualm, hesitancy: *His claims were greeted with distrust.*

distrustful *adj.* distrusting, untrusting, mistrustful, doubting, chary, °wary, °cautious, °suspicious, °sceptical, °doubtful, dubious, cynical, disbelieving, °unbelieving, uneasy, °nervous, °hesitant, hesitating, unsure, °uncertain, *Colloq* °leery: *She is distrustful of men who bring her flowers.*

disturb v. **1** °interrupt, °disrupt, °intrude (on), °inconvenience, °put out, °interfere (with); °bother, °pester, °annoy, °irritate, °irk, °upset, °plague, hector, harry, °harass, °worry, vex, °provoke, pique, peeve, get on (someone's) nerves, *Colloq* °bug, miff, get under (someone's) skin, get in (someone's) hair, drive nuts *or* °crazy *or* bats *or* batty *or* bananas *or* up the wall, hassle: *The sound of dripping water disturbed me. Please do not disturb the animals.* **2** °agitate, °stir *or* churn (up), °shake (up), unsettle, roil, °disorder: *The lake's surface was violently disturbed by an enormous creature.* **3** unsettle, °affect, °upset, °damage, °harm, °destroy: *We put the delicate mechanism where it wouldn't be disturbed by curious visitors.* **4** °trouble, disconcert, °discomfit, °perturb, °ruffle, °fluster, °upset, °agitate, °put off, °bother, discommode, °put out, unsettle, °distress; °alarm, *Colloq* °shake (up): *He was greatly disturbed by the death of his father.* **5** °affect, °upset, confound, °confuse, °change, °put off, °ruin, °destroy, °cancel, make °ineffectual *or* °ineffective, negate: *Any change in temperature will disturb the results of the experiment.*

disturbance n. **1** disruption, °disorder, disorganization, disarrangement, disarray; °upheaval, °interruption, °upset, intrusion, °interference: *She won't tolerate any disturbance to her schedule.* **2** commotion, °disorder, °upset, °outburst, °tumult, turmoil, turbulence, °violence, hubbub, hullabaloo, hurly-burly, °uproar, brouhaha, °rumpus, °brawl, mêlée *or* melee, °breach of the peace, Donnybrook, °fray, affray, °fracas, °trouble, *Colloq* ruckus, *Brit* spot of °bother, *Slang Brit* spot of bovver: *There was a disturbance at the pub yesterday.*

disturbed adj. **1** °upset, uneasy, uncomfortable, discomfited, troubled, °worried, bothered, °agitated, °anxious, °concerned, apprehensive, °nervous: *He's disturbed that Marie didn't come home last night.* **2** psychoneurotic, °neurotic, °unbalanced, psychopathic, °psychotic, maladjusted, °mad, °insane, out of one's °mind, depressed, *Colloq* °crazy, unable to cope, *Brit* bonkers, *Slang* nuts, screwy, batty, off one's rocker, off the deep end, messed-up, screwed-up: *She looks after her sister, who is disturbed.*

disturbing adj. upsetting, off-putting, perturbing, troubling, °unsettling, worrying, °disconcerting, disquieting, alarming, distressing: *There is disturbing news from the front.*

disused adj. °abandoned, neglected, °unused, discontinued, °obsolete, archaic: *We had to sleep in a disused railway carriage.*

diurnal adj. °daily, circadian; day-to-day, °regular, °everyday, quotidian; daytime: *Jet lag is a disturbance of the body's diurnal rhythms. Are these animals nocturnal or diurnal?*

dive v. **1** °plunge, nosedive, °sound, °descend, °dip, °submerge, °go under, °sink; °jump, °leap, °duck; °swoop, °plummet: *The submarine dived at once.* —n. **2** °plunge, nosedive: *The plane went into a dive.* **3** °bar, saloon, nightclub, bistro, °club, *Colloq* nightspot, *Slang* °joint, *US* °dump, honky-tonk, juke-joint: *He met the woman in a dive in Limehouse.*

diverge v. **1** °separate, °radiate, °spread (°apart), °divide, subdivide, fork, °branch (off *or* out), ramify, °split: *The roads diverge further on.*

2 °deviate, °turn aside *or* away, °wander, digress, °stray, °depart, °drift, divagate: *Our policy diverges from that set up by the committee.*

divergent adj. differing, °different, dissimilar, disparate, °variant, °separate, diverging, disagreeing, conflicting, discrepant: *There are divergent theories about the origin of the universe.*

divers adj. °various, °several, °sundry, °miscellaneous, multifarious, °manifold, °varied, assorted, °variegated, differing, °different; some, numerous, °many: *We have the divers statements of the witnesses.*

diverse adj. divers, °different, °varied, diversified, multiform, °various, assorted, °mixed, °miscellaneous, °distinctive, °distinct, °separate, varying, °discrete, °dissimilar, differing, °divergent, heterogeneous: *Diverse subjects are available for study.*

diversify v. °vary, variegate, °change, °mix; °spread, °distribute, °divide, °break up, °separate; °branch out: *We must diversify our investments to hedge against losses. Perhaps this is not a good time to diversify into other areas.*

diversion n. **1** °digression, deviation, departure, °distraction: *George created a diversion, while we robbed the safe.* **2** °detour, °sidetrack, deviation, °bypass: *Owing to roadworks, we had to take a diversion off the main road.* **3** °amusement, °distraction, °entertainment, °pastime, °recreation, divertissement, °game, °play, °relaxation: *She prefers chess for diversion.*

diversity n. **1** °difference, °dissimilarity, dissimilitude, unlikeness, °disparity, deviation, divergence, departure, distinctiveness, diverseness, °variation, °variety, individuality, inconsistency, contrariety, °discrepancy, °contrast: *Flowers are impressive in their diversity.* **2** °variety, °range, °extent, heterogeneity, multiplicity, multifariousness, variegation, multiformity: *Democracy encourages diversity of opinion.*

divert v. **1** °switch, rechannel, redirect; °change, °alter, °deflect: *Funds for the new civic centre have been diverted to housing. We must divert the course of the river.* **2** °turn away, °turn aside, avert, re-route, °deflect; °change course, °swerve (off *or* away), °shift, °sidetrack, °depart, °deviate: *Cars were diverted to avoid flooded areas. We should divert from our route because of the roadworks.* **3** °entertain, °amuse, °distract, °interest, °beguile, °engage, °occupy, absorb: *We found the stand-up comedian mildly diverting but not really funny.*

divest v. **1** °strip, denude, °rid, get °rid, °relieve, disencumber, °deprive, °dispossess; despoil, mulct: *The company has been divested of all its assets.* **2 divest oneself of**: °take *or* °put off, doff, °remove; °disrobe, unclothe, undress: *She divested herself of her fur coat.*

divide v. **1** °separate, °split (up), °break up, °cleave, °cut up *or* asunder, °partition, °segregate, subdivide, °disconnect, disjoin, °detach, °sever, sunder, °part: *Argyle divided his mountaineers into three regiments. A divided nation cannot stand. Some would like to see Britain divided from continental Europe.* **2** Sometimes, **divide up**: °distribute, °share (out), °measure out, °parcel out, °partition, °dole (out), °deal (out), °mete out, allocate, °allot, apportion, °dispense, °give (out): *The remaining food was divided among us.* **3** °separate, °split, cause to °disagree, °alienate, disunite, °set at °odds, sow °dissension (among), °pit *or* °set against one another, disaffect: *Racial issues still divide the people.* **4** °branch (out), ramify, °split, °separate: *The road divides there and passes on each side of that huge rock.* **5** °categorize, classify, °sort, assort, °grade, °group, (put in) °order, °rank, °organize, °arrange: *You have to divide the books into several piles according to size.*

divine *adj.* **1** °godlike, °godly, °holy, deiform, deific, angelic, °seraphic, °saintly; °heavenly, °celestial; °sacred, sanctified, hallowed, consecrated, °religious, °spiritual: *They believe in the divine right of kings. He receives divine inspiration at divine services.* **2** °superhuman, °supernatural, °gifted, °pre-eminent, °superior, °excellent, °supreme, °exalted, °transcendent, °extraordinary: *Even the divine Homer nods.* **3** °great, °marvellous, °splendid, °superlative, °glorious, °superb, °admirable, wonderful, °awesome, °perfect, °excellent, °beautiful, *Colloq* °super, °terrific, smashing, °fantastic, splendiferous, *Colloq Brit* ace, °magic: *They say that the new musical is simply divine.*
—*v.* **4** intuit, °imagine, conjecture, °guess, °assume, °presume, °infer, °suppose, hypothesize, °surmise, °suspect, °understand, °perceive, °speculate, °theorize, °predict, foretell, have foreknowledge of; °determine, °discover: *He had divined that she might be there.*
—*n.* **5** °holy man, °priest, °clergyman, cleric, ecclesiastic, °minister, °pastor, reverend, churchman, prelate: *At his club, he enjoys the company of bishops, archbishops, and other divines.*

division *n.* **1** dividing, °split, splitting (up), breaking up, °partition, partitioning, partitionment, °separation, separating, diremption, segmentation, segmenting, compartmentation, sectioning, apportioning, apportionment, °allotment: *In England a division between Church and State is not recognized.* **2** °section, °compartment, °segment; °partition, °separation: *Egg crates have 144 divisions.* **3** °branch, department, sector, °section, °unit, °group, arm; °part, °set, °category, °class, classification: *The textile division of the company lost money last year.* **4** °boundary (°line), °border, borderline, °frontier, °margin, °line, dividing °line: *Where is the division between good and evil?* **5** °discord, °disagreement, °upset, °conflict, °strife, disunity, disunion: *The issue of equal rights has led to much division within the movement.*

divorce *n.* **1** °separation, °split, split-up, °dissolution, severance, disunion, break-up: *Their divorce after twenty years surprised everyone.*
—*v.* **2** °separate, °divide, °split (up), °part, °sever, °detach, °dissociate, disassociate; °dissolve: *A splinter group has divorced itself from the main party. We were divorced last year.*

dizzy *adj.* **1** °giddy, vertiginous, light-headed, °faint, dazed, tottering, unsteady, reeling, tipsy, *Colloq* woozy: *I felt dizzy after going down the helter-skelter.* **2** °confused, °silly, °giddy, empty-headed, °scatterbrained, muddled, befuddled, °flighty, feather-headed, feather-brained, rattle-brained, °hare-brained, °frivolous: *He is dizzy with power.*

dock *n.* **1** wharf, °pier, berth, jetty, quay: *We went to the dock to see them off.*
—*v.* **2** (drop) °anchor, berth, °tie up, °moor, °land, °put in: *The ship docks at noon.*

doctor *n.* **1** °physician, medical practitioner, M.D., general practitioner, G.P., *Colloq* medic, medico, doc, sawbones, bones: *You ought to see a doctor about that cough.*
—*v.* **2** °treat, °attend, medicate; °cure, °heal; °practise °medicine: *She knows very little about doctoring children, in spite of having worked as a general practitioner.* **3** °mend, °repair, °patch (up), °fix: *We doctored the tyre as best we could.* **4** °falsify, °tamper with, °adulterate, °disguise, °change, °modify, °alter; °cut, °dilute, °water (down); °spike; °drug, °poison: *This sauce has been doctored.*

doctrine *n.* teaching, body of °instruction, °precept; °principle, °tenet, dogma, article of °faith, canon, °conviction, °creed, °belief, credo, °opinion, °idea, concept, theory, °proposition, °thesis, postulate: *Few believe the doctrine that all men are created equal.*

document *n.* **1** °paper, certificate, °instrument, °report, °chronicle, °record: *All the legal documents are at my lawyer's office.*
—*v.* **2** °record, °chronicle, particularize, °detail, °describe; °verify, validate, °certify, °authenticate, corroborate, °substantiate: *Detectives have documented every move you made since the murder.*

doddering *adj.* shaking, quaking, palsied, trembling, trembly, quivering, quavering, reeling, unsteady, °shaky, staggering, °shambling, °decrepit, faltering; °feeble, °weak, °frail, °infirm; °aged, °old, superannuated, °senile, anile: *Once a vigorous sportsman, his illness has reduced him to a doddering octogenarian.*

dodge *v.* **1** dart, °shift, °move aside, °sidestep, °duck, bob, °weave, °swerve, veer: *He dodged here and there across the traffic.* **2** °avoid, °elude, °evade, °escape from: *He neatly dodged the punches of his opponent.* **3** °escape from answering, °sidestep, °duck, °evade, hedge; °quibble, tergiversate, double-talk, *Colloq* °waffle: *She dodged the questions put to her by the interviewer.*
—*n.* **4** °trick, °subterfuge, ploy, °scheme, °ruse, °device, °stratagem, °plan, °plot, °machination, chicane, °deception, prevarication, contrivance, °evasion, *Slang* wheeze, °racket: *Crenshaw worked out a new dodge to avoid paying tax.*

dodgy *adj.* °tricky, °dangerous, °perilous, °risky, °difficult, °ticklish, °sensitive, °delicate, °touchy; °uncertain, °unreliable, °rickety, *Colloq* chancy, °hairy, *Brit* °dicky, °dicey: *Climbing up the sheer face of that rock could be a bit dodgy. You shouldn't be exerting yourself with your dodgy ticker.*

dogmatic *adj.* °arbitrary, °categorical, °dictatorial, imperious, °peremptory, °overbearing, doctrinaire, °authoritarian, °emphatic, °insistent, °assertive, °arrogant, °domineering; obdurate, °stubborn; °opinionated, °positive, °certain, *Rare* thetic(al), *Colloq* °pushy: *Patrick tends to be quite dogmatic when he is sure of his ground.*

dole *n.* **1** °portion, °allotment, °share, °quota, °lot, °allowance, °parcel; compensation, °benefit, °grant, °award, °donation, °gift, °largesse, alms, gratuity; *Slang* hand-out: *The prisoners received a daily dole of bread. If you've lost your job, are you eligible for the dole?* **2** °distribution, apportionment, allocation, dispensation: *The money was given to the disaster victims by dole.*

—v. **3** °give (out), °deal (out), °distribute, °hand out, °mete out, °share (out), °dispense, °allot, allocate, apportion, *Colloq* dish out: *They dole out the reparations on the basis of need.*

doleful *adj.* °sad, °sorrowful, °melancholy, °gloomy, °mournful, cheerless, °joyless, °sombre, depressed, disconsolate, °blue, down, distressed, °dejected, °downhearted, °forlorn, °unhappy, lugubrious, dolorous, °wretched, °miserable, °woebegone, °dreary, woeful, *Colloq* down in the °mouth, down in the dumps; distressing, °funereal, depressing, °grievous, °harrowing: *From his doleful expression I thought he would cry any minute. She lives in the most doleful surroundings.*

dolt *n.* °fool, ass, blockhead, dunce, dullard, idiot, nitwit, ignoramus, numskull *or* numb-skull, donkey, nincompoop, ninny, ninny-hammer, simpleton, dunderpate, dunderhead, bonehead, °twit, fat-head, goon, moron, imbecile, *Colloq* °dope, dumb-bell, dim-wit, chump, °dummy, °halfwit, birdbrain, pinhead, clot, °clod, chucklehead, *Brit* muggins, *US* thimble-wit, °jerk, knuckle-head, lunkhead, meat-head, lame-brain, dingbat, ding-a-ling, °flake: *The dolt actually tried to buy striped paint!*

domain *n.* **1** °realm, °dominion, °territory, °property, °land(s), °province, °kingdom, empire: *At one time his domain included most of Europe.* **2** °province, °realm, °territory, °field, bailiwick, °area, °department, °sphere, °discipline, °speciality *or US* specialty, specialization, °concern: *As a dentist, he considered diseases of the throat outside his domain.*

domestic *adj.* **1** °home, °private, °family, familial; residential, household: *Her domestic life is a shambles. This toaster is for domestic use.* **2** °tame, domesticated, house-trained, house-broken: *Tenants are forbidden to keep domestic animals.* **3** °home, °native, °indigenous, °internal, autochthonous: *The domestic market accounts for most of the company's income.* —n. **4** °servant, (hired) °help, housekeeper, major-domo, steward: *Her domestics left and she now does the cleaning herself.*

domicile *n.* **1** °dwelling (-place), °residence, °abode, °home, habitation, (living) quarters, °housing, °accommodation(s), °lodging(s), *Colloq Brit* digs, diggings, *Slang* °pad: *Domiciles in south-east England have increased enormously in value.* —v. **2** °locate, °quarter, °lodge, °settle, °establish, °situate, domiciliate: *She is domiciled abroad, hence pays no income tax here.*

dominant *adj.* **1** commanding, °authoritative, controlling, governing, ruling, °leading, reigning, °influential, °assertive, °supreme, °superior, ascendant: *He has taken a dominant role in promoting foreign language teaching.* **2** °predominant, °chief, °main, °principal, °primary, °prevailing, °outstanding, °pre-eminent, °paramount: *A large nose is a dominant characteristic in their family.*

dominate *v.* **1** °command, °control, °govern, °rule, °direct, °lead, °reign (over), exercise °command *or* °authority *or* °control *or* °rule over, have the whip *or* °upper hand (over), °run (things), be in *or* have under °control, °rule the roost *or* roast, *Colloq* call the shots *or* the tune, wear the trousers *or US* the pants, be in the driver's seat, °rule with an iron hand, have under

one's °thumb: *She clearly dominates the board of directors.* **2** °overlook, °look (out) over, °tower over *or* above, °rise above, °overshadow; °predominate: *The Eiffel Tower dominates the Parisian skyline.*

domination *n.* **1** °authority, °control, °rule, °power, °command, °influence, °sway, °supremacy, ascendancy, hegemony, the whip *or* °upper hand, °pre-eminence, mastery: *The tsar's domination lasted for more than thirty years.* **2** °oppression, °subjection, °repression, °suppression, subordination, enslavement, enthralment; dictatorship, °despotism, °tyranny: *The Allies finally brought to an end the Fascist domination of Europe.*

domineering *adj.* °overbearing, imperious, °officious, °arrogant, autocratic, °authoritarian, high-handed, high and mighty, °masterful, °arbitrary, °peremptory, °dictatorial, °despotic, °tyrannical, °oppressive, °strict, °hard, °harsh, °tough, *Colloq* °bossy, °pushy: *A classic character in humorous writing is the domineering spouse.*

dominion *n.* **1** °rule, °authority, °control, dominance, °domination, °grasp, mastery, °grip, °command, °jurisdiction, °power, °sovereignty, °sway, ascendancy, °pre-eminence, primacy, °supremacy, hegemony: *The magician claimed dominion over the entire universe.* **2** °domain, °realm, °territory, °region, °area, °country, °kingdom: *For six generations the dynasty ruled over its dominions on five continents.*

donate *v.* °give, °provide, °supply, °present, °contribute, °subscribe (to *or* for), °pledge, °award, °bestow, °confer, °grant, °vouchsafe, °will, °bequeath: *Lady Crayford donated two silver candlesticks to our charity drive.*

donation *n.* **1** °gift, contribution, °largesse, °present, °grant, °award, alms, °offering, °bequest: *Donations have exceeded our expectations.* **2** giving, contribution, bestowal, °allotment, °provision, °offer: *We are seeking the donation of a piano for our theatre group.*

donor *n.* giver, provider, supplier, °benefactor *or* benefactress, contributor, °supporter, °backer: *Blood donors receive a suitably inscribed certificate.*

doom *n.* °fate, karma, °destiny, °fortune, °lot, kismet; °downfall, °destruction, °death, °ruin, extinction, annihilation, °end, °termination, terminus: *The warrior had defied the Snake God, and his doom was sealed.*

doomed *adj.* **1** °fated, cursed, condemned, damned, °destined, ordained, foreordained, predestined: *She was doomed to live for ever.* **2** accursed, bedevilled, ill-fated, luckless, star-crossed, bewitched, condemned: *The doomed ship sank to the bottom of the sea.*

dope *n.* **1** See **dolt**, above. **2** °narcotic, °drug, opiate, hallucinogen, psychedelic, *Slang* °upper, downer: *He was caught trying to smuggle dope past customs.* **3** °information, °data, facts, °news, details, °story, °scoop, *Slang* info, °low-down, °score, *Brit* gen, *US and Canadian* poop: *The real dope on the minister is sensational!*

dormant *adj.* **1** asleep, sleeping, slumbering, resting, at °rest, °quiet, °inactive, °still, °inert, unmoving, motionless, stationary, immobile, quiescent, comatose, °torpid, hibernating, slumberous, somnolent, °sleepy, °lethargic, °dull, sluggish: *The bears are dormant during* *much of the winter.* **2** latent, °potential, °hidden, concealed, undisclosed, unrevealed, unexpressed: *The theory lay dormant for centuries and has only recently been revived.*

dose *n.* **1** °portion, °quantity, °amount, °measure, dosage: *How big a dose of the medication did the doctor prescribe?*
—*v.* **2** °dispense, °administer, °prescribe: *I was dosed with medicine and slept all day.*

dot *n.* **1** °spot, °speck, °point, °jot, °mark, iota, fleck, °dab; decimal °point, *Brit* full °stop, *US* °period: *Use three dots to denote text omissions.* **2 on the dot**: °exactly, °precisely, punctually, to the minute *or* second, *on* °time, *Colloq* on the button: *She arrived at noon on the dot.*
—*v.* **3** °spot, fleck, speckle, stipple, bespeckle: *The wallpaper is dotted with tiny squares of colour.*

dote *v.* Often, **dote on** *or* **upon**: be °fond of, be °infatuated with, °love, °idolize, hold °dear, °adore, °make much of; °coddle, °pamper, °spoil, °indulge: *I think she dotes on her husband at the expense of the children. What we need is a doting grandmother to babysit when we want to go out.*

double *adj.* **1** twofold, paired, coupled, °duplicate(d), doubled: *The forms banned and banning are spelt with a double n.* **2** folded *or* doubled *or* °bent over, overlapped, two-ply: *This wound needs a double bandage.* **3** dual, twofold, °ambiguous, double-barrelled: *He pronounced it 'de-seat', giving deceit a double meaning.* **4** twice: *The plant had grown to double its size.* **5** °deceitful, °dishonest, treacherous, °traitorous, °insincere, °hypocritical, double-dealing, °false: *It was Maria who exposed Fernando as a double agent.*
—*v.* **6** °duplicate, replicate; °copy; °increase, °enlarge; °magnify: *We'll have to double our milk order.*
—*n.* **7** °twin, °duplicate, °copy, °replica, °facsimile, clone, counterpart, *doppelgänger,* °look-alike, °stand-in, °understudy, *Slang* (dead) ringer, spitting °image *or* °spit and °image: *He could be Clint Eastwood's double.* **8 at** *or* **on the double**: °quickly, on the °run, at full °speed *or* tilt, briskly, °immediately, at °once, without delay, *Slang* p.d.q. (= 'pretty damned quick'): *Put down that book and come over here on the double!*

double-cross *v.* °cheat, °defraud, °swindle, °hoodwink, °trick, °betray, °deceive, °mislead, play °false with, *Colloq* two-time: *He swore he'd give me the money but he double-crossed me and kept it himself.*

doubt *v.* **1** disbelieve, °discredit, °mistrust, °distrust, have °misgivings (about), °question, °suspect: *I doubted his ability to beat the record.* **2** °hesitate, waver, vacillate, °fluctuate, °scruple, be °uncertain, entertain doubts, have reservations: *Who ever doubted her honesty?*
—*n.* **3** uncertainty, hesitation, °misgiving, °reservation(s), °qualm, °anxiety, °worry, apprehension, disquiet, °fear: *He has harboured doubts about the success of the enterprise.* **4** °distrust, °mistrust, °suspicion, incredulity, °scepticism, dubiousness, dubiety *or* dubiosity, lack of °faith *or* °conviction, irresolution: *Her doubts about his intentions have evaporated.* **5 in doubt**: See **doubtful**, below.

doubtful *adj.* **1** in °doubt, dubious, °questionable, open to °question, °problematic, °debatable, °disputable, °uncertain, unpredictable, indeterminate,

°unsettled, °unresolved, conjectural, °indefinite, unclear, °obscure, °vague, anybody's guess, *Colloq* up in the air: *The result is very doubtful.* **2** °sceptical, unconvinced, °distrustful, mistrustful, °suspicious, °uncertain, unsure, °hesitant, hesitating, vacillating, °indecisive: *I am doubtful whether an investigation will yield anything.* **3** dubious, °questionable, °shady, louche, °disreputable, °controversial: *Those are people of doubtful reputation.*

doubtless *adv.* **1** doubtlessly, °undoubtedly, no °doubt, indubitably, indisputably, unquestionably, °surely, for °sure, certainly, for °certain, °naturally, without (a) °doubt, beyond *or* without (a shadow of) a °doubt, °truly, °positively, °absolutely, *Colloq* absotively-posolutely, *US* make no mistake: *You doubtless remember my aunt.* **2** °probably, most *or* very °likely, in all °probability, °supposedly, °presumably: *He will doubtless be refused entry into the country.*

dour *adj.* **1** °sullen, °sour, unfriendly, °cold, °gloomy, morose, °dreary, °grim, cheerless, °dismal, °forbidding: *We went to Spain, away from the dour northern climate.* **2** °hard, °tough, austere, °severe, °hardy, °inflexible, °obstinate, °stubborn, unyielding, uncompromising, °strict, °rigid, obdurate, °stern, °harsh, adamant, *Colloq* hard-nosed: *Her father was a dour Scot who wouldn't let me in the house.*

dowdy *adj.* frowzy *or* frouzy *or* frowsy, frumpy, frumpish, °drab, °dull, °seedy, °shabby, °unseemly, °unbecoming; slovenly, °sloppy, messy, °unkempt; °old-fashioned, unfashionable, *Colloq US* °tacky: *Aunt Patience looked particularly dowdy in her dressing-gown and slippers.*

down and out *adj.* **1** °indigent, poverty-stricken, °poor, penniless, °destitute, °impoverished, *Colloq* °broke, *US* on the skids, on skid row, on the °bum, *Slang Brit* skint: *Those vagrants are down and out and need help, not pity.*
—*n.* **2 down-and-out**: °derelict, °beggar, °outcast, °tramp, vagrant, °vagabond, *US* °bum: *He took to drink and ended up a complete down-and-out.*

downfall *n.* °ruin, °undoing, débâcle, °collapse, °degradation, °defeat, °overthrow, °breakdown: *Selling the company to the conglomerate spelt its downfall.*

downgrade *v.* **1** demote, dethrone, °humble, °lower, °reduce, °displace, depose, °dispossess, disfranchise *or* disenfranchise, *US military* bust; *Colloq* bring *or* take down a °peg: *He was downgraded from supervisor to foreman.* **2** °belittle, °minimize, °play down, °disparage, decry, denigrate, °run down, *US and Canadian* downplay: *How could she downgrade her own sister?*
—*n.* **3** descent, °decline, declension, (°downward) °slope, gradient, °grade, °inclination: *Apply the brake as you approach the downgrade.* **4 on the downgrade**: on the °wane, waning, declining, falling, slipping, falling off, losing ground, going downhill, *US and Canadian* on the skids: *After the drug scandal, her popularity was on the downgrade.*

downhearted *adj.* discouraged, depressed, low-spirited, °miserable, °blue, °sad, downcast, °dejected: *Don't be so downhearted, we know you can win the gold medal.*

downpour n. rainstorm, deluge, inundation, cloudburst, thunder-shower, thunderstorm, °torrential °rain, °torrent; monsoon: *We got caught in that downpour without an umbrella.*

downright adj. **1** °direct, straightforward, °plain, °frank, °open, °candid, plain-spoken, °explicit, °blunt, °brash, °bluff, not roundabout or circuitous, unambiguous, °out-and-out, °outright, °categorical, °flat, unequivocal, °outspoken, unreserved, °unabashed, un-restrained, unconstrained, °bold: *She speaks with a downright honesty you have to admire.* —adv. **2** °completely, °entirely, °totally, °thoroughly, certainly, °surely, (most) assuredly, °definitely, °absolutely, uncon-ditionally, unequivocally, °very, °extremely, unqualifiedly, °perfectly, uncompromisingly, unmitigatedly, °utterly, unquestionably, °profoundly, °undoubtedly, indubitably: *It's downright stupid of you to leave in this weather.*

downtrodden adj. subjugated, oppressed, burdened, plagued, afflicted, exploited, over-whelmed, cowed, °overcome, beaten, °abused, mistreated, maltreated, tyrannized, Colloq °beat: *This poor, downtrodden wreck of a man had once been on top.*

downward adj. declining, sliding, slipping, spiralling, descending, going or heading or moving down: *This downward trend in the market will soon be reversed.*

downwards adv. down, °downward, °below, °lower: *We moved downwards, towards the centre of the earth.*

doze v. **1** Often, **doze off**: (take or have a) °nap, catnap, drowse, °sleep, slumber, Colloq snooze, have forty winks, °drop or °nod off, grab some shut-eye, Chiefly Brit (have or take a) zizz, Brit kip, US catch or log a few zees (Z's): *I was dozing in the sun when the phone rang.* —n. **2** °nap, catnap, siesta, °sleep; °rest; Colloq snooze, forty winks, shut-eye, Brit zizz, kip, lie-down: *I'll have a short doze before dinner.*

drab adj. °dull, °colourless, °dreary, °dingy, °lacklustre, lustreless, °dismal, cheerless, °grey, °sombre: *She wore drab clothes and no make-up.*

draft n. **1** °plan, sketch, °drawing, °outline, °rough (sketch), blueprint, diagram, °prospectus: *We must have the draft of the new design by morning.* **2** °bill of exchange, cheque, °money order, postal order; letter of credit: *Our customer issued a draft in full payment.* —v. **3** sketch, delineate, °outline, °design, °plan, °frame, °block out, °compose, diagram, °draw (up): *The art department has drafted the layout for the new encyclopedia.*

drag v. **1** °pull, °draw, °haul, °tow, °tug, °trail, °lug: *It took the two of us to drag the desk into the other office.* **2** °pull, °distract, °draw; °induce, °persuade, °coax, °wheedle: *She's been unable to drag him away from the TV.* **3** trudge, slog, °crawl, °creep, inch, °shuffle, shamble: *He's looking for a job and just drags along from one employment agency to another.* **4** °trail (behind), °linger, °dawdle, °lag (behind), °straggle, draggle, °potter or US putter, loiter, poke (along), dilly-dally, US lallygag: *She just drags along after us wherever we go.* **5** (be) °prolong(ed), (be) °extend(ed), (be) °draw(n) out, (be) protract(ed), (be) °stretch(ed) out, °spin out or be spun out: *Why drag out the agony of uncertainty any longer? His speech dragged on for another hour.* **6 drag**

one's feet or heels: °delay, °procrastinate, °hang back; °obstruct, °block, °stall: *The com-mittee is dragging its feet on the housing issue.* —n. **7** °bore, °nuisance, °annoyance; °pest; Colloq °drip, °pain (in the neck), °headache: *That course in botany is a real drag.*

drain n. **1** ditch, °channel, trench, culvert, con-duit, °pipe, gutter, °outlet, watercourse, sewer, cloaca: *The storm drains have overflowed.* **2** depletion, reduction, sapping, °sap, °exhaustion, °strain, °drag; outgo, outflow, withdrawal, disbursement, °expenditure: *The cost of the new roof was a drain on our resources.* **3 down the drain**: wasted, gone, thrown away, °lost, Slang up the °spout: *All that money spent on his education went down the drain.* —v. **4** °draw off, °tap, °extract, °remove, °take away, °withdraw, °pump off or out; °empty, °evacuate, °drink up or down, quaff, °swallow, °finish: *After washing the lettuce, drain off the water. He drained the glass in one gulp.* **5** °consume, °use up, °exhaust, °sap, deplete, bleed, °strain, °tax, °spend; °weaken, debilitate, °impair, °cripple: *The car repairs drained my bank account. After climbing to the top of the mountain, we were completely drained.* **6** seep, °trickle, °ooze, °drip, °leave, °go or °flow from or out of, °disappear (from), °ebb: *Let the pus drain from the boil. The blood drained from his face when he saw her.*

drama n. **1** °play, °stage °play, photoplay, screen-play, (°stage) °show, (°theatrical) °piece, (°stage) °production; °scenario: *He plays only in dramas, never in musicals.* **2** dramaturgy, stagecraft, °theatre °art(s), °Thespian or histrionic °art(s), acting, °theatre, °dramatic °art(s): *She has studied drama at RADA.* **3** histrionics, dramatics, theatrics, theatricalism, play-acting: *There's always a drama over who's going to wash up.*

dramatic adj. **1** theatric(al), dramaturgic(al), °Thespian, histrionic, °stage: *She was studying the dramatic works of Shakespeare. There will be a festival of dramatic arts at the centre next week.* **2** °vivid, °sensational, °startling, breathtaking, °sudden, °striking, °noticeable, °extraordinary, °impressive, °marked, °shocking, °expressive, °graphic, °effective; °complete, °considerable, °radical, °major: *A dramatic change has come over him since meeting her.* **3** °flamboyant, °melodramatic, colourful, °showy, °stirring, spectacular; °theatrical, histrionic, exaggerated, overdone: *His presentation was quite dramatic, well staged and with much arm-waving.*

dramatist n. °playwright, dramaturge, screen-writer, scriptwriter, scenarist, tragedian, melo-dramatist: *The actors failed to carry out the dramatist's intentions.*

dramatize v. °exaggerate, overplay, °overstate, °overdo, make a production or °show (out) of, Colloq °lay it on (thick), °pile it on, ham (some-thing or it) up: *He always dramatizes everything way out of proportion.*

drape v. **1** °hang, festoon, °swathe, deck, array, bedeck, adorn, °ornament, °decorate: *The coffin was draped with the national flag.* —n. **2** °drapery, curtain; hanging, tapestry: *The drapes match neither the carpet nor the wallpaper.*

drapery n. °drape, curtain; hanging, valance, pelmet, tapestry, arras, portière, lambrequin, °drop: *Which colour will you choose for the drapery?*

drastic adj. °violent, °severe, °extreme, °strong, °powerful, °potent, puissant, °fierce, °forceful, °vigorous, rigorous, °harsh, °radical, Draconian, °desperate, dire: I shall have to take drastic measures if this misbehaviour continues.

draught n. **1** °breeze, °breath (of °air), (light) °wind, °current (of °air), °puff (of °air or °wind): You'll get a cold sitting in the draught. **2** °dose, °portion, °measure, °quantity, °drink, °swallow, °sip, °nip, °tot, potation, dram, °gulp, Colloq swig, tipple: The doctor recommended a draught of this tonic before meals.

draw v. **1** °pull, °tug, °tow, °drag, °haul, °lug: The gypsy caravan was drawn by two horses. **2** °pull or °take out, °extract; unsheathe, unholster: The cowboy drew his gun and began firing. **3** draw off; °pour; °drain off or out: She drew two pails of water for the horses. **4** °attract, °gather, allure, °lure, °bring out or forth, °elicit, Colloq °pull: Anything will draw a crowd in New York. **5** depict, sketch, °portray, °outline, delineate, °design, limn, °paint: The artist was drawing pictures in chalk on the pavement. **6** °devise, draw up, °draft, °create, contrive, °frame, °compose, °prepare: The plans for the new civic centre have not yet been drawn. **7** °inhale, °breathe (in), °inspire; suck in: She's very ill and may draw her last breath any minute. **8** draw out, °withdraw, °take, °receive, °get, °acquire, °obtain, °secure, °procure, °extract, °remove: I have to draw some money from my bank account for groceries. **9** °choose, °pick, °select, °take: It is your turn to draw a card. **10 draw back**: °retreat, °recoil, °shrink (from), °withdraw: He drew back quickly when he saw the snake. **11 draw in**: °arrive, °pull in: The train drew in to the station. **12 draw off**: **a** °tap, °pour: The barmaid drew off two large beers from the keg. **b** °withdraw, draw or °go away, °depart, °leave: The Indians drew off and waited to see what we would do. **13 draw on**: **a** °employ, °use, make °use of, °exploit, have °resort or °recourse to, °resort to, °fall back on, °rely or °depend on: She drew on her years of experience as a doctor. **b** °come °close or °near, °near, draw nigh, °approach, °advance: With the cold season drawing on, we had to get in the crops. **14 draw out**: **a** °extend, °drag out, °prolong, protract, °lengthen, °stretch, °spin out: Her visit has been drawn out to a week. **b** °elicit, °evoke, °induce to talk: I drew him out on his feelings about social security. **c** See **8**, above. **15 draw up**: **a** °halt, °stop, °pull up or over: A taxi drew up and I got in. **b** °draft, °compose, °prepare, °put down (in °writing), °frame, °compile, °put together, °formulate: We drew up the agreement only yesterday. **c** °arrange, deploy, °position, °order, °rank, marshal: The troops were drawn up in full battle array. —n. **16** °magnetism, °attraction, °lure, °enticement, Colloq °pull, drawing °power: The draw of the rock concert was extraordinary. **17** °tie, °stalemate, dead heat, °deadlock: The race ended in a draw for second place.

drawback n. °disadvantage, °hindrance, °stumbling-block, °obstacle, °impediment, °hurdle, °obstruction, °snag, °problem, °difficulty, °hitch, °catch, °handicap, °liability, °flaw, °defect, °detriment, Colloq °fly in the ointment: Lack of education is a serious drawback to getting a good job.

drawing n. °picture, depiction, °representation, sketch, °plan, °outline, °design, °composition, black-and-white, monochrome: The book is illustrated by some delightful pen-and-ink drawings.

drawn adj. °haggard, °worn out, °tired, °fatigued, °strained, pinched, °tense, °exhausted: Sidonia looks a bit drawn after her ordeal.

dread v. **1** °fear, be °afraid of, apprehend, °anticipate, °flinch, °shrink or °recoil from, °cringe or quail or blench or wince at, view with °horror or °alarm: She dreads any kind of surgery. —n. **2** °fear, °fright, fearfulness, trepidation, apprehension, apprehensiveness, uneasiness, °anticipation, °alarm, nervousness, °qualm, queasiness, °misgiving, °dismay, °worry, °anxiety, consternation, °concern, °distress, perturbation, disquiet, °aversion, °horror, °terror, °panic, Colloq cold feet, butterflies (in the stomach), the °jitters; Slang the heebie-jeebies, the willies, the collywobbles: I regarded the history exam with dread. —adj. **3** feared, dreaded, °dreadful, °terrifying, °terrible: Before us, breathing fire, was the dread dragon of the Druids.

dreadful adj. **1** °bad, °awful, °terrible, Colloq °rotten, Slang °lousy: That TV soap opera is simply dreadful. **2** °grievous, dire, °horrible, horrendous, horrifying, horrid, °monstrous, °fearful, feared, °frightful, °dread, °frightening, °shocking, alarming, appalling, °fearsome, °hideous, °ghastly, °atrocious, heinous, °wicked, °evil, iniquitous, flagitious, °fiendish, diabolic(al), °devilish, demonic, malevolent, maleficent, malefic, Colloq °scary: They did the most dreadful things to political prisoners.

dream n. **1** °reverie, °day-dream, °delusion, °fantasy, °hallucination, °illusion, °vision, mirage, pipedream, (flight of) °fancy, °speculation: When I awoke I realized that my winning the lottery had just been a dream. —v. **2** °imagine, °fancy, conjure up, hallucinate: I dreamt I dwelt in marble halls.

dreamer n. fantasizer, °visionary, idealist, °romantic, romanticist, idealizer, Utopian; day-dreamer, escapist, star-gazer: If you think people change, you're a dreamer.

dreamlike adj. °unreal, °fantastic, °unbelievable, phantasmagoric(al), hallucinatory or hallucinative or hallucinational, surreal, delusionary or delusional, illusionary or illusional, delusive or delusory, °illusory or illusive, °insubstantial or unsubstantial, °imaginary, chimerical, °fanciful, °fancied, °visionary: His plans have a dreamlike quality about them that make them impractical.

dreamy adj. **1** °dreamlike, °vague, °indefinite, °indistinct, undefined, °intangible, °misty, °shadowy, °faint: He has a dreamy recollection of being awakened in the middle of the night. **2** °absent-minded, °absent, °far-away, abstracted, °pensive, °thoughtful; daydreaming, musing, occupied, in a °reverie, in a brown study, in the clouds; Colloq off somewhere: I was in a dreamy mood, my mind wandering through old memories. **3** relaxing, °soothing, calming, lulling, °gentle, °tranquil, °peaceful, °peaceable, °quiet; °lazy, °sleepy, °drowsy: It was one of those dreamy, hot midsummer days.

dreary adj. **1** °dismal, °joyless, cheerless, °gloomy, °bleak, drear, °sombre, °doleful, depressing, °wretched; °sad, °melancholy, downcast, depressed, °funereal, °glum, °unhappy, °forlorn, °mournful, morose, °blue, °miserable: *One more day on these dreary moors and I shall go mad. Caroline was again in a dreary mood.* **2** °boring, °lifeless, °colourless, ennuyant, °drab, °dull, arid, °dry, uninteresting, °dead, °monotonous, °prosaic, °tedious, °tiresome, tiring, wearisome, wearying, °humdrum, °ordinary, °vapid, run-of-the-mill, unstimulating, unexciting: *Do you mean to tell me that that dreary book is a best seller!*

dregs *n.pl.* **1** °sediment, °grounds, lees, °deposit, °residue, solids, °remains; °precipitate: *Filter the coffee to remove the dregs.* **2** °outcasts, pariahs, °rabble, °riff-raff, scum, °tramps, °down-and-outs, °losers: *That park is frequented by the dregs of society.*

drench *v.* °soak, °saturate, °wet, °flood, inundate, °immerse, °drown: *She had no coat or umbrella and got completely drenched in the storm.*

dress *v.* **1** °clothe, °put on (clothing *or* °clothes), attire, °apparel, °outfit, °fit out, garb, accoutre *or US also* accouter; array, bedeck, deck out, °rig out, smarten up: *They dressed him to look like a prince.* **2** array, °equip, adorn, °decorate, deck out, °arrange: *He has a job dressing shop windows.* **3** bandage, °treat, medicate, °doctor: *After dressing my wound they gave me a sedative.*
4 dress down: °reprimand, °scold, °berate, °castigate, °rebuke, °reprove, °upbraid, *Colloq* °tell off, haul (someone) over the coals, *Brit* tear (someone) off a strip, *US and Canadian* °chew out, *US* rake (someone) over the coals, tee off on (someone): *The colonel dressed us down and cancelled all leave.* **5 dress up: a** °put on dinner *or* °formal °clothes, °put on one's (Sunday) °best (°clothes), *Colloq* °put on one's °best bib and tucker *or* one's glad °rags: *On the cruise, we dressed up in our dinner-jackets every night.* **b** (°put on a) °costume, °disguise, °masquerade, °camouflage, °put on °fancy °dress: *The children dressed up as goblins for Hallowe'en.*
—*n.* **6** frock, gown, °outfit, °costume, *Colloq* °get-up: *Why not wear your new dress to the dance tonight?*

dressmaker *n.* seamstress, °tailor, couturier *or* couturière, modiste: *She's at the dressmaker's having a ball gown fitted.*

dressy *adj.* **1** °formal, dressed-up, °elegant, °fancy, °chic: *A black suit is too dressy to wear tonight—it's not a dressy party.* **2** °elegant, °smart, °stylish, *Colloq* classy, ritzy, *Brit* °swish: *That's a very dressy outfit, I must say!*

drift *v.* **1** °coast, °float, °waft: *A log drifted by on the tide.* **2** °wander, °roam, °meander, °stray, rove, °ramble, *Colloq* mosey: *He seems just to drift through life, without a purpose.*
—*n.* **3** °trend, °tendency, °direction, °course, °current, °bias, °inclination, °flow, °sweep, °bent: *The drift of the conversation seemed to be towards politics.* **4** °intention, °meaning, purport, °purpose, °aim, °object, °tenor, °tone, °spirit, °colour, °essence, °gist, °significance, °import: *Offended by the drift of her remarks, I excused myself.* **5** °accumulation, °pile, °heap, °mass, bank, °mound, dune: *After the snowstorm, a huge drift blocked the door.*

drifter *n.* vagrant, °tramp, °vagabond, beachcomber, rambler, wanderer, *Colloq* knight of the road, *US* °bum, hobo: *A drifter, he had no place to call home.*

drill *v.* **1** °bore, °penetrate, °pierce, °cut a °hole: *The thieves drilled into the safe.* **2** °rehearse, °train, °practise, °exercise, °teach, °instruct, °school, °tutor, °coach, °indoctrinate; °discipline: *We were thoroughly drilled in the Latin conjugations and declensions.*
—*n.* **3** auger, (°brace and) bit, gimlet: *The bit for this drill is no longer sharp.* **4** °practice, training, °repetition, °exercise, °rehearsal; °discipline: *Tomorrow there will be a complete drill of the parts of speech.*

drink *v.* **1** quaff, imbibe, °sip, °gulp, °swallow, °swill, guzzle, °toss off, °lap (up), *Colloq* wet one's whistle, swig, °knock back, *US* belt: *She prefers not to drink beer.* **2** tipple, °nip, °indulge, tope, chug-a-lug, °carouse, *Colloq* °booze, bend the elbow, hit the °bottle, go on a binge *or* °bender, drown one's sorrows, *US and Canadian* go on a toot, *Chiefly Brit* pub-crawl: *He threatened to leave her if she continued to drink.* **3 drink to:** °toast, °salute, °celebrate, °pledge: *Let's drink to friendship!*
—*n.* **4** beverage, potation, °liquid °refreshment, °liquid, potable, °draught: *After the match I was dying for a drink.* **5** °alcohol, spirits, °liquor, the cup that cheers; stirrup-cup; *Colloq* °booze, the °bottle, °hard stuff, mother's °ruin, eye-opener, nightcap, *US* hooch; *Slang* rot-gut, *US* the sauce, red-eye: *After the accident, he took to drink.* **6** °tot, °nip, °draught *or US also* °draft, schooner, pint, bumper, jigger, snifter, °sip, °taste, °glass, °gulp, °swallow, *Scots* (wee) deoch an doris *or* doch an dorris, (wee) dram, *Brit* sundowner; *Colloq* snort, slug, swig: *Granny likes a drink before retiring.* **7 the drink:** the °sea, the °ocean, the main, the °deep, *Nautical* Davy Jones's locker, *Colloq* the briny: *The canoe tipped and our picnic went right into the drink!*

drip *v.* **1** dribble, °trickle, °drop; drizzle, sprinkle: *The tap began to drip and kept me awake all night.*
—*n.* **2** dribble, °trickle, °drop, dripping: *Yes, it was the drip from the tap that kept me awake.* **3** °milksop, °bore, wet blanket, °killjoy, damper, *Colloq Brit* °wet, weed, *Colloq* wimp, *Slang* °pill, °drag, *US and Canadian* milquetoast: *Must you invite that drip George?*

drive *v.* **1** °push, °propel, impel, °urge, °press, °thrust, °move, °motivate, actuate, °prod, °spur, goad, °force, compel, coerce, constrain, °oblige, °pressure *or Brit* pressurize, high-pressure, °induce, °require; °demand: *What drove you to become a traitor?* **2** °operate, °conduct, °manoeuvre, °manipulate, °handle, °steer, °control; °pilot: *Have you a valid licence to drive this car?* **3** °ride, °travel, motor, °go, °move, °proceed, °journey, °tour, *Colloq* °tool along: *Luckily, when the tyre blew out, we were driving at only 20 m.p.h.* **4** °stab, °plunge, °thrust, °sink, °push, °send, °dig, °ram: *He has driven the dagger deep into the monster's heart.* **5** °herd, drove, °shepherd, °ride °herd (on): *We used to drive the cattle up the old Chisholm Trail to market in Abilene.* **6 drive at:** °hint (at), °suggest, °imply, °intimate, allude *or* °refer to, °intend, °mean, have in °mind, °indicate, *Colloq* °get at: *He was so naïve he had no idea what she was driving at.*
—*n.* **7** °ride, °trip, °outing, °journey, run, °tour, °excursion, *Colloq* °spin, whirl: *On Sundays we would go for a drive in the country.* **8** °energy, °effort, °impetus, °vigour, vim, °spunk, °enterprise, °industry, °initiative, °ambition, ambitiousness, °determination, °persistence,

°urgency, zeal, °enthusiasm, keenness, aggressiveness, *Colloq* get-up-and-go, °pep, zip, °push, °hustle: *She owes her success to her drive as well as her talent.* **9** driveway, °approach, (private) °road or °street, lane, byway, (scenic) °route: *The drive up to the house is lined with trees.* **10** °campaign, °effort, °appeal, °crusade: *The club has had a successful membership drive this year.*

drivel v. **1** dribble, drool, slobber, °slaver: *You're drivelling all over the front of your shirt!* **2** °babble, prate, °prattle, gibber, °jabber, burble, gabble, °chatter, blether or *US* blather, *Colloq* jibber-jabber, °gab, *Brit* rabbit or witter or natter on, *US* run off at the mouth: *She keeps drivelling on about her family.*
—n. **3** °gibberish, °rubbish, (°stuff and) °nonsense, twaddle, balderdash, hogwash, *Colloq* eyewash, tripe, °garbage, malarkey, hooey, °hot air, bosh, boloney or baloney, *Slang* crap, bull, bilge (water), codswallop, *US* horse feathers, *Taboo* bullshit, balls, *Brit* (load of old) cobblers: *I've never heard so much drivel from a candidate in my entire life!*

droop v. **1** °sag, °hang (down), °wilt, °dangle: *Flags drooped in the windless heat.* **2** languish, °weaken, °flag, °wilt, wither, be °limp, °slump, °sag: *Halfway through the marathon she began to droop a bit.*

drop n. **1** globule, bead, °drip, droplet, °tear: *A drop of sweat hung from his nose.* **2** °bit, °spot, °particle, °taste, dram, °sip, °nip, °pinch, °dash, °dab, *Colloq* smidgen or smidgin: *Add a drop of milk before kneading the dough.* **3** descent, °fall: *There was a sheer drop of a thousand feet from the ledge into the chasm below.* **4** °decline, °slope, fall-off, drop-off, declivity, °incline: *The drop is about 15 feet in 100.*
—v. **5** °drip, °trickle, dribble: *As the water drops, filling the tube, the float rises.* **6** °fall, °descend, °sink, drop away or down or off, °dive, °plunge, °plummet, °decline, °collapse: *The barometer dropped 10 millibars in 10 minutes. Near that rock, the road drops to the beach. At the first shot, we dropped to the ground.* **7** °desert, °forsake, °give up, °abandon, °leave, °quit, °throw over, °jilt, °discard, °reject, °repudiate, °renounce, *Colloq* chuck, ditch, °dump; °relinquish, °let °go, °discontinue, °stop, °cease, °end: *After what he said, she dropped him like a hot potato. I wish you'd drop the subject of my disability.* **8** °release, °let °go of, °shed, °cast off, °discard, doff: *Deciduous trees drop their leaves in winter.* **9** °omit, °leave out, °exclude, °eliminate: *To avoid confusion with his father, he dropped his middle initial.* **10** °dismiss, °let °go, °fire, °discharge, oust, *Colloq chiefly Brit* °sack, give (someone) the °sack: *They dropped her after a week's trial.* **11** °decline, °decrease, drop or °fall off, °diminish, slacken, °slack or °taper off, °subside, lessen: *Demand for swimsuits drops during the winter.* **12 drop in (on)** °visit, °call (on), °pop in (on), °come by, °stop in: *Viola dropped in for tea yesterday.* **13 drop out** °withdraw (from), °leave, rusticate, °depart, decamp, °go away or off, °take off, °turn off: *She dropped out of school. After winning the award, Crater dropped out and hasn't been seen since.*

drown v. **1** °flood, inundate, °swamp, deluge, °drench, °immerse, °submerge, engulf: *The village was completely drowned in the tidal wave.* **2** °overwhelm, °overcome, °overpower, engulf, °swamp, deluge, inundate: *We were almost drowned by the responses to our advertisement.*

drowsy adj. °sleepy, heavy-lidded, °groggy, somnolent, dozy, oscitant; °nodding, yawning; °torpid, sluggish, °tired, °weary, °listless, °lethargic, °lazy: *We all felt a bit drowsy after that big dinner.*

drudgery n. toil, °labour, moil, travail, (°hack) °work, donkey-work, chore, slog, slogging, °slavery, *Colloq* °grind, °sweat, *Brit* skivvying, °fag: *She wanted some relief from the sheer drudgery of housework.*

drug n. **1** medication, °medicine, medicament, pharmaceutical, °remedy, °cure, °treatment; cure-all, panacea: *My doctor prescribes too many drugs.* **2** opiate, °narcotic, °stimulant, °tranquillizer, antidepressant, hallucinogen(ic), psychedelic, hypnotic, soporific, °sedative, analgesic, °painkiller, *Slang* °dope, downer, upper: *Can they control the traffic in drugs?*
—v. **3** °dose, medicate, °treat: *I was drugged with antihistamines and unable to drive.* **4** anaesthetize, °dope, °deaden, °knock out, °sedate, stupefy, °numb, benumb, °dull, narcotize; °poison, *Slang* slip (someone) a Mickey (Finn): *The victim had been drugged and kidnapped.*

druggist n. °pharmacist, apothecary, *Brit* chemist: *Only a druggist is qualified to dispense this medication.*

drunk adj. **1** drunken, intoxicated, inebriated, besotted, tipsy, °groggy, sotted, crapulent or crapulous, in one's cups, under the weather, under the influence, °maudlin, ebriate, ebriose, ebrious, *Colloq* soused, pickled, °high (as a kite), °tight, boozed, boozy, lit (up), half-seas-over, three or four sheets to the wind, out (cold), under the table, *Brit* squiffy, *Slang* pie-eyed, °loaded, stoned, stewed (to the gills), (well-)oiled, bombed (out of one's mind), crocked, plastered, tanked, sloshed, polluted, stinko, smashed, blotto, pissed: *He was so drunk he tried to fly.* **2** exhilarated, °excited, °exuberant, invigorated, inspirited, °animated, °ecstatic; flushed, °feverish, °inflamed, aflame, °fervent, fervid, °delirious: *Since he became a director, he's been drunk with power.*
—n. **3** drunkard, drinker, toper, tippler, sot, °soak, bibber, winebibber; dipsomaniac, °alcoholic, problem drinker; *Colloq* guzzler, swiller, sponge, *Slang* wino, boozer, dipso, °lush, souse, alchy or alkic or alky, *US* juicer, juice-head, rummy: *The drunks who volunteered were registered for treatment.* **4** °carouse, bacchanal, carousal, bacchanalia, °revel, *Slang* °bender, °tear, °jag, bat, *US and Canadian* toot, *Chiefly Brit* pub-crawl: *I went off on a wild drunk the night before my wedding.*

drunkenness n. intoxication, insobriety, intemperance, sottishness, bibulousness, inebriety, crapulence, crapulousness, tipsiness, ebriety; dipsomania, alcoholism, ebriosity; *Colloq* boozing, *Slang* hitting the °bottle or *US* the sauce: *Only a psychiatrist could help cure his drunkenness.*

dry adj. **1** dehydrated, desiccated, arid, sear, parched, waterless, moistureless; °barren, °bare, °fruitless: *With no rain for a month, the dry earth yielded no crops.* **2** °dreary, °boring, °tedious, °tiresome, wearisome, wearying, tiring, °dull, uninteresting, °monotonous, °prosaic, commonplace, °stale, uninspired; °plain, °unadorned, unembellished: *The minister's speech was as dry as could be, a litany of dry*

statistics. **3** °witty, droll, °wry, cynical, °biting, °sarcastic, °cutting, °keen, °sly, ironic: *Oscar Wilde was known for his dry witticisms.*
—*v.* **4** dehydrate, desiccate, °parch: *As the rainfall subsided, the land dried and changed into a desert.* **5** dry up *or* out, wither, °shrivel, °shrink, °wilt: *The plants dried because they weren't watered.*

duck *v.* **1** bob, °dodge, °dip, °dive, °stoop, °bow, °bend, °crouch: *I ducked to avoid hitting my head on the beam.* **2** °plunge, °submerge, °immerse, dunk: *In the pool, she ducked me when I least expected it.* **3** °avoid, °sidestep, °evade, °dodge, °elude, °shun, °steer clear of, °shy away from; °shirk: *He is known for ducking his responsibilities.*

dud *n.* **1** °failure, *Colloq* °flop, lead balloon, lemon, washout, *Colloq US and Canadian* dog, clinker: *Her second novel certainly proved a dud—it sold only ten copies.*
—*adj.* **2** °worthless, valueless, °broken, unusable, °useless, inoperative, non-functioning, malfunctioning, *Colloq* kaput, bust(ed), *Brit* °duff: *They deliberately supplied us with dud ammunition.*

dude *n.* **1** °dandy, fop, °fancy dresser, Beau Brummell, popinjay, boulevardier, man about town, *Archaic* coxcomb, macaroni; *Slang* °swell, *Brit* toff: *He dressed like a real dude—zoot suit and all.* **2** °man, °fellow, °chap, *Colloq* °guy: *Hey, man, who's that dude in the tartan suit?*

due *adj.* **1** °payable, owed, owing, °unpaid, °outstanding, in arrears: *The rent is due tomorrow.* **2** °fitting, °right, °rightful, °correct, °proper, °appropriate, apropos, apposite, °suitable, apt, °meet; °deserved, (well-)earned, merited, °just, justified: *Was she treated with due respect?* **3** °necessary, needed, °adequate, °sufficient, °enough, °satisfactory; °ample, °plenty of: *I do not think my case was given due consideration.* **4** expected, scheduled, anticipated: *He was due on the two o'clock plane.*
—*adv.* **5** °directly, °exactly, °precisely, °straight: *Go due east to the river, then turn north.*

dues *n.pl.* (membership) °fee, °charge(s): *If you have not paid your dues, you may not use the club's facilities.*

duff *adj.* °bad, °useless, °worthless, unworkable, inoperable, inoperative, °broken, °fake, °false, °counterfeit, *Colloq* °dud, °phoney *or US also* phony: *We couldn't get that duff radio to work. We were provided with duff papers for crossing the border.*

duffer *n.* °incompetent, blunderer, bungler, oaf, *Colloq* ox, lummox: *He may be an expert at computers but he's a duffer at golf.*

dull *adj.* **1** °stupid, slow-witted, °dense, °stolid, bovine, cloddish, clod-like, °backward, °obtuse, doltish, crass, °dumb, *Colloq* °thick, °dim, dim-witted, *Brit* °dim as a Toc H lamp: *He might be a dull student but he's a brilliant artist.* **2** insensitive, °numb, °insensible, imperceptive *or* impercipient, unresponsive, °indifferent, unfeeling, °unsympathetic, °callous, hardened, °hard, inured, obtundent: *He knew that he could expect only a dull response to his pleading.* **3** °lifeless, °indifferent, unresponsive, sluggish, °slow, °listless, °inactive, °torpid: *The market for luxury cars is a little dull now.* **4** °boring, °tiresome, °tedious, °monotonous, uninspired, uninspiring, unoriginal, uninteresting, °humdrum: *All work and no play make Jack a dull boy.* **5** °dismal, °dreary, depressing, °sombre, °grey, °dark, °murky, °gloomy, cloudy, clouded, °overcast, °sunless:

If the day is dull, the photographs will show it. **6** blunted, °blunt; °obtuse: *I nicked myself with that dull razor.* **7** °hazy, blurry, °opaque, °drab: *Rub the dull film off that silver goblet.* **8** muffled, numbing, deadened, muted, °indistinct: *I've had a dull pain in my arm all day.*
—*v.* **9** allay, assuage, °relieve, °mitigate, lessen, °reduce: *Weeping dulls the inner pain.* **10** °dim, °tarnish, °obscure, bedim, °blur, cloud, becloud: *A mist dulled the rich colours of the glen.* **11** stupefy, narcotize, °numb, benumb, desensitize, °deaden, °blunt, obtund: *His war experiences had dulled his feelings towards others.*

duly *adv.* **1** °properly, fittingly, deservedly, °appropriately, suitably, befittingly, rightly, correctly, °accordingly: *Those elected were duly installed in office.* **2** punctually, on °time: *The train duly arrived.*

dumb *adj.* **1** °mute, °speechless, voiceless; °silent, °quiet, °taciturn, °mum, wordless; °inarticulate: *She was struck dumb with astonishment.* **2** °dull, °stupid, *Colloq* °thick: *He's too dumb to understand what you are saying.*

dumbfound *v.* dumfound, °amaze, °shock, °surprise, °startle, °astonish, °astound, °bewilder, °stagger, °stun, °floor, °nonplus, °confuse, confound, *Colloq* flabbergast, °bowl over: *Their offer for the house dumbfounded us.*

dumbfounded *adj.* dumfounded, amazed, shocked, surprised, startled, astonished, astounded, bewildered, staggered, floored, nonplussed, overwhelmed, °speechless, stunned, °thunderstruck, dazzled, dazed, dumbstruck, taken aback, °confused, confounded, bemused, perplexed, baffled, °disconcerted, *Colloq* bowled over, flabbergasted, knocked out, thrown (off), *US* thrown for a loss, *Brit* knocked for six, knocked sideways: *She is dumbfounded that he proposed marriage.*

dummy *n.* **1** mannequin, manikin *or* mannikin, °model, °figure: *I saw the coat on a dummy in the shop window.* **2** °sample, °copy, reprint, °reproduction, °likeness, °substitution, °imitation, °sham, mock-up, simulation, *Colloq* °phoney *or US also* phony: *Those aren't the real crown jewels, they're just dummies.* **3** °fool, idiot, dunce, blockhead, ninny, ass, °dolt, numskull *or* numbskull, simpleton, *Colloq* dim-wit, *US* thimble-wit: *They're such dummies they don't know that you're joking.* **4** *US* pacifier: *Give the baby the dummy to suck.*

dump *v.* **1** °unload, offload, °empty, °drop, °deposit, °throw *or* °fling down, °tip: *They dumped the topsoil all over the path.* **2** get °rid of, °throw away, °scrap, °discard, ditch, jettison, °dispose of, °reject, °tip, °toss out *or* away, *Colloq* °junk, chuck out *or* away: *We dumped all the food when the fridge broke down.*
—*n.* **3** junk-yard, °rubbish °heap *or Brit* °tip, *US* °garbage dump: *You'll have to take this garden refuse to the. dump.*

dumpy *adj.* °stocky, pudgy, squat, chunky, °chubby, tubby, °stout, °plump, portly, °fat: *No one with a dumpy figure looks good in shorts.*

dun *v.* °press, importune, °solicit, °plague, °nag, °pester, *Slang US* °bug: *The gas company has been dunning me to pay the bill.*

dung *n.* manure, °muck, droppings, cow-pats, fertilizer, guano, excrement, faeces *or US* feces, *US* cow *or* buffalo-chips, horse-apples, *Taboo* shit: *The dung is spread on the fields.*

dungeon n. donjon, °keep, °cell, °prison, lock-up, oubliette, black °hole, °stronghold: *Throw the infidels into the dungeon and give them twenty lashes!*

dupe n. **1** °fool, gull, °victim, fair °game, *Colloq* chump, *Chiefly US and Canadian* fall guy; *Slang* °sucker, °sap, boob, °pushover, pigeon, mark, *Brit* °mug, *Chiefly US and Canadian* patsy: *Swindlers often choose tourists as likely dupes.* **2** cat's-paw, °pawn, °tool, °puppet, *Slang* stooge: *I'm not going to be the dupe in your little game!* —v. **3** °deceive, °fool, °outwit, °cheat, °trick, °take in, °defraud, humbug, °hoax, °swindle, °hoodwink, bilk, gull, cozen, delude, °mislead, snooker, °victimize, *Colloq* bamboozle, flim-flam, °put one over on, pull a fast one on; *Slang* con, °rip off, rook, °take, *US and Canadian* snow, do a snow job on: *She was duped into believing she had won the lottery.*

duplicate adj. **1** °identical; °twin, °matching: *They sent me duplicate tickets by mistake.* —n. **2** (°exact *or* carbon) °copy, photocopy, machine °copy, °double, clone, (perfect) °match, °facsimile, °twin, °reproduction, °replica, replication, °look-alike, *Trade Mark* Xerox (°copy), *Slang* (°dead) ringer: *This painting looks like a duplicate of the one you bought.* —v. **3** °copy, photocopy, clone, °match, replicate, °imitate, °reproduce, °double, *Trade Mark* Xerox; °repeat, °equal: *Would you please duplicate this letter for me? Can he duplicate his performance in the Commonwealth Games?*

durable adj. °enduring, long-lasting, °stable, wear-resistant, heavy-duty, hard-wearing, long-wearing, °lasting, °persistent, °indestructible, °substantial, °sturdy, °tough, °stout, °strong, °firm, °sound, °fixed, fast, °permanent, dependable, °reliable: *The product is durable, guaranteed to last a lifetime.*

duress n. **1** coercion, °threat, °pressure, con-straint, compulsion; °force, °power: *The boys wash the dishes only under duress.* **2** confinement, °imprisonment, incarceration, °captivity, °restraint, *Literary* durance: *There were workhouses, prisons, and other forms of duress.*

dusk n. °twilight, sundown, nightfall, °evening, sunset, °dark, eventide: *The workers came in from the fields at dusk.*

dusky adj. **1** °dark, °black, ebony, sable, jet-black; °swarthy, swart, dark-complected, dark-complexioned: *'Dusky diamonds' is another name for coal. A dusky gentleman offered to see her home safely.* **2** °shadowy, °shady, °dim, °dark,

unilluminated, unlit, °murky, subfusc, sub-fuscous, °gloomy, °obscure: *An ominous figure was lurking in the dusky area under the stairs.*

dutiful adj. °obedient, compliant, °willing, °obliging, filial, °faithful, °conscientious, °reliable, °responsible, °diligent, °attentive, punctilious, °respectful, °polite, °considerate, deferential, °submissive, °yielding, acquiescent, malleable, °flexible, pliant, °accommodating, *Formal or archaic* duteous: *A dutiful son, he visits his parents weekly.*

duty n. **1** °responsibility, °obligation, °burden, onus, devoir, °office, °work, °task, °assignment, °job, °stint, chore, °occupation, °calling, °function, °role, °part, °bit, °charge: *Every man is expected to do his duty.* **2** °respect, °deference, °loyalty, fealty, fidelity, faithfulness, allegiance: *I think she did it out of a sense of duty to her family.* **3** °tax, excise, °tariff, impost, levy, customs: *You will have to pay duty on that whisky.*

dwarf v. °overshadow, °dominate, °diminish, °minimize: *The new tower dwarfs the older buildings.*

dwell v. **1** reside, °abide, °live, °lodge, °stay, °remain, °rest, *Formal* °domicile: *After the father's death, the mother dwelt with her daughter.* **2 dwell on** *or* **upon**: harp on, °ponder, °persist in, °emphasize, °stress, °focus on, °linger *or* tarry over, °elaborate (on); °labour: *Why must you always dwell on a person's shortcomings?*

dwelling n. °abode, habitation, dwelling-place, °house, °domicile, °lodging, quarters, °home, °residence, homestead: *His dwelling is a shanty in old shanty town.*

dwindle v. °diminish, °decrease, °shrink, lessen, °wane, °fade, °contract, condense, °reduce, peter out, °waste away, °die out *or* down *or* away, °ebb, °decline, °subside, °taper off, °shrivel (up *or* away): *The last days of summer dwindled away. His funds have dwindled until today he has nothing.*

dying adj. expiring, °sinking, slipping away, °going, °failing, fading (fast), at death's door, on one's deathbed, with one foot in the °grave, *in extremis;* °moribund: *The doctor said the dying man was in no pain.*

dynamic adj. dynamical, °vigorous, °active, °forceful, °energetic, °potent, °powerful, high-powered, °lively, spry, °vital, °electric, °spirited, zealous, °eager, °emphatic: *We are seeking a dynamic salesman for our Reading office.*

dynamism n. °energy, °vigour, °pep, °vitality, liveliness, °spirit, spiritedness, forcefulness, °power, °drive, °initiative, °enterprise, *Colloq* get-up-and-go, zip, °push: *That woman has the dynamism needed to get ahead in this organization.*

dynasty n. °line, °family, °heritage, °house: *The Ming dynasty ruled China for more than 300 years.*

E

eager *adj.* avid, zealous, °ardent, °earnest, °keen, °enthusiastic, °hot, °hungry, °fervent, fervid, °passionate, °spirited, inspirited, °energetic, energized, vehement, °animated, °excited, vitalized, stimulated; °desirous, yearning, desiring, craving, °wanting, °longing, itchy, °impatient; °anxious; *Colloq* dying, *Slang US* °hot to trot: *We were particularly eager to spend our holiday in Spain.*

eagerness *n.* **1** avidity, zeal, earnestness, keenness, °enthusiasm, °fervour, °hunger, vehemence, °animation, °vitality, °appetite, °zest, °relish, °spirit, spiritedness, °gusto, °verve, °dash, élan, vim, °vigour, °energy, *Colloq* get-up-and-go, zip, go: *Such eagerness for learning is rare. In his eagerness to please everyone he satisfies no one.* **2** °desire, °longing, wishing, yearning: *He observed the eagerness, the open hunger, with which she now waited for Mr Browning.*

eagle-eyed *adj.* °sharp-eyed, sharp-sighted, keen-eyed, keen-sighted, lynx-eyed, hawk-eyed; °perceptive, perspicacious, discerning, °sharp, watchful, °alert: *It would be impossible to deceive our eagle-eyed supervisor.*

ear *n.* **1** °attention, °heed, °notice, °regard, °consideration: *See if you can get his ear for a moment between meetings.* **2** °sensitivity, °appreciation, °taste, °discrimination: *She has an excellent ear for the right expression.*

early *adv.* **1** beforehand, ahead (of °time), °prematurely: *I arrived too early and had to wait.* **2** anciently, initially, °originally, at *or* near the °start *or* °beginning: *Plants appeared early in the development of life forms on earth.* **3** betimes, at cock crow *or* cock's-crow, at (the crack *or* break of) °dawn, at daybreak: *You're up early this morning!*
—*adj.* **4** untimely, °premature; °inopportune, °inappropriate: *The early fruit isn't as sweet.* **5** °initial, °beginning, °original, °first, °pioneer, advanced: *He was one of the earliest writers on the subject.* **6** primeval *or Brit also* primaeval, °primitive, primordial, °ancient, °old, °prehistoric, antediluvian, °original; °antique, °antiquated: *The Olduvai Gorge has yielded up many early humanoid fossils.*

earn *v.* **1** °merit, °deserve, be °worthy of, be °entitled to, °win, °warrant, °rate, °qualify for, have a °claim *or* °right to: *Peter has earned everyone's respect.* **2** °make, °pocket, °gross, °net, °clear, °realize, °receive, °get, °procure, °collect, °reap, °bring in, °take home; °draw, *Colloq US* °pull down: *It is still the case that most men earn more than their wives.*

earnest *adj.* **1** °serious, °solemn, °grave, °sober, °intense, °steady, °resolute, resolved, °firm, °determined, assiduous, °sincere, dedicated, committed, °devoted, °thoughtful: *He made an earnest promise to do his best.* **2** zealous, °ardent, °diligent, assiduous, °industrious, hard-working, °devoted, °eager, °conscientious, °keen, °fervent, fervid, °enthusiastic, °passionate: *Burbridge is an earnest pupil.* **3 earnest-money:** °deposit, down °payment, binder, handsel, °guarantee, °security, °pledge: *The company paid £10,000 earnest-money to secure the bid.*
—*n.* **4 in earnest:** °serious, °sincere: *She said she would come, but I doubt whether she was in earnest.*

earnings *n.pl.* °wages, °salary, °income, compensation, °pay, °stipend, emolument, °proceeds, °return, °revenue, °yield, takings, *Slang* °take: *The interest from tax-free bonds was not included in my earnings.*

earth *n.* **1** °globe, mother earth, planet, °world, blue planet, Terra: *Ozone depletion in the upper atmosphere may be threatening life on earth.* **2** °soil, °dirt, loam, sod, clay, °turf, °ground, °mould: *Pack the earth firmly around the roots.*

earthly *adj.* **1** °terrestrial, terrene, telluric: *Extraterrestrial beings might be unable to survive in our earthly atmosphere.* **2** °worldly, mundane, °material, °materialistic, °physical, non-spiritual, °sensual, °carnal, fleshly, corporeal, °base, °natural: *He has forsaken earthly pleasures in favour of spiritual pursuits.* **3** °human, °temporal, °secular, °profane, °mortal, °physical, non-spiritual, °material: *His earthly remains were committed to the sea.* **4** conceivable, imaginable, °feasible, °possible: *What earthly reason could she have had for kissing me?*

earthy *adj.* ribald, °bawdy, °unrefined, °coarse, °crude, °shameless, °wanton, °uninhibited, °abandoned, °vulgar, °lusty, °rough, °dirty, °indecent, °obscene: *She found Henry Miller's books a bit too earthy for her tastes.*

ease *n.* **1** °comfort, °repose, well-being, °relaxation, °leisure, °rest, contentment, calmness, tranquillity, °serenity, peacefulness, °peace, °peace and °quiet: *After 50 years of hard work, she felt entitled to a few years of ease.* **2** easiness, °simplicity, °facility, effortlessness, adeptness: *He passed the other runners with ease.* **3** affluence, °wealth, °prosperity, °luxury, opulence, °abundance, °plenty: *He has always led a life of ease, never having had to work.* **4** naturalness, informality, unaffectedness, ingenuousness, casualness, artlessness, insouciance, nonchalance, aplomb; unconcern: *I admire the ease with which she converses with complete strangers.*
—*v.* **5** °comfort, °relax, °calm, °tranquillize, °quiet(en), °still, pacify, soothe, disburden: *It eased his mind to learn that there was a reserve budget for emergencies.* **6** lessen, °diminish, abate, °mitigate, °reduce, °decrease, allay, alleviate, assuage, mollify, appease, palliate, °quiet(en), °relieve: *Her anxiety was considerably eased by the news that John would not need an operation after all.* **7** °manoeuvre, °manipulate, inch, °guide, °steer, °slip: *The helmsman eased the ship into dock.* **8** °facilitate, °expedite, °simplify, °smooth, °further, °clear, °assist, °aid, °advance, °forward, °help: *Having a wealthy father eased her way in life.*

easily *adv.* **1** smoothly, effortlessly, °readily, °simply, °handily, without a hitch, °hands down, without even trying, comfortably, with no *or* without difficulty, *Colloq* °easy as pie: *You can easily tackle the job yourself.* **2** by °far, beyond or without doubt or question, indisputably, indubitably, °undoubtedly, °doubtless(ly), unquestionably, °clearly, °far and away, °definitely, definitively, conclusively, certainly, °surely, undeniably, °obviously, patently: *He is easily the best lawyer in the firm.* **3** °probably, most or very °likely, °well, almost certainly: *We may easily be the first in Hampton to have plaster flamingos on the lawn.*

easy *adj.* **1** °simple, °effortless, °plain, °clear, straightforward, °hands down, uncomplicated, °elementary, °foolproof; easy as pie, easy as can be: *Feeding goldfish is an easy job that children can undertake for themselves.* **2** °carefree, °easygoing, °casual, °lenient, undemanding, °relaxed, °quiet, °serene, °restful, °tranquil, °peaceful, untroubled, undisturbed, unoppressive, °gentle, °mild, °calm, °comfortable, °cosy, °unhurried, leisurely: *He has a pretty easy life now that he's retired.* **3** °light, °lenient, undemanding, °mild, °flexible, °indulgent, °tolerant: *You really should be easy on him after what he's been through.* **4** °tractable, pliant, docile, compliant, °submissive, acquiescent, amenable, °accommodating, °soft, °suggestible, credulous, °trusting, °weak, °easygoing: *He was an easy victim for confidence tricksters. She has the reputation of being a woman of easy virtue.* **5** unstrained, °gentle, °moderate, °unhurried, leisurely, °even, °steady, undemanding, °comfortable, unexacting: *They kept up an easy pace of about five miles an hour.* **6** affable, °friendly, °amiable, °amicable, °agreeable, °outgoing, °informal, unceremonious, down-to-earth, unreserved, relaxing, °natural, °relaxed, °easygoing: *We found them easy to be with.* —*adv.* **7** effortlessly; calmly, unexcitedly, temperately, peacefully, tranquilly, serenely, nonchalantly, casually: *Take it easy and don't get so worked up about things.*

easygoing *adj.* °relaxed, °casual, °mellow, °carefree, undemanding, °easy, even-tempered, forbearing, °lenient, °tolerant, °permissive, over-tolerant, over-permissive, °lax, °weak, *Colloq* °wishy-washy, laid-back: *He's an easygoing sort of person.*

eat *v.* °dine, lunch, breakfast, sup, break bread, °snack, have a °bite; °consume, °devour, take (in) °nourishment, *Colloq* °put or pack away, *Slang* nosh, put or tie on the nosebag or *US and Canadian* feed-bag: *I'm not hungry, thank you: I've already eaten.*

eavesdrop *v.* °listen in, °tap, overhear, °snoop; °spy, °pry: *They were eavesdropping on our conversation, that's how they knew about Martha.*

ebb *v.* **1** °recede, °flow back, °subside, °go out, °go down; °fall back or away, °retreat, retrocede, °retire: *The tide ebbed, leaving the boat stranded.* **2** °decline, °flag, °decay, °wane, °diminish, °decrease, °drop, slacken, °fade (away), °drain (away), °dwindle, peter out, °waste (away), °deteriorate: *His enthusiasm for exercise is beginning to ebb.* —*n.* **3** °low tide, °low water, ebb tide, °low point: *The rocks appear when the sea is at its ebb.* **4** °decline, °decay, °decrease, diminution, °wane, °drop, slackening (off), dwindling, lessening, deterioration, degeneration: *She was no longer willing to contend with the ebb and flow of his temper.*

ebullient *adj.* bubbling, overflowing, °effervescent, °excited, °effusive, exhilarated, °elated, °buoyant, °exuberant, °enthusiastic, zestful: *The crowd was ebullient at the news from Mafeking.*

eccentric *adj.* **1** unconventional, °unusual, uncommon, idiosyncratic, anomalous, °unorthodox, out of the ordinary, °irregular, atypical, °incongruous, errant, aberrant, °exceptional, °individual, °singular, °unique; °abnormal, °odd, °peculiar, °strange, °curious, °bizarre, °outlandish, °queer, °quaint, quirky, °weird, °offbeat, *Colloq* far-out, °kinky, °cranky: *Yes, I would agree that walking a canary is a bit eccentric.* —*n.* **2** °original, °individualist, °nonconformist, °queer fellow, °odd fish, *Colloq* °character, °card, °freak, (nut) °case, °crank, oddball, °weirdo or weirdie, *US* oner: *In today's conformist society, anyone who isn't a carbon copy of his neighbour is regarded as an eccentric.*

eccentricity *n.* **1** unconventionality, unusualness, uncommonness, irregularity, nonconformity, individuality, individualism, °singularity, uniqueness, strangeness, oddness, bizarreness, distinctiveness, capriciousness, weirdness: *Why should someone be criticized for eccentricity?* **2** idiosyncrasy, °quirk, °peculiarity, °mannerism, crotchet, aberration, anomaly, °oddity, °curiosity, caprice: *Eating crackers in bed is only one of her eccentricities.*

echo *n.* **1** reverberation, °repercussion, °repetition, iteration, reiteration: *The echo of the church bells could be heard throughout the valley.* **2** °imitation, °copy, °replica or replication, duplication, °reproduction, simulation, °facsimile; °reflection, °mirror °image, °repetition: *Modern Rome is but a feeble echo of its glorious past.* —*v.* **3** °resound, reverberate, °ring: *The hall echoed with children's laughter.* **4** °imitate, ape, °parrot, °mimic, °copy, °duplicate, °reproduce, simulate, °repeat, emulate, °mirror, °reflect: *The poems are unoriginal and merely echo the works of others.*

eclipse *v.* **1** °conceal, °hide, °blot out, °obscure, °block, °veil, °shroud, °cover, darken: *A black cloud eclipsed the moon.* **2** °overshadow, °obscure, °surpass, °top, outshine: *His career was eclipsed by his wife's brilliant successes.* —*n.* **3** concealment, covering, hiding, blocking, blockage, occultation, obscuring, obscuration, darkening, shading, dimming: *Though good may suffer an eclipse, it can never be extinguished.* **4** °decline, downturn, °slump; °recession: *After the scandal, her career went into eclipse.*

economic *adj.* **1** °financial, °fiscal, pecuniary, °monetary, budgetary; commercial, °mercantile, °trade: *The economic indicators for July affected the markets.* **2** °profitable, cost-effective, money-making, remunerative, °productive, °solvent: *Increased demand for our products has made the company economic.*

economical *adj.* **1** cost-effective, money-saving, °thrifty, unwasteful; °cheap, °inexpensive, °reasonable; °economic: *This car is very economical to run.* **2** °provident, °thrifty, °sparing, economizing, °prudent, °conservative, °frugal; parsimonious, °penurious, stingy, °cheap, °miserly, niggardly, °tight, close-fisted, tight-fisted, °mean, penny-pinching, scrimping: *Aunt Gertrude was always a very economical house-keeper.*

economize v. °save, °cut back, °husband, retrench; tighten one's belt, °cut corners or costs, scrimp, skimp, °pinch pennies: *Without the extra income, we'll have to economize on something.*

economy n. **1** °thrift, husbandry, thriftiness, °conservation, conservatism, °saving, °restraint, °control, frugality: *We'll have to exercise economy to get through the winter.* **2** °brevity, briefness, succinctness, terseness, conciseness, concision, compactness, °restraint, curtness: *He manages to get his ideas across with an admirable economy of language.*

ecstasy n. **1** °delight, °joy, °rapture, °bliss, °transport, nympholepsy or nympholepsia, °happiness, gladness, elation, °pleasure, °enjoyment, °gratification; °heaven on earth: *The prospect of being with her again filled me with ecstasy.* **2** exaltation, °frenzy, °thrill, elation, °paroxysm, °excitement: *The ecstasy of space flight is impossible to describe.*

ecstatic adj. exhilarated, thrilled, °exultant, blissful, euphoric, °rapturous, enraptured, nympholeptic, °enchanted, transported, °rhapsodic, °excited, °elated, °delighted, °joyful, °gleeful, °overjoyed, °happy, °glad, beside oneself, °delirious, orgasmic, *Colloq* on cloud nine, *Brit* over the moon, in the seventh °heaven, cock-a-hoop, *US* in seventh °heaven, flying: *Our team had won an Olympic gold medal, and we were truly ecstatic.*

eddy n. **1** °swirl, whirl, vortex, gurgitation; °whirlpool, maelstrom, Charybdis; dust devil, °whirlwind, °twister, tornado, cyclone, typhoon, °hurricane; waterspout: *These treacherous eddies are caused by tidal changes.*
—v. **2** °swirl, whirl, °turn, °spin: *The wind eddied round us, driving the dinghy this way and that.*

edge n. **1** °brink, °verge, °border, °side, °rim, lip, °brim; °fringe, °margin, °boundary, °bound, °limit, bourn, °perimeter, °periphery: *I was hanging on to the very edge of the cliff. The edge of the handkerchief was trimmed with lace.* **2** acuteness, sharpness, keenness: *That hunting knife has quite an edge.* **3** harshness, sharpness, acrimony, pungency, °force, °urgency, effectiveness, incisiveness, causticity, °virulence, vehemence: *There was an edge to her voice when she told me not to bother her.* **4** °advantage, head °start, °superiority, °lead, °upper hand: *You're holding the gun, so I guess you have the edge on me.* **5 on edge** on tenterhooks, °nervous, °touchy, °sensitive, °prickly, itchy, °tense, irascible, crabbed, °irritable, °peevish, apprehensive, with one's heart in one's mouth, edgy, °anxious, °ill at ease, °restive, °restless, fidgety, *Colloq* uptight, like a cat on a hot tin roof: *She was on edge waiting for the exam results.*
—v. **6** inch, °move, °sidle, °crawl, °creep, °steal, worm, °work (one's way): *The burglar was edging along the wall, 30 storeys above the street.*

edible adj. eatable, esculent, palatable, °good or °fit (to °eat), °wholesome, *Rare* comestible: *After the sell-by date, fresh food is no longer considered edible.*

edification n. enlightenment, °improvement, uplifting, enlightening, °guidance, °education, °information, °tuition, teaching, °schooling, °instruction: *The exhibition is designed for both edification and enjoyment.*

edit v. **1** redact, copy-edit, rewrite, rephrase, °modify, °alter, °adapt, °change, °revise, °correct, emend, °style, restyle, °polish, °touch up: *His job is to edit the stories into idiomatic English.* **2** Often, **edit out**: blue-pencil, °cut (out), °delete, censor, °erase, bleep, blip; bowdlerize, expurgate, °clean up: *They edited out all his slanderous asides before broadcasting the interview.* **3** °cut, condense, compress, °shorten, crop, °reduce: *The story has to be edited so that it fits on one page.* **4** °prepare, °compile, °assemble, °select, °arrange, °organize, °order, reorganize, reorder: *Margoliouth edited the collected letters of Andrew Marvell.*

edition n. °number, °issue, printing, °print °run, °copy; °version: *The first Monday edition carried the news of the break-in, and a later edition reported the detention of a suspect.*

editor n. rewrite man or woman, rewriter, °copy editor, redactor, reviser; °writer, columnist, °journalist, °editorial °writer, *Brit* leader-writer; editor-in-chief, managing editor, senior editor; compiler, °collector: *The editor sent the reporter out to check the facts of the story.*

editorial n. op-ed article, think-piece, opinion piece, position statement; essay, article, column; *Brit* leader, leading article: *Did you see the editorial about the Middle East situation in today's paper?*

educate v. °teach, °train, °instruct, edify, °tutor, °school, °inform, °enlighten, °indoctrinate, inculcate, °coach, °drill, °prepare, °ready, °rear, °bring up, °cultivate, °develop, °civilize: *It is the responsibility of the state to educate the people.*

educated adj. **1** °cultivated, cultured, erudite, well-read, °lettered, °literary, °scholarly, °learned; (°well-) °informed, °knowledgeable, °enlightened: *There is no real evidence that educated people enjoy greater job satisfaction than those who leave school at 16. I haven't got the answer, but I could make an educated guess.* **2** °refined, °polished, °cultivated, civilized; discerning, °critical, °sensitive: *She has an educated palate and really knows her wines.*

education n. **1** teaching, °schooling, training, °instruction, °tuition, tutelage, °edification, tutoring, cultivation, °upbringing, indoctrination, drilling: *His education was in the hands of monks until he was twelve.* **2** °learning, °lore, °knowledge, °information, erudition: *Education is gained from the experience of others.* **3** °lesson, °course (of °study): *The inhabitants gave her an education in how to survive in the forest.*

educational adj. **1** °academic, scholastic, pedagogical, instructional: *This is one of the best educational centres in the world.* **2** °informative, °instructive, enlightening, edifying, eye-opening, revelatory, educative: *A year spent abroad is always educational.*

eerie adj. °frightening, °weird, °strange, uncanny, °ghostly, °spectral, °dreadful, °unearthly, °frightful *Poetic or Scots* eldritch, *Scots* °mysterious, *Colloq* °scary, creepy, spooky: *I had the eeriest feeling I was being watched.*

effect n. **1** °result, consequence, °outcome, conclusion, °upshot, aftermath, °impact: *The effects of the storm could be seen everywhere.* **2** effectiveness, efficacy, °force, °power,

°capacity, potency, °influence, °impression, °impact, *Colloq* clout, °punch: *His threats had no effect.* **3** °significance, °meaning, signification, purport, °sense, °essence, °drift, °implication, °import, °tenor, °purpose, °intent, °intention, °object, °objective: *She said 'Get lost', or words to that effect.* **4** °impact, °impression, °form, °sensation: *He didn't mean that, he just said it for effect.* **5 in effect**: effectively, °virtually, for (all) practical purposes, so to °speak, more or less; °actually, in (point of) °fact, °really, essentially, basically, at °bottom, in °truth, °truly, to all intents and purposes, at the end of the day, any way you look at it: *She always spoke of him as her adopted son and this, in effect, was what he was.* **6 take effect**: become °operative or operational, come into °force, °begin or °start to °work or °function or °operate: *The regulation doesn't take effect till next week.*
—*v.* **7** °bring about, °cause, °make °happen or take °place, °effectuate, °achieve, °accomplish, °secure, °obtain, °make, °execute, °carry out, °produce, °create: *The opposition was unable to effect any change in the law.*

effective *adj.* **1** °effectual, °efficacious, °productive; °capable, °useful, °serviceable, °competent, °operative, °able, °functional, °efficient: *The effective life of the battery is six months.* **2** °impressive, °remarkable, °noticeable, °conspicuous, °outstanding, °striking, °powerful, compelling, °moving, °telling, °effectual: *The stage setting was very effective.* **3** °operative, operational, in °operation, functioning, °real, °actual, °essential, °basic, °true: *The monthly interest may seem low, but the effective annual rate is much higher.*

effects *n.pl.* °belongings, (personal) °property, °gear, °possessions, °stuff, things, °paraphernalia, chattels, °goods, *Colloq* °junk, crap, *Brit* clobber, *Taboo slang US* shit: *His personal effects were left scattered around the house.*

effectual *adj.* **1** °effective, °efficacious, °efficient, °functional, °productive, °useful, °telling, °influential, °powerful, °forcible, °forceful; °capable, °adequate: *What is the most effectual way of stopping a take-over of the company?* **2** °effective, in °force, °legal, °lawful, binding, °sound, valid: *You must register the agreement for it to be effectual.*

effectuate *v.* °bring about, °effect, °carry out, °implement, °accomplish, do, °execute, °realize, °achieve; °cause, °make °happen: *It is unclear just how she will effectuate her escape.*

effeminate *adj.* unmanly, womanish, womanly; °gay, °homosexual; *All the following are offensive and derogatory* °sissy, °weak, campy; *Slang Brit* °bent, poncey, *US* limp-wristed, faggy, faggoty: *He's too effeminate to play the part of Othello.*

effervescent *n.* **1** bubbling, fizzy, carbonated, sparkling, fizzing, gassy; foaming, foamy, frothing, frothy, °bubbly: *I prefer effervescent mineral water to still.* **2** bubbling, °bubbly, high-spirited, °vivacious, °ebullient, °lively, °exuberant, °buoyant, °animated, °lively, exhilarated, °excited, °enthusiastic, °irrepressible: *Jeanette's effervescent personality endeared her to everyone who met her.*

efficacious *adj.* °effective, °effectual, °productive, °competent, °successful,

°efficient, °useful, °serviceable; °capable: *He was not very efficacious in getting the council to change their policy.*

efficiency *n.* **1** effectiveness, efficacy, competence, °capability, adeptness, °proficiency, expertness, °expertise, know-how, °experience, °skill, skilfulness, °dexterity, adroitness: *The efficiency of the staff has been greatly improved.* **2** productivity, effectiveness, efficaciousness: *How does the efficiency of a diesel compare with that of other engines?*

efficient *adj.* unwasteful, °economic, °thrifty; °effective, °efficacious, °effectual, °competent, °productive, °proficient, °operative: *The technique for producing electrical power from tidal action has not yet proved efficient.*

effort *n.* **1** °exertion, striving, °struggle, °strain, °labour, °pains, °energy, toil, °application, °trouble, travail, °work, *Colloq* elbow-grease: *He's gone to a lot of effort to please her. Getting the place cleaned up took a great deal of effort.* **2** °attempt, °endeavour, °essay, °try, °venture, *Colloq* °stab, crack: *Her efforts to be pleasant met with a stony response.* **3** °achievement, °accomplishment, °creation, °feat, °deed, attainment, °exploit: *Last year's fund-raising fair was a superb effort.*

effortless *adj.* °easy (as pie or as A, B, C, or as 1, 2, 3), °simple, °painless, °smooth, trouble-free, uncomplicated: *She admired the apparently effortless grace of the dancer.*

effrontery *n.* °impertinence, °impudence, audacity, °nerve, °presumption, presumptuousness, brazenness, boldness, insolence, temerity, brashness, rashness, °arrogance, °front, °indiscretion, *Archaic* frowardness, *Colloq* °gall, °brass, °nerve, cheek, lip, °mouth, *Slang Brit* °side: *He had the effrontery to call her 'Queenie'!*

effusive *adj.* °demonstrative, gushing, (over)-enthusiastic, unrestrained, unchecked, unreserved, °expansive, °emotional, °exuberant, °rhapsodic, °ebullient, °lavish, °voluble, °profuse; fulsome: *Her aunt greeted her with an effusive outpouring of affection.*

egoistic *adj.* egoistical, self-centred, egocentric, narcissistic, self-seeking, self-absorbed, °selfish, self-serving, °self-indulgent, °self-important: *She is too egoistic to consider anyone but herself.*

egotistical *adj.* egotistic, °conceited, °proud, overweening, bragging, °boastful, boasting, swelled-headed or swell-headed or swollen-headed, °vain, vainglorious, self-worshipping, self-admiring, vaunting, crowing: *Considering his poor track record, he has nothing to be so egotistical about.*

eject *v.* **1** °force or °drive out, °expel, oust, °remove, get °rid of, °evict, *Colloq* °throw or °kick or °boot out: *They were ejected for causing a disturbance.* **2** °expel, °emit, °throw up or out, °spew (forth), °discharge, °spout, disgorge, °vomit (up or forth), °send out or forth; °ooze, exude, extravasate: *The volcano ejected boulders the size of houses.* **3** °discharge, °dismiss, cashier, drum out, °lay off, °declare or make °redundant, *Colloq* °fire, °sack, °boot out, axe, give the °sack or boot or axe, give (someone) his or her marching orders or *US also* walking papers, °send packing: *He was ejected for stealing paper clips.*

ejection *n.* **1** °expulsion, casting out or up, disgorgement, vomiting forth, throwing out or up, °discharge, emission, disgorging: *The ejection* *of lava was preceded by loud rumblings.* **2** °exile, °expulsion, banishment, deportation, ouster, °removal; °eviction, dispossession: *His ejection from the meeting angered his supporters. My ejection by the landlord was illegal.* **3** °dismissal, °discharge, *congé,* cashiering, lay-off, *Colloq* firing, sacking, *Slang* the °sack, the boot, the axe, the (old) heave-ho, *US* the bounce: *Business was bad, and the entire staff was faced with ejection.*

elaborate *adj.* **1** °detailed, °painstaking, °meticulous, punctilious, °comprehensive, °thorough, °complete, °exhaustive, °intricate, °involved, °minute, °precise, °exact: *The escape had been worked out in elaborate detail.* **2** °complicated, complex, convoluted, °ornate, °fancy, Byzantine, °laborious, °laboured, °extravagant, °showy; ornamented, decorated, baroque, rococo, °busy, °fussy, gingerbread: *We marvelled at the elaborate mosaics. His plan is too elaborate and should be simplified.* —*v.* **3** °ornament, °decorate, °complicate, °embellish, garnish, adorn: *Later craftsmen elaborated the earlier Greek motifs.* **4** °enlarge, °expand (upon *or* on), expatiate, °develop, °cultivate, °flesh out, °enhance, °refine, °enrich, °improve, °better, ameliorate, emend, °polish: *Later on, I shall elaborate on the recruitment methods we used.*

elaboration *n.* **1** enhancement, °refinement, enrichment, °improvement, amelioration, melioration, betterment; °embellishment, adornment, garnish, garnishment, °decoration, over-decoration, gingerbread, *Slang* bells and whistles: *The customers always welcome elaboration of the equipment.* **2** enlargement, °development, amplification, °expansion: *The argument requires further elaboration.*

elapse *v.* °pass (by), °go (by), °slip by *or* away, °pass away, °slide by, °glide by, °transpire: *Three weeks have elapsed since I last saw her.*

elastic *adj.* **1** °flexible, stretchable, stretchy, °stretch, bendable, °pliable, springy, °plastic, extensile, extensible, expansible, expandable, contractile, resilient, bouncy, compressible: *Is it elastic enough to stretch round that box?* **2** adjustable, °adaptable, °accommodating, °flexible: *The schedule for our main project is elastic, so we can fit in additional tasks at very short notice.*

elasticity *n.* **1** °flexibility, °resilience, rubberiness, plasticity, ductility, springiness, stretchability, stretchiness, °stretch, suppleness, pliancy, *Colloq* °give: *Dry hair has no elasticity: it's brittle and breaks easily when brushed or combed.* **2** °flexibility, adjustability, adaptability, °tolerance, suppleness: *Their plan lacks the elasticity needed to accommodate changes.*

elated *adj.* exhilarated, uplifted, °elevated, °gleeful, °joyful, jubilant, joyous, °exultant, °ecstatic, blissful, °happy, °delighted, euphoric, °overjoyed, °excited, thrilled, transported, °pleased (as Punch), on °top of the world, on cloud nine, *Colloq* tickled, tickled °pink, *Brit* chuffed, over the moon, in the seventh °heaven, *US* in seventh °heaven: *We were elated to learn that our daughter had won first prize.*

elder *adj.* **1** older, °senior: *My elder brother was born in 1930.* **2** °venerable, respected, (pre-)°eminent; °experienced, °veteran: *Clemenceau was an elder statesman at the Geneva Convention.*

—*n.* **3** °senior, °superior; patriarch, elder statesman, dean, doyen *or* doyenne: *Everyone paid great respect to the elders of the tribe.*

elderly *adj.* **1** °old, past middle age, oldish, advanced in years, of advanced age, along in years, °grey, ageing, °aged, °venerable; hoary, °ancient, senescent, °decrepit, superannuated; °senile, anile; *Colloq* over the hill, past it, long in the tooth, having one foot in the grave, old-fogyish *or* old-fogeyish: *Today, a person isn't considered elderly till he's past 65.* —*n.* **2 the elderly**: the retired, the °old, °senior citizens, pensioners, O.A.P.'s, old-age pensioners, golden-agers, *Colloq* old-timers, (°old) geezers, (°old) fogies *or* fogeys, *Brit* wrinklies: *The elderly constitute an increasingly large body of voters.*

elect *v.* **1** °choose, °select, °pick, °vote (for), °determine, °designate: *We must elect a new chairperson at the next meeting.* —*adj.* **2** chosen, elected, selected, picked out: *The president-elect takes office next month.* **3** °select, °choice, °first-rate, first-class: *An elect few make up the executive committee.*

election *n.* °poll, °vote, referendum, °plebiscite; °selection, °choice, choosing, nomination, designation, °appointment; voting, electing: *They held an election and Michael lost. The election of a new social secretary is required.*

electioneer *v.* °campaign, °canvass, °support, °back, °promote: *They are busy electioneering for their candidate.*

electric *adj.* charged, °tense, energized, °stimulating, °exciting, °thrilling, galvanizing, electrifying, °moving, °stirring: *As the jury filed in, the atmosphere in the courtroom was electric.*

electricity *n.* °excitement, °verve, °energy, °tension, tenseness, fervency, °intensity, °ardour; vibrations: *I could feel the electricity between us.*

electrify *v.* **1** °startle, °shock, °stun, °jolt, °stagger, °astound, °jar, °astonish, °amaze: *We were electrified by the news of the disaster.* **2** °excite, galvanize, °animate, °move, °rouse, °stir, °stimulate, °vitalize, °fire, °thrill, °arouse: *His fiery oratory electrified the audience.*

elegance *n.* **1** °refinement, grace, tastefulness, good °taste, gentility, °polish, courtliness, °culture, politeness, politesse, °propriety, °dignity: *Where but in 18th-century France could one find such elegance?* **2** °luxury, °grandeur, luxuriousness, sumptuousness, exquisiteness, °splendour, °beauty: *The overwhelming elegance of the palace took our breath away.*

elegant *adj.* **1** °tasteful, °exquisite, °handsome, °beautiful, °comely, °dapper, °smart, °well turned out; °graceful, °choice, °superior, °fine, °select, °refined, °delicate, discerning, artistic; °dignified, °genteel, °sophisticated, °cultivated, °polished, urbane, Chesterfieldian, °suave, soigné(e), °debonair, courtly, to the manner born, °well-bred, well-born, high-born: *Desmond and Elizabeth are such an elegant couple!* **2** artistic, °stylish, modish, à la °mode, °chic, °fashionable, *Colloq* in, with it: *The newly refurbished rooms are very elegant.* **3** °luxurious, °sumptuous, °grand, °opulent, plush, *Colloq* °posh, swank, °swanky, ritzy, °fancy: *We stayed in a very elegant West End hotel.* **4** apt, °clever, °ingenious, °neat: *What is needed is a more elegant solution to the problem.*

element n. **1** component, constituent, °ingredient, °essential, °fundamental, °part, °unit, °piece, °segment, °feature, °factor, °detail, °particular: *Each element was carefully designed with a view to its place in the whole.* **2** °environment, °atmosphere, °situation, °locale, °territory, °sphere, °habitat, °medium, °domain: *Ordway is really in his element at a party.* **3 elements**: **a** (adverse or unfavourable) °weather, climatic conditions: *Stay here tonight—there's no need to brave the elements.* **b** °rudiments, basics, °fundamentals, °foundations, essentials, °principles: *It was she who taught me the elements of flying a helicopter.*

elemental adj. °basic, °fundamental, primal, °original, primordial, °primitive: *Elemental religion focused on worship of the sun and fertility.*

elementary adj. **1** °simple, °rudimentary, °easy, straightforward, uncomplicated, °clear, understandable, °plain: *This is an elementary mistake which most beginners make.* **2** °basic, °fundamental, °primary, °introductory, °initial, °beginning; °elemental: *She received her elementary education in France.*

elevated adj. **1** raised, upraised, uplifted, lifted (up): *Only three hands were elevated in opposition and the motion was carried.* **2** uplifted, °noble, °lofty, °high, °grand, °exalted, °dignified, °eminent, °pre-eminent, ennobled, °prominent, °notable, °illustrious, °distinguished, °imposing, °impressive, °sublime: *He has rather elevated notions of morality.* **3** °elated, °cheerful, °happy, exhilarated, °animated, °joyful, °glad: *Her elevated spirits and pleasant countenance make her a welcome guest.*

elevation n. **1** altitude, °height: *The elevation of Denver, Colorado, is one mile above sea level.* **2** °swelling, °lump, wen, eminence, °prominence; °hill, °height, °rise: *From this elevation, you can see seven counties.* *The doctor noticed a slight elevation in the skin near the eye.* **3** advancement, °promotion, uplifting, enhancement, °advance: *Since her elevation to the peerage, she has had less time for local community work.* **4** °grandeur, nobleness, loftiness, exaltation, sublimity, °distinction, °dignity, °refinement, cultivation: *The elevation of his style means that his work is not accessible to a mass readership.*

elfin adj. **1** elvish, elfish, elf-like, impish, puckish, °frolicsome, °sprightly, °arch, °playful, °mischievous, °tricky: *I suppose she has a certain elfin charm, but I don't like her.* **2** °small, °wee, °diminutive, °tiny, °little, °dainty, Lilliputian: *This is a delightful tale of elfin folk and magic birds.*

elicit v. °draw out, °call forth, °evoke, °bring out or forth, bring to °light, °extract, wring, wrest, °wrench: *They finally elicited the fact that she had been lying about his whereabouts.*

eligible adj. **1** °fit, °worthy, °qualified, °proper, °suitable, °appropriate, °fitting: *Is he an eligible candidate for the post?* **2** °single, °unmarried, unwed, °available: *He is one of the few eligible bachelors in the town.*

eliminate v. **1** °remove, °exclude, °rule out, °reject, °drop, °leave out, °omit: *Police have eliminated him from their enquiries.* **2** °take out or away, °omit, get °rid of, °dispose of, °expel, °knock out: *He was eliminated in the first heat of the 100-metre run.* **3** °erase, eradicate, expunge, °obliterate, °strike (out), °cross out or off, °cut

(out), °excise, °delete, °throw out, °edit (out), blue-pencil, °cancel: *The censors have eliminated all references to sex.* **4** °kill, °murder, assassinate, slay, °terminate, °exterminate, °dispose of, liquidate, °finish off, annihilate, °stamp out, °destroy, *Slang* °bump off, °polish off, *US* °rub out, take for a °ride, °bury, ice, °waste: *They used a sub-machine gun to eliminate the competition.*

élite n. **1** elite, °gentry, aristocracy, aristocrats, °elect, °upper °class, °nobility, °privileged °class, °blue bloods, *crème de la crème, haut monde,* jet °set, jet-setters, *US* Four Hundred, F.F.V., First Families of Virginia, *Colloq* °upper crust, beautiful people, *Brit* nobs: *The economic collapse had barely touched the wealthy élite.* —adj. °elite, aristocratic, °elect, °upper-class, °privileged, blue-blooded, °noble, °exclusive, °choice, °best, °top: *She socializes with rather an élite group of people.*

elixir n. **1** panacea, cure-all, nostrum, wonder °drug, miracle °drug, sovereign °remedy: *In the Middle Ages alchemists sought a universal cure, an elixir.* **2** °essence, °potion, °extract, tincture, °compound, °mixture: *Ophidia's Elixir was the name of a patent snake-oil medicine.* **3** °pith, °core, °kernel, °heart, °essence, °quintessence, °principle, °extract, °base, °basis, °soul: *The elixir of life is wisdom and its mystic ingredient is not knowledge but understanding.*

eloquent adj. **1** °expressive, articulate, silver-tongued, °fluent, well-spoken, °effective, °persuasive, convincing, cogent, °trenchant, °incisive, °graphic, °vivid, °striking, facile, °smooth, °glib, oratorical, °rhetorical: *He was an eloquent speaker. He rose and gave an eloquent speech.* **2** °suggestive, °meaningful, °pregnant: *His eyebrow was raised in eloquent scepticism.*

elsewhere adv. somewhere else, to another °place; in another °place, °abroad, °absent, away: *She's not in the office so I assume she's gone elsewhere. Elsewhere, winds have died down and temperatures are slowly rising.*

elude v. **1** °evade, °escape, °avoid, °dodge, °slip away from, *Colloq* °duck, give the °slip, °shake off: *The suspect has eluded the police for a year.* **2** °evade, °escape; baffle, °puzzle, °confuse, °bewilder, confound; °frustrate, °stump, °thwart: *The point of your argument eludes me.*

elusive adj. **1** °evasive, °slippery, °tricky, °shifty: *One of the world's most elusive guerrilla leaders was spotted in public yesterday.* **2** °evasive, evanescent, °fleeting, °fugitive, transitory, indefinable, elusory, °intangible, impalpable: *The notion of truth is always elusive.*

emaciated adj. emaciate, atrophied, shrivelled, °wizened, shrunken, °haggard, °gaunt, °drawn, pinched, bony, skeletal, cadaverous, withered, wasted, consumptive, phthisic, anorexic or anorectic, wasting (away), °scrawny, °skinny, °thin, °lean, °spare, undernourished, underfed, °starved, half-starved: *The inmates of the camp were so emaciated they could scarcely stand.*

emanate v. **1** °issue, °come (out), °emerge, °proceed, °flow, °ooze, exude; °radiate: *Black smoke emanated from the mouth of the idol.* **2** °radiate, °give off or out, °send out or forth, disseminate, °discharge, °put out, °emit; °exhale, °ooze, exude: *The idol's eyes emanated a blue light.*

emancipate v. °release, set °free, °liberate, enfranchise, manumit, °loose, °let °loose, °let go, disenthral, unfetter, unchain, unshackle; °deliver: *Britain emancipated the slaves almost 50 years before Lincoln's Emancipation Proclamation.*

embargo n. **1** °restraint, °block, blockage, °bar, °ban, stoppage, cessation, proscription, °prohibition, interdiction, °check, °restriction, °barrier; °hindrance, °impediment: *The government placed an embargo on the export of oil.* —v. **2** °restrain, °block, °bar, °ban, °stop, °cease, proscribe, °prohibit, interdict, °check, °restrict, °hold back, °prevent; °hinder, °impede, °retard, °hold up: *They may embargo oil shipments in case of war.*

embark v. **1** °board, go aboard; entrain; emplane *or* enplane: *We embarked and the ship sailed.* **2** Often, **embark on**: °commence, °begin, °enter (upon), °initiate, °launch, °start, °go into, °set about, °take up *or* on, °engage in, °assume, °tackle: *He will embark on the new enterprise next month.*

embarrass v. disconcert, °discomfit, chagrin, abash, °shame, °mortify, °humble, °humiliate, discountenance, discompose, °fluster, °upset, °distress, °disgrace, Colloq °show up: *He embarrassed his colleagues by his bad manners.*

embarrassed adj. **1** °ashamed, shamefaced, blushing, °disconcerted, discomfited, chagrined, abashed, shamed, mortified, humiliated, discountenanced, discomposed, flustered, distressed, red-faced, uncomfortable, °self-conscious, °sheepish, red in the face; humbled, disgraced: *She was extremely embarrassed by all the attention.* **2** in °debt, in the red, °straitened, °insolvent, Colloq °short, °hard up, °broke, Brit skint: *I'm financially embarrassed now but I'll pay you later.*

embarrassing adj. °awkward, humiliating, mortifying, shaming, °shameful, uncomfortable, discomfiting, °disconcerting, °touchy, distressing, worrying: *I had an embarrassing moment when I forgot the client's name.*

embarrassment n. **1** bashfulness, awkwardness, clumsiness, discomposure, abashment, uneasiness, °discomfort, self-consciousness, mortification, chagrin: *My embarrassment made me blush.* **2** °difficulty, °mess, °predicament, dilemma, °problem, °trouble, Colloq hot water, pickle, °fix, °scrape, °bind: *Finding them together presented me with a real embarrassment.* **3** °excess, °superfluity, super-abundance, over-abundance, *embarras de richesse, embarras de choix,* oversupply, °surplus, °profusion: *An embarrassment of options was open to me.*

embellish v. **1** °beautify, °improve, titivate *or* tittivate, °dress (up), °trick out *or* up, °enhance, °elaborate, °enrich, embroider, gild, furbish (up), garnish, °decorate, adorn, °ornament, deck, bedeck, °trim, caparison, rubricate, varnish; gild refined gold, paint the lily, Misquote gild the lily: *The saddles are embellished with silver studs.* **2** °elaborate, °exaggerate, °overdo, embroider, °enhance, °dress up: *His reports are so embellished that you cannot separate fact from fiction.*

embellishment n. **1** °decoration, ornamentation, °ornament, °elaboration, adornment, embroidery: *The basic design, which is shoddy, is unimproved by embellishment. Good pasta needs minimal embellishment.* **2** °exaggeration, enhancement, tinsel, garnish, gilding, °frill: *All the embellishments make her story totally unbelievable.*

embers n.pl. live coals; cinders, ashes; °remains, °remnants: *The dying embers of the fire symbolized her waning love for Darrin.*

embezzle v. °misappropriate, peculate, misapply, °misuse, °steal, °make off *or* away with, filch, °pilfer, purloin, Law defalcate; Colloq have one's hand in the till: *The treasurer had embezzled half a million from the company.*

embezzlement n. misappropriation, peculation, misapplication, °misuse, misusing, abstraction, °stealing, °theft, thievery, larceny, filching, purloining, pilferage, pilfering, Law defalcation: *Wanted for embezzlement, he fled to Brazil.*

embittered adj. °bitter, °resentful, °sour, soured, °caustic, acrimonious, acid, envenomed; °angry, choleric, °rancorous: *His conviction for fraud left him an embittered man.*

emblem n. badge, insigne, °symbol, °representation, °device, °seal, °crest, °token, °sign; trade °mark, logotype *or* logo: *The white knight's emblem was a pair of crossed flaming swords.*

emblematic adj. emblematical, °symbolical, °representative, representational: *The white dove is emblematic of peace.*

embodiment n. **1** incarnation, °realization, concretization, °manifestation, °expression, personification, materialization, actualization, reification, substantiation: *The golden section is the embodiment of an ancient principle of proportion.* **2** consolidation, °collection, unification, incorporation, °inclusion, integration, °combination, concentration, systematization, °organization, codification, °synthesis, °epitome: *This book is the embodiment of Arnolfo's theories of aesthetics.*

embody v. **1** concretize, °realize, °manifest, °express, °personify, °materialize, reify, actualize, externalize, incarnate: *Her feminist convictions are embodied in her lifestyle.* **2** °exemplify, °typify, °represent, °symbolize, °stand for: *Note how this painting embodies Longchamp's unique notions of form.* **3** consolidate, °collect, °unite, °unify, °incorporate, °include, °integrate, °combine, °concentrate, systematize, °organize, comprise, codify, epitomize, synthesize: *The teachings of the sect are embodied in their scriptures.*

embrace v. **1** °hug, °clasp, °grasp, °hold, enfold, °cuddle, °cleave together, Archaic °clip: *She embraced him warmly when they met again.* **2** °adopt, espouse, °take up *or* in, avail oneself of, °use, make °use of, °employ, °accept, °receive, °welcome: *They embraced Christian ideals.* **3** °include, comprise, °embody, °incorporate, °comprehend, encompass: *Their tribal territory embraces all areas south of the mountains.* —n. **4** °hug, °squeeze, °clutch, Slang °clinch: *He gave her a tender embrace and left.*

emerge v. **1** °appear, °come out, °come forth, °come up, °rise; °arise, °surface, °come into °view *or* °notice, come to °light, be °revealed, crop up, °turn out, °develop, become known, become °apparent, °transpire, °happen, evolve: *It emerged that she had bought a pistol that morning.* **2** °issue, °emanate, °come forth, °proceed: *The train emerged from the tunnel.*

emergence n. °rise, surfacing, °appearance; °development, materialization, °manifestation: *They were surprised by his emergence as leader.*

emergency n. °crisis, exigency, °danger, °predicament, °difficulty, °pinch: *In an emergency, put on lifebelts.*

emigrant n. émigré, expatriate, displaced person, DP, °refugee, boat person; colonist, °settler: *For millions of European emigrants, their first sight of the promised land was the Statue of Liberty in New York harbour.*

emigrate v. °migrate, °move, relocate, resettle; °leave, °quit, °depart, °forsake: *Her parents emigrated from Turkey and settled in Scotland.*

eminent adj. **1** °distinguished, esteemed, °exalted, respected, revered, honoured, °dignified, °notable, °noteworthy, °important, °noted, °outstanding, °prominent, °pre-eminent, °conspicuous, °superior, °great, °illustrious, °famous, °renowned, °well-known, °celebrated: *McLeod is an eminent meteorologist.* **2** °conspicuous, °outstanding, °marked: *His suggestion made eminent good sense.*

eminently adv. °very, °exceedingly, °extremely, exceptionally, remarkably, singularly, °notably, signally: *This man is eminently well suited for his job.*

emit v. °discharge, °eject, °expel, °emanate, °send out *or* forth, °pour out *or* forth, °give off *or* out, °issue, °vent, °radiate; °exhale; exude, °ooze: *The factory has been emitting toxic gases into the atmosphere.*

emotion n. °feeling, °passion, °sentiment, °sensation: *They say there is a fine line between the emotions of love and hate.*

emotional adj. **1** °passionate, °impassioned, °ardent, °enthusiastic, °heated, zealous, °heartfelt, °excited, °fervent, fervid: *She reacted in a very emotional way to the suggestions.* **2** °tense, °nervous, °excitable, highly-strung, high-strung, °temperamental, °volatile, °hotheaded, °demonstrative: *He is a very emotional person, who should not be driving a bus.* **3** °sensitive, °warm, °sentimental, °tender, °moving, °poignant, °stirring, emotive, affective, °touching: *Their meeting after 50 years was certainly emotional.* **4** °frantic, °agitated, irrational, °hysterical, °wild, ranting: *She became very emotional when the police took away her son.*

emphasis n. °importance, °stress, °significance, °prominence, °attention, °weight, °gravity, °force, °moment, °pre-eminence, °priority, underscoring, underlining, *Technical* paralipsis: *They place too much emphasis on the social aspects of school.*

emphasize v. °stress, accentuate, °accent, underscore, °point up, underline, call *or* draw °attention to, °mark, highlight, °play up, °spotlight, °feature: *The new procedures emphasize safety.*

emphatic adj. °firm, uncompromising, °determined, °decided, °resolute, dogged; °earnest, °definite, unequivocal, unambiguous, °distinct, °dogmatic, °categorical, °peremptory, °explicit, °incisive, °insistent, affirmative, °positive, °sure, °certain, unmistakable, °specific, °definitive, °direct; °forceful, °vigorous, °energetic, °assertive, °intense; °express, °pronounced, °strong: *She was emphatic about leaving then and there.*

empirical adj. empiric, experiential, °practical, observed, pragmatic, °experimental: *He has been there and has empirical knowledge of the system.*

employ v. **1** °hire, °engage, °enlist, °recruit, °enrol, °sign (up), °take on, °retain, commission: *I have employed a solicitor to look after my affairs while I am away. The company employed 120 engineers.* **2** °use, make °use of, utilize, °apply: *We plan to employ the most modern equipment.* **3** °occupy, °take (up), °engage, °involve: *He is employed with his stamp collection.*

employee n. °worker, °staff °member, wage-earner; °hand: *The employees are on strike.*

employer n. **1** °proprietor, °owner, °patron, °manager, °director, °chief, °head, *Colloq* °boss, *Brit* gaffer, governor, guv'nor, guv: *My employer comes in late every day.* **2** °company, °firm, corporation, °business, °establishment, °organization, *Colloq* °outfit: *She took her employer to court for unfair dismissal.*

employment n. **1** °occupation, °job, °trade, °work, °business, °profession, °vocation, °calling, livelihood, °pursuit, *métier*, °skill, °craft, *Colloq* °line, *Slang* °racket: *My employment for many years has been restoring antique furniture.* **2** °hire, hiring, °engagement, engaging, employing, taking on, retaining, enlistment, enlisting: *The employment of 50 people by the new firm will help the town.* **3** °use, utilization, °application, °operation, implementation: *The job involves the employment of specialized techniques.*

emptiness n. **1** voidness, hollowness, vacantness, °vacancy, vacuity, blankness, bareness, barrenness, °desolation, desertedness, vacuum, °void: *He was again alone in the vast emptiness of space. After she left, I felt a terrible emptiness.* **2** senselessness, meaninglessness, pointlessness, aimlessness, purposelessness, futility, uselessness, worthlessness, hollowness: *The emptiness of the candidate's words was apparent to all.* **3** vacuity, vacuousness, vacantness, blankness, expressionlessness, emotionlessness: *The emptiness of her facial expression told me that she hadn't understood a word.*

empty adj. **1** °void, unfilled, °hollow, °bare, °barren, °vacant, unfurnished, °unadorned, undecorated; emptied, drained, °spent, °exhausted: *That empty space on the wall needs a painting.* **2** °vacant, unoccupied, °uninhabited, untenanted: *He finally found an empty flat with two bedrooms.* **3** °deserted, °desolate, °uninhabited, °wild, °waste, °bare, °barren; forsaken: *He wandered for days on the empty moor.* **4** °trivial, °insincere, °hypocritical, °hollow, °cheap, °worthless, valueless, °meaningless, °insignificant, °insubstantial, unsatisfying, °idle: *His promises were merely words, empty words.* **5** °vacant, °blank, deadpan, expressionless, poker-faced; vacuous, fatuous, °stupid, °foolish, °inane: *He looked at me with that empty expression of his.* **6** °blank, °clean, °new, °unused, °clear: *On an empty page write your name and the date.* **7 empty of**: devoid of, lacking (in), °wanting, in °want of, °deficient in, °destitute of, without, sans: *Their hearts are empty of compassion.*
—v. **8** °clear, °remove, °take out *or* away, °put out, °cast *or* °throw out, °eject; °vacate, °evacuate; °dump, °drain, °exhaust, °pour out,

°void, °discharge, °unload: *Thieves emptied every-thing from the house. The police are emptying the building because of a bomb scare. Empty these bottles outside.*

enable *v.* **1** °qualify, °authorize, °entitle, °permit, °allow, °sanction, °approve, empower, °license, commission, °entrust, depute, °delegate, °assign, °charter, franchise: *An act was passed to enable them to build the rail-way.* **2** capacitate, °facilitate, °expedite, °help, °aid, °assist: *The grant enabled me to continue my studies.* **3** °permit, °allow, °approve, assent to, °go along with, °agree to, give the °go-ahead or green light, *Colloq* °OK or okay: *Her press pass enables her to get through police lines.*

enact *v.* **1** °pass, legislate, °ratify; ordain, °decree, °rule, °command, °order, °authorize: *The law was enacted to protect consumers.* **2** °act (out), °represent, °play, °portray, depict, °perform, °appear as: *She enacted the role of a modern Lady Macbeth.*

enchant *v.* **1** °bewitch, cast a °spell on, ensorcell or ensorcel, spellbind, °hypnotize, mesmerize, voodoo, *Brit* °magic, *US* hex, *Colloq* hoodoo: *Circe enchanted Ulysses' men and turned them into swine.* **2** °charm, °fascinate, °beguile, °captivate, enthral, °enrapture, °attract, allure, °delight, °entrance: *With her sultry looks she has enchanted the most cynical of men.*

enchanted *adj.* °pleased, °delighted, °happy, thrilled, French *enchanté(e)*: *I am enchanted to meet you at last, Mrs Thompson.*

enchanting *adj.* beguiling, bewitching, entran-cing, °spellbinding, charming, fascinating, cap-tivating, intriguing, °enthralling, alluring, °delightful, hypnotic, °attractive, appealing, winsome, °ravishing, °seductive: *Caesar found Cleopatra utterly enchanting.*

enchantment *n.* **1** witchcraft, °sorcery, °magic, wizardry, thaumaturgy, conjuration or conjury; °spell, °charm, °jinx, *US* hex: *Stories of enchant-ment and magic fail to interest today's sceptical five-year-old. When she worked her enchantment on me, I succumbed completely.* **2** °charm, beguile-ment, allure, °fascination, °rapture, mes-merism, °bliss: *She was completely carried away by the enchantment of the moment.*

encircle *v.* °surround, gird, °circle, °enclose, °ring, encompass, compass, confine, hem or °hold in; wreathe: *When the horde encircled the castle we thought we were doomed.*

enclose *v.* **1** inclose, confine, °shut in, °close or hem in, °surround, °pen, °encircle, encom-pass, °bound, °envelop, hedge in, °wall in, immure, °fence in or off, *US and Canadian* corral: *A high wall encloses the garden.* **2** °insert, °include, °contain; °wrap: *The cheque was enclosed in the same envelope.*

enclosure *n.* **1** °fold, °pen, cote, °run, sty, yard, farmyard, barnyard, courtyard, quadrangle or quad, °square, °compound, *Brit* °close, *US and Canadian* corral: *We had trouble keeping the dogs in the enclosure.* **2** °fence, °wall, °rail, railing, °barrier, hedge, barricade, °boundary: *The build-ings serve as an enclosure.*

encounter *v.* **1** °meet, °come upon, °run into or across, °happen upon, °chance upon, °hit upon, °light upon, °stumble upon, *Colloq* °bump into: *She encountered him again in the supermarket.* **2** °face, °experience, °meet with,

contend with, be °faced with, come into °contact with, °wrestle with: *She encounters such problems every day.* **3** come into °conflict with, contend with, assail, cross swords (with), °grapple with, °engage, joust with, do °battle with, confront, °clash with, °join, °meet: *The ballad tells how he encountered the black knight in single combat.*

—*n.* **4** °meeting: *It was a chance encounter that brought us together.* **5** confrontation, °brush, °quarrel, °disagreement, °dispute, altercation, °engagement, °action, °battle, °fight, °clash, °conflict, °skirmish, °contest, °competition, duel, contention, °struggle, °war, *Colloq* dust-up, °scrap, °run-in, set-to: *My uncle took part in the bloody encounter in the Ardennes.*

encourage *v.* **1** hearten, embolden, °reassure, °buoy (up), °stimulate, °animate, °support, inspirit, °inspire, °cheer (up), °urge or °spur on or onward(s), °incite, *Colloq* egg on, °pep up: *She encouraged him in his study of medicine.* **2** °promote, °advance, °aid, °support, °help, °assist, °abet, °foster, °forward, °boost, *Colloq* give a °shot in the arm: *The continued success of the team encouraged attendance at the games.*

encouragement *n.* **1** heartening, reassuring, reassurance, buoying up, °stimulating, stimu-lation, stimulus, animating, °animation, sup-porting, °support, promoting, °promotion, inspiring, °inspiration, cheering, urging, °spur, spurring, exhorting, exhortation, prodding, urging, innervation, inciting, °incitement: *With-out her encouragement, I could never have won.* **2** °boost, stimulus, °help, °aid, °support, *Colloq* °pep talk: *The team gets a lot of encour-agement from local merchants.*

encroach *v.* Often, **encroach on** or **upon**: °intrude, trespass, °infringe, invade, make inroads: *When you mention arctophily, you're encroaching on my territory.*

encumber *v.* **1** °burden, °weigh down, °load (up or down), °overload, overburden, °strain, °oppress, saddle, °tax, overtax: *Encumbered with intolerable taxes, the people revolted. She almost drowned because she was encumbered with her numer-ous petticoats.* **2** °hamper, °impede, °hinder, °handicap, °inconvenience, °trammel, °retard, °slow down: *Though encumbered by an invalid husband, she managed to qualify as a barrister.*

encumbrance *n.* °weight, °burden, onus, cross (to bear), albatross, millstone, °handicap, °impediment, °hindrance, °obstacle, °obstruction, °liability, °disadvantage, °drag: *The children were regarded merely as an encumbrance.*

encyclopedic *adj.* encyclopaedic, °comprehensive, °inclusive, °broad, °extensive, °universal, °thorough, °exhaustive, wide-ranging, °complete: *She has an encyclopedic knowledge of Chinese art.*

end *n.* **1** °extremity, °extreme, °extent, °bound, °boundary, °tip, °limit, terminus: *That fence marks the southern end of the property. At the end of the garden was a large shed.* **2** °close, °termination, conclusion, cessation, °expiration, °finish, °completion, finale, ending, wind-up; denoue-ment or dénouement: *At the end of the film, the lights came on.* **3** °aim, °purpose, °intention, °intent, °objective, °object, °goal, °point, °reason, *raison d'être*, °destination, °motive, motivation, °aspiration: *To what end does she per-sist so vehemently?* **4** consequence, °result,

°outcome, °effect, °upshot: *The end of the affair was that he had to leave town.* **5** °destruction, °death, °ruin, extermination, annihilation, °termination, conclusion: *That would spell the end to all life on earth.* **6 at a loose end** or *US and Canadian* **at loose ends**: °unsettled, unoccupied, °unemployed, uncommitted, undecided, °indecisive, ambivalent, vacillating, °purposeless, °aimless, adrift, drifting, betwixt and between, neither here nor there: *My wife has gone off to visit her mother and I'm at a loose end.* **7 on end: a** °upright, °erect, °standing: *He can balance a ruler on end.* **b** continuously, uninterruptedly, unceasingly, incessantly, consecutively: *It rained for days on end.* **8 the end: a** the worst, the °last straw, the °final blow, *Colloq* the °limit, too much: *Brian's winning first prize is the absolute end.* **b** the °best, the greatest: *That disc by The What is the living end.*
—*v.* **9** °terminate, conclude, bring to an end, °stop, °halt, °cease, °wind up or down, °settle, put an end to, °discontinue, °break off, °cut off, °close, °finish, culminate, end up, *Brit* put paid to; °die (out), °expire, °climax, peter out, vanish: *We have ended our relationship. The book ends with her returning to him. The year ends on December 31st.* **10** °kill, put to °death, annihilate, °exterminate, °terminate, °extinguish; °destroy, °ruin: *He ended his life last night with a bullet.* **11** °surpass, °outdo, outclass, outshine, °outstrip, °supersede: *It is a disaster film to end all disaster films.*

endanger *v.* imperil, °threaten, °jeopardize, °risk, put at °risk, °hazard, expose (to °danger), put in °jeopardy, tempt fate: *She endangered her life while trying to save him.*

endangered *adj.* imperilled, threatened, near extinction: *Every effort must be made to protect endangered species.*

endearing *adj.* °attractive, °engaging, °likeable, appealing, winsome, captivating, °winning: *He has a few endearing qualities, I suppose.*

endeavour *v.* **1** °try, °attempt, °strive, make an °effort, do one's °best, °struggle, °exert oneself, °undertake; °aim, °aspire; *Colloq* take a °stab at, have a °go or crack or whack or °shot at: *For years he's endeavoured to see her.* —*n.* °effort, pains, °attempt, °try, striving, °struggle, °venture, °enterprise, *Colloq* °stab, crack, whack, °shot: *Her endeavours to be published have come to naught.*

endless *adj.* **1** °limitless, °unlimited, °boundless, unbounded, °infinite, °immeasurable, °eternal, unending: *They found themselves in the endless reaches of outer space.* **2** ceaseless, uninterrupted, incessant, unceasing, unending, °constant, °perpetual, interminable, unremitting, °non-stop, °continuous, °continual, °everlasting: *I wish you two would stop your endless bickering.*

endorse *v.* **1** indorse, °approve, °sanction, °authorize, °advocate, °support, °back, °subscribe to, °sustain, °confirm, countenance, put one's °stamp or °seal (of °approval) on, set one's °seal (of °approval) to, give (something) one's °imprimatur, *Colloq* °OK, okay: *The council endorsed our application for planning permission.* **2** indorse, countersign: *Endorse the cheque to cash it.*

endorsement *n.* **1** indorsement, °approval, affirmation, °sanction, authorization, confirmation, ratification, °support, °backing, approbation, °seal or °stamp of °approval, imprimatur, *Colloq* °OK, okay: *He is acting with the full endorsement of his union.* **2** counter-signature: *His endorsement is on the back of the cheque.*

endowment *n.* **1** °grant, (°financial) °aid, °subsidy, subvention, °allowance, °allotment, contribution, °donation, °gift, °present, °award; °bequest, °inheritance, dowry: *The endowment was enough to support me for a year.* **2** °gift, °presentation, bestowal, °award, awarding, °settlement: *The endowment of the grant was approved by the college.* **3 endowments**: °qualities, talents, °gifts, °abilities, °aptitudes, °capabilities, °capacities, °qualifications, °strengths; °attributes, °properties, °characteristics: *She is a woman of considerable endowments.*

endurance *n.* **1** °stamina, staying °power, °perseverance, °persistence, °resolution, °fortitude, °tenacity, °patience, °tolerance, *Colloq US* stick-to-it-iveness: *He showed remarkable endurance in the pentathlon trials.* **2** °lasting quality, durability, longevity, lifetime, continuation: *In this film, he uses the river as a symbol of endurance and timelessness.*

endure *v.* **1** °last, °persist, °stay, °remain, °abide, °prevail, °survive, °continue, °hold, °live (on), *Colloq* go the distance: *Her fame as a poet will endure.* **2** °stand, °abide, °tolerate, °face, °survive, °withstand, °bear, °weather, °take (it), °suffer, °stomach, °undergo, °hold out (against), *Colloq* °hang in (there), °stick or °sweat (it or something) out: *He endured the pressure of his job as long as he could.* **3** °suffer, °undergo, °bear, °face, °stand, °put up with, °stomach, °take: *Consider the tyranny that Europe endured under Hitler.*

enduring *adj.* °lasting, long-lasting, °durable, °abiding, continuing, long-standing, persisting, °persistent, °remaining, °steady, °steadfast; °eternal, °immortal, °permanent: *Their enduring faith carried them through the ordeal.*

enemy *n.* foe, °antagonist, °adversary, °opponent, °rival, °competitor, °contestant, contender; the °opposition, the other side: *His enemies were running a smear campaign against him.*

energetic *adj.* °lively, °active, °vigorous, invigorated, °dynamic, °animated, °spirited, °untiring, °tireless, indefatigable, °sprightly, spry, °vital, high-powered, °brisk, vibrant, zesty, zestful, *Colloq* °hot, peppy, full of °pep, full of get-up-and-go, zippy, on one's toes, zingy, full of beans: *I feel most energetic at the start of the day.*

energize *v.* °enliven, °liven up, °stimulate, °animate, invigorate, °activate, actuate, °move, °motivate, galvanize, °electrify, °inspire, inspirit, °pep up, waken, °rouse, °stir, arouse, °excite, egg on, °urge: *Max's enthusiasm energized the whole of the research team.*

energy *n.* °vitality, forcefulness, vivacity, liveliness, °vigour, °animation, °spirit, °force, °dynamism, °drive, °verve, °dash, élan, °intensity, °power, °determination, puissance, °strength, °might, *Colloq* °pep, vim and °vigour,

US stick-to-it-iveness, get-up-and-go, zip, zing: *At seventy, she just couldn't put as much energy into her performance as she once did.*

enervate v. °weaken, °tire, °strain, enfeeble, debilitate, °fatigue, °exhaust, °drain, °sap, °wear out, devitalize, °break, °defeat: *I have always found the tropics quite enervating.*

enforce v. 1 °insist upon *or* on, °stress, °require, °impose, °support, put into °effect, °apply, °administer, °carry out, °inflict, bring to bear, °implement, °prosecute, °discharge; °reinforce; *Colloq* °crack *or* °clamp down: *The police will enforce the curfew tonight.* 2 °force, compel, °pressure *or Brit* pressurize, °press, coerce, lay °stress upon *or* on, °impose upon *or* on, °impress upon *or* on, °insist upon *or* on, °demand, °require; °intimidate, °browbeat, °bully, °railroad; *Colloq* °lean on, °twist (someone's) arm: *They hired thugs to enforce their claim.*

engage v. 1 °employ, °hire, °enrol *or US also* enroll, °enlist, °retain, °sign (up), °contract with *or* for, indenture; °rent, °book, °reserve, °secure, bespeak: *She was engaged on a part-time basis. We engaged rooms for the night.* 2 °occupy, engross, °busy, absorb, °involve, °tie up, preoccupy, °employ: *This task will engage all available resources until the end of next month.* 3 °pledge, °undertake, °bargain, °agree, covenant, °promise, °guarantee, °contract: *I engaged to complete the work by Tuesday.* 4 °attract, °hold, °capture, catch, °draw: *The museum has many exhibits that will engage the interest of children.* 5 °join (in) °combat *or* °battle with, °meet, °encounter, °fight, °combat, °attack, °battle, °clash with, °grapple with: *The enemy was engaged at dawn.* 6 **engage in**: °participate (in), °partake in, take °part (in), °enter (into), °undertake, °embark on: *She engages in many out-of-school activities.*

engaged adj. 1 betrothed, affianced, plighted, pledged, promised; °spoken for: *They got engaged on St Valentine's Day.* 2 °busy, occupied, tied up, °involved, employed, °absorbed, °preoccupied, wrapped up: *He is otherwise engaged and cannot meet me today.*

engagement n. 1 °appointment, °meeting, °date, rendezvous, °arrangement, commitment: *I'm sorry, I have a previous engagement.* 2 betrothal: *Their engagement was announced in all the papers.* 3 °agreement, °bargain, °obligation, °promise, °pledge, covenant, °contract: *The company undertook an engagement to provide the steel.* 4 °job, °position, °post, commission, booking; °employment, °work; *Colloq* °spot, *Slang (of a musician)* gig: *He has an engagement with the newspaper.* 5 °fight, °battle, °conflict, °encounter, °combat: *The naval engagement lasted three days and nights.*

engaging adj. charming, °pleasant, °attractive, winsome, °winning, appealing, °agreeable, °delightful, °pleasing, °likeable, °friendly, °open: *With her engaging personality, it is no wonder she has so many friends.*

engine n. motor, °machine, °mechanism, appliance, °apparatus; locomotive: *The invention of the internal combustion engine revolutionized modern transport.*

engineer n. 1 °designer, originator, inventor, contriver, architect, planner, °mastermind: *The engineer of this scheme was one David Jones.* 2 (°engine-) driver, conductor, °operator: *He was*

the engineer on the afternoon train out of Washington. 3 mechanic, technician, repairman: *The telephone engineers will be here on Monday to install a new phone system.* —v. 4 °devise, °plan, °develop, °originate, contrive, °invent, °mastermind, °construct, °build, °make: *It is said that Daedalus engineered the first man-made wings.* 5 °manipulate, °scheme, °plot, machinate, °intrigue, connive, conspire, °manoeuvre, °rig, °set up, °organize, °arrange, °put over, *Colloq* finagle, °wangle, °swing: *She tried to engineer the laundering of the money, but was caught.*

engrave v. 1 °cut, °carve, °chisel, inscribe; °etch: *The ring was a plain gold band, engraved with daisies.* 2 °impress, °stamp, °set, °lodge, °fix, embed, imprint, ingrain: *The horror of that night was forever engraved in his mind.*

engraving n. 1 intaglio, cameo, etching, dry-point, woodcut, linocut, wood *or* steel engraving, anaglyph, °block *or US also* °cut: *She uses a burin to make these engravings.* 2 °print, °impression, etching, dry-point: *The exhibition of Dürer engravings closes tomorrow.*

enhance v. °improve, °better, augment, °boost, °raise, elevate, °lift, °heighten, °exalt, °enlarge, °swell, °magnify, °increase, °add to, °amplify, °intensify, °enrich, °embellish, °complement, °reinforce, °strengthen: *His public image was greatly enhanced by his support of charities.*

enigma n. °puzzle, conundrum, °mystery, °riddle, poser, °problem: *How he escaped is an enigma to the police.*

enjoy v. 1 °delight in, °appreciate, °like, take *or* derive °pleasure *or* °satisfaction in *or* from, °relish (in), °fancy, °take to, *Slang* °dig, get a °kick *or* °lift *or* °charge out of, get °high on, °get off on: *Bernard really enjoys Wagner.* 2 °benefit *or* °profit from, take °advantage of, °use, utilize, make °use of, °use to advantage, °have, °possess: *He cannot be charged because he enjoys diplomatic immunity.* 3 **enjoy oneself**: have a good time, make °merry, *Colloq* have a ball *or* the time of one's life: *I enjoyed myself at your party.*

enjoyment n. 1 °pleasure, °delight, °joy, °gratification, °satisfaction, °relish, °zest, °delectation, °recreation, °entertainment, °diversion, °amusement: *The public has derived much enjoyment from Shaw's plays.* 2 °use, utilization, °exercise, °possession; °benefit, °advantage: *As a member, you are entitled to the enjoyment of all club privileges.*

enlarge v. 1 °increase, °expand, °magnify, °amplify, °extend, °swell, dilate, °spread, wax, °widen, broaden, °lengthen, elongate, °stretch, distend; °add to, °supplement, augment; °inflate; *Colloq* °blow up: *The government will enlarge the area devoted to public parks. Enlarge the photographs and details appear.* 2 **enlarge on** *or* **upon**: °expand on, expatiate on, °amplify, expound; °detail, °elaborate (on): *The speaker was asked to enlarge on her plans for building new hospitals.*

enlighten v. °inform, edify, °instruct, °teach, °tutor, °educate, °coach, apprise, make °aware, °advise, °counsel: *You must enlighten George on how to behave in public.*

enlightened adj. °well-informed, °informed, °educated, °aware, °knowledgeable, literate, °rational, °reasonable, °sensible, common-sense, commonsensical, broad-minded, open-minded, °liberal; °cultivated, civilized, °sophisticated, *Colloq* in the know: *In a democracy, the press serves an enlightened public.*

enlist v. **1** °enrol, °register, °join (up), volunteer, °sign up or on; °engage, °recruit, °induct, °muster, conscript, °impress, °call up, *US* °draft: *He enlisted in the navy at 17.* **2** °employ, °hire, °engage, °retain, make °available, °secure, °obtain, °get, °procure, °gather, drum up, °mobilize, *Colloq* °organize: *We must enlist all the help we can.*

enliven v. **1** invigorate, inspirit, °animate, °pep up, °stimulate, °energize, vivify, °vitalize, °quicken, exhilarate, arouse, °rouse, awaken, °wake up, °spark (off), °kindle, enkindle, °fire (up), °inspire: *Enlivened by the coach's talk, we were determined to win.* **2** °brighten, °cheer (up), °buoy (up), °gladden, uplift: *The room was considerably enlivened by the new curtains.*

enormity n. outrageousness, °outrage, atrociousness, °atrocity, wickedness, heinousness, flagitiousness, horribleness, °horror, °barbarity, savagery, monstrousness, horridness, °evil, viciousness: *The enormity of the crime shocked us all.*

enormous adj. °huge, °immense, °gigantic, elephantine, gargantuan, mammoth, titanic, °colossal, tremendous, °vast, °massive, stupendous, Brobdingnagian, °gross, °monstrous, °prodigious: *An enormous dragon blocked their way out of the cave.*

enormousness n. immensity, hugeness: *I was staggered by the sheer enormousness of the building.*

enough adj. **1** °sufficient, °adequate, °ample: *There isn't enough food to go round.*
—n. **2** sufficiency, adequacy, °ample °supply, °plenty: *I have enough for myself.*
—adv. **3** sufficiently, adequately, reasonably, satisfactorily, tolerably, passably: *Your word is good enough for me.*

enquire v. **1** °inquire, °ask, °question, °query: *The police enquired whether we had noticed any strange goings-on next door.* **2** See **inquire**, below.

enrage v. °anger, °infuriate, °madden, incense, °provoke, °inflame, make (someone's) blood boil, *Colloq* get (someone's) back or Irish or hackles or dander up, make (someone) see red, wave a red flag before (someone), *US* burn (someone) up, *Slang Brit* put (someone's) monkey up, *US* tick (someone) off, tee (someone) off, *Taboo slang US* piss (someone) off: *Lord Thimble was enraged at being made to wait his turn.*

enrapture v. °enchant, °entrance, °transport, °thrill, °bewitch, spellbind, °fascinate, °charm, enthral, °captivate, °beguile, °delight: *The soprano quite enraptured her audience.*

enrich v. **1** endow, °enhance, °improve, upgrade, °better, ameliorate, °refine, °add to: *His novels have enriched our literature.* **2** °ornament, adorn, °decorate, °embellish, °beautify, °grace: *Before us rose a lofty dome enriched with precious stones.*

enrol v. **1** °enlist, °register, °sign up or on (for), °join; volunteer; °recruit, *Colloq* °join up: *He enrolled at the university.* **2** °record, °register, °chronicle, °put down, °list, °note, inscribe, catalogue: *Their names will be enrolled forever in the Book of Heroes.*

ensemble n. **1** °outfit, °costume, clothing, °clothes, attire, °apparel, garb, °garments, coordinates, *Colloq* °get-up: *A black hat, gloves, and shoes completed the ensemble.* **2** °band, °combination, orchestra, °group; chorus, choir; *Colloq* combo: *A new chamber music ensemble is performing tonight at the town hall.* **3** assemblage, composite, aggregate, °collection, °set, °whole, °entirety, °totality; agglomeration, conglomeration: *A strange ensemble of objects was on display.*

enslave v. °subjugate, yoke, fetter, enchain, °shackle, °trammel, °dominate; °bind, indenture, *Archaic* enthral: *The enslaved masses rose and overcame their masters.*

ensure v. **1** insure, °assure, make °sure or °certain, °confirm, °certify, °guarantee; °secure, °effect: *He must ensure that there is no leak.* **2** insure, °protect, make °safe, °safeguard, °guard, °secure: *The captain is responsible for ensuring the safety of the passengers.*

entail v. °involve, °require, °call for, necessitate, °demand, °occasion, give °rise to, °impose; °lead to, °cause: *The post has entailed working an average 60-70 hours a week.*

entangle v. **1** °tangle, ensnarl, °snarl, enmesh, catch (up), entrap, °snag, °foul, °implicate, °knot (up), °twist; °impede; °involve, embroil: *The propeller became entangled in the seaweed so that the boat couldn't move.* **2** °confuse, °mix (up), °twist, °snarl, ensnarl, ensnare, °hamper, °complicate, confound, °bewilder, °perplex, °embarrass: *He became entangled in a web of social and business liaisons.*

enter v. **1** °go or °come (in or into), °pass (into): *Please enter at the left.* **2** °penetrate, °pierce, °stick (into), °stab (into), °puncture; invade, infiltrate: *The nail entered the tyre here. The iron entered into his soul.* **3** °insert, inscribe, °write, °set or °write or °put down, °note, °record, °take or °jot down, °register; log, °document, °minute: *Enter your name on the dotted line.* **4** enter on or upon, °begin, °start, °commence, °undertake, °set out on, °take up: *I didn't want to enter the marathon if I couldn't finish.* **5** °enrol, °enlist, °sign on or up, °join, become a member of: *He has entered the ranks of the unemployed.* **6** °present, °offer, proffer, °tender, °submit: *More than 100 poems were entered in the competition.* **7** °file, °register, °record, °submit: *The defendant entered a plea of 'Not guilty'.* **8** **enter into**: °engage or °participate in, °sign, be (a) party to, co-sign, countersign: *We entered into an agreement to buy the house.*

enterprise n. **1** °undertaking, °project, °venture, °adventure, °effort, °programme, °plan, °scheme: *His latest enterprise involves establishing a chain of pizza shops.* **2** boldness, °daring, °courage, mettle, adventurousness, audacity, °enthusiasm, zeal, °energy, °spirit, °drive, °vigour, °ambition, °initiative, °push, °eagerness, °determination, °resolve, purposefulness, °purpose; aggressiveness; *Colloq* get-up-and-go, zip, °pep, °gumption, °guts, *US* starch: *It takes a lot of enterprise to start your own business.* **3** °business, °operation, °firm, °company, °concern, °establishment: *We began this enterprise on a shoestring.*

enterprising adj. °resourceful, °venturesome, °adventurous, °daring, °courageous, °bold, °brave, mettlesome, °audacious, °enthusiastic,

°eager, °keen, zealous, °energetic, °spirited, °vigorous, °ambitious, °determined, resolved, °resolute, °earnest, °purposeful, purposive, goal-oriented; °aggressive, hard-working, indefatigable, °tireless, °diligent, assiduous, °industrious, persevering; *Colloq* °pushy, °go-ahead: *She is an enterprising young lawyer with her own practice.*

entertain v. **1** °amuse, °divert; °delight, °please; °occupy: *While we waited the boy entertained us with his juggling.* **2** °receive, °accommodate, °treat, be °host (to), °cater (for *or* to); have *or* see people *or* guests *or* visitors *or* company; *Colloq* °host: *We entertain on Tuesdays only.* **3** °contemplate, °consider, °have, °hold, °harbour, °foster, °tolerate, °allow, °maintain, °sustain, °support: *They felt that they could not entertain the idea of their daughter marrying the gardener's son.*

entertaining adj. amusing, diverting, °delightful, enjoyable, °pleasant, °fun, °pleasing, °pleasurable, °interesting, °engaging; °funny, °comic, °humorous, °witty: *We find Laurel and Hardy films entertaining.*

entertainment n. **1** °amusement, °diversion, °distraction, °pastime, °recreation, °sport, °play, °fun, °pleasure, °enjoyment, °relaxation, °relief: *What do you do for entertainment?* **2** °performance, °presentation, °diversion, °amusement, divertissement, °exhibition, °pageant, °spectacle, °show, °production, spectacular, °extravaganza: *They put on a lavish entertainment for the queen.*

enthralling adj. captivating, entrancing, °spellbinding, °enchanting, bewitching, beguiling, fascinating, gripping, °absorbing, intriguing, hypnotizing, mesmerizing, °riveting: *There was an enthralling melodrama on TV last night.*

enthusiasm n. **1** °eagerness, keenness, earnestness, °fervour, avidity, zeal, °excitement, °passion, °ardour, °interest, °relish, °devotion, devotedness, °gusto, °exuberance, °zest; °fanaticism, °mania, °rage: *No one matches her enthusiasm for grand opera.* **2** °rage, °passion, °craze; °hobby, °interest, °pastime, °diversion, °amusement; *Colloq* °fad: *His current enthusiasm is acid rock.*

enthusiast n. °fan, °devotee, aficionado, °lover, °admirer, °zealot, °addict, °fanatic, promoter, °supporter, °champion, °follower, °disciple, adherent, *US* booster, *Colloq* teeny-bopper, °bug, °hound, buff, °fiend, *Slang* nut, °freak, groupie, *US* °head: *They are model railway enthusiasts.*

enthusiastic adj. °eager, °keen, °fervent, fervid, °hearty, °ardent, avid, °energetic, vigorous, °devoted, °earnest, °passionate, °spirited, °exuberant, zealous, °fanatic(al), °unqualified, unstinting, °irrepressible: *He's an enthusiastic supporter of the prime minister's policies.*

entice v. °lure, allure, °tempt, °attract, °draw, °seduce, °coax, °persuade, °prevail (up)on, °beguile, °cajole, blandish, °wheedle, °decoy, °lead on, inveigle, *Colloq* sweet-talk, soft-soap, *Slang* suck in: *The prospectus enticed 3.15 million people to buy shares in the company.*

enticement n. **1** °temptation, allurement, beguilement, seduction, °cajolery, wheedling, blandishment, coaxing, °persuasion: *Do you approve of the system of enticement used to get you to buy time-share holidays?* **2** °lure, bait, °decoy,

°trap, °inducement, °attraction, °temptation, *Colloq* °come-on, soft soap: *Among the enticements offered was a free weekend in Paris.*

entire adj. **1** °complete, °whole, °total, °full, °undivided, °absolute, °thorough, unreserved, unrestricted, undiminished, unconditional, °express, unexceptional, unmixed, unalloyed: *That problem has occupied my entire attention all week.* **2** °intact, °whole, °sound, unbroken, undamaged, unimpaired, inviolate, without a scratch, °unscathed, in °one piece: *Twelve amphorae were recovered entire from the wreck.* **3** °continuous, °full, °whole, °complete, uninterrupted: *She has lasted an entire year in her new job.*

entirely adv. **1** °completely, °wholly, °altogether, fully, °totally, °utterly, unreservedly, unqualifiedly, unexceptionally, in every respect, in all respects, °thoroughly, to a T, *in toto*, exhaustively, all out, from head to toe *or* foot, (right) down to the ground, from A to Z, lock, stock and barrel, root and branch, without exception *or* reservation: *She was entirely satisfied. I agree with that entirely.* **2** solely, exclusively, °only, unambiguously, unequivocally; °positively, °definitely, °clearly: *It was entirely my fault.*

entirety n. **1** completeness, °unity, °totality, wholeness, fullness, °integrity, °perfection: *Any chance of completing his mission in its entirety had vanished.* **2** °whole, °sum °total, °everything, all: *The entirety of the bequest amounted to a million francs.*

entitle v. **1** °allow, °permit, °qualify, make °eligible, °authorize, °fit; enfranchise, °license, empower: *This document entitles her to half of the estate.* **2** °name, °title, °call, °label, °nickname, dub, °designate, °term; °christen, baptize: *His first novel was entitled Out of the Depths.*

entity n. **1** °thing, °object, being, °existence, °quantity, article, °individual, °organism: *The emergence of the youth movement as a separate entity posed problems for the party leadership.* **2** °essence, °real °nature, quiddity, °quintessence, *Metaphysics* ens: *Every living creature has a distinct entity.*

entrance[1] n. **1** (right of) °entry, access, °admission, °admittance, entrée, introduction: *You need security clearance to gain entrance.* **2** °entry, entry-way, access, door, °gate, °passage, °way (in); ingress: *The entrance is locked after midnight.* **3** °arrival, °appearance; coming, °entry, coming *or* °going in: *Her entrances were accompanied by cheers. He opposed our entrance into the war.* **4** °beginning, °start, commencement: *Today marks his entrance into his new duties.*

entrance[2] v. °enchant, °enrapture, °fascinate, °bewitch, spellbind, °transport, °delight, °charm, °captivate, enthral, °overpower, mesmerize, °hypnotize: *He was entranced by her beauty.*

entrenched adj. °rooted, deep-rooted, embedded, °fixed, (firmly) planted, established, °set, deep-seated, unshakeable *or* unshakable, ineradicable, °ingrained: *We were unable to combat their entrenched opposition to the proposals.*

entrust v. intrust, °trust, °charge, °assign, °delegate, confide: *I entrusted her with my secret.*

entry n. **1** access, °entrance, entrée, °admittance, °admission: *The burglar gained entry through the skylight.* **2** access, °entrance, entry-way, door,

inlet, °passage, °way in: *Both entries were
blocked.* **3** °entrance, °arrival, coming or °going
in: *His entry was met with jeers.* **4** °record, °item,
°memorandum, °note, °account, listing; registration; *Colloq* memo: *There is no entry in his
diary for the 15th of April.* **5** °competitor,
°contestant, °player, entrant, °participant,
°candidate; °rival, °adversary, °opponent: *Dennis
was a late entry in the marathon.*

entwine *v.* intwine, interlace, °braid, interweave, intertwine, °weave, °knit, plait, °twist,
°coil, °twine, °splice; °entangle, °tangle: *Her hair
was entwined with wild flowers.*

enumerate *v.* **1** °list, °name, °itemize, °specify,
°detail, °spell out, catalogue, tick off, take °stock
of, cite, °quote, °recite, °recount, °relate, narrate, *US* °check off: *I shall enumerate the reasons
why you may not go.* **2** °count, °calculate,
°compute, °reckon, °tally, °add, °number: *The
researcher could enumerate only seven different species.*

enunciate *v.* **1** articulate, °pronounce, utter,
°voice, °say, °speak, vocalize, °express, °deliver,
°present, *Formal* enounce: *Foreign names should
be enunciated clearly.* **2** °state, °proclaim, °declare,
promulgate, °announce, °broadcast,
°pronounce, °propound: *The party platform was
enunciated in last night's speech.*

envelop *v.* **1** °wrap, °enclose, enfold, enwrap,
°cover, engulf, °swathe, °shroud, enshroud,
swaddle: *The body was enveloped in a white
robe.* **2** °shroud, enshroud, °cover, °conceal,
°hide, °screen, °shield, °obscure, °veil, °cloak:
*The motive for the murder was enveloped in a mass
of misleading clues.*

enviable *adj.* °desirable, wanted, desired,
sought-after, covetable, in °demand: *He is in an
enviable financial position.*

envious *adj.* °jealous, covetous, °resentful,
begrudging, green-eyed, green (with °envy),
°desirous: *He is envious of his wife because she has
a better job.*

environment *n.* surroundings, environs,
°atmosphere, ecosystem, conditions, °habitat,
circumstances, °medium, °milieu; °territory,
°locale, °setting, *mise en scène*, °situation: *Car
exhaust fumes are ruining our environment.*

environmentalist *n.* ecologist, conservationist,
naturalist, preservationist, nature-lover, °green
or Green: *We have environmentalists to thank for
clean-air laws.*

envisage *v.* **1** visualize, °contemplate,
°imagine, °picture, °conceive (of), °fancy,
°think *or* °dream *or* conjure up, *Chiefly US*
°envision: *Envisage a city built entirely of
glass.* **2** °foresee, °see, °predict, °forecast,
°anticipate: *I envisage a time when all people will
be free.*

envision *v.* °envisage, visualize, °imagine,
°conceive of, °foresee, °anticipate, °predict,
°forecast, °prophesy: *I envision great success for
you.*

envoy *n.* °delegate, legate, °ambassador, diplomat, °minister, (papal) nuncio, attaché;
°representative, emissary, °agent; *Formal* envoy
extraordinary, °minister plenipotentiary: *The
government sent an envoy to discuss trade.*

envy *n.* **1** jealousy, enviousness, °resentment:
*She was consumed with envy of anyone who had
more money than she did.* **2** covetousness, °desire,
°longing: *Success excites my envy.*

—*v.* **3** covet, °begrudge, °resent: *He envies his
brother and his new car.*

epicure *n.* °gourmet, connoisseur, °aesthete,
°epicurean, °sybarite, hedonist, gastronome,
bon viveur, bon vivant, Lucullus; gourmand: *An
epicure, he refuses to eat any food not prepared by
his own chef.*

epicurean *adj.* **1** °sensual, sybaritic, °luxurious,
°voluptuous, °carnal, °self-indulgent,
pleasure-seeking, pleasure-oriented, hedonistic,
°gluttonous, intemperate, overindulgent,
crapulent *or* crapulous, swinish, porcine, piggish, °immoderate, orgiastic, libidinous, °wild,
unrestrained, unconfined, °dissolute, dissipated, Bacchanalian, Saturnalian: *The king's epicurean lifestyle contrasted with that of his starving
subjects.* **2** Lucullan, °gourmet: *That was truly an
epicurean repast.*
—*n.* **3** °epicure: *It was a meal that would have won
the approval of the greatest epicureans.*

epidemic *adj.* **1** widespread, °universal,
°prevalent, °prevailing, °rampant, °general,
wide-ranging, pandemic: *The disease has reached
epidemic proportions.*
—*n.* **2** °plague, °pestilence, °scourge, °rash,
°growth, upsurge, outbreak, °spread: *An epidemic of anthrax has affected the cattle.*

epigram *n.* **1** °witticism, bon mot, °quip, mot,
turn of °phrase, *jeu d'esprit*, Atticism; °pun,
°double entendre, *jeu de mots*, °play on words,
equivoque; paronomasia: *His epigram char-
acterizing Eskimos as 'God's frozen people' was widely
quoted.* **2** °proverb, aphorism, °maxim, °saw,
saying, adage, apophthegm *or* apothegm: *'Nothing succeeds like success' is his favourite epigram.*

epigrammatic *adj.* pithy, °terse, laconic,
°concise, °succinct, compendious, piquant,
°pungent, °trenchant, sententious, °witty,
°pointed, °proverbial, aphoristic, apophthegmatic *or* apothegmatic, *Colloq* °snappy,
punchy: *Oscar Wilde is known for his epigrammatic
sayings.*

episode *n.* **1** °event, °incident, °occurrence,
°happening, °experience, °adventure, °affair,
°matter: *Please do not remind me of the episode with
the chicken.* **2** chapter, °scene, instalment, °part:
*Don't miss tonight's episode of your favourite soap
opera.*

epitome *n.* **1** °essence, °quintessence,
°embodiment, personification, archetype,
exemplar, (°typical) °example, °model,
°prototype: *My secretary is the epitome of
laziness.* **2** °summary, °abstract, condensation,
°synopsis, °digest, compendium,
°abridgement, °abbreviation, conspectus,
résumé, contraction; °outline, °précis, syllabus:
*The chairman wants an epitome of the report by
lunch-time.*

equable *adj.* **1** even-tempered, °easygoing,
°serene, °calm, placid, composed, °cool, imperturbable, °collected, unruffled, °tranquil,
°peaceful, °level-headed, *Colloq* unflappable:
*With his equable temperament, Edgar is the man for
the job.* **2** °uniform, unvarying, unvaried,
°consistent, °stable, °steady, °regular, °even,
unchanging, °invariable, °constant: *We moved
to the Caribbean because of its equable climate.*

equal *adj.* **1** °identical, the °same (as), interchangeable, °one *or* the °same, coequal, self-
same; °like, °alike, tantamount, °similar (to),

°equivalent, commensurate: *This year's sales figures are equal to last year's.* **2** °uniform, °regular, corresponding, °correspondent, congruent, congruous, (evenly) balanced, (evenly) matched, °matching; °equivalent, °even; commensurate, comparable, proportionate, (evenly) proportioned, °harmonious, °symmetrical; *Colloq* fifty-fifty, *Brit* °level pegging, *US* even Steven: *Women are entitled to equal employment opportunities. The scores are equal.* **3 equal to:** up to, °capable of, °fit(ted) or suited or °suitable for, °adequate for, *Archaic or literary* °sufficient unto: *Are you sure that Renwick is equal to the responsibility?*
—*n.* **4** °peer, °colleague, °fellow, °brother, °mate, counterpart, °equivalent, °alter ego, compeer: *Constance is certainly anyone's equal in intelligence.*
—*v.* **5** °match, °meet, °even, °correspond (to), °square (with), °tally (with), °tie (with), °parallel, °come up to; °rival: *He will never be able to equal the world record.*

equality *n.* **1** °parity, sameness, °identity, coequality, °uniformity: *The equality of the two bids was very suspicious.* **2** similarity, °likeness, °resemblance, equivalence, correspondence, conformity, congruence, similitude, analogy, comparability, °comparison, °coincidence: *The equality between their performances is surprising.* **3** impartiality, fairness, °justice; egalitarianism: *Surely we all deserve equality of treatment under the law.*

equalize *v.* regularize, °even up, °square, °balance, equate, °match, °standardize, (make) °equal: *Equalize the amounts of liquid in all the containers.*

equip *v.* °furnish, °provide, °supply, °stock, °outfit, °fit (out or up), °rig (out or up), accoutre or *US also* accouter, array, attire, °dress, deck (out), caparison, °clothe, *Chiefly Brit* °kit out or up: *We can equip you with any scuba gear you may require.*

equipment *n.* °gear, °apparatus, furnishings, accoutrements or *US also* accouterments, appurtenances, °paraphernalia, °kit, materiel or *matériel*, °tackle, °outfit, °trappings, °tack, equipage, *Colloq Brit* clobber: *They spent a fortune on mountain-climbing equipment.*

equitable *adj.* °fair, even-handed, °just, °impartial, °objective, unbiased, °unprejudiced, °square, fair-minded, open-minded, °disinterested, °dispassionate, °neutral, °tolerant, unbigoted, °reasonable, °judicious, °ethical, °principled, °moral, °proper, right-minded, *Colloq* °fair and °square: *Suspects have the right to equitable treatment.*

equity *n.* fairness, impartiality, even-handedness, °justice, °fair play, °objectivity, disinterest, fair-mindedness, equitableness, open-mindedness, disinterestedness, neutrality, °tolerance, judiciousness, right-mindedness, high-mindedness: *This court recognizes the equity of your claim.*

equivalent *adj.* **1** tantamount, commensurate, °alike, °similar, °close, comparable, corresponding, interchangeable, °equal, °synonymous, of a °piece or a kind: *He didn't really believe that women's rights should be equivalent to men's.*
—*n.* **2** °match, °equal, °peer, counterpart, °twin: *The garage could not supply the same part but they offered an equivalent.*

equivocal *adj.* **1** °evasive, misleading, °roundabout, hedging, °suspicious, duplicitous, °questionable, °oblique, circumlocutory, °ambiguous, ambivalent, amphibolic or amphibolous, *Colloq* waffling, °wishy-washy: *When asked about the guarantee, they gave an equivocal answer.* **2** °ambiguous, °vague, °hazy, °indefinite, unclear, °indistinct, enigmatic(al), °puzzling, °perplexing, indeterminate, °uncertain, *Colloq* waffling: *Just say Yes or No—none of your equivocal responses.*

equivocate *v.* °evade, °mislead, hedge, °deceive, °quibble, °dodge, weasel out (of), double-talk, °fence, °sidestep, skirt, °avoid, tergiversate, prevaricate, *Colloq* °waffle, beat about the bush, °pussyfoot: *I wish she'd confirm or deny it and stop equivocating.*

era *n.* °age, °period, °time(s), °day(s), epoch, °stage, °generation, °cycle, °date: *They lived in an era of peace.*

erase *v.* **1** expunge, °rub or °scratch or °blot or °wipe out, °delete, °cancel, efface, °scratch, °cross or °strike out or off, °obliterate: *The scribe erased one line and substituted another.* **2** °abolish, °destroy, °obliterate, °remove, °eliminate, (get) °rid of, eradicate, efface: *We erased every trace of evidence that we had been there.*

erect *adj.* **1** °upright, °standing, upstanding, °straight, vertical, °perpendicular, °plumb: *There was a slight stoop now in what had previously been a notably erect body.*
—*v.* **2** °build, °construct, °put up, °raise; °pitch: *I could swear that they erected that building overnight!* **3** °establish, °found, °set up, °form, °institute, °organize, °create: *Their religion was erected on the principles of utilitarianism.*

erode *v.* °wear (down or away), °eat away, °grind down, abrade, °gnaw away (at), °consume, corrode, °wash away; °deteriorate, °destroy, deplete, °reduce, °diminish: *Water has eroded the rock. Their continued lying has eroded my confidence in their honesty.*

erosion *n.* °wear (and tear), wearing (down or away), wasting away, washing or grinding or rubbing away, corroding, corrosion, abrading, abrasion, eating or gnawing away, chafing, fraying, weathering, attrition: *Erosion by rainwater has washed away the topsoil.*

erotic *adj.* **1** °sensual, °stimulating, °suggestive, titillating, °risqué, °bawdy, ribald, °seductive, °voluptuous, °lustful, *Colloq* °sexy: *Some insist that there is a difference between pornographic and erotic literature.* **2** amatory, °venereal, amorous, anacreontic: *Many classical poets wrote erotic verse.* **3** erogenous, °naughty, °carnal, arousing, °rousing, aphrodisiac, libidinous, lubricious or lubricous, °prurient, °lascivious, °lewd, concupiscent, salacious, °obscene, °pornographic, °dirty, °filthy, °nasty, *Colloq* °blue: *He has a collection of photos that he calls erotic art.*

err *v.* **1** be °wrong, be in °error, be °mistaken, be °inaccurate, be °incorrect, be in the °wrong, go °wrong, go astray, make a °mistake, °miscalculate, (make a) °blunder, °bungle, °botch, °fumble, muff, make a °mess of, make a faux pas, °mess up, *US* bobble; *Colloq* goof (up), °slip (up), drop a clanger, °foul up, *Brit* drop a brick, °blot one's copybook, *Slang* °screw up, *Brit* boob, *Taboo slang* fuck up: *The referee erred* *in ruling that the ball was out.* **2** °misbehave, °sin, °transgress, trespass, °lapse, °fall, do °wrong: *She has erred many times in her long life.*

errand *n.* **1** °trip, °journey: *She was on an errand of mercy.* **2** °mission, °charge, °assignment, commission, °task, °duty: *Francis is out running some errands for me.*

erratic *adj.* **1** °irregular, unpredictable, °inconsistent, °unreliable, °capricious, °changeable, °variable; wayward, °unstable, aberrant, °flighty: *The buses run on an erratic schedule.* **2** °peculiar, °abnormal, wayward, °odd, °eccentric, °outlandish, °strange, °unusual, °unorthodox, °extraordinary, °queer, °quaint, °bizarre, °weird, unconventional: *He thinks that his erratic behaviour marks him as an individualist.* **3** wandering, °meandering, directionless, planetary, °aimless, °haphazard, °discursive, errant, divagatory: *Their course was erratic, following the loss of their compass.*

erroneous *adj.* °wrong, °mistaken, °incorrect, °inaccurate, °inexact, °imprecise, °amiss, awry, °false, °faulty, misleading, °flawed, botched, bungled, °unsound, °invalid, °untrue, fallacious, °spurious, °counterfeit, *Colloq* off the mark, off course, *Brit* off beam, *US* off the beam: *He gives the erroneous impression of being intelligent. 'Seperate' is an erroneous spelling of 'separate'.*

error *n.* **1** °mistake, inaccuracy, °fault, °flaw, °blunder, °slip, gaffe; °misprint, typographical error, erratum, °solecism; *Brit* literal, *Colloq* slip-up, goof, clanger, °fluff, boo-boo, °howler, *Brit* bloomer, *Slang* foul-up, boner, *Brit* boob: *I cannot accept a report so full of errors.* **2** °sin, °transgression, trespass, °offence, °indiscretion, wrongdoing, misconduct, iniquity, °evil, wickedness, flagitiousness: *He seems to have seen the error of his ways.* **3 in error: a** °wrong, °mistaken, °incorrect, at °fault: *She was in error about the date of the conference.* **b** mistakenly, incorrectly, by °mistake, erroneously: *I caught the earlier train in error.*

erupt *v.* **1** °eject, °discharge, °expel, °emit, °burst forth *or* out, °blow up, °explode, °spew forth *or* out, °break out, °spout, °vomit (up *or* forth), °throw up *or* off, °spit out *or* up, belch (forth), °gush: *The volcano erupted ash and lava.* **2** °appear, °come out, °break out: *A boil erupted on his chin.*

eruption *n.* **1** outbreak, °outburst, °discharge, °expulsion, emission, bursting forth, °explosion, spouting, vomiting (up *or* forth), belching forth: *The eruption of Vesuvius killed thousands in Pompeii.* **2** outbreak, °rash: *The doctor said the eruption would disappear in a day.*

escape *v.* **1** °get away, °break out *or* °free, °bolt, °flee, °fly, °run away *or* off, elope, decamp, abscond, °steal *or* °slip off *or* away, take to one's heels, take French °leave, °disappear, vanish, *Brit* levant, *Colloq* °take off, °clear out, cut and °run, °duck out, make oneself °scarce, do a disappearing act, *Brit* do a moonlight °flit, *US* vamoose, hightail it, skedaddle, *US and Canadian* °skip (town), °fly the coop, cut out; *Brit* do a bunk, °bugger off, mizzle off, *US and Canadian* scram, blow, lam out, take it on the lam, take a (run-out) powder, *Chiefly Australian* °shoot through: *They escaped when I wasn't looking.* **2** °evade, °elude, °avoid, °dodge: *They escaped detection for years by hiding in a deserted monastery.* **3** °drain, °leak, °issue, seep,

°discharge, °emanate: *Steam was escaping through a hole.* **4** °elude, °evade, baffle, °stump, °mystify, °puzzle, be °forgotten by, be beyond (someone): *How the thing started escapes me for the moment.*
—*n.* **5** °flight, °getaway, departure, decampment, °bolt, jailbreak, prison-break, *Colloq* °break, break-out: *The escape was planned for midnight.* **6** °distraction, °relief, °diversion, °recreation: *He watches westerns as an escape.* **7** leakage, leaking, seepage, seeping, drainage, draining, °leak, °discharge, °outpouring, outflow, effluence, efflux, effluxion: *An escape of radioactive waste from the nuclear power station had been reported earlier.*

escort *n.* **1** °guard, convoy, bodyguard, °protection, °guardian, °protector, chaperon, cortege *or* cortège, °retinue, entourage, safe °conduct, usher, °companion: *The king rode in with his armed escort.* **2** °guide, °attendant, conductor, °leader, cicerone: *The curator acted as our escort through the museum.* **3** °companion; °date, boyfriend, beau: *Donald is Thea's escort to the ball.*
—*v.* **4** °accompany, °shepherd, °squire, usher, °conduct, °guide, °attend: *Would you please escort Denise in to dinner?* **5** °guard, convoy, °protect, °watch over: *The oil tankers were escorted by destroyers.*

especially *adv.* **1** °particularly, °specially, specifically, exceptionally, conspicuously, singularly, remarkably, extraordinarily, unusually, uncommonly, peculiarly, outstandingly, uniquely, °notably, strikingly, noticeably, markedly, signally: *She was especially good at mathematics.* **2** °chiefly, °mainly, predominantly, °primarily, °principally, °first, firstly, °first of all, above all: *He is especially interested in music.*

essay *n.* **1** article, °composition, °paper, °theme, °piece; °thesis, dissertation, disquisition, °tract: *Her essay is on the life cycle of the flea.* **2** °attempt, °effort, °try, °endeavour, °venture; *Colloq* °shot, °go: *This is his first essay into the financial world.*
—*v.* **3** °try, °attempt, °endeavour, °strive, make an °effort, °undertake, °venture, °tackle, °test, °go about, *Colloq* take a crack *or* whack *or* °stab at, *Slang* give (it *or* something) a °shot, have a °go *or* bash (at): *Let him essay to do better.*

essence *n.* **1** °quintessence, quiddity, (°essential) °nature, °substance, °spirit, being, °heart, °core, °pith, °kernel, marrow, °soul, °significance, (active) °principle, crux, cornerstone, foundation-stone, *Colloq* °bottom line: *The essence of her argument is that animals have the same rights as people.* **2** °extract, °concentrate, distillate, °elixir, tincture: *The room smelled faintly of essence of roses.* **3 in essence:** essentially, basically, fundamentally, °materially, °substantially, at °bottom, °in the final analysis, *au fond; in* °effect, °virtually: *In essence, there is little to choose between Trotskyism and Stalinism.* **4 of the essence:** °essential, °critical, °crucial, °vital, °indispensable, requisite, °important: *In this job, time is of the essence.*

essential *adj.* **1** °indispensable, °necessary, requisite, required, °important, °imperative, °vital, °material, quintessential: *A strong defence is essential to peace.* **2** °fundamental, °basic, °intrinsic, °elemental, °elementary, °principal, °primary, °key, °main, °leading, °chief: *Yeast or baking powder is an essential ingredient of bread.*

establish v. **1** °found, °create, °institute, °set up, °start, °begin, °inaugurate, °organize, °form, constitute, °decree, °enact, ordain, °introduce: *The company was established in 1796. A new law was established to protect consumers.* **2** °secure, °settle, °fix, entrench, °install *or* instal, °seat, ensconce; °lodge, °locate, °station: *Hitler became established as dictator in 1933. Are you established in your new house?* **3** °prove, °confirm, °certify, °verify, affirm, °determine, °authenticate, °demonstrate, °show, °substantiate, corroborate, validate, °support, back (up): *It will be difficult to establish exactly how the crime was committed.*

establishment n. **1** °foundation, founding, °formation, °organization, construction, °creation, °origin, origination, °institution, inauguration, setting up: *We look forward to the establishment of a democratic government.* **2** °business, °concern, °firm, °company, °enterprise, °institution, °organization; °office; °shop, °store, °market: *He works for a retail establishment.* **3 the Establishment**: the °system, the °government, the authorities, the °administration, the °power structure, the ruling class, the (established) °order, the conservatives, the powers that be; the Church: *The press must not be under the control of the Establishment.*

estate n. **1** °property, holdings, °domain, demesne, °land, landed estate, manor, mansion: *They live on a large estate in the south of France.* **2** °property, holdings, °assets, °capital, resources, °wealth, °fortune; °belongings, °possessions, chattels: *The estate was divided among the heirs.* **3** estate of the °realm, °class, °caste, °order, °standing, °position, (social) °status, °state, °station, °place, °situation, °stratum, °level, °rank: *By virtue of her high estate, she is entitled to certain privileges.* **4** °development, Brit °housing *or* industrial *or* trading estate: *They live in a council house on an estate near Reading.*

esteem v. **1** °respect, value, °treasure, °prize, °cherish, °hold °dear, °appreciate, °admire, °look up to, °regard °highly, °venerate, °revere, °reverence, °honour, °defer to; °like, °love, °adore: *The novels of Virginia Woolf were greatly esteemed by a small intellectual group.* **2** °consider, °judge, deem, °view, °regard, °hold, °estimate, °account, °believe, °think, °rate, °rank, °reckon, °evaluate: *The Duke was esteemed throughout Europe as 'the perfect knight'.* —n. **3** °estimation, (°high) °regard, °respect, (°high) °opinion, °favour, °admiration, °appreciation, °approval, approbation: *He holds her talents in very high esteem. My esteem for your father's accomplishments is undiminished.*

estimable adj. esteemed, °respectable, respected, °admirable, admired, valuable, valued, creditable, °worthy, °meritorious, °reputable, honoured, °honourable, °laudable, °praiseworthy, commendable, °excellent, °good: *I want you to meet my estimable friend, Esterhazy.*

estimate v. **1** °approximate, °gauge, °determine, °judge, °guess; assess, appraise, value, °evaluate, °reckon, °calculate, °work out, Colloq guestimate *or* guesstimate: *Experts estimated the cost of restoration at £10,000.* **2** °consider, °think, °believe, °guess, conjecture, °judge: *I estimate our chances of success as very low.* —n. **3** approximation, °gauge, °guess, conjecture, assessment, appraisal, °evaluation,

°reckoning, °calculation, Colloq guestimate *or* guesstimate: *What is your estimate of the company's value?* **4** °estimation, °belief, °opinion, °judgement, °thinking, °feeling, °sentiment, °sense, (point of) °view, °viewpoint: *My estimate of his abilities is that he is not the man for the job.*

estimation n. **1** °opinion, °judgement, °view, (way of) °thinking, °mind: *In my estimation, the scheme will fail.* **2** °esteem, °regard, °respect, °admiration: *Her estimation of his talent is unflagging.* **3** °estimate, approximation, °guess, °gauge: *You must make an estimation of the value for insurance purposes.*

estranged adj. alienated, divided, separated, °withdrawn, disaffected, driven °apart, dissociated, disassociated: *Iain has had a lot of trouble with his estranged wife.*

etch v. **1** °engrave, incise, °carve, inscribe, °grave, °cut, °score, °scratch, corrode, °eat into: *After the design has been painted on, acid is used to etch the metal plate.* **2** °impress, imprint, °engrave, ingrain: *The scene will be etched into my memory forever.*

eternal adj. **1** °everlasting, °timeless, °infinite, °endless, °immortal, °limitless: *They pledged eternal love for one another.* **2** unending, °endless, ceaseless, unceasing, incessant, °perpetual, °constant, °continuous, interminable, uninterrupted, °non-stop, unremitting, °persistent, °relentless; °continual, °recurrent: *I'm sick and tired of my neighbours' eternal arguing.* **3** unchanged, unchanging, immutable, °invariable, unvarying, unalterable, °permanent, °fixed, °constant, °everlasting, °enduring, °lasting, undiminished, unfaltering, unwavering: *To the north there was only the eternal silence of the greatest desolation.*

eternity n. endlessness, everlastingness, unendingness, boundlessness, °perpetuity, timelessness, infinity: *Many religions believe in the eternity of the soul.*

ethical adj. °moral, °upright, °righteous, °right, °just, °principled, °correct, °honest, °proper, °open, °decent, °fair, °good, °virtuous, straightforward, high-minded, °noble: *It wasn't ethical of him to disclose details of the report.*

etiquette n. °code (of °behaviour), °form, °convention, °ceremony, formalities, °protocol, °rules, °custom(s), °decorum, °propriety, politesse, politeness, °courtesy, (good) °manners, °civility, seemliness: *Etiquette requires that you address me as 'Sir'.*

eulogize v. °praise, °extol, °laud, °applaud, °compliment, sound *or* sing the °praises of, acclaim; °appreciate, °honour; °flatter: *Kirk was eulogized for his contribution to space travel.*

eulogy n. °praise, commendation, acclaim, acclamation, °tribute, °compliment, °applause, °homage, plaudits, encomium, accolade, paean, panegyric: *The eulogy listed Wotton's many achievements.*

euphemism n. amelioration, mollification, mitigation, cushioning, Technical paradiastole: *Euphemism is saying 'not too good' when you mean 'bad' or 'awful'.*

evacuate v. **1** °empty, °clear (out), °exhaust, °drain, deplete, °purge, get °rid of, °void, °discharge, °vent; °divest, °deprive: *In cases of poisoning, they first evacuate the stomach.* **2** °vacate, °desert, °leave, °depart (from), °withdraw *or*

°retire (from), °go away (from), °quit, °relinquish, °abandon, decamp (from), °move or °pull out (of or from): *When the enemy approached, the troops evacuated the area.* **3** relocate, °move: *Thousands were evacuated to a safe distance when the bomb was discovered.*

evade *v.* **1** °avoid, °elude, °dodge, °sidestep, °escape (from); °get away (from), °get out of, °duck, circumvent, °shirk, *Colloq chiefly US and Canadian* weasel out (of): *The prisoner evaded capture. Don't evade your responsibilities.* **2** °quibble, °equivocate, tergiversate, °manoeuvre, hedge, °shuffle, fudge, °fence, parry, *Colloq* °waffle, *Slang* cop out: *The witness continued to evade the barrister's questions.*

evaluate *v.* **1** value, appraise, assess: *You must be an expert to evaluate netsuke.* **2** °judge, °rank, °rate, °gauge, °estimate, °approximate, °calculate, °reckon, °compute, °figure, quantify, °determine, ascertain: *How can they evaluate your importance to the project?*

evaluation *n.* **1** appraisal, valuation, assessment: *The insurance company refused to accept a higher evaluation on my house.* **2** °estimate, °estimation, approximation, rating, °opinion, ranking, °judgement, °reckoning, figuring, °calculation, computation, °determination: *The committee meets annually to discuss the evaluation of each employee's contribution.*

evaporate *v.* **1** vaporize; °boil off or out; dehydrate, desiccate: *Much of the surplus liquid will evaporate during cooking.* **2** °disappear, °disperse, °dissipate, vanish, evanesce, evanish, dispel; °fade (away), °melt away, °dissolve: *Opposition to his appointment seems to have evaporated.*

evaporation *n.* **1** vaporization, drying (up or out), dehydration, desiccation, exsiccation, parching, searing: *Clouds are formed by the evaporation of terrestrial water.* **2** disappearance, dispersion, dispelling, °dissipation, evanescence, dematerialization, °dissolution, fading (away), melting (away): *He was pleased to note the evaporation of all serious opposition.*

evasion *n.* **1** °escape, avoidance, shirking, dodging: *They disapproved of his evasion of his civic duties.* **2** °subterfuge, °deception, °deceit, chicane or °chicanery, °artifice, cunning, °trickery, sophistry, °excuse, dodging, prevarication, °lying, fudging, evasiveness, quibbling, equivocation, double-talk: *All the interviewers' questions were met with evasion.*

evasive *adj.* °devious, °indirect, equivocating, °equivocal, misleading, °oblique, °ambiguous, sophistical, casuistic, °shifty, dissembling, cunning, °tricky, °deceitful, *Colloq* cagey, Jesuitical: *When asked if he had visited her, he gave an evasive reply. She too was evasive about how she had spent the evening.*

eve *n.* **1** °evening or °day or °night before, °time or °period before; vigil: *It was Christmas Eve, and we went out carolling.* **2** °verge, °threshold, °brink: *We met on the eve of my departure for Hungary.*

even *adj.* **1** °smooth, °flat, °plane, °level, °regular, °uniform, °flush, °straight, °true: *Sand the edges till they are even.* **2** Sometimes, **even with**: °level or °uniform (with), coextensive (with), °flush (with), °parallel (with or to): *Make sure that the lines at the bottom of the columns are even. Is that board even with the others?* **3** °steady, °regular, °consistent, °constant, °uniform, unvaried, unvarying, °methodical, unchanging,

°set, °equable, °stable, °measured, metrical, rhythmic(al), °orderly, ordered, °monotonous, unbroken, uninterrupted: *We walked along at an even pace.* **4** even-tempered, °calm, °equable, composed, placid, °serene, °peaceful, °cool, °tranquil, unruffled, imperturbable, undisturbed, °impassive, °steady, °temperate, equanimous, °self-possessed, °sober, °staid, °sedate, sober-sided: *People of even disposition are unexcited, unexcitable, and unexciting.* **5** balanced, °equal, the °same, °identical, coequal, °level, °drawn, on a °par, tied, neck and neck; °equivalent, *Colloq* fifty-fifty, *Brit* °level pegging, *US* even Steven: *At half-time the scores were even. I have an even chance of getting the job.* **6** °square, quits, °equal: *If I pay for this round, we'll be even.* **7** °fair (and °square), °square, °impartial, °disinterested, °neutral, °just, even-handed, °equitable, straightforward, on the °level, °honest, °upright, unbiased, °unprejudiced: *See that you make an even distribution of the food parcels.* **8** °exact, °precise, °round, rounded off or out or up or down: *The bill came to an even fifty pounds.* **9 get even (with)**: °repay, °revenge oneself (on), even or °settle accounts or the score (with), °require, °reciprocate, °retaliate, be °revenged: *I'll get even with her for telling my mother. Whenever he feels that he's been insulted, he wants to get even.*

—*adv.* **10** °still, °yet; all the more, °indeed, (more) than ever: *He is even dumber than I thought. He is in debt to everyone, even his daughter.* **11** Sometimes, **even with** or **though**: °notwithstanding, °despite, in °spite of, disregarding: *Even with delays, we arrived on time.* **12 even so**: °nevertheless, °nonetheless, °still, °yet, °notwithstanding, all the °same, in °spite of that, °despite that: *He refused to attend; even so, we sent him an invitation.*

—*v.* **13** Usually, **even up** or **out**: °smooth, °flatten, °level, °equalize; align: *This road will be fine when they even out the bumps.* **14 even out** or **up**: °equalize, °balance (out), °settle; °compensate: *Unfortunately, our profits and our expenses evened out.*

evening *n.* nightfall, eventide, °dusk, sunset, sundown, p.m., *Literary* gloaming: *The Klincks will join us for dinner this evening.*

event *n.* **1** °occurrence, °happening, °incident, °episode, °occasion, °circumstance, °affair, °experience: *An event then took place that changed the course of his life.* **2** °issue, °outcome, consequence, °result, conclusion, °upshot, °end, °effect: *There is no merit in preparing for a disaster after the event.* **3 at all events** or **in any event**: come what may, in any °case, at any °rate, °regardless, anyhow, anyway: *At all events, we were ready and waiting when the raid started.* **4 in the event**: in the °reality or actuality, as it or things turned out, at the °time, when it happened: *In the event, we left as soon as we could.*

eventful *adj.* °busy, °full, °active, °lively, °exciting, °interesting; °important, °significant, °signal, consequential, °notable, °noteworthy, °momentous, °memorable: *What with your wedding and the birth of your son, it certainly has been an eventful week.*

eventual *adj.* **1** °ultimate, °final, °last, concluding, resulting: *The eventual cost is impossible to forecast.* **2** °due, expected, anticipated, °inevitable, °likely, consequent, resulting, resultant, foreordained, preordained, °unavoidable, °destined, predestined, ineluctable, °probable: *As they cannot afford the mortgage payments, they are faced with the eventual loss of their home.*

eventuality *n.* °circumstance, contingency, °event, °occurrence, °happening, °case; °likelihood, °chance, °possibility, °probability: *We must prepare for the eventuality of war.*

eventually *adv.* °ultimately, °finally, at °last, in the °end *or* long run, at the °end of the day, sooner or later, when all is said and done, in the °final analysis, in due course, in (the course of) °time, after all: *We must all die eventually.*

ever *adv.* **1** at all, (at) any °time, at any °point *or* °period, on any °occasion, in any °case, by any °chance: *Do you ever visit London?* **2** °always, °for ever, °yet, °still, °even, at all times, in all cases, eternally, perpetually, endlessly, everlastingly, constantly, continuously, continually, for ever and a day, till the end of time, till the cows come home, till doomsday; all the °time: *He is ever the one to make us laugh. Literacy is becoming ever more important.*

everlasting *adj.* °eternal, °deathless, undying, °immortal, °infinite, °timeless; never-ending, °perpetual, °constant, °continual, °continuous, °permanent, unceasing, incessant, interminable, °endless: *They believed in everlasting punishment after death. I wish that dog would stop its everlasting barking.*

everyday *adj.* **1** °daily, day-to-day, quotidian, °diurnal; circadian: *In our family a big breakfast was an everyday occurrence.* **2** commonplace, °common, °ordinary, °customary, °regular, °habitual, °routine, °usual, run-of-the-mill, unexceptional, °accustomed, °conventional, °familiar: *She found herself unable to cope with everyday tasks that she used to take in her stride.* **3** °prosaic, mundane, °dull, unimaginative, unexciting, °mediocre, °inferior: *These are very everyday paintings of little value.*

everyone *pron.* everybody, all (and °sundry), °one and all, each and every °one *or* °person, the °whole °world, everybody under the sun, every Tom, Dick, and Harry: *Everyone will want to come to my party.*

everything *pron.* all, all things, the aggregate, the (°whole *or* °entire) °lot, the °total, the °entirety, *Colloq* the °whole kit and caboodle, the °whole shooting match, *Chiefly US and Canadian* the °whole shebang: *Everything was destroyed in the earthquake.*

everywhere *adv.* in all places, in *or* to each *or* every °place *or* °part, in every nook and cranny, high and low, °far and wide, near and °far; ubiquitously, °universally, globally; °throughout: *She went everywhere searching for clues. The smell of jasmine was everywhere. Errors occur everywhere in his writings.*

evict *v.* oust, dislodge, °turn out (of house and home), °expel, °eject, °remove, °dispossess, °put out, *Law* disseise *or* disseize, *Colloq* °toss *or* °throw *or* °kick *or* °boot out, *Brit* °turf out: *The landlord evicted us for non-payment of rent.*

eviction *n.* ouster, dispossession, dislodgement, °expulsion, °ejection, °removal, *Law* disseisin *or* disseizin, *Colloq* the boot: *His eviction from the club was for refusing to wear a tie.*

evidence *n.* **1** °proof, °ground(s), °fact(s), °data, °basis, °support, verification, attestation, affirmation, confirmation, validation, corroboration, substantiation, documentation, certification: *Have we enough evidence to convict the suspects?* **2** °testimony, °statement, deposition, affidavit, averment, °assertion: *The prosecution will present its evidence tomorrow.* **3** °indication, °sign, °mark, °token, °manifestation, °demonstration, °hint, °suggestion, °clue, °trace, smoking gun: *There is evidence that there are mice in the house.* —*v.* **4** °demonstrate, °show, °display, °manifest, °signify, °exhibit, °reveal, °denote, °attest, °prove, evince, °testify, (bear) °witness: *The destruction of the forests is evidenced by the open plains.*

evident *adj.* °clear, °obvious, °plain, °apparent, °manifest, °patent, palpable, °conspicuous, clear-cut, °express, unmistakable, °incontrovertible, understandable, comprehensible, recognizable, °perceptible, perceivable, °discernible, °noticeable: *It was evident that someone had been tampering with the mechanism.*

evidently *adv.* **1** °clearly, °obviously, plainly, °manifestly, palpably, °apparently, patently, indubitably, °undoubtedly, °doubtless(ly), without a doubt, indisputably, incontestably, incontrovertibly, undeniably, unquestionably, °surely, certainly, to be °sure: *He is evidently the culprit.* **2** °apparently, °outwardly, °seemingly, it would °seem, so it °seems, as far as one can see *or* tell, to all appearances, °ostensibly: *Evidently, there were two people here, not just one.*

evil *adj.* **1** °bad, °awful, °wrong, °immoral, °wicked, °sinful, nefarious, iniquitous, °base, °corrupt, °vile, accursed, °damnable, °villainous, heinous, °infamous, flagitious, °foul, °nasty, °abominable, °atrocious, °horrible, horrid, °ghastly, °grisly, °dreadful, depraved, °vicious, malevolent, maleficent, malefic, black-hearted, °evil-minded: *He was an evil tyrant who killed anyone who opposed him.* **2** treacherous, °traitorous, °perfidious, insidious, °unscrupulous, unprincipled, °dishonest, °dishonourable, °crooked, °criminal, felonious, knavish, °sinister, underhand(ed), °dirty, °corrupt: *He thought up an evil plan for getting rid of his wife.* **3** °harmful, °destructive, °hurtful, °injurious, °mischievous, °detrimental, °ruinous, deleterious, °disastrous, catastrophic, pernicious, noxious, °malignant, malign, °virulent, toxic, °poisonous, °deadly, °lethal: *Evil policies were promulgated against minority groups, and racist attacks abounded.* **4** °unfortunate, unlucky, °ominous, °inauspicious, dire, unpropitious, °calamitous, infelicitous, woeful: *Their business had fallen on evil times.* **5** °bad, °offensive, °disgusting, °repulsive, °awful, °nasty, mephitic, noxious, °foul, pestilential, °putrid, °vile; °disagreeable, unpleasant: *An evil odour permeated the crypt.* —*n.* **6** badness, °sin, °vice, wickedness, iniquity, turpitude, immorality, °profligacy, depravity, degeneracy, corruption, °degradation, °devilry *or* deviltry, villainy, nefariousness, viciousness, vileness, heinousness, flagitiousness, baseness, foulness: *The evil that men do lives after them, the good is oft interred with their bones.* **7** °harm, °hurt, °injury, °mischief, °damage, °ruin, °calamity, °misfortune, °catastrophe,

°destruction, °disaster, cataclysm; °ill, °misery, °suffering, °pain, °sorrow, °woe, °agony, °anguish: *Evil befell the residents of Pompeii.*

evil-minded *adj.* **1** °dirty(-minded), smutty, °obscene, depraved, °lewd, °lascivious, °lecherous, salacious, licentious, °filthy, °nasty; foul-mouthed: *Those anonymous phone calls were made by some evil-minded degenerate.* **2** °wicked, °sinful, flagitious, °vicious, °hateful, malicious, °spiteful, malevolent, °evil, °bad: *The evil-minded old witch grabbed Hansel and Gretel.*

evoke *v.* °summon (up), °call up *or* forth, °elicit, conjure up, invoke, °recall, reawake(n), awake, °wake(n), (a)rouse, °raise: *Seeing her again evoked fond memories.*

evolution *n.* °development, °advance, °growth, °progress, °progression, phylogeny, evolvement, developing, growing, evolving, °formation, maturation, °production: *This book traces the evolution of the aeroplane. His treatise is on the evolution of insects.*

exact *adj.* **1** °precise, °accurate, °correct, °faithful, °true, °faultless, °identical, °literal, °perfect, consummate: *This is an exact copy of the original. Were those her exact words?* **2** °careful, °meticulous, °strict, rigorous, °accurate, °exacting, °severe, °fastidious, °scrupulous, °thorough, °painstaking, °rigid, punctilious: *He has conducted the most exact experiments.*
—*v.* **3** °demand, °extort, require, °enforce, °insist on *or* upon, °extract, °impose, wrest, compel, enjoin, °call for, °requisition, °claim: *The chief exacted tribute before releasing the prisoners.*

exacting *adj.* °demanding, rigorous, °difficult, °rigid, °stern, °hard, °tough, °severe, °harsh, °burdensome, taxing, stringent, °imperative, unsparing, °oppressive, °tyrannical: *I know of no more exacting job than that of air traffic controller.*

exactly *adv.* **1** accurately, °precisely, strictly, °perfectly, correctly, unerringly, faultlessly, faithfully, scrupulously, °literally, to the °letter, word for word, °verbatim, closely; methodically, systematically: *She translated the passage exactly, with no errors.* **2** °definitely, °absolutely, °positively, undeniably, °surely, certainly, unequivocally, °completely, in every respect, in all respects, °particularly, specifically, explicitly, °just, °quite, °expressly, °precisely, accurately, °truly, *Colloq Brit* bang on: *This is exactly the kind of house we want.*

exaggerate *v.* °overstate, °magnify, °inflate, overdraw, embroider, °embellish, °elaborate, °enlarge, °stretch, °romance, overemphasize, overstress, overplay, °overdo, °exalt, hyperbolize, °paint, *Colloq* °lay it on thick, °play up, °pile it on: *She exaggerates when she claims to be the best actress in the world. He believes the health risks are exaggerated.*

exaggeration *n.* overstatement, °magnification, inflation, embroidery, °embellishment, °elaboration, enlargement, °stretch, romanticization, °extravagance, overemphasis, °excess, exaltation, enhancement, hyperbole; °empty °talk, °bombast, bragging, boasting, boastfulness, magniloquence, *Literary* gasconade, rodomontade, *Colloq* fish °story, puffery, *Slang* bull(shit), °hot air: *It was a press agent's exaggeration to call the movie a 'colossal epic'.*

exalt *v.* **1** elevate, °raise *or* °lift (up *or* on high), upraise, uplift, upgrade, °boost, °promote,

°advance: *The goalkeeper was exalted to heroic status by the fans.* **2** °praise, °honour, °extol, °glorify, °idolize, °dignify, ennoble, °revere, °reverence, °venerate, pay °homage *or* °tribute to, °celebrate; lionize: *O magnify the Lord with me, and let us exalt His name together.* **3** °stimulate, °excite, °animate, (a)rouse, °fire, °inspire, °electrify, awaken, °spur, °stir (up), inspirit: *Certain drugs have the effect of exalting the imagination.*

exalted *adj.* **1** °elevated, °lofty, °high, °eminent, °notable, °noted, °prominent, °famous, famed, °celebrated, °distinguished, °dignified, honoured, °prestigious, °glorified, °sublime, °grand: *During his later life he enjoyed an exalted reputation.* **2** °elevated, °noble, °lofty, °superior, uplifting, heightened, high-flown; exaggerated, °pretentious, overblown, °inflated: *His writing is euphuistic, that is, flowery or exalted. She has an exalted notion of her importance.* **3** °elated, °excited, °exultant, °ecstatic, jubilant, °overjoyed, °joyful, °rapturous, transported, blissful, °happy, joyous, in seventh °heaven, uplifted, *Colloq* on cloud nine, *Brit* over the moon: *They were in too exalted a mood to be interested in such mundane matters.*

examination *n.* **1** °investigation, °scrutiny, °study, °analysis, inspection, °inquiry *or* enquiry, °probe, °search, °exploration, °research, °survey, going-over, check-up, °check(out), appraisal, assessment: *Examination of the finances revealed a secret Swiss bank account.* **2** testing, °test, °quiz, exam: *There will be a written examination on Friday.* **3** °interrogation, inquisition, °inquiry *or* enquiry, catechism, cross-examination, *Colloq* third degree, grill(ing): *Examination of the prisoners is left to intelligence officers.*

examine *v.* **1** °investigate, °scrutinize, °study, °peruse, °scan, pore over, °analyse, °sift, °inspect, °inquire *or* enquire into, °go over *or* through *or* into, °look over *or* into, °probe, °search, °explore, °research, °survey, °check up on, °check (out), appraise, assess, °weigh, *Brit* °vet, *Slang* °case: *The theory will be examined thoroughly.* **2** °test; interrogate, °quiz, catechize, cross-examine, °question, °sound out, *Colloq* grill, °pump: *The director closely examined all applicants for the position.*

example *n.* **1** °instance, °case, °sample, °specimen, °illustration: *If this is an example of your work, I'm afraid we aren't interested.* **2** °model, °prototype, °standard, archetype, exemplar, °pattern, benchmark, °norm, criterion: *You should set an example to the children.* **3** °warning, admonition, °lesson: *The judge made an example of him by giving him the maximum sentence.* **4 for example**: for °instance, as a °case in point, as an °illustration *or* example, by way of °illustration, to °illustrate, e.g. *or* eg, *exempli gratia*: *Consider, for example, the following poem by Wordsworth.*

exasperate *v.* **1** °anger, °infuriate, °enrage, incense, °madden, rile, drive °mad; embitter; °inflame; *Colloq* drive °crazy, drive up the °wall: *Dealing with a bureaucracy can be exasperating for anyone.* **2** °irritate, °irk, °annoy, °bother, °harass, pique, °gall, nettle, °rankle, °provoke, vex, °pester, °torment, °plague; hector, badger, *Colloq* °bug, needle, peeve, °get, °get under (someone's) skin, °rub (up) the wrong way,

°aggravate, *Slang* °get (someone's) goat, piss (someone) off: *The child's constant questions were beginning to exasperate me.*

excavate *v.* **1** °dig (out *or* up), °hollow *or* °gouge (out), °scoop out, °burrow *or* °cut (out): *They are excavating a great hole in the centre of the site.* **2** °unearth, uncover, expose, °clear, °lay °bare, °dig up, disinter, °bring up, exhume: *A large part of Pompeii has been excavated.*

excavation *n.* °cavity, °hole, °pit, crater, °cut, ditch, trench, trough, °burrow, °hollow, °shaft, °tunnel; °mine, °quarry: *Concrete for the foundations will be poured into the excavation.*

exceed *v.* **1** °surpass, °top, °excel, be °superior to, °go beyond, °beat, °overwhelm, °better, outdistance, °pass, °overtake, °outstrip, outrank, outrun, °outdo, outpace, °transcend, outshine, outreach, °overshadow, °eclipse: *The success of the new product exceeded our expectations.* **2** °overstep, °go beyond, overextend: *His behaviour exceeded the bounds of decency.*

exceeding *adj.* °great, °huge, °enormous, °extraordinary, °excessive, °exceptional, °surpassing: *The exceeding poverty of the people is heart-rending.*

exceedingly *adv.* °very, °extremely, °especially, exceptionally, considerably, incomparably, immeasurably, extraordinarily, remarkably; excessively, greatly, hugely, enormously: *She plays the violin exceedingly well. Even for a dog, that is an exceedingly ugly dog.*

excel *v.* °surpass, be °superior (to), °dominate, °top, °exceed, °go beyond, °beat, °outstrip, outrank, °outdo, outpace, outshine, °overshadow, °eclipse, °shine, be °pre-eminent: *Few places excel the Caribbean islands for beauty. He really excels when it comes to swimming.*

excellence *n.* °superiority, °merit, (°high) °quality, goodness, fineness, greatness, °prominence, eminence, °pre-eminence, °distinction, value, °worth, °supremacy: *Those who attain excellence often devote their lives to one pursuit.*

excellent *adj.* °superb, °outstanding, °exceptional, °superior, °matchless, °peerless, unequalled, without equal, °nonpareil, °supreme, °superlative, °sterling, °capital, first-class, °first-rate, °prime, °choice, °select, °distinguished, °noteworthy, °notable, °worthy, the °best, tiptop, °admirable, °splendid, °remarkable, °marvellous, °extraordinary, *Colloq* A-1 *or* A-one, °great, smashing, °super, °terrific, °fantastic, *Brit* °magic, *Dialectal* °champion, *Old-fashioned* top-hole, °ripping, tickety-boo, *US* A number 1, °major, *Australian* bonzer, *Slang* °cool, ripsnorting: *Thank you for an excellent dinner. He is an excellent pianist.*

except *prep.* **1** Sometimes **except for**: excepting, °save, but, excluding, °exclusive of, °barring, °bar, with the °exception of, omitting, not counting, °apart from, but for, other than, °saving: *There was no one there except us. Except for us, no one came.* —*conj.* **2 except that**: except *or* but (for the fact) that, but, °save that: *He would have gone except that he has no car.* —*v.* **3** °exclude, °omit, °leave out, °excuse: *As usual, the wealthy were excepted from the tax increase.*

exception *n.* **1** °exclusion, °omission: *With the exception of those who are absent, all members are entitled to a free T-shirt.* **2** debarment, blockage, lockout, shut-out: *His wife was deeply offended by his exception from membership of the country club.* **3** departure, anomaly, irregularity, °special case; °oddity, °freak, °rarity, °peculiarity, °quirk: *The exception proves the rule. Why does Viv always have to be an exception?* **4 take exception (to)**: make *or* raise (an) °objection (to *or* against), raise °objections (to *or* against) °object (to), demur (at), find °fault (with), take °offence *or* °umbrage (at), be offended (at); (call into) °question, °cavil, °quibble, °challenge, °oppose, °disagree (with): *She takes exception to everything I suggest. If you propose to ban smoking at the meeting, will some people take exception?*

exceptionable *adj.* objectionable, °disputable, °questionable, criticizable, °unacceptable, °unsatisfactory: *We found nothing exceptionable about the service.*

exceptional *adj.* **1** °special, °unusual, especial, out of the ordinary, °extraordinary, uncommon, °rare, °singular; °strange, °irregular, aberrant, °odd, °peculiar, anomalous: *The candlesticks turned out to be of exceptional value. He insisted that rainstorms in the Sahara were not exceptional.* **2** °gifted, °talented, °superior, °outstanding, above °average, °excellent, °prodigious, °extraordinary: *Your child is exceptional, Mrs Einstein.* **3** handicapped, below average, °deficient, *Brit* ESN (= 'educationally subnormal'): *The boy attends a school for exceptional children.*

excerpt *n.* **1** °extract, °selection, °quotation, citation, °passage, pericope: *The speaker read excerpts from well-known writers.* —*v.* **2** °extract, °select, °quote, cite, cull (out), °pick (out), °take: *Parts of this book were excerpted from his earlier writings.*

excess *n.* **1** °surplus, over-abundance, overflow, superabundance, nimiety, °superfluity, °surfeit, plethora, °glut, redundancy, over-sufficiency, supererogation, leftovers; overkill: *The excess of income over expenses constitutes profit. There is an excess of water on the road after a rainstorm.* **2** Often, **excesses**: debauchery, °extravagance, immoderation, °prodigality, overindulgence, intemperance, °dissipation, dissoluteness: *Because of their excesses they have been shunned by their friends.* —*adj.* **3** °surplus, °extra, °superfluous, °excessive, °leftover, °residual, °remaining: *After paying the bills, any excess money goes into savings.*

excessive *adj.* **1** °immoderate, °inordinate, °disproportionate, °extravagant, °exorbitant, °superfluous, °excess, undue, °enormous, °extreme, °unreasonable, °unwarranted, unjustifiable, °outrageous, °unconscionable: *This job is making excessive demands on my time.* **2** overdone, fulsome, cloying, nauseating, °disgusting: *I was sickened by her excessive sweetness.*

exchange *v.* **1** °trade, barter, °switch, °change, interchange, °reciprocate, °return, *Colloq* swap *or* swop: *We exchange gifts every Christmas.* —*n.* **2** °trade, barter, °change, °traffic, °commerce, dealing, °truck, °transfer, interchange, reciprocity, reciprocation, °switch, quid pro quo, tit for tat, *Colloq* swap *or* swop: *An exchange of prisoners was negotiated. What can I do for you in exchange?* **3** altercation, °argument, °quarrel, °disagreement, unpleasantness: *We had a brief exchange, then he struck me.* **4** °market, stock °market, Stock Exchange, securities exchange, the Market, the Board, the Big Board, the Exchange, the Bourse, Wall Street, *US* the Street: *The exchange reported little activity in anticipation of the finance minister's speech.*

excitable *adj.* °volatile, °jumpy, apprehensive, °nervous, °restive, °restless, fidgety, edgy, °touchy, highly-strung, high-strung, mercurial, °emotional, °quick-tempered, °testy, hot-blooded, °feverish, °hysterical, *US* on a short string: *The director becomes very excitable before each performance.*

excite *v.* **1** (a)rouse, °spur (on), °stir (up), °move, °animate, °enliven, °activate, °motivate, invigorate, °energize, °stimulate, °cause, °provoke, °prod, °agitate, °incite, °quicken, °urge, (a)wake, (a)waken, °call forth, °summon (up), °elicit, °inspire, inspirit, °rally, galvanize, °electrify, °foment, °fire (up), °inflame, °kindle, ignite, °initiate, instigate, °generate, °occasion, °begin, °start, °bring about, °effect, set in motion, *Colloq* get going, °spark, °wind up, get (someone) (all) steamed up, °hop up, *US* kick-start, light a fire under: *The speech excited the crowd's patriotic fervour.* **2** °agitate, °disturb, °perturb, °stir up, discompose, °fluster, °ruffle, °upset, disconcert: *Don't excite the horses.* **3** °thrill, °stir up, titillate, °work up, arouse, °inflame: *Risqué films are intended to excite viewers.*

excited *adj.* **1** (a)roused, stirred (up), stimulated, °agitated, °disturbed, perturbed, °upset, worked up, wrought up, °wound up, keyed up, °overwrought, discomposed, °disconcerted, discomfited, °nervous, edgy, on °edge, uneasy, flustered, ruffled, fidgety, °frantic, frenetic, aflame, °feverish, frenzied, °hysterical, beside oneself, *Colloq* itchy, (all) °hot and bothered, °high, on a °high, off the deep end, out of one's °mind: *Turner was in a very excited state by the time the police arrived. Don't get so excited just because he called you a name.* **2** °ardent, zealous, °impassioned, °passionate, °eager, energized, °energetic, °active, °brisk, °animated, °lively, °spirited, fervid, °fervent, vehement, stimulated, °enthusiastic, galvanized, electrified, intoxicated, *Colloq* turned on: *The excited children scrambled into the boat. She becomes excited listening to rock 'n' roll.*

excitement *n.* **1** restlessness, disquiet, disquietude, °tension, °agitation, °unrest, malaise, °discomfort, jumpiness, nervousness, freneticness, excitation: *He had to give the patient an injection to quell her excitement.* **2** perturbation, °upset, °action, ado, °activity, °ferment, °furore *or US* furor, turmoil, °tumult, to-do, °stir, commotion, hubbub, brouhaha, °fuss, hurly-burly, *Colloq* fireworks: *The robbery caused a lot of excitement at the bank.* **3** °animation, °eagerness, °enthusiasm, exhilaration, ebullience: *She could hardly contain her excitement at winning the lottery.*

exciting *adj.* **1** °stimulating, °intoxicating, heady, °thrilling, °stirring, °moving, inspiring, °rousing, °exhilarating, electrifying, galvanizing, energizing, °invigorating: °overwhelming, °overpowering, astounding, astonishing, fervid, °amazing, mind-boggling, *Colloq* far-out, rip-roaring, mind-blowing: *Orbiting the world in the space shuttle was the most exciting experience of my life.* **2** °seductive, °sensuous, °voluptuous, °ravishing, captivating, charming,

°tempting, enticing, alluring, °provocative, titillating, *Colloq* °sexy: *Fenella is truly an exciting young woman.*

exclaim *v.* °call *or* °cry (out), °proclaim, vociferate, utter, °declare, ejaculate, °shout, °yell, °bawl, °bellow, °burst out (with), °blurt out, *Colloq* holler: *'It's a girl!' he exclaimed.*

exclamation *n.* °outcry, °call, °cry, utterance, ejaculation, °interjection, vociferation, °shout, °yell, °bellow, *Colloq* holler: *She gave an exclamation of surprise at seeing me there.*

exclude *v.* **1** Often, **exclude from**: °keep out *or* away, °lock *or* °shut out, °ban, °bar, debar, °prohibit, interdict, °forbid, proscribe, °deny, °refuse, disallow: *Women are excluded from participating in certain religious ceremonies. Must we exclude Maria, too?* **2** °eliminate, °leave out, °reject, °omit, °except, °preclude, °repudiate, °count out: *Exclude them from consideration as candidates.* **3** °eject, °evict, °expel, oust, get °rid of, °remove, °throw out, *Colloq* °toss out, *Slang* bounce: *He was excluded from the club because of his behaviour.*

exclusion *n.* **1** lockout, shut-out, °ban, °bar, °prohibition, interdiction, forbiddance, °denial, °refusal, disallowance, proscription: *He would not join a club that supported the exclusion of women members.* **2** elimination, °rejection, °omission, repudiation, °exception, preclusion: *We must ensure the exclusion of unqualified candidates.* **3** °ejection, °eviction, °expulsion, ouster, °removal, riddance: *The exclusion of rowdies and hooligans is in the club's best interests.*

exclusive *adj.* **1** °incompatible, inimical, unshared, °unique, °absolute, restricted, °limited: *Exclusive concepts, like 'animal' and 'vegetable', do not coincide save in their both being 'alive'. Our newspaper printed the exclusive story of the disaster.* **2** °chic, clannish, °choice, °upper-class, aristocratic, closed, restricted, restrictive, °private, °snobbish, °fashionable, °elegant, °stylish, °select, *Colloq* °trendy, *Slang* classy: *They are seen in the most exclusive nightclubs.* **3** °only, °single, °one, °sole, °singular, °unique: *Boats are the exclusive means of transport here.* **4** Usually, **exclusive of**: excluding, excepting, °except for, omitting, ignoring, leaving aside, °apart from, (de)barring, not counting, eliminating: *Charges range from $220 to $350 a night, exclusive of meals.*

excruciating *adj.* tormenting, torturing, torturous, °agonizing, °painful, racking, °intense, °extreme, °unbearable, unendurable, °severe, °acute, °exquisite, °harrowing, distressful, distressing, °piercing, °insufferable: *She was racked with excruciating pain.*

excursion *n.* **1** °trip, °tour, °outing, airing, °expedition, voyage, °cruise, °journey, junket, jaunt; °ramble, °stroll, °walk, hike, trek, °drive, °ride, °sail: *We left the city and took an excursion into the mountains.* **2** °detour, deviation, side-trip, °diversion, °digression, excursus: *Forgive the excursion, but I'll return to the subject in a minute.*

excuse *v.* **1** °forgive, °pardon, °overlook, absolve, °clear, exonerate, acquit, exculpate, °pass over, °disregard, wink at, °ignore, be °blind to, look the other way, pay no °attention *or* °heed (to), find *or* prove °innocent (of): *Please excuse my tardiness.* **2** °release, °let go *or* off, °liberate, °free, °relieve, °exempt, absolve; °dismiss, *Colloq* °let off the °hook: *She was*

*excused from attending class today. You may be
excused.* **3** condone, °allow, °permit, °defend,
°apologize for, °justify, °warrant, °explain,
°vindicate, °rationalize, °mitigate, extenuate,
palliate: *Poverty does not excuse your stealing.*
—*n.* **4** apology, °explanation, °story, °reason,
justification, °defence, °plea, vindication, condonation, rationalization, extenuation, mitigation, palliation; °basis, °grounds,
°foundation, °cause: *Can you think of any excuse
for your behaviour?* **5** °forgiveness, °remission,
°pardon, °indulgence, °reprieve, clearing, exculpation, absolution, exoneration, acquittal,
°disregard, heedlessness, vindication,
°clearance, acquittance: *Ignorance of the law is not
an excuse.* **6** °evasion, °subterfuge, °pretence,
°pretext, °makeshift, °escape, °loophole, °way
out, *Colloq* °alibi, °stall, *Slang* cop-out: *He always
uses his grandmother's illness as an excuse for missing school.*

execute *v.* **1** °accomplish, do, °carry out *or* off
or through, °perform, °discharge, °dispatch *or*
despatch, °bring about *or* off, °implement,
°engineer, °cause, *Colloq* °pull off, °put over,
Slang US °swing, °cut, °hack (out): *She executes
her duties satisfactorily.* **2** °complete, °finish,
°deliver, °achieve, consummate, °fulfil, °effect,
°effectuate; °sign, °seal, validate, countersign:
*He executed the portrait in an hour. The contract was
executed yesterday.* **3** put to °death, °kill, put to
the sword, °butcher; liquidate, assassinate,
°murder, °remove, slay, *Slang* °bump off, °rub *or*
°wipe out, snuff (out), °knock off, *US* °waste,
ice: *Convicted murderers are no longer executed in
this country. The mob executed the rival gangleaders.*

execution *n.* **1** °accomplishment,
°performance, carrying out, doing, °discharge,
°dispatch *or* despatch, implementation,
prosecution, °realization, enactment: *His
drinking interferes with the execution of his
responsibilities.* **2** °completion, °fulfilment,
°consummation, °achievement, attainment,
implementation, bringing about,
°administration, pursuance: *The company will pay
ten thousand dollars upon execution of the
agreement.* **3** °killing, capital °punishment;
assassination, °murder, °removal, liquidation,
slaying: *The traitor's execution is tomorrow. There
has been another gangland style execution.* **4** °skill,
°art, mastery, °technique, °style, °manner,
°mode, °touch, °approach, °delivery,
°rendering, °rendition, °production: *The cellist's
execution was superb.*

executive *n.* **1** chairman (of the °board), chairperson, chairwoman, °director, managing
°director, °chief executive, president, °chief
(executive °officer), CEO, °manager, °head,
°leader, °principal, administrator, °official;
°supervisor, °foreman, °superintendent,
°overseer, °boss, °master, *Colloq* Mr Big, (°chief
or °head) honcho, number one, kingpin, *Slang*
°top banana, °big cheese, numero uno, °top
dog: *She is an executive in the local power
company.* **2** °administration, °management,
directorship, directorate, °government,
°leadership, supervision: *Five people form the
executive of the society.*
—*adj.* **3** administrative, managerial,
°supervisory, °official, governing, governmental, gubernatorial, regulatory: *He works in
the executive department of the government.*

exemplary *adj.* **1** illustrative, °typical,
°characteristic, °representative, archetypal;
paradigmatic: *The text contains passages exemplary
of good writing.* **2** °model, °meritorious,
°outstanding, °noteworthy, °admirable, commendable, °praiseworthy, °excellent, °superior:
Private Jones is an exemplary soldier. **3** cautionary,
admonitory, °warning, monitory: *In addition to
payment for the damage, we were awarded exemplary
damages.*

exemplify *v.* **1** °illustrate, °typify, °represent,
epitomize, °instance; °embody, °personify:
This painting exemplifies Picasso's blue period.
2 °demonstrate, °display, °show, °exhibit,
°model, depict: *Early Mediterranean civilization is
exemplified at Knossos.*

exempt *v.* **1** Often, **exempt from**: °free *or*
°liberate *or* °release from, °excuse *or* °relieve
from, °spare from, °let off, absolve, °except,
Colloq °let off the °hook: *The doctor exempted Becker
from strenuous activity.*
—*adj.* **2** exempted, °free, liberated, released,
excused, relieved, spared, °let off, excepted,
°immune, *Colloq* off the °hook: *It seems that Becker
is now exempt from doing any work.*

exemption *n.* °exception, °immunity, °freedom,
°release, impunity, dispensation, °exclusion: *This
document confirms his exemption from jury service.*

exercise *v.* **1** °employ, °use, °apply, °practise,
bring to bear, put to °use *or* °effect; °discharge,
°exert, °wield, °execute; utilize, °effect: *Try to
exercise better judgement next time. The chairman
exercises too much authority.* **2** °work out, limber
up, °warm up, °train, °drill: *She exercises for an
hour every day.* **3** °harass, °annoy, °irritate, vex,
harry, °distress, °worry, °concern, °burden, °try,
°trouble, °perturb, °disturb, °agitate, make
°nervous, *Colloq* drive °crazy, drive up the °wall:
*We have been much exercised over the issue of acid
rain.*
—*n.* **4** °activity, workout, working-out, warm-up,
warming up, callisthenics, aerobics, isometrics,
gymnastics; training, °drill, drilling: *Exercise is
good for the heart.* **5** °action, °application,
°practice, °performance, °discharge, °use, utilization, °employment, °execution, °operation:
We expect the exercise of your best endeavours.

exert *v.* **1** °exercise, °use, utilize, put to °use
or °work *or* °effect, °employ, °wield, bring to bear,
bring into play, °expend: *Please exert your influence
to have his conviction quashed.* **2 exert oneself**:
°attempt, °try, °endeavour, make an °effort,
°apply oneself, °strive, do one's °best, °work,
°strain, °struggle, toil, °push, °drive (oneself),
go all out, °give one's all, *Colloq* knock oneself
out, cudgel one's brains, beat one's brains out,
do one's damnedest, *Slang* bust a gut: *If Peter
exerted himself a bit more, we might see some results.*

exertion *n.* °action, °effort, striving, °strain,
°work, °struggle, toil, °drive, °push, diligence,
°industry, assiduity, assiduousness, sedulousness, sedulity, *Colloq US* stick-to-it-iveness:
*By considerable exertion, we finished on time. He was
tired after all his exertions.*

exhalation *n.* **1** °expiration, exhaling, °breath,
respiration, suspiration: *The doctor could detect
the wheezing only on exhalation.* **2** °vapour,
°breath, °air, °puff, whiff, °exhaust, emission,
steam, °mist, gas, °fog, °fume, emanation,

effluvium, °evaporation: *Poisonous exhalations from vents on the side of the volcano had destroyed all vegetation.*

exhale *v.* °breathe (out), °blow, °puff, °huff, °gasp, °evaporate, °pass off, °discharge, °emit, °emanate, °issue (forth), respire, suspire, °give forth, °blow off, °eject, °expel, exsufflate: *Please exhale into this balloon. The volcano continued to exhale noxious fumes.*

exhaust *v.* **1** °use (up), °expend, °consume, °finish, deplete, °spend, °dissipate, °run through, squander, °waste, °fritter away, *Slang* °blow: *In less than a year, he had exhausted all his funds.* **2** °tire (out), °fatigue, °weary, °wear out, °enervate, °fag, overtire, °sap, °strain, °tax, °weaken, °prostrate, debilitate, disable, *Colloq* frazzle: *Working sixty hours a week would exhaust anyone.* **3** °empty, °drain, °evacuate, °void, °clean *or* °clear out: *The pump is used to exhaust the chamber of air.* **4** °overdo, °overwork, treat thoroughly, deplete, °drain, °empty: *I think we've exhausted that topic.* **5** °empty (out), °drain (off *or* out), °vent, °issue, °escape, °discharge, °run out: *The fumes exhaust through this tube.* —*n.* **6** emanation, effluent, emission, fumes, gas: *Car exhausts are polluting the atmosphere.*

exhausted *adj.* **1** (°dead) °tired, °fatigued, °weary, wearied, °worn out, enervated, debilitated, overtired, °weak, weakened, °prostrate, °worn *or* fagged *or* played *or* burnt-out, °spent, all in, out on one's feet, *Colloq* dog-tired, °dead (on one's feet), wiped out, drained, knocked out, done in, frazzled, *Slang* (°dead) °beat, *Brit* knackered, *US and Canadian* pooped: *I must sleep: I'm exhausted.* **2** °empty, emptied, °bare; depleted, consumed, done, gone, at an °end, finished: *Our supply of paper-clips is exhausted.* **3** °spent, °worn out, depleted, °impoverished, °poor, °infertile, °barren: *It is impossible to grow anything in this exhausted soil.*

exhausting *adj.* **1** tiring, fatiguing, wearying, enervating, wearing, debilitating: *Proofreading these figures can be exhausting.* **2** °arduous, °laborious, back-breaking, °strenuous, °hard, gruelling, crippling, °difficult, °burdensome, onerous: *Harvesting sugar is exhausting work.*

exhaustion *n.* **1** emptying, drawing out *or* forth, °discharge, draining, evacuation, voiding, depletion, consumption, °finish(ing): *The exhaustion of air from the cylinder is accomplished by a powerful pump.* **2** tiredness, °fatigue, enervation, debilitation, weariness, lassitude: *The survivors were suffering from exposure and exhaustion.*

exhaustive *adj.* °complete, °comprehensive, all-inclusive, °thorough, all-encompassing, °encyclopedic *or* encyclopaedic, °extensive, thoroughgoing, far-reaching, °sweeping, full-scale, in-depth, maximal, °maximum, *Colloq* all-out: *The police conducted an exhaustive investigation of the company's finances.*

exhibit *v.* °show, °display, °present, °offer, expose; °show off, °parade, brandish, °flaunt, °demonstrate, °reveal, °betray, °manifest, °exemplify, evince, °evidence, disclose, °express: *Her paintings are widely exhibited. Such behaviour exhibits poor judgement.*

exhibition *n.* °exposition, °fair, °show(ing), °display, °demonstration, °presentation, °offering, *US* °exhibit, *Colloq* expo, demo: *The craft exhibition will be held at the civic centre.*

exhilarating *adj.* **1** °invigorating, °bracing, °stimulating, vivifying, enlivening, rejuvenating, °refreshing, vitalizing, fortifying, restorative, °tonic: *We took an exhilarating walk round the lake.* **2** cheering, uplifting, gladdening, elating, inspiriting, heartening, comforting, reassuring; °happy, °good, °delightful: *We received the exhilarating news of Phoebe's complete recovery.*

exile *n.* **1** expatriation, banishment, °expulsion, deportation, transportation; °separation: *Napoleon was sentenced to exile on Elba.* **2** expatriate, émigré(e), °emigrant, °outcast, deportee, pariah, displaced person, DP; °alien, °foreigner, °outsider: *Many of the exiles from Nazi Germany settled in Britain.* —*v.* **3** deport, °expel, °alienate, °banish, expatriate, oust, °eject, °displace, °transport, °drive *or* °run *or* °cast out, °outlaw, °exclude, oust, °evict, °bar, °ban; extradite; °maroon: *Many criminals were exiled to Australia.*

exist *v.* **1** be, °continue, °prevail, °endure, °abide; °live, °breathe: *Some believe that the universe exists only in our imagination.* **2** °survive, subsist, eke out a living *or* an °existence, °stay °alive, °get by *or* along: *How can the family exist only on his pension?* **3** °occur, °happen, be °found, be °present, °remain, °persist; °obtain, °prevail: *A two-foot gap exists between the wall and the roof. 'Status quo' refers to the circumstances that exist.*

existence *n.* **1** being, °presence, actuality, °fact: *Most cultures believe in the existence of one god or more.* **2** °life, living; continuance, continuation, °persistence, °permanence, duration, °endurance: *The early settlers had to struggle for existence.* **3** °entity, being, °creature; ens, quiddity, °essence: *In Hindu philosophy, there is no limit to the number of existences.*

exit *n.* **1** °way out, egress, door, °gate; °outlet, °vent: *Everyone left by the emergency exit when the alarm rang. This is the exit for the smoke.* **2** departure, leave-taking, withdrawal, leaving, °retreat, retirement; °flight, exodus, evacuation, °escape: *Terribly embarrassed, they made their exit. The villain's exit from the stage was marked by catcalls.* —*v.* **3** °go (out *or* away), (take one's) °leave, °depart, take *or* make one's departure, °retire, (beat a) °retreat, bid adieu, °withdraw, °run, (take a) °walk, °walk out (on), °quit, °escape, take to one's heels, show a clean pair of heels, vanish, °disappear, *Colloq* °take off, skedaddle, °kiss °goodbye, *US* °cut out; *Slang* °beat it, *US and Canadian* take it on the lam, lam (on) out of *or* from, take a (run-out) powder: *He exited from the party as soon as he could.*

exorbitant *adj.* °extraordinary, °excessive, °extravagant, °outrageous, °immoderate, extortionate, °extreme, °unreasonable, °inordinate, °disproportionate, °unconscionable, °preposterous, undue, °unwarranted, unjustifiable, unjustified: *The price of petrol in Britain is exorbitant.*

exotic *adj.* **1** °foreign, °alien, non-native, imported: *She raises exotic plants.* **2** °strange, °unfamiliar, °unusual, °bizarre, °odd, °peculiar, °unique, °singular, °extraordinary, °remarkable, out of the ordinary, °different, °outlandish, °weird, °crazy: *His exotic clothes make him stand out in a crowd.* **3** striptease, belly, go-go, topless, bottomless, °nude: *Her daughter is an exotic dancer at the new disco.*

expand v. **1** °enlarge, °spread (out), °extend, °increase, °open (out or up), °swell, °inflate, distend; °unfold: *His waistline began to expand as he approached middle age.* **2** °prolong, °lengthen, °stretch, dilate: *An elastic valve expands easily.* **3** °increase, °extend, °amplify, °magnify, broaden, °widen, augment, °heighten, °develop: *The minister sought to expand his influence.* **4** Often, **expand on**: °detail, °enlarge on, °embellish, °develop, °amplify, expatiate on or upon, °elaborate (on); °flesh out: *The speaker expanded on the topic of health insurance.*

expanse n. °stretch, °extent, °area, °space, °range, °sweep, °reach, °length and °breadth, °spread: *The vast expanses of space are yet to be explored.*

expansion n. **1** °increase, augmentation, °development, enlargement, °extension, burgeoning or bourgeoning, flourishing, °growth, °spread: *How will the company finance its expansion in other markets?* **2** dilatation or dilation, stretching, distension or distention, inflation, °swelling: *The animal moves by the alternate expansion and contraction of the muscle.*

expansive adj. **1** expansible or expandable or expandible, inflatable, dilatable, extensible or extendible or extendable; extending, expanding, enlarging, spreading, °opening or stretching (out): *Increased temperature causes the enlargement of expansive materials.* **2** °effusive, °open, °free, °easy, °genial, °amiable, °friendly, °warm, affable, °sociable, °outgoing, communicative, °outspoken, extrovert(ed) or extravert(ed), °talkative, loquacious, garrulous, °frank, unreserved: *William became relaxed, almost expansive over the meal.* **3** °broad, °extensive, far-reaching, wide-ranging; °comprehensive, widespread, all-embracing, (all-) °inclusive: *We stood on the edge of an expansive desert. The company has expansive interests in Europe.*

expect v. **1** °anticipate, °look forward or °ahead to, have or keep in view, await, °envisage, °watch or °look for, °wait for, °contemplate, °foresee, US °envision: *She expects to leave. He was expecting her at noon.* **2** °assume, °presume, °suppose, °imagine, °believe, °think, °trust, °surmise, conjecture; °foresee, US and Canadian °guess: *I expect you will be hungry when you return.* **3** °look for, °want, °require, °wish, °need, °demand, °reckon on or upon, °hope for, °calculate or °count on or upon: *What did you expect me to do?*

expectant adj. °expecting, (a)waiting, °ready, °eager, apprehensive, °anxious, with bated breath, °hopeful, looking, watchful, anticipating: *The understudy waited, expectant, in the wings.*

expectation n. **1** °anticipation, °confidence, hopefulness, watchfulness, apprehension, apprehensiveness, expectancy, °suspense: *There was an air of expectation in the room.* **2** °hope, assumption, °presumption, °surmise, °supposition, °belief, conjecture, US and Canadian °guess: *Our expectation is that he will come on the next train.* **3** °demand, °requirement, °wish, °desire, °want, insistence, °reliance: *I think your expectations might be too optimistic.* **4** °prospects, °outlook: *He had great expectations from his rich uncle.*

expecting adj. °pregnant, gravid, with child, enceinte, Brit in the family way, US in a family way, Colloq in the club, Brit preggers, Slang US with a bun in the oven: *Monica is expecting and will give birth any day.*

expedient adj. **1** °suitable, °appropriate, °fitting, °fit, °befitting, °proper, apropos, °right, °correct, °meet, °pertinent, °applicable, °practical, pragmatic, °worthwhile, °politic: *To cross the river, a bridge would prove expedient.* **2** °advantageous, °beneficial, °advisable, °desirable, recommended, °useful, °practical, utilitarian, °prudent, °wise, °propitious, °opportune, °helpful, °effective: *Count on him to do what is expedient and ignore what is honest.* —n. **3** °device, °resource, °means, °measure, contrivance, °resort, °recourse: *Life jackets are a useful expedient if the boat sinks.*

expedite v. **1** °hasten, °rush, °hurry, °speed or °step up, accelerate; °dispatch or despatch: *The shipment has been expedited and should reach you tomorrow.* **2** °advance, °facilitate, °promote, °forward, °ease, °enable: *The growing process can be expedited by adding this chemical.*

expedition n. **1** °exploration, °journey, voyage, field (trip), °tour, °excursion; °enterprise, °undertaking, °mission, °quest: *She went on an expedition up the Amazon to research herbal medicines.* **2** °speed, promptness, celerity, alacrity, °dispatch or despatch, °haste, °rapidity, swiftness, quickness: *He was ordered to complete his chores with expedition.*

expeditious adj. °ready, quick, °rapid, °swift, °fast, °brisk, °speedy, °fleet, °efficient, °diligent: *We make an expeditious passage round Cape Horn. The problem requires an expeditious solution.*

expel v. **1** °eject, dislodge, °throw or °cast out, °drive or °force out, °evict, °put or °push out, °remove, °run (someone) off or out, °displace, °dispossess, show the door, °suspend, °dismiss, °let °go, Colloq °fire, Brit °sack, °turf out: *They will expel the tenant at the earliest opportunity.* **2** °banish, deport, °exile, expatriate, °outlaw, °maroon; proscribe, °ban, °bar, debar, °dismiss, °exclude, blackball, drum out, cashier, °discharge, oust: *The leader of the opposition was expelled from the country. The committee voted to expel Horace from the club.*

expend v. **1** °pay out, °spend, disburse, °use, °employ, Slang °lay or dish out, fork or °shell out: *Reduce the money expended on entertainment.* **2** °use up, °consume, °exhaust, deplete, °finish (off), °dissipate, °sap, °drain: *I expended all my energies eking out a bare living.*

expendable adj. °dispensable, °disposable, °non-essential, inessential or unessential, °unnecessary, replaceable; unimportant, °insignificant: *In terms of military strategy, the commando unit was expendable.*

expenditure n. °outlay, outgoings, disbursement, spending, °payment, °expense, °cost; °price, °charge, °fee: *The financial director must closely examine all expenditures. I cannot justify that kind of expenditure for a car.*

expense n. **1** Often, **expenses**: °payment, °cost(s), °outlay, outgoings, disbursement, °expenditure, spending, out-of-pocket (expenses); °price, °charge, °fee, °rate: *Keep your expenses to a minimum. Expenses for travel and entertainment will be reimbursed by the* *company.* **2** °detriment, °sacrifice, °cost, °loss, °impairment, °ruin, °destruction: *They continue to smoke at the expense of their health.*

expensive *adj.* costly, °dear, high-priced, up-market, valuable, °precious, °priceless, °extravagant; overpriced: *Richard and Elizabeth flew off for an expensive holiday in the sun.*

experience *n.* **1** °knowledge, °contact, involvement, °practice, °familiarity, °acquaintance, °exposure; participation, °observation: *Her book on nursing is based on personal experience.* **2** °incident, °event, °happening, °affair, °episode, °occurrence, °circumstance, °adventure, °encounter; °trial, °test, °ordeal: *He has lived through some harrowing experiences.* **3** common °sense, °wisdom, sagacity, °knowledge, know-how, savoir faire, savoir vivre, °sophistication, °skill, °judgement, *Slang* savvy: *She is a woman of experience.*
—*v.* **4** °undergo, °live *or* °go through, °suffer, °endure, °sustain, °face, °encounter, °meet (with), °feel, °sense, °taste, °sample, be °familiar with, °know: *Your problem is that you have never experienced genuine hunger.*

experienced *adj.* **1** °adept, skilled, °skilful, °accomplished, °practised, °proficient, °knowledgeable, °knowing, °wise, °sage, sagacious, °shrewd, °prepared, (°well-)°informed, trained, (well-)°versed, °expert, °master, masterly, °qualified, °professional, °competent, °efficient, °capable, *au fait; Slang* on the ball, *US* savvy: *She is an experienced surgeon.* **2** °mature, °seasoned, °sophisticated, battle-scarred, °seasoned, °veteran; *Slang* in the know, *US* savvy: *We need an experienced leader.*

experiment *n.* **1** °test, °trial, °investigation, °inquiry *or* enquiry, °examination, experimentation, °research, °proof: *Experiment has shown that the ointment cures many minor skin ailments.* **2** °procedure, °policy: *Totalitarianism seems to have failed as a political experiment.*
—*v.* **3 experiment on** *or* **with:** °test, °try, °examine, °investigate, °research, °probe: *The time has come to experiment on human subjects. Artists now experiment with many media, from canvas to computers.*

experimental *adj.* **1** °hypothetical, °theoretical, °tentative, °speculative, conjectural, exploratory: *Man's first attempts at flying were purely experimental.* **2** °empirical, experiential: *She has profound experimental knowledge of what is involved.*

expert *n.* **1** °authority, °professional, °specialist, °scholar, °master, connoisseur, pundit, *Colloq* wizard, whiz, pro, ace, *Brit* °dab hand, boffin, *Slang US* maven *or* mavin: *We rely on experts to verify the age of works of art.*
—*adj.* **2** °skilful, skilled, trained, °knowledgeable, °learned, °experienced, °practised, °qualified, °adept, °proficient, °accomplished, *au fait*, adroit, °dexterous, °polished, finished, °masterful, masterly, °first-rate, °excellent, °superb, wonderful, °superior, °champion(ship), A-one, A-1, °virtuoso, *Colloq* top-notch, *Brit* whizzo, wizard, *US* crackerjack, °crack: *Davis is an expert snooker player.*

expertise *n.* expertness, °skill, °knowledge, know-how, °judgement, mastery; °dexterity, adroitness, *Slang* savvy: *You need a great deal of expertise to be a museum curator.*

expiration *n.* expiry, °finish, (coming to an) °end, °termination, running out, ending, conclusion, concluding, °close, closing, discontinuance, discontinuation: *The expiration of the option is in March.*

expire *v.* **1** °cease, (come to an) °end, °close, °finish, °terminate, °run out, conclude, °discontinue: *Your subscription expires with the next issue.* **2** °die, breathe one's last, decease, °perish, °pass away: *His grandmother expired only last year, at the age of 110.* **3** °exhale, °breathe out, °expel: *In the daytime we expire more carbon dioxide than during the night.*

explain *v.* **1** °interpret, °define, explicate, °detail, delineate, make °plain, °simplify, °spell out, °resolve, °get across, °clarify, °clear up, elucidate, °illustrate, expound, °describe, °disclose, °unfold, unravel, untangle: *The teacher explained the theory so that even I could understand it.* **2** Also, **explain away:** °justify, °account for, °excuse, °rationalize, °legitimate, legitimatize, extenuate, palliate: *You will be required to explain your absence.*

explanation *n.* **1** °interpretation, °definition, explication, delineation, simplification, °resolution, clarification, elucidation, °description, °illustration, °exposition, °account, disclosure; exegesis, commentary, °criticism, °analysis: *The encyclopedia contains detailed explanations of how machines work.* **2** °excuse, rationalization, justification, vindication: *What is your explanation for such outrageous behaviour?* **3** °cause, °motive, °reason, °key, signification, °solution: *The explanation for aberrant behaviour often lies in hormonal imbalance.*

explanatory *adj.* explanative, elucidative, revelatory, interpretive *or* interpretative, expository, descriptive; °critical, exegetic(al): *Please read the explanatory notes below.*

expletive *adj.* **1** °wordy, verbose, prolix, °repetitious, °redundant, tautological, iterative, reiterative, pleonastic; °unnecessary, unneeded, °needless, unessential, °non-essential, °gratuitous, °superfluous: *Her speech is punctuated by expletive words and phrases, like 'like, you know', and so forth.*
—*n.* **2** °oath, swear-word, °curse, obscenity, epithet, *Colloq* cuss-word, °dirty word, four-letter word: *Expletives sometimes lend an air of naturalness to written dialogue.* **3** filler, padding, redundancy, °tautology, pleonasm: *Some grammarians term the 'It' in 'It is raining' an expletive.*

explicit *adj.* **1** °specific, °categorical, (crystal-)°clear, °definite, well-defined, °distinct, unambiguous, °precise, °exact, unequivocal, °express, stated, °plain, °manifest, unmistakable, °positive, °absolute, °final, peremptory, °unqualified, unconditional: *The children had explicit instructions to keep away from the canal.* **2** °open, °outspoken, unreserved, unrestrained, °candid, °frank, °direct, °forthright, straightforward, °definite: *She was explicit in her orders.*

explode *v.* **1** °blow up, °burst, °blast, °fly °apart, °go off, °erupt, fulminate; °set off, detonate: *Police exploded the bomb after clearing the area. Rockets exploded in the night sky.* **2** °reject, °discredit, refute, °repudiate, °disprove, debunk, belie, give the lie to, *Slang* pick holes in, poke *or* shoot full of holes: *Ptolemy's geocentric theory has been thoroughly exploded.* **3** lose one's

°temper, °rant, °rave, °rage, °storm, throw a °tantrum, *Colloq* get into a tizzy, °blow one's top, °fly off the handle, go through *or* hit the roof, hit the ceiling; *Slang* °lose one's °cool, go up the °wall, *US* blow one's °stack *or* °cool, °flip (one's lid), freak out: *He exploded when he learned his car had been smashed up.*

exploit *n.* 1 °achievement, °deed, °feat, attainment, °accomplishment: *The speaker regaled them with tales of his exploits as an explorer.* —*v.* 2 °use, take °advantage of, °manipulate, make °capital out of, °profit from, utilize, turn to °account, °manoeuvre, °work: *Far from being your friends, they are exploiting you for their own purposes. They need capital to exploit the country's natural resources.*

exploration *n.* °examination, °investigation, °search, °probe, °inquiry *or* enquiry, °study, °research, °analysis, °review, °scrutiny, inspection, °survey, °reconnaissance, °observation; °expedition: *Exploration of the intestine revealed the presence of polyps. He is noted for his exploration of the sources of the Nile.*

explore *v.* 1 °survey, °tour, °travel, °reconnoitre, °traverse: *They are on safari, exploring the Congo.* 2 °investigate, °scrutinize, °examine, °inquire *or* °enquire into, °inspect, °probe, °search, °research, °look into, °study, °analyse, °review, °observe: *We ought to explore the possibility of your working for us.*

explosion *n.* 1 °blast, bang, °report, °burst, °boom, °clap, °crack, °eruption, °crash, °outburst, fulmination; detonation: *The explosion shook the entire house.* 2 °outburst, outbreak, °paroxysm, °upheaval, flare-up, °eruption, °burst, °fit, °spasm, °tantrum, *Colloq Brit* °paddy *or* paddywhack *or* paddywack, wax: *The unrest among the people is building up to an explosion.* 3 °increase, burgeoning *or* bourgeoning, °expansion, welling up, mushrooming: *The population explosion has caused a housing shortage.*

explosive *adj.* 1 °volatile, °sensitive, °delicate, °tense, °anxious, °fraught, touch-and-go, °touchy, °inflammable, (highly) charged, °unstable, °uncertain, °unsound, shaky, °hazardous, chancy, unpredictable, °precarious, °dangerous, °perilous, °critical, °nasty, °ugly, *Colloq* °dicey, iffy: *The explosive situation between the strikers and management may lead to bloodshed.* —*n.* 2 dynamite, TNT, gunpowder, gelignite, °plastic, plastique: *The car was blown up by a powerful charge of explosive.*

expose *v.* 1 (lay) °bare, °reveal, uncover, °show, °exhibit, °present, °display, °disclose; divulge, °unveil, unmask, °discover, °air, ventilate, °let out, °leak, °betray, bring to °light, °make known: *He unbuttoned his shirt, exposing his hairy chest. The facts of the case will be exposed tomorrow. Will he expose the names of his accomplices?* 2 °risk, imperil, °endanger, °jeopardize, °hazard: *Do not expose your house to danger of flooding by building it so close to the river.* 3 **expose to**: °subject to, °introduce to, °acquaint with, bring into °contact with: *Today children are not taught, but 'exposed to education'.*

exposition *n.* 1 °exhibition, °show(ing), °presentation, °display, °demonstration, *US* exhibit, *Colloq* expo: *There is a special exposition of medieval farming implements in the museum.* 2 °description, °declaration,

°statement, °explanation, explication, clarification, °interpretation, exegesis: *The exposition of his argument was remarkably lucid.* 3 °paper, °theme, article, °essay, °thesis, dissertation, treatise, disquisition, °study, critique, commentary: *She received high marks for her exposition on Zoroastrianism.*

exposure *n.* 1 baring, uncovering, laying °open, unveiling, disclosure, disclosing, unmasking, revealing, °revelation, exposé, airing, °publication, publishing, communicating, communication, leaking, °leak, divulging: *The exposure of the spy was part of the plan.* 2 °jeopardy, °risk, °hazard, endangerment, vulnerability, imperilment; °danger, °peril: *By diversifying your investments, you reduce your exposure to a loss in just one.* 3 °familiarity, °knowledge, °acquaintance, °experience, °contact, conversancy: *My exposure to Chinese philosophy has been negligible.* 4 °aspect, °view, °outlook, °orientation, frontage; °setting, °location, °direction: *She said that she preferred a bedroom with an easterly exposure.*

express *v.* 1 articulate, verbalize, °phrase, utter, °voice, °state, °word, °put (into words), °set *or* °put forth, °put *or* °get across, °communicate, depict, °portray; °say, °speak, °tell: *She expressed her thoughts on the subject very clearly.* 2 °show, °indicate, °demonstrate, °manifest, °exhibit, evince, °evidence, °reveal, expose, °disclose, divulge, °make known, °intimate, betoken, °signify, °embody, depict, °designate, °denote, convey: *His tone of voice expressed his resentment.* 3 °symbolize, °represent, °signify, °stand for, °denote, °designate: *The ratio can be expressed in the form of a fraction.* 4 °press *or* °squeeze *or* wring *or* °force out, °expel, °extract: *The oil is expressed from ripe olives.* —*adj.* 5 °explicit, °clear, °plain, unambiguous, unmistakable, °unqualified, °outright, °definite, °out-and-out, °downright, straightforward, °categorical, °direct, °specific, well-defined, °distinct, °precise, °accurate, °exact, °positive: *We had an express understanding not to enter into competition with one another.* 6 °specific, °special, °particular, clear-cut, °true: *Our express purpose in coming was to see you.* 7 quick, °speedy, °swift, °fast, °rapid, °prompt, °immediate; °direct, °non-stop: *The documents must be sent by express delivery.*

expression *n.* 1 verbalization, airing, °representation, °declaration, utterance, °assertion, enunciation, asseveration, °pronouncement, communication, voicing, °announcement: *Any expression of criticism of government is forbidden in many countries.* 2 °representation, °manifestation, °sign, °token, °symbol, °show, °demonstration, °indication, °evidence: *A curled lip is an expression of scorn.* 3 °look, mien, °air, °appearance, °face, °aspect, countenance: *He had long straight hair and a completely blank expression. Her smile twisted into an expression of frustration.* 4 °tone, °note, nuance, °intonation, °accent, °touch, shading, loudness, softness; expressiveness, °emotion, °feeling, °sensitivity, °passion, °spirit, depth, °ardour, °intensity, pathos: *There was much expression in her playing of the fugue.* 5 °word, °term, °phrase, °idiom, turn of °phrase, locution, saying: *Some find the expression 'Have a nice day' to be irritating.* 6 °wording, phrasing, phraseology,

°language, °style, °diction, °usage, °speech, °delivery: *Writers are not the only ones who should study effective expression.*

expressive *adj.* **1** indicative, °suggestive, allusive, °eloquent, revealing, °meaningful, °significant, denotative: *Her frown is expressive of her disapproval.* **2** °pointed, pithy, °explicit: *Leave it to him to make some expressive remark about Frieda's hat.* **3** °striking, °vivid, °telling, °pregnant, °loaded, °forceful, °moving, °emotional, °poignant, °provocative, thought-provoking: *His poetry contains much expressive language.*

expressly *adv.* **1** distinctly, °definitely, categorically, explicitly, °absolutely, °positively, °directly, unambiguously, unequivocally, unmistakably, plainly, pointedly, °exactly, °clearly: *He expressly denied the rumour.* **2** purposely, °especially, purposefully, °particularly, specifically, °specially; on °purpose: *The gift was intended expressly for you.*

expulsion *n.* expelling, °ejection, °eviction, repudiation, ouster, °removal, °dismissal, °discharge; *Colloq* the (old) heave-ho, *Brit* the boot, the °sack, sacking, *US* the bounce: *His expulsion from the pub was accompanied by cheers from the patrons.*

exquisite *adj.* **1** °delicate, °fine, °elegant, °graceful, °excellent, °choice, well-crafted, well-made, wellexecuted, °refined, °elaborate: *They have a collection of exquisite miniature portraits.* **2** °ingenious, °detailed, recherché, °rare, °subtle, °deep, abstruse; °far-fetched: *He is expert in the exquisite points of seduction.* **3** °beautiful, °perfect, °lovely, °attractive, °handsome, °comely, good-looking; °smart, °chic, °elegant, °striking: *In her youth, she was an exquisite blonde goddess. He wore an exquisite silk costume.* **4** °acute, °sharp, °keen, °excruciating, °agonizing, °intense; °elaborate: *The most exquisite pain I have known is occasioned by gout. Spies, subjected to exquisite torture, usually revealed their secrets.* **5** °superb, °superior, °peerless, °matchless, °incomparable, unequalled, °rare, °precious, °choice, consummate, °outstanding, °superlative, °excellent, °select, °flawless, °perfect, wonderful, °splendid, °marvellous: *She wore a tiara of exquisite diamonds.*

extemporaneous *adj.* unstudied, °unpremeditated, extempore, extemporary, impromptu, improvised, °spontaneous, unrehearsed, extemporized, °unprepared, unplanned, unscripted, °offhand, ad lib, *Colloq* off the cuff: *Though extraordinarily well-organized, Charlotte's speech was entirely extemporaneous.*

extend *v.* **1** °stretch or °spread (out), outstretch, outspread, °open (out), unroll, °unfold; °reach, °range; °carry on, °draw out, °continue, °develop: *The carpet extends from wall to wall. Her reputation extends worldwide. The city walls extended to the river.* **2** °lengthen, elongate, °widen, °continue; broaden, °enlarge, °add to, augment; °increase, °stretch (out), °supplement: *We are planning to extend the sitting-room. They asked the mortgage company to extend the repayment period.* **3** °last, °stretch, °continue, °go or °carry on; °perpetuate, °drag on or out, °keep up or on, °prolong: *Their visit extended until the following week.* **4** °offer, proffer, °give, °present, °hold out, °stretch forth, °tender; °bestow; °grant,

°impart, °confer, °accord, °advance: *She extended her hand. The store does not extend credit to any customers.*

extension *n.* **1** stretching, °expansion, °increase, enlargement, augmentation, °development, amplification, broadening, widening, lengthening, °spread, spreading: *The extension of the plan is scheduled for next year.* **2** °range, extensiveness, °scope, °extent, °magnitude, °gauge, compass, °sweep, °reach, °size, °volume, dimension(s), °proportions, °capacity, °span; °breadth, °width, °height, °length, °spread, °stretch: *The extension of the mind seems almost limitless.* **3** addendum, °addition, annexe, wing, adjunct, ell, appendage; appendix, °supplement: *We have built an extension to the house.*

extensive *adj.* **1** °broad, °wide, °expansive, far-reaching, far-ranging, wide-ranging, far-flung, °sweeping, widespread, °comprehensive, all-embracing; °national, nationwide, °international, intercontinental, cosmopolitan, worldwide, °global, °universal, °vast; cosmic; °catholic: *The storm is responsible for extensive crop damage. He has extensive business connections.* **2** °large, °big, °great, °huge, °substantial, °considerable, sizeable, °immense, °enormous, °vast, °gigantic, °massive; °voluminous, °spacious, commodious, capacious: *The extensive gold deposits were soon depleted. The cave contains several extensive chambers.*

extent *n.* **1** °magnitude, dimensions, compass, °size, °range, °scale, °sweep, °scope, °expanse, immensity, °enormousness, capaciousness, spaciousness, °space, amplitude: *The extent of space is unimaginably vast.* **2** °limit, bounds, limitation, °lengths; °range, °scope: *To what extent will he go to see justice done?* **3** °area, °region, °tract, °territory, compass: *In the whole extent of Europe you could find no better mushroom.*

extenuating *adj.* °mitigating, lessening, tempering, palliating, moderating, diminishing, qualifying: *Owing to extenuating circumstances, he could not be tried for murder.*

exterior *adj.* **1** outer, °outside, °external, °outward, °superficial, °surface: *The exterior covering of the capsule becomes very hot on re-entry into the earth's atmosphere.* **2** °external, °extrinsic, °extraneous, °foreign, °alien, °exotic, °outside: *The problem can be overcome without exterior help.* —*n.* **3** °outside, °surface, covering, coating, °facing, °face, °front, °skin, °shell, façade: *The exterior is of pink stucco.*

exterminate *v.* °destroy, °root out, eradicate, extirpate, annihilate, °eliminate, weed out, get °rid of, °wipe out, °obliterate, put an °end to, °terminate, liquidate, °massacre, °murder, °kill (off), °butcher, °slaughter, *Slang* °bump off, *US* °rub out, °waste: *It is his avowed intention to exterminate all the vermin of the criminal fraternity.*

external *adj.* **1** outer, °outside, °outward, °exterior: *This medication is for external use only.* **2** °outside, °exterior, °extrinsic, °extraneous, °alien, °foreign, °exotic: *Do not ignore the external influences on the nation's economy.* **3** °apparent, °visible, °perceptible, °superficial, °surface: *The external features of the planet barely suggest what lies within.*

extinct *adj.* **1** °defunct, °dead, died out, gone, departed, vanished: *These are the bones of an* *extinct species of flying mammal.* **2** dated, outmoded, °old-fashioned, °antiquated, °obsolete, archaic, out of °date, antediluvian, °ancient, °old hat, °passé, *démodé*: *High-button shoes and bustles have been extinct for almost a century.* **3** °out, extinguished, quenched, burnt- *or* °put *or* snuffed out; °inactive, °dormant: *The lake is in the caldera of an extinct volcano.*

extinguish *v.* **1** °put *or* snuff *or* °blow out, °quench; °turn off *or* out: *We are landing shortly, so please extinguish all smoking materials. Extinguish the lights before leaving.* **2** °kill (off), annihilate, °destroy, °obliterate, °abolish, °exterminate, °eliminate, do away with, nullify, eradicate, °remove, °banish, °wipe *or* °blot out: *The potion contained a drug that extinguished all memory of unhappiness.* **3** °obscure, °eclipse, °dim, °outdo, put in the °shade, °overshadow, adumbrate, *Colloq* °show up: *His personality is completely extinguished by the dazzle of his wife.*

extol *v.* °exalt, elevate, uplift, °glorify, °praise, °laud, °applaud, commend, acclaim, °cheer, °celebrate, pay °tribute *or* °homage to, sing the °praises of, °make much of, °honour, °congratulate, °compliment: *William is always extolling the talents of some dancer or other.*

extort *v.* °exact, °extract, °blackmail, °bully, coerce, °force, wring, wrest, *Colloq* °milk, bleed, put the arm on (someone): *Threatening to swear that it was my fault, she extorted a promise from me to keep silent about the body.*

extra *adj.* **1** additional, added, °auxiliary, °accessory, °supplementary, supplemental, °further, ancillary, °subsidiary, collateral, adventitious: *We had an extra person for dinner.* **2** °leftover, °excess, °spare, °surplus, °unused, °superfluous, supernumerary, °reserve: *After all were served, we had two extra desserts.* —*n.* **3** °addition, addendum, °accessory, appurtenance, °supplement, °bonus, °premium, dividend: *As an extra, each customer receives a free ball-point pen.* **4** °supplement, *US* mark-up, surcharge, *Slang US and Canadian* kicker: *There is an extra if you want bread and butter.* **5** supernumerary, walk-on, *Colloq* °super, spear-carrier: *One could scarcely call being an extra a 'Hollywood career'.* —*adv.* **6** uncommonly, unusually, exceptionally, unexpectedly, extraordinarily, remarkably, °notably, surprisingly, amazingly, °very, °particularly, °especially, °extremely, strikingly: *Teacher said that Philip was extra good today.* **7** additionally, again, more, in °addition: *They charge extra for room service.*

extract *v.* **1** °draw *or* °pull (out), °remove, °withdraw, °pluck *or* °take out, °draw forth, °extricate: *The dentist extracted two teeth. I extracted some important papers from your waste-paper basket.* **2** °draw, °derive, °deduce, °develop, glean, °extricate, distil, °get, °obtain: *I could extract little sense from her ramblings.* **3** °wrench, wring, wrest, °extort, °draw (forth), °evoke, °elicit, °extricate, winkle out, worm (out), prise (out), °force (out): *Using torture, they finally extracted a confession from him. She extracted money from her victims by threatening to tell their wives.* **4** °copy, °quote, cite, °abstract, °select, °choose, glean, cull: *We extracted useful material from some old encyclopedias.* —*n.* **5** °concentrate, distillate, °essence, distillation, °quintessence, concentration,

°extraction, decoction: *We boiled off the water and used the extract as a salve.* **6** °excerpt, °abstract, °quotation, citation, clipping, °cutting, °passage, °selection: *Extracts from other works are printed in smaller type.*

extraction *n.* **1** °removal, extrication, withdrawal, uprooting, eradication, extirpation, deracination: *The extraction of my tooth was completely painless.* **2** °extract, °concentrate, distillate, °essence, distillation, °quintessence, concentration, decoction, °separation, °derivation: *This syrup is an extraction from coffee beans.* **3** °origin, °birth, ancestry, descent, °lineage, °derivation, blood, °parentage, °breed, °strain, °race, stock, °pedigree: *The family is of Scandinavian extraction.*

extraneous *adj.* **1** unessential, °non-essential, inessential, °peripheral, °superfluous, °unnecessary, unneeded, °extra, added, additional, adventitious, supernumerary, °incidental, °needless: *Filter out all the extraneous substances.* **2** not pertinent, °impertinent, °inapplicable, inapt, unapt, unfitting, °inappropriate, °unrelated, °irrelevant, inapposite, unconnected, °remote, °alien, °foreign, °exotic, °strange, °outlandish, °external, °extrinsic, out of place, off the mark *or* point *or* subject, beside the point *or* mark: *Why must you constantly bring up extraneous matters?*

extraordinary *adj.* **1** °unusual, uncommon, °remarkable, °exceptional, °particular, °outstanding, °special, °rare, °unique, °singular, °signal, °unheard-of, °curious, °peculiar, °odd, °bizarre, °queer, °strange, °abnormal, unprecedented, °unparalleled: *She showed extraordinary courage in coming here.* **2** °amazing, surprising, astonishing, astounding, °remarkable, °notable, °noteworthy, °marvellous, °fantastic, °incredible, °unbelievable, °impressive, °fabulous, °miraculous, °unparalleled, *Colloq* °super, smashing, °lovely, °gorgeous, *Slang* far-out, °unreal: *This is an extraordinary example of the bookbinder's art.*

extravagance *n.* **1** wastefulness, °waste, lavishness, °profligacy, °prodigality, squandering, °dissipation, improvidence, exorbitance, recklessness, overspending, °excess: *Our present debts are the result of extravagance.* **2** immoderation, immoderateness, excessiveness, outrageousness, unrestraint, °superfluity, superfluousness, over-sufficiency, preposterousness, unreasonableness, irrationality, °absurdity; capriciousness, whim, °fantasy, flightiness: *His tawdry life belied the extravagance of his dreams.*

extravagant *adj.* **1** °wasteful, °lavish, °profligate, °prodigal, °improvident, °reckless, °excessive, °spendthrift, °profuse, °extreme, °immoderate: *She cannot afford to maintain her extravagant way of life for long.* **2** unrestrained, uncontained, °wild, °outrageous, °preposterous, °immoderate, °ridiculous, °foolish, °fanciful, °unreasonable, °absurd, °impractical; undeserved, unjustified, unjustifiable: *The speaker lavished extravagant praise on the award winners.* **3** °expensive, costly, extortionate, °unreasonable, overpriced, °exorbitant, °high; °dear; *Colloq* °steep: *That trip to Istanbul by private jet was extravagant to say the least.* **4** °gaudy, °garish, °ostentatious, °showy,

°ornate, °flashy, °loud, °flamboyant; exaggerated, high-sounding: *She appears at parties wearing the most extravagant costumes.*

extravaganza *n.* spectacular, °spectacle, °pageant, °production, °show, °exposition: *An extravaganza was staged to celebrate the opening of the World's Fair.*

extreme *adj.* **1** °unusual, uncommon, °exceptional, °outstanding, °notable, °noteworthy, °abnormal, °different, °extraordinary, °remarkable: *We experienced extreme difficulty driving home.* **2** °immoderate, °excessive, °severe, °intense, °acute, °maximum, worst: *This equipment is made to withstand extreme arctic conditions.* **3** outermost, endmost, farthest, °ultimate, utmost, uttermost, remotest, °last, far-off, far-away, °distant, °very: *She walked to the extreme end of the pier.* **4** °rigid, °stern, °severe, °strict, °conservative, °hidebound, °stiff, stringent, restrictive, constrictive, uncompromising, Draconian, °harsh, °drastic: *Grandfather favoured taking extreme measures against terrorists.* **5** unconventional, °radical, °outrageous, °wild, °weird, °bizarre, °queer, °outrageous, °offbeat, °exotic, °eccentric, °different, outré, *Slang* far-out, °way-out, *US and Canadian* kooky: *I find your outfit too extreme to wear in public.* **6** beyond the pale *or* limits *or* bounds, °extravagant, °inordinate, °excessive, °disproportionate, °outrageous: *Because of your extreme behaviour, you will be confined to the house for a week.*
—*n.* **7** Often, **extremes**: °limit(s), °bounds, utmost, °maximum, *Colloq* °swing: *Try to be more moderate and to avoid extremes.* **8** Often, **go to extremes**: °limit(s), °bounds, °maximum, °acme, °zenith, °pinnacle, °summit, °height, apex, apogee, °peak, °extremity; °depth, nadir: *Thea's moods varied between the extremes of joy and grief.* **9** **in the extreme**: °extremely, °very, exceptionally, °exceedingly, extraordinarily, unusually: *His table manners are rude in the extreme.*

extremely *adv.* °very, °exceedingly, outrageously, extraordinarily, unusually, uncommonly, exceptionally, damned, hellishly, to the nth degree, *Colloq Brit* bloody, *US* darned: *The service was extremely bad. They are extremely stupid.*

extremity *n.* **1** °end, °termination, °limit, °edge, °boundary, °bound, °border, °margin; °periphery; °frontier: *A fence marks the eastern extremity of our land.* **2** **extremities**: °fingers, fingertips, toes; °hands, feet; arms, °legs, limbs; paws, trotters, hooves, wings: *His extremities were numb with frostbite.* **3** °extreme, utmost, °maximum, °limit(s), °bounds: *The situation tested the extremity of my patience. They were driven to extremities in their search for food.*

extricate *v.* unravel, disentangle, untangle, °disengage, (set) °free, turn °loose, °release, °liberate, °rescue, °save, °deliver: *You helped extricate me from a terrible predicament.*

extrinsic *adj.* °external, °extraneous, °irrelevant, °exterior, °unrelated, °outside; outer, °outward: *Such extrinsic factors may be excluded from the discussion.*

exuberance *n.* **1** cheerfulness, °joy, joyfulness, ebullience, effervescence, exhilaration, buoyancy, °animation, °spirit, spiritedness, sprightliness, liveliness, °vitality, vivacity, °enthusiasm, °excitement, zeal, °zest, °energy, °vigour: *It is hard to imagine the dog's exuberance when he saw his master.* **2** °abundance, lavishness, effusiveness, flamboyance, copiousness, superabundance, °superfluity, °excess, °profusion, °prodigality, bounteousness, bountifulness: *Everything attests to the exuberance of the author's genius.*

exuberant *adj.* **1** °cheerful, °joyful, °ebullient, °effervescent, °buoyant, °animated, °spirited, spry, °sprightly, °lively, °vivacious, °enthusiastic, zealous, °energetic, °vigorous: *She enjoys exuberant good health.* **2** °happy, °glad, °delighted, °overjoyed, °joyful, °ecstatic, *Brit* in the seventh °heaven, *US* in seventh °heaven, *Colloq* on cloud nine: *She was exuberant at the news of Lyle's return.*

exult *v.* °rejoice, °revel, °glory (in), jump for °joy, °delight, °celebrate, make °merry: *We exulted in our new-found freedom.*

exultant *adj.* °delighted, jubilant, °overjoyed, °elated, °joyful, °gleeful, °glad, °ecstatic, °exuberant, in seventh °heaven, cock-a-hoop, *Colloq* on cloud nine, *Brit* over the moon: *We were exultant to learn that the war was over.*

eye *n.* **1** eyeball, °orb, *Colloq* optic: *The eye of the eagle is nearly as large as that of an elephant.* **2** °vision, (eye) sight, visual acuity, °perception: *Her eyes are weakened by so much reading.* **3** discernment, °perception, °taste, °judgement, °discrimination, percipience, perspicacity, °appreciation, °sensitivity; °knowledge, °recognition, comprehension: *Shirley has a good eye for Chinese antiques. Walmsley has the eye of an artist.* **4** °liking, °affection, fondness, °partiality, °appreciation; lustfulness: *Old Bisley still has an eye for the girls.* **5** °ogle, °leer, °look, wink, glad eye, sidelong °glance: *The barmaid gave me the eye as soon as I walked in.* **6** °view, °respect, °regard, °aim, °intention, °purpose, °design, °plan, °idea, °notion: *He lent me the money with an eye to asking a favour in return.* **7** °attention, °regard, °look, °scrutiny, °view, °examination, °observation; supervision: *All our comings and goings were under the watchful eye of Scotland Yard.* **8** °guard, °lookout, °watch, vigil: *The class monitor is expected to keep an eye on the younger children.*
—*v.* **9** °examine, °scrutinize, °look at, °regard: *My future mother-in-law eyed me up and down.* **10** °behold, °gaze *or* °look *or* °peer at *or* upon, °contemplate, °study, °regard, °view, °inspect, °watch, observe: *The doctor eyed the wound with concern.*

eyewitness *n.* °witness, °observer, °spectator, viewer, watcher; °bystander, °onlooker, passer-by: *The police sought eyewitnesses to the accident.*

fabric *n.* **1** °cloth, textile, °material, °stuff: *The chair is upholstered in traditional floral fabric.* **2** construction, constitution, °core, °heart, °foundation, °structure, framework, °organization, configuration, °make-up: *Extensive strikes threatened the very fabric of our society.*

fabricate *v.* **1** °erect, °build, °construct, °frame, °raise, °put *or* °set up, °assemble, °fashion, °form, °make, °manufacture, °produce: *The basic structure was fabricated of steel.* **2** °invent, °create, °originate, °make up, °manufacture, concoct, °think up, °imagine, °hatch, °devise, °design: *Numerous lies, fabricated by politicians, were already in circulation.* **3** °forge, °falsify, °counterfeit, °fake, feign, °manufacture; trump up, *Colloq* cook up, *Brit* cook: *He admitted to having fabricated the data in his application.*

fabrication *n.* **1** construction, °assembly, assemblage, making, fashioning, °production, °manufacture, putting together, °building, erection, °formation, formulation, structuring, constructing, °organization, forming, framing, architecture: *The fabrication of thousands of parts took only a month.* **2** °invention, °creation, origination, °make-up, °manufacture, hatching, concoction, contrivance, °design: *Only Vanessa could have been responsible for the fabrication of such a diabolical plot.* **3** °falsehood, °lie, °fib, prevarication, °story, °tale, untruth, fiction, °yarn, fable; falsification, °forgery, °fake, °sham, *Colloq* cock-and-bull °story, *Brit* fairy °story, fairy °tale: *His war record is a complete fabrication.*

fabulous *adj.* **1** fabled, mythic(al), °celebrated, °legendary, storied, °fictitious, °fictional, °unreal, °fanciful, °imaginary, story-book, fairy-tale: *Greek mythology tells us of a fabulous winged horse called Pegasus.* **2** °fantastic, °marvellous, °incredible, °unbelievable, °inconceivable, wonderful, astounding, astonishing, °amazing, wondrous, °extraordinary, °miraculous, °phenomenal: *Houses in London were selling at fabulous prices.* **3** °superb, °marvellous, °terrific, wonderful, *Colloq* °great, °super, smashing, °thumping, °whopping, thundering, rattling, howling, *US* °neat, °keen, *Slang* fab, °hot, far-out, °cool, *Old-fashioned* fantabulous, in the groove, groovy, ace, *Brit* °magic, *US and Canadian* copacetic: *I saw an absolutely fabulous new film the other night.*

face *n.* **1** visage, countenance, physiognomy, °features, lineaments, *Slang* °mug, mush, kisser, °pan, puss, *Brit* phiz, phizog, dial, clock: *I don't like the expression on your face.* **2** °look, °appearance, °aspect, °expression, mien: *He has the face of someone who is very proud of himself. Modern farming has changed the face of the countryside.* **3** °mask, °veneer, façade, °front, °camouflage, °pretence, °disguise, (°false) °impression, °semblance, °masquerade: *She puts on a bold face, but we know she was deeply hurt by your remarks.* **4** °dignity, °image, °self-respect, °standing, °reputation, repute, °name, °honour, °status: *You might lose face if you admit you were wrong.* **5** boldness, °daring, audacity, °effrontery, °impudence, °impertinence, °presumption, brashness, *Colloq*

°gall, °brass, °nerve, cheek, °guts, gutsiness, *Brit* °brass neck, *Slang US* balls: *Who would have the face to name such a hotel 'The Palace'?* **6** °surface, °exterior, °front, °outside, °cover, °facing, façade, °skin: *The building will have a face of white marble.* **7** right °side, obverse, °front; dial: *The card landed face up. The face of the clock is enamelled.* **8 face to face**: confronting, facing, °opposite, en face, vis-à-vis, °tête-à-tête, *à deux*, eye to eye, head to head, *Colloq* eyeball to eyeball: *We met face to face for the first time in the courtroom.* **9 in the face of**: in defiance of, °notwithstanding, °despite, in °spite of, confronting, in °opposition to: *Some experts attacked the report for flying in the face of received wisdom.* **10 make a face**: change one's °expression, murgeon: *When I said I would be there, she made a face.* **11 on the face of it**: to all *or* outward appearances, °seemingly, °apparently, superficially, °evidently: *On the face of it, he seemed guilty.* **12 show one's face**: °put in *or* make an °appearance, °appear, °arrive, be seen, °turn up, *Colloq* °show up: *I suppose I ought to show my face at the office party.* **13 to one's face**: °directly, brazenly, eye to eye, face to face, candidly, °openly, frankly: *I told him to his face that he was a liar.*
—*v.* **14** confront, °brave, °meet (with), °encounter, °experience, °deal *or* °cope with, °come *or* °go up against; °appear before: *In the jungle we faced grave danger from man-eating tigers. She faces her first audience tonight.* **15** °give (out) *or* °front on *or* on to, °front °towards, °overlook, °look out on *or* over; be °opposite: *Our rooms face the lake. Facing page 22 is a map of the area.* **16** °coat, °surface, °cover, clad, °dress, sheathe, overlay, °finish; °veneer: *The collar is faced with velvet.* **17 face down**: confront, °intimidate, cow, °subdue, °overawe, °browbeat: *I'll not be faced down by that impudent clerk.* **18 face up to**: **a** °admit, °accept, °acknowledge, °allow, °confess: *We must all face up to our own shortcomings.* **b** confront, °deal *or* °cope with, °come *or* °go up against, °brave, come to °terms with; °brazen through *or* out, bite (on) the bullet, grasp the nettle: *You wouldn't be able to face up to your wife if you'd forgotten her birthday.*

facilitate *v.* °ease, °expedite, °smooth, °further, °promote, °advance; °assist, °aid, °help: *It would facilitate transport if you would bring your own car.*

facility *n.* **1** °ease, smoothness, °fluency, effortlessness, °readiness, easiness, °skill, skilfulness, deftness, °dexterity, adroitness, °ability, °aptitude, °expertise, expertness, °proficiency, mastery, masterfulness, masterliness, °efficiency; quickness, alacrity, celerity, swiftness, °speed: *They praised her new-found facility with the Italian language.* **2** Often, **facilities**: **a** °plant, °system, °building(s), °structure, complex: *The company is building a new facility in France.* **b** convenience(s), °privy, °equipment, °lavatory, °toilet, powder-room, *Nautical* head, *Brit* water-closet, WC, loo, *US and Canadian* °rest room, men's room, ladies' room, *Colloq* the

Gents, the Ladies('), *Slang Brit* bog, karzy, *US and Canadian* john: *An American asked where he could find the facilities.*

facing *n.* façade, °front, cladding, °surface, overlay, °skin; coating: *The houses all have a colourful stucco facing.*

facsimile *n.* °copy, °reproduction, °print, carbon (°copy), °replica, °duplicate, photocopy, fax, *Trade Mark* Xerox (°copy), Photostat, *Colloq US* dupe: *Send a facsimile of the report to each field office.*

fact *n.* **1** °reality, actuality, °truth, °certainty: *The fact of the matter is that she didn't do it. Is there a basis in fact for your allegations?* **2** °accomplishment, *fait accompli;* °occurrence, °event, °happening, °incident, °episode, °experience, °act, °deed: *Supersonic travel has been a fact for many years.* **3** Often, **facts**: °data, °information, °particular(s), °detail(s), °point(s), °item(s), °factor(s), *Colloq* °low-down, (°inside) info, the °score, *Brit* the gen, *US and Canadian* the poop: *If I am going to defend you, I need all the facts of the case.* **4 in fact**: °indeed, to be °sure, as a matter of (°actual) fact, in °truth, °truly, truthfully, °actually, °really, in °reality, in point of fact, factually: *He didn't come; in fact, he had gone abroad the week before.*

faction *n.* **1** °group, °cabal, bloc, cadre, °camp, °splinter °group, °circle, camarilla, °clique, °set, coterie, °lobby, °pressure °group, °junta *or* junto, °ring, °gang, *Brit* ginger °group, *Colloq* °crowd: *There is a small faction plotting to assassinate the finance minister.* **2** °dissension, °intrigue, °strife, °sedition, disharmony, °discord, °disagreement, quarrelling, contention, °controversy, infighting, °rupture, °split, °rift, schism, °clash: *Faction within the party has no regard for national interests.*

factious *adj.* contentious, disputatious, litigious, refractory, divisive, conflicting, °discordant, °argumentative, at °odds, at loggerheads, °quarrelsome, °seditious, °mutinous, °rebellious: *A factious Congress spells trouble for the President.*

factitious *adj.* °fake(d), °bogus, °false, °mock, falsified, °artificial, °insincere, °unreal, °synthetic, fabricated, engineered, manufactured, °spurious, °counterfeit, °sham, simulated, °imitation, unauthentic, °set *or* got up, rigged, *Colloq* °phoney *or US also* phony: *We are all victims of factitious desires by which luxuries have become necessities.*

factor *n.* **1** constituent, °ingredient, °element, °part, °particular, °piece, component; °circumstance, °consideration, °aspect, °fact, °influence, determinant, °cause: *Which factors contributed to the decline of Mayan civilization?* **2** °agent, °representative, °proxy, middleman, °intermediary, °deputy, °go-between: *Our company has a factor handling all our exports.* **3** banker, °financier, °backer, moneylender, lender: *The factors lent us money to buy the stock needed to fill the orders.*

factory *n.* °works, °mill, °plant: *She has a job at the piano factory.*

factual *adj.* **1** °actual, °real, °true, °authentic, verifiable, °realistic, °true to life, °genuine, valid, bona fide: *The report is a forgery, but the letters are factual.* **2** °accurate, °correct, °true, °faithful, °precise, unbiased, undistorted, °unvarnished, unexaggerated, °objective, °unprejudiced, straightforward: *This is a factual account of the Battle of Marathon.*

faculty *n.* **1** °ability, °capacity, °skill, °aptitude, °potential, °talent, °flair, °knack, °gift, °genius; °dexterity, adroitness, cleverness, °capability: *She has a faculty for making people feel at home.* **2** °school, °department, °discipline: *Her graduate studies were in the Faculty of Philosophy.* **3** °staff, personnel, °members, *Brit* dons: *Each member of the faculty has a doctorate.* **4** °power, authorization, dispensation, °sanction, °licence, °prerogative, °privilege, °right, °permission, °liberty: *The government has the faculty to judge treasonable acts.*

fad *n.* °craze, °mania, °rage, °fashion, °trend, °fancy, °vogue: *Do you remember the hula-hoop fad?*

fade *v.* **1** (grow) °dim *or* °pale, grow °faint, cloud (over), °dull; °bleach, whiten, etiolate, °wash out, blanch *or* blench, discolour: *The scene faded in the distance. Look how the sun has faded the curtains!* **2** °droop, wither, °decline, °die out *or* away, °perish, °ebb, °flag, °wane, °wilt, °waste away, °sag, °diminish, °dwindle, languish, °deteriorate, °decay, °shrivel, peter out *or* away: *As he aged, his lust for life faded.*

fag *v.* **1** Often, **fag out**: °exhaust, °weary, °tire (out), °fatigue, °wear out, °jade, *Colloq Brit* knacker, *US* poop: *I am completely fagged out from studying all night.*
—*n.* **2** Brit bore, °nuisance, °drag, chore, °pain: *It's a bit of a fag having to fetch water from the garden.* **3** °servant, °menial, °flunkey, drudge, lackey, underling: *The seniors used to have fags to clean their shoes.* **4** See **homosexual, 1,** below. **5** cigarette, smoke, *Colloq* °butt, cig(gy), weed, coffin-nail, cancer stick, *Old-fashioned* gasper: *Got a fag?*

fail *v.* **1** not succeed, be °unsuccessful, °miss, °miscarry, °misfire, °fall short (of), °fall flat, °fall through, falter, be (found) lacking *or* °wanting, be °defective, be °deficient, be *or* prove °inadequate, come to °grief *or* °naught *or* °nothing, °go wrong, abort, °meet with °disaster, °founder, °run aground, *Colloq* °flop, °fizzle (out), go up in smoke, flunk: *Guy Fawkes's plot failed utterly. Gloria failed her history examination.* **2** °let down, °disappoint, °forsake, °desert, °abandon, °neglect, °ignore, °slight: *I was really counting on Mary, but she failed me.* **3** °decline, peter out, °dwindle, °diminish, °wane, °deteriorate, °weaken, °decay, °fade *or* °die (out *or* away), °disappear, °flag, °ebb, °sink, languish, °give out; gutter, °go out: *His health is failing. The light failed, leaving us in darkness.* **4** go bankrupt, go out of business, °go under, go into receivership, become °insolvent, °close up shop, °close up *or* down, °cease operation(s), *Brit* go to the °wall, *US* file for Chapter Eleven, *Colloq* °fold (up), go bust *or* °broke, *US* °drown in red ink: *According to the statistics, hundreds of businesses fail every week.*

failing *n.* **1** °weakness, °shortcoming, °foible, °flaw, °fault, °defect, °weak spot, °blind spot, °blemish, °imperfection: *Bigotry and prejudice are her most serious failings.*
—*prep.* **2** lacking, °wanting, in °default of, without, sans, in the °absence of: *Failing a favourable decision, we shall lodge an appeal.*

failure n. **1** °failing, °default, non-performance, remissness; °neglect, °omission, dereliction, deficiency: *His failure to do his duty resulted in a court martial.* **2** °breakdown, °collapse, discontinuance, °miscarriage, °loss; °decline, °decay, deterioration: *Power disruptions are caused by the failure of the national grid.* **3** °loser, non-starter, °incompetent, also-ran, nonentity, *Colloq* °flop, °fizzle, damp squib, °dud, lemon, °washout, dead duck, *US* lead balloon: *He was an utter failure as a violinist.* **4** bankruptcy, °ruin, insolvency, °downfall, °crash, *Colloq* folding: *Bank failures increased owing to bad loans and other poor investments.*

faint adj. **1** °dim, °dull, °pale, faded, °indistinct, °vague, °hazy, °imperceptible, indiscernible, unclear, blurred, blurry, muzzy, wavering, faltering, ill-defined, °weak, °feeble, flickering, °subdued; °low, °soft, °slight, hushed, muffled, muted, °inaudible, stifled: *A faint light burned in the corridor. I heard a faint noise.* **2** °dizzy, light-headed, unsteady, vertiginous, °giddy, *Colloq* woozy: *I felt faint after climbing the stairs.* —v. **3** °black out, °pass out, °lose consciousness, swoon, °drop, °collapse, *Colloq* keel over: *She fainted when they told her the news.* —n. **4** °loss of consciousness, blackout, unconsciousness, °collapse, swoon, *Medicine* syncope: *He dropped in a dead faint.*

faint-hearted adj. **1** °cowardly, timorous, °afraid, frightened, °scared, °faint, lily-livered, white-livered, pusillanimous; °timid, °shy, diffident; *Colloq* yellow (-bellied), chicken-hearted, chicken-livered, chicken: *He's too faint-hearted to ask her to marry him.* **2** °irresolute, °weak, °ineffectual, °feeble, °puny, feckless: *She made only a faint-hearted attempt at reconciliation.*

fair¹ adj. **1** °impartial, even-handed, °disinterested, °equitable, °just, °unprejudiced, unbiased, °objective, *Colloq* °square: *Judge Leaver is known for his fair decisions. We are counting on your sense of fair play.* **2** °honest, °above-board, °honourable, °lawful, °trustworthy, °legitimate, °proper, °upright, straightforward: *He won the trophy in a fair fight.* **3** °light, blond(e), fair-haired, flaxen-haired, tow-headed, tow-haired; light-complexioned, peaches and cream, °rosy; unblemished, °clear, °spotless, °immaculate: *She has fair hair and fair skin.* **4** °satisfactory, °adequate, °respectable, pretty °good, °tolerable, °passable, all °right, °average, °decent, middling, °reasonable, *comme ci, comme ça*, not bad; °mediocre, °indifferent, *Colloq* so so, °OK or okay: *The performance was fair but not outstanding.* **5** °favourable, °clear, °sunny, °fine, °dry, °bright, cloudless, °pleasant, halcyon, °benign: *Fair weather is promised for tomorrow's picnic.* **6** unobstructed, °open, °clear, °free: *Every spectator has a fair view of the football field.* **7** °attractive, good-looking, °handsome, °comely, pretty, °beautiful, pulchritudinous, °lovely, beauteous: *Faint heart never won fair lady.* **8** °civil, °courteous, °polite, °gracious, °agreeable: *She was not deceived by his fair words.*

fair² n. °fête or fete, °festival, kermis or kirmess, °exhibition, °exposition, °show; °market, bazaar, mart, *US* °exhibit: *Ashby will judge the sheep at the annual fair.*

fairly adv. **1** °quite, °rather, pretty, °somewhat, tolerably, adequately, sufficiently, passably,

°moderately, *Colloq* °sort of, °kind of: *I thought that the singing was fairly good.* **2** equitably, impartially, justly, °properly, °honestly, objectively: *Please make certain that everyone is treated fairly.* **3** °absolutely, °totally, °utterly, °completely, °positively, °really, °actually, veritably, °virtually: *The crowd fairly cheered themselves hoarse.*

fairyland n. dreamland, wonderland, never-never land, happy valley, °paradise, cloud-land, °enchanted forest, cloud-cuckoo-land, Nephelococcygia, Shangri-La: *Zuleika's thoughts are always off somewhere in fairyland.*

faith n. **1** °belief, credence, °confidence, °conviction, °trust, °certainty, certitude, °assurance, assuredness, sureness, °reliance, dependence: *His faith in God is unassailable. I have great faith in her ability.* **2** °belief, °religion, °creed, °persuasion, dogma, teaching, °doctrine, °denomination, °sect: *To which faith do you belong? She is of the Jewish faith.* **3** °duty, allegiance, °obligation, °promise, faithfulness, °loyalty, fidelity, °devotion, consecration, °dedication, fealty, °obedience: *Don't break faith with your electorate by supporting the bill.*

faithful adj. **1** °true, °loyal, °devoted, °steadfast, dedicated, °attached, unswerving, °firm, °staunch, unwavering, °constant: *He has always remained faithful to his wife.* **2** °close, °exact, °accurate, °true, °correct, °precise, °perfect, valid; °literal: *Jowett's is a faithful translation from the Greek.* **3** °conscientious, °dutiful, °scrupulous, °careful, °meticulous, °thorough, punctilious, °finicky or finical, °detailed, °fastidious, rigorous, °rigid, °severe, °particular: *He received a gold watch for fifty years of faithful attendance to his duties.* **4** °reliable, dependable, trusted, °trustworthy, trusty, °honest, °true, °truthful, °righteous, °right, °moral, °virtuous, °upright, veracious: *He has remained my faithful friend for many years.*

faithless adj. **1** °sceptical, doubting, °unbelieving, disbelieving, agnostic, atheistic, freethinking: *Faithless wretches are called Doubting Thomases.* **2** unfaithful, °disloyal, treacherous, °traitorous, °perfidious, shifting, °shifty, °fickle, °inconstant, untrustworthy, °unreliable, °false, °hypocritical, °insincere, °dishonest, °crooked, °unscrupulous, conscienceless, recreant: *With faithless friends like her, who needs enemies?*

fake v. **1** °falsify, °doctor, °alter, °modify, °counterfeit, °fabricate, °manufacture, °forge: *He faked the evidence in order to implicate his own sister.* **2** °pretend, make a °pretence of, dissemble, feign, °sham, °make believe, simulate, °affect: *She faked a headache to avoid gym classes.* —n. **3** °hoax, °counterfeit, °sham, °forgery, °imitation, *Colloq* °phoney or *US* also phony: *The experts agree that the painting is a fake.* **4** faker, °impostor, charlatan, °fraud, hoaxer, mountebank, °cheat, humbug, °quack, °pretender, *Colloq* °phoney or *US* also phony: *He isn't a doctor—he's a fake!* —adj. **5** °false, °counterfeit, forged, °sham, °fraudulent, °imitation, pinchbeck, °bogus, °spurious, °factitious, *Colloq* °phoney or *US* also phony: *He escaped the country using a fake passport.*

fall v. **1** °descend, °sink, °subside, °settle, °drop or °come (down), °plummet, °plunge, °dive, (take a) nosedive; cascade: *The bucket fell to the* *bottom of the well. A meteorite fell on my house. The water falls 100 metres over the cliff at this point.* **2** °tumble, °trip, °stumble, °slump, °collapse, keel over, °topple, °crumple: *Mother fell in the kitchen and hurt her knee.* **3** °diminish, (become) °lower, °sink, °decline, fall *or* °drop off, °drop, °decrease, °dwindle, °subside, °come *or* °go down: *The price of oil fell today to a new low.* **4** °slope, fall away, °decline: *Beyond the spinney, the meadow falls towards the river.* **5** °succumb, °surrender, °yield, °give up *or* in, °capitulate, be °defeated *or* °conquered, be °captured, be taken (°captive *or* °prisoner), be °overthrown, come *or* go to °ruin, be °destroyed, be °lost: *The castle fell after a year's siege.* **6** °die, °perish, °drop °dead, be slain *or* °killed: *His grandfather fell at the Battle of the Marne.* **7 fall apart**: °disintegrate, °crumble, °collapse, fall *or* come *or* go to °pieces, °break up, be °destroyed; °break °apart, °fragment, °shatter: *I knew she would fall apart on the witness stand. The gadget fell apart as soon as we used it.* **8 fall back**: °retreat, °retire, °withdraw, °draw back; °recede: *As the enemy advanced, we fell back.* **9 fall back on** *or* **upon**: have °recourse to, °rely *or* °depend on *or* upon, °return to, °count on *or* upon, °resort to, °call on *or* upon, make °use of, °use, °employ: *All the ready ammunition was gone and we had to fall back on our reserves.* **10 fall behind**: °drop back, °trail, °lag; be in arrears: *If you fall behind, I'll wait for you. We fell behind in our mortgage payments.* **11 fall down**: **a** °collapse, °drop: *She hit me so hard that I fell down.* **b** °fail, be (found) °wanting *or* lacking, be °unsuccessful, be °inadequate *or* °disappointing: *He had to be replaced because he fell down on the job.* **12 fall flat**: °collapse, °fail, *Colloq* °flop, *US* °bomb (out), lay an egg, go over like a lead balloon: *A hit in London might fall flat in New York.* **13 fall for**: **a** fall in °love with, be °infatuated with: *Some people will fall for anyone who tells them the right time.* **b** be °fooled *or* °duped *or* °taken in *or* °deceived by, °accept, °swallow, °succumb to, *Slang* be °sucker for, *US and Canadian* be a patsy for: *Did Beaseley really fall for that old confidence trick?* **14 fall in**: °cave in, °collapse, °sink inwards: *The walls were about to fall in on us.* **15 fall in with**: °join, °associate with, become associated *or* °allied with, befriend; °cooperate with, °go along with, concur with, °support, °accept: *He fell in with a gang of thieves and spent the next few years avoiding the police. She agreed to fall in with my plan.* **16 fall off**: °diminish, °decrease, °decline, °deteriorate: *Business falls off immediately after Christmas.* **17 fall on** *or* **upon**: °attack, °assault, assail, °set upon: *Three muggers fell on me and stole my wallet.* **18 fall out**: °disagree, °differ, °quarrel, °clash, squabble, wrangle, °dispute, °fight: *We fell out over politics.* **19 fall short**: prove *or* (turn out to) be °inadequate *or* °insufficient *or* °deficient *or* lacking *or* °wanting *or* °disappointing, °miss, °fail, °disappoint: *The results of the sales campaign fell short of expectations.* **20 fall through**: °fail, come to °nothing *or* °naught, °miscarry, °die, *Colloq* °fizzle (out), °flop: *The deal to buy the company fell through.* **21 fall to**: °start, °begin, °commence, °set *or* °go about, get under °way, °undertake, °tackle, °take on; get moving,

°attack, *Colloq* get the show on the road, get cracking, *US* get a wiggle on, °move it: *The washing-up had to be done so I fell to.*
—*n.* **22** °drop, descent, °dive, nosedive, °plunge, °tumble, dropping, falling: *How could he have survived a fall from such a height?* **23** *Chiefly in the US and Canada*: autumn: *They turn the clocks back one hour in the fall.* **24** °decline, °decay, °collapse, °downfall, °failure, °destruction, °ruin, deterioration, °eclipse: *Have you read Poe's classic Fall of the House of Usher?* **25** Usually, **falls**: cascade, cataract, °waterfall; rapids: *How many falls are there along the Limpopo River?* **26** depreciation, °sinking, diminution, °decrease, °decline, °lapse, downturn, down-swing, °drop, drop-off, lowering, abatement, °slump, °collapse: *On the Stock Exchange today, investors experienced sharp falls in share prices.* **27** °slope, declivity, descent, °decline, °drop, downhill, *Chiefly US and Canadian* °downgrade: *Note the smooth rise and fall of the land.* **28** °surrender, capitulation, °submission, °taking, °seizure, °capture, °overthrow, °defeat, °conquest, °downfall: *The fall of Khartoum in 1898 marked the re-establishment of British rule in the Anglo-Egyptian Sudan.*

fallacy *n.* °misconception, miscalculation, misjudgement, °mistake, °error, *non sequitur,* °solecism, °delusion; paralogism; sophism: *It is a fallacy to think that you could ever learn to play the violin as well as Susannah.*

false *adj.* **1** °untrue, unfactual, untruthful, °wrong, °amiss, °mistaken, °erroneous, °incorrect, °inaccurate, °inexact, °imprecise, °faulty, °flawed, °invalid, °unsound, °unreal, °imaginary, °fictitious, °spurious: *The explorers gave a completely false picture of the local inhabitants.* **2** °untrue, untruthful, °lying, misleading, fallacious, fabricated, made-up, concocted, mendacious, untrustworthy, °fraudulent, meretricious, °deceptive, °deceitful, treacherous, *Colloq* °phoney *or US also* phony: *The testimony of this witness is completely false.* **3** °counterfeit, °imitation, simulated, °sham, forged, °fraudulent, °fake, °artificial, °synthetic, manufactured, °unnatural, °spurious, °bogus, ersatz, °factitious, °mock, pseudo, *Colloq* °phoney *or US also* phony: *Your false teeth look almost real.* **4** °sham, feigned, affected, °insincere, faked, manufactured, °counterfeit(ed): *Don't shed any false tears over me when I'm gone.* **5** illogical, fallacious, °unsound, °invalid, °flawed, °faulty: *That conclusion could come only from false reasoning.*

falsehood *n.* °lie, °fib, prevarication, untruth, °fabrication, °misstatement, fiction, (fairy) °tale, °story, distortion, *Colloq* cock-and-bull °story, *Slang Brit* °load of codswallop: *That was a complete falsehood about the goings-on in the attic, wasn't it?*

falsify *v.* °fake, °alter, °distort, misstate, °misrepresent, °twist, *Colloq* fudge, trump up, *Brit* cook: *The tax inspector found that the accounts had been falsified.*

falsity *n.* untruthfulness, mendacity, mendaciousness, fraudulence, deceptiveness, °deceit, deceitfulness, dishonesty, spuriousness, speciousness, casuistry, °hypocrisy, insincerity, falseness: *The prosecution was unable to prove the falsity of her statement.*

fame n. °renown, repute, °reputation, °celebrity, illustriousness, °superiority, °pre-eminence, stardom, °prominence, eminence, °glory, °name, °notoriety, acclaim: *Randolph's fame has spread far and wide.*

familiar adj. **1** °well-known, °common, commonplace, °everyday, °ordinary, °current: *That's a familiar melody.* **2** °frequent, °usual, °customary, °habitual, °routine, °traditional: *He strolled along his familiar route through the trees.* **3** °friendly, affable, °close, °intimate, °sociable, °social, °free, °free and °easy, °relaxed; over-friendly, overfree, overfamiliar, °bold, °forward, °insolent, °impudent, °presumptuous, presuming, °disrespectful, unreserved, unrestrained; °informal, °casual, °cordial, unceremonious; *Colloq* °chummy, *Slang US and Canadian* buddy-buddy, palsy-walsy: *She began to get entirely too familiar.*
4 familiar with: °aware *or* °conscious *or* cognizant of, °knowledgeable about *or* of *or* in, conversant *or* °acquainted with, no stranger to, on speaking terms with, up on *or* in, (well-)°versed in, °informed *or* of *or* about, °privy to, in the know about, *au courant, au fait: Are you familiar with the latest theories in particle physics?*

familiarity n. **1** °knowledge, °acquaintance(ship), °grasp, °understanding, comprehension, °cognizance, awareness, conversance, °experience: *I have no familiarity at all with particle physics.* **2** friendliness, affability, sociability, neighbourliness, °fellowship, intimacy, intimateness, closeness, openness, naturalness, °ease, informality, unceremoniousness: *He prided himself on his familiarity with celebrities.* **3** boldness, presumptuousness, overfamiliarity, °presumption, °impudence, insolence, °impertinence, °impropriety: *He put his arm round her waist with offensive familiarity.*

familiarize v. Usually, **familiarize with**: °accustom (to), make °familiar *or* °acquaint (with), °initiate (in), °inform (about *or* on), °enlighten (about *or* as to), °teach (about), °educate *or* °instruct *or* °tutor (in): *I am trying to familiarize myself with the music of John Cage.*

family n. **1** (kith and) °kin, kinsmen, °kindred, kinsfolk *or US and Canadian* kinfolk, next of °kin, °relatives, °relations, household, °people, one's own °flesh and blood, one's nearest and dearest, ménage, *Colloq* folks: *We usually spend the holidays with my family.* **2** children, °offspring, °progeny, °issue, °brood, *Colloq* kids: *Large families were much more common in the 19th century.* **3** °ancestors, forebears, forefathers, °progenitors; ancestry, °parentage, descent, °extraction, °derivation, °lineage, °pedigree, genealogy, family tree, °house, °line, bloodline, °dynasty; blood, °stock, °strain: *He came from an old family of German bankers.* **4** °group, °set, °division, subdivision, classification, °type, °kind, °class, °genre, °order, species, genus: *English belongs to the Indo-European family of languages.*

famine n. starvation; °shortage, °dearth, °scarcity, deficiency, paucity, exiguity, barrenness, °lack: *In days of abundance, no one should die of famine.*

famished adj. starving, °starved, °voracious, °ravenous, ravening, craving, °hungry: *The survivors were famished after a fortnight in the lifeboat.*

famous adj. °renowned, °celebrated, famed, °well-known, °noted, °eminent, °pre-eminent, °conspicuous, °prominent, °illustrious, °notable, acclaimed, °venerable, °legendary, °distinguished, °praiseworthy, honoured, lionized: *A famous architect has been invited to address the convention.*

famously adv. excellently, (very) °well, superbly, marvellously, splendidly, capitally, spectacularly, superlatively: *The prince and I get on famously.*

fan n. °admirer, °enthusiast, adherent, °devotee, aficionado, °follower, °supporter, °lover, °zealot, *Colloq* buff, °fiend, °hound, °bug, °addict, nut, *US* booster, *Slang* junkie, °freak, groupie: *Avid fans of Ascot United, we go to all the matches.*

fanatic n. °maniac, extremist, °zealot, *Colloq* °fiend, nut, *Slang* °freak: *Religious fanatics killed 'heathens' or 'infidels' by the thousand.*

fanatical adj. °fanatic, °extreme, distracted, °maniacal, °mad, °rabid, zealous, frenzied, °feverish, °burning, °frantic, frenetic, °obsessive, °fervent, °compulsive, monomaniacal, fervid, perfervid, °passionate, °enthusiastic, °agog, °immoderate, °excessive: *The entire family are fanatical in their fundamentalism.*

fanaticism n. **1** °devotion, °dedication, devotedness; infatuation, °enthusiasm, °fervour, zeal, obsessiveness, franticness, °frenzy, hysteria: *Her fanaticism for rock musicians is getting a bit out of hand.* **2** monomania, single-mindedness, °mania, °madness, extremism, °intolerance, °bigotry, °bias, °partiality, °prejudice, narrow-mindedness, close-mindedness: *Some religious sects are characterized by virulent fanaticism.*

fancied adj. °imaginary, °unreal, °fanciful, imagined, °illusory, make-believe, °mythical, fairy-tale: *They support their king in the pursuit of his fancied rights.*

fanciful adj. **1** °whimsical, °capricious, °impulsive, °inconstant, °fickle, °changeable, °variable: *Those graffiti are products of a fanciful mind.* **2** °extravagant, chimerical, °fantastic, °fabulous, °mythical, fairy-tale, °imaginative, °fancied, make-believe, °unreal, °illusory, imagined, °visionary, °imaginary: *Some of the more fanciful ideas of science fiction have become realities.* **3** °curious, °odd, °peculiar, °bizarre, °unusual, °original: *The chalice was decorated with fanciful curlicues.*

fancy adj. **1** °ornate, decorative, decorated, °ornamental, ornamented, °elaborate, embellished, embroidered, °fanciful, °extravagant, rococo, baroque, gingerbread, Byzantine, °complicated, °intricate, complex: *The modern trend has been away from fancy architecture.* **2** °illusory, °capricious, °fanciful, °extravagant, °fantastic, °far-fetched, delusive, °whimsical, °visionary, °unrealistic, °grandiose: *He has some fancy ideas about building an undersea city.* **3** de luxe, °luxury, °luxurious, °choice, °select, °prime, °special, °elegant, °superior, °quality, °high-class; °posh: *They stock only fancy fruits and vegetables. She has a fancy suite at the Cardigan Hotel.* **4** °high, °exorbitant, °inflated, °outrageous: *One has to pay very fancy prices for haute couture.*
—n. **5** °imagination, °creation, °conception, inventiveness, creativeness, creativity: *These*

chimeras are entirely a product of his fancy.
6 °imagination, °fantasy, °hallucination,
°delusion, °illusion, unreality, make-believe,
°dream, day-dream, pipedream, mirage, phantasm, °phantom, figment (of the °imagination),
°impression: *Our plans for the future must be based
on fact, not fancy.* **7** °liking, °inclination, fondness, °taste, °penchant, °attraction,
°preference, °partiality, predilection, yearning,
craving, hankering, °wish, °desire, °longing:
*Miss Crow's fancy for younger men often causes her
some embarrassment.* **8** °idea, whim, caprice,
whimsy, °urge, impulse, °notion, vagary, °quirk,
crotchet, °peculiarity: *His fancy today is that he
invented electricity.*
—*v.* **9** °imagine, °conceive, °picture, visualize,
°envisage, °think *or* °make up, conjure up, *US*
°envision, *Colloq* °dream up: *He fancies himself on
a big yacht in the Mediterranean.* **10** °think,
°imagine, °understand, °believe, °suspect,
°guess, conjecture, °presume, °surmise,
°assume, °take it, °suppose, °infer, °reckon: *From
his costume I fancy he must be Superman. Fancy
Kim winning the Nobel prize!* **11** °like, be °attracted
to, take (a °liking) to, °desire, °want, crave,
°long *or* pine for, have a yen *or* craving for, have
an °eye for, °wish for, °hunger for, °favour,
°prefer, °lust after: *Terry has always fancied tall
women. I wouldn't fancy being 40 feet up a swaying
ladder like that.*

fanfare *n.* **1** °flourish, fanfaron, fanfaronade,
(trumpet-)°blast *or* °blare: *Following a loud fanfare, the toreador strutted into the ring.* **2** hullabaloo, hubbub, brouhaha, commotion, °stir,
ado, °show, °fuss, *Colloq* to-do, ballyhoo: *Despite
the enormous fanfare, the film was a failure.*

fantasize *v.* °dream, °imagine, day-dream,
°muse, °mull (over), build castles in the air *or* in
Spain, °speculate, °envisage, star-gaze; hallucinate, *US* °envision: *She often fantasized about
the kind of man she would marry.*

fantastic *adj.* **1** °fanciful, °strange, °weird,
°peculiar, °odd, °eccentric, °queer, °bizarre,
°quaint, °outlandish, °exotic, °extravagant,
°grotesque, °nightmarish, °alien, °remarkable:
*She wore the most fantastic costume to the fancy-dress
ball.* **2** °imaginary, °illusory, illusive, °unreal,
°visionary, °fanciful, °unrealistic, imagined,
irrational: *His books are inhabited by fantastic
creatures.* **3** °unbelievable, °incredible,
°preposterous, °extraordinary, °implausible,
°absurd, °unlikely: *At 85, he made the fantastic
decision to enter the marathon.* **4** °marvellous,
spectacular, °splendid, wonderful, tremendous,
°overwhelming, *Colloq* °great, °fabulous,
°terrific: *The Picasso exhibition is simply fantastic.*

fantasy *n.* **1** °imagination, °fancy, creativity,
inventiveness, °originality: *We encourage the children to give free rein to their fantasy.* **2** °vision,
°hallucination, °illusion, mirage, °delusion,
chimera, °dream, day-dream, (flight of) °fancy,
pipe-dream: *Her fantasy is to become prime
minister.* **3** make-believe, °invention, fabrication,
fiction, °masquerade, fable, concoction,
°pretence: *His story about being an orphan is pure
fantasy.*

far *adv.* **1** afar, far-away *or* -off, a good *or* great
or °long °way *or* °distance off *or* away: *We caught
sight of a sail far to the south.* **2** (very) much,
considerably, decidedly, incomparably: *She is a
far better swimmer than George.* **3 by far**: (very)

much, considerably, decidedly, incomparably,
(im)measurably, by a long °shot, far and away,
°clearly, plainly, °obviously, °doubtless(ly),
indubitably, °undoubtedly, °definitely, beyond
(the shadow of a) °doubt, without a °doubt,
Colloq Brit by a long chalk: *She's a better swimmer
than George by far. He is by far the wealthiest person
I know.* **4 far and wide**: °everywhere, near and
far *or* far and near, extensively, °widely, °high
and low; here, there, and °everywhere: *We
searched far and wide to find these specimens.* **5 far
gone**: **a** beyond *or* past help, advanced, deteriorated, °worn out, °dilapidated, near the °end:
*That shirt is too far gone to send to the laundry. My
house is so far gone it's beyond repair.* **b** °drunk,
besotted, *Slang* °loaded, pissed, paralytic, paralysed: *He's too far gone to walk.* **6 go far**:
a °progress, °advance, °succeed, go places, °get
ahead, °rise (in the world), make a name for
oneself, become °successful, set the world on
fire, *Brit* set the Thames on fire, *US* cut a swath:
*He is a very bright youngster and I'm sure he will go
far in whatever profession he chooses.* **b** °help,
°aid, °contribute, play a part: *The new law will go
far towards inhibiting child abuse.* **7 go too far**:
°go overboard *or* over the top, not know when
to stop, °go to extremes: °exceed, °overdo,
°overstep, °transcend, °go beyond: *Ambition is
one thing, but he went too far when he tried to get
his boss's job.* **8 so far**: **a** thus far, (up) to *or* till
or until °now *or* the °present *or* this °point, to
°date, to this °point in time: *So far, we have been
able to keep up with the mortgage payments.* **b** to
a certain °extent *or* °limit *or* °point: *She said she
would go just so far and no further.*
—*adj.* **9** (more) °remote *or* °distant, °far-away,
far-off; °extreme, °further, farther, farthest: *She
claimed the ability to see into the far future. He kicked
the ball to the far end of the field.*

far-away *adj.* **1** faraway, °distant, °remote,
far-off, °outlying, far-flung: *People came from
far-away places as news of the miracle spread.*
2 faraway, °dreamy, °detached, °absent,
°absent-minded, abstracted: *When you have that
far-away expression, I know you don't hear a word I
say.*

farcical *adj.* °ludicrous, laughable, risible,
°funny, °nonsensical, °ridiculous, °silly,
°preposterous, °absurd, °foolish; comical,
°humorous, droll, amusing: *His farcical attempts
at surfing fully dressed had us in hysterics.*

fare *n.* **1** °passenger, °traveller: *The taxi-driver
deposited his fare at the hotel.* **2** °charge, °price,
°cost: *What is the fare from Oxford to London?*
3 °food, °diet, victuals, °meals, viands, eatables, °provisions: *Prison fare consisted of bread
and water.*
—*v.* **4** do, make one's way, °manage, °get on *or*
along, °make out, °survive: *The children didn't
fare very well on their own.*

farewell *n.* **1** adieu, °goodbye: *We said our fare-
wells and left.* **2** departure, leave-taking, *congé*,
°parting, *Colloq* send-off: *I want to avoid a tearful
farewell.*
—*interjection.* **3** Adieu!, Goodbye!, So long!, God-
speed!, Adios!, Hasta luego!, Hasta la vista!, Auf
Wiedersehen!, Ciao!, Sayonara!, Aloha!, Vaya con
Dios!, *Colloq Brit* God bless!, *Old-fashioned*
Toodle-oo!, Pip! Pip!, Ta-ta!, *US old-fashioned* See
you later (alligator)!, Don't take any wooden
nickels!: *I said farewell and we went our separate
ways.*

far-fetched adj. °strained, stretched, °improbable, °implausible, °unlikely, °doubtful, dubious, °questionable, °forced, unconvincing, °unrealistic, °fantastic, °preposterous, hard to °believe, °unbelievable, °incredible, Colloq hard to °swallow, °fishy: They told some far-fetched tale about being robbed by a gang of midgets.

farm n. **1** farmstead, farmhouse, grange, homestead, holding; °land, farmland, acreage, arable; Brit steading, smallholding, °allotment, Scots farm-toun, croft: My grandfather owns a farm in Yorkshire. **2 buy the farm:** °die, be °killed: A MIG caught Johnson and he bought the farm.
—v. **3** °cultivate, °work the °land, °till the °soil: His family has been farming this land for centuries. **4 farm out:** °contract, subcontract, °lease, °delegate, °let (out): They cut staff and now farm out much of the work.

farmer n. husbandman, agriculturist, agronomist, yeoman, Brit smallholder, US dialect granger: The farmers here were hard hit by the drought.

farming n. agriculture, agronomy, husbandry, agribusiness, cultivation: Less than 8,000 years ago man turned from hunting and gathering to farming.

far-sighted adj. **1** far-seeing, foresighted, prescient, °provident, °prudent, °shrewd, °perceptive, discerning, insightful, °wise, sagacious, °acute, °sharp, °astute, °sensible, °imaginative: The committee drew up a far-sighted plan for the redevelopment of the town centre. **2** long-sighted, hyperopic or hypermetropic, presbyopic: I'm far-sighted, so I wear glasses only for reading.

fascinate v. °bewitch, °enchant, cast a °spell on or over, ensorcell, spellbind, °hold spellbound, put or have under a °spell, °charm, °captivate, °intrigue, °beguile, °hypnotize, mesmerize, °transfix, °entrance, engross, enthral, °enrapture, absorb, allure, °attract: Desmond is utterly fascinated by Elizabeth.

fascination n. °enchantment, °sorcery, °magic, attractiveness, °attraction, °draw, °pull, (animal) °magnetism, °charm, allure, captivation, °influence, witchcraft, entrancement: Blondes always held a strange fascination for him.

fashion n. **1** °style, °mode, °vogue, °trend, °look, °taste: That year there was a fashion for stiletto heels. **2** the °fad, °mania, the °craze, the °rage, the °latest (°thing), dernier cri, Colloq Brit the go: He remembers when upswept hair-dos were the fashion. **3** °manner, °mode, °way, °approach, °attitude: I'll always be true to you, darling, in my fashion. **4 in fashion:** See fashionable, below.
—v. **5** °make, °model, °style, °shape, °form, °frame, °mould, °fashion, °construct, °forge, °work, °manufacture: She fashions the most beautiful vases out of shapeless lumps of clay.

fashionable adj. in °fashion, °chic, à la °mode, modish, °stylish, °smart, in °vogue, up to the °minute, up to °date, Colloq °trendy, in, with it, Colloq Brit all the go: The couturiers insist that black will be fashionable this year.

fast¹ adj. **1** quick, °swift, °fleet, °speedy, °brisk; °brief, °hurried, °hasty, high-speed, accelerated, °expeditious, °rapid, °prompt: Reg is very fast on her feet. We need a fast turn-round on this job. **2** °loose, °profligate, °wild, °extravagant, dissipated, intemperate, °irresponsible, sybaritic, °self-indulgent, °dissolute, unrestrained,

indecorous, °rakish, licentious, °promiscuous, °immoral, °wanton, °lecherous, °lustful: They led quite a fast life till their divorce. **3** °firm, fastened, °secure(d), °fixed, tied, °bound, connected, °attached: The boat was fast to the pier. **4** °firm, °fixed, settled, °stable, °solid, °immovable, unshakable or unshakeable, °tight: The sword was fast in the stone. **5** °firm, °stable, °steadfast, °staunch, unwavering, °constant, °lasting, °close, °loyal, °devoted, °faithful, °permanent: We maintained a fast friendship over the years.
—adv. **6** °quickly, °swiftly, °rapidly, speedily, briskly, presto, °hastily, hurriedly, with all °speed or °haste, expeditiously, apace, °post-haste, like a °flash, in the blink of an eye, in a wink, before you can say 'Jack Robinson', in no °time (at all), Colloq like a bat out of hell, like a °shot, p.d.q. (='pretty damned quick'), Brit like the clappers (of hell), US and Canadian quick like a bunny or rabbit, lickety-split: Don't talk so fast. He ran out of there very fast. I'll be back very fast. **7** °firmly, fixedly, immovably, solidly, unshakeably or unshakably, °tightly, securely, soundly: The rope held fast. He is fast asleep. **8** closely, °close to, °immediately, °near, (°close) on, °right: Fast on the heels of the fugitive came the police. **9** loosely, wildly, recklessly, intemperately, irresponsibly, fecklessly, extravagantly, intemperately, sybaritically, self-indulgently, dissolutely, unrestrainedly, indecorously, rakishly, licentiously, promiscuously, immorally, wantonly, lecherously, lustfully: He's been living fast since inheriting that fortune.

fast² v. **1** abstain, go °hungry, °deny oneself, °diet, starve (oneself): Do you fast during Lent?
—n. **2** abstention, abstinence, fasting, °self-denial, °diet; °hunger °strike: She went on a two-week fast.

fasten v. **1** °attach, °tie, °bind, °bond, °stick, affix, °anchor, °fix, °lock, °hook (up), °secure, °join, °connect, °link, °fuse, cement, °clamp: Fasten your seat belts. The mussels fasten themselves by their byssi to underwater piles. **2** °fix, rivet, °focus, °concentrate, °direct, °aim, °point: He fastened his gaze on Kitty. She fastened her attention on the ceiling.

fastening n. fastener, catch, °clasp, latch, °lock, °tie, °bond: Can you see what kind of fastening is holding the cover?

fastidious adj. °squeamish, °delicate, over-nice, °fussy, °meticulous, °finicky, finical, pernickety or US also persnickety, °particular, °difficult, °critical, hypercritical, supercritical, over-precise, punctilious, Colloq nit-picking, picky: The Prioress was too fastidious to allow a morsel drop from her lip.

fat adj. **1** °obese, °stout, overweight, °heavy, °plump, °rotund, corpulent, portly, °well-fed, °chubby, podgy or chiefly US pudgy, roly-poly, tubby, °bulky, fleshy, paunchy, pot-bellied, overfed, °flabby, elephantine, Colloq °broad in the beam, °beamy, beefy, Slang US five-by-five: A fat man squeezed in beside me. **2** °oily, oleaginous, unctuous, °greasy, fatty, pinguid, sebaceous, adipose: His complexion is bad because he eats too much fat food. **3** °rich, °wealthy, °prosperous, affluent, well-to-do, well off, Colloq well-heeled, °loaded: They grew fat on their profits from the black market. **4** °profitable, lucrative, °fruitful, remunerative, Slang cushy: He has a fat job as a purchasing agent for the government.

—*n.* **5** °obesity, corpulence, stoutness, over-weight, heaviness, plumpness, rotundity, port-liness, chubbiness, podginess *or chiefly US* pudginess, tubbiness, fleshiness, paunchiness, flabbiness: *He leans a little towards fat because of lack of exercise.* **6** °riches, °wealth, °prosperity, fertility, °yield, °abundance, °plenty, plent-eousness: *He's living off the fat of the land.*

fatal *adj.* **1** °fateful, °deadly, °murderous, °lethal, °mortal, toxic, °terminal, °final; bane-ful, °poisonous: *She drank the fatal potion without a word. Who dealt the fatal blow?* **2** °destructive, °fateful, °ruinous, °calamitous, °dreadful, °disastrous, °devastating, cataclysmic, cata-strophic, °harmful, °mischievous, damaging: *Discovery by the police would prove fatal to our plan.* **3** °fateful, °fated, °destined, predestined, decreed, ordained, foreordained, preordained, °predetermined, °inevitable, °unavoidable, °necessary, °essential, inescapable, ineluctable: *The events fell into their fatal sequence.*

fatality *n.* **1** °catastrophe, °disaster, °calamity, cataclysm: *The eruption of Vesuvius was a relatively recent fatality.* **2** °death, °casualty: *Traffic fatalities are on the increase.*

fate *n.* **1** °fortune, °lot, °luck, °chance, °life, °destiny, God's °will, °providence *or* Providence, °doom, karma, kismet, toss *or* throw of the dice, *Colloq US and Canadian* the breaks, the way the cookie crumbles, the way the ball bounces: *Fate has brought us together. Our meeting this way was just fate.* **2** °doom, °destruction, °downfall, °undoing, °ruin, °disaster, °collapse, °death, nemesis, °end, °finish: *The defenders of Masada met their fate bravely.* **3** °end, °outcome, °future, °destination, °disposition: *There was no trace of the fate of the explorers. What is to be the fate of this obsolete equipment?*

fated *adj.* **1** °destined, predestined, °predetermined, decreed, °doomed, °fateful, ordained, foreordained, preordained, °decided: *The fated day of my trial arrived.* **2** °sure, °certain, °doomed, damned, cursed: *Was I fated to spend the rest of my life in this fetid dungeon?* **3** °fatal, °fateful, °unavoidable, inescapable, °inevitable, ineluctable: *Their fated punishment was to bail out the sea using sieves.*

fateful *adj.* **1** °significant, °momentous, °ominous, °major, consequential, °important, °critical, °crucial, decisive, °weighty, °portentous, earth-shaking, °pivotal: *The minister is faced with having to make a fateful decision.* **2** °deadly, °lethal, °fatal, °destructive, °ruinous, °disastrous, catastrophic, cataclysmic: *Failure to preserve the environment could have fateful consequences.*

father *n.* **1** sire, paterfamilias, *Colloq* dad, daddy, pa, papa, °pop, old man, old boy, *Brit* governor, pater: *His father is a chemist.* **2** forebear, °ancestor, forefather, °progenitor, primogenitor: *The father of the dynasty fought at Hastings.* **3** °creator, °founder, originator, inventor, °author, archi-tect, framer, initiator: *He regards Lavoisier as the father of modern chemistry.* **4** °priest, confessor, curé, abbé, °minister, °pastor, °shepherd, par-son, °clergyman, chaplain, *Colloq* padre, *Military slang* sky pilot: *We should see the Father about the funeral service.*

—*v.* **5** sire, beget, °get, engender, procreate, °generate: *He had fathered more than forty children in his harem.* **6** °originate, °establish, °found,

°invent, °author, °frame, °initiate, °institute, °create: *Galileo fathered modern astronomy by invent-ing the telescope.*

fatherland *n.* motherland, °native °land, °mother °country, homeland, (old) °country, birthplace: *They return to their fatherland for an annual visit.*

fatherly *adj.* °paternal, °kindly, °kind, °warm, °friendly, °affectionate, °protective, °amiable, °benevolent, well-meaning, °benign, caring, °sympathetic, °indulgent, °understanding; par-ental: *My nephew used to come to me for fatherly advice.*

fathom *v.* °probe, °sound, °plumb, °penetrate, °search (out), °investigate, °measure, °gauge, °determine, ascertain, °work out, get to the °bottom of, delve into, °understand, °grasp, °divine: *I never quite fathomed the purpose of this device.*

fatigue *n.* **1** weariness, tiredness, °weakness, °exhaustion, lassitude, listlessness, °lethargy, languor, °sluggishness, enervation: *She kept on tending the wounded till fatigue finally overcame her.*

—*v.* **2** °weary, °tire, °weaken, °exhaust, °drain, °enervate, *Colloq* °fag (out): *My morning's work had fatigued me.*

fatigued *adj.* °weary, wearied, °tired, overtired, °dead °tired, °weak, weakened, °exhausted, °listless, °lethargic, languorous, sluggish, ener-vated, °strained, wasted, *Colloq* whacked (out), knocked out, °dead, °beat, dead beat, all in, *Brit* knackered, jiggered, buggered, *US and Canadian* pooped, bushed: *The firemen were fatigued after being on duty round the clock.*

fatness *n.* °obesity, stoutness, corpulence, embonpoint, portliness, plumpness, chubbiness, rotundity, podginess *or chiefly US* pudginess: *His fatness is owing to a glandular condition, not over-eating.*

fault *n.* **1** °imperfection, °flaw, °defect, °blemish, deficiency, °shortcoming, °failing, °weakness; °frailty, °foible, °peccadillo: *The fault lies in this circuit. Using filthy language is only one of his faults.* **2** °mistake, °error, °blunder, °lapse, °failure, °offence, °oversight, °slip(-up), °indiscretion, gaffe, gaucherie, faux pas, *Slang* boner, °howler, goof, boo-boo, *Brit* boob: *People should be responsible for their faults. There are many faults in this manuscript.* **3** °responsibility, °liability, culpability, °blame, °accountability, answerability: *It wasn't my fault that the tree fell down. The fault lies with you, James.* **4** °sin, °transgression, trespass, °misdeed, °offence, mis-demeanour, °vice, °indiscretion, misconduct, °misbehaviour: *He will confess his faults to anyone who will listen.* **5 at fault**: to °blame, blameable, blameworthy, in the °wrong, °responsible, answerable, °accountable, °liable, culpable, °guilty: *You were at fault for failing to report the crime.* **6 find fault**: °criticize, censure, take °exception (to), °carp (at), °cavil (at), °pick at, °pick on, °pick apart, °pick holes in, °niggle, °fuss, *Colloq* nit-pick, °knock: *She constantly finds fault with everything I do.* **7 to a fault**: excessively, °extremely, to an °extreme, in the °extreme, unreasonably, °exceedingly, °unduly, dis-proportionately, immoderately, irrationally, *US* °overly: *She is modest to a fault.*

—*v.* **8** find fault with, censure, °blame, °criticize, call to °account, impugn, call into °question, hold (someone) °responsible *or* °accountable *or* to °blame, lay at (someone's) door, °accuse: *You cannot be faulted for not knowing the fuel tank was empty.*

fault-finding *n.* **1** °criticism, censure, carping, cavilling, captiousness, hypercriticism, quibbling, fussiness, °hair-splitting, pettifogging, *Colloq* nit-picking, pickiness: *Why continue to put up with the foreman's fault-finding?* —*adj.* **2** °critical, censorious, carping, cavilling, captious, hypercritical, °fussy, °hair-splitting, pettifogging, °niggling, contentious, °querulous, quibbling, *Colloq* nit-picking, picky: *She could no longer abide his fault-finding attitude.*

faultless *adj.* °perfect, °flawless, °immaculate, °ideal, °exemplary, °correct, °accurate, °foolproof, °irreproachable, unimpeachable, *Colloq Brit* bang on, °spot on: *Their performance was faultless.*

faulty *adj.* °defective, °unsound, °imperfect, °flawed, impaired, out of °order, malfunctioning, °broken, °bad; damaged; *Slang* on the °blink, *Chiefly US* on the fritz: *The carburettor is faulty.*

favour *n.* **1** °good °will, °approval, °support, approbation: *Father looked with favour on my marriage to Leslie.* **2** °courtesy, °good *or* °kind °deed, °good °turn, °kindness, °gesture, *beau geste;* °service: *As a favour, I'll walk your dog while you're away.* **3** °favouritism, °partiality, °prejudice, °bias, °preference, °patronage: *They show favour in repeatedly giving the contract to the same company.* **4** °grace, °esteem, °consideration, °view, °regard, °opinion, °account, (good *or* bad) books; °disposition, °taste, predisposition: *How does Rochester stand in the favour of the king?* **5 in favour (of):** °for, pro, on the °side of, in °support (of), at the back of, °backing, behind, on *or US and Canadian* in °behalf (of), in back of: *Please vote in favour of the resolution. Are you in favour or against?* —*v.* **6** °approve, °prefer, °like, have a °liking *or* °preference for, be °partial to, °advocate, espouse, °back, °endorse, °support, °champion, °recommend, °incline to *or* towards, °side with, take the °side *or* °part of, °go for, opt for, °fancy, °select, °choose, °elect, °single out, °sponsor, °adopt, °go in for: *Which candidate do you favour?* **7** °pamper, °coddle, °baby, °protect, °indulge, be °partial to: *Notice how Billie favours his left leg when walking?* **8** °advance, °forward, °promote, °facilitate, °expedite, °help, °benefit, °assist, °aid, °encourage, °accommodate, °smile upon: *The warm, moist climate favours the growth of mould.* **9** °resemble, °look °like, °take after: *Little Jimmy favours his father, I think.*

favourable *adj.* **1** °advantageous, °promising, auspicious, °fair, °beneficial, °suitable, °fitting, °appropriate, encouraging, facilitative, °helpful, °helping, °supportive, supporting, °convenient, °useful, °opportune, propitious, °accommodating, accommodative; facultative: *A favourable breeze sent our craft towards Cyprus.* **2** °good, °promising, °positive, encouraging, reassuring, affirmative, well-disposed, °sympathetic; commendatory, °laudatory, °enthusiastic, °eager, °ardent, zealous: *They concluded a very favourable deal to supply the army with boots. My latest book received favourable reviews.*

favourably *adv.* **1** graciously, indulgently, sympathetically, genially, °positively, agreeably,

enthusiastically, with °favour: *They reacted favourably to my suggestion.* **2** advantageously, affirmatively, °positively, in °favourable terms: *Your application has been considered favourably.*

favoured *adj.* **1** preferred, chosen, °choice, selected, °popular, °favourite, °pet: *The favoured explanation is that he is the boss's son.* **2** advantaged, °privileged, blessed, °prosperous, °wealthy, °rich, affluent, well off: *She is one of the favoured few who can afford to travel.*

favourite *n.* **1** °choice, °pick, °preference, preferred, esteemed, °darling, °pet, °ideal, apple of (someone's) eye, *Colloq Brit* blue-eyed boy *or* girl, flavour of the month, *US* white-haired *or* white-headed boy *or* girl, fair-haired boy *or* girl: *Raising interest rates doesn't exactly make the chancellor everyone's favourite.* —*adj.* **2** °beloved, chosen, picked, selected, preferred, best-liked, most-liked, °favoured, °choice, °pet, °ideal: *Which is your favourite flavour?*

favouritism *n.* °partiality, °bias, predisposition, prepossession, °prejudice, °bent, partisanship, nepotism, preferment; °preference, °leaning, °inclination, proclivity: *He openly admits to favouritism in selecting employees.*

fear *n.* **1** °dread, °terror, °fright, °panic, °horror, °alarm, trepidation, apprehension, fearfulness, apprehensiveness, °dismay, consternation, hesitation, qualms, diffidence, timidity, cravenness, °cowardice, °second thoughts: *His fear of going into the jungle alone is understandable.* **2** awe, °respect, °reverence, °veneration: *That'll put the fear of God into him!* **3** °horror, °spectre, nightmare, bogey *or* bogy, °phobia, bugbear, *bête noire,* °misgiving(s), °foreboding(s): *When they came to break the news, her worst fears were realized.* **4** °solicitude, °anxiety, angst, °foreboding(s), °distress, °misgiving(s), °concern, apprehension, °worry, uneasiness, unease: *Fear for her safety is shared by all of us.* —*v.* **5** be °afraid *or* °scared *or* °fearful *or* °frightened (of), °dread, quail *or* °tremble *or* °quake at, °shudder at, °shrink from, °quiver: *What man cannot understand he often fears.* **6** °revere, °respect, °venerate, be *or* stand in awe of: *If you fear the Lord as I do, you won't take his name in vain.* **7** °expect, °anticipate, °imagine, °suspect, °foresee: *I fear we are too late for dinner.*

fearful *adj.* **1** °afraid, °scared, frightened, terrified, alarmed, °panic-stricken, terror-stricken *or* terror-struck: *Of all disasters, I am most fearful of fire.* **2** °hesitant, °timid, timorous, °shy, diffident, unwilling, intimidated, °jumpy, °nervous, edgy, panicky, °anxious, apprehensive, °cowardly, pusillanimous, *Colloq* yellow, jittery: *Why is she so fearful of meeting her prospective in-laws?* **3** °awful, dire, °dreadful, °frightful, °frightening, °terrifying, °terrible, appalling, °ghastly, °atrocious, °horrible, horrifying, horrendous, horrific, °hideous, °gruesome, °grisly, °grim, baleful, °monstrous, unspeakable, °loathsome, heinous, °repugnant, °repulsive, °revolting, °disgusting, nauseating, °nauseous: *The fearful monster blocked our only way out.*

fearfully *adv.* **1** hesitantly, timidly, timorously, shyly, diffidently, unwillingly, nervously, edgily, anxiously, apprehensively: *Fearfully, she approached the altar.* **2** °very, °awfully, °terribly,

°extremely, °ex-ceedingly, °frightfully, tre-mendously: *It was fearfully considerate of you to come.*

fearless *adj.* °brave, °bold, °intrepid, valorous, °dauntless, °courageous, valiant, plucky, °daring, °audacious, °heroic, °venturesome, °gallant, °chivalrous: *These fearless commandos cared nothing for their personal safety.*

fearsome *adj.* °dreadful, °awesome, appalling, °formidable, daunting, °frightening, °frightful, aweinspiring, °menacing, °terrible, °terrifying, intimidating: *Last week's typhoon was the most fearsome storm of the century.*

feasibility *n.* practicability, workability, applicability, viability, practicality: *The feasibility of the scheme has yet to be assessed.*

feasible *adj.* °practicable, workable, doable, °applicable, °viable, °practical, °possible, realizable, achievable, attainable, °sensible, usable, °realistic: *The world needs a feasible method for disposing of nuclear waste.*

feast *n.* **1** °banquet, (°lavish) dinner, (°sumptuous) repast, (Lucullan *or* Epicurean) °treat, *Colloq* °spread, *Brit* beanfeast; *Slang* blow-out, *Brit* beano: *Dinner at Patrick's is no mere meal—it is a feast.* **2** °observance, °celebration, °rite, °ritual, solemnization, commemoration, memorialization, anniversary, birthday, jubilee, feast-day, °festival, °fête *or* fete, holy day, °holiday, red-letter day, °occasion, °event, °gala: *Church calendars list both movable and immovable feasts.* **3** °treat, °delight, °pleasure, °gratification: *Seeing you again was a feast for the eyes.*
—*v.* **4** °dine, wine (and °dine), °fare well *or* sumptuously, (over)indulge, °gorge (oneself), gormandize, °eat one's °fill: *We feasted on roast turkey with all the trimmings.* **5** °entertain, °feed, wine and °dine, °treat, °regale: *Visitors to Arthur's court were feasted with the finest viands available.* **6** °delight, °gratify, °please, °cheer, °gladden: *Ali Baba feasted his eyes on the vast treasure in the cave.*

feat *n.* °exploit, °deed, °act, attainment, °achievement, °accomplishment, *tour de force*: *Persuading your wife to let you go fishing was quite a feat.*

feature *n.* **1** °characteristic, °attribute, °trait, °mark, °hallmark, earmark, °property, °character, °quality, °aspect, facet, °peculiarity, °quirk, idiosyncrasy: *What are the identifying features of traditional Chinese architecture?* **2** (main) °attraction, °draw, °special °attraction, high °point *or* °spot, best *or* °memorable °part; °main °film; *US and Canadian* drawing card; column, °piece, article, °item: *The feature of the show was the appearance of Gracie Fields. He writes the gardening feature for a Sunday newspaper.* **3 features**: °face, visage, physiognomy, countenance, °looks, *Slang* °mug, kisser, chips and plaice: *Her features twisted into a frown.*
—*v.* **4** °present, °promote, °publicize, advertise, highlight, °spotlight, put into the limelight, °star, °stress, °emphasize, call °attention to, °play up, °puff up, *Colloq* headline, hype: *He was featured in many films.* **5** be, °act, °perform, take *or* have a °role *or* °part, °participate, be °involved *or* drawn in: *Novels feature prominently in our publishing programme.*

federation *n.* °combination, confederacy, confederation, °amalgamation, coalition, °league,

°alliance, °union, °association, *Bund,* °society: *The central government consists of a federation of states.*

fee *n.* **1** °charge, °price, °cost, °fare, °bill, °tariff, °toll, *Colloq* °damage(s): *The membership fee is £25.* **2** °pay, °payment, emolument, compensation, recompense, °honorarium, °remuneration, °rate, °wage(s), °stipend, °salary: *What is your fee per hour for proofreading?*

feeble *adj.* **1** °weak, °infirm, °frail, °puny, °slight, feckless; debilitated, enervated, °decrepit, enfeebled, °exhausted, weakened; effete, °delicate, °fragile, °powerless, °impotent, impuissant, languid, spiritless, °sickly, ailing, °unsound, °faint, °dizzy; *Colloq* woozy, *Brit* wonky: *The survivors were suffering from exposure and too feeble to walk.* **2** °flimsy, °weak, °ineffectual, °ineffective, namby-pamby, half-baked, °lame, unconvincing, °shoddy, °thin, °insubstantial, °poor, °unsatisfactory, °insufficient, °inadequate, unavailing, °meagre, °paltry, °insignificant, *Colloq* °wishy-washy, *Brit* °wet: *She gave her usual feeble excuse for being late.* **3** °weak, °obscure, °dim, °imperceptible, °faint, °distant, °indistinct, unclear: *He could see little in the feeble light from the one candle. We heard a feeble cry from under the rubble.*

feeble-minded *adj.* °stupid, °dull(-witted), witless, moronic, idiotic, imbecilic, °simple, °slow (on the uptake), slow-witted, weak-minded, dim-witted, addle-pated, °halfwitted, °deficient, subnormal, mentally °defective, retarded, atto-cerebral, *Brit* ESN (= 'educationally subnormal'), *Colloq* °dumb, °thick, °soft in the head, bone-headed, empty-headed, °vacant, *Brit* gormless, *US* °exceptional: *Why do you spend so much time with that feeble-minded twit?*

feed *v.* **1** °provision, °cater *or* °provide (for), victual, purvey, °provender, °supply, °maintain, nurture, °nourish, °board, °support, °sustain, wine and °dine: *Is there enough to feed everyone?* **2** °eat, °devour, graze, °pasture: *Cattle feed most of the day.* **3 feed on** *or* **upon**: subsist *or* °survive *or* °depend *or* °thrive on *or* upon, be °nourished *or* °gratified *or* °supported by: *Swindlers feed on others' gullibility.*
—*n.* **4** fodder, forage, pasturage, silage, °food, °provender: *What kind of feed are you giving the sheep?*

feel *v.* **1** °touch, °see, °note, °sense, °perceive, °experience, °determine; °handle, °manipulate, °finger: *Feel how rough the skin is at this spot.* **2** °stroke, °caress, °pet, °fondle: *I like to feel a bare carpet with my toes.* **3** °sense, be °conscious of, °perceive, be °aware *or* °sensible of, °experience: *I could feel the heat of the fire across the room.* **4** °sense, °believe, °think, °perceive, °judge, °consider, deem, °know, discern, intuit, *Colloq* get *or* have the °impression, have a °hunch, °guess, have a (funny) °feeling, feel in one's bones: *I feel I have outstayed my welcome.* **5** °undergo, °sense, °suffer, °bear, °endure, °withstand, °stand, °abide, °brook, °tolerate, °go through: *Let the other team feel the agony of defeat for a change.* **6** °seem, °appear, °strike one, give the °impression, have a *or* the °feeling: *It felt as if a great weight had been lifted from me. It feels like old times. That feels silky.* **7** °seem to be, be, °regard *or* °characterize oneself as, °take oneself to be: *I feel certain that*

we've met before. I felt a perfect fool. **8 feel for**: °sympathize *or* empathize with, commiserate with, bleed for, be °sorry for, °pity, have compassion for: *She feels for all mothers whose sons have died.* **9 feel like**: °incline *or* °lean to *or* °towards, °prefer, °fancy, °want, °desire, crave: *I feel like a cup of hot tea.*
—*n.* **10** °texture, °surface, °sensation, °touch, °finish: *This wood has the feel of satin.* **11** °feeling, °air, °atmosphere, °climate, ambience *or* ambiance, °sense, °note, °tone, °quality: *It's so cosy here—it has the feel of home.*

feeler *n.* **1** antenna, tentacle, palp, sensor: *Those moths have long, feathery feelers.* **2** °overture, °hint, °suggestion, foretaste, °probe, tester, sensor: *The questionnaire is a feeler put out to test public opinion.*

feeling *n.* **1** (°sense of) °touch, °sensitivity, °sense, °perception, °sensation, °sensibility: *I had no feeling in my left side.* **2** °intuition, °idea, °notion, °inkling, °suspicion, °belief, °hunch, theory, °sense; °premonition, °hint, presentiment, °sense of °foreboding, °sensation, °impression, °opinion, °view; °instinct, consciousness, awareness: *I have a feeling you're fooling. Do you ever have the feeling of being watched?* **3** °regard, °sympathy, empathy, °identification, compassion, tenderness, °appreciation, °concern, °understanding, °sensitivity, °sensibility: *He has a genuine feeling for animals.* **4** °ardour, °warmth, °passion, fervency, °fervour, ardency, °intensity, °heat, °sentiment, °emotion, vehemence: *She said she loved me with so much feeling that I thought she meant it.* **5 feelings**: °emotions, °sensitivity, °sympathies, °sensibilities, susceptibilities: *She hurt my feelings.* **6** °feel, °mood, °atmosphere, °climate, °sense, °air, ambience *or* ambiance: *There is a feeling of impending doom about this place.*
—*adj.* **7** sentient, °sensitive, °tender, tender-hearted, compassionate, °sympathetic: *Their behaviour did the soldiers honour as feeling men.*

feint *n.* °distraction, °mock °attack, °bluff, °dodge, °manoeuvre, °false °move, °pretence, °ruse, ploy, °subterfuge, °deception, °tactic, °stratagem, gambit, °artifice: *The attack on the flanks is merely a feint—the main thrust will be at the centre.*

fell *v.* °cut *or* °knock *or* °strike down, °floor, °prostrate, °level, hew (down), °flatten, °demolish, °mow (down); °kill: *He felled his opponent with one blow. All the trees in this area must be felled.*

fellow *n.* **1** °man, °boy, °person, °individual, gentleman, °one, *Colloq* °guy, °chap, °customer, kid, *Brit* bloke, *Slang* geezer, gink, *US old-fashioned* gazabo: *There was a fellow here asking for you today.* **2** °colleague, °associate, °comrade, °companion, °ally, °peer, compeer: *He is going to meet some of his fellows at the club.* **3** °mate, °match, counterpart, °partner, °complement, concomitant, °accessory: *I lost one glove last week and now have lost its fellow.* **4** boyfriend, °man, °sweetheart, °love, young °man; °lover, °paramour, *Formal* °suitor, *Old-fashioned* beau, *Archaic* swain, *Slang* °guy: *Bailey has been Sue's fellow for years.*

—*adj.* **5** °associate(d), affiliate(d), allied, °auxiliary, °related: *Ladies, not accorded membership in the men's club, belonged to a fellow organization. She shared her sandwiches with a fellow passenger.*

fellowship *n.* **1** °companionship, camaraderie, comradeship, amity, °brotherhood, fraternization, togetherness, °association, °friendship, companion-ability, sociability, intimacy: *I have always enjoyed the fellowship of my university colleagues.* **2** °society, °club, °association, °alliance, guild, °league, °union, sisterhood, sorority, °brotherhood, °fraternity, congregation, °circle, community, °order, °organization, consortium, partnership; °lodge, °clan, °company, coterie, °set, °clique, coalition, bloc, cartel, °trust: *They belong to the worldwide fellowship of artists.* **3** friendliness, clubbiness, sociability, intimacy, amicability, affability, kindliness, cordiality, °familiarity, °affinity, °belonging, congeniality, °warmth, °hospitality: *Being a club member gives him a feeling of fellowship.*

felon *n.* °criminal, °outlaw, lawbreaker, °offender, °culprit, °miscreant, malefactor, wrongdoer: *Only if convicted of a certain class of crime is a person technically a felon.*

feminine *adj.* **1** female, womanlike, womanly, °ladylike, °submissive, deferential, amenable, °gentle, docile, °tender, °soft, °delicate: *She is much more feminine than her sister.* **2** °effeminate, womanish, unmanly, unmasculine, °sissy *or Brit* cissy, sissified *or Brit* cissified, effete, °affected: *Barry's manner and behaviour seem to become more feminine every day.*

fence *n.* **1** °barrier, °enclosure, barricade, confine, °wall, °rampart; railing(s), palisade: *Maurice had a fence put up round his house.* **2 on the fence**: undecided, °indecisive, vacillating, uncommitted, °uncertain, °irresolute; °impartial, °neutral, °non-partisan, unbiased, °unprejudiced, unaligned, °non-aligned, °independent: *She is on the fence with regard to the issue of capital punishment.*
—*v.* **3** °enclose, °encircle, °surround, circumscribe, °bound, coop, °restrict, hedge, confine, °fortify, °protect, °separate: *The pasture is fenced both to keep the sheep in and the wolves out. Fence off this area for a garden.* **4** parry, °avoid, °fend off, °sidestep, °dodge, °evade, hedge, stonewall, °equivocate, palter, tergiversate, vacillate, °shilly-shally, °quibble, °cavil, °beat about the bush, °qualify, prevaricate, *Colloq Brit* °waffle: *Awkward questions were adroitly fenced by the chairman. Give a straight answer and stop fencing.*

fend *v.* **1 fend for oneself**: °get *or* °scrape along (on one's own), °make out, °get by, °make do, °shift for oneself, take °care of *or* °provide for *or* °support oneself: *Mother didn't believe I could fend for myself.* **2 fend off**: °discourage, parry, °keep *or* °hold at bay, °resist, °repel, stave *or* °ward *or* °fight off, °deflect, °turn aside, avert, °divert: *We fended off our attackers for three days.*

ferment *v.* **1** °boil, effervesce, °seethe, °bubble, °foam, °froth, °brew; °rise, °raise, °work, leaven: *A rebellion is fermenting in the northern counties. Adding yeast causes the bread to ferment.* **2** °excite, °stir up, °incite, instigate, °agitate, °foment, °inflame, °rouse, °provoke: *He helped to ferment a riot.*

ferocious adj. °fierce, °savage, °cruel, °vicious, feral, °fell, °brutal, bestial, °merciless, °ruthless, pitiless, °inhuman, barbaric, barbarous, °violent, °destructive, °murderous, °bloodthirsty, °sanguinary, °predatory, °fiendish, diabolic(al), °devilish, hellish, °monstrous: *Cerberus, a ferocious beast with three heads, guards the gates of hell.*

fertile adj. °fruitful, °prolific, fecund, °productive, bounteous, °profuse, °abundant, copious, fructuous, plenteous, generative, teeming, °rich, °luxuriant: *The land was fertile enough to grow anything. This book is a fertile source of ideas.*

fertilize v. 1 °impregnate, inseminate, pollinate, fecundate, fructify: *The flower should be fertilized by pollen from a different stock.* 2 manure, mulch, °feed, °nourish, °enrich, °dress, compost: *The earth can be fertilized at any time.*

fervent adj. 1 fervid, °fiery, °burning, °glowing, °hot, °intense, °passionate, °impassioned, °ardent, °hotheaded, °inflamed, °fanatic(al), °excited, °frantic, frenzied: *Only the most fervent acolytes were ordained as ministers of the faith.* 2 °eager, °earnest, °enthusiastic, zealous, °animated, °intense, °heartfelt, °emotional: *It is my fervent desire to see you happy.* 3 °ecstatic, transported, °rapturous, °rapt, enrapt, enraptured, captivated: *The fervent crowds cheered wildly when Caesar arrived.*

fervour n. fervency, °ardour, °warmth, °passion, vehemence, °glow, °intensity, zeal, °eagerness, earnestness, °enthusiasm, °animation, °gusto, ebullience, °spirit, °verve: *She went about her studies with a fervour we had not seen before.*

fester v. 1 ulcerate, suppurate, °run, °ooze, °putrefy, putresce, necrose, °mortify, °rot, °decay, °decompose: *His entire body was covered with festering sores.* 2 °rankle, °smoulder, °gall, °chafe, °inflame: *Bitterness over the way he had been treated festered inside him for years.*

festival n. 1 °holiday, holy day, fête or fete, °feast, commemoration, anniversary: *He wanted to be with his family for the Christmas festival.* 2 °celebration, °fête, festivities, carnival, °entertainment, red-letter day, gala day, anniversary, birthday: *The town organizes a festival every autumn.*

festivity n. 1 rejoicing, °gaiety, °mirth, jubilation, conviviality, joyfulness, °merriment, °revelry, merrymaking, °glee, jollity, jollification, felicity, Colloq Brit mafficking: *There were laughter and festivity in the air.* 2 **festivities**: °celebration(s), °festival, °party, °fun and games, °entertainment, °amusement, °hilarity, boisterousness, frivolity: *Come along and join the festivities at our house tonight.*

fetch v. 1 °get, °go after or for, °bring (back), °retrieve, °deliver, °obtain, °carry or convey (back): *Would you please fetch my slippers?* 2 °summon, °bring or °draw forth, °call, °elicit: *The doorbell fetched me from my bath.* 3 °sell for, °bring (in), °go for, °yield, °earn, °make, °cost, °realize: *These days a house near London fetches a high price.* —n. 4 °reach, °stretch, °range, °span, °extent: *It is quite a long fetch across the bay.*

fetching adj. °attractive, alluring, °taking, winsome, °winning, °cute, °enchanting, charming, captivating, intriguing: *Fingal's sister is a fetching young lass.*

fête n. 1 fete, °festival, °entertainment, °reception, levee, °gala, rejoicing, °celebration, °party, °festivities, °get-together, °social, °amusement, °revel, °fair, ball, °frolic, °spree, °jamboree, carnival, °event, °occasion, Colloq blow-out, shindig, bash, do, bust, Slang US and Canadian wingding, °blast: *You are invited to our annual fête on New Year's Eve.* —v. 2 °entertain, °feast, roll or bring out the red carpet for, wine and °dine, °celebrate, °honour, lionize, °fuss over, kill the fatted calf for: *Fiona's book was a great success and she was fêted all over Europe.*

fetish n. 1 °charm, °amulet, °talisman, totem, Rare periapt: *Round his neck he wore the dreaded fetish of the fish god.* 2 °obsession, compulsion, °fixation, °mania, idée fixe: *It's a fetish of hers to kiss only under the mistletoe.*

feud n. 1 °dispute, °conflict, °vendetta, °hostility, °strife, enmity, °animosity, hatred, °antagonism, °rivalry, °ill will, bad blood, °hard feelings, contention, °discord, °grudge, °dissension, °disagreement, °argument, °quarrel, bickering, squabble, falling out, estrangement: *A silly feud broke out over whose turn it was to bring the Christmas goose.* —v. 2 °dispute, °quarrel, °bicker, °disagree, °conflict, °row, °fight, °fall out, °clash, be at °odds, be at daggers drawn: *The Hatfields and McCoys feuded for decades.*

feverish adj. °inflamed, flushed, °burning, °fiery, °hot, °ardent, °fervent, hot-blooded, °passionate, frenzied, °frantic, °excited, frenetic, zealous; Pathology febrile, pyretic, pyrexic: *I was looking forward to our rendezvous with feverish excitement.*

few adj. 1 °hardly or °scarcely any, not °many, °insufficient; infrequent, °occasional: *Few people came to my party. He is a man of few words.* —n. 2 °handful, some, °scattering: *I invited a lot of people, but only a few came.* —pron. 3 (only) one or two, not °many: *Many apply but few are chosen.*

fiancé(e) n. betrothed, wife- or bride- or husband-to-be, intended: *He went out to buy a ring for his fiancée.*

fiasco n. °failure, °disaster, °muddle, °mess, abortion, °botch, Colloq °fizzle, °flop: *My effort to help Donald with his maths homework was a complete fiasco.*

fib n. 1 °falsehood, (little) white °lie, untruth, prevarication, °fabrication, °invention, misrepresentation, °story, (fairy) °tale, fiction; °lie; Colloq °tall °story, US °tall °tale, cock-and-bull °story, °whopper: *I told a little fib when I said my grandmother was ill.* —v. 2 prevaricate, °misrepresent, fudge, °falsify, palter; °lie; Colloq °waffle: *They admitted they had fibbed about who had thrown the egg.*

fibre n. 1 filament, °thread, strand, fibril, tendril: *This fabric is woven from cotton fibre.* 2 °texture, °structure, °material, °fabric: *The fibre of this rock is granular.* 3 °essence, °character, °nature, °mould, °composition, constitution, °substance, °quality, °stripe, °cast, °make-up: *Love for him is wrapped up in the very fibre of her being.*

fickle adj. °flighty, °capricious, °frivolous, unpredictable, °moody, °giddy, °fanciful, °whimsical, °fitful, mercurial, °volatile, °unstable, °changeable, mutable, °inconstant, changeful, unsteady, unsteadfast, °indecisive, undecided, vacillating *or rarely* vacillant, unsure, °uncertain, °irresolute, wavering, °erratic, °unreliable, undependable, °irresponsible, untrustworthy, °faithless, unfaithful, °disloyal, *Colloq* °wishy-washy: *That fickle woman has already taken up with someone else. You should know how fickle the tastes of the public are.*

fictional *adj.* °unreal, °imaginary, invented, made-up, °mythical, °fanciful; °legendary, °fabulous: *The newspaper article was a hoax— completely fictional. Lorna Doone is Janet's favourite fictional heroine.*

fictitious *adj.* 1 imagined, °imaginary, °non-existent, °unreal, made-up, invented, fabricated, °mythical, °fancied, °fanciful, fictive, °untrue, apocryphal: *The claim that an article had appeared was completely fictitious.* 2 °false, °counterfeit, °bogus, °artificial, °spurious; °assumed, improvised, made-up, invented, make-believe, °imaginary, *Colloq* °phoney *or US also* phony: *When arrested they gave fictitious names.*

fiddle *v.* 1 Often, **fiddle with**: °meddle (with), °tamper (with), °interfere (with), °alter, °falsify, °fix; °cheat, °swindle, flimflam; *Colloq* finagle, *Brit* cook: *The treasurer had been fiddling the accounts for years.* 2 Often, **fiddle with** *or* **about** *or* **around**: °toy *or* °trifle *or* °fidget (with), °twiddle *or* °play *or* °tinker (with), °fool *or* °fuss (with), *Colloq* °mess *or* °muck (about *or* around) (with), frivol (away), °monkey (around) (with): *He sat there nervously fiddling with his ear. Stop fiddling about and get on with your work.* —*n.* 3 *Brit* swindle, °fraud, °racket, thimblerig, *US* shell-game, *Slang* skin °game, °funny business, °monkey business: *The tax inspector caught him in some fiddle with his business expenses.* 4 violin, viola, viol, cello, violoncello, kit: *He played fiddle for the tsar.*

fiddlesticks *interj.* °Nonsense!, °Rubbish!, *Colloq* Fiddle-de-dee!, Balderdash!, °Stuff and Nonsense!, Poppycock!, Pish and tush!, Tommy-rot!, Hogwash!, Eyewash!, Boloney!, Bilge-water!, °Moonshine!, Humbug!, Bosh!, Fiddle-faddle!, Bull!, Rot!, *Brit* Codswallop!, *Taboo slang* Bullshit!, Balls!, Crap!, Horseshit!, *Brit* Bollocks! *or* Ballocks!: *When he said he'd pay what he owed, I just said, 'Fiddlesticks!'*

fidget *v.* 1 °squirm, twitch, °shuffle, °wriggle, wiggle, °fiddle, °fuss; °fret, °chafe: *Stop fidgeting and tell me the truth!* —*n.* 2 fusspot, fuss-budget, cat on hot bricks, *US* cat on a hot tin roof, *Colloq US* °nervous Nellie: *If her conscience is clear, why is she such a fidget?* 3 **the fidgets**: restlessness, fidgetiness, dither, uneasiness, the °jitters, nervousness, itchiness, *Colloq* heebie-jeebies, jim-jams, ants in one's pants: *Whenever he tells a lie he gets a bad case of the fidgets.*

field *n.* 1 °ground, °land, arable, °pasture, grassland, °meadow, °green, °lawn, °common, clearing, °tract, °area, acreage, *Literary* greensward, lea, sward; *Archaic* mead: *The house looks out over the fields.* 2 battlefield, battleground, airfield; (cricket) °pitch, football *or* hockey *or* soccer field, *American football* gridiron: *We marched onto the field prepared for anything.* 3 °competition, competitors, players, entrants, contestants, participants, candidates, possibilities, applicants: *Who can match you among today's field?* 4 °area, °domain, °realm, °department, °territory, °province, °sphere,

°scope, °division, °interest, °line, métier, °discipline, bailiwick, °speciality *or US* specialty, specialization, °expertise, °forte, °strength: *She is certainly the leading expert in her field. My field is biochemistry.* —*v.* 5 catch, °stop, °return, °retrieve, °pick up: *Did you see how Border fielded that ball?* 6 °answer, °reply to, °respond to, °handle, °manipulate, °deal with, °react to, °cope with: *The candidate adroitly fielded questions from the press.*

fiend *n.* 1 See devil, above. 2 °addict, °maniac, °fanatic; °fan, aficionado, °enthusiast, °devotee, °hound, °follower, *Colloq* buff, nut, *Slang* °freak: *He's a Welsh rarebit fiend.*

fiendish *adj.* °cruel, °savage, °inhuman, °monstrous, °ghoulish, °malignant, malevolent, malicious, °wicked, °evil, °bad, black-hearted, °satanic, °devilish, Mephistophelian, demonic, demoniac(al), °diabolic(al), cacodemonic, hellish, °infernal: *He sniggered with fiendish glee as he tightened the thumbscrew.*

fierce *adj.* 1 °ferocious, °savage, °wild, °truculent, brutish, feral, bestial, tigerish, °brutal, °cruel, °fell, °murderous, bloodthirsty, °sanguinary, °homicidal, barbaric, barbarous, °inhuman, °dangerous: *The fierce beasts will tear you limb from limb.* 2 intractable, °angry, °furious, °hostile, °aggressive, vehement, frenzied, °stormy, °violent, turbulent, °wild, °tempestuous, °tumultuous, raging, °merciless, uncontrollable: *The old curmudgeon is in a fierce mood again today. A fierce storm raged for three days.* 3 °severe, °awful, °dreadful, °intense, °keen, dire, °bitter, °biting, racking: *Wear warm clothes to protect you from the fierce cold.*

fiercely *adv.* °very, °extremely, °exceedingly, vehemently, intensely, impetuously, violently, furiously, ferociously, viciously, savagely: *She refuses to deal with anyone who is so fiercely competitive.*

fiery *adj.* 1 °burning, °flaming, blazing, °hot, red-hot, white-hot, overheated; afire, on °fire, in flames, °ablaze: *Fiery lava burst from the volcano.* 2 °glowing, red, °incandescent, °brilliant, °luminous, °glaring, gleaming, °radiant; aglow, afire: *We watched the fiery sunset fade into azure hues.* 3 °ardent, °eager, °spirited, °passionate, °excited, °excitable, peppery, irascible, °touchy, °irritable, edgy, °hotheaded, °fierce: *I had best not be late as my boss has a fiery temper.*

fight *v.* 1 contend (with), °battle, °conflict (with), °encounter, °war (against), °engage, °clash, °feud (with), °combat, bear *or* take up arms (against), °brawl, °struggle *or* °strive (with *or* against), cross swords (with), °close (with), °come to *or* °exchange blows (with), go to *or* °wage °war (with *or* against), joust (with), °grapple (with *or* against), °wrestle (with), °skirmish (with), tussle *or* scuffle (with *or* against); °box, °spar; *Old-fashioned* °broil: *He offered to fight anyone in the place. Why are the boys always fighting?* 2 °dispute, °question, confront, °contest, °oppose, °contradict, °defy, confute, °protest, °resist, °rail *or* °struggle against, °withstand, refute, oppugn, make *or* take a °stand against, contravene, confound: *He has sworn to fight prejudice wherever he finds it.* 3 °rise up, make *or* take a °stand, °struggle, take up arms: *It is better to fight for the good than to rail at the ill.*

4 °argue, °dispute, °bicker, °quarrel, wrangle, squabble, spat, °tiff, °fall out (over), have words, °disagree, °row, altercate, °debate: *I hear the neighbours fight every night.* **5 fight off**: °repel, °repulse: *Prepare to fight off anyone trying to come over the side!* **6 fight shy of**: °avoid, keep *or* remain °aloof from *or* of, keep away from: *She usually fights shy of going to cocktail parties.*
—*n.* **7** °battle, °conflict, °bout, duel, (single) °combat, monomachy, one-on-one, °action, warfare, °clash, hostilities, °war, °match, °struggle, °engagement, °meeting, °encounter, °contest, fighting, °brawl, Donnybrook, affray, °fray, °fracas, °disturbance, °riot, °row, mêlée *or* melee, tussle, scuffle, °scrimmage, °skirmish, °brush, *Colloq* free-for-all, set-to, °scrap, *Brit* scrum, bovver, *Slang US* rumble, *Old-fashioned* °broil: *Three policeman were injured in the hour-long fight.* **8** altercation, °argument, °quarrel, °feud, °dispute, °run-in, °disagreement, °dissension, dissidence, dissent, °difference (of opinion), squabble, bickering, spat, °misunderstanding, °row, °discord, *Colloq* ruckus: *Such fights between husband and wife happen all the time.* **9** pugnacity, mettle, militancy, belligerence, truculence, °spirit, °pluck, zeal, °enthusiasm, °zest: *She had enough fight left in her to go on to win.*

figure *n.* **1** °physique, °build, °shape, °form, configuration, conformation, °body, °outline, °silhouette; °cut, °cast; *Slang* bod, chassis: *It's exercise that gives Kathy such a fine figure.* **2** °appearance, °image, °likeness, °representation, °semblance: *The vision came to him in the figure of a dragon.* **3** °person, °individual, °human (being): *A burly figure loomed up out of the fog.* **4** °statue, effigy, °sculpture, bust, °mould, °cast, °image, °representation, °idol, icon: *Hundreds of figures are carved into the stone of the temple façade.* **5** °picture, °illustration, diagram, °drawing, sketch, °plate: *See Figure 12 for a graph showing the rate of inflation for the past decade.* **6** °personality, °celebrity, °somebody, °leader, °personage, °worthy, °notable, °individual, °presence, °force, °character: *Chaplin looms large as a figure in the history of comedy.* **7** °number, numeral, °cipher, digit; °character, °symbol, °device, °sign; °design, °pattern, °motif, °emblem: *His salary is in six figures.*
—*v.* **8** Often, **figure up**: °calculate, °compute, °reckon, °work out; °count, °enumerate, numerate, °total, °tot up, °tally, °sum: *Please figure up how much I owe you.* **9** °picture, °imagine, °think, °take, °reckon, °consider, °calculate, °judge, °believe, °assume, °presume, °suppose; °accept, °acknowledge, °concede: *I never figured her to be the guilty one.* **10** °act, °participate, take *or* play a °part *or* °role, °appear, °feature, have a °place; be included *or* mentioned, be featured *or* °conspicuous: *He does not figure in my plans.* **11 figure on** *or* **upon**: **a** °rely *or* °depend on *or* upon, °count on *or* upon, °trust in, put °faith in: *You mustn't figure on his help.* **b** °plan on *or* upon, take into °consideration *or* °account, °consider, make °allowance for: *They were figuring on consumer demand for a better mousetrap.* **12 figure out**: **a** °calculate, °reckon, °compute, °work out: *I haven't yet figured out last year's profits and losses.* **b** °decipher, °translate, °understand, °interpret, °solve, °grasp, °get, °fathom, °see, °perceive, *Colloq* °dig, make head(s) or tail(s) of, °get through one's head,

°get the hang *or* °drift of, catch on (to), get a fix on, *Brit* °twig, suss out: *Can you figure out what this article is trying to say?*

figurehead *n.* °puppet, °dummy, marionette, °mouthpiece, *Brit* man of straw, *US and Canadian* straw man, *Colloq* °front man, *Chiefly US* °front: *The king is a mere figurehead with no power at all.*

file *n.* **1** °document, documentation, dossier, °case, °data, folder, portfolio, °information: *Interpol has files on Cowdery's activities going back ten years.* **2** °line, °queue, column, °row, °rank: *The file of armoured vehicles stretched for miles.*
—*v.* **3** classify, °organize, systematize, °categorize, alphabetize, chronologize, °order, °arrange, pigeon-hole, interfile, °put *or* °place in °order, °register, °record, °enter: *Must all this correspondence be filed today?* **4** °submit, °send in, °complete, °fill in *or US and Canadian also* °fill out, °enter: *I have already filed my application for a transfer.* **5** °walk, °march, troop, °parade: *Please file into the classroom and take your seats.*

fill *v.* **1** °crowd, °stuff, °cram, °jam, °load, °burden, °pack, °squeeze: *A huge number of people filled the stadium.* **2** °top (off), °top up, fill up, make °full; °inflate, °swell, °stretch, °blow up, distend, °expand: *Pour in just enough to fill the bottle. See if you can fill the balloon. Wind filled the sails.* **3** Sometimes, **fill up**: °supply, °provide, °furnish: *Irena has filled her house with paintings.* **4** °meet, °satisfy, °fulfil, °answer: *Will a dozen fill your needs for a while?* **5** °satisfy, °satiate, bloat, sate, °gorge, °stuff; °stock: *The guests filled themselves with choice foods at the reception.* **6** °abound in, overflow, be °abundant *or* °plentiful in: *Trout filled the lake.* **7** °close, °stop (up), °block, °stuff, °plug, caulk, °seal: *The dentist had to fill two cavities.* **8** °occupy, take over, °discharge, °carry out, do, °execute: *Can you fill her job while she's away?* **9 fill in** *or US and Canadian also* **out**: **a** °make out, °complete, °answer: *Please fill in this application.* **b** take the °place, °stand in, °substitute: *Could you fill in during my secretary's absence?* **c** °inform, °tell, °advise, °let in on, °notify, bring up to °date, °share, °let in on: *Don will fill you in on the details later.* **10 fill out**: **a** °swell, °expand, °grow, distend, °stretch; fatten, °increase: *The sails filled out in the freshening breeze.* **b** *US* fill in. See 9a.
—*n.* **11 one's fill**: °plenty, °enough; °surfeit, sufficiency: *We ate our fill and left.*

filling *n.* filler, stuffing, padding, wadding; °contents, components, *Colloq* innards: *What kind of filling do you like in a pie?*

film *n.* **1** coating, °skin, °coat, membrane, °peel, integument, layer, overlay, covering, °cover, °sheet, dusting, °veil, *Technical* pellicle: *There is a film of grease over everything.* **2** motion °picture, °movie, °picture; videotape; *Colloq* flick, pic; video: *Why do they show the same films every Christmas?* **3** °veil, °screen, murkiness, °blur, smokescreen, haze, °mist, haziness, mistiness, cloud, °vapour, °fog, steam: *I could barely make out the road through the film on the windscreen.*
—*v.* **4** film over, °coat, °cover, °dim, °obscure, °fade (away), °veil, °screen, °blur, blear, °mist, cloud, °glaze: *The pond filmed over with bacteria. Her eyes filmed with tears.* **5** °photograph, °shoot, °take, (video)tape: *If the director insists, then the scene must be filmed again.*

filmy adj. **1** gauzy, gossamer(-like), °sheer, °delicate, diaphanous, °transparent, translucent, °flimsy, °light, cobwebby, °insubstantial, °see-through, peekaboo: *Phoebe looked very seductive in her filmy negligee.* **2** °murky, blurry, cloudy, °hazy, °misty, bleary, blurred, °dim, clouded, beclouded, milky, °pearly, °opalescent: *We inched down the cliff in the filmy light of the moon.*

filter n. **1** sieve, colander, °riddle, °screen, strainer, gauze, °cloth, cheesecloth, membrane: *To allow the liquid to pass through, a clean filter must be used.*
—v. **2** Sometimes, **filter out**: °strain, °screen, °sift, winnow, °refine, °purify, °clean; °separate, weed out, °exclude, °eliminate: *Some people filter tap water to improve its taste. This company would be improved if we could filter out the undesirable elements.* **3** leach, °percolate, °drip, seep, dribble, °trickle, °drain, °run or °pass through, °ooze: *The rainwater is filtered through fine sand to purify it.*

filth n. **1** sewage or sewerage, °dirt, slime, °muck, °sludge, sullage, effluent, °pollution, °trash, °rubbish, °garbage, °refuse, ordure, (night-)°soil, excrement, faeces, excreta, manure, droppings, guano, °dung, °foul °matter, filthiness, offal, leavings, carrion, °decay, putrescence, putrefaction, *Slang* crud, *Brit* gunge, *US* grunge, *Taboo slang* shit: *Cleaning the filth from the Augean stables was the fifth labour of Hercules.* **2** corruption, vileness, baseness, foulness, rottenness, debasement, defilement, °taint, °pollution, adulteration, °perversion, °degradation; sullying, besmirchment: *Sodom and Gomorrah were destroyed along with their filth.* **3** indecency, obscenity, smut, °pornography, corruption, nastiness, °vulgarity, grossness: *The censors forbade the showing of films with any hint of filth.*

filthy adj. **1** defiled, polluted, tainted, °foul, °nasty, °dirty, unclean, °vile, °putrid, °rotten, fetid or foetid, maggoty, fly-blown, purulent, feculent, faecal, scummy, °slimy, mucky, *Slang* cruddy, *Brit* gungy, *US* grungy: *That city's public lavatories are the filthiest I have ever seen.* **2** °dirty, °unwashed, begrimed, squalid, °sordid, °shabby, soiled, °low, stained, grimy, °bedraggled, °unkempt, slovenly, °sloppy, °mean, °scurvy, °disgusting, °miserable, °wretched, *Slang Brit* gungy, *US* grungy: *The filthy beggar turned out to be Holmes in disguise.* **3** °immoral, °taboo or tabu, °indecent, °impure, °obscene, smutty, °pornographic, X-rated, depraved, °corrupt, °dirty, °lewd, °lascivious, licentious, °gross, °offensive, °coarse, °bawdy, ribald, °blue, °suggestive, foul-mouthed, dirty-minded, filthy-minded: *Customs officers confiscated thousands of filthy books, magazines, films, and videos.*

final adj. **1** ending, concluding, terminating, finishing, closing, °last, °terminal, °ultimate, °end: *The final sentence needs rewriting.*
2 conclusive, decisive, unalterable, °irreversible, °irrevocable, °incontrovertible, irrefutable, °indisputable, unchangeable, immutable, °definitive; settled, °fixed, °absolute, °certain, °sure: *Those are my final words on the subject. We made a final series of measurements.*

finality n. conclusiveness, decisiveness, unalterability, irreversibility, irrevocableness, incontrovertibility, irrefutability, indisputability, unchangeability, immutability, definitiveness, °certainty, certitude, sureness, fixedness: *There is an air of finality in the way she gives orders.*

finalize v. conclude, °settle, °complete, °decide, *Colloq* °wrap up, °clinch, °sew up: *We finalized the agreement yesterday by signing the contract.*

finally adv. **1** at (long) °last, lastly, °eventually, in the °end, °ultimately, at °length, when all is said and done, in the long °run, at the °end of the day, at the °last °moment: *We finally arrived in port.* **2** conclusively, °once and for all, decisively, irrevocably, in °fine, °completely, inexorably, °absolutely, definitively, °definitely, for °good, °for °ever, for all °time: *I didn't want to commit myself finally till I'd seen the plans.*

finance n. **1** °resource(s), banking, accounting, economics, °money (°management), °business, °commerce, (°financial) affairs, investment: *Bendick is the officer in charge of finance for the company.* **2 finances**: °capital, °money, °cash, °funds, °resources, °assets, holdings, °wealth, wherewithal: *Have you the finances needed to buy the house?*
—v. **3** °fund, subvene, °invest in, °back, capitalize, °underwrite, °subsidize, °pay for, *Colloq US* bankroll: *The new enterprise is being financed entirely by small investors.*

financial adj. °monetary, pecuniary, °fiscal, °economic: *We must get the financial affairs of the country in order.*

financier n. capitalist, banker, plutocrat, investor, °backer, *US* money-man, *Colloq* angel: *The financiers suggest switching investment from shares to bonds.*

find v. **1** °discover, °come across, °happen or °come on or upon, °hit upon or on, °chance or °stumble on or upon; °encounter, °bump into: *We've found a tiny bistro on the Left Bank where we like to go.* **2** Often, **find out**: uncover, °discover, °unearth, °lay one's hand(s) on, °turn up, °come up with, °reveal, bring to °light, °light upon or on, °catch °sight of, °see, espy, descry, °detect, °learn, °spot, °locate, °track down; °identify, °become °aware of, °determine, ascertain, put one's °finger on, °point to, *Colloq* °tumble to, *Brit* °twig; *Slang* °finger, rumble, *Brit* suss out: *The police are trying to find the murderer. Can you find who did it?* **3** °discover, °perceive, °see, °understand, °notice, °mark, °remark, °note, °distinguish, discern: *I find nothing odd about her attire.* **4** °consider, °think, °regard, °view, °feel or °discover to be: *I have always found Lady Sharpless exceedingly dull. He finds it impossible to refuse her demands.* **5** °get, °obtain, °procure, °secure, °acquire, °win, °gain; °experience: *We despair of finding customers for our services in these hard times. He found relief only in painkillers.* **6** °recover, °locate, °get back; repossess, °recoup: *I hope you find the earring you lost.* **7** °summon (up), °call up, °command, °gather (up), °muster (up), °rouse, arouse, awaken: *I tried to find the courage to ask her to marry me.* **8** °set aside, °allot, °assign, °manage, °get: *Have you found the time to read Connie's new book?* **9** °judge, °decide or °determine to be, °pronounce, °declare: *A jury found her guilty. The judge found in favour of the plaintiff.*
—n. **10** °discovery, °catch, °bargain, °deal; °boon, °windfall: *The gold doubloon was the find of a lifetime.*

finding n. **1** °discovery, °find: *The findings from Pompeii are in the Museum of Portici.* **2** °judgement, °decree, verdict,

°decision, °determination, °pronouncement, °declaration, conclusion: *The findings of the Law Lords are final.*

fine¹ *adj.* **1** °superior, °excellent, °superb, °magnificent, °supreme, °marvellous, °exceptional, °splendid, °exquisite, °elegant, first-class, °first-rate, °prime, °choice, °select, top-grade, high-grade, top-drawer, °quality, °admirable, °good, °satisfactory, *Colloq* out of this °world, °great, °OK or okay, peachy, °keen, *Brit* tickety-boo, *US* °neat, *Australian* bonzer, *Slang* °swell, °cool, *Brit old-fashioned* °ripping, *Dialectal* °champion: *He is a connoisseur of fine paintings. She turned in a fine performance.* **2** °sunny, °fair, °bright, °clear, cloudless, balmy, °pleasant, °dry, °nice: *It was a fine day for a picnic.* **3** enjoyable, °satisfying, °entertaining, amusing, °good, °interesting, °pleasant, °nice: *Thank you for inviting us to such a fine party.* **4** °accomplished, °skilful, con-summate, °outstanding, masterly, °brilliant, °virtuoso: *Ann-Sofie is a fine pianist.* **5** °delicate, °subtle, °exquisite, well-made, °dainty, °elegant; °superior, °excellent, °outstanding: *What a fine example of miniature-painting!* **6** °delicate, °dainty, °thin, gossamer, dia-phanous, gauzy, °sheer, °slender, °frail, °flimsy, filamentous, threadlike: *The sword hung over Dam-ocles' head by a fine thread.* **7** powdered, powdery, pulverized, comminuted, crushed, fine-grained: *As soon as they touched the papyrus, it disintegrated into a fine powder.* **8** °sharp, °keen, keen-edged, razor-sharp, °pointed, °acute: *The points of the sea urchin's spines are so fine you don't feel them enter.* **9** °subtle, °delicate, °refined, °acute, °keen, °discriminating, °critical, °precise, °nice, °hair-splitting: *There is sometimes a fine distinction between pleasure and pain.* **10** good-looking, °handsome, °attractive, °striking, °beautiful, pretty, °lovely, °seemly, °fair, °comely, *Colloq US* °cute, *Scots* °bonny: *Jeanette married a fine young man.* **11** °meritorious, °worthy, commendable, °admirable, °excellent, °superb, °splendid, °good, *Colloq* °great: *She has displayed fine courage in the face of terrible family problems.* **12** °healthy, °well, healthful, °robust, all °right, *Colloq* °OK or okay: *I told the doctor that I was feeling fine.* **13** °close: *Arriving at the airport with only minutes to spare is cutting it pretty fine.*

fine² *n.* **1** °penalty, °charge, °fee, mulct, °forfeit, amercement; forfeiture: *He was unable to pay the parking fine.*
—*v.* **2** °penalize, °charge, mulct, amerce: *She was fined for parking at a bus stop.*

finery *n.* °decoration(s), °ornaments, °trappings, trinkets, frippery, °showy °dress, *Colloq* °best bib and tucker, Sunday °best, Sunday °clothes, °gear, glad rags: *They were all dressed in their finery at the reception.*

finesse *n.* **1** artfulness, °subtlety, cunning, craft-iness, cleverness, °strategy, shrewdness, °skill, °style, °dash, élan, °panache, °knack, skil-fulness, °talent, adroitness, expertness, °expertise, adeptness, °proficiency, °ability, °facility: *I admire the finesse with which she persuaded him to give the painting to the museum.* **2** °trick, °artifice, °stratagem, °wile, °ruse, °scheme, °machination, °intrigue, °device, °expedient, °manoeuvre, °deception, °deceit: *He used every finesse in the book to get her to work for him.* **3** °tact, °diplomacy, °discretion,

°grace, °taste, °delicacy, °polish, °refinement, °elegance: *With infinite finesse, Lord Lacey suggested that the duchess might like to stay the night.*
—*v.* **4** °manoeuvre, °manipulate, °bluff, °trick, delude, °deceive, °fool, °outwit, °hoodwink, *Colloq* finagle, *Slang* con: *She was finessed into making him heir to her fortune.*

finger *n.* **1** digit: *How many fingers am I holding up?* **2 have a finger in**: be or become or get °involved in, °figure in, have a hand in, °influence, °interfere in, °tamper or °meddle or °tinker or °monkey with: *I knew that Lightfoot must have had a finger in the deal.* **3 keep one's fingers crossed**: °hope or °pray for the best, touch or esp. *US* knock wood: *I'm sure you'll win, but I'll keep my fingers crossed just the same.* **4 lay** or **put a finger on**: (so much as) °touch, °strike, °hit, °punch: *If you lay a finger on her, you'll have to answer to me!* **5 lay** or **put one's finger on**: **a** °recall, °remember, °recollect, bring or call to °mind, °think of, °pin down: *I can't quite put my finger on the date when we met.* **b** °locate, °find, °discover, °unearth, °lay or °put one's hands on, °track down, °get °hold of, °come by, °acquire; °buy, °purchase: *I was finally able to put my finger on the book you asked for.* **c** °indicate, °identify, °point to, °pin down, *Colloq* °zero (in) on: *Frank put his finger on the problem at once.*
6 (not) lift or **raise (even) a (little) finger**: make an °attempt or °effort, °offer, make a °move, °contribute, do one's °part, do anything or something: *She didn't so much as lift a finger when I needed her.* **7 pull** or **get one's finger out**: °get on with it, stop delaying or procras-tinating, *Colloq* °get cracking: *He should have finished by now, and I wish he'd pull his finger out.* **8 put the finger on**: °accuse, °inform on or against, °tell or °tattle on, °betray, bear °witness, *Slang* snitch or squeal on, peach on: *After Louise put the finger on the kingpin, the cops arrested him.* **9 slip through one's fingers**: °elude, °escape, °get away, vanish, °disappear: *Despite the cordon round the house, the fugitive slipped through our fingers.* **10 twist** or **wrap around one's little finger**: °control, °dominate, °lord it over, have under °control, °manipulate, °manoeuvre, °wield °power or °authority over, have under one's °thumb, have the upper hand over, be °master of, °influence, make sub-servient: *She has her father twisted around her little finger, and can do no wrong in his eyes.*
—*v.* **11** °touch, °handle, °feel; °toy or °play or °fiddle with: *He was quite nervous and kept fingering his tie.* **12** °identify, °point out, °put the finger on: *It was too late, the mob had already fingered Slats for assassination.*

finicky *adj.* **1** finical, °fussy, °fastidious, °critical, °difficult, °meticulous, °hard to °please, (over-)°delicate, (over-)°dainty, (over-)°particular, over-nice, over-precise, niminy-piminy, punc-tilious, (over-)°scrupulous, *Colloq* pernickety or *US* persnickety, °choosy, nit-picking, picky: *No one can work for him—he's too finicky.* **2** °fussy, °elaborate, °detailed, °fine, °delicate: *Notice the tiny, finicky engraving on this watch-case.*

finish *v.* **1** °stop, conclude, °end, °cease: *When you have finished eating, please clear the table.* **2** °complete, °accomplish, °perfect, °achieve, °carry out, °fulfil, consummate, °clinch, write 'finis' to, *Colloq* °wrap up: *We finished the work on time.* **3** Sometimes, **finish**

off: °dispose of, °dispatch *or* despatch, °exhaust, °consume, °eat *or* °drink (up), °use (up), °devour, °drain, *Colloq* °polish off: *We finished the last of the beer last night.* **4** Sometimes, **finish off**: °kill, °exterminate, annihilate, °destroy, get °rid of, °dispose of, °dispatch *or* despatch, put an °end to, administer *or* deliver *or* give the *coup de grâce*, bring down, °overcome, °beat, °defeat, °conquer, °best, worst, *Colloq* °polish off, °terminate, *Slang* °bump off, °rub out, *US* °waste, ice: *The cavalry finished off the last of the enemy. The contender was finished in the third round.* **5** Sometimes, **finish up**: conclude, °close, °terminate, °wind up, °end, culminate: *He goes straight home when he finishes work. When will you finish?* **6** Sometimes, **finish up**: °end up, °settle: *Where did you finish up after the party?* **7** Sometimes, **finish off**: °perfect, put the °final touches on, °polish, put a finish on: *He finishes fine furniture for a living.* **8 finish with**: °release, °let °go, have *or* be done with, °let °loose, set °free: *I'll finish with you later, young man!*

—*n.* **9** conclusion, °termination, °end, °close, closing, °completion, culmination, ending, finale, *Colloq* winding up, *US* wind-up: *Tomorrow is the finish of the hunting season.* **10** °death, °killing, annihilation, extermination, °downfall, °destruction, °defeat: *A major catastrophe spelt the finish of the dinosaurs.* **11** °polish, °surface, °texture: *Just feel the finish on this gunstock!*

finite *adj.* °limited, bounded, °bound, restricted, delimited, numerable, countable: *It has been shown that there are a finite number of grains of sand in the universe.*

fire *n.* **1** °flame(s), °blaze; conflagration, °holocaust, inferno: *We gathered round the roaring fire.* **2** °feeling, °passion, °ardour, ardency, °fervour, fervency, °intensity, °vigour, °spirit, °energy, vim, vivacity, °sparkle, °animation, liveliness, °verve, °pep, élan, éclat, °dash, °vitality, °eagerness, °enthusiasm, fever, feverishness: *I have never seen the role of Carmen performed with such fire.* **3** firing, fusillade, °volley, barrage, bombardment, salvo, cannonade, shelling, broadside, °flak: *The fire from the guns shook the house.* **4 hang fire**: °delay, be delayed, be in °abeyance, be suspended, be shelved, be °put off, be postponed, be up in the °air, *Colloq* be put on °hold, be (put) on the back burner: *The decision is hanging fire till tomorrow.* **5 on fire**: afire, °burning, blazing, alight, aflame, °flaming; °ardent, °passionate, °fervent, fervid, hot-blooded, °intense, aroused, stirred, stimulated, °enthusiastic, fired up, °eager, inspired, °excited: *The building is on fire: you must leave at once. My very soul is on fire when I think of you.* **6 play with fire**: undertake a °risk *or* °hazard *or* °peril, run a °risk, °risk (something *or* everything), imperil *or* °endanger (something), tempt °fate, live °dangerously: *He warned people not to play with fire by stirring up racial hatred.* **7 set fire to**: See **8**, below.

—*v.* **8** a set fire to, set afire, set on fire, ignite, set alight, kindle, spark (off), put to the torch, °burn, *Slang US* torch: *Arsonists fired our headquarters last night.* **b** Sometimes, **fire up**: °inflame, impassion, °incite, °excite, °provoke, °foment, °whip up, arouse, °rouse, °work up, enkindle, °light a fire under, °stimulate, inspirit, °motivate, °move, °stir, °animate, °inspire, °awaken, °energize, °vitalize, vivify: *She fired*

the crowd's emotions with her impassioned speech. **9** °discharge, °shoot, °let °go (with), °launch, °propel, °throw, catapult, °hurl: *He fired the missile towards the enemy.* **10** detonate, °set off, ignite, °set fire to, °light, °let off: *It is against the law to fire any explosives in this area.* **11** °discharge, °dismiss, oust, °let °go, cashier, give (someone) °notice, *Brit* make *or* declare °redundant, *Colloq Brit* ask for *or* get (someone's) cards, *US* give (someone) a pink slip; *Slang* bounce, give (someone) the bounce, axe, give (someone) the axe, show (someone) the door, can, give (someone) the (old) heave-ho, °give (someone) his *or* her (*Brit*) marching orders *or* (*US*) walking papers, *Brit* °sack, give (someone) the °sack, °boot (someone) out, give (someone) the boot: *They fired me last month and I can't find work.*

firm *adj.* **1** °compact, °solid, °dense, compressed, condensed, concentrated, °rigid, °stiff, °hard, unyielding, °inflexible, inelastic: *I prefer a firm mattress.* **2** °stable, °fixed, °fast, °secure, °steady, °solid, stationary, anchored, moored, unmovable, °immovable: *This pole is firmer than that one.* **3** °steady, °strong, °sturdy, °tight, unwavering, unshakable *or* unshakeable, unswerving: *What we need is a firm hand at the controls.* **4** °resolute, °determined, dogged, °definite, resolved, °positive, decisive, °decided, °set on *or* upon, °steadfast, °constant, unflinching, °staunch, unshaken, unshakeable *or* unshakable, °immovable, °inflexible, °rigid, unwavering, undeviating, unchanging, unchangeable, °obstinate, obdurate, °stubborn, °strict, unyielding, unbending, unalterable: *Father was firm about my not staying out past midnight.*

—*v.* **5** Often, **firm up**: consolidate, °establish, °settle (down), solidify, °resolve, °determine, °set up: *We firmed up the terms of the contract. Sugar prices firmed today.*

—*n.* **6** °company, °organization, corporation, °limited °company, °public °limited °company, plc, partnership, proprietorship, °business, °enterprise, °concern, °house, conglomerate, multinational (°company), cartel, *Colloq* °outfit; *US jargon* CIA, Central Intelligence Agency: *He works for a firm in the City.*

firmament *n.* °heaven, the °heavens, °sky, the °skies, vault (of °heaven), *Literary* welkin, empyrean: *Sirius is one of the brightest stars in the firmament.*

firmly *adv.* **1** solidly, strongly, securely, °tightly, rigidly, °fast, immovably: *The column is set firmly into the concrete.* **2** resolutely, steadfastly, determinedly, staunchly, unwaveringly, decisively, unhesitatingly, constantly: *Jacquelyn firmly supports John in anything he says.*

first *adj.* **1** °foremost, °leading, °chief, °head, °premier, °prime, °primary, °principal, °pre-eminent: *The Kennedys were regarded as among 'the first people of Boston'. I heard that your son is now first violinist in the Philharmonic.* **2** earliest, °original, °senior, oldest, °initial, °beginning, °maiden, °opening: *The first clock in England was made about 1288. The first assault resulted in great loss of life.* **3** °fundamental, °elementary, °basic, °primary, °cardinal, °key, °essential: *It is necessary to return to first principles.*

—*adv.* **4** °before, in °front, earliest, beforehand, °ahead, sooner, °foremost: *Bannister came in*

first. **5** in the first °place, firstly, before all *or* anything else, initially, at the °outset *or* °beginning, to °begin *or* °start with, from the °start, *Colloq* first off: *First, I want to thank you all for coming to my party.*
—*n.* **6** °beginning, °start, inception, commencement, °outset, *Colloq* word go: *I knew you'd win from the first.* **7** first °place, blue ribbon, gold (medal), °triumph, °victory; °win: *Britain achieved three firsts in yesterday's athletics meeting.* **8 at first**: initially, in the °beginning, at the °start *or* °outset, *Colloq* from the word go: *I didn't believe him at first.*

first-rate *adj.* first-class, high-grade, °prime, °excellent, °superior, °superb, °great, °remarkable, °admirable, °fine, °exceptional, °outstanding, °extraordinary, °unparalleled, °matchless, unsurpassed, *Colloq* A-1 *or* A-one, top-notch, tiptop, °crack, °top, ace, *Brit* whiz-bang *or* whizz-bang, wizard: *Sarah is a first-rate pianist.*

fiscal *adj.* °financial, °economic, budgetary, pecuniary, °monetary: *It is against our fiscal policy to deal in off-shore securities.*

fishy *adj.* **1** piscine, fishlike, piscatory, piscatorial: *On the fishmonger's slab lay an array of fishy offerings, only a few of which I could recognize.* **2** dubious, °doubtful, °questionable, °unlikely, °far-fetched, °suspicious, not kosher, °peculiar, °odd, °queer, °strange, °suspect, °improbable, °implausible, *Colloq* °shady, °funny: *There is something fishy about this deal.*

fit[1] *adj.* **1** °fitting, °appropriate, °fitted, °suitable, suited, adapted, apt, °meet, apropos, °applicable; °befitting, °becoming, °convenient, °proper, °right, °correct: *Those books are not fit for children. It's not a fit night out for man or beast.* **2** °prepared, °ready, °able, °capable, °qualified, °worthy, °right, °adequate: *The question is, is such a man fit to lead men into battle?* **3** °healthy, °well, °hale, °hearty, °stalwart, °vigorous, °strong, °sturdy, °robust, strapping, able-bodied, in °good °shape *or* °trim *or* °condition, in °fine fettle: *Is she fit enough to run in the marathon?* **4** °ready, °angry, troubled, °upset, °inclined, °disposed, °ready *or* °likely *or* about to, °exhausted °enough: *I worked till I was fit to drop. Mr Barrett was coughing fit to burst.*
—*v.* **5** befit, °suit, °become, be suited to, be °suitable *or* °appropriate for, °answer, °satisfy: *This computer program does not fit my needs.* **6** °join, °conform, °go (together), °match, °correspond, dovetail, °tally: *I cannot make the parts fit.* **7** °adjust, °modify, °change, °adapt, °alter, °accommodate, °shape, °fashion: *You will just have to fit your schedule to conform to ours.* **8** °equip, °supply, °furnish, °provide, °outfit, fit out *or* up, °install *or* instal, °rig out, °gear up: *I am having my boat fitted with radar.*

fit[2] *n.* **1** °attack, °seizure, convulsion, °spasm, °spell, °paroxysm, °bout, °throe: *She has periodic fits of severe depression.* **2** °outburst, outbreak, °paroxysm, °spell, °period: *Occasionally, Gurning would go into a fit of hysterical laughter.* **3** °tantrum, °eruption, °explosion: *She throws a fit if I so much as mention Maria's name.* **4 by fits and starts**: sporadically, °occasionally, fitfully, spasmodically, intermittently, erratically, haphazardly, °now and then, irregularly, unsystematically; unreliably: *The fridge works only by fits and starts.*

fitful *adj.* °irregular, °sporadic, °intermittent, °occasional, °periodic, °erratic, °spasmodic, °haphazard, unsystematic, °changeable, °unstable, °capricious, varying, fluctuating, °variable, uneven: *The dying torch emitted a fitful light. No true patriot pays merely fitful allegiance to his country.*

fitness *n.* **1** aptness, appropriateness, suitability, suitableness, competence, pertinence, seemliness; eligibility, adequacy, °qualification(s): *There is some doubt about Henryson's fitness as a leader.* **2** °health, healthiness, (°good) (°physical) °condition, °vigour, well-being, (°good) °shape, (°fine) fettle, °tone, wholesomeness, salubriousness *or* salubrity: *Tony is a fanatic about physical fitness and exercises daily.*

fitted *adj.* custom-made, °tailor-made; tailored, bespoke: *The house boasts a fully fitted kitchen.*

fitting *adj.* **1** °fit, °befitting, °suitable, °appropriate, °meet, °becoming, °proper, *comme il faut,* °seemly, apt, apropos, apposite, germane, °relevant: *Is it fitting to send flowers? It was a fitting end to the story.*
—*n.* **2 fittings**: fitments, °attachments, °accessories, °elements, °pieces, °parts, °units, °fixtures; appointments, °extras, installations, furnishings, °trappings, °furniture, °equipment, accoutrements *or US also* accouterments, °paraphernalia, trimmings: *Gold-plated bathroom fittings are available at extra cost.*

fix *v.* **1** affix, °pin, °fasten, make °fast, °attach, °secure, °stick, °connect, °link, °tie, °couple, °clasp, °clamp, rivet, °cement, °weld, °fuse: *Fix this sign to the door.* **2** °establish, °set, °settle, °agree to, °determine, °organize, stabilize, °firm up, °solidify, °decide, conclude, °arrive at, °define, °specify, °resolve, °arrange, °install *or* instal, °institute: *The new limits must be fixed by tomorrow.* **3** °repair, °mend, fix up, °remedy, °rectify, °correct, emend, °adjust, °patch (up), °regulate, °put *or* °set to rights, °doctor, °straighten out: *My watch is at the jeweller's being fixed.* **4** °hold, °fasten, °focus, °direct, °level, rivet, °concentrate, °freeze; °fixate: *He fixed his attention on the ice-cream.* **5** °hold, rivet, spellbind, mesmerize, °hypnotize, °fascinate, °freeze, immobilize: *She fixed him with a baleful stare.* **6** °concentrate, °focus: *Fix your thoughts on how we're going to get out of here.* **7** °harden, congeal, °thicken, °set, consolidate, °solidify, rigidify, become °rigid, °stiffen, °freeze: *Mould the clay before it becomes fixed.* **8** °establish, °set, °settle, °organize, °install *or* instal, °situate, °locate, °position, °place: *Her family is comfortably fixed.* **9** °impose, °assign, allocate, °attribute, ascribe, °specify, °pin, °attach, °fasten, °establish: *They tried to fix the responsibility for the accident.* **10** °settle, °set, stabilize, °freeze, °solidify: *The introduction and spread of printing fixed many spellings.* **11** °bribe, suborn, °buy (off), °corrupt, °influence, °manipulate, *Colloq* grease (someone's) palm: *He attempted to fix a judge.* **12** °arrange, prearrange, predetermine, °set up, contrive, *Colloq* °fiddle, °pull strings, °rig: *We knew the winner as they had fixed the race.* **13** desexualize, desex, °alter, °cut; castrate, emasculate, see to, eunuchize, geld, caponize; spay, oophorectomize, ovariectomize: *Animals that have been fixed are usually more tractable.* **14** °retaliate against, °wreak °vengeance on, °hit *or* °strike *or* °get back at,

°get °even with, °even the °score with, make °reprisal against, avenge oneself against, take °revenge or °retribution on or against, °repay, °pay back, Colloq °settle (someone's) hash, cook (someone's) goose, °sort (someone) out: *I'll fix him for tattling to the teacher!* **15 fix on** or **upon**: °decide (on or upon), °set, °agree (on or upon), °choose, °select, °settle (on), °determine, °finalize: *We can't fix on a date till we know David's schedule.* **16 fix up: a** °furnish, °supply, °provide, °accommodate, °set up, *Brit* °lay on: *Her mother fixed her up with a nice young man. Can you fix me up with a room for the night?* **b** (re)decorate, °furnish, °renovate, °restore, furbish, °refurbish; °straighten out or up, °organize, do up, °set up: *I like the way you've fixed up the basement. Please fix up your room before the guests arrive.* **c** °clear up, °resolve, °reconcile, °sort out, °settle: *Have they fixed up their differences yet?* **d** °repair, °patch (up): *Fix up my car so it will run at least till I get home.* —*n.* **17** °dilemma, °predicament, °difficulty, corner, double °bind, catch-22, °quandary, °mess, (°bad) °situation, °strait(s), *Colloq* pickle, °jam, °hole, (°tight or °tough) °spot, °pinch, *US* °bind: *You could help me get out of a terrible fix.* **18** °arrangement, prearrangement, °fiddle; bribery, subornation; *Slang chiefly US and Canadian* °set-up: *The fix is on for her to win at roulette.*

fixation *n.* °mania, °obsession, compulsion, °fixed °idea, *idée fixe*, °fetish, monomania, preoccupation, infatuation, *Colloq* hang-up, °thing, °kick: *He has a health-food fixation.*

fixed *adj.* **1** fastened, °attached, anchored, °set, °secure(d), °firm, °stable, settled, °immovable, immobile, stationary, °rigid, °rooted, °solid; immobilized, stuck: *While this part rolls, the other remains fixed. There was a fixed smile on her face.* **2** established, °secure, unalterable, °steadfast, °set, °firm, unchangeable, unchanging, °persistent, unfluctuating, unflagging, unwavering, °inflexible, undeviating, unflinching, unblinking, °rigid, °rooted, immutable, °definite, °resolute, resolved, °determined, °intent; °obstinate, °stubborn: *I admire Philip's fixed determination to persevere.* **3** settled, resolved, agreed, °regular, °habitual, °decided, arranged, prearranged, °definite, established: *We have a fixed date on which we meet each month.* **4** arranged, prearranged, °set-up, framed; °crooked, °dishonest, °bent, *Colloq* rigged, °put-up: *He lost everything in a fixed poker game.*

fixture *n.* **1** °meet, °meeting, °event, °match, °occasion, °occurrence: *The Davis Cup tennis championship is an annual fixture.* **2** appliance, °accessory, °fitting, °equipment, °apparatus, °device, °instrument, °tool, °gadget, contrivance, appendage, fitment: *The landlord forbids the removal of any fixture.*

fizz *v.* **1** °bubble, effervesce, °sparkle, °froth, °fizzle; °hiss, sputter, sizzle: *The champagne fizzed in my glass.* —*n.* **2** effervescence, °sparkle, carbonation, bubbling, °froth, °fizzle, fizziness: *All the fizz is gone from my drink!* **3** °hiss, hissing, sibilance: *The steam escaped with a loud fizz.* **4** *US* soda, soda °water, °club soda, seltzer, *Dialect* plain; °soft °drink, °tonic: *May I have a little fizz with my scotch?* **5** champagne, *Colloq Brit* champers: *We celebrated with oysters and a bottle of fizz.*

fizzle *v.* **1** °fizz: *This headache powder makes the water fizzle.* **2** Often, **fizzle out**: °die (out or

away), °fizz out, °expire, peter out, come to °nothing or °naught, °fail, °fall through, °miscarry, abort, come to °grief, °misfire, °collapse, °cave in: *Her grandiose plans for staging an extravaganza quickly fizzled out.*

flabby *adj.* **1** °limp, °loose, °lax, flaccid, °slack, floppy, sagging, drooping, baggy, °pendulous, quaggy, °soft: *After forty, he began to get a bit flabby around the middle.* **2** °weak, °spineless, °feeble, °impotent, °ineffective, °ineffectual: *The critics found the characterizations flabby and the plot non-existent.*

flag[1] *n.* **1** °banner, ensign, °standard, °pennant, banneret, pennon, °streamer, bunting, jack, gonfalon, vexillum: *Our flag was raised over the fort.* —*v.* **2** Often **flag down**: °warn, °signal, °hail, °inform, °stop: *A workman flagged us down because the bridge was out.* **3** °mark, °tag, °label, °tab, °identify, *Brit* tick (off), *US and Canadian* °check (off): *Flag the supplies you need that are listed here.*

flag[2] *v.* **1** °droop, °sag, °dangle, °hang down, swag, festoon: *In the doldrums the sails flagged soggily about the masts.* **2** °weaken, languish, falter, °fail, °dwindle, °fade, °deteriorate, °waste away, °degenerate, °die, °decline, °diminish, °decrease, lessen, abate, peter out, °taper off, °let up, °ease (up), °subside, °slump, °fall off, °wane, °ebb, °sink, °lag: *As she approached the finish line she was alarmed to feel her energy flagging.*

flagrant *adj.* °blatant, °brazen, °bold, °barefaced, °audacious, arrant, °glaring, °outrageous, °shocking, °shameless, °scandalous, °atrocious, °infamous, °notorious, °defiant, egregious, °obvious, °conspicuous, °open, °complete, °out-and-out, utter, flagitious, °monstrous, heinous, °cruel, °villainous, treacherous, nefarious, °awful, °gross, °rank, °inconsiderate, °scornful, °contemptuous; reprehensible; °contemptible: *Speeding shows a flagrant disregard for the safety of others.*

flair *n.* **1** °talent, °ability, °aptitude, °feel, °knack, °genius, °skill, °mind, °gift, °faculty, propensity, °bent, proclivity, °facility: *He showed a flair for music at an early age.* **2** °chic, °panache, °dash, élan, éclat, °style, stylishness, °glamour, °verve, °sparkle, °vitality, °elegance, °taste, *Colloq* savvy, pizazz or pizzazz, *Old-fashioned* oomph: *She dresses with great flair.*

flak *n.* flack, °criticism, °disapproval, censure, °abuse, °blame, °aspersion, °complaint(s), disapprobation, condemnation, *Colloq* brickbats: *He took a lot of flak from the press for his comments.*

flake *n.* **1** snowflake; °scale, °chip, °bit, °piece, °scrap, °particle, tuft, °flock, scurf, °fragment, shaving, °sliver; wafer, lamina, *Technical* squama: *A flake of slate caught him in the eye.* —*v.* **2** Often, **flake off**: °scale, °chip, °fragment; *Technical* desquamate, exfoliate: *The paint is flaking off on this side.* **3** **flake out: a** °collapse, °go to °sleep, °fall asleep, °drop off (to °sleep), °pass out, keel over: *After the game, I flaked out on the couch for ten hours.* **b** become flaky, act °crazy: *He flaked out when he heard the new record.*

flamboyant *adj.* **1** °elaborate, ornamented, °ornate, decorated, embellished, baroque, rococo, florid: *We chose a flamboyant wallpaper with purple peacocks.* **2** °extravagant, °ostentatious, °showy, °gaudy, °flashy, °dazzling, °brilliant, °splendid, °dashing, °rakish,

°swashbuckling, °jaunty; high, wide, and °handsome: *With a flamboyant display of swordsmanship, d'Artagnan dispatched his attacker.*

flame *n.* **1** °fire, °blaze; conflagration: *The flame began to lick about my feet.* **2** °passion, °fervour, °ardour, °intensity, °warmth, °fire, zeal, feverishness, °enthusiasm, °eagerness: *The flame of love is still burning.* **3** boyfriend, girlfriend, °lover, heartthrob, °sweetheart, beau: *Linda is an old flame of Trevor's.*
—*v.* **4** °burn, °blaze, °glow, °flare: *Flaming embers from the chimney set fire to the roof. Here and there civil unrest flamed up in the countryside.*

flaming *adj.* °obvious, °conspicuous, °blatant, °flagrant, egregious, °extravagant, *Slang* bloody, bleeding, blasted, damned, blooming: *That flaming idiot was appointed to the Ministry of Defence!*

flammable *adj.* °inflammable, combustible, burnable: *The warning on the tin says the contents are flammable.*

flank *n.* **1** °side, °quarter; loin, haunch: *The enemy was about to attack our flank. The pony drew back with trembling flanks.*
—*v.* **2** °edge, °border, °line: *Armed guards flanked the entrance.* **3** skirt, outmanoeuvre, outflank, °circle, °go (a)round: *They have enough troops to flank our forces to the east.*

flannel *n.* **1** °flattery, humbug, °nonsense, blarney, °rubbish, prevarication, *Colloq* eyewash, hogwash, boloney, °soft soap, weasel words, sweet talk, bull, crap, *Brit* °waffle, cock, *US* bushwa; *Taboo slang* bullshit, horseshit, (load of) shit, *Brit* codswallop, bollocks or ballocks: *Don't believe a thing Fordyce says—it's all flannel.*
—*v.* **2** °flatter, hedge, °mislead, pull the wool over (someone's) eyes, *Colloq* soft-soap, sweet-talk, *Taboo slang* bullshit, horseshit, shit: *They aren't sincere—they're just flannelling you.*

flap *v.* **1** °slap, slat, °beat, flail, °wave, °wag, waggle, °flutter, thresh, thrash, °oscillate, °vibrate: *An ornithopter is an aeroplane that flaps its wings like a bird. The Union Jack was flapping in the breeze.*
—*n.* **2** flapping, °beat, °wave, °wag, waggle, °flutter, oscillation: *With a flap of its wings, the bird flew away.* **3** °fold, °fly, lappet, °lap, °tail, °tab: *Leave a flap of cloth to cover the pocket.* **4** °upset, °agitation, to-do, ado, commotion, °panic, °flurry, °fuss, °distress, *Colloq* °state, tizzy, °sweat, *Brit* kerfuffle: *She's in a flap about what to wear to the dance.* **5** °quarrel, °argument, °dispute: *There was a big flap over which car model to buy.*

flare *v.* **1** Often, **flare up**: °blaze *or* °flame (up), °flash, °erupt, °break out; °dazzle, °flicker, glimmer, °shimmer, °flutter: *The fire flared up briefly when he tossed the paper onto it.* **2** Often, **flare out**: °spread (out *or* outwards), °widen, broaden, °expand, °increase, °enlarge, °bulge, °swell: *The sides of the vase flare out near the top.* **3** Often, **flare up**: °anger, lose one's °temper, °chafe, °seethe, °fume, °rage, throw a °tantrum, become incensed *or* °angry (etc.); °blow up, °burst forth, °erupt, °explode: *Colloq* get one's back up, get one's Irish *or* dander up, see red, °get worked up, °fly off the handle, lose one's °cool, go out of *or* lose °control, get °hot under the collar, blow one's top: *He flares up at the very mention of her name. Tempers flared when we touched on the subject of politics.*

—*n.* **4** °blaze, °flame, °burst, °outburst, °flash, °glare, °dazzle, incandescence, °brilliance, luminosity: *A bright orange flare erupted from the mouth of the cave.* **5** °beacon, °light, °signal, torch, flambeau, °link: *We prayed that the rescue party would see our flares.* **6** °spread, broadening, widening, °expansion, °swelling, °bulge, °increase, enlargement: *I like that slight flare at the hem of the skirt.*

flash *n.* **1** °blaze, °flame, °flare, °burst, °dazzle, °spark, °sparkle, coruscation, fulguration, °glitter, °twinkle, °twinkling, °flicker, flickering, scintilla, scintillation, glint, °shimmer, glimmer, °gleam, °beam, °ray, °shaft: *There was a blinding flash of blue light and the little man was gone.* **2** (sudden *or* momentary) °display, °stroke, °show, °manifestation, °outburst, outbreak, °sign, °indication, °exhibition; °touch, °hint, °suggestion: *She has occasional flashes of insight bordering on genius.* **3** °moment, (split) °second, °instant, °twinkling (of an eye), trice, °minute, *Colloq* two shakes (of a lamb's tail), jiffy, °shake, before you can say 'Jack Robinson': *In a flash he was at her side.*
—*v.* **4** °burn, °blaze, °flame, °flare, °burst (out), °dazzle, °spark, °sparkle, coruscate, fulgurate, °glitter, °twinkle, °flicker, scintillate, °shimmer, glimmer, °gleam, °beam, °glare, °shine: *The light flashed every eight seconds.* **5** °race, °speed, °dash, °streak, flick, °tear, °rush, °hurry, °hasten, °fly, zoom, °shoot, °bolt, whistle; °run, sprint, dart, scuttle, scamper, *Colloq* scoot, skedaddle, °take off, whiz *or* whizz: *The train flashed by, doing about 100.*
—*adj.* **6** °dazzling, °showy, °ostentatious, °smart, °chic, *Colloq* °swish, classy, ritzy, snazzy: *Barbara's new car looks very flash.* **7** See **flashy, 1**, below.

flashy *adj.* **1** °flash, °gaudy, °flamboyant, °glaring, fulgurous, °showy, °ostentatious, °loud, °garish, °vulgar, °cheap, meretricious, °pretentious, °tawdry, °tasteless, *Colloq* °tacky, *Slang* jazzy, *US* glitzy: *He was attracted by her flashy appearance.* **2** °superficial, cosmetic, °skin-deep, °surface, °shallow, °glib, °slick, facile, °insubstantial, °thin: *The reviewer called it a flashy interpretation of the Bard.*

flat *adj.* **1** °level, °horizontal, °even, °smooth, °plane, unbroken, uninterrupted: *I looked out over the flat surface of the frozen bay.* **2** °prostrate, °prone, °supine, °lying (down), stretched out, °recumbent, outstretched, reclining, spread-eagle(d), °spread out, outspread: *I lay flat on my back staring up at the sky.* **3** collapsed, levelled, overthrown, laid °low: *The air raid had left all the buildings completely flat.* **4** °downright, °outright, °unqualified, unreserved, unconditional, °absolute, °categorical, °explicit, °definite, °firm, °positive, °out-and-out, unequivocal, °peremptory, unambiguous, unmistakable, °direct, °complete, °total: *The request for clemency was met with the judge's flat refusal.* **5** featureless, °monotonous, °dull, °dead, uninteresting, unexciting, °vapid, °bland, °empty, two-dimensional, insipid, °boring, °tiresome, °lifeless, spiritless, °lacklustre, °prosaic, stale, °tired, °dry, jejune: *The critics wrote that she turned in a very flat performance.* **6** deflated, collapsed, punctured, ruptured, blown out: *We had a flat tyre on the way.* **7** unchangeable, unchanging, °invariable, unvaried, unvarying, °standard, °fixed, unmodified, unmodifiable, *Colloq US* cookie-cutter: *They charge the same*

flat rate for children, the elderly, and all between. **8** °dead, insipid, °stale, °tasteless, flavourless, °unpalatable; decarbonated, non-effervescent: *My beer has gone flat.* **9** °exact, °precise: *It's a flat ten minutes from here to the railway station.* **10** °definite, °certain, °sure, °irrevocable: *I said I'm not going, and that's flat.* **11** °dull, °slow, sluggish, °inactive, depressed: *Business has been a bit flat since Christmas.* **12** °dull, mat *or* matt, unshiny, non-gloss(y), non-reflective, non-glare, unpolished: *The table looks better with a flat finish.* **13** lacking perspective, two-dimensional, °lifeless, °unrealistic: *Some of his paintings seem pretty flat to me.*
—*n.* **14** Often, **flats: a** *US* low shoes, loafers, sandals, *Colloq* flatties: *Cynthia said that wearing flats makes her feet hurt.* **b** lowland(s), °plain(s), tundra, steppe(s), savannah *or* savanna, heath, °moor, pampas; mud-flat(s); °shallow(s), shoal, strand; °marsh, °bog, fen, °swamp: *Before us was a large flat of barren ground.* **15** °rooms, °suite, apartment: *How can you afford to keep a flat in London?*
—*adv.* **16** °absolutely, °completely, categorically, °utterly, °wholly, uncompromisingly, irrevocably, °positively, °definitely, °directly; °exactly, °precisely, flatly: *He has come out flat in favour of the status quo. When he started drinking, she left him flat.* **17 flat out: a** at °maximum *or* °top *or* °full *or* °breakneck °speed, speedily, °quickly, apace, on the °run, °rapidly, °swiftly, at °full °speed *or* gallop, °post-haste, hell for leather, like a bat out of hell, like a °shot, like (greased) lightning, like the wind: *Someone shouted 'Fire!' and we headed flat out for the exits.* **b** flatly, unhesitatingly, °directly, at °once, °immediately, forthwith, without °delay; plainly, °openly, baldly, brazenly, brashly: *He asked to borrow some money and she told him 'No', flat out.*
—*n.* **18** °room(s), °suite (of rooms), chambers, tenement; garden °flat, maisonette, penthouse, studio, *Brit* bedsitter, bedsit; °accommodation, living quarters, *Colloq Brit* digs, *US and Canadian* apartment, furnished °room, walk-up, duplex, triplex, garden apartment: *We rented a two-bedroom flat in a good neighbourhood.*

flatten *v.* **1** °level *or* °even (off *or* out); °smooth (out), °press *or* iron (out), °roll: *The children's noses were flattened against the window of the toy shop. You will have to flatten the lawn if you want to play croquet on it.* **2** °knock down *or* over, °knock out, °floor, °prostrate: *Menges flattened the champion in the first round.* **3** °raze, °tear down, °demolish, °level: *The bomb flattened every house in the area.*

flatter *v.* **1** butter up, °play up to, °compliment, °praise, fawn (on *or* upon), toady to, °truckle to, court, curry °favour with, *Colloq* °flannel, soft-soap, °oil; *Slang* °shine *or* suck up to, boot-lick, *Taboo* °kiss (someone's) arse *or US* ass, brown-nose: *Flattering the boss won't get you a salary increase.* **2** °enhance, °complement, °suit, °show to °advantage: *That colour flatters her complexion.* **3** °cajole, °wheedle, °coax, inveigle, °beguile, sweet-talk: *He was flattered into signing that contract.*

flatterer *n.* toady, sycophant, fawner, wheedler, time-server, courtier, backscratcher, sponge, °parasite, leech, °hanger-on, sweet-talker, back-slapper, truckler, lickspittle, *Colloq* °yes-man; *Slang* bootlicker, *Taboo* brown-noser, *Brit*
arse-kisser, arse-licker, bum-sucker, *US* ass-kisser, ass-licker: *Don't believe anything that flatterer tells you.*

flattering *adj.* **1** °complimentary, °becoming, °kind, enhancing: *That is quite a flattering portrait of Dorian.* **2** adulatory, °laudatory, gratifying, fulsome, honeyed, sugary, fawning, °ingratiating, unctuous, °slimy, *Chiefly Brit* smarmy: *Authors once wrote the most flattering dedications to their patrons.*

flattery *n.* adulation, °cajolery, blandishment, sweet talk, beguilement, wheedling, gloze, *Colloq* soft soap, *Slang* boot-licking, *Taboo* brown-nosing, *Brit* arse-kissing, arse-licking, bum-sucking, *US* ass-kissing, ass-licking: *A judicious use of flattery moved him up the corporate ladder.*

flaunt *v.* °display, °show (off), °parade, °flourish, °exhibit, °sport, disport, °spotlight: *They were like all the other nouveaux riches who flaunt their wealth in the stylish continental resorts.*

flavour *n.* **1** °taste, °savour, °tang, piquancy, °zest; tastiness, savouriness; °essence, °extract, °seasoning, flavouring, °seasoning, °spice; °aroma, °odour, °scent; *Rare* sapor: *Overcooking destroys the flavour of food. This sweet has a minty flavour.* **2** °character, °spirit, °nature, °quality, °property, °mark, °stamp, °essence, °characteristic, °style, °taste, °feel, °feeling, ambience *or* ambiance, °sense, tinge, °aroma, °air, °atmosphere, °hint, °suggestion, °touch, soupçon: *We all agreed that the new play has a Shavian flavour.*
—*v.* **3** °season, °spice: *She flavours her teacakes with ginger.*

flaw *n.* **1** °fault, °defect, °imperfection, °error, °mistake, °blemish, °blot, °stain, °taint, (°black) °mark, °damage, disfigurement, °failing, °weakness, °weak °spot; °loophole: *Flaws in the casting give this bell a dull sound. I can see flaws in your argument.* **2** °crack, °break, °breach, °chink, °chip, °fracture, °rupture, fissure, cleft, °split, °slit, °cut, °gash, °rent, °rift, °tear, °rip, °puncture, °hole, perforation: *The tiniest flaw may reduce the value of a pot to a collector.*
—*v.* **3** °damage, °harm, °spoil, °ruin, °mark, °weaken, disfigure: *Careless workmanship has flawed many of the objects they produced.* **4** °discredit, °stigmatize, °damage, °hurt, °harm; °taint, °mar, °stain, °blot: *Her reputation has already been flawed.*

flawed *adj.* damaged, harmed, marred, weakened, tainted, stained, tarnished, °defective, °imperfect, °unsound, °faulty: *His flawed record prevented him from getting work.*

flawless *adj.* **1** °perfect, °pristine, °pure, uncorrupted, °chaste, virgin, °intact, °whole, °clean, °immaculate, unsullied, unspoiled *or* unspoilt, unsoiled, °impeccable, unblemished, °faultless, undamaged, unimpaired, °spotless, °untarnished: *Two flawless artefacts were found in the tomb. Many envied her flawless reputation.* **2** undeniable, unassailable, unimpeachable, °unquestionable, irrefutable, °foolproof, °sound, °demonstrable: *The prosecutor's evidence appears to be flawless.*

flecked *adj.* spotted, dappled, pied, (be)speckled, (be)sprinkled, dotted, °marked, stippled, dusted, specked, spattered, freckled: *His lank brown hair was flecked with grey.*

flee *v.* **1** °quit, °run away *or* off, °escape, °get away, °fly, °take °flight, °bolt, °go (away), decamp, abscond, seek safety, °avoid, °make off, make an °exit, °make (good) one's °escape, °make a (clean) °getaway, °beat a (hasty) °retreat, °take to one's heels, show a clean pair of heels, turn tail, °make tracks, make a °run for it, °cut and °run, vanish, °disappear, Brit levant, Colloq °take off, scoot, °make oneself °scarce, °beat it, °clear out, °fly the coop, skedaddle, scram, Brit scarper, Australian and New Zealand °shoot through, US and Canadian take a (run-out) powder, °skip (town), °cut out, hightail it, Old-fashioned skiddoo; Slang °split, Brit °bugger off, do a moonlight flit, do a bunk, US and Canadian vamoose, lam out, take it on the lam, °blow, bail out: He fled the town and was never seen again. When they saw what they had done, they fled. She fled to Brazil to avoid the tax authorities. **2** °avoid, °evade, °shun, °escape from, eschew: She fled the responsibilities of caring for her children.

fleece v. °cheat, overcharge, °swindle, bilk, °defraud, °victimize, °plunder, °strip, °milk, °rob, Colloq °take, flimflam, gyp, diddle, bleed, take for a °ride or to the cleaners, Slang °rip off, °chisel, °pluck, rook, °clip, °soak: The gang stole credit cards and fleeced the companies out of millions.

fleet[1] n. armada, flotilla, °navy, (naval) (task) °force, squadron, convoy, °division: A fleet of submarines was sent to harass shipping in the Atlantic.

fleet[2] adj. °swift, °rapid, °fast, °speedy, °quick, °nimble, °expeditious, °agile: Nowadays, the fleetest transportation in a large city is by bicycle.

fleeting adj. transitory, °fugitive, °transient, °temporary, °passing, ephemeral, fugacious, evanescent, °momentary, °short-lived, °fly-by-night, °short, °brief: I caught only a fleeting glimpse of the car as it sped by.

flesh n. **1** °meat; °tissue, muscle: We ate the flesh and threw away the fat, bones, and skin. **2** °body, corporeality, flesh and blood, °human °nature, physicality; mortality: The spirit is willing but the flesh is weak. **3** **flesh and blood**: °real, °physical, corporeal, °human, °natural: He pointed out that he was flesh and blood, not a robot. **4** **in the flesh**: °personally, in °person, °really, physically, bodily, °alive, living, in °life: She stood before me, in the flesh. **5** **one's (own) flesh and blood**: °kin, kinsfolk or US and Canadian kinfolk, °family, °stock, blood, kith and °kin, relatives, relations: How could she treat her own flesh and blood that way?
—v. **6** **flesh out**: °substantiate, °fill (in or out), give or °lend °substance or dimension to, °incorporate, °embody, °colour: The idea is good, but it needs fleshing out.

flex n. **1** wire, °lead, °cord, °cable, °extension: Replace this flex before you have a short circuit.
—v. **2** °bend, °give, °stretch, curve: The plastic tube can be flexed many times without breaking. **3** °exercise, °tense, °tighten, °contract: He flexed his muscles before lifting the weight.

flexibility n. **1** pliability, pliancy or pliantness, °elasticity, °resilience or resiliency, suppleness, flexibleness, bendability, limberness, °stretch, °give, °spring, springiness, ductility: Chemists improved the flexibility of the substance by adding more plasticizer. **2** conformability or conformableness, adaptability, versatility, adjustability or adjustableness, compliance or compliancy, manageability, tractability or tractableness, malleability, °obedience, submissiveness, docility, agreeableness, conformity: Fletcher has the flexibility needed to move from one department to another.

flexible adj. **1** °pliable, pliant, °elastic, resilient, °supple, bendable, limber, lithe, stretchy, stretchable, springy, extensible or extensile, ductile, flexile, tensile, °yielding, °willowy: The foil is a thin, flexible duelling sword. **2** modifiable, °adaptable, conformable, compliant, malleable, °obedient, °tractable, °manageable, cooperative, amenable, persuadable or persuasible: English seems to be an infinitely flexible language. Nicole is flexible in her attitude towards politics. **3** °easy, facile, °submissive, complaisant, docile: Discipline at the school might be a little too flexible.

flicker v. **1** °twinkle, °blink, waver, glimmer, glint, °sparkle, °shimmer, °flare, gutter: A slight draught made the candles flicker. **2** °flap, °flutter, °quiver, °twitter, °fluctuate, °oscillate, °shake, °tremble, °vibrate: Dozens of tiny flags flickered in the wind.
—n. **3** glimmer, glint, glimmering, °sparkle, °spark, °twinkle, °twinkling, °gleam, °flare, °glare: With a dying flicker the torch went out. **4** °hint, °suggestion, °trace, glimmer, °vestige, scintilla, °spark: I thought I detected a flicker of recognition when our eyes met.

flight[1] n. **1** flying, soaring, winging, °excursion: The flight above the mountains was exhilarating. He is subject to wild flights of the imagination. **2** (°air) voyage or °journey or °trip: We had a fine flight from New Delhi. **3** aeroplane, airliner, °plane, aircraft: Our flight was delayed in Istanbul. **4** °flock, °swarm, cloud, covey (of grouse or partridge), bevy (of quail), skein (of geese), exaltation (of larks): A flight of migrating birds passed overhead. **5** feather: The flights on this dart are broken.

flight[2] n. **1** °escape, °retreat, departure, °exit, exodus, °getaway, fleeing, bolting, Slang °split: Mohammed's flight from Mecca to Medina in 622 is called a 'hegira'. **2** **put to flight**: °chase or °drive (off or away), °disperse, °send off or away, °send packing, °dismiss, °rout, °stampede: They put the Saracens to flight in a decisive battle. **3** **take flight**: °flee, °go or °run away or off, abscond, °desert, °depart, (°beat a) °retreat, °exit, °bolt, decamp, °withdraw, take to one's heels, show a clean pair of heels, Colloq °light out, shove off, Brit scarper, US take a (run-out) °powder, °take it on the lam, lam out; Slang °split, Brit do a bunk, do a moonlight flit, °bugger off: The constable blew his whistle and the thief took flight.

flighty adj. **1** °fickle, °frivolous, °inconstant, °capricious, °fanciful, °changeable, °variable, mercurial, skittish, °volatile, °unstable, unsteady, °giddy, °wild: These flighty girls never stay in a job more than a month. **2** °irresponsible, light-headed, rattle-brained, °silly, °hare-brained, °dizzy, °crazy, °mad, °reckless, °thoughtless, Colloq nutty, screwy, dotty, dippy: It was flighty of Caroline to pour the brandy into the well.

flimsy adj. **1** °slight, °frail, °weak, °insubstantial or unsubstantial, °feeble, °makeshift, °fragile, frangible, breakable, °rickety, °ramshackle, °dilapidated, jerry-built, gimcrack, °delicate: That flimsy ladder will never support me. He lives in a *flimsy shack near the railway.* **2** °slight, trivial, °paltry, °feeble, unconvincing, °weak, °makeshift, °implausible, °unbelievable, °unsatisfactory, °insubstantial *or* unsubstantial, °poor, °inadequate: *Her flimsy excuse was that she had a headache.* **3** °sheer, °light, gauzy, °transparent, °thin, °filmy, diaphanous, gossamer, °delicate: *She was wearing a flimsy pink blouse.*

flinch *v.* wince, °draw back, °withdraw, cower, °cringe, °recoil, °start, quail, blench, °shrink (from), °shy (away) (from), °dodge, °duck: *Each time he raised the whip, I flinched.*

fling *v.* **1** °toss, °pitch, °throw, °cast, °hurl, °heave, °sling, °propel, °fire, °let °fly, °send, *Colloq* °lob, chuck: *The smugglers had flung the contraband into the sea.* —*n.* **2** °indulgence, debauch, binge, °spree, °party, *Colloq* blow-off: *This will be my last fling before going into the army.* **3** °gamble, °risk, °venture, °attempt, °try, °go, °shot, *Colloq* °crack, whirl, bash: *Her brief fling at an acting career was unsuccessful.*

flip *v.* **1** °toss, flick, °snap, °flop, °turn, °twist, °spin: *Flip a coin to see who goes first.* **2** °anger, become °angry *or* °furious, °go °mad, °go °crazy, °go °berserk, *US also* °flip out, *Colloq* °go off the deep end, °lose one's °cool, *Slang* °flip one's lid *or Brit* °top, *Brit* freak, *US* freak out, °lose it: *Father flipped when I said I was quitting college.*

flippancy *n.* **1** frivolousness, facetiousness, °levity, light-heartedness, frivolity, jocularity, offhandedness, unseriousness: *I was chagrined that she should treat my proposal of marriage with such flippancy.* **2** °disrespect, disrespectfulness, °impudence, °impertinence, irreverence, sauciness, rudeness, discourtesy, brazenness, brashness, pertness, insolence, *Colloq* cheek, cheekiness, lip, °mouth, *Slang Brit* °side: *The headmaster will not tolerate flippancy on serious subjects such as religion and race relations.*

flippant *adj.* **1** °frivolous, facetious, light-hearted, jocular, °offhand(ed), unserious, °shallow, °thoughtless, °superficial; °supercilious, belittling, °scornful, dismissive: *I don't appreciate your flippant remarks when I'm trying to be serious.* **2** °disrespectful, °impudent, °impertinent, °irreverent, saucy, °rude, °pert, °discourteous, °brazen, brash, °insolent, *Colloq* °cheeky, °flip: *He disapproves of Charles's flippant attitude towards the royal family.*

flirt *v.* **1** coquette, °play *or* °act the coquette, °tease, °tantalize, °toy, °lead on, dally, philander, *Colloq Brit* °chat up; *Slang US* °come on to: *Amanda enjoys flirting with the boys.* **2 flirt with:** °trifle *or* °toy *or* °play *or* °tinker with, °contemplate, °consider, °entertain, give a thought to, °think about *or* of, *Colloq Brit* °try on: *Many teenagers flirt with the idea of leaving home.* —*n.* **3** coquette, °tease, vamp, hussy, playgirl, minx; °philanderer, °playboy, *Slang* lady-killer, *Old-fashioned* wolf, sheik, masher, lounge lizard, *Taboo slang* cock-teaser, prick-teaser: *They are both such flirts, I can't tell if their advances are genuine.*

flirtatious *adj.* coquettish, vampish, °seductive, flirty, °coy, philandering, °provocative, enticing, alluring, amorous, come-hither: *They exchanged many flirtatious looks across the table.*

flit *v.* °move, °go, °fly, °flee, dart, °skip, °skim, flick, °hop, °whisk, °flutter, °flash: *As a bee flits from flower to flower, she flits from man to man.*

float *v.* **1** °hover, °poise, bob, °waft, be suspended, °hang; °sail, °drift, °glide, swim: *In the clear Caribbean waters, the boat seemed to float in mid-air.* **2** °launch, °establish, °set up, °organize, °found, °initiate, °get °going *or* °moving: *The financiers are trying to float a new company.* **3** °negotiate, °arrange, °transact, °bring *or* °carry off, °get, °effect, consummate, *Colloq* °pull off, °swing: *Were you able to float a loan on your house?* —*n.* **4** raft, *Brit* °platform: *I can swim out to the float.* **5** °buoy; pontoon: *The bridge is supported by floats.* **6** °(parade) °exhibit *or* °display: *Our parade float won first prize.*

flock *n.* **1** °body, °company, °group, °band, °pack, °bunch, troop, °set, °collection, °assembly, convoy, °gathering, congregation, °crowd, °mass, °mob, °throng, °gang, multitude, °number, °quantity, °host, horde, °swarm, drove; °herd, °flight, troupe, °fleet, °school; bevy: *A huge flock of buyers sought bargains in the post-Christmas sales.* —*v.* **2** °assemble, °meet, °collect, °gather, °come *or* °go together, congregate, °crowd, °mass, °mob, °throng, °pour, °flood, °swarm, °herd (together), °band together, °go: *People flocked around the speaker.*

flog *v.* **1** °whip, °lash, horsewhip, strap, flagellate, flay, °scourge, thrash, thresh, °beat; °chastise, °castigate, °punish: *He will be flogged, then drawn and quartered. He was flogged for stealing a loaf of bread.* **2** °sell; °promote, °publicize: *Her latest job is flogging encyclopedias door-to-door.*

flood *n.* **1** inundation, deluge, overflow(ing), débâcle: *The hurricane was accompanied by a devastating flood.* **2** °torrent, cataract, freshet, overflow, °stream, °spate: *A flood of lava poured down the mountain.* **3** °abundance, deluge, overflowing, °surge, °outpouring, °torrent, tide, tidal °wave, °stream, °rush, °flow, °glut, °surfeit, °satiety, °profusion, over-abundance, super-abundance, nimiety, plethora, °excess, °surplus, °superfluity: *A flood of invective poured from her lips.* —*v.* **4** inundate, °submerge, overflow, °swamp, °immerse, deluge, °pour over, °drown: *The water flooded everything in the basement.* **5** °overwhelm, °glut, oversupply, °saturate, °choke: *The market is being flooded with cheap imitations.* **6** °sweep, °flow, °swarm, °surge, °rush, °crowd, °pour: *As soon as the doors opened, the people flooded in.* **7** °permeate, °fill, engulf, °cover, °pour into *or* °throughout *or* over: *I open the curtain and sunlight floods the room.*

floor *n.* **1** flooring, parquet, boarding, planking, *Nautical or colloq* deck: *The floor is mopped once a week.* **2** °storey, °level; deck: *On which floor is your flat?* **3** °minimum, °bottom, °base, lower limit, lowest °(level): *Owing to inflation, the wage floor was raised. Share prices went through the floor in today's trading.* —*v.* **4** °knock over *or* down, °bowl over, °prostrate, °fell, °overthrow, °bring down, (make) °fall; °beat, °defeat, °conquer, °destroy, °rout, °overwhelm, °crush, °whip, trounce, thrash, drub, °best, worst: *The champion was floored by a blow to the head.* **5** °stump, °bewilder, baffle, °dumbfound *or* dumbfound, °confuse, confound, disconcert, °nonplus, °perplex, °puzzle,

°astound, °astonish, °amaze, °surprise, °shock: *Alexandra was floored when she received a gift from her ex-husband.*

flop v. **1** °collapse, °drop (down), °fall (down), °tumble, °topple, °plump down, plop down, °flounce down: *I was so exhausted that I flopped into bed at once.* **2** °flap, °wave, °swing: *The door, unfastened, flopped back and forth in the wind.* **3** °fail, °fall °flat, come to °naught or °nothing, °founder, Colloq °fold, US °bomb: *The musical flopped on the first night.*
—n. **4** °failure, °fiasco, °disaster, non-starter, débâcle, US °fizzle, Colloq °dud, °washout, clanger, US lead balloon, °bomb; Slang lemon, Brit cock-up, damp squib: *His idea for a new corkscrew was a complete flop.*

flounce n. **1** °frill, furbelow, peplum, °ruffle, °ornament, valance, trimming: *The dress has decorative flounces round the skirt.*
—v. **2** °fling, °toss, °bounce, °twist, °strut, °parade, °march, °storm, °stamp, US sashay: *She flounced out of the room in high dudgeon.*

flounder v. °grope, °blunder, °stumble, °tumble, °struggle, °stagger, °plunge about: *We floundered about in the dark till someone found the light switch.*

flourish v. **1** °prosper, °thrive, °grow, °develop, °luxuriate, bloom, blossom, °flower, °bear fruit, fructify, °boom, burgeon or bourgeon, °mature, °ripen, °increase, °succeed, °get °ahead, do or °fare °well, °make °good; °go up or °rise in the world; Slang °go °great guns: *We understand that Amy's medical practice has flourished.* **2** °wave, °wield, brandish, °wag, °swing, °twirl, °flaunt, vaunt, °swagger, °swish, °shake: *The band-leader flourished his baton.*
—n. **3** °decoration, °embellishment, floridness, floweriness, ornamentation, °elaboration, adornment, °frill, embroidery, curlicue, furbelow: *His signature is characterized by all these flourishes.* **4** °fanfare, °display, °show, showiness, °dash, gesturing, °wave: *With a flourish of his hand, the king signalled the tourney to begin.*

flourishing adj. °luxuriant, °lush, thriving, prospering, blooming, blossoming, °fruitful, flowering, burgeoning or bourgeoning, °successful, °prosperous, booming, growing, increasing: *Patel runs a flourishing flower shop in Bicester.*

flout v. °deride, °scorn, disdain, contemn, °spurn, decry, °denounce, misprize, °blaspheme, °depreciate, °degrade, abase, °belittle, °minimize, deprecate, °disparage, denigrate, °mock, °jeer, °guy, °ridicule, °scoff, °sneer, °gibe or jibe (at), °taunt, °twit, °insult, affront, Archaic fleer; Colloq °put down, °chaff, °rag, °knock: *When introduced in the sixties, miniskirts brazenly flouted convention.*

flow v. **1** °stream, °pour, °run, °rush, °course, °surge, °move, °go, °proceed, °progress, °drift; °gush, °glide, purl, °roll, °ripple, °trickle, °gurgle, °bubble; °swirl, whirl, °circulate: *People continue to flow past the window. The Thames flows silently to the sea.* **2** °rush, °gush, °surge, °well (forth), °stream, °spring, °issue, °spout, °spurt, squirt, °spew, °flood, cascade, °fall, °rain; °brim, overflow, °spill, °teem: *Open the gates to allow water to flow into the lock. A stream of insults flowed from his lips. Her tears flowed like wine.* **3** °issue, °originate, °come, °emanate, °rise, °begin: *With the dam repaired, water will once again flow from the reservoir. The authority of the* state constitutions does not flow from Congress. **4** °spread, overspread, °cover: *The paint flowed effortlessly onto the canvas.*
—n. **5** °rush, °gush, °surge; °current, °course, °stream, °run, °movement, °drift: *A dam blocks the flow of water here. The sound of a shot interrupted the flow of conversation.* **6** °abundance, superabundance, °flood, plethora, °excess, overflow(ing), deluge, tide, °supply; °plenty: *London experiences an unending flow of tourists.*

flower n. **1** blossom, bloom, floret or floweret, bud, Technical efflorescence: *He brought me flowers for my birthday.* **2** cream, °best, °pick, élite, crème de la crème, finest, choicest: *The flower of the city's youth were put to death by the wicked caliph.*
—v. **3** blossom, bloom, bud, burgeon or bourgeon, °come out, °open, °unfold, Technical effloresce: *The century plant was so called because it was thought to flower only once every hundred years.*

flowery adj. florid, °ornate, °fancy, °elaborate(d), decorated, ornamented, °overwrought, embellished, rococo, baroque, arabesque, euphuistic, Gongoristic, Ossianic, grandiloquent, °bombastic, °inflated, °pompous, °affected, °artificial, high-flown, showy: *Many find his flowery style of writing difficult to stomach.*

fluctuate v. °vary, °change, °alternate, °see-saw, °swing, vacillate, undulate, waver, °oscillate, °shift: *Prices fluctuate according to supply and demand.*

fluctuation n. Sometimes, **fluctuations**: °variation(s), °change(s), °alternation(s), °swing(s), vacillation(s), wavering(s), oscillation(s), undulation(s), ups and downs, instability, unsteadiness, °inconstancy: *We can expect fluctuation in temperatures during the coming week.*

fluency n. articulateness, eloquence, °control, °command, °ease, °grace, effortlessness, °facility, felicity, smoothness, °polish, slickness, glibness, volubility: *His extemporaneous speeches are marked by an enviable fluency.*

fluent adj. articulate, °eloquent, well-spoken, felicitous, °graceful, facile, °easy, °natural, °effortless, °ready, °smooth, °polished, flowing, °voluble, °glib, °slick; °expressive: *She is a fluent speaker of Spanish.*

fluff n. **1** down, fuzz, feather(s), thistledown, floss, lint, dust, dust-ball, fuzz ball: *Be sure you clean the fluff from under the beds.* **2 bit of fluff**: poppet, °girl (°friend), °mistress, Slang bit of all right, (bit of) crumpet, (bit of) skirt or stuff, Old-fashioned Brit popsy: *Bickerley keeps a bit of fluff on the side.* **3** °blunder, °error, °slip, °mistake, Colloq °howler, Brit bloomer, US and Canadian blooper: *They showed a video of the fluffs actors make during recordings.*
—v. **4** °muddle, °spoil, °ruin, make a °mess of, °bungle, °botch, Colloq °foul up, °screw up, °mess up, US snafu, Slang Brit cock up, balls up, US ball up, Taboo fuck up: *I have a funny story about how Barrymore fluffed Hamlet's soliloquy.* **5 fluff up**: °puff up, °shake out or up, aerate: *He doesn't like the pillows on his bed fluffed up.*

fluffy adj. **1** °soft, downy, puffy, whipped up, °light, airy, feathery, wispy: *Beat the egg whites till they are fluffy.* **2** °frivolous, °superficial, trivial, unimportant, airy, °thin, lightweight, °light, °insubstantial, gossamer, Brit airy-fairy: *Mr Piffle is too fluffy-headed to offer anything useful.*

fluid n. **1** °liquid, °solution, liquor, ichor; gas, °vapour: *It might surprise some to learn that physicists consider gases to be fluids.* —*adj.* **2** °liquid, flowing, °running, runny, °watery, aqueous: *Once the metal has become fluid, it is poured into the moulds.* **3** °changeable, mutable, °flexible, adjustable, °variable, pliant, unformed, formless, unfixed, unstatic *or* non-static, °plastic, °protean, mercurial, °mobile, °unstable, shifting, °uncertain, °indefinite, °unsettled: *The situation is fluid and the decision could go either way.*

fluke n. °lucky *or* °successful °stroke, °stroke of (°good) °luck, °lucky *or* °big °break, (°happy) °accident, °quirk *or* °twist of °fate, °windfall, fortuity, serendipity: *If he won first prize, it was by a fluke.*

flummox v. °confuse, baffle, °perplex, °bewilder, confound, °throw into °confusion, °stymie, °stump, °puzzle, °mystify, fox, °deceive, °hoodwink, °nonplus: *We were completely flummoxed by the licensing requirements.*

flunkey n. **1** °servant, retainer, lackey, footman, °menial, minion, hireling, underling, °subordinate, °inferior; °slave; *Colloq* dogsbody, *Slang US and Canadian* gofer: *A company flunkey drove me to the airport.* **2** toady, °hanger-on, °yes-man, jackal, doormat, stooge, lickspittle, sycophant, *Colloq US and Canadian* apple-polisher, *Taboo* brown-noser: *He has a collection of flunkeys waiting about for hand-outs.*

flurry n. **1** °activity, commotion, ado, to-do, °fuss, °upset, hubbub, pother, °stir, °excitement, °disturbance, °agitation, °tumult, whirl, °furore *or US* furor, bustle, °hurry, °hustle, °flutter, °fluster; °burst, °outburst; *Colloq* tizzy: *I was happy to leave the worry and flurry of the city. There was a brief flurry of activity at the Stock Exchange today.* —*v.* **2** °confuse, °bewilder, °agitate, °put out, °disturb, °excite, °fluster, disconcert, °upset, °perturb, unsettle, °shake (up), *Colloq* °rattle: *He was quite flurried by the arrival of the police.*

flush¹ v. **1** °blush, redden, crimson, °glow, °burn, °colour (up): *When he told her she was pretty she flushed a bit.* **2** Often, **flush out**: °rinse, °wash (out *or* away), douse, douche, hose down, °flood, °drench, °clean out, °cleanse, °purge, °discharge, °empty: *Oil tankers are flushed out far from shore.* **3** °animate, °stir, °inflame, impassion, °quicken, arouse, °excite, elate, °encourage, °cheer, °delight, °thrill, °gladden: *Suzie was flushed with the success of having got the job.* —*n.* **4** °blush, redness, bloom, rosiness, °colour, blood, °glow, °radiance: *When he was asked what had happened to the money, a flush rose to his cheek.* **5** °flood, deluge, drenching, °soaking, overflow, inundation, °rush, °gush, °surge, °stream, °flow: *The flush of water washed away all the debris.* **6** °thrill, °excitement, °passion, quickening, arousal, °stir, °stirring, °animation, elation, euphoria, °delight, °encouragement, tingle: *In the first flush of success, they were overwhelmed with orders. He felt a flush come over him when he won the race.*

flush² adj. **1** (on the °same) °plane *or* °level (with), °even, °smooth, °flat, °square, °true, °continuous; adjacent, next to: *See that the table-top is flush with the countertop. The mirror should be flush against the wall.* **2** °full, overflowing, °replete, °abundant: *Turn off the water when it is flush with the top of the basin.* **3** °solvent, well supplied, °comfortable; well-to-do, well off, well-found, °wealthy, °rich, °prosperous, affluent, moneyed, *Colloq* well-heeled, on Easy Street, in the °money, *US* in the chips; *Slang* °loaded, rolling (in °money *or* it): *He's flush enough to take us all out to dinner.* —*adv.* **4** °even(ly), °square(ly), levelly, °plumb, °directly: *Cut this branch off flush.*

fluster v. **1** °agitate, °stir (up), discompose, °discomfit, °discomfort, disconcert, °shake (up), °upset, disquiet, discommode, °bother, °put out *or* off, °disturb, °perturb, °flurry, °flutter, make °nervous, °throw off, °distract, °confuse, baffle, confound, °puzzle, °perplex, befuddle, °bewilder, °daze, °dazzle, *Colloq* °rattle, °throw, discombobulate, hassle, faze: *Don't be flustered by her rude manner.* —*n.* **2** °agitation, °upset, °discomfort, disquiet, °bother, °disturbance, commotion, perturbation, dither, °flurry, °flutter, nervousness, °distraction, °confusion, bafflement, befuddlement, °perplexity, bewilderment: *All this fluster came about through the absence of a coherent plan.*

flutter v. **1** °flap, °flop, °fluctuate, vacillate, °wave, waver, °oscillate: *The paper streamers fluttered in the breeze.* **2** °flit, °flicker, flitter, °hover, °dance; °fuss: *We shall never get done if you keep fluttering about.* **3** °tremble, °shake, °quiver, dither, °jump, °vibrate, twitch: *She is fluttering with anticipation waiting for the postman.* —*n.* **4** fluttering, flapping, flopping, °fluctuation, fluctuating, vacillation, vacillating, °wave, waving, oscillation, oscillating, trembling, °quiver, quivering: *The slightest flutter of her fan communicates volumes.* **5** See fluster, 2, above.

flux n. instability, °change, °mutation, modification, °fluctuation, °unrest, °swing, °swinging, wavering, °movement, °motion, oscillation, °indecision, indecisiveness: *The economic indicators are in a constant state of flux.*

fly v. **1** take wing, take °flight, take to the °air, wing, °soar, °sail, °hover, °flutter, °flit, °flap: *A stork flew overhead. Daedalus taught Icarus to fly.* **2** Also, **fly away** *or* **off**: take °flight, °depart, °leave, °flee, decamp, °bolt, °run away *or* off, °escape, make (good) one's °escape, take to one's heels, show a clean pair of heels, °rush *or* °nip off *or* out *or* away, (make a) °run (for it), °go *or* °get away *or* off, abscond, make a °getaway, °cut and °run, °beat a (hasty) °retreat, °take off, scoot, *Colloq* °light out, °beat it, °clear out *or* off, skedaddle, scram, *US* °cut out, hightail (it), take it on the lam, take a (run-out) powder, lam out, take to the hills, take to the woods; *Slang Brit* scarper, °bugger off, *US* vamoose, °blow: *She flew off before I could get her telephone number.* **3** °hasten, °hurry, °rush, °run, °race, °dash, sprint, °tear, scamper, scoot, *Colloq* make tracks: *I must fly if I'm to catch the train.* **4** °pass (by), °elapse, °go (by), °expire, °run its course, °slip *or* °slide by *or* away: *Time flies quickly when you're having fun.* **5** aviate, °pilot; jet: *Parker flies his own plane. I flew down to Paris with him.* **6 fly in the face of**: °flout, °defy, °go against, contemn, °scorn, °scoff at, °oppose, °go *or* °run °counter to, °counter, °counteract, countervail, countermine, °contradict, contravene, °thumb one's nose at, *Colloq Brit* cock a snook at: *His actions fly in the face of conventional behaviour.* **7 fly**

off the handle: fly into a °rage or °fury or °temper or °passion, lose one's °temper, have a °fit or °tantrum, be fit to be tied, °go °berserk, °go °crazy or °mad, °explode, *Colloq* lose or °blow one's °cool, °blow one's top, hit or °go through the roof, *US* hit the ceiling, °blow one's stack, get worked up (over); *Slang* °blow a fuse or a gasket, °flip (one's lid), have a haemorrhage, *Brit* °flip one's top: *Rudolf flies off the handle at the slightest provocation.* **8 let fly**: **a** °throw, °toss, °cast, °hurl, °fling, °heave, °pitch, °lob, °sling, chuck, °shoot, °fire (off), °let °rip, °discharge, °launch, °propel, °let °go or off: *They let fly a volley of arrows.* **b** °let °go with, °let (someone) have it, °lash out, °vent one's spleen, lose one's °temper, °burst out or forth, °burst into, *Colloq* pull no punches, °tear into: *That was the last straw, and she really let fly at him.*
—*n.* **9** Often, *Brit* **flies**: °flap, fly °front, *Brit* zip, *US* zipper: *He was embarrassed to find his flies were open.* **10 fly in the ointment**: °hitch, °snag, °impediment, °obstacle, °obstruction, °problem, °difficulty, °drawback, detraction, °rub, °hindrance, bugbear, bogey or bogy, bugaboo: *The one fly in the ointment is that my mother won't give me permission to go.*

fly-by-night *adj.* **1** °temporary, °short-lived, transitory, °fugitive, ephemeral, °transient, °fleeting, °passing, °brief, impermanent, here today, gone tomorrow: *That fly-by-night operation was in business for less than a month.* **2** °unreliable, untrustworthy, °disreputable, °irresponsible, dubious, °questionable; °shifty, dishonest, °sharp, °crooked, *Colloq* °shady, *Brit* cowboy: *Guarantees on double glazing are worthless if installed by some fly-by-night company.*

foam *n.* **1** bubbles, °froth, spume, °lather, suds; effervescence, °sparkle, carbonation, °fizz: *The foam leaves spots when it dries.*
—*v.* **2** °bubble, °froth, spume, °lather, suds, soap up: *Watch the solution foam when I drop this tablet into it.*

focal *adj.* °central, focused, concentrated, convergent, centred, centralized: *The light rays come together at this focal point. Harris's address was the focal point of the conference.*

focus *n.* **1** °centre, concentration, °focal °point, °heart, °core, °target, convergence, °hub, nave; cynosure: *Why should Anita always be the focus of attention?* **2 in focus**: °clear, °distinct, well- or °sharply defined: *With the telescope in focus, you feel as if you can almost touch the distant shore.* **3 out of focus**: unclear, °indistinct, blurred, blurry, °fuzzy, °woolly: *The photos are so out of focus that I can't tell who's who.*
—*v.* **4** °concentrate, °centre, °converge, °meet, pinpoint, °spotlight; bring into focus; *Colloq* °zero in: *Without distractions, we can focus on the problem at hand.*

fog *n.* **1** °mist, haze, smog, °vapour, cloud, *Colloq* pea-souper: *Our flight was grounded because of fog.* **2** °trance, °daze, °stupor, brown study, °confused state; coma: *He's in a fog and didn't hear a word you said.*
—*v.* **3** °dim, °obscure, cloud, bedim, becloud, °blind, °stifle: *The purpose of all that verbiage is merely to fog the issue.* **4** Usually, **befog**: °bewilder, °mystify, °perplex, °confuse, °muddle, °puzzle, °nonplus: *I was completely befogged by the technical language he used.* **5** Also,

fog up or **over**: °mist over or up, cloud up or over, °shroud: *My bathroom mirror fogs when I take a hot shower.*

fogy *n.* Usually, **old fogy** or **fogey**: fogey, °conservative, °relic, *Colloq* fuddy-duddy, fossil, °antique, °stick-in-the-mud, back number, °square: *That old fogy still dances the foxtrot.*

foible *n.* °weakness, °imperfection, °weak point, °fault, °frailty, °shortcoming, °flaw, °defect, °failing, °blemish, °infirmity; °peculiarity, idiosyncrasy, °quirk, crotchet, °eccentricity, preoccupation, °kink, *Colloq* hang-up, °bug: *One of her foibles is that she loves junk food.*

foil[1] *v.* °thwart, °offset, °defeat, baffle, balk, parry, °frustrate, °counter, °check, °impede, °hamper, °outwit, circumvent, checkmate, °daunt, disconcert, °discomfit, °disappoint, pull the rug out from under (someone), cut the ground from under someone's feet, nullify, °nip in the bud, countervail (against), *Brit* put a spoke in (someone's) wheel, *Colloq* clip (someone's) wings, cut (someone) down to size, °spoil (someone's) game, *Chiefly US and Canadian* faze: *The villain and his evil plan were again foiled by the arrival of the sheriff.*

foil[2] *n.* layer, lamina, lamination, °sheet, membrane, °film, coating, °flake, °scale, wafer: *Cigarettes once came packaged in tin foil.*

foist *v.* palm or °pass off, °impose, °unload, °put (off), °push (off), *Colloq* °lay (off), *Brit* fob off: *Don't try to foist those fake paintings on me!*

fold *v.* **1** °bend, °ply, °double (over or up), °overlap, crease, pleat, °gather, crimp: *Fold the letter before putting it into the envelope.* **2** °enclose, °envelop, enfold, °wrap, enwrap, °clasp, °clip, °embrace, °hug, °gather: *He folded her in his arms.* **3** °give °way, °collapse, °fail, °close (up or down), °shut down, °go out of business, °go bankrupt, *Colloq* °go under, °go °broke, °go bust, *Brit* go to the °wall: *The company folded and ten employees were made redundant.*
—*n.* **4** crease, °wrinkle, crinkle, °pucker, pleat, °gather, crimp, °overlap, °lap: *The folds will remain crisp if you use starch when ironing.*

folk *n.* °people, °tribe, (ethnic) °group, °clan, °race; °society, °nation, (°general) °public, °populace, °population, citizenry: *Archaeologists refer to these people as the 'Beaker Folk'. Some folks disliked the performance.*

follow *v.* **1** °go or °come after or next; °go or °walk or tread or °move behind, bring up the rear, *Colloq* °string or °tag along: *You go on ahead and I'll follow shortly. Please see the comments that follow.* **2** adhere to, °cleave to, °support, °believe in, °accept, °adopt, °conform to, °comply with, °obey, be guided by, be modelled after or on, °observe, °heed, °mind, °go along with, °reflect, °mirror, °echo, °imitate, °copy, °mimic, ape: *This newspaper follows strict party policy.* **3** °attend, °accompany, °escort, °go (along) with, °serve: *Mary's little lamb followed her everywhere.* **4** °chase, °pursue, dog, °hunt (down), °stalk, °run down, °track, °trail, °tail, °trace, °shadow: *The detective swore to follow him to the ends of the earth.* **5** °succeed, °supersede, °step into the shoes of, take the °place of, °replace, °supplant: *Who followed Henry VIII on the throne?* **6** °practise, °pursue, °engage in, °carry on, °occupy oneself with, °apply or °dedicate or °devote oneself to, °cultivate: *After the war he followed a career as a teacher.* **7** °result from, ensue, °issue, °flow, °arise, °develop: *The conclusion follows logically*

from the premise. **8** °understand, °fathom, °comprehend, °get, °grasp, °see, °catch, °appreciate, °take in, °keep up with, *Colloq* °dig: *Were you able to follow everything in that lecture?* **9** °watch, be a °fan *or* aficionado of, °pursue, take an °interest in, °keep up with, °keep abreast of, °cheer *or* °root for, °admire: *He follows international yacht racing.* **10 follow through (on)**: °persist *or* °persevere, °continue, °perform, conclude, °realize, consummate, °pursue, °carry out, °see through, °make good, °discharge, adhere to, °keep: *I only hope she follows this through and delivers the goods.*
11 follow up (on): **a** °pursue, °go after, °track, °investigate, °check (out), °check up (on), °inquire, make inquiries, °look into: *MacGregor is very good at following up on the most obscure references.* **b** °pursue, °prosecute, °reinforce, consolidate, °support, °buttress, augment, °bolster, °ensure: *The Romans followed up their success with an attack on Olbia.*

follower *n.* **1** °disciple, adherent, °student, °pupil, °apprentice, °protégé(e): *They were followers of Buddha.* **2** °attendant, °henchman, °servant, retainer, bodyguard, myrmidon: *Louie walked in with two of his followers.* **3** °supporter, °devotee, °fan, aficionado, promoter, °enthusiast, booster, °advocate, °proponent, *US* rooter, *Colloq* groupie: *She is a faithful follower of The Dirty Knees, a rock group.*

follow-through *n.* °perseverance, diligence, °persistence, steadfastness, °endurance, °stamina, indefatigableness, sedulousness, sedulity, pursuance, °tenacity, °resolve, °determination, *Colloq US* stick-to-it-iveness: *One needs imagination for new ideas but follow-through to make them succeed.*

follow-up *n.* °reinforcement, °support, backup, bolstering; consolidation: *The failure of the sales campaign was attributed to lack of follow-up.*

folly *n.* **1** foolishness, °nonsense, °absurdity, daftness, silliness, preposterousness, absurdness, senselessness, fatuousness, fatuity, rashness, °stupidity, asininity, inanity, nonsensicalness, idiocy, imbecility, irrationality, °lunacy, °insanity, °madness, craziness, °eccentricity, weak-mindedness, feeble-mindedness, simple-mindedness, muddle-headedness, thickheadedness, stolidity, stolidness, obtuseness, brainlessness, *Colloq* dumbness, dopiness, nuttiness, *US and Canadian* kookiness: *They saw the folly of fighting against such enormous odds. It would be folly to leave in this storm.* **2** °absurdity, °mistake, °blunder, °error, faux pas, gaffe, *Colloq* goof, °fluff: *What follies have been committed in the name of honour!*

foment *v.* °rouse, °stir *or* °whip up, °awaken, waken, °provoke, °incite, instigate, °initiate, °prompt, °start, °motivate, °inspire, °work up, °inflame, °fan the flames (of), °kindle, galvanize, °rally, °excite, °stimulate, °encourage, promote, °foster, °forward, °further, °advance, °cultivate, °sow the seeds of, °spur, goad, egg on, °urge: *He is always fomenting ill will against the management.*

fond *adj.* **1** °tender, loving, °affectionate, °warm, adoring, caring: *She clasped him in a fond embrace.* **2** °foolish, °bootless, °empty, °vain, °naïve: *She had fond hopes of his being elected.*
3 fond of: °partial to, (having a) °liking (for), °soft on *or* about, °affectionate towards,

°attached to, having a °fancy *or* °taste for, fancying, predisposed *or* °inclined to *or* towards; addicted to, *Colloq* hooked on: *She is inordinately fond of chocolate.*

fondle *v.* °caress, °stroke, °pet, °pat, °touch, °cuddle, °snuggle; °handle: *See that couple over there fondling one another? He fondled his dagger.*

fondly *adv.* affectionately, lovingly, tenderly, °warmly, adoringly, caressingly: *Martin regarded his wife fondly.*

food *n.* °nourishment, nutriment, aliment, °sustenance, °subsistence; foodstuffs, edibles, eatables, viands, bread, victuals, °rations, °provisions, comestibles, *Brit* commons, *Colloq* grub, eats, chow, *Brit* °scoff, prog: *Without any food for days, the survivors were near starvation.*

fool *n.* **1** simpleton, ninny, ninny-hammer, nincompoop, ass, jackass, dunce, °dolt, °halfwit, numskull *or* numbskull, blockhead, bonehead, pinhead, °silly, feather-brain, loon, goose, booby, jay, goon, mooncalf, idiot, ignoramus, dim-wit, nitwit, imbecile, moron, °clod, clodpole, clodpoll, clodpate, oaf, *Psychology* retardate, *Scots* gomerel, *Colloq* birdbrain, dumb-bell, fat-head, chump, °twit, knuckle-head, chuckle-head, nit, twerp *or* twirp, *Brit* pillock, *US and Canadian* °jerk, °retard; *Slang* °sap, °dope, *Brit* git, *Australian* boofhead: *He's such a fool he'll believe anything.* **2** (court) jester, °clown, °comic, °comedian *or* comedienne, entertainer, °zany, buffoon, °merry andrew, *farceur, farceuse*, °joker, jokester, droll, Punch, Punchinello, pierrot, harlequin: *In Shakespeare's plays, the fool is often the wisest character.* **3** °butt, °dupe, gull, °victim, cat's-paw, *Colloq* chump, °greenhorn, (easy) °mark, *US* fall guy; *Slang* pigeon, °sucker, stooge, *Brit* °mug: *His co-workers liked to make a fool out of him.*
—*v.* **4** °trick, °deceive, °take in, °swindle, °defraud, °hoax, °cheat, °fleece, cozen, °hoodwink, °bluff, °dupe, gull, humbug, delude, °mislead, make a fool of; pull the wool over (someone's) eyes, °have (someone) on, °pull (someone's) °leg, °tease, °twit, *Archaic* chouse; *Colloq* kid, con, snow, do a snow job on, bamboozle, °put one *or* something over on, pull something *or* a fast one on, *Brit* °twist, *Chiefly US and Canadian* josh; *Slang* °pluck, *Brit* nobble: *When he said the diamond was fake, he certainly fooled me. I think she was fooling when she said she'd inherited millions.* **5** °joke, jest, °banter, °tease, °twit, feign, °fake, °pretend, °make °believe, *Colloq* kid: *She insists that she is not fooling but dead serious.* **6 fool with** *or* **around** *or* **about (with)**: °play (around *or* about) (with), °toy *or* °trifle (with), °mess *or* °fiddle (around *or* about) (with), °monkey (around *or* about) with, °meddle (with), °tamper with, fribble (with): *Please stop fooling with the dials on the radio.* **7 fool around** *or* **about**: **a** °play *or* °mess around *or* about, gambol, °frolic, romp, °cavort: *Stop fooling around and get serious.* **b** °waste *or* °fritter away *or* squander *or* kill time, fribble, loiter, °dawdle, °idle, *Brit* °potter (about), °lark *or* °muck about *or* around, *US* putter around *or* about, *Colloq* footle: *She's always fooling around instead of getting on with her work.*

foolhardy *adj.* °rash, °imprudent, °impetuous, °reckless, °brash, °venturesome, °bold, °cheeky, °daring, °audacious, temerarious, °adventurous, °daredevil, incautious,

°hotheaded, °careless, °heedless, devil-may-care, °hasty, °thoughtless, °unthinking, °irresponsible, °wild, madcap, Colloq US and Canadian nervy, Slang gutsy: It is foolhardy to go scuba diving without a companion.

foolish adj. **1** °senseless, incautious, °imprudent, impolitic, °indiscreet, unwise, injudicious, ill-considered, °ill-advised, °misguided, °short-sighted, °impetuous, head-long, °rash, °brash, °reckless, °hasty, °heedless, °unwary, °foolhardy, °thoughtless, °mindless: Standing under a tree in a thunderstorm is foolish. **2** °nonsensical, °stupid, asinine, °inane, °silly, fatuous, fatuitous, dim-witted, °scatterbrained, °hare-brained, °crazy, °mad, °insane, demented, irrational, °erratic, °unstable, crack-brained, feather-brained, bird-brained, simple-minded, light-headed, muddle-headed, numskulled or numbskulled, addle-pated, rattle-brained, bemused, °confused, °feeble-minded, moronic, idiotic, imbecilic, °halfwitted, dull-witted, slow-witted, witless, brainless, empty-headed, blockheaded, boneheaded, thickheaded, °obtuse, °stolid, Colloq °dumb, balmy or Brit barmy, loony, nuts, nutty, batty, dopey or dopy, °soft (in the head), °dim, °thick, dippy, dotty, °dizzy, Brit potty, °daft, Slang cuckoo, goofy, screwy, wacky: Tracy was foolish to believe him when he said he loved her. **3** °preposterous, °ridiculous, °absurd, irra-tional, illogical, °unreasonable, °ludicrous, °wild: They have some foolish idea about building a hotel in Antarctica.

foolproof adj. °safe, °certain, °sure, °trustworthy, dependable, °reliable, °infallible, unfailing, guaranteed, warranted, Colloq sure-fire: She claims to have a foolproof way of preventing unwanted pregnancies.

footing n. **1** °foundation, °basis, °base, °ground(s): The events put our entire relationship on a new footing. **2** °standing, °status, °level, °condition, °position, terms, °state, °rank: The two departments are on an equal footing as far as funding is concerned. **3** foothold, toe-hold; °balance, °stability: She lost her footing on the icy pavement and down she went.

footstep n. **1** °step, footfall, tread: I recognized her footstep. **2** Usually, **footsteps**: footprint(s), °track, °trail, °trace, spoor, footmark(s); °tradition, °example, °way of life: He followed in his master's footsteps.

for prep. **1** representing, championing; in °favour of, Brit on or US and Canadian also in °behalf of, on the °side of, in °support of, in the °service of, as a °service to, for the °benefit of, pro: Are you for or against the candidate? She did it for herself. **2** in °search or °quest of, seeking, look-ing for or after, after, with a °view or an °eye to: We're just here for the beer. **3** °instead of, in °place of, representing, as a replacement for, Brit on or US and Canadian also in °behalf of; in °return or °exchange for, in compensation or recompense or °payment or repayment for, in °requital for: I am acting for my father. This cheque is for the toaster. Will you accept nothing for your pains? **4** for the °treatment of, as a °remedy for, against; for the °purpose or °object of: This medication is for skin infections only. It's for your own good. **5** for the °sake of, Brit on or US and Canadian also in °behalf of, in the °interest of: Would you really do that for me? **6** in the °direction of, to,

°towards, into: Head for the hills! **7** to °save, in the °interest or °benefit of, for the °sake or °benefit of, conducive to; because of, on °account of, by °reason of: Every summer, they went to Carlsbad for their health. She hated him for what he represented. **8** to °go to, °destined for: I am leaving for Tierra del Fuego tomorrow. **9** °suitable or suited for, °fit or °fitted or °fitting for, °appropriate for, °proper for: I am not sure that this colour is for you. Is it right for me to speak out now? **10** for the duration of; over (the °extent of), during, in the °course of, °throughout, °through: She stayed for a week. **11** °despite, in °spite of, °notwithstanding, allowing for: For all his complaining, he seemed satisfied. **12 as for**: °regarding, in °regard to, as regards, respecting, °concerning, as °far as (something or someone) is °concerned: As for Betty, let her do as she likes. —conj. **13** because, since, as, inasmuch as, °seeing that, owing or °due to the °fact that: I was unable to see him, for he was out of the office.

forbid v. °prohibit, °ban, °hinder, °stop, °exclude, debar, °preclude, °prevent; °outlaw, interdict, disallow, proscribe, °taboo; °veto: I was forbidden from entering. They forbid smoking in the classrooms.

forbidding adj. **1** °repellent, °repulsive, °offensive, odious, °abhorrent: In his long cloak and mask, he presented a forbidding appearance. **2** °hostile, unfriendly, °stern, °harsh, °menacing, °threatening, °ominous, °dangerous, °bad, °nasty, °ugly, unpleasant: The coast here is rocky and forbidding. The old crone gave him a forbidding look and we cringed.

force n. **1** °power, °might, °energy, °strength, potency, °vigour, °intensity, °violence, °impact; °dynamism, °pressure: The force of the blow knocked me down. **2** coercion, °pressure, constraint, °duress, compulsion, arm-twisting: When persuasion failed, the guards resorted to force. **3** troops, °soldiers, army: NATO forces are on manoeuvres. **4** °weight, persuasiveness, °persistence, cogency, effectiveness, efficacy, °strength, validity, °significance, value: The force of his argument was sufficient to convince us. **5** °meaning, °import, °significance: Are they able to cope with the full force of the word 'God'? **6 in force**: in °effect, °effective, in °operation, °operative, valid, binding, °current: The ancient customs still remain in force. The law came into force at midnight. —v. **7** °make, °oblige, °require, compel, coerce, °exact, constrain, °enforce, impel, °intimidate, °pressure or Brit also pressurize, °press, dragoon, °twist (someone's) arm, Colloq bulldoze, put the °squeeze on (someone): Each of us was forced to dig his own grave. **8** °push, °drive, °thrust, °propel; prise or °prize, °break, °wrench, °crack, jemmy, US °pry: The tornado forced the chair through the wall. He forced open the safe and took the money. **9** °exact, °extort, °extract, wrest, wring, °drag: The CIA tried to force a confession from her.

forced adj. °artificial, °unnatural, contrived, °stilted, °calculated, °studied, °laboured, °strained, °stiff, °false, feigned, °fake(d), °mannered, °affected, °self-conscious, Colloq °phoney or US also phony: Her forced joviality failed to conceal her contempt for those present.

forceful adj. **1** °vigorous, °energetic, com-pelling, °dynamic, °intense, °potent, °strong,

°mighty, °powerful, °aggressive, °weighty, °effective, convincing, °persuasive: *The colonel was known as a forceful leader of men.* **2** °effective, °efficacious, cogent, °logical, °impressive, °telling, convincing, °persuasive, °strong, °mighty, °forcible, °powerful, compelling, °irresistible; pithy, meaty: *The most forceful arguments came from Catherine towards the end of the discussion.*

forcible *adj.* **1** See forceful, 2, above. **2** °drastic, °forceful, °violent, °aggressive, coercive, °severe, stringent: *The plan involves the forcible repatriation of refugees.*

foreboding *n.* **1** apprehension, apprehensiveness, °feeling, °sense, °misgiving, °dread, °suspicion, °intuition, °anxiety, °fear: *An atmosphere of foreboding filled the crypt.* **2** °premonition, augury, °prophecy, °prediction, prognostication, °warning, foretoken, foreshadowing, presentiment, °omen, °sign, portent, intimation, forewarning, presage, °advance word: *I had a strange foreboding of horror as I entered the room.*

forecast *v.* **1** °predict, foretell, °prophesy, °prognosticate, °foresee, augur, presage, vaticinate, °anticipate; forewarn, °calculate: *Seers forecast coming events; meteorologists forecast the weather.* —*n.* **2** °prediction, °prophecy, °prognosis, prognostication, °foresight, augury, vaticination, °anticipation; forewarning, °calculation: *Have you heard the weather forecast for tomorrow?*

foregoing *adj.* °preceding, °above, °former, °previous, °precedent, °prior, antecedent; earlier, °preliminary, anterior; aforementioned, aforesaid: *The foregoing paragraph set forth the principles.*

foregone *adj.* Usually in **foregone conclusion**: °assumed, established, pre-established, °predetermined, °fixed, °inevitable, °set, accepted, °cut and dried: *His incarceration for the crime was a foregone conclusion.*

foreign *adj.* **1** °alien, imported, non-native, °overseas, °distant, tramontane, transalpine, transatlantic, transpacific: *Duty is payable on foreign goods. We holiday in a different foreign country each year.* **2** °strange, °outlandish, °exotic, °unfamiliar, °peculiar, °odd, °curious: *She regards anything except beans and toast as foreign food.* **3** °unknown, °unfamiliar, °strange, °inappropriate, °unrelated, unconnected, unassimilable, °remote, °extrinsic, °extraneous: *Their philosophy is completely foreign to my way of thinking.*

foreigner *n.* °alien, non-native, °immigrant, °newcomer, °new °arrival, °outsider, outlander, °stranger: *The word xenophobia means 'dread of foreigners'.*

foreman *n.* °superintendent, °manager, °boss, °supervisor, °overseer, *Brit* shopwalker, *US* floor-walker, *Colloq* °super, *Brit* gaffer, *US* straw °boss: *The foreman insists we use the time clocks.*

foremost *adj.* **1** °first, °primary, °prime, °leading, °pre-eminent, °supreme, °prominent, °notable, °noteworthy, °noted, °chief, °paramount, °main, °best, °superior: *She is one of the foremost eye surgeons in her country.* —*adv.* **2** °first, firstly, °primarily, in (the) °first place, before anything else: *First and foremost, we must consider the matter of safety.*

forerunner *n.* **1** °predecessor, °precursor, foregoer; herald, °harbinger, °envoy; forebear, °ancestor, forefather, °progenitor: *This dishwasher is better designed than its forerunners. The cuckoo is thought by many to be the forerunner of spring.* **2** °omen, portent, foretoken, °premonition, °sign, augury, °token: *A drop in the barometer is a forerunner of bad weather.*

foresee *v.* presage, foretell, °envisage, °picture, °forecast, °predict, °prophesy, augur, *US* °envision: *I don't foresee any problems.*

foreshadow *v.* presage, foretoken, portend, augur, °indicate, °prophesy, °predict, °bode, °signal, °signify, betoken: *The surrender of Ghent foreshadowed the fate of Flanders.*

foresight *n.* **1** °providence, °prudence, °care, far-sightedness, watchfulness, °caution, °precaution, long-sightedness, perspicacity, °wisdom, sagacity, °insight, circumspection: *The commander demonstrated foresight in ordering a retreat.* **2** prevision, °perception, °prospect, °vision, foreknowledge, prescience; °expectation: *A little foresight could have prevented the calamity.*

forestall *v.* °anticipate, °prevent, °obstruct, °hinder, obviate, °thwart, °preclude, °frustrate, avert, °ward or stave or °fend off, °intercept, parry, °stop, °delay: *The frigate effectively forestalled our plan to sail away secretly.*

forethought *n.* premeditation, planning, plotting, far-sightedness, long-sightedness: *Much forethought went into the assassination scheme.*

for ever *adv.* **1** forever, °always, for good, °ever, (for) evermore, forevermore, eternally, everlastingly, for °ever and a day, undyingly, for °eternity, till doomsday, till the °end of °time, *Colloq* till the cows come home, till hell freezes over: *They swore to be true for ever.* **2** forever, constantly, continually, continuously, all the °time, unceasingly, incessantly, without °cease or surcease, endlessly, °consistently, persistently, interminably, perpetually: *She was for ever watching soap operas on the telly.*

foreword *n.* °preface, prologue, prelude, prolegomenon, °preamble, *Literary* proem; introduction: *He set forth the purpose of the book in the foreword.*

forfeit *n.* **1** °penalty, °fine, °fee, °charge, damages, forfeiture, sequestration, amercement, mulct: *You will have to give me a kiss as a forfeit.* —*v.* **2** °lose, °yield (up), °give up or over, °relinquish, °surrender, be °stripped or °deprived of, °forgo, °renounce, °waive: *You have forfeited your right to trial and you will be hanged at dawn.* —*adj.* **3** surrendered, °lost, yielded, relinquished, forgone, waived, renounced: *His life was forfeit the moment he volunteered to defuse the bomb.*

forge *v.* **1** °make, °construct, °fashion, °fabricate, °manufacture, °shape, °mould, °cast, hammer out: *This plant forges heavy steel tools. He forged a new life for himself in the American West.* **2** °create, °invent, °conceive (of), °coin, °devise, °think up, °frame: *I have forged a new plan of escape.* **3** °counterfeit, °copy, °reproduce, °imitate, °falsify, °fake, *Slang US* hang paper: *She forged her employer's name on the cheque. The gang was caught because they forged three-pound notes.*

forgery *n.* **1** counterfeiting, falsification, °fraud, fraudulence: *He was sent to prison for ten years* for *forgery*. **2** °counterfeit, °fake, °sham, °imitation, *Colloq* °phoney *or US also* phony: *The police have found three forgeries of Dali paintings.*

forget *v.* **1** °fail *or* °cease to °remember *or* °recall *or* °think of, °lose, draw a °blank: *I forgot what I was supposed to buy at the market.* **2** °leave (behind), °omit *or* °neglect (doing *or* taking): *I forgot my umbrella this morning.* **3** °ignore, °dismiss from (one's) °mind *or* thoughts, °disregard, °overlook, consign to °oblivion: *Forget the fact that you ever met me.*

forgetful *adj.* amnesiac; °absent-minded, distracted, abstracted, °inattentive, °preoccupied, neglectful, negligent, °careless, °lax, °dreamy, dreaming, in dreamland, in the clouds, in cloud-cuckoo-land *or* cloud-land *or* Nephelococcygia, °remote, distrait(e), *Colloq* not turned on, turned off, out of it: *Franklin is so forgetful he'd lose his head if it weren't stitched on.*

forgive *v.* **1** °pardon, °excuse, °allow, make °allowance(s) for, °indulge, condone, °vindicate; °overlook, °ignore, °disregard, pay no °attention to, °pass over, *US* slough over: *Please forgive my curiosity, but where did you get that hat?* **2** °clear, acquit, absolve, exculpate, exonerate; °spare; *Colloq* °let off: *Father, forgive them, for they know not what they do.* **3** °cancel, °waive, °abolish, °void, nullify, °erase, °delete; *Colloq* °let off (the °hook): *Her dream was to awake one day and find all her debts forgiven.*

forgiveness *n.* **1** °pardon, °reprieve, absolution, °remission, °acquittal, acquittance, amnesty, °allowance, vindication, exculpation, exoneration, *Archaic* shrift: *Oh, Lord, I ask forgiveness for my sins.* **2** °mercy, mercifulness, compassion, °grace, leniency, clemency, °indulgence, °tolerance: *He begged her forgiveness for the way he had treated her.*

forgiving *adj.* °tolerant, °lenient, °sparing, forbearing, °merciful, compassionate, conciliatory, magnanimous, humane, °soft-hearted, clement: *In a forgiving mood, the judge gave her a light sentence.*

forgo *v.* **1** °give up, °renounce, forswear, °forsake, °abandon, °go without, °sacrifice, °eliminate, °omit, °leave out *or* °alone, °cede, °waive; °avoid, °shun, eschew, abstain from, °turn down, °pass up, °deny (oneself): *His new diet requires him to forgo all dairy produce.* **2** °resign, °give up, °yield, °surrender, °relinquish, °cede, °waive, °renounce, forswear, °abdicate, °abandon: *Did he not forgo all right to the throne by marrying a commoner?*

forlorn *adj.* **1** °miserable, °wretched, °desolate, °woebegone, °lost, °pitiable, °pitiful, °pathetic, woeful, cheerless, °joyless, °unhappy, depressed, °sad, disconsolate, °gloomy, lugubrious, °glum, °despondent, °dismal, °dejected, dispirited, low-spirited, comfortless, down, °melancholy, dolorous, °sorrowful, °mournful, °inconsolable: *She looked so fragile and forlorn as she struggled to hold back her tears.* **2** °abandoned, forsaken, °deserted, neglected, shunned, °outcast, °alone, °lonely, °lonesome, friendless, bereft: *We came upon a forlorn little village.*

form *n.* **1** °shape, configuration, conformation, °order, °organization, °arrangement, °formation, construction, °structure, °construct, °frame, °cut, °cast, °mould, °pattern, °appearance; °manifestation: *The equipment in the playground was in a variety of geometric forms. In what form will the jinnee appear next?* **2** °figure, °body, °build, °shape, °physique, anatomy; °silhouette, °aspect, °look, °appearance, °profile, contour; °carriage, °bearing, °attitude, °pose, *Slang US* bod, built: *She has the form of a wrestler.* **3** °type, °kind, °variety, °sort, °breed, species, genus, °genre, °character, °make, °brand, °colour, °tone, °tint, °texture, °fabric, °material, feather, °description, °manner, °way, °nature, °style, °stamp, °manifestation: *What forms of life are not of divine origin? He revelled in music in all its forms.* **4** °blank, °model, °format, °frame, framework, °course, °procedure, °order, regimen, °method, °system, °ritual, °formula, °rule(s), °practice, °technique, °way, °means, °approach, °mode, °fashion, °manner, °style: *Fill in the application form in ink. Please follow the proper form when submitting articles.* **5** °condition, °state, °shape, °trim, fettle: *He seems in unusually good form tonight.* **6** °decorum, °behaviour, deportment, °formality, °ceremony, °convention, °etiquette, manners, °conduct, °custom, °protocol, °propriety, °ritual: *Follow correct form when writing to the king. Spitting is considered bad form.*
—*v.* **7** °make, °fabricate, °forge, °shape, °mould, °fashion, °produce, °turn out, °manufacture, °construct, °assemble, °put together, °set up, °put up, °build, °erect, elevate, °raise; °organize, codify; °develop: *The architect takes the many elements and forms them into a coherent whole. Have you formed an opinion of the book?* **8** °create, °originate, °devise, °invent, °compose, °formulate, give form *or* °shape, °coin, concoct, °conceive, contrive, °dream up, °imagine, visualize, °envisage, *US* °envision: *His ideas of religion were formed when he was very young. A picture of the battle was formed in my mind.* **9** °make up, constitute, be made up of, comprise, be composed of; °serve as: *This compound is formed of many elements. Six fugues formed the main part of the programme.* **10** °acquire, °develop, °cultivate, °contract; °get: *In prison I formed the habit of rolling my own cigarettes. We formed a lasting friendship.* **11** °develop, °grow, °arise, °appear, °materialize, °show up, take °shape *or* form, °accumulate: *When the yeast is added, a barm forms on the surface.*

formal *adj.* **1** °standard, °conventional, °customary, established, prescribed, °regular, °normal, °correct, °proper; °strict, formulaic, °inflexible, punctilious, °exacting, unchanging, °methodical, °orderly, °systematic, °set, pro forma, °ritual, ritualistic, °ceremonial, °proper, °official, °routine, °fixed, °rigid, °stiff, °stilted, °stately, starched, unbending, °solemn; confining, °straitened, °limited; *Colloq* °straight, °square: *Formal rules of behaviour are observed.* **2** °explicit, °express, °definite, spelt *or* spelled out, formalized, °authorized, °official, °solemn, °legal, °lawful: *Formal demands have been made for the withdrawal of our ambassador.* **3** prim, °ceremonious, °dignified, °stuffy, °strait-laced, °stiff, °precise, °exact: *He made a formal bow and left our company.*

formality n. 1 Often, **the formalities**: °form, °convention, conventionality, °practice, °procedure, °custom, wont, °observance, °protocol, °ceremony, °rite, °ritual: *Observe the legal formalities by having this document witnessed. Formality requires that you walk backwards out of the room.* 2 strictness, punctilio, exactness, °precision, correctness, rigidity, stiffness, inflexibility: *We must maintain the formality of Sunday service.* 3 °etiquette, politesse, °decorum, punctilio, conformity, °propriety: *Formality prohibits casual conversation.*

format n. 1 °appearance, °look(s), °aspect, lay-out, °plan, °design, °style, °form, dimension(s), °shape, °size: *In its present format, the magazine resembles an academic journal.* 2 °composition, °content(s), °make-up, constitution, °arrangement, °plan, °organization, °order, °set-up: *Her TV programme has the format of a chat show.*

formation n. 1 °development, °appearance, materialization, °shape, °accumulation, °generation, °creation, crystallization, forming, genesis, °production: *The formation of bubbles indicates that the acid is working.* 2 °establishment, °institution, °creation, founding, °set-up, organizing, °organization, °development, °composition: *We met to discuss the formation of a new company.* 3 array, °display, °pattern, °arrangement, °structure, grouping, °organization, configuration, °disposition: *The vast military formation covered the entire valley.*

former adj. 1 °previous, earlier, °prior, ex-, one-time, °preceding, erstwhile, °late, °latest, °last, °recent, ci-devant, quondam, Archaic whilom: *I ran into a former girl-friend at the art show.* 2 °old, °past, °bygone, °ancient, (pre) historic, departed, antediluvian: *In former times, one could demand—and get—decent service.*

formerly adv. °once, °before, °previously, hitherto, °long ago, at °one °time, in the °old days, °once upon a °time, in days gone by, in days or °time °past, °time was, back then, when the world was young(er), Colloq °way back or US also °way back when: *Formerly, there were no tall buildings to block one's view.*

formidable adj. 1 alarming, appalling, °dreadful, °frightful, °awesome, awe-inspiring, °menacing, horrifying, °frightening, intimidating, daunting, petrifying, °terrifying: *A formidable, fire-breathing dragon blocked our exit.* 2 °terrific, °fantastic, °unbelievable, °incredible, °impressive, °prodigious, mind-boggling, °awesome, Colloq mind-blowing, freaky: *They are a formidable talent and will sell a million records this year.* 3 °arduous, °indomitable, °overwhelming, staggering, °powerful, °mighty, °difficult, challenging, °burdensome, onerous: *She has formidable obstacles to overcome before becoming a doctor.*

formula n. °recipe, rubric, formulary; °rule(s), °prescription, °directions, °instructions, blueprint, °method, °technique, °means, °way, °pattern, °procedure, modus operandi, Colloq US MO: *Ali Baba uttered the formula, 'Open sesame!', and the rock opened. Alchemists sought to discover a formula for making gold from lead.*

formulate v. 1 systematize, codify, °define, °specify, articulate, particularize, °denote: *You must try to formulate your ideas more clearly.* 2 °devise, °originate, °create, °think up or of, °dream up, °conceive, concoct, °invent, °improvise, Colloq cook up: *I have formulated a plan in my mind to deal with the problem.* 3 °develop, °forge, evolve, °work out, °design, map out, °block out, °draw up: *You have three days to formulate a workable procedure.*

forsake v. 1 °abandon, °desert, °quit, °leave, °flee, °depart, °vacate: *He forsook balmy California to dig for gold in the Klondike.* 2 °abandon, °desert, °leave, °jilt, °reject, °throw over, jettison, °cast off: *She has forsaken Michael for another man.* 3 °give up, °yield, °renounce, °repudiate, °relinquish, °forgo, forswear, °surrender, °resign, °abdicate, °recant, °deny, have or be done with, °turn one's back on: *Would you forsake a throne for the love of a woman?*

forte n. °talent, strong point, °gift, °speciality or US specialty, °strength, °aptitude, °genius, Colloq long suit: *His forte is carving ivory miniatures.*

forthcoming adj. 1 approaching, nearing, °impending, °imminent, coming, upcoming; °near or °close (by), (°near or °close) at °hand, in the offing, on the °horizon, Colloq Brit on the °cards, US in the °cards: *The forthcoming tax increase will affect everyone. A new regulation is forthcoming.* 2 awaited, expected, anticipated, looked-for, watched for, °prospective, foreseen: *The forthcoming payment will be a little late.* 3 °outgoing, °friendly, °amiable, affable, °sociable, °accessible, °expansive, chatty, °talkative, communicative, °informative, °open, °free, revealing, unreserved: *Barry was most forthcoming when questioned about his finances.*

forthright adj. straightforward, °direct, °blunt, °candid, °frank, °above-board, unambiguous, unequivocal, °open, °outspoken, °uninhibited, unreserved, unconstrained, unrestrained: *She has always been forthright and honest in her dealings with me.*

fortify v. 1 °strengthen, °reinforce, shore up, °buttress, °brace, °bolster, °secure: *Steel plates were used to fortify the walls.* 2 °cheer, °encourage, hearten, °buoy, invigorate, °energize, embolden, °reassure, °brace: *Her enthusiasm fortified him to face what was coming.* 3 °supplement, °enhance, °enrich, °boost, augment: *The drink was fortified by the addition of whisky.*

fortitude n. °strength, mettle, °backbone, °courage, °nerve, °resolution, resoluteness, °perseverance, °endurance, °tenacity, pertinacity, °grit, °determination, will-power, Colloq °guts: *His encouragement gave me the fortitude to carry on.*

fortunate adj. 1 °lucky, in °luck, fortuitous, blessed: *You were fortunate to have survived the crash.* 2 °favoured, °advantageous, °propitious, auspicious, °providential, °favourable, °opportune, °timely, °well-timed: *It was a fortunate time to be buying a house.*

fortune n. 1 °position, °worth, °means, °assets, holdings, °wealth, °property, °estate, °possessions; °riches, affluence, opulence, °treasure, °money, °prosperity: *Each member is liable to the full extent of his fortune. He acquired* *his fortune from oil.* **2** °luck, °chance, fortuity; °lot, °fate, kismet, °destiny, karma; °future; *US* happenstance: *It was just fortune that put me in the right place at the right time. She'll tell your fortune if you cross her palm with silver.* **3** Usually, **fortunes:** °circumstance(s), °experience(s), °adventures, °expectation(s), °lot: *My fortunes of late have been poor.*

fortune-teller *n.* °oracle, soothsayer, °prophet, diviner, augur, °seer, clairvoyant, prognosticator, sibyl, haruspex, crystal-gazer, tea-leaf reader, palmist, palm reader, star-gazer; futurologist: *The fortune-teller said to beware the Ides of March.*

forward *adj.* **1** °advance, °leading, °foremost, °front, °head, °first: *The forward contingents of the army moved into the town.* **2** °bold, °pert, °impudent, °brash, °insolent, °impertinent, °disrespectful, °brazen, °audacious, °rash, unashamed, °unabashed, saucy, °flippant, °presumptuous, °cheeky, *Colloq* °flip, °fresh, °pushy: *It was a bit forward of you to call the chairman by his nickname.* **3** (well-)advanced, (°well-)developed, °progressive, °precocious, forward-looking: *She was quite a forward girl at fifteen.*
—*adv.* **4** forwards, °ahead, °onward, along; clockwise, deasil: *I moved forward to the head of the queue. Set the clock forward an hour tonight.* **5** up, °out, forth, to the fore, into °consideration, into °view, into the °open, to the surface, on to the °table: *Cooper brought forward an interesting proposal.*
—*v.* **6** °advance, °further, °promote, °back, °foster, °support, °aid, °assist, °help; °patronize, °encourage, °nourish, °nurse along: *He did his best to forward her career.* **7** °dispatch or despatch, °send, °ship, °deliver, °transmit, °express, °post, °mail, consign, °remit; °send on: *The shipment will be forwarded as soon as payment is received. The post office will forward mail to my new address.* **8** °speed (up), accelerate, °advance, °hasten, °expedite, °hurry, °quicken, °step up: *This mixture is said to forward the flowering of plants.*

foster *v.* **1** °promote, °encourage, °stimulate, °further, °forward, °advance, °cultivate, nurture, °nourish, °support, °back, °assist, °help, °aid, succour, °patronize: *Cutting back these off-shoots fosters growth of the main stem. Representatives have fostered acceptance of our products throughout Europe.* **2** °bring up, °rear, °raise, take °care of, °maintain, °care for: *The Cartwrights have fostered eight orphans in their home.*

foul *adj.* **1** °offensive, °loathsome, °disgusting, °obnoxious, °revolting, °repulsive, °repellent, °repugnant, sickening, °nauseous, nauseating, °nasty, °beastly, *Archaic* fulsome: *The bartender makes a foul concoction he swears will cure a hangover.* **2** °filthy, unclean, °nasty, polluted, °putrid, putrescent, putrefactive *or* putrefacient, defiled, soiled, spoiled, °rotten, decayed, decomposed, °rancid, soured, turned, tainted, °mouldy, °impure, adulterated, contaminated, °stale, °bad, *Brit* off: *The hamburger place was closed when public health inspectors found foul food in the freezer.* **3** °smelly, °stinking, noisome, fetid *or* foetid, °rank, evil-smelling, foul-smelling, malodorous, °musty, mephitic, graveolent: *A foul odour emanated from the*

cabinet. **4** °wicked, °vile, °bad, °base, °abominable, °low, °sordid, iniquitous, °evil, flagitious, °atrocious, °monstrous, nefarious, °sinful, °immoral, amoral, °vicious, °villainous, °scandalous, °infamous, °dishonourable, °shameful, °disgraceful, ignominious; detestable: *They were finally brought to justice for their foul deeds.* **5** °dirty, °obscene, °filthy, °profane, scatological, °gross, smutty, foul-mouthed, °blue, licentious, salacious, °lewd, °indecent, °improper, °coarse, uncouth, °vulgar, °rude, °scurrilous, °rough, indelicate, °immodest, °risqué, off colour, °suggestive, °bawdy, ribald, Rabelaisian, Fescennine, *US* °raw, *Slang* raunchy: *My mother forbids my reading books containing foul language.* **6** °abusive, °offensive, affronting, insulting, disparaging, maligning, thersitical, calumnious *or* calumniatory, aspersive, °slanderous, defamatory, libellous, denigrating, °derogatory, deprecatory *or* deprecative, depreciatory *or* depreciative, denunciatory *or* denunciative, °derisory, derisive, °scornful, belittling, fulminous, objurgatory *or* objurgative, °vituperative, invective: *Keep your foul tongue to yourself.* **7** °dishonest, unfair, unjust, unsportsmanlike, °dishonourable, °fraudulent, underhand(ed), double-dealing, °two-faced, °corrupt, °venal, °dirty, treacherous, °perfidious, °traitorous, °unscrupulous, *Colloq* °crooked, °shady, *Slang chiefly Brit* °bent: *Thrupp will get his way by fair means or foul.* **8** °nasty, °dangerous, °rough, °disagreeable, unfavourable, °sloppy, °stormy, adverse; °windy, blustery; snowy, sleety, °wet, rainy: *We ran into a spot of foul weather at Dover.* **9** obstructed, blocked, choked, stopped (up), plugged (up), clogged (up): *The drain is foul with all that rubbish.* **10** tangled, entangled, caught, ensnared, enmeshed, snarled: *A foul anchor is a common nautical symbol.* **11** °illegal, prohibited, forbidden, interdicted, not °fair; °dirty: *In boxing a hit below the belt is a foul blow.*
—*v.* **12** °dirty, °pollute, °sully, befoul, defile, °soil, °contaminate, °adulterate, °taint: *Effluent from the factory was fouling the river.* **13** °tangle, °entangle, catch, °snare, ensnare, enmesh, °snag, °snarl, °jam, °twist: *We can't hoist the mainsail because the halyard is fouled.* **14** °disgrace, °dishonour, °sully, °taint, besmirch, defile, °soil, °stain, °smear, °tarnish, °blacken, denigrate, °debase, °degrade, abase, demean, °disparage, defame, derogate, asperse, devaluate, devalue, °depreciate, °vitiate, °belittle, °discredit, bring *or* call into disrepute: *That act of treachery will foul the family name for generations.* **15** °obstruct, °block, °choke, °stop *or* °plug *or* °clog (up): *Dead leaves fouled the downpipe.* **16 foul up: a** See 13, above. **b** mismanage, °mishandle, °botch, °bungle, make a °mess (of), °mess up, °spoil, °ruin, *Colloq* muff, *Brit* throw a spanner in(to) (the works), *US* throw a monkey wrench into (the machinery); *Slang* °muck up, goof (up), °blow, °screw up, louse up, *Chiefly Brit* °bugger (up), *US and Canadian* snafu: *Give him a chance and he's sure to foul up. She fouled up my hi-fi.*
—*n.* **17** °violation, °infringement, infraction, illegality: *The Rangers' forward has already been charged with two fouls.*
—*adv.* **18** °afoul, in °conflict, in °trouble, in °violation: *Curshaw has fallen foul of the law again.*

foul play n. treachery, °chicanery, °perfidy, perfidiousness, duplicity, double-dealing, °deception, guile, °crime, °sharp °practice, skulduggery, °dirty work or business, °dirty trick(s); °murder, homicide, manslaughter; Colloq °hanky-panky: The travellers suspected foul play when the aeroplane failed to arrive. The hacked up corpse suggested foul play to Detective Lemaître.

found v. 1 °establish, °originate, °institute, °set up, °organize, °inaugurate, °start, °initiate, °create, °bring about, °develop: The society was founded a hundred years ago. 2 °base, °ground, °establish, °set, °build; °rest: This charity was founded on love and concern for children.

foundation n. 1 °basis, °base, substructure, under-structure, underpinning, °bottom, foot, basement, °cellar: This foundation is of stone. 2 °basis, °base, °fundamental, (underlying or °fundamental) °principle, °grounds, °groundwork, °rationale, raison d'être, °purpose: Their morality finds its foundations in Judaeo-Christian culture. 3 founding, °establishment, instituting, °institution, °creation, origination, °setting up, organizing, °organization, inauguration, °endowment: We voted for the foundation of an institute to study the English language.

founder[1] n. originator, °creator, °progenitor, °author, framer, °father, architect, °designer, builder, initiator, establisher, institutor: Today we honour the founder of this great university.

founder[2] v. 1 °sink, °go down or under, °go to Davy Jones's locker, be wrecked or destroyed: Many a proud vessel has foundered on this rock. 2 °fail, °miscarry, °collapse, come to nothing or naught, °fall through, abort, falter, °break down, come to °grief, °die: After Alice left to get married, the business foundered. 3 °trip, °stumble, °stagger, °lurch, °fall, °topple (over or down), °collapse; go °lame: He drove the horse too hard and caused it to founder.

foundling n. orphan, waif; °stray, °outcast: We are trying to raise money for a hospital for foundlings.

fountain n. 1 fount, °spring, font, jet, °spout, °spray, well, well-spring, well-head, fountain-head: Bathing in the city fountains is forbidden. 2 °source, °origin, genesis: Miss Corbell was a fountain of wisdom on the subject of basket-weaving.

foxy adj. 1 °clever, °sly, cunning, °wily, °crafty, °tricky, guileful, °shifty, °devious, °slippery, °smooth, °slick, °artful, °resourceful, °ingenious, °calculating, °designing, plotting, °scheming, °disingenuous, °knowing, °shrewd, °sharp, °astute, °wise; foxlike, vulpine; Colloq cagey or cagy: Be careful dealing with him, for he can be foxy. 2 °attractive, alluring, °seductive, vampish, Colloq °sexy: Margo is a very foxy lady.

fracas n. 1 °trouble, °disturbance, commotion, °rumpus, °fuss, hubbub, °pandemonium, hullabaloo, °uproar, °disorder, °scramble, scuffle, °brawl, °rough-house, rough-and-tumble, turmoil, °tumult, free-for-all, °riot, °fray, brouhaha, mêlée or melee, Law affray; Brit scrum, US brannigan; Colloq ruckus, punch-up, Slang Brit bovver: It was football hooligans who caused the fracas after the game. 2 °argument, °disagreement, °quarrel, °dispute, °discord, wrangle, altercation, squabble, spat, °tiff, °fight, °row, tussle,

Donnybrook, °brawl, Colloq barney, °scrap: After the referee's ruling, a fracas broke out.

fracture n. 1 °break, breakage, breaking: An old fracture makes him walk with a limp. 2 °break, °crack, °split, °rupture, °breach, °separation, cleavage, °division, °rift: We can permit no fracture in the united front we present to the voters. —v. 3 °break, °rupture, °crack, °split, °breach, °separate, °cleave: He fractured three vertebrae in the accident.

fragile adj. °frail, breakable, °brittle, frangible, °delicate, °dainty, °thin, °light, °slight, °weak, °feeble, °infirm, °decrepit; °tenuous, °shaky, °flimsy, °rickety, unsubstantial or °insubstantial: Because of her great age, her bones had become fragile. The argument in favour of acquittal is very fragile, indeed.

fragment n. 1 °piece, °portion, °part, °chip, shard or sherd, °splinter, °sliver, °scrap, °bit, °speck, snippet, °morsel, °crumb, °particle, °remnant, °shred, °snatch: A fragment of the airliner was found twenty miles from the crash. 2 fragments: smithereens; debris, Literary disjecta membra: The car was blown into thousands of fragments. I tried to pick up the fragments of my former life. —v. 3 °shatter, °splinter, °break or °split (up), °explode, °disintegrate, °come or °go to °pieces, °come °apart: I picked up the skull and it fragmented in my fingers.

fragmentary adj. °disconnected, °piecemeal, °incomplete, scattered, °disjointed, °incoherent, °sketchy: Accounts of the disaster are still fragmentary.

fragrance n. fragrancy, °scent, °aroma, °smell, °odour, redolence, °perfume, °bouquet, balm: The fragrance of orange blossom filled the room.

fragrant adj. °aromatic, odorous, °redolent, perfumed, balmy, odoriferous, ambrosial, sweet-scented, sweet-smelling: A fragrant breeze wafted over the meadow.

frail adj. 1 See fragile, above. 2 ailing, unwell, °ill, °sick, °sickly, °poorly, °thin, °skinny, °slight, °puny, °scrawny, wasting or fading away, languishing, °infirm, °feeble; °crippled, consumptive, phthisic: She is too frail to see visitors.

frailty n. 1 °weakness, °infirmity, °delicate °condition, feebleness, fragility, °delicacy: The doctors are concerned about his frailty. 2 susceptibility, °liability, suggestibility, impressionability, vulnerability; fallibility, °foible, °flaw, °defect, °imperfection, °fault: You just said that to take advantage of my frailty. Her vanity is her greatest frailty.

frame n. 1 framework, °shell, °form, skeleton, °support, chassis, framing, °structure, °fabric, scaffolding, construction: We made a frame of sticks over which the canvas was stretched. 2 °border, casing, case-mounting, °mount, °edge, edging; °setting: This picture would look best in a gold frame. 3 °system, °form, °pattern, °scheme, schema, °plan, °order, °organization, framework, °structure, °construct, construction, °arrangement, blueprint, °design, layout, °composition, °context, °make-up, configuration: The proposed new department does not fit into the present frame of the company. 4 °physique, °build, bone °structure, °body, skeleton, °figure: He has an unusually large frame for a dancer. 5 **frame of mind**: °mood,

°humour, °state, °condition, °attitude, °bent, °disposition: *I am not in the right frame of mind to put up with your nonsense at the moment.* —*v.* **6** °construct, °build, °put together, °assemble, °set up, °put up, °erect, °raise, elevate: *We framed the entire house in two days.* **7** °make, °fashion, °form, °mould, °carve out, °forge, °originate, °create, °devise, °compose, °formulate, °put together, °conceive, °draw up, °draft, °shape, °block out, give °form *or* °shape to; contrive: *The founding fathers met to frame a new constitution.* **8** °enclose, °box (in); °set off: *I like the way you've framed that painting.* **9** °set up, °incriminate (fraudulently), °trap, entrap: *Did Dr Crippen kill his wife or was he framed?*

frank *adj.* **1** °open, °free, °candid, °direct, °outspoken, unreserved, °uninhibited, °honest, °sincere, °genuine, °truthful, plain-spoken, °forthright, °downright, °explicit, unrestrained, unchecked, unconstrained, unrestricted, °unabashed: *I asked for a frank appraisal of my work and, unfortunately, he gave it.* **2** °candid, °naïve, guileless, °artless, °ingenuous, °innocent, (°open and) °above-board, on the up and up, *Colloq* upfront, on the °level: *The boy's description of the events was completely frank.*

frantic *adj.* frenzied, °excited, frenetic, °nervous, °overwrought, °excitable, wrought up, distracted, °distraught, beside oneself, °hysterical, °wild, °berserk, °mad, running amok *or* amuck; °upset, °agitated, perturbed, at one's wit's end, °disconcerted, °confused; °hectic; *Colloq* in a °state, in a tizzy, up the °wall, in a dither, out of one's °mind, *Chiefly US and Canadian* discombobulated: *They are frantic because they haven't heard from Edmund in a week.*

fraternal *adj.* °brotherly, °platonic, °friendly, comradely, °idealistic, °intellectual: *He insists that his interest in her is purely fraternal.*

fraternity *n.* **1** community, °brotherhood, °crowd, °set, °clique, coterie, °circle, °society, *US* °club: *Rumours have been circulating in the academic fraternity for months.* **2** brotherliness, °kinship, °fellowship, camaraderie, sodality, comradeship, °friendship, °companionship, relatedness, closeness, °association, affiliation, °solidarity, °unity, esprit de corps, clannishness: *A sense of fraternity prevents them from betraying one another.* **3** °company, guild, °clan, °league, °club, °union, °society, °association: *She has joined the fraternity of legal clerks.*

fraternize *v.* consort (with), °associate (with), °socialize (with), °go (around *or* round) with *or* together, spend time with *or* together, keep °company (with), °hobnob with, °mingle (with), °mix (with), °take up with *or* together, keep up (with), °fall in with, °rub shoulders (with), *Colloq* °hang out (with *or* together), °hang about *or* around with *or* together: *Soldiers are forbidden to fraternize, which means they are not allowed to fraternize with local people.*

fraud *n.* **1** °deception, °trickery, cheating, °sharp practice, °chicanery, °deceit, swindling, double-dealing, duplicity, °artifice, °craft, guile, humbug, humbuggery, treachery, *Colloq* monkey business, funny business, °hanky-panky: *The company directors have been convicted of fraud.* **2** °trick, °hoax, °swindle, °deception, °cheat, °wile, °stratagem, °dodge, bilk, °ruse, °sham, °fake, °subterfuge, *Colloq* flimflam, *Slang*

gyp, °rip-off, scam: *The investigation exposed extensive fraud in the handling of local government funds.* **3** deceiver, trickster, °cheat(er), °impostor, °swindler, charlatan, humbug, sharper, shark, bilk(er), °quack, mountebank, °fake(r), °pretender, °bluff(er), confidence man, inveigler, defrauder; °scoundrel, °rogue, *Archaic* knave; *Colloq* con man *or* artist, °phoney *or US also* phony, flimflam man *or* artist, flimflammer, *US and Canadian* four-flusher; *Slang US* barracuda: *He is a fraud who extracts protection money from the elderly.*

fraudulent *n.* **1** °fake, °counterfeit, forged, °false, falsified, °spurious, °imitation, °sham, pinchbeck, *Colloq* °phoney *or US* also phony: *These banknotes are fraudulent.* **2** °deceitful, °dishonest, °criminal, °deceptive, °tricky, °artful, °crafty, double-dealing, duplicitous, °shifty, guileful, °sharp, *Colloq* °shady, °crooked, °bent: *Substituting paste for diamonds is a fraudulent act.*

fraught *adj.* **1** Usually, **fraught with**: filled *or* charged *or* °packed with, °loaded with, teeming *or* °replete *or* overflowing with, oversupplied with, abounding *or* °abundant in, attended *or* accompanied by: *The scene was fraught with emotion.* **2** °tense, °taut, stressful, °trying, °anxious, distressing, distressful, upsetting, °nerve-racking *or* nerve-wracking, °fretful, °strained, °traumatic: *Relations between the two countries became even more fraught following the incident.*

fray[1] *n.* °disturbance, °skirmish, °fight, °battle, °brawl, tussle, scuffle, °fracas, mêlée *or* melee, Donnybrook, wrangle, °rumpus, °row, °quarrel, °dispute, altercation, *Law* affray, *Colloq* ruckus, punch-up: *He leapt into the fray and fought like a tiger.*

fray[2] *v.* °shred, °wear (°thin *or* °threadbare), °wear out, °rub, abrade, °chafe, ravel, unravel, frazzle: *He saves his frayed shirts to wear at home.*

freak *n.* **1** °monstrosity, °monster, mutant, deformity: *The show features freaks such as a two-headed calf and a bearded lady.* **2** anomaly, °rarity, °abnormality, irregularity, °oddity, °curiosity, rara avis, °rare bird, *Brit* one-off, *Colloq* one-shot: *Biologists regard the albino giraffe as a freak of nature.* **3** whim, caprice, vagary, crotchet, °quirk, °eccentricity, °fancy, idiosyncrasy, °peculiarity: *The snow in New York in July was a freak.* **4** °enthusiast, °fan, °devotee, aficionado, °fanatic, °addict; *Colloq* buff, °fiend, nut: *She's been a jazz freak for years.* —*adj.* **5** freakish, freaky, °abnormal, anomalous, °extraordinary, °unique, °rare, atypical, unusual, °odd, °queer, °strange, °exceptional, °bizarre, °weird, °unparalleled, °unforeseen, unexpected, unpredicted, unpredictable, *Brit* one-off, *Colloq* one-shot: *He claims he had a freak experience with a lion that had a thorn in its foot.*

free *adj.* **1** °at °liberty, unfettered, unchained, unshackled, unconfined, untrammelled, unencumbered, unrestrained, unrestricted, unconstrained, °uncontrolled, free-born, °independent, self-governing, self-governed, self-ruling, autonomous, °democratic, °sovereign: *These people want to be free. It's a free country.* **2** liberated, at °large, °let °go, °let off, emancipated, delivered, manumitted, set free, unshackled, unfettered, released, freed, °loose, °out, *Colloq* sprung, on the °loose: *After ten years* *he was free at last.* **3** unoccupied, unengaged, at °liberty, not °busy, °available, °accessible; °unused, °vacant, °empty, °spare, °extra, °uninhabited, untenanted: *Are you free for dinner tonight? Here is a free room we can use for the meeting.* **4** cost-free, free of °charge, °complimentary, gratis, for °nothing, without °cost (or °obligation), unencumbered, *Colloq* for free, on the °house: *The food was free but we paid for our drinks.* **5** °unattached, unfastened, untied, °loose: *Tie the free end of the rope round your waist.* **6** °unasked for, °unsolicited, °gratuitous, unbidden, °voluntary, °spontaneous, unconditioned, unconditional: *Let me give you some free advice.* **7** °generous, °lavish, °open, °liberal, munificent, unstinting, °bountiful, open-handed, unsparing; °charitable: *Fred is quite free with his donations to good causes.* **8** °relaxed, °casual, °informal, free and °easy, °easy, °natural, unceremonious, *Colloq* laid-back: *He is quite free about letting me use his car.* **9** °open, °above-board, °honest, °direct, °outspoken, °uninhibited, unconstrained, un-restrained, °relaxed: *You can be free in your criticism.* **10** °unhindered, °unimpeded, unen-cumbered, unhampered, unobstructed, allowed, permitted, °able, °clear, unrestricted, unregulated: *She's free to do as she pleases. The two countries have signed a free-trade agreement.* **11 free of:** °rid of, °exempt(ed) from, relieved of, °safe from, not °liable *or* °subject to, °immune from, °unaffected by, °above, without, untouched by: *He thinks he is free of her influence.* —*adv.* **12** °freely, °openly, at °will, unrestrict-edly, °loose; loosely: *Our dog runs free on the farm. Let the rope hang free.* **13** gratis, at no °cost, free of °charge, without °charge: *They give new businesses advice free.* —*v.* **14** set free, set at °liberty, enfranchise, °release, °let °go, °liberate, °let out, °let °loose, unloose, unchain, unfetter, uncage; °emancipate, disenthral, manumit; °pardon, parole, furlough: *Bail was paid and we were freed. Lincoln freed the slaves. He was freed after six years in prison.* **15** °disengage, untie, unbind, °loose, unfasten, °undo, unshackle, unlock, °open, °release, disentangle, °loosen, °detach, °extricate: *Free the end of that rope.* **16** °relieve, °rid, unburden, disburden, disencumber, unbosom; °rescue, °redeem: *Free yourself of any preconceived notions on the subject.*

freedom *n.* **1** °liberty, °independence, °self-government, self-determination, self-direction, autonomy: *Democracy is based on the freedom of the individual.* **2** °release, deliv-erance, °liberation, emancipation, manu-mission: *Will these people ever get their freedom?* **3** °exemption, °immunity, deliverance, °liberation, °relief: *All citizens should enjoy free-dom from want.* **4** °range, latitude, °scope, °play, deregulation, non-interference, °discretion, °margin, °free hand, °facility, °ease, °licence, °permission, °right, °privilege, °authority, authorization, °power, *carte blanche*: *He must have the freedom to make decisions. I have the freedom to do as I wish.* **5** °free °time, °leisure, °spare °time: *I like a lot of freedom to do things in my own time.* **6** °candour, °honesty, openness, frank-ness, candidness, unrestraint, unconstraint, naturalness: *Freedom of speech is practised here.* **7** boldness, overfamiliarity, audacity,

audaciousness, forwardness, brazenness, °brass, °impertinence, °impudence, °disrespect, °arrogance, °presumption, presumptuousness, °nerve, °gall: *Where does she get the freedom to talk to you that way?*

freely *adv.* **1** candidly, frankly, °openly, un-reservedly, without °reserve, unrestrainedly, without °restraint, unconstrainedly, without constraint, unceremoniously, plainly: *Please speak freely.* **2** °willingly, spontaneously, °readily, °voluntarily, on (one's) own, independently, of (one's) own °accord, of (one's) own °volition *or* °free °will: *I didn't send for her—she came to me freely.* **3** unrestrainedly, unrestrictedly, without °restriction, without °let *or* °hindrance, with-out °interference: *He was allowed to move freely about the island.* **4** liberally, lavishly, un-reservedly, generously, unstintingly, open-handedly, ungrudgingly, munificently, °amply, plentifully, abundantly: *He has no money to donate but he gives freely of his time.* **5** °readily, °easily, smoothly, cleanly, unobstructedly: *With the obstacle removed, the water ran freely through the pipes.*

freeze *v.* **1** °chill, °refrigerate, ice, deep-freeze, flash-freeze, frost: *If you freeze the leftovers, they keep better.* **2** °solidify, congeal, °harden, °stiffen, ice up *or* over: *When the lake freezes, we can go skating.* **3** °fix, immobilize, °paralyse, °stop (dead *or* dead in one's tracks), °stay, °pin, °transfix, gorgonize; become °fixed, °stand (stock-)°still *or* motionless; °peg, °stick, °set: *She froze him with an icy stare. He froze to the spot in horror. Rates of exchange are no longer frozen.* **4 freeze out:** °exclude, debar, °ban, °reject, °ostracize; °eject, °drive away *or* out, °expel, °force out: *When he tried to join the club, he was frozen out.* —*n.* **5** frost, *Brit* freeze-up, *US* ice-up, deep-freeze: *There will be a freeze tonight in northern counties.* **6** °fix, immobilization: *The government has put a freeze on wages.*

freezing *adj.* °frigid, °icy, arctic, frosty, boreal, hyperboreal, numbing, Siberian, °polar, gla-cial, (ice-)cold, °wintry, bone-chilling, °bitter, °biting, °bitter(ly) °cold, perishing, °chill, tooth-chattering; chilled to the bone, frozen, shivering, *Archaic* frore: *The rescue was performed under freezing conditions. We were freezing in our thin jackets.*

freight *n.* **1** °transport, transportation, °carriage, conveyance, shipping, shipment, freightage, °delivery: *The charges for freight are included.* **2** °goods, °cargo, tonnage, freightage; °load, boatload, shipload, lorry °load, °haul, consignment, payload: *How much freight passes through here?*

frenzy *n.* **1** °excitement, °agitation, °fury, fever, *Brit* °furore *or* *US* furor, °passion, turmoil, °transport: *The crowd was whipped into a frenzy at the match.* **2** °distraction, paroxysm, °seizure, °outburst, °bout, °fit: *She went into a frenzy of despair after the death of her family.*

frequent *adj.* **1** °recurrent, recurring, °habitual, °regular, °familiar, °everyday, °customary, °usual, °ordinary, °normal, °common, repeated, iterative, reiterative, °persistent, continuing, °continual, °constant; °many, numerous, count-less, innumerable: *She was a frequent visitor at our house. She paid us frequent visits.*

—v. **2** °haunt, °patronize, °visit, °resort to, °go to or °attend regularly, *Colloq* °hang out or around at: *Yes, Inspector, I used to frequent the pub called The Saracen's Head.*

frequently adv. **1** °often, regularly, continually, °repeatedly, over and over (again), again and again, a °lot, °many times, °many a °time, °time after time, °time and (time) again, *Archaic* oftentimes, oft-times: *She has visited me frequently during the past weeks.* **2** °often, habitually, customarily, regularly, °usually, °ordinarily, °generally, commonly, every so °often, °many a °time, as °often as not, *Archaic* oftentimes, oft-times: *He frequently stops at The Golden Hind after work.*

fresh adj. **1** °new, today's, °brand-new; (most) °recent, °late(st): *Don't you love the smell of fresh bread? This is the product of fresh research.* **2** °new, °modern, up to °date, °novel, °original, new-fangled, °unusual, unconventional, °different, °alternative, °unorthodox: *We are seeking a fresh approach.* **3** °raw, °inexperienced, untested, °unsophisticated, °green, °untried, °unfledged, °immature, untrained, °naïve, °callow, (still) wet behind the ears, *Brit* still in nappies; *US* still in diapers: *These troops are too fresh to send into battle.* **4** additional, °new, °further, renewed, °extra, °supplementary: *We need a fresh supply of paper towels.* **5** °alert, refreshed, °vigorous, °energetic, invigorated, spry, °lively, full of vim and °vigour, fresh as a daisy, °keen, °bright, °brisk, °active, *Colloq* bright-eyed and bushy-tailed: *Put the horses through the dressage while they are fresh.* **6** °wholesome, °healthy, well, refreshed, °glowing, °fair, °rosy, ruddy, blooming, °flourishing: *She came back to work fresh from a week's rest.* **7** °moderate, °brisk, °strong; °cool, °clean, °pure, °clear, unpolluted: *Sailing conditions were ideal: a fresh breeze and good visibility. Open the window for some fresh air.* **8** °bold, °impudent, °impertinent, °brazen, °brassy, °forward, °disrespectful, saucy, °pert, °cheeky, °presumptuous, °insolent, °rude, *Colloq* smart-alecky or smart-aleck, *US* sassy, flip: *That fresh kid called her an old bag.*

freshen v. **1** °strengthen, °increase, °blow harder: *The wind began to freshen as we sailed past the headland.* **2** Sometimes, **freshen up**: invigorate, °revive, °refresh, °enliven, (re)vitalize, °stimulate, titivate, °rouse, °liven up: *I'll just freshen up before dinner. Freshen these flowers by changing the water.* **3** ventilate, °air out, deodorize, °purify: *We freshen the rooms by opening all the windows.* **4** °strengthen, °spike, °lace, °fortify: *May I freshen your drink?*

fret v. **1** °worry, be °concerned, agonize, lose sleep, be °upset or distressed or °anxious or °disturbed, °grieve, °brood, whine, °fuss, °complain, *Colloq* °stew, tear one's hair: *Your kitten is safe now, so stop fretting.* **2** °worry, °concern, °distress, vex, °annoy, °irritate, °torment, °provoke, *US* °rankle: *She fretted herself about Henry's health.*

fretful adj. °irritable, vexed, ill-tempered, bad-tempered, °peevish, edgy, °cross, °petulant, °testy, °touchy, tetchy, splenetic, irascible, choleric, crabby, fractious, °short-tempered, grumpy, sulky, °moody, °fault-finding, carping, °querulous, whining, complaining, captious, ill-natured, °disagreeable, °impatient,

°snappish, °waspish, °short, °abrupt, °curt, *US and Canadian* °cranky: *Are you always so fretful before breakfast?*

friction n. **1** abrasion, rubbing, abrading, chafing, fretting, attrition, scraping, °grating, °erosion: *Friction is always accompanied by heat.* **2** °disagreement, °discord, °conflict, contention, °dispute, °dissension, disharmony, °controversy, dissent, bickering, °argument, wrangling, °ill feeling, °ill will, bad blood, °animosity, °rivalry, °hostility, °antagonism, °strife: *Politics have always been a source of friction between them.*

friend n. **1** (boon) °companion, °partner, °comrade, crony, °familiar, confidant(e), °intimate, Achates, alter ego, °ally, compeer; °acquaintance, °playmate, pen-pal or *Brit* also pen-friend; *Colloq* °chum, °pal, *Brit* cocker, *Chiefly Brit and Australian and New Zealand* °mate, *Australian* cobber, *US and Canadian* (°bosom) buddy, *SW US* compadre; *Slang Brit* (old) china: *She is spending the weekend with some friends.* **2** °ally, °associate; °fellow, confederate, °colleague, co-worker, confrère, compatriot, consociate, *US* °cohort: *A friend from the office is coming to dinner.* **3** room-mate, bunk-mate, flat-mate, soul °mate, bedfellow, °lover, °sweetheart, °escort; °girl, °woman, girlfriend, concubine, °mistress, *Old-fashioned* doxy; °man, boyfriend, *Old-fashioned* beau; *Colloq US* alternative other, POSSLQ (= 'Person of the Opposite Sex Sharing Living Quarters'), roomie; *Slang* °baby, moll, sugar-daddy, *US* °squeeze, twist, *Chiefly Brit* bird: *Chris, why don't you introduce us to your new friend?* **4** °benefactor or benefactress, °patron, °supporter, °advocate, adherent, °backer, °financier, Maecenas; angel, investor: *He has long been associated with the Friends of the Library.*

friendly adj. **1** °amicable, congenial, °sociable, companionable, comradely, convivial, °familiar, well-disposed, °close, on °good terms, simpatico, °comfortable, at home, °neighbourly, clubby, °fraternal, °brotherly, sisterly, *Colloq* °chummy, pally, °thick, *Brit* matey, *US* palsy-walsy, buddy-buddy: *We've always been friendly with the people next door.* **2** °amiable, °affectionate, loving, demonstrative, °cordial, warm-hearted, °warm, °genial, °agreeable, °good-natured, °pleasant, °kind, °kindly, kind-hearted, affable, approachable, °accessible, unreserved, °open, *Brit* clubbable: *Clare can be very friendly when she wants to be.*

friendship n. **1** amity, congeniality, sociability, companionship, comradeship, °fellowship, conviviality, °familiarity, closeness, neighbourliness, °harmony, clubbiness, °fraternity, °brotherhood, sisterhood, °alliance: *I hope that this affair will not affect the friendship between our countries.* **2** friendliness, amiability, amicability, °esteem, °warmth, °devotion, °affection, fondness, °attachment, (deep) °regard, °rapport, intimacy, °love: *What can I do to regain your friendship?*

fright n. **1** °fear, °alarm, °terror, °dread, °horror, °panic, trepidation, °dismay, consternation, apprehension, *Colloq* (blue) funk: *He almost dies of fright at the sight of blood.* **2** °scare, °shock: *Here, sip this brandy; you've had a terrible fright.* **3** °spectre, °monster, eyesore, *Colloq* °sight, °mess: *He looked a perfect fright when I saw him after the accident.*

frighten v. °terrify, °scare, °alarm, °panic, °startle, °shock, °petrify, °horrify, °dismay, °appal, °unnerve, °distress, °daunt, cow, °intimidate, *Colloq* °scare out of one's wits, make one's hair stand on end, °scare the (living) daylights (*etc.*) out of, °scare °stiff, *Brit* put the °wind up (someone), put the frighteners on (someone): *She was frightened by the neighbours' vicious dog. Are you frightened of aeroplanes?*

frightening *adj.* °terrifying, alarming, °startling, °shocking, petrifying, horrifying, dismaying, appalling, unnerving, dire, distressing, daunting, intimidating, °formidable, °frightful, °fearful, hair-raising, °harrowing, °dreadful, *Colloq* °scary, spooky: *Skydiving can be a frightening experience. The sight of their mangled bodies was frightening.*

frightful *adj.* **1** See **frightening**, above. **2** °awful, °dreadful, °terrible, °disagreeable, °atrocious, °abhorrent, °loathsome, °grisly, °ghastly, °lurid, °macabre, °horrible, horrifying, horrid, horrendous, °nasty, °hideous, °vile, unspeakable, nauseating, °nauseous, °repugnant, °repulsive, °shocking, °revolting, °abominable, °offensive, °ugly: *Brixton police report a frightful crime of decapitation.*

frightfully *adv.* °awfully, °very, °extremely; amazingly, surprisingly: *We saw a frightfully good play last night.*

frigid *adj.* **1** °cold, arctic, frosty, frozen, glacial, °icy, hyperboreal, °polar, bone-chilling, boreal, Siberian, °freezing, °wintry, °chilly, °chill, *Archaic* frore: *We were huddled in that frigid alpine hut for two days.* **2** °cold, °cool, °cold-hearted, °forbidding, austere, unemotional, unfeeling, °stiff, °rigid, prim, °strait-laced, °stony, °callous, °steely, obdurate, °thick-skinned, impervious, °inaccessible, °remote, °unapproachable, unfriendly, °standoffish, °haughty, °aloof, °reserved: *His behaviour to his ex-wife has always been frigid.* **3** °unapproachable, unresponsive, °impassive, °passive, °indifferent, °cold; °impotent: *She says he's impotent and he insists that she's frigid.*

frill *n.* **1** trimming, °decoration, °ornament, furbelow, °flounce, °ruffle: *This dress would be suitable without the frill.* **2** ornamentation, frippery, falderal or fal de rol or folderol, frou-frou, showiness, °ostentation, °embellishment, °luxury, trimming, °extra, °addition, °superfluity, °gewgaw, (bit of) °paraphernalia, *Colloq US* foofaraw, bells and whistles, *Slang* jazz: *They ordered a computer system that has every imaginable frill.*

fringe *n.* **1** trimming, °edge, edging, °border, °frill, °flounce, °ruffle, purfle, purfling, ruff, ruche or rouche, ricrac or rickrack, °ornament, °decoration, furbelow: *The curtains would look better without that pink fringe.* **2** °border, °perimeter, °edge, °boundary, °bounds, °periphery, °limits, °margin, °outskirts, march(es); *Technical* fimbria: *We live on the fringes of Oxford.*

—*v.* **3** °edge, °border, °trim, °surround: *The grounds are fringed with trees.*

frisk *v.* **1** °caper, gambol, °cavort, °frolic, °skip, °trip, romp, curvet, °leap, °dance, °prance, °play, rollick: *She was frisking about like a lamb.* **2** °search, °inspect, °examine, °check (out), °go over: *At the airport, we were frisked for weapons.*

frisky *adj.* °lively, °frolicsome, rollicking, °playful, °active, °animated, (°high-)°spirited, coltish: *Tell Frances to calm down—she's getting a bit too frisky.*

fritter *v.* **fritter away**: squander, °waste, °idle away, misspend, °dissipate: *Stop frittering away your time watching television. She frittered away every penny of her inheritance.*

frivolous *adj.* **1** °trifling, °inconsequential, unimportant, trivial, nugatory, °insignificant, °minor, °petty, °paltry, °niggling, °peripheral, °superficial, °worthless, *Colloq* °small-time, *Brit* twopenny, two a penny, *US* two-bit, penny-ante, nitty-gritty: *Don't waste my time with frivolous details.* **2** °scatterbrained, bird-brained, °silly, feather-brained, °irresponsible, °flippant, °casual, °flighty, °giddy, °foolish, °childish, °puerile; airy, °light, °slight, *Brit* airy-fairy, *Colloq* °flip: *Try to be serious and less frivolous about such important matters.*

frolic *n.* **1** °merriment, merrymaking, °gaiety, °sport, °fun (and games), °high jinks, jollity, °mirth, jollification, °festivity, °celebration, °revelry, °play, horseplay, *Colloq* skylarking, partying: *After we won the cup there was great frolic in the town.* **2** romp, °party, °spree, °revel, gambol, °caper, gambado, antic; escapade, °prank: *The noise of our frolics echoed across the square.*

—*v.* **3** °frisk, °cavort, °caper, skylark, gambol, rollick, romp, cut capers, curvet, °play, °skip, °sport, have °fun, *Colloq* °party, make whoopee, horse around or about: *Gregory frolics about instead of getting on with his work.*

frolicsome *adj.* °playful, °merry, °frisky, °sportive, °gay, °lively, °sprightly, °animated, °spirited, coltish: *Irene may seem frolicsome but she has her sober side as well.*

front *n.* **1** °face, façade, °facing, fore-part, anterior; obverse: *The front of the door has a painting on it. This dress buttons up the front.* **2** frontage, forefront: *The front of the property measures only 40 feet.* **3** °beginning, °head, fore, vanguard, forefront, van: *At the front of the parade marched the mayor.* **4** °bearing, demeanour, mien, °air, °face, countenance, façade, °mask, °expression, °show, °appearance, °aspect, °look, °exterior: *Despite her grief, she put on a brave front at the wake.* **5** °disguise, °cover, °guise, °mask, cover-up, °show, °pretext, façade: *The restaurant was merely a front for a narcotics operation.* **6** °movement, °organization, °league, bloc, °party, °group, °faction, wing: *A new popular front was formed out of a coalition of several opposition groups.* **7** haughtiness, overconfidence, °effrontery: *He frightens away potential clients by showing so much front.* **8 in front**: °first, °leading, °ahead, to the fore, in the forefront, in the vanguard or van, in °advance, in the °lead, °before; °winning: *In this picture the man in front is my father. My horse was in front all the way.* **9 upfront: a** See **8**, above. **b** open, straightforward, °honest, °direct, forthright, °frank, °candid: *Why can't you be upfront instead of conspiring against me?*

—*adj.* **10** °first, °advance, °foremost, °leading, °head, °main: *The front carriage was smashed in the train wreck. Enter by the front door.*

—*v.* **11** °overlook, °face, °look out on or °towards, be °opposite: *Our house fronts the river. The flat fronts* *on the street.* **12 front for**: °act for, °represent; °substitute for, °replace: *I hate formal affairs and hoped that you might front for me.*

frontier *n.* °front °line; °border, °boundary, °bound(s), marches, (°far) reaches, °limit(s), °pale, °extreme(s), bourn: *We'll need our passports to cross the frontier into Italy.*

froth *n.* **1** °foam, spume, suds, °lather, bubbles; °head: *The froth tickles my nose.* **2** trivia, °rubbish, °nonsense, twaddle, °babble, °gibberish, °drivel, *Colloq* °hot air, gas, °gab, piffle: *His sermons were just so much froth.*
—*v.* **3** °foam, spume, °bubble, °fizz, effervesce, aerate: *You are supposed to drink the medicine while it is frothing.* **4** °foam, salivate; °lather: *He was so angry he began to froth at the mouth.*

frown *v.* **1** °scowl, glower, °glare, °knit one's brows, grimace, give a dirty °look, *Brit* °lour or *US* also °lower: *Don't frown so much or you'll get wrinkles.* **2 frown on** or **upon**: °disapprove (of), (°look on or °regard or °view with) °disfavour, discountenance, °look down on or upon, °look askance at, not take kindly to, not think much of, °look disapprovingly upon, *Colloq* take a dim °view of, be turned off by: *My parents frown on my seeing you.*
—*n.* **3** °scowl, glower, °glare, grimace, dirty °look, *Brit* °lour or *US* also °lower: *Her forehead is always furrowed by a frown.*

frugal *adj.* **1** °thrifty, °sparing, °economic(al), °careful, °prudent, °provident, °saving, °conservative, conservational, °moderate: *Mother had to become quite frugal when father fell ill.* **2** parsimonious, °penurious, penny-pinching, cheese-paring, °mean, °miserly, stingy, niggardly, °tight(-fisted), °close(-fisted), hand to mouth: *He led a frugal existence on his earnings as an artist.* **3** °meagre, °paltry, °poor, skimpy, scant(y), °small, °negligible, piddling: *His frugal meal consisted entirely of bread and water.*

fruit *n.* Often, **fruits**: °product(s), °result(s), °revenue(s), outgrowth, °outcome, consequence(s), °return(s), advantage(s), °benefit(s), °profit(s), emolument, °payment, °income, compensation, recompense, °desert(s): *He didn't live to enjoy the fruit of his work.*

fruitful *adj.* **1** °productive, °fertile, °prolific, fecund; fructiferous, frugiferous, fructuous: *The soil in this valley is extremely fruitful.* **2** °effective, °worthwhile, well-spent, °profitable, °successful, °useful, °rewarding, °advantageous, °beneficial, °productive, °fertile: *We had a fruitful meeting and accomplished a great deal.* **3** °plentiful, °abundant, bounteous, °bountiful, °prolific, plenteous, copious, °luxurious, °rich, °flourishing: *We expect another fruitful harvest this year.*

fruition *n.* °realization, °fulfilment, °consummation, °achievement, °success, materialization, °maturity, ripeness, maturation, °completion; °perfection: *I saw my plans for the town brought to fruition.*

fruitless *adj.* °barren, unfruitful, unproductive, °worthless, °bootless, °futile, °pointless, °useless, °vain, °idle, unavailing, °ineffectual, °ineffective, °unprofitable, for °naught, to no avail, °unsuccessful, unrewarding, abortive: *Our search for a new manager has so far been fruitless.*

frustrate *v.* **1** °thwart, °foil, °stymie, °block, baffle, °check, balk or baulk, °disappoint,

°discourage, °forestall, °prevent, °stop, °halt, °cripple, °hinder, °hamper, °impede, hamstring, °defeat, °counteract, °neutralize, nullify, °counter, °fight off, °repel, °repulse: *So far, we have been able to frustrate take-over bids for the company.* **2** °discourage, °disappoint, °upset, °exasperate: *I feel frustrated because mother won't let me help with the bills.*

fuel *n.* **1** tinder, combustible, kindling; fossil or °nuclear °fuel: *You must pay a lot for fuel to heat that big house.* **2** ammunition, °encouragement, stimulus, °incitement, °provocation: *Her teasing him only provided more fuel for his passion.* **3** °nourishment, nutriment, °sustenance, °food, nutrition: *The body needs more fuel on a cold day.*
—*v.* **4** °nourish, °feed, °sustain; °stimulate, °encourage, °incite, °provoke, °inflame, exacerbate, °excite: *U-235 is used to fuel the reactor. Frustration fuels the flame of desire.*

fugitive *n.* **1** °runaway, escapee, °deserter, °refugee, *Archaic* runagate: *Many fugitives from political oppression seek asylum in the UK.*
—*adj.* **2** fleeing, escaped, °running away, °runaway: *They police are able to devote little time to tracing fugitive children.* **3** °fleeting, °passing, °brief, °short-lived, transitory, °transient, ephemeral, evanescent, °momentary, °volatile, fugacious: *She once entertained the fugitive notion of becoming an opera singer.*

fulfil *v.* **1** °bring about, °achieve, °accomplish, °bring or °carry to °completion, °carry out, °complete, consummate, °discharge, °live up to, °abide by, °observe, °realize, °effect, °bring or °carry off, °carry through, °keep, °satisfy, do, °perform, °execute, °effectuate: *I trust that you will fulfil all your obligations. Will she ever fulfil her ambition to be a virtuoso pianist?* **2** °answer, °satisfy, °meet, °implement, °look or °see to, °conform to or with, °comply with, °obey: *This hammer will fulfil my needs for the moment. Will your new assistant be able to fulfil your requirements?*

fulfilment *n.* °completion, °consummation, °performance, carrying out or through, °discharge, °realization, implementation, °execution, °accomplishment, compliance, conformity or conformance, making °good, °meeting, °satisfaction, answering, °achievement: *You will be paid upon fulfilment of the contract.*

full *adj.* **1** filled, °replete, brimming, brim-full, °packed, jam-packed, °congested, °loaded, bursting, chock-a-block, chock-full or choke-full or chuck-full, jammed, crammed, °solid, well supplied, crowded, stuffed; gorged, saturated, sated, satiated: *The tank is full of petrol. Her Christmas stocking was full of toys. I'm full; I couldn't manage another bite.* **2** °complete, °thorough, °detailed, °comprehensive, °total, all-inclusive, °broad, °extensive, all-encompassing, °exhaustive, plenary: *The police are demanding a full investigation.* **3** °complete, °entire, °whole: *The recipe calls for a full dozen egg yolks.* **4** utmost, greatest, °maximum, highest, °top; °extreme: *Full speed ahead.* **5** °wide, °ample, °generous, °broad, copious, °loose(-fitting): *The tight bolero jacket is offset by a full skirt.* **6** occupied, engrossed, °absorbed, immersed, °preoccupied, obsessed, consumed, °engaged, °concerned: *She's entirely too full of herself to pay any attention to us.* **7** filled or rounded out, °round(ish), well-rounded,

°plump; °robust, °shapely, well-shaped, cur-vaceous, °buxom, busty, °voluptuous, full-bodied, well-proportioned, well-built, *Slang* stacked, *Brit* well-stacked, *US* zaftig, built: *His face is rather full, so wrinkles don't show. Her figure is what I'd call full.* **8** unrestricted, non-restricted, unconditional, °unqualified: *Payment of dues entitles you to full membership privileges.* **9** °sentimental, °emotional, overflowing: *His heart was so full he could say no more.* **10** unobscured, unshaded, undimmed, °open, °broad, °bright, shining, °brilliant, °dazzling, °glaring, °intense, blazing, blinding; °harsh, °vivid, revealing: *We emerged into full daylight. In the full light of day, the plan seems unworkable.* **11** °powerful, °resonant, °rich, °deep, °loud: *His full bass voice was unmistakable.* **12** °complete, °whole, °entire; °comprehensive, uncut, °unabridged, °intact, unshortened, unbowdlerized, uncensored: *We were to receive full pay for a half day's work. Is this a full deck of cards? I have a full set of the original engravings.* —*adv.* **13** fully, °completely, °entirely, °wholly, °thoroughly, °altogether: *That is not a full-grown horse.* **14** squarely, °directly, °right, °precisely, °exactly, bang, *Colloq* °slap, smack: *The ball hit him full in the eye.* **15** °very, °perfectly, °exceedingly, °quite, *Slang* damned: *You know full well why I am here.* —*n.* **16** °maximum, greatest °degree, fullest: *The moon is at its full tonight.* **17 in full**: °completely, fully, °entirely, °wholly, °thoroughly, in its °entirety, °totally, *in toto*: *Copy this report in full.* **18 to the full** *or* **fullest**: °completely, fully, °quite, °thoroughly, to the utmost, to the greatest *or* fullest °extent; a °great °deal, greatly, hugely, enormously: *We enjoyed our visit to the full.*

fumble *v.* **1** °grope, °feel, °stumble: *She fumbled about for the light switch.* **2** °mishandle, °drop, muff, °bungle, °botch, *Colloq US* bobble, flub: *Bosworth fumbled the ball and Fernpath scored again.*

fume *v.* **1** °seethe, °smoulder, °chafe, °boil, °rage, °storm, °rant, °flare up, °bluster, °lose one's °temper, °explode, *Colloq* get steamed (up) (over *or* about), °lose one's °cool, °flip one's lid, °flip (out), °fly off the handle, hit the roof, °raise the roof, blow one's top *or* stack, °get °hot under the collar, blow a gasket, °go off the deep end: *She was fuming because I was five minutes late.* **2** smoke: *The mixture fumes if you add these ingredients.* —*n.* **3** Usually, **fumes**: smoke, °vapour, efflu-vium, gas, °exhalation, °exhaust; °smell, °odour, °aroma, °fragrance, °stench, stink, miasma; °pollution, smog: *The fumes from O. C. Cabot's cigar spread through the building.*

fumigate *v.* °disinfect, °cleanse, °purify, sani-tize, °sterilize, decontaminate: *There have been no insects since the kitchen was fumigated.*

fun *n.* **1** °merriment, merrymaking, °gaiety, °glee, jollity, °mirth, °cheer, °high °spirits, °delight, °frolic, °festivity, °high jinks; °amusement, °diversion, °sport, °enjoyment, °recreation, °entertainment, °pastime, °joy, °pleasure, *Colloq* (making) whoopee: *Your party was great fun. We always have fun when we're together. Want to have some fun?* **2** tomfoolery, horseplay, joking, playfulness, clowning, °pranks, °sport,

jesting, jocularity, °nonsense, fooling around *or* about, *Colloq* skylarking: *This is no time for fun—we have to catch a train.* **3 in** *or* **for fun**: jokingly, teasingly, in jest, facetiously, with °tongue in cheek, playfully, as a °lark, for a °joke *or* °gag; not °seriously: *In fun, we told him that he had missed the last ferry.* **4 Like fun!** Under no circumstances!, No way!, *Colloq* Like hell!, *US* No way, Jose!: *Like fun will I go swimming in the nude!* **5 make fun of**: poke fun at, °tease, °deride, (hold up to) °ridicule, °scoff at, °lampoon, °parody, °satirize, make °sport *or* °game of, °taunt, °gibe, °rag, *Colloq* kid, rib, *Brit* °send up: *Kevin is always making fun of people by imitating them.*

function *n.* **1** °purpose, °aim, °use, °role *or* rôle, *raison d'être*, °responsibility, °mission, °charge, °concern, °business, °province, °duty, °job, °occupation, °work, °office, °task, chore, °assignment, commission, °activity: *A knife's function is to cut; a guard's is to stand watch.* **2** °reception, °gathering, °affair, °party, dinner, °banquet, °gala, °ceremony, °formality, °rite, °ritual; °occasion, °event: *We are attending a function at the embassy tonight.* —*v.* **3** °act, °operate, °perform, °behave, °work, °go, °run: *Are you sure the engine is functioning properly?* **4** °serve, take the °role *or* rôle of, °act the °part of, °act as, °work as: *Dunmow will function as host in my absence.*

functional *adj.* **1** utilitarian, °useful, °serviceable, °practical, °practicable, func-tioning, working; °essential, °important, °effective: *This gear is a functional part, not mere decoration.* **2** working, operating, operational, °running, °going: *Is this telephone functional?*

functionary *n.* °official, commissioner, bur-eaucrat, office-holder, °officer: *She is some sort of functionary at the Ministry of Information.*

fund *n.* **1** °supply, °stock, °reserve, °store, °pool, °cache, reservoir, repository, °mine: *Alison is a veritable fund of information about art.* **2** Often, **funds**: °money, (hard) °cash, °ready °money, °assets, °means, °wealth, resources, where-withal, savings, °capital, nest egg, °endowment, *Colloq* °loot, lucre, pelf, °green, bread, dough, *Brit* °ready, readies, lolly, *US* bucks, °scratch: *He has the funds to buy out his partners. Have you contributed to the fund for indi-gent lexicographers?* —*v.* **3** °finance, °back, capitalize, °stake, °support, °pay for, endow, °grant, °subsidize: *The company has funded a number of new businesses.*

fundamental *adj.* **1** °basic, °rudimentary, °elementary, °primary, °main, °prime, °first, °principal, underlying, °cardinal, °central, °essential, quintessential, constitutional, °inherent, °intrinsic, °important, °crucial, °critical, °organic, °vital: *Our fundamental aim is to provide employment.* —*n.* **2** °principle, °law, °rule, axiom, °essential, °element, *sine qua non*, cornerstone, °keystone: *Freedom of speech is a fundamental in a democracy.*

funeral *n.* obsequies, exequies; °burial, inter-ment, sepulture, entombment, inhumation; cremation: *It is fitting to wear black when attending a funeral.*

funereal adj. °grave, °solemn, °sad, °unhappy, morose, °sombre, °mournful, °doleful, °sorrowful, °melancholy, °gloomy, lugubrious, °dismal, °grievous, depressing, °dreary, woeful, °dark, sepulchral: Why are you in such a funereal mood?

funny adj. **1** comical, °humorous, °comic, °ludicrous, laughable, °ridiculous, risible, waggish, side-splitting, °hilarious, °uproarious, jocular, jocose, °merry, droll, facetious, °witty, °farcical, slapstick, °zany; amusing, °entertaining, diverting, Colloq °hysterical: A comedian's material may be funny but he relies on timing for much of his effect. **2** °peculiar, °odd, °unusual, °curious, °strange, °mysterious, mystifying, °puzzling, °queer, °weird, °bizarre, °remarkable, unconventional, °eccentric, Slang off-the-wall: She had a funny expression on her face. If you do love me, you have a funny way of showing it.

furious adj. **1** °angry, enraged, raging, infuriated, fuming, incensed, irate, maddened, °mad, boiling, wrathful, provoked, beside oneself, up in arms, in high dudgeon, on the warpath, foaming at the °mouth, Literary wroth, Colloq steaming, livid, in a tizzy, Slang up the °wall, pissed off, browned off, Brit cheesed off: Mark was furious at Betty for leaving without him. **2** °fierce, °wild, °violent, °savage, °intense, unrestrained, °frantic, frenzied: A few made a furious attempt to jump off the burning ship.

furnish v. **1** °supply, °provide, °afford, °equip, °outfit, °fit (out or up), °rig (out or up), °provision, °give, °stock up, Colloq Brit °kit out or up: The trading post furnished what we needed for a month in the wilderness. Can you furnish me with a blanket? **2** °decorate, °equip: She received a commission to furnish a ten-room house.

furniture n. **1** furnishings, household (°goods); movables, chattels, °paraphernalia, °effects, °possessions, °belongings, Colloq °gear, °things, °stuff, Slang shit: There wasn't any furniture in the room, not even a chair. **2** °fittings, fitments, °equipment, °fixtures, °apparatus, °devices, °tackle, °tack, °trappings, °gear, accoutrements or US also accouterments, °accessories, appliances, Colloq Brit clobber: The front door has some fine brass furniture.

furore n. **1** furor, °uproar, °outburst, °tumult, commotion, turmoil, brouhaha, ado, hurly-burly, to-do, hubbub, °stir, °fuss, °disturbance, °excitement: The deportation of the student caused a furore among his supporters. **2** °rage, °craze, °mania, °vogue, °enthusiasm, °obsession, °fad: The furore for antiques has driven up prices enormously.

furrow n. **1** °groove, °channel, °rut, trench, °track, ditch, gutter, trough, fosse, fissure, sulcus, sulcation, flute, °score, °cut, °gash, °scratch, °line; °wrinkle, crease, corrugation, crow's-feet, Technical sulcus: He can't even plough a straight furrow. The furrows in his brow come from worry. —v. **2** °groove, °channel, flute, °score, °cut, °gash, °scratch; °plough, harrow: This rock was furrowed by glacial action. **3** °wrinkle, crease, corrugate, °knit, °pucker, crinkle: A frown furrowed his forehead.

further adj. **1** more, additional, another, other, °new, supplemental, °supplementary, °accessory, °auxiliary, °extra, °spare, °fresh: Further invest-

ment by our group is out of the question. **2** farther, more °distant or °remote: Some day, we may travel to the further reaches of the galaxy. —adv. **3** furthermore, °besides, °moreover, too, also, additionally, in °addition, over and above, beyond, °above, what is more, to °boot, °yet, then (again), again: She told him he was rude and, further, ugly as well. **4** farther, at or to a greater °distance or °depth: She has looked into the matter much further than I. —v. **5** °advance, °promote, °favour, °push or °urge °onward(s) or forward(s), °forward, °foster, °back, °patronize, °support, °help, °assist, °aid: What can I do to further your efforts?

furtherance n. °promotion, advancement, °pursuit, °backing, boosting, °boost, fostering, championing, championship, advocating, advocacy, °patronage, °support, °help, °aid, °assistance, succour: The furtherance of anti-pollution laws is all to the good.

furtive adj. **1** °secret, °private, °secretive, clandestine, °surreptitious, °stealthy, underhand(ed), covert, °hidden, conspiratorial, skulking, °deceitful, under the table, under the counter, hugger-mugger, Colloq °sneaky: She gave me a furtive look to let me know she was on to me. **2** °sly, °foxy, cunning, °crafty, °wily, °shifty, untrustworthy, Colloq °sneaky: His furtive manoeuvres mark him as one not to be trusted.

fury n. **1** °anger, °rage, wrath, °indignation, ire, choler, °rancour: Hell hath no fury like a woman scorned. **2** impetuosity, ferocity, savagery, vehemence, fierceness, tempestuousness, turbulence, °violence: How can we stem the fury of his attack? **3** virago, °shrew, spitfire, hell-cat, termagant, vixen, she-devil, °hag, °witch, offensive slang °bitch, Archaic beldam: She is a fury when provoked.

fuse v. °blend, °merge, °unite, °combine, °compound, °mix, commingle, coalesce, °flow or °come together, consolidate, °amalgamate; °melt: The metals fuse at a relatively low temperature.

fuss n. **1** °bother, pother, dither, °fluster, °flurry, °fret, commotion, ado, bustle, to-do, °excitement, °furore or US furor, °unrest, (deal of) °trouble, disquiet, °upset, °stir, °uproar, °disturbance, hubbub, °agitation, brouhaha, Colloq hoo-ha, °flap, stink, Brit kerfuffle, Slang US hoop-la: Stop making such a big fuss over nothing. —v. **2** make a fuss, °rush about or around, °flutter, Colloq kick up a fuss: I do wish she'd stop fussing—the party is going very well.

fussy adj. **1** °particular, °finicky, finical, °dainty, °discriminating, °difficult, °fastidious, °exacting, °demanding, Colloq picky, °choosy, nit-picking, pernickety or US also persnickety: He's so fussy that he'll wear only custom-made shoes. **2** °fancy, °elaborate, over-decorated, gingerbread, rococo, °ornate, °detailed, Byzantine: The style is a bit too fussy for my taste.

futile adj. °unsuccessful, unavailing, °useless, °unprofitable, °vain, abortive, profitless, °bootless, °worthless, °empty, °sterile, °barren, unproductive, °impotent, °ineffective, °ineffectual; Chiefly literary sleeveless: After several futile attempts to get in touch with you, I gave up.

future n. **1** days or °time to °come; tomorrow: Who knows what the future may bring?

—*adj.* **2** coming, tomorrow's, later, °prospective, following, unborn, °subsequent, expected, approaching; to be to °come: *Future generations will appreciate what we have done here.*

fuzzy *adj.* **1** °woolly, downy, linty, fleecy, furry, °fluffy, frizzy, flossy, flocculent, floccose, floc-

cus; feathery: *Tiny bits from her fuzzy pullover kept coming off on my suit.* **2** °dim, °faint, °hazy, foggy, °misty, blurred, blurry, °indistinct, unclear, °vague, °shadowy, °indefinite, °obscure, ill-defined, °woolly, distorted: *The picture was too fuzzy to make out any details.*

G

gab v. **1** °jabber, gabble, °chatter, gibber, blather or blether, prate, °prattle, °blab, °gossip, Colloq Brit natter, witter, Slang jaw, ya(c)k, US run off at the mouth: Stop gabbing and get on with your work!
—n. **2** °chatter, chit-chat, °prattle, jibber-jabber, °jabber, °gossip, blarney, blather or blether, tittle-tattle; cackle, °moonshine, °nonsense, °drivel, twaddle, °rubbish, °gobbledegook or gobbledygook, °mumbo-jumbo, poppycock, bunk or bunkum, balderdash, °stuff and °nonsense, hogwash, eyewash, Colloq piffle, flummery, °rot, bull, codswallop, Slang bullshit, horseshit, shit, crap, °garbage, Chiefly Brit tosh, balls: He had nothing important to say—just a lot of gab.

gad v. Usually, **gad about** or **around**: gallivant, °run around, °flit about, traipse: He's never home, always gadding about from one party to another.

gadget n. contrivance, °device, appliance, °creation, °invention, °machine, °tool, utensil, °implement, °instrument, °mechanism, °apparatus, Colloq °contraption, widget, thingumabob or thingamabob or thingumbob, thingumajig or thingamajig or thingummy, whatchamacallit, what's-its-name, Brit doodah, US hickey, doodad, doohickey, whosis, whatsis, dingus, Chiefly US and Canadian gismo or gizmo: He invented a gadget for resealing fizzy drink bottles.

gag¹ v. **1** °silence, °stifle, °still, °muffle, °stop (up), muzzle, °quiet(en), °curb, °suppress, °repress, °restrain, throttle, strangle, °check, °inhibit, °discourage: The department gagged him, forbidding any press interviews. **2** retch, °choke, °heave; °gasp for air, °struggle for breath; US keck: That drink made me gag.
—n. **3** °restraint, °curb, muzzle, °check: MI5 tried to put a gag on the revelations of the former spy.

gag² n. **1** °joke, °witticism, jest, °quip, °pun, °gibe, Colloq °wisecrack, Slang °crack: He told some gags but nobody found them funny. **2** practical °joke, °hoax, °prank, °trick, Colloq fast one: For a gag, we put a snake in the sergeant's bed.

gaiety n. **1** cheerfulness, exhilaration, elation, °glee, joie de vivre, buoyancy, light-heartedness, blitheness, °happiness, felicity, °pleasure, °delight, °joy, joyfulness, joyousness, exultation, °merriment, °mirth, mirthfulness, jubilation, °good or °high spirits, sprightliness, liveliness, joviality, jollity, °hilarity: The gaiety of the celebration was becoming infectious. **2** °Often, **gaieties**: merrymaking, °festivity, festivities, °celebration, °revelry, °revels, rejoicing, conviviality, Old-fashioned Brit mafficking: We all joined in the gaiety of Mardi Gras. **3** °colourfulness, brightness, gaudiness, garishness, °brilliance, brightness, cheeriness: The gaiety of her costume was offset by her lugubrious expression.

gaily adv. **1** °showily, gaudily, brightly, splendidly, brilliantly, colourfully, flashily, flamboyantly, garishly: The dancers appeared in their gaily coloured dresses. **2** °happily, cheerfully, cheerily, gleefully, joyously, joyfully, jubilantly, merrily, blithely, light-heartedly, airily, jauntily, insouciantly: The revellers came cavorting gaily down the street.

gain v. **1** °get, °obtain, °acquire, °procure, attain, °achieve, °secure, °earn, °win, °capture, °bag, °net, °harvest, °reap, °garner, glean, °collect, °gather, °come by, °pick up: Any advantage we gain today may be lost tomorrow. **2** °make, °get, °profit, gain ground, °earn, °benefit, °realize, °clear, °bring in, °produce, °yield: Have you gained from the transaction? **3** °improve, °recuperate, °progress, rally, °get °better, °advance, gain ground: Her health has gained steadily since the cyst was removed. **4** °catch up (to or on or with), °approach, °get nearer (to), °overtake, °close with, °close in (on), °narrow the gap, gain ground: As we came to the finish line, Tom was gaining on me. Though he kept gaining, I won. **5** °leave behind, outdistance, °draw or °pull away (from), widen the gap, °get or °go or °move °further or farther °ahead, °get °further or farther away (from), °increase the °lead: I kept gaining on him till I was a mile ahead. **6** °reach, °arrive at, °get to, °come to: After paddling for hours, we finally gained the shore. **7** °increase, °move °ahead, °improve, °advance, °progress, gain ground: Shares gained again on the exchange.
—n. **8** °profit, °advantage, °margin, °yield, °return, °revenue, °income, dividend, °benefit, emolument, °payment, °pay, °money; proceeds, °earnings, winnings; Colloq chiefly US °take, payout, °pay-off: What was your gain on the sale of the house? He has seen gains of 20 per cent on his investment. **9** °increase, °increment, °improvement, °rise, °addition, enhancement, °elevation, augmentation, upward or forward °movement, °advance, °progress: Each month has seen a gain in share prices. **10** °acquisition, °achievement, attainment: My gain was at the expense of their sacrifice.

gainful adj. °advantageous, °profitable, °productive, °fruitful, °beneficial, °useful, valuable, °worthwhile, °rewarding, remunerative, lucrative, moneymaking: Your father thinks it about time you sought gainful employment.

gala n. **1** °feote or fete, °festival, °festivity, °feast, °celebration, °event, red-letter day, °holiday, holy day, carnival, °occasion, °happening, pageant, °party, ball; field-day: The annual gala is planned for Midsummer's Eve.
—adj. **2** °merry, festive, °joyful, joyous, °gleeful, jovial, °gay, celebratory, °jolly, convivial, °happy, °cheerful, cheery: Her home-coming was a gala occasion.

gale n. **1** wind-storm, °strong °wind, (big or hard) °blow, °blast, turbulence, °storm, °tempest: I refuse to take the boat out in that gale. **2** °outburst, °burst, °explosion, °eruption; °peal, °roar, °scream, °shout, °howl, °shriek: Bea Lillie needed merely to raise an eyebrow to send her audience into gales of laughter.

gall¹ n. **1** °bitterness, acerbity, acrimony, harshness, vitriol, asperity, bile, spleen, causticness or causticity, °bite, mordacity or mordaciousness, sharpness, rancidness or rancidity; °venom, °poison, °rancour: Once more he

experienced the gall of disappointment.
2 °impudence, insolence, °impertinence,
audacity, brashness, brazenness, sauciness,
°effrontery, temerity, overconfidence,
°front, *Colloq* °brass, °nerve, °guts, cheek, lip,
crust, °sauce, *US and Canadian* chutzpah,
moxie; *Slang* balls: *One student had the gall to
suggest that he would be a better teacher than I am.*

gall[2] *n.* **1** °sore (°spot), abrasion, °scrape, graze,
°scratch, °chafe: *This gall on my leg is from the
saddle.* **2** °irritation, °annoyance, °nuisance,
°bother, exasperation, vexation, *Colloq* aggravation: *One has to tolerate a lot of gall in this job.*
—*v.* **3** °irritate, °chafe, abrade, °fret, °scrape,
°rub, °grate, °scratch: *His shoe was galling his
heel.* **4** °irritate, °annoy, °bother, vex, °irk,
°exasperate, °harass, harry, °plague, °provoke,
goad, °nag, °pester, hector, badger, nettle,
needle, °ruffle, °fret, °anger, °enrage, °inflame,
°infuriate, incense, arouse, *US* °rankle: *It galls
me to think of all the animals killed just to make
fur coats.*

gallant *adj.* **1** °brave, °courageous, °bold, valiant, °daring, °dauntless, °intrepid, plucky,
°fearless, valorous, unafraid, undaunted,
°manly, manful, plucky, mettlesome,
stout-hearted, lion-hearted, °heroic, °dashing,
(high-)°spirited: *Three gallant soldiers held off the
enemy attack.* **2** °chivalrous, courtly, °courteous,
°polite, °attentive, gentlemanly, °noble,
°gracious, °considerate, °thoughtful, °well-bred,
mannerly: *What man is so gallant today as to give
up his seat on a bus to a lady?* **3** °dignified,
°elegant, °imposing, °grand, °noble, °glorious,
°fine, °splendid, °majestic, °stately,
°magnificent: *Overwhelmed by four enemy men o'
war, the gallant ship sank beneath the waves.*
—*n.* **4** °champion, °hero, knight, cavalier, paladin: *Which gallant wears her scarf on his sleeve in
today's jousts?* **5** °lover, Romeo, °sweetheart,
°beloved, °paramour, boyfriend, beau, °escort,
°suitor, °admirer, *Literary* swain: *In those days,
gallants continually sent their ladies gifts and
flowers.*

gallows *n.* gibbet: *Another name for gallows was
'Tyburn tree', after that at Tyburn, in London.*

galore *adv.* in °abundance, in °large °quantity
or numbers or amounts, in °excess,
°everywhere, aplenty, in °profusion: *There were
prizes galore for everything from swimming to
skittles.*

gamble *v.* **1** °risk, °venture, °hazard, °bet,
wager, °stake, °chance, °speculate; °play,
°game, *Brit* °punt: *I wouldn't gamble that he'll be
on time. I go to Monte Carlo to gamble.* **2 gamble
on**: °back, °bet *or* wager on, °stake *or* put
°money on, take a °chance *or* flier on, °try one's
°luck *or* °fortune on, lay *or* place *or* make a
wager *or* °bet on; °count on, °rely on: *We gambled
on the horse to win. I was gambling on his having
forgotten the debt.*
—*n.* **3** °chance, °risk, °venture; uncertainty,
°speculation, *Colloq US* crap-shoot: *I had to take
the gamble that the rope would hold. All of life is just
a gamble.* **4** °bet, wager, °stake, *Brit* °punt: *She
took a gamble on number 14.*

game *n.* **1** °amusement, °pastime, °diversion,
°distraction, °recreation, °play; °sport: *She
regards love as just a game.* **2** °contest,
°competition, °meeting *or US also* °meet,
°tournament *or US also* tourney, °match,

°encounter, °engagement, °event, °round;
regatta: *Would you like to see a football game? The
games are held annually.* **3** °scheme, °plan, °plot,
°design, °stratagem, °strategy, °tactic, °artifice,
°trick, °device(s), ploy: *Aha! I am on to your little
game!* **4** °occupation, °line (of °work), °job,
°position, °field, °business, °trade, °profession,
Slang °racket: *She is in the advertising game.*
5 °quarry, °prey; °victim, °target: *Game has been
plentiful this year, especially pheasant and quail. He
is fair game for any unscrupulous swindler.* **6 play
games**: dissemble, °dissimulate, be °deceitful
or underhand, °misrepresent, °pretend,
°practise °deceit *or* °deception, °fake, feign: *She
wasn't serious about selling, she was just playing
games.*
—*adj.* **7** °ready, °willing, °prepared; plucky *or*
°spirited *or* °daring *or* °adventurous enough:
*She's game for anything: I'm sure she'll jump at the
chance of scuba-diving lessons.* **8** °plucky, °spirited,
high-spirited, °daring, devil-may-care,
°adventurous, unflinching, °courageous,
°brave, °bold, °heroic, *Colloq* nervy, gutsy: *Entering the cave to rescue the dog was a game thing for
him to do.*
—*v.* **9** °gamble: *He has taken up gaming as a
hobby.*

gamut *n.* °range, °scale, spectrum, compass,
°spread, °sweep, °field, series: *Parker said that
Hepburn's acting ran the whole gamut of emotions
from A to B.*

gang *n.* **1** °group, °band, °crowd, °company,
°pack, °mob, °ring: *The police are looking for the
gang that robbed the mail train.* **2** °clique, °set,
coterie, °circle, °party, °company, °team,
troupe: *A whole gang of my friends came over
yesterday evening.*
—*v.* **3 gang up (on** *or* **against)**: conspire *or* °plot
against, °combine *or* °unite *or* °unify *or* °join
(against), °league *or* °ally *or* °club *or* °band
(against), °join forces (against), °overwhelm:
*When they all ganged up on me, I decided to change
my mind.*

gangster *n.* °criminal, °gang °member,
°racketeer, Mafioso, °soldier, hooligan, gunman,
°thug, mugger, °robber, °tough, ruffian, desperado, brigand, bandit, *Brit* skinhead,
Australian and New Zealand larrikin, *Chiefly US
and Canadian* °hoodlum, gunslinger, *Colloq*
crook; *Slang* hood, hit man, *US* gunsel, torpedo,
mobster, goon: *The gangsters were arrested for
smuggling cocaine.*

gap *n.* **1** °opening, °space, °aperture, °distance,
°hole, °void, °gulf, °cavity, °break, °breach,
°crevice, °chink, °crack, °split, °division, cleft,
°rift, °rip, °tear, °rent; °interruption, °interval,
lacuna, hiatus, discontinuity, disruption; °lull,
°pause, °rest, °recess, °halt, °stop, °suspension,
°delay, °wait, °intermission, °respite: *The gap
between the walls is just big enough for a child. I can
see through a gap in the curtain. There is a gap in
his payment record.* **2** °difference, divergence,
°disparity, °disagreement, inconsistency,
°discrepancy; °division, °distinction: *A gap
exists between your ideas of justice and mine.*

gape *v.* **1** °stare, °gawk, goggle, *Slang*
°rubberneck, *Brit* gawp *or* gaup: *She gaped when
they brought in the boar's head.* **2** yawn, °open
°wide, °part; °split: *The jaws of the huge shark
gaped to swallow the diver.*

garbage n. °rubbish, °refuse, °waste, °muck, offal, sweepings, °swill, °filth, slops, dross, scraps, °junk, °litter, debris, detritus, *Chiefly US and Canadian* °trash, *Slang* crap: *The garbage in the river is a health hazard.*

garble v. **1** °warp, °distort, °twist, °corrupt, °adulterate, °slant, °colour, °mangle, °mutilate, °pervert, °doctor, °falsify, °misrepresent, belie, misstate, misquote, misreport, mistranslate, misrender; °misunderstand, misconstrue, misread: *She has garbled the story and it makes no sense. I've garbled your message completely.* **2** °confuse, °mix up, °jumble, °mumble, °mutter: *He garbles his words so badly that I cannot understand him.*

garish adj. °gaudy, °flashy, °glaring, °cheap, °tawdry, florid, raffish, °vulgar, °harsh, °loud, meretricious, Brummagem, °showy, °crude, °tasteless, *Colloq* °flash, *Slang US* glitzy: *Their flat is filled with the most garish decorations.*

garland n. **1** wreath, festoon, °crown, chaplet, circlet: *Diana crowned the sleeping Endymion with a garland of flowers.* —v. **2** °wreathe, festoon, °crown, °decorate, °coil, °spiral, °encircle, °ring, °circle: *The columns were all garlanded with brightly coloured paper decorations.*

garments n.pl. garb, °clothes, clothing, raiment, °dress, attire, °apparel, °costume, °outfit, °habit, vestments, habiliment; °wardrobe; °uniform, livery; *Colloq* duds, °rig, togs, *Slang* rags, threads, °gear: *All his garments are custom-made in Savile Row.*

garner v. °gather, °collect, °accumulate, °assemble, °amass, °store (up), °stock (up), °husband, °lay in or up or down or by, °heap or °pile up, °put away or by, °stow (away), °cache, °store, °save, °reserve: *He garnered what he could from the family estate.*

gash n. **1** °cut, °slash, °wound, °score, cleft, °incision, laceration, °slit, °groove, °split: *The chisel slipped, cutting a deep gash in the table.* —v. **2** °cut, °slash, °wound, °score, °cleave, incise, °lacerate, °slit, °groove, °split: *I've gashed my hand on a rusty nail.*

gasp v. **1** °pant, °gulp for air, fight for air or breath; catch one's breath, snort, °huff, °puff: *I gasped when I saw the condition of the room.* —n. **2** °snort, °puff, °blow, °gulp, wheeze: *He gave a gasp of horror.*

gate n. **1** gateway, °barrier, doorway, door, access, °entrance, °exit, °passage, °opening: *The garden gate sagged on its hinges.* **2** °admissions, °attendance, °crowd, audience, assemblage: *We had the biggest gate of the year at yesterday's game.*

gather v. **1** °collect, °assemble, °accumulate, °amass, °muster, °heap or °pile (up), °garner, °pick, °harvest, glean, °get or °bring together, stockpile, °stock: *I gathered all the firewood I could find.* **2** °collect, °assemble, convene, °meet, °huddle, forgather or foregather; °get or °come together, congregate, °turn out, °flock or °herd (together), °group, °cluster, °throng, °crowd, °swarm, °rally: *We gathered round the old man's bed.* **3** °purse, shirr, °pucker, tuck, °ruffle, pleat, °draw or °pull together, °contract, constrict: *The fabric is gathered at the waist.* **4** °draw, conclude, °infer, °assume, °deduce, °understand, °learn, °hear, be led to °believe: *I gather that you'd prefer not to collect the award in person.* **5** °increase, °grow, °enlarge, °expand,

°extend, wax, °heighten, °deepen, °intensify, °build, °rise: *He stood, menacingly, in the gathering shadows.*

gathering n. °assembly, convocation, °convention, congress, assemblage, °meeting, °get-together, °turnout, conclave, °rally, aggregation: *There is a gathering of the clan once a year.*

gaudy adj. °garish, °flashy, °glaring, °tawdry, °loud, °cheap, florid, °showy, °ostentatious, raffish, °vulgar, °crude, °tasteless, Brummagem, meretricious, tinselly, gimcrack, °shoddy, trashy, *Brit* tatty, *US and Canadian* honky-tonk, *Colloq US* °tacky, chintzy: *The carnival stands were painted pink, purple, and other gaudy colours.*

gauge v. **1** °measure, °determine, °weigh, °calculate, °compute, °reckon, °figure, *US technical also* gage: *Try to gauge the height of that building.* **2** °judge, °evaluate, appraise, assess, °rate, °estimate, °guess, *US technical also* gage: *How can we gauge the strength of the opposition?* —n. **3** °standard, °yardstick, criterion, benchmark, °basis, °measure, °norm, °model, °example, °pattern, °rule, °touchstone, °test, °guide, guideline, *US* litmus °test, *Technical also* gage: *You cannot use your compulsive work habits as a gauge for others.* **4** °scope, °capacity, °amount, °extent, °measure, °size, dimension(s), °magnitude, °degree, °limit: *There are a number of narrow-gauge railways in Wales. What will be the gauge of your involvement in the enterprise?*

gaunt adj. **1** °emaciated, °scrawny, °raw-boned, bony, angular, °haggard, skeletal, wasted, starved-looking, cadaverous, scraggy, spindly, °meagre, hollow-cheeked, °spare, °skinny, lank(y), pinched, °thin, underweight: *We were shocked by the gaunt faces of the famine victims.* **2** °dreary, °dismal, °bleak, °bare, °barren, °deserted, °desolate, °harsh, °hostile, unfriendly, inimical, °stern, °forbidding, °stark, °grim, °forlorn: *Under the low cloud, the moor looked even more gaunt than usual.*

gawk n. **1** °oaf, lout, bumpkin, °clod, °boor, churl, °dolt, dunderhead or dunderpate, ninny, ninny-hammer, ignoramus, °fool, simpleton, ass, bungler, bumbler, *Colloq* clodhopper, lummox, *Slang chiefly US* old-fashioned galoot or galloot, °lug: *You big gawk, get out of my way!* —v. **2** °stare, goggle, °gape, *Colloq* °rubberneck, *Slang Brit* gawp or gaup: *Stop gawking and help me get him to a hospital.*

gay adj. **1** See homosexual, 1, below. **2** °happy, °blithe, jovial, light-hearted, °carefree, °debonair, °cheerful, °gleeful, °bright, °joyful, joyous, jubilant, high-spirited, °merry, °lively, °vivacious, °buoyant, °effervescent, °bubbly, bubbling, sparkling, *US* chipper: *In those days our hearts were young and gay.* **3** °garish, °gaudy, °flashy, °bright, °brilliant, °vivid, many-coloured: *The gay decorations added to the atmosphere to the party.* —n. **4** See homosexual, 2, below.

gaze v. **1** °look at or on or upon or over, °view, °regard, °contemplate, °stare; °wonder, °gape: *She stood gazing out to sea. I gazed at the screen in disbelief.* —n. **2** °fixed or °steady or °intent °look, °stare, °look: *His gaze faltered and he averted his eyes.*

gear n. **1** °cog, cog-wheel; gearbox, °mechanism, machinery; °works: *This gear operates the automatic doors.* **2** °equipment, °apparatus, appliances, °implements, °tools, °tackle, utensils,

supplies, °material(s), accessories, accoutrements *or US also* accouterments, appurtenances, °paraphernalia, panoply, °outfit, °trappings, °fixtures, materiel *or matériel*: *Have you taken all the camping gear?* **3** °clothing, °apparel, attire, °clothes, °garments, °habit, habiliments, vestments, raiment, °regalia, °uniform, livery, *Colloq* duds, togs, *Brit* clobber: *You should keep your gear in your locker.* **4** °belongings, °things, °stuff, °effects, °kit, chattels, °goods, impedimenta, (°bag and) baggage, accoutrements *or US also* accouterments, *Colloq* °junk, *Slang* shit: *Get your gear together and get out of here!*
—*v.* **5** °adjust, °adapt, °fit, °suit, °tailor, °accommodate: *You will have to gear your schedule according to our plans.*

gem *n.* **1** gemstone, °jewel, stone, °precious *or* semiprecious stone: *The crown was set with rubies and other precious gems.* **2** °ideal, °quintessence, °perfect °example; °pearl (of °great price), °marvel, °flower, élite, cream, *crème de la crème*, °pick, °nonpareil, °treasure, °prize, °masterpiece, *chef-d'œuvre*: *This is a perfect gem of a painting. The vale of Grasmere is a gem in the diadem of the Lake District.*

general *adj.* **1** °common, °prevailing, accepted, °popular, °public, communal, community, widespread, shared, °extensive, °prevalent, °universal, worldwide, °global; °comprehensive, °inclusive, all-inclusive, non-exclusive, °overall, unrestricted: *The general feeling is that she should resign. We demanded a general revision of the law.* **2** °ordinary, °common, °normal, °customary, °habitual, °regular, °usual, run-of-the-mill, °everyday, °familiar, °accustomed; non-specialized, unspecialized, non-specific, unspecific: *Indoor plumbing became general only in the twentieth century. Within the general area of ceramics there are scores of specialities.* **3** °mixed, assorted, °miscellaneous, heterogeneous, °encyclopedic *or* encyclopaedic, diversified, extended, °broad, °comprehensive, °inclusive, all-inclusive, non-exclusive, °overall, blanket, across the °board, °sweeping, °panoramic, °catholic, composite, combined, blended, °hybrid, °mongrel: *The plan is to prepare a general work of reference.* **4** °vague, °indefinite, °broad, ill-defined, °loose, °inexact, °imprecise, undetailed, non-specific, unspecific, generalized, °overall; °approximate: *This kind of general report fails to pinpoint problems.*

generality *n.* **1** generalization, abstraction, °abstract, °vague *or* °loose *or* °sweeping *or* °indefinite °statement, °imprecise *or* °vague notion: *His talks are characterized by empty generality, without detailed facts.* **2** °Often, **generalities**: °principle(s), °law(s), abstraction(s), generalization(s), universality *or* universalities: *You have given us the generalities, now we want the particulars.*

generally *adv.* **1** °usually, commonly, °ordinarily, in °general, customarily, habitually, conventionally, normally, typically, on °average, as a °rule, by and °large, for the most °part, mostly, °mainly, on the °whole, predominantly: *Generally, people do not have a healthy diet. He is generally in the office at noon.* **2** superficially, non-specifically, unspecifically, °roughly, broadly, in a °general way, loosely, °approximately, °largely, in the °main, °mainly, °principally: *He covered the subject generally, not dwelling on details.*

generate *v.* **1** °produce, °create, °originate, °make, °manufacture: *At these stations we can generate 1000 megawatts of electricity.* **2** °spawn, °father, sire, °bring into being, procreate, °breed, beget, engender, °propagate: *This one fish would generate millions of offspring if all survived.* **3** °produce, °create, °give °rise to, °inspire, °whip up, °cause, °initiate: *Her good fortune generated in him a feeling of envy.* **4** °produce, °create, °invent, °coin, °make up, °fabricate, °fashion, °devise, °develop, °form, °forge, °mould, contrive, °construct, °put together: *We must generate a new theory to account for these phenomena.*

generation *n.* **1** °production, °reproduction, propagation, procreation, begetting, fathering, siring: *In the lower animals, the generation of offspring is asexual.* **2** °time(s), °day(s), °age, °period, °era, epoch: *The trait did not appear till later generations. The 1950s and '60s spawned the yuppie generation of the '80s.* **3** °origination, °creation, genesis, inception, °initiation, °start, °beginning, °institution, °establishment, °formation, formulation: *The generation of legal systems can be traced to the oldest civilizations.* **4** °crop; °age (°group); contemporaries: *This generation of Americans has a rendezvous with destiny. He prefers to be with people of his own generation.*

generous *adj.* **1** °bounteous, °bountiful, magnanimous, °charitable, eleemosynary, °philanthropic, °lavish, open-handed, °free, °liberal, unstinting, ungrudging, beneficent, °benevolent, big-hearted, munificent: *Not everyone who has money is generous with it.* **2** °magnanimous, °benevolent, °charitable, °unselfish, °humanitarian, humane, °kindly, °noble, high-minded, °lofty, °good, °disinterested, °unprejudiced: *He was too generous in acknowledging the accomplishments of his political foes.* **3** °plentiful, °full, °lavish, over-flowing, °abundant, bounteous, °handsome, copious, °ample: *They certainly serve generous portions at that restaurant.*

genial *adj.* affable, °amiable, °cordial, °warm, °friendly, congenial, °agreeable, °good-natured, good-humoured, well-disposed, °neighbourly, °sociable, °kindly, °kind, °hospitable, °easygoing, °relaxed, °pleasant, °nice, °cheerful, cheery, convivial: *And here is your genial host, Sonny Gegenschein!*

genitals *n.pl.* genitalia, °sexual *or* reproductive organs, °sex organs, organs of procreation *or* °generation, °private parts, privates: *They wore loincloths to cover their genitals.*

genius *n.* **1** °mastermind, °master, °virtuoso, °intellect; maestro, °expert, °adept; *Colloq* °brain, Einstein: *At the age of nine, this genius entered university.* **2** °intelligence, °brilliance, °wit, °ingenuity, brains, °ability, °aptitude: *She is a woman of incredible genius.* **3** °talent, °gift, °knack, °faculty, °flair, °aptitude, °forte, °capacity, °ability, °capability: *He has a genius for saying the wrong thing.*

genre *n.* °kind, °sort, °type, °class, °style, °brand, °character, °category, genus, species, °variety, °fashion: *Her paintings are in the classicist genre.*

genteel adj. **1** °over-polite, °unnatural, °pretentious, °affected, °mannered, putting on airs, °pompous, overdone, Colloq °posh, la-di-da or lah-di-dah or la-de-da, °phoney or US also phony, Brit county: The Brumfits are a bit too genteel for my taste. **2** °courtly, °polite, °civil, well-mannered, °well-bred, °courteous, mannerly, °gracious, °proper, °respectable, °decorous, °ladylike, gentlemanly, °chivalrous, cavalier, °debonair, °suave, patrician, °high-class, °upper-class, aristocratic, thoroughbred, blue-blooded, °noble, °royal, Colloq classy, tony, °upper crust, US silk-stocking: His son married a woman from an ancient, genteel house. **3** °refined, °polished, °sophisticated, °debonair, °suave, urbane, cosmopolitan, °cultivated, cultured, °elegant, Colloq ritzy: Why small feet are considered genteel, I cannot say.

gentle adj. **1** °kind, °kindly, °mild, °tender, °benign, °moderate, °easy, °quiet, °calm, °still, °temperate, unruffled, untroubled, undisturbed, °tranquil, °restful, °peaceful, pacific, placid, °smooth, °lenient, °patient, °indulgent, °soothing, °thoughtful, °gracious, compassionate, humane, tender-hearted, °merciful; °soft, °light, balmy: Amy is very gentle with the patients. A gentle breeze barely stirred the leaves. The gentle waves belied the terror that lurked below. **2** °tame, °tractable, docile, °manageable, controllable; °broken: As he's a beginner, he's been given a gentle mare to ride. **3** °gradual, °easy, °moderate: The car rolled down the gentle slope and stopped.

gentry n. ladies and gentlemen, élite, aristocracy, landed gentry, gentlefolk, °upper class(es) or strata, cream, crème de la crème; landowners, Brit squirearchy, Colloq °upper crust or strata: He thinks he is privileged because he belongs to the gentry.

genuine adj. **1** °authentic, °real, bona fide, °veritable, °legitimate, °true, °original, °proper, not °counterfeit or °fake; °pukka or pukkah or pucka: Is that a genuine diamond? I know his feelings for her are genuine. Armstrong is a genuine leader of men. **2** °candid, °frank, °open, °sincere, °earnest, °honest, unfeigned: His art is much more genuine than the pretentious output of his contemporaries.

germ n. **1** °micro-organism, °microbe, bacterium, virus, Colloq °bug: Germs were not conceived of before Leeuwenhoek's invention of the microscope. **2** °source, °origin, fount, embryo, °seed, °root, rudiment, °beginning, °start, °base, °basis: The germ of romantic literature lies in folk-tales.

gesture n. **1** °movement, °motion, gesticulation, °signal, °indication, °action, Colloq US high °sign: She made a gesture of dismissal. **2** °formality, °move; gambit, ploy; °token, °indication, °symbol: Sending her flowers was a friendly gesture. Their burning the flag was a gesture of defiance.
—v. **3** °motion, gesticulate, °signal, °sign, °indicate, Colloq US give (someone) the high °sign: He gestured for me to step forward.

get v. **1** °obtain, °secure, °acquire, °come by or into (the) °possession of, °procure, °pick up; °collect; °buy, °purchase, °book, °retain, °hire, °engage, °rent, °lease; accede to, °inherit, °fall °heir to, °succeed to: Where did you get these beautiful prints? You had better get yourself a good lawyer. They got the furniture from his mother's estate. **2** °receive; be °given, °come by: He got a bicycle from his grandma. I got a job at the carwash. **3** °earn, °receive, °realize, °make, °take, °gross, °clear, °net, °pocket, be paid; °win, Colloq °take home, °pull down: He gets a lot of money for just standing there and answering questions. **4** °fetch, °go (to or and) get, °go for or after, °pick up; °bring (back), °retrieve: Please get me a cup of tea. **5** °catch, °contract, °have, °suffer from, °come down with, °fall °ill or °sick with, be afflicted with, °become infected with, °acquire: You'll get pneumonia if you go out without your coat. **6** °become, °fall: We got ill from eating too much chocolate. **7** °become, °turn, °grow: It got very cold last night. He got rich almost overnight. **8** °capture, °seize, °arrest, °take, apprehend, °grab, °pick up, °lay °hold of, °bag, Colloq collar, °nab, °pinch: Are the police sure that they got the right person? **9** °manage, °arrange, °come, °succeed; contrive, °fix it, °manoeuvre, °manipulate, Colloq °wangle: How did you get to be chairman? **10** °reach, °arrive (at), °come, °go, °travel, °journey: She got home by taxi. **11** °catch, °take, °enter, °make, °come or °go by, °travel or °journey by: He got the midnight train. **12** °reach, get in °touch with, °communicate with, get onto or through to, Colloq °contact: We finally got him just before he left for the day. **13** °receive, °pick up, °tune in to or on, °listen to or °watch: I cannot get that programme. **14** °persuade, °prevail (up)on, °coax, °induce, °influence, °cajole, °wheedle, °talk (someone) into, °sway, °bring (someone) round, °make, °cause: How did you ever get them to let you go? **15** °put, °place, °set, °fit, °manoeuvre, °manipulate, wiggle, °wriggle: I can't get this knob back on. **16** °affect, °stir, °move, °touch, arouse, °stimulate, °excite, °have an °impact or °effect on, °make an °impression on, °impress, °leave a °mark on, get to, Colloq °turn (someone) on: Those old romantic songs really get me. **17** get at, °irritate, °annoy, vex, °irk, nettle, pique, °provoke, °anger, °exasperate, °bother, °perturb, rile, Colloq °bug, get (someone's) goat, °rub (someone) (up) the wrong way, Sometimes non-standard °aggravate: Doesn't it get you to see people going unpunished for their crimes? **18** baffle, °confuse, confound, °puzzle, °perplex, °bewilder: You've got me! I don't know where it is! **19** °understand, °appreciate, °fathom, °see, °grasp, apprehend, °perceive, °follow, comprehend, °take in, °work out, make head(s) or tail(s) of: You just don't get the joke, do you? **20** °catch, °hear: I didn't get the name; please repeat it. **21** °derive, °learn, glean, absorb, °take in: Did you get anything from yesterday's lecture? **22** °have, °place, °put, °fix, pinpoint: Eventually, I'll get him where I want him! **23** get °even with, °revenge oneself on, °take °vengeance on, °pay (someone) back, °settle or °even the °score with, get back at: I'll get him for betraying me if it's the last thing I do! **24** °strike, °hit, °punch, smack; °shoot; °hurt, °harm, °damage, °injure; Slang sock, slug: She got him right between the eyes. **25 get about** or **around**: **a** °spread, become known, °leak (out), °circulate, be bruited about or around, be noised °abroad, °go about or around: He let the news get about that he needed a secretary. **b** be socially °active, °socialize, °go or get out; °run about or around, °gad about: Since his accident, he doesn't get around much any more. **26 get across**: get or °put over, °put across, get through, °communicate, make °clear, °impart: *She is trying to get across to you the fact that she despises television.* **27 get ahead**: °succeed, °prosper, be *or* become °successful, do well, °flourish, °thrive, °make good, °progress, °rise (up) in the world, *Colloq* °go places: *With his contacts, he's bound to get ahead.* **28 get along**: **a** be °friendly *or* compatible (with), °associate (with), °agree (with), be °agreeable, get on (with), *Colloq* °hit it off (with): *She gets along with most people quite well. Do you think they'll get along?* **b** °manage, °cope, °shift, °fare, °survive, make both ends meet, keep the wolf from the door, keep one's head above water, *Colloq* get by, °make out, °make do: *How are you getting along with your new novel?* **c** °leave, °depart, °go *or* °move away, get °going, get on, °go along, °proceed: *I have to get along now or I'll miss my train.* **d** °progress, °proceed, get on, °advance, °move °ahead *or* along *or* on: *How are you getting along with your new novel?* **e** get on, °age, get *or* become *or* °grow older, °advance: *They are getting along but you wouldn't guess that they're eighty.* **29 get around**: **a** See 25, above. **b** See 46, below. **30 get at**: **a** °gain access to, access, °reach, °put *or* °lay one's hands on, get to: *I can't get at the lock from there.* **b** °intend, °mean, °suggest, °hint (at), °insinuate, °imply, have in °mind *or* °view, °contemplate: *She just didn't understand what I was getting at.* **c** get, °tease, °taunt, °criticize, find °fault with, °carp, °nag, °pick on, *US* get to: *She is really beginning to get at me with her persistent criticism.* **d** get to, °influence, °intimidate, °corrupt, °bribe, °undermine, °subvert, suborn: *They tried to get at the judge.* **e** °learn, °find out, ascertain, °determine: *The police said they were only trying to get at the facts.* **31 get away**: **a** °escape, °leave, °break out *or* away, °flee, °depart, make good one's °escape, °elude one's captors, °break °free, °disappear: *He will never be able to get away now!* **b** °escape, take a °holiday *or US also* vacation, get *or* take a °rest *or* °respite: *I must get away for a few days.* **c** °start, get *or* °take off: *Black Flash got away from the starting gate at top speed.* **32 get back**: **a** °return, °come *or* °go back: *I'll try to get back before midnight.* **b** reacquire, °recover, regain, °retrieve, °recoup, repossess: *Can you get your money back for that hat?* **33 get back at**: See 23, above. **34 get behind**: °back, °support, °promote, °finance, °fund, °push, *Colloq* °plug, hype: *If you get behind the enterprise, I know it will succeed.* **35 get by**: See 28 b, above. **36 get down**: **a** dismount, alight, °descend, °come *or* °go down, °climb *or* °step down, get off: *He got down from his horse and drew his gun.* **b** °write (down), °note (down), °record, make a °note of: *She wasn't able to get down everything Shaw said.* **c** °depress, dispirit, °sadden, dishearten, °discourage, deject: *Don't let a little thing like that get you down.* **d** °swallow, °eat: *No sooner does he get some food down than it comes right back up again.* **37 get down to**: °concentrate *or* °focus on, °turn °attention to, °attend to: *Let's get down to business.* **38 get in**: **a** °enter, get into *or* on *or* onto, °embark, entrain, emplane *or* enplane, get *or* °go aboard: *We got in the car and were driven away. You can get in here.* **b** °enter, °arrive, °return, °come *or* °go in: *I got in at eight today.* **c** °fit *or* °squeeze in, °insert, °slip in, °include: *He got in my comment.*

The doctor got me in before anyone else. **d** °arrive, °come in, °land: *My flight got in at dawn.* **39 get into**: **a** put on, don, °dress in, get dressed in: *Here, get into this uniform.* **b** °go into, °discuss, become °involved in, °pursue, °treat, °describe, delineate, °detail, °follow up on, °penetrate: *Do you really want me to get into the nasty details?* **c** be into, be *or* become °involved in, °take up, °pursue, °enjoy, °like, become °enthusiastic about, *Slang* get off on, get *or* become °high on: *I could really get into farming.* **d** See 38 a, above. **40 get off**: **a** alight, °disembark, get down from, get out of, dismount, °descend (from), °climb *or* °step down off *or* from, deplane, detrain: *She got off her bike and came towards me.* **b** °leave, °depart, °go (off), °set out *or* off: *I hope to get off tomorrow morning.* **c** °remove, °take off, °shed, doff: *Can you get those boots off easily?* **d** cause to be °set *or* °go °free, be *or* cause to be acquitted *or* liberated *or* released *or* °set °free: *A clever lawyer could have got him off. He got off on a technicality.* **41 get off on**: See 39 c, above. **42 get on**: **a** See 28, above. **b** See 38 a, above. **c** See 39 a, above. **d** grow *or* become °late: *It's getting on and they'll be waiting.* **43 get onto**: **a** See 12, above. **b** See 38 a, above. **c** °discover, °learn about, become °aware of, °find out about, *Colloq Brit* °twig, *US* cotton (on) to: *If they get onto the missing stores we're in for it.* **44 get out (of)**: **a** °leave, °depart, °go out *or* away, be off, °retire: *We got out as quickly as we could.* **b** °escape, °extricate oneself; be released: *She thought she'd never get out alive.* **c** °extract, °draw, wrest, °force, °drag *or* °pry out, wring *or* get from: *They'll never get anything out of me!* **d** °gain, °profit: *Ask yourself what you will get out of the deal.* **e** °avoid, °evade, °sidestep, °escape: *Gabriela was somehow always able to get out of PE class.* **f** See 25 b, above. **45 get over**: **a** surmount, °cross, °climb, °pass, °traverse: *A dog can't get over a fence that high.* **b** °recover *or* °recuperate from, °survive: *Which takes longer, getting over a love affair or the measles?* **c** °finish, °complete, bring to an °end: *Let's get this over with as soon as possible.* **d** See 26, above. **46 get round *or* around**: **a** °bypass, circumvent, skirt, °avoid, °evade, °elude, °outsmart, °outwit, outmanoeuvre, outflank, steal a march on, *Colloq* give (someone) the °run-around: *Chris is always trying to get round the parking restrictions.* **b** °cajole, °wheedle, °flatter, °persuade, °coax, °win over: *I didn't want to propose, but she managed to get round me.* **c** See 25 b, above. **47 get round *or* around to**: get *or* °come to, °reach, °arrive at °(finally), °find °time for: *He said he would do the repairs if he got round to it.* **48 get through**: **a** (°help to) °succeed *or* °complete: *She got me through the ordeal. Without her help, I never could have got through.* **b** °reach, °contact: *The line is engaged and I cannot get through to mother.* **c** °finish, conclude: *When you get through, please put away the dishes.* **d** °communicate (with): *Parents sometimes have trouble getting through to their children.* **49 get (to)**: **a** °arrive at, °come to; °near, °approach: *What time did you get to the office? How did you get home?* **b** See 28 c, d, above. **50 get together**: **a** °gather, °accumulate, °collect, °assemble: *Get your things together and leave at once!* **b** °assemble, convene, °gather, °meet, congregate, °socialize: *Have you time to get together* on Friday? **c** °arrive at *or* °reach an °agreement *or* °settlement, °come to terms, °come to an °understanding: *I think we can get together on the question of wages.* **51 get up: a** °arise, °awaken, °wake (up): *I get up at dawn.* **b** °stand (up): *Get up and you'll be able to reach it.* **c** °mount, °climb (up), ascend: *Can we get up the next hill? She got up on the table and started to dance.* **d** °create, °devise, °organize, °arrange, °prepare: *We got up a cabaret for the after-dinner entertainment.* **e** °dress, °clothe, °apparel, °outfit, attire, °turn out, deck out, °rig out, °dress up, °fit out *or* up: *She got herself up as a cabaret dancer.* **f** °study, °learn, *US* get up on: *You'd best get up your history before the exam.* **52 get up to:** become *or* be °involved in, be up to: *If you don't watch her, she'll get up to no good.*

getaway *n.* °escape, °flight, °retreat: *The prisoners made their getaway in a van. Lady Fenella was so boring I couldn't wait to make my getaway.*

get-together *n.* °gathering, °meeting, °conference, °convention: *We had a get-together at my house. Can we arrange a get-together for all the members?*

get-up *n.* **1** °costume, °outfit; °rig: *He came in a diver's get-up.* **2** °format, layout, °arrangement, °structure, °look, °style: *Who is responsible for the magazine's new get-up?*

gewgaw *n.* trinket, °bauble, gimcrack, °trifle, knick-knack, bagatelle, kickshaw, °toy, °novelty, bijou, °vanity; bric-à-brac *or* bric-à-brac: *She has a huge collection of worthless gewgaws.*

ghastly *adj.* **1** °dreadful, °awful, °terrible, °terrifying, °frightful, °hideous, °horrible, horrendous, horrid, horrifying, °grim, °grisly, °loathsome, °gruesome, °ugly, °repellent, °repulsive, °shocking, appalling, *Colloq* °gross, °scary: *He was involved in a ghastly accident.* **2** °grim, cadaverous, °haggard, ashen, °wan, °pale, pallid, °pasty(-faced), °drawn, livid, °ghostly, °spectral, °macabre: *She looked ghastly after the surgery.* **3** °awful, °bad, °terrible, °ill, ailing, °sick: *We felt ghastly after eating the under-cooked chicken.*

ghost *n.* **1** apparition, °phantom, °spectre, phantasm, °shade, °spirit, wraith, poltergeist, banshee, double-ganger, *doppelgänger*, ghoul, manes, *No. Eng. dialect* boggart; °hallucination, °illusion, °vision; *Colloq* spook: *The ghost of his uncle appeared before him.* **2** °hint, °suggestion, °shadow, °trace, scintilla, glimmer: *Vera hasn't the ghost of a chance of meeting anyone suitable at the office.*

ghostly *adj.* **1** °spectral, ghostlike, wraithlike, phantasmal, °phantom, °eerie, °unreal, °unnatural, °supernatural, preternatural, °unearthly, °sinister, °strange, uncanny, °weird, *Colloq* spooky, °scary, creepy: *I heard a ghostly voice calling my name.* **2** See ghastly, 2, above.

ghoulish *adj.* **1** °devilish, demonic, °satanic, °diabolic(al), °fiendish, demoniac(al), caco-demonic, Mephistophelian; °infernal, hellish, malign: *The coven engage in the most ghoulish practices.* **2** °macabre, °grisly, °morbid, °gruesome, °disgusting, °monstrous, °abominable, °hideous, horrendous, °horrible, horrifying, horrid, °brutal, barbaric, °savage, °ruthless, pitiless, °merciless, °cruel, °vicious,

feral, °inhuman, bloodthirsty, °ferocious, *Colloq* °sick: *She has some ghoulish notions about being eaten alive by rats.*

giant *n.* **1** °superhuman, titan, colossus, Goliath; giantess, amazon, °ogre; behemoth, °monster, leviathan, mammoth: *Blocking the road in front of Jack was a giant nearly thirty feet tall.* —*adj.* **2** See gigantic, below.

gibberish *n.* °drivel, °nonsense, °rubbish, gibber, °prattle, twaddle, gabble, °jabber, balderdash, jibber-jabber, blather *or* blether, Jabberwocky, °gobbledegook *or* gobbledygook, °mumbo-jumbo, rodomontade, Gongorism, cackle, °chatter, °patter, °jargon, °babble, clap-trap, poppycock, *Colloq* tripe, codswallop, crap, bunk, piffle, *US* °garbage, horse feathers; *Taboo slang* balls, bull(shit), *US* crock (of shit): *If one listens to such gibberish long enough, one begins to believe it.*

gibe *v.* **1** jibe (at), °jeer (at), °scoff (at), °flout, °mock, °deride, make °fun of, °poke °fun at, °ridicule, °twit, °taunt, °sneer (at), °chaff, °tease, °rag, °heckle, *No. Eng. dialect* gird, *Colloq* kid, rib, *US and Canadian* razz: *All of us at school used to gibe at David because he wore fancy clothes.* —*n.* **2** jibe, °jeer, °taunt, °sneer, °dig, °cutting °remark, °thrust, °chaff, °raillery, scoffing, °derision, °ridicule, °mockery, *Rare* mycterism, *Slang* °crack, °wisecrack: *David paid no attention to his classmates' gibes.*

giddy *adj.* **1** °dizzy, °faint, unsteady, light-headed, vertiginous, reeling, *Colloq* woozy: *This medication may make you feel a bit giddy.* **2** °silly, °frivolous, °scatterbrained, °flighty, °capricious, °irresponsible, °erratic, °fickle, °volatile, °impulsive, °reckless, °whimsical: *You can't marry a giddy young girl like Peggy.*

gift *n.* **1** °present, °donation, °favour, °grant, °largesse, °bounty, benefaction, °offering, °honorarium, contribution, give-away, °premium, °bonus, °prize; alms, hand-out, °dole, °charity, °benefit; °tip, gratuity, baksheesh *or* backsheesh, *pourboire*, cumshaw: *Before we left, our neighbours made a gift to us of some local pottery.* **2** °talent, °ability, °aptitude, °genius, °flair, °knack, °facility, °forte, °strength, strong point, °bent, °capability, °capacity, °power: *Her family never recognized her special gifts.*

gifted *adj.* °talented, °able, skilled, °capable, °skilful, °outstanding, °excellent, °superior, °superb, °brilliant, °expert, °master, °masterful, masterly, °virtuoso, first-class, °first-rate, top-drawer, top-flight, °good, *Colloq* top-notch, ace, crackerjack, °crack: *Grants are available for gifted, indigent artists.*

gigantic *adj.* °big, °large, °huge, °enormous, °massive, °giant, °colossal, °immense, mammoth, tremendous, stupendous, °towering, staggering, °vast, titanic, gargantuan, elephantine, Cyclopean, Herculean, Brobdingnagian; king-size, extra-large, *Colloq* °jumbo, walloping, °whopping, °thumping, thundering, strapping, super-duper, *US* humongous: *The gigantic tower, reaching to the heavens, appeared before us.*

giggle *v.* **1** °titter, °snicker, snigger, °chuckle, °laugh, chortle, cackle, °twitter: *Stop that giggling at the rear of the classroom!*

—*n*. **2** °titter, °snicker, snigger, °chuckle, °laugh, chortle, cackle, °twitter: *Did I hear a giggle?* **3** °joke, °prank, °laugh: *Just for a giggle, we tied his shoelaces together.*

gimmick *n*. **1** °device, °strategy, °stratagem, ploy, °trick, °ruse, °wile, °subterfuge, °manoeuvre, °artifice, °deception, °trap, °snare, *US* °hook, *Colloq* °dodge: *We need some sort of gimmick to attract buyers.* **2** °device, contrivance, °gadget, °invention, *Colloq* °contraption, widget, thingumbob *or* thingumabob *or* thingamabob, thingumajig *or* thingamajig *or* thingummy, whatchamacallit, what's-its-name, *Brit* doodah, *US* doohickey, doodad, hickey, whosis, whatsis, dingus, Rube Goldberg (°invention), *Chiefly US and Canadian* gismo *or* gizmo: *He uses some kind of gimmick to break into cars.*

gingerly *adv*. **1** warily, cautiously, charily, carefully, delicately, °fastidious, daintily, squeamishly, tentatively, nervously, cannily, circumspectly, guardedly, watchfully, timidly, timorously, shyly: *Handle that nitroglycerine very gingerly.*
—*adj*. **2** °wary, °cautious, chary, °careful, °fastidious, °delicate, °dainty, °squeamish, °tentative, °nervous, canny, circumspect, °guarded, watchful, °timid, timorous, °shy: *Note the gingerly way he handles the nitroglycerine.*

girl *n*. **1** female, °woman, °lass, (°young) lady, °miss, mademoiselle, wench, *Fräulein*, °maid, °maiden, damsel, demoiselle, *Irish* colleen, *Australian and New Zealand* sheila, *Colloq* chick, filly, gal, *Slang* bird, frail, skirt, piece, mouse, *Brit* crumpet, bit of skirt *or* stuff, *Old-fashioned Brit* popsy, *US* dame, °broad, (bit of) San Quentin quail *or* jail-bait: *His mother wants to introduce him to a nice girl.* **2** girlfriend, °sweetheart; betrothed, fiancée; °mistress, °lover, °friend, live-in °lover, inamorata, tally, *US* POSSLQ (= 'Person of the Opposite Sex Sharing Living Quarters'), *Colloq Brit* popsy, *Slang* moll, *US* twist, °squeeze: *She's his girl and she'll stick by him.*

girth *n*. **1** circumference, °perimeter, ambit, °periphery, °circuit: *His girth steadily expanded as he approached fifty.* **2** °belt, girdle, °border, cincture, waistband, cestus, cummerbund, *Archaic* zone, *US and Canadian* cinch: *Tighten that girth or the saddle will come off.*

gist *n*. °essence, °core, °heart, °substance, °point, °theme, °quintessence, °pith, °meat, marrow, °focus, °nub, °significance, (°main *or* °basic) °idea; °direction, drift: *It will save time if I tell you the gist of the argument.*

give *v*. **1** °present, °deliver, °pass (over), °turn *or* °hand over, °confer, °vouchsafe, °provide, °supply, °furnish, °bestow, °donate, °accord, °afford, °award, °hand out, °contribute, °distribute, °grant, °allow, °transfer, °make over, °entrust: *Please give me the envelope. I have given the files to the tax inspector. Give freely to charity.* **2** °exchange, °pay, °transfer, °trade, barter, swap *or* swop: *Philippa gave a week's salary for that dress.* **3** °impart, °pass on, °communicate, °transmit, °send, convey, °express: *Give my regards to Broadway.* **4** °afflict with, °cause, °occasion: *Rock music gives me a headache.* **5** °sacrifice, °devote, °dedicate, °yield (up), °surrender, give up, °cede, °concede, consign, °apply (oneself) to: *Those monks have given their lives to the study of Scripture.* **6** °present,

°offer; °announce, °introduce: *Ladies and gentlemen, I give you Madja Kiziamainska, the Polish Nightingale!* **7** °present, °announce, °offer, °recite, °sing, °act, °perform, °read, °put on: *We were asked to give a performance for charity.* **8** utter, °emit, give out (with), °issue: *He gave a shout to warn us.* **9** °yield, °relax, give way, °fail, °collapse, °buckle, °break down, °fall *or* °come °apart: *If that pillar gives, the balcony will come down.* **10** °cause, °lead, °induce, °persuade, °make, °prompt, °move, °dispose: *I was given to understand that I was not welcome.* **11** °cede, °relinquish, °concede, °allow, °surrender, °yield: *He gave me the first game but I lost the second.* **12 give away: a** See 1, above. **b** °reveal, °betray, °let out, divulge, °disclose, expose, °inform on, uncover, °leak, °let °slip; °let the cat out of the bag; *Colloq* blow the whistle on, *Slang* rat on, *US* fink on: *The traitor gave me away, and I was arrested.* **13 give in:** °yield, °submit, give up, give ground, back away (from), back off, °capitulate, °surrender, °admit °defeat: *After trying for hours to make him change his mind, he finally gave in.* **14 give off:** give out, °emit, exude, °exhale, °discharge, °send *or* °throw out, °release, °smell of: *Her clothing gave off a scent of lavender.* **15 give out: a** See 14, above. **b** °distribute, °hand out, give, °deal (out), °pass out *or* around, disseminate, °dispense, °allot, apportion, allocate, °assign, °distribute, °issue, °mete out, °ration (out), °dole (out), °pay, *Colloq* dish *or* fork out, °shell out: *The prizes will be given out to the winners at a special ceremony. She was giving out handbills to passers-by.* **c** °publish, °announce, °make known, °broadcast, °impart, °issue, make °public, °reveal: *You shouldn't give out that kind of information.* **d** become °exhausted, be reduced *or* depleted, °fail, °run out: *What will we do when the food gives out?* **e** See 8, above. **16 give over:** °assign, °resign, °hand over, °surrender, °relinquish, °pass over, give up; °entrust: *We gave our dog over to Lambert's for training.* **17 give up: a** °abandon, °stop, °cease, °quit, °leave off, forgo, °forsake, °renounce, desist from, °swear off, abstain from; °reject; *Colloq* °cut out, chuck: *I am trying to give up smoking.* **b** °surrender, °capitulate, °yield, °cede, °concede, give in (to °defeat), °throw in the towel *or* sponge; °despair: *I've tried to convince him but finally gave up.* **c** See 4, above. **d** See 13, above. **e** See 16, above.
—*n*. **18** °slack, °play, leeway, °excess; °flexibility, °stretch: *There is very little give in the rules governing working hours. Nylon is used for boat anchor ropes because it has some give.*

give and take *n*. compromise, °cooperation, reciprocity, interaction, °fair °exchange, teamwork, °joint °effort, synergy: *There is a lot of give and take in our relationship—I give and she takes.*

given *adj*. **1** stated, accepted, agreed(-upon), delineated, confirmed, °noted, affirmed, specified, settled, °set, (pre)arranged, preordained, foreordained: *You must solve the problem using the given information.* **2** presupposed, °assumed, °understood, postulated, premised, conceded, acknowledged, allowed: *I think we can take her honesty as given.* **3** °prone, °accustomed, dedicated, addicted, °inclined, °disposed: *Our headmaster is not exactly given to flights of fancy.*
—*n*. **4** assumption, donnée; °fact, °certainty, °reality, actuality, °gospel, the °truth: *Can we accept her interest in the job as a given?*

glad *adj.* **1** °happy, °pleased, contented, gratified, satisfied; °delighted, thrilled, °joyful, °overjoyed, tickled, *Colloq* tickled pink or to death, °pleased as Punch, *Slang Brit* chuffed: *I am genuinely glad to see you.* **2** (°ready and) °willing, °happy, °keen, °eager, (well-)°disposed, °inclined, °ready: *I would be glad to help you, madam.*

gladden *v.* °cheer, °enliven, °brighten, °delight, hearten, exhilarate, elate, °buoy (up), °animate: *It certainly gladdened me to be home again.*

gladly *adv.* cheerfully, °happily, °readily, °willingly, with °pleasure: *I'd go with you gladly if I had the time.*

glamorous *adj.* **1** alluring, fascinating, charming, °attractive, °magnetic, captivating, °enthralling, °desirable, appealing, °enchanting, entrancing, intriguing, beguiling, bewitching, magical: *Esmé designs clothes for the most glamorous women in the world.* **2** °chic, °smart, °stylish, °fashionable, *Colloq* °trendy: *She always wears the most glamorous clothes.*

glamour *n.* allure, °fascination, °charm, attractiveness, °brilliance, °glitter, °attraction, °magnetism, charisma, captivation, desirability, °appeal, °enchantment, bewitchment, witchcraft, °sorcery, °magic: *Who today can match the glamour of the movie stars of the '30s?*

glance *v.* **1** glimpse, °peek, °peep, °scan, °look, *Colloq Brit* have a shufti or shufty at, take a dekko at: *I've only had time to glance at the report.* **2** °reflect, glint, °glisten, °shimmer, °twinkle, °gleam, °flicker, glimmer, °sparkle, scintillate, °glitter, °flash: *A ray of sunlight glanced off the windows opposite.* **3** °bounce (off), °reflect, ricochet, °rebound, carom: *The stone glanced off the pavement and struck my leg.*
—*n.* **4** glimpse, °peek, °peep, °look, *coup d'œil*, *Colloq* gander, *Brit* shufti or shufty, dekko: *She turned and gave him a questioning glance, As he fingered the tip of his fer-de-lance.* **5** °gleam, glint, glimmer, °shimmer, °twinkle, °sparkle, scintillation, °glitter, °flicker, °flash: *The silver light, with quivering glance, Played on the water's still expanse.*

glare *n.* **1** °dazzle, °brilliance, brightness, °splendour, resplendence, °radiance, effulgence, °lustre, °shine, °flame, °flare, °blaze: *We had to shade our eyes from the glare.* **2** °frown, °dirty or °nasty or °black °look, °scowl, °stare, glower, °lower or *Brit also* °lour: *She shrank from his fierce glare.* **3** garishness, gaudiness, floridity or floridness, flashiness, tawdriness, showiness, °ostentation, meretriciousness: *His writing is filled with the pomp and glare of rhetoric.*
—*v.* **4** °frown, give a °dirty or °nasty or °black °look, °scowl, °stare, glower, °lower or *Brit also* °lour, °look daggers (at): *He simply glared at him and he withered.*

glaring *adj.* **1** °blatant, °flagrant, egregious, °conspicuous, °obtrusive, °prominent, °evident, °obvious, °manifest, °patent, °overt, °clear, °visible, unconcealed, °outrageous, °gross, flagitious, °atrocious, heinous, °shameless, °disgraceful, °shocking, °scandalous: *They pointed out a glaring omission in the proposals.* **2** °garish, °dazzling, °brilliant, blinding, blazing, °vivid, °harsh, °strong: *I was blinded when we first walked out into the glaring sunlight.*

glass *n.* **1** glassware, crystal: *Use the best glass for the party.* **2** °mirror, looking-glass: *He constantly looks at himself in the glass.* **3** window, °pane, window-pane, plate glass: *The children pressed their noses against the glass of the toy shop.* **4** tumbler, drinking-glass, beaker, goblet: *May I have a glass of beer?.* **5** barometer: *The glass fell as the storm approached.* **6** lens, magnifying glass, °telescope, spyglass, microscope: *Look at this drop of water through the glass.* **7 glasses**: spectacles, eyeglasses, lorgnon, lorgnette, opera-glasses, binoculars, field-glasses, bifocals, trifocals, goggles, sun-glasses, *Colloq* specs: *These are my reading glasses.*

glassy *adj.* **1** shining, °shiny, gleaming, °smooth, °slippery, °glossy, °icy, mirror-like, *US* °slick: *We skidded on the glassy surface and crashed into a wall.* **2** °fixed, staring, trancelike, hypnotic, °vacant, °empty, expressionless, °blank, °void, vacuous, dazed, °dull, glazed, °cold, °lifeless: *His glassy stare made me very uncomfortable.*

glaze *v.* **1** varnish, lacquer, shellac, enamel, °coat, °cover; °polish, burnish, °shine, °gloss: *Many of the works of art had been glazed for protection.*
—*n.* **2** varnish, lacquer, shellac, enamel, coating, covering; °polish, °shine, °gloss, °lustre, patina: *The glaze distorts the design beneath.*

gleam *n.* **1** °light, glimmer, glint, °glow, °flicker, °shine, °shimmer, °glitter, °twinkle, °spark, °flare, °glare, °flash; °beam, °ray, °shaft: *I could just make out the faint gleam of a candle.* **2** °hint, °suggestion, °indication, °vestige, °trace, scintilla, °inkling, glimmer, °ray, °spark, °flicker: *There wasn't a gleam of hope of rescue.* **3** °look, glint: *He got a strange gleam in his eye when he talked about his inventions.*
—*v.* **4** glimmer, glint, °shimmer, °shine, °twinkle, °glitter, °glisten, °beam, °sparkle: *I could see the beast's eyes, gleaming in the dark. The shore was dotted with gleaming white houses.*

glee *n.* °delight, °exuberance, cheerfulness, °high or °good °spirits, °cheer, exhilaration, elation, exultation, °joy, °happiness, °rapture, gladness, felicity, °pleasure, joyfulness, °merriment, jubilation, joyousness, joviality, jollity, °gaiety, mirthfulness; °enjoyment, °satisfaction, *Schadenfreude*: *We watched with great glee as the villain was thwarted.*

gleeful *adj.* °happy, °merry, °joyful, °delighted, °exuberant, °ecstatic, °cheerful, in °high or °good °spirits, exhilarated, °elated, °exultant, °rapturous, °overjoyed, °pleased, jubilant, joyous, jovial, °jolly, °gay, mirthful: *He wrote a gleeful report of the chairman's conviction for insider trading.*

glib *adj.* °ready, °fluent, °smooth, °slick, facile, smooth-spoken, smooth-tongued, smooth-talking, fast-talking, °fluid, °easy, unctuous, °suave, °nonchalant, °superficial: *Why must obituary notices always be so glib?*

glide *v.* °slide, °slip, °coast, skate, °soar, °float, °sail, glissade, °stream, °flow: *The skiff glided peacefully down the river.*

glisten *v.* °shine, °reflect, glint, glimmer, °gleam, °sparkle, °glitter, wink, °blink; °glow, °twinkle: *The lamplight glistened on his wet coat. A tear glistened on her cheek.*

glitter *v.* **1** See glisten, above.
—*n.* **2** See gleam, 1, above. **3** See glamour, above. **4** showiness, gaudiness, garishness, °flash, flashiness, °ostentation, floridity or

floridness, °spectacle, °pageantry, °splendour, refulgence, °brilliance, Colloq pizazz or pizzazz, razzle-dazzle, razzmatazz, Slang US glitz: In those days, Hollywood was all glitter.

gloat v. Often, **gloat over**: °exult (in), °glory (in), °relish (in), °revel (in), crow (over or about), °delight (in): He is still gloating over the misery he caused her.

global adj. worldwide, °international, °broad, °extensive, wide-ranging, far-reaching, °epidemic, pandemic, °universal: Protection of the atmosphere is a global responsibility.

globe n. 1 °earth, °world, planet, Terra: Our family is scattered all round the globe. 2 °sphere, ball, °orb; globule: On the table was a lamp with a green glass globe.

gloom n. 1 shadowiness, gloominess, °shade, °shadow, murkiness, murk, dimness, °dusk, dullness, °dark, darkness, cloudiness, blackness, obscurity: We arose in the gloom of a midwinter's morning. 2 despondency, °depression, °sadness, dejection, downheartedness, °melancholy, °woe, °sorrow, moroseness, °desolation, °low spirits, blues, doldrums, °despair, dolour, °misery, Colloq dumps: The team suffered the gloom of defeat.

gloomy adj. 1 °shadowy, shaded, °shady, °murky, °dim, °dusky, °dull, °dark, cloudy, °overcast, °obscure, °black, inky, Literary Stygian: It is too gloomy a day to have a picnic. 2 depressed, °melancholy, °sad, °dejected, morose, °glum, lugubrious, °unhappy, cheerless, °dismal, °moody, down, downcast, °desolate, °doleful, °sorrowful, crestfallen, chap-fallen, °downhearted, °forlorn, °despondent, °miserable, °joyless, dispirited, despairing, °dreary, °sullen, °blue, distressed, down in the °mouth, in the doldrums, saturnine, Colloq (down) in the dumps: Both of them have been very gloomy since the divorce. 3 depressing, cheerless, °dreary, °dismal, dispiriting, °sad, disheartening: The décor is much too gloomy for a doctor's waiting-room.

glorified adj. 1 overrated, °pretentious, overdone, high-flown, high-sounding, °affected, °pompous, °exalted, Colloq jumped-up: You say he is a scholar, but he behaves more like a glorified schoolboy. 2 °sham, °pretend, °imitation, °counterfeit, °fake, °substitute, ersatz, Colloq °phoney or US also phony: In that outfit, she looks like a glorified chorus girl.

glorify v. 1 elevate, °exalt, °raise (up), upgrade, °promote, °advance, °boost, °enhance, °dignify, ennoble, °immortalize: Winning first prize glorified his reputation considerably. In her book she glorifies motherhood. These men are glorified by their heroism. 2 canonize, deify, °idolize, °revere, °venerate, °sanctify, °worship, pay °tribute or °homage to, ennoble, °idealize, apotheosize, °eulogize, panegyrize, °adore, °honour, °look up to, °celebrate, °extol, °praise, °laud, commend, °hail, lionize, °applaud, acclaim: The world glorified Lindbergh for the first solo flight across the Atlantic.

glorious adj. 1 °illustrious, famed, °famous, °renowned, °celebrated, °distinguished, honoured, °eminent, °excellent: England may be proud of her glorious literary heritage. 2 °outstanding, °splendid, °magnificent, °marvellous, wonderful, spectacular, °fabulous, °dazzling: They announced another glorious victory over enemy forces. 3 enjoyable, °delightful, °fine, °great, °excellent, °pleasurable, °superb, Colloq °heavenly: We had a glorious holiday in the Greek islands. 4 °beautiful, °splendid, °brilliant, °gorgeous, resplendent, °admirable, °superior, °excellent, °estimable: The walls are covered with frescos in glorious colour.

glory n. 1 °honour, °fame, repute, °reputation, exaltation, °celebrity, °renown, eminence, °distinction, illustriousness, °prestige, °dignity, immortality: Our soldiers fought for glory not for gain. Even today we sense the glory that was Rome. 2 °honour, °veneration, °reverence, °homage, °gratitude, glorification, exaltation, °worship, adoration, °praise, laudation, thanksgiving; benediction, °blessing: Glory be to God in the highest. 3 °splendour, °pomp, magnificence, °grandeur, °beauty, °brilliance, °radiance, effulgence, refulgence, °excellence, °pageantry, °nobility, °triumph, greatness: Her photographs depict the Amazonian rain forest in all its glory. 4 aureole, nimbus, °halo; °crown, circlet, corona: A glory surrounds the saint's head in the painting.
—v. 5 °revel, °relish, °delight, °exult, °pride oneself, crow, °rejoice, °gloat; °show off, °boast: She sat by the window, glorying in the magnificence of the scenery.

gloss[1] n. 1 °sheen, °lustre, °polish, °glow, °glaze, °shine, °gleam, burnish, brightness: I prefer a dull gloss to a high polish on furniture. 2 °show, °façade, °mask, °front, °surface, °veneer, °disguise, °camouflage, °false °appearance, °semblance: She soon saw through the gloss, and the honeymoon was over.
—v. 3 °glaze, °polish, burnish, °shine: Gloss up your shoes a bit. 4 Usually, **gloss over**: °veil, °cover up, °smooth over, °conceal, °hide, °disguise, °camouflage, °mask, Colloq °whitewash: He tried to gloss over his voting record.

gloss[2] n. 1 °explanation, °interpretation, exegesis, explication, °definition, elucidation, °comment, commentary, annotation, critique, °criticism, °analysis, footnote; °translation: Some editions of Shakespeare give glosses of difficult words and phrases at the foot of each page.
—v. 2 °comment on or upon, °explain, °interpret, explicate, °define, elucidate, annotate, °criticize, °analyse, °review, US critique, °translate: Johnson was not the first to gloss the word 'pastern'. 3 See gloss[1], 4, above.

glossary n. °gloss, (specialized or special-subject) °dictionary, wordbook, word-list: There is a useful glossary of terms at the end of the book.

glossy adj. 1 shining, °shiny, °smooth, °polished, glazed, °lustrous, burnished, °sleek, waxed, °glassy, glistening: Our magazine is printed on glossy paper. 2 °slick, °specious, °put-on, °artificial, meretricious, contrived, °pretended, simulated, feigned, °insincere, pseudo, °false, °unreal; °bogus, °counterfeit, °fraudulent, °imitation, Colloq °phoney or US also phony: It is only a glossy remake of the original film.

glow n. 1 luminosity, phosphorescence, incandescence, °light, lambency, °lustre: The surface of the flying saucer emitted a faint green glow. 2 °light, brightness, °gleam, luminousness, °brilliance, °radiance, resplendence, °splendour, effulgence: The glow in the east is from a forest fire. 3 °flush, °blush, redness, ruddiness,

°burning, °excitement, °warmth, °fervour, fervency, °enthusiasm, feverishness, °thrill, *Colloq* °rush: *I can feel a glow just thinking of you.*
—*v.* **4** °shine, °radiate, incandesce, phosphoresce, glimmer, °gleam, °light up: *The numerals on the clock were glowing in the dark.* **5** °heat, overheat, °burn; ablate: *The spaceship began to glow as it entered the atmosphere.* **6** °flush, bloom, °colour, °blush: *As you can see from her complexion, she simply glows with good health.* **7** °blush, °flush, redden, °colour, turn red or scarlet: *My cheeks glowed with embarrassment.*

glowing *adj.* **1** aglow, °incandescent, °burning, lambent, °luminous, candent; smouldering: *I stirred the glowing embers.* **2** °rich, °warm, vibrant, °bright, °brilliant: *Banners in glowing colours enlivened the hall. He is in glowing health.* **3** °laudatory, °complimentary, °enthusiastic, eulogistic, °rhapsodic, °favourable, encomiastic, panegyrical: *The critics described her performance in glowing terms.*

glue *n.* °cement, adhesive, mucilage, gum, paste: *You need a specialist glue to mend a break like that.*
—*v.* **2** °cement, paste, °stick, affix, °fix, °seal: *Let's glue this picture into the album.*

glum *adj.* °gloomy, °sullen, morose, dispirited, °woebegone, °dismal, °sad, sulky, °dour, °moody, °sour, crestfallen, °doleful, down, °low, °pessimistic, lugubrious, saturnine: *After Irena left, I was feeling rather glum.*

glut *n.* **1** °excess, °surplus, over-abundance, superabundance, °surfeit, oversupply, overflow, °superfluity, nimiety: *The glut of razor-blades in the market is due to increased production.* **2** saturation, glutting, satiation: *Glut leads to a lowering of prices.*
—*v.* **3** oversupply, °flood, °saturate, °swamp, inundate, deluge, °overload, overstock, °clog, °stuff, °gorge: *The markets will soon be glutted with mobile telephones.* **4** °satiate, sate, °choke, °cram, °overload, overfeed, °gorge, °surfeit, °pall, cloy, °jade, °sicken, °weary: *Everyone was thoroughly glutted before the wedding reception was over.*

glutton *n.* trencherman, gormandizer, gourmand or gormand, overeater, hog, pig, *Gran-gousier, Colloq* greedy-guts, *Slang Brit* gannet, *US* chowhound: *Like the glutton that he is, he asked for more after eating an enormous meal.*

gluttonous *adj.* °voracious, gormandizing, edacious, °greedy, °ravenous, insatiable, esurient, piggish, °hoggish, swinish: *She was so gluttonous that she ate my dinner after finishing her own.*

gluttony *n.* overeating, gormandizing, gormandism or gourmandism, °greed, hoggishness, piggishness, °rapacity, voraciousness, greediness, voracity, insatiability, edacity, crapulence, crapulousness, intemperance, immoderation, *Archaic* gulosity: *The Bible categorizes gluttony among the seven deadly sins.*

gnarled *adj.* twisted, knotty, °lumpy, °bumpy, knotted, °bent, °crooked, distorted, contorted, warped; arthritic: *I concealed myself in the gnarled branches of the old oak. The beggar reached out to me with his gnarled hand.*

gnaw *v.* **1** °chew, nibble, °eat, °bite, champ: *The marks were made by deer gnawing the bark.* **2** °erode, °eat away, corrode, °wear down or away, °fret, °consume, °devour: *The acid continues to gnaw away at the metal till it is*

gone. **3** °fret, °irritate, harry, hector, °pester, °worry, °bother, °plague, °trouble, °torment, torture, °distress, badger, °harass, °haunt, °nag, vex, °gall, nettle, °irk, peeve, °annoy: *The feeling that something was very wrong continued to gnaw at her.*

go *v.* **1** °move (°ahead or forward or °onwards), °proceed, °advance, °pass, make °headway, °travel, voyage, °set off, °tour, trek, wend, °stir, budge: *Would you go to the market for me?* **2** °leave, °depart, go out, °move (out or away), decamp, °make off, °withdraw, °repair, °retire, °retreat, *Colloq* °take off: *I wish he would go at once. She went to her country cottage for the weekend.* **3** °function, °operate, °work, °run, °perform: *I cannot get the engine to go properly.* **4** °lead, °open to, °give access to, °communicate to or with, °connect with or to: *Where does this door go?* **5** °lead, °communicate with, °run: *Does this road go to Oxford?* **6** °fit, °belong (together), °agree or °conform (with each other), harmonize, °blend, °match, be °appropriate or °suitable (for or to), °complement each other: *These colours don't go.* **7** °become: *He went mad when he learnt about the accident.* **8** °fit, °extend, °reach, °span, °stretch: *My belt would never go round your waist!* **9** be °disposed of or discarded or thrown away, be dismissed, be °rid of or abolished, be °given up, be °cast or °set or °put aside, be done with: *That out-dated computer has to go.* **10** °disappear (without a trace), vanish (into thin air), °evaporate: *Where has all the money gone?* **11** °pass, °elapse, °slip or tick away, °fly: *Time goes quickly when you're having fun.* **12** °fail, °fade, °decline, °flag, weaken, degenerate, °wear out, °give (out); °give °way, °collapse, °fall or °come or go to pieces, °disintegrate, °crack: *I'm afraid the tyres are going. When that last support goes, the roof will come down.* **13** °die, °expire, be gone, meet one's Maker, °pass on or away, shuffle off this mortal coil, go to one's reward, go to the happy hunting-grounds, go to that great cricket-pitch in the sky, *Slang* kick the bucket, snuff it: *By the time the doctor arrived, Graham had gone.* **14** °sound, °pronounce, °enunciate, articulate, °say, utter: *And this little pig goes 'Wee, wee, wee', all the way home.* **15** °survive, °last (out), °endure, °live, °continue: *How long can we go without water?* **16** be used up or consumed or finished: *The last of our food was gone.* **17** go to the °toilet or the °lavatory or the bathroom, °move (one's) °bowels, °urinate, °defecate, *Slang* pee, take a °leak or a crap, *Chiefly Brit* go to the loo, *Chiefly US* go to the john, *Taboo slang* (take a) piss or shit: *We stopped at a motorway filling station because Jane had to go.* **18 go about:** °approach, °tackle, °set about, °undertake, °begin, °start: *I don't like the way she goes about her work. How does one go about establishing a business?* **19 go ahead:** °proceed, °continue, °move or go forward, °advance, °progress, go on: *She told me I could go ahead with the scheme. The policeman motioned to go ahead.* **20 go along (with):** a °escort, °accompany: *We asked if we could go along with them to the cinema.* b °agree (to), concur (with), acquiesce (to), assent (to), °support: *Beverly would never go along with a plan like yours.* **21 go around** or **about** or **round (with):** a °move around, °circulate: *I wish he'd stop going round telling everyone about me. There's a lot of flu going* around. **b** °socialize (with), °frequent *or* °seek the °company of, °spend °time with, °associate with, *Colloq* °hang around *or* about (with), °hang out (with): *The boy is going around with that Collins girl.* **c** °wander *or* °move around: *He goes about picking through rubbish bins.* **22 go at**: °attack, °assault, assail: *We went at the enemy with all the fire power we could muster.* **23 go away**: go (off), °leave, °depart, °withdraw, °exit; °retreat, °recede, decamp: *The clouds went away and the sun came out. We are going away for the weekend.* **24 go back (to)**: **a** °return (to); °revert (to), °change back (to): *He went back to his old job after the war. Can we go back to the way things were before we were married?* **b** °originate (in), °begin *or* °start (with), °date back (to): *Our friendship goes back to our childhood.* **25 go back on**: °renege (on), °break, °retract, °repudiate, °forsake: *She's gone back on our agreement.* **26 go by**: **a** °pass (by), go °past, °move by; °elapse: *We used to watch the goods trains go by. The months went by quickly since our last meeting.* **b** °rely *or* °count *or* °depend *or* bank on, °put °faith in(to), be guided by, °judge from: *You cannot go by what Atherton tells you.* **27 go down**: **a** °sink, go under, °founder, °submerge: *The ship went down within minutes of striking the mine.* **b** °decrease, °decline, °drop, °sink: *The Nikkei Index went down 200 points.* **c** °fall, be defeated *or* beaten, °suffer °defeat, °lose, °collapse: *Our forces went down under an onslaught from the attacking armies.* **d** be remembered *or* memorialized *or* recalled *or* commemorated *or* recorded: *That day of infamy will go down in history.* **e** find °favour *or* acceptance *or* °approval, be accepted: *His ideas have not gone down well with the council.* **28 go for**: **a** °fetch, °obtain, °get: *Please go for help.* **b** °apply *or* °relate to, °concern, °involve: *The rule against smoking goes for you, too, Smedley.* **c** °fancy, °favour, °like, °admire, be attracted to, °prefer, °choose, *Slang* °dig: *I can tell that Peter really goes for Maria. I could go for a pint of beer right now.* **d** °attack, °assault, assail, °set upon: *The dog went for him as soon as he opened the gate.* **e** °set one's sights on, °aim for, °focus °attention *or* °effort(s) on: *I decided to risk all and go for Drogheda Boy at 100–8.* **29 go in for**: **a** °enter, °enrol, °start, °begin, °embark on, °pursue, °take up, °embrace, espouse, °undertake, °follow, °adopt, go into, *US* go out for: *He is going in for a career in boxing.* **b** °like, °fancy, °favour, °practise, do, °engage in: *I don't go in for mountain-climbing.* **30 go into**: **a** See 28 a, above. **b** delve into, °examine, °pursue, °investigate, °analyse, °probe, °scrutinize, °inquire into, °study: *I want to go into the subject of your absences with you, Fanshawe.* **c** °touch on, °discuss, °mention: *I should avoid going into the subject of money with Pauline if I were you.* **31 go off**: **a** go out, °cease to function: *I saw the lights go off at nine.* **b** °explode, °blow up, detonate, °erupt; °fire, be discharged: *The bomb is set to go off in an hour. The gun went off, killing the mouse.* **c** °occur, °happen, °take place: *The conference went off as planned.* **d** °depart, °leave, go (away), °set out, °exit, decamp, °quit: *She went off without another word.* **e** *Brit* deteriorate, °rot, moulder, go °stale, go °bad, °spoil, °sour, °turn: *After two days the milk goes off.* **f** Usually, **go off into**: °start *or* °break into *or* out in: *He goes off into gales of laughter whenever I mention your name.* **32 go on**: **a** °continue, °proceed, °keep

on, °carry on; °persist, °last, °endure, °persevere: *He went on coughing all night long. The party went on into the small hours.* **b** °happen, °occur, take place, °come about, *Colloq* °come off: *I have always wondered what went on in there.* **c** °come on, °begin *or* resume functioning: *The lights went on at midnight.* **d** °enter, make an °entrance: *She doesn't go on till the third act.* **e** going on. approaching, nearing, °nearly, °almost, not quite: *He's six going on seven. It's going on eight o'clock.* **f** gabble, °chatter, drone on, *Brit* natter, *Colloq Brit* witter (on), rabbit on: *He goes on endlessly about his cars.* **g** °rely *or* °depend on, °use: *The detective had very little to go on.* **33 go out**: **a** °fade *or* °die (out), °expire, °cease functioning, go off, be extinguished: *The lights went out, throwing the room into Stygian blackness.* **b** °depart, °leave, °exit: *He went out at six and has not been seen since.* **c** °socialize, °associate; court, go together, *Brit* °walk out, *US* °date: *Harry is going out with Annabel.* **34 go over**: **a** °review, °skim (through *or* over), go through, °scan, °look at, °read, °study; °inspect, °examine, °scrutinize, °investigate: *I went over your report last night. They are going over everyone's luggage with a fine-tooth comb.* **b** be received: *The first song went over very well.* **c** °clean, °tidy *or* °neaten (up): *I've just gone over the entire flat.* **d** °rehearse, °repeat, °reiterate, °review, go through: *We keep going over the same things, again and again.* **35 go round** *or US also* **around**: **a** °revolve, °rotate, °spin, whirl, °twirl: *The earth takes a year to go round the sun.* **b** °suffice, be °sufficient *or* °adequate *or* °enough, °satisfy: *Are there enough life jackets to go around?* **c** See 21, above. **36 go through**: **a** °experience, °suffer, °undergo, °bear, °take, °stand, °tolerate, °put up with, °brook, °submit to, °endure, °live through, °brave: *I don't think I could go through another war.* **b** be accepted *or* approved, °pass (°muster): *The bill went through without a hitch.* **c** See 34 a, above. **37 go together**: **a** harmonize, °accord, °agree, °fit, go, °suit each other, °belong (with each other): *I don't think that puce and vermilion go together.* **b** See 33 c, above. **38 go under**: **a** See 27 a, above. **b** °fail, °collapse, °subside, go bankrupt, °succumb, *Brit* go to the °wall, *Colloq* °fold, *US* go belly up: *Statistics show that more than 500 companies go under every week in the USA.* **39 go up**: **a** °rise, °increase: *If inflation goes up, the Chancellor will raise interest rates.* **b** °explode, °blow up: *The munitions factory went up, showering debris over the whole neighbourhood.* **40 go with**: **a** go together with, harmonize with, °blend with, be °suitable *or* suited for, °fit (in) with, °accord *or* °agree with: *That scarf does not go with the dress.* **b** °socialize with, °associate with, °accompany, court, *Old-fashioned Brit* °walk out with, *US* °date: *I hear that Connie is going with Don.* **41 go without**: do *or* °manage *or* °get by without, °lack, be °deprived of, °need; abstain from, °survive *or* °live *or* °continue without: *In the old days, if you could not afford something, you went without. She cannot go without a cigarette for more than an hour.* —*n.* **42** °chance, °turn, °opportunity, °try, °attempt, *Colloq* whack, crack, whirl, °shot, °stab: *I don't expect much, but I'll have a go anyway.*

go-ahead *n.* **1** °permission, °approval, °leave, authorization, °sanction, *Colloq* °say-so, okay *or* °OK, green light, *US* the °nod: *I have the go-ahead to proceed with the project.*

—*adj.* **2** °ambitious, °enterprising, °progressive, forward-looking, °resourceful: *The directors, all under thirty, make it a real go-ahead company.*

goal *n.* °object, °aim, °purpose, °end, °objective, °target, °ambition, °ideal, °aspiration: *Fletcher's goal is to be head of the company.*

gob *n.* chunk, °piece, °blob, °lump, gobbet, °morsel, °fragment, °bite: *She took a gob of peanut butter and spread it on the bread.*

gobbledegook *n.* **1** gobbledygook, °jargon, °nonsense, °gibberish, °moonshine, °rubbish, tommy-rot, °mumbo-jumbo, humbug, balderdash, eyewash, hogwash, poppycock, °drivel, *Colloq* bunk, °rot, °garbage, bosh, pish and tush, piffle, bilge (water), *Slang* crap, malarkey, bull, bullshit, *Brit* (load of old) cobblers *or* codswallop: *Can you make sense out of all that computer gobbledegook?* **2** gobbledygook, equivocation, double-talk, °deception, deceptiveness, vagueness, quibbling, circumlocution, obscurantism, obfuscation, ambagiousness, shiftiness: *Ordinary people are often confused by the gobbledegook of official pronouncements.*

go-between *n.* °intermediary, °agent, middleman, °medium, °mediator, °negotiator, °messenger, internuncio, °liaison; intercessor, interceder: *David served as go-between in our negotiations with the rebels.*

goblin *n.* elf, gnome, hobgoblin, °imp, kobold, leprechaun, °demon, brownie, pixie *or* pixy, nix *or* nixie: *On Hallowe'en the ghouls and goblins will get you if you don't watch out!*

god *n.* °deity, demigod, demiurge, divinity, °spirit, °immortal, °genius, °power, tutelary, numen: *Throughout man's sojourn on earth he has worshipped many gods.*

godless *adj.* **1** °wicked, °evil, iniquitous, °sinful, unrighteous, unholy, hellish; °impious, °blasphemous, °profane, °sacrilegious, °ungodly: *The prison was a godless place, where one was murdered for a crust of bread.* **2** atheistic, nullifidian, agnostic, °unbelieving, °sceptical: *In theory, communism is a godless ideology.*

godlike *adj.* **1** °divine, °godly, °sacred, °holy, °saintly, angelic, °seraphic, blest, blessed, sainted: *The tribe thought her a goddess and treated her with godlike reverence.* **2** °heavenly, °celestial, blissful, °rapturous, °ecstatic, beatific, ethereal: *For a decade, she lived a godlike existence with the tribe.*

godly *adj.* °religious, °pious, °devout, God-fearing, °good, °righteous, °holy, °virtuous, °moral, °pure, °saintly, reverent, pietistic, °devoted, °faithful: *The monks pursue a godly life in their mountain fastness.*

godsend *n.* °gift, °blessing, benediction, °boon, °windfall, bonanza, stroke of (°good) °fortune, piece *or* bit of (°good) °luck: *The Red Cross parcels were a godsend to the prisoners of war.*

goggle-eyed *adj.* °agog, awestruck, wide-eyed, thunderstruck, agape, open-mouthed, gawking, staring, °dumbfounded *or* dumfounded, astonished, astounded, amazed, stupefied, dazed, surprised: *His first time in the city, Eugene stood goggle-eyed at the skyscrapers.*

going *adj.* **1** thriving, °successful, succeeding, °prosperous, °wealthy, affluent, booming, prospering, °flourishing, growing: *The Davises took over a failing business and turned it into a going concern.* **2** °current, °present, °contemporary, °active, °effective, accepted, °prevailing, °prevalent, °universal, °common, °usual, °customary: *What is the going rate for a skilled cabinet-maker?*

golden *adj.* **1** yellow, yellowish, gold, blond *or* blonde, flaxen, aureate; tow(-haired): *Her golden tresses fell about her shoulders.* **2** gold, auriferous; gilded, gilt, aureate; *Technical* auric, aurous: *They drank together from a golden bowl.* **3** °bright, shining, °brilliant, °sunny, gleaming, °lustrous, °shiny, glittering, °dazzling, resplendent, °radiant, °glowing, sparkling: *We emerged from the black tunnel into golden sunshine.* **4** °happy, blissful, °delightful, °joyful, °glorious, joyous, °exuberant: *We can never recapture the golden days of our youth.* **5** °flourishing, halcyon, °prosperous, thriving, °favourable, °excellent, °outstanding, °productive, °fertile, blessed, blest, °good, °successful, palmy: *After the golden age of Greece and Rome, Europe was plunged into the dismal gloom of the Dark Ages.* **6** °gifted, °talented, °favoured, °special, °exceptional, °favourite, cherished, °pet, *Brit* blue-eyed, white-headed, white-haired, *US* fair-haired: *As long as the company's profits were increasing, Hamilton was the golden boy.* **7** °advantageous, °propitious, auspicious, °promising, °rosy, °opportune, °optimistic, °favourable: *She missed a golden opportunity by turning down the job.*

good *adj.* **1** °agreeable, °satisfactory, commendable, °acceptable, °fair, °adequate, admissible, °tolerable, all right, °passable, *Colloq* okay *or* °OK: *According to the reviews, the new opera is good but not great.* **2** °admirable, °outstanding, °first-rate, first-class, °fine, °superb, °superior, tiptop, °extraordinary, °exemplary, °choice, °excellent, °capital, °marvellous, wonderful, °splendid, °sterling, *Colloq* °super(-duper), °great, smashing, A-1 *or* A-one, *Brit* cracking, °brilliant, °amazing, ace, °knockout, brill, °fantastic, °terrific, °unbelievable, groovy, fab, °fabulous, °crucial, °serious, *Slang US* °bad, *Old-fashioned Brit* tickety-boo, *No. Eng.* °champion, *Chiefly US* A-OK: *I thought that was a really good dinner.* **3** °correct, °proper, °decorous, °orderly, °right, °seemly, °fit, °fitting, °suitable, °meet, °appropriate, allowable, °permissible, admissible, °passable, °satisfactory, °tolerable: *He should get time off for good behaviour.* **4** °obedient, well-behaved, °proper, well-mannered: *Why can't you be a good boy when we go out?* **5** °moral, high-minded, °righteous, °noble, °wholesome, °chaste, °pure, °honourable, °ethical, upstanding, °upright, °virtuous, °worthy, °lofty, °elevated, °saintly, angelic, °godly, °godlike: *Think only good thoughts and still you may not get to heaven.* **6** °kind, °benevolent, beneficent, °gracious, °gentle, °kindly, °nice, °considerate, °friendly, °solicitous, good-hearted, °sympathetic, °benign, °charitable, humane, kind-hearted, well-disposed: *Her parents have always been good to me.* **7** °fresh, unspoiled *or* unspoilt, °edible, consumable, palatable: *These eggs are good but the milk has gone off.* **8** °genuine, valid, °legitimate, °authentic, °proper, °reliable, °secure, dependable, °safe, creditable, °sound, °solid, °substantial, well-founded, °trustworthy, °honest, °actual, °real; credible, believable, convincing, compelling, cogent: *Have you a good reason for saying that?* **9** °honourable, esteemed, respected, °respectable, °well-thought-of,

°reputable, established, °solid: *They say that he comes from a good family.* **10** well-proportioned, °shapely, °attractive: *Yes, I'd say that Marilyn has a good figure.* **11** °thorough, °complete, °penetrating, °careful: *Has she had a good look at the defendant?* **12** °gifted, °talented, °competent, °capable, °skilful, °clever, °accomplished, °proficient, °adept, adroit, skilled: *Am I a good enough actor to audition for the part?* **13** °advantageous, °propitious, °opportune, °beneficial, °profitable, °favourable; °safe, °secure, °reliable, °sound, °sensible: *Are utilities a good investment? Is this a good time to buy shares?* **14** °healthy, salubrious, salutary, °beneficial, °wholesome: *We'll have to put you on a good diet.* **15** °best, company, Sunday, special-occasion, most °luxurious: *Should we use the good glasses tonight?* **16** °ample, °sufficient, °adequate, °considerable, °full, °extensive, sizeable, °large, °substantial: *We have a good supply of food available.* **17** approving, °complimentary, °flattering, °positive, °favourable, °enthusiastic, °laudatory, eulogistic, encomiastic: *His book received a very good review in the Sunday supplement.* **18** °great, °considerable, sizeable, °substantial, °fair: *We are still a good distance away from land.* —*n.* **19** °benefit, °advantage, °profit, °use, °usefulness, °gain, °worth, avail: *What good does it do to complain?* **20** goodness, °morality, °virtue, °merit, righteousness, °right, °rectitude, °worth, °probity, virtuousness, °integrity, °nobility, high-mindedness, honourableness, °honesty: *The evil that men do lives after them, The good is oft interred with their bones.* **21 goods: a** °possessions, (personal) °property, chattels, °things, °gear, °belongings, °effects, °paraphernalia, movables, °stuff: *He's gone and he's taken all his goods with him.* **b** °merchandise, commodities, °wares, °stock, °produce, tangibles, °assets: *We shall pay on delivery of the goods.* **c** *US and Canadian* (incriminating) °evidence *or* °proof *or* °information *or* documentation *or* °facts *or* °data: *The police have the goods on the murderer.* **d** °fabric, °cloth, textile, °material, yard goods, piece-goods: *My tailor said he had made it from the best goods available.* **e** °freight: *A goods train had broken down on the line between Oxford and Banbury.*

goodbye *interj.* Farewell!, Hawaiian Aloha!, *Italian* Arrivederci!, Ciao!; *German* Auf Wiedersehen!; *French* Au revoir!, Adieu!; *Japanese* Sayonara!; *Spanish* Adios!, Hasta la vista!, Hasta luego!; *Latin* Vale!; *Colloq* Bye! *or* 'Bye!, Bye-bye!, Toodle-oo!, So long!, *Brit* Ta-ta!, Cheers!, cheerio, *Old-fashioned* Pip! Pip!, *US* See you later (alligator)!: *We said our goodbyes and went on our way.*

good-for-nothing *adj.* **1** °worthless, °useless: *'You are asking too much for that good-for-nothing old lamp', Aladdin told the pedlar.* —*n.* **2** ne'er-do-well, °wastrel, waster, °idler, °loafer, layabout, lazybones, slugabed, sluggard, black sheep, *Colloq US* gold brick, goof-off: *Why doesn't that lazy good-for-nothing get a job?*

goodly *adj.* °considerable, sizeable, °substantial, °ample, °great, °large, °significant, consequential: *The museum attracts a goodly number of visitors each year.*

good-natured *adj.* good-humoured, °friendly, °agreeable, °genial, gracious, good-hearted, °pleasant, °mellow, °easygoing, °considerate,

°nice, °kind, °kindly, kind-hearted, tender-hearted, °charitable, °tolerant, °generous, °courteous, °cordial, °warm, warm-hearted, °amiable, °amicable, cooperative: *He seems a good-natured fellow, but not too bright.*

goody-goody *adj.* °smug, °sanctimonious, °self-righteous, °priggish, prim, holier-than-thou, Pecksniffian, °hypocritical: *She's one of those goody-goody people who never do anything wrong.*

gooey *adj.* **1** gluey, °sticky, °tacky, glutinous, mucilaginous, gummy: *The pudding was accompanied by an unpleasantly gooey sauce.* **2** °sweet, sugary, saccharine, °sentimental, unctuous, cloying, syrupy, mawkish, °maudlin, *Colloq* °mushy, slushy, °sloppy: *They like to watch those gooey soap operas.*

gore[1] *n.* blood, °carnage, butchery, °slaughter, °bloodshed: *The current crop of horror films have too much gore for my taste.*

gore[2] *v.* °pierce, °stab, °poke, horn, °penetrate, °puncture, spear, °gouge, °spit, °stick, °impale, disembowel: *The matador, severely gored by the bull, was carried away.*

gorge *n.* **1** °ravine, °canyon, defile, °pass, chasm, fissure, °crevasse, °gully *or* gulley, wadi *or* wady, °gap, *Brit* gill *or* ghyll, *US and Canadian* notch: *Water runs in this gorge only during the rainy season.* **2** °vomit, vomitus: *Injustice makes my gorge rise.* —*v.* **3** °fill, °stuff, °glut, °cram; °gulp, gobble (down), °devour, °bolt (down), wolf (down), gormandize, °swallow: *She acquired the habit of gorging on cream cakes.*

gorgeous *adj.* **1** resplendent, °splendid, °magnificent, °glorious, °exquisite, °sumptuous, °dazzling, °grand, °beautiful, splendorous, breathtaking, °radiant, refulgent, °brilliant, °showy, colourful, *Colloq* splendiferous: *The males are known for their gorgeous plumage.* **2** °great, °terrific, °fantastic, wonderful, °marvellous, °glorious, spectacular, °superb, °excellent, *Colloq* fantabulous, marvy, smashing, °super, °nifty, °neat, °swell: *He married a gorgeous fashion model.*

gory *adj.* bloody, °sanguinary, blood-soaked, bloodstained; °gruesome, °grisly, horrific, blood-curdling: *The scene was so gory as to turn the strongest stomach.*

gospel *n.* °truth, °fact, °certainty: *He swears that his story is gospel.*

gossip *n.* **1** °chat, °conversation, °talk, chit-chat, small °talk, °palaver; tittle-tattle, °prattle; *Scots* clishmaclaver; gup; *Colloq Brit* natter, chin-wag: *I was just having a little gossip with my neighbour.* **2** °rumour, °scandal, hearsay, °information, on dit, °word, *Colloq* °grapevine, (inside) info, tittle-tattle, *Slang* °dope, *Chiefly US* scuttlebutt, *US and Canadian* poop: *The latest gossip is that she left him for another woman.* **3** rumour-mill, rumour-monger, scandal-monger, gossip-monger, newsmonger, °busybody, tattle-tale, quidnunc, blabber, blatherskite, tell-tale, °talebearer, flibbertigibbet, *Colloq* big-mouth, chatterbox, °blabbermouth, Nosy Parker: *That old gossip will tell everybody your business.* —*v.* **4** Sometimes, **gossip about**: bruit, °tattle, °rumour, °whisper, blether *or US* blather, gabble, *Colloq* °blab, *Brit* natter, *Slang* jaw: *I was just gossiping to my friend about your new job.*

gouge v. **1** °chisel, °gash, incise, °scratch, °groove, °dig; °scoop or °hollow (out): *The screwdriver slipped and gouged a piece out of the table. She's so mad she wants to gouge out your eyes.* **2** °extort, °extract, bilk, °defraud, wrest, °wrench, °squeeze, °blackmail, *Colloq* °milk, bleed, °skin, °fleece, °cheat, °swindle: *The gang gouged money from Alice by threatening to tell the teacher she had cheated on her French exam.* —n. **3** °groove, °furrow, °scratch, °gash, °hollow; trench, ditch: *The retreating glacier cut a deep gouge in the landscape.*

gourmet n. °epicure, connoisseur, Lucullus, gastronome, gourmand, *bon vivant*, bon viveur: *My dear, that was a dinner fit for a gourmet!*

govern v. **1** °rule, °control, °direct, °reign, hold °sway (over), °lead, °conduct, °guide, °manage, °regulate, °run, °supervise, superintend, °oversee, °steer, captain, °pilot, °command, °head (up), °look after, sit on the throne, wield the sceptre, wear the crown, °run the show, be in °power, be in °charge (of), exercise or wield °power or °control (over), have or hold the whip hand, *Colloq* wear the pants, be in the saddle or driver's °seat: *Catherine governed with an iron hand.* **2** °control, °check, °bridle, °curb, °master, °subdue, °restrain, °contain, °hold in, °suppress, °repress: *You must govern the urge to scream out.*

government n. **1** °rule, °command, °authority, °regulation, °control, °management, °direction, °administration, °sway, superintendence, supervision, °oversight, °guidance, °domination: *His government of the island has led to disorder.* **2** °administration, °ministry, °regime: *The government intends to ban smoking in public places.*

grab v. **1** °snatch, °lay or °catch °hold of, °fasten upon, °grasp, °seize; °catch, °grip, °clutch; *Colloq* latch on to, °get one's hands or fingers on, °nab, *US* °snag: *The thief grabbed my purse and ran. She grabbed the railing to break her fall.* **2** °appropriate, expropriate, °seize, commandeer, °take over, usurp, arrogate: *The general grabbed the reins of government in the coup.* **3** °arrest, °capture, °catch, *Colloq* °nab, °pinch, collar: *The police grabbed him as he was leaving the scene of the crime.* —n. **4** °snatch, °clutch; °grasp, °grip: *I made a grab for the rope.*

grace n. **1** °elegance, gracefulness, suppleness, °finesse, °refinement, °ease, °polish, °poise: *She rides well, with an unconscious grace.* **2** tastefulness, (good) °taste, cultivation, suavity or suaveness, °culture, savoir faire, discernment, °discrimination, (good) manners, politeness, °breeding, °consideration, decency, °etiquette, °tact, °propriety, °decorum, mannerliness: *They had the grace to ignore my rough attire.* **3** °indulgence, °forgiveness, °mercy, mercifulness, leniency, compassion, clemency, °charity, goodwill, goodness: *We survived the fire only by the grace of God. The company gives you 30 days' grace to pay the bill.* **4** °kindness, °favour, kindliness, °benevolence, generosity, goodness, graciousness, becomingness, seemliness; °excellence, °virtue, strength of °character, considerateness: *At least he had the good grace to admit being wrong.* **5** °blessing, thanksgiving, °prayer, benediction: *Grace was said before each meal.* —v. **6** adorn, °embellish, °set off, °decorate, °ornament, °beautify, °enhance, garnish: *The*

table was graced by a huge silver candelabrum. **7** °dignify, °enhance, °distinguish, °enrich, °honour, °favour: *The dinner-party is graced by your presence.*

graceful adj. **1** °fluid, flowing, °supple, lissom or lissome, lithe, facile, °smooth, °nimble, °agile, deft: *How graceful a dancer she is!* **2** °tactful, well-mannered, °polite, °courteous, mannerly, °refined, °tasteful, °elegant, courtly, urbane, °polished, °refined, °suave: *In return for certain concessions, the chief was graceful enough to release the hostages.*

gracious adj. °kind, °courteous, °polite, well-mannered, °kindly, °benevolent, beneficent, °indulgent, kind-hearted, warm-hearted, °cordial, °warm, °friendly, °sociable, °good-natured, °amiable, affable, °benign, °accommodating, °obliging, °agreeable, °considerate: *It was gracious of you to grant me an audience.*

grade n. **1** °degree, °position, °rank, °status, °stage, °standing, °station, gradation, echelon, °class, °level, °category, °condition, °state, °estate, °situation, rung: *She is a singer of the first grade.* **2** rating, °mark, °score: *What grade did you get in physics?* **3** °class, °form, year: *My daughter is in the third grade.* **4** °hill, °slope, °rise, gradient, acclivity, declivity, °incline, °decline, ascent, descent, upgrade, °downgrade: *The car coasted down a gentle grade into the lake.* **5 make the grade**: °pass, °measure up, °succeed, °qualify, *Colloq US* °make it, *Slang US and Canadian and NZ* °hack or °cut it: *Do you think that Simpson can make the grade?* —v. **6** classify, °class, °order, °organize, °rank, °sort, °size, °group, categorize, °rate: *Her job is to grade pearls according to their size.* **7** °mark, °rate, °correct, °evaluate: *My teacher was up late grading our exams.*

gradual adj. °easy, °gentle, °even, °moderate, °slow, °piecemeal, inchmeal, °regular, °steady: *There is a gradual slope down to the garden wall. The acceleration was gradual. He became aware of a gradual erosion of his authority.*

gradually adv. slowly, evenly, °piecemeal, inchmeal, °drop by drop, °step by step, °bit by bit, °little by little, °piece by piece, gradatim: *The water gradually seeped through the filter. We advanced gradually through the forest.*

graduate n. **1** bachelor, postgraduate, *US* alumnus (*pl.* alumni) or alumna (*pl.* alumnae): *Even university graduates found it difficult to get a job.* —v. **2** gradate, °mark, °calibrate, °grade, °scale: *This thermometer is graduated in increments of one tenth of a degree.*

graft[1] n. **1** bud, scion, °shoot, °splice, implantation or °implant, °transplant: *New varieties were created by the implantation of grafts that have desirable qualities.* —v. **2** °implant, °splice, °insert, °join: *Fruit-bearing stems are grafted onto a sturdy rootstock.*

graft[2] n. corruption, jobbery; bribery, extortion, *Colloq* payola, °kickback: *After only five years, he retired on the takings from graft.*

grain n. **1** °seed, °kernel, stone, pip, °pit: *Grains from each crop are stored ready for sowing.* **2** cereal, corn, grist: *The grain harvest was sparse this year.* **3** °particle, °bit, °fragment, °crumb, °speck, granule, °morsel, mote, molecule, atom, fleck, iota, ounce, °scrap, °trace, scintilla, °hint,

°suggestion, whit, °jot (or tittle), °dab, soupçon, °taste, *Colloq US and Canadian* smidgen or smidgin: *There's not a grain of truth in anything that's been said.* **4** °texture, °pattern, °fibre, °weave, °nap: *Use a different kind of saw for cutting across the grain.*

grand *adj.* **1** °large, °great, °huge, °immense, °enormous, °impressive, °imposing, °splendid, °fine, °majestic, °stately, °lofty, °monumental, °lavish, °magnificent, °opulent, °luxurious, °palatial, °sumptuous, *Colloq* °posh: *We were led into a grand hall where thousands awaited the emperor.* **2** °dignified, °distinguished, august, respected, °eminent, °pre-eminent, °outstanding, °celebrated, °illustrious, °renowned, °notable, °legendary, °exalted, revered, °venerable, °immortal: *He is regarded as the grand old man of chemistry.* **3** °flamboyant, overdone, histrionic, °ostentatious, °pretentious, °grandiose, lordly: *The abysmal performance was punctuated by the actors' grand strutting and gesturing.* **4** °complete, °total, °sum, °comprehensive, (all-)°inclusive; bottom-line: *The grand total of expenses came to £12,467.22.* **5** °marvellous, wonderful, °outstanding, first-class, °first-rate, °splendid, °excellent, °superb, °admirable, *Colloq* °great, marvy, smashing, °terrific, °fantastic, °fabulous, fantabulous, °super: *Isn't it grand that Freda will be able to go!* **6** °principal, °chief, °main, °head, °leading, °foremost, highest: *The grand vizier was second only to the caliph.*

grandeur *n.* **1** °splendour, magnificence, majesty, sublimity, luxuriousness, °pomp: *The grandeur of the French court was never to be equalled.* **2** °nobility, augustness, nobleness, eminence, majesty: *The emperor received us with a grandeur befitting his station.*

grandiose *adj.* **1** °pretentious, °ostentatious, °showy, °flamboyant, °bombastic, histrionic, °extravagant, °pompous, fustian, high-flown, high-flying, overambitious, overdone, over-dramatic, °melodramatic, Ossianic, °inflated, °affected, florid, °flashy, *Colloq* high-falutin or hifalutin, °flash: *The council is unimpressed by your grandiose plans to redevelop the area, Mr Wren.* **2** °imposing, °impressive, °ambitious, °grand, °monumental, °magnificent, °lofty: *She has some grandiose ideas for a national symphony orchestra.*

grant *v.* **1** °give, °confer, °bestow, °present, °award, °offer; °supply, °furnish, °distribute, °donate; allocate, °assign: *She has been granted a sum that will enable her to complete the book.* **2** °concede, accede (to), °cede, °give (up), °agree (to), °consent (to), °allow, °permit, °admit; °let: *They granted my request for clemency.* —*n.* **3** °gift, °present, °endowment, °bequest, subvention, °subsidy, °award, grant-in-aid, °donation, contribution, concession, °allowance: *He received a government grant to study abroad.*

granular *adj.* grainy, granulated, particulate, comminuted, °gravelly, sandy, °gritty: *The sauce was somewhat granular and tasted too strongly of nutmeg.*

grapevine *n.* rumour-mill, jungle telegraph, grapevine telegraph, °rumour, °gossip: *According to the grapevine, you two are going to be married.*

graphic *adj.* **1** °vivid, °distinct, well-defined, °detailed, °explicit, °particular, °clear, lucid,

°plain, °manifest, crystal °clear, unmistakable, unambiguous, °accurate, °precise, well-drawn, °photographic, descriptive, °telling, °picturesque, °pictorial, °realistic, °lifelike, °true to °life, *Colloq* °gory: *He described his injuries in graphic detail.* **2** written, drawn, diagrammatic, delineated, °visible: *The magazine won a prize for graphic design.*

grapple *v.* **1** °grasp, °grab, °grip, °seize, °clasp, catch, °wrestle; °hold, °clutch, °snatch: *They grappled each other at the edge of the Reichenbach Falls.* **2 grapple with**: come to grips with, °cope with, contend with, °deal with, °struggle with, °tackle, °face, °take on: *The government is grappling with the problem of unemployment.*

grasp *v.* **1** °grip, °grab, °seize, °clasp, °clutch, °snatch, °hold, °take *or* °lay *or* °catch °hold of, *Colloq* °nab: *I grasped the rope and was pulled to safety.* **2** °understand, °comprehend, °appreciate, °catch (on), °get, get the °drift *or* °point of, °follow, °see, °realize, apprehend, °learn, *Colloq* °make head(s) or tail(s) of, *Slang* °dig: *I am trying to grasp the full import of what you are saying.* —*n.* **3** °hold, °grip, clutches, °clasp, °embrace, °lock: *He loosened his grasp on my throat and I could breathe again.* **4** °possession, °control, °power, mastery, °sovereignty, suzerainty, °hold: *By then, even the outer islands had fallen within his grasp.* **5** °understanding, comprehension, apprehension, awareness, °perception, °sense: *He has a poor grasp of the basics of the subject.*

grasping *adj.* °greedy, °avaricious, acquisitive, °rapacious, °mean, °miserly, stingy, °penurious, parsimonious, niggardly, °tight, tight-fisted, penny-pinching, close-fisted, °mercenary: *If the company weren't so grasping, they'd have less difficulty hiring staff.*

grass *v.* **1** °inform, °betray, °give away, *Slang* peach, squeal, snitch, squeak, °tattle, rat on, °sell out, *Brit* °blow the gaff, nark: *He received a shorter sentence for grassing on his accomplices.* —*n.* **2** °traitor, °informer, *Slang* stool-pigeon, stoolie, squealer, snitch, squeaker, rat, *Brit* nark: *A grass is treated roughly by fellow inmates.*

grate *v.* **1** °shred, °rasp, °scrape, °rub, triturate: *Peel six raw potatoes and grate them fine.* **2** °scrape, °rasp, °rub, °grind, °scratch, screech, stridulate: *The cricket grates its legs against its wing covers to produce the 'singing' sound.* **3** Often, **grate on** *or* **upon**: °annoy, vex, °irk, °irritate, °pester, set one's teeth on edge, °jar, °fret, °chafe, °rub (someone) (up) the wrong way, go against the grain, *Colloq* °get on one's nerves: *Her voice just grates on me.*

grateful *adj.* °thankful, appreciative: *I am grateful for any help I can get.*

gratification *n.* °satisfaction, °fulfilment, °enjoyment, °pleasure, °delight, compensation, recompense, °reward, °return, °requital: *She does it only for the gratification she gets from making the children happier.*

gratify *v.* °please, °satisfy, °fulfil, °delight, °compensate, recompense, °reward, °requite, °cheer, °gladden, °favour: *Albert would be gratified to see the good coming from his charitable bequests.*

grating *adj.* **1** jarring, °strident, °raucous, °harsh, °discordant, dissonant, unharmonious, °offensive, irritating, °irksome, annoying, vexatious, galling: *I find the noise of chalk squeaking on the blackboard very grating.* **2** grinding, °gritty, squeaky, jangling, screeching, creaking, °shrill, °piercing, squawking, croaking, rasping: *The grating noise you hear is my fridge motor.* —*n.* **3** °grate, grid, reticle *or* reticule, grille, lattice, trellis, °screen, °network, reticulation: *When a beam of light is directed through the fine grating, odd patterns are formed.*

gratitude *n.* thankfulness, °appreciation, gratefulness; °thanks, °return, compensation, thanksgiving: *Here is a box of chocolates in gratitude for looking after my cat.*

gratuitous *adj.* **1** gratis, °free, °complimentary, °spontaneous: *The earth is a machine which has, till now, yielded gratuitous service.* **2** °unasked for, unrequested, unsought for, °wanton, unprovoked, °unsolicited, unlooked-for, uncalled-for, °unwelcome, unjustified, °unwarranted, baseless, °groundless, °needless, °unfounded, ungrounded, unjustifiable, irrational: *He seems to derive some twisted pleasure from spreading gratuitous lies about me.*

grave[1] *n.* °crypt, °sepulchre, °tomb, vault, mausoleum, °last *or* °final resting-place, eternal °rest: *She began to sob as the coffin was slowly lowered into the grave.*

grave[2] *adj.* **1** °serious, °sombre, °solemn, °earnest, unsmiling, °staid, °sedate, °sober, °dour, °gloomy, °grim, grim-faced, grim-visaged, *Brit* °po-faced: *The doctor, looking very grave, said that he had done all he could.* **2** °serious, °critical, °vital, °dangerous, life and death, °crucial, °urgent, °weighty, °important, °pressing, °pivotal, °perilous: *Fenwick is in intensive care in a grave condition.*

graveyard *n.* burial-ground, churchyard, cemetery, God's acre, necropolis, potter's °field, *W US* Boot Hill, *Rare* Golgotha, *Slang* bone-yard: *Uncle Valentine is buried in the graveyard on the hill.*

gravity *n.* **1** gravitation; °attraction: *After middle age, the body obeys the laws of gravity but not of mutual attraction.* **2** seriousness, acuteness, immediacy, °importance, °significance, °weight, °magnitude, °severity, °urgency, exigency, momentousness, weightiness: *When I saw mother's expression I realized the gravity of the situation.* **3** °solemnity, °dignity, sombreness, staidness, sedateness, °sobriety, gravitas, soberness, °reserve; gloominess, grimness: *The ceremony was conducted with suitable gravity.*

greasy *adj.* **1** °oily, sebaceous, fatty, °fat, buttery, lardy, soapy, oleaginous, pinguid, butyraceous, saponaceous, waxy: *Before curing, the hide is greasy with natural oils.* **2** unctuous, °oily, °slippery, slithery, °smooth, °glib, fawning, °slick, toadying, sycophantic, *Slang Brit* smarmy: *Edna is so greasy, always trying to manoeuvre you into doing something for her.*

great *adj.* **1** °big, °large, °huge, °immense, °enormous, °gigantic, °giant, °grand, °extensive, °prodigious, °colossal, °massive, °vast, tremendous; °spacious, capacious, mammoth, gargantuan, °monstrous, titanic, Cyclopean, Brobdingnagian: *Europe was covered by a great forest. A great castle loomed before me.* **2** °large, °huge, °immense, °enormous, °gigantic, °prodigious, °vast, tremendous, °abundant, countless: *Plague killed a great number of people.* **3** °extreme, °considerable, °marked, °pronounced, °inordinate, °extraordinary, °significant; °excess, °excessive:

I have something of great importance to tell you. Your news created great confusion. **4** °critical, °important, °crucial, °momentous, °significant, °serious, °weighty, consequential: *Those were great days for the history of England.* **5** °important, °prominent, °major, °eminent, °celebrated, °distinguished, °famous, famed, °renowned, °notable, °noteworthy, °illustrious, °outstanding, °well-known, °weighty, °influential, *Rare* eximious: *What of the great universities, like Oxford and Cambridge? Our mayor thinks of himself as a great man.* **6** °talented, °gifted, °excellent, °outstanding, °exceptional, °major, °superlative, °superior, °leading, °best, °incomparable, °matchless, °peerless, °skilful, artistic, °brilliant, °first-rate, °remarkable, °top, °accomplished: *Flaubert was one of the greatest writers of his age. Tamara is a good dancer, but not a great dancer.* **7** °lofty, °elevated, °exalted, °noble, high-minded, °grand: *Great thoughts come from great minds.* **8** °talented, skilled, °skilful, adroit, °clever, °adept, °able, °proficient, °expert: *Daphne is really great at playing bridge.* **9** °keen, zealous, °eager, °active, °enthusiastic, °devoted, °ardent, °passionate: *Frank is a great stamp collector.* **10** °close, °devoted, dedicated, °fast, °faithful, °true, °loyal, °intimate, loving: *Graham and Pembroke quickly became great friends.* **11** °terrible, °bad, °awful, unforgivable, horrendous, heinous, °grievous, horrific, °horrible, °terrific, °huge, °colossal, °enormous, °gigantic, °significant, °cardinal, egregious, °basic, °profound, °flagrant, °glaring, arrant, consummate, °out-and-out: *Inviting her at the same time as her ex-husband was a great mistake.* **12** spectacular, °marvellous, °outstanding, °excellent, °superb, °grand, wonderful, °fine *Colloq* °fantastic, °terrific, stupendous, marvy, smashing, fantabulous, *Old-fashioned Brit* tickety-boo: *He says that we missed a truly great show.*

greed *n.* **1** greediness, °avarice, avariciousness, covetousness, acquisitiveness, cupidity, avidity, craving, yearning: *Greed accounts for most of man's dishonesty.* **2** meanness, stinginess, miserliness, selfishness, niggardliness, penuriousness, parsimony, close-fistedness, penny-pinching, tight-fistedness: *From a life of greed he had accumulated enormous wealth.* **3** °gluttony, voraciousness, edacity, esurience, voracity, overeating, gormandizing, ravenousness, insatiableness: *Obesity owes more to greed than to glandular disorder.*

greedy *adj.* **1** °ravenous, °voracious, °gluttonous, piggish, °hoggish, swinish, cormorant, edacious, esurient, insatiable, °unquenchable: *I'd love another slice, but I mustn't be greedy.* **2** °avaricious, acquisitive, covetous, °grasping, craving; °materialistic, money-hungry: *If some people were less greedy, there would be plenty for everyone.* **3** stingy, °miserly, °mean, °selfish, niggardly, parsimonious, °penurious, penny-pinching, °mercenary, close-fisted, tight-fisted, °close, *Colloq* near, °tight, *Brit* mingy: *He's so greedy that he asks beggars for receipts.*

green *adj.* **1** verdant, grassy, °fresh, °leafy; °rural, country-like: *Plans call for a green belt to be created around every major city.* **2** °immature, unripe, unripened; °naïve, °callow, untested, untrained, unversed, °inexperienced, °new,

°raw, unseasoned, °unsophisticated, °gullible, °amateur, unskilled, unskilful, amateurish, non-professional, inexpert, *Colloq* wet behind the ears: *This banana is still too green to eat. Isn't Piers a bit green to be given so much responsibility?* **3** environmental, conservationist: *The green activists appear to be gaining influence in governmental circles.* —*n.* **4** °lawn, sward, °common, grassland: *Let us meet on the village green at noon.* **5** °environmentalist, conservationist, preservationist: *The greens are opposed to draining the marshes.*

greenhorn *n.* °newcomer, beginner, °novice, tiro *or* tyro, neophyte, °initiate, °learner, tenderfoot, *Colloq* rookie: *They send all the greenhorns off to fetch a bucket of steam and a can of striped paint.*

greet *v.* **1** °welcome, °receive, usher in, °meet: *We were greeted warmly by the family.* **2** °hail, accost, °address, °salute: *People greeted him in the street with a wave and a smile.*

greeting *n.* **1** salutation, °hail, hello, °welcome, °reception: *She had a smile and a greeting for every passer-by.* **2** greetings °card, °card, °message, °note: *The Queen sent me a greeting on my 100th birthday.* **3 greetings**: °regards, °respects, best *or* °good wishes, devoirs, °compliments: *I sent you greetings from Barbados, where I took my holiday.*

grey *adj.* **1** ashen, °leaden, °colourless, °pale, pallid, °wan, livid, °pearly, griseous, smoky, sooty, bloodless: *The cadaver's skin was a dead, whitish grey.* **2** °gloomy, °dismal, °dull, depressing, °glum, °dreary, °sombre, °drab, cheerless, °dark, °murky, foggy, °misty, cloudy, °overcast, °sunless: *As if to mould her temperament, Kathleen was born on a grey December day in 1791.* **3** °aged, °elderly, hoary, °old, °venerable, °ancient: *A stooped, grey crone inched along, muttering to herself.* **4** °mature, °wise, °experienced: *Seventy years have spread their grey experience over his hoary head.*

grief *n.* **1** °anguish, °suffering, °agony, °misery, wretchedness, °pain, °hurt, °sadness, °sorrow, dejection, °depression, despondency, °melancholy, unhappiness, °woe, °torment, °desolation, heartbreak, °remorse, °regret, ruth, heartache: *Nothing equalled the grief I felt at the death of my dog, Whiffler.* **2** °distress, °trouble, °difficulty, tribulation, °trial, °burden, °load, onus, °ordeal, travail, °affliction, °worry, °bitterness, °curse; adversity, °misfortune, °evil days, °bad *or* °ill °fortune *or* °luck, °calamity, °disaster, °catastrophe, trauma: *The death of her only child was a lasting grief to Millie.* **3 come to grief**: °fail, go to °rack and °ruin, meet with °disaster, °miscarry, °fall *or* °come °apart, *Colloq* °come unstuck: *Our plans for retirement came to grief when my husband went bankrupt.*

grievance *adj.* **1** °wrong, °ill, °injustice, °disservice, unfairness, °injury, °damage, °harm, °outrage, affront, °indignity, °hardship, °calamity: *I had to listen to details of every grievance she had ever suffered.* **2** °complaint, °objection, °charge, plaint, °allegation, °grudge, *Colloq* °gripe, bone to pick, *Brit* crow to pluck, *Slang* beef: *Please register all your grievances at the office next door.*

grieve *v.* **1** °mourn, °bemoan, °lament, °regret, rue, deplore, °bewail, mope, eat one's heart out:

Sylvia is still grieving over the loss of her husband. **2** °weep, °cry, °mourn, °moan, °keen, °suffer, °sorrow, °shed tears, °complain: *Go in and try to comfort the grieving widow.*

grievous *adj.* **1** °severe, °heavy, °painful, °grave, °serious, distressing, °harmful; damaging, °hurtful, °acute, wounding: *The church buildings suffered grievous damage from the storm. He was charged with causing grievous bodily harm.* **2** egregious, °awful, °flagrant, °terrible, °outrageous, heinous, °dreadful, °atrocious, °monstrous, appalling, °shocking, °deplorable, °calamitous, °lamentable, intolerable, °shameful, °unbearable: *Missing that catch was a grievous error.*

grim *adj.* **1** °stern, °severe, unrelenting, °resolute, uncompromising, unyielding, °inflexible, adamant, °stony, iron, unbending, °firm, intractable, unflinching, unmoving, °unmoved, °implacable, inexorable, °determined, °steadfast, (dead) set, °fixed, °decided, °obstinate, headstrong, °stubborn, obdurate, dogged, unwavering: *By controlling the purse strings, she kept a grim hold over the family.* **2** °forbidding, °formidable, °harsh, °ferocious, °fierce, °cruel, °savage, °merciless, °heartless, °ruthless, pitiless, °vicious, °brutal, brutish, feral, °inhuman, °fiendish, °violent, °bloodthirsty, °murderous, °homicidal, °fell: *A grim pack of howling wolves loped after our sledge.* **3** dire, °dreadful, °ghastly, °awful, °frightful, °frightening, °sinister, °hideous, horrid, horrific, °horrible, horrendous, °terrible, °terrifying, °terrific, °harrowing, °dread, alarming, appalling, °grotesque, °gruesome, °eerie, °macabre, flagitious, heinous, °evil, °wicked, iniquitous, °atrocious, °monstrous: *Before me appeared the ghostly apparition of the Grim Reaper.*

grime *n.* °dirt, °filth, soot, °mud, °muck, slime, scum: *The lad began to rub the grime from the old oil lamp.*

grind *v.* **1** °pound, °powder, °pulverize, abrade, °crush, granulate, °mill, °grate, °rasp, °crumble, kibble, mash, triturate, bray, comminute: *The rock was soon ground to a fine powder.* **2** °sharpen, °whet; °file, °smooth, °polish: *He is grinding the edge to be razor sharp.* **3** gnash, °grit, °grate: *He grinds his teeth when he's angry.* **4** Also, **grind away**: °labour, toil, °slave (away); °study, lucubrate, burn the midnight oil, *Colloq* °cram, *Brit* swot: *George has been grinding away at the same job all his life. Languages came easily, but he had to grind away at the sciences.* **5 grind down**: °wear down *or* away, °crush, °oppress, °subdue, °suppress, °tyrannize, °persecute, maltreat, °ill-treat, harry, °harass, °hound, hector, °plague, badger: *Dictators first grind down all opposition, then destroy it.* **6 grind out**: °produce, °generate, °crank out, churn out, °turn out: *For 20 years he has been grinding out the daily gossip column.* —*n.* **7** toil, °labour, °drudgery, travail, °exertion, °task, chore: *Working at the checkout counter hour after hour is a terrible grind.*

grip *n.* **1** °hold, °grasp, °clutch, handgrip, °clasp, hand-clasp: *Losing his grip on the rope, he plummeted into the abyss.* **2** °control, °command, °hold, mastery, °authority, °influence, °power, °rule, °domination, °sovereignty, °tenure, °dominion, suzerainty, °custody: *Peter is losing his grip on reality. The dictator kept a tight grip on the people right up to his death.* **3** °grasp,

°understanding, apprehension, comprehension, °sense, °sensitivity, °feel, °feeling, awareness, °perception, °view, *Slang US* °handle: *Skerry is having trouble getting a grip on what you plan to do.* **4** handgrip, valise, (travelling *or* overnight) °bag, °case, satchel, °suitcase, *Brit* holdall, *US and Canadian* carry-all: *I got off the plane in New York, but my grip went on to Detroit.* **5 come** *or* **get to grips with**: °tackle, confront, °approach, °handle, °meet (head on), °undertake, °grapple *or* contend with, °cope *or* °deal with, °face: *We must come to grips with the problem of Cassandra.* —*v.* **6** °grasp, °clutch, °clasp, °hold, °seize: *He gripped the handle of the revolver more tightly.* **7** engross, °engage, °hold, °fascinate, enthral, °entrance, absorb, mesmerize, °hypnotize, spellbind, rivet: *Just at the gripping climax, the reel broke and the film stopped.*

gripe *v.* **1** °complain, °moan, grumble, whimper, whine, bleat, °nag, cavil, °carp, grouse, *Colloq* beef, *Brit* whinge, *Slang* °bitch, bellyache: *It's natural to gripe about the food in the army.* —*n.* **2** °complaint, °grievance, °objection, °protest; complaining, moaning, grumbling, whimpering, whining, °nagging, cavilling, carping, grousing, *Colloq* beef, *Brit* whinging, *Slang* bitching, bellyaching: *I don't want to hear any more gripes about the food!* **3** Usually, **gripes**: cramp, °twinge, °pang, °pain, °ache, colic, °distress, *Colloq* bellyache: *The gripes became so painful that he was sure he had appendicitis.*

grisly *adj.* °gruesome, °gory, °abhorrent, °abominable, °awful, appalling, °hideous, °shocking, °nasty, °dreadful, °repulsive, °repellent, °repugnant, °disgusting, sickening, nauseating, horrific, horrid, horrendous, horrifying, °terrible, °terrifying, °terrific: *A grisly scene greeted the soldiers who liberated the concentration camp.*

grit *n.* °courage, courageousness, valour, °bravery, °fortitude, °resolution, resoluteness, °resolve, toughness, mettle, °pluck, °spirit, °backbone, °nerve, gameness, intrepidity *or* intrepidness, dauntlessness, °tenacity, °determination, firmness, hardiness, hardihood, staunchness, stalwartness, doughtiness, fearlessness, *Colloq* °guts, gutsiness, °spunk, spunkiness, starch, *Brit* °bottle, *US and Canadian* chutzpah, moxie, stick-to-it-iveness: *Mountain-climbing requires more grit than you might think.*

gritty *adj.* **1** sandy, gravelly, °granular, grainy, °rough, abrasive, rasping, arenose: *The texture of the mud-pack felt somewhat gritty on her face.* **2** °courageous, valorous, °brave, °resolute, °tough, mettlesome, plucky, °spirited, °game, °intrepid, °dauntless, °tenacious, °determined, °persistent, °firm, °hardy, °staunch, °stalwart, doughty, °fearless, *Colloq* gutsy, spunky: *The band of gritty frontiersmen was led by Sheriff Boswell.*

groan *v.* **1** °moan, °sigh, °murmur, wail, whimper, whine: *Unattended patients were lying there, groaning in agony.* **2** °complain, grumble, grouse, °object, °protest, *Colloq* °gripe, beef, yammer, *Brit* whinge, *Slang* °bitch: *Now that he's rich, he's groaning about taxes.* —*n.* **3** °moan, °sigh, °murmur, wail, whimper, whine: *I thought I heard a groan coming from the attic.* **4** °complaint, grumble, grousing, muttering, *Colloq* °gripe, griping, beef, yammering, *Slang* bitching: *His announcement that the whole class would be punished was met by groans.*

groggy *adj.* unsteady, °shaky, wobbly, weak-kneed, °weak, staggering, stupefied, dazed, stunned, reeling, punch-drunk, °numb, numbed, benumbed, °faint, in a °trance *or* °stupor, muddled, addled, °confused, bewildered, confounded, puzzled, baffled, befuddled, *Colloq* dopey, punchy, woozy, *Brit* muzzy: *I was still groggy from the blow on the head.*

groom *n.* **1** stable-boy, stableman, *Brit* stable-lad, *Archaic* ostler *or* hostler, equerry: *The groom unsaddled the horses and began to curry them.* **2** bridegroom: *Let's drink to the bride and groom!* —*v.* **3** °spruce up, °dress, °tidy *or* °neaten up, smarten up, titivate *or* tittivate, °preen, °primp, °refresh: *Every time she passes a mirror Vivian stops to groom herself.* **4** °fit, °train, °prepare, °coach, °tutor, °brief, °drill, °prime, (get *or* make) °ready, °adapt, °shape: *McCusker is being groomed for a directorship.*

groove *n.* °slot, °cut, °channel, °furrow, °gouge, trough; flute, °scratch, striation *or* stria, rifling, °rifle, *Architecture* glyph, *Technical* sulcus: *The door slides in these grooves at the sides.*

grope *v.* °feel, °fumble, fish, °probe: *I groped for the switch in the dark.*

gross *adj.* **1** °fat, °obese, corpulent, overweight, °big, °large, °bulky, °great, °heavy, °ponderous, °massive, cumbersome, °unwieldy: *The gross detective eased his bulk onto a tiny chair.* **2** °total, aggregate, °entire, pre-tax, (all-)°inclusive, °overall, °whole: *The gross profit was up by 15 per cent this year.* **3** °coarse, °vulgar, °crude, °unsophisticated, uncultured, uncultivated, °earthy, crass, indelicate, °indecent, °inappropriate, °unseemly, °improper, °unrefined, °bawdy, ribald, Rabelaisian, °raw, °rude, °offensive, °obscene, °lewd, °dirty, smutty, °pornographic, °filthy: *That was too gross a story for mixed company.* **4** °outrageous, °flagrant, °obvious, °plain, °glaring, °shameful, °blatant, °monstrous, heinous, °manifest, °evident: *Her conviction was a gross miscarriage of justice.* **5** °disgusting, °repulsive, °repellent, °revolting, nauseating: *His table manners are truly gross.* —*v.* **6** °earn, °bring *or* °take in, °make: *We grossed over a million but netted only 50,000 after expenses.* —*n.* **7** (°overall) °total, °take, intake, takings, °receipts, °gate: *As I said, the gross was over a million.*

grotesque *adj.* **1** distorted, °bizarre, freakish, twisted, °misshapen, malformed, °deformed, °gruesome, °gnarled: *Victor Hugo created the character of Quasimodo, the grotesque bell-ringer of Notre Dame.* **2** °absurd, °incongruous, °weird, °odd, °fantastic, °strange, °queer, °peculiar, °curious, °outlandish, °offbeat, °abnormal, aberrant, anomalous, °ludicrous, °ridiculous, °preposterous: *The idea of marrying Leonard is too grotesque for even Gladys to contemplate.*

ground *n.* **1** °earth, °soil, °turf, sod, °dirt, loam, clay; °land, °terrain: *There is a great hole in the ground behind my house.* **2** °territory, °area, °range, °scope, compass: *We covered the ground quite thoroughly at our meeting.* **3** Often, **grounds**: °basis, °foundation, °base, °reason, °footing, justification, °rationale, °argument, °cause, °motive, °excuse: *What are her grounds for suing*

for divorce? **4 grounds**: °sediment, °dregs, lees, °deposit, settlings, *Brit* grouts: *Filter out the grounds before drinking the coffee.*
—*v.* **5** °base, °establish, °organize, °found; °settle, °set: *The school's philosophy is grounded on the principles of Maria Montessori.* **6** °instruct, °teach, °train, °coach, °tutor, °inform, °prepare, °initiate: *The purpose of the course is to ground students in basic mathematics.*

groundless *adj.* baseless, without °foundation, °unsound, °unfounded, unsupported, unjustified, unjustifiable, °unwarranted, uncalled-for, °gratuitous, unreasoned, °unreasonable, °speculative, suppositional, °hypothetical, °tenuous, °flimsy, °illusory, °imaginary, chimerical: *Assumptions that the boy is guilty are entirely groundless.*

groundwork *n.* °basis, spadework, °preparation(s), °base, °foundation, underpinning(s), cornerstone: *The report provided the groundwork for the research.*

group *n.* **1** °assembly, assemblage, °gathering, congregation, °company, °number, °alliance, °union, °association, °organization, °league, °society, coterie, °clique, °set, °band, °circle, °club, °party, °body, °faction, °crowd, °team, °corps, guild, troupe, °unit, troop, °platoon, °squad, °gang: *A group of revolutionaries meets nightly in a basement in Krakowskaya Street.* **2** °batch, aggregation, °set, grouping, °collection, assemblage, °bunch, °accumulation, conglomeration, agglomeration, °assortment, series; °pile, °heap, °bundle: *The entire group of abstract paintings was auctioned at double their estimated value.*
—*v.* **3** classify, °class, °sort, °bracket, °organize, °order, °rank, assort, °categorize, catalogue: *Books are grouped according to subject.* **4** °collect, °assemble, °arrange, °place, °dispose, °gather, °organize, °bring *or* °put together, °set °apart: *Group oversized books together on the lowest shelves.*

grovelling *adj.* °obsequious, fawning, toadying, toad-eating, sycophantish, subservient, slavish, °servile, °submissive, kowtowing, cringing, cowering, truckling, snivelling, scraping, tugging the forelock, abject, crawling, °base, °low, °mean, °sordid, *Colloq* boot-licking, *US* apple-polishing; *Slang* brown-nosing, *Brit* arse-kissing, *US* ass-kissing, ass-licking: *The grovelling coward threw himself to the ground, begging forgiveness.*

grow *v.* **1** °flourish, °develop, °increase, become larger *or* greater, °enlarge, wax, °swell, °expand, broaden, °thicken, °spread, °lengthen, multiply, burgeon *or* bourgeon, °thrive, °luxuriate, °prosper, °mature, °ripen, bloom, °flower, blossom, fructify, bear *or* yield °fruit: *The seeds he had planted grew abundantly. The population continues to grow.* **2** °develop, evolve, °arise, °issue, °stem, °spring (up), °originate: *A great friendship grew out of their association.* **3** °plant, °cultivate, °breed, nurture, °raise, °propagate, °produce; °sow: *Cathcart grows sorghum where he used to grow alfalfa.* **4** °become, °get: *I am growing fonder of you every day, Abbie.* **5 grow on**: °get *or* °become accepted by, °come *or* °begin to be liked by, gain *or* °increase in °interest *or* °attraction to, become more °pleasing to: *I didn't like her at first, but she grows on you.* **6 grow up**:

°mature, °reach *or* attain °maturity *or* adulthood, °come of °age, °reach one's °majority: *Those who grew up in the Great Depression knew real poverty.*

growth *n.* **1** °development, °evolution, evolvement, cultivation, nurturing, °increase, °expansion, broadening, °extension, enlargement, °spread, °proliferation, flowering: *The growth of education was a slow and painful process.* **2** vegetation, crop: *The area is covered with a dense growth of timber.* **3** °advance, advancement, °success, °improvement, °expansion, °rise, °progress: *The growth of the economy has slowed down in the last quarter.* **4** wen, excrescence, wart, °lump, °tumour, °swelling, intumescence: *He developed an ugly growth on his nose.*

grudge *n.* **1** °bitterness, °resentment, °rancour, °ill will, °hard feelings, °spite, °grievance, pique, °dislike, °aversion, antipathy, animus, °animosity, enmity, °venom, malice, malevolence, hatred: *He had harboured a grudge against her ever since she was promoted.*
—*v.* **2** °begrudge, °resent, °envy, °mind, covet: *She grudges other people their simple pleasures.*

gruesome *adj.* °ghastly, °repugnant, °horrible, horrid, horrific, horrendous, °grisly, °hideous, °revolting, °repellent, °repulsive, °loathsome, °grim, °grotesque, °macabre, °abominable, °frightful, °frightening, °fearsome, °shocking, °terrible, °awful: *She told a tale too gruesome to repeat here.*

gruff *adj.* **1** °surly, crusty, grumpy, curmudgeonly, °cantankerous, °sour, °peevish, churlish, °rude, uncivil, bearish, °testy, °querulous, °irritable, °cross, °petulant, crabbed, irascible, °sullen, sulky, °bluff, °abrupt, °curt, °blunt, °brusque, °short, °short-tempered, ill-humoured, ill-natured, bad-tempered, stinging, °cutting, °biting, acerb, acrimonious, acid, °caustic, *Colloq* grouchy, crotchety: *It is difficult to work for someone as gruff as he is.* **2** throaty, °deep, °rough, guttural, rasping, °low, °husky, hoarse, °harsh(-sounding): *Instantly I recognized father's gruff voice on the telephone.*

guarantee *n.* **1** guaranty, °warranty, °assurance, °pledge, °bond, °obligation, °promise; °word (of °honour), °oath, °undertaking: *The guarantee expires one month from the sell-by date. Have I your guarantee that this battery will last a year?*
—*v.* **2** guaranty, °warranty, °assure, °ensure, °pledge, °promise, °undertake, °stand behind, °vouch for, °certify, make °sure *or* °certain, °swear to, °attest to: *The manufacturer guarantees every car for three years or 50,000 miles.*

guard *v.* **1** °protect, °shield, °safeguard, (°keep *or* °stand) °watch (over), °defend, convoy, °escort, °police, °look after, °tend, °mind: *Only three men will be guarding the bullion when we make our move.* **2** °control, °mind: *Guard your tongue—the walls have ears.*
—*n.* **3** °sentinel, °watchman, sentry, °security guard, custodian, °guardian, °protector, °picket, °watch, bodyguard; evzone, bashibazouk; *Brit* warder, wardress, *Slang* screw, *Brit* °minder: *The guards go to eat at noon.* **4** °protection, convoy, °escort, °patrol: *A guard of six men will accompany the van along this route.* **5** °defence, °protection, °safety, °safeguard, °security, °shield: *This bandage will serve as a guard against infection.*

guarded adj. °careful, °cautious, heedful, °prudent, circumspect, °wary, °noncommittal, restrained, °mindful, °suspicious, °leery or Brit also leary, apprehensive; °loath or loth, °reticent, °reluctant, Colloq cagey: He became very guarded under close questioning. When I asked where she had been, she gave a guarded answer.

guardian n. °protector, defender, paladin, °champion; trustee, custodian, °keeper, preserver: She fancies him her guardian, her knight in shining armour. Do we really need guardians of the 'purity' of the language?

guerrilla n. guerilla, °partisan or partizan, °resistance or °freedom or °underground fighter, °irregular; insurgent, saboteur, °terrorist; US history Jayhawker, French history Maquis: The guerrillas continue to attack the government's supply convoys.

guess v. 1 conjecture, °estimate, hypothesize, °speculate, postulate, Slang guestimate or guesstimate: We guessed that he might try to come in through the window. 2 °think, °suppose, conclude, °assume, °believe, °dare °say, °surmise, °judge, deem, °reckon, °imagine, °fancy, °feel, °suspect, °divine: I guess you were right about her. —n. 3 conjecture, °estimate, °hypothesis, °speculation, °surmise, assumption, °judgement, °feeling, °suspicion, °supposition, postulate, theory; guesswork; Colloq °shot in the dark, Slang guestimate or guesstimate: My guess as to which card would turn up was wrong.

guest n. °visitor, °company, caller; °patron, °customer, lodger, boarder, roomer: Our guests get clean linen daily.

guidance n. 1 °leadership, °direction, °management, °government, °conduct, °control, °regulation, °charge, handling, °rule, °auspices: The company prospered under her guidance. 2 °counsel, °advice, counselling, advisement, °instruction, teaching: I have turned to you for guidance in the matter.

guide v. 1 °lead, °show or °lead the way, °conduct, °shepherd, °direct, usher, °steer, °orient or Brit orientate: She guided me to the proper office. What will guide your judgement in dealing with this situation? 2 °steer, °pilot, °manoeuvre, °navigate, °direct: He carefully guided the boat between the shoals. 3 °counsel, °advise, °influence, °sway; °supervise, °oversee, °handle, °manage, superintend, °direct, °control, °regulate, °govern: Mr Thrall guided my artistic development from the beginning. 4 °instruct, °teach, °tutor, °train: From early youth we were guided by the elders of the community. —n. 5 °leader, conductor, °director, cicerone, chaperon, mentor, °counsel, °counsellor, °adviser or advisor, guru, °master: He served as my guide through the financial jungle. Let your conscience be your guide. 6 °model, criterion, exemplar, °standard, °ideal, °example, °inspiration: She looked upon the life of Mother Theresa as a guide. 7 °beacon, °light, °signal, guiding °light, °landmark, lodestar, °sign, marker: The Southern Cross was our constant guide sailing round the Horn. 8 handbook, °manual, enchiridion, °vade-mecum, guidebook, Baedeker: Can you recommend a good guide to English usage?

guilt n. 1 culpability, guiltiness, criminality, °blame, °responsibility, blameworthiness; °crime, sinfulness, feloniousness, wrongdoing,

misconduct: Confronted by the evidence, Shillingworth admitted his guilt. 2 °remorse, self-reproach, °regret, °sorrow, contrition, repentance, °shame, contriteness, self-condemnation, °bad °conscience: That feeling of guilt would plague me for the rest of my life.

guilty adj. 1 °responsible, culpable, answerable, blameworthy, at °fault, °delinquent, °wrong; offending, reprehensible: Whoever was guilty will be prosecuted. First we must find the guilty party. 2 °remorseful, contrite, °regretful, °sorry, °apologetic, °repentant, °sorrowful, conscience-stricken, rueful, °penitent; °ashamed, shamefaced, °sheepish, °embarrassed, red-faced: Gavin felt terribly guilty for having insulted Tina.

guise n. 1 °appearance, °aspect, °semblance, °look, °image, °likeness, mien; °air, °behaviour, °conduct, deportment, comportment, °bearing, demeanour: This is nothing but an old political concept in a new guise. 2 °semblance, °disguise, façade, °front, °pretence: The treacherous Lothario assumed the guise of a knight in shining armour.

gulf n. 1 bay, bight, cove, inlet °sound, loch or °sea loch, firth or frith, fiord or fjord, Irish lough, Brit °creek: We sailed into the gulf to shelter from the wind behind the cliffs. 2 chasm, °deep, °depth, °abyss, abysm, °void, °space, °opening, °rift, °breach, °gap, °separation, °split: After the divorce, the gulf between us widened even further.

gullible adj. °innocent, °green, °simple, credulous, °unsophisticated, °naïve, °unsuspecting, °unwary, unsuspicious, wide-eyed, born yesterday, °inexperienced, °immature: He was gullible enough to fall for the old con game, three-card monte.

gully n. gulley, °channel, river-bed, watercourse, °gorge, °ravine, °canyon, °notch, °cut, °pass, defile, °deportment, wadi or wady, Brit gill or ghyll, W US arroyo, US and Canadian gulch: We rode along in the gully so as not to be seen.

gulp v. 1 °bolt, gobble, wolf (down), °devour, °gorge, °swallow, °throw down, °toss off, quaff, guzzle, °swill, Colloq °knock back, swig, US chug-a-lug: The boy gulped his dinner and ran out to play. 2 °swallow, °suppress, °stifle, °choke (back), °smother, strangle: She gulped back her tears as the coffin was lowered. —n. 3 °mouthful, °swallow, °draught, °swill, Colloq swig: He took a gulp of his drink before making another bid.

gumption n. 1 resourcefulness, shrewdness, cleverness, (mother) °wit, (common) °sense, astuteness, °judgement, Colloq horse °sense, brains, Slang Brit nous: It takes a lot of gumption to run a good cattle auction. 2 °backbone, °grit, °pluck, mettle, °enterprise, °initiative, °courage, °spirit, gameness, °nerve, °daring, °vigour, °energy, boldness, audacity, °stamina, Colloq °spunk, °guts, get-up-and-go, US moxie, Slang Brit °bottle, Taboo slang balls: He hasn't the gumption to go into business for himself.

gurgle v. 1 °bubble, burble, °babble, °ripple, °splash, plash, °lap, °murmur, purl: The cool brook gurgled merrily through the meadow. —n. 2 °babble, burble, bubbling, babbling, burbling, °splash, gurgling, splashing, plashing, murmuring, purl, purling: I lay back, listening to the gurgle of the spring among the rocks.

gush v. 1 cascade, °rush, °flood, °stream, °spurt, jet, °spout, °burst; °run, °flow: The water gushed

out of the pipe, soaking us all. **2** °bubble over, overflow, be °ebullient *or* °effusive *or* °effervescent, effervesce, °make much of, °fuss over, °prattle, °chatter, °babble, °jabber, blather *or* blether, *Colloq Brit* natter, witter: *It was impossible to stop them from gushing on about the performance.*
—*n.* **3** cascade, °rush, °flood, °flow, °stream, °spurt, jet, °spout, °burst, °torrent: *A gush of water hit me right in the face.* **4** °exuberance, effusion, bubbling over, °outburst: *After the first gush of enthusiasm, everything quieted down.*

gushy *adj.* gushing, fulsome, cloying, mawkish, °excessive, °effusive, overdone, (over-)°sentimental, (over) °enthusiastic, *Colloq* °sloppy, slushy: *It's another gushy film about a little girl and a lost kitten.*

gust *n.* **1** °puff, °blow, °wind, °breeze, °blast: *A gust of wind blew my hat off.*
—*v.* **2** °puff, °blow, °blast, °surge, °increase: *The wind gusted up to gale force overnight.*

gusto *n.* °enthusiasm, °relish, °zest, °appetite, zeal, zealousness, avidity, °eagerness, °enjoyment, °appreciation, °pleasure, °delight, °satisfaction: *We attacked the meal with great gusto and soon dispatched every scrap.*

gut *n.* **1** Often, **guts**: °bowels, intestines, entrails, viscera, °stomach, offal, vitals, °vital parts, gurry, *Brit (of a deer)* gralloch, *Colloq* insides, innards *or* inwards: *As soon as the game is killed, the guts must be removed.* **2** °stomach, abdomen, belly; beer-belly, bay window, corporation: *His enormous gut hung over his belt.*

3 guts: **a** °backbone, °bravery, boldness, audacity, °pluck, °courage, °determination, °daring, °spirit, °grit, mettle, °gumption, °nerve, intestinal °fortitude, *Colloq* °spunk, gutsiness, *Slang Brit* °bottle, *Taboo* balls: *He hasn't the guts to tell the boss what he thinks of him.* **b** °integrity, will-power, °stamina, °endurance, forcefulness, °dynamism: *It takes real guts to stand up for your rights.*
—*v.* **4** disembowel, eviscerate, °draw, °dress, °clean: *It will take hours to gut all these fish.* **5** °ransack, °pillage, °plunder, °sack, despoil, °strip, °ravage, °loot, °rifle, *Rare* depredate; °clean out, °devastate, °empty: *The building was completely gutted by the fire.*
—*adj.* **6** °basic, °heartfelt, °instinctive, instinctual, intuitive, visceral, deep-seated, deep-rooted, °emotional: *My gut reaction is to refuse the offer.*

guttersnipe *n.* waif, (street) Arab, (street) urchin, °ragamuffin, brat, gamin, °rogue, *Colloq Brit rare* mudlark: *That little guttersnipe stole my wallet!*

guy *n.* **1** °man, °lad, °youth, °boy, °fellow, °person, *Colloq* °chap, geezer, *Brit* bloke, *Slang* gink, cat, °customer, *US* °dude, *Old-fashioned* gazabo *or* gazebo: *Clarence is a pretty nice guy.*
—*v.* **2** °mock, °ridicule, make °fun of, °caricature, °satirize, °poke °fun at, °lampoon, *Colloq* rib, °take off, *Brit* °send up: *We put on a show at school in which we guyed the teachers.*

gyrate *v.* °rotate, °spin, °revolve, °turn (°round *or* about), whirl, °twirl, °swirl, °pirouette; °swivel: *The dancers were gyrating to the deafening music.*

H

habit n. **1** °custom, °routine, °practice, °convention, °policy, °pattern, °usage, °mode, °rule, wont, praxis: *Jogging every morning had become a habit. She is a creature of habit.* **2** °tendency, °disposition, °manner, °practice, °way, °custom, °inclination, °bent, predisposition, second nature, °frame of mind, °attitude, °penchant, propensity, proclivity; addiction, compulsion: *This kettle has a habit of leaking. Try to control your bad habits.* **3** attire, clothing, °dress, °apparel, °clothes, garb, °costume, °garments, vestments, °uniform, raiment, livery, °regalia, habiliment(s), *Colloq* °gear: *She was disguised in a monk's habit.*

habitable adj. liveable, inhabitable: *With some effort, two rooms were made habitable.*

habitat n. °abode, °home, °haunt, °domain, °range, °territory, bailiwick, °realm, °terrain, °element, °environment, surroundings, *Colloq* stamping-ground: *The winter habitat of the monarch butterfly is in northern Mexico. Curtis doesn't function well outside his natural habitat.*

habitual adj. **1** settled, °fixed, °customary, °usual, °conventional, °accustomed, °set, °rooted, established, °traditional, °standard, °routine, °ritual, °regular, °normal, wonted, °common, °ordinary, °natural: *He follows his habitual practice of rising at dawn.* **2** inveterate, established, °chronic, confirmed, hardened, °ingrained, °frequent, °persistent, °constant, °continual, °perpetual: *Many English people are habitual tea-drinkers.*

habitué n. frequenter, °patron, °regular °customer, *Colloq* °regular: *Larry has been a habitué of The Bell Inn for 20 years.*

hack¹ v. **1** °chop, hew, °lacerate, °gash, °slash, °cut; °mangle, °butcher, °mutilate, °ruin, °destroy, smash, °batter, °damage, °deface: *He hacked the furniture to pieces with an axe.* **2** bark, cough: *She was disgusted by the man's hacking and spitting.* —n. **3** °cut, °gash, °slash, °chop: *He took a hack at the log with his hatchet.*

hack² n. **1** drudge, penny-a-liner, scribbler, Grub Street °writer: *We made a mistake hiring that hack as a feature writer.* **2** plodder, drudge, toiler, °menial, °flunkey, lackey, °slave, *Brit* °fag, *Slang* °grind, *Brit* swot: *Fergus gets good grades because he's such a hack.* **3** saddle-horse, riding-horse, hackney, *Archaic* palfrey: *The hack was a fine bay mare.* —adj. **4** hackneyed, trite, °banal, overdone, commonplace, °routine, stereotyped, °stock, °tired, °tedious, °mediocre, overworked, °stale, unoriginal, run-of-the-mill, °humdrum, motheaten, °mouldy, *Colloq* old hat: *Haverstock keeps publishing hack romances.*

hag n. crone, °fury, °witch, ogress, gorgon, harpy, fishwife, harridan, °shrew, virago, termagant, vixen, hell-cat, maenad *or* menad, Xanthippe, *Archaic* beldam; dog, °beast, °monster; *Colloq* battleaxe, *Slang* °bitch, °bag, *US* two-bagger: *Perseus met the Graeae, three old hags with one eye that they passed among them.*

haggard adj. °gaunt, °drawn, wasted, °emaciated, hollow-eyed, hollow-cheeked, °scrawny, scraggy, °ghastly, cadaverous, °run-down, wearied, °weary, careworn, °spent, played out, °exhausted, toil-worn, °worn, shrunken, withered: *She looked haggard, as if she hadn't slept for a week.*

haggle v. wrangle, °bargain, higgle, °bicker, chaffer, palter, °dispute, squabble, °quibble, °negotiate; barter, °deal; *Colloq US* °dicker: *However little you ask for the lamp, she's sure to haggle over the price.*

hail¹ v. **1** °greet, accost, °address, °signal, °call: *Robert hailed us from across the road.* **2** °cheer, °salute, °applaud, °approve, °glorify, °praise, °laud, °honour, acclaim, °congratulate, felicitate, °acknowledge: *He was hailed by all for his charitable work.*

hail² v. **1** °rain *or* °beat *or* °shower (down) on, °bombard, °pelt, °volley, barrage: *Rocks and debris hailed down on us from the cliffs above.* —n. **2** °volley, °storm, °shower, °torrent, bombardment, barrage: *They were greeted by a hail of abuse when they entered the meeting hall.*

hair n. **1** tresses, locks, mane, curls, ringlets; braids, plaits: *You will recognize her by her red hair.* **2** hair's breadth, whisker, °trifle, fraction, skin of one's teeth: *He won the race by a hair.*

hairdo n. coiffure, hairstyle, °cut, coif: *Your hairdo is very becoming.*

hairless adj. bald, bald-headed, bald-pated, glabrous, calvous: *She finds hairless men rather sexy.*

hair-splitting adj. quibbling, (over-)°fussy, hypercritical, °petty, captious, carping, °fault-finding, °finicky, (over) °nice, °fastidious, cavilling, °niggling, *Colloq* nit-picking: *His hair-splitting attention to detail gets on my nerves.*

hairy adj. **1** hirsute, °shaggy, downy, fleecy, °fluffy, °woolly, lanate *or* lanose, languinose *or* lanuginose, bristly, setaceous, setal, hispid, comate *or* comose, fringy, crinite, trichoid, strigose *or* strigous, strigillose; whiskered, bewhiskered, bearded, barbate, unshaven: *The creature had a very hairy face.* **2** °tricky, °dangerous, °perilous, °risky, °uncertain, °precarious, °hazardous, °frightening, worrying, °nerve-racking *or* nerve-wracking, *Colloq* °scary: *The situation at the office has become very hairy.* **3** tangled, °intricate, knotty, complex, °complicated, °difficult, °problematic, °confused, confusing: *The exam contained some hairy questions.*

hale adj. °healthy, °hearty, °fit (as a fiddle), °sound, able-bodied, °hardy, °wholesome, °robust, °flourishing, in °good *or* °fine fettle, in the pink: *Her grandmother was as hale and hearty as ever.*

half-hearted adj. °indifferent, uncaring, unconcerned, °lukewarm, uninterested, °dispassionate, °cool, °unenthusiastic, half-baked, °nonchalant, °phlegmatic, °lackadaisical, insouciant: *The council has made only a half-hearted effort to solve the problem.*

halfwit n. dunce, °fool, idiot, simpleton, ninny, ass, ninny-hammer, moron, imbecile, °dolt,

dunderhead or dunderpate, rattle-brain, nincompoop, dullard, Colloq numskull or numbskull, nitwit, dim-wit, birdbrain, Brit nit, °twit:
He's such a halfwit, he can hardly expect me to give
him a job!

halfwitted adj. °stupid, °foolish, °silly, °simple,
°inane, asinine, moronic, imbecilic, doltish,
rattle-brained, °feeble-minded, attocerebral,
cretinous, °thick, non compos mentis, dim-witted,
weak-minded, Colloq °dumb, Brit dotty, barmy
(in the crumpet): She had some halfwitted idea
that she would win the lottery.

hall n. **1** °corridor, hallway, passageway,
°passage; foyer, °entry, entry-way, °lobby, vestibule: Let us step out into the hall for a brief
word. **2** auditorium, °assembly or meeting or
convention °hall, °theatre, amphitheatre, hired
hall; lecture-room, lecture-hall, classroom: We
hired a hall for the wedding reception.

hallmark n. **1** authentication, verification, °seal
or °stamp (of authenticity or approval), °mark,
°device, °sign, °symbol; plate-mark; assay-mark:
From this hallmark we know when and where the piece
was made, by whom, and its degree of purity. Surprise
endings are the hallmark of O. Henry's short
stories. **2** °feature, °stamp, °mark, earmark,
trade °mark, °characteristic, °identification:
From his hallmark, a tiny axe, you can tell that the
painting is a genuine Fellworthy.

hallow v. **1** consecrate, °bless, °sanctify,
°dedicate, °honour, enshrine, °glorify: Englishmen look upon this battlefield as hallowed
ground. **2** °venerate, °worship, revere,
°reverence, °respect, °honour, pay °homage or
°respect or °honour to, °exalt: We must observe the
hallowed traditions of the university.

hallucination n. °fantasy, mirage, day-dream,
°illusion, °delusion, °vision, °dream, aberration, chimera, phantasm, °phantom, figment
of the °imagination, apparition, °spectre,
°ghost; paræsthesia: Alone at sea for a fortnight, I
began having hallucinations.

halo n. nimbus, °aura, aureole or aureola, corona,
°radiance, Painting vesica, mandorla; °ring, disc,
°circle, annulation, annulus: The saints can be
identified by the golden halos round their heads.

halt n. **1** °stop, °standstill, °end, °termination,
°close, stoppage, cessation: We must call a halt
to absenteeism in the factory.
—v. **2** °stop, °quit, °end, °terminate, °cease,
°check, °curb, °stem, °discontinue, desist, bring
or come or °draw to an °end or °close, put an
°end or °stop to, conclude, °shut or °close down
or up: We halted when we came to the river. The
guerrillas halted the armoured column at the pass.

halting adj. °hesitant, hesitating, wavering,
shifting, uneven, faltering, stumbling, °faulty,
unsteady, °awkward, stammering, stuttering: He
told her in halting English that there was no news
of her friend.

hamper[1] v. °slow, balk or baulk, °delay, °hold
up, °retard, °inhibit, °encumber, °hinder,
°obstruct, °block, °impede, °prevent, °interfere
with, °frustrate, °restrict, °curb, °limit,
°handicap, °restrain, °trammel, °bar, barricade,
°shackle, °clog, °curtail, lessen, °reduce,
°diminish: Ice floes hampered their further progress.

hamper[2] n. basket, pannier, creel, Brit punnet;
hanaper, Dialectal skep: A hamper arrived from
Fortnum's, packed full of delicacies such as foie gras
and peaches in brandy.

hand n. **1** Slang mitt, paw, US lunch-hook: Keep
your hands off me, you oaf! **2** °help, °aid,
°assistance, °helping hand, °relief, °boost; °leg
up: Please give me a hand with this trunk.
3 °influence, °agency, participation, involvement, °part, °share: Did you have a hand in my
getting the appointment? **4** (manual) °labourer,
°worker, workman, °man, °help, °employee: It's
getting harder to find hands for the farm. **5** °pointer,
°indicator, °index: The minute hand covers the hour
hand at noon and midnight. **6** (round of)
°applause, °ovation, °clap: Give the lad a hand
for trying. **7** handwriting, °penmanship, °script;
calligraphy: The writing was in a hand that she
could not recognize. **8** Often, **hands**: °control,
°hold, °grasp, °possession, °custody, clutches,
keeping, °power, disposal, °jurisdiction,
°authority, supervision, °management, guardianship, °care: At last, the government is in the
hands of the people. **9 at hand**: °nearby, °close,
°near, °close by, °handy, (°readily) °available, to
or on hand, at one's fingertips, °convenient,
within (arm's) °reach, °accessible, °present;
approaching, °imminent, around the corner:
He always kept a pistol at hand. The Day of Judgement
is at hand. **10 hand in glove**: hand in hand,
in °league, together, in collusion, collusively,
connivingly, conspiringly, intimately, closely,
jointly, Colloq in cahoots: An informer is working
hand in glove with the police. **11 hand in hand**:
together, °side by side, hand in glove:
They walked hand in hand down the road.
12 hand-over-fist: °quickly, speedily,
°rapidly, °swiftly, steadily, like mad: He makes
money hand-over-fist in the stock market. **13 hands
down**: °easily, °readily, effortlessly: He can win
the marathon hands down.
—v. **14** °give, °pass, °deliver, °present to or with:
Please hand me the hammer. **15 hand down or
on or over**: **a** °bequeath, °will, °pass on;
°transfer, °turn over: The farm has been handed
down from father to son for seven generations.
b See 18 a, below. **16 hand in**: °submit, °give
in, °tender, proffer, °offer: I handed in my resignation. **17 hand out**: °distribute, disseminate,
°pass out or round or around, °give out, °deal
(out), °mete or °dole out, °dispense; disburse:
She was handing out leaflets to passers-by. **18 hand
over**: **a** °deliver, °submit, °yield, °give up,
°surrender, °turn over; °transfer: The man produced a gun and told the cashier to hand over the
money. See 15 a, above.

handcuffs n.pl. manacles, shackles, Colloq cuffs,
bracelets, Slang Brit darbies: The police put handcuffs on them all.

handful n. **1** °few, °couple, sprinkling, °small
°number; fistful: Only a handful of restaurants are
open that late. He gave the beggar a handful of
change. **2** (°behaviour or disciplinary) °problem,
°bother, mischief-maker, °troublemaker,
°nuisance: Timothy was a real handful when he
was five.

handicap n. **1** °hindrance, °restraint,
°encumbrance, °restriction, limitation,
°impediment, °barrier, °bar, °obstacle, (stumbling) °block, constraint, °check, °curb,
°trammel, °disability, °disadvantage: Did Douglas
Bader view the loss of his legs as a handicap?
—v. **2** °hinder, °hamper, °restrain, °encumber,
°restrict, °limit, °impede, °bar, °block, °check,
°curb, °trammel, disable, °disadvantage: He was
severely handicapped by the loss of his sword.

handily adv. 1 °readily, °easily, effortlessly, without °strain, comfortably, with both hands tied (behind one's back): *Donald handily won the first prize in the poetry competition.* 2 skilfully, capably, deftly, cleverly, dexterously, adroitly, expertly, proficiently, masterfully: *I could never do that intricate work as handily as she.*

handle n. 1 °grip, hilt, handgrip, haft, helve: *Hold it by the handle, not the blade.*
—v. 2 °feel, °touch, °finger, °hold; °caress, °fondle, °pat: *Be careful how you handle that knife.* 3 °manage, °run, °operate, °direct, °administer, °supervise, °oversee, °control, °command, °guide: *At the age of 26, she was handling all foreign business for the company.* 4 °steer, °control, °manage, °cope with, °manoeuvre, °manipulate: *Are you sure he can handle that horse?* 5 °deal or °trade or °traffic in, (°buy and) °sell, °market: *The gang was found to be handling stolen goods worth millions every month.* 6 °treat, °control, °deal with, °cope with: *She handled the customers with the utmost tact and respect.* 7 °treat, °employ, °use, utilize; °deal with, °wield, °tackle, °manipulate: *Don't you admire how she handled the perspective in this painting?*

handsome adj. 1 good-looking, fine-looking, °attractive, °fair, °comely: *He's handsome enough to be a movie star.* 2 °generous, sizeable, °large, °big, °substantial, °considerable, °good, °goodly, °ample, °abundant: *She has made a handsome profit on the painting.*

handy adj. 1 °nearby, °accessible, °available, at or on or to °hand, close (by), °convenient, at one's fingertips, within (easy) reach, (at the) °ready: *Because of the recent break-ins, she keeps a pistol handy.* 2 usable, °serviceable, manoeuvrable, °clever, °useful, °helpful, °practical: *A pair of pliers and a screwdriver are the handiest tools.* 3 deft, °clever, °dexterous, adroit, °adept, skilled, °skilful, °proficient, °expert: *Aunt Sara is very handy with a needle and thread.*

hang v. 1 °suspend, °depend, °dangle; be °poised or suspended, °hover, °swing: *Hang the lantern from this branch. The laundry was hanging on the line.* 2 gibbet, send to the °gallows, lynch, °execute, °kill, Colloq °string up, °stretch: *They hanged two murderers this morning.* 3 °drape, °fall: *The skirt isn't hanging straight.* 4 **hang about** or **around**: a loiter, °wait, °linger, dally, °idle, tarry, Colloq hang out: *He hangs about after school every day, waiting for Susan.* b Also, **hang about** or **around (with)**: °frequent, °haunt, °visit, °spend °time at; °associate with, °socialize with, °hobnob with, °rub elbows with, consort with, °fraternize with, °mix or °mingle with, Colloq hang out (with): *He hangs about the Golden Crown. I saw him hanging around with some pretty unsavoury characters.* 5 **hang back (from)**: be °reluctant, °recoil (from), °shrink (from), °hesitate, falter, °stay away (from): *Move to the front of the queue and don't hang back.* 6 **hang fire**: be delayed, °remain °unsettled or unfinished, be in °suspense or °abeyance; °stall, °hold up, °delay: *The decision will hang fire till after the election.* 7 **hang on**: a Also, **hang on to**: °hold on (to), °cling (to), °clutch, °grip, °grasp, °grab: *Hang on to me when we're crossing the street.* b °wait, °stay, °stop: *Hang on a minute—what did you call me?* c °wait, °persist, °remain, °carry on, °persevere, °go on, °hold out, °endure,

°hold the phone, Colloq US hang in there: *Hang on a minute, I have to put down the phone to get a pencil.* d Also, **hang on to** or **upon**: °listen carefully or attentively, give one's undivided °attention, be °rapt: *She hung on every word the guru uttered.* e °depend or °rely (on), be dependent or contingent (on), be °subject (to), be conditioned or conditional (on): *The entire project now hangs on their approval of the budget.* 8 **hang one's head**: be °ashamed or humiliated or abashed or humbled or °embarrassed: *She hung her head as the store detective confronted her with the stolen goods.* 9 **hang out**: See 5 a, above. 10 **hangover**: be °put off or postponed or delayed: *We must first deal with matters hanging over from our last meeting.* 11 **hang together**: a °unite, be °united, be as °one, °stick together, °join forces, °cooperate, act in concert or °harmony: *We must hang together or we shall hang separately.* b make sense, be °logical, be °consistent, °correspond, °match (up), cohere, be °coherent: *The statements issued yesterday and today just don't hang together.* 12 **hang up**: °break the connection, °disconnect, °cut off, put down the receiver: *Whenever a salesman phones, I simply hang up.*

hanger-on n. °follower, dependant, leech, °parasite, toady, sycophant, °yes-man, Colloq scrounger, US freeloader, Slang groupie, sponger or sponge: *The rock star came in, surrounded by his hangers-on.*

hangman n. executioner, Archaic Brit Jack Ketch: *The hangman, a black hood concealing his identity, slipped the noose over the prisoner's head.*

hanker v. Usually, **hanker after** or **for**: °yearn for, °long for, °thirst after or for, °hunger after or for, °itch for, pine for, °lust after or for, covet, crave, have a hankering for, °want, °desire, °fancy, Colloq have a yen for: *She hankered after a big box of chocolates.*

hanky-panky n. °mischief, °trickery, double-dealing, legerdemain, °deception, duplicity, °chicanery, naughtiness, foolishness, tomfoolery, Colloq °funny business, jiggery-pokery, °monkey business, shenanigans, goings-on, antics: *He'd best not try any of his hanky-panky with the tax inspector.*

haphazard adj. 1 °random, °arbitrary, °chance, fortuitous, aleatory, °accidental, °unforeseen, unlooked-for, unexpected, adventitious, serendipitous: *Her fate was to be decided by a haphazard throw of the dice.* 2 °casual, °offhand, hit-or-miss, unsystematic, slapdash, °slipshod, careless, disorganized, °disorderly: *He took some haphazard shots at the target.*

happen v. 1 °occur, take place, °come about, °go on, come to °pass, °develop; betide, °chance, °prove, °materialize, Colloq °transpire, °come off, Slang cook: *What is happening? As it happens, everyone has already left.* 2 befall, °become of: *What will happen to me if I refuse?* 3 **happen on** or **upon**: °come upon, °chance or °hit on or upon, °stumble on or upon, °find, °turn up, °encounter, °meet with: *It was then that I happened on an old letter of his.*

happening n. °event, °incident, °occurrence, °occasion, taking place, °circumstance, °chance, °episode, °phenomenon: *Such a conjunction of the planets is a very rare happening.*

happily adv. 1 fortunately, luckily, propitiously, providentially, opportunely: *Happily, she made* *a full recovery and was soon back at work.* **2** joyfully, joyously, delightedly, gleefully, cheerfully, °gaily, merrily, blithely; enthusiastically, heartily: *She waved happily as they drove off.* **3** °gladly, with °pleasure, agreeably, contentedly, °willingly, peaceably: *And they both lived happily ever after.*

happiness *n.* °pleasure, °delight, felicity, °enjoyment, °joy, joyousness, joyfulness, jubilation, cheerfulness, cheeriness, °cheer, blithesomeness, gladness, light-heartedness, exhilaration, elation, °exuberance, high spirits, °glee, °ecstasy: *My happiness at seeing you again was unbounded.*

happy *adj.* **1** °pleased, °delighted, °glad, joyous, °joyful, °overjoyed, jubilant, °cheerful, cheery, °blithe, blithesome, light-hearted, contented, exhilarated, °exultant, cock-a-hoop, °elated, °exuberant, thrilled, °gleeful, euphoric, °ecstatic, satisfied, gratified, *Colloq* on top of the world, on cloud nine, °pleased as Punch, tickled pink, *Brit* in the seventh °heaven, over the moon, *US* in seventh °heaven: *Her parents were happy that Georgina was married at last.* **2** °lucky, fortuitous, °propitious, °fortunate, auspicious, °advantageous, °beneficial, °favourable, felicitous, °opportune, °timely, °well-timed, apt, °appropriate: *By a happy chance, we were in Bermuda at the same time.*

harangue *n.* **1** diatribe, °tirade, °oration, peroration, declamation, philippic, screed, exhortation, vituperation, rodomontade, °speech, °address, *Colloq* spiel: *This morning he delivered a ten-minute harangue on the weakness of the coffee.* —*v.* **2** declaim, °hold forth, °preach, °lecture, sermonize, pontificate, °vituperate, °rant and °rave: *Our neighbour is always haranguing her husband about trimming the hedges.*

harass *v.* badger, harry, hector, °trouble, °torment, °bother, °exasperate, °hound, °plague, °persecute, vex, °annoy, °irritate, °pester, °worry, °beset, bait, °nag, °pick on *or* at, °tease, torture, *Brit* chivvy *or* chivy *or* chevy: *The police harass me by turning up at all hours for 'help with their inquiries'.*

harbinger *n.* °forerunner, herald, °precursor, °omen, foretoken, °sign, portent, augury: *The crowing cock is the harbinger of dawn.*

harbour *n.* **1** °port, (°safe) haven, anchorage, mooring: *We sailed into the harbour just as the storm broke.* —*v.* **2** °shelter, °keep °safe, °protect, °shield, °guard, °safeguard, °conceal, °hide: *They were found guilty of harbouring a known fugitive.* **3** °cherish, °foster, nurture, °nurse, °keep, °retain, °maintain, °hold, °cling to: *She harbours a grudge against whoever set the fire.*

hard *adj.* **1** °rigid, °stiff, °solid, °inflexible, °firm, °dense, condensed, compressed, °close, solidified, hardened; °stony, rocklike, °concrete, °petrified, granite(-like), flinty, °steely; °tough, °rugged, leathery, °callous; unyielding, adamant(ine), impenetrable, obdurate, impervious, °impregnable: *The cement gets hard in an hour. This steak is as hard as shoe-leather. The metal was so hard that I broke three drills trying to make a hole in it.* **2** °difficult, °laborious, °arduous, back-breaking, °burdensome, onerous, fatiguing, tiring, °exhausting, wearying, °strenuous, °tough, °toilsome: *Laying track for the railway is a very hard job.* **3** °difficult,

°perplexing, knotty, °puzzling, baffling, enigmatic, °intricate, °complicated, complex, tangled, °involved, °thorny, °incomprehensible, inscrutable, unsolvable, insoluble, *Colloq* °tough: *There were a lot of hard questions in the exam.* **4** °stern, °cold, °callous, intractable, °exacting, °strict, °demanding, hard-hearted, stony-hearted, °severe, °tyrannical, °despotic, °dictatorial, magisterial, °oppressive, °cruel, °ruthless, pitiless, °merciless, °savage, °brutal, brutish, °inhuman, °heartless, °harsh, °unkind, °implacable, °unsympathetic, °dispassionate, uncompassionate, unfeeling, obdurate, indurate; unsentimental, insensitive, °thick-skinned, °tough, hard-boiled, °stony, hardbitten, unfeeling, unsparing: *Hemel is a hard taskmaster. Of the prison warders, each was harder than the next. He advocates taking a hard line against white-collar crime.* **5** °bad, °difficult, °grievous, °calamitous, racking, °disastrous, °dark, °grim, distressing, °devastating, °agonizing, °painful, unpleasant, °severe, austere, *Colloq* °tough, °rough: *The years of the Great Depression were hard for everyone.* **6** °cool, unemotional, °calculating, uncompromising, °methodical, °critical, °systematic, °practical, pragmatic, businesslike, °realistic, °penetrating, searching, hard-headed, *Colloq* °tough, hard-nosed: *Shareholders should take a hard look at the annual report. Chapelle drives a hard bargain.* **7** sedulous, assiduous, °devoted, °conscientious, °industrious, indefatigable, °untiring, °persistent, dogged, °intent, °eager, zealous, °ardent, °energetic, °keen, avid: *Galpin is a very hard worker who gets a lot done.* **8** °cold, °bare, °plain, °straight, straightforward, °blunt, °unvarnished, °unquestionable, verifiable, °real, °indisputable, undeniable, incontestable, °incontrovertible, °strict, inescapable, ineluctable, °unavoidable, unalterable, immutable: *The hard fact is that the bill has never been paid.* **9** °angry, °bitter, acrimonious, °hostile, antagonistic, °harsh, unpleasant, unfriendly: *I'm afraid there were some hard words between us.* **10** spirituous, °alcoholic, °strong: *She won't touch hard liquor.* **11** addictive, habit-forming: *He later changed from marijuana to hard drugs.* **12** °sharp, well-defined, °clear, °distinct, °stark, °definite: *Note the hard edges of objects in Realist paintings.* —*adv.* **13** °vigorously, forcefully, forcibly, energetically, mightily, arduously, laboriously, strenuously, earnestly, actively, dynamically, eagerly, intensely, ardently, heartily, zealously, °intently, spiritedly, diligently, assiduously, sedulously, studiously, determinedly, steadfastly, conscientiously, industriously, devotedly, urgently, persistently, untiringly, indefatigably, persevering, unfalteringly, relentlessly, doggedly: *They always had to work very hard just to scrape by. He's hard at work writing his new book.* **14** violently, °deeply, intensely, °badly, distressingly, °painfully, °severely, agonizingly: *Failing the examination hit him quite hard.* **15** °intently, carefully, earnestly: *The judge thought long and hard before passing sentence.* **16** harshly, °severely, °badly, °ill: *It's going to go hard with her if she doesn't change her ways.* **17 hard up**: °poor, °indigent, poverty-stricken, °impoverished, penniless, impecunious, bankrupt, *Colloq* in the red, °broke, bust(ed), on one's uppers, *Slang Brit* skint: *He's so hard up he can't afford a decent meal.*

harden *v.* **1** °set, °solidify, °stiffen, °freeze: *The concrete will harden overnight.* **2** °intensify, °strengthen, °brace, °fortify, toughen, °reinforce, °stiffen: *The opposition have hardened their stand against privatization.*

hardly *adv.* °scarcely, °barely, °only, °just, °only °just; not quite, by no °means; °seldom, °rarely: *I hardly knew her. There was hardly enough to eat. He hardly ever visits his old mum any more.*

hardship *n.* °want, °privation, deprivation, °suffering, °misery, °distress, °affliction, adversity, austerity, °misfortune, unhappiness, ill fortune, bad luck, °difficulty, °trouble: *The hardship of frontier life has never been fully described.*

hardware *n.* **1** °tools, metal goods, *Brit* ironmongery: *Go down to the hardware shop for some nails.* **2** (computer) °equipment, components, °devices, machinery; arms, munitions, armament(s), *matériel*: *We need the personnel to operate the hardware.*

hardy *adj.* **1** °robust, °sturdy, °strong, °rugged, °tough, °durable, °sound, °stalwart, °stout, °vigorous, able-bodied, red-blooded, °fit, °hale, °healthy, *Colloq* °husky: *The pioneers were hardy souls.* **2** °bold, °courageous, °daring, valorous, valiant, °brave, °manly, °intrepid, °fearless, °heroic, plucky: *He was among the hardy sailors who went with Magellan.*

hare-brained *adj.* **1** °rash, °foolhardy, °wild, madcap, °reckless, °heedless, °improvident, °visionary, °fanciful, airy, *Colloq* crackpot: *Don't put money into any of Zenobia's hare-brained schemes.* **2** °foolish, °silly, °inane, asinine, °flighty, witless, bra111less, °mindless, °giddy, °frivolous, °scatterbrained: *Such hare-brained behaviour is not expected in two sober adults.*

harm *n.* **1** °injury, °damage, °mischief, °hurt, °abuse, °misfortune: *A bodyguard was hired to see that no harm would come to her.* **2** °evil, wrongdoing, wickedness, iniquity, °wrong, badness: *I meant no harm when I told Phoebe that her husband was having dinner with Kathy.* —*v.* **3** °hurt, °damage, °injure, °abuse, maltreat, °wound: *She insists that her pet viper would never harm her.*

harmful *adj.* °dangerous, pernicious, deleterious, °destructive, damaging, °bad, °detrimental, °injurious; °unhealthy, noxious, baleful, toxic, °poisonous, °venomous, *Archaic* baneful: *Do you really think that Barbara has had a harmful influence on him? That substance can be harmful if swallowed.*

harmless *adj.* °benign, innocuous, °inoffensive, °gentle, °mild, °innocent, °safe; non-toxic, non-poisonous, non-venomous: *Pay no attention to such harmless gossip. It is impossible to identify harmless snakes by sight.*

harmonious *adj.* °agreeable, compatible, congruous, consonant, in °accord, congenial, °complementary, °sympathetic, concordant, *Colloq* simpatico: *Our careers have always been harmonious.*

harmony *n.* **1** °agreement, °accord, concord, compatibility, °rapport, unanimity, °unity: *The purpose is to promote harmony among the warring factions.* **2** consonance, congruity, °balance, orderliness, closeness, togetherness, consistency, °fitness, parallelism: *A sense of harmony*

can be felt among the European nations. **3** melodiousness, euphony, tunefulness: *Their voices are in perfect harmony.*

harrowing *adj.* distressing, vexing, alarming, unnerving, °frightening, °terrifying, horrifying, °horrible, torturous, chilling, °heart-rending, °nerve-racking or nerve-wracking, °traumatic, °agonizing, °painful; °disturbing, upsetting, worrying, worrisome, °disconcerting, daunting, dismaying, disquieting: *Waiting for the rescue team to release me was a harrowing experience.*

harsh *adj.* **1** °rough, °coarse, bristly, °scratchy, °hairy, °crude; hoarse, °grating, °raucous, rasping, °husky, guttural; clashing, inharmonious or unharmonious, °discordant, atonal, dissonant, cacophonous, °strident, °shrill, grinding, °sour; °bitter, acrid: *He found harsh the sights, sounds, tastes, and smells of the Casbah.* **2** °stern, austere, °bleak, °dour, °unkind, unfeeling, comfortless, uncompassionate, unfriendly, °grim, °hard, Spartan, stringent, over-exacting, Draconian, °tyrannical, °stark, °severe, °cruel, °abusive, °punishing, °punitive, °brutal, brutish, °inhuman, °merciless, °ruthless, pitiless: *Simon is a very harsh taskmaster.* **3** unpleasant, °disagreeable, °impolite, °discourteous, uncivil, °rude, °nasty, °curt, °abrupt, °brusque, °bluff, °gruff, curmudgeonly, choleric, splenetic, °surly, °sullen, irascible, °short-tempered, °petulant, °peevish, °waspish, grouchy, °bilious, °cross, acrimonious, °sarcastic, acerbic: *Why is Maria so harsh to Alan?*

harvest *n.* **1** crop, °yield, °produce, °output, °fruit; °vintage: *If we get enough rain, the harvest should be good this year.* —*v.* **2** °reap, °gather, °pick, glean, °collect: *The oranges are harvested while they are still greenish.* **3** °earn, °make, °take in, °collect, °garner, °get, °receive, °obtain, °procure, °net: *They harvest huge profits from slot machines.*

hash *n.* **1** °mixture, °confusion, °hotchpotch or *US and Canadian* hodgepodge, °pot-pourri, gallimaufry, farrago, °mishmash, °jumble, °mess, °shambles, olla podrida, mélange, °medley: *The building is a hash of a dozen architectural styles.* **2** °fiasco, °disaster, °botch, °mess, *Slang Brit* balls-up, *US* snafu: *The council really made a hash of its housing policy.* —*v.* **3** Often, **hash up**: °mangle, °mess or °mix up, make a hash or °mess or °jumble of, °muddle, °bungle, °botch, °mishandle, mismanage, °ruin, °spoil, °butcher, *Colloq* °foul or louse up, °screw up, muff, *Brit* °bugger up: *Our plans for a holiday have been all hashed up.*

haste *n.* **1** swiftness, °rapidity, quickness, °speed, °velocity, °expedition, °urgency, °dispatch or despatch, alacrity, celerity, briskness: *We must return to Baker Street with all haste, Watson.* **2** °hurry, °rush, rashness, hastiness, °hustle, bustle, impetuousness or impetuosity, recklessness, precipitancy: *Haste makes waste.*

hasten *v.* **1** °hurry, °rush, make °haste, °fly, °run, sprint, °race, °bolt, °dash, °scurry, scamper, scuttle, °speed: *He hastened forward to greet her.* **2** °hurry (up), °speed (up), °dispatch or despatch, °send, °move, °quicken, accelerate, °expedite, °rush, impel, °urge: *Is there any way to hasten delivery of the mail?*

hastily *adv.* **1** °quickly, speedily, °swiftly, °rapidly, at °once, °immediately,

°instantaneously, °promptly, without °delay, °right away, °straight away, °post-haste, hurriedly, °directly, °suddenly, in °haste, precipitately, on the °spur of the moment, in a °flash or wink, before you can say 'Jack Robinson', Colloq pronto, like a °shot, like greased lightning, US lickety-split, Slang p.d.q. (= 'pretty damned quick'): She left hastily when I asked for the return of the loan. **2** impetuously, impulsively, rashly, recklessly, unthinkingly, thoughtlessly, heedlessly, incautiously: This is a trick question, so don't answer hastily.

hasty adj. **1** quick, °speedy, °swift, °rapid, °fast, °brisk, °prompt, °immediate, instantaneous: He made a hasty departure so as not to be late. **2** °careless, °rash, °precipitate, °impetuous, °impulsive, °reckless, °thoughtless, °unthinking, incautious, °heedless, ill-considered, °inconsiderate: His was a hasty decision. **3** °quick, °speedy, °cursory, °superficial, °fleeting, °passing, slapdash, °perfunctory, °momentary, °brief: I had a hasty look at the contract, which seemed all right. **4** °irritable, °quick-tempered, irascible, °testy, °passionate, °impatient, hot-tempered, °petulant, °waspish, °volatile, contentious, choleric, splenetic, bearish, °short-tempered, US and Canadian and Irish °cranky: Grandfather needn't have been so hasty with the poor child.

hatch v. **1** °breed, °brood, °incubate, °bring forth: The normal clutch of three eggs is hatched in a fortnight. **2** °devise, contrive, concoct, °design, °formulate, °originate, °invent, °dream up, Colloq cook up: Two of them hatched a scheme to discredit me.

hate v. **1** °loathe, °abhor, °detest, have an °aversion to, be °averse to, abominate, °dislike, execrate, °despise, °scorn: I hate the smell of petrol, it really turns my stomach. **2** be °loath, be °reluctant or unwilling or °disinclined; °resist, °shrink or °flinch from, °dislike: I hate to tell you what I really think. She hated revealing Bill's affair to his wife.
—n. **3** hatred, abhorrence, °loathing, odium, °animosity, animus, antipathy, °aversion, °hostility, °antagonism, malice, enmity, detestation: He didn't believe he could feel so much hate for one person.

hateful adj. **1** °loathsome, detestable, °abhorrent, horrid, °horrible, °abominable, odious, execrable, °despicable, °scurvy, °obnoxious, heinous, °foul, °contemptible, °repugnant, °repulsive, °repellent, °revolting, °vile: No vice is universally so hateful as ingratitude. **2** °malignant, malefic, malevolent, malicious, °evil, °mean, °spiteful, °contemptuous: She gave me a hateful glance.

haughty adj. °arrogant, °proud, °superior, °self-important, °smug, self-satisfied, complacent, °pretentious, °conceited, °egotistical, °snobbish, °overbearing, °lofty, °presumptuous, overweening, patronizing, °supercilious, °vain, °condescending, °contemptuous, belittling, derisive, °disdainful, °scornful, Colloq high-falutin or hifalutin, °hoity-toity, stuck-up, swell-headed or swelled-headed or swollen-headed, °high and °mighty, on (his or her) high horse, snooty, la-di-da or lah-di-dah or la-de-da, Slang snotty, °uppish, uppity: She's too haughty to have made any friends here.

haul v. **1** °drag, °pull, °tug, °tow, °trail, °lug, °heave, °draw: Are you sure that one horse can haul that load? **2** °cart, °transport, °carry, convey, °truck, °move: The new vehicles are equipped to haul bulk dry goods.
—n. **3** °pull, °tug, °drag, °draw; °heave; °attraction: The tides are greater under the haul of both sun and moon. **4** catch, °take, °yield, °harvest, °bag: We returned with quite a good haul of cod.

haunt v. **1** °visit, °frequent, °hang about or around, °spend °time at, US habituate: She haunts the yacht club, waiting for her ship to come in. **2** °beset, °obsess, °plague, °torment, °trouble, °possess, °prey on: He is haunted by the fear that she told the police everything.
—n. **3** gathering-place, meeting-place, stamping-ground, Colloq hang-out: She returned to Abergavenny to visit the haunts of her youth.

have v. **1** °possess, own, °keep; °maintain: Imelda had more shoes than you could count. **2** °receive, °take, °accept, °get, °obtain, °acquire, °procure, °secure: How many gifts did you say she had from him? **3** °entertain, be struck by: I have an idea! **4** °possess, °bear, °contain, °include, comprise: The night has a thousand eyes. **5** °suffer with or from, be °suffering with or from, be experiencing, be undergoing, be °enduring, be subjected to: My daughter was really ill when she had measles. **6** °arrange, °organize, °set up, °prepare; °hold: If I have a party, will you come? We shall have our next meeting on Saturday. **7** °partake of, °participate in, °experience, °enjoy; °eat; °drink: I hope you have a good time. **8** give birth to, °bear, °deliver, °bring into the world; beget, sire, °father: She had three children in as many years. How many children has he had? **9** °make, °demand; °force, °oblige, °cause, °induce, °press, °require, compel: We'll have the caterers come at noon. **10 had better** or **best**: ought to, °must, should: I had better not drink as I'm driving. **11 had rather** or **sooner**: °prefer to, would °rather or sooner: I'd rather be with you. **12 have on**: **a** be wearing, be dressed or clothed or attired in: I'll have on the silk nightgown you like so much. **b** be committed to, have planned, have in the offing, have on the agenda: I have something on next Tuesday evening. **c** °trick, °tease, °deceive, °pull (someone's) °leg, play a °joke on, °fool: Do you really love me or are you having me on?

havoc n. **1** °ruin, devastation, °destruction, °desolation, °rack or wrack or °ruin, despoliation, spoliation, °damage: Gales of more than 80 m.p.h. wreaked havoc right across the British Isles. **2** °confusion, °chaos, °upset, °disorder, °mayhem, °shambles, disruption: The railway slow-down created havoc with commuter schedules.

hazard n. **1** °peril, °danger, °risk, endangerment, °threat, °jeopardy: The greatest hazard in sailing single-handed round the world is the loneliness. **2** °chance, °gamble, uncertainty, °luck, °fortune: They banned all games that depended on hazard.
—v. **3** °venture; °dare; °gamble, °risk, °jeopardize, °endanger, °threaten, imperil, °stake: May I hazard a guess as to the origin of the word? He hazarded his entire fortune on the turn of a card.

hazardous adj. unsafe, °risky, °fraught with °danger, °questionable, °shaky, °dangerous,

°precarious, °uncertain, unpredictable, °parlous, °ticklish, °tricky, *Colloq chiefly Brit* °dicey, °dicky *or* dickey, *Slang* °hairy: *It took three months to make the hazardous overland journey in those days.*

hazy *adj.* **1** °misty, foggy, smoggy, cloudy, °overcast: *It was so hazy that we couldn't see the town a mile away.* **2** °indistinct, blurred, blurry, °dull, °dim, °faint, °nebulous, °vague, unclear, °fuzzy, °indefinite, muddled: *He has only a hazy idea of the plot.*

head *n.* **1** skull, pate, cranium, *Colloq* dome, *Slang* coco(nut), belfry, noggin, bean, nut, rocker, noodle, gourd, *Brit* conk, crumpet, noddle, °loaf: *She laid her head on the pillow and fell sound asleep.* **2** °chief, °leader, administrator, °chief °executive °officer, CEO, (managing) °director, MD, president, chairman, chairwoman, chairperson, °chair, °employer, °principal, °superintendent, °supervisor, governor, °prime °minister, headmaster, headmistress, *Colloq* °boss, headman, the °man, *Brit* guv'nor, guv, *US* (°chief) honcho; *Slang* °big cheese, *US* Mr Big: *The new head has called a meeting of the board of directors.* **3** °front, vanguard, forefront, van, fore-part: *At the head of the column marched the general himself.* **4** °aptitude, °intellect, °intelligence, °talent, °perception, perceptiveness, °mentality, °faculty, °flair, °genius, °brain, °mind, °wit, *Colloq* °brains, grey matter: *I have no head for figures.* **5** °crisis, apex, (°critical *or* turning) °point, °peak, °crest, (fever) °pitch, °climax, culmination, conclusion, crescendo: *Matters have been brought to a head because of the coming elections.* **6** °source, °origin, fount, font, fountain-head, well-spring: *We were trying to reach the head of the stream before nightfall.* **7** °top, °first place, °leading °position, °leadership, forefront: *Albert is at the head of his class in mathematics.* **8 head over heels:** °completely, °entirely, °deeply, °utterly, °wholly, fully, *Colloq* °madly, wildly: *The two of them are head over heels in love.* —*adj.* **9** °first, °chief, °main, °principal, °leading, °premier, °foremost, °prime, °pre-eminent, °cardinal, °paramount, °supreme, °superior, °senior: *Alphonse is our new head chef.* —*v.* **10** °go, °move, °proceed, °turn, °steer, °aim, °point, head for, °make a beeline for: *I shall head home when I leave here.* **11** head up, be in *or* take charge (of), °direct, °supervise, °oversee, °control, °govern, °run, (take the) °lead, °guide, °manage, °command, °rule, °administer, °conduct: *Who will head the organization if you resign?* **12** °lead, °precede, °top: *Charlotte heads the list of candidates.* **13 head off: a** °intercept, °divert; °cut off, °stop, °block: *The cavalry will head them off at the pass.* **b** °stop, °forestall, °prevent, °inhibit, avert, °ward *or* °fend off: *What can we do to head off inflation?*

headache *n.* **1** migraine, *Technical* cephalalgia: *Hazel says she has a headache and cannot come to work today.* **2** °worry, °bother, vexation, °inconvenience, °nuisance, °annoyance, °problem, °difficulty, °trouble, bane, *Colloq* °pain (in the neck), *Slang* °pain in the *Brit* arse *or US* ass: *The balance of payments deficit is a perpetual headache.*

headway *n.* **1** °progress, forward °motion, °improvement: *Headway against that current was almost impossible. Any headway to report?* **2 make**

headway: °advance, °progress, °move forward, °go, °gain (ground), get *or* go °ahead, °proceed, get going: *I tried to persuade her but haven't made much headway.*

heal *v.* **1** cure, °repair, °renew, revitalize, °rejuvenate, °restore; °mend, °recuperate, °recover, °improve: *The wounds have healed. The ointment healed his wounds. I heal quickly.* **2** °reconcile, °settle, °patch up, °put *or* set straight *or* °right, °remedy, °repair, °mend: *His only wish was to heal the rift with his brother.*

health *n.* **1** °condition, °fitness, °trim, fettle, °form, constitution: *My health has improved enough for me to return to work.* **2** healthiness, haleness, healthfulness, robustness, °vigour, vigorousness, salubrity, salubriousness, well-being, °strength: *The health of the economy is good.*

healthy *adj.* **1** °well, °fit, °trim, in °good *or* °fine fettle *or* °shape, in °good °health, °robust, °hale (and °hearty), °sturdy, °strong, °vigorous, thriving, °flourishing, *Colloq* in the pink: *How come he is so healthy if he smokes?* **2** °wholesome, healthful, salubrious, salutary, °beneficial, nourishing, °nutritious, °tonic, °bracing: *The answer lies in eating healthy food and living in a healthy climate.*

heap *n.* **1** °collection, °pile, °mound, °stack, °accumulation, aggregation, agglomeration, congeries, conglomeration, °hoard, °mass, °store, °mountain, stockpile, °supply, *Colloq US and Canadian* stash: *Donors contributed a huge heap of clothing for the sale.* **2** Often, **heaps**: °abundance, plethora, superabundance, °lot(s), °plenty, °great °deal, scores, peck, °sea, *Colloq* lashings, °load(s), °piles, ton(s), raft(s), pots, oodles, scad(s), *US and Canadian* slew: *It was served with heaps of chocolate sauce. Heaps of people bought your record. You're in for a heap of trouble.* —*v.* **3** °collect, °gather, °harvest, °reap, glean, °garner, °pile (up), °accumulate, cumulate, aggregate, °amass, stockpile, °save (up), bank, °lay by *or* up *or* in, °set aside, *Colloq* stash (away): *In autumn, squirrels heap up their supplies of nuts for the winter.* **4** °shower, °load, bestow, °give, °provide, °burden: *The grateful prince heaped us with treasure beyond imagination.*

hear *v.* **1** °perceive, °understand, °listen (to), °attend (to), pay °attention (to), °catch, °heed, hark (to): *Please hear what I have to say first.* **2** °understand, °learn, °discover, °find out, °gather, °get wind of, °pick up, ascertain, be told *or* advised *or* °informed: *I hear you're thinking of resigning.* **3 hear of:** °entertain, °consider; °approve (of), °sanction, condone, °agree *or* °consent *or* assent to: *I won't hear of your leaving.*

heart *n.* **1** *Colloq* ticker, °pump: *The doctor says I have a dicky heart.* **2** °stomach, °nerve, °courage, °bravery, mettle, °will, boldness, °pluck, °resolution, °determination; callousness, insensitivity, heartlessness; *Colloq* °guts, °spunk: *I haven't the heart to tell him that his hamster died.* **3** (basic) °nature, °core, °centre, °focus, °hub, °middle, marrow, °pith, °essence, °quintessence, °nucleus, °nub, crux, basics, fundamentals, *Colloq* nitty-gritty: *Let's get down to the heart of the matter.* **4** °sincerity, °sentiment(s), °feeling(s), °spirit, °verve, °enthusiasm: *She's going through the motions, but* *her heart isn't in her work.* **5** °humanity, human-itarianism, °sympathy, °understanding, °kindness, kindliness, compassion, empathy, goodness, °consideration, °concern, °soul, tenderness, magnanimity, generosity, °sensitivity, °sensibility, °sentiment, °pity, (brotherly) °love, °affection: *Mother Theresa is known for having a lot of heart. Have you no heart, Genghis?*

heartbroken *adj.* °broken-hearted, °downhearted, dispirited, °unhappy, °miserable, grief-stricken, °upset, °dejected, heartsick, crestfallen, °despondent, depressed, disconsolate, distressed, °woebegone, °doleful, °sorrowful, °mournful, morose, disheartened, °disappointed, crushed: *Lucy was heartbroken over the loss of her locket.*

heartfelt *adj.* °sincere, °honest, °genuine, unfeigned, °earnest, °serious, °wholehearted, °deep, °profound, dedicated, °devoted, °ardent, committed, °fervent, fervid, °hearty, °passionate: *It is my heartfelt wish that you should succeed.*

heartless *adj.* °cruel, hard-hearted, °callous, unconcerned, °inhuman, inhumane, °unkind, unfeeling, °unsympathetic, °brutal, °cold, °merciless, pitiless, °ruthless, °cold-blooded: *Taking away the child's toys was a heartless thing to do.*

heart-rending *adj.* °agonizing, distressing, °excruciating, °bitter, °painful, heartbreaking, °harrowing, °piteous, °tragic, depressing, °poignant: *Her distress was heart-rending to behold.*

heart-warming *adj.* **1** °moving, °touching, warming, affecting, uplifting, inspiriting, cheering, encouraging: *I heard the heart-warming news about Alan's recovery.* **2** °satisfying, gratifying, °pleasing, comforting, °pleasurable, °rewarding: *It was heart-warming to see the family together at Christmas.*

hearty *adj.* **1** °genial, °warm, kind-hearted, °affectionate, °amiable, °amicable, °friendly, affable, °cordial, °open, convivial: *I was greeted by a hearty welcome when I returned.* **2** °genuine, unfeigned, °authentic, °sincere, °heartfelt, °warm, °wholehearted, °honest, °earnest, °devout, °stalwart, °stout: *Please give Desmond my hearty congratulations.* **3** °enthusiastic, °vigorous, °energetic, °eager, zealous, °exuberant, °robust, °active, °animated, °strong: *They are hearty supporters of our cause.* **4** °abundant, °ample, °substantial, °solid, sizeable, °satisfying, °square; nourishing, °invigorating, strengthening: *On Sundays, we had a hearty meal at midday when we could afford it.* **5** °healthy, °hale, °vigorous, °robust, °strong, °sound: *Well, Eric, now that you're over your malaria you appear to be quite hearty.*

heat *n.* **1** °warmth, warmness, hotness, fever, fieriness, torridity *or* torridness: *The heat of the sun feels good after that cold swim.* **2** °passion, °ardour, °fervour, fervidness, °intensity, °fury, zeal, zealousness, earnestness, vehemence, °eagerness, °enthusiasm, °excitement, tenseness, °tension, °stress, °agitation, arousal, impetuosity, stimulation, exhilaration: *If I shouted at you in the heat of the moment, I apologize.* —*v.* **3** °warm (up): *It costs a lot to heat this house.* **4** Often, **heat up:** °excite, °intensify, impassion, °inflame, °kindle, ignite, °quicken, inspirit, °rouse, awaken *or* waken, °stir,

°animate, °stimulate, °warm (up), °activate, *Colloq Brit* °hot up: *It took a while for the debate to heat up.*

heated *adj.* °impassioned, °excited, intensified, aroused, quickened, stimulated, °inflamed, vehement, °fiery, frenzied, °frantic, frenetic, °passionate, °fervent, fervid, °ardent, °intense, °furious, °stormy, °tempestuous, °violent; °angry, °bitter: *There was a heated dispute over animal rights, which finally led to blows.*

heathen *n.* **1** unbeliever, °infidel, °pagan, idolater *or* idolatress, polytheist, atheist, nullifidian, °sceptic, agnostic, heretic: *One often finds more mercy in a heathen than in a brother Christian.* —*adj.* **2** °infidel, °pagan, atheist(ic), °godless, nullifidian, °sceptic(al), doubting, agnostic, °heretical, irreligious: *After the missionaries left, the tribe returned to their heathen practices.* **3** °savage, °barbarian, barbaric, °uncivilized, °primitive, unenlightened, uncultured, Philistine; polytheistic, pantheistic: *Each of these tribesmen carries with him a tiny sculptured image of the heathen god.*

heave *v.* **1** °raise, °lift, °hoist, °haul, °pull, °draw, °tug; °move: *We heaved in the anchor and made sail.* **2** °throw, °toss, °hurl, °fling, °cast, °sling, °pitch, let °fly, °send, °launch, *Colloq* °peg, chuck: *When he heaved the sword into the lake a hand rose from the waters and caught it.* **3** °breathe, utter, °sigh, °groan, °moan, °gasp: *We heaved a sigh of relief when we heard that they had been found.* **4** °gag, retch, °vomit, be °sick, °regurgitate, disgorge, *Colloq* °throw up, *Slang* puke, lose one's lunch, return one's dinner, *US* upchuck, spiff one's biscuits: *The smell of petrol always makes me heave.*

heaven *n.* **1** °paradise, °bliss, hereafter, nirvana, Abraham's °bosom, Elysian Fields *or* Elysium, Valhalla, Zion, °happy hunting-grounds, Avalon, Isles of the Blessed, the Blessed *or* Fortunate *or* Happy Isles *or* Islands: *Will I go to heaven when I die?* **2 heavens:** °sky, skies, °firmament, *Literary* welkin, empyrean: *The heavens opened and the rain started to pour down.* **3** °happiness, °bliss, °joy, °rapture, °ecstasy, °paradise, contentment, seventh heaven, Eden, Garden of Eden, °Utopia, heaven on earth, °paradise on earth: *Darby said that his years with Joan had been sheer heaven.*

heavenly *adj.* **1** °divine, angelic, °seraphic, °celestial, °holy, °immortal, blessed, beatific, beatified, °spiritual, °saintly; supernal, °unearthly, other-worldly, ultramundane, extramundane, extraterrestrial: *Alone on the mountain, she heard a heavenly voice calling her name.* **2** °delightful, wonderful, °marvellous, °sublime, paradisiac(al) *or* paradisaic(al), °glorious, °splendid, °superb, °exquisite, °perfect, °ideal, °excellent, °fantastic, °rapturous, entrancing, blissful, *Colloq* °gorgeous, °divine, smashing, °great: *André's serves a perfectly heavenly lobster thermidor.*

heavy *adj.* **1** °weighty, °ponderous, °massive, *Literary* massy, °compact, °dense: *This box is much too heavy for me to lift.* **2** °abundant, overflowing, °excessive, copious, °profuse, °prodigious, °ample, unmanageable: *We just crawled along in the heavy traffic.* **3** °serious, °grave, °important, °crucial, °critical, °acute: *You always bring up heavy topics at the end of the meeting.* **4** °burdensome, onerous, °oppressive,

°weighty, °unbearable, °severe, °grievous, distressful, °sore, intolerable, insupportable or unsupportable, °awful: *Teenagers often feel that they are weighed down with heavy responsibilities.* **5** °sad, °sorrowful, distressing, °grievous, upsetting, depressing, °gloomy, °sombre, °melancholy: *Some heavy news has been received from the front.* **6** °unhappy, °miserable, depressed, °melancholy, grieving, °sad, °dejected, °downhearted, disconsolate, downcast, °despondent, °gloomy, heavy-hearted, morose, crestfallen, cheerless: *Heavy at heart, he returned to his cheerless home.* **7** °ponderous, °tedious, °monotonous, °boring, uninteresting, °leaden, °dull, °prosaic, °dry, dry-as-dust, °stodgy, °staid, °stuffy, stifling, stultifying: *The critics found the style much too heavy for the subject being treated.* **8** °thick, °coarse, °broad, blunt, °clumsy, °ungraceful: *These heavy brush-strokes prove that the painting is not a Turner.* **9** °gloomy, cloudy, °overcast, °bleak, °dismal, °dreary, °leaden, °grey, °dark, louring or lowering, °threatening: *it was another of Scotland's heavy February days.* **10** °intense, concentrated, °severe, °forceful, °violent, °torrential: *The snowfall was the heaviest of the year.* **11** overweight, °fat, °obese, °stout, °chubby, °plump, corpulent, portly, paunchy, tubby, *Brit* podgy or *US* pudgy, *Colloq* beer-bellied: *The doctor did not say I was too heavy, only that I ought to be six inches taller.* **12** °weighty, °difficult, complex, °recondite, arcane, °deep, °profound, esoteric, °incomprehensible, impenetrable, unfathomable: *He specializes in some heavy subject like micro-palaeontology.* **13** burdened, laden, encumbered, °loaded, overloaded, weighed down: *We spied two Indiamen, heavy with cargoes of spices, sailing towards us.*

heavy-handed *adj.* **1** °awkward, °clumsy, °inept, maladroit, unskilful, °ungraceful, graceless, bungling: *She made a heavy-handed attempt to apologize.* **2** autocratic, imperious, magisterial, °overbearing, °despotic, °dictatorial, °tyrannical, °oppressive, °domineering, iron-handed, °harsh, °severe: *For more than 30 years he exercised heavy-handed control over the country.*

heckle *v.* badger, °pester, °annoy, °irritate, °bother, nettle, bait, °harass, harry, °plague, hector, °taunt, °jeer, *Colloq* hassle, °bug, *Brit and Australian and New Zealand* barrack: *One man kept heckling the speaker with persistent interruptions.*

hectic *adj.* °feverish, °excited, °agitated, °busy, bustling, rushed, hyperactive, over-active, frenzied, °frantic, °chaotic, °wild, °mad, frenetic, °riotous: *What with the new baby and everyone else having the flu, I've had a pretty hectic week.*

heed *v.* **1** pay °attention to, °attend, (take or make) °note (of), °listen to, °mark, °consider, bear in °mind; °take, °follow, °obey, °mind, °respect, °accept, °abide by: *I wish I had heeded her suggestions for redecorating the house. Heeding his advice, I joined the army.* —*n.* **2** °attention, °notice, °ear, °mind, °respect, °consideration, °thought: *Let us give heed to the speaker's admonitions.*

heedless *adj.* °inattentive, uncaring, unmindful, neglectful, unobservant, °regardless; °oblivious, °deaf, °blind: *Heedless of tradition, they replaced the older buildings with council housing.*

heel[1] *n.* **1** °end, °butt or °tail or °fag(-°end), °stump, °remainder, °remnant, °rind, crust: *You can always freeze the heel of a loaf to use at some later date for breadcrumbs.* **2** cad, °scoundrel, swine, °rogue, scamp, °philanderer, *Old-fashioned* worm, knave, *Chiefly Brit* blackguard, *Colloq Brit* rotter, *Old-fashioned* bounder, *Slang* bastard, *Brit* sod: *He's an absolute heel—he got her pregnant and then left her.* **3 down at heel**: *US also* down at the heels; °poor, °destitute, °impoverished, down and out, on (one's) uppers, in °straitened circumstances; °shabby, °seedy, °dowdy, °run-down, slovenly, *Brit* out at elbows, *US* out at the elbows, *Colloq* °broke, strapped: *Farrington looked down at heel, so I slipped him a fiver.* **4 take to (one's) heels**: take °flight, °flee, °escape, °run off or away, show a clean pair of heels, *Colloq* °split, *Brit* do a moonlight °flit, *US* take a (run-out) powder, °fly the coop, *Australian and New Zealand* °shoot through: *When I mentioned payment, she took to her heels.* —*v.* **5** dog, °follow (closely), °shadow, °chase, °pursue: *We have taught our puppy to heel.*

heel[2] *v.* °list, °lean (over), °tilt, °tip, °incline: *The boat heeled as we turned to beat into the wind.*

hefty *adj.* **1** °big, °large, °bulky, cumbersome, °awkward, °unwieldy, °clumsy, °substantial, °massive: *That's a pretty hefty box for one person to carry.* **2** °brawny, °strong, °powerful, °burly, °muscular, strapping, °rugged, °robust, *Colloq* °husky, beefy: *That hefty man over there is the Olympic weight-lifting champion.* **3** °substantial, °considerable, sizeable, °impressive, °enormous, °huge, *Colloq* °thumping or *Brit* socking °great: *I've just received a hefty increase in salary.*

height *n.* **1** altitude, °elevation, °level; tallness: *At what height is the second camp on Mount Everest? The height of the skyscrapers impressed me.* **2** °acme, °crest, °pinnacle, °top, °zenith, apogee, °peak, apex, °maximum, °high °point, °summit, °climax, culmination, °extreme: *Popularity of that style reached its height in the 1930s. His remark reflected the height of arrogance.* **3** Often, **heights**: °elevation, °mound, °hill, eminence, °prominence, °mountain, °peak, °crag, °summit; tor, °cliff, °bluff, promontory, escarpment, scarp, headland, *No. Eng. and Scots* fell: *As we gazed down from the heights, the villages seemed tiny.*

heighten *v.* **1** °raise, elevate, °build up, °increase, °lift (up), upraise: *A white ceiling gives the effect of heightening a room.* **2** °intensify, °deepen, °strengthen, reinforce, °amplify, °magnify, °increase, °enhance, augment, °add to, °supplement: *Adding some blue heightens the effect. The bribery scandal has only heightened distrust of the ruling party.*

heir *n.* heiress, beneficiary, inheritor, legatee, successor: *What if you are not the rightful heir to the estate?*

hell *n.* **1** Erebus, Hades, Acheron, Tartarus, Gehenna, Tophet, Abaddon, Pandemonium, Dis, Sheol, Avernus, °underworld, °infernal regions, °abyss, abode of the damned, inferno, hell-fire, lower world, nether regions, bottomless °pit, other place: *For his sins he was condemned to everlasting hell.* **2** °chaos, °misery, °torment, °agony, torture, °ordeal, nightmare, °trial: *The office has been an absolute hell since you left.*

3 °anguish, °pain, °agony, °torment, torture, °misery, °suffering, °affliction: *We have been through hell since Grenville's heart attack.*
4 °criticism, censure; scolding, castigation, °reprimand, upbraiding: *My mother gave me hell for getting home late.*

helm *n.* **1** tiller, °wheel, rudder, steering gear or apparatus: *I had to put the helm over hard to avoid hitting the pier.* **2** directorship, presidency, chairmanship, °leadership, °control, °rule, °command, *Colloq* driver's seat, saddle: *Arthur remained at the helm of the company for 40 years.*

help *v.* **1** °aid, °assist, °lend a hand, °support, °serve; succour: *Let me help you carry that package, Mrs Smith.* **2** °relieve, alleviate, °mitigate, °improve, °facilitate, °ease, °better, °remedy, °cure: *Complaining about it won't help the situation.* **3** °stop, °refrain from, °avoid, eschew, °resist, °keep from, forbear, °escape: *I know it was a secret but I couldn't help telling Sam.* **4** °assist, °serve, °advise, °inform: *May I help you, sir?* **5 help oneself**: °appropriate, °take, arrogate, commandeer, expropriate; °steal, purloin, usurp, plagiarize, °pirate, *Colloq* °pinch, °lift, *Brit* °nick, *US* °boost: *She helped herself to some money from the till.*
—*n.* **6** °aid, °support, succour, °assistance: *I need help in solving this problem.* **7** °employee(s), °worker(s), °staff, helper(s), °hand(s), °assistant(s), °labourer(s), °domestic(s), °servant(s), *Brit* °daily (help): *We have to hire more help to finish on time.* **8** °supporter, °aide, °assistant, helper: *You have been a great help to me.* **9** °relief, °remedy, °cure, balm: *This ointment has been a great help in stopping the itching.*

helpful *adj.* °useful, °serviceable, °practical, pragmatic, utilitarian, °beneficial, valuable, °profitable, °advantageous, °constructive, °productive, °supportive, reassuring, °sympathetic, °considerate, caring, °accommodating, °kind, cooperative, °neighbourly, °friendly, °benevolent: *A reference book might be helpful in answering that question. Mrs Carlyle gave me such helpful advice.*

helping *n.* serving, °portion, °ration, plateful, *Brit* help, *Colloq* dollop: *He has already asked for a third helping of potatoes.*

helpless *adj.* **1** dependent, °vulnerable, °weak, °helpless, °feeble, °infirm, °lame, °crippled, °disabled: *The disease has left him completely helpless.* **2** °confused, baffled, mystified, bewildered, perplexed, °at sea, confounded, muddled, nonplussed: *I am completely helpless when it comes to balancing my accounts.* **3** weakened, °weak, debilitated, °faint, enfeebled, °feeble, °worn out, °spent, °exhausted, °prostrate, enervated: *All of us were simply helpless from laughing so much.* **4** °worthless, °incapable, °incompetent, °useless, unavailing, °inefficient, °inept, unfit, °unqualified: *Dali said to be helpless without Gala to manage his affairs.*

helter-skelter *adj.* **1** °disorderly, disorganized, °confused, muddled, °haphazard, °careless, jumbled, °random, °topsy-turvy, *Colloq* higgledy-piggledy: *How can one find anything in this helter-skelter mess?*

—*adv.* **2** confusedly, °pell-mell, in all directions, recklessly, unsystematically, chaotically, erratically, aimlessly, *US* every which way, *Colloq* higgledy-piggledy: *When the giant appeared, the children ran away, helter-skelter.*

hence *adv.* **1** °therefore, °consequently, °thus, °accordingly, ergo, as a °result, for that or this °reason: *She has homework to do, hence cannot go to the cinema.* **2** away, from here or this place: *Get thee hence, you wicked witch!* **3** from °now, in the °future: *Where will I be two years hence?*

henceforth *adv.* hereafter, henceforward, from °now on, *Colloq US* from here on out: *Henceforth, make no more personal remarks.*

henchman *n.* (fellow-) mobster or °gangster or °hoodlum, °gangster, bodyguard, myrmidon, right-hand man, °associate, °attendant, °follower, °supporter, confidant, crony, *Colloq* sidekick, hooligan, *Brit* °minder, *US* buddy, °cohort; *Slang* °heavy, *US* torpedo, gunsel, goon: *Mr Big strutted in with his henchmen and wrecked the place.*

henpeck *v.* °nag, °harass, hector, °pester, °torment, °bully, °carp, °cavil: *She henpecked him so much that he finally left her.*

herd *n.* **1** °group, °pack, °bunch, °cluster, °flock, °crowd, multitude, °host, horde, °throng, °mass, °swarm, °press, °crush; assemblage, °collection: *A herd of protesters gathered before the embassy.* **2** °common °herd, °rabble, hoi polloi, great °unwashed, °riff-raff, °masses: *How can you expect the herd to understand these principles?*
—*v.* **3** °gather, congregate, °flock, °assemble, °collect: *The reporters herded round to interview the minister.* **4** °round up, °gather (together), °shepherd, °drive, *W US and Canadian* wrangle, corral: *Herd those cattle into the pen.*

hereditary *adj.* **1** heritable, inheritable, transmissible, transferable or transferrable, inherited, genetic, congenital, °inborn, innate; atavistic: *Green eyes and red hair are hereditary in our family.* **2** °traditional, handed down, inherited, bequeathed, willed; ancestral: *Priesthood was hereditary among Aaron's descendants. These are the hereditary lands that go with the castle.*

heretical *adj.* °unorthodox, heterodox, °impious, freethinking, heretic, apostate or apostatical, iconoclastic, °schismatic, °sceptic, agnostic, atheist(ic), idolatrous, °heathen, °pagan, °infidel, °godless: *The purpose of the Inquisition was to discover and suppress heretical views.*

heritage *n.* **1** °estate, °inheritance, legacy, patrimony, birthright: *The manor-house was included in the heritage that was passed on to me.* **2** °tradition: *The documentary examines our cultural heritage.*

hermetic *adj.* hermetical, airtight, sealed; impervious: *If the hermetic seal is broken, sterility is not guaranteed.*

hermit *n.* °recluse, eremite, anchorite or anchoret or anchoress, °solitary, stylite: *He retired from the world to become a hermit.*

hero *n.* **1** °heroine, °champion, exemplar, °star, superstar, °idol, °ideal, man of the hour, luminary, °notable, °celebrity; knight, paladin, warrior: *She was a hero to every aspiring woman lawyer. She expects a hero in shining armour on a white horse to sweep her off her feet.* **2** °protagonist, (male) °lead or °star, °leading man or actor, °principal: *Gérard Depardieu plays the hero in this lavishly produced film.*

heroic adj. **1** °brave, °courageous, °bold, valiant, valorous, undaunted, °dauntless, stout-hearted, °noble, °intrepid, °gallant, °chivalrous, °daring, plucky, °audacious, °fearless, °manly, virile, manful: *We published a book about Aylesworthy's heroic exploits.* **2** °noble, altruistic, magnanimous, °generous, upstanding, °honourable, °virtuous, °staunch, °steadfast, °stalwart, °determined: *This plaque commemorates Manzanilla's heroic work in curbing religious persecution.* **3** °desperate, °drastic, °extreme: *Despite heroic efforts, it was impossible to rescue the entire crew.* **4** °grand, larger than life, exaggerated, magniloquent, °grandiose, °extravagant; °giant, °gigantic, °enormous, °huge, titanic, °colossal, stupendous: *The heroic phrases of the demagogue still ring in my ears. Statues of heroic proportions have been moved from Abu Simbel.* **5** mythological, epic, Homeric, °legendary, °classical, °fabulous, wonderful, °miraculous: *He enjoyed tales of heroic demigods like Hercules.* **6** °majestic, °lofty, °elevated, °grand, august, °towering, °eminent, °distinguished, °prominent: *The entire court was silent as the heroic figure of the emperor entered.*

heroine n. (female) °lead, °leading actress *or* lady, prima donna *or* ballerina, *première danseuse*, diva: *The heroine was played by Mme Kropeczka.*

hesitant adj. **1** hesitating, undecided, °uncertain, °unsettled, °irresolute, vacillating, shilly-shallying, dithering, fluctuating, wavering, °unresolved, ambivalent, in *or* of two minds, °indefinite, *Brit* havering: *He was hesitant about whether to buy the blue or the green model.* **2** °halting, stammering, stuttering, faltering: *From her hesitant speech I'd say she was nervous.*

hesitate v. **1** °delay, °hold *or* °hang back, °pause, dilly-dally, °wait, temporize, think twice, balk, boggle at, °shrink from, demur, °scruple, *Brit* haver, jib, *Colloq* °stall: *He who hesitates is lost.* **2** °fumble, °equivocate, tergiversate, °fluctuate, °alternate, waver, dither, vacillate, °shilly-shally: *He hesitated between the doors—did this one conceal the lady or the tiger?* **3** °stammer, stutter, falter, sputter, splutter, °stumble, hem and haw: *She hesitated throughout the speech purely from stage fright.*

hidden adj. concealed, °secret, °obscure(d), °occult, °veiled, °cryptic, °recondite, arcane, covert, esoteric, unseen, °private: *Was this an ordinary shopping list or did it have some hidden meaning?*

hide[1] v. **1** °conceal, °secrete, °cache, squirrel away; °go °underground, take °cover, °lie low, go into hiding, °lurk, go to ground, drop out of °sight, hibernate, latibulize, *Colloq* °hide out, °hole up, °lie low, *Brit* °lie doggo: *Hide the sweets where the children won't find them. I found a place to hide under the stair.* **2** °conceal, °cover, °mask, °camouflage, °disguise, °veil, °shroud, °screen, °cover up, keep °secret: *He managed to hide his embarrassment.* **3** °eclipse, °blot out, °obscure, °block: *The clouds hid the moon as we made good our escape.* **4** °suppress, °hush (up), °repress, °silence, keep quiet *or* °secret: *She hid all knowledge of the crime.*

hide[2] n. **1** °pelt, °skin, °fell, leather, fur, °fleece: *Once tanned and dyed, the hide was made into clothing.*

—v. **2** °flog, °whip, °lash, flail, °beat, thrash: *The masters took great satisfaction in hiding the boys.*

hideaway n. °refuge, °retreat, °sanctuary, hide-out, hiding-place, °lair, °(safe) haven, *Colloq* °hole, *Brit* hidey-hole *or* hidy-hole: *My brother and I would crawl into our hideaway and pretend we were being held prisoner by pirates.*

hidebound adj. °strait-laced, °conventional, ultra-conventional, °conservative, °reactionary, °rigid, °set (in one's ways), °narrow-minded, close-minded, °inflexible, intractable, uncompromising, restricted, °cramped, °bigoted, °intolerant: *She's too much of a hidebound disciplinarian to rescind the punishment.*

hideous adj. **1** °grotesque, °ugly, °repulsive, °revolting, °repellent, °monstrous, °beastly, gorgonian, °unsightly, °ghastly, °disgusting, °grisly, nauseating, °nauseous, sickening, °gruesome: *Suddenly, a hideous face appeared at the kitchen window.* **2** foul, °abhorrent, heinous, horrifying, appalling, °outrageous, °abominable, °vile, °shocking, °loathsome, °contemptible, °hateful, odious, °atrocious, horrific, °beastly, °damnable, execrable: *Two hideous crimes were committed here last night.*

high adj. **1** °tall, °lofty, °elevated, °towering: *High mountains surround the valley.* **2** °extreme, °excessive, °extraordinary, °exorbitant, °outrageous, *Colloq* °steep, °stiff: *Houses in that district are fetching high prices.* **3** costly, °dear, °expensive, high-priced: *Shares are not as high as they were before the crash.* **4** °great, °huge, °enormous, °considerable, °strong; °violent, turbulent: *These wires carry high voltages. The high winds blew down trees.* **5** °exalted, °elevated, °lofty, °superior, °high-class: *With insider trading, theft became a high art in the financial world.* **6** consequential, °important, °grave, °serious, °weighty, °momentous, heinous; °capital: *His activities constitute high treason.* **7** high-pitched, high-frequency, squeaky, °acute, treble, soprano; °shrill, °strident, °sharp, °penetrating, °piercing, ear-splitting: *The higher notes make my radio speaker vibrate. She has an irritatingly high voice.* **8** °cheerful, °exuberant, °elated, °boisterous, exhilarated, °hilarious, °merry, °excited: *I find his persistent high spirits rather depressing.* **9** euphoric, intoxicated, inebriated, °drunk, drugged, *Colloq* °loaded, tipsy, turned on, on a °trip, *Slang* stoned, spaced out, *Brit* squiffy, *US* spacy, squiffed: *They got high sniffing glue.* **10** gamy, tainted, °aged, °ripe, *Slang Brit* pongy: *He likes to hang venison till it is quite high.* **11** °chief, °leading, °important, °principal, °foremost: *He regards himself as the high priest of women's fashion.* **12** °elaborate, °luxurious, °grand, °extravagant, °lavish, °rich, °prodigal, sybaritic: *With her millions she can now enjoy the high life.* **13** °considerable, °favourable, °great: *She is held in high esteem by her colleagues.*
—adv. **14** °far up; °great in °extent: *Daedalus warned Icarus not to fly so high. I was willing to go as high as 20,000 for the painting.*
—n. **15** °peak, °record, °height, °maximum, °acme, apex: *Employment is expected to reach a high next summer.* **16** intoxication, altered consciousness: *The high lasts till the drug wears off.* **17** anticyclone: *The high passing over the country will bring fair weather.*

highbrow n. **1** °scholar, °intellectual, savant, °sage, °mastermind, °genius; °aesthete, connoisseur, *Colloq* egghead, °brain: *Many who pretend to deride highbrows secretly envy them.* —adj. **2** °scholarly, °intellectual, °learned, erudite, °deep, bookish, cultured, °sophisticated, °cultivated, °aesthetic, *Colloq* brainy: *Books on philosophy are too highbrow for the market we cater to.*

high-class adj. **1** °first-rate, °superior, °better, top-drawer, *Colloq* tops, tiptop, A-one or A-1, °super, °great: *He has had the benefit of a high-class education.* **2** aristocratic, °upper-class, élite, °select, °exclusive; °upper crust, °fancy, *Brit* county, *US and Canadian* tony, *Slang* classy: *She says she comes from a high-class family.*

highly adv. **1** greatly, much, tremendously, well, enthusiastically, °warmly, immensely, hugely: *Her play was highly praised by all the critics.* **2** °very, °extremely, °quite, exceptionally, extraordinarily, incomparably, decidedly: *It is highly unlikely that I shall come to your party.* **3** °favourably, well, enthusiastically, approvingly, °warmly, praisefully: *They seem to think highly of him at the office.* **4** °well, influentially, powerfully, strongly, authoritatively, effectively, importantly: *I have the information from a highly placed government official.*

hilarious adj. °funny, side-splitting, °humorous, comical, amusing, °entertaining, mirthful; °merry, °gay, °jolly, jovial, °cheerful, cheery, joyous, °joyful, rollicking, °uproarious, *Colloq* °hysterical: *Binky told me a hilarious story about his aunt's pet boa constrictor. We had a hilarious time at your party.*

hilarity n. °laughter, °gaiety, joviality, jollity, °merriment, °mirth, °exuberance, °glee, boisterousness, cheerfulness, joyfulness, jubilation, elation, °revelry, conviviality, °high spirits, vivacity, exhilaration: *Thurgood did not join in the hilarity of his retirement party.*

hill n. **1** °elevation, °rise, highland, °mound, °prominence, promontory, eminence, °knoll, hillock, hummock, °height, foothill, tor, °mount, upland, downs or downland, *Scots* brae, *No. Eng. and Scots* fell, *W Eng.* tump, *US and Canadian* butte: *The house is on a hill overlooking the valley.* **2** °heap, °pile, °mound, °stack; °mountain: *By the autumn, the hill of compost had reached six feet in height.* **3** °slope, °incline or °decline, acclivity or declivity, gradient or esp. *US* °grade, *US* upgrade or °downgrade: *Are you sure this car can make it up the next hill?*

hinder v. **1** °hamper, °delay, °interrupt, °impede, °interfere with, °foil, °thwart, °frustrate, °forestall, °bar, °stymie, °check, balk or baulk, °encumber, °obstruct, °handicap, °set or °keep or °put or °hold back, °defer, °retard, °restrain, °slow, °postpone: *The difficulty of the task should not hinder the attempt.* **2** °stop, °prevent, °check, °preclude, °arrest; °discourage, °deter, °inhibit, obviate: *Does the threat of capital punishment hinder people from committing murder?*

hindrance n. **1** °obstruction, °impediment, °snag, °check, °obstruction, °barrier, °obstacle, °restraint, °drawback, °hitch, °stumbling-block, °deterrent, °encumbrance: *The only hindrance to the plan is Phyllis's disapproval of it.* **2** °prevention, °curb, limitation: *The presence of police cars serves as a hindrance to speeding motorists.*

hint n. **1** °suggestion, °clue, °implication, °inkling, °indication, °tip, tip-off, intimation, allusion, °innuendo, insinuation; °pointer, °help, °advice: *The quiz-master gave me a hint and I got the answer at once.* **2** °trace, °suggestion, °touch, °taste, °breath, °dash, soupçon, whiff, undertone, tinge, °whisper: *Which government has ever served without any hint of scandal?* —v. **3** °suggest, °imply, °indicate, °tip (off), °intimate, allude, °insinuate, °mention, °clue, °cue, °signal, °refer, advert: *She hinted that I might appeal to her sister.*

hip adj. °informed, °aware, °knowledgeable, °knowing, °perceptive, °alert, in or up on, onto, *Colloq* °wise (to), with it, °cool, *Old-fashioned* hep: *He's not hip to what they're saying about him and Carrie.*

hippie n. bohemian, *Old-fashioned* drop-out, beatnik, °beat, longhair, flower child or person, hipster: *A few hippies were playing their guitars at the street corner.*

hire v. **1** °engage, °employ, °take on, °appoint, °enlist, °sign on: *Alexandra had to hire more people to get all the work done.* **2** °rent, °lease, °engage, °charter: *We hired a car for the day.* **3 hire out**: °rent (out), °lease (out), °let (out), °charter (out): *I hire out my boat by the day.* —n. **4** °rent, °lease, °charter, letting: *Do you have bicycles for hire by the day?* **5** (hire) °charge, °cost, °fee, °price, °rate, °rent, rental: *How much is the hire of a horse by the hour?*

hiss n. **1** hissing, sibilance: *Serpents and geese make a sound like a hiss.* **2** catcall, °jeer, boo, hoot, *Slang* raspberry, *US* Bronx cheer: *The villain was greeted by hisses from the audience.* —v. **3** boo, hoot, °jeer, °deride, °mock, °taunt, decry, °disparage: *The workers hissed and booed the speaker.*

historic adj. °momentous, °important, °noteworthy, °significant, red-letter, °notable, °celebrated, °distinguished, °prominent, °great, consequential, °signal, unforgettable, °memorable: *We are gathered here to commemorate a historic event.*

historical adj. °factual, °true, verifiable, °reliable, °real, °authentic, recorded, documented: *The historical truth of what actually happened on that day has been obscured by legends.*

history n. **1** °account, °story, °record, °description, depiction, portrayal, °representation, °telling, retelling, °recital, °narration, °narrative, °relation, retailing: *Washington Irving's Knickerbocker's History of New York begins with the creation of the world.* **2** °news, °summary, recapitulation, °report, °intelligence, °information: *The history of these events is recounted in a book by Robinson.* **3** °past, °background, °life; °experiences, °adventures, °story, biography: *This woman appears to have had a rather curious history. The history of your years in Polynesia would make an interesting book.* **4** °record, °experience, °information, biography, CV or curriculum vitae, *US* résumé: *Your entire work history should be included in your application.* **5** °chronicle, annals, °record, °account: *The history of Parliamentary debate can be traced through Hansard.* **6** °ancient history, the °past, yesterday, the (good °old) days, days of yore, olden days, yesteryear, antiquity: *What can history tell* *us about the future?* **7** °dead letter, yesterday's news, old hat: *Any animosity I might have felt towards him is now history.*

hit *v.* **1** °strike, cuff, smack, °knock, whack, bash, bang, thump, thwack, °punch, buffet, °slap, swat, bludgeon, °club, smite; °spank, thrash, °beat, pummel, °batter, °flog, °scourge, birch, cane, °lash, °belabour, flagellate, °whip, horsewhip, cudgel, *Archaic* fustigate; *Colloq* °belt, wallop, clobber, clout, sock, °clip, °crown, bop, conk, paste, °lambaste, °zap: *She hit him on the jaw and he went down.* **2** °strike, bat, swat, °knock, °drive, °propel: *He hit the ball over the heads of the fielders.* **3** °strike, °collide or °impact with, °run or smash or °crash into, °bump or bang into: *The car went off the road and hit a tree.* **4** °affect, °touch, °stir, °move, °wound, °hurt, °strike or hit home, make or leave an °impression or a °mark on, (make an) °impact (on): *The new taxes hit the wealthy more than the poor.* **5** °dawn on, enter one's mind, °occur to, °strike: *It finally hit Graham that he had been insulted.* **6** °reach, attain, °arrive at, °gain, °achieve: *Those who have hit eighty know the meaning of old age. She hit the jackpot this week.* **7** °experience, °encounter, °meet (with): *It was at that point that we hit a snag in the negotiations.* **8** Also, **hit up**: importune, °beseech, °petition, °beg, implore, entreat, °ask for: *As usual, Guthrie hit me for a loan as soon as we met.* **9 hit on** or **upon**: **a** °come or °happen or °chance or °light on or upon, °discover, °find, uncover, °unearth, °stumble or °blunder on or upon, °arrive at: *After years of experimentation, the Curies hit upon pitchblende as a source of radium.* **b** °devise, °think of or up, °invent, °dream up, °come up with, °work out, °see, °perceive, °detect, discern, °find: *I have hit upon a way to counteract the force of gravity.* —*n.* **10** °impact, °collision; °blow, °punch, °knock, °strike, swat, °shot, smack, °bump, bang, *Colloq* whack, thwack, conk, bop, sock: *The weakness of the hit caused only a slight dent in my car door. The boxer reeled after a hard hit to the midriff.* **11** °success, °triumph, coup, °winner, °sensation, *Colloq* smash (hit), sell-out: *After opening in the West End the musical became a hit on Broadway.* **12** °kick, °jolt, °thrill, *Slang* charge, *US* °rush, bang: *Give me a hit off that reefer.*

hitch *v.* **1** °connect, °couple, °fasten, °attach, °join, harness, °tie, °unite, °hook (up), °link, °fix: *When I arrived, she was hitching the horses to the wagon.* **2** Often, **hitch up**: °raise, °pull up, hike (up), °tug (up), °hoist, °yank, °jerk, *Brit* hoick: *He hitched up his trousers, tucked in his shirt, and tightened his belt.* **3** hitchhike, °thumb a lift or ride, *Colloq US* °bum a ride: *I had no money and no car, so I hitched here from Newcastle.* —*n.* **4** °snag, catch, °difficulty, °trouble, °problem, °mishap, °handicap, entanglement, °interference, °impediment, °hindrance, °obstruction, °obstacle: *The entire plan went off without any hitch.*

hoard *n.* **1** °supply, °stock, store, stockpile, °reserve, °fund, reservoir, °accumulation, °collection, °cache: *They kept a hoard of food in the shelter in case of attack. Occasionally, farmers turn up a hoard of gold coins buried by the ancient Romans.* —*v.* **2** °amass, °collect, °accumulate, °pile (up), °assemble, °gather, °put away, stockpile, °store,

°reserve, °set aside, °save (up), squirrel away, °lay in or away or aside or up, *Colloq* stash away: *Hoarding food was against the law during rationing.*

hoax *n.* **1** °deception, °fraud, °swindle, °trick, flam or flimflam, imposture, °cheat, humbug, *Slang* con (°game), gyp, scam, °game, *US* snow job: *They perpetrated a hoax on you, and I am afraid there is no way of getting your money back.* —*v.* **2** °deceive, °defraud, °swindle, °trick, °fool, °dupe, °take in, cozen, °hoodwink, gull, °bluff, *Slang* con, gyp, bamboozle: *She was hoaxed into investing in Sicilian gold-mines.*

hobble *v.* **1** °limp, falter, dodder, °totter, °stagger, °reel, °weave, °stumble, °shuffle, shamble: *I hobbled about on crutches for weeks.* **2** °shackle, fetter, °restrain, °restrict, °hamper, °hinder, °impede, °trammel: *As hobbled horses do not stray, she tried to think of some way to hobble Clarence's errant ways.* —*n.* **3** °limp, °shuffle, shamble, claudication, °stagger: *With the leg-irons on, I could walk only with a jerking hobble.*

hobby *n.* °pastime, avocation, sideline, °recreation, °diversion, °relaxation: *Her hobby is collecting wedding rings.*

hobnob *v.* °associate, °fraternize, °socialize, consort, °mingle, °rub elbows or shoulders, °mix, °hang about or around, keep company: *He hobnobs with the aristocrats.*

hocus-pocus *n.* **1** °trickery, °chicanery, °deceit, °deception, °artifice, °cheat, duplicity, °mischief, °hoax, humbug, °trick, °swindle, °pretence, *Colloq* con (°game), jiggery-pokery, flimflam, °hanky-panky: *He tried some hocus-pocus on the company books but was caught.* **2** °mumbo-jumbo, abracadabra, incantation, °nonsense, °rigmarole, °gibberish, *Colloq* °gobbledegook: *The medicine man muttered some hocus-pocus over the body, which began to rise into the air.* **3** sleight of hand, legerdemain, prestidigitation, °magic, conjuring, jugglery: *From the earliest days religion has had its share of hocus-pocus.*

hoggish *adj.* piggish, °greedy, °avaricious, insatiable, °gluttonous, °voracious, edacious, acquisitive, °possessive, self-seeking, °selfish: *Don't be so hoggish; share the cake with the others.*

hoi polloi *n.* °riff-raff, °rabble, °mob, °common °herd, proletariat, °populace, °common °people, °crowd, masses, multitude, °rank and file, plebeians, bourgeoisie, °man in the street, *Brit* admass, °man on the Clapham omnibus, *US* John Q. Public, *Colloq* great °unwashed, proles, plebs, *US* silent °majority: *Much of what goes on in government is incomprehensible to hoi polloi.*

hoist *v.* **1** °lift (up), elevate, °raise, °heave, uplift, winch: *The lifeboat with the survivors aboard is now being hoisted onto the rescue vessel.* —*n.* **2** crane, °lift, elevator, davit, winch, °tackle: *The cable of the hoist broke, and the container dropped onto the pier.*

hoity-toity *adj.* °haughty, °arrogant, overweening, °snobbish, °disdainful, °supercilious, °conceited, °lofty, °superior, °self-important, *Colloq* °high and mighty, stuck-up, snooty, uppity or *chiefly Brit* °uppish, *Brit* toffee-nosed, *Slang* snotty: *Eleanor became very hoity-toity after her husband got his knighthood.*

hold *v.* **1** °grasp, °grip, °clasp, °seize, °clutch, °keep; °carry, *Colloq* °hang on to: *She asked me* to hold the baby for just a minute while she bought her railway ticket. **2** °hug, °embrace, °clasp, cradle, clench, °clutch, enfold: He held me in his arms briefly before the guards led him into the quad. **3** °maintain, °keep, °put: Hold up your hands and kick the gun over here to me. **4** °maintain, °keep, °sustain, absorb, °occupy, °engage, °involve, engross, °monopolize: You hold my attention while I try to get round behind him. **5** confine, °restrain, detain, °contain, coop up: Even a strait-jacket and chains couldn't hold Houdini. **6** °imprison, detain, confine, place into °custody, put behind bars, °jail: He is being held overnight for questioning. **7** °believe, deem, °judge, °consider, °regard, °look on or upon, °maintain, °think, °esteem, °take, °assume: What do you hold to be important in life? Father holds me responsible for every little dent in his car. **8** °accommodate, °support, °carry: That little nail won't hold this picture. **9** °contain, °include, comprise: This suitcase holds everything I own in the world. **10** °call, convene, °assemble, convoke, °run, °conduct, °engage in, °participate in, °carry on, °preside over, °officiate at: The next meeting will be held on Tuesday, at noon. **11** °apply, hold good, be in °effect or in °force, °stand or hold up, hold or °prove or be °true, be the °case, °function, °operate, be or °remain or °prove valid or °relevant or °applicable or °operative, Colloq hold °water, °wash: What may be in order for Manchester may not necessarily hold for another city. **12** °have, °possess: She holds two engineering degrees. He was holding four aces. **13** °remain or °keep (°fast), °stay, °stick: Screws are needed here—nails won't hold. **14 hold back: a** °restrain, °repress, °suppress, °curb, °inhibit, °control, °check, °keep back, °hinder: Many reasons hold me back from telling you what I think. **b** °withhold, °reserve, °deny, °keep back, °refuse: We ought to hold back payment till the work is completed. **15 hold down: a** °control, °restrain, °check; °reduce, °diminish: We must hold down inflation. **b** °keep, °maintain, °manage: He has to hold down two jobs to pay all the bills. **16 hold forth: a** Often, **hold forth on** or **upon:** °lecture (on), declaim, °harangue, °preach (on or about), orate, sermonize (on), discourse (on), speechify (on or about), expatiate or °expand on or upon, Colloq °go on (about), Brit rabbit or natter or witter on (about): As usual, Pinckley endlessly held forth on his pet subject, fishing. **b** hold out, °offer, proffer, °tender, °submit, °advance, °propose, °propound, °extend: The company has held forth a profit-sharing plan that we cannot refuse. **17 hold in: a** °control, °curb, °check, hold back, °restrain, °contain: I could hold myself in no longer and a scream escaped my lips. **b** °conceal, °hide, °suppress: How can I hold in my feelings for you? **18 hold off: a** °delay, °defer, °put off, °refrain from, °postpone, °avoid: We held off buying till we had the money saved up. **b** °repel, °keep off, °repulse, °fend off, °rebuff, °resist, °withstand: We held off the attackers till help came. **19 hold on: a** °grip, °grasp, hold, °clutch, °cling: Hold on to the rope and I'll pull you up. **b** °keep, °maintain, °cling, °hang on, °retain: Don't try to hold on to yesterday's dreams. **c** °stop, °wait, hold off, Colloq °hang on: Hold on a minute! I'm not finished. **20 hold out: a** °last, °carry on, °persist, °persevere, °continue, °hang on, °stand °firm or chiefly US

°pat, °endure: I hope that the good weather holds out for our trip. Can we hold out till reinforcements arrive? **b** °offer, proffer, °extend, hold forth, °present: I grasped the hand he held out. **21 hold over: a** °postpone, °delay, °defer, °put off, hold off, °suspend: The decision is to be held over till next year. **b** °continue, °retain, °extend, °prolong: The singer was popular enough to be held over a month. **22 hold up: a** °rob, °waylay, Colloq °mug, °stick up; °knock off or US over: Two men held up the bank courier last night. **b** °delay, °impede, °hinder, °slow (down or up), °set back, detain: I was held up by the infernal traffic again. **c** °last, °survive, °fare, °bear up, °endure: I am not sure that my car will hold up through another winter. **d** °present, °show, °exhibit, °display: Gibbons has been held up to ridicule since the scandal. **23 hold with:** °support, °sustain, °agree to or with, °favour, countenance, °approve (of), °subscribe to, condone, concur with: Being married to her doesn't mean you have to hold with all her ideas. —n. **24** °grasp, °grip, °clasp, °clutch: Take hold of the rope! **25** foothold, toe-hold, °purchase: She lost her hold and fell. He has a good hold on the subject. **26** °power, dominance, mastery, °control, ascendancy, °authority, °influence, leverage, °sway, Colloq °pull, clout: She has a hold over him that makes him do her bidding.

hold-up n. **1** (armed) °robbery, Colloq stick-up, mugging, US heist: The robbers escaped with my gold watch in the hold-up. **2** °delay, °set-back, °hitch, °snag, °interruption, lacuna, °gap, hiatus, °break, stoppage: The cause of the hold-up was an overturned van.

hole n. **1** °cavity, °pit, °hollow, °excavation, °burrow, crater, cavern, °cave, °recess, °niche, °nook, °pocket, °depression, °indentation, dent, °impression: The snake disappeared into a hole in the rock. **2** °opening, °aperture, orifice, perforation, °puncture, °slit, °slot, °breach, °rip, °tear, °rent, °break, °crack, fissure: The water poured through a hole in the pipe. **3** hole in the wall, °shack, °hut, shanty, °slum, °hovel, Slang °dump, °dive, °joint: How can anyone live in such a hole? She finally got a job dancing in some hole downtown. **4** °cell, °prison, °dungeon, donjon, °keep, °jail, oubliette, brig, °cage: When he refused to talk, they put him in the hole for a week. **5** °difficulty, °trouble, °dilemma, °predicament, °situation, °fix, corner, Colloq (tight) °spot, hot water, °scrape, box, °bind, pickle, catch-22, °mess, °muddle: She really got herself into a hole with the tax man. **6** °flaw, °shortcoming, inconsistency, °fault, °error, °mistake, °fallacy, °discrepancy, °loophole: He never offers anything original but is always ready to pick holes in any suggestion you make. —v. **7** °puncture, °pierce, °perforate: A floating log holed the hull and the boat went down with all aboard.

holiday n. **1** °time off, °break, °recess, °respite, °leave (of °absence), furlough, sabbatical, Chiefly US vacation: We spent our holiday in Ibiza this year. **2** °festival, °feast, °celebration, °fête or fete; °gala, °fair, red-letter day, °event: Where are you going over the Christmas holiday?

hollow adj. **1** °vacant, °empty, °void, unfilled: A hollow space in the wall concealed a secret passage. **2** °sunken, concave, indented, dented, recessed, depressed: Dust gathers in the hollow

places of the floor. **3** °hungry, °ravenous, °starved, °empty, °famished: *I'm feeling hollow and should prefer to eat now, not later.* **4** °insincere, °false, °hypocritical, °sham, °artificial, °counterfeit, feigned, °fraudulent, °spurious, °deceitful, mendacious, °deceptive, cynical: *Politicians campaigning for office often make hollow promises they do not intend to keep.* **5** °empty, °futile, costly, Pyrrhic, °worthless, °vain, unavailing, °bootless, °fruitless, profitless, °unprofitable, valueless, °ineffective, °pointless, °senseless, °meaningless: *Winning the lawsuit was a hollow victory, for the man was bankrupt.* **6** muffled, °dull, °flat, °low, sepulchral, toneless: *His voice sounded hollow, as if he were speaking into a metal bowl.*
—*n.* **7** °hole, °cavity, cavern, crater, basin, °depression, °excavation, °pit, trough, °furrow, °indentation, dent, °impression; °valley, dale, dell, glen, °dip: *We hid ourselves in a hollow in the ground hoping not to be seen. The dog herded the sheep into the hollow near the stream.*
—*v.* **8** °excavate, °dig (out *or* up), °gouge, °scoop, °furrow, dredge: *Huskies hollow out places for themselves to sleep in the snow.*

holocaust *n.* **1** conflagration, fire-storm, inferno, °fire; °destruction, devastation: *When the volcano exploded, few escaped the holocaust.* **2** genocide, mass °murder, °massacre, blood bath, pogrom, butchery, °carnage, annihilation, extinction, extermination, eradication, elimination: *Survivors of the Nazi holocaust hold periodic memorial services.*

holy *adj.* **1** °sacred, °religious, consecrated, sanctified, blessed, hallowed, venerated, °divine, °heavenly, supernal, °celestial: *The holy relics are kept in a silver casket.* **2** °godly, °godlike, °saintly, saintlike, °pious, °devout, reverent, reverential, °faithful, God-fearing, °chaste, °pure, unsullied, °clean, sinless, °spotless, °immaculate, undefiled, uncorrupted, untainted: *The holy men, in their saffron robes, sat in a circle, contemplating the master of the universe.*

homage *n.* °obeisance, °respect, °deference, °honour, °esteem, °admiration; °loyalty, allegiance, fidelity, °tribute: *Today we pay homage to those who fought and died so that we might be free.*

home *n.* **1** dwelling-place, °residence, °domicile, °abode, °dwelling, °house, (living) quarters, habitation, °lodging(s), *Brit* °accommodation *or US* accommodations, *Colloq* °place, *Chiefly Brit* digs, diggings: *He has been a guest in my home on many occasions.* **2** (home) °base, residency, °territory, °haunt, home °ground, bailiwick, *Colloq* stamping-ground: *As you travel so much, what do you call home these days?* **3** hospice, °retreat, nursing home, old folks' *or* people's home, retirement community, almshouse, poorhouse, °refuge, haven, °institution, °shelter, rest-home, *US* snug harbor: *His parents, who are very old and indigent, have been sent to a home.* **4 at home: a** °comfortable, at °ease, °relaxed, °cosy, composed, °tranquil, placid, °peaceful, °serene, untroubled: *The Harrises certainly do make one feel at home.* **b** in, °accessible, °available, welcoming: *You know that we are always at home to you, Frances.* **5 at home with** *or* **in:** °comfortable with, conversant with, °knowledgeable in *or* about, °familiar with, well-versed in, °competent in, °expert in, °proficient in, skilled in, up on, °current in, °adept in, adroit in,

°qualified in, (°well-)°informed in *or* on *or* about: *Widely read, she is at home in almost any subject you can name.*
—*adj.* **6** °domestic, °native, °national, °internal: *Buying more foreign than home goods upsets the balance of trade.* **7** °domestic, household: *She now sells home appliances for a big manufacturer.* **8** °family, °domestic: *What kind of home life has he had?*
—*adv.* **9** homeward(s): *When will you come home?* **10** to the °heart *or* °core, to the quick; effectively, tellingly, °profoundly, °deeply, stingingly, cuttingly, harshly, °severely, *Colloq* where it hurts, where one lives: *That remark really hit home.* **11 bring** *or* **drive home:** °stress, °emphasize, °impress upon, make clear: *I am trying to bring home to you the hardships people suffered during the war.*

homeless *adj.* **1** dispossessed, °outcast, exiled, °vagabond, °derelict, °unsettled; unhoused: *Their houses destroyed in the war, homeless people wandered everywhere.*
—*n.* **2 the homeless:** knights of the road, vagrants, vagabonds, tramps, *US* bums, hoboes: *There are not enough shelters for the homeless.*

homely *adj.* **1** homey, homelike, unpretentious, °modest, unassuming, °simple, °unaffected, °informal, °plain, °natural, °everyday, °unsophisticated, °homespun, commonplace, °ordinary, °familiar, °friendly, °amiable, °neighbourly, affable, congenial, *Colloq chiefly US* folksy: *Her success as a doctor is traceable in part to her homely approach.* **2** homey, homelike, °warm, °cosy, °snug, °domestic, °comfortable, °easy, °serene, °peaceful, °restful, °tranquil: *I like staying here for the homely atmosphere.* **3** °ugly, °plain, uncomely, unattractive, unlovely, ill-favoured: *Peggy-Jo's rather homely face is redeemed by her good-humoured nature.*

homesick *adj.* nostalgic, °longing, pining, °lonely, °lonesome; °wistful, °reminiscent: *I was homesick for the smell and taste of a good haggis.*

homespun *adj.* °rustic, °plain, °simple, °unrefined, unpolished, °unsophisticated, down-to-earth, °coarse, °rough, °rude, °crude, inelegant, °amateur, amateurish, non-professional, °unprofessional; handmade: *The furniture is not of museum standard, but it has a homespun quality.*

homicidal *adj.* °murderous, °lethal, °deadly, death-dealing, °mortal, bloodthirsty, °sanguinary, °ferocious, °maniacal, °berserk, amok *or* amuck, °mad, °insane: *The doctors say he is homicidal and should be institutionalized.*

homogeneous *adj.* °uniform, °consistent, unvarying, °identical, °constant; °similar, comparable, °alike, °akin: *The rock is ground up to make homogeneous powder.*

homosexual *n.* **1** °gay, homophile; lesbian, tribade, sapphist; *All the following are offensive and derogatory* °pervert, invert, *Slang* °queer, fairy, pansy, nancy *or* nancy boy, nance, °queen, drag °queen, homo; butch, (bull) dyke; *Brit* poof, poofter, ginger (beer), *US* °fruit, auntie, °fag, faggot: *Homosexuals prefer to be called 'gay'.*
—*adj.* **2** (of either sex) °gay, homoerotic, homophile; (of a female) lesbian, tribadic, sapphic; (of a male) °effeminate; *All the following are offensive and derogatory* °perverted, inverted, *Colloq chiefly Brit* °bent, *Slang* °queer, °camp, campy,

249

°kinky, *Chiefly US* fruity, limp-wristed, faggy, °swish, swishy: *We never knew of her homosexual tendencies.*

honest *adj.* **1** °trustworthy, °truthful, veracious, trusty, °honourable, creditable, °decent, law-abiding, uncorrupted, uncorrupt, incorruptible, °ethical, °moral, °virtuous, °principled, °upright, high-minded, dependable, °reliable, °reputable, on the up and up: *How often does one meet an honest person in politics?* **2** °above-board, °straight, °square, square-dealing, °fair, °just, on the up and up, straightforward, °proper, °genuine, bona fide, °real, °authentic, *Colloq* on the °level, *US* square-shooting: *I write because I cannot earn an honest living. Would Felix give me an honest deal on a used car?* **3** °candid, °frank, °open, °plain, straightforward, °forthright, °direct, °sincere, °ingenuous, °explicit, °uninhibited, unreserved, unrestrained, unconstrained, °above-board, plain-spoken, unambiguous, unequivocal, *Colloq* upfront: *To be completely honest, I cannot stand the sight of you.* **4** °fair, °just, °equitable, °legitimate, valid, °rightful, °sound, °proper: *He gets an honest day's pay for an honest day's work.*

honestly *adv.* **1** truthfully, honourably, creditably, decently, ethically, morally, uprightly, dependably, reliably, in good °faith, justly, °fairly, equitably, even-handedly, disinterestedly, objectively, impartially: *In general, the police deal honestly with suspects.* **2** candidly, frankly, °openly, straightforwardly, forthrightly, °sincerely, °truly, ingenuously, unreservedly, °above-board, unambiguously, unequivocally, plainly, °simply, °straight (out), to one's face, in °plain words *or* English, bluntly: *I tell you honestly that I have never heard of the man.*

honesty *n.* **1** trustworthiness, uprightness, °rectitude, °probity, °integrity, °virtue, virtuousness, °honour: *As he will deal with large amounts of money, his honesty cannot be in question.* **2** truthfulness, veracity, °candour, openness, frankness, forthrightness, directness, straightforwardness, outspokenness, °sincerity, guilelessness, ingenuousness, bluntness: *You might not like what he says, but you have to admire his honesty.* **3** fairness, °equity, equitableness, even-handedness, °objectivity, impartiality, disinterestedness, justness, °justice: *We rely on the honesty of judges in meting out punishment to convicted felons.*

honorarium *n.* (token) °fee, compensation, recompense, °pay, °payment, °remuneration, emolument: *Would you be willing to accept an honorarium in lieu of your usual fee?*

honorary *adj.* °nominal, °titular, in °name *or* °title only, ex officio: *She has several honorary doctoral degrees, which is not bad for someone who never went to university.*

honour *n.* **1** °integrity, °honesty, fairness, justness, °probity, uprightness, decency, goodness, righteousness, °rectitude, °justice, °morality, °principles, virtuousness, °virtue: *Doing the right thing is a matter of honour.* **2** °respect, °esteem, °reverence, °veneration, approbation, °deference, °admiration, °homage, °regard, accolade, °praise, °kudos, °fame, °glory, °celebrity, °distinction, °prestige, illustriousness: *Great honour accompanies the award of a Nobel prize.* **3** °privilege, °distinction, °pleasure, °joy, °delight; °credit, °blessing: *I*

have the honour to introduce tonight's speaker. It has been an honour to serve under you, Admiral. **4** virginity, °chastity, °virtue, °purity, innocence: *How did she manage to preserve her honour when fighting with the partisans?* —*v.* **5** °respect, °esteem, °revere, °venerate, adulate, °adore, °worship, °approve, °prize, value, °defer to, °admire, pay °homage to: *Albert Schweitzer was much honoured in the latter part of his life.* **6** °praise, °laud, °glorify, °celebrate, °eulogize, °salute, °hail, acclaim, ennoble, °dignify, °exalt: *We have come together to honour those who have died for their country.* **7** °keep, °maintain, °carry out, °live up to, °discharge, °fulfil, °observe, °meet: *She has done her best to honour her obligations.* **8** °pay, °redeem, °accept, °clear, °cash: *The bank refused to honour his cheque because of 'insufficient funds'.*

honourable *adj.* **1** °upright, upstanding, °trustworthy, trusty, °honest, °just, °fair, °moral, °principled, uncorrupt, uncorrupted, incorruptible, high-minded, °noble, °virtuous: *Mark Antony referred to Caesar as an honourable man.* **2** °right, °correct, °proper, °fitting, °appropriate, °virtuous, °ethical, °worthy, °respectable, °reputable, °decent, °square: *I think you can count on Cedric to do the honourable thing.* **3** °fair (and °square), °impartial, °equitable, °just, °honest, unbiased, °unprejudiced, non-prejudicial, even-handed, °straight, °disinterested, guileless, °ingenuous, °artless, °open, °sincere, °above-board, on the up and up, undeceiving, undeceitful, *Colloq* upfront, on the °level: *Eleanor is too honourable to accept payment for work she did not do.* **4** °distinguished, °prestigious, °eminent, °notable, °noteworthy, °noted, °illustrious, °famous, famed, honoured, °exalted, respected, °celebrated, °renowned, acclaimed, °well-thought-of: *Ian enjoys an honourable reputation as a publisher.*

hoodlum *n.* °gangster, °thug, °racketeer, mobster, desperado, °terrorist, ruffian, °tough, °rowdy, knave, *Colloq* hooligan, baddy, crook, *US* plug-ugly, *Slang* goon, *Brit* yob, yobbo, *US* mug, bad actor, roughneck, hood, gunsel, hit man, torpedo, *French* apache, *Australian* larrikin: *He has a few hoodlums on the payroll who do the dirty work.*

hoodwink *v.* °fool, °trick, °deceive, delude, °dupe, gull, °hoax, °defraud, °mislead, humbug, °outwit, *Colloq* bamboozle, pull the wool over (someone's) eyes, pull a fast one on, °lead (someone) up *or* down the garden path, °put one over on (someone), throw dust in (someone's) eyes, take (someone) for a °ride, °string (someone) along, *Slang* rook, con, suck in, *US* °sucker in, snow: *They are trying to hoodwink the voters into believing that the recession is over.*

hook *n.* **1** hanger, °peg, holder; fastener, catch, °clasp, °clip, °pin: *Hang your hat on that hook. I'm using a safety pin because the hook on my dress is gone.* **2** °snare, °trap; fish-hook: *What can we use as a hook to catch the fish?* **3 by hook or by crook:** °somehow (or other), someway, come what may, by fair means or foul, (by) one way or another: *I have to get out of this place by hook or by crook.* **4 hook, line, and sinker:** °completely, °entirely, all the way, through and through, °thoroughly, °totally, °utterly, °wholly: *She actually fell for that old routine hook,*

line, and sinker. **5 off the hook**: (set) °free, (in the) °clear, out of it; out of °trouble, acquitted, exonerated, cleared, °let off, vindicated, °off: *After paying them the extortion money, he still wasn't off the hook.*
—*v.* **6** °catch, °trap, entrap, °snare, ensnare; °grab, °capture, collar, °nab, °seize; *Chiefly US and Canadian* °snag, *Colloq* °pinch: *The petty crooks have been caught but we now want to hook the big fish himself.* **7** °steal, °pilfer, filch, palm, shoplift, °rob, *Slang* snitch, °rip off, *Euphemistic* °liberate, °remove, °borrow, °appropriate, *Brit* °nick, *Chiefly Brit* °pinch: *They used to hook sweets from Woolies'.*

hop *v.* **1** °jump, °leap, °bound, °spring, vault; °skip, °caper, gambol, °dance: *Here comes Peter Cottontail, Hopping down the bunny trail.* **2** take a (short) °trip *or* voyage, °travel, °come, °go, °proceed; °fly: *Those yuppies think nothing of hopping over to Paris just for dinner.*
—*n.* **3** °jump, °leap, °bound, °spring, vault; °skip, °caper, °dance: *In a few hops the bird was off the branch and onto my finger.* **4** (short) °trip *or* °flight *or* °journey *or* voyage: *The Bahamas are just a hop from Miami.*

hope *n.* **1** °desire, °wish, °expectation, yearning, hankering, craving, °longing, °fancy; °ambition, (day-)dream: *It was always my hope that you would go to university.* **2** °prospect, °promise, °expectation, expectancy, °confidence, °anticipation, assumption, °security, °faith, °conviction, °belief, °trust: *We had given up hope of being rescued.*
—*v.* **3** °aspire, °count *or* °rely on *or* upon, °anticipate, °contemplate, °foresee, °look forward to, °expect, await, °wait: *After all these years, he is still hoping to meet the girl of his dreams.* **4** °trust; °wish, °want, °desire; *Dialect* °expect: *I hope my ship will come in soon. I hope to see the last of her tomorrow.*

hopeful *adj.* **1** °expectant, anticipating, °optimistic, °sanguine, °confident, assured: *We are hopeful of victory in the forthcoming election.* **2** °promising, °bright, °rosy, reassuring, heartening, encouraging, auspicious, °propitious, inspiriting: *Today was a disaster, but tomorrow looks more hopeful.*

hopefully *adv.* **1** expectantly, optimistically, sanguinely, confidently: *Jocelyn set off hopefully for the party.* **2** with (any) °luck, if things go well, all being well, it is hoped, expectedly: *Hopefully, we shall arrive in time to catch the train.*

hopeless *adj.* **1** °desperate, beyond hope *or* saving, irreparable, beyond repair, irremediable, °lost, gone, °irretrievable; °incurable, °terminal, °deadly, °fatal, °lethal: *As their ship drifted into the intergalactic void, they saw that their situation was hopeless. They told me that her condition was hopeless.* **2** °bad, °poor, °incompetent, °inferior, °inadequate, °inept, °unqualified, unfit, unskilful, °deficient: *You might make a good surgeon, but as a judge of human nature you're hopeless.* **3** despairing, °despondent, °forlorn, °woebegone, disconsolate, °inconsolable, depressed, °dejected, °melancholy, downcast, °gloomy, °miserable, discouraged, °wretched, lugubrious, °funereal, °sorrowful, °sad, °unhappy: *Utterly hopeless after his script was rejected by Hollywood, he moped in his room.* **4** °futile, °vain, °bootless, unavailing,

°impossible, °impracticable, unworkable, °pointless, °worthless, °useless: *It would be hopeless to try to send out a lifeboat in this storm.*

horizon *n.* °view, purview, °range, °scope, vista, compass, °perspective, °prospect, ken, field of °vision, °limit(s): *This is something that lies beyond the horizon of present-day knowledge.*

horizontal *adj.* °level, °flat, °plane; °prone, °supine: *Make sure that the plank is horizontal before fastening it down. They say that dancing is merely a vertical expression of a horizontal desire.*

horrible *adj.* **1** °awful, horrendous, horrid, horrifying, horrific, °terrible, °terrifying, °dreadful, °abominable, °abhorrent, appalling, °frightening, °frightful, °ghastly, °grim, °grisly, °ghoulish, °gruesome, °loathsome, °hideous, °repulsive, °revolting, °disgusting, sickening, nauseating, °nauseous, °harrowing, blood-curdling, °macabre, unspeakable, °shocking: *The horrible sight of her father's mangled body haunted her for the rest of her days.* **2** °awful, °nasty, unpleasant, °disagreeable, horrid, °terrible, °dreadful, °obnoxious, °offensive, °atrocious, °monstrous, °contemptible, detestable, °despicable, *Colloq Brit* °beastly: *The food was perfectly horrible at our hotel. Take that horrible little dog away.*

horrify *v.* **1** °terrify, °frighten, °scare, °alarm, °intimidate, °panic, °scare *or* °frighten to death, °petrify, *Colloq* °scare *or* °frighten the living daylights out of, °scare stiff, make (someone's) hair stand on end, °make (someone's *or* the) blood run cold, curl (someone's) hair, °scare the pants off: *I was horrified to see the attack dogs racing towards me.* **2** °shock, °startle, upset, °put off, °outrage, °dismay, °appal, °distress, discountenance, disconcert: *I was horrified to hear that you weren't coming to my party.*

horror *n.* **1** °fear *and* °loathing, repugnance, °terror, °dread, hatred, °revulsion, detestation, abhorrence, °distaste, °dislike; °aversion, antipathy, °hostility, °animosity, animus, °rancour; odium, execration: *She has a horror of bats.* **2** °fear, °dismay, °distress, °dread, °fright, °alarm, °upset, perturbation, °panic, °terror, °fear and trembling, trepidation, °anxiety, angst, apprehension, uneasiness, queasiness, nervousness, awe: *The doctor helped me overcome my horror of flying.*

hors-d'œuvre *n.* appetizer, apéritif, antipasto, smorgasbord *or* smörgåsbord, °relish; *Chiefly Brit* starter; *Archaic* warner: *A Sauvignon was served with the hors-d'œuvre, which was gravadlax.*

hospitable *adj.* **1** welcoming, °gracious, °courteous, °genial, °friendly, °agreeable, °amicable, °cordial, °warm, congenial, °sociable, °generous: *It was most hospitable of you to invite me.* **2** open-minded, °receptive, amenable, approachable, °tolerant: *The director is always hospitable to suggestions for improving sales.*

hospital *n.* medical °centre, °health °centre, °infirmary, clinic, polyclinic, dispensary, sickbay; asylum, °sanatorium, nursing °home, convalescent °home *or* °facility, *US* sanitarium: *With that wound, you ought to be in a hospital.*

hospitality *n.* graciousness, °courtesy, courteousness, friendliness, amicability, cordiality, °warmth, congeniality, sociability, generosity: *I am grateful for the hospitality you showed my sister during her visit.*

host[1] *n.* **1** hostess, innkeeper, hotelier, hotel-keeper, hotelman, °landlord *or* °landlady, °manager *or* manageress, °proprietor *or* proprietress, *Brit* publican: *As host, it is my responsibility to greet the guests.* **2** entertainer, °master *or* °mistress of ceremonies, emcee, MC, °announcer, *Brit* presenter, compère, *US* tummler: *For twenty years he has been the host of popular TV quiz shows.*
—*v.* **3** °entertain, act *or* play the host *or* hostess, °have: *She hosts a dinner-party for close friends every Wednesday.*

host[2] *n.* army, °swarm, °crowd, horde, multitude, °throng, °mob, °pack, °herd, troop, legion, °body, °assembly, assemblage, drove: *The rock group turned up with a host of followers, their so-called groupies.*

hostage *n.* °pledge, °security, surety, °pawn, °captive, °prisoner, gage: *The terrorists threatened that if their demands were not met they would kill the hostages.*

hostile *adj.* **1** °opposed, antagonistic, °contrary, against, anti, adverse; °averse, °loath: *The government is hostile to curbs on business.* **2** unfriendly, inimical, °unsympathetic, °cold, °inhospitable; unfavourable: *Why do many social workers seem hostile to the people they are supposed to help? The polar regions are very hostile environments to man.* **3** warring, °belligerent, bellicose, °warlike, combative, °militant, °aggressive: *The UN units function as a buffer between the hostile forces.*

hostility *n.* **1** °antagonism, °opposition, enmity, °animosity, antipathy, animus, °ill will, malevolence, malice, °aversion, unfriendliness: *Do you still harbour the feelings of hostility towards them that you had during the war? The petty quarrels broke out into open hostility.* **2** **hostilities**: °war, warfare, fighting, °combat, °action, state of °war, °bloodshed: *Hostilities ceased when the factions agreed to parley.*

hot *adj.* **1** °fiery, white-hot, red-hot, piping hot, °burning, blistering, °scorching, roasting, frying, sizzling, searing, boiling, scalding, steaming, simmering, °torrid, °sweltering, °sultry, °heated: *The hot, molten steel is cast into ingots here. During the day it is hot, but it cools down at night.* **2** °spicy, peppery, °sharp, piquant, °pungent, °biting, acrid: *She likes very hot food, with plenty of chilli.* **3** °intense, °fervent, zealous, °ardent, °enthusiastic, °passionate, fervid, vehement, °excited, °animated; °impetuous, °fiery, °fierce, °inflamed, °sharp, °violent: *He had some hot words with the foreman who had dismissed him.* **4** °eager, °keen, avid, °anxious, °burning; °intense, °fervent, zealous, °ardent, °enthusiastic, °passionate, fervid, vehement, °excited, °animated, earnest, *Slang US* gung-ho: *Desmond set out in hot pursuit of the thief.* **5** °recent, °fresh, °new, °latest, °brand-new: *The hottest gossip is that she is marrying for the seventh time.* **6** °popular, sought-after, commercial, saleable, marketable: *The publisher believes Zenobia's Memoirs to be the hot property of the year.* **7** °lustful, °lecherous, libidinous, lubricous *or* lubricious, °sensual, concupiscent, °prurient, licentious, oversexed, sex-crazed, sex-mad, *Archaic* lickerish, horn-mad, *Slang* horny, *Chiefly Brit* °randy, *US* °hard up: *They were really hot, not having been with anyone of the opposite sex for months.* **8** °intense, °vivid,

°striking, °bright, °brilliant, °dazzling, °loud: *That hot pink lipstick looks good with your suntan.* **9** electrified, °live, charged, powered: *The hot wire connects to the other terminal—I think.* **10** °dangerous, °precarious, °risky, °sensitive, °delicate, °unstable, °touchy, unpredictable: *The situation is getting a bit too hot to handle.*
—*v.* **11** **hot up**: °intensify, °build up, °heighten, °increase, °worsen, °warm up, °heat up: *The environment is hotting up as a political issue.*

hot air *n.* blather *or* blether, bunkum, verbiage, °talk, °wind, pretentiousness, pomposity, °bombast, grandiloquence, magniloquence, flatulence, gasconade, rodomontade, *Colloq* claptrap, bosh, gas, guff: *Management's promises of pay increases were nothing but hot air.*

hotbed *n.* breeding ground, fertile source: *Slums are a hotbed of crime.*

hotchpotch *n.* °miscellany, °mixture, gallimaufry, °jumble, farrago, mélange, °mishmash, °mess, °tangle, °medley, °hash, conglomeration, agglomeration, olio, olla podrida, °pot-pourri, rag-bag, °welter, *US and Canadian* hodgepodge, *Colloq* omnium gatherum, mixed bag: *That hotchpotch of junk is scarcely what I should call an 'antiques collection'.*

hotel *n.* hostelry, inn, °lodging, caravanserai; motel, motor hotel, bed and breakfast *or* B & B, guest-house, °pension, *Australian and New Zealand* °pub, *US* tourist °house: *We are staying at a small hotel just outside of town.*

hotheaded *adj.* °impetuous, headlong, hot-tempered, °quick-tempered, °volatile, °rash, °hasty, °wild, °foolhardy, °reckless, °precipitate, °thoughtless, °heedless, madcap, °daredevil, devil-may-care: *He is too hotheaded to succeed in the diplomatic corps.*

hothouse *n.* **1** °hotbed, greenhouse, glasshouse, conservatory: *These tomatoes were grown during the winter in our hothouse.*
—*adj.* **2** °dainty, °delicate, °sensitive, °fragile, °frail, pampered, overprotected, sheltered, shielded, spoiled, coddled, babied: *She was glad to exchange the hothouse atmosphere of the university for the real world.*

hotly *adv.* intensively, energetically, doggedly, persistently, zealously, fervently, fervidly, ardently, °warmly, enthusiastically: *Hotly pursued by the police, I managed to hide in a culvert.*

hound *v.* °bully, °browbeat, °persecute, °nag, °harass, °annoy, °pester, harry, badger: *Although he was found innocent, his neighbours hounded him so much that he had to leave town.*

house *n.* **1** °residence, °dwelling, dwelling-place, °home, °abode, household, homestead, °domicile, °lodging(s), quarters, °building, edifice: *We are playing bridge at my house next Saturday.* **2** °family, °line, °lineage, °dynasty, °clan, ancestry, °strain, °race, blood, descendants, forebears: *She is a member of the royal house of Sweden.* **3** legislature, legislative °body, congress, °parliament, °assembly, °council, °diet: *Both houses of the legislature passed the bill.* **4** °establishment, °firm, °concern, °company, °business, °organization, °enterprise, °undertaking, *Colloq* °outfit: *He has gone from one publishing house to another with his manuscript.* **5** auditorium, °theatre, concert-hall: *The house is sold out.* **6** house of °ill repute *or* °ill fame *or* prostitution, °brothel, whore-house,

bagnio, bordello, *Archaic* bawdy-house, *Colloq* sporting house, crib, *Slang US* cat-house: *She used to run a house in Lambeth.* **7 on the house:** °free, gratis, for °nothing, as a °gift: *Drinks will be on the house tonight to celebrate the tenth anniversary of our opening.*
—v. **8** °shelter, °accommodate, °domicile, °lodge, °quarter, °put up, °take in, °board, billet, °harbour: *We have housed as many as ten people at a time in the cottage.* **9** °contain, °accommodate, °quarter: *This building houses our computer operations.*

housing *n.* **1** °homes, °houses, °lodging(s), quarters, °accommodation, habitation, °dwelling; °shelter, °protection: *The Council is trying to provide housing for the elderly.* **2** °case, casing, °cover, covering, °enclosure, container, °box, °shield: *We keep the sensitive equipment in a dust-proof housing.*

hovel *n.* °hole, °shack, shanty, (pig)sty, pigpen, coop, crib, °hut, *Colloq US* °dump: *The beggar lives in a hovel near the railway station.*

hover *v.* **1** °drift, °poise, °float, °hang, be *or* °hang suspended, °hang in the air: *The humming bird hovers over a flower, drinking its nectar.* **2** °linger, loiter, °wait, °hang about *or* around: *The waiter's constant hovering about is making me nervous.*

however *adv.* **1** °notwithstanding, °regardless, °nevertheless, °nonetheless, °despite that, in °spite of that, °still, but, °though, °yet, °even so, be that as it may, come what may, no matter what; at any °rate, anyway, anyhow, on the other hand, in all events, in any °event, in any °case, after all: *He insisted the council should give their approval; however, that is not their responsibility. I was ready to move to Cardiff; she didn't offer me the job, however.* **2** to whatever °manner *or* °extent *or* °degree, howsoever, no matter how, in any °way *or* °manner *or* °respect, anyhow, how, in whatever °way *or* °manner: *However you view it, he is still the boss. Spend the money however you see fit.*
—conj. **3** how, how on earth, how in the world, in what °way *or* °manner: *However do you manage with only three to help, you poor thing?* **4** no matter how, °regardless how, putting *or* °setting aside how, °notwithstanding how: *However much she earns, she is always short of money.*

howl *v.* **1** yowl, °cry, wail, ululate, bay; °shout, °yell, °bellow, °scream, °roar, *Colloq* holler: *The wolves were howling at the moon last night. He howled with pain when he caught his finger in the door.*
—n. **2** yowl, yowling, ululation, ululating, wail, wailing, yelp, yelping, °cry, °shout, °yell, °bellow, °scream, °roar, *Colloq* holler: *The wolf's howl is an eerie, chilling sound. I kicked him and he let out a howl.*

howler *n.* °blunder, °mistake, °error, gaffe; malapropism, Irish bull; *Brit* bloomer, *US* clinker, *Colloq Brit* clanger, *US* boner: *One paper contained the howler, 'Money is the route of all evil', which the author explained should be corrected to, 'The love of money is the root of all evil.'*

hub *n.* °centre, °focus, °focal °point, °pivot, °heart, °core, °nucleus, nave: *This is the hub of the city, around which everything else moves.*

huddle *n.* **1** °cluster, °group, °bunch, °clump, °pack, °herd, °crowd, °throng, °mass: *Everyone*

got into a huddle, trying to keep warm. **2** °meeting, °conference, °discussion, consultation: *They were in a huddle, deciding what to do next.*
—v. **3** °cluster, °gather, °crowd *or* °press together, °throng *or* °flock together, °nestle, °jam *or* °cram together, °squeeze together: *We huddled in basements during air raids.* **4** °meet, °discuss, °confer, °consult: *Let's huddle on this question of the advertising schedule.*

hue *n.* °colour, °tint, °shade, tinge, °tone, °cast, tincture, *Technical* chroma: *The dust in the atmosphere gives the sunsets a reddish hue.*

huff *n.* **1 in a huff:** piqued, peeved, °testy, irritated, angered, vexed, annoyed, in high dudgeon, provoked, exasperated, °petulant, in a °pet, *Colloq* (all) het up: *She went off in a huff because I didn't praise her painting.*
—v. **2** °puff, °blow, °bluster: *When I complained about the food, the manager simply huffed and puffed and walked away.*

hug *v.* **1** °embrace, °clasp, °squeeze, °cuddle, °snuggle, *Archaic or literary* °clip: *They hugged each other warmly, then kissed goodbye.* **2** °follow closely, °cling to, stay *or* keep °near *or* °close to: *We hugged the ground as the bullets whizzed by overhead.*
—n. **3** °embrace, °clasp, °squeeze, *Colloq* °clinch: *She saw me, ran over, and gave me a big hug.*

huge *adj.* °large, °great, °enormous, °gigantic, °giant, °immense, °massive, tremendous, gargantuan, °prodigious, mammoth, °colossal, °monumental, Brobdingnagian, titanic, stupendous, elephantine, leviathan, °mountainous, °vast, *Colloq* °jumbo, °whopping: *The red spot on Jupiter is so huge it could swallow the earth several times over.*

hulk *n.* **1** shipwreck, °wreck, °derelict, °shell, skeleton: *The rusting hulk of the once-proud ship is tied up at the dock.* **2** oaf, °clod, lout, ox, *Slang US* galoot *or* galloot, klutz: *Don't tell me that hulk of a man painted these delicate miniatures!*

hulking *adj.* °clumsy, °awkward, ungainly, lubberly, oafish, loutish; °unwieldy, cumbersome, °bulky, °ponderous, °massive, °ungraceful, inelegant: *Their great hulking son could no longer fit into his clothes. That hulking monolith of an office building dominates the entire neighbourhood.*

hull *n.* **1** framework, skeleton, °frame, °structure, °body: *The hull of the ship completed, we added the superstructure.* **2** °shell, pod, °case, husk, °skin, °peel, °rind, *US* shuck: *Squirrels carefully nibble through the hull of the nut to get at the kernel inside.*
—v. **3** °shell, °peel, °skin, husk, *US* shuck: *We hulled all the nuts and they are now ready for the fruit cake.*

hum *v.* **1** °buzz, drone, thrum, °murmur, whirr, purr, °vibrate, *Technical* bombinate *or* bombilate: *I want to smell the wild flowers and hear the bees hum once again.* **2** bustle, °stir, be °active, °move briskly, *Colloq* tick (over): *Within three months of completion, the new plant was humming.* **3** intone: *I said, 'Do you know your rock guitar is keeping me awake?', and he replied, 'No, man, but if you hum it I'll try to play it.'*
—n. **4** °buzz, buzzing, drone, droning, thrum, thrumming, °murmur, murmuring, murmuration, whirr, whirring, purr, purring, vibration: *From the other room came the hum of conversation.*

human *adj.* **1** °mortal, anthropoid, hominoid, android; hominid; *Possibly offensive* manlike: *The aliens from the spaceship had few human characteristics. It is human nature to think.* **2** °sensitive, °defenceless, °weak, fallible, °vulnerable: *She is human, too, and can be easily hurt.* **3** °kind, °kindly, kind-hearted, °considerate, °charitable, compassionate, °merciful, °benign, benignant, °tender, °gentle, °forgiving, °lenient, °benevolent, beneficent, °generous, magnanimous, °humanitarian, °understanding, °accommodating, °sympathetic, °good-natured, humane, °sensitive: *Human concern for others is in short supply these days.*
—*n.* **4** human being, °person, °individual, °woman, °man, °child, °mortal, °one, °soul, someone, °somebody: *Humans have long maltreated many of the animals on which they depend.*

humanitarian *adj.* **1** See **human**, 3, above.
—*n.* **2** Good Samaritan, °benefactor *or* benefactress, °philanthropist, altruist: *Because of her charitable works, Lady Pendleton is thought of as a great humanitarian.*

humanity *n.* **1** °human °race, °people, °society, humankind, Homo sapiens; the °public, the masses, community; *Possibly offensive* °man, mankind: *From what we are told, humanity took millions of years to evolve.* **2** humanness, °human °nature, mortality: *On his first voyage to Mars, Kollworth began to doubt his own humanity.* **3** °kindness, kindliness, kind-heartedness, °consideration, helpfulness, charitableness, open-heartedness, warm-heartedness, °good °will, °benevolence, compassion, mercifulness, °mercy, benignity, tenderness, °warmth, gentleness, leniency *or* lenience *or* lenity, beneficence, generosity, unselfishness, magnanimity, °understanding, °sympathy, °sensitivity: *It was owing to the humanity of our neighbours that we survived the bombing.*

humble *adj.* **1** °modest, °reserved, unpretentious, unostentatious, self-effacing, unassuming, unpresuming: *For someone who has accomplished so much, she is quite humble.* **2** °submissive, °meek, °servile, °obsequious, deferential, °mild, °respectful, subservient, °subdued: *Usually pompous, Nigel became humble in the presence of the chairman.* **3** °lowly, °low, °inferior, °mean, ignoble, °ordinary, °plebeian, °common, °simple, °obscure, unprepossessing, unimportant, °undistinguished, °insignificant; low-born, °base, base-born: *He lives in a humble cottage. Though she came from a humble background, she rose to become prime minister.*
—*v.* **4** °chasten, °bring *or* °pull down, °subdue, abase, °debase, demean, °lower, °degrade, °downgrade, °reduce, make (someone) eat humble pie, lose °face, °shame, °humiliate, °crush, °break, °mortify, chagrin, *Colloq* °put down, °take (someone) down a peg or notch: *He found army discipline a humbling experience.*

humdrum *adj.* °dull, °boring, °tedious, °tiresome, wearisome, °monotonous, unvaried, unvarying, °routine, undiversified, unchanging, °repetitious, uneventful, unexciting, uninteresting, °prosaic, mundane, °ordinary, commonplace, °common, °banal, °dry, insipid, jejune: *They saw no way of escaping from their humdrum lives.*

humid *adj.* °damp, °moist, °muggy, °clammy, °sticky, °steamy, soggy, °sultry, °wet: *The weather has been oppressively hot and humid all week.*

humiliate *v.* See **humble**, 4, above.

humiliation *n.* °disgrace, °shame, mortification, °dishonour, ignominy, °indignity, °discredit, loss of °face, obloquy, abasement, depreciation, detraction, °degradation, derogation, belittlement, disparagement, shaming, °embarrassment, humbling: *He had to suffer the humiliation of being drummed out of the corps.*

humility *n.* modesty, meekness, self-effacement, shyness, diffidence, timidity, timorousness, meekness, bashfulness, mildness, unpretentiousness, submissiveness, °servility, self-abasement, lowliness: *She sees humility as dissatisfaction with oneself on account of some defect or infirmity.*

humorous *adj.* °funny, comical, facetious, laughable, risible, °ludicrous, °farcical, side-splitting, °hilarious, °merry; droll, °whimsical, amusing, °witty, waggish, jocular, jocose, °playful, °pleasant, *Colloq* °hysterical: *The humorous parts of the play sent the audience into gales of laughter.*

humour *n.* **1** funniness, comedy, °wit, facetiousness, ludicrousness, drollery, jocoseness *or* jocosity, jocularity, waggishness, °raillery, °banter: *One writer defined humour as 'the happy compound of pathos and playfulness', another referred to the sense of humour as a 'modulating and restraining balance-wheel'.* **2** comedy, farce °jokes, jests, witticisms, °wit, *Slang* wisecracks, gags: *Milton was scarcely known as a writer of humour.* **3** °mood, °frame of mind, °temper; °spirit(s); °disposition, °nature, temperament: *She is in a bad humour till after breakfast.*
—*v.* **4** soothe, °gratify, placate, °please, mollify, °indulge, appease, °pamper, cosset, °coddle, mollycoddle, °jolly, °baby, °spoil: *They are trying to humour him because he's in a bad mood.*

hump *n.* **1** °bulge, °lump, °bump, protuberance, °protrusion, °projection, °knob, node, °mass, °hunch, enlargement, °swelling, °growth, excrescence, tumefaction, tumescence; °mound, barrow, °tell, hummock, hillock, tumulus, *Brit dialect* tump: *Digging into the hump near the trees, we uncovered an ancient burial-ground.*
—*v.* **2** °hunch, °arch, curve, crook, °bend: *Sulking in the corner, he humped his back and refused to speak to anyone.* **3** °drag, °lug, °haul, °carry, °heave: *She had to hump two heavy suitcases all the way from the railway station.*

hunch *n.* **1** (intuitive) °guess, °intuition, °feeling, °impression, °suspicion, °premonition, presentiment: *I had a hunch they would be late.* **2** See **hump**, 1, above.
—*v.* **3** See **hump**, 2, above.

hunger *n.* **1** hungriness, °emptiness, °appetite, ravenousness, voraciousness, voracity; °famine, starvation: *We ate leaves to stave off the pangs of hunger. Some optimists hope to eliminate hunger from the planet by the year 2000.* **2** yearning, °desire, craving, °itch, °thirst, °longing, hankering, °mania, cupidity, *Formal* cacoethes, *Colloq* yen: *She felt an insatiable hunger for intellectual companionship.*
—*v.* **3** Usually, **hunger for** *or* **after**: crave, °yearn, °desire, °thirst, °want, °hanker, *Colloq* yen, have a yen: *Blessed are they who hunger and thirst after righteousness.*

hungry adj. **1** °famished, °starved, starving, °ravenous, °voracious, °empty, °hollow, Colloq chiefly Brit peckish: I'm hungry enough to eat a horse. **2** craving, covetous, °eager, avid, °greedy, °keen, yearning, °desirous, °longing, hungering, thirsting, starving, °dying, Colloq hankering: Marooned for years, Crusoe was hungry for the sight of another human being. **3** acquisitive, °greedy, °thirsty, insatiable, °deprived: The parched, hungry earth drank up the rain.

hunt v. **1** °chase, °pursue, dog, °hound, °stalk, °trail, °track (down), °trace; °course: The jewel thieves were hunted across three continents. **2** Also, **hunt for** or **up** or **out** or **through**: °seek (out), °search (for), go in °search of or for, °look (high and low) for, °quest after, go in °quest of, °scour, °ransack, °investigate, °pry into, go over or through with a fine-tooth comb, °examine, °explore, Colloq US °check out: Detectives hunted the carpet for clues. She is hunting a job in publishing. I have hunted for the ring but cannot find it. Can you hunt up someone to fill the vacancy? Hunt through your pockets again for the key.
—n. **3** °chase, °pursuit, tracking (down), stalking, hunting; °course: The ten-year hunt for the thieves continues. **4** °search, °quest: My hunt ended when I found the ring.

hunter n. huntsman, huntswoman, stalker, tracker, Nimrod, Orion; huntress: An expert hunter, she bagged three tigers last year.

hurdle n. **1** °barrier, °obstacle, °impediment, °hindrance, °obstruction, °bar, °handicap, °restraint, °snag, (stumbling) °block, °check, °difficulty, °complication, °interference: Can she overcome the hurdle of prejudice against women?
—v. **2** °leap (over), vault (over), °jump (over): The fugitive easily hurdled the fence around the compound.

hurl v. °throw, °toss, °shy, °sling, °fling, °pitch, °cast, °send, °fire, °heave, °propel, let °fly, Colloq chuck: The fast bowler hurled the ball past the batsman.

hurricane n. cyclone, tornado, typhoon, °whirlwind, °twister, wind-storm, °storm, °gale, °blow: The 1985 hurricane destroyed millions of trees.

hurried adj. **1** °hasty, °feverish, °frantic, °hectic, °breakneck, frenetic, °impetuous, rushed, °precipitate, °swift, quick, °speedy; °brief, °short: We ate a hurried lunch before leaving to catch the train. **2** °superficial, °cursory, °offhand, °perfunctory, slapdash: Airport security guards made only a hurried examination of the hand luggage.

hurry v. **1** °rush, °hasten, °make °haste, °speed, °race, °dash, °hustle, °scurry, °tear, °fly, °run, °shoot, scoot, scamper, scuttle, hotfoot (it), Colloq shake a leg, get cracking, get a °move on, go hell for leather, skedaddle, °step on it, °step on the gas, Chiefly US hightail (it), go like greased lightning, get a wiggle on: You'll have to hurry to catch your bus. **2** °speed up, accelerate, °hasten, °rush, °push, °press, °expedite; °urge, egg: Such changes take time and can't be hurried. She hurried the children along so that they wouldn't miss the bus.
—n. **3** °haste, °rush, °urgency, °eagerness; °agitation, disquiet, °upset, dither, °fuss, bustle, ado, to-do, °furore or US furor, commotion, turmoil, °stir, pother; Colloq °stew, °sweat: Why all the hurry to finish before dark? He's in an awful hurry to get home.

hurt v. **1** °harm, °injure, °wound; °damage, °impair, °mar, °spoil, °vitiate, °ruin: She's so gentle she wouldn't hurt a fly. The scandal hurt the candidate's chances of election. **2** °ache, °smart, °pain, °pinch, °sting, °burn, °torment, °gripe: My elbow really hurts where I hit it. **3** °distress, °grieve, °affect, °afflict, aggrieve, °depress, °upset, °disappoint, °pain, °cut to the quick, affront, °offend: Sticks and stones may break my bones but names will never hurt me. You always hurt the one you love. **4** °injure, °maim, °wound, °cripple, °lame, disable, °incapacitate, °damage, °mutilate, °mangle: Three people have been badly hurt in a car crash on the motorway.
—n. **5** °harm, °injury, °damage, °detriment, °disadvantage: How much more hurt can you cause beyond what you have done already? **6** °ache, °pain, °pang, °distress, °discomfort, °suffering, °torment, torture, °agony; °anguish, °misery, °woe, dolour, °sadness, °depression: If you rub on this ointment, the hurt will go away. You cannot imagine the hurt we felt when he failed his examinations.
—adj. **7** injured, wronged, pained, rueful, grieved, °unhappy, aggrieved, °sad, °wretched, °woebegone, °sorrowful, °mournful, depressed, °dejected, °dismal, °gloomy, °melancholy: Whenever I mention getting a job she gets that hurt expression on her face. **8** damaged, °defective, marred, impaired, °broken, °worn, °dilapidated, shop-worn, scratched, bruised, scarred: They are holding a sale of hurt merchandise at the warehouse tomorrow.

hurtful adj. **1** °harmful, °injurious, °detrimental, pernicious, °prejudicial, disadvantageous, damaging, deleterious, °destructive, noisome, noxious, baneful, °mischievous: Efficient government is advantageous to many and hurtful to none. **2** °nasty, °cruel, °cutting, malicious, °mean, °unkind, wounding, °spiteful: He made some hurtful accusations about the librarian's efficiency.

hurtle v. °rush (headlong), °tear, °shoot, °race, °speed; °plunge: The car hurtled round the corner and crashed into a tree. Two bodies hurtled past me into the abyss below.

husband n. **1** °mate, spouse, °groom, bridegroom, °partner, Colloq old °man, hubby: My husband and I take turns cleaning the house.
—v. **2** °save, °keep, °retain, °hoard, °conserve, °preserve, °store; budget, °economize (on), °manage: If we husband our resources, we shall have enough for a rainy day.

hush interj. **1** Shush!, Quiet!, Be or Keep °quiet or °silent or °still!, Hold your °tongue!, Mum's the word!, Slang Shut up!, Clam up!, Shut your °trap!, Button your lip!, Shut your °gob!, Brit Belt up!, US Hush up!, Shut your °face!, US dialect Hush your °mouth!: Hush! You're in a library.
—v. **2** shush, °silence, °still, °quiet(en): I wish she'd hush the child's wailing. **3** °suppress, °mute, °soften, soft-pedal, °whisper: They spoke in hushed tones. **4** Usually, **hush up**: °suppress, °repress, °quash, °cover up, °hide, °conceal, °keep °quiet, Colloq °squelch: They tried to hush up the news about his extramarital affairs. **5** soothe, allay, °calm, °quiet(en), mollify, pacify, placate, °tranquillize: Our worst fears were hushed by father's comforting words.

—*n.* **6** °silence, °quiet, stillness, °peace, tranquillity: *A hush came over the crowd as she rose to speak.*

husky *adj.* **1** °brawny, strapping, °sturdy, °burly, well-built, °robust, °hefty, °rugged, °powerful, °strong, °stout, thickset, °muscular, °tough, *Colloq* beefy: *Two husky men arrived to move the piano.* **2** hoarse, °gruff, °dry, °harsh, rasping, °rough, °raucous: *She has a deep, husky voice I would recognize anywhere.*

hustle *v.* **1** °rush, °push, °hurry, °hasten, °run, °dash, scamper, scuttle, °scurry, sprint: *Mrs Grumble hustles off to the market every morning. He said that one must really hustle to make a living these days.* **2** shove, °push, °drive, °force, °hasten, °expedite, °press: *The bill was hustled through the legislature in just one day.* **3** shove, °crowd, °push, jostle, elbow, °thrust, °force: *She tried to hustle her way to the front of the queue.* **4** °push, °eject, °force, coerce, °drive, *Colloq* °bounce: *He was hustled out the back door.* —*n.* **5** pushing, jostling, buffeting, jarring, elbowing, shoving, nudging: *We always take taxis to avoid the hustle in the underground.* **6** °activity, °action, °stir, °movement: *I can't concentrate with all the hustle and bustle going on in the office.*

hut *n.* °cabin, °shack, shanty, °shed, lean-to, °shelter, cote, *Literary* cot, *Australian* gunyah: *We found a tiny hut where we could keep out of the storm.*

hybrid *n.* °mixture, cross-breed, half-breed, °mongrel, °cross, composite, °combination, °compound: *The best wheat for this region is a hybrid developed in our laboratory.*

hygienic *adj.* °clean, °sanitary, °sterile, disinfected, germ-free, aseptic, °pure: *It is essential that hygienic surroundings be maintained in hospitals.*

hypnotize *v.* °fascinate, mesmerize, °entrance, °cast a °spell over *or* on, °captivate, °enchant, °charm, spellbind, °bewitch, °enrapture, ensorcell, °transport: *Greg is completely hypnotized by that singer at Felipe's nightclub.*

hypocrisy *n.* °deceit, deceitfulness, duplicity, double-dealing, °deception, °chicanery, guile, quackery, charlatanism *or* charlatanry, falseness, fakery, °lying, mendacity, Pharisaism *or* Phariseeism, Tartuffery, insincerity, two-facedness, sanctimony, sanctimoniousness, *Colloq* phoneyness *or US also* phoniness: *I loath hypocrisy and double standards.*

hypocrite *n.* deceiver, double-dealer, °quack, charlatan, °impostor *or* imposter, mountebank, °confidence man *or* trickster, faker, °pretender, °liar, °Pharisee, whited sepulchre, Tartuffe, flimflammer, *Colloq* °phoney *or US also* phony, con man, flimflam man *or* artist, two-face: *It is incredible that so many were duped by that hypocrite.*

hypocritical *adj.* °deceptive, °deceitful, deceiving, °insincere, dissembling, feigning, dissimulating, double-dealing, °false, °fake, faking, °two-faced, pretending, °lying, °Pharisaic(al), °sanctimonious, °dishonest, underhand, treacherous, °perfidious, untrustworthy: *He regards the Victorians as nothing but smug prudes and hypocritical moralizers.*

hypothesis *n.* theory, °theorem, postulate, °premise *or* premiss, °proposition, assumption, °supposition, °speculation: *Cadwallader's Hypothesis is that television sets watch viewers while viewers are watching them.*

hypothetical *adj.* °assumed, °supposed, conjectural, conjectured, hypothesized, putative, surmised, °assumed, presumed, suspected, imagined, guessed, °speculative, speculated, °theoretical, suppositional, supposititious *or* supposititious: *Let us take the hypothetical case of someone, for example, who refuses to pay income tax.*

hysterical *adj.* **1** °raving, °mad, beside oneself, crazed, irrational, distracted, °rabid, °frantic, frenzied, °wild, °berserk, °uncontrolled, uncontrollable, unrestrained, unrestrainable: *They are subject to violent, hysterical outbursts.* **2** °hilarious, side-splitting, °uproarious, °farcical, comical, °funny: *The show we saw last night was absolutely hysterical.*

icing n. **1** frosting, glaze, coating: *Our favourite treat was chocolate cake with chocolate icing.* **2** °bonus, (fringe) °benefit, (°extra) added °attraction, °extra, °reward, dividend: *He clinched a seventh victory with his partner, putting the icing on the cake of their shared world championship.*

icy adj. **1** ice-cold, °frigid, arctic, °bitter, glacial, °freezing, frozen, °chill, hyperborean or hyperboreal, °polar, Siberian, °wintry, °raw, °cold, chilling, °chilly: *The icy wind cut through to the marrow of my bones.* **2** °cool, °chill, °chilly, °frigid, °distant, °aloof, °remote, °freezing, ice-cold, unemotional, unimpassioned, °stony, °steely, °callous, flinty, °formal, °reserved, °forbidding, unfriendly, °hostile: *She fixed him with an icy stare.*

idea n. **1** concept, °conception, °construct, °thought, °notion, °plan, °design, °scheme, °suggestion, °recommendation: *Is that your idea of a good singing voice? Peter has an excellent idea for increasing sales.* **2** °notion, °fancy, °impression, °picture, (°mental) °image, concept, °conception, °perception, °understanding, awareness, apprehension, °inkling, °suspicion, °hint, °suggestion, approximation, °clue, intimation, °guess, °estimate, °estimation: *I haven't the slightest idea what you are talking about. Can you give us any idea of the cause of the delay?* **3** °belief, °opinion, °sentiment, °feeling, teaching(s), °doctrine, °tenet, °principle, °philosophy, °view, °viewpoint, °outlook, °notion, °conviction, °position, °stance: *Western and Eastern ideas differ as to the role of women in society.* **4** °aim, °goal, °purpose, °objective, °object, °end, °point, °reason, raison d'être: *What was the idea of telling the teacher? The idea behind the scheme was to boost sales. The idea of the game is to capture your opponent's king.* **5** °hypothesis, theory, °notion, °dream, °fantasy or phantasy: *His invention is based on the idea of an anti-gravity device.*

ideal n. **1** °model, °paragon, °standard, criterion, paradigm, exemplar, °pattern, °example, °epitome: *She regarded Florence Nightingale as her ideal.* **2** °acme, (°standard of) °perfection, °nonpareil: *The ideal can rarely be achieved, so you had better settle for reality.* **3** ideals: °principles, °morals, °standards: *Everyone's ideals are compromised sooner or later.* —adj. **4** °perfect, °excellent, °supreme, consummate, °complete, °model, °idyllic: *This is an ideal home for a young couple.* **5** conceptual, imagined, °imaginary, °unreal, °visionary, °idealistic, °fictitious, Utopian, notional, °mythical or mythic, °fantasy, °dream, °romantic, chimeric(al), °illusory, °fanciful, °fancied: *In his ideal world there is no crime, so there is no need for police.*

idealistic adj. °visionary, °romantic, romanticized, °optimistic, starry-eyed, °quixotic, Panglossian, °impractical, °unrealistic: *He is idealistic enough to believe that people are basically good.*

idealize v. °exalt, elevate, °glorify, °worship, ennoble, deify, apotheosize, put on a °pedestal, romanticize: *Because she idealizes him, she cannot see his true nature.*

ideally adv. **1** under or in the °best of circumstances, at °best, in a °perfect world, all things being °equal: *Ideally, February is the time to holiday in the Caribbean.* **2** theoretically, in theory, in °principle: *Ideally, people ought to have money before they are too old to enjoy it.* **3** °perfectly: *John and Marsha are ideally suited to each other.*

identical adj. **1** °same, °twin, °duplicate, °indistinguishable, interchangeable; selfsame: *The two leaves look identical to me. The duchess and I had the identical suite at the hotel, but a week apart.* **2** °similar, °matching, °like, °alike, comparable, °equal, °equivalent, corresponding: *The children are dressed in identical clothing.*

identification n. **1** °connection, °recognition, distinguishing, °indication, °perception, detection, °selection, naming, labelling, pinpointing, designation, characterization, °denomination; authentication, verification, °establishment, certification, substantiation, corroboration, Colloq fingering: *Her identification of him as her attacker is not sufficient to convict him.* **2** classification, classifying, cataloguing, categorization, categorizing, pigeon-holing: *How much time is needed for the identification of the minerals in the moon rocks?* **3** ID, ID card, °identity card, badge, credentials: *Only up-to-date identification will be accepted as proof of ownership.* **4** °connection, °association, affiliation, empathy, °sympathy, °rapport, °relationship: *His continued identification with comic-book heroes is immature.*

identify v. **1** classify, °categorize, catalogue, pigeon-hole, °sort (out), °specify, pinpoint, home (in) on, °name, °label, °tag, °recognize, °place, °mark, pinpoint, °single out, °point out, Colloq °put one's °finger on: *We are unable to identify the butterfly you caught.* **2** °connect, °associate, °relate, °ally: *She is closely identified with the success of the enterprise.* **3** °diagnose, °specify, °name, °recognize: *From the symptoms, the doctor identified the disease as bubonic plague.* **4** Usually, **identify with**: empathize (with), °sympathize (with), °relate (to), Colloq °dig: *His problem is that he identifies too closely with his dog.*

identity n. **1** sameness, oneness, unanimity, indistinguishability, °agreement, °accord, congruence: *Identity of purpose held them together under stress.* **2** °personality, individuality, distinctiveness, uniqueness, particularity, °singularity: *Many who join the army lose their identity.*

ideology n. °belief(s), °convictions, tenets, credo, °philosophy, °principles, °creed, dogma, teachings, °doctrine: *Buddhism had a great influence on his ideology.*

idiom n. **1** °language, °tongue, °speech, °vernacular, °dialect, argot, patois, °jargon, °cant, idiolect, °parlance, façon de parler, phraseology: *The play is written in a rather old-*

fashioned idiom. **2** °expression, (°set) °phrase, phrasing, locution, °cliché: *The term red herring, an idiom meaning 'false trail', is used of something which is neither red nor a herring.*

idle *adj.* **1** °unused, °inactive, unoccupied, non-operative, stationary: *The looms were idle for months. The devil finds work for idle hands.* **2** °unemployed, out of °work, °redundant, jobless, workless, *Colloq* at °leisure, at °liberty, between assignments, resting, *US* on the beach: *Unable to find work, Gilbert has been idle for a year.* **3** °indolent, °lazy, °listless, °lethargic, loafing, °slothful, °shiftless, °lackadaisical, loitering, fainéant: *Since winning the lottery, Crouch has become one of the idle rich.* **4** °bootless, °fruitless, unproductive, abortive, unfruitful, °pointless, °vain, °trifling, trivial, °shallow, nugatory, °superficial, °insignificant, °meaningless, °senseless, unimportant, °frivolous, °worthless, °useless, otiose, unavailing, °futile: *We were passing the time at the pub in idle chatter when Michael walked in. He had no factual information to offer, only idle speculation.*
—*v.* **5** Often, **idle away**: °waste, °fritter away, while away, °kill: *They idle away the hours lying by the swimming-pool.* **6** laze (about), loiter, °kill time, °loaf, loll, °lounge, take it °easy, *Brit* °potter or *US* putter about or away, °mess around or about, °fool away, °fool around or about, *Colloq Brit* °muck around or about, °bugger around or about, *US* lallygag or lollygag, goof off or around, *Military slang US* gold-brick: *Stop idling and get down to work.*

idleness *n.* **1** °inactivity, inaction, °lethargy, °torpor, °indolence, laziness, °sluggishness, °sloth, slothfulness, shiftlessness, °inertia, lassitude, flânerie, dolce far niente; unemployment, *Colloq US* lallygagging or lollygagging, *Military slang US* gold-bricking: *The strike created enforced idleness for non-union workers as well.* **2** shirking, malingering, dawdling, loafing, time-wasting, lazing, *Colloq* dilly-dallying, shilly-shallying, *Brit* skiving: *The foreman warned that he would not tolerate idleness.*

idler *n.* °loafer, layabout, °slacker, shirker, sluggard, lazybones, slugabed, °laggard, dawdler, clock-watcher, drone, °slouch, ne'er-do-well, fainéant, *Colloq* lounge lizard, *Military slang US* gold brick or gold-bricker: *To fill out a crew we often recruited men from among waterfront idlers.*

idly *adv.* **1** unproductively, lazily, indolently: *She wanders about the shops, idly whiling away the hours.* **2** offhandedly, unconsciously, mechanically, thoughtlessly, unthinkingly, obliviously, insensibly, indifferently: *He sat quietly, his fingers idly drumming on the tabletop.*

idol *n.* **1** (graven) °image, icon or ikon, effigy, °fetish, tiki, °symbol: *Nebuchadnezzar's people worshipped golden idols.* **2** °hero or °heroine, superstar, °celebrity, luminary, matinée °idol, °favourite, °pet, °darling: *When he was a lad his idol was Quatermain, from the Rider Haggard novels.*

idolize *v.* °adore, °admire, adulate, °worship, °revere, °reverence, °venerate, put on a °pedestal, °exalt, °glorify, deify, lionize, °look up to, apotheosize: *She had always idolized her father, and his death came as a terrible blow to her.*

idyllic *adj.* Arcadian, paradisaic(al) or paradisiac(al), °heavenly, Edenic, halcyon, °ideal, idealized, °pastoral, °rustic, bucolic,
°picturesque, charming, unspoilt or °unspoiled, °peaceful, pacific: *He returned to the island to live out his life in idyllic repose.*

ignorance *n.* unfamiliarity, unawareness, unconsciousness, benightedness, unenlightenment, °inexperience, greenness: *Ignorance of the law is no excuse. Mistakes are often caused by ignorance rather than stupidity.*

ignorant *adj.* **1** unknowing, °uninformed, untaught, °uneducated, unschooled, unread, unlearned, unlettered, °illiterate: *Is there anyone so ignorant as not to know who Julius Caesar was?* **2** °unaware, °unfamiliar, °unconscious, °benighted, unenlightened, unwitting, in the °dark, °oblivious, *Formal* nescient: *She knows many things about which we are ignorant.* **3** °inexperienced, °green, °naïve, °innocent, °unsophisticated: *They used to tease ignorant young apprentices by sending them to find a left-handed hammer.* **4** uncouth, °ill-mannered, °discourteous, °impolite, uncivil, °boorish: *Don't be so ignorant and open the door for the lady!*

ignore *v.* **1** °disregard, °overlook, °pass over or by, turn a °blind eye to, be °blind to, turn one's back on, turn a °deaf ear to, wink at, °brush off or aside: *If you are over 65, you may ignore this paragraph.* **2** snub, give (someone) the cold °shoulder, °reject, °send to Coventry, °turn one's back on, *Colloq* give (someone) the °brush-off or go-by, °cut, °turn one's nose up at: *I don't care if you are cruel to me, just don't ignore me.*

ill *adj.* **1** ailing, °unsound, °sick, °indisposed, °infirm, °unhealthy, in a °bad °way, °diseased, afflicted, in °bad °health, °sickly, unwell, not well, out of commission; invalided, valetudinarian; *Colloq* under the °weather, in a °bad °way, °poorly, not up to snuff, out of sorts, on the sick-list, off one's feed, *Slang Brit* °dicky, °seedy: *Call a doctor—this man is ill. I was rather ill last night after eating that fish mousse.* **2** °bad, °wicked, °sinful, °evil, iniquitous, °immoral, depraved, °vicious, °vile, °wrong, °corrupt: *Police raided several houses of ill repute.* **3** °hostile, unfriendly, antagonistic, °belligerent, malevolent, malicious, ill-wishing, °unkind(ly), °harsh, °cruel: *The reading of the bequests sparked ill will amongst the heirs.* **4** °harmful, hurtful, °injurious, °detrimental, damaging, pernicious, °dangerous, adverse, deleterious, baleful, °bad, unfavourable, °destructive, °disastrous, catastrophic, °ruinous, cataclysmic: *He suffered no lasting ill effects from the accident.* **5** °bad, °miserable, °wretched, °disastrous, unfavourable, unpropitious, °untoward, °disturbing, °unfortunate, unlucky, °inauspicious, °ominous, °unpromising, °sinister, °unwholesome: *Ill fortune led Ulysses to our isle. It is an ill wind that blows nobody good.* **6 ill at ease**: uncomfortable, discomfited, uneasy, edgy, on °edge, fidgety, °nervous, °anxious, °disturbed, distressed, troubled, °awkward, unsure, °uncertain: *I felt ill at ease in the presence of so august a personage.*
—*n.* **7** °evil, °abuse: *Speak no ill of her in my home!* **8** °harm, °damage, °injury, °hurt, °mischief, °trouble, °misfortune, °misery, °affliction, °pain, °distress, °woe, woefulness, °discomfort, unpleasantness, °disaster, °catastrophe, cataclysm, °calamity, adversity, °suffering, °ruin, °destruction: *You will be held responsible if any ill*

befalls the children. **9** °injustice, inequity, °wrong, °evil, °sin, °transgression, °abuse, °mistreatment, maltreatment: He entered politics hoping to cure some of society's ills.
—adv. **10** °badly, adversely, unfavourably, °poorly, inauspiciously, unfortunately, unluckily: Don't speak ill of the dead. **11** °badly, adversely, unfavourably, critically, harshly, unkindly: Please don't think ill of me for failing to attend your wedding. **12** unkindly, harshly, unfairly, unjustly, improperly, °badly, wrongly, wrongfully, unsatisfactorily, °poorly, malevolently, maliciously: He insists that he was ill-treated when in prison.
13 °scarcely, °hardly, by no °means, in no °way: It ill behoves you to criticize other people's English.

ill-advised adj. **1** inadvisable, ill-judged, injudicious, ill-considered, °misguided, unwise, °imprudent, °inappropriate, unpropitious, inexpedient, impolitic, wrong-headed, °thoughtless; °indiscreet: It would be ill-advised to sell your house at this time. **2** °hasty, °rash, °reckless, °impetuous, °rash, °foolhardy, incautious, °short-sighted, °improvident: Driving without a seat belt is ill-advised.

illegal adj. °unlawful, °illegitimate, °criminal, felonious, outlawed, prohibited, interdicted, forbidden, proscribed, wrongful, °unauthorized, verboten, °illicit, Law actionable: The bookkeeper was prosecuted for illegal appropriation of funds.

illegible adj. unreadable, unintelligible, indecipherable or undecipherable, °incomprehensible: An illegible message was scrawled on the wall.

illegitimate adj. **1** See illegal, above. **2** bastard, °natural, fatherless, born out of wedlock, born on the wrong side of the blanket, misbegotten: Illegitimate children were often offered for adoption in those days. **3** °irregular, °improper, °incorrect, non-standard, °invalid, °unauthorized, °spurious: Purists consider the reason is because an illegitimate usage.

ill-founded adj. °groundless, baseless, without °foundation, unsupported, unsubstantiated, °empty, unjustified, unproven, uncorroborated, °unsound, °erroneous: He wasted a great deal of time refuting her ill-founded accusations.

illicit adj. **1** See illegal, above. **2** °wrong, °improper, underhand(ed), °secret, °furtive, clandestine, back-door, Colloq US °sneaky: They grew rich on the proceeds of illicit liquor.

illiterate adj. unlettered, analphabetic; unschooled, untaught, °uneducated, °benighted, °ignorant, unenlightened: She teaches illiterate people to read.

ill-mannered adj. °rude, °discourteous, °impolite, ill-bred, uncivil, °disrespectful, uncourtly, ungallant, °ungracious, indecorous, ungentlemanly, unladylike, °impudent, °insolent, insulting, °impertinent, °brazen: That ill-mannered oaf didn't even apologize for knocking me down.

illness n. sickness, °disease, °disorder, °affliction, °ailment, malady, °complaint, °infirmity, °disability, indisposition, °affection, Colloq °bug: His illness is serious but not contagious.

ill-treat v. °mistreat, maltreat, °abuse, °misuse, °harm, °hurt, °injure, °persecute, °mishandle: He is at last being punished for those years he ill-treated his wife.

illuminate v. **1** °light (up), °brighten, °lighten, °throw or °cast or °shed °light on or upon: She had only a single candle to illuminate her sewing. **2** °clarify, °throw or °cast or °shed °light on or upon, °enlighten, °clear up, elucidate, °explain, explicate, °reveal: The lectures on Heidegger illuminated his philosophy to some extent. **3** rubricate, °decorate, adorn, °embellish, °ornament: The museum has the best collection of illuminated manuscripts.

illumination n. **1** lighting, °light, brightness, °radiance, luminosity, incandescence, fluorescence, phosphorescence: The illumination from the fire was barely enough to read by. **2** enlightenment, °insight, °information, °learning, °revelation, °edification, °instruction, awareness, °understanding, clarification: It is astonishing what illumination his lectures brought to his audiences.

illusion n. **1** °deception, °delusion, °fancy, °misconception, misapprehension, °fallacy, °error, °mistake, °mistaken or °false °impression: He is labouring under the illusion that he is a great pianist. **2** °fantasy, day-dream, °hallucination, phantasm, °phantom, chimera, phantasmagoria, mirage, aberration, °vision, °spectre, figment of the °imagination, will-o'-the-wisp, ignis fatuus: For years after he died, she had the illusion of seeing her father everywhere.

illusory adj. illusive, °imaginary, °fictional, °unreal, °untrue, fallacious, °false, °mistaken, imagined, °fanciful, °fancied, hallucinatory, °deceptive, misleading, °apparent: Any financial gains that you perceive in the scheme are purely illusory.

illustrate v. **1** °instance, °exemplify, °demonstrate: Let me illustrate my point with the following example. **2** °picture, °illuminate, grangerize; °decorate, °embellish, emblazon, °ornament, adorn: We are looking for an artist to illustrate the book.

illustration n. **1** °example, °case (in point), °instance, °sample, °specimen, exemplar, Colloq for °instance: This film is an illustration of the film noir genre. **2** °picture, depiction, °representation, °figure: An illustration of a jet engine appears on page 32.

illustrious adj. °distinguished, °famous, °noted, °renowned, famed, °eminent, °well-known, °prominent, °important, °notable, respected, esteemed, °venerable, honoured, acclaimed, °celebrated, °great: He belongs in the same category as other illustrious generals, like Kitchener.

ill will n. °dislike, °animosity, hatred, °hate, °loathing, abhorrence, detestation, malevolence, malice, °hostility, enmity, animus, antipathy, °aversion, °rancour, acrimony, °spite, °venom, vitriol, acerbity: I bear her no ill will for the way she treated me. She incurred his ill will by refusing him access to the children.

image n. **1** °likeness, °representation, °picture, °sculpture, °statue, effigy, °figure, °portrait, simulacrum; icon or ikon, °idol, graven °image, °fetish, tiki: Images of Bolívar can be seen in every town square in Venezuela. The tribesmen still worshipped golden images of their gods. **2** °epitome, °duplicate, °copy, counterpart, °facsimile, °replica, °double, °twin, doppelgänger, clone, Colloq °spitting image or °spit and image, (°dead) ringer: He's the image of father. He stared at his image *in the mirror.* **3** °impression, concept, °conception, °perception, °idea, °perception, °notion, °mental °picture: *You are quite different from my image of you.* **4** °epitome, °representative, °model, (°typical) °example, °essence, archetype, °embodiment, incarnation, personification, materialization, reification, corporealization: *For us, she was the very image of what a leader should be.* **5** °figure (of °speech), trope, °metaphor, allusion, simile, °symbol: *The poem contains images that are obscure unless you know Greek myths.* **6** °form, °appearance, °likeness, °guise, °semblance, °aspect, °mould, °cast: *Man claims to be created in God's image.*

imagery *n.* figurativeness, allusion, symbolism: *Constance's poems are filled with ornate imagery.*

imaginary *adj.* °fictitious, °fanciful, °fancied, chimerical, imagined, fictive, °illusory *or* illusive, °visionary, made-up, °unreal, °untrue, °mythical *or* mythic, notional, °abstract, °legendary, mythological: *When he was a boy, he had an imaginary friend called Carbonario.*

imagination *n.* **1** mind's eye, °fancy; creativity, inventiveness, °ingenuity, °insight, °inspiration, °vision, imaginativeness, °creative °power(s): *His fertile imagination conjured up all kinds of terrifying pictures.* **2** °thought, °thinking, (°mental) acuity, °intelligence, °wit: *It doesn't take much imagination to see why you don't want to go to school this morning.*

imaginative *adj.* **1** °creative, °original, °clever, °ingenious, inventive, innovative, inspired, inspiring, °enterprising, °resourceful: *Richard is a highly imaginative computer programmer.* **2** °fanciful, °fantastic, °visionary, °poetic(al), °whimsical, contrived, °fictitious, °fictional: *The imaginative tale of Don Quixote sprang from the mind of Cervantes.*

imagine *v.* **1** °think of, °contemplate, °picture, °envisage, °consider, °ponder, °meditate on, °envision, visualize, °conceive (of), conceptualize, °create, °think up, concoct, °devise, *Colloq* °dream up, cook up: *I cannot imagine what you are referring to. Imagine, if you can, a world without conflict.* **2** °suppose, °guess, conjecture, °assume, °presume, °take it, °infer, °take (it) for granted, °take it as °given, °think, °fancy, °believe, °gather, °surmise, °suspect, °judge, deem: *I imagine that you won't want a drink if you are driving. You are imagining things if you think she is trying to undermine your authority.*

imitate *v.* **1** °mimic, °copy, ape, °parrot, °monkey, emulate, impersonate, do an °impression of; °echo, simulate: *Cruikshank was imitating the boss, who walked in at that very moment. His style imitates that of Carlyle.* **2** °copy, °mimic, °mock, °parody, °satirize, °burlesque, °caricature, travesty, *Colloq* spoof, °take off, *Brit* °send up: *In Hudibras, Samuel Butler imitated the style of the heroic epic.*

imitation *n.* **1** copying, mimicking, mimicry, aping, parroting, emulating, emulation, impersonating, impersonation, °impression: *Imitation is the sincerest form of flattery.* **2** impersonation, °parody, satirization, °burlesque, °caricature, °mockery, travesty, *Colloq* °take-off, *Brit* send-up: *In his nightclub act, he does scathing imitations of celebrities.* **3** °copy, °fake, °counterfeit, °forgery: *These are modern imitations of ancient coins.* **4** °copy,

°replica, replication, °reproduction, simulation, °facsimile, °duplicate, duplication, simulacrum: *We keep the original in a safe place and put the imitations on display.*
—*adj.* **5** °fake, °synthetic, °artificial, simulated, °sham, ersatz, °mock, °factitious, °reproduction, man-made, *Colloq* °phoney *or US also* phony: *It doesn't take an expert to see that this is an imitation diamond.*

immaculate *adj.* **1** °spotless, stainless, unblemished, °pure, °clean, °untarnished, unsullied, unsoiled, snow-white, spick and °span, °dapper, °spruce; °tidy, °neat: *Each morning he donned an immaculate uniform.* **2** °pure, °chaste, °innocent, virginal, °virtuous, vestal, °pristine, undefiled, untainted, °unspoiled *or* unspoilt, unblemished, stainless, unadulterated: *He remained convinced of his wife's immaculate reputation.* **3** °faultless, °flawless, °perfect, errorless, °impeccable: *His essay on Gibbon is an example of immaculate scholarship.*

immaterial *adj.* **1** unimportant, °inconsequential, nugatory, trivial, °trifling, °petty, °slight, °insignificant, °flimsy, °light, unessential, °non-essential, of °little °account or value: *Whether he stays or goes is immaterial to me.* **2** airy, incorporeal, °disembodied, ethereal, ephemeral, evanescent, unsubstantial: *The concept of immaterial matter, such as a gas, is difficult to comprehend.*

immature *adj.* **1** °premature, °undeveloped, unripe, °rudimentary, half-grown, unformed, °unfledged, fledgling *or Brit also* fledgeling, unfinished, °young, °new, °fresh, °incomplete: *The immature growth in the spring is not hardy enough to survive a frost.* **2** °green, °callow, °unsophisticated, °naïve, jejune, °inexperienced, babyish, °childish, °childlike, °puerile, °juvenile, °raw, *Colloq* wet behind the ears: *She is a bit immature to assume so many responsibilities.*

immeasurable *adj.* °vast, °infinite, °immense, °huge, °great, °limitless, °boundless, °endless, interminable, unbounded, °unlimited, measureless, °inestimable, unfathomable; innumerable, °numberless, uncountable, uncounted, incalculable: *The tiny ship hurtled through the immeasurable vastness of space. An immeasurable quantity of angels can dance on the head of a pin. He accomplished immeasurable good during his lifetime.*

immediate *adj.* **1** instantaneous, °instant, °abrupt, °sudden, °swift, °spontaneous, °instinctive, triggered, °unhesitating, °unthinking, °automatic, reflex, knee-jerk: *Why is your immediate reaction always to say 'It cannot be done'?* **2** °direct, nearest, next, closest, adjacent, proximate; °nearby: *Although he had cancer, the immediate cause of death was pneumonia. Is there a phone box in the immediate vicinity?* **3** existing, °present, °current, °actual, °pressing, °urgent: *The immediate problem is to find a way of getting out of here.*

immediately *adv.* **1** at °once, instantly, °instantaneously, °promptly, °right away, °right °now, without °delay, unhesitatingly, without hesitation, forthwith, this °instant, °directly, in a wink, in a °second, in a °minute, *tout de suite*, instanter, *Chiefly Brit* °straight away, *Colloq* pronto, in a jiffy, in two shakes of a lamb's tail, before you can say 'Jack Robinson', at the

drop of a hat: *Come here immediately. I shall be there immediately.* **2** °directly, closely, intimately: *These reactions are immediately concerned with the temperature.*
—*conj.* **3** when, as °soon as, the °moment (that), *Brit* °directly: *Immediately he heard the news, he hurried to her side.*

immense *adj.* °enormous, °gigantic, °extensive, °vast, °huge, °massive, °voluminous, tremendous, staggering, stupendous, mammoth, °colossal, °giant, titanic, Cyclopean, °jumbo, elephantine, Brobdingnagian, *Slang US* humongous: *Our exit from the cave was blocked by an immense boulder.*

immerse *v.* **1** °plunge, °sink, °submerge, °dip, dunk, °duck, inundate: *Immerse the device in the water before switching it on.* **2** °plunge, °sink, °submerge, °bury, absorb, engross, °engage, °occupy, °involve: *I immersed myself in my work and never noticed the time.*

immigrant *n.* °newcomer, °arrival, °settler, *Australian* °migrant; °alien, °foreigner, outlander, °outsider: *Her parents were immigrants from the Ukraine.*

imminent *adj.* °impending, looming, °threatening, °menacing, at °hand, nigh, °immediate, °close (by or at °hand), (forth)coming, drawing °near or °close or nigh, °momentary: *We face imminent disaster if steps are not taken now.*

immoderate *adj.* °excessive, °extreme, °exorbitant, °unreasonable, °inordinate, °extravagant, intemperate; °outrageous, °preposterous, exaggerated, unrestrained, undue: *Their immoderate demands for reparations cannot be met.*

immodest *adj.* **1** °indecent, °shameless, °shameful, indecorous, titillating, revealing; indelicate, °improper, °wanton, °loose, unrestrained, °provocative, °obscene, °lewd, smutty, °dirty, °lascivious, °bawdy, °coarse, *Colloq* °sexy: *The striptease was, to say the least, immodest. The streakers will be punished for their immodest behaviour.* **2** °brazen, °forward, °bold, °impudent, °impertinent, °brash, °arrogant, °insolent, °presumptuous, °disrespectful, *Colloq* °fresh, °cheeky: *Carl's immodest demand for a private office was ignored.*

immoral *adj.* **1** °corrupt, °bad, °wicked, °evil, iniquitous, °sinful, °impure, unethical, unprincipled, °abandoned, °base, °wrong, °vile, depraved, °dissolute, °degenerate, °reprobate, unregenerate, nefarious, flagitious, °villainous, treacherous, °unscrupulous, °dishonest: *Is it immoral to avoid paying one's taxes?* **2** °immodest, debauched, °indecent, °wanton, °libertine, °lecherous, °lustful, libidinous, °carnal, concupiscent, salacious, licentious, °lascivious, °lewd, °obscene, °pornographic, °dirty, smutty, °filthy: *He was convicted for living off immoral earnings.*

immortal *adj.* **1** undying, °eternal, °deathless, °everlasting, imperishable, sempiternal, never-ending, °endless, ceaseless, °perpetual, °timeless, °constant, °enduring, °indestructible: *Did the Egyptian pharaohs believe themselves immortal?* **2** °divine, °heavenly, °godlike: *The immortal wisdom of God guides man.* **3** remembered, °celebrated, unfading,

°famous, °renowned, °classic, lauded, praised, honoured, °timeless: *The immortal writings of Shakespeare inspire us still.*
—*n.* **4** Olympian, °god or goddess; °hero or °heroine, °legend, °genius, °great: *To be sure, we must consider Bach as one of the immortals.*

immortalize *v.* °celebrate, °honour, °glorify, °memorialize, °commemorate, apotheosize, canonize, beatify, °exalt, ennoble, °extol: *Dickens's father was immortalized as Mr Micawber.*

immovable *adj.* **1** unmovable, °fixed, °fast, °rooted, °set, immobile, stationary, motionless, °stable, riveted, anchored, frozen: *What happens when an irresistible force meets an immovable object?* **2** immutable, unchangeable, unalterable, settled, °set, unmovable, °fixed, °inflexible; unshakeable or unshakable, unswerving, °firm, °determined, °steadfast, °staunch, °rigid, dogged, obdurate, unyielding, unwavering, °resolute, unflinching, adamant(ine), °stony, °impassive, unbending, emotionless, °unmoved: *Christmas day, which always falls on December 25th, is an immovable feast. Despite pleas for mercy, the judge was immovable and she was hanged the next day.*

immune *adj.* inoculated, vaccinated; °exempt, °safe, protected, insusceptible or unsusceptible, invulnerable, untouched, °unaffected: *She never caught smallpox because a mild case of cowpox had made her immune. Rick mistakenly thought himself immune to Sally's charms.*

immunity *n.* **1** °exemption, non-liability, invulnerability, °protection, °excuse, °release, °exclusion, °privilege, °freedom, °indemnity, amnesty, exoneration, absolution: *In return for his testimony he was granted immunity from prosecution.* **2** insusceptibility or unsusceptibility, °protection, inoculation, vaccination: *Immunity to a number of diseases is conferred by this one injection.*

imp *n.* °devil(kin), °demon, sprite, °evil °spirit, hobgoblin, °goblin, elf, pixie or pixy, leprechaun, puck, brownie, fairy; scamp, urchin, gamin, °rogue, °rascal, mischief-maker, brat: *Sitting on my shoulder as I write is a tiny imp that inserts the misspellings. Give me a hug, you little imp!*

impact *n.* **1** °collision, °contact, °striking, °crash, smash, °bump, colliding, crashing, smashing, bumping: *The impact of the car against the stone wall was heard a mile away.* **2** °effect, °impression, °influence, °import, °meaning, °bearing, °force, °thrust, °weight, °burden, °brunt, repercussions, results, consequences: *It is becoming clear that technology is having an adverse impact on the environment.*
—*v.* **3** °strike, °hit, °collide with: *When its orbit decays, the satellite will impact the surface of the moon.* **4** °affect, °modify, °change: *I wonder how the news of the bankruptcy will impact share prices.*

impair *v.* °weaken, °cripple, °damage, °harm, °mar, °injure, °spoil, °ruin: *Standing too close to the speakers at a disco can impair your hearing.*

impairment *n.* lessening, weakening, °damage, °harm, °injury, °flaw, °imperfection, reduction, vitiation, deterioration, °decrease, diminution, enfeeblement, debilitation, undermining, worsening, marring: *The impairment to my eyesight was caused by reading in the dark.*

impale v. spear, °stab, °pierce, skewer, °spit, °stick, °transfix, °spike: *They impaled the heads of their enemies on poles as a warning.*

impart v. **1** °give, °cede, °lend, °bestow, convey, °confer, °grant, °afford, °accord, °contribute: *The dyes impart different colours to the ink.* **2** °communicate, °tell, °relate, °transmit, °reveal, divulge, °disclose, °pass on, °intimate, confide: *I've had a hard week imparting knowledge to bored schoolchildren.*

impartial adj. °fair, °just, even-handed, °disinterested, °neutral, °unprejudiced, unbiased, °objective, °equitable: *Judge Leaver can be relied on to render an impartial verdict.*

impasse n. °deadlock, °dead °end, °stalemate, stand-off, °block, blockage, *Colloq* °blind alley: *Negotiations reached an impasse and the meeting broke up.*

impassioned adj. °passionate, inspired, °spirited, °stirring, °fervent, °emotional, fervid, °ardent, °heated, °warm, °rousing, aroused, vehement, zealous, °eager, °earnest, °enthusiastic, °vigorous, °animated, °fiery, °inflamed, °glowing: *The barrister made an impassioned plea for the accused.*

impassive adj. °cool, apathetic, °calm, °serene, composed, °unmoved, °cold, °cold-blooded, °reserved, imperturbable, unimpressionable, unruffled, controlled, contained, °phlegmatic, °lackadaisical, °stoical, unemotional, °taciturn, unfeeling, °stolid, emotionless, uncaring, °indifferent, undisturbed, °callous, °unsympathetic, °stony, °dispassionate, °detached, °nonchalant, unconcerned, insouciant, °remote: *I could see nothing in the judge's impassive expression to hint at his decision.*

impatient adj. **1** uneasy, °nervous, fidgety, °agitated, °restless, °restive, unquiet, °eager, °fretful, °agog, chafing, °impetuous, athirst, *Slang* itchy, *US* antsy: *There is a short wait for seats, so please don't get impatient.* **2** °irritable, irascible, °testy, °short-tempered, °querulous, °waspish, °brusque, °curt, °short, hot-tempered, °snappish, °indignant, °demanding: *I don't mean to be impatient, but I have been waiting for three hours.*

impeach v. **1** °charge, °accuse, arraign, °indict, °incriminate, °implicate, inculpate, °blame, censure: *They were impeached for crimes against the state.* **2** (call into) °question, °challenge, °attack, °disparage, °discredit, impugn, deprecate, °belittle, asperse, cast aspersions on, declaim, °slander, malign, °vilify: *My daughter's character had been impeached by the witness.*

impeccable adj. °faultless, °flawless, °perfect, °ideal, °pure, °correct, °proper, °spotless, °immaculate, unblemished, unimpeachable, °blameless: *His lectures, though impeccable in content and style, lacked fire.*

impede v. °bar, °obstruct, °block, °thwart, °check, °hinder, °hamper, °slow, °retard, °restrain, °brake, °hold up, °delay, °foil, confound, °inhibit, °curb, °spike, °stop: *You can do nothing to impede the relentless march of time.*

impediment n. °bar, °barrier, °obstruction, °block, °check, °hindrance, °encumbrance, °restraint, °hold-up, °hitch, °snag, °restriction, °stricture, bottleneck, °delay, hang-up, °inhibition, °curb: *What are the impediments to a happy marriage?*

impending adj. °imminent, approaching, (°close or °near) at °hand, °close, nearing, forthcoming, brewing, to °come, in °view, in °prospect, in °store, in the offing, on the °horizon, in the air; looming, °threatening, °menacing; *Colloq Brit* on the cards, *US* in the cards: *The impending deadline made us work all the faster. We had a feeling of impending doom.*

imperative adj. **1** °mandatory, compulsory, °necessary, required, requisite, demanded, °obligatory, °indispensable, °essential, °crucial, °vital, °urgent, °pressing, exigent: *It is imperative that we catch the 5.04 to London.* **2** imperious, commanding, °authoritarian, °overbearing, °peremptory, autocratic, °domineering, magisterial, lordly, °arbitrary, °dictatorial, °dogmatic, °tyrannical, °despotic, *Colloq* °bossy: *We were all shaken into obedience by her imperative tone.*

imperceptible adj. **1** °invisible, indiscernible, °indistinguishable, undetectable, °obscure, °vague, ill-defined; °inaudible: *The differences between the twins are imperceptible.* **2** °indistinct, unclear, unnoticeable, °slight, °subtle, inconsiderable, inappreciable, °minute, °tiny, minuscule, infinitesimal, microscopic: *Her only response was an imperceptible flicker of her eyelid.*

imperfect adj. °wanting, unfinished, °undeveloped, °incomplete, °deficient, °defective, °faulty, °flawed, patchy: *This is an imperfect translation of the poem.*

imperfection n. °flaw, °failing, °fault, °error, °defect, °blemish, °damage; inadequacy, insufficiency, deficiency, °frailty, °weakness, °foible, °shortcoming, °peccadillo, shortfall, fallibility, °infirmity: *We have reduced the price because of tiny imperfections in the weave. Imperfections in her character make her unsuitable for the job.*

imperial adj. **1** kingly, kinglike, queenly, queenlike, °princely, princelike, °regal, °royal, °sovereign: *The imperial court was rich and splendid.* **2** °majestic, °royal, °regal, °lofty, °exalted, °supreme, august, °noble, °superior, °imposing, °splendid, °magnificent, °grand, °excellent: *Her imperial presence outshone all at the ball.*

impermeable adj. impenetrable, impassable, impervious, closed, sealed, °hermetic: *The floor has been damp-proofed by the insertion of an impermeable membrane under the concrete.*

impersonal adj. **1** °detached, °objective, °disinterested, °fair, °equitable, °dispassionate, °unprejudiced, unbiased: *The enforcement of the law should be entirely impersonal.* **2** °formal, °stiff, °strait-laced, °wooden, °rigid, prim, °stuffy, °cool, °detached, unfriendly, °cold, °mechanical: *Why does my bank manager have to be so impersonal?*

impertinence n. insolence, boldness, brazenness, °impudence, °presumption, presumptuousness, brashness, sauciness, pertness, °incivility, forwardness, impoliteness, discourtesy, °disrespect, audacity, rudeness, °effrontery, *Colloq* cheek, °brass, brassiness, °nerve, °gall, *Slang* chutzpah: *Why, the impertinence of that waitress to call you by your Christian name!*

impertinent adj. °presumptuous, °insolent, °bold, °brazen, °impudent, °brash, saucy, °pert, uncivil, °forward, °impolite, °discourteous, °disrespectful, °audacious, °rude, *Colloq*

°cheeky, °fresh, °brassy, *US* nervy: *That impertinent little upstart had the nerve to ask the lady's age!*

impetuous *adj.* °spontaneous, °unpremeditated, °impulsive, unplanned, °hasty, °abrupt, °precipitate, quick, °unthinking, unreasoned, °offhand, °rash, °reckless, spur-of-the-moment, unreflective, headlong: *Don't be impetuous and accept the first offer that comes along.*

impetus *n.* °drive, stimulus, °push, impulse, goad, °thrust, °energy, °momentum, stimulation, °incentive, motivation, °encouragement, °inspiration: *Roger's innovative ideas provided the impetus to develop new products.*

impious *adj.* irreligious, °irreverent, °ungodly, °sacrilegious, °blasphemous, °profane, unholy, °wicked, °sinful, iniquitous: *The priest said that he would be punished for his impious remarks.*

implacable *adj.* unappeasable, unmollifiable, unpacifiable, unforgiving, intractable, uncompromising, °inflexible, inexorable, unyielding, unrelenting, °ruthless, °cruel, pitiless, °merciless, °hard, °rigid, °unsympathetic, uncompassionate: *Ever since that incident at school he has been my implacable enemy.*

implant *v.* **1** °introduce, °instil, °insinuate, °inject; °indoctrinate, inculcate, °teach, °impress, imprint: *They spent months implanting that notion in his mind.* **2** °graft, °root, embed, inlay: *You must implant the scion nearer the main stem.*
—*n.* **3** °graft, scion, ingraft; °insert: *Are they really experimenting with brain implants to improve the memory?*

implausible *adj.* °improbable, °unlikely, °doubtful, dubious, °questionable, °unbelievable, °incredible, °far-fetched, unconvincing, °debatable, °unreasonable: *He told an implausible tale of having been raised by apes.*

implement *n.* **1** utensil, °tool, °instrument, °apparatus, °device, appliance, contrivance, °mechanism, (°piece of) °equipment, *Colloq* °gadget, °contraption: *You need the proper implement for measuring inside diameters.*
—*v.* **2** °carry out, °execute, °accomplish, °perform, °achieve, (°put into) °effect, °bring about, °cause, °fulfil, °realize: *You will need our help to implement the plan.*

implicate *v.* **1** °involve, °include, °associate, embroil, ensnare, entrap, enmesh, °entangle: *Don't implicate me in your hare-brained schemes!* **2** °incriminate, inculpate, °connect, °involve, °associate, °suspect, °concern: *Wasn't he implicated in that fraud case last year?*

implication *n.* **1** involvement, °connection, °inclusion, °association, entanglement: *My implication in that affair was minimal.* **2** °suggestion, °hint, insinuation, °innuendo, intimation: *I resent the implication that I had anything to do with the murder.* **3** °significance, purport, °drift, °meaning, denotation, conclusion, °inference, °import, connotation, °sense, °burden, °substance, °essence, °pith: *The implication of the article is that the government knew about the illegal exports all along.*

implicit *adj.* **1** implied, °indirect, inferable, °understood, unspoken, undeclared, °tacit, °inherent, inferential, latent: *Certain provisions are implicit in every legal contract and need not be*

expressed. **2** °absolute, unquestioning, unquestioned, °unqualified, °total, °sheer, °complete, °unmitigated, unalloyed, °undiluted, °unlimited, unconditional, unreserved, utter, °full, °wholehearted: *I have implicit faith in Nicole's judgement.*

imply *v.* **1** °suggest, °hint (at), °intimate, °insinuate: *Are you implying that I don't know what I'm talking about?* **2** connote, allude to, °refer to, advert to, °signify, °signal, betoken, °denote, °indicate, °mean, °express; °involve, °include, °evidence, °assume, °presume, °entail: *Silence sometimes implies consent. Discovery of the tools implies a more advanced culture.*

impolite *adj.* °discourteous, °ill-mannered, uncivil, °rude, °ungracious, ungentlemanly, unladylike, °pert, °disrespectful, saucy, °boorish, churlish, °crude, indecorous, indelicate, °unrefined, ill-bred, °vulgar, °coarse: *The waiter was so impolite that I refused him a tip.*

imponderable *adj.* unmeasurable, °inestimable, °inconceivable, °incomprehensible, °subtle: *There are too many imponderable questions to give you a definite answer.*

import *v.* **1** °introduce, °bring in: *We import the raw materials and export the finished product.* **2** convey, °mean, °signify, °denote, °imply, betoken: *He was a dictator, in all the senses that word imports.*
—*n.* **3** °meaning, °sense, denotation, signification, °gist, °drift, °thrust, °intention, °implication, purport, connotation, °suggestion, allusion, intimation: *It was difficult for me to catch the import of her words.* **4** °importance, °significance, °weight, consequence, °moment, °substance: *One could see at once that she was a personage of some import.*

importance *n.* **1** °significance, consequence, °import, value, °worth, °weight, °account, °concern, °moment, °substance, °matter: *How chemicals affect the ozone layer is of great importance to everyone.* **2** eminence, °distinction, °esteem, °standing, °status, °position, °rank, °prominence, °pre-eminence, °prestige, °power, °influence, °note: *His family is of considerable importance in the community.*

important *adj.* **1** °significant, consequential, °critical, °material, °vital, °urgent, °portentous, °weighty, °grave, °substantial, °momentous, °signal: *If it is important, put it in writing.* **2** °leading, °prominent, °notable, °noted, °noteworthy, °worthy, °eminent, °distinguished, respected, high-ranking, top-level, high-level, °superior, °outstanding, °foremost, °conspicuous, °impressive: *She is the most important member of the committee.* **3** °influential, °effective, well-connected, °powerful, °formidable, °mighty, °impressive: *With those important politicians supporting him, he might win.*

impose *v.* **1** °inflict, °force, °foist: *Stop imposing your standards on others.* **2** °interrupt, °interfere, °intrude, interpose, °insinuate: *I hope I am not imposing?* **3** levy, °place, °put, °exact: *A tax has been imposed on entertainment.* **4 impose on** or **upon: a** saddle, °burden: *He imposes on everyone with his demands for charity.* **b** °exploit, take °advantage (of), °misuse: *I hope I am not imposing on your good will in what I ask.*

imposing adj. °grand, °magnificent, °impressive, °stately, august, °majestic, °effective, commanding: *In his dress uniform, the general was an imposing presence at the reception.*

imposition n. **1** inflicting, infliction; applying, °application, enforcing, enforcement, levy, levying, promulgating, promulgation, introducing, introduction, placing, °placement, laying on: *People resent the imposition of a curfew.* **2** °burden, onus, °weight; intrusion, °misuse: *A flat-rate tax is a terrible imposition on the poor. Walking the dog is an imposition on my time.*

impossible adj. **1** °hopeless, °impracticable, °inconceivable, unimaginable, °unthinkable, unattainable, unsuitable, out of the °question, unachievable, unrealizable, unworkable, unresolvable, unsolvable: *Reading of the cipher is impossible without a key.* **2** °absurd, °ludicrous, °preposterous, °ridiculous, illogical, unworkable, °outrageous, °farcical, °outlandish, °crazy, °weird: *Inventors came up with the most impossible designs for aeroplanes.*

impostor n. imposter, impersonator, °pretender, deceiver, °cheat, °fraud, °swindler, trickster, °confidence man, shark, charlatan, mountebank, °hypocrite, Colloq con man, °phoney or US also phony, °tricky Dick, flimflam man or artist, US four-flusher: *It wasn't the bank manager but an impostor.*

impotence n. **1** °weakness, powerlessness, helplessness, °frailty, feebleness, enervation, debilitation: *The doctor said that his impotence was caused by exhaustion.* **2** impotency, inadequacy, inefficacy, ineffectualness, ineffectiveness, ineptness, °incompetence: *Georgiana was frustrated by her impotence in dealing with the situation.* **3** sterility, infertility: *Eating raw eggs and oysters does not cure impotence.*

impotent adj. **1** °weak, °powerless, °helpless, °frail, °feeble, enervated, debilitated, °infirm: *When it came to political influence, I was impotent.* **2** °inadequate, °ineffective, °ineffectual, °inept, °incompetent: *The attempted robbery was a half-hearted, impotent effort.* **3** °sterile, °barren, °infertile, infecund: *They never had any children because Dixon was impotent.*

impoverished adj. **1** °destitute, °poor, poverty-stricken, °penurious, beggared, °needy, necessitous, impecunious, in sore or bad °straits, °straitened, in °distress, °badly off, bankrupt, °insolvent, ruined, Colloq (°dead or °flat) °broke, stony-broke, °bad off, pinched, up against it, on one's uppers, °short, US strapped, wiped out, Slang Brit skint: *A series of failed harvests left many farmers impoverished.* **2** °stripped, °barren, °desolate, wasted, °empty, depleted, denuded, drained, °exhausted: *Two years of drought left the land impoverished.*

impracticable adj. **1** unworkable, infeasible or unfeasible, °impossible, unattainable, unachievable: *The new engine design proved impracticable because of its high fuel consumption.* **2** unsuitable, unfit, unusable, °useless, °inapplicable: *As we have no electricity, air conditioners are impracticable.*

impractical adj. **1** °visionary, starry-eyed, °unrealistic, °romantic, °quixotic, °wild: *Laura's solutions are very creative but quite impractical.* **2** °useless, °ineffective, °ineffectual,

unworkable, unavailing, °impracticable: *The idea looked good on paper but proved impractical when we tried it.*

imprecise adj. °inexact, °inaccurate, °wrong, inexplicit, °indefinite, ill-defined, °indistinct, °vague, °hazy, cloudy, blurred, °fuzzy, °woolly, °ambiguous: *The readings are imprecise because the needle wavers so much.*

impregnable adj. invulnerable, impenetrable, inviolable, unconquerable, °invincible, °unbeatable, °indomitable, °secure, °safe, °mighty, well-fortified: *The walls of the castle, sixteen feet thick, were impregnable.*

impregnate v. **1** °fertilize, inseminate, fecundate, make °pregnant: *The female can be impregnated only during one ten-day interval each year.* **2** imbue, °suffuse, °permeate, °penetrate, pervade, infuse, °saturate, °drench, °soak, °steep, °fill: *The preservative must be allowed to impregnate the wood.*

impress v. **1** °affect, °touch, °move, °reach, stir, °strike, °sway, °influence, °persuade, Colloq °grab, get under one's skin: *She was genuinely impressed by his sincerity.* **2** °print, imprint, °stamp, °mark, °engrave, emboss: *Before the bowl was placed in the kiln, the potter's seal was impressed in its underside.* **3** Often, **impress on** or **upon**: °stress, °emphasize, °urge, bring °home (to): *They tried to impress on them the gravity of the situation.*

impression n. **1** °sensation, °feeling, °sense, °suspicion, awareness, consciousness, °idea, °belief, °fancy, °notion: *I have the impression that I have been here before. She gave me the impression that she didn't like me.* **2** °impact, °effect, °influence: *Are you concerned about the impression of his speech on the crowd?* **3** dent, °indentation, °depression, °hollow, °mark, °stamp, °impress, °brand: *Look here, where the chair has made an impression in the carpet.* **4** printing, °issue, °print, °copy, °run: *This is the third impression from the original plates.* **5** impersonation, °imitation; °parody, °satire, Colloq °take-off, Brit send-up: *After dinner, Gerry did his impression of Churchill.*

impressionable adj. °suggestible, °susceptible, persuadable or persuasible, impressible, °receptive, °responsive: *They seek to enrol students who are at an impressionable age.*

impressive adj. evocative, °moving, affecting, °stimulating, °exciting, °stirring, °powerful, °provocative, arousing, awe-inspiring, °awesome, °imposing, °formidable, °portentous, redoubtable: *She has many impressive talents.*

imprison v. incarcerate, confine, detain, remand, °jail or Brit also gaol, °lock up, intern, °shut up, put behind bars, °put in or °throw into irons, °put away, Colloq Brit °send down, US °send up (the °river): *He was imprisoned for a crime he didn't commit.*

imprisonment n. incarceration, confinement, °detention, remand, °custody, Literary durance (vile): *The sentence is imprisonment for not less than one year.*

improbable adj. °doubtful, dubious, °unlikely, °questionable, °unrealistic, °far-fetched, °remote, °implausible, °unthinkable, °hard to °believe or °imagine, °inconceivable, °unbelievable, °fanciful, °incredible, °ridiculous, °ludicrous, °absurd, °crazy, °mad, °insane, °wild, °weird, °peculiar, °strange; °impossible; Colloq °fishy: *It is improbable that they will marry. He gave the most improbable excuses.*

improper adj. 1 °wrong, °mistaken, °erroneous, °false, °incorrect, °inaccurate, °inexact, °imprecise, °amiss, °faulty, °untrue, °irregular, °abnormal: *Sloppy research had led to improper conclusions.* 2 unfit, unsuitable, °inappropriate, inapt, °inapplicable, infelicitous, °incongruous, unsuited, °unseemly, un-befitting, unfitting, uncalled-for, inapposite, malapropos, out of keeping, out of °place, °incompatible, °inopportune: *Do you think it improper for shops to open on Sundays? His wedding was an improper occasion for comments about his philandering.* 3 indecorous, °indecent, indelicate, °immodest, °unseemly, °untoward, °unbecoming, °impolite, °suggestive, °risqué, off colour, °obscene, °corrupt, °immoral, °sinful, °wicked, °lewd, °lascivious: *Do you see anything improper in sex education for children?*

impropriety n. 1 improperness, erroneousness, incorrectness, °falsity, falseness, °inaccuracy, inaccurateness, inexactitude, inexactness, imprecision, impreciseness, irregularity, °abnormality: *I fail to see the impropriety in refusing to support capital punishment.* 2 unfitness, unsuit-ableness, inappropriateness, inaptness, in-applicability, infelicity, infelicitousness, incon-gruity, incongruousness, unseemliness, incom-patibility, inopportuneness: *The judge criticized the impropriety of allowing the child to testify.* 3 indecorousness, °bad *or* °poor °taste, indecency, °indelicacy, immodesty, unseem-liness, suggestiveness, immorality, sinfulness, wickedness, lewdness, lasciviousness: *In those days, the impropriety in wearing a brief bathing costume was thought shocking.* 4 °slip, °blunder, °mistake, °error, gaffe, gaucherie, faux pas: *She admitted to many improprieties during her term of office.*

improve v. 1 °better, ameliorate, upgrade, uplift, °amend, °enhance, °fix up, °reform, °redeem, °rehabilitate, redress, °repair, °correct, °rectify, °put *or* °set °right, emend; °modernize, update, °refurbish, recondition, °renovate, °repair, °overhaul, remodel: *We must improve procedures for dealing with small claims. The landlord refuses to spend any money to improve the property.* 2 °develop, °increase, °advance, °promote, °further, °benefit; °look up, °recover, °pick up, *Colloq* give a new lease of *or* US on life, take a °turn for the °better, US take a new lease on life: *How can I improve my chances of winning at snooker? Business has improved considerably.* 3 °convalesce, °recuperate, °recover, get °better, °mend, °rally, (make) °progress, °gain (strength *or* ground), °revive: *Mrs Costello is out of intensive care and improving daily.*

improvement n. 1 betterment, amelioration; °reform, rehabilitation, upgrading, enhance-ment, °repair: *The committee is working for the improvement of the neighbourhood.* 2 °recovery, °rise, °increase, °gain, °advance, upswing, °progress; recuperation, convalescence: *There was an improvement in share prices after release of the trade figures. The patient shows considerable improvement.* 3 °advance, °change for the °better: *This year's crop is an improvement over last year's.*

improvident adj. 1 °short-sighted, °imprudent, °wasteful, °profligate, °prodigal, °spendthrift, °extravagant, °lavish, °profuse, happy-go-lucky, penny wise and pound foolish, uneconomic(al), thriftless: *He who is improvident in his youth plans for a short life.* 2 incautious, °unwary, °rash, °reckless, °impulsive, °impetuous, headlong, °heedless, °careless, °unthinking, unthought-ful, unmindful: *The club's present financial straits are the result of having an improvident treasurer.*

improvise n. 1 ad lib, extemporize, *Colloq* °play (it) by ear, °fake it, wing it: *I like a comedian who improvises as he goes along.* 2 °invent, concoct, °devise, contrive, jury-rig; °make do: *We had to improvise a mast from parts of the boom. When you have nothing to work with, you have to improvise.*

imprudent adj. °indiscreet, °impulsive, °rash, °reckless, °hasty, incautious, °impetuous, °improvident, °careless, °heedless, °foolhardy, °irresponsible, injudicious, ill-judged, °thoughtless, ill-considered, °ill-advised, inad-visable, unwise, inexpedient, °foolish, °mad, °crazy, °insane, °inane, °silly, °perverse, °wrong, wrong-headed: *It would be imprudent to go out during the storm.*

impudence n. °impertinence, °effrontery, insolence, °disrespect, °presumption, pre-sumptuousness, audacity, shamelessness, pertness, sauciness, boldness, brazenness, °incivility, rudeness, impoliteness, *Colloq* lip, °gall, guff, °sauce, °mouth, *Brit* backchat, side, *US* back talk, *Slang* chutzpah: *He had the impu-dence to suggest that I was too old for the job!*

impudent adj. °shameless, °impertinent, °insolent, °disrespectful, °forward, °presumptuous, °audacious, °pert, saucy, °bold, °brazen, °cocky, cocksure, °arrogant, uncivil, °ill-mannered, °rude, °impolite, *Colloq* °fresh, °brassy, °cheeky: *Asked the simplest question, she is always ready with an impudent response.*

impulsive n. °impetuous, °emotional, unpre-dictable, °unpremeditated, unplanned, spur-of-the-moment, °extemporaneous, uncon-sidered, °offhand, °instinctive, °involuntary, °spontaneous, quick, °sudden, °precipitate, °immediate, °snap, °rash, headlong, °rash, °reckless, devil-may-care, °foolhardy, madcap, °wild: *You may say that it was impulsive of me to give her all that money, but I love her.*

impure adj. 1 °dirty, soiled, unclean, sullied, tainted, polluted, defiled, °foul, °filthy, fecu-lent, infected, scummy, °putrid, putrescent, °rotten: *The water is impure and not fit to drink.* 2 °mixed, alloyed, contaminated, adul-terated, debased, °unrefined: *Impure ore contains other substances which are removed during pro-cessing.* 3 unclean, unhallowed, forbidden, dis-allowed, *Judaism* tref *or* treif *or* treifa: *Certain foods are considered impure in some religions.* 4 °unchaste, °immoral, °sinful, °wicked, °evil, °vile, unvirtuous, unvirginal, corrupted, defiled, debased, vitiated, °degenerate, depraved, °loose, °wanton, °lustful, °promiscuous, libidinous, °dissolute, licentious, °obscene, °prurient, °dirty, °filthy, lubricious *or* lubricous, salacious, °lascivious, °lewd, °lecherous: *The book was condemned as 'likely to encourage impure thoughts'.*

impurity n. 1 °pollution, contamination, defilement, adulteration, dirtiness, unclean-ness, foulness: *The impurity of the water in our rivers is a cause for concern.* 2 Often, **impurities**: °dirt, contaminant, pollutant, °pollution, smut, °filth, °foreign °matter *or* °body: *This filter is* *guaranteed to remove impurities from the water.* **3** unchastity, immorality, sinfulness, wickedness, °evil, vileness, corruption, degeneration, depravity, looseness, wantonness, °lust, lustfulness, promiscuity, promiscuousness, libidinousness, dissoluteness, licentiousness, obscenity, prurience, dirtiness, filthiness, lubricity, salaciousness, lasciviousness, lewdness, lecherousness: *Children ought not to be exposed to the impurity encountered on everyday television.*

imputation *n.* °charge, indictment, °accusation, °allegation, °challenge, censure, °blame, reproach, °slur, °aspersion, °attribution, ascription, insinuation, °implication, °innuendo: *I resent the imputation that I broke the vase on purpose.*

impute *v.* ascribe, °assign, °attribute, °credit, °charge, °put *or* °set down to; °insinuate, °imply, °suggest, °hint at: *The critic imputed meanings to the book that the author had never intended.*

inability *n.* incapacity, incapability, °incompetence, unfitness, ineptness, °ineptitude, unqualifiedness, °impotence: *The inability of many school-leavers to perform simple arithmetical tasks is deeply worrying.*

inaccessible *adj.* **1** unavailable, unobtainable, unattainable, unreachable, °unapproachable: *The minister has made himself inaccessible for interviews.* **2** impenetrable, impassable, °out-of-the-way: *The tomb lies in a part of the jungle inaccessible except by air.*

inaccurate *adj.* °wrong, °incorrect, °erroneous, °mistaken, °inexact, °imprecise, °faulty, °flawed, °imperfect, °amiss, awry, °false, fallacious, illogical, °unsound, *Colloq* off the °mark, off the beam, °cold, *Chiefly US* all wet, *US* (way) off base *Slang* cock-eyed, full of °hot air: *Reports of my death were obviously inaccurate.*

inactive *adj.* **1** °passive, placid, °quiet, °tranquil, quiescent, °serene, °peaceful, pacific, resting, unmoving, motionless, immobile, immobilized, °still, °inert, °lifeless, °inanimate, sluggish, °listless, °lethargic, °lackadaisical, languid, °indolent, °lazy, °torpid, somnolent, °idle, °slothful, °supine: *Although there was plenty to do round the house, he remained inactive all summer.* **2** non-functioning, inoperative, °dormant; unoccupied, °idle, °unemployed, jobless, out of °work, out of a °job: *The volcano was inactive for a thousand years. These miners have been inactive for six months.*

inactivity *n.* **1** passiveness *or* passivity, placidity *or* placidness, °quiet, tranquillity, °serenity, °peace, peacefulness; motionlessness, immobility, stillness, °inertia, inertness, lifelessness, °sluggishness, listlessness, °lethargy, languidness, °indolence, laziness, °torpor, somnolence, °idleness, slothfulness, °sloth: *She alternates between periods of activity and inactivity.* **2** inaction, quiescence; hibernation, aestivation: *During repairs, the reactor will be in a state of inactivity. Some animals have a period of inactivity during certain times of the year.*

inadequate *adj.* **1** °insufficient, °deficient, not °enough, too °little, °scarce, °meagre, °scanty, skimpy, °sparse, (in) °short (supply); °unsatisfactory, °imperfect, °incomplete, °defective, unsuitable, °disappointing, °flawed, °faulty: *Funds are inadequate to meet her expenses. The terms of the agreement are inadequate.* **2 inadequate to**: unsuited to *or* for, unfit

for, °unqualified for, not up to, unequal to, °unworthy of, inapt for, °inept for, °incapable of: *He proved inadequate to the demands of the job.*

inadmissible *adj.* disallowed, unallowable, unallowed, forbidden, °unacceptable, prohibited, unsuitable, unsuited, °unqualified, °inappropriate, °inapplicable, °improper, objectionable, °exceptionable, °incorrect, °wrong: *Such evidence is inadmissible in court.*

inadvertent *adj.* **1** unintentional, unintended, °unpremeditated, °accidental, °unthinking, unwitting, °chance; °unconscious, unplanned, unstudied, undesigned, unintended: *She was an inadvertent witness to the murder. I assure you that the error was entirely inadvertent.* **2** °careless, °inattentive, negligent, °heedless, unobservant: *Inadvertent commentators failed to see the significance of her words.*

inalienable *adj.* untransferable, intransferable, °absolute, °inherent, unconsignable, sacrosanct, inviolable, non-negotiable, unnegotiable, unchallengeable, *Law* imprescriptible, entailed, indefeasible: *People have an inalienable right to life, liberty, and the pursuit of happiness.*

inane *adj.* °silly, asinine, °vapid, °vacant, vacuous, °absurd, fatuous, °foolish, °senseless, °nonsensical, °unreasonable, °preposterous, °ludicrous, °ridiculous, laughable, risible, °mad, lunatic, °crazy, °stupid, °dumb, idiotic, moronic, imbecilic, *Colloq* nutty, nuts, °daft, daffy, screwy, batty, dippy, wacky, cuckoo, loony, goofy, *Brit* bonkers, dotty: *Students seem especially prone to inane behaviour.*

inanimate *adj.* °lifeless, motionless, immobile, unmoving, °inactive, °inert, °still, spiritless, soulless, °dead, °defunct: *He just sits there, like an inanimate piece of furniture.*

inapplicable *adj.* °inappropriate, unsuitable, unsuited, inapt, °irrelevant, °unrelated, unconnected, inapposite, beside the °point *or* °question, °extraneous, off the °mark, *Colloq US* off base: *That law is inapplicable in your case.*

inappropriate *adj.* °improper, unfitting, unfit, unsuitable, unsuited, unbefitting, °incompatible, malapropos, ungermane, inapt, inapposite, out of keeping, °incongruous, infelicitous, °inopportune, untimely, °irrelevant, °inapplicable: *Your facetiousness was quite inappropriate to such a solemn occasion.*

inarticulate *adj.* **1** disjointed, unconnected, °incoherent, °incomprehensible, jumbled, unintelligible, unclear, illogical, °discursive, °rambling, scrambled, °wild, irrational, muddled, mixed-up, °confused, digressive: *She sat through an inarticulate lecture on Joyce's use of the subjunctive.* **2** mumbled, garbled, blurred, muffled, muttered, faltering, °halting, °indistinct, unclear, unintelligible: *They communicate with each other in inarticulate grunts.* **3** °speechless, °tongue-tied, (struck) °dumb, °mute, voiceless: *Ed is inarticulate when it comes to describing Vera.*

inattentive *n.* unobservant, °heedless, °careless, negligent, neglectful, °indifferent, uncaring, apathetic, °slack, °remiss, unconcerned, °detached, unmindful, distracted, distrait(e), °absent-minded, abstracted, in a brown study, day-dreaming, oscitant, wool-gathering, musing, °oblivious, (with one's head) in the clouds, in a world of one's own: *It was late and the children were getting restless and inattentive.*

inaudible *adj.* unheard, °imperceptible, °indistinct, °low, °faint, muted, °quiet, °soft, muffled, stifled: *The film was good, although some of the dialogue was inaudible.*

inaugurate *v.* **1** °initiate, °begin, °commence, °enter upon, °start, °introduce, usher in, °institute, °launch, °originate, °set up, °get under °way, °get °going: *A new programme of health services has been inaugurated.* **2** °install or instal, °induct, °invest, °establish, instate: *The President was inaugurated last week.*

inauspicious *adj.* °unpromising, unlucky, °unfortunate, unfavourable, unpropitious, °untoward, ill-starred, °ominous, ill-omened, ill-fated, °portentous, °menacing, °doomed, °sinister, °dark, °gloomy, cloudy, clouded, °black: *The middle of a recession is an inauspicious time to set up a business.*

inborn *adj.* innate, congenital, °inherent, in- herited, °hereditary, inbred, °natural, °native, constitutional, deep-seated, deep-rooted, °ingrained, °instinctive or instinctual, *Technical* connate: *A gift for music is inborn.*

incandescent *adj.* °glowing, red-hot, white-hot, alight, aflame, °flaming, °burning, °fiery, can- dent, flaring: *Light-bulbs contain an incandescent filament.*

incapable *adj.* **1** Often, **incapable of**: °unable (to), °powerless (to), °incompetent (to), unfit (to), °unqualified (to), °impotent (to), unequal to, not up to: *He seems incapable of completing his assignment.* **2 incapable of**: insusceptible to, °resistant to, impervious to, ill-disposed to, °disinclined to, not open to: *He is incapable of dishonesty.*

incapacitate *v.* disable, °cripple, °paralyse, °lame, °wound, °maim, °impair, °weaken, enfeeble, °enervate, °exhaust, devitalize; immobilize, inactivate, deactivate, put out of °action, indispose: *Severely incapacitated in the crash, John cannot walk without the aid of crutches. The power plant was incapacitated by one well-placed grenade.*

incentive *n.* °incitement, °impetus, °encouragement, goad, °prod, °provocation, °spur, impulse, °enticement, °lure, °inducement, stimulus, motivation, *Colloq* carrot: *The discount is offered as an incentive to buy a new car.*

incidence *n.* frequency, °rate, °degree, °extent, °occurrence, °prevalence; °quantity, °amount, °number: *The incidence of heart disease is high in Britain.*

incident *n.* **1** °event, °occasion, °occurrence, °proceeding, °circumstance, °fact, °happening, °experience, °episode: *A curious incident led to the discovery.* **2** °disturbance, °scene, °affair, °upset, commotion, °fracas, °skirmish, set-to, *Colloq* to-do, do: *The police were called because of an incident at the pub next door.*

incidental *adj.* **1** °casual, °chance, fortuitous, aleatory, °random, °haphazard, serendipitous, unpredictable, °accidental, adventitious, unplanned, unlooked-for, *Colloq* fluky: *Any good that came from the war was incidental.* **2** °subordinate, °secondary, ancillary, °minor, lesser, °non-essential, unimportant, trivial, °negligible, °inconsequential, °insignificant, °petty, °trifling, °paltry: *The incidental events were not covered by the press.*

incidentally *adv.* **1** by the °way, by the by, apropos (of), parenthetically: *Incidentally, I won't be able to go the party tonight.* **2** casually, as °luck would have it, accidentally, by °chance, per- chance: *In addition to being held for murder, he was incidentally charged with possession of an illegal weapon.*

incision *n.* °cut, °gash, °slit, °slash: *The surgeon made an incision in the abdominal wall.*

incisive *adj.* **1** °keen, °sharp, °acute, °piercing, perspicacious, °perceptive, percipient, °penetrating, °trenchant, canny, °shrewd: *Shirley offered some incisive observations on the matter.* **2** °sarcastic, °biting, mordant, °cutting, °caustic, °sardonic, ironic(al), °sharp, acid, °tart, acrid, acrimonious, °bitter, acerbic, cynical, stinging, °critical: *Your incisive comments are not really appreciated, George.*

incite *v.* °stimulate, °inspire, °prompt, °move, °stir, °stir or °whip or °work up, bestir, °excite, °fire, exhort, °agitate, °foment, °inflame, °provoke, °rally, goad, °spur, °prick, °prod, °drive, °push, egg on, °encourage, °urge, °influence, °wake, waken, awaken, °rouse, °arouse: *Who was it that incited the crowd to violence?*

incitement *n.* **1** stimulation, instigating, spur- ring, urging, influencing, awakening, waken- ing, arousing, prodding, prompting, °stirring, °whipping, °exciting, firing, exhorting, agitating, fomenting, inflaming, provoking, rallying, goad- ing, pricking, needling: *Certain rabble-rousers have been accused of incitement of the crowds at the football stadiums.* **2** stimulus, °incentive, °inducement, °enticement, °temptation, impulse, motivation, °influence, instigation, °provocation, °inspiration, °persuasion, exhor- tation, °agitation, fomentation, °inflammation, arousal, °encouragement, °excitement: *Greed is a powerful incitement to dishonesty.*

incivility *n.* rudeness, boorishness, coarseness, discourtesy, uncourtliness, unmannerliness, indecorum, indecorousness, discourteousness, impoliteness, tactlessness, ungentlemanliness, bad °breeding, ill °breeding, bad °manners, °misbehaviour: *The incivility with which the amba- ssador was treated is unforgivable.*

inclement *adj.* °extreme, intemperate, °severe, °harsh, rigorous; °stormy, °violent, rainy, squally, blustery, °raw, °bad, °tempestuous: *We are expecting inclement weather for the weekend.*

inclination *n.* **1** °bow, bowing, °bend, bending, °nod, °nodding, °tilt, tilting: *His tacit sign of recognition was an inclination of his head.* **2** °slope, °slant, °angle, °bend, °incline, °tilt: *The inclin- ation of the track is far too steep for such a vehicle.* **3** °disposition, predisposition, °tendency, °bent, °bias, °leaning, °preference, °turn, °cast, proclivity, propensity, °attitude, proneness, susceptibility, predilection, °partiality, °affection, °taste, °liking, °desire, velleity: *His inclination in favour of the offer is largely instinctive.* **4** °desire, °longing, craving, °appetite, °taste, °stomach, °sympathy, pre- dilection, °penchant, °fancy, °eagerness, °enthusiasm, zeal, °fervour, °ardour: *I have no inclination to watch open-heart surgery.*

incline *v.* **1** °tend, °lean, °bend, °bow, °slant, °tilt, °angle, bank, °slope, ascend, °rise, °descend: *The road inclines to the horizontal after a* *curve.* **2** °dispose, °influence, °persuade, predispose, °make, °lead, °prejudice, °bias: *Their accents might incline you to think of them as foreigners.* **3** °tend, °lean, gravitate, °show °favour *or* °preference, be attracted to, be °biased *or* °prejudiced, have a °mind; be °disposed *or* predisposed, °lean: *I incline towards the other candidate. He inclines towards corpulence.* —*n.* **4** °slope, °pitch, °grade, gradient, °slant, °ramp, °hill, °dip, descent, declivity, °rise, ascent, acclivity: *The car picked up speed going down one incline and slowed going up the next.*

inclined *adj.* **1** tending, °disposed, predisposed, °prone, °willing, °keen, °eager, *Colloq* of a °mind: *Though she is inclined to believe she has doubts.* **2** °likely, apt, °liable, minded, °prone: *He is equally inclined to kiss you as kill you.* **3** sloping, slanting, °leaning, bending, tilting, gravitating, °bearing, verging: *This wall is slightly inclined towards the river.*

include *v.* **1** °incorporate, °embody, comprise, °embrace, °cover, encompass, °take in, subsume, °comprehend, °contain: *Staff changes are included in the plan for reorganization.* **2** classify, °categorize, °group, °file, °list, catalogue, °tabulate, °register: *Did you include psychology among the social sciences?* **3** °involve, °count, °number, °allow for: *Please don't forget to include me in the invitation list.*

inclusion *n.* incorporation, involvement, counting, numbering, grouping, classification: *The inclusion of her name among the culprits was an error.*

inclusive *adj.* **1** °comprehensive, °general, all-encompassing, °wide, °broad, °extensive, °full, °umbrella, blanket, across the °board, all-in-one, unified: *We have an inclusive insurance policy that covers the entire family.* **2** inclusive of: including, embracing, comprising, °taking in, covering, incorporating, embodying: *Is this bill inclusive of service?*

incognito *adj.* **1** °unknown, disguised, concealed, °unidentified, in °disguise, unrecognizable, unrecognized: *I did not tell them who I was; I wanted to remain incognito.* —*adv.* **2** unrecognizably, in °disguise, °secretly, on the °sly, under °cover, clandestinely: *Why travel incognito if no one knows or cares who you really are?*

incoherent *adj.* °confused, garbled, °mixed up, disordered, jumbled, muddled, scrambled, °rambling, illogical, irrational, °wild, unstructured, disjoined, °disconnected, °disjointed, °loose, unconnected, uncoordinated, unintelligible, °inarticulate: *He arrived late with an incoherent excuse involving measles, his car, and a policeman.*

incombustible *adj.* °non-flammable, non-inflammable, fireproof, non-combustible; flame-proof: *She has to wear incombustible clothing at her job.*

income *n.* °return, °revenue(s), °receipts, proceeds, °profit(s), °gain(s), takings: *Most of his income is from investments.*

incoming *adj.* **1** arriving, entering: *Incoming passengers must pass through customs.* **2** °new, entering: *They are trying to predict the likely policies of the incoming government.*

incomparable *adj.* beyond °compare, unequalled, °matchless, °peerless, inimitable,

°unparalleled, unrivalled, °nonpareil, °transcendent, °surpassing, °supreme, °superior, °superlative, unsurpassed, unsurpassable: *Her performance as Lady Macbeth was incomparable.*

incompatible *adj.* °mismatched, unsuited, °discordant, clashing, jarring, °inconsistent, °contradictory, conflicting, uncongenial, irreconcilable, °incongruous; antithetic, °opposed, °opposite, °contrary, antipathetic, antagonistic, °hostile: *The colours in the carpet are incompatible with those in the curtains. My sister and I are totally incompatible and can never meet without arguing.*

incompetence *n.* °inability, incapacity, inadequacy, insufficiency, deficiency, °ineptitude, inefficiency, uselessness, faultiness: *The students' failure to perform well is often attributable to the incompetence of their teachers.*

incompetent *adj.* °unqualified, unfit, °unable, °incapable, unskilled, unskilful, °inept, maladroit, inexpert, °awkward, floundering, °clumsy, bungling, gauche, °useless, °inadequate, °insufficient, °ineffective, °ineffectual, °inefficient: *Incompetent managers need competent secretaries in order to survive.*

incomplete *adj.* unfinished, °undone, °imperfect, °undeveloped, °deficient, °defective, unaccomplished, °partial, °sketchy, °crude, °rough, °fragmentary, fragmented, °piecemeal: *An incomplete manuscript of a new novel was found in his desk.*

incomprehensible *adj.* unintelligible, unfathomable, impenetrable, °deep, abstruse, arcane, °recondite, indecipherable, undecipherable, inscrutable, °cryptic, °obscure, °opaque, °dark, °occult, °perplexing, °mysterious, mystifying, enigmatic, °puzzling, over (someone's) head, baffling, unimaginable, °inconceivable: *They spoke in Swahili, an incomprehensible language to me.*

inconceivable *adj.* °incredible, °unbelievable, °unthinkable, unimaginable, °incomprehensible, °unheard-of, undreamed of *or* undreamt of, unthought of, °impossible, °overwhelming, staggering, *Colloq* mind-boggling: *Putting a man on Mars before 2000 is inconceivable.*

inconclusive *adj.* °indecisive, °unresolved, °indefinite, °unsettled, °open, indeterminate, in °limbo, *Colloq* up in the air: *The test results are inconclusive, so we must continue our investigations.*

incongruous *adj.* °inconsistent, inharmonious, disharmonious, °discordant, dissonant, disconsonant, °incoherent, °incompatible, incongruent, conflicting, °unbecoming, °unseemly, unsuited, unsuitable, unapt, °inappropriate, misallied, unfitting, unfit, °improper, malapropos, unmeet, °absurd, discrepant, disparate, °different, °divergent, disagreeing, °contrary, °contradictory, °paradoxical, out of °step, out of keeping, out of °line: *That jacket looks incongruous with those trousers. It was incongruous to see two octogenarians dancing at the disco.*

inconsequential *adj.* unimportant, °insignificant, trivial, °trifling, nugatory, inconsiderable, inappreciable, °negligible, °minor, °paltry, °petty, °immaterial, °slight, lightweight, °worthless, *Colloq* piddling: *Why dwell on inconsequential details?*

inconsiderate *adj.* °thoughtless, unthoughtful, °unthinking, unconcerned, uncaring, unmindful, °heedless, unheeding, insensitive,

°unsympathetic, °tactless, °intolerant, °rude, °ungracious: *How could you be so inconsiderate as to work late on my birthday?*

inconsistent *adj.* **1** See **incongruous**, above. **2** °irregular, °capricious, °fickle, °erratic, °inconstant, uneven, unpredictable, °unreliable, undependable, °unstable, unsteady, °changeable, °variable: *Their behaviour is so inconsistent that I can't tell what they'll do next.*

inconsolable *adj.* disconsolate, °broken-hearted, heartbroken, °desolate, °forlorn, despairing, °miserable, °wretched, grief-stricken: *They are inconsolable over the death of their dog.*

inconspicuous *adj.* unnoticeable, °unnoticed, °unobtrusive, unostentatious, °insignificant, °indefinite, °indistinguishable, °undistinguished: °modest, unassuming, °discreet: *Wearing a grey coat and hat, he was quite inconspicuous in the crowd. He played an inconspicuous role in the entire affair.*

inconstancy *n.* changeableness, fickleness, irregularity, mutability, variability, unsteadiness, unsteadfastness, capriciousness, volatility, mercurialness *or* mercuriality, changeableness, unreliability; faithlessness, unfaithfulness, changeability: *How do you deal with inconstancy in one you thought a friend?*

inconstant *adj.* °changeable, mutable, °fickle, °capricious, mercurial, °volatile, vacillating, unsteady, unsteadfast, °irresolute, °unreliable, undependable, fluctuating, wavering, °erratic, °inconsistent, °flighty, °unstable, °unsettled, °fitful, °vague, °indefinite, °variable, °moody: *His supporters proved inconstant, and he fell from power. The inconstant wind blew their craft hither and thither.*

incontinent *adj.* **1** unrestrained, unconstrained, unrestricted, °uncontrolled, uncontrollable, ungoverned, °ungovernable, unbridled, uncurbed: *She must learn to suppress her incontinent tongue.* **2** °lecherous, libidinous, °lascivious, °libertine, °lustful, °lewd, debauched, °wanton, dissolute, °loose, lubricious *or* lubricous, salacious, °profligate, °obscene, °dirty, °filthy: *Members of the Hell-Fire Club were well known for their incontinent behaviour.* **3** self-soiling, bedwetting, *Medicine* enuretic: *Some old people lose control and become incontinent.*

incontrovertible *adj.* irrefutable, °indisputable, indubitable, undeniable, incontestable, °unquestionable, °sure, °certain, °definite, °definitive, established, °absolute, °positive: *The fingerprint was incontrovertible evidence that he had been there.*

inconvenience *n.* **1** °disadvantage, °discomfort, °pain, °trouble, °bother, °annoyance, °nuisance, awkwardness, °disturbance, disruption, °burden, °drawback, °hindrance, °impediment, °difficulty, °upset: *How are you coping with the inconvenience of walking with crutches?* **2** cumbersomeness, unwieldiness, burdensomeness, onerousness, troublesomeness, disadvantageousness, awkwardness, inappropriateness, untimeliness: *The delay has led to considerable public inconvenience.*

—*v.* **3** discommode, °trouble, incommode, °disturb, °disrupt, °upset, °put out, °bother, °annoy, °irritate, °irk: *Would it inconvenience you to meet me at the station?*

inconvenient *adj.* cumbersome, °unwieldy, °burdensome, onerous, °troublesome, bothersome, annoying, irritating, °irksome, °unsettling, °disturbing, upsetting, disrupting, disadvantageous, °awkward, °inappropriate; inexpedient, °inopportune, untimely, ill-timed: *Those large boxes of washing-powder are inconvenient because they're so heavy. It is inconvenient for me to go to the door now.*

incorporate *v.* °embody, °include, °combine, comprise, °embrace, °integrate, consolidate, °unite, °amalgamate, assimilate, coalesce, °unify; °merge, °mix, °blend: *The university incorporates several independent colleges. Gently fold in the egg whites, incorporating them into the mixture.*

incorrect *adj.* °wrong, °mistaken, °inaccurate, °untrue, °imprecise, °inexact, °erroneous, fallacious, °specious; °improper, °false, °faulty: *Your method is right but the answer is incorrect. That is the incorrect key for this lock.*

incorrigible *adj.* °bad, °naughty, °villainous, °wicked, °sinful, °hopeless; intractable, unchangeable, unalterable, °habitual, inveterate, °incurable, °stubborn, hardened, obdurate, °inflexible, uncontrollable: *When a teenager, Giles was absolutely incorrigible. Among other things, he was an incorrigible liar.*

incorrupt *adj.* **1** °moral, °upright, °righteous, °pure, upstanding, °honourable, °good, °virtuous, °honest, straightforward, °straight, unimpeachable, incorruptible, undefiled, °impeccable, °spotless, °immaculate, °faultless, °flawless: *Show me one nation run by a totally incorrupt government.* **2** error-free, °correct, uncorrupted: *He possesses the only incorrupt manuscript of the play.*

increase *v.* **1** °grow, °swell, °enlarge, dilate, wax, °expand, °extend, distend, °inflate, augment, snowball, °enhance, °heighten, °raise, °develop, multiply, burgeon *or* bourgeon, °flourish, °proliferate, °spread, broaden, °widen, °lengthen: *Since you left, my work has increased threefold.* **2** °prolong, °advance, °further, °improve, °better, °strengthen: *The more lottery tickets you buy, the more you increase your chances of winning.*

—*n.* **3** °growth, enlargement, °expansion, °extension, augmentation, enhancement, °development, multiplication, °proliferation, °spread: *The increase in scientific knowledge has been phenomenal.* **4** °addition, °increment, escalation, inflation, °gain, °rise, °boost: *Increases in costs are reflected in increases in prices.* **5 on the increase**: waxing, developing, growing, expanding, increasing, escalating, on the °rise, proliferating, spreading: *Trade with the Far East will be on the increase next year.*

incredible *adj.* **1** °unbelievable, beyond °belief, °inconceivable, unimaginable, °unthinkable, °improbable, °implausible, °far-fetched, °absurd, °preposterous, °ridiculous, °unlikely, °impossible, °unrealistic, °unreal, °fictitious, mythic(al): *Incredible as it may appear, continents move a few inches a year.* **2** °extraordinary, astounding, astonishing, °amazing, wonderful, awe-inspiring, °awesome, tremendous,

°marvellous, °prodigious, *Colloq* far-out, *US* humongous: *The incredible amounts spent on arms could be better spent on medical research.*

incredulous *adj.* disbelieving, °unbelieving, dubious, °doubtful, °sceptical, mistrustful, °distrustful, °suspicious: *We were incredulous when we learnt who had won the award.*

increment *n.* °increase, °addition, °gain, accrual *or chiefly Brit* accrument, augmentation: *The increment last year barely compensated for inflation.*

incriminate *v.* °accuse, °charge, °blame, °implicate, inculpate, °indict, °impeach, °involve, °entangle, *Colloq* °point the °finger at, *Chiefly US* put the °finger on, *Slang US* °finger: *The suspect confessed and incriminated two others.*

incubate *v.* °hatch, °brood; °nurse, nurture, °develop: *How long have you been incubating this plan?*

incumbent *adj.* **1** °obligatory, °necessary, required, °mandatory, compulsory, binding, °demanding, commanding, prescribed: *As their father, you ought to feel it incumbent on you to talk to the children's teachers.* **2** office-holding: *The incumbent chairman is not responsible for his predecessor's mistakes.*
—*n.* **3** office-holder, °official, °occupant: *As the incumbent, you have a better chance of being re-elected.*

incur *v.* °bring upon *or* on (oneself), °draw, °attract, °arouse, °provoke, invite, expose (oneself) to, lay (oneself) °open to: *For some reason he incurred the displeasure of his manager.*

incurable *adj.* **1** irremediable, °terminal, inoperable, °fatal, °hopeless: *The doctor told me yesterday that the condition is incurable.* **2** °hopeless, inveterate, °habitual, °incorrigible, dyed in the wool, unflagging, °relentless, irredeemable; irreparable, unrectifiable: *You are an incurable optimist if you think you will complete this book by the deadline.*

indebted *adj.* obligated, owing, °obliged, °beholden, °bound, °liable, °responsible: *I am indebted to the Salvation Army for their help.*

indecent *adj.* **1** indecorous, indelicate, °immodest, °improper, °unbecoming, unsuitable, unfit, °inappropriate; in °bad °taste: *When he proposed marriage she accepted with indecent haste.* **2** °unseemly, °shameless, °shameful, °offensive, °outrageous, °repellent, °repulsive, °distasteful, °ill-mannered, °rude, °suggestive, °coarse, °risqué, °vulgar, °blue, °obscene, °gross, °rank, °prurient, °dirty, °foul, °filthy, °pornographic, ithyphallic, scatological, salacious, °lascivious, licentious, °lewd, lubricious *or* lubricous, smutty, °vile, °degenerate, debauched: *There are always a lot of complaints about indecent language on television.*

indecision *n.* hesitation, wavering, indecisiveness, vacillation, irresolution, uncertainty, ambivalence, °shilly-shally *or* shilly-shallying, °fluctuation, tergiversation: *Her indecision stems from caution, not ignorance of the issues.*

indecisive *adj.* **1** hesitating, °hesitant, wavering, °doubtful, vacillating, undecided, °irresolute, °uncertain, of two minds, ambivalent, shilly-shallying, °wishy-washy, namby-pamby, fluctuating, tergiversating: *Why are you so assertive at the office yet so indecisive at home?* **2** °indefinite, indeterminate, undecided,

°inconclusive, °open, °unsettled, °moot, °doubtful: *The battle was indecisive, with both sides incurring heavy losses.*

indeed *adv.* **1** certainly, °surely, to be °sure, °doubtless(ly), °undoubtedly, undeniably, °definitely, °positively, °absolutely, °exactly, °just so, °actually, °truly, truthfully, °seriously, (all) joking aside, in (point of) °fact, of °course, °really, in °reality, to be °realistic, °naturally, upon my °word, on my °honour, on my °oath, *Brit* °rather, *Colloq* no kidding: *Indeed, that is the news he has been expecting.* **2** what is more, °still, not to say, as a matter of °fact, if the °truth be known, to say the least: *His had been a depressing, indeed miserable childhood.*
—*interj.* **3** Is that so!, You don't say!, Really!, By George!, By Jove!, (Upon) my word!, My goodness!, Goodness!, Gracious!, Mercy!, Good Lord!, Good heavens!, My stars!, Fancy that!, Imagine (that)!, Well, I'll be (damned)!, *Colloq Brit* Blimey!, Cor!, Crikey!: *'I've torn up the winning lottery ticket.' 'Indeed!'*

indefinite *adj.* **1** °uncertain, undetermined, undefined, °imprecise, °inexact, inexplicit, unspecified, °unsettled, unfixed, unspecific, non-specific, °vague, °general, indeterminate, undecided, *sub judice*: *The time of the meeting was indefinite.* **2** °vague, unclear, °obscure, °confused, confusing, °puzzling, baffling, °cryptic, bewildering, mystifying, °equivocal, °ambiguous, unspecific, non-specific, inexplicit, °inexact, °imprecise: *Your directions for getting here were too indefinite.* **3** ill-defined, undefined, blurred, blurry, °hazy, °indistinct, °obscure, °dim, °fuzzy, unrecognizable, °indistinguishable: *Indefinite shapes loomed in the fog.* **4** °unlimited, °unknown, uncounted, uncountable, undefinable, indeterminate, indeterminable, unbounded, °boundless, °immeasurable, incalculable, °limitless, °endless, °infinite: *He pondered the indefinite capacities of the mind.* **5** °hesitant, °vague, shilly-shallying, vacillating, °indecisive, undecided, °inconstant, wavering, unsure, °uncertain, *Colloq* °wishy-washy: *She is still indefinite about going to the party.*

indelible *adj.* ineradicable *or* uneradicable *or* non-eradicable, inerasable *or* unerasable *or* non-erasable, ineffaceable, inexpungible, °indestructible, uncancellable *or* non-cancellable, °enduring, °permanent, °lasting, °fixed, °ingrained, inextirpable: *The laundry marks are in indelible ink. Irena makes an indelible impression on everyone she meets.*

indelicacy *n.* coarseness, crudeness, roughness, °vulgarity, boorishness, churlishness, offensiveness, rudeness, immodesty, indecency, shamelessness; °incivility, indecorum, inelegance, uncourtliness, unmannerliness, impoliteness, unrefinement, unseemliness, tastelessness, °bad *or* °poor °taste, grossness: *She refuses to comment on the indelicacy of his proposal.*

indemnity *n.* **1** compensation, repayment, reimbursement, °remuneration, recompense, °consideration, °restitution, reparation(s), redress, indemnification, °return, quid pro quo, °restoration, °award, °reward, °payment, disbursement, °amends, °requital, °atonement, °reckoning, quittance: *The victors demanded indemnity for the losses they had suffered.*

2 °insurance, °protection, °security, °safety, °guarantee, °assurance, underwriting, °warrant, °endorsement, certification; °exemption, impunity, °privilege: *Am I covered for indemnity against third-party claims?*

indentation *n.* °notch, dent, °nick, °cut, °score, °mark, °depression, °impression, °hollow, dimple, °pit; *Typography* indention: *The chair legs had left small indentations in the parquet floor. The indentation of each paragraph should be five spaces.*

independence *n.* **1** °freedom, °liberty, autonomy, °sovereignty, self-rule, home °rule, self-determination, °self-government, self-direction, autarchy: *The colony gained independence from Portugal.* **2** °confidence, °self-confidence, self-sufficiency, self-reliance, self-assurance: *Edwina asserted her independence by taking over the company herself.*

independent *adj.* **1** °free, self-governing, autonomous, °sovereign: *In 1829 Greece was acknowledged as an independent state.* **2** unrestrained, unrestricted, unfettered, untrammelled, unregulated, °uncontrolled, °separate(d), unconnected, °disconnected, °unrelated, °distinct: *Air is made up of independent particles.* **3** self-reliant, °self-sufficient, self-assured, (self-)°confident, °bold, individualistic, °competent: *For a six-year-old, he is very independent.* **4** °voluntary, °non-partisan, °spontaneous, °unsolicited, unbidden, °unprejudiced, unbiased, °non-aligned, unaligned, °disinterested, °neutral: *Four independent witnesses testified to seeing him at the scene of the crime.* **5** °unlimited, unrestricted, affluent, °self-sufficient; unearned: *She is a woman of independent means.* **6** unallied, unaffiliated, uncommitted, individualistic, undecided: *Independent candidates outnumber those of the two main parties in this election.* **7** °outside, °external, unaffiliated, non-affiliated, unconnected, °disinterested: *An independent auditor was engaged to go over the company's books.* **8 independent of**: irrespective of, disregarding, °notwithstanding, ignoring, excluding; °exclusive of, °except for, °barring, °apart from, °besides, beyond, *US* aside from: *He insists on doing things his way, independent of others' feelings. Independent of you and me, no one cares what he does.*
—*n.* **9** °individual, °nonconformist, maverick, *Colloq* loner: *He is an independent, not affiliated to any political party.*

indestructible *adj.* °durable, long-lasting, °everlasting, °eternal, °endless, °perennial, °permanent, °fixed, unchanging, °changeless, unchangeable, °indelible, ineradicable, inextirpable, immutable, unalterable, °constant, undying, non-perishable, imperishable; unbreakable, non-breakable, shatter-proof: *The problem is that many plastics are virtually indestructible.*

index *n.* **1** °guide, directory, °list, listing, °table of contents, catalogue, °key, °thesaurus: *To find synonyms for a word in this book, look first in the index.* **2** °mark, °sign, °clue, °token, °hint, °pointer, °indicator, °indication, °guide: *An index to his feelings can be seen in the way he treats people.* **3** index °finger, forefinger, first °finger; °pointer, marker, needle, *Chiefly Brit typography* hand, *Chiefly US typography* fist: *Use an index to emphasize important paragraphs.* **4** °ratio,

°measure, °formula, °factor: *The cephalic index is the ratio of the width of a skull to its length multiplied by 100.*

indicate *v.* **1** °point out, °point to, °mark, °specify, °designate; call *or* direct °attention to, °show: *The thermometer indicated that the temperature was 22°C. Sally indicated the place where the dam would be built.* **2** °imply, °suggest, betoken, °manifest, °signify, bespeak, °reveal, evince, °evidence, °denote: *Measles is indicated by the presence of Koplik's spots.* **3** °suggest, °hint; °imply, °intimate; °say, °express, °state, °disclose, °tell, °make known, °make °clear, °register, °show, °display, °exhibit: *His frown indicated his doubts. She indicated her displeasure in a few, well-chosen words.* **4** °call for, °require, °demand, °need, °recommend: *The doctor advised that a surgical procedure is indicated in such cases.*

indication *n.* **1** °sign, °signal, °token, °suggestion, °hint, intimation, °inkling, °clue, °implication, °symptom: *A bullet-riddled corpse, said the detective, is usually a good indication of foul play.* **2** reading, °measure, °degree: *The indication on the pressure gauge is reaching the danger point.* **3** °omen, portent, forewarning, °warning, augury, foreshadowing, foretoken: *Those black clouds are an indication that a storm is brewing. Can't you give us any indication of what will become of us?* **4 indications**: °evidence, °data, °clues, °signs: *Indications are that she left on the last train.*

indicative of *adj.* signifying, indicating, indicatory of, suggesting, °suggestive of, hinting (at), °symptomatic of, denotative of, °characteristic of, °typical of, typifying: *Repeated stalling is indicative of some fault in the fuel.*

indicator *n.* °pointer, needle; °gauge, meter, °display: *The indicator reads exactly 67°C.*

indict *v.* Often, **indict for**: °charge (with), °accuse (with *or* of), arraign (for), °incriminate (in *or* for), inculpate (in *or* for), (for *or* with), °denounce (for), °blame (for *or* with); °summon, summons, subpoena: *She has been indicted for murder in the first degree.*

indifference *n.* **1** unconcern, apathy, listlessness, disinterest, coolness, nonchalance, insouciance, aloofness, °detachment, °disregard, inattention, pococuranteism *or* pococuratism, coldness, phlegm, stolidity, callousness, insensibility, impassiveness *or* impassivity: *I cannot believe the indifference she showed on learning about the tragedy.* **2** unimportance, insignificance, irrelevance, unconcern, inconsequence, °triviality: *Whether I go or stay is a matter of indifference to me.* **3** dispassion, disinterestedness, impartiality, neutrality, °objectivity, fairness, equitableness, even-handedness: *The judges demonstrated their indifference by awarding first prize to a novice.*

indifferent *adj.* **1** unconcerned, apathetic, uncaring, °listless, disinterested, uninterested, °cool, °nonchalant, °lukewarm, °lackadaisical, Laodicean, °dispassionate, insouciant, °aloof, °detached, °distant, removed, °inattentive, pococurante, °cold, °phlegmatic, °stolid, °callous, unemotional, uncompassionate, insensitive, unfeeling, °inconsiderate, °unsympathetic, °insensible, °impassive: *Joan remained totally indifferent to*

271

indigenous | indistinguishable

Charles's attentions. **2** °impartial, °neutral, °just, even-handed, °objective, °fair, °equitable, unbiased, °unprejudiced, °non-partisan, non-discriminatory, °dispassionate, °disinterested: *The problem is in reaching an indifferent judgement.* **3** °neutral, °average, °mediocre, °fair, °undistinguished, uninspired, lightweight, °passable, middling, °ordinary, commonplace, °everyday, so so, not bad; °poor, °inferior, not very *or* particularly *or* especially °good, *Slang Brit* naff: *He is a writer of indifferent quality. I held indifferent cards but lost little money.* **4** unimportant, °insignificant, trivial, °trifling, nugatory, °immaterial, °inconsequential, °minor, inappreciable, °slight, neither here nor there: *It is indifferent to him where she spends her money.*

indigenous *adj.* **1** °native, °local, autochthonous, endemic, °natural, °aboriginal, °original: *The indigenous inhabitants were displaced by marauding tribes.* **2** innate, °inborn, inbred, °inherent: *It is often difficult to distinguish between man's indigenous and his acquired characteristics.*

indigent *adj.* °needy, °poor, °destitute, poverty-stricken, in °want, penniless, °impoverished, °penurious, impecunious, necessitous, *Colloq* (dead *or* flat) °broke, stony-broke, °hard up, °short, on one's uppers, *Brit* skint, *US* strapped: *The two brothers made certain that their indigent parents were well looked after.*

indigestion *n.* dyspepsia, °upset °stomach, °stomach °distress; stomach-ache, gastralgia: *A bit of bicarbonate of soda cured my indigestion at once.*

indignant *adj.* provoked, exasperated, °disgruntled, piqued, irked, irritated, annoyed, vexed, °angry, °furious, irate, angered, enraged, incensed, wrathful, in high dudgeon, in a °temper, in a °rage, in a °pet, *Literary* wroth, *Colloq* peeved, riled, in a °huff, huffy, miffed, °mad, livid, °sore, *US* teed off, *Slang* pissed off: *Peter was quite indignant to learn that the publisher had lost his manuscript.*

indignation *n.* °anger, °fury, °rage, wrath, exasperation, irritation, °annoyance, vexation, °resentment, *Literary* ire, choler: *She was filled with righteous indignation at the treatment she received.*

indignity *n.* °insult, affront, °outrage, °injury, °offence, °humiliation, °disrespect, °slight, °dishonour, snub, obloquy, contumely, °scorn, reproach, °abuse, discourtesy, °aspersion, *Colloq* °slap (in the face): *The duchess had to suffer the indignity of arrest for shoplifting.*

indirect *adj.* **1** °roundabout, circuitous, circumambient, °devious, °tortuous, zigzag, winding, °rambling, roving, wandering, °erratic, °meandering, ambiguous, °crooked, °oblique, twisted, twisting; circumlocutory, periphrastic: *In an indirect way she told me that I was fired.* **2** °secondary, °incidental, ancillary, collateral, °accidental, °side, °subordinate, °subsidiary, °accessory, additional, adscititious, adventitious: *An indirect effect of winning the prize was an offer of more work.*

indiscreet *adj.* °imprudent, °tactless, incautious, impolitic, undiplomatic, °improvident, injudicious, °ill-advised, ill-judged, ill-considered, °rash, °reckless, °audacious, °bold, temerarious, °impulsive, °hasty, °impetuous, °thoughtless, insensitive, °heedless, °careless,

°unthinking, °mindless, unwise, °naïve, °foolish, °foolhardy: *Your reference to her plastic surgery was indiscreet to say the least.*

indiscretion *n.* **1** imprudence, tactlessness, improvidence, injudiciousness, rashness, recklessness, audacity, boldness, temerity, impulsiveness, hastiness, °haste, impetuousness, impetuosity, thoughtlessness, insensitivity, heedlessness, carelessness, °naïvety, foolishness, foolhardiness, °folly: *He was guilty of indiscretion in talking to the press about the confidential report.* **2** °blunder, °error, °mistake, °slip, °lapse, °misstep, gaffe, faux pas, °peccadillo, *Colloq* boner, *Brit* bloomer: *He spent much of his adult life paying for the indiscretions of his youth.*

indiscriminate *adj.* **1** undiscriminating, unselective, unparticular, uncritical, undiscerning, °careless, °promiscuous, °random: *Viola seems indiscriminate in her choice of companions.* **2** °confused, °haphazard, unorganized, °chaotic, disorganized, jumbled, disordered, disarranged, scrambled, mixed-up, °casual, °random, unsystematic, unsystematized, uncoordinated, unmethodical, wholesale, °erratic, *Colloq* higgledy-piggledy: *The Aztecs were victims of indiscriminate slaughter at the hands of the conquistadors.*

indispensable *adj.* **1** °crucial, °vital, °essential, °urgent, °imperative, °necessary, needed, needful, required, requisite, demanded, in °demand, called-for, of the °essence, °important, compelling: *A good television manner is indispensable in a national leader these days.* **2** °key, °unavoidable, inescapable, ineluctable, compulsory, °mandatory, sine qua non, °obligatory: *Are a black bowler and tightly furled umbrella still indispensable to doing business in the City?*

indisposed *adj.* **1** °ill, ailing, unwell, °sick, °sickly, °unsound, °unhealthy, in °bad °health, valetudinarian, out of commission, *Colloq* on the sick-list, (doing) °poorly, laid up, in a °bad °way, not up to snuff, off one's feed *or Brit* also grub, under the °weather: *Madam is indisposed and cannot have tea with you.* **2** °averse, °disinclined, °loath, unwilling, °reluctant, °resistant, °hesitant: *The judge was indisposed to leniency in such a serious case.*

indisputable *adj.* °unquestionable, °incontrovertible, incontestable, irrefutable, undeniable, indubitable, beyond °doubt, °sure, °certain, °positive, °definite, °definitive, °absolute, °fixed: *It was indisputable that the outlook was grim. The show was an indisputable success.*

indistinct *adj.* **1** °faint, °dim, °obscure, °vague, blurred, blurry, °filmy, °hazy, °misty, bleary, °shadowy, °fuzzy, foggy, °murky, °muddy, unclear, indiscernible, °illegible, muffled, unintelligible, °indistinguishable, indeterminate, °confused, °indefinite: *I could barely make out an indistinct figure in the dark. The writing on the matchbox was indistinct.* **2** °indistinguishable, °ambiguous, not °distinct, °equivocal, inseparable, ill-defined, undefined, °nebulous, °vague, °confused: *The identity of the three brothers is indistinct in my mind.*

indistinguishable *adj.* **1** Often, **indistinguishable from**: undifferentiated (from), °identical (to), °alike, °like two peas in a pod, °twin, inseparable: *He is indistinguishable from* *his brother. Her fingerprints and those found on the dagger are indistinguishable.* **2** indiscernible, °imperceptible, °indefinite, unclear, °indistinct: *His good qualities were indistinguishable to me.*

individual *adj.* **1** °single, °sole, °particular, °separate, °distinct, °discrete, °solitary, lone: *Consider the entire utterance, not just the individual words.* **2** °singular, °special, °specific, idiosyncratic, own, °characteristic, °distinctive, individualistic, °unique, °peculiar, °personal, °proper; unitary: *She has her individual style of dressing.*
—*n.* **3** °person, °human (being), (living) °soul, °mortal; °one, °party: *In a democracy each individual is entitled to one vote.*

individualist *n.* °independent, freethinker, °nonconformist, maverick, loner, lone wolf: *Nick is an individualist and seldom agrees with the majority.*

individually *adv.* °one at a time, °singly, °one by one, °separately, severally, °apart: *We must study each of these specimens individually.*

indoctrinate *v.* °train, °teach, °instruct, °school, °discipline, °drill, brainwash, propagandize; inculcate, imbue, °instil, °implant: *The children were indoctrinated to believe that they were members of the master race. He indoctrinated them with the idea that they were capable of anything.*

indolence *n.* laziness, slothfulness, °sloth, °sluggishness, °idleness, °lethargy, shiftlessness, languor, languidness, lassitude, listlessness, °torpor, torpidity, °inertia, inaction, °inactivity, fainéance, *dolce far niente,* oscitancy: *After winning the lottery, he spent his days in indolence.*

indolent *adj.* °lazy, °slothful, sluggish, °idle, °lethargic, °shiftless, languorous, languid, °torpid, °inert, °inactive, °stagnant, fainéant, °listless: *'Peel me a grape', she said in her most indolent manner.*

indomitable *adj.* °resolute, resolved, °determined, °steadfast, °staunch, °persistent, unstoppable, °irrepressible, indefatigable, °untiring, °tireless, unflagging, unyielding, unswerving, unwavering, unflinching, undaunted, °dauntless, °fearless, unafraid, °intrepid, °brave, °courageous, plucky, mettlesome; unconquerable, °unbeatable, °invincible: *She survived the prison camp by dint of indomitable strength of character.*

induce *v.* **1** °lead, °persuade, °influence, °prevail on *or* upon, °sway, °move, °convince, °get, °talk into, °prompt, °incite, instigate, actuate, °motivate, impel, °encourage, °inspire, °stimulate, °nudge, °push, °press, °urge, °prod, goad, °spur, egg on, °coax, °cajole, °lure, °entice, inveigle, °seduce: *He was induced to sell the secret plans to the enemy for a large sum.* **2** °cause, °bring about *or* on, °produce, give °rise to, engender, °create, °generate, °lead to; °effect, °occasion, °set in °motion: *Some drugs induce a state of euphoria.*

inducement *n.* °attraction, °lure, °incentive, stimulus, °enticement, bait, °encouragement, °incitement, °provocation, °spur, °premium, °consideration, °reward, *Colloq* carrot, *Chiefly US* °come-on: *What inducement were you offered to take out that subscription?*

induct *v.* **1** °install *or* instal, °inaugurate, °invest, instate, °establish, °swear in: *Crocker*

was inducted as president of the lodge last night. **2** °call up, °enlist, conscript, °enrol, °register, *US* °draft: *He was inducted into the army at 18.*

indulge *v.* **1** Often, **indulge in**: °yield (to), °succumb (to), °favour, °gratify, °humour, °oblige (with), °comply (with), °minister to, °cater to, °pander to, °treat (to), °pamper (with): *When it comes to chocolates, I indulge myself to the fullest. We indulge in an occasional beer. She indulges his every whim.* **2** °coddle, °baby, °pamper, cosset, mollycoddle, °spoil: *He doesn't believe in indulging children.*

indulgence *n.* **1** °tolerance, sufferance, °understanding, °patience, °good °will, °allowance, forbearance; acceptance, overlooking: *Genevieve's behaviour is testing the limits of Tom's indulgence.* **2** self-indulgence, °luxury, °extravagance, °profligacy, selfgratification, self-satisfaction: *A notorious pleasure-seeker, his capacity for indulgence is legendary.* **3** °treat, °luxury, °extravagance: *My sole indulgence is vintage port.*

indulgent *adj.* °tolerant, °permissive, °patient, °understanding, forbearing, °lenient, °easygoing, °relaxed, °liberal, °lax, °kind, °kindly, well-disposed, °agreeable: *Tony and Hazel are extremely indulgent parents.*

industrious *adj.* sedulous, assiduous, hard-working, °diligent, °intense, °conscientious, °energetic, °dynamic, °aggressive, °vigorous, °untiring, °tireless, indefatigable, unflagging, °persistent, pertinacious, dogged, °tenacious, *US* hustling: *The business was built up only because she was so industrious.*

industry *n.* **1** °production, °manufacture, °trade, °commerce, °business: *Competition in the car industry helps keep prices lower.* **2** diligence, assiduity, sedulousness, °energy, °exertion, °effort, °application, °perseverance, °persistence, °work, °labour, toil: *We were complimented on our industry by the teacher.* **3** indus-triousness, °energy, °activity, °vigour, °hustle, bustle, °dynamism, °enterprise, earnestness, °determination: *The sales office is a hive of industry.*

ineffable *adj.* **1** unutterable, unspeakable, °unmentionable, °taboo: *In certain religions, the name of the deity is ineffable.* **2** °inexpressible, indefinable *or* undefinable, indescribable *or* undescribable, beyond °description, beyond words: *The Royal Hotel had an ineffable air of serene affluence.*

ineffective *adj.* **1** unproductive, unfruitful, °bootless, °idle, °vain, °useless, °ineffectual, °inefficacious, inoperative, non-functioning, °inadequate, °insufficient, °worthless: *The anti-crime measures appear to have been ineffective.* **2** °inefficient, °incompetent, °incapable, unskilled, unskilful, °inept, unfit, unproficient: *The new office manager is totally ineffective.*

ineffectual *adj.* **1** °unsuccessful, unavailing, °futile, °bootless, °sterile, °barren, °fruitless, unproductive, °ineffective, °inefficacious, inoperative: *Our efforts to deal with pollution have been largely ineffectual.* **2** °weak, °feeble, effete, °impotent, °tame, °lame, °powerless,

°inefficient, °incompetent, °inadequate: *We tried to read the inscription by the ineffectual light of a match.*

inefficacious *adj.* See **ineffectual** and **ineffective**, above.

inefficient *adj.* **1** °ineffective, °incompetent, °incapable, °unqualified, inexpert, unskilled, unskilful, unfit, °inept, °ineffectual, °deficient: *Poorly paid labour is inefficient labour.* **2** uneconomic(al), °wasteful, disorganized, °slipshod: *For our purposes, the layout of the factory is quite inefficient.*

ineligible *adj.* °unqualified, °unacceptable, unfit, unsuited, unsuitable, °inappropriate, °improper: *He is ineligible for benefit as he left his job voluntarily.*

inept *adj.* **1** °clumsy, °awkward, bungling, maladroit, ungainly, bumbling, gauche, inexpert, unskilled, unskilful, °incompetent, °inefficient: *If he is inept at sailing, he'd better become proficient.* **2** °inappropriate, inapt, °unseemly, °improper, unfitting, unfit, unsuitable, impolitic, undiplomatic, injudicious, °imprudent, °indiscreet, ill-considered, ill-judged, °ill-advised, unadvised, unadvisable *or* inadvised, °misguided, inexpedient, out of °place, unwise: *She made some inept comment and blushed furiously.*

ineptitude *n.* **1** ineptness, clumsiness, awkwardness, maladroitness, ungainliness, gaucherie, °incompetence, inefficiency, unfitness, unsuitableness: *He displays a remarkable ineptitude for the pronunciation of French.* **2** inappropriateness, inaptness, °absurdity, unsuitability, unseemliness: *The ineptitude of her comments embarrasses everyone.*

inequality *n.* **1** °disparity, °difference, °discrepancy, unevenness, nonconformity, incongruence, incongruity, inconsistency, °dissimilarity, imbalance: *The inequality between their incomes made him resentful.* **2** °bias, °prejudice, °partiality, unfairness, °injustice, inequity: *Why should they have to tolerate any inequality of treatment?*

inert *adj.* **1** °inactive, unreactive, unresponsive, °neutral: *Argon, xenon, and neon are inert gases.* **2** motionless, immobile, °inanimate, °lifeless, °still, °quiet, quiescent, stationary, °static: *He was mute and inert: it was like talking to a zombie.* **3** sluggish, °slow, °torpid, °dull, °inactive, °idle, °indolent, °lazy, °slothful, °leaden, °slack, °passive, °supine, °dormant, otiose, °listless, languid *or* languorous: *I contemplated the inert bodies sunbathing around the swimming-pool.*

inertia *n.* inertness, °inactivity, °sloth, °sluggishness, °torpor, dullness, °idleness, °indolence, laziness, slothfulness, passivity, apathy, lassitude, dormancy, listlessness, languor, immobility, motionlessness: *Adele finds it difficult to overcome her feeling of inertia in the morning.*

inestimable *adj.* **1** incalculable, °immeasurable, measureless, °untold, incomputable; °priceless, °invaluable, °precious: *You have been of inestimable help in completing the project on time.* **2** countless, innumerable, °vast, °immense, °prodigious, °boundless, unfathomable, °infinite, incalculable, °immeasurable, measureless, °untold, incomputable: *An inestimable number of organisms have inhabited the earth.*

inevitable *adj.* °unavoidable, inescapable, ineluctable, unpreventable, °certain, °sure, °destined, °fated, assured, inexorable, °irrevocable, unchangeable, °absolute, ordained, decreed, °authoritative, incontestable: *The inevitable outcome of war is misery for all participants.*

inexact *adj.* °imprecise, °inaccurate, °erroneous, °incorrect, °wrong, °false, °faulty, °indefinite, fallacious, °fuzzy, muddled: *This gauge is giving an inexact reading.*

inexcusable *adj.* unjustifiable, unjustified, indefensible, unpardonable, unforgivable, intolerable, inexpiable: *Insulting your hostess was inexcusable.*

inexhaustible *adj.* **1** °limitless, °boundless, °unlimited, unbounded, unrestricted, °endless, measureless, indeterminate, °infinite, incalculable: *The supply of tasteless television programmes seems virtually inexhaustible.* **2** °untiring, °tireless, indefatigable, unflagging, unfailing, unfaltering, unwearying, unwearied: *Bartell is an inexhaustible practical joker.*

inexpensive *adj.* °cheap, °economical, low-priced, low-cost, °reasonable, budget-priced: *What might seem inexpensive to you is very costly for me.*

inexperience *n.* immaturity, innocence, °naïvety, greenness, callowness, unsophistication: *I attribute his mistakes to inexperience.*

inexperienced *adj.* °immature, °innocent, °naïve, °green, °callow, °unsophisticated, unworldly, °unfledged, °raw, uninitiated, untrained, unschooled, °uninformed, unseasoned, *Colloq* (still) wet behind the ears, born yesterday: *Isn't she too inexperienced to take on such a great responsibility?*

inexplicable *adj.* unexplainable, °unaccountable, unintelligible, inscrutable, °puzzling, enigmatic, mystifying, °perplexing, confounding, baffling, bewildering, °incomprehensible: *I find inexplicable their refusal to allow freedom of religion.*

inexpressible *adj.* unutterable, °ineffable, unspeakable, indescribable, indefinable: *I felt inexpressible joy at seeing my children again.*

inextinguishable *adj.* °unquenchable, °irrepressible, unsuppressible, °enduring, undying, imperishable, °eternal, °everlasting: *The teacher had to cope with inextinguishable giggling. Our hopes for freedom were inextinguishable.*

inextricably *adv.* inescapably, ineluctably, unavoidably, irretrievably, °completely, inseparably, indissolubly, °totally, complicatedly, intricately: *I found myself inextricably caught up in her emotional problems.*

infallible *adj.* **1** unerring, °faultless, °flawless, °perfect, oracular, unmistaken: *The infallible logic of computers sometimes defeats their users.* **2** unfailing, dependable, °sure, °secure, °certain, °reliable, foolproof: *The vaccination provides infallible protection against the virus.*

infamous *adj.* **1** °notorious, °disreputable, ill-famed, stigmatized, °scandalous, discreditable, °dishonourable, ignominious: *So this is the infamous house where the murders took place!* **2** °bad, °awful, °wicked, °evil, iniquitous, °villainous, heinous, °vile, °abominable, °outrageous, execrable, °abhorrent, opprobrious, °despicable, °loathsome, detestable, odious, °foul, °scurvy, °rotten, °atrocious, flagitious, °revolting, °monstrous, egregious, °base, °low, °shameful, °disgraceful: *A number of infamous criminals are portrayed in the Chamber of Horrors.*

infamy *n.* **1** °notoriety, °ill repute, °ill °fame, disrepute, °shame, ignominy, obloquy, °disgrace, °dishonour, °stigma, °discredit: *She has to suffer the infamy of her husband's treachery.* **2** wickedness, °evil, iniquity, villainy, heinousness, vileness, abomination, °outrage, abhorrence, opprobrium, loathsomeness, detestation, hatred, odium, °atrocity, °revulsion, °monstrosity, egregiousness, °shame, shamefulness, °disgrace, disgracefulness: *The infamy of his profligate behaviour is widely known.*

infancy *n.* **1** babyhood, early °childhood: *His limp was the result of polio, which he had contracted in infancy.* **2** °beginning(s), inception, °early or °initial °stage(s), commencement, °start, °emergence, °dawn, °rise: *When psychiatry was in its infancy it was marked by a notable lack of success.*

infantile *adj.* °childish, °immature, °puerile, babyish, °juvenile: *Ben behaves in the most infantile way whenever there are girls about.*

infatuated *adj.* fascinated, beguiled, °enchanted, bewitched, spellbound, °charmed, ensorcelled, enraptured, °possessed, hypnotized, mesmerized, captivated, besotted, °taken with, obsessed, °smitten, enamoured, °fond: *Francis is completely infatuated with the girl who moved in next door.*

infectious *adj.* contagious, °catching, communicable, transmissible: *There is also a highly infectious variety of the disease.*

infer *v.* °deduce, °derive, °draw, conclude, °understand, °gather, °surmise, °guess, °assume: *From the evidence, I infer that you were not at home last night.*

inference *n.* °deduction, conclusion, °understanding, °surmise, assumption, °presumption: *If this man's father is my father's son, the inference is that this man is my nephew.*

inferior *adj.* **1** °lower, nether: *We descended into the inferior regions of the cavern. The numeral in H_2O is called an inferior character.* **2** lesser, °lower, °subordinate, °secondary, °junior, °minor, unimportant, °insignificant, °lowly, subservient, °humble, °servile: *He occupies an inferior position in the company.* **3** °poor, °bad, low-quality, °mediocre, °indifferent, °imperfect, °defective, second-rate, second-class, substandard, low-grade, °shoddy, gimcrack, *Colloq* grotty, junky, crummy or crumby, °lousy, *Slang* crappy, *Brit* naff: *They tried to market an inferior product, but it was rejected by consumers.* —*n.* **4** °subordinate, underling, °junior, °menial, lackey, °flunkey, dogsbody, cat's-paw, doormat, stooge, °yes-man, lickspittle, bootlicker: *She is tired of being treated as an inferior.*

inferiority *n.* **1** unimportance, insignificance, lowliness: *The inferiority of his position rankled with him.* **2** inadequacy, deficiency, insignificance, unimportance, worthlessness: *Do not confuse modesty with a sense of inferiority.* **3** shoddiness, °imperfection, mediocrity: *Consumers are not fooled by the inferiority of a product for long.*

infernal *adj.* **1** hellish, °underworld, nether, Hadean: *Virgil was Dante's guide in the infernal regions.* **2** °devilish, °diabolic(al), demonic(al),

demoniac(al), °fiendish, °satanic, Mephistophelian; °damnable, damned, execrable, malicious, malevolent, maleficent, °wicked, °evil, iniquitous, flagitious, °villainous, heinous, dire, °sinister, °dreadful: *She tells everyone that there is an infernal plot against her.*

infertile *adj.* °sterile, °barren, infecund, unproductive, unfruitful, °non-productive: *The stony, infertile earth yielded only cactus and scrub grass.*

infest *v.* invade, °plague, °beset, °overrun, overspread, °flood, °swarm over, inundate, pervade, °permeate, °penetrate, infiltrate: *Mosquitoes infested this area before the swamp was drained.*

infidel *n.* unbeliever, °heathen, disbeliever, heretic, °pagan, agnostic, atheist, nullifidian, freethinker: *Thousands of the fanatics swarmed over the infidels, slaughtering them mercilessly.*

infidelity *n.* **1** unfaithfulness, faithlessness, treachery, traitorousness, disloyalty, °perfidy, falseness, apostasy, heresy: *The infidelity of his supporters brought about his downfall.* **2** adultery, cuckoldry; °affair, °liaison, amour, *Colloq* cheating: *Infidelity is a common cause of marriage break-up. She forgave him his many infidelities.*

infinite *adj.* **1** °boundless, °vast, °limitless, °unlimited, illimitable, °endless, interminable, indeterminable, indeterminate, °inestimable, astronomical, °numberless, multitudinous, uncountable, uncounted, innumerable, incalculable, °inexhaustible, °immense, °enormous, °immeasurable, measureless, °bottomless, unfathomable: *They hurtled through infinite space at the speed of light. We do what we can, but our resources are not infinite. In his infinite wisdom, God made the garden slug.* **2** °eternal, °everlasting, °perpetual, °endless, unending, °inexhaustible, undying, never-ending: *It is difficult to conceive of time as being anything but infinite, without beginning or end. With infinite patience she reassembled the pieces of the vase.*

infirm *adj.* **1** °ill, °indisposed, debilitated, °frail, °fragile, °weak, °feeble, weakened, ailing, °decrepit, enfeebled, °failing, wasted, on the °decline, °sick, °sickly, unwell, °lame, °crippled: *Campbell is infirm and unable to travel.* **2** °shaky, °flimsy, wobbly, wobbling, °doddering, °unstable, faltering, vacillating, wavering, unsteady, unsteadfast, °inconstant, °changeable, °irresolute: *We must find stalwart recruits, recruits who are not infirm of purpose.*

infirmary *n.* clinic, °hospital, sickbay, first-aid °station; dispensary, *Brit* nursing °home, surgery: *The infirmary is able to deal only with emergencies, not with long-term care.*

infirmity *n.* **1** °weakness, feebleness, frailness, °frailty, debility, °decrepitude, sickliness: *At 100, she finally succumbed to infirmity, and ceased going out altogether.* **2** sickness, °ailment, °disease, malady, °affliction, °disorder, °defect, °complaint: *What infirmity struck him down?*

inflame *v.* **1** °arouse, °incite, °touch off, ignite, enkindle, °provoke, °rouse, °excite, impassion, °foment, incense, °agitate, °stir (up), °fire (up), °heat, °anger, °enrage, °madden, °infuriate, °whip or °lash up, °work up, rile, °exasperate, °stimulate, °animate, °move, °motivate, °urge, °prod, goad, °spur (on), °rally, °drive: *The speakers inflamed the crowd to riot against the police.* **2** °aggravate, °intensify, °deepen, °heighten,

°fan, exacerbate, °increase, augment,
°fuel: *She inflamed his dislike of his brother into
hatred.*

inflamed *adj.* irritated, °sore, °angry, chafing,
chafed, red, °swollen, °heated, °hot, fevered,
°feverish, infected, septic: *The wound became
inflamed and we had no medicine to reduce the
infection.*

inflammable *adj.* burnable, combustible,
°flammable: *The plastic foam formerly used to stuff
furniture is highly inflammable.*

inflammation *n.* irritation, redness, °swelling,
°sore, infection: *The inflammation subsided as the
injection took effect.*

inflammatory *adj.* incendiary, °fiery, inflaming,
°explosive, °rousing, °provocative, °rabid,
rabble-rousing, °passionate, °fervent, fervid,
°frantic, frenzied, fomenting, demagogic, insurgent, °riotous, °mutinous, °seditious,
°rebellious, °revolutionary, °traitorous, treacherous: *His inflammatory speeches at the university
created tension between the students and the administration.*

inflate *v.* **1** °blow up, balloon, °expand, dilate,
°enlarge, °swell, °pump up, °puff up *or* out,
distend: *We inflated two plastic bags to use as
floats.* **2** °boost, °increase: *The price of the
company's shares was boosted by rumours of a
take-over bid.* **3** °exaggerate, °amplify, °magnify,
°blow up: *He tends to inflate to huge proportions
the small contribution he made to the project.*

inflated *adj.* **1** exaggerated, °conceited, overblown, °grandiose, puffed up, overstated, magnified, amplified, overdrawn, °smug,
egotistic(al), °immodest, °cocky, °vain,
°self-important, *Colloq Brit* swelled-headed *or*
swollen-headed, *US* swell-headed: *He has an
inflated idea of the importance of his work.* **2** grandiloquent, °bombastic, orotund, high-flown,
°pompous, °pretentious, °extravagant, magniloquent: *She always talks about her husband in
such inflated terms.*

inflexible *adj.* unbending, °stiff, °rigid, °firm,
rigorous, unyielding, adamant, °severe, Rha-
damanthine, inelastic, °hard (and °fast),
°determined, °fixed, obdurate, °immovable,
intractable, unvaried, unvarying, °invariable,
unchangeable, immutable, °obstinate,
°stubborn, pigheaded, mulish, dyed in the wool,
headstrong, refractory, °steely, °stony,
°resolute, resolved, unadaptable, unaccommodating, uncompliant, uncompromising,
unshakeable *or* unshakable: *The committee
remain inflexible about changing the rules of the club
to admit women.*

inflict *v.* °impose, °apply, °visit, °administer, levy,
°force on *or* upon; °trouble, °afflict: *The new
government is seeking ways of inflicting more taxes
on us. You ought not to inflict punishment on such
small children.*

influence *n.* **1** °power, °pressure, °weight,
°sway, °impact, °force, °effect, leverage,
potency; °hold, °control, mastery, ascendancy,
Colloq °pull, clout: *Would you use your influence
to see if you can get me a job? The boy is under the
influence of his tutor.* **2** connections, °favour,
°favouritism, *Colloq* °pull: *He got his position
through influence, not merit.*
—*v.* **3** °affect, °move, °change, °modify, °alter,
°bias, °sway, °persuade, °induce, °work on,
°impress (upon), °play *or* °act upon *or* on,

°incline; bring °pressure to bear on *or* upon,
°motivate, °manipulate, *Brit* pressurize, *US*
°pressure, *Colloq* pull strings *or US also* wires:
*She was able to influence the minister to drop the
scheme.*

influential *adj.* °powerful, °weighty, °strong,
°forceful, °effective, °effectual, °efficacious,
°instrumental, °telling, °significant,
°persuasive, °dominant, °leading, guiding,
°authoritative, °predominant, °important,
°substantial, °prestigious, controlling: *He comes
from an influential family. What factors were influential in reaching your decision?*

inform *v.* **1** °tell, apprise, °advise,
°communicate, °enlighten, °notify, °acquaint,
°brief; °impart, °disclose, divulge, °reveal,
°report, *Colloq* °tip (off): *I have informed everyone
about the storm warning.* **2** Usually, **inform
against** *or* **on**: °betray, °incriminate,
°implicate, °identify, *Colloq* °tell (on), °blab (on),
rat (on), *US* °blow the whistle (on); *Slang* peach
(on), snitch (on), squeal (on), put the °finger on,
°sing, °name names, *Brit* nark (on), °grass (on),
°split on, *US* °finger: *He informed on his accomplices
in return for a lighter sentence.*

informal *adj.* **1** unceremonious, °casual,
°natural, unstilted, °familiar, °ordinary,
°everyday, °unaffected, unassuming, unpretentious, °simple, °relaxed, °free, °free
and °easy, *Brit* °common *or* garden, *US*
garden-variety: *We had an informal dinner in the
kitchen.* **2** °unofficial, unconventional, unconstrained, °casual, °everyday, °simple: *On duty
he wore informal clothes—blue jeans and a denim
jacket.* **3** °vernacular, colloquial, °simple,
°unaffected, °ordinary, unpretentious,
°everyday: *He uses informal language devoid of scientific jargon.*

information *n.* °knowledge, °data, °facts,
°intelligence, °message, °word, °advice, °news,
tidings, °report, communication, *Colloq* info,
°low-down, *Slang* °dirt, °dope, *Brit* gen, bumf,
US poop: *I have little information regarding her
divorce.*

informative *adj.* communicative, °instructive,
°educational, edifying, revealing, illuminating:
*We found his report about the missiles very informa-
tive.*

informed *adj.* **1** °intelligent, °knowledgeable,
°enlightened, °educated, °learned, cultured,
°cultivated: *An informed public is democracy's greatest asset.* **2** °alert (to), °aware (of), advised, in
touch, *au fait*, briefed, °conversant (with), (well-)
°versed (up on), up to °date, *Colloq* in the °know,
°wise: *Keep me informed as to your whereabouts.*

informer *n.* °traitor, betrayer, tattle-tale, taleteller, informant, *Slang* stool-pigeon, snitch,
squealer, weasel, *Brit* °grass, *Chiefly US* rat, *US*
stoolie, canary, shoo-fly: *According to the informer,
the secret meeting is scheduled for tonight.*

infrequently *adv.* °rarely, °seldom, sporadically,
°occasionally, °now and then, irregularly,
exceptionally: *They were only infrequently seen in
public in later years.*

infringe *v.* **1** °violate, contravene, °break,
°disobey, °transgress, °overstep: *Publication of
this article has infringed her right to a fair
trial.* **2 infringe on** *or* **upon**: °intrude on,
impinge on, trespass on, °encroach on, invade:
Never let pleasure infringe on the domain of duty.

infringement n. °violation, °breach, contravention, infraction, disobedience, °non-compliance, breaking, °transgression: *Publication without permission constitutes infringement of copyright. The inventor sued the company for patent infringement.*

infuriate v. °enrage, °anger, °madden, incense, make (someone's) blood °boil, °provoke, °inflame, °work *or* °stir *or* °fire up, rile, arouse, vex, pique, °gall, °annoy, °irritate, °bother, °chafe, °agitate, °irk, nettle, °exasperate, raise (someone's) hackles, make (someone's) hackles rise, *Brit* have *or* get (someone's) blood up, *Colloq* miff, °bug, peeve, get under (someone's) skin, get *or Brit also* put (someone's) back up, make (someone) see red, *Chiefly US* get (someone's) Irish *or* dander up, *US* °burn up, *Slang* piss (someone) off, brown (someone) off, *Brit* cheese (someone) off: *It really infuriated him to see injustice done to anyone.*

ingenious adj. °clever, °skilful, skilled, °shrewd, cunning, °crafty, canny, °dexterous, adroit, °acute, °sharp, °keen, °resourceful, °adept, apt, °smart, °gifted, °bright, °brilliant, °talented, deft, °handy, inventive, Daedalian, °creative, °imaginative, °original, *Colloq* °neat, °keen, *US* crackerjack, *Slang* on the ball: *My friend here has come up with an ingenious solution to our problem.*

ingenuity n. ingeniousness, °genius, °brilliance, cleverness, °skill, shrewdness, cunning, °craft, °art, °knack, °flair, °dexterity, dexterousness, adroitness, acuteness, sharpness, keenness, resourcefulness, adeptness, aptness, smartness, canniness, °gift, °talent, °ability, °capability, °faculty, deftness, handiness, inventiveness, creativity, creativeness, °imagination, imaginativeness, °originality: *She displayed extraordinary ingenuity in preparing the case against the plaintiff.*

ingenuous adj. **1** °naïve, °simple, °innocent, °unsophisticated, °childlike, °suggestible, °artless, °sincere, °genuine, °trusting, guileless, °natural, °straight, uncomplicated, (°fair and) °square, °honest, °fair, °just, °open, undeceitful, °unaffected, undeceptive, undissembling, unfeigning, (°open and) °above-board, *Colloq* on the °level: *What ideas have you been implanting into the mind of this ingenuous young girl?* **2** °frank, °candid, °open, °trustworthy, °honourable, °forthright, °direct, straightforward, four-square, °honest, °outspoken, °blunt, °bluff, °bold, unreserved, °free, °uninhibited, °unabashed: *I shall be ingenuous enough to confess that what you heard about me is true.*

ingrained adj. engrained, deep-rooted, °fixed, inveterate, deep-seated, °fundamental, °basic, °essential, °inherent, °inborn, innate, inbred, inherited, °hereditary, °organic, °intrinsic, °native, °natural: *He has an ingrained fear of heights.*

ingratiating adj. fawning, °grovelling, sycophantic, toadying, toad-eating, °servile, °obsequious, °flattering, °time-serving, wheedling, cajoling, unctuous, °oily, buttery, sweet-talking, sugary, saccharine, *US* blandiloquent, *Colloq* boot-licking, °slimy, *Brit* smarmy, *US* apple-polishing, *Slang US* brown-nosing: *It is Crawley's ingratiating manner that none of us can abide.*

ingratitude n. unthankfulness, ungratefulness, thanklessness, unappreciativeness,

non-recognition: *Despite the favours they had received, they showed their ingratitude by refusing to contribute to the fund drive.*

ingredient n. constituent, °element, °part, component, °factor; (*pl.*) makings: *Humour is a necessary ingredient in any working relationship.*

inhabit v. °dwell in, reside in, °live in, °abide in, °occupy, °settle; °locate in, °populate, °people; colonize: *This bird inhabits northern Africa. North America was inhabited by emigrants from Europe.*

inhabitant n. °resident, dweller, °denizen, °citizen, °tenant, °occupant, occupier: *The inhabitants of the village refused to pay taxes.*

inhale v. °breathe in, °inspire, °draw *or* suck in: *I stepped outside and inhaled the fresh spring air.*

inherent adj. °intrinsic, indwelling, °essential, °basic, innate, connate, °ingrained *or* engrained, °native, congenital, inherited, °hereditary, °inborn, inbred, °indigenous, immanent, built-in: *It is difficult to tell which characteristics are derived and which are inherent.*

inherit v. °come into, fall *or* be *or* become °heir to, be bequeathed, °succeed to, be left, °receive, °acquire, *Colloq* °come by: *She inherited the property when her father died.*

inheritance n. patrimony, °heritage, legacy, °bequest, birthright; °property: *He came into his inheritance when he was 21.*

inhibit v. °discourage, °repress, °frustrate, °hold back, °bridle, °curb, °control, °govern, °hinder, °restrain, °impede, °obstruct, °interfere with, °check, °prevent, °bar, °stop: *Her sad look inhibited my expression of delight at seeing her again.*

inhibited adj. °reticent, restrained, repressed, °reserved, °self-conscious, °shy, abashed, °embarrassed, *Colloq* uptight: *He is much too inhibited to appear on television.*

inhibition n. self-consciousness, °restraint, constraint, °impediment, °hindrance, °bar, °barrier, °defence, °defence °mechanism, blockage, °interference, °check, °curb, °stricture: *Geoff overcame his inhibitions and went over to talk with Anne. She had no inhibitions about singing in public.*

inhospitable adj. **1** unwelcoming, unreceptive, °uninviting, unsociable, °unsocial, °aloof, °cold, °cool, °standoffish, unfriendly, inimical, antisocial, °hostile, xenophobic: *They were most inhospitable and refused to let me in.* **2** unfavourable, °forbidding, °hostile, °barren, °desert, °uninviting, uninhabitable: *They were marooned on an inhospitable reef in the middle of the Pacific.*

inhuman adj. **1** inhumane, °merciless, °cruel, pitiless, °ruthless, °heartless, °severe, °unsympathetic, unfeeling, °unkind, unkindly, uncompassionate, °cold-blooded, °vicious, stony-hearted, hard-hearted, °callous, insensitive, barbaric, barbarous, °savage: *Many refugees have suffered torture and other inhuman treatment.* **2** °animal, bestial, °brutal, brutish, °fiendish, diabolic(al), demonic: *The spectre, assuming an inhuman form, loomed over them.*

initial adj. **1** °original, °primary, °first; °prime, °beginning, incipient, inaugural, °opening, °introductory, commencing: *His initial plan, to take the children, was vetoed by his wife. It is best to tread cautiously during the initial stages of the programme.*
—v. **2** °sign, °approve, °endorse: *Please initial the clauses of the contract that we have changed.*

—*n.* **3** monogram: *The initial 'M' is on all their towels.*

initiate *v.* **1** °begin, °commence, °enter upon or on, °originate, °introduce, °set in °motion, °start, °give °rise to, °get under °way, °launch, °get or °set °going, trigger, °set off, actuate, °activate, instigate, °institute, °inaugurate: *The programme was initiated last spring with much fanfare.* **2** °admit, °accept, °introduce: *The new members were initiated last night, with due ceremony.* **3** °teach, °instruct, °train, °tutor, °drill, °coach: *His responsibility is to initiate recruits in the rudiments of jungle warfare.*
—*n.* **4** °novice, °beginner, °new boy or girl, °greenhorn, rookie, neophyte, tiro or tyro, °newcomer, tenderfoot, fledgling, °apprentice, (°raw) °recruit, abecedarian, noviciate or novitiate, catechumen, *Brit* fresher or *US* freshman, *Australian* °new °chum: *In the first weeks, initiates are drilled in the basics.*

initiation *n.* **1** °beginning, commencement, inauguration, origination, début, introduction, inception, °establishment: *April the first is the date for initiation of the new system.* **2** °admittance, °admission, °entrance, induction, °enrolment, instatement, investiture, ordination, °installation; °ceremony, °rite, °ritual: *The initiation of new members is scheduled for tomorrow at midnight.*

initiative *n.* **1** °first °move or °step, °lead, °opening °move: *Hogan took the initiative by winning the first set.* **2** °enterprise, aggressiveness, °drive, °ambition, ambitiousness, resourcefulness, °leadership, °dynamism, °energy, °vigour, °hustle, élan, *Colloq* get-up-and-go, °pep, °snap, zip, zing: *At least she had the initiative to get the company back on a profitable basis.*

inject *v.* **1** °introduce, °insert, °drive or °force (in), °shoot (in), intromit; inoculate: *The serum is injected into the upper arm. The doctor injected me with antibiotics.* **2** °introduce, °insert, imbue, °instil, °bring in, interject, °throw in: *Can't you inject a little more enthusiasm into your work?*

injunction *n.* **1** °prohibition, interdict, interdiction, °restriction, °restraint, *US law* restraining °order: *There is an injunction against picketing.* **2** °order, mandate, directive, °command, °direction, °instruction, ruling, °dictate, exhortation; °warning, admonition: *Mother's parting injunction was always to dress warmly.*

injure *v.* **1** °harm, °wound, °hurt, °damage, °impair: *He's sure to injure himself if he's allowed to play with a knife.* **2** °wrong, °offend, °abuse, °hurt, °wound, °outrage, °slight, insult, affront, °mistreat, °misuse, °ill-treat, maltreat: *She starts the arguments yet she invariably takes the role of the injured party.*

injurious *adj.* **1** damaging, °harmful, °hurtful, °bad, deleterious, unfavourable, °detrimental, °unhealthy, insalubrious, pernicious, °destructive; adverse, °ruinous: *Smoking is said to be injurious to health.* **2** °abusive, insulting, °scornful, °slanderous, libellous, defamatory, °scandalous, °scurrilous, °harsh, calumnious, calumniatory, disparaging, °derogatory, deprecatory, °contemptuous, denigrating, °offensive: *She speaks of her ex-husband in the most injurious terms.*

injury *n.* °damage, °hurt, °harm, °wound, °impairment; °wrong, °abuse, maltreatment,

°mistreatment, °mischief, °offence, °outrage; °mayhem: *The injury was less painful to his foot than to his self-esteem.*

injustice *n.* **1** unfairness, °favouritism, °discrimination, °bias, °inequality, °partiality, partisanship, °prejudice, °bigotry, one-sidedness, unjustness, inequity: *Class privilege has always condoned injustice.* **2** °wrong, °injury: *You do me an injustice if you think me capable of dishonesty.*

inkling *n.* °hint, °suggestion, glimmering, °suspicion, °whisper, intimation, °indication, soupçon, °clue, °notion, (faintest or foggiest) °idea, °tip, tip-off: *Can you give me an inkling of what you are getting at?*

inmate *n.* °prisoner, °convict, °captive, jailbird or *Brit also* gaolbird, *Slang Brit* lag; °patient, °case; °inhabitant, °occupant, °resident: *The inmates were fed on bread and water in those days. Inmates at the sanatorium are well treated.*

innocent *adj.* **1** not °guilty, guiltless, °blameless, °honest, (in the) °clear, unimpeachable, above °suspicion, above reproach, °faultless: *We all believe her innocent of extortion.* **2** °pure, sinless, °virtuous, °chaste, virgin(al), undefiled, untainted, unstained, unsullied, °pristine, °incorrupt, uncorrupted, °immaculate, °spotless, unblemished, unpolluted: *She is still a sweet child, innocent as the day she was born.* **3** °harmless, well-intentioned, °safe, innocuous, °inoffensive, unobjectionable: *What began as an innocent stroll became a dangerous expedition.* **4** °naïve, °unsuspecting, unsuspicious, °ingenuous, °unsophisticated, °trusting, trustful, °gullible, credulous, °green, °inexperienced, °childlike, unworldly, guileless, °artless, °simple, °open, unartificial, °sincere: *Youngsters would arrive in London directly from the farm, entirely innocent and unaware of the perils of city life.*
—*n.* **5** infant, babe (in arms or in the wood(s)), °child; ingénue, °novice, beginner, °newcomer, *Colloq* °greenhorn: *She's certainly no innocent when it comes to men.*

innovation *n.* **1** °novelty; °invention: *The flush toilet was a 19th-century innovation.* **2** modernization, °alteration: *Consumer product development is marked by a spirit of tireless innovation.*

innuendo *n.* insinuation, °imputation, °suggestion, °hint, intimation, °implication, allusion, °overtone; °reference, animadversion: *I resent your innuendo that I know more about the affair than I am letting on.*

inoffensive *adj.* °harmless, unobjectionable, innocuous, unoffending, °neutral, °retiring, °mild, °tame: *Bligh is so inoffensive, how could he possibly have upset you?*

inopportune *adj.* °inappropriate, malapropos, ill-timed, untimely, °inconvenient, unsuited, unsuitable, out of °place, unpropitious, unfavourable, °inauspicious, ill-chosen, °unseasonable, °unseemly, °untoward, °unfortunate: *Your call came at a most inopportune moment, as we were just sitting down to dinner.*

inordinate *adj.* **1** °immoderate, unrestrained, intemperate, °excessive, °disproportionate, °extravagant, overdone, °extreme, °exorbitant, °outrageous, °preposterous, °unconscionable, °unreasonable, undue, uncalled-for, °unwarranted: *Her inordinate appetite for scandal has made her a successful gossip columnist.*

2 °irregular, °disorderly, disordered, °uncontrolled, °unlimited, unregulated, unsystematic, °erratic, °haphazard: *Laws have been passed to limit the inordinate hunting of deer.*

inquire *v.* **1** Usually, **inquire into**: °search, °investigate, °probe, °examine, °research, °look into, °inspect, °study, °explore, °survey, °scrutinize: *Scientists are inquiring into the causes of the greenhouse effect.* **2** See **enquire**, above.

inquiry *n.* **1** enquiry, °investigation, °probe, °examination, °research, °search, inspection, °study, °exploration, °survey, °scrutiny, inquest; questioning, querying, °interrogation, cross-examination, inquisition: *The police have asked me to help them with their inquiry. They are conducting an inquiry into the cause of the accident.* **2** enquiry, °question, °query, °interrogation: *Would you please repeat the inquiry?*

inquisitive *adj.* **1** inquiring, °curious, probing, questioning, °interested, investigative, searching, exploring, analytical: *Children have a naturally inquisitive nature.* **2** prying, °intrusive, *Colloq* snooping, snoopy, °nosy *or* nosey: *Don't be so inquisitive about things that don't concern you!*

inroad *n.* **1** incursion, °raid, °attack, °invasion, °penetration, foray, encroachment, forced °entry, intrusion: *Our armoured units have made an inroad into enemy territory.* **2** Often, **inroads**: °advance(s), °progress, breakthrough: *Have researchers made significant inroads into the problem of AIDS?*

insane *adj.* **1** °mad, demented, °psychotic, schizophrenic, schizoid, *non compos mentis*, manic, °maniacal, lunatic, °deranged, °unbalanced, psychoneurotic, °neurotic, °eccentric, °crazy, of °unsound °mind, crazed, unhinged, out of one's °mind *or* °head, °mad as a hatter *or* a March hare, quirky, *Colloq* round the bend *or* °twist, off one's °rocker *or* chump, loopy, loony, certifiable, °mental, screwy, dotty, cuckoo, not all there, not have all one's marbles, off-the-wall, out of it, *Brit* potty, *Slang* °daft, nutty (as a fruit cake), nuts, spaced out, spacy, batty, have bats in one's belfry, not right upstairs, barmy (in the crumpet), crackers, have a screw loose, schizo, *Brit* bonkers, *US* bugs, bughouse, loco, °crazy as a bedbug, (gone) off the deep end, kooky, °kinky, out to lunch: *Witney was certified insane and institutionalized. You're insane if you think I am going out on that ledge.* **2** °stupid, °dumb, °dull, °silly, asinine, °ridiculous, idiotic, irrational, °absurd, fatuous, °ludicrous, °foolish, °nonsensical, °irresponsible, °reckless, °wild, imbecilic, moronic, °feeble-minded, °hare-brained, addle-pated, addle-brained, °scatterbrained, thimble-witted, attocerebral, *Brit* gormless, *Colloq* nutty, screwy, °crazy: *People in love sometimes do insane things.*

insanity *n.* **1** °madness, °lunacy, °mental °illness *or* °disorder, dementia (praecox), psychosis, schizophrenia, (°mental) derangement, °mania; psychoneurosis, neurosis: *Because of the plea of temporary insanity he never stood trial for the murders.* **2** °folly, foolishness, °stupidity, idiocy, imbecility, °lunacy, °absurdity, fatuity, fatuousness, °nonsense, senselessness, irresponsibility, irrationality, inanity: *What insanity it was to think I could win the lottery!*

insecure *adj.* **1** °uncertain, °afraid, unsure, unconfident, °nervous, °worried, °anxious, °disconcerted, apprehensive, uncomfortable, °shaky, °jumpy, unnerved, °fearful: *Harry is beginning to feel insecure about his job.* **2** unsafe, °dangerous, unprotected, °vulnerable, °unguarded, °defenceless, undefended, exposed, °open: *The machine-gun position is insecure and will soon be taken.* **3** °unstable, °shaky, wobbly, °precarious, °infirm, °weak, °flimsy, °frail, °rickety, unsubstantial, °rocky, °unsound, unsteady, °unreliable, °uncertain: *The structure collapsed because the footings were insecure.*

insensible *adj.* **1** insensate, °unconscious, insentient, °numb, benumbed, °senseless, °torpid, anaesthetized, *Colloq* out, out of it: *She was totally insensible for an hour after the blow on the head.* **2** Often, **insensible to** *or* **of**: insensitive, °callous, °indifferent, impervious, °impassive, apathetic, °cool, unsusceptible; °unaffected, °unmoved, untouched; °unaware, °deaf, °inconsiderate; hard-hearted, °thick-skinned, unfeeling, emotionless, °dispassionate, °thoughtless, *Colloq* cloth-eared: *He remained wholly insensible to her desires and needs.*

insert *v.* **1** °introduce, °place *or* °put *or* °stick in, intercalate; interpolate, interject, interpose: *Please do not insert comments of your own.* —*n.* **2** insertion, °addition, addendum, °supplement, °advertisement, broadside, °brochure, tip-in, handbill, °circular, *Colloq Brit* advert, *US* ad, flier *or* flyer; outsert, wraparound *or* wrapround: *The postage will be higher with this eight-page insert.*

inside *n.* **1** °interior, °centre, °core, °middle, °heart; contents; lining, °backing: *From the outside one could never guess what the inside looks like. Please paint the inside of the cabinet blue.* **2** Usually, **insides**: °bowels, entrails, viscera, °gut(s), °stomach, *Colloq* innards: *He has had trouble with his insides for years.* **3** **inside out**: everted, reversed; °backwards: *He is wearing his pullover inside out.* —*adj.* **4** °favoured, °advantageous, °favourable, advantaged, °privileged, preferred, °preferential, °propitious, °exclusive; °internal, °private, °secret, °confidential, °privy, clandestine: *She has an inside track to the chairman. He claims to have inside information about the successful bidder.* **5** °internal, °interior; arranged, prearranged: *The police think it was an inside job.* —*adv.* **6** fundamentally, basically, at °bottom, by °nature: *Despite her gruff exterior, inside she is quite sentimental.* **7** in °prison, in °jail *or Brit also* gaol, imprisoned, incarcerated, *Slang Brit* in quod, *US* up the river: *He'll be inside for another five years.* —*prep.* **8** within, *US* inside of: *Because of rain, the party was held inside the building.*

insight *n.* °perception, percipience, °sensitivity, perspicacity, perceptiveness, perspicaciousness, discernment, acuteness, acuity, acumen, sharpness, °understanding, °judgement, comprehension, °vision: *Chambers has brought his considerable insight to bear on this complex problem.*

insignificant *adj.* °paltry, °trifling, °petty, inconsiderable, °inconsequential, trivial, unimportant, °non-essential, °minor, °negligible, nugatory, unessential, °niggling, °puny, °insubstantial, unsubstantial, *Colloq* piddling: *These insignificant differences can be ignored. What you and I might do with our lives is, in the larger sense, insignificant.*

insincere adj. °hypocritical, °dishonest, dissembling, °deceptive, °disingenuous, °deceitful, untruthful, °false, °artificial, ungenuine, treacherous, °perfidious, °faithless, double-dealing, duplicitous, °two-faced, Janus-faced, °lying, mendacious, °sly, Machiavellian, cunning, °crafty, °slick, °foxy, vulpine, °wily, °artful, °evasive, °shifty, °time-serving, unctuous, °slimy, °slippery, °tricky, underhanded, °crooked, *Colloq* °phoney *or US also* phony: *From the first act I thought Iago insincere.*

insinuate v. 1 °impute, °suggest, °hint, °intimate, °imply, °whisper, °indicate; convey, °signify: *They insinuated that she married me for my money.* 2 °insert (oneself), °inject (oneself), worm *or* °work *or* inveigle *or* °manoeuvre (oneself *or* one's way); infiltrate, °intrude: *She insinuated herself into our group uninvited.* 3 °inject, infuse, °instil, °introduce: *Wild imaginings began to insinuate themselves into my mind.*

insist v. 1 °demand, °require, °call for, °command, importune, °urge, exhort, °argue, remonstrate, expostulate: *The chairman insisted that proper parliamentary procedure be followed.* 2 assert, °state, °declare, °emphasize, °stress, °maintain, °persist, °hold, °dwell on, °vow, avow, aver, asseverate: *He insisted that he wanted to see the last act but she insisted on leaving.*

insistent adj. °firm, dogged, °emphatic, °persistent, °tenacious, °resolute, °determined, °assertive, uncompromising, unfaltering, unwavering, persevering, perseverant, unrelenting, inexorable, °stubborn, °obstinate, unyielding, compelling, °urgent, importunate: *The judges were insistent that we should follow the rules to the letter.*

insolent adj. °impertinent, °impudent, °pert, saucy, °bold, °presumptuous, °brazen, °brash, °disrespectful, insulting, °contemptuous, °offensive, °rude, °crude, uncivil, °insubordinate, *Colloq* °fresh, °brassy, °cheeky, *Slang Brit* smart-arsed *or US* smart-ass(ed), *US* wise: *That insolent boor had the gall to call her 'Queenie'!*

insolvent adj. bankrupt, ruined, in receivership, penniless, °impoverished, °destitute, *US* in Chapter Eleven, *Colloq* °broke, wiped out, in the red, on the rocks, (gone) bust, gone to the °wall, *Brit* in Queer Street, skint: *A business is insolvent if its liabilities exceed its assets.*

inspect v. °examine, °scrutinize, °study, °scan, °survey, °vet, °check (up (on) or out), °investigate, °pore over; °peruse: *The customs man inspected every last inch of our luggage.*

inspiration n. 1 awakening, arousal, stimulus, °revelation, impulse, °feeling, afflatus, enlightenment, °insight, °spur, °incitement, °incentive; °spirit, °energy, élan, °passion, °ardour, zeal, °enthusiasm, °vigour, °gusto, ebullience, °sparkle: *Her extraordinary eyes gave me the inspiration I needed and I finished writing the song in an hour.* 2 °influence, stimulus, stimulation, °encouragement, °provocation, °suggestion, °guide, °education: *Kitchener's life was an inspiration to many a career soldier.*

inspire v. 1 °animate, °activate, actuate, °stimulate, invigorate, °stir, °move, waken, °awaken, arouse, °rouse, instigate, °prompt, °rally, °energize, °enliven, °vitalize, vivify, galvanize, inspirit, °excite, °spark (off), °quicken, °kindle, °fire, °provoke: *It was the inflammatory*

speeches that inspired the crowd to riot. His enthusiasm inspired her to take up writing as a profession. 2 °encourage, °strengthen, °support, °reinforce, °buoy (up), uplift, °boost, affirm, °confirm, °fortify, °buttress: *Your example has inspired many young people.*

install v. 1 instal, °invest, instate, °initiate, °establish, °inaugurate, °induct, °institute; °place, °put, °position, °introduce, °settle: *The new bishop will be installed in office next week.* 2 instal, °fit, °set up, °connect, °fix (in °place): *I installed our new air conditioner myself.*

installation n. 1 investiture, instatement, °initiation, °establishment, inauguration, induction, °institution, °placement, introduction, solemnization, swearing-in, consecration, *Ecclesiastical* ordination; crowning, coronation: *Will you attend the installation of the new vice-chancellor?* 2 °fitting, °placement, °connection, positioning: *The plumber will supervise the installation of the new heating system.* 3 °base, °post, °station, depot, °camp, °establishment: *Military installations all over the country are being picketed.*

instance n. 1 °case (in point), °example, exemplar, °illustration, °precedent, exemplification, °occurrence, °event: *The damage to the bus shelter is yet one more instance of hooliganism.* 2 **for instance**: for °example, as an °example, e.g., °say; in the °event, as it happens *or* happened: *Consider her, for instance: she managed to work and raise a family.*

instant n. 1 °moment, °point, °second, °time: *I was thinking of you at the very instant the phone rang.* 2 °moment, °second, °minute, °flash, °twinkling (of an eye), trice, *Colloq* jiffy: *I'll be with you in an instant, sir.* —adj. 3 instantaneous, °immediate, on the °spot, overnight: *His novel was an instant best seller.* 4 °urgent, crying, °pressing, °earnest, °imperative, °critical, exigent; split-second, °direct: *We have an instant need for a computer specialist.* 5 °ready-made, °ready-mixed, °prepared, ready-to-serve, pre-cooked: *This is an instant soup—just add hot water to the powder.*

instantaneously adv. instantly, °immediately, at °once, (°right) °now, °directly, forthwith, °promptly, this °minute *or* °second *or* °instant, without °delay, *tout de suite*, *Brit* °straight away *or US* °right away; *Colloq* pronto, *US* momentarily: *The results will be beamed instantaneously to 176 million people around the world.*

instead adv. 1 as an °alternative *or* a °substitute: *She wanted me to go but I stayed instead.* 2 **instead of**: alternatively, preferably, in °preference to, in °place of, in lieu of, °rather than, as a °substitute for; as contrasted with, as °opposed to: *Instead of going to the cinema we went to the theatre.*

instil v. instill, imbue, inculcate, infuse, ingrain *or* engrain, °implant; °insinuate, °impart: *From childhood a sense of justice was instilled in us.*

instinct n. °intuition, °feel, °feeling, empathy, °sensitivity, °tendency, propensity, °leaning, °bent, °skill, °talent, °faculty, sixth °sense, °knack, predisposition, °capacity, °aptitude; °subconscious: *She has an uncanny instinct for finding the most interesting person in a crowd.*

instinctive *adj.* **1** instinctual, intuitive, °natural, innate, °native, °inborn, inbred, congenital, constitutional, reflex, visceral, intestinal, °intrinsic, intuitional, °subconscious, *Colloq* °gut: *She has an instinctive flair for design.* **2** °immediate, °involuntary, irrational, °mechanical, °automatic, °spontaneous: *Harvey took an instinctive dislike to Percy when they met.*

institute *n.* **1** °society, °organization, °association, °league, °alliance, guild: *They tried to establish an institute for research on badgers.* **2** See **institution**, 2, below.
—*v.* **3** °establish, °found, °launch, °organize: *The principles of sportsmanship were instituted on the playing fields of England.* **4** °inaugurate, °introduce, °initiate, °set up, °start, °begin, °originate, °commence, °pioneer: *If you do not pay, we shall be obliged to institute proceedings against you.*

institution *n.* **1** establishing, °establishment, forming, °formation, origination, founding, °foundation, °installation, introduction, °creation, °organization: *Who was responsible for the institution of cricket as a national pastime?* **2** °establishment, °institute, academy, °foundation, university, college, °school: *He attended an institution of higher learning after leaving the army.* **3** °hospital, medical centre, °sanatorium or US also sanitarium, °home, asylum: *They spent their last days in an institution.* **4** °custom, °tradition, °habit, °practice, °routine, °rule, °order (of the day), °code (of °practice); °doctrine, dogma: *Throwing the coxswain into the river after the race has become an institution.*

instruct *v.* **1** °teach, °train, °tutor, °drill, °educate, °coach, °inform, °guide, edify, °prepare, °indoctrinate, inculcate: *My parents employed a tutor to instruct me in Latin.* **2** °direct, °order, °bid, °require, °tell, enjoin, °command, importune, °charge: *We were instructed to tell no one where we were going.*

instruction *n.* **1** Often, **instructions**: °order, °direction, °brief, briefing, directive, guideline, °advice, °recommendation, °rule; °information; *Colloq* °drill: *The next instruction is to insert the plug into the back of the receiver. Follow the instructions carefully.* **2** teaching, °education, °schooling, training, °drill, drilling, °tuition, °guidance, indoctrination, °preparation, lessons, classes, coaching, tutelage; tutorial: *Where did you receive instruction in first aid?*

instructive *adj.* °informative, informational, informatory, °educational, instructional, °helpful, revealing, edifying, enlightening, illuminating: *Studying the mistakes of others can be highly instructive.*

instructor *n.* °teacher, trainer, °tutor, °coach, mentor, °adviser, educator, pedagogue, scholastic, academe, academician, °doctor, docent, lecturer, professor, *Brit* °master, °mistress, don, preceptor, *US* docent: *Charlotte was not spending time with the tennis instructor just to improve her backhand.*

instrument *n.* **1** °implement, °tool, °device, °apparatus, utensil, appliance, contrivance, °mechanism, °gadget, *Colloq* °contraption, thingumabob, thingumajig, thingummy, thingy, whatsit, what's-its-name, whatnot, what-d'you-call-it, *Brit* gubbins, *US* gismo or gizmo: *Which instrument should I use to loosen this* bolt? *The doctor extracted the splinter with some sort of instrument.* **2** °agency, °means, °way, °factor, °mechanism, instrumentality, wherewithal, (°prime) mover, catalyst, °agent: *Summers refused to be the instrument of bringing free people into slavery.* **3** °contract, (°legal) °document, (written) °agreement, °pact, °compact, °paper: *After the signing, copies of the instruments were exchanged.*

instrumental *adj.* °helpful, °useful, utilitarian, contributory, of °service, °supportive, supporting, °advantageous, catalytic, conducive, °beneficial, valuable, °significant, °important; °accessory, ancillary: *Your presence will be instrumental in effecting a favourable settlement.*

insubordinate *adj.* °disobedient, °rebellious, °defiant, refractory, °mutinous, insurgent, insurrectional, insurrectionist, °revolutionary, °seditious, incompliant or uncompliant, uncooperative, °recalcitrant, contumacious, fractious, °unruly, °perverse, °contrary, °obstreperous, *Colloq Brit* stroppy: *The insubordinate officers have been court-martialled.*

insubstantial *adj.* **1** unsubstantial, °insignificant, °meagre, diaphanous, °small, °flimsy, °frail, °weak, °feeble, °paltry, °puny, °slight, °thin, °tenuous, °fragile, °light, gossamer, wispy, wisp-like, °fine: *Though the spider's thread appears insubstantial, for its weight it is enormously strong.* **2** °illusory, °unreal, illusive, °imaginary, imagined, °fanciful, °fancied, °visionary, °immaterial, °intangible, impalpable, incorporeal, airy, ethereal, °spiritual, chimerical, °phantom, phantasmal, phantasmagorical, hallucinatory, °fantastic; °false: *Through the mist London seemed insubstantial, a dream city of vapours rising from the Thames.*

insufferable *adj.* °unbearable, insupportable or unsupportable, intolerable, unendurable, °impossible: *The babysitter said she refused ever again to look after such an insufferable brat.*

insufficient *adj.* °inadequate, °deficient, °unsatisfactory, °meagre, °scanty, scant, °scarce; too °little, not °enough: *This light is insufficient for me to read by. We have insufficient skill to play the Brahms concerto.*

insulate *v.* **1** °detach, °separate, °isolate, °segregate, °shelter, °preserve, °set or °keep °apart, sequester, sequestrate, quarantine: *The rock star's aides did their best to insulate her from her screaming fans.* **2** °lag, °protect, °shield, °cushion, °wrap, °cover: *Insulate the pipes to prevent heat loss. Insulate the wire with this tape. Nitroglycerine must be insulated from shock.*

insult *v.* **1** °offend, affront, °slight, °outrage; °abuse, °dishonour, defame, °injure; °slander, °libel: *Don't be insulted if I arrive late and leave early. You insult her by suggesting that she has never heard of Keats.*
—*n.* **2** °offence, affront, °indignity, °slight, °outrage, barb, °dig, °slur, °dishonour, °abuse, defamation, discourtesy; °aspersion, °slander, °libel; *Colloq* °slap (in the face), °put-down: *Refusing to bow at a Japanese funeral is taken as an insult.*

insurance *n.* °assurance, surety, °indemnity, indemnification, °guarantee or guaranty, °warranty, °bond, °security, °protection, °cover: *The cost of insurance is higher owing to the increase in crime.*

intact *adj.* °whole, °entire, °perfect, °complete, °integral, °sound, unbroken, °solid, (all) in °one °piece, °undivided, uncut, together, untouched, unreduced, undiminished, unimpaired, inviolate, unblemished, °unscathed, uninjured, unharmed, undamaged, unsullied, undefiled, untainted: *The ancient city has been preserved virtually intact.*

intangible *adj.* impalpable, unperceivable, °imperceptible, incorporeal, unsubstantial, °insubstantial, °imponderable, °immaterial, ethereal, vaporous, airy, evanescent, °vague, °obscure, °dim, °imprecise, °indefinite, °shadowy, °fleeting, °elusive: *The architect must deal with intangible ideas of design, how people work and live, etc.*

integral *adj.* **1** °basic, °elementary, °elemental, °fundamental, °essential, °intrinsic: *The rhythm is an integral part of the music.* **2** See **intact**, above.

integrate *v.* °combine, °unite, °blend, °bring or °put together, °assemble, °merge, °amalgamate, °join, °knit, °mesh, consolidate, coalesce, °fuse; *US* desegregate: *We must integrate all the parts into a coherent whole. Several cultures have been well integrated into our community.*

integrity *n.* **1** °honesty, °probity, veracity, uprightness, °honour, °rectitude, °principle, °morality, goodness, trustworthiness, decency, °virtue, incorruptibility, righteousness: *He is a person of unimpeachable integrity.* **2** wholeness, °entirety, °unity, togetherness, soundness, completeness, coherence, oneness, °totality: *Care should be taken not to disturb the integrity of the protective film.*

intellect *n.* **1** rationality, °reason, reasonableness, (common) °sense, °understanding, °judgement, cleverness, °intelligence, °mind, *Colloq* brains: *You have the intellect, my boy, but it wants developing.* **2** See **intellectual**, 3, below.

intellectual *adj.* **1** °mental, cerebral: *The greatest minds have brought their intellectual powers to bear on the problem.* **2** °thoughtful, thought-provoking, °highbrow, °academic, bookish, °scholarly, *Colloq* brainy: *The professor did not find the subject intellectual enough for a dissertation.* —*n.* **3** °thinker, °intellect, °highbrow, °mastermind, °genius, *Colloq* °brain, egghead: *He enjoys associating with intellectuals at the university.* **4** °scholar, academician, professor, savant, °sage, °wise man, guru, polymath, pundit, °authority: *The editor of the journal is an intellectual who leaves the details of administration to her deputy.*

intelligence *n.* **1** °intellect, °understanding, °aptitude, °capacity, brainpower, cleverness, astuteness, quickness, alertness, keenness, brightness, shrewdness, °wit, °mother °wit, (common) °sense, °insight, perspicacity, °perception, discernment, °discretion, percipience, perspicaciousness, °wisdom, sagacity, *Colloq* brains, savvy, grey matter, *Slang Brit* nous: *He may not know anything about computer programming but he has the intelligence to learn how to do it.* **2** °information, °knowledge, °word, °data, °facts, °advice, °news, tidings, findings, *Colloq* °dope, °low-down, info, *Brit* gen, *US* °inside, poop: *Our agents are trying to gather intelligence on the Bulgarian situation.*

intelligent *adj.* °bright, °smart, °clever, discerning, perspicacious, °perceptive, percipient, °understanding, °rational, apt, °astute, quick, °quick-witted, °keen, °sharp, °alert, °shrewd, canny, insightful, °gifted, °sensible, °wise, °sage,

sagacious, °enlightened, °knowing, °aware, °knowledgeable, erudite, *au fait, Colloq* brainy, *Chiefly US* savvy: *She is certainly intelligent enough to be first in her class, if only she would study harder.*

intelligentsia *n.pl.* °intellectuals, literati, savants, illuminati, masterminds, highbrows, *Colloq* °brains, eggheads, brains trust: *The government stifled free speech and persecuted the intelligentsia.*

intelligible *adj.* understandable, comprehensible, fathomable, decipherable, °legible, °clear, °plain, lucid, unambiguous: *Crowther's notes are barely intelligible.*

intend *v.* °mean, have in °mind *or* in °view, °propose, °contemplate, °design, °plan, °aim, °purpose, °resolve, °determine: *I intend to give him a piece of my mind. She is intending to go, but I don't know if she will be able to.*

intense *adj.* **1** °extreme, °excessive, °severe, °strong, °great, °fierce, °harsh, °acute, °powerful, °profound, °deep: *The intense heat kept the firemen at bay.* **2** °eager, °enthusiastic, °keen, °earnest, °sincere, °heartfelt, °deep, °passionate, °impassioned, °ardent, zealous, °animated, °burning, consuming, °fervent, fervid, perfervid, vehement, °frantic, °fanatical, frenzied: *I had an intense desire to see the culprit brought to justice.* **3** highly-strung *or chiefly US* high-strung, °emotional, °temperamental, °tense, °touchy, °testy, °volatile, °hysterical, °hotheaded, °feverish, °nervous, (°high-)°spirited, °impetuous, °impulsive, *Colloq* uptight: *I appreciate his enthusiasm, but I wish Henshawe were a bit less intense about his politics.*

intensify *v.* °concentrate, °focus, °sharpen, °whet, °strengthen, °reinforce, °heighten, escalate, °deepen, °quicken, °emphasize, °magnify, °increase, augment, °double, redouble, °heat up, *Colloq* °step up, *Brit* °hot up: *We must intensify our efforts to effect a settlement of the crisis. The war is intensifying.*

intensity *n.* concentration, °focus, °strength, forcefulness, °force, °power; °vigour, °energy, vehemence, °fervour, zeal, °ardour, °passion, °sincerity: *The storm is diminishing in intensity. Political partisanship is often attended by great intensity of emotion.*

intensive *adj.* concentrated, focused, intensified, °comprehensive, °exhaustive, °thorough(-going), all-out: *The police have launched an intensive manhunt.*

intent *n.* **1** °intention, °aim, °goal, °target, °purpose, °object, °objective, °end, °design, °plan, °idea: *Was it your intent that I should go with you? The charge is assault with intent to kill.* **2** °inclination, °tendency, °desire, intending: *The mere intent to commit treason is often tantamount to treason.* **3 to all intents and purposes**: °virtually, °practically, for all °practical purposes, (°almost) as good as, (°almost) the °same as, more or less, in °effect: *Telling you that the position was being discontinued is, to all intents and purposes, the same as firing you.* —*adj.* **4** concentrated, focused, °fixed, °steady, °intense, °determined, °earnest, engrossed, °absorbed, °rapt, °steadfast, °resolute, °attentive: *Her intent stare unnerved many of her lecturers.* **5** °bent, °set, °resolute, committed, °decided, °firm, °keen; resolved, °eager, °determined, zealous, avid, °enthusiastic: *If you're intent on going, we won't try to change your mind.*

intention n. °aim, °purpose, °intent, °design, °goal, °end, °object, °objective, °target, °ambition: *Was it your intention to stay till the fat lady sings?*

intentional adj. °deliberate, intended, °premeditated, meant, °wilful, designed, planned, °preconceived, °studied, considered, contrived; °purposeful, on °purpose: *That slur was intentional and not just a slip of the tongue.*

intently adv. closely, attentively, concentratedly, earnestly, fixedly, unflinchingly, determinedly, °searchingly, steadily, steadfastly, continuously, assiduously, doggedly, unremittingly, eagerly, keenly, studiously: *They regarded one another intently across the table.*

intercept v. °interrupt, °deflect, °stop, °arrest, °check, °interfere (with), °head off, °block, °impede, °cut off, °seize, °grab, °catch, °trap: *He was intercepted as he was about to board a plane with the documents. Keeler intercepted the ball, preventing a goal.*

intercourse n. **1** °commerce, °traffic, °trade, °dealings, °exchange, communication, °contact, interaction: *In normal business intercourse our paths often cross.* **2** °sexual intercourse, coitus, coition, °sexual congress or °union, mating, copulation, °sexual relations, °carnal °knowledge, making °love, lovemaking, intimacy, °sexual °connection, Colloq °sex: *The plaintiff admits engaging in intercourse with the defendant.*

interest n. **1** °attention, attentiveness, °concern, °regard, °curiosity, °scrutiny, °notice, °engagement: *The way the puzzle fitted together drew my interest. She examined the books with interest. She shows interest in taking a writing course.* **2** °concern, °significance, °importance, °weight, °moment, °note, consequence: *Of what interest is a newly found painting by Tiepolo?* **3** Often, **interests**: °profit, °advantage, °benefit, °good, avail, °worth, value, °consideration, °behalf, behoof: *Is it in our interest to sell the business?* **4** °share, °portion, °stake, investment, °piece, °cut, °percentage, participation, involvement: *I have a small interest in an emerald mine.* **5** Often, **interests**: °business, °concern, °affair, °property; °hobby, °pastime, °diversion, avocation, °amusement, °entertainment, °pursuit, °relaxation, °occupation: *She travels abroad to look after her interests. Caroline has many interests besides business.* **6** (lending) °fee or °charge, °percentage, °rate, Slang US vigorish: *How much interest would the bank charge on a £40,000 mortgage?*
—v. **7** °engage, absorb, engross, °attract, °draw, °catch, °capture, °captivate, °hold, °fascinate, °intrigue, °excite, °incite, °provoke, arouse, °affect, °quicken, infect, °animate, °kindle, °fire: *At that time, our daughter was interested only in boys. There is something about astronomy that interests me.* **8** °influence, °induce, °persuade, °move, °tempt, °involve, °enrol, °enlist, °dispose, °incline, °prevail (up)on, °talk into, °concern: *Could I interest you in investing in my company?*

interested adj. **1** Also, **interested in**: °engaged, °absorbed, engrossed, °drawn (to), attracted (by), °involved (in), °curious (about), fascinated (by), °keen (on), stimulated (by), °responsive (to), °concerned (about): *We talked about investing in my plastics company, and he seemed interested. She has become interested in designing jewellery.* **2** °concerned, °involved, non-objective,

°partial, °biased, °prejudiced, °prejudicial, °partisan, predisposed: *You cannot get an honest appraisal of the painting's value from an interested party.*

interesting adj. °absorbing, °engaging, gripping, °riveting, engrossing, °attractive, compelling, intriguing, °provocative, °stimulating, °exciting, °inviting, fascinating, °enchanting, °spellbinding, captivating: *Nick has just told me the most interesting story about Tony.*

interfere v. **1** °meddle, °intrude, °butt in, °intervene, intercede, interpose, °interrupt, Colloq horn in, put or °stick in one's oar or one's oar in, °poke one's nose in, US kibitz: *Stop interfering in things that do not concern you.* **2** °hinder, °impede, °hamper, °block, °obstruct, °encumber, °slow, °retard, °handicap, °set back, get in the °way of, °frustrate, °conflict, °inhibit, °trammel, °subvert, °sabotage: *Allow nothing to interfere with the course of true love.*

interference n. **1** meddling, intrusion, intruding, intervention, interceding, intercession: *This interference in our personal affairs has gone far enough.* **2** °hindrance, °impediment, °block, °obstruction, °encumbrance, impedance, °difficulty, °snag, °hitch, °handicap, °set-back; frustration, °inhibition, °conflict, °opposition: *The lawsuit became an unwelcome interference in the smooth flow of our lives.*

interior adj. **1** °inside, °internal, inner, inward: *The interior surfaces are to be painted white.* **2** °internal, °domestic, °civil, °national, °local, °home: *We will not accept the interference of foreign governments in our interior affairs.* **3** inner, °private, °intimate, °personal, °individual, °secret, °hidden, °veiled: *Some of Hamlet's great speeches are in the form of interior monologues, or soliloquies.* **4** upland, inland, up-country, land-locked: *The most beautiful scenery is in the interior part of the country, away from the marshy coast.*
—n. **5** °inside: *The interior is coated with Teflon.* **6** °heart, °centre, °middle, °core, depths: *This is the story of a journey to the interior of the earth.* **7** uplands, up-country, heartland, hinterland: *The interior is covered with rocks and scrub pine.*

interjection n. °exclamation, ejaculation, °cry, interpolation, utterance: *Grammarians regard expressions like 'Hello' and 'Goodbye' as interjections.*

interlude n. °interval, entr'acte, °intermission, °pause, °stop, stoppage, °respite, °interruption, °break, hiatus, lacuna, °gap, °halt, °wait, breathing-space, °recess, °rest, °spell, °lull, Colloq °let-up: *There is a ten-minute interlude between the acts.*

intermediary n. °go-between, middleman, °agent, °representative, °broker, °intermediate, third °party, °mediator, arbitrator, arbiter, referee, °umpire, °judge: *Donaldson acted as intermediary and arranged the deal.*

intermediate adj. **1** °middle, in-between, medial, midway, halfway, transitional, intervening, °intermediary: *Middle schools cater for the age-range intermediate between primary and secondary schooling. In sublimation a substance changes from a gas to a solid (or vice versa), skipping the intermediate liquid state.* **2** See **intermediary**, above.

intermission n. See interlude, above.

intermittent adj. °irregular, discontinuous, °disconnected, °sporadic, °occasional, °random, °spasmodic, °fitful, °broken, °periodic, alternating, cyclic(al), °rhythmic(al), pulsating, seasonal, on-and-off, on-again-off-again, stop-and-go, stop-go: *Tomorrow, intermittent showers in the morning will yield to sunshine.*

internal adj. See interior, 1, 2, 3, above.

international adj. supranational, °global, worldwide, °universal, intercontinental, cosmopolitan, ecumenic(al) or oecumenic(al); °foreign: *An international conference is being held on disarmament. My father is engaged in international trade.*

interpret v. 1 °explain, explicate, °clear up, °clarify, elucidate, °illuminate, °throw or °shed °light on, °simplify, °decipher, decode, °define, °spell out, make °sense (out) of, °translate, °paraphrase: *Would you interpret this clause of the agreement for me?* 2 °understand, construe, °take (to °mean), °read, °figure or °work out, °sort out, unravel: *I haven't any idea how to interpret this poem.*

interpretation n. 1 °explanation, clarification, elucidation, simplification, decipherment, °solution, working-out, unravelling, sorting out, decoding, °definition, °illustration, °translation, paraphrasing: *Sharon's detailed interpretation of the data is quite easy to understand.* 2 °analysis, diagnosis, °examination, exegesis, explication, reading, construal, °inference, °understanding: *These figures are subject to individual interpretation.*

interrogation n. questioning, °examination, cross-examination, inquisition, °investigation, *Colloq* third degree, grilling: *Caught by the rebels, we were subjected to hours of interrogation.*

interrupt v. 1 °break in, °cut in, °intrude in, °butt in, °interfere in, °punctuate, °disturb, *Colloq* barge in, °chime in, horn in: *He keeps interrupting the discussion with his silly remarks.* 2 °discontinue, °break off, °cut off, °cut °short, °interfere with, °disrupt, °suspend, °hold up, °halt, °stop, °end, °terminate, °cease: *We interrupt this programme to bring you a news bulletin.*

interruption n. 1 °break, intrusion, °disturbance, °interference, disruption: *Please forgive this interruption, but you're wanted on the phone.* 2 °break, °gap, °interval, lacuna, hiatus, °respite, °rest, °pause, pausing, °intermission, stopping, °stop, °suspension, cessation, °cease, ceasing, surcease, hesitation, *Prosody* caesura, *Colloq* °let-up: *She talked for an hour without interruption.*

interval n. 1 °intermission, °interlude, entr'acte, °break, °pause; °recess, °rest (°period), °period, °time, °wait, °spell, °delay, °lapse: *The play was so bad we left in the interval. After a brief interval, the lights came on again.* 2 °meanwhile, °meantime, interim: *He returned later but found that in the interval she had changed her mind.* 3 °gap, °opening, °space, °hole, °void, lacuna, °distance, interstice, *Architecture* intercolumniation: *The interval between the columns is exactly three metres.*

intervene v. 1 °interfere, °intrude, °break in, °interrupt, intercede, °meddle, interpose, °butt in, *Colloq* °poke one's nose in, horn in, put in

one's oar, °step in: *If I had not intervened you might have been killed. She intervened on my behalf.* 2 °come or °go (between), °pass, °elapse: *A week intervened before we saw each other again.*

interview n. 1 °meeting, (°press) °conference, °discussion, °conversation, °talk, °question °period, audience: *The reporter phoned to ask for an interview.* 2 °evaluation, appraisal, vetting, assessment: *I have a job interview scheduled for tomorrow.*
—v. 3 °question, °examine, interrogate, °sound out, °talk with or to: *She interviewed the Prime Minister on television last night.* 4 appraise, °evaluate, °check (out), °vet: *The headmaster himself interviews the teachers.*

intimate[1] adj. 1 °close, °personal, °warm, °affectionate, loving, °dear, °bosom, cherished, °familiar, intime: *She had a party for intimate friends.* 2 °secret, °confidential, °private, °personal, °privy, °hidden, intime; °detailed, °penetrating, °deep, °profound, °thorough, °exhaustive: *In his autobiography he reveals intimate particulars of his marriage.* 3 °sexual; °carnal: *It is well known that Millie was on intimate terms with her chauffeur.* 4 °cosy, °informal, °snug, °friendly, °warm, °comfortable; intime, à deux, °tête-à-tête, *Colloq* comfy: *The two of us had an intimate dinner at home last night.*
—n. 5 °friend, °associate, °comrade, crony, °familiar, confidant(e), (°constant) °companion, Achates, alter ego, °colleague, confrère, *Colloq* sidekick, °chum, °pal, *Brit and Australian* °mate, *US* buddy, *Slang Brit* china (plate), mucker: *He and a few of his intimates like to get together now and then for a game of snooker.*

intimate[2] v. °hint, °imply, °suggest, °insinuate, °indicate, °refer to, allude to, °communicate, °make known, °give (someone) to °understand, °warn, °caution, *Colloq* °tip (off): *He intimates that my wife will be a widow if I tell the police.*

intimidate v. °frighten, °scare, °alarm, cow, °daunt, °dismay, abash, °appal, awe, °overawe, °browbeat, °menace, °threaten, °terrify, °petrify, terrorize, °tyrannize; *Slang* have or get (someone) by the short and curlies: *You can't intimidate me with your threats!*

intolerance n. °bias, °prejudice, °bigotry, °discrimination, °partiality, illiberality, narrow-mindedness, dogmatism; racism, racialism, sexism, classism, ageism, xenophobia: *The government has legislated against intolerance of minorities.*

intolerant adj. 1 °unsympathetic, unforbearing, unindulgent, °impatient, °inconsiderate, °inhospitable, uncharitable: *The present system seems intolerant of the aged.* 2 °biased, °prejudiced, °bigoted, discriminatory, °partial, illiberal, °narrow-minded, °parochial, °provincial, °jaundiced, warped, twisted, °one-sided, °opinionated, close-minded; racist, racialist, sexist, classist, ageist, xenophobic: *How can some religions be so intolerant of other people's beliefs?*

intonation n. °accent, accentuation, °speech or °sound °pattern, °delivery, modulation, articulation, °pronunciation, vocalization, °pitch, °tone, inflection: *You can tell the speaker's mood by his intonation.*

intoxicate v. 1 inebriate, make °drunk, addle, stupefy, °muddle, befuddle: *He tried to intoxicate me with his home-made brew.* 2 °stimulate, °excite,

°overwhelm, elate, exhilarate, °animate, °enliven, invigorate, inspirit, °thrill, galvanize, °electrify, make one's head °spin, take one's °breath away, infatuate, °entrance, °enchant, °enrapture, °fascinate, °bewitch, cast a °spell on, ensorcell: She was intoxicated by the atmosphere of the place.

intoxicating adj. **1** °alcoholic, spirituous, inebriant: Do not drink intoxicating beverages if you plan to drive. **2** °exhilarating, °invigorating, °thrilling, °exciting, heady, °stimulating, electrifying, entrancing, fascinating: Making a film of the life of Lola Montez is an intoxicating idea.

intrepid adj. °fearless, °brave, °bold, °daring, °dauntless, undaunted, °steadfast, °resolute, °courageous, unafraid, plucky, °gallant, valiant, valorous, doughty, °audacious, °heroic, °manly, manful, °dashing, °adventurous, °venturesome, stout-hearted, lion-hearted, °game: Quatermain was known to the enemy as an intrepid soldier.

intricate adj. **1** °involved, °complicated, convoluted, entangled, tangled, knotty, complex, twisted, winding, °tortuous, sinuous, anfractuous, °labyrinthine, °elaborate, Byzantine, °fancy, °ornate, rococo, Daedalian or Daedalean or Daedalic, Literary daedal or dedal: The plot was far too intricate and I became confused. **2** °perplexing, °puzzling, mystifying, enigmatic: The code was so intricate that even the computer needed hours to decipher the message.

intrigue v. **1** °fascinate, °beguile, °captivate, °attract, absorb, °charm, pique, °interest, titillate, arouse or °excite the °curiosity (of): It intrigues me to watch them put those ships into bottles. **2** conspire, °plot, connive, °scheme, °manoeuvre: She was sure that everyone was intriguing against her.
—n. **3** °conspiracy, °plot, °scheme, °manoeuvre, collusion, °stratagem, °trickery, °chicanery, double-dealing, guile, °subterfuge, °artifice, °machination, °deception: Many of those close to the government are engaged in intrigue of some kind. **4** °affair, °liaison, amour, °romance, intimacy; adultery: We all knew about the intrigue he was carrying on with the duke's wife.

intrinsic adj. °inherent, °basic, °fundamental, °essential, °proper, °elemental, °organic, °natural, °native, inbred, congenital, inherited, °hereditary, innate, °inborn, immanent, indwelling, underlying, constitutional; °real, °true, °actual, °genuine: As no painting has intrinsic worth, its value is arbitrary.

introduce v. **1** °acquaint, °present, °make known: Sandy introduced Gerald and Daphne to each other. **2** °bring in or up, °advance, °present, °broach, °put or °set forth, °put forward, °suggest, °offer, °propose, °mention: It was she who introduced the issue of bacteria in canned goods. **3** °announce, °present: Please introduce the next speaker. **4** °start, °begin, °originate, °launch, °establish, °set up, °pioneer, °initiate, usher in, °institute, °bring out or in, °organize: When was paper money first introduced? **5** °insert, °add, interpose, °inject, °put in, interpolate: Why introduce irrelevant matters into the discussion?

introductory adj. **1** °opening, °prefatory, °preliminary, °preparatory, °beginning, inaugural, °initial: His 'introductory' remarks lasted longer than the speeches! **2** °primary, °basic,

°fundamental, °elementary, °first, °rudimentary: Take an introductory course before enrolling for more advanced study.

intrude v. °interfere, °break in, °interrupt, °intervene, °push in, interpose, °butt in, °infringe, °encroach, °obtrude, Colloq horn in, barge in: They want to be alone and you are intruding. Forgive me for intruding into your conversation.

intruder n. **1** interloper, gatecrasher, uninvited °guest, °unwelcome °visitor; trespasser, encroacher, invader, infiltrator, squatter; °burglar, °thief: The intruders were quickly expelled by the guards. **2** meddler, Nosy Parker, Colloq °snoop(er), Nosy Parker, US kibitzer: You are an intruder into my private affairs.

intrusive adj. intruding, interfering, meddlesome, invasive, meddling, prying, °inquisitive, °obtrusive, importunate, °officious, °presumptuous, °forward; °unwelcome, uncalled-for, unwanted, unsought, Colloq °nosy, °pushy, snoopy: He said he apologized if he was being intrusive.

intuition n. °instinct, °insight, °hunch, sixth °sense, presentiment, °premonition, °foreboding; °perception, perceptiveness, percipience, perspicacity, common °sense, mother °wit: Intuition told me I should find the answer here.

invalid[1] adj. **1** ailing, °sick, sickly, °ill, °infirm, valetudinarian, °disabled: His invalid sister is confined to a wheelchair.
—n. **2** °patient, valetudinarian, °victim, sufferer, °incurable, °cripple, Chiefly US and Canadian shut-in: Many invalids have claimed complete recovery after a visit to Lourdes.

invalid[2] adj. **1** °void, null (and °void), nullified, annulled, repudiated, °untrue, °false, °faulty, °erroneous, °wrong, °spurious; °incorrect, °imperfect, impaired, °unsound, °untenable, °ineffective: He was driving with an invalid licence. Your reasons for quitting school are invalid.

invaluable adj. °priceless, valuable, °precious, of °inestimable or incalculable value; irreplaceable, irredeemable; costly, °expensive, high-priced, °dear: The thieves made off with several invaluable paintings.

invariable adj. **1** unchanging, °changeless, unvarying, invariant, unwavering, °constant, °steady, °stable, °regular; °fixed, °fast, °set, °rigid, °uniform, unfailing, unexceptional: She is invariable in her opinion of a woman's right to abortion. His invariable routine calls for a dawn swim, regardless of the weather. **2** immutable, unchangeable, unalterable, unmodifiable: The law of supply and demand is invariable. **3** °permanent, °fixed, °enduring, °abiding, °eternal, unaltered, unvarying, unchanged, unvaried, unmodified: The positions of the stars appear to be invariable.

invasion n. **1** incursion, °raid, foray, intrusion, °inroad, encroachment, trespass, infiltration; °infringement, infraction, °transgression, °violation: The poachers were charged with invasion of private property. Unauthorized publication of that material is an invasion of your rights. **2** °attack, °assault, onslaught, °aggression, °offensive, °drive, storming, blitzkrieg: The armoured divisions succeeded in stopping the invasion.

invent v. **1** °create, °devise, contrive, °originate, °think up, °dream up, °conceive, concoct,

°make up, °imagine, °formulate, °improvise, °design, °hit upon; °coin: *He claims to have invented the toothpaste tube.* **2** °fabricate, °make up, concoct, *Colloq* cook up: *She invented that story about having been a lion-tamer.*

invention *n.* **1** °creation, origination, contriving, devising, °conception, contrivance, introduction, °development: *The invention of the screwdriver has spared many a broken fingernail.* **2** °creation, contrivance, °device, °gadget, *Colloq* °contraption, *US* gismo *or* gizmo: *Thomas Edison held patents on a huge number of inventions.* **3** fiction, figment, °story, °fantasy, °fabrication, °tale, fable, °yarn, °fib, °tall °story *or* °tale, falsification, °fake, °sham, °falsehood, °lie, prevarication: *Her claim that the accident was my fault is a flagrant invention.*

invest *v.* **1** °venture, °lay out, °put in, °sink: *She was persuaded to invest her life savings in unit trusts.* **2** °devote, °allot, °spend, °contribute, °supply, °provide: *We have invested a lot of time in cleaning up local government.* **3** °install *or* instal, °inaugurate, °induct, °initiate, instate, °establish, ordain, °swear in, °seat: *He will be invested with the Order of Merit on Tuesday.*

investigate *v.* °enquire *or* °inquire into, °examine, °study, °consider, °explore, °probe, °look into, °research, °scrutinize, °analyse, °sift (through), winnow: *The laboratory is investigating the nature of the strange phenomenon.*

investigation *n.* enquiry *or* °inquiry, °examination, °study, °review, °exploration, °quest, °search, °probe, °research, °discovery °procedure, °scrutiny, °analysis, inquest, inquisition, °interrogation, questioning: *Has the investigation turned up any evidence of collusion?*

invigorating *adj.* °stimulating, °bracing, rejuvenating, °tonic, vitalizing, restorative, energizing, vivifying, enlivening, °exhilarating, °fresh, healthful, °healthy, salubrious, salutary: *Each morning I go for an invigorating walk. The doctor recommended the invigorating mountain air.*

invincible *adj.* **1** unconquerable, °unbeatable, °indomitable, insuperable, undefeated, unstoppable: *United look invincible, and are likely to retain the cup for a fourth successive season.* **2** °impregnable, invulnerable, impenetrable, °indestructible, unassailable: *The Romans believed the fortress to be invincible.*

invisible *adj.* **1** unseeable, °imperceptible, undetectable, imperceivable; °unseen: *The air we breathe is invisible.* **2** concealed, °hidden, disguised, camouflaged, masked, covered, unperceived, °veiled, indiscernible: *Once the part has been painted, the damage will be invisible.*

invitation *n.* **1** summons, °request, °call, °bidding, *Colloq* invite: *I am still waiting for my invitation to their wedding.* **2** °attraction, °inducement, allure, allurement, °enticement, °temptation, °magnetism, bait, °lure, °draw, °pull: *The possibility of going where no man had gone before was too great an invitation to ignore.*

inviting *adj.* alluring, °tempting, enticing, °attractive, beckoning, appealing, captivating, °engaging, intriguing, °irresistible, winsome, beguiling, bewitching, entrancing, fascinating, tantalizing, °seductive: *She gave him an inviting smile but he still approached cautiously.*

involuntary *adj.* °unconscious, unintentional, °unthinking, °impulsive, °spontaneous,

°unpremeditated, °instinctive, instinctual, unwitting; °automatic, reflex, °mechanical, conditioned, °uncontrolled, uncontrollable: *When I was struck, my involuntary reaction was to strike back at once. At the mention of his name she gave an involuntary start.*

involve *v.* **1** °include, °contain, comprise, °cover, °embrace, °incorporate, encompass, °take in, subsume, °embody, °comprehend, °number among, °count in: *The survey involved many people from all walks of life.* **2** °imply, °entail, °suggest, °mean, betoken, °require, necessitate, °presuppose: *Enrolling for a course involves doing homework as well as attending classes.* **3** Often, **involve in** *or* **with**: °implicate, °concern, °affect, °touch, °entangle, °draw in; °incriminate, inculpate; °associate with, °connect with, °catch (up) in: *I didn't know that Annette was involved. Are you involved in that murder investigation?*

involved *adj.* **1** implicated, °concerned, °affected, °interested, °active: *The public enquiry was attended by all involved members of the community.* **2** tangled, °complicated, complex, twisted, snarled, convoluted, °confused, confusing, °intricate, °tortuous, °elaborate, knotty, Byzantine, °labyrinthine: *The plot is too involved to be followed easily. The involved problems of adolescence cannot be treated in a one-day conference.*

3 involved with: associated with, entangled with, embroiled with, enmeshed with, *Colloq* °mixed up in *or* with: *Dennis is still very much involved with that singer from the Green Dragon.*

irk *v.* °irritate, °annoy, vex, °pester, °provoke, °chafe, nettle, °exasperate, *Colloq* needle, miff, °aggravate, °bug, peeve, °rub (someone) (up) the wrong way, °put out: *It really irks me to know that we lost because we didn't practise.*

irksome *adj.* irritating, annoying, vexing, vexatious, chafing, nettling, exasperating, bothersome, °troublesome, °burdensome, °tiresome, °tedious, °boring, wearisome, uninteresting, *Colloq* aggravating, pestiferous: *The mosquitoes are particularly irksome on muggy, windless evenings.*

irregular *adj.* **1** uneven, °bumpy, °lumpy, °coarse, °rough, unequal, unsymmetric(al), asymmetric(al), °pitted, potholed, °jagged, craggy, °lopsided: *The irregular surface of the road bounced us about in the car.* **2** °sporadic, uneven, °random, °erratic, unequal, °fitful, °haphazard, unsystematic, unsystematized, °disorderly, °uncertain, unmethodical; °occasional, °casual: *In the distance I could hear the staccato of irregular machine-gun fire.* **3** °extraordinary, °unusual, °eccentric, °abnormal, anomalous, aberrant, °unnatural, °peculiar, °queer, °odd, °weird, °bizarre, °strange, °singular, nonconforming, °nonconformist, °exceptional, unconventional, °offbeat, uncommon, freakish, *Colloq* freaky: *Don't you think that keeping a Komodo dragon as a pet is somewhat irregular?*

irrelevant *adj.* °inappropriate, °inapplicable, °impertinent, °unrelated, °alien, inapposite, malapropos, beside the °point, inapt, non-germane, unconnected, °extraneous, neither here nor there, out of °place, °gratuitous, uncalled-for, *Colloq* out of the blue, off the beam, *Slang* off-the-wall: *The name of the person who asked the question is entirely irrelevant.*

irrepressible adj. unrestrainable, irrestrainable, uncontainable, uncontrollable, unmanageable, insuppressible or unsuppressible, unstoppable, °ebullient, °buoyant, °effervescent, bubbling, °boisterous: *Nothing could dampen our irrepressible high spirits after winning the game.*

irreproachable adj. °blameless, unimpeachable, beyond reproach, unreprovable, °faultless, °innocent, above °suspicion, °impeccable, inculpable, °honest, °pure: *Till now, Forsyth's record in the army has been irreproachable.*

irresistible adj. **1** °irrepressible, unconquerable, °indomitable, °overpowering, °unbearable, °overwhelming, °overriding, unmanageable, °ungovernable, uncontrollable: *I had an irresistible desire to punch him in the nose.* **2** unstoppable, inexorable, °relentless, °unavoidable, ineluctable, inescapable: *What happens when an irresistible force meets an immovable object?*

irresolute adj. vacillating, wavering, faltering, °indecisive, °infirm of purpose, in or US only of two minds, undecided, °hesitant, hesitating, shifting, changing, °erratic, °uncertain, unsure, undetermined, °unresolved, °half-hearted, *Colloq* °wishy-washy: *You must act; this is no time to be irresolute.*

irrespective of prep. °regardless of, °notwithstanding, °despite, °apart from, in °spite of, without °regard to, ignoring, discounting: *We shall carry on irrespective of public opinion.*

irresponsible adj. °careless, °reckless, devil-may-care, unanswerable, °unaccountable, non-liable, °rash, °unruly, °wild; °unreliable, undependable, untrustworthy, °weak, feckless, °ineffectual: *Cyril is too irresponsible to take care of the children by himself.*

irretrievable adj. **1** non-retrievable, unretrievable, unrecoverable, irrecoverable, unsalvageable, unsavable, °lost, irreclaimable: *The data that was deleted is now irretrievable.* **2** irreparable, irremediable, uncorrectable, unrectifiable, irredeemable, °irreversible, °irrevocable: *The radiation from the atomic blast did irretrievable damage.*

irreverent adj. **1** °blasphemous, °impious, °profane, °sacrilegious, unholy, °ungodly, irreligious: *She was reprimanded for her irreverent attitude to morning prayers.* **2** °disrespectful, insulting, °insolent, °rude, °discourteous, uncivil, derisive, °impudent, °impertinent, saucy, °flippant, mocking, tongue-in-cheek, *Colloq* °flip, °cheeky: *The prince did not appreciate being the butt of the irreverent skit.*

irreversible adj. unreversible, non-reversible, °irrevocable, unchangeable, unalterable, °permanent, °fixed, °final, unrepealable, irredeemable, °irretrievable: *Burning, essentially the chemical process of rapid oxidation, is irreversible.*

irrevocable adj. °irreversible, unchangeable, immutable, °changeless, °fixed, unalterable, settled, unrecallable, °irretrievable, irrepealable, not undoable; irreparable, °permanent, °enduring, °everlasting: *The colonel says that his was an irrevocable order. That speech did you irrevocable harm.*

irritable adj. °impatient, °excitable, °testy, °touchy, °quarrelsome, grouchy, °fretful, °peevish, °cross, crabby, crusty, °short-tempered, °petulant, °prickly, irascible, °moody, °temperamental, °gruff, °cantankerous, curmudgeonly, dyspeptic, bad-tempered, ill-tempered, ill-humoured, °snappy or °snappish, grumpy or *Brit also* grumpish, *Colloq* crotchety, *US and Canadian and Irish* °cranky: *Why are you always so irritable before breakfast?*

irritate v. °annoy, vex, nettle, °pester, °provoke, °bother, °anger, °enrage, °chafe, pique, °exasperate, °ruffle, hector, °harass, harry, °nag, °plague, °worry, °fret, °fluster, °trouble, °pick at or on, *Colloq* needle, °get under (someone's) skin, °get in (someone's) hair, hassle, peeve, °get on (someone's) nerves, drive (someone) up the °wall, °get (someone's) hackles up, °get (someone's) back up, drive (someone) °crazy or °mad, °rub (someone) (up) the wrong way, *Brit* °get up (someone's) nose, *US* °burn (someone) up: *All these stupid questions are beginning to irritate me.*

island n. isle, islet, ait, cay, key; atoll; archipelago; *Brit dialect* eyot, holm: *There are actually about 1,500 islands in the Thousand Islands in the St Lawrence river.*

isolate v. °separate, °segregate, sequester, cloister, °detach, °cut off, send to Coventry, °ostracize, °maroon, °exclude, °shut out, °bar, debar, °banish, deport, °transport, °exile, °reject, °eject, °throw out, °expel, °shun, °spurn, °avoid, °ignore, snub; quarantine; *Colloq* cut, give (someone) the cold °shoulder: *You cannot isolate a child from the pressures of modern society.*

isolated adj. **1** lone, °solitary, °single, °singular, °unique, anomalous, °separate, °special, °particular, °individual, °exceptional, °unrelated: *In one isolated case they recommended a suspended sentence.* **2** °alone, separated, segregated, °secluded, sequestered, cloistered, unconnected, °detached, (set) °apart, removed, °cut off, excluded; °forlorn, °lonely, hermitic(al), eremitic(al), anchoretic(al), troglodytic(al), monastic: *Away from his friends and family, he felt totally isolated. After his wife died, he led an isolated existence.* **3** °secluded, °remote, °out-of-the-way, off the beaten track, unfrequented, °lonely, °secret, °hidden: *For twenty years we lived in that isolated shack in the wilderness.*

issue n. **1** outflow, °outgoing, °exit, egress, issuance, emanation, efflux, debouchment, °emergence, °outlet: *The river's colour changed abruptly at its point of issue into the sea.* **2** °outcome, conclusion, consequence, culmination, °result, °end, °effect, °consummation, °event, °climax, *Colloq* °pay-off: *Whatever the issue, it has been a brave effort.* **3** °point, °topic, °subject, °matter, °affair, °problem, °question: *That is an issue you should take up with the mayor.* **4** Usually, **major issue**: (°major or °big) °problem or °difficulty, °controversy, °fight, °dispute, cause célèbre: *He turns even walking the dog into a major issue.* **5** printing, °edition, °version, °copy, °number: *I have a copy of the Sunday issue. See if you can buy an issue of today's paper.* **6** °publication, promulgation, issuance, issuing, °distribution, °delivery, dissemination, broadcasting, °proclamation, °circulation: *There will be a special issue of stamps to commemorate his death.* **7** °offspring, °child or children, °descendant(s), °progeny, °young, scion(s), son(s), daughter(s): *According to the records, your*

uncle died without issue, making you his sole heir. **8 at issue**: in contention, in °dispute, °unresolved, °unsettled, °uncertain, up in the air, to be °decided: *The point at issue is which system will be the most efficient.* **9 take issue**: °disagree, °argue, contend, °dispute, °oppose, take °exception: *I feel that I must take issue with your conclusion.*
—v. **10** °proclaim, promulgate, °declare, °publish, °put out, °put *or* °set forth, °announce, °circulate, °distribute, °release, °deliver, °broadcast, disseminate, °get out: *The kidnappers have issued an ultimatum.* **11** °emerge, °come *or* °go forth, °exit, °emanate, °discharge, °stream, °flow, °pour; °appear, °originate, °spring, °stem, °arise: *The play ended, and people issued from the theatre. Where Pegasus stamped his foot the Pierian spring issued forth.*

itch v. **1** °tickle, tingle, °prickle: *These mosquito bites itch terribly.* **2** °desire, crave, °hanker, °hunger, °thirst, °yearn, pine, °wish, °want, °die: *I am itching to get my hands on whoever told you that I was dead.*
—n. **3** °tickle, tickling, tingle, tingling, °prickle, prickling, irritation: *My frustration is like having an itch I can't scratch.* **4** °desire, craving, hankering, °hunger, °thirst, yearning, °longing, *Colloq* yen: *I have a sudden itch to visit mother for the weekend.*

item n. **1** °detail, article, °point, °particular, °matter, °thing, °element, component, °ingredient: *There's one item I'd like you to keep in mind.* **2** °piece, °mention, °notice, °note, °memorandum, memo, filler, jotting: *We often publish short items to fill out a column.*

itemize v. °enumerate, °list, °specify, particularize, °detail, °document, °number, °record, °count, °tabulate: *Must I itemize every single book in the inventory?*

J

jab v. **1** °stab, °thrust, °poke, °dig, °prod; °plunge; °nudge; °tap: *The doctor jabbed a needle into my arm.* **2** °punch, °hit, °strike, °belt, smack, °rap, whack, thwack, cuff, thump, wallop; elbow; *Colloq* °clip, sock, slug, biff: *I jabbed him in the jaw with a quick left.*
—n. **3** °stab, °thrust, °poke, °dig, °prod, °nudge: *I felt the jab of her elbow signalling me to be quiet.* **4** °punch, °belt, smack, °rap, whack, thwack, cuff, thump, wallop, *Colloq* °clip, sock, slug, biff: *A hard jab in the stomach made the bully turn to pudding.*

jabber v. **1** blether *or US only* blather, °chatter, °babble, gibber, gabble, prate, °prattle, °patter, °drivel, °rattle, *Brit* natter, *Scots* yatter, *Colloq* °gab, gas, °yap, witter: *The couple behind me jabbered throughout the entire film.*
—n. **2** See **jargon**, 2, below.

jade n. **1** °nag, °hack, *Slang Brit* screw, *US* plug: *That old jade hasn't won a race in his last ten times out.* **2** °shrew, harridan, °nag, °hag, °drab, °witch, crone, hussy, minx, vixen, virago, termagant, beldam, slut, °slattern, trull, trollop, baggage, °tart, *Slang* battle-axe, °broad, °bitch, old °bag, floozie *or* floozy *or* floosie: *He was married to an expensive jade of a wife.*

jaded adj. **1** °exhausted, °weary, °tired, °dead °tired, bone-tired, bone-weary, dog-tired, °fatigued, enervated, °spent, *Colloq* (°dead) °beat, °dead, bushed, fagged, *US and Canadian* pooped: *The nightspot was full of jaded businessmen, who had gone there to relax after a heavy day at the office.* **2** sated, satiated, cloyed, °surfeited, glutted, gorged, fed up, °sick (and °tired) of, slaked; °dull, bored: *You need a little champagne and caviar to reawaken your jaded palate.*

jag n. °spree, °carouse, °orgy, °bout, *Colloq* binge, *US and Canadian* toot: *She was terribly hung-over after last night's jag.*

jagged adj. °rough, uneven, °notched, sawtooth(ed), °ragged, toothed, spiked, indented, denticulate, °serrated, chipped: *I cut myself on the jagged edge of that broken window.*

jail n. **1** gaol, °prison, lock-up, reformatory, *Brit* °Borstal, *US* penitentiary, °reform school, *Nautical* brig, *Slang* cooler, clink, can, °jug, °stir, slammer, *Brit* °nick, quod, choky *or* chokey, *US* calaboose, big house, °jug, °pen, coop, hoosegow, poky *or* pokey: *They were sent to jail for life.*
—v. **2** °imprison, °lock up, incarcerate, detain, confine, *Brit* °send down, *US* °send up (the river): *He was jailed for 30 days.*

jailer n. gaoler, turnkey, guard, *Brit* warder, governor, *US* warden, *Slang* screw: *The jailers let us out for exercise for an hour each day.*

jam v. **1** °cram, °force, °push, °wedge, °stuff, °press, °ram, °squeeze, shove, °pack, °crowd: *We were jammed in so tightly that we couldn't move.* **2** °block, °obstruct, congest, °fill up, °clog, °plug, °stop up: *The toilet is jammed with paper again.* **3** °slam, °activate, actuate: *I jammed on the brakes.*
—n. **4** °obstruction, blockage, blocking, °block, congestion, °tie-up, bottleneck, stoppage: *She was stuck in a traffic jam for an hour.* **5** °crush, °squeeze, °crowd, °mob, °swarm, multitude, °throng, °mass, horde, °pack, °press: *You wouldn't believe the jam of football fans at the cup final!* **6** °trouble, °difficulty, °predicament, °quandary, °dilemma, *Colloq* °bind, °fix, °hole, pickle, hot water, (tight) °spot, °scrape: *Harry helped me out of a jam once, and I won't forget it.*

jamboree n. °gathering, °get-together, °party, °celebration, °fête, °festival, °festivity, carnival, °frolic, °revelry, °spree, °carouse, jubilee, revels, charivari: *Everyone is invited to the annual jamboree in the village square.*

jangle v. **1** clatter, °clash, °rattle, clang, clank, °crash, °ring, °jingle: *The chains jangled as the prisoners marched to their cells.* **2** °jar, °upset, °irritate: *The continuous screaming of the sirens jangled my nerves.*
—n. **3** jangling, clatter, °clash, °rattle, jarring, clang, clanging, clank, clanking, °crash, clangour, °noise, °din, °racket, clamour, dissonance, cacophony, reverberation, *Literary* stridor: *I heard the jangle of the rag-and-bone man's cart in the next street.*

jar¹ n. crock; °receptacle, °vessel, container, urn, °pot, vase; °jug, pitcher, ewer, flagon, carafe, °bottle, amphora: *We always keep some small change in that blue jar.*

jar² v. **1** °shake, °agitate, °disturb, °stir, °shock, °jolt, jounce, °bounce, °jog, °jerk, °jiggle, joggle: *Don't jar the oven or the cake will collapse.* **2** °disagree, °conflict, °clash, °bicker, °quarrel, wrangle, °oppose, °discord: *She finds that her emotions about her ex-husband are jarring.* **3** °disturb, °upset, disconcert, unsettle, disquiet, °bother, °trouble, vex, °gall, °offend, °take aback, °irritate, °grate, °irk, nettle, °annoy: *It jars me to think that they got off with light sentences.*
—n. **4** °shock, °start, °jolt, °surprise: *Seeing Sam after all those years gave me quite a jar.*

jargon n. **1** °cant, argot, °parlance, °idiom, °vernacular, slang; patois, Creole, °dialect, pidgin; *Colloq* °lingo: *In the jargon of philately, this is known as a 'first day cover'.* **2** blether *or US also* blather, °chatter, °babble, °gibberish, °jabber, gabble, °gobbledegook *or* gobbledygook, °prattle, °patter, °drivel, cackle, jabberwocky, twaddle, (°stuff and) °nonsense, °rubbish, codswallop, balderdash, bunk, humbug, °palaver, bavardage, *Colloq* °rot, °garbage, hogwash, bosh, piffle, flapdoodle, chit-chat, °gab, claptrap, *Slang* bull, crap: *When I questioned my bank manager about the fee, he just gave me a lot of jargon.*

jaundiced adj. **1** coloured, tainted, distorted, twisted, °prejudiced, °opinionated, °biased, °preconceived, untrustworthy, °bigoted, °partial, unfair, °perverted; °dishonest, °corrupt: *Even the most jaundiced view must acknowledge the merits of the plan.* **2** splenetic, cynical, °bitter, °envious, °resentful, °jealous, °hostile, °spiteful, unfriendly, disapproving, °critical, unfavourable, disparaging, denigrating: *I can't say that I agree with Cartwright's jaundiced review of the play.*

jaunty adj. **1** °spirited, °lively, high-spirited, °buoyant, °brisk, °frisky, °sprightly, °free (and

°easy), °blithe, jovial, °happy, jubilant, °jolly, °merry, °cheerful, °gay: *It is heartening to see those pensioners in such a jaunty mood.* **2** °chic, °smart, °stylish, °dashing, °debonair, °elegant, colourful, °spruce, °flashy, °flash, °showy, °flamboyant, *Colloq* °sporty, natty: *Tipping his hat at a jaunty angle, the old boulevardier strolled off, twirling his walking-stick.*

jealous *adj.* **1** °resentful, °bitter, grudging, °envious, covetous, °green with °envy, green-eyed: *Brian is jealous of attention paid to anyone but himself.* **2** °distrustful, distrusting, mistrustful, mistrusting, °suspicious; °anxious, °insecure, threatened, imperilled, °vulnerable: *Ken is very jealous of Kathleen. If anyone so much as looks at her, he feels jealous.*

jealously *adv.* watchfully, carefully, guardedly, protectively, warily, vigilantly, scrupulously, zealously, eagerly, attentively, anxiously, suspiciously: *Victor jealously keeps all details of his business to himself.*

jeer *v.* **1** Often, **jeer at**: °mock, °laugh *or* °scoff *or* °sneer (at), °flout, °deride, °ridicule, make °fun of, °thumb one's nose at, °gibe *or* jibe, °chaff, decry, °twit, °taunt, *Colloq* °rag, bullyrag, roast, *Brit* cock a snook at, *Brit and Australian* barrack, *Slang* °knock: *Don't jeer at aromatherapy till you've tried it.* —*n.* **2** °taunt, °gibe *or* jibe, °aspersion, hoot, °hiss, boo, catcall; °derision, °ridicule, obloquy: *Just because he was fat, Christopher had to suffer the jeers of his classmates.*

jell *v.* **1** °set, congeal, °solidify, °harden, °coagulate, °thicken, °stiffen, gelatinize: *The mixture won't jell till you add hot water.* **2** (°take) °form, °take °shape, crystallize, °materialize, °come together, be °set: *Their plans for the shopping centre have not yet jelled.*

jeopardize *v.* °endanger, imperil, °threaten, °menace, °risk, °hazard, °venture: *You may jeopardize your freedom if you stand up for your rights.*

jeopardy *n.* Usually **in** (sometimes **at**) **jeopardy**: °danger, °peril; °threat, °menace, °risk, °hazard, °chance, uncertainty, vulnerability, °exposure, °liability: *She put her life in jeopardy by going into the lion's cage.*

jerk *v.* **1** °yank, °wrench, °pluck, °nip, °tug, °twist, °tweak: *I jerked the dagger out of his hand, leaving him defenceless.* **2** twitch, °lurch, °jolt, °jump, °start, jig, °jiggle, °wriggle, wiggle: *The creature jerked about convulsively, screaming, then lay still.* —*n.* **3** °yank, °pull, °wrench, °tug, °twist, °tweak: *With a sharp jerk, he pulled the plaster from the child's leg.* **4** °lurch, °jolt, °start, °bump: *The train stopped with a jerk, throwing me off balance.* **5** idiot, °fool, moron, imbecile, *Slang US* °dope, °creep, yo-yo, nerd, dweeb: *Why would she want to go out with a jerk like that?*

jewel *n.* **1** °gem, gemstone, °brilliant, °ornament, bijou, *Colloq* °rock, sparkler: *Thieves stole a diamond necklace and an heirloom brooch set with precious jewels.* **2** °treasure, °marvel, °find, °godsend, °gem, °pearl, °prize, °boon, *Colloq* °catch: *What would you do without your secretary— she's an absolute jewel!*

jewellery *n.* gems, °precious stones, °jewels, ornaments, °finery, bijouterie: *Alexandra keeps her jewellery in a bank vault.*

jiggle *v.* **1** °jog, joggle, jig, °shake, °agitate, wiggle, °wriggle, °jerk: *It's odd to see grown people jiggling about on the dance floor like that. Jiggle the key up and down—maybe then you can turn it.* —*n.* **2** °jog, joggle, jig, °shake, wiggle, °jerk: *I gave the line a few jiggles, hoping to attract a fish.*

jilt *v.* °throw over, °reject, °dismiss, °drop, °discard, °desert, °break (up) with, °forsake, °abandon, *Colloq* ditch, °dump, °brush off *or* give (someone) the °brush-off, *Chiefly US and Canadian* give (someone) his *or* her walking papers: *Angela met Tony and promptly jilted Mike.*

jingle *v.* **1** tinkle, °ring, tintinnabulate, clink, °chink, °chime: *She wore a dozen bracelets, which jingled when she walked.* —*n.* **2** tinkle, tinkling, °ring, ringing, tintinnabulation, clink, clinking, °chink, chinking, °chime, chiming: *I like to feel the jingle of change in my pocket.* **3** °tune, ditty, °melody, °song, °rhyme, verse, doggerel: *The only thing he ever wrote was a jingle for a dog-food commercial.*

jingoism *n.* chauvinism, flag-waving, superpatriotism, nationalism; hawkishness, warmongering, belligerence, bellicosity: *'Might makes right' is a basic tenet of jingoism.*

jinx *n.* **1** (°evil) °spell, °curse, evil eye, malediction, voodoo, *US and Canadian* hex: *I felt I had lost at roulette because she had put a jinx on me.* **2** nemesis, Jonah: *If we don't throw that jinx overboard we shall all die.* —*v.* **3** °curse, °bewitch, °damn, °doom, °sabotage, °condemn, *US and Canadian* hex: *My career was jinxed from the start.*

jitters *n.pl.* °shakes, °fidgets, °nerves, uneasiness, queasiness, nervousness, skittishness, restlessness, apprehension, apprehensiveness, *Slang* heebie-jeebies, willies, *US* whim-whams: *He always gets an attack of the jitters before an exam.*

job *n.* **1** °work, °employment, °position, berth, livelihood; °career, °occupation, °calling, °vocation, °appointment, °pursuit, °field, °trade, °craft, °profession, métier, °area: *What kind of job is she looking for? Harry has a new job.* **2** °assignment, °responsibility, °concern, chore, °task, °undertaking, °function, °duty, °role, °mission, °province, contribution, °charge: *It is my job to see that the machines run properly.* **3** °task, °undertaking, °procedure, °proceeding, °affair, °operation, °project, °activity, °business, °matter, chore: *The job of changing the gasket will take only a few minutes.* **4** °problem, °difficulty, °burden, °nuisance, °bother; toil, °grind, °drudgery; *Colloq* °headache, °pain (in the neck), hassle, *Slang* °pain in the *Brit* arse *or US* ass: *It was a real job getting them to pay for the damage.* **5** °crime, felony; °robbery, burglary, *Slang US and Canadian* °caper: *From the modus operandi, I'd say that the same gang did that job in Manchester.* —*v.* **6** Often, **job out**: °let out, °assign, apportion, °allot, °share out, °contract, °hire, °employ, subcontract, °farm out, consign, commission: *They undertake to do the work, but then they job it out to others.*

jog *v.* **1** °trot, lope, dogtrot, °run: *I jog around the reservoir every morning for exercise.* **2** °jar, °prod, °nudge, arouse, °stir, °stimulate, °prompt, °activate, °shake: *I jogged his memory by referring to the time the dog bit him.* **3** °bounce,

°shake, °jolt, joggle, jounce, °jerk: *I was being jogged about in the back of the van as we sped over the rocky terrain.*

join v. **1** °unite, °connect, °couple, °link, °marry, yoke, °combine, °fasten or °tie or °glue or °weld or solder (together), °unify: *These two pieces should be joined for greater strength.* **2** °ally or °league with, °associate (oneself) with, °team up with, throw (one's lot) in with, °enlist (in), °sign (up) (with), °enrol (in), °enter: *She was invited to join the bridge club.* **3** °go or be with, °associate with, °accompany, °attach (oneself) to, °participate with: *Would you care to join us for a game of bridge?* **4** °border (on or upon), °meet, °touch, abut, °butt, be adjacent (to), °extend to, °verge on, °coincide (with), juxtapose, be contiguous or conterminous (with), be coextensive (with): *The two properties join at the top of the ridge.*

joint n. **1** °seam, °union, °juncture, °connection, °junction, intersection: *The joint won't show after the whole thing's been painted.* **2** *Slang* dive, °dump, *US and Canadian* honky-tonk: *We went into a joint in Soho, looking for some action.* **3** roast: *Who carves the Sunday joint at your house?*
—adj. **4** shared, °mutual, combined, collective, cooperative, °common, communal, collaborative: *Our aims can only be achieved by joint effort.*

jointed v. articulated, segmented, sectioned, sectionalized, hinged: *The stick is jointed so that it can be folded for carrying in the pocket.*

joke n. **1** jest, °witticism, °quip, bon mot, °laugh, wordplay, °pun, °story, anecdote, *Colloq* °gag, °wisecrack, one-liner, °crack: *Ronnie comes up with the funniest jokes I have ever heard.* **2** laughing-stock, °butt, (fair) °game, buffoon: *After that incident, he became the joke of the regiment.* **3** farce, °mockery, °absurdity, travesty, °caricature: *My efforts to play the piano became a joke.*
—v. **4** jest, °quip, °pun, °frolic, °wisecrack, °tease, °taunt, °banter, °chaff, °fool, *Colloq* kid, *US* °crack °wise: *They joked about our predicament. You must be joking if you think I'm going to go out with him!*

joker n. **1** jokester, °comedian, comedienne, °funny man or woman, humorist, jester, °comic, °clown, °wag, °wit, punster, droll, °zany, °merry andrew, buffoon, trickster, prankster, *Colloq* °card, gagster, °gag man, kidder: *Give him a drink and a funny hat and Roger thinks he's the greatest joker in the world.* **2** *US* catch, °hitch, °snag, °drawback, °trap, °twist, °pitfall, fine or small print, *Colloq* catch-22, no-win °situation: *The joker is that whoever treats the patients catches the disease.*

jolly adj. **1** °merry, °cheerful, °frolicsome, °gay, jovial, °joyful, °sportive, convivial, jocund, jocose, jocular, °frisky, coltish, °playful, festive, jubilant, cheery, °exuberant, high-spirited, °animated: *Everyone was in a jolly mood at her birthday party.*
—v. **2** Often, **jolly along**: °humour, appease, °deceive, °string along, °fool, °hoax: *They're just jollying him along because they want him to invest in their scheme.*

jolt v. **1** °jar, °shake (up), jostle, °bump, °bounce, °jerk: *The cart jolted over the rough terrain.* **2** °butt, °strike, °hit, °push, °nudge, elbow, °knock, °jab: *He jolted me so hard he actually cracked a rib.* **3** °shock, °astonish, °astound, °amaze, °surprise, °startle, °stun, °dumbfound or dumfound, stupefy, °strike °dumb, °daze, °shake (up): *I was jolted to learn that my husband had been arrested for murder.*
—n. **4** °lurch, °jar, °jerk, °bump, °jump, °bounce, °start: *The train started with a jolt that almost knocked me over.* **5** °blow, °shock, °surprise, °bolt from the blue, °bombshell: *It was certainly a jolt to discover that she had left me.*

jot v. **1** Usually, **jot down**: make a °note of, °write or °note (down), °put or °set or °take down, °record: *Jot down this telephone number.*
—n. **2** °scrap, °grain, (°wee) °bit, °speck, mite, iota, whit, °particle, tittle, *Colloq* slightest, *US and Canadian* tad, smidgen or smidgin: *I don't care a jot what she thinks about the situation in Central America.*

journal n. **1** °periodical, °magazine, gazette, newspaper, °paper, newsletter, °review, tabloid; °daily, weekly, monthly, fortnightly, °quarterly, annual: *The journal contains information about every building permit awarded in the entire country.* **2** °diary, °chronicle, dossier, °record, °register, log, logbook, minute-book, minutes, documentation, album, °scrapbook, °memoir, almanac, annal, °history, yearbook, °record °book, °roll, catalogue, °list: *He kept a detailed journal of every event in his twenty-year exile.*

journalist n. °reporter, newspaperman, newspaperwoman, °correspondent, newsman, newswoman, °member of the fourth estate, gentleman or lady of the °press, stringer; columnist; °hack; newscaster, anchorman, anchorwoman, commentator, broadcaster, *Brit* pressman, paragraphist; newsreader, *Colloq* °scribe, newsmonger, *US and Canadian* legman, news-hawk, news-hound, news-hen: *Journalists crowded round the minister, urging her to make a statement.*

journey n. **1** °trip, voyage, °excursion, °tour, °travel, °outing, °expedition, junket, °cruise, jaunt, °pilgrimage, peregrination, odyssey, trek: *Did your wife accompany you on your journey to Tierra del Fuego?* **2** °way, °passage, °passing, °transit, °transition, °progress, °course, °trip, °route, °career: *On your journey through this life, Whatever be your goal, Keep your eye upon the doughnut, And not upon the hole.*
—v. **3** °travel, °tour, voyage, °go (°abroad or °overseas), make or take a °trip, make or wend one's °way, make a °pilgrimage, peregrinate, trek, rove, °range, °wander, °roam, °cruise, °gad (about), gallivant or galivant or galavant: *He journeyed to the far corners of the earth seeking an answer to life's mysteries.*

joy n. **1** °pleasure, °gratification, °satisfaction, °happiness, contentment, °enjoyment, gladness, °delight, felicity, elation, exaltation, °ecstasy, °bliss, exhilaration, exultation, °rapture: *We felt indescribable joy at seeing the children safe and sound.* **2** °gaiety, cheerfulness, °cheer, °glee, buoyancy, joviality, jollity, jocundity, joyfulness, joyousness, jubilation, °merriment, light-heartedness, blithesomeness: *Let me wish you joy in this holiday season.* **3** °delight, °pleasure, °treat, °blessing, °gratification, °satisfaction, °prize: *A thing of beauty is a joy forever.*

joyful adj. **1** °cheerful, °happy, °buoyant, °gleeful, °merry, jovial, °jolly, jocund, joyous, jubilant, °gay, light-hearted, °blithe, blithesome,

°sunny: *We are delighted that you have all come to help us celebrate this joyful occasion.* **2** °glad, °pleased, gratified, °delighted, °happy, °elated, °ecstatic, exhilarated, °exultant, °overjoyed, jubilant, in °heaven, *Brit* in the seventh °heaven, *US* in seventh °heaven, *Colloq* on cloud nine, tickled (pink), *Brit* over the moon: *Mark was joyful at the news that he was father of a boy.*

joyless *adj.* **1** °sad, °unhappy, °miserable, depressed, °dejected, °mournful, °downhearted, downcast, down, °despondent, dispirited, °melancholy, heavy-hearted, cheerless, °doleful, grief-stricken, disheartened, saddened, crestfallen, °wretched, disconsolate, °inconsolable, morose, heartsick, °sorrowful, woeful, °woebegone: *It was a joyless company that stood at the grave side. The cat died, the dog died, and my husband was ill—all in all, a joyless time.* **2** °gloomy, depressing, dispiriting, disheartening, °dreary, lugubrious, cheerless, °dismal, °bleak, °inhospitable, °desolate, °grim, austere, °severe: *The shuttered, joyless house loomed out of the misty moor ahead.*

judge *n.* **1** °justice, magistrate, jurist, *Isle of Man* deemster *or* dempster, *Slang Brit* beak: *The judge demanded order in the court.* **2** arbitrator, arbiter, °umpire, referee, adjudicator, judicator, °mediator, °moderator: *She served as a judge at Cruft's dog show last year.* **3** connoisseur, °expert, °authority, arbiter, appraiser, evaluator, reviewer, critic, *arbiter elegantiarum or elegantiae*: *Let me be the judge of which work I do best.* —*v.* **4** adjudicate, adjudge, arbitrate, °decide, °find, conclude, °settle, °determine, °decree, °pass °judgement, deem, °rule, °pronounce *or* °pass °sentence: *Do you think the jury will judge in Claus's favour?* **5** assess, °evaluate, appraise, °estimate, °rate, value, °weigh, °measure, °review, °consider, °size up, °appreciate: *A ballistics expert is required to judge this evidence.* **6** referee, °umpire, mediate, °moderate, arbitrate: *Mr Farnsworth agreed to judge the essay competition.* **7** °believe, °suspect, °think, °consider, °suppose, °guess, conjecture, °surmise, conclude, °infer: *Palaeontologists judge the age of the specimens to be 400 million years.*

judgement *n.* **1** °discretion, discernment, °discrimination, judiciousness, °prudence, °wisdom, °wit, sagacity, perspicacity, clear-headedness, °perception, perspicuousness, percipience, acumen, °intelligence, (°good) °sense, °common °sense, level-headedness, °understanding, shrewdness: *Charlotte's judgement is often sought in such matters.* **2** °decision, ruling, verdict, conclusion, °determination, °opinion, adjudication, °finding, °decree, °order; °outcome, °result, °upshot: *The judgement of the court is final. It was the judgement of Paris to award the golden apple to Aphrodite.* **3** °criticism, censure, °disapproval, °reproof, condemnation: *They offered a moral, not a legal judgement.* **4** °opinion, °view, °belief, (way of) °thinking, °mind, °perception; °sentiment: *In my judgement, she is innocent.* **5** °evaluation, valuation, appraisal, °estimation, assessment: *One critic's unfavourable judgement of a play can spell its doom.*

judicial *adj.* **1** °legal, judiciary, judicatory, juridic(al); °official: forensic: *A formal judicial procedure can be quite costly.* **2** °critical, analytical, °discriminating, distinguishing, discerning,

°keen, °sharp, °perceptive, percipient, perspicacious, differentiating, discriminatory, discriminative, °judicious: *Her decisions have always been judicial.* **3** judgelike, magisterial, °impartial, °fair: *He brought judicial procedures to bear on the handling of the problem.*

judicious *adj.* °sensible, commonsensical, °sound, °sober, °intelligent, °aware, °enlightened, °wise, °sage, sapient, °thoughtful, °reasonable, °rational, °sane, °logical, discerning, °discriminating, discriminative, °astute, °perceptive, percipient, perspicacious, °well-advised, (well-)°informed, °prudent, °discreet, °tactful, °diplomatic, °politic, °careful, considered, circumspect: *The treasurer was considered not to have made judicious use of the club's funds.*

jug *n.* pitcher, ewer, urn, carafe, °bottle, flask, decanter, °jar: *She came in from the barn carrying a jug of fresh milk.*

juggle *v.* °manipulate, °tamper with, °falsify, °fix, °rig, °distort, misstate, °misrepresent, °alter, °arrange, *Colloq* °doctor, cook: *The accountant refused a bribe to juggle the company's books.*

juice *n.* **1** °extract, °liquid, °fluid: *The recipe calls for the juice of one lemon.* **2** °essence, °pith, °extract, °vigour, °force, °vitality, °spirit, °strength, °power: *He really squeezed the juice out of my argument.*

juicy *adj.* **1** °succulent, °moist, °lush: *This is a very juicy pear.* **2** °interesting, °sensational, °lurid, colourful, °vivid, °exciting, °stirring, °thrilling, intriguing, fascinating, °provocative, °suggestive, °racy, °spicy, °risqué: *I've got such a juicy piece of gossip for you!*

jumble *v.* **1** °disorder, °mix (up), °mingle, °confuse, confound, °muddle, °shuffle, disarrange, disorganize, °tangle, °entangle: *I found my belongings all jumbled together.* —*n.* **2** °muddle, °tangle, °medley, °mess; °disorder, °confusion, disarray, °chaos, °clutter: *My clothes were in a jumble on the bed.*

jumbo *adj.* °huge, °gigantic, °enormous, elephantine, °immense, oversized, king-sized, *Colloq US* humongous: *Grandad brought us a jumbo box of chocolates.*

jump *v.* **1** °leap, °bound, °spring, °pounce, °hurdle, vault, °hop, °skip; °caper, °cavort, gambol: *Jack, jump over the candlestick! Lambs were jumping about in the meadow.* **2** °start, °jerk, wince, °flinch, °recoil: *The sudden noise made me jump.* **3** Sometimes, **jump over**: °skip (over), °omit, °pass over *or* by, °bypass, °avoid, °leave out, °ignore, °disregard, °overlook, °gloss over: *Jump the boring parts and read me the sexy bits.* **4** °pass, °move, °leap, °skip: *She jumped from one subject to another so quickly that I couldn't keep track.* **5** °advance, °increase, °rise, °gain, °surge, escalate: *The cost of living jumped again this month, causing fear of inflation.* **6 jump at**: °accept, °grab, °snatch, °swoop up, °leap at, °pounce on: *Most people would jump at the chance to better themselves.* **7 jump on**: °attack, °swoop down on *or* upon; °reprimand, °rebuke: *She jumps on anyone who suggests that she used influence to get her job.* —*n.* **8** °leap, °bound, °spring, °pounce, °hurdle, vault, °hop, °skip: *With one jump the cheetah was upon the gazelle.* **9** °rise, °increase, °boost, hike, °advance, °gain, °surge, escalation, upsurge, °increment, °elevation: *A jump in the Retail Price*

Index drove share prices lower again yesterday.
10 barricade, °obstacle, °hurdle, °fence, °rail, °obstruction: *My horse cleared the first jump easily.* **11** °start, °jerk, °spasm, twitch, °recoil, °lurch, °jolt: *When they called his name, he gave a little jump.* **12** °break, °gap, hiatus, lacuna, °space, °hole, °breach, °rift, °interruption: *There's a jump in continuity at the end of the fourth chapter.*

jumpy *adj.* °nervous, °agitated, °anxious, jittery, fidgety, °restless, edgy, on °edge, °tense, °shaky, skittish, °fretful, uneasy, °queasy, °restive, panicky: *Do you think he was jumpy because we were approaching Count Dracula's castle?*

junction *n.* °juncture, °union, °combination, joining, conjunction, °meeting, linking, °connection, conjoining, intersection, confluence; crossroads, interchange: *The train robbery took place at the junction of the two railways.*

juncture *n.* **1** See **junction**, above. **2** °point, °time, °moment, °stage, °period: *At this juncture, suggesting a merger seems premature.*

junior *adj.* °secondary, lesser, °lower, °minor, °subordinate, °inferior; younger: *Thompson has been offered a junior partnership in his firm.*

junk *n.* **1** °rubbish, °waste, °refuse, °litter, debris, °scrap; *US* °garbage, °trash: *A man came to cart away the junk that we had cleared out of the garage.* —*v.* **2** *Colloq* discard, °throw away, °scrap, °cast aside, jettison, *US* °trash: *We bought a new washing-machine and junked the old one.*

junta *n.* junto, °cabal, °clique, °faction, °gang, coterie, °band, °set, camarilla: *After the coup, the country was run by a military junta.*

jurisdiction *n.* °authority, °power, °prerogative, °dominion, °sovereignty, °say, °control, °rule, ascendancy, hegemony, °influence; °province, °district, °area, bailiwick, compass, °realm, °sphere (of °influence); °reach, clutches, °range, °orbit: *Tierra del Fuego seems a bit far to go just to be outside the jurisdiction of the Inland Revenue.*

just *adj.* **1** °fair, °equitable, °impartial, unbiased, °unprejudiced, °reasonable, fair-minded, even-handed, °neutral, °objective: *Do you think you can expect a just trial after all that publicity?* **2** °upright, °righteous, right-minded,

°honourable, °honest, °ethical, °moral, °principled, °straight, °decent, °good, upstanding, °virtuous, °lawful: *In our system of law, one must believe that juries are basically just.* **3** justified, justifiable, well-founded, well-grounded, °legitimate, valid, °reasonable, °rightful, (well-) °deserved, °due, °fitting, °proper; condign: *She has a just claim to her father's estate. His punishment was just.* —*adv.* **4** °only, °merely, °nothing but, solely, °simply, at °best, at most, no more than: *She said just that and nothing else.* **5** °exactly, °precisely, °perfectly; °barely, °only just, °hardly, °scarcely, by a hair's breadth, *Colloq* by the °skin of one's teeth: *My new car just fits into the garage, with only inches to spare.* **6** (only *or* just) °now, a °moment ago, (very) recently, °lately: *We have just returned from a holiday in Tenerife.*

justice *n.* **1** fairness, impartiality, °objectivity, objectiveness, °equity, equitableness, fair-mindedness, justness, even-handedness, neutrality, °fair play: *Justice triumphed on this occasion, and he was convicted of fraud.* **2** the °law, the °police; °punishment, °prison, °imprisonment, incarceration, °detention: *He is a fugitive from justice.* **3** °law, °right, °morality, lawfulness, rightfulness, legitimacy, judiciousness: *His conviction was a miscarriage of justice.* **4** See **judge, 1,** above.

justify *v.* °vindicate, °legitimate, legitimatize *or* legitimize, legalize, °rationalize, °substantiate, °defend, °support, °uphold, °sustain, validate, °warrant, °confirm; °excuse, °explain, absolve, acquit, exculpate: *My worst fears were justified. How can you justify owning three cars?*

jut *v.* °extend, °overhang, °project, °protrude, °stick out, beetle: *The balcony juts out over the lake.*

juvenile *adj.* **1** °young, youthful, under °age, °minor, teenage(d), °immature, °adolescent, °childish, °infantile, babyish, °puerile, °unsophisticated: *What could be more juvenile than painting graffiti on public buildings?* —*n.* **2** °youth, °boy, °girl, °adolescent, °minor, *Law* infant: *The police have arrested two juveniles for attacking an old lady in her own home.*

K

keen[1] *adj.* **1** °enthusiastic, avid, zealous, °devoted, °ardent, °fervent, fervid, °earnest, °impassioned, °passionate, °intense, °active; °agog, °eager, itching, °anxious: *They are keen fans of TV soap operas. I was keen to go swimming.* **2** °sharp, sharpened, razor-sharp, razor-like, knife-edged; °trenchant, °incisive, °cutting, rapier-like, °pointed, mordant, acid, vitriolic, acerbic, astringent, °biting, acrid, acrimonious, stinging, °scorching, °caustic, searing, °withering, °virulent, °pungent, °sarcastic, °sardonic: *This axe is very keen, so be careful. With his keen wit, the playwright answered his severest critics. His play is a keen satire on the government.* **3** °painful, °bitter, °acute, °poignant, °fierce, °grievous, °severe, distressing, distressful, °strong, °deep, °profound, °intense, °extreme, °heartfelt: *She felt keen resentment at the way she had been treated.* **4** °vivid, °detailed, °specific, unmistaken, unmistakable, °distinct: *He has a keen recollection of seeing the suspect on the bus.* **5** °sharp, °acute, °sensitive, °penetrating, °discriminating, °fine: *The bloodhound has an extremely keen sense of smell.* **6** °intelligent, °sharp, °acute, °perceptive, perspicacious, percipient, °sensitive, discerning, °astute, °smart, °bright, °discriminating, discriminative, °quick(-witted), °shrewd, °clever, canny, cunning, °crafty, °wise: *Philip has a keen understanding of what is required of him.* **7 keen on** *or* **about:** °fond of, enamoured of, °devoted to, °interested in: *Alan is almost as keen on Mary as on his stamp collection.*

keen[2] *v.* **1** °weep, wail, °moan, °lament, °mourn, °grieve; °bewail, °bemoan: *Finnegan's widow still keens over him.*
—*n.* **2** dirge, elegy, knell, °lament, °lamentation, Requiem, monody, threnody, thanatopsis, epicedium, *Scots and Irish* coronach: *The keens could be heard throughout the neighbourhood.*

keep *v.* **1** °retain, °hold, °hang on to, °preserve, °conserve, °have, °save, °maintain, °control: *The difficulty is not in making money but in keeping it.* **2** °hold, °have, take °care or °charge of, °mind, °tend, °care for, °look after, °guard, keep an °eye on, °watch over, °protect, °safeguard; °maintain, °feed, °nourish, victual, °board, nurture, °provide for, °provision: *Would you keep this parcel for me until I return? They keep chickens and ducks.* **3** °accumulate, °save (up), °amass, °hoard (up), °husband, °retain, °preserve, °put or °stow away: *My brother has kept all the toys he ever had.* **4** °maintain, °store, °preserve: *I keep woollen things in a cedar chest.* **5** Often, **keep on** or **at:** °continue, °carry on, °persist (in), °persevere (in); °prolong, °sustain: *How did you keep going after Elsa's death? She kept at it all night long. Keep on working till I tell you to stop.* **6** keep to, °abide by, °follow, °obey, °mind, adhere to, °attend to, pay °attention to, °heed, °regard, °observe, °respect, °acknowledge, °defer to, accede (to), °agree (to): *Only a stickler would keep the letter of such a law.* **7** °stay, °remain: *Keep off the grass. Keep to the left.* **8** °support, °finance, °provide for, °subsidize, °maintain: *He kept a mistress in Chelsea.* **9** confine, detain; °imprison,

incarcerate, °jail *or Brit also* gaol: *The police have kept him overnight.* **10** °celebrate, °observe, solemnize, °memorialize, °commemorate: *We always kept Easter at my mother's house in the country.* **11** °last, be preserved, °survive, °stand up, °stay °fresh: *Eggs keep longer in the refrigerator.* **12** °harbour, °maintain, °safeguard, keep °dark: *Can you keep a secret?* **13 keep from:** °prevent, keep or °hold back, °restrain, (hold in) °check, °restrict, °prohibit, °forbid, °inhibit, disallow, °block, °obstruct, °deny, °curb, °deter, °discourage: *How can I keep my plants from dying while I'm away?* **14 keep in: a** keep or °hold back, °repress, °suppress, °stifle, °smother, muzzle, °bottle up, °withhold, °conceal, °hide, °shroud, °mask, °camouflage: *She keeps in her true feelings. He could hardly keep in the tears.* **b** confine, °shut in or up, coop up, detain; °fence in: *Keith thought the teacher kept him in after school because she liked him.*
—*n.* **15** °upkeep, °maintenance, °support, °room and °board, °subsistence, °food, °sustenance, living: *He works hard to earn his keep.* **16** donjon, °tower, °dungeon: *He was imprisoned in the keep of the castle for twenty years.*

keeper *n.* custodian, °guardian, °guard, warden, caretaker; warder, °nurse, °attendant, *Brit* °minder: *The keepers are very strict about not letting people feed the animals. How come they let you out without your keeper?*

keepsake *n.* memento, souvenir, °token, °reminder, °remembrance, °relic: *The locket is a keepsake from those happy days in Antibes.*

keg *n.* cask, barrel, °butt, hogshead, tun, puncheon: *We bought a keg of beer for the party.*

kernel *n.* **1** °grain, °seed, pip, stone; nut, °meat, *US* nut-meat: *Try to extract the walnut kernel without breaking it.* **2** °centre, °core, °nucleus, °heart, °essence, °quintessence, °substance, °gist, °pith, °nub, quiddity: *Let's get down to the kernel of the problem.*

key *n.* **1** latchkey, skeleton °key, pass-key, opener: *Have you lost your car keys again? You will need a key to open the air valve on the radiator.* **2** °clue, °cue, °guide, °indication, °indicator, °explanation: *The key to his behaviour can probably be found in the way his mother treated him in his childhood.* **3** °pitch, °tone, °timbre, °level, tonality, frequency: *The song was originally written in the key of C.* **4** °legend, °explanation, °description, explication, clarification, °translation: *A key to the symbols appears on every other page.* **5** °mood, °tenor, °tone, °humour, °style: *In this passage there is a change to a more sombre key.*
—*adj.* **6** °important, °essential, °vital, °necessary, °crucial, °critical, °main, °pivotal: *Automatic reversal is a key feature of this cassette player. Roderick is a key man in the company.*

keystone *n.* °necessity, crux, linchpin, °basis, °principle, °foundation, cornerstone: *Predestination was the keystone of his religion.*

kick *v.* **1** °boot, °punt: *The basic aim in soccer is to kick the ball into the back of the net.* **2** °recoil, °backlash, °rebound: *The shotgun kicked when I fired it.*

—n. 3 °punt, drop-kick: *His kick sent the ball down the field.* **4** °recoil, °backlash, °rebound: *That gun has quite a kick!*

kickback *n.* °rebate, refund, °share, compensation, commission, °percentage, °reward; °bribe, °pay-off, *Colloq chiefly US* payola, *US* plugola: *We get a kickback on every computer sold. Some disc jockeys were accepting kickbacks for playing particular records.*

kidnap *v.* °abduct, °capture, °seize, °carry off, *Slang* °snatch: *He was kidnapped by guerrillas and held prisoner for over two years.*

kill *v.* **1** °execute, slay, °murder, assassinate, do away with, put to death, cause the death of, liquidate, °dispatch *or* despatch, take (someone's) life, °finish (off), put an end to, write 'finis' to, °silence, kill off, administer the *coup de grâce*, °eliminate, put (someone) out of (his or her) misery, °exterminate, °extinguish, °obliterate, eradicate, °destroy, annihilate, °massacre, °slaughter, decimate, °butcher, (of animals) °put down, put to sleep, *Slang* do in, °bump *or* °knock off, °hit, °polish off, snuff (out), take for a °ride, *US* °waste, °rub out, ice, fit with concrete overshoes *or* a wooden kimono: *He was the third police officer to be killed this year.* **2** °destroy, °ruin, °devastate, °ravage, °wreak *or* °work °havoc (up)on, °kill off: *The entire orange crop was killed by the sudden frost.* **3** °muffle, °neutralize, °deaden, °damp, °silence, nullify, °dull, absorb, °smother, °stifle, °suppress, °still: *This padding should kill the noise of the motor.* **4** °exhaust, °tire (out), °fatigue, °weary, *Colloq* °fag (out): *Pushing that mower all day nearly killed me.* **5** °hurt, °pain, °torment, torture: *These shoes are killing me.* **6** °quash, °suppress, °defeat, °veto, °cancel: *The tobacco interests campaigned to kill the bill to ban smoking in public places.* **7** °consume, °use up, °spend, while away, °occupy, °fill, °pass, °idle: *While waiting, I killed time doing a crossword puzzle.*
—n. 8 °game, °prey; °quarry: *The lioness allowed her cubs to eat part of the kill.* **9** °death, °killing, °end, °finish, deathblow, *coup de grâce*; °termination, denouement *or* dénouement, conclusion: *She wants to be in at the kill.*

killer *n.* **1** °murderer, assassin, slayer, °cutthroat, °butcher, exterminator, Bluebeard, (Jack the) ripper, *Slang US* torpedo, hit man, triggerman, gunsel, hooligan, gunfighter, iceman, hatchet man: *What are the statistics on the number of killers who are not caught?* **2** *Slang* old-fashioned bee's knees, *US* humdinger, doozy, killer-diller (from Manila), lallapalooza *or* lollapalooza, lulu, daisy, dilly: *The new show at the Odeon is a killer.*

killing *n.* **1** °murder, °carnage, butchery, °execution, °slaughter, °bloodshed, °death, °massacre, genocide, liquidation, mass °murder *or* °destruction, decimation, extermination, blood bath, manslaughter; slaying, homicide, °fatality: *The killing of dissidents must stop. There has been another killing in the park.* **2** coup, bonanza, °success, °windfall, stroke of °luck, °gain, °profit, *Colloq Brit* °bomb: *They've made a killing on the Stock Exchange.*
—adj. 3 °devastating, °ruinous, °destructive, °punishing, °exhausting, debilitating, fatiguing, tiring, enervating, °difficult, °arduous: *How can you keep up the killing pace of having two jobs?*

killjoy *n.* °spoilsport, damper, dampener, grouch, grump, malcontent, pessimist, cynic, prophet of °doom, Cassandra, *Colloq* °wet blanket, sourpuss, *US* party pooper, °gloomy Gus, picklepuss: *Go to the dance and stop being such a killjoy!*

kin *n.* **1** °family, °relative(s), °relation(s), °kindred, kinsfolk *or US and Canadian* kinfolk, kinsman, kinswoman, °stock, °clan, blood-relation(s), blood-relative(s): *We might have the same name, but he's no kin of mine. Grandmother says that too many people are thoughtless of their kin these days.*
—adj. 2 °related, °akin (to), °kindred, consanguineous, cognate, agnate: *One often forgets that all men are kin.*

kind¹ *adj.* °friendly, °kindly, °nice, congenial, affable, approachable, °amiable, °obliging, °accommodating, °amicable, well-disposed, °courteous, °good, °good-natured, °benevolent, well-meaning, well-wishing, °thoughtful, well-intentioned, °generous, big-hearted, °humanitarian, °charitable, °philanthropic, °gentle, °understanding, °sympathetic, °considerate, °lenient, °tolerant, °indulgent, compassionate, kind-hearted, °gracious, °warm, warm-hearted, °cordial, tender-hearted, °affectionate: *It was kind of you to stop and help us. I never thought of him as a kind man.*

kind² *n.* **1** °sort, °type, °variety, °style, °genre, species, °class, °breed; °brand, °make: *What kind of tree is the cypress? Do we always have to have the same kind of breakfast cereal?* **2** °nature, °character, °manner, °description, °sort, °persuasion, °stripe, feather, kidney: *What kind of person is she? Today's students are of a totally different kind.*

kindle *v.* ignite, °light, set alight, set °fire to, set afire, °inflame, °fire, °foment, °incite, instigate, °provoke, °prompt, °prick, goad, °spur, °whip up, °stir (up), °work up, °excite, °agitate, °shake up, °jolt, arouse, °rouse, (a)waken, °inspire, inspirit, °stimulate, °animate, °enliven, °energize, innervate, galvanize: *Kindling a fire in the rain is not easy. The wholesale pillaging kindled a feeling of deep resentment among the native population.*

kindly *adj.* **1** See **kind**, above.
—adv. 2 cordially, graciously, obligingly, amiably, amicably, politely, genially, courteously, thoughtfully, considerately, hospitably, agreeably, pleasantly: *He very kindly invited me in for a cup of tea.* **3** °please, be so °kind as to, be °good enough to: *Would you kindly pass the salt?*

kindness *n.* **1** friendliness, kind-heartedness, warm-heartedness, graciousness, goodness, good-naturedness, good-heartedness, °good °will, °benevolence, benignity, humaneness, °humanity, decency, tenderness, gentleness, kindliness, °charity, charitableness, generosity, °philanthropy, beneficence, compassion, °sympathy, °understanding, thoughtfulness, °consideration, cordiality, °hospitality, °warmth, geniality, °indulgence, °tolerance, °patience: *We shall always appreciate the kindness shown to us by our hosts during our visit.* **2** °favour, °good deed *or* turn, °service, act of kindness; generosity, °assistance, °aid: *She did me a great kindness in introducing me to you. How can I repay your kindness?*

kindred *adj.* **1** °close, associated, °united, allied, analogous, °like, °similar, °matching, °parallel, °common, °related; °akin: *Because we both like sports, Samantha's interests are kindred to mine.* **2** °related, consanguineous, consanguine, cognate, agnate: *Linguists regard the Romance languages as kindred tongues.* —*n.* **3** See **kin**, 1, above.

king *n.* prince, crowned °head, majesty, °sovereign, °monarch, ruler, regent, *Colloq Brit* °royal: *In former times, the king had power of life and death over his subjects.*

kingdom *n.* **1** °realm, empire, °sovereignty, principality, °monarchy: *He sought a suitable wife throughout the kingdom.* **2** °field, °area, °domain, °province, °sphere (of °influence), °territory, bailiwick, *Colloq* °turf: *The operating theatre is the surgeon's kingdom.*

kink *n.* **1** °twist, crimp, °tangle, °knot, °wrinkle, curl, °coil, curlicue, crinkle: *Those kinks wouldn't occur if you had coiled the rope properly.* **2** °pang, °twinge, °stab, °spasm, cramp, stitch, °tweak, crick: *I have a kink in my neck from constantly looking down.* **3** °difficulty, °complication, °flaw, °hitch, °snag, °defect, °imperfection, distortion, deformity: *There were several kinks that had to be ironed out before the plan was presented to the board.* **4** crotchet, °quirk, whim, caprice, °fancy, vagary, °eccentricity, idiosyncrasy: *He would win more support if he rid himself of certain kinks in his thinking.*

kinky *adj.* **1** °outlandish, °peculiar, °odd, °queer, quirky, °bizarre, crotchety, °eccentric, °strange, idiosyncratic, °different, °offbeat, °unorthodox, °capricious, °irregular, °erratic, unconventional, °unique, freakish, °weird, °fantastic, °whimsical: *This school is not interested in kinky notions of education.* **2** °perverted, °unnatural, °deviant, °degenerate, warped, °abnormal, depraved: *There is a rumour that they engage in kinky sex.* **3** °crisp, frizzy, frizzed, frizzled, curly, crimped, °wiry; knotted, tangled, twisted: *He has kinky red hair.*

kinship *n.* **1** consanguinity, (blood) °relationship, (°family) ties, (°common) descent, °lineage, one's (own) flesh and blood: *At that time, several of the royal houses of Europe were connected by kinship.* **2** °connection, correspondence, parallelism, °relationship, similarity, °association, °agreement, °alliance; °affinity: *There is a clear kinship among the Germanic languages. She felt a kinship with other adopted children.*

kiss *v.* **1** osculate, peck, *Colloq* smack, smooch, neck, *Old-fashioned* spoon, canoodle: *I kissed her on the cheek. A young couple were kissing on the park bench.* **2** °touch, °brush, graze: *The cue-ball barely kissed the black, toppling it into the pocket.* **3** **kiss goodbye**: °bid adieu, say °farewell to, °give up, °relinquish, °abandon, °forsake, °desert, °renounce, °repudiate, °forget (about), °dismiss, °disregard, °ignore: *With those marks, you can kiss goodbye to any thought of winning a scholarship.* —*n.* **4** osculation, peck, *Colloq* smack, smooch, *US and Canadian* buss, *Slang Brit* smacker: *He ran over and gave me a big hug and a kiss.*

kit *n.* °apparatus, °gear, °equipment, °paraphernalia, appurtenances, °rig, accoutrements *or US also* accouterments, °tackle, °trappings, °supplies, furnishings; °instruments, °tools, utensils, °implements: *Did you bring your tennis kit? The model aeroplanes were built from kits. The plumber left his tool kit behind.*

kitchen *n.* kitchenette, cookhouse; scullery, pantry, larder; *Nautical* galley, *Brit* caboose: *He was in the kitchen getting dinner ready.*

kittenish *adj.* °coy, °seductive, °flirtatious, coquettish, °sportive, °playful: *Barbara tends to get a bit kittenish when she's with men.*

kitty *n.* °pot, °pool, °collection: *Has he contributed anything to the kitty?*

knack *n.* °genius, °intuition, °talent, °gift, °facility, °skill, °aptitude, °bent; °ability, °flair, °dexterity, °capacity, adroitness, °proficiency, skilfulness: *He has an uncanny knack for saying the wrong thing. When it comes to gourmet cooking, Peggy certainly has the knack.*

knife *n.* **1** °blade: *This knife couldn't cut through warm butter.* —*v.* **2** °stab, °pierce, °slash, °cut, °wound: *There was a struggle, and one youth was knifed in the chest.*

knit *v.* **1** °join *or* °fasten *or* °weave (together), interweave, interlace, interconnect, intertwine, °link, °bind, °unite, °tie (up *or* together), consolidate, °combine, °compact: *He was the first king to succeed in knitting together the diverse elements of the empire.* **2** °grow (together), °heal, °mend, °join: *The broken bones will knit in about a month.* **3** °furrow, °contract, °wrinkle, °knot, crease: *He knit his brow and sighed.*

knob *n.* boss, stud, protuberance, °projection, °protrusion, °handle: *Turn the knob, then pull the drawer open.*

knock *v.* **1** °strike, °hit, °rap, thwack, whack, thump, bang, °tap: *Knock on the door. He knocked the man on the head with his walking-stick.* **2** criticize, deprecate, °carp *or* °cavil at, °disparage, °put down, °run down: *Don't knock something till you've tried it.* **3** **knock about** *or* **around**: **a** °wander, °roam, °ramble, rove, °travel, °gad about: *She's going to knock about the world for a bit before settling down.* **b** °associate with, consort with: *He was only knocking about with some of the boys.* **c** °discuss, °debate, °talk over, *Colloq* °kick about *or* around: *I have a business proposition that I want to knock around with you.* **d** °beat (up), maltreat, °mistreat, maul, °manhandle, °batter, °abuse, °hit, °strike: *He's been known to knock his wife about.* **4** **knock down**: **a** °raze, °demolish, °destroy, °level, °wreck, lay in ruins, °throw *or* °pull down: *They knocked down those beautiful old houses and erected an ugly office block in their place.* **b** °fell, °floor, °cut down: *As soon as he got up, McCloskey knocked him down again.* **5** **knock off**: **a** °stop °work(ing), °quit, °go home, clock off *or* out, °terminate, °lock up, °close down: *I think I'll knock off for a few hours' rest.* **b** °steal, °pilfer, thieve, °rob, *Colloq* °lift, *Brit* °pinch, *Slang Brit* °nick, *US* knock over: *Two men in balaclavas knocked off the bank in the High Street.* **c** See **kill**, 1, above. **d** make quick *or* short work of, complete, finish, bring to an end, *Colloq* polish off: *He knocked off that book in a week.* **e** °copy, °imitate: *They knock off expensive items, then sell them for much less than the originals.* **6** **knock out**: **a** knock *or* °render °unconscious, °floor, °prostrate, trounce, °whip, *Slang* °flatten, K.O. *or* kayo: *The smart money says that the challenger will knock out* *the champion in the third round.* **b** °overwhelm, °overcome, °daze, °stagger, °astound, °astonish, °bewilder, °stun, *Colloq* °bowl over, blow (someone's) mind, *Slang Brit* knock for six: *She'll really knock them out in that dress!* **7 knock up: a** knock *or* °put together, °improvise: *I think I can knock up something quickly that will pass muster.* **b** arouse, (a)waken, °wake up: *They knocked me up at dawn to go to work.* **c** impregnate, get with child, make °pregnant: *Her boyfriend knocked her up and then refused to marry her.* —*n.* **8** °blow, °rap, °tap, thump, pounding, hammering: *I was woken by a knock on the wall from my neighbour.* **9** °blow, °punch, °jab, smack, thwack, whack, right, left, cuff, *Colloq* clout, bop, biff, conk: *He gave me a knock on the nose, and it started to bleed.* **10** °slap (in the face), censure, °criticism, condemnation, °slur, °insult: *My latest novel took quite a few knocks from the reviewers.*

knock-off *n.* imitation, copy, simulation, replica, facsimile, duplication: *This cheap knock-off of a £1,000 watch is selling for £50.*

knockout *n.* **1** *coup de grâce, Slang* K.O., kayo: *Carnera won by a knockout in the first round.* **2** °success, °sensation, °triumph, *Colloq* °hit, °winner, smash, smash °hit, stunner: *She looks a knockout with her new hairstyle.*

knoll *n.* hillock, hummock, °mound, barrow, °hill, °elevation, °rise: *We climbed to the top of the knoll where we had a better view of the house.*

knot *n.* **1** °snarl, gnarl, °tangle; °tie, °bond: *I cannot loosen this knot.* **2** °collection, assemblage, aggregation, congregation, °crowd, °cluster, °bunch, °gathering, °company, °band, °gang, °crowd, °throng: *A small knot of people were standing in front of my painting.* —*v.* **3** °fasten, °tie, °bind, °secure, °lash, °tether, affix, °fix, °attach: *I knotted the rope around his neck.*

know *v.* **1** °understand, °comprehend, be °familiar with, °grasp, be °acquainted with, be °versed *or* skilled in: *Do you know anything about nuclear physics? I know Italian fairly well. She knows how to dance the tango.* **2** °recognize, °identify, °recall, °remember, °recollect: *I know him from somewhere.* **3** be °sure *or* °certain *or* °positive: *I knew I was right! I just know I'm going to win the first prize.* **4** °distinguish, °separate, discern,

°differentiate, °recognize, °identify: *Charles doesn't know right from wrong.* **5** be °aware *or* °conscious *or* cognizant of, be °informed *or* advised of, have °knowledge of: *He knows that he cannot fire her because she knows too much.*

knowing *adj.* **1** conspiratorial *or* conspiratory, °secret, °private; °significant, °meaningful, °eloquent, °expressive; °shrewd, canny, °artful, °sly, °wily, °crafty: *She gave him a knowing wink.* **2** °wise, °clever, °shrewd, (well-)°informed, °knowledgeable *or* knowledgable, °aware, °expert, °qualified, °astute, °perceptive, °intelligent, sagacious: *Harold is quite knowing about horses, why not ask him?*

knowledge *n.* **1** °knowing, awareness, apprehension, cognition, °grasp, °understanding, discernment, consciousness, °comprehension, °insight: *Miles's knowledge of history is extensive.* **2** facts, °information, °data, °intelligence: *They had no knowledge of any defections to the enemy.* **3** °acquaintance, acquaintanceship, °familiarity, °appreciation, conversance, °expertise, °experience, adeptness, °proficiency: *Has he any knowledge of their work on the DNA molecule?* **4** °schooling, °education, °scholarship, °instruction, °learning, erudition: *A little knowledge is a dangerous thing.*

knowledgeable *adj.* **1** °aware, *au fait, au courant,* up to °date, (well-)°informed, (well-)°acquainted, cognizant, °knowing, *Colloq* in the °know: *She is knowledgeable about events in eastern Europe.* **2** well-educated, erudite, °learned, cultured, well-read, °intelligent, °sophisticated, °worldly, °wise, °sage, sagacious: *Professor Evans is one of the most knowledgeable people I have ever met.*

kowtow *v.* Often, **kowtow to**: genuflect (before), salaam (to), °prostrate oneself (before), °bow (down) (to *or* before), pay court to, °scrape before, °cringe before, fawn (before), grovel (before), toady ((up) to), °pander to, °truckle ((up) to), dance attendance on, *Colloq* butter up, *Slang* suck up to, °play up to, shine up to, *Taboo slang US* brown-nose: *He kowtows to anyone who he thinks may be of use to him.*

kudos *n.* °praise, acclaim, °glory, °fame, °renown, °honour, plaudits, °applause, laudation, acclamation, accolade: *They got a lot of kudos out of funding a new opera-house.*

L

label n. 1 °identification, identifier, ID, °mark, marker, earmark, °tag, ticket, sticker, °stamp, imprint, °hallmark, °brand, Brit docket: *The label shows the weight, composition, and price of the contents. A proper shipping label should show both source and destination.* 2 °name, °denomination, designation, appellation, °nickname, epithet, sobriquet, classification, characterization, °description: *It is difficult to give a label to the kind of novels she writes.* 3 trade °name, trade °name, °brand, logo, °mark: *Many supermarket chains market products under their own label.*
—v. 4 °identify (as), °mark, °tag, earmark, ticket, °stamp, °hallmark, imprint, °brand, Brit docket: *In those days, every liberal was labelled a communist. Prepared food packages must be labelled with their ingredients.* 5 °name, denominate, °designate, °call, °term, dub, classify, °categorize, pigeon-hole, °class, °characterize, °describe, °portray, °identify, Colloq US peg: *We cannot label Voltaire either spiritualist or materialist.*

laborious adj. 1 °arduous, °burdensome, onerous, °strenuous, gruelling, back-breaking, Herculean, °exhausting, taxing, tiring, fatiguing, wearying, wearisome, °toilsome, °difficult, °tough, °hard, uphill, °stiff: *Few realize how laborious farm work can be.* 2 °painstaking, °detailed, °careful, °thorough, °diligent, °scrupulous, °exhaustive, °steady, °steadfast, °relentless, unrelenting, dogged, assiduous, sedulous, persevering, °persistent, °untiring, °tireless, indefatigable, unremitting: *After laborious research the virus was finally identified.* 3 °industrious, hard-working, dogged, °determined, unwavering, °obstinate, °stubborn, unflagging, obdurate: *He made a laborious effort to get ahead.* 4 °laboured, °strained, °forced, °ponderous, overworked: *The book contains some of the most laborious prose ever written.*

labour n. 1 toil, (°hard) °work, travail, °exertion, °effort, laboriousness, °strain, °drudgery, °pains, °industry, °slavery, donkey-work, Colloq °sweat, °grind, elbow-grease, Brit swot: *They know the labour involved in building a road.* 2 °employees, °workers, wage-earners, °labourers: *A meeting between labour and management is scheduled for today.* 3 °effort, °task, °job, chore, °undertaking: *Raising funds for the museum was a labour of love.* 4 travail, childbirth, parturition, labour pains, contractions, °delivery: *She went into labour at midnight, and the twins were born just after four.*
—v. 5 °work, toil, travail, drudge, °strain, °strive, °struggle, °slave, Colloq °sweat, °grind, Brit °peg away (at), swot: *We laboured hard to get where we are today.* 6 °dwell on, °overdo, overemphasize, harp on, overstress, °strain, Colloq °belabour: *I heard you the first time, so don't labour the point.* 7 **labour under**: be burdened or troubled or distressed by, be deluded or deceived by, be disadvantaged by, °suffer, °endure: *He is labouring under a misapprehension. She labours under the impression that she will not be affected by a lack of education.*

laboured adj. 1 °strained, °forced, °difficult, °hard, °laborious, °heavy: *His breathing became*
laboured. 2 overdone, °excessive, °overwrought, °ornate, °elaborate, overworked, over-embellished, contrived, °affected, °artificial, °unnatural: *Her writing style is very laboured and much too stiff.*

labourer n. °worker, workman, °hand, blue-collar °worker, working man, °manual °worker, drudge, Colloq Brit navvy: *Get some labourers to clear away that rubble.*

labyrinthine adj. labyrinthian, maze-like, mazy, °tortuous, sinuous, winding, convoluted, °complicated, confusing, °perplexing, °puzzling, enigmatic, baffling, confounding, complex, Daedalian or Daedalean or Daedalic, daedal, °intricate, Byzantine, twisted, °gnarled, snarled, tangled, knotted, knotty, Gordian: *The plot was so labyrinthine that the audience was unable to follow it.*

lace n. 1 lace-work, tatting, openwork, filigree, °mesh, °web, webbing, °net, netting, °network: *She wore a collar of handmade lace.* 2 shoelace, shoestring, bootlace, °cord, °string, thong, °tie, lacing: *They made me remove my belt, tie, and laces before locking me in a cell.*
—v. 3 °thread, °weave, °string, °twine, interweave, intertwine: *First lace the cord through the eyelets, then draw it tight.* 4 °spike, °fortify, °strengthen: *I saw her lace my punch with vodka, so I didn't drink it.* 5 **lace into**: **a** °attack, °assault, °beat, assail, thrash, °belabour, °fall on or upon, °set upon, °pounce on or upon, °lay into, Colloq °light into: *The brothers laced into one another with a fury.* **b** °berate, °scold, revile, °attack, °upbraid, °castigate, °rant or °rave at: *She really laced into me for being an hour late for dinner.*

lacerate v. °gash, °cut, °slash, °tear, °rip, °claw, °mangle, °wound, °rend, °hurt: *My feet were lacerated by the sharp stones. She suffered a lacerating attack from him for forgetting to pass on the message.*

lack n. 1 °want, deficiency, °dearth, °absence, °scarcity, °shortage, °need, insufficiency, paucity, °deficit, inadequacy: *We suffered from a severe lack of water. The orchestra is experiencing a serious lack of talent at the moment.*
—v. 2 °want, °need, °require, be °deficient in, be or fall °short of, be without: *He lacks the votes needed to win. Simon lacks the ability to paint any better.*

lackadaisical adj. 1 °lethargic, languorous, languid, °listless, °lazy, sluggish, spiritless, °idle, °indolent, °inactive, °slothful, fainéant: *She's much too lackadaisical to go out and get a job.* 2 °unenthusiastic, °dull, apathetic, insouciant, uncaring, unconcerned, °indifferent, °blasé, °cold, °cool, °lukewarm, °tepid, unexcited, °phlegmatic, unemotional, unexcitable, uninterested, unimpressed, uninspired, °unmoved, pococurante: *How can you explain the government's lackadaisical attitude towards the greenhouse effect?*

lacklustre adj. °drab, °dull, lustreless, °flat, °dingy, °colourless, °dismal, °dreary, unexciting, °boring, °prosaic, °tiresome, °tedious, wearisome, uninteresting, two-dimensional, insipid, °vapid, °bland, unimaginative, °thick, °slow, °dense, Colloq wishy-washy, blah: *He gave a very lacklustre performance as Shylock. She has been leading a lacklustre life since John left.*

lad *n.* °boy, °young °man, °fellow, schoolboy, °youth, °juvenile, youngster, hobbledehoy, °stripling, (street) urchin, (street) Arab, gamin, Colloq °guy, (little) shaver, kid, US sprout: *Round up a few of the lads for a game of football.*

ladylike *adj.* °well-bred, well-born, aristocratic, °noble, °refined, °respectable, cultured, °polished, °elegant, mannerly, °gracious, °genteel, °courteous, °polite, courtly, °dignified, °proper, °correct, °decorous: *I cannot believe that Mrs Gibson did not behave in a ladylike way.*

lag *v.* **1** °fall behind, °linger, loiter, °delay, °straggle, °trail, °hang back, dally, °dawdle, inch *or* poke along: *If you lag behind too far, you'll never catch up.* **2** °diminish, °decrease, slacken, abate, °slow (down *or* up), °flag, °wane, °ebb, falter, °fail, °let up, °fall (off *or* away), °ease (up), °lighten: *Contributions to the fund are lagging. Military preparations are lagging.*

laggard *n.* straggler, °idler, dawdler, loiterer, °slouch, sluggard, °loafer, snail, loller, Colloq Brit slowcoach, US slowpoke: *As a young boy he was always the laggard, dragging along behind everyone else.*

lair *n.* **1** den, °burrow, °hole, °nest, °tunnel, °cave, °hollow, covert: *We cautiously approached the lair of the man-eating tiger.* **2** hide-out, °hideaway, °retreat, hiding-place, °refuge, asylum, °sanctuary, Colloq hidey-hole *or* hidey-hole: *Oliver will not emerge from his lair before tea-time.*

laissez-faire *n.* laisser-faire, laissez-faireism, °free °enterprise, non-intervention, non-interference, °freedom, °free °trade, individualism, laissez-aller *or* laisser-aller, deregulation, decontrol, laxness: *The government's policy of laissez-faire has spurred business on.*

lambaste *v.* **1** °beat, °whip, °scourge, °flog, °lash, maul, horsewhip, cane, birch, thrash, bludgeon, trounce, drub, pummel, °batter, °belabour, cudgel: *Terry threatened to lambaste anyone who interfered.* **2** censure, °rebuke, °scold, °reprimand, chide, admonish, °reprove, °upbraid, °berate, °scold, revile, °attack, °castigate, flay, Colloq °dress down, get on (someone's) back, rake *or* haul over the coals, US °call down, Slang °chew *or* °bawl out: *The press lambasted the company for its unfair employment policies.*

lame *adj.* **1** °crippled, °disabled, handicapped, hobbled, limping, incapacitated, impaired, °halting, °halt, spavined, Colloq US gimpy: *The mare was found to be lame after the previous day's hunting.* **2** °feeble, °weak, °flimsy, °thin, unconvincing, unpersuasive, °awkward, °clumsy, °poor, °ineffective, Colloq half-baked: *Refusing to go because you have a headache sounds like a pretty lame excuse to me.*

lament *v.* **1** °mourn, °bemoan, °bewail, wail, °weep (over), °grieve (for *or* over), °keen (over), °sorrow (for *or* over): *A year later, and she is still lamenting the death of her hamster?!*
—*n.* **2** °lamentation, moaning, °mourning; °keen, dirge, elegy, knell, Requiem, monody, threnody, thanatopsis, epicedium, Scots and Irish coronach: *Laments for Kitty's late husband were heard throughout the village.*

lamentable *adj.* °deplorable, °wretched, °miserable, °terrible, distressing, °awful, °regrettable, °pitiful, °despicable, intolerable, °unfortunate: *The hall was left in a lamentable state after the party. His death was presaged by a lamentable series of events.*

lamentation *n.* °mourning, grieving, moaning, weeping, wailing, crying, sobbing, lamenting: *The lamentation went on far into the night.*

lampoon *n.* **1** °burlesque, °caricature, °satire, °parody, pasquinade *or* pasquil, squib, Colloq °take-off, Brit send-up: *The students published a hilarious lampoon of the teaching staff.*
—*v.* **2** °burlesque, °caricature, °satirize, °parody, pasquinade *or* pasquil, °mock, °ridicule, squib, US skewer, Colloq °take off, °put *or* °run down, Brit °send up: *The cows we hold most sacred are often lampooned by irreverent cartoonists.*

lance *n.* **1** spear, pike, javelin, assegai; lancet: *He transfixed the knight with his lance, and claimed victory in the joust.*
—*v.* **2** °pierce, °stab, °puncture, °prick, incise, °open, °slit: *The boil must be lanced at once to draw out the poison.*

land *n.* **1** °earth, (solid) °ground, terra firma: *After weeks in an open boat, Captain Bligh was relieved to have land under his feet again.* **2** °dirt, °earth, °soil, °turf, sod, loam, °mould: *Trumble tilled the land as his ancestors had done for generations.* **3** °property, grounds, real °property *or* realty *or* US and Canadian also real °estate, acreage; °estate: *How much land goes with the house?* **4** °fatherland, motherland, °nation, °country, homeland, °native land: *The land of our fathers flowed with milk and honey.*
—*v.* **5** °arrive, alight, °light, °touch *or* °come *or* °go down, splash down, °settle on *or* upon, come *or* °rest, berth, °dock, °disembark, debark, go ashore, deplane, dismount: *The plane was forced to land on the water. We land at dawn.* **6** catch, °capture, take °captive, Colloq °bag: *He was unable to land the shark unaided.* **7** get, °secure, °obtain, °win, °acquire: *He finally landed a job with his father-in-law. Sadie finally landed a millionaire!*

landing *n.* **1** touchdown, alighting, splashdown, docking: *The fog made landing quite dangerous.* **2** disembarkation, deplaning, °arrival: *After landing, passengers proceed through passport control.* **3** landing-place, °dock, °pier, jetty, wharf, quay: *We walked on to the landing to watch the ship come in.*

landlady *n.* **1** °proprietor *or* proprietress, lady of the house, mistress, °manager *or* Brit manageress, hostess: *My landlady owns three bed and breakfasts.* **2** See landlord, 2, below.

landlord *n.* **1** °host, publican, °proprietor, innkeeper, hotelier, °manager, restaurateur, Boniface: *Landlord! Two pints of your best bitter!* **2** °landlady, landowner, householder, (property) °owner, lessor, Brit freeholder: *My landlord has raised my rent claiming that his expenses have increased.*

landmark *n.* **1** °feature, °guide, guidepost; °identification: *The tower serves as a landmark for those seeking the castle.* **2** turning-point, watershed, milestone, °monument: *His essay remains a landmark in philosophical thought.*
—*attributive* **3** °critical, °crucial, °pivotal, °important, °historic, °significant,

precedent-setting, °momentous, °notable, °noteworthy, °major: *This stands out as a landmark decision in the annals of criminal law.*

landscape *n.* °prospect, °view, °scene, °aspect, vista, countryside: *Here and there the landscape is dotted with spinneys.*

language *n.* **1** °speech, °tongue, °idiom, °parlance, °dialect, idiolect, patois, °jargon, °cant, argot, °vernacular, *Colloq* °lingo: *How many languages do you speak?* **2** communication, °intercourse, interaction: *Karl von Frisch studied the language of the bees.* **3** °jargon, lingua franca, vocabulary, °terminology, °vernacular, *Colloq* °lingo: *In medical language, a head cold is called 'coryza'.* **4** °wording, °words, phrasing, phraseology, °style, °diction: *Guarantees, insurance policies, and other such things should be written in simple language.*

lanky *adj.* °thin, loose-jointed, lank, °lean, °gaunt, gangling, rangy, long-legged: *They recruited three tall, lanky youths for the basketball team.*

lap[1] *v.* **1** Often, **lap up**: lick up, °tongue; °sip, °drink: *In a moment, the cat had lapped all the cream from the saucer.* **2** °wash, °splash, °ripple, plash, purl: *The water rose till it was lapping at the doorstep.* **3 lap up**: **a** °consume, °drink, °eat: *The dog lapped up every last scrap of food.* **b** °accept, °believe, °credit, °fall for, *Colloq* °swallow (whole), °buy: *She lapped up Felix's sob story and invited him in at once.*

lap[2] *n.* **1** °circuit, °orbit, ambit, °circle, °tour, °trip, °revolution: *She runs four laps round the track every day for exercise.* **2** °flap, °fold, lappet, °projection, lapel, °overlap: *This lap hides the zip.*
—*v.* **3** °overlap, °fold, enfold, °envelop, °wrap: *Lap the fabric so as to cover the seam.*

lapse *n.* **1** °slip, °error, °mistake, °fault, °failing, °oversight, °blunder, °shortcoming, °omission, *Formal* lapsus, *Colloq* slip-up, °fluff, goof: *Apart from a brief lapse, the child behaved very well. Owing to a lapse, your payment was not credited.* **2** °gap, °break, °interval, °intermission, °interruption, °pause, lacuna, hiatus, *Prosody* caesura, *Colloq* °hold-up: *Listeners in Scotland experienced a lapse in transmission, for which we apologize.* **3** °decline, lowering, °fall, deterioration, °drop, diminution, descent: *There has been a serious lapse in church attendance.*
—*v.* **4** °decline, °lower, °fall, °drop, °diminish, °sink, °slip, °slump, °subside, °deteriorate: *Despite the doctor's best efforts, he lapsed into a coma.* **5** °run out, °expire, be discontinued, become °void, °terminate, °end, °cease, °stop: *Your option to sell the shares at the offering price lapses on Friday.* **6** °pass, °elapse, °go by, °slip away: *Three months had lapsed since she last saw him.*

large *adj.* **1** °big, °great, °broad, °stout, °heavy, thickset, chunky, °stocky, heavy-set, °brawny, °husky, °sturdy, °hefty, °muscular, strapping, °burly, °solid, °weighty, corpulent, °fat, °obese, °rotund, portly, adipose, °beamy, overweight: *Two large gentlemen came up and offered to help me find the door.* **2** °big, °generous, °bountiful, °charitable, eleemosynary, °philanthropic, open-handed, magnanimous, °munificent, °unselfish, big-hearted, large-hearted, °substantial, °considerable, °ample, beneficent, °liberal; °goodly, °kind, °good; *Colloq* °tidy: *We have to thank Mr Wilson for large donations to our*

Christmas fund. **3** °big, °huge, °ample, °enormous, °gigantic, °immense, °colossal, °monumental, °massive, mammoth, Brobdingnagian, gargantuan, elephantine, °monstrous, staggering, sizeable, °substantial, °wide, °broad, capacious, °extensive, *Colloq* °jumbo, *US* humongous, ginormous: *The house has a large dining room. Supertankers are the largest ships afloat.*
—*adv.* **4** °big, prominently, overwhelmingly, imposingly, °eminently, °pre-eminently: *The problem looms large in the history of biology.*
—*n.* **5 at large: a** °free, unfettered, at °liberty, on the °loose, unconfined, unrestrained: *One of the robbers is still at large.* **b** °generally, °mainly, in °general, °chiefly, as a °whole, in a body, °altogether, in the °main: *The people at large support reductions in taxes.*

largely *adv.* °chiefly, °mainly, as a °rule, by and °large, °generally, in °general, to a °great extent, mostly, in °great part, in °great measure, in the °main, on the °whole, °pretty much, essentially, at °bottom, basically, fundamentally: *The voters are largely in favour of keeping the present government.*

largesse *n.* largess, °gifts, alms, °grants, °bonuses, endowments, °presents, contributions, °donations, hand-outs; °support, subvention, °aid, °subsidy, °charity, °philanthropy, generosity, munificence, °bounty, liberality, open-handedness: *The church depends on the largesse of its members.*

lark *n.* **1** °frolic, °spree, escapade, °caper, °fling, romp, °adventure, °revel, jape, °game, antic, horseplay, shenanigans, °mischief, °prank, practical °joke: *The boys say they took the horse just as a lark.*
—*v.* **2** Often, **lark about**: °frolic, °caper, romp, °revel, °play, °sport, °cavort, gambol, *Colloq* skylark: *We spent a lot of time larking about after our exams.*

lascivious *adj.* **1** °lustful, °randy, °lecherous, licentious, °lewd, °prurient, salacious, libidinous, °erotic, °sensual, lubricious *or* lubricous, ruttish, goatish, hircine, satyr-like, °wanton, Cyprian, debauched, *Slang* horny, °hot: *I wouldn't let that lascivious old man near my daughter.* **2** °pornographic, °obscene, °blue, °lurid, °indecent, smutty, °dirty, Fescennine, °filthy, °vile, ribald, °bawdy, °gross, °coarse, °offensive: *He said that such lascivious novels should be banned and certainly not read in schools.*

lash[1] *n.* **1** °whip, °scourge, cat-o'-nine-tails, cat, quirt, knout, bull-whip, thong; rope's end: *The bosun gave him twenty of the best with his lash.* **2** °stroke, °blow, °strike, °slash, °cut: *Few could stand up after five lashes with his whip.*
—*v.* **3** °flog, °beat, thrash, °switch, °whip, °scourge, horsewhip, °lambaste, flail, smite, thwack, *Colloq* whack: *Any boy was liable to be lashed for the most trivial misdemeanour.* **4 lash out**: °attack, flay, °lambaste, °belabour, °punish; °criticize, °berate, °scold: *She often lashes out at her critics quite virulently.*

lash[2] *v.* °fasten, °tie, °bind, °secure, °rope, °fix, strap, make °fast: *His crew lashed Odysseus to the mast as they sailed past the land of the Sirens.*

lass *n.* °girl, °young °woman, °miss, mademoiselle, schoolgirl, *Old-fashioned* °maiden, °maid, damsel, demoiselle; *Scots* lassie, *Irish* colleen: *He has married a young lass from Arbroath.*

lasso n. **1** lariat, °rope, SW US reata or riata: The cowboy tossed the lasso round the calf's neck. —v. **2** °rope: He lassoed steers to practise for the rodeo.

last[1] adj. **1** hindmost, rearmost, aftermost; °final: I was the last person to board the plane. **2** °latest, newest, most °recent or up to °date: What was the subject of his last novel? During the last week I have seen seven films. **3** °final, concluding, °terminal, °ultimate, terminating: The last train to London leaves at eleven. She was the last speaker of Cornish. **4** °definitive, conclusive, decisive, closing: That is my last word on the subject. —adv. **5** behind, at or in the °end, in or at the °rear, after: My horse always seems to come in last. —n. **6** °end, °termination, °finish: That was the last we ever saw of Charlie. **7 at last**: °finally, °eventually, °ultimately, at °length: At last we shall see the results of our work.

last[2] v. **1** °continue, °endure, °survive, °keep on, °persist, °remain, °stay, °abide, °carry on, °hold out, Colloq go the distance: He wouldn't last a day in my job. **2** °wear, °stand up, °endure, °survive: This shirt has lasted through innumerable washings.

last[3] n. °mould, matrix, °form, °model, °pattern: These shoes were not made on the same last as those.

lasting adj. °permanent, °enduring, °durable, °everlasting, long-term, undying, °eternal: She made a lasting contribution to ophthalmology.

late adj. **1** tardy, delayed, °overdue, behindhand, dilatory, unpunctual; °belated, US °past due: He was even late for his own wedding. Better late than never. Your mortgage payment is late again. **2** °recent, °last, °new, °fresh, °current, up to °date: Have you got a copy of a late edition of today's newspaper? **3** deceased, departed, °dead; °former, °past, ex-, °recent, °previous, °preceding, °old (see also **5**, below): Here is a song by the late, great Bing Crosby. He has a meeting with Lord Pamby, late chairman of United Oxidation. **4 of late**: See **5**, below. —adv. **5** recently, °lately, °previously, °formerly, °once, heretofore, in °recent or °former °time(s), of late, latterly (see also **3**, above): They are dining tonight with Sir Keith, late of Scotland Yard. **6** °till or at an advanced hour or °time: I was up late last night. She married late. **7** tardily, unpunctually, belatedly: We arrived too late for the first act. **8** recently, °lately: As late as a week ago they were still holding the job open for her.

lately adv. See **late**, **5**, above.

latest adj. **1** See **last**[1], **2**, above. **2** °fashionable, °current, °modern, up to the °minute, Colloq in: She drives the latest model. —n. **3** most °recent or up-to-date or °modern development or news or example: What's the latest? Have you seen the latest in scuba gear?

lather n. **1** suds, °froth, °foam: He spread lather on his face and began to shave. **2** °sweat; dither, °fuss, pother, °flutter, Colloq tizzy, °state, °flap: He got into a real lather when he missed the train. —v. **3** soap (up); °foam, °froth: The barber lathered my chin thoroughly. **4** thrash, °beat, °belabour, maul, drub, °flog, whack, pummel, buffet, °whip, flail, °lash: If he dared to swear, his father would lather him.

laud v. °praise, commend, °celebrate, sing or speak or sound the praises of, °honour, acclaim, °extol, °glorify, °promote, °advance, °recommend, °exalt: Bramble's paintings have been lauded by leading art critics the world over.

laudable adj. °praiseworthy, °meritorious, creditable, °admirable, °outstanding, °excellent, °noteworthy, °notable, commendable, °estimable: He has made a laudable effort to keep up in his work.

laudatory adj. laudative, praiseful, eulogistic, panegyric(al), encomiastic(al), °complimentary, °favourable: None of the laudatory comments made in the introduction was true.

laugh v. **1** °titter, °giggle, snigger, °snicker, °chuckle, chortle, guffaw, split one's sides, Colloq break or crack up, roll on the floor, go into hysterics, °roar with °laughter, hoot: Whenever he wore his hat, they couldn't stop laughing. **2** Often, **laugh at**: **a** °deride, °ridicule, °mock (at), °jeer (at), make a °mockery of, poke °fun (at), make °fun or °sport (of), make an ass or a °fool (out) of, °tease, °taunt, pull (someone's) °leg, °satirize, pasquinade or pasquil, °parody, lampoon, jest (at), °joke (about), °scoff (at), °scorn, Colloq Brit take the mickey out of, US roast: They laughed when I sat down—I didn't know the chair was broken. Why did the other children laugh at you? **b** laugh away or off, °spurn, °dismiss, °brush aside, °minimize, shrug off, °reject, °ignore, °disregard, °deny, °belittle, Colloq pooh-pooh: He laughed off his injury and insisted on continuing to work. —n. **3** °titter, °giggle, snigger, °snicker, °chuckle, chortle, guffaw, horse laugh: She would do anything for a laugh.

laughter n. laughing, tittering, giggling, sniggering, snickering, chuckling, chortling, guffawing: Children's laughter filled the air.

launch v. **1** °start (off), °set in °motion, °set or °get °going, °begin, °embark upon or on, °initiate, °inaugurate: The council is about to launch a scheme for dockside development. The attack was launched at dawn. **2** °originate, °establish, °organize, °set up, °found, °open, °start: Robson is talking about launching a new company. **3** °shoot, °fire, °discharge, °hurl, °throw, °sling, °pitch, °fling, catapult, °send, °dispatch or despatch: The enemy launched ground-to-air missiles against our planes. **4** °float, °set afloat: Two frigates will be launched today. —n. **5** inauguration, °start, °initiation, °opening: The launch of the offensive is scheduled for noon tomorrow. **6** °boat, skiff, °tender, motor °boat, runabout, gig, dinghy: The launch will shuttle passengers between the pier and the cruise ship.

launder v. **1** °wash, °clean, °scrub, °cleanse: The chambermaid laundered three shirts for me. **2** legitimize, legitimatize, °legitimate, legalize: The money from heroin was being laundered through several car dealerships.

laurels n.pl. °honour(s), °distinction(s), °fame, °awards, °tributes, °rewards, acclaim, acclamation, °glory, °renown, °celebrity, °popularity, °reputation; °successes, °accomplishments: With no new fields to conquer, he is resting on his laurels.

lavatory n. water-closet, WC, °toilet, bathroom, Colloq Brit the Gents('), the Ladies('), Men's (Room), rest room, °privy, Chiefly military or institutional latrine; Nautical head; Brit (public) convenience, US equipment, outhouse; Colloq (little) boys' or girls' room, powder-room, *Brit* loo, lav, *US* can; *Slang Brit* bog: *Our new house has two upstairs bathrooms and a downstairs lavatory.*

lavish *adj.* **1** °profuse, °abundant, °liberal, copious, °plentiful, °prolific, °opulent: *He wore a silk tunic with lavish gold embroidery.* **2** °generous, °liberal, open-handed, unstinting, °bountiful, unsparing, °unselfish, °effusive, °free: *She showered the most lavish gifts on her children.* **3** °extravagant, °wasteful, exaggerated, °prodigal, °improvident, °excessive, °unreasonable, °immoderate, °profligate, uncurbed, unrestrained, intemperate: *The council was accused of lavish overspending on the civic centre.* —*v.* **4** squander, °waste, °throw away, °dissipate, °spend, °expend, °sink: *We lavished a fortune on the gardens.* **5** °shower, °bestow, °thrust, °heap, °pour: *Granny always lavished gifts on us.*

law *n.* **1** °rule, °regulation, ordinance, statute, °act, enactment, by(e)-law, °measure, edict, °decree, °order, directive, °injunction, °command, commandment, canon, mandate, ukase: *They have a law that forbids smoking on aeroplanes.* **2** corpus juris, (°legal) °code, constitution, °rules and °regulations, °charter, *Law* °equity: *The law must be applied equally to all citizens.* **3** °principle, °proposition, theory, °theorem, °formula, axiom, °deduction, corollary, postulate, conclusion, °inference: *Not every observable phenomenon obeys the laws of physics.*

lawful *adj.* **1** °legal, licit, °legitimate, de jure, constitutional, °just, °rightful, valid, °proper: *I am the lawful heir.* **2** °permissible, allowable, justifiable, authorized, allowed, permitted: *It is not lawful to let your dog foul the footpath.*

lawless *adj.* **1** anarchic(al), anarchist(ic), °chaotic, °unruly, unregulated: *There was a lawless period between the revolution and the establishment of government.* **2** °illegal, °illicit, °unlawful, °criminal, felonious, larcenous, °dishonest, °corrupt, °venal, *Colloq* °crooked: *Holding a demonstration without a permit is a lawless act.* **3** °villainous, nefarious, °wicked, °sinful, flagitious, iniquitous, treacherous: *He was once a member of a lawless motor-cycle gang.*

lawn *n.* sward, greensward, °turf, sod, °green: *I lay back on the lawn and gazed at the sky.*

lawyer *n.* °counsel, °advocate, member of the °bar, °legal practitioner, *Brit* °solicitor, barrister, Queen's *or* King's °counsel, bencher, *US* attorney(-at-law), counselor(-at-law), *Slang US* °mouthpiece: *We have turned the case over to a lawyer.*

lax *adj.* **1** °loose, °slack, °casual, °slipshod, °easygoing, °careless, negligent, °permissive, °weak, °indulgent, °flexible, °relaxed: *Law enforcement has always been lax in that city.* **2** °imprecise, °undefined, °indefinite, non-specific, unspecific, °vague, °shapeless, amorphous, °general, °broad, °inexact, hit-or-miss, °careless, °untidy, *Colloq* °sloppy: *His ideas about tactics are too lax for a military man.*

lay[1] *v.* **1** °place, °put (down), °set (down), °position, °deposit; °spread: *Lay the cloth on the table, then lay the book on top of it.* **2** °set, °arrange: *The table was laid for four.* **3** Often, **lay down**: °establish, °build, °construct: *Before I can argue my case, I must lay a firm foundation of trust.* **4** °stake, °bet, wager, °gamble, °hazard, °risk: *I'll lay ten to one that you won't be able to move that crate.* **5** °destroy, °suppress, exorcize: *Did Edward*

ever *succeed in laying that ghost of a rumour that haunted his career for so long?* **6** °present, °offer, °submit, °set *or* °put forth, °advance, °bring *or* °put forward, °set out: *We have laid our proposal before the board.* **7** charge, °impute, °direct, °lodge, °prefer, °aim, °attribute, ascribe: *There is no justification for laying the blame on Leonard.* **8** copulate (with), couple (with), have (°sexual) °intercourse (with), °sleep (with), °lie (with), bed, go to bed (with), °mate (with), have °sex (with), go all the way (with), service, *Slang* °screw, °shack up (with), *Brit* roger, *Taboo* fuck. **9 lay bare**: expose, °reveal, uncover, °disclose, divulge, bring to °light, °show, °unveil, lift the °veil from: *She laid bare the most intimate details of their relationship.* **10 lay down**: °stipulate, °require, °demand, °insist on, °dictate: *She laid down the conditions on which he could return home.* **11 lay hold of**: °seize, °grab, °snatch, °nab, catch *or* °get °hold of, °get: *I have been trying to lay hold of that book for weeks.* **12 lay in**: See **19 a**, below. **13 lay into**: °attack, °assault, °set about, assail, °lambaste, °belabour: *We laid into the gang and gave them a sound drubbing.* **14 lay it on**: °exaggerate, °overstate, embroider: *Don't believe what Frank tells you—he really lays it on pretty thick sometimes.* **15 lay low**: See **18 c**, below. **16 lay off**: **a** °suspend; °dismiss, °discharge, °fire, °let go, cashier, drum out of the corps, *Colloq* (give the) °sack, (give the) axe, °kick out, (give the) °boot, °boot out, give (someone) his *or* her walking papers: *Fifty workers were laid off because business was slack.* **b** °let up, °quit (it), °stop (it), °cease, desist, °leave off, °leave °alone, *Colloq* °knock (it) off, °cut (it) out, come off (it): *I wish you'd lay off for a while and stop bothering me. You must lay off phoning your mother twice a day.* **17 lay on**: **a** °provide, °cater (for), °supply: *The company laid on quite a Christmas party.* **b** °impose, °charge, assess; °demand, °require: *In addition to enforcing payment of back taxes, they laid on a penalty of 20 per cent.* **18 lay out**: **a** °design, °plan, °outline, sketch, °arrange, °set up: *The art department laid out the advertisements for the new campaign.* **b** °advance, disburse, °spend, °expend, °pay, °give, °contribute, *Colloq* °shell out, ante up, kick in with, fork out: *The salesmen often lay out the money for their expenses and are then reimbursed.* **c** lay low, °floor, °prostrate, °knock down *or* out, °strike *or* °cut down, °flatten, °fell, *Colloq* °knock for six, kayo *or* K.O.: *He laid out the challenger with a blow to the solar plexus.* **19 lay up**: **a** lay in, °amass, °accumulate, °save (up), °hoard, °preserve, °store, °keep, °put away, °put by: *We laid up a supply of canned goods for the winter.* **b** hospitalize, °incapacitate, disable, confine to bed, keep indoors: *She has been laid up with a virus all week.*

lay[2] *adj.* **1** °secular, non-clerical, laic, non-ecclesiastical: *He served as a lay preacher for many years.* **2** °amateur, non-professional, non-specialist: *Members of the lay public did not immediately understand the dangers of the greenhouse effect.*

lay[3] *n.* ballad, °song, °air, °refrain, °strain, °melody; °poem, ode, °lyric, °rhyme, ballade: *Macaulay wrote a book entitled* Lays of Ancient Rome.

lazy *adj.* **1** °indolent, °slothful, dilatory, °idle, °shiftless, °inactive, °listless, fainéant, otiose, °slack, °lax, °lethargic: *He's so lazy and so rich that* *he pays someone just to walk his dog.* **2** °slow, languid, °easy, °easygoing, sluggish, slow-moving, languorous: *The hot lazy summer days were whiled away fishing.*

lead *v.* **1** °conduct, °escort, usher, °guide, °show the °way, °pilot, °steer: *If you lead, I'll follow.* **2** °cause, °influence, °prompt, °bring, °incline, °induce, °persuade, °move, °dispose, °convince: *What led you to suspect the butler?* **3** °head (up), °direct, °govern, °command, °supervise, superintend, °preside (over), take the lead, take *or* assume °command (of), °manage, captain, *Colloq* °skipper: *The orchestra would like you to lead. Who is going to lead the men into battle? Nicole leads a weekly discussion group on alcoholism.* **4** come *or* be *or* go °first, °excel, °surpass, °exceed, °precede, be °ahead (of), °outstrip, °distance, outrun, °outdo: *They lead the world in the production of sugar.* **5** °live, °experience, °spend, °pass; while away: *He is leading a life of ease on the French Riviera.* **6** be conducive to, °create, engender, °cause, °contribute to, °result in, °bring on *or* about, °produce: *Your stubbornness can lead only to frustration.* **7** **lead astray**: lead on, °mislead, misguide, °misdirect, °deceive; °fool, °decoy, °hoodwink, *Colloq* bamboozle: *She might have been led astray by that wolf in sheep's clothing.* **8** **lead off**: °start (off *or* in *or* out *or* up), °begin, °commence, get °going *or* °moving, get under °way, °initiate, °inaugurate, *Colloq* kick off: *The proceedings will lead off with the national anthem. Who is going to lead off the singing?* **9** **lead on**: **a** See 7, above. **b** °lure, °entice, °seduce, °beguile, inveigle, °tempt: *They led me on with offers of a huge salary.* **10** **lead up to**: **a** °prepare *or* °pave *or* °clear (the °way), do the °groundwork *or* spadework, °precede: *The events leading up to the overthrow of the government may never be known.* **b** °approach, °broach, °bring up, °present, °introduce, °work up *or* °round *or* around to, get (up) to: *I should lead up to the subject delicately, if I were you.*
—*n.* **11** °front, vanguard, van, lead *or* °leading °position *or* °place, °advance *or* advanced °position *or* °place: *The horse that he had bet on was in the lead coming down the home straight.* **12** °advantage, °edge, °advance, °supremacy, °margin, °priority, primacy, °pre-eminence: *She has the lead over all her competitors. Our team had a two-point lead at half-time.* **13** °direction, °guidance, °leadership, °precedent, °example, °model, exemplar, °pattern, °standard: *We decided to follow his lead.* **14** °tip, °clue, °hint, °suggestion, °cue, intimation; °prospect, °possibility, °potential; *Colloq* tip-off: *Barry is following up some leads for a new job. The advertisement produced some new sales leads.* **15** leash, °tether, °restraint, °cord, °chain: *The dog fetches his lead himself when he wants to go out.* **16** °protagonist, °hero *or* °heroine, °leading *or* starring °role *or* °part, °leading *or* lead actor *or* actress, °leading lady *or* man, male *or* female lead, °principal; prima donna, diva, prima ballerina, *première danseuse*, °*premier danseur*: *She has the lead in the new production of* Giselle. **17** wire, °cable, *Brit* °flex: *Connect this lead to the power source.*
—*adj.* **18** °leading, °foremost, °first; °main, °chief, °principal, °premier, °paramount: *The lead climber fell when the rope broke. The lead story*

in today's paper is about an American take-over bid for the longest-standing British car-manufacturing company.

leaden *adj.* **1** °heavy, onerous, °ponderous, °dense, °burdensome: *Exhausted, he dragged his leaden feet to the next meeting.* **2** °heavy, °dull, numbing, °oppressive: *I was happy to escape the leaden atmosphere of the theatre.* **3** °grey, °dull, °dingy, °gloomy, glowering, lowering, °dreary, °dismal, °oppressive, °dark, °sullen, °sombre: *The leaden sky seemed to forebode disaster as he fled across the moor.* **4** °inert, °lifeless, °listless, sluggish, °inanimate, °inactive, °lethargic, languid, languorous, °torpid, spiritless, °stagnant, °static, °dormant, soporific, °sleepy: *The refugees trudged along at a leaden pace.*

leader *n.* **1** °chief, °head, commander, ruler, °superior, °director, chairman, chairwoman, chairperson, chieftain, captain, commandant, °principal, *Colloq* °boss, bossman, kingpin, °big cheese, number one, numero uno, *Brit* gaffer, *Chiefly US* Mr Big, *Slang US* the man: *The police can identify the leader of the gang. The leader of the assembly is elected for a year.* **2** bandmaster, °band leader, °director, *US and Canadian* conductor, bandleader, concert-master: *The leader tapped his baton for silence.*

leadership *n.* °direction, °guidance, °management, directorship, °administration, supervision, °command, °regulation, °control, °operation, °influence, °initiative; governorship, superintendence, °running: *The company made huge profits under Katherine's leadership. The leadership of the country at this time was in the hands of the privileged class.*

leading *adj.* **1** °important, °influential, °chief, °prime, °cardinal, °foremost, °paramount, °primary: *A leading politician hinted today that interest rates might go down soon.* **2** °best, °outstanding, °pre-eminent, greatest, °supreme, °peerless, °matchless, unequalled, unrivalled, unsurpassed: *He was the leading writer of his time.*

leaflet *n.* folder, °circular, °brochure, handbill, bill, booklet, °advertisement, *US and Canadian* throw-away, flier *or* flyer, *Colloq Brit* advert: *The candidate gave out leaflets urging us to vote for him.*

leafy *adj.* °green, verdant, bosky, °shady, shaded, arborescent: *We lay beneath the leafy bowers and dreamed of summers past.*

league *n.* **1** confederation, °association, °alliance, °combination, coalition, °federation, confederacy, guild, °society, °fraternity, °union, °band, °fellowship, °club: *The teams in the south favour forming a football league of their own.* **2** **in league (with)**: allied (with), °united (with), associated (with), leagued (with), federated (with), collaborating (with), conspiring (with), in collusion (with), *Colloq* in cahoots (with): *The suspects are said to be in league with saboteurs.*
—*v.* **3** °ally, °unite, °associate, °band, °combine, °collaborate, °join (forces), conspire, collude: *Did most people league with the rebels or the official government?*

leak *n.* **1** leakage, leaking, °discharge, °trickle, °escape, seepage, seeping, oozing, exudation: *We have to stop leaks of radioactive waste from power plants.* **2** °hole, fissure, °crack, °chink, °crevice, °aperture, °opening, °puncture, °cut, °break, °split, °gash, °rent, °tear, °gap, °flaw: *There was*

a leak in the balloon and it began to descend.
3 disclosure, °revelation: *The press knew about his defection because of a security leak.*
—*v.* **4** °escape, °discharge, °spill, °trickle, °drip, seep, °ooze, exude, extravasate: *Oil was leaking out through a hole in the container.* **5** °disclose, divulge, let °slip, °release, °give away (the game), °make known *or* °public, let (something *or* it) be known, *Colloq* °spill the beans (about); let the cat out of the bag: *Someone as yet unidentified leaked the scandal to a reporter.* **6 leak out:** °transpire, become known, °come out, be revealed: *Their secret relationship has leaked out.*

lean[1] *adj.* **1** °thin, °slim, °slender, rangy, °spare, °wiry, °lanky, lank, °skinny, angular, bony, °raw-boned, °gaunt, gangling, gangly, °meagre, skeletal, scraggy, °scrawny, °haggard, °emaciated, pinched, wasted, shrunken, macilent: *He has the lean leggy build typical of a runner.* **2** unfruitful, unproductive, °barren, °infertile, °poor, °meagre, °scanty, °bare, arid, °sparse, °impoverished: *The Kanes tried for years to eke a living from the lean soil.* **3** °impoverished, °destitute, °needy, poverty-stricken, °penurious, °indigent, necessitous, °hard, °bad, °difficult: *The Depression was a lean period for most people.*

lean[2] *v.* **1** °rest (against *or* on *or* upon), be held up *or* supported by: *She leant her head on his shoulder.* **2** °incline, °slant, °tilt, °bend, °tip: *Isn't that pole leaning over too much?* **3** Often, **lean towards:** °favour, gravitate towards, °tend towards, be °disposed towards, °prefer, show a °preference for, °incline towards, be *or* lean on the °side of, be °biased towards, be (°prejudiced) in °favour of: *She leans towards conservatism when it comes to morality.* **4 lean on: a** °rely on, °depend on, °count on, °believe *or* °trust in, °pin one's hopes *or* °faith on *or* upon: *You can lean on me if you need help.* **b** °pressure, bring °pressure to bear on, °intimidate, °threaten, cow, terrorize, °terrify, °scare, °frighten, °warn, °menace, °endanger, imperil, *Brit* pressurize: *Sometimes the gang would lean on a shopkeeper who refused to pay for 'protection'.*

leaning *n.* °bent, °inclination, °bias, °prejudice, °favouritism, °partiality, predilection, °liking, °taste, °preference, °penchant, °sympathy, °tendency, tendentiousness: *The judges' leanings in favour of short-haired dogs are well known.*

leap *n.* **1** °spring, °bound, °jump, vault (into); °hurdle, °clear, °hop over, °skip over, °negotiate: *He leapt into the saddle. Superman leaps tall buildings at a single bound.* **2** °jump, °cavort, gambol, °dance, °frisk, °caper, °frolic, romp, °prance, curvet: *He leapt for joy at the news that he had won first prize.* **3** °jump, °rush, °hasten, °form hastily, accept (prematurely *or* without question): *The speaker kept leaping from one subject to another. Don't leap to conclusions about her strange behaviour.* **4 leap at:** °jump at, °accept, be °eager for, move °quickly, °take: *I leapt at the chance to apply for a scholarship.*
—*n.* **5** °spring, °bound, °jump, vault, °hurdle, °hop, °skip: *With one leap I was on the other side.* **6** °jump, °increase, (up)surge, °rise, upswing, °growth, escalation: *The figures show a leap in inflation for the month.* **7 by leaps and bounds:** °rapidly, °quickly, °swiftly, speedily: *The plans for the new theatre are progressing by leaps and bounds.*

learn *v.* **1** Often, **learn of:** °find out, °discover, °hear (of), °chance *or* °hit upon, °understand,

°gather, have revealed to one; °determine, ascertain, uncover: *I learned today that you are leaving. I learned of your plans yesterday.* **2** be taught, be instructed in, °master, become °proficient (in), °acquire °knowledge (of): *I learned German at school.* **3** °understand, see the °light, °get the picture, *Colloq* catch on, °get the idea, °get it, *Brit* °twig: *No matter how often they are told, some people never learn.* **4** °memorize, commit to memory, learn by heart: *Bolton was told to learn his part by the next day.*

learned *adj.* (°well-)°informed, erudite, °knowledgeable, *au fait*, cultured, °intellectual, °highbrow, (well-)°educated, °scholarly, °academic, scholastic, °lettered, °experienced, skilled, °practised, °accomplished, °expert, literate, well-read, (well-)°versed, (well-)°trained, (well-)°grounded: *The consultants to the encyclopedia are all learned people.*

learner *n.* °student, °pupil, °scholar, trainee, °apprentice, °novice, tiro *or* tyro, abecedarian, beginner, °initiate, neophyte: *Learners of English as a second language will benefit from this book.*

learning *n.* °knowledge, erudition, °culture, °scholarship, °lore, °information, °wisdom: *You have the advantage of being able to draw on centuries of learning.*

lease *n.* **1** rental °agreement *or* °contract, sublease, sublet: *A new ten-year lease will be signed tomorrow.*
—*v.* **2** °rent (out), °let (out), sublet (out), sublease (out), °charter (out), °hire (out): *They leased their home to us for the summer. We arranged to lease their boat for the weekend.*

leave[1] *v.* **1** °go (away *or* off), °depart, °set off, be off, °get away *or* off, °retire, °retreat, °withdraw, decamp, (make an) °exit, °run, be gone, bid (someone *or* something) °goodbye, say °goodbye *or* adieu (to), take (one's) leave (of), °quit, °desert, °pull out, °check out, °fly, *Colloq* °push *or* shove off, °take off, skedaddle, °flit, °disappear, do a disappearing act, pull up stakes, up-anchor, *Slang* °beat it, scram, vamoose, °split, *Brit* beetle off, do a bunk, do a moonlight flit, °hop it, *Taboo slang Brit* °bugger off: *Please leave at once. May I leave the room? She left him alone.* **2** °go *or* °run off, °deviate from: *The car left the road and hit a tree.* **3** °forget, °mislay, °lose: *I left my car keys somewhere in the house.* **4** °abandon, °desert, take leave of, °wash one's hands of, °turn one's back on; °quit, °resign from, °give up, °renounce, °drop (out of): *She left him because he mistreated her. I left school at sixteen.* **5** °make, °render, °cause to be *or* become *or* remain: *The beauty of the place left me speechless.* **6** °bequeath, °will, °hand down, °devise, demise, °transfer: *Her aunt left some valuable paintings to my wife.* **7** °entrust, °commit, °assign, °cede, relinquish, °give over *or* up, consign, °resign: *They are leaving all the responsibility to me.* **8** °cause *or* °allow to °remain, have as a °remainder, °yield, °give: *Seven from eleven leaves four.* **9 leave off:** °stop, °cease, desist, forbear, °give up, °refrain from, °discontinue, abstain (from), °renounce: *He won't leave off gossiping about her.* **10 leave out:** °omit, °disregard, °ignore, °neglect; °count out, °reject, °exclude, °eliminate, °bar, °except: *You left out the best part. Don't leave me out of the fun!*

leave[2] *n.* **1** °permission, authorization, °consent, °freedom, °liberty, °licence,

°sanction, dispensation: *Who gave you leave to borrow my car?* **2** furlough, leave of °absence, °time off, sabbatical, °recess, °holiday, vacation: *I am overworked and badly in need of some leave.* **3** departure: *He took his leave of us at last.*

lecherous *adj.* °lewd, °lascivious, salacious, libidinous, °sensual, lubricious *or* lubricous, °lustful, concupiscent, licentious, °prurient, dirty-minded, filthy-minded, °carnal, goatish, hircine, °randy, °libertine, °wanton, °profligate, depraved, °degenerate, °decadent, °dissolute, *Slang* horny: *The lecherous villain dared to proposition my wife.*

lecture *n.* **1** °speech, °address, °talk, discourse, disquisition, treatise, dissertation, °paper, °lesson, °instruction, °sermon, declamation, °harangue, diatribe, philippic, screed: *The preacher delivered a lecture on the evils of drink.* **2** °reproof, °reprimand, °rebuke, °criticism, censure, reproach, scolding, upbraiding, chiding, berating, °tongue-lashing, remonstration, *Colloq* dressing-down, telling-off, *Slang Brit* wigging, *US and Canadian* chewing-out: *I had to listen to another lecture about staying out late.* —*v.* **3** °make *or* °deliver *or* °give a °speech *or* °address *or* °talk, discourse; sermonize, °hold forth, moralize, pontificate, orate, °preach, declaim, expound, °go on about, °harangue: *She lectures on Chinese art of the 18th century. He insists on lecturing to everyone he meets.* **4** °reprove, °reprimand, °rebuke, reproach, °scold, °upbraid, °berate, chide, tongue-lash, remonstrate with, °rail at, fulminate against; admonish, °warn; *Colloq* °dress down, °tell off, °send (someone) away *or* off with a flea in his *or* her ear, *Slang Brit* wig, *US and Canadian* °chew out: *She is always lecturing me about keeping my room tidy.*

ledge *n.* shelf, °projection, °step, mantel *or* °mantle, mantelpiece *or* mantelpiece, °overhang, sill: *We stood on a small ledge of rock unable to move.*

leer *v.* **1** °ogle, °eye: *He leers at every pretty girl.* —*n.* **2** °ogle, the °eye, *Colloq* once-over, *Slang* glad °eye: *She was repelled when he gave her a leer.*

leery *adj.* °suspicious, °sceptical, dubious, °doubtful, doubting, °distrustful, °wary, °cautious, chary, °careful: *I was very leery of his story.*

leeway *n.* °space, elbow-room, °room, °play, °scope, °slack, latitude, °wide berth; °freedom: *We allowed him some leeway to make changes in the manuscript.*

left *adj.* **1** left-hand, sinistral, *Nautical* °port, *Formerly* larboard, *Heraldry* °sinister: *In most countries, the driver sits on the left side.* **2** leftist, left-wing, °progressive, °liberal, socialist(ic), °pink; °radical, communist(ic), red: *The party's platform has become a bit too left for my taste.* —*n.* **3** left side *or* hand *or* fist, *Nautical* °port, °port side, *Formerly* larboard: *The fort is on the left as you enter the bay. The champion has a powerful left.*

left-handed *adj.* **1** °clumsy, °awkward, gauche, fumbling, maladroit, cack-handed: *He has a left-handed way of doing things.* **2** insulting, disparaging, derisive, uncomplimentary, °paradoxical, °ambiguous, °questionable, dubious, °doubtful: *Calling her piano-playing 'not bad' was a left-handed compliment.*

leftover *n.* **1** Usually, **leftovers**: °remainder(s), °remnant(s), °rest, °residue, residuum, °balance, °surplus, °excess, °superfluity, overage; °scrap(s), leavings, crumbs, °odds and ends, debris, °refuse, °waste, °rubbish, rubble, detritus, *Archaic* orts: *I'm just having leftovers for dinner tonight.* —*adj.* **2** °remaining, °residual, °extra, °excess, °unused, uneaten: *Save some of the leftover ice-cream for later.*

leg *n.* **1** limb, °member, *Colloq* pin, peg, stump, *Slang* gam: *I have a touch of arthritis in my left leg.* **2** °support, °brace, °prop, °upright, °standard, column, °pillar: *One of the legs of this table is about to collapse.* **3** °part, °portion, °segment, °stretch, °stage, °section, °length, °lap: *The first leg of my journey passed without incident.* **4 a leg up**: °boost, °assistance, °push, °help, °helping °hand, °advance, °support, *US and Canadian* °assist: *Let me give you a leg up over the wall. Gordon might give you a leg up in getting a job.* **5 leg it**: °run, °hurry, °hasten, °scurry, *Colloq* scoot, skedaddle: *He legged it down the street to catch the bus.* **6 not a leg to stand on**: °defenceless, unsupported, insupportable *or* unsupportable, indefensible, unjustifiable, °untenable, °invalid: *She insists she's right, but she hasn't got a leg to stand on.* **7 on one's** *or* **its last legs**: °decrepit, °failing, °exhausted, °dying, °worn out, °run-down, falling °apart *or* to °pieces, broken-down, the worse for °wear; °dilapidated, °rickety, °shabby, °ramshackle, crumbling, °tumbledown: *George looked as if he was on his last legs. My car is on its last legs.* **8 pull someone's leg**: °tease, °mock, °jeer at, °taunt, °gibe, make °fun of, °chaff, °guy, °fool, °deceive, *Chiefly Brit* °twit, *Colloq* rib, kid, °rag: *We were just pulling his leg, but he took it seriously.* **9 shake a leg**: **a** °hurry (up), °hasten, °rush, *Colloq* get °going *or* °moving *or* cracking, look alive *or* lively: *You'll have to shake a leg to catch that train.* **b** °dance, °trip the light fantastic (toe), *Slang* hoof it, *US* cut a rug: *What do you say we go out and shake a leg tonight?* **10 stretch one's legs**: (take *or* go for a) °walk, (take some) °exercise: *After sitting for so long, I have to stretch my legs.*

legal *adj.* **1** °lawful, licit, statutory, °acceptable, °permissible, permitted, admissible, authorized: *The police officer was found to have exceeded his legal authority.* **2** °legitimate, °proper, °right, °rightful, °sound, constitutional, authorized, *Slang* legit: *I question whether his business is legal. Who is the legal heir?* **3** °judicial, juridical, judiciary, forensic: *The case is without legal precedent.*

legalistic *adj.* °narrow(-minded), disputatious, contentious, litigious, °literal, °strict, °niggling, °hairsplitting, cavilling, quibbling, Jesuitical, pettifogging, °nice, °fine, °subtle, *Colloq* nit-picking: *Her argument is legalistic and ignores the spirit of the law.*

legend *n.* **1** epic, °saga, °myth, °story, (°folk) °tale, °romance, °narrative, fable, °tradition, fiction, *Scandinavian* Edda: *There are scores of legends woven into the cultural fabric of our lives.* **2** °celebrity, °phenomenon, °tradition, °wonder, luminary, °personage, °somebody: *Someone said that Rudolph had become a legend in his own mind.* **3** °key, °table of symbols, °code, °explanatory °note: *Refer to the legend for explanations of symbols used in the map.* **4** °motto, °slogan, inscription, caption, °title: *The legend reads, 'Dieu et mon droit'.*

legendary adj. **1** fabled, storied, °traditional; °heroic, epic, mythic: Legendary tales have been identified in every culture. **2** °fanciful, °imaginary, °fabulous, °mythical, °romantic, °fictional: Was King Arthur a real person or a legendary figure? **3** °famous, °celebrated, °noted, famed, °well-known, °renowned, °illustrious, °immortal, °prominent, °eminent, °great, acclaimed, °noteworthy: Irena became known for her legendary dinner parties.

legible adj. °readable, decipherable, °clear, understandable, °plain, °distinct: The handwriting is legible, but I don't know what language it's in.

legitimate adj. **1** valid, °proper, °right, °rightful, authorized, °legal, °genuine, °real, °true, °authentic: Which one of them was the legitimate Anastasia? **2** °lawful, licit, °legal, by °law, de jure, statutory: Bonnie Prince Charlie claimed to be the legitimate ruler of Scotland. **3** commonsensical, °sensible, °reasonable, °proper, °correct, °acceptable, valid, °logical, justifiable, °just, °fair: The question is perfectly legitimate and deserves a proper answer.
—v. **4** legitimize, legitimatize, legalize, °authorize, °sanction, °warrant, validate, °certify: By signing before two witnesses, she legitimated her will.

leisure n. **1** °spare or °free °time, °time (off), °liberty, °freedom, °opportunity: How many people these days have the leisure to do what they like? **2** °holiday, vacation, °respite, °relief, °rest, °recreation, °relaxation, °ease, breathing-space, °quiet, tranquillity, °repose, US military °rest and °recreation, R and R: Everyone needs a few days of leisure now and then. **3 at leisure:** **a** unoccupied, °inactive, retired, resting, °free, on °holiday or chiefly US and Canadian vacation; at °liberty, °available, °unemployed: I have been at leisure for a year now. **b** Often, **at one's leisure:** at one's convenience, when °convenient, unhurriedly, in one's own °time: I shall mow the lawn at my leisure.
—adj. **4** recreational: The 'leisure industry' is booming with theme parks opening throughout the country. **5** °free, unoccupied, non-working, unencumbered, °idle, °holiday, vacation: How do you usually spend your leisure time?

leisured adj. °wealthy, °rich, affluent, °prosperous, moneyed or monied, well-to-do: Yachts of that size are strictly for the leisured classes.

lend v. **1** make a °loan of, °loan, °advance: The bank agreed to lend me the money for a boat. **2** °impart, °furnish, °bestow, °give, °confer, °contribute, °add: The silk scarf lends cachet to the whole outfit. **3 lend itself to:** °suit, °fit, be °fitted or °appropriate or °suitable (to or for), be °applicable or °adaptable (to or for): The book lends itself well to film adaptation.

length n. **1** °extent, °measure, °span, °reach, °size, °magnitude, dimension, °measurement: What is the length of a piece of string? The pool is 25 metres in length and 15 metres in width. **2** duration, °stretch, °term, °period, °space: What length of time did he spend in prison? **3 at full length:** fully, °completely, to the fullest °extent: They were stretched out at full length on the floor. **4 at length: a** °finally, at °(long) °last, °eventually, after a (°long) °time or while, °ultimately; in the °long °run: At length, the doctor

emerged from his office. **b** for a °long °time, interminably, for ages: He read to her at length, till she dozed off. **c** in °depth, °thoroughly, °completely, exhaustively, extensively, to the fullest or greatest °extent, in °detail: I haven't the time to go into the story at length just now.

lengthen v. make longer, °extend, elongate; °stretch, °drag out, °draw out, °prolong, protract, °expand, °continue: I need to lengthen the skirt an inch. The ten-minute interview lengthened into an hour. They lengthened the playing field.

lengthy adj. °long, over-long, long-drawn(-out), °protracted; °endless, interminable, prolonged, long-winded, °wordy, prolix, verbose, garrulous, °talkative, loquacious, °boring, °dull, °tedious: He underwent a lengthy operation for removal of the clot. She launched into a lengthy description of the life cycle of a frog.

lenient adj. °gentle, °kind, °kindly, °easy, °sparing, °merciful, °tender, humane, tender-hearted, kind-hearted, °indulgent, °permissive, °forgiving, °easygoing, °tolerant, °patient, compassionate, forbearing, °understanding, magnanimous, °generous, °charitable: Do you think they were lenient in their treatment of prisoners caught while escaping?

lesson n. **1** °exercise, °drill, reading, °lecture, °recitation; °assignment, homework, °task: The pupils are having an English lesson at the moment. You must finish your lessons before you can go out and play. **2** °class, °session; °instruction, teaching, tutoring, °schooling; °practice: I take piano lessons on Tuesday afternoons. **3** °example, exemplar, °model, °guide, °maxim, °paragon, °message, °deterrent, discouragement; °warning, admonition; °moral, °precept: Norman's punishment should be a lesson to you. **4** °punishment, chastisement, chastening, castigation, scolding, chiding, °rebuke, °reprimand, °reproof: If she does that again, I'll give her a lesson she won't forget in a hurry!

let¹ v. **1** °allow (to), °permit (to), °sanction (to), give °permission or °leave (to), °authorize (to), °license (to), °suffer (to): Don't let him go alone. Let George do it. **2** °cause (to), °arrange for, °enable (to): Let me know if you have any difficulty. Let me help you. Let the police know of any crime. **3** Sometimes, **let out:** °rent (out), °hire (out), °lease (out), °charter (out); °contract (out), subcontract (out), °farm (out), °job (out): Mrs Finney lets rooms by the week. Much of the work is let out to people who work at home. **4 let down:** °disappoint, °fail, °frustrate, disenchant, dissatisfy, °disillusion: He promised to be here at nine, but he let me down. **5 let in:** °admit, °allow in; °include, °take in, °receive, °welcome, °induct, °install or instal: I'll just open a window and let in some fresh air. I wouldn't want to be a member of a club that would let in someone like me. **6 let off: a** °pardon, °forgive, °excuse, °release, °discharge, let go: They let him off with only a severe reprimand. **b** exonerate, absolve, °clear, acquit, °vindicate, Slang let off the °hook: When the real culprit confessed, she was let off. **c** detonate, °explode, °discharge, °fire, °set off: Don't let off those fireworks so near the haystack. **d** °emit, °give out or off, °release, °throw off or out, let °loose, exude: Some plastics let off an awful smell when they burn. **7 let on: a** °confess, °admit, °disclose, divulge, °reveal, expose, let it be known, let out, °say, °tell, °give away, let °slip, °betray; °leak:

I'll never let on that you are to blame. **b** feign, °affect, °pretend, °fake, (°put on an) °act, simulate, dissemble, °dissimulate: He let on that he had a bad leg and couldn't play in the match, when in fact he just wanted to go away for the weekend. **8 let out: a** See 7 a, above. **b** (let) °loose, °liberate, (°set) °free, °release, let go, °discharge: He served three years before being let out. Let the cat out, will you. **c** °emit, give °vent to, °produce: She let out a scream that could have woken the dead. **d** °end, °stop, °break up, °finish, °close, °terminate: When does school let out for the Christmas holidays? **9 let up:** °decrease, abate, °ease (up), slacken, °diminish, lessen, °mitigate, °subside, °moderate: Perhaps we can still go if the rain lets up soon. **10 let up on:** °ease up on, °slack off on: He didn't let up on haranguing us for an hour.

let² n. °hindrance, °impediment, °obstruction, °obstacle: People can now cross the border without let or hindrance.

let-down n. °disappointment, disillusionment, disenchantment: She had practised so hard that losing was all the more of a let-down.

lethal adj. °deadly, °fatal, °mortal: The lethal blow was delivered by a blunt instrument.

lethargic adj. **1** lethargical, sluggish, °slow, °dull, °heavy, °lazy, °indolent, °phlegmatic, °slothful, °idle, languid, languorous, °listless, fainéant, °inactive, °torpid, stuporous, comatose; °indifferent, apathetic: They were so lethargic that they did absolutely nothing about it. **2** °weary, °tired, fagged out, °fatigued, enervated, °weak, °exhausted, °drowsy, °sleepy, somnolent: I have a bad cold and feel very lethargic.

lethargy n. **1** °sluggishness, °sloth, dullness, heaviness, laziness, °indolence, phlegm, °idleness, languidness, languor, listlessness, dolce far niente, °inactivity, °inertia, °torpor, °stupor; °indifference, apathy: After taking the medicine, a feeling of lethargy overtook me. **2** weariness, tiredness, °fatigue, °weakness, °exhaustion, drowsiness, sleepiness, somnolence: The strident persistence of my alarm clock dragged me out of my lethargy.

letter n. **1** °character, °symbol, °sign: Epsilon is a letter in the Greek alphabet. **2** °missive, epistle, communication, °note, °line, °message, °dispatch or despatch; correspondence: Write me a letter when you get there. **3 letters:** °literature, the humanities, belles-lettres, the classics; erudition, °culture, the world of letters, °learning, °scholarship: He is a widely known man of letters. **4 to the letter:** °precisely, °literally, °exactly, accurately, strictly, sic, °thus, letter for letter, literatim, °word for word, °verbatim: The document has been copied to the letter.
—v. **5** inscribe, °write, °spell (out): She carefully lettered the caption under the picture.

lettered adj. literate, °literary, (well-)°educated, erudite, °scholarly, °learned, °well-informed, °enlightened, °knowledgeable, (well-)°versed, well-read, cultured, °cultivated: He was greatly influenced by the lettered men of his time.

let-up n. °cease, °stop, stopping, ceasing, cessation, surcease, °break, °interruption, °pause, °intermission, °suspension, °time out or off;

moderation, lessening, abatement, diminution, °relief, hesitation, °respite, °relaxation: I was nagged without let-up about getting the work done by the end of the month.

level adj. **1** °even, °smooth, °plane, °uniform, °plain, °flat, °flush, °straight, °true: The plaster is not level enough to apply the wallpaper. **2** °horizontal, °prone, °supine: Make sure the playing field is level. Try to keep the body level when doing this exercise. **3** °uniform, °constant, °steady, °consistent, °invariable, unvarying, unalterable, unchanging, unfluctuating; °very: I did my level best to warn him, but he wouldn't listen. **4** °parallel, °even, °equal, °equivalent, °consistent: The top floor of my house is level with the roof of the one across the street. The problem arises because wages are not level with inflation. **5** up (on), °informed (about or on), up to °date (on or with), au fait (with), au courant (with): He does his best to keep level with what is going on in the world. **6** °even, tied, °equal, neck and neck: The scores are level. So at half-time, it's level pegging between Arsenal and Liverpool. **7** See level-headed, below.
—v. **8** level off, °even, °smooth (out), °flatten (out): The concrete is levelled by dragging a straight-edge over it. **9** °destroy, °demolish, °raze, lay °waste, °devastate, °knock down, °tear down, °pull down, °wreck, bulldoze: The building was levelled in a matter of minutes. **10** °aim, °point, draw a bead on, °direct, °train, °focus: He levelled his gun at her and she screamed. **11 level with:** be or play °fair with, be °honest or °straight with, be °open or °frank or straightforward with, Colloq be upfront with: I am going to level with you—I find you very difficult to work with.
—n. **12** °plane, °horizontal, °elevation, °height; altitude: The windows are at the same level. **13** °floor, °storey: On which level is Mr Stone's office? **14** °plane, °position, °status, °standing, °rank, °stage: She functions at a higher level, both administratively and intellectually. **15 on the level:** °straight, straightforward, °honest, °direct, °sincere, °square, °open, °above-board, Colloq upfront, on the up and up, US straight-shooting: You haven't been on the level with me about your plans for the company.

level-headed adj. (well-)balanced, °sensible, °sane, °reasonable, commonsensical, °level, unruffled, undisturbed, unperturbed, imperturbable, even-tempered, composed, °calm, °cool, °collected, °tranquil, °serene, unflappable, °poised, °relaxed, °selfpossessed: Even when she was a teenager, Fran was quite level-headed.

levity n. light-heartedness, lightness, frivolity, frivolousness, °flippancy, trivialization, °triviality, facetiousness: Politics is a weighty business and should not be treated with levity.

lewd adj. °lascivious, salacious, °lecherous, °lustful, licentious, °carnal, goatish, hircine, satyric(al), ruttish, concupiscent, libidinous, lubricious or lubricous, °indecent, °offensive, °wild, debauched, °obscene, smutty, °crude, °dirty, °foul, °filthy, °rude, °pornographic, °prurient, °gross, °dissolute, Fescennine, °bawdy, ribald, °scurrilous, °raw, °blue, °erotic, °suggestive, °unchaste, unvirtuous, Colloq °randy, Slang °hot, horny: He is said to have chronicled the lewd goings-on at the Hellfire Club.

liability n. **1** answerability, °responsibility, °burden, onus, °accountability: Who bears the liability for the company's losses? **2** °obligation, °debt, indebtedness, arrear(s), debit: *Outstanding shares are treated as a liability of the corporation.* **3** °disadvantage, °drawback, °hindrance, °impediment, °encumbrance, °snag, °hitch, °barrier, °obstacle, °obstruction, °burden, onus: *Her biggest liability is her inability to read.* **4** °exposure, susceptibility, vulnerability: *The insurer's liability is spread amongst many underwriters.*

liable *adj.* **1** °likely, apt, °prone, °inclined, °disposed: *She is liable to want payment for her contribution.* **2** answerable, °responsible, °accountable, obligated, blameable, blameworthy, *Law* actionable: *An owner is liable for damage done by his dog.* **3** exposed, °susceptible, °vulnerable, °open, °subject: *Certain kinds of plants are more liable to disease.*

liaison *n.* **1** °connection, communication, °contact, linkage, affiliation, °relationship, relations: *Liaison between the ministries is improving.* **2** °contact, °intermediary, °link, °tie, °medium, °go-between, °agent: *She acts as liaison between the heads of research and manufacturing.* **3** (°love) °affair, amour, °relationship, *affaire d'amour, affaire de cœur,* °intrigue, °romance, entanglement, flirtation: *David's wife soon found out about his liaison with the girl in the typing pool.*

liar *n.* fabricator, prevaricator, perjurer, falsifier, teller of tales, °false witness, Ananias, Baron von Münchhausen, *Colloq* fibber: *He's a liar if he says he saw me that night—I was ill in bed.*

libel *n.* **1** defamation, vilification, denigration, denunciation, deprecation, depreciation, belittlement, disparagement, derogation, °disgrace, °ill repute, °dishonour, obloquy, °shame, °humiliation, mortification: *His entire conversation is a perpetual libel on his acquaintances.* **2** °slander, calumny, °lie, °falsehood, prevarication, untruth, misrepresentation, °aspersion, °innuendo, insinuation, °slur, °smear, °blot, °stain, smirch, °stigma: *For years he suffered the libels circulated by his ex-mistress.*
—*v.* **3** defame, °vilify, denigrate, °denounce, deprecate, °depreciate, °belittle, °disparage, derogate, °disgrace, °dishonour, °shame, °humiliate, °mortify: *He claims to have been libelled by an article in the newspaper.* **4** °slander, calumniate, °lie about, °misrepresent, asperse, °insinuate, °slur, °smear, malign, °stain, °blacken, °discredit, besmirch, °stigmatize, traduce, °vilify, *Rare* vilipend, *Colloq chiefly US* bad-mouth: *There is often a fine line between libelling a person and exercising freedom of speech.*

liberal *adj.* **1** °generous, °bountiful, °free, open-hearted, °open, open-handed, bounteous, °charitable, °philanthropic, munificent, magnanimous, °big, big-hearted, unstinting, °unselfish, unsparing, °lavish, °abundant, °ample, °large, °handsome, °plentiful, copious: *Lady Browning is a liberal benefactor of our cause. Thank you for your liberal contributions.* **2** °progressive, libertarian, reformist, humanistic, °left (of centre), latitudinarian, °non-partisan, unaligned or °non-aligned, individualistic, *South African* verligte: *The liberal voters found little to attract them in the latest election.* **3** °free, not literal, °flexible, °lenient, °loose, °broad, °open, °disinterested,

°impartial, °dispassionate, °fair, broad-minded, open-minded, °unprejudiced, unbigoted, unjaundiced, unopinionated, °tolerant: *That judge is known for his liberal interpretation of the law.*
—*n.* **4** °progressive, libertarian, reformer, progressivist, latitudinarian, °independent, freethinker, leftist, left-winger, *South African* verligte: *They think of themselves as liberals, not as conservatives.*

liberalize *v.* **1** broaden, °widen, °extend, °expand, °stretch, °enlarge: *The purpose of the law is to liberalize the functions of solicitors.* **2** °loosen, °ease, slacken, °relax, °modify, °change, °moderate, °soften: *The police really ought to liberalize the parking regulations in this area.*

liberate *v.* **1** (set) °free, °release, set at °liberty, disenthral, °emancipate, manumit, °deliver, enfranchise, (°let) °loose, °let go, °let out, °let off: *When the enemy retreated, the army liberated the prisoners of war. After her divorce, she felt like a liberated woman.* **2** °steal, °pilfer, purloin, °take, °appropriate: *She was caught liberating some books from the library.*

liberation *n.* freeing, liberating, deliverance, emancipation, enfranchisement, enfranchising, °delivery, °rescue, rescuing, °release, releasing, loosing, unfettering, unshackling, unchaining: *The liberation of the prisoners occurred on May Day, 1945.*

libertine *n.* **1** lecher, °reprobate, °profligate, °rake, rakehell, °roué, debaucher, womanizer, °seducer, fornicator, adulterer, debauchee, whoremonger, °philanderer, Don Juan, Lothario, Casanova, *Colloq* wolf, lady-killer, (old) goat, dirty old man: *He fancied himself a libertine, but women shunned him like the plague.*
—*adj.* **2** licentious, °lecherous, °reprobate, °profligate, °rakish, rakehell, philandering, °dissolute, °immoral, °degenerate, depraved, debauched, °decadent, °dirty, °filthy, amoral, °wanton, °lewd, °lascivious, °prurient, lubricious or lubricous, salacious, Paphian, libidinous, ruttish, goatish, hircine, satyric(al), °carnal, bestial, *Colloq* randy, *Slang* horny: *A paragon of prudery to his family, Viscount Guarnier secretly led a life of wild, libertine abandon.*

liberty *n.* **1** °freedom, °independence, self-determination, autonomy, self-rule, °self-government, self-direction, °sovereignty: *People have always been willing to die for their liberty.* **2** °right, °freedom, franchise, *carte blanche,* °privilege, °prerogative, °licence, °leave, °permission, authorization: *I was given the liberty to go where I pleased.* **3** °freedom, °licence, °initiative, °exemption, °exception, °privilege: *On a strict diet, she allowed herself no liberties whatever.* **4 at liberty**: °free, °uninhibited, unfettered, unconstrained, unrestricted, unrestrained, liberated: *I was at liberty to do as I pleased.* **5 take a liberty** or **the liberty** or often **liberties**: be unrestrained or °presumptuous or °bold or °uninhibited or overfamiliar or forward or °aggressive or °impudent or °impertinent or °audacious or °improper; display or exercise boldness or °impropriety or °presumption or presumptuousness or indecorum or unseemliness or boldness or °arrogance: *She thought he was taking liberties in asking her to dance. I took the liberty of asking her to accompany me.*

licence n. **1** °leave, °permission, °liberty, authorization, °authority, entitlement, dispensation, °right, *carte blanche*, °freedom, latitude, °free °choice, °privilege, °charter: *Merely being eighteen does not give you licence to do exactly as you please.* **2** °permit, certificate, credential(s), °paper(s): *Bring along your driving licence.* **3** °disregard, deviation, departure, nonconformity, °non-compliance, divergence: *Such grammatical abnormalities are an exercise of poetic licence.*

license v. **1** °authorize, °allow, °permit, °certify, °sanction, °approve, commission: *The government once had the power to license books for publication.* **2** °certify, °document, accredit, °entitle, validate, °enable, empower: *Whoever licensed him to drive a car made a grave mistake.*

lie[1] v. **1** °prevaricate, °fabricate, °misrepresent, °invent, commit °perjury, perjure *or* forswear oneself, *Colloq* °fib: *If he says that I ate the last cake, he's lying.*
—n. **2** °falsehood, untruth, falsification, misrepresentation, fiction, °invention, prevarication, °fib, °fabrication, *Colloq* °story, cock-and-bull °story, (tall) °tale, whopper, *US* fish °story, fish °tale: *His claim of having been attacked was found to be a lie.*

lie[2] v. **1** °recline, °stretch out, be °prostrate *or* °recumbent *or* °prone *or* °supine: *I'm going to lie down for a nap before dinner.* **2** °rest, °repose; can be found, be, be situated: *The book is lying on the table. The land lies on the Berkshire–Surrey border.* **3** °rest, °repose, be, reside, °dwell, °abide, °remain, °belong: *The responsibility lies with you.* **4** °press, °burden, °weigh, °rest, be: *The onus for the crime lies heavily on him.* **5 lie low:** °hide, remain concealed *or* in hiding, keep out of sight, *Colloq Brit* lie doggo: *You'd better lie low till the affair is forgotten.*
—n. **6 lie of the land:** °state, °status, °condition, °situation, °atmosphere, °mood, °spirit, °temper, °character: *You ought to determine the lie of the land before submitting your proposal.*

life n. **1** °existence, °entity, being; sentience, viability: *Who can imagine the possible forms of life in the universe?* **2** °existence, survival, living, °subsistence, °sustenance: *Certain nutriments are necessary to life on earth.* **3** °existence, living, °way of life, lifestyle: *What kind of life does he lead? I enjoy country life.* **4** °existence, lifetime, °time; duration: *She did much during her short life. The life of a light-bulb depends on how often it is switched off and on.* **5** °person, °mortal, °human (being), °individual, °soul: *The new drug might save millions of lives.* **6** biography, autobiography, °memoir(s), (life) °story: *He has written a life of Mozart.* **7** °soul, °spirit, °spark of life, °vital °spark, °moving °spirit, life-force, *élan vital*; lifeblood; °animation, °vitality, liveliness, sprightliness, vivacity, °sparkle, °dazzle, °dash, élan, °vigour, °verve, °zest, °flavour, pungency, freshness, effervescence, brio, °flair, vim, °energy, °exuberance, °enthusiasm, *Colloq* °pep, zing, get-up-and-go: *We must breathe some life into these people. Eva is always the life of the party.* **8** °obsession, preoccupation, °passion, °fixation, compulsion: *Model railways are his life.* **9** °bounce, °resilience, °spring, °elasticity: *There's no life in this old tennis ball.*

lifeless adj. **1** °dead: *I stared at the lifeless body of the man.* **2** °unconscious, °inanimate, insensate, °inert, unmoving, °dead, °insensible: *At the news of the accident, she sank, lifeless, to the floor.* **3** °dull, °boring, °tiresome, °heavy, °lacklustre, °torpid, °tedious, °flat, °stale, uninteresting, °colourless, uninspiring, °vapid, °wooden: *The production was a success apart from Ellen's lifeless performance as Portia.* **4** °barren, °desert, °desolate, °bare, °sterile, °bleak, °empty, °uninhabited, unoccupied, °dreary, °waste: *We gazed at the lifeless landscape of the moon.*

lifelike adj. °authentic, °realistic, °natural, °true to life, °real, °faithful, °graphic, °vivid: *She painted a very lifelike picture of her cat.*

lift v. **1** °raise, elevate; °hoist, °heave (up): *She lifted her eyes to the heavens. The pallbearers lifted the coffin to their shoulders.* **2** Often, **lift up**: °exalt, °raise, elevate, uplift, °boost, upgrade, °promote, °advance; °improve, ameliorate, °better, °dignify, °enhance, ennoble, enshrine, deify, °immortalize: *His unusual talents lifted him up from the ranks of ordinary mortals.* **3** °discontinue, °end, °terminate, °stop: *The siege was lifted after six months.* **4** °withdraw, °cancel, °confiscate, °take away, rescind, °void, annul: *They charged him with driving while intoxicated and lifted his licence.* **5** °rise, °disappear, °dissipate, vanish: *When the fog lifted, I saw that we were about to run aground.* **6** °steal, °appropriate, °pilfer, °pocket, thieve, °take, purloin; plagiarize, °copy, *Colloq* °pinch, crib, °liberate, *Slang Brit* °nick, *Old-fashioned* half-inch: *He went into the supermarket and lifted a bottle of scotch. This passage was lifted from my book in its entirety.*
—n. **7** °ride: *She looked tired so I gave her a lift home.* **8** *In US and Canada:* elevator: *Take the lift to the tenth floor.* **9** °encouragement, °boost, stimulus, °inducement, °inspiration, reassurance, cheering up, *Colloq* °shot in the arm: *Winning first prize has given Susan the lift she needed to continue with her writing.*

light[1] n. **1** °illumination, brightness, °daylight, lamplight, candlelight, firelight, gaslight, °torchlight, starlight, moonlight, sunlight; gegenschein, counterglow: *There is just enough light for me to read the label.* **2** lamp, light-bulb, torch, °beacon, lantern, candle, °flare, headlight *or* headlamp, street-light *or* street lamp, *US and Canadian* flashlight: *I saw a light in the distance. Someone turned off the lights.* **3** °radiance, °radiation, luminescence, °glare, °gleam, °glow, °reflection, luminosity, °shine, °sparkle, scintillation, incandescence, phosphorescence, fluorescence: *The light of the full moon shone through the window.* **4** daybreak, °dawn, sunrise, *US* sun-up: *We leave at first light.* **5** clarification, enlightenment, °insight, °understanding, elucidation, simplification, °explanation: *After an hour's talk with his lawyer, he finally saw the light and confessed. Can you shed a little light on this problem, Robyn?* **6** window, window-pane: *The west wall has three windows of six lights each.* **7** °match, lighter, spill, taper, fire, flame, ignition: *Can you give me a light for my cigarette?* **8** highlight: *Note the chiaroscuro effect from the lights and shadows in the drawing.* **9 bring to light**: °reveal, °unearth, °find, uncover, °unveil, °discover, expose, °disclose, °make known: *A vital fact has recently been brought to light.* **10 come to light**: be revealed, be unearthed, be uncovered, be unveiled, be discovered, be exposed, be disclosed, °appear, °come out, °turn up, °transpire, °develop, evolve, °emerge:

The truth about her parents has finally come to light. **11** *Brit* **in the light of** or *US* **in light of**: considering, in view of, in consideration of, taking into account, keeping or bearing in °mind: *In the light of his condition, he has decided to pull out of the competition.* **12 shed** or **throw (some, a little) light on**: °explain, elucidate, °simplify, °clarify: *Perhaps you could throw some light on the reason why she refuses to leave the house.* —*adj.* **13** (well-)illuminated, °bright, alight, (well-)lit, (well-)lighted, shining, °luminous, effulgent, °brilliant, beaming, °incandescent, phosphorescent, fluorescent: *The lightest room in the house is the kitchen.* **14** °pale, light-hued: *Put the light blue chair over here.*
—*v.* **15** ignite, set alight, set or put a match to, °kindle, °burn, °touch off, set °fire to, °fire: *It's getting chilly, so you'd better light the fire. When the bomb was in place, they lit the fuse.* **16** °illuminate, °light up, °lighten, °brighten: *Take this candle to light your way to the bedroom.* **17** °turn on, °switch on, °put on: *Light the lamps.* **18 light up**: °lighten, °brighten, °cheer up, °liven up: *The moment she walked in, the whole room lit up. Her face lit up when she saw him.*

light[2] *adj.* **1** lightweight, °portable: *I bought some light garden furniture.* **2** underweight, °skinny, °slight: *Isn't Ted a bit light for his height?* **3** °faint, °dim, °obscure, °indistinct, unclear, faded, °imperceptible: *There is a very light pencil mark on the paper.* **4** °faint, °gentle, °mild, °slight, °delicate, °insignificant: *A light breeze rippled the surface of the pool.* **5** °dainty, °graceful, °delicate, °gentle, °slight: *He felt the light brush of her lips on his.* **6** not °weighty, °frivolous, unimportant, °insignificant, °inconsequential, inconsiderable, trivial, °trifling, evanescent, unsubstantial, °slight, °superficial: *The party was a very light affair.* **7** °nimble, °agile, °active, °swift, spry, lithe, °sprightly, lightsome, light-footed, limber, lissom or lissome: *When dancing, he may be light on his feet, but he's not very light on mine.* **8** simple-minded, light-headed, °scatterbrained, rattle-brained, bird-brained, feather-brained, °hare-brained, °flighty, °giddy, °dizzy, °silly, °inane, °foolish, °frivolous, empty-headed, °vacant, vacuous, °shallow, °superficial: *Featherstone is a bit too light in the head to be a good manager.* **9** °cheerful, °happy, °gay, °sunny, °merry, light-hearted, happy-go-lucky, °easygoing, °joyful, jovial, °jolly: *Noël has written another light drawing-room comedy.* **10** °easy, not °burdensome, endurable, °bearable, °tolerable, °supportable, undemanding, °effortless, untaxing, °moderate: *After my surgery, I was able to resume light duties at the office. The tax on such a small income is very light. You should take some light exercise every day.* **11** amusing, °entertaining, °witty, diverting: *The book hasn't much substance, but it makes good light reading.* **12 make light of**: °dismiss, °write off, shrug off; °trivialize; °ridicule: *The teacher made light of my attempts to play the concerto.*
—*v.* **13** alight, °land, °come or °go down, °descend, °settle; deplane, °disembark or debark, detrain, dismount: *The bird was so tame it lighted on my finger.* **14 light into**: °attack, assail, °lambaste, °assault, °pounce or °fall on or upon, °beat, °belabour, °abuse, tongue-lash, °harangue, °upbraid, °scold, °berate, *Colloq* °lace into; *Slang* clobber: *He really lit into the challenger in the third round. Her mother lit into her for not*

doing her homework. **15 light on** or **upon**: °chance or °happen or °stumble or °hit on or upon, °come across, °encounter, °find, °meet up with: *She claimed she lit upon the formula when reading some ancient hieroglyphics.*

lighten[1] *v.* **1** °illuminate, °brighten, °light up: *Opening the curtains would lighten up the room.* **2** °cheer (up), °brighten, °gladden, °shine; °smile: *Her face lightened when he said he would be home for the holidays.*

lighten[2] *v.* disencumber, disburden, °relieve, alleviate, °reduce, lessen, °mitigate: *To lighten my load, I had left my suitcase at the hotel.*

like[1] *adj., adv.* **1** °similar (to), °akin (to), allied (to), °parallel (to or with), comparable (to or with), °equivalent (to), °equal (to), °identical (to), cognate (with), analogous (to), corresponding (to), °correspondent (to), °close (to), homologous (to or with), of a piece (with), (much) the °same (as), along the °same lines (as), not °unlike: *We hold like opinions. Her opinions are like mine. Her pies are like the ones my mother used to bake. Problems like this give me a headache. Opposite charges attract, like charges repel.* **2** in the °mood for, °disposed to: *Do you feel like a walk in the park? He felt like going with me.*
—*adv.* **3** as if, as °though: *He ran like mad.*
—*prep.* **4** °similar to, °identical to or with: *Her daughter looks like one. He makes her feel like a perfect fool.* **5** in the °same °way as, in the °manner of, similarly to: *Sometimes she acts like a maniac. The jacket fits him like a glove. He laughed like a drain. He treats his mother like a child.* **6** such as, for °example, for °instance, e.g., that is (to say), i.e., in other words, °namely, to wit, viz.: *Mistletoe grows on various trees, like oaks and birches.*
—*n.* **7** °match, °equal, °peer, °fellow, °opposite °number, counterpart, °twin: *It is doubtful that we shall see his like again.* **8** °same or °similar °kind or °sort or ilk or °type or kidney or °breed or °mould or °cast or °strain: *The book deals with music, literature, theatre, painting, and the like.*

like[2] *v.* **1** be °fond of, °approve of, °appreciate, be °partial to, °have a fondness or °liking for, have a °weakness for, °take to, °delight in, °take °pleasure in, °derive or get °pleasure from, find °agreeable or congenial, feel attracted to, be or feel °favourably impressed by, °relish, °love, °adore, adulate, *Colloq* take a °shine to, *Slang* °go for, °dig, get a kick out of, *US* °get off on, °groove on, get a bang or a charge out of: *She likes a day at the seaside. He likes chocolate ice-cream. I think she likes me.* **2** Usually, **would** or **should like**: °prefer, °want, °wish, °ask: *I would like you to try to get to work on time in future. I'd like a drink.*
—*n.* **3** Usually, **likes**: °preference, °partiality, predilection, °liking: *We all have our different likes and dislikes.*

likeable *adj.* °likeable, °genial, °amiable, congenial, °pleasant, *simpatico*, °agreeable, °pleasing, °attractive, appealing, °nice, °friendly, °winning, charming, °engaging, °good-natured, winsome: *He is likeable enough, but not my ideal son-in-law.*

likelihood *n.* °probability, strong or distinct °possibility, good °chance: *We must consider the likelihood that she will refuse to go.*

likely *adj.* **1** °probable, °liable, expected: *Three o'clock is the likely arrival time.* **2** °probable, conceivable, °reasonable, credible, °plausible,

°tenable: *It seemed likely that Holmes would solve the case.* **3** °fitting, °able, °suitable, °probable, °seemly, °meet, °right, °proper, °qualified, °acceptable, °appropriate, apposite; °favourite, odds-on, °favoured, °promising: *Peters is the likely man for the job.* **4** °disposed to, apt to, °inclined to, °liable to: *It's likely to rain. You're likely to think me mad, but I have my reasons for going.*
—*adv.* **5** °probably, °undoubtedly, indubitably, no °doubt, in all °probability, *Colloq* like as not: *You would most likely say that I am wrong. He will very likely win the election.*

liken *v.* °compare, equate, °match, juxtapose: *How can you liken him to Mahatma Gandhi?*

likeness *n.* **1** similarity, °resemblance, correspondence, analogy, °agreement, parallelism: *The artist has caught her likeness in the second painting.* **2** °copy, °replica, °facsimile, °duplicate, °reproduction, °model, °representation, °portrait, painting, °picture, °drawing, °photograph, °sculpture, °statue, statuette, °image, simulacrum, icon *or* ikon: *He sells miniature likenesses of the Eiffel Tower to tourists.* **3** °appearance, °face, °figure, °image: *The premier's likeness appears on posters throughout the country.*

likewise *adv.* **1** similarly, in the °same *or* °like °manner *or* °way: *Penny is sitting quietly and you should do likewise.* **2** as well, too, also, furthermore, °further, °besides, in °addition, °moreover, to °boot: *There are many ways to take exercise and, likewise, many ways to avoid it.*

liking *n.* **1** °affinity, fondness, °affection, °love, °partiality, °bias, °preference, °bent, predilection, predisposition, °inclination, °appreciation, °penchant; °eye, °appetite, soft spot, °weakness: *He has a liking for good claret and beautiful women.* **2** °taste, °pleasure, °fancy, °preference: *The chef will prepare the steak to your liking.*

limbo *n.* **in limbo**: up in the air, consigned to °oblivion, in °abeyance, suspended, hanging (°fire), neither here nor there, *Colloq* on hold, treading water, holding one's breath, *US* in a holding pattern, on the shelf, on the back burner: *My career is in limbo till I learn the result of the interview.*

limit *n.* **1** Sometimes, **limits**: °extent, °bound(s), °end, limitation, °check, °curb, °restriction, °restraint: *Is there no limit to how far you will go to get your own way?* **2** Often, **limits**: °border, °edge, °end, °extent, °boundary, °bound(s), (°boundary *or* °border *or* °partition) °line, °frontier, °perimeter, °periphery: *That row of poplars marks the limit of the property to the east.* **3** Often, **limits**: °area, °territory, confines, °zone, °region, °quarter, °district, °precinct(s): *Stay outside the three-mile limit. We have jurisdiction only within city limits.* **4 the limit**: **a** the °end, the °last straw, the straw that broke the camel's back, all (that) one can °take, °enough, too much, *Colloq* it: *Your presumption is the absolute limit—you can't seriously expect me to lend you money.* **b** °outrage, °joke, °surprise, *Colloq* caution: *Wasn't Nigel the limit in that hat!?*
—*v.* **5** °check, °curb, °bridle, °restrict, °restrain, °hold in °check: *We must limit spending on arms. The shackles limited my movements.* **6** °restrict, confine, delimit, °narrow, °focus, °guide, °channel: *Please limit your questions to the subject*

at hand. **7** °set, °define, °determine, °fix: *The bank manager has limited my overdraft to half what it was.*

limited *adj.* **1** circumscribed, restricted, °fixed, °predetermined; °small, °little, reduced, °minimal: *The theatre seats a limited number of people. She was awarded limited access to the children.* **2** °narrow, restricted, restrictive, °meagre: *Few original ideas presented themselves to his limited imagination.*

limitless *adj.* unrestricted, unrestrained, unconfined, unbounded, °boundless, °extensive, °vast, °immense, °enormous, °unlimited, illimitable; interminable, unceasing, incessant, undefined, °immeasurable, innumerable, °numberless, countless, myriad, unending, °perpetual, °everlasting, °eternal: *Dickens possessed a seemingly limitless capacity for characterization. In the depths of space exist limitless numbers of stars. God's love is limitless.*

limp[1] *v.* **1** °hobble, °stagger, °totter, dodder, falter: *He limped slowly along the road.*
—*n.* **2** °hobble, hobbling, °stagger, staggering, °totter, tottering, dodder, °doddering, falter, faltering, claudication, *Slang US* gimp: *He was easy to recognize at a distance because of his limp.*

limp[2] *adj.* **1** flaccid, °flabby, °lax, °slack, °soft, drooping, °relaxed, unstarched, unstiffened, °flexible, °pliable, floppy, °loose: *The banners hung limp in the still, sultry air.* **2** °exhausted, °tired, °fatigued, °worn out, °spent, enervated, wasted, debilitated, °weak, °feeble, °frail: *He felt limp with exhaustion after the day's hiking.* **3** °weak, °feeble, °ineffective, °ineffectual, °flimsy, °half-hearted, °lukewarm, °spineless, thewless, namby-pamby, *Colloq* °wishy-washy, *Slang* gutless: *Having to visit her grandmother seemed a pretty limp excuse to me.*

line[1] *n.* **1** °mark, pencil-mark, pen-mark, °rule, °score; °stroke, underline, underscore; diagonal, °slash, virgule, shilling-mark, solidus, separatrix, °oblique: *The lines on this paper are very faint. Draw a red line under your name. A line separates the numerator from the denominator.* **2** °strip, °belt, °stripe, °band, °border, °edge, edging: *Do you see that line of trees? Put a heavy black line round the obituary notices.* **3** °wrinkle, crease, crinkle, °furrow, crow's-foot: *He has many lines on his face. The palmist said I have a long lifeline.* **4** °border, borderline, °frontier, °limit, °boundary; demarcation, °threshold: *We crossed the line into Italy. I don't mind cooking dinner, but I draw the line at washing the dishes. There is a fine line between genius and insanity.* **5** °outline, °silhouette, contour, °figure, °profile: *The line of the skirt is too straight.* **6** °row, °rank, column, °file, °train, °parade, cortege *or* cortège, °procession, *Brit* °queue, *Colloq Brit* crocodile, tailback: *I stood in line for six hours for tickets. The line wound all the way round the block.* **7** °field, °area, °activity, °forte, °speciality *or chiefly US and Canadian also* specialty, specialization, °business, °profession, °occupation, (line of) °work, °job, °vocation, °pursuit, °trade, °calling, °employment, *Colloq* °racket, °game: *Saying that he was a computer programmer, he asked me my line.* **8** °note, °word, °card, postcard, °letter, *US* postal °card: *Drop me a line when you get there.* **9** °course, °direction, °path, °way, °route, °road, °track, °procedure, °tack, °policy, °strategy, °tactic(s), °approach,

°plan: *What line will our competitors take to win the account? I adopted the line of least resistance.* **10** °information, °data, °word, °lead, °clue, °hint: *Interpol is trying to get a line on where he might be found.* **11** °cord, °string, °thread, °twine, °yarn, strand, filament, °rope, °cable, hawser: *The anchor line became entangled. Hang the clothes out on the line.* **12** °track, °railway *or US and Canadian also* °railroad: *The accident on the southern line is delaying all the trains.* **13** telephone, wire, °cable: *We have three lines at the office. He tried all day to get you on the line.* **14** °front (line), vanguard, °formation: *These men have been in the line for weeks. Captain Hughes was given command of a ship of the line.* **15** ancestry, descent, °stock, °lineage, °succession, °family, °parentage, °extraction, °heritage, genealogy: *She comes from a long line of horsewomen.* **16** °assortment, °stock, °merchandise, offerings, °goods, °brand, °make, °type, °kind, °variety: *What line of lawnmower do you distribute?* **17** Often, **lines**: °part, °role, °speech, °script, °words, *Theatre US* sides: *I know my lines by heart for the school play. She has one line in the third act.* **18** °story, (sales) pitch, blarney, *Colloq* spiel, °song and dance, *Slang* con: *He handed her a line about being lonely, but she soon found out why.* **19** **in** *or* **into line**: **a** aligned, in alignment, °true, °straight, in a °row, °plumb: *Bring the balusters for the railing in line.* **b** in °agreement, in °accord, in accordance, in conformity, in °step, in °harmony, *US* lined up: *We are bringing the staffing requirements into line with the council's recommendations.* **c** Usually, **into line**: under *or* in °control: *Were you able to bring the other board members into line?* **20 in line for**: °ready for, short-listed for, on the short list for, up for, being considered for, under °consideration for, a °candidate for, in the °running for: *We all think she's in line for a promotion.*
—*v.* **21** °rule, inscribe, °score, underline, underscore: *If you use lined paper, your writing won't be so wavy.* **22** °edge, °border, °fringe: *Millions lined the streets for the parade.* **23 line up**: **a** °organize, °prepare, °ready, °assemble, °set up, °put *or* °set in °place, °develop, °formulate, °arrange (for), °coordinate: *Everything is all lined up for the big event.* **b** °arrange for, °secure, °get (°hold of), °obtain, °contract for; uncover, °dig up, °acquire, °engage, °hire, °sign (up), °contract with, °employ: *We lined up an excellent after-dinner speaker.* **c** °queue (up), °form a line, °get in line, °form ranks *or* columns: *Hundreds of us lined up for meals three times a day.* **d** align, array, °straighten, °order: *These paragraphs should line up. Line up the troops for inspection at 0600.*

line² *v.* **1** interline, °cover, °face; ceil: *The coat is lined with fur.* **2 line one's pockets**: accept °bribes, °graft, *US* °sell out, *Colloq US* be on the take: *He was secretly lining his pockets during his years on the council.*

lineage *n.* **1** °extraction, ancestry, °family tree, °pedigree, descent, °stock, bloodline, °parentage, genealogy: *She has spent a lot of time tracing the lineage of the village's families.* **2** forebears, forefathers, foremothers, °family, °people, °clan; descendants, °succession, °progeny, °offspring: *Does Debrett list his lineage? Peerages were confined to the lineage of the person ennobled.*

linen *n.* Often, **linens**: bedclothes, bed linen(s), °sheets and pillowcases; table linen(s), napery, tablecloths and napkins; bath linen(s), towels and wash-cloths: *The soiled linen is sent to the laundry.*

linger *v.* **1** Sometimes, **linger on**: °stay (behind), °remain, °tarry, loiter, °persist, °hang on, °endure, °persevere, °survive, *Colloq* °hang *or* °stick about *or* around: *The smell of tobacco lingered for hours after he had gone. He lingered on for a day, then died from his wounds.* **2** °pause, °dawdle, dally, °lag, °idle: *She lingered for a moment at the jeweller's window.* **3** Often, **linger on** *or* **over**: °dwell on, °elaborate, harp on, °labour: *I shall not linger over the details of the crime.* **4** °procrastinate, dither, °shilly-shally, temporize: *You must stop lingering and decide today.*

lingering *adj.* **1** °long, °persistent, °protracted, °remaining: *I was left with the lingering feeling that I had forgotten to tell her something.* **2** °slow, long-drawn-out, °gradual: *She died a lingering, painful death.*

lingo *n.* °jargon, argot, °cant, patois, pidgin, Creole, °parlance, °vernacular, °dialect, °idiom, °language, °talk, °speech; °gobbledegook *or* gobbledygook, °gibberish, °mumbo-jumbo: *In medical lingo, he is suffering from coryza—in other words, a cold.*

link *n.* **1** °tie, °bond, coupling, connector, vinculum; °element, constituent, component: *A chain is no stronger than its weakest link.* **2** °connection, °tie-up, °tie-in, °relation, °relationship, °association, affiliation, interdependence: *What is the link between her arrival and his sudden departure? He thinks he's identified the missing link.*
—*v.* **3** Often, **link up**: °couple, °join, °fasten (together), °unite; concatenate: *They linked arms to form a barrier.* **4** °connect, °tie (up *or* in *or* together), °associate, °relate, °identify with: *I cannot help feeling that this murder links up with the others.*

liquid *n.* **1** °fluid, °liquor, °juice, °solution: *Mixing these two liquids could be dangerous.*
—*adj.* **2** °fluid, flowing, °running, runny, °fluent, liquefied, °watery, molten, melted: *The Saturn V was the first space vehicle to be fuelled by liquid hydrogen and liquid oxygen.* **3** °bright, shining, °brilliant, °clear, °transparent, translucent, limpid: *The surface of the lake gleamed like liquid sunshine.* **4** convertible, °solvent, °profitable: *Government bonds are regarded as liquid assets. The company remains liquid despite losses.*

liquor *n.* **1** spirits, °alcohol, (strong) °drink, intoxicants, John Barleycorn, schnapps, °whisky *or US and Irish* whiskey, demon rum, °moonshine, *US* white lightning, white mule; *Colloq* °booze, pick-me-up, hard stuff, fire-water, juice, mother's ruin (= 'gin'), *US* Kickapoo mountain joy juice; *Slang* rot-gut, *Chiefly US and Canadian* hooch *or* hootch, *US* sauce, red-eye, mountain dew: *I don't drink liquor, but I will have some tea.* **2** °liquid, °fluid, °extract, °broth, °stock, distillate, °concentrate, infusion: *After poaching the fish, pour off the liquor and save it.*

list¹ *n.* **1** listing, roster, °roll, rota, catalogue, directory, °register, °index, °record, °schedule, °muster, slate, beadroll, laundry list, shopping list, inventory, °file, tabulation; bibliography, liber veritatis, catalogue raisonné: *Select what you need from this list.*

—v. **2** catalogue, °register, °index, °record, °note, °itemize, °enumerate, °schedule, °tabulate, °chronicle, °book, °enter, °enrol: *Those eligible to vote are listed in this computer printout.*

list² v. **1** °lean (over), °tilt, °slant, °heel (over), °tip, °career, °cant, °incline: *The ship suddenly listed to starboard and I was thrown onto the deck.* —n. **2** °lean, °tilt, °slant, °heel, °tip, °cant, °slope, °inclination: *The leak caused a severe list to port.*

listen v. **1** °hear, pay °attention (to), °attend, lend an ear (to), prick up one's ears, keep one's ears open, *Archaic* hark (to), hearken *or US also* harken (to): *I was listening to the radio when you phoned.* **2** °obey, °heed, °mind, pay °attention (to), do as one is told: *You wouldn't be in this trouble if you'd listened to me.*

listless adj. sluggish, °lethargic, °weary, °weak, enervated, °spent, languid, °lifeless, °heavy, °phlegmatic, unemotional, °impassive, °unenthusiastic, °indifferent, apathetic, unconcerned, °lukewarm, °tepid, °cool, uncaring, insouciant; pococurante, Laodicean: *She was just over an illness and feeling quite listless.*

litany n. **1** °prayer, invocation, °supplication, °petition: *The monks trudged through the streets, chanting their litany.* **2** °recitation, °recital, enumeration, listing, °list, cataloguing, catalogue, inventorying, inventory: *We had to sit through an interminable litany of the names of contributors to the fund.*

literal adj. **1** word-for-word, °verbatim, line-for-line, letter-for-letter, literatim, °exact, °precise, °faithful, °strict: *In a literal translation the spirit of the original is often lost.* **2** denotative, etymological, semantic, dictionary, lexical, °basic, °essential, °true, °simple, simplistic, °real, °objective, °true, °genuine, bona fide, °unvarnished, unadulterated, unembellished, simple-minded, uncomplicated, unbiased, °unprejudiced, *Colloq* honest-to-goodness, honest-to-God: *'Female parent' may be the literal definition of* mother, *but it doesn't convey the emotional and connotative senses of the word.* **3** °prosaic, °matter-of-fact, °colourless, °dull, down-to-earth, literal-minded, unimaginative, °humdrum, °boring, °tedious: *His literal approach to everything spoils the conversation for those who have any spirit.*

literally adv. **1** word for word, °verbatim, line for line, letter for letter, literatim, faithfully, strictly, °exactly, °precisely, closely; °thus, *sic*: *Generally* cordon sanitaire *means 'buffer zone', but literally it means 'sanitary line'.* **2** °actually, °truly, in °fact, °really: *When I said he'd spilled the beans, I meant it figuratively, not literally.*

literary adj. **1** erudite, well-read, cultured, °learned, bookish, °scholarly, °lettered, °cultivated, °refined, °educated; literate: *Her latest book has been scorned by the literary élite.* **2** written, °formal, °scholarly, °pedantic, °learned, °academic, scholastic, school-marmish: *His writing contains literary words rarely heard in ordinary conversation.*

literature n. **1** °writing(s), °letters, belles-lettres, °creative °writing(s): *These works are representative of the literature of the period.* **2** °information, °facts, °data, publicity; °propaganda; °brochures, °pamphlets,

hand-outs, handbills, °leaflets, circulars: *As a member, you will be sent literature about future events. They print subversive literature.*

litigant n. litigator, °party, plaintiff, appellant, °suitor, petitioner, suer, defendant, appellee, accused: *The judge suggested that the litigants settle out of court.*

litigation n. lawsuit, °suit, °action, °case, °legal °remedy: *The costs of litigation are extremely high.*

litter n. **1** °rubbish, debris, °refuse, fragments, °odds and ends, *US and Canadian* °trash, *Colloq* °junk: *The room was strewn with food wrappers, cigarette butts, and other litter.* **2** °brood, °issue, °offspring, °young: *Note the differences in the young of the same litter.* **3** stretcher, palanquin *or* palankeen, sedan °chair: *The potentate was borne in on a litter carried by four huge slaves.* —v. **4** °clutter, °strew, °scatter: *The streets were littered with bricks and broken glass.*

little adj. **1** °small, °short, °slight, °tiny, °minute, °diminutive, °miniature, mini, °baby, doll-sized, °undersized, °dwarf, midget, pygmy, °elfin, °toy, bantam, °petite, °wee, infinitesimal, minuscule, Lilliputian, teeny, teeny-weeny, teensy-weensy, itty-bitty, itsy-bitsy, microscopic: *I live in a little house. A little red-faced man suddenly appeared. They sat drinking coffee out of little white cups.* **2** °young, °small, youthful: *You are asking a lot from a little boy.* **3** °small, °sparse, skimpy, °meagre, scant, °insufficient, °inadequate, not enough, °scanty, °barely *or* °hardly any: *A little crowd gathered round us. You will get little help from her. There's too little milk for us to make custard.* **4** °short, °brief: *We had only a little time together before he was sent overseas.* **5** °trifling, trivial, °small, °minor, °petty, °paltry, °insignificant, inconsiderable, unimportant, °inconsequential, °negligible: *He seemed to consider my safety of little importance. He does a little business on the side. You are too concerned about little things.* **6** °small(-minded), °petty, picayune, °mean, ungenerous, illiberal, °cheap, °narrow(-minded), unimaginative, °shallow: *What is going on in his cunning little brain?* —adv. **7** °seldom, °rarely, °hardly ever, °scarcely: *I travel very little these days.* **8** (but *or* only) °slightly, °barely, °hardly, °scarcely, no, not any, not much: *She arrived with little more than what she was wearing.* **9** °scarcely, °hardly: *Little does he care whether he wins his wager.* —pron. **10** °bit, °dab, dollop, °particle, spoonful, °taste, thimbleful, °speck, °spot, °scrap, °crumb, °particle, *Colloq* smidgen *or* smidgin: *If you could spare me a little of your time, I'd be grateful.*

live adj. **1** living, breathing, °animate, °viable, existent; °material, °physical, °tangible, °real, °actual, palpable: *She said she'd rather be a live beggar than a dead countess. My cat brought a live mouse into the house the other day.* **2** °energetic, °lively, °spirited, °vigorous, °active, °dynamic, °busy; °current, °contemporary: *Our new advertising agency seems to have some live ideas. The other party made nuclear disarmament a live issue in the election.* **3** °burning, °glowing, °flaming, alight, red-hot, white-hot: *A live coal popped out of the grate onto the carpet.* **4** °loaded, °explosive, unexploded, combustible: *Builders have dug up a live bomb in London.* **5** charged, electrified: *Don't touch a live wire or you'll get a shock.* —v. **6** °breathe, °exist; °function: *There has never lived a more gifted scholar. She lives as a* recluse. **7** °survive, °persist, °last, °persevere, °endure; °spend, °continue, °live out, °complete, °end, conclude, °finish: *He lived out his days happily in Torquay.* **8** reside, °dwell, be; °abide, °stay, °remain, °lodge, °room: *He normally lives in Acton, but at the moment he's living with his mother in Kent.* **9** subsist, °get along, °survive, °fare: *Many old-age pensioners complain that they have barely enough to live on.*

lively *adj.* **1** full of °life, °vigorous, °energetic, °vivacious, °spirited, °brisk, spry, °active, °animated, °frisky, °sprightly, °agile, °nimble, °perky, chirpy, bouncy, °buoyant, °gay, cheery, °cheerful, *Colloq* chipper, full of °pep, peppy: *His speech sparked off a lively discussion. The carriage was drawn by a pair of lively horses.* **2** °strong, °intense, °vivid, °keen, °pointed, °eager, °energetic, °active: *She takes a lively interest in current affairs.* **3** °active, °busy, bustling, °stirring, °eventful, swarming, teeming; astir, °alive: *We joined the lively crowd at the antiques fair. The streets near the square were lively with people rushing to and fro.* **4** °vivid, °bright, °gay, °cheerful, °glowing, °brilliant, °gorgeous, °rich: *Some lively colours in the upholstery and curtains would brighten up the sitting-room.*

liven *v.* Often, **liven up**: **1** °brighten, °cheer, °enliven, °perk up: *You need some fresh paint to liven up the outside of the house.* **2** invigorate, °stimulate, °energize, inspirit, °activate, °animate, °fire, °stir (up), put (some) °life into, °enliven, °perk up, *Colloq* °pep up: *We need a good dance band to liven up the place in the evenings.*

load *n.* **1** °weight, °burden; onus, °pressure, °encumbrance, millstone, °cross, albatross, °responsibility, °care, °anxiety, °worry, °trouble: *He put down his load and rested. Seeing her safe is a load off my mind.* **2** shipment, consignment, °cargo, °weight: *That load is too heavy for the van.* —*v.* **3** °pack, °pile, °stack, °heap, °fill, lade, °stuff, °cram, °jam, °squeeze: *Load all the boxes you can in the truck.* **4** Often, **load down**: °weigh down, °burden, °encumber, saddle with, °overwhelm: *I was loaded down with too many responsibilities.*

loaded *adj.* **1** overloaded, overwhelmed, burdened, laden, weighted (down), filled (up), chock-full, chock-a-block, stuffed, jammed, °packed, crowded, brimming, brim-full, crammed: *A fully loaded lorry has overturned near exit 5. The train was loaded with commuters.* **2** charged, primed, °ready: *Be careful—the gun is loaded.* **3** charged, °tricky, manipulative, insidious, °prejudiced, °prejudicial, °trap, °devious: *'When did you stop beating your wife?' is what anybody would call a loaded question.* **4** °rich, °wealthy, affluent, moneyed, well-to-do, °well off, *Colloq* °flush, well-heeled, *US* in the chips, *Slang* rolling in it: *I hear that her new husband is really loaded.* **5** °drunk: *He was loaded before he even went to the party.*

loaf[1] *n.* **1** °brick, °cake, °block, chunk; °lump, cube: *We could do with an extra loaf of bread.* **2** °head, °sense, brains, *Colloq* noggin, noodle, block, bean, *Brit* noddle, *Slang Brit* chump: *Use your loaf!*

loaf[2] *v.* **1** °lounge (about *or* around), loiter, °idle, laze, °lie about *or* around, take it °easy, vegetate, watch the grass grow, *Colloq US* lally-gag *or* lollygag, *Slang Brit* skive, *Military* scrim-shank, *US* goof around *or* off, *US military*

gold-brick, *Taboo slang US* fuck off, fuck the dog: *There are always some youngsters loafing about in the park.* **2 loaf away**: °waste, °fritter away, °idle away: *He loafs away all his time watching the telly.*

loafer *n.* °idler, layabout, °wastrel, shirker, *flâneur,* ne'er-do-well, °tramp, vagrant, *Old-fashioned* °lounge lizard, slugabed, *Colloq* lazybones, *Brit* drone, *US* °bum, (ski *or* tennis *or* surf) °bum, *Slang Brit* skiver, *Military* scrim-shanker, *US military* gold brick *or* gold-bricker, *Taboo slang US* fuck-off: *Why did she marry that good-for-nothing loafer?*

loan *n.* **1** °advance, °allowance, °credit, °accommodation: *We needed a loan to pay for Melissa's education.* —*v.* **2** °lend, °advance, °allow, °credit: *The bank loaned us enough money to buy a car.*

loath *adj.* loth, unwilling, °reluctant, °averse, °disinclined, °indisposed: *I was loath to tell my wife where I had been.*

loathe *v.* °detest, °hate, °despise, °abhor, abominate, execrate, °shrink *or* recoil from, °shudder at: *I love broccoli but loathe cauliflower.*

loathing *n.* hatred, abhorrence, °aversion, °hate, odium, detestation, antipathy, repugnance, °horror, °revulsion: *She treated her critics with loathing.*

loathsome *adj.* detestable, °abhorrent, odious, °hateful, °disgusting, execrable, °abominable, °despicable, °contemptible, noisome, °offensive, °horrible, °repulsive, °repugnant, nauseating, sickening, °revolting, °nasty, °vile: *Without warning, the loathsome beast attacked me. She died shortly of a loathsome disease.*

lob *v.* **1** loft, °toss, °pitch, °shy, °heave, °fling, chuck, °hurl, °throw: *He lobbed the ball high in the air over the net.* —*n.* **2** °toss, °throw, °bowl, °pitch, °hit, *US* °fly: *I misjudged the slow lob and swung too soon.*

lobby *n.* **1** foyer, entrance-hall, vestibule, °entry, *US* entry-way; °reception (room *or* area), °waiting-room, °corridor, °hall, hallway: *We were to meet in the main lobby of the arts centre.* **2** special-interest °group, °pressure °group, lobbyist: *A powerful lobby has been formed to influence farming legislation.* —*v.* **3** (bring) °pressure (to bear), (exert) °influence, °persuade, °pull strings *or* wires, put one's weight behind, °sway, °press, °push, °promote, °urge, *Brit* pressurize: *Environmentalists are lobbying for a ban on chlorofluorocarbons.*

local *adj.* **1** °neighbourhood, °neighbouring, °nearby, °close by; °adjoining: *She works for a local butcher. The law affects only the local area.* **2** °provincial, regional, °district, °state, county, shire, °municipal, °city, °town, village, °neighbourhood; restricted, °limited, °specific, °particular, °peculiar: *Clean water is a general, not a local problem.* —*n.* **3** °resident, °native, townsman, townswoman, townsperson: *The locals all voted against the proposition.* **4** neighbourhood °pub: *He stopped in at his local on the way home.*

locale *n.* °site, °location, °spot, °place, °setting, venue, °neighbourhood, °situation, locality: *We moved the locale of the film to Spain.*

locate *v.* **1** °situate, °place, °site, °position, °set (up), °fix, pinpoint, °establish, °settle, °base: *Where is your office located? We located our warehouse* *close to the railway.* **2** °find, °come across, °discover, °unearth, lay *or* put *or* get one's hand(s) *or* °finger(s) on, °chance *or* °hit upon, °turn up, °track down: *Where can I locate a good piano player?*

location *n.* **1** °site, °place, °locale, °spot, °setting, °situation, °position: *We have just moved to a new location.* **2** °finding, °discovery, laying *or* putting *or* getting one's hand(s) *or* °finger(s) on, unearthing, turning up, tracking down: *The location of the other half of the coin became an obsession with him.*

lock[1] *n.* **1** padlock, hasp, °bolt, latch, °bar, °hook, °clasp, catch: *Why put a lock on the door if there is nothing worth stealing inside?* **2** °hold; °control, °power, °sway, °authority, °command, supervision: *The bureau has a complete lock on the issue of licences.*
—*v.* **3** Often, **lock up**: padlock, °bolt, latch, °bar, °secure, °seal: *Lock the doors before leaving for the day.* **4** °clasp, °entangle, °engage, °join, °entwine, °close; °clutch, °grasp, °grapple: *For six hours the knights were locked in battle.* **5 lock away**: See 9, below. **6 lock in**: a °secure, °retain, °fix, °plant, °implant, stabilize: *What does the maker mean by 'the flavour is locked in'?* **b** °commit, °oblige, constrain, °bind: *We are locked in to the promises we made to our employees.* **c** lock up *or* away, confine, °restrain, coop up: *You'd better lock in the dogs before you leave.* **7 lock on**: °fix on *or* upon, °track, °follow, °pursue, keep °track of: *Our sights are locked on the target.* **8 lock out**: °exclude, °shut out, °close out, °keep out, °bar, debar: *During the strike, the management locked out all employees.* **9 lock up** *or* **away**: confine, °jail *or Brit also* gaol, °imprison, coop up, incarcerate, detain, impound, put behind bars, °restrict, °cage: *They threatened to lock him up and throw away the key.*

lock[2] *n.* tress, curl, ringlet: *As a love token, she sent him a lock of her hair.*

lodge *n.* **1** hunting-lodge, °cabin, chalet, °cottage, °house; gatehouse, °shelter, °hut: *I have a small lodge in the mountains.* **2** °branch, chapter: *He belongs to the Manchester lodge of the Masons.*
—*v.* **3** reside, °live, °dwell, °abide, °stay, °stop, °room, °occupy rooms: *For years they lodged together at 221B Baker Street.* **4** °accommodate, °board, °put up, billet, °quarter, °house, °take in; °shelter, °harbour: *Mrs Mulrooney is lodging a student in her spare room. Her house cannot lodge more than three.* **5** °stick, °wedge, catch, °deposit, become stuck *or* wedged *or* °fixed *or* caught *or* deposited, embed itself, become embedded: *I've got an apple pip lodged in one of my back teeth.* **6** °register, °enter, °record, °submit, °bring forward, °set forth *or* out, °file: *We lodged a complaint against our neighbours because of the noise.*

lodging *n.* Often, **lodgings**: °accommodation(s), °shelter, °quarters, °rooms, apartment, °housing, °house, °dwelling, dwelling-place, °residence: *I found a night's lodging in Cranberry Street.*

lofty *adj.* **1** °tall, °high, °elevated, °towering, soaring: *The lofty skyscrapers of New York always impress visitors on first sight.* **2** °exalted, °majestic, °imposing, °grand, °magnificent, °noble, °regal, °imperial, blue-blooded, thoroughbred, aristocratic, magisterial, august, °stately, °venerable, °distinguished, °dignified,

°elevated, °eminent, °celebrated, honoured, °honourable, respected, °renowned, °famous, °prominent, °illustrious, °notable, °leading, °pre-eminent, °sublime, °immortal: *He is heir to one of England's loftiest peerages.* **3** °elevated, °honourable, °superior, °exalted, °noble: *Public servants should adhere to lofty principles of morality.* **4** °grand, °grandiose, °haughty, °arrogant, °disdainful, °condescending, °contemptuous, °scornful, °supercilious, contumelious, patronizing, °superior, overweening, vainglorious, °pompous, °snobbish, *Colloq* °high and °mighty, snooty, uppity, *Brit* °uppish, *Slang* snotty, *Brit* toffee-nosed: *Her lofty attitude made her unpopular with the voters.*

logic *n.* **1** °reasoning, °deduction, dialectics, ratiocination, inferential *or* °scientific °reasoning: *Mill defined logic as the science of proof, or evidence.* **2** (good *or* common) °sense, °sound °judgement, °wisdom, °presence of mind: *According to Disraeli, England was not governed by logic.* **3** reasonableness, °intelligence, judiciousness, practicality, rationality: *Your logic is valid, but you are forgetting the human factor.*

logical *adj.* **1** syllogistic(al), inferential, deductive, inductive: *Her argument follows basic logical criteria.* **2** °reasonable, °plausible, °sensible, °sound, valid, °intelligent, °judicious, °practical, °rational, °wise, °proper: *Is it logical to assume that people will believe you?* **3** well-organized, °sound, °coherent, °consistent, °sensible, °rational, °reasonable, well-reasoned, well-thought-out: *The proposal is set forth in a logical fashion, from premise to conclusion.*

lonely *adj.* **1** °single, °solitary, °sole, lone, °one; °unaccompanied, °alone: *The lonely survivor of the crash struggled out of the jungle. She walked for miles, lonely and desolate.* **2** °desolate, °uninhabited, °deserted, °barren: *Robinson Crusoe's world was a lonely place.* **3** friendless, °lonesome, °abandoned, °outcast, forsaken; °solo, hermit-like, eremitic(al), °reclusive, °secluded, °retiring, °withdrawn, °unsocial: *He felt lonely in the strange city. She leads a lonely existence with only her cat for company.*

lonesome *adj.* **1** °alone, forsaken, friendless, rejected, °unpopular, °unwelcome, °outcast, °deserted, °abandoned, °estranged: *She was terribly lonesome and homesick before meeting Patrick.* **2** See **lonely**, 2, above.

long[1] *adj.* **1** °extensive, extended, elongate(d), °large, °great, °big: *That is a very long snake!* **2** °lengthy, prolonged, °protracted; °extensive, extended, °sustained: *I waited for a long time.*

long[2] *v.* °wish, crave, °want, °yearn, °desire, °hunger, °fancy, covet, °dream of, °hanker, eat one's heart out: *I am longing for a good roast beef dinner. I long to see you once more.*

longing *n.* craving, °wish, yearning, °hunger, °fancy, °desire, hankering, *Colloq* yen: *I have a longing to be home again.*

look *v.* **1** Usually, **look at**: °see, °observe, °consider, °contemplate, °regard, °view, °survey, °inspect, °scrutinize, °study, °scan; pay °attention, °attend, °notice, °watch, °witness; *Literary* °behold, *Slang US* eyeball: *Look at what you've done! Look at the way I do it.* **2** °seem (to be), °appear (to be): *That looks like a useful utensil. You certainly look healthy.* **3** °face, °front (on), °overlook, look out on: *The house looks over the sea at the back.* **4 look after**: °care for, take

°care of, be °responsible for, °attend, °mind, °watch, °serve, °wait on, °nurse, °protect: *Rose will look after your house while you're away. I need someone to look after me.* **5 look down on** or **upon** or *US* **at**: disdain, °despise, contemn, °scorn, °disparage, derogate, °spurn, °sneer, misprize, *Colloq* turn one's nose up at, look down one's nose at: *They look down on anyone with less money.* **6 look for: a** °seek, °demand, °require: *We aren't looking for the same things in a person.* **b** °hunt for, forage for, °search for: *I am looking for a cup to match my set.* **c** °expect, °hope, °anticipate, °count on, °reckon on: *I am looking for a better school report next term.* **7 look forward to: a** °anticipate, await, °wait for: *I am looking forward to Sunday's match.* **b** °expect, °count or °rely on or upon: *We were looking forward to your help.* **8 look into:** °examine, °study, °investigate, °inspect, delve into, °dig into, °probe, °scrutinize, °explore, °go into, °research, °check (out), °check into: *I shall have to look into the matter.* **9 look out:** be °careful, be °alert, be °vigilant, be on the qui vive, be watchful, °watch out, °beware, pay °attention, be on °guard: *If you don't look out, you'll bang your head.* **10 look over:** look at, °examine, °read, °scan, °study, °check (out or over), *Slang US* eyeball: *I haven't had a chance to look over the material you gave me.* **11 look up: a** °seek, °search for, °hunt for, try to find, °track or °run down: *I meant to look up the etymology of 'picnic'.* **b** get in touch with, (tele)phone, °ring (up), °visit, °call on, °call up, look or °drop in on, go to °see: *I looked up a friend of mine when I was in Chicago.* **c** °improve, get °better, °pick up, show °improvement, °progress, °gain, make °headway or °progress: *He was pleased to see that business was looking up.* **12 look up to:** °admire, °regard °highly, °respect, °esteem, °honour, °revere, °extol, °worship, °idolize, °venerate: *The boy really looks up to you.*
—*n.* **13** °gaze, °glance: *Her look was inviting. He gave me a dirty look. Let me have a look at you.* **14** looks, °appearance, °aspect, °bearing, °manner, °air, demeanour, °expression, countenance, °face, mien: *I just didn't like the look of the man. He had a nasty look.*

look-alike *n.* °twin, °double, °exact or °perfect °likeness or °match, clone, *Colloq* spitting °image or °spit and °image; doppelgänger; *Slang* (°dead) ringer: *She is such a perfect look-alike of Princess Di's that people follow her in the street.*

lookout *n.* **1** °guard, sentry, °sentinel, °watchman: *The lookout reported that the fort was surrounded by Cochise's braves.* **2** °alert, qui vive; °guard, °watch: *Be on the lookout for shoplifters.* **3** °responsibility, °worry, °concern, °problem, °difficulty, *Colloq* °headache: *How he wastes his free time is his lookout, how he spends his working time is ours.*

loom *v.* **1** °appear, °emerge, take °shape or °form, °materialize, °arise: *A huge figure loomed out of the fog.* **2** °menace, impend, °threaten, °overshadow, °tower, °dominate, °hang or °hover over: *Count Dracula's dark castle loomed over us.* **3 loom large:** °dominate, °predominate, play a big or an important role or part: *Sales to children loom large in your predictions.*

loop *n.* **1** hoop, noose, °ring, °circle, °bow, eye, eyelet, °coil, whorl, *Nautical* bend: *I caught my toe in a loop of rope and fell on the deck.*

—*v.* **2** °twist, °coil, °wind, °tie, °circle, curl, °entwine, °turn, °ring, *Nautical* bend: *Loop the thread round the crochet hook and pull it through.*

loophole *n.* °outlet, °way out, means of °escape, °escape, °subterfuge, °pretext, °evasion, °quibble, *Colloq* °dodge: *They couldn't prosecute him because he found a loophole in the law.*

loose *adj.* **1** °unattached, unconnected, °disconnected, °detached, °free, unsecured, unfastened, °movable: *I have a loose tooth. The vacuum cleaner will pick up any loose bits.* **2** unconfined, untied, unfettered, released, freed, unshackled, unchained, °free, at °liberty, at °large, on the loose, untrammelled: *In Pamplona, they allow loose bulls to run through the streets to the arena.* **3** unconfining, free-flowing, flowing, baggy, °slack, hanging: *That skirt is loose on you since you lost weight.* **4** disordered, disorganized, unbound, untied, messy; strewn or °spread or tossed or thrown about or around, scattered (about or around), in °disorder, in disarray, dispersed: *On the desk was a loose pile of papers.* **5** °rambling, °disconnected, unstructured, unconnected, discontinuous, non-specific, unspecific, °indefinite, °imprecise, °inexact, °inaccurate, °free, °broad, °rough, °offhand, °casual, °careless, °untidy, °sloppy, slapdash, °general, °vague: *He gave a loose description of his assailant. A loose translation does not convey the flavour of the original.* **6** °lax, °relaxed, negligent, °careless, °sloppy: *Discipline has been quite loose around here lately.* **7** °wanton, °dissolute, debauched, °immoral, °promiscuous, °abandoned, °fast, °libertine, °profligate, licentious, °lewd, °perverted, °corrupt: *She was quickly gaining a reputation for being a loose woman.*
—*adv.* **8 break loose:** °escape, °flee: *The boy broke loose from my grasp and ran to greet his mother.* **9 hang** or **stay loose:** °relax, stay or keep °calm or °cool, °cool off or down, °sit back, take it °easy: *Hang loose and everything will be all right.* **10 let** or **set** or **turn loose:** °discharge, let go (with); °emit, °give out (with), °fire: *They let him loose after questioning. She let loose a stream of invective like a fishwife.*
—*v.* **11** let go, (set) °free, °release, let or set or turn loose; °liberate, °deliver: *Ten thousand balloons were loosed in the celebration.* **12** untie, °undo, unfasten, let go, °disengage, °relax, °ease, °loosen, slacken; cast off: *Loose these ropes, please.* **13** let go, let °fly, °fire, °discharge, °shoot, unleash, °deliver: *We loosed a devastating barrage at the enemy.*

loosen *v.* **1** °loose; °undo, unfasten, unhook, unbutton, unlace, untie, unbind, unbuckle; unscrew: *Quick! Loosen his collar!* **2** °weaken, °detach, °separate, °sever, °break or °cut (°apart): *The vibration has loosened the rivets.*

loot *n.* **1** °booty, spoils, °plunder, °prize, °haul, *Slang* swag, boodle: *They divided up the loot amongst the gang.*
—*v.* **2** °plunder, °sack, °ransack, °rob, °pillage, despoil, °raid, °ravage, maraud, *Rare* depredate: *The soldiers looted every house in the city.*

lop *v.* Often, **lop off:** °chop off, °trim, °top, °head, crop, °prune, °dock, °clip, °snip off, shear off, °cut off, °pare, °shorten, °hack off, amputate: *Lop the lower branches off close to the trunk.*

lopsided adj. **1** uneven, askew, °one-sided, awry, unsymmetric(al), asymmetric(al), unequal, °crooked, °unbalanced, °irregular, Colloq cock-eyed: *That lopsided bookcase is the sole product of Ed's cabinet-making class.* **2** uneven, unequal, °one-sided, °biased, °disproportionate, unfair, warped, twisted: *Four against two—I'd call that lopsided, wouldn't you?*

lord n. **1** °master, °monarch, ruler, °sovereign: *Harry considers himself lord of all he surveys.* **2** °noble, nobleman, °peer, aristocrat; earl, duke, °count, viscount, baron: *He was made a lord in recognition of his achievements.* **3 The** or **Our Lord**: God, the Almighty, God Almighty, the Creator, the Supreme Being, Christ, Jesus, Jehovah: *The Lord moves in mysterious ways his miracles to perform.*
—v. **lord it over**: domineer, °swagger, be °overbearing, Colloq °boss (around), act °big, pull °rank: *He lords it over everyone in the office.*

lore n. **1** folklore, °beliefs, °culture, °tradition(s), °mythology, °myths, mythos, ethos, teaching(s), °doctrine, °wisdom: *According to their lore, the American Indians go to the Happy Hunting Ground when they die.* **2** °knowledge, °learning, erudition: *He was acquainted with medical lore through his reading.*

lose v. **1** °mislay, misplace, °displace, °part with; suffer the °loss of, be °deprived of: *I lost my pen. He lost a leg in the war.* **2** °forfeit, °yield: *He says he lost the rent money gambling.* **3** °give up, °yield, °capitulate, °admit °defeat, °succumb, °bow to, be defeated or conquered, °suffer °defeat, be beaten or °overcome or worsted or bested, Colloq lose out: *It was a good game, but we lost.* **4** °waste, let °slip, squander, °dissipate, °fritter or °trifle away, °run out of; °consume, °use (up), °expend, °spend: *We lost a lot of time waiting for him to decide.* **5** °elude, °evade, °escape, °throw or °shake off, give the °slip: *I managed to lose the sinister-looking man who was shadowing me.*

loser n. also-ran, °misfit, °failure, °fiasco, non-starter, Colloq °flop, °dud, °washout, bummer, lead balloon, lemon, born loser, Brit damp squib, Brit and Australian no-hoper, US clinker, nebbish, schlemiel or schlemihl or shlemiel, schlimazel or shlimazel or shlimazl, schnook, sad sack: *Dick is a real loser and will never amount to anything. His idea for a company newsletter was a loser.*

loss n. **1** deprivation, bereavement, °privation, °denial, °sacrifice, forfeiture, disappearance: *We must be constantly vigilant to watch for any loss of our liberty.* **2** diminution, °erosion, reduction, impoverishment, depletion, shrinkage: *New policies are in place to stem the loss of parkland.* **3** °disadvantage, °detriment, °harm, °impairment, °injury, °damage: *I don't regard Wentworth's resignation as any great loss.* **4** °waste, wastage, wasting, squandering: *The loss of time was owing to a train delay.* **5** °defeat, °set-back, °disadvantage, °disappointment, °failure, °downfall, °collapse, °breakdown, °ruin; drubbing, trouncing: *His loss is my gain.* **6** Often, **losses**: debit(s), °liability (liabilities), negative cash flow: *The company wrote off the losses.* **7** Often, **losses**: °death, °dying, °passing, demise, °destruction, extermination, extinction, annihilation: *The loss from disease was overwhelming. What losses did they suffer in the battle?*

lost adj. **1** gone, departed, vanished, strayed; missing, mislaid, misplaced, irrecoverable: *They found my lost dog. The airline told me that my bag was lost.* **2** wasted, °misspent, gone by the board, squandered, down the °drain, °spent, °exhausted, Colloq out of the window: *The new arrangement is resulting in a lot of time lost. I watched another lost opportunity slip by.* **3** °confused, baffled, perplexed, puzzled, mystified, bewildered, confounded, adrift, °helpless, disoriented, at °sea, astray: *I am totally lost when it comes to high finance.* **4** forgotten, °bygone, °extinct, °past, °obsolete, vanished, buried: *Good writing needn't be a lost art.* **5** °dead, °extinct, departed, fallen, °late: *We held a memorial service for our lost comrades.* **6** destroyed, demolished, devastated, ruined, wrecked, irreparable, unsalvageable, irreclaimable, irremediable: *After the exposé in the newspaper, his name was consigned to the limbo of lost reputations.* **7** damned, cursed, accursed, °abandoned, °corrupt, fallen, °wanton, °unchaste, °dissolute: *Unrepentant sinners are lost souls.* **8** °hopeless, °distraught, distracted, °desperate, °frantic, frenzied: *He had the lost look of a cornered fugitive.*

lot n. **1** °collection, °batch, consignment, °assortment, °group, °portion, °set, °quantity, grouping, apportionment: *They are expecting a new lot of furniture this afternoon.* **2** °luck, °fortune, °destiny, °fate, kismet, °plight, °doom, °end: *It seems to be my lot to stay in the same place all my life.* **3** °lottery, °drawing, °raffle, drawing lots or straws: *The winner will be decided by lot.* **4** °share, °portion, °division, °interest, °part, °allotment, °assignment, apportionment, °ration, °allowance: *Marguerite was bequeathed the house, while my lot included the paintings.* **5 a lot** or **lots: a** a good or great °deal: *You have a lot of nerve! I'd give a lot to be able to paint like you. He got into a lot of trouble.* **b** much, loads or a °load, mountains or a °mountain, tons or a ton, barrels or a barrel, stacks or a °stack, °piles or a °pile, heaps or a °heap, masses or a °mass, °oceans, Colloq oodles, scads, US gobs: *She has lots of money.* **c** °many, myriad, numerous, countless, reams, °infinite or an infinity, quantities or a °quantity, °enormous numbers or an °enormous °number, Colloq oodles, scads, °loads, tons, °masses: *There are lots of fish in the sea.* **6 the lot**: °everything, Colloq the whole kit and caboodle, all: *I'll give you a fiver for the lot.*

lotion n. cream, liniment, balm, °salve, °ointment, embrocation, unguent, pomade: *The doctor said to rub in some of this lotion twice a day.*

lottery n. °raffle, sweepstake, drawing, °pool, Brit tombola: *I've never known anyone who won anything in the national lottery.*

loud adj. **1** deafening, ear-splitting, booming, blaring, stentorian, thundering, °thunderous, sonorous, °noisy, clamorous, °piercing, fortissimo: *The hi-fi is so loud I can't hear myself think. A loud crash came from the kitchen.* **2** °tawdry, °garish, °flashy, °gaudy, °tasteless, °extravagant, °showy, °ostentatious, Colloq splashy, snazzy, jazzy: *He was wearing a check suit and the loudest shirt and tie I had ever seen.*

lounge v. **1** °idle, °loaf, laze, loll, languish, vegetate: *After dinner, we lounged till midnight, sipping port.*
—n. **2** sitting-room, salon, front room, °parlour: *Mother insisted that we entertain visitors in the*

lounge. **3** °lobby, foyer, waiting-room, °reception (room), vestibule: *I was waiting in the lounge when the doctor returned.* **4** cocktail lounge, (lounge *or* saloon) °bar: *We went into the lounge and ordered a drink.* **5** sofa, °couch, divan, studio °couch, day-bed, settee, settle, love-seat, *chaise longue;* causeuse, tête-à-tête; *US and Canadian* Davenport: *The psychoanalyst has a lounge on which you lie while talking to him.*

lour *v.* **1** lower, darken, °threaten, °menace, °loom: *The clouds loured: she suddenly began to feel afraid.* **2** lower, °frown, °scowl, glower; °sulk, °pout, mope: *He said nothing, but loured at me from beneath his beetled brow.*

lousy *adj.* **1** °awful, °terrible, °mean, °contemptible, °low, °base, °hateful, detestable, °despicable, °vile, °wretched, °miserable, °scurvy, °dirty, °vicious, *Colloq* °rotten: *Telling tales to the teacher was a lousy thing to do.* **2** °bad, °poor, °awful, °terrible, °inferior; low-quality, °shoddy, °shabby, °miserable, second-rate, °wretched: *We had lousy seats for the theatre last week. The dealer seems to have sold you a really lousy car.* **3** pedicular, pediculous, *Brit* lice-infested, lice-ridden, *US* louse-infested, louse-ridden: *Even lice are lousy—they have their own parasites.* **4 lousy with**: °alive with, overloaded with, swarming with, teeming with, *Colloq* crawling with, knee-deep in: *In five minutes the place was lousy with cops.*

lovable *adj.* loveable, °adorable, °darling, °dear, cherished, °likeable, °attractive, °engaging, °cute, °fetching, °taking, alluring, °endearing, appealing, winsome, °sweet, °tender, cuddly, °affectionate, charming, °enchanting: *She has the most lovable little baby boy.*

love *n.* **1** °warmth, °affection, °attachment, fondness, tenderness, °devotion, °attraction, °friendship, amity, °regard, °admiration, °fancy, adoration, adulation, °ardour, °passion, °fervour, °rapture, infatuation: *Her love for him grew over the years.* **2** °liking, °delight, °enjoyment, °pleasure, fondness, °attraction, predilection, °bent, °leaning, proclivity, °inclination, °disposition, °weakness, °partiality, °preference, °taste, °relish, °passion: *In his retirement, Charles has developed a love for golf.* **3** °darling, °beloved, °sweetheart, sweetie, °sweet, honey, °dear one, dearest, angel, turtle-dove, true-love, light of one's life, °lover, °paramour, °mate, intended, betrothed; girl-friend, inamorata, lady-love, young lady, fian-cée; boyfriend, beau, inamorato, °suitor, swain, young man, fiancé, *Archaic* leman, tally, *US* POSSLQ (= 'Person of the Opposite Sex Sharing Living Quarters'), *Colloq* girl, woman, guy, man: *Let me tell you something, my love. Come live with me and be my love.* **4** °sympathy, tenderness, °concern, °charity, °care, °solicitude, °affinity, °rapport, °harmony, °brotherhood, sisterhood, fellow-feeling: *He has great love for his fellow human beings.* **5 love affair: a** amour, °liaison, °affair, °romance, °relationship, *affaire de cœur,* °intrigue: *He's been having a love affair with his secretary.*
b °passion, °mania, *Colloq* °thing: *George allows nothing to interfere with his love affair with tennis.* **6 make love (to)** *or* **(with)**: °embrace, °cuddle, °caress, °fondle, have °sexual °intercourse, *Archaic* take, know, *Colloq* neck, °pet, canoodle, °romance, have °sex, make the

beast with two backs, *US and Canadian* make out; *Taboo slang* °screw, fuck, hump, bang, *Brit* roger, bonk: *He still makes love to his wife even though they are both in their eighties.*
—*v.* **7** °cherish, °admire, °adore, be in love with, lose one's heart to, °worship, °idolize, °dote on, °treasure, be °infatuated with, think the world of, adulate, hold °dear, °like, *Colloq* be hung up on, be °crazy *or* nuts *or* °wild *or* °mad about, have a crush on: *Only after ten years of friendship did she discover that she loved him.* **8** °delight in, take °pleasure in, derive °pleasure *or* °enjoyment from, °relish, be °partial to, have a °passion *or* °preference *or* °taste for, be attracted to, be captivated by, be °fond of, °like, °enjoy, °appreciate, value, *Colloq* get a kick from *or* out of, be °wild about, be thrilled by, *US* get a bang *or* charge from *or* out of: *She loves chocolates. I just love your new dress! Love me, love my dog.*

love-letter *n.* billet-doux, *Archaic* mash °note: *She saved all his love letters.*

lovely *adj.* **1** good-looking, °pretty, °handsome, °attractive, °comely, °fair, °fetching, °engaging, captivating, alluring, enticing, bewitching, °ravishing, °gorgeous, °beautiful, beauteous, pulchritudinous: *Larry has two lovely daughters. The house has a lovely view of Lake Windermere.* **2** °satisfying, °satisfactory, °agreeable, enjoyable, gratifying, °nice, °pleasing, °pleasant, °pleasurable, °engaging, °delightful: *What a lovely way to spend an evening!*

lover *n.* See love, 3, above.

low[1] *adj.* **1** °short, squat, °little, °small, stubby, stumpy, °stunted; low-lying: *The terrain has many low shrubs, not more than two feet tall.* **2** °inadequate, °insufficient, °deficient, down, °short, °sparse, °scanty, scant, °limited: *The air in the tyres is a bit low. Our water supply ran low.* **3** °coarse, °unrefined, indelicate, °improper, °naughty, °risqué, °indecent, °unseemly, °vulgar, °crude, °common, °rude, °offensive, °gross, ill-bred, °lewd, °obscene, rib-ald, °bawdy, °scurrilous, smutty, °pornographic, °dirty: *The old burlesque acts were characterized by their low humour.* **4** °weak, °frail, °feeble, debili-tated, enervated, °sickly, °unhealthy, °infirm, °shaky, °decrepit, °ill, °sick: *He's very low and sinking fast.* **5** °ineffectual, °ineffective, °weak: *Her resistance to disease is low. I have a low pain threshold.* **6** °miserable, °dismal, °wretched, °abysmal, °sorry, abject, °destitute: *I seem to have reached a low point in my career.* **7** °humble, °poor, low-born, °lowly, °base, °inferior, base-born, °plebeian, proletariat, ignoble: *He rose from those low beginnings to a peerage.* **8** °unhappy, depressed, °dejected, °sad, °gloomy, °melancholy, °miserable, °despondent, disconsolate, °blue, downcast, down, °glum, °wretched, morose, crestfallen, °broken-hearted, heartbroken, °tearful, lachry-mose, °sorrowful, °mournful, heavy-hearted: *I felt low for weeks after the death of my kitten.* **9** °inferior, second-rate, °poor, °bad, not up to °par, °worthless, °shoddy, °shabby, °mediocre, substandard: *Their products are of low quality.* **10** °inferior, °lower, lesser, °small, smaller: *Play a low card.* **11** low-cut, décolleté, revealing, *Colloq US* low and behold in the front and vie de Bohème in the back: *Gilda wore a low, strapless black satin evening gown.* **12** °base, °vile, abject, °contemptible, °despicable, °mean,

°menial, °servile, ignoble, degraded, °vulgar, °foul, dastardly, depraved, °nasty, °sordid: *That was a low trick he played telling on his friends. I didn't know that anyone could sink to such a low level.* **13** °quiet, hushed, °soft, °subdued, °gentle, muted, muffled, stifled, °indistinct, whispered, murmured, murmurous: *Her low voice was sweet.* **14** unfavourable, °critical, adverse: *She has a rather low opinion of his singing.*

low[2] v. moo, °bellow; °bawl: *The lowing herd moved slowly into the pasture.*

low-down n. °information, °intelligence, °data, the °facts, °inside story, *Colloq* info, °dope, °dirt, *Brit* bumf: *I have the low-down on the scandal.*

lower[1] v. **1** °drop, °reduce, °decrease, °mark down, °discount, lessen, °diminish, °downgrade, °cut, °slash: *Prices on all goods have been lowered.* **2** °let or °move or °bring or °put down, °drop: *The drawbridge was lowered and the knights rode across. They lowered the coffin into the grave.* **3** °cut or °lop off, °cut or °take down, °reduce, °diminish, crop, °trim: *We lowered the hedge by a foot.* **4** abase, °debase, °degrade, °discredit, °shame, °disgrace, demean, °belittle, °humble, °humiliate, °stoop, °deign, °condescend: *I wouldn't lower myself to so much as speak to him.* **5** °turn down, °quieten, °moderate, °modulate, °soften, °tone down: *He lowered his voice to a whisper.*
—adj. **6** °further or farther down: *My mother has a flat on a lower floor of the building.* **7** earlier: *These primitive amphibians are from the Lower Carboniferous.* **8 lower case**: °small, minuscule: *Use capitals for the first letters and lower case for the rest in these names.*

lower[2] v. See lour, above.

lowly adj. See low[1], 7, above.

loyal adj. °faithful, °true, dependable, °devoted, °trustworthy, trusty, °steady, °steadfast, °staunch, trusted, °reliable, °stable, unswerving, unwavering, dedicated, °constant, °patriotic: *Give me twelve men loyal and true and we shall rout the enemy.*

loyalty n. faithfulness, fidelity, dependability, devotedness, °devotion, allegiance, patriotism, trustworthiness, steadfastness, staunchness, firmness, °resolution, °resolve, reliability, °stability, °dedication, constancy: *I hope that we can rely on the loyalty of everyone in your unit, Colonel.*

luck n. **1** °fortune, °chance, °destiny, °fate, °accident, fortuity, serendipity; °fluke, stroke of luck, *US* happenstance: *Luck brought us together.* **2** good °fortune, (good) °break: *It takes a lot of luck to get the kinds of roles you want as an actor.* **3** °chance(s), °success rate, °fortune(s): *I hope that my luck improves soon.*

lucky adj. **1** °fortunate, blessed, °favoured, °charmed: *She was very lucky to get the job.* **2** °providential, °timely, °opportune, °propitious, °favourable, auspicious, °advantageous, °convenient, fortuitous: *It was lucky that you were at the swimming pool to save her.*

ludicrous adj. °ridiculous, laughable, °absurd, °farcical, °nonsensical, °preposterous, °incongruous, asinine, °foolish, °silly, °zany, °crazy, comical, risible; °funny, facetious, droll, waggish, jocular, jocose: *The explanations*

of the new tax laws have been carried to ludicrous extremes. You can count on Billy to come up with some ludicrous prank on All Fools' Day.

lug v. °drag, °tug, °tow, °haul, °heave; °carry, tote, °transport: *You're mistaken if you think I'm going to lug that case round everywhere.*

luggage n. baggage, °bags, °gear, impedimenta, °paraphernalia, °things, °belongings: *When I arrived in Torremolinos, I found my luggage was missing.*

lukewarm adj. **1** °tepid, room temperature, °warm: *I like my bath-water lukewarm.* **2** °cool, °indifferent, °half-hearted, °chill, °chilly, °phlegmatic, unresponsive, °unenthusiastic, °nonchalant, °lackadaisical, apathetic, insouciant, Laodicean, °unmoved, *US* half-baked, *Colloq* laid-back: *My ideas for improving efficiency continued to receive a lukewarm reception from the board.*

lull n. **1** °pause, °respite, °interlude, °intermission, °interval, °break, hiatus, °interruption, °stop, °halt, °lapse, °delay, *Literary* caesura, *Colloq* °let-up: *After a brief lull, the hurricane resumed in all its ferocity.* **2** °quiet, quiescence, °hush, °calm, calmness, stillness, °silence, °peace, peacefulness, tranquillity: *There was a lull, then the noise of the artillery again shattered the night.*
—v. **3** soothe, °calm, °quiet, °hush, pacify, mollify, °tranquillize: *Do not let her sweet words lull you into a sense of false security. I was lulled to sleep by the crickets and the bees.*

lumber n. **1** °odds and ends, °junk, °clutter, °jumble, °rejects, white elephants; °rubbish, °litter, *Chiefly US* °trash: *The small room off the kitchen is for lumber.* **2** °timber, wood, °beams, °planks, °boards: *I have ordered the lumber for building the garage.*
—v. **3** °encumber, °burden, °load, °overload, saddle, °impose upon, land: *We have been lumbered with looking after our neighbours' six cats.*

luminous adj. **1** °shiny, shining, °bright, °brilliant, lighted (up), lit (up), illuminated, °radiant, alight, resplendent, °lustrous, gleaming, shimmering, glistening, sparkling, °dazzling, refulgent, effulgent: *The moon shone with a luminous beauty.* **2** °glowing, aglow, luminescent, °incandescent, phosphorescent, fluorescent: *He had a watch with luminous hands.* **3** °clear, lucid, perspicuous, percipient, perspicacious, °penetrating, discerning, °perceptive, clear-eyed, clear-headed, °keen, °acute, °sharp, °explicit, °incisive, °specific, °express; understandable, °intelligible: *His latest novel provides another example of his luminous style.*

lump[1] n. **1** °mass, °piece, °gob, gobbet, °clod, chunk, clot, °wad, °clump, hunk, nugget; cube, °wedge, °cake: *There was a lump of earth clogging the drain. May I have two lumps of sugar, please?* **2** °bump, °growth, °swelling, protuberance, °protrusion, °prominence, °bulge, excrescence, tumescence, nodule, °knob; wen, cyst, °boil, carbuncle, blister, wart, corn: *You ought to see a doctor about that lump on your foot.*
—v. **3** Often, **lump together**: °combine, °join, consolidate, °collect, °bunch, °group, °unite, °mass, aggregate, °blend, °mix, °throw or °put together: *Don't lump me together with everyone else, without even asking my opinion.*

lump[2] v. Usually, **lump it**: °allow, °tolerate, °suffer, °put up with, °bear, °stand, °brook, °endure: *I'm afraid you'll just have to lump it, whether you like it or not.*

lumpy adj. chunky, °bumpy, uneven, °granular, grainy: *Mix the batter till it is no longer lumpy.*

lunacy n. **1** °madness, °insanity, dementia, craziness, derangement, psychosis, °mania: *Formerly, it was believed that lunacy fluctuated in accordance with the phases of the moon.* **2** °folly, foolishness, bad or poor °judgement, illogicality, illogic, senselessness, ridiculousness, irrationality, foolhardiness, °stupidity: *It would be sheer lunacy to confess to something you did not do.*

lunge n. **1** °thrust, °jab, °strike: *He was impaled by the first lunge of the sword.* **2** °dive, °plunge, °rush, °leap, °jump, °spring, °pounce: *I made a lunge for the knife but missed.*
—v. **3** °dive, °plunge, °charge, °pounce, °dash, °bound, °jump; °thrust, °stab, °strike, °hit, °jab, °cut: *He lunged at her with his machete.*

lurch[1] n. **leave in the lurch**: °desert, °abandon, °forsake; °drop, °jilt: *He left her in the lurch, waiting at the church.*

lurch[2] n. **1** °stagger, °sway, °pitch; °list, °tilt, °toss: *The man gave a sudden lurch, knocking the vase from my hands.*
—v. **2** °stagger, °sway, °stumble; °roll, °tilt, veer, °pitch, °list, °heel, °wallow: *He lurched into the room, a dagger protruding from his back. The ship lurched dangerously in a heavy sea.*

lure v. **1** °tempt, °attract, °induce, °coax, inveigle, °seduce, °draw in, °entice, °lead on, °decoy, °charm, °persuade, allure, catch: *She lured me into the trap of believing that she loved me.*
—n. **2** bait, °decoy, °attraction, °temptation, °inducement, magnet, °siren song, °charm, *US* drawing card, *Slang* °come-on: *Too many naïve people fall for the lure of easy money.*

lurid adj. **1** °sensational, °vivid, °shocking, °startling, °graphic, °melodramatic: *The tabloids delight in a lurid scandal.* **2** °ghastly, horrid, horrifying, horrendous, °gory, °grisly, °gruesome, °macabre, °revolting, °disgusting, appalling, °frightful, °terrible, °awful: *Every lurid detail of the massacre was shown on TV.* **3** °pale, ashen, sallow, °wan, pallid, °ghastly, baleful: *From the lurid shade of his skin, I could see he had some horrible affliction.* **4** °glaring, °fiery, °flaming, °burning, aglow, °glowing, glowering: *The burning city cast a lurid light in the sky.*

lurk v. skulk, °slink, °prowl, °steal, °sneak, °hide, (°lie in) wait, °lie low: *The muggers were lurking in the shadows, waiting for a victim.*

luscious adj. delectable, °delicious, mouth-watering, °tasty, toothsome, °savoury, appetizing, °rich, °sweet, °epicurean, ambrosial, palatable, °pleasant; °succulent, °juicy, *Colloq* scrumptious, °yummy: *My grandmother used to make the most luscious pies and tarts.*

lush adj. **1** °luxuriant, °thick, °lavish, °flourishing, verdant, °green, °dense, °overgrown, °exuberant: *The walls were covered with a lush growth of ivy.* **2** °juicy, °succulent, mouth-watering, °fresh, °moist, °ripe: *We ate lush pears that we picked straight from the tree.* **3** °palatial, °extravagant, °elaborate, °luxurious, °opulent, °sumptuous, *Colloq* ritzy, °plush: *The bridal suite is the lushest accommodation they offer.*

lust n. **1** sensuality, libido, libidinousness, sexuality, lustfulness, concupiscence, °sexual °appetite, *Slang* horniness: *The nouveaux riches spend much of their time and money satisfying their lust.* **2** °desire, °drive, °energy, voracity, avidity, avidness, °ambition, ravenousness: *Henry has an infectious enthusiasm and lust for life.*
—v. **3 lust after**: °desire, crave, °hunger or °thirst or °hanker for or after, °ache for: *Barney was lusting after the barmaid at The Two Magpies.*

lustful adj. libidinous, °carnal, concupiscent, licentious, °lewd, °prurient, °lascivious, salacious, *Colloq* horny, °randy: *On her way to work she was forced to endure daily the lustful calls of the construction workers.*

lustre n. **1** °sheen, °gleam, °glow, °gloss, luminosity, luminousness, °radiance: *A good waxing should restore the lustre to the table.* **2** °glory, °renown, °brilliance, °celebrity, °honour, °distinction, °fame, illustriousness: *Winning first prize lent a little lustre to his tarnished reputation.*

lustrous adj. °glossy, °shiny, shined, °polished, burnished: *French polishing gives the furniture a lustrous finish.*

lusty adj. **1** °vigorous, °healthy, °strong, °energetic, °robust, °hale and °hearty, °lively; °buxom: *The sailors were accompanied by a couple of lusty young women.* **2** °vigorous, °substantial, °strong, °husky, °powerful: *He sang in a lusty voice.*

luxuriant adj. **1** °abundant, °profuse, copious, °lush, °rich, bounteous, overflowing, full, °luxurious: *Her luxuriant hair hung down to her waist.* **2** °lavish, full, °rank, °prolific, thriving, rife, °exuberant, °lush, abounding, plenteous, °abundant, superabundant, °dense, °fruitful, teeming: *The luxuriant orange groves are yielding a bumper crop this year.* **3** °ornate, °elaborate, decorated, °fancy, rococo, baroque, °flowery, frilly, florid, overdone, °flamboyant, °showy, °ostentatious, °gaudy, °garish, *Colloq* °flashy: *The elders disapproved of the luxuriant ornamentation of the churches.*

luxuriate v. **1** Often, **luxuriate in**: °wallow in, swim in, bask in, °indulge in, °delight in, °relish, °revel in, °enjoy oneself, °savour, °appreciate, °like, °love: *She luxuriates in her new-found wealth.* **2** live in °luxury or °comfort, be in the lap of °luxury, have a good or great or marvellous time, take it °easy, °enjoy oneself, live the life of Riley, live off the °fat of the land, *Colloq* have the time of one's life, have a ball, *US* live high off the hog: *Their postcard says that they are luxuriating on Capri for a week.*

luxurious adj. **1** °opulent, °sumptuous, °grand, °extravagant, °lavish, °magnificent, °splendid, de luxe, °fancy, °epicurean, °gourmet; *Colloq* °swanky, swank, ritzy, °plush, °posh: *We had a luxurious room overlooking the sea and ate the most luxurious meals.* **2** °self-indulgent, °voluptuous, voluptuary, sybaritic, hedonistic, pampered: *We lived a truly luxurious life for two years till the money ran out.*

luxury n. **1** opulence, °splendour, sumptuousness, °grandeur, °extravagance, magnificence, richness, luxuriousness: *I cannot describe the overwhelming luxury of the maharaja's palace.* **2** °indulgence, self-indulgence, hedonism, sybaritism, voluptuousness: *He had been living* a life of luxury in Tahiti. **3** °security, °confidence; °gratification, °satisfaction, °enjoyment, °pleasure, °delight, °comfort: *He has the luxury of knowing that his dog will be well looked after.* **4** °frill, °extravagance, °extra, °indulgence, °non-essential, °expendable, °treat: *He showered her with luxuries from the finest shops.*

lying *n.* **1** prevarication, fibbing, mendacity, mendaciousness, falsification, untruthfulness, °perjury; dishonesty, °deceit, duplicity: *She was accused of lying while under oath.*
—*adj.* **2** untruthful, °false, mendacious, °hypocritical, °dishonest, °deceitful, °deceptive, duplicitous, treacherous, °perfidious: *Whoever told you they had found the solution is a lying scoundrel.*

lyric *adj.* **1** melodic, song-like, °musical, °melodious, °lyrical: *Lyric drama is no longer fashionable.* **2** °personal, °subjective, °individual, idiosyncratic; °sentimental, °rhapsodic: *He expresses his own feelings in the lyric poems.* **3** °sweet, dulcet, °graceful, silvery, lilting, mellifluous, °mellow, °light: *This song sounds best when sung by a lyric tenor.*
—*n.* **4 lyrics**: libretto, °book, °words: *Ira Gershwin wrote the lyrics for much of George Gershwin's music.*

lyrical *adj.* **1** See **lyric**, 1, above. **2** °enthusiastic, °ecstatic, encomiastic, °rapturous, °rhapsodic, °effusive, °impassioned, °emotional, °ebullient, °exuberant, panegyrical: *He waxed lyrical whenever he spoke of his children.*

M

macabre *adj.* °grim, °ghastly, °grisly, °gory, °gruesome, °grotesque, °ghoulish, °fiendish, °dread, °eerie, °fearsome, °frightful, °frightening, °terrifying, °terrible, °dreadful, dire, °morbid; deathly, °deadly, deathlike, °ghostly, cadaverous: *He told a macabre story of how they survived by resorting to cannibalism. The crypt had a macabre eeriness about it.*

Machiavellian *adj.* °deceitful, cunning, °shrewd, °crafty, °wily, °foxy, °scheming, °tricky, °perfidious, nefarious, treacherous, °sneaky: *Mr Williams has concocted a truly Machiavellian plan for getting the pensioners to move out.*

machination *n.* plotting, °scheming, intriguing, manoeuvring, °designing, manipulating; °plot, °scheme, °intrigue, °manoeuvre, °design, °stratagem, °ruse, °trick, °trickery, °artifice, °dirty °trick(s), °wile, manipulation, ploy, °tactic(s), °move, gambit: *He escaped from the machinations of his enemies. Must you resort to such machinations merely to get them to listen?*

machine *n.* **1** °mechanism, °device, °apparatus, contrivance, appliance, °instrument, °implement, °tool, utensil, °gadget, *Colloq* °contraption, *US* gismo or gizmo: *What kind of machine is used to make a corkscrew?* **2** °engine, motor, prime mover, °vehicle; °car, automobile, motor °car, *US* auto: *We used to get into the machine and go for Sunday picnics.* **3** °organization, °system, °ring, °gang, °cabal, °clique, °party, °faction: *The entire council is run by a political machine.*
—*v.* **4** °shape, °make, °manufacture: *In this department we machine the castings to a tolerance of one ten-thousandth of an inch.*

machismo *n.* masculine °pride or °arrogance, manliness, virility, masculinity, °grit, *Colloq* guts, *Slang* balls: *He is just trying to impress you with his machismo.*

macho *adj.* °manly, masculine, virile, °proud, °arrogant: *He's afraid his macho image will be destroyed if he admits to enjoying ballet.*

mad *adj.* **1** °insane, °deranged, °crazy, crazed, demented, lunatic, unhinged, °delirious, out of one's °mind, °psychotic, °maniacal, (mentally) °unbalanced, mentally °ill, of °unsound °mind, *non compos mentis, Chiefly Brit* °daft, *Colloq* out of one's head, touched (in the head), screwy, cuckoo, °mental, certifiable, having a screw loose, dotty, cracked, mad as a March hare, mad as a hatter, not all there, off-the-wall, stark °raving mad, *Chiefly Brit* potty, *US* nutty as a fruit cake; *Slang* nuts, loony, goofy, loopy, crackers, batty, off one's rocker or trolley, bananas, *Brit* round the bend or twist, twisted, off one's chump, barmy or balmy, bonkers, *US* out to lunch, bughouse, bugs, °crazy as a bedbug or a coot, loco, wacky, out of one's tree, meshuga: *You're mad if you think I'm going in there with that lion.* **2** °foolish, °silly, °childish, °immature, °puerile, °wild, °nonsensical, °foolhardy, madcap, °heedless, °senseless, °absurd, °imprudent, unwise, °indiscreet, °rash, °ill-advised, ill-considered, °reckless, °extravagant, irrational, fatuous: *I did many mad things when I was a student. Hitching to Inverness is a mad idea.* **3** °wild, °ferocious;

°rabid: *Have they caught that mad dog yet?* **4** °furious, °angry, infuriated, incensed, enraged, irate, fuming, °berserk, irritated, provoked, wrathful, exasperated, *Literary* wroth: *Will you get mad if I ask you a question? Please don't be mad with me—I wrecked your car.* **5** **like mad**: °madly, feverishly, in a °frenzy, frenziedly, desperately, excitedly, violently, wildly, hysterically, furiously; enthusiastically, fervently, ardently; *Colloq* like °crazy: *He's been running about like mad trying to find her.* **6** **mad (about** or **for)**: °crazy, °infatuated, °ardent, °enthusiastic, °eager, avid, zealous, °passionate, °fervent, fervid, °keen, °fanatical, °wild, *Colloq* hooked, *Brit* dotty, *Slang* nuts: *She's absolutely mad about cricket.*

madden *v.* **1** °infuriate, °anger, °enrage, incense, °provoke, °inflame, °excite (someone) to (a) °frenzy or °rage, make (someone's) blood °boil, raise (someone's) hackles, make (someone) see red, get (someone's) back up, drive (someone) °crazy, *Literary* raise (someone's) ire, *Colloq* drive (someone) up the °wall, *Brit* drive (someone) round the bend or twist, *US* tick (someone) off, burn (someone) up, tee (someone) off, °bug: *Their getting away with something like that maddened us all.* **2** °irk, vex, pique, °exasperate, °irritate: *He has the maddening habit of affecting a lisp.* **3** bait, badger, °torment, °plague, bedevil, *US* rile, hassle: *The dog was maddened into attacking anything that moved.*

madly *adv.* **1** insanely, hysterically, dementedly, wildly, distractedly, frenziedly: *The patient keeps screaming madly, day and night.* **2** foolishly, stupidly, inanely, ridiculously, ludicrously, idiotically, absurdly, irrationally, senselessly: *The king madly spurned the proffered aid and was soundly defeated.* **3** furiously, wildly, ferociously, °fiercely, energetically, desperately, like °mad, vehemently, feverishly, excitedly, fanatically, violently, impetuously: *He dashed about madly trying to get help.* **4** excessively, °extremely, desperately, intensely, passionately, wildly, ardently, fervently, fervidly, °exceedingly: *She was madly in love with George.*

madman *n.* madwoman; lunatic, psychopath, °psychotic, °maniac, *Colloq* crackpot, psycho, loony, screwball, *US* kook, *Slang* nut, nutcase, *Brit* nutter: *I am working like a madman to finish the book by the deadline.*

madness *n.* **1** °insanity, °lunacy, °mania, dementia, psychosis, °mental °illness: *That form of madness is called schizophrenia.* **2** craziness, °lunacy, °folly, foolishness, °nonsense, senselessness, ridiculousness, pointlessness, illogicality, illogic, illogicalness, impracticality, preposterousness, futility: *He soon realized the madness of trying to stem the tide of public opinion.*

magazine *n.* **1** °periodical, °journal, °publication: *We publish a quarterly magazine about language.* **2** arsenal, ammunition or munitions dump, armoury: *Saboteurs infiltrated the camp and blew up the magazine.*

magic *n.* **1** witchcraft, °sorcery, wizardry, °black magic, necromancy, °black °art, voodoo, obeahism, °devilry or deviltry, diabolism, demonolatry, occultism; sortilege, theurgy, white

magic; °spell: *As the magic began to work, he slowly changed into a horrible ghoul.* **2** legerdemain, conjuring, prestidigitation, sleight of hand, °illusion, °hocus-pocus, °trickery: *He performs tricks of magic, including sawing a woman in half.* **3** °enchantment, allure, allurement, °charm, bewitchment, °spell, witchery, witchcraft, wizardry, °glamour, °fascination, °magnetism, ensorcellment: *She worked her magic on every man she met.*
—*adj.* **4** magical, °miraculous: *The magic ointment made her young again.* **5** necromantic, °occult, mystic, shamanistic, theurgical: *Using a magic spell, she turned him into a toad.* **6** magical, °enchanting, entrancing, bewitching, fascinating, hypnotic, mesmerizing, °spellbinding, charming, °magnetic, ensorcelling: *The music had a magic effect on them.*

magician *n.* **1** conjuror *or* conjurer, illusionist, wizard, °sorcerer, sorceress, magus, necromancer, enchanter, enchantress, Merlin, Houdini, Circe, °witch, warlock; thaumaturge, theurgist: *The court magician changed the pebbles into precious stones by a wave of his wand.*
2 °marvel, miracle-worker, °virtuoso, wizard, °genius, °master, *Colloq* whiz: *Mary Lou Williams is a magician on the boogie-woogie piano.*

magnetic *adj.* °attractive, attracting, °engaging, captivating, °enthralling, °seductive, alluring, entrancing, bewitching, beguiling, °arresting, °spellbinding, °irresistible, charismatic, °winning, winsome, °inviting: *Because of Amy's magnetic personality, men flock about her.*

magnetism *n.* °attraction, °draw, °appeal, allure, °magic, °lure, attractiveness, °charm, °pull, seductiveness, irresistibility, °drawing °power, charisma, *duende*, likeableness, °sex °appeal: *JFK's personal magnetism won him millions of votes.*

magnification *n.* enlargement, amplification; build-up, strengthening, enhancement, aggrandizement, raising, °elevation, °increase, °expansion, heightening, glorification, ennoblement: *The microdot can be read only at a magnification of X260. The advertising agency worked on the magnification of the candidate's record of achievement.*

magnificent *adj.* °great, °excellent, °splendid, °superior, °superb, °marvellous, °glorious, °grand, °fine, °impressive, °imposing, awe-inspiring, °brilliant, commanding, august, °noble, °majestic, °regal, °distinguished, °elegant, °exalted, °sublime, °outstanding; °sumptuous, °resplendent, °opulent, °rich, °luxurious, °lavish: *She lives in a magnificent country house.*

magnify *v.* **1** °enlarge, °expand, °amplify, °inflate, °increase, augment, °exaggerate, °heighten, °build up, °boost, °dramatize, °aggravate, °worsen, exacerbate; °overstate, *Colloq* °blow up, make a mountain out of a molehill: *Tiny errors in the beginning are magnified later on. I fear that he has magnified its importance out of all proportion.* **2** °enlarge, °blow up: *They had to magnify the photograph to read the registration number of the stolen car.*

magnitude *n.* **1** greatness, °size, °extent, bigness, immensity, °enormousness, dimensions: *You cannot imagine the magnitude of the unemployment problem in our area.* **2** °importance, °significance, consequence, °note: *This is a matter of sufficient magnitude to warrant a board meeting.*

maid *n.* **1** °girl, °maiden, °lass, °miss, nymphet, nymph, wench, damsel, mademoiselle, demoiselle, *Scots* lassie; virgin, *virgo intacta*: *A lovely young maid was milking the cow.* **2** housemaid, maidservant, °domestic, chambermaid, lady's maid, *Archaic or literary* abigail, *Brit* daily, *Archaic colloq Brit* tweeny: *When she rang, the maid brought in the tea.* **3 old maid**: spinster, bachelor girl: *She never married and now is an old maid.*

maiden *n.* **1** See maid, 1, above.
—*adj.* **2** virgin, virginal, undefiled, °intact, °chaste, (*virgo*) *intacta*: °unmarried, unwed: *His maiden aunt was visiting for the weekend.* **3** inaugural, °first, °initial, *Colloq US* shakedown: *The Titanic sank on her maiden voyage.*

mail *n.* **1** °post, correspondence; °letters: *Has the mail arrived?*
—*v.* **2** °post, °send, °dispatch *or* despatch: *Please mail this letter tonight.*

maim *v.* °cripple, °mutilate, °lame, disable, °incapacitate, °wound, wing, °impair, hamstring, put out of action *or* commission; °injure, °harm, °damage: *Their daughter was badly maimed in the fire.*

main *adj.* **1** °chief, °primary, °prime, (most) °important, °principal, °cardinal, °paramount, °first, °foremost, °leading, °pre-eminent, °predominant, predominating, °dominant, ranking, °major; °outstanding: *The main cause of traffic deaths is drunken driving. In Britain, the main street of a town is called 'the High Street'. We arrived late and missed the main entertainment.* **2** largest, biggest, greatest, strongest: *The main part of the strike force landed in Normandy.* **3** °necessary, °essential, °basic, °particular, °fundamental, °critical, °crucial, °vital: *Economic recovery is the main thrust of our programme for reform.* **4** °sheer, °brute, utter, °pure, °out-and-out, °absolute, °mere, °plain: *He lifted that block by main force!*
—*n.* **5** °pipe, duct, °channel, °line, °pipeline, water *or* gas main, *Brit* (electric) °cable, mains, power (°supply), conduit: *Water reaches the city through a huge underground main.* **6** °strength, °power, °might, °effort, °energy, °vigour: *With all his might and main he tried to move the stone blocking the cave.* **7 in the main**: See mainly, below.

mainly *adv.* in the °main, °chiefly, °principally, predominantly, °generally, above all, on the °whole, in °general, mostly, most of all, effectively, essentially, at °bottom, °first and °foremost, for the most part, °largely, by and °large, °primarily, as a °rule, °usually, all in all, on °balance, for all practical purposes, in the long °run: *We are concerned mainly with safety. The tourists are mainly from Italy.*

mainstay *n.* °main *or* °chief *or* °principal °support, °anchor (to windward), sheet °anchor, °bulwark, °buttress, linchpin, °main *or* greatest °strength: *David remains the mainstay of the sales force.*

maintain *v.* **1** °continue, °preserve, °persevere in, °keep going, °persist in, °keep (up), °carry on, °retain, °perpetuate, °prolong, °sustain, °uphold: *Sarah maintained friendly relations with her ex-husband. Try to maintain your composure.* **2** °look after, take °care of, °care for, °preserve, (°keep in) °service, °keep up, °keep in °repair; nurture, °support: *It is expensive to maintain a vintage car. Allison maintains an ancient aunt* *in Piddlington.* **3** °hold, °state, °say, °declare, °claim, assert, °allege, °testify, contend, aver, avow, °announce, °proclaim, °vouchsafe, °profess, °insist (on), affirm: *Despite evidence to the contrary, he maintains that he is innocent.* **4** °defend, °stand by, °keep, °fight for; take up the cudgels for, make a case for, °advocate, °champion, take *or* make a °stand for, °plead for, back (up), °support, °vindicate, °justify, *Colloq* go to bat for: *He maintained his ground in the face of virulent attacks.*

maintenance *n.* **1** °upkeep, °care, °preservation, °conservation, °support, sustention, sustentation: *I can no longer afford the maintenance of a large country estate.* **2** continuation, continuance, perpetuation, prolongation, °persistence, maintaining: *His maintenance of an untenable position will lose him votes.* **3** °upkeep, livelihood, °subsistence, °support, °allowance, living, °sustenance, °stipend, subvention, contribution, alimony, °keep: *How much maintenance does he pay to his ex-wife and children?*

majestic *adj.* **1** °regal, °dignified, °grand, °imperial, °royal, °noble, lordly, °lofty, °elevated, °exalted, °glorious, °magnificent, °monumental, °impressive, °striking, °imposing, °awesome, °splendid, °marvellous, kingly, queenly, °princely: *With majestic ceremony, the procession entered the cathedral.* **2** °pompous, °supercilious, °disdainful, °superior, °arrogant, °haughty, magisterial, imperious, °grandiose, °affected: *She dismissed him with a majestic wave of her hand.*

major *adj.* **1** larger, greater, bigger, °main, °chief, °important: *Henderson grabbed the major portion of the credit.* **2** °vital, °important, °critical, °crucial, °principal, °foremost, °paramount, °primary, °prime, °main, °big, biggest, °pre-eminent, °notable, °noteworthy, °significant, °outstanding, °dominant, dominating; °serious, °grave, worst: *The major problem in commercial kitchens is sanitation.*

majority *n.* **1** °bulk, °preponderance, °mass, more than half, the °better *or* °best °part, the greater °part *or* °number, lion's °share: *The majority of shares were bought by existing shareholders.* **2** adulthood, °maturity, seniority, womanhood, °manhood: *They reach their majority in 1999.*

make *v.* **1** °build, °assemble, °construct, °erect, °put together, °set up, °fashion, °form, °mould, °shape, °frame, °create, °originate, °fabricate, °manufacture, °produce, °put out, °forge, contrive, °devise: *She makes her own dresses. They make TV sets here. The Colossus of Rhodes was said to be made of bronze.* **2** °cause, compel, °force, impel, coerce, °provoke, °urge, exhort, °press, °pressure, °require, °command, °order, °induce, °persuade, °prevail (up)on, °insist (up)on, °oblige, *Brit* pressurize: *The devil made me do it.* **3** °bring about, °occasion, °cause, give rise to: *The new regulation is going to make trouble for you.* **4** make out *or* up, °draw (up), °create, °write, °sign, °frame: *I made a new will leaving everything to my children.* **5** °produce, °cause, °create, °generate: *The engine made a funny noise, then died.* **6** °enact, °pass, °frame, °establish, °institute: *He thinks that laws were made to be broken.* **7** °earn, °return, °reap, °garner, °take in, °get, °procure, °gather, °clear, realize, °gross, °net, °pocket, °acquire, °obtain, °receive;

°win, °gain, *Slang US* °pull down: *Has her invention made money? He makes a good living out of his shop. He made £25 playing poker.* **8** °amount to, constitute, °represent, °add up to, °total, °come to: *He knows how many beans make five. Three and two do not make four. One singer does not make an opera.* **9** °change, °turn, °alter, °modify, °transform, °convert; transmute, mutate, metamorphose: *He made him into a star. The alchemists tried to make base metal into gold.* **10** °become, be, °change *or* °turn *or* °grow into, °perform as: *I think Quentin will make a brilliant surgeon one day.* **11** °serve as *or* for, be °suitable for, be, °prove to be, °turn out to be, °turn into, °become: *This cut of meat will not make a good roast.* **12** °fetch, °realize, °earn, °return: *The locket made £1,000 at the auction.* **13** °score, °earn, °secure: *The West Indies made 654 in their first innings.* **14** °reach, °arrive at, attain, °get (to), °win, °achieve, °accomplish; °come in, *Brit* be placed, *US* °place: *Fran might make first place in the marathon.* **15** °prepare, °arrange, rearrange, °tidy (up), °neaten (up): *You have made your bed, now you will have to lie on it.* **16** °record, °arrange, °fix, °decide (on *or* upon), °agree (to): *I made an appointment to see the doctor.* **17** °prepare, °fix, cook: *I made what you like for dinner.* **18** °deliver, °present: *Janet made a good speech.* **19** °traverse, °cover, do, °travel, °navigate: *We cannot make more than 100 miles a day over this terrain.* **20** do, °go, °travel *or* °move at, °move: *His old banger could hardly make 40 m.p.h.* **21** °judge, °think, °calculate, °estimate, °reckon, °gauge, °suppose: *What do you make of Sidney's new book?* **22** °establish, °set up, °organize: *We made our headquarters in the farmhouse.* **23** °appoint, °name, °select, °choose, °elect, °vote (in as), °designate, °authorize, commission, °delegate, depute, deputize, °assign, °sanction, °approve, affirm, °certify, °confirm: *They made him their leader.* **24** °seduce, make it with: *Kenneth tried to make Sharon last night.* **25 make as if** *or* **as though**: °pretend, feign, °act as if *or* as °though, °affect, make a °show *or* °pretence of, give the °impression of: *He made as if to strike me.* **26 make away**: °run off *or* away, °flee, °fly, make off, abscond, take to one's °heels, decamp, °beat a (hasty) °retreat, *Colloq* °run for it, make a °run for it, °beat it, °clear out, °cut and °run, skedaddle, °take off, °cut out, °skip (town), make tracks, *US* °fly the coop, *Slang* scram, vamoose, *US* hightail it, take a (run-out) °powder: *Taking the jewels, he made away as fast as he could run.* **27 make away with**: °steal, °rob, filch, °pilfer, purloin, °walk away *or* off with, *Colloq* °borrow, °liberate, *Slang* °pinch, °hook, °swipe, °rip off, °lift, *US* boost: *That boy has made away with my cherry tarts!* **28 make believe**: °pretend, °fancy, play-act, °dream, °fantasize, °imagine, °act as if: *We used to make believe we were grown-ups.* **29 make do**: °get by or along, °cope, °scrape by *or* along, °manage, °muddle through, °survive, *Colloq* make out: *We have to make do on the pittance Randolph gets from the university.* **30 make for**: **a** °head for *or* towards, °aim for, °steer (a course) for, °proceed towards, be °bound for: *After this is done, I am making for the nearest pub.* **b** °assault, °attack, °set upon, °charge, °rush (at), °pounce upon, °fall upon *or* on, °go for, °lunge at, °storm, assail: *The big fellow was making for me with a*

knife when the lights went out. **c** °promote, °contribute to, be conducive to, °favour, °facilitate: *Good fences make for good neighbours.* **31 make good**: **a** make up (for), °pay (for), °compensate for, recompense (for), °repay, °offset, make °restitution for, °settle, °square, °rectify, put to rights, set °right, °remedy, °correct, °restore: *He agreed to make good any losses.* **b** °succeed, °prosper, °flourish, °thrive, *Colloq* make it: *In later life he made good as a property developer.* **c** °fulfil, °carry out, *Colloq* °deliver (the goods): *She made good on her promise to return my book.* **32 make it**:
a °succeed, °prosper, °triumph, °win, make good, *Colloq* make the °grade: *Do you think she will make it as a doctor?* **b** °get (somewhere), °show up, °appear, °turn up: *They are hoping to catch the 5:03 to Ipswich but I doubt if they will make it.* **33 make known**: °tell of, °impart, °disclose, °reveal, divulge, °mention, °communicate, °announce, °declare, promulgate, °publish, let °slip, *Colloq* °tip off: *She made known her demands.* **34 make much of**:
a °exaggerate, °overstate, °colour, hyperbolize, *Colloq* make a big deal of, °blow up: *He made much of his new title.* **b** °coddle, cosset, °baby, °pamper, °dote on, °flatter, toady (up) to, °cajole, °humour, °indulge, *Colloq* butter up: *Henry makes much of his grandchildren.* **35 make off**: See make, 26, above. **36 make off with**: See make, 27, above. **37 make out**: **a** °see, discern, descry, espy, °detect, °discover, °distinguish, °perceive: *I made out a dim figure in the gloom.* **b** °complete, °fill in, *Brit* °fill up, *US and Canadian* °fill out: *I made out an application for the job.* **c** °draw (up), °write (out or down), °record, *Colloq US* cut: *Please make out a list of your complaints. Make out the cheque to me, personally.* **d** °understand, °fathom, °comprehend, °figure out, °perceive, °follow, °grasp, °see, °decipher, °read: *She mumbles so, I cannot make out what she's saying. Can you make out this name?* **e** °suggest, °imply, °hint, °insinuate, °indicate, °impute, °intimate, make to °appear, °pretend, make as if or as °though, °represent, °present, °show, °demonstrate, °establish: *She tried to make out that I was a fool. He made out a strong case for dog licensing.* **f** °get on, °survive, °manage, °fare, °thrive, °succeed: *How are you making out in your new house?*
38 make over: **a** do over, remodel, redecorate, °alter: *We are making over our kitchen.* **b** °transfer, °hand over, °sign over, convey, °assign, °turn over: *The property has been made over to me.* **39 make up**: **a** °complete, °fill out, °finish (out), °flesh out: *We need another player to make up the team.* **b** °compose, °form, constitute, be comprised of: *The gang is made up of ex-convicts.* **c** °hatch, °invent, concoct, °devise, °create, °construct, °dream up, °originate, °coin, °compose, *Colloq* cook up: *He made up that story about the murder.* **d** be reconciled, make °peace, °settle amicably, come to °terms, bury the hatchet: *The litigants have kissed and made up.* **e** °construct, °build: *The shack is made up of scrap boards.* **40 make up for**: °compensate, redress, make good, atone, make °amends: *How can I make up for all the bad things I said about you?* **41 make way**: °move aside, °clear the °way, allow to pass, make °room or °space: *Make way for the Lord High Executioner!*

—*n.* **42** °kind, °brand, °style, °sort, °type, °mark: *Foreign makes of car currently dominate the market-place.* **43 on the make**: °aggressive, °assertive, °go-ahead, °enterprising, °vigorous, °energetic, *Colloq* °pushy: *The book is about a young man on the make in today's financial world.*

makeshift *adj.* **1** °temporary, °stopgap, °expedient, °emergency, jury-rigged, improvised, °tentative, °stand-by, slapdash: *We were able to fashion a makeshift rudder out of an oar.* —*n.* **2** °stopgap, °expedient, improvisation, °substitute: *The heater broke down and we had to get along with a makeshift.*

make-up *n.* **1** cosmetics, *maquillage*, greasepaint, *Colloq* warpaint: *Do you think I am wearing too much make-up?* **2** constitution, °character, °cast, °disposition, °personality: *There is not an ounce of sympathy in Janet's make-up.* **3** constitution, °arrangement, construction, °composition, °format, configuration, °build, °form: *What is the chemical make-up of the plastic?*

male *adj.* masculine, man's; virile, °manly, manful; *Archaic* spear: *His is bound to be a male point of view.*

malignant *adj.* **1** °virulent, pernicious, °deadly, °fatal, toxic, °poisonous, °harmful, life-threatening: *The tumour proved to be malignant.* **2** malign, malevolent, °evil, malicious, pernicious, °vicious, invidious, °spiteful, °bitter, °hateful, °venomous: *The exposé was full of malignant insinuations.*

man *n.* **1** gentleman, °male, °fellow, *Colloq* °guy, °chap, *Brit* bloke, °squire, *Slang* gink, geezer, *US* gazabo: *Have you met the man she is going to marry?* **2** °people, °human beings, mankind, °mortals, *Homo sapiens*, °humanity, humankind, the °human °race: *Man wants but little here below.* **3** valet, manservant, gentleman's gentleman, °servant, retainer, houseboy, houseman: *Humberson sent his man round with a note.* —*v.* **4** °staff, °people, °crew; °cover: *Who will man the office while I am away?*

manacle *n.* **1 manacles**: shackles, fetters, °handcuffs, gyves, °chains, irons, *Colloq* cuffs, *Slang* bracelets, *Brit* darbies: *The manacles are cutting into his wrists.* —*v.* **2** °shackle, fetter, handcuff, °restrain, put or throw or °clap in irons, °chain, *Colloq US* cuff: *The manacled prisoner was led away.* **3** confine, °inhibit, °restrain, °curb, °check, °control, °hamper: *They felt manacled by the nine o'clock curfew.*

manage *v.* **1** °handle, °administer, °run, °supervise, °look after, °watch over, °direct, °head, °oversee, superintend, °preside over, be in charge (of), take °care of, °control; °rule (over), °govern, °regulate: *Mr Grant manages the glove department.* **2** °handle, °cope or °deal with, °control, °govern, °manipulate: *Will you be able to manage such a frisky horse?* **3** °conduct, °carry on, °carry out, °bring off, °control, °undertake, take °care of, °look after, °handle: *Is she old enough to manage her own affairs?* **4** °succeed, °function, °make do, make it, °shift (for oneself), °get along or by or on, °make out, °muddle through, °survive: *Will you be able to manage from here on?*

manageable *adj.* controllable; °tractable, compliant, amenable, docile, tameable, °tame, trainable, teachable, manipulable, °submissive: *Keep your spending within manageable limits. The dog is quite manageable.*

management *n.* **1** managing, °control, supervision, manipulation, handling, °direction, directing, directorship, °administration, °government, °conduct, governance, °operation, °running, superintendence, °command, °guidance, stewardship: *The management of the company is in your hands.* **2** °administration, °executive(s), °bosses, °directors, °board (of °directors), directorate, *Colloq* (°top) brass: *The management believes that you are the right person for the job.*

manager *n.* °supervisor, °superintendent, °director, °executive, °head, °proprietor, °overseer, °foreman, forewoman, administrator, *Chiefly Brit* manageress, *US* straw °boss, *Colloq* °boss, °chief: *The position of manager entails a lot of responsibility.*

mandatory *adj.* compulsory, °obligatory, requisite, required; °essential, commanded, demanded, °necessary, needed: *The wearing of safety belts in cars is mandatory.*

mangle *v.* °destroy, °mutilate, °butcher, deform, disfigure, °spoil, °mar, °ruin, °wreck; °cut, °hack, °lacerate, °chop (up), °crush, °damage, °cripple, °maim: *Don't you hate the way they mangle the English language? His hand was badly mangled in the accident.*

mangy *adj.* scruffy, °dirty, °sleazy, °wretched, °miserable, °repulsive, °sorry, squalid, slovenly, °unkempt, °filthy, °dingy, °seedy, °poor, °shabby, °mean, °low, ignominious, °base, abject, odious, °disreputable, moth-eaten, °contemptible, °despicable, °nasty, °scurvy: *That mangy beggar was once a top athlete.*

manhandle *v.* maul, paw, °rough up, °batter, °beat (up), pummel, °abuse, °mistreat, maltreat, °ill-treat, trounce, °belabour, *Slang* °knock about or around, clobber: *His captors manhandled him into a car and drove off.*

man-hater *n.* °misanthrope, misanthropist: *He says he prefers to live alone because he's a man-hater.*

manhood *n.* **1** masculinity, manliness, manfulness, virility, *Colloq* °machismo: *He felt that looking after the children at home somehow compromised his manhood.* **2** °bravery, °pluck, boldness, °determination, °resolution, °fortitude, °grit, °spirit, °force, *US* intestinal °fortitude, *Colloq* guts: *He joined the army to test his manhood.*

mania *n.* **1** °rage, °craze, °passion, °obsession, compulsion, °urge, °fascination, preoccupation, °furore *or US* furor, yearning, craving, °desire, cacoethes, *Colloq* °fad, yen: *By that time, the hula hoop mania had died down. She has a mania for collecting apostle spoons.* **2** °madness, °lunacy, °insanity, dementia, derangement, hysteria, *Technical* manic °disorder: *The psychiatrists diagnosed his problem as a mania.*

maniac *n.* **1** °madman, madwoman, lunatic, psychopath, °psychotic, *Colloq* crackpot, *Slang* nut, *Brit* nutter, loony, *US* kook: *In former times, maniacs were scorned and maltreated.* **2** °fanatic, °fan, °enthusiast, °zealot, *Slang* °freak, °fiend: *Since his retirement, he has become a golf maniac.*

maniacal *adj.* **1** manic, °maniac, °insane, lunatic, °mad, demented, °deranged, °hysterical, mentally °ill, of °unsound °mind, *non compos mentis*, °psychotic: *He had to be hospitalized because*

of his maniacal behaviour. **2** °hysterical, °wild, °crazy, *Slang* loony: *His maniacal outbursts frightened us.*

manifest *adj.* **1** °apparent, °clear, °evident, °obvious, °plain, °patent, °blatant, °conspicuous, unmistakable, °discernible, recognizable, comprehensible, °distinct, palpable, °definite, °explicit, unambiguous, °unquestionable, indubitable, °indisputable: *He lost his job because of his manifest dishonesty.* —*v.* **2** °show, °demonstrate, °exhibit, evince, °reveal, °disclose, °display, °betray; °express, °declare: *Fitzsimmons had been manifesting signs of dissatisfaction with his assignment.* **3** °prove, corroborate, °substantiate, °attest: *His distaste for cauliflower was manifested by the look on his face.*

manifestation *n.* °display, °exhibition, °demonstration, °show, disclosure, °appearance, °exposure, °presentation, °sign, °indication, °mark, °expression, °example, °instance; °declaration, avowal, °publication, °announcement: *The police feared that the crime wave was a manifestation of civil unrest. The first manifestation of thought is speech.*

manifestly *adv.* °evidently, °clearly, °obviously, plainly, °apparently, patently, unmistakably, palpably, unquestionably, indubitably, °undoubtedly, indisputably: *The treaty is manifestly to England's advantage.*

manifold *adj.* °diverse, diversified, multifarious, °varied, °various, assorted, multiplex, °miscellaneous, °sundry, many-sided, °many °different, *Literary* °divers; °many, numerous, multitudinous: *I have manifold reasons for wishing you to stay.*

manipulate *v.* **1** °manage, °handle, °control, °manoeuvre, orchestrate, choreograph, °influence, °use, °exploit, °play on, utilize: *He knows how to manipulate people to make them do what he wants.* **2** °handle, °control, °operate, °direct, °work, °use, °employ, °negotiate: *The controls can be manipulated to make the robot imitate human motion.* **3** °rig, °falsify, °juggle, °tamper with, °doctor, *Colloq* cook, *Chiefly Brit* °fiddle: *He's been manipulating his expense account for years.*

manly *adj.* manful, virile, °courageous, °bold, °brave, °intrepid, valorous, valiant, °dauntless, °fearless, plucky, °daring, °venturesome, stout-hearted, °resolute, °stable, °steadfast, unflinching, unwavering, unshrinking, °chivalrous, °gallant, °noble, °heroic; masculine, °male, *Colloq* °macho, red-blooded: *Emerson characterized the English as manly rather than warlike.*

manner *n.* **1** °way, °mode, °style, °technique, °procedure, °method, °fashion; °means, °approach: *Her incisive manner of reporting is widely admired.* **2** °air, °behaviour, mien, demeanour, °bearing, deportment, comportment, °conduct, °attitude, °aspect: *His manner is overbearing and dictatorial.* **3 manners**: °etiquette, °decorum, (°good) °form, politeness, proprieties, °protocol, politesse, °civility, °ceremony, °social code, °social graces, °formalities, niceties, amenities, °social °conventions; °behaviour, °conduct: *Can't you teach him some manners?*

mannered *adj.* °artificial, contrived, °stilted, °stiff, °affected, °insincere, °pompous, °pretentious, posed, °unnatural, °hypocritical,

Colloq °phoney *or US also* phony, pseudo, high-falutin *or* hifalutin, la-di-da *or* lah-di-dah *or* la-de-da, °hoity-toity, on one's high horse, high-hat, uppity *or Brit* °uppish: *Alice's speech is too mannered for anyone to feel close to her.*

mannerism *n.* °quirk, peculiarity, idiosyncrasy, °trait, °characteristic, °habit: *She has the irritating mannerism of pulling on her ear lobe.*

manoeuvre *n.* **1** °move, °stratagem, °tactic, °trick, gambit, ploy, °subterfuge, °ruse, °dodge, °artifice, °device, °wile, *démarche,* °strategy, °plan, °plot, °scheme, °intrigue, °machination: *That manoeuvre will never work on a clever woman.* **2** °exercise, °operation, °drill, war-game, kriegspiel, training: *We were out on manoeuvres for a week.* —*v.* **3** °manipulate, contrive, °plot, °scheme, machinate, °intrigue, °trick, °devise, °engineer, °finesse, °manage, *Colloq* finagle, °wangle: *He manoeuvred his way out of going on that mission.* **4** °manipulate, °operate, °run, °drive, °guide, °navigate, jockey: *She manoeuvred the car into a surprisingly tiny space.*

mantle *n.* **1** °cloak, °cape, °wrap, shawl, pelisse, pelerine: *Over his armour he wore a mantle embroidered with his bearing.* **2** covering, °cover, °sheet, °veil, blanket, °screen, °cloak, °shroud, °pall, canopy, curtain: *A mantle of snow lay on the ground.* —*v.* **3** °cover, °clothe, °envelop, °surround, °encircle, °shroud, °veil, °screen, °obscure, °cloak, °conceal, °hide, °mask, °wrap, °disguise: *The mountains were brilliantly mantled and capped with snow.*

manual *n.* handbook, °vade-mecum, enchiridion; directions, instructions, °guide: *Follow the manual carefully to avoid mistakes.*

manufacture *v.* **1** °make, (°mass-)°produce, °construct, °build, °assemble, fabricate, °put together, °turn out, °create, °originate: *The company manufactures windscreen wipers.* **2** concoct, °create, contrive, °invent, °make up, °fabricate, °think up, *US and Canadian* °create out of *or* from whole cloth, *Colloq* cook up: *She manufactured that tale about being an orphan.* —*n.* **3** making, (°mass) °production, construction, °building, °assembly, °fabrication, turning *or* putting out, putting together, °creation, origination: *The manufacture of durable goods increased 0.02% in the last quarter.*

manufacturer *n.* maker, °producer, industrialist, fabricator: *Manufacturers of computers usually buy components from specialized firms.*

many *adj.* **1** numerous, multitudinous, myriad, °profuse, innumerable, °numberless, uncountable: *Many people have an irrational fear of spiders.* **2** °diverse, multifarious, °varied, °various, assorted, °sundry, *Literary* °divers: *There are many kinds of courage.* —*n.* **3** horde(s), °crowd(s), °lot(s), °swarm(s), °throng(s), °mass(es), °profusion, multitude(s), °abundance, °plenty, shoal(s), °flock(s), drove(s), °torrent(s), °flood(s), °number(s), °score(s), hundred(s), (thousand(s), etc.); *Colloq* ton(s), scads: *A great many will turn out to vote next week. Many are picked but few are chosen.*

mar *v.* **1** °damage, °ruin, °mutilate, °deface, °spoil, °scar, disfigure: *The surface of the table was marred by a deep scratch.* **2** °damage, °wreck, °ruin, °impair, °harm, °hurt, °blight, °blot, °taint, °stain, °tarnish: *She claims that her reputation was marred by the article.*

march *v.* **1** °parade, °step, stride, °strut, tread, °pace, °walk: *They marched from Baxter Street to the Town Hall.* —*n.* **2** °parade, °procession, °demonstration, cortege *or* cortège, °walk: *The march was organized to protest against the government's nuclear arms policy.* **3** °walk, trek, slog, hike: *We had a long march ahead of us to get to Hastings.*

margin *n.* **1** °edge, °border, °perimeter, °periphery, °rim, lip, °side, °brink, °verge: *Leave a one-inch margin at the left side of the page. Trees grew at the margin of the pond.* **2** °limit(s), °bound(s), °boundary (°line), °border, °frontier, °line, °partition °line: *These streets form the margin of the inner city.* **3** °allowance, °play, °leeway, latitude, °scope, °freedom, °room, °space; compass: *These calculations do not provide much of a margin for error.*

marginal *adj.* **1** borderline, °minimal, °small, °slight, °negligible, °insignificant, °tiny, infinitesimal: *There are marginal differences in policy on this issue.* **2** borderline, on the °edge, °disputable, °questionable, °doubtful, dubious: *His qualifications for the job are marginal.*

marine *adj.* **1** maritime, °nautical, naval, °seafaring, seagoing, ocean-going, °sea: *Marine commerce has declined during recent decades.* **2** maritime, °sea, °oceanic, aquatic, salt-water, pelagic, thalassic: *Many groups are concerned about the conservation of marine life.*

mark *n.* **1** °spot, °stain, °blemish, °smear, smudge, °trace, °impression, dent, °nick, °scratch, pock-mark *or* pock, °streak, °line, *Brit* splodge, *US* splotch: *One of the children had made a mark on the newly painted wall.* **2** °sign, °symbol, insigne, °emblem, °device, °hallmark, earmark, fingerprint, badge, °characteristic, °token, °brand, °stamp, °label, °identification, °indication, °feature, °attribute, °trait, °quality, °property: *This work bears the mark of true genius.* **3** °standard, criterion, °norm, °yardstick, °level, °measure: *I'm afraid your son's work has not come up to the mark.* **4** rating, °grade, grading: *I'd give her a low mark for originality but high marks for technique.* **5** °influence, °impression, °effect: *Her innovations have left their mark on all music composed since 1900.* **6** °target, °goal, °objective, °aim, °purpose, °end, °object: *Her criticisms fell wide of the mark.* **7** marker, °indicator, °guide, signpost, °landmark: *The next mark, a bell-buoy, should be left to port.* **8** consequence, °importance, °note, noteworthiness, notability, °distinction, eminence, °dignity, °prestige, °standing, °account: *Granada was a place of little mark as compared with Cordova.* **9 make one's mark**: °succeed, get °ahead, °triumph, °distinguish oneself, attain °distinction, bring °honour upon oneself, acquit oneself, bring °credit to oneself, have an °effect, *Colloq* °make it °big, make the °grade: *Randolph has made his mark in the world of scholarship.* —*v.* **10** Sometimes, **mark up**: °spot, °stain, °blemish, °smear, smudge, °streak, dent, °trace, pock-mark, °nick, °scratch, °cut, °chip, °pit, °bruise: *That glass has marked the finish on the table.* **11** °signify, °specify, °indicate, °designate, °identify, tick, °label: *Mark your choice with an 'X' next to the candidate's name.* **12** pay °attention to, °attend (to), pay °heed to, °note, °notice, take °notice of, °watch, °see, °look at, °observe; °respect, °mind, °heed, °obey: *Mark the way she swings the golf club. Mark my words or you'll be sorry.* **13** °brand, °stamp, °identify, °characterize, °distinguish: *His music is marked by long atonal passages.* **14** °correct; °grade, °evaluate, assess, appraise: *The teachers are busy marking exam papers.* **15 mark down: a** °write (down), °record, °register, make (a) °note of, °note (down): *Mark down these numbers in your book.* **b** °decrease, °reduce, devalue, devaluate, °cut, °slash, °discount: *We marked down the prices for a quick sale.* **16 mark up: a** See **10**, above. **b** °increase, °raise, hike, up: *Prices were marked up to keep pace with inflation.*

marked *adj.* °noticeable, °conspicuous, °decided, °pronounced, °considerable, °remarkable, °significant, °signal, unmistakable, °prominent, °obvious, °patent, °evident, °apparent: *There is a marked improvement in your work.*

market *n.* **1** market-place, °exchange, Stock Exchange: *There are some excellent buys on the market.* **2** °shop, °store, bazaar, supermarket, *Chiefly US* superstore: *If you are going to the market, please buy some milk.* **3** °demand, °customer °base, °call: *The market for computers is still growing rapidly.* —*v.* **4** °sell, °merchandise, retail, vend, °peddle, hawk, make available, °furnish; °trade (in), °buy and °sell, °deal in: *We market these computers worldwide.*

maroon *v.* °abandon, °cast away, °desert, strand, °forsake; °isolate, seclude: *They were marooned on a desert island.*

marriage *n.* **1** matrimony, wedlock: *Their marriage has lasted over forty years.* **2** nuptials, °wedding: *The marriage took place at noon.* **3** °association, °alliance, confederation, °federation, affiliation, °connection, coupling, °union, °merger, °amalgamation, integration, *Colloq* hook-up: *Would a marriage of the companies benefit the shareholders?*

marry *v.* **1** °wed, °join in matrimony *or* wedlock, become man and wife, *Colloq* get hitched *or* spliced, tie the knot: *They married and lived happily ever after.* **2** °match (up), go *or* °fit together, °fit; °unite, °unify, °bond, °weld, °fuse, °put together, °couple, °join, °link; °league, affiliate, °ally, °amalgamate, °combine: *The marble head, found in London, married perfectly with the torso, found in Crete. The best qualities of each earlier model are married in this new product.*

marsh *n.* °swamp, °bog, fen, slough, quagmire: *The marsh teems with new life in the spring.*

martial *adj.* **1** °warlike, °belligerent, bellicose, °pugnacious, °militant: *We had no suspicion of their martial intentions. He is an expert in the martial arts.* **2** °military, soldierly, °courageous, °brave, valorous, valiant, °staunch, °stalwart, stout-hearted: *The speech was intended to rouse the soldiers' martial spirit.*

marvel *v.* **1** °wonder (at), °gape (at), be awed *or* amazed (by), be °agog *or* astonished (at): *We marvelled at the way the homing pigeons found their way home.* —*n.* **2** °wonder, miracle, °phenomenon: *Tammy was a marvel at fixing electrical equipment.*

marvellous *adj.* wonderful, astonishing, °amazing, astounding, surprising,

°remarkable, °extraordinary, °phenomenal, °glorious, °splendid, °superb, °excellent, spectacular, breathtaking, °miraculous, °unbelievable, °incredible, °sensational, mind-boggling, °unparalleled, *Colloq* °terrific, °great, °fantastic, °fabulous, smashing, *Slang* far-out, °crazy, °wild, groovy, °super, out of this °world, fantabulous, *Brit* spot *or* bang on, *US* marvy: *It was a marvellous show, and Renfrew is a marvellous actor.*

mask *n.* **1** °false °face, domino: *She wore a mask, and I don't know who she was.* **2** °disguise, °guise, °camouflage, °show, °semblance, °pretence, °cover, cover-up, °false colours, °false flag, concealment, °cloak, façade, °veil: *He wormed his way into her confidence under the mask of friendship.* —*v.* **3** °disguise, °camouflage, °cover (up), °conceal, °hide, °obscure, °veil, °screen, °shroud: *She was unable to mask her true feelings for him.*

masquerade *n.* **1** masked ball, masquerade ball, °costume °party, *ballo in maschera, bal masqué: He went to the masquerade as Lorenzo di Medici.* **2** °disguise, °deception, °pose, °dissimulation, °bluff, °subterfuge, °false °show, °outward °show, fakery, imposture, play-acting, °false °front, cover-up, °camouflage, *Colloq* °act, °front, *Slang* °put-on: *How long will she continue her masquerade as a wealthy widow?* —*v.* **3** Usually, **masquerade as**: °pretend (to be), °pass oneself off (as), impersonate, simulate, °pose (as), °imitate, °mimic: *He is a conservative masquerading as a liberal to garner votes.*

mass *n.* **1** °pile, °heap, °mountain, °load, °stack, °mound, °bunch, °bundle, °lot, °batch, °quantity, °hoard, °store, °collection, °accumulation, aggregation, agglomeration, congeries, °assortment, °miscellany, assemblage, conglomeration: *There was a mass of boulders at the bottom of the cliff.* **2** °abundance, °quantity, °profusion, °volume, multitude, horde, °host, °mob, °crowd, °throng, drove(s), °herd(s), °swarm(s), legion(s), °score(s), °number(s), *Colloq* °bunch(es), ton(s), °mountain, °piles, bags, barrels, oodles, °lots, °oceans, loads, scads, *US* °mess, slew(s): *A mass of bills awaited my return from a trip abroad. Masses of people greeted us at the airport.* **3** °block, concretion, chunk, °lump, hunk, nugget: *A mass of sludge was clogging the valve.* **4** °majority, °best *or* °better *or* greater °part, °bulk, °body, °preponderance, almost all, lion's °share: *The great mass of the votes was still uncounted.* **5** dimension, °size, °magnitude, °bulk, bigness, massiveness, °enormousness, immensity: *The very mass of the elephant made it a hard target to miss.* **6 the masses**: the °common °people, the (°common) °herd, the proletariat, the plebeians, hoi polloi, the °lower °class(es), the man *or* woman in the street, *Brit* the man *or* woman on the Clapham omnibus, A. N. Other, *US* John Q. Public, John *or* Jane Doe *or* Roe: *The taxes became burdensome and the masses rebelled.* —*v.* **7** °amass, °pile *or* °heap up, °gather: *Thunderclouds began to mass over the mountains.* **8** aggregate, °accumulate, °collect, °assemble, congregate, °meet, °get *or* °come together, °gather, forgather *or* foregather, °throng, convene, °flock together, °rally, °group, °cluster, marshal, °muster, °mobilize: *Thousands of people massed in front of the embassy. The massed bands made a tremendous noise.*

massacre n. **1** °slaughter, slaughtering, °carnage, annihilation, annihilating, blood bath, °killing, °execution, extermination, exterminating, butchery, butchering, (°mass) °murder, murdering, slaying, liquidation, pogrom, genocide: *The massacre of millions of innocent people followed the coup.*
—v. **2** °slaughter, annihilate, °kill, °execute, °exterminate, °butcher, °murder, slay, liquidate, °destroy, °eliminate, °obliterate, eradicate, put to the sword, decimate, *Colloq* °mow down, *Slang* °bump off: *It was their policy to massacre all the men and take captive all the women and children.*

massage n. **1** rub-down, °rub, manipulation, kneading: *I felt really relaxed after the massage and steam bath.*
—v. **2** °rub down, °manipulate, knead, palpate: *She gently massaged my temples with her fingertips.* **3** °manipulate, °handle, °manoeuvre, *Colloq* finagle, *Brit* °fiddle: *He massaged the figures to make it look as if the company was solvent.*

massive adj. °big, °large, oversized, °huge, °bulky, °enormous, °hulking, °immense, °gigantic, °towering, mammoth, °colossal, titanic, °vast, tremendous, °prodigious, °mountainous, gargantuan, Brobdingnagian, Cyclopean, elephantine, °jumbo, stupendous, °mighty, °weighty, °ponderous, *Literary* massy, *Colloq* walloping, °whopping, °monster, *Brit* whacking (°great), *US* ginormous, humongous: *They built a massive wall round the city. Massive beams support the roof.*

master n. **1** °owner, °head, °chief, °leader, chieftain, commander, °lord, governor, °director, controller, °employer, °manager, °overseer, °supervisor, °superintendent, taskmaster, slave-driver, °principal, °sovereign, °monarch, ruler, *Colloq* °lord high muck-a-muck, Pooh Bah, kingpin, °boss, °skipper, *Brit* gaffer, *US* king-fish, the man, °big fish, °big °boss, bossman, *Slang US* °big cheese, °big wheel, Mr Big, °chief *or* °head honcho: *He is master of all he surveys. Decisions about punishment are referred to the master.* **2** °expert, °authority, °genius, craftsman, °adept, maestro, °mastermind, past master, old hand, °virtuoso, ace, °professional, *Colloq* pro, wizard, *Chiefly Brit* dab hand, *US* crackerjack; *Slang US* maven *or* mavin: *He is a master in the art of chicanery.* **3** °teacher, °tutor, °instructor, °guide, °leader, guru, swami: *She studied under the master for years.*
—adj. **4** °adept, °ingenious, °expert, °masterful, masterly, °skilful, skilled, °proficient: *After twenty years, he became a master craftsman.* **5** °overall, controlling, °principal, °main, °prime, °basic, °chief: *Only the leader knows the master plan for conquering the planet. This is the master switch that turns off all the power.* **6** °main, biggest, °principal, owner's: *The master bedroom had a bathroom en suite.*
—v. **7** °learn, °grasp, become °expert in, °know inside out and backwards, °know, °understand: *He claims to have mastered the art of levitation.* **8** °control, °overcome, °repress, °suppress, °subdue, °bridle, °check, °quell, get the better of, *Colloq* get a °grip on: *You must learn to master your emotions.*

masterful adj. **1** masterly, °adept, °expert, °excellent, °superior, °superb, adroit, °exquisite, °superlative, °supreme, consummate, °accomplished, °peerless, °matchless, °first-rate, °proficient, °dexterous, deft, °skilful, skilled, *Colloq* crack: *She gave a masterful performance of Bruch's violin concerto.* **2** °authoritarian, °dictatorial, °tyrannical, °despotic, °arbitrary, °domineering, imperious, °overbearing, °arrogant, dominating, autocratic, high-handed, magisterial, overweening, °self-willed, *Colloq* °bossy: *I dislike Ian's masterful attitude, always telling everyone what to do.*

mastermind v. **1** °plan, °devise, °conceive, °think up, °engineer, °design, °generate, °create, °manage, °organize, °develop, °work up *or* out: *It was probably Fu Manchu who masterminded this diabolical plot.*
—n. **2** planner, contriver, conceiver, °creator, architect, °genius, °mind, °intellect, *Colloq* °brain(s): *it would take a mastermind to get even a pass mark on that exam.*

masterpiece n. master-work, magnum °opus, chef-d'œuvre, tour de force, °jewel, °work of °art, °work of °genius, pièce de résistance: *Among his many fine paintings, I consider this his masterpiece.*

match n. **1** °equal, °equivalent, °peer, °fellow, °mate; °parallel, °replica, °copy, °double, °twin, °look-alike, °facsimile, counterpart: *When it comes to punning, Crosby has finally met his match.* **2** °contest, °competition, °game, °meet, tourney, °tournament, °bout, duel, °rivalry, °trial: *The match was between the top-seeded players.* **3** °marriage, betrothal, °alliance, °combination, °compact, °contract, partnership, °union, affiliation: *It was a match made in heaven.* **4** °prospect, °candidate: *With his inheritance, he's considered a good match.*
—v. **5** match up, °join, °marry, °unite, °link, °combine, °put together, °pair up *or* off, juxtapose, conjoin: *However did you manage to match names and faces? Glynis matched them up at the dinner table.* **6** °equal, be °equivalent (to), °resemble, °compare (with), °tie, °measure up (to), °compete (with), °vie (with), °rival: *His skill on the flute will never match hers.* **7** °fit, °go with, °suit, °accord, °agree, harmonize, °go (together), °coordinate, °blend, °correspond: *Who will notice that your socks match your tie? Your eyes don't match.*

matching adj. **1** corresponding, homologous, comparable, °equivalent, complementary: *Birds' wings and fishes' fins are matching parts.* **2** analogous, °like, corresponding, °identical: *He wore a pink jacket and matching shoes. She bought a set of matching luggage.*

matchless adj. °unique, °original, °peerless, unequalled, without °equal, inimitable, unmatched, °incomparable, °unparalleled, beyond °compare: *Stefania has a contralto voice of matchless quality.*

mate n. **1** °companion, °associate, °colleague, °fellow, °chap, co-worker, °comrade, crony, °ally, °friend, alter ego, *Colloq* °chum, °pal, *US* buddy, °cohort, *Slang Brit* cully, china: *After work, my mates and I stop off for a beer or two (or three).* **2** spouse, °partner, helpmeet, helpmate, consort, °husband *or* wife, better half, *Colloq* hubby, old man *or* lady *or* woman, lord and master, *US* bride, *Slang* trouble and strife (= 'wife'): *He scarcely seems a worthy mate for the winner of a Miss World contest.* **3** °fellow, °twin, counterpart, °parallel, one of a °pair: *Have you seen the mate to this sock anywhere?*

—v. **4** °pair (up), °match (up), °marry, °wed, °join, °unite, °couple, °link (up): *People should be free to mate with whom they wish.* **5** °breed, °couple, copulate, °pair (up): *The zoo was able to get the rhinoceroses to mate. A lion was mated with a tiger to produce a tigon.* **6** °match (up), °fit (together), synchronize, °join: *I cannot get these gears to mate.*

material n. **1** °substance, °matter, °stuff, °fabric: *It is hard to tell what material this is made of.* **2** °cloth, °fabric, textile, °stuff: *This material is too sheer for a dress.* **3** constituents, °elements, components: *We import the raw materials and make the finished product here.* **4** °information, °data, °facts, statistics, figures, °documents, documentation, °papers, °notes, °resources, °means, °research, °apparatus, °supplies: *I have not yet gathered enough material for the article.*
—adj. **5** °physical, °tangible, °concrete, °solid, °real, substantive, °substantial, palpable, corporeal, bodily: *It was many years before scientists could persuade people that air is a material substance.* **6** consequential, °important, °significant, °serious, °substantial: *How could one horseshoe nail be material in the outcome of a battle?* **7** °worldly, °earthly, mundane, °temporal, non-spiritual, °secular, °lay, °materialistic: *He ponders the abstract, not the base, material things of everyday life.*

materialistic adj. °expedient, money-oriented, possession-oriented, °greedy, *Slang* yuppy: *He's very materialistic and only married her for her money.*

materialize v. **1** °appear, °turn up, become °visible, become °manifest, be revealed, take °shape or °form, °form, °emerge: *A hulking shape began to materialize out of the fog.* **2** °happen, come to pass, take place, °occur, become °manifest or °real, be realized, become an actuality, be actualized: *The dream of a united Europe is finally materializing.*

materially adv. °substantially, palpably, significantly, °seriously, essentially, basically, considerably, greatly, much, in the long °run, at °bottom: *I doubt that his criticism will materially affect the success of the play.*

maternal adj. motherly, °warm, nurturing, caring, °understanding, °affectionate, °tender, °kind, °kindly, °devoted, °fond, doting; maternalistic: *Her interest in him is strictly maternal.*

maternity n. **1** motherhood, parenthood, pregnancy: *Maternity brings about great changes in a woman's life.* **2** parenthood, motherhood: *The maternity of the child was not questioned until the hospital revealed that there had been a mix-up in the nursery.*

mathematical adj. arithmetical; °precise, °exact, rigorous: *He went about his plans with mathematical precision.*

matrimonial adj. marital, °marriage, °wedding, conjugal, °nuptial; married, °wedded, connubial: *She obtained a court injunction banning him from the matrimonial home. They enjoy matrimonial bliss.*

matter n. **1** °material, °substance, °stuff, °sum and °substance: *Some yellowish matter oozed out of the wound. It is a question of mind over matter.* **2** °situation, °issue, °question, °affair, °business, °subject, °topic, °condition, °thing, °fact, °concern; °occurrence, °episode, °incident, °event, °occasion, °proceeding: *It was a matter of life and death. His loss of face is not a*

matter that need involve you. **3** °problem, °difficulty, °trouble, °complication, °worry, °upset, °dilemma, °quandary, °enigma, °puzzle: *What is the matter?* **4** °content, °essentials, °pith, °context, °theme, °argument, purport, °implication; signification, °meaning, meaningfulness, °import, °importance, °significance, °moment, °weight, consequence: *Pay attention to the matter in his speech, not his manner. It is of little matter to me whether you go or not.* **5** °amount, °sum, °quantity, °question: *It was only a matter of a few pennies' difference.*
—v. **6** be °important or of °importance, °count, be of consequence, make a °difference, °mean something: *What you think matters a great deal.*

matter-of-fact adj. straightforward, °direct, °forthright, °sober, °factual, unimaginative, unartistic, °prosaic, unpoetic, °dry, dry-as-dust, °dull, °boring, °tiresome, °flat, mundane, °lifeless, featureless, °unvarnished, °colourless, unembellished, °unadorned: *The report contained a matter-of-fact description of the events.*

mature adj. **1** °adult, grown (up), full-grown, fully grown, of °age, fully fledged, full-fledged, fully developed, matured, °experienced, °knowledgeable, °sophisticated: *At twenty-two, she is mature enough to be on her own.* **2** °ripe, °ready, ripened, °mellow, °aged, °seasoned: *A good wine, like fruit, should not be consumed till it is mature.* **3** °complete, matured, °perfect, perfected, °polished, °refined, °ready, fully developed, consummated: *Our plans are not yet mature.*
—v. **4** °grow up, °age, °develop, come of °age; *Brit* be one's °age, *US* °act one's °age: *Has he matured sufficiently to be trusted alone in the house for the weekend? I wish he'd mature a bit more.* **5** °ripen, °mellow, °age, °season; maturate: *Fruit that has matured on the plant tastes best.* **6** °develop, °perfect, °refine, °polish, maturate, °bring to °fruition: *Their plans for major changes in company structure have not yet fully matured.*

maturity n. **1** adulthood, °majority, full °growth or °development: *Maturity is as much a state of mind as a matter of age.* **2** ripeness, °readiness, mellowness; maturation: *Different wines need ageing for different periods to attain maturity.* **3** °readiness, °perfection, °completion, fullness, °consummation, operability, applicability; maturation: *Their plans were brought to maturity.*

maudlin adj. °sentimental, (over)emotional, mawkish, °romantic; °tearful, lachrymose, weepy, teary(-eyed); *Colloq* °mushy, slushy, *Brit* soppy, *US* soupy: *He gets maudlin thinking about his childhood in the countryside.*

maxim n. saying, °proverb, axiom, aphorism, adage, °byword, °saw, apophthegm or apothegm, °epigram, °motto, °slogan; mot, °witticism; °cliché, °truism: *Her maxim is, 'What you don't know, can't hurt you'.*

maximize n. **1** °increase, broaden, °improve, °magnify, augment, °add to, °expand, °build up, °enlarge: *He maximizes his chances for winning by betting on several numbers. To compete, you must maximize your productivity.* **2** °inflate, overplay, °overdo, °overstate, °exaggerate, oversell, make much of, overstress, (over)colour, °enhance, embroider (on), °embellish, °elaborate, °magnify: *Roland tends to maximize his role while minimizing others'*.

maximum n. **1** most, utmost, uttermost, greatest, °peak, °extreme, °extremity, °pinnacle, °top, highest, (°upper) °limit: *Turn the volume up to the maximum.* **2** °zenith, °pinnacle, °peak, °limit, apex, °acme, apogee, °climax, °crest, °high(est) °point, °top, °summit: *Her career reached its maximum in the 1930s.*
—adj. **3** maximal, greatest, most, utmost, uttermost, °superlative, °supreme, °paramount, °extreme, highest, °top, topmost, climactic, crowning: *The maximum amount that I can afford for a car is £2,000.*

maybe adv. °perhaps, °possibly, *Literary* perchance, *Archaic or dialect* mayhap, *Archaic* peradventure: *We could go and see a film tonight, or maybe have a meal somewhere.*

mayhem n. maihem, °violence, °havoc, °destruction, °disorder, devastation, °chaos; °fracas, commotion, °confusion: *Someone screamed 'Fire!', and the ensuing mayhem was unbelievable.*

maze n. labyrinth, complex, intricacy, twistings and turnings, convolutions: *His application has been lost in the maze of bureaucratic bungling.*

meadow n. °field, meadow-land, °pasture, °pasture °land, *Archaic or literary* lea, mead: *The entire meadow was dotted with little puffy clouds of white sheep.*

meagre adj. **1** °scanty, scant, °poor, °paltry, °inadequate, skimpy, scrimpy, °sparse, °spare, °insufficient, °bare, °puny, piddling, °trifling, °pathetic, exiguous, *Colloq* °measly: *Angela scraped out a meagre living as a shop assistant. The meagre supplies wouldn't last another day.* **2** °spare, °skinny, °scrawny, bony, °emaciated, °gaunt, °thin, °lean, bare-boned, (half-)°starved, underfed, undernourished, starving: *The meagre faces of the survivors told of their ordeal.* **3** °spare, °plain, bare-boned, °unadorned, unembellished, unelaborate, unelaborated, °simple, simplified, oversimplified, °bare, °inadequate, °deficient, undetailed, °indefinite, non-specific, °general, °broad, °loose, °vague: *The police have only a meagre description to go on.* **4** unfruitful, °infertile, °barren, °deficient, °poor, unproductive: *This land is too meagre to provide the people with a living.*

meal n. **1** °food, repast, victuals, °nourishment, °spread, collation, refection; dinner, supper, breakfast, lunch, luncheon, *Brit* tea: *Meals will be served in the main dining room.* **2 make a meal of:** °overdo, overplay, go overboard, go or carry to °extremes, carry or go too °far, do to °excess: *Perkins is bound to make a meal of the slightest thing.*

mealy-mouthed adj. °mincing, °reticent, °reluctant, °hesitant, °equivocal, equivocating, °ambiguous, °indirect, unwilling to call a spade a spade, euphemistic, °roundabout, °vague, circumlocutory, periphrastic, °hypocritical, °deceitful, °artful, °slick, °oily, unctuous: *All you'll get from that mealy-mouthed hypocrite is platitudinous twaddle.*

mean[1] v. **1** °intend, °design, °purpose, °plan, °aim, have in °mind, °contemplate, have in °view; °want, °wish, °expect, °hope; be motivated by, have as justification: *I did mean to phone you but had no time. I am sure she meant nothing by her remark.* **2** °denote, °signify, °indicate, °note, °specify, °designate, °represent, betoken, °signal, °carry, convey, °drive at, °refer to, allude to, °communicate, °express, °bring out, °get over or across; °imply, °suggest, connote, °intimate, °hint (at): *What does 'canicular' mean? It depends on what you mean by 'liberty'. The footprints meant that someone had already been here.* **3** portend, °show, foretell, °foreshadow, °promise, presage, augur, herald: *Those clouds mean that it will soon rain.* **4** carry or have the °weight or °significance or °importance of: *Money means little to someone in her circumstances.*

mean[2] adj. **1** stingy, °miserly, °tight, °close, °cheap, parsimonious, °penurious, stinting, niggardly, penny-pinching, tight-fisted, close-fisted, °mercenary, uncharitable, ungenerous, mean-spirited, unaccommodating, °small, °petty, *Colloq* near, money-grubbing, °measly, *Brit* mingy: *He is far too mean to buy anyone a Christmas present. It seems rather a mean contribution to the fund, given his wealth.* **2** °lowly, °low, °base, °inferior, abject, °menial, °servile, degraded, °degenerate, undignified, ignoble, °plebeian, proletarian, °modest, °humble, °common: *He rose to a position of great power in spite of his mean background.* **3** °disgraceful, °run-down, °poor, °sorry, °miserable, scruffy, °seedy, °scurvy, °shabby, squalid, °wretched, °vile, °mangy, °sordid, °contemptible, °dismal, °dreary, °abysmal: *They live in very mean circumstances.* **4** °unkind, malicious, °cruel, unaccommodating, disobliging: *It was very mean of you to steal that toy from the baby.* **5** °cantankerous, churlish, °nasty, °hostile, ill-tempered, bad-tempered, °sour, unpleasant: *That mean old lady would never even talk to us.* **6** °excellent, wonderful, °marvellous, °great, °exceptional, °effective, °skilful, skilled, *Slang* far-out, *US* bad: *The saxophonist in that combo is one mean cat.*

mean[3] n. **1** °average, °middle, °norm, (happy) °medium: *We are attempting to achieve the mean between the two extremes.* **2 by all means:** **a** °absolutely, °definitely, certainly, °surely, assuredly, of °course, °positively: *By all means, do tell us what you think is wrong.* **b** in any °event, at all events, no matter what, without °fail, at any °cost, in any °case: *By all means, you must do what you think is right.* **3 by means of:** by dint of, via, °through, by °way of, with the °help or °aid of, employing, using, utilizing: *She gained access to her victims by means of the telephone directory. We entered by means of the front door.* **4 means: a** °instrument, °agency, °method, °process, °technique, °mode, °manner, °way(s), °approach, °course, °procedure, avenue, °medium, °vehicle: *If you can find the means, then get the job done at once.* **b** °resources, °funds, °money, wherewithal, °capital, °finances, °backing, °support: *I wanted to go to Australia to see my brother, but I simply didn't have the means.* **c** °substance, °wealth, °property, °position, °financial °stability: *She is a woman of considerable means.* **5 by no means:** by no manner of means, in no °way, not at all, °definitely or °absolutely not, on no °account, not conceivably, not in one's wildest dreams or fantasies, not by any stretch of the imagination, *Colloq* no way, *US* no way José: *This is sometimes but by no means always the case. He is by no means a great artist.*

—*adj.* **6** °middle, °centre, °intermediate, medial, °medium, median, °average, middling: *The mean temperature for the year has increased.*

meander *v.* **1** °wander, °ramble, zigzag, °snake, °wind, °twist, °turn; °stroll, amble, rove, *Colloq* mosey, *Brit* swan around *or* about: *The river meandered with a mazy motion through the meadows. We meandered through the forest.*
—*n.* **2** Often, **meanders**: °meandering(s), °turn(s), turning(s), °twist(s), twisting(s), winding(s), curve(s), curving(s), °loop(s), looping(s), °bend(s), °coil(s), zigzag(s), convolutions; tortuosities, flexuosities, anfractuosities: *We followed the river's meanders till we came to the ruined church.*

meandering *adj.* wandering, °roundabout, circuitous, sinuous, °tortuous, winding, °serpentine, °indirect, flexuous, curvy, °crooked, convoluted, °labyrinthine, mazy, anfractuous: *The meandering road followed the river through the valley.*

meaning *n.* **1** °sense, °import, °content, signification, denotation, °message, °substance, °gist: *The meaning of the word 'lucid' is clear.* **2** purport, °implication, °drift, °spirit, connotation, °significance, °intention: *You understand my meaning, so I need not explain.* **3** °interpretation, °explanation: *What is the meaning of my dream about being attacked by my philodendron?*

meaningful *adj.* **1** °significant, °important, consequential, °serious, °sober, °deep, °substantial, pithy, substantive, °telling, °weighty, valid, °relevant: *Tired of casual encounters, he was ready for a meaningful relationship.* **2** °suggestive, °pregnant, tell-tale, °pointed, sententious, °significant, °expressive, °eloquent: *She gave him a meaningful look.*

meaningless *adj.* **1** °empty, °hollow, vacuous, unsubstantial, °absurd, °silly, °foolish, fatuous, asinine, °ridiculous, °preposterous, °nonsensical: *He gave some meaningless excuse for having forgotten the appointment. This gibberish is entirely meaningless to me.* **2** °ineffective, °ineffectual, °inefficacious, °bootless, unavailing, to no avail, trivial, nugatory, °trifling, °puny, °paltry, °worthless, not °worth anything *or* a straw *or* a rap, valueless, °inconsequential, unimportant, of no °moment, °insubstantial, °vain, °pointless, °senseless, °purposeless, undirected, °irrelevant, °insignificant: *Considering the enemy forces, anything we could do would be meaningless.*

means *n.* See mean³, 4, above.

meantime *n., adv.* See **meanwhile**, below.

meanwhile *n.* **1** interim, °meantime, °interval: *In the meanwhile, you could study for the exam.*
—*adv.* **2** in the meanwhile, °meantime, in the °meantime, in the interim, for the °moment, °temporarily, for °now, for the °time being, during the °interval, in the intervening °time: *Ruth was watching TV; meanwhile George was washing up.*

measly *adj.* °sparse, scant, °scanty, °meagre, °paltry, °pathetic, skimpy, °puny, piddling, °miserly, niggardly, °miserable, beggarly, stingy, *Colloq Brit* mingy: *'Nouvelle cuisine' is the name given to a restaurateur's design to serve decorative, but measly, portions.*

measure *n.* **1** °amount, °quantity, °magnitude, amplitude, °size, °bulk, °mass, °extent, °reach, dimension, °scope, proportions, °range, °spread; °capacity, °volume; °width, °length, °breadth, °height; °weight: *It is difficult to calculate the measure of an irregularly shaped object.* **2** °scale, °gauge *or technical* gage, °yardstick, °rule, *US* litmus °test: *I cannot determine the length without a proper measure.* **3** °system, °standard, criterion, °rule, °method; barometer, Richter °scale: *The measure by which ice-cream is sold ought to be weight, not volume. What sort of measure do you apply when judging character?* **4** assessment, °evaluation, valuation, appraisal, value, °gauge *or US* gage, °rank, rating, °measurement, °stamp, °estimation: *It is not easy to get the measure of a man who wants to marry your daughter.* **5** °quota, °allotment, °ration, °share, °amount, °degree, °proportion, °quantity, °allowance; °portion, °part: *He was accorded a measure of freedom in choosing the method for getting the job done. She has had her measure of praise.* **6** Often, **measures**: °step(s), °procedure, °proceeding, °action, °course (of °action), °plan, °method, °means, avenue, °tactic(s), °way, °direction, °approach, °technique: *They took measures to ensure that it never happens again.* **7** °bill, °resolution, legislation, °act, statute, °law; °plan, °proposal: *A measure to change the speed limit is before the council.* **8** °bound, °limit, °end, °extreme, °extent, limitation, moderation, °control, constraint, °restraint: *Drug trafficking has gone beyond all measure in some countries.* **9** °beat, °rhythm, °cadence, metre, °time; °melody, °tune, °bar, °theme, °motif: *The ambassador entered, and the band played in stately measures.* **10 for good measure**: to °boot, in °addition, additionally, as a dividend, into the °bargain, °besides, as *or* for a °bonus, °moreover, furthermore: *The job includes a company car and, for good measure, free medical insurance.*
—*v.* **11** °rank, °rate, °gauge *or US* gage, meter, °weigh, °calculate, °reckon, °compute, °calibrate, °determine, ascertain, °figure out *or* up, assess, appraise, °estimate, °evaluate, °judge, value; °survey, °find out: *We must measure the effect of the new safety regulations on our equipment budget. Public acceptance of the new product may be difficult to measure.* **12** °proportion, °pace, °adapt, °gauge *or US* gage, relate, °tailor, °fit, °adjust, °regulate, °control: *Teachers should measure homework assignments according to pupils' available time. Measure your words when speaking to young children.* **13 measure off** *or* **out**: °mark off *or* out, °limit, delimit, °fix, °pace off *or* out, °lay off: *Now measure off exactly 122.5 metres due north.* **14 measure out**: °mete out, °dole out, °ration (out), °parcel out, apportion, °allot, °share out, °assign, allocate, °give out, °deal out, °distribute, °issue, °pass out, °hand out, °dispense, °disperse, °spread around *or* about: *The relief workers measured out food and water to the victims of the famine.* **15 measure up (to)**: **a** °meet, °equal, °fulfil, °match, °reach, attain: *The first eleven have not measured up to their coach's expectations. Will they ever measure up?* **b** °qualify (for), be °suitable (for), be °equal to, be °fit *or* °fitted for, be °adequate (to), be up to, *Colloq* °make the °grade, come up to °scratch, be up to snuff, *US* cut the mustard: *If Clive gets the assignment, are you sure that he'll measure up? No one else measures up to the job.*

measured *adj.* **1** °slow, regulated, °unhurried, leisurely, °stately, °majestic, °dignified,

°sedate, °solemn: *The silent procession moved through the streets at a measured pace.* **2** °careful, °cautious, °prudent, °calculated, °studied, considered, °deliberate, °systematic, °sober, °intentional, planned, regulated, °premeditated, well-thought-out, reasoned: *He planned the murder with the same measured deliberation he used in writing computer programs.* **3** °rhythmic(al), °regular, cadenced, °steady, °uniform, °even, °monotonous: *The measured marching of the soldiers echoed through the night.* **4** °precise, regulated, °exact, °predetermined, modulated, quantified; clockwork: *A measured amount of each ingredient is automatically added at each stage of the manufacturing process.*

measurement *n.* **1** measuring, °reckoning, gauging *or US* gaging, ascertainment, °determination, assessment, °estimation, appraisal, °evaluation, valuation, °judgement, °calculation, computation, mensuration, commensuration; metage: *The measurement of astronomical distances can only be approximate.* **2** dimension, °extent, °size, °amount, °magnitude, amplitude; °length, °breadth, °height, °width, °depth; °area; °volume, °capacity; °weight, tonnage; (elapsed) time, period; (square *or* cubic) footage, (square) yardage, mileage, acreage: *I need the measurements of the room to order the fitted carpet.*

meat *n.* **1** °flesh; °food, °nourishment, °sustenance, viands, victuals, nutriment, °provisions, °provender, comestibles, edibles, eatables, *Colloq* eats, chow, grub: *She's turned vegetarian and won't touch meat in any form.* **2** °pith, °core, °heart, marrow, °kernel, °vital °part, °essence, °gist, °substance, °basics, °essentials, crux: *The sub-plot seems to swamp the real meat of the play.*

mechanical *adj.* **1** °automatic, automated, machine-driven; machine-made: *Early mechanical toys are sometimes quite intricate. This is a mechanical, not a hand-crafted device.* **2** °automatic, reflex, °involuntary, °instinctive, °routine, °habitual, °unconscious, °perfunctory, machine-like, robot-like: *Good manners ought to be mechanical. Blinking is a mechanical reaction to bright light.* **3** °impersonal, °distant, °cold, °matter-of-fact, unfeeling, °insensible, ritualistic, °lifeless, spiritless, °dead, °inanimate, unanimated, unemotional, unartistic, mechanistic, °colourless, uninspired, businesslike: *The girl at the check-out gave us a mechanical smile.*

mechanism *n.* **1** °device, appliance, contrivance, °apparatus, °instrument, °machine: *This mechanism will detonate the bomb at the right moment.* **2** machinery, workings, °works, °structure, °system, °organization, °arrangement: *Astrophysicists can offer only an imperfect account of the mechanism of the universe.* **3** °way, °means, °method, °procedure, °approach, °technique, °medium, °process, °agency: *We shall use every mechanism at our disposal to have the case heard by a different judge.* **4** materialism, mechanicalism, physicalism, °logical positivism, °identity theory, monism: *His notions of mechanism reject the idea of free-thinking individualism.*

meddle *v.* °interfere, °intrude, °butt in, °pry, °intervene, interlope, °tamper, °snoop, *Rare*

intermeddle, *Colloq* °stick *or* °poke one's nose in, have a *or* one's °finger in the pie, kibitz: *Why are you always meddling in things that don't concern you?*

mediator *n.* arbitrator, arbiter, referee, °umpire, °judge, °negotiator, °intermediary, °go-between, middleman, °moderator, °liaison, intercessor, interceder, conciliator, appeaser, °peacemaker: *To avoid a lawsuit, they agreed to allow a mediator to settle their differences.*

medicinal *adj.* healing, remedial, °therapeutic, curative, restorative, sanative; medical, iatric(al), *Medicine* roborant, analeptic, alexipharmic: *The doctor prescribed a medicinal ointment for the rash.*

medicine *n.* medication, medicament, °remedy, °drug, pharmaceutical, °prescription, *Archaic* physic; nostrum, panacea, cure-all: *There is no medicine that can cure your affliction.*

mediocre *adj.* middling, °indifferent, °ordinary, commonplace, °average, °medium, °everyday, run-of-the-mill, °pedestrian, °undistinguished, uninspired, unimaginative, unexceptional, °tolerable, °fair, not (that *or* too) good, not bad, second-rate, third-rate, °inferior, °poor, *Brit* common-or-garden variety, *US* garden-variety, *Colloq* °so so, °fair to middling, nothing to brag *or* to write home about, no °great shakes: *It was a mediocre play, and we couldn't be bothered to sit through it.*

meditate *v.* **1** °reflect, °think, °muse, °ponder, °study, ruminate, cogitate, °contemplate, cerebrate, be °lost in °thought, be in a brown study: *Please don't interrupt me while I'm meditating.* **2** Often, **meditate on** *or* **upon**: °consider, °contemplate, °mull over, °reflect on *or* upon, °ponder on *or* over, °chew over, °plan, °scheme, °devise, °design, °conceive, °frame, °think up, have in °mind: *She was meditating revenge, while I was meditating on how to discourage her.*

meditative *adj.* °thoughtful, °pensive, contemplative, °reflective, °studious, cogitative, excogitative, abstracted, °rapt, engrossed, °lost *or* °deep in °thought, ruminative, brooding: *She suddenly stopped talking and became meditative, looking at me with a curious expression.*

medium *adj.* **1** °average, °middle, mid, medial, median, °normal, °standard, °usual, °everyday, °ordinary; mid-sized: *His wife has an estate car of medium size—nothing extravagant.* **2** See **mediocre**, above.
—*n.* **3** °average, °middle, mid-point, compromise, °centre, °mean, °norm, mediocrity: *Instead of going to extremes, try for the happy medium.* **4** °atmosphere, °environment, ambience *or* ambiance, °milieu: *The air serves as a medium of sound. The light is refracted as it passes into a denser medium.* **5** °means, °method, °mode, °approach, instrumentality, °device, °mechanism, intermediation, °technique, contrivance, °agency, °expedient, °way, °course, °route, °road, avenue, °channel, conveyance, °vehicle: *Latin and Greek were the media of the scholarship, the science, and the theology of the Middle Ages. Television is a powerful advertising medium.*

medley *n.* °mixture, °assortment, °combination, °miscellany, mélange, °collection, conglomeration, agglomeration, °hotchpotch *or US-*

and Canadian hodgepodge, olio, °blend, gallimaufry, omnium gatherum, °pastiche, °pot-pourri, salmagundi, olla podrida, °mishmash, °jumble, °mess, farrago, °stew, goulash, *Colloq* °mixed bag: *The programme consisted of a medley of show tunes.*

meek *adj.* **1** °modest, °humble, °submissive, unassuming, unambitious, unpretentious, °mild, °bland, °patient, deferential, °shy, °retiring, °lowly: *The meek shall inherit the earth.* **2** °tame, °timid, °weak, docile, compliant, °submissive, °yielding, acquiescent, unaggressive, non-militant, °tractable, °manageable, °subdued, repressed, spiritless, suppressed, °broken, *Colloq* wimpish: *The people are meek and will not offer any resistance to such dictatorial government.*

meet[1] *v.* **1** °encounter, °come across, °chance on *or* upon, °happen on *or* upon, °stumble on *or* into, °see, *Colloq* °run across *or* into, °bump into: *Guess who I met in the park this morning!* **2** Often, **meet with**: rendezvous (with), °get together (with); convene, °assemble, °gather, °collect, forgather *or* foregather, congregate: *I met with the mysterious stranger as arranged. The board meets at 9.00 a.m.* **3** make the °acquaintance of, be introduced to, first °encounter, °come across, °find: *Where did you meet your wife?* **4** °link up, °join, °come together, °unite, adjoin, abut, °touch, intersect: *The horizon is where the sky meets earth.* **5** °answer, °deal with, °handle, °satisfy, °fulfil, take °care of, °dispose of, °heed, °observe, °carry out; °gratify, °pay, °settle, °defray, liquidate: *Will these precautions meet the requirements of the Department of the Environment? The police advised the parents not to meet the kidnapper's demands.* **6** **meet with**: °encounter, be met by, °experience; °undergo, °endure, °suffer, °have, °go through: *All our efforts met with little or no response. Gary met with an accident yesterday.*
—*n.* **7** °competition, °contest, °meeting, °match, tourney, °tournament; °muster, °rally: *The track meet was won by our team.*

meet[2] *adj.* °fitting, °suitable, °appropriate, °proper, °fit, congruous: *It is meet to offer praises to God.*

meeting *n.* **1** °appointment, °engagement, rendezvous, °encounter, assignation, tryst, *Slang US* meet: *She arranged a meeting with her ex-husband.* **2** °assembly, °convention, °conference, °gathering, congress, conclave, °session, congregation, convocation, *US* caucus, *Colloq* °get-together: *Nominations for next year's officers will be presented at the next meeting.* **3** convergence, converging, confluence, joining, °union, °junction, conjunction, intersection: *The earliest settlement was at the meeting of the two rivers.* **4** See meet, 7, above.

melancholy *adj.* **1** °sad, morose, depressed, °unhappy, °dejected, °despondent, °blue, °downhearted, °glum, °gloomy, woeful, °woebegone, lugubrious, disconsolate, downcast, dispirited, low-spirited, cheerless, crestfallen, chap-fallen, °forlorn, °heartbroken, °mournful, °sorrowful, °miserable, °dismal, *Colloq* down in the °mouth, (down) in the dumps, °low: *Harold has been melancholy ever since Lucy left.*
—*n.* **2** °sadness, °sorrow, °misery, °woe, °gloom, unhappiness, blues, moroseness, °depression,

dejection, dejectedness, despondence, despondency, downheartedness, glumness, gloominess, woefulness, lugubriousness, disconsolateness, dispiritedness, cheerlessness, mournfulness, sorrowfulness, miserableness, dolour, °anguish: *Getting Harold's mind off his problems may relieve his melancholy.*

mellow *adj.* **1** °soft, °juicy, °luscious, °delicious, °rich, °sweet, flavourful, full-flavoured, °ready, °ripe, °mature, ripened, °aged: *She set before us a dish of mellow peaches. Amontillado sherry is noted for its mellow taste.* **2** °musical, °melodious, °full, °pure, °rich, °sweet, dulcet, mellifluous, euphonious, vibrant: *Her voice was low, mellow, and suggestive.* **3** °soft, softened, °subtle, muted, pastel: *The mellow shades of this painting would fit well into the décor.* **4** °easygoing, °genial, °gentle, °good-natured, °easy, °cordial, °friendly, °warm, °amiable, °agreeable, °pleasant, °cheerful, °happy, jovial, felicitous: *Patrick seems to have become more mellow with age.*
—*v.* **5** °mature, °ripen, °age, °season, °sweeten, °develop, °improve (with °age), °soften: *Frank has mellowed since taking up golf.*

melodious *adj.* °sweet(-sounding), dulcet, °tuneful, euphonious, °harmonious, melodic, °lyrical, °musical, mellifluous, mellisonant, silvery, °golden: *I agreed with her father that Sylvia has a most melodious voice.*

melodramatic *adj.* °sensational, sensationalistic, °dramatic, stagy, °theatrical, emotionalistic, (over-)°sentimental, (over-)sentimentalized, overdrawn, overworked, °overwrought, overdone, exaggerated, blood-and-thunder, histrionic, *Colloq* hammy, *US* schmaltzy, hokey: *The slightest thing that happened to him he blew up with melodramatic effect to elicit Maria's sympathy.*

melody *n.* **1** °song, °tune, °air, °strain, °measure, °theme, °refrain: *Isn't that the melody from Mimi's aria in La Bohème?* **2** tunefulness, melodiousness, euphoniousness, euphony, °harmony, musicality, sweetness: *The older music seems to be marked by so much more melody than rock 'n' roll.*

melt *v.* **1** °soften, °thaw, liquefy, °fuse, °dissolve, liquidize, deliquesce: *You'd better eat that ice-cream before it melts.* **2** °soften, °thaw, mollify, assuage, °touch, °move, °disarm, °mellow: *The look on the child's face melted his icy reserve.* **3** Usually, **melt into**: °blend, °fade, °merge, °disappear, °dissolve, °shrink: *As soon as the police arrived, Phyllis tried to melt into the background.* **4** **melt away**: °disappear, °dissolve, vanish, °evaporate, °go away, °fade, °pass, °decline, °decrease, °shrink, °dwindle, °diminish: *When the company began to make a profit, all his previous reservations melted away.*

member *n.* °colleague, °associate, °fellow: *I am going to propose Fred as a member of the club.*

memento *n.* **1** souvenir, °keepsake, °remembrance, °relic, °trophy, °token: *I kept his medals as a memento of our time together.* **2** **mementos**: memorabilia: *There will be an auction of war mementos next week.*

memoir *n.* **1** °account, °report, reportage, °narrative, °essay, dissertation, disquisition, °paper, °journal, °record, biography, °life: *They found her memoir about life in the jungle very exciting.* **2** **memoirs**: autobiography, °reminiscences, °recollections, °memories,

°diary, confessions, °letters, °life °story; annals, °history, °account(s), °record(s), °chronology: *She was reading the memoirs of Henry Kissinger.*

memorable *adj.* unforgettable, catchy, never-to-be-forgotten, °noteworthy, °notable, °remarkable, °significant, °important, °worthy, °momentous, °eventful, °historic, °illustrious, °celebrated, °great: *His first book contains many memorable and quotable passages.*

memorandum *n.* °note, °record, °minute, °reminder, °message, *Brit* chit or chitty, *Colloq* memo: *Send a memorandum reminding them of the meeting.*

memorial *adj.* **1** commemorative: *A memorial plaque will be dedicated to him tomorrow.*
—*n.* **2** °monument, marker, °plaque, cenotaph, °statue, °memento, °remembrance, °reminder, souvenir: *Let this serve as a memorial to those who died in the wars. Wreaths were laid at the foot of the memorial.*

memorialize *v.* °honour, °commemorate, pay °homage or °respect or °tribute to, °remember, °eulogize, °celebrate, °mark: *His life, devoted to botany, is memorialized in these beautiful gardens.*

memorize *v.* °learn by heart or rote, °commit to °memory, °learn word for word, °retain; °remember: *He memorized the entire Rime of the Ancient Mariner.*

memory *n.* **1** °recall, °recollection, retention: *My memory of the incident is very vivid. She has a poor memory for faces.* **2** °recollection, °reminiscence, °thought: *The interviewer was drawing on grandfather's memories of the 1920s.* **3** °remembrance, °honour, °homage, °respect, °tribute, °celebration: *He wrote a sequence of poems in memory of a dear friend.*

menace *v.* **1** °threaten, °intimidate, °daunt, terrorize, °terrify, cow, °bully, °frighten, °scare, °alarm: *The loan sharks menaced him when he refused to pay.*
—*n.* **2** °threat, °danger, °peril, °hazard, °risk: *The sunken wreck is a menace to navigation.* **3** intimidation, °scare, °threat, °warning, commination: *According to law, a menace alone does not constitute an injury.*

menacing *adj.* °threatening, looming, °impending, °ominous, °frightening, °terrifying, intimidating, minacious, minatory or minatorial, louring or lowering; °dangerous, °perilous, °hazardous, °risky, chancy: *Menacing storm clouds scudded across the darkening sky.*

mend *v.* **1** °repair, °fix, °patch (up), °rectify, °correct, °remedy, °restore, rehabilitate; °heal: *When will you get round to mending the roof?* **2** °correct, °improve, °better, ameliorate, °reform, °revise, °rectify, set or put °right, emend: *When are you going to mend your ways?* **3** °heal, °improve, °recover, °convalesce, °recuperate, get °better: *It took me a few months to mend after the accident.*
—*n.* **4** °repair, °patch: *You can hardly see where the mend is.* **5 on the mend**: recovering, recuperating, convalescing, convalescent, improving: *The good news is that father is on the mend after his attack.*

menial *adj.* **1** °lowly, °servile, °humble, subservient, °base, °low, °mean, slavish, demeaning, °degrading, ignoble; °routine, unskilled: *He took a number of menial jobs to pay for his daughter's wedding.* **2** °servile, fawning, °grovelling, toadying, sycophantic, °obsequious, cringing,

°time-serving, °flattering, snivelling, *Colloq* boot-licking, *Taboo slang* brown-nosing: *His insecurity makes him surround himself with menial hangers-on.*
—*n.* **3** lackey, °flunkey, serf, °slave, underling, minion, *Brit* °fag, *Colloq Brit* dogsbody, skivvy, *US* gofer: *He works as one of the menials in the hotel kitchen.* **4** toady, sycophant, °yes-man, lick-spittle, leech, °parasite, time-server, *Colloq* boot-licker, *Taboo slang* brown-nose(r): *The film star was attended by a retinue of menials, all anxious to keep in her favour.*

mental *adj.* **1** °intellectual, cognitive, cerebral, perceptual, °rational, conceptual, °theoretical, noetic, °abstract: *The boy staggered us with his ability to perform rapid mental arithmetical calculations.* **2** lunatic, °mad, °crazy, °psychotic, demented, mentally °ill, °unstable, °unbalanced, °deranged, °disturbed, °daft, certifiable, *Slang* off one's rocker, nutty, batty, balmy or barmy, loony, screwy, bonkers, crackers, nuts, bananas, loco: *My great-aunt has gone a bit mental in her old age.*

mentality *n.* **1** °intelligence, °brain, °capacity, °intellect, °wit, °sense, °judgement, acuity, acumen, I.Q., rationality, °understanding: *I'd say that Frank is a man of average mentality.* **2** °inclination, °attitude, °bent, mind-set, °disposition, °frame of °mind, temperament, °outlook, °view: *The news betrays little about what is actually happening, but much about the mentality of the leadership. They criticized Britain's 'island mentality'.*

mention *v.* **1** °speak or °write about, °refer to, allude to, °touch on or upon, make mention (of), °bring up or in, °introduce, °broach, call or direct attention to, °note, °name, cite, °acknowledge; °point out, °indicate, °make known, adduce, °report, °quote: *Sergeant Payne was mentioned in dispatches from the front. He mentions the works of Conrad in support of his thesis.* **2** divulge, °reveal, °intimate, °disclose, °impart, °suggest, animadvert on or upon, °hint (at), °imply, °insinuate: *Did he mention that Liz was present?*
—*n.* **3** °reference, allusion, °note, naming, citation, mentioning, *Colloq* cite: *There was a mention of you in the newspaper today.* **4** °recognition, °tribute, °acknowledgement, °kudos, °praise: *She won no prize but came in for an honourable mention.* **5** °announcement, °reference, referral, °remark: *The speaker's mention of the conference reminded me of something.*

mercantile *adj.* commercial, °business, °trade, marketing, °market: *The book dealt with the mercantile affairs of the Hanseatic League.*

mercenary *adj.* **1** money-oriented, °grasping, °greedy, acquisitive, covetous, °predatory, °avaricious, °venal, *Colloq* money-grubbing: *She objected that the 'financial world' ought to be renamed the 'mercenary world'.* **2** °venal, bribable, °corrupt, bought, *Colloq US* on the take: *They found themselves a mercenary judge and the indictment was quashed.*
—*n.* **3** hireling, legionnaire, °soldier of fortune: *The highly trained task force was made up entirely of mercenaries.*

merchandise *n.* **1** °goods, commodities, °products, °stock, °staples, °produce: *The merchandise you ordered was shipped yesterday.*

—v. 2 °trade, °deal in, °traffic in, °market, °distribute, retail, (°buy and) °sell, °promote, advertise: *We are merchandising the new product line via direct mail.*

merchant *n.* 1 °dealer, retailer, °seller, shopkeeper, °store °owner, °trader, °tradesman *or* tradeswoman, vendor: *High Street merchants are complaining about a decline in sales.* 2 °pedlar, hawker; (travelling) salesman, (sales) °representative, commercial traveller, huckster, door-to-door salesman, *US old-fashioned* drummer, *Colloq* (sales) rep: *His work as an itinerant merchant took him away from home most of the week.* 3 distributor, wholesaler, jobber, °broker, °agent, forwarder; businessman *or* businesswoman, merchant prince, °mogul, °tycoon, magnate, industrialist, *US* baron: *She comes from a family of steel merchants.*

merciful *adj.* compassionate, °sympathetic, °forgiving, °kind, °kindly, clement, kind-hearted, forbearing, °sparing, °lenient, °tender, humane, °liberal, °mild, tender-hearted, °soft-hearted, °gracious, °generous, magnanimous, benignant, beneficent, °charitable, °thoughtful, °considerate, °indulgent, °big: *She begged the governor to be merciful and to spare her life.*

merciless *adj.* °cruel, pitiless, °ruthless, °heartless, °unmerciful, inhumane, °inhuman, °brutal, °savage, barbarous, barbaric, °barbarian, °crude, °rude, °rough, °harsh, °tough, °callous, °hard, hard-hearted, illiberal, °tyrannical, stony-hearted, °cold, °severe, unsparing, insensitive, °indifferent, °unsympathetic, unforgiving, °ungracious, malevolent, °thoughtless, uncharitable, °inconsiderate, °unmoved, unbending, °inflexible, °relentless, unrelenting, inexorable: *Their captors proved to be utterly merciless. The merciless sun beat down on the desert outpost.*

mercy *n.* compassion, °pity, forbearance, °quarter, °tolerance, °sympathy, °favour, °forgiveness, °kindness, kindliness, leniency, tenderness, °humanity, humaneness, liberality, kind-heartedness, tender-heartedness, soft-heartedness, graciousness, generosity, magnanimity, benignity, beneficence, °charity, thoughtfulness, °consideration, °indulgence: *May the Lord have mercy on your soul. We could expect no mercy from that slave-driver.*

mere *adj.* °bare, °basic, scant, °stark, °sheer; °absolute, unmixed, °only, °just, °nothing but, °pure (and °simple), °unmitigated, °undiluted: *She was a mere slip of a girl. We need something more to go on than mere hearsay evidence.*

merely *adv.* 1 °only, °simply; basically, purely, essentially, fundamentally, at °bottom: *I was merely going to ask if you'd like to go to the cinema.* 2 °only, no more than; °barely, °scarcely, °simply, solely, °entirely: *She was merely the scullery-maid. We can't unlock the safe merely on your authority.*

merge *v.* °combine, coalesce, °unite, °join, °amalgamate, consolidate, °pool, °blend, °mix, °mingle, commingle, °fuse: *If we merge our companies, we shall save on overhead costs.*

merger *n.* °combination, coalescence, °union, merging, °amalgamation, consolidation, coalition, pooling, blending, mixing, mingling, commingling, fusing, fusion: *A merger of the two firms might result in a monopoly.*

merit *n.* 1 °worth, worthiness, value, °excellence, °quality, °virtue, °good, goodness: *Philip's plan has a good deal of merit.* 2 Often, **merits**: °assets, strong point, °advantage, rights and wrongs: *What exactly are the merits of his approach over mine? The case should be tried on its own merits.*
—v. 3 °earn, °deserve, °warrant, °rate, have a °right *or* °claim to, be entitled to, be °qualified for, be °worthy of: *What gave you the idea that you merited any special consideration?*

meritorious *adj.* °honourable, °laudable, °praiseworthy, commendable, creditable, °admirable, °estimable, °excellent, °exemplary, °outstanding: *Penny has won the company award for meritorious service five months in a row.*

merriment *n.* jollity, joviality, merrymaking, °revelry, °gaiety, °high *or* °good spirits, °mirth, mirthfulness, joyfulness, felicity, jubilation, °festivity, exhilaration, buoyancy, °exuberance, °cheer, cheerfulness, °glee, °fun, °hilarity, °enjoyment, °happiness, blithefulness, blithesomeness, frolicking: *Everyone joined in the merriment at the office party.*

merry *adj.* 1 °cheerful, °happy, °gay, cheery, °jolly, jovial, in °high *or* °good spirits, mirthful, °joyful, joyous, °hilarious, jubilant, rejoicing, festive, °exhilarating, °exuberant, °vivacious, convivial, °buoyant, °gleeful, °blithe, blithesome, °carefree, light-hearted, °delighted: *Didn't we have a merry old time at the Christmas party!* 2 **make merry**: °revel, °celebrate, °carouse, °frolic: *The guests made merry till the wee hours of the morning.*

mesh *n.* 1 mesh-work, °network, netting, °net, °web, webbing, lattice, lattice-work, °screen, screening, interlacing, lace-work, grid, °grate, °grating, grater, sieve, strainer, trellis, trellis-work, decussation, *Technical* rete, reticle *or* reticule *or* graticule, reticulation, plexus, plexure, reticulum; interstice: *The mesh of the hammock broke and I fell to the ground.* 2 Often, **meshes**: °grip, °clutches, °grasp, toils, °web, °trap, entanglement, °tangle, complex, °complexity, intricacy: *Her papers were lost in the meshes of the filing system.*
—v. 3 catch, °entangle, enmesh, °grab, °trap, entrap, °snare, ensnare, °involve: *I became meshed inextricably in the complexities of her life.* 4 °engage, °fit (together), dovetail, °knit, enmesh, °match, interlock: *After they were aligned, the gears meshed perfectly.*

mess *n.* 1 °chaos, °disorder, disarray, disorganization, °shambles, °muddle, disarrangement, °clutter, °hotchpotch *or US also* hodgepodge, °litter, °tangle, °jumble, °confusion, °mishmash; untidiness: *Would you help me clean up this mess? Drugs have made a mess of his life.* 2 concoction, °mixture, °medley, °miscellany, °hash, gallimaufry, farrago, olio, olla podrida, °pot-pourri, smorgasbord *or* smörgåsbord, kedgeree: *They presented us with a huge mess of things from which we must select what we want.* 3 °predicament, °difficulty, °plight, °pinch, °trouble, °dilemma, °quandary, imbroglio, *Colloq* foul-up, °stew, °fix, hot water, (pretty *or* fine) kettle of fish, pickle, °jam, *Slang* screw-up, *Brit* balls-up, can of worms, *US* snafu: *You have got yourself into a fine mess this time!*
—v. 4 **mess about** *or* **around (with)**: a °potter *or US* putter, °fool (around), dally, °busy oneself, °fiddle about *or* around, °play: *He enjoys*

messing about in boats. **b** philander, °trifle, °toy, °flirt, °seduce, °sleep around, °fool around, °run around: *She doesn't want him to mess about with other women.* **5 mess up: a** disarrange, disarray, dishevel, °tousle, *Colloq US* muss (up): *He always messes up my hair when he kisses me.* **b** °ruin, °destroy, make a °shambles of, °wreck, °bungle, °botch, °foul up, *Colloq* make a °hash of, *Slang* °muck up: *Making that one little mistake messed up his whole career.* **c** °dirty, °clutter up, make °untidy, turn upside down, °pull to °pieces, °upset: *The police messed up my whole house looking for the pistol.* **6 mess with:** °interfere in *or* with, °intervene, °meddle with *or* in, °intrude in, °butt in *or* into, °tinker with, °tamper with, get °involved in *or* with: *They ought to learn not to mess with things that don't concern them.*

message *n.* **1** communication, °bulletin, °report, communiqué, °news, °dispatch *or* despatch, °information, °word, °intelligence, tidings; °note, °missive, °letter, °memorandum: *The message reached us by carrier pigeon.* **2** °speech, °address, °presentation, °statement, °declaration: *His message was delivered via television to people everywhere.* **3** °idea, °point, °import, °meaning, °essence, °implication: *The message that he isn't liked around here still hasn't penetrated his thick skull.*

messenger *n.* °envoy, emissary, legate, nuncio, °intermediary, °go-between; °page, errand-boy, errand-girl, messenger-boy, messenger-girl, courier, °runner, dispatch-rider, Pheidippides, Mercury, Hermes; herald, °harbinger; *Colloq US* gofer: *If you don't like the message, don't take it out on the messenger.*

Messiah *n.* deliverer, liberator, emancipator, °saviour, rescuer: *They believe in a Messiah who will release them from earthly bondage.*

metaphor *n.* figure (of °speech), allusion, analogy, analogue, °reference, °image, trope, °symbol; simile, parabole; metonymy, symbolism, °imagery: *When she said she was blue, she was using 'blue' as a metaphor. Poetry is rife with metaphor.*

metaphoric *adj.* metaphorical, non-literal, allusive, analogic(al), analogous, figurative, °symbolic, referential, parabolic(al), metonymic, metonymous, tropological: *I meant 'filthy' in a metaphoric, not a literal, sense.*

mete *v.* Usually, **mete out:** °deal (out), apportion, °distribute, °dole (out), °allot, °assign, allocate, °parcel out, °share out, °ration (out), °measure out, °dispense, °hand out, °give out, °pass out, *Colloq* dish out: *Punishment was meted out to those who deserved it.*

meteoric *adj.* **1** °brief, °short-lived, °temporary, transitory, °transient, ephemeral, evanescent, impermanent, °fleeting, °momentary, °swift, overnight: *She enjoyed a meteoric rise as a singer, but after two years at the top she disappeared without a trace.* **2** °brilliant, °dazzling, flashing, spectacular, °sensational: *His meteoric career was launched in 1974.*

method *n.* **1** °way, °means, °procedure, °approach, °route, avenue, °road, °mode, °manner, °technique, °process, °routine, *modus operandi;* °plan, °scheme, °programme, °course, °practice, °pattern, °system, methodology; *Colloq US* M.O.: *What method was used to arrive at the answer?* **2** °arrangement, °order, °system, °structure, °organization, °design, °pattern,

orderliness, neatness, °regularity, °discipline: *There is a discernible, underlying method to what seems superficially chaotic.*

methodical *adj.* organized, ordered, °systematic, structured, businesslike, °orderly, °neat, °tidy, °regular, °routine, balanced, disciplined, °painstaking, °meticulous, °deliberate, paced, °laborious, plodding, °laboured: *The weaver resumed his methodical throwing of the shuttle, back and forth, back and forth.*

meticulous *adj.* °careful, °precise, °accurate, °exact, °fastidious, °scrupulous, °thorough, °particular, °painstaking, punctilious, °fussy, °finicky, °demanding, °strict, °critical, °exacting, °perfectionist: *His work is noted for its meticulous attention to detail.*

metropolis *n.* °capital, (°capital) °city; metropolitan °area, urban °sprawl, megalopolis, °municipality: *Street crime has become a problem in every major metropolis.*

microbe *n.* micro-organism, microzoon, °germ; bacterium, virus, *Colloq* °bug: *Only recently has science learnt that diseases are caused by microbes.*

midday *n.* °noon, noontime, twelve (o'clock) °noon, *US* high °noon: *By midday, the temperature had reached 34° Celsius.*

middle *adj.* **1** °central, °centre, halfway, mid, midway, °mean, medial, *Technical* mesial: *We had reached the middle stage of our journey. Her index finger and middle finger are almost exactly the same length.* —*n.* **2** °centre, mid-point, °midst, halfway °point; °heart, bull's-eye: *He lives in the middle of the city. The arrow found the very middle of the target.* **3** midriff, waist, mid-section, °stomach: *She wore a red sash round her middle.*

midst *n.* °middle, °centre, mid-point, halfway °point: *In the midst of life we are in death. They live in a fairy-tale château in the midst of beautiful Breton countryside. This proved a welcome boost in the midst of a difficult election campaign.*

midwife *n.* accoucheur *or* accoucheuse: *Most babies in the world are delivered by midwives.*

might *n.* **1** °strength, °power, °energy, °force, muscle, potency, *Literary* puissance: *I hit my attacker with all my might. Might doesn't always make right.* **2** °influence, °authority, °weight, °sway, °dominion, ascendancy, °superiority, mightiness, °capability, °capacity, °power, °effect, effectiveness, *Colloq* clout: *It was not till the 20th century that the might of the United States was felt outside its borders.*

mighty *adj.* **1** °powerful, °strong, °potent, °influential, °dominant, °predominant, ascendant, °weighty, doughty, °authoritarian, autocratic, °indomitable: *The pen is mightier than the sword. He should have thought twice before challenging such a mighty opponent.* **2** °strong, °muscular, °powerful, °robust, strapping, °sturdy, °brawny, °burly, well-built, able-bodied, °hardy, *Colloq* °husky, °hefty: *The smith a mighty man was he, With large and sinewy hands.* **3** °big, °large, °huge, °grand, °great, °enormous, °gigantic, tremendous, °towering, °monumental, °prodigious, °massive, °bulky: *The giant plucked a mighty tree from the earth and flung it across the sea.* —*adv.* **4** °very, °extremely: *It was mighty nice of you to visit me here in the Ozarks.*

migrant *n.* **1** wanderer, °rover, °drifter, gypsy, nomad, itinerant, °transient, migrator, wayfarer, bird of °passage, peregrinator, °traveller; vagrant; *Colloq US* wetback: *The townspeople were having difficulty finding accommodation for the migrants.* —*adj.* **2** °transient, migratory, itinerant, peripatetic, drifting, nomadic, °travelling, gypsy, floating; vagrant: *The farmers depend on migrant workers to bring in the harvest.*

migrate *v.* **1** °go, °move, °travel, °settle, resettle, relocate, °move °house; °emigrate, immigrate, expatriate: *During the potato famine, many migrated from Ireland to America.* **2** °wander, °roam, voyage, rove, °drift, °range: *Some say that the American Indians migrated across the Bering land bridge from Asia.*

mild *adj.* **1** placid, °peaceful, °calm, °tranquil, °bland, °mellow, °inoffensive, °gentle, °serene, °good-natured, affable, °amiable, °kind, °kindly, °equable, °easygoing, °temperate, non-violent, conciliatory, °indulgent, °merciful, °forgiving, compassionate, °lenient, forbearing, °peaceable, pacific, °passive, °submissive, °yielding, °tractable, °meek, unassuming, °modest, °quiet, °subdued: *Judge Leaver is known for his mild disposition.* **2** clement, balmy, °warm, °fair, °pleasant, °temperate, placid, °moderate: *We've had a succession of mild winters here.* **3** °bland, °soothing, lenitive, mollifying, demulcent, emollient, °gentle, calming, softening: *The doctor recommended a mild laxative.*

milieu *n.* °environment, °climate, surroundings, environs, °background, ambience *or* ambiance, °sphere, °setting, °atmosphere, °medium, °element, °precincts: *The British Library was the perfect milieu in which to pursue his research and writing.*

militant *adj.* **1** °aggressive, combative, °pugnacious, °belligerent, °hostile, contentious, antagonistic, °offensive, °truculent, °fierce, °ferocious, °warlike, bellicose, °martial, jingoistic, hawkish: *Those who have experienced war are not likely to be militant.* **2** warring, fighting, combatant, combating, embattled; at °war, up in arms: *The militant members of the council refused to discuss terms.* —*n.* **3** fighter, °aggressor, combatant, °belligerent, warrior, °soldier: *Anyone who experiences the hardships of a long strike may think twice before being a militant.*

military *adj.* **1** °martial, soldierly, naval, army, fighting, °service: *The military machine was poised to strike.* —*n.* **2** (armed) °services *or* °forces, army, °navy, air °force, military establishment, soldiery: *The military will oppose any reductions in spending for arms.*

militate *v.* **1** Usually, **militate against**: °discourage, °work *or* °go *or* °operate against, °foil, °counter, countervail, °cancel (out), °reduce (possibility of), °prevent, °hinder, °resist, °oppose: *His poor prison record militates against his early parole.* **2** Usually, **militate for** *or* **in favour of**: be on the °side of, °favour, °further, °promote, °help, °aid: *The same reasoning that militated in favour of lower taxes then persists today.*

milk *v.* °drain, bleed, °extract, °tap, °exploit, wring, °draw off *or* out, °withdraw: *The comic milked the joke for yet another laugh. The taxman is milking me dry.*

milksop *n.* °sissy *or Brit also* cissy, °coward, °weakling, namby-pamby, mollycoddle, cry-baby, nancy (boy), nance, dastard, poltroon, caitiff, (little) Lord Fauntleroy, *Archaic* caitiff, *US* milquetoast, *Colloq* chinless wonder, *Brit* mother's *or* mummy's boy, *US* mama's boy, pantywaist, *Slang* pansy: *We want men, not milksops, in the Marines.*

mill *n.* **1** grinder, quern, crusher, °roller: *In many parts of the world, corn is still ground by hand in a stone mill.* **2** °plant, °factory, °works, workshop, °shop, foundry: *This mill turns out rolled steel.* **3 been through the mill**: °experienced, °knowledgeable, °sophisticated, toughened, hardened, °seasoned, battle-scarred, *Colloq* been through the wringer, in the know: *He's been through the mill and knows what to expect.* **4 run-of-the-mill**: °average, unexceptional, °ordinary, °common, unremarkable, °everyday, °basic, °simple, *Brit* common-or-garden variety, *US* garden-variety: *Critics found her voice pleasant but rather run-of-the-mill.* —*v.* **5** °grind, °crush, comminute, °powder, °pulverize, °grate, granulate, °pound, triturate, masticate, bray; °crunch, mince: *Flour milled to a very fine consistency is more suitable for pastries than for breads.* **6 mill about** *or* **around**: °meander, °wander, °walk, °stroll, amble, °move about *or* around, °crowd, °throng, °swarm: *There were quite a few people milling about our stand at the trade fair.*

mimic *v.* **1** °imitate, ape, °copy, simulate, °mirror, °echo: *The image in the mirror mimicked every move I made.* **2** °reproduce, °duplicate, °copy: *This frieze mimics one on the Parthenon.* **3** °mock, °ridicule, °satirize, °caricature, °parody, make °fun of, °lampoon, impersonate, *Colloq* °take off: *It is rude to mimic your elders.* —*n.* **4** impersonator, imitator, impressionist, caricaturist, parodist, *Colloq* copycat: *Professor Eidolon, the greatest mimic in the world, is here to entertain you!* —*adj.* **5** imitative, °imitation, °mock, simulated, mimetic, °sham, make-believe, °pretend(ed); °fake, °counterfeit, feigned: *Naumachia is the name given to the mimic sea battle staged in ancient Rome.*

mincing *adj.* °effeminate, °dainty, °delicate, niminy-piminy, foppish, dandyish, over-dainty, °affected, °put-on, °pretentious, °precious, *Brit* °twee, *Colloq* la-di-da *or* lah-di-dah *or* la-de-da: *His mincing speech sets my teeth on edge.*

mind *n.* **1** °intelligence, °intellect, °wit(s), °mentality, °brain, brains, brainpower, °sense, sagacity, °wisdom, °perception, percipience, °reason, astuteness, °insight, shrewdness, sapience, *Colloq* grey matter: *There is nothing wrong with your son's mind, Mr Field; he just doesn't want to apply it to school work.* **2** °memory, °recollection; °remembrance: *Keep in mind what I am about to tell you.* **3** °aptitude, °head, °perception, °capacity, °brain: *She has a great mind for dates—for figures of all kinds.* **4** °intellect, °intellectual, °sage, °genius, °thinker, *Colloq* °brain: *There is no doubt that your daughter is one of the great minds of all time.* **5** °intention, °disposition, °temper, temperament, °humour, °fancy, °tendency, °bent, °inclination, °bias, °persuasion: *I was of a mind to let him have his own way.* **6** °opinion, °sentiment, °attitude, (°point of) °view,

°feeling, °judgement, °belief, °viewpoint, °position: *She has a mind of her own. To my mind, the process could be greatly speeded up.* **7** °feeling, °position, °will, °wish, °desire, °plan(s): *Won't you change your mind and stay to dinner?* **8** °attention, °thoughts, concentration, °thinking: *Try to keep your mind on your work.* **9 bear** or **keep in mind**: °remember, do not forget or overlook, °recall, °retain, be °aware or cognizant or °mindful of, °consider: *Bear in mind that the post office is closed tomorrow.* **10 give someone a piece of one's mind**: °castigate, °scold, °rebuke, °reprimand, °rail at, °reprove, reproach, °chastise, °upbraid, °berate, read (someone) the riot act, Colloq °tell off, °dress down, haul or rake over the coals, °skin alive, US °bawl out; Slang give someone °hell, US °chew out: *This time my father really gave the maître d'hôtel a piece of his mind.* **11 in** or **of two minds**: vacillating, undecided, ambivalent, °uncertain, shilly-shallying, unsure, wavering: *Sam was in two minds about ordering a new computer.* **12 know one's (own) mind**: be °decided or resolved, be °firm or °resolute, be °sure or °certain or °positive, be (self-)assured or (self-)°confident, be in touch with oneself: *He knows his own mind when it comes to his career.* **13 make up one's (own) mind**: °decide, °choose, conclude, form an °opinion; °determine, °consider, °weigh, °judge, deem: *Sally hasn't yet made up her mind about marrying Jim. Let her make up her own mind.* **14 out of one's mind**: °insane, °mad, °crazy: *You're out of your mind if you think I'll go swimming in that shark-infested bay!*
—v. **15** °object to, °resent, take °offence at, be offended by, °dislike, be troubled or annoyed by, °care, have any °objection to, °disapprove of, be bothered or affronted by: *Do you mind not smoking? Yes, I mind very much. Would you mind moving your car, you're blocking the drive.* **16** °heed, °attend to, pay °attention to, °obey, °listen to, make or take °note of, °mark, °note: *Please mind what your mother says.* **17** °watch, be °careful of, take °care with, be °cautious of: *Mind your head at that low doorway!* **18** °watch over, take °care of, °care for, °look after, °sit with, babysit, °guard, keep an eye on or out for, have or take °charge of, °attend: *Suzie is minding the children so that we can get some work done.* **19 never mind**: °ignore, °disregard, °forget, pay no °attention to, do not °think twice about, do not give a second °thought to, °erase or °obliterate or °cancel from the mind, slough off: *Never mind what that naughty boy calls you!*

minder *n.* **1** child-minder, babysitter, sitter, nanny, °nurse, governess: *The minder will put the children to bed.* **2** bodyguard, °escort, °protector: *Arthur hired an ex-fighter as his minder.*

mindful *adj.* Often, **mindful of**: °aware, °alert, °attentive to, °alive, °conscious, heedful, °conscientious, watchful, °vigilant, on the qui vive, on the °lookout, circumspect, °cautious: *I am ever mindful of the way you like things done. She was always mindful of keeping the plants well watered.*

mindless *adj.* **1** °stupid, asinine, °thick, thick-headed, °obtuse, idiotic, imbecilic, moronic, °thoughtless, witless, °senseless, brainless, °feeble-minded, fatuous, addle-brained, addle-pated, feather-brained, Colloq Brit gormless: *Many of the programmes on television are mindless twaddle.* **2** °inattentive, °unthinking, °thoughtless, °unaware: *He plunged into the pool, mindless of any of the perils that awaited him.*

mine *n.* **1** °pit, °excavation, lode, °vein; colliery, coalfield: *My father worked in a mine from the age of 14.* **2** °source, mother-lode, °vein, °store, °storehouse, °supply, °deposit, depository or depositary, repository, °reserve, °hoard, °treasure trove, reservoir, well-spring; °abundance, °fund, gold-mine, °wealth, °treasury: *This encyclopedia is a rich mine of information.*
—v. **3** °excavate, °dig, °quarry, °extract, °scoop out or up, °remove, °unearth; °derive, °extract, °draw: *He claims to have mined coal in Wales and gold in South Africa. Analysis shows this ore was mined in Pennsylvania.* **4** °ransack, °search, °rake through, °scour, °scan, °read, °survey, °look through, °probe: *Several directories were mined to compile our list of sales prospects.*

mingle *v.* **1** °mix, °blend, intermingle, commingle, intermix, °combine, °amalgamate, °merge, °compound, °marry, °join, °unite: *The stories cleverly mingle gravity and levity, the mundane and the magical. There was loud applause, mingled with a few chuckles and gasps.* **2** °mix, °socialize, °associate, °join, °circulate, °fraternize, °hobnob, consort, °go, °spend time, Colloq °hang about or around or out, °rub shoulders, Brit °pal up, US °pal around: *I asked Fred to mingle with the guests and make them feel at home.*

miniature *adj.* °small, small-scale, °little, °tiny, °diminutive, °minute, °wee, minuscule, mini, microscopic, °micro, midget, °dwarf, bantam, °baby, pygmy, °pocket, Lilliputian, US vest-pocket, Colloq °minimal: *This miniature TV fits in the palm of your hand.*

minimal *adj.* least, smallest, minutest, littlest, tiniest, slightest; °minimum, °nominal, °token: *As a house plant, the cactus requires minimal attention. There is a minimal charge for service.*

minimize *v.* **1** °reduce, °shrink, lessen, °diminish, °prune, °abbreviate, °pare (down), °cut (down), °curtail, °abridge, °shorten, °decrease, minify: *Our stringent safety measures minimize the chance of an accident.* **2** °belittle, de-emphasize, downplay, °play down, make °little or °light of, °disparage, decry, deprecate, °depreciate, misprize, devalue, devaluate, undervalue, underrate, °underestimate, US °talk down: *Being modest, she minimizes her role in the organization.*

minimum *n.* **1** least, lowest, nadir: *The hotel offered the minimum of comfort for the maximum price.*
—adj. **2** °minimal, °nominal, reduced, minutest, littlest, least, slightest, lowest: *What is the minimum deposit the travel agent will accept? He refused to make even the minimum effort needed to save himself.*

minister *n.* **1** cleric, °clergyman, clergywoman, ecclesiastic, °pastor, vicar, °priest, °father, reverend, churchman, °divine, parson, °preacher, man or woman of the °cloth, evangelist, °missionary, dean, curate, curé, abbé, chaplain, Colloq padre, Slang US military sky pilot, Holy Joe: *The marriage was performed by a visiting minister.* **2** °envoy, °delegate, legate, diplomat,

°ambassador, emissary, plenipotentiary, minister plenipotentiary, °envoy °extraordinary, minister °resident, consul, °agent, chargé d'affaires, *Brit* °cabinet °officer *or* °member: *The minister himself signed the treaty.*
—v. **3** Usually, **minister to**: °attend (to *or* on *or* upon), °wait on, °care for, °look after, °see to, °accommodate; °serve, °supply, °aid, °help, °assist, °support: *In his last days, she ministered to him in every way.*

ministry n. **1** priesthood, °sacred °calling, the church, the pulpit, the °cloth; °religion, °holy orders: *Burt retired from the ministry to write tracts.* **2** clergy, clergymen *or* clergywomen, clericals, the °cloth, church elders *or* elders of the church: *During his regime, the ministry exercised great influence on the government.* **3** °department, °office, °bureau, °agency: *Military affairs are the responsibility of the Ministry of Defence.*

minor *adj.* **1** lesser, smaller, °secondary, °subordinate, °subsidiary: *The minor planets are bodies orbiting the sun in the asteroid belt.* **2** °insignificant, °obscure, °inconsequential, unimportant, °trifling, trivial, °negligible, inconsiderable, °slight, °petty, °paltry, °small, *Colloq* °small-time, one-horse, *Brit* two a penny, *US* minor-league, bush-league, penny-ante, two-bit, picayune: *It is a minor matter to me whether you stay or go. She is only a minor player in this game.*
—n. **3** °child, youngster, °youth, °stripling, °teenager, °adolescent, schoolboy, schoolgirl, °boy, °girl, °lad, laddie, °lass, lassie, *Law* °ward, infant: *At your age, you are still a minor in the eyes of the law.*

minstrel n. bard, troubadour, balladeer, jongleur, skald *or* scald, minnesinger, Meistersinger: *The medieval minstrels wandered the countryside, entertaining as they went.*

mint n. **1** (small) °fortune, °lot, king's ransom, millions, billions, *Colloq* °bundle, °pile, °heap, °wad(s), °packet, °pot(s), loads, ton, *Slang Brit* bomb, *US* (big) bucks: *He lost a mint at roulette last night. She made a mint on her inventions.*
—v. **2** °make, °coin, °produce, °earn: *Special commemorative coins were minted to celebrate the Coronation.*

minute[1] n. **1** °instant, °second, split °second, °flash, °moment, before you can say 'Jack Robinson', °blink *or* wink *or* °twinkling of an eye, coup d'œil, trice, *Colloq* °one sec, two secs, bat of an eye, shake, jiffy, tick, *Brit* half a mo, two shakes (of a lamb's tail): *I'll be with you in a minute.* **2 minutes**: log, °record, °journal, °transcript, °notes, °summary, résumé, °proceedings, °transactions, °memorandum: *Have you the minutes of the last meeting?* **3 up to the minute**: °latest, newest, °modern, up to °date, °trendy, °fashionable, °smart, all the °rage, in °vogue, °stylish, in °style, in °fashion, à la °mode, *Colloq* in, with it, hep *or* °hip, °hot, °cool, *US* °now: *She always wears the most up-to-the-minute clothes.*
—v. **4** °record, °transcribe, °take down, °write down, °note, °make (a) °note of, °document, log: *We need someone to minute the meeting.*

minute[2] *adj.* **1** °small, °little, °tiny, tiniest, minuscule, °miniature, °wee, infinitesimal, microscopic, micro, °diminutive, mini, °baby, pint-sized, bantam, Lilliputian, *Colloq* teeny,

teensy-weensy, itty-bitty, itsy-bitsy: *The minute furniture in the doll's house was made entirely by hand.* **2** unimportant, °petty, °insignificant, least, °slight, °mere, °meagre, °trifling, trivial, °minor, °small, °little, *Colloq* piddling, *US* picayune: *The painting was a perfect copy, down to the minutest detail.*

miraculous *adj.* °marvellous, wonderful, wondrous, °incredible, °unbelievable, °inexplicable, unexplainable, °extraordinary, spectacular, °amazing, astounding, astonishing, mind-boggling, °remarkable, °phenomenal, °fantastic, °fabulous; magical, °supernatural, preternatural, °superhuman, *Colloq* out of this °world, *Slang* far-out, °crazy: *Langley has made a miraculous recovery from yellow fever.*

mire n. **1** °swamp, °bog, fen, °marsh, quagmire, °morass, slough, *Brit dialect* sump: *The horse stumbled into the mire and began to flounder.* **2** °mud, °ooze, °muck, slime, °dirt: *I had to wade through muck and mire to get to your front door.*
—v. **3** enmire, °bog down, become entangled *or* tangled, become enmeshed *or* meshed, become °involved: *Sorry I'm late; I got mired in a problem at the office.* **4** °dirty, °soil, begrime, °muddy, befoul, besmirch, °sully, °tarnish, °smear, °blacken, defile, smudge: *My boots were badly mired. The scandal badly mired his reputation.*

mirror n. **1** looking-glass, °glass, speculum, reflector: *She stared at her reflection in the mirror, wondering whether she should grow her hair.* **2** °reflection, °reproduction, °picture, °representation, replication, (mirror) °image: *Language is the mirror of society, reflecting every social change.*
—v. **3** °reflect, °reproduce, °represent, depict, °repeat, °echo, °send back: *The calm lake mirrored the moonlight. The people's misery was mirrored in their faces.*

mirth n. °merriment, merrymaking, jollity, °gaiety, °fun, °laughter, °amusement, °frolic, frolicking, joviality, joyousness, °revelry, rejoicing, °glee, high spirits, mirthfulness, °hilarity, buoyancy, *Formal* jocundity: *Life without mirth is a lamp without oil. Christmas is a time for mirth.*

misalliance n. mésalliance, mismarriage, mismatch, mismatchment, bad match, mismating: *No one is surprised that John and Marsha's misalliance has ended in divorce.*

misanthrope n. misanthropist, mankind-hater; °man-hater, woman-hater, misogynist; loner, °hermit, °recluse, anchorite *or* anchoret, *Colloq* lone wolf: *The longer he lived and the more he learned of his fellow-man, the more of a misanthrope he became.*

misanthropic *adj.* man-hating; antisocial, °unsocial, unfriendly, egocentric, °egoistic: *In his misanthropic moods, Joel disdains human company.*

misappropriate v. **1** °embezzle, °steal, filch, expropriate, °pocket, *Formal* peculate, defalcate: *He was found guilty of misappropriating club funds.* **2** misapply, °misuse, °pervert, misemploy: *The money intended for the health service was misappropriated for the war effort.*

misbehave v. °disobey, behave °badly *or* improperly, be °bad *or* °naughty *or*

°mischievous, *Colloq* °carry on, act up, *Slang* raise hell, raise Cain: *The teacher sent for me because Robyn misbehaved in class.*

misbehaviour *n.* naughtiness, badness, misconduct, misdemeanour(s), disorderliness, disobedience, delinquency, °disorderly °conduct, °rowdyism: *She was severely reprimanded for persistent misbehaviour in class.*

miscalculate *v.* misjudge, °err, misevaluate, misestimate, misreckon, miscompute, miscount, misappreciate, misread; °underestimate, undervalue, underrate; overestimate, overvalue, °overrate: *She miscalculated the effect of her resignation.*

miscarriage *n.* °failure, abortion, °collapse, °breakdown, °failing, mismanagement, non-fulfilment, °defeat, non-success, frustration: *Her acquittal was a miscarriage of justice.*

miscarry *v.* abort, °fail, °fall through, °break down, go °wrong, °founder, °come to nothing or naught or nought, go awry, come to °grief, go °amiss, °misfire, go up or end up in smoke, °perish, °die: *The plan to steal the crown jewels miscarried.*

miscellaneous *adj.* °varied, heterogeneous, °diverse, °mixed, diversified, °divers, motley, °sundry, assorted, °various, varying, multifarious, multiform, many-sided, multiplex, °manifold: *A large part of the exhibition is devoted to miscellaneous paintings and prints from his early period.*

miscellany *n.* °mixture, °assortment, °variety, °medley, °diversity, °mixed bag, job °lot, rag-bag, mélange, °pot-pourri, gallimaufry, motley, °hotchpotch or *US and Canadian* hodgepodge, salmagundi, olio, olla podrida, smorgasbord or smörgåsbord, °odds and ends, omnium gatherum, °hash, °mess, *Brit* lucky dip, °jumble, *US* grab-bag: *A miscellany of household goods was contributed for the jumble sale.*

mischief *n.* **1** °misbehaviour, naughtiness, impishness, elfishness or elvishness, roguishness, rascality, °devilry or deviltry, mischievousness, playfulness, devilment, badness, *Colloq* °monkey business, shenanigans, *Brit* °monkey tricks or *US* monkeyshines: *That boy is always up to some mischief.* **2** °harm, °injury, °damage, °detriment, °trouble, °hurt, °wrong, °difficulty, disruption, °destruction, °misfortune, °evil: *He didn't realize the mischief a casual remark could do. She was accused of malicious mischief when she punctured his car tyres.*

mischievous *adj.* **1** °naughty, impish, roguish, rascally, °devilish, elfish or elvish, puckish, scampish, °frolicsome, °playful, °sportive: *Tying his cousin's shoelaces together was a mischievous prank and not malicious.* **2** °harmful, °injurious, °hurtful, damaging, pernicious, °detrimental, °destructive, deleterious, °dangerous, °spiteful, malicious, °vicious, malign, baleful, baneful, noxious, °wicked, °evil, °bad: *The government regards as mischievous the detention of any Foreign Office personnel.*

misconceive *v.* °misunderstand, misconstrue, misjudge, °mistake, misapprehend, °misinterpret, misread, get or have the wrong idea, get or have (hold of) the wrong end of the °stick: *He has misconceived the purpose in banning firearms.*

misconception *n.* °false or °wrong °notion or °idea, °misunderstanding, misconstruction,

misconstrual, misjudgement, miscalculation, misapprehension, °mistaken °belief, °error, °mistake, °delusion: *The confused wording of the warranty could result in a misconception of one's rights.*

miscreant *n.* **1** °villain, °wretch, mischief-maker, scamp, °rascal, °criminal, evil-doer, °felon, malefactor, °rogue, °reprobate, °scoundrel, wrongdoer, °good-for-nothing, ne'er-do-well, blackguard, hooligan, ruffian, °hoodlum, °thug, °rowdy, *Archaic* knave, caitiff, varlet, rapscallion, *Colloq* crook, roughneck, scallywag or scalawag, *Slang* hood, *Brit* °mug, °rough, *Australian* larrikin, *US* baddy, bad actor: *The police have apprehended the miscreant who had been attacking passers-by.*
—*adj.* **2** °villainous, °wretched, °mischievous, rascally, °criminal, felonious, °corrupt, malefic, malevolent, °evil, depraved, °base, nefarious, iniquitous, °vicious, unprincipled, ne'er-do-well, °reprobate, scoundrelly, °wicked: *The miscreant terrorists may be hiding in Greece.*

misdeed *n.* Often, **misdeeds**: °offence, °crime, felony, wrongdoing, misdoing, °transgression, misdemeanour, °fault, misconduct, °sin, trespass, °wrong, °peccadillo: *Who will punish him for his misdeeds now that he is safe in Argentina?*

misdirect *v.* misguide, misadvise; misaddress: *He misdirected us by saying the lavatory was downstairs. The letter, misdirected, was returned.*

miser *n.* skinflint, hoarder, niggard, penny-pincher, pinchpenny, cheese-parer, Scrooge, *Colloq* cheapskate, *US* tightwad: *For that old miser, charity begins and ends at home.*

miserable *adj.* **1** °wretched, °unhappy, depressed, woeful, °woebegone, °sad, °dejected, °forlorn, disconsolate, °despondent, °heartbroken, °sorrowful, °broken-hearted, °mournful, °desolate, °desperate, despairing, °downhearted, °melancholy, °glum, low-spirited, °gloomy, °dismal, lachrymose, °tearful, *Colloq Brit* °cut up: *Tanya is miserable because no one invited her to go to the dance.* **2** unpleasant, °inclement, °inconvenient, °untoward, °bad, unfavourable, °awful, °terrible, adverse, *Colloq* °rotten, °lousy: *The weather was miserable throughout the weekend.* **3** °inadequate, °unworthy, °poor, deplorable, °contemptible, °bad, despicable, °sorry, °pitiful, °pathetic, °lamentable, *Colloq* °rotten, °lousy: *That was the most miserable play I have ever had the misfortune to sit through.* **4** squalid, °wretched, °bad, abject, °deplorable, °shabby, °mean, °vile, shameful, °scurvy, °awful, °disgraceful, °contemptible: *He lives in a cellar in the most miserable conditions.*

miserly *adj.* stingy, °penurious, niggardly, penny-pinching, parsimonious, °mean, °cheap, cheese-paring, °tight, tight-fisted, °close, close-fisted, °mercenary, °avaricious, °greedy, covetous, *Colloq* moneygrubbing, *Brit* mingy, *US* chintzy: *Flynn is too miserly to lend you a penny.*

misery *n.* **1** unhappiness, °distress, °discomfort, wretchedness, °woe, °sadness, °melancholy, °sorrow, dolour, heartache, °grief, °anguish, °anxiety, angst, °depression, °despair, °desperation, °desolation, despondency, °gloom: *Worn out by grief and misery, she collapsed into a chair.* **2** squalor, °poverty, destitution, °privation, indigence, penury, wretchedness, sordidness: *The misery of those slums is unbelievable.*

3 °hardship, °suffering, °calamity, °disaster, °curse, °misfortune, °ordeal, °woe, °trouble, °catastrophe, °trial, tribulation, adversity, °burden, °affliction: *She cannot bear the twin miseries of illness and poverty.*
4 °spoilsport, damper, °killjoy, dampener, Job's comforter, grouch, grump, malcontent, pessimist, cynic, °prophet of doom, Cassandra, *Colloq* wet blanket, sourpuss, *US* party pooper, °gloomy Gus, picklepuss: *How can you stand living with such a misery?*

misfire *v.* **1** °fail, abort, °miscarry, go °wrong, °fizzle (out), °fall through, *Colloq* °flop, come a cropper, *Brit* go phut, *US* go pfft or phft: *The plan to take over the conglomerate misfired when the shares soared in price.*
—*n.* **2** °miscarriage, °failure, °fizzle, °dud, *Colloq* abort, °flop: *After two misfires, we gave up trying to buy a time-share in the Algarve.*

misfit *n.* oner, °eccentric, °individual, °nonconformist, maverick, square peg in a round hole: *People regard him as one of society's misfits and tend to steer clear.*

misfortune *n.* **1** °bad °luck, °ill °luck, °ill °fortune, °hard °luck, infelicity, adversity, °loss: *He had the misfortune to marry the wrong woman.* **2** °accident, misadventure, °mishap, °calamity, °catastrophe, mischance, °disaster, contretemps, °tragedy, °blow, °shock, °reverse, stroke of °bad °luck, *Colloq* °bad news: *With the death of his father, then his illness, then the loss of his business, one misfortune followed another.*

misgiving *n.* apprehension, °mistrust, °worry, °concern, °anxiety, °qualm, °scruple, disquiet, hesitation, °doubt, °question, uncertainty, °suspicion, unease, uneasiness, °discomfort, °dread, °premonition, °foreboding, *Colloq* °funny °feeling: *I had grave misgivings about driving all that way on my own.*

misguided *adj.* misled, °wrong, misdirected, °foolish, °unreasonable, °erroneous, °mistaken, misplaced, °imprudent, unwise, impolitic, °ill-advised, fallacious, uncalled-for, labouring under a misapprehension, °wide of the mark, *Colloq* off (the mark), barking up the °wrong tree: *Her helpfulness is often misguided, ending in disaster for all concerned.*

mishandle *v.* **1** °abuse, °mistreat, maltreat, °ill-treat, °beat (up), brutalize, maul, °molest, °injure, °hurt, °harm, °handle or °treat °roughly, °manhandle, *Colloq* °knock about or around: *The poor child was mishandled by her parents.*
2 mismanage, °bungle, °botch, misconduct, °mangle, °mess up, °muddle, °wreck, °ruin, °destroy, *Colloq* muff, make a °mess or °hash of, *Slang* °screw up, °bugger up, *Taboo* fuck up: *Forster mishandled the deal so badly that it cost the company millions.*

mishap *n.* See **misfortune**, 2, above.

mishmash *n.* °mess, °medley, °hash, gallimaufry, farrago, °pot-pourri, °jumble, °pastiche, °mixture, salmagundi, °hotchpotch or *US and Canadian* hodgepodge, °tangle, omnium gatherum, *mélange*, olio, olla podrida, goulash, °stew: *His paper is nothing more than a mishmash of other people's ideas.*

misinform *v.* misguide, °mislead, misadvise, °misdirect, delude, °deceive, °dupe, °defraud, °fool, gull, °lead astray, throw someone off the scent, *Colloq* con, slip or put something over on someone, pull a fast one on, *US* give (someone)

a bum °steer, throw someone a curve: *If you think you have a right to compensation, you've been misinformed.*

misinformation *n.* disinformation, misintelligence; red herring, °false trail, °false °scent: *When we uncover an enemy agent in our midst, we allow him to collect misinformation.*

misinterpret *v.* °misunderstand, °mistake, misconstrue, °misconceive, misread, misjudge, misapprehend, *Slang* °screw up, °bugger up: *He misinterpreted what I said and stepped off the ledge.*

mislay *v.* misplace, °lose, mislocate; misfile: *I have mislaid my reading spectacles.*

mislead *v.* °misinform, °lead astray, misguide, °misdirect, throw off the scent or track, pull the wool over someone's eyes, °fool, °outwit, °bluff, °hoodwink, °trick, humbug, bamboozle, °deceive, °dupe, gull, cozen, *Colloq* con, °take in, lead up the garden path, flimflam, slip or put or pass one over on, *Slang* °take, *US* give someone a bum °steer: *I was misled into believing that she loved only me. He is misleading you if he says that the shares will soon increase in value.*

mismatched *adj.* mismated, ill-matched, ill-mated, °incompatible, unfit, °inappropriate, unsuited, unsuitable, °incongruous, misallied, disparate, uncongenial, °inconsistent, inharmonious, °discordant: *With her interest in art and his in football, they made a mismatched pair.*

misprint *n.* °error, °mistake, erratum, typographical °error, printer's or printing °error, *Brit* literal, *Colloq* typo: *We cannot publish a book containing so many misprints.*

misrepresent *v.* °distort, °twist, °pervert, °garble, misstate, °mangle, °falsify, belie, °disguise, °colour: *In his report, he misrepresented everything I said.*

miss¹ *v.* **1** °skip, °forgo, °absent oneself from, be °absent from, fail to keep; °avoid, °evade, °escape, °dodge, *Colloq* °pass up: *I missed my dentist's appointment. I missed school because my grandmother was ill.* **2** °long for, °yearn for, pine for, °feel nostalgic for, be nostalgic for or about, °want, °need, °wish for: *I miss those long summer evenings by the lake.* **3** °misunderstand, °misinterpret, misconstrue, misapprehend, fail to understand or perceive, °mistake: *You have completely missed the point.* **4** Sometimes, **miss out (on)**: °pass up, °omit, °leave out, °slip up (on), °overlook, let °slip (by), let °pass, °pass over, °disregard, °ignore: *You can be sure that Frobisher would never miss a free meal.*
—*n.* **5** °omission, °oversight, °slip, °failure, °mistake, °error, °blunder, *Colloq* slip-up: *A miss is as good as a mile.*

miss² *n.* Ms, °girl, °lass, lassie, °maid, °maiden, young lady, young °woman, schoolgirl, mademoiselle, nymphet, °teenager, virgin, spinster, old °maid, *Brit* bachelor °girl, *Irish English* colleen, *Literary* nymph, *Archaic* demoiselle, damsel, *Colloq* old-fashioned gal, *US* coed, Valley °girl, bachelorette, *Slang* teeny-bopper, groupie, *Chiefly Brit* bird, *Old-fashioned US* bobby-soxer: *She's a pretty young miss, isn't she?*

misshapen *adj.* distorted, twisted, contorted, °crooked, °deformed, °crippled, malformed, °grotesque, awry, warped, °gnarled, ill-proportioned, ill-made, °monstrous, *Technical* acromegalic: *The misshapen bell-ringer in The Hunchback of Notre Dame was named Quasimodo.*

missile *n.* °projectile, brickbat; guided missile, ballistic missile: *Bottles, stones, and other missiles were thrown at the police during the riot.*

mission *n.* **1** °task, °duty, °function, °purpose, °job, °office, °work, °assignment, °errand, °charge, °business, commission, °undertaking, °pursuit, °activity, °aim, °objective: *He accepted the mission to convert the natives to Christianity.* **2** °calling, °occupation, °vocation, °trade, °line (of °work), °profession, métier: *It has become my mission in life to see that you learn how to do sums.* **3** delegation, legation, deputation, commission, °committee, °group, °ministry: *She has been sent on a governmental trade mission to Botswana.*

missionary *n.* evangelist, °preacher, °minister, proselytizer: *During the 19th century, many missionaries were dispatched to spread the faith in Africa.*

missive *n.* °letter, communication, °message, °dispatch, °note, °line, postcard, °card, epistle: *I have just received a missive from great-aunt Cecilia that took me an hour to read.*

misspent *adj.* wasted, squandered, °idle, dissipated, thrown away, profitless, °prodigal: *Proficiency at billiards is a sign of a misspent youth.*

misstatement *n.* **1** falsification, misreport, misquotation, miscitation, distortion, misrepresentation, misconstruction, misinterpretation, °perversion, °lie, °falsehood, untruth, °fabrication: *The prosecutor's indictment is a misstatement of the charges against the defendant.* **2** °solecism, °error, °mistake, gaffe, faux pas, °slip of the °tongue, lapsus linguae, °blunder, *Slang* °howler, *Brit* bloomer, *US and Canadian* blooper: *For an educated man his speech is sprinkled with too many grammatical misstatements.*

misstep *n.* **1** °false °step, °blunder, °mistake, °error, °bad or °wrong or °false °move, °trip, °stumble, °slip: *One misstep meant a fall into the abyss.* **2** °indiscretion, °mistake, °lapse, faux pas, °oversight, °error, gaffe, *Colloq* slip-up, *Slang* °howler, *Brit* bloomer, *US and Canadian* blooper, goof: *Her misstep was telling her fiancé's mother that she had formerly been an artist's model.*

mist *n.* **1** °fog, haze, smog, (low-hanging) cloud, °vapour; drizzle, *Brit dialect* mizzle: *I could scarcely make out the road in the mist.*
—*v.* **2** Usually, **mist up** or **over**: cloud (up or over), becloud, °fog, befog, °dim, °blur, °film, steam up: *The mirror in the bathroom had misted up when I was having a shower.*

mistake *n.* **1** °misconception, misapprehension, °error, °fault, miscalculation, misjudgement, °blunder, °botch, °fumble, °bad °move, °misstep, °slip, erratum, gaffe, faux pas, *Colloq* boo-boo, clanger, muff, °howler, *Brit* boob, bloomer, *US* blooper, goof, goof-up, flub: *Giving Aston a salary rise was a mistake.* **2** °indiscretion, °misstep, °false °step, °wrong °move: *It was a mistake not to stand up when she entered.*
—*v.* **3** °misunderstand, °misinterpret, misjudge, misconstrue, °take the °wrong way, get °wrong, misread, misapprehend: *The fool mistook my remark as a compliment.* **4 mistake for:** °mix up in or with, misidentify as, °confuse with, °take for: *In the dark, she mistook him for her husband.*

mistaken *adj.* **1** (all or completely) °wrong, °amiss, incorrect, in °error, °wide of the mark, in the °wrong, °inaccurate, out of °order, *Colloq*

barking up the °wrong tree, °off, (way) off the beam, on the °wrong track, *US* full of °hot air, *Slang* full of it (= *Taboo* 'full of shit'), *US* all wet: *I may be mistaken, but I thought I saw your wife with your squash partner.* **2** °erroneous, °faulty, °false, fallacious, misinformed, °incorrect, °wrong, °inaccurate, °flawed, warped, distorted, twisted, °misguided, *Slang* cock-eyed: *You have a mistaken impression of me.*

mistreat *v.* °abuse, maltreat, ill-use, °ill-treat, °misuse, °damage, °manhandle, °harm; °hurt, °injure, °molest, maul, °rough up, brutalize: *He was found guilty of mistreating his dogs. She was mistreated by her husband for years.*

mistreatment *n.* °abuse, maltreatment, °ill °use, ill-treatment, brutalization, °misuse; manhandling, molestation, mauling, roughing-up, °rough handling, battery, °assault: *This mistreatment of employees must stop at once. The children complained of their parents' mistreatment.*

mistress *n.* **1** °lover, girlfriend, live-in °lover, kept °woman, concubine, inamorata, °paramour, *Literary* odalisque, *Archaic* doxy, *Colloq US* alternative other, POSSLQ (= 'Person of the Opposite Sex Sharing Living Quarters'): *She was the mistress of a leading politician.* **2** schoolmistress, instructress, governess; headmistress: *She had a rewarding career as a mistress in a girls' school in Lancashire.*

mistrust *v.* **1** °suspect, °distrust, be °suspicious of, °doubt, be or feel °wary or °suspicious or °doubtful of or about, have (one's) doubts about, °question, have reservations; °beware; *Slang* be or feel °leery of or about: *He has not done anything specifically bad, but I mistrust his motives.*
—*n.* **2** °suspicion, °distrust, °doubt, °scepticism, wariness, °reservation, chariness, °misgiving(s), uncertainty, unsureness, apprehension, apprehensiveness: *Is there nothing I can say to dispel your mistrust of me?*

misty *adj.* cloudy, foggy, °hazy, °murky, °fuzzy, °dim, blurred, blurry, unclear, °indistinct, °vague, °dark, °opaque, °shadowy, °obscure, unintelligible: *It is very misty, so drive carefully. I have only the mistiest idea of what you mean.*

misunderstand *v.* °misconceive, misconstrue, °misinterpret, misapprehend, get (it or it all) wrong, get the wrong idea (about), misread, misjudge, °miscalculate, °miss the point (of): *He understood your words but misunderstood your meaning.*

misunderstanding *n.* **1** °misconception, misconstruction, misinterpretation, misapprehension, misreading, misjudgement, miscalculation, °wrong °idea, °wrong or °false °impression, mistaking, *Technical* parasynesis: *Misunderstanding of the law is no excuse for flouting it.* **2** °disagreement, °discord, °dispute, °argument, °difference, °dissension, °controversy, °quarrel, °rift, *Colloq* falling out: *We had a slight misunderstanding about who was to pay the restaurant bill.*

misuse *n.* **1** misapplication, misusage, misappropriation, misemployment, diverting, °diversion, perverting, °perversion: *He was accused of the misuse of public funds for his personal gain.* **2** misusage, °abuse, corruption, °solecism,

malapropism, barbarism, catachresis, ungrammaticality, infelicity: *His misuses of English have made him a laughing-stock.* **3** See **mistreatment**, above.
—*v.* **4** °abuse, misapply, misemploy, °misappropriate; °pervert: *I broke the knife blade misusing it as a screwdriver. He was accused of misusing the courts to his own ends.* **5** See **mistreat**, above.

mitigate *v.* °moderate, °temper, °reduce, abate, lessen, °decrease, °relieve, °ease, °ease up (on), °relax, alleviate, °remit, assuage, allay, °let up (on), slacken, slacken up (on), °tone down, °lighten, appease, palliate, mollify, °calm, °tranquillize, soothe, placate, °quiet *or chiefly Brit* °quieten, °still, °soften, °dull, °blunt, take the edge off, *US* °lighten up (on): *The pain was mitigated by taking aspirin. The relief organizations did their best to mitigate the effects of the disaster.*

mitigating *adj.* °extenuating, justifying, excusatory, palliating, vindicating, qualifying: *Were there mitigating circumstances in her taking the money?*

mix *v.* **1** °mingle, °combine, intermingle, °blend, °incorporate, °put together, °merge, °unite, °alloy, commingle, °amalgamate, coalesce: *Mix the ingredients to a creamy consistency.* **2** °socialize, °fraternize, consort, °hobnob, °go round *or* around *or* about (together), °get together, keep °company, °join (with), °associate (with), *Colloq* °hang out *or* about *or* round *or* around (with): *The Hatfields and the McCoys do not mix very well, so you'd best invite them separately.* **3 mix in**: °add, °stir in, °combine, °fold in: *Mix in the chocolate at the very end.* **4 mix up**: **a** See 1, above. **b** °confuse, confound, °bewilder, °muddle, °perplex, °puzzle, °fluster, °upset; addle, °disturb; *Colloq US and Canadian* discombobulate: *She mixed me up so that I cannot decide what to do.* **c** °snarl, ensnarl, °tangle, °entangle, °scramble, °jumble: *The treasures were all mixed up with the rubbish at the church sale.* **d** °confuse, interchange, °exchange: *Have they mixed up our room keys again?* **5 mix up in**: °involve, °implicate, °include, °connect, °draw *or* °drag into: *Wasn't Wilcox mixed up in that scandal last year?* **6 mix up with**: °confuse, °mistake, misidentify, confound; interchange, °exchange: *I think you must have me mixed up with somebody else. The porter mixed up my bag with someone else's.*
—*n.* **7** °mixture, °blend, °compound; °amalgam, °combination, °alloy, °assortment, °distribution: *Was this cake made from a mix or from scratch? The centre party has a good mix of liberals and conservatives.*

mixed *adj.* **1** °hybrid, half-bred, °mongrel, interbred, cross-bred; °impure, tainted, adulterated: *This horse has mixed blood.* **2** °confused, muddled; °varied, °various, °diverse; conflicting, °contradictory, °opposing, clashing, °opposite: *He had mixed feelings about ending his relationship with her.* **3 mixed up in** *or* **with**: °involved, connected, associated: *Wasn't she mixed up in that scandal last year? He doesn't want his children mixed up with people who take drugs.*

mixture *n.* **1** °assortment, °amalgam, °amalgamation, °medley, °combination, mingling, intermingling, composite, °blend, °jumble, °mix, °miscellany, *mélange*, °mess, °mishmash, °hotchpotch *or US and Canadian* hodgepodge,

gallimaufry, farrago, olio, olla podrida, °hash, °pot-pourri, ragout, goulash, omnium gatherum, salmagundi: *The design is an unfortunate mixture of many incompatible styles.* **2** mixing, °amalgamation, amalgamating, combining, mingling, intermingling, °combination, °blend, blending, °association, associating, °compound, compounding, °synthesis, interweaving, merging, °merger, fusion, fusing, °alloy, alloying: *The mixture of household ammonia and bleach creates noxious fumes.*

mix-up *n.* °confusion, °mess, °muddle, °hotchpotch *or US also* hodgepodge, °tangle, °jumble, *Colloq* °botch, °mishmash, foul-up, *Slang US* screw-up, snafu, *Taboo slang Brit* balls-up: *The mix-up in the files is due to a computer malfunction.*

moan *n.* **1** °complaint, °lament, °lamentation, °groan, wail, moaning, °grievance: *Disregard his moans about money—he has plenty.*
—*v.* **2** °complain, °lament, °groan, wail, °bewail, grumble, °bemoan, deplore, whine, whimper, *Colloq* grouse, °gripe, beef, °bitch, *Brit* whinge: *She's always moaning about the way people take advantage of her.* **3** °sigh, °mourn, °weep, °sorrow, °cry, wail, °keen, °grieve, °sob, °snivel, °bawl, mewl, pule, ululate: *The women, all in black, moaned and tore their hair as they neared the coffin.*

mob *n.* **1** horde, °host, °press, °throng, °crowd, °pack, °herd, °swarm, °crush, °jam, multitude, °mass, °body, assemblage, °collection, °group: *The mob surged forward, hurling sticks and stones at anyone in uniform.* **2** °rabble, °riff-raff, proletariat, °populace, the masses, great °unwashed, *hoi polloi*, canaille, bourgeoisie, °lower classes, scum (of the earth), °dregs of society: *The mob cheered when the king was beheaded.*
—*v.* **3** °crowd (round *or* around), jostle, °throng, °surround, °beset, clamour over, °swoop down on *or* upon: *Thousands of screaming teenagers mobbed the singer.*

mobbed *adj.* crowded, °packed, thronged, °congested, teeming, swarming, full, filled: *They tried to leave by the emergency exit, but that was mobbed, too.*

mobile *adj.* **1** °movable, non-stationary, unstationary, unfixed, °travelling, °portable, transportable: *A mobile display was designed for industrial fairs.* **2** motorized, °mechanical, transportable, °movable: *They live in a mobile home. The mobile library comes round every Wednesday.* **3** °expressive, °sensitive, °animated, °plastic, °flexible, *US* facile: *Her mobile face at once reflected her thoughts.* **4** °agile, °versatile, °nimble, quick, °alert, °active, °responsive: *You need your wits about you to keep up with Randolph's mobile mind.* **5** ambulatory, ambulant: *After the artificial joint surgery, Keith was once again completely mobile.*

mobilize *v.* °assemble, marshal, conscript, °enrol, °enlist, °organize, °muster, levy, °rally, °activate, °call up, °prepare, °ready, *US* °draft: *A huge army was mobilized, virtually overnight.*

mock *v.* **1** °deride, °ridicule, make °fun of, °tease, °taunt, °tantalize, °jeer (at), °gibe (at), °thumb one's nose at, °chaff, °laugh at, °poke °fun at, make °sport of, °guy, °scorn, °flout, °abuse, °defy, °scoff (at), °sneer (at), disdain, °disparage, decry, *Archaic* fleer (at), *Colloq* °rag, rib, kid, °put (someone) on, *Brit* take the mickey

out of, cock a snook at: *He was taken in for questioning only because he mocked a police officer. Jealousy is the green-eyed monster that mocks the meat it feeds on.* **2** ape, °mimic, °imitate, °caricature, °lampoon, °satirize, °parody, °burlesque, travesty, *Colloq* spoof, °take off, *Brit* °send up: *The political cartoonist mocks governments daily on the pillory of his pen.*
—*adj.* **3** °substitute, °artificial, simulated, °fake, °synthetic, °imitation, °false, forged, ersatz, °sham, feigned, °counterfeit, °fraudulent, °bogus, make-believe, °pretend, *Colloq* °phoney or *US also* phony, pseudo: *By means of a mock car accident they demonstrated how to rescue victims. Mock turtle soup, though good, does not taste like real turtle soup.*

mockery *n.* **1** °ridicule, °derision, disdain, taunting, disparagement, °abuse, °scorn, °contempt, contumely, decrial: *John was expelled for his mockery of the headmaster.* **2** °semblance, °imitation, impersonation: °caricature, °parody, °burlesque, travesty, °lampoon, °satire, pasquinade, farce; °miscarriage; *Colloq* spoof, °take-off, *Brit* send-up: *That wasn't a trial, it was a mockery of justice.* **3** °disappointment, °joke, °laugh, °absurdity: *It is a mockery to speak of that wretched sadist and humanity in the same breath.*

mode[1] *n.* **1** °way, °manner, °method, °approach, °form, °course, °fashion, °procedure, °technique, °system, °wise, *modus operandi*, methodology, standard operating °procedure, SOP: *What mode of teaching foreign languages do you use?* **2** °status, °condition, °state, configuration, °set-up: *The computer is now in printing mode.*

mode[2] *n.* °fashion, °style, °look, °vogue; °trend, °rage, °craze, *Colloq* °fad: *We went to the ball dressed in the mode of the 1920s.*

model *n.* **1** °representation, °replica, mock-up, maquette, scale model, working model, °miniature, °dummy, °image, °likeness, °facsimile, °copy: *This is a model of the house he is planning.* **2** °original, °mould, archetype, °prototype, °pattern, °paragon, °ideal, exemplar, °example, °standard: *When the wax model is finished, we cast it in bronze using the cire perdue process. Their government was established after the Roman model.* **3** °ideal, °paragon, exemplar, °epitome, *beau idéal*, cream, *crème de la crème*, *ne plus ultra*, °nonpareil, nonsuch *or* nonesuch: *He is the very model of what a father should be.* **4** °subject, sitter, poser: *Dali's wife served as his model for many paintings.* **5** mannequin; °dummy: *She is tall and thin enough to be a fashion model. May I see the hat that is on that model in the window?* **6** °design, °kind, °type, °style, °version, °variety, °sort, °form, °fashion, configuration; °brand, °mark: *I'm intending to trade my car in for a newer model.*
—*v.* **7** °fashion, °mould, °shape, °form, sculpt, °carve (out), °make, °fabricate, °produce: *She modelled these figures out of fine clay.* **8** °pose in, °display, °show (off), °wear, *Colloq* °sport: *She makes a fortune modelling swimwear.* **9 model after** *or* **on:** °imitate, °copy, °pattern on *or* after, emulate, °follow: *Architects often used to model public buildings after the temples on the Acropolis.*
—*adj.* **10** °copy, °imitation, °facsimile, °representative, °miniature: *He enjoys building model aeroplanes.* **11** °ideal, °exemplary, °perfect, archetypal, unequalled, consummate, inimitable: *Oliver has been a model student.*

moderate *adj.* **1** °temperate, °calm, °reasonable, °cool, °judicious, °rational, balanced, unexcessive, °modest, °sober, °sensible, commonsensical, controlled, °deliberate, °steady: *In view of the conflicting interests expressed, the council has adopted a moderate policy regarding parking.* **2** °centre, middle-of-the-road, non-radical, non-reactionary: *Bella's political outlook is said by some to be moderate.* **3** °fair, middling, °average, °ordinary, °medium, °middle, °modest, mediocre, unexceptional, *Colloq* °fair to middling: *They have a good range of clothing, all sold at very moderate prices.*
—*n.* **4** middle-of-the-roader, non-radical, non-reactionary, centrist: *Where do the moderates stand on the issue of constitutional reform?*
—*v.* **5** abate, °calm, mollify, soothe, °ease, °relax, alleviate, °mitigate, °soften, °dull, °blunt, °cushion, °relieve, °reduce, lessen, °remit, slacken, °diminish, °decrease, defuse, °temper, *Colloq* °let up (on): *He would get along better if he moderated the violence of his reactions and learned to relax.* **6** mediate, arbitrate, referee, °judge, °chair, °supervise, °preside (over), °coordinate, °run, °regulate, °manage, °direct: *Professor Gill will moderate the panel discussion.*

moderately *adv.* °somewhat, °rather, °quite, °fairly, °pretty, comparatively, °slightly, passably, more or less; to some °extent, within °reason, to a certain °extent, to a °degree, to some °degree, in some °measure, in moderation, within limits; temperately; *Colloq* °sort of, kind of: *Clifford is moderately well off. It was a moderately hot day.*

moderator *n.* °mediator, arbiter, arbitrator, °judge, referee, °umpire; *Chiefly US* °chair, chairperson, chairman, chairwoman, presiding °officer, president, coordinator, (discussion) °leader; anchorman, anchorwoman; °master of ceremonies, toastmaster, *Brit* compère, *Colloq* emcee, MC: *Lady Felicia was chosen as the moderator of next year's panel.*

modern *adj.* up to °date, °current, °contemporary, today's, °new, °fresh, °novel, °brand-new, up to the °minute, present-day, °latest, new-fashioned, newfangled; à la °mode, modish, in °vogue, °fashionable, in °fashion, °stylish, in °style, chic, *Chiefly Brit* flavour of the month, *Slang* °trendy, in, with it, mod, °hip, °hot: *Elaine has little patience with modern electronic gadgets.*

modernize *v.* °renovate, streamline, redo, redecorate, °refurbish, refurnish, update, do over, °rejuvenate, °refresh, °revamp, redesign, remodel, refashion, remake: *We installed air conditioning when we modernized our offices.*

modest *adj.* **1** unassuming, unpresuming, °humble, unpretentious, °unobtrusive, °reserved, °retiring, diffident, °shy, °bashful, demure, °coy, shamefaced, self-effacing, °self-conscious, °reticent, °reluctant, °timid, °meek, timorous, *Rare* verecund: *Caroline is quite modest about her accomplishments.* **2** °humble, °simple, °plain, °ordinary, unpretentious, °homely, °lowly, unexceptional, unostentatious, °inconspicuous, °unobtrusive: *They live in a modest little cottage.* **3** °moderate, °limited, °understated, unimportant, unexaggerated,

°reasonable, °sensible, constrained, restricted, restrained: *The workers' demands seem modest enough.*

modicum *n.* °bit, °trifle, °jot, °jot *or* tittle, atom, scintilla, °spark, °particle, iota, °speck, °grain, whit, °scrap, °shred, snippet, °sliver, °fragment, °splinter, °morsel, °crumb, ounce, dram, °drop, °dash, °spot, °touch, tinge, °hint, °suggestion, *Colloq* smidgen *or* smidgin: *One must exercise a modicum of judgement in affairs of the heart.*

modify *v.* **1** °adjust, °adapt, °change, °transform, °alter, °revise, °amend, redo, remake, remould, reshape, reconstruct, °reform, °revamp, refashion, remodel, rework, °reword, reorient, reorganize: *They are modifying the car to increase its performance. He should modify his views on censorship.* **2** °reduce, °decrease, °diminish, lessen, °moderate, °temper, °soften, °lower, abate, °tone down, °modulate; °qualify, °limit, °restrict: *The severity of the winter is modified by our proximity to the sea. We shall have to modify our demands.*

modulate *v.* °adjust, °regulate, °set, °tune, °balance, °temper, °moderate, °modify; °lower, °tune *or* °tone *or* °turn down, °soften: *Modulate the volume to suit the size of the auditorium. Please modulate your voice—everyone can hear you!*

mogul *n.* magnate, °tycoon, baron, mandarin, *Colloq* °big shot, °big gun, °big cheese, Pooh Bah, °bigwig, °big wheel, °big (White) Chief, °big Daddy, hotshot, VIP, °big noise, nabob, *Slang US* Mr Big: *In the old days, he was one of the moguls in Hollywood.*

moist *adj.* **1** °damp, wettish, dampish, dewy, dank, °humid, °clammy, °muggy, °steamy, °misty, foggy: *During the monsoon everything becomes so moist that your clothes never seem to dry.* **2** °damp, °wet, rainy, drizzly, soggy, moisture-laden: *The moist climate keeps Ireland green.* **3** °tearful, teary, °misty, lachrymose: *Every eye in the theatre was moist at the end of that scene.*

molest *v.* **1** °annoy, °irritate, vex, °disturb, °pester, badger, needle, °provoke, nettle, °tease, °harass, harry, °worry, hector, °irk, °bother, °gall, °chafe, roil, °torment, °plague, beleaguer: *For weeks people on the beach have been molested by green flies.* **2** accost, °meddle with, °interfere with, °annoy, °abuse, °bother, °attack, °ill-treat, maltreat, °manhandle; paw: *The police are looking for a man who has been molesting girls in the park.*

moment *n.* **1** °instant, °second, °minute, half a °second, two seconds, °flash, °twinkling, °blink *or* wink of an eye, °twinkling of an eye, trice, *Colloq* jiffy, shake, two shakes (of a lamb's tail), before you can say 'Jack Robinson', *Brit* mo, half a mo, tick: *I'll be with you in a moment, Madam.* **2** °instant, °time, °second, °minute, hour, °point (in time), °juncture, °stage: *At that very moment, the phone rang.* **3** °importance, °weight, consequence, °significance, °import, °gravity, seriousness, °prominence, °concern, °note, °interest, °consideration: *What you decide to do is of no great moment.*

momentary *adj.* °fleeting, °temporary, ephemeral, evanescent, impermanent, °fugitive, °passing, transitory, °brief, °short-lived, quick, °short, °hasty: *The medicine afforded only momentary relief from the pain.*

momentous *adj.* °important, °weighty, consequential, °significant, °grave, °serious, decisive, °crucial, °critical, °vital, °pivotal, °portentous, charged, laden, °fraught, of °concern: *The Augustan Age was a momentous period in Latin literature.*

momentum *n.* °energy, °force, °drive, °strength, °impetus, °power, °inertia, impulse, °thrust, °push: *The car's momentum carried it over the cliff. Her encouragement has given me the momentum needed to carry on.*

monarch *n.* **1** ruler, °sovereign, potentate, crowned °head; °queen, °king, empress, emperor, tsar *or* czar: *Mary was the monarch of Scotland from 1542 to 1567.* **2** ruler, °sovereign, °chief, °lord, °master, °owner, *Colloq* °boss: *He is monarch of all he surveys.*

monarchy *n.* **1** °kingdom, empire, °domain, °dominion, principality; °state, °nation, °country: *According to Gibbon, a hereditary monarchy presents the fairest scope for ridicule.* **2** monocracy, autocracy, absolutism, royalism, monarchism, °sovereignty, totalitarianism, authoritarianism, °despotism, °tyranny: *Those who are discontented with monarchy call it tyranny.*

monastery *n.* abbey, cloister, priory, friary, charterhouse, hospice, *Buddhism* vihara, *Hinduism* ashram, *Tibetan Buddhism* lamasery: *In later life he retired to a monastery to contemplate the world.*

monetary *adj.* pecuniary, °cash, °money, °fiscal, °financial, °capital; numismatic, *Technical* nummular, nummary: *Monetary shortages result from the government's tightening its hold on the economy by raising interest rates.*

money *n.* **1** currency, legal °tender, medium of °exchange, specie, (hard) °cash, °ready money, banknotes, paper money, *Brit* notes, *US* °bills, °coin(s), °change, small °change, *Derogatory* (filthy) lucre, pelf, *Colloq* shekels, *Brit* dosh, lolly, *US* folding money, cold (hard) °cash, *US and Canadian and Australian* shin-plasters; *Slang* °loot, dough, bread, spondulicks *or* spondulix, boodle, readies *or* the °ready, moolah, *Brit* rhino, *US* (long) green, greenbacks, mazuma, wampum, simoleons, bucks, scratch, gelt, kale, cabbage, lettuce, spinach: *He makes daily rounds to collect the money from the launderettes he owns.* **2** °resources, °wealth, fortune, °funds, °capital, wherewithal, affluence, °means, (liquid) °assets, °riches: *All the family money is invested in long-term bonds.* **3** °gain, °profit, °net, *Colloq* °take, °percentage, *Slang* °rake-off: *How much money does the shop take in at the end of the day?* **4 in the money:** °rich, °wealthy, affluent, moneyed *or* monied, °well off, well-to-do, °prosperous, *Colloq* °flush, in clover, in *or* on Easy Street, *Slang* °loaded, well-heeled, rolling in it *or* in money *or* in dough, filthy °rich, stinking °rich, °fat: *They have been in the money since their uncle died.*

mongrel *n.* cur, mutt, cross-breed, °mixed °breed, °hybrid, half-breed, *Technical* bigener; lurcher: *There is little chance of that mongrel winning a prize in the dog show.*

monitor *n.* **1** watchdog, °supervisor, °sentinel, °guard, °guardian, custodian; *Brit* invigilator, prefect, *Rare* prepositor *or* praepostor; *US* proctor: *The government has appointed a committee to monitor oil prices.* **2** (°television) °screen,

cathode-ray tube °screen, CRT, °display, *Chiefly Brit* visual display unit, VDU: *Do you prefer an amber, green, or black-and-white monitor?*
—*v.* **3** °watch, °oversee, °observe, °check (out or up on), audit, °supervise, superintend, °scan, °examine, °study, °follow, °keep an °eye on, °survey, keep °track of, °track, °trace, °record, *Brit* °vet: *Before a drug is approved, it must be monitored through thousands of tests.*

monk *n.* °brother, °religious, coenobite, monastic, *Loosely* friar: *He was accepted into the Benedictine order, also called the black monks.*

monkey *n.* **1** simian, ape, primate, *Colloq* monk: *The monkeys' antics forever delight the children.* **2** °fool, ass, laughing-stock, °butt, °victim, °target, (fair) game, *Colloq* goat, *Slang* °sucker: *The teacher should not have made a monkey out of Hubert in front of his classmates.* **3** °imp, °devil, mischief-maker, °rascal, scamp, rapscallion: *She's a real little monkey: you wouldn't believe what she got up to this morning.*
—*v.* **4** °mimic, mime, °imitate, impersonate, °copy, ape, °duplicate: *He monkeys everything you do.* **5** Usually, **monkey around** or **about (with)**: °fool around (with), °play (with), °fiddle (about or around) with, °meddle (with or in), °interfere (with or in), °mess (about or around) (with), °tinker (with), °tamper (with), *Colloq US* °screw around (with): *Stop monkeying around with that switch or the light will fuse. Colin is always monkeying around in class.*

monograph *n.* treatise, dissertation, disquisition, °essay, °paper: *Entwhistle's monograph is the definitive work on Hawthorne.*

monolithic *adj.* °massive, °huge, °enormous, °monumental, °imposing, °colossal, °gigantic, °giant; featureless, °uniform, undifferentiated, characterless; °rigid, impenetrable, invulnerable, unbending, °inflexible, °solid, °stolid, intractable, °immovable: *These monolithic international conglomerates, assembled with the aid of junk bonds, staffed by yuppies, and controlling markets worth hundreds of billions, resemble the monolithic glass towers that house them.*

monopolize *v.* corner (the °market in), °control, °dominate, own, *Slang* hog: *Till recently, one company monopolized the telephone business in the US.*

monotonous *adj.* °boring, °tedious, °dull, °tiresome, °humdrum, sleep-inducing, soporific, wearisome, wearying, tiring, monotonic, °repetitious, °prosaic, °banal, °dry, dry-as-dust, uninteresting, °dreary, °colourless, unexciting, run-of-the-mill, °ordinary, commonplace, °routine, uneventful, °everyday, °mechanical, banausic, *Colloq* ho-hum: *Working in an assembly line became monotonous, so I took a job in advertising.*

monster *n.* **1** °beast, °fiend, °ogre, °giant, dragon, °brute, °demon, troll, bog(e)yman: *Why are so many children's fairy tales populated by monsters?* **2** °monstrosity, (living) abortion, mutant, °mutation, °freak, deformity, *lusus naturae*, eyesore, °horror, miscreation, missing link: *Monsters of every description were the main features of circus sideshows for centuries.*
—*adj.* **3** See **monstrous**, 3, below.

monstrosity *n.* **1** See **monster**, 2, above.
2 monstrousness, heinousness, horribleness, horridness, hideousness, awfulness, nightmarishness, dreadfulness, frightfulness,

°horror, hellishness, ghoulishness, fiendishness, °barbarity: *The monstrosity of the concentration camps was not widely known till after the war.*

monstrous *adj.* **1** °awful, °horrible, horrid, horrific, horrendous, horrifying, °hideous, °ugly, °nightmarish, °dreadful, heinous, °grisly, °gruesome, °disgusting, °nauseous, nauseating, °repulsive, °repellent, °revolting, °frightful, °grotesque, hellish, °ghoulish, freakish, °fiendish, barbaric, barbarous, °savage, °inhuman, °merciless, °ruthless, °brutal, brutish, °beastly: *How could anyone treat another human being with such monstrous cruelty!* **2** °outrageous, °shocking, °scandalous, °atrocious, appalling, °wicked, °villainous, °evil, °vile, insensitive, °cruel, °base, debased, °shameful, °shameless, °infamous, °disgraceful, nefarious, egregious, °foul, °vicious, flagitious, °loathsome, depraved: *It is monstrous to suggest that money could compensate for the loss of a child. It was a monstrous trick to make him think he had failed the exam when he'd got the top mark.* **3** °gigantic, °giant, °huge, °vast, °enormous, °colossal, °monster, gargantuan, °jumbo, °immense, tremendous, titanic, °prodigious, °massive, °towering, elephantine, mammoth: *They are planning to build a monstrous shopping mall in the town centre.*

monument *n.* **1** °marker, cairn, °memorial, °tablet, shrine, commemoration; °sepulchre, gravestone, °tombstone, headstone, °tomb, mausoleum, cenotaph: *Many monuments have been established in memory of those who died in the war.* **2** °testimony, °testimonial, testament, °token, °witness, °record, °evidence, °example, exemplar: *The book will survive as a lasting monument to her scholarship.*

monumental *adj.* **1** staggering, awe-inspiring, °outstanding, °prominent, stupendous, °vast, °awesome, epoch-making, °historic, history-making, °memorable, °lasting, °permanent, unforgettable, °significant, °notable, °noteworthy, °impressive, °marvellous, °prodigious, wonderful, wondrous, spectacular, °magnificent, °grand, °striking, °glorious, °enduring, °classic: *This work is a monumental contribution to linguistic theory.* **2** °massive, °huge, °gigantic, °enormous, °prodigious, °colossal, °immense, °vast, tremendous: *These monumental stones, each as big as a house, were dragged from a quarry hundreds of miles away.* **3** commemorative, °memorial: *A monumental obelisk will be raised to mark the battle.* **4** egregious, catastrophic, °calamitous, °huge, °enormous, °awful, abject, °terrible, unforgivable, °unbelievable, °monstrous, *Colloq* °whopping: *Announcing our plans in advance could prove to be a monumental blunder.*

mood *n.* **1** °humour, °attitude, °inclination, °disposition, °nature, °temper, °frame of °mind, °spirit, °atmosphere, °sense, °feeling: *The mood of the people is rebellious. She's in a bad mood.* **2 in the mood**: °ready, °willing, °eager, °keen, (well-)°disposed, °inclined, °sympathetic, minded: *I'm not in the mood for a film tonight, but I am in the mood to go dancing.*

moody *adj.* **1** °sullen, °melancholy, °blue, °sad, °unhappy, °dejected, depressed, crestfallen, downcast, °despondent, chap-fallen, in the doldrums, °downhearted, °gloomy, °glum, moping, mopy, mopish, sulky, sulking, morose, brooding, broody, heavy-hearted, °dour, cheerless,

°dismal, °desolate, disconsolate, lugubrious, disheartened, saturnine, *Colloq* down in the
°mouth, (down) in the dumps, out of sorts, *US*
off (one's) feed: *He's been moody the past few days,
and I don't know how to cheer him up.* **2** °testy,
crotchety, °short-tempered, °abrupt, °short,
°curt, °impatient, crabby, crusty, huffy, huffish,
crabbed, °cantankerous, curmudgeonly,
ill-humoured, ill-tempered, °cranky, °petulant,
°waspish, °temperamental, °snappish, °snappy,
°irritable, °peevish, °touchy, piqued; in a (fit of)
pique, in high dudgeon: *If I were you, I shouldn't
ask her for a favour today as she's very
moody.* **3** °fickle, °volatile, °capricious, mercurial, °unstable, °fitful, °flighty, unsteady,
°changeable, °erratic, uneven, °inconstant,
undependable, °unreliable, unpredictable: *Being
artists, they are moody, and there's no telling if they
will want to be interviewed today.*

moonshine *n.* **1** moonlight, moonbeams: *Her
hair reflected silver in the moonshine.* **2** (stuff and)
°nonsense, °rubbish, taradiddle, humbug,
°drivel, twaddle, balderdash, blather *or* blether,
Colloq °hot air, claptrap, pack of lies, con, bosh,
gas, eyewash, hogwash, bunk, guff, piffle,
hokum, °rot, malarkey, bilge (water), tripe, (the
old) °song and dance, °line, *Brit* tommy-rot, *US*
apple-sauce, razzmatazz, jive, *Slang* crap, bull,
hooey, *Brit* tosh, *US* °garbage, BS, *Taboo slang*
horseshit, bullshit: *He fed her a load of moonshine
about owning a big yacht.* **3** poteen, *Colloq chiefly
US and Canadian* hooch *or* hootch, white lightning, white mule, home-brew, bootleg: *Government agents raided a still that produced 100
gallons of moonshine a day.*

moor[1] *n.* heath, moorland, wasteland, *No. Eng.
and Scots* fell: *The police pursued the escaped prisoner across the moor, but they lost him.*

moor[2] *v.* °secure, °tie up, make °fast, °dock,
berth, (drop) °anchor; °fix: *The vessel was soon
moored and the passengers disembarked. The huge
aerial is moored by cables.*

moot *adj.* **1** °debatable, arguable, undecided,
undetermined, °controversial, °doubtful,
°disputable, °open to debate, at °issue,
°indefinite, °problematic(al), °questionable,
°open (to °question *or* to °discussion), con-
futable, confuted, contestable, contested,
°unsettled, °unresolved, up in the air, unconcluded: *Whether he would be found innocent was
still a moot point.*
—*v.* **2** °bring up *or* forward, °introduce, °broach,
°put forward, proffer, °posit, °propound,
°advance, °submit, °suggest: *It has been mooted
that she was with the victim just before the murder.*

moral *adj.* **1** °ethical; °right, °good, °pure,
°honest, °proper, °upright, °honourable, °decent,
moralistic, °respectable, high-minded,
°virtuous, upstanding, °righteous, °principled,
°scrupulous, incorruptible, °noble, °just: *She is
one of the most moral people I have ever met.*
2 °ethical, moralizing, moralistic: *Questions
of right and wrong are a subject for moral philosophy.
It is a moral, not a legal, issue.*
—*n.* **3** °lesson, homily, teaching, °point,
°message; aphorism, °maxim, °precept, apophthegm *or* apothegm, adage, °saw, °proverb,
°epigram, °motto, °slogan: *The moral of the story
is, 'Do unto others before they do unto you'.* **4 morals**
°behaviour, °conduct, mores, °belief, °habit(s),
°custom(s), °practice(s), °principle(s), °scruples,

ethics, °ideals, °standards; °probity, °morality,
°rectitude, °integrity: *For this appointment, we
require a person of the highest morals.*

morale *n.* °dedication, °spirit(s), °unity, *esprit de
corps*, °disposition, °attitude, °confidence,
°selfconfidence, °self-esteem: *The team's morale
improved after they won their first game in five
weeks.*

morality *n.* **1** ethics, °morals, ethicalness, moral-
ness, °principle(s), mores, °integrity, °propriety,
standards, °ideals, °honesty, °right, rightness,
righteousness, °rectitude, °justice, °fair play, fairness, decency, uprightness: *Morality should not be
conditioned by expediency.* **2** °behaviour, °conduct,
°habit(s), °custom(s): *Are you suggesting that utilitarianism is a guide for morality?*

morass *n.* **1** °bog, °marsh, °swamp, fen, quagmire, slough, marshland, moorland, *No. Eng.
and Scots* moss: *The land not under cultivation was
morass or forest.* **2** entanglement, °confusion,
°muddle, °mess, quagmire, °tangle, quicksand:
*It took years to extricate the company from the legal
morass of the bankruptcy courts.*

moratorium *n.* °halt, hiatus, °suspension, °stay,
°respite, °freeze, waiting-period,
°postponement: *The arts commission requests a
six-month moratorium on sales to foreign purchasers.*

morbid *adj.* **1** °unhealthy, °unwholesome, disordered, °unsound, °sick, pathological, patho-
genic: *Inhalation of fumes containing lead has caused
this morbid condition.* **2** °grim, °ghoulish,
°macabre, °monstrous, °ghastly, °grotesque,
°grisly, °gruesome: *At an early age, Glynis exhibited a morbid interest in cadavers. Spare me the
morbid details—please!* **3** °gloomy, lugubrious,
°glum, morose, °sombre, °blue, °sad,
°melancholy, °despondent, depressed,
°dejected, downcast: *With Charley again in one of
his morbid moods, we can anticipate another cheerless visit.*

moreover *adv.* furthermore, °further, °besides,
not °only that, more than that, what is more;
to °boot, into the °bargain, in °addition, additionally, as well, too: *She was pleased that I had
brought some wine—it was, moreover, her favourite
burgundy.*

moribund *adj.* **1** °dying, *in extremis*, at death's
door, °failing, fading, with one foot in the °grave,
half-dead, breathing one's last, expiring, on
one's last legs, on one's deathbed: *Apparently
moribund for weeks, he suddenly revived when he saw
her.* **2** ending, declining, °obsolescent, °weak,
on the way out, waning, on the °wane, °dying
out; stagnating, °stagnant: *At the time, the Ottoman
Empire was already moribund.*

morning *n.* **1** forenoon, a.m., °dawn, daybreak,
sunrise, *Literary* morn, *Archaic* cock crow,
day-spring, morrow, *Chiefly US* sun-up: *The meeting will be at nine o'clock in the morning.*
—*adj.* **2** matutinal, matinal, a.m., forenoon: *I
prefer a morning meeting.*

morsel *n.* **1** °mouthful, °bite, gobbet, spoonful,
forkful, °chew, °taste, °sample, nibble, °bit,
°drop, dollop, soupçon: *She delicately ate tiny
morsels of the banana.* **2** °bit, °crumb, °fragment,
°scrap, °sliver, °splinter, shard *or* sherd, °shred,
°remnant, °particle, atom, °speck, whit, fraction, °grain, granule, °pinch, °piece, *Colloq*
smidgen *or* smidgin: *There wasn't the slightest morsel
of evidence to connect me with the crime.*

mortal *adj.* **1** °human; transitory, °temporal, °transient, ephemeral: *It finally dawned on him that the king was mortal, like other men.* **2** °physical, bodily, corporeal, corporal, fleshly, °earthly, °worldly, perishable: *Her mortal remains are buried at Bognor Regis.* **3** °deadly, °fatal, °lethal, °terminal, °destructive, °disastrous: *The admiral lay dying from a mortal wound.* **4** °relentless, °implacable, unrelenting, °bitter, sworn, °deadly, unremitting, unappeasable, unceasing: *Halifax was the mortal enemy of despotism.* **5** abject, °extreme, °awful, °great, °enormous, °intense, °terrible, °inordinate, dire: *Giles lived in mortal fear of offending his mother.*
—*n.* **6** °human (being), °man, °woman, °person, °soul, °individual, °creature, earthling: *The novel depicts a lifestyle far removed from that of ordinary mortals. We mortals have nothing to fear from intergalactic aliens.*

mortify *v.* **1** °humiliate, °shame, °humble, °embarrass, abash, chagrin, °rebuff, °crush, °discomfit, deflate, °bring down, °degrade, °downgrade, °reduce, °chasten, °subdue, °suppress, make someone eat °humble pie, teach someone his *or* her °place, *Colloq* °put down: *She was mortified to learn that she had been disqualified.* **2** °punish, °castigate, °discipline, °control, °subdue, °subjugate: *Repentance was considered insufficient penance, so the flagellants mortified the flesh with scourges.* **3** gangrene, °fester, necrose, °putrefy, °rot, °decompose, °decay, putresce: *After a fortnight, the flesh mortifies and falls away.*

mother *n.* **1** dam, materfamilias, (female) °parent, *Old-fashioned or formal or jocular* mater, *Formal* progenitrix; matriarch, *Colloq* ma, old lady, old °woman, *Brit* mummy, mum, *US* mom, mommy, mama, mamma, maw, mammy, mam: *He runs crying to his mother whenever anyone teases him.* **2** °source, °origin, genesis: *Necessity is the mother of invention.* **3** nourisher, nurturer, °nurse: *Poverty was the mother of anarchy.*
—*adj.* **4** °native, °natural, innate: *She has the mother wit to know better.*
—*v.* **5** nurture, °nourish, °nurse, °care for, °look after, °protect, °shelter, °watch over, take °care of: *She mothered me when I needed her, and I won't desert her now.* **6** °pamper, °baby, °coddle, °spoil, °indulge, °fuss over, overprotect: *You mother the child too much.*

motif *n.* °theme, °idea, °topic, °subject, concept, leitmotif; °pattern, °figure, °refrain, °device, °ornament, °decoration, °element, °convention: *The painter repeats the motif throughout his pictures in much the same way that a composer repeats a bar of music.*

motion *n.* **1** °movement, °moving, °change, °shift, shifting, °action, °going, °travelling, °travel, °progress, °passage, °transit; °activity, commotion, °stir, °agitation, turmoil, turbulence: *One could barely sense the slow motion of the train. The leaves of the aspen appear to be in constant motion.* **2** mobility, movability, motility: *I could feel the motion gradually returning to my numbed limbs.* **3** gait, °bearing, °carriage, tread, °walk, °step: *The machine works with alternate upward and downward motions.* **4** °gesture, gesticulation, °signal, °sign: *She made a motion for me to come nearer.* **5** °proposal, °suggestion, °proposition, °recommendation, °offering, °submission: *A motion must be seconded by a member in good standing.*

—*v.* **6** °gesture, gesticulate, °beckon, °signal, °sign, °wave: *The cashier motioned to me and I went over to the window.*

motivate *v.* °prompt, °activate, °move, °inspire, °incite, °induce, actuate, °stimulate, °provoke, °influence, °encourage, °occasion, °bring about, °cause; °excite, egg (on), °urge, °prod, °spur, galvanize, goad, °rouse, °arouse, °stir (up), °wheedle, °coax, °persuade, °cajole, °tempt, °push, impel, °drive, instigate: *The biggest problem is motivating students to apply themselves to academic subjects.*

motive *n.* **1** °inducement, °incentive, motivation, stimulus, motivating °force, stimulation, °incitement, °influence, °cause, °reason, °rationale, grounds; °attraction, °lure, °enticement, goad, °spur, °urge, °prod: *It is thought that jealousy was his motive for murder.* **2** °purpose, °aim, °intention, °intent, °object, °objective, °goal, °end, *arrière pensée* (= 'hidden motive'); °ambition, °desire; *Colloq* °angle: *I asked the chairman what his motive was in trying to expand the company.*
—*adj.* **3** driving, impelling, propelling, propulsive, °moving, kinetic, activating, °operative: *The motive power used in the ultra-light aircraft is provided entirely by the pilot's pedalling.*

mottled *adj.* dappled, brindled, marbled, streaked, splodgy *or US* splotchy, blotched, blotchy, freckled, spotted, °spotty, patchy, °speckled, °flecked, sprinkled, spattered, splashed, streaky, stippled, pied, piebald; multicoloured, °variegated, particoloured, *Colloq* splodged *or US* splotched: *Do you like that mottled effect on the wallpaper?*

motto *n.* °maxim, °proverb, saying, adage, °saw, aphorism, apophthegm *or* apothegm, gnome, °slogan, °byword, catchword, battle-cry, °guide, °moral, °principle, °rule, °precept: *The motto of the Order of the Garter is* Honi soit qui mal y pense, *'Shame on whoever thinks ill of it'.*

mould¹ *n.* **1** °form, °cast, matrix, °die; °template *or* templet, °pattern, °form: *He broke the mould to prevent the casting of a duplicate statuette.* **2** °form, °shape, °pattern, °format, °structure, °build, construction, °design, °arrangement, °organization, configuration, °kind, °brand, °make, °line, °type, °stamp, °cut: *Was man made in the same mould as his God, or vice versa?* **3** °character, °nature, °stamp, °type, °kind, kidney, ilk, °sort: *Grandpa said that he wouldn't want someone of her mould in the family.*
—*v.* **4** °shape, °form, °make, °work, °fashion, configure, °sculpture or sculpt, °model, knead, °construct: carve, cut: *The artist moulded the original design in clay.* **5** °forge, °cast, °stamp, die-cast: *These beads are moulded from solid gold.* **6** °influence, °shape, °form, °affect, °make, °control, °direct, °guide, °lead: *The speech-writer's job is to mould the language to fit his client's ideas. The candidate is trying to mould public opinion in his favour.*

mould² *n.* mildew, fungus, °blight, smut: *A mild solution of bleach will clean that mould off the bathroom tiles.*

mould³ *n.* °soil, °earth, loam, topsoil, °dirt, humus: *Add some rich mould to the house-plants periodically and they will flourish.*

mouldy *adj.* °aged, °ancient, out-dated, °old-fashioned, antediluvian, °unused, °stale,

decayed, decaying, carious, mildewed, mouldering, °musty; spoilt or spoiled, °rotten, rotting,
°putrid, putrescent, putrefying, °rancid, °rank,
decomposed, decomposing, mucid: *Digging about
in the files, he unearthed some mouldy old plans of
the house. All the food in the fridge had gone mouldy
while they were away.*

mound n. **1** hillock, °rise, hummock, °hill,
°hump, bank, °elevation, °knoll, °knob, °swell,
dune, °slope, tor, *Chiefly W US and Canadian*
butte: *We stood on a high mound from which we
could see for miles.* **2** °heap, °pile, °stack,
Archaeology tumulus, °tell, barrow, (kitchen)
midden: *Excavation of the mound yielded scores of
Iron Age artefacts.*

mount n. **1** See **mountain, 1,** below.
—v. **2** °climb (up), °go up, ascend, °scale, clamber
up, make one's way up: *We mounted the ladder
to the roof. The speaker mounted the dais.* **3** °rise
(up), °arise, °soar, °fly (up), °rocket (upwards):
*With the salmon in its grasp, the eagle mounted to
the sky.* **4** °climb or °get or clamber up on,
bestride, straddle, bestraddle: *The gunfighter
mounted his horse and rode off.* **5** (put on) °display,
(put on) °exhibit, put on °exhibition, °present,
°install or instal, °stage, °prepare, °ready, °put
on, put in °place, °set up; °arrange, °coordinate,
°compose, °organize, set in °motion, °launch:
*The gallery will mount a show of John's sculpture next
spring. They have mounted a major advertising
campaign for their face cream.* **6** °frame, mat or
matt, °set off: *This print should be mounted using
an olive green paper.* **7** °increase, wax, °rise,
escalate, °intensify, °swell, °expand, °grow,
°mount up, multiply, °pile up, °build up,
°accumulate: *Complaints have been mounting
against the vulgar language heard on prime-time TV.*
—n. **8** °backing, °setting, °support, mounting,
°background, °set, °arrangement, backdrop,
°scene: *This style of mount sets off the ruby to its
best advantage.* **9** horse, steed, charger, palfrey:
Her mount was a grey mare.

mountain n. **1** °height, °elevation, °mount,
eminence, °prominence, °peak, alp, tor, °summit,
No. Eng. and Scots fell, *Scots and Irish English*
ben: *Her favourite sport is climbing
mountains.* **2** °heap, °pile, °stack, °mound,
°accumulation, °abundance, °mass, *Colloq*
ton(s), °heaps, °piles, °stacks: *I have a mountain
of laundry to do.*

mountainous adj. **1** craggy, alpine, Himalayan:
*It was very slow going through the mountainous
parts of the country.* **2** °huge, °towering, °high,
°steep, °enormous, °immense, °formidable,
°mighty, °monumental, °prodigious, staggering:
*Their tiny craft was almost engulfed by the moun-
tainous seas.*

mourn v. °grieve (over), °lament, °sorrow (over),
°bemoan, °bewail, °keen, °weep for or over,
°regret, rue, deplore: *We all mourned the loss of a
great leader. After his death, the nation mourned for
a month.*

mournful adj. **1** °sad, °sorrowful, °dismal,
°melancholy, °blue, afflicted, °doleful, dolorous,
grief-stricken, rueful, °forlorn, °woebegone,
°sombre, lugubrious, °funereal, °joyless, dispirited, cheerless, °unhappy, °downhearted,
heavy-hearted, disconsolate, °heartbroken,
°inconsolable, °despondent, °desolate, despairing, heartsick, °overcome, °prostrate: *The
mournful crowd filed past the bier to pay their last

respects.* **2** °deplorable, °sorrowful, °grievous,
distressing, upsetting, °tragic, saddening, disheartening, depressing, °lamentable, catastrophic, °calamitous, °disastrous: *The mournful
news of the great loss of life in the explosion was
broadcast round the world.*

mourning n. **1** °grief, °lament, grieving,
°lamentation, sorrowing, keening, weeping, wailing: *The Highlanders are wont to mingle a degree of
solemn mirth with their mourning.* **2** bereavement,
°loss, °anguish, °sorrow, °misery, °grief,
°sadness, °woe, woefulness, °melancholy,
heartache, despondency, °despair, °desolation:
In China people wear white as a sign of mourning.
3 °black, widow's weeds, sackcloth and ashes:
*It was customary at that time to spend at least one
month in mourning.*

mousy adj. **1** mousey, mouse-coloured, °dun,
°grey, greyish-brown, brownish-grey, brownish,
brown, °dull, lustreless, °lacklustre, °drab, °flat,
°plain, °colourless: *Her lank, mousy hair hung down
over her shoulders.* **2** °timid, cowering, timorous,
°shy, self-effacing, diffident: *Adrian is far too
mousy to ask for an increase in salary.*

mouth n. **1** lips; maw, jaws, °oral °cavity,
Technical stoma, *Slang* °trap, kisser, muzzle,
°gob, chops, °yap, *US* bazoo: *I want to hear
that you don't love me from your own
mouth.* **2** °opening, °aperture, doorway, door,
gateway, °gate, access, °entrance, inlet, °entry,
entry-way, °way in, entrée; °passage, passageway, °way, orifice; °exit, °way out, °vent,
°outlet, outfall, *Technical* debouchment or
debouchure, debouch or débouché, embouchure: *We stood at the mouth of the cave. An enormous
delta formed at the mouth of the river.* **3** bragging,
boasting, braggadocio, empty or idle °talk,
°bombast, rodomontade, fustian, *Slang* claptrap, °hot air, gas: *The fellow is all mouth and no
action.* **4** °disrespect, °impudence, insolence,
sauciness, rudeness, °impertinence, pertness,
boldness, audacity, presumptuousness, brashness, °flippancy, *Colloq* lip, cheek, backchat,
°sauce, freshness, *US* sass, back °talk: *He'd better
not give me any of his mouth or I'll have his guts for
garters.* **5** grimace, °pout, moue, °face: *She made
a mouth when I said she couldn't go.* **6 down in** or
at the mouth °dejected, °despondent, °sad,
°sorrowful, °unhappy, °melancholy, °blue, crestfallen, dispirited, disheartened, downcast,
Colloq (down) in the dumps, °broken up: *He was
very down in the mouth after seeing the results of
the laboratory tests.*
—v. **7** utter, °say, °speak, °pronounce,
°announce, °enunciate, articulate, °voice,
°sound, °express, vocalize; declaim, orate: *He
mouthed each word with excruciating care. Who
wants to hear some pompous fool mouthing plati-
tudes?*

mouthful n. °morsel, °bite, spoonful, forkful,
°lump, chunk, °gob, hunk: *He took a mouthful
of food.*

mouthpiece n. **1** embouchure; bit: *I need a new
mouthpiece for my clarinet.* **2** spokesman, spokeswoman, spokesperson, °agent, °representative,
intermediary, °mediator, °delegate: *He is
always quoted through his mouthpiece, never
directly.* **3** °lawyer, attorney, *Slang US* shyster:
A good mouthpiece could get me out of this fix.

movable adj. moveable, floating, °variable,
°changeable, unfixed; °portable, transportable,

transferable or transferrable: *Easter Sunday is a movable feast and has no fixed date on the calendar. Recent developments have produced computers that are smaller than an attaché case and easily movable.*

move v. **1** °shift, °stir, budge, make a move, °go; °proceed, °advance, °progress: *It is difficult to move in a strait-jacket. The train is moving at a rate of sixty miles an hour. Don't move—I have a gun.* **2** move house, move out, °remove, move away, relocate, decamp, °depart, °change residence, °emigrate, °go or °make off, °transfer, *Colloq* °take off (for), pull up °stakes, *Brit* up sticks, *Slang US* °split (for): *When did you say you were moving to London?* **3** °shake (up), °disturb, °stir (up), °agitate, °affect, °touch: *We moved heaven and earth to find a proper place for her to stay.* **4** °affect, °touch, °stir, °shake up, °agitate, °hit (hard), °upset, °strike, smite, °disturb, °ruffle, disquiet, have an (or a profound) °effect (on), make a (deep) °impression (on): *The pictures of starving children moved everyone.* **5** °provoke, °arouse, °excite, °stir up, °lead, °rouse, °stimulate: *At the end of the film, when she died, I was moved to tears.* **6** °arouse, °rouse, °provoke, actuate, °lead, °prompt, °spur, °motivate, °influence, impel, °prod, °remind, °inspire, °make: *His mention of families moved me to ask when he had last seen his father.* **7** °propose, °put forward or forth, °forward, °advance, °submit, °suggest, °advocate, °propound: *The question of budget was moved at the last meeting.*
—n. **8** °change, change-over, relocation, °transfer, °shift, °removal: *My supervisor suggested a move to a different department.* **9** °manoeuvre, °device, °trick, °caper, °dodge, ploy, °stratagem, °artifice, °ruse, °action, °act, °deed, *Colloq* °gimmick: *Getting Diana to invite Colin was a very good move.* **10** °turn, °time, °opportunity: *I have had my turn, now it's your move.* **11** °gesture, gesticulation, °action, °motion, °stirring: *One move and you're a dead man!* **12 get a move on: a** get °moving, °begin, °start, °commence, get °going, get under °way, get started, °stir or bestir oneself, *Colloq* get or °start the ball rolling, get the show on the road, °break the ice, get cracking, °step on it or the gas: *He doesn't usually get a move on till noon.* **b** °hurry, °hasten, °make °haste, °rush, °run: *Get a move on down to the supermarket before it closes.* **13 on the move: a** °travelling, in °transit, on the °way, on one's °way, on the °road, on the °go, °moving: *She is always on the move and it is difficult to catch her.* **b** on the go, working, on the °run, °busy, occupied: *I have been on the move since six this morning.* **c** °proceeding, progressing, advancing, °moving °ahead, succeeding, on the go: *It looks as if the industry is again on the move after a brief decline.*

movement n. **1** repositioning, °move, °motion, relocation, °moving, migration, °shift, °transfer, °flow, displacement: *Population movement increased dramatically in the Middle Ages.* **2** °action, °activity, °move, °moving, °stir, °stirring: *There was a sudden movement in the bushes.* **3** °gesture, gesticulation, °move, °flicker, °sign, °signal; °manoeuvre, change of attitude or position: *Only the slightest upward movement of his eyebrow indicated his surprise. Every little movement has a meaning all its own.* **4** °mechanism, °works, workings, °moving parts, machinery, °action, gears, *Colloq* innards: *Technically, the movement of a watch does not include the escapement.* **5** °campaign, °crusade, °drive; °front, °faction, °party, °group, wing: *The 1960s saw many successes for the civil rights' movement in America.* **6** °change, °activity, °action, °shift, °advance or °decline, °increase or °decrease, upward or °downward movement, stirring; °development, °progress: *Shares displayed little movement in today's trading.* **7** °drift, °trend, °tendency, °course, °swing: *They have noted a growing movement towards religious fundamentalism.*

movie n. **1** motion picture, °film, moving picture, silent (picture), talking picture, *Colloq* talkie, flick: *Her grandfather was one of the first actors in silent movies.* **2** Usually, **movies**: picture °show, cinema, flicks, *Colloq* big or large °screen, silver °screen: *Why don't we go to the movies instead of watching television tonight?*

moving adj. **1** °touching, °poignant, emotive, affecting, °stirring, °heart-rending, °emotional, °telling, °effective, °impressive, °striking, compelling; °pathetic, °exciting, °thrilling, inspiring, inspirational, impelling, °persuasive: *He related a moving story of his years in various concentration camps.* **2** °active, °mobile, unfixed, unstationary, motile, going, operating, working, in °motion, on the °move: *Be careful not to touch any of the moving parts inside the clock.*

mow v. **1** °cut (down), scythe, °trim, shear: *You don't need to mow the lawn so much during a dry spell.* **2 mow down**: annihilate, °kill, °massacre, °butcher, °slaughter, °exterminate, liquidate, eradicate, °wipe out, °cut down, °cut to °pieces, °destroy, decimate: *The first platoon was mowed down by machine-gun fire.*

muck n. **1** ordure, manure, °dung, excrement, faeces, droppings; guano: *The muck is saved for use as fertilizer.* **2** °dirt, °filth, bilge, slime, °sludge, °ooze, scum, sewage, °mire, °mud, feculence, *Colloq* gunge, gunk, *US* grunge: *Give me a chance to get the muck off my shoes.*
—v. **3 muck about**: °fool around, °waste time, °idle, loiter, °mess around or about: *She told me to stop mucking about and get a job.* **4 muck up**: °ruin, °wreck, °destroy, make a °mess of, °botch, °mess up, °bungle, *Colloq* °screw up, *Slang* °bugger up, make a muck of: *She's mucked up her own life, and, given the chance, she'll muck up mine.*

mud n. °muck, °ooze, slime, °mire, clay, °sludge, °silt, °dirt, *US and Canadian* gumbo or gombo: *The mud came up to my ankles.*

muddle v. **1** °bewilder, °confuse, confound, °mystify, baffle, °mix up, disorient, befuddle, °perplex, °bemuse, °puzzle, befog: *I am totally muddled by your explanation of differential calculus.* **2** °confuse, °mix up, °jumble, °scramble, °entangle, °tangle, °mess up, °disorder, disarrange, disorganize, °bungle, mismanage, *Colloq* muff: *My financial affairs got hopelessly muddled when I changed banks.* **3 muddle through**: (barely) °manage, °cope, °make it, °scrape through or along, contrive, °make do, °get by, °get along: *We were just muddling through when James was offered this wonderful job.*
—n. **4** °mess, °confusion, °mix-up, °jumble, °tangle, °disorder, °hotchpotch or *US* also hodgepodge, °mishmash, °chaos, °disaster, *Colloq* °stew, *Slang US* screw-up, snafu, *Taboo slang Brit* balls-up: *A lot of muddles, mix-ups, and misunderstandings ensued.*

muddy *adj.* **1** fouled, befouled, muddied, mud-spattered, °dirty, grubby, grimy, soiled, mud-caked, °slimy, mucky, miry; oozy, squelchy, squashy, boggy, fenny, marshy, swampy; *Formal* feculent; *Colloq* squishy, squushy, squooshy: *Take off those muddy boots before you come into the house. The walk up to the house has become all muddy in the rain.* **2** °confused, unclear, °vague, °obscure, °dull, °dim, °fuzzy, muddled, addled, mixed-up: *Greg has only a muddy idea of what you're talking about.* **3** °drab, °subdued, blurred, °dingy, °flat, °murky, mat *or* matt, washed out: *The colours in her paintings look very muddy to me.*
—*v.* **4** °obscure, °dull, °dim, °confuse, °mix up, befog, cloud: *His argument muddied the issue rather than clarifying it.* **5** °dirty, °soil, begrime, smirch, besmirch, °spatter, bespatter: *A passing car muddied my new skirt.*

muffle *v.* **1** Often, **muffle up**: °wrap, °swathe, swaddle, °cloak, °envelop, °cover (up), enfold, °shroud, enshroud, °conceal, °protect: *Make sure your neck is muffled when you're out in that icy wind.* **2** °deaden, °silence, °suppress, °stifle, °subdue, °damp, °dampen, °mute, °hush, °quiet(en), °tone down, °still: *A few more thicknesses of flannel will muffle the noise of the motor.*

muffler *n.* scarf, boa; shawl, °wrap: *Wrap this muffler round your neck for added warmth.*

mug *n.* **1** °jug, tankard, stein, toby (°jug), °pot, beaker, cup: *The relief workers passed round mugs of hot coffee to the homeless.* **2** °face, visage, features, countenance, *Slang* puss, kisser, mush, *Brit* clock, dial, *Archaic* phiz *or* phizog, *US* °pan: *The ex-boxer has a mug that only a mother could love.* **3** °fool, °duffer, simpleton, °dupe, gull, °innocent, *Colloq* chump, °mark, soft *or* easy touch, *Brit* muggins, *Slang* °sucker: *The mug thought he had found a full wallet.*
—*v.* **4** make a °face *or* faces, grimace: *Here are some pictures of the twins mugging for the camera.* **5** °attack, °set upon, °rob, °assault; garrotte, throttle: *Anyone who walks through the park at night risks getting mugged.* **6 mug up (on)**: °study, *Formal* lucubrate, *Colloq* °cram, burn the midnight oil, °get up (on), *Brit* swot, bone up (on): *I have to mug up on my Latin for tomorrow's examination.*

muggy *adj.* °humid, °damp, °sticky, °sultry, °oppressive, °clammy, °steamy, °close, °stuffy, °moist, soggy: *It was so muggy that every night the bedlinen was completely soaked.*

mull *v.* Usually, **mull over**: °ponder, °consider, °study, °think (over *or* about), cogitate (on *or* over *or* about), con, °evaluate, °turn over, °weigh, °deliberate (on *or* over), °reflect (on), °muse (on), °review, °examine, °contemplate, °meditate (on), °chew over, ruminate (on *or* over): *I have been mulling over your suggestion that I should join the navy.*

mum *adj.* **1** °silent, °mute, close-mouthed, °quiet, °tight-lipped: *She swore she would keep mum about where the money was hidden.*
—*n.* **2 Mum's the word**: Don't tell a soul, Keep °silent, Keep °secret, Keep °quiet, Keep (something) to oneself, Keep (something) under one's hat, Say nothing, Tell no-one, Play dumb: *He told who stole the bell, but mum's the word.*

mumble *v.* °murmur, °mutter, °say inarticulately, utter indistinctly, swallow one's words: *He mumbled the name of the person who had shot him, but she didn't catch it.*

mumbo-jumbo *n.* **1** °gibberish, °nonsense, °rubbish, °gobbledegook *or* gobbledygook, °drivel, humbug, bunkum, double-talk, °rigmarole *or* rigamarole, jabberwocky, blather *or* blether, poppycock, *Colloq* eyewash, °rot, tommy-rot, hogwash, bilge, bosh, bull, malarkey, claptrap, piffle, *US* hooey, °moonshine, bunk *Slang* crap, *Brit* tosh, *Taboo slang* bullshit: *Before he would give me the cheque, the lawyer made me sign something full of legal mumbo-jumbo.* **2** °spell, incantation, °chant, °formula, °charm, abracadabra, °hocus-pocus, °rite, °ritual, conjuration, °magic: *She had to sit through all the mumbo-jumbo of her husband's investiture.*

munch *v.* °chew, °crunch, masticate, champ, chomp, scrunch: *He just sat there munching peanuts.*

municipal *adj.* civic, °civil, metropolitan, urban, °city, °town, village, borough, parish, *Brit* °council: *Voting takes place in the municipal elections next week.*

municipality *n.* °city, °metropolis, °town, village, borough, °district, township; suburb, exurb: *The recreational facilities offered by the municipality are in need of refurbishing.*

murder *n.* **1** homicide, manslaughter, regicide, patricide, matricide, parricide, fratricide, sororicide, uxoricide, infanticide; °killing, slaying, assassination: *In many countries, murder is a crime punishable by death.* **2** °slaughter, butchery, genocide, °massacre, liquidation, decimation, extermination, eradication, wiping out, murdering, slaying, °killing, °bloodshed, °carnage: *Their wanton murder of thousands of prisoners of war has been proven.*
—*v.* **3** °kill, slay, assassinate, put to °death, °end the life of, °put away *or* down, °put out of one's misery, °wipe out, °destroy, °butcher, °massacre, liquidate, °exterminate, eradicate, annihilate, °extinguish, °slaughter, lay low, *Slang* °eliminate, °bump off, °knock off, do in, °polish off, °blow away, *US* °rub out, °waste, ice, take for a ride, fit with a concrete overcoat *or* with concrete overshoes, snuff (out): *the drug dealers were murdered, one by one, by a rival gang.* **4** °spoil, °ruin, °mar, °destroy, °wreck, °kill, °mangle, °butcher, °mutilate: *She murdered the song by singing it far too fast.*

murderer *n.* murderess, °killer, slayer, assassin, homicide, °cutthroat, liquidator, executioner, °butcher, *Slang* hit man: *The police have arrested someone they are certain is the murderer.*

murderous *adj.* **1** °fatal, °lethal, °deadly, deathly, °mortal, °destructive, °devastating, °sanguinary, bloody, °brutal, °savage, °bloodthirsty, barbarous, °fell, °cruel, °inhuman: *The tolling of the bell signalled that the murderous deed had been done.* **2** °killing, °strenuous, stressful, °difficult, °arduous, °exhausting, hellish, °harrowing, rigorous, intolerable, °unbearable: *You cannot keep up such a murderous pace, without any rest, and remain healthy.*

murky *adj.* °dark, °gloomy, °threatening, °dim, clouded, cloudy, °overcast, °grey, °dismal, °dreary, °bleak, °sombre, °grim, °funereal, °shady, °shadowy: *I could barely make out her face in the murky corner of the chapel.*

murmur *n.* **1** °undercurrent, undertone, background °noise *or* °sound, rumble, rumbling, °mumble, mumbling, drone, droning, °buzz,

buzzing, murmuration, murmuring, °hum, humming, whispering, *Formal* susurration *or* susurrus: *They spoke in low voices, barely audible above the murmur of the mourning doves.* **2** muttering, complaining, °complaint, grumble, grumbling, *Colloq* grousing, grouse: *We have heard not a murmur since everyone had an increase in salary.*
—v. **3** °mumble, °mutter, °whisper: *He murmured into her ear something about being pleased to see her.* **4** °complain, grumble, °mutter, °moan, °lament, wail, *Colloq* grouse: *Employees will always find something to murmur about.*

muscular *adj.* °sinewy, °brawny, °burly, °powerful, powerfully built, strapping, °rugged, °husky, °robust, athletic, °sturdy, well-muscled, broad-shouldered: *We all envied Nick's muscular physique.*

muse *v.* cogitate, °meditate, °reflect, °contemplate, ruminate, °think over, °think about, °consider, °chew over, °deliberate, °revolve, °weigh, °evaluate, °study, °mull over, °brood (over), °ponder; be °absorbed (in °thought), be in a brown °study, °dream, °day-dream, be in a °trance *or* °reverie: *Asked for a decision, Michael mused for a while before answering.*

mushy *adj.* **1** °soft, pulpy, doughy, squidgy, spongy; swampy, boggy, miry; *Colloq* squishy, squushy, squashy, squooshy: *The peach was over-ripe and mushy. The bottom of the pond is all mushy and feels awful when you stand up.* **2** mawkish, °maudlin, °sentimental, °romantic, saccharine, sugary, syrupy, *Colloq* corny, °sloppy, °gooey, slushy, *Brit* wet, *Slang* schmaltzy: *She cried three handkerchiefs-full over the mushy parts of* Gone With The Wind.

musical *adj.* °tuneful, melodic, °harmonious, lilting, °lyrical, °melodious, mellifluous, dulcet, euphonious: *Many modern compositions, while technically competent, are not as musical as the old-fashioned pieces.*

must *v.* **1** ought (to), should, °have to, be °obliged or obligated to, be compelled *or* °forced to, be required to: *I must get this work done before lunch-time. Must you go? Yes, I must.*
—n. **2** °necessity, requisite, °requirement, °obligation, sine qua non, °essential: *Patience is an absolute must in this job.*

muster *v.* **1** °call *or* °come together, °assemble, convoke, convene, °collect, °mobilize, °rally, °round up, °gather, marshal, °summon (up): *Within a month he had mustered a force of thousands to fight the invaders. I mustered up enough courage to ask Joan out to dinner.*
—n. **2** °rally, °assembly, assemblage, convocation, °meet, °meeting, °convention, congress, °round-up, °turnout, °gathering, congregation, aggregation, aggregate: *We attended the annual muster of bagpipe marching bands.* **3 pass muster**: come up to °scratch, make the °grade, °measure up, be °acceptable, *Colloq* come *or* be up to snuff: *Are you sure that your new design will pass muster with the art director?*

musty *adj.* **1** °mouldy, °damp, mildewed, mildewy, °sour, °rancid, spoilt, decayed, °rotten, °putrid, fetid *or* foetid, fusty, °stale: *Open the windows to get rid of that musty odour.* **2** °stale, °old-fashioned, °antiquated, antediluvian, °ancient, out of °date, °bygone, °passé, °old hat,

°obsolete, archaic, °tired, hoary, °worn out, trite, clichéd, stereotypical: *I've heard all those musty jokes of his a thousand times before.*

mutation *n.* **1** °change, changing, °alteration, altering, modification, modifying, °transformation, transforming, metamorphosis, transmutation, transmuting, transfiguration, transfiguring, °evolution, evolving, °variation, varying: *For years he studied the mutation of the sweet pea.* **2** °variant, °variation, deviation, °deviant, mutant, anomaly, departure: *The mutations exhibited marked differences over the generations.*

mute *adj.* **1** °silent, °dumb, °speechless, voiceless, wordless, °tight-lipped, °taciturn, °tacit, °reserved, °quiet, *Colloq* °mum: *Though I persisted in asking his name, he remained mute.* **2** unspoken, unsaid, °tacit, °silent: *The stain on the floor was a mute reminder of the crime.*
—v. **3** °deaden, °silence, °muffle, °stifle, °dampen, °damp, °subdue, °suppress, °quiet *or Brit also* °quieten, °hush, soft-pedal, °turn down, °tone down: *The carpet muted her footsteps as she crept up behind him.*

mutilate *v.* **1** °maim, disfigure, °mangle, °cripple, °lame, °butcher, disable; dismember, amputate, °hack off, °cut off, °lop off, °tear off, °rip off: *Formerly, the hands of thieves were mutilated as an example to others.* **2** °spoil, °mar, °ruin, °damage, °deface, vandalize, °destroy: *As the book had been mutilated, he had to buy the library a replacement.*

mutinous *adj.* **1** °rebellious, °revolutionary, °subversive, °seditious, insurgent, insurrectionary: *The mutinous crew was finally subdued and clapped in irons.* **2** °recalcitrant, refractory, contumacious, °obstinate, °defiant, °insubordinate, °disobedient, °unruly, unmanageable, °ungovernable, uncontrollable: *Whenever we told Clare to work harder at school she became mutinous.*

mutiny *n.* **1** °revolt, °rebellion, °revolution, °subversion, subversiveness, insurgency, insurgence, insurrection, °uprising: *The crew are threatening a mutiny.*
—v. **2** °rebel, °rise up (against), °strike, °revolt; °disobey, °subvert, °agitate (against): *The crew of the Bounty mutinied and set Captain Bligh adrift.*

mutter *v.* **1** °mumble, °murmur, grunt: *He was muttering something to himself that I didn't catch.* **2** grumble, °complain, *Colloq* grouch, grouse, *Brit* chunter: *She has been muttering about cuts in the postal service ever since I can remember.*

mutual *adj.* **1** °reciprocal, reciprocated, requited, interactive, complementary: *I love her and I hope that the feeling is mutual.* **2** °common, communal, °joint, shared: *Gerald is our mutual friend.*

mysterious *adj.* **1** °puzzling, enigmatic, baffling, insoluble, unsolvable, bewildering, confounding, confusing, °perplexing, mystifying, °weird, °bizarre, °strange, uncanny, °curious: *A mysterious force makes the saucer rise off the ground and fly at incredible speeds.* **2** °cryptic, arcane, °secret, inscrutable, covert, hidden, °furtive, unclear, °dark, concealed, °occult, °inexplicable, °incomprehensible, mystic(al), °unknown, unfathomable, °mystical, °recondite, abstruse: *It is mysterious how the agency accomplishes its ends.*

mystery *n.* **1** °puzzle, °enigma, conundrum, °riddle, °question: *How he escaped from the locked room is a mystery.* **2** °obscurity, °secrecy, indefiniteness, vagueness, nebulousness, °ambiguity, ambiguousness, inscrutability, inscrutableness: *The identity of the beautiful lady in the green dress is shrouded in mystery.* **3** detective story *or* novel, murder (story), *Colloq* whodunit: *Joel, who once fancied himself an intellectual, now reads nothing but mysteries.*

mystical *adj.* **1** allegorical, °symbolic(al), mystic, cabbalistic, arcane, unrevealed, °secret, °occult, °supernatural, esoteric, other-worldly, preternatural, °cryptic, concealed, hidden, clandestine, °private, °veiled, °ineffable, °mysterious: *A mystical spirit dwells in the raven that sits on his shoulder.* **2** See **mysterious**, 2, above.

mystify *v.* °fool, °hoax, humbug, °confuse, confound, °mix up, °bewilder, °stump, °puzzle, baffle, *Colloq* bamboozle, °flummox, *Slang* °beat: *We were totally mystified by the unfamiliar symbols on the wall.*

mystique *n.* °mystery, °magic, charisma, °aura, inscrutability, supernaturalism, preternaturalism, strangeness: *She has a certain mystique about her.*

myth *n.* **1** °legend, fable, allegory, °parable, °tradition, °saga, epic, (°folk) °tale, °story, mythos; °history: *The ancient myths have provided sources for much of modern literature.* **2** fable, °lie, (tall) °tale, °fib, prevarication, fiction, untruth, °falsehood, °fabrication, cock-and-bull °story, *Colloq* whopper: *He told her some myth about his being a multimillionaire and she believed it.*

mythical *adj.* **1** mythic, mythological, fabled, °legendary, °traditional, folkloric, storied, °romantic, fairy-tale, story-book; allegorical, °symbolic, parabolic(al): *Campbell has demonstrated astounding similarities amongst the mythical tales of unrelated cultures.* **2** mythic, °fanciful, °imaginary, °fictitious, make-believe, made-up, chimerical, °untrue: *When she was about seven, my daughter had a mythical friend named Theodosia.*

mythology *n.* (body of) °myths, folklore, °tradition, °lore, °stories, mythos: *After only one generation, an extraordinary mythology has been created about Marilyn Monroe.*

N

nab v. catch, °capture, °arrest, put or place under °arrest, °seize, apprehend, °pick up, °bring in, take into °custody, Colloq °pinch, collar, °run in, °nail, Brit °nick: They finally nabbed that cat burglar in Hampstead.

nag[1] v. **1** Sometimes, **nag at**: °annoy, °irritate, °irk, °pester, °criticize, °ride, °scold, °carp (at), °upbraid, badger, °harass, harry, vex, °henpeck, °torment, hector, °pick at, goad, °pick on, find °fault with, °berate, nettle, °bully, °provoke, °plague, °worry, °bother, Brit chivvy or chivy or chevy, Colloq needle: He nags her day and night about going on a diet.
—n. **2** °scold, harpy, °pest, °shrew, virago, termagant, °fishwife: You certainly can be a terrible nag, can't you?

nag[2] n. °jade, Rosinante; horse, °hack, pony, dobbin, racehorse, thoroughbred, Slang gee-gee, US hayburner, plug, bangtail, gee-gee: That old nag wouldn't be able to clear the fence.

nagging adj. distressing, °chronic, °continuous, °continual, °persistent, unrelenting, °relentless, recurring: He complains of a nagging pain in his shoulder. I have a nagging feeling that I have an appointment to be somewhere.

nail n. **1** fastener, °fastening, °spike, °pin: The pieces were held together by several nails. **2** fingernail, toenail, °claw, talon: The detective found some fibres under the victim's nails. **3 bite one's nails**: °worry, agonize, °fret, lose sleep (over), °chafe, °suffer, Colloq °stew (over or about): Carl is biting his nails over the result of his cholesterol test. **4 hard** or **tough as nails**: **a** °tough, °vigorous, °hardy: After years of mountain-climbing, René is as hard as nails. **b** °cold, unsentimental, °unsympathetic, unfeeling: The boss, as hard as nails, doesn't care what you sacrifice to get the job done. **5 hit the nail on the head**: be °accurate, be °correct, be °precise, be °right, put (one's) °finger on it: When you said they were fools, you really hit the nail on the head. **6 on the nail**: °immediately, at °once, °straight or °right away, °promptly, without °delay, on the spot, Colloq US on the barrel-head: He has always paid his bills right on the nail.
—v. **7** °attach, °secure, °join, °pin, °tack, °clinch or clench, °fasten, °fix, °focus, rivet, °glue: The door to the mysterious room was nailed shut. His eyes were nailed to the pressure gauge. **8** See nab, above. **9** °hit, °strike; °punch; °shoot: She nailed him with a left hook and he sank like a stone. **10 nail down**: °settle, °secure, °resolve, °complete, conclude, make °final; °finalize: Let's celebrate: I nailed down the order for 10,000 air-conditioning units.

naïve adj. naive or naïf, °ingenuous, °innocent, credulous, °childlike, born yesterday, °unaffected, °unsophisticated, °inexperienced, °green, unworldly, °unsuspecting, unenlightened, unsuspicious, °trusting, trustful, °gullible, °artless, guileless, °simple, simplistic, simple-minded, unpretentious, unpretending, °candid, °natural: Is Chatterley naïve enough to believe that the gamekeeper's meetings with his wife were to discuss fox-hunting?

naïvety n. naïveté, ingenuousness, innocence, credulity, credulousness, °inexperience, (blind)

°trust, gullibility, artlessness, callowness, guilelessness, °simplicity, unpretentiousness, °candour, naturalness, frankness, openness, °sincerity: I hope that no one takes advantage of her naïvety.

naked adj. **1** stark naked, unclothed, undraped, °bare, exposed, stripped, undressed, unclad, uncovered, bared, °nude, in the °nude, Colloq in the altogether, in one's birthday suit, in the buff, in the raw, au naturel, in a state of nature, Brit starkers, in the nuddy: The two of them stood there, completely naked. **2** unaided, unassisted: Stars of the seventh magnitude or brighter are visible to the naked eye. **3** °plain, °unadorned, unembellished, °stark, °overt, °patent, °obvious, °conspicuous, °manifest, °sheer, °undisguised, °unvarnished, °unmitigated, °evident, palpable, unconcealed, in °plain sight or view, °blatant, °barefaced, undeniable, °glaring, °flagrant, unmistakable, unalloyed, unmixed, °blunt, unadulterated, °pure: He told her the naked truth about how he felt. **4** unsheathed, unprotected, °bare, exposed: How dare he show a naked sword in the presence of the Emperor?!

name n. **1** designation, °label, appellation, °term, °tag, °style, Colloq moniker or monicker, handle: His name is Chauncy but they call him Rusty. **2** °reputation; repute, °honour, °esteem, (high) °regard, °respect, °rank, °standing, rating, °pre-eminence, °superiority, eminence, notability, °prominence, °prestige, °favour, °distinction, °renown, °fame, °popularity, °celebrity: She has made a name for herself as a clever business executive. He thinks he has to protect his name as a ladies' man. **3** °personage, °somebody, °celebrity, °star, superstar, °hero, VIP, °dignitary, luminary, Colloq °big shot, °bigwig, °big cheese, °big name: The programme included some well-known names in the entertainment world.
—v. **4** °label, °tag, °style, °entitle; °call, dub, °christen, baptize: They named their book 'The Alien Tongue'. Why would people want to name their child 'Quercus'? **5** °choose, °elect, °select, °delegate, °nominate, °designate, °appoint; °identify, denominate, pinpoint, °specify: She has been named 'Woman of the Year'. I asked her to name our wedding day. She refuses to name her attacker. **6 name names**: °identify, °specify, °mention, cite: In exchange for a lighter sentence, the witness agreed to name names.

nameless adj. **1** unnamed, innominate, °unidentified, anonymous, pseudonymous, °incognito, °unknown, °unheard-of, °unsung: How much we owe the nameless inventor of the wheel! **2** °inexpressible, indefinable, unidentifiable, unspecified, unspecifiable: A nameless dread seized him as he entered the cave. **3** °ineffable, unutterable, unspeakable, °unmentionable, °abominable, °horrible, indescribable, °repulsive: Paganism allowed man to sink beneath a flood of nameless sensualities.

namely adv. specifically, to °wit, that is (to say), id est, i.e., videlicet, viz., scilicet, sc.; for °example, for °instance, *exempli gratia,* e.g. *or* eg: *We visited three countries, namely, France, Italy, and Switzerland.*

nap[1] *v.* **1** °doze, °nod (off), catnap, *Colloq* catch forty winks, °drop off (to °sleep), get some shut-eye, snooze, zizz, *US* catch *or* log a few zees (Z's): *I nap every afternoon.*
—*adv.* **2 napping**: °unawares, off °guard, unexpectedly, in an °unguarded moment: *The ball, hit to his backhand, caught him napping.*
—*n.* **3** °doze, catnap, siesta, *Colloq* forty winks, shut-eye, snooze, zizz, *Brit* lie-down: *Take a short nap before dinner.*

nap[2] *n.* °pile, °fibre, °texture, °weave, down, shag: *Choose a carpet with a short nap for areas of heavy wear.*

narcotic *adj.* **1** soporific, stuporific, hypnotic, °sedative, somnolent, sleep-inducing, opiate, dulling, numbing, anaesthetic, stupefacient, stupefying, stupefactive, tranquillizing, Lethean: *Most narcotic drugs may be sold only with a doctor's prescription.*
—*n.* **2** °drug, soporific, stuporific, hypnotic, °sedative, opiate, anaesthetic, stupefacient, °tranquillizer: *Many doctors are reluctant to prescribe narcotics.*

narrate *v.* °relate, °tell, °recount, °report, give an °account (of), °recite, °rehearse, °repeat, °review, °unfold, °chronicle, °describe, °detail, °reveal, retail: *She narrated a bone-chilling story of intrigue and murder. Please narrate the events leading up to your finding the body, Mrs Easton.*

narration *n.* **1** °telling, relating, unfolding, recounting, chronicling, recording, describing; °report, °recital, °recitation, °rehearsal, °relation, °chronicle, °description, portrayal, detailing, °revelation, °story, °tale, °narrative: *His narration was accompanied by nervous gestures. Her narration disagrees with her husband's in certain essential respects.* **2** reading, voice-over: *The narration did not seem to be coordinated with the pictures on the screen.*

narrative *n.* **1** °story, °tale, °chronicle, °description, °revelation, portrayal, °account, °report, °record, °history, °recital, °statement: *The characterizations were poor, but the narrative was fascinating.*
—*adj.* **2** storytelling, chronicling, anecdotal: *One of her long, narrative poems has been published in a collection.*

narrator *n.* °reporter, storyteller, °raconteur, taleteller, teller of °tales, anecdotist *or* anecdotalist, relator, annalist, chronicler, describer, °author; voice-over: *We sat spellbound waiting for the narrator to continue.*

narrow *adj.* **1** constricted, °slender, °slim, °thin, restricted, °straitened, attenuated, narrowed; narrowing, tapering: *We squeezed through the narrow passage to freedom.* **2** confined, confining, °limited, °cramped, °close, °meagre, pinched, °tight, incommodious: *I awoke in a cell so narrow I could scarcely move.* **3** °strict, °careful, °close, °precise, °exact, °exacting, °demanding, °finicky, finical, °sharp, °meticulous, °scrupulous, °fussy, °rigid, searching, °critical: *The suspected forgeries were submitted to the narrow scrutiny of several experts.* **4** restricted, °limited, circumscribed, proscribed, denotative: *I learnt the meaning of charity in its narrowest sense.* **5** See **narrow-minded,** below. **6** °close, hairbreadth, °lucky: *I'd had a very narrow escape, for the bullet just*

grazed my scalp. **7** stingy, niggardly, parsimonious, °miserly, °tight, °sparing, tight-fisted, °mean, °mercenary *Brit* mingy, *Dialect*al near, *Colloq* °close: *He was so narrow he barely allowed himself the essentials.*
—*v.* **8** constrict, °limit, °qualify, °reduce, lessen, °diminish, °decrease: *She narrowed her chances of winning by buying only one lottery ticket.* **9** °limit, °restrict, °focus, confine, °concentrate, °narrow down: *They have narrowed the search for the boy to the area near Chester.*
—*n.* **10 narrows**: °strait(s), °channel, °passage: *The vessel approached the narrows at dead slow speed.*

narrowly *adv.* **1** °barely, (only) °just, °scarcely, °hardly, by a hair's breadth; by the °skin of one's teeth, *Colloq* by a whisker: *The speeding lorry narrowly missed those children.* **2** closely, carefully, meticulously, scrupulously, °searchingly, critically: *She regarded him narrowly before speaking.*

narrow-minded *adj.* °bigoted, °prejudiced, illiberal, °narrow, °biased, °opinionated, °one-sided, °intolerant, non-objective, °conservative, °reactionary, °parochial, ultra-conservative, stiff-necked, °conventional, °hidebound, fundamentalist, literal-minded, narrow-spirited, mean-minded, mean-spirited, °petty, pettifogging, °small-minded, puritanical, unprogressive, °old-fashioned, old-fogyish *or* old-fogeyish, °strait-laced, *Colloq* °stuffy, *US* close-minded, °square, screed-bound, red-necked: *The vote reflected a reasonable balance between broad-minded and narrow-minded factions.*

nasty *adj.* **1** °foul, °filthy, °dirty, unclean, °offensive, °disgusting, nauseating, °revolting, °horrible, °loathsome, °repugnant, °repellent, °vile, odious, °obnoxious, objectionable, °nauseous, sickening, vomit-provoking, fetid *or* foetid, noisome, mephitic, °rank, malodorous, °rancid, noxious: *The nasty stench of rotting vegetation assailed our nostrils.* **2** unpleasant, °disagreeable, °unsavoury, °painful, objectionable, annoying, °untoward, °awkward, °difficult, °bad, °serious: *He had some very nasty experiences in the war.* **3** °obscene, °dirty, °pornographic, °blue, smutty, °lewd, °vulgar, °sordid, °indecent, licentious, °gross, °coarse, °crude, °rude, ribald, °bawdy, °risqué, °off colour, °suggestive, *Colloq* X-rated, raunchy: *The shops are selling some rather nasty videos that I don't want the children to watch.* **4** unpleasant, °disagreeable, °ugly, bad-tempered, °vicious, currish, °surly, °abusive, °spiteful, irascible, ill-natured, ill-tempered, °cruel, °inconsiderate, °rude, churlish, °obnoxious, crotchety, curmudgeonly, °cantankerous, crabbed, °cranky, *US and Canadian* °mean: *Why is your father so nasty to everyone who wants to go out with you?* **5** °bad, °severe, °acute, °painful, °serious; °dangerous, °critical: *I got a nasty shock when I opened the cupboard door. That's a nasty wound you have there.*

nation *n.* °country, °state, °land, °political entity, polity, °domain, °realm: *The countries of Europe are unlikely to become one nation.*

national *adj.* **1** nationwide, country-wide, °state, governmental, °civil; °public, °popular, *US* federal: *It took years to enact national clean-air laws.* **2** °nationalistic, nationalist, °patriotic, jingoistic, chauvinistic: *During the war, national feelings ran high.*

—*n.* **3** °citizen, °subject, °inhabitant, °resident; °native: *Stephenson left England years ago and is now an Australian national.*

nationalistic *adj.* nationalist, °patriotic, jingoist(ic), chauvinist(ic), xenophobic, isolationist: *As communications improved, nationalistic feelings were eroded.*

nationality *n.* **1** citizenship: *Some countries allow their citizens dual nationality.* **2** °race, °nation, ethnic °group, ethnos, °clan, °tribe; °strain, °stock, °pedigree, °heritage, °roots, °extraction, bloodline, °breed: *The country became a melting-pot of myriad nationalities.*

native *adj.* **1** innate, natal, °inborn, °natural, °inherent, congenital, indwelling, inherited, °hereditary, in the blood, °intrinsic, constitutional: *Early in life, Carla demonstrated a native ability for music.* **2** °domestic, °local, home-grown; °indigenous, autochthonous, °aboriginal: *The native oysters in this area are superb.* **3** °basic, °first, °best, °original, °exclusive: *Can you tell that my native language is Hungarian?* **4** °national, ethnic, °clan, tribal: *We visited a Dutch town where the people wear traditional native dress.* **5** °aboriginal, °provincial, °local: *We soon fell in with the native custom of taking a siesta.* **6** born; by °birth: *Are you a native Glaswegian?*
—*n.* **7** aborigine, indigene, autochthon; °national, °citizen, °resident, °inhabitant: *It is not difficult to distinguish the natives from the tourists in London.*

natural *adj.* **1** °ordinary, °common, commonplace, °normal, °standard, °regular, °usual, °customary, unexceptional, °routine, °habitual, °typical, °everyday; °reasonable, °logical, °sensible, accepted: *They say that Count Dracula could not die a natural death. The natural thing to do in case of attack is to defend oneself.* **2** °normal, °ordinary, °regular, expected; °spontaneous: *The natural motion of the waves carried the bottle out to sea.* **3** °simple, °basic, °fundamental, °real, unartificial, °genuine, unembellished, °unadorned, unpretentious: *She has great natural beauty and needs no cosmetics.* **4** unstudied, unconstrained, °candid, °frank, °spontaneous, °unaffected, °easy, °honest, °straight, straightforward, °artless, guileless, °impulsive, °unpremeditated, °ingenuous, °unsophisticated, unsophistic(al): *His kindness is quite natural.* **5** See **native, 1,** above: *She has a natural gift for painting.* **6** °true, °real, °genuine, °actual, °authentic, bona fide: *That, believe it or not, is his natural hair.* **7** °lifelike, °true to life, °realistic: *Note the natural colours of the sea in this painting by Whistler.* **8** °illegitimate, bastard: *He was the duke's natural son and had no claim on the estate.* **9** °consistent, consonant, consequent, °logical, °reasonable, °fitting, °appropriate, °proper, expected, not °incongruous, understandable: *In the circumstances, it would have been natural for her to despise Jonathan.* **10** °organic, organically grown, non-chemical, °health: *They eat only natural foods, which they grow themselves.*
—*n.* **11** °genius, artist, °talent: *When it comes to chess, Boris is a natural.* **12** *Archaic* idiot, imbecile, simpleton, °fool, °halfwit: *One would have to be a natural to give money to that crook.*

naturally *adv.* **1** (as a matter of) °course, °needless to say, to be °sure, certainly, °surely, not unexpectedly, as expected *or* anticipated, °obviously, °clearly, logically, °consequently, as a consequence *or* °result: *He treated her badly, so, naturally, she refuses to see him again.* **2** normally, by °nature, by °character, °really, °actually, genuinely; inherently, instinctively, innately, congenitally: *My hair is naturally curly. He is not aloof, just naturally shy.* **3** unaffectedly, unpretentiously, °easily, candidly, °openly, °simply, plainly, °honestly, straightforwardly, uncomplicatedly: *If only politicians expressed themselves naturally and not pompously.*

nature *n.* **1** °quality, properties, features, °character, °personality, °make-up, °essence, constitution, °identity, attributes, °disposition, temperament, complexion: *Only detailed analysis will reveal the nature of this compound. It is not in his nature to be envious.* **2** °universe, cosmos, °world, °creation, °environment: *Science fiction deals with phenomena and contrivances that defy the laws of nature.* **3** scenery, countryside, wildness, primitiveness, °simplicity: *I often enjoyed sitting by the river, communing with nature.* **4** °kind, °variety, °description, °sort, °class, °category, °type, °genre, species; °stamp, °cast, °mould, feather, kidney, °colour, °stripe: *The duties of the position are largely of a ceremonial nature.* **5 by nature:** See **naturally, 2,** above.

naught *n.* nought, °nothing, °nil, °zero, aught *or* ought; °ruin, °destruction, °disaster, °collapse, °failure: *All my efforts had come to naught.*

naughty *adj.* **1** °mischievous, impish, puckish, roguish, scampish, °devilish; °frolicsome, °playful: *The children would get naughty the minute the teacher turned her back to the class.* **2** °disobedient, refractory, °insubordinate, °bad, °perverse, °wicked, fractious, °unruly, wayward, unmanageable, °ungovernable, °undisciplined, °defiant, °obstreperous: *Naughty pupils in this school are birched.* **3** °improper, °offensive, °vulgar, °indecent, °immoral, °risqué, °off colour, ribald, °bawdy, °blue, °pornographic, smutty, °lewd, °obscene, °dirty, *Colloq* X-rated, raunchy: *The teacher caught Keith reading a naughty book.*

nauseate *v.* °sicken, °disgust, °repel, °revolt, °offend: *Your hypocrisy nauseates me. When you get used to it, eating snails no longer seems nauseating.*

nauseated *adj.* sickened, °disgusted, repelled, revolted, offended, °sick (to one's stomach), °queasy, °squeamish; seasick, carsick, airsick: *They were nauseated when they saw the cadavers. I became nauseated by the rocking of the boat.*

nauseous *adj.* nauseating, °loathsome, sickening, °disgusting, °repellent, vomit-provoking, °offensive, °revolting, °repugnant, °repulsive, °abhorrent, °nasty, °foul, unpleasant, stomach-turning, *Technical* emetic: *A nauseous odour emanated from the crypt.*

nautical *adj.* maritime, °marine, °seafaring, seagoing; naval; °boating, yachting, sailing; navigational: *Britain has always been a nautical nation. One must observe the nautical rules of the road.*

navel *n. Technical* umbilicus, omphalos, *Colloq* belly button: *The dancer wore a ruby in her navel.*

navigable *adj.* **1** °passable, traversable, negotiable, unblocked, unobstructed, °clear: *The Thames is not navigable above Lechlade.*

2 manoeuvrable, sailable, controllable, steerable, yare: *My boat is navigable when under way at about four knots.*

navigate *v.* **1** °sail, voyage, °cruise, °journey; °cross, °traverse: *After navigating the Indian Ocean for a month, we reached the Seychelles.* **2** °manoeuvre, °handle, °sail, °guide, °pilot, °steer, °direct, °skipper, captain, *Nautical* con: *It was tricky navigating through the shoals. Richard has navigated the company through rough waters over the years.*

navigation *n.* pilotage, helmsmanship, seamanship, steersmanship, steering, sailing: *The navigation of a small vessel in such a storm is no mean task.*

navigator *n.* °pilot, helmsman, seaman, tillerman, wheelman, steersman, °skipper: *The navigator without knowledge of local waterways must engage a pilot.*

navy *n.* °fleet, flotilla, naval °force(s), armada, *Literary* argosy: *The entire navy sailed across the Channel to Le Havre.*

naysayer *n.* denier, refuser, disdainer, rejecter or rejector; °prophet of doom, pessimist, °sceptic, dissenter, defeatist: *Don't expect any encouragement from a naysayer like Raymond.*

near *adv.* **1** °close (by or at °hand), not °far (off or away), °nearby, nigh, in or into the °vicinity or °neighbourhood, within (easy) °reach: *Draw near and listen to my tale.* **2** °close to, next to: *Don't go near the edge!* **3** °nearly, °almost, °just about, wellnigh, °close to being; not °quite, °virtually: *She was damn near killed in the car crash.* —*adj.* **4** °close, °imminent, °immediate, °impending, looming, coming, approaching, °forthcoming; in the offing, at °hand: *We hope to settle the pollution problem in the near future. The time is near for me to go.* **5** °nearby, °close (by), adjacent, next-door, °adjoining, abutting, °neighbouring, contiguous: *My nearest neighbours live a mile away.* **6** stingy, °mean, niggardly, °miserly, parsimonious, °penurious, °cheap, penny-pinching, cheese-paring, °selfish, °close, tight-fisted, close-fisted: *He is so near he begrudged me even a cup of tea.* **7** °close, °intimate, connected, °related, °attached: *In case of emergency, list the name and address of a near relative.* **8** °close, °narrow, hairbreadth: *Although I escaped, it was a near thing.* —*prep.* **9** °close to, in the °vicinity or °neighbourhood of, next to, adjacent to, within °reach of, within a mile of; a stone's throw from, not °far (away) from: *She wouldn't allow the doctor to come near her. I live near the railway.* —*v.* **10** °approach, °draw near or nigh, come °close or closer, °verge on, °approximate on, °lean °towards: *As summer nears, I think of going on holiday. The ship neared port. His estimate is beginning to near mine.*

nearby *adv.* **1** °close by, °close at °hand, not far-off or -away, in the °vicinity or °neighbourhood, within (easy) °reach, °about, °around: *Hyenas loitered nearby waiting for the lions to leave the kill.* —*adj.* **2** °close, within °reach, °handy, °accessible, at or to °hand, adjacent: *Nearby villagers helped put out the fire. We always kept a gun nearby because of pirates.*

nearly *adv.* **1** °almost, not quite, °about, °approximately, all but, °just about, °virtually, wellnigh, °practically, as good as, more or less;

°around, approaching, nearing, °barely, °hardly, °scarcely, °close to: *We were nearly there but couldn't make it. She was nearly ninety when her first book was published.* **2** closely, identically, °exactly, °precisely: *Her opinions agree most nearly with his. His painting most nearly resembles Picasso's.*

near-sighted *adj.* **1** myopic, °short-sighted: *Being near-sighted, I must wear spectacles for driving.* **2** *Chiefly US* short-sighted, °narrow-minded, blinkered, °narrow, close-minded, illiberal, °unthinking, °heedless, insular, °partial, °one-sided, °parochial, °unsophisticated, unimaginative, °biased, unobjective, °opinionated, °dogmatic, °prejudiced, °intolerant, °bigoted: *They maintain a near-sighted attitude towards associating with anyone outside their immediate clique.*

neat *adj.* **1** °tidy, °orderly, °clean, uncluttered, °trim, °spruce, natty, °fastidious, spick and span, °shipshape (and Bristol fashion), organized, well-organized, well-ordered, °systematic, *Brit* dialect trig, *Colloq* neat as a pin, *Brit* dinky: *His room was always neat—very odd for a teenager.* **2** °straight, unadulterated, unmixed, °undiluted, uncut, unblended, °pure: *He drinks his whisky neat.* **3** unembellished, °unadorned, unornamented, °simple, °elegant, °graceful, °smart, uncomplicated, °regular, °precise, copperplate; calligraphic: *An invitation in her neat handwriting awaited my return from abroad.* **4** deft, adroit, °clever, °efficient, °ingenious, °expert, °practised, °skilful, °dexterous: *He contrived a neat plan to avoid paying taxes.* **5** °fine, wonderful, °marvellous, °great, °splendid, °excellent, °exceptional, °capital, °grand, first-class, *Colloq* cool, smashing, keen, °nifty, top-notch, A-1 or A-one, *Brit* top-hole, *Chiefly US* A-OK or A-okay, *Slang* °swell, far-out, boss, *Brit* topping, *US and Canadian* spiffy: *She found a really neat way to get boys to ask her out. Gordon has a neat new car.*

neaten *v.* Often, **neaten up**: °tidy (up), °straighten (up or out), °clean (up), °spruce up, (put in) °order, *Brit* dialect trig: *If you don't neaten up your room, Mandy, you may not borrow the car.*

nebulous *adj.* °vague, °hazy, clouded, unclear, °obscure, °indistinct, °fuzzy, °muddy, ill-defined, °shapeless, amorphous, blurred, indeterminate, °murky, °opaque, turbid, °dim, foggy, °faint, °pale: *He has only the most nebulous idea of what the lecture was about.*

necessarily *adv.* inevitably, unavoidably, inescapably, axiomatically, inexorably, ineluctably, irresistibly, incontrovertibly, automatically, °naturally, (as a matter) of °course, as a °result, certainly, °surely, to be °sure, like it or not, °willy-nilly, perforce, of °necessity, by definition: *If you accept his premise, then you must, necessarily, accept his conclusion. You don't necessarily need to be rich to be happy.*

necessary *adj.* **1** °indispensable, °essential, required, needed, compulsory, requisite, °vital, demanded, °imperative, °obligatory, needful, of the °essence, °important, of the utmost °importance, top-priority, high-priority, °urgent, exigent, compelling, life-and-death or life-or-death: *A good diet is necessary for good health. It is necessary that you come at once. Take the necessary steps to get the job done.* **2** °inevitable, °unavoidable, inescapable, ineluctable: *In the circumstances, we find it necessary to ask for your*

resignation. **3** °sure, °certain, °predetermined, predestined, °fated, inexorable; resulting, resultant: *The necessary outcome of the affair was that the child was returned to her natural parents.*
—*n.* **4** See **necessity, 1,** below.

necessity *n.* **1** °requirement, °essential, °necessary, requisite, °need, °prerequisite, °basic, °fundamental, *sine qua non,* desideratum, constraint: *I was marooned for a year with only the bare necessities of life. We regard honesty as a necessity in a bank manager.* **2** indispensability, unavoidability, needfulness, inexorability: *The necessity for exercise is often met by private health clubs.* **3** °poverty, °want, indigence, °need, destitution, penury, straits, °difficulty, °difficulties, pauperism, neediness: *The extreme necessity of the unemployed demands that the government act quickly.* **4** °urgency, °emergency, °crisis, °misfortune, exigency, °pinch, °extreme, matter of life and death: *She has made a virtue of necessity. Electric power is no longer a matter of choice but of necessity.*

need *v.* **1** °require, °demand, °want, be in °want of, °call for, have need of or for; °lack, °miss, have °occasion for: *This room needs a coat of paint. Although she may want more money, she doesn't need it. Do you need anything to make you more comfortable?*
—*n.* **2** °necessity, °requirement; °call, °demand, constraint: *There's no need to shout—I can hear you. There is a need to keep this matter confidential. This facility will meet our electricity needs for decades.* **3** °essential, °necessary, requisite, °prerequisite, °necessity, °basic, °fundamental, *sine qua non,* °necessary, desideratum: *I am perfectly capable of taking care of my family's needs.* **4** °distress, °difficulty, °trouble, (dire or °desperate) straits, °stress, °emergency, exigency, °extremity, neediness, needfulness; °poverty, penury, impecuniousness, destitution, °privation, deprivation, indigence, beggary: *She was very supportive in his hour of need. The need of the people in that district is heart-rending.* **5** °want, °lack, °dearth, °shortage, paucity, °scarcity, insufficiency, desideratum: *The need for medical supplies was most sharply felt in areas that were already ravaged by famine.*

needless *adj.* **1** °unnecessary, °non-essential, unessential, unneeded, unwanted, °useless, uncalled-for, °gratuitous, °superfluous, °redundant, °excess, °excessive, tautological, °dispensable, °expendable, supererogatory, *de trop,* pleonastic: *He went to a lot of needless trouble to change the tyre. It is needless to raise further questions.* **2 needless to say**: °naturally, (as a matter of) °course, °obviously, it goes without saying: *Needless to say, he will have to resign when this comes to light.*

needy *adj.* °poor, °indigent, poverty-stricken, °destitute, °impoverished, penniless, impecunious, necessitous, underprivileged, °deprived, disadvantaged, below the °poverty level, in dire straits, in or on the way to the poorhouse, in reduced circumstances, down-and-out, *Colloq* °insolvent, on one's uppers, °dead or °flat or stony-broke, °hard up, strapped, pinched, on the breadline, up against it, *Brit* on the °dole, *US* °dead °broke, on welfare, on °relief: *It is not enough to look after needy families only at Christmas time.*

negative *adj.* **1** °contradictory, anti, °contrary, dissenting, dissentious, disputing, disputatious, °argumentative, adversarial, adversative, antagonistic, antipathetic, adverse, *US* °adversary: *He has adopted a very negative attitude towards his job. Few negative voices were heard on the issue.* **2** °pessimistic, °unenthusiastic, °cool, °cold, uninterested, unresponsive: *The reaction to our offer has been largely negative.* **3** nullifying, annulling, neutralizing, voiding, cancelling: *The laws are mainly negative, listing only things one must not do.* **4** negating, refusing, denying, gainsaying, °opposing: *The judge came to a negative decision regarding bail.* **5 in the negative**: negatively, 'No': *Asked if she wanted to go, she replied in the negative.*

neglect *v.* **1** °disregard, °ignore, °slight, pay no °attention to, be °inattentive to, °overlook, °pass by, °spurn, °rebuff, °scorn, disdain, contemn, *Colloq* cold-shoulder: *Scholars neglected his work for years.* **2** °fail (in), °omit; °disregard, let °slide or °pass, be °remiss (about or in or regarding), °abandon, °lose sight of, °forget, °shirk: *Have I neglected telling you how much I love you? Sybil has neglected her obligations.*
—*n.* **3** °disregard, °disrespect, inattention, °indifference, slighting, unconcern, °oversight, heedlessness, neglectfulness, carelessness, inadvertence: *We lost business to our competitor through simple neglect.* **4** °negligence, laxity, laxness, slackness, neglectfulness, passivity, passiveness, °inactivity, inaction, dereliction, °default, °failure, °failing, remissness: *She has been accused of neglect in not looking after her children properly.*

negligence *n.* inattention, inattentiveness, °indifference, carelessness, unconcern, dereliction, °failure, °failing, heedlessness, laxity, laxness, °disregard, °oversight, °omission, inadvertence, °neglect, remissness, forgetfulness, oscitancy or oscitance: *The car crash was attributed to the lorry driver's negligence.*

negligible *adj.* °insignificant, °minor, unimportant, °trifling, trivial, °inconsequential, piddling, inappreciable, °small, °slight, °paltry, nugatory, °worthless, °petty, °niggling, not worth mentioning or talking about: *The differences between the two plans are negligible.*

negotiate *v.* **1** °deal, °bargain, °dicker, °haggle, chaffer, palter; °discuss, °debate, mediate, °consult, °parley, °speak, °talk, °transact, come to °terms: *A conglomerate is negotiating to buy our company. The company asked me to negotiate on our behalf.* **2** °arrange (for), °organize, orchestrate, °conduct, °handle, °manoeuvre, °manage, °engineer, °work out, °settle, °get, °obtain, °bring off or about, °carry off, °accomplish, do, °execute, °effect, °complete, conclude, *Colloq* °pull off: *Will you be able to negotiate a loan for the car?* **3** °manoeuvre, °clear, °get through or past or round or over, °pass, °cross, *Colloq* °make (it (through or past or round or over)): *Will you be able to negotiate the barbed-wire fence?*

negotiation *n.* **1** °discussion, mediation, arbitration, bargaining, °parley, parleying, °talk, coming to °terms: *The disarmament negotiations have dragged on for years.* **2** °deal, °bargain, °transaction, °agreement, °arrangement, °understanding, °determination, °decision, °settlement; °contract, °pact, °compact, covenant, concordat, °treaty: *All parties seem pleased with the final negotiation.*

negotiator *n.* arbitrator, arbiter, °mediator, °moderator, diplomat, °ambassador, °go-between, middleman, intercessor, interceder, intervener, °agent, °broker: *An independent negotiator was invited to the bargaining table with the union and management representatives.*

neighbourhood *n.* **1** locality, °area, °region, °vicinity, vicinage, environs, °quarter, °district, °precinct(s), purlieus, °locale; surroundings, confines: *Houses in the neighbourhood of the blast were levelled.* **2 in the neighbourhood of:** °approximately, °about, °around, °nearly, °practically, °close to, °almost, more or less, *Colloq* in the ballpark of, *Brit* getting on for, not far off, *US* within an eyelash of, *Slang* as °near as dammit to: *The playground will cost in the neighbourhood of £5,000.*

neighbouring *adj.* °nearby, °near, °around, adjacent (to), °surrounding, °adjoining, contiguous (to), °touching, bordering (on), next (to), nearest: *Owners of properties neighbouring the nuclear power plant worry about radiation. The neighbouring villages will participate in the fête at Long Norton.*

neighbourly *adj.* °friendly, °cordial, °warm, °amiable, °agreeable, affable, companionable, welldisposed, °kindly, °kind, well-wishing, °genial, °sociable, °social, °harmonious, °considerate, °thoughtful, °helpful, °gracious, °courteous, °civil: *It was quite neighbourly of the Constables to look after our cat.*

neologism *n.* neoterism, coinage, neology, nonce-word; °blend, portmanteau °word: *Lexicographers must decide the neologisms to be added to their dictionaries.*

nerve *n.* **1** °courage, coolness, boldness, °bravery, intrepidity, °determination, valour, °daring, fearlessness, dauntlessness, °pluck, mettle, °spirit, °fortitude, °will, °tenacity, steadfastness, staunchness, firmness, doughtiness, resoluteness, *Colloq* guts, °grit, °gumption, °spunk, *US* sand, *Brit* °bottle, *US* moxie, *Taboo slang* balls: *It took a lot of nerve to go back into that burning building.* **2** °effrontery, brazenness, °gall, °impertinence, °brass, °impudence, insolence, audacity, brashness, °presumption, presumptuousness, temerity, *Colloq* cheek, °sauce, chutzpah, *Slang* crust: *You have a lot of nerve, talking to your mother that way!* **3 get on someone's nerves:** °annoy, °irritate, °upset: *That loud rock music gets on my nerves.* **4 nerves:** °tension, nervousness, hysteria, °anxiety, fretfulness, °stress, °worry, apprehension, °fright, *Colloq* the °jitters, *Slang* the willies, the heebie-jeebies, *US* the whim-whams: *I had a bad case of nerves before learning the doctor's diagnosis.*

nerve-racking *adj.* nerve-wracking, °harrowing, °agonizing, distressing, °trying, vexing, vexatious, °troublesome, worrisome, °irksome, irritating: *Waiting for the names of the survivors was the most nerve-racking experience of my life.*

nervous *adj.* **1** highly-strung, °excitable, °sensitive, °tense, °agitated, wrought up, worked up, °upset, flustered, ruffled, °disturbed, perturbed, distressed, °worried, °anxious, troubled, °concerned, disquieted, edgy, on °edge, on tenterhooks, fidgety, °fretful, uneasy, apprehensive, frightened, °fearful, °shaky, °scared, skittish, *US* on a tightrope, *Colloq* °jumpy, jittery, flappable, in a °stew, in a dither,

in a °sweat, in a tizzy, in a °flap, uptight, *Brit* nervy, *US* on pins and needles, *Slang* strung out: *Thomas is nervous because he has to give a speech.* **2** °difficult, °tense, °critical: *There were a few nervous moments before we knew if the rope would hold.*

nest *n.* **1** roost, °perch, eyrie *or US also* aerie, den, °lair: *The birds, which mate for life, return to the same nest each year.* **2** snuggery, °retreat, °refuge, °haunt, °hideaway, hide-out; °resort: *We have a little nest in the country which we escape to at weekends.*

nestle *v.* °cuddle (up), °snuggle (up), °huddle, curl up, nuzzle (up): *They nestled close together to keep warm.*

net[1] *n.* **1** °network, netting, °mesh, mesh-work, °web, webbing, openwork, lattice, lattice-work, trellis, trellis-work, lace-work, reticulum, reticle, rete, plexus, grid, grid-work, grille, °grate, °grating, fretwork; sieve, °screen, strainer, sifter: *They watched the fishermen mending their nets.* —*v.* **2** °catch, °capture, °trap, entrap, °snare, ensnare, °bag: *As I bring the fish close to the boat, you net it with this.*

net[2] *n.* **1** nett, (net) °profit, °gain, °earnings, °return(s), *Colloq US* °take: *The net for the first quarter was 15 per cent higher than last year's.* —*adj.* **2** °clear, after deductions, after taxes, take-home, °final, bottom-line: *The tax increase was greater than my salary increase, so my net income was lower this year.* **3** °final, °end, closing, concluding, conclusive, °effective, °ultimate: *The net result of the advertising campaign was a sales increase of 18 per cent.* —*v.* **4** °make, °realize, °clear, take home, °bring in, °earn, °pocket, °take in, °get: *How much did you net last year—after taxes, that is.*

network *n.* **1** See net[1], 1, above. **2** °system, °arrangement, °structure, °organization, complex, grid, criss-cross, °web, plexus; °maze, labyrinth, jungle, °tangle: *She has developed a worldwide network of contacts for her business. Before transistors, the back of a radio was a network of multicoloured wires.*

neurotic *adj.* psychoneurotic, °unstable, °disturbed, °confused, irrational, disordered, maladjusted, °distraught, °overwrought, °anxious, °nervous, °obsessive, °deviant, °abnormal: *Many people are neurotic about something.*

neuter *adj.* **1** asexual, sexless, epicene: *Worker bees are neuter, neither male nor female.* —*v.* **2** desex *or* desexualize, °doctor; castrate, emasculate, geld, capon *or* caponize, eunuchize; spay, ovariectomize, oophorectomize; *Colloq* °fix, cut, *US* alter: *We had our cat neutered after her first litter.*

neutral *adj.* **1** non-belligerent, non-combatant, unaligned, °non-aligned, unaffiliated, uninvolved, unallied, non-allied, °non-partisan, °impartial, °disinterested, °indifferent, °dispassionate, unbiased, uncommitted, °noncommittal, °aloof, °withdrawn, °detached, °remote, removed: *Switzerland has remained neutral during both world wars.* **2** °dull, °drab, °colourless, achromatic, toneless, washed out, °pale, °indefinite, °indistinct, °indistinguishable, indeterminate, °vague, beige, ecru: *A neutral wallpaper colour won't clash with the paintings.*

neutralize v. °void, annul, °cancel (out), nullify, invalidate, negate, °delete, °undo, make or render °ineffective, counterbalance, °counteract, °offset, °equalize, °even, °square, °compensate for, °make up for: *The forces on both sides of the sail, being equal, neutralize each other.*

never adv. 1 at no °time, not °ever, not at any °time, on no °occasion, under no °circumstances or condition(s), on no account, not at all, *Colloq* not in a million years, not till hell freezes over: *You are never to use such language again!* 2 in no way, not in any way, not in the least, not in any °degree, not under any condition, not: *Never fear, for I am near.*

nevertheless adv. °still, °notwithstanding, °yet, in °spite of that, °despite that, °nonetheless, °regardless, be that as it may, for all that, °even so, but, °however, °just or all the °same, °everything considered, at any °rate, anyway, in any °case, in any °event, at all events, *Literary* withal: *He said he dislikes sweets; nevertheless, he ate a whole bar of chocolate.*

new adj. 1 °novel, °original, °unique, °unusual, °different, °fresh, °creative, °imaginative, °brand-new: *Ruth has a new idea for the sales campaign.* 2 °latest, °late, °modern, °contemporary, modish, °stylish, °fashionable, °chic, °recent, advanced, up to °date, °brand-new, late-model, *Colloq* °trendy, *Slang* mod, °hip: *Mac-Gregor buys a new car every year: it has to be equipped with the newest gadgets.* 3 °fresh, °further, additional, supplemental, °supplementary: *Has the new issue of* Verbatim *come out yet?* 4 °unfamiliar, °unknown, °strange, °different; °unique, unheard-of: *I hear there's a new girl in your office. I want to introduce my new friend, Dan Hammond. Every year they discover a new virus.* 5 revitalized, reborn, renewed, rejuvenated, changed, altered, redone, restored, redesigned, remodelled: *I saw before me a new Marie. They published a new version of the Bible.* 6 °inexperienced, °green, °fresh, °callow, °unfledged, budding, °immature, unripe, untrained: *Let us look over the new recruits, Sergeant.* 7 °late, °young, °recent: *We found newer fossils at higher levels.* 8 °uncharted, unexplored, untrodden, °unknown, °experimental: *Astronomers are breaking new ground in the analysis of pulsars.*

newcomer n. 1 °alien, °immigrant, °foreigner, outlander, °stranger, °settler, colonist, °outsider: *The newcomers quickly established themselves and became self-sufficient.* 2 beginner, °amateur, °novice, proselyte, neophyte, tiro or tyro, °initiate, trainee, °learner, fledgling or *Brit* also fledgeling, *Brit* fresher or *US* freshman, *Colloq* °greenhorn: *Though experienced in book publishing, he was a newcomer to magazine publishing.*

news n. 1 tidings, °word, °information, °advice, °intelligence; °rumour, °talk, °gossip, hearsay, °dirt, °scandal, exposé, *Colloq* info, °low-down, °scoop, *US* scuttlebutt, *Slang* °dope: *What's the latest news about the situation in the Middle East?* 2 °dispatch or despatch, °report, °account, °story, communication, °bulletin, communiqué, °announcement, °information, °message, °word, °statement, (°press) °release, (news)flash: *The news from our correspondent contains no mention of finding a cache of arms.* 3 newscast, news °broadcast or telecast, news °programme; newsflash: *Please be quiet so that I can listen to the news.* 4 (good) °copy, front-page news, (hot) °item: *The royal family is always news.*

nice adj. 1 °pleasant, °agreeable, °amiable, °amicable, °friendly, °cordial, °warm, °gracious, warm-hearted, °kind, °kindly, °outgoing, charming, °genial, °delightful, °courteous, °polite, °refined, gentlemanly, °ladylike, winsome, °likeable, °attractive: *They are one of the nicest couples I have ever met.* 2 °good, °satisfactory, commendable, °worthy, °worthwhile: *The manager said that I had done a nice job in preparing the specifications.* 3 °good, °fine, °superb, °superior, °attentive, °sharp, °acute, °keen, °careful, °exact, °exacting, rigorous; °precise, °accurate, unerring, °scrupulous, °meticulous, punctilious, °discriminating, discriminative, °perceptive, °delicate, °fastidious, °flawless, °faultless, °subtle, °strict, °close, °small, °slight, °minute, complex, °complicated, °intricate: *A diamond cutter must have a nice eye for detail. It is difficult to maintain nice distinctions of meaning among certain words, given that people are so careless with their speech these days.* 4 °delicate, °subtle, °sensitive, °exquisite, °hair-splitting, over-nice, °fine, °critical, °ticklish, °dangerous, °precarious, °perilous, *Colloq* °hairy: *The matter of Hong Kong requires some nice political negotiations.* 5 °trim, °well turned-out, °tidy, °neat, °fine: *Don't you want to look nice for your birthday party?* 6 **nice and** — : pleasantly, delightfully, pleasingly, agreeably, enjoyably, gratifyingly, satisfyingly, comfortably: *It's nice and warm by the fire.*

niche n. 1 °recess, °hollow, alcove, °nook: *A small statue of Buddha stood in a niche in the wall.* 2 °place, °position, *Colloq* °slot, pigeon-hole: *Humphrey has finally found a niche for himself working as a tax inspector.*

nick n. 1 °cut, °notch, °chip, °gouge, °gash, °scratch, dent, °indentation, °flaw, °mark, °blemish, °defect: *Be careful of that nick in the rim of the glass.* 2 °jail or *Brit* also gaol; police station: *The police took him to the nick to help them with their inquiries.*
—v. 1 °steal, purloin, °take, °appropriate, °make off with, *Colloq* °pinch: *Who nicked my biro?* 4 °arrest, °nab, °take in, *Colloq* collar: *Alan was nicked for possession of marijuana.* 5 **nick off**: °depart, °go or °run off or away, °take off, take to one's °heels, show a clean pair of °heels, beat a (hasty) °retreat, *Colloq* scarper, make tracks, °beat it: *The cops were coming so I nicked off.*

nickname n. 1 °pet °name, sobriquet, epithet, agnomen, *Colloq* moniker or monicker, handle: *Her real name is Josephine, but her nickname is Dusty.* 2 °diminutive: *A common nickname for Terence is Terry.*

nifty adj. 1 °smart, °stylish, modish, °chic, °spruce: *I borrowed a nifty outfit from Grandma for the flapper's costume ball.* 2 °healthy, in °good °form, spry, °energetic, °agile, quick: *I'm not as nifty as I was in 1950.* 3 °excellent, °neat, °great, °splendid, °fine, °clever, °skilful, apt, °suitable: *Having a picnic was a nifty idea. That was as nifty a bit of bargaining as I've ever seen.* 4 °satisfactory, °satisfying, °good, °profitable, °substantial, °considerable: *He made a nifty profit on the sale of his house in Chelsea.*

niggle v. °find °fault, °nag, °carp, °fuss, °cavil, °criticize; °complain, Colloq grouse, Slang °bitch, US kvetch: I do wish she would stop niggling when we cannot do anything about the situation.

niggling adj. **1** irritating, worrying, worrisome, °irksome, vexing, vexatious, °troublesome: There are a few niggling matters that I must see my accountant about. **2** °petty, nugatory, °trifling, trivial, °fussy, °insignificant, unimportant, °inconsequential, °frivolous, Colloq piddling, nit-picking, US and Canadian picayune: Bill always ignores the core of a problem and occupies himself with the niggling details.

night n. **1** (Stygian or Cimmerian) °dark or darkness or blackness or °gloom; night-time, shades of night, Formal tenebrosity or tenebrousness: The strange creature slunk off into the night. **2** nightfall, gloaming, °twilight, °dusk, eventide, °evening, evensong, edge of night, sunset, sundown, end of day, vespers: When night comes, one can hear the frogs calling from the pond. **3 night and day**: all the °time, continually, incessantly, unceasingly, continuously, unendingly, endlessly, round-the-clock, ceaselessly, °non-stop: Those animals keep up their caterwauling night and day.

nightly adj. **1** every °night, each °night, each and every °night, °night after °night: The watchman does his nightly rounds. **2** night-time, nocturnal, bedtime: A nightly glass of warm milk promotes sound sleep. —adv. **3** every °night, each °night, nights, after °dark, after sunset; nocturnally: The bird sings nightly outside my window.

nightmarish adj. °frightening, °terrifying, alarming, horrific, °horrible, °dreadful, °awful, °ghastly, dismaying, °agonizing, worrisome, exasperating, frustrating, Kafkaesque, Colloq creepy, °scary: Dealing with officialdom can be a nightmarish experience when abroad.

nil n. °nothing, °zero, nought or °naught, aught or ought, Tennis, table tennis, etc. love, Cricket duck, US goose-egg, Slang US zip: Oxford United: 4; Queens Park Rangers: Nil.

nimble adj. **1** °agile, °lively, °active, °light, lithe, limber, spry, °sprightly, °brisk, °smart, °energetic, °rapid, quick, °swift, adroit, deft, °dexterous; nimble-fingered; nimble-footed: She's as nimble as a cat on a hot tin roof. **2** °agile, °alert, °acute, nimble-witted, °quick-witted, ready-witted, °intelligent, °keen, °sharp; °smart, °brilliant, sparkling, °scintillating, coruscating: Despite his inability to make decisions, Desmond has quite a nimble mind.

nip[1] v. **1** °bite, nibble; °pinch, °snip, °clip, °cut, °snap, °tweak, twitch, °trim, °lop, crop, shear; °grip, °squeeze: The dog nipped the postman's ankle. Nip off the suckers to promote healthy growth of the tomatoes. **2 nip in the bud**: °stop, °arrest, °check, °thwart, °frustrate, °stymie, °forestall; °quash, °squelch, °suppress, °extinguish, °put down: The revolt of the army officers was nipped in the bud. —n. **3** °bite, nibble, °morsel, °pinch, °snip: The deer had taken nips off the tips of the shrubbery. **4** °chill, coldness, iciness, sharpness, °tang, °bite: There's a definite wintry nip in the air tonight.

nip[2] n. °taste, °drop, °sip, soupçon, °portion, °swallow, °gulp, °mouthful, °finger, Brit peg, °tot, °draught, Scots dram, US draft, Colloq snort, °shot: I had a few nips of brandy to ward off the cold.

nobility n. **1** nobleness, °dignity, °grandeur, illustriousness, greatness, °glory, °influence, °authority, °leadership, °distinction, °probity, °integrity, °excellence, goodness, °character, °rectitude, righteousness, ethics, °honesty, honourableness, decency, justness, high-mindedness, magnanimity, °prestige, loftiness, primacy, °significance: The man's nobility was evident from his mien and bearing. **2** °rank, °position, °class, °birth, blue blood: Their nobility is recognized only at court and in fashionable society. **3 the nobility**: the °gentry, the °élite, the aristocracy, Colloq the °upper crust, the ruling °class(es), the Establishment, US the Four Hundred: With a name like Hohenzollern, her family must be from the European nobility.

noble n. **1** nobleman, noblewoman, aristocrat, patrician, °lord, lady, °peer; gentleman, gentlewoman, Colloq blue blood: The nobles united and forced King John to sign the Magna Carta. —adj. **2** high-born, °high-class, °upper-class, aristocratic, titled, high-ranking, lordly, patrician, Colloq blue-blood(ed): She came from a noble Austrian family. **3** °dignified, °eminent, °distinguished, august, °grand, °lofty, °elevated, °illustrious, °prestigious, °pre-eminent, °noted, honoured, esteemed, °celebrated, °renowned, acclaimed, respected, venerated: The noble Knights of the Round Table have become legend throughout the world. **4** °upright, °righteous, °honourable, °honest, °virtuous, incorruptible, °chivalrous, °staunch, °steadfast, °true, °loyal, °faithful, °trustworthy, °true, °principled, °moral, °good, °decent, self-sacrificing, magnanimous, °generous: The qualities that make a noble friend make a formidable enemy. **5** °splendid, °magnificent, °imposing, °impressive, °stately, °exquisite, °sublime, °grand, °striking, °stunning, °superb, °admirable, °elegant, °rich, °sumptuous, °luxurious: The Taj Mahal is probably one of the noblest works of man.

nobody pron. **1** no one, not anyone, no person: We had to wait because nobody was in the shop when we entered. —n. **2** nonentity, °unknown, °zero, cipher, Colloq °nothing: Overnight, Tony went from being a celebrity to being a nobody.

nod v. **1** °greet, °acknowledge, °recognize: The maître d'hôtel nodded to me as I entered the restaurant. **2** say yes; °consent, assent, °agree, concur, acquiesce: Asked if she had seen Nick, the barmaid nodded. I asked permission to leave the room and the teacher nodded. **3** °doze (off), °nap, drowse, °drop off, °fall asleep: Exhausted travellers nodded in their chairs waiting for their flights to be announced. **4** °slip (up), °err, make a °mistake, be °mistaken or °wrong; be °careless or negligent or °lax or °inattentive: Sometimes, even Homer nods. —n. **5** °signal, °sign, °cue, °indication, °gesture: I saw him give a nod to the barber, who suddenly held a cutthroat razor to my throat. **6** °approval; °consent, acquiescence, concurrence, assent, °agreement, Colloq OK or okay: The company has given me the nod to open an office in Acapulco.

nodding adj. °casual, °slight, °superficial, °distant; °incomplete: I know Graham slightly—he's a nodding acquaintance. It was clear that the violinist had only a nodding acquaintance with Mozart's concerto.

noise n. **1** °sound, clamour, °crash, °clap, °clash, clangour, °din, °thunder, thundering, rumble, rumbling, °outcry, hubbub, °uproar, hullabaloo, °racket, charivari or US and Canadian also shivaree, °rattle, caterwauling, °rumpus, °blare, °blast, blasting, bawling, babel; commotion, °bedlam, °fracas, °tumult, °pandemonium, turmoil; discordance, dissonance, cacophony; Archaic alarms or alarums and excursions, Colloq ruckus, ruction, ballyhoo: I couldn't sleep because of the unbearable noise from the party next door. You may call acid rock music, but she calls it noise. **2** °sound, °disturbance: Did you just hear that strange noise? It's only the noise of the crickets.
—v. **3** Often, **noise about** or **around**: °circulate, °spread, °rumour, bruit (about): It is being noised about that John and Marsha are getting a divorce.

noiseless adj. muted, °quiet, °soft, hushed, muffled, deadened, dampened, damped; °silent, °mute, °still, °inaudible, soundless: We watched the noiseless boats gliding past.

noisy adj. °loud, deafening, ear-splitting, jarring, °grating, °harsh, °piercing, °shrill, °discordant, unmusical, dissonant, cacophonous, resounding, clarion, clamorous, clangorous, °thunderous, °uproarious, blaring, blasting, °obstreperous, vociferous, °boisterous, °tumultuous, °riotous: I could hear nothing over the noisy aeroplane engines. When she arose to speak, the noisy crowd fell silent.

nominal adj. **1** °titular, in °name only, °formal, °pretended, °so-called, °self-styled, soi-disant, °professed, purported, °supposed, would-be, representational, represented, supposititious; proposed, propositional; °puppet: Elliot is the nominal chairman, but Foster actually runs the company. **2** °insignificant, trivial, °trifling, °minor, minuscule, °tiny, °small, °insubstantial, °minimal, inconsiderable, °token: We charge a nominal fee for the analysis if you refuse our recommendation.

nominate v. °choose, °select, °name, °appoint, °designate, °suggest, °offer, °submit, °recommend, °propose, °present, °put up or forward; °forward; Formal put forth: Baker has been nominated for the presidency.

nominee n. °candidate, office-seeker, designee, selectee, appointee, assignee: We must choose a nominee to run in the next election.

non-aligned adj. uncommitted, non-allied, non-affiliated, unaligned, unaffiliated, unallied; °neutral, °impartial: There are several non-aligned nations that remain independent of the influence of the superpowers.

non-believer n. unbeliever, disbeliever, cynic, doubting Thomas, doubter, °sceptic, freethinker, agnostic, atheist, nullifidian; °infidel, °heathen, °pagan: During his reign, thousands of non-believers were put to the sword.

nonchalant adj. °cool, unexcited, unexcitable, unperturbed, imperturbable, undisturbed, untroubled, unflappable, unruffled, °dispassionate, unemotional, °detached, °distant, unconcerned, °indifferent, pococurante, insouciant, uninterested, °aloof, °blasé, °offhand, °calm, °collected, composed, °easygoing, °free and °easy, happy-go-lucky, °casual, °relaxed, at °ease; °unenthusiastic, apathetic; Colloq laid-back, together: How can you be so nonchalant about important issues that affect all our lives?!

noncommittal adj. °wary, °cautious, °careful, °gingerly, °guarded, (playing it) °safe, circumspect, watchful, °prudent, canny, °tentative, on °guard, °reserved, °cool; precautionary or precautional, precautious; Colloq playing it °cool, playing it °safe, playing it or one's cards close to the chest: The company is still noncommittal about the take-over of the American company.

non-completion n. non-fulfilment, unfulfilment, non-performance, incompleteness, deficiency: We regret the non-completion of the work on your house and will refund in full the amount already paid.

non-compliance n. disobedience, nonconformity, non-observance, °disregard, disregarding, °failure, non-cooperation, uncooperativeness, unresponsiveness, °rejection, °refusal, °denial: If you fail to provide the records requested by the tax inspector, you can be charged with non-compliance.

nonconformist n. **1** nonconformer, °renegade, maverick, °rebel, °radical, °individualist, heretic, dissenter, °dissident, iconoclast, loner, °exception, anomaly: In the 1960s, Alastair counted himself among the nonconformists who wore unconventional clothes and flouted conventional behaviour.
—adj. **2** nonconforming, °renegade, maverick, °rebellious, °radical, °individualist(ic), °heretical, dissentient, °dissident, iconoclastic: Suffragists were ridiculed for their nonconformist ideas.

nondescript adj. indescribable, unclassifiable, unclassified, °ordinary, common-or-garden variety, °common, commonplace, unremarkable, °colourless, °drab, °everyday, °bland, uninteresting, insipid, characterless, undistinctive, unexceptional: He was wearing nondescript clothing and blended into the crowd.

none pron. no one, not anyone, °nobody, no person; no one; not any; °nil: Of all the people I met, none impressed me more than Kathy. I'd give you a sweet if I had one, but I have none. I'd even give you money, but I have none.

non-essential adj. **1** non-vital, unessential, unneeded, °unnecessary, °needless, °inconsequential, °insignificant, unimportant, °superfluous, °dispensable, °expendable, °gratuitous, uncalled-for, °extraneous, °peripheral, °extra, de trop, adventitious, additional, supplemental, adscititious, °redundant, °accessory, °subordinate, °secondary, °subsidiary: The non-essential industries were converted to the war effort during the 1940s.
—n. **2** unessential, inessential, nonentity, cipher, °zero, °nobody; °extra, supernumerary, spear-carrier, Colloq °nothing, Slang US nebbish: She used him as a lackey, a non-essential whom she could dispose of at will.

nonetheless adv. See nevertheless, above.

non-event n. anticlimax, Colloq non-starter, lead balloon, °dud, Brit damp squib: Jeremy's party turned out to be the non-event of the year.

non-existent adj. °unreal, °imaginary, imagined, °fictional, fictive, °fanciful, °fancied, °mythical, °fabulous, fabled, °illusory, chimerical, delusive: Although the entire Graeco-Roman pantheon became non-existent overnight, its gods and goddesses continue to pervade our culture.

non-flammable adj. non-combustible, °incombustible, non-inflammable, unburnable; fire-retardant: *The government recently passed regulations requiring that non-flammable materials be used in upholstered furniture.*

no-nonsense adj. °serious, unfrivolous, businesslike, °practical, non-trivial, untrivial: *Customs officials take a no-nonsense approach to drug trafficking.*

nonpareil n. °paragon, °model, °standard, *ne plus ultra*, exemplar, °ideal, *Literary* nonsuch *or* nonesuch, *Colloq* oner, one in a million, *Brit* one-off: *Annabelle was a nonpareil among the artists of her day.*

non-partisan adj. **1** non-partizan, °non-aligned, unaligned, unaffiliated, °independent, non-committed, uncommitted, °neutral, uninvolved, °free, (sitting) on the °fence: *Choose between non-partisan and coalition candidates.* **2** °impartial, even-handed, °fair, °just, °objective, unbiased, °unprejudiced, °equitable, °dispassionate, °disinterested: *One could not find a more non-partisan judge than Sir Ronald.*
—n. **3** °independent, °neutral, mugwump: *I am a non-partisan on the subject of privatization of public utilities.*

nonplus v. confound, °perplex, °puzzle, °confuse, °dismay, baffle, °stop, °check, °stun, °shock, °dumbfound *or* dumfound, °take aback, °astonish, °astound, *US* faze, *Colloq* bring up short, °flummox, °stump: *She was nonplussed to learn that Simpson had been arrested.*

non-productive adj. **1** unproductive, °barren, °sterile, °infertile, unfertile, unfruitful, infecund: *Non-productive land was left uncultivated.* **2** °ineffectual, °bootless, °ineffective, °impractical, unavailing, °pointless, °useless, °worthless, °wasteful, time-consuming, time-wasting: *Executives should spend more time working and less in non-productive meetings discussing the work to be done.*

nonsense n. **1** °rubbish, °drivel, °gibberish, °gobbledegook *or* gobbledygook, twaddle, °trash, °babble, balderdash, °moonshine, °bombast, fustian, rodomontade, puffery, flummery, blather *or* blether, bunkum, poppycock, stuff and nonsense, double-talk, °jargon, °mumbo-jumbo, jabberwocky, cackle, gas, °palaver, *Colloq* bunk, piffle, °rot, bosh, eyewash, hogwash, malarkey, bilge (water), boloney *or* baloney, claptrap, °hot air, *Brit* tosh, *Old-fashioned Brit* gammon, °waffle, *US* apple-sauce, horse feathers, °garbage, bushwa; *Slang* crap, tripe, bull, hooey, double Dutch, *Taboo slang* bullshit, horseshit, *Brit* (a load of old) cobblers: *Watson's speech on the benefits of tobacco was unmitigated nonsense.* **2** °mischief, clowning, antics, capering, horseplay, pranks, °tricks, °jokes, silliness, foolishness, inanity, frivolity, tomfoolery, joking, jesting, waggishness, buffoonery, shenanigans, *Colloq* °monkey business, *Brit* °monkey tricks, *US* monkeyshines: *Keep up this nonsense and you'll get into a lot of trouble!*

nonsensical adj. °senseless, °meaningless, °absurd, °ridiculous, °ludicrous, laughable, °preposterous, irrational, warped, askew, °crazy, °mad, °silly, °foolish, °hare-brained, asinine, idiotic, moronic, imbecile, °stupid, °dumb, *Colloq* nutty, screwy, cock-eyed, °fool, screwball, *Slang* loony: *What is your nonsensical excuse for being late this time?*

non-stop adj. **1** uninterrupted, °continuous, unbroken, °direct: *Is this a non-stop flight to New York?* **2** unending, °endless, interminable, unceasing, ceaseless, °continual, °continuous, uninterrupted, unbroken, °persistent, °relentless, °constant, unremitting, °steady, round-the-clock, ongoing, continuing, °unhesitating, unfaltering, °tireless; °regular, °habitual: *I told my neighbour that his non-stop rock 'n' roll music was driving me mad.*
—adv. **3** unendingly, endlessly, interminably, unceasingly, ceaselessly, continually, continuously, uninterruptedly, persistently, relentlessly, constantly, unremittingly, steadily, round-the-clock, day in and day out, tirelessly; regularly, habitually: *He continues to play his hi-fi non-stop.*

nook n. **1** °cranny, °recess, °niche, alcove, corner, °cavity, °crevice, °crack, °opening: *Flowers grew from the nooks in the wall.* **2** °retreat, hide-out, °hideaway, °nest; inglenook: *I curled up with a book in my nook next to the fireplace.*

noon n. twelve o'clock (noon), °midday, 1200 hours, noontime, high noon, *Archaic* noontide; noonday: *We sit down to lunch promptly at noon. The noon sun is terribly hot in the tropics.*

norm n. **1** °usual, °average, °mean, °normal: *The norm for the day is 12 degrees Celsius.* **2** °model, °standard, °type, °pattern, criterion, °rule, °measure, °gauge, °yardstick, benchmark: *That style of window became the norm for many years.*

normal adj. **1** °standard, °regular, °average, °conventional, °usual, run-of-the-mill, °ordinary, °routine, °universal, °general, °common, °customary, °natural, °typical, conformist, °orthodox; °healthy: *If living in this mess seems normal to you, we clearly have different standards. His temperature and pulse are normal.* **2** °sane, °rational, °reasonable, well-adjusted: *After he had set fire to his school, Julian's parents began to wonder if he was quite normal.*

normalize v. regularize, °standardize, °regulate, °control; °conform: *The program is directed at normalizing the codes used in keyboarding text.*

nosy adj. nosey, °curious, °inquisitive, prying, meddlesome, °spying, peeping, eavesdropping, *Colloq* snooping, snoopy: *Mind your own business and don't be so nosy.*

notable adj. **1** °noteworthy, °noted, °famous, famed, °well-known, °renowned, °illustrious, °important, °prominent, °eminent, °outstanding, °great, °distinguished, °celebrated, acclaimed: *Many notable people attended my college.* **2** °remarkable, °different, °distinctive, °singular, °unusual, uncommon, °pre-eminent, °peerless, °matchless, unmatched, unequalled, °unparalleled, °extraordinary, °conspicuous, °outstanding, °memorable, unforgettable, °striking: *She enjoyed a notable reputation as a cellist. Last night's notable performance was enjoyed by a capacity audience.*
—n. **3** °dignitary, °personage, °worthy, VIP; °celebrity, luminary, *Colloq* (°big) °name, °big shot: *Many notables attended the charity ball.*

notably adv. **1** °particularly, °especially, markedly, °noticeably, signally, distinctly, remarkably, unusually, uncommonly, outstandingly, conspicuously, °clearly, °obviously, °evidently, °manifestly, specifically, curiously, oddly, uniquely, strangely, strikingly, shockingly, surprisingly, stunningly: *In the temperate zones, the* seasons vary notably in length. **2** meaningfully, significantly, importantly, prominently: *The viruses changed in notably different ways.*

notation n. **1** °note, °memorandum, jotting, °record, °reminder, °minute(s), °abstract, *Colloq* memo: *I shall make a notation of that in my diary.* **2** symbols, signs, °code, characters, symbolism: *In musical notation, a minim represents two crotchets.*

notch n. **1** °nick, °cut, dent, °indentation, °groove, cleft, °score, °mark, °gouge, °gash: *For every man he killed, the gunfighter cut a notch in the barrel of his gun.* **2** °step, °grade, °level, rung, °peg, °degree, °stage, gradation: *Gillian's promotion moves her up another notch towards the chairmanship.*
    —v. **3** °nick, °cut, dent, indent, °groove, °score, °mark, °gash, °gouge: *You notch the end of the arrow to admit the bowstring.* **4 notch up**: °gain, °win, °accomplish, °achieve, °score, °register, °mark (up): *The All-India cricket team has notched up another win.*

notched adj. serrate(d), sawtooth(ed), crenellate(d), crenate, serriform, pinked, scalloped, zigzag, toothed, dentate, denticulate(d), dentiform: *The flower has notched yellow petals. The vase was decorated with a notched pattern.*

note n. **1** See **notation**, 1, above. **2** °message, °letter, communication, (piece of) correspondence, °memorandum, epistle, postcard or (postal) °card, fan °letter, love-letter, billet doux, bread-and-butter °letter, °word, °line, thank-you note, *Colloq* memo, *US old-fashioned* mash note: *She sent Rob a note only last week asking him to attend the meeting.* **3** °comment, commentary, °remark, °observation, °explanation, annotation, footnote, side-note, marginalia (pl.), °gloss, critique, °criticism, *Literary* scholium, exegesis, eisegesis, *Technical* shoulder-note: *Her notes on insect behaviour are of great interest.* **4** banknote, °money, °bill, currency, °treasury note; promissory note, °demand note, °bill of °exchange, °letter of °credit, (bank) °draft, note of hand; *Colloq* folding °money: *I found a packet of notes dropped by the bank robbers. The bank is holding my note for £10,000.* **5** °theme, °characteristic, °motif, °element, °quality, °mood, °tone, °tenor: *There is a note of angry frustration that runs through her writing.* **6** °signal, °cue, intimation, °hint, °inkling, °suspicion, °clue, °suggestion, °idea, °tip, *Slang* tip-off: *Her greeting, though warm, contained a note of suspicion. On that note, I decided to leave.* **7** °heed, °attention, °notice, °regard, °respect, °thought, *Colloq US* °mind: *Note of the prosecutor's objection to that line of questioning has been taken.* **8** °mark, consequence, °substance, °importance, °moment, °weight, °distinction, °merit, °prestige, (°high) °rank or °standing, eminence, °prominence, repute, °reputation, °renown: *People of note have been entertained at our table.* **9** °tone, °sound, °key: *He knows the music but gets the notes wrong.* **10 notes**: jottings, impressions, °record(s), °report, (°thumbnail) sketch, (°rough) °draft, °outline, °synopsis: *The entire account is based on the notes she made during the trial.*
    —v. **11** °notice, °observe, °perceive, °see, °mark, °think about, give °thought to, °consider, °contemplate, °study, pay °attention to, °attend to; °look into, °investigate, °check out: *Have you*

ever noted how people try to avoid you because of your bad temper? Note how quickly the days seem to grow shorter towards the end of summer. A detective has been assigned to note every move the suspect makes.* **12** °record, °register, °write down, °put or °set down, put on °record, °jot down, put in °writing, °chronicle: *The traffic warden noted down the number-plate of the car.* **13** call °attention to, °remark on or about, °mention, °report, °touch on, °comment on or about: *The report failed to note the disappearance of the murder weapon.*

noted adj. respected, °eminent, °distinguished, °illustrious, esteemed, acclaimed; °well-known, °famous, famed, °prominent, °celebrated, °notable, °popular; °notorious: *We are pleased to welcome the noted violinist, David Popov. Was it his aunt or his mother who ran the noted house of ill repute near Brighton?*

noteworthy adj. °notable, °exceptional, °extraordinary, out of the °ordinary, °unusual, °rare, uncommon, °singular, °unique, °different: *Miss Byrne has made many a noteworthy contribution to our knowledge of local Roman sites.*

nothing n. **1** °naught or nought, °nothing at all or whatsoever, no thing, not anything, *Taboo slang Brit* bugger-all, (sweet) Fanny Adams or F.A., SFA: *Nothing that you tell me can be held against you in court. You may think it important, but I tell you it is nothing.* **2** cipher, °zero, °nobody, nonentity: *If it weren't for her, he would be nothing.* **3** °trifle, bagatelle, *Colloq* peanuts: *A million is nothing to him.*

notice v. **1** °note, take or make °note (of), take notice (of), pay or give °attention to, °attend (to), °heed, take °heed (of), give °heed to, °mark, °remark, °mind, °observe, °perceive, °see: *Notice how quickly he retracted his remarks when challenged. I waved to them, but they didn't notice me.* **2** °mind, °observe, °perceive, discern, °see, detect, °make out, °identify, °recognize, *Colloq* °spot: *I noticed signs of illness when I visited her.*
    —n. **3** °attention, awareness, consciousness, °perception, °observation, °cognizance: *Let me bring to your notice the second paragraph on page six.* **4** °regard, °consideration, °respect, °observation, °attention, °note, °heed: *They have published many books worthy of notice. He considers matters of money beneath his notice.* **5** notification, °announcement, °information, °advice; °warning, intimation: *A notice showing the currency exchange rates is posted in the bank. The company let Corbett go without notice.* **6** °criticism, critique, °review, °comment, commentary: *The play has enjoyed excellent notices in the London newspapers.* **7 give notice**: °warn, admonish, °notify, °announce, °advise, °inform: *British Rail gave notice of a curtailment of service to this station. Barry gave notice today of his resignation.*

noticeable adj. **1** °discernible, perceivable, °observable, °perceptible, recognizable, distinguishable, °visible, palpable, °manifest, °distinct, °evident, °clear, clear-cut, °conspicuous, °obvious, °patent, unmistakable, °undisguised, unconcealed: *Is the scratch noticeable? Wrinkles around the eyes are one of the first noticeable signs of ageing.* **2** °noteworthy, °notable, °significant, °signal, °remarkable, °important, °singular, °exceptional, °pronounced, °distinct, especial, °considerable, °major: *After the reprimand, there was a noticeable improvement in his work.*

notify v. **1** °inform, °tell, °advise, °alert, apprise, °warn: *She notified us that she might come in late today. They wrote to notify shareholders of the new share offer.* **2** °announce, °publish, °declare, °proclaim, give °notice of; °intimate, °hint: *The arrival of the first salmon notified to us the change of season.*

notion n. **1** °idea, °thought, concept, °conception, °image, °impression, general °idea, (°mental) °picture, °inkling: *She has a pretty good notion of who did it. I haven't the slightest notion of what you are talking about.* **2** °fancy, whim, crotchet, whimsy, caprice, impulse, °inclination, vagary, °conceit, °quirk, °kink: *She suddenly took a notion to fly to New York and left.*

notoriety n. notoriousness, disrepute, °dishonour, °disgrace, °infamy, °shame, °discredit, °scandal, °stain, °blot, obloquy, ignominy, opprobrium: *The notoriety attending his latest escapades displeased the prime minister.*

notorious adj. **1** °disreputable, °dishonourable, °disgraceful, °infamous, °shameful, shaming, °embarrassing, discreditable, °scandalous, °naughty, °flagrant, ignominious, opprobrious: *Charles was yet again seen in public with a notorious arms dealer.* **2** °celebrated, °renowned, °famous, °well-known, fabled, °legendary, °memorable: *Annie was notorious for riding her horse to victory in every event.*

notwithstanding adv. **1** °nevertheless, °nonetheless, °despite that, in °spite of that, °yet, anyway: *He was refused permission to go but he left notwithstanding.*
—prep. **2** °despite, in °spite of, °regardless of, in the °face of, against: *Notwithstanding his mother's objections, George married Marsha.*
—conj. **3** although, °though, °even °though, °despite the fact that: *The product was almost totally unknown, notwithstanding it had been on the market for years.*

nourish v. **1** °feed, °sustain, °support, °maintain, °keep, °provide for, °care for, take °care of, °look after, nurture, °nurse: *The child seems to be thriving and well nourished.* **2** °foster, °cherish, °nurse, °maintain, °harbour, °keep, nurture, °sustain: *Iago nourished a terrible hatred for Othello.* **3** °strengthen, °fortify, °encourage, °promote, °stimulate, °cultivate, °help, °advance, °aid: *These malcontents continue to nourish trouble in the party ranks.*

nourishment n. °food, °sustenance, °nutriment, nutrition, victuals: *You must take nourishment to maintain your strength.*

novel adj. **1** °new, °unusual, °unfamiliar, unconventional, °fresh, °different, °original, °creative; untested, °untried: *I have a novel idea for the design of an ultralight aircraft.*
—n. **2** °story, °tale, °narrative, °romance; novella, novelette, best-seller, Colloq blockbuster: *The members of our company board behave like characters out of a novel.*

novelty n. **1** °originality, newness, uniqueness, freshness, innovativeness: *We are enthusiastic about the novelty of the new sales campaign.* **2** °gimmick, gimcrack, °trifle, °gewgaw, °bauble, knick-knack, °toy, trinket, °ornament, °plaything, Brummagem, kickshaw: *New subscribers receive as a premium some novelty, like a ball-point pen or a cheap clock.*

novice n. beginner, neophyte, °newcomer, proselyte, tiro or tyro, noviciate or novitiate,

°learner, °amateur, °initiate, °apprentice, trainee, probationer, fledgling or Brit also fledgeling, Brit fresher or US freshman, Colloq °greenhorn, rookie: *She is a mere novice at parachuting.*

now adv. **1** at °present, °just now, °right now, at the °present °time or °moment, at this (°very) °moment or °minute or °second or °instant: *He's in the shower and cannot come to the phone now.* **2** these days, °nowadays, today, in these times, at the °moment, in this day and age, under or in the °present circumstances or conditions, in the °present °climate, things being what they are, contemporarily, any more, any longer; for the °time being, for the nonce: *What makes you say that the minimum wage is enough to live on now? Selling now might bring the highest price.* **3** at °once, °immediately, °right away, without °delay, instantly, °promptly, Chiefly law instanter, Chiefly Brit °straight away: *I want you here now—not in five minutes, but now!* **4 now and then** or **again**: °occasionally, from time to time, at times, on °occasion, °sometimes, sporadically, °once in a while, every now and then or again, randomly, intermittently; °infrequently, °seldom, °rarely, °once in a blue moon: *There was a power cut now and then. He visits his mother only now and then.*
—adj. **5** °contemporary, up to °date, °modern, °stylish, °fashionable, °trendy, Colloq in, with it: *Advertisers must appeal to the yuppies of the now generation.*

nowadays adv. See **now, 2**, above.

nub n. **1** °projection, protuberance, °knob, boss, °lump, °bump, knop, °protrusion, °bulge, node, °knot; excrescence, °swelling, tumescence: *Press the small nub on the side to open the door.* **2** °essence, °core, °heart, °nucleus, crux, °point, °gist, °pith, °kernel, °nucleus, °meat, (°sum and) °substance, °main °issue, gravamen: *Let's get to the nub of the argument.*

nuclear adj. atomic: *He joined the protest march against nuclear weapons.*

nucleus n. °core, °heart, °centre, °kernel, °pith, °focus, °nub: *We already have the nucleus of a very good team. The market square was the nucleus around which many towns were built.*

nude adj. unclothed, undressed, uncovered, au naturel, °bare, °naked, in the nude, stark °naked, undraped, without a stitch (on), Colloq in the buff, in the altogether, in one's birthday suit, Brit starkers, Brit and Australian in the nuddy: *A nude man streaked across the football pitch.*

nudge v. **1** °jog, °poke, elbow, °jab, °dig, °bump, °prompt, shove; °prod, °push, US °encourage: *I had to nudge him to stay awake for the film's thrilling climax.*
—n. **2** °jog, °poke, elbow, °jab, °dig, °bump, shove; °prod, °push, °encouragement: *Nigel just needs a nudge in the right direction.*

nuisance n. **1** °annoyance, °inconvenience, °trial, °ordeal, °burden, irritation, irritant, °thorn in the flesh or side, °difficulty, °bother, US bur(r) under the saddle, Colloq °pain (in the neck or rear), °headache, hassle, Slang US and Canadian °pain in the butt, Taboo slang °pain in the Brit arse, or US ass: *Having to paint the room again was a terrible nuisance.* **2** °bore, °pest, °nag, °tease, tormentor or tormenter: *James has made a nuisance of himself by telephoning every fifteen minutes.*

numb adj. **1** numbed, benumbed, °insensible, insensate, °dead, deadened, without °feeling, sensationless, °senseless; asleep: My feet are numb from the cold.
—v. **2** benumb, anaesthetize, °drug, °deaden, °dull, °freeze, °paralyse, immobilize, °stun: The doctor numbed my hand before removing the wart. Fear numbed her, and she felt nothing as the monster approached.

number n. **1** numeral, integer, °figure, digit: The columns of numbers were entered in a neat hand. **2** °few, °handful, °crowd, slew, °gang, °bunch, °party, bevy, covey, troop, °company, °platoon, °swarm, horde, multitude, °mob, °host, army, °mass, hundred, thousand, million, billion; °several, °many, numbers, legions, US and Canadian slew(s), Colloq loads, tons: A number of people attended the meeting. An enormous number of viruses could fit on the head of a pin. **3** °issue; °edition, °copy: The fourth number of the quarterly is published at the end of the year.
—v. **4** °count, °enumerate, °compute, °calculate, °tally, °figure (up), °add (up), °include, °total, tot (up), °reckon, °sum (up): Who can number the stars?

numberless adj. uncountable, uncounted, countless, innumerable, incalculable, °immeasurable, numerous, °untold, myriad, °infinite: Although seemingly numberless, the number of grains of sand in the universe is calculable.

nuptial adj. °bridal, °matrimonial, °wedding, spousal, °wedded, marital; connubial, conjugal, Literary hymeneal: The nuptial arrangements have been made.

nurse n. **1** angel of mercy, Florence Nightingale, Brit sister: I awoke to see two nurses bending over me.
—v. **2** °care for, °look after, °tend, °attend, °minister to, °treat; nurture, °foster, °coddle, °baby, °pamper, °cherish, °preserve, °keep alive, °cultivate, °develop: During his illness, she nursed him night and day. We nursed the company along through the first year. **3** wet-nurse, suckle, breast-feed, °nourish: Nursing mothers must be careful about what they eat. **4** °preserve, °harbour, °keep alive, nurture, °foster: She has nursed a grudge against him for ten years.

nutritious adj. healthful, °healthy, nutritive, °wholesome, life-giving, °beneficial, salutary, nourishing, alimentary, nutrimental: Be sure you eat a nutritious breakfast every day.

O

oar *n.* **1** °paddle, scull: *The ancient galleys sometimes had six men on each oar.* **2** oarsman, oarswoman, bencher, sculler, rower, paddler: *With Hanson out because of his back, we'll need a new oar for tomorrow's race.*

oasis *n.* **1** °fertile °patch, watering-hole: *In the desert, you cannot always be sure whether you are looking at an oasis or a mirage.* **2** haven, °refuge, (°safe) °harbour, °sanctuary, °retreat, asylum, °resort, °sanctum: *We escaped to the cottage, a tiny oasis away from the city's frenetic activity.*

oath *n.* **1** °vow, avowal, °pledge, °promise, °word (of °honour), °promise, °plight, °guarantee or guaranty, °warrant or °warranty, (sworn) °statement, *Archaic* troth: *She has taken an oath to tell the whole truth.* **2** °curse, °profanity, °blasphemous language or expression or word, imprecation, malediction, swear-word, °expletive, four-letter word, obscenity, °dirty word: *The door slammed on his finger and he muttered a foul oath.*

obedience *n.* compliance, dutifulness, °observance, °respect, respectfulness, tractability, conformity or conformance, °yielding, conformability, adaptability, °agreement, agreeability, agreeableness, acquiescence, submissiveness, °submission, subservience, docility, passiveness, passivity: *The abbot demanded unquestioning obedience with regard to every rule of the monastic order.*

obedient *adj.* compliant, °dutiful, duteous, °observant, °respectful, °tractable, °yielding, conformable, °adaptable, °agreeable, amenable, acquiescent, °submissive, subservient, docile, °passive, °timid, biddable, pliant: *Prunella was always an obedient child. All matter and energy is obedient to the laws of physics.*

obeisance *n.* °deference, °respect, respectfulness, °homage, °submission, °reverence, °honour: *As she entered the chamber, she made obeisance to the king.*

obese *adj.* °fat, overweight, °stout, fleshy, °gross, corpulent, °heavy, °plump, portly, tubby, pudgy, °chubby, paunchy, °rotund, pot-bellied, *Rare* abdominous: *I sat down next to an obese person who occupied nearly two chairs.*

obesity *n.* corpulence, plumpness, tubbiness, chubbiness, grossness, embonpoint, rotundity, portliness, paunchiness, °size, °bulk, °weight, avoirdupois: *Risk factors with respect to heart disease include smoking, bad diet, obesity, and family history of heart disease.*

obey *v.* **1** °comply (with), °agree (to), °consent (to), °submit (to), °abide (by), °observe, °respect, adhere to, °follow, °conform (to or with), acquiesce (to or in), °mind, °accept, °heed, °defer to, °yield (to), knuckle under (to), give °way (to), °surrender (to), °succumb (to), °give in (to), °truckle to, °bow to, °bend to, take or °accept orders from: *Unfortunately, Ogilvy has obeyed his baser instincts in making the punishment fit the crime. Everything must obey the laws of nature. Harold obeys Millie's slightest whim.* **2** °discharge, °execute, °effect, °carry out, °fulfil, °meet, °satisfy, do, °perform; °serve, °act: *We obeyed the colonel's orders to the letter. It is your function to command, mine to obey.*

obituary *n.* necrology, °death notice, °eulogy, necrologue, *Colloq* obit: *Mark Twain is one of the few people ever to have read his own obituary.*

object *n.* **1** °thing, °tangible, °item; °reality, °entity, °fact, °phenomenon: *A number of objects lay on the table. Thoughts may be considered as objects of the imagination.* **2** °focus, °target, °butt, °aim, °destination, °quarry, °goal: *The object of my affection has married someone else.* **3** °purpose, °end, °intention, °objective, °reason, °intent, °idea, °goal: *The object of our visit is to ask you a few questions.* —*v.* **4** °protest (to or against), °interfere (with), °raise °objection(s) (to), °argue (against), °oppose, be against, take °exception (to), °disapprove (of), draw the line (at), °complain (about), remonstrate (over or about), take a °stand (against), °refuse: *I won't object if you want to bring the wine. Would you object to rereading that passage? If they ask me, I cannot object.*

objection *n.* °protest, °opposition, °exception, °argument, °challenge, °interference, demur or demurral or demurrer, °question, °doubt, °disapproval, °interference, °complaint, remonstrance, remonstration, °stand, °refusal, °dislike, antipathy: *The meeting proceeded without further objection from the audience. If you have no objection, I'd like to leave now. The secretary has raised an objection to the method of procedure.*

objective *adj.* **1** °fair, °impartial, °just, °judicious, °equitable, °neutral, °disinterested, °dispassionate, open-handed, open-minded, °detached, unbiased, °unprejudiced, unbigoted, even-handed, uncoloured, unjaundiced: *How can you be objective about the guilt or innocence of your own child?* —*n.* **2** °target, °goal, °object, °aim, °purpose, °end (in view), °intent, °intention, °design, °aspiration, °ambition, °hope: *If we capture the flag, we shall have gained our objective. My objective is to win the pentathlon.*

objectivity *n.* impartiality, fairness, fair-mindedness, equitableness, equitability, even-handedness, neutrality, disinterest, °detachment, °indifference, dispassion: *The jury's objectivity was never in doubt.*

obligate *n.* °oblige, °pledge, °commit, °bind; °require, compel, constrain, °force: *I feel deeply obligated to her for her kindness to our children. We are obligated to do what we are told.*

obligation *n.* **1** °responsibility, °duty, charge, °burden, onus; °accountability, °liability, °trust; °demand, °requirement, compulsion, *Literary* devoir: *It was Frank's obligation to get the children home safely. Civil servants have an obligation to serve the people. I could never fulfil all my obligations.* **2** constraint, °requirement, °contract, °promise, °pledge, °bond, °agreement, covenant: *The company is under no obligation to replace a product because the customer dislikes its colour. I am under an obligation to her for introducing*

obligatory | obscurity

us. **3** °debt, °liability: *Denby may be unable to meet all his obligations.*

obligatory *adj.* required, demanded, °necessary, requisite, compulsory, °mandatory; °incumbent; °indispensable, °essential: *Has she been able to meet all the obligatory qualifications?*

oblige *v.* **1** °accommodate, °indulge, °favour, °serve, °please, °cater to, °gratify: *The hotelier obliged us with every luxury he had to offer. Please oblige us by keeping your dog on a lead.* **2** °make, °require, °demand, °force, compel, coerce, °bind, °obligate: *What hold has she over you that obliges you to do her housework?*

obliged *adj.* **1** °thankful, °grateful, appreciative, °beholden, °indebted, obligated: *We are deeply obliged to you for lending us your car.* **2** °bound, required, compelled, °forced, made, obligated: *Under the terms of the agreement, I am obliged to repay the debt by May.*

obliging *adj.* °accommodating, °willing, °indulgent, °gracious, °courteous, °civil, °considerate, °polite, °agreeable, amenable, °kind, °kindly, °helpful, °friendly, °amiable, °neighbourly, °supportive: *It was very obliging of you to look after my cat while I was gone.*

oblique *adj.* **1** slanting, slanted, sloping, aslant, °inclined, diagonal, inclining, angled, angling, canted, canting, banked, banking, cambered, °crooked, askew, °divergent, diverging, tilted, atilt, tilting: *The roof joins the wall at an oblique angle.* **2** awry, °devious, °roundabout, °indirect, circuitous, circumlocutionary, °evasive, °sly, °sidelong, °offhand, °surreptitious, °furtive, implied, clandestine, underhand(ed), °deceitful, °deceptive, °false: *She made some oblique comments about the candidate's wife.*

obliterate *v.* **1** °erase, expunge, °rub out, efface, eradicate, °wipe out, °delete, dele, °strike off or out, °strike from, °rule out, °eliminate, °write off: *After the scandal, that name was obliterated from the roll of honour.* **2** annihilate, °destroy, °kill, °exterminate, °wipe out, °eliminate, °blot out, eradicate, extirpate: *The entrance to the cave was completely obliterated by the explosion.*

oblivion *n.* **1** blankness, blackness, darkness, °obscurity, nothingness, nihility, anonymity, extinction, non-existence, °void, °limbo: *The rock band enjoyed brief fame, then sank into oblivion.* **2** unawareness, obliviousness, forgetfulness, heedlessness, °disregard, unconsciousness, insensibility: *I sank back into the sweet oblivion of deep sleep.*

oblivious *adj.* °unaware, °unconscious, unmindful, disregardful, °insensible, insensitive, °distant, unconcerned, °detached, removed, unfeeling, abstracted, °absent-minded, °forgetful, Lethean: *Many are completely oblivious to the plight of the starving millions in Africa.*

obnoxious *adj.* °revolting, °repulsive, °repugnant, °disgusting, °offensive, objectionable, fulsome, noisome, °vile, °repellent, °nauseous, nauseating, sickening, °foul, noxious, mephitic, °unsavoury, execrable, °abominable, °abhorrent, °loathsome, detestable, °hateful, odious, °scurvy, °base, °obscene, °despicable, °awful, °terrible, °unpalatable, °distasteful, unlikeable, unpleasant, °nasty, *Colloq chiefly Brit* °beastly: *Mary's obnoxious sister even has obnoxious table manners.*

obscene *adj.* **1** inelegant, °improper, °rude, °impure, °unchaste, °shameless, °shameful, °indecent, °immodest, °off colour, indecorous, indelicate, °risqué, °vulgar, °immoral, °degenerate, amoral, °dissolute, °broad, °suggestive, °erotic, °sensual, ribald, debauched, °wanton, °loose, °libertine, °bawdy, °blue, scabrous, °coarse, °dirty, °filthy, smutty, °pornographic, libidinous, °lewd, licentious, °lecherous, °lustful, goatish, °carnal, ruttish, °lascivious, salacious, °prurient, °disgusting, °offensive, °repulsive, °foul, °abominable, °vile, °loathsome, °gross, foul-mouthed, °scurrilous, scatological, *Literary* Cyprian, Paphian, Fescennine, thersitical: *In the cinema business, 'adult' and 'obscene' seem to be synonyms.* **2** °evil, °wicked, heinous, °atrocious, °awful, °outrageous, °repulsive, °shocking, °repellent, °obnoxious, off-putting, objectionable, °beastly, intolerable, °insufferable, °unpalatable, °distasteful, °nauseous, nauseating, sickening, execrable, °despicable, °nasty: *The obscene monster dashed the brave warriors to the rocks far below.*

obscure *adj.* **1** °dark, unlit, °gloomy, °sombre, °dismal, °murky, °dusky, °black, Cimmerian, tenebrous, °dim, °faint, blurred, °veiled, °shadowy, subfusc, subfuscous, umbral, °shady, °hazy, foggy, befogged, clouded, °nebulous, °overcast, cloudy: *The traveller's lantern was barely seen in the obscure reaches of the wood.* **2** unclear, °uncertain, °ambiguous, °vague, °hazy, °doubtful, dubious, °equivocal, °indefinite, °indistinct, °fuzzy, blurred, °confused, confusing, Delphic, °puzzling, enigmatic, °perplexing, baffling, mystifying, °mysterious, °cryptic, °incomprehensible, °unfamiliar, °foreign, °strange: *The sorcerer muttered some obscure words, and a golden horse stood prancing before them.* **3** °secret, concealed, hidden, °remote, °out-of-the-way, °inconspicuous, unnoticeable, °secluded, °unnoticed: *The caped figure scurried down the alley and disappeared into some obscure doorway.* **4** °unknown, °unheard-of, anonymous, unnamed, °insignificant, unimportant, °inconsequential, °humble, °lowly, °mean, inglorious, °inconspicuous, °undistinguished, °unnoticed, °unsung, °minor, little-known: *Though extremely popular, the song was written by an obscure composer.* **5** abstruse, arcane, °recondite, esoteric, °intricate, complex, °occult, out of the ordinary, °unfamiliar, *Colloq* far-out: *He is an authority on some obscure subject like Coptic calligraphy.*
—*v.* **6** °cover, °conceal, °hide, °veil, °shroud, °cloak, °mask, °screen, °disguise, °keep from: *Her link with military intelligence was obscured from her family.* **7** °dim, bedim, cloud, becloud, °dull, °shroud, °shade, adumbrate, °overshadow, darken, obfuscate, °block, °eclipse: *The street lamp was obscured by trees.*

obscurity *n.* **1** dimness, darkness, °gloom, murk, murkiness, duskiness, °dusk, blackness, faintness, blurriness, °shade, °shadow, haze, °fog, cloudiness, nebulousness: *The two of them vanished into the obscurity of the night.* **2** abstruseness, ambiguousness, intricacy, °complexity, unintelligibility, °mystery, arcanum, °secret, esoterica (*pl.*): *Can he truly believe that he has fathomed all the obscurities of Scripture?* **3** insignificance, unimportance, ingloriousness, inconspicuousness, anonymity, namelessness, °limbo: *After a fleeting surge of popularity, punk rock sank into obscurity.*

obsequious *adj.* °low, cringing, toadying, toadyish, sycophantic, sycophantish, unctuous, truckling, °grovelling, crawling, fawning, deferential, °ingratiating, °menial, °flattering, °servile, slavish, subservient, °submissive, abject, °mealy-mouthed, °slimy, *Colloq* boot-licking, *Chiefly Brit* smarmy, *Taboo slang* brown-nosing, *Brit* arse-kissing, arse-licking, *US* ass-licking, ass-kissing: *He is surrounded with obsequious followers who cater to his every whim.*

observable *adj.* °perceptible, perceivable, °noticeable, °discernible, recognizable, detectable, °visible, °apparent, °distinct, °evident, °manifest, °plain, °obvious, °clear, °explicit, °transparent, °patent, °tangible, unmistakable: *A marked change in public sentiment became at once observable.*

observance *n.* **1** °observation, observing, °obedience, obeying, compliance, complying, conformity, conforming, adherence, adhering, keeping, accordance, °regard, °recognition, recognizing, °respect, respecting, °heed, heeding, °attention: *Observance of the rules by everyone makes for a happier community.* **2** °ceremony, °celebration, °ceremonial, °practice, °rite, °ritual, °service, °performance, °form, °custom, °convention, °tradition, °formality, °usage, °habit, wont, °institution: *Almost all the fine arts derived their origin from religious observances.* **3** °observation, °examination, inspection, °scrutiny, looking, watching: *His observance of the passing scene was chronicled in his diary.*

observant *adj.* **1** watchful, °alert, °attentive, °vigilant, on the °lookout, on the qui vive, on °guard, wide °awake, regardful, °mindful, °aware, °keen, keen-eyed, °sharp-eyed, eagle-eyed, °perceptive, °sharp, °shrewd: *Hannay was observant of all who passed him on the way to the train. How very observant of you to spot the man in the crowd!* **2** Usually, **observant of**: °obedient (to), compliant (with), °respectful (of), heedful (of), °attentive (to *or* of), conformist (to), adherent (to): *One must be always be observant of the rules of the road.*

observation *n.* **1** watching, °examination, °scrutiny, inspection, viewing, °survey, °surveillance; °notice, °discovery, °attention, awareness: *The police put the house under 24-hour observation. The smuggled weapon escaped the guard's observation.* **2** °comment, °remark, °note, °reflection, °opinion, °sentiment, point of °view, °impression, °feeling, commentary, °criticism; utterance, °word, °announcement, °pronouncement, °proclamation, °declaration: *She made a number of trenchant observations concerning life in Britain today.*

observe *v.* **1** °obey, °abide by, °comply with, be heedful of, °attend to, °conform to, °regard, °keep, °follow, adhere to, °respect, pay °attention to: *We observed the prohibition against swimming.* **2** °watch, °look at, °examine, °monitor, °scrutinize, °study, °regard, °view, °inspect, pore over, °contemplate, consider; *Colloq* °check (out *or* up on), °check over, °size up, *Slang* case: *The naturalists went to the Arctic to observe the polar bears.* **3** °see, °mark, °notice, °look, °perceive: *Observe how swiftly the skin forms pustules when this substance is applied.* **4** Sometimes, **observe on** *or* **upon**: °comment (on *or* upon), °remark (on *or* upon), °mention, °say, °note, °refer (to), make °reference to, animadvert on *or* upon *or* to; °state, °declare: *It is impolite to observe on others' manners. He couldn't help observing to his cell-mate how easy it would be to escape.* **5** °celebrate, °keep, solemnize, °respect, °keep holy, °mark, °commemorate, °memorialize, °remember, °recognize: *We always observe the sabbath.*

observer *n.* °witness, °eyewitness, °spectator, viewer, °onlooker, beholder, watcher, looker-on; non-participant: *UN observers reported that the battle was over.*

obsess *v.* °haunt, °harass, °plague, bedevil, °torment, °take over, preoccupy, °dominate, °control, °grip, °possess, °hold: *He was obsessed by the conviction that he could design a successful flying machine.*

obsession *n.* °fixed °idea, idée fixe, °fixation, °conviction, preoccupation, prepossession, °passion, °mania, °phobia, *Colloq* hang-up, °thing: *Thoughts of death became his constant obsession.*

obsessive *adj.* haunting, harassing, tormenting, dominating, controlling, possessing, all-encompassing, °passionate, unshakeable *or* unshakable: *She has an obsessive fear of heights.*

obsolescent *adj.* fading, waning, on the °wane, declining, °dying, on the way out, on the °decline, going *or* passing out of °use *or* °fashion *or* °style: *Much of yesterday's newest slang is obsolescent today.*

obsolete *adj.* out of °date, out of °fashion, out-dated, °passé, °out, °dead, outmoded, °old, °antiquated, antediluvian, °ancient, superannuated, dated, archaic, °old-fashioned, démodé; °unused, °disused, discarded, superseded, °extinct, *Colloq* °old hat: *The expression 'tickety-boo' is obsolete. He plays his 78-rpm records on an obsolete gramophone.*

obstacle *n.* °impediment, °hindrance, °obstruction, °hurdle, °hitch, catch, °snag, °stumbling-block, °barrier, °bar, °check: *The obstacles in the road prevented our proceeding further. One must often overcome many obstacles before achieving success.*

obstinacy *n.* obstinateness, stubbornness, doggedness, °tenacity, °persistence *or* persistency, mulishness, pigheadedness, wilfulness, contrariness, perverseness, perversity, cantankerousness, recalcitrance, uncooperativeness, rebelliousness, contumacy, contumaciousness, refractoriness, intractability, intransigence, pertinacity, pertinaciousness, obduracy, fixedness, stolidity, inflexibility, firmness, *Archaic* frowardness, *Colloq Brit* bloody-mindedness: *His obstinacy and narrow-mindedness made it impossible to work with him in any cooperative way.*

obstinate *adj.* °stubborn, dogged, °tenacious, °persistent, mulish, °perverse, headstrong, pigheaded, °single-minded, °wilful, strong-willed, °self-willed, °contrary, °recalcitrant, uncooperative, °rebellious, contumacious, refractory, intransigent, pertinacious, obdurate, °fixed, °inflexible, °stony, adamant, °set, unmoving, °immovable, inexorable, intractable, unchangeable, °resolute, °steadfast, unyielding, persevering, °stiff, °rigid, °hard, *Archaic* froward, *Colloq Brit* bloody-minded: *The obstinate man does not hold opinions—they hold him.*

obstreperous *adj.* vociferous, clamorous, °noisy, °loud, °raucous, °riotous, °uproarious, °tumultuous, °boisterous, °rowdy, rumbustious, °tempestuous, °unruly, °disorderly, unmanageable, uncontrollable, °uncontrolled, unrestrained, °irrepressible, out of control, °undisciplined, roisterous, °wild, turbulent, *Colloq* rambunctious, *Brit* mafficking: *The party was getting rough and some of the guests a bit too obstreperous.*

obstruct *v.* **1** °block, °bar, °check, °prevent, °stop (up), °arrest, °halt, °clog, make impassable; bring to a °standstill: *The vein is obstructed by a large blood clot. A clogged drain is obstructing the water.* **2** °hamper, °slow, °impede, °interfere with, °retard, °hinder, °interrupt, °delay, °stay, °stall: *An overturned truck obstructed traffic on the motorway.* **3** °preclude, °prevent, debar, °block, °prohibit, °forbid, °stop, °stand in the °way of: *They are manoeuvring to obstruct her from taking over the company.*

obstruction *n.* **1** °obstacle, °barrier, °bar, °check, °stumbling-block, °hindrance, °impediment, °hurdle, °hitch, °snag, catch, bottleneck, limitation, constraint, °restriction: *The fallen trees created an almost impassable obstruction.* **2** checking, stopping, cessation, proscription, °forbidding, forbiddance; hindering, impeding, limiting, °halting, slowing: *The obstruction of the bill's passage can be blamed on the Tories.*

obtain *v.* **1** °get, °procure, °acquire, °come by, °come into (the) °possession of, °secure, °get hold of *or* one's °hands on, °grasp, °capture, take °possession of, °seize, °buy, °purchase: *She has been unable to obtain the job she wants. You can obtain that kind of soap at the supermarket.* **2** °earn, °gain: *We talked to the manager about obtaining an increase in wages.* **3** °prevail, be in °force, be in °vogue, °exist, subsist, have (a) place, be °prevalent, be established, be °customary, °apply, be °relevant, °relate: *A different set of regulations obtains here.*

obtrude *v.* °thrust (oneself) forward *or* forth, °intrude, °impose (oneself), °force (oneself): *The best writers never obtrude between the reader and the story.*

obtrusive *adj.* interfering, °intrusive, meddling, °officious, meddlesome, importunate, °forward, °presumptuous, °forceful, *Colloq* °pushy: *She found him somewhat obtrusive—always giving advice when she least needed it.*

obtuse *adj.* **1** rounded, unpointed, °blunt: *When mature, the leaves become more obtuse.* **2** °dull, insensitive, unfeeling, imperceptive, °thick-skinned, °stolid, °thick, °dense, doltish, cloddish, thickheaded, dull-witted, dim-witted, slow-witted, (mentally) retarded, boneheaded, lumpish, loutish, oafish, °simple, simple-minded: *Luke is a bit too obtuse to get the point of the story.*

obvious *adj.* °clear, °plain, °apparent, °patent, °perceptible, °evident, °self-evident, clear-cut, °manifest, palpable, (much) in °evidence, °conspicuous, °open, °visible, °overt, ostensible, °pronounced, °prominent, °glaring, undeniable, unconcealed, unhidden, unsubtle, °distinct, °simple, bald, bald-faced, straightforward, °direct, self-explanatory, °indisputable, unmistakable: *There are obvious flaws in the fabric. The reason you were refused seemed obvious to me.*

obviously *adv.* °clearly, plainly, °apparently, patently, °evidently, °simply, certainly, of °course, undeniable, unmistakably, indubitably, °doubtless(ly): *You are obviously the right person for the assignment.*

occasion *n.* **1** °time, °moment, °circumstance, °incident, °occurrence, °opportunity, °chance, °opening, °advantage: *I took the occasion of the inquiry to leave town.* **2** °reason, °cause, °call, justification, °ground(s), °warrant, °provocation, prompting, impulse, stimulus, °incitement, °inducement: *Tom gave David no occasion to doubt his honesty.* **3** °event, °function, °happening, °affair, °observance, commemoration, °ceremony, °celebration, °gala, °party: *Grandpapa's ninetieth birthday was a great occasion. This hall is saved for important occasions.* **4 on occasion**: See occasionally, below. —*v.* **5** give °rise to, °bring about, °cause, °bring on, °effect, °prompt, °provoke, °evoke, °call forth, °elicit, °call up, °induce, impel, °create, °generate, engender, °produce, °make (for): *An increase in the inflation rate occasions a decrease in the value of money.*

occasional *adj.* **1** °intermittent, °irregular, °periodic, °random, °sporadic, infrequent, °casual, °incidental: *They staged occasional raids on the arsenal. He works as an occasional farm hand.* **2** additional, °extra, °spare, °supplementary, °incidental, °auxiliary, °accessory: *We bought a few occasional chairs in case we have company.* **3** °special, °particular, °ceremonial, °ritual: *She writes occasional verses for memorial services.*

occasionally *adv.* °sometimes, on °occasion, (every) °now and then, from time to time, at times, (every) °now and again, °once in a while, every so often, periodically, intermittently, sporadically, irregularly, off and on: *We go up to the Lake District for a weekend occasionally. Trevor occasionally drops in at the local pub for a beer.*

occult *adj.* **1** °secret, °dark, concealed, °private, °privy, hidden, °obscure, °veiled, obscured, shrouded, °vague, abstruse, °shadowy, °mystical, °mysterious, cabbalistic, esoteric, °recondite, arcane: *Printing was kept an occult art for generations.* **2** magical, °mystical, alchemic(al), unexplained, unexplainable, °inexplicable, °puzzling, baffling, °perplexing, mystifying, °mysterious, °incomprehensible, inscrutable, indecipherable, impenetrable, unfathomable, transcendental, °supernatural, preternatural, mystic: *They dress in odd clothes and participate in occult rituals at peculiar times of the day and night.* —*n.* **3** Usually, **the occult**: the °supernatural, the °unknown, the °black arts; arcana, cabbala *or* kabbala; cabbalism *or* kabbalism, occultism, °sorcery, witchcraft, °black °magic: *Keith has studied the occult for many years.*

occupant *n.* °resident, °inhabitant, occupier, °tenant, lessee, leaseholder, renter, °owner, householder, indweller, dweller, °denizen, lodger, roomer, boarder; addressee; °incumbent: *The occupant of the flat upstairs is rarely home.*

occupation *n.* **1** °job, °position, °post, °situation, °appointment, °employment, °vocation, °line (of °work), °career, °field, °calling, °trade, métier, °craft, °skill, °profession, °business, °work: *Claverton pursued* *his occupation as a miniaturist for some fifty years.* **2** °possession, °tenure, occupancy, °control, suzerainty, subjugation, °subjection, °oppression, °bondage: *Terrible atrocities were committed while the land was under the occupation of the Mongols.* **3** °conquest, °seizure, appropriation, take-over: *Francisco Pizarro was responsible for the occupation of Peru.*

occupy *v.* **1** °capture, °seize, °take °possession of, °conquer, invade, °take over, °overrun, garrison, °dominate, °hold: *Rebel forces had occupied the capital and toppled the governor.* **2** °live or reside or °dwell in, °tenant, be established or ensconced or situated in, °establish or ensconce or °situate oneself in, °inhabit, be settled in or into, °settle in or into, °take up residence in, make one's °home in, °move in or into; be located in: *She occupies a luxurious flat in Belgravia.* **3** °engage, °busy, absorb, °monopolize, °hold, °take up or over, catch, °grab, °seize, °grip; °divert, °amuse, °entertain, °distract, °beguile, preoccupy, °hold (someone's) °attention, °interest, engross, °involve: *Other matters occupied my attention last Sunday. While one man was keeping the shopkeeper occupied, the other man was robbing the till.* **4** °fill (in or up), °take up, °cover, °extend over, °consume, °use (up), *Colloq* °eat up: *The car occupies more garage space than I thought it would. Housework occupies very little of my time.*

occur *v.* **1** °happen, take place, °arise, °come about, befall, come to pass, °chance, °appear, °surface, °materialize, °develop, become °manifest, °manifest itself, *Colloq* °transpire, crop up, °come off, °turn up: *We reported to the police all that had occurred. What occurred to make you late this time?* **2 occur to**: °dawn on, °strike, °hit, °come to, °suggest itself to, cross (someone's) mind, enter (someone's) head, be brought to (someone's) °attention: *Has it occurred to you that she might not like opera?*

occurrence *n.* **1** °happening, °event, °incident, °phenomenon, °affair, °matter, °experience: *Earthquakes are frequent occurrences in California.* **2** °existence, °instance, °manifestation, materialization, °appearance, °development: *The occurrence of mutations diversifies the species.* **3** frequency, °incidence, °rate; °likelihood, °chance: *What is the recorded occurrence of typhoons in the South China Sea?*

ocean *n.* **1** (deep blue) °sea, (bounding) main, high °seas, the °deep, Davy Jones's locker, the depths, *Colloq* the briny, the °drink: *The sails filled, and our tiny craft was swept out into the open ocean.* **2** Often, **oceans**: °flood, °abundance, multitude, °profusion, plethora, *Colloq* scads, loads, tons, °lots, oodles, gobs, zillions: *The direct mail campaign yielded oceans of responses.*

oceanic *adj.* °marine, pelagic, thalassic; salt-water, deep-water, aquatic, maritime, °sea, °ocean: *These creatures are chiefly oceanic, coming ashore only to breed.*

odd *adj.* **1** °strange, °peculiar, °unusual, uncommon, °different, unexpected, °unfamiliar, °extraordinary, °remarkable, atypical, untypical, °exotic, out of the ordinary, °unparalleled, unconventional, °exceptional, °unique, °singular, °individual, anomalous, idiosyncratic, °rare, °deviant, °outlandish, uncanny, °queer, °curious, °bizarre, °weird, °eccentric, °funny, °quaint, °fantastic, °freak, °abnormal, freakish,

Colloq °offbeat, screwy, °kinky, freaky, *Slang Brit* barmy, °bent, rum, *US and Canadian* kooky: *Ebenezer is an odd name for a dog. Where did you get that odd hat? I cannot account for his odd behaviour.* **2** °occasional, °casual, part-time, °irregular, °random, °sporadic, discontinuous, °disconnected, °various, °varied, °miscellaneous, °sundry, °incidental: *After being made redundant, he worked at odd jobs for a year or so. The odd shower can be expected during the afternoon.* **3** °leftover, °surplus, °remaining, °unused, °spare, °superfluous, °extra: *After the patterns were cut, we were allowed to take the odd scraps of fabric.* **4** uneven, unmatched, unpaired: *This gallery has an odd number of columns.*

oddity *n.* **1** °peculiarity, strangeness, unnaturalness, curiousness, incongruity, incongruousness, °eccentricity, outlandishness, extraordinariness, unconventionality, bizarreness, weirdness, queerness, oddness, unusualness, individuality, °singularity, distinctiveness, anomalousness, anomaly, *Colloq* kinkiness, *US and Canadian* kookiness: *What caught my attention was the oddity of the clothes worn by the students.* **2** °peculiarity, °curiosity, °rarity, °freak, °original, °phenomenon, °character, °eccentric, °nonconformist, fish out of water, odd bird, *rara avis*, °misfit, square peg in a round hole, maverick, *Colloq* °card, °crank, weirdie or °weirdo, oner, *Brit* odd fish, *US and Canadian* kook, oddball, screwball: *The townspeople thought Albert an oddity, but we knew he was a genius.* **3** °peculiarity, irregularity, anomaly, idiosyncrasy, °eccentricity, deviation, °quirk, °mannerism, °twist, °kink, crotchet: *I suppose people all have their own oddities when it comes to food.*

odds *n.pl.* **1** chances, °likelihood, °probability: *The odds are that Janet will finish the job in time.* **2** °edge, °advantage, °lead, °superiority: *We have won before against greater odds.* **3** °difference, °inequality, °disparity, unevenness, °discrepancy, °dissimilarity, °distinction: *It makes no odds who you are, you may not go in there.* **4 at odds**: at °variance, at loggerheads, at daggers drawn, at sixes and sevens, at cross purposes, at each other's throats, in °disagreement, in °opposition, on bad terms, not in keeping, out of line, inharmonious, conflicting, clashing, disagreeing, differing: *Teenagers have been at odds with their parents since time immemorial.* **5 odds and ends**: oddments, °fragments, debris, °leftovers, leavings, °remnants, °bits (and pieces), °particles, °shreds, snippets, scraps, °rubbish, °litter, *Colloq Brit* odds and sods: *We managed to pack everything into boxes except for a few odds and ends.*

odour *n.* **1** °smell, °scent, °aroma, °bouquet, °fragrance, °perfume, redolence; °stench, stink, fetor or foetor: *The air was filled with the odour of orange blossoms. The odour of rotting vegetation assailed our noses.* **2** °air, °breath, °hint, °suggestion, °atmosphere, °spirit, quality, °flavour, °savour, °aura, °tone: *She would never allow the odour of scandal to touch her family.*

off *adv.* **1** away, °out, °elsewhere: *His secretary said that he'd gone off for the weekend.* **2** °distant, away, afar, far-off: *The U-boat was a mile off. Christmas is only a month off.* —*adj.* **3** °incorrect, °wrong, °inaccurate, in °error, °mistaken, °misguided, misled, off the mark: *I'm afraid you're off on the question of the best way to approach him.* **4** °mad, °insane, °crazy, °eccentric, touched (in the head), *Colloq* dotty, dippy, nutty, potty: *Underwood's aunt is slightly off.* **5** °remote, °distant, °improbable, °unlikely: *He went to the station on the off chance that she would be on the midday train.* **6** off work, at °leisure, °idle, °free, °open; on °holiday: *Can you get the day off tomorrow to go on a picnic with me?* **7** °sour, °mouldy, °bad, °rotten, °rancid, turned, °high: *The cream smells a bit off.* **8** °bad, unpropitious, °disappointing, °unsatisfactory, disheartening, displeasing, °slack, °slow, substandard, below °par, below °average, °quiet: *It has been an off year for the local football team.* **9** cancelled, postponed: *The meeting is off till next week.* **10** situated, °fixed, supplied: *Is he really that well off? She was much worse off when they were married.*

offbeat *adj.* °strange, °eccentric, °bizarre, °weird, °peculiar, °odd, °queer, unconventional, °unorthodox, °Bohemian, idiosyncratic, °unusual, unexpected, °outré, °outlandish, °deviant, °novel, innovative, *Colloq* °kinky, °way-out, far-out, off-the-wall, freaky, °weirdo: *Jasper's offbeat, satirical humour has made him a popular comedian.*

off colour *adj.* **1** unwell, °ill, off °form, out of sorts, °queasy, °sick, °run down, °awful, °seedy, *Colloq* under the °weather, °poorly, *Slang* °lousy, °rotten: *I have been feeling off colour since eating that fish.* **2** indelicate, °risqué, ribald, °bawdy, °indecent, °suggestive, °broad, inelegant, °improper, °inappropriate, °unseemly, °blue: *My mother does not tolerate off-colour remarks at the dinner table.*

offence *n.* **1** °violation, °breach, °crime, felony, misdemeanour, infraction, °transgression, trespass, °wrong, wrongdoing, °sin, °peccadillo, °misdeed, °fault, °infringement, malefaction; dereliction, °lapse, °slip, °error: *He was accused of offences against the rights of others. Some regard the splitting of an infinitive an offence against the Queen's English.* **2 give offence**: incur °displeasure, create °annoyance *or* irritation *or* °resentment *or* pique, evoke °indignation *or* °anger; °slight, °injure, °hurt, °harm, °offend, °insult, °outrage, *Colloq* °put (someone) down: *He denied that he meant to give offence in his criticism of the play.* **3 take offence**: take °umbrage, feel °displeasure *or* annoyance *or* °resentment *or* pique *or* °indignation, be angered *or* enraged: *Why should you take offence at what a fool says?*

offend *v.* **1** °hurt (someone's) feelings, affront, °insult, °slight, snub, give °offence, °hurt, °pain, °displease, disgruntle, chagrin, °humiliate, °embarrass; pique, °fret, °gall, vex, °annoy, °irritate, nettle, needle, °rankle, °provoke, °ruffle, °outrage, rile, anger, *Colloq* miff, put (someone's) back up, put (someone's) nose out of joint, tread *or* step on (someone's) toes, °put (someone) out, °rattle: *I hope you weren't offended by my saying that you could do with losing some weight.* **2** °disgust, °sicken, turn (someone's) stomach, °nauseate, °repel, °repulse, °revolt, *Colloq* °turn (someone) off: *I, for one, am offended by seeing explicit sex on television.*

offender *n.* °criminal, malefactor, lawbreaker, °outlaw, wrongdoer, °culprit, °miscreant, °transgressor, °sinner, evil-doer, *Slang* crook: *I don't know if they apprehended the offender.*

offensive *adj.* **1** antagonistic, °hostile, contentious, °quarrelsome, attacking, °aggressive, °threatening, °provocative, combative, °martial, °belligerent, °warlike, bellicose: *The minute the enemy made an offensive move, we attacked.* **2** insulting, °rude, °disrespectful, uncivil, °insolent, °discourteous, °impolite, unmannerly, °impertinent, °impudent, objectionable, displeasing: *Nigel has been asked to leave because of his offensive behaviour.* **3** °disgusting, °unsavoury, °unpalatable, nauseating, °nauseous, noisome, noxious, °obnoxious, °repugnant, °repulsive, °repellent, °revolting, °abominable, °foul, °loathsome, °vile, sickening, fetid *or* foetid, °rank, malodorous, mephitic, °putrid, putrescent, putrefying, °rancid, °rotten: *An offensive stench emanated from the stagnant pond.*
—*n.* **4** °attack, °offence: *At last, our team was on the offensive.* **5** °attack, onslaught, °drive, °assault, °offence, °push: *The offensive to capture the arsenal will be launched at dawn tomorrow.*

offer *v.* **1** proffer, °propose, °tender, °bid: *They offered twice what I had paid for it. She offered to buy my old car.* **2** make °available, °present, °tender, put on the °market, °sell, put up for °sale, °put up, °furnish: *The supermarket is offering lettuce at half price.* **3** proffer, °provide, °submit, °put forward *or* forth, °advance, °tender, °extend, °make; °suggest: *Can you offer a suggestion for improving office efficiency? He offered to forget the whole thing if I paid him £1,000.* **4** volunteer, °present oneself, °step *or* °come forward: *I offered to help with her luggage.*
—*n.* **5** °proposal, °bid, °tender, °offering: *She said she would double any offer we have already had for the painting.* **6** °proposal, °presentation, proffer, °proposition: *The company said they could entertain no offers past the deadline. My offer to lend the money was contingent on being repaid.*

offering *n.* °sacrifice, oblation, contribution, °donation, °gift, °present: *They made offerings to the gods in order to propitiate them.*

offhand *adj.* **1** offhanded, °casual, °informal, °nonchalant, °cool, °distant, °aloof, °easygoing, °blasé, unceremonious, °relaxed, °easy, °smooth, unconcerned, insouciant, light-hearted, uninterested, °superficial, °cursory, cavalier, °careless: *His offhand reaction shows that he doesn't care as much about her as we thought.* **2** °curt, °brusque, °abrupt, °perfunctory, °ungracious, °glib, °smooth: *When asked when he expected to pay, he gave an offhand reply.* **3** extempore, impromptu, °unpremeditated, unstudied, °extemporaneous, °informal, off the cuff, ad lib: *She rose to make some offhand comments about the accomplishments of the guest of honour.*
—*adv.* **4** extempore, impromptu, extemporaneously, informally, off the cuff, ad lib, on the °spur of the moment, at the drop of a hat: *That was a pretty good speech considering it was made offhand.* **5** casually, informally, °incidentally, by the °way, offhandedly, by the by, parenthetically, in °passing, *en passant*, cursorily, superficially: *Offhand, I'd say that the two of them deserve each other.*

office *n.* **1** °business, °organization, °department, °firm, °house, °establishment, °company, corporation: *Whenever I'm travelling, I always try to phone the office once a day.* **2** commission, °department, °branch; °section,

°division: *He was with the overseas office for years.* **3** workplace, offices; °room, °area: *Our new office is completely air-conditioned. My office is next to the board room.* **4** °duty, °obligation, °responsibility, °charge, commission, °service, °employment, °occupation, °position, °post, °appointment, °assignment, chore, °task, °job, °place, berth, °work, °role, °function, °purpose, °part, bit, *Colloq* °thing, *Slang* shtick: *He was appointed to the office of Minister of Health. In her office as Minister of Finance, she wields great power.* **5 offices**: °indulgence, intermediation, °auspices, °support, advocacy, aegis, °help, °aid, intercession, mediation, °patronage, °favour, °backing, backup: *She appealed to the police chief's good offices to allow her to visit her son.*

officer *n.* **1** (°public) °official, °dignitary, office-holder, °public °servant, office-bearer, (°political) appointee, (°government) °agent, bureaucrat, °functionary, commissioner, administrator, °manager, °director; apparatchik: *He was stopped by customs officers who demanded to search his baggage. The bailiff is an officer of the court.* **2** policeman, policewoman, °police officer, officer of the law, °constable, *Old-fashioned* catchpole, *US* lawman, peace officer, G-man, T-Man, *Colloq* gendarme, *Slang* cop, copper, fuzz, *US* dick, narc, *Brit* Old Bill, tec: *The officer standing at the door was there to serve a writ.*

official *adj.* **1** authorized, °legitimate, °lawful, °legal, °authentic, bona fide, °proper, °true, accredited, valid, documented, licensed, sanctioned, endorsed, certified, verified, recognized, accepted: *I won't believe I've won till I hold the official notification in my own hands.* **2** °ceremonial, °formal, °solemn, ritualistic, °ceremonious, °pompous, °stiff, °proper, °seemly, °decorous: *She has to make an acceptance speech at the official dinner.* —*n.* **3** See **officer**, 1, above.

officiate *v.* °preside, °direct, °manage, °chair, °conduct, °oversee, °head (up), °run, °lead, °supervise, superintend; °umpire, referee, °judge, adjudicate, °moderate, mediate: *Who will officiate at the annual meeting? Dennis has been invited to officiate at the football match on Saturday.*

officious *adj.* °dictatorial, °intrusive, intruding, meddlesome, meddling, °obtrusive, °forward, °bold, interfering, °aggressive, °insistent, °persistent, °demanding, importunate: *Hamish is one of those officious little men who are always ready to give unasked-for advice.*

offset *v.* **1** °compensate, counterbalance, countervail, counterpoise, °counteract, °balance (out), °equalize, °even (out *or* up), °square, °cancel (out), °neutralize, nullify, °make up (for), °atone (for), redress; recompense, °repay, °make amends *or* °restitution, °make good, °reimburse, indemnify: *The votes from the Centre offset those lost to the Far Left. How are you going to offset losses resulting from pilferage by shop assistants?* —*n.* **2** compensation, counterbalance, counteraction, °check, equalizer, neutralizer: *The bank manager considered the money owed to the company as sufficient offset for the money owed by it.*

offshoot *n.* **1** °branch, °spur; °shoot, limb, bough, °twig, °stem, appendage, °sucker, °sprout, sprig, tendril, scion: *There is an offshoot of this road that goes up the hill. The offshoots*

are trained to grow along the arms of the espalier. **2** °descendant, °relation, °relative, °kin, °kindred, °offspring, scion, °heir: *One offshoot of the family later emigrated to the United States.* **3** outgrowth, °development, °branch, spin-off; by-product, °derivative: *An offshoot of the company manufactures optical instruments. The sale of gravel for concrete is an offshoot of our mining operations.*

offspring *n. Often used as plural*: °child, °progeny, °issue, °seed, youngster, °brood, °young, successor, °heir: *None of the earl's offspring ever amounted to much.*

often *adv.* °frequently, regularly, much, °many times, °usually, habitually, commonly; °ordinarily, again and again, over and over again, °time after °time, °repeatedly, °time and (°time) again, in °many cases *or* instances, on numerous occasions, day in (and) day out, continually, *Literary* oftentimes, oft: *How often do you visit your mother? We often went to the seaside for our summer holiday. She was often warned not to go too near the edge.*

ogle *v.* **1** °leer, °eye, make °eyes at, *Colloq* give (someone) the glad °eye, give (someone) the once-over, make sheep's eyes at: *The old lecher is always ogling the pretty young secretaries.* **2** °gape, °gaze, goggle, °gawk, °stare, *Slang Brit* gawp *or* gaup: *We took turns ogling the rings of Saturn through the telescope.* —*n.* **3** °leer, °stare, °gape, goggle, oeillade, *Colloq* once-over, glad °eye: *They all crowded round the paper for an ogle at the pin-ups.*

ogre *n.* ogress, °monster, °giant, °fiend, °demon, troll, man-eater, bogey *or* bogy, bogeyman *or* bogyman, bugbear, °spectre, Minotaur, Cyclops, gorgon, Caliban; °brute, sadist, °villain, cad, °scoundrel: *The ogre chased Jack to the beanstalk. The persistent ogre of poverty threatened him all his life.*

oil *n.* **1** lubricant, grease, lubricator, unguent: *A little oil will stop that squeak.* **2** °fuel: *Miraculously, the lamp burned for eight days with only one day's supply of oil.* —*v.* **3** lubricate, grease: *Oil the bearings or they will burn out.*

oily *adj.* **1** °greasy, oleaginous, °fat, fatty, adipose, pinguid, sebaceous, soapy, saponaceous, buttery, butyraceous, lardaceous; °slippery, °slimy, slithery, °smooth, unctuous: *The cars slid about as the tyres failed to grip the oily surface.* **2** °glib, °smooth, unctuous, °servile, °obsequious, sycophantic, °ingratiating, °flattering, °hypocritical, °suave, urbane, °sophisticated, *Colloq* smarmy: *Sarah found Curtis's approach sickeningly oily.*

ointment *n.* unguent, balm, °salve, emollient, embrocation, demulcent, pomade, pomatum, petrolatum; °lotion, cream: *A little ointment will keep the sore moist till it heals.*

OK *interj.* **1** O.K.!, Okay!, Fine!, Yes!, Definitely!, Agreed!, Very °well!, All right!: *'Would you have dinner with me?' 'OK!' 'I think you ought to leave.' 'OK!'* —*adj.* **2** °satisfactory, °acceptable, °correct, °suitable, all °right, °fine, °good, in °order: *Is it OK if I go the cinema tonight? That dress is OK to wear to the dance.* **3** °adequate, °mediocre, °fair, middling, °passable, °tolerable, *Colloq* °so so, °pretty good, not bad, not great: *The film was OK, I suppose.* **4** °well, °healthy; °sound, in °good

°condition, in °fine fettle, °fine, all °right: *Now that he's on the proper medication, Sam is OK. The mechanic assured me that my car would be OK.*
—*v.* **5** °approve, °sanction, °ratify, °authorize, °endorse, °support, °agree to, °allow, °consent to, °agree to, *Colloq* give the °go-ahead *or* green light to, give the thumbs up *or* the °nod to, rubber-stamp: *A department head must OK your expense account before you can be reimbursed.*
—*n.* **6** °approval, °sanction, ratification, authorization, °endorsement, °agreement, °support, °permission, °consent: *You need an OK from the security guard to enter the restricted area.*
—*adv.* **7** all °right, satisfactorily, °well (enough), adequately: *She can get along OK without me.*

old *adj.* **1** °elderly, ageing, °aged, advanced in years *or* °age, long-lived, past one's °prime, °grey, full of years, getting on (in years), hoary, superannuated, *Colloq* over the hill, °past it: *Bill is too old to continue working in the mine.* **2** °ancient, °antiquated, antediluvian, fossil, °prehistoric, Noachian, °obsolete, °antique, out-dated, out of °date, old-time, dated, archaic, °stale, out-moded, °passé, *Literary* Ogygian: *The archaeological dig has turned up some interesting old artefacts.* **3** °time-worn, decayed, °dilapidated, °ramshackle, disintegrated, crumbling, °shabby, °worn out, dusty, broken-down, °tumbledown, °disused, °unused, °cast off, °cast aside: *They have torn down the old mill near the river.* **4** long-standing, °well-established, °enduring, °lasting, age-old, °time-honoured: *It is hard to see an old friendship die.* **5** °former, olden, °bygone, °early, primordial, °primitive: *In the old days, it took a week to travel from London to Edinburgh.* **6** °previous, °preceding, °prior, °former, quondam, erstwhile, one-time, ex-: *The West End was my old stamping-ground when I lived in London.* **7** °experienced, °veteran, °practised, (well-)°versed, °knowledgeable, °proficient, °accomplished, °adept, skilled, °expert, old-time: *Charles is an old hand at steam engines.* **8** °dear, °beloved, loved, esteemed, valued, °precious, °well-known, °intimate, °close, °familiar: *Penelope is an old friend of the family's.*

old-fashioned *adj.* °antiquated, °antique, °passé, out-moded, out-dated, unfashionable, °stale, dated, out of °date, °tired, old-time, °obsolete, °obsolescent, °dead, superseded, replaced, °disused, °out, old-fangled, °old hat: *Whoever thought we would see the day when miniskirts were old-fashioned?*

omen *n.* portent, augury, °sign, °token, foretoken, °indication, °harbinger, forewarning, °premonition, foreshadowing, writing on the wall, prognostic, presage: *Solar eclipses were once regarded as omens, sometimes good, sometimes bad.*

ominous *adj.* **1** °foreboding, °threatening, °fateful, °dark, °black, °gloomy, lowering *or* louring, °menacing, °sinister; unpropitious, unfavourable, ill-omened, ill-starred, °unpromising, star-crossed, °inauspicious: *With ominous solemnity, the judge placed a black cloth square on his head before passing the death sentence.* **2** minatory, °warning, admonitory, cautionary: *The whispering had taken on ominous overtones.* **3** °portentous, °prophetic, oracular, vaticinal, predictive, prognostic, augural, mantic, sibyllic, °meaningful, premonitory,

foreshadowing, foretelling, foretokening, indicative: *Virtually everything was regarded as ominous in ancient times.*

omission *n.* **1** non-inclusion, omitting, leaving out *or* off, excluding, eliminating, dropping, skipping; °exclusion, °exception, deletion, elimination, excision: *The omission of your name from the list was a mistake. Allowing for inadvertent omissions, the inventory is complete.* **2** °failure, °default, °neglect, dereliction, °oversight, °shortcoming, °negligence: *She is being punished for her innocent omission in failing to notify the police, while he is at liberty despite his deliberate commission of a crime.*

omit *v.* **1** °leave out, °exclude, °skip, °except, °pass over; °delete, °erase, °cancel, eradicate, °edit out, °strike (out), dele, °cut (out), °cross out, °obliterate: *She was offended because he omitted any mention of all that she had contributed.* **2** °neglect, °disregard, °fail, °forget, °overlook, let °slide, °ignore: *I omitted to tell you that your sister telephoned yesterday.*

once *adv.* **1** once upon a °time, °formerly, (at) one °time, on a °former °occasion, °previously, °before, in days gone by, in olden days, in the (good) °old days, long ago, some °time ago, years *or* ages *or* aeons ago, in days of yore: *Your hair is as long as mine once was. He was once a famous film star. That once revered leader has fallen.* **2** °one °time, on °one °occasion, a °single °time: *He has visited his family only once in all these years.* **3 once and for all**: °finally, °positively, °definitely, decidedly, conclusively, for good: *We must settle the itinerary once and for all before we can make the bookings.* **4 once in a while**: °occasionally, (every) °now and then, °now and again, at °times, °sometimes, periodically, from °time to time, at intervals, sporadically: *We go to the theatre once in a while.*
—*conj.* **5** (if) ever, as soon as, at any °time: *Once the bus comes, you'd best get on it straight away.*
—*n.* **6 at once**: **a** °immediately, °straight away, °right away, °directly, without °delay, °promptly, instantly, °post-haste; in a wink, in the twinkling of an eye, in a °minute *or* °moment *or* °second *or* split °second, in no time (at all), before you can turn around, before you can say 'Jack Robinson', in a trice, *Colloq* in a jiffy, in two shakes of a lamb's tail: *Watson, come here at once. I'll be there at once.* **b** together, at the same time, simultaneously, at a °stroke, in the same °instant, in the same breath, *Colloq* at °one go, at a go, in °one go: *You cannot be in two places at once.*

oncoming *adj.* **1** advancing, arriving, coming, nearing, approaching, onrushing, °imminent: *He swerved and just managed to avoid the oncoming lorry.*
—*n.* **2** °onset, °beginning, nearing, °arrival, °advance, °approach: *With the oncoming of spring, the birds returned.*

one *adj.* **1** °single, lone, °solitary, °individual, °sole, °only: *The one time I kissed Margie it was heaven.* **2** unified, °united, inseparable, joined, °undivided, one and the °same, °identical, °equal, at one, °harmonious, in °unison, °whole, °entire, °complete: *When he went into a trance, he felt one with his God.* **3** a °particular, a °certain, a given, a °specific: *I recall one occasion when she brought all her dogs into work.*

—pron. **4** a °person, an °individual, a °man *or* a °woman, everybody, °everyone, anybody, anyone; °people; *Possibly offensive* °man: *One ought to treat others as one would like to be treated. One cannot be too careful these days.*
—n. **5** °joke, °story, anecdote, chestnut, one-liner; limerick, °rhyme, ditty, °song; bromide: *Have you heard the one that begins, 'There was a young man from Loch Ness'?*

one-sided *adj.* **1** °partial, °biased, °partisan, °prejudiced, °bigoted, unfair, unjust, inequitable, close-minded, °narrow-minded, °intolerant: *His is a one-sided view of the problem.* **2** °lopsided, °unbalanced, unequal, unequalized, uneven, °disproportionate, *Slang* cock-eyed: *The swelling on his left cheek made Tom's face look very one-sided.* **3** unilateral, °independent, exclusionary, °exclusive: *They made a one-sided decision to halt production of nuclear weapons.*

ongoing *adj.* **1** continuing, continued, °continuous, °continual, ceaseless, unbroken, uninterrupted, °constant, °perpetual, °non-stop, °relentless, °persistent, unending, °endless, interminable, °running: *There has been an ongoing dispute with the museum over the authenticity of the sculpture.* **2** developing, evolving, growing, °successive, unfolding, progressing, °progressive: *Rather than come to a hasty decision, we decided to monitor ongoing developments.*

onlooker *n.* °spectator, °observer, looker-on, °eyewitness, °witness, watcher, viewer; °bystander, passer-by: *She was merely an onlooker, not a participant. Onlookers reported that the driver had run away from the accident.*

only *adj.* **1** °sole, °single, °solitary, lone, °one and only, °exclusive: *He is the only one who can identify the murderer.*
—adv. **2** solely, °just, exclusively, °alone: *He has a face that only a mother could love. They have been here only twice. She gets her own way only because she has a tantrum if anyone crosses her. Harry was correct in one respect only.* **3** °merely, °simply, °barely, at °best, at worst, at most, °just, purely, not *or* no more than, not *or* no greater than: *She is only seventeen. I received your note only today. Don't get excited, it's only a small present.*
—conj. **4** but, °however, on the other hand, on the °contrary, contrariwise: *The flowers are lovely, only they have no scent.*

onset *n.* **1** °attack, °assault, onrush, onslaught, °charge, °strike, °hit, °raid, storming, sally, sortie: *These troops had to bear the brunt of the onset.* **2** °beginning, °start, °outset, °initiation, inauguration, commencement, inception, °dawn, °birth, °origin, genesis, °appearance, début: *We must leave before the onset of the monsoon season. The sudden onset of a new policy will throw the ministers into a panic.*

onward *adj.* °forward, advancing, °progressive, progressing, °moving onward *or* forward: *They resumed their onward march, laying waste to the countryside as they went.*

onwards *adv.* °onward, forwards *or* forward, °ahead, in °front, on, forth: *They marched onwards through the dismal valley. From this day onwards afternoon visiting hours will be from two to four o'clock.*

ooze *n.* **1** slime, °muck, °mud, °mire, °silt, °sludge, °sediment, slush, *Colloq* goo, gunk, guck, *Slang US* glop, goop: *I stepped into the bog and the ooze rose over the tops of my shoes.*

—v. **2** exude, °weep, seep, °secrete, bleed, °leak, °drain, °trickle; °emit, °discharge: *Sap continues to ooze from the gash in the tree.*

opacity *n.* **1** opaqueness, darkness, murkiness, dimness, °obscurity, impermeability, impenetrability: *The opacity of the lens increases automatically in the presence of sunlight.* **2** °obscurity, density, impenetrability, unintelligibility, indefiniteness, vagueness, reconditeness, abstruseness, °ambiguity, equivocation, mystification: *For centuries scientists were unable to penetrate the opacity of the question of what occurred when substances burned.* **3** °stupidity, dullness, denseness, thickness, obtuseness: *A light finally dawned through the thick opacity of his brain.*

opalescent *adj.* opaline, iridescent, nacreous, °pearly, °lustrous: *The sea was opalescent in the moonlight.*

opaque *adj.* **1** °dark, °murky, °dim, turbid, °muddy, cloudy, °obscure, obscured, obfuscated, °black, °impermeable, impenetrable, clouded, non-transparent, untransparent, non-translucent, °hazy, blurred, blurry, smoky: *Solar eclipses should be viewed directly only through special opaque glass.* **2** unclear, °vague, °indefinite, °obscure, unfathomable, unplumbable, baffling, mystifying, °ambiguous, °equivocal, impenetrable, °cryptic, enigmatic, °puzzling, °perplexing, °mysterious, °elusive, abstruse, arcane, °recondite: *Despite years of study, the inscriptions on the tomb have remained opaque to scholars.* **3** unintelligent, °dense, °thick, °dull, °obtuse, °stupid, dull-witted, °stolid, thickheaded, dunderheaded, dunderpated, °slow, doltish, °backward, cloddish: *He was too opaque to notice the jeers of his colleagues.*

open *adj.* **1** ajar, gaping, agape, unfastened, unlocked, unbarred, unbolted, unlatched, unclosed: *Come on in—the door is open.* **2** yawning, agape, uncovered, revealed, unsealed, exposed, °bare: *Her uncle escaped by hiding for three nights in an open grave.* **3** unwrapped, unsealed, unfastened: *The package was open and the contents gone.* **4** °free, °accessible, °public, °available, obtainable; unrestricted, unobstructed, unencumbered *or* unincumbered, °unimpeded, unhindered, unhampered, unregulated, unconditional, °unqualified: *The parks are open to all. We were allowed open access to the library stacks.* **5** unprotected, unenclosed, unsheltered, °bare; uncovered, exposed: *They spent a week in an open boat before being rescued. The roof can be retracted, leaving the interior completely open to the sky.* **6** °unsettled, unagreed, unsigned, unsealed, unclinched, unestablished, unconcluded, undecided, °pending: *As far as I am concerned, the deal is open till the contract is signed.* **7** undecided, °unsettled, °unresolved, °debatable, arguable, °problematic, °moot, *US* up in the air: *Whether they should get married is a question that will remain open until he returns from abroad.* **8** unscheduled, unbooked, unspoken for, unreserved, uncommitted, °free, unpromised: *The doctor has an hour open at noon on Friday.* **9** °clear, unobstructed, wide open, uncluttered, °roomy, °spacious, °extensive, °expansive; treeless, uncrowded, unfenced, unenclosed; ice-free, °navigable, unblocked, °passable: *We travelled through open country for days. In the spring the shipping lanes will again be open.* **10** °available, unfilled, °vacant, untaken:

There are not many jobs open in this part of the country. **11** °receptive, open-minded, °flexible, amenable, persuasible *or* persuadable, pliant, °willing, °responsive: *The management is open to suggestions for improving its products and services.* **12** exposed, °public, °well-known, °widely known, unconcealed: *That they are living together is an open secret.* **13** °evident, °obvious, °conspicuous, °manifest, °clear, unconcealed, unequivocal, °plain, palpable, °apparent, °patent, °downright, °out-and- out, °blatant, °flagrant, °glaring, °brazen: *He operates with open disregard for the law.* **14** °generous, °liberal, °charitable, unreserved, open-handed, munificent, magnanimous, big-hearted, beneficent, bounteous, °unselfish, unstinting, °humanitarian, altruistic: *They are quite open when it comes to giving to charity.* **15** unreserved, °candid, °frank, °outspoken, straightforward, °forthright, °direct, °honest, °sincere, guileless, °artless, °fair: *He found it difficult to be open with his wife.* **16** °free, unrestrained, unconstrained, °uninhibited, unreserved, unrestricted: *They have an open marriage, each aware of the other's affairs.* **17** unfolded, extended, °spread (out), outstretched, outspread: *She ran into my open arms.* **18** °liable, °subject, °susceptible, exposed, °inclined, predisposed, °disposed: *These fraudulent shipping documents may well leave the captain open to prosecution for barratry.* **19** unprotected, undefended, unfortified, exposed: *With the invaders at the gates, Paris was declared an open city.* —*v.* **20** °begin, °start, °initiate, °commence, get under way, °inaugurate, °launch, °put in *or* into °operation, °activate, get going, °set in °motion; °establish, °set up; *Colloq* get *or* °start the ball rolling, get *or* put the show on the road, kick off: *The minister opened the proceedings with an interminable speech. Jeremy is planning to open a restaurant in Pebble Lane. The show opens in Manchester next week.* **21** unlock, unbar, unlatch, unbolt, unfasten; uncover; uncork, unseal; °undo, untie, unwrap; °pull out: *Open the door. Open the box. Open the bottle. Open your present. He opened the drawer.* **22** unblock, °clear, unobstruct, unclog, unstop: *They had to dig up the yard to open the drain. The new law has opened the way for increased exports.* **23** °disclose, °unveil, uncover, °expose, °display, °show, °exhibit, °reveal, divulge, bring to °light, °communicate, °bring out, unbosom, °explain, °present, °announce, °release, °publish, °air, °make known, advertise: *The wonders of the language were opened to me by my first dictionary.* **24** °expand, °spread (out), °stretch out, °open up *or* out, unfurl, °extend: *The flag opened to the breeze.* **25** °present, °offer, °furnish, °provide, °afford, °yield, °reveal, uncover, °raise, °contribute, °introduce: *Expansion of technology opens new business opportunities every day.*

opening *n.* **1** °break, °breach, °rent, °rift, cleft, °crack, °crevice, fissure, °cranny, °chink, °pit, °gap, °split, °slit, °slot, °aperture, °hole, orifice, °separation: *Flowers grew from openings in the wall.* **2** °opportunity, °chance, °occasion, toe-hold, foothold, *Colloq* °break, toe *or* foot in the door, *Brit* look-in: *I was waiting for an appropriate opening to make my presentation.* **3** °job, °position, °opportunity, °vacancy: *Is there likely to be an opening in the art department of your company?* **4** °beginning, commencement, °start,

°birth, °origin, °outset, °onset, inauguration, °launch, send-off, °initiation, °presentation, début; vernissage, *US* start-off, start-up: *The opening of the autumn social season was marked by Malcolm's birthday party. Aren't you going to the opening at the museum tonight?*

openly *adv.* **1** brazenly, brashly, flagrantly, unabashedly, unashamedly, unreservedly, boldly, audaciously, flauntingly: *She has openly defied the direct orders of her employer.* **2** frankly, unreservedly, plainly, forthrightly, candidly, °directly, °outright, °freely, outspokenly: *The man admitted openly that he had stolen the plans for the missile.*

operable *adj.* workable, °practicable, °serviceable, usable, °functional, °fit, operational, in working order *or* condition: *Aircraft engines that rely on oxygen for burning fuel are not operable where the air is too thin.*

operate *v.* **1** °go, °run, °perform; °work, °function, °serve, °act: *This watch operates even under water. The drug operates to reduce blood pressure.* **2** °manage, °run, °direct, °conduct, °control, °carry on, °ply, °manipulate, °handle; *US* °drive: *Katherine has been operating as an antiques dealer for years. It is unsafe to operate this machinery without goggles.*

operation *n.* **1** °function, functioning, working, °running, °performance, °action, °motion, °movement: *The operation of the internal combustion engine is very simple.* **2** manipulation, handling, °direction, °running, °control, °management, managing, manoeuvring: *The operation of the aircraft is under the control of the captain.* **3** °undertaking, °enterprise, °venture, °project, °affair, °deal, °procedure, °proceeding, (day-to-day) °business, °transaction: *Who will be in charge of the operation while the president is abroad?* **4** Often, **operations**: °action, °manoeuvre, °mission, °task, °campaign, °exercise: *The generals directed military operations from positions close to enemy lines.* **5 in** *or* **into operation**: functioning, °operative, in °effect, in °force, operating, operational, °functional, °effective, °efficacious: *Is the factory in operation yet? The new regulations went into operation last week.*

operative *adj.* **1** See **operation**, **5**, above. —*n.* **2** °worker, °hand, °employee; craftsman, craftswoman, artisan, mechanic, machinist: *We hired two more lathe operatives today.* **3** private °detective, (private) investigator, *Colloq* private eye, °sleuth, *Brit* sleuth-hound, *US* P.I., gumshoe, *Slang* (private) dick, *US* shamus, eye: *Our operatives reported that Jones had been seen in the company of a known enemy agent.* **4** espionage *or* °intelligence °agent, counter-espionage *or* counter-intelligence °agent, °spy, counter-spy, °undercover °agent *or* man, (FBI *or* CIA) °agent, *US* G-man, *Colloq US* company man, member of the firm: *We had an operative at the top level of the NKVD.*

operator *n.* **1** (bus *or* taxi *or* °train) driver; °worker, °operative, manipulator, practitioner: *These operators are required to take safety courses.* **2** °director, administrator, °manager, °supervisor, °superintendent: *Shaughnessey is the operator of a roofing business in Tring.* **3** machinator, faker, °fraud, manipulator, manoeuvrer, *Colloq* finagler, °wise guy, *Slang* smooth *or* slick operator, smoothie, wheeler-dealer, bigshot, big-time operator, *Chiefly US and Canadian* big wheel: *Claude is a cunning operator who always gets what he goes after.*

opinion *n.* **1** °belief, °judgement, °thought, °sentiment, (°point of) °view, °viewpoint, °conviction, way of °thinking, °perception, °idea, °impression, °notion, °conception, theory, *idée reçu;* °mind: *It is my opinion that sickness benefits ought to be increased. In her opinion all men are chauvinists.* **2** °evaluation, °estimation, °estimate, appraisal, °appreciation, °impression: *Myra has a very low opinion of Ray's taste in architecture.*

opinionated *adj.* **1** °stubborn, pigheaded, °obstinate, doctrinaire, °inflexible, °dogmatic, °single-minded, cocksure, obdurate, °dictatorial, dogged, mulish, bull-headed, °overbearing: *Felix is too opinionated to change his mind even if he knows he is wrong.* **2** °prejudiced, °biased, °bigoted, °one-sided, °jaundiced, coloured, °partial, °partisan: *You can count on Joan for an opinionated view of social values.*

opponent *n.* °antagonist, °adversary, disputant, °contestant, °competitor, contender, °rival, foe, °enemy; the °opposition: *He may be my opponent in the chess competition, but we are the best of friends.*

opportune *adj.* **1** °favourable, °advantageous, auspicious, °good, felicitous, °happy, °propitious, °beneficial, °helpful, °fortunate, °lucky, °profitable: *As I need money, and you have it to invest, our meeting is most opportune.* **2** °timely, °well-timed, °seasonable, apt, °appropriate, germane, °pertinent, °convenient, °fitting, °suitable, °becoming: *If this is not an opportune time to bring up the matter of the money you owe me, just say so.*

opportunistic *adj.* °expedient, °selfish, taking °advantage, exploitive *or* exploitative, unprincipled, Machiavellian, opportunist: *Don't you agree that it was opportunistic of him to inform on his own brother for a reward?*

opportunity *n.* °chance, °occasion, °opening, °possibility, °moment, °time, *Slang* °break: *She has taken advantage of every opportunity to vilify her ex-employers.*

oppose *v.* **1** °resist, °counter, °object (to), °defy, take a °stand against, °withstand, °resist, °combat, °contest, °attack, counter-attack, °fight, °grapple with, contend with *or* against: *If it comes to that, we must oppose force with force.* **2** °check, °bar, °obstruct, °block, °hinder, °impede, °stop, °slow, °curb, °restrain, °inhibit, °interfere with, °restrict, °prevent, obviate, °preclude, °thwart, °foil, °frustrate: *Labour seeks to oppose the privatization of industry.* **3** °match, °offset, counterbalance, °contrast, °pit *or* °set against, °play off (against), °set off: *What can they call upon to oppose the power of the Devil?*

opposed *adj.* Often, **opposed to**: against, in °opposition (to), °opposing, in °conflict (with), antipathetic, conflicting, °contrary (to), at °variance (with), antithetical (to), °hostile (to), inimical (to), °opposite (to), contrasting: *Harvey is among those opposed to abortion. All those who are opposed to the motion raise your hands.*

opposing *adj.* °opposite, conflicting, °contrary, antithetical, antagonistic, antipathetic, °hostile, inimical, contrasting, °rival, °contradictory, °incompatible, irreconcilable, °dissident, discrepant: *Those with opposing views will be heard from later.*

opposite *adj.* **1** °facing, vis-à-vis, *en face*: *The sniper was on the roof of the building opposite.* **2** °opposing, conflicting, °contrary, contrasting, °contradictory, antithetical, differing, °different, °divergent, °diverse, antagonistic, °inconsistent, irreconcilable: *William and his wife hold diametrically opposite political views.*
—*n.* **3** °reverse, °converse, °contrary, antithesis: *Whatever you tell teenagers to do, their first reaction is to do the opposite.*

opposition *n.* **1** °hostility, °antagonism, unfriendliness, °resistance, counteraction, °disapproval, °objection, °conflict, defiance, °contrast, antipathy, adversity, *Colloq* °flak: *There is strong opposition to plans for an amusement arcade.* **2** °competition, °opponent, °adversary, °competitor, °antagonist, °enemy, foe, °rival, other °side: *We must overcome the opposition in order to win.* **3 in opposition**: competing, competitive, antagonistic, °hostile, conflicting, in °conflict, antithetic(al), °opposed, at daggers drawn, in deadly embrace: *Although they agree on some points, the parties are in opposition on others.*

oppress *v.* **1** °burden, °afflict, °trouble, °weigh down, °overload, °encumber, °wear (down), °press, °weary, overburden, °overwhelm, *Brit* pressurize, *US* °pressure: *He was oppressed by the heavy burden of responsibility.* **2** °crush, °repress, °put down, °suppress, °subjugate, °tyrannize (over), °subdue, °overpower, °enslave, °persecute, maltreat, °abuse, harry, °harass, °trample underfoot, ride roughshod over: *The Russian serfs had been oppressed for centuries before they finally rose up against tyranny.*

oppression *n.* °repression, °suppression, subjugation, °subjection, °tyranny, °despotism, enslavement, °persecution, maltreatment, °abuse, °torment, torture, °hardship, °injury, °pain, °anguish, °injustice: *People who have not known oppression cannot imagine the agonies suffered by the oppressed who once were free.*

oppressive *adj.* **1** °burdensome, °overpowering, °overwhelming, onerous, °heavy, cumbersome, °exhausting, racking, °unbearable, intolerable, °agonizing, unendurable, °harsh, °brutal, °severe, °tyrannical, °repressive; dispiriting, depressing, disheartening, discouraging, °grievous, distressing, dolorous, °miserable, °harrowing, °wretched: *The conquerors resorted to oppressive measures to keep the people subjugated.* **2** suffocating, stifling, °stuffy, °close, airless, unventilated, uncomfortable: *The atmosphere in the tiny cell quickly became oppressive, and a couple of people fainted.*

oppressor *n.* °bully, °tyrant, taskmaster, taskmistress, °despot, autocrat, persecutor, slave-driver, °dictator, overlord, iron hand, °scourge, tormentor *or* tormenter, torturer, intimidator: *The citizens finally banded together and overthrew their oppressors.*

optimistic *adj.* °sanguine, °positive, °cheerful, °buoyant, °bright, °hopeful, °expectant, °confident, bullish, °idealistic, Pollyannaish: *We have every reason to be optimistic that the venture will succeed.*

optimum *n.* **1** °best, finest, most °favourable, °ideal, °perfection, °model, °paragon, exemplar: *In all work, the optimum is difficult to achieve.* —*adj.* **2** °best, finest, most °favourable, °ideal, °perfect, choicest, optimal, °first-rate, first-class, °sterling, °prime, °capital, °excellent, °exceptional, °superlative, °extraordinary, °unique, °peerless, unequalled, unexcelled, unsurpassed: *These instruments keep the chamber at the optimum temperature. After months of training, Guy is in optimum condition to win the marathon.*

option *n.* **1** °choice, °selection, °alternative, °recourse, °opportunity, °way out: *There are fewer employment options open to the uneducated.* **2** °choice, °privilege, °election, °opportunity, °chance: *Investors pay for the option to buy at a fixed figure if the price of the shares goes up.*

optional *adj.* °voluntary, discretionary *or* discretional, elective, facultative, °free, °spontaneous, uncoerced, unforced, non-compulsory, uncompulsory, non-mandatory, unmandatory, non-requisite, unrequisite: *Life insurance is optional for those who have our hospitalization policy.*

opulent *adj.* **1** °wealthy, affluent, °rich, °prosperous, well-to-do, °well off, °comfortable, *Colloq* °flush, well-heeled, °loaded, rolling in it, made of °money, in clover, on Easy Street, *Brit* on velvet, *US* in velvet, in the chips: *Timothy was fortunate in having met and wed an opulent widow.* **2** °luxurious, °lavish, °sumptuous: *That poor little rich girl was raised in the most opulent of surroundings.* **3** °abundant, copious, °bountiful, °plentiful, °prolific, °profuse, plenteous: *We enjoyed a most opulent harvest this year.*

opus *n.* °work, °composition, °production, œuvre, °creation; *magnum opus: Her most important opus will be performed at the Albert Hall next week.*

oracle *n.* **1** °prophet, sibyl, °seer, soothsayer, augur, °fortune-teller, diviner, prognosticator, *US* reader (and °adviser *or* advisor), Cassandra, Nostradamus; °authority, guru, °mastermind, mentor, wizard: *He insists on consulting his oracle before making any final decision.* **2** °prophecy, augury, °prediction, divination, °advice, prognostication, °answer, °message, °divine utterance: *According to the oracle, the travellers would survive the perils of their journey.*

oral *adj.* °spoken, said, °verbal, uttered, voiced, vocal, vocalized, enunciated, °pronounced, articulated, word-of-mouth, viva voce: *Tomorrow James must make an oral presentation of his plan to the entire staff.*

oration *n.* °speech, °declaration, °address, °lecture, °recitation, discourse, monologue, declamation; valedictory, °eulogy, homily, panegyric; *Colloq* spiel: *Bentley delivered a long oration on the future of the economy.*

oratory *n.* °public speaking, speech-making, eloquence, °rhetoric, way with words, °command of the °language, °fluency, glibness, grandiloquence, magniloquence, declamation; elocution, °diction, enunciation, articulation, °address; *Colloq* gift of the gab: *The crowds who thronged to hear Churchill's oratory were seldom disappointed.*

orb *n.* °sphere, ball, °globe: *The golden orb of the sun sank into the sea.*

orbit *n.* **1** °circuit, °course, °path, °track, °revolution, °circle, °round, °cycle: *The earth's orbit round the sun is elliptical.* —*v.* **2** °revolve, °go °round, °circle, °encircle, °turn: *The earth orbits the sun in a year. Electrons orbit the nucleus of an atom.*

ordeal *n.* °trial, °test, tribulation(s), °hardship, °affliction, °trouble(s), °suffering, °distress, °anguish, nightmare, °misery, °grief, °misfortune, adversity, °tragedy, °disaster: *She never fully recovered from her ordeal at the hands of the kidnappers.*

order *n.* **1** °organization, °arrangement, grouping, °disposition, °form, °structure, categorization, systematization *or* systemization, classification, codification, disposal, layout, array, °sequence, *Colloq* °set-up: *The order of the library is of crucial importance if we are to find anything.* **2** °organization, °uniformity, °regularity, °system, °pattern, °symmetry, °harmony, tidiness, orderliness, neatness: *Some believe that there is an order of things in the universe, others that the universe tends to chaos.* **3** °category, °class, °caste, °level, °kind, °sort, °rank, °group, °scale, °importance, hierarchy, °position, °status, °degree, *Colloq* pecking °order: *Gregory's musical talents are of a very high order.* **4** °command, °direction, directive, °instruction, commandment, °dictate, mandate, edict, behest, °request, °demand, ukase, °decree, fiat, °proclamation, °pronouncement, pronunciamento; °rule, °regulation, °law, ordinance, statute, °requirement: *The police have issued an order to surrender all hand guns.* **5** °procedure, °proceeding(s), °discipline, °conduct: *The order of the meeting was breached by some rowdies.* **6** °condition, °state (of affairs): *Please leave everything in the order in which you found it.* **7** °purchase °order, °request, °requisition, commitment, commission, °instruction: *We received a large order for office furniture.* **8** °calm, °peace, peacefulness, tranquillity, °quiet, °serenity, °law and °order, °discipline, lawfulness: *After a brief commotion, order was restored.* **9** °brotherhood, °fraternity, sisterhood, sorority, °fellowship, sodality, °association, °organization, °society, guild, °sect, °company, community, °lodge, °body, knighthood: *One of her ancestors was a Knight of the Teutonic Order.* **10 in order: a** °neat, °clean, °tidy, °shipshape, °orderly, (°well-)organized, °ready, °prepared, arranged: *Is everything in order for the wedding tomorrow?* **b** °fitting, °suitable, °appropriate, °correct, °right, apt, called-for; required, demanded, needed: *I think that an apology is in order for the way you behaved.* **11 in order that**: so (that), with the °aim *or* °purpose that, to the °end that: *We invited him in order that you might meet him.* **12 in order to**: to, for the °purpose of: *In order to get there, you have to drive up the hill.* **13 out of order: a** disordered, non-sequential, out of °sequence, non-alphabetical, disorganized, unorganized, in °disorder: *The cards in this catalogue are out of order and I cannot find anything.* **b** °unseemly, out of °place, °improper, uncalled-for, unsuitable, indecorous, *Colloq chiefly Brit* not cricket: *Your remark about her religion was completely out of order.* **c** out of commission, °broken, in °disrepair, non-functioning, non-functional, not working, broken-down, inoperative, out of kilter *or Brit also* kelter, *Colloq* (gone) haywire,

kaput, bust(ed), *US* out of whack, on the fritz, shot; *Slang* on the °blink, *Brit* wonky, gone phut: *The telly is out of order again.*
—*v.* **14** °direct, °command, °instruct, °charge, °tell, °bid, °require, enjoin; °demand, ordain; °force, °make: *The sergeant ordered the men to run around the drill field with full packs. The council ordered that garden rubbish should be packed in special bags.* **15** °requisition, °ask for, °send (away) for, °call for, °apply for, °reserve, °engage, commission, °contract for; °purchase, °buy: *Have you ordered breakfast for tomorrow? Let's order a take-away from the Chinese restaurant.*
16 °organize, systematize, °arrange, classify, °categorize, codify, °lay out, °sort (out), °straighten (out *or* up): *The bottles were ordered in neat rows along the wall.*

orderly *adj.* **1** in (°good) °order, (°well-)organized, °neat, °shipshape, °tidy, arranged, °methodical, °systematic, systematized *or* systemized, °harmonious, °symmetrical, °regular, °uniform: *Before you leave, make sure that your room is orderly.* **2** well-behaved, disciplined, °decorous, law-abiding, well-mannered, °peaceable, °tranquil, mannerly, °polite, °courteous, °civil, civilized, non-violent: *Everyone left the burning theatre in an orderly fashion.*
—*n.* **3** °assistant, adjutant, °attendant, °messenger; °menial, °servant; nurse's °aide; *Military Brit* batman; *US* candystriper; *Slang US and Canadian* gofer: *An orderly arrived with dispatches from the general. She has a job as a hospital orderly.*

ordinarily *adv.* °usually, normally, as a °rule, commonly, °generally, in °general, customarily, routinely, typically, habitually, by and large, for the most °part: *Ellie is ordinarily at her desk by nine o'clock.*

ordinary *adj.* **1** °usual, °normal, expected, °common, °general, °customary, °routine, °typical, °habitual, °accustomed, °traditional, °regular, °everyday, °familiar, °set, °humdrum: *This wine is quite good for ordinary drinking. Just display ordinary good manners when you meet the Queen.* **2** °common, °conventional, °modest, °plain, °simple, °prosaic, °homespun, commonplace, run-of-the-mill, °everyday, °average, unpretentious, workaday, °mediocre, °fair, °passable, °so so, °undistinguished, unexceptional, unremarkable, uninspired, °pedestrian, °bourgeois, °peasant, °provincial, °unrefined, *Colloq Brit* °common *or* garden, *US* common-or-garden variety, garden-variety: *They bought a rather ordinary house in an inferior neighbourhood.*
—*n.* **3** °standard, °norm, °average, °status quo, °convention, expected: *Saint-Gaudens' architectural designs are far from the ordinary.* **4 out of the ordinary**: °extraordinary, °unusual, uncommon, °strange, °unfamiliar, °different, unexpected, unconventional, °curious, °eccentric, °peculiar, °rare, °exceptional, °original, °singular, °unique, °odd, °bizarre, °weird, °offbeat, °outlandish, °striking, °quaint, °picturesque: *She was looking for a gift that was a little out of the ordinary, so I suggested a pet tarantula.*

organ *n.* **1** °device, °instrument, °implement, °tool; °member, °part, °element, °unit, component, °structure, *Technical* process: *The eye, come to think of it, is a truly miraculous*

organ. **2** °medium, °vehicle, °voice, °mouthpiece, forum, °publication, °paper, °magazine, newsletter, house organ, newspaper, annual, semi-annual, °quarterly, monthly, fortnightly, weekly, hebdomadal, daily, °journal, °periodical: *The official organ of the Society is published in Abergavenny.*

organic *adj.* **1** living, °natural, biological, biotic, °animate, breathing: *Though coal may seem to be a mineral, it is organic, for it was formed from plants.* **2** °basic, °elementary, °essential, innate, °inborn, °natural, °native, °ingrained, °primary, °fundamental, visceral, constitutional, °inherent, structural, °integral: *The organic differences between the styles of writing are obvious.* **3** organized, °systematic, °coherent, coordinated, integrated, structured, °methodical, °orderly, °consistent: *The various elements of the painting blend into an organic whole.*

organism *n.* living thing, °structure, body; being, °creature: *It is the work of natural scientists to classify all kinds of organisms.*

organization *n.* **1** organizing, structuring, assembling, °assembly, putting together, coordination, systematizing, systematization, classifying, classification, categorizing, categorization, codifying, codification: *The organization of the school timetable took hours to complete.* **2** °structure, °pattern, configuration, °design, °plan, °scheme, °order, °system, °organism, °composition, °arrangement, constitution, °make-up, grouping, framework, °format, °form, °shape: *One must consider the organization as a whole, not merely its constituent elements.* **3** °body, °system, °institution, °federation, confederacy, confederation, °society, °group, °league, coalition, conglomerate, °combine, consortium, °syndicate, °organism: *The organization is a coherent structure made up of an enormous number of disparate elements.*

organize *v.* **1** °structure, °coordinate, systematize, systemize, °order, °arrange, °sort (out), classify, °categorize, codify, catalogue, °group, °tabulate, pigeon-hole, °standardize: *These files ought to be organized so that you can find something when you need it.* **2** °form, °found, °set up, °establish, °institute, °start, °begin, °create, °originate, °initiate, °put together, °build, °develop, *US* pull together: *In 1969, we organized a company to publish reference books.*

orgy *n.* **1** bacchanalia, bacchanal, saturnalia, Dionysia, debauch, carousal, °carouse, °spree, °revel, °party, *Colloq* binge, °bender, °drunk, bust, *Slang* °jag, *US and Canadian* toot, tear: *The journalist represented the earl's party as a wild orgy.* **2** overindulgence, °splurge, °spree, °fling, *Slang US* °bender: *Trying to lift himself out of depression, Roger went on a spending orgy.*

orient *n.* **1** east: *Harriet is in the orient on business.* —*adj.* **2** *Literary* oriental, eastern: *The grass was sown with orient pearls.*
—*v.* **3** °adjust, °adapt, acclimatize *or* acclimate, habituate, °accommodate, °condition, °accustom, °familiarize, feel one's °way, assess, get one's °bearings, *Colloq* orientate: *It is a new job and she needs a few days to orient herself.*

orientation *n.* **1** °placement, bearings, °attitude, alignment, °lie, placing, °situation, layout, °location, °position, positioning,

°arrangement, °set-up: *The orientation of the buildings is such that the windows face south.* **2** introduction, training, °initiation, briefing, familiarization, assimilation, acclimatization, °preparation, °instruction: *The orientation of the new employees is scheduled for next week. We were given orientation lectures.*

origin *n.* **1** °source, °derivation, °rise, fountain-head, °foundation, °basis, °base, well-spring, fount, provenance, *Chiefly US* provenience: *The origins of many English words are unknown.* **2** °creation, genesis, °birth, birthplace, cradle, dawning, °dawn, origination, °start, °beginning, commencement, °outset, °launch, launching, inception, inauguration: *The origin of the notion of democracy can be traced to ancient Greece.* **3** Often, **origins**: °parentage, ancestry, °extraction, descent, °lineage, °pedigree, genealogy, °stock, °heritage: *We have traced our family's origins back to the Middle Ages.*

original *adj.* **1** °initial, °first, earliest, °primary, °beginning, starting, °basic: *The original report made no mention of any missing jewellery.* **2** °native, °indigenous, autochthonous, °aboriginal, primordial, primeval *or Brit. also* primaeval, °primitive: *At first, we could only find slight traces of the original inhabitants.* **3** °master, °actual, °primary, °authentic, °true, °genuine, °real, °basic; prototypic(al), archetypal, °source: *I have the original document and my lawyer has a copy.* **4** °creative, °novel, innovative, °unique, °imaginative, °unusual, inventive, °ingenious; firsthand, °fresh, underived, unprecedented: *The film is based on a highly original story by Daphne du Maurier. The author has some original insights into Hamlet's relationship with Ophelia.* —*n.* **5** °prototype, archetype, °source, °model, °pattern; °master: *The original hangs in the National Gallery.* **6** °eccentric, °nonconformist, °individualist, *Colloq* case, °card, °character, *Brit* °queer fish: *True to his reputation as an original, Wilde sauntered down the Strand with a lily in his hand.*

originality *n.* creativeness, creativity, inventiveness, °ingenuity, innovativeness, °innovation, °novelty, newness, unorthodoxy, unconventionality, cleverness, °daring, resourcefulness, °independence, individuality, uniqueness, nonconformity: *One must admire Dali for his originality.*

originally *adv.* in *or* at *or* from the °beginning, (at) °first, from the °first, initially, to °begin with, at *or* from the °outset, at *or* from the °start, in the °first place *or* instance, *Colloq* from the word go, from day one: *Originally, we were to have gone in Patrick's car.*

originate *v.* **1** °create, °bring about, engender, give °birth to, beget, °conceive, °initiate, °inaugurate, °start, °begin, °introduce, °launch, °found, set up, °institute, °establish, °invent, °coin, °devise, °pioneer, °design, contrive, concoct, °mastermind, °compose, °organize, °formulate, °form, °generate, °produce, °develop, evolve: *Wasn't it the Chinese who originated free public health schemes?* **2** °arise, °rise, °begin, °start, °come, °spring, °stem, °flow, °issue, °emerge, °emanate, °proceed, °grow, °develop, evolve, °derive, °result: *Where did the idea of the democratic form of government originate?*

ornament *n.* **1** enhancement, °embellishment, adornment, °decoration, ornamentation, gingerbread, trimming, garnish, garnishment, °frill, embroidery, beautification, °accessory; frippery; knick-knack, furbelow, °bauble, °gewgaw, *Slang US* tchotchke: *We spent a pleasant afternoon putting ornaments on the Christmas tree. The ornaments on the mantelpiece needed dusting.* —*v.* **2** °decorate, °embellish, °enhance, adorn, °trim, garnish, embroider, °elaborate, °beautify, accessorize, deck (out), °dress up: *The cabinet is ornamented with ormolu fittings in the Empire style.*

ornamental *adj.* decorative, beautifying, adorning, garnishing, embellishing: *Nothing in the house is ornamental, everything is functional.*

ornate *adj.* °elaborate, florid, overdone, °laboured, rococo, baroque, gingerbread, arabesque, °fancy, °lavish, °rich, °flowery, °busy, °fussy, frilly, °intricate; high-flown, euphuistic, Ossianic, °bombastic, °pompous, °pretentious, °affected, °grandiose, fulsome, highfalutin *or* hifalutin, grandiloquent, °flamboyant: *Louis Quinze style is far too ornate for my tastes. We find his writing, with its contorted artificialities, far too ornate to appeal to the modern reader.*

orthodox *adj.* conformist, accepted, °authoritative, authorized, recognized, received, °official, standard, °prevailing, °prevalent, °common, °regular, °popular, °ordinary, doctrinal, established, °traditional, traditionalist, °accustomed, °conventional, °customary, °conservative: *The orthodox view is that he was killed by an assassin acting on his own.*

oscillate *v.* °fluctuate, °vibrate, waver, °see-saw, °swing, °sway; vacillate, °equivocate, °shilly-shally, hem and haw, tergiversate: *The needle is oscillating between the 'Safe' and 'Danger' marks. I wish he'd stop oscillating and make up his mind.*

ostensibly *adv.* °outwardly, externally, superficially, patently, ostensively, demonstrably, °apparently, °evidently, °seemingly; °clearly, plainly, °manifestly, conspicuously, °obviously, patently, noticeably, prominently: *Ostensibly, he was visiting his aunt, but we all know he went to see Stella.*

ostentation *n.* °show, °display, °exhibition, exhibitionism, showing off, °pretension, pretentiousness, flaunting, flashiness, °flourish, flamboyance, °parade, window-dressing: *His clothes are elegant without ostentation.*

ostentatious *adj.* °showy, °boastful, °braggart, vaunting, °vain, vainglorious, flaunting, °pretentious, °flamboyant, °theatrical, *Colloq* °flash: *It's terribly ostentatious of Lady Penny to wear her diamond tiara to the disco.*

ostracize *v.* blackball, blacklist, °banish, °exile, °boycott, °isolate, °segregate, °exclude, excommunicate, snub, °shun, °avoid, *Chiefly Brit* send to Coventry, *Colloq* °cut, cold-shoulder, give (someone) the cold °shoulder: *Marcus has been ostracized at the club ever since the court case.*

otherwise *adv.* **1** if not, or else, under other circumstances, in another °situation, on the other hand: *I learned something about you tonight that otherwise I should never have guessed.* **2** differently, in another °manner *or* °way: *You may travel unless the doctor advises otherwise.*

out *adv.* **1** °outside, outdoors, in *or* into the open °air: *If you go out take an umbrella.* **2** away (from), °abroad, °elsewhere, not (at) °home, gone (from), gone away (from), °absent (from): *She was out of the house when I phoned.* **3** in *or* into the open, to *or* into °public °notice, for all to see, out of the closet: *Everything will be brought out at the trial.* **4** revealed, exposed, °visible, °discernible, °manifest, in °sight, in °view: *Are the stars out tonight?* **5** °short, minus, missing, in °default, out of pocket: *He is out the £2,000 he invested in a Welsh diamond mine.* **6** °free, at °liberty, at °large, °loose, unconfined: *They let Matilda out after she served her sentence.* **7** °completely, °thoroughly, effectively, °entirely: *I was tired out after that long swim.* —*adj.* **8** °unconscious, °senseless, °insensible, *Colloq* out °cold, out like a light: *He has been out for almost an hour.* **9** dated, out-dated, out-moded, °passé, °old-fashioned, °antiquated, °old hat, *démodé,* °obsolete, unfashionable: *Longer skirts were out in the mid-1960s.* **10** °often, **outer**: outlying, °distant, far-off, °peripheral: *He was planning to travel to the outer reaches of his empire. Let's sail to some of the out islands.* **11** °exhausted, gone, finished, ended; over, completed: *Our food was out. Rescue came before the day was out.* **12** °inaccurate, °incorrect, °wrong, at °fault, °faulty, °off, °wide of the mark: *Your figures are out by a factor of four.* **13** °unacceptable, forbidden, prohibited, not allowed, *Colloq* not on: *Smoking is out in the dining room.* **14** extinguished, unlit; °off, doused; inoperative, non-functioning, out of °order *or* commission, unserviceable, °broken: *Make certain that all camp-fires are completely out. The light is out in the corridor.* —*n.* **15** °alibi, °excuse, °escape, °loophole, °evasion: *She used your visit as an out to avoid calling on her mother.*

out-and-out *adj.* °complete, °unmitigated, un-alloyed, °undiluted, °pure, utter, °perfect, consummate, °outright, °total, °downright, °unqualified, °thorough, thoroughgoing, through-and-through, dyed in the wool: *She was an out-and-out fool to turn down his marriage proposal.*

outburst *n.* outbreak, °eruption, °explosion, blow-up, flare-up, fulmination; upsurge, °surge, °outpouring, welling (forth), upwelling, outflow(ing), °rush, °flood, effusion, effluence *or* efflux; °fit, access, °attack, °spasm, °paroxysm, °seizure, °tantrum: *Another outburst like that, young man, and you'll be sent home.*

outcast *n.* pariah, °exile, °reject, *persona non grata,* leper, untouchable, expatriate, °refugee, displaced person, DP, evacuee: *In 1946, Europe swarmed with outcasts, the detritus of the war.*

outcome *n.* °result, consequence, °end (°result *or* °product), after-effect, °effect, °upshot, °sequel, °development, outgrowth, aftermath, °wake, °follow-up, *Medicine* sequela (usually *pl.* sequelae), *Colloq* °pay-off, bottom line: *One outcome of the new safety regulations will be higher fares. We eagerly awaited the outcome of the race.*

outcry *n.* °protest, protestation, decrial, °complaint, °indignation, °uproar, vociferation, clamour, clamouring, commotion, °outburst, °noise, hullabaloo, °howl, howling, hoot, hooting, boo, booing, °hiss, hissing: *The public outcry against terrorism was heard round the world.*

outdo *v.* °exceed, °surpass, °excel, °transcend, °beat, °outstrip, outshine, °top, °cap, trump, °overcome, °defeat, °outweigh: *Their prices are lower because they outdo us in cheapness of labour.*

outdoor *adj.* °outside, out of doors, alfresco, open-air: *Both of them enjoy outdoor activities like hiking and bicycling.*

outfit *n.* **1** °gear, °rig, °equipment, equipage, °apparatus, accoutrements *or US also* accouterments, °paraphernalia, °trappings, °tackle, °tack, utensils: *His mountain-climbing outfit turned out to be extremely expensive.* **2** °clothes, °costume, °ensemble; attire, garb, clothing, °dress; *Colloq* °get-up, togs: *She was wearing a very weird outfit that attracted a lot of stares.* **3** °firm, °concern, °business, °organization, °company, (military) °unit, corporation; °party, °set, °group; *Colloq* °set-up: *I joined the outfit when it consisted of only a hundred people.* —*v.* **4** °fit (out *or* up), °equip, °kit out, °provision, °stock, accoutre *or US also* accouter, °rig (out *or* up), °supply, °furnish: *The shop is prepared to outfit anyone for anything from a walk in the country to an African safari or an Arctic expedition.*

outgoing *adj.* **1** departing, °retiring, ex-, °former, °past, emeritus, leaving, withdrawing: *It is our custom to honour the outgoing president with a banquet.* **2** °genial, °friendly, °amiable, °cordial, °warm, °expansive, approachable, affable, °accessible, amenable, °easygoing, °amicable, °sociable, congenial, extrovert, °familiar, °informal, communicative: *Because of his outgoing attitude, Keith gets along well with most people.*

outing *n.* jaunt, junket, °excursion, °trip, °expedition, °tour, °ride, *Colloq* °spin: *This year, the annual church outing will again be to Torquay.*

outlandish *adj.* °unfamiliar, °strange, °odd, °queer, °offbeat, °peculiar, °curious, °exotic, °foreign, °alien, °unknown, °unheard-of, °different, °exceptional, °extraordinary, °quaint, °eccentric, °bizarre, *outré,* °weird, °fantastic, °unusual, °singular, °unique; freakish, °grotesque, barbarous; *Colloq* °camp(y), °kinky: *Those youngsters wear the most outlandish hair-dos you have ever seen.*

outlast *v.* °survive, outlive; outwear; °weather: *Considering her condition, it seems doubtful that she will outlast her husband.*

outlaw *n.* **1** °criminal, °gangster, °robber, desperado, bandit, highwayman, brigand, footpad, picaroon *or* pickaroon, °pirate, °fugitive (from justice *or* the law), °renegade, *US* road-agent: *In Westerns, the sheriff always wins out over the outlaws.* —*v.* **2** °forbid, disallow, °ban, interdict, °bar, °exclude, °prohibit, proscribe: *Some countries have outlawed prostitution, but with little effect.*

outlay *n.* °expense, °cost, °expenditure, spending, disbursement, °payment: *The city council refused to approve the outlay for a new swimming-pool.*

outlet *n.* **1** °way out, °exit, egress, °loophole, °relief, °escape, °escape hatch, °vent, °opening, °release, safety-valve, °discharge: *There seemed to be no outlet for his anger but to throw the cushion at her. The main outlet of the Great Lakes is the St Lawrence river.* **2** retailer, °shop, °store, °market: *The company is having difficulty finding outlets that will stock its products.*

outline n. 1 °profile, °silhouette, contour, °periphery, °boundary, footprint: *This outline is of the desk area occupied by the keyboard and monitor.* 2 °précis, °synopsis, résumé, °summary, °digest, °abstract, conspectus, °survey, overview, °run-down, recapitulation, °review, (°thumbnail) sketch, skeleton, (°overall) °plan, layout, framework, °draft, °scenario: *O'Brien presented an outline of what his company planned to do after the take-over.*
—v. 3 °trace, °draft, sketch, °rough out, °profile, °block (out), °plan (out), °lay out, °define, delineate: *None of the divers was particularly enthusiastic about the procedure outlined for bringing up the wreckage.*

outlook n. 1 °view, °position, °point of °view, °viewpoint, °prospect, °perspective, °slant, °angle, °standpoint, °attitude, °opinion: *His outlook on the situation in the Middle East is bound to be somewhat biased.* 2 °prospect, °forecast, °expectation(s): *What is the outlook for the value of the pound sterling over the next year?*

outlying adj. °distant, far-off, far-flung, outer, outermost, °out-of-the-way, °remote, °far-away, °peripheral, furthest or farthest: *In those days it took weeks for the news to reach the outlying parts of the empire.*

out-of-the-way adj. 1 untravelled, unfrequented, °isolated, °lonely, °outlying, °obscure, hidden, °secluded, °inaccessible: *She now lives in some out-of-the-way village in the Himalayas.* 2 °unusual, °odd, °peculiar, °extraordinary, °far-fetched, °remarkable, °outré, °exceptional, °outlandish, °strange, °rare, uncommon, °exotic, °unheard-of, unconventional, °queer, °weird, °bizarre: *His latest book is a treatise on some out-of-the-way subject.*

outpouring n. effusion, outflow, °flow, °outburst, °flood, deluge, °torrent, °spate, emanation, spouting, °spurt, gushing, efflux, effluence, outrush, tide, cascade, cataract, Niagara, *Technical* debouchment: *We scarcely expected such an outpouring of grief at her death. This writing appears to reflect the outpourings of his soul.*

output n. 1 °production, °result, °yield, crop, °harvest: *Nobody was quite ready for such a massive output.* 2 productivity, °achievement, °efficiency: *Job insecurity has diminished her output.*
—v. 3 °put out, °produce, °generate, °create, °manufacture, °yield, °achieve: *Our new laser printer outputs about ten pages a minute.*

outrage n. 1 °violence, °atrocity, inhumanity, barbarism, °enormity, °evil, °barbarity, savagery, brutality, malignity, malefaction, wrong-doing, evil-doing, maltreatment, °abuse, cruelty, °injury, °harm, °damage: *Wherever there is war there is misery and outrage.* 2 °resentment, affront, °bitterness, °indignation, °hurt, °shock, °anger, wrath, ire: *The minister felt outrage at being given a parking ticket.* 3 °insult, °indignity, °slight: *Contributors to the charity considered it an outrage that the fund-raisers should keep so much of the money.*
—v. 4 °offend, °insult, affront, vex, °displease, °distress, nettle, °chafe, °infuriate, °anger, °enrage, °madden, make one's blood °boil, raise (someone's) hackles, rile: *He was outraged to discover that the wretch had proposed to his daughter.* 5 °violate, °desecrate, defile, do

violence to, °injure, °harm, °abuse, °damage: *Such deeds outrage human feelings.* 6 °rape, °violate, °ravage, °ravish, deflower, °attack: *He seized the unhappy girl and outraged her.*

outrageous adj. 1 °excessive, °extravagant, °immoderate, °exorbitant, °enormous, °unreasonable, °preposterous, °shocking, °extreme, °unwarranted, exaggerated, °unconscionable, °inordinate, intolerable, °disgraceful, °shameful, °scandalous: *The prices at that restaurant are absolutely outrageous.* 2 °vicious, °cruel, heinous, °atrocious, barbaric, °inhuman, °abusive, °beastly, °horrible, horrid, horrendous, iniquitous, °villainous, °wicked, °evil, egregious, °flagrant, °grievous, °infamous, execrable, °abominable, °grisly, °hideous, °monstrous, °vile, °unthinkable, °foul, °awful, unspeakable, appalling, °offensive, °indecent: *The captives suffered the most outrageous treatment at the hands of their conquerors.* 3 °indecent, °offensive, °immoral, °rude, indelicate, °obnoxious, °profane, °obscene, °dirty, °filthy, °lewd, salacious, °foul, smutty, scatological, °pornographic, objectionable, °repellent, °repulsive, nauseating, °nauseous, °nasty, °gross, °revolting, °shocking, °repugnant, °disgusting, fulsome, °perverted, depraved, °dissolute, °degenerate, dissipated, debauched, °profligate; °explicit, unrestrained; foul-mouthed, thersitical, insulting; °unseemly, °inappropriate, indecorous, °improper, °naughty, appalling, °embarrassing; *Literary* Fescennine, *US* shy-making: *The sermon denounced the outrageous films, books, magazines, and television programmes to which children are exposed. Warren sometimes says the most outrageous things.*

outré adj. unconventional, °unusual, °extravagant, °bizarre, °weird, °strange, °odd, °peculiar, °grotesque, °outlandish, freakish, °out-of-the-way: *The attention of the media was turned upon the singer's outré behaviour on stage.*

outright adj. 1 °unqualified, °total, unreserved, unrestricted, full, °complete, unconditional, unequivocal, °clear, °direct, °definite, unmistakable: *The duke is the outright owner of the property.* 2 °undisguised, °unmitigated, utter, consummate, °pure, °out-and-out, all-out, °sheer, °absolute, °stark, bald, °thorough, arrant, thoroughgoing, through-and-through, °downright, °direct, °definite, unmistakable: *Her outright refusal to provide further help was met with dismay.*
—adv. 3 °directly, at °once, °immediately, °instantaneously, instantly, then and there or there and then, °straight or °right away, on the °spot, °right off: *One passenger was killed outright, the other died later in hospital.* 4 °completely, °entirely, °exactly, °precisely, °totally, *in toto,* °utterly, baldly, starkly, consummately, purely, °thoroughly, °directly, unhesitatingly, °quite, °absolutely, explicitly, categorically, straightforwardly, plainly, °openly, forthrightly, unequivocally, unambiguously, candidly: *I wish that Henry wasn't so reticent and would say outright what he means.* 5 unrestrictedly, unqualifiedly, unreservedly, unconditionally: *The duke owns the property outright.*

outset n. °beginning, °start, inauguration, inception, °first, *Colloq* kick-off: *Had you let them know who you were at the outset, this wouldn't have happened.*

outside *n.* **1** °exterior, °face, °facing, °shell, °skin, °case, casing, °surface, °front; façade: *What is that on the outside of the box? The outside of the house is painted white.* **2** °aspect, °appearance, °look, demeanour, °face, °front, façade, mien, °mask, °disguise, °false °front, °pretence: *One cannot tell what people are really like from the outside they present to the world.* **3** °extreme, °limit, most, °maximum, utmost, best, worst, longest: *At the outside, you shouldn't pay more than half your income for housing. I'll wait for her for an hour at the outside.* **4** the world at °large: *We had to bring in someone from the outside to complete the work.*
—*adj.* **5** °exterior, °external, out-of-doors, °outdoor: *They have added an outside swimming-pool to the house.* **6** °maximum, maximal, highest, best, worst, greatest, most, largest, longest, furthest *or* farthest: *What was their outside estimate for replacing the roof? The outside time for driving here from London is about an hour.* **7** °private, °home, cottage, °secondary, °peripheral, °independent, freelance: *Her outside job pays more than her regular work.* **8** °unlikely, °remote, °faint, *Colloq* °slim: *He has an outside chance of beating the world record.* **9** °foreign, °alien, °outward; unconnected, excluded, uninvolved, disinvolved, °independent, °separate, °different: *I'm worried that Phil might be subject to outside influences. An outside contractor is doing the work.*
—*adv.* **10** outdoors, out of doors: *Perhaps you'd like to step outside to discuss the matter further?*

outsider *n.* non-member, non-initiate, °foreigner, °alien, outlander, °stranger, °newcomer, °guest, °visitor, trespasser, interloper, °intruder, squatter, invader, *Colloq* gate-crasher: *The others always treated Peter as an outsider. Why do I feel an outsider in my own home?*

outskirts *n.pl.* °periphery, °edge, environs, outer reaches, °vicinity, °border(s), suburb(s), exurb(s), general °area *or* °neighbourhood, purlieus, °fringes, vicinage, faubourg(s): *The university is on the outskirts of the city.*

outsmart *v.* °outwit, outfox, out-think, out-manoeuvre, outmanipulate, outplay, steal a march on, get the better *or* best of, °trick, °dupe, °hoodwink, °fool, °deceive, °hoax, gull, make a °fool of; °swindle, °cheat, °defraud, cozen, *Colloq* °put one over on, pull a fast one on, °take in, make a °monkey (out) of, bamboozle, con, *Brit* nobble, *Slang* °slip *or* °put one *or* something over on (someone): *'I have been outsmarted by bigger fools than you!', Mr White shouted.*

outspoken *adj.* °candid, °frank, °open, °free, °direct, unreserved, unreticent, straightforward, °forthright, °explicit, °specific, plain-spoken, plain-speaking, unequivocal, unceremonious, unambiguous, unsubtle, °uninhibited, unshrinking, °blunt, °bold, °brusque, °brash, undiplomatic, °tactless, °crude: *Linda was always quite outspoken in her opinions of her neighbours. Her outspoken observations are a fruitful source of gossip.*

outstanding *adj.* **1** °prominent, °eminent, °renowned, °famous, famed, unforgettable, °memorable, °celebrated, °distinguished, °special, °choice, °noteworthy, °notable, °noted, °important, °conspicuous, °exceptional, °excellent, °superior, first-class, °first-rate, °superb, °remarkable, °extraordinary, °marvellous, °sensational, *Colloq* smashing,

°super: *Liszt was the outstanding pianist-composer of his time.* **2** °unsettled, on-going, °unresolved, °unpaid, °due, owed *or* owing, receivable *or* °payable; °remaining, °leftover: *The company has a few outstanding debts.*

outstrip *v.* °overcome, °surpass, °outdo, outperform, outshine, outclass, °better, °beat, °transcend, °best, worst, °exceed, °excel, out-distance, °overtake, °top, °cap, put in the °shade, °eclipse: *Bannister again outstripped everyone in the race.*

outward *adj.* °external, °exterior, outer, °outside, °outlying, °manifest, °obvious, °evident, °apparent, °visible, observable; °superficial, °surface, °extrinsic, °skin-deep, °shallow, °pretended, °false, ostensible, °formal, °physical, bodily, fleshly, °carnal, mundane, °worldly, °secular, °temporal, °terrestrial, °material, non-spiritual: *She gave every outward sign of being the bereaved widow. Whatever outward trappings money may buy, A man's true wealth lies deep inside.*

outwardly *adv.* externally, °apparently, visibly, superficially, °ostensibly, °evidently, °seemingly, on the °surface, to all appearances, to all intents and purposes: *Though the town was outwardly quiet, we had a feeling of ominous foreboding.*

outwards *adv.* °outward, °outside, away, °out, without: *The towns of the early twentieth century centred on the railway station and radiated outwards.*

outweigh *v.* °overcome, outbalance, over-balance, overweigh, tip the scales, preponderate (over), °surpass, °prevail (over), override, take °precedence (over), °compensate (for), °make up for: *His feeling for his wife outweighed all else in his life.*

outwit *v.* See outsmart, above.

oval *adj.* egg-shaped, ovoid, ovate, oviform, obovoid, obovate; elliptical, ellipsoid(al): *His mother's picture hung in an oval frame over the mantel.*

ovation *n.* °applause, acclamation, acclaim, plaudits, °cheers, cheering, clapping, laudation, °praise, °kudos, *Colloq* (big) °hand: *At the conclusion of the concerto, the pianist was given a standing ovation.*

over *prep.* **1** above, on, upon, on °top of, atop (of): *She spread a tarpaulin over the boat to protect it.* **2** more than, greater than, upwards *or* upward of, in °excess of, (over and) above, (over and) beyond; °exceeding: *Of the 2,000 people questioned in our survey, over half said they think prunes are funny. The thieves took over £50,000-worth of paintings.* **3** across, to *or* from *or* on the other °side of; beyond: *The children crossed over the river to play in the woods on the other side.* **4** °for, during, in *or* over *or* during the °course of, °through, °throughout: *Over the next week she will be working in the Paris office.* **5** (all) through, °throughout, (all) about, all over: *We travelled over the entire country in the course of our holiday.*
—*adj.* **6** done (with), finished, terminated, concluded, ended, °past, settled, closed, at an °end, over with: *I'm afraid it's all over between us, Carrie.*
—*adv.* **7** °to, onto, °past, beyond, across: *This room looks out over the sea.* **8** °remaining, as a °remainder, as °surplus, °outstanding: *When we finished eating, there wasn't much left over.* **9** (once) again, once more, one more time: *This pot will have to be cleaned over again.* **10** down, to the ground *or* floor: *You almost knocked over the lamp.*

overall adj. °total, °complete, °comprehensive, all-inclusive, °inclusive, °whole, °entire, all-embracing, blanket: *The overall cost, including materials and labour, came to more than I had expected.*

overawe v. °overwhelm, °intimidate, cow, °daunt, awe, °bully, hector, °browbeat, °dominate, domineer, °frighten, °scare, °terrify, disconcert, °discomfit, °upset, abash: *The children were overawed by their father's slightest sign of displeasure.*

overbearing adj. °repressive, °domineering, bullying, imperious, °officious, °high and °mighty, high-handed, overweening, magisterial, lordly, °authoritarian, °wilful, °despotic, °dogmatic, autocratic, °tyrannical, °dictatorial, °peremptory, °arbitrary, °assertive, °arrogant, cavalier, °haughty, °superior, °supercilious, °pretentious, *Colloq* °bossy, °pushy, °hoity-toity, highfalutin *or* hifalutin, snooty, *Slang* snotty: *His temper was harsh and severe, his manner haughty and overbearing.*

overcast adj. cloudy, clouded, °sunless, moonless, starless, °murky, °grey, louring *or* lowering, °dull, °dark, darkened, °dreary, °sombre, °gloomy, °dismal, °threatening, °menacing: *The sky was overcast this morning, but the sun is now beginning to shine through.*

overcome v. **1** °beat, °defeat, °conquer, °overpower, °subdue, worst, °best, °triumph over, °win (out) (over), °prevail (over), °overthrow, °overwhelm, vanquish, get the better *or* best of, °whip, drub, °rout, °break, °subjugate, °suppress, °crush, °master, *Colloq* lick: *If we do not overcome these temptations, they will overcome us. The superior force easily overcame the tiny group of defenders.*
—adj. **2** beaten, defeated, overwhelmed, °subdued, worsted, bested; °affected, °speechless, swept off one's feet, rendered °helpless, overpowered, moved, influenced, at a loss (for words), *Colloq* bowled over: *The victim's parents were overcome with grief when the casualty list was published. Colin was too overcome to speak at the award presentation.*

overconfident adj. **1** °brash, °arrogant, cocksure, °cocky, °brazen, hubristic, swaggering, °audacious, °overbearing, vainglorious, *Colloq* °pushy: *It is harmful for a sportsman's morale to be overconfident of winning.* **2** °heedless, °foolhardy, °thoughtless, °short-sighted, °hasty: *Rock-climbers should not be overconfident and rely entirely on their ropes.*

overcritical adj. supercritical, hypercritical, captious, carping, °niggling, cavilling, °querulous, °fault-finding, °finicky, °fussy, °hair-splitting, °difficult, °fastidious, °harsh, °severe, °demanding, °exacting, small, °small-minded, *US and Canadian* picayune, *Colloq* picky, nit-picking, pernickety *or US also* persnickety: *You should not be overcritical of Maddy—she's only a child.*

overcrowded adj. jammed, °packed, °congested, °populous, over-populous, jam-packed, overpopulated; swarming, crawling, choked, °packed to the gunwales: *The planet is becoming overcrowded. We squeezed into an already overcrowded train.*

overdo v. **1** carry to °excess, overindulge, be intemperate, go *or* carry to °extremes, overact, °exaggerate, carry *or* go too far, overreach, not know when to stop, paint the lily, gild refined gold, out-Herod Herod, *Colloq* go overboard, do to death, lay it on thick, °lay it on with a trowel; go off the deep end: *Exercise a little judgement and try not to overdo it.* **2** °overwork, do too much, overtax, °exhaust, °fatigue, °overload, overburden, *Colloq* bite off more than one can chew, burn the candle at both ends: *Don't overdo it or you'll feel the results tomorrow.*

overdue adj. °late, °tardy, behindhand, behind, unpunctual, °belated, *US* past °due: *As it is now December, payment is long overdue. I've got an overdue library book to return.*

overeat v. °gorge, binge, gormandize, °stuff oneself, overindulge, guzzle, °feast, wolf down, overfeed, do the gavage, *Colloq* pack away, *Brit* pig, *US* pig out: *People not only overeat but they tend to eat the wrong foods.*

overgrown adj. covered, °overrun, overspread, °luxuriant, weedy, °abundant: *The walls are all overgrown with ivy.*

overhang v. **1** °jut (out), beetle, °bulge (out), °project (out), °protrude, °stick out, °loom (out), °extend (out), °hang (out) over: *The balcony overhangs the sea.* **2** impend, °threaten, °menace, imperil, °loom: *His life was overhung by the threat of blackmail.*
—n. **3** °ledge, °projection, °bulge, °protrusion, °extension: *A swallow nested under the overhang of the roof.*

overhaul v. **1** °overtake, °pass, °gain on *or* upon, °draw °ahead of, catch up with, get ahead of, °outstrip, outdistance, °leave behind, °lap: *We overhauled the ketch and were beginning to close on the yawl when the squall hit us.* **2** °renovate, °refurbish, recondition, rebuild, °restore, °repair, °service, °adjust, °patch (up), °mend, °fix (up): *The car engine needs to be thoroughly overhauled.*
—n. **3** reconditioning, overhauling, refurbishing, rebuilding, renovation, servicing, °adjustment, mending, fixing (up): *The overhaul of the die-stamping machine will require two months to complete.*

overhead adv. **1** (up) above, (up) in the °air *or* °sky, °high up, on °high, °aloft, skyward: *The aeroplanes passed overhead at dawn.*
—adj. **2** °elevated, raised, °upper: *The crane travels on an overhead track.*
—n. **3** *Brit* overheads, *US* overhead (basic *or* fixed) costs, operating °cost(s), °expense(s), °outlay, disbursement(s), °running °cost(s), °expenditure(s), °maintenance, °cost(s) of doing °business: *One way to increase profits is by reducing overheads.*

overjoyed adj. °delighted, °ecstatic, °elated, °happy, °rapturous, euphoric, jubilant, thrilled, cock-a-hoop, transported, *Colloq* tickled pink, in seventh °heaven, on cloud nine, *Brit* over the moon: *We were overjoyed to hear your news and to receive the invitation to your wedding.*

overlap v. **1** °lap (over), overlie, overlay, shingle, *Technical* imbricate, strobilate: *Note how the upper tiles overlap the lower to keep the rain out.* **2** °coincide, °correspond, intersect: *Our work shifts overlap by four hours.*
—n. **3** °lap, °flap, overlay, °fly (front) *or Brit* flies, imbrication: *The overlap conceals the buttons that close the skirt on the side.*

overload v. **1** °weigh down, °burden, overburden, °load (up), overtax, saddle with, °tax,

°strain, °impede, °handicap, °oppress, °encumber, cumber, overcharge: *They overloaded me with so much work that I'll never finish.* —*n.* **2** surcharge, overcharge, overburden, dead °weight, °oppression, °handicap, °tax, °load, °encumbrance, °impediment, °hindrance: *We had to hire extra people at Christmas to help deal with the overload.*

overlook *v.* **1** °miss, °slip up on, °omit, °neglect, °slight, °disregard, °fail to notice, °ignore, °pass over, °leave out, °forget, *Colloq* °pass up: *You overlooked an error on the first page.* **2** °blink at, wink at, °let go (by), °let pass, °let ride, turn a blind eye to, °shut (one's) eyes to, pretend not to °notice, take no °notice of, °ignore, °disregard, °forgive, °pardon, °excuse, °permit, °allow, °forget about, °write off, condone, make allowances (for), °let bygones be bygones, °gloss over: *I shall overlook your slowness if you will work late to compensate for it.* **3** °front on (to), °face, °give upon, °command *or* °afford a °view of, °look out on *or* over, have as a vista *or* °view: *My room overlooks the lake.*

overly *adv.* excessively, too, °exceedingly, immoderately, disproportionately, °unduly, inordinately, extraordinarily, °very, *Colloq* damned: *She seemed overly anxious for us to leave.*

overpower *v.* **1** °overcome, °overwhelm, °beat, vanquish, °conquer, °defeat, °crush, °put down, worst, °best, °prevail, °master, °quell, °subdue, °subjugate: *The thugs easily overpowered the elderly couple and took their money.* **2** °overcome, °overwhelm, °dumbfound *or* dumfound, °daze, °stagger, °amaze, °stun, stupefy, °nonplus, °strike, *Colloq* °floor: *I was quite overpowered by the grandeur of the house.*

overpowering *adj.* °overwhelming, °irresistible, °powerful, °telling, compelling, unendurable, °unbearable, °oppressive: *They presented an overpowering argument against the use of asbestos as an insulator.*

overrate *v.* overvalue, °make too much of, °exaggerate the °worth *or* value of, °attach too much °importance to, overprize, assess too °highly: *They insist that his value to the company is overrated and that he should be dismissed.*

overreact *v.* °exaggerate, make much ado about nothing, °make too much of (something), make a mountain out of a molehill, lose all *or* one's sense of proportion, °blow (up) out of (all) proportion: *I'd say that she overreacted by leaving him because he forgot her birthday.*

overriding *adj.* °dominant, dominating, °predominant, predominating, compelling, °prevailing, °primary, °prime, most °important, overruling, °overwhelming, °paramount, preponderant, °principal, °cardinal, °main, °chief: *His overriding reason for buying the larger dictionary was that it made a better doorstop.*

overrun *v.* invade, °defeat, °attack, °ravage, °destroy, °overwhelm, °conquer, harry, vandalize, °plunder, maraud, °scourge, despoil, °sack, °strip, °pillage, °storm, *Colloq* blitz: *Within a week the armies had overrun the country and captured the capital city.*

overseas *adv.* °abroad: *Did you serve overseas during the war?*

oversee *v.* °direct, °manage, °watch (over), °keep an °eye on, °administer, superintend, °run,

°supervise, °operate, °manipulate, °handle, °control: *We employed Gertrude to oversee our offices in Frankfurt.*

overseer *n.* °superintendent, °supervisor, °manager, °foreman, forewoman, °superior, *Colloq* °boss, °chief, °super, *Brit* gaffer, *US* straw °boss, (°head *or* °chief) honcho: *Simon is too hard a taskmaster to be overseer of that sensitive operation.*

overshadow *v.* **1** °dominate, outshine, °eclipse, °dwarf, °diminish, °minimize, put in *or* throw into *or* leave the °shade, steal the limelight from, °tower over *or* above, °excel: *The Crown, overshadowed by the great barons, turned for aid to the Church.* **2** °spoil, °blight, °ruin, °mar, take (all) the pleasure from, put a damper on, take the edge off, °impair, take the enjoyment out of: *The news from the east overshadowed everyone's spirits at the party.*

oversight *n.* **1** °omission, inadvertence, °neglect, laxity, laxness, °fault, °failure, dereliction, °error, °mistake, °blunder, carelessness, heedlessness: *It was owing to an oversight by a clerk that the flight booking was not made.* **2** supervision, superintendence, °surveillance, °management, °direction, °guidance, °administration; °charge, °care, °custody, keeping, °hands, °protection, °auspices: *The matter of expenses must be left to the oversight of the committee established to deal with such things.*

overstate *v.* °exaggerate, °magnify, hyperbolize, embroider, overstress, °colour, °make (too) much of, overdraw, overemphasize, °stretch, °enlarge, °inflate, °blow up: *They might have overstated the problem by asking for a 24-hour police guard.*

overstep *v.* °exceed, °transcend, °surpass, °go beyond: *Again Hortense has overstepped the bounds of propriety by inviting herself to the reception.*

overt *adj.* °apparent, °evident, °plain, °clear, °obvious, °manifest, clear-cut, unconcealed, °patent, °open, °visible, °observable, °public: *Moving the troops to the border may be considered an act of overt hostility.*

overtake *v.* **1** catch (up with *or* to), °reach, draw °level *or* °even with, °overhaul, °gain on *or* upon, °move by *or* °past, °pass, °leave behind, °outstrip, outdistance: *The express train overtakes the local one at Amersham.* **2** °come upon, °seize, catch (unprepared), befall, °strike, °hit, °overwhelm: *The weaknesses of old age overtook the actress before she could finish writing her memoirs.*

overthrow *v.* **1** °defeat, °beat, °rout, °conquer, °overpower, °master, °bring down, depose, oust, °overwhelm, unseat, unhorse, °topple, °overturn, dethrone, thrash, worst, °best: *The new leader was overthrown by the partisans in two weeks. Cotswold Rangers overthrew Kent United in last night's match at Hurley.* —*n.* **2** °defeat, °rout, °conquest, deposing, ousting, unseating, toppling, °overturn, overturning, °downfall, °end, °ruin, °fall, collapse, °destruction, °suppression, quashing, crushing, subjugation, *US* ouster: *The overthrow of the military regime was followed by weeks of rioting and looting.*

overtone *n.* undertone, connotation, °hint, °suggestion, °innuendo, insinuation, intimation, °indication, °implication: *Do I detect overtones of regret now that you are finally leaving?*

overture n. Often, **overtures**: °approach, °advance, °offer, °proposal, °proposition, °tender: *While they were winning, they rejected all peace overtures.*

overturn v. **1** °turn over, °knock down or over, °tip over, °capsize, up-end, °upset, °turn turtle, °turn upside down, °turn °topsy-turvy, invert: *The tanks overturned when they tried to drive past the huge concrete barriers. On his first day as a waiter, he overturned the soup in a guest's lap.* **2** °bring down, °overthrow, °throw over, °upset, depose, unthrone, unseat, oust, °eject: *The dictatorship was overturned and the country returned to being a democratic republic.*
—n. **3** overturning, °overthrow, unseating, ousting, toppling, °fall, °destruction, °ruin, °defeat, US ouster: *Could the overturn of the present regime be effected without force of arms?*

overwhelm v. **1** °overpower, °overcome, overtax, °devastate, °stagger, °crush, °defeat, °destroy, °subdue, °suppress, °quash, °quell, °conquer, °beat, °bring down, °prostrate, °weigh down, °oppress: *Overwhelmed by grief, she dissolved into tears.* **2** inundate, °overcome, engulf, °submerge, °flood (over); deluge, °swamp, °bury, °immerse: *A feeling of terror suddenly overwhelmed me as I watched my safety rope fray and break. In only a few hours the rising waters had completely overwhelmed the house.* **3** °overcome, °stagger, °astound, °astonish, °dumbfound or dumfound, °shock, °stun, °bewilder, °confuse, confound, °nonplus, °surprise, °take aback, Colloq °bowl over, °knock off one's feet or pins, blow one's °mind, discombobulate, Brit °knock for six: *We were overwhelmed by the friendly reception that awaited our return.*

overwhelming adj. **1** °overpowering, uncontrollable, °irresistible, °devastating, unendurable, °unbearable, crushing, °burdensome, °formidable: *He had an overwhelming sense of shame for what he had said.* **2** °awesome, awe-inspiring, stupefying, astounding, astonishing, staggering, bewildering, mind-shattering, °prodigious, mind-boggling, Colloq mind-blowing: *When I first went to live in London, I found its sheer size totally overwhelming.*

overwork v. **1** overexert, overstrain, overburden, °oppress, overtax, °overload, overuse: *We were so overworked that the quality had to suffer.* **2** °slave (away), burn the midnight oil, lucubrate: *She insisted on overworking in order to get the project finished on time.*
—n. **3** overexertion, overstrain, °strain: *I was ready to drop from overwork.*

overwrought adj. **1** °tense, °nervous, jittery, °jumpy, fidgety, °touchy, in a dither or °twitter, all a-twitter, overexcited, on °edge, over-stimulated, °frantic, frenetic, distracted, Brit strung up, US strung out, Colloq (all) worked up, edgy, in a tizzy, wound up, uptight: *They were quite overwrought worrying about the children's safety.* **2** overworked, °ornate, °elaborate, baroque, rococo, florid, °flowery, °fussy, °ostentatious, °busy, °gaudy, °garish: *Some of the Victorian houses were characterized by overwrought gingerbread decoration. A few of his poems are overwrought and difficult to digest.*

owe v. **1** be in °debt to, be °indebted to, be °beholden to: *It must be a good feeling not to owe anyone any money at all.* **2 owing to**: because of, on °account of, thanks to; °through, as a °result of, resulting from, Colloq °due to: *Owing to my schedule, I cannot stay the night. The higher tides are owing to the positions of the sun and moon.*

owner n. possessor, holder; °proprietor, proprietress: *The papers have been returned to their rightful owner. Who is the owner of the property?*

P

pace *n.* **1** °step, stride: *Please walk forward two paces.* **2** °rate (of °speed), °tempo, °speed, °velocity, *Colloq* °clip: *We were proceeding at a pace of five miles per hour.* —*v.* **3** °walk, stride, tread; °traverse: *Alistair paced up and down nervously, waiting for word from the surgeon.* **4** °measure, °gauge *or* gage, °judge, °rate, °estimate, °determine, °reckon, °figure, °compute: *I was trying to pace myself to conserve some energy for a sprint finish.*

pack *n.* **1** °parcel, °package, °packet, °bundle, bale, backpack, knapsack, rucksack, haversack, kitbag, °kit, duffle *or* duffel °bag: *The stranger hoisted his pack onto his shoulder and loped off.* **2** °load, °lot, °bunch, multitude, °heap, °pile, °accumulation, °mass, amassment, °mess, barrel, peck: *She told the jury a pack of lies.* **3** °group, °collection, °assembly, assemblage, congregation, °gathering, °crowd, °number, °throng, horde, °mass, °crew, °gang, °body, °lots, loads, °band, company, °party, °set, °flock, °herd, drove, °mob, °swarm, bevy, covey, °circle, coterie, °clique: *A huge pack of people were waiting at the stage door for the star to emerge.* **4** deck: *We ought to have two packs of cards for bridge.* —*v.* **5** Often, **pack in** *or* **into**: °package, bale, °bundle, °compact, °crowd, °cram, °jam, °fill, °stuff, °squeeze, °ram, °press, °wedge, tamp: *They packed us into the train like sardines. I packed as much as I could into the short time I had left.* **6 pack it in**: °stop, °cease, °end, °finish, °quit, °wind up, °terminate, °give up, call it a day, *Colloq* chuck: *Edward finally packed it in because they were giving him too much trouble.* **7 pack off**: °dismiss, °send off *or* away, °bundle off *or* out, °hustle off *or* out *or* away, get °rid of, °drive off *or* away, °order off *or* away *or* out, °send (someone) about his *or* her business: *At the beginning of the war, Sally's mother packed her off to America to stay with her aunt.* **8 pack up**: **a** °get *or* °gather together, °put away, °store: *Pack up your troubles in your old kit bag and smile, smile, smile.* **b** °quit, °stop, °break down, °fail, °give out, °stall, °die, give up the ghost, *Colloq* conk out, have had it: *After three days crossing the desert, the engine finally packed up.*

package *n.* **1** °packet, °parcel, °box, container, °case, carton, °bundle: *I am donating a package of clothing to the relief fund.* **2** °combination, °unit, package °deal: *Included in the package from the car dealer are several luxury features.* —*v.* **3** °wrap, °pack, containerize, carton, °case, encase, °enclose, °include; °combine, °unite, coupled, °incorporate: *More and more merchandise comes packaged in plastic these days. A special sponge is packaged with the cleaning liquid.*

packed *adj.* filled, full, °loaded, crowded, stuffed, jammed, crammed, brim-full, chock-a-block, chock-full, jam-packed, overloaded, overflowing, °loaded *or* filled to the gunwales, up to there, bursting, groaning, °swollen, °replete, *Colloq* wall-to-wall: *The gallery was packed with the soprano's relatives, who cheered every note. The publicity for the show promised a packed programme of mirth and merriment.*

packet *n.* **1** °package, °parcel, °pack, °batch: *We found a packet of your old love-letters in a trunk in the lumber room.* **2** loads, °lot(s), °great °deal, °fortune, °mint, *Colloq* °bundle, pretty penny, °pile(s), °tidy °sum, king's ransom, *Brit* bomb: *He lost a packet on that property when they built a sewage plant alongside it.*

pact *n.* °agreement, °treaty, °bargain, °alliance, °contract, °compact, concord, covenant, concordat, entente, °understanding, °arrangement, °deal: *The companies entered into an illegal pact not to compete in the same markets.*

pad *n.* **1** °cushion, pillow, °wad, wadding, stuffing, padding, °filling, filler: *Wrap a soft cotton pad over the wound to protect it.* **2** writing-pad, note-pad, memo pad, °block (of paper), jotter, *US* filler: *You'd best take a pad with you to make notes at the lecture.* **3** °flat, apartment, °room(s), °home, °place, °quarters, *Colloq* hang-out, *Brit* digs *or* diggings, *Slang US* flop: *A few friends are crashing at my pad while they're in town.* —*v.* **4** °cushion, °wad, °stuff, °fill; upholster: *The chair seats are padded with foam rubber, but the arms are bare.* **5** Sometimes, **pad out**: °expand, °inflate, °stretch, dilate, °lengthen, protract, °extend, °blow up, °flesh out, °puff up, augment, °spin out, °amplify: *He pads his weekly newspaper column with trivia in order to fill the space.*

paddle *n.* **1** °oar, °sweep, scull: *A 'crab' occurs when you catch the water with the paddle blade on the return stroke.* —*v.* **2** °row, scull, °oar: *Deftly she paddled the canoe over to the pier.* **3** °wade: *The children were paddling at the water's edge.* **4** °spank, thrash, °beat, °whip, °flog, *Colloq* paddywhack: *Dad threatened to paddle me if he caught me playing hookey again.*

paddy *n.* °rage, (fit of) °temper, °fit, °tantrum, *Colloq Brit* paddywhack *or* paddywack, wax: *She was in a proper paddy when she found out what you'd done.*

pagan *n.* **1** °heathen, unbeliever, idolater, polytheist, °infidel, Gentile: *He joined the religion of the pagans and worshipped the golden calf.* —*adj.* **2** °heathen, °infidel, idolatrous, polytheistic, heathenish, Gentile: *Many churchmen condemned Renaissance scholars for their interest in pagan and pre-Christian writers.*

page[1] *n.* **1** leaf, folio, °side, °sheet, verso *or* recto: *On which page does the index begin?* **2** °episode, °phase, °period, °time, °stage, °point, °era, epoch, °age, chapter: *The early 1940s were among the darkest pages in Britain's history.* —*v.* **3** paginate, folio, °number: *Roman numerals were used in paging the preface to the book.*

page[2] *n.* **1** °attendant, page-boy, °servant, errand-boy, °messenger, *Brit* foot-boy, *US* bell-man, bellhop, *Offensive used of an adult* bellboy: *Please have a page deliver this message to Mr Simmonds.* —*v.* **2** °announce, °summon (forth), °send for *or* after, °call, °call for, °call out: *They are paging your wife now to give her your message.*

pageant n. °spectacle, °display, °grandeur, °tableau, °show, °parade, °procession, °ceremony, °formality, °ritual, °event, °affair, °extravaganza, °presentation, °gala: *The children stage a medieval mystery play as a part of the annual Christmas pageant.*

pageantry n. °pomp, °ceremony, °display, magnificence, °extravagance, panorama, showiness, °show: *The pageantry of the Oberammergau passion play should be experienced at least once.*

pain n. **1** °hurt, °suffering, °discomfort, soreness, °ache, aching, °pang, °spasm, smarting, cramp: *I feel the pain in my back from lifting that box.* **2** °anguish, °agony, °affliction, °distress, °grief, °woe, °suffering, °misery, travail, wretchedness, °despair, °torment, tribulation, °trial, torture, dolour, discomposure, °ordeal, disquiet: *No one who has not experienced it can imagine the pain of losing a child.* **3** irritation, vexation, °annoyance, °bother, °nuisance, °pest, *Colloq* °pain in the neck, °headache, °drag, °bore, *Taboo slang* °pain in the *Brit* arse *or US* ass: *What a pain it is that you have forgotten your keys again! David can really be a pain when he goes on about the book he's writing.* **4 pains**: °effort, °trouble, °exertion, toil, °labour: *She went to great pains to make our stay comfortable.* —v. **5** °hurt, °distress, °grieve, °wound, °injure; °trouble, °depress, °sadden, °sorrow, °cut to the quick: *It pained us to learn of Mrs McArthur's illness.*

painful adj. **1** hurting, °grievous, °hurtful, °sore, distressing, distressful, °excruciating, torturous, °agonizing, smarting, stinging, aching, achy, throbbing, °burning, °piercing, stabbing, °sharp, °tender, °sensitive, °raw, °bitter, *Formal* nociceptive: *The bullet caused a painful wound in the knee. Mother's arthritis can be quite painful at times.* **2** vexing, vexatious, annoying, harassing, irritating, °irksome, aggravating, galling, exasperating, unpleasant, afflictive, °harrowing, worrisome, worrying, troubling, disquieting, °disturbing, distressing: *Fighting in the front lines was a painful experience for Rupert.* **3** °painstaking, °laborious, °careful, rigorous, °arduous, assiduous, sedulous, °diligent, °earnest, °conscientious, °meticulous, °scrupulous, °detailed, °thorough, thoroughgoing, °exacting, °demanding: *A great deal of painful research went into discovering the cause of yellow fever.*

painfully adv. agonizingly, distressingly, disagreeably, unpleasantly, unfortunately, °sadly, woefully, lamentably, ruefully, unhappily: *I became painfully aware that much of the relief destined for the poor never reached them.*

painkiller n. anodyne, analgesic, anaesthetic, °sedative, palliative: *When he wrenched his back, the doctor gave him a painkiller so that he could walk.*

painless adj. trouble-free, °easy, °simple, °comfortable, °effortless, *Colloq* °easy as 1, 2, 3 or as ABC, °easy as pie, a °piece of cake, °pushover, child's play, *Slang* cinch, no °sweat: *The procedure for assembling the bicycle is relatively painless.*

painstaking adj. See painful, 3, above.

paint n. **1** °colour, °tint, dye, colouring, pigment, °stain: *I bought the paint and brushes, and started work on the kitchen walls.* **2** coating, °coat, °surface; enamel: *The rust has come through the paint here and there.* **3** °make-up, cosmetics, maquillage, greasepaint, *Colloq* warpaint, face: *Sheila is in her room putting on some paint before we go out.* —v. **4** depict, °portray, °picture, °show, °represent, delineate, °render, °draw, limn, °characterize, °describe: *Whistler painted a portrait of my grandmother. Correspondents painted a very grim picture of the plight of the hostages.* **5** °coat, °brush, °apply, °cover, daub: *The doctor painted the area with some medication that soothed the pain.* **6** °colour, °tint, dye, °stain, °decorate: *We are planning to paint the nursery pale blue.* **7 paint the town red**: make merry, °carouse, °revel, go on a °spree, go out on the town, *Colloq* whoop it up, live it up, (go on a) pub-crawl, °step out, *Slang* make whoopee, go on a °bender *or* °drunk *or* binge, °booze it up: *Saturday nights a few of the boys would go out and paint the town red till the wee hours.*

pair n. **1** °couple, twosome, two of a kind, °set of two, matched °set, duo, dyad, twins, °double, doublet; °brace, °span, yoke, °team, tandem: *A pair of silver candelabra disappeared during the party.* —v. **2** °match (up), °mate, °pair off *or* up, °team (up), °put together, °partner, °twin, °double, °join, °unite, yoke; °wed, °marry, °join in wedlock *or* in holy matrimony: *Pair these gloves for me, would you? Husbands may not pair off with wives for the next dance.*

pal n. **1** °friend, consort, °comrade, *alter ego*, crony, °companion, amigo, °playmate, classmate, *Colloq* °chum, sidekick, °mate, *Chiefly US and Canadian* buddy: *Jim left a little while ago with a few of his pals.* —v. **2 pal (up) with** *or* **about** *or US* **around (with)**: °associate (with), be *or* become °friendly *or* °friends (with), be *or* get *or* become on °friendly *or* °intimate terms (with), °go (around *or* about) with, °fraternize (with), consort (with), spend time together *or* with, keep °company (with), *Colloq* °hang out *or* about *or* around (with), °knock about *or* around (with): *Fiona and Isabel palled up last year. Do you still pal about with Timothy?*

palace n. mansion, °castle, °stately *or* °palatial °home *or* °residence, manor (house), (°country) °estate, château, palazzo, villa: *After the wedding, they went to the prince's palace and lived happily ever after.*

palatial adj. °luxurious, de luxe, °magnificent, °splendid, °stately, °sumptuous, °opulent, °majestic, °grand, °elegant, palatine, *Slang* °posh, ritzy, °swanky, classy: *After winning the pools, they moved into a palatial house in Belgravia.*

palaver n. **1** °nuisance, °procedure, red tape, to-do, °rigmarole *or* rigamarole, *Colloq* °song and dance, °bother, °nonsense, °business, carry-on, °performance: *He lost the certificates, so she now has to go through all the palaver of getting new ones.* **2** °chatter, °babble, °jabber, (°empty *or* °small) °talk, blather *or* blether, °gossip, prating, °prattle, prattling, palavering, *Brit* natter, nattering, *Scots* clishmaclaver, *Colloq* jawing, °hot air, *Colloq Brit* witter, wittering: *There is so much palaver at the annual meeting that nothing important ever gets said.* **3** °parley, °talk, °conference, °discussion, colloquy, °conversation, confabulation, °meeting, °get-together, round table, powwow, *Colloq* confab, °huddle, chin-wag: *The annual palaver of the regional general managers is scheduled for next week.*

—*v.* **4** °chatter, °babble, °jabber, blather *or* blether, °gossip, °prattle, prate, chit-chat, gabble, *Brit* natter, witter, *Colloq* jaw, chin-wag, *US and Canadian* shoot the breeze, *Slang* ya(c)k, ya(c)kety-ya(c)k: *Peter and I were palavering outside the supermarket when Sophie came along.*
5 °confer, °consult, °discuss, °parley, °talk, °converse, powwow, °meet, °get together, °sit down (together), confabulate, °negotiate, *Colloq* confab, °huddle, chew the fat *or* the °rag: *Management and union representatives will palaver tomorrow.*

pale[1] *adj.* **1** °colourless, °white, °wan, sallow, waxen, livid, ashen, ashy, pallid, bloodless, whitish, °pasty, whey-faced, washed out, anaemic, blanched, drained, °ghostly, °ghastly, °peaky *or* peakish, peaked, cadaverous: *If you had been through an ordeal like that, you'd look pale, too.* **2** °faint, °light, °dim, washed out, pastel: *She was wearing a pale green evening gown tonight.* **3** °feeble, °weak, °flimsy, °meagre, enfeebled, °ineffective, °ineffectual, °puny, °insignificant, °paltry, °lame, °poor, °inadequate, °half-hearted, °tame, spiritless, whey-faced, °empty, °sterile, °lifeless, uninspired, anaemic, *Colloq* half-baked: *The sequel was a pale imitation of the original film.*
—*v.* **4** blanch, blench, °dim, whiten: *He paled when they told him of the car crash.* **5** °diminish, lessen, °fade (away), °decrease, abate: *The works of most modern writers pale in comparison with those of the Elizabethans.*

pale[2] *n.* **1** paling, palisade, °picket, °upright, °post, °stake: *The pales are attached to horizontal rails to form a fence.* **2** °boundary, °limit(s), °restriction, °bounds, °border(s), confines: *Nothing is outside the pale of the imagination of a great novelist.* **3 beyond the pale:** °improper, °irregular, °unseemly, unsuitable, °indecent, °unacceptable, °inadmissible, forbidden, anathema, disallowed, prohibited, *verboten*, interdicted; *US* °unusual, °bizarre, °peculiar, °outré, °weird, °abnormal, °strange: *The committee have found your behaviour to be beyond the pale, Frances, and we demand your resignation.*

pall[1] *n.* **1** °shroud, covering, °mantle, °cloth, °veil: *A black velvet pall covered the coffin.*
2 °gloomy *or* °melancholy *or* °sombre *or* °grave *or* depressing °air *or* °mood *or* °atmosphere; damper, cold water, *Colloq* wet blanket: *The recently uncovered scandals have cast a pall over his successes in office.*

pall[2] *v.* **1** Often, **pall on** *or* **upon**: °bore, °tire, °weary, °jade, °irk, °irritate, °sicken: *His position lost all its charm when the work began to pall on him.* **2** sate, °satiate, cloy, °glut, °surfeit, °gorge: *I had reached the point where even the finest foods began to pall me.*

paltry *adj.* °trifling, trivial, °petty, °small, °insignificant, °worthless, °pitiful, °pathetic, °pitiable, °puny, °sorry, °wretched, °miserable, °inconsequential, inconsiderable, unimportant, °meagre, °mean, beggarly, °base, °low, °contemptible, *Colloq* piddling, *Brit* twopenny, twopenny-halfpenny, mingy, *US* penny-ante, *Slang* Mickey Mouse: *Despite his wealth, his charitable contributions are paltry. We all recognize Denison for the paltry pedant he is.*

pamper *v.* °baby, °coddle, cosset, (over)indulge, °spoil, mollycoddle, °cater to, °pet, *Rare* cocker, *Irish* cosher: *The Simpsons pamper their children far too much.*

pamphlet *n.* booklet, °brochure, °tract, °essay, folder, °leaflet, °circular; handbill, °bill, °notice, °bulletin, °advertisement, hand-out, ad, *Brit* advert, *US* flyer, throw-away: *He was arrested for printing a pamphlet that denounced the government's repression of free speech. Yesterday we received our sixteenth pamphlet promoting replacement windows.*

pan *n.* **1** saucepan, frying-pan, skillet, °pot, casserole, *US* spider: *Melt a teaspoonful of butter in the pan, add the mixture, and stir briskly over a medium heat.* **2** °face, visage, mien, façade, *Slang* kisser, °mug, puss: *The worst part of Alf's not working is that I have to look at his ugly pan all day.* **3** °depression, °indentation, concavity, °cavity, °hollow, °pit, °hole, crater: *In a rain-shower, the pans fill with water and the desert blooms.*
—*v.* **4** °wash, °separate, °sift: *For years prospectors have panned for gold in these hills.* **5** °criticize, censure, find °fault, °put down, °reject, flay, excoriate, *Brit* hammer, *Colloq* °knock, roast, slate, *Slang Brit* °rubbish, *US* trash: *The critics panned the play and it closed after a week.* **6 pan out**: °succeed, °thrive, °prosper, °flourish, fare well, °make it; °work out, °turn out, °result, °come out, °end (up), conclude, culminate, eventuate: *Your grandiose plans for irrigating the Sahara didn't pan out, either! How did the election pan out?*

panache *n.* °flourish, °dash, élan, éclat, °chic, °sophistication, savoir faire, savoir vivre, flamboyance, °verve, °style, cultivation, (good) °taste, °flair, smartness, boldness, self-assurance, °swagger, °vigour, liveliness, °spirit, brio, °gusto, °zest, °animation, °enthusiasm, °energy: *Whatever needs to be done, you can count on Irena to carry it off with panache.*

pandemonium *n.* °bedlam, °chaos, turmoil, °disorder, °tumult, °frenzy, °uproar, *Brit* °furore *or US* furor, °confusion: *Pandemonium reigned after the first bomb struck.*

pander *v.* **1** Usually, **pander to**: °satisfy, °gratify, °humour, °indulge, °fulfil, °bow to, °yield to, °truckle to, °cater to: *She is tired of pandering to his every wish.* **2** °procure, °pimp, °solicit: *I didn't believe he would sink so low as to pander for his business clients.*
—*n.* **3** panderer, °pimp, °procurer, °solicitor, whoremonger, White °slaver, *Slang* flesh-pedlar *or US also* flesh-peddler *or* flesh-pedler, *Brit* ponce, mack: *The word pander is an eponym for Pandarus, who acted as a sycophantic go-between for Troilus in Chaucer's Troilus and Criseyde.*

pane *n.* panel, °sheet, °glass, window-pane, °light, quarrel, bull's-eye: *Ring up the glazier and have that pane replaced in the door.*

pang *n.* **1** °pain, °stab, °ache, °pinch, °twinge, stitch, °spasm: *I felt a sharp pang of hunger.* **2** °qualm, hesitation, °scruple, °misgiving, °remorse, °regret, contrition, contriteness, self-reproach, mortification, °guilt, °anguish, °discomfort, malaise: *Does Claire feel the slightest pangs for treating him badly?*

panic *n.* **1** °terror, °alarm, °fear, °fright, °dread, °horror, °dismay, consternation, hysteria; °anxiety, apprehension, apprehensiveness, nervousness: *As the speeding car veered towards us, a feeling of panic gripped me.*
—*v.* **2** be terrified *or* alarmed *or* °fearful *or* frightened *or* terror-stricken *or* terror-struck, °dread, °fear, lose one's °nerve; °frighten, °scare;

Colloq go to °pieces, °fall apart, *Brit* lose one's °bottle: *I panicked, turned the wheel the wrong way, and crashed the car into a tree. Gregory panics at the slightest sign of danger.* **3** °frighten, °scare, °alarm, °terrify, °unnerve: *Something panicked the horses and one kicked out his stall door.*

panic-stricken *adj.* panic-struck, terrified, alarmed, horrified, aghast, terror-stricken *or* terror-struck, panicky, frenzied, in a °frenzy, °hysterical, °beside oneself with °fear *or* °terror, °fearful, °afraid, °scared (stiff), °petrified, horror-struck *or* horror-stricken, frightened *or* °scared out of one's wits, appalled, stunned, stupefied, perturbed, unnerved, °nervous, distressed, °upset, jittery, °jumpy, (all) worked up, *Colloq* in a cold sweat, in a °flap, in a tizzy, *Taboo slang* °scared shitless, shitting green: *At the news of the leak at the nuclear plant, hundreds of panic-stricken people fled from the area.*

panoramic *adj.* °sweeping, commanding, °extensive, °comprehensive, °wide, °overall, °scenic, far-reaching, all-embracing, far-ranging, all-encompassing, °inclusive, bird's-eye, °general: *This room affords a panoramic view of the sea-coast.*

pant *v.* **1** °gasp, °huff (and °puff), °blow, °heave, °breathe hard, wheeze: *He was panting when he came into the room, having run up the stairs.* **2** Usually, **pant for** *or* **after**: °crave, °hanker after, °hunger *or* °thirst for *or* after, °yearn for, °ache for, °want, °desire, covet, °wish for, °long *or* pine *or* °sigh for, have one's heart set on, °die for, be dying for, *Colloq* have a yen for, give one's eye-teeth *or* right arm for: *Margery was the girl that all the boys panted after when we were ten.*

pants *n.pl.* **1** *In Britain*: (men's) drawers, small-clothes, underpants, boxer shorts, trunks, undershorts, Y-fronts, briefs, *Colloq* smalls; (women's) knickers, camiknickers, panties, bloomers, pantalettes, °tights, pantihose, undies: *The baby was dressed in a frilly dress and matching pants.* **2** *In US*: trousers, slacks, breeches, (Oxford) bags, knickerbockers, flannels, shorts, Bermuda shorts *or* Bermudas, pedal pushers, bell-bottoms, peg-tops, hip-huggers, (blue) jeans, dungarees, denims, *Trade Mark* Levis, *Scots* trews; *Scots and No. Eng.* breeks, *US* knickers, *Colloq* cut-offs: *Americans who go into British shops asking for a pair of pants are embarrassed to be offered only underwear.*

paper *n.* **1** newspaper, tabloid, daily, weekly, °journal, gazette, °publication, °periodical, newsletter, °organ, *Colloq* °rag, °sheet: *She is feature editor of a paper in Manchester.* **2** Often, **papers: a** °document(s), °instrument, °legal papers, °form, certificate, °deed, ownership papers; credential(s), °identification: *Bring the papers to my office for signing. His papers are not in order. Many people lost their papers during the war.* **b** docket, files, dossier, °record(s), archive(s): *Your papers seem to have disappeared from our office.* **3** °stationery, letterhead, writing-paper, letter-paper, notepaper; foolscap; °scrap *or* US also scratch paper; wrapping paper, gift-wrapping, gift-wrap; wallpaper: *She wrote to me on the most beautiful engraved paper. We buy our Christmas paper from a museum shop.* **4** article, °composition, °essay, °assignment, °report, °thesis, °study, °tract, °analysis, critique, exegesis, treatise, dissertation, disquisition, manuscript, MS *or* ms, autograph, holograph,

typescript, °script, °speech: *Adelaide will present her paper at the meeting of the Royal Academy this year.*
—*v.* **5** (hang) wallpaper, line; °post, °distribute: *The entire area was papered with posters announcing the meeting.*

par *adj.* **1** °standard, °normal, °average, expected: *A success rate of two per cent is par for these candidates.*
—*n.* **2** °level, °rank, °standing, °scale, °standard: *How can you place yourself on a par with her as a tennis player?* **3 above par**: above °average, °superior, °outstanding, °excellent, °exceptional; °choice, °select, °prime: *Since I stopped taking that medication, I've been feeling above par. I am pleased to announce that the test results were above par for the school as a whole.* **4 at par**: °average, °level, °even, °equal, °equivalent, °standard; °par value: *The shares are selling at par, or below their true market value.* **5 below** *or* **under par: a** below °average, substandard, °inferior, second-rate, °mediocre, middling, not up to par, °poor, °inadequate, °unsatisfactory, °wanting, °bad, °wretched, °miserable, °awful, °terrible, *Colloq* °lousy, not up to snuff *or* °scratch: *Ian's goal-keeping has been below par all season.* **b** °ill, °sickly, °unhealthy, unwell, not (very) well, not oneself, not in good *or* the best °shape, in bad °shape, *Brit* °off form, °off colour; *Colloq* under the weather, °poorly, not up to snuff: *I was feeling below par.* **6 up to par**: all °right, °adequate, °average, °satisfactory, °good enough, °passable, °acceptable, *Colloq* °OK *or* okay, up to °scratch *or* snuff, °fair to middling: *If your game had been up to par, Davis would not have won.*

parable *n.* allegory, fable, °lesson, °morality °tale: *When we first read Aesop's Fables we didn't know they were parables.*

parade *n.* **1** °procession, °march, °train, °file, °promenade, cortège, column; entourage: *They held a parade to celebrate the soldiers' safe return from the war.* **2** °exhibition, (ostentatious) °display, °show, °spectacle, array, °pomp, °splash: *She often makes a parade of her knowledge of architecture.* **3** °promenade, °walk, (pedestrian) °way, mall, esplanade: *Let's meet in the Parade when you have finished shopping.*
—*v.* **4** °march, pass in °review, °promenade, °walk, °file: *The generals saluted smartly as the troops paraded past.* **5** °strut, °flaunt, °show (off), brandish, °wave, vaunt, °display, °air: *Why does he feel it necessary to parade every new girlfriend in front of all the neighbours?*

paradise *n.* **1** °heaven, City of God, Zion, Elysium, Elysian Fields, °happy hunting-grounds, Abraham's bosom, °heavenly kingdom, Promised Land, Celestial City, New Jerusalem, Avalon, Valhalla, Hesperides, Isles *or* Islands of the Blessed, seventh °heaven: *People all have their own ideas of paradise, but everyone agrees it's a nice place to be.* **2** °heaven on earth, (Garden of) Eden, (land of) Goshen, °Utopia, Shangri-La, Land of Beulah: *Early settlers of California thought it a paradise.* **3** °bliss, °happiness, °rapture, °heaven, °delight, blessedness, °ecstasy, seventh °heaven, °joy, dreamland, nirvana: *Being with you has been sheer paradise.*

paradox *n.* contradiction, self-contradiction, incongruity, inconsistency, °absurdity, °ambiguity, °enigma, °puzzle, °mystery,

°quandary, °problem, °dilemma: *Can you explain away Zeno's paradox of Achilles and the tortoise? The paradox was that although it was Edward's fifth birthday, he was 20 years old.*

paradoxical *adj.* °contradictory, self-contradictory, conflicting, oxymoronic, °impossible, °improbable, °incongruous, illogical, °inconsistent, °absurd, °ambiguous, confusing, °equivocal, enigmatic, °puzzling, baffling, °incomprehensible, bewildering, °perplexing, °mysterious, °problematic: *It would be true, though it might sound paradoxical, to say that the Norman Conquest made England Saxon.*

paragon *n.* °epitome, archetype, °model, °prototype, °quintessence, °pattern, °standard, exemplar, °ideal, *beau idéal*, criterion: *He had previously regarded Michael as a paragon of virtue and was deeply shocked by the revelations.*

parallel *adj.* **1** °similar, corresponding, congruent, analogous, analogic(al), °correspondent, °like, °matching, homologous, °coordinate, °equivalent, coequal, °proportional, proportionate, *pari passu, mutatis mutandis*, in °proportion, °uniform; °contemporary *or* cotemporary, contemporaneous *or* cotemporaneous: *The situation in Northern Ireland could be compared with a parallel situation in Lebanon.*
—*n.* **2** analogue, °match, homologue, °equivalent, °complement, counterpart, °equal, coequal: *Campbell found many parallels among the legendary heroes of other cultures.* **3** analogy, parallelism, equivalence, complementarity, °relationship, °kinship, correspondence, °resemblance, °likeness, similarity, °symmetry, °equality, coequality, °parity, correlation; °proportion, °balance, equiponderance, equipoise, counterbalance, °offset: *One can draw parallels between the human arm, the fish's fin, and the bird's wing. By way of parallel, consider the flood in the Bible and that in the Gilgamesh epic.*
—*v.* **4** °correspond to *or* with, °match, equate to *or* with, be likened to, correlate to *or* with, °compare with *or* to, °imitate, °repeat, °echo, iterate, °reiterate, °duplicate, °follow, °agree with; keep °pace with, °conform (to), °balance, °set off, °offset, °even off *or* up, be accompanied by, °coincide with, *Colloq* jibe with: *In many respects, your attitudes towards life parallel mine when I was your age. A decrease in the rate of inflation supposedly parallels a rise in interest rates.*

paralyse *v.* **1** immobilize, inactivate, deactivate, °transfix; °halt, °stop: *The stroke paralysed his entire left side. As the thing approached, the children became paralysed by fear.* **2** °deaden, °numb, °freeze, anaesthetize, benumb, °render °insensible: *This injection will paralyse your thumb so that we can operate on it.* **3** disable, °cripple, °incapacitate, disenable: *His left leg was paralysed in the accident.*

paramount *adj.* °pre-eminent, °chief, °supreme, °dominant, °main, °predominant, °cardinal, °first, °prime, °primary, °principal, °essential, °vital, requisite, °basic: *The company feel that the independence of researchers is paramount. It is of paramount importance that you study trigonometry before calculus.*

paramour *n.* °lover, °love, inamorato *or* inamorata, amorist, °mistress, gigolo, concubine, cicisbeo, kept °woman, *Colloq* °flame, sugar-daddy, *US* POSSLQ (= 'Person of the

Opposite Sex Sharing Living Quarters'), *Slang* fancy man *or* woman: *At eighty, she liked to reminisce about her many paramours.*

paraphernalia *n.* Usually *pl.* equipment, apparatus, °accessories, outfit, appliances, utensils, gear, rig, °material(s), *matériel*, °things, tackle, equipage, accoutrements, °effects, chattels, °possessions, °belongings, appurtenances, °trappings, property, baggage, impedimenta, °supplies, stuff, *Colloq* junk, *Brit* rubbish, clobber, *Slang* crap, *Taboo slang US* shit: *Bring along your scuba paraphernalia. It took us a month just to pack up all the paraphernalia we had in the flat.*

paraphrase *n.* **1** rephrasing, rephrase, rewording, restatement, rewriting, rewrite, °rehash, °rendition, °rendering, °version, *Technical* paraphrasis: *The editor wanted a revision, not merely a paraphrase of the original.*
—*v.* **2** rephrase, °reword, restate, rewrite, explicate, °explain: *Please paraphrase the specialized jargon to make it understandable to non-professionals.*

parasite *n.* leech, °hanger-on, *Colloq* freeloader, sponger *or* sponge, °bloodsucker, cadger, scrounger *or* °scrounge, barnacle, jackal, hyena *or* hyaena: *That parasite lives off Gemma's money and has never worked a day in his life.*

parcel *n.* **1** °package, °packet, carton, °box, container, °case: *We are sending food parcels to the needy.* **2** °portion, °plot, plat, °lot, piece, °section, °tract: *We have bought a small parcel of land and plan to build on it next year.* **3** °lot, °group, °batch, °collection, °pack, °bundle, °set: *She gathered a parcel of drawings and published them as a travel sketchbook.*
—*v.* **4** Often, **parcel out**: apportion, °allot, °deal (out), °dole (out), °mete (out), °hand out, °distribute, °share (out), °divide, *Colloq* divvy (up): *Before he died he parcelled out his fortune amongst his grandchildren.*

parch *v.* °dry (out *or* up), desiccate, dehydrate, exsiccate; °scorch, sear, °burn, bake; °shrivel (up), wither: *The earth was parched by the unrelenting sun.*

pardon *n.* **1** °forgiveness, °forgiving, amnesty, °remission, °release, reprieval, absolution, °indulgence, °excuse, excusal, °allowance, overlooking, condonation, exoneration, exculpation: *Should there be any pardon for crimes against humanity?*
—*v.* **2** °forgive, °remit, °release, °reprieve, absolve, °indulge, °allow, °overlook, °let off, °excuse, condone, exonerate, exculpate: *There are some crimes that ought not be pardoned.*

pare *v.* **1** °trim, °peel, °skin, °shave (off), shuck, decorticate, excoriate: *Pare the apples and then grate them coarsely.* **2** Often, **pare down**: °reduce, °diminish, °decrease, °cut (back *or* down), °curtail, °slash (back), °lower, lessen: *Since his illness, Bob has pared down his time at the office. We'll have to pare our prices to stay competitive in the present climate.*

parent *n.* **1** °father *or* °mother, °progenitor, progenitrix, procreator, begetter, materfamilias *or* paterfamilias; foster-parent, stepmother *or* stepfather, °guardian, *Colloq* old lady *or* old man, *Brit old-fashioned or facetious* mater *or* pater: *Most teenagers clash with their parents sooner or later.* **2** °source, °origin, originator, well-spring, fountain-head, °root: *The liturgy of St James is undoubtedly the parent of the Armenian Rite.*

parentage *n.* °lineage, ancestry, °line, °family, °extraction, descent, °origin, °pedigree, °stock, °birth, °strain, bloodline, °heritage, roots: *As he was separated from his mother at birth, he knows nothing of his royal parentage.*

parenting *n.* (of children) rearing, °upbringing, raising, nurturing: *Brian and Betty take their parenting very seriously.*

parity *n.* **1** °equality, equivalence, consistency, °uniformity, °par, °likeness, similarity, analogy, congruity, similitude, conformity, congruence: *The ministers agreed that they would observe parity of power amongst themselves at the conference.* **2** °proportion, parallelism, analogy, °balance, correspondence: *We are trying to maintain parity between the Deutschmark and the pound sterling.*

park *n.* **1** garden, °green(s), °common(s), °preserve, °reserve, greensward, parkland, woodland, °estate, *Chiefly Brit* °reservation: *Twice a day he strolls through the nearby park.* **2** *Brit* car park, *US and Canadian and New Zealand* parking-lot: *I shall meet you in the car park at the railway station.*
—*v.* **3** °leave, °put, °deposit, °store: *It is illegal to park in this street.*

parlance *n.* way *or* manner of speaking, *façon de parler,* phrasing, phraseology, °speech, °wording, °language, °idiom, °dialect, °jargon, *Colloq* °lingo: *In the parlance of the yuppies, that's a ballpark figure.*

parley *n.* **1** °conference, °discussion, °dialogue, °palaver, deliberation, °meeting, colloquy, colloquium, confabulation, powwow, °talk(s), *Colloq* °huddle, confab: *The issue will be decided at the executive council's parley.*
—*v.* **2** °confer, °discuss, °palaver, °deliberate, °talk (over), °negotiate, °deal, *Colloq* °huddle: *Would Sitting Bull parley with General Custer?*

parliament *n.* **1 Parliament**: Houses of Parliament, House of Lords and House of Commons, Westminster, the House, Mother of Parliaments: *The new health bill got its second reading in Parliament today.* **2** legislature, °council, congress, °diet, °assembly, Upper and Lower House *or* °chamber: *The United States parliament consists of the Senate and the House of Representatives.*

parliamentary *adj.* °formal, ordered, °orderly, procedural, conforming, conformist, *US* according to *Roberts Rules of Order*: *The debate must follow parliamentary procedure.*

parlour *n.* living-room, *Old-fashioned or Brit* drawing-room, *Chiefly Brit* sitting-room, °reception (room), °lounge: *She invited us into the parlour where tea was laid out.*

parlous *adj.* °perilous, °risky, °precarious, °uncertain, °dangerous, °hazardous, °difficult, °ticklish, °awkward, *Colloq* chancy, iffy, *Slang* °hairy: *These are parlous times in the Middle East.*

parochial *adj.* regional, °provincial, °narrow, °local, insular, °isolated, °limited, restricted, °narrow-minded, °petty, °short-sighted, °hidebound, °conservative, °conventional, illiberal, °bigoted, °prejudiced, °intolerant, °one-sided, °partial, °biased, °stubborn, °opinionated, °dogmatic, °rigid, °stiff,

stiff-necked, °immovable, intractable, unchangeable, unchanging, close-minded, °unsophisticated, unworldly, uncultivated, uncultured: *Uneducated and untravelled, Mr Shriver maintained a very parochial view of the world.*

parody *n.* **1** °burlesque, °lampoon, °satire, °caricature, °mockery, mimicry, *Colloq* °take-off, spoof, *Brit* send-up: *The more serious the intent of the original author's work, the easier it is to write a parody of it.* **2** travesty, °mockery, feeble *or* poor °imitation, distortion, °perversion, corruption, debasement: *The Inquisition was a parody of justice and of religion.*
—*v.* **3** °burlesque, °lampoon, °satirize, °caricature, °mock, °mimic, ape, °ridicule, °deride, °laugh at, °poke °fun at, °guy, °scoff at, °sneer at, rib, °tease, °twit, roast, pillory, make a laughing-stock (of), make °sport of, make °fun of, make a °monkey (out) of, *Archaic* fleer, *Colloq* °take off, spoof, kid, *Brit* °send up: *Swift parodied English political figures and policies of the day in Gulliver's Travels.*

paroxysm *n.* °fit, convulsion, °spasm, °throe, °seizure, °spell, °outburst, °eruption, °explosion, *Colloq* flare-up: *At the sight of George dressed as Madame Pompadour Melissa rolled on the floor in a paroxysm of hysterical laughter.*

parrot *n.* **1** imitator, °mimic, *Colloq* copycat: *She never has an original idea of her own: she's a mere parrot of others' fashions and fancies.*
—*v.* **2** °imitate, °mimic, ape, °copy, °echo, °repeat, °reiterate: *Mick doesn't understand the issues and just parrots what he hears on TV.*

part *n.* **1** piece, °portion, °division, °allotment, °share, °percentage, participation, °interest; °parcel, °fragment, °scrap, shard; some: *I bought a part of the company when it was available. I want no part of the deal now.* **2** °portion, component, °factor, constituent, °element, °ingredient: *A part of her problem is that she doesn't speak Japanese.* **3** °role, °function, °duty, °responsibility, °share; °say, °voice, °influence, participation, involvement, °business: *Every man must do his part. Don't thank me! I had no part in your getting the contract.* **4** °role, °character: *He plays the part of Tweedledum in the school play.* **5** °side, °interest, °cause, °behalf, °faction, °party: *Which part did you support in the argument? No explanation has been offered on either part.* **6** °neighbourhood, °quarter, °section, °district, °region, °area, corner, °vicinity, vicinage, *Colloq* neck of the woods: *I come from the same part of the country as you.* **7** °piece, °portion, °segment, °section; °department, °division, component, °unit: *Which part of the turkey do you prefer? In which part of the company do you work?* **8 for the most part**: mostly, °generally, °usually, °mainly, in the °main, by and large, on the °whole, °chiefly, °principally, essentially, for all practical purposes, to all intents and purposes, in most cases *or* instances: *The shops are for the most part closed on Sunday.* **9 in part**: °partly, °partially, to some °extent *or* °degree, in some °measure, °relatively, comparatively, °somewhat: *He is himself in part responsible for the present state of affairs.* **10 on the part of (someone)** *or* **on (someone's** *or* **one's) part**: °by, on *or* *US also* in °behalf of, (as) for, as regards, as far as (someone) is concerned, in the °name of, for the °sake of, in °support of: *Tyrannical acts on the part of the king were not condoned. For my part, I want*

nothing to do with it. **11 take (a) part (in)**: °participate (in), °join (in), be (a) °party to, °play a part *or* °role (in), be °involved (in *or* with), °associate oneself (with), have *or* take a °hand in, °partake (of), °contribute (to): *Why insist that she take part in your nefarious plot? People began to sing, but she didn't feel like taking part.*
—*v.* **12** °separate, part company, °split up, °go his *or* her (*or* their) °separate °way(s), °break up, say *or* bid °goodbye (*or* adieu, etc.); °leave, °depart, °go (away *or* off): *We parted on the best of terms.* **13** °separate, °divide, °put *or* °pull °apart, °put asunder: *I saw a pale hand part the curtains for a brief moment. A fool and his money are soon parted.* **14 part with**: °give up, °yield, °relinquish, °release, °sacrifice, °forgo, °renounce, °forsake, °let go, °surrender: *I doubt that you'll persuade Rover to part with his bone.*
—*adj.* **15** °partial, fractional, °limited: *Ronald is a part owner of the company.*

partake *v.* **1** Usually, **partake in**: °share (in), °participate (in), take (a) °part (in), °enter (in *or* into): *We share each other's burdens and partake in each other's joys.* **2** Usually, **partake of**: **a** °receive, °get, have a °share *or* °portion *or* °part (of), °share: *We were invited to partake of a meagre repast.* **b** °evoke, °suggest, °hint at, °intimate, °imply, °possess *or* have the °quality of: *Greater knowledge often partakes of insolence.*

partial *adj.* **1** °incomplete, °fragmentary, not °total *or* °whole, °imperfect: *They were able to afford only a partial restoration of the house. There will be a partial solar eclipse at noon.* **2** °prejudiced, °biased, °partisan, °inclined, influenced, °one-sided, °jaundiced, unfair, discriminatory: *It will be difficult to find a judge who is not partial.* **3 partial to**: in °favour of, predisposed to, °fond of, having a soft spot *or* °weakness for, having a °liking *or* °taste *or* predilection for, having a fondness for, feeling an °attraction *or* °affinity to *or* toward(s), °finding °enjoyment in: *She used to be partial to punk rockers. I am partial to Scotch beef.*

partiality *n.* **1** °prejudice, °bias, °inclination, °favouritism, predilection, predisposition, °leaning, °preference: *The losers of the contest accused the judges of partiality.* **2** °preference, °taste, °relish, °liking, fondness, °appreciation, °fancy, °love, °eye, °weakness, soft spot, °penchant; °fetish *or* fetich: *Alas, my wife has acquired a partiality for emeralds.*

partially *adv.* °partly, in °part, to some °extent *or* °degree, to a °limited *or* a °certain °extent *or* °degree, not °totally *or* °wholly *or* °entirely, restrictedly, incompletely, in some °measure, °relatively, comparatively, °moderately, (up) to a (given *or* certain) point, °somewhat: *Jon found the meal only partially satisfying and ordered another bread pudding.*

participant *n.* **1** participator, partaker, sharer, °party, contributor, prime mover: *The chief participants in the recent terrorist attack are in custody.*
—*adj.* **2** Usually, **participant in** *or* **of**: participating, partaking, sharing: *As a shareholder, he will be participant in the profits.*

participate *v.* Often, **participate in**: take °part (in), °share (in), °partake (in *or* of), °join (in), °engage (in), get *or* become °involved (in), be *or* become associated (with), °enter (in *or* into),

°contribute (to): *We invited her to join the group, but she refuses to participate. I would like to participate in the venture.*

particle *n.* atom, molecule, scintilla, °spark, mote, °suggestion, °hint, °suspicion, °gleam, °bit, °crumb, °jot, tittle, whit, mite, °speck, °dot, °spot, iota, °grain, °morsel, °shred, °sliver, °scrap, *Colloq* smidgen *or* smidgin: *There isn't the slightest particle of evidence linking them with the murder.*

particular *adj.* **1** °certain, °specific, °special, °peculiar, °singular, °single, °isolated, °individual, °distinct, °discrete, °separate, °definite, °precise, °express: *These are not his particular sentiments but those of thousands of his followers. In this particular instance your theory does not apply.* **2** °marked, °special, especial, °exceptional, °remarkable, °noteworthy, °notable, °outstanding, °unusual: *The commendation is for her particular contribution to the treatment of nervous disorders. Vintage port is a particular favourite of mine.* **3** °detailed, itemized, item-by-item, °thorough, °minute, °precise, °exact, °exacting, °painstaking, °nice, rigorous, °close, blow-by-blow: *The inscriptions reveal the particular care taken in keeping daily records.* **4** °fussy, °meticulous, °finicky, finical, °fastidious, °discriminating, °selective, °demanding, hypercritical, °critical, *Colloq* pernickety *or US also* persnickety, °choosy, picky: *Daphne is very particular about whom she invites to dinner.*
—*n.* **5** Usually, **particulars**: °detail, minutia, fine °point, °item, °specific, °element, °fact, °circumstance, °information: *The particulars may never be revealed, but we know in general what took place that fateful night.* **6 in particular**: °particularly, specifically, °precisely, °exactly, °especially, °specially; °particular, °specific, °special, °definite: *I told mother that I was just going out, not anywhere in particular.*

particularly *adv.* **1** °especially, °specially, exceptionally, peculiarly, singularly, distinctively, uniquely, unusually, uncommonly, °notably, outstandingly, markedly, extraordinarily, °very, °extremely, strikingly, surprisingly, amazingly: *Susannah went through a particularly bad patch but she's better now. Holroyd is a good writer, particularly of biography.* **2** in °particular, specifically, °especially, °principally, °mainly, exceptionally, °expressly, explicitly, °notably, markedly; °only, solely: *Maeterlinck was particularly interested in bees.*

parting *n.* **1** separating, splitting, dividing, breaking (up *or* °apart), sundering, cleaving; °separation, °split, °division, break-up, °rift, °rupture: *The high point of the film was the parting of the Red Sea. The parting between Harriet and Sam after twenty turbulent years was to be expected.* **2** leave-taking, °farewell, saying °goodbye, departure, leaving, going (away), making one's adieus *or* adieux; valediction: *Parting is such sweet sorrow.*
—*adj.* **3** closing, °final, concluding, °last, departing, valedictory; deathbed, °dying: *Her parting comment was, 'If you're leaving, take the rubbish'.*

partisan *n.* **1** partizan, °devotee, °follower, °supporter, adherent, °backer, °champion, °enthusiast, °fan, °zealot, °fanatic, *Chiefly US and Canadian* booster, *Colloq US* rooter: *He has long been a partisan of surrealism.* **2** °guerrilla *or*

guerilla, °freedom fighter, °underground or
°resistance fighter, irregular: *During the war the
Yugoslav partisans were led by Marshal Tito.*
—*adj.* **3** °one-sided, factional, °biased, ten-
dentious, °sectarian, °opinionated, °partial,
°bigoted, °prejudiced, °parochial, myopic,
°short-sighted, °near-sighted, °narrow,
°narrow-minded, °limited: *She refuses to become
involved in partisan politics.* **4** °guerrilla or
guerilla, °freedom, °underground, °resistance,
irregular: *They were both members of the Maquis,
the French partisan group who fought against the
Nazis.*

partition *n.* **1** °separation, °division, splitting
(up), split-up, partitionment, break-up, breaking up, segmenting, segmentation: *One of the
results of World War II was the partition of
Germany.* **2** °allotment, allotting, apportionment, apportioning, °distribution, distributing, meting out, doling out, rationing
(out), sharing (out), dividing (up), giving or
handing or passing out, parcelling out, *Colloq*
divvying up: *The partition of the estate is in the
hands of our solicitors.* **3** (°room) divider, (dividing)
°wall, °barrier, °screen, separator: *Let's put
up a partition to divide this office into
two.* **4** °compartment, °room, °chamber,
°section, °part, °area, °division, subdivision,
°cell, °stall, °booth: *In open floor planning, furniture, plantings, and other movables are used to
create the partitions where people work.*
—*v.* **5** °divide (up), °separate, °cut up, subdivide,
°split (up): *It is always a mistake to partition a
country into smaller, potentially quarrelsome
units.* **6** Often, **partition off**: °divide, °separate,
subdivide, °wall off, °screen (off), °fence off: *We
must partition off the machine room so that the
office staff are not disturbed by the noise.*

partly *adv.* See partially, above.

partner *n.* **1** sharer, partaker, °associate,
°colleague, °participant, °accomplice, °accessory,
confederate, °comrade, °ally, collaborator,
°companion, team-mate, °fellow, *alter ego*,
°friend, *Colloq* °pal, sidekick, °mate, *US and
Canadian* buddy, °cohort: *His partner in the bank
robbery was arrested this morning.* **2** wife or
°husband, spouse, °mate, helpmate, helpmeet,
consort: *She became my life partner more than 50
years ago.* **3** °companion, fellow-dancer: *Won't you
change partners and dance with me?*

party *n.* **1** (social) °gathering, cocktail or dinner
party, °celebration, °fête or fete, °function,
°reception, soirée, levee, °festivity, festivities,
°festival, °frolic, °spree, romp, carousal or
°carouse, saturnalia, bacchanalia, debauch,
°orgy, *Colloq* °get-together, bash, bust, shindig
or shindy, ball, at-home, do, *Brit* beanfeast,
beano, knees-up, *US* blow-out, *Slang Brit* °rave or
rave-up, *Chiefly US and Canadian* wingding,
bust-up, *US* °hop: *Campbell said he had a marvellous time at your birthday party.* **2** °group,
°company, °band, °body, °corps, °gang, °crew,
°team, °squad, troop, °platoon, °detachment,
°detail, cadre, °unit, *Colloq* °bunch, °outfit: *A
small party of men is trapped on the other side of
the river.* **3** °side, °interest, °faction, °league,
°club, coalition, bloc, °division, °sect,
°denomination, °clique, coterie, °set, °cabal,
°junta or junto, partisans, adherents, confederacy, confederation, °federation, *Chiefly US
and Canadian* caucus: *The proliferation of political*

parties confuses the electorate. **4** °participant, participator, confederate, °associate, °ally,
°accomplice, °accessory, approver, ratifier,
upholder, contributor, °supporter, °advocate,
°backer, °aid, helper, seconder, promoter,
°partisan, defender, exponent, °proponent,
°champion: *I refuse to be a party to any illegal
act.* **5** °individual, °person, °litigant, plaintiff,
defendant, °side, °interest, signer, signatory,
co-signatory, °participant, *US* co-signer: *The party
of the first part accuses the party of the second part
of infidelity. How many parties are there to this
contract?*

parvenu *n.* **1** parvenue, °upstart, *arriviste*, *nouveau riche*, °intruder, °adventurer, social
climber: *Usually one generation has to pass before
a parvenu is accepted by the class with which his
money associates him.*
—*adj.* **2** *nouveau riche*, °upstart, °intrusive: *This
parvenu industrialist tried to use his wealth to make
up for his lack of refinement.*

pass *v.* **1** Often, **pass by**: °proceed or °move
°past, °go by or °past: *She passed me in the street. I
didn't recognize her till she had passed. We met like
ships that pass in the night.* **2** °proceed, °move
(°onwards), °go (°ahead), °progress, °extend, °lie,
°run, °flow, °fly, °roll, °course, °stream, °drift,
°sweep: *A flock of geese passed overhead.* **3** °let
pass, °let °go (by), °overlook, °disregard,
°ignore, pay no °heed, °omit, °skip: *I think I'll
pass on making a °decision till the proper time
comes.* **4** °qualify (in), pass °muster (in), °get or
°come through, °succeed: *Deirdre didn't believe she
would pass chemistry, but pass she did.* **5** °spend,
°devote, °use (up), °expend, °employ, °occupy,
°fill, while away, °take (up); °dissipate, °waste,
°fritter away, °kill: *He passed his time on Devil's
Island planning ways to escape.* **6** °surpass,
°exceed, °outdo, °transcend, °go beyond, overshoot, °outstrip, outrun, surmount, outdistance: *She passed her own expectations in
winning the scholarship. How Alan ever got a degree
passes all comprehension.* **7** °allow, °tolerate,
°permit, °approve, °sanction, °accept,
°authorize, °endorse, °carry, °agree to,
°confirm: *The customs inspectors passed my luggage
without question. The bill passed the committee and
came up for voting.* **8** °give, °hand °round or
along or over, °transfer, pass on or over, °deliver,
convey, *Sports US* hand off, *Colloq* °toss, °throw,
°reach: *Please pass the salt. The sweeper passed the
ball back to the goalkeeper.* **9** utter, °express, °issue,
°declare, °pronounce, °deliver, °set forth,
°offer: *Who is she to pass judgement on abstract
paintings?* **10** °go away, °disappear, vanish,
°evaporate, °fade away, °melt away, evanesce,
°cease (to exist), (come to an) °end, °die out,
go by the board, °terminate, *Literary* evanish,
Colloq °blow over: *For an instant I was gripped
by a horrible fear, but the feeling passed.* **11** °go
(by), °expire, °elapse; °slip by or away, °fly;
°crawl, °creep, °drag: *Weeks have passed since we
last met. Time passes quickly when you're having
fun.* **12** °evacuate, °void, °eliminate, excrete,
°defecate, °urinate: *The tests showed that he had
passed some gravel in his urine.* **13 come to pass**:
befall, °happen, °occur, °take °place, °come
about, °arise, *Colloq* °come off: *And it came to
pass that a great pestilence was abroad in the
land.* **14 pass away: a** °die, °expire, °perish,
°succumb, breathe one's last, pass on, go to
one's reward, go to one's final or last

resting-place, (go to) meet one's Maker, *Colloq* go west, give up the ghost, *Slang* croak, kick the bucket, *Chiefly US* bite the dust, turn up one's toes: *He was the sole beneficiary when she passed away.* **b** vanish, °disappear, °go away, °stop, °cease, °end: *The feeling of vertigo simply passed away when the plane landed.* **15 pass by**: See 1, above: *The strikers were urging people to pass by the shop.* **16 pass for** *or* **as: a** be °taken for, be °mistaken for, be regarded as, be accepted as: *He wrote a book about being a man who passed for a woman.* **b** impersonate, °imitate, °mimic, °pass (oneself) off as, °come *or* °go as, be disguised as, °disguise oneself as, °assume the °guise of, °masquerade as, °pose as, °assume the °role of, °act the part of, °pretend to be, °play: *Using her best cockney accent, she tried to pass as a Londoner.* **17 pass off**: °evaporate, °disappear, evanesce, be emitted: *The water passes off as steam, leaving the distillate in the flask.* **18 pass on: a** °proceed, °continue, °progress: *Let us now pass on to the next lesson.* **b** °bequeath, °hand down *or* on, °transfer, °make over, °will, °cede, °give: *The old gambler passed on to me the secret of never losing—Don't gamble.* **c** See 14 a above. **19 pass (oneself) off as**: See 16 b, above. **20 pass out: a** °faint, °collapse, swoon, black out, °drop, *Colloq* conk out, keel over: *When they told her of the accident, she passed out on the spot.* **b** °distribute, °dole out, °mete out, °deal (out), °hand out: *After we took our seats, the cabin staff passed out glasses of champagne.* **21 pass over**: See 3, above: *I shall pass over his latest misdeeds without comment.* **22 pass up**: °reject, °decline, °refuse, °waive, °turn down, °dismiss, °spurn, °renounce, °deny (oneself), °skip, °give up, °forgo, °let °go (by), °abandon, forswear, °forsake, °let pass, °ignore, pay no °heed, °disregard, °omit: *If you don't buy this car, you are passing up an opportunity of a lifetime.* —*n.* **23** defile, °gorge, col, cwm, cut, °canyon, notch, °gap, °gully *or* gulley, couloir; °passage, °opening, °way, °route, °road: *We had mined the pass to prevent the enemy's advance.* **24** authorization, °permit, °licence, °approval, safe conduct, green light, °go-ahead, °permission, °freedom, °liberty, °authority, °clearance; *Colloq* °OK *or* okay: *He bribed an official for a pass to leave the country.* **25** °free pass, °complimentary ticket, *Slang US* twofer, Annie Oakley: *I have two passes to the opera tonight—Want to go?* **26** °state (of affairs), °condition, °situation, °stage, °juncture, °status, crux; °predicament, °crisis: *At that critical pass, it was too late to change policy. Things had come to a pretty pass.* **27** °attempt, °trial, °try, °effort, °endeavour: *Anita's first pass at a perfect score resulted in disaster. We made a pass at docking while under sail.* **28** (°sexual *or* °indecent) °overture *or* °advance(s), °proposition, °indecent °proposal: *That lecher has made a pass at every secretary he's ever had.* **29** °manoeuvre, °approach; °passage, °flight, fly-by, °transit: *The pilot's first pass over the airfield was at 500 feet.* **30** °transfer, °toss, °throw, *US* hand-off: *A forward pass is illegal in rugby.*

passable *adj.* **1** °satisfactory, °acceptable, °tolerable, all right, °adequate, admissible, allowable, °presentable, °average, °fair (enough), °fair to middling, °fairly °good, middling, not bad, unexceptional, °sufficient, °indifferent, *Colloq* °OK *or* okay, °so so: *I thought*

the play passable, but not up to his usual standard.* **2** traversable, °navigable, °open, unobstructed, unblocked: *The channel is passable till October, when the river freezes over.*

passage *n.* **1** °movement, moving, going, °transition, °transit, traversal, °traverse, °progress, crossing, °passing: *The Queen's passage through the town was attended by much jubilation. We observed the passage of Mercury across the sun's disc.* **2** °extract, °excerpt, °selection, °section, °part, °portion, °text, paragraph, canto, stanza, verse, °line, °sentence, °phrase, citation, °quotation: *I recognize this passage from* The Faerie Queene. **3** °way, °route, avenue, °course, °channel; °road, thoroughfare: *Amundsen found a navigable passage between the Atlantic and Pacific across North America.* **4** °corridor, °hall, passageway, hallway, vestibule, °lobby, foyer: *As I stepped into the passage outside my room I heard a door slam.* **5** °change, °mutation, °shift, conversion, °progression, passing: *In sublimation, the passage is directly between the solid and gaseous or vaporous states, without an intermediate liquid stage.* **6** °passing, °elapse, °progress, °progression, °flow, °march, °advance: *She may become more tractable with the passage of time.* **7** voyage, °trip, °journey, °cruise, crossing, °sail, °run, °travel, travelling; *Brit* °accommodation *or US* °accommodations, °arrangement(s), facilities: *In 1942 the trans-Atlantic passage was fraught with danger. The refugees were guaranteed safe passage to the border. We have been unable to book a passage to Majorca for tomorrow.* **8** safe conduct, °permission, °privilege, °liberty, °freedom, visa, authorization, °allowance: *Our troops were denied passage through Nepal.* **9** enactment, ratification, °sanction, °approval, acceptance, passing, adoption, °endorsement, endorsing, legitimatization *or* legitimization, legalization, legislation, constitutionalization, ordainment: *It appears that there is enough support to ensure passage of the bill.* **10** °traffic, trafficking, dealing, shipment, shipping, °commerce, °trade, °exchange, °transaction: *Representatives of several governments discussed putting a halt to the passage of narcotics from Colombia.* **11** °aperture, °hole, orifice, °opening, °entry, access, inlet; °exit, °outlet: *We found a tiny passage through which the termites were entering and leaving.*

passé *adj.* °old-fashioned, unfashionable, dated, out of °date, behind the °times, outmoded, °obsolete, °obsolescent, °antiquated, archaic, démodé, °quaint, °antique, superseded, *Colloq* out, not *or* no longer in, °old hat, back number: *She persisted in dressing in a style that had been passé at the turn of the century.*

passenger *n.* rider, °fare, °traveller, voyager, commuter: *The cruise ships have very comfortable accommodation for their passengers.*

passing *adj.* **1** disappearing, vanishing, ephemeral, °brief, going, fading (away), slipping away, °short-lived, expiring, °transient, transitory, °temporary, °momentary, °fleeting, transitional, impermanent: *I hope that Anne's obsession with acid rock is a passing fancy.* **2** °hasty, °superficial, °cursory, °casual, quick, °fleeting, °brief, °summary, °abrupt, dismissive; glancing: *The speaker paid only passing attention to those he disagreed with.* **3 in passing**: by the °way,

°incidentally, by the by, parenthetically, *en passant: I might mention, in passing, that my train was late owing to the strike.*
—*n.* **4** °death, °dying, demise, °end, °loss, expiry, °expiration, °dying out, extinction, disappearance, vanishment: *Her passing is a great sorrow to all of us. Who thought we would live to see the passing of the steam engine?*

passion *n.* **1** Often, **passions**: °ardour, °ardency, °eagerness, °intensity, °fervour, fervency, fervidness, zeal, zealousness, avidity, avidness, °zest, zestfulness, vivacity, vivaciousness, °gusto, °verve, °emotion, °feeling, °animation, °spirit, spiritedness, °vigour, °enthusiasm; °zealotry, °fanaticism, feverishness: *The passions of the mob are uncontrollable. Passion and prejudice govern the world. Passions ran high at the political convention.* **2** °fit, °outburst, °frenzy, °paroxysm, °seizure, °spasm, convulsion, °eruption, °whirlwind, °tempest, °storm, °ferment, °fury, °furore or US furor: *Henry fell on his knees in a passion of grief.* **3** infatuation, °mania, obsession, °craze, craving, °lust, (unquenchable) °thirst, (insatiable) °hunger, °itch, yearning, °longing, °desire, concupiscence, °love, °affection, °enthusiasm, compulsion, fondness, predilection, keenness, °fancy, °fascination, °partiality, °liking, °interest, °weakness, *Colloq* yen: *Would the world be a better place if the passion for spiritual values were as great as for material things? She has a passion for chocolates.* **4** °love, heart's °desire, °beloved, °idol, °hero or °heroine, °obsession, *Colloq* heartthrob, dream-girl or dream-boy: *He may not look much to you but he is the passion of every teenage girl.* **5** Usually, **Passion**: °pain, °suffering, °agony, martyrdom: *Christ underwent his Passion at Calvary.*

passionate *adj.* **1** °ardent, °eager, °intense, fervid, zealous, avid, °earnest, zestful, °feverish, °fanatic(al), vehement, °impassioned, °emotional, °animated, °spirited, °enthusiastic, °vigorous, invigorated, °energetic: *Passionate environmentalists campaign for better governmental control of carbon dioxide emissions.* **2** aroused, °lustful, °lecherous, °erotic, °sexual, amorous, °sensual, *Colloq* °hot: *She tried to resist his passionate advances.* **3** °quick-tempered, irascible, °hotheaded, °fiery, °testy, huffy or huffish, °peevish, °cranky, peppery, choleric, °touchy, °bilious, °snappish, °volatile, °cross, °temperamental, °irritable, °quarrelsome, °pugnacious, °argumentative, contentious, °belligerent, *Rare* atrabilious or atrabiliar: *Valerie gets into a passionate mood whenever she thinks she is being treated unjustly.*

passive *adj.* **1** °inactive, non-aggressive, °inert, motionless, unresponsive, °quiet, °calm, °tranquil, °serene, placid, °still, °idle, unmoving, °unmoved, °impassive, untouched, °cool, °indifferent, °phlegmatic, uninterested, uninvolved, °dispassionate, apathetic, °lifeless, °listless, quiescent, unperturbed, °unaffected, imperturbable, unshaken, *Colloq* laid-back, out of it: *The comic was unable to get a reaction from the passive audience.* **2** °submissive, repressed, deferential, °yielding, compliant, complaisant, °receptive, °flexible, malleable, °pliable, °tractable, docile, °subdued, °sheepish, ovine, lamblike, cow-like, bovine, °tame, °gentle, °meek, °patient, unresisting, unassertive, forbearing, °tolerant, resigned, long-suffering,

Colloq US excuse-me-for-living: *People tend to bully those of a more passive nature.* **3** unexpressed, °tacit, unrevealed, undisclosed, °implicit, unasserted: *We can no longer take a passive position regarding crime. Your passive support, while welcome, is not as effective as active campaigning.*

password *n.* watchword, °shibboleth, open sesame, countersign: *If you don't know the password, the guard won't let you in.*

past *adj.* **1** over, done, finished, (over and) done with, gone (and forgotten), °dead (and buried or gone), °defunct: *The day of the horse and carriage is past.* **2** °late, °former, one-time, °sometime, °previous, °prior, erstwhile, quondam, whilom; °last, °recent: *Past owners of the house had no idea that this treasure was buried in the basement.*
—*adv.* **3** on, °(close) by, °nearby: *I was standing here when he ran past.* **4** ago, °before, heretofore, since: *The previous owners moved out two years past.*
—*n.* **5** °history, °background, °life, lifetime, °existence, °career, lifestyle, biography: *She reveals all about her past in her new book.* **6** days or years or times gone by, days of yore, °old times, olden times or days, °former times, (good) °old days, days of °old, days beyond recall: *In the past, life proceeded at a more leisurely pace.*

pastiche *n.* °mixture, °medley, °blend, °compound, composite, °patchwork, olla podrida, °pot-pourri, motley, °miscellany, omnium gatherum, *mélange*, gallimaufry, farrago, °mishmash, °hotchpotch or US and Canadian hodgepodge, °tangle, *Colloq* °mess: *The room was furnished in a pastiche of styles from every imaginable period.*

pastime *n.* °hobby, avocation, °recreation, °diversion, °distraction, °amusement, °entertainment, °fun, °play, leisure-time °activity, °relaxation, °leisure, °sport, divertissement: *As a pastime, she collects books.*

pastor *n.* vicar, °clergyman, clergywoman, parson, °minister, churchman, churchwoman, rector, canon, reverend, °father, °divine, ecclesiastic, °priest, bishop: *The pastor led the congregation in prayer.*

pastoral *adj.* **1** bucolic, °idyllic, Edenic, °innocent, °simple, °tranquil, °serene, °quiet, °restful, °peaceful, °peaceable, placid, pacific, °harmonious, un-complicated, *Literary* Arcadian, georgic: *After a week in those pastoral surroundings, she felt inspired. Theocritus is noted for his pastoral poetry.* **2** °country, °rural, °rustic, °provincial, °farming, agricultural, agrarian; °humble: *He has chosen a pastoral setting for the play, which contrasts sharply with the emotional intensity of the characters.* **3** °clerical, ministerial, ecclesiastic(al), church(ly): *Our vicar discharges his pastoral duties with energy and sincerity.*
—*n.* **4** idyll, eclogue, georgic: *Flambeau did these marvellous engravings for a book of pastorals.*

pasture *n.* °meadow, meadow-land, pasture °land, grassland, °grass, lea, °range; pasturage: *How much pasture is needed for 200 head of cattle?*

pasty *adj.* °wan, pallid, pasty-faced, sallow, °pale, pale-faced, whey-faced, °sickly, anaemic: *He had the pasty complexion of a child raised in an industrial city.*

pat[1] *v.* **1** °tap, °touch, °dab, °pet, °stroke, °caress: *Being short, he hated it when people affectionately patted him on the head. Pat down the coverlet to smooth out the wrinkles.* **2 pat on the back**:

°congratulate, commend, °praise, °compliment, °encourage, °reassure: *The sales manager patted me on the back for clinching the contract.*
—*n.* **3** °tap, °touch, °dab, °stroke, °caress: *Give the dog a pat and he'll leave you alone.* **4** (°small) piece, patty, °lump, °cake, °portion; patty: *The waiter put a pat of butter on my plate.* **5 pat on the back**: commendation, °praise, °compliment, °flattery, °encouragement, °credit, reassurance, °approval, °endorsement, °recognition; honeyed words: *I was expecting a big bonus, but all I got was a pat on the back.*

pat[2] *adv.* **1** °perfectly, °exactly, °precisely, faultlessly, flawlessly, °just so *or* °right, *Brit* off pat: *She has the new technique pat.* **2** aptly, suitably, appositely, °readily, °appropriately, fittingly, relevantly: *His reply came out a little too pat.*
—*adj.* **3** apt, °suitable, apposite, °ready, °appropriate, °fitting, °relevant: *The poet made a very pat comparison.*

patch *n.* **1** °piece, °scrap, °reinforcement; °shred, °snip, snippet, °tatter; pad: *Mother sewed colourful patches over the holes in my jeans.* **2** °area, °section, °segment, plat, °plot, °lot, °tract, °ground, °parcel, °field: *All he ever wanted was a little house on a little patch of land.* **3** °responsibility, °area, bailiwick, °territory: *The handling of customer complaints is in your patch, Gordon.* **4** °period, °interval, °spell, °stage, °episode, °time; °experience: *She went through a bad patch shortly after Starkey died.*
—*v.* **5** °patch up *or* over, °mend, °repair, vamp, °revamp, darn, °sew (up), °reinforce, °cover: *I had my trousers patched where the dog bit me. Her father always wore the same patched jacket to the club.* **6** Often, **patch up**: °fix (up), °doctor, jury-rig, °improvise, °knock together *or* up: *Can you patch it up so I can drive it home?* **7 patch up**: °settle, set °right *or* °straight, °straighten out, °reconcile, °resolve, °heal; come *or* bring to °terms, bury the hatchet, kiss and °make up, °call a °truce: *Will the two girls ever patch up their differences?*

patchwork *n.* °pastiche *or* pasticcio, °mixture, °confusion, °hotchpotch *or* US also hodgepodge, gallimaufry, olio, olla podrida, °mishmash, °jumble, *mélange*, °medley, °hash, US crazy quilt, *Colloq* mixed bag: *The landscape is a patchwork of ploughland and pasture, with little copses and rivers. The concerto by Lindslade is 'derivative'—that is, it is a patchwork.*

patent *n.* **1** certificate of °invention, letters patent, °trade °name, °trade °mark, copyright, US service °mark; °licence, °permit, °charter, franchise, °grant; °control: *My brother holds the patent on a new piece of laboratory equipment. You think you have a patent on misery, but I have news for you.*
—*adj.* **2** °obvious, °clear, °transparent, °manifest, °apparent, °plain, °evident, °self-evident, unmistakable, °explicit, palpable, °tangible, °physical, °conspicuous, °flagrant, °blatant, °prominent: *The results are as patent as the fact that two and two make four.*

paternal *adj.* **1** °fatherly, °kindly, °indulgent, °solicitous, °fond, °concerned, °devoted, loving; patriarchal: *Uncle Charles takes a paternal interest in the welfare of his nieces and nephews.*

2 patrilineal *or* patrilinear, patriclinous *or* patroclinous *or* patriclinal *or* patroclinal *or* patriclinic *or* patroclinic, patrilateral, patrimonial: *She resembles her paternal grandmother. His fortune is partly paternal, partly acquired.*

paternity *n.* fatherhood, fathership; °parentage, descent, °heritage, °line, °lineage, °extraction, °family, °stock, °strain, blood, patrilineage: *The child's paternity was established through DNA tests.*

path *n.* **1** footpath, pathway, tow-path, °track, °trail, °walk, walkway, *Brit* footway: *A little kitten was sitting on the garden path.* **2** °way, °course, °track, °route, °road; °orbit, °trajectory, °circuit: *She had to overcome many obstacles in her path to the directorship. The path of the missile will take it outside the atmosphere.* **3** °course, °approach, °channel, °direction, °procedure, °process, °way, avenue, °means, °method, °technique, °strategy, °scheme, °plan, *Colloq* US game °plan, °scenario: *What path would you follow to accomplish your ends?*

pathetic *adj.* **1** °moving, °stirring, affecting, affective, °touching, °emotional, emotive, °poignant, °tragic, °heart-rending, heartbreaking, °pitiful, °pitiable, °piteous, plaintive, °wretched, °miserable, °sorrowful, °grievous, °sad, °doleful, dolorous, °mournful, woeful, °lamentable: *The boat people told a pathetic tale of the hardship of weeks in the open sea.* **2** °meagre, °paltry, °feeble, °inadequate, °poor, °petty, °puny, °sorry, piddling, *Colloq* °measly, *Slang* crummy: *He made a pathetic effort to pull himself together. A return of three per cent a year is pathetic.*

patience *n.* **1** °tolerance, forbearance, °restraint, toleration, sufferance, leniency, °submission, °resignation, °self-control, imperturbability, even °temper, unflappability, composure, calmness, °serenity, equanimity: *Many parents lose their patience when dealing with children.* **2** diligence, °tenacity, doggedness, indefatigability, °endurance, assiduity, °perseverance, constancy, °persistence, steadfastness, pertinacity, °determination, °resolve, °resolution, firmness, °stoicism, °fortitude, *Colloq* US stick-to-it-iveness: *Where do you get the patience to wait in those long queues?*

patient *adj.* **1** resigned, °submissive, °stoical, long-suffering, compliant, acquiescent, °passive, °self-possessed, °philosophical, °serene, unaggressive: *The staff who handle complaints must be extremely patient.* **2** °diligent, dogged, °tenacious, °persistent, assiduous, sedulous, °steadfast, °staunch, perseverant, unwavering, unswerving, °constant, unfaltering, unfailing, °untiring, °tireless, indefatigable, pertinacious, °determined, resolved, °resolute, °firm, unyielding: *Be patient, and don't do anything rash.* **3** forbearing, °tolerant, °forgiving, °lenient, °accommodating: *We have been patient long enough and must now put a stop to the vandalism.*
—*n.* **4** °invalid, sufferer, °case, valetudinarian: *Doctors were called in to treat patients who developed the symptoms.*

patriot *n.* nationalist, loyalist; flag-waver, jingo, jingoist, chauvinist: *She was among the patriots ready to do battle for their country.*

patriotic *adj.* nationalist(ic), loyalist; flag-waving, jingoist(ic), chauvinist(ic): *The fact that they criticize the government may show that they are more rather than less patriotic.*

patrol n. 1 °guard, sentry, °watch, °watchman, °sentinel, patrolman: *The patrol passes here once every hour.* 2 °rounds, policing, patrolling, °beat; protecting, °protection, guarding, safeguarding, defending, watchfulness, °vigilance: *The patrol must be maintained night and day.* —v. 3 °police, °guard, °protect, °defend, °watch over, walk a °beat, make (the) °rounds, stand or keep °guard or °watch (over), keep vigil: *Some of the local residents have taken to patrolling the neighbourhood at night.*

patron n. 1 patroness, °benefactor, benefactress, °philanthropist, Maecenas, °protector, °supporter, defender, °advocate, °champion, °guardian (angel), °sponsor, °backer, promoter, °sympathizer, °friend, °friend at court; *Colloq* angel: *Lady Agnes is a well-known patron of the arts.* 2 °customer, °client, purchaser, °buyer, patronizer, °habitué, °regular, frequenter: *The patrons habituate her shop because of the bargains to be found there.*

patronage n. 1 sponsorship, °support, °backing, °promotion, °encouragement, boosting, °aid, °help, °sympathy, financing, °auspices, °protection, guardianship, aegis: *The exhibition was organized with the duke's patronage.* 2 °trade, °business, °custom, trading, °traffic: *The shop could never succeed with our patronage.* 3 condescension, disdain, °scorn, °contempt, contumely, °superiority, patronizing, stooping, deigning, °humiliation: *There is an air of patronage about him when he finally does allow me a visit.* 4 °favouritism, °partiality, °preference, °bias, nepotism, political patronage, granting of indulgences, *US* °spoils (system): *Politicians have always used patronage to reward support.*

patronize v. 1 °look down on, °scorn, °look down one's nose at, °treat condescendingly, °talk down to, °treat as (an) °inferior, disdain, demean, °put down, °humiliate, *Formal* contemn: *He patronizes people by patting them on the head.* 2 bring °trade to, °deal or °trade with, do or °transact °business with, °buy or °purchase from, °frequent, °shop at, be a °customer or °client of: *You should patronize the local merchants in your town.* 3 °sponsor, °support, °back, °promote, °encourage, °boost, °aid, °assist, °help, °fund, °contribute or °subscribe to, °underwrite, °foster: *The fund has patronized the arts in this town for many years.*

patter[1] v. 1 tiptoe; °scurry, scuttle, °skip, °trip: *I could hear the squirrels pattering across the metal roof.* 2 °spatter, pitter-patter, °tap, pit-a-pat; °beat, °pelt: *The rain pattered on the tent with increasing intensity.* —n. 3 °spatter, spattering, pit-a-pat, pitter-patter, tattoo, drum, thrum, °beat, beating, °tap, ratatat, tap-tap: *The rhythmical patter of the rain lulled me to sleep.*

patter[2] n. 1 °pitch, sales °talk, spiel, °line: *Anyone listening to his patter might be inclined to buy a time-share holiday.* 2 °chatter, °prattle, prate, babbling, °babble, gabble, gabbling, cackle, cackling, °palaver, °jabber, jabbering, chit-chat, °small °talk, °gossip, blather or blether, °gibberish or gibber, *Chiefly Brit* natter, nattering, *Scots* clishmaclaver, *Colloq* °gab, gabbing, *Slang* gas, °hot air, ya(c)kety-ya(c)k, ya(c)k: *The chap tapping our phone had to listen to the teenagers' patter for hours on end.* —v. 3 °chatter, °prattle, prate, °babble, gabble, cackle, °palaver, °jabber, °rattle (on), chit-chat,

chaffer, °gossip, blather or blether, gibber, *Chiefly Brit* natter, witter (on), *Colloq* °gab, *Slang* gas, ya(c)kety-ya(c)k, ya(c)k, jibber-jabber: *They just patter on about nothing in particular.*

pattern n. 1 °model, °original, archetype, °prototype, exemplar, °paragon, °ideal, °standard, °yardstick, criterion, °gauge, °measure: *Their life together could serve as a pattern for any couple.* 2 °figure, °motif, °design, °device, °decoration, °ornament: *The pattern of the wallpaper clashes with that of the curtains.* 3 °system, °order, °arrangement, °plan, °theme; °repetition, consistency, orderliness, °regularity, °sequence, °cycle: *By carefully noting the movements of the heavenly bodies, ancient observers were able to detect a pattern.* 4 blueprint, diagram, °plan, layout, °design, °draft, °guide, °template or templet, stencil, °mould, matrix: *These new lighting fixtures are made to a 19th-century pattern.* 5 °sample, °example, °instance, °specimen, °representation: *Were you able to match up your fabric pattern with one of those in the tailor's book?* 6 layout, configuration, °figure, °formation, °composition: *The geese often flew in a V-shaped pattern.* —v. 7 Often, **pattern on**: °model on, °imitate, °copy, °mimic, °duplicate, °follow, emulate, simulate: *She tried to pattern her behaviour on that of her older sister.* 8 °decorate, °figure, °ornament: *Cynthia's gifts were wrapped in a beautifully patterned paper.*

paunch n. belly, pot-belly, *Colloq* corporation, *US* bay window, *Slang* beer-belly: *Capitalism is often conventionalized as a top-hatted older man, in tails, with a huge paunch and a cigar.*

pauper n. have-not, °indigent, °down-and-out(er), bankrupt, °insolvent; °beggar, mendicant, °tramp, hobo, vagrant, *US* °bum: *The mortgage payments on such a lavish house soon made him a pauper.*

pause v. 1 °hesitate, °interrupt, °delay, °hold up, °discontinue, °break, °wait, mark time, °suspend, intermit, falter, °rest: *He paused for a moment to allow late-comers to take their seats.* —n. 2 hesitation, °interruption, °delay, °lull, °lapse, °moratorium, °hold-up, °wait, °break, breather, breathing-space, discontinuity, lacuna, hiatus, °abeyance, discontinuation, discontinuance, *Prosody* caesura, *Music* fermata, *Colloq* °let-up: *There was a brief pause, then the altercation in the neighbouring flat resumed.*

pave v. 1 macadamize, tarmac, asphalt, tile, flag, °concrete, °cover, °surface: *Europeans thought that the streets of America were paved with gold.* 2 **pave the way for** or **to**: °prepare or °smooth the °way for, °open the door for, make °easy or easier for; °facilitate, °ease: *If I talk to him first, perhaps I can pave the way for you to make your proposal.*

pawn[1] v. 1 °pledge, mortgage, hypothecate, °plight, °deposit, *Formal* pignorate, *Archaic* gage, *Colloq Brit* pop, *Chiefly US and Canadian* hock: *I had to pawn my watch to get enough money to eat.* 2 °venture, °stake, °risk, °gamble, °hazard, °chance, °jeopardize: *By agreeing to donate one of his kidneys, he pawned his life to save hers.* —n. 3 collateral, guaranty or °guarantee, °pledge, surety, °security, °assurance, °bond, bail, °deposit: *She gave her jewels as pawn for the safe return of the children.*

pawn² *n.* °tool, cat's-paw, °puppet, instrument, °dummy, °dupe, *Colloq* stooge: *He's not important: he's just being used as a pawn by the powerful interests involved.*

pay *v.* **1** recompense, °compensate, remunerate, °reward, indemnify; °repay, refund, °reimburse; pay off, pay out, pay up, °satisfy, °clear, °remit, °discharge, liquidate, °settle, °honour, °meet: *Do you think that nurses are poorly paid? You have 30 days to pay this invoice.* **2** °reward, °benefit, recompense, °requite, °compensate: *Thurlow has been amply paid by having his name engraved on the roll of honour.* **3** °extend, °bestow, °transmit, °pass on, °give, °deliver: *Please may my respects to your wife.* **4** °benefit, °profit, avail, (turn out to) be or prove °profitable or °worthwhile, °yield a °return, °repay, °benefit, °advantageous, produce results, pay off: *It no longer pays to complain about the service in the shops. Honesty pays.* **5** pay back, °repay, °retaliate, °settle (accounts) (with),°reciprocate, °requite, take or get °revenge on, avenge oneself for or on, °treat in kind, °hit or °strike or °get back (at), °settle or pay off or °even a °score or the °score (with), °exact one's pound of flesh (from), make (someone) pay (for), °punish, °chastise, °castigate, *Brit* pay out, *Colloq* get °even (with): *If I catch him, I'll pay him for turning informer.* **6** °suffer (the consequences), °answer (for), make °amends (for), °atone (for), get one's (just) deserts, °undergo °punishment (for), be punished (for): *If I catch him, I'll make him pay. Society requires that he pay for his crime.* **7** °produce or °make or °generate or °earn °money, °yield a °return, pay off: *His vending-machine business certainly pays well.* **8 pay back: a** recompense, °compensate, remunerate, °reward, indemnify; °repay, pay off, refund, °reimburse: *I paid back every penny I borrowed from the bank. I'll pay her back if it's the last thing I do.* **b** See 5, above. **9 pay for:** See 6, above. **10 pay off: a** See 4 and 7, and 8a, above. **b** °bribe, suborn, °buy off, grease (someone's) palm, give (someone) a °bribe or a °rebate, *Colloq* give (someone) a °kickback, slip (someone) something: *Did he really pay off the judges to select his daughter as Miss Tyneside?* **11 pay out: a** °distribute, °deal out, °give out, °disperse, disburse: *The managing director paid out bonuses to the entire staff.* **b** disburse, °expend, °spend, °contribute, *Colloq* °shell out, °lay out, *US and Canadian and Australian and New Zealand* kick in with, *Slang* cough up, fork out or over or up: *In the office, we are forever paying out for leaving presents.* **c** °release, °loosen, °let out, °slack or slacken off (on): *Pay out more rope so that he can reach it.* **d** See 5, above: *We'll pay him out for everything he's done to you, never fear!* —*n.* **12** °payment, compensation, recompense, °settlement, °return; °remuneration, °consideration, °reward, °money, wages, °salary, °fee, °honorarium, °remittance, °stipend, °income, takings, take-home (pay), °gain, °profit, *Colloq US* °take: *His sole pay for painting the kitchen was a big hug and a kiss. The work is tedious, but the pay isn't bad.*

payable *adj.* °due, owed, owing, °outstanding, °unpaid, receivable, °mature: *This bill is payable at the end of the month.*

payment *n.* **1** See pay, 12, above. **2** °expenditure, disbursement, °distribution, °outlay, °fee, contribution, °charge, °expense, payout: *You are not authorized to make payment of any amount over £100.*

pay-off *n.* **1** See pay, 12, above. **2** °result, °outcome, °upshot, conclusion, wind-up, °settlement, final °reckoning, *Colloq* punch-line, °crunch, grand finale, *Slang US and Canadian* kicker: *The pay-off was that permission to march on Sunday was denied.* **3** °bribe, °graft, °rebate; °ransom, blood-money, *Colloq* °kickback, °hush °money, *Chiefly US* payola, *US* plugola: *The pay-off was always made in cash, in used notes.*

peace *n.* **1** °serenity, tranquillity, °calm, calmness, placidity or placidness, peace of mind, °quiet, peacefulness, peaceableness, stillness: *For a summer holiday, we enjoy the peace of the Lakes.* **2** °harmony, °accord, harmoniousness, concord, amity, peacefulness, peacetime; cease-fire, armistice, °truce: *Since the Second World War, Europe has enjoyed more than 45 years of relative peace.*

peaceable *adj.* **1** See peaceful, 1, below. **2** pacific, °inoffensive, dovish, peace-loving, °mild, non-violent, non-belligerent, unbelligerent, unwarlike, non-warring, non-combative, °temperate, °agreeable, compatible, congenial, °genial, °friendly, °amiable, °amicable, °cordial, °civil: *Despite cultural differences, the two countries maintained peaceable relations.*

peaceful *adj.* **1** °peaceable, °serene, placid, °calm, °quiet, quiescent, °gentle, °restful, °tranquil, untroubled, undisturbed, unruffled: *After our week-end guests left, the house was again peaceful.* **2** See peaceable, 2, above.

peacemaker *n.* conciliator, pacifier, reconciler, propitiator, placater, pacificator, °mediator, arbitrator, intermediator, °intermediary, diplomat, appeaser, interceder, °go-between, referee, °umpire, adjudicator; peacemonger: *The ambassador was called upon to act as peacemaker between the warring nations.*

peak *n.* **1** °top, °pinnacle, °crest, °ridge, tor, °mountain °top, °summit, °mountain, eminence, °elevation, °hill: *We were just able to make out the snow-capped peaks in the distance.* **2** °top, °tip, tiptop, apex, °acme, culmination, apogee, °zenith, °high °point, °crown, °extreme, utmost, uttermost, °perfection, ne plus ultra, °consummation, °climax: *Irene has brought the office to a peak of efficiency.* **3** visor, °brim, *US* bill, nib: *The peak of the fisherman's cap serves as an eyeshade.* —*v.* **4** °rise, °crest, culminate, (°reach a) °climax, °top (out): *Prices peaked during the Christmas shopping season.*

peaky *adj.* peakish, pinched, °unhealthy, °sickly, ailing, °ill, unwell, °infirm, °unwholesome, °pale, pallid, °wan, waxen, anaemic, °pasty, sallow, whey-faced, ashen, washed out, drained, °emaciated, wasted, °gaunt, hollow-eyed, °haggard, °drawn, °weak, °feeble, *US* peaked: *Paul has been looking a bit peaky of late.*

peal *n.* **1** ringing, °ring, carillon, °chime, chiming, °toll, tolling, clang, clangour, tintinnabulation, clamour, reverberation; knell; °clap, °crash, °roar, rumble, °thunder: *The constant peal of the bells nearly drove him mad. The doleful peal rang out for yet another fisherman lost at sea. A resounding peal of thunder shook the house.* —*v.* **2** °ring, °toll, °chime, clang, tintinnabulate, reverberate, resonate, °resound; knell; °boom,

°crash, °roar, °roll, rumble, °thunder: *The cow-bells pealed plaintively, reminding me of my youth in the Alps. Lightning flashed, and the echoing thunder pealed through the valley.*

pearl *n.* °gem, °treasure, °prize, cream, °flower, °wonder, °nonpareil: *Wasn't Cuba once called the Pearl of the Antilles?*

pearly *adj.* nacreous, pearl-like, perlaceous, °lustrous, mother-of-pearl: *The dress was trimmed with pink lace and little pearly buttons.*

peasant *n.* °rustic, countryman, country-woman, °farmer, °provincial, (°farm) °worker, (°country) bumpkin, bucolic; peon, fellah, muzhik *or* mouzhik *or* mujik; *Historical* esne, serf, *Archaic* swain, hind, churl, *Derogatory* yokel, hill-billy, bog-trotter, oaf, °lump, lout, °boor, churl, °clod, clodhopper; *Colloq US and Canadian* hick, galoot *or* galloot, *Derogatory* hay-seed, rube, *Derogatory and offensive US* poor white (trash): *Regimes came and went, but the life of the medieval peasant endured.*

peccadillo *n.* °slip, °error, °lapse, °mistake, infraction, °violation, °misdeed, °shortcoming, °misstep, °blunder, *faux pas*, °indiscretion, gaffe, °botch, °stumble, °fault, °petty °sin, (°minor) °transgression, trespass, *Colloq* slip-up, goof: *We have to forgive the occasional peccadillo.*

peculiar *adj.* **1** °odd, °curious, °strange, °queer, °bizarre, °weird, °unusual, °abnormal, anom-alous, aberrant, °deviant *or* °deviate, °eccentric, uncommon, °outlandish, °exceptional, °extraordinary, out of the °ordinary, °offbeat, °unorthodox, atypical, idiosyncratic, uncon-ventional, °out-of-the-way, °quaint, °unique, °singular, °one of a kind, *sui generis*, °distinct, °distinguished, °special, °particular, quirky, °funny, freakish, *Slang* far-out, freaky, *Brit* rum: *Don't you agree that anyone who by choice goes barefoot in winter is a bit peculiar? She enjoys a peculiar immunity to colds.* **2** Usually, **peculiar to**: °typical of, °characteristic of, characterized by, °natural to, °symptomatic of, °appropriate to *or* for, °distinctive of, restricted to, °specific to, indicative of, denotative of, °limited to, °individual to, °personal to, °special to, °unique to; seen *or* observed (°only) in, °local to, °native to, °indigenous to: *Such behaviour is peculiar to those who have served long prison sentences.*
—*n.* **3** *Typography* arbitrary, sort: *Characters with diacritical marks are called 'peculiars' in the printing trades.*

peculiarity *n.* **1** idiosyncrasy, °oddity, °eccentricity, °abnormality, irregularity, °quirk, °kink, crotchet, caprice: *Keeping alligators was only one of Jess's peculiarities.* **2** °feature, °characteristic, °property, °quality, °trait, °attribute, earmark, °hallmark, °mark, par-ticularity, °singularity, *Brit* °speciality, *US* spe-cialty: *One of the peculiarities of the books is their wide margins.*

pedantic *adj.* **1** didactic, doctrinaire, donnish, pedagogic, pedantical, preachy, professorial, bookish, °ostentatious, °pretentious, sen-tentious, °pompous, °vain, °stuffy, °stilted, °stiff, °dry: *A pedantic approach to marketing may be all right in the classroom, but it doesn't sell products.* **2** °perfectionist, °scrupulous, over-scrupulous, °finicky *or* finical, °fussy, punctilious, °fastidious, °meticulous, °exact, chop-logic,

°hair-splitting, quibbling, *Colloq* nit-picking: *His secretary left because of his pedantic criticisms of her work.*

peddle *v.* °sell, hawk, °market, vend, huckster, *Colloq* °push, °flog: *He is a publishing tycoon today, but he started by peddling books door-to-door.*

pedestal *n.* **1** °foundation, °base, °platform, °stand, substructure, mounting, °pier, foot, °support, *Technical* plinth, socle, dado: *The statue crumbled away and only its pedestal remained.* **2 put** *or* **place** *or* **set on a pedestal**: °glorify, °exalt, °worship, deify, °revere, °idolize, °dignify, apotheosize, ennoble, elevate, °raise: *No woman is worth putting on a pedestal.*

pedestrian *n.* **1** walker, stroller, ambler, ram-bler, footslogger; itinerant, peripatetic: *A special crossing has been installed for pedestrians.*
—*adj.* **2** °boring, °dull, °banal, °tiresome, com-monplace, mundane, °tedious, unimaginative, uninteresting, °monotonous, run-of-the-mill, °humdrum, °stock, °prosaic, insipid, °dry, °flat, jejune, °colourless, °dreary, °pale, °ordinary, hackneyed, trite, (as) °dull as ditch-water *or US* also dishwater, °vapid, °stale, uninspired, un-inspiring, spiritless, °lifeless, °dead: *The dean delivered his customary pedestrian lecture to the new students.* **3** walking, strolling, ambulatory, on foot, rambling, peripatetic: *We were exhausted after taking a pedestrian tour of London.*

pedigree *n.* (°line of) descent, ancestry, gene-alogy, blood, bloodline, °line, °extraction, °lineage, °stock, °heritage, °family, °derivation, °birth, °parentage, °strain, °roots: *His pedigree is all right, but does he have brains as well as money?*

pedlar *n.* hawker, (door-to-door) salesman *or* saleswoman *or* °salesperson, vendor, huckster, °seller, colporteur, *US* peddler, drummer, *Archaic* chapman, *Colloq* cheapjack: *How can you expect the watch to work if you bought it from a street pedlar?*

peek *v.* **1** °peer, °peep, glimpse, °look, squint (at), squinny (at), *Scots* keek, *Colloq* take *or* have a gander (at), *Brit* take a dekko (at): *A small boy peeked out from under the blanket.*
—*n.* **2** °look, glimpse, °peep, °glance, *Scots* keek, *Colloq* gander, look-see: *I've had a peek at what Father hid in the cupboard.*

peel *v.* **1** Sometimes, **peel off**: °skin, °strip (off), °pare, flay, °flake off, descale, decorticate; shuck, °hull, bark, °scale; desquamate: *Beulah, peel me a grape.* **2** °strip, undress, °disrobe; do a striptease: *In the last act, everyone peels to the bare skin.* **3 peel off**: °take off *or* doff, °strip off: *I peeled off my coat and dived into the canal to save her.*
—*n.* **4** °skin, °rind, coating, peeling: *Don't you like candied orange peel?*

peep *v.* **1** °chirp, tweet, cheep, squeak, °twitter, °pipe, chirrup: *The birds peeped excitedly when they saw the cat.*
—*n.* **2** °chirp, tweet, cheep, squeak, °twitter, °pipe, chirrup, chirr *or* chirre *or* churr: *The night was filled with the peep of the frogs at the pond.* **3** °sound, °complaint, °outcry, °protest, protestation, grumble, °murmur: *The students didn't let out a peep when ordered to remain after class.*

peer[1] *n.* **1** °noble, nobleman *or* noblewoman, °lord *or* lady, aristocrat; duke *or* duchess, mar-quess *or* marchioness, earl *or* countess, viscount *or* viscountess, baron *or* baroness: *As a peer of* *the realm, she had certain rights.* **2** °equal, coequal, compeer, °like, °match, confrère, °associate, °colleague: *Under law, he is entitled to trial by a jury of his peers.*

peer[2] *v.* **1** °peep, °peek, squint (at), squinny (at), °look, °examine; °spy: *Scrooge peered closely at the accounts ledger.* **2** °appear, °peep through or out, °break through, °show, become °visible, °emerge: *Now and then, the moon peered through the clouds.*

peerless *adj.* without °equal, unequalled, °matchless, unmatched, unrivalled, °unique, °incomparable, beyond °compare, °unparalleled, °nonpareil, inimitable, unexcelled, unsurpassed, °superior, °superb, °excellent, °supreme, °superlative, finest, °best, ne plus ultra, °sovereign, consummate, °pre-eminent, °paramount: *James's mother was a peerless beauty and the toast of her generation.*

peevish *adj.* °irritable, °testy, °touchy, °fretful, ill-humoured, °waspish, °petulant, crabbed, churlish, °querulous, °short-tempered, ill-natured, tetchy, °cross, bad-tempered, ill-tempered, °fault-finding, captious, carping, cavilling, crusty, curmudgeonly, crotchety, °cantankerous, grumpy or grumpish, pettish, ·acrimonious, splenetic, *Colloq* °bilious, *US and Canadian and Irish* °cranky: *He's very peevish today, so don't get on his wrong side.*

peg *v.* **1** °pin, dowel, °rod, °stick, °bolt; thole or thole-pin; clothes-peg, °hook: *Pegs and glue are often used for fastening good furniture together. Hang your coat on the peg.* **2 off the peg:** °ready-made, ready-to-wear, °stock: *As bespoke clothing is so dear, I buy mine off the peg.* **3 take down a peg (or two):** °humble, °diminish, °lower, °subdue, °suppress, °downgrade, °dishonour, °mortify, °humiliate, °put down, abase, °debase, devalue or devaluate: *He was acting a bit high and mighty, so she took him down a peg or two.* —*v.* **4** °fasten, °secure, make °fast, °fix, °attach, °pin: *They pegged the tent firmly to the ground.* **5** °fix, °attach, °pin, °set (by), °control by, °limit by, °restrict, confine, °freeze, °bind, °regulate, °govern: *In indexing, the rate of inflation is often used for pegging wages.* **6** °toss, °throw, °shy, °flip, °sling, °cast: *I'll bet a fiver you can't peg that stone across the river.* **7 peg away** or *US* also **along:** °work (away) (at), °persevere (at), °apply oneself (to), °persist (in or at), °go to or at (it), °keep at (it), °stick to or at (it), °stay with or at (it), °carry on (with or at), *Colloq* °plug away (at), beaver away (at), hammer or bang or peck away (at): *Trevor pegs away at his homework every evening.*

pell-mell *adv.* **1** °helter-skelter, slapdash, rashly, feverishly, incautiously, confusedly, chaotically, wildly, impulsively, recklessly, slap-bang, impetuously, °hastily, hurriedly, precipitately, spontaneously: *The ice-cream vendor pedalled down the street with the children running pell-mell after him.* —*adj.* **2** °helter-skelter, slapdash, °rash, °feverish, incautious, °confused, disordered, °disorderly, disorganized, °wild, °mad, °chaotic, °tumultuous, panicky, °impulsive, °reckless, °precipitate, °impetuous, °hasty, °hurried: *Quick action by the soldiers was responsible for the pell-mell rout of the attackers.* —*n.* **3** °confusion, °disorder, °chaos, °tumult, °pandemonium, turmoil, mêlée or melee, °furore

or *US* furor, commotion, °bedlam, brouhaha, hubbub, °excitement: *In the pell-mell that followed, several bystanders were injured.*

pelt[1] *v.* **1** °bombard, °shower, °bomb, °pepper, strafe, °batter, °shell, assail, °assault, °attack, *US* pummel or pommel, °belabour, °pound, *Old-fashioned* °lay about, *Slang US* clobber, wallop, paste, work over: *The hooligans pelted the crowd with sticks and stones.* **2** Often, **pelt down:** °beat, °dash, °pound, °hit; °come down, °teem, °pour, *Colloq* °rain cats and dogs, bucket down, *US* °rain pitchforks: *The rain came pelting down just as we were ready to go out.* **3 pelt along** or **over:** °hurry, °rush, °run, °dash, °shoot, scoot, °scurry: *The constables pelted along after the escaping thief.* —*n.* **4** °stroke, °blow, whack, °hit, smack, °slap, thwack, bang, thump, *Colloq* wallop, °belt: *Chris received a pelt on the head from a rock.*

pelt[2] *n.* °skin, °hide, °coat, fur, °fleece: *The trappers traded the fox pelts for supplies.*

pen[1] *n.* **1** °writing °instrument, fountain-pen, ball-point (pen), *Brit trade mark* Biro, *Old-fashioned* quill: *Dearest, I have finally found time to put pen to paper. I prefer a pen with a fine point.* —*v.* **2** °write (down or up or out), °jot down, (make a) °note (of), °draft, °draw up, °compose, put on °paper, commit to °paper, commit to °writing, put in °writing, scribble, °scrawl, °scratch, *Formal* indite: *While he was in prison, he penned letters to many men of influence.*

pen[2] *n.* **1** coop, °enclosure, hutch, (pig)sty, pound, fold, °stall, confine, *US and Canadian* corral: *We kept the geese in a pen by the barn.* —*v.* **2** Often, **pen up:** °enclose, confine, coop up, °shut up, impound, °round up, *US and Canadian* corral: *It took three of us to pen the sheep. During the blockade, the ships remained penned up at Gibraltar.*

penal *adj.* correctional, °punitive, disciplinary: *Crime and its punishment are covered in the penal code. He was sent to a penal colony for life.*

penalize *v.* °punish, °discipline, mulct, °fine, °handicap, impose or invoke a °penalty against, impose a °penalty on, *Formal* amerce; °sentence: *This judge penalizes speeders mercilessly.*

penalty *n.* °punishment, °discipline, °penance, °sentence; °forfeit, °fine, °handicap, °price, mulct, *Formal* amercement; °imprisonment, incarceration: *The prosecution demanded the maximum penalty allowable under law for the crimes.*

penance *n.* **1** °punishment, °penalty, reparation, °amends, °atonement, self-punishment, self-mortification, °regret, repentance, contrition, °suffering, °penitence: *A year of public service was fair penance for the offence.* **2 do penance:** °pay, °suffer, make °amends or reparation(s), °atone, wear sackcloth and ashes or a hair-shirt: *She has done penance enough for her crime.*

penchant *n.* °inclination, °bent, proclivity, °leaning, °bias, predisposition, predilection, °partiality, proneness, propensity, °tendency, °affinity, °liking, °preference, fondness, °taste: *Agnes has a penchant for tennis and for men who play tennis.*

pendant *n.* °ornament, tassel, lavaliere or lavalière, medallion, locket, necklace, rivière, ear-drop, tear-drop, drop, *Old-fashioned* carcanet: *I recognized the pendant she wore at her neck as my mother's.*

pending *prep.* **1** awaiting, waiting (for), depending on, °till, until, 'til, °till such time as; while, during: *Pending the outcome of the trial, he was remanded in custody.*
—*adj.* **2** °unsettled, undetermined, undecided, unconfirmed, unfinished, °inconclusive, up in the air, hanging °fire, in the °balance, in °abeyance; °forthcoming, °imminent, °impending, in the offing, *Colloq US* in a holding pattern, on hold: *The pending negotiations on the rent will determine whether we stay or move house. While the matter is pending, we can do nothing.*

pendulous *adj.* **1** pendent, hanging, drooping, sagging, dangling, suspended, pensile: *The weaver-bird's pendulous nest is a marvel of engineering.* **2** °swinging, swaying, waving, undulating, undulatory, oscillating, oscillatory: *I was hypnotized by the pendulous motion of the bell.*

penetrate *v.* **1** °enter, °go *or* °pass through *or* into, °pierce, °bore (into), °lance, spear, °probe, °stab, °puncture, °perforate, °drill: *The shell penetrated the tank's heavy armour.* **2** °permeate, °diffuse, °suffuse, pervade, °filter *or* seep through, °percolate through: *The soothing balm penetrated my aching body and I relaxed into a deep sleep.* **3** °reach, °get to, °get at, °touch, °affect, °hit, °strike: *Her cruel words penetrated the darkest recesses of my soul.* **4** °sink in, be °absorbed, be °understood, °register, °come *or* °get through, become °clear, °come across, be realized, *Colloq* °soak in, seep in: *It took a while for it to penetrate that she did not wish to see him again.* **5** °understand, °sense, become °aware *or* °conscious of, °see (through), gain °insight (in)to, discern, uncover, °discover, °find (out), °comprehend, °grasp, °work out, unravel, °fathom, °perceive, *Colloq* °get, °figure out, °dig, *Brit* suss out: *Will we ever penetrate all of nature's secrets?*

penetrating *adj.* **1** °incisive, °trenchant, °keen, searching, °deep, °acute, °sharp, °perceptive, perspicuous, percipient, quick, °discriminating, °intelligent, °sensitive, °clever, °smart, discerning: *This is a penetrating analysis of the situation which clarifies many of the issues.* **2** °piercing, °shrill, °strident, ear-splitting, ear-shattering, °pervasive; °pungent, °harsh, °biting, mordant, °strong, stinging: *I was awakened by a penetrating scream. The penetrating odour of ammonia assailed my nostrils.*

penetration *n.* **1** °piercing, perforation, puncturing, °incision, °puncture, °penetrating; °inroad, °entry, °entrance: *Penetration of the skull required great effort on the part of the surgeon. Tentatively we attempted the penetration of the jungle.* **2** °insight, keenness, °perception, percipience, °intelligence, perspicacity, perspicuity, perspicaciousness, perceptiveness, incisiveness, °sensitivity, sentience, °understanding, acuteness, discernment, °discrimination, cleverness, shrewdness, °wit, quick-wittedness: *We all admired the penetration that was shown by the examiner in the questions she asked.*

penitence *n.* °penance, contrition, °regret, repentance, regretfulness, °compunction, °remorse, °sorrow, sorrowfulness, ruefulness, °grief, °sadness, °shame, self-reproach: *Brendan's penitence for his former misdeeds was shown by his selfless devotion to good causes.*

penitent *adj.* contrite, °regretful, °repentant, °remorseful, °sorrowful, °sorry, rueful, grief-stricken, °sad, shamefaced, self-reproachful, °apologetic, conscience-stricken: *He said that he was truly penitent for all the heinous crimes of his youth.*

penmanship *n.* calligraphy, °hand, fine Italian *or* Italic °hand, handwriting, °script, °writing, longhand, chirography: *One must admire the penmanship of the medieval scribes.*

pennant *n.* °flag, °banner, pennon, °streamer, banderole, gonfalon, ensign, °colours, °standard, labarum, *Chiefly nautical* jack, *Nautical and yachting* burgee, *Technical* vexillum: *We saw from her pennant that she was a Spanish frigate.*

pension *n.* **1** °benefit, °allowance, annuity, subsistence, superannuation, °allotment, old-age pension, *US* social security, *Colloq* golden handshake: *She finds that her pension is not enough to live on.*
—*v.* **2** Usually, **pension off**: (cause to) °retire, superannuate; °dismiss; *Colloq* °shelve, °put out to pasture: *The company cut back on staff by pensioning off everyone over 60.*

pensioner *n.* retiree, °veteran, °senior citizen, *Brit* OAP (= 'old-age pensioner'), *US* golden-ager, *Colloq Brit* wrinkly: *The housing units were specially designed for pensioners' needs.*

pensive *adj.* °thoughtful, °meditative, musing, in a brown °study, cogitative, contemplative, °reflective, °preoccupied, ruminative, °wistful, day-dreaming, in a °trance, in a °reverie, brooding, °sober, °serious, °grave: *I found the professor in a pensive mood, staring out the window.*

pent-up *adj.* restrained, constrained, repressed, stifled, bottled-up, corked-up, held in, checked, held back, curbed, °inhibited, restricted: *After weeks of frustration, he wanted to release his pent-up emotions in a scream. They went jogging to try to work off their pent-up energy.*

penurious *adj.* **1** stingy, °mean, penny-pinching, °miserly, °tight, tight-fisted, close-fisted, cheese-paring, niggardly, °cheap, ungenerous, parsimonious, skinflinty, °thrifty, begrudging, grudging, Scrooge-like, *Colloq* near, *Brit* mingy, *US* chintzy: *Even today, he is so penurious that he gives his children an allowance of only 50 pence a week.* **2** °poor, poverty-stricken, °destitute, °impoverished, penniless, °indigent, °needy, impecunious, necessitous, beggarly, bankrupt, *Colloq* (°dead *or* °flat) °broke, stony-broke, °hard up: *They lived in penurious circumstances.*

people *n.pl.* **1** °persons, °individuals, °men and °women, ladies and gentlemen, males and females, living souls; °mortals; bodies: *How many people can this aeroplane carry?* **2** °relations, relatives, °kin, kinsmen, kinsfolk *or US and Canadian* kinfolk, °family, kith and °kin; °ancestors, forebears: *His people left Russia in 1917.* **3** masses, (general) °public, hoi polloi, consumers, multitude, °populace, °common people, °common °man *or* °woman, commoners, °subjects, citizenry, °plebeians, grass roots, proletariat, rank and file, the °crowd, commonalty *or* commonality, *mobile vulgus*, bourgeoisie; °man *or* °woman in the street, Everyman, Everywoman, Mr *or* Mrs Average, *Brit* A. N. Other, Joe

Bloggs, °man or °woman on the Clapham omnibus, US John or Jane Doe or Roe, Mary Doe, Richard Roe, John Q. Public; *Colloq* and often derogatory proles, the °rabble, ragtag and bobtail, silent °majority, °common °herd, *Brit* plebs, admass: *Politicians unable to communicate with the people are seldom elected.*
—*n.sing.* **4** °race, community, °clan, °tribe, °folk, °nation, °population, °society: *On the subject of religion, they were a people divided. The anthropologists were studying the peoples south of the Sahara.*
—*v.* **5** °populate, colonize, °settle, °occupy: *The area was once peopled with Berber tribesmen.*

pep *n.* **1** °vigour, vim (and °vigour), °spirit, °animation, vivacity, °energy, °verve, °zest, °fire, sprightliness, °life, effervescence, °sparkle, ebullience, °dash, °enthusiasm, brio, *élan*, *Colloq* zip, zing: *He certainly has a lot of pep for an octogenarian.*
—*v.* **2 pep up**: °stimulate, invigorate, °animate, °enliven, °vitalize, vivify, °energize, exhilarate, °quicken, °arouse, breathe (some) °life into, °inspire, °activate, actuate, °fire, °cheer up, *Colloq* buck up, °spark, °work or °fire up, US °wind up: *After those defeats, the team needed to be pepped up.*

pepper *v.* sprinkle, °scatter, °dot, speckle, fleck, °spot, °spray, bespeckle, °spatter, stipple, mottle: *The letter was peppered with ink-spots. Their speech was peppered with swear-words.*

perceive *v.* **1** °see, °make out, discern, catch °sight of, glimpse, °spot, espy, apprehend, °take in, °notice, °note, °discover, descry, °observe, °mark, °remark, °identify, °distinguish, °detect: *I perceived his hesitation when a solo flight was suggested. She perceived a strange odour emanating from the cupboard.* **2** °appreciate, °grasp, °feel, °sense, apprehend, °understand, °gather, °comprehend, °deduce, °infer, °figure out, ascertain, °determine, conclude, °decipher, *Colloq* °dig, catch on: *She perceived that he was going to renege on his promise to take her to the Riviera.* **3** Often, **perceive of**: °regard, °view, °look on, °consider, °contemplate, °judge, deem, °believe, °think: *Calthorpe perceives of himself as a great actor, but he is dreadful. This gesture is often perceived as threatening.*

percentage *n.* °share, °part, °portion, °proportion, °interest, °piece, *Colloq* °cut: *We are to get a percentage of the profits in return for our investment.*

perceptible *adj.* °discernible, detectable, °observable, perceivable, °noticeable, distinguishable, recognizable, °apparent, °evident, °notable, °obvious, °patent, °manifest, palpable, °plain, °clear, °prominent, unmistakable: *There are perceptible differences between your playing and Heifetz's.*

perception *n.* **1** °appreciation, °grasp, apprehension, °understanding, comprehension, °knowledge, °perspective, °view: *Mrs Hart's perception of the situation is quite different from mine.* **2** °intuition, °insight, °instinct, °feel, °feeling, °sense, °impression, awareness, °idea, °notion, consciousness, °realization: *Norton hasn't the slightest perception of what is going on behind his back at the office.*

perceptive *adj.* °astute, °alert, °attentive, quick, °alive, °quick-witted, °intelligent, °acute, °sharp, °sensitive, °sensible, percipient, discerning, °observant, perspicacious; on the qui vive; *Colloq* on the ball: *No one was sufficiently perceptive to predict the full extent of the recession. She is perhaps the most perceptive journalist writing on French politics today.*

perch *n.* **1** roost, °rest, °seat; °spot, °location, °position, °place, °site, vantage °point, °perspective: *From his perch at the top of the cliff, Martin had a clear view of the cave entrance.*
—*v.* **2** roost, °rest, °sit, °nest; °place, °put, °set, °situate, °locate, °position, °site: *The owl was perched in the tree, waiting for the vole to appear from its burrow.*

percolate *v.* seep, °steep, °transfuse, leach, °drip, °drain, °strain, °filter, pervade, infuse, °ooze, transude, filtrate, °trickle, °permeate, °suffuse, °penetrate: *The earth is too hard for the rainwater to percolate to the roots below. It slowly percolated through to me that Clare had told the police where I was hiding.*

perdition *n.* damnation, °hell, hell-fire, °doom, °ruin, condemnation, °destruction, ruination, °downfall: *If what divines call lust be punished with perdition, who is pure?*

peremptory *adj.* **1** commanding, °imperative, compelling, °obligatory, °mandatory, irrefutable, °incontrovertible, decretal: *After the sound of marching came a peremptory knock at the door.* **2** decisive, °final, preclusive, °arbitrary, °categorical, unequivocal, °dogmatic, unconditional, unreserved, °flat, °out-and-out, °outright, °unqualified, °unmitigated: *The juror was subject to peremptory dismissal because he was the defendant's cousin.* **3** imperious, °authoritative, °tyrannical, °despotic, °dictatorial, autocratic, °emphatic, °positive, °firm, °insistent, *Colloq* °bossy: *How dare you take such a peremptory tone when speaking to your father!*

perennial *adj.* **1** °durable, °lasting, continuing, °enduring, °constant, °stable, lifelong, °persistent, incessant, uninterrupted, °continual, °continuous, °chronic: *Once we expected our rivers to yield a perennial supply of fresh water. Bing Crosby has been a perennial favourite since the 1930s.* **2** °permanent, unfailing, never-failing, °endless, unending, ceaseless, unceasing, imperishable, undying, °perpetual, °everlasting, °timeless, °eternal, °immortal, *Literary* sempiternal: *The artificial flowers at her grave symbolize Ingrid's perennial youth.*

perfect *adj.* **1** °complete, °absolute, finished, (fully) realized, fulfilled, consummate, °pure, °entire, °whole, perfected, °best, °ideal: *Many have called the building a perfect example of the Palladian style.* **2** °sublime, °ideal, °superb, °supreme, °superlative, °best, °flawless, °faultless, °pre-eminent, °excellent, °exquisite, unexcelled, unrivalled, unequalled, unmatched, °matchless, °incomparable, °nonpareil, °peerless, inimitable: *At her throat she wore the most perfect emerald I had ever seen.* **3** °blameless, °righteous, °holy, °faultless, °flawless, °spotless, °immaculate: *Nobody's perfect.* **4** °fitting, °appropriate, (°just) °right, apt, °suitable, °correct, °proper, made to order, °best, *Brit* spot on: *Arthur would be perfect for the role of Quasimodo.* **5** °precise, °exact, °accurate, °correct, unerring, °true, °authentic, °lifelike, °right on, °excellent, °superlative, °superb, °reliable, *Brit* spot on: *These copies are perfect replicas of the original.* **6** utter, °absolute,

°complete, °mere, °thorough, °out-and-out, through-and-through; 24-carat *or esp. US* 24-karat, °categorical, °unqualified, unalloyed, °unmitigated: *We were perfect strangers at the time. Once again, he's shown himself to be a perfect idiot.* **7** °expert, °proficient, °accomplished, °experienced, °practised, °skilful, skilled, °gifted, °talented, °adept, deft, adroit, °polished, °professional, masterly, °masterful: *The admirable Crichton was the perfect butler.*
—*v.* **8** °complete, °finish, °realize, °fulfil, consummate, °accomplish, °achieve, °effect, °execute, °carry out *or* through, bring (to °perfection): *The design of the bicycle was not to be perfected for several years.* **9** °rectify, °correct, emend, (put *or* set) °right, °improve, °refine, °polish, °cultivate, °better, ameliorate: *Viniculture has been perfected in the Bordeaux region of France.*

perfection *n.* **1** °purity, flawlessness, faultlessness, sublimity, °superiority, °excellence, °pre-eminence, transcendence: *Though we strive for perfection, we never can achieve it.* **2** °completion, completeness, °achievement, °fulfilment, °realization, °consummation, °accomplishment, attainment: *The building doesn't reach perfection till the last roof-tile is in place.* **3**°ideal, °paragon, °model, archetype, °pattern, °mould, °standard, idealization, °essence, °quintessence, °acme, °pinnacle, °summit: *Machiavelli probably achieved the perfection of political cunning.*

perfectionist *n.* **1** °purist, pedant, precisian, precisionist, stickler, *Colloq* fusspot, *US* fuss-budget: *The foreman is such a perfectionist that there's no satisfying him.*
—*adj.* **2** °meticulous, °precise, punctilious, °scrupulous, °exacting, °particular, °demanding, °fastidious, °fussy; °obsessive; *Colloq* picky, nit-picking: *She takes a perfectionist attitude towards everything she does.*

perfectly *adv.* **1** °completely, purely, °entirely, °absolutely, °utterly, °totally, °wholly, consummately, °thoroughly, °quite, °definitely, °positively, unambiguously, unequivocally, unmistakably, explicitly, °truly, °very, °extremely, extraordinarily, remarkably: *Your instructions for finding the house were perfectly clear.* **2** superbly, superlatively, flawlessly, faultlessly, impeccably, inimitably, incomparably, sublimely, exquisitely, marvellously, admirably, wonderfully: *Sally plays that Chopin étude perfectly.* **3** °exactly, °precisely, flawlessly, faultlessly, accurately, °literally, line for line, word for word, °verbatim, letter for letter, to the letter, literatim: *He knows the entire Koran perfectly.* **4** °very, full, °quite, *Dialect* °right, *Brit* jolly, *Slang* damned, bloody: *You know perfectly well that I hate cauliflower.*

perfidious *adj.* treacherous, °deceitful, °traitorous, treasonous, treasonable, °disloyal, °faithless, °false, unfaithful, °untrue, insidious, °hypocritical, °two-faced, Janus-faced, °corrupt, °dishonest: *His perfidious brother betrayed him to his enemies.*

perfidy *n.* perfidiousness, treachery, °deceit, traitorousness, treason, disloyalty, faithlessness, falseness, °falsity, unfaithfulness, °infidelity, insidiousness, °hypocrisy, °betrayal: *The name of Judas is a byword for perfidy.*

perforate *v.* °riddle, °puncture, °pierce, honeycomb, °drill, °bore, °punch; °enter, °penetrate, °pass into: *A perforated metal screen let through a pattern of light. The bullet perforated his lung but he survived.*

perform *v.* **1** °execute, °complete, °bring off *or* about, °accomplish, °effect, °carry out, °discharge, °dispatch, °conduct, °carry on, do, °fulfil, *Colloq* °pull off, °knock off, °polish off; put up *or* shut up: *Postmen perform their duties despite hazards such as vicious dogs.* **2** do, °act, °behave, °operate, °function, °run, °work, °go, °respond: *How does your new car perform?* **3** °present, °stage, °produce, °put on, °mount, do; °act, depict, °take, °play, °appear as: *The repertory group performs six shows weekly. He is performing the role of Scrooge.*

performance *n.* **1** °execution, °completion, bringing off *or* about, °accomplishment, effectuation, carrying out, °discharge, °dispatch, °conduct, carrying-on, doing, °fulfilment: *The soldiers acquitted themselves nobly in the performance of their duties.* **2** °show, °exhibition, °exhibit, °play, playing, °engagement, °act, °appearance, *Colloq* gig: *She does three performances nightly at the Blue Angel.* **3** playing, acting, °interpretation, °presentation, portrayal: *His performance in the courtroom scene was outstanding.* **4** °behaviour, °conduct, deportment, demeanour: *Her performance in the pub last night was outrageous.* **5** °scene, °show, °exhibition, °display: *The lad put on quite a performance till threatened with punishment by the headmaster.*

performer *n.* actor *or* actress, artiste, °Thespian, trouper, °player: *They received their training as performers in a repertory company.*

perfume *n.* **1** °essence, °extract, *parfum*, eau-de-Cologne, toilet water, °scent, °fragrance, °aroma, °odour, °smell, °bouquet, nose: *What is that wonderful perfume you're wearing? The perfume of the wine wafted over to me.*
—*v.* **2** °scent: *Orange blossoms perfumed the air.*

perfunctory *adj.* **1** °routine, °mechanical, °automatic, robot-like, °unthinking, businesslike, unspontaneous, °formal, dismissive, °inattentive, uninvolved, apathetic, °indifferent, unconcerned, removed, °distant, *dégagé*, °offhand, °heedless, uninterested, °hasty, °hurried, °superficial, °cursory, °fleeting, rushed: *I don't care for the perfunctory service in those fast-food restaurants.* **2** °careless, °slipshod, slovenly, negligent, °sketchy, °spotty: *The bill, made out in a perfunctory fashion, was incorrect.*

perhaps *adv.* °maybe, °possibly, it is °possible that, conceivably, as the case may be, it may be, *Archaic or literary* perchance, peradventure, *Archaic or dialect* mayhap: *Perhaps she'll be on the next train.*

peril *n.* °danger, °threat, °risk, °jeopardy, °exposure, vulnerability, susceptibility, uncertainty, insecurity: *You enter there at your peril. It was a time of peril for us all. The child's life was in peril.*

perilous *adj.* °dangerous, °risky, °hazardous, °vulnerable, °susceptible, °uncertain, °insecure, unsafe, unsure: *Why undertake such a perilous journey alone?*

perimeter *n.* °boundary, °border, borderline, °margin, °periphery, °limit(s), °bounds, ambit, circumference, °edge, °verge, °fringe(s), *Archaic or literary* bourn *or* bourne: *The perimeter of the military base is patrolled by sentry dogs.*

period *n.* **1** °interval, °time, °term, °span, duration, °spell, °space, °stretch; while; *Colloq chiefly Brit* °patch: *During the period of his absence, his children had grown up. I waited a short period, then phoned again. We went through a bad period last year.* **2** °era, °days, epoch, aeon, °age, years: *During the Old English period, very little was written down.* **3** full stop: *Place periods at the ends of sentences.*

periodic *adj.* °periodical, °intermittent, °regular, °recurrent, °repetitive, iterative, cyclic(al), repeated; episodic, °sporadic, °occasional: *We called in the plumber because of the periodic hammering in the pipes. The next periodic return of Halley's comet is expected in 2061–62.*

periodical *n.* °magazine, °journal, °paper, °publication, newsletter, °organ, serial, weekly, fortnightly, semi-monthly, monthly, bimonthly, °quarterly, semi-annual, annual, yearbook, almanac, *Rare* hebdomadal *or* hebdomadary: *Nicole's story will soon be published in an important literary periodical.*

peripheral *adj.* **1** °incidental, unimportant, °minor, °secondary, inessential *or* unessential, °non-essential, °unnecessary, °superficial, °tangential, °irrelevant, beside the point: *Let's ignore the peripheral issues for the time being and concentrate on the important ones.* **2** circumferential, °external, perimetric, °outside, outer: *The peripheral measurement of the figure is seven inches.*

periphery *n.* **1** °perimeter, circumference, °border, °edge, °rim, °brim, ambit, °boundary, °bound, °margin: *Trees will be planted along the periphery of the car park.* **2** °surface, °edge, °superficies: *Your analysis deals with the periphery, not the core, of the problem.*

perish *v.* °die, °expire, lose (one's) °life, be killed, be °lost, meet (one's) °death, be destroyed: *Three gnus perished in the fire at the zoo.*

perjury *n.* °lying, mendacity, mendaciousness, forswearing, prevarication, bearing °false °witness: *The defendant was acquitted and the prosecution witnesses charged with perjury.*

perk *n.* See **perquisite**, below.

perk up *v.* °cheer up, become °jaunty, °brighten, °liven up, invigorate, smarten up, °quicken, (re)vitalize, °pep up, °revive, inspirit, *Colloq* buck up: *The old lady perks up when her grandchildren come to visit. To perk up the party, Peter suggested we should all play a game.*

perky *adj.* °lively, cheery, °cheerful, °jaunty, bouncy, °bright, invigorated, °vigorous, vitalized, peppy, °spirited, °sprightly, °frisky, °animated, °vivacious, °effervescent, °bubbly, °buoyant, °gay, *Colloq* bright-eyed and bushy-tailed, full of °pep: *Sue's been quite perky since she started going with Trevor.*

permanence *n.* permanency, °stability, durability, fixedness, changelessness, °lasting quality, longevity, °endurance, °persistence, dependability, reliability, survival: *The new roofing material is being tested for permanence.*

permanent *adj.* °everlasting, °eternal, unending, °endless, °perpetual, unceasing, °constant, undying, imperishable, °indestructible, °stable, °abiding, long-lasting, °lasting, °enduring,

°perennial, long-lived, °durable: *The satellite is in permanent orbit around the earth.* **2** unchanging, °invariable, °changeless, °fixed, unchangeable, immutable, unalterable, °stable, °persistent: *This stain is permanent and will not come out in the wash. Bonham is a permanent member of the executive committee.*

permanently *adv.* for ever, for good, °once and for all, forevermore, °always, eternally, everlastingly; perpetually, constantly, incessantly, °non-stop, continuously, endlessly, ceaselessly, unendingly, interminably: *Is the boy permanently disabled? According to one theory the universe will not continue to expand permanently.*

permeate *v.* imbue, °diffuse, °penetrate, pervade, infiltrate, °enter, °spread through(out), °saturate, seep through(out), °percolate through, °soak through: *He felt the warmth permeate every limb. Greed seemed to permeate every level of society.*

permissible *adj.* allowable, admissible, °acceptable, allowed, permitted, °tolerable, °legal, licit, °lawful, °legitimate, authorized, °proper, (all) °right; pardonable, excusable, °venial, *Colloq* °OK *or* okay, kosher, legit: *Some things that are permissible are not necessarily honourable.*

permission *n.* °consent, assent, °leave, acquiescence, sufferance, °tolerance, laxity, leniency *or* lenience, °leave, °licence, °sanction, acceptance, authorization, °approval, approbation, countenance, °allowance, °liberty, °indulgence; franchise, enfranchisement: *Have you permission to watch television? She eats anything she likes with the doctor's permission.*

permissive *adj.* assenting, consenting, °indulgent, °lenient, latitudinarian, acquiescent, °lax, °easygoing, °liberal, °tolerant, non-constraining, non-restrictive, libertarian: *Allison grew up in the permissive society of the 1960s.*

permit *v.* **1** Often, **permit to**: °allow (to), °consent (to), give °permission *or* °leave (to), °authorize, °sanction, °license, °tolerate, countenance, °suffer, °brook, °admit, °grant, °enable, empower, franchise, enfranchise; °let: *He permitted me to use his name as a reference. Do they permit smoking here?* —*n.* **2** °licence, °authority, authorization, franchise, °warrant; °pass, passport, visa: *Your parking permit expired last week. Shirley has a permit to visit Tibet.*

perpendicular *adj.* **1** °erect, °upright, vertical, °plumb, °straight (up and down): *The plumb-line shows that the wall isn't perpendicular.* **2** Often, **perpendicular to**: at right angles (to), at 90 degrees (to): *The two paths are perpendicular to one another.*

perpetrate *v.* °commit, °execute, °perform, °carry out *or* through, °effect, °effectuate, °accomplish, do, be °responsible for, °practise, *Colloq* °pull (off): *Atrocities were perpetrated on both sides in the war.*

perpetual *adj.* **1** °eternal, °infinite, °everlasting, never-ending, unending, °perennial, ageless, °timeless, long-lived, °permanent, unceasing, °lasting, °enduring, unvarying, unchanging, immutable, °invariable, undeviating, *Literary* sempiternal: *They declared their perpetual love for each other.* **2** °constant, uninterrupted, °continuous, unfailing, incessant, °persistent, unremitting, unending, °non-stop, °endless, °recurrent, °continual, °repetitive: *Why should we have to listen to the neighbours' perpetual bickering?*

perpetuate *v.* °continue, °maintain, °extend, °keep (on or up), °keep going, °preserve, °memorialize, °immortalize, eternalize: *Thoughtless jokes can perpetuate damaging stereotypes.*

perpetuity *n.* °permanence, constancy, timelessness; °eternity: *The estate was bequeathed to the townspeople in perpetuity.*

perplex *v.* °confuse, °bewilder, °puzzle, °mystify, °distract, baffle, befuddle, confound, °muddle, disconcert, °stump, °nonplus, °stymie, stupefy, °stun, °daze, °dumbfound or dumfound, flabbergast, *Colloq* bamboozle, hornswoggle, *Chiefly US and Canadian* discombobulate, °throw for a loop: *The more I tried to understand bathymetric semiotics, the more perplexed I became. Anne-Marie's reticence perplexed us all.*

perplexing *adj.* confusing, bewildering, °puzzling, mystifying, baffling, confounding, °disconcerting, stupefying, flabbergasting, enigmatic, °paradoxical, °incomprehensible, unfathomable, impenetrable, °recondite, arcane, °labyrinthine, complex, °complicated, Byzantine, °intricate, °involved, convoluted, twisted, knotty, Gordian: *The writing is filled with perplexing references to the author's personal experiences, of which the reader is told nothing.*

perplexity *n.* **1** °confusion, bewilderment, bafflement, °distress, °doubt, °difficulty: *My perplexity grew as he related his version of the event.* **2** intricacy, °complexity, complicatedness, arcaneness, reconditeness, impenetrability, impenetrableness, involvement, unfathomability, °obscurity, °difficulty: *The more deeply the enigma was probed, the greater its perplexity.* **3** °puzzle, °enigma, °mystery, °dilemma, °problem, °paradox, catch-22, °quandary, °predicament, °bind: *Because of the interlocking directorships of the companies, we faced many perplexities in trying to sort out what had happened to the funds.*

perquisite *n.* °consideration, emolument, °bonus, (fringe) °benefit, °extra, dividend, gratuity, °tip, douceur, baksheesh, token (of appreciation), *US* lagniappe or lagnappe, *Colloq* °perk: *It was traditional to provide each director with a company car as a perquisite.*

persecute *v.* **1** °oppress, °suppress, °subjugate, maltreat, °ill-treat, °abuse, °outrage, °molest, °victimize, °tyrannize, °afflict, °punish, martyr, °torment, torture: *For years black people had been persecuted.* **2** °bother, °annoy, °pester, °plague, hector, °bully, badger, harry, °harass, °irritate, °worry, vex, °trouble, importune, °hound: *Her lawyers continually persecuted him for non-payment of alimony.*

persecution *n.* **1** °oppression, °suppression, subjugation, maltreatment, ill-treatment, °abuse, °outrage, molestation, victimization, °tyranny, °affliction, °punishment, °torment, torture: *They suffered persecution because of their difference of religion.* **2** °bother, °annoyance, hectoring, bullying, badgering, harrying, harassing, irritation, °worry, vexation, °trouble: *The press is often guilty of the persecution of famous people.*

perseverance *n.* °persistence, steadfastness, °determination, °resolution, °resolve, decisiveness, °decision, firmness, purposefulness,

pertinacity, staying power, °stamina, sedulousness, assiduity, °grit, °pluck, tirelessness, indefatigableness, indefatigability, °patience, °endurance, diligence, °devotion, °tenacity, doggedness, stubbornness, inflexibility, °obstinacy, obstinateness, obdurateness, *Colloq* guts, *US* stick-to-it-iveness: *Perseverance is essential for success in the theatre.*

persevere *v.* Often, **persevere in** or **with** or **at**: °persist, °resolve, °decide, °endure, °continue, °carry on or through, °keep at or on or up, be °steadfast or °staunch or °constant, °keep going, stand °fast or °firm, °see through, be or °remain °determined or resolved or °resolute or °stalwart or °purposeful or uncompromising, be °tenacious or °persistent or °constant or pertinacious or assiduous or sedulous, be °tireless or °untiring or indefatigable, show °determination or °pluck or °grit, be plucky, be °patient or °diligent or °stubborn or °inflexible or adamant or °obstinate or obdurate, show or exhibit or demonstrate °patience or diligence or stubbornness or inflexibility or °obstinacy or obduracy, °remain dogged, °pursue doggedly, be intransigent or intractable, °cling to, °stick to, °support, stop at nothing, °sustain, *Colloq* °stick with, °stick (it) out: *We must persevere if we are to win. I shall persevere in my loyalty.*

persist *v.* **1** Often, **persist in** or **at**: °persevere, be °persistent, °insist (on), stand °firm or °fast, be °steadfast or °staunch, °strive, toil, °labour, °work (°hard) (at): *She persists in arguing her innocence. Only those who persist will succeed.* **2** °remain, °continue, °endure, °carry on, °keep up or on, °last, °linger, °stay: *The bad weather persisted through the weekend.*

persistence *n.* °perseverance, °resolve, °determination, °resolution, steadfastness, °tenacity, constancy, assiduity, °stamina, tirelessness, indefatigability, indefatigableness, °pluck, °grit, °patience, diligence, pertinacity, doggedness, stubbornness, °obstinacy, obduracy: *By sheer persistence he got his own way.*

persistent *adj.* **1** persisting, persevering, °tenacious, °steadfast, °firm, °fast, °fixed, °staunch, °resolute, resolved, °determined, unfaltering, unswerving, undeviating, unflagging, °tireless, °untiring, indefatigable, dogged, unwavering, °stubborn, °obstinate, obdurate, °inflexible, °rigid: *He was persistent in his demands for justice. The inspector never gave up his persistent pursuit of criminals.* **2** continuing, °constant, °continuous, °continual, unending, interminable, unremitting, unrelenting, °perpetual, incessant, unceasing, °non-stop: *The persistent rainy weather began to depress us. At last he gave in to her persistent complaints and bought a washing machine.*

person *n.* **1** °individual, °human (being), being, °man or °woman or °child, (living) °soul; °mortal: *Not a single person knew the answer to my question.* **2 in person**: physically, °personally, bodily, °actually, myself or yourself or himself or herself or ourselves or yourselves, or themselves, *Colloq* in the °flesh: *The correspondent visited the battlefield in person to see for himself the extent of the carnage. I know their records, but I have never seen them in person.*

persona n. °face, °front, façade, °mask, °guise, °exterior, °role, °part, °character, °identity, self: *Her office persona is quite different from the one she displays at home.*

personage n. °celebrity, luminary, VIP, °name, °notable, °somebody, °personality, °star, superstar, magnate, °mogul, *Colloq* °big shot, °big wheel, hotshot, °hot stuff, *Brit* °big noise, *Theatre US* headliner: *My cousin is fast becoming a personage in the financial world.*

personal adj. **1** °individual, °physical, bodily, °actual, °live; in °person, in the °flesh: *The star is scheduled to make a personal appearance on tonight's chat show.* **2** °intimate, °exclusive, °private, °special, °particular: *Would you do me a personal favour? I hear they are having personal problems.* **3** °intimate, °close, °dear, °bosom, °familiar, °special: *Wendy happens to be a personal friend of ours.* **4** °intimate, °individual; disparaging, slighting, °offensive, °derogatory, °critical, deprecating, belittling, adverse, unfriendly, insulting: *He should confine his criticism to her acting and avoid personal remarks.*

personality n. **1** °character, °nature, temperament, °disposition, °make-up, °persona; °identity, °psyche: *Miles has an extremely abrasive personality that has upset many people.* **2** °celebrity, luminary, °star, superstar, °name, headliner, °somebody: *Whom shall we get as a personality to attract the crowds?*

personalized adj. monogrammed, initialled, individualized; signed: *They ordered personalized stationery with their new address on it.*

personally adv. **1** in °person, °alone, by oneself, on one's own, myself *or* yourself *or* himself *or* herself *or* ourselves *or* yourselves *or* themselves, *Colloq* in the °flesh: *She has not met them personally, but we have. They will see to the matter personally.* **2** in one's own °view *or* °opinion, for one's °part, for oneself, as far as one is concerned, from one's own °viewpoint, from where one stands, as one sees it *or* things, as for oneself: *Personally, I wasn't sure I would make it.* **3** as an °individual, as a °person, privately, in °private: *I like him personally but would never have him as my dentist.*

personify v. **1** °embody, °typify, °exemplify, epitomize, be the °embodiment of, °manifest, °represent, °stand for, °symbolize, *Archaic* impersonate, personate: *In my view, he personifies everything that is evil.* **2** humanize, personalize: *In literature, personifying inanimate things in nature with human attributes is called the pathetic fallacy.*

perspective n. **1** (°point of) °view, °viewpoint, °standpoint, °prospect, vantage °point, °position, °angle, *Colloq* where one is coming from: *I can see that my view would be illogical from his perspective.* **2** °attitude, °position, °angle, °approach, °sentiment, °outlook, °lookout: *Management has a different perspective on what is good for the company.*

perspiration n. °sweat, dampness, wetness; sweating; *Technical* sudor; diaphoresis: *I could feel the perspiration stand out on my forehead. They say that perspiration makes one cooler on a hot day.*

persuade v. **1** °urge, °induce, °prevail (up)on, °influence, exhort, importune, °dispose, °incline, °prompt, °sway, °press: *The officer persuaded him to surrender.* **2** °bring round,

°convince, °win over, °talk *or* °argue into, °convert: *We persuaded her to open the door. He was persuaded to vote Labour.*

persuasion n. **1** °inducement, inducing, °influence, influencing, exhortation, exhorting, persuading: *At the bank's persuasion, the company tightened up its cashflow management. She has extraordinary powers of persuasion at her command.* **2** °opinion, °belief, °creed, °faith, °set of °beliefs, °religion, (°religious) °conviction; °sect, °denomination, °faction, °school (of thought), affiliation: *Till he met Maggie, he had always been of the Baptist persuasion.*

persuasive adj. convincing, °telling, °influential, °effective, °productive, °impressive, °efficacious, cogent, °weighty, compelling, °forceful, valid, °winning, °authoritative, °dynamic: *His most persuasive argument for our leaving was that if we stayed we'd be shot.*

pert adj. **1** °forward, °brash, °brazen, °cheeky, °insolent, °impertinent, °flippant, saucy, °bold, °presumptuous, °impudent, °disrespectful, °audacious, °rude, °impolite, uncivil, °ill-mannered, unmannerly, *Archaic* malapert, *Colloq* °fresh, °flip, out of line, °brassy, big-mouthed, wise-guy, *Slang Brit* smart-arsed, *US* smart-ass(ed), wise-ass(ed): *He's a clever child, but I don't like his pert manner.* **2** °lively, °jaunty, °ebullient, °vivacious, °enthusiastic, bouncy, °sprightly, °brisk, °cheerful, °jolly, °bright, °perky, °animated, °nimble: *She is usually quite pert in the morning, becoming depressed as the day wears on.*

pertain v. Often, **pertain to**: °concern, °refer to, °regard, have °reference *or* °relation (to), °apply (to), °relate (to), °include, °cover, °affect, appertain (to), be °appropriate (to), be °fitting (for), befit, °bear on, have °bearing (on): *The sign, 'Keep Off the Grass', does not pertain to the people who mow the lawn, Morris.*

pertinent adj. pertaining, °appropriate, °fitting, °suitable, apt, °relevant, germane, apropos, apposite: *Try to keep your comments pertinent to the subject under discussion.*

perturb v. °upset, °disturb, °fluster, °ruffle, unsettle, disconcert, make uneasy, °discomfit, vex, °worry, °agitate, °shake up, °alarm, disquiet, °confuse, discompose, °unnerve, addle, disorganize: *He became quite perturbed when the police asked him to help with their inquiries.*

perusal n. reading, °scrutiny, °check, °examination, °study, inspection, scanning, °review: *I saw nothing blasphemous in my perusal of the text.*

peruse v. °read, °study, °scan, °scrutinize, °examine, °inspect, °review, °browse, run one's °eye over: *As Gregory was perusing the ancient manuscript, a sudden draught blew out the candle.*

pervasive adj. °penetrating, pervading, omnipresent, °general, inescapable, °prevalent, °universal, widespread, ubiquitous, permeating, permeative: *A pervasive sense of doom in the castle made everyone feel uneasy.*

perverse adj. **1** °wrong, wrong-headed, awry, °contrary, wayward, °incorrect, °irregular, unfair, °improper, °contradictory: *It was most perverse of you to change your mind after all the arrangements had been made.* **2** °cantankerous, °testy, curmudgeonly, churlish, crusty, bad-tempered, °petulant, captious, °cross,

cross-grained, °peevish, °waspish, °snappish, °bilious, splenetic, fractious, ill-tempered, °quarrelsome, irascible, °sullen, contentious, °touchy, °obstreperous, crabby, crabbed, °irritable, °surly, *Colloq* grouchy, *Brit* stroppy, *US and Canadian* °cranky: *With everything going wrong, Catherine feels particularly perverse today.* **3** °stubborn, °self-willed, wrong-headed, intractable, °wilful, obdurate, °obstinate, pigheaded, adamant, °inflexible, unbending, refractory, unyielding: *I refuse to give in to a perverse child just because he has a tantrum.*

perversion *n.* **1** deviation, irregularity, misdirection, corruption, °subversion, distortion, twisting, falsification, misrepresentation, °diversion, sidetracking: *The conduct of this trial has been a perversion of the course of true justice.* **2** °unnatural act, deviation, deviance or deviancy, °abnormality, depravity, °vice, aberration, debauchery, *Colloq* kinkiness, *Brit* °kink: *Every kind of perversion flourished in ancient Rome.*

pervert *v.* **1** °deflect, °divert, °sidetrack, °turn aside *or* away, °subvert, °misdirect, °distort, °twist, °abuse, °falsify, misapply, misconstrue, °misrepresent, °corrupt: *By withholding evidence, you have perverted the course of justice.* **2** °seduce, °lead astray, debauch, °degrade, °corrupt, °demoralize, °subvert: *He was accused of perverting young girls.*
—*n.* **3** °deviant, °degenerate, debauchee, *US* °deviate, *Colloq* °weirdo: *I worry about your being out late, when there are so many perverts about.*

perverted *adj.* °deviant, °deviate, °abnormal, amoral, unmoral, °immoral, °bad, depraved, °unnatural, warped, twisted, °profligate, °dissolute, °delinquent, °degenerate, °evil, °wicked, malign, malicious, malefic, malevolent, °evil-minded, °sinful, iniquitous, °base, °foul, °corrupt, unprincipled: *Members of the Hell-Fire Club yielded themselves up to the most perverted, abandoned behaviour.*

pessimistic *n.* °gloomy, °negative, despairing, °hopeless, °inauspicious, depressed, °despondent, °dejected, °melancholy, °downhearted, heavy-hearted, defeatist, °glum, °sad, °blue, °unhappy, cheerless, °joyless, cynical, °bleak, °forlorn: *The bears in the Stock Exchange take a pessimistic view of share prices.*

pest *n.* °nuisance, °annoyance, °nag, irritant, °bother, gadfly, brat, trial, heckler, vexation, °curse, °thorn in one's flesh, *Colloq* °pain (in the neck), *Slang US* nudge *or* noodge *or* nudzh, nudnik, *Taboo slang* °pain in the *Brit* arse *or US* ass: *That man is such a pest, I wish he'd leave me alone.*

pester *v.* °annoy, °nag, °irritate, °irk, °bother, °get at *or* to, badger, °plague, vex, °fret, hector, °harass, harry, °heckle, nettle, °chafe, peeve, pique, °provoke, °exasperate, bedevil, °get *or* °grate on (someone's) °nerves, °get under (someone's) skin, °get in (someone's) hair, °try (someone's °patience, °torment, °persecute, *Brit* chivvy, *Colloq* drive (someone) up the °wall, needle, give (someone) the needle, hassle, °ride, give (someone) a °hard *or* °bad time, °bug: *Please stop pestering me about going to the football game.*

pestilence *n.* **1** °plague, °epidemic, pandemic, Black Death, *Rare* pest: *The pestilence raged throughout all Europe, killing 50 million*

people. **2** °scourge, °blight, °curse, cancer, canker, bane, °affliction: *How are we to overcome the pestilence of greed?*

pet[1] *n.* **1** °darling, °favourite, °idol, apple of (one's) eye, *Colloq Brit* blue-eyed boy, *US* fair-haired boy: *You know that you were always Father's pet.*
—*adj.* **2** °tame, trained, domesticated: *Doesn't the landlord take a dim view of your keeping a pet alligator in the bath?* **3** °favourite, °favoured, preferred, cherished, °special, °particular; indulged, prized, treasured, °precious, dearest, adored, °darling: *Building the summer-house was Desmond's pet project. Elizabeth's pet pupil is Anne.*
—*v.* **4** °caress, °fondle, °stroke, °pat; °cuddle, nuzzle, °nestle, °snuggle, *Colloq* neck, smooch *or Australian and New Zealand also* smoodge *or* smooge, *Chiefly US and Canadian* make out: *Small children need to be petted a lot. Two teenagers were petting in the back seat of the car.* **5** °humour, °pamper, °favour, °baby, °coddle, cosset, mollycoddle, cocker, °spoil, °indulge, °dote on: *His mother pets him far too much.*

pet[2] *n.* (°bad *or* ill) °temper, pique, °sulk, (bad) °mood, °fume, *Colloq Brit* °paddy *or* paddywhack *or* paddywack: *He's in a terrible pet because they forgot to cancel the milk when they went on holiday.*

peter out *v.* °diminish, °evaporate, °wane, come to nothing *or* naught *or US also* nought, °die out, °disappear, °fail, °fade (out *or* away), °dwindle (into nothing), °run out, °give out, °flag, °melt away: *The path petered out after a mile or so and they realized that they had lost their bearings.*

petite *adj.* °delicate, °dainty, *mignon(ne)*, °diminutive, °small, °little, °slight, °tiny, small-boned, *Colloq Brit* dinky: *It was incongruous to see the basketball player with a petite blonde.*

petition *n.* **1** °request, °application, solicitation, °suit, entreaty, °supplication, °plea, °appeal: *An anti-pollution petition, signed by thousands of people, was delivered to the Department of the Environment.*
—*v.* **2** °request, °ask, °apply to, °apply for, °solicit, °sue, °call upon, entreat, supplicate, °plead, °appeal (to), °appeal (for), °beseech, implore, importune, *Rare* obsecrate: *The shopkeepers petitioned the council for better police protection.*

petrified *adj.* **1** horrified, horror-stricken or -struck, terrified, terror-stricken, °panic-stricken, frightened, °afraid, paralysed, numbed, benumbed, frozen: *The maiden stood petrified as the dragon, breathing fire, approached.* **2** shocked, °speechless, °dumbfounded *or* dumfounded, dumbstruck, stunned, °thunderstruck, astonished, astounded, confounded, stupefied, appalled, aghast, *Colloq* flabbergasted: *The firemen rescued three petrified children who were huddled in a corner.* **3** ossified, fossilized: *These were not stones but the petrified remains of ancient trees.*

petrify *v.* **1** °frighten, °scare, °horrify, °terrify, °paralyse, °numb, benumb: *I was petrified by the noise of the explosion.* **2** °shock, °dumbfound *or* dumfound, °stun, °astonish, °astound, °amaze, confound, disconcert, stupefy, °appal, *Colloq* flabbergast: *The sight of so much destruction petrified even hardened reporters.* **3** ossify, fossilize, turn to stone: *Over thousands of years the desert conditions petrify the wood.*

petty adj. **1** °insignificant, trivial, °paltry, °minor, °inferior, °niggling, °trifling, °negligible, °puny, inessential, °non-essential, °inconsequential, unimportant, °slight, nugatory, of no °account, US dinky, Colloq piddling, °measly, no great shakes, no big deal, °small-time, Brit twopenny-halfpenny or tuppenny-halfpenny, US and Canadian picayune: He has been convicted only of petty crimes. **2** °miserly, °mean, mingy, stingy, cheese-paring, grudging, °small-minded, °cheap, niggardly, parsimonious, °tight, tight-fisted, close-fisted: It was very petty of you to refuse the beggar a few pence.

petulant adj. °peevish, pettish, °impatient, ill-humoured, °testy, °waspish, irascible, choleric, °cross, captious, ill-tempered, bad-tempered, splenetic, °moody, °sour, °bilious, crabby, crabbed, °irritable, huffish, huffy, °perverse, °snappish, crotchety, °cantankerous, curmudgeonly, grouchy, grumpy: With a petulant gesture she hurled the rose away.

phantom n. **1** apparition, °spectre, °ghost, °spirit, phantasm, °shade, wraith, revenant, °vision, Formal eidolon, phantasma, Colloq spook: The so-called phantom of the opera turned out to be a real person. **2** figment (of the °imagination), °illusion, °delusion, chimera or chimaera, °hallucination, °fancy, mirage: She was a phantom of delight When first she gleamed upon my sight.

Pharisaic adj. Pharisaical, °hypocritical, °insincere, °self-righteous, °pretentious, holier-than-thou, °sanctimonious, pietistic(al), formalistic, canting, unctuous, °oily, °slimy, Literary Tartuffian, Pecksniffian, Colloq goody-goody, Chiefly Brit smarmy: I cannot tolerate his Pharisaic preaching.

Pharisee n. °hypocrite, °pretender, dissembler, humbug, °fraud, whited sepulchre, pietist, formalist, canter, Literary Tartuffe, Pecksniff, Colloq °phoney or US also phony: She is such a Pharisee with her pious little anecdotes.

pharmacist n. pharmacologist, Rather old-fashioned or formal apothecary, Brit (pharmaceutical) chemist, US and Canadian °druggist, Formal posologist, Colloq °pill pusher, US °pill roller: The pharmacist said that those pills have bad side-effects.

pharmacy n. **1** dispensary, Rather formal or old-fashioned apothecary, Brit chemist's (°shop), US and Canadian drugstore, druggist's: Stop off at the pharmacy and get me something for this headache, please. **2** pharmaceutics, pharmacopoeia: Research has vastly expanded modern pharmacy.

phase n. **1** °stage, °period, °development, °step: The boy is just going through a phase. **2** °time, °moment, °juncture, °occasion: At this phase of the discussion, I should like to introduce a new subject. **3** °state, °form, °shape, configuration, °aspect, °appearance, °look, °condition, °status: Here is a diagram of the phases of the moon at various points in its orbit. **4** facet, °side, °angle, °viewpoint, °point of °view, Colloq °slant: Only one phase of the argument has so far been presented. —v. **5 phase in**: (°gradually) °introduce, usher in, °work in, °inject, °insert, °insinuate, °include, °incorporate: The new work schedules will be phased

in over the next month. **6 phase out**: °ease out or off, °taper off, °wind up, put a °stop to, (°gradually) °eliminate, °remove, °withdraw, °discontinue, °end: The use of non-biodegradable and non-recyclable packaging is being phased out.

phenomenal adj. °outstanding, °remarkable, °exceptional, °extraordinary, °unusual, freakish, °rare, uncommon, °singular, °unorthodox, unprecedented, °unheard-of, °unparalleled, °unbelievable, °incredible, °marvellous, wonderful, °amazing, astonishing, astounding, staggering, °stunning, °prodigious, °miraculous, °fantastic, Colloq mind-boggling, mind-blowing: She made a phenomenal recovery and can walk again.

phenomenon n. **1** °event, °happening, °occurrence, °incident, °occasion, °experience, °fact: Everyone knows the phenomenon of the souring of milk. **2** °wonder, °curiosity, °spectacle, °sight, °sensation, °marvel, °rarity, °exception, miracle, Slang stunner: An eight-year-old chess champion is truly a phenomenon, even in Russia.

philanderer n. °flirt, °gallant, °roué, °rake, Casanova, Lothario, Don Juan, Romeo, °lover, °playboy, °gay dog, Colloq lady-killer, womanizer, Old-fashioned wolf, Slang stud: In his memoirs it emerged what a philanderer he had been, often dallying with six women at once.

philanthropic adj. °charitable, eleemosynary, °generous, magnanimous, munificent, °benevolent, open-handed, ungrudging, unstinting, beneficent, °humanitarian, altruistic, humane: Finlay was always philanthropic, and spent much of his fortune on worthy causes.

philanthropist n. contributor, °donor, °benefactor or benefactress, °patron or patroness, °sponsor, Maecenas, Good Samaritan, °humanitarian, altruist: Some anonymous philanthropist provided the funds for the new school swimming-pool.

philanthropy n. **1** generosity, °benevolence, °charity, °patronage, magnanimity, charitableness, public-spiritedness, big-heartedness, thoughtfulness, alms-giving, kind-heartedness, beneficence, benignity, liberality, open-handedness: Carnegie's philanthropy was focused on libraries and education. **2** °donation, contribution, °largesse, °aid, °grant, °assistance, °help: Mrs Ander's recent philanthropy allows us to offer six new scholarships.

philistine n. **1** °boor, °barbarian, yahoo, lowbrow, Boeotian, vulgarian, ignoramus, °bourgeois, US Babbitt: Charlotte never could abide the philistines who put love of money above love of culture. —adj. **2** uncultured, uncultivated, °tasteless, commonplace, unenlightened, °unrefined, unread, unlettered, °uneducated, untutored, unlearned, °narrow-minded, anti-intellectual, °boorish, lowbrow, °dull, °prosaic, °boring, °bourgeois, crass, commercial, °materialistic: The television companies were accused of pandering to the basest appetites of the philistine viewer.

philosophical adj. **1** philosophic, °abstract, esoteric, °learned, °scholarly, erudite, °theoretical, °rational, °logical, °impractical: The person who is out of a job cares nothing about philosophical reasons for unemployment. **2** °detached, unconcerned, unemotional, unimpassioned, composed, °thoughtful,

°reflective, °meditative, cogitative, contemplative, °judicious, °sober, °level-headed, °realistic, °practical, pragmatic(al), down-to-earth, °cool, °calm, °serene, placid, °stoical, °patient, unruffled, cool-headed, °tranquil, unperturbed, even-tempered, °temperate, °moderate, °equable, equanimous, imperturbable: *Over the years, Evelyn had learned to take a philosophical attitude towards her husband's shortcomings.*

philosophy *n.* **1** metaphysics, epistemology, °logic, °natural *or* °moral *or* metaphysical philosophy, rationalism, °thinking, aesthetics: *He views philosophy as the attempt to describe and codify universal truths.* **2** °viewpoint, (°point of) °view, °outlook, °opinion, °attitude, °feeling, °sentiment, °idea, °notion, °ideology, (set of) °beliefs *or* values, °tenets, Weltanschauung, world-view: *Harold's philosophy of life is 'Live and let live'.* **3** °stoicism, °sang-froid, °control, °self-control, °restraint, coolness, composure, calmness, °serenity, placidity, cool-headedness, equanimity, thoughtfulness, imperturbability, self-possession, aplomb, dispassion, °patience, °resignation: *You may be sure that Paul allows nothing to disturb his philosophy.*

phlegmatic *adj.* **1** phlegmatical, stoic(al), unemotional, °unenthusiastic, unanimated, sluggish, apathetic, uninvolved, °lethargic, unfeeling, uncaring, °cold, unresponsive, °stolid, °unmoved, insensitive, °unaffected, °insensible, °indifferent, unconcerned, uninterested, °listless, °torpid, °indolent, °inactive, °passive, *Rare* hebetudinous: *Hutton is far too phlegmatic to be stirred by the fervour of the revolutionaries.* **2** phlegmatical, °self-possessed, self-controlled, controlled, restrained, composed, °calm, °serene, °tranquil, placid, cool-headed, equanimous, °cool, undisturbed, unperturbed, unruffled, imperturbable, even-tempered, °philosophical, °temperate, °moderate: *One has to learn to be phlegmatic about things going wrong at the office.*

phobia *n.* °fear, °horror, °terror, °dread, hatred, detestation, abhorrence, °loathing, execration, °aversion, °revulsion, repugnance, °dislike, °distaste, antipathy; disquiet, nervousness, °qualm, °distrust, °suspicion, apprehension, °worry: *He suffers from claustrophobia, which means that he has a phobia of enclosed places, and he avoids lifts and telephone booths.*

phoney *adj.* **1** °unreal, °fake, °synthetic, °artificial, °factitious, °false, °fraudulent, °imitation, °bogus, °spurious, °counterfeit, °mock, ersatz, paste, trumped up; °sham, °pretended, °insincere, °hypocritical, dissimulating, °deceitful, °dishonest; *US also* phony, *Colloq* pseudo *or Brit* pseud: *They were caught trying to collect insurance on the theft of a string of phoney pearls. Every time she wanted something, she'd turn on the phoney charm.* —*n.* **2** °fake, °fraud, °imitation, °counterfeit, °forgery, °hoax, °sham, *US also* phony: *The diamond she's wearing is a phoney.* **3** trickster, faker, humbug, °impostor, °pretender, charlatan, mountebank, double-dealer, °counterfeiter, °quack, deceiver, *US also* phony, *Colloq Brit* pseud, *Slang US* paper-hanger: *Madame Tatiana claims to be able to communicate with the dead, but I think she's a phoney.*

photograph *n.* **1** snapshot, °print, °picture, slide, transparency; negative, positive, *Colloq* photo, snap, °shot, pic (*pl.* pix): *Heinrich has taken some marvellous photographs of the children.* —*v.* **2** take a °picture (of), shoot, °film, take, *Colloq* °snap: *He photographed Jennifer holding her kitten.*

photographer *n.* lensman, lenswoman, cameraman, camerawoman, cinematographer, paparazzo (*pl.* paparazzi), *Old-fashioned* photographist: *The photographers clustered round the prime minister.*

photographic *adj.* **1** °vivid, °natural, °realistic, °graphic, °accurate, °exact, °precise, °faithful, °detailed, °lifelike, °true to life: *Many such neo-realist paintings are virtually photographic.* **2** cinematic, filmic, °pictorial: *Uncannily, a photographic image appeared on the Shroud under certain light.*

phrase *n.* **1** clause, noun phrase, verb phrase, prepositional phrase, adverbial phrase, adjectival phrase: *When asked for an example of a verb phrase, the student responded, 'Shut up'.* **2** °expression, word-group, collocation, locution, °idiom, idiomatic °expression, collocution, °proverb, °motto, °slogan, saying, catch-phrase, adage, °maxim, axiom, °saw, colloquialism, °cliché, platitude, commonplace, *Colloq* chestnut: *Do you know the source of Churchill's famous phrase, 'Blood, toil, tears, sweat'?* **3** phraseology, phrasing, °wording, °language, °usage, way *or* manner of speaking, °diction, °parlance, façon de parler, modus loquendi, modus scribendi, °speech habit, °style, choice of words, °word choice, syntax, vocabulary: *He was to 'let slip', to use Shakespeare's phrase, 'the dogs of war'.* —*v.* **4** °express, °term, °word, °put, °frame, °formulate, °couch, °put into words, °put *or* °set forth, verbalize, articulate, °voice, utter, °say, °write; °describe, delineate: *I am pondering over the best way to phrase this example.*

physical *adj.* bodily, corporeal, corporal, fleshly, incarnate, °carnal, °mortal, °earthly, °natural, somatic, °material, °tangible, palpable, °real, °actual, °true, °concrete, °manifest, °solid: *Curtis doesn't have the physical strength to lift that weight. As a chemist, James deals with the physical, not the spiritual universe.*

physician *n.* °doctor, medical °doctor, M.D., °doctor of °medicine, medical practitioner, general practitioner, G.P., medical man *or* woman, °specialist, diplomate, *Brit navy* surgeon, *Colloq* doc, medico, medic, *US* man, *Slang* sawbones, bones: *You ought to see a physician if the pain persists.*

physique *n.* °build, °figure, °body, °frame, °shape, bodily °structure, °form, *Slang* chassis, *US* bod, built: *She has the physique of an Amazon but the disposition of a lamb.*

pick *v.* **1** Often, **pick out**: °select, °choose, cull, °sort out, hand-pick, °single out, opt for, °fix *or* °decide upon *or* on, °elect, °settle upon *or* on, °screen (out), °sift (out): *Melanie was picked to succeed Hubert as president.* **2** °pluck, °gather, °collect, °harvest, °bring *or* °take in, °garner: *Scores of extra workers were brought in to pick apples.* **3** °provoke, °foment, °start, °initiate, °work *or* °stir up: *He tried to pick an argument with me about who is taller.* **4 pick at**: **a** °criticize, °carp at, find °fault with, °cavil (at *or* about), °quibble (at *or* about), °pick on, °nag (at), °niggle (at), °harass, °pester, °annoy, °irritate, °bother: *Stop picking at your brother!* **b** nibble (at), peck at: *We can't get him to eat a thing, he just picks at his food.* **5 pick off**: °shoot (down), °kill: *We picked them off one by one as they emerged from the trench.* **6 pick on**: °bully, °ride, °intimidate, °abuse, °browbeat, badger, harry, hector, °harass, °tease, °taunt, needle, °torment: *Robert must learn not to pick on the smaller boys.* **7 pick out: a** See 1, above. **b** discern, °distinguish, °tell apart, °make out, °recognize, °separate, °discriminate: *I was able to pick out a distant rider, approaching swiftly. From amongst the forest sounds she picked out the song of the nightingale.* **8 pick up: a** °raise (up), °lift (up), °hoist, °take up: *The stone is too heavy to pick up. Please pick up that piece of paper.* **b** °gather, °collect, glean, °take up: *I wish you would pick up your clothes.* **c** °tidy (up), °neaten, °straighten up *or* out, °clean (up): *She refuses to continue to pick up after him.* **d** °acquire, °learn, become °acquainted with; °master; *Colloq* get the hang of: *We picked up a little Spanish on our holiday.* **e** °acquire, °find, °come by, °get hold of, °obtain; °buy, °purchase, °get: *Basil picked up a few bad habits in the army. Let's pick up a bottle of wine on the way.* **f** °improve, get °better, °gain, °make °headway, °recover, °perk up, °rally, °recoup, (make) °progress, move °ahead, °increase, *Colloq* make a comeback: *Business usually picks up before Christmas.* **g** accelerate, °speed up: *The pace picked up as they approached the finish line.* **h** °arrest, apprehend, take into °custody, *Colloq* °pinch, collar, °nab, bust, °run in, °pull in, *Brit* °nick: *Two men were picked up trying to break into the bank.* **i** °call for, give a °lift *or* ride to, °collect, °go for *or US also* after, °go to get: *I'll pick you up at the railway station at noon.* **j** °meet, °introduce oneself to, °strike up an °acquaintance with, accost, make advances to: *I think she picked him up in a wine bar.* **k** catch, °come down with, °contract, °get: *He picked up a mystery virus in the Tropics.* —*n.* **9** °selection, °choice, °option, °preference: *She could have had the pick of any man in the place. Take your pick.* **10** choicest, °best, *crème de la crème,* cream: *The early shoppers had already taken the pick of the crop.*

picket *n.* **1** °stake, °pale, °post, °peg, stanchion, °upright, vertical, palisade, paling: *The walls of the fort were of strong pickets tapered to a point at the top.* **2** demonstrator, protester *or* protestor, striker: *The police prevented the pickets from attacking workers who entered the factory.* **3** picquet, °sentinel, °watchman, °guard, °observer, °patrol, vedette *or* vidette *or* vedette boat: *The picket reported no unusual activity.* —*v.* **4** °enclose, °shut in, °wall in, °fence (in), hem in, °box in: *We picketed the camp for the night.* **5** °protest, °demonstrate, blockade: *Strikers picketed the factory 24 hours a day.*

picnic *n.* **1** garden °party, fête champêtre, °meal alfresco, barbecue, *US* clam-bake, *US and Canadian* cookout: *The clouds had gone, and it was a great day for a picnic.* **2** child's play, *Colloq* °pushover, °snap, cinch, °piece of cake, walk-over, *US and Canadian* °breeze, lead-pipe cinch: *Sailing home with a quartering wind—it was a picnic all the way.* **3 no picnic**: °difficult, °arduous, torture, torturous, °agony, °agonizing, °painful, °disagreeable, discomfiting, °misfortune, *Colloq* °tough, °tough

luck, °tough going, °rough, a °pain in the neck, *US* °tough sledding, *Taboo slang* °pain in the *Brit* arse *or US* ass: *Being marooned on a desert island for a month was no picnic, I assure you.*

pictorial *adj.* **1** °graphic, °picturesque, °vivid, °telling, °striking, °expressive, °plain, °explicit, °clear, lucid: *Many of the poet's images are amazingly pictorial.* **2** illustrated: *They published a pictorial history of biblical lands just for children.*

picture *n.* **1** °drawing, painting, °representation, °portrait, depiction, artwork, °illustration, sketch, °photograph: *Here is a picture of our cottage in the Cotswolds.* **2** °image, (perfect *or* exact) °likeness, (carbon) °copy, °double, °duplicate, °twin, (exact) °replica, °look-alike, °facsimile, *Colloq* spitting °image *or* °spit and °image, *Slang* (dead) ringer: *Isn't she just the picture of her mother?* **3** °impression, °idea, °notion, °understanding, °image: *I think I have a pretty good picture of the situation.* **4** °model, °prototype, °epitome, °essence, °embodiment, incarnation, personification, perfect °example: *From her autobiography, you might believe her to be the picture of sweet innocence.* **5 put (someone) in** *or* **into the picture**: °inform *or* °advise fully, *Colloq* °fill (someone) in: *Put me into the picture about what went on here last night.* —*v.* **6** °envision, °envisage, visualize, °imagine, °fancy, °conceive of, °see in the mind's eye: *Picture yourself lying on a beach in the Bahamas.* **7** depict, °draw, °portray, °paint, °represent, °show, °illustrate, °display: *In this fresco, Salome is pictured dancing before Herod Antipas.*

picturesque *adj.* **1** colourful, °interesting, intriguing, °unusual, °unique, °original, charming, °idyllic, °fetching, °attractive, °pretty, °lovely, °quaint, °delightful, °pleasing, °scenic: *We came upon a picturesque village in which all the houses were half-timbered Tudor style with thatched roofs.* **2** colourful, °graphic, °realistic, °vivid, °striking: *Bernard has written a picturesque account of a walking trip through Bavaria.*

piece *n.* **1** °bit, °morsel, °scrap, chunk, hunk, °sliver, °lump, °portion, °particle, °fragment, °shred, shard *or* sherd, °remnant, °quantity: *All the beggar wanted was a piece of bread. A piece of shrapnel is still embedded in my arm.* **2** °wedge, °slice, serving, °helping, °portion: *You may not have a piece of pie till you've eaten your vegetables.* **3** °share, °portion, fraction, °part, °division, °segment, °section, °interest, holding, °percentage, °proportion: *It turned out that a piece of the company had been sold without shareholders' approval.* **4** (short) °story, article, °essay, °report, °theme, °draft; °poem; music, °opus, (°musical) number, °composition, °arrangement, °tune, °melody, °song, °air, °jingle, ditty, °production, °play, °drama, sketch, °show: *I read that piece about cholesterol in yesterday's paper. He wrote a piece for the flute. Which piece by Strindberg will you put on next?* **5** man, °token, chessman, chess-piece, chequer, *Brit* draughtsman: *Once you have touched a piece you must move it.* **6 go to pieces**: °fall °apart, °disintegrate, °crumble, °shatter; be shattered, be °upset, be °disturbed, have a nervous °breakdown, go out of *or* lose °control, °break down, *Colloq* °crack up: *Another earthquake and this wall will go to pieces. At the news of his son's death, Joe simply went to pieces.* **7 in**

pieces: smashed, destroyed, ruined, shattered, °broken, in smithereens: *The vase lay in pieces at my feet. Though I had won the case, my life was in pieces.* **8 of a piece (with)**: °similar, similarly constituted, °alike, of the °same °sort *or* °kind *or* °type, °uniform, the °same, °part and parcel (of the °same thing), °identical; in °harmony, °agreement, °harmonious, in keeping: *This book is of a piece with the others in the same series. All his paintings are of a piece.* **9 piece of cake**: *Colloq* snap, cinch, *US and Canadian* lead-pipe cinch, °breeze: *The French exam was a piece of cake.* **10 piece of (one's) mind**: scolding, °rebuke, °lecture, °reprimand, °tongue-lashing, chiding, °rap over *or* on the knuckles, *Colloq* °hell, what for, dressing-down, *US* bawling-out, chewing-out: *She gave him a piece of her mind about the amount of time he spent in the pub.* **11 piece of the action**: °share, °portion, °interest, °stake, °percentage, holding, °quota: *For £1,000 you can have a piece of the action.* **12 speak (one's) piece**: °have (one's) °say, °express (one's) °opinion, °say what is on (one's) mind; °vent (one's) spleen, *Colloq* get a load off (one's) mind *or* °chest: *All were given a chance to speak their piece.*
—*v.* **13 piece together**: °assemble, °put together, °connect, °gather, °compose; °fix, °unite, °restore, °mend: *We pieced together what happened from the witnesses' accounts. You'll never be able to piece together the bits of that lamp.*

pièce de résistance *n.* highlight, (°special *or* °main) °feature *or* °attraction, *spécialité (de la maison)*, °masterpiece, *chef-d'œuvre, Brit* °speciality, *US* specialty: *The pièce de résistance of the meal was a magnificent gateau.*

piecemeal *adv.* **1** °piece by piece, °little by little, inch by inch, inchmeal, °gradually, by °degrees, slowly, in °bits and °pieces, by °fits and starts, fitfully, intermittently, sporadically, disjointedly: *The ministry insisted that the plans should remain as one package and not be introduced piecemeal over the next two years.* **2** into fragments *or* shreds *or* °pieces: *He angrily took the cheque and tore it up piecemeal.*
—*adj.* **3** °fragmentary, °bit by bit, inchmeal, °gradual, °disjointed; °sporadic: *The South-east could become one huge traffic jam unless the Government drops its piecemeal approach to planning.*

pier *n.* **1** wharf, °landing (-stage *or* -place), jetty, quay, floating °dock, *Technically inaccurate* °dock: *The ship is tied up at the pier.* **2** °pile, piling, °post, °upright, column, °support, °buttress: *Owing to lack of maintenance, the piers supporting the building have crumbled.*

pierce *v.* **1** °stab, °puncture, °penetrate, °thrust *or* °poke into, °lance, spear, °spit, °run through *or* into, skewer, °impale, °fix, °transfix: *The arrow pierced his heart and he dropped down dead.* **2** °bore into *or* through, °penetrate, °drill, °perforate, °riddle, °punch through, °hole, °tunnel into: *The wall is pierced to provide ventilation.* **3** °penetrate, °fathom, °see, °understand, °comprehend, °grasp, °discover, °realize: *His keen analytical mind allowed him to pierce the mysteries of nature.* **4** °affect (keenly), °touch, °move, °melt, °stir, °rouse, °pain, °cut to the quick, °wound, °strike: *It pierced my heart to hear the child weep.*

piercing *adj.* **1** °strident, °shrill, °harsh, ear-splitting, ear-shattering, high-pitched,

screaming, shrieking, screeching, °loud, blaring: *The piercing sound of the police siren made me sit bolt upright in bed.* **2** probing, searching, °penetrating, °sharp, °keen; °arresting, gripping, °spellbinding, °enthralling, fascinating, entrancing: *I was completely transfixed by her piercing green eyes.* **3** °penetrating, °icy, frosty, °frigid, chilling, °freezing, °cold, numbing, °keen, °wintry, arctic, °raw, °bitter, °fierce, °biting, nipping, nippy: *Shivering in that piercing wind I thought I'd never be warm again.* **4** stabbing, shooting, °excruciating, °exquisite, °acute, °sharp, °severe, °agonizing, °fierce, °intense, °painful, racking: *I suddenly felt a piercing pain in my left ear.*

piety *n.* **1** °devotion, devotedness, °respect, °deference, °dedication, dutifulness, °loyalty, °affection: *In filial piety he hung the painting of his parents prominently over the mantelpiece.* **2** piousness, °reverence, °veneration, devoutness, holiness, godliness, pietism, devotedness, °devotion, °observance, religiousness, °grace, °sanctity: *His life of piety had marked him out as a likely candidate for sainthood.*

pile¹ *n.* **1** °heap, °mound, °stack, °accumulation, stockpile, °mass, °supply, °deposit, °collection, assemblage, °batch, °hoard, aggregation, congeries, conglomeration, °assortment, agglomeration, concentration, amassment: *A huge pile of gravel was delivered today for the builders.* **2** °money, °fortune, °wealth, holdings, *Colloq* bundle, °loot, °mint, *Slang* °packet, °tidy °sum, *US* bankroll, °roll, °wad: *She made her pile selling arms to terrorists.* **3** Usually, **piles**: °abundance, over-abundance, superabundance, °plenty, °great °deal, °quantity, °ocean(s), °lot(s), °stack(s), plethora, *Colloq* oodles, ton(s), °bag(s), °heap(s), °bundle(s): *He made piles of money in the black market.* **4** See **pier, 2**, above.
—*v.* **5** Often, **pile up**: °stack (up), °heap (up), °mound, °accumulate, stockpile, °amass, °collect, °assemble, °hoard, aggregate, cumulate: *Please pile the cartons in the corner.* **6 pile in** *or* **into**: °enter, °get in *or* into, °crowd in *or* into, °pack in *or* into, °flood in *or* into, °jam in *or* into, °crush in *or* into, *Colloq* °jump in *or* into: *All of us piled into my car to go to the cinema.* **7 pile it on**: °exaggerate: *Ronnie was really piling it on about how much his new job pays.* **8 pile on** *or* **onto**: **a** °get in *or* into *or* on *or* onto, °crowd on *or* onto, °jump on *or* onto: *We piled on the train after the game. They piled onto the hay wagon for a ride home.* **b** °attack, °assault, °jump on, °overwhelm: *They all piled on me and I had to give up.* **9 pile out**: °leave, °get out (of) *or* down (from), °exit: *When we arrived, we all piled out of the bus. Hordes of people piled out of the theatre.* **10 pile up**: °accumulate, °amass, °collect: *The rubbish kept piling up during the strike.*

pile² *n.* °nap, shag, °plush; fuzz, bristles, °fleece: *The feet of the chairs have left marks in the carpet pile.*

piles *n.pl.* haemorrhoids.

pile-up *n.* **1** (road) °accident, smash, °crash, (multiple) (rear-end) °collision, *Colloq* smash-up: *Thirty cars were involved in that pile-up on the motorway.* **2** °accumulation, °heap, °stack, °mass, *Colloq* °mountain: *How will you ever get through that pile-up of work on your desk?*

pilfer *v.* °steal, °rob, °plunder, thieve, filch, °embezzle, °misappropriate, purloin, °take, walk off with, palm, *Colloq* °appropriate, °pinch, °snatch, °grab, °lift, borrow, *Brit* °nick, snaffle, *US* boost, *Slang* °hook, snitch, °swipe, °rip off: *The auditors found that he had pilfered small sums from the company for years.*

pilgrim *n.* hajji *or* hadji *or* haji, *Medieval history* palmer; crusader: *The pilgrims visited holy places in and near Jerusalem.*

pilgrimage *n.* hajj *or* hadj, holy °expedition, °crusade; °expedition, °journey, trek, voyage, °tour, °trip, °excursion: *Every year the entire family made a pilgrimage to grandfather's grave.*

pill *n.* **1** °tablet, capsule, bolus, pellet, pilule; °medicine, medication, medicament, °drug, pharmaceutical, °remedy, °cure; cough drop, pastille, lozenge, troche: *Doctor, can't you give me some kind of pill for this headache?* **2** °nuisance, °bore, °pest, *Colloq* °pain (in the neck), °crank, °drag: *I don't understand what she sees in Leonard—he's such a pill.*

pillage *v.* **1** °plunder, °raid, °ravage, °sack, despoil, °rob, °loot, °ransack, °rifle, maraud, depredate, °devastate, vandalize, °ruin, °demolish, °raze, °level, °strip: *The Goths pillaged every community they conquered and carried off the booty.*
—*n.* **2** °plunder, rapine, despoliation, looting, °robbery, °sack, sacking, ransacking, marauding, brigandage, piracy, freebooting, buccaneering, banditry, °depredation, devastation, vandalization, defilement, laying °waste, °destruction, razing, demolition, levelling, °ruin, stripping: *Pirates from Tripoli were responsible for the pillage of one coastal town after another.* **3** °plunder, °loot, °booty, spoils: *In the cave Ali Baba found the pillage from a thousand robberies.*

pillar *n.* **1** column, pilaster, °pile, piling, °pier, °upright, °post, °shaft, °prop; atlas, caryatid: *The roof is supported by a single pillar. Lot's wife was turned into a pillar of salt.* **2** °mainstay, °supporter, °worthy, upholder, °backbone, (°tower of) °strength, °leader: *Cummings has been a pillar of strength in our community.*

pilot *n.* **1** aviator, aviatrix, flier, airman, air-woman, aeronaut, captain: *The pilot announced that we would land in five minutes.* **2** steersman, helmsman, °navigator, *US* wheelman *or* wheelsman; °guide, °leader, cicerone, conductor: *The pilot knows his way through the shoals. A student acted as our pilot in our tour of Oxford.*
—*v.* **3** °guide, °steer, °run, °direct, °shepherd, °control, °lead, °navigate, °drive; °fly: *Only someone with local knowledge can pilot the ship into that harbour. The chairman piloted the company through turbulent times.*

pimp *n.* **1** procurer, panderer *or* °pander, White °slaver, whoremonger, *Slang US* hustler: *The police rounded up the pimps and prostitutes for questioning.*
—*v.* **2** °procure, °pander, °solicit, *Slang US* °hustle: *He was well known as having pimped for three generations of the nobility.*

pimple *n.* pustule, papula, °boil, °swelling, °eruption, blackhead *or* *Technical* comedo, excrescence, *Brit* °spot, *Scots* plouk *or* plook, *US* whitehead, *Old-fashioned US* hickey: *The old witch had a pimple at the end of her nose.*

pin *n.* **1** °peg, dowel, °bolt, thole, thole-pin, °spike, rivet; *Brit* drawing-pin, *US* push-pin: *The table is held together by wooden pins. We need some*
more *pins for the notice-board.* **2** °brooch, °clip; stickpin, tie-pin, scarf-pin, *US* tie tack: *She is wearing the cameo pin that her mother gave her. I had George's pin made into a brooch.*
—*v.* **3** °attach, °fix, affix, °fasten, °secure, °tack; °hold, °staple, °clip: *Let's play 'Pin the tail on the donkey'. Pin these papers together.* **4 pin down**: **a** °force, °make, compel, coerce, constrain, °press, *Brit* pressurize, *US* °pressure: *We must pin him down to give his decision by tomorrow.* **b** °define, °specify, pinpoint, °name, °identify, °determine, put *or* lay one's °finger on, home *or* °zero in on, °focus on: *The doctor was unable to pin down what is wrong with her.* **c** confine, °hold (down), °fix, immobilize, °tie down, constrain: *We were pinned down by enemy fire.* **5 pin on**: °blame, °hold °responsible *or* °accountable, point the °finger at, °accuse; °lay at (someone's) door: *They'll never be able to pin the murder on Drayton.*

pincers *n.pl.* pliers, nippers, tweezers: *Can you get the nail out with these pincers?*

pinch *v.* **1** °squeeze, °nip, °tweak, °press, compress, °grip, °grasp: *I pinched my finger in the drawer.* **2** °squeeze, cramp, confine, °crush, °hurt: *These shoes really pinch badly.* **3** °steal, thieve, °rob, °take, shoplift, filch, °pilfer, purloin, *Colloq* °lift, *Brit* °nick, *US* boost, *Slang* °swipe, °knock off: *I think it was Andrew who pinched my book.* **4** °arrest, apprehend, take into °custody, *Colloq* °nab, °run in, collar, bust, *Brit* °nick: *She was pinched for driving while under the influence.* **5 pinch pennies**: scrimp, °save, skimp, °economize: *We're pinching pennies now so that we can afford a nice holiday later.*
—*n.* **6** °squeeze, °nip, °tweak, °twinge: *Montrose gave the girl's cheek an affectionate pinch.* **7** °touch, (°tiny *or* °wee) °bit, soupçon, °jot, mite, °taste, *Colloq US* tad, smidgen *or* smidgin: *Add a pinch of salt to the boiling water.* **8** °predicament, °emergency, °crisis, °difficulty, °dilemma, (°ticklish *or* °delicate) °situation, °complication, *Colloq* pickle, °jam, °scrape, *Chiefly Brit* °crunch: *Sue will help me out in a pinch.*

pink[1] *n.* **1 in the pink**: at one's °best, °healthy, °hearty, in the °best of °health, in °top °form, in °good °shape, *Colloq US* up: *I saw Rob the other day, and he's in the pink.*
—*adj.* **2** °rosy, rose, rose-coloured, pinkish, flesh-colour(ed), salmon(-colour(ed)): *The designer suggests pink curtains for the bedroom.*

pink[2] *v.* serrate, °notch, scallop; °perforate, °puncture, °prick: *Pink the edge of the fabric to prevent fraying.*

pinnacle *n.* °top, °peak, apex, °acme, °summit, °zenith, °maximum, °climax, crowning °point, °consummation, utmost, °extreme, °perfection; °tip, °cap, °crest, °crown: *Being elected chairman was the pinnacle of Mark's career. The climbers reached the pinnacle, where they will rest overnight.*

pioneer *n.* **1** pathfinder, frontiersman, frontierswoman, trail-blazer, explorer, colonist, (early) °settler; ground-breaker, °forerunner, °precursor, °predecessor, innovator, °leader, trend-setter, pacemaker, pace-setter: *The pioneers who explored and settled the American west were daring men and women. Marconi was a pioneer in the development of radio.*
—*v.* **2** °create, °originate, °invent, °initiate, take the first °step, °introduce, °institute, actuate, trigger, °set off, °inaugurate, °start, °begin,

°launch, °establish, °found, °set up, °develop,
lay the °groundwork or °foundation, set or put
in motion, take the °lead, °lead or show the
way, blaze the trail, be a °prime mover, °open
up, Colloq kick off, get the ball rolling: Our
company has pioneered systems for automatic type-
setting.

pious adj. **1** °devout, °religious, reverent, reverential, worshipful, °dutiful, God-fearing,
°godly, °faithful, °holy, dedicated, °devoted,
°spiritual, °moral, °good, °virtuous,
right-minded, °saintly, angelic, °seraphic,
Christ-like, °godlike: Francis is a pious boy who
attends church regularly. **2** °hypocritical,
°sanctimonious, pietistic, °self-righteous,
°Pharisaic, °mealy-mouthed, °pretended,
°fraudulent, °goody-goody, unctuous, °oily,
Colloq Brit smarmy: You are rationalizing your bad
behaviour with a lot of pious cant.

pipe n. **1** °pipeline, tube, duct, hose, °line,
°main, conduit, °passage, conveyor, °channel:
The pipes are inspected regularly for corrosion.
2 briar, meerschaum, corn-cob, calabash,
clay pipe, water-pipe, hookah, narghile,
chibouk or chibouque, peace-pipe or pipe of
peace or calumet, brier, Brit hubble-bubble, US
bong: He slowly tamped down the tobacco in his
pipe, then lit it. **3** pan-pipe, whistle, boatswain's
pipe, tooter, horn, wind, wind °instrument,
woodwind, brass: They play the pipes in the London
Symphony.
—v. **4** tootle, tweet, skirl, warble, whistle, °peep,
cheep: One was piping away on a flute, the other
was dancing a jig. **5** °transmit, °deliver, °channel,
°conduct, convey, °supply: The gas is piped directly
into our homes. **6** US °look at, °notice, °spot,
°note, Colloq get a load of: Pipe the guy trying to
climb up the outside of that building. **7 pipe down**:
become quieter, °quiet(en) down, make less
°noise, °hush (up), shush (up), °whisper, Colloq
°belt up, °shut up: I wish they'd pipe down, I can't
sleep. **8 pipe up**: °speak (up), °say, raise one's
voice, make oneself heard, °offer, volunteer:
Sally piped up with the correct answer from the back
of the classroom.

pipeline n. **1** °pipe, tube, duct, hose, °line,
°main, conduit, °passage, conveyor, °channel:
Pipelines carry gas from the North Sea throughout
Britain. Very little information was flowing through
the pipeline from Beirut. **2 in the pipeline**: on
the °way, under °way, in the offing, °ready,
°imminent, coming, Colloq in the °works, cooking, US in °work: They said that the contract was
in the pipeline and should arrive soon.

pirate n. **1** buccaneer, sea °rover, corsair, privateer, freebooter, sea-robber, filibuster, Archaic
pic(k)aroon: Captain Kidd and Blackbeard were
actual pirates who looted shipping in the Americas in
the 17th century. **2** plagiarist, plagiarizer,
infringer: Some of these pirates offer unauthorized
cheap reprints of expensive textbooks.
—v. **3** plagiarize, °infringe, °copy, °reproduce,
°steal, °appropriate, poach, Colloq °lift, °pinch,
crib: Our government has no jurisdiction over those
who pirate books in countries with which we have
no treaty.

pirouette n. **1** °spin, whirl, °twirl, °turn,
°revolution, pivoting: Antoinette did a beautiful
pirouette followed by a pas de chat.
—v. **2** °spin, whirl, °turn (°round), °revolve,
°pivot: He was so happy that he fairly pirouetted
round the room.

pistol n. gun, handgun, °revolver, automatic,
Slang rod, piece, shooting-iron, Chiefly US gat,
US Saturday-night special, heater, roscoe: In the
United States, law enforcement officers are required
to carry a pistol.

piston n. plunger: The piston in a bicycle pump is
worked by hand.

pit[1] n. **1** °hole, °excavation, °shaft, °cavity,
°mine, mine-shaft, °quarry, working, ditch,
trench, trough: Pits had been dug for the extraction
of gravel. **2** pothole, °hollow, °depression, dent,
°indentation, dimple, pock-mark: His face was
disfigured by the pits left by teenage acne. **3** °abyss,
chasm, °well, °crevasse, crater: We found a bottomless pit that led to the centre of the earth. **4 the
pits**: °awful, °terrible, the worst, Slang °lousy:
That TV show last night was the pits. He thought that
going to school was the pits.
—v. **5** dent, pock-mark, °dig, °scar, °hollow out,
°gouge: The salt air has pitted the metal parts of my
car. **6** Often, **pit against**: °match, °oppose, °set
against; °contrast: Shirley doesn't stand a chance
if you pit her against Maria.

pit[2] n. stone, °seed, pip: I prefer seedless grapes, the
ones without pits.

pitch[1] v. **1** °toss, °throw, °cast, °fling, °hurl,
°heave, °sling, °fire, °launch, °shoot, °send, let
°fly, Cricket °bowl, Colloq chuck, °peg, °lob, Brit
bung: He rolled the paper into a ball and pitched
it into the basket. **2** °erect, °raise, °set or °put
up, °position, °fix, °place: We ought to pitch the
tent in a level area. **3** °plunge, °fall (headlong),
°dive, °drop, °plummet, (take a) nosedive: I
caught my toe on the kerb and pitched forward onto
the pavement. **4** Chiefly nautical °toss about,
°lurch, °plunge, °flounder, go °head over heels,
go keel over truck, °pitchpole or pitchpoll: The
wind reached force ten as we pitched and rolled and
yawed in the heavy seas. **5 pitch in**: °contribute,
°cooperate, °help, °assist, Colloq °chip in: Everyone pitched in to make the church fair a success.
6 pitch into: **a** °attack, °lay into, assail,
°lash out at, °abuse, °rail against, Colloq °lace
into, °tear into, jump down (someone's) throat,
°jump on: Reggie's wife really pitched into him about
going out with other women. **b** °attack, °assault,
°set upon, °belabour, Colloq °light into, sail into,
°tear into: They pitched into each other and fought
like Kilkenny cats. **7 pitch on** or **upon**:
°determine, °decide on, °select, °pick, °choose,
opt for, °elect, °nominate, °name, Colloq °light
on: They pitched on Carrie to be the best candidate
for treasurer.

pitch[2] n. tar, bitumen, asphalt: Peter patched pot-
holes with pitch.

pitch-black adj. °black, °dark, ebon(y), Stygian,
inky(-black), unlit, unlighted, pitch-dark,
coal-black, jet-black; raven, sable: The cellar was
pitch-black. Her pale complexion was in stark contrast to her pitch-black hair.

pitched adj. organized, planned, °deliberate,
coordinated, arranged, systematized: The two
armies fought a pitched battle on the plain.

piteous adj. °pitiable, °pathetic, °pitiful, plaintive, °miserable, °heart-rending, °poignant, distressing, °grievous, heartbreaking, °mournful,
°sad, °doleful, dolorous, °tearful, °lamentable,
°deplorable, °regrettable, rueful, woeful,
°moving, °emotional: We heard the piteous wailing
of the mothers who had lost children in the disaster.

pitfall n. 1 °trap, °pit: *Pitfalls were often used in Burma for trapping tigers.* 2 °danger, °peril, °hazard, catch, °difficulty, °snag: *You might well encounter pitfalls, but don't be discouraged.*

pith n. 1 °core, °heart, °kernel, °nucleus, crux, °gist, °focus, °focal °point, °essence, °meat, marrow, °nub, °point, °spirit, °substance, °quintessence: *As usual, Randolph came immediately to the pith of the argument.* 2 °weight, °burden, gravamen, °gravity, °force, °moment, °import, °importance, °significance, °substance, °depth, °matter: *I have something of great pith to tell you about.*

pitiable adj. See piteous, above.

pitiful adj. 1 See piteous, above. 2 °small, °little, °insignificant, °trifling, unimportant, beggarly, °sorry, °mean, °contemptible: *Does Hodges seriously expect us to praise him for that pitiful contribution of his?*

pittance n. mite, shoestring, *Slang* peanuts, chicken-feed, small potatoes: *The miserable pittance that she receives does not even cover the necessities of life. He's trying to run that business on a pittance.*

pitted adj. eaten away, corroded, eroded, pock-marked, defaced, marred, pierced, perforated: *The chrome plating is all pitted where the acid splashed.*

pity n. 1 °sympathy, commiseration, °sorrow, condolence, compassion, tenderness, *Archaic* ruth: *I really feel pity for Betty, being married to such a brute.* 2 (crying or damned) °shame, °sad thing, °disgrace, °misfortune, °sin, °sacrilege, *Colloq* crime: *It's a pity that no one can do anything.* —v. 3 °sympathize, °feel for, commiserate with, °feel °sorry for, °feel or have compassion or tenderness for, bleed for, °weep for: *I pity any mother whose son goes off to war.*

pivot n. 1 pintle, gudgeon, hinge, °swivel, °pin, kingpin, spindle, fulcrum: *Use this stone as a pivot for the lever to lift the rock.* 2 °centre, °heart, °focal °point, °hub, nave, crux: *The finance minister regards the interest rate as the pivot on which the economy turns.* —v. 3 °rotate, °revolve, °turn, °spin, °twirl, whirl, °swivel: *The flywheel pivots on a bearing that requires constant lubrication.* 4 hinge, °depend, °hang, be contingent, °revolve around, °rely: *The whole deal pivots on the cooperation of the banks.*

pivotal adj. °critical, °central, °focal, °crucial, °significant, °important, °essential, °vital, °pressing, °urgent, °radical: *The attitude of the judge is pivotal in the jury's decision.*

place n. 1 °location, °site, °position, °point, °spot, locus, °area, °locale, °scene, °setting: *This looks like a nice place for a picnic. She likes to see a place for everything and everything in its place.* 2 °locale, °area, °neighbourhood, °vicinity, °district, °section, °part of the country, °quarter, °region; °city, °town, village, hamlet: *She comes from some place near Glasgow.* 3 °status, °station, °standing, °grade, °rank, °position, °niche, °slot, °situation, °estate, °state, °circumstance(s): *Angela was just saying how difficult it is today to find a servant who knows his place.* 4 °function, °role, °part, °purpose, °duty, °obligation, °task, °responsibility, °charge, chore, °burden, °concern, °mission: *It is scarcely my place to remind you of your appointments with the dentist.* 5 °position, °job, °post, berth, °appointment, livelihood; °employment, °occupation, *Colloq* billet: *Is there a chance of my earning a place in your new company?* 6 °home, °house, °flat, apartment, °room(s), °quarters, °lodgings, *Rather formal* °residence, °domicile, °dwelling, °abode, *Colloq* digs or diggings, °pad: *Why not stop by my place for tea on Sunday?* 7 stead; lieu: *As I cannot go, would you go in place of me?* 8 °position, °situation, circumstances, °condition: *Put yourself in my place and I think you would have done exactly the same.* 9 °seat, °chair, °position: *Kevin, please take your place at the head of the table.* 10 **go places**: °succeed, become °successful, °get ahead, °advance, °prosper, °thrive, °flourish, go up in the world, °make good, strike it rich, *Colloq* °arrive, make a °splash, *US and Canadian* hit pay dirt, luck out: *That boy will go places one day.* 11 **in place**: a °fitting, °suitable, °appropriate, °right, °proper, °correct, good °form: *I don't think it in place for you to tell me what to do.* b *in situ*, in (the right or proper or correct) °position, °ready, all °set, °set up, in °order, all °right, *Colloq* °OK or okay: *Is everything in place for tonight's party?* 12 **out of place**: °awkward, uncomfortable, unsuitable, °inappropriate, °wrong, °improper, misplaced: *Compassion is out of place when dealing with war criminals.* 13 **put (someone) in his** or **her** or **their place**: °humble, °mortify, °bring down, °embarrass, °squelch, *Colloq* °cut down to size, take down a °peg (or two): *Aunt Agatha used to put Uncle Wilfred in his place by reminding him who held the purse-strings.* 14 **take place**: °happen, °occur, °go on, °come about; °arise, *Colloq* °transpire: *We shall never know what took place behind those locked doors.* —v. 15 °put (out), °position, °situate, °locate, °dispose, °arrange, °order, °set (out), °lay, °deposit; °station, °post, °spot, pinpoint, *Colloq* °stick, *Brit* bung: *Place the forks on the left and the knives on the right. They placed guards at the door of my room.* 16 °class, classify, °sort, °order, °arrange, °rank, °group, °categorize, °bracket, °grade; °regard, °view, °see, °consider: *She places love of family above love of country. Critics place him among the best writers of the century.* 17 °identify, put one's °finger on, °recall, °remember, °recognize; °associate: *I just can't place her for the moment. He finally placed me with those who had ragged him at school.* 18 °put, °set, °assign, °give: *People place too much importance on material things.*

placement n. 1 °arrangement, placing, °position, °distribution, array, °disposition, deployment, positioning, stationing, °organization, °order, ordering, °location, locating, arraying, emplacement, emplacing: *The placement of the chairs is all wrong for tonight's meeting.* 2 °employment, °appointment, °engagement, hiring: *Placement of qualified engineers has not been a problem.*

plagiarism n. plagiarizing, plagiary, piracy, pirating, °theft, purloining, °stealing, copying, appropriating, appropriation, thievery, usurpation, infringing, °infringement, °imitation, *Euphemistic* borrowing, *Colloq* lifting, cribbing: *The similarities between the two books could only be explained by plagiarism.*

plague n. 1 °scourge, °epidemic, °pestilence, °affliction, pandemic, °calamity, °curse, °evil, bane, °blight, °visitation: *The inhabitants turned a plague of locusts to advantage by eating them.*

2 irritation, °annoyance, °nuisance, °pest, vexation, °bother, °thorn in one's side or flesh, °torment, torture, Colloq °pain (in the neck), °headache, aggravation, Slang °drag, °bitch, hassle, Taboo slang °pain in the Brit arse or US ass: It's a plague trying to find a place to park the car.
—v. **3** badger, harry, °hound, °pester, °annoy, vex, °irritate, °bother, °harass, °nag, nettle, °exasperate, °gall, °irk, °torment, torture, °anguish, °distress, Brit chivvy or chivy or chevy: I wish the police would stop plaguing me with questions about Jonathan's whereabouts.

plain adj. **1** °flat, °smooth, °even, featureless, °level, °plane: I'd rather have a paper with a plain surface, not an embossed one, for the bedroom walls. **2** °clear, °evident, °simple, °distinct, crystal °clear, lucid, °vivid, °transparent, °apparent, °obvious, °patent, °self-evident, °manifest, unmistakable, unequivocal, unambiguous, understandable, °intelligible, °graphic, °direct, in black and white: His intentions regarding my daughter are plain enough. The plain fact is that she despises him. **3** °open, °honest, straightforward, °forthright, °direct, °frank, °candid, °blunt, °outspoken, °ingenuous, °sincere, guileless, °artless, unreserved: I want to see some plain talk between the two of us. **4** °simple, °unadorned, undecorated, unembellished, °basic, austere, °stark, unostentatious, °colourless, °drab, °bare, °unvarnished, °Spartan: Don't you find the average business suit a very plain affair? **5** °homely, unattractive, ordinary-looking, unlovely, °ugly: Who would believe that such a plain child could become such a beautiful woman?
—n. **6** prairie, grassland, °pasture, meadow-land, veld or veldt, pampas, campo, llano, savannah or savanna, steppe, tundra, champaign or campagna; heath; °moor, moorland; °plateau, flatland; down, downland, Literary wold, Archaic or literary mead: The plain stretched out before us as far as the eye could see.

plan n. **1** °design, layout, blueprint, °scheme, °method, °procedure, °system, °arrangement, °programme, °project, °formula, °pattern, Colloq °script, °scenario: The plan called for monthly progress meetings. The best laid plans of mice and men gang aft agley. **2** °drawing, sketch, °design, layout, blueprint, °chart, map, diagram, °representation: This plan shows where the furniture will be placed.
—v. **3** °lay out or down, °design, °arrange, °devise, °outline, °organize, °plot, map out, delineate, °develop: She has been invited to plan the new shopping mall. **4** °intend, °expect, °envisage, °envision, °foresee, °aim, °contemplate, °propose: Were you planning to go to the cinema tonight?

plane n. **1** °flat or °level (°surface): The lines meet in the same plane. **2** aeroplane, aircraft, airliner, jet (plane): I caught the next plane for Marrakesh.
—adj. **3** °flat, °even, °level, °smooth, °plain, °regular, unbroken, uninterrupted, °uniform, °horizontal: We landed on the plane surface of the glacier.
—v. **4** °glide, °skim, skate, skid, °slip, °slide: I swiftly planed along on my sailboard.

plank n. °board, °timber, °slab: The flooring was made up of wide planks laid side by side.

plant n. **1** °flower, vegetable, herb, bush, shrub, tree, vine, weed: Because of all the rain, the plants are flourishing this summer. **2** °factory, °mill, °shop, °works, workshop, foundry: The new plant in Crawley is hiring lathe operators. **3** °equipment, machinery, °apparatus; °gear, °fixtures: The plant includes heavy cranes, JCBs, earth movers, and bulldozers. **4** °spy, (°undercover or °secret) °agent, °informer, informant: The new assistant is a plant, sent in by management to report on union activities.
—v. **5** bed (out), °sow, °seed, °set (out), °transplant: We planted a herbaceous border along the south wall of the garden. **6** °implant, °establish, °root, °fix, ingrain, °lodge, °instil, °insinuate, °inject, °introduce, °impress, imprint: Who planted the idea in your mind that you were a gifted writer? **7** °place, °put, °position, °station, °assign, °situate: Watch-towers are planted at 50-foot intervals around the prison. **8** °hide, °secrete, °conceal: The company has planted detectives in the store to watch out for shoplifters.

planter n. flowerpot, cache-pot: He poured the drugged wine into a nearby planter.

plaque n. **1** °tablet, medallion, °plate, panel, marker, °slab, plaquette: The plaque on the house marks it as the birthplace of Thomas Carlyle. **2** badge, °brooch, °pin, °patch, medallion, medal, insignia or insigne: The plaque shows him to be a member of the Royal Yacht Squadron. **3** °prize, °honour, °award, °trophy: At the annual dinner, she was presented with a plaque to mark her many years of service.

plaster v. °smear, daub, bedaub, °spread, °coat, °cover, overlay, superimpose: The mud was plastered all over my boots. They plastered the walls with posters.

plastic adj. **1** mouldable, shapable or shapeable, fictile, °soft, malleable, workable, ductile, °flexible, pliant, °supple, °pliable, clayey, waxy: The clay must be worked into the desired form while it is still plastic. **2** °impressionable, °receptive, °open, persuadable or persuasible, °susceptible, °tractable, compliant, °responsive, °manageable, unformed, °inexperienced: One encounters the children at an age when their minds and personalities are still plastic enough to be influenced. **3** °artificial, °synthetic, °imitation, °fake, °counterfeit, ersatz, paste, °bogus, meretricious, °sham; °cheap, pinchbeck, °shoddy; Colloq °phoney or US also phony, crummy, US chintzy: She was wearing a tawdry plastic brooch.

plate n. **1** °platter, dish, Archaic trencher, charger: I left the cold mashed potato on my plate. **2** °course, serving, °portion, dish, °platter: I ordered their speciality, a plate of spaghetti. **3** layer, leaf, °sheet, °pane, panel, lamina, °slab: In the condenser, insulation separates the thin metal plates. **4** coating, °coat, plating, layer, lamination: The plate on our cutlery is wearing thin. **5** °illustration, °picture, °print, US °cut: The book contains many beautiful colour plates of flowers.
—v. **6** °cover, °coat, overlay, °face, laminate: All the serving dishes were plated with gold.

plateau n. **1** tableland, upland, highland, mesa: We climbed till we reached a grassy plateau. **2** °level, °lull, °pause, levelling off: At 39, Julia seemed to have reached a plateau in her career.

platform n. **1** °stand, dais, °stage, podium, °rostrum: After the introduction, the speaker mounted the platform. **2** °policy, party °line,

°principle(s), °tenet(s), °programme, plank: *The main elements of our platform will be revealed at the party conference.*

platonic *adj.* non-physical, asexual, non-sexual, °celibate, °chaste, °dispassionate, °detached, °spiritual, °ideal, °intellectual: *Some say that their relationship has not always been purely platonic.*

platoon *n.* °company, °squad, squadron, °group, °patrol, °team, cadre, °body, °formation, °unit, *Colloq* °outfit: *A platoon of soldiers was marched to the barracks in close-order drill.*

platter *n.* serving dish, server, salver, tray, °plate, dish: *Waiters walked among the guests with platters of hot hors-d'œuvres.*

plausible *adj.* **1** °likely, believable, °reasonable, credible, °tenable, conceivable, °thinkable, °probable, imaginable, admissible, °sound, °sensible, °rational, °logical, °acceptable, °trustworthy, °presentable: *The police regarded our alibi as plausible.* **2** °specious, °deceptive, meretricious, misleading, °deceitful, casuistic, sophistical, Jesuitical, °smooth, °empty: *He was a cunning, plausible sort of fellow.*

play *v.* **1** °amuse oneself, °frolic, °frisk, °cavort, gambol, °caper, °sport, have °fun, have a good time, °enjoy oneself, disport (oneself), °carouse: *Ken's mother won't let him go out and play.* **2** °participate (in), take °part (in), °join (in), be occupied (in or with); °engage in, contend in, °take up, °occupy oneself in or with, °undertake: *He was invited for a game of poker, but he refused to play. I understand that you play bridge.* **3** °engage, contend with, °compete with or against, °challenge, °vie with, °pit oneself against, °take on, °rival: *The stranger played me at snooker, and I lost three games out of three.* **4** °portray, depict, °perform, act or take the °role or °part of, °act: *In the new production of Othello she plays Desdemona.* **5** perform (upon or on); put on: *Play 'Misty' for me. She plays the piccolo very well. Could you play that Caruso record?* **6** °operate: *I wish they wouldn't play their hi-fi so loud.* **7** °gamble, °bet, wager, °stake, °place, °put: *He played his last chip on number 14.* **8 play along**: **a** Often, **play along with**: °cooperate, °participate, °go along (with), do or play one's °part, be a °party to: *I agreed to play along with her charade.* **b** °manipulate, °jolly along: *She played him along till he bought her a car.* **9 play around**: **a** °fool around, °tease, *Colloq* °monkey about or around, horse around or about: *Stop playing around and get to work.* **b** dally, °flirt, be unfaithful; philander, womanize; *Colloq* °fool around, °run around, °sleep around, play the field: *She found out about his playing around and filed for divorce.* **10 play at**: °pretend, make °believe, °fake, feign, simulate, °affect: *She's merely playing at enjoying skiing to please you.* **11 play ball**: °cooperate, °agree, °work together, work °hand in glove, play along: *They want him to smuggle diamonds, but he won't play ball.* **12 play by ear**: °improvise, extemporize, ad lib, *Colloq* wing it: *She can't read music and just plays by ear. With no definite plan of action, I'll just play it by ear.* **13 play down**: °belittle, °minimize, °diminish, °disparage, make °light of, deprecate, decry, de-emphasize: *He has always played down his role in the affair.* **14 play for time**: °delay, °procrastinate, °stall (for time), temporize, °hesitate, *Colloq* °drag one's feet: *They don't yet have the money to pay, so they are playing*

for time. **15 play on** or **upon**: °use, °misuse, °abuse, °trade on, °exploit, take °advantage of, °impose on: *He plays on women's affections then persuades them to give him money.* **16 play the game**: °behave, °conduct oneself, deport oneself, °act: *It makes no difference whether you win or lose, it's how you play the game.* **17 play up**: **a** °stress, °emphasize, underscore, underline, accentuate, call °attention to, highlight, °spotlight, °dramatize, °build up: *Always try to play up your assets and play down your liabilities.* **b** °act up, °misbehave, give or cause °trouble, malfunction, *Colloq* go on the °blink or *US* fritz, *Brit* be wonky: *The bloody engine started playing up again, right in the middle of a rainstorm.* **18 play up to**: curry °favour with, °flatter, toady to, ingratiate oneself with, butter up, °truckle to, court, *Colloq* soft-soap, suck up to, boot-lick, *US* apple-polish, *Taboo slang* brown-nose: *Ray is always playing up to the teacher, trying to get a better mark.* **19 play with**: **a** °toy with, °trifle with, treat cavalierly or lightly, make °light of, think nothing of, dally with, °amuse oneself with: *He's just playing with her till he gets what he's after.* **b** °consider, °think about, °toy with, not treat seriously: *We were playing with the idea of a winter holiday this year.* **c** °mess with, °fiddle with, °toy with, °fidget with: *Stop playing with your food!*
—*n.* **20** °drama, °stage play, °show, °piece, °production, °entertainment: *We have tickets to a different play for every night this week.* **21** °behaviour, °actions, deportment, °conduct, demeanour: *In the game of life, many have no regard for the rules of fair play. The police suspect foul play.* **22** °amusement, frivolity, °entertainment, °recreation, °fun, °pleasure, °sport, merrymaking, °revelry, tomfoolery, *Colloq* horseplay, skylarking, °monkey business, *Brit* °monkey tricks or *US* monkeyshines: *The time for play is past, and we must get down to serious business.* **23** °move, °manoeuvre, °action: *That last play might have won you the game.* **24** °flexibility, looseness, °freedom, °leeway, °margin, °room, °space, °movement, °motion, *Colloq* °give: *There's too much play in this gear lever.* **25** °treatment, coverage, °attention: *The newspapers gave Connie's new book a big play.*

playboy *n.* man about town, °roué, °rake, debauchee, °gay dog, womanizer, Don Juan, Casanova, Lothario, Romeo, *Colloq* wolf, lady-killer: *He fancies himself as a playboy, but no women seem to agree.*

player *n.* **1** °contestant, °participant, °competitor, contender; athlete, sportswoman, sportsman, *Colloq US* jock: *Chess players from all over the world came together for the championship. The referee sent three players off.* **2** actor or actress, °performer, entertainer, trouper, °Thespian: *The local drama group is the Allen Arts Players.* **3** gambler, °better or *especially US* bettor, gamester, speculator, *Brit* °punter: *J.B. is a big player in the commodities market.* **4** musician, instrumentalist, °performer, °virtuoso: *Gladys is one of the best tuba players in the band.*

playful *adj.* **1** °(high-)spirited, °cheerful, °frisky, °frolicsome, °kittenish, °sprightly, fun-loving, °sportive, coltish, °mischievous, puckish, impish, elfish, °devilish: *The cat didn't mean to scratch you, she was just being playful.* **2** joking, facetious, teasing, roguish, waggish, jesting, °humorous, tongue-in-cheek: *Cleo's in a playful mood today, isn't she?*

playmate *n.* playfellow, °friend, °comrade, *Colloq* °pal, °chum, *US and Canadian* buddy: *Some of Molly's playmates are asking if she can come out to play.*

plaything *n.* 1 °toy, °game, knick-knack, °pastime: *Please pick up your playthings before supper.* 2 °tool, cat's-paw, °dupe, pigeon, °pawn, *Colloq US and Canadian* fall guy: *She had no use for Gerry except as a plaything.*

playwright *n.* °dramatist, dramaturge *or* dramaturgist, scriptwriter, screenwriter, scenarist: *The playwright has deftly caught the way people talk to each other.*

plea *n.* 1 °request, entreaty, °appeal, °petition, °supplication, °suit, °cry, solicitation: *Teenagers' mischievous behaviour is an earnest plea for attention.* 2 °answer, °defence, °argument: *She entered a plea of 'not guilty' to the charge.* 3 °excuse, °reason, °explanation, justification; °pretext: *His plea was that he had not received the bill and therefore couldn't pay it.*

plead *v.* 1 Often, **plead for**: °request, °appeal (for), °cry (for), °ask (for), °seek, °beg (for), °pray (for), supplicate (for): *It was a hot day and the children were pleading for ice-creams every half hour.* 2 Usually, **plead with**: °request (of), entreat, °appeal to, °petition, °ask, °apply to, implore, °beseech, °beg, importune, °solicit; °demand: *Bryan pleaded with us to let him go to the rock concert.* 3 assert, °say, aver, °allege, °argue, °maintain, °offer, °put forward, °declare, affirm, avow, °swear: *She pleaded that she was unaware that the goods she was selling had been stolen.*

pleasant *adj.* 1 °pleasing, °pleasurable, °nice, enjoyable, °satisfying, °good, °lovely, °attractive, °inviting, gratifying, °delightful, charming, °agreeable, °suitable, °fitting, °appropriate; °harmonious, euphonious, melodic, mellifluous; °delicious, delectable, palatable, °savoury, toothsome: *Travelling on the Orient Express was a most pleasant experience. The bedroom is decorated in a combination of pleasant colours. He simply doesn't find sunbathing particularly pleasant. That sauce has a very pleasant taste.* 2 °friendly, affable, °amiable, °amicable, gregarious, companionable, °sociable, °engaging, °attractive, °winning, °open, approachable, °outgoing, welcoming, °hospitable, °agreeable, °gracious, charming, congenial, °genial, °nice, °likeable, urbane, °cultivated, °genteel, °polite, °courteous, well-mannered, °suave, °debonair, °polished, °well-bred, cultured: *Murray always has a pleasant expression on his face. He is quite a pleasant fellow, once you get to know him.* 3 °fair, °sunny, °clear, °bright, cloudless, balmy, °nice, °fine: *What a pleasant day for an outing in the country!*

please *v.* 1 °delight, °gratify, °satisfy, °suit, °humour, °content, °cheer, gladden, °amuse, °divert, °interest, °entertain: *I cannot tell you how much it pleases me to see you again.* 2 °like, °prefer, °choose, °desire, °want, see fit, °wish, °will, °elect, opt: *She may have her birthday party wherever she pleases.*

pleased *adj.* °happy, °delighted, °glad, gratified, satisfied, contented, thrilled; *Colloq* tickled

pink, °pleased as Punch, on cloud nine, in seventh °heaven, on top of the °world, walking on air, *Brit* over the moon, chuffed: *His pleased look comes from his having won first prize.*

pleasing *adj.* 1 See pleasant, 1, above. 2 See pleasant, 2, above.

pleasurable *adj.* See pleasant, 1, above.

pleasure *n.* 1 °enjoyment, °happiness, °delight, °joy, °satisfaction, °fulfilment, contentment, °gratification; °comfort, °recreation, °amusement, °entertainment, °diversion: *It is a pleasure to meet you at last. Fred derives so much pleasure from tinkering with his model railways.* 2 °choice, °option, °desire, °wish, °preference, °fancy, °inclination, discretion: *Feel free to come and go at your pleasure.*

plebeian *adj.* 1 proletarian, working-class, blue-collar, low-class, lower-class, °lowly, low-born, °common, °mean, °humble, °inferior, peasant-like, *Colloq* non-U: *What would you expect from someone with such a plebeian background?* 2 °unrefined, °coarse, °vulgar, ignoble, low-brow, unpolished, uncouth, crass, brutish, gauche, °provincial, °rustic, °popular, commonplace, °undistinguished: *The entertainment caters to the most plebeian tastes.* —*n.* 3 proletarian, °common °man *or* °woman, commoner, °man *or* °woman in the street, (any *or* every) Tom, Dick, *or* Harry, *Brit* °man *or* °woman on the Clapham omnibus, *Colloq* pleb, prole: *This art exhibition is not going to mean very much to the plebeians.*

plebiscite *n.* popular °vote *or* ballot, referendum, °poll: *The plebiscite revealed that the people were in favour of joining the Common Market.*

pledge *n.* 1 °promise, °oath, °vow, °word (of honour), covenant, °assurance, guaranty, °guarantee, °warrant, °warranty: *They have our solemn pledge that we will return within the hour.* 2 bail, surety, collateral, °security, °deposit, °earnest (money), °pawn, gage, °bond, guaranty, °guarantee: *They wanted something besides my signature as a pledge for the money.* 3 °toast, °tribute, °cheer, health: *They drank a pledge to the success of the voyage.* —*v.* 4 °swear, °vow, °promise, give one's °word (of honour), °contract, °undertake, °agree, °vouch, °vouchsafe: *I pledge allegiance to the nation.* 5 °deposit, °pawn, mortgage, *Archaic* gage, *Colloq US and Canadian* hock: *He pledged his gold watch to pay for her birthday present.* 6 °toast, °drink (to), °drink (someone's) health: *Drink to me only with thine eyes And I will pledge with mine.*

plentiful *adj.* 1 °ample, °abundant, °profuse, copious, °lavish, plenteous, °bountiful, °generous, bounteous: *We found a plentiful supply of food in the markets.* 2 °fertile, °fruitful, °productive, bumper, °luxuriant, thriving, °prolific: *We thanked the Lord for a plentiful harvest.*

plenty *n.* 1 °abundance, more than °enough, °great °deal, °mass(es), °quantity *or* quantities, multitude(s), °number(s), °load(s), °mess, °scores, *Colloq* °lot(s), °mountain(s), °heap(s), °stack(s), °pile(s), °load(s), ton(s), °ocean(s), oodles, *US and Canadian* slew(s): *There is plenty of food, so it is just as well that plenty of people are coming. There's plenty of time before your bus arrives.* 2 plentifulness, fertility, copiousness, °abundance, plenteousness, °wealth, °profusion, lavishness, °prodigality, plenitude, bountiful-ness: *It was a land of plenty, a land of milk and honey.*

pliable *adj.* **1** °flexible, pliant, °elastic, °plastic, fictile, malleable, workable, bendable, bendy, ductile, flexuous, °supple; lithe, limber: *This substance remains pliable only while it is warm.* **2** °tractable, °adaptable, °flexible, pliant, compliant, persuadable *or* persuasible, °impressionable, °susceptible, °responsive, °receptive, docile, °manageable, °yielding: *The other directors may not be as pliable when it comes to improving employee benefits.*

plight *n.* °condition, °state, circumstances, °situation, °case; °difficulty, °predicament, °quandary, °dilemma, catch-22, °straits, °trouble, °extremity, *Colloq* °hole, °jam, pickle, °spot, °scrape, °fix, °bind, hot water, °mess, fine kettle of fish, fine °state of affairs: *As soon as Elliott's sorry plight became known, we all rallied round to help.*

plod *v.* **1** Often, **plod along**: trudge (along), °tramp, slog, °drag, tread, lumber, °labour, *Colloq* stomp, galumph: *We plodded wearily up the road carrying our heavy packs.* **2** Often, **plod along** *or* **away**: °labour, °work, drudge, toil, moil, °slave (away), °grind (away *or* along), grub (on *or* along), °plug (along *or* away), *Brit* °peg away (at) *or* along: *Plodding through the compilation of the Oxford Thesaurus, he was only halfway through the letter P.*

plot[1] *n.* **1** °scheme, °plan, °intrigue, °machination, °cabal; °conspiracy: *The plot to blow up the Houses of Parliament was uncovered at a late stage.* **2** °story(-line), °chain of events, °theme, °outline, °scenario, °thread, skeleton: *Most operas have weak plots, but the music can be sublime.* —*v.* **3** °scheme, °plan, °intrigue, machinate, °cabal, collude, conspire, °hatch, °devise, °design, °arrange, °organize, concoct, °dream up, °conceive, *Colloq* cook up: *Martin's wife had been plotting to murder him since their wedding night.* **4** °draw, °plan, diagram, °lay down, °outline, °calculate, °compute, °figure, °chart, map (out), °find, °determine, depict, °show: *The navigator plotted our position as being in the Strait of Malacca.*

plot[2] *n.* °lot, plat, °patch *or* °parcel (of °land), °tract, acreage, °area, *Brit* °allotment: *I have a small plot by the canal which is ideal for growing potatoes.*

plough *v.* **1** °till, °cultivate, °furrow, harrow, *Literary* delve: *They ought to finish ploughing the south field by tomorrow.* **2** °drive, °plunge, °push, bulldoze, °lunge, °dive, shove, °hurtle, °crash: *Out of control, a bus ploughed through the fence and into my garden.*

pluck *n.* **1** °courage, °spirit, °bravery, °grit, boldness, intrepidity, °backbone, mettle, °determination, gameness, °resolve, °resolution, steadfastness, hardiness, sturdi-ness, stout-heartedness, stoutness, °fortitude, °nerve, *Colloq* guts, °spunk, *US* sand, *Slang Brit* °bottle, *US* moxie: *She certainly showed pluck standing up to the boss like that.* —*v.* **2** °pick, °remove, °withdraw, °draw out, °extract: *The children plucked flowers in the garden and made posies.* **3** °snatch, °grab, °yank, °jerk, °tear (away): *She was plucked from the jaws of death by Tarzan, who happened to be swinging by on*

a vine. **4** °tug (at), °pull (at), catch (at), °clutch (at); vellicate: *An ancient crone plucked at his sleeve as he passed.*

plug *n.* **1** °stopper, stopple, bung, cork: *If you pull the plug out, the water will run out.* **2** chew, twist, quid, °wad, pigtail, cavendish: *As they forbade smoking, he would take snuff or chew a plug of tobacco.* **3** publicity, °mention, °promotion, °recommendation, °puff, blurb, PR; °advertisement, *Colloq* advert, hype: *His book was given a plug on yesterday's evening news.* —*v.* **4** Often, **plug up**: °stop (up), °close (up *or* off), °seal (off *or* up), cork, °stopper, bung, °block, °jam, °stuff, °clog, °obstruct, dam (up): *A piece of soap has plugged the drain.* **5** °publicize, °mention, °promote, °push, advertise, °puff, commend, *Colloq* °boost, beat the drum for: *It wasn't right to plug her brother's company in her article on double glazing.* **6** See **plod**, **2**, above.

plum *n.* °find, catch, coup, °prize, °treasure; °bonus, cream: *Harvey's landed a plum job as overseas buyer.*

plumb *n.* **1** weight, (plumb-)bob, plummet, lead, sinker: *The plumb holds the string taut and exactly vertical.* —*adj.* **2** vertical, °perpendicular, °straight up and down: *Make sure the jamb is plumb before hanging the door.* —*adv.* **3** vertically, perpendicularly, °straight up and down: *The cord doesn't hang plumb because the shelf is in the way.* **4** °exactly, °precisely, °dead, °right, accurately, *Colloq* °slap, *Brit* bang, spot: *The navigator checked our position and we were plumb on course.* —*v.* **5** °sound, °fathom, °measure, °probe, °explore, °measure, °gauge, delve, °penetrate: *The bathyscaphe has plumbed the deeps of the Indian Ocean. I plumb the depths of depression thinking of starving people everywhere.*

plummet *v.* See **plunge**, **1**, below.

plump[1] *adj.* **1** °chubby, °stout, fleshy, °ample, full-bodied, portly, tubby, °rotund, squat, chunky, °buxom, corpulent, roly-poly, °fat, °obese, overweight, steatopygous, *Brit* podgy *or* *US* pudgy, *Colloq* busty, °beamy, hippy, beefy, well-upholstered: *They went on a diet because they were getting a bit plump.* —*v.* **2** °puff up *or* out: *When you get up, please plump up the pillows on the sofa.*

plump[2] *v.* **1** °drop, °plummet, °fall, °plunge, °dive, °sink, °collapse, °flop: *I was so tired that all I could do was plump down in an armchair and watch TV.* **2** °deposit, °set *or* °put (down), plunk, plop: *She plumped down the defective mixer on the counter and asked for a refund.* **3** **plump for**: °support, °choose, °select, °back, °side with, °campaign for: *Given the choice, they plumped for a film rather than the circus.* —*n.* **4** °drop, plunk, °flop, thump, clunk, °clump, °thud, °bump: *He dropped the book on the floor with a plump.* —*adv.* **5** abruptly, °suddenly, °directly, unhesi-tatingly, at °once, unexpectedly, surprisingly, without °warning, (all) of a °sudden, plunk, bang: *As I came out of the bank, I ran plump into a policeman.* —*adj.* **6** °direct, unequivocal, unmistakable, unambiguous, °definite, °definitive, °blunt, °simple, °plain, °forthright, °downright, °straight, °matter-of-fact: *He asked her to marry him and she gave him a plump 'no'.*

plunder v. **1** °pillage, °loot, °rob, °ravage, °ransack, °rifle, despoil, °spoil, vandalize, °sack, °strip, maraud, °devastate, °desolate, lay °waste: *The attacking army plundered the villages.* **2** °prey on *or* upon, °pirate, °capture, °seize: *The buccaneers plundered the Spanish treasure ships on the high seas.*
—*n.* **3** °pillage, looting, °robbery, °depredation, rapine, despoliation, spoliation, vandalization, °sack, vandalism, vandalizing, sacking: *It is said that the plunder of Rome took no more than a fortnight.* **4** °booty, °loot, °spoils, °prizes, *Slang* boodle: *The police displayed an Aladdin's cave of plunder recovered from the thieves.*

plunge v. **1** °descend, °drop, °plummet, °dive, °pitch, nosedive, °fall (headlong): *They lost their footing, and both Holmes and Moriarty plunged into the abyss.* **2** °submerge, °sink, °immerse; engulf, °overwhelm: *I plunged my hand in the icy water to retrieve the keys. She plunged herself into her work to try to forget him.*
—*n.* **3** °dive, nosedive, °fall, °pitch, °plummet, °drop, descent; submersion, immersion: *After the scandal his career took a plunge from which it never recovered. Every winter they take a plunge into the icy waters of the Serpentine.* **4** °gamble, wager, °bet, °risk: *Are you taking the plunge with an investment in South America?*

plus *prep.* **1** and, added to, increased by, with the °addition of, with an °increment of, (coupled) with, together with: *Two plus three equals five. Your initial deposit plus accumulated interest will make a substantial sum.*
—*adj.* **2** added, additional, °supplementary, °extra: *One must take into account the plus value of the good publicity.* ·
—*n.* **3** °addition, °bonus, °extra, °gain, °benefit, °asset, °advantage, °profit, °return: *Improvements constitute a big plus in evaluating the building.*

plush *adj.* °luxurious, °posh, costly, (de) luxe, °palatial, °lavish, °rich, °opulent, °sumptuous, °regal, °elegant, *Colloq* ritzy, classy, *Old-fashioned* swank(y): *I had no idea that you lived in such plush surroundings.*

ply *n.* layer, leaf, thickness, °fold: *These seams are sewn through two plies of fabric.*

pocket *n.* **1** °pouch, °sack, °bag, °receptacle, reticule, satchel: *You should always have a clean handkerchief in your pocket.* **2** °cavity, °pit, °hollow, crater: *We found water that had collected in pockets in the surface of the rock.* **3** °area, °island, °camp, °centre, °cluster, concentration: *Leaders encountered pockets of resistance to the new policies among the farmers.*
—*v.* **4** °take, °appropriate, °keep; filch, °embezzle, °steal, purloin, thieve, °pilfer, °help oneself to, palm, *Colloq* °walk off *or* away with, °pinch, °swipe, °rip off, °hook, °lift, snitch, *Brit* °nick, snaffle: *While collecting for charity, Johnson was known to have pocketed occasional contributions.*

poem *n.* verse, °lyric, °rhyme *or Archaic* rime, °song, ode, rhapsody, °jingle, ditty: *The anthology contains poems by politicians.*

poet *n.* poetess, versifier, metrist, lyricist *or* lyrist, versemaker, sonneteer, elegist, bard, °minstrel; rhymester *or* rimester *or* rhymer *or* rimer, poetaster: *A widely published poet, Constance is often invited to give readings.*

poetic *adj.* **1** poetical, °lyric(al), metrical, °musical, melodic; °idyllic, elegiac, georgic,

°rhapsodic, epic, dithyrambic: *She bought a volume of the poetic works of John Keats.* **2** artistic, °aesthetic, Parnassian, Hippocrenian, °melodious: *The novel contains some poetic passages of surpassing quality.*

poetry *n.* verse, versification, metrical composition, metrics, °rhyme, *Archaic* poesy: *Modern poetry is often rather obscure.*

po-faced *adj.* stern-visaged, austere, °dour, disapproving, frowning, °grave, saturnine, °solemn, °sombre, humourless, °grim, °forbidding, °severe, °strait-laced, uncompromising, puritanical, prim, °prudish, °gruff, °bluff, curmudgeonly: *Despite having a po-faced approach to his work, William has a keen sense of humour when off duty.*

poignant *adj.* **1** distressing, upsetting, °agonizing, °grievous, °painful, woeful, °melancholy, °blue, °sad, °sorrowful, °tragic, °disastrous, °heart-rending, heartbreaking, °excruciating, °bitter, °pathetic, °pitiable, °piteous, °pitiful, °miserable, °moving, °touching: *The biography also covers the poignant early years, spent largely in orphanages and foster homes.* **2** °keen, °acute, °intense, °incisive, °sharp, stinging, °pointed, °piercing, °penetrating, barbed, °cutting, °caustic, acid, acerbic, °bitter, °biting, mordant, °sarcastic, °sardonic, °severe: *The headmaster's poignant remarks about honesty and loyalty really hurt.* **3** °sincere, °earnest, °heartfelt, °deep, °profound, °dramatic, deeply felt, °stirring, °moving, °touching, °emotional: *The reunion of the little boy and his dog was the most poignant moment in the film.*

point *n.* **1** °dot, °mark, °speck; (full) stop, °period; decimal point: *The writing is smudged, but that looks like a point at the end of the line.* **2** °tip, °peak, apex, °spike, °spur, prong, °sharp end: *Be careful of the point of that knife.* **3** °spot, °place, °stage, °position; °site, °station, °location, °locale: *We have reached the point of no return on that subject. I stopped at a few points along the way to admire the view.* **4** °time, °moment, °instant, °juncture: *At that point, we were summoned by the dinner bell.* **5** °focus, °essence, °meat, °pith, quiddity, °substance, °heart, °nucleus, crux, °nub, °core, °bottom, °details, *Colloq* guts, nitty-gritty: *I wish he would stop all the palaver and get to the point.* **6** °purpose, °intent, °intention, °aim, °goal, °object, °objective, °sense: *What was the point of bringing that piece of gossip into the discussion?* **7** °thrust, °drift, °theme, purport, °burden, °import, °implication, °significance, signification, °sense, °meaning: °application, applicability, relevancy, appropriateness: *We found it difficult to see the point of the argument.* **8** promontory, °projection, headland, °cape, peninsula: *It may take us a day to sail round the point.* **9** °brink, °verge: *We were on the point of leaving when the guest of honour finally arrived.* **10** °detail, °particular, °item, °element, nicety, °aspect, facet, °matter, °issue, °subject, °question; specifics: *Some of the points in her speech need clarification.* **11** °pointer, °hint, °suggestion, piece of °advice, °tip: *The golf pro at the club gave me some good points on improving my swing.* **12** °thought, °idea, °consideration; °notion, °view, °plan, °tactic; something: *That's a point to keep in mind if you buy another sailing-boat.* **13** °unit, °tally, °score: *She made her*

point and went on to win the match. **14** °attribute, °characteristic, °feature, °aspect, °trait, °quality, °side, °property: *I suppose he has his good points, too.* **15 beside the point:** °irrelevant, inapt, °inappropriate, malapropos, °incidental, °immaterial, unimportant, °pointless, °inconsequential: *The fact that she's my sister is beside the point.* **16 in point of:** in °reference to, °regarding, as regards, in the °matter of, °concerning, with °respect to: *In point of date, the two events coincide perfectly.* **17 make a point of** *or US also* **make (it) a point to:** make an °effort (to), put *or* place °emphasis on, go out of one's way (to); °emphasize, °single out, °stress: *He made a point of apologizing to the hostess for his behaviour. She made a special point of forgiving him.* **18 to the point:** °relevant, °pertinent, °appropriate, °fitting, apropos, germane, apt, °applicable, apposite: *The speech was short and to the point.*
—v. **19** Often, **point to:** °indicate, call *or* °direct attention to: *Desirée pointed to the building and asked what it was.* **20** °direct, °level, °aim, °train: *I awoke to find her pointing a gun at my head.* **21 point out: a** °designate, call *or* °direct attention to, °show, °exhibit, °indicate, °identify: *The taxi driver pointed out all the sights as we drove along.* **b** °say, °bring up, °mention, allude to, °emphasize, °stress, point up, °single out; call attention to, °remind: *I'd like to point out that you have rarely won at bridge. She pointed out the fallacy in his argument.* **22 point up:** °emphasize, °stress, accentuate, underline, underscore, °accent, °spotlight: *Such errors point up the need to double-check everything.*

point-blank *adj.* **1** °direct, °straight, °blunt, °flat, straightforward, °abrupt, °categorical, °explicit, uncompromising, °unmitigated, unalloyed, °downright, °outright, to the °point, °straight from the shoulder, (open and) °above-board, unreserved: *I asked her out to dinner and got a point-blank refusal.* **2** °close, °short, °nearby: *He was shot at point-blank range.*
—adv. **3** °directly, °straight (away), °right away, bluntly, °flat, flatly, abruptly, categorically, unqualifiedly, explicitly, uncompromisingly, unmitigatedly, °outright, unreservedly, plainly, frankly, °openly, candidly: *He turned her down point-blank when she offered him the job.* **4** °directly, °straight: *He fired point-blank at the target.*

pointed *adj.* **1** needle-shaped, °sharp, °acute, barbed, peaked, spiked, spiky, *Technical* acuminate, cuspidate, aciform, acicular, aciculiform, aculeous, apiculate, spiculate, serrate(d), mucroniform, mucronulate, mucronate(d), muricate, hebetate: *The child was poking holes in the sand with a pointed stick.* **2** °incisive, °piercing, °cutting, °sharp, °pungent, °keen, °penetrating, °telling, °trenchant, °biting, unmistakable: *The critic made a few pointed remarks about the actors' reading of the lines.*

pointer *n.* **1** °indicator, °rod, °stick; °index, °sign, arrow, *Typography* fist: *The pointer is used to call attention to something important.* **2** °tip, °advice, °hint, °suggestion, °recommendation, piece of °advice: *McLeod gave me a few pointers on how to improve the restaurant service.*

pointless *adj.* °purposeless, °aimless, °worthless, °ineffective, °meaningless, °ineffectual, °futile, unproductive, °fruitless, °bootless, °useless, °vain, °senseless, °absurd,

°silly, °stupid, °inane, asinine, fatuous, °preposterous, °nonsensical, °ridiculous, °empty, °hollow: *After her paper, someone rose and wasted half an hour making pointless remarks.*

point of view *n.* **1** °viewpoint, °perspective, °approach, °position, °angle, °slant, °orientation, °outlook, °stance, °standpoint, vantage °point: *From his point of view, I can see why Fred thinks the research is a waste of time.* **2** °opinion, °view, °belief, (way of) °thinking, °principle, °doctrine: *Shouldn't everyone be entitled to express a point of view?*

poise *n.* **1** °balance, equilibrium, equipoise, equiponderance, °parity, °par: *The chariots of the gods in even poise, obeying the rein, glide rapidly.* **2** composure, °control, self-possession, aplomb, °assurance, °dignity, equanimity, °sang-froid, cool-headedness, imperturbability, °presence of mind, coolness, staidness, °reserve, sedateness, calmness, °serenity, tranquillity, *Colloq* °cool: *Jane's poise is remarkable, despite the heckling by the audience.*
—v. **3** °balance, be balanced, °hover, °hang, °float; make *or* be *or* get °ready, °prepare: *The boulder was poised on the edge of the cliff.*

poised *adj.* **1** composed, controlled, °self-possessed, unflappable, (self-)°confident, (self-)assured, °dignified, cool-headed, imperturbable, unruffled, °cool, °staid, °reserved, °sedate, °calm, °serene, °tranquil, *Colloq* together: *For a lad of eleven, Richard is quite poised.* **2** °ready, standing by, waiting, °prepared: *Our commando unit is poised to attack at your signal.* **3** teetering, hovering, tottering, wavering, suspended, trembling, wobbling, balanced: *In the present business climate, the company is poised on the brink of bankruptcy.*

poison *n.* **1** toxin, °venom, bane; miasma, mephitis: *The chemical plant was found to be releasing poisons into the atmosphere. He kills rats using poison.* **2** virus, bane, cancer, canker, °corrupt *or* °evil influence, °pestilence, °plague, °blight: *The drug barons continue to spread their poison throughout the world.*
—v. **3** defile, °adulterate, infect, °taint, °pollute; °contaminate, °debase, °pervert, °vitiate, °subvert, °warp, envenom: *Chemicals from the nearby plant have poisoned the drinking-water. Why have you poisoned the child's mind against eating spinach?* **4** °murder, °kill, do away with, °destroy, °dispatch *or* despatch: *Lucrezia Borgia poisoned her enemies in ingenious ways.*

poisonous *adj.* **1** °lethal, °deadly, °fatal, °mortal, toxic, septic, °virulent, noxious *or Rare* nocuous, °venomous, °malignant, pernicious, miasmic, mephitic: *Poisonous effluents were leaked into the rivers by the chemical plant.* **2** malicious, malevolent, °malignant, corruptive, °vicious, baleful, °evil, °foul, °diabolic(al), defamatory, libellous, °slanderous, °dangerous, deleterious: *They have been spreading poisonous gossip about him again.*

poke *v.* **1** °jab, °stick, °prod, °dig, goad, °stab, °thrust, °push, elbow, °nudge, °jog, jostle, °butt, shove: *Be careful not to poke someone in the eye with your umbrella. He tells a joke, then pokes me in the ribs to make sure I've got it.* **2** °punch, °hit, °strike, °box, cuff, smite, smack: *I made a suggestive remark and she poked me in the jaw.* **3** °pry, nose (about *or* around), stick one's nose into, °intrude, °dig, °probe, °investigate;

°meddle, °interfere, °butt in, °tamper; *Colloq* °snoop: *I wish they would stop poking into my affairs.* **4 poke fun (at):** °tease, °ridicule, °mock, make °fun of, °jeer (at), °chaff, °taunt, °twit, make °sport of, needle, *Colloq* kid, rib, *Brit* °send up, take the mickey out of: *People who don't understand something often poke fun at it. Stop poking fun at my hat.*
—*n.* **5** °jab, °prod, °dig, °stab, °thrust, °push, elbow, °finger, °nudge, °jog, jostle, °butt, shove: *Every time Rodney wants to emphasize a point, he gives you a poke.* **6** °punch, °hit, °box, °jab, cuff, smack, °blow: *If anyone says anything bad about you, I'll give him a poke in the nose.*

polar *adj.* **1** arctic, Antarctic, °frigid, °icy, glacial, °freezing, frozen, numbing, Siberian, hibernal, hyperborean, brumal, °wintry: *It is positively polar in the house without the heat turned on.* **2** °opposite, °opposed, antithetical, °contrary, °contradictory, diametric, antipodal, antagonistic, °hostile: *Dante felt Good and Evil to be the two polar elements of the Creation, on which it all turns.*

pole¹ *n.* °rod, °stick, °staff, °spar, °shaft, mast, °standard, °upright; flag-pole, flagstaff, jack-staff; beanpole, hop-pole: *We had to use a long pole to get the kite down from the tree.*

pole² *n.* **1** °extremity, °end, °limit, °extreme: *Their views are at opposite poles and they cannot agree.* **2 from pole to pole:** °everywhere, all over, °far and °wide, high and low, leaving no stone unturned, °throughout the world *or* the length and breadth of the land, *Colloq US* every-place: *He searched for her from pole to pole.* **3 poles apart:** (very *or* completely) °different, worlds apart, at °opposite extremes, at °opposite ends of the earth, at °odds, irreconcilable: *I'm afraid that the union and management remain poles apart on the issue of working hours.*

police *n.* **1** constabulary, policemen, police-women, police officers, *Colloq* boys in blue, the (long arm of the) °law, the cops, the gendarmes, *Slang* the coppers, the fuzz, *Brit* the (Old) Bill, *US* the heat: *There was a bit of an argument, so we called the police.*
—*v.* **2** °patrol, °guard, °watch, °protect: *Additional officers were assigned to police the neighbourhood.* **3** °enforce, °regulate, °administer, °oversee, °control, °observe, °supervise, °monitor: *A unit was established to police the terms of the agreement.*

police officer *n.* °officer, policeman, police-woman, °constable, *Brit* °police °constable, PC, WPC, *Chiefly US* peace °officer, patrolman, patrolwoman, *Colloq* cop, gendarme, *Brit* bobby; *Slang* copper, fuzz, flatfoot, *Brit* rozzer, Old Bill, *Offensive and derogatory* pig, *Historical* peeler, *US* bull, fuzz ball: *The police officers then asked if I wouldn't mind helping with their inquiries.*

policy *n.* °approach, °procedure, (game) °plan, °design, °scheme, °programme, °method, °system, °management, °conduct, °behaviour, °strategy, °tactic(s), °principle(s), °protocol, °regulation, °rule, °custom, °way, °practice, ways and °means, °action: *What policy should we follow regarding interest rates?*

polish *v.* **1** °shine, °brighten, burnish, buff, furbish, wax, °clean, °smooth, °rub, °gloss: *He polished up the handles so carefully That now he is the ruler of the Queen's navy.* **2** Often, **polish up:** °refine, °improve, °perfect, °finish, °cultivate,

ameliorate, °enhance; °correct, emend: *If you polish up the article we might consider it for publication.* **3 polish off: a** conclude, °end, °terminate, °finish: *Ned polished off his homework in less than an hour.* **b** °kill, slay, °murder, °dispatch *or* despatch, °destroy, °dispose of, do away with, liquidate, °eliminate, *Slang* °bump off, °rub out, do in, take for a °ride: *Three platoons were polished off quickly.* **c** °dispose of, °put away, °eat, °consume, wolf (down): *In a few minutes, MacGregor had polished off the entire meal.* **4 polish up:** °study, °review, °learn, *Archaic* con, *Colloq* bone up (on), *Slang Brit* swot up (on): *If you're going to Málaga, you'd better polish up your Spanish.*
—*n.* **5** °gloss, °shine, °lustre, °sheen, °glaze, smoothness, °brilliance, °sparkle, °gleam, °glow, brightness, °radiance: *You cannot imagine what a fine polish she put on that old table.* **6** wax, °oil: *The new polish really put a shine on the desk.*

polished *adj.* **1** °accomplished, °adept, °proficient, °expert, °fine, °outstanding, °skilful, °gifted, °masterful, masterly, °virtuoso, °excellent, °superior, °superb, °superlative; °flawless, °faultless, °perfect, °impeccable: *Edna is quite a polished cellist. She gave a polished performance.* **2** °refined, °elegant, °cultivated, °graceful, °debonair, °sophisticated, urbane, soigné(e), courtly, °genteel, cultured, civilized, °well-bred, well-mannered, °polite: *Under her guidance, James has become a polished gentleman.*

polite *adj.* **1** °civil, °respectful, well-mannered, mannerly, °courteous, deferential, °diplomatic, °tactful, °formal, °proper, °cordial: *We asked our new neighbours to tea but were met with a polite refusal.* **2** See **polished, 2,** above.

politic *adj.* **1** °ingenious, °shrewd, °crafty, canny, cunning, °designing, °scheming, °clever, °wily, °foxy, °tricky, °artful, °Machiavellian, °evasive, °shifty, *Colloq* cagey: *Daniel is politic enough to know how to manoeuvre situations to his benefit.* **2** °tactful, °diplomatic, °discreet, °prudent, °judicious, °wise, °sage, sagacious, °sensible, °intelligent, percipient, °discriminating, °far-sighted, °expedient, °perceptive: *It was politic of the winner to share the prize with those who had helped him most.*

political *adj.* **1** governmental, civic, °civil, °public, °state, °national, federal; administrative, bureaucratic: *The movement began as an attempt to gain political freedom.* **2** °partisan, °factious, factional: *A coalition government was formed by the major political parties.*

politician *n.* legislator, lawmaker, statesman, stateswoman; °minister, *Brit* Member of Parliament, MP, *US* public *or* civil °servant, administrator, °official, bureaucrat, office-bearer, senator, congressman, congresswoman, °representative, assembly-man, assembly-woman, selectman; *Colloq US* derogatory politico, (°political) boss *or* hack, °machine politician, ward-heeler, wirepuller: *Some politicians have given a bad name to the art of politics.*

politics *n.* **1** °public affairs, °political science, civics, °civil affairs, °government, statecraft, °diplomacy, statesmanship: *Hume viewed politics as people united in society and dependent on each other.* **2** manoeuvring, manipulation, wire-pulling, °machination: *Office politics are such that they wouldn't dare dismiss that department head.*

poll *n.* **1** voting, °vote, returns, °tally, figures: *The poll shows that the incumbents are not as secure as they thought.* **2** opinion poll, °survey, °canvass, census, ballot, °count: *A poll of home-owners shows that most would like to own washing machines.* —*v.* **3** °sample, °survey, °question, °canvass, ballot, °ask, °interview; °count, °enumerate, °tally, °register, °record: *We polled teenagers to determine their reaction to a youth centre; those in favour polled 73 per cent.* **4** °receive, °get, °win, °register, °tally: *Cavendish polled more than 60 per cent of the votes cast.*

pollute *v.* **1** °contaminate, °adulterate, befoul, °foul, °soil, °spoil, °taint, °stain, °dirty, °sully, °blight, °poison: *These factories must be prevented from continuing to pollute the atmosphere.* **2** °corrupt, °desecrate, °profane, defile, °violate: *The altar was polluted because it had been touched by a non-believer.*

pollution *n.* contamination, adulteration, corruption, polluting, fouling, befouling, soiling, spoiling, tainting, staining, dirtying, sullying, blighting, poisoning, vitiation: *Laws were passed to prosecute those responsible for the pollution of the environment.*

pomp *n.* °glory, °grandeur, magnificence, °splendour, °show, °extravaganza, °pageantry, °ceremony, °spectacle, °brilliance, ceremoniousness: *The Chinese court's pomp and display of wealth had never before been seen by a westerner.*

pompous *adj.* **1** °vain, vainglorious, °proud, °arrogant, °pretentious, °ostentatious, °showy, °grandiose, °haughty, °overbearing, °conceited, °egotistical, °self-important, °boastful, °braggart, °inflated, °snobbish, magisterial, imperious, pontifical, °affected, exhibitionist, *Colloq* uppity, highfalutin *or* hifalutin, °hoity-toity, high-hat, *Slang* snooty, snotty: *Don't you despise the pompous way Marshall struts about in that ridiculous uniform?* **2** °bombastic, °flowery, grandiloquent, °pedantic, °stuffy, fustian, orotund, °ornate, embroidered, flatulent, °windy, turgid, °inflated, high-flown, euphuistic: *He's always making long-winded, pompous speeches because he loves the sound of his own voice.*

ponder *v.* °consider, °muse (over *or* on), °brood (over *or* upon *or* on), °mull over, °deliberate (over), °meditate (upon *or* on), °think (over *or* on *or* about), °weigh, ruminate (over), °chew over, cogitate, excogitate, °reflect (on *or* over), °contemplate: *I shall need a while to ponder the answer to that question. Give me a little more time to ponder.*

ponderous *adj.* **1** °weighty, °unwieldy, °heavy, °massive, °huge, °big, °large, °awkward, °clumsy, cumbersome *or* cumbrous: *A ponderous juggernaut bore down on us, completely out of control.* **2** °dull, °tedious, °laboured, °laborious, °tiresome, turgid, °boring, °dreary, °pedestrian, °stilted, °windy, °inflated, long-winded, °wordy, verbose, prolix, elephantine, °pompous, grandiloquent, overdone: *Many students faced with textbooks written in ponderous prose become disenchanted with learning.*

pool *n.* **1** pond, lake, tarn, mere, lagoon; swimming-pool, °leisure pool, *Brit* paddling pool, *US* wading pool, *Formal* natatorium: *We found an icy mountain pool where we went for a swim.* **2** °collection, °fund(s), °purse, stakes, °reserve(s), bank, *Colloq* °pot, jackpot, °kitty: *So far we have too little money in the pool for an office*

party at Christmas. **3** °syndicate, °trust, °group, consortium, cartel, °combine: *The object of the pool was the private regulation of market prices, which is illegal.* —*v.* **4** °accumulate, °collect, °gather, °combine, °merge, consolidate, °amalgamate, °league, bring *or* come *or* °band *or* °get together, °team (up) with: *We would do better if we pooled our resources.*

poor *adj.* **1** °needy, °destitute, °indigent, in °want, in °need, penniless, poverty-stricken, °impoverished, °badly off, necessitous, poor as a church-mouse, °straitened, pinched, in reduced °circumstances, impecunious, financially °embarrassed, down and out, out of pocket, ruined, °insolvent, bankrupt, *Colloq* °broke, °hard up, on one's uppers, °short, *US* wiped out, *Brit* in Queer Street, *Slang Brit* skint: *They were poor and didn't know where their next meal was coming from.* **2** °low, °bad, skimpy, °meagre, scant, °scanty, °inadequate, °deficient, °insufficient, °sparse: *How can a family of five survive on such a poor salary? These days, 3 per cent would be considered a poor return on investment.* **3** °barren, unproductive, unfruitful, °fruitless, °infertile, °sterile; depleted, °exhausted, °impoverished: *This is poor soil, and no amount of cultivation is likely to make it productive.* **4** °bad, °awful, °inadequate, °unsatisfactory, °unacceptable, bumbling, °inefficient, amateurish, °unprofessional, °inferior, second-rate, third-rate, low-grade, °shabby, °shoddy, °mediocre, °defective, °faulty, °flawed, substandard, °sorry, not up to °par *or* snuff, °slipshod, below *or* under °par, *Colloq* °rotten, °lousy: *They did a poor job repairing my car. Her latest recital was pretty poor.* **5** °insignificant, °slight, °paltry, °inconsequential, °mean, °modest, trivial, °trifling: *They made only a poor attempt to correct the problem.* **6** °unfortunate, unlucky, °pathetic, luckless, °pitiful, °pitiable, ill-fated, °miserable, °wretched, ill-starred, star-crossed, jinxed, hapless: *The poor chap lost his entire family in the disaster.* **7** °bad, °ill: *Aunt Theresa has been in poor health lately.*

poorly *adv.* **1** °badly, inadequately, unsatisfactorily, incompetently, inexpertly, improperly, crudely, unprofessionally, amateurishly: *The decorators you recommended have done their work very poorly indeed.* —*adj.* **2** unwell, °indisposed, ailing, °sick, below °par, *Colloq* °rotten, under the °weather: *Charles is rather poorly, I'm afraid.*

pop *v.* **1** °burst, °explode, bang, °go off: *The balloon popped, making me jump.* **2** Often, **pop in** *or* **out** *or* **by**: °visit, °stop, °call, °appear, *Colloq* °drop in, *Brit* °nip in: *Guess who popped in to see me on his way to the airport.* **3** °bulge, °protrude, °stick out, *US* bug out: *The little boy's eyes popped when they brought in the birthday cake.* —*n.* **4** °explosion, bang, °report, °crack: *The Christmas cracker went off with a loud pop.* **5** soft °drink, soda (water); cola, *Brit* fizzy °drink, lemonade, *US* soda pop: *A bottle of pop for my daughter and a pint of bitter for me, please.*

populace *n.* °people, masses, commonalty *or* commonality, (general) °public, commoners, multitude, hoi polloi, °crowd, °throng, °rabble, peasantry, proletariat, °common °folk, rank and file, working °class, bourgeoisie, °mob, *Derogatory* great °unwashed, °riff-raff, °rabble, canaille, ragtag and bobtail: *Some MPs act on behalf of their own constituencies rather than the populace at large.*

popular *adj.* **1** °favourite, °favoured, in °favour, accepted, well-received, approved, (°well-)liked, °fashionable, in °fashion, °stylish, in °vogue, °celebrated, °renowned, acclaimed, °famous, in °demand, sought-after, all the °rage, *Colloq* °trendy, in, °hot: *You would become a millionaire overnight if you could accurately predict the popular music of the coming year.* **2** °conventional, °stock, commonplace, °public, °normal, °standard, °general, °universal, °average, °everyday, °ordinary, °routine, °common, °habitual, °prevalent, °current, °prevailing, °dominant, °predominant, predominating, °customary: *His films cater to popular tastes in science fiction.* **3** °lay, non-professional, °amateur, understandable, °accessible, popularized, simplified: *He presents a popular astronomy programme on TV.*

popularity *n.* °favour, acceptance, °approval, °esteem, °regard, repute, °reputation, °vogue, °trend, stylishness, °renown, acclaim, °fame, °celebrity, lionization, (hero-)°worship, *Colloq* trendiness: *The immense popularity of her novels in America has made her very rich.*

popularly *adv.* commonly, °generally, °ordinarily, °usually, °universally, °widely, regularly, customarily, prevalently, habitually: *It is a popularly held belief among the French that their wine is the best in the world.*

populate *v.* colonize, °settle, °people, °occupy; °inhabit, °dwell in, reside in, °live in: *Shiploads of families braved the voyage to populate the New World.*

population *n.* °people, °populace, °inhabitants, °residents, °natives, °denizens, citizenry, °citizens, °folk: *In those days there was no one to look after the legal rights of the population.*

populous *adj.* crowded, (heavily) populated, peopled, teeming, thronged, crawling, swarming, jammed, jam-packed, °packed: *The populous cities contrast with the sparsely inhabited rural areas.*

pore[1] *v.* **pore over**: °study, °examine, °scrutinize, °peruse, °read, °go over, *Colloq* con: *Hamilton sits in the library, day after day, poring over books of forgotten lore.*

pore[2] *n.* °opening, orifice, °hole, °aperture, °vent, perforation, *Technical* spiracle, stoma: *A hot bath opens the pores in the skin.*

pornographic *adj.* obscene, °lewd, °offensive, °indecent, °prurient, smutty, °taboo, °blue, °dirty, salacious, licentious, °nasty, X-rated, *Colloq* porno, *US* raunchy: *Some prudes consider anything concerning sex to be pornographic.*

pornography *n.* obscenity, smut, °filth, °dirt, erotica, *Colloq* porn: *The council voted to forbid the sale of pornography within the town precincts.*

porous *adj.* spongy, spongelike, permeable, pervious, penetrable: *The rainwater runs through the porous rock and collects in the pools below.*

port *n.* °harbour, haven, seaport; °mooring, anchorage; °refuge: *We were bound east for the port of Cardiff.*

portable *adj.* transportable, °manageable, carriable, °handy, °light, lightweight, °compact, °pocket, pocket-sized, °little, °small, *US* carry-on, vest-pocket, shirt-pocket: *He needs a*

van just to transport his portable television, portable radio, portable hi-fi, portable typewriter, portable computer, and portable calculator.

portentous *adj.* **1** °ominous, °threatening, °momentous, °sinister, °fateful, alarming, °menacing, °foreboding, ill-omened, °inauspicious, unfavourable, ill-starred, ill-fated, star-crossed, lowering *or* louring, °gloomy, °unpromising, unpropitious: *Precisely at midnight they appeared with the most portentous news.* **2** °extraordinary, °amazing, astonishing, astounding, °prodigious, °awesome, awe-inspiring, °remarkable, °marvellous, °phenomenal, °fabulous, °fantastic, mind-boggling, wondrous, °miraculous: *The coronation of a British monarch is truly a portentous event.*

porter[1] *n.* bearer, (baggage) °carrier *or* °attendant, *US airports* skycap, *US railways* redcap: *I tipped the porter to carry our bags to a taxi.*

porter[2] *n.* **1** concierge, cleaner, caretaker, *Chiefly US and Canadian* janitor, °superintendent, *Colloq US* super: *When we are away, the porter keeps our mail for us.* **2** door-keeper, °watchman, doorman, gatekeeper, concierge, *US* tiler: *He went to my club, but the porter would not let him in.*

portico *n.* porch, veranda *or* verandah, gallery, colonnade, galilee: *At the front of the mansion, six Corinthian pillars support a wide portico.*

portion *n.* **1** °segment, °part, °section, °division, subdivision, °parcel, °piece, hunk, chunk, °lump, °wedge, °slice, °sliver, fraction, °fragment, °bit, °morsel, °scrap: *A portion of the masonry fell into the street in the earthquake.* **2** °share, °part, °allotment, °quota, °ration, apportionment, °allowance, allocation, °assignment, °percentage, °measure, °division, °quantity: *The size of an investor's portion depends on the amount invested.* **3** °helping, serving; °ration, °plate, °platter: *He complained that the portions in nouvelle cuisine are too small.*

—*v.* **4** Often, **portion out**: apportion, °share out, allocate, °ration, °allot, °partition, °assign, consign, °dole out, °deal (out), °parcel out, °distribute, °administer, °dispense, °disperse, °divide, °split up, °carve up, °cut up, °break up, °section, *Colloq* divvy up: *The conquered territories were then portioned out among the victors.*

portrait *n.* °picture, °likeness, °image, sketch, °rendering, vignette; °representation, °description, °profile, °thumbnail sketch, portrayal, picturization, depiction; °account, °story, characterization, °study, °record, °file, dossier: *We have the culprit's portrait in our rogues' gallery. We need a more accurate portrait of the kidnapper.*

portray *v.* **1** °represent, °picture, °show, depict, °paint, °render, °characterize, °describe, delineate: *She is portrayed wearing the Castelli tiara. Why must I always be portrayed as the villain?* **2** °act *or* °play (the part *or* role of), take the part *or* role of, °represent, °pose as, impersonate: *She portrays an aged crone who regains her youth in the last act.*

pose *v.* **1** °sit, °model; °position, °place, °arrange, °set (up), °put: *Would you let your husband or wife pose in the nude? She posed the model standing, looking out of the window.* **2** Usually, **pose as**: °portray, °act *or* °play (the part *or* role of), take the part *or* role of, °represent, impersonate, be disguised as, °masquerade as, °pretend *or* °profess to be, °pass (oneself off) as, °pass for,

°imitate, °mimic; attitudinize, °posture, put on °airs, *Colloq* °show off: *She posed as an art expert from Switzerland. She thinks him a roué, but he's only posing.* **3** °set, °put, °ask, °submit, °broach, °posit, °advance, °present, predicate, postulate: *The interviewer posed some questions that were quite embarrassing.* —*n.* **4** °position, °attitude, °posture, °stance: *Her profile is not shown to best advantage in that pose.* **5** °affectation, °act, °pretence, attitudinizing, affectedness, °display, façade, °show, °ostentation: *His interest in art is just a pose to impress her.*

poseur *n.* posturer, exhibitionist, °pretender, °impostor, masquerader, attitudinizer; °fake, faker, dissembler, °fraud, *Colloq* °show-off, °phoney *or US also* phony: *He talks about literature, but he's a poseur who just spouts the opinions of others.*

posh *adj.* (de) luxe, °luxurious, °elegant, °sumptuous, °lavish, °opulent, °rich, °royal, °regal, °luxury, °grand, °fashionable, *Colloq* swank(y), classy, ritzy, *Slang* snazzy: *You ought to see what a posh office my son has!*

posit *v.* postulate, hypothesize, °propound, °put *or* °set forth, °put forward, °advance, °propose, °pose, °offer, °submit, predicate: *If we posit a downturn in prices next year, how does that affect our profit forecasts?*

position *n.* **1** °posture, °attitude, °stance, °pose; °disposition, °arrangement, disposal: *Once in a while, he would change his position so that he faced the sun. With the pieces in this position the chess game is a draw.* **2** °site, °placement, °situation, °whereabouts, placing, emplacement, °location: *Those bearings put his present position about 20 miles west of Cádiz.* **3** °viewpoint, °point of view, °outlook, °attitude, °angle, °slant, °stance, °stand, °opinion, °inclination, °leaning, °bent, °sentiment, °feeling, way of °thinking: *My solicitor is pessimistic about my position in this case.* **4** °status, °condition, °state, °circumstances, °situation: *Our financial position vis-à-vis investment in gilt bonds has changed.* **5** °class, °caste, °place, °rank, °standing, °station, °status, °importance: *They insist on knowing the social position of the girl's family.* **6** °job, °occupation, °situation, °post, °office, °function, °appointment, °capacity, °place, °role, *Colloq* billet, berth, *Australian* possie *or* possy: *My mother's position as managing director had nothing to do with my getting a promotion.* **7** °hypothesis, °thesis, °principle, contention, °assertion, predication, °belief, °proposition, postulate: *His position is based on the implications of the third law of thermodynamics.* —*v.* **8** °put, °place, °situate, °site, °set, °fix, °settle, °dispose, °arrange: *The pointer is again positioned at zero. Position your forces along this ridge and stay on full alert.* **9** °place, °locate, °establish, °determine, °fix, localize: *The scientists positioned the seismic activity as being along the San Andreas fault.*

positive *adj.* **1** °sure, °certain, °definite, unequivocal, °categorical, °absolute, °unqualified, unambiguous, unmistakable, clear-cut, °clear, °explicit, °express, decisive, °indisputable, indubitable, °unquestionable, unquestioned, incontestable, uncontested, undeniable, °reliable, °persuasive, convincing, irrefutable: *The police have positive evidence that the men are*

innocent of any crime. Spending this evening with you has been a positive delight.* **2** °definitive, °emphatic, °decided, °forceful, °firm, °peremptory, °definite: *He gave a positive denial when asked if he had agreed to let the hostages go. She made a positive commitment to meet me here at noon.* **3** °sure, °certain, °confident, convinced, satisfied: *Are you positive that the last train is at midnight?* **4** °beneficial, °favourable, °complimentary, °productive, °useful: *I heard many positive things about the way she handled herself at the interview.* **5** °overconfident, °dogmatic, doctrinaire, pontifical, °opinionated, pigheaded, °stubborn, °obstinate, obdurate, °arbitrary, overweening, °arrogant, °assertive, °dictatorial, °despotic, imperious, *Rare* thetic(al): *His problem is that he is quite positive about things that simply are not so.* **6** °practical, °realistic, utilitarian, °productive, °functional, pragmatic(al), °matter-of-fact, *Colloq* hard-nosed: *They have taken a positive approach to studying the economics of small businesses.* **7** encouraging, °supportive, °constructive, reassuring, °enthusiastic, °favourable, affirmative, yes, confirming: *Our plan to buy out the company has received a positive reaction from our bankers. Asked if they would buy our product, businessmen gave a positive response.* **8** auspicious, °promising, °propitious, encouraging; °optimistic, °favourable, °cheerful, °confident; *Colloq* bullish, °upbeat: *In the long run, the picture for home-owners looks positive. It pays to maintain a positive outlook and not get depressed.* **9** °complete, utter, °total, °perfect, °out-and-out, consummate, °unmitigated, °thorough, thoroughgoing; egregious, °glaring, °stark, °sheer, °outright, °unqualified, unequivocal: *You were a positive idiot not to let me know you needed help. All attempts at reconciliation ended in positive disaster.*

positively *adv.* °definitely, °absolutely, unquestionably, certainly, (most) assuredly, undeniably, °undoubtedly, °surely, to be °sure, emphatically, unmistakably, unqualifiedly, categorically, indisputably, beyond *or* without (a °shadow of) a °doubt, indubitably, beyond °question: *The wine list at Le Maître's is positively the best in the area.*

possess *v.* **1** be °possessed *or* in °possession of, °have, own, °enjoy, be blessed *or* endowed with: *In the 19th century, the family possessed great wealth.* **2** °have, be born *or* °gifted *or* endowed with, °contain, °embody, °embrace, °include: *He possesses a talent to amuse people. Man does not possess as keen a sense of smell as many animals.* **3** °dominate, °control, °govern, °consume, take °control of, preoccupy, °obsess; °charm, °captivate, °enchant, cast a °spell on *or* over, °bewitch, enthral: *What possessed her to think that I could help? He behaves as if he is possessed by the devil.* **4 be possessed with** *or* **of**: °have, be held *or* influenced *or* dominated by, be imbued *or* inspired *or* permeated *or* °affected with: *She became possessed with the notion that she could sing. Fiona believes herself the only person possessed of reason.* **5 possess oneself of**: °acquire, °achieve, °get, °come by, °gain, °come into, °win, °obtain, °procure, °secure, °take, °seize, °take *or* °gain °possession of: *Kevin has possessed himself of the only comfortable bed in the place.*

possessed *adj.* obsessed, driven, controlled, dominated, ridden, bedevilled, consumed, haunted, pressed, maddened, crazed, demented, frenzied, *Colloq* eaten up: *He behaved like a man possessed.*

possession *n.* **1** ownership, °title, proprietorship, °control, °hold, °tenure, keeping, °care, °custody, guardianship, °protection: *The paintings are now in my possession.* **2** holding, °territory, °province, °dominion, colony, protectorate: *How long will the Falkland Islands remain a possession of the Crown?* **3 possessions**: °belongings, °property, °effects, chattels, °assets, worldly °goods, °things: *The prison clerk placed all my possessions in an envelope, explaining that they would be returned when I was released.* **4 take** *or* **gain possession of**: °seize, °capture, °take, °conquer, °occupy, °acquire, °win, °possess oneself of, °secure, °obtain; repossess: *The raiding party gained possession of the port and surrounding area. The finance company has taken possession of my car.*

possessive *adj.* **1** °greedy, unyielding, °selfish, ungiving, ungenerous, stingy, niggardly, °materialistic, covetous, acquisitive: *He refuses to see anyone, as he is very possessive of his time.* **2** overprotective, controlling, °grasping, dominating, °domineering, °overbearing: *Anyone with a possessive parent finds it difficult to leave home.*

possibility *n.* **1** °chance, °odds, °prospect, conceivability, °feasibility, plausibility, °likelihood, admissibility: *There is a possibility of my leaving work early to meet you. What is the possibility that he might be honest? They deny even the possibility of God's existence.* **2** Often, **possibilities**: °opportunity, potentiality, °potential, °capacity, °promise: *The old house has many large rooms and offers great possibilities.*

possible *adj.* **1** °feasible, °plausible, imaginable, conceivable, °thinkable, credible, °tenable, °reasonable, admissible: *It is remotely possible, though improbable, that she committed the crime.* **2** realizable, °practicable, workable, °practical, doable, achievable, attainable, reachable, accomplishable, °viable, *Colloq* on: *In the present state of the art, a fully interactive computer, operating in real time, is still not possible.*

possibly *adv.* **1** °maybe, °perhaps, God willing, *Deo volente*, if °possible, *Archaic or literary* perchance, mayhap, peradventure: *She is possibly the best person for the job.* **2** in any °way, under any circumstances, by any °chance, by any °means, at all: *Could you possibly help me find my contact lens? The weather forecast couldn't possibly be correct.*

post[1] *n.* **1** °pole, °stake, °upright, column, °pillar, °pale, °picket, °shaft, standard, newel, °pier, pylon, °pile, piling, °strut, shore, stanchion, °leg, °prop, °stay, °support, °brace: *A huge central post held up the roof.*
—*v.* **2** advertise, °announce, °proclaim, °publish, °circulate, °propagate, promulgate; °put *or* °pin *or* °tack *or* °stick *or* °hang up, affix: *The notice of the meeting has been posted for all to see.*

post[2] *n.* **1** °assignment, °appointment, °position, °situation, °job, °place, °duty, °role, °function, °employment, °work, °task, chore: *Clarke was given a post as consul in some forgotten country.*
—*v.* **2** °place, °put, °station, °assign, °appoint, °position, °situate, °set, °locate: *Guards have been posted around the enclosure.*

post[3] *n.* **1** postal service, °mail; °delivery; collection: *I am expecting an important letter in the post. It hasn't come in the first post.*
—*v.* **2** °send, °dispatch *or* despatch, °transmit, *Chiefly US and Canadian* °mail: *I posted your cheque this morning.* **3** °record, °enter, °register, °list: *We post the daily receipts in this ledger.* **4 keep (someone) posted**: °inform, °advise, °brief, °notify, *Colloq* °fill (someone) in on: *Our observers have kept me posted as to your whereabouts every step of the way.*

poster *n.* placard, °notice, bill, °advertisement, °announcement, broadside, broadsheet; circular, flier: *Who designed that striking poster for the new play?*

posterior *adj.* **1** hind, °rear, °back, after, °hinder, rearward, *Nautical* aft: *The posterior legs are somewhat longer.* **2** later, after, latter, ensuing, following, succeeding, °subsequent: *Analysis has yielded evidence of the posterior origin of the lava.*
—*n.* **3** °buttocks, °bottom, rump, °seat, *derrière*, behind, °rear, backside, *Colloq Brit* °bum, *US* hinie, tush *or* tushy *or* tushie, tokus *or* tochis *or* tuchis, °tail; *Taboo slang Brit* arse, *US* ass: *The term describing a person with a fat posterior is 'steatopygous'.*

posterity *n.* descendants, successors, heirs, children, °offspring, °issue, °progeny: *It is good that these buildings will be preserved for posterity. Posterity will be the judge of our success.*

post-haste *adv.* °quickly, at °once, without delay, °immediately, °directly, straight away, °right away, °promptly, speedily, °swiftly, instantly, before you can say 'Jack Robinson', before you can say 'knife', °rapidly, at full tilt, in a wink, in a trice, in the °twinkling of an eye, *Colloq* pronto, chop-chop, p.d.q. (= 'pretty damned quick'), *US and Canadian* lickety-split, like greased lightning: *He got me the report post-haste.*

post-mortem *n.* **1** autopsy, necropsy: *We'll know the cause of death after the post-mortem.* **2** °review, °analysis, *Slang US* Monday-morning quarterbacking: *We can do without the post-mortem on every bridge hand.*

postpone *v.* °delay, adjourn, °defer, keep in °abeyance, °put off *or* aside, °lay aside, °suspend, °shelve, put *or* keep on ice, temporize, dally, *Colloq* put on the back burner, *US* °table: *We ought to postpone further discussion till we have the facts.*

postponement *n.* °delay, adjournment, °abeyance, °suspension, °stay, deferment, deferral, °moratorium: *There has been a postponement of the meeting till Monday.*

posture *n.* **1** °pose, °position, °attitude, °stance, °appearance, °carriage: *She stood there in a defiant posture, with arms akimbo.* **2** °position, °condition, °situation, °state, °disposition; °arrangement, °organization, layout, array, °format: *The government adopted a conciliatory posture in the matter.* **3** °attitude, °stance, °position, °feeling, °sentiment, °outlook, (°point of) °view, °viewpoint, °orientation, °disposition, °frame of mind, °mood: *The interviewer tried to determine the general's posture on disarmament.*
—*v.* **4** °pose, attitudinize, °affect, put on a °show, do for °effect, *Colloq* °show off: *Despite all her posturing, we believe her to be sincere.*

pot n. **1** °pan, saucepan, cauldron, cook-pot, stewpot; kettle: *How many politicians have promised the people 'a chicken in every pot'?* **2** jackpot, bank, °kitty: *You will have to add £5 to the pot to see my hand.* **3** pot-belly, °paunch, °gut, *Colloq* corporation, beer-belly, °spare tyre, *US* bay window: *If he exercised more, Patrick wouldn't have such a pot.*

potent adj. **1** °powerful, °strong; °mighty, °vigorous, °forceful, formidable, °authoritative, °influential, *Literary* puissant: *A potent poison will kill those weeds. We have to reckon with an enemy that is quite potent.* **2** °effective, convincing, cogent, °persuasive, compelling, °efficacious, °telling, °sound, valid, °impressive: *Their argument is potent enough to convince the biggest sceptics.*

potential adj. **1** °possible, °likely, °implicit, implied, °imminent, developing, budding, embryonic, °dormant, hidden, concealed, covert, latent, quiescent, °passive, °future, unrealized, °undeveloped: *We are dealing with a potential threat to our liberty.*
—n. **2** °capacity, °capability, °possibility, °aptitude, potency, *Colloq* the (right) stuff, what it takes: *All teenagers have potential; the problem is to teach them to exploit it to the best advantage.*

potion n. °draught, °brew, beverage, °drink, philtre, potation, °elixir, °tonic, cup, °dose, concoction, decoction: *The old crone gave him a tiny bottle containing the love potion.*

pot-pourri n. °mixture, °medley, °miscellany, °assortment, olla podrida, smorgasbord *or* smörgåsbord, gallimaufry, salmagundi, °patchwork, °collection, °hotchpotch *or US and Canadian* hodgepodge, *mélange*, motley, °pastiche *or* pasticcio, °mishmash, °jumble, °mess: *What a pot-pourri of styles is represented in that art gallery!*

potter v. °dabble (in *or* with), °toy with, °trifle with, fribble, °fool (with *or* about *or* around), °fritter (away), °mess (about *or* around *or* with), °tinker (with), meddle (with), °monkey (about *or* around *or* with), fidget (with), *US* putter (around *or* with), *Colloq* °fiddle (about *or* around *or* with), footle (around *or* about): *On Sundays I like to potter about in the garden.*

pottery n. earthenware, ceramics, terracotta, crockery, stoneware, porcelain, china, delftware: *Ornamented pottery has been found in pre-Columbian digs.*

pouch n. °pocket, °sack, °bag, °purse, reticule, *Dialect* poke: *A Highlander's pouch is called a sporran. As I was going out, I filled my tobacco pouch.*

pounce v. **1** Often, **pounce on** *or* **upon**: °spring (on *or* upon), °leap (at *or* on), °swoop down (on *or* upon), °fall upon, °jump (at *or* on), °strike, take by °surprise *or* °unawares, °attack, °ambush, *Colloq* °mug: *As I rounded the corner, three youths pounced on me, stole my bag, and ran off.*
—n. **2** °spring, °leap, °swoop, °jump: *The cat was on the mantel shelf in a single pounce.*

pound[1] v. **1** °beat, °batter, °pelt, hammer, pummel; thump, °belabour, thrash, bludgeon, cudgel, maul, °strike, *Colloq* °lambaste, *Slang* paste, clobber, work over, give (someone) the °works *or* a pasting: *She pounded on the door till someone came. It was satisfying to see him pound the class bully into submission.* **2** °crush, °powder, °pulverize, bray, comminute, triturate, mash, °pulp: *The corn must be pounded into a fine meal before use.* **3** °beat, throb, hammer, °pulse, °pulsate, palpitate: *My heart was pounding, waiting to see if the tiger would attack.* **4 pound into**: °instil, °din into, °drill into, drub into, hammer into, °beat into: *Her parents have pounded into her that she must show respect to her elders.* **5 pound out**: °rid, °expel, °clear, °cleanse, °empty, °purge, °beat out, hammer out: *The last bit of stubbornness was pounded out of me at school.* **6** °beat out; hammer out, °produce: *The jungle drums pounded out the message that Tarzan was coming.*
—n. **7** pounding, °beat, beating, thump, °thumping: *The pound of horses' hooves heralded the arrival of the cavalry.*

pound[2] n. °enclosure, °pen, °compound, confine, yard: *My car was towed to the pound, and it cost a fortune to retrieve it.*

pour v. **1** °flow, °run, °gush, °rush, °flood, °stream, °course, °spout, °discharge, °spurt, °spew out, cascade: *Water was pouring from a crack in the dam.* **2** °empty, °discharge, °let out: *Pour the boiling water over the tea leaves and let them steep for a few minutes.* **3** °rain, °teem, *Colloq* come down in buckets *or* by the bucketful, bucket down, °rain cats and dogs, *US* °rain pitchforks: *It poured all night.* **4** °stream, °swarm, °crowd, °throng, °teem, °emerge, sally forth, °issue (forth), °go (forth): *The show over, people poured into the streets.*

pout v. **1** mope, °brood, °sulk, make a moue, pull a long °face, °frown, °lour *or* lower, °knit one's brows: *Don't pout—I'll buy you an ice-cream.*
—n. **2** °frown, moue, long °face: *Her pout was occasioned by her father's scolding.*

poverty n. **1** °want, penury, indigence, insolvency, destitution, pauperism, impecuniousness, neediness, beggary: *Her childhood was spent in poverty.* **2** °scarcity, scarceness, °want, °need, °lack, meagreness, insufficiency, °shortage, °dearth, paucity, inadequacy: *They criticized the poverty of talent among the current crop of actors.*

powder n. **1** dust; talc: *I couldn't remember whether the jar contained cornflour or baking powder. She dabbed her body all over with scented powder.* **2 take a (run-out) powder**: °run away, abscond, °escape, vanish, °disappear, *Slang Brit* scarper, do a moonlight flit, *US* take it on the lam: *The cops are coming, so I'm taking a powder.*
—v. **3** °pulverize, bray, °grind, °crush, °pound, granulate, triturate, comminute, levigate: *The rocks must first be crushed, then powdered.* **4** sprinkle, besprinkle, dust, dredge, °cover, °coat: *Lightly powder the top of the cake with icing sugar, and it is ready to serve.*

power n. **1** Sometimes, **powers**: °capacity, °capability, °ability, °potential, °faculty, competency *or* competence, potentiality, *Colloq* what it takes, *US* the (right) °stuff, the goods: *Fishes have the power to change their buoyancy. He has remarkable powers of observation.* **2** °control, dominance, °authority, mastery, °rule, °influence, °sway, °command, ascendancy, °sovereignty, °dominion, °weight, clout, *Colloq* °pull, *US* drag: *He maintains a Svengali-like power over her. The prime minister has the power to appoint and dismiss cabinet ministers.* **3** °control, °command, °authority: *The party might not be in power for very long.* **4** °strength, °might, °vigour,

°energy, °force, mightiness, potency, force-fulness, °brawn, muscle, *Literary* puissance: *His speech was delivered with great power and a certain wit. Has she the power it takes to toss the caber?*　**5** °talent, °skill, °ability, °faculty, °gift, °aptitude, °genius, °knack: *They say that she has the power to see into the future.*　**6** °authority, °licence, °right, authorization, °privilege, °warrant, °prerogative: *By the power vested in me, I now declare you man and wife. It is within her power to grant a stay of execution.*　**7** Often, **powers**: °activity, effectiveness, °effect, °ability, °capacity, °active °ingredient(s): *This mushroom has hallucinogenic powers.*　**8** °energy, °momentum, °impetus, °drive, °force, °inertia: *The car rolled halfway up the next hill under its own power.*　**9** (mechanical *or* electrical *or* atomic) energy, °electricity, °fuel: *Yesterday there was another demonstration against the use of nuclear power.*　**10 powers that be**: °government, °administration, authorities, °incumbents: *It is up to the powers that be to investigate corruption.*

powerful *adj.*　**1** °potent, °strong, °mighty, °vigorous, °robust, °energetic, °sturdy, °stalwart, °tough, resilient, °dynamic: *Leslie has a powerful physique. The cities of the Hanseatic League had powerful economies.*　**2** °influential, °strong, com-pelling, °forceful, °potent, °substantial, °weighty, °authoritative, °effective; °important, °impressive, °telling, °effectual, °formidable, °persuasive: *Powerful arguments have been brought to bear against taking such action. She has many powerful friends.*　**3** °strong, °potent; °intense, °substantial, °great, °high: *The drug is too powerful to be taken regularly. A powerful electrical charge was sent through the wire to test the connection.*

powerless *adj.*　**1** °helpless, °incapable, °unable, unfit, °incompetent, °ineffectual, °ineffective: *Without his wand, the magician was powerless.*　**2** incapacitated, °helpless, °weak, °feeble, debilitated, °crippled, paralysed, °disabled: *He is completely powerless without the use of his right hand.*

practicable *adj.* doable, °feasible, workable, performable, achievable, attainable, accom-plishable, °possible, °viable: *We climbed up the glacier as far as was practicable. At last we had a practicable flying machine.*

practical *adj.*　**1** pragmatic, °useful, usable *or* useable, °functional, °realistic, °reasonable, °sound, utilitarian, °applicable, °serviceable, °empirical, °efficient: *Whether the device is prac-tical will depend on its cost effectiveness.*　**2** °sensible, °reasonable, common-sense *or* common-sensical, °everyday, °ordinary, down-to-earth, °expedient, °matter-of-fact, mundane, business-like, hard-headed, °judicious, *Colloq* hard-nosed: *Put theory aside and focus on a prac-tical solution to the problem.*　**3** applied, °field, hands-on, °personal, °everyday: *She has had prac-tical experience in nursing the elderly.*

practically *adv.*　**1** °almost, (very) °nearly, well-nigh, °virtually, in °effect, °just about, essen-tially, fundamentally, at °bottom, basically, when all is said and done, at the end of the day, to all intents and purposes: *We are practically there. I have practically finished the ironing.*　**2** realistically, matter-of-factly, °clearly, °simply, reasonably, rationally, sensibly: *Practically, there was nothing to be done except let the fire burn itself out.*

practice *n.*　**1** °custom, wont, °habit, °routine, °convention, °tradition, °rule, °procedure, °usage, °mode, °style, °way, modus operandi, °technique *or* technic, *Formal* praxis, *Colloq* MO (= 'modus operandi'): *She makes a practice of swimming for an hour every day. It is our practice to get patients out of bed as soon as possible after surgery.*　**2** °exercise, °discipline, °drill, prac-tising, °repetition, °rehearsal, training, °preparation, workout, warm-up; °application, °study: *She needs more practice on the beginner's slope before going down the main piste.*　**3** °pursuit, °exercise, °work, °profession, °career, °vocation, °conduct; °business, °office: *He genuinely enjoys the practice of law. I heard of a veterinary practice for sale in Yorkshire.*　**4 in practice**: °practically, °actually, day-to-day, realistically, in real life: *In practice no one would ever treat an injury the way this book recommends.*　**5 out of practice**: °inexperienced, unpractised, °unaccustomed, rusty: *I once played a good game of chess, but I'm out of practice now.*

practise *v.*　**1** °drill, °exercise, °work out, °train, °prepare, °rehearse, °run through, °repeat, °study, *US* practice: *I am practising for Sunday's tennis tournament. She practises the piano every day. You should practise your routine for the show.*　**2** °carry on, make a °practice of, °perform, do, °act, °carry out, put into °practice, *US* practice: *She practises law. You should practise what you preach.*

practised *adj.*　**1** °accomplished, °proficient, °expert, skilled, °experienced, °capable, °adept, °seasoned, °able, °qualified, °gifted, °talented, °skilful, °masterful, consummate, °superb, °superior, *US* practiced: *She is a practised liar.*　**2** trained, rehearsed, °versed, °cultivated, schooled, finished, perfected, *US* practiced: *He greeted them with the practised air of a veteran diplomat.*

praise *n.*　**1** acclaim, °approval, approbation, °applause, plaudits, °kudos, °endorsement, acclamation, °tribute, accolade, compliments, commendation, encomium, °eulogy, pan-egyric, °ovation: *Sheila has received well-deserved praise for her work with paraplegic children. Would you expect me to sing the praises of my rival?*　**2** °honour, glorification, adoration, exaltation, °devotion, °homage, °worship, °veneration, adu-lation, °reverence, °glory, hymn *or* song of praise, paean, hosanna: *The king rejoiced and said, 'Praise be to God'.*　—*v.*　**1** acclaim, °approve, °laud, °applaud, °endorse, pay °tribute to, °compliment, com-mend, °eulogize, °extol, °honour, sing the praises (of): *The speaker praised Read for his many contributions to linguistics.*　**4** °worship, °revere, °reverence, °exalt, °glorify, °adore, pay °homage to, °venerate, give °thanks to, °hallow: *Praise the Lord and pass the ammunition.*

praiseworthy *adj.* commendable, °laudable, °admirable, creditable, °worthy, °meritorious, °deserving, °exemplary: *However praiseworthy your motives were, you did not stop to consider the consequences.*

prance *v.* °caper, °dance, gambol, °skip, °cavort, romp, °leap, °frisk, °jump, °spring, °bound, *Dressage* curvet, capriole: *Ahead of the royal coach came a dozen riders on prancing horses.*

prank *n.* °trick, (practical) °joke, °frolic, escap-ade, antic, °caper, °stunt, °lark, jest, jape,

°monkey tricks or esp. US monkeyshines, °mischief: *Those schoolboy pranks we once thought hilarious now seem quite silly.*

prattle v. **1** prate, °babble, blather or blether, blither, gibber, °jabber, jibber-jabber, °palaver, °tattle, twaddle, gabble, °chatter, °patter, °drivel, °twitter, °rattle on, °go on (and on), maunder, *Brit* natter, *Colloq* witter (on), gas, °gab, °spout, °gush, °run (on), *US* run off at the mouth, *Slang* jaw, ya(c)k, ya(c)kety-ya(c)k, shoot off one's mouth: *Do I have to listen to him prattle on and on about his grandchildren?* —n. **2** prate, prating, °babble, babbling, blather or blether, blathering or blethering, gibber, gibbering, °jabber, jabbering, °palaver, palavering, °tattle, tattling, twaddle, °chatter, chattering, gabble, gabbling, °patter, °drivel, °twitter, twittering, rattling on, going on, maundering, cackle, *US* jibber-jabbering, twattle, clack, *Colloq* gas, °gab, running off at the mouth, *Slang* jawing, ya(c)kety-ya(c)k: *We were treated to constant prattle about eating healthy foods.* **3** jabberwocky, °gobbledegook or gobbledygook, °mumbo-jumbo, °rubbish, balderdash, (°stuff and) °nonsense, humbug, bunkum, tommy-rot, °trash, °rot, foolishness, *Colloq* pish and tush, °hot air, flapdoodle, °rigmarole or rigamarole, bunk, piffle, °moonshine, poppycock, claptrap, bull, hogwash, °swill, *Brit* tosh, fiddle-faddle, boloney, *Chiefly US* °garbage, horse feathers, *Slang* crap, hooey, guff, *Taboo slang* bullshit, *US* crock (of shit): *What they told you about guaranteeing your job is just a lot of prattle.*

pray v. **1** °beseech, °ask, °call upon or on, entreat, implore, °request, °appeal to, °plead (with), °beg (for), importune, °solicit, °petition, supplicate, *Rare* obsecrate: *I pray you to find it in your heart to approve my work.* **2** say one's °prayers, offer a °prayer: *We prayed for her safe return.*

prayer n. **1** °petition, °supplication, °request, entreaty, °plea, °suit, °appeal, *Rare* obsecration: *Our prayers were answered, and she returned safely.* **2** °devotion, praying, invocation, (°divine) °service, *Literary* orison: *Man ascends to God through prayer.*

preach v. **1** °deliver a °sermon, evangelize, °spread the Word or the Gospel; catechize: *The Most Reverend John Attwood will preach next week at Winchester.* **2** moralize, sermonize, °advise, °counsel, admonish, °reprimand, °lecture, °harangue, pontificate, °urge, inculcate, °advocate: *Mother used to preach to us about being charitable. Father preached restraint in all things.*

preacher n. °minister, evangelist, °clergyman, clergywoman, cleric, ecclesiastic, reverend, °divine, *Colloq* tub-thumper: *He studied for many years to become a preacher.*

preamble n. introduction, °foreword, prologue, °preface, *Formal* proem, prolegomenon, exordium: *As a preamble to today's proceedings, I should like to welcome our honoured guests.*

precarious adj. °uncertain, °unreliable, unsure, °risky, °hazardous, unpredictable, °insecure, °unstable, unsteady, °unsettled, °shaky, °doubtful, dubious, °questionable, °tricky, °delicate, °ticklish, °sensitive, °slippery, touch-and-go, (hanging) in the °balance, hanging by a thread, Damoclean, °perilous, treacherous, °dangerous, °difficult, °problematic, *Colloq* chancy, *Brit* °dodgy, °dicey, *US* iffy, *Slang*

°hairy: *If sales continue to drop, the company will be in a precarious condition. We followed a precarious trail down the mountainside.*

precaution n. **1** °provision, °preventive °measure, °safety °measure, °safeguard, °insurance, °protection, °cover, °escape: *Unfortunately, he had failed to take any precautions against storm damage.* **2** °foresight, °prudence, °providence, °forethought, °caution, cautiousness, circumspection, °care, °attention, watchfulness, °vigilance, alertness, wariness, chariness, apprehension, far-sightedness, °anticipation: *Precaution is wiser than hindsight.*

precede v. °come or °go or °proceed before or °first, °go °ahead or in °advance (of), °lead (the way), °pave the °way (for), herald, usher in, °introduce, antecede; °foreshadow, antedate, predate: *His wife preceded him into the room. The Decameron preceded The Canterbury Tales by about fifty years.*

precedence n. precedency, °priority, °pre-eminence, °superiority, °supremacy, °preference, °privilege, °prerogative, °importance, °rank, °position, primacy: *Your school work must take precedence over football practice.*

precedent n. °prototype, °model, °example, exemplar, °pattern, paradigm, °yardstick, criterion, standard, °lead: *The French considered the War of American Independence a precedent for their revolution.*

preceding adj. °foregoing, °former, °previous, above, °prior, earlier, above-mentioned, aforementioned, above-stated, above-named: *The defendant in the preceding action was remanded in custody for a week.*

precept n. **1** °rule, °guide, °principle, unwritten °law, canon, guideline, °dictate, °code, °injunction, °law, commandment, °instruction, directive, °prescription, mandate, °charge; statute, °regulation, edict, ukase, °decree, °order, fiat, ordinance: *The Ten Commandments provide basic precepts of moral behaviour.* **2** °maxim, °proverb, axiom, °motto, °slogan, saying, °byword, aphorism, apophthegm or apothegm: *Does anyone follow the precepts set forth in Scripture?*

precinct n. **1** Usually, **precincts**: °area, °territory, °region, °province, environs, purlieus, °borders, °bounds, confines: *Does he have any authority outside the precincts of the city?* **2** °sphere, °neighbourhood, °zone, sector, °section, °quarter, °district, °locale: *In some US cities, the area covered by a police station is called a precinct.*

precious adj. **1** °dear, dearest, costly, °expensive, high-priced, valuable, °invaluable, prized, °priceless, irreplaceable, *Colloq* °pricey or pricy: *The entire cabinet was filled with precious jewels.* **2** esteemed, °choice, cherished, °beloved, idolized, adored, loved, valued, prized, revered, venerated, °venerable, hallowed: *The church keeps its most precious relics in a special vault.* **3** °precise, °exquisite, overrefined, chichi, over-nice, °studied, °artificial, effete, °affected, overdone, °pretentious, euphuistic, alembicated, *Colloq Brit* °twee, *Slang US* cutesy: *His style is characterized by somewhat precious language.*

precipice n. °cliff, escarpment, °bluff, °crag: *We looked nervously over the edge of the precipice at the raging sea below.*

precipitate v. **1** accelerate, °hasten, °speed (up), °advance, °hurry, °quicken, °expedite,

°bring on *or* about, trigger, °provoke, instigate, °incite, °facilitate, °further, °press, °push forward(s): *The rise in interest rates precipitated many bankruptcies.* **2** °hurl, °fling, °cast, °launch, °project: *The force of the impact precipitated him through the windscreen.*
—*adj.* **3** headlong, °violent, °rapid, °swift, quick, °speedy, °meteoric, °fast: *A powerful counter-attack brought about the enemy's precipitate rout.*
4 °sudden, °abrupt, unannounced, unexpected, unanticipated: *Today's fall in share prices was as precipitate as yesterday's rise.* **5** °rash, °impetuous, °hasty, °volatile, °hotheaded, °careless, °reckless, incautious, injudicious, °foolhardy, °impulsive, unrestrained: *The selection of a career should not be a precipitate decision.*

precipitation *n.* showers, drizzle, °downpour, °rain, rainfall, snow, snowfall, hail, sleet: *Precipitation can be expected in advance of the low-pressure area pushing down from the north.*

precipitous *adj.* **1** °abrupt, °steep, °perpendicular, °sheer, bluff, acclivitous, declivitous: *I cannot see how anyone can climb up the precipitous face of that crag.* **2** See **precipitate**, 5, above.

précis *n.* °outline, °summary, °synopsis, *aperçu*, résumé, conspectus, °survey, overview, °abstract, °abridgement, °digest, compendium, recapitulation; °table of contents: *As I haven't the time to read the entire study document, let me have a précis of it.*

precise *adj.* **1** °correct, °exact, °definite, well-defined, °explicit, word-for-word, °verbatim, °literal, letter-for-letter, *literatim*, °faithful, °specific, unambiguous, unequivocal, °strict, °authentic, °perfect, °true, veracious, °truthful, unerring, error-free, °accurate: *Errors show that medieval scribes did not always succeed in making precise copies.* **2** °strict, °meticulous, °scrupulous, °careful, °conscientious, °exact, unconditional, rigorous, °rigid, puritanical, unbending, °inflexible, unyielding, °demanding, °severe, prim, °absolute: *He has been very precise about dates and facts. Margaret is precise in insisting on obedience to her orders.*
3 °fastidious, °particular, °finicky, finical, °fussy, °meticulous, °scrupulous, °careful, °conscientious, °nice, °exacting, °critical, °demanding: *Painting miniatures is very precise work.* **4** °exact, °very: *This is the precise spot where I found the body.*

precisely *adv.* **1** °exactly, °just, strictly, *Colloq* on the °nail, smack, °slap, on the nose, *Brit* bang on, spot on: *His view is precisely the opposite of hers. We left precisely at five o'clock. You phoned, and that is precisely why I came. The two paintings are not precisely the same.* **2** °exactly, exactingly, correctly, rigorously, °absolutely, punctiliously, minutely, carefully, meticulously, scrupulously, conscientiously, strictly, rigidly, inflexibly; in all respects, in every °way: *This judge follows the letter of the law precisely.*

precision *n.* **1** correctness, exactness, fidelity, faithfulness, exactitude, preciseness, °accuracy, °rigour, °perfection, flawlessness, faultlessness, literalism, unerringness: *This copy follows the original with precision.* **2** definiteness, °care, nicety, meticulousness, rigorousness, °rigour, fastidiousness, punctiliousness, scrupulousness, unambiguousness, strictness, explicitness: *The precision of the wording leaves no doubt about what the writer intended.*

preclude *v.* obviate, °bar, °prevent, °stop, °exclude, °prohibit, °shut out, °forestall, °rule out, debar, °check, °block, °obstruct, avert, °avoid, °thwart, °frustrate, °impede, °inhibit, °hinder, °interfere with: *To preclude misunderstanding, please repeat what you said. They may not engage in activities that preclude them from performing their regular duties.*

precocious *adj.* advanced, °mature, °bright, °gifted, °intelligent, °smart, quick: *It is hard to believe that Oliver was a precocious child.*

preconceived *adj.* beforehand, predisposed, prejudged, °predetermined, °prejudiced, °biased, anticipatory: *He has many false preconceived notions about people.*

preconception *n.* predisposition, prejudgement, predetermination, °prejudice, °bias, °presumption, °presupposition, assumption, *idée fixe,* prepossession, °preconceived notion *or* idea: *This production of* King Lear *will challenge your preconceptions of the play.*

precondition *n.* °prerequisite, °stipulation, °condition, °essential, °must, *sine qua non,* °imperative, °requirement, °proviso, °provision, °qualification, °necessity: *The release of the prisoners is a precondition for talks. Is great humanity a precondition of great music, or is it just a matter of the notes?*

precursor *n.* **1** °harbinger, herald, vanguard: *The glow on the eastern horizon is the precursor of another day.* **2** See **predecessor**, 1, below

predatory *adj.* **1** predacious *or* predaceous, carnivorous, preying, raptorial: *Despite domestication, dogs and cats are predatory animals.* **2** °rapacious, °ravenous, plundering, robbing, pillaging, marauding, despoiling, looting, piratical, vulturine, °avaricious, °greedy, °voracious, larcenous, thieving, extortionate, usurious: *Predatory pirates once ravaged the Mediterranean. Keep out of the hands of predatory money-lenders, my son.*

predecessor *n.* **1** °forerunner, antecedent: *I could not match the accomplishments of my predecessor in this post.* **2** forebear, forefather, °ancestor, antecedent: *Can you name the Tudor predecessors of Elizabeth I?*

predestination *n.* °destiny, °future, °lot, °fortune, kismet, karma; °doom, °fate; foreordainment, foreordination: *Meeting like this must have been predestination.*

predetermined *adj.* **1** °fixed, prearranged, pre-established, °set (up), °foregone, pre-planned, pre-set: *A predetermined amount of milk is automatically poured into each cup of coffee.*
2 °fated, °doomed, °destined, ordained, foreordained, *Colloq* °cut and dried, *Brit* on the cards, *US* in the cards: *One gets the feeling that the outcome was predetermined.*

predicament *n.* °dilemma, °quandary, °difficulty, °trial, °situation, °state, °condition, imbroglio, °emergency, °crisis, °impasse, *Colloq* pickle, °jam, °fix, °pinch, °scrape, °spot, °bind, corner, °hole, °mess, *US* box: *I was hoping that you might help me out of a very awkward predicament.*

predict *v.* foretell, °prophesy, °forecast, °foresee, augur, °prognosticate, forewarn, presage, vaticinate; portend, °foreshadow, foretoken, forebode; °intimate, °hint, °suggest: *My mother predicted that there would be moments like this. If only I could predict the winner of the 2.30!*

predictable *adj.* foreseeable, foreseen, °probable, °likely, °liable, expected, anticipated, (reasonably) °sure *or* °certain, *Colloq Brit* on the cards, *US* in the cards: *Her angry reaction at being dismissed was quite predictable.*

prediction *n.* °forecast, °prophecy, augury, °prognosis; intimation, °hint, °suggestion: *The weatherman's predictions are more accurate than one might think. The prediction that he might be released the next day did not come true.*

predominance *n.* predominancy, °superiority, °influence, dominance, °pre-eminence, °preponderance, ascendancy, °precedence, °power, °supremacy, °hold, °sway, hegemony, °leadership, mastery, °control, °dominion, °sovereignty, transcendence *or* transcendency, °authority, the °upper hand, the whip hand, °advantage, the °edge: *We must re-establish the predominance of intellectual vigour over crass commercialism.*

predominant *adj.* °dominant, predominating, controlling, °sovereign, ruling, °pre-eminent, preponderant, ascendant, °superior, °supreme, °leading, °paramount, °main, °chief, transcendent, °important, °telling, °influential, °primary, °prevailing, °prevalent: *England was the predominant power in the world during the 19th century. The phlogiston theory was once predominant among scientists.*

predominate *v.* Often, **predominate over**: °dominate, °control, °rule, °reign, preponderate, °outweigh, °obtain, °prevail, °overshadow, get *or* have the °upper hand, °lord it over, hold °sway, overrule: *Though the American president is a Republican, the Democrats predominate in Congress.*

pre-eminence *n.* **1** See predominance, above. **2** peerlessness, magnificence, °excellence, °distinction, eminence, inimitability, °superiority: *There is no gainsaying the pre-eminence of Shakespeare as a poet and playwright.*

pre-eminent *adj.* **1** See predominant, above. **2** °peerless, °excellent, °distinguished, °eminent, inimitable, °superb, unequalled, °matchless, °incomparable, °outstanding, °unique, unrivalled, unsurpassed, °supreme, °superior: *In her opinion, Craig is the pre-eminent authority on the subject.*

pre-eminently *adv.* °primarily, °principally, by °far, °far and away, °manifestly, °eminently, °notably, conspicuously, prominently, signally, uniquely, extraordinarily, °supremely, superbly, matchlessly, incomparably, outstandingly: *There is no doubt that Nathalie is pre-eminently qualified to direct the play.*

pre-empt *v.* °appropriate, usurp, arrogate, °take over, °assume, °take °possession of, °seize, °acquire, °take, °possess, expropriate: *All the seats on the committee had been pre-empted by the ruling faction.*

preen *v.* **1** °trim, °clean, plume, °groom: *The gliding swans stopped now and then to preen their feathers.* **2** °primp, °dress up, titivate *or* tittivate, prettify, °beautify, prink, °spruce up, deck (out), *Colloq* doll up, *Brit* °tart up: *He made Sonia wait while he preened himself before the mirror.*

preface *n.* **1** introduction, °foreword, prologue, °preamble, *Formal* proem, prolegomenon, exordium: *By way of preface, I should like to say how happy I am to be here. The preface to the book is far too long.*

—*v.* **2** °precede, °introduce, prefix, °begin, °open: *The speaker prefaced his acceptance speech with a tribute to his predecessor.*

prefatory *adj.* °opening, °introductory, °preliminary, °preparatory: *Would you like to make a few prefatory remarks introducing this evening's speaker?*

prefer *v.* **1** °favour, °like better, °fancy, °lean *or* °incline towards *or* on the side of, be °inclined, be °partial to, °pick, °select, opt for, °choose, °single out, take a °fancy to, °embrace, espouse, °approve, °esteem: *Which flavour do you prefer, chocolate or coffee? I should prefer to take my own car.* **2** °present, °offer, °propose, proffer, °advance, °submit, °tender, °put forward, °file, °lodge, °enter: *They preferred charges against the hooligans for criminal damage.*

preference *n.* **1** °favourite, °choice, °selection, °desire, °option, °pick: *My preference is the Dover sole meunière.* **2** °partiality, proclivity, °prejudice, °favouritism, predilection, °liking, °fancy, predisposition, °bent, °inclination, °leaning: *She shows a marked preference for short men.*

preferential *adj.* °advantageous, °biased, °prejudiced, °favourable, °privileged, °partial, °better, °favoured, °superior: *What entitles her to preferential treatment?*

pregnant *adj.* **1** gravid, parturient, °expectant, (heavy) with child, enceinte, *Colloq* °expecting, in a family way, *Brit* preggers, *Slang* having a bun in the oven, *Brit* in the (pudding) club, up the spout: *Her twins are only seven months old and now she's pregnant again.* **2** charged, °fraught, °loaded, °weighty, °significant, °meaningful, °suggestive, °eloquent, °expressive, °pointed: *Although she said nothing, her smile was pregnant with meaning.* **3** °fruitful, teeming, °fertile, fecund, °rich, abounding, °replete, °productive: *My mind was so pregnant with ideas that I couldn't wait to get down to work.*

prehistoric *adj.* **1** primordial, primal, primeval *or Brit also* primaeval, °primitive, earliest, °early, antediluvian, Noachian *or* Noachic, fossil, °ancient: *The prehistoric remains of yet another skeleton have been found in the peat bogs.* **2** °antiquated, out-dated, °old-fashioned, °passé: *My mother makes me wear these absolutely prehistoric clothes to school.*

prejudice *n.* **1** °partiality, °preconception, pre-judgement, °bias, °leaning, °warp, °twist, °preconceived notion, predisposition, predilection, °jaundiced eye, jaundice: *The judge showed an unfortunate prejudice against my client.* **2** °bigotry, unfairness, °bias, partisanship, °favouritism, cronyism, °discrimination, °intolerance, °inequality; racism, racialism, apartheid, Jim Crowism, sexism, (male) chauvinism: *There is still prejudice against many minority groups in society.*
—*v.* **3** °bias, °influence, °warp, °twist, °distort, °slant; °colour, jaundice, °poison: *Stop trying to prejudice me against the book, and let me form my own opinion. Are you prejudiced in favour of Anita's getting the job?*

prejudiced *adj.* **1** unfair, °one-sided, °biased, °jaundiced, °opinionated, predisposed, °partial, °partisan, non-objective, unobjective: *The prosecution objected to him as a prejudiced witness.* **2** °bigoted, °intolerant,

°narrow-minded, closed-minded, °parochial, sexist, racist, chauvinistic: *We have no room in our organization for people who are prejudiced.*

prejudicial *adj.* °injurious, damaging, °detrimental, °harmful, unfavourable, inimical, deleterious, disadvantageous, counter-productive, pernicious: *Such an investment decision might prove prejudicial to her financial security.*

preliminary *adj.* **1** °advance, °prior, °introductory, °beginning, °initial, °opening, °preparatory, °prefatory, °preceding, antecedent, forerunning; premonitory; *Formal or technical* prodromal *or* prodromic: *The preliminary design for the swimming-pool is ready. After some preliminary remarks, the ceremonies got under way.* —*n.* **2** introduction, °beginning, °opening, °preparation, °groundwork, prelude, °precedence; °overture: *We insist on rigorous training as a preliminary to working in the field.* **3 prelims**: *rarely,* **preliminaries**: introduction, °preface, °foreword, °preamble, prologue, front matter, *Formal* proem, exordium, prolegomenon, prodromus, prodrome: *The manuscript is finished and we are waiting for the prelims.*

premature *adj.* **1** °immature, °undeveloped, underdeveloped, °unfledged, untimely, unready, °early, unripe, °green: *Much premature fruit has been blown down in the winds.* **2** °hasty, untimely, ill-timed, too °early, too °soon, beforehand, °unseasonable, overhasty, °impulsive, °inopportune: *The post may be slow, but still I think September a bit premature to send Christmas cards. The discovery that money was missing accounts for his premature departure.*

prematurely *adv.* **1** untimely, too °soon, too °early: *He died prematurely at the age of 46.* **2** rashly, (over-)°hastily, at half-cock, half-cocked: *She dismissed him prematurely, before he had the time to prove himself. The gun went off prematurely, with no chance to aim it.*

premeditated *adj.* planned, °conscious, °intentional, intended, °wilful, °deliberate, °studied, purposive; contrived, preplanned, °calculated, °preconceived: *The murder was coldly premeditated. I admit to being wrong, and I have no premeditated excuses.*

premier *n.* **1** °prime °minister, PM, °head of °state, °chief °executive, president, chancellor: *The premiers of the Commonwealth met at Kuala Lumpur in 1989.* —*adj.* **2** °first, °prime, °primary, °chief, °principal, °head, °main, °foremost, top-ranking, highest-ranking, ranking, °leading, °top, °pre-eminent: *He is the premier expert in his field.*

première *n.* **1** premiere, °first night, °opening (night), début: *The première of Aïda was at the opening of the Suez Canal.* —*v.* **2** °open, début: *The film will première at the Festival Cinema tomorrow.* —*adj.* **3** °opening, début, °first, °original, °initial: *The première West-End performance is scheduled for May after a provincial tour.*

premise *n.* premiss, assumption, °proposition, postulate, °hypothesis, conjecture, °assertion, °supposition, °thesis, °presupposition, °proposal, °theorem, °surmise, °basis, °ground: *He started out with the premise that time had a beginning and will have an end.*

—*v.* **2** °assume, °propose, postulate, hypothesize, hypothecate, conjecture, °posit, assert, °suppose, °presuppose, °theorize, °surmise, °put *or* °set forth, predicate, °argue: *If you accept what Einstein premised in the Special Theory of Relativity, then you accept that space is curved.*

premium *n.* **1** °bonus, °extra, dividend, °prize, °award, °reward, °perquisite: *In our slimming competition, a premium will be paid for each pound that you lose beyond five.* **2** °incentive, °inducement, stimulus, °incitement, °lure, bait, °spur, goad, °reward, *Colloq* °come-on, *Slang US and Canadian* freebie: *Many Building Societies offer premiums to first-time buyers.* **3** value, °importance, °regard, °stock, °store, °appreciation: *We place a premium on the way our staff treat customers.* **4 at a premium**: **a** °scarce, °rare, scant, °scanty, °sparse, hard to °come by, in °short supply, *Colloq* °scarce as hen's teeth, *Chiefly Brit* °thin on the ground: *Proficient, literate, experienced editors are at a premium these days.* **b** costly, °expensive, °dear, high-priced, *Colloq* °steep, °stiff: *The convertible model of this car is at a premium.*

premonition *n.* °intuition, °foreboding, presentiment, forewarning, °suspicion, °feeling, °hunch, *Colloq* funny °feeling, °sneaking °suspicion: *I had a premonition that something terribly evil was lurking in store for me.*

preoccupied *adj.* **1** engrossed, °lost in °thought, °rapt, °thoughtful, °pensive, °absorbed, cogitating, cogitative, meditating, musing, reflecting, °reflective, contemplative, contemplating, pondering, brooding, ruminating, in a brown study: *John is preoccupied, thinking about the speech he has to deliver tonight.* **2** °vague, °offhand, °far-away, °absent-minded, abstracted, °oblivious, °unaware, wrapped up, immersed, °inattentive, distracted, distrait(e), *Colloq* turned off, *US* out of it: *From her preoccupied air it was obvious that something was wrong.*

preparation *n.* **1** *Often,* **preparations**: **a** °groundwork, spadework, °provision(s), °foundation, preparing, measures, °proceedings: *Nothing will interfere with our preparation for the royal visit.* **b** °plans, °arrangements: *We are making preparations to leave tomorrow.* **2** °fitness, °readiness, readying, preparing, training, °education, teaching, °instruction, instructing, °tuition, briefing, grooming, *Colloq* gearing up, prep, *US* prepping: *The preparation of the students was your responsibility.* **3** °drawing up, draughting, planning, °setting up, putting together, organizing, °organization, composing, making: *How is your preparation of the new proposal coming along?* **4** °work, preparing, getting °ready, °study, studying, practising, °practice, *Colloq* cramming, *Brit* swotting: *All my preparation for the exam was to no avail.* **5** °substance, °compound, concoction, °mixture, °product, °material, °stuff, °composition: *This preparation is a furniture wax, not a suntan lotion.*

preparatory *adj.* **1** preparative, °preliminary, °introductory, °prefatory, °opening: *After some preparatory warnings about safety, the scuba-diving lessons began.* **2** °elementary, °basic, °essential, °fundamental, °primary, °rudimentary: *His preparatory training left him ill-equipped to deal with* *such a major problem.* **3 preparatory to**: °before, in °preparation for, °preceding: *Preparatory to the mission, we were briefed by MI5.*

prepare *v.* **1** (get *or* make) °ready, °prime, °arrange, (put in) °order, °organize, °provide for, make °provision(s) for, lay the °groundwork (for), make °fit, °fit (out), °equip, °outfit, °adapt: *Have you prepared adequately for the meeting? We prepared the house to receive guests.* **2** °train, (get *or* make) °ready, °study, °practise, *Colloq* °cram, *Brit* swot, °get up: *He is preparing to take an exam.* **3** °train, °educate, °teach, (get *or* make) °ready, °groom, °brief, °develop: *Her mother is preparing her for the next Olympics.* **4** cook (up), °make, do, *Colloq* °whip up, *US and Canadian* °fix: *I shall prepare dinner for eight o'clock.* **5** °manufacture, °fabricate, °produce, °make, °put out, °build, °construct, °assemble, °put together, °turn out, °fashion, °forge, °mould: *Our company prepares components for the printing industry.* **6** °brace, °strengthen, °steel, °fortify, °ready: *When I saw the doctor's face, I prepared myself for bad news.* **7** °process, °produce, °make, °treat, °change, °modify, °transform: *This fabric has been specially prepared to repel stains.*

prepared *adj.* **1** °ready, °set, °advance, pre-arranged, planned: *We have six prepared questions for the interview.* **2** treated, processed, modified, changed: *Using an etching needle, incise the lines on the prepared surface of the steel plate.* **3** °willing, °disposed, predisposed, °able, °inclined, of a °mind; °ready, (all) °set: *Are you prepared to apologize?* **4** oven-ready, microwave-ready, microwavable, °instant, convenience, ready-to-eat, ready-to-serve, precooked, °ready-made: *He lives alone and usually buys prepared dinners that just need reheating.*

preparedness *n.* °vigilance, alertness, °readiness, °fitness: *The armed forces were kept in a continuous state of preparedness.*

preponderance *n.* **1** °majority, greater °part, °bulk, °mass, lion's °share: *The preponderance of voters want a change of government.* **2** °weight, °influence, weightiness, °superiority, °supremacy, °predominance, primacy, ascendancy, °sway, °strength, °force, °power, °advantage, °control, °authority, hegemony, °leadership, °rule: *Good has always appeared to have an incontestable preponderance over evil.*

prepossessing *adj.* °attractive, appealing, °pleasing, °favourable, °engaging, charming, captivating, fascinating, winsome, °winning, °magnetic, alluring, bewitching, °taking, °fetching, °inviting, good-looking, °handsome, °lovely, °beautiful: *She is a woman of prepossessing appearance and a delightful nature.*

preposterous *adj.* °absurd, °ridiculous, °ludicrous, laughable, risible, asinine, °foolish, °senseless, irrational, °nonsensical, fatuous, fatuitous, °mindless, °insane, °crazy, crack-brained, °mad, idiotic, moronic, imbecilic, °incredible, °unbelievable, °outrageous, °extravagant, °extraordinary, °extreme, °exorbitant, °outlandish, *outré*, °weird, °bizarre, *Slang* barmy, nutty, screwy, batty, dotty, wacky, loony, cuckoo, *US* balmy: *To claim that it is all my fault is simply preposterous!*

prerequisite *adj.* **1** °essential, °necessary, requisite, °imperative, °indispensable, °obligatory, required, called-for, demanded: *Naval service is a prerequisite condition for joining the club.*
—*n.* **2** °precondition, °requirement, °qualification, requisite, °condition, *sine qua non*, °proviso, °provision, °necessity: *A thorough grounding in mathematics is a prerequisite for the study of advanced physics.*

prerogative *n.* °privilege, °right, °liberty, °power, °due, °advantage, °licence, franchise, °claim, °sanction, °authority, authorization: *As managing director, she exercises her prerogative to park her car closest to the door.*

prescribe *v.* ordain, °order, °direct, °dictate, °demand, °decree, °require, enjoin, °rule, °set (down), °stipulate, °command, °instruct, °define, °specify, °impose, °lay down, °exact, constrain: *The doctor prescribed rest. An independent journalist, Healey would not let anyone prescribe what he could or could not write.*

prescription *n.* **1** °formula, °recipe, °instruction, °direction: *The prescription is for three tablets a day, and this dose must not be exceeded.* **2** °remedy, medication, °medicine, °drug, °preparation, medicament: *That prescription had no effect at all on my headache.*

prescriptive *adj.* °dictatorial, constrictive, didactic, restrictive, °dogmatic, °authoritarian, °overbearing, autocratic, imperious: *As grammar is a description of how language works, it cannot be prescriptive.*

presence *n.* **1** °proximity, nearness, closeness, adjacency, °vicinity, *Formal* propinquity: *The presence of a hospital near her home made Aunt Mary feel more secure.* **2** °attendance, °company, °companionship, °society, °association, °existence, °manifestation, manifestness, being: *The Queen honoured us by her presence at the unveiling of the plaque.* **3** °poise, self-assurance, °bearing, self-possession, °confidence, mien, °carriage, comportment, deportment, °air, °personality, °aspect, °aura, °appearance: *When Geoffrey entered, his presence created quite a stir.* **4** °spirit, wraith, °spectre, °shade: *I had the vague but pervading sense that an unidentifiable presence was with me in the empty room.* **5 presence of mind**: aplomb, °sophistication, coolness, cool-headedness, composure, imperturbability, phlegm, °sang-froid, self-possession, self-assurance, °calm, equanimity, level-headedness, quick-wittedness, alertness, *Colloq* °cool: *With great presence of mind, Grainger walked up to the man and took the gun from him.*

present¹ *adj.* **1** °current, °contemporary, present-day, existing, existent, up to °date, *Colloq* °now: *Do you understand the present generation?* **2** °nearby, nearest, °immediate, closest, adjacent, proximate, propinquitous; °close, °remaining; accounted for: *Everybody has been awful to me—present company excepted. All those present heard what she said to me.*
—*n.* **3 at present**: (right *or* just) °now, for the °time being, for the present, today, these days, *Non-Standard* °presently, *Colloq* at this °point in °time: *I am not ready to invest at present.* **4 the present**: the °time being, the °moment, the hour, the nonce, this °juncture, these days, our times; today, (right) °now, °nowadays; *Colloq* this °point in °time: *She lives for the present, and never thinks of the consequences.*

present² n. **1** °gift: *May I open my birthday presents now?* **2** °donation, °offering, °bounty, °grant, °largesse, contribution, °endowment: *I'll make you a present of the painting if you like it.* **3** °tip, gratuity, *pourboire*, baksheesh or backsheesh, °bonus; alms, hand-out, °dole, °aid, °allowance: *She gave the maître d'hôtel a present for looking after us so well.*
—v. **4** °introduce, °acquaint with, °make known: *I'd like to present my wife, Cordelia, who has been looking forward to meeting you.* **5** °offer, °give, °stage, °show, °exhibit, °put on (°show), °mount, °produce: *The local players will present a new production of Blithe Spirit tonight.* **6** °give (out), °award, °confer (on), °bestow (on), °turn or °hand over, °grant, °provide, °furnish; °dispense, °distribute, °dole out, °pass out, °deal out, °mete out: *They presented her with a prize for the best poem. Is it tonight that they present the awards?* **7** °offer, °bring (in or up), proffer, °tender, °introduce, °produce, °submit, °set or °put forth, °put forward, adduce; °register, °file, °record: *The lawyer for the defence presented evidence of his client's alibi.* **8** °introduce, °announce, *Brit* compère, *Colloq* emcee: *And here, to present our show, is the inimitable Reginald Norton!*

presentable adj. **1** °fit, °fitting, °suitable, °acceptable, °satisfactory, °adequate, °passable, °tolerable, admissible, all °right, allowable, up to °par or °standard or the °mark, °good enough, *Colloq* up to °scratch, °OK or okay, up to snuff: *Whether that argument is presentable in a court of law is disputable.* **2** °decent, °proper, °polite, °decorous, °respectable, °well-bred, well-mannered, °fit to be seen: *After a bath, shave, and change of clothing he looked quite presentable.*

presentation n. **1** giving, bestowal, °offering, proffering, presenting, °award, awarding, conferral, conferring, °delivery; °donation: *The presentation of the prizes will be at the annual dinner.* **2** °appearance, °image, °display, visual(s), °spectacle, °show, °performance, °demonstration, °production: *The text of the proposal was fine, but the presentation could be improved.* **3** début, °launch, introduction, unveiling, disclosure: *We attended the presentation of the latest electric car.*

presently adv. °soon, by and by, in a little while, °shortly, after a short time, in due course, after a while or a time, before long, in a °moment or a °minute or a while, *Archaic or literary* anon, *Colloq* in a jiffy, in two shakes (of a lamb's tail), *Non-Standard* °now, at °present: *The show opens presently in the West End. I shall be with you presently.*

preservation n. **1** °upkeep, °maintenance, °care, °conservation: *The preservation of old paintings has become an art in itself.* **2** keeping, retention, retaining, perpetuation, perpetuating, continuation, °safe keeping, °security, safeguarding, °protection, protecting, °conservation: *Several charities are dedicated to the preservation of our heritage.*

preserve v. **1** °keep °safe, °protect, °guard, take °care of, °care for, °safeguard, °watch over, °shield, °shelter, °defend, °spare: *What can we do to preserve ourselves from this terrible pestilence? May God preserve me, I never expected to see you again!* **2** °keep (up), °maintain, °conserve, °spare, °perpetuate, °continue, °support, °sustain, °save: *We developed a technique to preserve antique furniture. The sea preserves much of the*

heat it absorbs in the summer. It is difficult to preserve one's sanity in this madhouse. **3** °conserve, °put up, pickle, °cure, smoke, kipper, °salt, corn, marinate, can, °freeze, freeze-dry, °refrigerate, °dry, dehydrate, vacuum-pack; embalm, mummify: *The berries were preserved by bottling and freezing. Some of the remains were preserved for hundreds of years.*
—n. **4** Often, **preserves**: °conserve(s), °jam, jelly, confiture, marmalade: *Susan likes thick toast with butter and preserves for tea.* **5** (°game) °reserve, °reservation, °sanctuary, *Brit* °park: *No hunting is allowed in this preserve.*

preside v. °supervise, °run, °oversee, °direct, °operate, °lead, °head (up), °govern, °rule, °manage, °handle, °control, °direct, °chair, °administer, administrate, °regulate, °officiate: *Melissa presides over the meetings of the board.*

press v. **1** °subject to or °exert °pressure or °force, °force, °push, impel, °thrust, °bear (on), °weigh on or upon, °jam, °cram, °crush; °pressure or *Brit* also pressurize: *The crowd was pressing against the door. Although hard pressed at first, we eventually won.* **2** °squeeze, compress, °depress, °push: *When the picture is in focus, press this button to release the shutter.* **3** °squeeze, °crush, compress, mash: *After harvesting, the grapes are pressed to extract the juice.* **4** iron, °smooth, °flatten, put through a mangle; steam: *I shall have to press my jacket before going out to dinner.* **5** °clasp, °embrace, °hug, °hold (°close or °tight(ly)), take in one's arms, throw one's arms about or around, °cleave to, *Archaic* clip: *She pressed the child to her with great affection.* **6** constrain, °urge, °force, °pressure, compel, °demand, °persuade, °induce, °prod, °provoke, importune, °beseech, °ask, °request, °beg, entreat: *They pressed me to tell where the money was hidden.* **7** °crowd, °flock, °gather, °mill, °swarm, °throng, °seethe, °cluster, congregate, °meet, °converge, °huddle: *The reporters pressed round the chancellor to catch every word.*
—n. **8** crowding, °gathering, thronging, converging, convergence, °crowd, °throng, °swarm, °cluster, °huddle, °pack, °herd, °host, multitude, horde, °mob, °crush: *When the doors opened, the huge press of people pushed onto the train.* **9** °urgency, °haste, °hurry, °hustle, bustle, °pressure, °stress: *The press of business required me to postpone my trip to Paris.* **10 the press: a** newspapers, °papers, Fleet Street, the fourth estate, the media, the wire or °news services, broadcasting, °television, °radio: *The press will have a field-day when this news gets out.* **b** newspaper people, newspapermen or newspaperwomen, newsmen or newswomen, °reporters, °correspondents, ladies or gentlemen of the press, °journalists, commentators, paparazzi, *Brit* leader-writers, *US* °editorial °writers, *Colloq* news-hounds, *Brit* journos: *The doors were opened and the press were invited in.*

pressing adj. °urgent, compelling, °crucial, °pivotal, °burning, °grave, °serious, °major, °important, °vital, high-priority, °critical, °portentous, °momentous, °profound, °significant: *Some pressing matters kept me late at the office.*

pressure n. **1** °force, compression, °weight, °power, °strength: *The air pressure in your tyres is low. The pressure of the water burst the pipe.* **2** compression, °pressing, squeezing, compressing,

°tension, °stress, crushing: *The pressure of a tourniquet has to be loosened now and then.* **3** °affliction, °oppression, °press, °weight, °burden, °load, albatross, °strain, °stress, °urgency, demands, exigency *or* exigencies, vexation, °distress, °trouble(s), adversity, °difficulty *or* difficulties, °straits, constraint(s), °problem(s): *Pressure of work prevents me from taking any time away from the office. When interest rates increase, we all feel financial pressure.* **4** °influence, °power, °sway, constraint, insistence, coercion, intimidation, arm-twisting, °inducement, °persuasion, urging, °pressing: *Without more pressure from local residents, the roadworks will not be completed in time.*
—*v.* **5** °persuade, °influence; °prevail upon *or* on, °press, °urge, °sway, °intimidate, bring pressure to bear (on), apply pressure (on *or* to), coerce, °force, compel, constrain, °require, °demand, °make, °insist upon *or* on, *Brit* pressurize, *Colloq* twist (someone's) arm, °lean on, turn the heat on, *Slang* put the screws on *or* to: *They pressured him to take the assignment in New Zealand.*

prestige *n.* °status, °reputation, °standing, °rank, stature, °importance, °significance, eminence, °esteem, °pre-eminence, °prominence, °predominance, primacy, °superiority, °supremacy, ascendancy, °distinction, °renown, °regard, °fame, °cachet, repute, °celebrity, °glamour, stardom: *To raise money, someone with prestige must be found to serve as director of the charity.*

prestigious *adj.* °important, °significant, °eminent, °estimable, °imposing, °impressive, °pre-eminent, °prominent, °distinguished, august, °dignified, °renowned, °famous, famed, °well-known, °illustrious, acclaimed, respected, °celebrated, °noted, °notable, °noteworthy, °outstanding, °glorious, honoured, °glamorous: *She may be a prestigious author, but she does not live at a very prestigious address.*

presumably *adv.* °probably, in all °likelihood, (very *or* most) °likely, in all °probability, °seemingly, °doubtless(ly), indubitably, no doubt, °undoubtedly, unquestionably, without a doubt, °surely, certainly, on the °face of it, all things considered, all things being equal: *Presumably, you have heard the one about the colonel's poodle.*

presume *v.* **1** °assume, take for granted, °suppose, °surmise, °infer, °presuppose, °take it, °gather, °understand, °think, °believe, °imagine, °suspect, °fancy, conjecture, postulate, °posit, °theorize, °speculate, hypothesize, hypothecate, *US and Canadian* °guess: *For some unaccountable reason, we presumed that your train would arrive on time. Dr Livingstone, I presume?* **2** °dare, take the °liberty, be so °presumptuous as, make (so) °bold (as), have the audacity *or* °effrontery, go so °far as, °venture: *Who is he to presume to judge others?* **3** Often, **presume on** *or* **upon**: °encroach (on *or* upon), °impose (on *or* upon), take liberties (with), °intrude (on *or* upon *or* into): *I hate to presume on our friendship, but could you lend me some money?*

presumption *n.* **1** °arrogance, °pride, °effrontery, audacity, boldness, brazenness, °impudence, °impertinence, insolence, temerity, overconfidence, presumptuousness, forwardness, immodesty, *Colloq* pushiness, cheek, cheekiness, °nerve, °gall, chutzpah, °brass, *Brit* °brass neck: *He had the presumption to ask my age.* **2** assumption, °supposition, °presupposition, °preconception, °premise *or* premiss, °surmise, °proposition, postulation; °probability, °likelihood, plausibility, °feasibility: *The presumption of the innocence of a person accused of a crime is established in law.* **3** assumption, °stand, °position, °inference, °feeling, °deduction, conclusion, °conviction, °bias, °guess, theory, °hypothesis, conjecture, °belief, °thought; °suspicion: *Having examined the evidence, the pathologist's presumption was that the victim had died of natural causes.* **4** °ground(s), °reason, °basis, °evidence: *What is your presumption for thinking that you might win the lottery?*

presumptive *adj.* **1** °likely, °reasonable, °plausible, °tenable, believable, credible, conceivable, °acceptable, justifiable, °sensible, °rational, °sound: *There is strong presumptive evidence, but we need proof.* **2** inferred, presumed, °assumed, °supposed, °understood, predicted, predicated: *As King Richard was childless, his brother was heir presumptive to the Crown.*

presumptuous *adj.* °arrogant, °proud, prideful, °audacious, °bold, °brazen, saucy, °impudent, °impertinent, °insolent, temerarious, °brash, °overconfident, overweening, °forward, presuming, °immodest, °egotistical, *Colloq* °pushy, °cheeky, too big for one's boots, *Brit* °uppish: *He is presumptuous enough to think he can do no wrong.*

presuppose *v.* See presume, **1**, above.

presupposition *n.* See presumption, **1**, **2**, above.

pretence *n.* **1** °show, °display, °pretension, °ostentation, °airs, °front, façade, °appearance, make-believe, fiction, °hypocrisy, fakery, faking, feigning, humbuggery, humbug, °deception, °artifice, °pretext, posturing, pretentiousness, pretending, °camouflage, cover-up: *Her charming manner was all pretence, for in reality she despised him.* **2** °hoax, humbug, °artifice, °pretext, °sham, °show, °pose, façade, °front, cover-up, °cover, °cloak, °veil, °mask, °masquerade, °disguise, °guise, °deception, °ruse, °dodge, °blind, °fabrication, °invention, fiction, °story, fable, make-believe, fairy °tale, figment, falsification, °impression: *His loyalty was a pretence under which he carried on many liaisons.* **3** °excuse, °pretext, °pretension: *They would ring for the butler on the slightest pretence, just to impress us.*

pretend *v.* **1** feign, °profess, °represent, °allege, °make °believe, °make out: *Let's pretend that we are royalty. Often, he pretends to be me.* **2** °try, °attempt, °endeavour, °venture, °presume, °undertake: *I could not pretend to guess the number of people attending last night's meeting.* **3** °make °believe, °act *or* °play, play-act, °fake, feign, put on an °act, dissemble, °sham, sail under false °colours: *Is she serious about wanting you to leave or was she just pretending?*

pretended *adj.* °so-called, °alleged, asserted, °reputed, °professed, ostensible, purported, °imaginary, make-believe, °fictitious, °fictional, °sham, °false, °fake, feigned, °bogus, °counterfeit, °spurious, *Colloq* °phoney *or* *US* also phony, pseudo, °pretend: *So this is the pretended hero of yesterday's battle!*

pretender *n.* claimant, aspirant, °candidate, °suitor, °rival, seeker: *He was the pretender to the Scottish throne.*

pretension *n.* **1** Often, **pretensions**: °claim(s), °pretence(s), °aspiration(s), ambitiousness, °ambition(s): *He is known to have pretensions to the chancellorship.* **2** °pretext, °pretence, pretentiousness, °ostentation, pretending, °affectation, °hypocrisy: *Gladys has behaved without pretension and with great sincerity.*

pretentious *adj.* **1** °ostentatious, °showy, °superficial, °pompous, °arrogant, °bombastic, °inflated, high-flown, exaggerated, vainglorious, fastuous, °grandiose, grandiloquent, °extravagant, magniloquent: *The minister's pretentious language is a bit too much to take.* **2** °snobbish, °lofty, °haughty, flaunting, *Colloq* high and °mighty, highfalutin *or* hifa-lutin, °hoity-toity, high-hat, *Slang* snotty, *Brit* toffee-nosed: *That new couple next door are so pretentious—they think that nobody is good enough to associate with them!*

pretext *n.* **1** °pretence, °excuse, °camouflage, °guise, °disguise, °cover, °veil, °cloak, °colour: *They carried on the surveillance under pretext of working on the sewer.* **2** °ruse, red herring, °cover (°story), °rationale, °pretence, rationalization, °explanation: *What pretext did the thief use that made you let him in?*

pretty *adj.* **1** °comely, °attractive, good-looking, nice-looking, appealing, °lovely, °cute, mignon(ne), °graceful, °fair, °bonny, °fetching, charming, winsome, °beautiful, pulchritudinous, *Colloq* easy on the eye(s): *A pretty girl is like a melody. That's a very pretty cottage.* **2** °tuneful, melodic, °melodious, dulcet, °musical, °lyrical, °harmonious, catchy, mellifluous, euphonious: *He played a pretty tune on the piano.*
—*adv.* **3** °rather, °quite, °fairly, °moderately, reasonably, tolerably; °somewhat; °very, °extremely, unbelievably, incredibly: *The children put on a pretty good performance, I thought. He had become pretty fat since we last saw him.*

prevail *v.* **1** hold °sway, °win (out), °predominate, °succeed, °triumph, gain *or* achieve a °victory, prove °superior, gain mastery *or* °control: *It is sometimes disappointing to learn that right does not always prevail.* **2** °predominate, be °prevalent *or* widespread *or* °current, preponderate, °dominate, be the order of the day: *As usual during Oktoberfest in Bavaria, revelry prevailed.* **3** **prevail on** *or* **upon**: °persuade, °induce, °influence, °sway, °dispose; °incline, °win over, °bring round, °convince: *We prevailed on the guard to let us through the gate.*

prevailing *adj.* **1** °dominant, °predominant, °prevalent, °main, °chief, °principal, °common(est), °usual, °customary, °universal: *The prevailing winds are westerlies.* **2** °influential, °effective, °effectual, dominating, affecting, °powerful, °potent, °forceful, ruling, °telling, °main, °principal: *The prevailing religion there is Buddhism.*

prevalence *n.* **1** prevalency, frequency, commonness, currency, universality, ubiquitousness, ubiquity, pervasiveness, omnipresence, extensiveness; °predominance, °practice, acceptance, °popularity: *The prevalence of disease among the population is distressing.* **2** °sway, °control, °rule,

primacy, ascendancy, mastery, °predominance: *The prevalence of bushido in Japan has diminished little since 1945.*

prevalent *adj.* °universal, °catholic, °common, °frequent, °prevailing, °current, ubiquitous, °pervasive, omnipresent, °general, °usual, °customary, commonplace, °extensive, widespread, established, ascendant, °dominant, °predominant, governing, ruling: *A desire for change is prevalent throughout the country.*

prevent *v.* °anticipate, °preclude, obviate, °forestall, avert, °avoid, °prohibit, °ban, °bar, °forbid, interdict, °taboo, enjoin, proscribe, °foil, °frustrate, °obstruct, debar, °intercept, °nip in the bud, abort, °thwart, °check, °block, °ward *or* °fend *or* stave off, baffle, balk *or* baulk, (put a) °stop (to), °arrest, (bring to a) °halt, °hinder, °impede, °curb, °restrain, °hamper, °inhibit, °delay, °retard, °slow, °mitigate, °control: *Some diseases can be prevented by inoculation or vaccination. There is nothing to prevent us from leaving. The barrier was built to prevent flooding.*

prevention *n.* preventing, °anticipation, preclusion, obviation, forestalling, avoidance, avoiding, °prohibition, prohibiting, °ban, banning, °bar, °barring, forbiddance, °forbidding, interdiction, interdicting, °taboo, tabooing, enjoining, °injunction, proscription, proscribing, foiling, frustration, frustrating, °obstruction, obstructing, debarment, debarring, interception, intercepting, abortion, aborting, thwarting, checking, °check, blocking, °block, warding *or* fending *or* staving off, balk *or* baulk, balking *or* baulking, stopping, °arrest, °arresting, °halt, °halting, °hindrance, hindering, impedance, impeding, °curb, curbing, °restraint, restraining, hampering, °inhibition, inhibiting, °delay, delaying, retardation, retarding, slowing, mitigation, °mitigating, °control, controlling: *The first item on the agenda is the prevention of cruelty to children. As the total prevention of crime is impossible, we must at least try to curb it.*

preventive *adj.* **1** preventative, preventing, hindering, impeding, restraining, hampering, inhibitive *or* inhibitory, inhibiting, restrictive: *We must take preventive steps to ensure the stability of the rate of exchange.* **2** preventative, prophylactic, precautionary, anticipatory *or* anticipative, °protective, counteractive: *Preventive means are available to limit heart disease.*
—*n.* **3** preventative, °hindrance, °curb, °inhibition, °impediment, °block, °barrier, °obstacle, °obstruction: *Caffeine is one of the most powerful preventives of sleep that exists.* **4** preventative, prophylactic, °protection, °shield, °safeguard, °prevention, countermeasure, counteractant, counter-agent, inoculum *or* inoculant, vaccine, serum, °antidote, °remedy: *Heart specialists have recommended an aspirin every other day as a preventive to arterial blood clotting.*

preview *n.* °advance showing, °private showing; °opening, *vernissage*: *We saw the Picasso exhibition at a preview held for friends of the gallery.*

previous *adj.* **1** °former, °prior, °past, earlier, one-time, °foregoing, °sometime, erstwhile, °preceding, *Literary* quondam, *Archaic* whilom: *A previous owner of the house filled in the fish-pond.* **2** °prior, °former, °foregoing, above, °preceding, *Formal* antecedent, anterior, aforementioned, above-mentioned, before-mentioned, aforesaid, above-named: *Please see the previous examples in the Foreword.* **3** °premature, untimely, too °soon or °early: *Isn't putting up Christmas decorations in October being a bit previous?* **4 previous to**: °previously to, °before, °prior to, °preceding, anterior to, antecedent to: *Previous to the advent of motor cars, we had traffic jams of horse-drawn vehicles.*

previously *adv.* °before, °once, °formerly, earlier, at one °time, then, beforehand, heretofore, theretofore, hitherto, thitherto, in the °past, in days gone by, in days of old, in days or time °past, in the °old days, some time ago, a while ago, °once upon a time, yesterday, *Literary* in days of yore, in olden days *or* times: *The same thing had happened previously when I was in London. Previously, people lived more relaxed lives—or so we like to think.*

prey *n.* **1** °quarry, °kill, °game, °objective, °target: *The lioness singled out her prey from the herd of zebra.* **2** °victim, °target, °objective; °dupe, *Colloq* mark, *Slang* fall guy, °pushover, *Brit* °mug: *A public company with huge cash reserves, United Vector seemed easy prey for a take-over bid.* —*v.* **3 prey on** *or* **upon: a** °live off, °feed on *or* upon, °eat, °consume, °devour, °kill, °destroy, °stalk, °pursue, °hunt, °seize: *These snakes prey mostly upon other snakes.* **b** °victimize, °go after, °exploit, °use, take °advantage of, °intimidate, °bully, °cheat, °dupe, °swindle, gull, °trick, snooker, °defraud, °outwit, °outsmart, outfox, °hoodwink, *Literary* cozen, *Colloq* rook, bamboozle, flimflam: *An unscrupulous gang is preying on the elderly, persuading them to invest in non-existent properties.* **c** °oppress, °weigh on *or* upon, °burden, °depress, °distress, °strain, vex, °worry: *His wretched condition preyed very much on her mind.*

price *n.* **1** charge, °cost, °expense, °expenditure, °outlay, °payment, °amount, °figure, °fee; °quotation, appraisal, value, valuation, °evaluation, °worth: *The price of this lamp is too high. What is the price of that box? Can he afford the price of a ticket? The current price of a London flat is out of my reach.* **2** °sacrifice, °toll, °penalty, °cost, consequence: *Loss of his freedom was too high a price for standing by his principles.* **3** °reward, °bounty, °premium, °prize, °payment, °bonus, °honorarium, *Literary* guerdon: *The gunfighter had a price of $1,000 on his head.* **4 without price**: See priceless, 1, below. —*v.* **5** value, °evaluate, °rate, assay, assess, °cost (out): *How would you price a piece of furniture like this chair?*

priceless *adj.* **1** costly, °dear, °expensive, high-priced, valuable, °invaluable, °precious, °inestimable, incalculable; irreplaceable, °unique: *The vaults in the Vatican contain a king's ransom in priceless jewels.* **2** °hilarious, °riotous, (screamingly) °funny, side-splitting, °hysterical, droll, comical, amusing: *The expression on his face when he realized it was a joke was priceless.*

pricey *adj.* pricy, °expensive, °dear, costly, °exorbitant, °outrageous, °excessive, extortionate, *Colloq* °steep, *Brit* over the odds: *The restaurant where she took him was certainly pricey, but the food was excellent.*

prick *n.* **1** °puncture, pinhole, pinprick; °hole, perforation: *For the blood test, the doctor made a tiny prick in my finger with a needle.* **2** °sting,

°pinch, °twinge, °prickle, tingle, °pain: *The teacher leapt from her chair the instant she felt the prick of the tack.* —*v.* **3** °puncture, °pierce, °stab, °jab, °punch, °perforate, °riddle; °lance: *Using a pin, prick tiny holes in the paper to let the steam escape. The doctor pricked a boil on my neck.* **4** °stab, °sting, °hurt, °prickle, °pinch, °bite, °smart: *The hypodermic needle really pricked me when it went in.*

prickle *n.* **1** °spine, °bristle, barb, °thorn, bur *or* burr, needle, tine, °spike, °spur, prong: *The prickles make the brambles cling to your clothes.* **2** pricking, prickliness, °itch, itchiness, °sting, tingling, tingle: *I felt the prickle of the rough wool against my skin.* —*v.* **3** tingle, °sting, °itch, °smart: *Sloane complained that the beard he had to grow for the pirate role made his face prickle.* **4** °stick, °jab, °prick: *The child's hands had been prickled by the chestnuts.*

prickly *adj.* **1** bristly, °thorny, brambly, spiny, barbed, briery *or* briary, spinous, spiky, *Technical* setaceous, setose, acanthoid, aciculate, aculeate, muricate, spiculate: *Dad's face is all prickly when he hasn't shaved.* **2** tingling, stinging, pricking, prickling, itchy, crawly, crawling: *The squeak of the chalk on the blackboard gives me a prickly feeling.* **3** °touchy, °irritable, °petulant, °cantankerous, °testy, °waspish, bad-tempered, °peevish, fractious, °short-tempered, curmudgeonly, *Colloq* °cranky: *Moira gets a bit prickly if you ask her why she married Noel.* **4** nettlesome, °thorny, °ticklish, °touchy, °troublesome, °intricate, °complicated, complex, knotty, °hard, °difficult, contentious: *The prickly problem of how to pay for the university must still be faced.*

pride *n.* **1** °honour, proudness, °self-esteem, °self-respect, *amour propre*, °dignity: *It is gratifying to be able to look with pride on one's children's achievements.* **2** °conceit, egotism, self-importance, °vanity, hubris, °arrogance, overconfidence, overweeningness, self-admiration, self-love, smugness, haughtiness, hauteur, °snobbery, snobbishness, *Colloq* uppitiness: *Pride goeth before a fall. Her pride stems from an exaggerated notion of her own worth.* **3** °boast, °flower, °best, °prize, °pride and °joy, °treasure, °jewel, °gem: *Those model railway trains are Eustace's pride and joy.* —*v.* **4** Usually, **pride oneself on**: be °proud of, take °pride in, °delight in, °revel in, °celebrate, °glory in: *Irena prides herself on having made her own way in life, without anyone's help.*

priest *n.* priestess, °clergyman *or* clergywoman, ecclesiastic, cleric, churchman *or* churchwoman, reverend, vicar, °divine, man *or* woman of the °cloth, man *or* woman of God, curate, confessor, °minister (of the Gospel), servant of God, °father, mother, °holy man *or* woman, °preacher, °missionary, evangelist, abbé, abbot *or* abbess, *Colloq* padre: *The oak tree was sacred to Druid priests.*

priestly *adj.* °clerical, ecclesiastical, °pastoral, hieratic, sacerdotal; ministerial, canonical, °missionary: *She has taken her priestly vows.*

prig *n.* (ultra-)°conservative, °prude, °purist, pedant, school-ma'm, °puritan, (Mrs) Grundy, Grundyite, Grundyist, precisionist, precisian, conformist, formalist, *Colloq* stuffed shirt, °stick-in-the-mud, °goody-goody: *A terrible prig, the headmaster forbade even the slightest hint of slang usage.*

priggish *adj.* (ultra-)°conservative, prim, demure, °prudish, °purist, puristic, °pedantic, school-marmish, °strait-laced, °hidebound, stiff-necked, puritanical, conformist, (Mrs) Grundyish, punctilious, °formal, formalistic, °strict, °severe, °fastidious, °fussy, °particular; °precious, *précieux* or *précieuse*, niminy-piminy, over-nice, *Colloq* °stick-in-the-mud, °goody-goody, °prissy, old-maidish, stuffed-shirt, °stuffy, uptight, nit-picking, *Brit* °twee: *Victorians were less priggish in their private behaviour than in their public image.*

primarily *adv.* **1** °principally, °mainly, °chiefly, °especially, at °bottom, °particularly, °first of all, °pre-eminently, basically, essentially, fundamentally, on the °whole, for the most °part, mostly, predominantly or predominately, °generally: *The rain in Spain falls primarily in the plain.* **2** initially, °originally, from or at the °start, °first (and °foremost), in the °first instance, *ab initio: The colonists, primarily refugees from England, began to settle the New World in the 17th century.*

primary *adj.* **1** °first, °prime, °principal, °chief, °main, °leading, °pre-eminent, °cardinal, °fundamental, °basic, °essential, °predominant, °elementary, °elemental, underlying: *The primary reason I want to see you is to discuss your future with the company. The primary meaning of a word is given first.* **2** earliest, °first, °original, °initial, °primitive, primeval or *Brit also* primaeval, primordial, embryonic, germinal, °beginning, °ultimate: *The primary source of life was possibly a sort of soup containing proteins and other molecules.* **3** firsthand, °direct, °immediate: *Bauxite is the primary source of aluminium ore.* **4** °elementary, °basic, °rudimentary, °fundamental: *One of the primary lessons we are taught is consideration for others.* **5** unmixed, unadulterated, °pure, °simple, °rudimentary, °fundamental, °principal: *The primary colours in art are red, yellow, and blue.*

prime *adj.* **1** See **primary, 1,** above. **2** °best, °foremost, °chief; °first-rate, first-class, °choice, °select, °superior, °pre-eminent, °leading, ranking, °predominant, °unparalleled, °matchless, °peerless, °noteworthy, °outstanding, °admirable, °worthy, °exceptional, °excellent, °extraordinary: *She is a prime example of the results of a modern education. Arthur is certainly a prime candidate for the position.* **3** °original, °fundamental, °basic, °elemental, °elementary: *The prime cause of scurvy is lack of fresh fruit and vegetables.*
—*n.* **4** °youth, springtime; °best years, heyday, °pinnacle, °acme, °peak, °zenith: *Some people reach the prime of life at 60.*
—*v.* **5** (make or get) °ready, °prepare, °educate, °teach, °instruct, °coach, °train, °tutor, °drill: *Has Sonia been fully primed to take over the chairmanship when Sir William steps down?* **6** °inform, °advise, °notify, apprise, °brief: *Having read your book, I am fully primed on American history.*

primitive *adj.* **1** °first, °original, °aboriginal, earliest, primordial, primal, primeval or *Brit also* primaeval, °pristine, °prehistoric; antediluvian, Noachian or Noachic, °old, °ancient: *In its most primitive state, life probably originated from some random strings of molecules. The most primitive farming tools date from some 10,000 years ago.* **2** °crude, °rude, °unrefined, °raw, barbaric, uncultured, °barbarian, °coarse, °rough,

°uncivilized, °savage, uncultivated, °unsophisticated, uncouth: *I cannot tolerate Nigel's primitive table manners.* **3** °simple, °basic, simplistic, °naïve, °childlike, °unsophisticated, uncultivated, °unrefined, unpolished, °rough, untutored, untaught, untrained, unschooled, °undeveloped: *Gary collects paintings of the primitive school and has one by Grandma Moses.*

primp *v.* °preen, prink, prettify, titivate or tittivate, plume, °dress up, °groom, *Colloq* doll up, get (all) dolled up, °spruce up, put on one's °best bib and tucker, *Chiefly Brit* °tart up, get (all) tarted up, *Slang* deck out, trick out or up, put on one's glad °rags, *Brit* fig out, *US* gussy up, get (all) gussied up, °dude up: *She was primping before the mirror, awaiting the arrival of her beau.*

princely *adj.* **1** °lavish, °bountiful, °generous, °liberal, °ample, °substantial, °huge, °enormous: *They paid a princely sum for their stately home in Surrey.* **2** °lavish, °magnificent, °splendid, °luxurious, °majestic, °royal, °regal, °sumptuous, °superb, *Colloq* ritzy, swank(y), °posh, °plush: *The hotel laid on princely accommodation for us with rooms overlooking the sea.* **3** °royal, °noble, °regal, °sovereign, of °royal or °noble blood or rank: *Who would have thought that our humble home would ever shelter a princely guest?*

principal *adj.* **1** °chief, °primary, °prime, °paramount, °main, °first, °foremost, ranking, °pre-eminent, °predominant, °dominant, °prevailing; °leading, starring: *The principal reason I'm here is to see you. The principal food of the people is corn. The principal role was sung by Pavarotti.* **2** °important, °prominent, °leading, °key, °cardinal: *Cuba is a principal source of sugar.*
—*n.* **3** °owner, °proprietor, chairman, chairwoman, chairperson, (managing) °director, °head, president, °chief, chief °executive officer, CEO, °manager or *Brit* manageress, °superintendent, °supervisor, *Colloq* °boss, *US* (°head or °chief) honcho: *We should talk to the principals about buying that company.* **4** dean, °director, *Chiefly Brit* headmaster, headmistress, °master, rector, (vice-)chancellor: *His appointment as principal is for a two-year period.* **5** (working) °capital, °capital funds, resources, investment, °backing, (cash) °reserve(s), °assets; °money: *She is fortunate to be able to live on the income from her investments, without touching the principal.* **6** °star, °lead, °heroine, °hero, °leading lady or man, °leading role, °main °part; diva, *première danseuse, premier danseur,* prima donna, prima ballerina: *The principal in the ballet company was a Russian.*

principally *adv.* °chiefly, °mainly, °first (and °foremost), °primarily, above all, in the °main, mostly, for the most °part, °largely, predominantly, on the °whole, at °bottom, in °essence, essentially, basically, fundamentally; °especially, °particularly: *He seems to be interested principally in money, with little regard for anything else.*

principle *n.* **1** °truth, °given, °precept, °tenet, °fundamental, °grounds, °law, °rule, dictum, canon, °doctrine, teaching, dogma, °proposition, (°basic) assumption, postulate, axiom, °maxim, truism, °guide, °standard, criterion, °model: *The perpetual-motion machine violates a basic principle of physics.* **2** Often, **principles**: °philosophy, °code, °attitude, (°point of) °view, °viewpoint, °sentiment, °belief, credo, °creed, °idea, °notion, ethic, sense of right and wrong: *He cynically conducts his life on the principle, 'Do unto others before they do unto you'. I am not sure I can condone his principles.* **3** (sense of) °honour, uprightness, °honesty, °morality, morals, °probity, °integrity, °conscience: *If you don't think him a man of principle, don't do business with him.* **4 in principle**: on principle, in theory, theoretically, basically, fundamentally, at °bottom, in °essence, essentially, °ideally: *I like your plan in principle, but in practice it cannot be accomplished that way.*

principled *adj.* °moral, °righteous, right-minded, °virtuous, °noble, high-minded, °ethical, °honourable, °proper, °correct, °right, °just, °upright, °honest, °scrupulous: *Michael is too highly principled to take bribes.*

print *v.* **1** °impress, imprint, °stamp, °publish, °issue, °run off, °put out; °copy; (pull a) proof: *We decided to print 500 copies of the book. You may have your name printed on the cover for an additional amount.* —*n.* **2** °reproduction, °copy, °replica, °facsimile; positive, °photograph, etching, (steel or wood-) °engraving, lithograph, woodcut, linocut, silk screen, rotogravure, *Trade Mark* Xerox; °picture, °illustration; *Colloq* photo, °cut, pic (*pl.* pix): *Today, a good print of a Picasso costs more than an original did fifty years ago.* **3** °text, printed matter, °type, °writing; °language, °wording, (choice of) °words, phrasing: *You'd be well advised to read the small print before signing the agreement.*

prior *adj.* **1** °former, °previous, earlier, one-time, ex-, erstwhile; °old, °last, °late, °latest, *Literary* quondam, whilom: *If you overdraw your account without prior arrangement, you will automatically be charged a higher rate of interest.* **2 prior to**: °before, °previous to, °previously to, °till, until, °preceding: *Prior to the earthquake, Valdivia was a river port.*

priority *n.* °precedence, precedency, primacy, °urgency, immediacy, °predominance, °pre-eminence, °preference, °rank, °superiority, °prerogative, °right, seniority, °importance, °weight: *The applications for aid will be processed in order of priority.*

prison *n.* °jail or *Brit* also gaol, °dungeon, oubliette, lock-up, °penal °institution, house of °correction, correctional °institution, reformatory, house of °detention; confinement, °detention; *Old-fashioned* °reform school, *Military* guardhouse; *Brit* remand centre, °detention centre, remand home, community home, *Military* glasshouse, *Formal* CHE (= 'community home with education on the premises'), *Old-fashioned* approved school; *US* penitentiary, *Military* brig; *Archaic Brit* bridewell; *Slang* clink, can, cooler, jug, °stir, *Brit* quod, chokey or choky, *US and Canadian* pokey or poky; *US* pen, calaboose, slammer, hoosegow, *Old-fashioned* big house: *He was released from prison last Friday after serving six months for burglary.*

prisoner *n.* °convict, trusty; internee, detainee; *Colloq* jailbird or *Brit* also goalbird, lifer, *Slang* con, *Brit* (old) °lag, *Old-fashioned* ticket-of-leave man, *US* two-time or three-time loser: *Prisoners' letters were censored.*

prissy *adj.* °fussy, °precious, over-nice, °finicky or finical, °strait-laced, school-marmish, prim

(and °proper), °prudish, °squeamish, °fastidious, *Colloq* old-maidish: *He is awfully prissy about changing on the beach.*

pristine *adj.* **1** °original, primal, °basic, primeval or *Brit* also primaeval, °primitive, primordial, earliest, °first, °initial: *It is impractical to try to return the world to what some regard as its pristine purity.* **2** uncorrupted, °pure, unsullied, undefiled, virginal, virgin, °chaste, untouched, °unspoiled or unspoilt, unpolluted, °untarnished, °spotless, °immaculate, °natural: *One must travel far today to experience the pristine beauty of nature. The car was in pristine condition.*

privacy *n.* **1** °seclusion, retirement, °solitude, isolation, °retreat, sequestration, reclusiveness, reclusion, solitariness; monasticism: *Coleman very much enjoys the privacy of living alone.* **2** °secrecy, secretiveness, clandestineness, confidentiality, surreptitiousness, covertness, concealment: *Many feel that the questions on census forms invade their privacy.*

private *adj.* **1** (top) °secret, °confidential, undisclosed, hidden, clandestine, concealed, covert, °surreptitious, off the °record, not for publication, °unofficial, *Colloq* hush-hush: *I think our relationship should be kept private for the time being. What I am about to tell you is strictly private.* **2** °privileged, restrictive, restricted, °exclusive, °special, °reserved, °personal, °inaccessible, non-public; °hidden, °secluded, concealed, °secret, °sneaking: *The house is situated on a private road. I had a private suspicion that they would cancel their trip.* **3** °personal, °individual, own, °intimate, °particular: *My private affairs are none of your business.* **4** °solitary, seclusive, °reclusive, °withdrawn, °retiring, °reticent, ungregarious, non-gregarious, °unsocial, unsociable, antisocial, °reserved, uncommunicative, hermitic(al), hermit-like, eremitic(al); sequestered, °secluded, retired: *You have to bear in mind that Edmund is a very private person.* —*n.* **5** private °soldier, infantryman, foot-soldier, *US* enlisted man, *Colloq Brit* Tommy, Tommy Atkins, squaddie, *US* GI (Joe), *Slang US* grunt: *Before cashiering him, they reduced him from colonel to private.* **6 in private**: in °secret, °secretly, privately, *sub rosa*, °personally, confidentially, behind closed doors, in camera, off the °record, *US* on the q.t. or Q.T.; clandestinely, secretively, sneakily, sneakingly, surreptitiously, furtively, covertly, on the °sly: *Family matters should be discussed only in private. They met in private with agents of the rebel forces.* **7 private parts** or **privates**: °genitals, °sexual or °sex organs, genitalia: *The natives wore loincloths to cover their private parts.*

privation *n.* °need, neediness, °want, deprivation, °hardship, indigence, °necessity, °poverty, penury, destitution, °strait(s), pauperism, beggary; °distress, °misery: *The lower classes in Victorian England suffered terrible privation.*

privilege *n.* °benefit, °advantage, °right, °prerogative, concession, °allowance, °indulgence, °immunity, °exemption, dispensation, °freedom, °liberty, franchise, °permission, °consent, °leave, authorization, °sanction, °authority, °licence, *carte blanche*: *The children were given the privilege of choosing where the family should go on holiday.*

privileged adj. **1** °favoured, advantaged, indulged, entitled, °élite, °special, honoured: John was one of the privileged few to be told her private telephone number. **2** protected, °exempt(ed), °immune; licensed, empowered, admitted, permitted, sanctioned, authorized, enfranchised, chartered: This is a privileged institution as far as the dispensation of grants is concerned. **3** °powerful, ruling; °wealthy, °rich: He despised the privileged class till he became wealthy enough to be a member of it. **4** °confidential, °secret, °private, °privy, °inside, off the °record, not for publication, restricted, Colloq hush-hush: What I am about to tell you is privileged information.

privy adj. **1** See privileged, 4, above. **2 privy to**: °aware of, in on, on to or onto, sharing (in), cognizant of, apprised of, °informed or advised about or of, °informed on, °knowledgeable about, Colloq in the know about, Slang °hip to, °wise to, Old-fashioned hep to: Was the minister's wife privy to what was discussed at cabinet meetings?
—n. **3** °lavatory, (outside or outdoor) °toilet, latrine, water-closet, WC, US outhouse, Colloq chiefly Brit loo, Slang Brit bog, US crapper, Taboo slang US shithouse: In those days, almost every home had an outside privy, as there was no interior plumbing.

prize[1] n. **1** °reward, °award, °trophy, °premium; °honour, accolade, Literary guerdon: The first prize was a week's holiday in the Bahamas. **2** winnings, jackpot, °purse, receipts, °gain, °windfall, stakes, Colloq °haul, Chiefly US °take: He used his prize from winning the lottery to buy a new car. **3** °aim, °goal: The prize they all strove for was a grant to carry on lexicographic research. **4** °loot, °booty, °spoil(s), °trophy, °plunder, pickings: The pirates took the galleon as their prize.
—adj. **5** °choice, °excellent, (prize)winning, °best, °champion, °outstanding, °select, °superior, °superlative, °first-rate: This dairy owns a prize herd of Guernseys.

prize[2] v. value, °treasure, °esteem, °cherish, °appreciate, °rate highly, hold °dear: I prize your friendship above all things.

probability n. °likelihood, likeliness, °odds, °expectation, °chance(s), (distinct) °possibility, °presumption: There is a high probability that it will rain.

probable adj. (most) °likely, apt, (quite) °possible, presumed, °plausible, undoubted, indubitable, °apparent, °unquestionable, °evident, ostensible, odds-on, °feasible, believable, credible: The probable cause of the flooding was a blockage in the drains. It is probable that most medieval churches had paintings round the walls.

probably adv. (very) °likely, in all °likelihood, in all °probability, °undoubtedly, doubtlessly, indubitably, unquestionably, °presumably, all things considered, to all intents and purposes, °possibly, °perhaps, Colloq °as likely as not, °quite: She is probably the best tennis player in the world at the moment.

probe v. **1** °explore, °examine, °scrutinize, °investigate, °search (into), °look into, °go into, °study, °dig into, delve into, °poke about or around, Colloq °poke into: They probed his background thoroughly but found nothing unusual.

2 °poke, °prod, °explore, °examine; °plumb, °dig: Snipe use their long bills to probe for worms in soft mud.
—n. **3** °investigation, °examination, °exploration, °scrutiny, °search, °study, °inquiry or enquiry, inquest: There will be a governmental probe into the mismanagement of the department.

probity n. °integrity, uprightness, °honesty, °morality, °rectitude, °virtue, goodness, decency, righteousness, right-mindedness, °sincerity, trustworthiness, °honour, °equity, justness, °justice, fairness: Lord Chancellors have consistently been men of unquestioned probity.

problem n. **1** °difficulty, °trouble, °question, °dilemma, °quandary, °predicament, °complication, hornet's nest, imbroglio, °mess, °muddle, °stew, Colloq can of worms, fine kettle of fish, (pretty) pickle, Brit facer: The Chancellor must constantly deal with the problems of the country's economy. **2** °puzzle, conundrum, poser, °riddle, °question, °enigma, puzzler, Colloq mind-boggler, hard or tough nut to crack: The problem is how to get the yolk out without breaking the shell.
—adj. **3** °unruly, unmanageable, intractable, uncontrollable, °difficult, °ungovernable, refractory, °incorrigible, °obstreperous, °delinquent, maladjusted, °disturbed, emotionally °upset: He teaches at a school where most of the students are problem children.

problematic adj. problematical, °difficult, °uncertain, °questionable, questioned, °doubtful, doubted, °debatable, °disputable, disputed, °unsettled, °moot, undecided, °controversial, °tricky, °touchy, °sensitive, Colloq °hairy, iffy: The value of treating colds with massive doses of vitamin C is problematic.

procedure n. °way, °conduct, °course, °action, °course of °action, °method, methodology, °mode, °form, °system, °approach, °strategy, °plan (of °action), °scheme, modus operandi, °operation, °policy, ways and °means; °routine, °tradition, °practice, °custom, wont, standard operating procedure, Colloq MO (= 'modus operandi'), SOP (= 'standard operating procedure'), Chiefly Brit drill: What procedure will you follow to regain the stolen property? The procedure in ballroom dancing has always been for the man to lead.

proceed v. **1** Sometimes, **proceed with**: °go or °move (on or ahead or forward), °advance, °continue, °progress, °carry on, °get or °move along, get going or moving or under °way, °start, °pass on, make °progress or °headway, °push or °press on or °onward(s), forge ahead; resume, °renew, °go on with, pick up (where one left off): Proceed to the T-junction, then turn left. If the membership committee has finished, let us proceed to the report of the finance committee. After the break, the performance will proceed. **2** Often, **proceed from** or **out of**: °result from, °arise (from), °come (from), °stem from, °spring from, °develop (from), °issue (from or forth), °derive from, be derived (from), °descend from, °emerge (from), °grow (from or out of), °originate (in or from or with), °begin (with), °start (with or from): The outcropping proceeds from glaciation and erosion. They say that more than half of a person's happiness proceeds from hope.
—n. **3 proceeds**: °profit(s), °gain, °yield; °income, °receipts, °return(s), °gate, box office, US °take: The proceeds from the charity auction were better than ever this year.

proceeding n. **1** °measure, °act, (°course of) °action, °move, °step, °undertaking, °deed, °procedure, °process, °operation, °transaction, °manoeuvre, °feat, °accomplishment: *Grace Darling's rescue of the shipwrecked men was truly a heroic proceeding.* **2 proceedings**: **a** °transactions, °report(s), °minutes, °record(s), annals, °affairs, °dealings, °business, °account(s), archives, *Formal* acta: *The proceedings of the Society are published annually.* **b** °events, goings-on, doings; °celebration(s); °performance(s): *The proceedings were briefly interrupted while the hecklers were ejected from the hall.*

process n. **1** °procedure, °proceeding, °operation, °system, °method, °approach, °technique; °course of °action: *I am sure you understand how the process works. What process do they use to make paper out of wood?* **2** °activity, °function, °development: *The process of photosynthesis is the means by which plants synthesize carbohydrates.*
—v. **3** °treat, °prepare, (make or get) °ready, °change, °modify, °transform, °convert, °alter: *This is the room where the ingredients are processed before mixing.* **4** °handle, take °care of, °organize, °deal with, °manage; °dispose of, °answer, °manipulate: *After the earthquake the insurance companies processed thousands of claims.*

procession n. **1** °parade, °march, cavalcade, motorcade, cortege or cortège, column, °line, °file, °train, °march past: *A strange procession of thousands of beggars silently wound its way through the city.* **2** °succession, °cycle, °sequence, °string, °train, °chain, series, °course, °run, °progression, cavalcade: *He began to recount the procession of events that led up to the murder.*

proclaim v. **1** °announce, advertise, °circulate, °declare, °broadcast, °pronounce, °make known, bruit (about), trumpet, °publish, promulgate, herald; °profess, °protest, °enunciate, articulate: *Edgar was proclaimed king. She proclaimed her innocence.* **2** °brand, °accuse of being, °stigmatize as, °pronounce, °rule, °decree, °characterize, °report: *She found herself proclaimed a traitor.*

proclamation n. **1** °announcement, °advertisement, °declaration, °publication, promulgation, °statement, manifesto, pronunciamento, notification, °notice: *A proclamation was issued granting amnesty to all political prisoners.* **2** proclaiming, announcing, advertising, declaring, broadcasting, publishing, promulgating, heralding, making known, bruiting about: *The proclamation of his appointment as Chancellor came at a bad time.*

procrastinate v. **1** temporize, act evasively, °play for time, dally, °delay, °stall; °postpone, °defer, °put off or aside, °shelve, *US* °table: *I wish he would stop procrastinating and say what he plans to do.* **2** °hesitate, °pause, waver, vacillate, be undecided, °equivocate, tergiversate, °shilly-shally: *Helen procrastinates every time she is faced with making a decision.*

procure v. **1** °obtain, °acquire, °get, °come by, °secure, get or lay one's hands on, get (a) hold of, °gain, °win, °come into, °pick up, °find, °appropriate, °requisition; °buy, °purchase: *I have been trying to procure early editions of Defoe's works.* **2** °accomplish, °bring about, °effect, °cause, °produce: *Using every resource available to her, she finally procured his release.*

procurer n. °pander or panderer, °pimp, White °slaver, flesh-pedlar or *US also* flesh-peddler or flesh-pedler, *Archaic* whoremaster, bawd; madam, procuress: *He became a procurer for the wealthy men in the village.*

prod v. **1** °jab, °dig, °poke, °nudge, elbow: *Every time the comedian said something risqué, Aunt Flora would giggle and prod me in the ribs.* **2** °spur, °urge, impel, egg on, °push, °thrust, °prompt, °rouse, °stir, °incite, °move, °motivate, actuate, °activate, °provoke, °encourage, °stimulate: *My uncle keeps prodding me to continue with my studies.* **3** °incite, goad, needle, °irritate, °irk, °annoy, °pester, °harass, hector, badger, °plague, °nag, °hound, °carp at, °cavil; °henpeck: *My parents are constantly prodding me to go out and get a job.*
—n. **4** °jab, °dig, °poke, °nudge, elbow, °push: *I was quite black and blue from those prods I was getting from Aunt Flora.* **5** goad, °spur; needle, rowel: *These days electrified cattle prods are available.* **6** stimulus, °push, °prompt, °reminder, °signal, °cue: *Calvin needed that prod to make him finally go home after the party.*

prodigal adj. **1** °wasteful, °extravagant, °spendthrift, °lavish, °excessive, °profligate, squandering, °immoderate, intemperate, °wanton, °improvident, °reckless: *If the government were less prodigal, it would be possible to have a balanced budget.* **2** °generous, °bountiful, copious, °profuse, bounteous, °lavish, °liberal, °luxuriant, °sumptuous, °abundant, abounding, °rich, °plentiful, plenteous, superabundant, thriving, swarming, teeming: *He was prodigal of both compliments and criticism.*
—n. **3** °wastrel, °spendthrift, °profligate, squanderer, waster, big spender: *That prodigal went through his inheritance in less than a year.*

prodigality n. **1** wastefulness, °waste, °extravagance, °excess, excessiveness, immoderation, intemperateness, wantonness, recklessness, °profligacy, improvidence, °dissipation, squandering: *Surely his contemporaries must have condemned Shah Jehan's prodigality in building the Taj Mahal.* **2** lavishness, profuseness, °luxury, luxuriousness, luxuriance, °abundance, °plenty, °bounty, bountifulness, bounteousness, copiousness, °profusion, profuseness, sumptuousness, richness, plentifulness, plenteousness, superabundance, °exuberance: *The prodigality of Nature is unbounded.*

prodigious adj. **1** °vast, °immeasurable, °colossal, °enormous, °huge, °giant, °gigantic, °immense, mammoth, °monumental, tremendous, stupendous, titanic, Brobdingnagian, gargantuan, Herculean, Cyclopean, leviathan, °monstrous, °extensive, *Colloq US* ginormous, humongous: *There is a prodigious amount of water vapour contained in a cloudy sky. You may accuse her of being a workaholic, but consider the prodigious amount she gets done in a day.* **2** °amazing, astonishing, astounding, °startling, °extraordinary, °exceptional, °marvellous, wonderful, wondrous, °fabulous, °miraculous, °phenomenal, spectacular, °fantastic, °sensational, °unusual, staggering, °striking, dumbfounding or dumfounding, °remarkable, °noteworthy, °notable, *Colloq* flabbergasting, mind-boggling, mind-blowing: *In those days, running a mile in four minutes was considered a prodigious feat.*

prodigy n. **1** (child or girl or boy) °genius, wonder child, Wunderkind, °mastermind, °talent, °intellect, °intellectual or °mental giant, wizard, °virtuoso, Colloq °brain, Einstein, whiz-kid or whizz-kid, whiz or whizz, walking dictionary or encyclopedia or encyclopaedia: She was a prodigy at the age of six and went on to become a great concert performer. **2** °wonder, °marvel, °phenomenon, °sensation, miracle: Some regarded the painting Nude Descending a Staircase a prodigy of cubist art.

produce v. **1** °make, °develop, °turn out, °put or °bring out, °manufacture, °fabricate, °generate, °create; °construct, °assemble, °put together, °compose; °mould, °cast; extrude: This machine is capable of producing 10,000 units an hour. **2** °yield, give °rise to, °cause, °bring up, °bring forth, °spark, °initiate, °occasion, °bring about, °prompt, °evoke, °start, °create, °generate, beget, °originate: He was unprepared for the laughter produced by his slip of the tongue. **3** °generate, beget, °create, °put out or forth, °breed, °propagate, °bear, give birth to, °hatch, °grow: See how the plant is producing buds at these nodes? **4** °bring forward or in or out, °introduce, °present, °offer, °show, °exhibit, °display, °stage, °put on, °mount: She was the first to produce Japanese Noh drama in the west. **5** °disclose, °reveal, bring to °light, °show, °display, °draw: When I refused to give him the money, he produced a gun. **6** °supply, °furnish, °provide, °deliver, °distribute: They are accused of continuing to produce fluorocarbons despite the government ban.
—n. **7** vegetables, fruit, Chiefly Brit greengrocery: The produce is delivered to the markets from the farms at the crack of dawn.

producer n. **1** maker, °manufacturer, fabricator, processor, °creator; °grower, farmer: That company is the largest producer of microchips in the world. **2** In Britain: °director, auteur, impresario, regisseur; In US and Canada: entrepreneur, (business or financial) °manager, organizer: He was a producer of TV soap operas.

product n. **1** °result, consequence, °output, °outcome, °issue, °effect, fallout, °yield, °upshot; spin-off, °offshoot, by-product: It is evident that this work is the product of much thought. One product of her interest in literature is a new publishing company. **2** artefact or US artifact, °good(s), °produce, commodity, °output, °merchandise, °offering, °work: It doesn't matter how good the product is if nobody knows about it.

production n. **1** producing, °manufacture, manufacturing, making, °fabrication, °preparation, origination, °creation, °output, putting out, °development; °formation, forming, forging, shaping, moulding, casting, °assembly, °building, construction: Our business is the production of insulating materials. **2** °product, (°end) °result, °work, °effort, handiwork, °output, °opus, œuvre: These paintings are clearly productions of a fertile imagination. **3** In Britain: artistry, °direction, staging; In US and Canada: °display, °presentation, mise en scène, °setting: Both the acting and the production were superb. **4** °drama, °play, (°stage or °television or °radio) °show, °performance; °film, motion or moving picture, °movie: Our repertory company is putting on a production of Othello next week.

productive adj. **1** °fruitful, °fertile, °rich, fecund, °plentiful, plenteous, °abundant, °bountiful, bounteous, °prolific, °dynamic: Owing to a perfect balance of rain and sunshine, the earth has proved productive this year. **2** °imaginative, °creative, inventive, °resourceful, generative, °ingenious, °fertile, °vigorous: Her latest science-fiction trilogy is certainly evidence of a highly productive mind. **3** °profitable, remunerative, °rewarding, valuable, °worthwhile: Years ago he made an investment in computer shares that has turned out to be very productive. Discussing sales strategy is not as productive as getting out there and selling.

profane adj. **1** °irreverent, °sacrilegious, °blasphemous, idolatrous, irreligious, °infidel, °heathen, °unbelieving, disbelieving, °pagan, atheist(ic), °impious, °godless, °ungodly, °sinful, °wicked, iniquitous, °contemptuous, °disrespectful: The faithful attacked anyone who was seen to perform a profane act. **2** unsanctified, unholy, unconsecrated, defiled, °impure, unclean, unhallowed, non-religious, non-sacred, unsacred; °lay, non-clerical, °secular, °temporal; Judaism tref or treif or treifa, non-kosher: The missionaries persuaded them to abandon their profane rites and practices. **3** °bad, °dirty, °filthy, smutty, °foul, foul-mouthed, °obscene, °vulgar, °coarse, uncouth, °low, °taboo, °blasphemous, °bawdy, ribald, °scurrilous, °off colour, °immodest, °improper, °naughty, °indecent, unprintable, °unmentionable, indecorous, indelicate, °common; °abusive, °vituperative, °venomous, thersitical, Literary Fescennine, Colloq °blue: The boy was sent home from school for using profane language.
—v. **4** °debase, °contaminate, °pollute, °taint, °vitiate, °degrade, defile, °desecrate, °violate, °pervert, °corrupt: They swore undying retribution against those who had profaned their temple.

profanity n. blasphemy, obscenity, cursing, curse-word(s), swearing, swear-word(s), °foul or °bad or °dirty or °vulgar or °coarse or °filthy or smutty or °taboo °language, four-letter word(s), billingsgate: The film was held to be unfit for broadcasting as it contained so much obscenity and profanity.

profess v. **1** assert, °claim, aver, asseverate, °state, affirm, °confirm, °confess, °declare, °say, °hold, °maintain, °present, °offer, proffer, °tender, °set forth, °put forward, °pronounce, enounce, °enunciate, °announce, utter, °vow, avow: He professed himself satisfied with the judge's decision. **2** °pretend, lay °claim, make a °pretence, purport, °act as if, simulate: They professed to be legitimate businessmen, but I was always suspicious.

professed adj. **1** °pretended, ostensible, °apparent, °alleged, purported, °so-called, would-be, °self-styled, soi-disant: He was a professed wine 'expert' but the bottle he recommended turned out to be awful. **2** confessed, avowed, sworn, admitted, acknowledged, confirmed, certified, declared: What do you do when a professed friend betrays you?

profession n. **1** °occupation, °calling, °work, °field, °vocation, °employment, métier, °trade, °business, °craft, °line, °sphere, °speciality or US specialty, °job, °position, °post, °situation, Slang °racket: I know that she's a doctor, but what is her husband's profession? **2** confession, affirmation, °statement, avowal, °assertion, asseveration, °declaration, °acknowledgement,

°testimony, averment, °admission, °announcement: *I was uncertain whether to believe his professions of love.*

professional *adj.* **1** trained, °educated, °practised, °veteran, °experienced, °seasoned, °able, skilled, °skilful, °gifted, °talented, °qualified, °knowledgeable, licensed, °official, °expert, °masterful, masterly, °master, °efficient, °adept, °proficient, °competent, °polished, finished: *He is a professional ambulance driver who has to work as a plumber to make ends meet.* **2** °excellent, °proficient, °efficient, °skilful, masterly, °thorough, °prompt, °conscientious, °authoritative, businesslike: *She did a very professional job of repairing my car.*
—*n.* **3** °master, °expert, maestro, °virtuoso, past °master *or* mistress, °specialist, °authority, *Colloq* wizard, pro, whiz *or* whizz, *US* maven *or* mavin, *Brit* °dab hand: *You can always tell when the work has been done by a professional.*

proficiency *n.* °facility, °skill, °talent, adeptness, °expertise, expertness, skilfulness, °aptitude, °capability, °ability, °dexterity, competence *or* competency, °ingenuity, °knack, *savoir faire, Colloq* know-how: *The proficiency he displayed as a racing-car driver was second to none.*

proficient *adj.* °skilful, skilled, °talented, °adept, °gifted, °expert, °experienced, °practised, *au fait,* °veteran, well-versed, (highly) trained, °professional, °qualified, °capable, °able, °accomplished, °dexterous, °competent, °knowledgeable, top-notch, °first-rate, *Colloq* ace, crack, whiz-bang *or* whizz-bang, *Brit* wizard: *She is an extremely proficient surgeon.*

profile *n.* **1** °outline, °silhouette, contour, side-view: *His aquiline nose shows up prominently in this profile.* **2** biography, (biographical *or* °thumbnail *or* °character) sketch, °life, °portrait, vignette: *That profile of Allen in a well-known magazine did not do him justice.* **3** °analysis, °study, °survey, °examination; graph, diagram, °chart, °list, statistics: *The profile of the average newspaper reader revealed some interesting anomalies.*
—*v.* **4** °describe, °draw, sketch, limn: *The editor phoned to say that they want to profile you in the Gazette's Sunday colour supplement.*

profit *n.* **1** Often, **profits**: °gross *or* °net profit, °net *or Brit also* nett, °return(s), °gain, °yield, °revenue, proceeds, bottom line, °surplus, °excess, *US* °take, *Slang* gravy, *US* vigorish: *The profits are down in the third quarter owing to the higher interest rate.* **2** °advantage, avail, °good, °benefit, °welfare, °gain, value, °interest, °use, °usefulness, *Archaic or literary* behoof: *Let me recommend a book that you will find of some profit.*
—*v.* **3** °advance, °further, be of profit to, °benefit, °promote, °aid, °help, be °advantageous *or* of °advantage, °serve, avail, °improve: *A few lessons from the club professional could profit your golf game.* **4** Often, **profit from**: take °advantage of, °use, turn to °advantage *or* °account, °exploit, utilize, make (good) use of, make °capital (out) of, capitalize on, °benefit, make the most of, *Slang* cash in on: *I hope you profit from the experience.* **5** clear, °realize, °earn, °gain, *Colloq* make a °killing, clean up, °rake it in, make a °bundle *or* a °packet: *Ernestine profited to the tune of £100,000 on the sale of her house.*

profitable *adj.* **1** °beneficial, °productive, lucrative, °fruitful, (well-)paying, well-paid, °worthwhile, °effective, cost-effective, °gainful, remunerative, money-making, °rewarding: *I had never thought of being a pavement artist as a profitable enterprise. Playing professional golf can be very profitable—if you win tournaments.* **2** °beneficial, °helpful, °useful, utilitarian, valuable, °worthwhile, °advantageous, °productive, °rewarding: *She gave me a lot of good advice that I found profitable in my professional life.*

profiteer *n.* **1** °racketeer, exploiter, extortionist, extortioner, blackmarketeer: *The profiteers turned to selling sugar at exorbitant prices.*
—*v.* **2** overcharge, °fleece, °exploit, °milk, make the most of; °extort; *US* °gouge: *The arms dealers are profiteering by selling banned* matériel *to guerrillas.*

profligacy *n.* **1** debauchery, °vice, immorality, °sin, sinfulness, wickedness, °evil, °dissipation, dissoluteness, degeneracy, licentiousness, depravity, corruption, promiscuity, lechery, lasciviousness, lewdness, indecency, °perversion, carnality, libertinism, wantonness, unrestraint, eroticism, sybaritism, voluptuousness, sensuality: *Soho's reputation for profligacy is now much less deserved.* **2** °prodigality, °extravagance, °excess, °waste, wastefulness, recklessness, exorbitance, lavishness, improvidence, squandering: *The profligacy of the French court at the end of the 17th century was remarkable.*

profligate *adj.* **1** debauched, vice-ridden, °immoral, unprincipled, °sinful, °shameless, °evil, iniquitous, °wicked, dissipative, °dissolute, °degenerate, °loose, licentious, depraved, °corrupt, °promiscuous, °lecherous, °lascivious, °lewd, °indecent, °perverted, °carnal, °libertine, °wanton, unrestrained, °erotic, sybaritic, °voluptuous, °sensual, °wild, °abandoned: *The duke suddenly gave up his profligate life and became a monk.* **2** °extravagant, °prodigal, °wasteful, °reckless, squandering, °improvident, °spendthrift, °immoderate, °excessive: *As the family fortunes waned, my aunt had to curb her profligate ways.*
—*n.* **3** debauchee, °sinner, °degenerate, °pervert, sodomite, °reprobate, °rake, rakehell, °libertine, lecher, whoremonger, °roué, °wanton, °sybarite, voluptuary, °sensualist: *With the restraints removed, the profligate abandoned himself to every excess imaginable.* **4** °prodigal, °spendthrift, °wastrel, waster, squanderer: *Such are the extravagances indulged in by the profligates who never learnt the value of money.*

profound *adj.* **1** °deep, unfathomable, abstruse, °recondite, arcane, esoteric, °intricate, knotty, °involved, °tricky, inscrutable, indecipherable, cabbalistic, °incomprehensible, °obscure, °subtle, °occult, °secret, °cryptic, °puzzling, enigmatic, mystifying, °mysterious: *Some aspects of the theory of thought are even too profound for many specialists.* **2** °learned, °scholarly, °intellectual, erudite, discerning, °astute, sagacious, °sage, °wise, °penetrating, °sharp, °keen, insightful, analytical, °knowledgeable, °informed, °well-informed, well-read: *Russell was one of the most profound thinkers of his day.* **3** °deep, °great, °intense, °sincere, °heartfelt, °keen, °acute, utter, °extreme, °overpowering, °overwhelming: *He gave a profound sigh and fell asleep at once. It is with profound regret that I must tender my resignation.* **4** utter, °complete, °total, °perfect, °absolute,

°thorough, thoroughgoing, °out-and-out, °downright, consummate; °awful, °terrible: *Her casual attitude stems from her profound lack of awareness of how important the work is. I was immediately struck by the profound silence in the house. Profound changes are under way.*

profoundly *adv.* °very, °extremely, °deeply, greatly, keenly, acutely, intensely, °sincerely; °terribly, °awfully: *We are profoundly sorry to have been so much trouble to you.*

profundity *n.* **1** °depth, profoundness, abstruseness, reconditeness, arcaneness, intricacy, °subtlety, °complexity, complicatedness, °difficulty, inscrutability, involvement, involvedness; indecipherability, incomprehensibility, incomprehensibleness, °obscurity: *I wouldn't claim to have fully grasped the profundity of his ideas.* **2** erudition, discernment, °scholarship, scholarliness, sagacity, °wisdom, sharpness, keenness, astuteness, acumen, insightfulness, knowledgeableness, knowledgeability: *I was amazed by the profundity of the argument of one so young.*

profuse *adj.* **1** °abundant, °ample, °plentiful, copious, unstinting, unsparing, ungrudging: *My profuse apologies if I have offended you in any way.* **2** °extravagant, °lavish, °bountiful, bounteous, °prolific, °luxuriant, °abundant, °exuberant, superabundant, °lush, °thick, teeming, overflowing, bursting, thriving, °productive, °fruitful, °rich: *From the seventh year onwards, the trees yielded profuse crops of pears and plums.* **3** °excessive, copious, °considerable, °prolific, °liberal, °lavish, °free, °abundant, °ample: *This stage of the fever is accompanied by profuse sweating.* **4** °generous, °abundant, °plentiful, copious, unsparing, °unselfish, unstinting, °exuberant, magnanimous, °liberal: *The audience was profuse in its applause and cries of 'Bravo!' and 'Encore!'*

profusion *n.* profuseness, °quantity, °abundance, °plenty, plentifulness, plenteousness, °bounty, copiousness, superabundance; °mass, °host, °hoard, °number, multitude, °lot, °mountain, °load, °mess, °stack, °pile, °heap, agglomeration, conglomeration, °accumulation, °wealth, °glut, °surplus, oversupply, °surfeit, plethora, °superfluity, *Formal* nimiety: *Ivy grew in profusion over the front of the house. We had never seen such a profusion of bric-à-brac as they had collected.*

progenitor *n.* **1** progenitrix, °ancestor, forefather, forebear: *They regarded the snake god as the progenitor of the human race.* **2** °predecessor, °forerunner, °precursor, antecedent, foregoer, °source, originator; °origin, °original, °prototype, archetype, °pattern, °guide: *The ancient philosophers were progenitors of many modern ideas. Some regard da Vinci's designs as the progenitors of some of today's machines.*

progeny *n.* °offspring, °children, °descendants, °issue, °young, °posterity, °heirs, scions, successors, sons and daughters, *Colloq* kids, °spawn, fry, *US* sprouts: *He dreamed that his progeny might have a freer, healthier life than his.*

prognosis *n.* °forecast, forecasting, °prediction, °prophecy, prognostication, °projection: *The doctor has recorded his prognosis for the course of the disease.*

prognosticate *v.* **1** °predict, foretell, °prophesy, °forecast, presage, °divine, forebode: *Those prophets of doom are always prognosticating disaster.* **2** betoken, augur, herald, °foreshadow, foretoken, °announce, °harbinger, °signal, portend: *The freshening breeze from the east prognosticates some rainy periods ahead.*

programme *n.* **1** °schedule, °plan, °scheme, agenda, °order of the day, °routine, °protocol, slate, °list, listing, °description, °outline, °abstract, °précis, °calendar, menu, bill of fare, curriculum, syllabus, °synopsis, °summary, °prospectus: *The programme shows the sequence of events. You cannot tell what is being offered without a programme.* **2** °performance, °production, °show, °presentation, (°radio or °television) °play, telecast, °broadcast, °recital, concert: *Television programmes seem to cater to lower levels of taste and intelligence every year.* **3** °proceedings, °events, °affairs, °activities: *The programme includes an hour of exercise before breakfast every day.* —*v.* **4** °organize, °arrange, prearrange, °plan, °lay out, map (out), °design, °formulate, °set (up), °schedule, °book, *US* slate: *The solo pianist is programmed to follow the chamber orchestra.*

progress *n.* **1** (forward) °movement, going forward, °progression, °advance, °headway, advancement: *Progress through the dense underbrush was very slow.* **2** advancement, °advance, °promotion, °improvement, betterment, °elevation, °rise, °development, °furtherance: *Her progress in the company might have been impeded by the fact that she was a woman.* **3** advancement, °course, °development, °growth, °expansion, °increase, °evolution, maturation, ripening, burgeoning or bourgeoning, amplification, enlargement, °spread, °extension, broadening, °promotion, °furtherance, °advance, °encouragement: *Our publishing credo is that every book must contribute to the progress of culture or knowledge.* **4 in progress**: under °way, ongoing, going on, °happening, occurring, taking °place, at °work, in °operation, being done, °proceeding, *Colloq* in the °works: *Some of the plans for reorganization are already in progress.* —*v.* **5** °advance, °move or °go (forwards or °onwards), °proceed, °continue, °go or forge °ahead, °go or °move along, make (one's) °way, make °headway, °travel, °go or °push or °press on: *Throughout the 19th century wagon trains of pioneers progressed across the prairies to settle the American West. I haven't progressed far enough in my reading to say whether I like the book or not.* **6** °advance, °improve, get °well, get °better, °develop, °grow, °expand, °increase, evolve, °mature, °ripen, burgeon or bourgeon, °amplify, °enlarge, °spread, °extend, broaden, °rise, °move up, upgrade: *Sarah's condition progressed to the point where she could get out of bed. Christmas sales of the new toy are progressing nicely. In only ten years, Michael progressed to a directorship in the company.*

progression *n.* **1** °movement forward or forward °movement, °advance, advancement, (making or gaining) °headway, °progress, ascension, °rise, °elevation: *This mode of progression requires enormous effort. It was interesting to watch her progression through the corridors of power.* **2** °progress, °development, °advance, advancement, °spread, spreading, °extension, extending, broadening, enlargement, °headway, intensification, °rise: *It seemed impossible to halt* the progression of the disease. **3** °order, °sequence, °succession, °train, °chain, concatenation, °course, °flow: The report traces the progression of events leading up to the war.

progressive adj. **1** advancing, continuing, developing, increasing, growing, ongoing, °continuous, °step by step, °gradual: The doctors noted the progressive deterioration in his condition. With the onset of spring, we shall see progressive improvement in the weather. **2** reformist, revisionist, °liberal, °radical, °revolutionary, °avant-garde, advanced, °dynamic: Carrie was soon regarded as one of the more progressive thinkers of her day.
—n. **3** reformist, reformer, revisionist, °liberal, leftist, left-winger: Once a conservative, he did a complete volte-face after the war and became a progressive.

prohibit v. **1** °bar, °ban, °forbid, disallow, interdict, °outlaw, °taboo, debar, proscribe: Fishing without a permit is prohibited. **2** °prevent, °stop, °preclude, °rule out, °obstruct, °block, °impede, °hinder, °hamper, °inhibit, °frustrate, °foil, °thwart, °restrain, °check: A turnstile prohibits entry through the exit doors.

prohibition n. **1** forbiddance, °barring, °bar, banning, °ban, disallowance, disallowing, interdiction, interdicting, outlawing, outlawry, °taboo, debarment, debarring, proscription, proscribing: Did the members vote for the prohibition of smoking on club premises? **2** °bar, interdict, °injunction, debarment, °embargo, proscription, °ban: Imposition of an excessively high tariff on imported computer components has amounted to the prohibition of their use in this country.

prohibitive adj. **1** discouraging, suppressive, °repressive, restrictive, prohibitory, inhibitory, restraining: Prohibitive legislation has forced capital out of some profitable areas and into others less productive. **2** °excessive, °exorbitant, °outrageous, °dear, °high, °outlandish, °abusive, extortionate, insupportable, criminal: The prices of new designer dresses are prohibitive.

project n. **1** °proposal, °plan, °scheme, °design, layout: The project for housing low-income families had to be modified to allow for car parking. **2** °activity, °enterprise, °programme, °undertaking, °venture, °assignment, commitment, °obligation, °contract, °engagement; °occupation, °job, °work: What project will you move on to when you complete this one?
—v. **3** °plan, °scheme, °prepare, °devise, conjure up, concoct, °think up, °contemplate, contrive, °invent, °work up or out, °propose, °present, °outline, °design, °draft, °draw up, delineate, °describe, °put forth or forward, Colloq cook up: In his theory, he projects a quite different causal relationship. **4** °cast, °hurl, °fling, °throw, °toss, °launch, °propel, °discharge; °shoot, °transmit; Colloq chuck, °lob: A body projected into space will keep on travelling unless it strikes something. This device projects stereoscopic pictures on a screen. **5** °jut out, °stick out, °protrude, °stand out, °bulge (out), °extend (out), °poke out, beetle (out), °overhang: The cornice projects a full six feet over the street. **6** °estimate, °reckon, °calculate, °predict, °forecast: The economists projected a decline in inflation over the coming months.

projectile n. °missile, °shell, bullet, °rocket: Projectiles rained down on the enemy gun emplacement.

projection n. **1** °protrusion, protuberance, °bulge, °extension, °overhang, °ledge, flange; °ridge, eminence, °prominence, °spur, °crag, outcropping: The safety line caught on a projection of the building, and the man was saved. That projection off to the north is covered with ice all year long. **2** °proposal, outlining, mapping, mapping out, presenting, °presentation: The projection of the plan for the new development must be effective for the council to accept it. **3** °plan, °scheme, blueprint, °programme, °design, °proposal, °outline, diagram, map, °representation, planning: The council has approved the projection for the development of the waterfront. **4** °estimate, prognostication, °forecast, °prediction, °calculation, °reckoning: These sales projections for next year are quite optimistic.

proliferate v. °grow, °increase, burgeon or bourgeon, multiply, mushroom, snowball; °breed, °reproduce: Fast-food restaurants are proliferating everywhere. Failure to disinfect the wound allows germs to proliferate.

proliferation n. °growth, °increase, burgeoning or bourgeoning, °expansion, °spread, escalation, build-up, °rise: Some attribute the increase in violent crime to the proliferation of hand-guns.

prolific adj. **1** °fertile, fecund, °productive, °fruitful, °abundant, copious, °bountiful, bounteous, °profuse, °plentiful, plenteous, °lush, °rich, rife: The more perilous its natural survival, the more prolific a species is likely to be. **2** °productive, °creative, °fertile: He is a prolific author, and has more than 200 novels to his credit.

prolong v. °extend, °lengthen, elongate, °stretch (out), °draw or °drag out, °drag (on), keep up, °string out, protract: Not wishing to prolong the agony, we left after the first act. Aunt Caroline prolonged her visit by yet another week.

promenade n. **1** °walk, °parade, esplanade, boulevard: We strolled along the promenade as far as the pier. **2** °walk, °stroll, °saunter, °ramble, °turn, constitutional, airing, turn: After a brief promenade round the garden, she returned to the house.
—v. **3** °walk, °stroll, °saunter, amble, °ramble, °parade, perambulate, take a °walk or °stroll: Every Sunday, regardless of the weather, he promenades for an hour in the park. **4** °flaunt, °show (off), °display, °parade, °strut: Why he promenaded that awful person before all his friends is beyond me!

prominence n. **1** °celebrity, eminence, °fame, °distinction, notability, °reputation, °pre-eminence, °standing, °position, °rank, °prestige, °renown, repute, °importance, °weight, °influence, °account, °name, consequence: They are a family of considerable prominence in the county. She rose to prominence as an actress just last year. **2** °hill, hillock, °rise, hummock, outcrop, outcropping, °spur, tor, °crag, areote, °spine, °ridge, °peak, °mount, °pinnacle; headland, °point, promontory: We planted our flag on the prominence and constructed a small cairn. **3** protuberance, °projection, °protrusion, °growth, excrescence, °swelling, tumefaction, tumescence, extrusion, outshoot, outgrowth, °spur, °bulge: If that prominence on your elbow doesn't disappear in a day or so, I should see a doctor.

prominent adj. **1** °conspicuous, °obvious, °evident, recognizable, °pronounced,

°discernible, distinguishable, identifiable, °noticeable, °remarkable, °noteworthy, eye-catching, °striking, °outstanding, °chief, °main, °principal, °significant, °important; °apparent, unmistakable, °patent, °glaring, °salient, °flagrant, egregious: *The most prominent peak in the region is Annapurna. Some of the prominent shortcomings of the plan can be rectified easily.* **2** °eminent, °pre-eminent, °distinguished, °notable, °noteworthy, °noted, °leading, °foremost, °first, °outstanding, °well-known, famed, °illustrious, °famous, °celebrated, °renowned, acclaimed, honoured, °honourable, respected, °well-thought-of, °prestigious, °reputable, creditable: *A prominent politician is to be invited to cut the ribbon opening the new bridge.* **3** °protuberant, protruding, protrusive, projecting, jutting (out); excrescent, bulging, raised, °elevated: *She has a rather prominent chin. There is one prominent spot on the tabletop that needs more sanding.*

promiscuous *adj.* **1** °indiscriminate, undiscriminating, unselective, non-selective, non-discriminatory, unconscientious, °heedless, °haphazard, °indifferent, uncaring, uncritical, unfussy, unfastidious, disregardful, neglectful, negligent, °slipshod, slovenly, °irresponsible, °careless, °cursory, °perfunctory, °unthinking, °thoughtless, unconsidered: *The promiscuous massacre of civilians caused an international outcry.* **2** °lax, °loose, °unchaste, °wanton, °wild, °uninhibited, unrestrained, ungoverned, °uncontrolled, unbridled, uncurbed, °immoderate, °abandoned, amoral, °immoral, °indecent, °libertine, licentious, dissipated, °dissolute, depraved, °profligate, debauched, °fast; unfaithful, °faithless, °dishonourable: *Nothing you say could persuade me to condone your promiscuous behaviour.* **3** °mixed, °miscellaneous, heterogeneous, °random, intermixed, jumbled, °disorderly, disordered, °confused, °chaotic, motley, intermingled, scrambled, unorganized, disorganized, unsystematic, unsystematized, °helter-skelter, higgledy-piggledy, °hotchpotch *or US also* hodgepodge: *There is a somewhat promiscuous collection of books in his library that well reflects the eclecticism of his tastes.*

promise *n.* **1** °assurance, (solemn) °word (of °honour), °pledge, °vow, °oath, °undertaking, °engagement, °bond, commitment, guaranty, °guarantee, °warranty; °agreement, °contract, covenant, °compact: *You have my promise that the book will be completed by the deadline. She broke her promise to marry him. Unlike a contract, a promise does not imply a mutual commitment.* **2** °expectation, °potential, °capability; °likelihood, °probability: *This first novel shows a lot of promise. There is little promise that compensation will be paid to the victims by the government.* —*v.* **3** °assure, give one's °word (of °honour), °pledge, °swear, °vow, take an °oath, °undertake, °engage, °commit oneself, °guarantee *or* guaranty, °warrant, cross one's °heart (and hope to die): *Harold promised to do what cannot be done. We were promised a free ride on the roundabout. She promises she will repay the loan promptly. Make him pay for the damage as he promised.* **4** give °indication of, °hint at, °suggest, foretell, augur, °indicate, °show signs of, be in store for, look like, °seem *or* °appear °likely *or* °probable, *Brit*

be on the cards, *US* be in the cards, *Literary* bid fair, betoken, bespeak: *Though the economic situation promised to improve, many were disappointed that it took so long.*

promising *adj.* °hopeful, encouraging, °favourable, auspicious, °positive, °rosy, °optimistic, °propitious, cheering, full of °promise, reassuring, heartening: *I see a promising future for you as a dancer.*

promote *v.* **1** °help, °further, °encourage, °assist, °advance, °support, °forward, °back, °sanction, °abet, °aid, °boost, °foster, °patronize, nurture, °develop, inspirit, °strengthen, °stimulate, °inspire: *Their continual bickering did little to promote domestic harmony. The sale of portable appliances has done much to promote the battery business.* **2** °advance, °move up, °raise, upgrade, elevate, °exalt, *Colloq* °kick upstairs: *He is to be promoted to floor manager next month.* **3** °recommend, °endorse, °sponsor, °support, espouse, commend, °advocate, °advance, °champion, °talk up, °speak for, °side with, °present, call °attention to: *She is promoting the cause of ecology in her campaign.* **4** advertise, °publicize, °push, °sell, *Colloq* beat the drum for, °plug, *Slang* hype, *Chiefly US* ballyhoo: *They are promoting the new chewing-gum by giving out free samples in Trafalgar Square.*

promotion *n.* **1** °furtherance, advancement, °advance, °encouragement, °support, °backing, °sanction, sanctioning, abetting, aiding, °helping, assisting, boosting, fostering, nurturing, cultivation, °development, developing, °improvement, improving, °inspiration, inspiriting, strengthening, stimulation, °stimulating: *The Society exists for the promotion of learning in a number of subjects.* **2** advancement, °advance, upgrading, upgrade, °rise, °elevation, preferment, exaltation: *He was envied for his promotion to the highest ranking post in the department.* **3** promoting, °recommendation, °presentation, espousal, commendation, advocacy, championing: *I am grateful for your promotion of my name for the job.* **4** advertising, publicity, public relations, °propaganda, selling, hard *or* soft °sell, °fanfare, plugging, *Colloq* puffery, *Slang* (media) hype, *Chiefly US* ballyhoo, hoop-la: *The manufacturer spent millions on the promotion of the new cola.* **5** °advertisement, advertising, °circular, °brochure, handbill, °bill, hand-out, °leaflet, °poster, affiche, placard, publicity, °space, (publicity) °release, hoarding, *US and Canadian* flier *or* flyer, billboard, broadside, *Colloq US* °puff piece, poop sheet: *The promotions for the new detergent use the celebrity endorsement technique.*

prompt *adj.* **1** quick, °ready, °immediate, instantaneous, °unhesitating, °rapid, °fast, °swift, °speedy, °punctual, °timely, on °time, °instant, °summary, °brisk, alacritous: *No matter what the question, Gemma gave a prompt response.* **2** alert, °eager, °ready, quick, °expeditious, °ready and °willing, °disposed, predisposed, °unhesitating, °keen, avid: *Slow to praise, Alan was always prompt to criticize.* —*v.* **3** °urge, egg (on), °prod, °nudge, °spur, exhort, °incite, °induce, impel, °provoke, °rouse, °arouse, °encourage, °work *or* °stir *or* °fire up, °move, °motivate, °cause, °influence, °put (someone) up to (something), °coax, °persuade, °cajole, °prevail upon *or* on, °talk

(someone) into (something): *If he hadn't prompted her, she never would have apologized.* **4** °cue, °remind, feed lines (to), °help: *She never could remember her lines and needed to be prompted.* **5** °bring about, °inspire, °occasion, give °rise to, °elicit, °evoke, °provoke, °call forth, °stimulate, °awaken: *The mention of hostages prompted a question about what was being done to gain their release.*
—*n.* **6** °reminder, °cue, °hint, stimulus: *He always needs a prompt to remind him to send his mother flowers on her birthday.*

promptly *adv.* °quickly, at °once, *or* °straight away, °directly, °right away, °immediately, without °delay *or* hesitation, unhesitatingly, °swiftly, speedily, °readily, instantly, °instantaneously, punctually, expeditiously, with celerity, with alacrity, *Colloq US and Canadian* momentarily: *If this bill is not paid promptly, we shall have to discontinue your credit arrangements.*

prone *adj.* **1** face down *or* °downwards *or chiefly US* °downward, °prostrate, °lying down, reclining, °recumbent, °horizontal, procumbent, *Formal or technical* decumbent, accumbent: *She was lying prone, resting between push-ups.* **2** °inclined, apt, °likely, °liable, °disposed, predisposed, of a °mind, °subject, °given, tending, °leaning: *They are prone to petty squabbles.*

pronounce *v.* **1** °declare, utter, °say, °voice, °express, articulate, °enunciate, vocalize, put into words: *He pronounced a curse on the family. Try to pronounce it one syllable at a time.* **2** °declare, affirm, °proclaim, °announce, °decree, °judge, aver, °state, asseverate, assert, °say to be: *I now pronounce you man and wife. The doctor pronounced mother to be out of danger.* **3** °announce, °proclaim, promulgate, °publicize, °publish, °deliver, °broadcast, °make known, °let (something) be known, °put out *or* forth, °set forth; °pass: *The judge will pronounce sentence tomorrow.*

pronounced *adj.* **1** °definite, °clear, °plain, well-defined, °decided, °conspicuous, °noticeable, recognizable, identifiable, °obvious, °striking, °prominent, °notable, °distinct, unmistakable, °marked, °strong: *There was a pronounced odour of bitter almonds in the room. Sophie spoke with a pronounced lisp.* **2** °definite, °distinct, unequivocal, unambiguous, °specific, °unqualified, °undisguised, °downright, °outright, °out-and-out, °decided, °complete, °total, °unmitigated, °strong, utter, unalloyed, unmixed, °clear, clear-cut, unmistakable: *A pronounced prejudice against fuzzy thinking emerges from his writings.*

pronouncement *n.* **1** °statement, °assertion, °observation, °comment, °opinion, °announcement, °proclamation, pronunciamento, manifesto, °declaration, avowal, affirmation, asseveration, averment, promulgation: *Occasionally he would issue a pronouncement on the sad state of English usage.* **2** °judgement, °decree, edict, °proclamation, dictum, °command, ukase, (papal) bull, °imperative, °order, ordinance: *The authorities made several official pronouncements regarding travel restrictions.*

pronunciation *n.* enunciation, articulation, elocution, °diction, °speech, °speech pattern,

°manner of speaking, °delivery, °accent, accentuation, °intonation, inflection, modulation: *Standard pronunciations of English are so diverse that it is sometimes difficult for one native speaker to understand another. Rock singers seem always to imitate a Texan pronunciation.*

proof *n.* **1** °evidence, verification, corroboration, confirmation, validation, authentication, ratification, substantiation; documentation, °document, °facts, °data, certification, °testimony, *Colloq* ammunition: *Is there any proof that she was with you? The prosecution claims to have enough proof of his guilt to convict him of embezzlement.* **2** °test, °trial, °measure, °standard, °touchstone, criterion: *Do you intend to put his loyalty to the proof? The proof of the pudding is in the eating.*
—*adj.* **3** impervious, impenetrable, able to °withstand *or* °resist, °protective, °strong, °tough, °impregnable, °resistant, tempered: *They maintain that this armour is proof against a nine-inch shell.*

prop *v.* **1** Often, **prop up**: °support, °brace, °hold (up), °buttress, °stay, °bolster, °uphold, °bear, °sustain, shore up, °keep up: *A longer post is needed to prop up this end of the roof.* **2** °lean, °stand, °rest: *Do you mind if I prop my crutches against the desk while I sit down?*
—*n.* **3** °support, °brace, truss, °stay, °buttress, °mainstay, °upright, vertical, shore: *Can you use this broomstick as a prop to support the shelf temporarily?*

propaganda *n.* **1** agitprop, disinformation, Newspeak, rumours, lies: *The state-controlled media spread propaganda about minorities to foster nationalism.* **2** advertising, °promotion, publicity, °public relations, °puff, °fanfare, *Colloq* puffery, ballyhoo, *Slang* hype, *US* hoop-la, whoop-de-do *or* whoop-de-doo: *All that propaganda was merely to launch a new washing-powder!*

propagate *v.* **1** °breed, °generate, °reproduce, multiply, °proliferate, °deliver, °bring forth, °bear, procreate: *Biologists are studying ways of making the species propagate at a faster rate.* **2** multiply, °increase, °spread, °grow, °develop: *These plants propagate very rapidly.* **3** °publicize, °promote, disseminate, °dispense, °distribute, °spread, °publish, °broadcast, °circulate, °make known, °transmit, °disperse, propagandize, °proclaim, promulgate, bruit about, noise abroad, herald: *The purpose of the organization is to propagate information about the state of the environment.*

propel *v.* °drive, impel, °move, actuate, set in °motion, get moving, °push, °thrust, °force, °send, °launch, °start: *Each galley was propelled by huge oars. The capsule is propelled by a rocket. Job opportunities propelled her to move to Bristol.*

proper *adj.* **1** °right, °appropriate, apropos, apt, °suitable, °fit, °fitting, °befitting, °becoming, suited, *de rigueur, comme il faut,* adapted, *Literary* °meet: *Is this the proper time to ask for a salary increase?* **2** °correct, °accurate, °exact, °right, °precise, °orthodox, °formal, expected, °normal, °usual, accepted, established, *Old-fashioned Brit* tickety-boo: *Some insist that the only proper way to pronounce 'controversy' is with the stress on the first syllable.* **3** °decorous, °dignified, °genteel, °fitting, °right, *de rigueur,* °appropriate, °becoming, °suitable, °decent,

°seemly, °due, °correct, apt, *comme il faut*, conformist; gentlemanly, °ladylike, °polite, °refined, punctilious, °respectable: *Jeans are not proper attire for dinner at La Hacienda. Do you call that proper behaviour for the president of a learned society?* **4** °fitting, °suitable, °correct, °right, °satisfactory, °good, °sensible: *The kitchen is a proper place for the dishwasher, not the garage. Proper nutrition is very important.* **5** °complete, °perfect, utter, °thorough, thoroughgoing, °out-and-out, °unmitigated: *He felt a proper fool for having locked his keys inside his car.* **6** own, °individual, °separate, °distinct, °correct, °specific, °special, °particular, °respective; °characteristic, °distinctive, °peculiar, °singular, °unique: *When you have finished, return each book to its proper place.*
—*quasi-adv.* **7** strictly speaking *or* °so-called, in the °strict(est) *or* °narrow(est) °sense, °only, solely, °alone, on (its *or* someone's) own: *Does the deed refer only to the house proper or are the outbuildings also included?*

properly *adv.* **1** °appropriately, fittingly, correctly, °well, becomingly, suitably, politely, decently, decorously, nicely: *If you cannot behave properly I shall have to ask you to leave.* **2** °duly, °appropriately, °well, suitably, rightly, correctly, aptly: *Are they properly equipped for the rescue mission?*

property *n.* **1** °possessions, °belongings, °effects, °gear, °paraphernalia, chattels: *All his worldly property fitted into the small Gladstone bag he carried everywhere.* **2** °assets, °means, °resources, holdings, °capital (°goods), °fortune, °riches, °estate, °worth: *We look on all our shares, personal belongings, and real estate as part of our property.* **3** °land, acreage, realty, real °estate *or* °property: *That property on the high street was recently sold to developers.* **4** °characteristic, °attribute, °quality, °feature, °trait, °mark, °hallmark, idiosyncrasy, °peculiarity, °oddity, °quirk, *Formal* haecceity, quiddity: *A property of iodine is that it changes directly from a solid to a vapour—and vice versa—without first liquefying.*

prophecy *n.* **1** forecasting, foretelling, °prediction, fortune-telling, divination, soothsaying, augury, prognostication, crystal-gazing, *Formal* vaticination: *The prophecy of future events lies outside the realm of science.* **2** °prediction, °forecast, °prognosis, °revelation: *Her prophecy warned of ice storms that would ravage the earth.*

prophesy *v.* **1** °predict, foretell, °forecast, forewarn, °prognosticate, vaticinate: *His father prophesied that he would come to no good if he quit college.* **2** augur, foretell (of), presage, °foreshadow, portend, °bode, °harbinger, herald, °promise, vaticinate: *The early disappearance of the swallows prophesies a long, cold winter.*

prophet *n.* prophetess, °oracle, forecaster, °seer, soothsayer, clairvoyant, prognosticator, °fortune-teller, augur, diviner, °witch, warlock, sibyl, haruspex, vaticinator; (*of doom*) Cassandra: *Statistically, the weather prophets have a fair record of accuracy.*

prophetic *adj.* predictive, prognostic, divinatory, oracular, inspired, prescient, sibylline, *Literary* fatidic, vatic: *His warnings of a drought proved to be prophetic.*

propitiatory *adj.* **1** conciliatory, pacifying, appeasing, expiatory, placative, propitiative, pacificatory, placatory: *He said that he was truly sorry and held out a propitiatory hand.* **2** deferential, °ingratiating, °obliging, obeisant, acquiescent, compliant, °tractable: *He was most propitiatory in his treatment of his stepchildren.*

propitious *adj.* °advantageous, °timely, °well-timed, °opportune, °lucky, °fortunate, °happy, °providential, °favourable, °bright, encouraging, auspicious, °promising, °rosy: *It was not a propitious moment to ask her to marry him.*

proponent *n.* proposer, promoter, °supporter, upholder, °backer, subscriber, °patron, espouser, adherent, °enthusiast, °champion, °friend, °partisan, defender, °advocate, exponent, pleader, apologist, spokesman, spokeswoman, spokesperson: *Ashley is a staunch proponent of the literacy movement.*

proportion *n.* **1** °ratio, (comparative) °relation, °relationship, °comparison: *The proportion of men to women on the course is three to one. The demand is out of all proportion to the supply.* **2** °balance, °agreement, concord, °harmony, suitableness, °symmetry, congruity, correspondence, correlation, °arrangement, °distribution: *The beauty of the building is at once apparent in the elegant proportion of its parts.* **3** °portion, °division, °share, °part, °percentage, °quota, °allotment, °ration, *Colloq* °cut: *Water covers a large proportion of the surface.* **4 proportions:** °size, °magnitude, dimensions, °measurements, °extent; °volume, °capacity, °mass, °bulk, °area, °expanse, °scope, °range, °degree: *The dragon suddenly assumed gigantic proportions.*
—*v.* **5** °adjust, °modify, °change, °modulate, °poise, °balance, °shape, °fit, °match, °conform, equate: *The punishment should be proportioned to the crime.*

proportional *adj.* proportionate, proportioned, comparable, analogous, analogic(al), °relative, °related, correlated, balanced, °symmetrical, corresponding, compatible, °harmonious, °consistent, commensurate, in accordance with: *The zeal with which their ideals are defended is directly proportional to the fierceness with which they are attacked.*

proposal *n.* **1** °offer, °presentation, °bid, °tender, °proposition, °recommendation, °suggestion, *Literary* proffer: *Her proposal was to provide the funding if we would do the work.* **2** °plan, °scheme, °outline, °draft, °design, layout; °programme, °proposition, °project: *The proposal for the new civic centre was rejected as too expensive.*

propose *v.* **1** °offer, °tender, proffer; °present, °introduce, °submit, °advance, °set forth, °put forward, °propound, °bid, °recommend, °suggest, °come up with, call °attention to, °broach, *Brit* °table: *Management proposed a wage increase of five per cent. The architect proposed that we consider an addition to the north wing.* **2** °offer, °mean, °intend, °plan, °expect, °aim: *We propose to make a start on the decorating once we have had our lunch.* **3** °nominate, °name, °put forward *or* forth, °suggest, °introduce, °submit, °put up: *His boss proposed him for membership of the golf club.*

proposition *n.* **1** See proposal, 1, above. **2** See proposal, 2, above.
—*v.* **3** accost, °solicit, make an °indecent *or* °sexual °advance *or* °proposal *or* °overture,

449

propound | prostitution

Colloq make a °pass at: *She said she had been propositioned by him, but we never learnt if she accepted or not.*

propound v. °put or °set forth or forward, °propose, °offer, proffer, °suggest, postulate: *It was she who first propounded the idea of a unified country.*

proprietor n. **1** proprietress, °owner, landowner, °landlady, °landlord, landholder, title-holder, deed-holder, property °owner: *He is the proprietor of a large house in Chiswick.* **2** °owner, °partner, °landlord, restaurateur, innkeeper, hotel-keeper, hotelier, licensee, °manager, *Brit* publican: *The proprietor greeted us warmly and showed us to our rooms.*

propriety n. **1** correctness, properness, conformity, suitableness, appropriateness, suitability, aptness, °fitness, seemliness, °decorum; advisability, °wisdom: *I questioned the propriety of concealing this information from shareholders.* **2** °protocol, °good or °proper °form, punctilio, °etiquette, politeness, °courtesy, politesse, °refinement, sedateness, °dignity, modesty, °decorum, decency, °breeding, respectability, gentility, °grace, mannerliness: *He always behaved with the utmost propriety in the presence of his aunt.* **3 the proprieties**: the social graces, the amenities, the civilities, °formality or the formalities, social °convention or social conventions, social °procedure or °codes, accepted °practice, °tradition, °ceremony, °ritual: *He only observes the proprieties when he wants to make a good impression.*

propulsion n. °drive, impulse, °impetus, °thrust, °power, driving or propelling or propulsive °force, °pressure, °momentum, °push: *Enormous propulsion is required to lift the space shuttle into orbit.*

prosaic adj. °dull, °banal, overdone, °tedious, clichéd, commonplace, stereotyped, °pedestrian, °flat, stereotypical, hackneyed, °stock, °routine, °everyday, °ordinary, °common, workaday, °mediocre, °undistinguished, °bland, characterless, °homely, °plain, trite, °stale, °threadbare, °tired, °lifeless, °dead, °dry, jejune, °boring, °tiresome, unimaginative, unpoetic, unromantic, uninspiring, uninspired, insipid, uninteresting, °humdrum, °monotonous, *Literary* ennuyant, *Colloq* ho-hum, run-of-the-mill, °mouldy: *She found the law too prosaic and trained to become a jockey.*

prose n. (expository) °writing, °text, °language: *It came as a great revelation to learn that he had been speaking prose all his life.*

prosecute v. **1** arraign, °indict, °charge, put on or bring to °trial, °try, take to court, °sue, bring °suit or °action against, °accuse, *Brit* put in the °dock: *She threatened to prosecute him for slander.* **2** °pursue, °follow up or through, °see or °carry through, °persist, °go on with: *Will the same policy be prosecuted in other countries?* **3** °carry on or out, °perform, do, °exercise, °conduct, °follow, engage in, °practise, °continue: *The government needs popular support if it is to continue to prosecute the war successfully.*

prospect n. **1** °view, °scene, panorama, °landscape, seascape, °outlook, vista, °sight, °spectacle, °perspective, °aspect: *The sitting-room window offered a splendid prospect of the sea and cliffs below.* **2** °anticipation, contemplation,

°outlook, °promise, °plan, °design, °intention, expectancy, °expectation, °thought, °likelihood: *The prospect of spending the Christmas holidays with your family is quite daunting.* **3** Often, **prospects**: °future, °outlook, °chance(s), °hope(s), °possibility or possibilities, °likelihood, °opportunity or opportunities: *The prospects for her advancement are excellent.* **4 in prospect**: in °sight or °view, in the offing, on the °horizon, in °store, in the °wind, projected, °likely, °probable, °possible, *Brit* on the cards, on the table, *US* in the cards: *As a doctor, he has a number of opportunities in prospect.* —v. **5** Often, **prospect for**: °explore, °search (for), °look (for): *In 1896, his grandfather went to the Klondike to prospect for gold.*

prospective adj. anticipated, expected, awaited, looked-for, °future, °forthcoming, coming, approaching, °imminent, nearing, °pending, °impending, °destined, °potential, incipient: *Jane's prospective wedding had excited the entire family.*

prospectus n. °announcement, °plan, °scheme, °programme, °outline, conspectus, °description: *According to the prospectus for the fund, the minimum investment is £1000.*

prosper v. °flourish, °thrive, °succeed, °fare °well, °progress, get ahead, °grow, °develop; °profit, °gain, become °wealthy, grow °rich, make one's °fortune, °make good, *Colloq* °make it, make one's °pile: *With hard work, thrift, and perseverance, MacIntosh prospered and was soon able to buy the house he wanted.*

prosperity n. °success, (°good) °fortune, °wealth, °riches, affluence, °money, °luxury, °plenty, prosperousness, opulence, °bounty, *Colloq* life of Riley: *The basis of the family's prosperity was huge land holdings in Australia.*

prosperous adj. **1** °rich, °wealthy, moneyed or monied, affluent, well-to-do, °well off, *Colloq* well-heeled, °loaded, °flush, in the money, rolling in it or °wealth or °money, in clover, on Easy Street, *Slang* stinking °rich: *Anyone who owns six houses and four yachts must be prosperous.* **2** °successful, thriving, °flourishing, booming, prospering: *Frank owns a prosperous chain of video shops.*

prostitute n. **1** whore, call-girl, streetwalker, strumpet, trollop, harlot, lady of the night or *US also* evening, fallen or loose woman, demi-mondaine, *Archaic* cocotte, fille de joie, painted woman, woman of °ill repute, camp-follower, *Archaic* catamite, *Literary* hetaera or hetaira, courtesan or courtezan, *Brit* rent-boy, toy boy, *US* boy toy, *Archaic* bawd, quean, trull, cotquean, *Colloq* °tart, hustler, *Slang* pro, moll, *Brit* brass, hooker, *US* bimbo, working girl, chippy or chippie, roundheels: *There was a terrible scandal when the MP was found to have consorted with prostitutes.* —v. **2** Often, **prostitute oneself**: °degrade, demean, °lower, cheapen, °debase, °profane, defile, °desecrate, °pervert, °abuse, °misuse, devalue, *Colloq* °sell out: *To ward off starvation, he prostituted his talent by drawing comic strips.*

prostitution n. **1** whoredom, harlotry, the oldest profession, Mrs Warren's profession, streetwalking, °vice: *They argued strongly against the legalization of prostitution, saying that it would lead to a decline in public morals.* **2** °degradation, debasement, profanation, defilement, desecration, °misuse, °abuse, devaluation, lowering, °perversion, corruption: *Don't you regard pornography as a prostitution of the principle of freedom of expression?*

prostrate v. **1** Usually, **prostrate oneself**: °lie down, °kowtow, °bow (down), °bow and °scrape, grovel, kneel, °fall to or on one's knees, °truckle, °crawl, °cringe, °submit, abase oneself: *The captives were forced to prostrate themselves before the emperor.* **2** °overwhelm, °overcome, °overpower, °crush, °lay or bring low, °paralyse, °fell, °bowl over, °floor, °bring down, °humble, make °helpless, °ruin; °exhaust, °fatigue, °weary, °wear down or out, °tire (out): *They were prostrated by grief at the loss of their son. Having been prostrated for months by glandular fever, she finally recovered and returned to work.*
—adj. **3** °prone, °horizontal, °lying down, laid low, stretched out, procumbent, °recumbent, *Formal or technical* accumbent, decumbent: *The prostrate bodies of the worshippers in their multicoloured garb resembled a huge patchwork quilt.* **4** overwhelmed, °overcome, overpowered, crushed, brought or laid °low, paralysed, felled, bowled over, brought down, humbled, °helpless, ruined, brought to one's knees, °powerless, °impotent, °defenceless, disarmed, *Colloq* floored: *She was prostrate at the news of the car crash. After the long war, the countries were struggling to revitalize their prostrate economies.* **5** °exhausted, drained, °fatigued, °spent, °worn out, wearied, °weary, °tired (out), °dead °tired, dog-tired, played out, *Colloq* fagged out, knocked out, all in, °beat, bushed, *US* wiped out, *Slang* shagged out, *US and Canadian* pooped (out): *We were prostrate after the long climb.*

prostration n. **1** genuflection or *Brit also* genuflexion, kowtowing, °kowtow, kneeling, bowing, °bow, salaaming, salaam, °submission: *Prostration before a superior was a mark of honour.* **2** °servility, °veneration, °worship, °humiliation, °respect, adulation, °deference, °obeisance, °homage: *Their silence betokened the profound prostration they felt before her superior intellect.* **3** °despair, °misery, °desolation, °desperation, dejection, °depression, despondency, wretchedness, unhappiness, °grief, °woe, woefulness: *Years of poverty created in him a spiritual prostration from which he never recovered.* **4** weariness, °exhaustion, °weakness, debility, feebleness, enervation, lassitude, paralysis, °collapse, °breakdown: *The diagnosis was nervous prostration and the treatment was bed rest for a week or more.*

protagonist n. **1** °hero, °heroine, anti-hero, anti-heroine, °principal, °leading °character; °lead, °leading role, °title role: *Mother was always the protagonist in our little domestic dramas.* **2** °leader, °supporter, °advocate, °backer, °prime mover, moving °spirit, °champion, °mainstay, standard-bearer, exponent: *He is considered the chief protagonist of reformist policies in the party.*

protean adj. °variable, ever-changing, multiform, mutable, °changeable, labile, polymorphous or polymorphic, kaleidoscopic: *The magic ring gave him protean powers to appear now as an eagle, now as a serpent.*

protect v. **1** °defend, °guard, °safeguard, keep °safe, °shield, °cover, °screen: *Company rules require the wearing of safety goggles to protect the eyes when operating any machine.* **2** °care for, °preserve, °keep, °shelter, °watch over, °safeguard, take °care of, °conserve, take under one's wing, °foster, nurture, °tend, °mind: *The best way of protecting wildlife is to conserve natural habitats.*

protection n. **1** °defence, °screen, °shield, °barrier, °guard, °safeguard, °immunity, °bulwark, buffer, °shelter, °refuge, haven, °sanctuary, °security, °safe keeping, °safety, °preservation: *They have not yet developed any protection from the common cold. How can we offer these fledglings protection against predators?* **2** °care, guardianship, aegis, °custody, °charge, °safe keeping, °patronage, sponsorship, keeping: *Even under the protection of the government, elephants continue to be slaughtered.* **3** extortion, °blackmail, °protection °money: *If we refuse to pay protection, they say that they will bomb the restaurant.*

protective adj. defensive, °jealous, °vigilant, watchful, heedful, °careful, °possessive; preservative, shielding, sheltering, safeguarding: *She is fiercely protective of her independence and will not accept help. Many animals rely on protective colouring as a defence against predators.*

protector n. protectress, defender, °benefactor, benefactress, °patron, patroness, °guardian (angel), °champion, knight in shining armour, paladin, bodyguard, *Slang Brit* °minder: *She came to regard him as her friend and protector.*

protégé n. protégée, °ward, °charge, dependant; °discovery, °student, °pupil: *He became her protégé and she has taught him everything he knows.*

protest n. **1** °objection, °opposition, °complaint, grumble, °grievance, dissent, °disapproval, protestation, °exception, °disagreement, demur or demurral, demurrer, disclaimer, °denial, °scruple, °compunction, °qualm, *Colloq* °gripe, grouse, °squawk, *US* kick, *Slang* beef, °bitch: *The Home Office has received many protests about the treatment of prisoners.*
2 under protest: unwillingly, reluctantly, involuntarily: *I paid the fine under protest.*
—v. **3** °object, °oppose, °complain, grumble, dissent, °disapprove, take °exception, take °issue with, °disagree, demur, disclaim, °deny, °scruple, *Colloq* °gripe, grouse, °squawk, *Brit* °kick (against), *US* °kick, *Slang* beef, °bitch: *Bank employees protested at being expected to work on Saturday mornings.* **4** assert, °confirm, °declare, aver, asseverate, affirm, °announce, °profess, °insist on, avow, avouch: *The convicted man went to the gallows protesting his innocence.*

protocol n. **1** °rule(s) or °code(s) or °standard(s) of °behaviour or °conduct, °convention(s), °custom(s), °diplomacy, °formality, formalities, °form, °etiquette, politesse, manners, °practice, °usage, °authority: *According to protocol, the lady stands at the right of the gentleman. Which protocol are you following, the British or the French?* **2** °treaty, °pact, °compact, covenant, °agreement, concordat; °memorandum, °minute, °note, °draft, °outline: *The original protocol must be checked before the ministers attach their signatures.*

prototype n. **1** °model, archetype, °first, °original, °pattern, exemplar, °precedent, °mould: *Many improvements were made as a result of tests on the original prototype.* **2** °example, °instance, °illustration, °sample, °norm,

°paragon, °epitome, °model, °standard, analogue, referent, °metaphor: *Mrs Grundy is a common prototype for narrow-mindedness and prudishness.*

protracted *adj.* °long, long-drawn-out, interminable, prolonged, over-long, never-ending, extended, stretched out, marathon, °endless, °everlasting, long-winded: *The protracted union negotiations delayed the start of the work by six months.*

protrude *v.* °stick out, °jut (out), °project, °extend, °poke out, °stand out, °thrust out *or* forward, °start (from), exsert, *Rare* extrude; °bulge, balloon, °bag (out), belly (out); (of the eyes) °pop, goggle, *Colloq US* °bug (out): *Only the very tops of the plants protruded from the snow.*

protrusion *n.* °projection, protuberance, °prominence, °swelling, excrescence, tumescence, °bump, °lump, °knob, °bulge; (*condition of the eyes*) *Technical* exophthalmic goitre: *I can feel the slight protrusion of the nail-heads above the smooth surface.*

protuberant *adj.* protrusive, protruding, bulging, gibbous, jutting, bulbous, °swelling, °swollen, turgid, tumescent, distended, tumid, extrusive, excrescent, extruding, projecting, beetling, overhanging, °prominent: *She has large brown eyes that are a little protuberant.*

proud *adj.* **1** Often, **proud of**: °pleased (with), satisfied (with), contented (with), °glad (about), °happy (with *or* about), °delighted (with *or* about), °elated (with *or* about); honoured, gratified: *He is very proud of his children and what they have achieved. I am proud to be your friend.* **2** °conceited, °boastful, self-satisfied, narcissistic, °self-important, °egotistical, °vain, vainglorious, prideful, self-centred, complacent, °snobbish, °haughty, °supercilious, °smug, °arrogant, °cocky, cocksure, °boastful, °braggart, *Colloq* high and mighty, snooty, stuck-up, *Slang* snotty, *Brit* toffee-nosed: *She's far too proud to have anything to do with the likes of us.* **3** °lofty, °dignified, lordly, °noble, °great, respected, honoured, °honourable, °important, °glorious, august, °illustrious, °estimable, creditable, °eminent, °prominent, °distinguished, °reputable, °worthy, °notable, °noted, °noteworthy: *His will always be a proud name in British military history.* **4** °stately, °majestic, °magnificent, °splendid, °grand: *Proud Edinburgh earned the sobriquet, 'Athens of the north'.*

prove *v.* **1** °verify, °authenticate, °confirm, °make good, corroborate, °demonstrate, °show, validate, °establish, °substantiate, °certify, affirm; °support, °sustain, back (up), °uphold: *Prove that he lied under oath, and we shall have him for perjury. If you cannot prove her guilt, she must be presumed innocent.* **2** °try, °test, °examine, °check, °analyse, assay: *Division can easily be proved by multiplication, and vice versa. The proving ground for military vehicles is off limits to the public. Come live with me and be my love, And we shall all the pleasures prove.* **3** °turn out, be °found, be °shown, be °established, °end up; °develop, °result: *The child proved to be his long-lost grandson.* **4** °show, evince, °demonstrate: *He proved his love many times over during their fifty years of marriage.*

provender *n.* **1** °provisions, °food, °supplies, victuals, rations, foodstuffs, groceries, eatables, edibles, comestibles, aliment, °nourishment,

°sustenance, *Colloq* grub, eats: *The armies relied for their provender on farms they passed on the march.* **2** fodder, forage, °feed, hay, silage, corn, °grain: *Provender for the livestock was running low because of the long winter.*

proverb *n.* saying, °maxim, aphorism, °saw, adage, apophthegm *or* apothegm, axiom, °moral, moralism, homily, dictum, gnome, °epigram, commonplace, platitude, °truism, °cliché, bromide: *According to the old proverb, 'A fool and his money are soon parted'.*

proverbial *adj.* **1** axiomatic, aphoristic, °epigrammatic, apophthegmatic *or* apothegmatic, homiletic, moralistic; acknowledged, °well-known, accepted, °time-honoured, °traditional: *The language is full of proverbial sayings reflecting popular wisdom.* **2** °typical, archetypal, °exemplary: *The humanitarianism of Albert Schweitzer is proverbial.*

provide *v.* **1** °supply, °furnish, °equip, °outfit, fix up (with) °provision, °contribute, °accommodate, purvey, °cater, °stock (up), victual, °provender: *After providing us with a map and a compass, they sent us off across the moor.* **2** °produce, °yield, °afford, °lend, °give, °present, °offer, °accord: *The fertile land provided food in plentiful abundance. During those bleak years, the radio provided us not only with news but also entertainment.* **3** °stipulate, °lay down, °require, °demand, °specify, °state: *The lease provided that the rent be reviewed every five years.* **4 provide for**: °look after, °care for, °support, take °care of, take under one's wing, °minister to, °attend (to): *The bequest ensured that his widow would be amply provided for.* **5 provide for** *or* **against**: °arrange for, °prepare for, °anticipate, forearm, make *or* get °ready for, °plan for, take °precautions, take °measures: *It would seem that you have provided for any eventuality.*

providence *n.* **1** °foresight, °forethought, °preparation, °anticipation, °readiness, far-sightedness, °caution, °precaution, °discretion, °prudence, °care; °thrift, frugality, husbandry, thriftiness, °conservation, °economy: *Because of the providence of our founders, we were able to weather severe financial setbacks.* **2** Usually, **(divine) Providence**: °protection, °care, °concern, beneficence, °direction, °control, °divine intervention, °guidance; °destiny, °fate, °lot, °fortune, karma, kismet: *Providence is always on the side of those who help themselves.*

provident *adj.* **1** °cautious, °wary, °discreet, canny, °prudent, °careful, °vigilant, °prepared, °far-sighted, °thoughtful, °wise, °shrewd, sagacious, °sage, °judicious: *In the fable, the grasshopper learns from the ant what it means to be provident.* **2** °frugal, °economic(al), °thrifty, °prudent: *Because he is not a provident man, he will always be poor.*

providential *adj.* °fortunate, °lucky, blessed, felicitous, °happy, °opportune, °timely: *It is providential that we left the house just before the earthquake.*

providing *conj.* Sometimes, **providing that**: provided (that), on (the) °condition (that), if (only), only if, as long as, in °the event (that), with the °proviso (that), in °case, with the °understanding (that): *Simon is always ready to go out to dinner, providing someone else pays for it.*

province n. **1** °territory, °state, °zone, °region, °quarter, °area, °district, °domain, dependency or US also dependancy, °division, °section: *Quebec is one of the administrative provinces of Canada*. **2** °country, °territory, °region, °dominion, °realm, strand, °tract: *During the war, those who escaped fled to distant provinces*. **3** °sphere or °area (of °responsibility), °responsibility, bailiwick, °concern, °function, °charge, °business, °field; *Colloq* °thing, °headache, °worry: *The payroll falls within the province of my department*. **4 provinces**: °outlying districts, countryside, hinterland(s), *Chiefly US* exurbia, *Slang US and Canadian* boondocks, boonies, hicksville: *Once a year, people flock into London from the provinces to do their Christmas shopping*.

provincial adj. **1** °local, regional: *Provincial administration is the responsibility of the sheriff*. **2** uncultured, uncultivated, °unsophisticated, °limited, °uninformed, °naïve, °innocent, °ingenuous, unpolished, °unrefined, °homespun, °rustic, °rude, °country, °parochial, insular, °narrow-minded, °boorish, loutish, cloddish, °awkward, °ungraceful, oafish, backwood(s), *Brit* parish pump, *US* small-town, *Colloq US and Canadian* hick, hick-town: *These paintings are unlikely to appeal to provincial tastes*.
—n. **3** °rustic, °country cousin, (°country) bumpkin, yokel, *US and Canadian* out-of-towner, hick, hayseed: *One could tell they were provincials by the cut of their clothes*.

provincialism n. **1** dialectalism, localism, regionalism; °idiom, patois, °dialect: *His northern speech is peppered with provincialisms unfamiliar to those who live in the south*. **2** narrow-mindedness, insularity, parochialism, narrowness, benightedness; unsophisticatedness, °simplicity, lack of awareness, °naïvety, ingenuousness, innocence, °inexperience: *Their provincialism made them suspicious of city people. There was something charming about the provincialism of this rough man from the outback*.

provision n. **1** °providing, supplying, furnishing; catering, victualling, provisioning, purveyance, purveying, equipping, °fitting out, outfitting, accoutrement or US also accouterment, °equipment: *The school is responsible for the provision of textbooks. The provision of a cruise ship of that size requires days*. **2** °stipulation, °proviso, °condition, °restriction, °qualification, clause, °term, °exception, °demand, °requirement, °prerequisite, *Colloq* °catch, °string, *US* hooker: *This provision of the contract calls for a penalty for each day's delay beyond the guaranteed completion date*. **3** °preparation, prearrangement, °arrangement, °measures, °steps: *They had failed to make provision for so many customers and soon ran out of food*. **4** Usually, **provisions**: °supplies, °stores, stockpile, °stock(s), °quantity; °food, foodstuffs, eatables, edibles, drinkables, potables, victuals, viands, comestibles, °rations, groceries, °provender, °staples: *We had enough provisions to last a year*.
—v. **5** stockpile, °stock, °supply, victual, °cater, purvey: *They provisioned the expedition for a three-month period*.

provisional adj. **1** °temporary, interim, provisionary, transitional, °stopgap, *pro tempore*, *Colloq* pro tem: *The provisional government was expected to be in place for less than a month*. **2** conditional, contingent, provisory, °qualified, stipulatory, provisionary, probationary: *The appointment is provisional and will be reviewed in six months*.

proviso n. See **provision, 2**, above.

provocation n. **1** grounds, °reason, °cause, justification, instigation, °initiation, °incitement, stimulus, °incentive, motivation, °motive, °inducement: *What was the provocation for that unpleasant outburst?* **2** °insult, °offence, °taunt, irritation: *After a series of provocations, the final straw was his remark about my mother*.

provocative adj. **1** °inviting, alluring, °tempting, charming, tantalizing, teasing, intriguing, fascinating, °seductive, °stimulating, °voluptuous, °sensual, °sensuous, °suggestive, °erotic, arousing, °exciting, entrancing, °irresistible, bewitching, *Colloq* °sexy: *The council found the film too provocative to be shown to schoolchildren*. **2** irritating, annoying, galling, °irksome, nettlesome, harassing, plaguing, exasperating, infuriating, angering, incensing, maddening, enraging, vexing, vexatious, disquieting, challenging, upsetting, distressing, °disturbing, °outrageous, wounding, stinging, °offensive, humiliating, mortifying: *She is given to making provocative remarks that drive him to distraction*.

provoke v. **1** °stir (up), °stimulate, °move, °motivate, °push, impel, °drive, °get, °spur (on), egg on, goad, °force, compel, °prompt, °rouse, °arouse, waken, °awaken, °enliven, °animate, °activate, °induce, °encourage: *She did her best to provoke him to start his new novel*. **2** °start, °incite, instigate, °produce, °promote, °foment, °kindle, °work up: *Are you trying to provoke an argument?* **3** °irritate, °annoy, °irk, °pester, vex, pique, °anger, °enrage, °madden, incense, °infuriate, °gall, rile, nettle, °harass, hector, °plague, badger, °exasperate, get on one's °nerves, °try one's °patience, °frustrate, °upset, °disturb, °perturb, °distress, °outrage, °offend, °insult, affront: *If he continues to provoke me I shall punch him*.

prowess n. **1** °ability, °skill, skilfulness, °aptitude, adroitness, °dexterity, dexterousness, adeptness, °facility, °finesse, °expertise, mastery, °genius, °talent, know-how, °ingenuity, °capability, °proficiency: *Her prowess as a sculptor is unquestioned*. **2** °bravery, valour, °courage, boldness, °daring, intrepidity, dauntlessness, mettle, stout-heartedness, valiance, lion-heartedness, fearlessness, gallantry, doughtiness, °fortitude: *He was famed for his prowess in single combat*.

prowl v. **1** °lurk, °sneak, skulk, °steal, °slink: *I thought I saw someone prowling about in your back garden*. **2** °scour, scavenge, °range over, rove, °roam, °patrol, °cruise, °cover: *The police continued to prowl the waterfront looking for smugglers*.
—n. **3 on the prowl**: lurking or sneaking or skulking or stealing or slinking about or around, searching, seeking, hunting, tracking, stalking: *The lioness was on the prowl for wildebeest. After a few drinks, the boys went on the prowl for some female companionship*.

proximity n. nearness, closeness, adjacency, °neighbourhood, °vicinity, vicinage, contiguity, contiguousness, propinquity: *The proximity of the airport kept housing prices relatively low.*

proxy n. °substitute, °agent, °delegate, surrogate, °representative, °factor: *As I was unable to attend the owners' meeting, I sent Jane as my proxy.*

prude n. °prig, °puritan, Mrs Grundy, Colloq °goody-goody, US bluenose: *He was a bit of a prude and disapproved of anything even slightly suggestive.*

prudence n. **1** °discretion, °wisdom, sagacity, °judgement, °discrimination, common °sense, canniness, °presence of mind, awareness, wariness, °care, °tact, carefulness, °caution, cautiousness, circumspection, watchfulness, °vigilance, heedfulness: *You should proceed with prudence in this hazardous business.* **2** planning, °preparation, °preparedness, foresightedness, °forethought, °foresight, °providence, °precaution, far-sightedness; °economy, husbandry, °thrift, (good or careful) °management: *Owing to the prudence of her investments, Clara had accumulated a substantial nest egg.*

prudent adj. **1** °careful, °cautious, °discreet, discerning, °wise, °sage, sagacious, °politic, °judicious, °discriminating, °sensible, °reasonable, canny, °shrewd, °cautious, circumspect, watchful, °vigilant, heedful, °wary, °attentive, °alert, °guarded: *James had always found it prudent to listen to others before speaking his mind.* **2** °provident, °thrifty, °economic(al), °frugal, prudential: *Father favours prudent, conservative management of the family business.*

prudery n. prudishness, priggishness, puritanicalness, puritanism, squeamishness, Grundyism, primness, stuffiness, old-maidishness, precisianism: *She said that censorship was the result of prudery rather than concern for moral welfare.*

prudish adj. °priggish, puritanical, old-maidish, °prissy, prim, °fussy, °squeamish, °strait-laced, °stiff, °rigid, over-nice, over-modest, over-coy, °proper, demure, °decorous, °formal: *Victorian society was both prudish and prurient.*

prune v. °clip, °cut back, °lop, °dock, °pare (down), °trim: *If you prune fruit trees, they bear more abundantly. We have to prune the entertainment budget.*

prurient adj. **1** libidinous, °lecherous, °lascivious, °lewd, lubricious or lubricous, salacious, °lustful, concupiscent, licentious, °carnal, debauched, rakehell, °sensual, °randy, °voluptuous, °loose, goatish, ruttish, Literary Cyprian, Paphian, Archaic lickerish or liquorish, Slang horny, °hot: *The press takes a prurient interest in the private lives of famous people.* **2** °dirty, °lewd, °filthy, °pornographic, smutty, °obscene, °foul, °scurrilous, °vile, °indecent, °gross, °lurid, °blue, °bawdy, ribald, titillating, °suggestive, °coarse, °vulgar, °low, °crude, Literary Fescennine: *The police raid uncovered a store of prurient literature, films, and videos.*

pry v. **1** °investigate, ferret about, °examine, °peer, °peek, be °inquisitive, °inquire or °enquire: *They pried into her past but found nothing revealing.* **2** °intrude, °meddle, °interfere, Colloq °poke or °stick one's nose in or into, °snoop, be °nosy, nose about or around, °poke about or around: *They have no right to pry into my private affairs.*

pseudonym n. *nom de plume, nom de guerre,* alias, pen-name, stage °name, °incognito: *'George Eliot' was the pseudonym of Mary Ann Evans.*

psyche n. °soul, °spirit, °mind, *élan vital,* divine °spark, life-force, anima, self, °subconscious, °unconscious, °personality, (°essential) °nature, inner man or woman or °person, Philosophy pneuma: *To Homer, the psyche was more like an alter ego, or conscience.*

psychic adj. **1** psychical, °mental, °spiritual, psychologic(al), °subjective, psychogenic, cognitive, metaphysic(al), °intellectual, cerebral; philosophic(al): *The psychic effect of losing a loved one can have physical repercussions.* **2** psychical, extrasensory, °supernatural, °occult, magical, telepathic, telekinetic, preternatural, spiritualistic, °unearthly, extramundane, supermundane: *Many psychic phenomena have never been satisfactorily explained.*
—n. **3** °medium, spiritualist, clairvoyant, mind-reader, telepathist, °seer, seeress, crystal-gazer, soothsayer, astrologer, °fortune-teller, °prophet, prophetess, sibyl: *We were disturbed to learn that our political leaders consulted psychics.*

psychological adj. °mental, °intellectual, cerebral, cognitive, °psychic(al), °spiritual, °subjective, °subconscious, °unconscious, °subliminal, psychogenic; philosophic(al): *He has plenty of money, so there must be psychological reasons for his stealing.*

psychology n. (°mental) °make-up, constitution, °attitude, °behaviour, °thought processes, °thinking, °psyche, °nature, °feeling(s), °emotion(s), °rationale, °reasoning: *I cannot understand the psychology of fascism.*

psychotic adj. **1** °mad, °insane, psychopathic, °deranged, demented, lunatic, paranoiac or paranoid, °abnormal, °unbalanced, (mentally) °ill or esp. US °sick, °disturbed, *non compos mentis,* of °unsound mind, °exceptional, certifiable, °daft, unhinged, °raving, Slang °crazy, nuts, nutty, loony, off one's rocker or trolley or chump or head, cracked, crack-brained, °mental, out to lunch, batty, bats, having bats in one's belfry, having a screw loose, not all there, touched (in the head), bonkers: *The doctors diagnosed him as psychotic and insisted he be hospitalized.*
—n. **2** °madman, madwoman, °maniac, psychopath, lunatic, paranoid or paranoiac, schizophrenic, bedlamite, Slang nut, nutter, screwball, crackpot, °crazy, loony or looney or luny, schizo, US kook: *How many psychotics do you think are wandering about loose?*

pub n. public house, alehouse, tavern, inn, °bar, cocktail °lounge, saloon, taproom, hostelry, Brit saloon or °lounge °bar, US bar-room, Colloq Brit °local, Slang boozer, watering-hole, °joint, °dive, Chiefly Brit gin-palace, US barrelhouse, gin-mill, honky-tonk: *We went down to the pub for a pint and a game of darts.*

puberty n. pubescence, °sexual °maturity, adolescence, juvenescence, teens; nubility: *The anxiety of parents for the health of an infant is as nothing compared with their concerns when their child reaches puberty.*

public adj. **1** communal, community, °common, °general, collective, °universal, °catholic, °popular, worldwide: *One need only compare early and new films to see how public taste has*

changed. **2** °civil, civic, °social, societal, community, communal: *Although they may seem restrictive, these laws are for the public good.* **3** °accessible, °open, °free, unrestricted, non-exclusive, communal, community, °available: *He does much of his research in the public library.* **4** °open, °manifest, exposed, °overt, projected, °plain, °obvious, °apparent, °patent, °clear, clear-cut, acknowledged, known, admitted, °visible, viewable, °conspicuous: *Her public image is quite different from her private persona.* **5** °visible, viewable, °conspicuous, unconcealed, unshrouded, °flagrant, °blatant: *Has Alfie made a public spectacle of himself again?* **6** °well-known, °prominent, °eminent, °celebrated, °famous, °renowned, °noted, °notable, °influential, °illustrious; °notorious, °disreputable, °infamous: *Invite a well-known public figure to open the exhibition if you can.* **7 make public**: See publish, below.
—*n.* **8** community, °people (at °large or in general), citizenry, °citizens, °nation, °populace, °population, °society, °masses, multitude, hoi polloi, bourgeoisie, °plebeians, proletariat, °rank and file, middle class, third °estate, commonalty or commonality, voters, °man or °woman in the street, *Brit* admass, *US* John Q. Public, Mr or Mrs Average, *Colloq* (any or every) Tom, Dick, and Harry: *The public has responded generously to the charity appeal.* **9** °clientele or *Brit also* clientage, °customers, °custom, °patrons, °followers, °supporters, °buyers, consumers, purchasers, following, °business, °trade: *How can you expect to attract the public without advertising?* **10** sector, °segment, special-interest °group, °portion: *The commuting public will no longer tolerate these excessive train delays.* **11 in public**: publicly, °openly, in the °open, *Colloq* out of the closet: *Jarvis has finally confessed in public what we long suspected privately.*

publication *n.* **1** dissemination, promulgation, publicizing, publishing, °proclamation, issuance, reporting, °announcement, °advertisement, advertising, °pronouncement, airing, putting out, °revelation, declaration, °appearance: *The publication of the news about the sale of the company was no surprise to us.* **2** °book, booklet, °pamphlet, °brochure, °leaflet, broadside or broadsheet, flier or flyer, handbill, hand-out; °periodical, °magazine, °journal, newsletter, newspaper, °paper, tabloid; annual, semi-annual, °quarterly, bimonthly, monthly, semi-monthly, fortnightly, biweekly, weekly, hebdomadal or hebdomedary, semi-weekly, °daily: *He buys every publication he can find dealing with model railways.*

publicize *v.* °promote, advertise, give publicity to, *Colloq* beat the drum for, °plug, °puff, *US* °push, *Slang* hype: *They once hired an elephant to publicize a huge department-store sale.*

publish *v.* make °public, °put out, °broadcast, °spread (about or around), advertise, °make known, let (something) be known, °announce, °publicize, °report, °proclaim, promulgate, bruit about, °reveal, divulge, °disclose, °break the °news (about), *Colloq* °leak: *The minister resigned the day the news of the scandal was published.*

pucker *v.* **1** °gather, °draw together, compress, °purse, crinkle, ruck, shirr, °ruffle, corrugate, °furrow, °wrinkle, crease, °screw up, °tighten, °contract, °squeeze: *Pucker up your mouth and*

give me a kiss. The shirring is done by puckering up the fabric and stitching it through with decorative thread.
—*n.* **2** °gather, tuck, pleat, pleating, shirr, shirring, °ruffle, ruck, ruche, ruckle, °wrinkle, wrinkling, °fold, crinkle, crinkling: *The curtains have some puckers that need ironing.*

puerile *adj.* °childish, °immature, babyish, °infantile, °juvenile, °silly, asinine, °foolish, trivial, °ridiculous, °irresponsible, °shallow, °inconsequential, °insignificant, *US* sophomoric: *Stop that puerile horseplay and settle down.*

puff *n.* **1** °blow, °breath, °wind, whiff, °draught, °gust, °blast, °huff: *A slight puff through the open window stirred the curtains.* **2** °draught, °draw, °pull, *Colloq* drag: *She took a puff from her cigarette and blew the smoke in his face.* **3** °advertisement, °praise, °mention, °word, °item, °review, °notice, publicity, puffery, *Colloq* °plug, blurb, *Slang* hype: *The late editions of the papers carry puffs for your new restaurant.*
—*v.* **4** °blow, °breathe, °huff, °pant, °gasp, wheeze: *Victor came huffing and puffing up to the finishing line.* **5** °draw, °pull (at or on), °inhale, suck, smoke, *Colloq* drag: *Holmes was puffing silently on his pipe.* **6** Usually, **puff up** or **out**: °inflate, distend, bloat, °swell (up or out), °stretch, balloon, °expand, °pump up, °enlarge: *Calvin swaggered in, all puffed up with pride about his new job.* **7** °publicize, advertise, °promote, °push, trumpet, ballyhoo, °extol, commend, °praise, *Colloq* °plug, beat the drum (for): *He has been shamelessly puffing his book on every radio and TV show.*

pugilism *n.* boxing, prizefighting; the manly art of self-defence, fisticuffs; *Colloq* the boxing or °fight game: *His career in pugilism came to an abrupt end in the second minute of the third round.*

pugilist *n.* boxer, prizefighter, fighter, contender, °contestant, battler, combatant, *Colloq* °bruiser, scrapper, champ, *Slang* slugger, pug: *The pugilists came out of their corners and at once started jabbing away at each other.*

pugnacious *adj.* °aggressive, °belligerent, combative, °quarrelsome, bellicose, antagonistic, °argumentative, °hostile, litigious, contentious, disputatious, °disagreeable, fractious, °petulant, °testy, irascible, hot-tempered, choleric, unfriendly, curmudgeonly, °irritable, °short-tempered: *The Gothic tribes were very pugnacious, always ready to fight with little or no provocation.*

pukka *adj.* **1** pukkah or pucka, °well done or made, °properly or °perfectly done, °first-class: *That was a pukka meal.* **2** pukkah or pucka, °genuine, °good, °authentic, °reliable, °honourable, °fair, °right, °proper, °thorough, °out-and-out: *They always referred to him as 'pukka sahib'.*

puling *adj.* whining, wailing, °querulous, whimpering, snivelling, weeping, caterwauling: *The third-class carriage was filled with chickens, pigs, and puling infants.*

pull *v.* **1** °draw, °haul, °drag, °lug, °tow, °trail: *Do you think the car is strong enough to pull that load?* **2** °tug, °jerk, °yank, °wrench, °pluck: *He suddenly pulled on the door and it opened.* **3** Sometimes, **pull out** or **up**: °pluck (out), °withdraw, °extract, °uproot, °pick (up or out), °snatch out or up, °tear or °rip out or up, cull, °select, °draw out, °take out, °remove: *We pulled out all the*

weeds and threw them on the compost heap. He has a collection of jokes pulled from his speeches.
4 Often, **pull apart**: °tear or °rip (up or °apart), °rend, pull asunder, °wrench (°apart), °stretch, °strain: This fabric is so weak it pulled apart as soon as I touched it. I think I pulled a muscle in my calf. **5** Often, **pull in**: °attract, °draw, °lure, °entice, allure, °catch, °captivate, °fascinate, °capture: We need something besides the 'Sale' sign to pull the customers into the shop. **6 pull apart**: pull to pieces or shreds, °criticize, °attack, °pick or take °apart or to pieces, flay, °run down, Colloq °put down, °pan, °knock, °devastate, °destroy, slate, Slang °slam: The critics really pulled apart her new play. **7 pull away**: °withdraw, °draw or drive or °go or °move away; outrun, outpace, °draw °ahead of: She pulled away abruptly when he touched her hand. The green car is pulling away from the others. **8 pull back**: **a** °withdraw, °draw back, back off or away, °recoil, °shrink (away or back) from, °shy, °flinch (from), °jump, °start: The burglar pulled back when he saw the ferocious dog. **b** °withdraw, (beat a) °retreat, take °flight, °flee, °turn tail, °drop or °fall back, back out: We cheered when we saw the enemy troops pulling back. **9 pull down**: **a** °demolish, °raze, °level, °destroy, °wreck: It takes only hours to pull down a house that it has taken generations to build. **b** °draw, °receive, °get, be paid, °earn: He pulls down much more at his new job. **c** °lower, °debase, °diminish, °reduce, °degrade, °dishonour, °disgrace, °discredit, °humiliate: When his fortunes declined, he pulled down all his friends with him. **10 pull for**: °hope or °pray for, be °enthusiastic for, be °supportive of, °support, °campaign for, °cheer for, °encourage, °boost, US °root for: We are all pulling for you to win. **11 pull in**: **a** °drive up, °arrive, °come, °draw up or in, °reach: The train finally pulled in at midnight. We need petrol, so pull in at the next filling station. **b** °arrest, apprehend, take into °custody, Colloq °pinch, °nab, collar, °nail, Brit °nick, Slang bust: The cops pulled him in for possession of narcotics. **12 pull off**: **a** °detach, °rip or °tear off, °separate, °wrench off or away: When he was cashiered from the army, they pulled off all his insignia and medals. **b** °accomplish, do, °complete, °succeed, °carry out, °bring off, °manage, °perform: Three men pulled off the robbery in broad daylight. **13 pull oneself together**: °recover, get a °grip on oneself, °get over it, °recuperate, Colloq °snap out of it, buck up: Try to pull yourself together and stop crying. **14 pull out**: **a** °uproot, °extract, °withdraw: In the ensuing scrap, someone tried to pull out his hair. Two survivors were pulled out of the rubble. **b** °withdraw, °retreat, beat a °retreat, °recede, °draw back, °leave, °depart, °go or °run away or off, °evacuate, Colloq beat it, do a bunk, Brit do a moonlight flit: The artillery unit pulled out yesterday. **c** °leave, °go, °depart, °take off: When that train pulls out, I want you on it! **d** °withdraw, °quit, °abandon, °resign (from), °give up, °relinquish: You can still pull out of the deal if you want to. **15 pull someone's leg**: °tease, °chaff, rib, °have on, °rag, °twit, poke °fun at, make °fun of, °hoodwink, °ridicule: He said that I'd just eaten a fly, but he was pulling my leg. **16 pull strings**: use °influence or connections, US use pull, pull wires: His uncle pulled strings to get him the job. **17 pull through**: °survive, °recover, °improve, get °better, °get

over (it), °rally; °live: Murphy was at death's door, but luckily he pulled through. **18 pull up**: **a** °stop, °halt, come to a °standstill: We pulled up in a lay-by for a few minutes' rest. **b** °uproot, °root out, °dig out, deracinate, eradicate: Your dog has pulled up all the flowers in my garden. **c** draw °even or °level with, °come up to, °reach: On the fifth lap, Manson pulled up to, then passed Sabbatini. —n. **19** °draw, °tug; °yank, °jerk: Give the bell-rope a strong, steady pull, and try not to yank it suddenly. **20** °attraction, °draw, °magnetism, °appeal, drawing or pulling °power, seductiveness, seduction, °lure: The pull that golf has on certain people is hard to explain. **21** °influence, °authority, °connections, °prestige, °weight, leverage, Colloq clout, muscle: You'd better treat her nicely, for she has a lot of pull with the boss. **22** °puff, °draw, inhalation, Colloq drag: He took a long, meditative pull on his cigarette and blew some smoke rings.

pulley n. sheave, °block: The rope is run through a system of pulleys, called a tackle, for lifting weights.

pulp n. **1** marrow, °pith, °heart, °soft part, °flesh: After removing the seeds, add two tablespoonfuls of sugar and mix into the pulp. **2** mush, paste, mash, pap, pomace, °mass, Technical triturate: Water is added to the waste paper, which the machines then reduce to a pulp. —v. **3** mash, squash, °pulverize, Technical levigate, triturate: The entire print run of the book was pulped after she threatened to sue the publishers. —adj. **4** °lurid, °sensational, trashy, °cheap: What he considers great literature you would call pulp fiction.

pulsate v. °beat, °pulse, throb, °pound, thrum, drum, thump, °thud, reverberate, hammer, palpitate, °vibrate; °oscillate, °quiver: Throughout the voyage, I could feel the ship's engines pulsating.

pulse n. **1** °beat, beating, throb, throbbing, pulsing, pulsating, pulsation, pounding, thrumming, drumming, °thumping, thudding, reverberation, reverberating, hammering, palpitation, palpitating, vibration, vibrating: The pulse of the jungle drums became louder and faster. —v. **2** See pulsate, above.

pulverize v. **1** °powder, comminute, °grind, °crush, °mill, granulate, °crumble, °break up, bray, °pound, Technical triturate, levigate: This machine pulverizes the rock, after which the binding agents are added. **2** °devastate, °destroy, °demolish, °crush, smash, °shatter, °ruin, °wreck, annihilate: The four battalions were pulverized in the attack.

pump v. **1** °send, °force, °deliver, °push: The heart pumps blood around the body. **2** interrogate, °question, °examine, cross-examine, °quiz, °probe, Colloq grill, give (someone) the third degree: They pumped her for hours, but she told them nothing about my whereabouts. **3 pump out**: pump °dry or °empty, °empty, °drain, bail out, °draw or °drive or °force out, siphon (out): After the flood it took two days to pump out my basement. **4 pump up**: **a** °inflate, °blow up; dilate, °swell, bloat, °expand, °puff out or up: If you don't repair the tyre, pumping it up will accomplish nothing. **b** °excite, °inspire, °stimulate, °animate, inspirit, °electrify, galvanize, °energize, °motivate, Colloq enthuse: The coach is talking to the team, trying to pump them up *before the big game.* **c** °intensify, °concentrate, °emphasize, °stress, °increase: *We ought to pump up our promotion campaign just before Christmas.*

pun *n.* play on words, °quip, (*bon*) *mot*, °witticism, double entendre, *Literary* equivoque, *Technical* paronomasia: *Dennis made some awful pun on 'nose' and 'knows' that nobody got.*

punch[1] *v.* **1** °hit, °clip, °jab, whack, thwack, °knock, smack, °box, pummel, °strike, cuff, *Colloq* clout, bop, slug, wallop, thump, °lambaste, °slam, *Slang* sock, biff, °plug, °belt, °lace (into), *US* paste: *Anyone says anything about my girl, I'll punch him in the jaw!*
—*n.* **2** °clip, °jab, whack, thwack, °knock, smack, °box, cuff, upper-cut, °left *or* °right, *Colloq* clout, bop, slug, wallop, thump, °slam, *Slang* sock, °belt, biff, haymaker, °plug, paste: *The punch knocked him down.* **3** °effect, °impact, effectiveness, °force, forcefulness, °power, °vitality, °gusto, °vigour, °life, vim, °zest, ginger, *Colloq* it, oomph, what it takes, *Slang* zing, zip: *These advertisements are pretty, but they are lacking in punch.*

punch[2] *n.* **1** awl, auger, bodkin, perforator; °drill, °brace and bit: *Use the punch to make another hole in your belt.*
—*v.* **2** °pierce, °stab, °puncture, °perforate; °bore, °drill: *She uses a needle to punch a tiny hole in each end of the egg.*

punctual *adj.* on °time, °timely, °prompt, *Colloq* on the °dot: *Please be punctual, as I don't fancy waiting about in the street.*

punctuate *v.* **1** °interrupt, °break, intersperse; °pepper, sprinkle: *The speeches were punctuated by frequent shouts from the audience.* **2** °accent, accentuate, underline, underscore, °emphasize, °stress, °mark: *He punctuated each element of his argument with a sharp rap of his pencil on the lectern.*

puncture *n.* **1** °hole, perforation, °opening, °leak; °flat (tyre): *I haven't the tools needed to patch the puncture in the tyre.* **2** perforation, perforating, holing, puncturing, °piercing, stabbing, punching: *The puncture of the balloon means that we shall have to postpone our trip.*
—*v.* **3** °perforate, °hole, °pierce, °stab, °penetrate, °go through, °prick, °nick, °rupture: *An arrow punctured the side of the tent.* **4** deflate, °disillusion, bring up °short, °discourage, °humble, °dash, °destroy, °ruin: *Any hopes I had of winning the marathon were punctured when I tripped and fell, spraining my ankle.*

pungent *adj.* **1** °spicy, °hot, °sharp, °strong, °penetrating, °aromatic, °seasoned, peppery, piquant, tangy, flavourful, °tasty, sapid: *The pungent odours of devilled kidneys dominated the dining-room.* **2** °sharp, °biting, stinging, °caustic, °severe, astringent, °stern, acrid, °harsh, °sour, acid, °tart, acrimonious, °bitter, °cutting, °keen, barbed, °trenchant, °scathing, °incisive, mordant, °sarcastic: *This week's Review carries a pungent criticism of his new novel.* **3** distressing, upsetting, °poignant, °painful, °hurtful, °penetrating, °piercing, stabbing, °intense, °severe, °acute, °agonizing, °oppressive, °excruciating, racking, consuming: *Only when surgery eased the pressure was he relieved of the pungent pain.*

punish *v.* **1** °penalize, °chastise, °castigate, °discipline, °chasten, °scold, °rebuke, take to °task, °reprove, °dress down, admonish, °correct, teach someone a °lesson, °give a °lesson to, throw the book at, °rap (someone's) knuckles, °slap (someone's) wrist, have *or US* call on the carpet, *Colloq* take it out on (someone): *A child's first taste of injustice is being punished for something she did not do.* **2** °imprison, °jail *or Brit also* gaol, incarcerate, °lock up; °fine, mulct, amerce; °lash, °flog, °beat, °scourge, °spank, °whip, cane, birch, put across *or US also* turn over (one's) knee, *US* °paddle; pillory, crucify; tar and feather, °exile, °banish, excommunicate, cashier, drum out of the corps; °hang, °execute, electrocute, draw and quarter, send to the gas chamber, *Colloq* °put away, *Slang Brit* °send down, *US* °send up: *They were punished for their crimes.* **3** °hurt, °harm, °injure, °damage, °abuse, maltreat, °rough up, °knock about *or* around, maul, thrash, °beat, trounce, °manhandle, °batter, *Slang* °beat up: *The challenger punished the champion so badly that he could not come out for the tenth round.*

punishing *adj.* gruelling, °hard, °arduous, °strenuous, °laborious, °exhausting, tiring, wearying, fatiguing, wearing, taxing, °demanding, °burdensome, back-breaking, torturous: *Laying railway track was the most punishing job I ever had. This punishing schedule is beginning to tell on me.*

punishment *n.* **1** chastisement, chastising, castigation, castigating, °discipline, disciplining, chastening, scolding, °rebuke, °reproof, dressing-down, admonishment, admonition, °correction, °punitive measures: *Every society must continually revise its approach to the punishment of criminals.* **2** °penance, °penalty, °sentence, sentencing, °just °deserts; °imprisonment, incarceration, jailing *or Brit also* gaoling; lashing, flogging, beating, °whipping, scourging, °spanking, caning, birching, *US* paddling; °exile, banishment, excommunication, cashiering; hanging, °execution, electrocution, drawing and quartering: *Her punishment is to perform 20 hours a week of public service for a year. Stop whimpering and take your punishment like a man.* **3** °injury, °harm, °damage, °abuse, maltreatment, mauling, beating, °thrashing, trouncing, manhandling, battering, torture: *How are professional wrestlers able to withstand so much punishment?*

punitive *adj.* chastening, castigatory, disciplinary, retributive, punitory, retaliatory, correctional: *A punitive expedition was sent there to quell the colonists' uprising.*

punk *n.* **1** ruffian, °hoodlum, hooligan, °delinquent, °tough, °thug, vandal, yahoo, °barbarian, *Colloq* goon, °mug: *A couple of young punks were standing at the bar, trying to look important.*
—*adj.* **2** °inferior, °rotten, unimportant, °worthless, °bad, °poor, °awful, *Colloq* °lousy: *I thought that the lead in the play was a punk actor.*

punt *v.* **1** °bet, wager, °stake, °gamble, °speculate, °lay a °bet *or* °stake *or* wager: *Herbert spends all the grocery money punting at the races.*
—*n.* **2** °bet, wager, °stake, °gamble: *In roulette, Janet always placed her punt on number 14.*

punter *n.* **1** *Brit* better *or US also* bettor, gambler, gamester, °player, speculator, °backer, wagerer, *Brit* °punt, *Colloq* crap-shooter: *The punters are putting all their money on United to win the cup.* **2** °fellow, °chap, °person, °individual, °man or °woman in the street; °customer, °client, °buyer, *Colloq* °guy, *Brit* bloke, geezer: *The average punter likes a beer now and then.*

puny *adj.* **1** °small, °little, °insignificant, °petty, unimportant, °inconsequential, °paltry, trivial, °trifling, °minor, °negligible, nugatory, of °little or no account, °inferior, °worthless, °useless, *Colloq* piddling, *Slang Brit* not much cop: *Farr's contribution to the success of the business was really quite puny.* **2** °small, °little, °diminutive, °tiny, °minute: *Mattson looks so puny alongside that sumo wrestler.* **3** °weak, °feeble, °frail, °sickly, weakly, underfed, undernourished, °undersized, underdeveloped, °stunted, °dwarf, midget, pygmy: *You cannot expect such a puny chap to lift such a great weight.*

pup *n.* puppy, whelp, °upstart, whippersnapper, popinjay, cub, jackanapes, °show-off, °braggart: *That young pup had the gall to tell me I was too old to be running the company.*

pupil *n.* °student, °learner, °scholar, schoolchild, schoolgirl, schoolboy, °disciple, °apprentice; beginner, °novice, neophyte, tiro *or* tyro, *Chiefly ecclesiastical* catechumen: *A number of Geoffrey's former pupils have organized a dinner to honour him.*

puppet *n.* **1** hand-puppet, finger-puppet, glove puppet, doll; marionette, string puppet: *The children built a little theatre and put on a puppet show.* **2** °figurehead, cat's-paw, °pawn, °dupe, °tool, hireling, °yes-man *Colloq* °front (man), *Slang* stooge, °sucker, patsy: *He is without authority and is merely a puppet of the drug dealers. The army of occupation set up a puppet government to rule the country.*

purchase *v.* **1** °buy, °acquire, °procure, °obtain, °get, °secure, °pay for: *He recently purchased a new personal computer and cannot get it to work. Not long ago, a shilling purchased a loaf of bread.* **2** °win, °gain, °achieve, °realize, attain, °obtain: *His liberty was purchased by the betrayal of his colleagues.* —*n.* **3** °acquisition, acquiring, buying, purchasing, °obtaining, securing, procurement: *The purchase of books for the university library is the responsibility of Ms Turnbull.* **4** °buy, °acquisition: *Tom returned from the shop carrying his purchases.* **5** °grip, °hold, °support, toe-hold, foothold, °grasp; leverage, °position, °advantage, °edge: *The climber was having trouble getting a good purchase on the icy ledge.*

pure *adj.* **1** unmixed, unadulterated, unalloyed, simon-pure; 24-carat *or US also* 24-karat, °sterling, °solid; °real, °genuine, °authentic, °flawless, °faultless, °perfect, °natural, °true, °simple: *We have made every effort to keep the blood-line of these horses completely pure. Pure gold is not used for coins or jewellery because it is too soft. She wore a dress of the purest white.* **2** uncontaminated, °clear, °clean, °wholesome, °sanitary, uninfected, disinfected, pasteurized, sterilized, °sterile, antiseptic, unpolluted, °spotless, °immaculate, unsullied, unbesmirched, unblemished, unmarred, unstained, untainted: *It was refreshing to breathe pure air again. Stringent tests ensure that the substances are pure before they go on the market.* **3** °chaste, virginal, virgin, °intact, maidenly, vestal, undefiled, °innocent, guileless, °virtuous, °modest, °moral, °correct, °proper, °decent, °decorous, uncorrupted, °blameless, sinless, °impeccable: *As far as we can tell, she led a totally*

pure life. **4** °theoretical, °hypothetical, conjectural, °speculative, °abstract, conceptual, notional, °philosophical, °academic(al): *His field is pure science, and he cares little how the results of his work might be applied to everyday life.* **5** unalloyed, °simple, °unmitigated, °sheer, utter, °absolute, °unqualified, °complete, °total, °perfect, °thorough, °outright, °downright, °out-and-out, °mere: *Many regarded the notion that man could ever fly as pure nonsense. Any resemblance to a living person is pure coincidence.* **6** °honourable, (highly) °principled, °righteous, °upright, °honest, straightforward, high-minded, °pious, °worthy, °good, °ethical, °virtuous, °sincere, above °suspicion, above reproach, like Caesar's wife: *Can anyone doubt that their motives in striving for international peace are pure?*

pure-bred *adj.* full-blooded, thoroughbred, pedigreed: *We raise only pure-bred Angus cattle.*

purgative *n.* **1** laxative, cathartic, aperient, °purge, physic, depurative: *The doctor prescribed a mild purgative, and she felt much better next day.* —*adj.* **2** laxative, cathartic, aperient, evacuant, diuretic, depurative; abstergent: *We were totally unprepared for the purgative effects of the spicy food.*

purge *v.* **1** °cleanse, °purify, °clean (out), °clear, °scour (out), depurate, deterge, °wash (out): *The tanks must be purged before filling them with the new fuel.* **2** °eject, eradicate, °expel, °eliminate, get °rid of, °dismiss, °clear out or away, °sweep away or out, oust, °remove, °rout out, weed out, °root out; do away with, °exterminate, liquidate, °kill, °destroy: *After the coup, the old guard was purged from all the governmental agencies. The rebels purged the entire council of elders.* **3** °clear, exonerate, absolve, °forgive, °purify, °pardon, exculpate: *He was given every opportunity to purge himself of the charge of contempt of court.* —*n.* **4** °ejection, eradication, °expulsion, elimination, °dismissal, clearing out *or* away, ousting, ouster, °removal, routing out, weeding out, rooting out, unseating; defenestration; extermination, liquidation, °killing, °murder, °slaughter: *The bloody purge of dissidents was carried out by the secret police.* **5** See **purgative**, **1**, above.

purify *v.* **1** °cleanse, °clean, °clarify, °wash, sanitize, depurate, decontaminate, °freshen, °disinfect; °fumigate: *The water is then purified by passing it through sand.* **2** exonerate, exculpate, absolve, °clear, °redeem, shrive, lustrate, acquit, °pardon, °forgive, °excuse: *Before the aspirants can be admitted to the church they must be purified.*

purist *n.* pedant, precisian, formalist, stickler, blue-stocking, dogmatist, °Pharisee, °fanatic, *Colloq* die-hard, stuffed shirt: *Language purists are often unaware of their own grammatical and semantic blunders.*

puritan *n.* **1** moralist, pietist, religionist, °fanatic, °zealot, °purist: *It seems to me that all religions have their puritans.* —*adj.* **2** °prudish, puritanical, prim, °proper, °strait-laced, ascetic, austere, moralistic, pietistic, °intolerant, disapproving, °bigoted, °narrow-minded, °stuffy, stiff-necked, °rigid, uncompromising, hard-line, °stern, °severe, °strict, *Colloq* uptight, hard-nosed: *Puritan notions about women's clothing have often put propriety before practicality.*

purity n. **1** pureness, faultlessness, correctness, flawlessness, °perfection, spotlessness, cleanness, cleanliness, °clarity; healthfulness, wholesomeness, salubrity; innocuousness, harmlessness: *The purity of the drinking-water has been affected by the nearby chemical plant.* **2** °chastity, chasteness, virginity, virtuousness, °virtue, °morality, °propriety, °honesty, °integrity, °rectitude, properness, innocence, guilelessness, decency, decorousness, modesty, blamelessness, sinlessness: *We never had any reason to doubt the purity of their character.*

purpose n. **1** °object, °intention, °intent, °end, °goal, °ambition, °objective, °target, °aim, °principle, °point, °rationale, °reason; °scheme, °plan, °design, °motive, motivation, °view: *What purpose was served by her confession? If your purpose in inviting me was to insult me, I shall leave now. I fail to understand Laura's purpose in warning me against David.* **2** °resolution, firmness, °determination, °persistence, °drive, single-mindedness, deliberation, deliberateness, purposefulness, steadfastness, °tenacity, doggedness, °will, °resolve, resoluteness, °perseverance, stubbornness: *She admired the strong purpose behind his refusal to compromise with quality.* **3** °use, practicality, avail, °effect, utility, °usefulness, °outcome, °result; °advantage, °profit, °gain, °good, °benefit: *To what purpose are you planning to put this knowledge? I cannot see the purpose in pursuing this line of questioning.* **4 on purpose: a** purposely, intentionally, °deliberately, wilfully, by °design, consciously, knowingly, designedly, wittingly: *That was no accident: you kicked me on purpose!* **b** °especially, °specially, °expressly, °exactly, °precisely, specifically, in °particular: *He kicked me on purpose, Mum, just to make me cry!*
—v. **5** °plan, °intend, °design, °resolve, °mean, °aim, have in °mind or °view, have a °mind, °propose, °consider, °contemplate, °aspire, long, °yearn: *They purpose to open an office of their own.*

purposeful adj. °intentional, intended, planned, °deliberate, resolved, settled, °determined, °resolute, °decided, confirmed, affirmed, °sure, °certain, °positive, °definite, °staunch, °steadfast, °persistent, strong-willed, dogged, °tenacious, pertinacious, unfailing, unfaltering, °firm, °fixed: *Her purposeful manner inclines other people to defer to her.*

purposeless adj. °pointless, °bootless, °meaningless, °empty, vacuous, °senseless, °aimless, °rambling, °discursive, wandering, disorganized, unorganized: *He made what we thought was a purposeless trip to the branch office, but it ultimately proved invaluable.*

purse n. **1** °pouch, (money-)°bag, °wallet, °pocket, *Dialect* poke, *Highland dress* sporran, *US and Canadian* (woman's) handbag, pocketbook: *The money goes out so fast I think there is a hole in my purse.* **2** °money, °wealth, °resources, °funds, °finances, exchequer, °treasury, °capital, °revenue, °income, °means, °cash, °riches; pounds, shillings, and pence, l.s.d., dollars, shekels, *Derogatory* Mammon, pelf, (filthy) lucre, *US* almighty dollar, *Slang Brit* °ready or readies, lolly, dosh, °loot, dough, *US and Canadian* bucks, °scratch: *The spread of capitalism shows that the power of a man's purse can*

transcend his political idealism. **3** °prize, °reward, °award, °present, °gift: *The purse for the next race will be 5,000 guineas.*
—v. **4** °pucker (up), °contract, °wrinkle, compress, °press together: *Robert pursed his lips thoughtfully.*

pursue v. **1** °follow, °chase, °go or °run after, °hunt (after or down or for or up), °trace, °trail, °track, °run down, °take off after, dog, °stalk, °shadow, *Brit* chivvy or chivy or chevy, *Colloq* °tail: *The police pursued the escaped convicts across the moor.* **2** °follow (up or on with), °trace, °carry on with, °continue, °conduct, °devote or °dedicate oneself to, °cultivate, °undertake, °practise, °persist or °persevere in, °maintain, °exercise, °proceed with, adhere to, °stay with, °apply oneself to, *Colloq* °stick with: *If you pursue such a course, you are certain to land in jail.* **3** °aspire to, °aim for, °work for or toward(s), °try or °strive for, °purpose, °seek, °search for, °go in °search of, °quest after or for, be °intent on, be °bent upon or on: *Jonathan is pursuing a doctorate in history at Oxford.* **4** woo, (pay) court (to), °seek the hand of, *Formal* °press (one's) °suit with, pay °suit or court or (one's) °addresses to, *Colloq* set one's cap for, *Slang* °chase (after): *Jack is pursuing Jacquelyn with matrimony in mind.*

pursuit n. **1** pursuing, chasing, following, hunting, °hunt, going or °running after, tracing, trailing, tracking, °running down, dogging, stalking, shadowing, *Brit* chivvy or chivy or chevy, *Colloq* tailing: *We all joined in the pursuit of the animal. The police set off in hot pursuit of the thieves.* **2** pursuance, striving after, seeking, searching, °search, looking for: *Many think that the pursuit of wealth is the only worthwhile thing in life.* **3** °work, °line (of °work), °employment, °field, °area, °speciality or *US and Canadian only* specialty, specialization, °business, °profession, °trade, °vocation, °calling, °career, life-work, °activity; °hobby, °pastime, avocation, °interest; *Slang* °racket: *What pursuits are open to Jack Ketch now that hanging has been abolished?*

push v. **1** °thrust, shove, °drive, °move, set in °motion, get °moving, °propel; °press: *Push the boat away from the pier. He pushed the door shut.* **2** °press, °depress: *Push the button if you want anything.* **3** shove, °thrust, elbow, °shoulder, °force, jostle, °nudge: *We pushed our way through the crowd.* **4** °urge, encourage, °press, °induce, °ask, °persuade, °get, egg on, °prod, °spur, goad, °rouse, °prompt, °incite, °move, °motivate, °stimulate, °influence, impel, °make, compel, °force, dragoon, coerce, constrain; badger, °hound, °pester, °harass, °plague, °nag, °browbeat, °beg, importune, entreat: *His family is pushing him to find work. I'll soon have the work done, but stop pushing me.* **5** °force, °strain, overstrain, °tax, overtax, °burden, overburden: *You might have got away with it this time, but don't push your luck.* **6** °promote, °publicize, advertise, °boost, propagandize, °puff, *Colloq* °plug, *Slang* ballyhoo, hype: *Because we have too much stock, we are pushing suntan oil this week.* **7 push about** or **around** °intimidate, °bully, cow, domineer, °tyrannize, bullyrag, °torment, °force, coerce: *Don't push people about if you want them to do what you want.* **8 push away** °reject, °deny, °brush off or aside, give (someone) the cold °shoulder, °rebuff, °distance oneself from: *She pushes everyone away and then wonders why she*

has no friends. **9 push off**: **a** shove off, °sail away *or* off: *We stepped into the dinghy and pushed off.* **b** °leave, °depart, °go away, *Colloq* light out, °take off, hit the road, skedaddle, scram, make oneself scarce, *Slang* °beat it: *I have to push off now if I'm to make that train.* **10 push on** *or* **forward(s)** *or* **along**: °move °onwards *or* °onward *or* °ahead *or* forward, °continue, °proceed, °advance, press on *or* °onwards *or* °onward: *If we stay the night here, we shall have to push on first thing in the morning.* **11 push through**: °force, °press, *Colloq* °railroad: *The bill was pushed through committee without delay.* **12 push (up) daisies**: be °dead (and buried), be six feet under: *Her husband's pushing up daisies.*
—*n.* **13** shove, °thrust, °nudge: *My car needs a push to get it started.* **14** °effort, °energy, °dynamism, °drive, °force, °enterprise, °ambition, °vigour, °determination, °initiative, °eagerness, °spirit, °enthusiasm, zeal, °verve, *Colloq* get-up-and-go, zing, zip, °gumption, °go: *If he had a bit more push, he might succeed.* **15** °campaign, °attack, °assault, °advance, °offensive, °charge, onslaught, foray, sortie, °invasion, incursion, °raid, sally, blitz-krieg, blitz, °strike: *The troops were massed along the coast, ready for the big push inland.* **16 the push**: °dismissal, °notice, *Colloq* marching orders, *Chiefly Brit* the °sack, the °boot, *Chiefly US and Canadian* walking papers, a pink slip: *He'd been with the company for twenty years, but they still gave him the push when sales fell.*

pushover *n.* **1** °sure thing, *Colloq* °piece of cake, child's play, °snap, °picnic, walk-over, *US* °breeze, *Slang* cinch, *Brit* doddle, *US* lead-pipe cinch: *The Latin exam was a pushover.* **2** *Colloq* walk-over, chump, °soft touch, °soft *or* °easy mark, °easy °prey *or* °game, *Slang* patsy, °sucker, stooge, °sap, *Brit* °mug, *US and Canadian* milquetoast: *I spotted him at once as a pushover for the find-the-lady con.*

pushy *adj.* °forward, (self-)°assertive, °forceful, °aggressive, °obnoxious, °arrogant, bumptious, °brassy, °brazen, °impertinent, °insolent, pushing, °presumptuous, °officious, °loud, °showy, °cocky, °brash, °offensive, °bold, *Colloq* °cheeky: *I hate pushy salesmen who won't take 'No' for an answer.*

pussyfoot *v.* **1** °sneak, °creep, °slink, °prowl, °steal, tiptoe: *I wish she'd stop pussyfooting about the house.* **2** beat about the bush, hem *or* hum and haw, °equivocate, °hesitate, be °evasive, °evade the °issue, prevaricate, tergiversate, be °noncommittal, be *or* sit on the °fence, °blow hot and cold: *Don't pussyfoot with me—just come out and say what you really think.*

put *v.* **1** °place, °position, °situate, °set, °lay, °station, °stand, °deposit, °rest, °settle; °locate: *Please put all books where they belong.* **2** °assign, °commit, °cause, °set, consign, °subject: *I joined the army to fight for my country, and they put me to work peeling potatoes.* **3** °subject, cause to °experience *or* °undergo *or* °suffer, consign, °send: *He was put to death for his beliefs, not his actions.* **4** °express, °word, °phrase, °say, utter, °write: *How did they put it?—'We hold these truths to be self-evident, that all men are created equal...' To put it to you straight, shape up or ship out! Can you put that into French?* **5** °offer, °advance, °bring

forward, °present, °propose, °submit, °tender, °set before: *I put it to you that you have been lying to the court and that you did leave your house that night.* **6** °bet, °gamble, wager, °stake, play, °chance, °risk, °hazard: *I put two pounds on the horse to win.* **7** °throw, °heave, °toss, °fling, °cast, °pitch, °bowl, °lob, °send, °shy, °shoot, °snap, catapult: *How far did you say you can put a 10-pound shot?* **8** °place, °assign, °attribute, °lay, °pin, °attach, °fix: *They try to put the blame on me for everything that goes wrong around here.* **9 put about**: °broadcast, °publish, °make known, °publicize, °announce, °spread about *or* around: *They have been putting about some story linking the two of us romantically.* **10 put across** *or* **over**: make °clear, °get across, make (something *or* oneself) °understood *or* under-standable, °explain, °spell out, convey, °communicate: *She is quite adept at putting across her ideas.* **11 put aside**: °set *or* °lay aside, °ignore, °disregard, pay no °heed to, °push aside, shrug off: *They put aside their differences and discovered they had much in common. Isn't it time you put aside childish things?* **12 put aside** *or* **by** *or* **away**: °lay aside *or* by, °set aside; °save, °store, °stow *or* °store *or* °salt *or* squirrel away, °lay away, °cache, bank: *You ought to put a little money aside for a rainy day.* **13 put away**: **a** See 12, above. **b** °jail *or* *Brit also* gaol, °imprison, incarcerate, *Colloq* °send, °jug, confine, °commit, institutionalize, remand, *Brit* °send down, *US* °send up: *She wants rapists and child molesters put away for a long, long time.* **c** See 16 d, below. **d** °consume, °gorge, gormandize *or* *US also* gourmandize: *It is unbelievable how much that man can put away in one sitting.* **14 put back**: °return, °replace, °restore: *He insists that he put back all the money he took. Put the pictures back where they belong.* **15 put by**: See 12, above. **16 put down**: **a** °record, °register, °write down, °set down, °enter, °list; log, °note (down), °jot down, make a °note *or* °notation of: *You may put me down for a contribution of £5. Please put down your name and address in the box provided.* **b** depose, put an °end to, °topple, °crush, °overthrow, °subdue, °suppress, °check, °quash, °quell: *The loyalists put down the rebellion in short order.* **c** ascribe, °assign, °attribute: *The doctor put my feelings of fatigue and listlessness down to anaemia.* **d** °kill, °exterminate, °destroy, put to death, put to sleep, put away, do away with: *We had to have our cat put down, which was very upsetting for us all.* **e** abash, °humiliate, °crush, °silence, °mortify, °lower, take down (a °peg *or* a notch), °shame, snub, deflate, °slight, °reject, °dismiss: *Waiters have a way of putting people down if they behave presumptuously.* **f** °take for, °reckon, °account, °count, °categorize, °regard: *Don't put Martin down as a dunce just because he acts the fool now and then.* **g** °belittle, °diminish, °disparage, deprecate, °depreciate, °criticize, disdain, °look down on, °despise, con-temn: *They deny being prejudiced, but they put down everyone who isn't exactly like them.* **17 put forth**: **a** °propose, °offer, °set forth, °advance: *Several theories have been put forth on the function of mitochondrial DNA.* **b** °grow, °produce, °send out *or* forth, bud, °flower: *When the plant puts forth suckers, they must be pinched back.* **c** °begin, °set out, °set forth, °start: *We put forth on our voyage with great enthusiasm.* **d** promulgate,

°issue, °publish, °make known, °make °public: *The committee have not put forth any suggestions for improving traffic flow.* **18 put forward:**
a °propose, °present, °tender, °nominate, °name; °recommend: *Your name has been put forward as chair for next year's committee.*
b °suggest, °offer, °propose, °set forth, put forth, °present, °submit, °tender, proffer, °introduce, °advance, °propound, °air, °make known, °announce: *No new solutions to the problem were put forward.* **19 put in: a** °insert, °introduce: *Why did you put in a reference to your mother?* **b** °spend, °devote: *During the holiday season I plan to put in a lot of time reading.*
c °make: *So, you finally decided to put in an appearance.* **20 put in for: a** °apply for, °request, °ask for, °petition for: *He has put in for a transfer twice and has been refused both times.* **b** °seek, °apply for, °pursue, °file: *Do you really think that Jamieson will put in for re-election?*
21 put off: a °postpone, °delay, °defer, put back, °stay, °hold off, °shelve, put or °set aside, *Chiefly US* put over, °table: *Consideration of your request has been put off till tomorrow.* **b** °dismiss, get °rid of, °send away, °turn away; °discourage, *Colloq* give (someone) the °brush-off, *US* °brush off: *The manager put me off when I went in to ask about a salary increase.* **c** °dismay, disconcert, °upset, °confuse, °disturb, °perturb, abash, °distress, *Colloq* °throw, °rattle: *Curiously, Michael didn't seem a bit put off to learn about the murder.* **d** °repel, °disgust, °sicken, °revolt, °nauseate: *That television programme on open-heart surgery really put me off.* **e** °leave, °depart, °go (off), °set off: *We put off tomorrow morning for Rockall.* **22 put on: a** don, °clothe or attire or °dress (oneself) in, get dressed in, change or slip into: *We put on our best clothes to come to your party.* **b** °assume, °take on, °pretend, °affect, feign, °bluff, make a °show of: *She puts on an air of indifference, but she really does care.* **c** °add, °gain: *Bill put on quite a bit of weight when he stopped smoking.* **d** °stage, °mount, °produce, °present, °perform: *Our local repertory group is putting on Hedda Gabler this weekend.* **e** °tease, °mock, *Colloq* kid, pull (someone's) °leg, rib, °rag, *Brit* °have on: *When he told you that all holidays had been cancelled he was only putting you on.* **23 put out: a** °inconvenience, discommode, °disturb, °embarrass, °trouble, °bother, °impose upon or on, *Colloq* put on the °spot: *Her arriving an hour early didn't put me out one bit.* **b** °annoy, vex, °irritate, °anger, °exasperate, °irk, °perturb, °provoke, *Slang* °bug: *Donald was very much put out to discover that the appointment had gone to someone else.* **c** snuff out, °extinguish, °blow out, douse, °quench, °smother: *We put out the fire on the stove before it could spread.* **d** °exert, °put forth, °expend, °use, °exercise: *We put out considerable effort moving the furniture before she decided she liked it the way it had been.* **e** °publish, °issue, °broadcast, make °public, °circulate, °spread, °make known, °release: *The information office put out the news that the summit meeting had been a great success.* **24 put out of (one's) misery:** °release, °relieve, °free, °deliver, °rescue, °save, °spare: *Just tell him what they said and put him out of his misery.* **25 put over: a** put or °get across, convey, °communicate, °set or put forth, °relate: *I am trying to put the point over to you that I cannot leave now.* **b** See 21a, above. **26 put (one**

or **something) over on (someone):** °fool (someone), °pull (someone's) °leg, °deceive (someone), °mislead (someone), pull the wool over (someone's) eyes, °trick (someone), °hoodwink (someone): *She really put one over on me when she said she loved me. I think that Manfred is trying to put something over on you.* **27 put through: a** °carry out or through, °execute, (put into) °effect, °bring off, °accomplish, °complete, °finish, conclude, *Colloq* °pull off: *If they succeed in putting through their plan, the company will be bankrupt.* **b** °process, °handle, °organize, °see to, °follow up on: *I will personally see that your application is put through the proper channels.* **c** °connect, °hook up: *I asked the operator to put me through to the chairman himself.* **28 put up: a** °erect, °build, °construct, °raise, °set up, °put together, °fabricate: *They demolished a row of Georgian houses and put up some ugly County offices in their place.*
b °accommodate, °lodge, °board, °house, °take in, °quarter, *Chiefly military* billet: *As our house is small, we were able to put up only three people.* **c** °preserve, can; °cure, pickle: *There are many foods that can be put up for later consumption.* **d** °contribute, °pledge, °offer (as collateral), °stake, mortgage, °post: *We put up the house as security for the loan.* **e** °contribute, °give, °supply, °donate, ante (up), °advance, °pay, °invest: *We put up all our savings to secure our retirement pension.* **f** °increase, °raise, °boost, elevate: *As soon as there is a hint of an oil shortage, they put up the price of petrol.* **g** See 18 a, above. **h** °offer, °tender, put or place on the °market: *They put their house up for sale and are planning to move to the Riviera.* **29 put up to:** °incite, °urge, goad, °spur, egg on, °encourage, °prompt, instigate: *Was it you who put Reggie up to playing that prank on the teacher?* **30 put up with:** °tolerate, °abide, °take, °brook, °stand (for), °stomach, °accept, °resign oneself to, °bear, °endure, °swallow: *Why do you put up with his outrageous behaviour?*

put-down *n.* °dig, °sneer, snub, disparaging or denigrating °remark, °slight, °offence, °insult: *The worst put-down was to tell her she looks like her sister, whom she hates.*

put-on *n.* **1** °deception, °hoax, °trick, leg-pull, jest, (practical) °joke, °prank, °pretence, *Colloq* spoof: *He was completely taken in by my put-on about being from the Nobel prize committee.* **2** °take-off, °parody, °satire, °burlesque, °caricature, °act, *Brit* send-up, *Colloq* spoof: *You shouldn't be offended, it was only a put-on.*

putrefy *v.* °rot, °decompose, °decay, moulder, °go °bad, °spoil, °deteriorate, °go off: *We traced the smell in the larder to a putrefying leg of lamb.*

putrid *adj.* °rotten, rotting, decomposed, decomposing, decayed, decaying, °mouldy, mouldering, spoilt or spoiled, putrefied, putrescent, putrefying, °foul, fetid, °rank, tainted, °corrupt: *Only the vultures continued to hover about the putrid carcass.*

put-up *adj.* (secretly) °preconceived, prearranged, plotted, preconcerted: *If the butler had a hand in it, you know it was a put-up job.*

put-upon *adj.* imposed upon, inconvenienced, put out, taken °advantage of, exploited, °abused: *I shall be happy to help, and I don't feel put-upon at all.*

puzzle v. **1** baffle, °bewilder, °confuse, confound, °mystify, °flummox, °perplex, °nonplus, °stymie, °stump: *I am completely puzzled by what you wrote in your last letter.* **2** Usually, **puzzle over**: °study, °ponder (over), °mull over, °contemplate, °meditate on *or* upon *or* over, °consider, °muse over *or* on, °reflect on *or* over, °think about *or* over *or* on: *If you puzzle over it long enough, the problem may vanish of its own accord.* **3 puzzle out**: °solve, °decipher, °crack (the °code), unravel, °work out, °figure out, °think through, °sort out, unlock: *I finally*

puzzled out the inscription on this old coin. It might take a while, but I can puzzle out the solution to this crossword.
—*n.* **4** °enigma, °problem, °question, °paradox, poser, °mystery, °riddle, conundrum, *Colloq* brain-teaser: *The puzzle is how the murder was committed when the door was locked from the inside.*

puzzling *adj.* mystifying, enigmatic(al), bewildering, baffling, confounding, °perplexing, confusing, °ambiguous, °contradictory, abstruse: *It is a bit puzzling to see Catherine so often in the company of the husband she recently divorced.*

Q

quack *n.* **1** charlatan, °impostor, °pretender, °fake(r), °fraud, *Colloq* °phoney *or US also* phony: *The quack diagnosed Franny as having appendicitis, but it turned out that she was pregnant.* —*adj.* **2** °fake, °fraudulent, °sham, °counterfeit, *Colloq* °phoney *or US also* phony: *Are you still going to see that quack doctor—the one who told you to take aspirin to relieve the pain from your ulcer?*

quaint *adj.* **1** °curious, °odd, °strange, °bizarre, °peculiar, °unusual, °queer, uncommon, °singular, °unorthodox, °eccentric, °whimsical, °offbeat, °fanciful, °outlandish, unconventional, °fantastic: *Her sitting-room was furnished in a quaint mixture of Gothic and Victorian styles.* **2** °old-fashioned, archaic, °antiquated, out-dated, °picturesque, °antique: *A rotund little figure appeared, dressed in the quaint clothing of another era.*

quake *v.* **1** °tremble, °shake, °quiver, °shudder; °vibrate, °stagger: *The children were quaking with fear as they crept past the abandoned house.* **2** earthquake, tremor, temblor *or* trembler *or* tremblor, seismic(al) activity, *Rare* seism: *In a few moments the quake levelled three cities that had stood for thousands of years.*

qualification *n.* **1** Often, **qualifications**: °fitness, °ability, °aptitude, °capability, competence *or* competency, °capacity, suitableness, suitability, eligibility, °proficiency, °skill, °knowledge, *Colloq* know-how: *You cannot persuade me that Powell has the qualifications needed to do the job.* **2** limitation, °restriction, modification, °reservation, caveat, °condition, °stipulation, °proviso, °prerequisite, °requirement: *The only qualification for use of the club's facilities is that one must be a member. My support for the proposal is without qualification.*

qualified *adj.* **1** °able, °suitable, °capable, °competent, °fit, °fitted, equipped, °prepared, °ready, trained, °proficient, °accomplished, °expert, °talented, °adept, °skilful, skilled, °experienced, °practised, °knowledgeable, °well-informed: *Is Kimble qualified to become foreman?* **2** contingent, conditional, restricted, modified, °limited, °provisional: *The chairman has given his qualified approval to the scheme.*

qualify *v.* **1** °equip, °fit (out), °ready, °prepare, °condition, make °eligible; °certify: *His training in the air force qualified him to be a pilot.* **2** be °eligible, meet the °requirements, be °fit *or* °suitable *or* equipped *or* °ready *or* °prepared, make the °grade: *Sue will qualify as a doctor if she passes just one more exam.* **3** °temper, °mitigate, °modify, °moderate, °modulate, °restrict, °limit: *In the light of their later behaviour, I shall have to qualify my recommendation that you accept them as students.*

quality *n.* **1** °property, °attribute, °characteristic, °mark, °distinction, je ne sais quoi, °trait: *Can you describe the qualities needed to be a good musician?* **2** °grade, °calibre, °rank, °status, °importance, value, °worth: *In the curiosity shop items of high and low quality are mixed*

together haphazardly. **3** *Old-fashioned* eminence, °prominence, °importance, °excellence, °superiority, °distinction, °standing, °supremacy, °dignity, °grandeur, °nobility, blue blood: *Despite her shabby appearance, one could see from her bearing and speech she was a person of quality.*

qualm *n.* second thought, °doubt, uncertainty, °misgiving, hesitation, °scruple, uneasiness, °compunction, °reluctance, disinclination, queasiness, apprehension, apprehensiveness, °twinge, °pang, °worry, °concern, *Colloq* °funny °feeling, °sinking °feeling: *He had some qualms about leaving the town where he had lived for over thirty years.*

quandary *n.* °dilemma, °predicament, °difficulty, °plight, cleft stick, uncertainty: *The management is in a quandary: should it risk overstretching the company by making further capital investment, or should it risk being left behind by its competitors by playing safe?*

quantity *n.* °amount, °extent, °volume; °sum, °number, °total; °weight, °measure: *There seemed to be no limit to the quantity of gold in the mine. The person who most accurately guesses the quantity of beans in the jar wins a prize. What quantity of flour should I buy to make enough cakes for fifty people?*

quarrel *n.* **1** °dispute, °argument, °disagreement, °debate, °controversy, °discord, °difference (of opinion), contention, °misunderstanding; wrangle, °tiff, °row, squabble, altercation, set-to, scuffle, °feud, °fight, °fray, °fracas, °brawl, Donnybrook, mêlée *or* melee, °riot, °battle (royal), *Colloq* dust-up, barney, °scrap, *US* spat: *I have no quarrel with my accountant—it's the tax man that's the problem. A quarrel broke out over whose turn it was to wash the dishes.* —*v.* **2** °argue, °disagree, °dispute, altercate, have an altercation, °differ, wrangle, be at °odds *or* loggerheads, °clash, squabble, °feud, °fight, °brawl, °battle, *Colloq* °fall out, °scrap: *When we were children, my sister and I quarrelled all the time, but we still loved each other.*

quarrelsome *adj.* °testy, °petulant, irascible, °irritable, °disagreeable, fractious, °querulous, °peevish, °cross, choleric, curmudgeonly, °contrary, dyspeptic, °cranky, grouchy, °argumentative, combative, squabbling, disputatious, °hostile, antagonistic, dissentious, dissentient, °dissident, °pugnacious, bellicose, °belligerent, contentious: *I have to listen to the continual bickering of my quarrelsome neighbours.*

quarry[1] *n.* °prey, °game, °prize, °object: *The hunter's dogs had run their quarry to ground. Wealthy widows were regarded as fair quarry by the swindlers.*

quarry[2] *n.* **1** °mine, °pit, °excavation: *Only one quarry yielded the statuary marble needed by those sculptors.* —*v.* **2** °mine, °extract, °obtain, °get: *Gault's ideas were all quarried from the jottings of obscure writers.*

quarter n. **1** fourth: *Statistics showed that a quarter of the population attended church regularly.* **2** three-month period, three months, ninety days, thirteen weeks; fifteen minutes; °phase (of the moon), quadrature: *The first quarter's rent is now due. We waited a quarter of an hour. The moon is in its third quarter.* **3** °area, °region, °part, °section, °district, °zone, °division, °territory, °place, °neighbourhood, locality, °locale, °location, °point, °spot; °direction: *The army was called in to patrol the quarter of the city where looting had occurred. It was difficult to tell from which quarter the wind was blowing.* **4** °mercy, compassion, mercifulness, clemency, leniency, °forgiveness, °favour, °humanity, °pity: *The hostages expected no quarter from their captors.* **5 quarters**: living quarters, °lodging(s), dwelling-place, °dwelling, °accommodation(s), rooms, chambers, °residence, °shelter, habitation, °domicile, °home, °house, °abode; *Military* billet, barracks, cantonment, casern or caserne: *We found comfortable quarters in which we remained during our stay in the area.*
—v. **6** °lodge, °accommodate, °house, °board, °shelter, °put up; *Military* billet, °post, °station: *The tour guide stayed at the best hotel, while we were quartered in a youth hostel.*

quarterly adj. **1** trimonthly, three-monthly: *She is editor of a quarterly medical journal.*
—adv. **2** every three months, every ninety days, every thirteen weeks, four times a year: *The landlady insisted on being paid quarterly, in advance.*

quash v. **1** annul, nullify, °void, declare or render null and °void, invalidate, °revoke, °vacate, °set aside, rescind, °cancel, °reject, °throw out, °reverse, °overthrow, °discharge, overrule: *When the real culprit confessed, my conviction was quashed and I was set free.* **2** °suppress, °subdue, °quell, °put down, °squelch, °repress, °overthrow, °crush, °overwhelm: *The rebellion was quashed by the secret police.*

quasi- adv. **1** Sometimes, **quasi**: as if, as it were, °seemingly, °apparently, °partly, to some °extent, to all intents and purposes, more or less, °virtually, °almost: *Her apology seemed only quasi-sincere to me. His function in the proceedings was quasi-judicial.*
—adj. **2** Often, **quasi**: so to °speak, °kind of, °sort of; °pretended, °fake, pseudo, °so-called, °supposed, °artificial, °mock, °sham, *Colloq* °phoney or *US also* phony: *His quasi excuse does not diminish the horror of what he did.*

quaver v. **1** °tremble, °quiver, °shake, °shiver, °vibrate, waver, °shudder, °fluctuate, °oscillate, °flutter: *His voice quavered with emotion as he described his rescue.*
—n. **2** trembling, °tremble, °quiver, quivering, tremor, shaking, vibration, wavering, °break, °fluctuation, oscillation: *Only a slight quaver in her voice betrayed her feeling of panic.*

queasy adj. **1** uncomfortable, uneasy, °nervous, apprehensive, °ill at ease, troubled, °worried, discomfited; °doubtful, °hesitant: *I had a queasy feeling that I was being watched. The manager was a bit queasy about giving Denis so much responsibility.* **2** °sick, °nauseous, °nauseated, °ill, °bilious, °queer, *Colloq* green around or about the gills, °groggy, woozy: *Catherine felt very queasy after the ride on the roller coaster.*

queen n. **1** °sovereign, °monarch, ruler; empress; queen consort; queen mother; queen dowager: *She was absolutely thrilled when she was invited to a garden party at Buckingham Palace and met the Queen.* **2** beauty queen, movie queen, °star, prima donna, diva; °epitome, °model, °idol, °leading light, cynosure, °leader: *At the height of her career, she was known as 'the Queen of the Silver Screen'. 'Queen of the Antilles' was once a nickname of Cuba.*

queer adj. **1** °odd, °strange, °different, °peculiar, °funny, °curious, uncommon, unconventional, °unorthodox, atypical, °singular, °exceptional, anomalous, °extraordinary, °unusual, °weird, °bizarre, uncanny, °unnatural, freakish, °remarkable, °offbeat, °irregular, °unparalleled, °incongruous, °outlandish, °outré, °exotic, °eccentric, fey, °quaint, °absurd, °ridiculous, °ludicrous, unexampled: *How do you explain Basil's queer behaviour at the office party? Her attire could only be described as queer, given her age and status.* **2** °questionable, dubious, °suspicious, °suspect, °doubtful, °puzzling, °mysterious, *Colloq* °fishy, °shady: *We had a feeling that something queer was going on when the clocks started running backwards.* **3** (slightly) °ill, °queasy, °sick, unwell, °poorly, °faint, uneasy, °dizzy, °giddy, vertiginous, light-headed: *It's not surprising that you feel queer after drinking all that wine.* **4** °mad, °unbalanced, unhinged, demented, °deranged, °insane, °daft, touched, *Colloq* dotty, potty, nutty, nuts, loony, batty, cracked: *Francis seems to have gone a bit queer—fancies himself a reincarnation of Cicero.*
—v. **5** °ruin, °spoil, °bungle, °botch, °muddle, muff, °mar, °wreck, °destroy, *Colloq* make a °hash or °mess of, gum up (the works), *Slang* °muck up, °screw up, louse up, *US* balls up, *Taboo slang Brit* balls up: *Grimstone queered the deal by telling the buyer the company was worth half what we were asking.*

quell v. **1** °suppress, °put down, °repress, °subdue, °quash, °overcome, °crush, °squelch: *The army arrived to quell the uprising at the prison.* **2** °moderate, mollify, soothe, assuage, alleviate, °mitigate, allay, °quiet(en), °calm; pacify, °tranquillize, °compose: *Any feelings of bitterness were quelled by her comforting words.*

quench v. **1** °satisfy, °slake, sate, °surfeit, °satiate, allay, appease: *My thirst isn't quenched by those sweet fizzy drinks.* **2** °put out, °extinguish, douse, °smother, snuff out, °stifle, °kill, °destroy, °suppress, °squelch, °repress, °overcome, °subdue: *Even the most totalitarian regime cannot entirely quench the fire of freedom in the hearts of the oppressed.*

querulous adj. complaining, carping, °critical, criticizing, hypercritical, °fault-finding, °finicky, finical, °fussy, over-particular, censorious, °petulant, whining, murmuring, grumbling, °peevish, °testy, °touchy, °irritable, irritated, annoyed, piqued, in a pique, irascible, fractious, °perverse, °quarrelsome, ill-natured, ill-humoured, °cantankerous, curmudgeonly, crusty, crotchety, °fretful, bad-tempered, ill-tempered, °waspish, crabby, °cross, splenetic, choleric, °sour, dyspeptic, grumpy, *Colloq* grousing, pernickety or *US also* persnickety, *Slang* bitching: *He objected to almost all the television programmes and sent querulous letters to the broadcasters telling them so.*

query *n.* **1** °question, °inquiry *or* enquiry: *The information office will answer any query you may have about social security benefits.* **2** °doubt, uncertainty, °scepticism, °reservation, °problem: *She wants to see the manager about some query concerning her bank balance.*
—*v.* **3** °ask (about), °inquire *or* °enquire (about), °question; °challenge, °doubt, °dispute: *I am writing to query the third item on your latest bill.*

quest *n.* **1** °search, °pursuit, °exploration, °expedition, voyage (of °discovery), °pilgrimage, °mission, °crusade; °chase, °hunt: *When a child, he was inspired by the legend of Sir Launcelot's quest for the Holy Grail.*
—*v.* **2** Usually, **quest after** *or* **for**: °seek (after *or* for), °search after *or* for, °hunt (for), °track down, °pursue, °stalk: *In 1928, joined by his father, he quested for gold along the Orinoco river.*

question *n.* **1** °query, °inquiry *or* enquiry: *I asked you a simple question, 'Where were you last night?', and I expect a civil answer.* **2** °problem, °difficulty, °confusion, °doubt, dubiousness, uncertainty, °query, °mystery, °puzzle: *Is there some question about the qualifications of the new employee?* **3** °matter, °issue, °point, °subject, °topic, °theme, °proposition: *Whether you stay is not the question. The question remains, How are you going to earn a living?* **4 beyond** (**all** *or* **any**) **question**: beyond (the °shadow of) a °doubt, without °question, without a °doubt, indubitably, °undoubtedly, doubtlessly, °definitely, certainly, assuredly: *He is guilty beyond all question.* **5 call in** *or* **into question**: °question, °doubt, °query, °challenge, °dispute, harbour *or* entertain *or* have doubts *or* suspicions about, °suspect, cast °doubt *or* °suspicion on: *I cannot see why he has called into question his loyalty into question.* **6 in question**: **a** under °discussion *or* °consideration: *The person in question never worked for this company.* **b** °questionable, °debatable, at °issue, in °doubt, °doubtful, open to °debate: *Her honesty was never in question.* **7 out of the question**: °unthinkable, °impossible, °absurd, °ridiculous, °preposterous, °inconceivable, beyond °consideration, insupportable: *An increase in salary at this time is out of the question.* **8 without question**: See **4**, above.
—*v.* **9** °ask, °examine, interrogate, °query, °interview, °sound out, °quiz, *Colloq* °pump, grill, *Slang* give (someone) the third degree: *He was questioned for six hours as to his whereabouts.* **10** call in *or* into question, °doubt, °query, °mistrust, °distrust, cast °doubt upon, °dispute, °suspect: *Investigators have long questioned the relationship between the banks and the drug barons.*

questionable *adj.* °doubtful, dubious, °debatable, °moot, °disputable, borderline, °suspect, °suspicious, °shady; open to °question, in °question, in °dispute, °problematic(al), °uncertain, arguable, unsure, °unreliable, °ambiguous: *The evidence shows that the defendant engaged in questionable banking practices while a director of Offshore Ltd. The advantages of quick divorce are questionable.*

queue *n.* **1** °line, °row, °file, column, °string, °train, cortege *or* cortège, °retinue, °procession, °succession, °chain, concatenation, series, °order, cordon, *Brit* tailback, *Colloq Brit* crocodile, *Military* °picket: *There were dozens of people in*

the queue in front of me. **2** pigtail, °braid, plait; °tail, pony-tail: *Not long ago, Chinese men wore their hair in a queue.*
—*v.* **3** Often, **queue up**: °line up, get in *or* into or form a °line *or* queue *or* °file, get into *or* in °line, *Military* fall in: *All he remembers about the war is that everyone had to queue up for everything and wait.*

quibble *v.* **1** °equivocate, split hairs, °evade, be °evasive, palter, chop logic, bandy words, °cavil, pettifog, *Colloq* nit-pick: *While people continued to be kept in slavery, the politicians quibbled over the difference between 'liberty' and 'freedom'.*
—*n.* **2** quibbling, equivocation, °hair-splitting, splitting hairs, °evasion, paltering, sophistry, *Colloq* nit-picking: *Lawyers often become involved in a quibble over the mot juste and forget their clients.* **3** °cavil, sophism, °subtlety, nicety: *It's a quibble whether you say 'either' and 'neither' to rhyme with 'peek' or 'pike'.*

quick *adj.* **1** °rapid, °fast, °speedy, °swift, °fleet; °expeditious, °express: *We made a quick descent to reach the camp before dark. The hand is quicker than the eye. Can you arrange the quick delivery of this parcel to Aylesbury?* **2** °sudden, °precipitate, °hasty, °brisk, °short, °abrupt, °hurried, °perfunctory, °summary; °immediate, °prompt, °timely, instantaneous: *There is no quick answer to your question about the causes of World War II. Don't be so quick to criticize others. I had a quick response to my letter complaining about service.* **3** °agile, °lively, °nimble, °energetic, °vigorous, °alert, °animated, °keen, °sharp, °acute, spry, °spirited, °vivacious, °rapid, °swift: *In three quick steps she was at my side. Antonia is known for her quick mind.* **4** °intelligent, °bright, °brilliant, facile, °adept, adroit, °dexterous, apt, °able, °expert, °skilful, deft, °astute, °clever, °shrewd, °smart, °ingenious, °perceptive, perspicacious, discerning, °far-sighted, °responsive; nimble-witted, °quick-witted: *You can rely on Rob's quick thinking to come up with a solution to the problem.* **5** °excitable, °touchy, °testy, °petulant, irascible, °irritable, °impatient: *She said that I have a quick temper because of my red hair.*

quicken *v.* **1** accelerate, °hasten, °speed up: *As we neared the house, our pace quickened.* **2** °expedite, °hurry, accelerate, °hasten, °speed (up): *We did everything we could to quicken her departure.* **3** °stimulate, °arouse, °kindle, °spark, invigorate, °excite, °animate, °vitalize, vivify, galvanize, °enliven, °awaken, °energize, °revive, resuscitate, reinvigorate: *Olivia's inspiring lectures quickened the imagination of everyone who heard them.*

quickly *adv.* **1** °rapidly, °swiftly, speedily, °fast: *Although share prices dropped in the morning, they recovered quickly during afternoon trading.* **2** °rapidly, °swiftly, speedily, °fast, with °dispatch *or* despatch, apace, °post-haste, at *or* on the °double, with all °speed, °quick, *Colloq US and Canadian* lickety-split: *Run quickly, and you'll get there before the shop closes.* **3** instantly, °promptly, °hastily, at °once, °immediately, °straight away, °right away, °shortly, without °delay, (very) °soon, hurriedly, °quick, *Colloq* pronto: *You'll have to leave quickly to catch your train.*

quick-tempered *adj.* °excitable, °impulsive, °temperamental, hot-tempered, °waspish, choleric, splenetic, °impatient, °short-tempered,

°touchy, irascible, °irritable, °snappish, °abrupt, °short, short-spoken, °quarrelsome, °testy, °volatile, hot-blooded, bad-tempered, ill-tempered, churlish, highly-strung, US high-keyed: *Len is very quick-tempered these days and flies into a rage at the slightest provocation.*

quick-witted *adj.* °acute, °sharp, °clever, °smart, nimble-witted, °alert, °keen, °astute, °perceptive, perspicacious: *Hallam is known for his quick-witted responses to hecklers in the audience.*

quiet *adj.* **1** °silent, soundless, °noiseless, hushed, °still: *We have to be very quiet so as not to wake the children.* **2** °still, °serene, °silent, °peaceful, unperturbed, °calm, °tranquil, placid, pacific, °smooth, °mild, °restful, unagitated: *The sea was very quiet as we rowed towards the beach.* **3** °dormant, quiescent, °inactive, retired, °withdrawn, °unobtrusive: *His last days were spent living a quiet life in the Outer Hebrides.* **4** °still, motionless, unmoving, °fixed, stationary, at °rest, °inactive, composed, °temperate, unexcited, °calm: *There was a knock at the door and everyone suddenly became quiet.*
—*n.* **5** °silence, stillness, soundlessness, noiselessness, °hush, quietness, quietude, °ease, °rest, calmness, °serenity, tranquillity, °peace, °peace of mind, °repose: *In the quiet of the cave I could hear my heart beating.*
—*v.* **6** See **quieten**, below.

quieten *v.* Often, **quieten down**: °quiet (down), °still, °silence, °hush, °calm, °tranquillize, °lull: *He gradually quietened down the audience, and the curtain rose.*

quietly *adv.* **1** °silently, soundlessly, noiselessly, inaudibly, in °silence, softly: *She tiptoed quietly out of the room.* **2** in hushed tones, in whispers: *In a corner of the room a young couple were quietly conversing.* **3** peacefully, calmly, serenely, peaceably, meekly, mildly: *When the police explained they only wanted him to help in their inquiries, he went with them quietly.* **4** modestly, humbly, demurely, unpretentiously, unostentatiously, unobtrusively, unassumingly, sedately: *The applicants sat quietly, waiting to be called in for the interview.*

quintessence *n.* °essence, °heart, °core, quiddity, essentiality, essentiality, °pith, marrow, °sum and °substance, °epitome, °nonpareil, °embodiment, personification, °model, °prototype, exemplar, *beau idéal*, °paragon: *Hernandez considered the ancient Greek temple the quintessence of classic design.*

quip *n.* **1** (bon) *mot*, °witticism, sally, jest, ad lib, °joke, °gibe, barb, aphorism, °epigram, apophthegm *or* apothegm, °pun, °double entendre, equivoque *or* equivoke, *Colloq* °gag, one-liner, crack, °wisecrack, wheeze, chestnut: *In his worst quip he attributed the breakdown of his computer to a slipped diskette.*
—*v.* **2** °joke, jest, °gibe, *Colloq* °wisecrack, US crack wise: *As Mae West quipped, 'It's not the men in my life that count; it's the life in my men'.*

quirk *n.* °peculiarity, caprice, vagary, °eccentricity, °fancy, °twist, °warp, aberration, idiosyncrasy, °oddity, °kink, °characteristic, crotchet, whim, °trick: *By some strange quirk of fate, after weeks in an open boat I was cast ashore at Cap d'Antibes.*

quit *v.* **1** °leave, °depart from, °go (away) from, °get away from, decamp, °exit, °desert, °flee, °forsake, °abandon, *Colloq* °take off, °beat it, °skip: *They think that he will try to quit the country if he is released on bail.* **2** °resign, °give up, °relinquish, °leave, °renounce, °retire from, °withdraw from: *Would you really quit your job to sail around the world?* **3** °cease, °stop, °discontinue, °leave off, desist from: *They would always quit laughing when I walked into the room.*
—*adj.* **4** °free, °clear, discharged, °rid of, released (from), °exempt (from): *When my ex-wife remarried I was quit of the burden of paying alimony.*

quite *adv.* **1** °completely, °very, °totally, °utterly, °entirely, from head to toe, from A to Z, fully, °wholly, °thoroughly, unequivocally, °absolutely, °perfectly, °altogether, unreservedly: *Her trouble is that she is quite certain of many things that are simply not the case. The last time I saw him, he was quite drunk.* **2** °rather, °fairly, °moderately, °somewhat, °relatively, to some *or* a certain °extent *or* °degree, noticeably: *I thought that the paintings were quite well done.* **3** °rather: *We had quite a good dinner last night.* **4** °very much, °totally, °entirely, °wholly, °altogether, °really, °actually, °truly, °definitely, °positively, °undoubtedly, indubitably, °absolutely, unequivocally, certainly, °surely, unreservedly, °honestly: *What you are talking about is quite another matter. Your home-made chutney is quite the best I have ever tasted.*

quiver *v.* **1** °shake, °tremble, °vibrate, °shiver, °quaver; °shudder, tremor, °oscillate, °fluctuate, wobble: *He felt his lips quivering as he told her that he was dying. The outcome of the contest quivered in the balance.*
—*n.* **2** °tremble, °quaver, °shudder, °spasm, °shake, tremor, °shiver: *Pierced by the dart, the tiny bird fell to the earth, gave a little quiver, and lay still.*

quixotic *adj.* °idealistic, °impractical, °impracticable, °unrealistic, unrealizable, °visionary, °romantic, °fantastic, chimerical, °fanciful, °dreamlike, °dreamy, nephelococcygeal, starry-eyed, °optimistic, °rash, °absurd, °mad, °foolhardy, °reckless, °wild, °preposterous, °ridiculous: *When he was young, he had a quixotic notion that he could improve the world.*

quiz *n.* **1** °examination, °test, *Colloq* exam: *We have a ten-minute quiz every week on our reading assignment.*
—*v.* **2** °question, interrogate, °ask, °examine, *Colloq* grill, °pump: *The police have quizzed everyone in the neighbourhood about what they might have seen.*

quizzical *adj.* °curious, °queer, °odd, inquiring *or* enquiring, questioning, puzzled: *The interviewer had a quizzical expression, as if he didn't quite understand his own questions.*

quota *n.* apportionment, °portion, °allotment, allocation, °allowance, °ration, °share, °part, °proportion, °percentage, °equity, °interest, *Colloq* °cut: *Each shareholder is allowed a quota of the new shares based on the number now held.*

quotation *n.* **1** °quote, °passage, citation, °reference, allusion, °extract, °excerpt,

°selection: *For many years Frances collected quotations from the speeches of politicians.* **2** °quote, (bid *or* asking *or* offer *or* market) °price, °charge, °fixed °price, °rate, °cost; value: *The quotation for Universal General International stood at 486 pence at the close of the market on Friday.*

quote *v.* **1** cite, °mention, °recite, °repeat, retell, °reproduce, °duplicate, °call up, °bring up, °bring in, °instance, °exemplify, °refer to, °reference, °extract, °excerpt: *Let me quote to you the relevant passage from* Paradise Lost. —*n.* **2** See **quotation**, above.

R

rabble *n.* **1** °mob, °crowd, horde, °throng, °swarm, °gang: *We narrowly escaped the wrath of the rabble fighting the police in the square.* **2 the rabble**: *Derogatory* °masses, proletariat, hoi polloi, commoners, peasantry, ragtag and bobtail, vermin, °outcasts, °riff-raff, scum, °dregs (of society), lower °classes, *canaille*, commonalty or commonality, *Colloq* °trash, the great °unwashed: *He always refers to blue-collar workers as 'the rabble'.*

rabble-rouser *n.* °agitator, demagogue, instigator, inciter, firebrand, incendiary, °radical, °troublemaker, *agent provocateur,* °revolutionary, insurrectionist, *Colloq* hell-raiser: *The crowd was whipped into a frenzy by a rabble-rouser who was not identified.*

rabid *adj.* **1** °unreasonable, unreasoning, °extreme, °fanatical; raging, °furious, °violent, crazed, frenzied, °maniacal, °wild, °mad, infuriated, frenetic, °berserk: *Please don't mention politics to Nigel—he gets rabid on the subject.* **2** hydrophobic, °mad: *Animals from abroad are kept in quarantine to make sure they are not rabid.*

race[1] *n.* **1** foot-race, horse-race, marathon, °rally or rallye; °competition, °contest, °rivalry, contention: *How many will be running in Saturday's race? Several countries had joined the race to complete a workable anti-gravity device.* **2** sluice, flume, °chute, watercourse, °course, °channel, bed, mill-race, raceway, spillway; °track: *The water in the race enabled us to wash the sand in order to extract the gold. The ball-bearings don't fall out because they are retained in the race.* **3 the races**: horse-races, dog-races, the dogs, the °track, the °turf, *Brit* racecourse, race °meeting, *US* racetrack: *We're off to the races at Newmarket.* —*v.* **4** °speed, °hurry, °hasten, °dash, sprint, °fly, °rush, °scramble, °step lively, *Colloq* °tear, °rip, zip, °step on the gas, °step on it, °hop to it, get a °move on, *Brit* hare, *US* get a wiggle on: *You're going to have to race to catch the last bus.* **5** °compete (with): *I'll race you to the gate and back.*

race[2] *n.* **1** °stock, °line, °lineage, °type, °tribe, °nation, °people, °folk, °clan, °family: *The citizens constitute a mix of all imaginable races.* **2** blood, descent, °breed, °kin, °family, °stock, °line, °lineage: *You say you are liberal, but how would you feel about your daughter's marrying someone of a different race?*

racial *adj.* ethnic, genetic, genealogical, ethnological, °folk; tribal; °national: *Bigots emphasize racial differences rather than racial similarities.*

rack *n.* **1** framework, °frame, trestle, holder, °support; °stand, scaffold, scaffolding, °structure, hat-rack, hatstand, coat-rack, *Technical* stretcher, tenter, *US* hat-tree: *The fish are hung out on long racks in the sun to dry. Please take your luggage off the seat and put it on the overhead rack.* **2** °suffering, °torment, torture, °agony, °anguish, °pain, °misery, °distress, °affliction, °scourge, adversity: *Only those who have experienced it can know the severe rack of gout.*

—*v.* **3** °distress, °torment, torture, agonize, °oppress, °pain, °persecute, °anguish, beleaguer, °plague, °harass, harrow, °hurt: *Gruber was racked by the feeling that he had been responsible for the road accident. Quentin has been racked by the pain of arthritis for ten years.* **4** °beat, °strain, °wrench, °tear at, °lash (at), °batter, °shake, °damage: *Winds of hurricane force racked villages along the coast last night.*

racket *n.* **1** °noise, °din, °uproar, °disturbance, clamour, hubbub, °row, °rumpus, hullabaloo, °fuss, ado, commotion, to-do, hue and °cry, °outcry, brouhaha, °tumult, babel, °pandemonium, *Elizabethan theatre* alarums and excursions, *Colloq* ballyhoo: *How can you sleep through the racket from your neighbour's all-night parties?* **2** (organized) °crime, °criminal *or* °illegal activity *or* enterprise, °trickery, °trick, °dodge, °scheme, °swindle, °stratagem, °artifice, °game, °ruse, *Slang* °caper, scam, gyp: *Their racket is selling 'protection' to shop-owners.* **3** °business, °line, °profession, °occupation, °trade, °vocation, °calling, °job, °employment, livelihood: *I'm in commodities; what's your racket?*

racketeer *n.* mobster, °gangster, Mafioso: *The Chicago racketeers of the 1930s seem tame compared with today's terrorists.*

raconteur *n.* storyteller, anecdotalist *or* anecdotist, °narrator, relater *or* relator, *Colloq* spinner of yarns: *The after-dinner speaker was a marvellous raconteur with a wealth of stories about the theatre.*

racy *adj.* **1** °fresh, °lively, °animated, °spirited, °sprightly, °buoyant, °vivacious, °energetic, °vigorous, °dynamic, zestful, °stimulating, mettlesome *or* mettled, *Colloq* full of vim and °vigour, peppy, full of °pep, full of beans: *Tabloid journalists are told that their writing must be racy—straightforward reporting is out of fashion.* **2** °risqué, ribald, °bawdy, °naughty, °lusty, °earthy, °gross, °off colour, salty, °suggestive, °sexual, °immodest, indelicate, °indecent, °blue, smutty, °lewd, salacious, °vulgar, °dirty, °filthy, °pornographic, °obscene, sex-oriented, °adult, °rude, °crude, °coarse, *Colloq* raunchy, °sexy, °spicy, °hot: *By mistake my name got on the mailing list of some company selling racy videos.* **3** °spicy, piquant, °tasty, flavourful, °pungent, °strong, °savoury, °sharp, zesty, tangy, °tart, °hot: *That curry you served last night had quite a racy flavour.*

radiance *n.* **1** radiancy, °splendour, brightness, °brilliance, resplendence, luminosity, luminousness, °dazzle, °sparkle, coruscation, scintillation, °twinkle, effulgence, refulgence, incandescence, °glow, phosphorescence, °gleam, °lustre, °shimmer, °shine: *As Aladdin rubbed the ring, it began to glow with an inner radiance and then—suddenly—a genie appeared.* **2** °warmth, gladness, °joy, °pleasure, °happiness, cheeriness, °delight: *It was good to see again the radiance of the family at Christmas dinner.*

radiant *adj.* **1** shining, °bright, beaming, °burning, °ablaze, blazing, °brilliant,

°luminous, resplendent, °splendid, splendorous, °lustrous, gleaming, °glowing, phosphorescent, shimmering, °shiny, °glossy, glistening, °incandescent, alight, effulgent, refulgent, sparkling, °dazzling, glittering, coruscating, °scintillating, °twinkling; aglow: *In her hair she wore a diamond tiara, a radiant crown whose glory was diminished only by her beauty. The room was radiant with sunshine.* **2** °happy, °overjoyed, °ecstatic, °rapturous, °delighted, °joyful, °blithe, blithesome, blissful, beatific, °glad, °gleeful, joyous, °gay, bubbling, °bubbly, jubilant, °elated, °rhapsodic, °exultant, exhilarated, in seventh °heaven, in °heaven, *Colloq* on cloud nine, *Brit* over the moon: *Carrie was absolutely radiant when she learned she was pregnant.*

radiate *v.* **1** °shine, °beam, °burn, °blaze, °gleam. °glow, °shimmer, °glisten, °sparkle, °dazzle, °glitter, coruscate, scintillate, °twinkle: *The jewel seemed to radiate with an inner light.* **2** °emanate, disseminate, °disperse, °spread, °diffuse, °shed, °send out, °emit, °give off *or* out, *Rare* irradiate: *He radiated goodwill the way a fire radiates heat and light.*

radiation *n.* emission, emanation, diffusion, dispersal, shedding: *Because the night was cloudless, unhindered radiation of the earth's heat rapidly cooled the air.*

radical *adj.* **1** °basic, °fundamental, °elementary, °inherent, constitutional, °elemental, °essential, °cardinal, °principal, °primary, °deep, deep-seated, deep-rooted, °profound, underlying, °organic, °natural, °rudimentary: *There is a radical error in your approach to the problem. There are radical differences in the ways we regard the English language.* **2** °thorough, thoroughgoing, °complete, °entire, °total, °exhaustive, °sweeping, (all-)°inclusive, °comprehensive, all-embracing, °out-and-out, °drastic, °severe, °extreme, extremist, °revolutionary: *We have made radical changes in the way we live. Every political party that is not in power promises radical reform.* **3** extremist, °revolutionary, °fanatic(al), °militant, anarchist(ic), °immoderate: *A staunch conservative, Vincent regarded as radical anyone who disagreed with him.* —*n.* **4** extremist, °revolutionary, °fanatic, °zealot, °immoderate, anarchist, °militant: *The radicals favour reform, the conservatives the status quo—but there is nothing new in that.* **5** communist, leftist, left-winger, red, Bolshevik, Bolshevist, pink, *Slang US* pinko: *Carlo, recently arrested as a spy, had been a radical since his days at university.*

radio *n.* **1** receiver, °portable (radio), *Old-fashioned* crystal °set, *Brit and US old-fashioned* wireless, *Colloq* transistor, *Slang* ghetto-blaster, *Brit* tranny *or* trannie, *US* boom box: *He listens to BBC World Service on his short-wave radio.* —*v.* **2** °transmit, °broadcast, °air, disseminate, °announce, °present: *Weather reports are radioed continuously to ships at sea and aircraft.*

raffle *n.* °lottery, °draw, sweepstake *or US* sweepstakes, sweep *or US* sweeps: *The church is holding a raffle for a new car next week.*

rag[1] *n.* **1** °tatter, °piece, °shred, °scrap, °fragment, °bit, *Dialect* clout: *Take a clean rag and dust the bookshelves when you get the chance.* **2** newspaper, °periodical, °magazine,

°publication, °journal: *You can't believe anything you read in that rag.* **3 rags**: *Facetious* clothes, clothing, attire, °dress, °garments, *Old-fashioned* duds: *I bought some new rags at the post-Christmas sales.* **4 rag trade**: garment-industry, clothing °business, °fashion °industry: *Peggy has been a model in the rag trade for years.* **5 chew the rag**: **a** °converse, °talk, °gossip, °chat: *We bought a bottle of wine and just sat about chewing the rag all evening.* **b** *Brit* argue, wrangle: *They are constantly chewing the rag over trivial nonsense.*

rag[2] *v.* °tease, °taunt, °belittle, °twit, °ridicule, °mock, make °fun of, °pull (someone's) °leg, *Brit* °rally, *Colloq* kid: *The boys at school were always ragging him about his lisp.*

ragamuffin *n.* (street) urchin, (street) Arab, waif, mudlark, gamin, little lost lamb, babe in the wood, °stray, °guttersnipe, scarecrow: *We took in a poor little ragamuffin who was shaking from the cold.*

rage *n.* **1** °anger, °fury, wrath, ire, high dudgeon, exasperation, vehemence, °passion: *Imagine her rage when Simon phoned to say that he couldn't make it home for dinner!* **2** °fury, °passion, °frenzy, hysterics, °tantrum, °fit, °temper, *Colloq Brit* °paddy *or* paddywhack *or* paddywack, wax: *He flies into a rage if Grace is as little as five minutes late for an appointment.* **3** °fashion, °craze, °vogue, the (°latest *or* newest) °thing, last word, *dernier cri*, °mode, *Colloq* °fad: *Miniskirts were all the rage in the 1960s.* —*v.* **4** °rant, °rave, °storm, go °mad *or* °crazy *or* bonkers *or* °wild *or* out of one's °mind, go °berserk, run amok *or* amuck, behave *or* act *or* be like one °possessed, °fret, be beside oneself (with °anger *or* °fury), lose one's °temper, have a °tantrum, fulminate, °explode; °fume, foam at the mouth, °stew, °smoulder, °boil, °seethe, °simmer, *Colloq* have kittens, lose one's cool, °fly off the handle, go off the deep end, *Slang* get into *or* work oneself up into a °lather *or* °stew *or* °sweat, get all worked up, °blow one's top, °blow a gasket, °blow up, °flip one's top *or* lid, hit the ceiling *or* roof, °freak out, be fit to be tied, be ready for a strait-jacket, *Brit* throw a wobbly, *US and Canadian* °blow one's °stack, °flip one's wig, °blow a fuse, have a haemorrhage, go ape, do a slow burn, have a conniption °fit: *Father raged for hours when he found that Donald had borrowed the car without permission.*

ragged *adj.* **1** °rough, °shaggy, °shabby, °seedy, °tattered, °unkempt, scraggy, torn, rent, ripped, frayed, °worn (out), °threadbare, patched, patchy, ravelled, *Chiefly Brit* tatty, *Brit* down at °heel, *US* down at the °heel(s), *Colloq US* frazzled, beat-up: *On weekends, Charles put on his most ragged clothes to work in the garden.* **2** °rough, uneven, °irregular, nicked, °jagged, °serrated, sawtooth(ed), zigzag, °notched, toothed, denticulate(d), ridged: *Every morning on his way to work, his first sight of the factory was the ragged edge of its roof.* **3** °worn out, °tired, °exhausted, on one's last legs, the worse for °wear, °dead °tired, overtired, °fatigued, °weary, fagged out, °spent, *Colloq* all in, dog-tired, *Slang* °dead (on one's feet), (°dead) °beat, *Brit* knackered, *US and Canadian* pooped (out): *The emergency crew was run ragged by thirty hours on duty without rest.* **4** °bad, °rough, patchy, °imperfect, °shabby, messy, disordered, °disorderly, °run-down, battered, broken-down, neglected, deteriorated, °dilapidated, *Colloq* beat-up: *From its ragged condition, it's clear that the building isn't properly maintained.* **5** °rough, °harsh, °discordant, °grating, rasping, hoarse, °scratchy, croaking: *His voice, once a beautiful lyric tenor, was ragged after years of alcoholism.* **6** uneven, °bad, °poor, °shabby, patchy: *The guests gave a ragged rendition of 'Happy Birthday' as their host entered the room.*

ragman *n.* rag-dealer, rag-picker, °scrap °dealer, *Brit* rag-and-bone man, knacker, *US* °junk °dealer, junkman: *When the ragman comes round, give him those old curtains.*

raid *n.* **1** (°surprise) °attack, incursion, °invasion, °onset, onslaught, blitz, sortie, sally, °expedition, *Slang* (police) bust: *The partisans made a raid on the arsenal last night and got away with guns and ammunition.*
—*v.* **2** °attack, invade, °assault, °storm, °set upon, °descend upon, °swoop down on *or* upon, °pounce upon, *Military* forage; °sack, °plunder, °pillage, °loot, °ransack, °rifle, °strip, maraud, depredate, *Slang* bust: *The commandos raided the enemy stronghold and destroyed it.*

rail[1] *n.* **1** °bar, °rod, handrail, foot-rail , towel-rail; railing, banisters, balustrade, baluster, °fence: *Don't lean on the rail or it will break.* **2** by *or* via rail: by °train, by °railway *or US also* °railroad: *We travelled by rail from Paris to Geneva.*

rail[2] *v.* Usually, **rail at** *or* **against**: °vituperate, vociferate, fulminate, be *or* become °abusive, revile, °attack, °berate, °scold, °upbraid, °criticize, censure, decry, °condemn, °denounce: *She continues to rage and rail against those who would deny equal rights to women.*

raillery *n.* °banter, badinage, persiflage, °repartee, frivolity, joking, jesting, chaffing, teasing, °ridicule, *Colloq* kidding: *You shouldn't get upset over what was nothing more than some good-natured raillery.*

railroad *n.* **1** See railway, below.
—*v.* **2** °force, compel, °expedite, coerce, °intimidate, °push (through), *Brit* pressurize, *US* °pressure, °bully, hector, °tyrannize, dragoon, °browbeat, bullyrag, *Colloq* bulldoze, °squeeze, °lean on: *Clayton was railroaded into appointing Pinbury to head the committee to investigate corruption.*

railway *n.* °train, °rail, rolling-stock, *Archaic* iron horse, *US* °railroad: *Railway service could be improved on some suburban lines. Diamond Jim Brady, the American millionaire, made his money from the railway.*

rain *n.* **1** °precipitation, drizzle, sprinkle, °downpour, °shower, thunder-shower, cloudburst, rainstorm, squall, deluge, *US* sunshower: *After the rain the sun came out.* **2** rainfall, °precipitation: *The rain in Spain falls mainly in the plain.* **3** °flood, °torrent, °shower, °volley, °stream, °outpouring: *Arriving home, she could barely shield herself from the rain of children's kisses.*
—*v.* **4** come down, °pour, °teem, sprinkle, drizzle, °spit, *Brit dialect* mizzle, *Colloq* come down in buckets *or* by the bucketful, rain cats and dogs: *The weatherman said it would rain today, so take an umbrella.* **5** °trickle, °pour, °run, °fall: *Tears rained down her sallow cheeks.* **6** °descend, °shower: *Blows rained down on him from the tiny fists of the furious child.* **7** °bestow, °lavish, °shower: *He rained kisses on her upturned face.*

raise *v.* **1** °lift (up), elevate; °hoist, °pull up, °haul up, run up, *Literary* upraise: *She raised the glass to her lips. We raised the mainsail and sailed out of the harbour.* **2** °erect, °put up, °construct, °build, °produce, °create, put together, °assemble, °frame: *With the help of some neighbours, the barn was raised in less than a day.* **3** °farm, °grow, °cultivate, °plant, °bring up, nurture, °harvest, °propagate: *During that year's mild winter, we were able to raise three crops.* **4** °bring up, nurture, °rear; °mother, °father, °parent: *His grandmother raised ten children, six girls and four boys.* **5** °assemble, °gather, bring *or* °gather *or* °get together, °muster, °mobilize, °round up, °rally, °collect, convene, °recruit, *Colloq* pull together: *Do you think you could raise an army quickly enough to defend us against attack?* **6** °increase, °boost, °advance, °put up, jack up, run up, °inflate, escalate: *Why are consumer petrol prices always raised at the vaguest hint of an increase in oil prices?* **7** °cultivate, °foster, nurture, °heighten, °stimulate, °buoy, °lift, uplift, °boost, °arouse, °quicken, °encourage, °develop: *The news about the new company raised our hopes of finding jobs.* **8** °open, °introduce, °initiate, °broach, °bring up, °bring *or* °put forward, °present, °suggest, °mention, °moot: *It is regrettable that you saw fit to raise such a delicate issue.* **9** °remove, °relieve, °lift, °abandon, °eliminate, °discontinue, (bring to an) °end, °terminate: *Restrictions on travel to south-east Asia were about to be raised.* **10** °cause, °provoke, °evoke, °occasion, put *or* set in °motion, °institute, °prompt, engender, °stir up, instigate, °inspire, give °rise to, °bring about, °arouse, °originate: *Objections to the relaxation of safety regulations were raised by relatives of the victims of the earlier disaster.* **11** utter, °express, °bring up, °put forward, °shout, °call: *Was it you who raised the alarm at the first sign of smoke?* **12** °assemble, °obtain, °get, °collect, °amass, °solicit: *We raised twice as much for charity as last year.* **13** invigorate, °animate, °vitalize, vivify, °buoy, °lift, uplift, °cheer (up), exhilarate, elate: *Our spirits were raised considerably by the news from head office.*

rake[1] *v.* **1** Often, **rake up**: °scrape together, °gather (together *or* up), °collect, °draw together: *You really must rake up the leaves from the lawn and burn them.* **2** °scrape, comb, °scratch, °grate, graze: *Don't you just hate the sound of a fingernail being raked across a blackboard?* **3** rake in: °collect, °gather (up *or* in), pull in, °make: *Pamela is raking in the royalties from her latest thriller.* **4** rake it in: °coin °money, °make °money (hand-over-fist), *Brit* °coin it in: *The new record shop in the mall is really raking it in.* **5** rake out: °sift (out), °screen, °remove, °clear, °eliminate: *Please rake out the cinders from the grate.* **6** rake over *or* through: °search, °probe, °ransack, °scour, comb, °rummage through, °pick through *or* over, °go through *or* over (with a fine-tooth(ed) comb), °rifle (through): *The police raked through her entire flat but found nothing incriminating.* **7** rake up: **a** See 1, above. **b** °revive, resuscitate, °resurrect, °raise, °bring up, °recall: *Must you persist in raking up those bad memories?* **8** rake up *or* together: °gather, °scrape up *or* together, °collect, °drag together, °pick up, °dig up, dredge up, °find, °unearth: *Were you able to rake up the others for a game of poker tonight?*

rake² *n.* °libertine, womanizer, lecher, °roué, °playboy, ladies' man, Don Juan, Casanova, Lothario, debauchee, voluptuary, °profligate, °prodigal; °scoundrel, °rascal, cad, *Archaic* rakehell, masher; *Colloq* lady-killer, *Colloq* old-fashioned wolf, *Brit* bounder: *Lady Anne was led astray by some young rake, a friend of the Prince Regent's.*

rake-off *n.* °kickback, commission; °discount, mark-down, °rebate, *Colloq* °cut, °piece: *Does Mac get a rake-off for every buyer he sends to the shop?*

rakish *adj.* °dashing, °jaunty, °dapper, °spruce, °debonair, raffish, °smart, °breezy, °flashy, °chic, °fashionable, °elegant; °dandy, foppish: *Adjusting his trilby to a rakish angle, Peter strode along the boulevard.*

rally *n.* **1** °gathering, (mass) °meeting, °meet, convocation, °convention, assemblage, °assembly, °muster: *There is to be a political rally tonight in the town square. Are you taking your Daimler to the vintage car rally?* **2** °recovery, °improvement, °revival, °turn for the °better, recuperation, renewal: *His doctors said that the rally might be only temporary.*
—*v.* **3** Often, **rally round**: bring or call or °get together, °round up, °assemble, convene, °group, congregate, °organize, come together, troop; marshal, °mobilize, °summon, °gather, °muster: *All Sally's friends rallied round her when her father died. She rallied every last ounce of strength in the dash for the finishing line.* **4** °revive, °rouse, °recover, °improve, get better, take a °turn for the °better, °recuperate, °perk up, °pick up, *Colloq* °snap out of it, make a comeback: *According to the nurse, he rallied during the night and asked for something to eat.*

ram *v.* **1** °jam, °force, °drive, °cram, °crowd, °pack, compress, °stuff, °squeeze, °thrust, tamp, °pound, hammer: *We rammed as much filler as we could into the crevices.* **2** °butt, °bump, °strike, °hit, °collide with, °dash, °crash, °slam: *Their car rammed into mine in the garage.*

ramble *v.* **1** amble, °wander (off), °stroll, °saunter, °walk, perambulate, °go (off or away), °travel, °drift, °range, rove, °go or °move about, hike, trek, *Colloq* mosey: *Don't ramble too far as dinner will be ready soon. We used to ramble over those hills, but the area is now an industrial site.* **2** °meander, °wander, digress, maunder: *Fiona tends to ramble off the main topic of conversation.* **3** Sometimes, **ramble on**: °babble, °chatter, gibber, °rave, °go on (and on), °rattle on, *Colloq Brit* witter on, rabbit on or away: *If you didn't stop him, Hugh would ramble on for ever about his grandchildren.*
—*n.* **4** °stroll, amble, °saunter, °walk, °promenade, constitutional, walkabout, °tour, °tramp, hike, trek: *We went on a short ramble through the park.*

rambling *adj.* **1** °discursive, °roundabout, circuitous, °tortuous, °incoherent, °diffuse, °unsettled, °disconnected, °disjointed, disorganized, unorganized, illogical, maundering, °aimless, °confused, muddled, jumbled, scrambled, unintelligible, °inarticulate, periphrastic, circumlocutory, circumlocutional, circumlocutionary, ambagious, °wordy, verbose, prolix, °endless, interminable: *We couldn't make heads or tails of the professor's rambling lecture.* **2** unplanned, straggling, °irregular, sprawling, °spread out, spreading, straggly: *The Wilsons live in that big old rambling Victorian house down the road.* **3** roving, wandering, °travelling, peripatetic, itinerant, wayfaring, migratory, nomadic: *For five years he led a rambling life as a folk-singing banjo player.*

ramification *n.* **1** consequence, °result, °effect, °upshot, °implication, °subtlety; °complication, °difficulty: *Have you considered the ramifications of your decision to retire?* **2** °branch, °extension, outgrowth, subdivision, °offshoot: *Courier services may be considered a ramification of services that were once performed by the post office.*

ramp *n.* °slope, °grade, gradient, °incline; °rise, ascent, acclivity; descent, °dip, declivity: *There is a special ramp in the theatre for wheelchair access.*

rampage *n.* **1** °excitement, °agitation, recklessness, °riot, °tumult, °uproar, °frenzy, °fury, °rage, °furore or US furor, turmoil: *His latest rampage was prompted by their serving him a cup of cold coffee.* **2** *Brit* **on the rampage**, *US* **on a rampage**: berserk, °mad, °crazy, amok or amuck, °wild, out of control: *Pete regularly drank too much whisky and then went on the rampage.*
—*v.* **3** °storm, °rage, °rant, °rave, go °berserk, run amok or amuck: *He rampaged like a man possessed when he got his second parking ticket of the day.*

rampant *adj.* **1** unchecked, °uninhibited, unrestrained, °wild, °uncontrolled, out of control, out of hand, frenzied, unbridled, uncontrollable, °violent: *He was a victim of rampant jealousy. Jennie could hardly be described as a rampant feminist.* **2** °profuse, unbounded, abounding, °flourishing, rife, widespread, °everywhere, °epidemic, pandemic, °prevalent, unrestrained, unchecked, running °wild, °uninhibited, °indiscriminate, °wild, °uncontrolled; in °control, holding °sway, in full °sway, °dominant, °predominant, °paramount, °rank, °luxuriant: *Before Masterson became sheriff, vice and crime were rampant in the town.*

rampart *n.* °defence, bastion, °guard, fortification, °security, °stronghold, °bulwark, barricade, °wall; earthwork, breastwork, parados, gabion: *The old town is surrounded by seven rows of ramparts leading up to the cathedral at the summit. They regard religion as an impenetrable rampart against immorality.*

ramshackle *adj.* °dilapidated, °tumbledown, crumbling, broken-down, °rickety, unsteady, jerry-built, °decrepit, °flimsy, shaky, °unstable, tottering, unsubstantial or °insubstantial, ruined, in °disrepair, beyond repair, °run-down, neglected, °derelict: *He lives in a ramshackle hut on the outskirts of town.*

rancid *adj.* °stinking or reeking (to high heaven), foul-smelling, ill-smelling, evil-smelling, noisome, mephitic, miasmic or miasmal or miasmatic(al), °smelly, °rank, malodorous, fusty, °nasty, °disagreeable, odious, fetid or foetid, °rotten, decayed, spoilt or spoiled, turned, °bad, °awful, °sour, tainted, °high, gamy, °ripe, °putrid, °corrupt, °stale: *To rid your fridge of that rancid smell, wash it out with a solution of baking soda.*

rancorous *adj.* °hateful, °spiteful, °resentful, °hostile, malign, °malignant, °bitter, malevolent, malicious, °venomous, vindictive, vengeful, splenetic, acrimonious: *Olivia felt rancorous towards her brother-in-law when he refused to lend her money.*

rancour n. hatred, °hate, antipathy, °spite, °resentment, resentfulness, °antagonism, °hostility, malignity, °bitterness, malevolence, malice, venomousness, °venom, vindictiveness, vengefulness, spleen, acrimony, animus, °animosity, enmity, bad feeling, bad blood: *Owing to the rancour between them, the brothers had not exchanged a word in forty years.*

random adj. **1** °haphazard, °chance, fortuitous, serendipitous, aleatory, °arbitrary, °casual, °stray, °occasional, °indefinite, °indiscriminate, non-specific, unspecific, unspecified, unordered, unorganized, undirected, °unpremeditated, unplanned, °accidental, uncalculated, unsystematic, adventitious, °incidental, hit-or-miss: *He used a computer program to generate random numbers. A random selection of slips was drawn from the drum and Madelaine's name was on one of them.* **2 at random**: randomly, haphazardly, fortuitously, by °chance, serendipitously, arbitrarily, casually, °occasionally, (every) °now and then, (every) °once in a while, irregularly, indefinitely, erratically, indiscriminately, unsystematically, adventitiously, °incidentally, unpremeditatedly: *They picked names from a hat at random. They drove up and down the road, firing at random.*

randy adj. aroused, °lustful, °lecherous, *Brit* on °heat *or US* in °heat, *Brit* in oestrus *or US* in estrus, *Slang* °hot, horny, in rut, rutting, at stud: *Seeing Betty always made Len feel terribly randy.*

range n. **1** °scope, °sweep, °reach, °limit, °extent, °span, °area, radius, °distance, compass, latitude, °stretch, °sphere, °orbit: *The gun has a range of about 200 yards. This radio transmitter is effective only within a thirty-mile range. The minister is trying to broaden the range of his influence.* **2** °assortment, series, °collection, °lot, °spread, °selection, °choice, °number, °variety, °kind, °sort, °scale, °gamut, °register: *The courses offered cater to a wide range of interests.* **3** °rank, °row, °tier, °line, °file, series, °string, °chain: *From my window I could see the range of hills stretching away into the distance.* **4** kitchen range, (cooking-) stove, *Chiefly Brit* cooker, *Brit trade mark* Aga, *US* cook-stove: *In every French farmhouse there was always a pot of soup on the range.* —v. **5** line up, °rank, °order, align, °order, array: *The teacher ranged the children according to their height.* **6** °vary, °fluctuate, °spread, °run the °gamut, °extend, °stretch, °run, °go: *The students range in age from eight to eighty.* **7** °organize, °categorize, catalogue, °arrange, classify, °sort, °class, °group, °rank, °bracket, pigeon-hole, °file, °index, °break down, °grade, °distribute: *The books are ranged according to their subject-matter.* **8** °cover, °traverse, °roam, °travel over *or* across, °go *or* °pass over, °drift, °migrate, °wander, °move, °extend: *The wildebeest ranges far and wide over vast tracts of grazing land in Africa.*

rank¹ n. **1** °status, °standing, °position, °place, °level, °stratum, °class, °caste, circumstances, echelon, °grade: *It is virtually impossible to determine rank simply by looking at a person.* **2** °weight, °authority, °power, °superiority, seniority, ascendancy, °priority, °influence, eminence: *Caldwell uses the privilege of rank to cover up some of his more questionable transactions.* **3** °nobility, °title, high °birth, aristocracy, °dignity, °prestige, (blue) blood; peerage: *Gentlemen of rank*

should behave with honour, my boy. **4** °line, °row, column, °queue, series, °formation; °sequence: *We gazed on the serried ranks of warriors, golden shields glistening in the sun.* **5 ranks**: °soldiers, °workers, °staff, °employees: *Smithers rose from the ranks to become chief executive officer.* —v. **6** °grade, °rate, classify, °class, °categorize; °dispose, °organize, °order, °sort, assort, °arrange, array, align, °range, °graduate: *He was ranked among the best in the school. The applicants are ranked according to their test scores.* **7** °rate, °count, °stand, have °standing or value or °prestige, be °important or °distinguished: *To Janet, character ranks far above wealth. Phil is so mean that Scrooge would rank high on a list of charitable men in comparison with him.*

rank² adj. **1** °lush, °luxuriant, °abundant, °flourishing, °profuse, °prolific, °dense, superabundant, °exuberant, °fertile, °productive, fructuous: *The expedition could hardly make its way through the rank undergrowth of the jungle.* **2** °corrupt, °foul, °low, °base, °gross; °downright, utter, °sheer, °absolute, °complete, °out-and-out, °blatant, °flagrant, unalloyed, °unmitigated, °undiluted: *I cannot understand the rank treachery of the man after all that we have done for him. I ventured my opinion, even though a rank outsider.* **3** °offensive, °loathsome, °disgusting, °gross, °foul, °corrupt, °indecent, °shocking, °immodest, indecorous, °shameless, °risqué, °lurid, °off colour, °outrageous, °blue, °nasty, °vulgar, °vile, °dirty, °filthy, smutty, scatological, °pornographic, °obscene: *Those bigots always resort to the rank vocabulary of malice and hate. In a secret cupboard was a collection of the rankest literature.* **4** °offensive, °loathsome, °disgusting, °gross, °foul, foul-smelling, °smelly, °rancid, noisome, °stinking, reeky, reeking, mephitic, miasmic or miasmal or miasmatic(al), fetid or foetid, noxious, °rotten, °putrid, °musty, °stale, °disagreeable, °strong, °pungent: *The rank stench from the open sewers pervades the air in those pockets of poverty.*

rank and file n. (general) membership, °members, °majority: *The union's rank and file must now vote on whether to accept management's pay offer.*

rankle v. °gall, °fester, °irk, vex, °plague, °chafe, °grate, nettle, °torment, °pain, °hurt, °provoke, °anger, °exasperate, °get (to), °upset: *Although she had forgiven him, the insult still rankled.*

ransack v. **1** °search, °examine, °go through or over (with a fine-tooth(ed) comb), comb, °rake or °rummage through, °scour, °explore, °scrutinize, turn inside out: *I ransacked the second-hand bookshops for a copy but had no success.* **2** °rob, °plunder, °pillage, °sack, despoil, °loot, °strip; burgle, *US and Canadian* burglarize: *The thieves who ransacked the shop apparently missed the most valuable jewel.*

ransom n. **1** redemption, °rescue, deliverance, °release, °liberation: *The envoy was held to ransom by a fanatical band of zealots.* **2** °payment, payout, °pay-off, °price: *The police refuse to reveal the amount of the ransom given to the kidnappers.* —v. **3** °redeem, °rescue, °release, °deliver: *The boy was ransomed for £10,000.*

rant v. **1** declaim, °hold forth, expound, expatiate, orate, perorate, pontificate, trumpet, °preach, °harangue, °lecture, deliver (oneself of) a °tirade or diatribe or °speech, °speak: *The* minister ranted pompously about his accomplishments. **2** vociferate, °bluster, °rave, rant and °rave, °bellow, °rage: *The master kept ranting on about his newspaper having been creased.* —*n.* **3** °tirade, philippic, °bluster, flatulence, °rhetoric, °bombast, pomposity, turgidity, gasconade, rodomontade, theatrics, histrionics, °act: *As he carried on his rant, the theatre gradually emptied till he was alone.*

rap *v.* **1** °knock, °strike, °tap, °hit: *The policeman rapped smartly at the door with his truncheon.* **2** °criticize, °rebuke, °scold, °reprimand, rap over the knuckles, *Colloq* °knock, *Brit* tick off: *We were severely rapped for dropping litter on the pavement.* **3** °converse, °talk, °chat, °gossip, *Colloq* °gab, *Slang* °chew the fat or the °rag: *That guy was so fascinating—we could rap with him for hours.* —*n.* **4** °knock, °tap, °hit, °blow, °crack, °stroke, cuff, whack, thwack, °punch, *Colloq* °belt, clout, *Slang* sock, slug, biff: *The punishment for failing to complete the assignment was a severe rap on the knuckles.* **5** °conversation, °discussion, °chat, confabulation, °talk, °dialogue, discourse, colloquy, *Colloq* confab, *Slang chiefly US and Canadian* bull session, rap session: *We used to get together for a nice long rap now and then.* **6** °responsibility, °blame; °punishment, °sentence; °charge, °accusation, indictment: *Why should I have to take the rap for something you did? The witness failed to show up, so Baxter beat the rap.*

rapacious *adj.* °greedy, covetous, °grasping, °avaricious, °mercenary, usurious, acquisitive, °predatory, predacious, °ravenous, ravening, °voracious, insatiable, insatiate, wolfish, wolflike, lupine, vulturine, raptorial: *That rapacious swindler took everything they had in the world.*

rapacity *n.* °greed, greediness, cupidity, covetousness, °avarice, acquisitiveness, predaciousness, ravenousness, voracity, voraciousness, insatiability, insatiableness, rapaciousness: *The rapacity of the invading hordes of Mongols knew no bounds.*

rape *n.* **1** ravishment, defloration, deflowering, °violation, sexual °assault, defilement: *The police are investigating reports of rape by a masked man.* **2** rapine, despoliation, spoliation, despoilment, °pillage, °depredation, ravagement, ravaging, °plunder, plundering, °sack, sacking, looting, ransacking: *He travelled in disguise to document the rape of the war-torn areas.* **3** abduction, carrying-off, kidnapping, °seizure, °capture, snatching: *History debates whether the ancient Romans were truly responsible for the rape of the Sabine women.* —*v.* **4** °violate, °ravish, °assault sexually, deflower, defile, force to submit to sexual intercourse, have one's way with, take advantage of: *The defendant raped three women before he was caught.* **5** despoil, spoliate, °pillage, depredate, °ravage, °plunder, °sack, °loot: *Throughout history the city has been raped by marauding tribes.*

rapid *adj.* °quick, °fast, °swift, °speedy, high-speed, °brisk, °expeditious, °prompt, °express, °fleet, lightning(-fast), alacritous; °hurried, °hasty, °precipitate, °impetuous, °immediate, instantaneous, °instant, °sudden: *The company we use offers rapid delivery service. What do you suppose occasioned Flannery's rapid departure?*

rapidity *n.* quickness, swiftness, °speed, speediness, briskness, expeditiousness, promptness, promptitude, alacrity, celerity, immediateness, °dispatch or despatch, instantaneousness: *The rapidity with which they responded to our request is truly commendable.*

rapidly *adv.* **1** °quickly, °fast, °swiftly, speedily, briskly, expeditiously, like a °shot, at the speed of light, double-quick, at full °speed, like one °possessed, at a gallop, tantivy, *Colloq* like blazes, like (greased) lightning, *US* lickety-split, *Slang* like a bat out of hell, like °mad: *He cycled down the High Street as rapidly as he could go.* **2** °promptly, instantly, °instantaneously, instanter, without °delay, at °once, °straight away, °right away, in a °moment, in a trice, like a shot, in a wink, in (less than) no °time, double-quick, in a °flash, at the °speed of light, before you (can) turn around, *Colloq* in a jiffy, in two shakes (of a lamb's tail), like (greased) lightning, before you can say 'Jack Robinson', *US and Canadian* (right) off the bat, lickety-split, *Slang* like a bat out of hell: *When I mentioned that you were coming, she left rapidly.*

rapport *n.* empathy, °relationship, °sympathy, °harmony, °affinity, °accord, °bond, °relationship, (mutual) °understanding, camaraderie: *The minute we met we established a rapport.*

rapprochement *n.* °reconciliation, °understanding, °settlement: *The party needs to bring about a rapprochement between the radicals and the reactionaries.*

rapt *adj.* **1** entranced, fascinated, spellbound, mesmerized, hypnotized, engrossed, enthralled, bewitched, °absorbed, transported, captivated, °delighted: *She gave her last performance of 'Giselle' before a rapt audience.* **2** enraptured, °rapturous, °delighted, °elated, °happy, °ecstatic, blissful, °overjoyed, joyous, °joyful, beatific: *You should have seen the rapt expression on the child's face when Santa Claus appeared.*

rapture *n.* °ecstasy, °delight, °joy, joyfulness, joyousness, °pleasure, exaltation, elation, °thrill, °enchantment, euphoria, beatitude, °transport: *Nothing could compare with the rapture he felt at seeing his daughter win the Nobel prize.*

rapturous *adj.* °ecstatic, °delighted, °joyful, joyous, °elated, thrilled, °enchanted, euphoric, in seventh °heaven, °overjoyed, °rhapsodic, *Colloq* on cloud nine, *Brit* over the moon: *He was rapturous over qualifying for the Olympics.*

rare[1] *adj.* **1** uncommon, °unfamiliar, °unusual, °exceptional, out of the °ordinary, °extraordinary, atypical; °scarce, °unparalleled, °choice, recherché, °phenomenal, infrequent, °few and far between, °sparse, °scanty, °limited, °seldom encountered or met with or seen; °unique, °singular, one of a kind; *Chiefly Brit* °thin on the ground: *It was rare to see Liz in such good humour. Specimens in such perfect condition are rare. A copy of the first edition in this condition is rare.* **2** °fine, °good, °admirable, °excellent, °choice, °select, °special, °first-rate, first-class, °exquisite, °superior, °superlative, °peerless, unequalled, °matchless, °incomparable, in a °class by itself or herself or himself or themselves, *sui generis*, °outstanding; collectible or collectable: *O, rare Ben Jonson! On exhibit was a black pearl of rare beauty and remarkable size. Consideration for others seems a rare quality these days.*

rare² *adj.* underdone, undercooked, *bleu(e)*, *saignant(e)*: *Do you want your steak rare, medium, or well-done?*

rarefied *adj.* **1** °thin, °lean, attenuated, diluted, °sparse, scant, °scanty: *As we climbed higher, the rarefied atmosphere made breathing more difficult.* **2** °exalted, °lofty, °elevated, high, °sublime, °noble: *I feel out of place in the rarefied atmosphere of academia.* **3** cliquish, clannish, °exclusive, °private, °select, esoteric: *Clarence copes well in the rarefied atmosphere of Whitehall's corridors of power.*

rarely *adv.* °seldom, °infrequently, on °rare occasions, °hardly (°ever), °scarcely (°ever), °almost °never, *Colloq* °once in a blue moon: *He rarely attends formal dinners at his club.*

rarity *n.* **1** °curiosity, °oddity, curio, collector's item, °find, °treasure, conversation piece, *Brit* one-off, *Colloq Brit* oner: *Among the rarities in his collection is a stuffed dodo.* **2** unusualness, uncommonness, rareness, uniqueness, °scarcity: *The rarity of the first edition makes this book all the more valuable.*

rascal *n.* °imp, °devil, scamp, mischief-maker; rapscallion, °rogue, °scoundrel, cad, °villain, blackguard, knave, °good-for-nothing, ne'er-do-well, °wastrel, scapegrace, dastard, °wretch, *Colloq* scallywag *or* scalawag, *Brit* rotter, blighter, bounder: *That little rascal has eaten all the cherry tarts. They've caught the rascals who were vandalizing parked cars.*

rash¹ *adj.* °impetuous, °impulsive, °unthinking, °thoughtless, °foolhardy, unconsidered, ill-considered, °ill-advised, injudicious, °imprudent, °indiscreet, °precipitate, °hasty, °careless, °heedless, °reckless, headlong, °wild, madcap, °hare-brained, °hotheaded, °adventurous, °quixotic, °venturesome, °audacious, °bold, °dashing, °brash, devil-may-care: *It was rash of him to try to sail round the world single-handed, but he did it.*

rash² *n.* **1** °eruption, eczema, redness, efflorescence, dermatitis: *One of the symptoms of measles is a skin rash.* **2** °number(s), °quantity, °lot(s), multitude, °profusion, °outbreak, series, °succession, °spate, °wave, °flood, deluge, °plague, °epidemic: *There's been a rash of burglaries in the neighbourhood.*

rasp *n.* **1** °grating, °scrape, scraping, °scratch, scratching, stridulation: *One could hear the rasp of the file as they tried to cut through the door.* **2** °file, grater: *The coarser rasp is for use on wood.*
—*v.* **3** °scrape, abrade, °grate, °file: *First, rasp the horseradish, then combine the gratings with a little vinegar.* **4** °irritate, °jar (upon), °grate upon or against, °rub (someone) (up) the wrong way, nettle, °irk, °annoy, vex, °wear on, °get, *Literary* gride: *She has a rasping metallic voice that gets on my nerves.* **5** croak, °squawk, screech: *The sergeant rasped out another command and the company marched forward.*

rate¹ *n.* **1** °measure, °pace, gait, °speed, °velocity, *Colloq* °clip: *We moved along at a pretty fast rate. Rates of production must increase.* **2** °charge, °price, °fee, °tariff, °figure, °amount; °toll: *The rate for a hotel room has increased enormously in the past few years.* **3** °percentage, °scale, °proportion: *What is the current rate of interest on government savings bonds?* **4** Usually, **-rate**: °rank, °grade, °place, °standing, °status, °position, °class, classification, °kind, °sort, °type, rating, worth, value, valuation, °evaluation: *After a few years, he had improved from a second-rate typist to a first-rate secretary.* **5 at any rate**: in any °case, in any °event, anyway, at all events, anyhow, under any circumstances, °regardless, °notwithstanding: *At any rate, with their last child out of university, they have no more worries about paying education costs.*
—*v.* **6** °rank, °grade, °class, classify, °evaluate, °estimate, °calculate, °compute, °count, °reckon, °judge, °gauge, assess, appraise, °measure: *How do you rate your chances of beating the champion?* **7** °merit, be entitled to, °deserve, be °worthy of, have a °claim to: *The play doesn't rate all the attention it's been getting in the press.* **8** °count, °place, °measure: *She rates very high among her friends.*

rate² *v.* °scold, °berate, °reprimand, °rebuke, reproach, °reprove, take to °task, °upbraid, censure, *Colloq* °bawl out, °dress down, *US and Canadian* °chew out: *I was rated severely for staying out after midnight.*

rather *adv.* **1** °quite, °very, °somewhat, °fairly, °moderately, to a certain °extent *or* °degree *or* °measure, to some °extent *or* °degree *or* °measure, more or less, pretty, °slightly, *Colloq* °sort of, kind of: *I suppose she was rather good-looking, but at that age I didn't pay much attention to girls. This coffee tastes rather strange.* **2** preferably, sooner, °instead, more °readily *or* °willingly: *Given an option, I choose to live alone rather than marry.* **3 would** *or Colloq US* **had rather**: °prefer, °choose: *Given a choice, I would rather live alone.*

ratify *v.* °approve, °sanction, °endorse, °support, corroborate, °uphold, °back (up), °sustain, °establish, validate, °substantiate, °verify, °authenticate, °guarantee, °warrant, °certify, affirm, °ensure, °clinch, °settle: *The pact was ratified by all members.*

ratio *n.* °proportion, °relationship, correlation, correspondence: *What is the ratio of male to female students at Oxford University? In that area, the ratio of tenants to home-owners is about two to one.*

ration *n.* **1** °share, °quota, °allotment, °portion, °helping, °part, °provision, °measure, °dole, °percentage, °amount: *Each person is permitted a weekly fixed ration of butter, sugar, coffee, meat, etc. We shall have to go on short rations till we are rescued.* **2 rations**: °supplies, provisions, °food, °provender, victuals, viands, eatables, edibles, comestibles, *Brit* commons: *It was not till the third week with our rations running low that we really began to worry.*
—*v.* **3** Often, **ration out**: °allot, apportion, °dole (out), °give out, °distribute, °deal out, °mete out, °parcel out, °measure out, °hand out: *As water was in short supply, we had to ration it. One cup was rationed out to each of us every morning.* **4** budget, °schedule, °restrict, °control, °limit: *Water had to be rationed to one cup a day for each of us.*

rational *adj.* **1** °well-balanced, °sane, °sound, °normal, °reasonable, °reasoning, °logical, ratiocinative, clear-headed, clear-eyed, °sober; of °sound mind, *Colloq* all there: *Desmond is a rational human being who would be able to advise you about your problem.* **2** °discriminating, °intelligent, °thinking, °enlightened, °prudent,

°wise, °knowledgeable, °informed: *We could not have elected a more rational representative for our cause than Robert Brown.* **3** °sensible, common-sense, commonsensical, °practical, pragmatic, down-to-earth, °everyday, °acceptable, °reasonable, °logical: *Philippa thinks she has a rational explanation for the strange light we saw in the sky last night.*

rationale *n.* °reason, °explanation, °logical °basis, grounds, °logic, °reasoning, °philosophy, °principle, theory: *Do you understand the rationale of a policy for curbing inflation that sets interest rates at a level where business, initiative, and productivity are stifled?*

rationalize *v.* **1** make °plausible *or* believable *or* understandable *or* °acceptable *or* °reasonable, make °allowance(s) *or* excuses for, °vindicate, °account for, °justify, °excuse, °reason away, °explain away: *How can you rationalize taking my car without my permission?* **2** °think through, °reason out; apply °logic to, ratiocinate: *He warps the statistics to rationalize his argument. The fundamentalists make no attempt to rationalize their literal interpretation of the Scripture.*

rattle *v.* **1** clatter: *An acorn dropped from an overhanging tree and rattled down the tin roof.* **2** °shake, °vibrate, °jar, joggle, °jiggle: *The wind was strong enough to rattle the windows in their frames.* **3** °unnerve, disconcert, °discomfit, °disturb, °perturb, °shake, discountenance, °upset, °agitate, °put off, *Chiefly US and Canadian* faze: *They are only trying to rattle us by saying that we might lose our jobs if we strike.* **4** jounce, °bounce, °bump, °jolt, °speed, °hurtle: *The stagecoach came rattling down the road, swaying wildly.* **5 rattle off**: °recite, °list, utter, °reel off, run through, °enumerate, call off: *The announcer rattled off a long list of trains cancelled because of the storm.* **6 rattle on**: °chatter, °babble, °jabber, gibber, prate, °prattle, blabber, cackle, blather, °ramble, *Chiefly Brit* witter, natter, *Slang US* run off at the mouth: *The speaker kept rattling on and on about the delights of collecting beer cans.*
—*n.* **7** clatter, °racket, °noise; rale *or* raole, crackle, crackling; death-rattle: *I heard the rattle of the beans and knew you were about to grind the coffee. The doctor said he didn't like the rattle in my chest.* **8** °clapper, sistrum, *US* noise-maker: *Rattles have been used as musical instruments for thousands of years.*

rattletrap *n.* flivver, rattler, *Colloq* jalopy, tin Lizzie, *US* Model T: *This old rattletrap won't get us all the way to Hawkhurst.*

ratty *adj.* **1** °irritable, °cross, °testy, °touchy, annoyed, crabbed, irritated, °angry, °short-tempered, °impatient, °disagreeable: *He's always ratty in the mornings when he has a hangover.* **2** °dirty, °greasy, straggly, °unkempt, matted: *His hair was all ratty and he hadn't bathed in a month.*

raucous *adj.* °harsh, rasping, °rough, °husky, hoarse, °grating, scratching, °scratchy, °discordant, dissonant, jarring; °strident, °shrill, °noisy, °loud, ear-splitting, °piercing: *You could hear Ramsay's raucous voice above the others. A raucous scream came from the parrot's cage.*

ravage *v.* **1** lay °waste, °devastate, °ruin, °destroy, °demolish, °raze, °wreck, °wreak °havoc (up)on, °damage: *The hurricane ravaged outlying*

areas but did little damage in the city. **2** °pillage, °plunder, despoil, °ransack, °sack, °loot: *The police tried to prevent hooligans from ravaging the shops in the town centre.*
—*n.* **3** Usually, **ravages**: °destruction, °damage, °depredation(s), devastation, wrecking, °ruin, demolition: *All about us we saw the ravages of war.*

rave *v.* **1** °rant, °rage, °storm, fulminate, °roar, °thunder, °howl, °yell, caterwaul, yowl, °bellow, °shout, °scream, °fly off the handle, *Colloq* °flip one's °top *or* lid, *Slang* raise hell: *He kept raving on about his coffee mug having been pinched.* **2 rave about**: °praise, °laud, rhapsodize over, °applaud, °gush over: *Bernard can't stop raving about that new Thai restaurant.*
—*n.* **3** °praise, acclaim, °favour, °enthusiastic °reception, °tribute, °testimonial, encomium, °bouquet, plaudits, accolade, °admiration, *US* hosanna: *The play got raves in all the newspapers when it opened.* **4** °rage, °fashion, °vogue, °trend, °thing, last word, *dernier cri*, °craze, °mania, *Colloq* °fad: *The rave that year was for stiletto heels.* **5** °party, °fête *or* fete, soirée, *Colloq* do, *Slang* bash, blow-out, *Brit* rave-up, *US* wingding, °blast: *Monica threw quite a rave to celebrate her new job.*

ravenous *adj.* **1** °hungry, °famished, starving, °starved: *We were ravenous after the long hike.* **2** °voracious, °gluttonous, °greedy, insatiable, ravening, swinish, piggish, °hoggish, edacious, wolfish: *With my family's ravenous appetites, there are rarely any leftovers.*

ravine *n.* °gorge, °canyon, °pass, cleft, defile, °gully *or* gulley, °valley, *Brit dialect* clough, *Scots* linn, *US* °gap, gulch, arroyo: *At the spring thaw, torrents filled the ravines.*

raving *adj.* **1** °mad, °insane, °berserk, raging, °crazy, crazed, irrational, manic, °maniacal, °frantic, frenzied, °delirious, °hysterical; out of one's °mind *or* head: *He stood there shouting and screaming, like a raving lunatic.* **2** °extraordinary, °outstanding, °unusual, °rare, uncommon, °phenomenal, °great, °striking, °ravishing, *Colloq* °stunning: *Diana had been a raving beauty in her time.*
—*n.* **3** Often, **ravings**: °rant, ranting, °bombast, pomposity, grandiloquence, magniloquence, rodomontade, °rhetoric, °bluster, blustering, claptrap, balderdash, puffery, bunkum, flatulence, hyperbole, vapouring, fustian, *Colloq* °hot air, bunk: *Why must we be subjected to the ravings of this politician?* **4** gabble, °babble, babbling, °gibberish, *Colloq* °gab: *This is nothing more than the raving of a maniac.*

ravish *v.* **1** °enrapture, °delight, °captivate, enthral, °fascinate, °charm, °entrance, spellbind, °bewitch, °transport: *I was ravished at the prospect of seeing you again.* **2** °rape, °violate, have one's °way with, deflower, defile: *The soldiers attacked the village and ravished the women.*

ravishing *adj.* °dazzling, °beautiful, °gorgeous, °striking, °radiant, charming, alluring, °attractive, entrancing, captivating, °enthralling, bewitching, °spellbinding, *Colloq* °stunning: *Daphne was even more ravishing than her sister Diana.*

raw *adj.* **1** uncooked, °unprepared, °fresh: *Many vegetables can be eaten raw.* **2** unprocessed, untreated, °unrefined, unfinished, °natural, °crude: *The raw sugar is shipped to the plant where it is refined. The raw statistics revealed that many*

women had refused to respond to the questionnaire. **3** °new, °inexperienced, unseasoned, °immature, °green, °untried, °fresh, untrained, unskilled, untested: *They sent us raw recruits who had never seen battle.* **4** exposed, unprotected, uncovered, °open; °sore, °tender, °inflamed, °painful, °sensitive: *When he mentioned her name, it was as if he had touched a raw nerve.* **5** °chill, °chilly, chilling, °cold, °damp, °frigid, °freezing, °biting, stinging, nippy, nipping, °sharp, °keen, °piercing, °penetrating: *You should wrap up warmly if you're going out in that raw wind.* **6** °brutal, °frank, °candid, °blunt, °direct, °unvarnished, unmollified, unembellished, °realistic, °honest, °plain, unreserved, unre-strained, °uninhibited, °bluff, straightforward: *The producer felt that no domestic audience could stomach a raw depiction of the horrors of war.*
—*n.* **7 in the raw**: °naked, °stark °naked, undressed, unclothed, °nude, in the °nude, *Brit* starkers, *Colloq* in the buff, in the altogether, in one's birthday suit: *For punishment, they made us stand outside, in the freezing cold, in the raw.*

raw-boned *adj.* °gaunt, °lean, gangling, °thin, °skinny, °spare, °meagre, °scrawny, underfed, bony, °emaciated, half-starved, wasted, hollow-cheeked, cadaverous: *They'll take that raw-boned youngster into the army and put some meat on him.*

ray *n.* **1** °beam, °shaft, °bar, °streak, pencil, °gleam, °flash: *A single ray from the setting sun illuminated the head of the statue.* **2** glimmer, °trace, °spark, scintilla, °flicker: *As he had not been rejected outright, there was still a ray of hope that he might be accepted.*

raze *v.* °tear *or* °pull *or* bring *or* °knock *or* throw down, °demolish, °destroy, °level, °flatten, bull-doze: *As usual, beautiful old buildings were razed to make way for a new shopping centre.*

reach *v.* **1** Often, **reach out**: °hold out, °extend, °stretch (out), °stick out, °thrust out, out-stretch, outreach: *He reached out his hand and grasped mine warmly.* **2** °arrive at, °get to, come to, go to, end up at *or* in; °land at *or* in, *Colloq* °make (it to): *I won't reach the office till noon today. Have we reached the point of no return?* **3** °get, °get in touch with, °communicate with, establish *or* make °contact with, °get through to, °get (a) hold of: *I tried to reach her at home, but she was out.* **4** attain, °achieve, °accomplish, °make, °get *or* go to, °get *or* go as far as: *Do you think that McClintock will reach the semi-finals?* **5** come *or* go *or* get up to, °amount to, attain, °climb to, °rise to, °run to, °equal, °match: *It looks as though the trade deficit might reach last year's figure.* **6** °get through *or* across to, °register with, °communicate with, reach into the mind of, °impress, °influence, °sway, °move, °stir, °carry °weight with: *It is very difficult for teachers to reach teenagers, who have a natural suspicion of adults.*
—*n.* **7** °range, ambit, °scope, °orbit, compass, °sphere, °territory: *Those outlying areas are beyond our reach. Padua is within easy reach of Venice.* **8** °capability, °capacity: *Tragedy often occurs when one's ambition exceeds one's reach.*

react *v.* **1** °act, °behave, °conduct oneself, °proceed; °retaliate, °reciprocate, °get °even: *I wonder how you would have reacted if someone had insulted you!* **2** °respond, °answer, °reply,

°retort: *The crowd reacted to the police presence by becoming very nasty. She reacted with surprise on learning of his arrest.*

reaction *n.* **1** °response, °reply, °answer, °effect, feedback: *Did you get any reaction when you told her I had been arrested? Her reaction was to turn over and go back to sleep.* **2** repulsion, °resistance, counteraction, counterbalance, compensation: *A rocket derives forward thrust by reaction against its own exhaust, hence can operate in a vacuum.* **3** retaliation, reciprocation, °reprisal, °revenge: *He shot her in reaction to her announce-ment that she was leaving him.*

reactionary *adj.* **1** (ultra-)°conservative, °right, rightist, right-wing, blimpish; traditionalist; *South African* verkrampte: *Reactionary governments tend to reduce social services.*
—*n.* **2** (ultra-)°conservative, rightist, right-winger, Colonel Blimp; traditionalist; *South African* verkrampte: *As a reactionary, he feels that the status quo is fine and change unnecessary.*

read *v.* **1** °peruse, °scan, °skim, °review, °study, °look over, °pore over: *I have read the article twice but still cannot understand it.* **2** °understand, °know, be °familiar with, °comprehend, °interpret, °decipher: *Can you read Greek? Madame Sonja reads tea leaves.* **3** °announce, °present, °deliver: *Anna reads the news on TV at six o'clock every evening.* **4 read into**: °assign to, °impute (to), °infer (from), °assume (from), °presume (from), conclude (from): *You might be reading too much into that letter of commendation.*

readable *adj.* **1** °intelligible, comprehensible, understandable, °easy to °understand, °easily °understood, °plain: *Surprisingly, the instructions for operating the computer are fairly readable.* **2** °entertaining, °easy to °read, enjoy-able, °pleasurable, °absorbing, °interesting, °engaging, °stimulating, °worthwhile: *Her latest thriller is so readable that I stayed up all night to finish it.* **3** °legible, decipherable, °distinct: *The print on that microfiche is too small to be readable.*

readily *adv.* **1** cheerfully, °willingly, eagerly, ungrudgingly, unhesitatingly, °freely, °gladly, °happily, agreeably, graciously, charitably: *He always gave readily of his time to anyone who sought his help, and we shall miss him sorely.* **2** effortlessly, °easily, smoothly, without °difficulty: *I was able to get the wheel off readily enough, getting it back on was the problem.* **3** °promptly, °quickly, speedily, °swiftly, apace, at °once, without °delay, in no °time, °immediately, instantly, °instantaneously, instanter, °straight away, °right away, at *or* on short notice, *Colloq* pronto: *The police came readily but were unable to catch the thieves, who had already escaped.*

readiness *n.* **1** willingness, cheerfulness, good °will, °eagerness, agreeableness, graciousness: *Her readiness to help marked her as truly charit-able.* **2** promptness, quickness; °facility, °ease, °skill, adroitness, expertness, °proficiency: *The readiness with which he gave expert advice on gar-dening made him very popular with his neigh-bours.* **3 in readiness**: See **ready**, **1**, below.

ready *adj.* **1** °prepared, (all) °set, in °readiness, in (°proper) °shape; up, primed, °ripe, °fit, °condition; *Colloq* psyched (up): *The charge is ready for detonation. I'm ready for a good run in the park. Are these apples ready for eating? Are you ready to meet the girl of your dreams?* **2** °agreeable, consenting, acquiescent, °willing, °content,

°eager, °keen, °happy, °cheerful, °genial, °gracious, °cordial, °friendly, well-disposed, °enthusiastic, *Colloq* °game: *Tim was always a ready accomplice to any mischief devised by his brother.* **3** apt, °likely, °inclined, °disposed, °given, °prone: *She was all too ready to believe anything she was told.* **4** about, °liable, °likely, apt; on the °verge of, °subject to, in °danger of, on the °brink of, on the °point of, °close to: *The volcano seemed ready to erupt at any moment.* **5** °prompt, °rapid, quick, °immediate, °speedy, °swift, °punctual, °timely: *Alistair seems to have a ready answer for everything.* **6** °clever, °keen, °sharp, °agile, deft, °skilful, adroit, °alert, °bright, °intelligent, °perceptive, °quick: *It was Carlotta's ready wit that first attracted me.* **7** on or at *or* to °hand, °handy, °available, °accessible, at (one's) fingertips, at the ready, °close at °hand, °convenient: *I don't have the ready cash for a new car at the moment.*
—*n.* **8 readies**: °money, °cash, wherewithal: *If you have the readies, please pay me what you owe me.* **9 at the ready**: **a** waiting, on °tap, °expectant, in °position, °poised: *Keep your pistol at the ready in case there's trouble.* **b** See **7**, above.
—*v.* **10** °prepare, make *or* get ready, °set, °fit out, °equip, °organize, psych up: *He readied himself as best he could for the ordeal.*

ready-made *adj.* **1** ready-to-wear, finished, pre-fabricated, *Brit* off the °peg: *Ready-made clothes fit me better than custom-made.* **2** °convenient, °expedient, °serviceable, usable, °handy, °useful, °suitable, °adaptable; °plausible, credible, believable: *The storm provided a ready-made excuse for cancelling the appointment.* **3** stereotyped, stereotypic(al), hackneyed, °time-worn, trite, °stale, °conventional, unoriginal, °stock, °pedestrian, °routine, run-of-the-mill: *His speeches are always full of ready-made clichés.*

real *adj.* **1** °genuine, °true, °actual, °authentic, verified, verifiable, °legitimate, °right, bona fide, °official; °legal, licit, °natural, valid, °veritable: *He says that his name is Smith, but what is his real name? Her diamonds are not real. It has been proved beyond the shadow of a doubt that he is the real father.* **2** °genuine, °actual, °true, existent, °authentic, °natural; °material, °physical, °tangible, palpable, corporeal: *How can one distinguish between the real object and what one sees, which is merely its image?* **3** °genuine, °sincere, °heartfelt, °true, °actual, unfeigned, °unaffected, °earnest, °honest, truthful, °legitimate, valid: *Deirdre's face is so impassive that it is impossible to tell what her real feelings are. What's the real reason that you're here?* **4** °genuine, °actual, °true, °loyal, °trustworthy, trusted, °honest: *You are a real friend, and I know I can count on you.* **5** °intrinsic, °actual, °true, °genuine, °proper, °essential: *The £150 million sale of the company fell significantly below its real value.*
—*adv.* **6** See **really**, below.

realistic *adj.* **1** °practical, °matter-of-fact, down-to-earth, pragmatic, common-sense, °sensible, °reasonable, °level-headed, °rational, °sane, hard-headed, businesslike, °no-nonsense, unromantic, unsentimental, °tough, tough-minded, *Colloq* hard-nosed, hard-boiled: *Kevin's realistic grasp of the problems may make the company profitable at last.* **2** °natural, °lifelike, °true to °life, natural-

istic, °vivid, °genuine, °real, °graphic: *This painting is so realistic that it looks like a photograph. Harriet's description was so realistic that I felt I had actually been to Benidorm.*

reality *n.* **1** actuality, °fact, °truth, genuineness, authenticity, *Aristotelianism* entelechy: *It is important to deal with the reality not the potentiality of the situation.* **2 in reality**: See **really**, below.

realization *n.* **1** °conception, °understanding, comprehension, apprehension, awareness, °appreciation, °perception, °recognition, °cognizance: *Full realization of what he had done finally dawned on him.* **2** actualization, °consummation, °accomplishment, °achievement, °establishment, °fulfilment, materialization, effectuation: *The realization of the dream of a united Europe seems possible in the last decade of the 20th century.*

realize *v.* **1** make °real, °effect, °bring about, make happen, make a °reality, actualize, °accomplish, °produce, °achieve, °fulfil, °materialize, °effectuate: *Many of Leonardo da Vinci's inventions were not realized in his lifetime.* **2** °understand, °appreciate, °comprehend, be °aware of, °conceive of, °grasp, °perceive, discern, be *or* become °conscious *or* °aware *or* appreciative of, °recognize, °see, *Colloq* °catch on (to), cotton (on) to, *Brit* °twig: *Did Clare fully realize the consequences of her actions?* **3** °return, °gain, °clear, °profit, °make, °earn, °bring *or* take in, °net, °produce, °get: *We have realized a substantial profit on the sale of the shares bought when the company was privatized.*

really *adv.* **1** genuinely, °actually, °truly, °honestly, in °reality, in actuality, in (point of) °fact, as a matter of °fact, °surely, °indeed, °absolutely, °definitely: *Is he really going to do the high-wire act without a net?* **2** °indeed, °actually, °absolutely, unqualifiedly, °positively, categorically, unquestionably, °definitely, undeniably: *She is really the musical one in the family.* **3** in °effect, in °reality, °actually, in °fact, de facto, in the end, at °bottom, in the final analysis, at the end of the day, *Colloq* deep down: *Despite the sergeant's protests to the contrary, it was really Andrews who saved the platoon.* **4** °very, °extremely, °quite, exceptionally, remarkably, unusually, uncommonly, extraordinarily, °exceedingly, *Non-Standard* °real: *I saw a really good film last night.*

realm *n.* **1** °domain, °kingdom, empire, °monarchy, principality, palatinate, duchy *or* dukedom: *They searched the realm for a girl whose foot would fit into the glass slipper.* **2** °territory, °area, bailiwick, °department, °responsibility, °jurisdiction: *Collecting taxes is not within the realm of our office.* **3** °area, confines, °sphere, °limits: *Cooperation with foreign companies is certainly well within the realms of possibility.*

ream *v.* °drill (out), °bore (out), °open up, °tap: *The carpenter reamed three holes in the beam.*

reap *v.* **1** °harvest, °garner, glean, °gather (in), °mow, °take in *or* up: *The land was fertile, and a bountiful crop was reaped. As ye sow, so shall ye reap.* **2** °profit, °bring in, °gain, °procure, °acquire, °get, °obtain, take in: *It is impossible to reap much when there is so small a margin between cost and selling price.*

rear[1] *n.* **1** °back (part), °end, hind part, *Nautical* °stern, *Colloq* °tail (end), fag-end, *US and Canadian* tag end: *The rear of the column was attacked as it*

marched through the defile. We took seats at the rear of the auditorium. **2** hindquarters, °posterior, rump, °buttocks, bottom, behind, backside, rear end, Colloq Brit °bum, US hinie, tush or tushy or tushie, tokus or tochis or tuchis, Taboo Slang Brit arse, US ass: As he left, he felt someone give him a pat on the rear.
—adj. **3** °back, °last, end, rearmost, Nautical aft, after, °stern: The rear window is all misted over.

rear[2] v. **1** °raise, °bring up, °care for, nurture, °nurse; °cultivate, °educate, °train; °breed, °produce: They reared six children in that tiny house. Is this where they rear Aberdeen Angus cattle? **2** °erect, °raise, °build, °put up, °construct, °fabricate, °create: The family reared an elaborate mausoleum in memory of Lord Percy. **3** °raise, °lift, °put up, upraise, uplift, °hold up: He said that élitism was rearing its ugly head again, and that equality of opportunity was proving a myth.

reason n. **1** justification, °argument, °case, °explanation, °rationale, °ground(s), °pretext, vindication, °defence, why (and wherefore), Literary apologia, apology: What reason did they give for confiscating our luggage? **2** °judgement, common °sense, °intelligence, °sanity, °sense(s), saneness, °insight, perspicacity, percipience, °understanding, rationality, °reasoning, °mind, °intellect: He must have lost his reason to accuse you of embezzlement. **3** °purpose, °aim, °intention, °object, °objective, °goal, °motive, °end, °point: His reason for leaving now is to be on time for the curtain. **4** °excuse, rationalization: Ignorance of the law is not an accepted reason for breaking it. **5 by reason of**: because of, on account of, owing to, by °virtue of, as a °result of; °due to: He was declared unfit to stand trial by reason of insanity. **6 within** or **in reason**: °reasonable, °sensible, justifiable, °rational, °fitting, °proper, °acceptable: We will consider any offer for the house that is within reason.
—v. **7** °think, conclude, °calculate, °reckon, °estimate, °figure (out), °work out, °deduce, act or °think rationally or logically, ratiocinate, use (one's) °judgement or common °sense, use (one's) °head, put two and two together: I reasoned that she would be arriving at the station at that very moment. Roy certainly hasn't lost his powers of reasoning. **8 reason with**: °argue with, remonstrate with, °debate with, °discuss with, °talk over with, °plead with, °convince; °persuade, dissuade, °urge, °prevail (up)on: George is very stubborn and can't be reasoned with.

reasonable adj. **1** °sensible, °rational, °sane, °logical, °sober, °sound, °judicious, °wise, °intelligent, °thinking: I had always thought Philip a reasonable man. **2** credible, believable, °plausible, °tenable, reasoned, arguable, well-thought-out, well-grounded: Her story about having found the child wandering in the street doesn't sound very reasonable to me. **3** °moderate, °tolerable, °acceptable, within °reason, °equitable, °fair; °inexpensive, unexcessive, unextravagant, °economical, °conservative: Considering inflation, we thought the price increases were reasonable. **4** °appropriate, °suitable, °proper, °sensible, °right: The car was travelling at a reasonable speed, considering conditions.

reasoning n. **1** °thinking, °logic, °analysis, rationalization: The entire argument falls to pieces because of faulty reasoning. **2** reasons, arguments,

premises, °rationale, postulate, °hypothesis, theory, °explanation, explication: His reasoning had no effect on her—she simply refused to listen.

reassure v. °comfort, °encourage, hearten, °buoy (up), °bolster, °cheer, uplift, inspirit, °brace, °support, restore °confidence to, set or put (someone's) mind at rest, set or put (someone) at ease, °settle (someone's) doubts: The minister reassured the public regarding the safety of public transport.

rebate n. **1** °discount, reduction, °deduction, °allowance, mark-down, cut-back, refund, repayment, Colloq US °rake-off: This coupon entitles you to a rebate of ten per cent on the purchase of four new tyres. **2** °kickback, °percentage, °rake-off, commission, °cut, °bribe, °graft, Colloq chiefly US payola, US plugola: He gets a rebate of five per cent on every client he refers to the solicitor.
—v. **3** °discount, °reduce, °deduct, °mark down, refund, °repay; kick back: Periodicals rebate fifteen per cent of their gross advertising revenue to the agencies that place ads.

rebel v. **1** °revolt, °mutiny, °rise up: The people will rebel if subjected to more oppression. **2** Often, **rebel against**: °defy, °flout, °dare, °challenge; °disobey, dissent: It is in the nature of young people to rebel against authority and the status quo.
—n. **3** °revolutionary, revolutionist, insurgent, insurrectionist, mutineer, resister, °resistance fighter, freedom fighter: We call ourselves fighters for justice, but the unjust call us rebels and traitors. **4** heretic, °nonconformist, apostate, dissenter, recusant, °schismatic: James's problem was that he was a rebel without a cause.

rebellion n. **1** °uprising, °revolution, °mutiny, insurrection, °revolt, insurgence or insurgency: Rebellion is the last recourse against tyranny. **2** insubordination, disobedience, defiance, °resistance, rebelliousness, contumacy: Her rebellion against parental authority led her to leave home at sixteen.

rebellious adj. **1** °insubordinate, °defiant, °mutinous, °revolutionary, contumacious, insurgent, insurrectionary, °seditious: The more rebellious students organized mass meetings against the university authorities. **2** unmanageable, °disobedient, °incorrigible, °ungovernable, °unruly, °difficult, refractory, °stubborn, °obstinate, °recalcitrant: They resented being treated as rebellious children.

rebirth n. °renaissance or renascence, °revival, renewal, reawakening, °resurgence, revitalization, resurrection, regeneration, rejuvenation, °restoration, new °beginning, reincarnation; metempsychosis, palingenesis: The 15th century marked the rebirth of learning in Europe after the so-called Dark Ages.

rebound v. **1** °spring back, °bounce, °recoil, ricochet, resile: The ball rebounded from the goalpost.
—n. **2** °bounce, °recoil, ricochet, °return, comeback, °repercussion, °backlash, reflex: Carter caught the ball on the rebound.

rebuff n. **1** °rejection, snub, °check, °denial, °repulse, °refusal, °dismissal, °defeat, repudiation, °slight, discouragement, Colloq cold °shoulder, °cut, °put-down, °brush-off, Slang US °brush: Ellie's friendly approach was met with an abrupt rebuff.
—v. **2** °reject, snub, °check, °deny, °repel, °drive away, °spurn, °repulse, °refuse, °dismiss,

°defeat, °repudiate, °slight, °ignore, send (someone) to Coventry, *Colloq* give (someone) the cold °shoulder, °cut, °put (someone) down, °brush (someone) off, give (someone) the °brush-off, tell (someone) where to go *or* get off, tell (someone) where to get lost, *Slang* give (someone) his *or* her walking papers, °freeze (someone) out, *US* give (someone) the °brush, show (someone) the door: *She rebuffed everyone who proposed marriage to her, preferring to remain a spinster.*

rebuke v. **1** °scold, reproach, admonish, °reprove, °reprimand, °lecture, censure, chide, reprehend, °berate, °castigate, °criticize, take to °task, °upbraid, revile, *Colloq* °dress down, °bawl out, give (someone) a piece of one's °mind, haul (someone) over the coals, let (someone) have it, give (someone) hell *or* what for, °tell (someone) off, tell (someone) where to get off, *Brit* carpet, tear (someone) off a strip, tick (someone) off, wig, °blow (someone) up, give (someone) a wigging, *US and Canadian* rake (someone) over the coals, give (someone) the business, °chew out: *The headmaster severely rebuked those boys who had violated the school curfew.* —n. **2** scolding, reproach, admonition, °reproof, °reprimand, °lecture, censure, chiding, reprehension, berating, castigation, °criticism, upbraiding, revilement, °tongue-lashing, *Colloq* dressing-down, what for, *Brit* wigging, blow-up *or* blowing up, *Slang* °hell: *Rawlings was let off with nothing more than a rebuke.*

rebut v. refute, °deny, °disprove, confute, invalidate, negate, °discredit, belie, °contradict, controvert, °puncture, expose, °destroy, °ruin, °devastate, *Colloq* shoot full of holes, knock the bottom out of, shoot down, blow sky-high: *We have all the evidence needed to rebut the contention that our client was anywhere near the scene of the crime.*

rebuttal n. °answer, °reply, °retort, °response, rejoinder, counter-argument, riposte, retaliation, °denial, refutation, contradiction, confutation, *Colloq* comeback: *In rebuttal, the defence tried to prove that the witness for the prosecution had been bribed.*

recalcitrant adj. °stubborn, °obstinate, °wilful, °defiant, refractory, headstrong, °perverse, °contrary, contumacious, °mutinous, °rebellious, fractious, °unruly, unmanageable, °ungovernable, uncontrollable, wayward, °insubordinate, intractable, unsubmissive, unyielding, unbending, adamant, °immovable, °inflexible, °stiff, °firm: *Recalcitrant students who refuse to obey the rules risk expulsion.*

recall v. **1** °remember, °recollect, °think back to, °reminisce over *or* about, call to °mind: *I like to recall the happy days we had at Biarritz.* **2** °withdraw, °retract, °call back, °summon: *The legions guarding the frontier provinces were recalled to Rome.* **3** rescind, °cancel, annul, nullify, °retract, °withdraw, °revoke, °recant, °take back, call back; disavow, disown, °deny: *Despite the fact that you might have been hasty, you cannot recall your promise.* —n. **4** °memory, °recollection, remembering, °remembrance: *He had a loving and near-photographic recall of their holiday in the Alps.* **5** withdrawal, recantation, °cancellation, revocation, annulment, nullification, recision, rescission, retraction, °repeal, disavowal,

°denial: *The decision was made without any possibility of recall.* **6** withdrawal, retraction, °return: *The manufacturer's recall of the shipment of defective toasters was voluntary.*

recant v. °recall, forswear, °deny, rescind, °repudiate, disavow, disclaim, °withdraw, °revoke, °retract, °forsake, °abandon, apostatize, °renounce, abjure, °take back: *He was given three days to recant: otherwise, he would be executed for heresy.*

recapitulate v. summarize, °sum up; °repeat, °go over (again), °reiterate, restate, °review; °recount, °enumerate, °recite, °relate, °list, *Colloq* recap: *I shall begin by recapitulating some of the issues which I covered in my last lecture.*

recede v. **1** °ebb, °subside, °fall *or* °go *or* move back, abate, °return, °withdraw, °retreat, back up: *As the flood waters receded, people began to go back to their homes.* **2** °diminish, lessen, °decline, °dwindle, °shrink, °wane, °fade, °become more °distant *or* less likely: *The likelihood of our being rescued receded with each passing day.*

receipt n. **1** sales receipt, register receipt, sales °slip, ticket, °stub, counterfoil, °proof of °purchase, voucher: *Any request for a return or exchange must be accompanied by a receipt.* **2** °delivery, acceptance, °reception, °arrival: *He has acknowledged receipt of the merchandise.* **3 receipts:** °income, °proceeds, °gate, takings, °gains, °return, *Colloq* °take: *The receipts from ticket sales were below expectations.*

receive v. **1** °get, °obtain, °come by, °collect, °take (into one's °possession), °accept, be given, °acquire, °come into, °inherit, °gain, °profit, °make: *She received a large sum of money from the sale of the house. What will he receive when his aunt dies?* **2** °earn, be paid, °make, °draw, °gross, °net, °clear, °pocket, *Colloq* °take, walk off *or* away with, *US* °pull down: *He receives a bigger weekly salary than I make in a year.* **3** °greet, °meet, °welcome; °show in, give entrée, °let in, °admit: *We received our guests in the foyer.* **4** °experience, °undergo, °endure, °suffer, °bear, °sustain, be subjected to, °meet with: *In return for helping him all I received was a punch in the nose.* **5** °gather, °hear, °learn, ascertain, be told, be informed *or* notified of, °find out, °pick up: *We only received the information yesterday that you were coming to stay for a month.*

recent adj. °late, °latest, °new, °just out, °brand-new, °fresh; °current, °modern, up to °date, late-model: *This feature is now supplied as standard on all our more recent models. Recent arrivals will be interviewed by the committee.*

receptacle n. container, holder, repository; °box, tin, can, °case, °casket, °chest, reliquary, °vessel, °bag, basket: *Please put the rubbish into the receptacle. She kept the diamond in a velvet-lined receptacle which she always carried with her.*

reception n. **1** °welcome, °greeting, °treatment, °reaction, °response: *My suggestion that we open a bottle of champagne met with a warm reception.* **2** °party, levee, °social, soirée, °function; °opening, °preview, vernissage, *Colloq* do: *Would you like to go to a reception at the new art gallery next week?*

receptive adj. **1** °open, °hospitable, amenable, pervious, persuasible, °tractable, °flexible, pliant, °interested, °willing, °responsive: *I have always found Peggy receptive to suggestions on* *improving productivity and efficiency.* **2** °quick, °alert, °perceptive, °astute, °intelligent, °keen, °sharp, °bright, °sensitive: *Julia has a receptive mind.*

recess *n.* **1** alcove, °niche, °nook, °cranny, bay, °hollow: *The statuette fits perfectly in that recess outside the library.* **2** °respite, rest, °interlude, time off, °break, °intermission, breather, breathing-space, °pause; °holiday, vacation: *A brief recess has been scheduled to allow us to relax before continuing.* **3 recesses**: innermost reaches, corners, °secret places, °depths, penetralia: *I searched for her name in the recesses of my mind.*

recession *n.* °set-back, (economic) downturn, °slump, °decline, °dip, °depression: *The slowing of the economy led to a recession which soon deepened into a depression.*

recipe *n.* **1** °formula, °prescription: *Elizabeth gave me a marvellous recipe for chocolate cake.* **2** °plan, °procedure, °method, °approach, °technique, °way, °means, °system, °programme, modus operandi, *Colloq US* MO: *The minister insists that his recipe for conquering inflation will work.*

recipient *n.* receiver, beneficiary, °heir *or* heiress, legatee: *Who is the current recipient of her favours?*

reciprocal *adj.* °mutual, exchanged, returned, complementary, correlative, °common, shared, °joint, requited: *The reciprocal courtesies enjoyed among our neighbours benefit us all.*

reciprocate *v.* °repay, recompense, °requite, °exchange, °return, °trade, °match, °equal, °correspond: *You have always been very kind to me and I want to reciprocate in any way I can.*

recital *n.* **1** (°solo) concert, °performance, musicale, °presentation, °show, °entertainment: *We have tickets to a recital for that night.* **2** °report, °narration, °account, °recitation, °description, °relation, °telling, recounting, °narrative, °rendition, °interpretation, °version, recapitulation, °rehearsal, °repetition, *Colloq* recap: *A reporter who was on the flight provided us with a recital of the events leading up to the crash.*

recitation *n.* **1** reciting, °performance, reading, monologue: *At the age of four Simon delighted his parents with his recitation of 'The Charge of the Light Brigade'.* **2** See *recital, 2*, above.

recite *v.* **1** °quote, °repeat, °present: *In the old days, children were often called upon to recite poems they had learned by heart.* **2** °report, °narrate, °recount, °relate, °tell, °describe, °detail, °chronicle, °list, °share, °recapitulate, °repeat, *Colloq* recap: *Again I recited every particular of the hold-up that I could recall.*

reckless *adj.* °careless, °rash, °thoughtless, incautious, °heedless, °foolhardy, °imprudent, unwise, injudicious, °impulsive, °irresponsible, negligent, unmindful, °foolish, devil-may-care, °daredevil, °wild, °breakneck, °dangerous, madcap, °mad, °hare-brained: *I won't go with Oliver because he's a reckless driver.*

reckon *v.* **1** Often, **reckon up**: °calculate, °compute, °add (up), °figure (up), °tally (up), °sum up, °total (up), °work out *or* up: *If you reckon up the bill, I'll pay it at once.* **2** °include, °count, °number, °enumerate, °list, °name, °consider, °account, °judge, deem, look upon, °regard, °view, °think of, °hold, °gauge,

°estimate, appraise, value, °rank, °rate, °class: *I have always reckoned Arthur as being among my closest friends.* **3** °suppose, °think, °assume, °presume, °dare say, °venture, °imagine, °fancy, °consider, conclude, be of the °opinion, *US or colloq* °guess: *She reckoned that no one could accuse her of idle chatter.* **4 reckon on** *or* **upon**: °count on, °rely on, °depend on, °lean on, °trust in, take for granted, *Colloq* bank on: *I was reckoning on your help, and I hope you won't disappoint me.* **5 reckon with**: **a** °settle (accounts) with, take °care of, °look after, °see *or* °attend to, °deal with, °handle, pay °attention to, °think about: *I have to go now, but I'll reckon with you later.* **b** take into °account *or* °consideration, °consider, °contemplate, °account for, °remember, bear in °mind: *He thought he had got away with it, but he failed to reckon with Inspector Harris of the CID.*

reckoning *n.* **1** counting, calculating, °calculation, computation, enumeration, °addition: *The reckoning of Old Style dates used the Julian calendar.* **2** °bill, °account, invoice, *US* °check, *Colloq chiefly US and Canadian* °tab: *If you let me have the reckoning, I'll pay it with my credit card.* **3** (last) °judgement, °retribution, final °account(ing) *or* °settlement, °doom: *On the day of reckoning we must all face the music.*

reclaim *v.* °restore, °recover, °rescue, °redeem, °salvage, °save, regain, °retrieve, regenerate, °rejuvenate: *Much of the farmland was reclaimed from the sea.*

recline *v.* °lie (down), °lie back, °lean back, °lounge, °rest, °repose, °sprawl, loll, °stretch out: *Just recline on the sofa and make yourself comfortable.*

recluse *n.* °hermit, anchorite *or* anchoress, °monk *or* nun, eremite: *For the past ten years, he has been living the life of a recluse.*

reclusive *adj.* °solitary, lone, °secluded, °isolated, eremitic(al), hermitic(al), anchoritic, monastic, cloistered, sequestered, °retiring, °shut off: *She insists that she enjoys her reclusive existence.*

recognition *n.* **1** °identification, detection: *Her recognition of the man on TV led to his arrest.* **2** °acknowledgement, °notice, °attention, °cognizance, acceptance, awareness, °perception, °admission; °honour, °appreciation: *The award was a recognition of his contributions to scientific knowledge.*

recognize *v.* **1** °identify, °detect, °place, °recall, °remember, °recollect, °know (again): *I recognized him from seeing his picture in the newspaper.* **2** °acknowledge, °perceive, °understand, °realize, °see, °admit, °accept, own, °concede, °allow, °grant, °appreciate, °respect, be °aware of: *He refuses to recognize that he is responsible for his own actions.* **3** °approve, °sanction, °endorse, °accept, validate, °ratify: *A totalitarian government refuses to recognize the rights of the individual.* **4** °honour, give °recognition to, °salute, show °gratitude *or* °appreciation, °reward, °distinguish, pay °respect, do °homage: *The society recognizes Dr Jackson for his many contributions to science.*

recoil *v.* **1** °jerk *or* °jump *or* °spring back, °start, °flinch, wince, °shrink, blench, balk *or* baulk, shy (away) (from): *He recoiled when confronted with the evidence of the gruesome experiments with live*

animals. **2** °rebound, °bounce back, resile, °kick back: *When fired, the gun recoiled, bruising his shoulder.*
—*n.* **3** °kick, °rebound, °repercussion, °backlash: *He was unprepared for the violent recoil of the old gun.*

recollect *v.* °recall, °remember, call to °mind: *Now that you mention it, I do recollect your asking me to buy some milk when I went out.*

recollection *n.* °memory, °recall, °remembrance, °impression, °reminiscence: *My brother's recollection of our grandparents is quite different from mine.*

recommend *v.* **1** °counsel, °advise, °guide, °urge, exhort, °suggest, °advocate, °propose, (°put) °forward, °propound, °persuade: *He recommended that the entire system should be changed.* **2** °endorse, °praise, commend, °mention °favourably, °vouch for, °second, °subscribe to, °back, °push, °favour, °approve, °underwrite, °stand up for, °support, °promote, *Colloq* °tout, °plug: *I wish Charles would stop recommending his brother-in-law for a job with us.* **3** make °attractive *or* °advisable *or* °interesting *or* °acceptable: *Wendover has little to recommend it as a tourist spot.*

recommendation *n.* **1** °counsel, °advice, °guidance, urging, exhortation, °direction, °encouragement, °suggestion, prompting, advocacy, °proposal: *It was on your recommendation that we tried that restaurant.* **2** °endorsement, °praise, commendation, °favourable °mention, °backing, °blessing, °approval, approbation, °support, °promotion, good word, °testimonial, °say-so: *The chairman of the board gave Caswell's brother-in-law his personal recommendation.*

reconcile *v.* **1** °get *or* bring (back) together, °unite, reunite, °settle *or* °resolve differences between, °restore °harmony between, make °peace between, placate, make compatible: *Do you think that a marriage counsellor could help reconcile John and Martha?* **2** °resign, °submit, °accommodate, °adjust: *Lady Mary Wortley Montague wrote that she was reconciled to being a woman when she reflected that she was thus in no danger of ever marrying one.*

reconciliation *n.* **1** conciliation, appeasement, propitiation, pacification, placation, *rapprochement*, reconcilement, °understanding, détente, reunion, °harmony, concord, °accord, amity, °rapport: *It was with great effort that the reconciliation between the two families was finally arranged.* **2** compromise, °settlement, °agreement, arbitration, conformity, compatibility, °adjustment: *Reconciliation of their differences seems difficult but not impossible.*

recondite *adj.* abstruse, arcane, °obscure, esoteric, °deep, °profound, °incomprehensible, unfathomable, impenetrable, undecipherable, °opaque, °dark, °occult, cabbalistic *or* kabbalistic, °inexplicable, enigmatic: *I have difficulty following the more recondite aspects of information theory.*

reconnaissance *n.* °survey, °examination, scouting, °exploration, reconnoitring, °investigation, inspection, °scrutiny, *Slang Brit* recce: *Their reconnaissance showed that the enemy forces had withdrawn.*

reconnoitre *v.* °survey, °examine, °scout (out), °scan, °explore, °investigate, °inspect, °scrutinize, °check out, °check up (on), *Slang Brit* recce: *We reconnoitred the territory and reported the enemy troop movements.*

record *v.* **1** °write (down), °transcribe, °document, °register, °note, make a °notation (of), °take down, °put *or* °set down, log, °chronicle, °report, °itemize, °list, °enumerate: *I recorded the events of the day in my diary.* **2** °tell of, °relate, °recount, °narrate, °recite: *The chronicle records an eyewitness account of the battle.*
—*n.* **3** recording, °report, °document, log, °journal, °memorandum, °note, °notation, °minute(s), transactions, archive(s), annal(s), °chronicle, °diary, °account, dossier, °register, °list, catalogue: *Patricia has kept a careful record of all the men whose books she has ever read.* **4** documentation, °data, °information, °evidence; °memorial, °memento, souvenir: *There is no record of your birth in the church archive. I took away a piece of the Berlin Wall as a record of my visit.* **5** (°best) °performance, track record, °accomplishment; time; distance; °height: *Her records for the 110-metre hurdles and the high jump still stand.* **6** °accomplishment(s), °deed(s), °history, °reputation, curriculum vitae, CV, *Colloq* track record: *He has a record of being late everywhere. His criminal record is none too savoury.* **7** disc, recording, album, release, LP (= 'long playing'), 78, 33⅓, 45, EP (= 'extended play'), compact disc, CD, *Brit* gramophone record, *US* phonograph record, *Colloq* single, *Slang US* platter: *We put a jazz combo together and cut a few records last year.* **8 off the record**: °confidential(ly), °private(ly), not for publication, °secret(ly), in °confidence, °unofficial(ly), sub rosa: *We cannot publish his statement, which was off the record. Off the record, I'll tell you where Hazel is staying.*
—*adj.* **9** record-breaking, °extreme: *Last week we had a record snowfall.*

recount *v.* **1** °relate, °narrate, °tell, °recite, °report, °communicate, °impart, °unfold: *The old man recounted for us the legend of the two-headed lamb.* **2** particularize, °review, °detail, °describe, °enumerate, °specify: *Must I recount every particular all over again?*

recoup *v.* regain, °make good, °make up, recompense, °repay, °recover; refund, °redeem, °reimburse, remunerate: *From his profits on the Culpepper deal, he recouped all the losses he had sustained when Cranston Ltd failed.*

recourse *n.* **1** °resort, access, entrée, °admittance, availability: *They are completely isolated and without recourse to help from the outside world.* **2** °resource, backup, °reserve, °refuge, place to turn, °alternative, °remedy: *The company has no recourse against the authorities.*

recover *v.* **1** regain, °get *or* °take *or* °win *or* make back (again), °recoup, repossess, retake, recapture, °restore, °retrieve, °reclaim, °redeem: *It was impossible to recover the time lost. After a fierce battle, the territory was recovered.* **2** get °well *or* °better, °recuperate, °convalesce, °mend, °return to °health, regain one's °strength *or* °health, be on the °mend, °heal, °improve, °revive, °rally, take a °turn for the °better, get back on one's feet, °pull through: *It took me a week to recover from the operation. Lucy had a virus, but she's recovering now.* **3** °save, °salvage, °deliver, °rescue, °return, °bring back, °reclaim, °retrieve: *They never did recover the gold from the sunken ship.*

recovery n. **1** recuperation, convalescence, °restoration, °improvement, healing, °rally, °turn for the °better; °rise, °revival, °increase, amelioration, bettering, betterment, °advance, °gain, advancement, Colloq pick-up, comeback: After so serious an illness, Bentley has made a remarkable recovery. Share prices staged a recovery after the reduction in interest rates. **2** retrieval, recouping, repossession, retaking, °restoration, reclamation; recapture, redemption: The recovery of the stolen gems was credited to excellent detective work. Hard fighting resulted in the recovery of the land west of the river. **3** °salvage, °delivery, deliverance, °rescue, °return, °saving, reclamation, retrieval: Recovery of the climbers' bodies from the ravine was very hazardous.

recreation n. °entertainment, °amusement, °enjoyment, °diversion, °distraction, °fun and games, °leisure (°activity), °pastime, °relaxation, °sport, °play: What do you like to do for recreation? His favourite recreation is building model aeroplanes.

recrimination n. counter-accusation, countercharge, retaliation, counter-attack, blaming, °aspersion, °reprisal: Recriminations for real and imagined ills were continually exchanged throughout their marriage.

recruit v. **1** °draft, °induct, °enlist, °enrol, °muster, °raise, °call up, conscript, °mobilize, impress, levy: Owing to the nefarious enemy attack, there was little time to recruit men for a strong fighting force.
—n. **2** conscript, trainee, beginner, °apprentice, °initiate, °novice, neophyte, tiro or tyro, US draftee, enlistee, Colloq °greenhorn, rookie: The new recruits have to be issued with their uniforms and other gear.

rectify v. °correct, °revise, redress, put or set °right, °cure, °repair, °remedy, °improve, emend, °fix, °adjust, °square, ameliorate: What do you intend to do to rectify the damage you have done?

rectitude n. °propriety, correctness, °morality, uprightness, °probity, °virtue, decency, goodness, °honesty, °integrity, incorruptibility, righteousness, °principle, °good °character, respectability, unimpeachability: Fred's unquestioned moral rectitude makes him an outstanding candidate for membership.

recumbent adj. reclining, °lying down, °flat on one's back, °horizontal, °lying, reposing, accumbent, decumbent, °supine, stretched out; °leaning (back): Oscar resumed his recumbent posture, sprawled out on the cushions.

recuperate v. °improve, °recover, °convalesce, get °better, °rally, °revive, °mend, °heal, get back on one's feet, regain one's °health or strength, °pull through, °survive, take a °turn for the °better: Paul went to Ibiza to recuperate from his illness.

recur v. °return, °happen or °occur again, reoccur, °repeat, come (back) again, reappear: The condition recurred after a year, and he was obliged to have another operation.

recurrent adj. repeated, recurring, returning, reoccurring, reappearing, °frequent, °periodic, cyclical, °regular, °repetitive, °repetitious, °persistent, incessant, °continual, °intermittent, °habitual, iterative: She told the psychiatrist about her recurrent dream of flying.

redeem v. **1** °reclaim, °recover, regain, repossess, °retrieve, °get back, °buy back, repurchase; °pay off, Brit °clear: He went into the pawn shop to redeem the gold watch. **2** °rescue, °ransom, °deliver, °free, °save, °liberate, set °free, °emancipate, °release: He was able to redeem the boy only after paying the kidnappers. **3** °exchange, °cash (in), collect on, °trade in: These coupons must be redeemed before the end of the month. **4** °rehabilitate, °save, °reform, °convert, absolve, °restore to °favour, reinstate: She can be redeemed only by atoning for her sins. **5** make °amends for, °make up for, °atone for, redress, °compensate for, °offset, make °restitution for: Do you think that 200 hours of community service was enough to redeem his crime of snatching handbags in the shopping centre? **6** °perform, °fulfil, °keep, °make good (on), °discharge, °satisfy, °abide by, keep °faith with, be °faithful to, hold to, °carry out, °see through: Helen is here to redeem her promise to help at the charity bazaar.

red-handed adj. in the (very) °act, (in) flagrante delicto, Colloq with one's hand in the till, US with one's hand in the cookie-jar: There's no doubt that Rick did it—he was caught red-handed.

redolent adj. **1** °fragrant, sweet-smelling, °aromatic, perfumed, odorous, scented, °savoury: The entire house was redolent with the odour of pine needles. **2 redolent with** or **of**: °reminiscent of, °suggestive of, evocative of, remindful of, °characteristic of, having the earmarks or °hallmark of: The style of the film is redolent of 1930s Hollywood.

reduce v. **1** °cut (back), °cut down (on), °decrease, °diminish, °moderate, abate, lessen, °shorten, truncate, °abbreviate, °abridge, °curtail, crop, °trim, compress, °restrict, °limit, °stunt: We must reduce expenses this year. **2** °ease (up on), °let up (on), °decrease, °mitigate, °tone down, slacken up (on): It will reduce the burden of your costs if you share with me. **3** lose weight, °slim (down), °diet, °trim down, Chiefly US slenderize: You'll have to reduce to fit into that dress, Betty. **4** °change, °modify, °adjust, °turn, °convert; °break down or up, °grind, °rub, triturate, °pulp, °powder: Payment of the debt reduced me to poverty. The first step is to reduce the liquid to a thick extract. **5** °cut, °decrease, °trim, °bring down, °lower, °drop, °mark down, °slash, Colloq °knock down: The prices on these shoes have been reduced for a quick sale. **6** demote, °degrade, °lower, °downgrade, °break; °humble; Military US and Canadian bust: He was reduced in rank from sergeant to private. **7** °diminish, lessen, °bring down, °depreciate, °subdue, °belittle, °minimize: He was reduced in her estimation when she saw the deprecating way his friends treated him. **8** Medicine set, °adjust, reset: The doctor caused little pain when he reduced her dislocated finger.

redundant adj. **1** °superfluous, °unnecessary, °surplus, inessential or unessential, °non-essential, unneeded, unwanted, de trop, in °excess, °excessive: He was made redundant at the age of forty-five and was unable to find another job. **2** °wordy, verbose, prolix, over-long, long-winded, °repetitious, tautological or tautologous, circumlocutory, °roundabout: The book would be improved if certain redundant passages were removed.

reek v. **1** stink or °smell (to high heaven), Slang Brit pong, hum: Allie reeks from cleaning out the stable. **2** smoke, steam: It is because it used to reek so badly that Edinburgh acquired its nickname, 'Auld Reekie'.

—n. **3** stink, °stench, fetor or foetor, miasma, mephitis, °odour, °smell, Slang Brit hum, pong: The reek of rotting vegetation permeated the atmosphere. **4** °fumes, smoke, steam, °vapour, °exhalation, cloud, °mist: He delighted in the redolent reek that arose from the haggis.

reel v. **1** °stagger, °totter, waver, °stumble, °lurch, falter, °roll, °rock, °sway, °flounder, °pitch: Chris came reeling down the lane, dead drunk. **2 reel off**: °list, °recite, °rattle off, °enumerate, °review, °itemize, °name, °read off, °call off, °run through, °run over: Under questioning, the suspect began to reel off the names of his accomplices.

refer v. **1** Often, **refer to**: allude to, make °reference to, °mention, make mention of, °touch on, °bring up, advert to, °speak of, turn or call or direct °attention to, °direct to, °point to, °indicate, °specify, °name, °concern, °quote, cite, make a °note of, take °note of, °note: A footnote refers to the author's article on netsukes. **2** °assign, °hand over, °pass on or over, °send, °direct, °commit: I was referred to your office for information about rates. The question will be referred to committee. **3** Usually, **refer to**: °look at, °use, °study, °check, °consult, °resort to, have °recourse to, °turn to, °appeal to, °confer with; °talk to, °ask, °inquire or °enquire of, °apply to: For information about words, you should refer to a dictionary. Refer to the departmental office for Professor Clarke's address. **4** Usually, **refer to**: °mean, °signify, °denote, °say: What are you referring to?

reference n. **1** allusion, °mention, °remark, referral, °direction, °indication, °specification, naming, °quotation, citation, °note, °notation, notification, °hint, intimation, °innuendo, insinuation: I can't find a reference in any footnote. Few readers make use of the bibliographical references in scholarly articles. Her persistent references to my baldness embarrass me. **2** °regard, °concern, °connection, °respect, °relation, °relevance, pertinence: People are selected without reference to race, creed, colour, sex, or age. **3** °endorsement, °recommendation, °testimonial, certification; credentials: I relied on my former employer to give me a good reference. We shall not be needing to take up your references.

refine v. **1** °purify, °cleanse, °clear, °clarify, decontaminate: They continued to refine the liquid till all the impurities were gone. **2** °cultivate, °civilize, °polish, °improve, elevate, °perfect: He is trying to refine his speech by getting rid of his country accent. **3** hone, °sharpen, °concentrate, °focus, subtilize: We ought to refine our argument for higher wages before approaching the management.

refined adj. **1** °cultivated, cultured, civilized, °polished, °sophisticated, urbane, °elegant, °well-bred, °genteel, courtly, °ladylike, gentlemanly, °polite, °courteous, mannerly, well-mannered, °gracious, °gentle, °noble, aristocratic, °dignified, °elevated, Colloq °posh: It is seldom that I find myself in such refined company. **2** °subtle, °discriminating, discerning, °sensitive, °fastidious, °nice, °precise, °exacting, cultured, °educated, °cultivated, °knowledgeable, advanced, °sophisticated: Her taste in the visual arts is fairly refined, but she knows little about music. **3** °exact, °precise, °fine, °subtle, °sensitive, °nice, °sophisticated: In his poetry one encounters an extremely refined use of

metaphor. These new devices are far more refined than any previously available. **4** purified, clarified, cleansed, °pure, °clean; distilled: Only refined chemicals may be used in pharmaceuticals.

refinement n. **1** °culture, °polish, °elegance, °sophistication, urbanity, urbaneness, °breeding, cultivation, gentility, °propriety, courtliness, °civility, politeness, politesse, °delicacy, °tact, °diplomacy, °finesse, suavity, suaveness, °taste, tastefulness, °discrimination, discernment, °sensitivity: He drank thirstily, with no pretence at refinement. **2** °subtlety, nicety, nuance, °distinction, °detail, °fine °point, °delicacy, minutia, fastidiousness, finickiness: The latest version contains refinements that are beyond the appreciation of all but a few. **3** °refining, purification, purifying, clarification, clarifying, cleaning, cleansing; filtration, distillation: The sugar must undergo refinement before being sold commercially. **4** °improvement, betterment, bettering, enhancement, °development, °perfection: She is working on the refinement of her technique before performing in public.

reflect v. **1** °mirror, send or throw back, °reproduce, °return; °echo: The smooth surface of the lake reflected the sunlight. The radio waves are reflected and focused by this parabolic dish. **2** °show, °demonstrate, °exhibit, °illustrate, °exemplify, °reveal, °lay °bare, expose, °display, °disclose, bring to °light, uncover, °point to, °indicate, °suggest, °evidence: They say that your true emotions are reflected in your dreams. His crime reflects the depths of depravity to which a person can sink. **3** Often, **reflect about** or **on**: °think (about or over or on), °contemplate, °muse (about or on), °consider, °ponder (about or over or on), °deliberate (on or over), ruminate or °meditate (about or on or over), cogitate (about or on or over); °mull over, °weigh, °evaluate, °examine: I was just sitting here reflecting. I was reflecting on what you said about wanting to quit your job. **4 reflect on** or **upon**: °result in, °end in, °bring, °attract, °cast, °throw: The success of the team reflects credit on the coach.

reflection n. **1** °image, °echo, Brit reflexion: Sonar works by detecting the reflection of generated sound waves. **2** °thought, °thinking, meditation, meditating, °consideration, cogitation, rumination, deliberation, deliberating, pondering, °study, cerebration: After a moment's reflection, I arrived at the same conclusion as you had. **3** °aspersion, °imputation; °effect: Any reflection on his reputation might harm his career. **4** °result, °sign, °token, °symbol, °mark; °evidence, °testimony, testament, °proof, substantiation, corroboration: Her tears are a reflection of how she feels about having betrayed me.

reflective adj. reflecting, °thoughtful, °pensive, contemplative, meditating, musing, °meditative, cogitating, cogitative, ruminating, deliberative, deliberating, pondering: I found Alan in a reflective mood, staring out of the window.

reform v. **1** °improve, °better, ameliorate, meliorate, emend, °rectify, °correct, °mend, °repair, °fix, °remedy, redo, °revise, revolutionize, °rehabilitate, remodel, refashion, °renovate, reorganize, rebuild, °recover: The first thing to be done was to reform the political system. **2** °mend one's ways, turn over a new leaf, *Colloq* go °straight: *After three convictions in as many years, there seemed little chance that he would reform.* —*n.* **3** °improvement, betterment, amelioration, melioration, emendation, rectification, °correction, rehabilitation, °change, modification, perestroika, reorganization, renovation, °recovery: *Many believe that prison reform would reduce crime by second offenders. The many reforms introduced by the president were condemned by hard-line party members.*

reform school *n. Brit* youth custody centre, CHE (= 'community home (with education on the premises)'), *Formerly* Borstal, approved school, *US* reformatory: *He was sent to a reform school because of his persistent misbehaviour.*

refrain[1] *v.* **1** Usually, **refrain from**: °keep (from), forbear, abstain (from), eschew, °avoid: *Whatever you do, refrain from whistling on board his boat.* **2** °stop, °cease, °give up, °discontinue, desist, °quit, °leave off, °renounce: *You must refrain from calling the headmaster 'Pops', even if he is your father.*

refrain[2] *n.* °melody, °song, °tune, chorus, °burden, reprise: *It was one of those long boring folk songs with a refrain that we all supposed to join in.*

refresh *v.* **1** °enliven, °renew, °revive, °freshen (up), resuscitate, bring back to °life, breathe °new °life into, invigorate, °vitalize, °energize, °brace, °fortify, exhilarate, revitalize, reinvigorate, reanimate: *I felt fully refreshed after a short nap.* **2** °arouse, °rouse, °awaken, waken, reawaken, °stimulate, °jog, °prod, °activate: *Would you mind refreshing my memory as to when and where we last met?* **3** °fix up, °repair, redo, °revamp, °overhaul, °spruce up, recondition, °renovate, °refurbish, refurnish; °renew, restock, °restore: *We took the opportunity of the ship's arrival to refresh our supplies.*

refreshing *adj.* °invigorating, °stimulating, °bracing, °exhilarating, °fresh, inspiriting, fortifying, °tonic, like a breath of °fresh air, rejuvenating, enlivening, vitalizing, revitalizing; cooling, thirst-quenching, slaking: *It's refreshing to be around young people. I would love a cool refreshing glass of beer right now.*

refreshment *n.* **1** Usually, **refreshments**: °nourishment, nutriment, °sustenance, restorative, °food, °drink(s), edibles, eatables, °bite, °snack(s), °titbit(s), *Slang* grub, eats, chow, nosh: *Will they be serving refreshments after the meeting?* **2** stimulation, invigoration, exhilaration, °tonic, rejuvenation, enlivenment, °revival, °restoration, renewal, resuscitation, fortification, °reinforcement: *The library provides an oasis of mental refreshment.*

refrigerate *v.* °cool, °chill, keep °cool or °cold or chilled, ice, °freeze: *The soufflé must be refrigerated for three hours to allow it to set.*

refuge *n.* **1** °sanctuary, °shelter, haven, asylum, °protection, °cover, °retreat, °harbour, °security, °safe °house, °stronghold, citadel, bolt-hole, °hideaway, hide-out, *Colloq* hidy-hole or hidey-hole: *The abandoned mine served as a refuge from the storm.* **2** °excuse, °pretext, °resort, °recourse, °ruse, °trick, °stratagem, °subterfuge, °dodge, °evasion, °expedient: *Patriotism is often the last refuge of a scoundrel.*

refugee *n.* °fugitive, °runaway, escapee, displaced °person, DP, °exile, émigré: *The problem of the refugees was most acute after the war.*

refurbish *v.* °restore, refurnish, redecorate, °clean (up), °polish, °renew, °renovate, °spruce up, remodel, refit, °overhaul, °repair, recondition, °revamp, rebuild, *Colloq* do up, *US* °fix up: *The person who bought the house refurbished it completely, at enormous expense.*

refusal *n.* **1** °denial, °rejection, °disapproval, turn-down: *She pleaded against the grand vizier's refusal to grant amnesty to her brother.* **2** °option, °choice, °privilege, disposal: *We were promised first refusal on the house should it come on the market.*

refuse[1] *v.* **1** °decline, °reject, °spurn, °repudiate, °turn down, °rebuff, give (something) the °thumbs down, *US* °turn °thumbs down on, *Colloq* °pass by or up: *They refused our application to build a hotel here. Did he actually refuse a knighthood?* **2** °deny, °deprive (of), °withhold, disallow, not °allow or °permit: *They refused me my right to vote.*

refuse[2] *n.* rubbish, sweepings, °waste, °litter, dust, °dirt, °dregs, dross, °garbage, debris, detritus, cast-offs, °junk, *Chiefly US* °trash: *Refuse collection is scheduled for once a week.*

regal *adj.* **1** °royal, kingly, queenly, °princely, °fit for or °befitting a °king or °queen, °noble, lordly, °sovereign, °majestic, °imperial, °stately, °splendid, °magnificent, °grand, resplendent, °palatial, °exalted: *The regal throne was decorated with gold and precious stones.* **2** °disdainful, °haughty, °proud, °scornful, contumelious, °contemptuous, °derisory, derisive, °pompous, lordly: *She was dismissed with a regal wave of the hand.*

regale *v.* °entertain, °amuse, °delight, °divert, °indulge, °please, °gratify, °captivate, °fascinate, °entrance, °enchant, spellbind, °bewitch, °charm, °enrapture: *She regaled them with entertaining tales of her travels.*

regalia *n.* °finery, °decorations, insignia, °emblems, accoutrements or *US also* accouterments, furnishings, °apparatus, °gear, °paraphernalia, °trappings, °tackle, appurtenances, °equipment, equipage: *The Bishop was dressed in full regalia with mitre and crook.*

regard *v.* **1** °view, °look at or upon or on, °observe, °note, °notice, °watch, °eye, keep an °eye on, °gaze at or upon, °stare at: *The children regarded the magician's performance with great interest.* **2** °contemplate, °consider, °perceive, °view, °look upon or on, °treat: *The lion looked at me as if he regarded me as his dinner. Smith appears to regard his appointment as treasurer as a licence to steal.* **3** °respect, °esteem, value: *Gwen's friends regard her very highly indeed.* **4** °consider, °view, °look upon or on, °think (of), °judge, deem, °rate, °believe (to be), °gauge, °see, pay °heed or °attention to, °esteem, °account, take into °account, °imagine, °reckon, °evaluate: *I don't regard her as a likely suspect. He regards his professor as his mentor.* **5** °concern, °relate to, be °relevant to, °pertain to, °apply to, °refer to, °affect, have (a) °bearing on, °bear on or upon, °involve, °have to do with, °go for: *Our discussion regarded the disappearance of £10 from petty cash.* —*n.* **6** °reference, °relation, °relevance, relevancy, °association, pertinence, °application, °bearing, °connection, °link, °tie-in: *We would like to talk to you with regard to your application* for the post of assistant editor. **7** °respect, °consideration, °attention, °reverence, °veneration, awe, °deference, °honour, °favour, °esteem, high °opinion, °approval, approbation, °appreciation, °admiration, °affection, fondness: *They have no regard for the law.* **8** °point, °particular, °respect, °aspect, °detail, °matter: *In this regard, I must take your past record into consideration.* **9** °care, °concern, °thought, °consideration, °respect, °sympathy, °feeling, °sentiment; °heed, °attention, °notice, °mind: *The police behave as if they have no regard for the safety of the hostages. This work reflects the artisan's regard for detail.* **10 regards**: °best wishes, °good wishes, °compliments, °greetings, °respects, salutations, *Archaic* devoirs: *Please give my regards to your father.*

regarding *adj.* °concerning, °about, respecting, with °regard to, with °respect to, in *or* with °reference to, in the °matter of, pertaining to, on the °subject of, apropos, re, *Law* in re, *Archaic or Scots* anent, *Dialect* anent: *We have received your letter regarding poor service. Regarding your claim, the processing of it has been delayed because you failed to sign the form.*

regardless *adj.* **1** Sometimes, **regardless of**: °despite, °notwithstanding; in °spite of, °heedless of, *Non-Standard* irregardless: *Regardless of her father's protestations, she continued to go out with William.* —*adv.* **2** °notwithstanding, °nevertheless, no matter what, in °event, in any °case, at all events, anyway, anyhow, *Non-Standard* irregardless: *She heard his threats but is going out with William regardless.*

regime *n.* régime, regimen, °reign, °government, °rule, °regulation, °administration, °direction, °order, °leadership, °management, °system, °discipline: *Persistent offenders were given harsh penalties under the new regime.*

regiment *v.* °discipline, °order, °organize, systematize, whip into °shape, °standardize, °regulate, °control: *I dislike the way management regiments people in this establishment, as if they were schoolchildren.*

region *n.* **1** °district, °area, °zone, °territory, °division, locality, sector, °section, °tract, °part, °dominion, °precinct, °province, °quarter, °department: *Each region is under the suzerainty of a powerful dictator.* **2** °sphere, °territory, °domain, °province, °field, ambit, °pale, °jurisdiction, bailiwick: *She is an expert in the region of climatology.*

register *n.* **1** °record, °roll, roster, rota, catalogue, annal(s), archive(s), °journal, daybook, °diary, appointment °book, °calendar, °chronicle, °schedule, °programme, directory, ledger, °file, °index, inventory, °list, listing, °poll, °tally: *The council holds a register of all houses sold since 1900 with the names of both sellers and buyers.* **2** cash register, cash-drawer, °till, °money °box, cash-box: *The money in the register does not agree with the figures for receipts.* —*v.* **1** °record, °write *or* °jot *or* °take *or* °put *or* °set down, °list, °enrol, °sign in *or* on *or* up, °enter, catalogue, log, °index, °chronicle, °note, make *or* take °note (of): *All transactions must be registered.* **4** °show, °display, °express, °indicate, °manifest, °reveal, °betray, divulge, °record, °reflect: *James pretended to like my book, but his*

contempt for it was registered on his face. **5** °make known, °inform of, °advise, °transmit, °communicate, °record, °note, make °note of, °report, °write down, °minute: *I wish to register my disapproval of the way prisoners are treated here.* **6** °check in, °sign in *or* on, log in: *In the US, all aliens are required to register each year in January. We registered in the hotel as man and wife.* **7** Sometimes, **register with** *or* **on**: °sink in, °impress, become °apparent (to), make an °impression (on), come °home (to), °get through (to); °dawn on *or* upon, °occur to: *I heard what you said, but it just didn't register. The name didn't register with me at first, but I now know who you are.* **8** °indicate, °read, °mark, °represent, °measure, °point to, °specify, °exhibit, °show, °manifest: *The earthquake registered 7 on the Richter scale.*

regret *v.* **1** rue, °mourn, °lament, °bemoan, °bewail, °repent, be *or* feel °sorry for, feel °remorse for, feel *or* be °remorseful over, be *or* feel °upset, never forgive oneself, deplore, deprecate, °weep *or* °cry over: *You will regret speaking to me that way! The management regrets any inconvenience caused by the redecoration of the restaurant.* —*n.* **2** Sometimes, **regrets**: repentance, °guilt, °sorrow, °disappointment, contrition, °remorse, regretfulness, (°pang *or* pangs of) °conscience, self-reproach, self-condemnation, °qualm, second thoughts, rue, ruefulness, °grief, °woe, °sadness, mournfulness, *Literary* dolour: *He felt no regret for his evil deeds. Do you ever have any regrets over the way you treated him?* **3 regrets**: °refusal, non-acceptance, non-consent, *US* turn-down: *Thank you for the invitation, but I must tender my regrets.*

regretful *adj.* rueful, °mournful, °sad, °repentant, °guilty, °sorry, °sorrowful, °disappointed, contrite, °remorseful, °apologetic, °penitent: *He was most regretful for the way he had behaved.*

regrettable *adj.* °lamentable, °deplorable, woeful, °sad, distressing, upsetting, °unhappy, °unfortunate, unlucky, too °bad, °awful, °terrible, execrable, reprehensible, °wrong, °shameful, shaming, *Colloq* °tough, °rough: *It is regrettable that he had the car crash, but he had been warned about drinking and driving.*

regular *adj.* **1** °routine, °ordinary, °common, °everyday, °customary, °accustomed, wonted, commonplace, °normal, °usual, °traditional, °time-honoured, °conventional, °typical, °habitual, °natural, °familiar, °standard, °predictable, scheduled, °fixed, unvarying, °invariable, °methodical: *The attack occurred while Eric was taking his regular evening stroll.* **2** scheduled, °routine, °systematic, ordered, °steady, °consistent, °rhythmic(al), °automatic, °uniform, °periodic, cyclic(al); hourly, °daily, weekly, hebdomadal, semi-weekly, biweekly, fortnightly, semi-monthly, monthly, bimonthly, seasonal, °quarterly, semi-annual, annual: *The patrol made their regular rounds, as usual. The printers' strike might delay regular publication of the magazine.* **3** °symmetrical, °uniform, °even, even-sided, equal-sided, equilateral, equal-angled, equiangular; °harmonious: *Any six-sided plane figure is a hexagon, but if it has six equal angles and six sides equal in length, it is a regular hexagon.* **4** undistorted, °even, well-proportioned, °proportional, °symmetrical,

°classic: *He was classically good-looking, with regular features.* **5** °even, °smooth, °level, °straight, °uniform, uninterrupted, unvarying, °continuous, °flat, °plane, °plumb: *The surface of the wing is regular except for the spoilers.*
6 dependable, °methodical, (well-)regulated, (well-)ordered, °orderly; °proper, °correct, °legal, °official, bona fide, °legitimate, established, recognized, °orthodox, approved, *Colloq* kosher, °OK *or* okay: *Everything about the council election was entirely regular.* **7** °usual, expected, °normal, °habitual, °accustomed, °familiar: *Our regular doctor was on holiday, and we had to see a locum.* **8** °acceptable, accepted, °estimable, °fine, °good, °likeable, °popular, °pleasant: *We all consider Bob to be a regular fellow and a friend.* **9** °complete, utter, thoroughgoing, °unmitigated, unalloyed, °unqualified, consummate, °perfect, °thorough, °absolute, °well-known, acknowledged: *The man is a regular dunce when it comes to repairing cars.*
10 °permanent, °career: *She's in the regular navy.* **11** °conventional, °usual, °common, conformable, °ordinary, °systematic, *Colloq US* ruly: *Regular English verbs form their past by the addition of -d or -ed to the infinitive.*
—*n.* **12** °fixture, °habitué, (°steady) °customer, °patron, °client, frequenter: *Jan has been a regular at the Star and Garter pub for years.*

regularity *n.* **1** consistency, constancy, °uniformity, evenness, sameness, °symmetry, °balance, °harmony, harmoniousness, orderliness, °order, °stability, predictability: *To the casual observer, nothing interferes with the regularity of planetary movement.* **2** °routine, reliability, dependability, steadiness, invariability: °pace, °rhythm, °cadence: *Mr Warbridge listens to the six o'clock evening news with unfailing regularity. Our business depends on the regularity of the postal service. The regularity of the ticking of the clock is driving me mad.*

regulate *v.* **1** °adjust, °modify, °modulate, °control, °balance, °set, °fix, °order, °govern, °organize, °maintain, °manage: *The mixture of air and fuel in modern cars is regulated by an injection system. The responsibility of this department is to regulate prices.* **2** °control, °monitor, °govern, °run, °operate, °administer, °handle, °guide, °steer, °conduct, °direct, °supervise, superintend, °oversee, °manage: *The foreman's job is to regulate the work on the assembly line.*

regulation *n.* **1** °adjustment, modification, modulation, °control, °balance, balancing, °setting, fixing, °organization, °maintenance: *The regulation of the temperature is accomplished by the thermostat.* **2** °rule, ruling, °law, °code, by-law *or* bye-law, edict, °order, ordinance, statute, °decree, directive, °dictate: *There are strict regulations governing the sale, disposal, and movement of radioactive materials.* **3** edict, ukase, °pronouncement, fiat, (papal) bull, °proclamation: *A regulation was issued against meetings of more than five people.*
—*adj.* **4** °standard, accepted, °official, required, prescribed, °mandatory: *The soldier was not wearing a regulation uniform.* **5** °usual, °normal, °ordinary, °customary, °typical: *If you use anything but regulation accessories, the guarantee will be null and void.*

regurgitate *v.* °vomit, disgorge, return one's dinner, °spew up, (*of birds of prey*) cast; retch,

°gag; *Colloq* °throw up, upchuck, *Slang* puke, *US* spiff one's biscuits, barf: *The child regurgitated its dinner all over the inside of the car.*

rehabilitate *v.* **1** °restore, °save, °reclaim, °rescue, °redeem, re-establish, reinstate, re-educate, reorient, °reform, *US* °straighten out, *Colloq US* rehab: *They have had marked success at rehabilitating criminals.* **2** °renew, redecorate, °renovate, °refurbish, °restore, °fix (up), °repair, reconstruct, rebuild, °change, °transform: *Sam has plans to rehabilitate vintage cars for a living.*

rehash *v.* **1** rework, °go over again, restate, redo, rearrange, reshuffle, reuse: *Heverton has nothing new to offer—he just keeps on rehashing the same old material.*
—*n.* **2** reworking, restatement, redoing, rearrangement, reshuffle, reshuffling, reuse, rewording: *Her speech was a mere rehash of what she's said scores of times already.*

rehearsal *n.* **1** °practice, °exercise, dry run, °drill, °run-through, read-through, dress rehearsal, *Technical* undress rehearsal: *Is there a rehearsal of the school play scheduled for tonight?* **2** °narration, recounting, °relation, °recital, °telling, °description, enumeration, °account, °repetition, °repeat: *Do we have to listen to yet another rehearsal of your great-uncle's exploits in the war?*

rehearse *v.* **1** °practise, °exercise, °run through, °read through, °study, °repeat: *Sorry, Annie, but we are going to have to rehearse the scene till you get it right.* **2** °repeat, °relate, °recite, °tell, °describe, °recount, °review, °go through *or* over, °report, °recapitulate, *Colloq* recap: *I shall go mad if I hear him again rehearse the events leading up to the final acceptance of his novel.*

reign *n.* **1** °rule, °sovereignty, ascendancy, °power, hegemony, °influence, °command, suzerainty, °administration, °jurisdiction, °leadership, °government, °direction, °control, °domination, mastery; °kingdom, °monarchy, empire: *During her reign, the kingdom saw its greatest prosperity.*
—*v.* **2** °rule, °control, °command, °govern, °lead, °direct, °dominate, °supervise, °manage, hold °sway, wear the °crown, °wield the sceptre, occupy the throne, *Colloq* °run the show, °rule the roost, *Slang* call the shots: *During the sixth Egyptian dynasty, Pepi II Nefektare reigned for 94 years, the longest in recorded history.* **3** °prevail, be *or* become °prevalent, °predominate, hold °sway, °obtain, be *or* become °rampant, be *or* become °universal: *An argument broke out, which developed into a fist fight, and soon pandemonium reigned.*

reimburse *v.* °repay, recompense, refund, °pay back, °compensate, remunerate, indemnify: *Don't worry—we'll reimburse you for any money you spent.*

rein *n.* **1** °check, °curb, °control, °restraint, constraint, limitation, harness, °bridle, °brake: *You are going to have to put a rein on your expenses.* **2 reins:** °control, °command, °administration, °running, °leadership, °power, °rule, tiller, °helm: *He should hand over the reins to a younger person.*
—*v.* **3 rein in:** °check, °curb, °control, °restrain, °limit, harness, °bridle, °restrict, pull back on: *You will have to rein in your passions: it is not becoming to behave in this way at your age.*

reinforce v. °strengthen, °buttress, °bolster, °support, °fortify, °prop (up), shore up, augment, °brace, °stay, °steel: *The bookshelf needs to be reinforced with another bracket, or it'll fall down.*

reinforcement n. **1** °buttress, °support, °prop, °brace, °stay, °bolster: *This iron reinforcement ought to be strong enough to support the wall.* **2** strengthening, buttressing, bolstering, shoring (up), augmentation, °bracing: *This shelf is wobbly and in need of reinforcement.* **3 reinforcements**: °reserves, auxiliaries, men, soldiers, °forces, personnel: *We cannot hold out till reinforcements arrive.*

reiterate v. °repeat, restate, iterate, °labour, harp on, °dwell on, °rehash, °recapitulate, *Colloq* recap: *I must reiterate my warning to you to be careful.*

reject v. **1** °decline, °refuse, disallow, °spurn, °veto, °turn down, give (something) the °thumbs down, °set aside, *US* turn °thumbs down (on); °deny, °repudiate, °renounce, °rebuff, °shun, °brush aside, turn a °deaf ear to, will not °hear of: *Jim has rejected my plan for a holiday in Torremolinos. She rejects any suggestion that she might be wrong.* **2** °refuse, °repel, °repulse, °spurn, °rebuff, say no to, °turn down, °decline, °brush aside; °jilt, °drop, °dismiss, °throw over, give (someone) the cold °shoulder, show (someone) the door, send (someone) away or on his or her or their way, turn one's back on, *Slang* give (someone) the °brush-off or *US also* the °brush, give (someone) his or her walking papers, *Brit* give (someone) the boot: *Ted proposed, but Alice rejected him.* **3** °throw away or out, °discard, disown, jettison, °eliminate, °scrap, *Colloq* °junk, °scratch: *The inspector rejects all defective merchandise.*
—n. **4** °second, °irregular, °discard, cast-off: *The rejects are sold at reduced prices in the factory shop.*

rejection n. °refusal, °denial, repudiation, °rebuff, °dismissal, spurning, renunciation, turn-down; cold °shoulder, *Slang* °brush-off or *US also* °brush, the (old) heave-ho: *The union voted for the rejection of management's offer of a 9.2 per cent increase. Her advances were met with rejection.*

rejoice v. °delight, °exult, °glory, °celebrate, °revel, be °happy or °delighted or °pleased or °overjoyed or °elated or °glad, *Colloq* be tickled (pink): *We all rejoiced to be home once again after the ordeal.*

rejuvenate v. °restore, °refresh, reinvigorate, revitalize, revivify, °renew, reanimate, regenerate, recharge, breathe new °life into: *I think a week in Barbados would rejuvenate me.*

relapse v. **1** get back, backslide, °fall back, °lapse, °slip back, regress, retrogress, recidivate; °go back, °return, °retreat, °revert: *Lottie has relapsed into her bad habits.* **2** °decline, °deteriorate, °weaken, °degenerate, °fail, fade, °sink, °sicken, °worsen, get or become worse: *Just when we thought he was improving, he relapsed into a coma and died.*
—n. **3** backsliding, falling or going back, °lapse, lapsing, °return, returning, reversion, reverting, regression, regressing, retrogression, retrogressing, recidivism, apostasy: *The church's main concern was a relapse into idolatry.* **4** °decline, deterioration, weakening, degeneration,

°failing, °failure, fading, °sinking, worsening: *Barry was getting better but has now suffered a relapse.*

relate v. **1** °associate, °connect, °couple, °link, °tie, °ally, correlate, °coordinate: *Volta first enabled us to relate the forces of chemistry and electricity.* **2** °recount, °narrate, °tell, °report, °present, °describe, °recite, °detail, °set forth, °communicate, divulge, °impart, °reveal, delineate, make known, give an °account of, °rehearse: *It was not till years later that Olivia related to me the strange events of that night.* **3** °apply to, °coordinate with, °respect, °regard, °bear upon or on, have a °bearing on, have °reference to, have to do with, °pertain to, °refer to, appertain to, °belong with or to: *Does your comment really relate to the matter in hand?* **4** Often, **relate to**: be in or en °rapport with, °understand, empathize, °sympathize, °communicate with, °identify with, °grasp, °comprehend, be in °tune with, °deal with, °handle, °cope with, *Colloq* °dig, °tune in to, be °hip to, be turned on to, be or get into: *I have been having trouble relating to my new psychiatrist. Your favourite music is reggae? —Man, I can relate to that.*

related adj. **1** °associate(d), affiliate(d), connected, coupled, linked, tied up, allied, correlated, °coordinate(d), interconnected, interrelated, interdependent, °mutual, °reciprocal, °common, °joint, cognate: *She and her husband work for related companies.* **2** °kin, °kindred, consanguineous, cognate, agnate; °akin: *Just how are you two related? Are you cousins?*

relation n. **1** °relationship, °connection, affiliation, °association, °bearing, °link, °tie, °tie-in, °reference, pertinence, interconnection, interdependence, correspondence, °kinship: *The relation between time and money is rarely disputed these days.* **2** °kinship, °relationship: *Just what is your relation to this lady?* **3** °relative, kinsman or kinswoman, blood °relative, in-law, °family member: *Is she a relation of yours?* **4** °narration, °narrative, °telling, recounting, °description, °report, °recital, °recitation, delineation, portrayal, °story, recapitulation: *She amused them all with her relation of what had happened to her that night.* **5 in relation to**: °concerning, °about, °regarding, respecting, pertaining to, with °regard to, with °respect to, referring to, in or with °reference to, in the °matter or °subject of, apropos, re, *Archaic or Scots* anent, *Dialect* anenst: *I should like to talk to you in relation to the matter of company expenses.* **6 relations: a** sexual °intercourse, coitus, °sex, criminal conversation; carnal °knowledge: *It is well known that he had relations with his secretary.* **b** °dealings, °intercourse, °link(s), °association(s), °liaison, °relationship, *Colloq* doings, °truck: *We have no relations with that company.*

relationship n. See relation, 1, 2, above.

relative adj. **1** °related, connected, associated, allied, °affiliated, interconnected, interrelated, °pertinent, °relevant, germane, °applicable; apropos: *Your comments are not relative to the matter at hand.* **2** Sometimes, **relative to**: comparative, comparable, proportionate, °proportional, commensurate; analogous to, contingent on, dependent on, reliant on, conditioned by, °subject to, °attendant on, °correspondent or corresponding to, °provisional on, appurtenant to; °subordinate to, ancillary to: *Well, as they say, everything is relative. Relative humidity depends on the temperature of the air. The yield is relative to the effort.* —*n.* **3** See **relation**, **3**, above.

relatively *adv.* more or less, °somewhat, comparatively, °rather, to some °degree *or* °extent: *Business has been relatively quiet lately.*

relax *v.* **1** °loosen, let go, °release, °let up (on), °relieve, °ease, °reduce, °moderate, slacken, °remit, *Colloq* °ease up on, slacken up on: *He relaxed his grip on the rope and fell to his death on the rocks below.* **2** °diminish, °decrease, lessen, °reduce, abate, °weaken, °mitigate, °modify, °tone down, °moderate, °modulate, °lighten (up on), °check, °temper, °curb: *We must not relax our vigilance. I hope that they don't relax the regulations concerning smoking in the office.* **3** °ease up, °slow down, °loosen up, put one's feet up, °rest, unbend, *Colloq* take it °easy, unwind: *Why not come for a weekend and relax a bit?* **4** °calm down, °cool down, °quiet(en) down, stay °calm, °cool and °collected, *Colloq* take it °easy, *Slang* °cool it: *You ought to relax and not get so excited.*

relaxation *n.* **1** °ease, °repose, °rest, °leisure, °recreation, °amusement, °entertainment, °fun, °pleasure, °diversion, *Colloq* R and R ('rest and relaxation'): *For relaxation we usually charter a boat and go sailing.* **2** easing (up *or* off), relief, alleviation, abatement, diminution, lessening, mitigation, moderation, slackening, °remission, weakening, letting up, *Colloq* °let-up: *What do you think about the proposed relaxation of the laws against pornography?*

relaxed *adj.* °nonchalant, °easygoing, °calm, °peaceful, °tranquil, °serene, pacific, °carefree, insouciant, °blasé, languorous, languid, devil-may-care, °free and °easy, happy-go-lucky, °mellow, at °ease, composed, °cool: *Richard takes a relaxed view of life.*

release *v.* **1** °let °go, (set) °free, °liberate, (set *or* °let *or* turn) °loose, unloose, untie, unchain, unfetter, unshackle, °deliver, °let out, disenthral, °discharge, °let off, °emancipate, manumit, °rescue, °save: *They kept up a strenuous campaign until all the political prisoners were released.* **2** °issue, °publish, make °available, °put out, °pass out, °hand out, °come out with, °circulate, °distribute, disseminate; °launch, °unveil, °present: *The government refuses to release information that is considered harmful to its interests. The band's new album will be released tomorrow.* —*n.* **3** freeing, releasing, liberating, loosing, unloosing, delivering, emancipating, manumitting, rescuing, °saving, °freedom, °liberation, deliverance, °discharge, emancipation, manumission, °rescue, °remission, salvation: *The release of the prisoner is scheduled for noon. It would be a great release to be rid of housework.* **4** °press *or* publicity release, °announcement, publicity, °notice, °story, °report: *The press office sent out a release to the media about Randolph's appointment.*

relegate *v.* **1** consign, °banish, °exile, °transfer, °dispatch *or* despatch: *Owing to his disagreement with the Foreign Office, Kendall was relegated to some outpost in the Indian Ocean.* **2** °downgrade, demote: *I fear that Corporal Jones has been relegated to private.* **3** °assign, °commit, °hand over, °refer, °transfer, °pass on: *She relegates most of her everyday correspondence to her secretary for reply.*

relent *v.* °relax, °soften, °yield, °give, °give °way *or* ground, °bend, °comply, acquiesce, compromise, °capitulate, come round, be °merciful, show °pity *or* compassion, °melt, show °mercy, °succumb: *They finally relented and allowed me to have visitors.*

relentless *adj.* **1** unyielding, inexorable, unstoppable, unrelenting, dogged, °implacable, °inflexible, unbending, unmoving, °unmoved, unrelieved, °stiff, °hard, stiff-necked, °rigid, °obstinate, adamant, obdurate, intransigent, °determined, unswerving, undeviating, intractable, persevering, °steely, °tough, unsparing, uncompromising, pitiless, unforgiving, °ruthless, °merciless, °cruel, °unmerciful, °remorseless: *The novel is about the relentless horde of Mongols that swept across Europe in the 13th century.* **2** °non-stop, °persistent, incessant, unrelenting, unremitting, unstoppable, °perpetual, unfaltering, unfailing, unflagging, unrelieved, unabated, unbroken, °continual, °continuous, ceaseless, °constant, unceasing, °steady, °habitual, °regular: *Won't you ever stop your relentless nagging?*

relevance *n.* relevancy, appropriateness, aptness, pertinence, °bearing, °connection, °affinity, °tie-in, °relation, °significance, suitability, suitableness, applicability, °application, applicableness: *What you just said has no relevance whatsoever to the issue under discussion.*

relevant *adj.* °pertinent, °appropriate, apt, °related, °relative, °significant, suited, °applicable, °fitting, °proper, germane, °akin, allied, associated, apposite, to the °point: *Alan's suggestion is not strictly relevant to our plans.*

reliable *adj.* dependable, °trustworthy, °honest, trusty, trusted, °principled, °conscientious, punctilious, °honourable, credible, believable, °safe, °sure, °certain, °secure, °sound, °responsible, °predictable, °stable, unfailing, °infallible, °reputable: *Would a reliable employee like Susan abscond with the money?*

reliance *n.* °confidence, °trust, °faith, dependence: *You may be placing too much reliance on the smoke alarm.*

relic *n.* **1** °memento, °keepsake, °memorial, °remembrance, souvenir, heirloom, °token, artefact *or* artifact: *It has been argued again and again that the Turin shroud, though old, is not a genuine relic of Christ.* **2** °remains; °fragment, °trace, °scrap, shard *or* sherd, °remnant: *Deep in the jungle, archaeologists unearthed relics of a previously unknown civilization.*

relief *n.* **1** °ease, easing, abatement, easement, deliverance, °remedy, redress, alleviation, °release, °remission, assuagement, °liberation, °recess: *We would all welcome relief from this blistering heat. Contributions for the relief of famine in Africa would be most welcome.* **2** °aid, °help, °support, °assistance, succour; °comfort: *How many troops can we send for the relief of the besieged garrison?* **3** °elevation, °projection, °contrast, °prominence; bas-relief *or* basso-rilievo ('low relief'), mezzo-rilievo ('medium relief'), alto-rilievo ('high relief'): *The Greek reliefs brought to England by Lord Elgin are on display at the British Museum.* **4** °substitute, surrogate, replacement, °alternate, locum (tenens), °stand-in; °understudy, °double: *I wish that my relief would arrive so I could go home.*

relieve v. **1** °ease, lessen, °reduce, °diminish, abate, °lift, °raise, alleviate, °mitigate, palliate, °soften, soothe: *Business will suffer if nothing is done to relieve the burden of high interest rates. The doctor gave me something to relieve the pain.* **2** disburden, °free, °rid, °liberate, disencumber, unburden, °rescue, °save, °release: *Winning the lottery relieved me of any immediate worries of poverty.* **3** °help, °aid, °assist, °support, succour, °rescue, °save, °deliver: *Will the cavalry arrive in time to relieve the fort, which is under attack?* **4** °stand in (for), °replace, °substitute for, take over for or from, *US* °spell, *Colloq* sub for: *I thought you were coming to relieve me at noon.*

religion n. °creed, °belief, °faith; °doctrine, dogma: *People must be treated equally, regardless of their religion.*

religious adj. **1** °devout, churchgoing, °pious, God-fearing, °holy, spiritual-minded: *You never struck me as a particularly religious person.* **2** °scrupulous, °exact, °precise, °conscientious, rigorous, °strict, °fastidious, °meticulous, °faithful, punctilious, unerring, unswerving, undeviating: *Edmund's work is characterized by religious devotion to detail.*

relinquish v. **1** °yield, °give up, °cede, °waive, °leave, °quit, °abandon, °drop, °forsake, forswear, °desert, °abdicate, °resign, °renounce, let go, °surrender, °vacate, °retire from: *Richard was forced to relinquish the throne.* **2** let go, °give up, °release, unloose, °loose, °free: *He refused to relinquish his grasp on her arm.*

relish n. **1** °enjoyment, °pleasure, °delight, °gusto, °eagerness, avidity, °anticipation, °taste, °appetite, °zest, °liking, °appreciation, fondness, °fancy, °partiality, °preference: *The children attacked the birthday cake with great relish.* —v. **2** °enjoy, °delight in, take °pleasure in, °fancy, be °partial to, °appreciate, °savour, °look forward to, °anticipate: *After all that dining out, I'd really relish a home-cooked meal. I don't relish having to tell her she is being made redundant.*

reluctance n. unwillingness, disinclination, °aversion, °dislike, disrelish, hesitancy: *Cooper's reluctance to leave before the end of the play was understandable.*

reluctant adj. unwilling, °disinclined, °averse, °hesitant, °loath, °unenthusiastic, °indisposed, °opposed, antagonistic; °cautious, chary, °wary, °leery, circumspect, °careful: *I remember how reluctant you were to try raw oysters, and then you couldn't get enough of them.*

rely v. **rely on** or **upon**: °depend on or upon, °lean on or upon, °count on or upon, bank on or upon, have °confidence in, °bet on, °trust in, °swear by, be °sure or °certain of: *You can rely on Philippa to come through when you need a friend. I am relying on the fact that interest rates are likely to stay at their present levels.*

remain v. **1** °stay (behind), be °left, °tarry, °linger, °wait, *Colloq* °stay put: *I remained to help with the washing-up.* **2** be °left, be there: *How many days remain before your trip?* **3** °stay, °continue, °carry on, °abide; °endure, °persist, °last, °persevere: *She refuses to remain with him another minute. His last book will remain a monument to his scholarship.* —n. **4 remains: a** leavings, °remnants, °crumbs, debris, detritus, °remainder, °balance, °residue, leftovers, °scraps, °vestiges, °traces, °fragments, oddments, °odds and ends:

The remains of a half-eaten meal were on the table. **b** °body, °cadaver, °corpse; carcass: *The remains of the impala were being picked over by vultures.*

remainder n. **1** °rest, °balance, °remains, °residue: *He spent the remainder of his life in penury.* **2** °excess, overage, °surplus, °residue, residuum, leftovers: *I have used all I needed and don't know what to do with the remainder.*

remaining adj. **1** °left (over), extant, °outstanding: *I did as much as I could in the time remaining.* **2** °leftover, surviving, °residual; °unused, uneaten, unconsumed: *The remaining books will be sold at auction.*

remark v. **1** °note, °notice, °observe, °perceive, °regard, °look at, take °notice or °note of: *His friends remarked his tired and overworked appearance and suggested that he should take a holiday.* **2** °comment (on or upon), °say, °observe, °reflect, °mention, °declare, °state, assert: *Carrie remarked that she had seen Ted the night before.*

remarkable adj. **1** °extraordinary, °unusual, °singular, °exceptional, °noteworthy, °notable, uncommon, °incredible, °unbelievable, °impressive, °phenomenal, astonishing, astounding, surprising: *With remarkable swiftness the falcon dropped on its prey.* **2** °striking, °distinguished, °signal, °special, wonderful, °marvellous, out of the °ordinary, °unique, °significant, °outstanding, °rare, °memorable, unforgettable, never-to-be-forgotten: *This novel is truly a remarkable achievement.* **3** °strange, °different, °odd, °peculiar, °curious: *Contortionists can do truly remarkable things with their bodies.*

remedy n. **1** °cure, °treatment, °therapy, °antidote, counteractant, countermeasure, medication, medicament, °medicine, °prescription, °drug, pharmaceutical, cure-all, panacea, nostrum, restorative, °specific: *What remedy did the doctor recommend?* **2** °cure, °antidote, cure-all, panacea, nostrum, countermeasure, relief, redress, °answer, °solution: *Knowledge is the only remedy for superstition.* —v. **3** °cure, °treat, °heal, °mend, °restore, °relieve, soothe, °control, °ease, °mitigate, alleviate: *The ointment will remedy the itching but not the infection causing it.* **4** °correct, °rectify, °reform, °improve, ameliorate, redress, °repair, put or set °right, °straighten out: *How can I remedy a situation that has already gone too far?*

remember v. **1** call to °mind, bear in °mind; °recall, °recollect: *Can you remember her funny little laugh? Yes, I remember.* **2** °muse (on or about), °reminisce over or about, °think back on or about, °memorialize, °commemorate, °recognize: *He will be remembered for his many achievements.* **3** °retain, keep in °mind, °recall: *He was unable to remember his own name or where he lived.* **4** °tip, °reward: *The Elliotts always remembered the servants at Christmas.*

remembrance n. **1** °memory, °recollection, °reminiscence: *My remembrance of her is quite different from yours.* **2** °memento, °reminder, souvenir, °keepsake, °memorial: *I keep this piece of shrapnel as a remembrance of being wounded in the war.*

remind v. °prompt, °cue, cause to °remember, °jog the °memory, put in °mind of: *Remind me to set the clock back an hour tonight.*

reminder *n.* mnemonic, refresher; °cue, °prompt: *I tied this string round my finger as a reminder, but I don't know of what.*

reminisce *v.* Sometimes, **reminisce about**: °remember, °recollect, °think back, °look back, turn one's °mind *or* thoughts back; call to °mind, hark back, °return: *Most of the time we just sit about and reminisce. The other day we were reminiscing about the time Alex was arrested for shoplifting.*

reminiscence *n.* Usually, **reminiscences**: anecdote(s), °memory *or* memories, °reflection(s), °memoir(s): *The Sunday Clarion has paid a six-figure sum to Charlotte for her reminiscences as a cleaner at Whitehall.*

reminiscent *adj.* Usually, **reminiscent of**: recalling, °redolent of, evocative of, indicative of, °suggestive of, °similar to, comparable with *or* to: *The odour of burning cabbage is reminiscent of my husband's cooking.*

remiss *adj.* °slack, °careless, negligent, neglectful, °heedless, unheeding, °inattentive, unmindful, °thoughtless, °forgetful, °unthinking, °slow, °indolent, °lazy, dilatory, °delinquent: *You were remiss in failing to turn off the bath water.*

remission *n.* **1** °forgiveness, °pardon, deliverance, amnesty, °reprieve, exoneration, °release, absolution, exculpation, °indulgence, °excuse, °exemption, acquittal: *As we were granted remission of our crimes, we were freed.* **2** diminution, abatement, °decrease, lessening, subsidence, alleviation, mitigation, assuagement, ebbing, °relaxation, easing: *Remission of the disease may occur, but most sufferers deteriorate rapidly.*

remit *v.* **1** °send, °transmit, °forward, °dispatch *or* despatch; °pay, °compensate, °settle, liquidate: *We have remitted in full the amount requested.* **2** abate, °diminish, slacken, °decrease, lessen, °subside, alleviate, °mitigate, assuage, °ebb, °dwindle, °reduce, °relax, °ease (up *or* off), °fall off: *The fever ought to remit on the sixth day.*

remittance *n.* °payment, °settlement: allowance, consideration: *Remittance was made regularly on the tenth of the month. He lives on remittances he receives from home.*

remnant *n.* **1** °scrap, °shred, °fragment, °end, °bit, °piece, °trace, °vestige, °relic: *A silver button was the only remnant of the splendid uniform.* **2** °leftover, °remainder, °residue, °rest, remains, °part: *The surviving remnant of the battalion made its way across the desert to Djibouti.*

remorse *n.* °regret, repentance, ruefulness, °sorrow, °woe, °anxiety, °guilty *or* °bad °conscience, °pangs of °conscience, °humiliation, °embarrassment, °guilt, self-reproach, mortification, °shame, contrition, contriteness, °penitence, °compunction, °bitterness: *It is impossible to describe the remorse he felt at having run over the little girl's puppy.*

remorseful *adj.* °regretful, °repentant, rueful, °sorry, °apologetic, °sorrowful, woeful, °anxious, °guilty, °bad, conscience-stricken, guilt-ridden, humiliated, humbled, °embarrassed, mortified, °shamefaced, °shameful, °ashamed, shamed, contrite, °penitent, °bitter: *Harold made a remorseful confession of all his sins.*

remorseless *adj.* **1** °cruel, °heartless, °callous, °harsh, hard-hearted, stony-hearted, °savage, °merciless, °unmerciful, pitiless, °ruthless: *The heavyweight champion administered a remorseless beating to the challenger.* **2** °relentless, unrelenting, unremitting, unstoppable, inexorable, °implacable: *The remorseless storm thrashed at our tiny vessel, tearing away every last shred of rigging.*

remote *adj.* **1** °distant, °far-away, far-off, removed, °outlying, °inaccessible: *The more remote the transmitter, the weaker the signal.* **2** °lonely, °isolated, God-forsaken, °secluded, °out-of-the-way, sequestered, tramontane, ultramontane: *They spent their holiday on a remote island in the Indian Ocean.* **3** °unfamiliar, °obscure, arcane, °recondite, °subtle, °alien, °far-fetched, °unusual, °unlikely: *Her writing is scattered with references remote to the average reader's experience.* **4** °unrelated, °irrelevant, °inappropriate, unconnected, °outside: *Her conclusions were not remote from what we now know to be the truth.* **5** °slight, °faint, foggy: *I haven't the remotest idea what you're talking about.* **6** °slight, °faint, °slender, °insignificant, °slim, °small, °meagre, °outside, °poor, inconsiderable, °negligible, °improbable, °unlikely, °implausible: *There is only a remote chance that the experiment will succeed.* **7** °aloof, °detached, °withdrawn, °reserved, °indifferent, °standoffish, abstracted: *He keeps himself quite remote from the hurly-burly of everyday life.* **8** °early, °ancient, far-removed, °distant: *The archaeopteryx is a remote ancestor of modern birds.*

removal *n.* **1** elimination, removing, eradication, taking away: *The removal of the wallpaper revealed that the plaster underneath was in very poor condition.* **2** extermination, °murder, elimination, °killing, slaying, assassination, °execution, liquidation, eradication, °massacre, °slaughter, °purge, doing away with, *Slang* bumping off, rubbing out, doing in, *US* rub-out, wasting: *The removal of the finance minister was accomplished by the secret police.* **3** °dismissal, °transfer, transference, transferral, shifting, °discharge, throwing over, throwing out, deposition, unseating, dethroning, dethronement, displacement, °expulsion, ouster, ousting, riddance, °purge, *Colloq* firing, sacking: *The company functions better since the removal of the former chairman.* **4** °move, °transfer, departure, °moving: *Her removal to a branch office was requested by top management.* **5** moving, house-moving: *We hired a removal van when we moved to Shropshire.*

remove *v.* **1** °take off, doff, °shed, °cast off: *Gentlemen are requested to remove their hats in her presence.* **2** °take away, get °rid of, °carry away *or* off, °shift; °transfer: *When I arrived this morning, my desk had been removed. The threat of war has been removed. Kindly remove your elbows from the table.* **3** °obliterate, °delete, °erase, expunge, eradicate, efface, °eliminate, °take off, °wipe *or* °rub out, °wipe *or* °rub off, get °rid of: *Use chemicals to remove the graffiti from the wall.* **4** °murder, assassinate, °kill, slay, °execute, °exterminate, °eliminate, liquidate, eradicate, °massacre, °slaughter, do away with, °dispose of, get °rid of, °purge, *Slang* °rub *or* °wipe out, do in, °bump off, *US* °waste: *We brought in some of the boys to remove the competition.* **5** °discharge, °dismiss, depose, unseat, °displace, °expel, oust, °turn out, get °rid of, °purge, *Colloq* °fire, °sack, °kick out: *Andrews must be removed from his job before he does any more harm.* **6** relocate, °move,

°transfer, °shift: *I removed to a quieter place where I could write in peace.* **7** °take out, unfasten, °detach, °disconnect, °separate, °undo: *They have to remove the transmission to overhaul it.* —*n.* **8** °distance, °space, °interval, °separation: *They tried to keep the girls and the boys at some remove from one another.*

remuneration *n.* **1** °payment, compensation, °salary, wages, °earnings, emolument, °income, °pay, °stipend, °consideration, °reward: *What remuneration will she expect to receive if appointed?* **2** recompense, repayment, reimbursement, °restitution, reparation(s), damages, °indemnity, indemnification, redress: *Have they received any remuneration for their loss of property during the earthquake?*

renaissance *n.* renascence, °rebirth, °revival, reawakening, °restoration, resumption, renewal, °resurgence, °return, regeneration, rejuvenation, °new °dawn, °new °birth: *The Renaissance is so called because of the return to classical tradition. Hugh seems to have undergone a renaissance since taking that rest cure.*

rend *v.* **1** °rip *or* °tear *or* °pull (to pieces *or* apart *or* asunder), °wrench, °mangle, °shred: *The bully threatened to rend me limb from limb.* **2** °split, °tear, °rip, °rupture, °cleave, rive, °separate, °slice, °lacerate: *When the balloon was rent from top to bottom, the basket fell to the ground.* **3** °pain, °distress, °pierce, °stab, smite, °wound, °afflict, °torment, wring, °hurt: *My heart was rent by conflicting emotions.*

render *v.* **1** depict, °picture, °represent, °reproduce, °portray, °create, °produce, do, °execute, °make, °accomplish, °achieve: *The artist rendered this portrait of the family from a photograph.* **2** °make, °cause to be *or* °become: *The news of winning the lottery rendered me speechless.* **3** °give (up), °yield (up), °surrender, °relinquish, °resign, °cede, °deliver, °hand over, °tender, °offer, proffer, °present, °furnish, °provide: *The inscription on the tomb has still not rendered up its secret. To Caesar will I render my legions and my horse.* **4** °play, °perform: *She rendered a fugue most beautifully on a harpsichord.* **5** °deliver, °return: *The jury rendered a verdict of Guilty.* **6** °translate, decode, °decipher, °transcribe, °convert, °explain, °interpret, °put, restate, °reword, rephrase: *She rendered the passage into idiomatic English.* **7** °deliver, °hand in, °present, °offer, proffer, °furnish, °provide, °tender: *They rendered their invoice for the work already done.* **8** Usually, *Brit* **render down**: °melt, °clarify, °extract: *The fat must be rendered down before it can be used for making soap.*

rendering *n.* depiction, showing, °presentation, °interpretation, °conception, °version, °rendition, °representation, delineation, portrayal, °picture: *This is the architect's rendering of what the building will look like when completed.*

rendition *n.* **1** °performance, °interpretation, °execution, °conception, concept, °understanding, construction, reading, °rendering: *I have never before heard such an exquisite rendition of a Bach cantata.* **2** See **rendering**, above.

renegade *n.* **1** °deserter, °turncoat, heretic, °defector, °traitor, apostate, *Archaic* renegado: *The renegade has organized a conspiracy against us.*

—*adj.* **2** °traitorous, treacherous, °perfidious, treasonous, apostate, °heretical, °disloyal: *A renegade band of deserters has turned against the army leaders.*

renege *v.* **1** *Cards* revoke: *When you renege you fail to follow suit.* **2** °go back on, back out, °default, °repudiate, °go back on *or* °break (one's) °promise *or* °word, °recant, abrogate, abjure, *Slang* welsh (on): *You swore you would keep your word, and now you're reneging.*

renew *v.* **1** °restore, °refresh, °rejuvenate, revitalize, reinvigorate, resuscitate, °revamp, redo, °rehabilitate, °transform, regenerate, °refurbish, refurnish, °renovate, refit, °overhaul, recondition, °modernize, redecorate, do over: *The entire interior of the hotel has been renewed at considerable expense.* **2** resume, °resurrect, restart, °pick *or* °take up again, recommence, °return to, reopen: *They renewed their argument in favour of the teaching of Latin.* **3** °restore, °replace, restock, °replenish: *We must renew our supply of claret.* **4** °repeat, °reiterate, reaffirm, °confirm, reconfirm, restate, reassert: *Each autumn she renews her promise to return in the spring.*

renounce *v.* °give up, forswear, °surrender, °abandon, °desert, abjure, °reject, °repudiate, °spurn, °swear off, abstain from, °deny, °forgo, °forsake, eschew, disown, °throw off *or* out, °shun, °avoid: *He renounced his claim to the throne and retired to a monastery.*

renovate *v.* redecorate, °modernize, do over, °refurbish, refurnish, refit, remodel; recondition, °rehabilitate, °restore, °repair, °revamp, °overhaul, °patch up, *Colloq* do up, *US* °fix up: *We are having the entire house renovated by an interior decorator. It was quite costly to have those paintings renovated.*

renown *n.* °fame, °celebrity, °glory, °distinction, °esteem, acclaim, °reputation, °prominence, eminence, °note, °mark, °honour, °prestige, repute, éclat, °lustre, illustriousness, stardom: *She enjoys great renown as a rock star.*

renowned *adj.* °famous, famed, °celebrated, °distinguished, acclaimed, °prominent, °eminent, °well-known, °noted, °notable, honoured, °illustrious: *He was one of the most renowned authors of the 19th century.*

rent¹ *v.* **1** °let (out), °lease, °hire (out), °charter (out), °farm out: *Eric owns a three-bedroom house that he rents out. I should like to rent a yacht for a cruise this summer.*
—*n.* **2** rental, °hire, °lease, °fee: *The rent comes to about a quarter of my salary.*

rent² *n.* °tear, °rip, °split, °gash, °slash, °hole, °slit: *The skirt has a six-inch rent in it.*

repair *v.* **1** °mend, °patch (up); °renew, put *or* set °right, °restore, °fix (up), °service, put (back) in *or* into working order, vamp, °revamp, °adjust: *Can you repair the tear in my trousers? I must remember to ask the garage to repair the brakes on my car.*
—*n.* **2** °mend, °patch; °restoration, fixing (up), servicing, °improvement, °adjustment, renovation, revamping, renewal: *The cost of the repairs to our roof after the storm was covered by our insurance.* **3** °form, °condition, fettle, °state, working °order, *Colloq* °shape, *Brit* °nick: *The engine, I'm afraid, has not been kept in good repair.*

repartee *n.* °banter, badinage, persiflage, °patter, (°witty) °conversation, wordplay,

°raillery, °give and take, *Literary* deipnosophism: *Simon's witty repartee makes him a most welcome dinner guest.*

repay *v.* °pay back, recompense, °compensate, °requite, °reciprocate, °return the °favour *or* °compliment, °reward, °square with, °settle (up) with; refund, °give back, °return, °reimburse, °restore: *How can I ever repay you for what you have done? Alan repaid the money he borrowed from me.*

repeal *v.* **1** °revoke, °recall, rescind, °reverse, °cancel, annul, nullify, invalidate, °void, °set aside, °abolish, abrogate, *Law* °vacate: *They have repealed the rule forbidding guests to wear shorts in the restaurant.*
—*n.* **2** revocation, °recall, rescission, rescindment, °reversal, °cancellation, annulment, nullification, invalidation, voiding, °abolition, abrogation: *Alcoholic beverages were forbidden in the US until the repeal of Prohibition.*

repeat *v.* **1** °reiterate, restate, °echo, retell, °recite, °quote, °rehearse, °recount, °recapitulate, *Colloq* recap: *Would you please repeat to Anne what you told me?* **2** °duplicate, °reproduce, replicate: *History repeated itself on the playing field here today, when Queens Park Rangers defeated Manchester United, 2–0.*
—*n.* **3** °repetition, °duplicate, °copy, duplication, replication, °reproduction, °replica, rerun, rebroadcast, replay, encore, reprise: *This is a repeat of a show we saw last year.*

repeatedly *adv.* again and again, over again, over and over, °frequently, °often, °time and (time) again, °time after time, recurrently, repetitively, repetitiously: *The needle stuck, and the record player kept playing the same thing repeatedly.*

repel *v.* **1** °repulse, °drive back *or* away *or* off, °reject, °fend off, parry, °ward off, °hold off, °rebuff, °resist, °withstand, keep at bay *or* arm's length: *They were completely defenceless and unable to repel attackers.* **2** °revolt, °offend, °disgust, °sicken, °nauseate, turn one's stomach, make one's skin crawl, *Colloq* give one the creeps, turn one off: *The idea of eating sheep's eyes repels me.*

repellent *adj.* °repulsive, repelling, °revolting, °disgusting, nauseating, °nauseous, stomach-turning, sickening, °offensive, °loathsome, °repugnant, °distasteful, vomit-provoking, sick-making, °disagreeable, °obnoxious, off-putting: *He described some of the more repellent examples of vivisection he had encountered.*

repent *v.* °regret, feel contrition, °lament, °bemoan, °bewail, be °sorry, rue, feel °remorse, feel °remorseful *or* °penitent, show °penitence: *She repented having reported him to the police. Now that the evil deed is done he can but repent.*

repentant *adj.* °regretful, contrite, rueful, °remorseful, °apologetic, °sorry, °ashamed, °embarrassed, °penitent: *It was terrible that she wasn't the least bit repentant for what she had done.*

repercussion *n.* Often, **repercussions**: °reaction, °response, °effect, °outcome, consequence, reverberation, °result, aftermath, after-effect, °upshot, fallout, °backlash, °echo: *We were dealing with the repercussions of that decision long afterwards.*

repertory *n.* repertoire, °store, reservoir, °collection, °hoard, °cache, repository, °stock,

°supply, inventory, stockpile: *Cosgrove felt compelled to run through his entire repertory of jokes at dinner.*

repetition *n.* **1** Often, **repetitions**: reiteration(s), duplication(s), redundancy *or* redundancies, °repeats, °tautology *or* tautologies: *The book is full of boring repetitions.* **2** reiteration, °repeat, °echo, echoing, repeating, duplication, duplicating, °rehearsal, recapitulation, restatement, replication, rereading, retelling, relisting, °recital, reprise, rerun, rerunning: *We sat through a repetition of every name for the benefit of any who might have missed it the first time.*

repetitious *adj.* °tiresome, °tedious, °boring, °redundant, prolix, °windy, long-winded, °wordy, tautological, pleonastic: *Streatham's lectures are very repetitious—he makes the same point over and over again.*

repetitive *adj.* iterative, °repetitious, incessant, °monotonous, repeated, °redundant, °humdrum, unceasing, ceaseless, °relentless, unremitting, °persistent, °recurrent, °non-stop, uninterrupted, °continual, °constant, °continuous: *The repetitive beat of that rock music is driving me mad.*

replace *v.* **1** °change, put in °place of, °substitute, °supplant, °renew: *If the toy won't work, try replacing the batteries.* **2** °succeed, °supersede, °substitute for, °take over from, °supplant: *Tim will be replacing David as department head.* **3** °restore, °return, °put back, make good (on), °repay, refund, make °restitution for: *Are you going to replace the money you took?*

replenish *v.* refill, restock, °restore, °renew, °replace, °fill, °top up; °furnish, °provide: *They stopped off in Bordeaux to replenish their supplies.*

replete *adj.* **1** Often, **replete with**: °full (of), filled up (with), overflowing (with), well supplied *or* well provided *or* well stocked (with), chock-full (of), crammed *or* jammed *or* jam-packed (with), brim-full (with), chock-a-block, bursting, teeming, °loaded, overloaded (with), gorged (with), stuffed (with), *Colloq* up to the eyes *or* ears (in), up to here *or* there (in), *US* up to the old wazoo (in), *Slang* °lousy (with), *Taboo slang* up to the *Brit* arse (in) *or* *US* ass (in): *His speech was replete with names, dates, and precise quotations, all delivered without a note of any kind.* **2** satisfied, sated, satiated: *After a meal like that, anybody would feel replete.*

replica *n.* °copy, °duplicate, °facsimile, °reproduction, °likeness, °imitation, carbon °copy, photocopy, duplication, *Colloq* °dupe, *US* °knock-off: *The hall was dominated by a replica of Michelangelo's David.*

reply *v.* **1** °answer, °respond, rejoin, °retort, °return, come back, °acknowledge: *When I asked where he had been, he refused to reply and walked out of the room.*
—*n.* **2** °answer, °response, rejoinder, °retort, comeback, riposte, °reaction, *US* rise: *I have written to the prime minister but as yet have had no reply.*

report *n.* **1** °account, °description, °story, article, write-up, °piece, °statement, °dispatch *or* despatch, communication, communiqué, °announcement, °narrative, °record; °news, °information: *Stanley hasn't yet sent in the full report of his meeting with John. Is there any report from the front?* **2** °explosion, bang, °boom, °shot, gunshot, gunfire, backfire, °discharge, °crack, °blast, detonation: *In the distance we heard the report of a gun, and later a muffled explosion.* —*v.* **3** °relate, °recount, °describe, °narrate, °tell of, °detail, give an °account of, °write up, °document: *Our man in Kuala Lumpur reported a disturbance in a remote village.* **4** °publish, promulgate, °publicize, °put out, °announce, °set forth, °reveal, °disclose, divulge, °circulate, make °public, °broadcast: *Two newspapers and a television station reported the arrest of the suspect.* **5** °arrive, °appear, °surface, °check in, °sign in, clock in *or* on, °turn up, °come in, *US* report in: *We were asked to report for duty at 0800 on Friday.* **6** report on: °investigate, °cover, °examine, °explore, °look into, °inquire into, °check into *or* on, °check (up) on, °research, °study, °probe, °scrutinize, *Slang* °check out, *Brit* suss out: *The new journalist was assigned to report on allegations of bribery in the council.*

reporter *n.* °journalist, newspaperman, newspaperwoman, newsman, newswoman, °correspondent, columnist, newswriter, gentleman *or* lady of the °press, gentleman *or* lady of the fourth estate, *Brit* pressman, presswoman; newscaster, news-presenter, commentator, broadcaster, anchorman, anchorwoman; photojournalist, cameraman, camerawoman, *Colloq* news-hound, news-hawk, news-hen, stringer: *Reporters swarmed around the footballers who had returned home with the World Cup.*

repose *n.* **1** °rest, °inactivity, °calm, °respite, tranquillity, °quiet, restfulness, °peace, °relaxation: *A half hour's repose would be welcome after a long day coping with lively toddlers.* **2** °sleep, °nap, °doze, catnap, siesta, slumber, *Slang* forty winks, snooze, *Slang* zizz, shut-eye: *The short repose refreshed, and she felt ready to tackle anything.* **3** composure, calmness, °calm, °serenity, equanimity, °poise, self-possession: *He became angry in a flash, his face changing from quiet repose to livid distortion.* —*v.* **4** °lie, °abide, be, °lodge, rest: *The power to make the modifications reposes with you.*

represent *v.* **1** °substitute for, °stand (in) for, °replace, °act for: *I have appointed her to represent me in all legal matters.* **2** Often, **represent oneself as**: °present (oneself), depict (oneself), °put *or* °set (oneself) forth, °masquerade as, take (on) *or* assume the °guise *or* role *or* °part of, °characterize as, impersonate, °pretend to be, °pose as, °imitate, °mimic: *He represents himself as a plumber in order to get into houses to rob them. His wife was represented to me as a social worker.* **3** °describe, delineate, °reproduce, °report, assert, °state, °put *or* °set forth, °show, °reflect, °mirror, °characterize, °define, °note, °outline, sketch, depict, °picture, °portray, °draw, °paint; °pretend: *What took place that fateful day is not as represented in Inspector Taylor's testimony.* **4** °symbolize, °stand for, °typify, °exemplify, °embody, epitomize; °illustrate: *He represents all that is good in the world today.*

representation *n.* **1** °reproduction, °image, °likeness, °portrait, °picture, depiction, portrayal, °semblance, °model, °manifestation: *This is an accurate representation of the town's appearance in the 18th century.* **2** °agency: *The sales representation for this area is under Wright's direction.* **3** °statement, °account, °exposition, °declaration, deposition, °assertion,

°presentation, °undertaking: *Certain representations have been made concerning harassment by the police.* **4** °replica, °reproduction, °figure, figurine, °statue, statuette, bust, °head, °model, effigy: *This representation of the goddess Athena was found in Kios.*

representative *adj.* **1** °symbolic, °typical, °characteristic, °emblematic, archetypal, evocative, illustrative: *Is this a representative sample? These poems are not representative of your best work.* **2** elected, chosen, °democratic: *They are struggling to establish a representative form of government.* —*n.* **3** °agent, °deputy, legate, °ambassador, (papal) nuncio, spokesman, spokeswoman, °proxy, °delegate, °envoy, emissary, °missionary, commissioner; Member of Parliament, MP, Councillor, Congressman, Congresswoman, Assemblyman, Assemblywoman: *We like to think that our representatives are acting on our behalf.* **4** °agent, (travelling) salesman *or* saleswoman, *Colloq* rep: *We have hired a new representative to sell refrigerators in the north of the country.*

repress *v.* °suppress, °put down, (keep in) °check, °curb, °quash, °stifle, °overcome, °squelch, (keep under) °control, °contain, °restrain, constrain, °limit, °keep back, °quell, °hold back *or* in, °subdue, °inhibit, °hamper, °hinder, °deter, °frustrate, °discourage, disallow: *The government tried to repress freedom of expression.*

repression *n.* **1** °restraint, °suppression, subjugation: *Increasing repression of their liberties finally led the people to revolt.* **2** °check, squelching, °control, °inhibition, hampering, hindering, °hindrance, stifling, deterring, frustration, frustrating: *The repression of the revolt was unsuccessful.*

repressive *adj.* °tyrannical, °oppressive, °dictatorial, °despotic, °brutal, suppressive, °authoritarian, °totalitarian; Fascist(ic): *In some countries, the people were unable to rebel against the repressive regime.*

reprieve *v.* **1** °respite, °rescue, °save; °let off, °spare: *The Home Secretary reprieved the prisoner from execution pending further investigation.* —*n.* **2** °delay, °postponement, °suspension, °remission, °respite, °stay, amnesty: *The governor granted the condemned man a reprieve at the eleventh hour.*

reprimand *n.* **1** scolding, °reproof, °rebuke, admonition, upbraiding, castigation, reproach, °lecture, censure, °criticism, °disapproval, remonstrance, remonstration, reprehension, °tongue-lashing, *Colloq* dressing-down, talking-to, telling-off, ticking-off, rap over *or* on the knuckles, slap on the wrist, *Brit* slating, *US and Canadian* chewing-out, *Slang Brit* wigging: *Brown received a severe reprimand for violating the curfew.* —*v.* **2** °scold, chide, °reprove, °rebuke, admonish, °upbraid, °castigate, reproach, °berate, °lecture, censure, °criticize, find °fault with, °attack, flay (alive), reprehend, read (someone) the riot act, slap on the wrist, rap over the knuckles, take to °task, *Colloq* °bawl out, °dress down, give a dressing-down, °tell off, tick off, haul over the coals, give (someone) a °piece of (one's) °mind, *Brit* slate, give (someone) a row, send (someone) away *or* off with a flea in his *or* her ear, tell (someone) a thing or two, carpet, wig, skin (alive), *US and Canadian* °chew out, rake over the coals, call on the carpet, pin (someone's) ears back: *Nigel deserves to be reprimanded for what he did.*

reprisal *n.* retaliation, °revenge, °retribution, redress, °requital, °vengeance, repayment, recompense, vindication, getting °even, °indemnity: *She refused to be named because she feared reprisals. How many hostages did they shoot in reprisal?*

reproachful *adj.* °fault-finding, °critical, censorious, disapproving, disparaging, upbraiding, reproving, scolding, admonitory, condemnatory, hypercritical: *She was quite reproachful after seeing what I had written about her in my book.*

reprobate *adj.* **1** unprincipled, °immoral, amoral, °abandoned, depraved, °despicable, °dissolute, °low, low-life, °base, °mean, debased, damned, accursed, cursed, °degenerate, °profligate, °shameful, °shameless, °vile, °evil, °wicked, °villainous, °sinful, irredeemable, °foul, iniquitous, reprehensible: *Such reprobate behaviour soon brought him to the attention of the church fathers.*
—*n.* **2** °scoundrel, blackguard, °miscreant, °rake, °profligate, °roué, °villain, °wastrel, °wretch, °degenerate, unprincipled person, °villain, evil-doer, debauchee, °libertine, °good-for-nothing, ne'er-do-well, cur, rapscallion, scamp, knave, °rascal, *US* low-life, *Colloq* scallywag *or* scalawag: *I can't understand what she sees in that old reprobate.*

reproduce *v.* **1** °duplicate, °copy, replicate, °match, recreate, °repeat, °imitate, simulate: *The printer thinks he can reproduce successfully the colours of the original picture in a print.* **2** °breed, multiply, °propagate, procreate, °spawn, °produce *or* °bring forth *or* beget °young; regenerate: *These animals normally reproduce twice a year.*

reproduction *n.* **1** duplication, copying, printing: *Unlicensed reproduction of this film is against the law.* **2** °duplicate, °copy, °print, clone, carbon (°copy), °facsimile, °replica, °look-alike, °double, °twin, °imitation: *The reproductions look better than the original.* **3** propagation, °breeding, spawning, °proliferation, °production: *Today's lecture concerns the reproduction and breeding habits of large sea-mammals.*

reproof *n.* See reprimand, 1, above.

reprove *v.* See reprimand, 2, above.

repudiate *v.* °reject, °scorn, °turn down, °renounce, °retract, rescind, °reverse, °abandon, abrogate, forswear, °forgo, °deny, disown, °discard: *The government has repudiated its earlier policy of refusing to negotiate with the strikers.*

repugnant *adj.* °repulsive, °abhorrent, °disgusting, off-putting, °offensive, °repellent, °revolting, °vile, °abominable, °loathsome, °foul, °distasteful, °unpalatable, °unsavoury, execrable, intolerable, °obnoxious, noisome, nauseating, °nauseous, sickening, unpleasant, objectionable: *I find the very thought of seeing them again repugnant.*

repulse *v.* **1** °repel, °rebuff, °drive back, °ward off, °fight *or* °beat off, °check: *With a mighty effort, they were able to repulse the attacking forces.* **2** °refuse, °spurn, snub, °reject, °rebuff, °fend off, °resist, °turn down, give the cold °shoulder to: *She repulsed his offer of marriage, and he left, never to see her again.*

—*n.* **3** °rejection, °rebuff, °refusal, °denial, snub, cold °shoulder, spurning: *Alistair told himself he could not accept another repulse.*

repulsive *adj.* °disgusting, °revolting, °abhorrent, °loathsome, °repugnant, °repellent, °offensive, °obnoxious, objectionable, °gross, °unsavoury, °distasteful, °nasty, unpleasant, displeasing, °disagreeable, °ugly, off-putting, sickening, nauseating, °nauseous, °beastly, °vile, °dreadful, °awful, °rotten, feculent, °foul, odious, °horrible, horrid, °abominable, execrable, fulsome: *I have seldom had so repulsive an experience as the tour of that abattoir. The repulsive sights and smells were more than I could bear.*

reputable *adj.* °respectable, °honourable, °well-thought-of, °estimable, respected, °trustworthy, trusted, °honest, °reliable, dependable, °principled, °virtuous, °good, °worthy: *Alan is one of Aylesbury's most reputable businessmen.*

reputation *n.* **1** repute, °name, °standing, stature, °position, °status: *Jean is a woman of excellent reputation in the community.* **2 have a reputation for**: be known *or* °noted *or* °notorious *or* °famous for: *The company has a reputation for dismissing employees without notice.*

reputed *adj.* °alleged, purported, °supposed, °assumed, presumed; rumoured, said, deemed, held, regarded, viewed, looked on *or* upon, judged, considered, thought, believed: *The police arrested three reputed gang members. They are reputed to be international drug dealers.*

request *v.* **1** °ask for, °seek, °plead for, °apply for, °put in for, °requisition, °call for, °demand, °insist on, °solicit, °beg, entreat, °beseech, importune: *They request my cooperation. I requested to be excused. He requested her to open the door for him.*
—*n.* **2** °plea, °petition, °application, °requisition, °call, °demand, solicitation, entreaty: *We receive many requests for information.*

require *v.* **1** °order, °command, °ask (for), °call (for), °press (for), °instruct, coerce, °force; °insist, °demand; °make: *I am required to appear in court on Monday. The teacher required that I bring my mother to school.* **2** °need, °want, °lack, be lacking, be missing, be °short (of); °desire: *We require one more trainee in order to fill our quota.*

requirement *n.* **1** requisite, °prerequisite, °demand, °precondition, °condition, °qualification, °stipulation, *sine qua non*, °provision, °proviso, °necessity, °essential, desideratum, °must: *It is a requirement of the loan agreement that you maintain an account with this bank.* **2** °need, °want, °demand: *We hope the new design will meet all your requirements.*

requisition *n.* **1** °request, °order, °demand, °call, authorization, mandate, voucher: *A requisition was issued by headquarters for the delivery of 200 desks and chairs.*
—*v.* **2** °request, °order, °demand, °call, °authorize, mandate: *Have you requisitioned the office furniture we need?* **3** °seize, °appropriate, commandeer, °confiscate, °take °possession of, °take (over), °occupy; expropriate: *The army of occupation has requisitioned all available sleeping accommodation in the town.*

requital *n.* **1** repayment, °return, recompense, redress, °restitution, reparation, °remuneration, quittance, °amends, °satisfaction, compensation, °payment: *I look* *forward to an opportunity to make requital for all the favours you have done for me.* **2** °revenge, retaliation, °retribution, °reprisal, °vengeance; quid pro quo, Roland for an Oliver: *In requital for his shameful treachery, MacFallon was sent into exile.*

requite v. **1** °repay, °reward, °reciprocate, recompense, °compensate for, °respond to: *Her years of tender care were requited with abuse and scorn.* **2** °retaliate for, °revenge, avenge, make °restitution for, redress, °pay back for, give tit for tat for, make °amends for: *Who can requite the wrongs inflicted on these poor people?*

rescue v. **1** °save, °deliver, (°set) °free, °liberate, °let °go (°free), °release, (°let) °loose: *We rescued all the men who were being held prisoner. Jane was rescued by a very handsome lifeguard.*
—*n.* **2** deliverance, °saving; freeing, liberating, °release: *The seaman's rescue was conducted by a navy helicopter team. Because of the heavy guard, the prisoners' rescue is out of the question.*

research n. **1** °investigation, investigating, °exploration, delving, digging, enquiry or °inquiry, fact-finding, scrutinization, °scrutiny, °examination, inspection, probing, °analysis, experimentation: *Her research into the causes of the disease have yielded good results. The government no longer supports much research.*
—*v.* **2** °investigate, °explore, delve into, °dig into, °enquire or °inquire into, °scrutinize, °examine, °study, °analyse, °inspect, °check in or into or (up) on, °probe, °experiment with, *Colloq* °check out: *We are researching ways in which the virus attacks the blood cells.*

resemblance n. °likeness, similarity; correspondence, congruity, °coincidence, conformity, °accord, °agreement, equivalence, comparableness, comparability, °comparison: *There is a striking resemblance between your wife and mine. Any resemblance is purely a matter of chance.*

resemble v. °look or °sound or °taste or °seem or be °like or °similar to, °bear (a) °resemblance to, °approximate, smack of, °correspond to, have (all) the °hallmarks or earmarks of, °take after, *Colloq* °favour: *You are right, the taste does resemble that of liquorice. Does she resemble her mother?*

resent v. feel °embittered or °bitter about, feel °envious or °jealous of, °begrudge, have hard feelings about, be displeased or °disgruntled at, be °angry about: *I resent having to go to work while you sit about the house all day.*

resentful adj. °embittered, °bitter, acrimonious, °spiteful, °envious, °jealous, begrudging, °vindictive, °indignant, displeased, °disgruntled, °dissatisfied, unsatisfied, °unhappy, peeved, irritated, irked, annoyed, provoked, riled, °angry, piqued, irate, °furious, incensed, °agitated, °upset, worked up, antagonistic, °hostile: *Ronald is resentful because you got the promotion that he considered rightfully his.*

resentment n. °bitterness, acrimony, °rancour, °envy, jealousy, °grudge, °indignation, °displeasure, °dissatisfaction, unhappiness, irritation, °annoyance, °provocation, pique, °anger, ire, °fury, °agitation, °upset, °anxiety, °ill will, malice, °antagonism, °hostility, °animosity, enmity, antipathy, °hate: *Some believe that inequality among people provokes resentment.*

reservation n. **1** keeping or holding back, withholding, reticence, °reluctance, hesitation, hesitancy, hedging: *It was not without some*

reservation that I gave the book my endorsement. **2** °qualm, °scruple, °qualification, hesitancy, limitation, °exception, °objection, demur or demurral or demurrer, °condition, °proviso, °provision: *He has no reservations about revealing the most intimate details in his autobiography.* **3** booking, °appointment, °arrangement: *I'll make a reservation for dinner for the two of us.* **4** °preserve, °sanctuary, °reserve, °area, °tract, °territory, °region, °section, °plot: *In North America, many Indians still live on reservations.*

reserve v. **1** °keep or °hold (back), °withhold, °save, °set or °put aside, °conserve, °preserve, °retain, °keep (to or for oneself), °hold over, °postpone, °delay, °put off, °defer: *Reserve judgement till you have heard all the facts. I shall reserve my answer to that question for another day.* **2** °hold, °keep, °book, °register, °save, °put or °set aside, °charter, °engage, °secure, °contract for: *I have reserved two seats for the matinee.*
—*n.* **3** Often, °reserves: °store, °stock, stockpile, inventory, °supply, nest egg, reservoir, °fund, °hoard, °cache: *We prayed for rain, as our water reserves were getting low.* **4** reticence, (self-) °restraint, (self-)°control, taciturnity, aplomb, °formality, coolness, aloofness, guardedness, standoffishness, remoteness, °detachment: *I had to admire Paul's reserve in the face of such insults.* **5** Often, °reserves: °auxiliary, °alternate, °substitute, reinforcements, backup, °spare: *If the battle goes badly, we shall have to call out the reserves.* **6** See reservation, 4, above. **7** °reservation, °restriction, °restraint, hesitancy, hesitation, °limit, limitation, hedging, avoidance, °evasion, dodging, fudging: *The lawyer acknowledged without reserve that the case was weak.* **8 in reserve**: °ready, in °readiness, on °hand, °available, on °call, °accessible, as backup, in °store, on °tap, at (one's) fingertips: *We have huge resources in reserve should we require them.*

reserved adj. °reticent, restrained, controlled, °silent, °taciturn, uncommunicative, unforthcoming, close-mouthed, unresponsive, undemonstrative, unemotional, poker-faced, °cool, °formal, °aloof, °guarded, °standoffish, °unsocial, antisocial, °distant, °remote, °detached, °retiring, °withdrawn, °sedate, demure, °dignified, prim, °rigid, °strait-laced, °icy, °frigid, ice-cold: *She was always very reserved, not showing any emotion.*

residence n. **1** °abode, °home, °domicile, °dwelling, dwelling-place, °place, °house, habitation, (living) quarters: *A crowd was waiting to greet them outside their residence.* **2** residency, °stay, °sojourn, °visit, °tenancy: *During his residence in Cape Province, he became bilingual in Xhosa.* **3** mansion, villa, manor (°house), stately °home, °estate, château, °castle, °palace, *Brit* °hall: *The ambassadorial residence was a very imposing structure.*

resident adj. **1** in °residence, residing, living, staying, °abiding, °dwelling, °remaining: *Is he resident in this country?* **2** °local, °neighbourhood, °district, regional, °neighbouring: *Our resident astronomer mentioned there would be an eclipse of the moon tonight.*
—*n.* **3** °denizen, dweller, °inhabitant, °citizen, householder, home-owner, °tenant, °local: *Parking permits are available only to residents.*

residual *adj.* °remaining, °leftover, °surplus, °spare, °extra, residuary: *Residual units of the army are still bivouacked in the field. How would we survive nuclear fall-out and the subsequent residual contamination?*

residue *n.* °remainder, °leftover, °surplus, remains, rest, °excess, °dregs, residuum: *The residue of the tatterdemalion force escaped into the forest.*

resign *v.* **1** °quit, °leave, °go, °abdicate, give °notice; °retire (from), °abandon, °give up, °forsake, °hand over, °yield up, °renounce, °relinquish, let go, °release, °vacate, °surrender, °deliver up, °turn over: *Amanda resigned because she was offered a better job elsewhere. Anthony refused to resign the last of his responsibilities till he was ninety.* **2 resign (oneself) (to):** °reconcile (oneself) (to), be *or* become resigned *or* reconciled (to), °accommodate (oneself) (to), °adjust (oneself) (to), °adapt (oneself) (to), acclimatize *or* acclimate (oneself) (to), °submit (oneself) (to): *Knowing that no one had ever escaped from the prison, he resigned himself to his fate.*

resignation *n.* **1** °notice; abandonment, abdication, resigning, renunciation, forgoing, relinquishment: *After the incident in the boardroom, Kim was asked for her resignation. Stuart's resignation of his responsibilities led to a severe reprimand.* **2** °reconciliation, reconcilement, °adjustment, °adaptation, acclimatization *or* acclimation, °submission, acceptance, compliance, capitulation, abandonment, acquiescence, passivity: *His resignation to his fate won admiration from those around him.*

resilience *n.* °rebound, °recoil, °bounce, °elasticity, springiness, °spring, buoyancy, °flexibility, suppleness, °ability to °recover: *The resilience of youth is astonishing, and William was soon on his feet again.*

resist *v.* **1** °stop, °hinder, °prevent, °hold out (against), be °proof (against), °keep *or* °hold at bay, °hold the line (against), °thwart, °impede, °block, °obstruct, °inhibit, °restrain, °preclude, °check, °control, °curb, °stem, °bridle, °hold back, °withstand, °weather, °last (against), °endure, °outlast, °stand up (to or against); °combat, °fight (against), °battle, countervail (against), °counteract, °oppose, °rebuff, °defy: *He was jailed for attempting to resist arrest. It is pointless to resist.* **2** °refuse, °deny, °turn down, °forgo: *I cannot resist a rich sweet for dessert.*

resistance *n.* **1** °opposition, defiance, °refusal, °denial, °obstruction, intransigence, rebelliousness, recalcitrance, stubbornness: *The child puts up considerable resistance to any form of discipline.* **2** °defences: *My resistance is low, I can deny you nothing.* **3 Resistance:** °underground, partisans, °freedom fighters, °guerrilla *or* guerilla °movement, guerrillas *or* guerillas, irregulars, Maquis, *US* resisters: *During the war, he was a member of the Resistance and engaged in sabotage against the invaders.*

resistant *adj.* **1** °opposed, against, °defiant, °averse, unsubmissive; impervious, °unaffected: *The organisms are resistant to any change.* **2** °recalcitrant, °stubborn, °obstinate, intransigent, °rebellious, °immovable, intractable, refractory, °wilful, °ungovernable, unmanageable, °unruly, uncompliant, uncooperative: *We have run up against a highly resistant group of activists.* **3** Often, **resistant to:** impervious (to),

impenetrable (to), °repellent (to); °proof (against); shedding: *You need a more resistant material. This fabric is resistant to rain and snow.*

resolute *adj.* resolved, °determined, °purposeful, °steadfast, °firm, °stubborn, adamant, °set, °decided, °staunch, °bold, dogged, undaunted, °dauntless, persevering, persisting, °persistent, perseverant, pertinacious, °tenacious, °single-minded, dedicated, °devoted, bulldog, purposive, °deliberate, °inflexible, unwavering, unshakeable *or* unshakable, unshaken, unflagging, °untiring, indefatigable, °tireless, unfaltering, °unhesitating, unhesitant, unswerving, °irreversible, undeviating, unchanging, °changeless, unchangeable, immutable, unalterable: *We remain resolute in our determination to end injustice.*

resolution *n.* **1** °resolve, resoluteness, °determination, °purpose, purposefulness, steadfastness, firmness, decidedness, °decision, staunchness, boldness, doggedness, dauntlessness, stubbornness, °obstinacy, °perseverance, °persistence, relentlessness, pertinacity, °tenacity, single-mindedness, °dedication, °devotion, constancy, devotedness, deliberation, deliberateness, inflexibility, inflexibleness, unshakeability *or* unshakability, fixedness, indefatigability, indefatigableness, irreversibility, changelessness, unchangeability, immutability, immutableness, unalterability, *Colloq US* stick-to-it-iveness: *The boys showed extraordinary resolution in deciding to continue despite the hardships.* **2** °promise, commitment, °pledge, °word (of honour), °oath, °vow, °undertaking, °obligation; °intention: *I find that my New Year's resolutions last till about January 5th.* **3** °motion, °resolve, °proposal, °proposition, °plan, °suggestion, °idea, °notion; °determination, verdict, °decision, °judgement: *The committee votes today on the resolution to increase membership fees.* **4** °answer, answering, °solution, solving, unravelling, disentanglement, sorting out, explication; °outcome, °issue, °result, °end (°result): *The resolution of a family problem is seldom easy. Can there be a final resolution of the question of a free market economy?* **5** acutance, sharpness, °precision, °accuracy, exactness, exactitude, fineness, °discrimination, detailing, distinguishability: *The new optical system provides for a much better resolution.*

resolve *v.* **1** °determine, °decide, make up one's °mind, °agree, °undertake, °settle, °fix, conclude: *When did you resolve to move to Australia? Let us resolve never to let this happen again.* **2** °work out, °figure out, °solve, °clear up, °answer: *How have you resolved the problem of looking after the cats while you are away?* **3** °adopt, °pass, °approve, °decide: *It was resolved that membership fees should be raised.* **4 resolve into:** °change into, °convert into, °alter into, °transform into, transmute into, metamorphose into, be °convert(ed) into, °become, °dissolve into, °break down into, liquefy into, °disintegrate into, °reduce to *or* into: *O, that this too too solid flesh would melt, Thaw, and resolve itself into a dew!*

—*n.* **5** See **resolution, 1,** above. **6** See **resolution, 2,** above: *She kept her resolve never to marry again.*

resonant *adj.* vibrating, vibrant, resounding, (re-)echoing, reverberating, reverberant, pulsating, ringing, booming, thundering, °thunderous, °loud: *The resonant pealing of the bells almost drove me mad.*

resort *n.* **1** spa, °retreat, *Chiefly Brit* watering-place: *We go to a lovely resort in the Alps every summer.* **2** °resource, backup, °reserve, °refuge, place to turn, °alternative, °remedy: *He will see a doctor only as a last resort.*
—*v.* **3 resort to**: have °recourse to, °turn to, °look to, °fall back on, °repair to, °take to, °frequent, °patronize, °attend; °visit, °haunt, °hang out in: *I have to resort to father for a small loan. She was said to be resorting to the lowest dens in the Casbah.*

resound *v.* °boom, resonate, °ring (out), °boom (out), (re-)°echo, reverberate, °pulsate, °thunder: *The laughter resounded around the entire office.*

resource *n.* **1** Often, **resources**: °initiative, °ingenuity, °talent, inventiveness, °imagination, imaginativeness, cleverness, quick-wittedness, °capability, resourcefulness, °aptitude, °qualifications, °strength, °quality, °forte, *Colloq Brit* °gumption, *Slang* °guts: *Has he the inner resources for the job that lies ahead?* **2** Often, **resources**: °capital, °assets, °money, °possessions, °own, °wealth, °property, °cash, °funds: *She has sufficient resources to retire at fifty if she wants to.*

resourceful *adj.* °ingenious, inventive, °imaginative, °clever, Daedalian, °creative, °skilful, °smart, °slick: *Sylvia is resourceful enough to get out of any situation.*

respect *n.* **1** °regard, °consideration, °admiration, °esteem, (high) °opinion, °appreciation: *We have great respect for Samuel Simpson, our president.* **2** °regard, °consideration, °courtesy, politeness, °civility, attentiveness, thoughtfulness, °etiquette, °deference, °reverence, °veneration: *Few treat Alastair with the respect he deserves.* **3** °reference, °relation, °connection, °comparison, °regard, °bearing: *What are they planning to do with respect to the flooding?* **4** °detail, °point, °element, °aspect, °characteristic, °feature, °quality, °trait, °particular, °matter, °attribute, °property: *Describe the respects in which the War of American Independence and the French Revolution were similar.* **5 respects**: °regards, °good or °best wishes, °greetings, compliments, *Formal* salutations, *Formal or archaic* devoirs: *I went to pay my respects to my aunt on her 90th birthday.*
—*v.* **6** °consider, °admire, °esteem, °honour, °appreciate, value, °defer to, pay °homage to, °think °highly or °well of, °look up to, °revere, °reverence, °venerate: *I am not sure that I like Mrs Horne, but I certainly respect her for what she has done for the poor.* **7** °heed, °obey, show °consideration or °regard for, °pay °attention to, °attend to, be °considerate or °polite or °courteous to, °defer to: *Children are no longer taught to respect their elders.*

respectable *adj.* **1** °proper, demure, °decorous, °seemly, °estimable, °worthy, °dignified, °decent, °upright, °honest, respected, °genteel, °refined, °reputable, °above-board, unimpeachable, law-abiding: *Patricia Smythe is a very respectable member of the community. I'll have you know that I run a respectable boarding house!*
2 °moderate, appreciable, °goodly, °reasonable, °fair, not inconsiderable, °considerable, °tolerable, °satisfactory, sizeable, good-sized, °substantial, not °insignificant, °significant, *Colloq* °tidy: *She earns a respectable living. A respectable number of people showed up. Climbing Annapurna, though it is not Everest, is a respectable feat.* **3** °presentable, °moral, °decent, °proper, °modest, °chaste, °innocent, °pure, °clean: *The board decided that the film is not respectable enough to be shown to schoolchildren.*

respectful *adj.* °courteous, °polite, well-mannered, well-behaved, mannerly, °civil, °cordial, gentlemanly, °ladylike, °gracious, °obliging, °accommodating, °considerate, °thoughtful: *On entering, Captain Gregory made a respectful bow to the ladies.*

respective *adj.* °separate, °individual, °particular, °pertinent, °specific, °special, °personal, °own, °relevant, corresponding, °several: *Each retired to his respective room for the night. All of you know your respective duties.*

respectively *adv.* °separately, °individually, °singly, severally, *mutatis mutandis*, each to each: *Ron and Daniel are, respectively, president and secretary of the association.*

respite *n.* **1** °interval, °intermission, °break, °interruption, °recess, breather, °rest; °holiday, *Chiefly US and Canadian* vacation: *I haven't had a moment's respite since six o'clock this morning. We are planning a brief respite from work in August.* **2** °pause, °delay, hiatus, °stay, °extension, °reprieve, °postponement: *After a ten-minute respite, the infernal noise began again.*

respond *v.* **1** °answer, °reply, °come back, °return, °react, °reciprocate, °counter; rejoin, °retort: *When Sean insulted her, Una responded with a slap to his face. I said, 'Good morning!' and Adrian responded, 'What's good about it?'* **2** Often, **respond to**: be °responsive (to), °react (to), empathize (with), °sympathize (with), commiserate (with), °feel for, °pity, be °affected or moved or touched (by): *Many respond to those charity appeals for the crippled and disabled.*

response *n.* °answer, °reply, °retort, rejoinder; °reaction, °effect, feedback, °return, *Colloq* comeback: *Whatever you say to Ronnie Farrago, he always has a snappy response. The response to our advertising has been quite good.*

responsibility *n.* **1** °accountability, °liability, chargeability, answerability, °obligation: *Responsibility is one of the burdens a parent must undertake.* **2** °charge, °duty, onus, °burden, °trust, °job, role, °task: *Has Ted taken on more responsibilities than he can handle? It is your responsibility to see that the children are awakened in time for school.* **3** °blame, °guilt, °fault, culpability: *Professor Davies assumed full responsibility for the failure of the experiment.* **4** dependability, reliability, trustworthiness, °stability, °accountability, creditability: *Before accommodating you with a loan, Mr Stokes, we must confirm your financial responsibility.*

responsible *adj.* **1** °accountable, answerable, °liable, chargeable: *The court determined that she was not responsible for her actions.* **2** °reliable, °trustworthy, dependable, °stable, creditable, °accountable, °ethical, °honest: *If teenagers can show that they are sufficiently responsible, the bank will lend them money for their enterprise.* **3** °executive, °leading,

°authoritative, administrative, °important, decision-making, managerial, directorial, °principal, °chief, °top, US front-office: *Oliver played a responsible role in the running of the company.* **4** °guilty, to °blame, at °fault, culpable: *We never found out who was responsible for putting the frog in the teacher's desk.*

responsive *adj.* °alert, °alive, (wide-)°awake, reactive, communicative, °sharp, °keen, °receptive, °sensitive, °open, °sympathetic: *I was delighted to find students who were so responsive to the ideas put forth in my lectures.*

rest[1] *n.* **1** °repose, °sleep, °nap, °doze, siesta, slumber, *Chiefly Brit* lie-down, *Colloq* forty winks, zizz, snooze; shut-eye: *I think I'll have a bit of a rest before dinner.* **2** °relaxation, °intermission, °interval, °interlude, entr'acte, rest °period, cessation, (tea *or* coffee) °break, °recess, breather, breathing-space, °respite, °time off, °holiday, *Chiefly US and Canadian* vacation: *Why don't you take a rest for a while?* **3** °ease, °relaxation, °leisure, °indolence, °idleness, °inactivity, loafing, dozing: *His well-deserved rest was disturbed by an urgent request from Interpol to investigate a smuggling operation.* **4** °prop, °support, holder, °brace, trestle, shelf, °bracket: *Those old guns were too heavy to hold and fire without using a rest.* **5 come to rest**: °stop, °end up, °turn up, °arrive: *The ball rolled down the slope and came to rest in a puddle.* —*v.* **6** (go to) °sleep, °doze, °relax, take a rest, (take one's) °repose, °lie down, °recline, go *or* take to one's bed, take one's °ease, unwind, loll, languish, laze about, be °idle, °idle about, °lounge, (take a) °nap, put one's feet up, *Colloq* take it °easy, snooze, count sheep, have a zizz, catch *or* grab some shut-eye, get *or* take forty winks, US catch *or* log a few zees (Z's), *Slang Brit* kip, doss down, hit the °sack, hit the hay, US °sack out: *Rest now—you'll feel better tomorrow.* **7** reside, be situated, be lodged, °lie, be placed, hinge, be found, °remain, °stay: *The responsibility for passenger safety rests with the captain and the crew. The blame for this fiasco rests on you.* **8** °place, °position, °put, °lay, °set, °lean, °prop: *Rest your head on my shoulder.* **9** °lie, °remain, °stay: *Can't you let the matter rest?* **10** allay, °calm, °quiet, °still, °stay: *Rest your fears—I shall let nothing happen to you.*

rest[2] *n.* **1** °remainder, °balance; °remains, °remnants, leftovers, °residue, residuum, °excess, °surplus, overage: *If you carry these bags, I'll take the rest. Martin bought up all the best books and left the rest for us.* —*v.* **2** (°continue to) be, °remain, °keep on being: *Rest assured, the situation is bound to get easier as we go along.*

restful *adj.* **1** relaxing, °soothing, comforting, tranquillizing, °sedative, calming, sleep-inducing, hypnotic, soporific, somnolent: *Don't you find the sound of the waves restful?* **2** °tranquil, °calm, °peaceful, °quiet, °still, °serene, pacific, °comfortable, °relaxed, reposeful: *After a hectic day in the city, I was happy to return to the restful atmosphere of the country.*

restitution *n.* **1** °amends, compensation, redress, recompense, °remuneration, reparation, °requital, indemnification, °indemnity: *It was agreed that victims of the raids were entitled to restitution for what had been taken from*

them. **2** °restoration, °return, re-establishment, reinstatement, °recovery: *A commission is to investigate the restitution of plundered property.*

restive *adj.* See restless, below.

restless *adj.* °restive, uneasy, edgy, on °edge, on tenterhooks, fidgety, °nervous, skittish, °excitable, highly-strung, high-strung, worked up, °agitated, °fretful, °jumpy, apprehensive, itchy, *Colloq* jittery, *Slang* uptight, US antsy, hyper: *The crowd in the square were becoming restless as they waited for the speeches to start.*

restoration *n.* **1** See restitution, 2, above. **2** renovation, refurbishment, rehabilitation, renewal, °repair, rejuvenation, reconstruction, resurrection, reconversion, °revival: *The programme for the restoration of ancient buildings suffers from lack of funding.*

restore *v.* **1** °give *or* °hand back, °return, make °restitution, bring back: *We must restore to the people the land that is rightfully theirs.* **2** °revive, °rejuvenate, reestablish, °renew, bring back, °give (someone) back, resuscitate, °resurrect, rekindle, reinvigorate, °refresh, °stimulate, revitalize, °strengthen: *Your kindness has restored my faith in mankind.* **3** °renovate, °refurbish, °renew, °repair, °rejuvenate, °resurrect, °revive, reconstruct, °rehabilitate, rebuild; °mend, °fix, °retouch, °touch up; *Colloq US* °fix up: *They live in a 17th-century cottage that has been lovingly restored. Antiques often lose their value entirely if they are restored.* **4** °replace, reinstate, °put back; °return, bring back: *They said that they would not rest until they had restored the rightful king on the throne. The doctor said she would soon be restored to good health.* **5** °replace, °reimburse, °repay, °return, °pay *or* °put *or* °give back: *Even though he has restored all the money he took, she refuses to forgive him.*

restrain *v.* **1** (keep under *or* in) °control, (keep *or* hold in) °check, °hold (back *or* in), °curb, °govern: *A poor rider, he was unable to restrain his horse. Something must be done to restrain the general's power.* **2** °limit, °restrict, °inhibit, °regulate, °suppress, °repress, °bar, debar, °curtail, °stifle, °hinder, °interfere with, °hamper, °handicap: *Trade between the two countries was restrained because of tariff disputes.* **3** (place under) °arrest, confine, °imprison, incarcerate, detain, °hold, °lock up, °jail *or Brit also* gaol, °shut in *or* up: *For his most recent offence, he was restrained for two months.*

restraint *n.* **1** °control, °check, °curb, °rein, °bridle, °restriction, constraint, °limit, limitation, curtailment, °taboo, °ban, interdict *or* interdiction, proscription, delimitation, °bound(s), °embargo: *The law places restraints on executives' buying and selling shares in their own companies. In 1863, a bill for the restraint of the press was brought before the House of Commons.* **2** °control, °restriction, constraint, confinement; °bondage, °bonds, fetters, °shackles, °handcuffs, gyves, bilboes, pinions, manacles, ball and °chain, strait-jacket, *Colloq* cuffs, bracelets: *Despite the restraints to his liberty, he felt a free man. He became violent and had to be put under restraint.* **3** °control, °reserve, °self-control, self-possession, °poise, equanimity, self-discipline, self-restraint: *Heather Gorse exhibited admirable restraint in remaining silent when teased about her name.*

restrict v. °limit, confine, °bound, circumscribe, delimit, °mark off, demarcate, °regulate; °qualify, °restrain, °impede: *Smoking is allowed only in restricted areas. The opposition party said that they would restrict the movement of heavy goods by road.*

restriction n. **1** °condition, °provision, °proviso, °qualification, °stipulation: *One restriction is that purchasers of shares in the utility must be resident in the UK.* **2** See **restraint**, 1, above.

result n. **1** °outcome, consequence, °effect, °end (result), °fruit; conclusion, °upshot, °issue, °development, °sequel, °follow-up, denouement or dénouement: *It will take years to evaluate the results of the new educational curriculum. As a result of his speeding ticket, his driving licence was suspended.*
—v. **2** Often, **result from**: °develop, °emerge, °follow, °happen, °occur, °come (about), °come to °pass, °arise, evolve, be produced: *Severe burns can result from allowing children to play with matches. The mixture that results may be highly volatile.* **3 result in**: °end, conclude, culminate, °terminate: *The explosion resulted in a heavy loss of life. The experience gained often results in better safety devices.*

resume v. °continue, °carry on, take up again, °pick up (where one left off): *After prison, it is not easy to resume one's life where it left off. When the audience quieted, the speaker resumed.*

résumé n. **1** °summary, °digest, °abstract, °synopsis, °précis, °outline, °review, recapitulation, °epitome, *Colloq* °run-down, recap: *Give me a résumé of what went on at the board meeting.* **2** curriculum vitae, CV, °summary, biography, °work or °job °history, °career °description, *Formal* prosopography, *Colloq* bio, *US* vita: *Suitably qualified candidates are invited to send their résumés to the address below.*

resurgence n. °renaissance, renascence, °rebirth, °revival, reawakening, °restoration, renewal, resumption, °return, resurrection, regeneration, rejuvenation, new °dawn, new °birth: *Simone is banking her entire future on a resurgence of interest in seventies' fashion.*

resurrect v. °revive, bring back, °return, reawaken, °restore (to °life), reintroduce, °renew, regenerate, °rejuvenate, °raise (from the dead), resuscitate, breathe new °life into, re-animate, reincarnate: *Some antiquated law was resurrected in order to prevent their using the land for grazing.*

retain v. **1** °keep (°possession of), °hold (on to), °save, °preserve, *Colloq* °hang on to: *Retain the receipt in case you wish to exchange the merchandise.* **2** °engage, °hire, °employ, commission, °take on: *We have retained a caretaker to look after the estate.* **3** °hold, absorb, °contain, °soak up, °preserve: *This type of soil retains little water.* **4** °remember, °keep or bear or have in °mind, °recall, remain aware of, °memorize, impress on the °memory, °recollect: *As he aged, he found it increasingly difficult to retain even the simplest information such as names and dates.*

retaliate v. °repay, °pay back (in kind), °counter, °strike back (at), take °revenge (on), °wreak °vengeance (on), °revenge oneself (on), avenge, °reciprocate, °settle a °score (with); give a Roland for an Oliver, give tit for tat, take an eye for an eye (and a tooth for a tooth), give as good as one gets, give (someone) a taste of

his or her or their own medicine, °pay (someone) back in his or her own coin; *Colloq* get °even (with), °get back (at): *After government forces bombed their mountain headquarters, the guerrillas retaliated by destroying bridges and railway lines.*

retard v. **1** °slow (down or up), °hold up or back, °set back, °hinder, °impede, °delay, °keep back, °stall, °thwart, balk, °block, °restrict, °hold in °check, °frustrate, °interfere with: *Growth of the economy was severely retarded by the war.*
—n. **2** *Offensive and derogatory*: idiot, moron, °fool, imbecile, dunce, *Slang chiefly US and Canadian* °jerk: *Why she invites that retard to her parties I can't imagine.*

reticent adj. °quiet, °shy, °timid, °retiring, °reserved; °taciturn, °silent, unresponsive, °tight-lipped, unforthcoming: *If you are proud of your accomplishments, why be reticent about saying so? Colin is reticent about how he acquired his gold earring.*

retinue n. entourage, °escort, convoy, cortège, °company, °train, °suite, followers, attendants, following, hangers-on, *Colloq* groupies: *The rock band arrived at the airport accompanied by a retinue of flunkeys.*

retire v. **1** °withdraw, rusticate, °go off or away, °take off, °retreat; hibernate, aestivate or *US* estivate, seclude or sequester or cloister oneself: *I think I'll retire to some mountain-top to finish my book.* **2** °stop or °give up work(ing), be pensioned off, (be) put out to grass or pasture, take the golden handshake, be given the gold watch, go on social security, go on a pension, be super-annuated, go out of circulation: *Gemma Frobisher has retired from her job in the bakery, and is now living with her daughter in Norfolk.* **3** go or take to (one's) bed or bedroom, (go to) °sleep, °lie down, (take one's) °repose, (take a) °nap, put one's feet up, *Colloq* take it °easy, snooze, count sheep, have a zizz, catch or grab some shut-eye, get or take forty winks, *US* catch or log a few zees (Z's), *Slang* hit the °sack, °sack out, hit the hay, *Brit* kip, doss down: *I usually retire around midnight.*

retiring adj. °shy, °bashful, °coy, demure, °modest, diffident, °timid, unpretentious, unassuming, °humble, self-effacing, timorous, °meek, °reticent, °reserved, °unsocial, unsociable, °aloof, removed, °standoffish, °distant, °reclusive, eremitic(al): *Howard is of a retiring disposition, preferring to keep to himself.*

retort n. **1** °response, °reply, rejoinder, °answer, riposte, °rebuttal, *Colloq* comeback: *Faced with criticism of the novel, the author's retort was a four-letter word.*
—v. **2** °fling or °hurl back, rejoin, °answer back, riposte, °rebut, °counter, come back with, °return, respond, °answer, °reply, °retaliate: *'And don't expect a Christmas present from me, either!', she retorted vehemently.*

retouch v. °touch up, °correct, °restore, °repair, recondition, °refresh, °brush up, °adjust, °improve, °finish, put the finishing touches on: *Only an expert restorer could have retouched the damaged painting so skilfully.*

retract v. **1** °withdraw, °pull or °draw back: *The instant he felt the heat, he retracted his hand.* **2** °take back, °withdraw, rescind, °revoke, °repeal, °deny, disavow, °recant, °renounce, abjure, °cancel, forswear, °repudiate, disclaim, disown, °reverse: *If they refuse to retract their statement, I shall sue them for libel.*

retreat *n.* **1** retirement, withdrawal, pulling *or* falling *or* drawing back, giving ground, evacuation, °flight: *The regiment's retreat in the face of overwhelming odds is complete.* **2** retirement, °seclusion, withdrawal, isolation, °solitude, rustication: *Since her retreat from public life, she has devoted herself to painting.* **3** °sanctuary, °sanctum (sanctorum), °refuge, °shelter, den, haven, asylum, °resort, °hideaway, hide-out: *Antonia insisted on having her own retreat where she could occasionally escape from the children.* —*v.* **4** °withdraw, decamp, °run (away), °turn tail, °depart, give *or* lose ground, °pull *or* °fall *or* °draw back, °retire, °evacuate, °flee, take °flight: *We must retreat to the shelter of the hills, where we can regroup.* **5** °ebb, °draw *or* move back, °recede: *The waves, constantly advancing and retreating across the pebbly strand, lulled me to sleep.*

retribution *n.* °vengeance, °revenge, °reprisal, retaliation, °requital, redress, quid pro quo, °satisfaction, °punishment, °justice, just °deserts, recompense, compensation: *It is a moral question whether society's treatment of malefactors should be an act of retribution or the setting of an example to others.*

retrieve *v.* **1** bring *or* °get (back), °fetch, come back with: *Simon trained his dog to retrieve his slippers.* **2** °recover, °save, °rescue, °take back, °recoup, regain, °reclaim: *I tried using a fishing line to retrieve my hat from the lake.* **3** °make up, make °amends for, °recover, °cover, °redeem, °repay, °pay for, °return, °get back, regain, be repaid *or* reimbursed for: *Will we be able to retrieve our losses when we sell the business?*

retrospect *n.* hindsight, reconsideration, °review, remembering, afterthought, °recollection, looking back: *In retrospect, I am not sure we did the right thing.*

return *v.* **1** come *or* °go back, °revert, °turn back: *She is returning to her old habits. I shall return to this subject later if I have time.* **2** come back, reappear, resurface, crop up again, °turn *or* °show up again, put in an °appearance again; °recur, reoccur, *Colloq* pop up again: *Will he return before March? The symptoms returned.* **3** °replace, °put back, °restore, give back, bring *or* carry back: *The missing books have mysteriously been returned.* **4** °exchange, bring back *or* carry back: *You may return any merchandise, for any reason, for refund or exchange, within ten days of its purchase.* **5** °yield, °earn, °gain, °profit, °benefit: *Where else can you find a secure investment that returns more than 15 per cent?* **6** °deliver, °render, °give, °offer, °turn in, proffer, °report: *The jury returned a verdict of Not Guilty.* —*n.* **7** recurrence, reappearance, °repetition, renewal, recrudescence, resurfacing, re-emergence: *There was a return of the symptoms when I stopped taking the medicine.* **8** replacement, replacing, °restoration, restoring, °restitution: *We shall see to the return of the stolen items to their rightful places.* **9** Sometimes, **returns**: °yield, °earnings, °profit, °gain, °benefit, °income, °revenue, °proceeds, °interest, takings, °results: *The return on my investment was almost 100 per cent!* **10** °arrival, advent, coming, home-coming: *A small crowd had gathered to await his return.* **11** reciprocity, reciprocation, repayment, recompense, reimbursement, compensation, °payment, reparation, °indemnity, indemnification, °consideration, °amends, redress, °requital: *If I give you my bike, what will I get in return?*

revamp *v.* °overhaul, redo, recondition, °renovate, °repair, °fix, do up, refit, °refurbish, °restore, °rehabilitate, *US* °fix up: *To bring it into line with the 21st century, the constitution may need to be revamped completely.*

reveal *v.* expose, °display, divulge, °disclose, °show; make known, °let on, °let out, let it be known, let °slip, °communicate, give °vent to, °air, ventilate, °leak (out): *The increasing light of dawn revealed a no-man's-land of utter devastation. The book is said to reveal everything you would prefer not to know about factory-farming.*

revel *v.* **1** Usually, **revel in**: (take) °delight (in), take °pleasure (in), °rejoice (in), °luxuriate (in), bask (in), °wallow (in), °lap up, crow (about *or* over), °glory (in), °savour, °relish: *Gavin revelled in the news that his ex-wife was remarrying and he would no longer have to pay her alimony.* **2** make °merry, °carouse, °celebrate, cut loose, go on a °spree, *Colloq* live it up, °whoop it up, make whoopee, paint the town red, °party, *Brit* push the boat out, *Slang Brit* have a °rave *or* rave-up: *The night after exams finish, the students traditionally revel till dawn.* —*n.* **3** °spree, °party, merrymaking, debauch, °carouse, °festival, °fête *or* fete, carousal, °celebration, °gala, ball, romp, °fling, carnival, °jamboree, bacchanal, saturnalia: *Everyone joined in the revels on New Year's Eve, and had a good time.*

revelation *n.* °news, °information, °proclamation, °publication, °bulletin, communiqué, °announcement, °pronouncement, °declaration, °statement, °leak; °admission, confession; °discovery, unveiling, uncovering, °exposure, disclosure, exposé: *We were shocked at the revelation that they had been married all these years. Scientists' revelations about the depletion of the ozone layer are causing widespread concern.*

revelry *n.* merrymaking, °fun, revelling, carousal, carousing, °gaiety, °festivity, jollity, °mirth, °celebration, ball, high jinks *or* hijinks, °spree, *Colloq* partying, *Slang Brit* rave *or* rave-up: *The revelry went on into the wee hours of the morning.*

revenge *n.* **1** °vengeance, retaliation, °reprisal, °retribution, vindictiveness, spitefulness, repayment, °satisfaction: *They think he set fire to the place in revenge for having been dismissed.* —*v.* **2** avenge, get °even for, take revenge for, make °reprisal for, exact °retribution *or* °payment *or* repayment for: *She was seeking ways to revenge the murder of her brother.* **3** **revenge oneself (on)**: settle a °score *or* an old °score (with), °pay (someone) back in his *or* her own coin, give a Roland for an Oliver, give tit for tat, take an eye for an eye (and a tooth for a tooth), °punish, *Colloq* °get, °get °even (with), give (someone) his *or* her *or* their comeuppance, give (someone) a taste of his *or* her *or* their own medicine: *He found ways to revenge himself on them for all that they had done to him.*

revenue *n.* (gross) °income, °proceeds, °receipts, °return(s), °yield, °interest, takings, net (°income), °gate; °profits, °gain, *Colloq chiefly US* °take: *The revenue from the drugs operation must run into billions.*

revere v. °adore, adulate, °reverence, °venerate, °worship, °idolize, enshrine, °sanctify, beatify, °glorify, °esteem, °admire, °respect, °honour: *He was revered as the founding father of British psychology.*

reverence n. **1** °honour, °respect, °esteem, °admiration, glorification, beatification, sanctification, idolization, °worship, °veneration, adulation, adoration, °homage, fealty, °obeisance, °deference, awe: *Their totalitarian discipline was able to succeed because of the people's reverence for authority.*
—v. **2** See **revere**, above.

reverie n. °day-dream, °fantasy, brown study, wool-gathering, absent-mindedness; meditation, °thought: *I shouldn't disturb Kevin—he's deep in a reverie.*

reversal n. **1** °reverse, °turn-about, turn-round, U-turn, °change, volte-face, (complete) °switch, Brit °about-turn, US about-face: *This represents a reversal of former policy, doesn't it?* **2** See **reverse**, 8, below. **3** annulment, nullification, nulling, °cancellation, revocation, °repeal, rescission: *The present case is an appeal against the reversal of an earlier judgement.*

reverse adj. **1** °opposite, °contrary, inverse, °converse; inverted, upside down, °mirror, reversed, °backward: *Now try turning the wheel in the reverse direction. What appears on the retina is a reverse image, which the brain inverts.*
—v. **2** invert, °overturn, °turn upside down, °turn °topsy-turvy, °turn over, up-end; °exchange, °change, interchange, °transpose: *Using your finger to keep the mercury from running out, reverse the tube in the dish of mercury. Perhaps the car will start if you reverse the leads to the battery.* **3** °overturn, °overthrow, °upset, °set aside, °quash, override, annul, nullify, °vacate, °abandon, °revoke, negate, °veto, declare null and °void, disaffirm, invalidate, °cancel, °repeal, rescind, overrule, countermand, °undo: *The superior tribunal reversed the decision of the lower-court judge.* **4** °alter, °change, °modify; °renounce, °recant, °take back: *Reverse the polarity of the wiring. I reversed my opinion after hearing her sing.* **5** °back up, move or go °backwards or US also °backward, backtrack, Nautical make sternway: *You will be in the right spot if you reverse a yard or two.*
—n. **6** °opposite, °contrary, °converse, antithesis: *Whatever she tells you, I suggest you do the reverse.* **7** °back, °rear, wrong side, verso, underside; flip side, B-side; tail side: *Read what it says on the reverse.* **8** °set-back, °disappointment, °misfortune, °reversal, °mishap, misadventure, °trouble, °problem, °difficulty, °vicissitude, adversity, °defeat; °disaster, °catastrophe, débâcle, °rout, Colloq °washout: *We suffered a temporary reverse or two in business, but we're all right now. United suffered a humiliating reverse against Wanderers in the cup last week.*

revert v. °return, come or °go back, take or pick up again, °lapse, backslide, regress, °relapse, °retreat: *He reverted to his old beliefs about male superiority.*

review v. **1** °survey, °examine, °regard, °look at, °study, con, °consider, °weigh, °inspect, °look over, °scrutinize: *Would you be good enough to review the work of the new employees? She is coming to review the troops this weekend.* **2** re-examine, reconsider, °go over again, °look at or over again, reassess: *Billings*

reviewed once more all the bad things he had done in his lifetime. **3** °criticize, critique, assess, °judge, °evaluate, give one's °opinion of, °comment on or upon, °discuss: *Who reviewed your latest book?*
—n. **4** °criticism, critique, review article, assessment, °judgement, °evaluation, commentary, °study, °comment, °notice: *The play received rave reviews from almost all the critics.* **5** °survey, °examination, °study, °consideration, inspection, °scrutiny, °analysis; reviewing, reading: *After a detailed review of the circumstances, we have decided to let you off easy this time, Finnegan.* **6** re-examination, reconsideration, rehashing or °rehash, °post-mortem, reassessment, rethinking, rethink: *Why do you always insist on a review of all the bidding on every hand, whenever we play bridge?* **7** °periodical, °journal, °magazine: *Have you read Stonehouse's article in the latest Birmingham Review?* **8** °parade, °procession, array, cavalcade, °march past, fly-past or chiefly US flyover: *A great naval review was held at Spithead.*

revise v. **1** °edit, emend, °improve, °correct, °rectify, °modify, °revamp, redact, rework, °overhaul, update; rewrite: *A revised edition of the dictionary has been published every ten years.* **2** °alter, °change, °amend: *Since hearing him sing, I have been forced to revise my taste in music.*

revision n. editing, revising, emendation, °improvement, °correction, rectification, modification, revamping, reappraisal, re-examination, reinterpretation, reassessment, redaction, reworking, °overhaul, overhauling, updating, update; rewrite, °edition, °version, °rendition: *Her revision of the text is based on a newly discovered manuscript. The fourth revision will be available next April.*

revival n. **1** resurrection, resuscitation, renewal, °restoration, revitalization, resurfacing, °return, returning: *How much more often we see the revival of out-moded fashions than the introduction of new ideas!* **2** °rebirth, °renaissance or renascence, °resurgence, awakening, quickening, reanimation: *Do you regard the current trend towards fundamentalism as a genuine revival of religion?* **3** °recovery, °improvement, °increase, upsurge, upturn, °boost, upswing, °advance, advancement, °progress, °rise, escalation, Colloq pick-up, comeback: *This week saw a revival in the metals market.*

revive v. **1** (re)awaken, °wake (up), come or °bring (a)round, waken, resuscitate; °recover, (re)gain consciousness: *Dashing cold water in his face revived him at once. I revived to find her leaning over me.* **2** reawaken, °stir up again, °renew, resume, reopen, °refresh: *You can blame Andy for reviving the feud between our families.* **3** bring back, reactivate, °renew, °resurrect, re-establish, resume, reopen, revitalize, breathe life into, reinvigorate, °rejuvenate: *Perhaps we ought to revive the practice of putting hooligans, vandals, and delinquents into stocks in the market square.*

revoke v. °cancel, °deny, invalidate, annul, declare null and °void, °void, nullify, negate, °repudiate, °renounce, rescind, °repeal, °recall, °recant, °quash, °veto, °set aside, abrogate, °abolish, °withdraw, °take back, °retract: *He warned that if they refused to comply with local authority rulings he had the power to revoke their licence.*

revolt *n.* **1** °rebellion, °revolution, °uprising, °mutiny, insurrection, *coup d'état*, putsch, take-over: *The council ordered the secret police to suppress the revolt.*
—*v.* **2** °rebel, °rise up, °mutiny; °protest, dissent: *After years of oppression, the people revolted and deposed their leaders.* **3** °repel, °offend, °disgust, °shock, °horrify, °repulse, °nauseate, °sicken: *I was revolted by the poverty and sickness I saw in that country.*

revolting *adj.* °disgusting, sickening, nauseating, °nauseous, stomach-turning, stomach-churning, vomit-provoking, sick-making, °foul, °loathsome, °abhorrent, horrid, °horrible, °nasty, °vile, °obnoxious, °repulsive, appalling, °abominable, °repellent, °offensive, objectionable, off-putting, °beastly, °gross, °rotten, °rancid, inedible, °disagreeable, unpleasant, *Slang* icky, °yucky: *Rick served up some revolting mess for dinner and then took offence when we didn't eat it.*

revolution *n.* **1** °mutiny, °revolt, °rebellion, coup, *coup d'état*, °uprising, insurgency, insurrection, putsch, take-over, °overthrow: *If the government fails to ensure that the people have food, there will be a revolution.* **2** °upheaval, cataclysm, °transformation, (°drastic *or* radical *or* major) °change, sea °change, metamorphosis: *Recent successes of capitalism have sparked a revolution in the political philosophies of communist nations.* **3** rotation, °turn, °orbit, °circuit, °spin, °lap, °round, °cycle, °circle, gyration; °wheel, whirl, °pirouette: *At each revolution of the gear (A), the ratchet (B) moves one notch. The rapid revolutions of the ice-skater dissolved her into a blur of colour.*

revolutionary *adj.* **1** °mutinous, °rebellious, insurgent, insurrectionist, insurrectionary, °radical, °rebel, °seditious; °subversive: *They had dreamed for years of the revolutionary overthrow of the government.* **2** °novel, innovative, °creative, °new, °different, °original, °avant-garde: *The firm hopes that its revolutionary new product will make a clean sweep in the market-place.*
—*n.* **3** °rebel, mutineer, insurgent, insurrectionist, insurrectionary, revolutionist, sansculotte *or* sansculottist, anarchist, °radical, extremist, °terrorist: *In his younger days at university, Charles fancied himself a revolutionary, without quite knowing what he might rebel against.*

revolve *v.* **1** °spin, °turn, °pivot, °rotate, °gyrate, whirl, °twirl, °reel, °wheel, °go (a)round, °circle, °cycle, °orbit; °swivel: *As the earth revolves on its axis, the moon revolves round the earth.* **2** °turn, °depend, °pivot, °rely: *His decision to buy a new car revolves on his finances.* **3** °turn over (in one's mind), °ponder, °weigh, °consider, °meditate upon *or* on, °think about, °reflect upon *or* on, ruminate over *or* on, °chew over, °contemplate: *I have been revolving in my mind your most attractive proposal, but I regret I must turn it down.*

revolver *n.* °pistol, gun, side-arm, firearm, *Chiefly US and Canadian* handgun, *Colloq US* six-gun, six-shooter, *Slang US* rod, gat, roscoe, piece, Saturday-night special, shooting-iron: *How do you explain the fact that your fingerprints were found on the revolver with which she was shot?*

revulsion *n.* °loathing, detestation, °disgust, repugnance, abomination, abhorrence,

°aversion, hatred, antipathy, odium, execration: *I cannot describe the revulsion I felt at seeing those elephants slaughtered for their ivory.*

reward *n.* **1** °award, °favour, recompense, compensation, °return, °payment, °pay, °requital: *For your good deeds you will have to seek your reward in heaven; dishonesty is recompensed here on earth.* **2** °prize, °award, °tribute, °honour, *Literary* guerdon: *The Victoria Cross was instituted as a reward for military valour in 1856.* **3** °retribution, °punishment, just °deserts, *Colloq* comeuppance: *Hanging was the reward of treason.*
—*v.* **4** recompense, °compensate, °pay, °repay, remunerate, redress, °requite, (some-thing *or* it) worth someone's while: *Only if they reward him will Fuller give information leading to the capture of the thief.*

rewarding *adj.* °satisfying, gratifying, °worthwhile, enriching, enriched, °fruitful; °profitable, °advantageous, °productive, °gainful: *Laurence says that his most rewarding experience has been seeing his children again.*

reword *v.* °paraphrase, rephrase, put into different words, put another way, express differently, °revise, recast, rewrite: *Perhaps if you reworded your request in politer terms it might get more sympathetic consideration.*

rhapsodic *adj.* rhapsodical, °ecstatic, °enthusiastic, °elated, °overjoyed, °effusive, °rapturous, thrilled, blissful, transported, orgasmic, intoxicated, euphoric, walking on air, °delighted, °happy as a sandboy, °happy as a pig in clover, (sitting) on top of the °world, *Brit* in the seventh °heaven, *US* in seventh °heaven, °happy as a cow in clover, *Taboo slang US* °happy as a pig in shit: *What kind of society have we that is scornful of intellect and rhapsodic about celebrities?*

rhetoric *n.* **1** eloquence, expressiveness, elocution, way with words, *Colloq* gift of the gab: *His rhetoric, though it defied analysis, exactly reflected the emotions of the Labour movement.* **2** °bombast, °bluster, fustian, rodomontade, grandiloquence, magniloquence, °oratory, windiness, high-flown poppycock, wordiness, sesquipedality, verbosity, prolixity, long-windedness, turgidity, flatulence, gasconade, *Colloq* °hot air, puffery: *Her threats are mere rhetoric and I refuse to take notice of them.*

rhetorical *adj.* **1** stylistic, linguistic, °poetic, °expressive, oratorical: *Zeugma, hysteron proteron, and anacoluthon are all terms for rhetorical devices.* **2** °artificial, contrived, for °effect, unanswerable, not °literal: *The question, 'Why don't you drop dead', was purely rhetorical.* **3** °pretentious, °bombastic, °flamboyant, °extravagant, florid, fustian, high-flown, °inflated, °grandiose, euphuistic, turgid, grandiloquent, magniloquent, long-winded, °windy, orotund, °wordy, prolix, sesquipedalian, *Colloq* highfalutin *or* hifalutin: *The rhetorical style of Crampton's parliamentary speeches appear to be doing the party more harm than good.*

rhyme *n.* **1** rime, °poem, °poetry, verse, versification, metrical composition, °song: *The art of rhyme may well be coincident with the earliest stages of language.* **2 rhyme or reason**: (common) °sense, °logic, °intelligence, °meaning, °wisdom, rationality, °rationale, soundness, °organization, °structure: *There appears to be no rhyme or reason behind the bombing of the library.*

rhythm *n.* °tempo, °beat, °cadence *or* cadency, throb, throbbing, °accent, accentuation, °time, timing, °stress *or* rhythmic(al) pattern, °measure, metre, °pulse, lilt, *Music* downbeat, thesis, upbeat, arsis: *The song is in samba rhythm.*

rhythmic *adj.* rhythmical, °measured, cadenced, throbbing, pulsing, pulsating, °regular, °steady, beating: *The rhythmic sound of the waves soon sent me to sleep.*

ribaldry *n.* °vulgarity, immodesty, °indelicacy, indecency, coarseness, bawdiness, earthiness, wantonness, raciness, naughtiness, shamelessness, lustfulness, rakishness, rascality, dissoluteness, lubricity, lasciviousness, looseness, scurrility *or* scurrilousness, lewdness, salaciousness, licentiousness, grossness, offensiveness, rankness, rudeness, smuttiness, smut, °dirt, °filth, foulness, obscenity: *The ribaldry of some of Chaucer's tales makes them not altogether suitable for schoolchildren.*

rich *adj.* **1** °wealthy, affluent, °prosperous, well-to-do, °well off, well provided for, °opulent, moneyed, in clover, on velvet, *Colloq* °flush, °loaded, on Easy Street, rolling in it *or* °money *or* °wealth, in the chips *or* the dough *or* the °money, well-heeled, *US* well-fixed: *A year ago Montmorency was a rich man, but that was before Blue Thursday on the Stock Exchange.* **2** Sometimes, **rich in**: °abundant (in), overflowing (with), °fertile (in), fecund (in), °productive (of), copious (in), abounding in, well supplied (with), well stocked (with), rife (with), °replete (with), °profuse (in *or* with): *The rich prairie land was soon yielding abundant harvests. The surrounding mountains were rich in minerals of all kinds.* **3** valuable, °precious, °invaluable, °priceless: *For centuries the islanders have enjoyed the rich bounty of the seas. The thieves who broke into the vaults got a rich haul.* **4** costly, °expensive, °dear, valuable, °invaluable, °precious, °priceless, °lavish, °sumptuous, °lush, °luxurious, °palatial, °elaborate, °splendid, °exquisite, °superb, °elegant: *The caravans returned laden with rich treasures of the Orient—silks, jewels, spices, rare woods, and other luxuries.* **5** °intense, °dark, °deep, °warm, vibrant, °strong, °lustrous: *At the rajah's court the rich colours of the carpets and hangings dazzle the eye.* **6** °fat, fattening, °heavy, creamy, °succulent, °savoury, mouth-watering, °luscious, sapid, °delicious: *When Vicky complained that her sweet was too rich, Arthur ate hers, too.* **7** °mellow, mellifluous, °resonant, sonorous, °full: *Edgar's rich basso filled the cavernous amphitheatre.* **8** °aromatic, ambrosial, °savoury, °fragrant, °redolent, °pungent, °strong: *The house was filled with the rich odour of freshly made coffee.* **9** °productive, °plentiful, °abundant, °ample, °bountiful, °prolific, °fruitful, °fertile, fecund, copious, °profitable, °potent: *The letters proved a rich source of intimate details about their private life.* **10** laughable, °funny, °hilarious, °comic(al), °humorous, amusing, *Colloq* side-splitting: *He had many rich anecdotes to relate about the practical jokes they used to play on one another.* **11** °ridiculous, °preposterous, °outlandish, °ludicrous, °absurd, °nonsensical: *One particularly rich episode involved a chimpanzee.*

riches *n.pl.* °wealth, affluence, opulence, °plenty, °prosperity, °abundance, °fortune,

°means, °resources; lucre, pelf: *It was rumoured that the family had acquired its apparently endless riches in the slave trade, in the 18th century.*

richly *adv.* **1** sumptuously, lavishly, luxuriously, splendidly, elaborately, exquisitely, elegantly, superbly: *The flat was richly appointed with Chinese antiques, thick oriental carpets, and silk hangings.* **2** °well, °thoroughly, °amply, fully, °appropriately, fittingly, condignly: *Shirley's work was at last given the recognition it so richly deserved.*

rickety *adj.* wobbly, unsteady, broken-down, °decrepit, °shaky, tottering, teetering, °ramshackle, °flimsy, °frail, °precarious, °dilapidated, in °disrepair, °tumbledown, insecure: *Don't put such a heavy lamp on that rickety table!*

rid *v.* **1 rid of**: °deliver from, °relieve of, °free from *or* of, °rescue, °save: *What can we do to rid ourselves of that appalling smell?* **2 be** *or* **get rid of**: °banish, °exile, °eject, °expel, °dispose of, °throw out *or* away, °eliminate, °dispense with; °refuse, °reject, °dismiss, shrug off: *If she had wanted to be rid of him, she would have divorced him long ago. I am having a spot of bother trying to get rid of my old car: nobody wants to buy it.*

-ridden *adj.* afflicted *or* harassed *or* °affected *or* dominated by, infected *or* infested with: *They were shocked when they first came to this drought-ridden province of Northern Ethiopia. Only foreign aid can salvage the debt-ridden economy of this state.*

riddle¹ *n.* conundrum, °puzzle, °enigma, poser, °question, °mystery, °problem, brain-teaser *or Brit* brain-twister: *The cracker contained a whistle, paper hat, and the inevitable riddle.*

riddle² *v.* **1** °perforate, °pepper, °puncture, °pierce, honeycomb: *The back of the bookcase was riddled with tiny worm-holes.* **2** °penetrate, °infest, infect, pervade, °permeate, °fill, °spread: *An investigation revealed that the entire department was riddled with corruption.* —*n.* **3** sieve, colander *or* cullender, strainer, °grating, °screen, sifter, °filter: *He shovelled the dirt through the riddle to sift out the larger stones.*

ride *v.* **1** °sit on *or* in, °travel *or* °journey *or* °go *or* °proceed on *or* in, be borne *or* carried *or* conveyed (on *or* in), °take; °propel *or* °control *or* °drive (a horse *or* a bicycle *or* a motor cycle): *They ride the bus to work each day. The film began with a witch riding a broomstick. Do you know how to ride a motor bike?* **2** °float, °lie: *The yacht is riding at anchor off Portsmouth.* **3** °tyrannize, terrorize, °intimidate, °dominate, °oppress; °bully, °rag, harry, °harass, hector, °nag, °provoke, °heckle, badger, °plague, °pester, °annoy, °irritate, *Colloq* hassle: *He has been ridden by obsessive ambition all his life.* —*n.* **4** °drive, °journey, °trip, °excursion, °tour, jaunt, °outing, °expedition, *Colloq* °spin: *Let's go for a ride in the country!* **5 take for a ride**: **a** delude, °swindle, °trick, °deceive, °defraud, humbug, gull, °take in, °cheat, bamboozle: *Those tricksters with the loaded dice certainly took Charlie for a ride last night!* **b** (°kidnap and) °murder *or* °kill *or* °execute *or* do in, *Slang* °bump off, *US* (°snatch and) °rub out *or* °waste: *They said that if he identified them, they would take him for a ride.*

ridge *n.* °crest, °line, °strip, °top edge, areote: *The mountain ridge was partly obscured by clouds.*

ridicule *n.* **1** °derision, deriding, °jeer, jeering, °taunt, taunting, °mockery, mocking, °gibe *or* jibe, gibing or jibing, °raillery, *Colloq* ribbing, *US and Canadian* razzing, joshing: *Nick was often subjected to ridicule because of his outlandish clothes.* —*v.* **2** °deride, °jeer at, °taunt, °tease, °mock, °gibe or jibe, °guy, °chaff, °laugh at, °caricature, °poke °fun at, make °fun or °sport of, °lampoon, °burlesque, travesty, °parody, make a laughing-stock (of), *Colloq* rib, roast, *Brit* °send up, take the mickey out of, *US and Canadian* razz, josh: *In a democracy, it is an inalienable right of the people to ridicule their leaders and government.*

ridiculous *adj.* °absurd, laughable, °preposterous, °weird, comical, °funny, °humorous, °ludicrous, °farcical, droll, amusing, mirthful, °hilarious, side-splitting, risible; °silly, °inane, °nonsensical, °foolish, °stupid, °outlandish, °bizarre, °grotesque, °queer, °crazy, °insane, °zany, °wild, *Slang* far-out: *You look absolutely ridiculous in that outfit! Where did she ever get the ridiculous notion that she would marry a prince?*

riff-raff *n.* °rabble, hoi polloi, ragtag and bobtail, scum, *canaille*, masses, °dregs (of society), *Colloq* great °unwashed: *I am shocked that you continue your membership in a club to which riff-raff like Barnes belong.*

rifle *v.* **1** °rob, °loot, °ransack, °plunder, despoil, burgle, °pillage, *US* burglarize: *We caught the man who had rifled the till.* **2** °search, °ransack, °go through, °rummage through: *She rifled through the files till the will was found.*

rift *n.* **1** °separation, °break, °split, °schism, cleft, °gulf, °gap; °disagreement, °conflict, disruption, °difference, °breach, break-up, °division, °distance, alienation: *The continued bitterness served only to intensify the rift between them.* **2** °tear, °rent, °opening, °hole, °crack, °chink, °crevice, cleavage, °fracture, °flaw, °fault: *Water was pouring through an ever-widening rift in the dam.*

rig *v.* **1** Often, **rig out** or **up**: °fit (out or up), °equip, °set up, °outfit, °supply, °provision, accoutre or *US also* accouter, caparison, *Chiefly Brit* °kit out: *Good Sports was the shop that rigged us out completely for our Himalayan climbing expedition.* **2** °falsify, °manipulate, °doctor, °juggle, °fix, °tamper with, °fake, *Colloq* °fiddle (with), cook: *The accountants rigged the books to make the company appear profitable enough to merit a bank loan.* —*n.* **3** °equipment, equipage, °gear, °tackle, °apparatus, °outfit, °kit, accoutrements or *US also* accouterments, °paraphernalia, appurtenances, *Colloq* °things, °stuff: *It cost a fortune to transport his diving rig by plane.*

right *adj.* **1** °just, °moral, °good, °proper, °correct, °legal, °lawful, licit, °honest, °upright, °righteous, °virtuous, °ethical, °fair, °true, °honourable, right-minded, °principled, °open, °above-board: *There is no doubt in my mind that Simon can be relied on to do the right thing.* **2** °correct, °fitting, °suitable, °proper, °accurate, °exact, °precise, °perfect; °factual, °truthful, veracious, valid, °sound, *Colloq Brit* bang on: *Have you bought the right kind of nail to go into plaster? Jennie had nine right answers out of ten. How many of yours are right?* **3** °propitious, °convenient, °strategic, °advantageous, °beneficial, °favourable, auspicious, preferred, preferable, °promising: *I waited for the right moment to ask his*

advice. **4** °sound, °sane, °normal, °rational, lucid, °healthy: *Is she right in the head, letting him drive in his condition?* **5** right-hand, dextral, dexter, *Nautical* starboard: *In the United Kingdom, drivers sit on the right side.* **6** rightist, right-wing, °conservative, °reactionary, Tory: *The right wing of the liberal party is not so very different from the left wing of the conservatives.* **7** °face, °upper, °principal, °front: *Have you laid the tablecloth right side up?* **8** utter, °complete, °perfect, °unmitigated, unalloyed, °out-and-out, °thorough, thoroughgoing, 24-carat or *esp. US* 24-karat, dyed in the wool, °pure, °absolute, °real, *Brit* °proper: *I've been a right idiot not to realize that he loved only her.* —*n.* **9** °privilege, °prerogative, °licence, °power, °claim, °title, °freedom, °liberty: *We must allow nothing to interfere with our democratic rights, such as our right to vote.* **10** °justice, °reason, °fact, °truth, fairness, °equity, °good, goodness, °integrity, °virtue, virtuousness, °honesty, honourableness, °morality, °propriety, °rectitude, right-mindedness, high-mindedness, °nobility, uprightness: *He believes that he has right on his side.* **11** right side or hand or fist, *Nautical* starboard: *She stood on his right. She gave him a quick right to the jaw.* **12 by rights**: °properly, °fairly, justly, to be °just, to be °fair, in fairness, °honestly, in all °honesty, to be °honest: *By rights, because I paid for it, the house is mine.* —*adv.* **13** °directly, °straight, straight away, right away or off, in a beeline, as the crow flies, forthwith; unhesitatingly, °immediately, °promptly, at °once, instantly, without hesitating or hesitation, without °delay, °quickly, °swiftly, speedily, *Colloq* pronto, °straight off: *The minute he walked into the room, he went right to the wall-safe. Please come over right now.* **14** °exactly, °precisely, unerringly, accurately; °just: *She hung the paintings right where they belonged.* **15** °just, °only: *I stopped right now—when you walked in.* **16** °well, satisfactorily, advantageously, profitably, °favourably, opportunely: *I hope that everything turns out right for you.* **17** correctly, accurately, °properly, °precisely, °well, sensibly, fittingly, suitably, aptly: *If you can't do it right, why bother doing it at all!* —*v.* **18** °straighten (up or out), set °upright or aright: *I righted all the chairs the children had knocked over.* **19** put or set or make right, put or set to rights, °correct, °straighten out, redress, °amend, °make up for, °rectify, °sort out, °repair, °fix: *She has always felt that her mission in life was to right wrongs.* **20** avenge, °retaliate for, °vindicate, °repay, °revenge, °settle, *Colloq* get °even for: *Langdon swore that he would right the injury done to his father's name.*

righteous *adj.* **1** °moral, °just, °virtuous, upstanding, °upright, °good, °honest, °ethical, °honourable, °fair, °reputable, °trustworthy: *He insists that his father was a righteous man who had been unjustly accused.* **2** °right, °correct, justifiable, justified, °appropriate, condign, °fitting, apt, °self-righteous: *Her righteous indignation at being criticized stems from her overweening pride.*

rightful *adj.* **1** °legal, °lawful, °legitimate, licit, de jure, °correct, °proper, bona fide, valid, °true, authorized, °right: *If the deed is in his name, then he is the rightful owner.* **2** °just, °fair, °equitable, °right: *Emily has supported rightful causes all her life.*

rigid adj. **1** °stiff, unbending, unbendable, °firm, °hard, °strong: *Are those brackets rigid enough to support such a heavy shelf?* **2** °inflexible, inelastic, unyielding, undeviating, unalterable, °set, °firm, °hard, adamant, hard-line, unbending, adamantine, °steely, iron, °strong, uncompromising, unrelenting, intransigent, stringent, °severe, °strict, rigorous, °stern, °harsh, austere: *Frank is known to favour rigid discipline in the classroom.* **3** rigorous, °exact, °precise, unwavering, °unqualified, unswerving, undeviating, °demanding, °strict, °hard and °fast, °literal, °nice, °close, °thorough, °scrupulous, °careful, °conscientious, °painstaking, °meticulous, punctilious, °exacting, °strait-laced: *Rigid observance of the regulations produced the desired results. Pinwell's rigid parsimony met with little favour from his family.* **4** °obstinate, °stubborn, pigheaded, °inflexible, °immovable, adamant, adamantine, °fixed, °set, obdurate, °wilful, headstrong, dogged, persevering, °determined, °resolute, °steadfast, resolved, °tenacious, °relentless, unrelenting, uncompromising, unadaptable, mulish, close-minded: *Candida remained rigid in her opposition to birth control.*

rigmarole n. rigamarole, motions, °complication(s), formalities, red tape, °bureaucracy, punctilio; ceremoniousness, °ceremony, °ritual, °procedure, °mess, °mumbo-jumbo, °gobbledegook or gobbledygook, bunkum or buncombe, °bother, balderdash, °rubbish, °nonsense, foolishness, *Colloq* hassle, bunk, *Slang* crap, *US* meshugaas or mishegaas: *Why must one go through such a rigmarole just to get a driving licence?*

rigour n. **1** Usually, **rigours**: °severity, harshness, °hardship, inhospitableness, bleakness, inclemency or inclementness, °bitterness, °cold: *I am not sure that my grandmother can endure the rigours of another Scottish winter.* **2** strictness, rigidity, °precision, preciseness, punctilio, literalness, exactness, meticulousness, stringency, inflexibility, rigorism, harshness, °severity, °hardship, asperity, austerity, sternness: *If you work with radioactive materials, safety regulations must be observed with rigour. The rigour of monastic life has toughened him over the years.*

rim n. °edge, °brim, lip, °border, °periphery, °perimeter: *To make a margarita, you first coat the rim of a cocktail glass with coarse salt.*

rind n. °peel, °skin, husk: *Cut the thin outer part of the rind of a lemon into thin strips and soak them in brandy.*

ring[1] n. **1** °loop, hoop, °band, °circle, ringlet, circlet, annulus, grommet, eyelet, quoit, noose, cincture, °belt, girdle, cestus, °border, °halo, aureole, nimbus, corona, cuff, collar, necklace, neckband, bandeau, fillet, bracelet, armlet, torque or torc, °crown, coronet, tiara, diadem, (laurel-)wreath, °garland, *Mechanics* gland, bearing, *US and Canadian* bushing or *Brit also* bush, washer, O-ring, *Nautical* thimble, *Architecture and heraldry* annulet, *Literary* roundlet, *Anatomy* cingulum: *The rings brought up from the wreck of the ancient Greek trading vessel are worth a great deal.* **2** rink, °enclosure, arena, circus, bullring, *Spanish* plaza de toros, boxing ring: *I would no sooner get into the ring with him than with a bull!* **3** °circle, °organization, °gang, °band, °pack, °cell, °team, °crew, confederacy, confederation, °combination, cartel, °mob, bloc, coterie, °set,

°clan, °clique, °fraternity, °brotherhood, sorority, sisterhood, guild, (secret) °society, °junta or junto, °cabal, °faction, °group, °league, °alliance, °federation, coalition, °union, affiliation, camorra, camarilla, Bund: *She was running an international ring of jewel thieves who worked only in the most exclusive resorts.*
—v. **4** °encircle, °surround, °bind, gird, girt, °circle; °loop, compass, °envelop, encompass, °embrace: *The swimming-pool is ringed with dense shrubbery. After the vase is fired, I intend to ring the base with a gold band.*

ring[2] v. **1** °peal, °chime, °toll, knell, tintinnabulate, ding-dong, gong, °sound, resonate, °resound, °echo, re-echo, reverberate; clang, °jangle; tinkle, clink, °jingle, ding-a-ling, ring-a-ding-ding, *Archaic or dialect* knoll: *The bells rang out their joyous announcement of peace on earth.* **2** °telephone, ring up, phone, °call, give (someone) a ring, *Colloq* (give someone) a °buzz, give (someone) a tinkle, °get (someone) on the blower or horn, *US* (give someone) a jingle: *I'll ring you when I am next in town.*
—n. **3** ringing, °peal, pealing, °chime, chiming, °toll, tolling, tintinnabulation, knell, sounding, resonating, °echo, echoing, re-echo, re-echoing, reverberation, reverberating; clang, clanging, °jangle, jangling; tinkle, tinkling, clink, clinking, °jingle, jingling, ding-a-ling, ring-a-ding-ding, *Archaic or dialect* knoll: *I couldn't hear the ring at the door because the water was running.* **4** (telephone or phone) °call, *Colloq* °buzz, tinkle, *US* jingle: *Don't forget to give your mother a ring on Sunday.*

rinse v. **1** °wash (out or off), °wash up, °clean, °cleanse, bathe, °drench, °flood, °flush, irrigate, *Chiefly Brit* °swill (out), *Literary* lave: *Use plenty of fresh water to rinse all the soap out of the clothes.* **2** °tint, dye, °touch up, highlight: *The hairdresser rinsed a little blue into Martine's greying hair.*
—n. **3** rinsing, °wash, washing, bath, bathing, cleaning, cleansing, ablution, drenching, °flood, flushing, irrigation, *Medicine* lavage, *Literary* laving: *The softening agent should be added in the final rinse.* **4** °tint, dye: *I had no idea that she used a rinse—I thought her hair was naturally reddish.*

riot n. **1** rioting, °riotous behaviour, °disturbance, °uproar, °tumult, turmoil, (civil) °disorder, lawlessness, hubbub, °rumpus, turbulence, °fracas, °fray, affray, mêlée or melee, °pandemonium, Donnybrook, °brawl, °row, °unrest, commotion, °bother, imbroglio, °outburst, anarchy, disruption, °violence, °strife, *Colloq* ruckus, ruction, to-do, do, *Brit* bovver, punch-up: *The government is unable to quell the food riots, which have become more frequent and more violent.* **2** °funny man or woman, °comedian or comedienne, °hilarious event or bit or shtick or thing or piece of business, *Colloq* gas, *US* °panic, laugh-riot: *Benny's closing routine with the model is an absolute riot.*
—v. **3** mount the barricades, take to the streets, °rebel, °revolt, create or cause a °disturbance, °brawl, °fight, (go on the or US also a) °rampage, run riot, °storm: *The prisoners rioted to protest against the crowded conditions.*

riotous adj. **1** °tumultuous, unrestrained, °wild, °noisy, °uncontrolled, uncontrollable, unmanageable, °chaotic, °disorderly, disordered,

°lawless, turbulent, °violent, brawling, °obstreperous: *The headmaster warned that he would not tolerate such riotous behaviour.* **2** °rowdy, °boisterous, °unruly, °uproarious, rollicking, roisterous, °wild, rumbustious, unrestrained, °uninhibited, *Archaic* robustious, *Colloq* rambunctious, no-holds-barred: *Bernard's retirement party was certainly a riotous affair.*

rip v. **1** °tear (apart *or* asunder), °rend, be torn or rent, °split, °cut (apart): *I ripped my trousers on that nail. The paper ripped because you yanked it out of my hand.* **2 rip off: a** °steal, purloin, °rob, °snatch, °pilfer, filch, °take, shoplift, *Colloq* °pinch, *Brit* °nick, *Slang* °lift, °swipe, *US* boost, promote: *They broke into my car and ripped off my tape deck.* **b** °cheat, °swindle, °trick, °fleece, bilk, °dupe, °deceive; °defraud, °embezzle, *Colloq* con, bamboozle, *Slang* skin, gyp, rook: *A smooth couple got £100 by using the old 'stuffed wallet' trick to rip me off.*
—n. **3** °tear, °rent, °split, °gash, °slash; °rift, cleft, °rupture: *The vandals tore a foot-long rip in the top of my new convertible.*

ripe adj. **1** °mature, matured, °seasoned, (fully) grown, (well-)ripened, developed, °mellow, °ready, °fit, *US* (fully) °aged, well-aged: *The grapes are ripe for picking.* **2** °prepared, °ready, °fit, °appropriate, °experienced, °veteran, °seasoned, °sage, °wise, °sophisticated, °mature, °informed, °qualified, dependable, °reliable: *Henry is ripe in judgement and understanding.*
3 ripe for: a °timely, °opportune, °propitious, °favourable, auspicious, °ideal, °right, °suitable, apt, °proper, suitably advanced: *Is the time yet ripe for another revival of Heartbreak House?* **b** °ready, °eager, °enthusiastic, °prepared, °fit, in °readiness: *The mob is ripe for revolt.*

ripen v. °develop, °mature, °age, °season, maturate, bring *or* come to °maturity; °perfect: *The peaches need another day to ripen.*

rip-off n. **1** °stealing, purloining, robbing, pilfering, °taking, filching, pilferage, °theft, °robbery, larceny; shoplifting, *Colloq* pinching, *Brit* nicking, *Slang* lifting, swiping, *US* boosting: *The rip-off of books from the library is a disgrace.* **2** °swindle, confidence °trick, swindling, cheating, °cheat, °fraud, °deception, defrauding, defalcation; °embezzlement, *Colloq* con (°job *or* °trick): *A husband-and-wife team are being sought for executing a rip-off of thousands from the Outland Bank using a forged letter of credit.* **3** overcharging, exploitation, *Colloq* highway *or* chiefly *Brit* daylight °robbery: *It's a rip-off to charge two pounds for something that costs only three pence to make.*

ripping adj. fine, splendid, marvellous, excellent, exciting, thrilling, stirring, spine-tingling: *Buchan and Henty and Haggard all wrote ripping adventure novels.*

ripple n. **1** wavelet, °wave, °ruffle, ruffling, cat's-paw, purl, purling, undulation, *US* riffle, riffling: *There wasn't even the slightest breath of air to cause a ripple on the mirror-like surface of the lake.* **2** (slight) °disturbance, °upset, perturbation, °agitation, °flurry, °flutter, °suggestion, °hint, soupçon: *The divorce occasioned only a ripple of dissent in the royal family.*
—v. **3** °ruffle, purl, undulate, °wave; °splash, °wash, *US* riffle: *I sat musing, watching the water ripple over the stones in the brook.*

rise v. **1** °get up, °arise, °stand (up), °get to one's feet, *Brit* be upstanding: *All rise when the judge enters the court.* **2** °get up, °arise, °awaken, waken, °wake up, start *or* begin the day, *Nautical or colloq* hit the deck, *Colloq* turn out: *We usually rise at about six o'clock.* **3** ascend, be °elevated, °arise, °climb, °lift, °go up, °mount: *The smoke slowly, almost furtively, rose from the camp-fire into the still night air. The morning star can be seen tomorrow rising in the sky just before dawn. Some of those skyscrapers rise to a height of 110 storeys.* **4** Often, **rise (up) (against)**: °rebel, °revolt, °mutiny, kick over the traces, take up arms, mount the barricades, take to the streets: *If the food shortages persist, the people are sure to rise up and overthrow the present regime.* **5** °swell, °flood, °increase, °grow; wax: *Owing to the heavy rains, the river is rising rapidly.* **6** °slant *or* °incline *or* °slope (upwards), ascend, °climb, go uphill: *The path rises steeply just beyond the cwm.* **7** °fly, take °flight, take wing, take to the air, °take off, °arise, °lift, °climb, °soar, °mount: *At the roar of the gun, tens of thousands of flamingos rose from the lakes.* **8** °advance, °improve one's lot *or* position, °progress, °get °ahead, go *or* get somewhere, °succeed, make something of oneself, be promoted, °prosper, °thrive, °make good, *Colloq* °make it, °make the °grade, go places: *Fielding could well have risen in the company had his attitude been different.* **9** °start, °begin, °originate, °arise, °occur, °happen, take °place: *I cannot explain how so much bad feeling rose between us.* **10** °increase, be °elevated *or* lifted *or* boosted, °grow, °go up, move upwards, °climb, escalate, ascend, snowball: *When interest rates rise, they contribute to the inflation that raising them was supposed to reduce.* **11** °arise, be nurtured, be produced, be generated, be created, °spring up, be engendered: *The feelings that rose within him were spurred on by sheer hatred of the man.* **12 rise to: a** °arise, come up, °meet, be °equal to, prove °adequate to: *If you need a good man, you can count on Michael to rise to the occasion.* **b** come *to* get, °take, °swallow, °react to, °respond to, °succumb to, be tempted by: *Sue rose to the bait of a company car and accepted our offer.*
—n. **13** ascent, °hill, hillock, °knoll, eminence, °prominence, °elevation, upland, highland, (upward) °slope *or* °incline, acclivity, *US* upgrade: *As we climbed a slight rise, we saw the mountains gleaming in the distance.* **14** °increase, °increment, °gain, °addition: *In return for only a slight rise in wages, they are being asked to take on much more responsibility.* **15** ascent, ascension, °elevation, °flight, °climb, °take-off: *The balloon's rise was suddenly halted when the basket caught in a tree.* **16 get** *or Brit also* **take a rise out of (someone)**: °provoke, °stimulate, °incite, instigate, °foment, goad, °encourage, °press, °push, °shake up, waken, °awaken, °move, °motivate, °activate, °agitate, °stir (up), °inflame, impassion: *We finally got a rise out of Sidney by threatening to charge him for cleaning his room.* **17 give rise to**: °start, engender, °generate, °begin, °commence, °produce, °bring out, °cause, °bring about, bring into being: *We never discovered what gave rise to Tom's dislike of dogs.*

risk n. **1** °danger, °peril, °jeopardy, °hazard, °chance, °gamble: *I would take up skydiving, but my mother won't let me because of the risk.*

—v. **2** °endanger, imperil, °jeopardize, °hazard, °chance, °gamble: *Would you really risk all your money on one roll of the dice?*

risky *adj.* °dangerous, °perilous, °hazardous, chancy, touch-and-go, °precarious, *Colloq* iffy, °dicey, °dodgy, °touchy: *Futures trading is a very risky business, as many have discovered to their dismay.*

risqué *adj.* indelicate, °unrefined, indecorous, °indecent, °improper, °broad, °naughty, °spicy, salty, °off colour, °racy, °bawdy, °erotic, °suggestive, °wicked, °blue, ribald, °daring, salacious, °gross, *Colloq Brit* near the knuckle: *Some of those photographs of beauty contest queens are pretty risqué.*

rite *n.* °ceremony, °ritual, °ceremonial, °observance, °formality, °custom, °practice, °routine, °procedure, °solemnity, solemnization, liturgy: *This weekend I have to perform the annual rite of having tea with great-aunt Elizabeth at the Ritz.*

ritual *adj.* **1** °ceremonial, °ceremonious, sacramental: *The celebrants undergo ritual washing before preparing the sacrifice.* **2** procedural, °formal, °conventional, °customary, °habitual, °routine, prescribed, °usual, °automatic, °perfunctory: *Each time they meet, Harold and Bill have to go through a ritual handshaking routine—a hangover from their school-days, I think.*
—n. **3** °formality, °routine, °custom, °practice, °convention, °protocol: *If everyone goes through this tea-drinking ritual twice a day, how do you get any work done?* **4** See **rite**, above.

rival *n.* **1** °competitor, °opponent, contender, challenger, °antagonist, °adversary; °opposition: *This year there are many formidable rivals for the championship.*
—v. **2** °compete with *or* against, contend with *or* against, °oppose, °challenge, °contest, °struggle with *or* against, °vie with, °combat, °compare with, °equal, °measure up to, (be a) °match (for): *Jan's prowess at tossing the caber rivalled that of anyone else in Craigie.*

rivalry *n.* °competition, competitiveness, contention, vying; °dispute, °feud, feuding, °conflict, °struggle, °strife, °controversy, °dissension, °discord, °difference(s): *Once again the two local teams meet in a rivalry that has been traditional for over a century. It appeared unlikely that the rivalry between the brothers would be settled amicably.*

river *n.* **1** watercourse, °branch, °tributary, °stream, waterway, estuary, rivulet, °creek, °brook, streamlet, runnel, rill, *Scots and No. Eng.* burn, *Brit* beck, *US* kill: *We used to sail our toy boats on the river here when I was a lad.* **2** °stream, °flood, °torrent, °quantity, cataract, °flow, cascade: *Rivers of sweat poured down me as I toiled in the humid heat of the jungle.*

riveting *adj.* °spellbinding, engrossing, hypnotic, hypnotizing, transfixing, fascinating, °enthralling, gripping, captivating, °absorbing: *The programme was absolutely riveting—one of the best I have ever seen.*

road *n.* **1** °way, °means, °approach, °route, °procedure, °technique, °method, °passage, °street, avenue, °course, °track, entrée, access, °direction: *Our researchers arrived at the identical results via a completely different road.* **2** thoroughfare, °way, byway, highway, roadway, high road, low road, avenue, boulevard, °street, lane,

alley(way), *Brit* motorway, carriageway, *US* turnpike, expressway, freeway, parkway, throughway *or* thruway, *German* Autobahn, *Italian* autostrada, *French* autoroute, *Colloq US* pike: *The roads are jammed with traffic on Sunday evenings during the summer.*

roam *v.* °wander, rove, °ramble, °range, °walk, °drift, dally, °dawdle, °cruise, °stroll, amble, °meander, °saunter, °stray, °prowl, perambulate, °travel, voyage, peregrinate, circumambulate, traipse, gallivant, jaunt, *Colloq* mosey, swan: *They spent a year roaming about the continent, staying wherever they pleased.*

roar *v.* **1** °bellow, °thunder; °howl, °bawl, squall, °cry, °yell, yowl; bay, °snarl, growl: *A train roared by. The crowd roared appreciation. A lion roared once in the night.* **2** °laugh, guffaw, °howl (with °laughter), hoot: *They fell about roaring when he told the joke about the egg and the taxi.*
—n. **3** roaring, °bellow, °thunder, rumble, °boom; °howl, °bawl, squall, °cry, °yell, yowl, clamour, °outcry; °snarl, snarling, growl, growling: *The roar of the falls could be heard miles away. There was a roar of indignation at the proposal. The beast's roar was enough to strike terror into our hearts.* **4** guffaw, °outburst, °howl, hoot: *Everything she said was met by a roar of laughter from the gallery.*

rob *v.* **1** burgle, °loot, °rifle, °ransack, °plunder, depredate, °raid; hijack; °pillage, °sack; *US* burglarize, *Colloq* °hold up, *Slang* °stick up, °rip off: *They robbed a jeweller's shop last week.* **2** °prey upon *or* on, *Colloq* °hold up, °mug, *Slang chiefly US* °stick up, °rip off, *Chiefly US and New Zealand* °roll: *These hooligans rob old ladies in the street.* **3 rob (someone) (of):** °deprive (of), °cheat *or* °swindle (out of), °defraud (of), °strip (of), °fleece (of), bilk (of), °victimize, mulct (of), *US* euchre ((out) of), *Colloq* rook ((out) of), do *or* diddle (out of), gyp (out of), *Slang Brit* nobble (of): *I was robbed of my last penny by those confidence men. We were robbed by a taxi driver who offered to change our money. She robbed me of my self-respect.*

robber *n.* °thief, pickpocket, shoplifter, °burglar, bandit, housebreaker, sneak-thief, cat °burglar, safe-breaker, highwayman, gentleman of the road, brigand, °pirate, freebooter, buccaneer, privateer, corsair, *Colloq* mugger, °hold-up man, *Slang* cracksman, °rip-off artist, safe-cracker, safe-blower, *Chiefly US* stick-up man, *US* second-story *or* second-storey man: *The police were making every effort to catch the robbers.*

robbery *n.* robbing, °theft, thievery, thieving, burglary, burgling, pilfering, pilferage, °stealing, plundering, °plunder, looting, °sack, sacking, ransacking, °depredation, °pillage, pillaging, hijacking, hijack, larceny, breaking and entering, *Colloq* pinching, °hold-up, holding up, mugging, *Slang* °rip-off, ripping-off, *Chiefly US* stick-up, sticking-up, *Brit* nicking, *US* heist: *The robbery of the paintings took place in broad daylight. The robbery of the shop was aided by a former employee. The robbery of elderly persons is on the increase.*

robe *n.* **1** °cloak, °dress, garment, vestment, °habit, frock, cassock, caftan, muu-muu, surplice, bathrobe, dressing-gown, lounging °robe, housecoat, kimono, house-dress, peignoir, °wrapper, *French* robe de chambre, °costume: *A woman wearing a green robe came to the door and asked what I wanted.* **2 robes:** °costume, °habit,

°uniform, garb, attire, vestments, °apparel, raiment, livery, clothing, °garments, °outfit, accoutrements *or US also* accouterments, °regalia, °finery, °trappings, panoply, °gear, °paraphernalia, appurtenances, equipage, °rig, *Archaic* vesture: *She looked absolutely splendid decked out in the full robes of state.*
—*v.* **3** °cloak, garb, °dress, °cover, enrobe, °clothe: *The dish consists of ladyfingers topped with fresh strawberries robed in chocolate, with whipped cream spread over the top.*

robot *n.* **1** automaton, °mechanical man *or* monster, android: *In the future, much of the drudgery will be taken over by electronic robots.* **2** drudge, °clod, °tool, °puppet, cat's-paw, myrmidon, °mechanical man, automaton: *The company has a number of robots on its payroll who carry out orders without question.*

robust *adj.* **1** °healthy, °fit, °sound, °hale (and °hearty), °sturdy, °hardy, °hearty, °strong, °stout, °tough, able-bodied, strapping, °brawny, °sinewy, °rugged, °muscular, °powerful, well-knit, athletic, °staunch, °vigorous; in fine *or* good fettle, *Colloq* °husky: *Kelly was such a robust chap one might have thought he'd live forever.* **2** °pungent, °strong, flavourful, sapid, °rich, full-bodied, nutty, fruity: *He gave me a glass of an excellent robust tawny port.*

rock[1] *n.* **1** stone; boulder: *In the avalanche, the rocks thoroughly destroyed the ski lodge.* **2** °crag, tor, escarpment, scarp, *Brit* outcrop, *US* out-cropping: *We used to go rock climbing when I had the strength.* **3 on the rocks: a** on ice: *I'd like a whisky on the rocks, thanks.* **b** in (a) °shambles, destroyed, in ruins, ruined, finished, broken-down, beyond repair: *He lost his job and his marriage went on the rocks.* **c** °destitute, poverty-stricken, °indigent, penniless, bank-rupt: *Unable to find another job, he's been on the rocks for a year, now.*

rock[2] *v.* **1** °sway, °swing, °lull: *Her father used to rock her to sleep in his arms.* **2** °roll, °reel, °lurch, °toss, °swing, °sway, wobble: *The building rocked so during the earthquake that I thought it was going to fall down.* **3** °astound, °astonish, °shock, °surprise, °jar, °stagger, °amaze, °stun, °dumbfound *or* dumfound, °daze, stupefy, °overwhelm, disconcert, °unnerve, *Colloq* set (someone) back on his *or* her *or* their heels, °throw, °rattle, °shake up: *I was really rocked by the news that Sue was marrying Craig.*

rocket *v.* zoom, °take off, sky-rocket, °shoot up, °climb, °rise rapidly, °soar, °spiral upwards, *Colloq* go through the roof: *The day controls were lifted, prices rocketed, almost doubling overnight.*

rocky[1] *adj.* **1** °stony, pebbly, shingly, boulder-strewn, craggy; °bumpy, °difficult, °hard, uncomfortable, °arduous: *The beach at Nice might be romantic, but it's very rocky to lie on. The road to love can be very rocky indeed.* **2** °stony, adamant, adamantine, °firm, unyielding, rock-like, °tough, unbending, flinty, °solid, °steadfast, °steady, unfaltering, °staunch, unflinching, °determined, °resolute, unwaver-ing, unchanging, unvarying, invariant, °invariable, °reliable, dependable, °sure, °certain: *I knew we could depend on Charles's rocky determination to see the project through.* **3** °stony, flinty, unfeeling, °unsympathetic, unemo-tional, emotionless, °impassive, °cold, °cool,

apathetic, °indifferent, uncaring, °detached, *dégagé*, callous, °thick-skinned, °tough, °hard: *Beneath that rocky exterior beats a tender heart.*

rocky[2] *adj.* °unstable, tottering, teetering, unsteady, °shaky, °rickety, unsure, °uncertain, °unreliable, °weak, °flimsy, wobbly, wobbling, vacillating, dubious, °doubtful, °questionable, *Colloq* iffy: *The project will be very rocky till we are assured proper funding.*

rod *n.* **1** °bar, °pole, baton, °wand, °staff, °stick, dowel, cane, °shaft: *Steel rods are used to reinforce the concrete in modern buildings.* **2** cane, birch, °switch, °scourge, °lash: °punishment, chas-tisement, castigation, °discipline, chastening, °correction: *As they say, spare the rod and spoil the child.*

rogue *n.* **1** trickster, °swindler, °cheat, cad, ne'er-do-well, °wastrel, °good-for-nothing, °miscreant, *Rather old-fashioned* scamp, °scoundrel, blackguard, knave, °rascal, rap-scallion, scapegrace, dastard, cur, churl, °wretch, °villain, charlatan, mountebank, *Brit* bounder; *Colloq* louse, °stinker, rat, °creep, *Brit* rotter, blighter, *Chiefly US and Canadian* son of a gun, *Slang* bastard, *Chiefly US and Canadian* son of a bitch, SOB *or* s.o.b., °bum: *She met some clever rogue in Capri who conned her out of fifteen thousand lire.*
—*adj.* **2** °independent, °undisciplined, uncon-trollable, °ungovernable, unmanageable, unpre-dictable, °disobedient, °incorrigible, fractious, °self-willed, °unruly, intractable, unrestrained, °wild, °lawless, strong-willed, headstrong, refractory, contumacious, °recalcitrant, cross-grained, rampageous: *Part of the village was destroyed when a rogue elephant ran amok. Perkins quit the company to start up his own rogue concern.*

role *n.* **1** roole, °part, °character, impersonation; lines: *She had the role of Maria in a recent production of Twelfth Night.* **2** °function, °position, °situation, °place, °post, °capacity, °job, °duty, °task, °responsibility: *Hermione's role in the com-pany is that of managing director.*

roll *v.* **1** °rotate, °cycle, °turn (over (and over)), °wheel, trundle, °revolve, °go (a)round, °orbit, °tumble, somersault *or* somerset *or* sum-mersault *or* summerset: *The landlord rolled another barrel beer into the pub. The children loved rolling about in the ride at the fun fair.* **2** °pass, °go, °flow, °slip, °flit, °glide, °slide, °move (on); °expire, °elapse, °disappear, vanish, °evaporate: *The time certainly rolls by quickly when you're having fun.* **3** °move, °drive, °bowl, be carried *or* conveyed, °cruise, °sail, °coast, °ride, °float, °fly: *We rolled down the road, singing and laugh-ing.* **4** undulate, billow, °rise and °fall: *The countryside rolled away before us as far as the eye could see.* **5** °roar, °echo, re-echo, rumble, rever-berate, °resound, °sound, °boom, °peal, res-onate, °thunder: *The roar of the explosion rolled over us as we ran for cover.* **6** °rob, °steal from: *They got their money by rolling drunks.* **7** Often, **roll out**: °flatten, °level (off *or* out), °smooth (out), °even (out), °grade: *After cutting, the lawn ought to be rolled.* **8** Usually, **roll over**: °turn (over), °rotate, °spin: *Roll onto your stomach so I can examine your back.* **9** Usually, **roll up**: furl, °coil, curl, °wind (up), °wrap (up); enwrap, °swathe, enfold, °envelop, °shroud, enshroud: *Every night he takes down the banner and carefully rolls it. Cleopatra was rolled up in a rug to be smuggled* *past the guards.* **10 roll in: a** °arrive, °come in, °pour in, °flow in, °turn up, °show up: *The contributions really started to roll in after the appeal.* **b** °luxuriate in, °revel in, °wallow in, °savour, bask in, °delight in, take °pleasure in, °indulge in, °rejoice in, °relish: *Basil has been rolling in unaccustomed wealth since his aunt died.* **11 roll out**: unroll, unfurl, °spread (out), °unfold, uncoil, uncurl, unwind, °open (out): *Roll out the bolt of cloth so that we can measure it.* —*n.* **12** °reel, spool, cylinder, scroll; tube: *The message was written on a long roll of paper.* **13** °list, rota, °register, °record, directory, listing, roster, slate, docket, catalogue, inventory, °muster, °index, census, annal(s), °schedule, °chronicle(s), *Sports* line-up: *With great ceremony, the clerk read the roll.* **14** rolling, billowing, waving, °wave action, °wave, billow, °swell, undulation, pitching, rocking, tossing: *With each roll of the boat, I felt more seasick.* **15** °peal, rumble, reverberation, °boom, °echo, °thunder, °roar: *A roll of thunder drowned out her shouts.* **16** rotation, °spin, °toss, whirl, °twirl: *I decided to bet everything on one last roll of the dice.* **17** bun; scone, croissant; *Brit* bread-roll, bap, split: *Waiter, would you please bring some more rolls?* **18** bankroll, °money, °wad, °bundle: *He took out a roll of notes and peeled off five twenties.*

roller *n.* **1** drum, cylinder, barrel, calender; tube; windlass; rolling-pin; mangle, wringer: *Make certain that the roller is clean.* **2** billow, °wave, comber, breaker, °swell: *After the storm, the heavy rollers continued to pound the sea wall.*

romance *n.* **1** (°love) °affair, amour, °affair of the heart, *affaire (de cœur or d'amour)*, °liaison, °relationship, dalliance, °intrigue: *Wasn't Rick the one from Canada with whom Diana had a romance?* **2** (true) °love: *You are lucky if you find romance even once in your lifetime.* **3** °novel, °narrative, fiction, °story, °mystery, thriller, horror °story, ghost °story, science fiction, °fantasy, Western, melodrama, gothic *or* Gothic *or* Gothick °novel *or* °tale, (fairy) °tale, love °story, idyll, epic, °legend: *It is probably accurate to say that the romance is the most popular form of fiction.* **4** °sentiment, nostalgia, °mystery, °intrigue, °fantasy, °imagination, imaginativeness, °adventure, °excitement, °fascination, exoticism, °glamour, °colour, colourfulness: *It was the romance of Morocco that entranced me.* **5** °tall °tale *or* °story, °fantasy, °fabrication, fairy °tale, °exaggeration, prevarication, concoction, flight of °fancy, °fib, (white) °lie, balderdash, fiction, °nonsense, °imagination: *That episode with the girl on the train that David told you about was all romance.* —*v.* **6** make °love to; woo, court: *Steve has been romancing Maria ever since they met.* **7** °pander to, °flatter, curry °favour with, toady (up) to, *Colloq* butter up, soft-soap, *Taboo slang* brown-nose: *The new restaurant is romancing neighbourhood office executives, and luring them in for business lunches.*

romantic *adj.* **1** °imaginary, imagined, °fictitious, °fictional, °ideal, idealized, °fancied, °fabulous, made-up, dreamed-up, dreamt-up, fantasized, °fanciful, fairy-tale, °mythical, °idyllic, Utopian, °illusory: *Vivian isn't a real person—she's just Howard's romantic notion of the girl he wants to marry.* **2** °impractical, °visionary, °fictitious, unpractical, °unrealistic, °ideal, °abstract, °quixotic, chimerical, °absurd,

°extravagant, °wild, crackpot, °mad: *She had romantic notions of how she would be running her own international business by the time she was thirty.* **3** nostalgic, °sentimental, °emotional, °sweet, °tender, °picturesque, °exotic, °glamorous; mawkish, °maudlin, saccharine, *Colloq* soppy, sugary, °mushy, °sloppy: *I can think of a lot more romantic places to eat on our anniversary. Fred hates it when I get too romantic.* **4** amorous, °affectionate, aroused, °impassioned, °passionate, libidinous, °lustful, over-friendly, *Colloq* lovey-dovey; °fresh: *After a drink or two Mike starts getting romantic—if you know what I mean.* —*n.* **5** romanticist, °dreamer, Don Quixote, °visionary, idealist, sentimentalist: *I've never lost my taste for soft lights and sweet music—I suppose I'm just a romantic at heart.*

room *n.* **1** °space, °area, °scope, °extent, °allowance, latitude, elbow-room, °range, °leeway, °margin: *There is room for one more inside.* **2** °chamber, apartment, °compartment, °office, °cell, cubicle: *For years Pablo occupied a small room on the top floor.* **3 rooms**: °quarters, °lodgings, °accommodation, °flat, °dwelling: *We had rooms in an old house downtown.* —*v.* **4** °live, °lodge, °dwell, °abide, reside, °stay: *Did you really room with the daughter of a prime minister?*

roomy *adj.* °spacious, capacious, commodious, °large, sizeable, °big, °ample: *For what appears to be a small car, it has a surprisingly roomy interior.*

root¹ *n.* **1** °base, °basis, °foundation, °source, °seat, °cause, fountain-head, °origin, fount, well-spring: *Love of money is the root of all evil.* **2** rootstock, rootstalk, °tap root, rootlet; tuber; *Technical* radix, radicle, radicel, rhizome, rhizomorph: *When transplanting seedlings, special care should be taken not to damage the roots.* **3 root and branch**: radically, °completely, °utterly, °entirely, °wholly, °totally: *The Romans sought to destroy Carthage root and branch.* **4 roots**: °origins, °heritage, °family, °lineage, °house, antecedents, forefathers, foremothers, descent, genealogy, °family tree, forebears, ancestors, predecessors, °stock, °pedigree; birthplace, motherland, °fatherland, °native °land *or* °country *or* °soil, cradle: *Carlotta spent years tracing her roots to ancient Rome. The roots of civilization first appeared in Mesopotamia.* **5 take root**: become °set *or* established *or* settled, germinate, °sprout, °grow, °develop, °thrive, burgeon, °flourish, °spread: *Good work habits should take root at an early age; then they will last a lifetime.* —*v.* **6** °plant, °set, °establish, °found, °fix, °settle, embed *or* imbed; entrench, °anchor: *The cuttings failed to grow because they were not properly rooted. Hilary's fear of heights is rooted in a childhood fall from a tree.* **7 root out: a** °Sometimes, **root up**: °uproot, eradicate, °eliminate, °destroy, extirpate, °exterminate: *Any subversives in the organization must be rooted out.* **b** °find, uncover, °discover, °dig up *or* out, °unearth, °turn up, bring to °light: *The survey of accounts is aimed at rooting out customers who are slow in paying.*

root² *v.* rootle, forage, °dig, °pry, nose, °poke, ferret, °burrow, °rummage, delve, °search, °ransack: *Harvey has been rooting about in the garage looking for his tennis racket.*

root[3] *v.* Usually, **root for**: °cheer (for), °applaud (for); °boost, °support, °encourage, °urge on: *I'm rooting for our side to win.*

rooted *adj.* °firm, established, °set, °fixed, °fast, settled, deep-rooted, deep-seated, °entrenched, °ingrained *or* engrained, (°firmly) embedded *or* imbedded, implanted, instilled; °chronic, inbred, °inherent, °intrinsic, °essential, °fundamental, °basic, °radical: *Have you any rooted objections to the principle of living with someone of the opposite sex without being married?*

rope *n.* **1** °line, °cord, °cable, hawser; strand, °string: *This rope is too light for mooring the boat. She wore a rope of baroque pearls.* **2 the ropes**: the °routine, the °procedure, one's way around, the ins and outs; the °truth, the (real) °situation; *Colloq* what's what, the °score, *Brit* the gen: *It didn't take her long to learn the ropes.* —*v.* **3** °tie, °bind, °lash, °hitch, °fasten, °secure; °tether, °attach: *Rope these two crates together. The horses were roped to the post.* **4 rope in**: °attract, °draw (in), °tempt, °entice, °lure, °persuade: *They are going to use a lottery to rope the customers in to supporting our cause.*

ropy *adj.* **1** ropey, viscous, °stringy, viscid, glutinous, mucilaginous, gluey, gummy, thready, fibrous, filamentous: *The plastic resin emerging from the vat looks somewhat ropy, like mozzarella cheese.* **2** °questionable, °inadequate, °inferior, °deficient, °indifferent, °mediocre, substandard, °unsatisfactory, °poor, °sketchy: *Greenwood's plan for increasing profit margins looks pretty ropy to me.* **3** °sickly, °ill, unwell, hung-over, below °par, out of sorts, *Colloq* under the °weather, °poorly, °rough, not up to snuff, off one's feed: *I was feeling pretty ropy on Saturday morning after that do at your place on Friday.*

rostrum *n.* °platform, °stage, dais, podium, °stand; pulpit; lectern, reading-stand: *As the crowd hooted and booed, the speaker descended from the rostrum.*

rosy *adj.* **1** °pink, rose-coloured, red, roseate, reddish, pinkish, cherry, cerise, ruddy, flushed, °glowing, blushing, ruby, rubicund, florid; rose-red: *During the skiing holiday, they all developed healthy rosy complexions.* **2** °optimistic, °promising, °favourable, auspicious, °hopeful, encouraging, °sunny, °bright: *Caldwell has a rosy future ahead of him.*

rot *v.* **1** °decay, °decompose, °fester, °spoil, °go °bad *or* °off, be tainted, be ruined, °mould, moulder, °putrefy; corrode, rust, °disintegrate, °deteriorate, °crumble *or* go *or* °fall to °pieces: *When the power went off, all the food in the freezer rotted. The piers holding up the far end of the bridge have all rotted away.* **2** °waste away, wither away, languish, °die, moulder, °decline, °deteriorate, °degenerate, °decay, atrophy: *Despite repeated appeals for clemency, he's been rotting away in jail all these years.* —*n.* **3** °decay, decomposition, °mould, putrefaction, putrescence, °blight, corrosion, corruption, disintegration, deterioration: *Once the rot has set in, the job of revitalization can be overwhelming.* **4** (°stuff and) °nonsense, balderdash, °rubbish, bunkum, tommy-rot, twaddle, °drivel, hogwash, eyewash, °trash, *Colloq* claptrap, bunk, baloney *or* boloney, bosh, malarkey, °moonshine, poppycock, tosh, *Slang*

crap, bull, codswallop, *Brit* (a load of (old)) cobblers, *Taboo* balls, bullshit: *He knows nothing whatsoever about linguistics and is just talking a lot of rot.*

rotate *v.* **1** °turn, °revolve, °go °round, °spin, °gyrate, °pirouette, whirl, °twirl, °wheel, °pivot, °reel: *As the gear rotates, its teeth mesh with those of the other gear, causing it to turn in the opposite direction.* **2** °change, °exchange, °alternate, interchange, °switch, °trade places; take °turns, *Colloq* swap *or* swop: *Rotate the positions of the tyres for more even wear. We rotate the chores in our family.*

rote *n.* **1** °routine, °ritual: *He acquired a rote knowledge of the words, without knowing what they mean.* **2 by rote**: **a** by heart, from °memory: *He can recite the entire Prologue of* Canterbury Tales *by rote.* **b** unthinkingly, automatically, mechanically: *She learned the French dialogue by rote but doesn't understand a word of it.*

rotten *adj.* **1** rotted, decayed, decomposed, decomposing, °putrid, putrescent, putrescing, °mouldy, mouldering, spoilt *or* spoiled, mildewed, °rancid, fetid *or* foetid, °stale, °rank, °foul, feculent, tainted, contaminated, festered, festering, °corrupt, °bad, °off, turned, overripe, soured, °sour: *One rotten apple in the barrel can spoil the rest. The stench of rotten meat filled the room.* **2** rotted, rusted, corroded, deteriorating, disintegrating, crumbling, crumbly, falling to pieces, friable: *He stepped on a spot where the wood was rotten and his foot went right through the stair.* **3** °immoral, °corrupt, °dishonest, °deceitful, °venal, °shameless, °degenerate, °villainous, iniquitous, °evil, °wicked, °vile, debased, °base, °perverted, depraved, °unscrupulous, unprincipled, amoral, warped, *Slang* °bent: *These drug dealers are rotten at the core.* **4** heinous, °evil, °vile, °base, °miserable, °despicable, °wretched, °awful, °terrible, °horrible, horrific, °nasty, °contemptible, °filthy, °mean, low, *Colloq* °lousy, °stinking, °low-down, dirty-rotten: *Pairing me off with Vera at the dance was a rotten trick.* **5** °ill, unwell, °sick, °nauseated, °awful; hung-over, *Colloq* °lousy, °ropy *or* ropey, rough: *I feel really rotten—maybe it was those mushrooms I ate last night.*

rotund *adj.* **1** °round(ed), °circular, orbicular, globular, °spherical: *His rotund, cherubic little face simply invited a pinch of the cheek.* **2** °full, full-toned, °deep, °resonant, reverberant, reverberating, sonorous, °rich, °round, °mellow; pear-shaped: *They thrilled to hear the rotund notes issuing from Caruso's lips as he sang 'Vesti la Giubba'.* **3** °chubby, podgy *or chiefly US* pudgy, (pleasingly) °plump, portly, tubby, °heavy, fleshy, corpulent, °stout, °fat, °obese, overweight, *Colloq* roly-poly: *Jack's rotund figure was easily recognizable waddling up the street.*

roué *n.* °playboy, womanizer, ladies' man, °rake, lecher, Lothario, Don Juan, Romeo, Casanova, °charmer, °flirt, °libertine, debauchee, *Old-fashioned* masher, gay dog, *Colloq* wolf, lady-killer, dirty old man, *Taboo slang* gash-hound: *Alistair was quite a roué in his youth but has settled down since turning 50.*

rough *adj.* **1** uneven, °irregular, °coarse, °jagged, °rugged, °bumpy, °lumpy, °broken: *The next mile or so we slogged over some very rough terrain.* **2** °agitated, turbulent, choppy, °stormy,

storm-tossed, °tempestuous, roiled: *We negoti-*
ated a very rough patch of water before sailing
into the calm, sheltered bay. **3** °brusque, °bluff,
°curt, °short, °abrupt, unpleasant, churlish,
°discourteous, °impolite, rough-spoken,
°ungracious, °surly, °disrespectful, °rude,
uncouth, loutish, °unrefined, uncivil,
°uncivilized, uncultured, °vulgar, unladylike,
ungentlemanly, °coarse, °ill-mannered, ill-bred,
°inconsiderate: *Ian can be a bit rough, I know, but*
underneath he is a true and loyal friend. **4** °tough,
rough-and-tumble, roughneck, °rowdy: *There*
are some very rough characters frequenting that
pub. **5** °harsh, °violent, unfeeling, unjust,
°severe, °cruel, °tough, °hard, °brutal, °extreme;
ungentle: *They were subjected to very rough treat-*
ment when being questioned by the police. **6** °dirty,
°obscene, smutty, °pornographic, °vulgar,
°crude, °raw, °rude: *After midnight they watch the*
rough shows beamed by satellite from Italy. **7** °hard,
°tough, °Spartan, °difficult, °arduous,
°laborious, °rugged, unpleasant: *It was pretty*
rough going with almost no money and all those
expenses. **8** °harsh, °grating, cacophonous,
°discordant, jarring, °strident, °raucous, rasping, unmusical, inharmonious, °gruff, °husky:
In acknowledgement he made a rough, growling
noise. **9** unfinished, °incomplete, uncompleted,
°imperfect, °rudimentary, °crude, °rude, formless, unformed, °raw, rough-and-ready,
rough-hewn, roughcast, °undeveloped,
unshaped, unworked, unwrought, unprocessed,
°unrefined; uncut, unpolished; °shapeless,
undressed: *I only saw the sculpture in its rough state*
and cannot say how it looked when finished. The
stones are rough, as they were when taken from the
ground. **10** °general, °approximate, °inexact,
°cursory, °quick, °hasty, °sketchy, °vague,
°hazy; foggy, *Colloq* ballpark: *Can't you give me*
even a rough idea of how much you want for the house?
11 unfair, unjust, °bad, °tough; unlucky,
°unfortunate: *We went through a spell of rough*
luck last year. This is a rough time for everyone. **12** See
rotten, 5, above.
—*n.* **13** °rowdy, °tough, hooligan, ruffian, °thug,
brawler, yahoo, *Slang* roughneck, *Australian*
larrikin, *US* mug: *Phil will get into trouble if he*
continues to associate with those roughs at the
Lantern. **14** sketch, (rough) °draft, mock-up,
°outline: *Let me see roughs of the presentation before*
the meeting with the client.
—*v.* **15 rough out** *or* **in**: sketch, °draft, mock-up,
°outline, °mark out, °trace, °block out: *Our*
escape plan was roughed out by Captain Gallagher.
16 rough up: °beat (up), thrash, °attack, °batter,
°assault, pummel *or* pommel, lay on, °knock
about, °belabour, °lambaste, *Colloq* wallop: *Some*
of the boys roughed him up a bit when they learned
that he was an informer.
—*adv.* **17** violently, savagely, brutally, brutishly:
You'd best not mention Cassie or Henry might cut
up rough.

rough-house *n.* **1** boisterousness, rowdiness,
°rowdyism, °violence, brawling, disorderliness,
°disorderly conduct, ruffianism: *The police were*
called in to quell the rough-house that broke out at the
dance.
—*v.* **2** °brawl: *If you want to rough-house, do it*
outside!

roughly *adv.* **1** °approximately, °around; °about,
°nearly: *The British Museum is roughly in the same*
direction as Euston. It cost roughly two weeks' wages.

Roughly two years later I saw her again. **2** harshly,
unkindly, °severely, sternly, unsympathetically,
brutally, violently, savagely, inhumanly, mercilessly, unmercifully, ruthlessly, pitilessly,
cruelly, heartlessly: *The police were accused of deal-*
ing too roughly with those suspected of harming a
fellow officer. **3** clumsily, rudely, crudely, awk-
wardly, primitively, inexpertly, amateurishly,
maladroitly, heavy-handedly, ineptly, inef-
ficiently, unskilfully, inartistically: *This roughly*
hewn block of local granite is what the council paid
a fortune for as 'sculpture'.

round *adj.* **1** °circular; disc-shaped, discoid,
disc-like: *I prefer a round table to a square one. She*
made a round motion to demonstrate the
shape. **2** ring-shaped, annular, hoop-shaped,
hoop-like: *The track is oval, not round.* **3** °spherical,
ball-shaped, ball-like, globular, spheroid, spher-
oidal, globe-shaped, globelike, globate,
orb-shaped, orb-like, orbicular: *You will never con-*
vince me that the earth is round—I know what I
see. **4** curved, curvilinear, rounded, arched: *The*
round chisel is used to cut these grooves. **5** °exact,
°precise, °complete, °entire, °full: *That makes a*
round hundred times you have asked me the same
question. **6** °approximate, °rough, rounded (off
or up *or* down), °whole: *In round numbers, that*
makes 40 per cent For and 60 per cent Against. **7** rounded, °mellow, °full, vibrant, reverberant, reverberating, sonorous, °rich, mellifluous, orotund,
pear-shaped: *Couldn't you listen forever to those*
beautiful round tones sung by Fischer-Dieskau?
8 °plain, °honest, straightforward, °direct,
°unvarnished, unembellished, unelaborated,
°outspoken, °candid, °truthful, °frank, °open,
°blunt, *Colloq* upfront: *They delivered what they*
had to say in round, assertive statements. **9** *Chiefly*
Brit return: *We made the round trip to Bristol in*
less than three hours.
—*n.* **10** °circle, disc; °ring, hoop, annulus; ball,
°sphere, °globe, °orb, bead: *The moulding has a*
repeated pattern of a round alternating with three
vertical grooves. **11** °cycle, series, °sequence,
°succession, °bout, °spell: *The current round of*
talks on the economy is expected to last for three
days. There was the usual round of parties on New
Year's Eve. **12** Often, **rounds**: °beat, °route,
°routine, °circuit, °course, °tour, °turn, ambit:
The milkman still makes his daily rounds in
England. **13** °heat, °stage, °level, °turn: *After*
each round in the tournament, the losers are elim-
inated, reducing the competitors by half. **14** °spell,
°period, °run, °spate, °bout, °outburst, °burst,
°volley: *Each new acrobat who added to the human*
pyramid got a round of applause. **15** bullet,
cartridge, charge, °shell, (single) °shot: *Each man*
was given only ten rounds of ammunition.
—*v.* **16** °turn, °go (a)round: *The car rounded the*
corner on two wheels. **17** °orbit, circumnavigate,
°go (a)round, °circle, °encircle: *He rounded the*
earth in the fastest recorded time. **18 round off**
or **out**: °complete, °close, °end, bring to an °end
or °completion *or* a °close, °finish: *Tim suggested*
we round off the evening with a rubber of
bridge. **19 round up**: °gather, °assemble,
°muster, draw *or* pull *or* °get together, °collect,
°herd, marshal, *US and Canadian* (of cattle *or*
horses) corral, wrangle: *The police are rounding up*
witnesses who might have seen the shooting. More than
10,000 head of cattle have been rounded up for the
drive.

—*prep.* **20** °about, °around, encircling, enclosing; orbiting: *The fence round the site ought to keep out the curious. The new bypass round town ought to reduce local traffic.* **21** here and there in, °about, °around, °throughout, all over, °everywhere in: *Dad used to smoke and kept dozens of ash trays round the house.* **22** °about, around, °nearby, in the °neighbourhood or °vicinity or (general) °area of: *Whenever I want to see you alone, there are always people round you. Just look round you if you don't believe me.*
—*adv.* **23** around, °about, in a °circle or °ring, on all sides: *Gather round and I'll tell you a story. Pass the hat round for Harry's farewell party.* **24** from beginning to end, from start to finish, °through: *He now lives in France the year round.* **25** in °perimeter or °periphery, °around: *The indoor track is exactly one fifth of a mile round.* **26** °about, °around, in the °neighbourhood or °vicinity or (general) °area: *There isn't a soul for miles round.* **27** around, in a °circle or °circuit, in or by a °circular or circuitous route or path, circuitously: *This road goes round to the other side of the lake.*

roundabout *adj.* **1** circuitous, °circular, °indirect, °long: *We had plenty of time so we came the more scenic, roundabout way.* **2** °devious, circuitous, °evasive, °indirect, °oblique: *If you wanted to borrow some money, asking me for tax advice was quite a roundabout way of asking.*
—*n.* **3** merry-go-round, carousel or carrousel, *Old-fashioned or dialect* whirligig: *The children weren't the only ones who enjoyed themselves on the roundabout.* **4** *Brit* mini-roundabout, *US and Canadian* rotary, traffic circle: *When you come to the roundabout, turn right and keep going till you come to a traffic light.*

round-up *n.* **1** °gathering, °assembly, °rally, °collection, herding, *US and Canadian* (of cattle or horses) corralling, wrangling: *The round-up of suspects by the police was focused on the Bournemouth area.* **2** °summary, °synopsis, °digest, °outline, recapitulation, °review, °survey, *Colloq* recap: *And now, with a round-up of the news, here is Moira Lawley.*

rouse *v.* **1** °arouse, °call, waken, °awaken, °wake (up), °get up, °arise: *I was roused from a deep slumber by a dog's barking.* **2** °stir (up), °arouse, bestir, °stimulate, inspirit, °animate, invigorate, °electrify, °excite, °provoke, °prompt, goad, °prod, galvanize, °incite, °whet, °move, °work up, °fire up: *Bruce's unquenchable enthusiasm roused many to become involved in the campaign.*

rousing *adj.* °stimulating, inspiriting, animating, enlivening, energizing, inspiring, °invigorating, vitalizing, electrifying; °fervent, °vigorous, °energetic, °enthusiastic, °spirited, °brisk, °lively, °animated, *Colloq* peppy: *The huge crowd gave the team a rousing cheer as they jogged out onto the field.*

rout *n.* **1** °defeat, trouncing, °ruin, °overthrow, subjugation, vanquishment, débâcle, °conquest, °thrashing, drubbing, beating; dispersal, °retreat, °collapse; *Colloq* licking, hiding, *US and Canadian* shellacking: *Owing to the government's overwhelming forces, there was a complete rout of the rebels.*
—*v.* **2** °defeat, °win (out) over, trounce, °ruin, °overthrow, °bring down, °subjugate, °subdue, °suppress, vanquish, °conquer, °overwhelm,

°overpower, put to rout or °flight, worst, °best, °trample, °overrun, thrash, °trim, °whip, drub, °beat, °crush, °batter, smash, °shatter, °cut to pieces or ribbons or shreds, °destroy, °devastate, °wipe out, °eliminate, °put down, seal the °doom or the °fate of, eradicate, °obliterate, *Colloq* lick, wipe the floor with, °polish off, °knock off, *Hyperbolic sports jargon* °pulverize, make mincemeat of, ride roughshod over, °demolish, °mangle, °ravage, °mutilate, °flatten, squash, °topple, lay °waste, wreak °havoc (up)on, °massacre, °murder, °exterminate, annihilate, liquidate, °smother, °stifle, do away with, *Slang* clobber, do in, *US* skunk, *Chiefly US and Canadian* cream: *Queens Park Rangers routed Manchester United 6–0.*

route *n.* **1** °way, itinerary, °course, °direction, °path, °road, avenue: *If you have the time, take the scenic route. John's route to the chairmanship is strewn with his colleagues' corpses.*
—*v.* **2** °direct, convey, °carry: *Goods destined for Cleveland will be routed through Northampton.*

routine *n.* **1** °custom, °habit, °procedure, °practice, °method, °schedule, °plan, °programme, °formula, °pattern, °way, °usage, wont, *Colloq chiefly Brit* °drill: *Chalmers has always been a stickler for routine. What's the routine here when you want to order a new chair?* **2** °act, °piece, °bit, °performance, °number, °part, *Colloq* °thing, shtick: *The fat lady doesn't sing till after Joe Miller finishes his routine.*
—*adj.* **3** °customary, °habitual, °usual, °rote, °accustomed, °familiar, °conventional, °regular, °ordinary, °everyday; programmed, assigned, designated, scheduled: *Her routine responsibilities include proofreading.* **4** °boring, °tedious, °tiresome, unimaginative, uninteresting; hackneyed, trite, stereotypic(al), clichéd, run-of-the-mill, °ordinary; unvaried, unvarying, unchanging, °monotonous, uneventful, °rote, °automatic, °mechanical, °perfunctory: *He has a routine job on the assembly line.*

rover *n.* wanderer, bird of passage, itinerant, °traveller, rolling stone, nomad, gypsy, wayfarer, gadabout, sojourner, °tourist; °drifter, °tramp, °vagabond, vagrant, *US* hobo, °bum: *He's a born rover and will never settle down.*

row¹ *n.* °line, °rank, °tier, bank, °string, series, °file: *A row of trees serves as a wind-break along one side of the farm.*

row² *n.* **1** altercation, °argument, °dispute, °quarrel, °disagreement, squabble, spat, °tiff, °conflict, °fracas, *Colloq* shouting match, °scrap, falling-out, *Brit* slanging-match: *We had a silly row about where we should spend the Christmas holidays.* **2** commotion, °disturbance, clamour, hubbub, °racket, °din, °rumpus, °tumult, °uproar, brouhaha, °fuss, °stir, turmoil, hullabaloo, °bedlam, pandemonium, °chaos; *US* foofaraw, *Colloq* ruckus: *There was a tremendous row over the increase in membership fees.*
—*v.* **3** °dispute, °quarrel, °argue, °disagree, wrangle, cross swords, have words, °bicker, °tiff, *Colloq* °scrap, °fall out: *They are constantly rowing over something, usually some insignificant detail.*

rowdy *adj.* **1** °boisterous, °uproarious, °disorderly, °noisy, °loud, °obstreperous, °unruly: *It only takes a couple of rowdy youths to start trouble at a match.*

—*n.* **2** ruffian, °tough, hooligan, yahoo, brawler, lout, *Brit* lager lout, skinhead, *Chiefly US and Canadian* °hoodlum, hood, *Slang Brit* bovver boy: *The police arrested three of the rowdies involved in last night's fight.*

rowdyism *n.* rowdiness, ruffianism, hooliganism, °rough-house, barbarism, troublemaking, brawling, unruliness, boisterousness, *Slang Brit* bovver: *Have you any suggestions about what to do to curb rowdyism at football matches?*

royal *adj.* **1** queenly, kingly, queenlike, kinglike, °regal, °imperial, °sovereign, °princely, °majestic: *The Royal Family usually spend their summer holidays at Balmoral. The establishment proudly boasts royal patronage.* **2** °grand, °splendid, °stately, °impressive, august, °imposing, °superior, °superb, °magnificent, °majestic: *She arrived at the ball in a royal coach drawn by six white horses.* —*n.* **3** °king, °queen, prince, princess, duke, earl, duchess, viscount, viscountess, baron, baroness, °noble, nobleman, noblewoman, °peer: *Her greatest ambition is to meet a royal in the flesh.* **4 royals**: °royalty, °nobility, °nobles, peerage: *He writes the daily column reporting on the activities of the royals.*

royalty *n.* **1** queenship, kingship, °royal °house or °line or °family, °sovereignty: *Royalty does have its privileges, doesn't it?* **2** °percentage, commission, °share, °payment, compensation: *He receives a royalty every time his song is played or sung commercially, anywhere in the world.* **3** °nobility, °nobles, peerage, *Colloq Brit* °royals: *It is ironic that Americans are more impressed than the British with royalty.*

rub *v.* **1** °massage, knead, °stroke; °scour, °scrub, °scrape, abrade, °chafe, °clean; °wipe, °smooth, °polish, °shine, buff, burnish: *Rub my back, would you?—Not there, a little lower down. You are not supposed to rub those plastic baths with abrasive cleansers. Before the guests arrived, we rubbed the silver till you could see yourself in it.* **2 rub in** *or* **on**: °apply, °smooth, °smear, °spread, °put: *The ache may be relieved a bit if you rub on some liniment.* **3 rub (it** *or* **something) in**: °emphasize, °stress, make an °issue of, harp on, °reiterate, °dwell on, hammer away, °dramatize: *It's bad enough that Caroline did better than I did—you don't have to keep rubbing it in.* **4 rub off** *or* **out**: expunge, °erase, °remove, °delete, °cancel, °eliminate, eradicate: *It's a pity, Peter, that you rubbed out the right reply and wrote in the wrong one. The boys were released on the condition that they would rub the graffiti off the wall.* **5 rub off (on)**: °affect, be transferred (to), be communicated or transmitted (to), be passed on or along (to), be imparted to: *Your mother and I had hoped that some of our love of music might have rubbed off on you.* **6 rub out**: °murder, °kill, °execute, slay: *The Godfather ordered all witnesses to be rubbed out.* **7 rub shoulders with**: °rub elbows with, °associate with, °socialize with, °mix with, °fraternize with, keep °company with, consort with, *Colloq US* °run or °pal or °chum around with: *Since getting his knighthood Charles no longer rubs shoulders with the likes of us.* **8 rub (someone) (up) the wrong way**: °annoy, °irritate, °irk, °anger, °provoke, go against the grain, *Colloq* °bug, get under one's or someone's skin, peeve: *I don't know what it is about Underbridge, but every time we meet he manages to rub me up the wrong way.*

—*n.* **9** °wipe, °stroke, rubbing: *You will have to give that stain a good rub to make it come out.* **10** °massage, rub-down: *After exercising, Jane always has an alcohol rub.* **11 the rub**: the or a °catch or °hitch or °snag or °hindrance or °set-back, the or an °obstacle or °impediment, the or a °difficulty or °problem or °trouble: *The only rub I can see is that Warren may not agree to resign.*

rubberneck *v.* **1** °gape, °stare, goggle, °gawk: *They spent a weekend in New York, rubbernecking at the skyscrapers.* —*n.* **2** °tourist, °sightseer, rubbernecker, *US* out-of-towner: *Buses for the rubbernecks leave Trafalgar Square every hour or so.*

rubbish *n.* **1** °refuse, °waste, debris, rubble, detritus, °litter, °garbage, sweepings, dross, °dregs, °residue, °leftovers, °remnants, lees, °scraps, °fragments, leavings, residuum, °junk, °rejects, *Chiefly US* °trash *Slang chiefly US* dreck: *Private companies are now contracted to remove household rubbish weekly.* **2** (°stuff and) °nonsense, balderdash, °moonshine, °gibberish, °gobbledegook or gobbledygook, tommy-rot, bunkum, °trash, °garbage, twaddle, *Colloq* °rot, flapdoodle, crap, hokum, codswallop, bosh, piffle, hooey, bunk, malarkey, poppycock, boloney or baloney, eyewash, hogwash, bilge-water, bull, *Scots* havers, *Brit* tosh, gammon, *US* a crock, horse feathers, gurry, *Brit* (a load of (old)) cobblers, *Taboo slang* bullshit, horseshit, *US* a crock of shit: *What she told you about how I treated her is absolute rubbish.* —*v.* **3** °criticize, °attack, °destroy, *Colloq* clobber, °pan, *Chiefly US* °trash, *Slang* °jump on, *Chiefly US and Canadian* bad-mouth, °jump all over: *In his latest book he rubbishes the newspaper that had given his previous book a bad review.*

rude *adj.* **1** °impolite, °discourteous, °disrespectful, °ungracious, ungallant, unmannerly, °ill-mannered, uncivil, bad-mannered, ungentlemanly, unladylike, ill-bred, °unrefined, unpolished, uncouth, °boorish, churlish, oafish, loutish, °coarse, °uncivilized, uncultured, unceremonious: *It was rude of him not to get up when she came in, but he doesn't know any better.* **2** °impertinent, °impudent, °discourteous, insulting, °insolent, °offensive, saucy, °bold, °disrespectful, uncivil, °flippant, °brusque, °curt, °gruff, °tactless, °outrageous, *Colloq* °fresh: *I simply asked the chambermaid to make up my room early and she responded with a rude remark.* **3** °naughty, °unrefined, ribald, °bawdy, °indecent, indelicate, °vulgar, °obscene, °dirty, °filthy, lubricious or lubricous, °lewd, °gross, smutty, °taboo, °pornographic: *Chris has an extensive collection of rude photographs.* **4** °crude, °rough, °clumsy, °awkward, unskilful, unskilled, °artless, inartistic, °imperfect, unpolished, °inaccurate, gauche, bumbling, °raw, inelegant, °makeshift, °homespun, °primitive, °misshapen, ill-formed, unfinished, rough-hewn, °simple, °basic, °bare: *The replica on view in the local museum is only a rude approximation of the original.*

rudimentary *adj.* **1** °basic, °essential, °elementary, °fundamental, rudimental, °primary, °introductory, abecedarian, formative, °first, °initial, °elemental, primal, °seminal: *The purpose of the course is provide students with a rudimentary knowledge of computer* *programming*. **2** °crude, °coarse, unshaped, unfinished, °imperfect, °primitive, °undeveloped, °vestigial, embryonic, primordial, °immature: *These fish, which spend their lives in darkness, have only a rudimentary organ for an eye.*

rudiments *n.pl.* basics, °elements, essentials, °fundamentals, °first °principles: *She learnt the rudiments of musical composition from the maestro himself.*

ruffle *n.* **1** trimming, °flounce, °frill, ruff, peplum, °flare, smocking, ruche, ruching, gather, gathering: *Doesn't that ruffle at the back of the skirt make it look a bit old-fashioned?* **2** °ripple, wavelet, °disturbance, °flurry, bustle, °stir, perturbation, wrinkle: *The news of the divorce caused a slight ruffle at court.*
—*v.* **3** °agitate, disconcert, °confuse, discompose, °discomfit, °upset, °disturb, °stir up, °perturb, unsettle, disorient, °unnerve, °fluster, °affect, °bother, °intimidate, unstring, °put out, vex, °trouble, °worry, *Colloq* °rattle, °throw, °shake up, *Chiefly US and Canadian* discombobulate, voodoo, hex, psych out, *Slang chiefly US and Canadian* get (someone) all shook up, spook: *She was ruffled by questions concerning her relationship with the deceased.* **4** disarrange, dishevel, °disorder, °rumple, °mix up, °tousle, °tangle, *Colloq* °mess or muss (up): *His unpleasant attitude ruffled quite a few feathers in the department.*

rugged *adj.* **1** °rough, uneven, °broken, °stony, °rocky, °irregular, °bumpy, °pitted, °jagged, °ragged: *The horses picked their way slowly across the rugged terrain.* **2** °tough, °rough, °severe, °hard, °harsh, °difficult, °arduous, °Spartan, rigorous, onerous, °stern, °demanding, °burdensome: *It is amazing how that small band of pioneers withstood the rugged life in the untamed West.* **3** °hardy, °durable, °strong, °sturdy, °hale, °robust, °tough, °vigorous, °hard, rough-and-ready, °stalwart; °independent, individualistic, self-reliant, °self-confident, °self-sufficient, °bold: *WANTED: Five rugged pioneering types to join an expedition to the source of the Amazon river.* **4** °rude, uncouth, uncultured, °uncivilized, °unrefined, unpolished, °crude, °ungraceful, churlish: *I admit that Charlie's manners are a bit rugged, but he's one of the best men we have.*

ruin *n.* **1** °downfall, °destruction, devastation, °havoc, °breakdown, breakup, débâcle, °collapse, °fall, disintegration, ruination, °dissolution, wiping out, °failure, °decay, °undoing, °end; °conquest, °defeat, °overthrow; bankruptcy, liquidation: *Alexander was responsible for the ruin of the Persian empire. Overwhelming debts spelt Theo's financial ruin.* **2** degradation, °dishonour, debasement, °defilement, corruption, vitiation, seduction, °degrading, dishonouring, debasing, defiling, corrupting, vitiating, seducing; deflowering, defloration: *Who was the libertine who brought about the ruin of Lord Harecombe's daughter?* **3** nemesis, °curse, °end, bane: *That boy will be my ruin!* **4** gin, mother's ruin, blue ruin, *Slang* rot-gut: *After eating, we sat down and polished off a bottle of mother's ruin.* **5** °hag, °witch, crone, beldam; dotard, (old) °fogy or fogey, fossil, fuddy-duddy, °antique, *Brit* OAP (= 'old-age pensioner'), *Chiefly US* retiree, *Colloq* (old) geezer, °wreck, *Slang* dodo: *It's hard to understand what those two*

old ruins see in each other. **6** **ruins**: debris, °wreckage, °fragments, rubble, °remains: *He stood among the ruins of the burnt-out house wondering what to do next. She was trying to piece together the ruins of her disastrous marriage.*
—*v.* **7** °destroy, °devastate, °demolish, annihilate, °dissolve, °wipe out, °undo, °overthrow, lay °waste, °raze, °shatter, °wreck, °crush, °flatten, wreak °havoc (up)on, °reduce to °nothing or °naught, °pulverize, smash, bring to °ruin: *The bomb ruined the entire centre of the city.* **8** °spoil, disfigure, °damage, °botch, °mess up, make a °mess of, °mar, uglify: *The county office building completely ruins the Aylesbury skyline.* **9** °spoil, °destroy, °wreck, nullify, °damage, °harm, °hurt, °impair, °poison, *Slang* louse up, °screw up, put the kibosh on, *US* bollix up, *Taboo slang chiefly Brit* make a balls-up of: *I think that your behaviour at the office party may just have ruined your prospects for promotion.* **10** bankrupt, pauperize, impoverish, reduce to penury or °poverty or destitution or indigence: *Paying off the loan virtually ruined me.* **11** °violate, deflower, °ravish, °seduce, °lead astray, °dishonour, defile, °corrupt, °debase: *She claimed that it was the local squire who ruined her, despite evidence to the contrary.*

ruinous *adj.* °disastrous, °destructive, catastrophic, °calamitous, deleterious, pernicious, crippling, cataclysmic, baleful, °fatal, toxic, °poisonous, noxious, °harmful, °injurious, °nasty, *Archaic* baneful: *Smoking can be ruinous to your health. Who was behind the ruinous decision to move the factory to the north-east?*

rule *n.* **1** °regulation, °order, °law, ordinance, ruling, °decree, ukase, statute, °principle, °direction, °guide, guideline, °precept: *We go by the Golden Rule here, Jim, 'Do unto others before they do unto you'.* **2** °dominion, °authority, °control, °sovereignty, °sway, °command, ascendancy, °direction, °oversight, supervision, mastery: *How could such a despised monarch maintain rule over a people for so long?* **3** °fact, °standard, customs, °practice, °form, °routine, °convention, °policy, way things are: *Honesty and integrity among our students are the rule rather than the exception.* **4 as a rule**: °generally, °usually, normally, customarily, for the most °part, mostly, °ordinarily, °mainly, in the °main, °chiefly, on the °whole, commonly, more often than not: *As a rule, we require payment in advance.*
—*v.* **5** Sometimes, **rule over**: °reign (over), °govern, be in °control or °charge or °command (of or over), be in °power (over), hold °sway (over), °wield the sceptre, wear the °crown, °run; °prevail, °dominate, °predominate, °control: *The hand that rocks the cradle rules the world. Supposedly, the majority rules in a democracy.* **6** °direct, °guide, °manage, °control, °lead, °head (up), °preside (over), superintend, °oversee, °supervise, °regulate, °govern, °run: *The company is ruled by a committee made up of employees and directors.* **7** °decide, °judge, hand down a °judgement or °decision, °decree, deem, °resolve, °settle, °determine, °find, °declare, °pronounce: *The referee ruled that Jones had committed a foul.* **8 rule out**: °ban, °bar, °prohibit, °exclude, °eliminate, °forbid, °preclude, proscribe, negate, °dismiss, °disregard, °bypass, °ignore, °overlook: *The programme committee ruled out Birmingham as the site of next year's conference.*

rummage v. **1** °search, °hunt, comb, °scour, scrabble, °look through, °sift through, °turn inside out or upside down, °examine, Colloq °scrounge: *We rummaged about in four dustbins before finding the discarded receipt.*
—n. **2** °jumble, miscellanea, knick-knacks, °odds and ends, °hotchpotch or US also hodgepodge: *May we borrow your car to collect items for the church rummage sale?*

rumour n. **1** °news, °gossip, hearsay, °information, °scoop, tidings, °chat, chit-chat, tittle-tattle, on dit; °grapevine, jungle telegraph, Colloq °low-down, info, US and Canadian poop, Slang chiefly US nautical scuttlebutt: *The rumour is that they are moving from Reading to Exeter. Rumour has it that you are not going with them.*
—v. **2** bruit about, °noise abroad, °circulate, °pass around, °intimate, °breathe, °suggest, °whisper, °leak, °reveal, °make known, °put about, °say, °report, °tell: *It has been rumoured that she is going to have his baby.*

rumple v. Sometimes, **rumple up**: °wrinkle, °crumple, °crush, crease, °fold, crinkle, dishevel, °ruffle, °tousle, scrunch (up), °pucker, muss (up), °mess (up): *When she stood up, the back of her dress was all rumpled.*

rumpus n. commotion, °disturbance, °fuss, °confusion, °uproar, °tumult, to-do, ado, °mayhem, °bedlam, brouhaha, °stir, pother, affray, °fracas, °row, mêlée or melee, °rough-house, °brawl: *You have no idea what a rumpus he created just because my dog went in his garden.*

run v. **1** sprint, °race, scamper, °scurry, °scud, dart, °bolt, °dash, °flit, °tear (along), scoot, scuttle, zip, whiz or whizz, gallop, °jog, °trot, lope; °rush, °hurry (up), °hasten, °scramble, °hustle, °step °lively, hop (to) it, °step on it, put on some °speed, Archaic hie, Colloq get a °move on, hoof it, °leg it, hotfoot (it), °stir one's stumps, Brit hare, US °step on the gas, hump (it), Slang get cracking, US get the lead out (of one's pants or taboo ass), Chiefly US get a wiggle on: *If you run, you might catch her before she gets on the train.* **2** run away or off, °flee, °escape, take °flight, take to one's °heels, °bolt, decamp, °make off, °clear out, show a clean pair of °heels, abscond, cut and run, (beat a (hasty)) °retreat, °retire, make a °getaway, (make a) run for it, Colloq °beat it, scram, skedaddle, °take off, °skip (out), take French °leave, °fly the coop, Slang head for the hills, Brit scarper, do a bunk, US and Canadian take a (run-out) °powder, lam out of (somewhere), take it or go on the lam, US vamoose: *The minute the enemy appeared, the entire troop ran. Cavendish ran, hoping the police wouldn't catch him.* **3** °go, °cover, °pass over, sprint, °race: *He ran the mile in just under four minutes.* **4** °wander, rove, °roam, °meander, °drift: *Some farmers allow their animals to run free, rather than penning them up.* Often, **run for**: °compete (for), be a °candidate (for), °vie, °struggle, contend, °fight (for), °stand (for): *As she has already said she would not stand again, I doubt that she will run for re-election in the council elections.* **6** °pass, °flow, °pour, °stream, °flood, °gush, °spill, dribble, °spurt, °issue, °move, °trickle, seep, °discharge, cascade, °spout: *You can see where the rainwater has run down this crack in the roof and into the room below.* **7** °flow, °diffuse: *The colour ran when he washed his red underwear with some white shirts in*

very hot water. **8** °melt, liquefy, °dissolve, °fuse: *It was so hot that the icing on top of the cake began to melt and run down the sides.* **9** °keep, °maintain, °support, °sustain, °manage: *It is very expensive to run a large house.* **10** °operate, °manage, °direct, °supervise, °oversee, °conduct, superintend, °control, °handle, °manipulate, °head, °carry on, °lead, °regulate, take °care of, °look after, °administer, be in °charge of, °coordinate: *She must be a terrifically high achiever to run a huge international conglomerate like that!* **11** °operate, °perform, °function, °work, tick, °go: *Even after all that abuse, the watch kept running and kept good time.* **12** °extend, °stretch, °reach; °amount, °add up, °total up, °come (up): *The balance of payments deficit is running to twice last year's figure. His bill at the restaurant last night ran to more than £200.* **13** convey, °transport, give (someone) a °lift, °drive, °take, °bring: *Tom said he would run me home in his new car.* **14** bootleg, smuggle, °deal or °traffic in, Chiefly US and Canadian rustle: *During Prohibition, his father ran whisky from Canada to the US.* **15** be in °effect or °force, be °effective, have °force or °effect: *This lease has another year to run.* **16** °incur, invite, °encourage, °attract, be subjected to: *Aren't you running a risk asking Sheila to handle your money?* **17** °propel, °drive; °steer, °guide, °navigate: *If you are inept enough to run a boat aground, at least have the sense to do it at low tide.* **18** unravel, come °undone, Chiefly Brit ladder: *My stocking ran just before I had to leave for the dance!* **19** Sometimes, **run off**: °print, °offset, lithograph, °reproduce, °publish, °display; imprint, °position, °place, °locate, °lay out: *They are going to run his story in the next issue of* The Londoner! *We'll run the photographs of the fire alongside the article on page one.* **20 run across**: °meet (up with), run into, °come across, °find, °stumble on or upon, °hit or °chance or °happen upon, Colloq °bump into: *Guess whom I ran across at Harrods yesterday.* **21 run after**: °chase, °pursue, °go after, court, woo, Colloq set one's cap for: *The City is filled with young men and women running after big money. Mick is running after this girl half his age, and he hasn't a clue that she's leading him on.* **22 run along**: °go away, °leave, Slang get °lost: *Sue wanted to get rid of Wayne and told him to run along.* **23 run around**: philander, be unfaithful, gallivant, Colloq sleep around, play the field: *How does she cope with his constant running around?* **24 run around with**: °associate with, spend time with, dally with, consort with: *Cynthia is running around with a bad crowd these days.* **25 run away**: See **2**, above. **26 run down**: **a** °trace, °track, °hunt, °stalk, °follow, °pursue, dog, °shadow; °find, °locate, °track down, °discover: *We ran down the suspect in an abandoned barn in Little Fakenham.* **b** °criticize, decry, defame, °vilify, °disparage, deprecate, °depreciate, denigrate, Colloq °knock, °pan: *If you keep running him down like that he'll develop an inferiority complex before he's seven.* **c** °weaken, °tire, °expire, play (itself) out, °burn out, run out, °fail, Colloq peter out: *Once the batteries have run down, we will no longer be able to transmit a distress-signal.* **d** °strike, °hit, smash or °crash or °slam into, run over, °knock over or down, °collide with: *On the way home, he almost ran down a boy on a bicycle.* **27 run in**: °arrest, take into °custody, °jail, apprehend, take or bring in, Colloq °pinch, °nab, °pull in, bust, collar, Brit

°nick: *This is the third time this week that Minette has been run in for soliciting.* **28 run into**: See 20, above. **29 run off**: **a** See 2, above.
b °duplicate, °print, °copy, °turn out, °produce, °make, °manufacture, °generate, *Colloq* do, churn out: *How quickly can you run off 1,000 copies of this brochure?* **30 run out**: **a** be °exhausted, °expire, °terminate, (come *or* draw to a) °close, °end, °cease: *The time for renewing your subscription has run out.* **b** °finish, °go, be °exhausted, be used up, *Colloq* peter out: *The food had run out and we had no water when we were rescued.* **31 run out of**: °use up, °consume, °eat up, °exhaust, be out of: *We've run out of milk—can you nip down to the shop and get some?* **32 run out on**: °desert, °abandon, °leave high and dry, °forsake, °leave in the lurch, °leave holding the baby: *Despite all his promises, Edgar ran out on her when she became pregnant.* **33 run over**: **a** See 26 d, above. **b** °scan, run through, °go over, °look over, °flip *or* leaf *or* °thumb through, °look at, °skim (through), °browse through, °dip into, °review: *I promised Casey I would run over his article if I had the time.* **c** overflow, °spill (over), °brim over, slosh over, °pour over; °extend, °reach, °spread over, °stretch over; °exceed, go beyond, overreach, overshoot, °surpass, °transcend: *She accidentally let the bath run over, ruining the ceiling below. This article will run over onto the next page. McClelland always runs over the time allotted to his part of the proceedings.*
d °rehearse, run through, °repeat, °practise, °review, °go over, °study, °learn, °memorize: *You'd best run over your speech again before the banquet.* **34 run through**: **a** °pierce, °stab, °transfix, °stick, °spit: *In the last scene, the hero runs the villain through with his sword before succumbing to his own wounds.* **b** squander, °consume, °use up, °waste, °fritter away, °exhaust, deplete, °spend, °dissipate, °throw away, *Slang* °blow: *It didn't take Hugh more than a year to run through his inheritance.* **c** See 33 b, above.
—*n.* **35** sprint, °dash, °race, °jog, °trot: *They go for a two-mile run every morning before breakfast.* **36** °trip, °journey, °visit, °drive, °expedition, trek, °outing, °excursion, jaunt, junket, °sojourn, *Colloq* °spin, joyride: *He has to make a run over to Paris for the weekend, supposedly on business.* **37** °route, °routine, °circuit, °passage, °trip, °cycle, °round; °beat: *I was on the Murmansk run during the war.* **38** °period, °spate, °interval, °time, °spell, °stretch, °course; °engagement, booking, *Colloq* °patch: *Roger has had a run of bad luck and could use some help. The show had a long run on Broadway.* **39** access, °freedom, °liberty: *The children had the run of the house for a week while their parents were away.* **40** °return, °satisfaction, °reward, recompense, compensation, °requital, expiation, °atonement, repayment, °remuneration: *Although the money is never in your favour, you get a good run for your money at Diamond Lil's Gambling Emporium.* **41** series, °sequence, °stream, °spate, °string, °succession, °progression: *Will attributed his poor showing at the tournament to a bad run of cards.* **42** °stream, °brook, runnel, °creek, rill, rivulet, *Brit* beck, *Scots* burn, *US* branch, kill: *There is a small run at the bottom of the hill.* **43** °demand, °call, °request: *Bouillon cubes seem to have enjoyed quite a run lately.* **44** °type, °category, °class, °kind, °sort: *Mark*

seems to be a bit more refined than the usual run of guest at Lisa's parties. **45** °trail, °track, piste, °path, °slope; °way, runway: *She skied down the north run in record time.* **46** °enclosure, yard, °pen, °compound, runway; paddock; °pound: *There is a good-sized run at the kennel where we board the dogs when we go on holiday.* **47** *Music* roulade, cadenza, arpeggio, riff: *The soprano treated us to a marvellous run in which each note was distinct and pure.* **48 in the long run**: °eventually, °finally, after all, °ultimately, in (due) °time, in due course, in fine, in the °end, at the °end of the day, in the °final °analysis, all things considered, when all is said and done: *Regardless of early troubles, things always seem to turn out all right in the long run in his plays.* **49 on the run**: **a** °hastily, in °haste, hurriedly, while under °way, in a °hurry, at °speed, in a °rush: *It isn't supposed to be good for you to eat breakfast on the run every day.* **b** on the °loose, fleeing, escaping, in °flight, °running (away), *Slang US* on the lam: *He was on the run from the police and desperate to find Duncan.* **c** °running, retreating, on the °move *or* the °go: *They kept the enemy on the run for a week.* **50 the runs**: diarrhoea, dysentery, °upset °stomach, *Jocular* tummy rot, Delhi belly, Aztec hop, turista *or* tourista, Mexican foxtrot *or* two-step *or* toothache, Montezuma's revenge, curse of Montezuma, Rangoon runs, Tokyo trots, Lambeth run(s): *I came down with the runs when we got to Ankara.*

run-around *n.* °evasive treatment; °slip: *Every time he applied for help he was given the run-around.*

runaway *n.* **1** °fugitive, escapee, °refugee, °deserter, °truant, absconder: *The lad is a notorious runaway who has escaped four times before.* —*adj.* **2** °wild, °uncontrolled, unchecked, °rampant, °renegade, unsuppressed; driverless, riderless, °loose; escaped: *Runaway inflation is ruining the economy of the country. The runaway horses were finally brought back.* **3** °easy, °effortless, °overwhelming, uncontested: *The incumbent enjoyed a runaway victory in yesterday's election.*

run-down *adj.* **1** wearied, °exhausted, debilitated, weakened, °worn out, peaked, °fatigued, enervated, °tired, drained, °spent, out of °shape *or* °condition, below °par, in °bad °shape; °unhealthy, °sickly, °ill: *He was found in a badly run-down condition, but was soon back on his feet.* **2** °ramshackle, °dilapidated, °tumbledown, °decrepit, °rickety, broken-down: *The family lives in a run-down cottage on the edge of the moor.* —*n.* **3** °run-through, °synopsis, °summary, °survey, °précis, résumé, (°thumbnail) sketch, °outline, °rough °idea, °review, recapitulation, briefing; °highlights, high points: *Give me a quick run-down of what happened while I was gone.*

run-in *n.* °disagreement, °argument, °dispute, altercation, °quarrel, confrontation, contretemps: *We had a run-in with our neighbour about playing his hi-fi too loud.*

runner *n.* **1** sprinter, racer, jogger, hurdler, miler: *Gordon is one of our best runners and ought to make the Olympic team.* **2** °messenger, courier, errand-boy, errand-girl, messenger-boy, messenger-girl, °page, dispatch-bearer *or* despatch-bearer, dispatch-rider *or* despatch-rider, *Colloq US* gofer: *The runner said that the package fell off his motor cycle and he lost it.* **3** sucker, tendril, creeper, °shoot, °branch,

°stem: *Tie these runners to the frame in order to train the vine.* **4** °blade: *The runners on your skates need sharpening.*

running *n.* **1** °operation, °management, °direction: *Who attends to the everyday running of the business while you are away?* **2** °competition, °contest, °meet, °tournament, °race, °match; °event, °game: *If he is found to take steroids, he'll be out of the running.*
—*adj.* **3** °continuous, on-going, °continual, °perpetual, °sustained, °constant, uninterrupted, ceaseless, unceasing: *Where do they get the energy to keep up a running argument on the same silly subject?*

runt *n.* °dwarf, pygmy, midget: *Save the runt of the litter for me.*

run-through *n.* **1** °rehearsal, °practice, °trial, °test: *Let's have one more run-through before tomorrow's dress rehearsal.* **2** See **run-down**, above.

rupture *n.* **1** °break, °rift, °split, fissure, °fracture, cleavage, bursting; breaking, splitting, break-up, °breach, °schism, disunity, breaking up, severance, °division, °separation: *The rupture was caused by the expansion of the water on freezing. There was no rupture in friendly relations between the families.* **2** hernia: *He is to undergo surgery for a rupture.*
—*v.* **3** °break (up *or* apart), °split, °fracture, °cleave, °divide, °breach, °separate; °disrupt, °part, sunder: *The fabric of the balloon ruptured, the gas escaped, and the basket plummeted earthward.*

rural *adj.* **1** °country, °pastoral, sylvan, bucolic, °rustic, Arcadian, exurban; agricultural, agrarian, *Literary* georgic: *They always preferred rural life to life in the city. Constable painted mainly rural scenes. He sells farm equipment, strictly a rural business.* **2** See **rustic**, 2, below.

ruse *n.* °trick, °device, °deception, °manoeuvre *or chiefly US* maneuver, °dodge, °pretence, °pretext, °subterfuge, °stratagem, ploy, °hoax, °wile, °artifice, imposture: *His feigned friendship was only a ruse to get them to reveal their next move.*

rush *v.* **1** °hurry (up), °hasten, °run, °race, °hustle, bustle, make °haste, °dash, °speed, °scurry, °scramble, scoot, °jump, sprint, scamper, scuttle, *Colloq* °move (it), hotfoot (it), skedaddle, °step on it, make it °snappy, *US* hightail (it), °step on the gas, *Slang* get °moving, get cracking, get a wiggle on, go like a bat out of hell, shake a °leg: *If you want the job, you'll have to rush to send in your application. Don't rush—*

there's plenty for everyone. **2** °attack, °assault, °charge, °storm, blitz: *If we rush them, we might take them by surprise.*
—*n.* **3** °hurry, °haste, °hustle, bustle, °dash, °speed, turmoil, turbulence, °flurry, commotion, °ferment, pother, ado, to-do, °excitement, °pell-mell, harum-scarum: *What's the rush?* **4** °surge, °sensation, °thrill, °charge: *I felt a rush of pleasure when I saw her coming down the street.*
—*adj.* **5** °urgent, hurry-up, exigent, high-priority, top-priority, °emergency: *This is a rush job that must be completed today.*

rustic *adj.* **1** See **rural**, 1, above. **2** °peasant, °plain, °simple, uncomplicated, °unsophisticated, °naïve, °ingenuous, guileless, °artless, °unrefined, unpolished, countrified, uncultivated, uncultured, °boorish, °crude, °rough, unmannerly, hill-billy, backwoods, °awkward, ungainly, cloddish, plodding, oafish, gawky, lumpen, loutish: *Who could dream that such a rustic homebody would some day be famous for the most fashionable literary salon in London?*
—*n.* **3** °peasant, bumpkin, °boor, yokel, hill-billy, countryman, countrywoman, °country boy *or* girl, oaf, °country cousin, *Colloq* clodhopper, *Derogatory and offensive* bog-trotter, *US and Canadian* hayseed, hick: *In those days, few rustics ever even visited a city.*

rustle *v.* **1** °whisper, °swish, sibilate, susurrate: *Outside my window, the leaves rustled in the evening breeze.*
—*n.* **2** °whisper, whispering, rustling, °swish, swishing, sibilation, sibilance, susurration, susurrus: *I heard the faint rustle of satin and knew she was listening at the door.*

rut *n.* **1** °groove, °furrow, wheel-mark, °track, trough: *In the winter the ruts in the lane fill with water and freeze, making driving difficult.* **2** °pattern, °habit, °routine, °groove, °grind, treadmill, dead end, *Colloq* rat race: *After 27 years as a horse groom, I'm beginning to feel I'm stuck in a rut.*

ruthless *adj.* pitiless, unpitying, °cruel, °unsympathetic, °merciless, °unmerciful, °harsh, °fierce, °remorseless, uncompassionate, °vicious, °savage, °ferocious, hard-hearted, °callous, unfeeling, °tough, °severe, °heartless, °inhuman, °brutal, brutish, unrelenting, °relentless, *Chiefly US and Canadian* °mean: *The jail houses some of the country's most ruthless criminals. In all of history there was no more ruthless a tyrant.*

S

sabotage n. **1** °destruction, °damage, wrecking, °impairment: *Enemy infiltrators were responsible for the sabotage of our radar.* **2** °subversion, treachery, treason: *When the radar was found damaged, sabotage was suspected.*
—v. **3** °undermine, °subvert, °disrupt, °spoil, °ruin, °cripple; °damage, °incapacitate, disable, °destroy, °wreck, *Colloq Brit* throw a spanner in(to) the works, *US* throw a monkey wrench into the machinery, *Slang Brit* °queer (someone's pitch): *Only someone who had something to lose would have sabotaged our plan for reorganization. The engine had been sabotaged by pouring sand into the fuel tank.*

sack n. **1** °pouch, °bag, *Scots and US dialect* poke; *Technical* sac: *She bought a 10-pound sack of potatoes.* **2 hit the sack**: °retire, °turn in, go to bed *or* to °sleep, *Slang* hit the hay, *Brit* kip (down), *US* sack out: *I need my beauty sleep so I'm going to hit the sack.* **3 the sack**: °dismissal, °discharge, firing, *Colloq* heave-ho, the axe, marching orders, *US* pink slip, bounce, *Chiefly US and Canadian* walking papers, *Slang Brit* the boot, the chop, the °push: *Ten of us got the sack when the new management took over.*
—v. **4** °dismiss, °discharge, °fire, let go, °lay off, *Brit* make *or* declare °redundant, *Colloq* give (someone) the axe *or* the (old) heave-ho, give (someone) his *or* her marching orders, *Brit* give (someone) the sack, *US* bounce, *Slang Brit* give (someone) the boot *or* the chop *or* the °push: *Now that he's been sacked, Norman will be able to spend more time with the children.*

sacred adj. **1** consecrated, dedicated, hallowed, °holy, blessed, blest, sanctified, revered, °divine, awe-inspiring, °venerable, venerated, sainted, heaven-sent: *This is a most sacred Islamic site.* **2** inviolable, inviolate, untouchable, protected, sacrosanct: *They held nothing sacred as they ransacked the temple.* **3** °religious, °spiritual, °ceremonial, church(ly), ecclesiastical, °priestly, hieratic, °ritual, °solemn, sacramental, liturgical: *He continued to carry out his sacred duties despite the war.*

sacrifice n. **1** immolation, °surrender, forfeiture, forgoing, giving up, yielding up, °offering (up), °offer, *Christian religion* oblation: *The Aztec religion demanded the sacrifice of human beings.* **2** forfeiture, forgoing, giving up, relinquishment, °loss: *Mrs Clinton continues her charitable work at the sacrifice of much of her time.*
—v. **3** immolate, °offer (up), °yield (up), °give up: *In their religion, they were required to sacrifice small animals to propitiate the gods.* **4** °give up, °forgo, °forfeit, °relinquish, °surrender, °let °go, °lose, °yield, °renounce, forswear; forbear, desist, °cease, °stop, °refrain from: *She was quite ready to sacrifice her inheritance to see justice done. If you sacrificed smoking you could give the money you save to charity.*

sacrificial adj. **1** sacrificed, immolated, surrendered, given up, yielded: *They led the sacrificial lamb to the slaughter.* **2** atoning, expiatory, °propitiatory, conciliatory: *The solemn sacrificial ceremonies were carried out by the high priestess.*

sacrilege n. **1** desecration, profanation, debasement, °violation, °prostitution, dishonouring, vitiation, defilement, befouling, fouling, contamination, befoulment, °misuse, °abuse, °perversion, maltreatment: *The horrendous Buckinghamshire county office building is an example of architectural sacrilege.* **2** impiety, heresy, profanation, °outrage, °violation, °profanity, blasphemy, impiousness, irreverence, °disrespect, secularization: *It was an unscrupulous sacrilege to appropriate to his own use the offerings to the gods.*

sacrilegious adj. °profane, °impious, °heretical, °blasphemous, °irreverent, °disrespectful: *The inscription contains a curse on any who perpetrate any sacrilegious act against the remains of the pharaoh.*

sad adj. **1** °unhappy, °melancholy, downcast, °dejected, depressed, °low, °sorrowful, °gloomy, morose, °glum, lugubrious, °mournful, heartsick, crestfallen, chap-fallen, disheartened, °downhearted, °blue, °despondent, °broken-hearted, °heartbroken, °woebegone, °miserable, °wretched: *Danny was so sad when his dog died that he wept for a week.* **2** depressing, °gloomy, disheartening, °dreary, °dismal, °funereal, °sombre, lugubrious, saddening, heartbreaking, °bleak, distressing, dispiriting, °calamitous: *It was a sad day for all of us here when the England team lost the semifinal.* **3** °unfortunate, °unsatisfactory, °awful, °bad, °shabby, °dirty, °lamentable, °miserable, °sorry, °wretched, °pathetic, °pitiful, °pitiable, °deplorable, °terrible, *Colloq* °lousy, °rotten: *After two weeks under water, the sofa was in pretty sad shape.*

sadden v. °depress, deject, °sorrow, dishearten, °distress, dispirit, °discourage, °grieve, aggrieve: *It saddens me to think of all the starving people.*

sadistic adj. °cruel, °monstrous, °brutal, brutish, °beastly, °ruthless, °perverse, *Technical* algolagnic: *She derives sadistic pleasure from reminding me of all my failures. The scars and bruises confirmed the sadistic treatment he had undergone.*

sadly adv. **1** unfortunately, alas, unhappily, unluckily, lamentably, regrettably, deplorably, °sad to relate: *Sadly, all our oldest oaks were uprooted in the hurricane.* **2** unhappily, gloomily, morosely, mournfully, despondently, miserably, wretchedly, dejectedly, dismally, sombrely, lugubriously: *He told me sadly that he did not expect to return to England again.*

sadness n. unhappiness, dolour, °misery, °sorrow, dispiritedness, °grief, °depression, dejection, dejectedness, sorrowfulness, despondency, °melancholy, °gloom, gloominess: *It is hard to describe the sadness we all felt when she left.*

safe adj. **1** unharmed, °whole, uninjured, unhurt, (safe and) °sound, °secure, protected, shielded, sheltered, out of harm's way, all right, *Colloq* °OK or okay: *You'll be safe here with me.* **2** °harmless, non-toxic, non-poisonous, innocuous; unpolluted: *This medication is safe if you do not exceed the recommended dosage. Is the water safe to drink?* **3** °sure, °secure, °sound,

protected, risk-free, riskless, safe as the Bank of England, °reliable, dependable, °solid, bona fide, °conservative, tried and °true, *Brit* safe as houses: *It was previously thought that an investment in Alfordyce Ltd was safe.* **4** all right, allowable, °permissible, °acceptable, °satisfactory, °appropriate, °suitable, °timely, °right, °correct, °proper, justifiable, justified, *Colloq* °OK or okay: *Is it safe to come out now?* **5** secured, protected: *The children are safe in bed. Your secret is safe with me.*
—*adv.* **6** safely, securely: *I won't breathe easy till he's safe behind bars.*
—*n.* **7** vault, °crypt, strongbox, safe-deposit or safety-deposit °box, coffer, °chest, repository: *The necklace is kept in the safe and I never get a chance to wear it.*

safeguard *n.* **1** °protection, °defence, °security: *Such a flimsy fence is hardly a sufficient safeguard.*
—*v.* **2** °protect, °defend, °shield, °shelter, keep °safe, °guard; °conserve, °save, °keep, °care for, °look after: *What is being done to safeguard the passengers from attacks by bandits?*

safe keeping *n.* °charge, °protection, keeping, °custody, °care, guardianship: *The deed to the house is in the safe keeping of Mr Williams, my solicitor.*

safety *n.* safeness, °protection, aegis, °cover, °shelter, °security, °refuge; °sanctuary, °safe keeping: *There's safety in numbers, so the more the merrier. We retreated to the safety of the castle dungeon.*

sag *v.* **1** °droop, °sink, °slump, °bend, °dip; swag, °bag: *The board sagged precariously under his weight. Without a breath stirring, the banners sagged in the humid air.* **2** °drop, °decrease, °decline, °go or come down, °fall, °slide, °slip, °weaken, °slump, °descend, °diminish, lessen, °droop, °subside, °flag, falter, °wilt: *The value of the dollar sagged in world markets today.*
—*n.* **3** sagging, °drop, °droop, °sinking, sinkage, subsidence, °dip; reduction, °decrease, °decline, °fall, °slide, weakening, °slump, lessening, flagging, faltering: *If you stand over here you can see a definite sag in the roof. The sag in profits was attributed to a poor response to the new model.*

saga *n.* (heroic) °legend, °narrative, epic, Edda, °chronicle, °romance, *roman-fleuve*, °story, °tale, °adventure: *Are you really interested in the continuing saga of the inhabitants of Coronation Street?*

sage *adj.* **1** °wise, sagacious, °prudent, °sensible, perspicacious, °profound, °intelligent, discerning, °reasonable, °logical, °judicious, common-sense, commonsensical: *The old woman gave her some sage advice about men, which she promptly forgot.*
—*n.* **2** °wise man, savant, °expert, °elder, doyen or doyenne, guru, Nestor, pundit, Solomon, philosopher, °oracle, °authority: *The sage whose counsel you seek lives deep in the forest.*

sail *v.* **1** °navigate, °pilot, °steer: *Sail as close to the shore as possible to avoid the whirlpool.* **2** go sailing or boating or yachting, °cruise, set sail, put (out) to sea: *Would you like to sail to the Isle of Wight for the weekend?* **3** °drift, °move lightly, breeze, °flow, °waft, °sweep, °coast, °float, °scud, °glide, °slide, °slip, °plane, °skim, °fly, °flit: *It was delightful to watch the tiny boats sailing, tacking, beating, and running in the brisk wind.*
—*n.* **4** canvas: *The schooner was carrying all the sail she could.*

sailor *n.* seaman, seafarer, °seafaring man or woman, seagoing man or woman, mariner, (old) °salt, sea dog, bluejacket, shellback, yachtsman, yachtswoman, boatman, boatwoman, deck-hand, captain, °skipper, *Literary* Jack Tar, *Colloq* tar, *Naval US* swab, swabbie, gob: *When she said she had married a sailor I didn't know she meant that he had a 100-foot yacht.*

saintly *adj.* °holy, blessed, blest, beatific, °godly, sainted, angelic, °seraphic, °pure, °righteous, °virtuous, °blameless: *Donald was such a saintly man, it was impossible to think ill of him.*

sake *n.* **1** °benefit, °welfare, well-being, °good, °advantage, °behalf, °profit, °gain, °account: *Joe and I stayed together for the sake of the children. She felt pleased, for his sake, that he had managed to get away.* **2** °purpose(s), °reason(s), °objective(s): *Just for the sake of comparison, let us now look at the situation in Taiwan.*

salary *n.* °income, °pay, °earnings, compensation, °remuneration, emolument; °wage(s): *I can't afford a new car on my present salary.*

sale *n.* **1** selling, °traffic, vending, marketing, trafficking, trading; °trade, °exchange, °transaction: *The sale of alcoholic beverages on Sundays is prohibited. Provide a receipt for each sale.* **2** °trade, °purchase; trading, buying, purchasing: *We must do something to boost sales. The house is very reasonably priced for a quick sale.* **3** sales event, mark-down, white sale, jumble sale, *Brit* car-boot sale, *US* rummage sale, garage sale, tag sale, yard sale, *Colloq* sellathon, sales marathon: *We are having a sale to clear out things we no longer want or need.* **4** °transaction: *She hasn't made a sale in a week.* **5 on sale**: *US* marked down, cut-price, bargain-priced; reduced (in price): *Bacon is on sale this week at half price.* **6 (up) for sale**: on the market, °available, in stock, *Chiefly Brit* on sale, on offer, *US* on the block: *Their house is for sale to the highest bidder.*

salesperson *n.* salesman, saleswoman, saleslady, salesgirl, sales-clerk, clerk, *Chiefly Brit* shop-girl, *Brit* shop °assistant, *Old-fashioned* counter-jumper: *The shop is noted for its wide range of merchandise and the efficiency and courtesy of its salespeople.*

salient *adj.* °conspicuous, °outstanding, °pronounced, °noticeable, °prominent, °significant, °important, °marked, °impressive, °striking, °remarkable, distinguishing, °distinctive, °unique, °eminent, °noteworthy, °notable, °principal, °chief, °primary: *A salient feature of this policy is that it can be converted at any time from a straight life to an endowment policy.*

salt *n.* **1** common or table salt, sodium chloride, sea salt, rock-salt: *A little salt will bring out the flavour.* **2** °spice, spiciness, °zest, zestiness, pungency, °vigour, °vitality, liveliness, °pep, °pepper, poignancy, piquancy, °relish, °bite, °savour, °seasoning, °taste, *Colloq* zip, zing, °punch: *Yes, do invite Randolph, for he can be relied on to add a little salt to the dinner conversation.* **3** (Attic) °wit, Attic salt, °dry °humour, °sarcasm: *Her conversation is sprinkled with the salt of clever aphorisms.* **4** See sailor, above. **5 with a grain** or **pinch of salt**: *cum grano salis*, warily, cautiously, qualifiedly, qualifyingly, doubtfully, sceptically, suspiciously, reservedly, with °reservation(s) or °qualification(s): *You have to take what he says with a grain of salt.*

—v. **6** °season, °spice, °flavour, °pepper: *The pirate's speech was salted with expressions like 'Shiver me timbers!', 'Avast there!', and 'Blow me down!'* **7** pickle, °cure, °preserve, corn, marinate, souse: *The book gives several recipes for curing ham and salting beef.* **8 salt away:** °save (up), °hoard, °put or °lay or °set by or aside, squirrel away, °store up, stockpile, °amass, °accumulate, °pile up, *Colloq* stash away, *US and Canadian* sock away: *They were always terribly stingy, claiming they were salting something away for their old age.* *—adj.* **9** salty, saline, brackish, briny: *The water had a salt taste.* **10** pickled, kippered, marinated, soused; corned; cured: *Do you like salt herring?*

salute *v.* **1** °greet, °hail, °address, accost: *The moment I stepped in at the door I was saluted with the peremptory question, 'Where have you been?'* **2** pay °respects or °homage or °tribute to, °honour, °recognize, °acknowledge: *Wherever she went she was saluted as a heroine.* *—n.* **3** °greeting, °address, salutation: *He returned my salute with a nod.*

salvage *v.* **1** °save, °recover, °rescue, °redeem, °deliver, °retrieve, °reclaim: *Were you able to salvage anything of value after the fire?* *—n.* **2** °recovery, °rescue, retrieval, redemption, deliverance, reclamation, salvation: *The salvage of a vessel or cargo at sea invests the salvager with legal rights under certain conditions.*

salve *n.* **1** balm, °ointment, unguent, dressing, cream, °lotion, demulcent, embrocation, liniment: *The doctor applied a salve to the wound and bandaged it.* **2** emollient, balm, palliative, °tranquillizer, opiate, anodyne, °narcotic, relief, assuagement: *The money was more a salve to his conscience than a token of his charity.* *—v.* **3** °mitigate, °relieve, °ease, alleviate, assuage, palliate, soothe, mollify, °comfort, appease: *There must be something you can do to allow them to save face and to salve their wounded pride.*

same *adj.* **1** °identical, °exact (same), selfsame; °very: *When I said they were wearing the same dress I meant that they were wearing identical dresses. That's the same tie you wore when we first met.* **2** unchanged, unchanging, °changeless, unmodified, unaltered, °constant, °uniform, unvaried, unvarying; word-for-word, °verbatim: *As you can see, it's the same old Charley you used to know and love. Professor Spicer is still giving the same lecture that he has given all these years.* **3 all the same:** at the same time, °nevertheless, °nonetheless, °even so, °yet, but, anyway, anyhow, in any °case, in any °event, at any °rate, °regardless, °still (and all), in °spite of or °despite the fact, °notwithstanding, for all that, that (having been) said, having said that, after all is said and done, just the same: *Of course you have a right to go; all the same, I wish you had let me know.*

sample *n.* **1** °specimen, °example, °representative, °representation, °illustration, sampling, sampler, cross-section; swatch; °bite, nibble, °taste: *I should like to see a sample before deciding whether to place an order with you.* *—v.* **2** °test, °try, °taste, °experience: *Anyone is welcome to sample the merchandise on request.* *—adj.* **3** °representative, °specimen, illustrative, representational, °trial, °test: *A sample copy of the book is available for examination.*

sanatorium *n.* rest-home, convalescent °home, nursing °home, clinic, health farm, *US also* sanitarium: *After spending a month recuperating in a Swiss sanatorium, Gladys was as good as new.*

sanctify *v.* **1** consecrate, °hallow, make °sacred or °holy, °glorify, °exalt, canonize, enshrine; *Rom Cath Ch* beatify: *The site was sanctified and is visited by pilgrims throughout the year.* **2** °purify, °cleanse: *According to Scripture, some are sanctified before birth.* **3** °confirm, °sanction, °ratify, °justify, °legitimate, legitimatize or legitimize, legalize, °license: *Her family insisted that the marriage be sanctified at the church in Suffolk, where they live.*

sanctimonious *adj.* °hypocritical, °self-righteous, canting, °mealy-mouthed, holier-than-thou, Pharisaical, pietistic, unctuous, Tartuffian, *Colloq* °goody-goody, *Chiefly Brit* smarmy, *Slang Brit* pi: *I wondered what happened to all that sanctimonious talk about putting his family first?*

sanction *n.* **1** confirmation, ratification, secondment, authorization, legalization, legitimatization or legitimization, validation, °licence, certification, °approval, °permission, imprimatur, °seal or °stamp (of °approval), signet: *If you get the sanction of the rest of the members, then I shall agree.* **2** °help, °aid, °encouragement, °support, advocacy, °backing, sponsorship, °favour, countenance: *You will need the sanction of the entire committee in order to win a vote of confidence.* **3** °agreement, concurrence, acceptance, affirmation, assent, acquiescence, compliance, °approval, °OK or okay: *He would never have proceeded with the invasion without the sanction of his generals.* **4** °ban, °penalty, °punishment, °retribution, °discipline, retaliation, redress: *The government decided to introduce sanctions against the regime on account of their atrocious record on human rights.* *—v.* **5** °confirm, °ratify, °second, °authorize, legalize, legitimatize or legitimize, validate, °license, °certify, °approve, °permit, °allow, notarize, °vouchsafe, °subscribe to, commission, °consent to: *If the board sanctions the purchase of the company, it is then up to the shareholders to vote.* **6** °support, °encourage, °advocate, °back, °sponsor, °favour, countenance, °help: *You know I cannot be seen to sanction your plan in preference to others.*

sanctity *n.* °piety, holiness, saintliness, divinity, °grace, sacredness, godliness, °devotion, °dedication: *The arguments of the anti-abortionists were based on a belief in the sanctity of all human life.*

sanctuary *n.* **1** °sanctum, shrine, chapel, °temple, church, house of °worship, house of God; synagogue, mosque, pagoda: *All of us retire at this time to the sanctuary for evening prayer.* **2** asylum, °refuge, °retreat, °protection, °shelter, °safety: *Formerly, criminals could seek sanctuary in churches.* **3** (nature or wildlife) reserve or °preserve, °reservation, conservation area, national °park: *If housing is built here, it will destroy the bird sanctuary.*

sanctum *n.* **1** °sanctuary, holy of holies, shrine: *No one is allowed into the sanctum except the high priestess.* **2** sanctum sanctorum, den, °study, °retreat; hiding-place, hide-out, °hideaway, cubby-hole: *After dinner Roger goes to his sanctum to write.*

sane adj. °normal, of °sound mind, °rational, compos mentis, °well-balanced, right-minded, °level-headed, °reasonable, °sensible, °judicious, Colloq °right in the head, all there: They decided that the killer was sane and fit to stand trial.

sang-froid n. cold-bloodedness, coolness, cool-headedness, °indifference, composure, phlegm, self-possession, °self-control, °poise, imperturbability, equanimity, Colloq unflappability, °cool, coolth: What amazed us was the remarkable sang-froid displayed by even the smallest children in the face of bullying.

sanguinary adj. **1** °bloodthirsty, °cruel, °brutal, brutish, °gory, °merciless, °remorseless, °ruthless, pitiless, °heartless, °savage, barbarous, slaughterous, °grim, fell, °murderous, °homicidal: The axe murder was the most sanguinary crime that the division had ever been required to investigate. **2** bloody, sanguineous, sanguinolent: I am unsure how I survived such a sanguinary battle.

sanguine adj. °optimistic, °rosy, °confident, °hopeful, forward-looking, anticipatory, °expectant, °enthusiastic, fervid, zealous: Some experts took a more sanguine view, saying that they expected to see the start of an economic upturn in the next few months.

sanitary adj. °clean, °sterile, °hygienic, antiseptic, disinfected, aseptic, germ-free, bacteria-free; °healthy, unpolluted, salubrious, healthful, salutary, °wholesome: With such shortages of personnel and equipment, it was impossible to maintain a sanitary hospital environment.

sanity n. saneness, °reason, mental °health or soundness, normality, rationality, reasonableness, °stability, °balance: Have you any reason for suspecting her sanity?

sap[1] n. **1** (vital) °juice or °fluid, bodily or US also body °fluid, lifeblood, °essence, Literary ichor: He apostrophized about how the sap of youth had shrunk from his veins. **2** °fool, idiot, nincompoop, ninny, ninny-hammer, simpleton, ignoramus, nitwit, dim-wit, dunce, ass; °dupe, gull, US thimble-wit; Colloq chump, °drip, Brit (right) charlie, noddy, noodle, °wet, Chiefly Brit °twit, Slang patsy, °sucker, (easy) mark, °pushover, sap-head, Brit muggins, US schnook, schlemiel or schlemihl or shlemiel, fall guy: You certainly were a sap to fall for that old line! —v. **3** bleed, °drain, °draw, °tap, °rob, °milk: I could feel the strength being sapped from my body.

sap[2] v. °undermine, °sabotage, °weaken, °cripple, °wreck, devitalize, deplete, °drain, °erode, °enervate, debilitate: They did everything they could to sap my self-confidence.

sarcasm n. °scorn, contumely, °derision, °ridicule, °bitterness, acrimony, acrimoniousness, acerbity, harshness, acridity, acridness, asperity, °venom, °poison, venomousness, poisonousness, °virulence, °spite, spitefulness, malice, maliciousness, malevolence, °satire, irony, cynicism, disdain: Kathy was too thick-skinned to appreciate the sarcasm of Tom's cutting commentary on her acting.

sarcastic adj. °scornful, contumelious, derisive, °derisory, ridiculing, °bitter, °biting, °cutting, °trenchant, °incisive, acrimonious, acerbic, acid, acidic, acidulous, °harsh, acrid, aspersive, °venomous, °poisonous, °virulent, °spiteful, malicious, malefic, malevolent, satiric(al), ironic(al), cynical, °disdainful, mocking, °contemptuous, °critical, censorious, captious,

carping, cavilling, °sardonic, °scathing, °caustic, °nasty: I don't think he knows how hurtful his sarcastic remarks can be.

sardonic adj. ironic(al), derisive, °derisory, mocking, cynical, °sarcastic: She said that she was leaving him, but his only response was a sardonic smile.

satanic adj. **1** °diabolic(al), °fiendish, °devilish, Mephistophelian, demonic, demoniac(al), cacodemonic, °ghoulish, hellish, °infernal, °evil, °wicked, iniquitous, °corrupt, depraved, °perverted, °perverse, °godless, °ungodly, °impious, unholy, °sinister, °dark, °black, °immoral, amoral: They practise witchcraft and other satanic inventions. **2** dire, °monstrous, heinous, °atrocious, °hideous, °horrible, horrendous, horrid, horrifying, °loathsome, °vile, °abhorrent, unspeakable, unutterable, °damnable, °despicable, °abominable: The miners worked under positively satanic conditions.

satellite n. **1** moon, spacecraft, Old-fashioned sputnik: The sky is crowded with artificial satellites orbiting the earth. **2** °follower, °attendant, retainer, °disciple, acolyte, °aide, aide-de-camp, minion, lieutenant, °assistant, helper, °hanger-on, dependant, °shadow, right-hand man, vassal, °parasite, sycophant, Colloq sidekick: Boswell became the obsequious satellite of Samuel Johnson.

satiate v. **1** °stuff, °glut, °gorge, cloy, °surfeit, overfill, overstuff, °pall, overindulge, °saturate, °choke, deluge, °flood, suffocate, °weary, °exhaust, °bore, °tire, °jade: The travellers were so satiated with food and drink that nothing could wake them. **2** °slake, °satisfy, °quench, °content, °gratify, sate: I felt it would take at least a gallon of water to satiate my thirst.

satiety n. °surfeit, °glut, superabundance, overindulgence, saturation, nimiety, °excess, °superfluity: The painting exudes a mood of sexual languor and satiety.

satire n. **1** °ridicule, irony, °sarcasm, °mockery, spoofing, °exaggeration, °caricature: Often, the best way to comment on a distasteful political situation is through satire. **2** °burlesque, °lampoon, °parody, travesty, pasquinade, spoof, cartoon, °caricature, Colloq °take-off, Chiefly Brit send-up: For several years he wrote mainly satires of life among the wealthy.

satirical adj. satiric, ironic, °sarcastic, mocking, spoofing, °irreverent, exaggerating, Hudibrastic, derisive, disparaging, °abusive, °scornful, °flippant, ridiculing, chaffing: After a number of satirical plays, he returned to writing novels, which, he felt, reached a wider audience.

satirize v. °lampoon, °burlesque, °parody, °caricature, travesty, °poke °fun at, (hold up to) °ridicule, make °fun or °sport of, pillory, °deride, °mock; °mimic, °imitate; Colloq °take off, °put down, Brit °send-up: Since ancient times writers have satirized the follies of their age.

satisfaction n. **1** °gratification, °comfort, °fulfilment, contentment, °delight, °joy, °enjoyment, °pleasure, °happiness: They get a great deal of satisfaction out of seeing their children happily married. **2** °payment, °requital, repayment, compensation, recompense, °remuneration, reparation, °indemnity, indemnification, °restitution, vindication, °damages,

°amends, redress, °atonement, expiation: *The purpose of the lawsuit is to demand satisfaction for the wrongs done to our family.*

satisfactory *adj.* °adequate, °sufficient, °acceptable, °passable, all right, not bad, °good enough, °fair, *Colloq* °OK or okay: *I'd say that the food at Michelle's is satisfactory but not outstanding.*

satisfy *v.* **1** °gratify, °fulfil, °comfort, °please, °content, placate, appease, pacify: *It takes a lot to satisfy him: he is one of the fussiest men I have ever worked with.* **2** °fill, °meet, °fulfil, °provide for, °look after *or* to, °serve, °answer, °comply with, °resolve, solve, °gratify, °indulge; °slake, °quench, sate, °satiate: *Your desire for better working conditions can probably only be satisfied by a change of job. What will it take to satisfy your thirst for adventure?* **3** °convince, °persuade, °reassure, °assure, put (someone's) mind at rest, °content: *He was satisfied that emigration to Australia was the only option open to him.* **4** °pay, °repay, redress, °make good, indemnify, °write off, liquidate: *I shall see to it that the debt is satisfied at once.*

satisfying *adj.* gratifying, °satisfactory, fulfilling, °filling, satiating; comforting, °pleasing, pacifying, °pleasurable: *That was a very satisfying meal. It is a satisfying feeling to know that you are happy.*

saturate *v.* °soak, °wet, °drench, °steep, °fill, imbue, souse, °suffuse, °impregnate, °permeate; waterlog; *Technical* ret: *I got caught in the rain and came home saturated. Make sure that you saturate the earth round the tree once you have finished planting.*

sauce *n.* **1** gravy, condiment: *That sauce on the meat was truly delicious.* **2** °impertinence, sauciness, °impudence, audacity, insolence, brazenness, pertness, °disrespect, disrespectfulness, *Colloq* cheek, cheekiness, lip, back °talk, backchat, °brass, °nerve, °gall, *Slang* crust, *US and Canadian* sass, sassiness: *She had the sauce to tell me to pay at once or get out.*

saunter *v.* °walk, °stroll, amble, °meander, °ramble, °wander, *Colloq* mosey, traipse: *An oddly dressed man sauntered over and asked if I had ever bet on a horse before.*

savage *adj.* **1** °wild, °untamed, undomesticated, feral, unbroken: *These savage beasts had never seen a man before.* **2** °vicious, °ferocious, °fierce, °beastly, bestial, brutish, °bloodthirsty, °brutal, °cruel, °ruthless, pitiless, °merciless, °harsh, bloody, °unmerciful, fell, barbarous, barbaric, °murderous, demonic, demoniac, °sadistic: *The boy was subjected to a savage attack by the defendant's dog. The king's guards were selected for their savage nature.* **3** °wild, °uncivilized, uncultivated, °primitive, °inhuman, bestial, barbaric, barbarous, °untamed, °rude: *The savage behaviour of some New Guinea tribes included cannibalism.*

—*n.* **4** °wild man *or* woman, °brute, °barbarian; Caliban: *When the explorers landed on the island, they were welcomed by the savages who lived there.*

save *v.* **1** (come to someone's) °rescue, °deliver; (set) °free, °liberate, °release, °redeem, bail (someone) out; °recover, °salvage, °retrieve: *What can be done to save me from the drudgery of doing the laundry? She saved only one thing of value from the fire.* **2** °keep, °preserve, °guard, °safeguard, °protect, °conserve, °secure, °shelter, °shield: *One way to save dried flowers is*

to press them between the leaves of a book. **3** lay *or* °put aside, lay *or* °put by, lay *or* °put away, °keep, °retain, °save, °set °apart, °hold, °reserve, °preserve, °conserve; °economize, scrimp, °scrape: *Soon he had saved enough money to buy a new car. If you keep on saving, you may soon have enough for a new suit.* **4** obviate, °preclude, °spare, °prevent: *A little extra care taken now will save a lot of trouble later on.*

saving *adj.* **1** redeeming, redemptory *or* redemptive *or* redemptional, compensating, °compensatory, qualifying, °extenuating, extenuatory: *His one saving grace is that he has a lot of money.* **2** parsimonious, °economical, °thrifty, °provident, °frugal, °sparing, °prudent: *It was only because of Alison's saving nature that we had enough to live on during the strike.*

—*n.* **3** economizing, economization, °economy, °thrift, °providence, frugality, °prudence, scrimping, scraping, sparingness: *It was only by her saving that we survived.* **4** **savings**: °resources, °reserve, °cache, °hoard, nest egg: *Our savings are pay for your education, not for having a good time.*

saviour *n.* **1** rescuer, salvation, °friend in need, Good Samaritan, liberator, redeemer, deliverer, emancipator, °champion, knight errant, knight in shining armour: *Because he gave her a job when she most needed it, she regarded him as her saviour.* **2** **the** *or* **our Saviour**: *Christian religion* Christ (the Redeemer), Jesus, the °Messiah, Lamb of God, Our Lord, Son of God, King of Kings, Prince of Peace, *Islam* Mahdi.

savoir faire *n.* °tact, tactfulness, °sophistication, °finesse, urbanity, °discretion, knowledgeability, °diplomacy, smoothness, °polish, suavity *or* suaveness, °poise, °grace, °style, °skill, adroitness, °knowledge, comprehension, *Slang* savvy: *She felt a vague sense of social inferiority, an uneasy lack of savoir faire.*

savoir vivre *n.* °breeding, °upbringing, comity, °knowledge, °sophistication, °polish: *He has at least enough savoir vivre to know that one doesn't drink red wine with oysters.*

savour *n.* **1** °taste, °flavour, °zest, °tang, smack, piquancy: *These poached peaches have a savour of brandy about them.* **2** °hint, °suggestion, °odour, °scent, °fragrance, °smell, °perfume, redolence, °bouquet, °breath, °trace, °quality, soupçon, °dash: *He preferred talking about the savour rather than the odour of sanctity, for alliteration's sake.*

—*v.* **3** °taste, °sample, °perceive, °detect, °sense, discern, °mark, descry, °observe, °notice, °note, °identify; °enjoy, °luxuriate in, °relish, °indulge in, bask in, °appreciate, °revel in, °delight in, value, °cherish, *Colloq* lick *or* smack one's lips *or* chops over: *One could savour a trace of honey in the wine. For a week we savoured the delights of the Costa Brava.*

savoury *adj.* **1** palatable, °delicious, delectable, °tasty, toothsome, appetizing, °flavourful, flavorous, flavoursome, ambrosial, °luscious: *Pettigrew bit greedily into the savoury flesh of the ripe melon.* **2** °tasteful, °honest, °proper, °decent, °reputable, °respectable, °honourable, creditable, °upright, °decorous, °seemly, °wholesome, °innocent: *I am not sure that Victoria is travelling in particularly savoury society.*

—*n.* **3** appetizer, °hors-d'œuvre; °dessert, °sweet; °morsel, °dainty, °titbit *or US* tidbit, *Chiefly Brit* starter, *Archaic* warner: *I think I'd like the Welsh rabbit as a savoury.*

saw *n.* °proverb, °maxim, (old) saying, aphorism, apophthegm *or* apothegm, axiom, adage, °epigram, gnome; °slogan, °motto, catchword, catch-phrase, °byword; dictum, platitude, °truism, °cliché, commonplace: *She always quoted to him the old saw, 'A fool and his mother are soon parted'.*

say *v.* **1** °state, affirm, °declare, °maintain, °hold, aver, °remark, assert, °claim, asseverate, °announce: *She said that I had to go at once, and I said, 'I shall never leave you!'* **2** assert, °allege, °report, °mention, °rumour, °reveal, bruit about, °disclose, divulge, bring to °light, °put about, °noise abroad, °suggest, °hint, °whisper: *It was said that spies had already infiltrated the party.* **3** °pronounce, articulate, utter; °phrase, rephrase, °translate: *How do you say gemütlich? How do you say it in English?* **4** °tell, °put, °express, verbalize, °communicate, °explain, °reveal, °bring up, °break, °impart: *I don't quite know how to say this, Harry, but you have bad breath.* **5** °reply, °respond, °answer: *What have you to say to her allegation that it is all your fault?* **6** °guess, °estimate, conjecture, °venture, °judge, °imagine, believe, °think: *I'd say you look about 60 years old.* **7** mean *or* intend *or* try to say, °think, °contemplate, °imply, °suggest: *Are you saying that you would steal if you had the opportunity?* **8** °predict, °prognosticate, foretell: *The newspaper says that shares will go down.* **9** °signify, °denote, °symbolize, °communicate, °indicate, convey, °suggest, °imply, °mean: *What does a red light say to you?* **10** °order, °require, °demand, °bid, °stipulate, °command, give the word: *If I say that you are to go, then you go—and quickly.* **11** °deliver, utter, °speak: *Say your lines and exit stage left without waiting for a reply.* —*n.* **12** °voice, °authority, °influence, °power, °weight, °sway, clout: *Does she have that much say about how the money should be spent?* **13** °turn, °chance, °opportunity, °vote: *You've had your say, now let's hear from Ackroyd.* —*adv.* **14** °approximately, °about, °roughly, circa, °nearly: *The snake was, say, twenty feet long.* **15** for °example, for °instance, as *or* for an °illustration, eg *or US* e.g.: *Take any novel, say, Wuthering Heights, and analyse the characters.*

say-so *n.* °authority, °word, °say, °order, dictum; authorization: *I shouldn't do it just on his say-so if I were you.*

scale[1] *n.* Often, **scales**: °balance: *We need new bathroom scales: the old one gives too high a reading.*

scale[2] *n.* **1** °flake, imbrication; scurf, dandruff; *Technical* squama, °plate, scute *or* scutum, lamina, lamella: *Scrape the scales off the fish with a sharp knife before gutting it.* **2** coating, encrustation *or* incrustation, crust, overlay, layer, cake, caking, tartar, °plaque: *The hardness of the water causes the scale inside the kettle.*

scale[3] *n.* **1** °range, compass, °rank, ranking, gradation, graduation, °register, spectrum, calibration, °progression, hierarchy, °scope, °gamut: *As we ascend in the scale of life we rise in the scale of longevity.* **2** °proportion, °ratio: *The scale of these drawings is One Foot = One Centimetre.*

—*v.* **3** °climb, ascend, °mount, clamber up, surmount, °go up, escalade: *Using grappling hooks and ropes, we scaled the wall in minutes.* **4** °regulate, °adjust, °proportion, *Chiefly US and Canadian* prorate: *The size of the cable is scaled to the weight it must carry.* **5 scale up** *or* **down**: °increase, °enlarge, °raise; °decrease, °reduce, °diminish, °lower: *Depending on the expanse of the façade, the windows ought to be scaled up or down accordingly.*

scaly *adj.* **1** °rough, imbricated, shingly, *Technical* lamellar, laminar, lamellate, scutate: *The scaly covering of reptiles and fishes is related to the feathers of birds.* **2** scabby, scabrous, squamous, squamulose, squamosal, squamose, scurfy, furfuraceous, scruffy: *The medication causes the skin to dry and become temporarily scaly.*

scan *v.* **1** °glance at *or* through, °look over, °skim, °read over, °flip *or* °thumb *or* leaf through: *I didn't have time to read it thoroughly, but I did scan it.* **2** °study, °pore over, °examine, °investigate, °scrutinize, °inspect, delve into, °research, °explore (in depth), °sweep, *Archaic* con: *Scan the horizon for hostile planes.* —*n.* **3** °look, °survey, inspection, °examination, overview: *A microscopic scan revealed no trace of blood.*

scandal *n.* **1** °shame, °disgrace, embarrassment, °sin, °outrage: *It is a scandal how much of the money raised for charity goes into the pockets of the fund-raisers.* **2** °discredit, °damage, calumny, ignominy, obloquy, °dishonour, °degradation, disrepute, °infamy: *The scandal resulting from their being found together could never be lived down. The breath of scandal never touched her.* **3** °slander, °libel, °aspersion, °innuendo, insinuation, °abuse, °dirt, defilement, defamation, °slur, °smear, °taint, °blemish, °spot, °stigma, smirch, black °mark *or* °spot, °blot (on the escutcheon), (badge of) °infamy, skeleton in the cupboard, *Brit* °blot on one's copybook: *His cowardice brought scandal to the name that could never be lived down.*

scandalize *v.* °appal, °shock, °outrage, affront, °offend, °horrify, upset, °disturb; °rankle, stick in (someone's) °craw *or* throat, °gall: *They were scandalized to learn the truth about Cooksley's father.*

scandalous *adj.* **1** °shocking, °disgraceful, ignominious, °improper, indecorous, °unseemly, °infamous, °outrageous, °shameful, °immodest, °dishonourable, °disreputable, °sordid, °despicable, flagitious, °wicked, °sinful, °evil, iniquitous, °profligate, °immoral, °indecent, °lewd, °lascivious, °lustful, licentious, °lecherous, °atrocious, heinous, °disgusting, fulsome, °taboo, °unmentionable, unspeakable: *The scandalous goings-on at the Hellfire Club are well documented.* **2** defamatory, libellous, °slanderous, calumnious, calumniatory, aspersive, °abusive, °scurrilous, °injurious: *The newspaper published a scandalous article about him which they refused to retract.*

scanty *adj.* **1** scant, °sparse, °scarce, °little, °meagre, °minimal; °barely adequate *or* sufficient, °limited, restricted, *Colloq* °measly: *The news from the front was scanty. We received only scanty support from the Arts Council.* **2** skimpy, °short, °small, °sparse, °minimal, °meagre, in °short supply, *Colloq chiefly Brit* °thin on the ground: *Investor interest in the new share offering seemed to be scanty.*

scapegoat n. °victim, °front, °dupe, gull, cat's-paw, whipping-boy, Brit man of straw, Aunt Sally, US straw man, Colloq fall guy, Slang °sucker: We have to find a scapegoat to take the punishment for us.

scar n. **1** °blemish, °mark, °damage, disfigurement, °wound, °injury, °scratch, °mar, °cut, °burn, °brand, cicatrix: Fortunately, the cut is shallow and shouldn't leave a scar.
—v. **2** °blemish, °mark, °damage, disfigure, °wound, °injure, °scratch, °mar, °cut, °burn, °brand; dent: The blow scarred him for life.

scarce adj. °scanty, scant, °insufficient, °inadequate, °deficient, °wanting, lacking, °rare, °unusual, at a °premium, in °short supply, °meagre, °few and far between, °seldom met with, hard to come by, Chiefly Brit °thin on the ground: Good editors are very scarce.

scarcely adv. **1** °hardly, °barely, (only) °just, not quite: He had scarcely uttered the magic words when the rock split open. **2** (probably or certainly or surely or definitely) not, in no way, not at all, not in the least, by no °means, on no °account, under no circumstances, nowise, Colloq US noway: I scarcely need remind you that you are getting married tomorrow.

scarcity n. °lack, °want, °need, paucity, °dearth, insufficiency, °shortage, inadequacy, inadequateness: The teaching of foreign languages is not improved by the scarcity of qualified teachers.

scare v. **1** °frighten, °alarm, °startle, °shock, °dismay, °daunt, °appal, give (someone) a °shock or a °fright, °terrify, terrorize, °threaten, °menace, cow, °intimidate, °horrify, US and Canadian spook, Colloq scare the pants off, scare the life or the living daylights or the hell out of, scare out of one's wits, make one's hair stand on end, make one's flesh creep or crawl, give one goose bumps or goose-pimples, US scare the bejesus out of, Taboo slang scare or °frighten the shit out of, scare shitless, US scare shitty: A sudden noise scared me, and I ran out of the cave as fast as I could. **2** scare up: °scrape together or up, °find, °gather, °collect, °raise, °dig up, °get, °come by, °scrounge (up): I can't scare up that much money in one day!
—n. **3** °fright, °shock, °surprise, °start: I had a terrible scare when I saw what I thought was blood.

scared adj. frightened, alarmed, °afraid, appalled, shocked, terrified, horrified, startled: Don't be scared, I won't hurt you.

scary adj. °frightening, °eerie, °terrifying, °frightful, hair-raising, unnerving, blood-curdling, horrifying, spine-chilling, intimidating, daunting; horrendous, horrid, °horrible, creepy, crawly, Colloq spooky: Aren't you afraid to watch scary movies on TV when you're home alone?

scathing adj. searing, °withering, damaging, °harmful, °severe, °harsh, °stern, °nasty, °biting, acrid, acrimonious, mordant, °incisive, °cutting, °sharp, °keen, °virulent, vitriolic, acid, °scorching, °burning, °fierce, °savage, °ferocious: She was totally unprepared for the critics' scathing attack on her book.

scatter v. **1** °spread, °diffuse, °shower, °litter, sprinkle, °strew, °circulate, °distribute, disseminate, °sow, °broadcast: As the seeds of dissent were scattered far and wide, we became aware of a ground swell of hatred for the regime. **2** °disperse, °separate, °dissipate, dispel, °disband, °break up, °go off: My notes were scattered all over the floor. Immediately after dividing up the loot, the gang scattered to the four winds.

scatterbrained n. °hare-brained, rattle-headed, rattle-brained, °frivolous, flibbertigibbet, °giddy, dazed, °flighty, wool-gathering, Colloq dippy, °dizzy, dopey or dopy, slap-happy: It irritates me to think that our lives might depend on such a scatterbrained fool.

scattering n. smattering, sprinkling, °trifle, °bit, °suggestion, soupçon, °hint: It is true, there was a scattering of rebellious sentiment in the town.

scenario n. **1** (master or ground or floor) °plan, (grand) °scheme, °plot, schema, °design, °outline, layout, framework, °structure; °sequence of events, °routine: According to this scenario, the bank will provide the financing and we shall organize the take-over. **2** (plot) °summary, °précis, résumé, °synopsis; (working or shooting) °script, screenplay: The scenario for the film was a joint venture between the director and the author of the book on which it was based.

scene n. **1** °location, °site, °place, °area, °locale, °spot, locality, °whereabouts, °sphere, °milieu, backdrop, °background: The scenes of my youth are always in my mind. **2** °action, °episode, °part, chapter, °section, °segment; (stage) °setting, mise en scène; scenery: The next scene takes place in Venice. Is the Venice scene ready? **3** commotion, °upset, °exhibition, °display, °row, brouhaha, °disturbance, °furore or US furor, °tantrum, °argument, altercation, uncomfortable or disagreeable situation, °episode, °incident: She made an unpleasant scene in the restaurant when he refused to sit next to her. **4** °view, scenery, °sight, °landscape, seascape, panorama, vista, °picture, °prospect: The scene from the terrace was completely tranquil. **5 behind the scenes**: °secretly, privately, clandestinely, confidentially, surreptitiously, on the q.t. or Q.T.: Sigrid operated behind the scenes and her identity was never revealed to MI5. **6 make** or **do the scene**: °socialize, °appear, °get around or about, °go out, °participate: We used to make the scene in the Village back in the forties, but no more.

scenic adj. °picturesque, °panoramic, pretty, °beautiful, °grand, °awesome, awe-inspiring, °impressive, °striking, spectacular, breathtaking: The train passes through some incredibly scenic routes in Switzerland.

scent n. **1** °fragrance, °aroma, °perfume, redolence, °smell, °odour, °bouquet, whiff, °trace: The room was filled with the scent of wild flowers. **2** °trail, spoor, °track: In drag hunting, the scent is laid down by a sack dragged along the ground.
—v. **3** °perceive, °detect, °find out, °determine, discern, °distinguish, °recognize, °sense, °smell, °sniff (out), get °wind of, °learn or °hear about: Scenting possible trouble, he decided he had better take along my revolver. **4** °perfume: She had left behind her handkerchief, scented with Chanel No. 19.

sceptic n. doubter, questioner, doubting Thomas, disbeliever, nullifidian, agnostic, scoffer, cynic: You'll always find some sceptics who don't believe that a woman could be a good prime minister.

sceptical adj. doubting, dubious, °doubtful, questioning, disbelieving, °incredulous, agnostic, scoffing, cynical, mistrustful,

°distrustful: *We were sceptical at first whether anything would come of it, but then things began to happen.*

scepticism *n.* °doubt, dubiety, dubiousness, doubtfulness, disbelief, incredulity, incredulousness, agnosticism, cynicism, °mistrust, °distrust, mistrustfulness, distrustfulness: *At first, the entire matter was greeted with some scepticism; but then the Berlin Wall came tumbling down.*

schedule *n.* **1** °programme, °timetable, °plan, °calendar, agenda, °outline, °list, listing, °record, °register: *I'd like a complete schedule of your work for the next month on my desk tomorrow.* —*v.* **2** °programme, °organize, °plan, °outline, °list, °record, °register, °arrange, °book, °time, slate, °appoint, °assign, °allot, °dedicate, earmark: *Schedule the next meeting for the 15th of the month. Alistair is scheduled to speak tomorrow.*

schematic *adj.* **1** diagrammatic(al), representational, °graphic, charted: *We have the schematic drawings showing the placement of the equipment.* —*n.* **2** diagram, blueprint, layout, (floor *or* °game) °plan, °scheme, °design, °representation, graph, (flow *or* PERT) °chart: *Give copies of the schematics to the electricians so that they can plan where to put the wiring.*

scheme *n.* **1** °plan, °plot, °design, °programme, °system, °course (of action), schema, °outline, °exposition, °projection, °draft, °method, °technique, °approach, °game °plan, °scenario: *In my scheme, compensation would be dependent on productivity, merit, and length of service.* **2** °pattern, °arrangement, layout, °design, diagram, blueprint, °chart, map, °drawing, °schematic, °disposition, °order, °organization, schema: *This alternative scheme shows the executive offices on the second floor.* **3** °plot, °plan, ploy, °manoeuvre, °strategy, °stratagem, °tactic, °machination, °subterfuge, °trick, °device, °dodge, °wile, °ruse, °intrigue, *Colloq* °racket, °game, °move: *Ashton's scheme was to lure the security guards into the outer room, then lock them in.* —*v.* **4** °plan, °plot, °devise, contrive, °intrigue, °organize, °formulate, °hatch, conspire, machinate, °manoeuvre, connive, concoct, *Colloq* cook up: *Clifton had been scheming to get his revenge on them ever since the Manchester episode.*

scheming *adj.* conniving, plotting, nefarious, treacherous, °crafty, cunning, °artful, °sly, °wily, °devious, Machiavellian, intriguing, °slick, °calculating, °tricky, °foxy, °slippery, underhanded, duplicitous, °deceitful: *Wait till I lay my hands on the scheming little thief!*

schism *n.* °split, °rift, °break, °breach, °division, °rupture, °separation, disunion: *The schism was caused by a group of left-wing idealists.*

schismatic *adj.* schismatical, separatist, breakaway, divisive, °dissident, °heretical: *The schismatic movement in art was marked by one faction's abandonment of realism.*

scholar *n.* **1** °academic, professor, °teacher, pedagogue, °authority, °expert, pundit, savant, bookman, book-woman, man *or* woman of letters, °intellectual, °highbrow, °bookworm, *Colloq* egghead, °brain, *US* longhair: *Professor Read is one of the most respected linguistics scholars in the world.* **2** °student, °pupil, schoolboy, schoolgirl, undergraduate: *Cosgrove was a failure as a scholar, preferring football to physics.*

scholarly *adj.* °learned, erudite, °lettered, scholastic, °profound, °deep, °intellectual, °academic, °highbrow(ed), ivory-tower(ed), *Colloq* egghead, brainy, *US* longhair, long-haired: *Her scholarly achievements are not limited to scholarly articles for learned journals.*

scholarship *n.* **1** °learning, erudition, °knowledge, °lore, °education, °schooling, training, °preparation, *Colloq* know-how: *Elsa Cairn brings to her appointment as headmistress considerable scholarship and experience.* **2** °grant, °endowment, °award, °fellowship, *Brit* °exhibition, *Chiefly Scots and New Zealand* bursarship: *Without the scholarship, I should never have been able to continue my education.*

school *n.* **1** (°educational) °institution, kindergarten, nursery school, primary *or* grammar *or* secondary *or* high school, °institute, college, university, °seminary; Alma Mater; boarding-school, day-school; public school, private school, *Brit* State school; lycée; Lyceum, *Brit* first *or* middle school, *US* junior high school: *His mother was very upset when he hinted that he might quit school.* **2** °set, coterie, °circle, °clique, °group, °denomination, °faction, °sect, °followers, °devotees, adherents, votaries, °disciples; °style, °kind, °form, °manner, °fashion: *Burne-Jones belonged to the Pre-Raphaelite School of painters.* **3** °philosophy, principles, °creed, set of beliefs, way of life, °persuasion, credo, dogma, teaching, °view, °opinion, °faction, °approach: *Regarding the creation of the universe, do you support the big-bang school or the steady-state school?* —*v.* **4** °teach, °educate, °drill, inculcate, °instil, °indoctrinate, °instruct, °tutor, °train, °discipline, °coach, °prepare, °prime, °equip, °ready; °mould, °shape, °form; imbue with, infuse with: *Young ladies were schooled in all the social graces.*

school-book *n.* °text(book), primer, grammar (-°book), reader, °manual, handbook, exercise °book, notebook, copybook, *Rare* enchiridion, *Old-fashioned* hornbook, abecedarium: *All I did was ask if I could carry her school-books!*

schooling *n.* °education, teaching, °instruction, tutelage, °tuition, °guidance, training, °preparation, indoctrination, °edification, enlightenment; °learning, °study, °research: *How many years of schooling are needed to become a doctor?*

schoolteacher *n.* °teacher, professor, °instructor, °tutor, pedagogue, schoolmaster, schoolmistress, *Scots* dominie, *Colloq* school-ma'm: *It is not often realized what a profound influence schoolteachers have on one's entire life.*

science *n.* **1** (body of) °knowledge *or* °information, (body of) °laws *or* °principles, °discipline, °study, °branch, °field, °area, °subject, °realm, °sphere: *Many new sciences have sprung up even in the past fifty years. DNA research falls properly into the science of microbiologic genetics.* **2** °skill, °art, °technique, °expertise, °proficiency, °method, °system: *He made a science of brewing tea.*

scientific *adj.* (well-)organized, (well-)regulated, (well-)controlled, (well-)ordered, °orderly, °systematic, °methodical, °precise, °meticulous,

°thorough, °painstaking, °detailed: *A scientific approach to the problem would start with a complete analysis of present conditions.*

scintillating *adj.* **1** sparkling, coruscating, flashing, °dazzling, gleaming, glittering, °twinkling, shimmering, glistening, shining, °lustrous, °radiant, effulgent, °brilliant, *Literary* nitid: *Madame Irena appeared wearing a scintillating silver lamé gown.* **2** °exciting, °engaging, °lively, °effervescent, fascinating, entrancing, °stimulating, °invigorating, °dynamic, °vivacious: *I cannot remember when I last found myself in such scintillating company.*

scoff[1] *v.* Often, **scoff at**: °deride, °belittle, °dismiss, °disparage, °mock, make °light of, °sneer (at), °poke °fun (at), °ridicule, spoof, °lampoon, °jeer (at), °chaff, °tease, °twit, rib, kid, *Brit* °rag: *It's easy for you to scoff at Clare's tantrums—you don't have to live with her. Don't scoff: your turn might come next.*

scoff[2] *v.* **1** °devour, °put away, °gorge oneself on, wolf (down), °bolt, °stuff (oneself with), gobble (up *or* down), guzzle, °gulp (down), *Brit* gollop: *The two of them scoffed every crumb they could find.* —*n.* **2** °food, victuals, °rations, edibles, °provisions, *Colloq* grub, eats, chow, *Slang Brit* prog: *In no time at all, they had cleared out every last bit of scoff in the larder.*

scold *v.* **1** °reprimand, chide, °reprove, °upbraid, °criticize, censure, find °fault (with), °rebuke, reproach, °lecture, °berate, °rate, °castigate, take (someone) to °task, °rap (someone's) knuckles, °slap (someone's) wrist, *Colloq* °bawl out, °dress down, give (someone) hell, give (someone) what for, °jump on (someone), °jump down (someone's) throat, call (someone) to account, bring (someone) to book, let (someone) have it with both barrels, give (someone) a °piece of (one's) °mind, give (someone) a °tongue-lashing *or* a talking-to, give (someone) a hard time, rake *or* haul (someone) over the coals, °tell (someone) off, tick (someone) off, skin (someone) alive, call *or* have (someone) on the carpet, °light *or* °rip *or* tear *or* °lace *or* sail into (someone), *US* °chew out, °jump all over (someone), *Brit* carpet: *When their mother scolded them, they began to cry.* —*n.* **2** °nag, °shrew, termagant, virago, fishwife, beldam, harridan, hell-cat, °fury, amazon, tigress, Xanthippe, *Colloq* battleaxe: *In the old days, they used to take scolds, tie them in a chair at the end of a pole, and dunk them in a pond till they cooled off.*

scoop *n.* **1** ladle, dipper, bailer, spoon: *Use the scoop to skim the fat off the soup.* **2** °exclusive: *Fergus's story on the minister's illegal business dealings was a real scoop for the paper.* **3** (°latest) °news, (°inside) °story, °revelation, °truth, *Colloq* °latest, °low-down, info, °dope, *Brit* gen, *US* poop: *What's the scoop on that man who moved in next door?* —*v.* **4** Often, **scoop up**: bail, °dip, ladle, spoon: *They scooped up some sand and spread it on the ice for traction.* **5 scoop out**: °gouge out, °excavate, spoon out, °hollow out, °dig, °cut: *Scoop out some melon balls for the fruit salad.* **6 scoop up**: °pick up, °gather (up), °sweep up *or* together, °take up *or* in: *He scooped up the money and ran out of the bank.*

scope *n.* **1** °range, °reach, °field, °area, °extent, compass, °expanse, °breadth, °sphere, °orbit,

°span: *The scope of her interests includes both the sciences and the arts.* **2** °leeway, °space, °room, elbow-room, °freedom, °opportunity, °capacity, °stretch, latitude, °spread: *Have you allowed enough scope for growth?*

scorch *v.* sear, °blacken, °burn, roast, °singe, char: *Though scorched in the fire, the papers were saved intact.*

scorching *adj.* **1** °hot, °torrid, searing, parching, shrivelling, tropical, hellish, sizzling, broiling, boiling, °sweltering: *Scorching heat waves are dangerous for the very young and the elderly.* **2** °critical, °caustic, °scathing, mordant, °vituperative, excoriating, °harsh, acrimonious, °bitter: *The shadow minister for finance issued a scorching condemnation of the government's tax policies.*

score *n.* **1** °record, °account, °reckoning, °register, °tally, °amount, °number, °count, °sum, °total; °mark, °grade: *What was your best golf score? Chester got a score of 80 in the French test.* **2** °nick, °groove, °scratch, °line, °mark, °stroke, °notch, °cut, *Archery* nock: *Every time he won, he made a score on his walking-stick.* **3** twenty: *And the days of our lives shall be three score years and ten.* **4** Often, **scores**: dozens, hundreds, (tens *or* hundreds of) thousands, millions, °number(s), drove(s), horde(s), °host(s), multitude(s), °herd(s), legion(s), °lot(s), °mass(es), myriad(s), shoal(s), °pack(s), covey(s), bevy *or* bevies, °swarm(s), °flock(s), army *or* armies, °crowd(s), °throng(s): *Passengers by the score angrily protested against the airline's policy of overbooking flights. Scores of animals were fleeing before the forest fire.* **5** music, accompaniment, *Technical* full *or* short *or* vocal score: *Boito might have written the libretto, but the score was by Verdi.* **6** °situation, °story, °news, °status (quo), °condition, °word, *Colloq* °latest, °scoop, *US* poop: *What's the score on your applications to medical school?* **7** °dupe, gull, °victim, °greenhorn, *Colloq* fall guy, chump, goat, sitting duck, *Slang* °sucker, patsy, mark, *Brit* °mug: *That fellow in the Hawaiian shirt looks a likely score for our little scam.* **8** °ground(s), °basis, °account, °reason, °rationale, °provocation, °cause: *On what score can you justify eliminating him from the competition?* **9 settle** *or* **pay off** *or* **even a score** *or* **the score** *or* **old scores**: get °revenge, °retaliate, get °even, avenge, °repay, get an eye for an eye, give tit for tat, give measure for measure, °pay (someone) back in his *or* her own coin, give (someone) a taste *or* a dose of his *or* her *or* their own medicine, *Colloq* get one's own back: *He tried to find out where MacTavish had moved to as he had an old score to settle with him.* —*v.* **10** °mark, °line, incise, °scratch, °nick, °notch, °cut, °groove, °graduate; °scrape, °deface, °mar, °gouge, °slash: *The dipstick is scored at intervals to indicate how much oil is in the crankcase.* **11** gain *or* make a °point *or* points, °record, °tally, °account for: *George scored a hat trick in the game against Hotspurs.* **12** °count (for), °reckon for *or* as: *The ace scores either 1 or 11 in vingt-et-un.* **13** °succeed, be °successful, °triumph, °win, make an °impression, have an °impact, *Colloq* make a °hit: *Your plan really scored with the boss.* **14** succeed in seducing, *Slang* make out, get laid: *Did you score with Ava last night?*

scorn *n.* **1** contumely, °contempt, contemptuousness, disdain, deprecation;

°rejection, °dismissal: *He treated their demands with the utmost scorn.* **2** °mockery, °derision, derisiveness, sneering, °ridicule, scoffing, jeering, taunting: *The crowd's scorn was directed at the politicians who failed to deliver what they had promised.*
—*v.* **3** °reject, °rebuff, disown, disavow, °disregard, °ignore, °shun, snub, °flout, contemn, treat with *or* hold in °contempt, have no use for, disdain, °spurn, °despise, turn up one's nose at, curl one's lip at, °look down on *or* upon, °look down one's nose at, °thumb one's nose at, *Colloq* pooh-pooh, °put down, *Brit* cock a snook at: *His parents offered to finance his education, but he scorned their help.* **4** °mock (at), °deride, °sneer at, °ridicule, °scoff at, °jeer at, °taunt, °poke °fun at, make °fun of, °laugh at: *People scorned him because he said the earth was round.*

scornful *adj.* contumelious, °contemptuous, °disdainful, deprecative, disparaging, °derisory, derisive, snide, °supercilious, mocking, sneering, scoffing, °haughty, overweening, high-handed, °superior, *Colloq* snooty, *Slang* snotty: *The people were scornful of his attempt to reassure them, and continued to demand action.*

scoundrel *n.* °villain, °rogue, °wretch, °good-for-nothing, scapegrace, blackguard, °rascal, scamp, cur, *Old-fashioned* bounder, cad, knave, *Colloq* °heel, *Slang* louse, *Brit* rotter: *Politicians tend to treat their opponents as liars and scoundrels.*

scour *v.* **1** °scrub, °clean, °cleanse, °wash, °rub, abrade, °polish, burnish, buff, °shine: *The pots were scoured until they shone.* **2** °scrape (about *or* around), °rake, comb, turn upside down, °search, °ransack: *I scoured the shops looking in vain for the coffee filters you wanted.*

scourge *n.* **1** °curse, °misfortune, bane, °evil, °affliction, °plague, adversity, °torment, °misery, °woe: *He questions whether AIDS should be considered the scourge of the 20th century. Was it Attila who proved himself the scourge of Rome?* **2** °whip, °lash, cat-o'-nine-tails, knout, quirt, horsewhip, bull-whip: *They saw fit to punish themselves with scourges.*
—*v.* **3** °whip, °flog, °beat, °lash, horsewhip, whale, °belt, flagellate: *Some medieval sects scourged themselves as they went in procession through the cities.* **4** °punish, °castigate, °chastise, °discipline, °afflict, °torment: *In the old days, students were scourged if they made a mistake.*

scout *v.* **1** Often, **scout about** *or* **around**: °reconnoitre, °investigate, °study, °research, °examine, °explore, °spy, °search *or* °look (about *or* around) (for), °hunt (about *or* around) (for), °cast around *or* about (for), *Colloq* °check (about *or* around): *I am going to scout about to find a key that fits.* **2 scout up** *or* **out**: °discover, °find, °locate, uncover, *Colloq* °dig up: *I was finally able to scout up a key that fits.*

scowl *v.* **1** glower, °frown, grimace, °glare, look daggers, °lower *or* °lour: *It's hard to tell if he's ever pleased because he's always scowling.*
—*n.* **2** °frown, grimace, °glare, dirty °look: *I do wish she would wipe that scowl off her face and try to look more pleasant.*

scramble *v.* **1** °climb, clamber, °crawl, scrabble, °struggle: *We scrambled up the rocky hillside with the big cat in pursuit.* **2** °rush, °hurry, scamper, °run, °hasten, °race, °scurry, scoot, scuttle,

°dash, hotfoot (it), °hustle, *Chiefly US and Canadian*, hightail (it), *Colloq* skedaddle: *When the siren sounded, we scrambled down to the air raid shelter.* **3** Often, **scramble up**: °mix up, °confuse, °jumble, intermingle, °mingle, commingle: *Contestants, spectators, and officials were all scrambled together.*
—*n.* **4** °scrimmage, °struggle, tussle, contention, °clash, °competition, °contest, °race, °rush, °conflict, °disorder, commotion, °riot, mêlée *or* melee, °pandemonium, *Colloq* free-for-all, hassle, *Brit* scrum *or* scrummage: *Thousands were involved in the scramble for tickets to the rock concert. In the scramble for a directorship Jeremy lost.* **5** °struggle, °climb: *She twisted her ankle in the scramble over the rocks.*

scrap[1] *n.* **1** °mite, °bit, °shred, °bite, °morsel, °piece, °fragment, shard *or* sherd, °particle, °sliver, snippet, °snip, °crumb, whit, iota, °jot *or* tittle, °snatch, °drop, °drip, °grain, °speck, molecule, atom, °dab, °trace, scintilla, °hint, °suggestion: *There wasn't a scrap of evidence to link him with the crime.* **2 scraps**: °remnants, °remains, °leftovers, leavings, °residue, °vestiges, °traces, scrapings, °discards, rejections, °rejects: *In the alley, two cats were fighting over some scraps of garbage.* **3** °waste, debris, °rubbish, *Colloq* °junk: *Any computer more than five years old isn't even worth its weight as scrap.*
—*v.* **4** °discard, °throw away, °reject, °abandon, °give up, consign to the scrap heap, °forsake, °forget, get °rid of, °dispose of, °dispense with, *Colloq* °junk, *US* °trash: *If I were you, I would buy a new car and scrap this one.*

scrap[2] *n.* **1** °fight, °brawl, °fracas, °fray, affray, °rumpus, scuffle, Donnybrook, °battle (royal); °row, °dispute, °argument, °quarrel, °disagreement, wrangle, squabble, °tiff, spat, *Colloq* ruckus, set-to, dust-up: *A terrible scrap broke out in the pub last night and the police were called in. Our neighbours were having a scrap about who should take the dog for a walk.*
—*v.* **2** °fight, °brawl, °spar, scuffle, °battle, °row, wrangle, °argue, °disagree, squabble, °bicker: *Let's not scrap over trifles—only important things.*

scrapbook *n.* album, portfolio, °collection: *She keeps a scrapbook of reviews of her stage triumphs.*

scrape *v.* **1** abrade, graze, °scratch, bark, scuff, °skin, °bruise, °damage, °injure: *I scraped my knee on the pavement when I fell.* **2** Often, **scrape off** *or* **away** *or* **out**: °remove, °rub off *or* away, °scour *or* °scrub *or* °clean (off *or* away), °scratch off *or* away, °claw (at *or* away *or* out), °gouge out, scrabble (at), °dig out *or* away at: *As I scraped away the grime, a beautiful mosaic was revealed. Each sled dog scraped out a hole in the snow and snuggled into it.* **3** skimp, scrimp (and °scrape), °save, °stint, be °frugal *or* stingy *or* parsimonious *or* °thrifty, °pinch and °save *or* scrape, °economize; °struggle, *US* scrabble: *Only by scraping were we able to pay the increased taxes.* **4 bow and scrape**: make °obeisance, °kowtow, salaam, genuflect, kiss the feet *or* hem *or* ring, grovel, demean *or* °lower oneself, °prostrate oneself, toady, *Colloq* boot-lick: *He can bow and scrape all he likes, but Jones will get nowhere with the foreman.* **5 scrape by** *or* **through**: °get by, °cope, (barely) °manage, °survive, scrape *or* °get along, *Colloq* squeak by, barely make it: *We are just about able to scrape by on the little that Nigel-*

is making. **6 scrape together** *or* **up**: glean, °garner, scratch *or* °get *or* °rake together *or* up, dredge up, scrabble for, °gather, °save (up), get hold of, marshal, °amass, °muster, °accumulate, aggregate, °compile, °pile up, °stack up, °assemble, *Colloq* °scrounge (up): *By the time we finally managed to scrape up enough for a down payment on a house, the prices had gone up.*
—*n.* **7** abrasion, °bruise, °scratch, graze, scuff, °damage, °injury: *He was very annoyed when he found a scrape on his brand-new car.*
8 °predicament, °difficulty, °quandary, °dilemma, °plight, (fine) kettle of fish, °muddle, °stew, °situation, °position, °pinch, *Colloq* pickle, °fix, °mess, the °crunch, (tight *or* tough) °spot: *I got into a terrible scrape by forgetting our wedding anniversary. Can you lend me some money to help me out of a scrape?*

scratch *v.* **1** °mar, °mark, °gouge (out), °gash, abrade, graze, scuff, °grate against, °bruise, °damage, °injure: *If you glue some felt to the bottom, the lamp won't scratch the table.* **2** °chafe, °rub: *If you scratch those mosquito bites you might get an infection.* **3** Often, **scratch out** *or* **off**: °erase, °obliterate, °rub out *or* off, °cross out, °delete, °strike out *or* off, expunge; °exclude, °eliminate, *US* x out: *You can scratch my name from the list of candidates. She scratched out what she had written and started again.*
—*n.* **4** °mark, °gouge, °gash, abrasion, °scrape, graze, scuff, °bruise, °damage, °injury; °line: *Where did you get that scratch on your face? 'It's only a scratch', Sandy protested as they tried to remove the spear from his shoulder.* **5 up to scratch**: up to °standard *or* °par, °adequate, °sufficient, good enough, °competent, °satisfactory, competitive, *Colloq* up to snuff: *Cynthia's performance is not yet up to scratch, so she might not make the team.*
—*adj.* **6** °hasty, °hurried, impromptu, unplanned, °haphazard, °rough, °casual, °informal, °unprepared, °unpremeditated, °makeshift, extempore, *Colloq* off the cuff, *US* pick-up: *We didn't have time to practise, so we are racing with a scratch crew.*

scratchy *adj.* **1** itchy, irritating, °prickly: *The pullover was as scratchy as a hair shirt.* **2** °rough, hoarse, °raw, °grating, °sore, raspy, °dry: *My throat feels a bit scratchy and I need something to drink.*

scrawl *n.* **1** scribble, *Colloq* squiggle, *US* hen-scratch, chicken-scratch: *I can't read that scrawl of his.*
—*v.* **2** scribble, °scratch, doodle: *How do pharmacists read the prescriptions that doctors scrawl?*

scrawny *adj.* bony, °skinny, °spare, °drawn, reedy, °haggard, °lean, lank(y), scraggy, °gaunt, °raw-boned, angular, °emaciated, cadaverous; anorectic *or* anorexic: *She certainly has changed from that scrawny kid I used to know.*

scream *v.* **1** °shriek, screech, squeal, yowl, wail, caterwaul, °howl, °cry: *She screamed when I applied iodine to the cut.* **2** °laugh, °roar, hoot, °howl, guffaw: *The women screamed hysterically as the male stripper got down to the bare essentials.*
—*n.* **3** °shriek, screech, squeal, yowl, wail, caterwaul, °howl, °cry: *When she saw what had happened, she let out a blood-curdling scream.*
4 *Colloq* card, °panic, °riot, thigh-slapper: *Phyllis is such a scream when she talks about the silly things that happen to her.*

screen *n.* **1** °partition, (room) divider, paravent, °wall: *In their one-room flat a bookcase serves as a screen to separate the living area from the sleeping area.* **2** °shelter, °protection, °shield, °cover: *A row of poplars acts as a screen against the wind.* **3** curtain, °blind, °shroud, °cloak, °cover; concealment, °camouflage: *The gauze fabric was too transparent to act as a screen.* **4** sieve, °mesh, strainer, °filter, colander, °riddle: *The sand has to be shovelled through a screen to get rid of the stones.* **5** motion pictures, movies, silver screen; °television, small screen, home screen, *Colloq* box, telly, *US* boob tube: *She is a star of both the big and small screens.*
—*v.* **6** °partition (off), °separate, °divide, °wall off: *Why not use a beaded curtain to screen the kitchen area from the dining-room?* **7** °shelter, °protect, °shield, °cover, °guard, °conceal, °camouflage, °mask, °veil, °hide: *A decorative pierced wall screens the ladies of the harem from the prying eyes of visitors.* **8** °sift, °separate (out), °sort (out), °filter, °select, cull, °process, °interview, °evaluate, °grade, °gauge, °qualify, °examine, °scan, *Chiefly Brit* °vet: *The agency screens all candidates before sending them to see a client.*

screw *n.* **1** °bolt, screw-bolt, machine screw, lag-bolt, lag-screw: *This screw is too small to hold that door hinge.* **2** helix, °spiral, corkscrew: *The screw of a spiral staircase should not be too small for safety.* **3** sexual °intercourse; sexual °partner, *Slang* °lay, *Taboo slang* fuck: *When arrested for kerb-crawling, he said that he was just looking for a screw.* **4 put the screws on (someone)**: °pressure, °influence, °force, constrain, °press, °oblige, °require, °demand, coerce, compel, apply °pressure, bring °pressure to bear (on); °insist; *Chiefly Brit* pressurize, *Colloq* °twist (someone's) arm, put the °squeeze on (someone): *I believe that someone put the screws on him to leave town.*
—*v.* **5** °twist, °turn, °rotate: *Screw the bolt in clockwise.* **6** Often, **screw out of**: °defraud, °cheat, °swindle, gull, bilk, do out of, *Slang* °take, °clip, °fleece: *They screwed him by convincing him that the bonds were real. He was screwed out of all his savings.* **7 screw up**: **a** °raise, °increase, °stretch, °strain; °summon, °call up, °call upon, °tap, °draw on *or* upon: *I screwed up my courage to ask for a salary increase.* **b** °ruin, °destroy, make a °mess of, °botch, °bungle, °muddle, mismanage, °mishandle, *Colloq* make a °hash of, *Slang* louse up, *Brit* make a muck-up of, *US* bollix up, *Taboo slang* fuck up, *Brit* °bugger up, ballocks *or* bollocks up, make a balls-up of: *It is hard to see how they could have screwed up such a simple operation.* **c** contort, °twist, deform, °warp: *At the suggestion of cauliflower, Ambrose screwed up his face in displeasure.*

scribe *n.* **1** copyist, copier, transcriber, *Archaic* scrivener; amanuensis, clerk, secretary: *Before the invention of movable type printing, copies of books and documents were prepared by scribes.* **2** °writer, °author, penman, scrivener, wordsmith, scribbler, °hack, penny-a-liner; °dramatist, dramaturge, °playwright, °poet, novelist, essayist, columnist, technical °writer; °journalist, gentleman *or* lady of the °press, newspaperman, newspaperwoman, °reporter, rewrite man *or* woman *or* person, °editor, reviewer, commentator, newswriter, sob sister, agony aunt *or* uncle, Miss Lonelyhearts, gossip columnist, member of the fourth estate, *Brit* paragraphist,

leader-writer, US Grub Streeter, Colloq Brit journo: In a general way, he refers to all writers as 'scribes', but particularly those he considers a bit old-fashioned.
—v. **3** inscribe, incise, °etch, °engrave, °mark, °scratch, °score, grave, scrimshaw, °carve, chase or enchase: The shotgun was scribed with the most beautiful designs, some inlaid in gold.

scrimmage n. °skirmish, scuffle, °fray, affray, °disturbance, brouhaha, mêlée or melee, °riot, °row, °brawl, °struggle, °scramble, tussle, °fracas, °rumpus, Donnybrook, °battle, °fight, Colloq ruckus, set-to, dust-up, free-for-all, °scrap, Brit scrum or scrummage, Slang Brit (bit of) bovver: The police were called when what started as a minor scrimmage began to develop into a riot.

script n. **1** handwriting, °hand, (cursive) °writing, °penmanship; calligraphy: These love-letters are written in an unusually beautiful script. **2** manuscript, °scenario, °book, °play, screenplay, teleplay, libretto, continuity: Stick to the script—I don't want you ad libbing!
—v. **3** °write, °pen, °prepare, °create: The new series was scripted by the same writer who wrote 'Out in the Outback'. **4** °plan, °organize, °design, °arrange, °lay out, °order, configure, °pattern: The take-over of the company had not been scripted in their business forecasts.

Scripture n. Scriptures, °sacred writings, Bible, Good Book, Holy Writ or Scripture(s), Word of God, Gospel(s); Book of Mormon; Koran; Upanishad(s), Bhagavad-Gita: Throughout his life, he did only those things approved in Scripture.

scrounge v. **1** ferret out, °seek out, nose or °smell out, come up with, °scrape together or up, °scratch up; importune, cadge, °beg (, °borrow, or °steal), Colloq US freeload, °bum: Did Hedley try to scrounge some money from you, too?
—n. **2** scrounger, cadger, °parasite, Colloq sponger, US freeloader: Hedley, that scrounge, has just asked me for a cigarette.

scrub v. **1** See scour, 1, above. **2** °cancel, °call off, abort, °scratch, °drop, °terminate, °give up, °end, °abandon, °stop, °cease, °discontinue, do away with: Something went wrong with the fuel computer, so they scrubbed today's satellite launch.

scruple n. **1** °compunction, °qualm, °reluctance, °misgiving, second thoughts, °doubt, (twinge of) °conscience, hesitation, uneasiness, °discomfort, squeamishness: Peter hadn't the slightest scruple about taking the money from his aunt.
—v. **2** °pause, falter, °hesitate, vacillate, have °doubts or °compunction (about), demur, waver, °shrink from or at, have °misgivings or °qualms (about or over), be °loath or loth (to), think twice (about), °stick at, be °reluctant, balk (at), have scruples (about): Susan didn't scruple for a moment about keeping the money she found in the street.

scrupulous adj. **1** °careful, °cautious, °meticulous, °exacting, °precise, over-nice, °strict, °rigid, rigorous, °severe, °critical, °fastidious, °neat, conscientious, °finicky or finical, °fussy, °painstaking, punctilious: Andrew has always been scrupulous about his toys, his books, his clothes, etc. **2** °ethical, °honourable, upstanding, °moral, °righteous, °principled, high-minded, °just: Meg was always scrupulous in her business dealings.

scrutinize v. °examine, °analyse, dissect, °investigate, °probe, °study, °inspect, °sift, °go over or through, °check: I have scrutinized the results of the blood tests and can find nothing abnormal.

scrutiny n. °examination, °analysis, °investigation, °probe, probing, °study, inspection, sifting, °inquiry or enquiry, °exploration, °check: The tax inspectors have subjected the company books to close scrutiny but have found nothing amiss.

scud v. °fly, °skim, °race, scoot, °speed, °shoot: We scudded along in the catamaran at a good 30 knots.

sculpture n. **1** °figure, figurine, °statue, statuette, group, head, bust, °relief; bronze, marble: His favourite sculpture is Rodin's Burghers of Calais.
—v. **2** sculpt or sculp, °model, °chisel, °carve, °cast, °form, °fashion: The students are learning how to sculpture in clay.

scurrilous adj. foul-mouthed, thersitical, °gross, °indecent, °profane, Fescennine, °vulgar, °obscene, licentious, Sotadean or Sotadic, °foul, °vituperative, °low, °coarse, scabrous, °vile, °nasty, defamatory, °derogatory, disparaging, vilifying, calumnious or calumniatory, malign, aspersive, opprobrious, °offensive, °abusive, insulting: Clifford was an inveterate collector of scurrilous limericks.

scurry v. °dash, °scramble, scamper, scoot, dart, °fly, °race, sprint, scuttle, °hurry, °hasten, °speed, °hustle, °rush, °tear, zoom, zip, °bolt, °rip, °scud: A rat scurried across the floor. We went scurrying round the shops on Christmas Eve.

scurvy adj. °low, °miserable, °contemptible, °vile, °base, °despicable, °rotten, °sorry, °bad, ignoble, °dishonourable, °mean, °worthless, °shabby: Robbing poor old ladies is a pretty scurvy activity.

sea n. **1** °ocean, °deep blue sea, high seas, Literary (briny) °deep, (bounding) main, Neptune's or Poseidon's kingdom or domain, Nautical blue °water, Davy Jones's locker, Colloq briny, °drink, pond (= 'Atlantic Ocean'): For years he sailed the seas in search of adventure. **2** °swell, breaker, °wave: As the wind increased, huge seas began to wash over the boat. **3** plethora, °quantity, °abundance, °surfeit, °profusion, °flood, multitude, °spate, legion, °mass, Colloq °lot(s), °heap(s), °pile(s), ton(s), °mountain(s), °load(s), oodles, gobs, scads: Hamlet's sea of troubles was nothing compared to mine if this book isn't completed soon! **4 (all) at sea**: °confused, disoriented, at sixes and sevens, bewildered, perplexed, baffled, mystified, °lost, adrift: They were clearly not expecting her and were completely at sea as to what to do.

sea-coast n. seashore, shore, °coast, seaside, seaboard, shoreline, coastline, littoral, sand(s), °beach, strand: The people in the villages along the sea-coast depend mainly on fishing for their livelihood.

seafaring adj. maritime, °nautical, naval, °marine: Britain was at one time the largest seafaring nation in the world.

seal n. **1** °symbol, °token, °mark, insigne (pl. insignia), °sign, signet, °crest, °bearing, coat of arms, escutcheon, °emblem, badge, monogram, °identification, cartouche, °design, imprint,

°stamp: *The seal on his ring showed a crouching lion.* **2** authentication, confirmation, verification, validation, affirmation, attestation, ratification, corroboration, °assurance, °guarantee *or* guaranty, °endorsement, substantiation, °evidence, °notice, notification: *Management set their seal of approval on the plans.* —*v.* **3** Sometimes, **seal off** *or* **up**: °close (off *or* up), °shut (off), zip up, °plug (up), °stop (up), °lock, °bolt, °secure, batten down, make airtight *or* waterproof; cork: *All exits had been sealed off. They sealed up the windows so that no air could get in.* **4** °authenticate, °confirm, °verify, validate, affirm, °attest, °ratify, °clinch, corroborate, °assure, °ensure, °guarantee, °endorse: *The peace treaty was sealed by the marriage of the king to the emperor's daughter.*

seam *n.* **1** °junction, °juncture, °joint, suture, *Technical* commissure; °scar, °ridge, °line, cicatrix: *It is easy enough to see the seam where the parts meet.* **2** lode, °vein, °stratum, bed, layer, thickness: *The miners have been working on a new seam discovered at the end of Tunnel 4.*

seamy *adj.* °sordid, °nasty, °dark, °disreputable, °shameful, °unwholesome, °unpalatable, °unsavoury, °distasteful, °unseemly, squalid, °low, depraved, °degenerate, degraded, °foul, °vile, odious, °abhorrent, °contemptible, °scurvy, °rotten, unattractive, °ugly, °repulsive, °repellent: *In his later work, he painted the seamy side of life in the slums.*

search *v.* **1** Often, **search through**: °examine, °scrutinize, °check, comb (through), °explore, °go through, °investigate, °scout out, °inspect, °look at *or* into, °probe, °scour, °sift through, °pry into, °hunt *or* °rummage through; °inquire *or* °enquire of, *Colloq* plough through: *She searched through several encyclopedias but could not find the information she was looking for. Search your conscience to determine the best course.* **2** Often, **search for**: °look (about *or* around), °cast about, °seek, leave no stone unturned: *I searched high and low but couldn't find my key.* —*n.* **3** °hunt, °pursuit, °quest: *The search for the killer went on for years.* **4** researching, °analysis; °exploration, °examination, °scrutiny, °probe, °study, °perusal, sifting, inspection, scouring, °inquiry *or* enquiry: *A thorough search of the documents failed to turn up anything useful. The police made a house-to-house search of the neighbourhood.*

searchingly *adv.* penetratingly, piercingly, °intently, °deeply, fixedly, concentratedly, eagerly: *She looked searchingly into my eyes for some glimmer of hope.*

season *n.* **1** °time, °period, °occasion, °opportunity: *This is the season when the birds migrate north. Is the silly season upon us again so soon?* **2 in season**: °ripe, °ready, °edible, °seasoned, °seasonable, °available: *Fresh strawberries will be in season soon.* —*v.* **3** °spice, °salt, °flavour, °pep up, °enliven: *One of the great things about chicken is that you can season it in many different ways.* **4** °ripen, °mature, °age, °condition, °mellow: *The wood should be well seasoned before being made into furniture.*

seasonable *adj.* °appropriate, °opportune, °suitable, apt, °timely, °fitting, °providential, °well-timed, °proper, °fit, °propitious, °welcome, well-suited, °happy, °lucky, °fortunate, °convenient, auspicious, °favourable,

°advantageous, °expedient: *The success of the book was owing largely to its seasonable publication, just at the end of the cold war.*

seasoned *adj.* °experienced, trained, long-standing, long-serving, °practised, well-versed, habituated, acclimatized *or* acclimated, °accustomed, familiarized, °prepared, established, °veteran, tempered, hardened, toughened, inured: *It was a pleasure to be working with so seasoned a performer as Margie.*

seasoning *n.* °spice, °zest, °flavour, °relish, °sauce: *The fact that a former film star was running for office lent just the right seasoning to the campaign.*

seat *n.* **1** °place, °chair, bench, sofa, settee, °settle, stool, throne: *He found a seat and waited to be called.* **2** °focus, °base, °centre, °heart, °hub, °site, °capital, cradle, headquarters, fountain-head: *In those days, Paris was the main seat of learning in western Europe. Istanbul was established as the seat of the Turkish empire.* **3** membership, °position, incumbency: *His grandfather held a seat in the House of Commons.* **4** °bottom, °buttocks, °posterior(s), rump, hindquarters, fundament, *derrière,* behind, backside, °rear (end), *Colloq Brit* °bum, *US* hinie, tush *or* tushy *or* tushie, tokus *or* tochis *or* tuchis, butt, °tail, *Taboo slang Brit* arse, *US* ass: *He needs a swift kick in the seat to get him to move.* **5** °abode, °residence, °home, °domicile, °estate, mansion: *The duchess used to spend the summer at her country seat in Norfolk.* —*v.* **6** °hold, °accommodate, have room *or* °space *or* capacity for, °contain, °sit: *The new auditorium will seat more than four thousand.* **7** °install *or* instal, enthrone, ensconce, instate, °invest, °establish, °place, swear in: *Once the new judge has been seated, it will be difficult to get rid of him.*

seating *n.* °accommodation, °capacity, °space, °room: *At present, the auditorium has seating for only 500.*

secede *v.* °withdraw *or* °resign *or* °retire (from), °abandon, °forsake, apostasize, °break with *or* away (from), °drop *or* °pull out (of), turn one's °back to *or* on, °quit, °separate from, °leave, °wash one's hands of, have nothing further to do with: *The City of New York occasionally threatens to secede from the United States.*

secession *n.* withdrawal, seceding, defection, °break, breaking, disaffiliation, retirement, °separation, splitting off *or* away, apostasy: *The secession of the splinter group was welcomed by virtually all the other members.*

secluded *adj.* **1** °private, °separate, °isolated, °lonely, cloistered, sequestered, °detached, °solitary, retired, eremitic, monastic: *He lives a very secluded life on an island in the Outer Hebrides.* **2** off the beaten track, °out-of-the-way, °remote, °far-away, far-off, °separate, segregated, °private: *He chose a secluded island in the Outer Hebrides for his vacation.*

seclusion *n.* °privacy, °private, °separation, isolation, loneliness: *He prefers to live in complete seclusion.*

second¹ *adj.* **1** °subsequent, following, next: *He let the first target go by and aimed for the second one.* **2** °subordinate, next: *If the colonel isn't here, who is the second officer?* **3** °alternative, second-best: *She refuses to settle for second choice.* **4** °alternate, other: *The laundry is picked up and delivered every second Tuesday. His second*

language is Italian. **5** other, later, younger, newer, more recent: *After his first wife died, he took her nurse as his second wife.* **6** another, °duplicate: *The boy is a second Einstein.*
—*n.* **7** °defective *or* °imperfect *or* damaged *or* °faulty *or* °deficient *or* °flawed *or* impaired *or* marred *or* blemished *or* bruised *or* °inferior °merchandise: *The prices of these shirts have been reduced because they are seconds.* **8** °subordinate, °assistant, number two, lieutenant, aide-de-camp, man Friday, girl Friday, right hand; °understudy, °stand-in, °substitute, surrogate, °double, °alternate, °backer, °supporter; *Colloq US* gal Friday: *Not being ambitious, Helen would prefer to be a second to the person who runs the business.*
—*v.* **9** °support, °back, °aid, °help, °assist, °approve (of), °advance, °promote, °subscribe to, espouse, °sponsor, °patronize, °favour, °encourage, °go along with: *Madam Chairwoman, I would like to second this proposal.*
10 °transfer, °move, °assign, °shift, relocate: *After the Falklands War, he was seconded to fleet headquarters for a year.*
—*adv.* **11** secondly, in the second place, secondarily, (number) two, b *or* B: *I want to go: first, because it'll be interesting, and second, because Jake'll be there.*

second[2] *n.* °moment, °instant, °flash, °minute, °twinkling *or* wink *or* bat (of an eye), split second, *Colloq* sec, jiffy, two shakes (of a lamb's tail), *Brit* tick, half a mo: *I'll be with you in a second, as soon as I finish writing this letter.*

secondary *adj.* **1** less important, unimportant, inessential *or* unessential, °non-essential, non-critical, °subsidiary, ancillary, °minor, °inferior, °subordinate: *These secondary matters can be dealt with after the important ones.* **2** °derivative, derived, °indirect, °second-hand, unoriginal, not °original; copied, imitated: *His biography of Queen Victoria was based entirely on secondary sources.* **3** °auxiliary, second-line, backup, °extra, °reserve, °spare, °provisional, supporting, °supportive, °alternate, °alternative: *We were forced to rely on our secondary defences after the enemy cavalry broke through.*

second-hand *adj.* °used, old, °worn, *Colloq* hand-me-down: *When we were children our parents could only afford to dress us in second-hand clothes. His much-vaunted novels are for the most part based on second-hand ideas.*

secrecy *n.* **1** °mystery, concealment, confidentiality, °stealth, secretiveness, surreptitiousness, °privacy, furtiveness, covertness, clandestineness: *Why was there so much secrecy surrounding the publication date of Jennie's book?*
2 in secrecy: °secretly, mysteriously, confidentially, stealthily, secretively, surreptitiously, privately, furtively, covertly, clandestinely, sneakily: *They carry on much of their business in secrecy.*

secret *adj.* **1** concealed, °hidden, °private, covert, shrouded, clandestine; °confidential, °quiet, under cover, °secretive, unpublishable, unpublished, *Colloq* hush-hush: *There is a secret passageway leading from the cave to the cove. Keep secret what I shall tell you. She revealed to me her most secret desires.* **2** °cryptic, °private, arcane, °mysterious, °incomprehensible, esoteric,

°recondite, abstruse; cryptographic, encrypted, encoded: *We used to communicate by secret code. Did you receive my secret message?*
—*n.* **3** °private *or* °confidential matter *or* affair, °mystery: *If I tell you my secret will you tell me yours?*
4 in secret: privately, confidentially, °secretly, on the q.t. *or* Q.T.; surreptitiously, under cover, by °stealth, stealthily, furtively, °quietly, on the °sly, clandestinely: *The office manager told me in secret that John was going to resign. They see one another in secret.*

secrete[1] *v.* °hide, °conceal, °cache, °bury, °cloak, °shroud, enshroud, °camouflage, °mask, °disguise, *Slang* stash away: *They secreted the haul from the robbery in the cellar of a house in Balham.*

secrete[2] *v.* °yield, excrete, °pass, °generate, °release, °ooze, seep, exude, °discharge, °leak, °drip, °drop, dribble, °trickle, °run, °drain, °emit, °give off, °emanate, transude, *Technical* extravasate: *The ants herd aphids for the substance they secrete. The wound will secrete pus for a while.*

secretion *n.* secreting, °release, °escape, oozing, seeping, seepage, °discharge, discharging, °leak, leaking, leakage, °drip, dripping, °drop, dropping, dribbling, trickling, °trickle, °running, °drain, draining, emission, emitting, giving off, exudation, transudation, excretion, excreting, emanation, emanating, °generation, *Technical* extravasation; transudate, excreta, *Technical* extravasate: *The secretion of perspiration may be profuse under such circumstances. The secretion is highly acid in content.*

secretive *adj.* °reticent, °silent, close-mouthed, °taciturn, uncommunicative, °reserved, °tight-lipped, °close, *Colloq* °mum: *Robert is very secretive about where he goes every day at lunch-time.*

secretly *adv.* surreptitiously, °quietly, privately, covertly, on the q.t. *or* Q.T., furtively, stealthily, mysteriously, clandestinely, in °secret, confidentially, on the °sly, slyly, sub rosa, sub sigillo: *I can tell you secretly that she is wanted by the police. Henry secretly rents videotape cartoons to watch at weekends.*

sect *n.* **1** °religious °order *or* °group *or* °denomination *or* °body *or* cult *or* °persuasion *or* subdivision: *At times it seems as if there are as many sects as worshippers.* **2** °school (of thought), °faction, ism, °set, °clique, °cabal: *He belonged to a small sect that promulgated the Ptolemaic cosmogony.*

sectarian *adj.* **1** cultist, cultish, clannish, cliquish, °partisan, °partial, °dogmatic, doctrinaire, factional: *They seldom mingle with others, maintaining their sectarian existence.* **2** °parochial, °narrow, °narrow-minded, °limited, insular, °provincial, °rigid, °fanatic(al), °prejudicial, °prejudiced, °bigoted: *Because they refused to consider ideas other than their own, they gradually became more and more sectarian in their views.*
—*n.* **3** adherent, °member, sectary, votary, cultist, °partisan: *They tried to banish Anabaptists, Lutherans, Calvinists, and other sectarians.* **4** (true) believer, dogmatist, °fanatic, bigot, °zealot, extremist, *Slang* nut, °bug, °fiend: *Some of the sectarians engage in the ritualistic handling of live rattlesnakes.*

section *n.* **1** °part, °division, °department, °branch, sector, °group, °detachment, °segment, °portion, subdivision, component, °element: *Sadler has been assigned to work in the*

research section. *I never read the sports section in the Sunday papers. Which sections of the country will vote for you? The string section needs practice before tonight's concert.* **2** °sample, °slice, cross-section, fraction: *It can be faulty to assume that the characteristics of the whole are necessarily represented in a small section of it. I examined a section of tissue under the microscope.* **3** °part, °stage, °segment, °portion, °leg: *The first section of the journey was more comfortable than the last.*
—*v.* **4** °cut (up), °divide (up), °segment, °split, °cleave, °measure out, apportion, °allot, allocate: *The land was sectioned into four-acre parcels.*

secular *adj.* °worldly, °terrestrial, mundane, °temporal, °material, °lay, laic *or* laical, non-clerical, non-ecclesiastic(al), non-spiritual, non-religious, °civil, °state: *Once he had taken his vows, he put aside secular matters.*

secure *adj.* **1** °safe, shielded, sheltered, protected, °immune, unthreatened, unexposed, unimperilled, °snug, °cosy: *Fiona feels quite secure in her new house. Considering the success of the company, Bill's job looks secure.* **2** °firm, °steady, °stable, °fixed, °fast, moored, anchored, °immovable, closed, °shut, fastened, locked (up), °tight, °sound, °solid, °sturdy, °strong: *That button on your jacket doesn't look very secure. Make sure that the house is secure before you go to sleep.* **3** °reliable, °safe, °good, °profitable, °healthy, °solid: *Telephone shares looked like a secure investment at the time.* **4** °sure, °certain, assured, ensured, °definite, °inevitable, °assumed, °evident, °obvious, °unquestionable, established, °probable, °easy: *With only two minutes left to play, victory seemed secure for Rangers.*
—*v.* **5** °obtain, °get (hold of), °come by, °acquire, °procure, °win; °gain, °get *or* °take °possession of, arrogate: *Tim has secured a responsible position at the bank. She always manages to secure the sympathy of older men.* **6** °guarantee, °underwrite, hypothecate, collateralize: *We used our house to secure the loan.* **7** °protect, °shelter, °shield, °defend, °guard, °safeguard, °preserve: *It seems impossible to secure young children from bullying at school.* **8** °fasten, make °fast, °fix, affix, °attach, °anchor: *Secure the cases to the roof-rack with strong rope.*

security *n.* **1** °safety, °shelter, °protection, fastness, °refuge, °safe keeping, °sanctuary, asylum: *During the air raids, we retired to the security of the basement.* **2** °confidence, °certainty, surety, °assurance, °conviction: *He has the security of knowing that he is right in this instance.* **3** °guarantee *or* guaranty, collateral, °deposit, gage, °pledge, °insurance: *What are you going to offer as security for the loan?* **4** °surveillance, safeguarding, guarding, °safe keeping, °protection, °custody, custodianship, °care: *What plans does the company have for the security of the office building?*

sedate *adj.* **1** composed, °serene, °peaceful, °calm, °tranquil, °cool, °collected, even-tempered, °detached, imperturbable, unruffled, undisturbed, unperturbed, controlled, placid, °grave, °serious, °sober, °solemn, *Colloq* unflappable: *Despite all the turmoil round her, Sarah remained quite sedate.* **2** °dignified, °decorous, °refined, °formal, °stiff, °staid, °proper, °strait-laced, °prudish, °fussy, prim, °conventional, °old-fashioned: *Donald prefers a sedate waltz to boogying and jiving.*

sedative *n.* **1** °narcotic, °tranquillizer, opiate, sleeping-pill, soporific, calmative, anodyne, depressant, hypnotic, barbiturate, lenitive, *Colloq* downer, knock-out drop, *Slang* Mickey (Finn): *The doctor has given him a sedative and he should sleep now.*
—*adj.* **2** °narcotic, tranquillizing, relaxing, °soothing, calming, allaying, opiate, soporific, sleep-inducing, calmative, anodyne, lenitive, depressing, hypnotic: *I found that listening to a recording of surf splashing on a beach has a sedative effect.*

sedentary *adj.* seated, sitting, stationary, °fixed, immobile, unmoving, housebound, desk-bound: *You should find a more sedentary occupation to follow while you recover. As a writer, I lead a sedentary existence and get little exercise.*

sediment *n.* lees, °dregs, °deposit, °grounds, °precipitate, °remains, °residue, settlings, residuum, detritus: *Periodically, the sediment must be cleaned out of the filters.*

sedition *n.* °agitation, °incitement (to °riot), rabble-rousing, fomentation, instigation, firing-up, stirring up, °whipping up; °mutiny, insurrection, insurgency *or* insurgence, °rebellion; treason, treachery: *Because he had organized the strike in the munitions plant during wartime, he was accused of sedition.*

seditious *adj.* °rebellious, °mutinous, °revolutionary, insurgent, °inflammatory, rabble-rousing, insurrectionist, insurrectionary, refractory, °subversive, treacherous, °dissident, °disloyal, °turncoat, unfaithful: *One seditious action on the part of the colonists was to dump tea into the harbour at Boston, Massachusetts.*

seduce *v.* **1** °lure, °entice, °attract, allure, °tempt, °mislead, °beguile, °deceive, °decoy, draw on, °charm, °captivate, vamp, entrap, ensnare, °trap, *Colloq* sweet-talk: *He was seduced into giving her his life's savings.* **2** °dishonour, °ruin, °corrupt, °lead astray, defile, debauch, deflower, °violate, °ravish: *How many girls have been seduced in the name of undying love?*

seducer *n.* See also **seductress**, below; °rake, °libertine, °roué, °playboy, lady-killer, lecher, debauchee, debaucher, °lover, cicisbeo, Don Juan, Lothario, Casanova, *Colloq* wolf: *She can't really be going out with that wretched seducer!*

seductive *adj.* alluring, °attractive, °tempting, tantalizing, enticing, °inviting, seducing, °enchanting, entrancing, bewitching, fascinating, °flirtatious, coquettish, captivating, beguiling, °provocative, °siren, °irresistible, °winning, appealing, °prepossessing, *Colloq* °sexy: *He was lured into the whirl of the financial world by the seductive five-letter word—money. Never had Helena looked more seductive than on that night in Rio.*

seductress *n.* See also **seducer**, above; °temptress, °siren, *femme fatale*, enchantress, Circe, Lorelei, Jezebel, vamp: *That clever seductress will soon have him eating out of her hand.*

see *v.* **1** °perceive, °note, °notice, °mark, °spot, °watch, °witness, °recognize, °behold, discern, °distinguish, °observe, °look at, °regard, °sight, catch °sight of, descry, espy, °spy, °make out, °look upon, °view, glimpse, catch a glimpse of, *Slang* get a load of, *US* glom: *I saw him buy a bottle of whisky. We saw two yellow-bellied sapsuckers in one day! Can you see the sea from your suite? Did you see the Houses of Parliament when you were in*

London? **2** °understand, °comprehend, apprehend, °perceive, °appreciate, °fathom, °grasp, °take in, °realize, °know, be °aware or °conscious of, °get the °idea or °meaning of, *Colloq* °dig, °get, °get the °drift or the °hang of: *I see what you are saying, but I don't agree. After her speech, I saw Gladys in a new light.* **3** °foresee, foretell, °imagine, °envisage, °envision, visualize, °picture, °divine, °conceive (of), °dream of, conjure up, °accept: *I can see a day when warming from the greenhouse effect will make the sea level rise. Ted said he can't see you as a married man.* **4** °determine, ascertain, °find out, °investigate, °discover, °learn: *See if the bakery has any macaroons. I'll see what she thinks.* **5** Often, **see to it**: °ensure, °assure, make °sure or °certain, °mind, be °vigilant: *It's cold outside, so see that you dress warmly.* **6** °accompany, °escort, °show, °lead, °conduct, usher, °take, convoy, °bring, °walk, °drive: *I was seeing Nellie home from a soirée at Aunt Dinah's.* **7** °go out with, °socialize with, keep °company with, consort with, °associate with; court, woo; *Colloq* go °steady with, *Chiefly US* °date: *Are you still seeing that boy you met at the school dance?* **8** make up one's °mind, °think over, °mull over, °consider, °ponder (on or over), °contemplate, °decide, °reflect (on), °meditate (on or over or about), ruminate (on or over), °brood over: *Mother said she'd see whether I could go. Then I asked father, and he said he'd see.* **9** °receive, °meet (with), °talk or °speak with, °confer with, °consult (with), have a word with, sit down with, °visit with, °interview; °welcome, °greet: *The ambassador will see you now.* **10** °undergo, °experience, °go through, °endure, °survive: *He saw service overseas during the war.* **11** °help, °aid, °assist, °support, °finance, °pay the way for; °guide, °shepherd: *She saw three children through university without anyone's help.* **12 see about**: **a** see to, °attend to, °look after, take °care or °charge of, °look to, °organize, °manage, do, °undertake, °sort out; °think about, °consider, give some °thought to, pay °attention or °heed to: *Could you please see about feeding the horses while I am away? I asked Martin and he said he'd see about it.* **b** °investigate, °study, °probe, °look into, make enquiries or °inquiries, °enquire or °inquire about: *The teacher said she would see about letting us out early before the holiday.* **13 see off**: bid adieu or bon voyage: *We went to the airport to see them off.* **14 see through**: **a** °penetrate, °detect, °perceive, *Slang* be °wise to: *She saw through your subterfuge at once.* **b see (something) through**: °persevere, °persist, °manage, °survive, °last, °ride out, *Colloq* °stick out: *Once you start on something, I wish you'd see it through.* **c see (someone) through**: provide with °help or °aid or °assistance, °help, °aid, °assist, °last: *We'll give you enough money to see you through.* **15 see to**: See 12 a, above.

seed *n.* **1** °grain, spore, °kernel, °pit, tuber, bulb, corm, *Technical* ovum, ovule, embryo, egg, °germ: *Add water and the seeds will soon germinate.* **2** °origin, °source, °cause, °root, °provocation, °reason, °basis, °grounds; °motive, motivation, motivating factor: *The seeds of suspicion were sown by the continuous police presence in the neighbourhood.* **3** °offspring, °children, °progeny, °young, °issue, °descendants, °heirs, successors: *Yea, and verily I say unto you that his seed shall populate the*

earth. **4 go** or **run to seed**: °run down, become °dilapidated or °worn out or °shabby, °decay, go downhill, °decline, °degenerate, °deteriorate, go to rack and °ruin, *Colloq* go to pot: *If he doesn't start to look after it, the entire place will go to seed.* —*v.* **5** °scatter, °sow, °distribute: *Don't walk on the freshly seeded lawn.*

seedy *adj.* **1** °shabby, °dilapidated, °worn (out), decayed, deteriorated, °run-down, broken-down, °mangy, grubby, decaying, tatty, scruffy, squalid, °sleazy, *Colloq* °ratty: *They live in a seedy little shack on the other side of town.* **2** °tired, °weary, wearied, °run-down, °worn out, unwell, out of °sorts, ailing, °ill, °sickly, *Colloq* °poorly, under the °weather, off one's feed: *I begged off at dinner time because I was feeling a bit seedy.*

seeing *conjunction.* in °view of (the fact that), whereas, in (the) °light of, inasmuch as, since, °considering: *Seeing that you are here, you might as well tell her yourself.*

seek *v.* **1** °look (for), °search (for), °hunt (for), go or be after, °quest after, °pursue: *They are seeking a really good site for a grand luxury hotel. Seek and ye shall find.* **2** °hope, °aim, °aspire, °try, °essay, °endeavour, °undertake: *They are seeking to recruit members for the new party.* **3** °ask for, °request, °beg, °solicit, invite; °demand: *He sought her help and she refused him.*

seem *v.* °appear, °look (as if or like), °sound, °feel, have (all) the hallmarks or earmarks of, give every °indication or °appearance of: *He seems all right to me. She seems to have forgotten her key again. It seems as if I've never been away at all. He seemed frightened.*

seeming *adj.* °apparent, °evident, ostensible, °outward, °superficial, °surface, °assumed, feigned, °pretended, °false, °so-called, °alleged, °specious, purported, °professed: *She was shocked by his seeming indifference to her problems.*

seemingly *adv.* °apparently, °evidently, °ostensibly, °outwardly, superficially, falsely, allegedly, speciously, purportedly, professedly, on the °face of it, °possibly, feasibly, conceivably, plausibly, believably: *The purpose of this seemingly honest confession was to throw the detectives off the scent.*

seemly *adj.* **1** °proper, °fitting, °appropriate, °becoming, suited, °suitable, °fit, °befitting, apt, *comme il faut*, °right, apropos, apposite, °characteristic, °meet, °reasonable, °sensible: *You can count on Felix to do the seemly thing in such cases.* **2** °decent, °decorous, °proper, °dignified, °genteel, gentlemanly, °ladylike, °diplomatic, °discreet, °prudent, °politic: *She behaved in a seemly manner, in keeping with what was expected of a princess.*

seer *n.* soothsayer, °fortune-teller, sibyl, °oracle, °prophet, prophetess, augur, vaticinator, prophesier, clairvoyant, °psychic, crystal-gazer, star-gazer: *The seer foretold a grave famine and much suffering in the land.*

see-saw *n.* **1** teeter: *The children were playing on the see-saw.* —*v.* **2** °teeter, °totter, waver, °vary, vacillate, °oscillate, °alternate, °fluctuate, °swing, °switch: *He couldn't make up his mind and kept see-sawing between staying and going.*

seethe *v.* **1** °boil, °stew, °simmer, °foam: *In the kitchen, a large pot of stew seethed on the* stove. **2** °stew, °simmer, °foam (at the mouth), °fume, °smoulder, °burn, °rage, °rant, °rave, become livid *or* °feverish, be in °ferment, be °furious *or* incensed, *Colloq* °blow one's °stack *or* top, carry on, take on, get °hot under the collar, get red in the face, get all steamed up: *The ball sailed through Mr Griffiths' new greenhouse and he came out seething with rage.*

see-through *adj.* °sheer, diaphanous, gauzy, °transparent, translucent, gossamer, °filmy, peekaboo: *She was wearing a see-through negligée when she appeared at the door.*

segment *n.* **1** °section, °part, °division, °portion, component, °element; °piece, fraction, °fragment, °length, °joint, °slice, °wedge: *Only a narrow segment of the population supports the new measures. She divided the orange into three equal segments.* —*v.* **2** °divide, °partition, °section, °separate, °part, °cleave, °split, subdivide, °fragment: *The department was then further segmented into smaller units, each with its own manager.*

segregate *v.* °separate, °segment, °partition, °isolate, seclude, sequester, °set apart, compartmentalize, °exclude, °ostracize, °discriminate against: *In the sorting process, each size must be segregated into its own compartment. Their policy was to segregate the Blacks from the rest of the population.*

segregation *n.* °separation, segmentation, °partition, isolation, °seclusion, sequestration, setting apart, compartmentalization, °exclusion, ostracism, °discrimination, apartheid, *US* Jim Crowism: *No modern culture can long survive a segregation of the races.*

seize *v.* **1** Sometimes, **seize on**: °grab, °grasp, °clutch, °take (hold of), °grip, °snatch: *Robin felt that he had to seize every opportunity that presented itself. The dog seized the robber by the seat of the pants.* **2** °capture, °catch, °arrest, take into °custody, take °prisoner, apprehend, °round up, *Colloq* °pinch, °nab, collar, °pick up, *Brit* °nick, *Slang* bust: *The police seized him as he was trying to leave the country.* **3** °catch, °transfix, °stop, °hold, °possess, take °possession of, °afflict, °beset, °visit, °subject: *I was seized by a sudden desire to kiss those quivering, pouting lips.* **4** take °advantage of, make good use of: *When their attention was diverted, I seized the opportunity to escape.* **5** °confiscate, °take (away), commandeer, °appropriate, °capture, °take °possession of, impound: *Ten tons of cannabis was seized in the raid.* **6** Sometimes, **seize up**: °bind, °jam, °stop, °lock (up), °stick, °freeze (up): *Because of the excessive heat, the gears seized and the engine stalled.*

seizure *n.* **1** seizing, confiscating, confiscation, appropriation, impounding, commandeering, °capture, taking, °possession, annexation, sequestration, usurpation: *Police today announced the seizure of a shipment of 2,000 pounds of cocaine.* **2** °spasm, °attack, °fit, °paroxysm, convulsion, *Technical* ictus: *He has had another seizure and is not expected to live.*

seldom *adv.* °rarely, °infrequently, not °often, °hardly ever, very °occasionally: *Since they moved away, we seldom see the Pattersons.*

select *v.* **1** °choose, °pick, °show (a) °preference for, °prefer, opt for, °single out, hand-pick, °distinguish: *Select any two books from this pile. Anne was delighted to be selected from hundreds of candidates.* —*adj.* **2** selected, chosen, hand-picked, °choice, °special, preferred, preferable, °favoured, °favourite, °exceptional, °excellent, °first-rate, first-class, °superior, °supreme, °prime, °better, °best, finest, tiptop: *We have set aside some of our select jewels for you to consider, Your Ladyship.* **3** °limited, restricted, restrictive, °exclusive, °privileged, °élite, closed: *He belongs to one of those select clubs that accept you only if your family can be traced back five hundred years.*

selection *n.* **1** °choice, °pick, °preference, °option: *Please make your selection from the merchandise in this display.* **2** °assortment, °variety, °collection, °range, °batch, °number, °set, series, °group: *Tonight I shall play for you a selection of jazz recordings made at the Savoy.* **3** selecting, choosing, picking, singling out, electing, settling on, voting for, opting for, °choice, °pick, °election: *Selection has been delayed till tomorrow.* **4** °extract, °quotation, °excerpt, °abstract, °passage, °piece, °quote: *I shall read you a selection from Blake's* Songs of Innocence and Experience.

selective *adj.* °particular, discerning, discriminative, °discriminating, discriminatory, eclectic, °exacting, °demanding, °choosy, *Colloq* picky: *Thea has been very selective in her choice of partners.*

self-abuse *n.* masturbation, onanism, self-gratification, auto-eroticism *or* auto-erotism, self-stimulation, self-manipulation, self-pollution, self-defilement, self-contamination, *Technical* manustupration: *Victorian schoolboys were punished if suspected of self-abuse.*

self-confidence *n.* °confidence, self-assurance, °self-respect, °self-esteem, °assurance, °poise, aplomb, self-reliance, self-sufficiency: *Harrigan has demonstrated that he has the self-confidence to run the department.*

self-confident *adj.* °confident, self-assured, assured, °poised, self-reliant, °secure, °sure of oneself, °positive, °definite, °assertive, °independent: *She seems much more self-confident, relaxed, and contented these days.*

self-conscious *adj.* °embarrassed, °coy, diffident, °shy, °modest, self-effacing, °sheepish, shrinking, °retiring, unsure, apprehensive, °reserved, °insecure, °affected, °awkward, °nervous, uncomfortable, °hesitant, °timid, timorous: *Phil felt a bit self-conscious about asking Maria to the dance.*

self-contained *adj.* **1** °self-possessed, unemotional, self-controlled, in °control, composed, °serene, °peaceful, °calm, °tranquil, °cool, °collected, even-tempered, °detached, imperturbable, unruffled, undisturbed, unperturbed, controlled, placid, °grave, °serious, °sober, °solemn, *Colloq* unflappable: *Sometimes I think Frank is a little too self-contained.* **2** °reserved, controlled, °distant, °aloof, °formal, °withdrawn, °reticent, °standoffish: *Gregory is so self-contained that he did not tell anyone that he was ill, not even his wife.* **3** °whole, °entire, °complete, stand-alone, unitary: *The house has been divided into five self-contained apartments.*

self-control *n.* **1** self-discipline, self-restraint, °restraint, °self-denial, °control, will-power,

°strength (of character *or* of mind *or* of
°will), mettle, °fortitude, moral °fibre,
°determination, self-possession, resoluteness,
°resolve, °will, constancy, steadfastness,
°perseverance, doggedness, obduracy,
°persistence, *Facetious US* won't-power: *Can I
exercise the self-control needed to stop smoking?*
2 calmness, tranquillity, °serenity, placidity,
imperturbability, cool-headedness, coolness,
°poise, level-headedness, °patience, aplomb,
°dignity, equanimity, forbearance, °control,
°restraint, self-restraint, °even °temper: *You
exhibited marvellous self-control by not losing your
temper when you were insulted.*

self-denial *n.* **1** self-sacrifice, self-abnegation,
renunciation, selflessness, °altruism,
unselfishness, magnanimity: *His contributions
must have been made at the cost of some
self-denial.* **2** °hardship, °suffering,
self-mortification, asceticism, °privation, renunciation, renouncing, abstemiousness, abstinence, abstention, self-deprivation, keeping
away from, °refusal, refusing, giving up, desist-
ing, *Colloq* swearing off: *As far as certain foods are
concerned, a little self-denial is good for one's
health.* **3** See **self-control, 1**, above.

self-esteem *n.* **1** °conceit, °vanity, egoism,
narcissism, self-centredness, egotism, *amour
propre,* self-approbation, self-satisfaction,
self-admiration, self-love, self-adulation,
self-idolatry, smugness, self-importance,
self-regard: *The arrogant, overweening self-esteem
of some of the club members is unbearable.* **2** See
self-confidence, above.

self-evident *adj.* °evident, °obvious, °patent,
°clear, °incontrovertible, °definite, °express,
°distinct, clear-cut, °apparent, unmistakable,
undeniable, inescapable, incontestable, °plain,
axiomatic, °proverbial, °manifest, °true, palpable, °tangible: *Her guilt seemed self-evident at first.
The gradual destruction of the beaches is self-evident.*

self-government *n.* **1** self-rule, °independence,
self-determination, home rule, autonomy,
°freedom: *The satellite countries, one by one, voted
for self-government.* **2** See **self-control, 1**, above.

self-important *adj.* °conceited, self-centred,
self-seeking, self-absorbed, °vain, egotistic(al),
self-satisfied, °smug, °pompous,
swollen-headed, swell-headed *or* swelled-headed,
°arrogant, overweening, °overbearing, vainglorious, self-glorifying, self-engrossed,
°presumptuous, °snobbish, °haughty, *Colloq*
snooty, *Slang* snotty, stuck-up: *That self-important
little cockalorum ought to be taken down a few pegs.*

self-indulgent *adj.* self-gratifying, °selfish,
°extravagant, °sensual, intemperate, over-
indulgent, °greedy, °immoderate, hedonistic,
sybaritic, °epicurean, °gluttonous, gormandizing, pleasure-bound, pleasure-seeking,
°dissolute, dissipating, licentious, °profligate,
debauching: *David's self-indulgent habits take no
account of his wife and children.*

selfish *adj.* **1** °greedy, covetous, °grasping,
°avaricious, °self-indulgent, self-aggrandizing,
acquisitive, self-seeking, self-loving,
self-centred, self-absorbed, self-interested,
self-serving, egotistic(al), °egoistic(al): *They pursue
success for their own selfish ends.* **2** stingy, °mean,
°mercenary, °tight, tight-fisted, °narrow,
°penurious, parsimonious, °miserly, niggardly,
penny-pinching, cheese-paring, ungenerous,

illiberal, grudging, uncharitable, °possessive,
°inconsiderate, °thoughtless: *He is so selfish that
he won't even give you the right time.*

selfless *adj.* °open, °charitable, °unselfish,
self-denying, °generous, altruistic,
ungrudging, magnanimous, °considerate,
°thoughtful; self-sacrificing: *Always ready to help
anyone with a need, Archer is the most selfless man
I know.*

self-made *adj.* °independent, self-reliant, entre-
preneurial, °self-sufficient: *She is a self-made
woman and has accomplished it all without anyone
else's help.*

self-possessed *adj.* composed, °cool, °serene,
placid, °collected, self-assured, °peaceful,
°calm, °tranquil, even-tempered, °detached,
imperturbable, unruffled, undisturbed, unperturbed, controlled, °dignified, °refined, *Colloq*
unflappable: *Considering what she has been
through, Tanya is quite self-possessed for a teenager.*

self-respect *n.* °honour, °dignity, °integrity,
self-regard, °self-esteem, °pride, *amour propre,*
°morale: *He managed to maintain a semblance of
his self-respect despite the accusations hurled at him.*

self-righteous *adj.* °Pharisaic(al),
°sanctimonious, holier-than-thou, pietistic,
°mealy-mouthed, °hypocritical, complacent,
°smug, self-satisfied, °priggish, °superior, Tartuffian, canting, *Colloq* °goody-goody, *Slang Brit*
pi: *Butter would not melt in the mouth of that
self-righteous hypocrite!*

self-styled *adj.* would-be, self-called, *soi-disant,*
°professed, self-appointed, self-christened,
°so-called, °quasi-: *The building has been designed
by a firm of self-styled 'neo-traditionalist' architects.*

self-sufficient *adj.* °independent, self-reliant,
self-supporting, self-sustaining: *Agriculture will
soon reach the point where the country is self-sufficient
for food.*

self-willed *adj.* headstrong, °determined,
°forceful, refractory, °stubborn, °obstinate, pigheaded, °wilful, °ungovernable, uncontrollable,
°unruly, unmanageable, intractable, °contrary,
°perverse, uncooperative, contumacious,
°recalcitrant, stiff-necked, vexatious, °difficult,
°incorrigible, °disobedient: *That self-willed, over-
indulged little brat needs a good spanking.*

sell *v.* **1** vend, °transfer, convey (title), °trade,
barter, °exchange, °dispose of: *Sorry, but I sold
that car last week.* **2** °market, °deal in,
°merchandise, °trade in, °traffic in, °peddle,
vend, hawk, °handle, retail, °carry, °stock,
°furnish, °supply, °offer, *Colloq* °push, *Slang Brit*
°flog: *We no longer sell that model. She has a shop
selling second-hand clothes.* **3** Often, **sell out**:
°betray, °inform against, °deliver up, °give away,
Slang rat on, °grass on, °tell on, °tattle on, sell
down the river, blow the whistle on,
°double-cross, *Brit* °shop: *He swore he'd get the
man who sold him.* **4** °promote, °push, °put
across *or* over: *He couldn't sell sand to a beach
flea.* **5 be sold on**: persuaded, convinced, won
over: *After seeing that film, I was sold on a holiday
in Mexico.*

seller *n.* °dealer, vendor, °merchant, retailer,
shopkeeper, °salesperson, salesman, saleswoman, saleslady, sales °agent, °representative,
°traveller, travelling salesman, peddler, hawker,
colporteur, sutler, chandler, *Old-fashioned*
counter-jumper, *Brit* shop °assistant, -monger

(*as in* costermonger, ironmonger, fishmonger, etc.), *US and Canadian* sales-clerk, clerk, shop-girl, *Colloq* rep, *US* drummer: *Time ran out on his job as a seller of water-clocks and hourglasses.*

semblance *n.* **1** °appearance, °image, °likeness, °resemblance, °form, °figure, °bearing, °aspect, °air, °look, mien, °exterior, °mask, façade, °front, °face, °show, °veneer: *Beneath that semblance of tranquillity lies a turbulent, tortured mind.* **2** °guise, °face, °front, façade, °air, °show, °veneer, °look, °pretence, °cloak, simulation, °impression, °affectation, *Rare* °superficies: *You might try to give the sculpture at least a semblance of reality.*

seminal *adj.* **1** °original, °basic, °creative, °primary, °prime, formative, innovative, °imaginative, °new, unprecedented, precedent-setting, °landmark, benchmark, °important, °influential, °telling: *Michaelson's paper is considered the seminal work on the subject. It sets forth many seminal ideas.* **2** embryonic, germinal, °potential, °undeveloped, incipient: *Each seed contains a seminal plant.*

seminary *n.* academy, °school, °institute, °institution, college, university, training ground: *His three daughters had all attended an exclusive seminary on the East Coast.*

send *v.* **1** Sometimes, **send off**: °dispatch *or* despatch, commission, °charge, depute, °delegate, °assign: *The Pope sent an emissary to London.* **2** °communicate, °transmit, convey, °deliver, consign, °address to, °mail, °post, fax, °remit, °ship, °forward; °broadcast, telecast, televise, °radio, telegraph: *The message is being sent to all concerned.* **3** °release, °discharge, °shoot, °propel, °fire, °fling, °project, °hurl; °cast, °throw, °toss, let °fly: *With a great burst of flame the satellite was sent into orbit.* **4** °delight, °please, °charm, °enrapture, °stir, °thrill, °move, °electrify, *Slang* °turn (someone) on: *That saxophone solo really sends me.* **5 send down**: °imprison, incarcerate, send away, °jail *or Brit also* gaol *Slang US* send up (the river): *If she doesn't mend her ways, she'll be sent down.* **6 send for**: °call for, °summon, °order, °request, °ask for: *I have sent for a taxi which should be here shortly.* **7 send forth** *or* **out**: °emit, °radiate, °discharge, °give off, exude, °grow: *The object sent forth a strange phosphorescent glow. In the spring, the vine sends forth tendrils.* **8 send off**: send (someone) away, send (someone) away *or* off with a flea in his *or* her ear, °dismiss, °discharge, send (someone) packing, send (someone) about his *or* her business, *Colloq* give (someone) his *or* her walking papers, *Slang* give (someone) the °brushoff, *US* give (someone) the °brush: *I went to the office as you instructed, but they just sent me off with no explanation.* **9 send up: a** °lampoon, °satirize, °burlesque, °parody, make °fun of, *Colloq* °take off, spoof, *Brit* take the mickey out of: *In Britain one of the enduring forms of humour is in sending up the government.* **b** °imprison, incarcerate, send away, °jail *or Brit also* gaol, *Slang US* send up the river: *He was sent up for insider trading.*

senile *adj.* (*of a woman*) anile; senescent, °decrepit, declining, °failing, in one's dotage, doting, °doddering, in one's second childhood, dotty, °simple, °feeble-minded; °forgetful, *Colloq* past it: *He's senile and needs constant care.*

senility *n.* (*of a woman*) anility; °senile dementia, Alzheimer's disease, senescence, °decrepitude, °decline, dotage, second childhood, loss of one's faculties: *Senility has robbed my grandmother of her memory.*

senior *adj.* °elder, older, *Brit* (*postpositive*) °major; (higher-)ranking, °superior, °chief: *The senior members of the club are impossibly stuffy. You must not address your senior officer in such a manner.*

senior citizen *n.* °elderly person, retired person, °pensioner, *Brit* OAP (= 'old-age pensioner'), °grey panther, *Chiefly US* °retiree, golden-ager: *Special tax provisions have been made for senior citizens.*

sensation *n.* **1** °feeling, °sense, °impression, °perception, °foreboding, presentiment, prescience, awareness, °suspicion, *Colloq* sneaking °suspicion, funny °feeling, °hunch: *I had the distinct sensation of having been there before.* **2** commotion, °stir, °thrill, °furore *or US* furor; °excitement: *The news of the wedding caused a sensation.* **3** °hit, coup de théâtre, °success, *Colloq* show-stopper, crowd-puller, crowd-pleaser: *Edith Piaf was a sensation at Le Théâtre de la Verdure in Nice.*

sensational *adj.* **1** °exciting, °stimulating, electrifying, galvanizing, °shocking, hair-raising, spine-tingling, °thrilling, °stirring, breathtaking, °amazing, astonishing, astounding, staggering, mind-boggling, °unbelievable, °incredible, spectacular, *Slang* mind-blowing: *They certainly put on a sensational show—the best I have ever seen.* **2** °lurid, °vivid, overdone, overdrawn, °extreme, °melodramatic, exaggerated, °dramatic, °extravagant: *The weekly I worked for insisted that each issue's first page carry a sensational story—whether it was true or not.* **3** (very) °good, °great, °marvellous, wonderful, °superior, °superb, °matchless, °peerless, unequalled, °nonpareil, °extraordinary, °terrific, °phenomenal, °splendid, °fabulous, °fantastic, stupendous, *Colloq* °super, smashing, *Slang* far-out: *Suzanne Peters's performance in Carmen was sensational.*

sense *n.* **1** °faculty: *It's not always easy to tell if Brown's senses are all functioning.* **2** common sense, °intelligence, °perception, quick-wittedness, quickness, (mother) °wit, °judgement, °reason, °wisdom, sagacity, °discrimination, discernment; °sanity, *Colloq* °brains, *Slang Brit* nous: *Fancy doing something like that!—she hasn't the sense she was born with!* **3** See **sensation, 1,** above. **4** °meaning, intelligibility, coherence, head or tail, °drift, °gist, °import, purport, nuance, °significance, °message, °substance: *I was unable to get any sense out of what she was saying. Yes, I wasn't able to make sense out of it either.* **5** °sentiment, °atmosphere, °impression, °intuition, °sensation: *I had a sense of being de trop—that I was not wanted.* —*v.* **6** °feel, °perceive, °detect, °divine, intuit, have a °hunch *or* °feeling, have *or* get *or* be under the °impression that, °suspect, *Colloq* have a funny °feeling that, °feel (something) in one's bones, pick up: *I sensed a certain antagonism in that last remark. I sensed that he was getting bored with me.*

senseless *adj.* **1** °insensible, °unconscious, (knocked) °out (cold), stunned, insensate, comatose: *Agatha's head hit the fire-grate and she was* borne senseless to her room. **2** °numb(ed), insensate, unfeeling, benumbed, °insensible, anaesthetized, °dead, deadened, insentient: *My feet are senseless from the cold.* **3** °pointless, °purposeless, °ridiculous, °ludicrous, unintelligent, illogical, irrational, °incongruous, °meaningless, °absurd, °wild, °mad, °crazy, demented, °insane, asinine, °nonsensical, imbecilic *or* imbecile, idiotic, moronic, simple-minded, fatuous, °stupid, °foolish, °silly, °dizzy, °halfwitted, °mindless, brainless, witless, empty-headed, thimble-witted, pea-brained, bird-brained, °hare-brained, feather-headed, rattle-brained, addle-pated, muddle-headed, *Colloq* °daft, *US* daffy, nutty, batty, *Slang* wacky, dippy: *Many of the government's objections to the plan are just senseless posturing. He is promoting some senseless plan for double-decker motorways.*

sensibility *n.* **1** See sensitivity, 3, below. **2** Often, **sensibilities**: °feelings, responsiveness, responsivity, °emotions, °sentiments: *Personal events are more likely to affect our sensibilities than major disasters in which we are not involved.*

sensible *adj.* **1** °reasonable, °realistic, °logical, common-sense, commonsensical, °rational, reasoned, ·°sound, °practical, °prudent, °judicious, °discreet, °intelligent, °sage, °wise, °sane; down-to-earth, °matter-of-fact, well-thought-out: *Do you really think it sensible to go out in this storm? Andrew has a very sensible way of dealing with junk mail—he returns it to sender.* **2** perceivable, °perceptible, detectable, °evident, °discernible, recognizable, ascertainable, apprehensible, cognizable, °manifest, palpable, °physical, °tangible, corporeal, substantive, °material, °visible, °observable, seeable: *Some maintain that in addition to the sensible world there is another world, an anti-world, that we do not normally encounter.* **3** sentient, °feeling, °sensitive, °live, °conscious, °aware: *Who among us ever regards microbes as sensible creatures?* **4** Usually, **sensible of** *or* **to**: °conscious (of), °aware (of), °acquainted (with), cognizant (of), °sensitive (to), °alive to, °mindful (of), understanding (of), in °touch (with), °observant (of), °awake (to), °alert (to), *Slang* °wise (to), °hip *or* old-fashioned hep (to): *The people of the village are ever sensible to the needs of their neighbours. There are some things to which we are not at all sensible.* **5** appreciable, °significant, °considerable, °substantial, substantive, °noticeable: *The theory is that an increased interest rate will have a sensible effect on the rate of inflation.*

sensitive *adj.* **1** °delicate, °tender, °sore, °susceptible: *My arm is still sensitive where I got the injection.* **2** °touchy, °susceptible, susceptive, reactive, °responsive, attuned, °impressionable, thin-skinned, °vulnerable, supersensitive, hypersensitive, °testy, irascible, °quarrelsome, °irritable, °volatile, °excitable, °temperamental, °petulant, hot-tempered, °quick-tempered: *Liz is very sensitive on the subject of being unmarried, and I shouldn't bring it up.* **3** finely tuned, °delicate, °responsive, °subtle, °acute, reactive, °receptive: *We need a more sensitive test to detect neutrinos. This radio is not sensitive enough to receive distant stations.*

sensitivity *n.* **1** sensitiveness, °delicacy, touchiness, over-sensitivity, hypersensitivity, supersensitivity; soreness, irritability: *The sensitivity of*

teenagers to criticism is well known to teachers and parents. She complained of sensitivity and pain in the pelvic region.* **2** compassion, °concern, °sympathy, tenderness, tender-heartedness, kind-heartedness, kindliness, °warmth, °feeling: *The nurses exhibit a genuine sensitivity for the problems of the handicapped.* **3** awareness, consciousness, acuteness, °perception, °understanding, °intuition, °feeling, °sense, sensitiveness, receptivity *or* receptiveness, receptibility, °appreciation, appreciativeness, susceptibility, susceptivity *or* susceptiveness: *Harvey has a keen sensitivity for the feelings of others. Sometimes I think the duke lacks the sensitivity needed to sympathize with the needy.*

sensual *adj.* °physical, appetitive, °voluptuous, °carnal, bodily, fleshly, °erotic, °sexual, °lustful, °unchaste, °abandoned, °dissolute, °profligate, dissipated, licentious, °lewd, °lascivious, lubricious *or* lubricous, goatish, hircine, °lecherous, libidinous, salacious, °prurient, °rakish, °wanton, debauched, Cyprian, °loose, °dirty, *Slang* °randy: *Cranston pursued his sensual pleasures with no regard for morality.*

sensualist *n.* lecher, °profligate, °wanton, debauchee, °roué, °rake, Romeo, Don Juan, Casanova, Lothario, °libertine; voluptuary, hedonist, °sybarite, bon viveur, *bon vivant*, °epicure, °epicurean, °gourmet, gourmand, gastronome, pleasure-seeker: *The main character in the film is a self-seeking sensualist who betrays every woman in his life.*

sensuous *adj.* sensory, sybaritic, °epicurean, hedonist(ic), °sumptuous, °luxurious, °rich: *She felt sensuous delight in the scents and sounds of the island.*

sentence *n.* °judgement, °decision, ruling, verdict, °decree, °determination; °punishment, *Slang* °rap: *It is up to the judge to announce the sentence of the court. Asked by his teacher for an example of a short sentence, Johnny replied, 'Thirty days'.*

sentiment *n.* **1** °attitude, °feeling, °sensibility, °emotion, susceptibility, tenderness, tender-heartedness, °sentimentality, sentimentalism: *He wanted to preserve the old village square more out of sentiment than because it was historically important.* **2** Often, **sentiments**: °view, °outlook, °opinion, °position, °attitude, °judgement, °thought, °belief, °feeling, °emotion: *His sentiments regarding apartheid are better left unexpressed.*

sentimental *adj.* **1** °emotional, °sympathetic, compassionate, °tender, warm-hearted, tender-hearted: *Has he returned for sentimental reasons or for practical and mercenary ones?* **2** °romantic, nostalgic, °emotional, °maudlin, mawkish, over-emotional, °tender, °tearful, weepy, sickening, nauseating, simpering, °sweet, saccharine, *Colloq* °sloppy, °gooey, °sticky, °tacky, °mushy, slushy, °gushy, soppy, drippy, tear-jerking, ill-making, sick-making, *Slang* corny, schmaltzy, icky, °yucky *or* yukky: *His last tune is always some sentimental ballad like 'Good Night, Sweetheart'.*

sentimentality *n.* romanticism, nostalgia, pathos, emotionalism, maudlinism, bathos, mawkishness, over-emotionalism, tenderness, tearfulness, weepiness, sweetness, *Colloq* sloppiness, gooeyness, mushiness, slushiness, gushiness, soppiness, drippiness, *US* stickiness, ackiness, *Slang* corn, corniness, schmaltz, schmaltziness, ickiness, yuckiness *or* yukkiness: *The role of the bereaved mother was overplayed with enough gushing sentimentality to make one sick.*

sentinel *n.* sentry, °guard, °watchman, °watch, °picket, °lookout, °patrol: *The sentinels measured out the ramparts of the fortress with their regular paces.*

separable *adj.* distinguishable, segregable, detachable, divisible, severable, removable, fissile, scissile: *Unfortunately, as history demonstrates, morality and religion are separable.*

separate *v.* **1** disjoin, °pull *or* take *or* °break °apart, °come *or* °fall °apart, °fall *or* °take *or* °break to pieces, °split *or* °divide *or* °break (up), °split *or* break (off *or* away), °disconnect, °disengage, °part, °partition, °sort (out), uncouple, disarticulate, disassemble, unhook, °detach, disunite, unyoke, disentangle, unravel: *In order to clean it, I first have to separate all the individual elements of the motor. The glue didn't hold, and the vase separated into a dozen fragments. Separate this yarn into different piles.* **2** °distinguish, °discriminate, °analyse, °sort, °break down, classify, °segregate, °single out, sequester, °type, codify, °organize, °split up; °group, collate: *What criteria are used to separate the men from the boys, the sheep from the goats, or the wheat from the chaff?* **3** °split *or* °break up, °part (company), °divide (up), °disband, °divorce: *After ten years we separated, and each went our own way.* **4** fork, °split (up *or* off), bifurcate, °diverge, °branch: *Beyond the river, the road to Norton separates from the main road.* —*adj.* **5** divided, separated, disjoined, °disconnected, °detached, °isolated, °discrete, °distinct, °individual, °independent, °solitary, °different: *Sort these books by subject into separate piles.* **6** °different, °independent, °unrelated, other: *How you behave when you are not at home is a separate matter.* **7** °withdrawn, °solitary, °alone, °shut *or* closed off *or* away, °apart, °detached, removed, cloistered, °secluded, sequestered, °isolated, separated: *He prefers a separate existence, far away from the rest of the world.*

separately *adv.* °individually, independently, °singly, one by one, one at a time, °personally, °alone, severally: *Each child approached separately to wish her Bon Voyage.*

separation *n.* **1** °rift, °break, °split, split-up, °divorce, break-up, disunion, estrangement: *Their separation, after forty years, was a surprise.* **2** °partition, °division, °split, °schism, dividing line, dissociation, disassociation, severance: *The United States constitution provides for the separation of church and state.* **3** disintegration, shattering, break-up, fragmentation, dismemberment, taking *or* keeping °apart, °segregation, °division, disjoining, disjunction, fission, scission, °rupture, °schism, splitting, °split, fracturing, °fracture, °break: *After a crash, investigators supervise the separation of the aeroplane into its tens of thousands of component parts.*

sepulchre *n.* °tomb, mausoleum, burial-vault, °grave, °crypt, pyramid, burial-place: *Beneath the floor of the church are the sepulchres of important people.*

sequel *n.* °follow-up, °upshot, °issue, °result, consequence, °development, °supplement: *The ruling went against him, but there was a curious*

sequel *when he was suddenly offered an out-of-court settlement. They are showing the film* Jean de Florette*, together with its sequel* Manon des Sources.

sequence *n.* °succession, °progression, °order, series, °chain, °string, °course, °cycle, °arrangement, °organization, °train, °line, °set, °run, concatenation, °system: *His description conflicts with the sequence of events as recorded by the video camera. Some of these dates are out of sequence.*

sequential *adj.* °successive, ordered, °orderly, serial, °progressive, organized, °systematic, cyclic, °continuous: *Would you please put these periodicals into sequential order?*

seraphic *adj.* angelic, °celestial, °divine, °heavenly, blissful, °sublime, empyrean, Elysian, ethereal, °holy, °saintly, °godly: *In her later years, Anna's beauty took on a detached, seraphic quality.*

serene *adj.* **1** °peaceful, °tranquil, °calm, pacific, °peaceable, °restful, halcyon, °idyllic, bucolic, °pastoral, undisturbed, unruffled, imperturbable, unperturbed, untroubled, °quiet, °still: *With the turmoil of the love affair behind her, Sharon looked ahead to a more serene life.* **2** °calm, °cool, °collected, placid, composed, °self-possessed, °poised, unexcitable, even-tempered, °temperate, °nonchalant, °easygoing, cool-headed, °easy, *Colloq* unflappable: *William's serene exterior disguised his violent nature.*

serenity *n.* **1** peacefulness, °peace, tranquillity, °calm, calmness, restfulness, °quiet, stillness: *The serenity of the warm summer's evening was shattered by an enormous explosion.* **2** tranquillity, peacefulness, peaceableness, unexcitability, calmness, °calm, composure, self-possession, °poise, aplomb, even-temperedness, °temperance, nonchalance, cool-headedness, placidity, *Colloq* unflappability: *The serenity of her nature was like a safe harbour to the friends who sought comfort from the turbulence of their lives.*

serious *adj.* **1** °grave, °solemn, °earnest, unsmiling, poker-faced, straight-faced, °sedate, °sober, °pensive, °thoughtful; humourless, °sombre, °grim, °dour, °severe: *One should be wary of the person who is always serious, who cannot see the ludicrous side of life.* **2** °grave, °important, °vital, °dangerous, °weighty, °significant, °momentous, °crucial, consequential, life-and-death *or* life-or-death, °urgent, °pressing; no laughing matter, of consequence *or* °moment *or* °importance: *Things like the greenhouse effect and the hole in the ozone layer are serious concerns for all mankind.* **3** °sincere, straightforward, not joking *or* fooling, °genuine, °honest: *Is he serious about wanting me to fetch him a left-handed wrench?* **4** °acute, °critical, life-threatening, °bad, °dangerous, °nasty, °perilous, alarming, °grave, °severe, °precarious: *His condition is serious and we might have to operate tonight. She had no idea that measles could be such a serious illness.*

seriously *adv.* **1** gravely, °badly, °severely, critically: *Two men were seriously injured in the explosion.* **2** °really, °honestly, Scout's honour, °sincerely, °truly, candidly, °openly, *Colloq* joking *or* kidding aside, no joking *or* kidding *or* fooling, cross one's heart (and hope to die): *Seriously, kids, I meant what I said about going to bed on time, or no treats tomorrow at the beach.* **3** soberly, earnestly, unquestioningly, without a doubt, at face value: *What teacher takes seriously that old story about a grandmother's illness as an excuse for absence?*

sermon *n.* **1** °lecture, °lesson, preaching, °reprimand, reproach, °reproof, remonstration, remonstrance, scolding, °harangue, *Colloq* talking-to, dressing-down: *Mother gave me a long sermon last night about getting home late.* **2** homily, °address, exhortation, °lesson, °lecture, °speech, °talk, discourse: *We thought that Father Keiller's sermon on vanity was especially appropriate.*

serpentine *adj.* **1** °evil, °bad, diabolic(al), °satanic, Mephistophelian, reptilian, °devilish, °wily, cunning, conniving, °sneaky, °shrewd, °artful, °crafty, °slick, °sly, insidious, °shifty, °tricky, °scheming, plotting, Machiavellian: *With serpentine deceit she swore that she had returned the ring.* **2** twisting, winding, °tortuous, snaking, snakelike, sinuous, anfractuous, °roundabout, °meandering, ambagious, °indirect, °devious, °crooked, °labyrinthine, vermicular, vermiculate, complex, °complicated, Byzantine: *The amulet was traced through a serpentine trail of ownership back to Xerxes.*

serrated *adj.* sawlike, saw-shaped, sawtooth(ed), toothed, °notched, zigzag, °jagged, serrate, serriform, serratiform, serrulate(d), crenellated, crenulate, crenate, denticulate: *A knife with a serrated edge would cut the meat more easily.*

serried *adj.* ranked, tiered, row on row, ranged, assembled, °packed, °close, compacted, °compact: *The serried army of brightly clad warriors stretched as far as the eye could see.*

servant *n.* **1** °domestic (servant), °help, retainer; °maid, maidservant, parlour-maid, upstairs °maid, lady's °maid, cleaner, cleaning °man, cleaning °woman, amah; housekeeper, chatelaine, major-domo, factotum, steward, seneschal, butler, houseman, houseboy, °boy; °page; valet, °man, gentleman's gentleman, manservant, serving-man, footman, foot-boy, chauffeur, driver, °attendant, °groom; governess, au pair (°girl), °nurse, nursemaid, ayah; cook, chef, °waiter, waitress, stewardess, wine steward, *sommelier* (*des vins*); °menial, lackey, dogsbody, *Archaic* servitor, *Historical* coachman, postilion, serving-woman, serving-girl, servant-girl, serving-wench, scullery-maid, scullion, *Literary* cup-boy, Ganymede, *Chiefly Brit* nanny, *Brit* boots, charwoman, charlady, daily, tweeny, *US* scrubwoman: *Who can afford to keep domestic servants these days?* **2 civil servant**: civil-service employee *or* worker, public servant, (°government *or* State) °official, office-holder, °government worker: *In his capacity as a civil servant, Richard has worked for several different governments.*

serve *v.* **1** °attend (to), °wait on *or* upon, °minister to, °look after (the needs of), be at (someone's) beck and call, °assist, °help, be of °assistance *or* °help, be in the °service of, °oblige, °accommodate, °gratify: *After a patron is seated and settled, approach him and ask, 'May I serve you, Sir (or Madam, as the case may be)?' We serve all customers with equal consideration.* **2** °fulfil *or* °carry out *or* °perform *or* °discharge (a °function *or* a °duty *or* one's °duty), °work (for), do (°duty) (as *or* for), do one's °part, °suffice, be °used *or* of °use *or* °useful (to *or* for), °function (as *or* to), °act (as *or* to), fill the bill, be °serviceable (as *or*

for), be °available (for), °answer (for), be °sufficient *or* °adequate *or* °suitable, °suit, be °advantageous *or* of °advantage (to); fight (for), be °obedient (to), take one's part: *This catch will serve to keep the door closed. I had no screwdriver, but a coin served just as well. They also serve who only stand and wait.* **3** °distribute, °deal out, °dole out, °give out, °present, °set out, °provide, °supply, °offer, °pass out *or* about *or* around, make °available, come (a)round with, dish up *or* out: *They will serve hors-d'œuvres at seven-thirty. Dinner is served, Madam.* **4** be °convenient *or* °opportune *or* °favourable (to): *If the opportunity serves me, I shall repay you many times over.* **5** not fail, not play tricks (on), °work *or* °function (for), be °accurate *or* °correct: *If memory serves, he was last here about ten years ago.* **6** °go through, °complete, °spend, °last, °endure, °survive: *Henryson served ten years in Dartmoor for that crime.*

service *n.* **1** °help, °assistance, °aid, °use, °usefulness, utility, °benefit, °advantage: *May I be of service to you? You could do me a great service by not saying anything of this to my mother.* **2** °maintenance, °overhaul, servicing, checking, °repair, mending: *Must we send the copier out for service or can they do it in the office?* **3** serving, °accommodation, amenities, waiting, °care: *The food is good but the service leaves much to be desired.* **4** °employment, °employ: *How long have you been in my service, Jones?* **5** °use, utilization, °usage, handling: *This old teapot has seen much service.* **6** °assignment, °post, °appointment, *Military Brit* secondment: *Oscar was on service in the Far East during the war.* **7** °rite, °ceremony, °ritual, °worship: *I shall be attending a memorial service for Grimes on Saturday.* **8** Often, **services**: army, °navy, air force, marines; armed forces *or* services, °military: *He was a pianist before joining the service.* **9** Often, **services**: °talents, °help, professional °care, °work, °advice: *You will need the services of a good accountant.* **10** °serve, serving; putting into play: *Clarke's tennis service is faster and more accurate than before.*

serviceable *adj.* **1** workable, working, °functional, functioning, usable, °useful, °operative, operating: *It seems unlikely that the old tractor will still be serviceable.* **2** hard-wearing, long-wearing, °durable, utilitarian, long-lasting, °tough, wear-resistant: *I need to buy a serviceable pair of hiking boots.*

servile *adj.* °submissive, subservient, °menial, craven, acquiescent, abject, cringing, slavish, °mean, fawning, deferential, mean-spirited, °vile, °low, °base, °ingratiating, °grovelling, °obsequious, toadying, toadyish, sycophantish, sycophantic, truckling, wheedling, unctuous, °slimy, °flattering, °time-serving, boot-licking, *Colloq chiefly Brit* smarmy, *US and Canadian* apple-polishing, *Slang Brit* arse-kissing, *US* ass-kissing, *Taboo slang* brown-nosing, *Brit* arse-licking, *US* ass-licking: *Victor is constantly trying to gain favour with the directors in the most servile way.*

servility *n.* submissiveness, °submission, subservience, servileness, acquiescence, abjectness, abjection, cringing, slavishness, meanness, fawning, mean- spiritedness, vileness, baseness, °grovelling, obsequiousness, obsequence, toadying, toadyism, sycophancy, sycophantism, truckling, wheedling, unctuousness, sliminess, °flattery, boot-licking, *Colloq chiefly Brit* smarminess, *US and Canadian* apple-polishing, *Slang*

Brit arse-kissing, *US* ass-kissing, *Taboo slang* brown-nosing, *Brit* arse-licking, *US* ass-licking: *We are sick of the servility with which Victor treats the directors.*

servitude *n*. °bondage, °slavery, thraldom, serfdom, subjugation, enslavement, °subjection, vassalage: *They were sentenced to ten years' penal servitude.*

session *n*. **1** sitting, °seating, °assembly, °conference, °meeting, hearing: *Parliament is in session at this very moment.* **2** °term, °period: *The bill will be introduced again at the next session of Parliament.*

set *v*. **1** set down, °place, °put, °situate, °locate, °site, °plant, °position, °station, °stand, °lay, °install *or* instal, °lodge, °mount, °park, °deposit, °plump, °drop, plunk *or* plonk (down): *Please set that blue box over here.* **2** °go down, °sink, °decline, °subside: *The sun is setting.* **3** °jell *or* gel, congeal, °freeze, °solidify, °stiffen, °harden, clot, °coagulate, °thicken, °cake: *The concrete takes a long time to set in this weather.* **4** °establish, °fix, °fasten on, °appoint: *The date of the wedding has been set for May 23rd.* **5** °focus on, home *or* °zero in on, pinpoint, °pin down: *When Ivor sets his mind on doing something, it usually gets done.* **6** °adjust, °regulate, °turn, synchronize, °fix, °calibrate, °coordinate: *Set your watches to Greenwich Mean Time. Set the counter back to zero.* **7** °present, °introduce, °establish, °determine, °stipulate, °lay down, °define, °indicate, °designate, °specify; set *or* °mark off, delineate: *Who set the pattern for such behaviour? You'll have to set the rules.* **8** °prepare, set up, concoct, °lay, °arrange, °fix: *I think we ought to set a trap for the burglar.* **9** set forth, °propound, °present, °devise, °work out *or* up, °make up, °select, °choose, °decide, °settle, °establish: *Who is going to set the questions for the examination?* **10** °arrange, °lay, °spread: *If you set the table, I'll serve dinner.* **11** °adjust, °move, °tilt, °fix, °place, °position, °lodge: *He set his hat at a jaunty angle and strode out of the restaurant.* **12 set about**: **a** get *or* make ready, °start, °begin, get to work, set in motion, get under °way, °start the ball rolling, break the ice, °undertake, °launch, °tackle, °address oneself to, °enter upon, *Colloq* get cracking: *It's time you set about deciding what you want to do for a living.* **b** °attack, assail, °assault, °beat up: *The gang set about him with clubs.* **13 set against**: **a** °compare, °evaluate, °rate, °balance, °weigh, juxtapose, °contrast: *If you set his assets against his liabilities, he comes off pretty well.* **b** antagonize, set at °odds, °alienate, °divide, disunite: *They succeeded in setting brother against brother.* **14 set apart**: **a** °distinguish, °separate, °differentiate: *His talent for language sets him apart from the others.* **b** °reserve, °put *or* set aside, °store, earmark, °put away, °lay away, set by, °save, °keep back: *I set apart this piece of chocolate just for you.* **15 set aside**: **a** See 14 **b**, above. **b** annul, °cancel, nullify, declare *or* render null and °void, °reverse, °repudiate, abrogate, °quash, °overturn, overrule, °discard: *The judge set aside the ruling of the lower court.* **16 set back**: put back, °hinder, °slow, °hold up, °retard, °delay, °impede, °obstruct, °stay, °thwart, °frustrate, °inhibit: *Completion has been set back because the materials failed to arrive.* **17 set down**: **a** °write (down), put in °writing, °put down, °record, °register, °mark

or °jot down, °list: *The secretary laboriously set down every word the official said.* **b** ascribe, °assign, °attribute, °impute, °charge: *She set down her failure to win promotion to prejudice on the part of management.* **c** °put down, °land: *See if you can set the plane down in that field over there.* **18 set forth**: **a** °express, °voice, °propose, °propound, °state, °offer, °submit, °suggest, °broach, make a °motion, °move: *Hugo set forth various proposals for the expansion of the company.* **b** set out *or* off, °put forth *or* out, °begin, °start (out), get under °way, °go, °embark, sally forth, °push off, °depart, °leave: *After much hemming and hawing, Clive finally set forth on his big adventure.* **c** set out, °present, °declare, °describe, °propose, °state, articulate, °enunciate: *Hermione's theory is set forth in a lengthy report.* **19 set in**: °begin, become established, °arrive, °come: *Winter has set in quite early this year.* **20 set off**: **a** ignite, °kindle, detonate, °light, °touch off, trigger, °trip: *That little spark set off an explosion that destroyed the entire plant.* **b** °dramatize, °enhance, highlight, throw into °relief, °show (off), °display: *The engraving is beautifully set off by the new mat and frame.* **c** See 18 **b**, above. **21 set on**: set upon, °attack, °assault, °pounce on *or* upon, °fall on *or* upon, °fly at: *You were set on by a pack of dogs in the park?* **22 set out**: **a** See 17 **b** and **c**, above. **b** put out, °lay out, °arrange, °dispose, °display: *The stallholders are all setting out their wares for the jewellery fair this morning.* **23 set up**: **a** °build, °put up, °erect, °assemble, °construct, °raise, elevate, °put together, °arrange, °prepare: *They are setting up the Christmas displays over the weekend.* **b** °start, °begin, °initiate, °organize, °establish, °found; °finance, °fund, °invest in, °back, °subsidize: *The Crockers are setting up their third shop in Halsted. His father set him up in business.* **24 set upon**: °attack, °assault, °ambush, °beat up, °fall upon, set about, *Colloq* °mug: *The gang set upon him as he was getting home from work.*

—*n*. **25** °collection, °group, °combination, °number, grouping, °assortment, °selection, °arrangement, series: *Brackenhall bought a set of Hogarth etchings from the gallery.* **26** °clique, coterie, °group, °company, °circle, °ring, °crowd, °faction, °sect, °gang: *The set she associates with think nothing of flying to Rio for the weekend.* **27** °kit, °outfit, °rig, °equipment, °apparatus: *When I was ten, my father bought me a chemistry set.* **28** °setting, stage set *or* °setting, °scene, *mise en scène*, mounting, scenery: *Hunter's set for* Waiting for Godot *won a prize.*

—*adj*. **29** °fixed, established, °determined, °predetermined, arranged, prearranged, °decided, °customary, °usual, °normal, °regular, agreed, °conventional, °habitual, °definite, defined, °firm, unvarying, unvaried, unchanging, wonted, °rigid, °strict, settled, scheduled: *There is a set order in which these things are done.* **30** stereotyped, trite, hackneyed, °routine, °standard, °traditional, unchanged, unvaried, °invariable: *He made his set welcoming speech, as usual dripping with condescension, to the incoming classes.* **31** °prepared, °ready, °fit, primed: *Are you all set to go?*

set-back *n*. °hindrance, °hitch, °check, °reverse, °reversal, °impediment, °block, °obstruction, °defeat, °hold-up, °delay, °check, °rebuff, °upset;

°relapse; *Colloq* hiccup: *The reduction in arts funding has resulted in some severe set-backs in certain programmes. Derek has suffered a set-back and will remain in hospital for a while.*

setting *n.* mounting, scenery, °background, backdrop, °locale, °location, surroundings, °habitat, °home, environs, °environment, °milieu, °frame, °context, °site, °placement; stage °set *or* setting, *mise en scène,* °scene: *It is quite interesting to see how the animals live in their natural setting. The setting of Hardy's novels is in the West Country.*

settle *v.* **1** °arrange, °order, °dispose, °organize, °straighten out, put in *or* into °order, °compose, °sort out, classify, °coordinate, °resolve, set to rights, °reconcile: *Ben settled his affairs before undergoing surgery.* **2** Often, **settle on** *or* **upon**: °fix (on), °decide (on), °establish, °appoint, °set, °confirm, affirm, conclude, make °sure *or* °certain (of), °determine, °agree (upon *or* on), °pick, °choose, °select: *Have you been able to settle on a suitable time to visit Max and Maddy?* **3** °decide, °reconcile, °resolve, put an °end to, conclude, °clear up, °patch up, °adjust, °negotiate, mediate: *We have settled our differences.* **4** Often, **settle down**: take up °residence, go *or* come *or* °move to, °dwell, reside, make one's °home, °abide, °remain, °stay, °live, set up °home *or* °house, put down roots, °locate, °inhabit, *US* °set up housekeeping, °locate: *They have decided to settle in Australia after George retires.* **5** Sometimes, **settle down**: °light, alight, °land, °come down, put down, °set down, (come to) °rest *or* roost, °descend, °perch: *The butterfly settled on the tip of Alice's nose.* **6** °populate, °people, colonize, °pioneer: *That part of the country wasn't settled till late in the 19th century.* **7** Usually, **settle down**: °calm down, °subside, °quiet down, be *or* become °tranquil, *Chiefly Brit* °quieten (down): *The class settled down and we began the lesson. I must settle down and get back to work.* **8** °calm, °quiet, soothe, °tranquillize, °relax, *Chiefly Brit* °quieten: *He drank some camomile tea to settle his nerves.* **9** °subside, °sink, °decline, °fall: *A great crack appeared in the wall when the house settled a bit.* **10** Often, **settle up**: °pay, °square, °dispose of, °clear, °balance, liquidate, °discharge: *If you settle the bill, we can leave.* **11** Often, **settle out**: gravitate, °sink, °fall, °precipitate (out): *Stop shaking the container and let the sand settle to the bottom.* **12** °clarify, °clear: *After a few days the pond will settle.*

settlement *n.* **1** colony, outpost, °post, °camp, community, encampment, village, hamlet: *The first colonists established a small settlement on the bank of the river.* **2** colonization, settling, populating: *The settlement of the valley was mainly by Scandinavians.* **3** °agreement, °rapprochement, °resolution, °adjustment, elimination, °reconciliation, working-out, °accommodation, arbitration, °arrangement: *Settlement of the dispute was supervised by a union representative.* **4** °payment, defrayal, °discharge, liquidation, °satisfaction, settling, quittance, clearing, °clearance: *The settlement of our debts is of paramount importance.* **5** deciding, settling, °setting, °decision, conclusion, confirmation, affirmation, °establishment, stabilization, °determination, °agreement, °choice, °selection: *The only thing on his mind was the settlement of their holiday destination—should it be France or Thailand?*

settler *n.* colonist, frontiersman, frontierswoman, °pioneer, °immigrant: *The early settlers cleared the land for farming.*

set-up *n.* **1** °arrangement, °system, °organization, layout, regime, °structure, °make-up, °composition, framework, °frame, construction; °conditions, °circumstances: *This set-up of interlocking directorships makes it difficult to see who answers to whom and who owns what. What, exactly, is the set-up between you and Eustace?* **2** prearrangement, °trap, *Slang* °put-up job: *As soon as I saw the police car, I knew we had walked into a set-up.*

sever *v.* **1** °cut off *or* °apart *or* in two, °lop *or* °chop *or* hew *or* °hack off, °slice *or* shear off, °cleave, dock, bob, dissever, °split, °separate, °divide, disjoin, °detach, °disconnect: *The animal's foot was severed by the trap.* **2** °separate, disunite, °dissolve, °break off *or* up, °terminate, °end, °cease, °stop, °discontinue, °suspend, °abandon, put an °end to: *The final divorce decree severed us from one another once and for all.*

several *adj.* **1** some, a °few, not too *or* very °many, a °handful *or* a sprinkling *or* a °number of: *Several people asked for you at the party last night.* **2** °various, °sundry, a °variety of, °diverse, °divers, °different, °respective, °individual, °distinct, disparate, °particular, °certain, °specific, °discrete, °dissimilar: *There are several stages one must go through before reaching the end.*

severe *adj.* **1** °strict, °harsh, rigorous, austere, °hard, °stony, stony-hearted, hard-hearted, flinty, inexorable, iron-handed, °oppressive, unbending, °rigid, uncompromising, °relentless, unyielding, obdurate, pitiless, °punitive, °merciless, °unsympathetic, unfeeling, °cruel, °brutal, °mean, °savage, °inhuman, °beastly, °ruthless, °despotic, °dictatorial, °tyrannical, autocratic, °demanding, °exacting, °painstaking, °fastidious, exigent, taxing: *Nicholas Nickleby was subjected to extremely severe treatment at Dotheboys Hall. Mr Bradshaw was a severe taskmaster.* **2** °stern, °forbidding, °dour, glowering, °grave, °grim, °stiff, °strait-laced, °serious, unsmiling, °sober, °cold, °frigid, °aloof, austere: *If he so much as dropped a spoon the master would give Nicholas a severe look.* **3** °dangerous, °critical, °dreadful, °awful, life-threatening, °acute, dire; °mortal, °fatal, °terminal: *She has had a severe attack of the flu.* **4** stringent, °punitive, °harsh, °punishing, °burdensome, °tough, onerous, °grievous, °painful, Draconian *or* Draconic: *There are severe penalties for breaking the parking laws in this city.* **5** °harsh, °bitter, °cold, °inclement, °keen, °violent, °stormy, °intense, turbulent, °fierce, °wicked: *Granny couldn't live through another severe winter at Fort William.* **6** °stark, °bare, °plain, austere, °Spartan, ascetic, °primitive, °simple, °sparse, °spare, monastic, °modest, °unadorned, unembellished, °crude, undecorated, unembroidered: *The severe décor in the servants' quarters gave the appearance of a prison.*

severely *adv.* **1** acutely, °seriously, °badly, °dangerously, dreadfully; °permanently, fully, °entirely: *The accident left him severely handicapped.* **2** strictly, harshly, rigorously, austerely, oppressively, relentlessly, mercilessly, cruelly, brutally, savagely, inhumanly, tyrannically: *The boys were severely maltreated at the school.* **3** sternly, forbiddingly, dourly, gloweringly, gravely, °seriously, grimly, unsmilingly, soberly, coldly, coolly, austerely: *Mrs Gladwin regarded me severely over the top of her pince-nez.* **4** stringently, punitively, harshly, onerously, grievously, °painfully: *One is punished severely for the slightest infraction of the law.* **5** °dangerously, acutely, critically, dreadfully, °awfully; mortally, fatally, terminally: *I am afraid to say that your mother is severely ill.* **6** starkly, plainly, °barely, modestly, austerely, ascetically, monastically, primitively, °simply, crudely, sparsely, sparely: *The room is furnished a bit severely for my taste.*

severity *n.* **1** strictness, harshness, °rigour, rigorousness, austerity, hardness, flintiness, inexorability, inexorableness, stringency, °oppression, oppressiveness, rigidity, inflexibility, relentlessness, obduracy, obdurateness, pitilessness, mercilessness, cold-bloodedness, abusiveness, cruelty, brutality, meanness, savagery, inhumanity, beastliness, ruthlessness, °despotism, °tyranny, fastidiousness, exigency: *The severity of the discipline was almost unbearable.* **2** coldness, aloofness, sternness, °gravity, grimness, frigidity, austerity, °solemnity: *The severity of his look froze me to the spot.* **3** dangerousness, acuteness, seriousness, °gravity, ferocity, fierceness, °virulence, °violence, °intensity: *The severity of the fits has diminished since we put the patient on new medication.* **4** stringency, punitiveness, °punishment, harshness, onerousness, grievousness, painfulness, burdensomeness, oppressiveness: *The severity of the sentence is not inappropriate to the heinousness of the crime.* **5** harshness, inclemency, °violence, storminess,- °intensity, ferocity, fierceness, °fury, furiousness, tempestuousness: *The severity of the weather has interfered with our maintenance of the electrical power lines.* **6** plainness, starkness, austerity, asceticism, bareness, modesty, °simplicity, primitiveness, spareness, sparseness, monasticism, crudeness: *The severity of the cells at the monastery was equalled by the austerity of the regimen.*

sew *v.* sew up, stitch, darn, °mend, °repair; sew on, °attach, °fasten; °tack, baste, hem: *Would you sew up a hole in my sweater for me and, while you're at it, would you mind sewing on a button on my shirt?*

sex *n.* **1** gender: *It is difficult to determine the sex of some of the lower animals.* **2** sexual °intercourse *or* relations, coitus, coition, mating, copulation, (sexual) congress *or* °union, intimacy, lovemaking, making °love, coupling, *Colloq* making out, going to bed, shacking up, *Slang* having it away, *Taboo slang* screwing, shafting, shagging, fucking, *Chiefly Brit* bonking: *They feel that there is too much sex and violence on television these days.*

sexual *adj.* **1** sex, reproductive, genital, procreative *or* procreant, propagative: *Their current project is an investigation of sexual behaviour in young adults.* **2** °sensual, °sensuous, °erotic, °carnal, fleshly, °voluptuous, libidinous, °earthy, bodily, °physical, °lustful, °animal, *Colloq* °sexy: *They have a deep sexual attraction to one another.*

sexy *adj.* **1** °erotic, arousing, °exciting, °sensual, °sensuous, °seductive, °suggestive, °provocative, °inviting, alluring, bedroom, °flirtatious, appealing, fascinating, °striking,

°tempting, captivating, °enchanting, °stunning, *Colloq* come-hither: *She thought he had a sexy smile.* **2** sex, °dirty, °pornographic, °obscene, °filthy, smutty, °lewd, °foul, °lascivious, °indecent, °explicit, °gross, X-rated, °vulgar, °rude, °coarse, °off colour, °risqué, titillating, °bawdy, ribald, °lusty, °immodest, °rough, indelicate, °suggestive, °unseemly, °improper, indecorous, °naughty, °shameless, *Slang* raunchy: *They sat there leering over a sexy magazine.*

shabby *adj.* **1** °worn, °dingy, faded, °worn out, °threadbare, tatty, °tattered, frayed, raggedy, °ragged, scruffy, °dilapidated, °ratty, °dirty, °bedraggled, °mangy, °run-down, °seedy, (much) the worse for wear, *Brit* down at °heel, *US* down at the °heel(s), *Colloq* grubby, scrubby, gungy, °tacky, *US* grungy: *He was wearing a shabby suit and down-at-heel shoes.* **2** °poor, °peremptory, unpleasant, °nasty, °disagreeable, °mean, °contemptuous, demeaning, grudging, ungenerous, °impolite, °rude, unfriendly, unhelpful, °shoddy, ungentlemanly, unladylike, °dishonourable, °unworthy, °scurvy, *Colloq* °rotten: *We were subjected to very shabby treatment at the office where we applied for work.* **3** °dilapidated, °tumbledown, broken-down, shattered, battered, °run-down, °ramshackle, °seedy, neglected, °dirty, squalid, slum-like, slummy, *Colloq* beat-up, crummy: *Sam lives in a shabby little house near the canal.* **4** °mean, stingy, ungenerous, niggardly, °contemptible, °low, °lowly, °base, mean-spirited, °despicable, °vile, uncouth, discreditable, °inferior, °disreputable, °infamous, °abominable, °dishonourable, ignoble, °atrocious, ignominious, odious, detestable, opprobrious: *The shabby apology for their behaviour fell on deaf ears.*

shack *n.* °hut, °hovel, shanty, °cabin, lean-to, *Colloq* °dump: *The shack was built out of scrap lumber and cardboard boxes.*

shackle *n.* **1** Often, **shackles**: fetter(s), leg-iron(s), °chains, iron(s), bilboes, gyve(s), ball and °chain, °manacle(s), handcuff(s), °restraint(s), °bond(s), °trammel(s), *Colloq* cuff(s), *Slang* bracelet(s), *Brit* darbies: *When those shackles went round his ankles, he thought he'd never see them taken off.* **2** Usually, **shackles**: °restriction, °restraint, °deterrent, °impediment, °check, °obstacle, °obstruction, °barrier, °hindrance, °bar, °encumbrance: *When shall we throw off the shackles of ignorant prejudice and see a truly free world?*
—*v.* **3** °chain, fetter, °manacle, handcuff, °bind, °restrain, °tie, °secure, truss, pinion, °tether: *He was shackled to the mast and whipped for disobedience. In this glorious spring weather I resent being shackled to a desk.* **4** °restrain, °hold back, °check, °deter, °hinder, °discourage, °hobble, °handicap, °restrict, °curb, °rein, °bridle, °control, fetter, °inhibit, °limit: *Freedom of expression has been shackled during all those years of oppression.*

shade *n.* **1** °shadow, shadiness, dimness, duskiness, semi-darkness, gloominess, murkiness, °dusk, °gloom, murk, darkness, °obscurity, *Literary* shades: *We rested in the shade of an old oak to get out of the hot sun.* **2** °tint, tinge, °tone, °colour, °hue, °intensity: *The curtains should be of a lighter shade to match the wallpaper.* **3** °hint, intimation, tinge, °suggestion, °modicum, sprinkling, soupçon, °trace, °suspicion, undertone, °overtone, °touch, °speck, °dash, nuance,

atom, °grain, scintilla, iota, °jot or tittle: *Did I detect a shade of sarcasm in your voice, Aloysius?* **4** °ghost, °spectre, apparition, °phantom, phantasm, °spirit, wraith, °vision, banshee, *Colloq* spook: *As night came on, horrifying shades took shape amongst the leafless trees.* **5** °blind, window-blind, curtain, venetian °blind; lampshade; °screen, °cover, covering, °protection, °veil, awning, canopy, °shield, °shelter, °umbrella, parasol: *We need shades to reduce the glare of the light. We had only a light tent as a shade against the broiling sun.* **6** fraction, hair's breadth, °bit, °hair, *Colloq* smidgen or smidgin: *Try moving the picture a shade to the left.* **7** °variation, °variety, nuance, °degree: *Do you really think his approval would make a shade of difference to me?*
8 put (someone) in or **into the shade**: °overshadow, °exceed, °surpass, °outstrip, outclass, °eclipse, outshine, °best, °better, °beat, put to °shame, outplay, outperform, °outdo, *Colloq* run rings or circles around, °show up: *Your record time in the 1000-metre put other contenders in the shade.* **9 shades**: sun-glasses: *Take off those shades so I can see what you are thinking.*
—*v.* **10** °screen, °protect, °shield, °shelter, °cover: *You should shade your eyes from the direct sunlight.* **11** darken, °opaque, black out, °blacken: *She shaded in parts of the diagram to give a better effect.* **12** °dim, °shadow, °veil, °blot out, cloud, °conceal, °hide, obscure, °shroud, °screen, °mask, °camouflage, °disguise: *The house is shaded from view by trees on the south side.*

shadow *n.* **1** darkness, °gloom, dimness, °dusk, °obscurity: *In the shadow I could make out the dim outline of a figure.* **2** °cover, °screen, covering, °shield, °veil, curtain, °protection, concealment: *He stole past the sentry under the shadow of darkness.* **3** °hint, intimation, °suggestion, °suspicion, °trace, °vestige, °remnant: *I do not have the slightest shadow of doubt that she is telling the truth. Martin is merely a shadow of his former robust self.* **4** cloud, °blight, °curse: *A terrible shadow has fallen upon the family name.* **5** See **shade**, 4, above. **6** °companion, alter ego, °comrade, *Colloq* sidekick, crony, °chum, (°bosom) °pal, *US* (°bosom) buddy: *Boswell was Johnson's shadow for almost twenty years.*
—*v.* **7** °follow, °trail, °track, dog, °stalk, °pursue, °trace, *Colloq* °tail, *US and Canadian* bird-dog: *For a month detectives shadowed the suspect.*

shadowy *adj.* **1** °dark, °shady, bowery, °leafy, shaded, °gloomy, °dusky, °dim, *Literary* bosky: *The hotel bar was a shadowy place with pink lights on the tables.* **2** °vague, °dim, °dark, °obscure, °faint, °indistinct, °indefinite, °hazy, ill-defined, unclear, indeterminate: *The photograph was too shadowy for us to identify anyone in it. The years before he came to London are part of his shadowy past.* **3** °spectral, °ghostly, °phantom, phantasmal, wraithlike, phantasmagoric(al), °illusory, °dreamlike, °imaginary, °visionary, chimerical, hallucinatory, °unreal, unsubstantial, °fleeting, impalpable, transitory, ethereal, °immaterial: *He saw shadowy figures lurking near the tomb. The plaintiff's case is shadowy, to say the least.* **4** See **shady**, 2, below.

shady *adj.* **1** See **shadowy**, 1, above.
2 °indistinct, °indefinite, °questionable, °doubtful, °uncertain, °unreliable, °suspicious, °suspect, dubious, °shifty, °disreputable; °devious, °tricky, °slippery, underhand(ed), unethical, °unscrupulous, °dishonourable,

°dishonest, *Colloq* °fishy, °crooked, °bent, not (strictly) kosher: *The minister's shady past will be revealed in the next issue of* Tribune. *She got involved with some shady character who had just come out of prison.*

shaft *n.* **1** °pole, °rod, °staff, °stick, °stem, shank, °handle, helve; °pillar, column, °post, stanchion, °upright: *The shaft of the harpoon splintered as the whale suddenly plunged downwards. These shafts help support the upper storey.* **2** °beam, °ray, °gleam, °streak, pencil: *At exactly noon on the winter solstice a shaft of light struck the altar at the centre of the stone circle.* **3** °thrust, barb, °sting, dart, °gibe or jibe, *Colloq* °slap (in the face), °knock, °put-down: *After the episode in the restaurant, Barbara had to suffer the shafts of her colleagues and their teasing.* **4** mine-shaft, °tunnel, adit, °well, °pit; air-shaft, duct, flue: *How many men went down the shaft in the first shift? The screen over the ventilating shaft must be kept clean.*

shaggy *adj.* °hairy, °woolly, °unkempt, unshorn, uncut, hirsute, dishevelled, matted, °untidy: *They had a large black dog with shaggy hair and a great bushy tail.*

shake *v.* **1** °quiver, °quake, °shudder, waver, wobble, °tremble, °shiver: *The poor child is shaking from the cold.* **2** wiggle, °wriggle, °squirm, shimmy, twitch, joggle, °jiggle, waggle, °sway, °swing, °roll, °bump, °grind, °vibrate, oscillate, °pulsate, °gyrate: *When Lola shakes her hips the strongest men have been known to weaken.*
3 °weaken, undermine, °impair, °harm, °damage, °discourage; disenchant, °disappoint, disaffect: *The incident shook my faith in the political party I had supported all my voting life.* **4** °wave, brandish, °flourish, °display, °show off, °parade, °exhibit, vaunt, waggle, °flap, °flutter: *It was thrilling to see the once-banned flag being shaken under the noses of the deposed leaders.* **5** Often,
shake up: °agitate, °stir (up), °mix (up); °upset, °distress, °frighten, °scare, °shock, °disturb, °unnerve, unsettle, disconcert, °discomfit, °worry, °fluster, disquiet, confound, °confuse, °perplex, °puzzle, *Colloq* °rattle, get to, *US* °throw (for a loop): *Shake the medicine before taking it. I was really shaken by the news that Sheila had quit.* **6 shake down: a** °break in, °condition, °test, °prove, *Colloq* debug: *We shook down the submarine on a 30-day cruise.* **b** °blackmail, °extort or °extract or °squeeze or wrest money from, °hold up, °squeeze, °threaten: *The shopkeepers were so frightened that the gang easily shook them down.* **7 shake off**: get °rid of, °discard, dislodge, °drop, °brush off, °elude, °evade, °lose, °throw off, °rid oneself of, give the °slip to: *We finally shook off our pursuers: at last we felt safe.*
—*n.* **8** shaking, quivering, quaking, shuddering, wavering, wobbling, trembling, shivering, °quiver, °quake, °shudder, waver, wobble, °tremble, °shiver, wiggle, °wriggle, twitch, joggle, °jiggle, °sway, °swing, °roll, gyration: *The dog gave a shake of its tail and bounded towards them.* **9** agitating, °agitation, shaking, stirring (up), °jolt, °jar, jarring, jounce, jolting, jouncing: *Give him a good shake and he'll wake up.* **10 the shakes**: trembling, tremors, delirium tremens, *Colloq* D.T.'s: *She's had so much to drink that she's got the shakes.*

shake-up n. reorganization, rearrangement, °overhaul, °revamp, restructuring, rehabilitation, make-over, realignment: *With new owners you can expect a complete shake-up of top management.*

shaky adj. **1** °uncertain, wobbly, °unstable, °precarious, °unsound, °flimsy, °weak, unsteady, unsupported, unsubstantiated, undependable, °unreliable, °tenuous, untrustworthy, dubious, °questionable, °doubtful, Colloq iffy: *The evidence against him is very shaky indeed.* **2** wobbly, wobbling, °unstable, °precarious, °dilapidated, °ramshackle, on its last °legs, °decrepit, falling down or °apart, °rickety, °flimsy, unsteady, °insecure, °unsound, unsubstantial, °insubstantial, °feeble: *Surely, you can't expect that shaky old chair to support your weight!*

shallow adj. **1** °surface, °skin-deep, °superficial, °thin, °empty, °flimsy, trivial, unimportant, °slight, °frivolous, °idle, °foolish: *If you read only comic books, your thoughts are bound to be shallow.* —n. **2** Often, **shallows**: shoal(s), sand °bar, sandbank, bank, shelf: *This boat draws too much water to go fishing in the shallows.*

sham n. **1** °fake, °fraud, °counterfeit, °imitation, °hoax, humbug, °pretence, °forgery, °copy, imposture, Colloq °phoney or US also phony: *Their call for reform is a sham, as they have no intention of disturbing the status quo.* —adj. **2** °fake, °fraudulent, °counterfeit, °imitation, paste, simulated, °false, make-believe, °fictitious, made-up, °bogus, °spurious, °mock, ersatz, °artificial, °synthetic, Colloq °phoney or US also phony, pseudo: *He sat there feigning interest, a sham smile on his face.*

shambles n. °chaos, devastation, °mess, °disaster, Augean stables, pigsty, °muddle, pigpen: *I can't find anything in this shambles. The campaign degenerated into a complete shambles.*

shambling adj. shuffling, lumbering, dragging, scuttling, °awkward, °clumsy, lurching, unsteady, faltering: *The old beggar hobbled off with a shambling gait.*

shame n. **1** °embarrassment, °humiliation, mortification, chagrin, ignominy, shamefacedness, loss of °face, abashment: *Watts felt abysmal shame at being discovered stealing from petty cash.* **2** °disgrace, ignominy, °dishonour, disrepute, °degradation, opprobrium, vilification, calumniation, °infamy, obloquy, odium, °contempt, °scandal, denigration, loss of °face, defamation, °discredit, disesteem, °disfavour, derogation, disparagement: *To think that one knight's single act of cowardice in 1249 could have brought such shame to all his descendants.* **3** °pity, °calamity, °disaster, °catastrophe; °outrage: *What a shame that Gerry failed the exam!* **4** °humility, modesty, (sense of) decency or °decorum or °propriety, respectability, decorousness, diffidence, shyness, coyness, prudishness, timidity, shamefacedness: *The people who wear bathing suits like that obviously have no shame at all.* **5 put to shame**: **a** °surpass, °eclipse, outclass, °overshadow, cast into the °shade, °outdo, °outstrip, outshine, °show up: *Cochrane put his opponents to shame when they failed to score a single point against him.* **b** See 8, below. —v. **6** °embarrass, °humiliate, °mortify, °humble, chagrin, disconcert, discountenance, °put down, bring down, abash, °chasten, Colloq bring (someone) down a °peg, °suppress, °subdue: *He*

hated the teacher because she had shamed him in front of his friends. **7** coerce, °force, °drive, °bully, °push; °embarrass, °humiliate, °mortify, °humble: *The other boys shamed him into admitting that he had done it.* **8** °disgrace, °embarrass, °dishonour, °scandalize, calumniate, °degrade, °debase, defame, °discredit, °stigmatize; °smear, °blacken, °stain, °taint, besmirch, °tarnish: *I am sure, son, that nothing you ever do would shame the family or me.*

shamefaced adj. **1** °bashful, °shy, °modest, self-effacing, diffident, °timid, °meek, °coy, °sheepish, timorous: *He felt shamefaced as a schoolboy when they awarded him a medal for bravery.* **2** °ashamed, shamed, abashed, °embarrassed, humiliated, dishonoured, mortified, humbled, chastened, chagrined, uncomfortable, discomfited, °remorseful, red-faced: *Shamefaced, she finally admitted the truth about where she had been.*

shameful adj. °disgraceful, °dishonourable, °base, low, °mean, °vile, °degrading, °indecent, inglorious, °deplorable, discreditable, °corrupt, °disreputable, °infamous, ignominious, humiliating, °embarrassing, mortifying, humbling, chastening, discomfiting, shaming, blameworthy, °scandalous, °outrageous, unprincipled: *Quentin was known for his shameful behaviour both at school and in the army.*

shameless adj. °wild, °flagrant, unreserved, °uncontrolled, °immodest, °wanton, indecorous, °indecent, °rude, °improper, °forward, °bold, unembarrassed, unblushing, °audacious, °brazen, °brash, °unabashed, unashamed, °impudent, °shocking, °outrageous: *He was roundly condemned for his shameless neglect of his responsibilities. Her behaviour was shameless, even wanton.*

shape n. **1** °form, °figure, °build, °body, °physique; lines, °profile, °silhouette, contours: *I've never heard anyone complain about Marilyn Monroe's shape.* **2** °form, °pattern, configuration, °structure, °aspect: *The discussion is on the shape of things to come in the double-glazing trade. The new swimming-pool will be in the shape of a figure of eight.* **3** °form: *Gradually, the shopping mall began to take shape.* **4** °state, °condition, fettle, °status, (°state of) °health, °order, °trim: *When I saw Wayne yesterday, he seemed in very good shape indeed.* **5** °guise, °disguise, °form, °appearance, °likeness, °image: *Zeus visited Danäe in the shape of a golden shower, and fathered Perseus on her.* —v. **6** °form, °fashion, °mould, °cast, °make, °model, °sculpture, sculpt; °cut, °carve, hew, °hack, °trim: *Using primitive tools, they were able to shape the clay into bowls. The topiary shrubs were shaped into the forms of birds.* **7** °determine, give °form to, °control, °govern, °regulate, °affect, °condition, °influence, °decree, °frame, °define,: *There are many factors that shape our future.* **8** °word, °express, °embody in words, °put, °formulate, °form: *Perhaps you could shape your question differently.* **9** °change, °modify, remodel, °accommodate, °fit, °adapt, °adjust: *The box was shaped especially for this bottle.* **10 shape up**: **a** take °form, take shape, °develop, evolve, °proceed: *The plan is shaping up very nicely.* **b** °improve, °progress, go or move or °come along, show °improvement, °come up to snuff; behave better: *Those who cannot shape up will have to ship out.*

shapeless *adj.* **1** amorphous, formless, °nebulous, unformed, °indefinite, unstructured, °vague: *Sculptors start with a shapeless mass of clay.* **2** unshapely, °deformed, °misshapen, distorted, twisted, °bent, battered: *The wreckage was a shapeless tangle of steel and mortar.*

shapely *adj.* curvaceous, °comely, well-proportioned, °graceful, °neat, well turned out, good-looking, °pleasing; °voluptuous, *Colloq* °sexy: *That slinky black dress certainly sets off her shapely figure to advantage.*

share *n.* **1** °portion, °allotment, °division, apportionment, allocation, °ration, appropriation, dispensation, °allowance, °part, due, °percentage, °interest, dividend, °quota, °helping, serving, *Colloq* °cut: *Each of us is entitled to a share in the profits. We made sure that all participants got their shares.* **2** °interest, °piece, °part, °stake, °equity, °slice: *Do you own any shares in the stock market? My share in United Telephone is worth twice what I paid for it.*
—*v.* **3** share out, °divide up, °allot, apportion, allocate, °ration, °appropriate, °share in, °split, °partition, °parcel or °deal or °dole out, °pay out: *Ownership in the company is shared equally among the employees. Let's just take one car, and share the expenses.*

sharp *adj.* **1** °acute, °keen; razor-sharp, knife-like, knife-edged, sharpened; °pointed, needle-sharp: *How do you keep the telescope in sharp focus? You need an extremely sharp knife for boning fish. This pencil isn't sharp enough.* **2** °abrupt, °sudden, °precipitous, °sheer, vertical, °marked: *Just round the corner is a sharp dip in the road. There was a sharp rise in prices on the London Stock Exchange today.* **3** °keen, keen-witted, keen-minded, sharp-witted, °shrewd, °intelligent, °smart, °alert, °bright, quick, °agile, °astute, °clever, on the qui vive, °penetrating, °observant: *Penny has a very sharp mind and a good eye for detail.* **4** °caustic, °bitter, °biting, acrid, °hot, °spicy, °pungent, piquant, tangy, °harsh, °sour, acid, acidulous, °tart: *That lemon sorbet is a little too sharp for my taste.* **5** acid, acidulous, acerbic, vitriolic, acrimonious, °cutting, piquant, °biting, bitter, °unkind, °strict, °hurtful, °spiteful, °virulent, °sarcastic, °sardonic, °trenchant, °severe, °scathing, malicious, °nasty, °malignant, °venomous, °poisonous: *How does one escape the sharp comments of the critics? She was unprepared for the sharp exchange between the guests on her chat show.* **6** °clever, °shrewd, °artful, °crafty, °sly, cunning, °foxy, °calculating, °unscrupulous, °dishonest, *Colloq* °sneaky, fly: *There is evidence that the stock manipulators were engaged in very sharp practice.* **7** high-pitched, °shrill, °penetrating, °piercing, °strident, °harsh, ear-splitting, °loud: *Jane gave a sharp cry when she felt the ice break under her feet.* **8** °poignant, °severe, °cutting, °intense, °sudden, °piercing, °extreme, °acute, °fierce: *Complaining of a sharp pain in his chest, he fell down.* **9** °chic, °dapper, °spruce, °stylish, °smart, °fashionable, °dressy, *Colloq* °snappy, natty, classy, °nifty, °swell, °swanky: *If you want to see the latest collection of sharp clothes, go to the disco.*
—*adv.* **10** °sharply, °precisely, °exactly, punctually, on the °dot, *Colloq* on the button, *US* on the nose: *Our appointment was for seven o'clock sharp.* **11** °sharply, °suddenly, abruptly: *I was pulled up sharp by her mention of the Black Rose.* **12** °sharply, alertly, attentively, vigilantly, watchfully, carefully: *Listen sharp to what I tell you.*

sharpen *v.* hone, °grind, strop, °whet: *Of what use is a knife if you don't sharpen it periodically?*

sharp-eyed *adj.* sharp-sighted, °eagle-eyed, hawk-eyed, lynx-eyed, gimlet-eyed, keen-sighted, wide °awake, °wakeful, watchful, °observant, (on the) °alert, on the qui vive, °wary, circumspect, Argus-eyed, °cautious, °careful: *It takes quite a sharp-eyed person to check the accuracy of these circuits.*

sharply *adv.* **1** °severely, sternly, harshly, cuttingly, acerbically, peremptorily, angrily, strictly, °firmly: *Her teacher sharply rebuked Hilary for smiling.* **2** °suddenly, °quickly, abruptly, precipitously, precipitately: *Prices increased sharply for the third day in succession.* **3** acutely, distinctly, °definitely, definitively: *These new cameras automatically remain sharply focused on the object.*

shatter *v.* **1** °disintegrate, °burst, °pulverize, °shiver, smash, °demolish, °break (to smithereens), °splinter, °fragment, °fracture, °dash to pieces: *If you hadn't caught the vase, it would have shattered into a million pieces.* **2** °destroy, °ruin, °devastate, °wreck, °dash, °crush, °demolish, torpedo, °undermine, °blast: *Any dreams he might have had of being published were shattered by the rejection letter.* **3** °upset, °disturb, °perturb, °trouble, °unnerve, °overcome, °overwhelm, °crush, °devastate, °depress, deject, °rattle, °shake (up), unsettle, °agitate, confound, °confuse, stupefy, °daze, °stun, °paralyse, *Colloq* °throw: *He was shattered by the news of Mill's death.*

shave *v.* **1** shear (off), °cut (off), °trim, °clip, crop, °snip off, °remove: *He made a mistake in shaving off his beard, as it hid his weak chin.* **2** °pare, °scrape, °plane, °whittle: *If you shave just a hair off this side, it will fit into the hole.*
—*n.* **3** close shave: °narrow °escape, *Colloq* °narrow or °near squeak, *US* squeaker: *That was a close shave!—You almost fell out the window!*

shed¹ *n.* lean-to, °shelter, °structure, °addition, penthouse, °hut, °shack, °stall, °booth, °pen, cote, hutch: *The tools are in the shed alongside the barn.*

shed² *v.* **1** °spill: *Much blood has been shed in the name of freedom.* **2** °shine, °spread, °scatter, °throw, °cast, let fall, °impart, °release, °focus, °pour forth, °radiate: *Can you shed a little light on a matter that has puzzled me for years?* **3** °pour or °stream or °flow or °surge or °spill (out or forth), °discharge, °emanate, °emit, °drop; exude, °ooze, °weep: *The clouds shed their snow and the world below turned white. Don't shed any tears over me.* **4** °cast off, doff, °drop, °abandon; moult, defoliate, desquamate, °peel (off), °flake (off): *The trees shed their leaves. She rushed into the bathroom, shedding her clothes as she went.*

sheen *n.* °shine, °gleam, °polish, °lustre, shininess, burnish, brightness, °gloss, °glow, glimmer, °shimmer, °radiance, glint, °dazzle: *The sheen of the horse's coat glistened in the sunlight.*

sheepish *adj.* **1** °timid, °withdrawn, °passive, docile, °obedient, compliant, sheeplike, manipulable, °tractable, °pliable, °meek, amenable: *Dashworth might seem sheepish but he doesn't like to be bullied.* **2** See shamefaced, above.

sheer *adj.* **1** °steep, °precipitous, °abrupt, °perpendicular, °bluff, vertical: *There is a sheer drop of 2000 feet to the valley below.* **2** °absolute, °unmitigated, °unqualified, °downright, °out-and-out, unalloyed, unadulterated, °pure, unmixed, °plain, °simple, °rank, °total,

°complete, arrant, °thorough, thoroughgoing, utter: *Johnson said that he had got his definition of 'pastern' wrong out of 'sheer ignorance'.*
3 °transparent, °see-through, °thin, diaphanous, °filmy, gauzy, gossamer, translucent, peekaboo: *Kathryn was wearing the sheer nightgown he had given her for her birthday.*

sheet *n.* **1** bed-sheet, crib-sheet, fitted sheet, flat sheet, *US* contour sheet: *How often do you change the sheets on your bed?* **2** leaf, folio, °page: *He tore a sheet of paper from the notebook.* **3** °pane, panel, °plate, °slab: *The desk has a sheet of glass on top for protection.* **4** lamina, lamination, layer, °stratum, °veneer, membrane: *Plywood is made up of a number of thin sheets of pressed wood bonded together for strength.* **5** °area, °expanse, °stretch, layer, °film, °coat, coating, covering, blanket, °cover, °surface, °skin, °veneer: *The sheet of ice on the road made driving hazardous.* **6** newspaper, °journal, °paper, tabloid, gazette, daily, weekly, monthly, *Colloq* °rag: *Have you got a copy of the sheet that published the article about you?*

shell *n.* **1** cartridge, °projectile, °shot: *We huddled in the foxhole as the shells whistled overhead.* **2** °exterior, °outside, façade, framework, °frame, chassis, externals, skeleton, °hull: *After the earthquake, only the shell of the building was left standing.*
—*v.* **3** shuck, husk, °peel, °hull, excorticate, decorticate: *Would you mind shelling the peas while I peel the potatoes?* **4** °fire on *or* upon, °bombard, barrage, °attack, °bomb, blitz, cannonade, *Slang Brit* prang: *The enemy shelled our position relentlessly.* **5 shell out**: °pay out, °give out, disburse, °spend, °expend, °hand over, °hand out, *Colloq* °lay out, fork out, dish out, *Chiefly US* ante up: *I had to shell out a month's salary for that suit.*

shelter *n.* **1** °protection, °cover, °refuge, asylum, °sanctuary, haven, °safety, °security: *During the hailstorm, we sought shelter in a cave.* **2** °cover, covering, concealment, °screen, °umbrella: *Under the shelter of a moonless night, they stole quietly past the guards.* **3** dwelling-place, habitation, °home, °dwelling, °housing, °accommodation: *He feels that everyone is entitled to food, clothing, and shelter.*
—*v.* **4** °protect, °screen, °shield, °safeguard, °guard, °keep, °secure, °harbour: *The parapet sheltered the guards from the icy wind.* **5** seek *or* take °refuge *or* shelter, °hole up, *Colloq* °lie *or* °lay low: *Mike sheltered in a mountain hut until the hue and cry died down.*

shelve *v.* °postpone, °defer, °put off *or* aside *or* on ice *or* on the shelf, pigeon-hole, °lay aside, hold in °abeyance, *US* °table: *We will have to shelve this matter until we have more information.*

shepherd *v.* °lead, convoy, °escort, °conduct, °guide, usher, °take, °pursue: *I want you, personally, to shepherd Miss Jones through the plant. As this project requires special care, I shall shepherd it through personally.*

shibboleth *n.* °password, catchword, catch-phrase, buzz-word, °byword, watchword, °jargon: *As Simon knew none of the shibboleths of teenagers' slang, he remained an outsider to his classmates.*

shield *n.* **1** °protection, °guard, °safeguard, °defence, °screen, °bulwark, °shelter: *Education is a poor shield against poverty.*
—*v.* **2** °protect, °guard, °safeguard, °keep, °defend, °screen, °shelter: *The mother bear will shield the cubs from harm or die in the attempt.*

shift *v.* **1** °move, °change position; °edge, budge, relocate, rearrange, °transpose, °switch: *Shift the picture slightly to the left. Marla shifted over closer to me on the bench. I almost broke my leg because you shifted the chair as I was about to sit on it.* **2** Usually, **shift for (oneself)**: °manage, °succeed, °make do, °look after, take °care of, °get *or* °scrape by *or* along, °fend for (oneself), °make it, paddle one's own canoe: *Cyril prefers to live alone and shift for himself.* **3** °sell, °market, move: *The object of advertising is to shift merchandise.*
—*n.* **4** hours, °stint, °schedule; workforce, relay, °crew, cadre, °staff, workers, °squad, °team, °corps, °group, °party, °gang: *I prefer to work the morning shift. The night shift comes on at 1600.* **5** °change, °movement, °switch, °transfer, °swerve, deflection, veer: *Owing to a wind shift, it became impossible to manoeuvre among the rocks.* **6** smock, chemise, muu-muu; caftan *or* kaftan: *A light cotton shift is the most comfortable thing to wear in such scorching weather.*

shiftless *adj.* unambitious, °lazy, °indolent, uninspired, unmotivated, °idle, °lackadaisical, °irresponsible, uncaring, unenterprising, °aimless, °slothful, otiose, °ineffective, ne'er-do-well, °good-for-nothing, fainéant, pococurante: *He calls Geoff a shiftless vagabond, virtually a tautology.*

shifty *adj.* °tricky, °artful, °shrewd, canny, cunning, °foxy, °wily, °sharp, °devious, °slick, °evasive, °smooth, °slippery, °scheming, °designing, conniving, °calculating, underhand(ed), conspiratorial, treacherous, °traitorous, °deceitful, deceiving, duplicitous, °two-faced, Janus-faced, °dishonest, °crooked, untrustworthy, *Colloq* °bent: *The shifty scoundrel gave me a bad cheque and did a moonlight flit.*

shilly-shally *v.* hem and haw, dilly-dally, teeter-totter, °see-saw, yo-yo, vacillate, waver, °alternate, °fluctuate, dither, falter, tergiversate, *Brit* haver, hum and haw, *Scots* swither; °delay, °hesitate, °dawdle: *Stop shilly-shallying and decide whether you want chocolate or strawberry!*

shimmer *v.* **1** °shine, °gleam, °glow, glimmer, glint, °glisten, °ripple, °flicker: *The desert shimmered like a lake under the relentless sun.*
—*n.* **2** shimmering, °shine, °gleam, °glow, glimmer, glint, °gloss, °flicker, °light: *As Julia slunk up to the microphone, the spotlight picked up the shimmer from her black satin gown.*

shin *v.* Usually, **shin up**: °climb, clamber up, °scramble up, °scale, *US* shinny up: *The lad shinned up the flag-pole carrying the banner.*

shine *v.* **1** °gleam, °glow, °shimmer, °radiate, °beam, °glare, °flare, °glisten, °glitter, coruscate, °twinkle, °sparkle, scintillate, glint, °flash, °flicker: *The light of a candle shone from her window. The stars are shining brightly. I want that brass polished till it shines.* **2** °polish, burnish, °rub (up *or* down), buff, °brush, °brighten: *You'd best shine your shoes before going for the job interview.* **3** °excel, °surpass, °stand out, outshine, be °outstanding *or* °pre-eminent *or* °excellent *or* °prominent *or* °conspicuous: *She had shone at tennis from a very early age, and first entered Wimbledon when she was twelve.*

—*n.* **4** °gleam, °glow, °shimmer, °sparkle, brightness, °radiance, °gloss, °lustre, °sheen, °glaze, patina: *That shine was achieved with a little wax and elbow-grease.* **5 take a shine to**: °like, be attracted to, take a °fancy to, °fancy: *Her Great Dane has taken a shine to me and likes to sit on my lap.*

shiny *adj.* gleaming, °glowing, shimmering, °glossy, shimmery, °lustrous, °glassy, °radiant, °bright, beaming, glistening, °polished, burnished, glittering, °dazzling, coruscating, °twinkling, sparkling, °scintillating, glinting, flashing, °flashy, flickering, lambent, fulgent: *She loves riding about in her shiny new car.*

ship *n.* **1** °vessel, (ocean *or* passenger) liner, steamer, wind-jammer, cutter: *The statue is dedicated to the men who go down to the sea in ships.*
—*v.* **2** °send, °move, ferry, °transport, °deliver, °carry, °dispatch *or* despatch, °freight, °haul, °truck, °cart: *You need a specialized company that ships computers and other delicate equipment.* **3 ship out**: °leave, °depart, °embark, set °sail, °take off, °get out, °quit, *Slang* scram: *You'll ship out if you know what's good for you.*

shipshape *adj.* °neat, °trim, °spotless, °orderly, Bristol fashion, spick and °span, °tidy: *Pick up your clothes and make this room shipshape at once!*

shirk *v.* °avoid, °evade, °dodge, °get out of, °shrink from, *Colloq* °duck (out of), *Brit* skive, *Military Brit* scrimshank, *US* gold brick: *Stop shirking your responsibilities and get to work! Is Callum shirking again?*

shiver[1] *v.* **1** °shake, °quake, °tremble, °shudder, °quiver: *We sat in our wet clothes, shivering in the cold. The old shack shivered in the wind.* **2** °vibrate, luff, °flap, °flutter, °chatter, °rattle, °shake, wallop: *The sails shivered violently in the stiff breeze.*
—*n.* **3** °shake, °quake, °tremble, °shudder, °quiver, °thrill, *frisson,* trembling, tremor, °flutter: *She gave a little shiver and then snuggled into my arms.* **4 the shivers**: trembling, shivering, goose-pimples *or* goose bumps, *Colloq* the shakes, *US* the chills: *He's had malaria and occasionally gets the shivers. Those horror films give me the shivers.*

shiver[2] *v.* °shatter, °fragment, °splinter, °disintegrate, °rupture, °explode, implode, smash (to smithereens), °crash: *The light-bulb fell and shivered into a million fragments.*

shock *v.* **1** °startle, °surprise, °stagger, °jar, °jolt, °shake (up), °stun, °numb, °paralyse, °daze, stupefy, °dumbfound *or* dumfound, °bowl over, °appal, °astonish, °astound, °frighten, °scare, °petrify, traumatize, °horrify, °outrage, °disgust, °nauseate, °repel, °revolt, °sicken, °upset, disquiet, °disturb, °perturb, discompose, unsettle, *Colloq* °throw, *US* °throw for a loop, flabbergast, give (someone) a °turn: *He shocked us when he announced his resignation. We were shocked to learn of the train wreck.*
—*n.* **2** trauma, °stupor, paralysis, °prostration, °breakdown, °collapse, nervous °exhaustion: *He is in a state of shock after the accident.* **3** °surprise, thunderbolt, °bolt from the blue, °bombshell, °revelation, shocker, eye-opener, °jolt: *It came as a shock to a woman whom I had been talking to so casually. The death of her husband was a terrible shock.* **4** tingle, °jolt, °impact: *You'll get a nasty shock if you touch those wires.*

shocking *adj.* **1** surprising, astounding, astonishing, °amazing, °striking, stupefying, numbing, °sudden, unexpected, electrifying, °startling, *Colloq* mind-boggling, mind-blowing:

It was shocking to see the way the neighbourhood had deteriorated. **2** °disgusting, °revolting, nauseating, °nauseous, sickening, °repulsive, °abominable, °hideous, °horrible, horrifying, horrific, horrid, °foul, °loathsome, °abhorrent, °ghastly, unspeakable, °dreadful, distressing, °outrageous, appalling, °monstrous, °scandalous: *The conditions in the concentration camps were shocking.*

shoddy *adj.* °shabby, tatty, °inferior, °poor, rubbishy, °cheap, pinchbeck, meretricious, °tawdry, °gaudy, Brummagem, °plastic, °artificial, tinsel, tinselly, second-rate, trashy, junky, *Colloq* crappy, cheapjack, °tacky, *US* chintzy: *They can't get away for long with selling such shoddy merchandise.*

shoo *interjection.* **1** Scat!, Go away!, Away with you!, Be off!, Get out!, Begone!, *Colloq* Get lost!, Beat it!, Scram!: *I shouted 'Shoo!' and the chickens scattered.*
—*v.* **2** Often, **shoo away** *or* **off**: °scare off, °frighten away, °drive away, force to leave: *She shoos away anyone who disturbs her while she is painting.*

shoot *v.* **1** scoot, dart, °whisk, °speed, °bolt, °run, °race, °rush, °flash, °fly, °dash, °hurtle, °streak, scuttle, °bound, °leap, °spring, *Colloq* zip, whiz: *The instant the baby cried out, its mother shot over to protect it.* **2** °discharge, °fire, open °fire; let °fly, °launch, °propel, °project, °fling, hurl, °throw, °toss: *Don't shoot till you see the whites of their eyes! With all his strength he shot the arrow into the beast's neck.* **3** °wound, °hurt, °harm, °injure; °kill, slay, assassinate, °execute, *Slang* fill *or* pump full of lead, °plug, °blast, °zap, °knock off, snuff (out): *He insulted her, so she shot him. He's to be shot at sunrise.* **4** °sprout, germinate, burgeon, °flourish, °grow, °spring up, mushroom, °develop: *Owing to the perfect weather, the corn shot up very quickly.*
—*n.* **5** °sprout, °stem, bud, °branch, °offshoot, °slip, scion, °sucker: *If you want fruit, the new shoots have to be pinched back.*

shop *n.* **1** °store, boutique, department °store: *Would you stop at the shop and buy some lettuce?* **2** workshop, machine shop: *Henry gained experience in operating a lathe at my father's shop.*
—*v.* **3** °betray, °inform on *or* against, *Slang* peach on, rat on, snitch on, blow the whistle on: *The police persuaded Luke to shop his accomplices in exchange for a lighter sentence.* **4 shop for**: °buy, °purchase, °seek, °look for, °research: *I've been shopping for a new dishwasher.*

short *adj.* **1** °small, °little, °slight, °petite, °diminutive, °wee, °tiny, °elfin, minuscule; midget, dwarfish, squat, °dumpy, runty, stubby, °stunted, *Colloq* pint-sized, knee-high to a grasshopper, sawn-off: *Did you know that Queen Victoria was quite short?* **2** shortened, °brief, °concise, compressed, compendious, °compact, °pocket, *US* vest-pocket; °abbreviated, abridged, °cut: *A short version of the book was published in paperback.* **3** laconic, °terse, °succinct, pithy, sententious, °epigrammatic: *He made a few short remarks that were very much to the point.* **4** °abrupt, °curt, °terse, °sharp, °blunt, °bluff, °brusque, °offhand, °gruff, °testy, °snappish, °discourteous, uncivil, °impolite: *It is unnecessary to be so short with the staff.* **5** °direct, °straight, straightforward, short and sweet: *In reply to your request for permission to leave early, the short answer is 'No'.* **6** Usually, **short of**: °deficient (in), lacking (in), needful (of), °wanting, °inadequate, °shy (of),

°low (on): *The hotel is short of clean linen because the laundry failed to deliver.* **7** °brief, °limited; transitory, °temporary, °short-lived, °momentary, °quick, °transient: *HQ had a short life but a happy one. I'll just make a short stop in here and will join you in a moment.* **8** impecunious, °straitened, pinched, underfunded, °poor, penniless, °deficient: *I'm a bit short today and wonder if you could lend me some money?* **9 in short supply**: °rare, °scarce, °scanty, unplentiful, °meagre, °sparse, *Colloq chiefly Brit* °thin on the ground: *Good editors are in short supply these days.* **10 short of**: °before, °failing, excluding, °exclusive of, °barring, eliminating, precluding, excepting, °except for, leaving out, °apart from, setting aside: *Short of killing him, I am not sure what she could have done in the circumstances.*
—*adv.* **11** abruptly, °suddenly, peremptorily, without warning, instantly, unexpectedly, hurriedly, °hastily, out of the blue: *She stopped short in the middle of the road and made me get out.* **12 cut short**: **a** °trim, °curtail, °shorten, °abbreviate, °cut: *I must cut my visit short because I have a train to catch.* **b** °stop, °cut off, °terminate, °cut in on, °break in on, °interrupt; °butt in: *I am sorry to cut you short, but it is getting on for midnight.* **13 fall** *or* **come short**: °fail, be *or* prove °inadequate *or* °insufficient: *These grades fall short of our expectations, Bobby.*
—*n.* **14 in short**: °briefly, in a °word, all in all, to make a long story short, in a nutshell: *He told me, in short, that there was no job and there never had been one.* **15 shorts**: Bermuda shorts, knee-breeches, knee-pants, hot °pants: *I usually wear shorts to play tennis.*

shortage *n.* °deficit, deficiency, shortfall, °dearth, °scarcity, °lack, °want, paucity: *They are predicting a shortage of water again this summer.*

shortcoming *n.* °failure, °defect, deficiency, °weakness, °frailty, °drawback, °liability, °imperfection, °weak point, °flaw: *One might justifiably regard colour-blindness as a shortcoming in an interior decorator.*

shorten *v.* **1** °cut, °curtail, °cut off *or* down *or* °short, °reduce, °diminish, °trim; °lop off, °dock, °prune; hem: *Please shorten the time you spend in the bathroom in the mornings. This skirt has already been shortened.* **2** condense, °abridge, °abbreviate, °digest, compress: *Can one shorten the book without losing too much of the characterization?*

short-lived *adj.* ephemeral, evanescent, °temporary, °fleeting, transitory, °transient, °passing, fugacious, °volatile: *He enjoyed a short-lived reputation that died with him.*

shortly *adv.* **1** °soon, °presently, anon, before long, in a (little) while, by and by, *Archaic* ere long: *I'll see you shortly.* **2** °just, °immediately, °soon, °right: *We had dinner with him shortly before he went abroad.* **3** abruptly, °briefly, peremptorily, curtly, brusquely, °sharply, tersely, testily, gruffly, rudely, tartly: '*Leave me alone', said Bill shortly.*

short-sighted *adj.* **1** °near-sighted, myopic, dim-sighted: *He wears thick spectacles because he's so short-sighted.* **2** unimaginative, unprogressive, °improvident, °imprudent, injudicious, °rash, °brash, °impulsive, °reckless, impolitic, °limited, °unwary, incautious, °careless, °thoughtless, unmindful: *Lewis's short-sighted view makes no provision for the future.*

short-staffed *adj.* undermanned, short-handed, understaffed: *We are usually short-staffed during the summer because of the holiday schedules.*

short-tempered *adj.* °testy, irascible, °short, °curt, °abrupt, °gruff, °peremptory, °bluff, °rude, °tart, acid, acidulous, °terse, °brusque, crabbed, crabby, °irritable, °touchy, °petulant, °peevish, bearish, °snappish, °waspish, shrewish, curmudgeonly, crusty, °surly, °discourteous, grouchy, °disagreeable, °caustic, acrimonious, acerbic: *Henry is often short-tempered if he has slept badly.*

short-winded *adj.* short of *or* out of breath, winded, °breathless, panting, huffing (and puffing), gasping (for air *or* for breath), *Technical* dyspnœal: *He is very short-winded because he smokes too much.*

shot *n.* **1** °discharge, shooting: *The town was captured without a shot being fired.* **2** bullet, ball, slug, cannon-ball, buckshot, pellet, °projectile, °missile: *A dumdum bullet is a piece of soft shot with a hollowed-out nose.* **3** °attempt, °try, °opportunity, °chance, °go, °essay, °endeavour, °guess, conjecture, *Colloq* °stab, °crack, whack: *You are allowed three shots at the answer.* **4** marksman, markswoman, sharpshooter, sniper, rifleman: *Geraghty is an excellent shot and favourite for an Olympic gold.* **5** °photograph, snapshot, °picture, *Colloq* °snap, photo: *Miller took some excellent action shots using stroboscopic lighting.* **6** injection, inoculation, vaccination: *The doctor gave me a flu shot this morning.* **7** °drink, jigger, °tot, dram, °nip, spot, °swallow, *Colloq* finger, swig, slug, snort: *Will you have a shot of whisky with me, Muldoon?* **8** (space) °launch *or* launching: *The moon shot scheduled for today has been postponed owing to technical difficulties.* **9 call the shots**: °run *or* °direct *or* °manage *or* °administer *or* °control things *or* affairs *or* matters, °run the show, °rule the roost, be in °command *or* the driver's seat: *Ravelli calls the shots around here, and don't you forget it.* **10 like a shot**: °quickly, °swiftly, °rapidly, speedily, hurriedly, °hastily, at °once, like a °flash, °immediately, instantly, °instantaneously, *Colloq* in two shakes of a lamb's tail, like greased lightning, before you can say 'Jack Robinson': *All I had to do was mention ice-cream, and the children were in here like a shot.* **11 (not) by a long shot**: no way, under no circumstances, by no °means, on no account, by no chance, °never: *You ask if he can get elected and my response is, 'Not by a long shot'.* **12 shot in the arm**: °boost, stimulus, °encouragement, °incentive, °inducement, °provocation, motivation: *The team needs a shot in the arm to improve morale.*

shoulder *n.* °side, °edge, °verge, °margin; breakdown lane: *If you have a flat tyre, drive onto the hard shoulder and phone for help.* **2 give (someone) the cold shoulder**: °rebuff, snub, °ostracize, send (someone) to Coventry, cold-shoulder, °put (someone) down, °reject, °exclude, °freeze (someone) out, °shun, °avoid, *Colloq* °cut (dead): *After his court case, they gave Nicholas the cold shoulder at his club.* **3 put (one's** *or* **the) shoulder to the wheel**: make every °effort, make an °effort, °strive, °work hard, °pitch in, °apply oneself, roll up one's sleeves, set *or* get to °work, *Colloq* knuckle down, °buckle down: *If we put our shoulders to the wheel, we ought to be able to get our candidate elected.* **4 rub**

shoulders (with): °associate (with), °hobnob (with), °socialize (with), consort (with), °mix (with), °fraternize (with), keep °company (with): *Once in a while, she condescends to come down and rub shoulders with the common people.* **5 shoulder to shoulder**: °side by °side, °united, as one, cooperatively, jointly, arm in arm, °hand in °hand, in partnership: *If we fight shoulder to shoulder, we can defeat this menace and regain our freedom.* **6 straight from the shoulder**: °directly, straightforwardly, candidly, frankly, °honestly, °openly, unabashedly, unashamedly, unambiguously, unequivocally, plainly, bluntly, man to man, (with) no holds barred, °outright, *Colloq* without beating about the bush, without pulling (any) punches: *I want to tell you, straight from the shoulder, Willie, you're the best pal in the world.*
—*v.* **7** °push, shove, jostle, °hustle, °thrust aside, elbow, °force: *She shouldered everyone aside roughly to fight her way to the bargain counter.* **8** °support, °carry, °bear, °take upon oneself, °take on, °accept, °assume: *Are you ready to shoulder the responsibilities of caring for a family?*

shout *v.* **1** °yell, °scream, °bellow, °bawl, °howl, °roar, °cry (out), °call (out), °whoop, *Colloq* holler: *We lined up when the sergeant shouted out our names.*
—*n.* **2** °yell, °scream, °bellow, °howl, yelp, °roar, °cry, °call, °whoop, *Colloq* holler: *Nobody on shore could hear the boys' shouts when their boat capsized.*

show *v.* **1** °display, °present, expose, °demonstrate, °indicate, °exhibit, °manifest, (°lay) °bare, °disclose, °reveal, °betray, °make known, divulge, °register, °express, °make °clear or °plain or °manifest, elucidate, °clarify, °explain: *Show your identification as you enter. Your persistent refusal to associate with Dominic shows how you feel very clearly. They showed me how the new machine works.* **2** °escort, °accompany, °conduct, usher, °lead, °guide, °direct; °steer: *Please show Mr Sorenson to his table.* **3** °prove, °demonstrate, °confirm, corroborate, °verify, °substantiate, °bear out, °certify, °authenticate: *This signature shows that the will was signed personally by your father.* **4** °teach, °instruct, °tell, °inform, let (someone) in on, give (someone) an idea of: *Would you please show me how to use this washing-machine?* **5** °appear, become or be °visible, °peek through, can or may be seen: *The floor was showing through a hole in the carpet.* **6** °exhibit, °reveal, °indicate, °display, °register: *A thermometer shows the temperature, a barometer the atmospheric pressure.* **7** make an °appearance, °appear, show up, °arrive, °come: *Do you really think that the Jack Nicholson will show at the club tonight?* **8** °represent, °symbolize, depict, °portray, °picture, °illustrate: *This drawing shows what happens to children who bite their fingernails.* **9** °present, °play, °put on, °stage, °screen; be (being) presented or played or playing or °put on or staged or screened: *They are showing The Maltese Falcon at the local cinema. What is showing there tomorrow?* **10** °grant, °accord, °bestow: *They finally showed mercy and let the hostages go.* **11 show off**: make an °exhibit or a °spectacle of, °flaunt, advertise, °display, °parade; °pose, °swagger, °posture, °boast, °brag, *US and Canadian* grandstand: *They invited us to show off their new house. Quilty shows off too much for my taste.* **12 show up**: **a** expose, °give away, °reveal: *His collection of animal trophies shows him*

up for what he really is. **b** °stand out, be °conspicuous, be °noticeable, °contrast: *The white dress shows up nicely against your suntan.* **c** °embarrass, (put to) °shame, °mortify, upstage, °overshadow, outshine, °eclipse: *John only runs in the marathon to show me up.*
—*n.* **13** °display, °demonstration, °exhibition, °exposition, °fair, °presentation, *Colloq* expo: *There will be a computer show at the convention centre next week.* **14** °production, °presentation, °drama, °musical, °entertainment: *We flew to New York for a week to see a few Broadway shows.* **15** °ostentation, °display, °appearance, pretentiousness, °pretension, °affectation: *Those paintings are there just for show, not because they enjoy art.*

showdown *n.* confrontation, °climax, moment of truth, final °settlement, moment of decision, *US* face-off: *It's come to the point where we must have a showdown about who's boss.*

shower *n.* **1** sprinkle, sprinkling, drizzle: *Scattered showers are predicted for this afternoon.* **2** deluge, °torrent, °flood, °stream, barrage, overflow, °abundance, °profusion: *Showers of confetti rained on the parade from the offices.*
—*v.* **3** sprinkle, °rain, °pour, °spray, °bombard, °fall, °descend, °drop: *Debris and ash from the volcano showered down on the village.* **4** °lavish, inundate, °overwhelm, °heap, °load (down): *On return from her triumphant tour, Sylvia was showered with gifts and praise.*

showman *n.* °producer, impresario, °director: *P. T. Barnum was possibly the greatest showman in modern history.*

show-off *n.* °braggart, exhibitionist, swaggerer, egotist, boaster, *Colloq* blowhard, windbag: *Sit down and stop being such a show-off, Tetsworth.*

showy *adj.* °flashy, °garish, °flamboyant, °conspicuous, °ostentatious, °pretentious, bravura, °gaudy, *US* °show-off; °elaborate, °fancy, florid, °ornate, °fussy, °intricate, baroque, rococo, Byzantine, arabesque: *Their house is very showy, with gargoyles and lions and unicorns everywhere you look.*

shred *n.* **1** °scrap, °fragment, °bit, °tatter, °sliver, snippet, °rag, °remnant, °chip, °piece; atom, °trace, whit, °grain, °jot or tittle, scintilla, °hint, °suggestion, iota, °speck: *We found shreds from his shirt caught on the thorn-bushes. There isn't a shred of evidence to suggest that she killed him.*
—*v.* **2** °fragment, °tear (up), °tatter, °rip (up); °destroy, °demolish; °throw away, °dispose of, °scrap, *US* °trash: *At the news of the break-in, he dashed to his office and shredded the incriminating evidence.*

shrew *n.* harridan, virago, termagant, vixen, °scold, fishwife, °nag, °fury, spitfire, maenad, harpy, °witch, °hag, crone, hell-cat, beldam, °bitch, banshee, Xanthippe, Thyiad or Thyad, *Colloq* battleaxe, dragon: *His mother is an old shrew who does nothing but complain all the time.*

shrewd *adj.* °clever, °smart, °astute, cunning, canny, °acute, °sharp, keen-minded, °keen, °quick-witted, °crafty, artful, manipulative, °calculating, °calculated, °foxy, °sly, °wily, °perceptive, percipient, perspicacious, discerning, °wise, °sage, sagacious, long-headed, °intelligent, °ingenious, Daedalian, inventive, °resourceful: *He is a shrewd politician, very good at knowing exactly what people want to hear him say.*

shriek *n.* **1** °scream, °cry, screech, squeal, °squawk, squall: *The girls collapsed in shrieks of laughter.*
—*v.* **2** °scream, °cry, screech, squeal, °squawk, squall: *It is very boring to listen to one's neighbours shrieking at each other day and night.*

shrill *adj.* high-pitched, ear-splitting, °piercing, ear-piercing, °sharp, piping, screeching, screechy, °penetrating: *She let out a shrill cry when she saw what had happened.*

shrink *v.* **1** wither, °shrivel (up), °contract: *My woollen pullover shrank because you washed it in hot water.* **2** Often, **shrink from**: °withdraw (from), °draw back, °recoil (from), back away (from), °retreat (from), cower, °cringe, °flinch, °shy away (from), wince, balk (at): *Once committed to a responsibility, nothing could persuade Ella to shrink from it.*

shrivel *v.* Often, **shrivel up**: °shrink, °wrinkle, °pucker (up), curl (up), wizen, °contract; wither, °wilt, °dry up, desiccate, dehydrate: *The soil had dried up and all the plants had shrivelled.*

shroud *v.* **1** °screen, °veil, °mask, °disguise, °camouflage, °cover, °shield, blanket, °shade, °hide, °conceal, °protect, °cloak, °swathe, °wrap, °envelop: *The tanks were shrouded from view in the forest. His activities were shrouded in mystery.*
—*n.* **2** winding-sheet, cerement, cerecloth, grave-clothes: *They wrapped his body in a shroud and buried him in the churchyard.* **3** °veil, °cover, °shield, °cloak, blanket, °mask, °mantle, °pall, °screen, covering, cloud: *A shroud of secrecy descended over the Morocco affair.*

shrubbery *n.* shrubs, planting(s), hedge(s), hedging, hedgerow, °thicket, underbrush, brake, bracken, undergrowth, coppice *or* copse: *The fox lay low in the shrubbery till the dogs flushed him out.*

shudder *v.* **1** °quiver, °shake, °tremble, °shiver, °jerk, convulse, °quaver, °quake; °vibrate, °rattle: *I shudder to think what he might do next. Olive slammed on the brakes and the ancient car shuddered to a stop.*
—*n.* **2** °quiver, °shake, °tremble, twitch, °shiver, convulsion, °paroxysm, °spasm, °quaver, °quake; vibration, °rattle: *He gave a shudder at the prospect of having to clean out the stable.*

shuffle *v.* **1** °mix (up), intermix, disarrange, rearrange, interfile, intersperse, °jumble, °confuse; °shift (about), °mess up, °turn topsy-turvy, °scatter, disorganize: *I shall cut the cards after you have shuffled them. Osbert shuffled the papers on his desk.* **2** scuff *or* °drag (one's feet), °scrape along, shamble: *The boy shuffled into the headmaster's office, guilt written all over his face.* **3** °equivocate, hem and haw, bumble, shift, °cavil, °fence, be °evasive *or* °shifty, °dodge, °niggle, split hairs, °quibble, prevaricate, *Brit* hum and haw, *Colloq* °waffle: *The suspect shuffled when asked the names of his accomplices.*
—*n.* **4** shamble, °shambling, scuffling, scraping: *Whenever he was lying, he did a funny little shuffle with his feet.* **5** °sidestep, °evasion, °subterfuge, °trick, °dodge, °shift, prevarication, °quibble, shuffling: *Tell me what you've done with the money— and no shuffle!*

shun *v.* °avoid, keep *or* °shy away from, °steer °clear of, eschew, °shrink from, °fight °shy of, °run *or* °turn (away) from, °flee *or* °escape from; °forgo, °give up; disdain, °spurn, °rebuff,

°reject, cold-shoulder, give the cold °shoulder to: *After her experience, Penelope shunned the company of men for several years.*

shut *v.* **1** °close, °fasten, °secure, shut up; °lock, °bolt, °seal: *Come in and shut the door.* **2 shut down**: °close down, °discontinue, °cease, °suspend, °halt, °leave off, shut up; °switch *or* °turn *or* shut off, °stop: *We shut down operations at the Enfield factory last week. Make sure you shut down the machinery before leaving.* **3 shut in**: **a** confine, seclude, °keep in, °pen, °fence in, °secure: *We shut the dog in before we went out.* **b** See 6 a, below. **4 shut off**: **a** °switch *or* °turn off, shut down, *Colloq* °kill, douse, °cut (off): *They shut off the lights while I was shaving.* **b** °separate, °isolate, seclude, °segregate, sequester, °bar, shut out, °cut off, send to Coventry: *The more violent cases are shut off in another wing.* **c** °close (off), °shut (down): *To save on heating, we shut off part of the house in the winter.* **5 shut out**: **a** °exclude, °eliminate, °bar, debar, °lock out, °ban, °keep out *or* away, disallow, °prohibit: *Aliens without work permits are shut out from employment. We shut out all hooligans and rowdies.* **b** °keep out, °screen, °exclude, °block out, °cut out: *This window shade shuts out the direct sunlight.* **c** °screen, °mask, °hide, °conceal, °veil, °cover: *The house is shut out from view by the hedge.* **6 shut up**: **a** confine, shut in, coop (up), °cage (in), °bottle up, °box in; °imprison, °jail, incarcerate, intern, immure: *People suspected of being subversives were shut up during the war.* **b** °silence, keep °quiet, °stifle, °mute, °gag, shush, *Chiefly Brit* °quieten: *As soon as Colin wants to say something, Sidonie shuts him up.* **c** See 1, above. **d** See 2, above.
—*adj.* **7** closed (up), sealed (up), locked (up), bolted, fastened: *There is not much hope of penetrating their shut minds on this issue.*

shuttle *v.* commute, °alternate: *He shuttles daily between London and Paris.*

shy *adj.* **1** diffident, °coy, °bashful, °retiring, °withdrawn, withdrawing, °reserved, °timid, °meek, °modest, °sheepish, unconfident, °self-conscious, introverted, °nervous, apprehensive, timorous, *Rare* verecund: *Casey is quite shy and you have to draw him out gently.* **2** timorous, °cautious, °wary, chary, °leery, °guarded, °afraid, °fearful, frightened, °anxious, °worried, °suspicious, °distrustful, °cowardly, craven, uncourageous: *The local people are shy of anyone or anything unfamiliar.* **3** missing, lacking, °deficient in, °short of: *The shipment is shy a few dozen shoelaces we ordered.*
—*adv.* **4 fight shy of**: °avoid, be unwilling *or* °reluctant *or* °averse *or* °loath *or* loth *or* °disinclined *or* not disposed; be °wary *or* °cautious *or* watchful: *The children fight shy of talking to strangers.*

sick *adj.* **1** *Chiefly Brit* nauseated, °queasy, sick to one's stomach, °squeamish, qualmish; seasick, carsick, airsick, *Colloq* green around the gills: *Patrick felt a bit sick after the rough ferry crossing.* **2** °ill, unwell, °unhealthy, °sickly, °indisposed, °infirm, ailing, °diseased, afflicted, *Colloq* under the °weather, on the sick-list, °poorly, laid up, not (feeling) up to snuff: *If you feel sick, you'd best see a doctor. I've been sick for a week.* **3** °affected, troubled, °stricken, heartsick, °wretched, °miserable, burdened, weighed down: *I was sick with worry to learn of the problems*

you have been having with your business. **4** °mad,
°crazy, °insane, °deranged, °disturbed,
°neurotic, °unbalanced, psychoneurotic,
°psychotic, *Colloq* °mental, *US* off ((one's) rocker
or trolley): *Anyone who could have committed such
a crime must be sick.* **5** °peculiar, unconventional, °strange, °weird, °odd, °bizarre,
°grotesque, °macabre, °shocking, °ghoulish,
°morbid, °gruesome, stomach-turning, °sadistic,
masochistic, sado-masochistic, *Colloq* °kinky,
°bent, far-out, *US* °off: *In 30 years as a policeman,
I've seen some sick things, but this is the end.*
6 sickened, shocked, put out, °upset, appalled,
°disgusted, revolted, repulsed, offended,
repelled, °nauseated; annoyed, chagrined, irritated: *She was sick at what she saw in the army field
hospital. The way you do things sometimes makes
me sick.* **7** Sometimes, **sick of**: (sick and) °tired,
bored, °weary, *Colloq* fed up with: *Don't you get
sick of telling them the same thing so many times?*

sicken *v.* **1** fall °ill, take °sick, °contract, be
°stricken by, °come down with *or* °catch something *or* a °bug, °fail, °weaken: *After he seemed
to be recovering so well, he suddenly sickened and
died.* **2** make °ill *or* °sick, °afflict, °affect,
°disgust, °nauseate, turn one's stomach, °upset,
°appal, °shock, °repel, °revolt, °repulse, °offend,
make one's gorge rise; °put out: *The scene in the
abattoir sickened me.*

sickly *adj.* **1** See sick, 2, above. **2** ailing, °feeble,
°delicate, °wan, °weak, pallid, °pale, °drawn,
peaked, °peaky, peakish: *Jennie looks sickly and
must build up her resistance.* **3** °mushy, mawkish,
°maudlin, cloying, insipid, °weak, °watery: *The
sickly sentimentality of the episode about the boy and
his lost puppy was unbearable.*

side *n.* **1** Sometimes, **sides**: °flank(s), °edge(s),
°verge, °margin(s), °rim, °brim, °brink,
°border(s); bank; °boundary *or* boundaries,
°perimeter, °periphery, °limit(s): *This side of the
road is in West Sussex, the other in East Sussex. The
sides of the swimming-pool are tiled.* **2** °surface,
°face, °plane; facet: *The smallest possible number
of sides of a pyramid is four.* **3** °faction, °interest,
°party, °part, °sect, °camp, (point of) °view,
°viewpoint, °aspect, °opinion, °standpoint,
°stand, °cause, °angle, °position, °attitude,
°school, °philosophy: *Which side do you support
in the controversy?* **4** °team; string, °squad;
American football and *Association Football or
Soccer* and *Cricket* eleven, *Australian Rules football*
eighteen, *Baseball* nine, *Basketball* five, *Gaelic
football* and *Rugby Union* fifteen, *Rugby League*
thirteen: *Whichever side Craig is on seems likely to
win. The local side is now coming out onto the
field.* **5** °affectation, °pretension, haughtiness,
°arrogance, insolence, pretentiousness, °airs:
*Chauncy puts on a bit too much side for my
taste.* **6 side by side**: together, jointly, cheek
by jowl: *These paintings should not have been hung
side by side.* **7 take sides**: show °preference,
be °partial, show °favouritism: *A judge must
avoid taking sides.*
—*adj.* **8** °secondary, °incidental, °subordinate,
°tangential, °subsidiary, °indirect, ancillary,
°marginal, lesser, °minor, unimportant,
°inconsequential, inconsiderable,
°insignificant: *The main point is that he refuses to
cooperate, and his reasons are entirely a side
issue.* **9** °auxiliary, °secondary: *We live in a quiet
side-road just off the High Street.*

—*v.* **10 side with**: take sides with, show
°preference for, be °partial to, °show
°favouritism to *or* for, °support, °favour, °prefer,
°go in *or* along with, °join ((up) with), °ally
with, be *or* become allied with, *Colloq US* throw
in with, °team up with: *You can be sure that Kenneth
will always side with the favourite candidate.*

sidelong *adj.* °oblique, °indirect, °sideways, covert, °surreptitious: *He marched straight ahead, without so much as a sidelong glance in her direction.*

sidestep *v.* °avoid, °dodge, circumvent, skirt,
°evade, °shun, °steer °clear of, *Colloq* °duck:
*The minister neatly sidestepped all questions about
her retirement.*

sidetrack *v.* °divert, °deflect, °draw off *or* away,
°distract, °turn aside; shunt: *Where was I? I got
sidetracked by your comment about being overweight.*

sidewalk *n.* °walk, *Chiefly Brit* pavement, footpath, footway: *You may play on the sidewalk, but
don't you dare step into the street.*

sideways *adv.* obliquely, laterally, edgeways,
edge on, °sidelong, crabwise, indirectly, *US and
Canadian* edgewise: *The dresser will go through the
door if you turn it sideways.*

sidle *v.* °edge: *She sidled towards the door, opened
it, and was gone.*

siege *n.* **1** blockade, encirclement, belea-
guerment, besiegement: *The siege of Troy lasted
ten years.*
—*v.* **2** lay siege to, °besiege, blockade, beleaguer,
cordon off, °encircle, °box *or* °pen *or* °shut in,
°bottle up: *They sieged the city and the inhabitants
surrendered when they ran out of food and water.*

sift *v.* **1** °strain, sieve, °riddle, °filter, °screen,
bolt; winnow, °separate, weed out, °sort out,
°select, °choose, °pick: *It is not easy to sift out the
promising manuscripts.* **2** °examine, °analyse,
°study, °probe, °screen, scrutinize, °investigate:
The police are sifting the evidence of the witnesses.

sigh *v.* **1** °breathe, sough; suspire: *Troilus sighed
forth his soul to the tent where sleeping Cressid
lay.* **2 sigh for**: °bemoan, °lament *or* °mourn
or °grieve *or* °weep for, °bewail; °yearn *or* pine
for: *Now and then, all of us sigh for the good old
days.*
—*n.* **3** °murmur, °exhalation, °sound; suspiration: *I gave a sigh of relief as the train left the
station.*

sight *n.* **1** eyesight, °vision, °eyes: *His sight was
completely restored by the operation.* **2** field of
°view *or* of °vision, °range of °vision, ken,
°perception, °view, eyeshot, °gaze: *We turned a
corner, and at last the welcoming lights of the pub
came into sight.* **3** °spectacle, °scene, °show;
°rarity, °marvel, °wonder, °phenomenon;
°pageant: *I shall never forget the sight of Joe wearing
a strapless ballgown in the pantomime. We went to
Rome to see the sights.* **4** °mess, °disaster, eyesore,
°monstrosity, *Colloq* °fright, °atrocity: *The flat
looked a sight after the boys finally moved
out.* **5 catch sight of**: °spot, °notice, descry,
°spy, espy, °glance at, (catch a) °glimpse (of),
(get a) °look *or* °peep *or* °peek at, *Colloq* take a
gander at, get a look-see at, *Slang* get a load
of, *US* glom, pipe: *We caught sight of a
sinister-looking person slipping behind a pillar.*
6 out of sight: **a** °remote, °distant,
°far-away, unseeable, °imperceptible, °invisible:
*She soon walked out of sight down the road. The
mortar emplacement is out of sight, over the*

hill. **b** °unusual, °rare, °extraordinary, °outrageous, °imaginative, awe-inspiring, °incredible, °shocking, °unreal, °moving, jolting, *Colloq* °neat, °cool, *Brit* °brilliant, brill: *The gig last night was out of sight, man.* —*v.* **7** °look, °view, (take) °aim, °peer, °peek, °peep, draw a bead: *Sight along this stick and you'll see a cluster of stars called the Pleiades.* **8** °spot, °see, catch sight of, °mark, °observe, °behold, °view, °distinguish, discern, °identify, °note, °notice, °remark, glimpse, descry, espy, °spy: *A group of bird-watchers have sighted a golden eagle recently in the Grampians.*

sightseer *n.* °tourist, °traveller, globe-trotter, *Colloq* °rubberneck(er), *Brit* tripper, day-tripper: *As usual, the streets of Oxford were crowded with sightseers and tourists.*

sign *n.* **1** °token, °symbol, °indication, °mark, °signal, °indicator; °notice: *I interpreted the shouts of the crowd as a sign that I had won the race.* **2** °movement, °gesture, °motion, °signal, °cue, gesticulation: *She made a sign motioning me to come over.* **3** °trace, °indication, °evidence, °mark, °clue, °hint, °suggestion, °vestige: *She waited for an hour but there was no sign of him.* **4** °device, °mark, °symbol, °representation, °emblem, trade °mark, badge, °brand, °stamp, °seal, ideogram, ideograph, lexigram, phonogram, grapheme, hieroglyph, cartouche, rebus, logo(type), colophon, ensign, °standard, °banner, °flag; monogram, °initials, cipher *or* cypher: *Sir Roger fought under the sign of a rampant lion.* **5** signboard, °advertisement, placard, °poster, *US* broadside; shingle, °notice, °announcement: *You can't miss the huge supermarket sign at the corner.* **6** °omen, augury, °warning, forewarning, °foreboding, portent, °indication, writing on the wall, °prophecy, prognostication, foreshadowing: *We took the rumbling as a sign of an imminent earthquake.* —*v.* **7** autograph, put one's signature on *or* to, inscribe, countersign, °endorse, °witness, put *or* set one's hand to, °mark; sign on the dotted line; *Colloq US* put one's John Hancock on *or* to: *I have already signed the petition, have you? The painting is valueless unless signed by the artist.* **8 sign away**: °forgo, °relinquish, °give up, °abandon, °abandon *or* °quit claim to, °waive, °release, °surrender, °dispose of, °sacrifice, get °rid of: *With one stroke of the pen, he signed away most of his fortune.* **9 sign off**: °close down, °discontinue (broadcasting, writing a letter, *etc.*): *It is midnight, time for us to sign off till tomorrow.* **10 sign on** *or* **up**: **a** °enrol, °enlist, °register, volunteer, °join (up), °contract: *I signed on to be a bodyguard, not a nursemaid.* **b** °enrol, °enlist, °hire, °employ, put under °contract, °retain, °engage, °take on, *Colloq* °take on board, °bring aboard: *We signed up three new engineers this week.* **11 sign over**: °assign, consign, °transfer, °make over, °deliver, °give, °donate, °present, °dispose of, turn over: *Aunt June was persuaded to sign over the ownership of the business to her nephews.*

signal *n.* **1** See sign, 1, above. **2** °incitement, stimulus, °spur, °impetus, goad, °prick: *The waving of the flag will be the signal to advance.* —*adj.* **3** °remarkable, °conspicuous, °striking, °extraordinary, °unusual, °unique, °singular, °special, °noteworthy, °notable, °exceptional, °significant, °important, °outstanding,

°momentous, consequential, °weighty: *The British forces won a signal victory at Khartoum that day. Winning the competition is a signal accomplishment.* —*v.* **4** °motion, °indicate, °gesture, gesticulate, °communicate, °announce, °notify; whistle, wink, °blink, °nod, °beckon, °wave, °sign: *When your turn comes, a clerk will signal you to approach the counter. Peter raised his hand as a request to leave the room and the teacher signalled his assent.*

significance *n.* **1** °meaning, °sense, signification, denotation, °message, °idea, °point, °import, purport, °implication, portent, °content, °pith, °essence; °gist, °drift, °vein, °impression, connotation: *The significance of words like God and love is different for almost everyone who uses them.* **2** °importance, °weight, weightiness, consequence, °moment, °relevance, value: *The significance of the agreement lay not in its wording but in the fact that it was drawn up at all.*

significant *adj.* **1** °important, °weighty, °momentous, consequential, °critical, °substantial, substantive, °noteworthy, °notable, valuable, valued, °meritorious, °outstanding, °impressive, °historic, °relevant, °signal: *Appleton made significant contributions to knowledge about the ionosphere.* **2** °meaningful, °eloquent, pithy, °expressive, °pregnant, °suggestive, °informative: *It is significant that they prefer the term* Britain *to* England, Scotland, *and* Wales.

signify *v.* **1** °sign, °signal, °indicate, °communicate, °make known, convey, °symbolize, betoken, °represent, °express, °announce, °declare, °denote, °say, °mean, °specify; connote, °intimate, °suggest, °reveal, °disclose, °impart: *She signified her agreement by a nod. What does the phrase 'pursuit of happiness' signify to you?* **2** °matter, °count, be °significant *or* °important *or* consequential, be of °significance *or* of °importance *or* of consequence, carry °weight, °impress, °stand out, deserve *or* merit consideration: *It signifies little that they were found innocent of a crime we all believe they committed.*

silence *n.* **1** °quiet, quietness, stillness, soundlessness, noiselessness, °calm, calmness, °hush, quietude, tranquillity, °peace, peacefulness, °serenity: *The silence was so complete that I could hear my heart beating.* **2** speechlessness, muteness, dumbness, reticence, taciturnity, uncommunicativeness: *Do not construe his silence as agreement.* —*v.* **3** °quiet, °mute, °hush, °still, shush, °calm, °tranquillize, soothe, *Chiefly Brit* °quieten: *The audience was silenced by the start of the overture.* **4** °mitigate, °temper, mollify, take the sting out of, propitiate, pacify, °blunt, °suppress, °repress, °restrain, °subdue, draw the fangs *or* teeth of, °inhibit, °put down, °damp, °mute, °squelch, °quash, emasculate, muzzle, °muffle, °shut off, °gag, °stifle, °smother, °deaden (the effect of): *Only a full account of what lay behind these events will silence criticism in the media.*

silent *adj.* **1** °quiet, °still, soundless, °noiseless, °tranquil, hushed, shushed, °mute; °calm, °serene, placid, °peaceful, pacific, unagitated, unruffled, untroubled, undisturbed, *Literary* stilly: *After the children left the house fell silent. Not a mouse stirred in the silent city.* **2** uncommunicative, °mute, close-mouthed, °taciturn,

°reticent, °reserved, °mum, °tight-lipped, °secretive: *Millie told me a great deal about her children but was silent on the subject of her own activities.* **3** unspeaking, unspoken, °mute, unexpressed, °tacit, °understood, °implicit, implied, unstated, unsaid: *There is a silent agreement among the islanders not to reveal where the whisky is hidden.* **4** °inactive, non-participating, °passive, quiescent, *Brit* sleeping: *Although John runs the company, he has several silent partners.* **5** unpronounced, unuttered, not sounded, *Technical* aphonic: *The g in sign is silent, like the k in know and the l in could.*

silently *adv.* °quietly, soundlessly, noiselessly, with catlike tread, as °quietly as a mouse, stealthily; wordlessly, speechlessly, mutely: *They fold their tents like the Arabs, And silently steal away. He stood by silently, allowing his brother to do all the talking.*

silhouette *n.* °outline, °profile, contour, °form, °figure, °shape, °shadow, configuration, °periphery, °perimeter: *I could see the silhouette of a person on the window-blind.*

silky *adj.* silken, silklike, °delicate, °sleek, °soft, °smooth, satiny, °shiny, °glossy, °lustrous, *Technical* sericeous: *Her long, silky black hair hung below her shoulders.*

silly *adj.* **1** °senseless, °nonsensical, °absurd, °ridiculous, °ludicrous, laughable, risible, asinine, °inane, °preposterous, idiotic, °childish, °puerile, °foolish, foolhardy, °irresponsible, °unreasonable, illogical, irrational, °pointless, fatuous, °stupid, unwise, imbecilic, °crazy, °mad, °insane: *It would be silly to pay for it if you can get it for nothing.* **2** stunned, stupefied, dazed, °giddy, °dizzy, muzzy, benumbed: *Culley said something rude and the girl knocked him silly with a karate chop.* —*n.* **3** °fool, nincompoop, idiot, dunce, ninny, °halfwit, simpleton, numskull *or* numbskull, dim-wit, booby, °dolt, jackass, °twit, blockhead, bonehead, nitwit, ignoramus, °clod, *US* thimble-wit, *Colloq* °dope, °dummy, knuckle-head, goose, °drip, silly billy, *Brit* clot, *Slang US and Canadian* °jerk, nerd: *Warren is such a silly to spend so much money on a girl who cares nothing for him.*

silt *n.* **1** °deposit, °sediment, alluvium, °ooze, °sludge: *The irrigation pumps get clogged up with silt.* —*v.* **2** Usually, **silt up** *or* **over**: become clogged *or* choked *or* obstructed *or* dammed *or* °congested: *The channel silts up and has to be dredged yearly so that the boats can pass through.*

silver *n.* **1** silverware, °sterling, (silver) °plate; cutlery, *US* flatware; holloware: *Guests are coming so I'll have to polish the silver.* **2** °white, greyish, whitish-grey, greyish-white, °grey: *When your hair has turned to silver, I will love you just the same.* —*adj.* **3** silvery, °shiny, shining, °polished, burnished, °lustrous, °pearly, nacreous, °bright, gleaming, *Literary or heraldry* argent; °white: *The moon's silver crescent hung low in the sky. Her hair is more silver than grey.* **4** silvery, silver-toned, silver-tongued, °sweet, pretty, euphonious, °melodious, mellifluous, mellifluent, dulcet, °musical: *The silver tones of the muezzin echoed in the streets, calling the faithful to prayer.*

similar *adj.* **1** °like, almost °identical, comparable, °equivalent, nearly the °same; °alike: *That brooch is similar to the one I bought for my*

mother. *The two may be similar, but they are not the same.* **2 be similar to**: °resemble, be °like, °correspond to, °compare favourably with: *This letter is very similar to the one I received yesterday.*

simmer *v.* **1** °seethe, °stew, cook, °boil, °bubble: *A huge cauldron of soup simmered on the fire.* **2** °chafe, °seethe, °stew, steam, °smoulder, °fume, °rage, °burn, *Colloq US* do a slow burn: *Father is still simmering because you scratched his car.* **3 simmer down**: °calm *or* °cool down, °cool off, °calm oneself, become °quiet, °control oneself, get °control of *or* over oneself, *Chiefly Brit* °quiet(en) down, *Slang* °cool it: *Yesterday he was in a towering rage, but he has simmered down a bit today.*

simple *adj.* **1** uncomplicated, °plain, uninvolved, °unsophisticated, understandable, °intelligible, (easily) °understood, comprehensible, °clear, lucid, straightforward, °easy, °elementary, °basic: *At the age of four, Jan was able to do simple mathematical calculations.* **2** °plain, °unadorned, undecorated, unembellished, °basic, °fundamental, °elementary, °elemental, °mere, unostentatious, unassuming, unpretentious, °modest, °classic, uncluttered, °stark, °clean, °severe, austere, °Spartan, °homely; °unvarnished, °naked, °honest: *Thea was stunning in a simple black dress with a colourful scarf and gold jewellery. The simple truth is that he came home from work to find the house broken into and his wife gone.* **3** °sincere, °frank, °candid, °open, °unaffected, uncomplicated, unpretentious, straightforward, °above-board, simple-hearted, uncontrived, °direct, °upright, °square, °forthright, four-square, °righteous, °honest, °naïve, guileless, °artless, undesigning, °childlike, °ingenuous, °unsophisticated, °innocent, °green: *The colonel was a simple man who was respected because he always said just what he meant. A simple heart may be its own best guide.* **4** °unsophisticated, °naïve, °slow, slow-witted, °stupid, °thick, thickheaded, simple-minded, °feeble-minded, oafish, bovine, °dense, °obtuse, °dull, dull-witted, witless, °halfwitted, brainless, °backward, imbecilic *or* *chiefly Brit* imbecile, cretinous, *Colloq* °dumb, moronic: *That chap Dawson is far too simple to understand what you are asking him.* **5** °lowly, °humble, °inferior, °mean, °base, subservient, °common, °subordinate: *The lord of the manor regarded his tenants as simple folk, a breed apart from himself and his family.*

simplicity *n.* **1** uncomplicatedness; understandability, comprehensibility, lucidity, straightforwardness, °clarity, intelligibility, decipherability: *Consider the simplicity of some life forms in contrast to the complexity of others. The simplicity of the Bible can be deceptive.* **2** plainness, cleanness, °clarity, °severity, starkness, austereness, asceticism, °restraint, bareness, °purity: *She prefers the simplicity of classical or very modern design to baroque and rococo clutter.* **3** °sincerity, openness, artlessness, °candour, guilelessness, frankness, unsophisticatedness, ingenuousness, straightforwardness, forthrightness, unaffectedness, unpretentiousness, modesty, °naïvety; plainness, directness, inelegance, rusticity, pastoralism: *Many have been charmed by the simplicity of the local folk art.* **4** °stupidity, slow-wittedness, thickheadedness, simple-mindedness, feeble-mindedness, oafishness, cloddishness, obtuseness, dullness, dull-wittedness, witlessness, halfwittedness, imbecility, brainlessness: *The simplicity of some of those yokels is incredible.*

simplify v. °clarify, °clear up, make °easy, °paraphrase, °explain, explicate, disentangle, untangle, unravel, streamline: *Simplify your request and we shall be able to do what you ask.*

simply adv. **1** °merely, °barely, purely, °only, solely, °just, °entirely, fully, °totally, °wholly, °altogether, °absolutely, °really: *Is it true that they met regularly simply to discuss politics?* **2** °totally, °completely, °altogether, °entirely, °just, plainly, °obviously, °really, unreservedly, unqualifiedly: *If you believe that, you're simply too stupid for words!* **3** naïvely, artlessly, guilelessly, °openly, innocently, ingenuously, unaffectedly, unpretentiously, plainly, °naturally: *He asked her very simply what she did as a 'working girl'.* **4** plainly, modestly, starkly, °severely, sparely, sparsely, austerely, ascetically: *His home is simply furnished, without paintings or any other decoration.* **5** distinctly, unambiguously, plainly, °obviously, unmistakably: *The instructions must be written simply so that they are understandable to anyone.*

simultaneous adj. coincident, coinciding, concurrent, contemporaneous, synchronous; °contemporary: *The simultaneous appearance of two books on such an obscure subject was very unusual.*

sin n. **1** trespass, °transgression, °offence, °wrong, impiety, °misdeed, profanation, desecration, iniquity, °evil, °devilry, °sacrilege, °crime, infraction, °misdeed, dereliction, °infringement, °violation, misdemeanour, °fault, °foible, °peccadillo: *How many sins have been committed in the name of righteousness! It's a sin to tell a lie. The seven deadly sins are anger, covetousness, envy, gluttony, lust, pride, and sloth.* **2** wickedness, sinfulness, °vice, corruption, ungodliness, badness, °evil, wrongfulness, iniquity, iniquitousness, immorality, depravity, impiety, irreverence, impiousness, °sacrilege: *His brother Edmund was conceived in sin, and sin ruled his entire life.* —v. **3** °transgress, °offend, °fall (from grace), °lapse, go °wrong, °stray, go astray, °err, *Biblical or archaic* trespass: *Strictly speaking, we can sin only against God.*

sincere adj. °honest, °truthful, °true, veracious, °genuine, °heartfelt, true-hearted, undissembling, unfeigned, °open, (°open and) °above-board, straightforward, °direct, °frank, °candid, guileless, °artless, *Colloq* upfront, on the °level, on the up and up: *I took her criticism as a sincere desire to see improvement in my work. You have always been sincere in your emotional involvements.*

sincerely adv. °truly, °honestly, °really, wholeheartedly, candidly, frankly, unequivocally, °seriously, earnestly, genuinely, °deeply, fervently: *When they say they love each other, they mean it sincerely.*

sincerity n. °honesty, truthfulness, straightforwardness, openness, forthrightness, frankness, °candour, candidness, seriousness, genuineness, uprightness: *Everyone appreciates sincerity in dealings with others.*

sinew n. **1** ligament, tendon; muscle, thew: *After the climb, I ached in every sinew.* **2** Usually,

sinews: °strength, °force, °power, °energy, °brawn, °vigour, °might, °stamina, °vitality: *The sinews of his argument were considerably weakened by her disarming candour.*

sinewy adj. °strong, °powerful, °muscular, °mighty, °stout, °wiry, °robust, °tough; strapping, °brawny, °burly: *She looked so tiny and fragile cradled in his huge sinewy arms.*

sinful adj. °corrupt, °evil, °wicked, °bad, °wrong, wrongful, iniquitous, °vile, °base, °profane, °immoral, °profligate, depraved, °criminal, °sacrilegious, °ungodly, unholy, demonic, irreligious, °impious, °irreverent: *Anything that you like as much as you like chocolate must be sinful. They would never condone such sinful behaviour in our church.*

sing v. **1** °chant, intone, carol, vocalize, trill, croon, °pipe, °chirp, warble; chorus; yodel: *It was a wonderful spring day and Barbara felt like singing. Can you sing On the Road to Mandalay?* **2** whistle, °pipe, °peep: *I have just bought a singing kettle.* **3** °tell, °tattle, °name names, *Slang* rat, snitch, squeal, blow the whistle, peach, °spill the beans: *They found out that Johnny had been singing to the cops about the bank job.*

singe v. char, °blacken, sear, °scorch, °burn: *Unfortunately, I singed the tail of my shirt while ironing it.*

singer n. °vocalist, soloist, songster, crooner, *chanteuse*, nightingale, °minstrel, troubadour, balladeer, caroller, chorister, choirboy, choir girl, choir member, chorus-boy, chorus girl, chorus-member, *Colloq* songbird, canary, thrush: *She used to be a professional singer.*

single adj. **1** °unmarried, unwed, °unattached, °free; °celibate: *She remained single till she was twenty-two.* **2** °singular, °individual, °distinct, °solitary; °one, °only, °sole, lone, °unique, °isolated: *There wasn't a single person there who could think for himself. A single shot rang out.* **3** °separate, °distinct, °individual, °solitary: *Every single hair is rooted in its follicle.* —v. **4** **single out**: °select, °choose, °pick, °separate, take *or* °put *or* °set aside *or* °apart, °distinguish, cull, °segregate, °fix *or* °fasten on: *Why was she singled out for special treatment?*

single-handed adj. **1** °solo, lone, °solitary, °independent, unaided, unassisted: *Chichester was the first winner of the single-handed transatlantic sailing race.* —adv. **2** single-handedly, by oneself, °alone, °solo, on one's own, independently: *He sailed round the world single-handed.*

single-minded adj. dedicated, °devoted, °resolute, °steadfast, persevering, °firm, °determined, dogged, unswerving, unwavering, °tireless, °purposeful: *Single-minded perseverance saw him through the completion of the work in eight years.*

singly adv. one at a time, °separately, °individually, one by one, successively, one after the other, seriatim: *Taken singly, the facts are not hard to assimilate.*

singular adj. **1** °unusual, °different, atypical, °eccentric, °extraordinary, °remarkable, °special, uncommon, °strange, °odd, °peculiar, °bizarre, °outlandish, °curious, °queer, outré, °offbeat, *Slang* far-out: *Ideas that yesterday were considered singular have today become quite commonplace.* **2** °outstanding, °prominent,

°eminent, °pre-eminent, °noteworthy, °significant, °important, °conspicuous, °particular, °notable, °signal, °exceptional, °superior: *Stempel made a singular contribution to the development of microscopy.* **3** lone, °isolated, °single, °separate, uncommon, °rare, °unique, °distinct, one of a kind: *Some medieval philosophers denied the existence of general realities, and claimed that all things that exist were particular and singular.*

singularity *n.* **1** individuality, distinctiveness, uniqueness, idiosyncrasy: *Personality demonstrates its singularity even in handwriting.* **2** °eccentricity, °peculiarity, strangeness, oddness, queerness, outlandishness, uncommonness: *The singularity of the marriage ceremony among these tribes was often remarked on by anthropologists.* **3** *Technical* black hole: *The ultimate collapse of the star results, theoretically, in a singularity.*

sinister *adj.* **1** °fateful, °inauspicious, unfavourable, °foreboding, °threatening, °menacing, minacious, minatory *or* minatorial, °portentous, °ominous, unpropitious, °disastrous, °dark, °gloomy: *There was a sinister meaning in the look he gave her.* **2** °evil, °bad, °corrupt, °base, malevolent, °malignant, malign, °harmful, pernicious, treacherous, nefarious, °wicked, °diabolic(al), baleful, °villainous, insidious, °sneaky, °furtive, underhand(ed): *The poor girl fell under the sinister influence of a real-life Svengali.*

sink *v.* **1** °founder, °submerge, °go down, °go under, °plunge, °descend, be engulfed: *The ship was struck below the water-line and sank in minutes.* **2** °subside, °cave in, °collapse, °settle, °drop, °fall in, °go down, °slip away: *The earth suddenly sank beneath our feet.* **3** °descend, °go down, °drop, °fall, move down *or* °downward(s), °go down to *or* on: *The parachute slowly sank to the ground. When he saw the statue move, he sank to his knees, terrified.* **4** °decline, °weaken, °worsen, degenerate, °subside, deteriorate, °flag, °fail, °diminish, °die, °expire; languish; *Colloq* go downhill: *Grandfather, sinking fast, summoned the family to his bedside.* **5** °disappear, vanish, °fade away, °evaporate; °set, °go down, °descend, °drop: *After a meteoric rise, many rock stars sink into oblivion. As the sun sank slowly in the west, we returned to our hotel to reminisce about our day at the pyramids.* **6** °settle, °precipitate, °descend, °drop: *After a few minutes, the sand sinks to the bottom.* **7** °bore, put down, °drill, °dig, °excavate, °drive: *A special shaft will be sunk just for ventilating the mine.* **8** °submerge, °immerse, °plunge: *He sank his hand deep into the mud and came up with a small box.* **9** °stoop, °bend, °get, °go, °lower *or* °humble oneself: *I never dreamt that he would sink so low as to beg in the streets.* **10** °invest, °venture, °risk, °put: *He sank his life's savings into his son's business, only to see it go bankrupt.* **11 sink in**: be °understood, °penetrate, °register, make an °impression on, °get through to: *How many times do I have to tell you in order for it to sink in?*
—*n.* **12** basin, wash-basin, wash-bowl, lavabo; *Church* font, stoup, piscina: *The kitchen has a large double sink.* **13** cesspool, cesspit, °pit, hell-hole, den of iniquity, sink-hole, *Colloq* °dive: *We found him playing piano in some sink frequented by the worst element of society.*

sinking *adj.* **1** °queasy, °nervous, uneasy, °tense, apprehensive, unquiet, °fretful, °shaky, jittery,

°jumpy, °anxious: *Just thinking about the way they treat hostages gave me a sinking feeling in the pit of my stomach.* **2** depressed, °dejected, °miserable, dolorous, °doleful, °mournful, °forlorn, woeful, °desolate, despairing, °stricken, heavy-laden: *I had a sudden sinking feeling when she announced that she had something important to tell me.*

sinner *n.* °transgressor, wrongdoer, °miscreant, °offender, evil-doer, malefactor, °reprobate, *Biblical or archaic* trespasser: *Few people nowadays believe that sinners are punished in hell for all eternity.*

sip *v.* **1** °taste, °sample, sup: *She was sitting on a bar stool, sipping a cocktail.*
—*n.* **2** °taste, °sample, soupçon, °drop, °bit, °swallow, °mouthful, spoonful, thimbleful, °nip, dram, *Colloq* swig: *She took a sip, savoured it, then turned to me with a smile.*

siren *n.* **1** whistle, warble, wailer, horn, foghorn; °signal, °alarm, °warning, °alert, tocsin: *The air raid siren sounded and everyone ran for shelter.* **2** °temptress, °seductress, enchantress, °charmer, sorceress, *femme fatale*, Circe, Lorelei, *Colloq* vamp, *US* mantrap: *Have you seen the latest siren to whom John has fallen prey?*

sissy *n.* °milksop, mama's boy, mummy's boy, namby-pamby, °weakling, °baby, cry-baby, mollycoddle, *US* milquetoast, *Colloq* softie *or* softy, *Brit* °wet: *The boy you remember from school as a sissy is now a football star.*

sit *v.* **1** be seated, °settle, sit down, take a °seat, rest, *Colloq* take the weight *or* a load off one's feet: *Come in and sit with me for a while. If you sit on that chair it will break.* **2** hold a °session, be in °session, °assemble, °meet, convene; °gather, °get together: *The Supreme Court of the United States will be sitting next week.* **3** Often, **sit on**: have *or* hold *or* occupy a °seat (on), °participate (in), be a °member (of): *Kathy sits on the board of directors.* **4** °remain, °stay, °lie, rest; °relax, mark time, °abide, °dwell: *Let the dough sit a while to rise. Anita sat in Vienna awaiting her instructions.* **5** °seat, °contain, °hold, °accommodate, have seats *or* °seating for, have °room *or* °space *or* °capacity for seating: *The auditorium sits only 600.* **6 sit in**: **a** Often, **sit in on**: °play, °join (in), °participate (in), take °part (in); °observe, °watch: *Mind if I sit in on your poker game? We invited Mary Lou to sit in during our discussion.* **b** °substitute, °fill in, °stand in, °double, *Colloq* °cover, sub, *US* pinch-hit: *Mary Lou often sat in for our pianist if he had another gig.* **7 sit out**: °wait out, outwait, outstay, °outlast, outlive, °last through, °live through: *Will sat out endless dances. He sat out the whole evening merely waiting to walk home with Lily.* **8 sit tight**: °wait, °hang back, °hold back, be °patient, bide (one's) time, play a waiting game, take no action, °delay, temporize, *Colloq* hold (one's) horses: *Just sit tight till you hear from them—don't jump the gun.* **9 sit up**: °awaken, pay °attention, °notice, become °alert *or* °interested *or* °concerned: *Jennie's performance in the hurdles made many track coaches sit up.* **10 sit (with)**: Often, **sit well** *or* **right (with)**: °agree with, be °agreeable to; °seem, °appear, °look: *The way Ashton handled the matter did not sit well with the directors.*

site *n.* **1** °location, °place, °plot, plat, °spot, °locale, °area, °milieu, °neighbourhood, locality,

purlieus, °placement, °position; °situation, °orientation: *A site near that of ancient Pergamum has been acquired for the building. The site alongside the river has much to recommend it.*
—v. **2** °locate, °position, °place, °put, °situate, °install *or* instal: *The building has been sited to take maximum advantage of the sun.*

situate *v.* °place in a °position *or* °situation *or* °location, °place, °position, °locate, °set, °spot, °put, °install *or* instal: *Harwood is very well situated to learn what the high command is planning. The greenhouse should be situated on the south side of the house.*

situation *n.* **1** °place, °position, °location, °spot, °site, °locale, °setting: *The situation of the monastery, high on the mountain, makes it almost inaccessible.* **2** °state (of affairs), °condition, °circumstances, °case, °status (quo), lay of the land, °picture; °plight, °predicament; *Colloq* ball game; kettle of fish: *The present situation calls for careful planning. The chancellor's policies have done little to improve the economic situation.* **3** °position, °place, °job, °employment, °post, *Colloq* berth: *Jenkins likes his new situation as Lord Fortescue's valet.*

size *n.* **1** °magnitude, largeness, bigness, °bulk, °extent, °scope, °range, dimensions, °proportions, °measurement(s), °expanse, °area, square footage, °volume, °mass, °weight; hugeness, immensity, greatness, vastness, °enormousness: *How do astronomers determine the distance and size of stellar objects? A shape of extraordinary size suddenly loomed up in the darkness.*
—v. **2** dimension, °measure: *The furnishings are sized in proportion to these miniature room displays.* **3 size up**: assess, °judge, °evaluate, °measure, take the °measure of, appraise, assay, make an °estimate of, °estimate, value, °gauge, °rate: *She looked him up and down, sizing him up as a prospective husband.*

sketchily *adv.* cursorily, superficially, incompletely, patchily, °roughly, perfunctorily, skimpily, °vaguely, imperfectly, crudely, °hastily, hurriedly: *His account of the event was sketchily written.*

sketchy *adj.* °cursory, °superficial, °incomplete, patchy, °rough, °perfunctory, skimpy, °imperfect, °crude, °hasty, °hurried, °vague, ill-defined, °fuzzy, °indistinct, °inexact, °imprecise, °unrefined, unpolished, rough-hewn, unfinished: *We received only sketchy reports of what was going on in the capital. This will do as a sketchy outline, but eventually the details will need to be filled in.*

skilful *adj.* skilled, °accomplished, °adept, adroit, °dexterous, °expert, °proficient, masterly, °masterful, °gifted, apt, °able, °clever, °talented, °capable, °professional, trained, °qualified, °experienced, °practised: *Julio is a skilful enough driver to race tomorrow. I have to admire the skilful way he handles people.*

skill *n.* **1** °talent, °ability, °aptitude, expertness, °expertise, °facility, skilfulness, °art, artistry, cleverness, adeptness, adroitness, mastery, °dexterity, handiness, °ingenuity, °experience, °proficiency, °finesse, °knack, quickness, deftness, °technique: *It requires great skill to operate this machine.* **2** °accomplishment, °forte,

°strength, °gift, °capability, know-how, °faculty: *Her skill is in teaching others how to be skilful sales people.*

skim *v.* **1** Often, **skim off**: °separate, cream, °scoop *or* ladle off, °take off, °remove: *After the water has come to a boil, skim off the scum that has collected on top.* **2** Often, **skim through** *or* **over**: °scan, °flip *or* °thumb *or* leaf through, °skip through, °glance at *or* through, °dip into: *I only had time to skim through your report, but at a glance it looks good.* **3** °soar, °glide, skate, °slide, °sail, °fly: *Along came Calabro on his sailboard, skimming along the tops of the waves.*

skin *n.* **1** epidermis, derma, integument, °hide, °pelt, °fleece, fell: *Her skin reddens in the sun. How many skins are needed to make a coat?* **2** °coat, °film, coating, crust, incrustation, husk, °peel, °rind, °outside, °shell, pellicle, °veneer, outer layer, lamina, overlay: *The frame is first covered with a tough plastic skin to make it waterproof.*
—v. **3** flay, °strip, decorticate, excoriate: *I shall skin that boy alive if I catch him!* **4** °peel, °hull, husk, °shell: *This machine skins the fruit automatically.* **5** abrade, °scrape, graze, bark: *She skinned her knee on the edge of the coffee table.*

skin-deep *adj.* °superficial, °shallow, °surface, °slight, °external, unimportant, trivial, unprofound, °insubstantial: *The impression he makes on people is only skin-deep.*

skinny *adj.* °thin, underweight, °gaunt, bony, scraggy, lank, °lanky, gangly, gangling, °raw-boned, °meagre, °spare, °emaciated, half-starved, undernourished, pinched, hollow-cheeked, wasted, shrunken: *Two skinny children were clinging to their mother's skirts.*

skip *v.* **1** °leap, °cavort, °caper, gambol, °frisk, °prance, °jump, °hop, romp, °bound, °dance: *Eleanor came skipping down the walk to the house.* **2** °omit, °leave out, °pass by, °overlook, °pass over, °avoid, °ignore, °disregard, °steer clear of, °cut: *In my haste, I skipped over your name. Please skip the reading of the roll today.*
—n. **3** °leap, °cavort, °caper, gambol, °frisk, °prance, °jump, °bound, °dance, °hop, romp: *He had a curious way of walking, giving a little skip before each step.* **4** lacuna, °gap, °omission, avoidance, °disregard, °miss, *Colloq* go-by: *There was a skip of 32 pages after page 64. If you take my advice, you will give that restaurant a skip.*

skipper *n.* captain, °master, commander; °boss, °leader, chief: *The skipper gave orders to put him in irons.*

skirmish *n.* **1** °fight, °encounter, °fray, °brush, °clash, °engagement, confrontation, °showdown, °combat, °battle, °conflict, °struggle, set-to, °contest, °scrimmage, °fracas, tussle, mêlée *or* melee, *Law* affray, *Colloq* °scrap, dust-up, *Brit* scrum: *There was a brief skirmish when the troops met a band of partisans.*
—v. **2** °fight, °clash, °struggle, °battle, tussle: *At the edge of the convoy a destroyer skirmished with a submarine.*

sky *n.* **1** °heaven(s), skies, arch *or* vault of °heaven, °firmament, (wild) blue (yonder), ether, *Archaic or literary* welkin, empyrean, azure: *The dour, overcast sky gave the bleak moor a chilling sense of foreboding.* **2 to the skies**: °overly, excessively, extravagantly, fulsomely, profusely, inordinately, °highly: *If I praise him to the skies people will get the idea that I benefit from his success.*

slab *n.* °slice, °wedge, °piece, hunk, chunk, tranche, *Colloq Brit* wodge: *The keeper threw a large slab of meat into the lion's cage.*

slack *adj.* **1** °remiss, °careless, °indolent, negligent, °lax, °lazy, °idle, neglectful, °delinquent, °inattentive, otiose, dilatory, cunctatory, °laggard, °easygoing, °slothful, sluggish, °lethargic, °shiftless, do-nothing, fainéant, *Colloq* asleep at the switch or the wheel, asleep on the job: *Production has fallen off because the workers are getting slack.* **2** °loose, °flabby, flaccid, °soft, °limp, baggy, drooping, droopy, bagging, sagging, floppy: *The flag hung down, slack in the still air.*
—*v.* **3** Often, **slack** or **slacken off** or **up**: **a** let go, let run, let °loose, °release, slacken, °loose, °loosen, °relax, °ease (out or off), °let up (on): *Slack off the stern line a bit.* **b** °slow (down or up), °delay, reduce speed, °tire, °decline, °decrease, °diminish, °moderate, abate, °weaken: *Barnes could not keep up his terrific pace and is beginning to slack off. Business has slackened off since Christmas.* **4** °neglect, °shirk, *Colloq Brit* skive (off), *US* goof around or off, *Chiefly military* gold-brick, *Taboo slang US* fuck the dog: *Don't let the foreman find you slacking.*
—*n.* **5** °lull, °pause, °inactivity, cut-back, lessening, reduction, abatement, drop-off, downturn, diminution, °decline, fall-off, °decrease, dwindling: *How do you compensate for the slack in sales of ski equipment during the summer?* **6** °room, looseness, slackness, play, °give: *There's too much slack in that mooring line.*

slacker *n.* shirker, °loafer, °idler, *Slang Brit* skiver, *Military* scrimshanker, *US* gold brick, goof-off: *We have tight deadlines to meet, so there is no room for slackers on the team.*

slake *v.* °satisfy, °quench, °gratify, allay, assuage, °ease, °relieve: *Nothing would slake my thirst better right now than a pint of ice-cold lager.*

slam *v.* **1** °shut, fling closed, bang: *Gillian said that she hated encyclopedias, and slammed the door in the salesman's face.* **2** °crash, smash, smack, °dash, °ram, bang, °slap: *Not looking where he was going, Newland slammed his car into a street lamp.* **3** °criticize, °attack, °vilify, pillory, °run down, °disparage, denigrate, °denounce, °put down, flay, °pounce on or upon, *Colloq* °shoot down, °pan, *Chiefly Brit* slate: *The critics slammed his play because of the way it portrayed women.*

slander *n.* **1** defamation (of character), calumny, obloquy, misrepresentation, °slur, vilification; °libel: *He spread lies about me and I am suing him for slander.*
—*v.* **2** defame, calumniate, °disparage, °slur, traduce, malign, °smear, °vilify, decry; °libel: *He must be stopped from slandering people and ruining their reputations.*

slanderous *adj.* defamatory, calumnious, calumniatory, disparaging, smear, deprecatory, depreciative, discrediting, decrying; libellous: *I understand that she made some slanderous remarks about your relationship with your ex-wife.*

slant *n.* **1** °angle, °viewpoint, (point of) °view, °standpoint, °approach, °twist, °idea, °aspect, °attitude: *The article reflects a new slant on why governments are sometimes out of touch with the electorate.* **2** °bias, °prejudice, °partiality, one-sidedness, °turn, °bent: *Carla's reporting has a feminist slant which occasionally distorts the facts.* **3** °slope, °incline, °tilt, °ramp, gradient, °pitch, °lean, °leaning, deflection, °angle, °rake, °cant, camber: *A window sill normally has an outward slant. The road has a slant downwards to the right on right-hand curves.*
—*v.* **4** °tilt, °angle, °incline, °pitch, °cant, °slope, °bend, °lean, °list, °tip, bevel, °shelve: *The land slants downwards near the lake. Notice how his writing slants upwards at the ends of the lines. Cut the edges to slant outwards.* **5** °bend, °distort, °deviate, °twist, °warp, °colour, °weight, °bias: *The editor slanted the story to put the minister in a favourable light.*

slap *v.* **1** smack, cuff, whack, °rap; °spank; *Colloq* clout, wallop: *He said something extremely rude so she slapped him.* **2** °flap, slat, °whip, °beat, bat: *Can't you stop that blind from slapping in the wind?* **3** °fling, °toss, °splash, °hurl, °throw, °sling: *If you slap some paint on it, no one will know the difference.*
—*n.* **4** smack, °blow, cuff, whack, °rap, *Colloq* clout, wallop: *He got a hard slap on the cheek for using foul language.* **5** Often, **slap in the face**: °reprimand, °reproof, °rebuff, °criticism, censure, °rebuke, shot, °thrust, °attack, °put-down, °insult, °offence, smack in the eye: *The speaker's reference to Anne's paper as 'trivial' was a severe slap in the face.*
—*adv.* **6 slap on**: °exactly, °directly, °precisely, °straight, °point-blank, °right, squarely, °plumb, smack, bang: *As usual, Barry's comments were slap on the mark.*

slash *v.* **1** °cut, °gash, °hack, °score, °slit, °knife, °lacerate; °wound; °scar: *The guide slashed away at the undergrowth with his machete.* **2** °lash, °whip, °scourge, °flog, °beat, horsewhip, flail, flagellate, flay, °lambaste, thrash: *In those days, a convicted felon was beaten and slashed in front of a crowd in the market-place.* **3** °cut, °reduce, °decrease, °drop, °mark down, °trim, °lower: *Prices were slashed to clear out last season's styles.*
—*n.* **4** °cut, °gash, °incision, °slit, °slice, °gouge, °rent, °rip, °score, laceration: *There is a slash in each sleeve that reveals the colourful fabric underneath.* **5** °cut, reduction, °decrease, mark-down: *The department stores continued their price slashes to the end of January.*

slattern *n.* slut, °tramp, sloven, trollop, hussy, °wanton, whore, °prostitute, harlot, streetwalker, lady of the evening, woman of ill repute, °loose or fallen woman, trottoise, *Colloq* call-girl, pro, *Slang* °tart, hooker, hustler, *US* roundheels, bimbo: *His reputation will not be enhanced if he associates with slatterns.*

slaughter *n.* **1** butchery, butchering, *Rare* abattage: *Most of the cattle were sent for slaughter.* **2** °massacre, °killing, °bloodshed, blood bath, °murder, homicide, manslaughter, °carnage, extermination, °execution, liquidation, slaying, blood-letting, butchery, pogrom, genocide, mass °murder or °execution or extermination, °sacrifice, hecatomb: *1940 to 1945 saw the slaughter of millions in Europe and the Far East.*
—*v.* **3** °butcher, °kill, °murder, slay, °execute, °exterminate, °massacre, put to the sword, put to death, liquidate, °destroy: *How many more must be slaughtered before war is made obsolete?* **4** °defeat, °beat, °win (out) over, vanquish, °overcome, °overwhelm, smash, °crush, thrash, °destroy, °rout, °upset, trounce, *Colloq* clobber: *Our school soccer team slaughtered the visitors 10–0.*

557

slave | slide

slave *n.* **1** lackey *or* lacquey, scullion, serf, slave-girl, slaveling, odalisque, bondservant, bondslave, bondsman *or* bondman, bondswoman *or* bondwoman, bondmaid, vassal, *Derogatory chiefly Brit* skivvy, *Archaic* esne, helot, hierodule, *Colloq Brit* slavey: *In ancient times, captured peoples and those of lower social status were kept as slaves.* **2** drudge, workhorse, °hack, °grind, toiler, °labourer, *Chiefly Brit* °fag, dogsbody, *Colloq US* gofer: *Susan was a slave to her job for years, only to be sacked without a pension by the new owners.*
—*v.* **3** °labour, toil, moil, °grind, grub, drudge, °sweat, burn the midnight oil, lucubrate, °work one's fingers to the bone, °work like a Trojan *or* a horse, *Brit* skivvy: *He was slaving over an essay that was due the following morning.*

slaver[1] *v.* **1** drool, salivate, slobber, °drivel, dribble, °spit, *Dialect* slabber: *The wolf opened its slavering jaws.*
—*n.* **2** drool, saliva, °drivel, dribble, °spit, spittle, *Dialect* slabber: *The slaver formed on his lips as he raged on.* **3** °nonsense, °drivel, °rubbish, twaddle, piffle: *The slaver spewed forth by the critics set her teeth on edge.*

slaver[2] *n.* **1** slave ship, slave-trader: *Conditions were so bad aboard the slavers that many of the poor souls died before reaching their destination.* **2** blackbirder, slave-trader; White slaver, °pimp, panderer: *He was ashamed that his grandfather had been a South Sea slaver.*

slavery *n.* **1** enslavement, °bondage, thraldom, thrall, enthralment, °servitude, serfdom, vassalage, yoke; subjugation, °captivity, *Historical US* peculiar institution: *All of those ancient cultures that we venerate practised slavery.* **2** slave-trade, blackbirding: *No one ever mentions that the family fortune had been made from slavery.* **3** toil, moil, °drudgery, travail, °grind, °strain, (hard) °labour: *She remembered the years of slavery she had spent at the kitchen sink.*

sleazy *adj.* **1** unsubstantial *or* °insubstantial, °flimsy, °slight, °shabby, °poor, gimcrack, jerry-built, °tawdry, °cheap, tatty, °ramshackle, °rickety, °slipshod, *Colloq US* chintzy: *Her garish dress was made from some sleazy synthetic material.* **2** °disreputable, low-class, low-grade, squalid, °dirty, °base, °seedy, °sordid, °contemptible, trashy, °run-down, °mean, °cheap, *Colloq* crummy, slummy, *Slang* crappy, cheesy: *He was lying low in a sleazy hotel while the police searched for him.*

sleek *adj.* **1** °smooth, °slick, velvety, °lustrous, °shiny, shining, °glossy, °silky, silken: *The seals' sleek fur glistened in the sunlight.* **2** °graceful, °trim, °streamlined: *For her birthday Edmund gave her a sleek convertible.* **3** °suave, unctuous, °slimy, fawning, °oily, °specious, °hypocritical, *Chiefly Brit* smarmy: *His explanations sounded plausible enough, but we soon found out what a sleek rogue he really was.*

sleep *v.* **1** °doze, (take a) °nap, catnap, °rest, °repose, slumber, drowse, °drop *or* °nod off, be in the land of Nod, be in the arms of Morpheus, snore, *Colloq* snooze, saw wood, catch *or* log a few zees (Z's), take *or* have a zizz, catch forty winks: *I was so tired, I slept for a full ten hours.*
—*n.* **2** °nap, °doze, slumber, rest, siesta, *Colloq* forty winks, snooze, zizz, beauty sleep: *As she grew older, she found she needed less sleep.*

sleepless *adj.* **1** °restless, °wakeful, insomniac, °disturbed: *Your mother and I spent a sleepless night worrying about you.* **2** °alert, watchful, °vigilant, unsleeping: *Mark's wife kept a sleepless vigil at his bedside.*

sleepwalking *n.* **1** noctambulism, somnambulism, noctambulation, somnambulation: *Because of his sleepwalking, he had to be strapped in at night.*
—*adj.* **2** noctambulant, somnambulant: *Proper drugs will control her sleepwalking activities.*

sleepy *adj.* **1** °drowsy, somnolent, °tired, °nodding, dozy, °lethargic, °torpid, slumberous, sluggish, oscitant; °weary, °fatigued, °exhausted, *Colloq* °dead on one's feet, (knocked) out, °beat, *US and Canadian* pooped: *All that exercise has made me sleepy.* **2** °boring, °inactive, °dull, °quiet, soporific, °slow, sluggish: *He grew up in a sleepy little village in the Outer Hebrides.*

slender *adj.* **1** °slim, °lean, °willowy, sylphlike, svelte, lissom *or* lissome, lithe, °graceful, snake-hipped, °thin, °spare, °slight, °lanky: *By exercising regularly, she has retained her slender figure.* **2** °slim, °narrow, °slight, °poor, °unlikely, °small, °little, °scanty, °remote, °meagre, °weak, °feeble: *Prospects for a quick recovery of the stock market are slender.* **3** °slim, °slight, °little, °scanty, °inadequate, °insufficient, °insignificant, °trifling: *The evidence against the defendant was too slender for a conviction.*

sleuth *n.* (private) °detective, (private) investigator, *US* P.I., *Colloq* private eye, Sherlock, °snoop, *Brit* tec *or* 'tec, *US* hawkshaw, *Slang US* dick, shamus, *US and Canadian* gumshoe: *Dissatisfied with the progress of the police, we hired a private sleuth to investigate the theft.*

slice *n.* **1** °slab, °piece, rasher, collop, shaving, layer, *Cookery* scallop, escalope, scaloppine (*pl.* of scaloppina) *or* scaloppini (*pl.*): *May I have another slice of ham?* **2** °portion, °piece, °part, °wedge, °share, °sliver, °helping: *He wants to make certain he gets his slice of the pie.* **3** spatula; slicer: *The Cabots gave us a silver fish slice for a wedding present.*
—*v.* **4** °cut, °carve, °divide: *They watched their mother slicing bread for sandwiches.*

slick *adj.* **1** °smooth, °sleek, °glossy, °silky, silken, °shiny, shining, °glassy, °slippery: *His slick hair looked as if it had been greased.* **2** °smooth, urbane, °suave, smooth-spoken, °glib, °smug, °plausible; sycophantic, unctuous, *Colloq* smarmy: *Thomas was a slick operator and managed to worm his way into a position of power.* **3** °smooth, °clever, °skilful, adroit, °dexterous, °professional, °ingenious, °imaginative, inventive, °creative, *Colloq* °neat: *The performance was slick and well-rehearsed.* **4** °superficial, °shallow, meretricious, °specious, °glib: *They have made a lot of money publishing slick magazines for the yuppy market.*
—*v.* **5** Often, **slick down**: °smooth, °plaster down, grease, °oil: *He likes his hair slicked down to look like Valentino's.*

slicker *n.* **1** confidence man *or* woman, °cheat, °swindler, mountebank, *Colloq* con man, city slicker: *That slicker she met in Paris tricked Harriet out of a lot of money before he disappeared.* **2** oilskin (raincoat): *Best wear your slicker if you're going out in this storm, James.*

slide *v.* **1** °glide, °slip; °coast, °skim, glissade, skate, °plane, skid, toboggan, °slither: *The drawer* slid smoothly out on its runners. Terry came sliding down the icy hill, arms and legs flailing. **2** °creep, °steal, °slip, °slink, °move: My contact slid into the seat beside me and slipped me a note. **3** °decline, °decrease, °drop, °fall: Shares slid to an all-time low on this morning's market. **4 let slide**: °forget, °ignore, °neglect, °gloss or °pass over, pay no °heed or °mind (to): When Mr Bartlett borrowed my lawnmower, I let the matter slide till he began to think of it as his own, and offered to lend it to me! —n. **5** landslide, earth-slip, avalanche, mud-slide: A dozen houses were destroyed in the slides caused by the recent torrential rains.

slight adj. **1** °small, °little, °minor, °negligible, °unlikely, °insignificant, °inconsequential: There is always a slight chance that you might be wrong, you know. **2** °trifling, °tiny, °slender, °minute, infinitesimal; trace, °perceptible: He didn't attach the slightest importance to the rumours that were going round. You'd best wash it again, as there is still a slight odour of garlic. **3** °small, °short, °petite, °thin, °slim, °slender, °delicate, °diminutive, °tiny, °miniature, bantam, °wee, °pocket, pocket-sized, US vest-pocket, Colloq pint-sized: Charlotte's slight build seems totally unaffected by the amount she eats. **4** °insubstantial or unsubstantial, °weak, °feeble, °delicate, °dainty, °frail, °unstable, °fragile, °flimsy, lightly made or built, °precarious, °inadequate, °rickety, °insecure: This table is too slight to support the computer and the printer. His arguments were far too slight to carry conviction. —v. **5** °disregard, °ignore, disdain, °scorn, snub, °rebuff, °cut, °disrespect, cold-shoulder: He thought she had slighted him deliberately at the dance. **6** °insult, °offend, affront, °mortify, °diminish, °minimize, °deprecate, °disparage: Siobhan felt slighted by Harry's inattention. —n. **7** °insult, affront, °slur, °indignity, °outrage, °offence, °disrespect: It is hard to understand why she tolerates his persistent slights. **8** inattention, °neglect, °disregard, °indifference, snub, cold °shoulder, coldness, ill-treatment: Perhaps she misinterprets his obsessive occupation in his work as a slight to her.

slightly adv. a °little, °somewhat, to a certain or slight or minor extent or °degree or measure, marginally: Yes, I do feel slightly better, thank you.

slim adj. **1** See **slender**, 1, above. **2** See **slender**, 2, 3, above. —v. **3** reduce, lose or shed weight, °diet, Chiefly US slenderize: I really must slim if I am to fit into my summer clothes.

slimy adj. **1** oozy, °slippery, mucky, squashy, squishy, viscous, °sticky, gluey, mucilaginous, uliginous, glutinous, mucous, °clammy, °mushy, US squashy or squooshy, Colloq °gooey, gunky, US gloppy: He had cleverly buried the bag of diamonds in a mass of slimy waste where no one would want to look. **2** °slippery, unctuous, °obsequious, sycophantic, toadying, °servile, creeping, °grovelling, abject, Colloq smarmy: I don't mind his trying to sell me insurance, but why does he have to be so slimy about it?

sling v. **1** °toss, °throw, °cast, °propel, °hurl, °shy, °fling, °fire, °shoot, °pitch, let °fly, °launch, °heave, °lob, Colloq chuck: He slung his briefcase onto the desk and flopped into a chair. —n. **2** slingshot, catapult, trebuchet or trebucket: It is said that David slew Goliath with a stone from his sling. **3** °support, strap, °band; °belt: The

doctor ordered him to keep his sprained arm in a sling for a few days. The military rifles are supplied with leather slings.

slink v. °sneak, °creep, °steal, °prowl, skulk: The dog slunk out of the room with its tail between its legs.

slip¹ v. **1** °slide, skid, °glide, °slither: Waxing the runners helps the sleigh slip along more easily. **2** °stumble, lose one's °footing or °balance, miss one's °footing, °trip, °fall, °tumble: Mother slipped on the ice but luckily didn't fall down. **3** Often, **slip up**: °err, °blunder, make a °mistake, °miscalculate, go °wrong, °botch (up), Slang °screw up: He slipped up again by failing to give you your telephone messages. **4 let slip**: °reveal, divulge, °blurt out, °leak, °let out, °disclose, °expose, Colloq come out with, °blab: He accidentally let slip the news that you were back in town. **5 slip away** or **by**: °pass, °elapse, vanish, °go by: The hours just slipped away when I was with Irena. **6 slip away** or **off** or **out**: °escape, °disappear, °leave, vanish, °steal, °go or °run away or off or out, °break away, °get away, give (someone) the slip; °sneak away or off or out: After the speech, he slipped away before we could interview him. **7 slip in**: °enter, °get in, °sneak in; °put in: A field mouse slipped in past the wire netting. I managed to slip in my suggestion before the meeting was adjourned. —n. **8** °blunder, °error, °mistake, °fault, °oversight, slip of the tongue or pen, inadvertence, °indiscretion, °impropriety, °transgression, °peccadillo, faux pas, Colloq slip-up, Chiefly US blooper, Slang Brit boob, bloomer: She made so many slips in the letter that she had to retype it.

slip² n. **1** °piece, °scrap, °strip, °sliver; °paper, °note, chit, °permit, °permission, °pass, °document: I'll put my phone number on this slip of paper. To go on the outing, each child will have to bring in a slip signed by a parent. **2** °shoot, scion, °cutting, sprig, °twig, °sprout, °runner, °offshoot: After the slip is inserted, the branch must be bandaged up firmly.

slippery adj. **1** °slick, °sleek, °slimy, °icy, °glassy, °smooth, °greasy, °oily, lubricated, Colloq skiddy: Be careful! Those stairs can be slippery when they're wet. **2** °evasive, °devious, °shifty, °unreliable, undependable, °questionable, untrustworthy, °dishonest, treacherous, °disloyal, °perfidious, °slick, °crafty, °sly, °foxy, cunning, °tricky, °sneaky, °false, reptilian, °faithless, Colloq °shady: I have dealt with some very slippery characters over the years, but this one is downright evil.

slipshod adj. °careless, slovenly, slapdash, °haphazard, messy, °untidy, disorganized, °lax, unorganized, Colloq °sloppy: We refused to pay the bill because of the slipshod way they did the repairs.

slit v. **1** °split, °cut, °slash, °gash, °knife, °slice: The bark of the log is first slit open, then carefully peeled back. —n. **2** °split, °cut, °gash, °incision, fissure, °groove, °slash, cleft, °aperture, °opening: Off-stage, the rest of the actors are watching the audience through a slit in the curtain.

slither v. °slide, worm, °snake, °slip, °slink, °glide, skitter, °creep, °crawl: After regarding me for a moment, the cobra turned and slithered away.

sliver *n.* °fragment, °piece, shard, °shred, °splinter, °slip, shaving, paring, °flake, °chip, °bit, °scrap, snippet, °snip: *Two weeks later, we were still finding tiny slivers of glass from the broken vase.*

slob *n.* oaf, °boor, pig, lout, churl, yahoo, *Slang Brit* yob, yobbo, *Chiefly US* galoot *or* galloot, Slobbovian: *He was a complete slob—he never tidied his room, and hardly ever washed.*

slogan *n.* war °cry, battle-cry, rallying °cry, catchword, watchword; °motto: *The magazine's slogan was 'If you love words, you'll love Word'.*

slope *v.* **1** °incline, °decline, ascend, °descend, °rise, °fall, °dip, °sink, °drop (off), °angle, °slant, °pitch, °tilt, °tip: *The lawn slopes downwards from the house, then upwards towards that grove of trees.* —*n.* °incline, °decline, ascent, descent, acclivity, declivity, °rise, °fall, °ramp, °dip, °sink, °drop, °angle, °slant, °pitch, °tilt, °rake, °tip, camber, °cant, bevel, °hill, bank, °mount, gradient, *US* °grade, upgrade, °downgrade: *Sheep can be seen grazing on the grassy slopes.*

sloppy *adj.* **1** messy, °dirty, slovenly, °careless, °slipshod, °untidy, disordered, °disorderly; draggle-tailed, °bedraggled, dishevelled, °unkempt, °dowdy, frumpy, frumpish, °shabby, scruffy, *Colloq US* grungy: *She is certainly a sloppy housekeeper. John's teacher complained about his sloppy work.* **2** °wet, slushy, °watery, soggy, soppy, sopping, sodden, sloshy, °muddy, rainy: *The roads were sloppy after all the rain. You're lucky you don't have to go out in this sloppy weather.* **3** °sentimental, °gushy, gushing, mawkish, °maudlin, °mushy, over-emotional, *Colloq* slushy, *Brit* °wet, soppy: *She starts to cry whenever she watches a sloppy film on TV.*

slot *n.* **1** °groove, fissure, °notch, °slit, °opening, °hollow, °depression, °channel, sulcus: *Each of these pieces fits into its own slot. Drop a coin in the slot and watch what happens.* **2** °opening, °position, °vacancy, °job, °place, °assignment, °niche, °space, °spot, pigeon-hole: *We filled that slot in the sales department. They scheduled the new programme into the half-hour slot after the six o'clock news.* —*v.* **3** °groove, fissure, °notch, °slit, °hollow out: *We slotted the stanchions to accommodate the shelf brackets.* **4** °assign, °schedule, °place, °position, pigeon-hole, °fit: *Can we slot this interview into the documentary on China?*

sloth *n.* °idleness, laziness, °indolence, slothfulness, °inertia, apathy, °indifference, accidie, °torpor, fainéance, pococurantism *or* pococuranteism, torpidity, °sluggishness, languor, languidness, °lethargy, phlegm, *Rare* hebetude: *The maharajahs lived a life of sloth and luxury at the expense of their poverty-stricken subjects.*

slothful *adj.* °idle, °lazy, °indolent, apathetic, °indifferent, °torpid, °inert, pococurante, °slack, °lax, °shiftless, fainéant, °inactive, do-nothing, sluggish, sluggard(ly), °slow, °laggard, languorous, languid, °lethargic, °lackadaisical, °phlegmatic, hebetudinous: *One cannot pursue a slothful attitude and expect to get anywhere in life.*

slouch *v.* **1** °droop, °sag, °stoop, loll, °slump, °hunch: *Sit up straight and stop slouching.* —*n.* **2** °stoop, °sag, °droop, °slump, °hunch: *He seems to have developed a slouch from the burden of*

his responsibilities. **3** Usually, **no slouch**: sloven, °loafer, sluggard, °laggard, °loafer, °idler, malingerer, lazybones: *Nellie is certainly no slouch when it comes to exercising to keep fit.*

slow *adj.* **1** lagging, °laggard, dawdling, sluggish, sluggard(ly), slow-moving, °leaden, °ponderous, °unhurried, plodding, snail-like, tortoise-like, °torpid, leaden-footed, creeping, crawling; °deliberate, slow-paced, leisurely, °gradual, °easy, °relaxed, °lax, °lackadaisical, °lazy, *US* lallygagging *or* lollygagging: *They walked at a slow pace back to the house. Philip has become a little slower in his old age.* **2** °gradual, °progressive, °moderate, perceptible, almost imperceptible, measurable: *The church elders have noted a slow decline in moral standards.* **3** °unhurried, slow-moving, slow-paced: *The slow funeral cortege crept through the streets.* **4** behindhand, unpunctual: *I missed the train because my watch is five minutes slow.* **5** °late, °tardy, behindhand, dilatory, delayed, unpunctual: *You were so slow in getting here that everyone has gone.* **6** °slack, °inactive, °quiet, sluggish, unproductive: *Business is always a bit slow after the holidays.* **7** °dense, °dull, slow-witted, dull-witted, °obtuse, °backward, bovine, °dim, dim-witted, °stupid, unresponsive, blockish, cloddish, unintelligent, doltish, °simple, °stolid, unimaginative, Boeotian, *Colloq* slow on the uptake, °thick, °dumb: *I'm afraid I'm a bit slow when it comes to particle physics.* **8** °conservative, unprogressive, °old-fashioned, out of °date, °backward, old-fogyish *or* old-fogeyish, behind the times, *Colloq* °square, not with it, past it, *US* out of it: *The council has been rather slow in realizing the needs of the community.* **9** °boring, °dull, °tiresome, ennuyant, °tedious, °sleepy, somnolent, °torpid, soporific, wearisome, °tame, uneventful, °humdrum, *Colloq* ho-hum, °dead, *Brit* dead-and-alive: *This town becomes really slow in the autumn, till the tourists reappear in the spring.* **10** °reluctant, not quick, unwilling, °hesitant, °disinclined, °averse, °loath *or* loth, °indisposed: *Even when provoked, Cassie tends to be slow to anger.* —*adv.* **11** slowly, unhurriedly, carefully, circumspectly: *He failed his test because he drove too slow.* **12** behindhand, tardily, °late, unpunctual: *All the trains seem to be running a bit slow tonight.* **13** slowly, °easy, leisurely, °easily: *They told him to take things slower or he'd have another heart attack.* —*v.* **14** Often, **slow down** *or* **up**: °slack *or* slacken off, °reduce speed, hold back, put on the brakes, take it easy: *You'd better slow down before you come to Deadman's Hill.* **15** °relax, take it easy, *Colloq* °ease up: *The doctor suggested that at my age I ought to slow down a little.*

sludge *n.* °muck, °mire, °ooze, °mud, slime, °dregs, °silt, °residue, °precipitate, *Colloq* goo: *The mechanic said that there was a lot of sludge in the engine.*

sluggishness *n.* °sloth, laziness, slothfulness, languor, lassitude, °lethargy, languidness, laggardness, °torpor, phlegm, lifelessness, stagnation, slothfulness, pococurantism *or* pococuranteism, fainéance, accidie, *Rare* hebetude: *A few days' golfing in Scotland will help to shake off the sluggishness of your Caribbean holiday.*

slum n. Often, **slums**: ghetto, warren, shanty town, US skid row or Skid Road: *Many very famous men emerged from the slums of the Lower East Side in New York.*

slump n. **1** °dip, trough, depreciation, °decline, downturn, downslide, °recession, °depression, falling-off, fall-off, °fall, °drop, °plunge, descent, °crash, °collapse, °failure; nosedive, tailspin: *A slump in the housing market was one of the early signs of the impending recession. The market went into a slump this morning from which it barely recovered before closing.* —v. **1** °decline, °slip, °recede, °fall (off), °drop, °plunge, °descend, °sink, °crash, °collapse, °dive, °plummet, take or go into a nosedive or tailspin: *Prices on the stock market slumped following announcement of a rise in interest rates.* **3** See **slouch**, 1, above.

slur n. **1** °smear, °insult, calumny, °aspersion, affront, °stigma, °stain, °blot, °spot, (black) °mark, °discredit, insinuation, °innuendo, °imputation, °slander, °libel, °slight, Colloq °put-down: *She resents any slur on her husband's character.* —v. **2** °mumble, misarticulate, °garble, stutter, lisp: *Some people nowadays slur their speech so badly that one can hardly understand them.* **3 slur over**: °gloss over, °pass over, °disregard, give short shrift to, °ignore: *The eulogies at the memorial service slurred over his faults and focused on his accomplishments.*

sly adj. **1** cunning, °artful, °crafty, °clever, °wily, guileful, underhand(ed), °deceitful, treacherous, °foxy, °scheming, plotting, °designing, conniving, °furtive, °shrewd, °sneaky, °stealthy, insidious, °devious, °disingenuous, °tricky, °shifty, °sharp, canny, Colloq °shady: *It was devilishly sly of him to manoeuvre you into paying for his party.* **2** impish, elfish, roguish, °mischievous, puckish, °devilish, scampish, °naughty, °arch, waggish: *Even as he was flirting with Allison he was giving Antonia sly, conspiratorial winks.* —n. **3 on the sly**: slyly or slily, °quietly, surreptitiously, covertly, stealthily, furtively, sneakily, underhandedly, clandestinely, Colloq on the q.t. or Q.T., on the side: *Although her parents had forbidden her to see him again, Antonia continued to meet Kevin on the sly.*

small adj. **1** °little, °tiny, °short, °diminutive, °petite, mignon(ne), °wee, teeny, °elfin, Lilliputian, midget, °miniature, °minute, minuscule, °baby, bantam, °pocket(-sized), mini; °undersized, °immature, °young, under age; Colloq pint-sized, US peewee: *She was once small enough to fit into a size 7. When I was very small, my father took me to my first cricket match.* **2** °slight, °secondary, °insignificant, trivial, °inconsequential, lesser, °puny, °negligible, °minor, °trifling, unimportant, °paltry, nugatory: *The opinions of other people were not of the smallest importance to him.* **3** unimaginative, °shallow, unoriginal, mundane, °everyday, °limited, unprofound, uninspired, commonplace, °matter-of-fact, °flat, two-dimensional: *With their small minds they were incapable of fully appreciating the scope of the project.* **4** skimpy, niggardly, stingy, uncharitable, ungenerous, °scanty, °meagre, °cheap, °petty, parsimonious, grudging, stinting, °selfish, °miserly, °tight, tight-fisted, close-fisted,

°close; °poor, °insignificant, °inadequate, °insufficient, °unsatisfactory, °negligible, °trifling, °humble, small-scale, °modest, unpretentious, Colloq piddling, °measly: *With all your money, it was very small of you not to contribute more to the scholarship fund. We all thought their cheque was too small.* **5** °insignificant, °limited, °negligible, °trifling, °tiny; °little, °minor, diminished, reduced, °slight: *Only a small number of people came to the opening night. It was small consolation to be told that he had come a good second.* **6 feel small**: feel °embarrassed or °ashamed or shamed or humiliated or °foolish, feel discomfited or °disconcerted or uncomfortable, feel mortified or chagrined, Colloq feel °put down: *Doreen always managed to make some remark that made Andrew feel small.*

small-minded adj. °small, °petty, °selfish, stingy, grudging, niggardly, ungenerous, °mean, °narrow-minded, °narrow, close-minded, uncharitable, °hidebound, °rigid, °intolerant, unimaginative, °short-sighted, °near-sighted, myopic: *Charging members of staff for local telephone calls seems rather small-minded.*

small-time adj. °small, small-scale, unimportant, °petty, piddling, °minor, °insignificant, °trifling, trivial: *In less than ten years he succeeded in building a small-time used-car business into a national chain.*

smart adj. **1** °intelligent, °clever, °bright, °brilliant, °quick-witted, °sharp, °acute, °astute, °capable, °adept, apt, °quick, °ingenious: *Emily is one of the smartest children in the class.* **2** canny, perspicacious, °perceptive, percipient, discerning, °knowledgeable, au fait, well-educated, well-read, erudite, °learned, well-versed, °aware, °shrewd, streetwise, Slang °hip, tuned in, US savvy: *Brendan is smart enough to avoid trouble.* **3** °elegant, °chic, °fashionable, °stylish, modish, à la °mode, °smart, °trim, °neat, °dapper, °spruce, soigné(e), Colloq °snappy, natty: *You must admit that both Della and Paul are smart dressers.* **4** °pert, °pointed, saucy, °witty, nimble-witted, °poignant, °trenchant, °effective: *I wish he would stop making smart remarks when I am trying to explain something.* **5** °brisk, °vigorous, °animated, °active, °energetic, °spirited, °lively; °quick, °alert, °jaunty, °perky, °breezy: *The enemy launched a smart counter-attack at dawn. He set off down the road at a smart pace.* **6** °quick, °swift, °stiff, smarting, stinging, °sharp, °severe: *The mugger gave him a smart blow on the back of the neck.* —v. **7** °sting, °hurt, °pinch, °pain, °ache, tingle, °prickle, °burn, throb, °stab, °pierce: *The antiseptic may smart a bit when it is put on the cut. The smoky atmosphere made her eyes smart.* —n. **8** °injury, °harm, °pain, °pang, °twinge, °affliction, °suffering, smarting: *For years he silently endured the smart of his colleagues' ridicule.*

smear v. **1** daub, °rub, anoint, °spread, °cover, °coat, °wipe, °plaster, bedaub; besmirch, °dirty, smudge, °stain, °soil, begrime: *The baby smeared ice-cream all over his face. The car windows were smeared with dirt from the road.* **2** °blacken, besmirch, °soil, °sully, calumniate, °slander, °discredit, °tarnish, defile, °vilify, °scandalize,

°stigmatize, *Colloq* drag through the mud: *Politicians regularly smear their opponents with all sorts of accusations.* —*n.* **3** smudge, daub, °stain, splodge *or chiefly US* splotch, °blot, °taint, °spot: *These outrageous lies constitute a smear on my good reputation. There was a smear of blood on his collar.* **4** °slander, °scandal, °libel, vilification, mud-slinging, defamation, calumny, °aspersion, °reflection: *The article contains several smears on the character of an MP.*

smell *n.* **1** °odour, °scent, °aroma, °perfume, °fragrance, °bouquet, °breath, whiff: *Don't you love the smell of freshly brewed coffee in the morning?* **2** stink, °stench, fetor *or* foetor, fetidness, mephitis, effluvium, *Colloq Brit* pong: *The smell from the rubbish tip was overpowering.* —*v.* **3** °scent, °sniff, *Colloq* get a whiff of: *The moment I smelt that perfume I knew that Nicole had been there.* **4** stink, °reek, *Colloq Brit* pong, hum: *The milk had gone off and smelled to high heaven.*

smelly *adj.* malodorous, evil-smelling, foul-smelling, °foul, mephitic, fetid, °putrid, reeky, °stinking, noisome, °rank, °offensive, miasmic *or* miasmatic *or* miasmatical *or* miasmal, odoriferous, °rancid, high, gamy, *Slang Brit* whiffy: *She hid the diamond in a washing basket full of smelly clothes.*

smile *v.* **1** grin, °beam: *He smiled and said he was pleased to meet me.* —*n.* **2** grin: *Georgina bestowed on me a sweet, wistful smile.*

smirk *n.* **1** °leer, °sneer, grin, grimace, simpering °smile: *Wipe that conceited smirk off your face.* —*v.* **2** °sneer, grimace, °leer: *Instead of saying, 'I told you so', he just stood there smirking.*

smitten *adj.* **1** °affected, afflicted, °beset, °stricken, troubled, distressed, burdened, crushed, plagued, haunted, °worried, bothered, vexed: *Offers of help for the smitten town came pouring in.* **2** captivated, enthralled, struck, bewitched, °enchanted, beguiled, °charmed, enraptured, °infatuated, enamoured, ensorcelled, swept off one's feet, *Colloq* bowled over, gaga: *Anthea met some rock star and was totally smitten. They were so smitten by the beauty of the island that they returned every year.*

smooth *adj.* **1** °regular, °even, °flush, °flat, °level, °plane, unruffled, unbroken, unwrinkled, undisturbed, °tranquil, °peaceful, °calm, °serene, °glassy: *A light breeze rose to ripple the smooth surface of Alan's martini.* **2** °slick, °sleek, °shiny, °glossy, °glassy, mirror-like, °uniform, °polished, burnished; °silky, silken, velvety, satiny: *Optical mirrors for telescopes must be as smooth as modern technology can make them. He ran his fingers over the smooth fabric.* **3** unobstructed, °easy, °effortless, °free, uncluttered, °even, °orderly, well-ordered, uneventful, flowing, °fluent, unconstrained, uninterrupted: *There were no obstacles in the way of a smooth return to normal operations. The road to ruin is short and smooth.* **4** °hairless, bald, °bare, °naked, clean-shaven, smooth-shaven, depilated, glabrous: *His smooth pate shone in the moonlight.* **5** °soothing, °mellow, °pleasant, °bland, °mild, °soft: *That is a very smooth whisky indeed.* **6** °suave, °slick, °slippery, unctuous, silken, °silky, °glib, urbane, soigné(e), °agreeable, °winning, °plausible, facile, °nonchalant, courtly, °eloquent,

honey-tongued, smooth-spoken, °persuasive, °oily, °slimy, syrupy, *Colloq chiefly Brit* smarmy: *With his quick understanding and smooth manner, Edward was a very successful salesman.* **7** °sweet, dulcet, pear-shaped, °mellow, well-modulated, silver-tongued: *The smooth tones of his serenade wafted through the evening air.* **8** °slick, °scheming, conniving, °crafty, °shrewd, cunning, °tricky, °shifty, °sly, °foxy, Machiavellian, °sophistic(al), °plausible, credible, believable, *Colloq* cagey: *Robinson came up with a very smooth plan to bilk wealthy widows out of their money.* —*v.* **9** Often, **smooth out** *or* **away**: °flatten, °even, °level, iron, °press, °mangle, calender: *Please smooth the wrinkles out of this shirt so that I can wear it tonight.* **10** °prepare, °lay, °pave, °ease, °ready, °clear, °open, °prime, lubricate, °facilitate: *What is your policy for smoothing the way for employees joining the firm?* **11** sand, °plane, °polish, buff, burnish: *The wood is smoothed to a glassy finish before being used for the cabinets.* **12** Often, **smooth over**: ameliorate, assuage, allay, °calm, °gloss over, °minimize, °mitigate, lessen, soothe, °reduce, °temper, mollify, smoothen, °soften, palliate, appease: *An otherwise uncomfortable situation was smoothed over by her quiet words.*

smother *v.* **1** suffocate, °stifle, °choke, asphyxiate; throttle, strangle, snuff (out), °kill: *He was accused of trying to smother his wife with a pillow.* **2** be suffocated *or* stifled *or* asphyxiated, be choked *or* strangled, be killed: *The infant apparently smothered in the blanket.* **3** °overwhelm, °overcome, blanket, inundate, °cover, °shower, °envelop, °wrap, enshroud, °surround: *The children crowded round and smothered her with kisses. The banquet table was smothered in white roses.* **4** °repress, °subdue, °suppress, °conceal, °hide, keep *or* °hold back, °cover up, °mask, °choke back *or* down, °check; °stifle, °muffle, blanket, °blank out: *He managed to smother his grief and put on a brave face. Our whispers were smothered by the noise of the hi-fi.* **5** °extinguish, °put out, snuff out: *The foam from the fire extinguisher smothered the blaze in a few moments.*

smoulder *v.* °burn, °seethe, °simmer, °chafe, °rage, °fume, °foam, °boil, °stew, °fester, *Colloq* get hot under the collar, get (all) steamed up, see red, *US* do a slow burn, get (all) burnt up: *The fire continued to smoulder, then flared up again a week later. He has been smouldering ever since his wife confessed she was going out with another man.*

smug *adj.* self-satisfied, complacent, holier-than-thou, °self-important, °overconfident, °conceited: *She is a bit too smug about the security of her job and might get a nasty shock some day soon.*

snack *n.* **1** °bite, nibble, °morsel, °titbit *or chiefly US* tidbit, °refreshment(s), *Brit* elevenses, *Colloq* nosh: *Have a little snack or you'll be hungry later.* —*v.* **2** °bite, nibble, *Colloq* nosh: *He gained all that weight just from snacking between meals.*

snag *n.* **1** °hitch, °catch, °problem, (stumbling) °block, °stricture, bottleneck, °complication, °obstacle, °impediment, °obstruction, °hindrance, °difficulty, *US* hang-up: *A snag developed that prevented my keeping my promise to you.* —*v.* **2** °catch, °tear, °rip: *He snagged his new jacket on a nail.*

snake *n.* **1** reptile, serpent, ophidian, viper: *A specialist in snakes is called a herpetologist.* **2** snake in the grass, °traitor, °turncoat, Judas, quisling, betrayer, double-crosser, °informer, rat, *US* Benedict Arnold, *Slang chiefly US and Canadian* fink, ratfink: *Eventually they caught the snake who was giving away their plans to the enemy.* —*v.* **3** °slither, °glide, °creep, °crawl, worm: *To avoid being seen, he snaked along on his stomach for a few yards.* **4** °twist, °wind, curve, °bend, °turn, zigzag, worm, °wander, °loop, crook, °meander: *The road snakes through the jungle for 50 miles or more.*

snap *v.* **1** °break (off), °separate, °crack; °cleave, °split, °fracture, °give °way, °part: *The wind snapped off tree branches like matchsticks. The back legs of the chair snapped in two as she sat on it.* **2** click; °pop; °crack: *The door snapped shut.* **3** Often, **snap at: a** °bite (at), °nip, gnash or °snatch at: *The postman ran down the street, the dog snapping at his heels.* **b** °attack, °lunge at, °lash out (at), °snarl at, growl (at), bark (at), be °brusque *or* °short *or* °curt (with), *Colloq* jump down (someone's) throat, °fly off the handle (at): *Robin is in a bad mood today, snapping at everyone.* **4** Usually, **snap up** *or US also* **off**: °grab (up), °snatch (up), °seize, °pluck, °pounce on *or* upon, °make off with, °take (away), °capture, °catch, °get, °secure: *The people who arrived early at the sale had snapped up all the bargains.* **5** °shoot, snapshot, °photograph, click, °catch: *He always has his camera with him so that he can snap anything interesting.* **6 snap one's fingers at**: disdain, °scorn, °flout, °dismiss, contemn, °disregard, °ignore, °defy, °mock, °deride, °thumb one's nose at, *Brit* cock a snook at: *He merely snapped his fingers at the dangers when I mentioned them.* **7 snap out of it**: °recover, °come °round or around, °revive, °awaken, °wake up, °perk up, °liven up, °cheer up; get a grip *or* (a) hold on *or* of oneself, °pull oneself together, (re)gain control of oneself: *I was feeling very blue yesterday but managed to snap out of it.* —*n.* **8** °crack, crackle, °pop, click: *The lid shut with a snap.* **9** °spell, °period, °interval, °wave: *During that cold snap we thought we were in for a terrible winter.* **10** °catch, spring °catch, (snap-) fastener, °fastening, °clasp: *Do you want snaps or buttons sewn on this shirt?* **11** °energy, °vigour, °animation, liveliness, °vitality, °bounce, alertness, sprightliness, élan, °dash, °sparkle, °verve, *Colloq* zip, zing, get-up-and-go, °pep, pizazz *or* pizzazz: *Granny certainly has a lot of snap left in her.* **12** easy job, *Slang* °picnic, *US and Canadian* °breeze: *There had been no need for her to worry, for the exam turned out to be a snap.* —*adj.* **13** °abrupt, °sudden, °precipitate, °hurried, hasty, incautious, °rash, °unpremeditated, unplanned, not well-thought-out, °quick, instantaneous, °instant: *This is too important a matter for a snap decision.*

snappish *adj.* **1** °short-tempered, °testy, °petulant, °peevish, °irritable, °prickly, °touchy, irascible, quick to anger, °quick-tempered, hot-tempered, °waspish, *Brit* °snappy, *US* on a short string *or* tether: *He fancies that being snappish goes with his 'artistic' temperament.* **2** °curt, °short, °abrupt, °brusque, curmudgeonly, °cantankerous, °sharp, °cross, grouchy, °gruff, °cranky, crusty, crabby, crabbed,

acid, °tart, acerbic, churlish, dyspeptic, choleric, splenetic, ill-humoured, ill-tempered, °temperamental, °moody, *Brit* snappy: *Grandad tended to be snappish when he became impatient with our lack of experience.*

snappy *adj.* **1** °quick, °sharp, °brisk, °smart, °crisp, °lively, °rapid, °speedy: *If you want to come with us, you'd better make it snappy.* **2** °fashionable, °chic, °sharp, °smart, °stylish, °dapper, modish, *Colloq* natty, *Brit* °trendy: *Your new friend is a very snappy dresser, isn't he?*

snare *n.* **1** °trap, °net, springe, noose, gin: *They had caught only a pigeon in the snare.* —*v.* **2** °trap, °catch, entrap, °seize, °capture, ensnare: *Using a different bait, William snared some partridges.*

snarl[1] *v.* **1** growl; °snap: *I admit I found three snarling Dobermans a bit off-putting. The clerk snarled at me when I asked for a form.* —*n.* **2** growl: *With a snarl the dog leapt at his throat.*

snarl[2] *v.* **1** Often, **snarl up**: °tangle, °entangle, °complicate, °confuse, °scramble, °muddle, °twist, °mix *or* °mess up, *Colloq* ball up, °screw up: *This situation is so snarled up that we'll never straighten it out.* **2** °tangle, °entangle, °knot, °twist, ravel, °jam, °kink: *The rope won't feed through the pulley because it's all snarled.* —*n.* **3** °tangle, entanglement, °complexity, °snag, °problem, °difficulty, °complication, °muddle, °mess, °predicament, °fix, °quandary, °dilemma, *Colloq* snarl-up, °tight °spot, pickle: *The situation was full of snarls and problems.* **4** jungle, °maze, labyrinth, °knot: *The drain was clogged by a snarl of hair.*

snatch *v.* **1** °grab, °grasp, °seize, °clasp, °clutch, °pluck, °take (hold of), °catch, lay hold of, wrest, latch on to, °capture, °snap up, °win, °get, lay *or* get one's hands on: *The thief snatched her purse and ran away. One must snatch every available opportunity for happiness.* **2** *Chiefly US* kidnap, °abduct: *They snatched the kid and are holding him for ransom.* **3** °save, °rescue, °deliver, °remove: *At the very last moment, we were snatched from the jaws of death.* —*n.* **4** °grab, °clutch, °grasp: *He made a snatch for her necklace, but she managed to duck out of the way.* **5** °scrap, °bit, °fragment, snippet, °segment, °morsel, °specimen, °sample: *We were able to hear only brief snatches of their conversation through the closed door.*

sneak *v.* **1** °lurk, °slink, °steal, °creep, skulk, cower, °lurk, °pad, °prowl, °sidle, *Colloq* °pussyfoot: *We caught Francis sneaking about the house last night.* —*n.* **2** °informer, *Colloq* tattle-tale, *Brit* °grass, *Slang* stool-pigeon, snitch, *Brit and Australian* nark, *US* stoolie, shoo-fly. *Chiefly US and Canadian* fink, ratfink: *Frank picked up a little money acting as a sneak for the police.*

sneaking *adj.* **1** °persistent, °lingering, lurking, °nagging, worrying, worrisome, °niggling, intuitive, deep-rooted, deep-seated, *Slang* °gut: *She had a sneaking suspicion that Stephen was a police informer.* **2** innate, intuitive, °inherent, °private, °secret, suppressed, °hidden, unexpressed, undeclared, unvoiced, unavowed, unconfessed, unrevealed, unadmitted, undivulged, undisclosed, covert: *I have a sneaking sympathy with the underdog.*

sneaky *adj.* underhand(ed), °devious, °furtive, °sly, °slippery, °disingenuous, °deceitful, °dishonest, °unscrupulous, °shifty: *He took a sneaky look at his friend's homework before starting his own.*

sneer *v.* **1** °smirk, curl one's lip, °sniff: *Don't sneer—you might be the next to lose your job.* **2** °scorn, disdain, °despise, contemn, turn up one's nose (at), °sniff (at), °jeer (at), °laugh (at), °deride, °mock, °ridicule; underrate; *Colloq* °sneeze at, *Slang* °knock: *They sneered at her ambition to become a serious athlete.*

—*n.* **3** °scorn, °jeer, disdain, °contempt, °derision, °mockery, °ridicule; sneering, jeering: *Barry endured his classmates' sneers without a word.*

sneeze *v.* **1** sternutate: *I was about to sneeze, so I grabbed a tissue.* **2 sneeze at**: See sneer, 2, above.

—*n.* **3** sternutation; sneezing: *The sneeze is an involuntary convulsive action.*

snicker *v.* **1** snigger, °chuckle, °giggle, °titter, °laugh up one's sleeve, °mock, °scorn, °laugh (at), °jeer (at): *It was embarrassing when the audience began to snicker at the ineptitude of the juggler.*

—*n.* **2** snigger, °chuckle, °giggle, °titter: *The villain gave a little snicker when he thought he had her in his clutches.*

sniff *n.* **1** whiff, °breath, °odour, °scent: *I got a sniff of her perfume as she walked by.* **2** °hint, °spirit, °feeling, °suggestion: *There is the sniff of spring in the air.*

—*v.* **3** °smell, snuffle, snuff: *Why is your dog always sniffing at my shoes?* **4** sniff (**at**): See sneer, 2, above.

snip *v.* **1** °nip, °clip, crop, °cut, °lop, °prune, °dock: *When the blossoms begin to fade, snip them off.*

—*n.* **2** °cut, °slit, °gash, °slash, °incision, °nick: *We could watch the audience through a small snip in the curtain.* **3** °bit, °scrap, °shred, snippet, °fragment, °cutting, clipping, °remnant, °morsel: *You are welcome to the leftover snips of fabric.* **4** snips: scissors, shears, tinsnips: *This duct can be cut with the snips.*

snipe *v.* Usually, **snipe at**: °shoot at, °fire at; °attack, °criticize, °deride, find °fault with, °carp at, °pick apart: *Newby has been sniping at the organization for years and we simply ignore him.*

snivel *v.* sniffle, snuffle, blubber, whimper, whine, mewl, pule; °cry, *Colloq Brit* whinge: *I'll buy some of your matches, little girl, but only if you stop snivelling.*

snobbery *n.* snobbism, snobbishness, pretentiousness, °pretension, hauteur, haughtiness, superciliousness, condescension, loftiness, contemptuousness, presumptuousness, lordliness, disdainfulness, disdain, pompousness, pomposity, °affectation, inflatedness, self-importance, °conceit, vainness, °vanity, narcissism, self-admiration, self-centredness, egotism, smugness, *Colloq* uppishness, uppitiness, snootiness, snottiness: *It is commonplace to criticize the nouveau riche for their snobbery.*

snobbish *adj.* °condescending, °superior, patronizing, °arrogant, °haughty, lordly, °lofty, putting on airs, °disdainful, °supercilious, °contemptuous, °pretentious, °smug, °scornful, °self-important, °affected, °conceited, egotistic(al), °vain, self-satisfied, complacent, °pompous, *Colloq* snooty, snotty, highfalutin *or*

hifalutin, on one's high horse, uppity, °hoity-toity, high and mighty, stuck-up, *Brit* °uppish, *Chiefly US* high-hat, *Slang Brit* toffee-nosed: *Since he got his knighthood, Cathcart has become so snobbish he'll have nothing to do with us.*

snoop *v.* **1** °pry, °spy, °interfere, °meddle, °intrude, °butt in(to), *Colloq* stick *or* °poke one's nose; be °nosy, nose around *or* about: *He couldn't stop snooping into other people's affairs.*

—*n.* **2** °busybody, Paul Pry, meddler, °spy, °intruder, snooper, peeper; private °detective *or* investigator; *Colloq* Nosy Parker, *US* buttinsky *or* buttinski; private eye, *US* shamus: *There was a snoop here today, asking a lot of personal questions.*

snug *adj.* °cosy, °comfortable, °intimate, relaxing, °restful, °warm, sheltered, °friendly, °easy, °homely, °casual, *Colloq* comfy: *Curled up on the sofa, Chris looks as snug as a bug in a rug.*

snuggle *v.* °cuddle, °snug down, °nestle, nuzzle: *The puppies snuggled up close to their mother for warmth and protection.*

soak *v.* **1** °drench, °saturate, °wet, °immerse, souse, douse *or* dowse, bathe, °steep, inundate, ret: *You'd better let the tablecloth soak for a while to get out those wine stains.* **2 soak up**: absorb, °take in, sponge up; assimilate, °learn: *The parched earth soaked up the water like a sponge. Let me just lie here and soak up some sunshine. She spent years soaking up the culture of the Cameroons.*

—*n.* **3** °alcoholic, drunkard, °drunk, dipsomaniac, drinker, tippler, toper, sot, *Slang* sponge, souse, boozer, *US* dip, lush, juicer: *You'll never get a straight answer out of that old soak.*

soaking *n.* **1** drenching, wetting, dousing *or* dowsing, immersing, saturating: *We got a thorough soaking when we were caught in the storm.*

—*adj.* **2** °wet, sopping, drenched, dripping, saturated, soaked, wringing °wet, streaming, sodden, waterlogged: *Take off your soaking clothes and sit by the fire in this robe.*

soar *v.* **1** °rise, °fly, °hover, °float, °hang: *The glider soared over the hills, catching every updraught.* **2** °rise, °increase, escalate, °climb, °spiral upwards, °shoot up *or* upwards, °rocket, sky-rocket: *To counteract inflation, interest rates began to soar.*

sob *v.* °cry, °weep, blubber, °shed tears, °snivel, whimper, °sniff, snuffle, pule, wail, °moan, boohoo, mewl, °bawl, °howl, yowl: *The poor, lonely child sobbed quietly.*

sober *adj.* **1** teetotal, °temperate, *US* °dry, *Colloq* on the (water-) wagon: *Because he was driving, he stayed sober at the party while everyone else got drunk.* **2** °serious, °solemn, °earnest, °dispassionate, unruffled, unflustered, unexcited, unperturbed, °steady, °sedate, °staid, composed, °dignified, °cool, °calm, serene, °tranquil, °collected, cool-headed, °level-headed, °sane, balanced, °practical, °realistic, °rational, clear-headed, *Slang* together: *We invited you because we respect your sober judgement.* **3** °sedate, °sombre, °plain, °simple, °subdued, °quiet, repressed, °dreary, °dark, °drab, °colourless, °neutral: *At the funeral the widow wore a sober black costume.*

—*v.* **4 sober up**: detoxify, °recover, *Colloq* dry out: *When she finally sobered up she awoke to find herself in custody.*

sobriety *n.* **1** teetotalism, abstemiousness, abstention, abstinence, non-indulgence,

°temperance: *Since taking the pledge, Oscar has been a model of sobriety.* **2** seriousness, soberness, solemnity, staidness, °gravity, temperateness, sedateness, °formality, °dignity: *They made him promise to do nothing to upset the sobriety of the memorial service.*

so-called *adj.* **1** styled, °self-styled, designated, soi-disant, called, °professed: *They found themselves fighting for Kolchak, the so-called supreme ruler of all the Russias.* **2** °alleged, °pretended, °supposed, ostensible; misnamed, misdesignated; °suspect: *She bought it through the so-called Honest Used Car Dealers Association.*

sociable *adj.* °friendly, affable, approachable, °social, gregarious, °outgoing, extrovert(ed) *or* extravert(ed), companionable, °accessible, °amiable, °amicable, °genial, congenial, convivial, °warm, °cordial, °neighbourly, hail-fellow-well-met, *Colloq* °chummy, °cosy: *The people in this area are quite sociable, and we get together often.*

social *adj.* **1** communal, community, °common, collective, °group, °public, °popular, societal: *In many New England towns, the business of government is a social activity. Crime is a social, not an individual problem.* **2** °sexual, sexually transmitted, °venereal: *The clinic was established specifically to deal with social diseases.* **3** See **sociable**, above.

socialize *v.* °mix, °get together, °fraternize, keep °company, °go out, °get out; °associate: *They haven't had much time for socializing since the birth of their baby.*

society *n.* **1** °fellowship, °brotherhood, °association, °intercourse, °companionship, °company, camaraderie, °friendship: *Few people can be happy for long without the society of others.* **2** mankind, °people, the °public: *I fear that Bob is not yet ready to mingle with society again. Do you believe that society demands too much?* **3** °culture, °civilization, community, way of life, °world; °organization, °system: *The hunting society was replaced largely by the agricultural some 10,000 years ago.* **4** high society, haut monde, beau monde, °upper classes, polite society, °élite, °gentry, *Colloq* °upper crust: *The purpose of the debutante ball is to introduce young ladies of about 18 to society.* **5** °organization, °club, °association, °circle, °league, °institute, academy, °alliance, guild, °group, °fraternity, sorority, °brotherhood, sisterhood, °fellowship, °union, consociation, sodality, *Verein*, bund *or* Bund: *The society, founded to advance and support linguistic scholarship, is now 100 years old.*

soft *adj.* **1** °yielding, cushiony, plushy, spongy, squeezable, compressible, squashy, squashable, °flexible, °plastic, °pliable, pliant, °supple, flexile, flexuous, unstarched: *This mattress is much too soft for my back.* **2** °easy, °comfortable, undemanding, *Colloq* cushy: *His uncle got him a soft job at the Labour Ministry.* **3** °gentle, °mild, balmy, °pleasant, °moderate, °warm, halcyon, springlike, summery, °restful, °tranquil, relaxing, °lazy: *Alexandra was looking forward to a week in the soft Caribbean climate.* **4** °subdued, toned *or* turned down, muted, °low, °quiet, °melodious, mellifluous *or* mellifluent, °mellow, °gentle, °faint, softened, °soothing, °smooth: *Riley thought she might succumb to the influences of the wine and the soft music and lights.* **5** °easygoing, °tolerant, °kind, compassionate, °gentle,

°merciful, °lenient, °indulgent, °permissive, °liberal, °lax, °easy, docile, °tame, °submissive, deferential, °benign, tender-hearted, °sympathetic, kind-hearted, °kind: *Some believe that the jailers were too soft with the criminals. His parents were far too soft.* **6** Usually, **soft in the head**: °foolish, °silly, °simple, *Colloq chiefly Brit* °daft, *US* °off: *Kevin must have gone a bit soft in the head if he thinks that Clara still loves him.* **7** depressed, declining, in °decline, in °recession, °slow, °unprofitable, borderline, °questionable, °weak: *Owing to the stormy, cold summer, the resort business has been soft this year.* **8** downy, °silky, silken, satiny, furry, °fluffy, feathery, fleecy, °fuzzy, velvety, °smooth (as a baby's bottom): *The wool from the lambs is much softer.* **9** pastel, °pale, °delicate, °fine, °subdued, °light, mat *or* matt, °quiet, °diffuse(d), °soothing: *He wanted the bedroom painted in soft shades of greenish blue.* **10** °harmless, non-addictive: *Some consider cannabis a soft drug.* **11** °fuzzy, °woolly, blurred, blurry, foggy, °diffuse(d): *The soft focus photos of the wedding looked very romantic.* **12** °weak, °feeble, °frail, effete, °delicate, non-physical, non-muscular, °puny, °flabby, out of training *or* °condition *or* °shape, pampered; namby-pamby, °effeminate, unmanly, unmanful, *Colloq* sissified, °sissy: *He had been out of the marines for so long they thought he had gone soft.* **13** °easy, °luxurious, pampered, °rich, °opulent, °plush, °posh, *Colloq* ritzy, swank(y): *Since selling his business, Aubrey has been living the soft life on the Costa del Sol.*

soften *v.* **1** Often, **soften up**: °melt, °affect, mollify, °mellow, palliate, soothe, °relax, appease: *Nothing would soften the heart of that cruel tyrant.* **2** °mitigate, assuage, °diminish, °moderate, °reduce, °cushion, lessen, °weaken, allay, °ease, °lighten, abate, °temper, °relieve: *Can't you think of some way to soften the blow of such bad news?* **3** °muffle, °deaden, damp, soft-pedal, °lower, °still, °quiet, °tone down, lessen, °diminish, °lighten, °turn down, °quell, *Chiefly Brit* °quieten: *Try to soften the high notes and bring up the bass.* **4** °give in, °succumb, °surrender, °yield, °agree, °consent, concur, assent, give °way, °relax, °ease (up), °let up: *The committee finally softened and allowed the park to be used for games.*

soft-hearted *adj.* tender-hearted, compassionate, °tender, warm-hearted, °sentimental, °charitable, °generous, giving, °sympathetic, °indulgent, °kind, kind-hearted, °responsive: *Alison is quite soft-hearted when it comes to animal causes and contributed willingly.*

soil[1] *v.* **1** °dirty, °stain, begrime, °muddy, °smear, °spot: *His shirts were returned by the laundry still soiled.* **2** °pollute, °contaminate, °sully, defile, °foul, befoul, °tarnish, besmirch, °disgrace, °muddy, °smear, °blacken; °blot: *The scandal soiled his previously spotless reputation.* —*n.* **3** °dirt, °filth, °muck, °mire, °mud, °sludge, °dregs, °refuse; excrement, °waste (matter): *The soil is carried away by these pipes into the main sewer.*

soil[2] *n.* earth, loam, °dirt, °ground, °turf, humus; clay: *The men who dug the swimming-pool took away the soil from the pit.*

sojourn *n.* **1** °stay, °stop, stopover, °visit, °rest, °holiday, vacation: *We had a very pleasant sojourn in Toronto on our way home.*

—v. **2** °stay, °stop (over), °visit, rest, °holiday, vacation, °tarry: *Next year we plan to sojourn in Bermuda for a while.*

solace n. **1** °comfort, consolation, condolence, relief, balm, °support, °help, succour; reassurance, °cheer: *The children brought her solace in her bereavement.*
—v. **2** °comfort, °console, condole, °support, °help, succour, soothe, allay, alleviate, ameliorate, °mitigate, assuage, °relieve; °cheer (up), °reassure, hearten: *There was little to solace James's misery.*

soldier n. **1** serviceman, servicewoman, °recruit, fighter, infantryman, foot-soldier, trooper, warrior, military man, man-at-arms, *Brit* Tommy (Atkins), *US* enlisted man *or* woman, *Colloq Brit* squaddie, *US* GI *or* G.I. (Joe), *Old-fashioned (WWI)* doughboy: *Enemy soldiers had been reconnoitring our position during the night.* **2** fighter, °stalwart, °supporter, °militant: *He has been a soldier in the fight against poverty all his life.*
—v. **3** °serve (in the army): *In his family the men have been soldiering for generations.* **4 soldier on**: °continue, °persist, °persevere, °endure, °drive, °keep going, °keep on *or* at, °grind, drudge: *Despite the set-backs, they soldiered on to complete the project in time.*

sole adj. lone, °only, °singular, °unique, °solitary; °particular, °exclusive, °individual, °personal: *As Susan is the sole surviving heir, she has the right to sell the house if she wishes.*

solecism n. °error, °slip, °impropriety, °fault, °breach, °violation, °lapse, °mistake, misusage, incongruity, inconsistency, barbarism, °blunder, gaffe, °bungle, °fumble, gaucherie, faux pas, °botch *or* botch-up, *Colloq* flub, *Slang* boner, *Brit* boob, bloomer, *Chiefly US and Canadian* blooper: *Solecisms in his writing include failure of subject and verb to agree.*

solemn adj. **1** °serious, °sober, °reserved, °grave, °earnest, °sedate, °staid, °taciturn; morose, °morbid, mirthless, unsmiling, °gloomy, °sombre, °grim; °glum, long-faced, saturnine: *We observed a moment of solemn silence in memory of our fallen comrades. They knew from their father's solemn expression that something was wrong.* **2** °ceremonial, ritualistic, liturgical, °religious, ecclesiastical, °holy, °divine, °sacred, hallowed, sacramental, reverential, devotional: *We attended a solemn service to celebrate the return of the hostages.* **3** °ceremonious, °ritual, °formal, °dignified, °stately, °grand, august, °imposing, °impressive, awe-inspiring, °awesome, °important, °momentous: *The Trobriand islanders regarded the rites of passage as most solemn.*

solemnity n. solemnness, °gravity, seriousness, soberness, °reserve, sedateness, taciturnity, staidness, earnestness, impressiveness, °grandeur, °importance, momentousness, consequence: *All who attended the service were affected by the solemnity of the lighting of the eternal flame.*

solicit v. **1** entreat, °beseech, °ask (for), implore, °petition, importune, °appeal for *or* to, °call on *or* upon, °beg, supplicate, °pray, crave: *He has solicited my help on more than one occasion.* **2** accost, °approach, °entice, °lure, °pander to, *Slang* °hustle: *You can't go out in that neighbourhood without being solicited.*

solicitor n. °lawyer, attorney, *US* counselor-at-law: *I have turned the matter over to my solicitor.*

solicitous adj. **1** °concerned, caring, °considerate, uneasy, troubled, °anxious, apprehensive, °worried: *She seemed genuinely solicitous over the state of my health.* **2** °eager, °earnest, zealous, °keen, °anxious, °desirous, °ardent, avid: *She seems sincerely solicitous to please the firm's customers.*

solicitude n. °concern, °consideration, °regard, disquiet, disquietude, uneasiness, °anxiety, apprehension, °worry, nervousness, °fear, fearfulness, °alarm: *As she had not yet made him her sole heir, his solicitude over her health was understandable.*

solid adj. **1** three-dimensional, cubic: *The perspective drawing is a representation of a solid object.* **2** filled (in *or* up), °packed, jammed, crowded, teeming, °congested, crammed, swarming, compressed, concentrated, *Colloq* chock-a-block, jam-packed, chock-full: *By the time I arrived, the gallery was solid with people.* **3** °compact, °firm, °hard, °stable; unshakeable *or* unshakable, unshaky, °substantial, °concrete, °sturdy, °sound, °stout, °strong: *The vessel floated through the air before coming to rest on solid ground. His theories rest on a solid foundation.* **4** °consistent, °homogeneous, °uniform, unalloyed, unmixed, °pure, °continuous, unbroken, °real, °authentic, °true, °genuine, 24-carat *or esp. US* 24-karat, unadulterated, *Slang* honest-to-God: *This mountain seems to be solid iron all the way through. John gave me a solid gold necklace for my birthday.* **5** law-abiding, upstanding, °upright, °decent, °stout, °substantial, °powerful, °reliable, °regular, °steady, °steadfast, °stalwart, °straight, °estimable, °sure, trusty, °trustworthy, true-blue, °worthy, dependable, °sober: *Mr Hart is one of the solid citizens of this town. He has always been a solid defender of the underdog.* **6** °steady, °stable, °stalwart, dependable, °sturdy, °strong, °substantial, °sound, °firm, well-built, well-constructed, well-made, °tough, °durable, °rugged, °stout: *That chair is not solid enough for you to stand on.* **7** cogent, °sound, °concrete, °weighty, proved, provable, valid, °reasonable, °sensible, °rational, °sober, well-founded, °authoritative, °indisputable, °incontrovertible, irrefutable, incontestable, °good, °powerful, °potent, °forceful, convincing, °persuasive: *He presents a solid argument for a sales tax.* **8** °firm, °downright, °vigorous, °telling, °effective, °forceful, °potent, °powerful, °mighty, °dynamic, °thorough, through-and-through, °intensive: *Jan struck a solid blow against the supporters of abortion.* **9** See solvent, 1, below. **10** °entire, °complete, °whole, °continuous; uninterrupted, °undivided, unbroken, unrelieved, °blank, windowless: *I had to wait at the dentist's for a solid hour. Around the park they erected a solid wall.*

solidarity n. °unity, unanimity, unification, °accord, concord, concordance, °harmony, concurrence, like-mindedness, °agreement, mutuality, single-mindedness, singleness (of purpose), community of interest, esprit de corps, camaraderie, comradeship, sodality, *Solidarność*: *It was through solidarity, not the pursuit of individual interest, that freedom was achieved.*

solidify v. **1** °harden, °freeze, °set, °cake, °compact, compress, crystallize; °jell *or* gel, clot, congeal, °coagulate, °thicken, *Technical* inspissate; sublime: *The lava flowed round the bodies of* those who died and solidified, preserving them in their final attitudes. **2** consolidate, °unite, °unify, pull or draw together: *Studying the speeches of politicians enables me to solidify my own views.*

solitary *adj.* **1** lone, °single, °sole, °individual; unattended, °solo, companionless, friendless, °lonesome, °lonely, °unsocial, cloistered, °secluded, °reclusive, °separate, eremitic(al), hermitic(al), °remote, °withdrawn, °distant, °out-of-the-way, unfrequented, °desolate: *There is not a solitary exception to the rule. Flora's solitary style of living allows her to concentrate on her writing. There is a solitary little inn where we go for weekends.* —*n.* **2** solitary confinement: *The prisoner has been in solitary for striking a guard.*

solitude *n.* **1** solitariness, aloneness, isolation, °seclusion, °privacy: *Peter enjoys the solitude of living on an island.* **2** loneliness, remoteness; °emptiness, wilderness: *How long could one person survive in the solitude of interstellar space?*

solo *adv.* **1** °alone, °unaccompanied, on one's own: *Jack flew solo for the first time yesterday.* —*adj.* **2** °individual, °unaccompanied, °solitary: *Let Eugene play the solo trombone part.*

solution *n.* **1** solving, working *or* figuring out, °discovery, °finding out, unravelling, explication, deciphering, decipherment, elucidation, °revelation, clarification, °explanation; °answer, °key: *The solution of the problem should be left up to the experts. Several solutions have been found through computer analysis.* **2** °settlement, settling, °resolution, °result, denouement *or* dénouement, °outcome, conclusion: *It seems unlikely that we shall be able to bring this matter to a solution in a one-day meeting.* **3** °mixture, °blend, °compound, infusion; °liquid, °fluid; *Technical* emulsion, °suspension, colloid *or* colloidal solution *or* colloidal °suspension: *After mixing the powder with water, use the solution to bathe the wound.* **4** dissolving, °dissolution, mixing, °mixture: *The solution of these ingredients in alcohol was first accomplished in ancient times.*

solve *v.* °work *or* °figure out, unravel, disentangle, untangle, °clarify, °clear up, make °plain *or* °clear, °interpret, explicate, °decipher, °crack, °explain, elucidate, °reveal, °answer, °resolve: *Oedipus' problems began in earnest when he solved the Riddle of the Sphinx.*

solvent *adj.* creditworthy, (financially) °sound, °solid, °reliable; debt-free; °profitable: *The auditors rate the business as solvent.*

sombre *adj.* **1** °gloomy, morose, lugubrious, °funereal, °morbid, louring *or* lowering, °melancholy, °sad, °dismal, °unhappy, cheerless, °joyless, °serious, °sober, °doleful, dolorous, °mournful, depressed, depressing, °grave, °grim, grim-faced, grim-visaged, *Literary* melancholic, darksome: *Despite his sombre appearance, Sid was one of the funniest men I've ever met.* **2** °dark, °gloomy, °foreboding, °bleak, depressing, °shadowy, °murky, °leaden, °grey, °black, °dismal, °dreary, °overcast, °dusky, °dim, °dingy, darkling, °dull, subfusc *or* subfuscous: *The sombre sky set the mood for the proceedings that were to follow.* **3** °staid, °sedate, °sober, °solemn, °dark, °dull, subfusc: *A young person like you ought to dress in less sombre colours.*

somebody *pron.* **1** °one, someone, some person: *There must be somebody who will take you to the dance.*

—*n.* **2** °personage, °celebrity, °dignitary, VIP, luminary, °notable, °star, superstar, *Colloq* hotshot, °bigwig, °big wheel, °big gun, °big noise, °big White Chief, °big Daddy, °big Chief, big-timer; hot stuff; *Old-fashioned* °big cheese; *US* Mr Big: *He must be a somebody to merit such treatment.*

somehow *adv.* someway, in one °way or another, in some °way, somehow or other, by °hook or by crook, by fair means or foul, *Colloq* come hell or high water: *Somehow, we have to get into the vault for those papers.*

sometime *adj.* **1** °former, erstwhile, °past, °recent, one-time, quondam: *Crawford was a sometime student of the occult.* —*adv.* **2** at some °time or other, someday, one day, any °time, on a future occasion, when *or* if the opportunity arises, °soon, by and by, one of these days: *Come up and see me sometime.* **3** sooner or later, in (due) °time, in the fullness of °time, in the long °run, one fine day, *Un bel di*, °eventually, when all is said and done, before long, before you know it: *You can be sure that the tax man will find out about it sometime.*

sometimes *adv.* °occasionally, on occasion, (every) °now and then, °now and again, off and on, at times, from °time to °time, every so often, (every) °once in a while: *Sometimes Ambrose used to visit his grandchildren twice a week.*

somewhat *adv.* °rather, °quite, °relatively, more or less, °moderately, pretty, °fairly, to some *or* a certain °extent *or* °degree *or* °measure, °slightly, a bit, a °little, *Colloq* °sort of, kind of: *Ingrid was somewhat put out by my refusal.*

song *n.* **1** °tune, °air, °melody, ditty, °number: *Together, they wrote some of the most popular songs of this century.* **2 for a song** cheaply, inexpensively, at a °bargain price: *That old book you wanted went for a song at the auction.* **3 (old) song and dance: a** °fuss, to-do, commotion, °bother, ado, *Colloq* °flap, °performance, *Brit* kerfuffle: *I cannot see why they made such a song and dance of telling us they couldn't come.* **b** °evasion, °tale, prevarication, (long) °story, (long) °explanation: *To excuse his absence he gave me the old song and dance about his grandmother being ill.*

soon *adv.* **1** before long, °presently, ere long; in the near future, any minute (now), before you know it, in good time, in a little while, in a °minute *or* a °moment, momentarily, °shortly, anon, in a °second, *Colloq* in a jiffy: *Soon another year will have passed. The doctor will be with you soon.* **2** °quickly, speedily, at °once, °promptly, °immediately, °directly, without delay, °straight away, °right away, forthwith, in short order, at the °double, in two shakes (of a lamb's tail), in a wink, *tout de suite*, *Colloq* pronto, *US and Canadian* lickety-split: *If he doesn't come soon, dinner will be spoilt.* **3** °quickly, speedily, °promptly, °swiftly: *I'll be there as soon as I can.* **4** °willingly, lief, °gladly, °happily, °readily: *I'd just as soon be left alone, if you don't mind.* **5 sooner or later:** at some °time or other, some °time, one day, in °time, in due course, °eventually, °ultimately, in the end, when all is said and done, at the end of the day, in the last *or* final analysis, at °bottom: *Don't worry, she'll come home sooner or later. Sooner or later they will have to yield.*

soothing *adj.* **1** relaxing, °restful, °serene, °peaceful, pacifying, °calm, calming, °quiet, °soft, quieting: *I put on some soothing music and offered her a cocktail.* **2** mollifying, comforting, palliative, lenitive, demulcent, balsamic, emollient: *The doctor prescribed a soothing ointment to relieve the pain.*

sophistic *adj.* sophistical, °specious, fallacious, °deceptive, °hypocritical, °false, °unsound, baseless, °groundless, casuistic(al), Jesuitic(al), captious, misleading, °bogus, °sham, °untenable: *The politicians advanced their usual sophistic arguments for continuing a war that no one wanted to support.*

sophisticated *adj.* **1** °cultivated, cultured, °refined, °experienced, °worldly, cosmopolitan, °polished, °elegant, urbane, worldly-wise, °knowledgeable, °knowing, °suave, soigné(e), °blasé, chichi, °slick, *Slang* °hip *or* hep, °cool, with it: *The Gordons mix with a pretty sophisticated crowd.* **2** advanced, complex, °complicated, °intricate, °elaborate, °subtle, °refined, multifaceted: *The desk-top computers of today are much more sophisticated than most older main-frame systems.*

sophistication *n.* **1** worldliness, urbanity, °culture, °refinement, °knowledge, knowledgeability, cosmopolitanism, °polish, °elegance, °poise, suavity *or* suavité, savoir faire, savoir vivre, °finesse, °discrimination, discernment, awareness, °taste, tastefulness, °style: *They want him on the board of directors of the museum because he lends it sophistication.* **2** °complexity, intricacy, °subtlety, °refinement: *There is a staggering amount of sophistication built into modern integrated circuits.*

sorcerer *n.* sorceress, magus, necromancer, wizard, °witch, warlock, enchanter, enchantress, °magician, thaumaturgist, shaman, witch-doctor, medicine man: *The law demanded death for the sorcerers and for those who dealt with them.*

sorcery *n.* witchcraft, °enchantment, sortilege, necromancy, wizardry, (black *or* white) °magic, shamanism, black art, diabolism: *Once Vera works her sorcery on you, you obey her every whim.*

sordid *adj.* **1** °base, °vile, °corrupt, °low, ignoble, debased, degraded, abased, °mean, ignominious, °dishonourable, °despicable, °disreputable, °shabby, °shameful, °scurvy, °rotten, execrable: *He forced his family to do the most sordid things to raise money.* **2** °avaricious, °greedy, °grasping, °mercenary, piggish, °hoggish, °selfish, °rapacious, money-grubbing, stingy, parsimonious: *His most sordid plan was to pretend he was collecting money for the handicapped.* **3** °dirty, °foul, °filthy, squalid, unclean, °untidy, °mean, slummy, °seamy, °seedy, °wretched, unsanitary, insanitary, °offensive, defiled, polluted, fetid, feculent, mucky, maggoty, °putrid, fly-blown, °slimy: *The conditions of some of the homes the social workers visit are indescribably sordid.* **4** °wretched, °miserable, °poor, poverty-stricken, down-and-out, °impoverished, °ramshackle, hovel-like, °tumbledown, °dingy, °seamy, °seedy, slummy, deteriorated, °sleazy, back-alley: *When he first came to town, he lived in a sordid shack lent him by a farmer.*

sore *adj.* **1** °painful, °sensitive, °tender, °raw, °angry, °burning, stinging, smarting, hurting; irritated, °inflamed, chafed: *My finger is still sore round the cut.* **2** °sensitive, °delicate, °tender, °embarrassing, °awkward, °ticklish, °touchy, °thorny, °prickly: *Failing to complete medical school is a sore point with her.* **3** dire, °serious, °acute, °extreme, °critical, °urgent, °pressing, °desperate: *He is in sore need of some good advice.* **4** °angry, angered, annoyed, irritated, vexed, irked, °upset, *Colloq* peeved: *Don't get sore at me because you got low marks in your exams.* **5** °painful, °troublesome, °grievous, aggrieved, distressing, distressful, °harrowing, °severe, °agonizing, °bitter, °fierce, °burdensome, onerous, °heavy, °oppressive: *Melanie's marital troubles proved a sore trial for her friends.* **6 sore straits:** °difficulty, °trouble, °distress, °danger, °dangerous *or* °precarious condition: *The business is in sore straits, I fear.* —*n.* **7** °injury, °damage, °swelling, rawness, infection, °inflammation, °bruise, abrasion, °cut, laceration, °scrape, °burn, canker, °ulcer: *If that sore on your arm doesn't heal, you'd better see a doctor.*

sorrow *n.* **1** °sadness, heartbreak, °grief, unhappiness, dolour, °misery, °woe, °anguish, °distress, °suffering, °torment, °agony, wretchedness, heartache, °desolation, desolateness: *How can one deal with the sorrow of the loss of a child?* **2** °affliction, °trouble, °trial, tribulation, °misfortune, °hardship, adversity, bad *or* hard luck, °cares, °pressure, °strain, travail: *It is unbelievable that anyone could survive a life filled with such sorrow.* —*v.* **3** °grieve, °lament, °mourn, °regret, °keen, °bemoan, agonize, °moan, °bewail: *She is sorrowing over the loss of her nephew.*

sorrowful *adj.* **1** °sad, °unhappy, °regretful, °sorry, depressed, °dejected, crestfallen, chap-fallen, °gloomy, downcast, °blue, dispirited, °melancholy, in the doldrums, °wretched, °woebegone, °miserable, heartsick, disheartened, °piteous, heavy-hearted, °broken-hearted, rueful, woeful, °tearful, disconsolate, °inconsolable, grief-stricken, *Colloq* down in the °mouth, down in the dumps: *The entire family was sorrowful to learn of Carriston's death.* **2** distressing, °lamentable, °doleful, °unfortunate, °bitter, distressful, troublous, °grievous, unlucky, hapless, afflictive: *What a sorrowful life some of those miners' families have led!*

sorry *adj.* **1** °regretful, °penitent, °remorseful, contrite, conscience-stricken, guilt-ridden, °repentant, °apologetic, penitential: *I am sorry if I offended you.* **2** abject, °miserable, depressing, °wretched, °pitiful, °pitiable, °pathetic, °deplorable, °stark, °grim, °sordid, °dismal, °base, star-crossed, ill-starred: *Crackham has led a rather sorry life, most of it as a vagrant. Agnes again made a sorry spectacle of herself at the Christmas party.* **3** See sorrowful, 1, above: *I was indeed sorry to learn that you are moving away, Peggy.*

sort *n.* **1** °kind, °variety, °type, °class, classification, °group, °category, °brand, °make, °mark, °stamp, °description, °mould, °stripe, ilk, feather, kidney, °character, °nature; °manner, species: *A 1928 Alfa-Romeo coupé is not exactly the right sort of car for a family. Lewis is a person of a different sort. What sort of person is he?* **2** °kind, °type, °manner: *This sort of behaviour must stop.* **3** species, genus, °family, phylum, subgenus, subspecies, °race, °breed, °strain,

°stock, °kind, °variety, °type: *Aberdeen Angus is a better sort of beef for steaks.* **4** °person, °individual, °lot; °thing: *He is not really such a bad sort.* **5 of sorts**: of a sort, of a °mediocre or °passable or admissible or not (too) bad or °fair or sufficiently good or °adequate or °undistinguished or °indifferent kind or quality or proficiency: *Yes, one might say that he is a violinist of sorts.* **6 out of sorts**: not oneself, not up to snuff, unwell, ailing, °indisposed, (slightly) °ill, °low, *Colloq* off one's feed, under the °weather: *He is out of sorts after last night's revelries.* **7 sort of**: See somewhat, almost.
—*v.* **8** assort, classify, °file, °order, °rank, °grade, °class, °categorize, °separate, °divide, °combine, °merge, °arrange, °organize, systemize, systematize, catalogue, °group, sort out: *Sort these names into alphabetical order.* **9** °describe, °characterize, °categorize, °cast, °throw, °combine, °mould, type: *I did not enjoy being sorted together with thieves and murderers.* **10 sort out**: **a** °organize, set or put °straight, °straighten out, °resolve, °tidy (up), °clarify, °clear up, °solve; °decide: *Someone will have to sort out how we are to proceed.* **b** °choose, °select, °separate, °divide: *Sort out all the books that you want to keep from those to be donated to the library.*

so so *adj.* °mediocre, all right, °average, °undistinguished, °passable, not (too) bad or good, °adequate, °fair (to middling), middling, °indifferent, °ordinary, °tolerable, *comme ci, comme ça*, °modest: *Sabrina, whose singing is just so so, will never be a star.*

soul *n.* **1** (vital) °spirit or °force, being, (inner or true) self, °essence, °psyche, °heart, °mind, °intellect, °reason, anima: *He finally surrendered, body and soul.* **2** °person, °individual, °man, °woman, °mortal, (°human) being: *I won't tell a soul about our conversation. What a sweet old soul she is!* **3** incarnation, °embodiment, personification, typification, °essence, °quintessence: *You can count on me as the soul of discretion.* **4** °emotion, °feeling, °sentiment, °sincerity, °fervour, °ardour, °warmth, °dynamism, vivacity, °energy, °spirit, °vitality, °force: *Alice puts a lot of soul into her singing, and that comes across to the audience.*

soulful *adj.* °sincere, °deep, °profound, °moving, °emotional, °warm, °ardent, °intense, °fervent, °expressive: *The lovers exchanged soulful looks.*

sound[1] *n.* **1** °tone; °noise; °din; cacophony; °report: *This piano has a tinny sound. We could hear the sound of laughter from below. I heard nothing over the sound of the crowd. Sounds of gunfire echoed in the valley.* **2** °ring, °tone, °impression, °characteristic, °quality, °effect, °aspect, °look: *I didn't like the sound of that remark.* **3** hearing, °range, earshot: *Anyone within the sound of his voice could tell that he was angry.*
—*v.* **4** °resound, reverberate, °echo, resonate: *The noises sound very close.* **5** °seem, °appear, °look; °strike °one, give one the °impression or °feeling or °sense (that); °resemble, °seem or °look °like: *It sounds as if you don't want to come to my party. That sounds like Russian to me.* **6** °ring, (be) °activate(d), (be) °set or °touch(ed) off, °signal: *Anyone walking into the room sounds the alarm. The alarm sounds when the beam is broken.* **7** Sometimes, **sound out**: articulate, °pronounce, °enunciate, utter; °voice, vocalize: *I was taught to speak clearly, to sound each consonant and vowel.* **8** Sometimes, **sound out** or **off**: °shout

(out), °cry out, °yell (out): *Sound out those numbers loud and clear!* **9 sound off**: °vituperate, °complain, °bluster, grumble, *Slang* °bitch: *Today Mr Morrison was again sounding off about the service in the café.*

sound[2] *adj.* **1** undamaged, uninjured, °whole, unmarred, in °good °condition or °shape, °intact, unimpaired, °unscathed: *When the vase was sold to you it was sound.* **2** °healthy, °hale (and °hearty), °fit (as a fiddle), °robust, °vigorous, blooming, °rosy, ruddy: *Old Tom is as sound as ever.* **3** °firm, °solid, °substantial, °strong, °sturdy, °tough, °rugged, °durable, well-built, well-constructed, dependable: *A business, like a building, must be built on sound foundations if it is to last.* **4** °sane, balanced, °normal, °rational, °wholesome, °reasoning, °reasonable, clear-headed, lucid, right-minded, °responsible, °practical, °prudent, °politic, °wise, °sensible, °logical, common-sense, commonsensical, °astute, °far-sighted, °perceptive, perspicacious, percipient; valid, °good, °judicious, °reliable, °useful: *As Juvenal said, 'Mens sana in corpore sano,' or 'A sound mind in a sound body'. My old teacher gave me a lot of sound advice.* **5** °safe, °secure, °good, °conservative, non-speculative, °solid, riskless; °profitable: *Are you sure that utilities are a sound investment now?* **6** unbroken, uninterrupted, undisturbed, untroubled, °peaceful, °deep: *I drank the potion and at once fell into a sound sleep.*

sound[3] *v.* **1** Often, **sound out**: °plumb, °probe, °test, °check (out or into), °fathom, °inquire or °enquire or °question, °poll, °canvass, °investigate, °examine, °survey: *Sound out the membership on their feelings about increasing the dues.* **2** °dive, °plunge, °submerge: *The great whale sounded, almost taking the tiny boat down with it.*

sound[4] *n.* inlet, °strait(s), fiord or fjord, bight, (sea) loch, bay, arm of the sea, cove, *Scots* firth: *The breeze freshened as we sailed across the Sound of Mull.*

sour *adj.* **1** acid, acidic, °tart, vinegary, lemony, acidulous or acidulent, acidulated, acescent, acerbic: *This apple has a pleasant, slightly sour taste. Do you like sour dill pickles?* **2** turned, °bad, (gone) °off, fermented, curdled, °rancid, spoilt or spoiled: *If the food is sour, throw it away.* **3** °disagreeable, unpleasant, °distasteful, °bad, °nasty, °bitter, °terrible: *The poor service and facilities made the entire holiday a very sour experience.* **4** acrimonious, °bitter, °embittered, unpleasant, churlish, ill-natured, ill-tempered, bad-tempered, crusty, curmudgeonly, crabbed, crabby, grouchy, °cross, °cranky, °testy, °petulant, °impatient, °abrupt, °nasty, °curt, °caustic, °brusque, °peevish, °snappish, edgy, °sullen, morose, °gloomy, °discontented: *The waitress's sour expression matched her sour disposition.*
—*v.* **5** °turn, °spoil, curdle, go °bad or °off, °ferment: *Milk sours quickly in this climate if you don't refrigerate it.* **6** embitter, acerbate, disenchant, °exasperate, vex, *Colloq* peeve: *Being forced to practise for hours when a child was what soured my enjoyment of playing the piano.*

source *n.* **1** fountain-head, well-spring, °origin, provenance, provenience, inception, °start, °outset, °beginning, °root(s), commencement, °rise: *We set out to find the source of the Blue Nile.*

The mineral bauxite is the source of aluminium.
2 originator, °author, °creator, begetter:
Who is credited as the source of this quotation?
3 °authority, documentation; informant,
Colloq horse's mouth: *To verify the information, go to the source.*

sovereign *n.* **1** °monarch, ruler, emperor, empress, °king, °queen, prince, princess, potentate, °chief, °master, °mistress, shah, sultan; Akund (of Swat), Gaekwar (of Baroda), Nizam (of Hyderabad), Mehtar (of Chitral), Nucifrage of Nuremberg, Sheikh of Araby, *Colloq* supremo: *She is the sovereign and must be obeyed.*
—adj. **2** °supreme, °paramount, highest, °principal, °foremost, greatest, °predominant, °dominant, ranking, °leading, °chief, °superior, °pre-eminent, ruling, regnant, reigning, governing, all-powerful, °absolute, °unlimited: *The first-born of the monarch is vested with sovereign authority upon the monarch's death.* **3** °royal, °regal, °majestic, °noble, lordly, aristocratic, kingly, queenly: *He was hailed as the sovereign ruler of all the islands.*

sovereignty *n.* suzerainty, hegemony, °dominion, °rule, °pre-eminence, °power, °jurisdiction, °authority, °leadership, °command, °sway, °supremacy, ascendancy, primacy: *Anyone who doubted his sovereignty was seized and thrown into a dungeon.*

sow *v.* °seed, disseminate, °broadcast, °plant: *The grand vizier sowed the seeds of dissension amongst the subjects of the caliph.*

space *n.* **1** spaciousness, °room, °place, °expanse, elbow-room, °leeway, °margin, latitude, °play: *There was no space for another desk.* **2** °blank: *When the spaces are filled in, the puzzle is done.* **3** °interval, °lapse, °period, °time, hiatus, lacuna, °span, while, duration, °extent, °spell, °stretch, °pause, °wait, °intermission, °gap, °break, °interruption: *After a short space we were home again.* **4** °accommodation, °seat, berth, °room, °place: *Luckily, I got the last available space on the plane.*
—v. **5** °arrange, °organize, array, °set out, align, °range, °order, °rank, °lay out, °measure (out): *Space the trees about eight feet apart.*

spacious *adj.* °vast, °large, °extensive, °enormous, °wide, °broad, commodious, °ample, °expansive, °roomy, °huge, sizeable, capacious, °great, °immense, outsized, °voluminous, oversize(d): *The house was more spacious than it looked from the outside. Siberia offers spacious territory, ripe for habitation over the next century.*

span *n.* **1** °bridge, °link, °stretch, overpass, *Chiefly Brit* flyover: *We drove across the entire span in less than five minutes.* **2** °course, °extent, °interval, °stretch, °period, °time, °term, °spell: *In the short span of six hours we had crossed the Atlantic.*
—v. **3** °cross, °stretch over, °reach over, °extend over, °go over, °bridge: *A rude bridge spans the river at Lexington. Their lives spanned more than a century.*

spank *v.* °slap, smack, put *or* take over one's knee, thrash, °paddle, °chastise, °punish, °castigate; *Colloq* wallop, tan, (someone's) °hide, paddywhack, whack, give (someone) a (good) licking *or* hiding: *In those days when you misbehaved you were spanked.*

spanking *adj.* **1** spick and span, °smart, °bright, °snappy, gleaming, °brand-new, °fine,

°remarkable, °outstanding, °big, °large, °great: *You ought to see Jim Trowbridge's spanking new yacht.* **2** °brisk, °lively, °crisp, °bracing, °fresh, freshening, rattling, °strong, °invigorating, blustery: *A spanking breeze blew up from the west.* **3** °quick, °rapid, °swift, °lively, °snappy, °fast, °smart, °energetic, °vigorous, °brisk: *The pony drew the dogcart at a spanking pace.*

spar[1] *n.* mast, yard, yard-arm, boom, boomkin, gaff, jigger, mizzen, *Colloq* °stick, °pole: *The first gusts of the storm tore the remaining canvas from the spars.*

spar[2] *v.* **1** °fight, °box, exchange blows; shadow-box: *He was once the champion's sparring partner.* **2** °dispute, °argue, °bicker, squabble, wrangle, bandy words, have words; °fight, *Colloq* °scrap: *I have better things to do than spar with you over breakfast every day.*

spare *adj.* **1** °extra, °surplus, supernumerary, °auxiliary, °supplementary, additional; °odd, °leftover; in °reserve, in °addition: *We got a puncture, so Dad stopped and put on the spare wheel. Give them the spare room. Have you a spare cigarette?* **2** unoccupied, °leftover, °leisure, °free, °surplus, °extra; not spoken for: *Her demanding job left her very little spare time.* **3** °thin, °skinny, °scrawny, cadaverous, °gaunt, °raw-boned, °meagre, gangling, lank(y), °wiry, °slim, °slender; all skin and bones: *The spare, ragged figure crouched in the shadows, his hand outstretched in supplication.* **4** See **sparing**, below. **5** °meagre, °frugal, °small, skimpy, °modest, °scanty: *Their meals were spare but wholesome.*
—v. **6** °save, °rescue, °deliver, °redeem: *Bill spared me from a fate worse than death. Spare me the embarrassment of having to ask for my money back.* **7** °pardon, °let go, °release, have °mercy on, °let off, °free, °liberate: *At the last moment, the judge spared him.* **8** °allow, °relinquish, let go (of), °give, °award, °bestow, let have, °donate, °part with, °yield: *She decided she could spare a couple of pounds for the disaster appeal. Buddy, can you spare a dime?* **9** °avoid, °dispense with, manage *or* do without, °give up, °forgo, °forsake, °surrender, °sacrifice: *We spared a great deal of trouble by settling the dispute. Spare the rod and spoil the child.*

sparing *adj.* **1** °thrifty, °saving, °frugal, °spare, °careful, °prudent, parsimonious, °economical, °penurious, °mean; penny-pinching, stingy, niggardly, °miserly, °close, close-fisted, °cheap, *Colloq* °tight, tight-fisted, *Brit* mingy: *As sparing in his praise as he was in his purse, General Waller rarely complimented his troops.* **2** See **sparse**, 2, below.

spark *n.* **1** scintilla, °flicker, glimmer, glint, °sparkle, °speck, °hint, °suggestion, °vestige, atom, whit, °jot (or tittle), iota: *As long as a spark of life remained in his body he fought for freedom and justice.*
—v. **2** Often, **spark off**: °set *or* °touch off, ignite, °kindle, enkindle, °electrify, °animate, trigger, °energize, galvanize, °activate, °excite, °stimulate, set in °motion, °bring about, °start (up), °begin, °initiate, °inspire, inspirit, °provoke, °precipitate: *Was there any single factor that sparked the Renaissance?*

sparkle *v.* **1** °glitter, scintillate, glint, °flicker, °shine, °twinkle, wink, °blink, glimmer, °flash, coruscate, °blaze, °burn, °flame: *The setting sun*

sparkled on the sea. *Brian's eyes sparkled with an inner fire.* **2** effervesce, °fizz, °bubble: *We ordered a jeroboam of sparkling Burgundy.*
—*n.* **3** °glitter, scintillation, °twinkle, coruscation, °dazzle, °spark, °gleam, brightness, °brilliance, °radiance: *I fear that the sparkle has gone out of her smile.* **4** vivacity, liveliness, °fire, brightness, wittiness, effervescence, ebullience, °excitement, °animation, °vigour, °energy, °spirit, °cheer, °joy, light-heartedness, élan, zeal, °gusto, °dash, °life, °gaiety, °cheer, cheerfulness; certain something; *Colloq* vim, zip, zing, pizazz or pizzazz, oomph: *It is easy to see that she gets her sparkle from her mother.*

sparse *adj.* **1** °thin (on the °ground), °few (and far between), °meagre, °scanty, (widely) dispersed or scattered, °spread out, °spotty, in °short supply, °scarce: *Tourists are sparse in Scotland in January. Sparse blooms appeared on the rose-bushes this year.* **2** °little, °limited, °meagre, scant, °sparing, inappreciable, not much, °insignificant: *Sparse use was made of the new tennis court because of the rain.*

Spartan *adj.* austere, °strict, °severe, °harsh, °hard, °stern, rigorous, °rigid, ascetic, stringent, controlled, disciplined, self-denying, abstinent, abstemious: *He gave up all luxuries and today lives a Spartan life in the forest.*

spasm *n.* **1** convulsion, °throe, °fit, twitch, °paroxysm: *Deprived of his medication, Brian might go into spasms.* **2** °fit, °seizure, convulsion, °paroxysm, °spell, °outburst, °burst, °eruption: *After that, every time he said 'furniture', the crowd went into spasms of laughter.*

spasmodic *adj.* **1** spasmodical, paroxysmal, convulsive, jerky, jerking, °sudden, *Technical* spastic: *John was quite uneasy, unaware that Cynthia's spasmodic winking was due to a tic.* **2** °fitful, °irregular, °intermittent, arrhythmic, °random, interrupted, °sporadic, °erratic, °occasional, °periodic, unsustained, discontinuous, pulsating, cyclic(al), °broken: *Spasmodic peals of thunder shook the house.*

spate *n.* °flood, inundation, onrush, °onset, °rush, deluge, °outpouring, outflow, outflowing, °flow: *What did I say to provoke that spate of foul language?*

spatter *v.* °splash, splatter, speckle, bespatter, °spray, °dabble, daub, bedaub, sprinkle, besprinkle, *Brit* splodge, *US* splotch: *When she dropped the pan the grease spattered all over my new white flannels.*

spawn *v.* give birth to, °yield, °bear, °bring forth, °breed, beget, °create, °father, sire, °produce, °generate, engender, give °rise to, °bring about, °cause: *Donald's arrogance over his wealth spawned a great deal of resentment.*

speak *v.* **1** °talk, °converse, discourse: *We were not allowed to speak during lessons.* **2** °talk to, °converse or discourse with, °address, °say (something or anything) to: *She was speaking quietly to the children. That is no way to speak to your elders.* **3** °talk, °communicate in, discourse or °converse in, utter in, articulate in, °use: *Can you really speak Chinese?* **4** °express, utter, °say, °state, °tell, °pronounce, °enunciate, °voice; articulate, °make known, °communicate, °reveal, °indicate: *He is speaking the truth.* **5** °symbolize, betoken, °signify, °communicate, convey, °indicate: *Her refusal to return your love-letters speaks volumes.* **6 so to**

speak: as it were, in a manner of speaking, figuratively or metaphorically (speaking): *When it comes to employee benefits, the boss is Scrooge himself, so to speak.* **7 speak for**: **a** °support, °uphold, °defend, °stand up for, °plead for, make a plea for, °recommend, *Colloq* °stick up for: *Be quiet and let Simon speak for himself.* **b** act on or in behalf of, act for, °represent, act as agent for: *He is speaking for the whole staff when he expresses worries about the cuts.* **c** °demand, °require, °beg, °request, °ask for: *The situation speaks urgently for an effective drug rehabilitation programme.* **8 speak for itself**: be °self-evident, be °obvious, be °significant: *The fact that both your son and the ring are missing speaks for itself.*
9 speak of: °mention, advert to, allude to, °refer to, make °reference to, °comment on, speak or °talk about: *I begged you not to speak of her again in my presence.* **10 speak on**: °discuss, °address, discourse upon or on, speak to, °treat (of), °deal with, °examine, °touch upon or on: *In his presentation Dr Andrews spoke on the role of natural predators in pest control.* **11 speak out** or **up**: **a** °talk (more) loudly or °clearly, make oneself heard: *I cannot hear you unless you speak up a bit.* **b** °talk °freely or unreservedly, °express one's opinion, speak one's mind, °declare, come out, °state one's position, take a stand: *I heard a mother of ten speak out against birth control.*
12 speak to: **a** °reprove, °scold, °reprimand, °rebuke, admonish, °warn, °lecture: *After his father spoke to him, Nicholas stopped staying out so late.* **b** be °meaningful to, °appeal to, °influence, °affect, °touch: *Constance's poetry effectively speaks to the heart.* **c** accost, °address, °talk to, *Formal* apostrophize: *I have to speak to the teacher after class.* **d** See **10**, above. **13 spoken for**: °reserved, °engaged, bespoke, °set aside, accounted for, chosen, selected: *I'm afraid that the purple dress has already been spoken for, madam.*

speaker *n.* orator, lecturer; keynoter; °rabble-rouser, demagogue, *Colloq* tub-thumper, spieler: *It was my function to introduce the speaker.*

spearhead *v.* **1** °launch, °initiate, °lead (the way), take the °initiative, °pioneer, blaze the trail, break the ice, take the °lead, be in the van or vanguard: *He spearheaded medical research into arthritis.*
—*n.* **2** vanguard, advance guard, van, forefront, cutting edge: *They claim to be the spearhead of space technology.*

special *adj.* **1** °particular, °specific, °exceptional, uncommon, especial, °rare, °unusual, out of the °ordinary, °extraordinary, °different, °unorthodox, unconventional, °unique, °precise, °individual, °singular, °distinctive, specialized, °certain, °remarkable, inimitable, idiosyncratic, °curious, °peculiar, °odd, °strange, °bizarre, °weird, one of a kind, °distinguished, °notable, °noteworthy: *They have a special way of communicating with each other. I bought something very special for your birthday. A special relationship sprang up between us.* **2** °significant, °important, °momentous, earth-shaking, °memorable, red-letter; °gala, festive, celebratory: *The fifth of September is a special day in our family.* **3** °pointed, concerted, °deliberate, °particular, °extra, °determined: *After I had made a special effort to get there, nobody was home.* **4** °exclusive, °express, °individual, °extra: *Send the packet by special messenger.*
5 °dear, °intimate, °particular, °good,

°close, °bosom, °staunch, °loyal, °faithful,
°devoted, °steadfast; dearest, °best, closest;
esteemed, valued: *I wasn't aware that John Spencer
was a special friend of yours.* **6** °prime, °primary,
°major, °prominent, °paramount: *I shouldn't
attach any special importance to her demands.*
—*n.* **7** See **speciality**, 2, below.

specialist *n.* °expert, °authority, °professional,
°master, connoisseur, maestro, artiste, artist,
°adept: *Pierre Legrand is a specialist in matching
antique furniture finishes. Such work requires specialist
knowledge.*

speciality *n.* **1** °expertise, °talent, °genius,
°gift, °skill, °aptitude, °trade, °craft,
°accomplishment, °ability, °strength, °forte,
strong point, °capability, adeptness, °art,
°sphere, °field, °area, °subject, concentration,
specialization, métier, *Chiefly US and Canadian*
specialty, *Colloq* °bag, °thing, cup of tea, baby,
claim to fame: *Dr Mann's speciality is tropical
diseases.* **2** pièce de résistance, spécialité de la maison,
°special, *Chiefly US and Canadian* specialty, *US*
blueplate °special: *Today's speciality is calves' brains
au beurre noir.*

specially *adv.* °especially, °particularly,
°custom, °expressly, exclusively: *I had this suit
specially made for me.*

specific *adj.* **1** °definite, °precise, °exact,
°particular, °explicit, °express, unambiguous,
°definitive, clear-cut, unequivocal, (well-)
defined, °determined, specified, °individual,
°peculiar, °certain, °limited, indicated,
°predetermined, established, spelt *or* spelled
out, delineated, °set, °distinct, °fixed, circumscribed, restricted: *Each part has its specific
function.* **2** Often, **specific to**: °characteristic
(of), °unique to, °individual (to), *sui generis*,
°proper (to), °typical (of), °peculiar to, identified with, °personal (to), °discrete (to), °special
(to), associated with: *The disease is specific to one
area only. Are these problems group-specific?*

specification *n.* **1** °identification, identifying,
°description, describing, particularization, par-
ticularizing, specifying, naming: *The police were
relying on a specification of the ringleaders by an
informer.* **2** itemization, itemizing, °list, listing,
check-list, inventory, °list of °particulars,
°detail, enumeration: *When can you let me have
the specifications for the new building?*
3 °requirement, °qualification, °condition,
°restriction, °stipulation, °consideration: *The
specification called for green marble and no substitute.*

specify *v.* particularize, °enumerate, °itemize,
°name, denominate, °list, °indicate, °mention,
°identify, cite, °define, °detail, °stipulate, °spell
out, °set out *or* forth, individualize, be °specific
about, delineate, °determine, disambiguate,
°establish: *You must specify the source of each
quotation.*

specimen *n.* °sample, °example, °instance,
exemplar, °representative, °representation;
°illustration, °case (in point), °type, °model,
°pattern: *This is a specimen taken from the
Pre-Cambrian strata. Using this as a specimen, can
you reproduce the entire fabric?*

specious *adj.* °deceptive, °superficial, casuistic,
ostensible, misleading, °apparent, °seeming,
fallacious, °sophistic(al), °plausible, °likely, conceivable, °possible, °supposed, purported, presumed, presumable, °alleged, °so-called: *The

candidate affected a specious show of liberality
merely to attract votes. Do not be misled by specious
reasoning.*

speck *n.* °spot, °dot, fleck, mote, speckle, °mark,
°bit, °particle; °crumb, iota, °jot (or tittle), whit,
atom, molecule, °touch, °hint, °suggestion,
°suspicion, tinge, °modicum, °amount, °grain,
smidgen *or* smidgin: *There's a speck of soot on your
collar. Is there a speck of truth in what she says
about you?*

speckled *adj.* spotted, °mottled, dotted,
sprinkled, °flecked, stippled, °dapple(d),
freckled, brindle(d); discoloured, spattered,
bespattered: *I can see by looking at it that it's a
speckled trout.*

spectacle *n.* **1** °show, °display, °sight,
°performance, °event, °presentation,
°exhibition, °exhibit, °exposition,
°demonstration, °extravaganza, °marvel,
°wonder, °sensation: *Instead of criticizing everything in life, why not just sit back and enjoy the
spectacle?* **2** °fool, laughing-stock, °curiosity: *Joan
makes a spectacle of herself by her solo dancing when
she gets a little tipsy.* **3** **spectacles**: eyeglasses,
°glasses, *Colloq* specs: *He wears spectacles only for
reading.*

spectator *n.* °witness, °eyewitness, °observer,
viewer, °onlooker, looker-on, watcher,
beholder: *There were more spectators than participants at the spring dance.*

spectral *adj.* °ghostly, ghostlike, °phantom,
°eerie, wraithlike, incorporeal, °unearthly,
°supernatural, °weird, *Colloq* spooky: *I could have
sworn there was a spectral figure, dressed in white,
standing near the window.*

spectre *n.* **1** °ghost, °phantom, wraith, apparition, °vision, °spirit, °shade, revenant, doppelgänger, chimera, *Colloq* spook, bogeyman *or*
bogyman: *Each year the spectre appeared to her on
Christmas Eve.* **2** °image, °vision, (mental)
°picture: *Again the horrible spectre of war and
pestilence arose.*

speculate *v.* **1** Often, **speculate on** *or* **upon**
or **about** *or* **over**: °reflect (on *or* about *or* over),
°consider, °muse (on *or* about *or* over), °meditate
(on *or* over *or* about), °contemplate (on *or*
about), cogitate (on *or* about *or* over), °think (about *or*
over *or* on), °ponder (over *or* about), °mull over,
°chew on *or* over, ruminate (on *or* over *or* about),
°wonder (about), °deliberate (over *or* on *or*
about), °weigh, °judge, °evaluate, °theorize (on
or about), conjecture (on *or* about), postulate,
hypothesize: *I have been speculating about whether
I should take a holiday in the Algarve. Why not go
and enjoy yourself instead of speculating on the world's
injustices?* **2** °gamble, wager, take a °chance,
Colloq have a flutter, play the market, take a
°plunge: *She is too conservative to speculate in the
stock market.*

speculation *n.* **1** conjecture, °guess,
°hypothesis, theory, guesswork, postulation,
°surmise, °supposition, °opinion: *My speculations
have often proved true. Both the steady-state and the
big-bang theories of the origins of the universe are
pure speculation.* **2** °thinking, rumination, cogitation, °reflection, meditation, contemplation,
°consideration, cerebration, pondering, wondering, deliberation, °evaluation: *All serious philosophers engage in idle speculation.* **3** gambling,

°gamble, wagering, wager, taking (a) °chance(s) or °risk(s), chance-taking: *Her speculation on the market paid off handsomely.*

speculative *adj.* **1** °intellectual, ideational, °abstract, cogitative, notional, °theoretical, °hypothetical, conjectural, suppositional, suppositious *or* suppositious, suppositive, °rational, ratiocinative, °ideal, idealized, °idealistic, °unrealistic, unpractical, °impractical, analytical: *Frank's theories about climate change were entirely speculative and substantially wrong.* **2** °risky, °hazardous, °uncertain, °unreliable, untrustworthy, °doubtful, dubious, untested, unproven, unproved, *Colloq* iffy, chancy, *Slang* °dicey: *You ought to invest your money in less speculative enterprises.*

speech *n.* **1** speaking, talking, articulation, °diction, °language, °expression, enunciation, elocution, speech pattern; communication: *His speech is marred by a lisp. Martha studied speech at a well-known drama school.* **2** °oration, °address, °lecture, °talk, discourse, disquisition, °sermon, homily; °tirade, °harangue, philippic; (sales) pitch, °line, °song and dance; *Colloq* spiel, blast: *Her speech left her audience awed with her knowledge of the subject. When the householder opens the door, you launch into your speech about the encyclopedia.* **3** °dialect, idiolect, °jargon, °parlance, °idiom, façon de parler, °language, °tongue, *Colloq* °lingo: *English speech varieties range from Scots to Cockney to Texan to Jamaican.*

speechless *adj.* **1** °mute, °dumb, voiceless: *He was speechless and in shock for two days following the accident. They claim to speak for animals who are, of course, speechless themselves.* **2** °dumbfounded *or* dumfounded, dumbstruck *or* dumbstricken, wordless, struck °dumb, °tongue-tied, °thunderstruck, shocked, dazed, °inarticulate, paralysed, nonplussed, *Slang Brit* gobsmacked: *He was speechless with fury to find his car missing.*

speed *n.* **1** °rapidity, fleetness, quickness, speediness, swiftness, °velocity, °dispatch *or* despatch, °hurry, hurriedness, °haste, hastiness, celerity, alacrity, expeditiousness, °expedition, briskness, promptness, timeliness; suddenness, precipitateness, precipitousness, abruptness: *We reached a speed of Mach 2. What is the speed of your new computer? The speed of her reactions will be recorded during the experiment.*
—*v.* **2** Often, **speed up**: accelerate, °move, °expedite, °forward, °advance, °facilitate, °boost, °further, °promote, °help, °assist, °aid, *Colloq* give a °leg up: *He vowed to do anything he could to speed the troops' return from the battlefield.* **3** °hasten, make °haste, °hurry, °rush, °charge, dart, °bolt, °shoot, °run, °race, sprint, °fly, °streak, °scurry, °tear, °hustle, °scramble, scamper, °career, °bowl along, °go *or* °fly like the wind, *Colloq* °go °hell for leather, °go like a bat out of hell, belt along, °step on it, put one's foot down, zip, zoom, skedaddle, °go like a °shot, *US* hightail it, step on the gas, °go like greased lightning, make tracks, *Slang US* burn rubber: *Where the road is straight, cars speed along at up to 120 miles per hour.*

speedy *adj.* **1** °quick, °rapid, °swift, °brisk, °expeditious, °fast, °immediate, °prompt: *What happened to the form of justice under which the accused were guaranteed a speedy trial?* **2** °hasty,

°precipitate, °precipitous, °hurried, °summary: *Some of the townspeople favoured the wrong kind of speedy justice—by lynching.* **3** °fleet, °nimble, wing-footed, winged, °fast, °quick, °rapid, °swift: *Carol is one of the speediest sprinters on our team.*

spell¹ *n.* **1** °period, °interval, °time, °term, °season; °stint, °turn, °run, °course, °shift, °tour (of duty), °watch, °round: *We had a spell of bad weather. Each of us had a spell at the tiller during the crossing.*
—*v.* **2** °relieve, °replace, °substitute for, °take over for *or* from: *After 36 hours of uninterrupted duty, I needed someone to spell me for a while.*

spell² *n.* **1** °enchantment, allure, °charm, °magic, witchcraft, witchery, °fascination, captivation, enthralment: *She had them all under her spell.* **2** incantation, °formula, °charm: *The priest uttered some spell and I found myself unable to move.* **3** °attraction, °lure, allure, °appeal, °draw, °pull, °magnetism, °fascination, °influence, mesmerism, hypnotic effect: *We were drawn ever onward by the spell of the jungle.*

spell³ *v.* **1** augur, portend, presage, °promise, hold °promise of, °signify, °point to, °indicate, °omen, °bode, look like, °amount to, °mean: *Harry's conviction will spell the end of his career as a bank robber.* **2 spell out**: °specify, delineate, make °clear *or* °plain *or* °explicit, °clarify, elucidate: *She despises you—I can't spell it out for you more plainly than that.*

spellbinding *adj.* fascinating, °enchanting, °enthralling, captivating, enrapturing, bewitching, mesmerizing, charming, °overpowering: *The preacher put on one of his most spellbinding performances.*

spend *v.* **1** °pay out, disburse, °expend, °lay out, *Colloq* fork out, dish out, °shell out, *Brit* splash out: *That man spends more for a suit than you earn in a year.* **2** squander, °throw away, °fritter away, °waste, °go through, °splurge, °lavish, °dissipate: *He spends money as if it's going out of style.* **3** °devote, °allot, °assign, °invest, °put in, °pass: *If you don't spend more time with the children they'll forget they have a father.*

spendthrift *n.* **1** °profligate, °wastrel, (big) spender, squanderer, °prodigal: *Because her nephew is such a spendthrift, she put his inheritance in a trust fund.*
—*adj.* **2** °wasteful, free-spending, °prodigal, °profligate, squandering, °extravagant, °improvident: *The chancellor's spendthrift budget will increase inflation.*

spent *adj.* **1** drained, °exhausted, °prostrate, °tired, °fatigued, fagged out, °weary, wearied, °worn out, *Colloq* (°dead) °beat, done in, done for, all in, dog-tired, played out, burnt- *or* burned-out, °used up, *Brit* knackered, done up, *US* pooped: *He was totally spent after sitting in the airport all night during the storm.* **2** °exhausted, °used up, emptied, gone, expended, finished, fini, consumed, depleted: *At 70, he was wrong to feel that his life was spent.*

spew *v.* Often, **spew forth** *or* **out** *or* **up**: belch (up *or* out *or* forth), °vomit (up *or* forth), °regurgitate, °spit up *or* out, °spout, °discharge, °emit, °eject, °send forth, °spurt, °gush, °throw up *or* out, disgorge, *Slang* puke: *The volcano spewed forth lava for six days and nights.*

sphere *n.* **1** °globe, °orb, globule, spherule; °drop, droplet, °bubble: *Flotation is provided by* *thousands of hollow plastic spheres.* **2** °society, °class, °level, °caste, °rank, °domain, walk of life, °station, °stratum, °position: *They did not belong to the same social sphere.* **3** °area, °field, °province, °subject, °discipline, °range, °speciality *or US* specialty, °forte, *Colloq* bailiwick, °territory, °department, °thing, °bag: *Are Gregorian chants within Stanley's sphere of interest?*

spherical *adj.* spheric, globular, °round, ball-shaped, ball-like, globelike, globe-shaped, globose *or* globous, globoid, globate(d), spheroid(al): *They chose simple, spherical lampshades for the sitting-room.*

spice *n.* **1** condiment, °relish, °seasoning, °flavour(ing); herb: *Much of the purpose of early explorers was to search for spices.* **2** °zest, spiciness, piquancy, °tang, pungency, °bite, sharpness, poignancy, °gusto, °excitement, °seasoning, °dash, élan, °colour, °life, °vigour, °interest, stimulation, °stimulant, °spirit, *Colloq* vim, zip, °pep, °kick, pizazz *or* pizzazz, °punch, ginger, °pepper: *A holiday in the Bahamas will add a little spice to our lives.*
—*v.* **3** °season, °flavour: *Highly spiced food does not agree with many people.* **4** Often, **spice up**: °enliven, inspirit, °stimulate, invigorate: *The proprietor felt that the new editor should try to spice up the magazine.*

spicy *adj.* **1** zesty, zestful, piquant, tangy, (well-)spiced, (well-)°seasoned, °hot, peppery, °sharp, °pungent, °snappy, °biting, full-bodied, °aromatic, °savoury, flavoursome, flavourful: *This curry is a little too spicy for my taste.* **2** °off colour, indelicate, °suggestive, °risqué, °improper, °indecent, indecorous, ribald, °racy, °bawdy, °unseemly, °offensive, titillating, °sexy, *Colloq* °hot: *This magazine often publishes spicy nude photos.* **3** °scandalous, °sensational, °outrageous, °notorious, revealing, revelatory, °intimate: *She likes to read about the spicy goings-on in Hollywood.*

spike *n.* **1** skewer, °stake, prong, treenail, °nail, °peg, °picket, °pin, pike, °spine: *To subdue a vampire, drive a wooden spike through its heart.*
—*v.* **2** °impale, °stab, °stick, spear, °pierce, °spit, °lance: *He was spiked through the thigh by a bayonet.* **3** disable, °thwart, nullify, °disarm, °block, °frustrate, °foil, °void, balk, °check, °cancel, annul: *Our plans for the picnic were spiked by the weather.* **4** °strengthen; °drug, °poison, *Slang* slip in a Mickey (Finn): *I passed out because my drink was spiked.*

spill *v.* **1** °pour (out *or* over), overflow, slop *or* °run *or* °brim over: *The milk spilt all over the floor.* **2** °waste, °throw out, °lose: *Don't cry over spilt milk.* **3 spill the beans**: °reveal *or* °tell *or* °disclose *or* divulge all *or* everything, °blab, °tattle, let the cat out of the bag, °confess, *Slang* squeal, be a stool-pigeon *or* stoolie, spill one's guts, °sing (like a canary), *Brit* blow the gaff: *Finnegan spilled the beans to the cops.*
—*n.* **4** °outpouring, °flood, °leak, leakage: *Don't tell me there's been another oil spill!* **5** °fall, °tumble, °accident, *Colloq* cropper, header: *Crutchley had a nasty spill at the third fence in the Grand National.*

spin *v.* **1** °revolve, °turn, °rotate, °gyrate, °twirl, whirl, °twist, °reel, °pirouette, °pivot: *The car spun out of control on the ice. Fred spun Ginger around the dance floor.* **2** °invent, concoct, °make up, °devise, °produce, °fabricate, °weave, °relate,

retail, °recount, °narrate, °tell, °unfold: *Each night, father would spin a new chapter in the yarn of the vagabond princess.* **3** be °dizzy, suffer °vertigo, swim, whirl, be °giddy: *My head was spinning from so much attention by the media.* **4 spin off**: °separate, °derive: *The manufacturer spun off two new companies specializing in parts and service.* **5 spin out**: °prolong, protract, °drag *or* °draw out, °stretch out, °perpetuate, °continue, °extend, keep alive, keep going: *The case was spun out for years in the courts.*
—*n.* **6** whirl, whirling, °twirl, twirling, °turn, turning, gyration, °reel, °pirouette, °revolution, revolving, rotation, rotating: *He puts a spin on the ball when he throws it. Is the spin of all planets in the same direction?* **7** °drive, whirl, joyride, °ride, °tour, °excursion, °outing, jaunt: *On Sunday afternoons we sometimes went for a spin in the car.*

spine *n.* **1** °backbone, spinal column, vertebrae: *He can't stand up straight—he has curvature of the spine.* **2** °thorn, needle, barb, °spike, °spur, prong, quill, °ray, barbel, °bristle, °prickle, *Technical* barbule, spicule *or* spiculum *or* spicula: *The surface of the sea urchin is covered with needle-like spines.*

spineless *adj.* **1** *Technical* invertebrate: *There are more species of spineless creatures than those with internal backbones.* **2** °weak, °feeble, °flabby, °irresolute, weak-willed, °indecisive, °ineffectual, °ineffective, °impotent, °powerless: *After her reign, any king would appear spineless.* **3** °cowardly, dastardly, pusillanimous, timorous, lily-livered, white-livered, craven, °fearful, °timid, spiritless, °squeamish, *Colloq* yellow, chicken-hearted, chicken, yellow-bellied, °wimpish: *She said you were spineless because you refused to go into the lions' cage.*

spiral *n.* **1** helix, °coil, corkscrew, °screw, scroll; whorl, volute, °turn, curl: *In earlier Greek motifs, the spiral is commoner than the rectangular fret.*
—*adj.* **2** helical, coiled, screw, corkscrew, cochlear *or* cochleate; scrolled, volute(d), whorled: *A spiral staircase is attractive and space-saving, but hard to use.*

spire *n.* **1** column, °tower, belfry; steeple, *flèche*: *The spire of the church was repeatedly struck by lightning that night.* **2** °top, °pinnacle, apex, °peak, °summit, °acme, °tip, °crest, °crown, °vertex: *We climbed till we stood on the highest spire above the valley.*

spirit *n.* **1** anima, °breath, °life, °vitality, vital spirit, pneuma, °soul, consciousness, °psyche, self, °heart, °essence: *Though past eighty, Mr Wilkins has a great deal of spirit. Even though she is gone, Annabel's spirit is still with us.* **2** °character, temperament, °temper, °persona, °disposition, °mind, °will, will-power, °attitude, °bent, °inclination, °energy, °ardour, °desire, °impetus, °drive, °urge, eagerness, °zest, zeal, zealousness, °fire, °passion(s), °enthusiasm, motivation, mettle, °resolution, resolve, °intention, °enterprise: *We have always admired the spirit of the early pioneers. Bill has shown a lot of the right spirit.* **3** °zest, pungency, piquancy, °warmth, °fire, °animation, °life, liveliness, vivacity, vivaciousness, °panache, élan, °dash, °spice, *Colloq* °sauce, °pepper: *He needs to put more spirit into his sales presentation.* **4** See **spectre, 1**, above. **5** °bravery, °courage, °grit, °backbone, valour, °pluck, °daring,

stout-heartedness, manfulness, manliness, gameness, resoluteness, °will, will-power, *Colloq* vim, °spunk, get-up-and-go, (right) °stuff, °guts, *US* sand: *Johnston has the spirit to be a marine.* **6** °meaning, °sense, °tenor, signification, purport, °intent, °intention, °purpose, °aim, °implication, °message, °essence, °quintessence, °core, °heart, °meat, °pith, °substance, marrow: *The spirit of the agreement is different from the way the lawyers worded the contract. Is it in keeping with the spirit of the law?* **7** °attitude, °principle, °thought, °idea, °inspiration, °notion, °feeling, °inclination, impulse: *Christmas is associated with the spirit of giving.* **8** Often, **spirits**: °temper, °mood, °sentiments, °feelings, °cheer, °humour, °frame of °mind; °morale: *I hope he took my criticism in good spirit. You seem to be in pretty good spirits today. My spirits are quite low.* **9 spirits**: **a** °feelings, °mood, °temper, °sentiments; °morale, esprit de corps, team spirit: *Spirits were high at the annual boat races.* **b** °alcohol, °liquor, °whisky, strong °drink, *Colloq* °booze, fire-water, *Slang chiefly US and Canadian* hooch or hootch: *It is illegal to sell spirits to minors.*
—*v.* **10 spirit away** *or* **off**: °abduct, °make off or away with, °carry off, °transport, °take away, °kidnap, °steal (off *or* away with), °whisk away, abscond with; make °disappear: *A thief spirited away a painting from the exhibition. She was spirited away by a band of elves.*

spirited *adj.* °lively, °sprightly, °energetic, °vigorous, °animated, sparkling, °dynamic, °buoyant, °effervescent, °vivacious, °ardent, mettlesome: *The horse I chose was a bit too spirited. The barrister presented a spirited defence for his client. The 1970s saw spirited revivals of art nouveau and art deco styles.*

spiritual *adj.* **1** °sacred, ecclesiastic(al), churchly, °clerical, °priestly, devotional, °holy, °divine, sacerdotal, °religious, non-secular: *Father Craig was in charge of the spiritual aspects of our lives.* **2** non-material, incorporeal, °psychic(al), °mental, psychological, inner: *Spiritual needs are less easily satisfied than physical needs.*

spit *v.* **1** expectorate; dribble, salivate, drool, °slaver, sputter, splutter; °discharge, °spew (forth), °eject: *Spitting is forbidden. Don't you hate people who spit when they talk? The volcano spat huge boulders into the sky.* **2 spitting image** *or* **spit and image**: °twin, °duplicate, clone, °image, counterpart, °likeness, °copy: *She is the spitting image of her mother.*
—*n.* **3** spittle, saliva, drool, *Technical* sputum: *A large gobbet of spit clung to his beard.*

spite *n.* **1** spitefulness, maliciousness, malice, malevolence, malignity, °ill will, °venom, spleen, °rancour, °animosity, °gall (and wormwood), °resentment, °bitterness, °hostility, °antagonism, hatred, °hate, *Colloq* bitchiness: *Just out of spite, Marian saw to it that he didn't get the job.* **2 in spite of**: °despite, °notwithstanding, °regardless of, ignoring, in defiance of: *In spite of his efforts to be helpful, she despises him.*
—*v.* **3** °annoy, °irritate, vex, °upset, disconcert, °offend, °provoke, °discomfit, pique, °put out, °hurt, °injure, °wound, *Colloq* peeve, get under (someone's) skin, needle, *US* do a number on:

He would cut off his nose to spite his face. He told her he was happy only to spite her for having divorced him.

spiteful *adj.* °rancorous, °bitter, acrimonious, malevolent, malicious, °venomous, °hateful, invidious, °hostile, antagonistic, unfriendly, unforgiving, retaliative *or* retaliatory, °punitive, retributive *or* retributory: *Cutting off Colin's allowance because he forgot your birthday was a spiteful thing to do.*

splash *v.* **1** °spatter, bespatter, splatter, °shower, °spray, sprinkle, besprinkle, *Brit* splodge *or US also* splotch; mottle, °spot: *The painters splashed paint all over the floor. My freshly washed car was soon splashed with mud again.* **2** blazon, °spread, °plaster: *Was that your picture splashed across the front page of yesterday's paper?*
—*n.* **3** °spatter, °spray, splatter, sprinkle, °spot, °stain, °smear, smudge, *Brit* splodge *or US also* splotch: *There's a splash of tomato sauce on the tablecloth.* **4** °impression, °show, °uproar, ado, brouhaha, °sensation, commotion, °excitement, *US* foofaraw, *Colloq* to-do: *After all the advance publicity, he was sure to make a big splash in the theatre.*

splendid *adj.* **1** splendorous, °magnificent, resplendent, °dazzling, °gorgeous, °showy, °dashing, °marvellous, spectacular, °grand, °glorious, °lavish, °ornate, °sumptuous, °majestic, °brilliant, °extraordinary, °exceptional, °superb, °supreme, °imposing, °impressive, awe-inspiring, °awesome, °lush, °plush, °rich, °luxurious, *Colloq* splendiferous, °posh, swank(y), ritzy: *The mausoleum built by Shah Jehan for his wife was far more splendid than his own palace.* **2** °impressive, °marvellous, °brilliant, °eminent, °prominent, °superior, °noteworthy, °notable, °celebrated, °illustrious, °famous, °distinguished, °exemplary, °remarkable, °admirable, °conspicuous, °outstanding, °sublime, °striking, °extraordinary, °successful, °meritorious, creditable: *His splendid victory at Waterloo was the climax of his military career.* **3** °excellent, °superior, °pre-eminent, °fine, °marvellous, °extraordinary, °exceptional, °unbelievable, °incredible, first-class, °unequalled, unsurpassed, °fabulous, °peerless, °matchless, °nonpareil, °superlative, °praiseworthy, °laudable, *Brit* °brilliant, *Colloq* °great, °colossal, supercolossal, stupendous, fab, °fantastic, °super, smashing, A-1 *or* A-one, tiptop, °capital, *Brit* brill, *Slang* far-out, °way-out, °dandy, °cool, keen, *US* solid, out of °sight, fantabulous, boss, °neat, major: *Bill is a splendid dancer.*

splendour *n.* **1** magnificence, °grandeur, °brilliance, °display, °radiance, resplendence, sumptuousness, stateliness, majesty, panoply, °spectacle, °show, °glory, °pomp, gorgeousness, °dazzle, refulgence, °beauty, splendidness, exquisiteness, luxuriousness, richness, lavishness, °luxury, *Colloq* swankiness, poshness, swank, ritziness: *There was nothing to match the splendour of the court of Louis XIV.* **2** °brilliance, °shine, °lustre, °light, effulgence, brightness, °glitter, °dazzle, refulgence, luminosity, luminousness, °gloss: *The splendour of the city's golden domes was reflected in the setting sun.*

splice *v.* **1** °join, °unite, °marry, °bind, conjoin; °knit, °entwine, intertwine, °braid, plait, °twist, interlace: *After the two rope ends are spliced together, they should be seized with marline.*

—*n.* **2** joining, °union, splicing, °joint, °connection *or Brit* connexion, °tie, °bond, binding, °fastening, linking, linkage: *A proper splice will probably be stronger than the single cable.*

splinter *n.* **1** °sliver, °fragment, °piece; °scrap, shard, °shred, °chip: *A splinter of glass is stuck in my finger.*
—*v.* **2** °shatter, °break, °fragment, °split, °disintegrate, smash to smithereens: *The lamp hit the floor and splintered into a million pieces.*

split *v.* **1** Often, **split up** *or* **apart**: °divide, °separate, °cleave, °cut *or* °chop apart, °cut *or* °chop in two, °pull *or* °tear °apart, °rend, °break *or* °snap apart *or* in two, °break up, °come apart, °rupture, °partition, °detach, become °detached; bisect, dichotomize: *He split the log with one blow of his axe. The ship split apart on the reef. The party may split on the tax issue.* **2** Often, **split up**: °divorce, °separate, go °separate ways, °break up, °part company: *After 30 years, the Hitchcocks have decided to split up.* **3** Often, **split up**: °branch, fork, °diverge, °separate: *The road splits to pass round the pond.* **4** Often, **split up**: °divide (up), apportion, °deal out, °dole out, °distribute, °allot, °share *or* °parcel out, °carve up: *Why don't we split the dinner bill five ways?* **5** °burst, °crack *or* °break up, °fall apart *or* about, *Slang* bust: *I laughed so much I thought I'd split!* **6** °leave, °depart, °go, *Slang* take a (run-out) °powder, take it on the lam, °beat it, scram, skedaddle: *When they heard the sirens of the police cars, they split.*
—*n.* **7** °crack, cleft, fissure, °chink, °cranny, °slit, °slot, °crevice, °groove, °furrow, °channel, sulcus; °gap, hiatus, lacuna, °opening, °separation, °division, chasm; °rift, °break, °rupture, °fracture; °slash, °gash, °tear, °rip, °rent: *The edges of the tectonic plates mark splits in the earth's crust. Pressure caused the splits in these plaster columns. I had to borrow a tablecloth to cover up the split in my trousers.* **8** °division, dichotomy, °schism, °breach, °rupture, °partition, disunion, °discord; °break, °separation: *Don't you think that the issue will cause a split within the party?*
—*adj.* **9** divided, separated; halved, bisected, cleft; °cut, °broken, fractured: *The result was a split vote along party lines. Their first containers were of split bamboo.*

splurge *n.* **1** °display, °show, ostentatiousness, °extravagance, °indulgence, access, °splash, °burst, °outburst, °spree: *In his final splurge he bet everything on the number 14.*
—*v.* **2** Often, **splurge on**: squander *or* °dissipate *or* °waste *or* °burn (up) *or* °throw away money (on), °show off *or* °flaunt one's money, *Slang* °blow everything (on): *Victor splurged on toys for the children.*

spoil *v.* **1** °ruin, °destroy, °wreck, °queer, °mess up, °upset, °demolish, °harm, °damage, *Colloq* °kill: *You really spoiled everything by telling Mum about my pet frog. Spare the rod and spoil the child.* **2** °damage, °mar, °injure, °harm, °deface, disfigure, °scar, °blemish: *The painting was spoiled by some fanatic who slashed it.* **3** °baby, mollycoddle, °coddle, °indulge, °pamper, °dote on, spoonfeed, *Rare* cocker: *Barbara really spoils her family terribly by indulging their every whim.* **4** °turn, °go °off *or* °bad, curdle, moulder, °decay, °decompose, become addle(d), °rot, °putrefy, mildew: *The milk will spoil if not refrigerated.* **5 be spoiling for**: °itch (for *or* after),

°yearn (for), be °eager (for), be °keen (for), °look for, be °bent on, be °desirous of, crave, be after: *If you give Tom a drink he'll be spoiling for a fight.*
—*n.* **6 spoils**: °loot, °booty, °plunder, °pillage, °prizes, pickings, *Slang* swag, °take, °goods, boodle: *The Nazis took the paintings as spoils of war.*

spoilsport *n.* °killjoy, damper, dog in the manger, *Colloq* wet blanket, *US* party pooper: *Some spoilsport tipped off Jane about her surprise birthday party.*

spoken *adj.* **1** °oral, vocal, °verbal, viva voce: *My spoken commentary was recorded for later broadcast. He has an excellent command of spoken French.* **2 spoken for**: See speak, 13, above.

sponsor *n.* **1** °backer, °supporter, promoter, angel, °patron, Maecenas, subsidizer: *Make a contribution and we will list you as a sponsor of the games.* **2** (radio *or* television) advertiser: *The American broadcasting catch-phrase 'A word from our sponsor' is not to be taken literally.*
—*v.* **3** °back, °support, °promote, °fund, °patronize, °subsidize, °finance, °underwrite: *Hughes agreed to sponsor a campaign to clean up the environment.*

spontaneous *adj.* **1** unannounced, °unpremeditated, unplanned, impromptu, °extemporaneous, extempore, °unprepared, unrehearsed, °offhand, ad lib, spur-of-the-moment, *Colloq* off the cuff: *Miss Malkin's spontaneous speech could not have been written out.* **2** °natural, unforced, unbidden, °instinctive, instinctual, °unconscious, reflex, °automatic, °mechanical, °immediate, °offhand, °unguarded, °unthinking, unwitting, °involuntary, °impetuous, °impulsive, *Slang* knee-jerk: *How could you doubt the sincerity of such an outburst of spontaneous affection? My spontaneous reaction is to beg you not to take up sky-diving.*

sporadic *adj.* °occasional, °intermittent, °random, °irregular, uneven, °erratic, °chance, unexpected; °spasmodic(al), °fitful, °periodic(al): *There has been sporadic unrest in that area of the city.*

sport *n.* **1** °recreation, °diversion, °pastime, °amusement, °entertainment, °play, °distraction, °relaxation, divertissement, °pleasure, °enjoyment, °fun: *I fish for sport, not to earn a living.* **2** jest, °humour, °fun, °mockery: *They often call him rude names, but only in sport.* **3 make sport of**: °tease, °deride, make a laughing-stock (of), (hold up to) °ridicule, make a °fool of: *She doesn't like it when you make sport of her husband.*
—*v.* **4** °frolic, gambol, °cavort, romp, °caper, °play, °frisk, °lark, rollick, °skip about: *These octogenarians are sporting about like young foals.* **5** °show off, °exhibit, °flaunt, °display, °wear: *Keith arrived, sporting the latest in Italian footwear.*

sportive *adj.* °frisky, gambolling, cavorting, frolicking, romping, capering, rollicking, °sprightly, coltish, °spirited, °frolicsome, °buoyant, gamesome, °gay, °kittenish, °merry, °playful, °gleeful, light-hearted, °blithe, prankish, waggish: *He watched a sportive group of children playing hide-and-seek.*

sportsmanship *n.* °fair °play, sportsmanliness, fairness, honourableness, °honesty, °honour,

°probity, scrupulousness, °integrity, uprightness, °justice, justness: *Good sportsmanship
requires that the loser congratulate the winner.*

sporty *adj.* °informal, °casual, °stylish, °chic,
°smart, °trendy, °fashionable, modish, à la
°mode, up to °date, °showy, °rakish, *Colloq*
swank(y), °loud, *Slang* classy, °swell, °flashy,
snazzy, °sharp, *US and Canadian* spiffy: *He came
to dinner wearing sporty clothes. Yes, I suppose you
might call Fred a sporty dresser.*

spot *n.* **1** °mark, °patch, °speck, °blot, blotch,
°blemish, speckle, fleck, °particle, mote, macula, smudge, °stain, °stigma, discoloration, *Brit*
splodge *or US also* splotch: *There's a spot of ink on
your shirt.* **2** °site, °place, °locale, °location,
locality, °scene, °setting, °section, °area,
°neighbourhood, °quarter: *The Coopers picked out
a lovely spot to build their new house.* **3** °morsel,
°bit, °bite, *Colloq* smidgen *or* smidgin: *Let's stop
in here for a spot of tea.* **4** °predicament, °situation,
°quandary, °mess: *John said he was in a bit of a
spot, and needed to borrow £20 until the end of the
week.* **5 spots**: eruptions, °pimples, acne, pustules, blackheads, comedos *or* comedones,
whiteheads; °boils, blains, wens; pock-marks;
Old-fashioned US and Canadian hickeys: *Teenagers
often get spots.*
—*v.* **6** °see, catch °sight of, glimpse, discern,
°identify, °pick out, °distinguish, °single out,
°detect, °sight, °recognize, °make out, descry: *I
think I spotted Molly in the crowd.* **7** °mark, °stain,
fleck, speckle, °spray, °splash, °spatter, bespatter, °sully, °soil, °dirty, °taint, besmirch,
smudge: *The car's shiny new paintwork was spotted
with mud.*

spotless *adj.* **1** °immaculate, °clean, gleaming,
°shiny, °polished, unspotted, spick and span:
The floor is so spotless you could eat off it. **2** °pure,
unsullied, unassailable, °flawless, °faultless,
°untarnished, °blameless, °irreproachable: *Samantha has a spotless reputation.*

spotlight *n.* **1** arc °light, searchlight, *US* pin
spotlight, *Colloq US* (pin) spot: *I couldn't see the
audience with the spotlight shining in my eyes.*
2 °focus (of attention), limelight, public
eye: *How does it feel to have been in the spotlight
most of your life, Miss Hallward?*
—*v.* **3** °light (up), °illuminate, °focus (light)
upon *or* on, °shine *or* °shed *or* °throw *or* °cast
light upon *or* on, °emphasize, highlight, draw
attention to, °feature, give °prominence to,
°stress, accentuate, °accent, °point up, underscore, underline: *The students held a sit-in to spotlight
the cuts in their grants.*

spotty *adj.* **1** spotted, dotted, °speckled,
freckled, °flecked, blotched, blotchy, stained,
°marked, pied, piebald, brindle(d), skewbald,
°mottled, motley, °dapple(d), macular, foxed;
soiled, °dirty; *Brit* splodgy, splodged *or US also*
splotchy, splotched: *Pages of some old books are
spotty with brown stains.* **2** pimply, pimpled,
blotched, blotchy, acned, pock-marked, pocky,
bad, *Scots* plouky *or* plooky: *Ian used to have a
spotty complexion, but it's clear now.* **3** patchy,
°irregular, uneven, °erratic, °sporadic,
°capricious, °fitful: *Radio reception in our area is
spotty during electrical storms.*

spout *v.* **1** °discharge, °emit, squirt, °spurt, jet,
°shoot, °gush, °erupt, °spew (up *or* out *or* forth),
°spit, °eject, disgorge, °vomit (up *or* forth), °pour
(out *or* forth), °flow, °stream: *Steam spouts from

many vents in Iceland. The water came spouting out
of the hose and drenched me.* **2** °ramble on, °rant,
°rave, carry on, pontificate, orate, declaim, °hold
forth, maunder (on), witter on, expatiate,
speechify, °talk, *Colloq* °go on, *Brit* rabbit on:
*Harry, as usual, was spouting about his golf handi-
cap.*
—*n.* **3** waterspout, gargoyle, downspout, duct,
°drain, °outlet, conduit: *The rainwater drains
into the gutters, then into the spouts.* **4 up the
spout**: gone, °lost, destroyed, beyond hope *or*
°recovery, to be written off *or* °abandoned: *Our
dream of finding the treasure was now up the spout.*

sprawl *v.* **1** °spread (out), °stretch (out), straddle,
°ramble, °meander, °wander, °straggle,
°branch out: *Greater Los Angeles sprawls over a
huge area of some 450 square miles.* **2** °spread
out, °stretch out, loll, °lounge, °slouch, °slump,
°recline, °lie about *or* around: *A dozen guests
were sprawled on blankets at the beach party.*
—*n.* **3** °spread, °stretch, °expansion, °extension:
*Some suburbs of large cities have been swallowed up
in urban sprawl.*

spray[1] *v.* **1** sprinkle, °spatter, °scatter, °shower,
°disperse, °diffuse, atomize, °spread: *Try to spray
the insecticide evenly over the plants.*
—*n.* **2** °shower, sprinkling, drizzle, °mist,
sprinkle, spindrift *or* spoondrift: *The strong wind
carried the spray from the whitecaps right up into
the streets of the town.* **3** atomizer, sprayer,
sprinkler, vaporizer, aerosol: *Richard bought me
a cologne spray for Mother's Day.*

spray[2] *n.* flower *or* floral arrangement, nosegay,
posy, °bouquet, sprig, °branch, bough: *The scores
of tiny roses were interspersed with sprays of
baby's-breath.*

spread *v.* **1** Often, **spread out**: °diffuse,
°distribute, °disperse, disseminate, °broadcast,
°sow, °scatter, °strew, °shed, dispel, °dissipate:
*Spread the mulch as evenly as possible to a depth of
several inches.* **2** Often, **spread out** *or* **around**:
°broadcast, °publicize, °make known, bruit
about, °air, televise, °circulate, °publish,
°distribute, disseminate, trumpet, °announce,
°pronounce, promulgate, advertise, enounce,
make °public, °tell the world, herald, °repeat,
°recite: *Start spreading the news: I'm leaving
today.* **3** Often, **spread out**: °unfold, °draw out,
°display, °stretch out, °open out, °extend, °lay
out, °fan out, unroll, unfurl: *Please spread the
cloth on the table.* **4** Often, **spread out**: °stretch
(out), °extend, protract, °prolong, °drag out,
°distribute, °disperse: *The bank said I could spread
the payments over twenty years.* **5** Often, **spread
out**: °stretch, °extend, °separate, put apart *or*
out, °part: *He spread his arms and Lorna rushed
into them.* **6** °grow, °develop, °increase, broaden,
°expand, °extend, °widen, °enlarge, mushroom,
°proliferate, °sprawl, °branch out; metastasize:
*To meet the demand for the pies, bakeries began to
spread throughout the country. The cancer, unchecked,
was bound to spread.* **7** °smear, °apply, °smooth,
°put, °rub, °cover, layer, °plaster, °plate, °coat,
°wash, °glaze, °paint, varnish, overlay, overspread; °cloak, °mantle, swaddle, °wrap, blanket: *I was careful to spread the paint evenly, avoiding
streaks. When the cake has cooled, spread the chocolate icing over it.*
—*n.* **8** spreading, °extension, extending,
°expansion, expanding, enlargement, enlarging, °development, developing, °increase,

increasing, °proliferation, proliferating, broadening, °growth, widening, mushrooming, dispersion, dispersal, dispersing, dissemination, disseminating, °distribution, distributing, dispensation, dispensing: *The spread of the disease is uncontrolled. One of the functions of a university is to encourage the spread of knowledge.* **9** °extent, °expanse, °area, °span, °sweep, vastness, °stretch, °reach, °breadth, °depth, °size, dimensions, compass, °limits, °bounds, °boundary or boundaries: *As our craft accelerated past the moon, we were awed by the spread of empty space that lay before us.* **10** °range, °extent, °scope, °span, °difference: *There was too much of a spread between the cost and the selling price.* **11** °feast, °banquet, °meal, dinner, repast, barbecue; °table; *Colloq* °feed: *I have never seen a spread like the one laid on for the returning champions.* **12** butter, margarine, °jam, jelly, °preserve, °conserve, confiture, paste, *US old-fashioned* oleo: *What kind of spread do you like on your toast?* **13** ranch, landholding, holding, °property, °place, plantation, °farm, homestead: *His spread in Texas eventually amounted to 10,000 acres.* **14** bedspread, counterpane, coverlet, bed-cover, °cover, quilt, eiderdown, duvet, afghan, *US* comforter, *US and Canadian* throw: *Leave the spread off the bed, Carlotta, as I want to take a nap.*

spree *n.* °frolic, romp, °lark, °outing, escapade, °revel, wild °party, °fling, debauch, °orgy, bacchanalia; drinking-bout, carousal, *Colloq* °bender, binge, °jag: *Bruce has gone off on another of his sprees.*

sprightly *adj.* °lively, chipper, spry, °vivacious, °cheerful, °gay, °brisk, °animated, °sportive, °active, °alert, °nimble, °agile, °energetic, °jaunty, °perky, playful, °spirited: *She is quite sprightly for a grandmother of 78.*

spring *v.* **1** °leap, °bound, °jump, °hop, vault, dart, °fly, °bounce: *He sprang to his feet when she came into the room. When Tom came to the stream, he sprang over it. The leprechaun sprang out from behind a tree.* **2** °arise, °appear, °grow, °come up, °rise, °come into being or °existence, be born, °emerge, °sprout, °shoot up, °burst forth: *Where the dragon's teeth were sown, an entire army sprang up.* **3** Often, **spring up** or **from**: °originate, °begin, °start, evolve; °proceed from, °stem from, °descend from, °derive from, °come from, °develop from: *He learned how the practice of scratching the head in perplexity had sprung up. I wondered where the term* horse latitudes *sprang from.* **4** start or begin or experience or cause to occur or appear or happen °suddenly or unexpectedly, °broach, °pop, introduce or divulge or reveal or disclose °suddenly or unexpectedly: *The canoe sprang a leak and started to sink. He likes to spring trick questions at candidates in an interview.* **5 spring for**: °pay for, °treat (someone) to, assume the °expense(s) of: *If you go to a place I choose, I'll spring for dinner.* —*n.* **6** °leap, °bound, °jump, °hop, vault, °bounce, °skip: *In one spring the cat cleared the garden wall and was off.* **7** bounciness, °bounce, resiliency, °resilience, springiness, buoyancy, °elasticity, sprightliness, airiness, °flexibility: *Despite her age, there's still a lot of spring in her step.* **8** °source, fount, fountain-head, well-spring, °well, °origin, °beginning, °root: *From what secret spring does his understanding arise?* **9** springtime, Eastertide, Maytime: *At 35, James is still in the spring of life.*

—*adj.* **10** vernal: *We exulted in the spring sunshine.*

sprout *v.* bud, germinate, °come up, °arise, °begin, bloom, blossom, °flower: *With this warm weather, everything in my garden is beginning to sprout.*

spruce *adj.* **1** °neat, °dapper, °smart, °trim, well turned out, °well-groomed, °elegant, *Colloq* natty: *Peter Thornton turned up for dinner looking as spruce as can be.* —*v.* **2 spruce up**: °tidy (up), °neaten (up), °primp, °clean (up), °straighten out or up, smarten (up), titivate or tittivate: *Some people are coming to dinner, so first spruce up your room and then spruce yourself up.*

spunk *n.* °nerve, °courage, °pluck, °spirit, gameness, °resolve, °resolution, mettle, °heart, °grit, spunkiness, °backbone, marrow, *Colloq* °guts, °gumption, *Brit* °bottle, *US* sand: *Frances has shown she has tremendous spunk to have got this far despite her handicap.*

spur *n.* **1** goad, °prod, urging, impulse, °incitement, instigation, prompting, °pressure, stimulus, stimulation, °incentive, °provocation, °inducement, °encouragement, °motive, motivation: *The company paid the workers a bonus for each piece they completed as a spur to productivity.* **2** °projection, prong, °spike, °spine, gaff, barb, quill, tine, barbel, barbule, process: *The hook has a spur that prevents the fish from disengaging.* **3 on the spur of the moment**: impetuously, impulsively, unthinkingly, unpremeditatedly, impromptu, on the spot; rashly, thoughtlessly, recklessly, °hastily, brashly, incautiously, unexpectedly, °suddenly: *On the spur of the moment, we decided to fly to Cap d'Antibes for the weekend.* —*v.* **4** goad, °prod, °urge, egg on, impel, °incite, °prompt, °press, °push, °pressure or *Brit* pressurize, °stimulate, °drive, provoke, °induce, °encourage, °motivate, °excite, °animate: *The sales force are spurred on by the huge bonuses the company offers.*

spurious *adj.* °false, °counterfeit, °sham, °fake, °fraudulent, °bogus, °mock, °imitation, simulated, unauthentic, ungenuine, forged, feigned, °pretended, °deceitful, meretricious, contrived, °factitious, °artificial, ersatz, °synthetic, *Colloq* pseudo, °phoney or *US also* phony: *His brother was jailed for peddling spurious Egyptian burial artefacts to archaeologists.*

spurn *v.* °reject, disdain, °scorn, contemn, °despise, °rebuff, °repudiate, °refuse, °sneer at, snub, °brush off, °turn down, turn one's °back on or upon, °look down on or upon, *Colloq* cold-shoulder, turn one's nose up at, °sneeze at: *Judith spurned her father's offer of a loan.*

spurt *n.* **1** °burst, access, °effort, outbreak, °spell, °interval, °spate, °moment, °instant: *With a sudden spurt of speed he caught up with me.* **2** °increase, °advance, acceleration, °rise, °improvement: *After a brief spurt in business in January, everything stopped.* —*v.* **3** °gush, °spew, squirt, jet, °shoot, °erupt, °burst, °surge: *The minute the plumber left, water began spurting out of the drain again.*

spy *n.* **1** double °agent, foreign °agent, secret(-service) °agent, intelligence °agent, °undercover °agent, mole, fifth-columnist, CIA man or woman or °agent, MI5 or MI6 man or woman or °agent; °informer, informant, *Colloq*

mole, *Slang* stool-pigeon, stoolie, fink, ratfink:
*In those days, everyone was a spy and you could trust
no one.*
—*v.* **2** Usually, **spy on** *or* **upon**: °follow, °shadow,
°trail, °watch, °observe, °reconnoitre, keep
under °surveillance, *US* surveil, *Colloq* °tail,
°check out, case: *Why should anyone from a foreign
government be spying on my mother?* **3** espy,
glimpse, °spot, catch °sight *or* a glimpse of,
descry, °note, °notice, °see, discern: *I spied him
getting into a yellow convertible.*

spying *n.* espionage, °undercover work, secret
service; detection, °intelligence, °surveillance:
Virtually every government engages in spying.

squad *n.* °unit, °team, °band, °company, °crew,
°force, troop, cadre, °gang, °section, °group,
squadron, °platoon, °party: *They decided to call in
the drugs squad. Has the work squad returned to
base yet?*

square *adj.* **1** equilateral, quadrangular, rectangular, right-angled, quadrilateral, four-sided,
cubic, cubed, six-sided, boxy: *She bought a work
of art consisting of three square pieces of red plastic
on a mauve ground. He keeps trying to put square
pegs into round holes.* **2** °equal, on a °par, °even,
on °equal terms, settled, balanced: *With this
payment, our accounts are now all square.* **3** °even,
°true, °exact, °straight, °accurate, °precise,
°correct: *Make sure that the corners are perfectly
square.* **4** °honourable, °upright, °honest,
straightforward, °fair (and square), °decent,
°ethical, °open, (°open and) °above-board,
°right, (°right and) °proper, °clean, °just,
°equitable, *Colloq* °level, on the °up and
up: *I have never had anything but square dealings
with Fred Latham.* **5** healthful, °healthy,
°nutritious, °substantial, °solid, °full,
°generous, °satisfying, °filling, unstinting: *You
could always count on three square meals a day when
staying at Auntie Maisie's.* **6** °naïve, °innocent;
°bourgeois, °conservative, conventional,
°unsophisticated, °provincial, °old-fashioned,
conformist, °strait-laced, unimaginative,
°predictable, *Colloq* antediluvian, uptight, out
of it, not with it, not in the know, not °hip *or*
hep, unhip, °stuffy, behind the times, °straight,
US L-7: *We were at the age when anyone over 25 was
considered square.*
—*n.* **7** rectilinear figure, rectangle; cube, °block:
*He took a square of wood and quickly carved it into
the shape of a duck.* **8** plaza, piazza, place, °park,
(village) °green, market-place, °market (square),
agora, quadrangle: *We like to sit on the benches in
the square outside my house and chat with the
neighbours.* **9** °bourgeois, °conservative, conformist, traditionalist, (old) °fogy *or* fogey,
die-hard; °outsider; *Colloq* stuffed shirt,
fuddy-duddy, *US* longhair, L-7, *Slang US* nerd,
dweeb: *My parents did not understand me—they were
real old squares.*
—*v.* **10** °stiffen, throw back, °straighten (up),
°tense: *I squared my shoulders and prepared for the
worst.* **11** Usually, **square with**: °meet, °match
(with), °conform to *or* with, °obey, °correspond
to *or* with, °tally with, °accord with, °agree with,
°reconcile with *or* to: *These activities do not square
with the plans set out by the directors.* **12** °adapt,
°adjust, °change, °modify, harmonize,
°accommodate, °arrange, °comply with, °fit: *Ronald was unable to square his beliefs with what they
were teaching him at the seminary.* **13** °settle,

°arrange, come to °terms, °patch up, °clear up,
°satisfy, °fix: *Don't worry about the customs officials—I'll square it with them later on.*

squawk *v.* **1** cackle, screech, °shriek, °yell, yowl,
°whoop, hoot, °scream, °call, °cry: *The parrot
kept squawking 'Where is the treasure? Where is the
treasure?'* **2** °complain, grumble, whine, grouse,
°protest, °object, (make a) °fuss, °yap, yowl,
Slang bellyache, °bitch, kick, beef, °gripe, kick
up a °fuss: *Oh, stop squawking and get on with your
work!*
—*n.* **3** °complaint, grouse, grumble, °protest,
Colloq kick, beef, °gripe: *If you have a squawk,
take it up with the sergeant.*

squeamish *adj.* **1** °dainty, °delicate, °prudish,
punctilious, °demanding, °critical, °exacting,
°difficult, °fussy, °scrupulous, °fastidious,
°meticulous, °painstaking, °finicky *or* finical,
Colloq persnickety *or* pernickety, fuddy-duddy:
*The museum directors were too squeamish to put on
an exhibition of nudes.* **2** °nauseous, qualmish,
easily °disgusted *or* revolted *or* °nauseated: *Sam
was too squeamish to watch open-heart surgery on
the TV.*

squeeze *v.* **1** °press, compress, °compact,
°crush, squash, wring, °pinch, °nip, °grip, °tweak:
*Each morning Anne squeezes an orange to make fresh
juice for Edgar. Everyone knows that squeezing the
nose between the thumb and forefinger means that
something smells.* **2** °extract, wrest, °exact,
°extort, °milk, °wrench, °pry (out), °tear, *Colloq*
bleed: *It is doubtful that they will be able to squeeze
a contribution out of old Scrooge.* **3** °milk, *Colloq*
°shake down, bleed, °lean on, put the °screws
to, put the squeeze on, °twist (someone's) arm,
US put the arm on: *You'll have to squeeze Fletcher
if you want to get paid.* **4** °ram, °jam, °pack,
°stuff, °cram, °crowd, °force, °press, °wedge: *We
were squeezed into the train so tightly that I could
hardly breathe.* **5** °clasp, clench, °embrace, °hug,
°hold, enfold, °fold, °clutch, *Archaic* clip: *She
squeezed him close as they bade goodbye.*
6 squeeze through *or* **by**: °get through
or by, °pass, (barely) °succeed, *Colloq* squeak
through *or* by, (barely) °make it: *He managed to
squeeze through the exam with a pass mark, but it
was touch-and-go.*
—*n.* **7** °clasp, °embrace, °hug, °clutch, *Colloq*
°clinch: *She gave me a little squeeze to signal her
affection.* **8** °pressure: *I was beginning to feel the
squeeze between inflation and high interest
rates.* **9** °crush, °jam, °crowd, squash, °press:
*There was such a squeeze of people at the sale that
I couldn't get in.* **10** girlfriend, °mistress,
°sweetheart, *Colloq* sweetie, *Slang* moll, °broad,
Archaic doxy: *Willie showed up with his current
squeeze.* **11 put the squeeze on**: °press, bring
°pressure to bear on, °urge, °influence, *Brit* pressurize, *US* °pressure: *The bank was beginning to
put the squeeze on me to repay my overdraft.*

squelch *v.* **1** °suppress, °subdue, °put down,
°quell, °quash, °defeat, °overcome, °outdo,
°humiliate, *Colloq* shoot *or* slap down, take down
a °peg (or two), take the °wind out of (someone's) sails, settle (someone's) °hash: *The slightest
sign of disapproval from Noël was enough to squelch
the most arrogant toady.*
—*n.* **2** riposte, °retort, comeback, °quip, sally,
°gibe *or* jibe, barb, *Colloq* °wisecrack,
°put-down: *One of the best squelches was when Oscar*

Wilde said, referring to a bon mot, 'I wish I'd said that', to which Whistler said, 'You will, Oscar. You will.'

squire v. **1** °escort, °accompany, °conduct, °go with, °take; convoy: Who will squire my sisters to the prince's ball?
—n. **2** esquire, gentleman, landowner, landholder, landed °proprietor: The old squire held his head high among the county aristocracy.

squirm v. °wriggle, writhe, °twist, °flounder, °shift, °fidget, be (very) uncomfortable, agonize, Colloq °sweat: The boy squirmed under the stern gaze of the headmaster.

stab v. **1** °stick, °puncture, °prick, °lance, °jab, °pierce, °run through, °impale, °gore, °transfix, °knife, bayonet, skewer, °spike, °spit, spear, °pin; °plunge, °poke, °thrust: In the melee, George was stabbed in the arm. It is said that she stabbed a fork into his hand. **2 stab in the back**: °harm, °betray, °sell out, °double-cross, give the Judas kiss, play false with: As soon as he had left, they stabbed him in the back by phoning the authorities.
—n. **3** °puncture, °jab, °thrust, (stab-)°wound: The coroner's office reported that the body had six stabs in the abdomen. **4** °attempt, °try, °essay; °guess, conjecture: Even if you are wrong, you lose nothing by making a stab at the right answer. **5** °pang, °twinge, °pain, °ache, °hurt, stitch: Doctor, I get a terrible stab of pain in my side when I turn that way. **6 stab in the back**: treachery, °betrayal, °double-cross, Judas kiss, kiss of death, duplicity: Informing on someone to the tax inspector is a really nasty stab in the back.

stability n. **1** steadiness, solidity, firmness, soundness, sturdiness, °strength: These flimsy structures are not known for their stability. **2** steadfastness, constancy, dependability, reliability, °tenacity, °resolve, resoluteness, °perseverance, °determination, °persistence, durability, °lasting quality, solidity, °permanence: The stability of the government was in doubt as the crisis continued.

stable adj. **1** °steady, °solid, °firm, °sound, °sturdy, °strong, °durable, well-founded, °fast, °sure, established, deep-rooted, °stout: The building is designed to remain stable even in a severe earthquake. **2** °lasting, °enduring, long-lasting, long-standing, °secure, °steadfast, °steady, °strong, unchanging, unchanged, unchangeable, unalterable, °fixed, °invariable, unwavering, immutable, °permanent: A stable relationship has existed between our countries for generations. The relationship you and I enjoy has remained stable all our lives. **3** °sane, (°well-)balanced, °responsible, °reasonable, °sensible, °competent, °accountable: He seemed a nice, stable young man, and nobody would have guessed that he had a drugs habit.

stack n. **1** °pile, °heap, °mound, °mass, °accumulation, °hill, °mountain, °store, °stock, bank, °deposit, °supply, stockpile, °hoard, °load, °bundle, bale, Colloq US and Canadian stash: This stack of paper ought to be enough to last through the next printing. **2** haystack, cock, haycock, rick, rickle, hayrick, Brit clamp: The stacks were covered with a tarpaulin before it started to rain. **3** °collection, aggregation, °accumulation, agglomeration, amassment, °mass, °load, °pack, °amount, °abundance, °plenty, °profusion, °volume, array, °sea, °throng, multitude, °swarm, °host, °number, °quantity,

°pile-up: We have a huge stack of orders to process this morning. **4** smokestack, chimney, chimney-stack, funnel; Building soil stack: They built the stack very tall to carry the fumes away from the town below. **5 blow one's stack**: °anger, become °angry, become °furious or infuriated, °rage, °rant, lose one's °temper, Slang °blow or lose one's cool, get hot under the collar, °blow one's top: The boss will blow his stack if we miss the deadline.
—v. **6** Often, **stack up**: °pile (up), °heap, °accumulate, °amass, °store, °stock, stockpile, °hoard, °collect, aggregate, agglomerate, Colloq stash (away), squirrel away: Stack those boxes neatly in the corner. Has he stacked up enough points to qualify? **7 stack up**: **a** make sense, add up, °agree, jibe, be verifiable, Colloq °check out: The ledgers don't stack up with the cheque-book. The two sets of figures simply don't stack up. **b** °compare, °measure up, hold a candle to, be on a °par (with), be as good as: He could never stack up to Olivier.

stadium n. arena, °ground, amphitheatre, hippodrome, coliseum or colosseum, circus: The new football stadium can accommodate 60,000 spectators.

staff n. **1** °stick, °pole, °standard, baton, °rod, pikestaff, pike, °stake, cane, stave, °shaft, alpenstock, shillelagh, °club, truncheon, mace, crook, crozier, sceptre, °wand, caduceus: Carrying the ceremonial staff and dressed in full regalia, the officer impressively opened the royal court proceedings. **2** personnel, °employees, °help, workforce, °crew, °team, °organization: Before we introduced computers, we had a staff of fifty doing nothing but filing.

stage n. **1** °position, °situation, °grade, °level, °stratum, °tier, echelon, °step, °station, °place, °point, °spot, °juncture, °division, °phase, °lap; °status, °condition: We have to reach the third stage before going on to the fourth. **2** °platform, dais, podium; °rostrum: After the performance, the audience threw flowers onto the stage. **3 the stage**: show business, the °theatre, the boards, the footlights, Broadway, Chiefly Brit the West End; acting, Thespianism; Colloq showbiz: That first burst of applause decided her to make the stage her career.
—v. **4** °put on, °produce, °present, °mount, °exhibit: If we can't get the theatre, why don't we stage the show in Mr Kimble's barn? **5** °put on, contrive, °organize, °originate, °devise, °make up, concoct, °fake, trump up, stage-manage, °manipulate, °manoeuvre: It seems that the enthusiastic reception given his wife was staged solely for his benefit.

stagger v. **1** °totter, °reel, °lurch, °teeter, °sway, walk unsteadily or shakily, °pitch, °rock, wobble: When he staggered in, they thought he was drunk till they saw the knife in his back. I was already staggering under the burden of a heavy mortgage and three children and two elderly parents to care for. **2** °surprise, °amaze, °astound, °astonish, °overwhelm, °overcome, °dumbfound or dumfound, °shock, stupefy, °stun, °nonplus, °floor, confound, °bewilder, °startle, °jolt, °shake (up), take one's °breath away, make one's head swim, °take (someone) aback, throw (someone) off balance, °tax, °burden, Colloq flabbergast, °flummox, °bowl over, Slang blow (someone's) mind: The cost of *cleaning up the oil spill will be staggering. He was staggered by her announcement.* **3** °alternate, °space (out), °vary, rearrange, zigzag, *US* change off: *Working hours will be staggered during the holiday period. We could strengthen the structure by staggering the positions of the columns.*

stagnant *adj.* motionless, °standing, °still, °quiet, sluggish, unmoving, immobile, °flat; °stale, °foul, °putrid, putrescent, putrefied, polluted, °dirty, contaminated, °filthy: *The malarial mosquitoes thrive in pools of stagnant water in the tropical swamps.*

stagnate *v.* languish, °idle, vegetate, °deteriorate, °degenerate, °decline, go to °seed or pot, °decay, rust, moulder, °decompose, °spoil, °rot: *He felt he had stagnated in a backwater of civilization for far too long.*

staid *adj.* °sedate, °rigid, °stiff, prim, °dignified, °sober, °calm, composed, °quiet, restrained, °solemn, °serious, serious-minded, °grave, sober-sided: *One expects a judge to be rather staid in his behaviour.*

stain *n.* **1** °blot, °mark, °spot, discoloration, blotch, smutch, smirch, °speck, *Brit* splodge or *US also* splotch: *There's a stain on your tie.* **2** °mark, °blot (on the escutcheon), °stigma, °blemish, *Brit* °blot on one's copybook, *Colloq US* black eye: *His cowardice in battle was a permanent stain on his reputation.* **3** dye, °colour, colouring, °tint, tinge, pigment: *An indigo stain was used to bring up certain features in microscopy.*
—*v.* **4** °blot, °mark, °spot, discolour, blotch, speckle, dye, °spatter, splatter, tinge, smudge, smutch, °splash: *The tablecloth was stained red from the spilt wine.* **5** °spoil, defile, °ruin, smirch, besmirch, °taint, °tarnish, °stigmatize, °shame, °disgrace, °sully, °contaminate, °soil, °corrupt: *Her reign was stained with the blood of the thousands she had tortured and executed.*

stake[1] *n.* **1** °stick, °post, °spike, °picket, paling, °pale, °pole, pike, stave; palisade, °upright, °pillar, column: *They tied the goat to a stake and hid, waiting for the tiger to catch the scent.* **2 pull up stakes** °move (house), resettle, °move on, °migrate, °emigrate, °leave, °depart: *It was time to pull up stakes and find a new camp-site.*
—*v.* **3** °tether, °tie (up), °secure, °fasten, °picket, °lash, leash, °hitch, °chain: *The ponies were staked out in the pasture.* **4** Usually, **stake out**: **a** °fence (in or off), confine, °pen, °enclose, °close in or off, hem in, °shut in, impound, °cage, °wall in: *We hired a man to stake out a large enough area to keep the horses.* **b** °mark off or out, °define, delimit, °outline, demarcate, delineate, circumscribe: *The pioneers had already staked out the land they planned to cultivate.*

stake[2] *n.* **1** °bet, wager, ante, °risk, °hazard: *If you want to make the game interesting, you'll have to raise the stakes.* **2** investment, °interest, °share, involvement, concern: *Myra has a considerable stake in the outcome of the shareholders' meeting.* **3 at stake**: at °hazard, hazarded, at °risk, risked, on the table, in °jeopardy, jeopardized, °concerned, °involved: *Don't take the matter lightly, as Tom's reputation is at stake.*
—*v.* **4** °risk, °jeopardize, °venture, put (money) on, °chance, °hazard, °gamble, wager, °bet: *I had staked my last penny on that gold-mine.*

stale *adj.* **1** old, past its prime, unfresh, °dry, dried-out, hardened, °limp, wilted, withered, °flat, °sour, turned, (gone) off, °mouldy, °musty,

spoiled, °rotten: *All the food is stale because you failed to wrap it carefully.* **2** °old, °banal, overused, °antiquated, °old-fashioned, °threadbare, trite, clichéd, unoriginal, hackneyed, stereotyped, °tired, °weary, °boring, °tiresome, warmed-over, shop-worn, °familiar, °stock, °well-known, *Colloq* hand-me-down, *Brit* reach-me-down: *These comedians come up with the same old stale jokes year after year.*

stalemate *n.* °impasse, °deadlock, stand-off, °standstill, (dead or full) °stop, °tie; °check, checkmate, mate; *US* Mexican stand-off: *As both parties refused to back down, the situation was a stalemate.*

stalk[1] *v.* °follow, dog, °haunt, °shadow, °trail, °track (down), °hunt (down), °pursue, °hound, °chase, *Colloq* °tail: *The leopard stalked its prey in complete silence.*

stalk[2] *n.* °stem, °trunk, cane, main axis, leaf-stalk, °shaft, °spike: *The leaves cluster at the very top, leaving the entire stalk of the plant bare.*

stall[1] *v.* **1** °stop, °halt, °die, °quit, °shut down, °fail, cease operating, come to a °standstill, *Colloq* conk out: *My car stalled in the middle of rush-hour traffic—isn't that typical?*
—*n.* **2** °compartment, °stand, °booth, cubicle, alcove, °section, °space, °area, °slot, °enclosure, °quarters; °counter, table: *Several antiques dealers had hired stalls in the market.* **3** °shed, pen, cote, fold, coop, sty, corral, °enclosure, cowshed, barn, stable: *The animals belong in their stalls at night.*

stall[2] *v.* **1** °delay, °dawdle, dilly-dally, dally, loiter, °linger, temporize, °equivocate, °hesitate, prevaricate, play for time, waste time, stonewall, be obstructive, °put (someone or something) off; vacillate, dither, hedge, °procrastinate; *Brit* haver, *Colloq* beat about the bush, °drag one's feet, give (someone) the run-around: *He managed to stall for a while before handing over the money.*
—*n.* **2** stalling, °delay, hedge, hedging, °pretext, °subterfuge, °wile, °trick, °ruse, °artifice, °stratagem, °manoeuvre, °move, stonewalling, obstructionism, playing for time, procrastinating, procrastination, *Colloq* beating about the bush, °run-around, foot-dragging: *Her claim that she was dressing was nothing but a stall to give her time to hide the pistol.*

stalwart *adj.* **1** °robust, °stout, °strong, °mighty, °powerful, °rugged, °staunch, °hardy, °sturdy, °vigorous, °lusty, °indomitable, °solid, able-bodied, °brawny, °sinewy, °muscular, °fit, °healthy, °hale, (°hale and) °hearty, *Colloq* °husky, °hefty, beefy: *We shall need a dozen stalwart men to carry out the raid.* **2** redoubtable, °intrepid, undaunted, °resolute, °firm, °determined, unbending, °steadfast, °tenacious, unswerving, unwavering, unfaltering, unflinching, uncompromising, unyielding, persevering, °persistent, unflagging, °relentless, °tireless, °untiring, indefatigable: *Although they lost, their lawyers put up a stalwart defence.* **3** °brave, °courageous, °daring, °intrepid, valiant, °heroic, °manly, manful, °fearless, °indomitable, stout-hearted, °bold, °audacious, °game, red-blooded, plucky, mettlesome, lion-hearted, °spirited: *These stalwart knights met at dawn on the battlefield.*
—*n.* **4** °supporter, upholder, sustainer, °partisan, loyalist, (party) °faithful, trouper, °hero,

°heroine: *And most of all I want to thank those stalwarts who have supported me throughout this victorious campaign.*

stamina *n.* ruggedness, °vigour, vigorousness, (intestinal) °fortitude, robustness, indefatigability, staying °power, °endurance, °energy, °power, °might, mettle, (inner) °strength, staunchness, stalwartness, °courage, indomitability, *Colloq* °grit, °guts, starch, *US* stick-to-it-iveness, sand, *Taboo slang* balls: *Even at the age of 70, she still had the stamina to run in the marathon.*

stammer *v.* **1** stutter, °hesitate, hem and haw, °stumble, falter, °pause, *Brit* hum and haw: *Is he stammering from embarrassment or because he has a speech defect?*
—*n.* **2** stutter: *Many young people who have a stammer lose it when they get out of their teens.*

stamp *v.* **1** °trample, bring down one's foot; tread, °step, °tramp; *Colloq* stomp (on): *He flew into a rage and stamped on the floor, like a petulant child.* **2** °impress, °mark, imprint, °print, °record, °document, °register, log; °engrave, emboss, inscribe; °sign, °initial: *That last night in Rio is stamped forever in my memory. Their passports were stamped at the frontier.* **3** °brand, °label, °mark, °tag, °term, °name, °style, °identify, °categorize, classify, °characterize, °designate, denominate, °show to be: *The episode on Friday stamped him as someone not to be trifled with.* **4 stamp out**: °eliminate, eradicate, °abolish, get °rid of, annihilate, °exterminate, °kill, snuff out, °terminate, °end, put an °end to, °destroy, °put down, °put out, °extinguish, extirpate; °quell, °subdue, °suppress, °squelch, °repress: *Something must be done to stamp out the drug traffic.*
—*n.* **5** °mark, °sign, °hallmark, earmarks, °traits, °features, °characteristics: *Her work bears the stamp of genius.* **6** die, block, punch, °seal, matrix, °plate, die-stamp, stereotype, °mould; signet(-ring): *The stamps for the binding are not quite ready.* **7** °seal, (trade *or* service) °mark, °brand, logo, logotype, °symbol, °representation, colophon, imprint, °emblem, insigne (*singular of* insignia), °label, monogram, °sign, °crest, coat of arms, escutcheon, cartouche, signature, initials: *As it bears his stamp, it must belong to him.* **8** °character, °kind, °sort, °make, °fashion, °type, °cast, °mould, °grade, °style, °cut, °genre, °class, °level, kidney, feather, °stripe, classification, species, genus, °variety, °description: *Men of Randolph's stamp are hard to find amongst gentlemen and scholars alike.*

stampede *n.* **1** °rout, °flight, °scattering, °panic, °rush, °dash: *When the store opened its doors for its annual sale, we were nearly trampled in the stampede.*
—*v.* **2** °panic, °frighten, °rush, °scatter, °rout: *Millions of buffalo were killed by stampeding them off cliffs.* **3** °rush, °run, °race, °charge, take to one's °heels, °flee, take °flight: *At the cry of 'Fire!', the audience stampeded for the exits.*

stance *n.* °carriage, °bearing, deportment; °position, °posture, °attitude, °standpoint, °stand, °viewpoint, °point of °view: *Legs apart and arms akimbo, she assumed a defiant stance at the door. Her stance was that she must protect the children at all costs.*

stanch *v.* °staunch, °stop, °stem, °halt, °check, °arrest, °stay, °end, °cease; °prevent: *Apply pressure with a pad to stanch the flow of blood from the wound.*

stand *v.* **1** °rise, °arise, °get up, *Brit* be upstanding: *We all stood when the master of ceremonies proposed a toast to McArthur.* **2** Sometimes, **stand up**: **a** °set, °place (°upright), °position, °put, °move; up-end: *Please stand the cabinet in the corner.* **b** °stay, °remain (°standing): *Just for that you can go and stand in the corner!* **3** °endure, °survive, °tolerate, °brook, countenance, °face, confront, °last through, °abide, °allow, °accept, °take, °suffer, °bear, °withstand, °undergo, °experience, °cope with, °brave, stand *or* °bear up under, stand for, °withstand, °stomach, °weather, °handle, *Colloq* °put up with: *I could not stand another year in the tropics. She can stand neither hypocrites nor vanilla ice-cream.* **4** °continue, °remain, °persist, be *or* °remain in °effect *or* in °force, °prevail, °obtain, °apply, °exist: *The law will stand as it is till it is rescinded or modified by the court.* **5 stand by**: **a** °support, °defend, °back, stand *or* °stick up for, stand behind, be *or* °remain °loyal *or* °faithful to, °uphold, take the °side of, °side with, °sympathize with, *US* go to bat for: *No matter what he did, she always stood by him.* **b** °wait (in the wings), stand *or* °wait *or* stay *or* remain on the sidelines, be *or* stand °ready *or* °available *or* °accessible, be *or* stand in °readiness: *Would you mind standing by in case we need your help?* **c** °stick to, adhere to, °support, °maintain, °persist in, affirm, reaffirm, °confirm, °abide by: *We shall stand by every word of the agreement.* **6 stand down**: °resign, °quit, °step aside, °withdraw: *When it was revealed that she was taking steroids, she agreed to stand down from the team.* **7 stand for**: **a** °symbolize, betoken, °represent, °signify, °mean, be °emblematic of, °exemplify, epitomize, °illustrate, °typify, °refer to, allude to: *The initials in P. G. Wodehouse's name stand for 'Pelham Grenville'.* **b** °support, °advocate, °favour, °sponsor, promote, espouse (the cause of), °subscribe to, °back, °champion, lend support *or* one's name to, °second: *Norma has always stood for the principles of democratic freedom.* **c** °campaign for, be *or* °present (oneself) as a °candidate for, *US* °stump for, °run for: *Who will stand for chairman this year?* **d** See **3**, above. **8 stand in**: °substitute (for), °understudy (for), °replace, °relieve, °double for, take the place of, *US and Canadian* pinch-hit (for), *Colloq* °cover for: *If you can't get to the rehearsal, I'll stand in for you.* **9 stand out**: **a** be °prominent *or* °conspicuous *or* °noticeable, be °notable *or* °noteworthy: *With her green spike hairdo and a safety pin through her cheek, Kylie really stands out in a crowd. His farewell speech stands out in my mind as one of his best.* **b** °protrude, °project, °stick out, °jut out, °bulge, °obtrude, beetle, °overhang, °extend: *The balcony stands out over the village square.* **10 stand up**: **a** °stand, °rise, °arise, get to one's feet, °get up: *The boys had been taught to stand up when a woman entered the room.* **b** °endure, °last, °wear (well), °survive: *Today's products, with their built-in obsolescence, don't stand up to long use.* **c** °jilt, °break *or* fail to keep an °appointment with: *After waiting for two hours, he realized that he had been stood up.* **11 stand up for**: °support, °defend, take the °side of, °side with, °champion, °uphold, *Colloq*

°stick up for: *I shall never forget how you stood up for me when they accused me of cheating.* **12 stand up to**: **a** confront, °brave, °challenge, °encounter, °dispute, °question, °resist, °defy, °withstand: *He's a coward when it comes to standing up to authority.* **b** °resist, °defy, °withstand, °endure, °outlast, °last through, °suffer: *This material will stand up to years of abuse.* —*n.* **13** °position, °attitude, °stance, °posture, °policy, °philosophy, °point of °view, °viewpoint, °standpoint, °belief, °opinion, °sentiment, °feeling, °line: *I disagree completely with the Chancellor's stand on the economy.* **14** °defence, °resistance, °effort: *This campaign will be our last stand in trying to retrieve some of the market we lost.* **15** °stop, stopover, °halt, °stay; °performance, °show: *We do some one-night stands in the country before returning to Manchester.* **16** °counter, °booth, °stall, table; wagon *or Brit* waggon, barrow, °cart: *He sells fruit from a stand in the street.* **17** °rack, °frame, °bracket; hatstand, coat-rack: *This stand is for displaying a china plate. I left my hat on the stand in your office.* **18** staging, °platform, dais, °stage, bandstand, summer-house: *We like to go to the stand in the park to hear the band play.* **19** copse, grove, wood, °thicket, brake, *Brit* spinney, coppice: *Near the house was a small stand of beeches.*

standard *n.* **1** criterion, °measure, benchmark, °model, °pattern, archetype, °touchstone, °yardstick, °gauge, °guide, guideline, paradigm, °paragon, exemplar, °example, °sample, °type, °ideal, *beau idéal*, °rule, canon, °law, °requirement, °precept, °principle: *The metric system has become the standard in many countries. People resent having imposed on them the standards of another culture.* **2** °mean, °average, °norm, °par, °level, rating: *With many luxuries now necessities, the standard of living has improved enormously. The course was for students of intermediate standard.* **3** °flag, °banner, ensign, °emblem, °pennant, burgee, insigne (*singular of* insignia), guidon, gonfalon *or* gonfanon, labarum: *The black knight bore a curiously coloured standard into battle.* **4** °pole, °post, stanchion, lamppost, column, °pillar, °support, °pedestal, °pier, °footing, (upright) °bar *or* °rod *or* timber: *The car went out of control and knocked down two lighting standards.* —*adj.* **5** accepted, approved, °definitive, defined, °authoritative, °official, required, regulative, regulatory, textbook: *Must we follow standard procedure? The tests were conducted according to the standard methods.* **6** recognized, °prevailing, °prevalent, °usual, °customary, °habitual, °orthodox, °set, established, °regular, °familiar, °ordinary, °traditional, °classic, °stock, °typical, °normal, °staple, °conventional, °universal: *People in the south usually regard themselves as speakers of standard English.*

standardize *v.* °regiment, systematize, codify, °normalize, homogenize: *We could save money if we standardized the dimensions of the books we publish.*

stand-by *n.* **1** °supporter, defender, °backer, upholder, °partisan, °sympathizer, adherent, °stalwart: *His mother had always been his stand-by against the severity of his father.* **2** °substitute, surrogate, replacement, backup, °understudy, °second, *US and Canadian* °alternate: *They had a second ambulance as a stand-by in case the first* broke down or needed servicing. **3** °resource, °support, replacement: *I knew I could always count on you as a stand-by in case I had trouble.*

stand-in *n.* °double, °substitute, stunt man *or* woman; surrogate, replacement, °stand-by, backup, °understudy, °second, *US and Canadian* °alternate: *Any time they had to shoot a dangerous scene, my stand-in went through the motions.*

standing *adj.* **1** established, °set, °standard, °conventional, °customary, °usual, °normal, °regular, °fixed, °permanent, continued, continuing: *The club has standing rules concerning use of the card-room.* **2** °stagnant, motionless, unmoving, stationary, °still, °static: *Insects bred in the standing pools of rainwater.* **3** °continuous, °fixed, °ongoing, °perpetual, unbroken: *Michael placed a standing order for six cases of Beaujolais Nouveau every November.* **4** °erect, °upright, on one's feet, vertical, unseated: *Please remain standing till the signal is given to be seated.* —*n.* **5** °status, °rank, °station, °position, °place, °grade, °order, °level, °stratum: *Considering her standing in the party, Mrs Miller ought to win the nomination easily.* **6** eminence, °prominence, repute, °reputation: *Foster is a surgeon of considerable standing.* **7** Usually, **long standing**: (considerable) °age *or* longevity *or* °experience *or* seniority *or* duration: *Ivan is an art expert of long standing.*

standoffish *adj.* °aloof, °haughty, °unsocial, °reserved, °cool, frosty, °withdrawn, °remote, removed, °distant, °detached, °unapproachable, °inaccessible, uncongenial, unfriendly, unsociable; Olympian, lordly, °pompous, *Colloq* highfalutin *or* hifalutin, snooty: *Oliver is much too standoffish to deign to come to my party.*

standpoint *n.* °viewpoint, °point of °view, vantage point, °perspective, °position, °angle, °view: *From the standpoint of mice, cats do not make good pets.*

standstill *n.* (dead *or* full) °stop, °halt: *The car came to a standstill with the front wheels overhanging a cliff.*

staple *adj.* **1** °basic, °elementary, °essential, °necessary, requisite, required, °vital, °indispensable, °critical, °fundamental, °primary, °principal, °main, °chief: *These people cannot afford even staple commodities like flour and salt.* **2** °standard, °usual, °habitual, °ordinary, °customary, °prevailing, °normal, °conventional, °universal: *The staple fare on television seems to consist of old and new sitcoms.* —*n.* **3** Often, **staples**: °necessities, essentials, basics, °fundamentals: *Supermarkets disperse low-cost staples such as bread, tea, and milk to force shoppers to pass luxury items. Marital and financial problems are the staples of soap operas.*

star *n.* **1** °celestial *or* °heavenly body; evening star, morning star, falling star, shooting star, comet; nova, supernova: *It was a beautiful clear night and the sky was full of stars.* **2** °celebrity, °personage, °dignitary, VIP, °name, °somebody, luminary, °leading light, °leading man *or* woman *or* lady, °lead, °principal, diva, prima donna, °hero, °heroine, °idol, superstar, *Colloq* big shot, (big) draw, celeb, big °name, *Slang* top banana, headliner: *Clancy knows many of the big stars personally.* —*adj.* **3** °principal, °major, °leading, °important, °celebrated, °famous, famed, °prominent, °eminent, °pre-eminent, °distinguished,

°brilliant, °illustrious, unequalled, °peerless, °matchless, °incomparable, unrivalled, inimitable, unmatched, °unparalleled, °top, °foremost: *A new local rock band was the star attraction at the Hippodrome.*
—v. **4** °feature *or* be featured; play *or* act *or* take the °lead *or* the °leading part *or* role: *He began his career starring in spaghetti westerns.*

stare v. **1** °gaze, °gape, goggle, °gawk, °watch, *Colloq* °rubberneck, *Slang Brit* gawp: *The people were powerless to do anything but stare as the molten lava engulfed the city.*
—n. **2** °fixed *or* °blank °look; goggle, °gaze: *The teacher fixed her with a stare and she blushed with guilt.*

stark adv. **1** °completely, °utterly, unqualifiedly, °wholly, °absolutely, °entirely, °totally, fully, °altogether, plainly, °obviously, °clearly, certifiably: *Is that an elephant on the beach, or am I going stark staring mad? The children were running around stark naked.*
—adj. **2** °plain, °simple, °Spartan, °severe, unembellished, °unadorned, °cold, °bare, °harsh, °hard, °grim, bald, °blunt: *The room looks less stark with curtains. Just give me the stark facts without all the elaboration.* **3** °harsh, °severe, °bleak, austere, °barren, °desolate, °dreary, °grey, depressing, ravaged, °empty, °vacant, *Literary* drear, *Colloq US* spooky: *As day dawned, I looked out over the stark landscape of the nuclear winter.* **4** °sheer, °complete, utter, °absolute, °perfect, °pure, °thorough, thoroughgoing, arrant, °unmitigated, °out-and-out, °downright, °outright, °total, unconditional, °unqualified, °clear, °plain, °evident, °obvious, °patent, °flagrant, °gross, °rank: *They were shocked by the stark poverty they saw in the rural areas.*

start v. **1** Often, **start off** *or* up: °begin, °commence, get (something) going, get off the ground, °originate, °initiate, °open, set in motion, °activate, °embark on; °turn *or* °switch on, °crank up, *Colloq* kick off: *They started operations at once. I can't start my car.* **2** Often, **start off** *or* up *or* in: °arise, °come up, come to be *or* into being, °emerge, crop up, °develop, °begin, °commence, get under °way, °originate: *How did this situation start?* **3** Often, **start off** *or* up *or* in: °go, °leave, °depart, get going, °move (off *or* out *or* on), get under °way, °set off *or* out *or* forth, *Colloq* hit the road, get the show on the road: *You start and I'll follow shortly.* **4** Often, **start in**: °begin, °commence, get *or* start the ball rolling, get things under °way, be on one's °way, get going: *When I went in I found that she had started without me.* **5** °jump, °flinch, blench, quail, °shy, °recoil, wince, °shrink, °draw back: *He started when he saw her suddenly behind him in the mirror.* **6** cause to °spring *or* °leap or dart *or* °jump *or* °bound: *Any abrupt movement will start the plovers from cover.* **7** °establish, °found, °begin, °set up, °initiate, °institute, °create, °father, give birth to, beget: *It was her ideas that started the current trend in mystery novels.* **8** °bulge, °protrude, °stick out; *Colloq US* bug out: *Warping caused these boards to start from the floor. When he saw what was in his swimming-pool, his eyes started from their sockets.*
—n. **9** °beginning, °opening, °move: *This is not very good, but it's a start.* **10** °beginning, commencement, °opening, °outset, °onset, inception, start-up: *The start of the race is set for ten o'clock.* **11** °beginning(s), inception, °birth,

°initiation, °onset, °rise, genesis, °creation, °emergence, °origin: *The start of the blues can be traced to New Orleans.* **12** °opportunity, °chance, °beginning; °help, °assistance, °aid, °backing, financing, sponsorship, °encouragement, *Colloq* °break: *Her father-in-law gave her the start she needed in business.* **13** head start, °advantage, °edge, °lead, *Colloq* (the) °jump, *US and New Zealand* drop (on someone): *Having the inside track gave her a start on the competition. If he has a ten-minute start, we'll never catch him.* **14** inauguration, °opening, °beginning, °initiation, *Colloq* kick-off: *When is the start of the salmon fishing season this year?* **15** °beginning(s), founding, °foundation, °establishment, inception, °birth, °origin: *This company had its start in 1781.*

startle v. °frighten, °surprise, °scare, °disturb, unsettle, °upset, discompose, make (someone) °jump, °jolt, °jar, °dismay, °perturb, °stun, °take (someone) aback, °shock, °astound, °astonish, *Colloq* °shake up, give (someone) a turn, *US* discombobulate: *He jumped out from behind the door and startled me. She was startled when she was told that she had to leave at once.*

startling adj. °shocking, °terrifying, °frightening, astounding, astonishing, °awesome, staggering, jarring, °disturbing, °unsettling, upsetting, °amazing, surprising: *Monica fainted when told the startling news.*

starved adj. **1** starving, (extremely) °hungry, °famished, °ravenous: *Harry came in from the fields, declaring he was starved and ready to eat a horse.* **2** **starved** *or* **starving for**: yearning for, dying for, hankering for, °hungry *or* hungering for, pining for, °longing for, °burning for, craving, thirsting for *or* after, °desirous of, aching for, *Colloq* hurting for: *I was starved for a pint of cold lager.* **3** **starved of**: °deprived of, in °need *or* °want of, lacking, bereft of: *The children seemed starved of affection.*

state n. **1** °condition(s), °circumstance(s), °situation, state of affairs, °status, °shape, °position: *He was concerned about the state of the company's finances.* **2** °structure, °form, constitution, °shape, °phase, °stage: *One does not see iodine in its gaseous state outside the laboratory.* **3** °grandeur, °pomp, °style, °splendour, magnificence, °glory, °brilliance: *The prince was met at the airport and escorted in state to the palace.* **4** °nation, °country, °land, body politic: *No longer a colony, it became an independent state in 1952.*
—adj. **5** governmental, °government, °national, federal: *The State schools in the town had a good reputation.* **6** °ceremonial, °formal, °dignified, °stately, °solemn, °official; °royal, °regal, °imperial, °majestic: *We attended a state dinner at the White House. The Queen travelled in the state coach from Buckingham Palace to Westminster.*
—v. **7** aver, assert, asseverate, °declare, affirm, °express, °report, articulate, °voice, °specify, delineate, °claim, °maintain, °allege, °submit, °confirm; °say, °testify, °hold, have: *He has often stated his firm belief in democracy. He stated firmly that he was not in the house on the night of the murder.*

stately adj. °dignified, august, °solemn, °distinguished, °impressive, °striking, °imposing, °awesome, °grand, °lofty, °elevated, °noble, °majestic, °regal, °royal, °imperial: *The stately procession wound through the streets of the capital.*

statement n. °assertion, °allegation, °declaration, °expression, °report, °account, affirmation, asseveration, averral, °announcement, annunciation, °proclamation, utterance, communication, communiqué, disclosure: *Your statement is subject to interpretation. He made a long and detailed statement about the future of the project.*

static adj. **1** °immovable, immobile, unmoving, motionless, stationary, °fixed, °stagnant, °inert, °still, unchanging, unchanged, °changeless, unvarying, °invariable, °constant: *The situation remained static for years. A living language is not static but dynamic.*
—n. **2** °interference, °noise, atmospherics; °difficulty or difficulties, °trouble, °problem(s), Colloq °flak: *With all the static, I couldn't understand what she was saying. You can expect some static about being late for your wedding.*

station n. **1** °place, °position, °spot, °post, °site, °location: *The sentry is not to leave his station till relieved.* **2** °position, °place, °status, °rank, °caste, °standing, °class, °level: *As a doctor, he attained a station in life far above that of his father.* **3** railway station, train station, passenger station, bus station, US and Canadian depot: *Let's meet in the waiting-room in the station.*
—v. **4** °position, °place, °spot, °post, °site, °locate, °assign, °appoint, garrison, °install or instal, Colloq billet: *He was stationed in three different places in four years.*

stationery n. writing-paper, letterhead(s), °paper and envelopes, writing implements or supplies; °office supplies or equipment: *We consider stationery costs as part of overheads.*

statue n. °sculpture, °figure, figurine, statuette, carving, casting, °model, bronze, °image, icon or ikon, effigy, °representation; bust, atlas, caryatid, colossus, °figurehead, Biblical graven °image: *A statue of Disraeli stands in the market square of Aylesbury.*

statuesque adj. °imposing, °impressive, °majestic, °regal, °stately, °magnificent, °noble, °dignified, august, °grand, well-proportioned, °comely, °handsome, queenly, Junoesque: *Julie's statuesque figure was well set off by the draped silk gown.*

status n. **1** eminence, °prominence, °pre-eminence, °standing, stature, °importance, °significance, repute, °reputation, °rank, °station: *Few could approach Keith's status as a pathologist.* **2** See **standing**, 5, above.

staunch adj. **1** °steadfast, °loyal, °firm, unflinching, °steady, unshrinking, unswerving, dependable, °reliable, (tried and) °true, °devoted, true-blue, trusty, trusted, °faithful, unfaltering, undeviating, unwavering: *Charles has always been a staunch supporter of the party.* **2** °strong, °solid, °sturdy, °sound, well-built, °stout, °substantial, well-constructed, well-made, °tough, °rugged, long-lasting, °watertight, seaworthy: *The ship's staunch oaken hull has withstood much abuse over the years.*

stay¹ v. **1** °remain, °stop, °continue, °tarry, °wait, °stand, Colloq °freeze: *Stay where you are or I'll shoot!* **2** °remain, °stop, °lodge, °sojourn, °abide, reside, °dwell, °live, °visit: *I heard that Sheila was back in town, staying at her aunt's.* **3** °keep, °remain, °continue to be: *I was having trouble staying awake.* **4** °stop, °arrest,

°thwart, °prevent, put an °end to, °halt, °interrupt, °block, °check; °curb, °retard, °slow, °impede, °foil, °obstruct, °hamper, °hinder, °discourage, °deter, °delay, °postpone, °put off, °discontinue, °defer, Technical prorogue: *Only one man has the authority to stay the execution. What can be done to stay the advance of the killer bees?* **5** °linger, loiter, °wait, °tarry, °stop, °remain, Archaic bide: *I like this part of the world and plan to stay here a while.*
—n. **6** °stop, stoppage, °arrest, °set-back, °check, °halt, °prevention, discontinuance, discontinuation, °interruption, blockage, °delay, °postponement, deferment, deferral, °reprieve: *Have you been able to arrange a stay in carrying out the sentence?* **7** stopover, °sojourn, °visit, °stop: *We really enjoyed our stay at Fred's house in Fort Lauderdale.*

stay² n. **1** guy, °line, °rope, °cable, °chain, °support, °brace, °reinforcement; Technical head-stay, (running) backstay, forestay, °mainstay, mizen-stay: *If one of those stays gives way, the entire structure may fall.*
—v. **2** °support, °strengthen, °secure, °reinforce, °brace, °buttress, gird, shore (up): *The mast is stayed by two steel cables, fore and aft.*

steadfast adj. °resolute, °determined, persevering, resolved, °single-minded, °steady, unflinching, unfaltering, unwavering, unswerving, indefatigable, dependable, °immovable, °stable, °firm, °fixed, °constant, °persistent, unflagging, °tireless, °enduring, dedicated, deep-rooted, °faithful, °true, °loyal, °staunch: *For years Janet has been steadfast in supporting the cause. Stephen was a steadfast friend and will never be forgotten.*

steady adj. **1** °stable, °firm, °solid, °substantial, °sound, °stout, °strong: *Is this chair steady enough to stand on?* **2** °even, °regular, °uniform, °habitual, °invariable, unvarying, unfluctuating, unwavering, undeviating, °changeless, unchanging, °continuous, °constant; °perpetual, °non-stop, round-the-clock, °persistent, uninterrupted, unbroken, unrelieved, unceasing, ceaseless, incessant, °relentless, unremitting, never-ending, unending, °endless: *Steady trade winds could be relied on to carry vessels to the Caribbean. Inflation has remained steady for a year. How do the children manage to survive on a steady diet of junk food? The economists fear a steady rise in inflation.* **3** unflinching, unblinking, °fixed, °constant, unfaltering, °continuous, °direct: *The boy began to quail under the headmaster's steady gaze.* **4** °calm, °cool, balanced, °equable, controlled: *Steady nerves are needed to handle this new breed of fighter plane.* **5** °devoted, °firm, °staunch, °faithful, °loyal, long-standing, inveterate, °consistent, confirmed, °persistent: *The Pendergasts have always been steady supporters of the museum.* **6** °staid, sedate, °sober, °dignified, °poised, °sophisticated, civilized, °sensible, down-to-earth, settled, °serious, °level-headed, °reliable, Colloq unflappable: *WANTED: Steady person as housekeeper to eccentric editor.*
—adv. **7** °firmly, solidly: *His wife was holding the ladder steady while he mended the gutter.* **8 go steady**: keep company, °date, °socialize: *Is Jane still going steady with Hubert?*
—n. **9** boyfriend, girlfriend, (regular) °fellow or °girl, °sweetheart, Colloq guy, gal, woman, man:

Yes, Hubert is still Jane's steady. **10** °regular, °habitué, °customer, frequenter, familiar face: *Gil has been a steady here ever since we opened.* —*v.* **11** stabilize, hold fast; °brace, °secure, °support, °strengthen: *Prices steadied after the first hour of trading. To steady the table, merely tighten the screws holding the legs.*

steal *v.* **1** °take (away), °appropriate, filch, shoplift, °pilfer, purloin, °make *or* walk off *or* away with, get away with; °embezzle, °misappropriate, peculate; *Colloq* °lift, °pinch, °hook, snitch, borrow, *US* boost, °liberate, heist, hijack, *Slang* °swipe, *Brit* °nick, prig, *US* hoist: *The thieves stole only the emeralds, leaving the diamonds. The bookkeeper stole the money by diverting it into his own account.* **2** plagiarize, °pirate, °copy, °imitate, °appropriate, usurp, °take: *He claims that the story of the film was stolen from his short story.* **3** °sneak, °creep, °slip, tiptoe, °prowl, °lurk, skulk, *Colloq* °pussyfoot: *Silently, we stole into the garden at the rear of the house.* —*n.* **4** °bargain, (good) °buy, *Colloq* give-away: *At that price, the rug was a steal!*

stealing *n.* °theft, °robbery, robbing, larceny, pilferage, shoplifting, poaching, °embezzlement, peculation, thievery, thieving, filching, burglary, °plagiarism, plagiarizing, piracy, pirating: *Stealing from the church poor-box must be one of the lowest things a person can do.*

stealth *n.* furtiveness, °secrecy, clandestineness, surreptitiousness, sneakiness, slyness, underhandedness: *What the thieves lacked in stealth they compensated for in knowledge of art.*

stealthy *adj.* stealthful, °furtive, °secretive, °secret, °sly, clandestine, °surreptitious, °sneaky, °sneaking, skulking, covert, °undercover, underhand(ed), backstairs, hugger-mugger, closet: *He was as stealthy as a cat in his movements. They were stealthy collectors of pornography.*

steamy *adj.* **1** °humid, steaming, °damp, °moist, °muggy, °sticky, dank, sweaty, °sweltering, sodden, °sultry, boiling, °wet: *We were not prepared for the steamy jungle of equatorial Africa.* **2** steamed (up), fogged (up), befogged, °misty, misted, °hazy, clouded, cloudy, beclouded, °dim, blurred: *Every time I take a hot shower, the bathroom mirror gets all steamy.* **3** °erotic, °passionate, (sexually) °exciting, arousing, °hot, *Colloq* °sexy, *Slang* horny: *The film was notorious for its steamy scenes.*

steel *n.* **1** sword, °dagger, °blade, °knife, dirk, stiletto: *He saw the flash of the cold steel in the moonlight.* —*v.* **2** °brace, °nerve, °stiffen, °fortify, grit one's teeth, °bear up, bite the bullet, screw up one's courage (to the sticking point); inure, °insulate, °protect: *People must learn to steel themselves against criticism in this business.*

steely *adj.* **1** greyish, °grey: *His steely blue eyes pierced deep into her soul.* **2** iron, °tough, indurate, adamant, adamantine, °hard, °strong, °rugged, unyielding, flinty, °sturdy: *She was a woman of steely determination.*

steep[1] *adj.* **1** °sheer, °abrupt, °precipitous, °bluff, °sharp, nearly vertical *or* °perpendicular *or* °upright: *In those days, a car had to be in first gear to climb such a steep hill.* **2** °expensive, °dear, high, overpriced, °exorbitant, °excessive, °extravagant, extortionate, *Colloq* °stiff: *The house prices in the city centre were much too steep for all but the highest-paid executives.*

steep[2] *v.* **1** °soak, °submerge, souse, °drench, °immerse, °saturate, douse, °wet, ret; pickle, marinate: *Before cooking, the meat has to be steeped in brine for at least six hours to tenderize it.* **2** imbue, °fill, °saturate, °immerse, inundate; °bury: *He learnt Japanese by steeping himself in the language for six months.*

steer *v.* **1** °guide, °pilot, °conduct, °direct; °manage, °control, °channel: *Steer the boat closer to the pier. David has steered the company to greater profits than ever before.* **2 steer clear of**: °avoid, °dodge, keep away from, °shun, circumvent, give (something *or* someone) a wide berth: *You'd best steer clear of Melissa when she's angry.* —*n.* **3** Usually, **bum steer**: (bad *or* poor) °tip *or* °suggestion *or* °hint; (bad *or* poor) °guidance *or* °advice *or* °information: *He avoids me because I once gave him a bum steer on a horse.*

stellar *adj.* **1** astral, star, sidereal: *The sidereal year is based on stellar calculations.* **2** °chief, starring, °principal, °leading, °main, headlining: *For years Lee has been a stellar performer on the golf circuit.*

stem[1] *n.* **1** °trunk, °stalk, °stock; *Technical* peduncle, pedicel, petiole, °shoot: *Three white blossoms are borne on each stem of the plant.* **2** bows, prow, stem-post: *The ship shook from stem to stern.* —*v.* **3** °come, °arise, °develop, °derive, °issue, °flow, °generate, °originate, °spring, °emanate, °sprout, °grow, °descend, °result, °proceed: *The dispute stems from basic differences in the ways the parties regard property.*

stem[2] *v.* **1** °check, °stop, °halt, °stanch *or* °staunch, °arrest, °stay, °curb, °control, °quell, °suppress; °retard, °slow, lessen, °diminish, °reduce, °cut (back (on)): *The government introduced legislation to stem immigration. I was able to stem the bleeding by applying the tourniquet.* **2 stem the tide (of)**: °resist, °withstand, go *or* make °headway *or* °advance *or* make °progress against, °prevail over *or* against: *They were unable to stem the tide of public opinion.*

stench *n.* stink, °reek, noisomeness, mephitis, fetor *or* foetor, foul °odour, effluvium, *Colloq Brit* pong: *A terrible stench emanated from the cupboard. For decades their government has wallowed in the stench of corruption.*

stenographer *n.* secretary, amanuensis, stenotypist, tachygrapher, phonographer: *The court stenographer read back part of the testimony.*

stenography *n.* shorthand, stenotypy, tachygraphy, speedwriting: *Her qualification in stenography proved most useful.*

step *n.* **1** °movement, °move: *The steps of the dance were very intricate.* **2** footfall, °footstep, tread: *I think I hear father's step on the stair.* **3** °footstep, footprint, °trace, spoor, °track, mark, °impression; imprint, °vestige: *In his master's steps he trod, where the snow lay dinted.* **4** °action, °initiative, °measure, °activity, °procedure, °move, °motion: *What steps are needed to improve the situation?* **5** °stage, °move, gradation, °degree, °progression: *Can we not proceed from one to the other in easy steps?* **6** °pace, °footstep, stride: *My mother's cottage is just a few steps away, at the bottom of the garden.* **7 in step (with)**: in keeping (with), in °harmony *or* °agreement (with), °harmonious (with),

°agreeable (with), according (with or to), concordant (with), attuned (to), in °tune (with), consonant (with), °consistent (with), °appropriate (to), °fitting (for); °conventional, °traditional, °routine: *Do you think that her ideas of discipline are in step with the times? I am not sure they are in step at all.* **8 out of step (with)**: out of keeping (with), out of or not in °harmony or °agreement (with), not °harmonious (with), not °agreeable (with), not according (with or to), °discordant (with), not concordant (with), not attuned (to), out of °tune (with), not consonant (with), °inconsistent (with), °inappropriate (to), not °fitting (for); °offbeat, unconventional, °eccentric, *Slang* °kinky: *You must admit that her views are out of step with the committee's.* **9 step by step**: °gradually, a step at a time, slowly, steadily: *The way to unravel the problem is to analyse it step by step.* **10 steps**: **a** °course, °way, °route, °direction, °path, °movement, °passage; °journey, journeying, °travels, °travelling: *After leaving the village, I directed my steps southward, towards the coast.* **b** stairway, stairs, stair, staircase, stepladder, *US and Canadian* stoop: *Claire walked down the steps to greet me.* **11 take steps**: °proceed, °move, °begin or °start or °commence to act or to take action, do something: *We must take steps to prevent this from happening again.* **12 watch one's step**: tread carefully or cautiously, be °cautious or °careful, exercise °care or °caution, be °wary or °discreet, be on the qui vive, be or remain °alert, be on one's °guard, have or keep one's wits about one, take care or heed, *Colloq* °pussyfoot about: *You must really watch your step with Marnie to avoid upsetting her.*
—*v.* **13** °move, °walk, look; °pace, stride: *Step lively or you'll miss your last chance to see the elephants.* **14 step down**: **a** °resign, °abdicate, °quit, bow out, °retire: *Don't you think it time you stepped down from the chairmanship?* **b** °decrease, °diminish, °reduce: *Using this transformer, we can step down the voltage gradually.* **15 step in**: °intervene, °interfere, intercede, become °involved: *It seemed the right time for us to step in and take over the company.* **16 step on it**: °hurry (up), make °haste, °hasten, °speed up: *He'd better step on it if he is going to catch his plane.* **17 step out**: **a** °go °outside or out of doors, °leave: *Would you mind stepping out for a few minutes while we settle this in private?* **b** °go out, °socialize: *Notice how quickly Genevieve has started stepping out again after her bereavement.* **c** become disinvolved, °withdraw, °secede: *Our firm stepped out of the negotiations when we saw who was bidding.* **18 step up**: **a** °improve, °progress: *George has certainly stepped up in the world since I knew him at university.* **b** °increase, accelerate, °raise, °intensify, °boost, escalate, up, °speed up: *They stepped up the pace until she could no longer keep up with them.*

sterile *adj.* **1** °barren, °fruitless, unfruitful, childless, unproductive, °infertile, infecund: *The first great disappointment of Napoleon's life was that Josephine was sterile.* **2** °pure, aseptic, uninfected, unpolluted, uncontaminated, disinfected, °sanitary, sterilized, germ-free, antiseptic: *Make sure that you always use a sterile bandage for a wound.* **3** °barren, unproductive,

°stale, effete: *Vanessa's greatest fear was that her mind would become sterile and she would run out of ideas.*

sterilize *v.* **1** °purify, °disinfect, °cleanse, °clean, °fumigate, depurate, *Technical* autoclave: *Sterilize the instruments before using them.* **2** castrate (males), emasculate (males), geld (horses), spay (female animals), alter (animals), °neuter (animals), caponize (male fowl), eunuchize (males), *Technical* ovariectomize (females), vasectomize (males), *Colloq* fix (animals), cut (male animals), *Slang* tie (someone's) tubes: *Steers—that is, sterilized bulls—yield tenderer meat.*

sterling *adj.* **1** °genuine, °authentic, °real, °true, °pure: *Is this candle-snuffer sterling silver?* **2** °excellent, °superior, °superb, °superlative, first-class, °exceptional, °matchless, °peerless, unequalled, °nonpareil, °incomparable, °fine, very °good, °worthy, °estimable, °admirable: *Commander Johnston has acquitted himself as an officer of sterling character.*

stern *adj.* **1** austere, °severe, °strict, stringent, °demanding, °critical, °rigid, rigorous, flinty, °steely, °authoritarian, uncompromising, °hard, °tough, °inflexible, °firm, °immovable, °unmoved, unrelenting, unremitting, °steadfast, °resolute, °determined, unyielding, adamant, adamantine, obdurate, hard-hearted, °stony, stony-hearted, unsparing, unforgiving, °unsympathetic, °harsh: *Discipline in the French Foreign Legion is said to be quite stern.* **2** °serious, frowning, °grim, °forbidding, °grave, °gloomy, °dour, °sombre, saturnine, lugubrious, °gruff, °taciturn, crabby, crabbed, crusty, churlish, °sour: *Beneath that terribly stern exterior he really is a pussy-cat.*

stew *n.* **1** gallimaufry, goulash, salmagundi, °hash, °mess, olla podrida, olio, °mixture, °mishmash, *Brit* °hotchpotch, *US also* hodgepodge: *His book is a stew of many different opinions, none of them his own.* **2** state of °excitement or °alarm or °anxiety, dither, pother, °bother, °lather, °sweat, *Colloq* tizzy, state: *She really worked herself up into a stew over the boy Paula is engaged to.*
—*v.* **3** °simmer, °seethe, agonize, °fret, dither, °chafe, °burn, °smoulder, *Colloq* get steamed (up) (over or about), °work (oneself) (up) into a °sweat or °lather or state (over): *Paula's father is all stewed up over her leaving school to get married.*

stick¹ *v.* **1** °pierce, °thrust, °stab, °transfix, °pin, °spike, °impale, spear, °spit, °run through, °poke, °gore, °jab, °prick, °puncture, °punch, °penetrate, °drill, °bore, °riddle, °perforate: *He stuck the wild boar with his spear.* **2** °put, °drop, °place, °deposit, *Colloq* shove, plonk, plunk, plop: *Stick another ice cube in my drink, would you?* **3** °put, °poke, °push, °thrust, °prod, °dig; °insert: *She stuck her head out of the window to get a better look. Stop sticking your finger in my ribs!* **4** °attach, °fasten, affix, °fix, °nail, °pin, °tack; °glue, °cement, paste, gum, °weld, solder, °bind, °tie, °tape, wire; °bond, °melt, °fuse, °unite, °join: *What shall we use to stick the poster to the wall? How can I stick the pieces of the vase together again?* **5** Often, **stick together**: cohere, adhere, °stay or °remain or °cleave or °cling together: *I cannot make these parts stick together.* **6** °hold, °last, °endure, °go through, be upheld, be or remain effective, remain attached:

The prosecutor was unable to make a charge of murder stick. **7** °linger, °dwell, °remain (fixed), °continue, °stay; be *or* become lodged *or* stopped *or* °fixed *or* °fast *or* °immovable *or* stationary, be *or* become entangled *or* enmired *or* bogged down: *Something sticks in my mind about your leaving next week. We were stuck in the Sunday traffic for hours. The wheel is stuck in the sand.* **8** °burden, °weigh down, °encumber, saddle with, °charge, °impose on, °force on: *We stuck Tony with the nasty job of changing the tyre.* **9** baffle, °puzzle, °bewilder, °perplex, °confuse, °stump, stop, °nonplus: *I was totally stuck for a solution.* **10** °stand, °abide, °tolerate, °endure, °bear: *I can't stick people watching me while I am painting.* **11 stick around** *or* **about**: °wait, °tarry, °linger, °stay, °stand by, °remain, *Colloq* °hang around *or* about *or* on: *Can you stick around for a few minutes after the meeting?* **12 stick at**: °stop at, °hesitate at, °pause at, °scruple at, be deterred *or* °put off by, take °exception to, °shrink from *or* at, balk at: *Barnes sticks at nothing to get his way.* **13 stick by**: °support, be °loyal *or* °faithful to, °stand by: *Arnold will stick by you, come what may.* **14 stick it (out)**: °persevere, °persist, stand fast, °bear it, be °resolute, °soldier on, hold (one's) ground, grin and °bear it, °see it through, °weather it, *Colloq US* tough it out: *It was a very hard job, but I stuck it out to the very end.* **15 stick out** *or* **up**: °protrude, °jut (out), °extend, °project, poke (out); °bulge, °obtrude, °stand out, °overhang, beetle: *Stick out your tongue. What is sticking out of your ear? Balconies stick out from all sides of the building.* **16 stick together: a** °unite, °unify, °join (forces), consolidate, °merge, confederate, °amalgamate, °cooperate, work together: *The family always sticks together at times of crisis.* **b** See 5, above. **17 stick up: a** °rob, °mug, *Colloq* °hold up, *US* heist: *They stuck up a bank courier this morning, in broad daylight!* **b** °put up, °post, affix, °display: *We went round town sticking up posters for our candidate.* **18 stick up for**: rally to the °support of, °support, °stand by *or* up for, °defend, °speak for *or* on *or* in behalf of, take up the cudgels for; put one's money where one's mouth is, have the courage of one's convictions: *A person must stick up for what he thinks is right.* **19 stick with**: °persevere, °persist, °stay *or* °remain *or* °continue with, not change one's mind about: *Stick with me, kid, and you'll wear diamonds. I'll stick with the smoked eel as a starter.*

stick[2] *n.* °stake, °twig, °branch, baton, °wand, °staff, °rod, cane, °pole, pike, walking-stick: *We put a stick in the ground to mark the place.* **2** °person, °man, °fellow, °chap, *Colloq* °guy, *Brit* geezer, bloke: *Desmond isn't such a bad old stick after all.* **3 the sticks**: the °country, the °provinces, the countryside, the backwoods, the bush, *Brit* the hinterland *or US* the hinterlands, *Australian* the outback, *US* the boondocks, the boonies: *He hates the city and now lives somewhere in the sticks.* **4 wrong end of the stick**: °misunderstanding, misreading, misconstruction, misinterpretation: *When it comes to understanding a regulation, Ed always seems to get hold of the wrong end of the stick.*

stick-in-the-mud *n.* (old) °fogy *or* fogey, °conservative, °anachronism, *Colloq*

fuddy-duddy, fossil, °square, back number: *Her husband was a terrible stick-in-the-mud and would never try anything new.*

sticky *adj.* **1** gluey, gummy, viscous, °tacky, glutinous, viscid, *Colloq* °gooey: *Children, please keep your sticky fingers off the car windows.* **2** °awkward, °ticklish, °tricky, °sensitive, °delicate, uncomfortable, discomfiting, discomforting, °embarrassing, *Slang* °hairy: *Inviting Steve with his ex-wife might be a bit sticky, don't you think?* **3** °humid, °clammy, dank, °damp, °muggy, °close, °sultry, °oppressive, °sweltering: *The weather was oppressive and sticky, and they kept the fan on constantly.*

stiff *adj.* **1** °firm, °rigid, inelastic, unbending, °inflexible, °hard, unbendable, °tough, °solid, solidified, stiffened, unyielding, °brittle: *The table napkins were so stiff with starch that I almost cracked one.* **2** °severe, °harsh, °punitive, °hurtful, °punishing, °abusive, torturous, distressing, afflictive, °painful, °overwhelming, °unbearable, tormenting, °merciless, excruciating, °cruel, °drastic, *US* °cruel and unusual: *The government here has stiff penalties for drug traffickers.* **3** °strong, °potent, °powerful, °overpowering, °alcoholic: *After that kind of an ordeal, you could use a stiff drink, I'm sure.* **4** °vigorous, °energetic, °staunch, dogged, °tenacious, °resolute, resolved, °determined, °stubborn, °obstinate, unyielding, °indomitable, °relentless: *They met with stiff opposition in trying to capture the fort.* **5** °strong, °steady, °powerful, °fresh, °brisk, °spanking, gusty, °forceful, howling: *We had to reduce sail because of a stiff westerly wind.* **6** °excessive, °exorbitant, °high, °steep, °expensive, °dear: *They are asking a pretty stiff price these days for a bottle of good vintage port.* **7** °cool, °haughty, °rigid, °wooden, °stuffy, °aloof, °tense, °intense, unrelaxed, °forced, °pompous, °stilted, °mannered, °ceremonious, austere, °formal, °chilly, °cold, unfriendly, °standoffish, °reserved, °snobbish, *Colloq* snooty, *Slang* uptight: *Vince is warm and friendly, but his wife is as stiff as a poker.* **8** °stilted, unrelaxed, °wooden, °forced, °artificial, °laboured, °pedantic, turgid, °formal, prim, *Colloq* °stuffy: *I have always found her writing to be rather stiff.* **9** °difficult, °hard, °steep, uphill, °laborious, °arduous, tiring, fatiguing, °exhausting, °harrowing, °toilsome, rigorous, challenging, *Colloq* °rough, °tough: *It is quite a stiff climb to the top of the pyramid of Cheops. That was a stiff homework assignment.* **10** °solid, semi-solid, °firm, °hard, °thick, °dense, °compact: *If you add a bit more water the next time, the jelly won't get quite so stiff.* —*n.* **11** °corpse, °body, °cadaver: *Barry had to go down to the morgue to identify some stiff they hauled out of the river.* **12** skinflint, °miser, *Colloq* cheapskate, *Slang* piker, *US and Canadian* tightwad: *A stiff is a customer who fails to leave a tip.*

stiffen *v.* **1** °thicken, °coagulate, clot, °harden, °jell, °set, °solidify, congeal, crystallize: *Beat the egg-whites with a whisk until they stiffen.* **2** °brace, °reinforce, tauten, rigidify, toughen, °strengthen: *The weak support was stiffened by means of a steel bar.*

stifle *v.* **1** suffocate, °smother, °choke, strangle, throttle, asphyxiate: *The firemen were almost stifled by the smoke from the chemical fire.* **2** °choke back, keep *or* °hold back, °withhold, °repress,

°suppress, °hold in, °restrain, °prevent, °curb, °cover up, °control: *I stifled a yawn as John went on about his grandchildren.* **3** °destroy, °crush, °demolish, °extinguish, °stamp out, °kill, °quash, °silence, °stop, °check: *Under his tyrannical rule all artistic creativity was stifled for fifty years.*

stigma *n.* °brand, (bad) °mark, °blot, smirch, °stain, °spot, °taint, °blemish, demerit, °blot on the escutcheon, *Brit* °blot in one's copybook: *Bankruptcy is no longer the social stigma that it used to be.*

stigmatize *v.* °brand, °mark, °scar, °blemish, besmirch, °sully, °disparage, °depreciate, °denounce, °condemn, calumniate, defame, pillory, °slander: *His foul treachery stigmatized his entire family.*

still *adj.* **1** °quiet, °serene, placid, °calm, °tranquil, motionless, unmoving, °peaceful, pacific, at rest, quiescent, °even, °flat, °smooth, °inert, stationary, undisturbed, unruffled: *In the moonlight, the lake lay still and dark.* **2** °silent, °quiet, °noiseless, soundless, hushed, °restful, *Literary* stilly: *Be still or they'll hear you! In the still night I heard the distant sound of an owl.*
—*n.* **3** stillness, °hush, °quiet, °silence, tranquillity, noiselessness, peacefulness, °calm: *In the still of the evening came the call of the nightingale.*
—*adv.* **4** even now, to or till or until this or that time, (up) till or until now, °yet: *Henry came for dinner five years ago, and he's here still. Do you still smoke?* **5** °even, in °addition: *Hugh weighed twenty stone when you last saw him, but he's heavier still today.* **6** °notwithstanding, °yet, °even then: *Are you still going to Sue's party, despite what she said?.* **7** motionless(ly), °quiet(ly), °silent(ly), stock-still: *Lie still while I put on this bandage.*
—*conj.* **8** °however, but, °notwithstanding, °nevertheless, °even so, in any °event, in any °case: *She said she'd be here; still, you never know, she may come later.*
—*v.* **9** °calm, allay, assuage, alleviate, °relieve, °silence, °lull, °quiet(en), pacify, soothe, mollify, appease, °subdue, °suppress: *A few kind words and she had stilled my fears.*

stilted *adj.* °awkward, °ungraceful, graceless, °clumsy, °wooden, °stiff, turgid, °affected, °artificial, °unnatural, °mannered, °laboured; °pretentious, °formal, °pompous, °lofty, °bombastic, grandiloquent, high-flown, °inflated: *Francis has a stilted way of expressing himself.*

stimulant *n.* **1** stimulus, °incentive, °provocation, °spur, °prompt, goad, °urge, °prod, fillip, °impetus, °incitement, °drive, impulse, °push, °pull, °draw: *She yielded readily to the stimulants of literature, science, and the fine arts.* **2** energizer, antidepressant, °tonic, restorative, *Colloq* bracer, pick-me-up, shot in the arm, *Slang* °pep pill, upper, bennie, speed: *He found he couldn't get through the day without a stimulant.*

stimulate *v.* **1** °rouse, °arouse, waken, °awaken, °wake up, °excite, °incite, °inspire, °encourage, °spur, °quicken, °fire, °fuel, °nourish, °activate, °whip or °stir up, goad, galvanize, °jolt, inspirit: *What can be done to stimulate students to study history? Their teacher eventually found a way to stimulate their interest.* **2** °increase, °encourage, °prompt, °provoke, °quicken: *This drug stimulates the circulation of the blood.*

stimulating *adj.* °exciting, inspirational, inspiring, arousing, °stirring, animating, °exhilarating, °provocative, thought-provoking: *I cannot recall having spent a more stimulating evening in the theatre.*

sting *v.* **1** °prick, °stab, °pierce, °stick; °bite: *Bees, wasps, and scorpions, sting you, but mosquitoes, spiders, and snakes bite.* **2** °hurt, °wound, °pain, °injure, °distress, nettle, °cut to the quick: *He was really stung by Maria's callous remarks.* **3** See stimulate, 1, above: *We were stung into action by the minister's inspiring speech.* **4** °cheat, overcharge, °swindle, °fleece, °defraud, *Slang* °rob, °soak, °rip off, take for a °ride: *You really stung if you paid that much for such an old piano.*

stinker *n.* °wretch, °villain, °scoundrel, cad, °heel, °beast, cur, viper, °snake in the grass, skunk, swine, polecat, *Rather old-fashioned* blackguard, °rogue, *Archaic* knave, varlet, dastard, (base) caitiff, *Colloq* stinkpot, louse, °creep, rat, *Brit* °nasty °piece of °work, sod, *Old-fashioned* rotter, bounder, blighter, *Slang* (rotten) bastard, son of a bitch, *Brit* toerag, °bugger, *US* SOB or s.o.b., °bum, stinkeroo or stinkaroo, *Taboo slang* shit, *Brit* arse-hole, *US* ass-hole: *They were a lovely couple, but their son was a real stinker.*

stinking *adj.* **1** foul-smelling, °smelly, fetid or foetid, mephitic, °rank, noisome, malodorous, reeking, °putrid, miasmal or miasmatic(al) or miasmic, °rancid, gamy, *Colloq Brit* pongy, whiffy: *They were kept in a stinking dungeon with little food for a month.* **2** °wretched, °villainous, °beastly, °vile, °contemptible, °low, °despicable, °mean, °nasty, °disgusting, °rotten, °terrible, °awful, *Old-fashioned* dastardly, *Colloq* °lousy, *Taboo slang* shitty: *Taking my clothes while I was swimming was a stinking thing to do.* **3** drunken, °drunk (as a lord or *US* also a skunk), intoxicated, inebriated, (be)sotted, under the °influence, over the limit, °high, °maudlin, tipsy, woozy, *Colloq* pie-eyed, °loaded, in one's cups, under the °weather, three sheets to the wind, *Slang* sozzled, soused (to the gills), potted, plastered, smashed, bombed, pissed, boozed, boozy, tanked, stoned, canned, *US* in the bag: *The last time I saw Bob, he was so stinking I had to pour him onto his train.*

stint *n.* **1** °share, °quota, °allotment, °bit, °assignment, °stretch, °shift, °term, °time, °job, chore, °task, °routine, °turn, °tour, °duty, °responsibility, °obligation, °charge: *She had done her stint of washing-up and refused to do any more.* **2** °control, °curb, °limit, limitation, °restriction, °check, °restraint, constraint, °condition, °qualification, °reservation: *The committee is free to exercise without stint its power to raise membership fees.*
—*v.* **3** °control, °curb, °limit, °restrict: *Don't stint yourself, lunch is on the firm.* **4** skimp, scrimp, be stingy or °cheap or °penurious or parsimonious or °sparing or °frugal, °hold back (on), °withhold, °economize, °pinch (pennies), cut corners, *Colloq Brit* be mingy: *They certainly didn't stint on the food and drink at Andrea's party.*

stipend *n.* °pay, °salary, °payment, °remuneration, °remittance, recompense, compensation, °reward, emolument, °earnings, °income, °grant, subvention, °scholarship, °subsidy, °allowance, °allotment, (financial) °support: *His stipend barely covers his basic expenses.*

stipulate v. °specify, °demand, °require, covenant, °set forth, °agree (to), °provide (for), °guarantee, °warrant, °promise, °insist (upon or on); °call for: *The agreement stipulates that the goods be received prior to payment. The compensation stipulated in the contract has been paid.*

stipulation n. °condition, °demand, °essential, °given, °requirement, requisite, °prerequisite, °specification, °undertaking, °obligation, covenant, clause, °proviso, °term, °agreement, °provision, °guarantee, °warranty, °promise: *This stipulation calls for payment on delivery in full and in sterling.*

stir v. **1** Often, **stir up**: °agitate, °shake (up), °mix (up), °scramble, °amalgamate, °mingle, commingle, intermingle, °merge, °blend, °fold (in), churn (up), °beat, °whip (up): *Stir all the ingredients together.* **2** °move, °rise, °arise, °get up, bestir (oneself), be up and about, *Colloq* get a °move on, get moving, get a wiggle on, shake a °leg, look or step lively, look alive, stir one's stumps: *It is about time you were up and stirring.* **3** °disturb, °trouble, °affect, °upset, °stimulate, °activate: *The play stirred the conscience of the king. Mention 'diet' to Roberta and you'll stir up a wasp's nest.* **4** Often, **stir up**: °motivate, °encourage, °stimulate, °energize, galvanize, °electrify, °animate, °excite, °inspire, °provoke, °move, °rouse, °arouse, °get, °prompt, °urge, °incite, °spur, °prod, °induce, °persuade, °convince: *What will it take to stir the council to take action? The usual rabble-rousers were there, stirring up the crowd.* **5** Often, **stir up**: °awaken, °rouse, (cause to) °recall or call to mind, °revive, resuscitate: *Those photographs stir up so many old memories!*
—n. **6** bustle, °activity, °movement, °stirring, °action, commotion, °flurry, °confusion, °tumult, ado, to-do, °fuss, °disturbance, °excitement, hubbub, *Colloq Brit* kerfuffle: *There was a stir at the door, which was flung wide to allow Kitty to sweep in. The news of her marriage caused quite a stir.* **7** °prison, °jail or *Brit also* gaol, jail-house, clink, penitentiary, lock-up, *Military Brit* glass-house, *US* brig, *Slang chiefly Brit* quod, *US* big house, °pen, slammer, can, calaboose: *He claims he's in stir for something he didn't do.*

stirring adj. °moving, °telling, °emotional, emotive, emotion-charged, °rousing, °stimulating, inspiring, gripping, evocative, °exciting, °thrilling, °melodramatic, °dramatic, heady, °intoxicating, °spirited, inspiriting, °exhilarating, awe-inspiring: *He was treated to the stirring experience of hearing fifty thousand people shouting his name in unison, again and again.*

stock n. **1** °supply, °store, inventory, stockpile, °reserve, reservoir, °cache, °hoard; °wares, °merchandise, °goods, °selection, °assortment, °range, °variety, array: *One can select something suitable from the stock at the local wine shop.* **2** °pedigree, bloodline, °house, °dynasty, (°line of) descent, genealogy, °extraction, °roots, °lineage, °family, ancestry, °parentage, °breeding, °heritage: *Her mother was concerned that she should marry someone of good stock.* **3** °source, °progenitor, °creator, °father, begetter, forefather, °ancestor, °precursor, °forerunner, forebear, forebear, °founder: *He might well provide the stock for a new line of kings.* **4** livestock, (domestic or farm) animals, °cattle, beasts; horses, cows, oxen, sheep, goats: *Don't forget to water the stock before driving to the village.* **5** °share, ownership, investment, °capital, °funds; °property, °assets: *He owned ten shares of stock in the corporation. The company's stock is worth next to nothing today.* **6 take stock**: °weigh (up), °estimate, °review, appraise, °look at, *Colloq* °size up: *We must take stock of the situation and decide what to do.*
—adj. **7** °routine, stereotyped, °banal, clichéd, commonplace, °usual, hackneyed, °ordinary, °stale, °staple, run-of-the-mill, °tired, old, °everyday, °customary, °set, °standard, °traditional, trite, °worn out, *Colloq* corny: *Ask him how he is and you always get his stock reply, 'Fair to meddling'.* **8** °standard, °ordinary, °regular, °routine, °staple: *The shop does not carry 'extra tall' or 'extra short', only stock sizes.*
—v. **9** °carry, °have, °have or make °available, °handle, °deal in, °market, °sell, °supply, °furnish, °provide, °offer, °trade in, °keep: *The shop stocked a wide range of hardware.* **10** Often, **stock up (on)**: °accumulate, °amass, °pile up, stockpile, °hoard, °store (up), °cache, °lay in, inventory: *Everyone stocked up on food in case the village was blocked by snow.*

stocky adj. thickset, °sturdy, chunky, °dumpy, °solid, stumpy, °burly, beefy, heavy-set, squat, pyknic, mesomorphic: *He is stocky and powerfully built.*

stodgy adj. °stuffy, °dull, °heavy, °ponderous, elephantine, °boring, °tedious, °humdrum, °tiresome, turgid, uninteresting, unimaginative, dry-as-dust, jejune, °vapid, °dreary, °flat, °colourless, °bland, *Colloq* ho-hum, blah, °deadly: *The speaker was boring and gave the stodgiest talk I have ever heard.*

stoical adj. stoic, °impassive, resigned, apathetic, °cool, unemotional, emotionless, °frigid, imperturbable, °calm, °dispassionate, °indifferent, °phlegmatic, long-suffering, °stolid, disciplined, °self-possessed, (self-)controlled, *Colloq* unflappable: *Bertram remained stoical as the judge read out the sentence of death.*

stoicism n. °indifference, self-possession, austerity, °self-control, °fortitude, calmness, °calm, coolness, imperturbability, longanimity, forbearance, °patience, fatalism, °resignation, *Colloq* unflappability: *The people accepted the news of one defeat after another with increasing stoicism.*

stole n. tippet, scarf, boa, shawl: *Mandy was too embarrassed to wear her mink stole to the charity ball.*

stolid adj. °impassive, °dull, doltish, °obtuse, °thick, °dense, bovine, °wooden, °slow, lumpish, unemotional, clod-like, °phlegmatic, °lethargic, apathetic, °indifferent, uninterested: *He was a stolid character, very different from his dynamic younger brother.*

stomach n. **1** abdomen, belly, °gut, pot-belly, °pot, °paunch, *Colloq* corporation, bay window, tummy, bread basket, spare tyre: *His huge stomach hung over and concealed his belt.* **2** °tolerance, °taste, °appetite, °desire, °hunger, °thirst, craving, °need, °inclination, °relish, °longing, yearning, hankering: *I have no stomach for those TV sitcoms featuring precocious four-year-olds.*
—v. **3** °abide, °tolerate, °endure, °stand, °bear, °suffer, °take, °accept, °swallow, °resign or °reconcile oneself to, °put up with, °countenance, °brook, *Brit* °stick: *He walked out when he could no longer stomach her continual criticism.*

stony *adj.* **1** °rocky, pebbly, shingly, shingled: *Some of the beaches along the Riviera are too stony to lie on directly.* **2** °hard, obdurate, adamant, adamantine, °heartless, stony-hearted, hard-hearted, °indifferent, °unsympathetic, °implacable, intractable, insensitive, °insensible, unfeeling, unsentimental, °merciless, pitiless, °cold, °cold-hearted, °chilly, °frigid, °icy, °tough, °callous, °steely, °inflexible, unresponsive, *Colloq* hard-boiled: *He listened to her pleadings in stony silence.* **3** bankrupt, penniless, °indigent, poverty-stricken, °poor, *Colloq* °broke, *Chiefly Brit* stony-broke, skint: *At the time, I was so stony I didn't have two pennies to rub together.*

stoop *v.* **1** Sometimes, **stoop down**: °bend (down), °bow, °duck (down), °lean (down), °hunch (down), hunker (down), °crouch (down), scrunch down: *She had to stoop down to talk to the child.* **2** Often, **stoop low**: °condescend, °deign, °lower or abase or °degrade oneself, °sink, °humble oneself; be demeaned or diminished: *She had to stoop pretty low to accept a job paying only half of what she had demanded.* —*n.* **3** °hunch, °slouch, scrunch, °crouch, stooping, slouching, *Technical* lordosis, curvature of the spine, torticollis, wryneck: *The orthopaedist thought his stoop could be corrected by a back brace.*

stop *v.* **1** °discontinue, °halt, °terminate, °cease, °break off, °end, put an °end or a stop to, bring to a stop or a °halt or an °end or a °close, °give up, °quit, °leave off, °finish, conclude, desist (from), °refrain (from), °abandon; draw to a °close, be over, come to a stop or a °halt or an °end or a °close; *Colloq* °cut (out), °lay off, *Brit* °pack in: *Stop shouting, I'm not deaf. The car stopped suddenly. Will the fighting ever stop?* **2** bring to a stop or a °halt or a °standstill, °check, °cut off; °arrest, °suppress, °restrain, °thwart; °block, °bar, °obstruct, dam, keep or °hold back, °prevent, °hinder, °slow, °impede, °stem, °stanch or °staunch: *The main problem was how to stop drug trafficking. Can we stop the river from flooding? This tourniquet will stop the bleeding.* **3** Often, **stop up**: °obstruct, °block (up), °jam (up), °plug (up), °clog (up), °choke (up), °stuff (up), °fill (up), °close (up or off): *The drain was all stopped up with paper.* **4** peter out, be over, °end: *He gave me an injection and the pain finally stopped.* **5** °pause, °break, take a °break, °interrupt, °tarry; °sojourn, rest, °stay, °put up, °lodge, °visit, stop off or in or over; pull over, °pull up: *I'd like to stop for a cup of coffee. I stopped at The Bell Inn on my way here. We stopped short at the sign.* —*n.* **6** °halt, °end, cessation, °termination, °ban, °prohibition; °close, °standstill, conclusion: *The new law put a stop to door-to-door selling. We must bring that practice to a stop.* **7** °stay, °sojourn, °visit, °break, °rest, stopover, *US* layover: *We thoroughly enjoyed our stop in Brighton.* **8** stopping-place, °station, °terminal, °stage, terminus, *US and Canadian* depot: *There is a bus stop in the next street.* **9** blockage, blocking, stopping (up), stoppage, closing up, °obstruction, °block: *A stop in the water supply was soon cleared up.*

stopgap *n.* **1** °makeshift, improvisation, °substitute: *The wire served as a stopgap until they could get the proper part.* —*adj.* **2** °makeshift, °temporary, improvised, impromptu, °substitute, °emergency, °provisional, °stand-by; jury-rigged: *A broomstick served as a stopgap mast for the dinghy's sail.*

stopper *n.* stopple, cork, °plug, bung: *I had problems getting the stopper out of the barrel.*

store *v.* **1** °stock, °collect, °accumulate, °put by, lay away, °set aside, °pile (up), aggregate, °amass, cumulate; °hoard; °assemble: *The corn is stored in huge silos.* **2** °keep, °hold, °stow (away), °preserve, °warehouse, stockpile: *Apples should be stored in a cool, dry place.* —*n.* **3** °supply, inventory, °collection, °accumulation, °stock, stockpile, reservoir, °cache, °fund: *We keep a large store of dry foods for an emergency. Grandfather has an endless store of tales about the sea.* **4** °shop, department store, °market, retailer, °outlet, cooperative (store), *Colloq* co-op: *You might get a good fridge at a department store.* **5 set** or **lay store by**: give credence to, °believe (in), °have °faith or °trust in, °trust (in), bank or °rely on, °depend on or upon, °count on, value: *I shouldn't set much store by what that old gossip tells you.*

storehouse *n.* °warehouse, depository or depositary, repository, storeroom, bank, °store, (*In Asia*) godown; arsenal, °magazine, armoury: *The company maintains storehouses in a dozen countries to better supply their customers.*

storey *n.* °floor, °level, °tier, *Chiefly US* story: *The new building is five storeys high.*

storm *n.* **1** °tempest, °disturbance, turbulence; wind-storm, mistral, °gale, °whirlwind, °hurricane, tornado, typhoon, cyclone, *US and Canadian* williwaw; °shower, cloudburst, °downpour, rainstorm, deluge, monsoon, thunder-shower, thunderstorm, electrical °storm; dust-storm, sandstorm, simoom or simoon or samiel, harmattan, khamsin, sirocco; snowstorm, blizzard; hailstorm, ice-storm: *People were evacuated from the area where it was thought the storm would strike.* **2** °outburst, °outcry, °explosion, °eruption, °outpouring, °furore or *US* furor: *The proposed taxes were met by a storm of protest.* **3** °disturbance, °rumpus, °stir, commotion, °agitation, °furore or *US* furor; turbulence, °strife, turmoil, °disorder: *I am not sure the company could weather another serious financial storm.* —*v.* **4** °rage, °rant, °rave, °bluster, °fume, °explode, °thunder, °roar, raise the roof, raise hell, raise Cain, *Colloq* °fly off the handle, °blow one's top, *US* °blow one's °stack: *When she found out where Laura had gone, mother stormed round the house.* **5** °blow, °rain, °hail, snow, sleet, °rage, °bluster, squall, °howl: *It stormed for a week, and much property was destroyed.* **6** °attack, °assault, assail, °raid, blitz, blitzkrieg, °bombard, barrage, °fire upon or on, °shell; °besiege, lay °siege to, °siege: *The enemy stormed the castle again and again without effect.*

stormy *adj.* **1** °violent, °tempestuous, blustery, turbulent, °wild, howling, raging, roaring, °foul, °nasty, °bad, not fit for man or beast, °inclement: *It was always stormy along the eastern coast of the island.* **2** °violent, °tempestuous, turbulent, °fierce, °fiery, frenetic, °nerve-racking or nerve-wracking, frenzied, °feverish, °raving, °wild: *He and Kate enjoyed—if that is the right word—a stormy relationship for thirty years.*

story n. **1** °narrative, °tale, recounting, anecdote, °yarn; °account, °recital, °chronicle, °record, °history; °legend, °myth, fairy °tale or story, °romance, gest or geste, fable, fabliau; epic, °saga, Edda; °joke, Colloq °gag; °mystery, detective story, whodunit, thriller; horror story; allegory, °parable; °piece, article: In olden days, the historians were the story tellers. George really knows how to tell a story. Have any of your stories been published? **2** contention, °testimony, °assertion, °version, °statement, °representation, °allegation: That's his story and he's sticking to it. **3** °fib, confabulation, (white or black) °lie, °alibi, °excuse, untruth, °falsehood; °tall °tale, fishing or fish story: He told us some story about having sailed round the world single-handed in a dinghy. Did you believe her story about being of royal blood? **4** article, °item, °report, °dispatch, °news, tidings, °release, °information, °copy, °feature; °scoop, °exclusive: A story about China appears on page two. **5** story-line, °plot, °scenario, (°plot) °outline, °summary, °book: The story needs some revision before the dialogue can be rewritten. **6** biography, curriculum vitae, °life (story); °facts, °experiences, °adventures, °fortunes: His story is going to be made into a film.

stout adj. **1** °fat, °obese, tubby, overweight, thickset, heavy-set, °big, °burly, corpulent, fleshy, °heavy, °plump, portly: She squeezed onto the seat between the door and a rather stout man. **2** valiant, °brave, undaunted, °dauntless, °hardy, °courageous, °gallant, plucky, valorous, °staunch, °resolute, doughty, °bold: 'Stout fellow!' exclaimed the colonel, the ultimate compliment he was ever heard to utter. **3** °strong, °tough, °substantial, °durable: Tie the stout cord round the box before posting it. **4** °brawny, °sturdy, °healthy, °robust, strapping, °stalwart, °lusty, °hulking, athletic, Colloq beefy, °husky: Two stout bouncers flanked the entrance to the club.

stow v. °pack, °store, °load, °deposit, °put (away), °place; °cram, °stuff, °wedge, °bundle, °jam; °hide, °secrete, °conceal, °cache, Colloq stash (away): We stowed our gear the moment we went aboard. They couldn't stow another thing in the basement. Where did he stow the pistol when the police searched the place?

straggle v. °stray, °ramble, loiter, rove, °prowl, °range, °drift, °wander, °meander, (be) °spread, Colloq mosey: Thousands of refugees straggled along the road away from the bombed village.

straight adj. **1** °direct, unbending, undeviating, uncurved, °regular, linear: The tracks are straight for as far as the eye can see. **2** °erect, vertical, °upright, upstanding, °perpendicular; °plumb: Stop slouching and stand up straight. He stood straight as a ramrod. **3** °even, °square, °true, °right, °flat, °smooth, °horizontal, °level: Are you sure that the billiard table is straight? **4** °honest, °frank, straightforward, °direct, °forthright, °legitimate, (°fair and) °square, °fair, °equitable, °just, °above-board, °upright, °respectable, °decent, °trustworthy, °honourable, dependable, °reliable, Colloq upfront: Sternway seems to be perfectly straight in his business dealings. **5** unequivocal, unambiguous, straightforward, °candid, °plain, °simple, °explicit, °blunt, unembellished, unelaborated, °unqualified, °outright, °accurate: The straight facts are given in this article. The police cannot get

a straight story out of him as to his whereabouts last night. **6** °direct, °point-blank, straightforward, straight from the shoulder, °candid, °outright, °plain, °frank, °no-nonsense: Do you mind answering a straight question? **7** °shipshape, °orderly, °neat, °tidy, in °order, arranged, organized, sorted out, °spruce, straightened out: I wish Leonard would put his room straight before the guests arrive. **8** °sober, °staid, °sedate, °serious, unsmiling, unemotional, °impassive, emotionless, °taciturn, composed, mask-like: It was impossible to keep a straight face during the school play. **9** °undiluted, °neat, unmixed, °pure, unadulterated, uncut, unmodified, unaltered, unalloyed: He likes his whisky straight. **10** °even, °square, settled, straightened out, agreed: The account will be straight when Dick makes the last payment. **11** heterosexual, °normal, Slang hetero: Till Evelyn came out of the closet, I thought he was straight.
—adv. **12** °directly, °right, undeviatingly, unswervingly; as the crow flies, in a beeline: I should have known she would go straight to the police. **13** (straight) °ahead: Go straight for a mile and you'll see it on the right. **14** Sometimes, **straight out**: °directly, °unequivocally, unambiguously, forthrightly, straightforwardly, °point-blank, candidly, plainly, °simply, in °plain or °simple English, explicitly, °outright, °honestly, accurately: Just give me the story straight, without beating about the bush. **15** Often, **straight away** or **off**: °immediately, at °once, without °delay, instantly, °summarily, °directly, °right (away or off), °right off the bat, °promptly, Colloq p.d.q. (= 'pretty damned quick'): She went back to work straight after having the baby. I told him straight off to leave town. **16 straight up**: without ice: I like my gin straight up.

straighten v. **1** Often, **straighten out**: uncurl, untangle, disentangle, unsnarl, unravel, unkink; °clear (up), °settle, °resolve, °sort out, set or put °straight or °right or to rights, °correct, °adjust, °rectify: She decided to have her hair straightened. They are busy straightening out the matter of father's will. **2** Often, **straighten out**: °reform, °rehabilitate, °organize, reorganize: Perhaps psychotherapy will straighten him out. **3** Often, **straighten out** or **up**: °tidy (up), °arrange, rearrange, °neaten, °spruce up, put in °order, °clean (up): Would you help me straighten up the place before you leave?

strain[1] v. **1** °stretch, °force, °tax, overtax, °burden, overburden, °overwork, °push; °exceed, °surpass: His story that a bushy-haired intruder had shot her strained the jury's credulity. **2** °push, °pull, °tug, °heave, °stretch, °twist, °wrench, °struggle: As he strained at his bonds the rope cut more deeply into his wrists. **3** °injure, °hurt, °harm, °impair, °damage, °overwork, °tax, °pull, °tear, °twist, °wrench: I strained my back lifting that box of books. **4** °stretch, crane, °twist; °try (hard), °struggle, °strive, labour, toil, °push, make an °effort, °exert oneself: She strained to catch a glimpse of the prince. They strained to hear every word. **5** °filter, °sift, °drain, °screen, sieve; winnow, °draw off, °separate; °purify, seep, °percolate: Strain the soup to remove the bones. Strain the dregs from the wine. The water is then strained through sand.

—n. **6** °sprain, °injury, °damage, °harm, °wrench: *Strains often hurt more than broken bones.* **7** °anxiety, °worry; °effort, °exertion, °stress, °tension, °pressure, °burden; °tax, °demand, °obligation: *The strain began to tell on all of us. Another rope was needed to relieve the strain on the first. This advertising budget will put a great strain on our resources.* **8** Often, **strains**: °air, °melody, °tune, °song, °sound, music: *In the distance I made out the faint strains of skirling bagpipes.* **9** °tenor, °tone, °drift, °inclination, °tendency, °quality, °spirit, °mood, °humour, °character, complexion, °cast, °impression, °thread, °vein, °theme: *I detected a mellowing strain in her letters.*

strain² *n.* **1** °family, °stock, ancestry, °roots, °extraction, °derivation, (°family) °background, °heritage, descent, °parentage, °lineage, °pedigree, bloodline, °race, °line, descendants: *This sample of sweet pea came from an entirely different strain.* **2** °trace, °hint, °suggestion, °suspicion, soupçon, °streak, °trait, °mark, °indication, °vestige, °evidence, °sign: *There was a definite strain of ruthlessness in her character.*

strained *adj.* °laboured, °forced, °artificial, °stiff, °tense, °awkward, uneasy, uncomfortable, °difficult, tension-ridden, °self-conscious, °unnatural, °insincere, °put-on: *His already strained relations with his wife scarcely improved when he met Lisa.*

strait *adj.* **1** °narrow, °tight, constricted, constricting, confining, confined, restricting, restricted, °limited, limiting, rigorous, °demanding, °exacting; °difficult, °straitened: *Strait is the gate and narrow is the way which leadeth unto life, and few there be that find it.* *—n.* **2** Usually (except in gazetteers), **straits**: narrows, °channel: *We coasted through the Straits of Magellan with all sails flying.* **3** dire or **desperate** or **sore straits**: bad or poor °state or °condition, °trouble, °predicament, °plight, °mess, °dilemma, °tight °spot, hot water, *US* °bind, *Colloq* pickle, °jam, °scrape, pretty or fine kettle of fish, *US* box: *We shall be in dire straits if father's cheque doesn't come soon.*

straitened *adj.* °inadequate, °insufficient, reduced, oppressed, distressed, °needy, necessitous, °poor, poverty-stricken, °indigent, °impoverished, °destitute, penniless, °insolvent, *Colloq* °hard up, *US* strapped: *As a writer, he was accustomed to living in straitened circumstances between sales of his stories.*

strait-laced *adj.* °priggish, prim, °conservative, °old-fashioned, Victorian, old-maidish, °proper, °prudish, puritanical, moralistic, °strict, °narrow-minded, (over-)°scrupulous, °fussy, *Colloq* pernickety or *US also* persnickety, °stuffy, °goody-goody: *Her aunt has the strait-laced notion that girls ought to be home by ten o'clock.*

strange *adj.* **1** °odd, °peculiar, °bizarre, °weird, °curious, uncommon, °unusual, °rare, °singular, °exceptional, °eccentric, °funny, °quaint, °fantastic, out of the °ordinary, °extraordinary, °out-of-the-way, °queer, °outlandish, °unheard-of, °grotesque, °abnormal, °remarkable, surprising, °inexplicable, °unaccountable, uncanny, *Colloq* °offbeat, far-out, *Slang* °kinky, *Brit* rum, *US* kooky: *I had a strange dream last night.* **2** °unfamiliar, °unknown, °unaccustomed: *The children were*

warned not to get into strange cars. She was overwhelmed by the strange culture of her husband's country.

stranger *n.* °foreigner, outlander, °alien, °newcomer, °visitor: *The people in these parts don't take kindly to strangers.*

stratagem *n.* °trick, °artifice, °device, °dodge, °subterfuge, °lure, °wile, °ruse, °plan, °scheme, °plot, °intrigue, °manoeuvre, ploy, °tactic: *What stratagem did they use to tempt you to attend this boring affair?*

strategic *adj.* °tactical, °key, °crucial, °principal, °cardinal, °critical, °vital, °key: *That line of supply is of strategic importance. Sending in the landing force was a strategic manoeuvre.*

strategy *n.* °plan, °tactic(s), °design, °policy, °procedure, °scheme, blueprint, *Colloq* game or master °plan, °scenario: *The enemy's strategy calls for quick air strikes by low-flying bombers.*

stratum *n.* **1** layer, °level, stratification, °table, °vein, °seam; °plane: *These coal strata have been mined for hundreds of years.* **2** °level, °caste, °class, °rank, °station, °standing, °status, °bracket, °group, °estate: *She married someone from a higher stratum of society.*

stray *v.* **1** °wander, °roam, rove, °range, °straggle, °drift, °meander: *They found the ponies straying up the valley and across the moor.* **2** °deviate, °diverge, °wander, digress, °ramble, divagate, get or go off on a tangent, get sidetracked: *She let her mind stray from the matter in hand.* *—n.* **3** straggler, vagrant, waif, *US* dogie: *They have always taken in and cared for strays.* *—adj.* **4** vagrant, °lost, roving, roaming, wandering, °homeless, °derelict, °abandoned: *The problem with stray pets increases when people abandon them on returning home after the summer.* **5** °random, °casual, °chance, °accidental, °haphazard, °singular, °freak, unexpected: *A stray bullet caught him in the leg.* **6** °isolated, °separate(d), lone, °odd, °single: *She brushed a stray hair from her face.*

streak *n.* **1** °stripe, striation, °strip, °stroke, °bar, °band, °line, °mark, °smear, °slash, °dash, °touch, daub, °fleck, °trace; °vein, layer, °seam, °stratum: *The male bird is marked with a streak of bright reddish-orange on its throat. A red streak marks the iron deposit.* **2** °flash, °bolt: *I saw the dark figure in the light from a streak of lightning.* **3** °spell, °spate, °period, °stretch, °run: *They were celebrating their streak of good luck at the roulette table.* *—v.* **4** °stripe, striate, °line, °bar, °mark, °smear, daub, °slash: *Dawn was beginning to streak the sky when she left the party.* **5** °race, °run, °rush, °dash, sprint, dart, °hurtle, °fly, scoot, °speed, °hasten, °hurry, °tear, whistle, zip, zoom, *Colloq* whiz or whizz: *The gang streaked through the village on their motor cycles and were gone.*

stream *n.* **1** °brook, brooklet, streamlet, rivulet, °tributary, °river, freshet, °run, watercourse, waterway, °channel, *Chiefly literary* rill, runnel, *Literary or No. Brit dialect* beck, burn, *Archaic NE US except in placenames* kill, *US* °creek, °branch: *If the streams continue to swell, flooding can be expected in low-lying areas.* **2** °flow, °current, °outpouring, effluence or efflux, effusion, °rush, °spurt, °surge, °fountain, geyser, °torrent, °flood, deluge, cataract, cascade: *A stream of bubbles showed where the diver was swimming. A*

stream of obscenities poured from his lips. **3** °flow, °rush, °swarm, tide, °flood, deluge, °succession, series, °row, °line, °string, °chain, barrage, *Brit* °queue: *Simon has had a constant stream of visitors all morning.*
—*v.* **4** °run, °flow, °course, °glide, °rush, °slide, °slip, °surge; °pour, °issue, °emanate, °gush, °flood, °spout, °well up *or* out *or* forth, squirt, °spurt, °shoot, jet; cascade: *The rain streamed down the windows.* **5** °issue, °emanate; °rush, °surge, °pour, °flood, °file, °proceed, °march, °walk, °move: *People streamed in and out of the building all day long.*

streamer *n.* °pennant, °banner, pennon, °flag, bannerette *or* banneret, banderole *or* banderol *or* bannerol, gonfalon *or* gonfanon, jack, burgee: *A long streamer fluttered from the mast.*

streamlined *adj.* **1** aerodynamic, hydro-dynamic, curved, curvilinear; °smooth, flow-ing: *Streamlined design began to appear in cars and boats in the 1930s.* **2** °modern, ultra-modern, modernistic, modernized, up to °date, time-saving, labour-saving, °compact, (°well-)organized, °efficient, automated: *Mother always dreamt about having a streamlined kitchen.* **3** well-run, °smooth, °efficient, automated, labour-saving, time-saving, °profitable, °productive, simplified: *He designed a fully stream-lined manufacturing process for us.*

street *n.* **1** thoroughfare, °way, °road, roadway, high °road, avenue, concourse, boulevard, lane, °drive, terrace, °circle, °row, °passage, alley, byway: *I don't know the name of the street where she lives.* **2 up (someone's)** *Brit* **street** *or US* **alley:** (someone's) cup of tea, in (someone's) baili-wick, suiting (someone) to a T: *Crossword puzzles are very much up Eugene's street.*

strength *n.* **1** °power, °might, °force, mighti-ness, robustness, toughness, stoutness, sturdi-ness, °brawn, brawniness, muscle, °sinew: *Do you have the strength to lift that by yourself?* **2** °fortitude, °backbone, °stamina, °tenacity, tenaciousness, will-power, °perseverance, °persistence, resoluteness, °resolution, per-tinacity, °nerve, °grit, °pluck, °determination, gameness, intrepidity, firmness, °stability, *Colloq* °guts, gutsiness, °spunk, *US* intestinal °fortitude, stick-to-it-iveness: *Sally was a tower of strength when I needed her the most.* **3** °talent, °ability, °aptitude, °gift, °strong point, °asset: *One of his strengths is being able to sight-read music.* **4** concentration, concentratedness, °intensity, potency: *Coffee of that strength would keep me awake all night.* **5** °vigour, °force, °energy, °power, potency, °intensity: *The strength of the wind was great enough to pick up cars and toss them about.* **6** durability, °power, toughness, °stability, reliability, °resistance, solidity, °stamina, rug-gedness, °endurance, soundness: *The manu-facturer claims that his product has the strength to resist wear for a hundred years.* **7** persuasiveness, cogency, °weight, °force, convincingness, inci-siveness, soundness: *There is no disputing the strength of the argument against smoking.*

strengthen *v.* **1** °reinforce, °renew, °bolster, °fortify, °support, °confirm, corroborate, °substantiate, °buttress, °step up, °boost: *A thou-sand troops were sent to strengthen the garrison at Fort Old.* **2** °encourage, hearten, invigorate, °fortify, °rejuvenate, °nourish, °energize,

°vitalize, toughen, °brace (up), °steel, innervate, °stiffen: *Whatever she said seems to have strengthened his determination to succeed.*

strenuous *adj.* **1** °demanding, taxing, °tough, °arduous, °laborious, °toilsome, °burdensome, tiring, °exhausting, °difficult, °hard, uphill: *Hauling the fishing nets was strenuous work.* **2** °energetic, °active, °vigorous, °enthusiastic, zealous, °earnest, °dynamic, °intense, indefatigable, °tireless, °persistent, dogged, °determined, °tenacious, pertinacious, °resolute, °sincere, °eager: *He has made a strenu-ous effort to be more accommodating.*

stress *n.* **1** °emphasis, °force, °pressure, force-fulness, °accent, accentuation, °prominence, *Technical* ictus: *Many people place the stress on the first syllable of 'controversy'.* **2** °emphasis, °significance, °importance, °weight, °force, insistence, °urgency: *She lays too much stress on looks.* **3** (stress and) °strain, °burden, °anxiety, °worry, °distress, °pain, °grief, °suffering, °anguish, °pressure, tenseness, °tension: *She has four elderly people to care for, and the stress is beginning to show.*
—*v.* **4** °emphasize, °accent, accentuate, lay stress *or* °emphasis on, underscore, underline, °mark, °note, make a °point of, bring °home, °focus on, bring into °prominence, °spotlight, °feature, highlight: *The conference succeeded in stressing the importance of a good home life.* **5** °strain, put under °strain *or* stress, °upset, °disturb, °burden, °worry, °distress, *Brit* pres-surize *or US* °pressure: *Duncan was terribly stressed after a few months in the new job.*

stretch *v.* **1** °extend, °reach; °span, °spread: *Her memory stretches back to the first World War. His Texas ranch stretches as far as the eye can see.* **2** distend, °lengthen, elongate, °widen, broaden, °swell, °draw *or* °pull out, balloon, °inflate, °enlarge, °expand, °increase, dilate, °blow up: *Stretch the netting to cover the frame.* **3** overtax, overextend; °warp, °strain, °distort, °bend, °break: *We like to stretch our employees in this company. He is stretching the rules by allowing undergraduates to take his course.*
—*n.* **4** °elasticity, °give, °resilience, resiliency, stretchability, stretchiness: *There isn't much stretch left in this old rubber band.* **5** °extent, °reach, °span, °spread, °expanse, °sweep, °area, °tract, *US* °section: *There is a stretch of desert just south of the coast.* **6** °time, °stint, °period, °spell, °term, °tour (of duty), *Colloq US and Canadian* °hitch: *He signed up for a two-year stretch in the navy. He once did a six-month stretch in prison for assault.*

strew *v.* °scatter, bestrew, sprinkle, °disperse, °spread, °toss, °distribute; °litter: *Rubbish was strewn all over the floor.*

stricken *adj.* **1** Usually, **stricken by**: struck (down) (by), °hit (by), laid °low (by *or* with), °affected (by *or* with), afflicted (with), racked (by *or* with): *He was stricken by pneumonia but is recovering.* **2** °affected (by), °smitten (by), over-whelmed (by *or* with), °overcome (by *or* with), plagued (by *or* with), tormented (by); °broken, crushed, demoralized, °broken-hearted, grief-stricken: *He was stricken by her beauty. During the plague year, commerce virtually ceased with the stricken city of London.*

strict *adj.* **1** rigorous, °narrow, °close, undevi-ating, confining, constricting, constrictive,

°rigid, defined, °precise, °exact, °exacting, stringent, °meticulous, °compulsive, punctilious,
°finicky or finical, °scrupulous, °attentive,
°conscientious, °faithful, °thorough,
°complete: *The judge's strict interpretation of the
law left no room for leniency or sympathy.* **2** °severe,
austere, °authoritarian, autocratic, °stern,
°firm, °hard, °tough, uncompromising,
°inflexible, °cold-blooded, iron-fisted,
°tyrannical, °harsh, °ruthless, pitiless,
°unsympathetic: *Miss Wells is remembered by all
her students as a strict disciplinarian.*

stricture *n.* **1** interdiction, blockage,
°restriction, °restraint, constraint, °deterrent,
°impediment: *The strictures imposed on credit have
throttled trade.* **2** °criticism, censure: *He deplored
conservative strictures against anything new in the
arts.*

strident *adj.* °shrill, °raucous, °harsh, °loud,
°grating, stridulous, stridulant, scraping, scratching, °scratchy, grinding, hoarse, °rough, guttural, °husky, gravelly, rasping, jarring,
°discordant, unharmonious, unmelodious,
unmusical, cacophonous, croaking, creaking:
Her strident voice could be heard all over the building.

strife *n.* **1** °discord, disharmony, °disagreement,
°difference, °conflict, °rivalry, °competition,
contention, °dispute, °dissension, °struggle,
squabbling, bickering, arguing, quarrelling: *The
nation is torn by the strife of perpetual labour
disputes.* **2** °animosity, °friction, hard feelings,
bad feeling(s), bad blood, °antagonism, °ill will,
hatred, enmity, °hostility, unfriendliness: *The
strife between us will continue because our philosophies differ so radically.*

strike *v.* **1** °hit, deal a °blow to, °knock, smack,
thump, thwack, °crown, cuff, °punch, smite;
°beat, hammer, °belabour, °batter, pummel *or*
pommel, °pelt, buffet, thrash; cudgel,
bludgeon, °club, °whip, horsewhip, °scourge,
°lash, cane, °flog, birch, °slap, *Colloq* wallop, slug,
whack, clout, sock, conk, °belt, bash, °lambaste,
bop: *Small wonder he struck you after what you
called his wife.* **2** °deliver, °deal, °aim, °direct:
He struck a blow for freedom. **3** °hit, °collide
with, °land on *or* in *or* against, smash *or* °bump
or bang *or* °crash *or* °dash into, °go *or* °run
into, °impact: *Mrs Humphrey's car went out of
control and struck a tree.* **4** °remove, °take away,
°take apart, dismantle, °knock down; °take *or*
°pull *or* °haul down: *Stage-hands struck the set. As
the wind piped up we struck the mainsail.* **5** Usually,
strike off *or* **from** *or* **out**: °obliterate, expunge,
°erase, eradicate, °blot out, °delete, °scratch,
°eliminate, °rub out, °cross (out), °cancel, °wipe
out, *US* x out: *After the scandal, his name was
struck off the register. Strike out any references that
might be thought libellous.* **6** °light, ignite: *He
struck a match to see where he was going.* **7** °affect,
°impress, °influence, °afflict, *Colloq* °hit: *The
death of her kitten struck Mandy to the heart.*
8 °make, °reach, attain, conclude; °agree
or °settle (on), °ratify, °confirm: *We struck a bargain on the sale of the car.* **9** °occur *or* °come to,
°dawn on *or* upon, *Colloq* °hit, °register (with):
*It suddenly struck me that you are leaving
tomorrow.* **10** °impress, °print, °stamp, °punch,
°mint, °make: *They have struck a new gold coin
for collectors.* **11** °instil, °implant, °induce: *Horror
films struck fear into our hearts when we were
children.* **12** °assume, °adopt, °put on, °display,

°affect, °take on, feign: *He struck a supercilious
pose of insouciant hauteur that annoyed her
intensely.* **13** Often, **strike down**: °afflict,
°affect, °attack, indispose, °incapacitate, disable, °cripple, °invalid: *Polio struck her down in
the prime of life.* **14** °encounter, come *or* °happen
or °hit upon, °come across, °chance upon,
°discover, °stumble on, °find: *The news is that
they've struck oil in the North Sea.* **15** °revolt,
°rebel, °mutiny, °walk out (of the job), walk off
the job: *The machinists struck at midnight, bringing
the industry to a halt.* **16 strike on** *or* **upon**:
°dream up, °devise, conjure up, °improvise,
°work out, °invent, contrive, come up with, °hit
on *or* upon, °arrive at: *The alchemist never did strike
upon a way to turn lead into gold.* **17 strike out**:
a °fail, get nowhere, *Colloq US* miss the boat,
°flop, come a cropper, *Slang US* °blow it, blow
the gaff, come to nothing *or* naught *or* nought:
Tim always strikes out when it comes to girls.
b See 5, above. **18 strike up**: (cause to)
°begin *or* °start *or* °commence: *The band struck up.
We struck up an acquaintance aboard ship.*
—*n.* **19** °attack, °assault: *A dawn air strike is
planned.* **20** walk-out, sit-down (strike), job
action, slow-down, go-slow, work-to-rule: *They
will call a strike if negotiations break down.*

striking *adj.* °remarkable, astounding, astonishing, °amazing, wondrous, awe-inspiring,
°awesome, °stunning, °impressive, °imposing,
°fabulous, out of the ordinary, °unusual, °rare,
°exceptional, °marvellous, °extraordinary,
°magnificent, °superb, °splendid, stupendous,
Colloq °great, smashing, *Slang old-fashioned Brit*
°ripping, ripsnorting, top-hole, topping: *I met
the most striking girl at the golf club.*

string *n.* **1** °line, °cord, °thread, °twine, °fibre,
°rope, °cable, ligament, strand, filament: *To fly a
kite one needs the right weight of string.* **2** leash,
°lead, °leader: *Why does he let her drag him around
on the end of a string?* **3** °line, °row, series,
°sequence, °succession, °chain, °procession,
°stream, °train, °file, *Chiefly Brit* °queue: *A string
of coincidences led to their meeting again after
twenty years.* **4** necklace, °chain, °loop, strand,
dog-collar, choker, chaplet, wreath, rivière
Archaic carcanet: *In her hair was a string of
pearls.* **5 pull strings** *or* **wires** use *or* exert
°influence, *Colloq* throw one's weight around:
*He had to pull strings to get his son a job on the
paper.* **6 pull the strings**: be in °control,
°control, °run, °operate, °dominate, be in
°command, be in the driver's seat, hold the
reins, °manipulate: *She is the one who pulls the
strings when it comes to new investments.* **7 strings**:
°conditions, °stipulations, provisos,
°qualifications, °requirements, °prerequisites,
°terms, °obligations, limitations, °provisions,
°musts, *Colloq* °catches: *I might have known that
there would be strings attached to their offer of a
free holiday in Corfu.*
—*v.* **8** °thread, °join: *The children were busy
stringing beads to make necklaces.* **9** Often, **string
together** *or* **up**: °loop, festoon, °link, °drape,
°suspend, °sling, °hang, array, concatenate,
°chain together: *At holiday time, coloured lights are
strung round the town square.* **10 string along**:
a °follow, °go along (with), °agree, concur,
°collaborate: *I said I would string along with the
plan for the time being.* **b** keep waiting *or* dangling,
keep on a string, keep on tenterhooks, *Colloq*
play fast and loose with (someone): *She's just*

*stringing you along till her boyfriend comes
back.* **c** °fool, °deceive, °bluff, °dupe, °cheat,
°trick, °hoax, *Colloq* take someone for a ride,
put one or something over on (someone): *They
strung Harold along for months before they made
off with his life savings.* **11 string out: a** °stretch,
°reach, °extend: *The line of refugees strung out as
far as one could see.* **b** °delay, °postpone, °drag
out, protract, °spin out: *He strung out the repayment for as long as possible.* **12 string up:** °hang,
lynch: *He knew that if the jury didn't convict him the
townspeople would string him up.*

stringy *adj.* fibrous, chewy, °sinewy, gristly,
°ropy, leathery, °tough: *The beef was somewhat
stringy and the potatoes were overcooked.*

strip[1] *n.* °band, ribbon, fillet, °belt, °swath or
°swathe, °stripe: *She wore a strip of embroidered
silk tied round her head. They began farming the
strip of land near the lake.*

strip[2] *v.* **1** °peel, °skin, °bare, uncover, denude,
°lay, °bare, decorticate, excoriate, flay: *The wood-
work will need stripping before you repaint
it.* **2** °disrobe, undress, get undressed,
unclothe, strip down to nothing or to the skin
or to the buff or to (one's) birthday suit, °take
off or °peel off or °divest (oneself) of or °shed
(one's) clothes or clothing, get °naked: *The doctor
told me to go behind the screen and strip.* **3** (do a)
striptease, *US* work the runway: *Sugar Caine says
she enjoys stripping for an appreciative
audience.* **4** °remove, °take away, °confiscate,
°seize, expropriate, *Slang* °rip off: *He was accused
of stripping the assets from the companies he
purchased.* **5** °rob, °pillage, despoil, °plunder,
°ransack, °loot, °sack: *Armies could be raised only
by letting them strip the cities they conquered.*

stripe *n.* **1** °band, °bar, striation, °strip, °streak,
°line, °stroke, °slash, °length: *Each railway car has
a bright orange stripe along each side.* **2** °style,
°kind, °sort, °°class, °type, complexion,
°character, °nature, °description, °persuasion,
kidney, feather: *These new students are of a completely different stripe.*

striped *adj.* streaked, lined, striated: *Why not
wear your striped dress to the party?*

stripling *n.* °lad, °boy, °adolescent, °juvenile,
°minor, schoolboy, youngster, °teenager,
°youth, °young fellow or °man, fledgling or *Brit
also* fledgeling, *Dialect* gossoon, °young 'un,
Archaic hobbledehoy: *The police cadet was a callow
youth, a mere stripling.*

strive *v.* **1** °endeavour, °strain, °struggle, make
every °effort, °attempt, °try (hard), do one's
°best or utmost, °exert oneself, °work at, *Colloq*
give (it) one's all, go all out: *Jim strove to keep
his self-control. Jennie strives for perfection in all she
does.* **1** °compete, contend, °fight: *One must
often strive against unbelievable odds to achieve a
goal.*

stroke *n.* **1** °blow, °rap, °tap, thump, °knock,
smack, whack, °swipe, °slam, °strike, *Colloq*
wallop: *One stroke of the hammer and the nail went
in.* **2** °action, °motion, °go, °move, °movement,
°feat, °achievement: *She won the leading role and
defeated her shyness at one stroke.* **3** °flourish,
°movement, °gesture; °mark, °dash, *Colloq*
°splash: *With a stroke of the pen the man's fate was
sealed.* **4** °beat, throb, °pulse, pulsation, thump:
*His heart was beating at exactly 72 strokes a
minute.* **5** °attack, °seizure, °fit, apoplexy, apo-
plectic °fit, °spasm, paralytic attack or °fit;

Technical embolism, thrombosis, cerebro-
vascular accident, aneurysm: *Gerry has been incapacitated since he had a stroke.* **6** °pat, °touch,
°caress: *A few strokes of her fingers on my brow
and the headache was gone.* **7** °achievement,
°accomplishment, °feat, °act, °action, °work;
°example; °touch: *Your idea of having a jazz concert
to raise money is a stroke of genius.* **8** °bit, °jot
or tittle, °scrap, iota, °touch, stitch, °hint,
°suggestion: *You haven't done a stroke of work all
morning.* **9** °occurrence, °happening, °matter:
*It was just a stroke of luck that I came along when
I did.*
—v. **9** °caress, °pet, pat, °fondle; °massage, °rub,
soothe: *His heart beat faster when she stroked his
hand lightly with her fingertips.*

stroll *v.* **1** amble, °saunter, °ramble, °walk,
°wander, °promenade, °meander, °stray, *Colloq*
mosey: *think I'll stroll over and buy a newspaper.*
—n. **2** amble, °ramble, °saunter, °walk, °wander,
°promenade, °meander, constitutional: *Father
rarely missed his Sunday stroll in the park.*

strong *adj.* **1** °powerful, °muscular, °mighty,
°brawny, strapping, °robust, °sturdy, °stalwart,
°burly, °stout, °sinewy, athletic, °wiry, *Colloq*
beefy, °hefty, °husky: *He was so strong he carried
both wounded men 500 yards to safety.* **2** °powerful,
concentrated, °intense, °pungent, °potent,
°sharp, piquant, acrid, heady, °penetrating,
°aromatic, °fragrant, °hot, °spicy: *There was a
strong odour of ammonia. The flavour is a little too
strong for my taste.* **3** °smelly, odoriferous,
noisome, °stinking, °foul, mephitic, miasmic,
°putrid, putrescent, °rotten: *There is a strong
smell of rotting flesh.* **4** concentrated, °undiluted,
°potent, intensified: *How can you drink such strong
coffee and still sleep?* **5** °vigorous, °active,
°dynamic, °energetic, °eager, unflagging,
°tireless, unfailing, °diligent, indefatigable,
°staunch, true-blue, °steadfast, dedicated,
°enthusiastic, °ardent, °fervent, fervid, vehement, °rabid, zealous, °resolute, °determined,
unwavering, unswerving, °firm, uncompromising, °regular, °persistent, °tenacious,
sedulous, assiduous, hard-working: *We could
use other strong party supporters like
Sandy.* **6** °competent, °talented, skilled,
°qualified, °knowledgeable, °able,
°experienced, well-versed, trained, °efficient,
°capable: *We are looking for someone who is
particularly strong in writing advertising
copy.* **7** °influential, °persuasive, convincing,
compelling, °trenchant, unmistakable, °telling,
°great, °profound; °effective, °efficacious,
°effectual, °powerful, °formidable: *His evidence
had a strong effect on the jury. She was taking very
strong medicine for her migraine.* **8** well-supported,
irrefutable, well-substantiated, cogent, °forceful,
°substantial, convincing, conclusive: *The police
made out a very strong case against her for premeditated murder.* **9** °well-established, well-
founded, redoubtable, °substantial, °powerful,
°formidable: *The position inside the fortress was quite
strong.* **10** °likely, °definite, °substantial, °good,
better than average, °reasonable, sizeable: *There
is a strong possibility that she will be elected. Sales
of cars were strong during the first
quarter.* **11** °stable, °sound, °solvent,
°prosperous, °flourishing, thriving, affluent:
*The economists think that the economy will remain
strong.* **12** °solid, °sturdy, °substantial, °tough,
well-built, reinforced, heavy-duty, °durable;

hardwearing: *Is the cage strong enough to hold the beast?* **13** °drastic, °extreme, Draconian, high-handed, °severe, °forceful, rigorous, °harsh, stringent, °aggressive, °strenuous, °stiff, °tough, *Colloq* hard-nosed: *We had to resort to strong measures.* **14** numerous, °large, °considerable, °great; numerically, in number, in °strength: *They arrived on the battlefield with a strong force of ten thousand men. Their army was ten thousand strong.* **15** °vivid, °graphic, etched, engraved, imprinted, impressed; °definite, clear-cut, °clear, °pronounced, °distinct, °striking, °marked: *The memory of her embrace was still strong in my mind. He bears a strong resemblance to his brother.* **16** °wilful, °aggressive, combative, defensive, °difficult, °assertive, °incisive, °dogmatic, doctrinaire, °opinionated, °self-willed, hard-headed, °strong-minded, °recalcitrant, °stubborn, °obstinate, °emphatic, *Colloq* °pushy: *One cannot deny that Caroline has a strong personality.* **17** °vigorous, °forceful, °powerful, °heavy: *Strong winds lashed the west coast last night.* **18** °rugged, craggy, °rough, weather-beaten: *She was attracted by Martin's strong, suntanned good looks.* **19** °dazzling, °glaring, °bright, °garish, °brilliant, °vivid, °bold, blinding: *The strong sunlight made her blink. Shocking pink is too strong a colour for a small room.* **20** °urgent, strongly-worded, °emphatic, °assertive: *A proposal to repeal the tax was met by strong protests.* **21** °unvarying, the °same, °steady, °stable, °firm, balanced: *The market has remained strong all day.* **22** °emotional, deep-felt, deep-rooted, °basic, °intense, °fervent, °passionate, °deep, °earnest: *Doris has very strong feelings on the subject of feminism.*
—*adv.* **23** °overbearingly, overenthusiastically, offensively, aggressively, antagonistically, truculently: *He always comes on a bit strong when he's enthusiastic about something.*

strong-arm *adj.* °threatening, °menacing, bullying, high-pressure, thuggish, °violent, °brutal, brutish, °aggressive, terrorizing, °terrorist, initimidating, minacious: *The gang used strong-arm tactics to force shop-keepers to buy protection.*

stronghold *n.* fortress, °bulwark, bastion, fastness, fortification, citadel: *The eastern district was one of the last strongholds of the Labour Party.*

strong-minded *adj.* strong-willed, °obstinate, °firm, °determined, uncompromising, °resolute, resolved, °independent: *He found he was dealing with a very strong-minded young woman.*

structure *n.* **1** °form, °shape, configuration, °organization, °arrangement, °make-up, framework, °order, °design, °formation, °system, °nature, °character: *The career structure of the company has served as a model for similar firms.* **2** °building, edifice, °house, construction: *Planning regulations allow only a certain kind of structure in the residential areas.*
—*v.* **3** °construct, °build, °organize, °design, °form, °shape, °arrange, systematize: *Their language seems to be structured in an unusual way.*

struggle *v.* **1** °strive, °strain, °expend °energy, °exert oneself, °labour, °endeavour, °try, °attempt: *He struggled to keep his head above water.* **2** °contend, °fight, °wrestle, °battle: *They*

struggled against the twin odds of poverty and sickness. **3** °wriggle, wiggle, °squirm, writhe, °twist, worm: *She finally struggled free of the ropes.*
—*n.* **4** °effort, °exertion, °strain, toil, °work, travail, °labour, °drudgery, striving, struggling: *Earning even a humble living was a struggle in those days. Was the outcome worth the struggle?* **5** °contention, °competition, °contest, °battle, °fight, tussle, °match, °clash, °encounter, °strife: *The struggle between good and evil continues.*

strut *v.* °swagger, °parade, °promenade, peacock, °prance: *She goes strutting about the office as if she were the boss.*

stub *n.* **1** °butt, °end, °stump, °tail (°end), °remnant, *Colloq Brit* fag-end: *He produced a stub of pencil from his pocket and began to make notes.* **2** counterfoil; °receipt: *You will need your ticket stub for any claim.*

stubborn *adj.* °obstinate, unyielding, °inflexible, intransigent, intractable, uncompromising, mulish, pigheaded, refractory, wayward, adamant, °recalcitrant, bull-headed, °persistent, °tenacious, pertinacious, unrelenting, dogged, °determined: *He remains stubborn in his refusal to join the group.*

student *n.* **1** °pupil, °learner, °scholar, undergraduate, schoolboy, schoolgirl, schoolchild, trainee, °apprentice, °disciple; *Colloq Brit* swot or swotter, *US* °grind: *Only students of advanced standing are admitted to this class.* **2** °devotee, °follower, °admirer, °observer, evaluator, commentator, critic: *Nicole is a perceptive student of human nature.*

studied *adj.* °premeditated, °deliberate, °calculated, planned, °intentional, °wilful, well-thought-out, °conscious, contrived, feigned, °forced, °laboured: *He treated even the greatest crisis with a studied air of insouciance.*

studious *adj.* **1** °assiduous, sedulous, °diligent, °industrious, °attentive, °careful, °painstaking, °thorough, °tireless: *Miniaturists must pay studious attention to detail.* **2** °scholarly, bookish, °academic: *She refused to allow her athletic achievements to interfere with her studious pursuits.*

study *v.* **1** °learn (about), °read, con, °memorize, burn the midnight oil, lucubrate, *Colloq* bone up (on), °cram, *Brit* swot, °mug up: *I want to study music. She has to study for an exam.* **2** °contemplate, °consider, °reflect on, °think over *or* about, ruminate on, °chew over, °turn over, °weigh, °ponder, °deliberate over *or* on *or* about, °muse about *or* on, °mull over, °meditate on *or* about *or* over: *I want to study the problem before deciding what to do.* **3** °look *or* °go into *or* over, °look at, °scan, °examine, °analyse, °inspect, °investigate, °scrutinize, °survey, °observe: *The crime squad studied every square inch of the murder scene. Avoiding the issue as usual, Joyce silently studied her fingernail.*
—*n.* **4** °analysis, °review, °examination, °survey, °inquiry *or* enquiry, °investigation, °scrutiny, °research, °exploration: *Government funds are paying for a study of the ecosystem of the Norfolk Broads.* **5** °learning, lessons, bookwork, °work, reading, contemplation, °investigation, *Colloq* boning up, cramming, *Brit* swotting: *The study of anthropology is what led him to his theory of linguistic universals.* **6** library, reading *or* writing-room, °sanctum (sanctorum), °haunt, studio, °retreat, den, workroom, °office: *Let's go into the study and talk business.*

stuff n. **1** °substance, °material, °matter, °fabric, ingredients, °essence, essentials, fundamentals, building blocks, makings: *This is the stuff that dreams are made on. Is hydrogen the basic stuff of the universe?* **2** °equipment, °goods, °gear, °trappings, °kit, °tackle, °accessories, °paraphernalia, accoutrements *or US also* accouterments, °effects, °belongings, °possessions, °things, °bits and °pieces, impedimenta, baggage, °property, chattels, °furniture, *Brit* °lumber, *Colloq* °junk, °rubbish, crap, *Brit* clobber, *Taboo slang* shit: *Graham left all his stuff with his mother when he went west.* **3** °spirit, °attitude, °grit, °substance, makings, °talent(s), °abilities, °capabilities, °qualities, °attributes: *Is Simon the stuff of which commandos are made?* **4** °nonsense, °trash, °rubbish, stuff and nonsense, twaddle, humbug, bunkum, tommy-rot, balderdash, *Colloq* °rot, °garbage, bunk, tripe, poppycock, crap, malarkey, boloney *or* baloney, bosh, hogwash, °swill, claptrap, piffle, °hot air, flapdoodle, fiddle-faddle, codswallop, bull, *US* horse feathers, *Taboo slang* bullshit, horseshit: *You don't believe all that stuff you've been reading about me do you?* **5** °creations, °accomplishments, °things, °works, °materials, °matter: *Without the attributions, I'd have trouble telling their stuff apart.*
—v. **6** °jam, °ram, °cram, °crowd, compress, °pack, °press, °squeeze, squash, shove, °thrust, °force: *You couldn't stuff another handkerchief into that suitcase.* **7** °line, °fill, °pack: *Stuff the chicken with the following mixture.* **8** °overeat, °gorge, overindulge, gormandize, gluttonize, *Colloq* make a pig *or* hog of oneself: *They really stuffed themselves at the wedding reception.* **9 stuff up:** °clog, °plug, °obstruct, °choke, °block (up), °stop *or US also* °pack up: *Phone the plumber: the drain is stuffed up again. The cold has given her a headache and a stuffed-up nose.*

stuffy adj. **1** °close, airless, unventilated, °oppressive, stifling, suffocating, °stale, °musty, fusty, °mouldy, mildewy, °muggy, fetid *or* foetid, frowzy *or* frouzy *or* frowsy, *Brit* frowsty: *It was stuffy in the ancient tomb.* **2** °pompous, °pedantic, °self-important, self-centred, °stodgy, old-fogeyish, °old-fashioned, °straitlaced, °staid, °conventional, prim (and °proper), °priggish, niminy-piminy, °stilted, °stiff, rigid, *Colloq* fuddy-duddy, uptight: *What a bore to be trapped for an entire evening with those stuffy old codgers!*

stumble v. **1** falter, °blunder, °slip, °trip, °miss one's footing, °stagger, °lurch, °flounder: *Minnie caught her heel in the grating and stumbled.* **2** falter, °pause, °hesitate, °trip, °slip, °blunder: *He was very nervous and stumbled his way through his speech.* **3 stumble on** *or* upon: °chance *or* come of °happen on *or* upon, °hit upon, °come *or* °run across, °find, °discover, °encounter, *Colloq* °bump into: *I stumbled on a great new pub when I was out on Saturday.*

stumbling-block n. °impediment, °obstacle, °bar, °block, °obstruction, °hurdle, °hindrance, °barrier, °difficulty, °snag: *It was often labour unions that proved the stumbling-blocks to technological progress.*

stump n. **1** °stub, °butt, °end: *The branches were lopped off, leaving only the stumps.*
—v. **2** °mystify, °confuse, °perplex, °bewilder, °flummox, °foil, °puzzle, baffle, confound,

dumbfound *or* dumfound, °stop, °stymie, °nonplus, bring up short: *I am completely stumped as to how the trick was done.* **3** °campaign, °electioneer, °canvass, *US and Canadian* barnstorm: *The candidates are out stumping in the farm areas in Iowa.* **4 stump up:** °pay up *or* out, °contribute, °donate, *Colloq* cough up, °chip in, °shell *or* fork out: *Everyone at the office stumped up for Peter's leaving present.*

stun n. **1** °daze, °numb, benumb, °knock out: *I was stunned by an unexpected blow to the solar plexus.* **2** °astonish, °daze, °paralyse, °stagger, stupefy, °overcome, °overwhelm, °astound, °jar, °shock, °jolt, strike °dumb, °amaze, confound, °bewilder, take (someone's) breath away, *Colloq* °shake up, °bowl over, discombobulate, flabbergast: *The children were stunned to hear that their mother had been arrested.*

stunning adj. **1** stupefying, paralysing, staggering, benumbing, numbing; °knockout: *Another stunning punch to the head and McGinty went down.* **2** °beautiful, °dazzling, °brilliant, °gorgeous, spectacular, °ravishing, °sensational, °extraordinary, °remarkable, °marvellous, stupendous, °fabulous, wonderful, °superb, °grand, °divine, °heavenly, °sublime, °lovely, °exquisite, °glorious, astonishing, astounding, °amazing, °striking, °splendid, staggering, °overpowering, mind-boggling, earth-shaking, °magnificent: *There stood the most stunning creature I had ever laid eyes on. The team won a stunning victory in the county tournament.*

stunt[1] n. °caper, °act, °deed, °feat, *tour de force* °exploit, °trick, *US* dido: *The dangerous stunts are done by a stand-in for the star.*

stunt[2] v. **1** °stop, °stunt, delimit, °restrict, °check, °arrest, put an °end to, °end; °impede, °hamper, °hinder, °slow, °retard: *My parents always told me that smoking would stunt my growth.*

stunted adj. dwarfed, shrunken, °undersized, °small, °tiny, °diminutive, °little, °wee: *We saw a bonsai—a stunted Japanese potted tree—that was hundreds of years old.*

stupid adj. **1** unintelligent, fatuous, °obtuse, bovine, °dull, °dense, lumpish, doltish, °simple, simple-minded, moronic, imbecilic, cretinous, Boeotian, sub-normal, °feeble-minded, weak-minded, °stolid, dull-witted, °dim, dim-witted, °halfwitted, °thick, thick-witted, thickheaded, slow-witted, witless, brainless, °mindless, empty-headed, bird-brained, feather-brained, feather-headed, rattle-brained, rattle-headed, ox-like, boneheaded, addle-pated, addle-headed, addled, *Chiefly Brit* imbecile, *Chiefly US* °dumb, jerky, thimble-witted, *Colloq* dopey, *Brit* dozy: *He seemed really stupid in comparison with his precocious younger sister.*. **2** °foolish, °silly, °frivolous, asinine, °hare-brained, °crazy, °insane, °mad, crack-brained, °scatterbrained, °absurd, °inane, idiotic, °ridiculous, risible, laughable, °ludicrous, °nonsensical, °senseless, °bootless, °irresponsible, irrational, °ill-advised, °fool-hardy, half-baked, *Colloq* cuckoo, cock-eyed, damn-fool, *Chiefly Brit* °daft, barmy *or* balmy, *US* cockamamie *or* cockamamy: *He came up with one stupid plan after another.* **3** insipid, °dull, °tedious, °boring, °tiresome, °humdrum, °prosaic, °monotonous, unimaginative, uninspired, uninteresting, °vapid, vacuous, *Colloq* ho-hum: *Most sitcoms feature stupid characters doing stupid things.*

stupidity *n.* **1** fatuity, obtuseness, dullness, denseness, lumpishness, doltishness, °simplicity, simple-mindedness, imbecility, cretinism, feeble-mindedness, weak-mindedness, stolidity, dull-wittedness, dimness, dim-wittedness, halfwittedness, thick-wittedness, slow-wittedness, thimble-wittedness, witlessness, brainlessness, mindlessness, empty-headedness, feather-headedness, rattle-headedness, boneheadedness: *In public affairs stupidity is more dangerous than knavery.* **2** foolishness, °folly, asininity, craziness, °insanity, °madness, °absurdity, absurdness, inanity, idiocy, ridiculousness, risibility, ludicrousness, °nonsense, senselessness, bootlessness, irresponsibility, irrationality, foolhardiness: *The stupidity of such a venture is obvious when you consider the enormous risk and the minuscule return.*

stupor *n.* insensibility, stupefaction, °torpor, °lethargy, listlessness, languor, laziness, lassitude, lifelessness, supineness, °inertia; inertness, coma, °trance, unconsciousness, numbness: *His stupor might be caused by the medication he is taking for his cold.*

sturdy *adj.* **1** °strong, °solid, °stout, °rugged, °tough, well-built, °substantial; strapping, °muscular, °powerful, °brawny, °burly, °robust, well-muscled, athletic, °hardy, *Colloq* °husky, °hefty: *This ladder should be sturdy enough to hold you. James got that sturdy build from exercise.* **2** °stalwart, °staunch, °steadfast, °resolute, °firm, °vigorous, °determined, uncompromising, unyielding, unwavering, unswerving, unfaltering, °enduring, °indomitable: *One must admire her sturdy independence in the face of all that criticism.*

style *n.* **1** °type, °kind, °variety, °category, °genre, °sort, °manner, °mode, °make, °design, °fashion, °look, °period, °pattern, configuration, °line, °cut, °shape, °form: *That style of jacket looks really good on you. They are planning to build the house in the pointed Gothic style.* **2** °fashion, °trend, °vogue, °mode, °look, °rage, °craze, *Colloq* °fad, (latest) °thing: *The current style is for shorter skirts.* **3** °luxury, high style, °comfort, opulence, °splendour, °elegance: *Now that he's won all that money, they live in style on the Costa Smeralda.* **4** °chic, stylishness, °taste, smartness, °flair, °dash, élan, °panache, °cachet, tastefulness, fashionableness, °elegance, °refinement, °polish, °sophistication, sophisticatedness, cosmopolitanism, *Colloq* pizazz or pizzazz; ritziness: *Irena has more style in her little finger than you have in your whole body.* **5** °quality, °character, °mode of °expression, °approach, °treatment, °vein, colouring, °spirit, °mood, °form, °technique; °tenor, °tone, °wording, phraseology, phrasing, °language, vocabulary, word choice, °diction, sentence °structure: *The pointillist style of painting appeals to many. His style of writing is reminiscent of Stevenson's.* **6 in style**: see stylish, below. —*v.* **7** °characterize, °designate, denominate, °call, °name, °term, °label, °tag, °brand: *The use of the indicative for the subjunctive is no longer styled a solecism in British English.* **8** °fashion, °design, °arrange, °set, do, °cut, °tailor, °shape, °form: *Antoine styled my hair in a page-boy for the reception.*

stylish *adj.* °chic, °fashionable, °smart, à la °mode, modish, in °style *or* °fashion *or* °vogue,

°elegant; chichi; *Colloq* in, with it, °swanky, *Chiefly Brit* °trendy, *Slang* °swell, °neat, classy, snazzy, *US* spiffy: *Nicole always looks so stylish.*

stymie *v.* °thwart, °obstruct, °block, °frustrate, snooker, °defeat, °spike, °ruin, °foil, confound, °stump, °nonplus, °hinder, °impede, *Colloq* °flummox: *The government has stymied all efforts to have him extradited.*

styptic *adj.* astringent: *The styptic effect of alum stops bleeding.*

suave *adj.* °debonair, °sophisticated, urbane, cosmopolitan, °worldly, °smooth, °gracious, °nonchalant, civilized, °cultivated, °courteous, °diplomatic, °polite, charming, °agreeable, affable, °bland: *Fictional detectives range from the suave Simon Templar to the earthy Philip Marlowe.*

subconscious *adj.* **1** °subliminal, °unconscious, suppressed, °hidden, latent, repressed, inner, innermost, underlying, deep-rooted, *Colloq* Freudian: *Despite his belligerence, he has a subconscious desire to be loved.* —*n.* **2** (collective) °unconscious, inner self; °heart: *Her subconscious tells her that all confined areas are dangerous.*

subdue *v.* **1** °put *or* °beat down, °quell, °repress, °suppress, °quash, °crush, °control, °master, °overpower, gain mastery *or* °control *or* the °upper hand over, get the °better of, °dominate, °triumph over, hold *or* keep in °check, °bridle, °tame: *Having subdued the uprising, government forces are again in control.* **2** °conquer, vanquish, °defeat, °overcome: *The Mongol horde subdued all the people in their path.* **3** °quiet(en) *or* °tone down, °moderate, °mellow, °temper, °soften, soft-pedal, °check, °curb, °control: *His anger was subdued by her calm words.*

subdued *adj.* **1** °quiet, °mellow(ed), toned down, °moderate(d), tempered, hushed, muted, low-key, °unenthusiastic, repressed, restrained, °peaceful, °tranquil, placid, °calm(ed), °temperate, °reserved: *There was a little subdued criticism at first, but the bill was passed.* **2** chastened, °sober, sobered, °solemn, saddened, °dejected, °sad, down in the °mouth, crestfallen, downcast, °grave, °serious: *He looked subdued when he emerged from the headmaster's office.*

subject *n.* **1** (subject-)°matter, °topic, °issue, °theme, °angle, °thesis, °gist, °substance, °business, °affair, °point: *What is the subject of conversation today? The subject under discussion was of crucial importance.* **2** °course (of °study), °field, °area, °discipline, °branch of °knowledge: *In which subject did Frank take his doctorate?* **3** °cause, °ground(s), °motive, °reason, °basis, °source, °rationale; °excuse: *Increased taxes are always a subject of complaint.* **4** °participant, °case, guinea-pig, testee: *The subjects of the experiment were all in their thirties.* **5** °citizen, °national; taxpayer, voter; liegeman, vassal: *She became a British subject after her marriage to Frank.* —*adj.* **6** Usually, **subject to**: exposed (to), °open (to), °vulnerable (to), °susceptible (to), °prone (to), °disposed (to), at the °mercy (of), °liable (to suffer *or* undergo): *She is subject to asthma attacks. This kind of wood is subject to worm infestation.* **7** discussed, under °discussion, referred to, above: *The subject book was not returned before the due date.* **8 subject to**: **a** answerable to, °responsible for, °bound by, °obedient to, subservient to, °submissive to, controlled by, under the °control of: *You are subject to the same laws as*

everyone else. **b** dependent on, conditional on, contingent on: *All leave is subject to the approval of the departmental head.*
—*v.* **9 subject to**: expose, lay °open, °submit, °put through, °impose on, cause to °undergo: *How could anyone subject another human being to such cruelty?* **10** °conquer, °subjugate, °dominate, °subdue, °enslave, enthral, °crush, °humble: *The peoples subjected by the Romans sometimes fared better than when independent.*

subjection *n.* subordination, °domination, °conquest, subjugation, enslavement, enthralment, humbling, °humiliation: *Their goal was the subjection of all peoples in the Mediterranean area.*

subjective *adj.* **1** personal, °individual, idiosyncratic, °prejudiced, °biased: *His review of the play was entirely subjective.* **2** self-centred, °egoistic, egocentric, °selfish, self-serving: *Your approach is much too subjective to be of interest to others.*
—*n.* **3** *Technical* nominative: *The subjective of 'me' is 'I'.*

subjugate *v.* °dominate, °enslave, enthral, °crush, °humble, °subject, °oppress, °suppress, °put down, °tyrannize, °subdue, °reduce, °quell, °overcome, °overpower, make subservient *or* °submissive, °humiliate: *Few peoples have been subjugated so ignominiously as the American-Indians.*

sublimate *v.* transmute, °alter, °transform; °channel, °divert: *He sublimates his aggressions by jogging and marathon running.*

sublime *adj.* **1** °lofty, °high, °supreme, °exalted, °elevated, empyrean *or* empyreal, °heavenly, °noble, °glorious, °grand, high-minded; °honourable, ennobled, °eminent, °glorified, beatified, canonized, sanctified, °great, °good: *Her poetry evokes sublime emotions.* **2** °awesome, °overwhelming, inspiring, mind-boggling, °overpowering, humbling, awe-inspiring, °majestic, °splendid, empyrean: *The architecture of the cathedral was truly sublime.*

subliminal *adj.* °subconscious, °unconscious, °suggestive: *Advertisers know that subliminal techniques can be very effective in TV commercials.*

submerge *v.* **1** °plunge, submerse, °immerse, inundate, °dip, °wash, °soak, °drench, °saturate, °wet, douse, *Colloq* dunk: *To cleanse, submerge the garment in a basin of warm water for ten minutes.* **2** °dive, °plunge, °go down, °descend, °sink, °sound, °plummet: *The order to submerge was given as soon as the planes were spotted.* **3** °flood, °immerse, inundate, °swamp, °bury, engulf, °overwhelm, deluge, °drown; °conceal, °hide, °camouflage, °obscure, °cloak, °veil, °shroud: *He was quickly submerged under an enormous pile of correspondence.*

submission *n.* **1** concession, acquiescence, capitulation, °surrender, °yielding, °deference, giving in, °obedience, compliance, °resignation, submissiveness, tractability; meekness, docility, passivity, timidity, unassertiveness: *After years of oppression their abject submission to a new tyrant was not altogether surprising.* **2** submittal, °offering, °tender, contribution, °entry: *Submissions for the essay competition should be sent to the address given below.*

submissive *adj.* **1** °yielding, acquiescent, deferential, compliant, °obedient, °tractable, amenable, °agreeable, °accommodating, °passive, unresisting, pliant, °flexible, °manageable,

unassertive, docile, °meek, °timid, resigned, uncomplaining: *As a child she was very submissive but she rebelled in adolescence.* **2** °obsequious, abject, subservient, °servile, °humble, deferential, slavish, °ingratiating, truckling, biddable, sycophantic, toadying, *Colloq* boot-licking, *Taboo slang* brown-nosing, *Brit* arse-kissing, arse-licking, *US* ass-kissing, ass-licking: *She keeps a few submissive lackeys about to do her bidding.*

submit *v.* **1** Often, **submit to**: °surrender (to), °yield (to), °capitulate (to), °give in *or* up (to), °comply (with), °agree (to), °concede (to), °consent (to), accede (to), °defer (to), °bow *or* bend (to), °succumb (to), °truckle (to), knuckle under (to), °resign (oneself) (to), be *or* become resigned (to); °respect, °accept, *Colloq* °put up with: *Despite the threats, he refused to submit. The government eventually submitted to the union's demands.* **2** °offer, proffer, °tender, °enter, °propose, °present: *Many of the suggestions that Alan submitted have been accepted.*

subordinate *adj.* **1** Often, **subordinate to**: °minor; °inferior (to), °lower (than), lesser (than), °secondary (to), °second (to), °junior (to), °subsidiary (to); next to, °below, °beneath, °under: *He had to accept a subordinate position in the new company. His new job is subordinate to that of purchasing director.*
—*n.* **2** °assistant, °aide, °junior, subaltern, °staff °member; underling, hireling, °inferior, lackey, °servant, °slave, vassal; *Colloq US* staffer: *She is a subordinate to the editor-in-chief.*
—*v.* **3** make (something) °secondary: *Too many subordinate community interest to personal greed.*

subscribe *v.* **1** Often, **subscribe to**: °endorse, °support, °underwrite, °advocate, back (up), °approve (of), °agree (with *or* to), °accept, °consent (to), assent (to), countenance, °tolerate, condone, °allow, °permit, °brook: *I sympathize with many of their arguments but I cannot subscribe to terrorism.* **2** Often, **subscribe to**: °contribute (to), °support, °give (to), °donate (to), °pledge, °promise, °sign (up) (for), *Colloq* °chip in (to *or* for): *Mrs Donaldson has subscribed thousands to Amnesty International.*

subscription *n.* **1** °payment, °remittance, investment; commitment, °dues, °fee, °price, °cost: *The subscription is now £100 a year.* **2** °obligation, °pledge, °promise, underwriting: *If we get enough subscriptions, we shall be able to print the book.*

subsequent *adj.* **1** succeeding, following, ensuing, next, °future, later, °successive; resultant, resulting, consequent: *Subsequent governments have failed to solve the problem.*
—*prep.* **2 subsequent to**: after, following, succeeding, in the °wake *or* aftermath of: *Further problems arose subsequent to their second term of office.*

subsequently *adv.* later (on), afterwards *or US* also afterward: *Subsequently, the law was changed to protect witnesses.*

subside *v.* **1** °sink (down), °drop (down), °go down, °recede, °descend, °decline; °lower, °settle: *The waters of the swollen river subsided. The volcano's centre subsided, leaving a caldera.* **2** abate, °quiet(en) (down), °calm (down), °moderate, °let up, °decrease, °diminish, lessen, °die (down *or* out), °pass (away), °wear off: *His enthusiasm* *for sky-diving subsided a bit after he broke both legs. When the clamour had subsided, the president rose to speak.*

subsidiary *adj.* Often, **subsidiary to**: ancillary (to), °secondary (to), °auxiliary (to), lesser (than), additional (to), °supplementary or supplemental (to), complementary (to), °accessory (to), °subordinate (to), adjuvant (to): *The company offers removal of hazardous waste as a subsidiary service.*

subsidize *v.* °fund, °finance, °support, °aid, °sponsor, subvene, °maintain, °underwrite; capitalize, *Slang US and Canadian* bankroll: *Bill and Sue can only afford to live in that big house because her parents subsidize them.*

subsidy *n.* funding, financing, subsidizing, sponsoring, sponsorship, °assistance, °aid, contribution, °support, °grant, subvention, °maintenance, underwriting, capitalization: *Farmers are hoping for increased subsidies.*

subsistence *n.* **1** °existence, living, survival, subsisting, being: *You are worried about buying beer when I feel my very subsistence threatened!* **2** °food, rations, victuals, °provision, °sustenance, °board, °nourishment, nutriment, aliment; °maintenance, °keep, °upkeep: *We depend on your salary for our subsistence, so forget about quitting your job.*

substance *n.* **1** °material, °matter, °stuff; °fabric, °composition, °make-up: *She couldn't recognize the substance in the bottle. The comet's substance is mainly ice and dirt.* **2** °essence, °pith, °heart, °core, °gist, °burden, °theme, °meat, °kernel, °nub, crux, °sum total, °sum and substance, °point, gravamen, haecceity, °quintessence, quiddity: *Explain, in 500 or fewer words, the substance of Hegel's dispute with Kant.* **3** °meaning, °import, °significance, purport, signification, °point: *Our visit to San Francisco gave substance to all we had read about it.* **4** °reality, corporeality, solidity, actuality, concreteness: *You must learn to deal with the substance, not the shadows.* **5** °means, °wealth, °property, °possessions, °riches, °resources, affluence, assets: *John Culver was a citizen of some substance in this town.*

substantial *adj.* **1** °material, °considerable, °significant, °great, °worthwhile, consequential, °ample, °goodly, °respectable, °abundant, °generous, °big, °large, sizeable, °major, *Colloq* °tidy, °healthy: *We understand that he made a substantial payment to keep his name out of the papers.* **2** °strong, °solid, well-built, °durable, °sound, °stout, °sturdy; °big, °large, °massive, °huge, sizeable, °impressive, °vast; numerous, °numberless: *A substantial mausoleum was constructed for his family. A substantial crowd had gathered.* **3** well-founded, °sound, °weighty, °solid, °well-established, °telling, °good, valid, °actual: *Many economists produced substantial arguments in favour of another cut in interest rates.* **4** °wealthy, well-to-do, °rich, affluent, °prosperous, °profitable, °successful; landed, propertied: *The Trevelyan Ironworks is a substantial business, and Mr Trevelyan is one of our more substantial businessmen.*

substantially *adv.* in °substance, essentially, at °bottom, fundamentally, basically, in °essence, intrinsically, in °reality, at °heart, °sincerely, °truly, °actually, in °truth, veritably, °indeed, in °fact, as a matter of °fact; °largely, to a °large extent, in °large measure, °materially, °practically, in the °main, for the most °part, mostly, °virtually, to all intents and purposes; *Archaic* verily: *The article was substantially sound. Do you agree substantially with the ruling of the court?*

substantiate *v.* °confirm, affirm, corroborate, °support, °sustain, back up, °bear out, °authenticate, °show (clearly), °prove, °document, °verify, °certify, validate: *Do not make accusations that cannot be substantiated by evidence.*

substitute *v.* **1** Sometimes, **substitute for**: °replace, °exchange, °displace, °relieve, °supplant, °switch; take the °place of, °stand in for, °double for, *Colloq* sub for, °cover for, swap or swop, *US and Canadian* pinch-hit for: *She substituted the real diamond with a paste replica. I will substitute for you while you are away.* —*n.* **2** °substitution, replacement, °alternative, °relief, °representative, °deputy, °delegate, °stand-in, °stand-by, °understudy, surrogate, succedaneum, *Brit* locum (tenens), *US and Canadian* °alternate: *In those days a man could hire a substitute to serve in his place in the militia.*

substitution *n.* **1** °exchange, exchanging, °change, changing, replacement, replacing, supplanting, °switch, switching, interchange, interchanging, *Colloq* swap or swop, swapping or swopping: *The substitution of certain words distorted the sense.* **2** See substitute, 2, above.

substratum *n.* substrate, °foundation, under-layer, °basis, fundament, °base, substructure, °groundwork: *The agreement rests on a substratum of mutual trust and respect.*

subterfuge *n.* °artifice, °trick, °device, °stratagem, °manoeuvre, ploy, °evasion, °deception, °dodge, °feint, °shift, °excuse, °expedient, contrivance, °intrigue: *Although he told no lies, he used every subterfuge to avoid telling the truth.*

subtle *adj.* **1** °delicate, °fine, °refined, °exquisite, °nice, *Archaic* subtile: *I became aware, almost subconsciously, of the subtle odour of jasmine. These subtle shades of green are so peaceful.* **2** abstruse, arcane, °recondite, °remote, °deep, °profound, concealed, °hidden, °shadowy, °nebulous, °vague, °obscure, °veiled, °thin, airy, °insubstantial, °elusive, °faint; °sophistic(al): *The symbolism is so subtle as to be meaningful to the poet alone. A subtle hint gave me to understand that I ought to go.* **3** °tricky, °shrewd, cunning, °wily, °sly, °devious, °crafty, °smart, °clever, °foxy, °artful, °scheming, °designing, underhand(ed), °deceptive, Jesuitical, Machiavellian, °ingenious, °skilful, °strategic, insidious, casuistic, °shifty, °slick, °slimy, *Chiefly Brit* smarmy: *You were a fool to allow that subtle serpent to insinuate himself into your confidence.*

subtlety *n.* **1** °refinement, nicety, °delicacy, exquisiteness, intricacy, fineness, acuteness, °elegance, °sophistication: *The subtlety of the detail in this work is quite unique. One must admire the subtlety of expression in her writing.* **2** treachery, guile, insidiousness, casuistry, cunning, artfulness, craftiness, deviousness, slyness, deceptiveness: *The subtlety of her deception was revealed only after the war.*

subtract *v.* **1** °deduct, °take away, °take off, °take (something) from: *First calculate the discount, then subtract it from the price.* **2** Sometimes,

subtract from: °detract (from), °diminish, °take away (from): *Nothing could subtract from the exhilaration of that moment.*

subversion *n.* °overthrow, °ruin, °destruction, undermining, °upheaval, displacement: *The dictator used extreme tactics to avoid the subversion of his leadership.*

subversive *adj.* **1** subversionary, °seditious, seditionary, treasonous, treacherous, °traitorous, °revolutionary, insurrectionary: *The government regarded as subversive anything and anyone disagreeing with their policies.* —*n.* **2** °traitor, insurgent, saboteur, fifth-columnist, collaborator, collaborationist, quisling, °radical, °revolutionary, insurrectionist, insurrectionary; °dissident, °defector: *The security agencies were removing subversives from sensitive jobs.*

subvert *v.* °overthrow, °ruin, °destroy, °undermine, °topple, °demolish, °wreck, °sabotage: *The regime was subverted from within, not by outside forces.*

subway *n.* **1** *In US*: underground (°railway), tube: *She takes the subway to work.* **2** *In Britain*: tunnel, underpass: *Use the subway to cross the road in safety.*

succeed *v.* **1** °follow, °come after, supervene: *The end of the war in the Pacific succeeded the surrender in Europe.* **2** be successor (to), °follow, be °heir (to), °replace, take the °place of, °inherit or °take over from: *Elizabeth I succeeded Mary in 1558.* **3** Often, **succeed in** or **at**: °make good, °thrive, °prosper, °flourish, be a °success, be °successful, °progress, °advance, °get ahead or on, attain or °gain or °achieve °success, °win, °triumph, *Colloq* °make it, °arrive, °get to the °top: *Has she succeeded in persuading you to sing? He always wanted to make a lot of money and now he has succeeded. They have succeeded at whatever they have tried.*

success *n.* **1** °good or °happy °result or °outcome, good °fortune, °achievement, °triumph, attainment, ascendancy, °prosperity: *The success of the fast food business is evident everywhere.* **2** °star, °celebrity, (big) °name, °sensation: *She was a great success as a singer, dancer, and actress.*

successful *adj.* **1** °wealthy, °rich, °prosperous, °fortunate, °lucky, °flourishing, thriving, prospering, well-to-do, affluent, *Colloq* °loaded, well-heeled, °flush, in the °money, *US* well-fixed: *He is a very successful investor.* **2** lucrative, booming, °profitable, °fruitful, money-making, remunerative: *The shares they bought proved to be a successful investment. How successful was last year for the company?* **3** °famous, °well-known, famed, °celebrated, °renowned, °eminent; °prominent, °pre-eminent, °popular, °leading, °top, best-selling: *Constance is one of our most successful poets. That book of mine was also successful.* **4** °victorious, °triumphant; °first; °winning: *Henry was successful in his bid for the chairmanship. I want to see a successful conclusion to the tour.*

succession *n.* **1** °passing (on), handing down or on, transmittal, °transmission, °transfer, transferral, °shift, conveyance, conveyancing: *According to her will, the succession of the property is via her first-born.* **2** °sequence, °progression, °order, series, °turn, °course, °flow, °chain, °train, °procession: *The succession of events was as*

he described. **3** accession, assumption, attainment, °elevation, °promotion; °inheritance: *What was the year of Charles II's succession to the Spanish throne?* **4** °lineage, descent, birthright, °dynasty, ancestry, descendants, bloodline: *The 18th century began with the War of the Spanish Succession.* **5 in succession**: one after or behind the other, at intervals, successively, consecutively, in a °row, °running, without °interruption, uninterruptedly, in °order, in °line: *They published several historical novels in quick succession.*

successive *adj.* uninterrupted, °continuous, unbroken, °continual, consecutive, succeeding: *Last season he scored in sixteen successive matches.*

succinct *adj.* °compact, °brief, °concise, pithy, °terse, °short, compressed, condensed, °epigrammatic: *He prefers a succinct style of writing, one that gets to the point.*

succulent *adj.* °juicy, °rich, °luscious, mouth-watering, toothsome: *He was eating a succulent peach with evident enjoyment.*

succumb *v.* °yield, °give up, °give °way, °surrender, accede, °submit, °capitulate: *I finally succumbed and agreed to their request for help.*

sucker *n.* °dupe, goat, gull, °victim, °butt, cat's-paw, °fool, *Colloq* °easy °mark, °easy or fair °game, chump, °pushover, soft touch, *Chiefly US and Canadian* fall guy, *Slang* °sap, pigeon, *Brit* °mug, *Chiefly US and Canadian* patsy: *He's asking far too much for his car, but some sucker will buy it.*

sudden *adj.* unexpected, unannounced, unanticipated, °unforeseen; °unwonted, surprising, °startling; °precipitate, °abrupt, quick, °immediate, °rapid, °swift, °brisk; °impetuous, °hasty, °rash, °impulsive: *His sudden turn caught us off balance. Your change of heart was quite sudden.*

suddenly *adv.* **1** in a °flash or a °moment or a split °second, all at °once, instantly, °instantaneously, momentarily, fleetingly, in the °twinkling of an eye, in a trice; °quickly, abruptly, °swiftly, speedily, °rapidly: *Suddenly, my whole life flashed before me. He suddenly realized why the head of MI6 had summoned him.* **2** all of a °sudden, out of the blue, unexpectedly, without °warning, on the °spur of the moment, °hastily, hurriedly, feverishly: *Suddenly, she turned on her heel and stormed out.*

sue *v.* **1** proceed or move or act (against), take (°legal) °action or bring °suit or °prefer charges (against); °summon(s), °charge, °accuse: *He threatened to sue. They are suing him for the injuries they sustained.* **2** °petition, °beg, °plead, entreat, °pray, °request, °solicit, °apply, °beseech, implore, supplicate: *After five years of constant warfare, the country is suing for peace.*

suffer *v.* **1** Sometimes, **suffer from** or **with**: agonize, °smart, °hurt, writhe, °sweat, °ache: *He is suffering with a stomach virus. How terribly they suffered when their child was kidnapped!* **2** °endure, °undergo, °experience, °bear, °live or °go through, °tolerate, °withstand, °sustain, °take, °submit to, °abide, *Colloq* °put up with: *He suffered years of ill health before he finally died.* **3** °allow, °tolerate, °permit, °let, °admit, °humour, °indulge: *They suffer the storks to build their nests on their chimneys.* **4** °deteriorate,

°diminish, °decline, °go down, °fall off, be reduced or diminished: *If you discontinue advertising, sales will suffer.*

suffering *n.* °pain, °agony, °distress, °misery, °affliction, °hardship, °torment, torture, tribulation, °trial: *The man's suffering is written in his face.*

suffice *v.* °satisfy, °serve, do, be °sufficient or °enough or °adequate, °answer, sate, °satiate, °quench: *If you are merely thirsty, water should suffice.*

sufficient *adj.* °adequate, °enough: *Have we sufficient food to last through the winter?*

suffix *n.* **1** ending, desinence, °addition; affix: *The suffix -ness is added to many English adjectives to form nouns.*
—*v.* **2** °add (on), °join, °fasten to, subjoin, °amend, *Colloq* °tack on: *One can suffix -ness to a huge number of adjectives to form nouns.*

suffrage *n.* (°right to) °vote, voting °right(s), franchise, °voice, °say, ballot, °option, °choice: *They campaigned for universal adult suffrage.*

suffuse *v.* overspread, imbue, °pour or °spread over, bathe, °cover, °permeate, pervade, °flood, °flush, °penetrate, °saturate, °mantle, infuse, °transfuse, imbrue or embrue: *A rosy glow suffused her face.*

suggest *v.* **1** °propose, °advance, °recommend, °urge, °advocate, °support, °offer, proffer, °put or °set forward, °present, °mention, °introduce: *He suggested going out to a pub for dinner. Can you suggest an alternative?* **2** call to °mind, °bring up, °hint (at), °imply, °insinuate, °intimate, make one think, °lead one to believe, °indicate: *His silence suggested that this was not the right time to pursue the matter.*

suggestible *adj.* °impressionable, °susceptible, °receptive, impressible, susceptive, °open, mouldable, fictile: *Patricia was very suggestible at that age and readily believed everything that she was told.*

suggestion *n.* **1** °proposal, °proposition, °recommendation, °plan, °advice, °counsel, °idea, °notion, °opinion; prompting, urging: *The committee rejected your suggestion that membership fees should be increased.* **2** °indication, °trace, °whisper, insinuation, °innuendo, °implication, intimation, °hint, soupçon, °touch, tinge, °suspicion, °breath, iota, °jot or tittle: *There wasn't the slightest suggestion of animosity in her criticism.*

suggestive *adj.* **1** Often, **suggestive of:-** °reminiscent (of), evocative (of), indicative (of): *To me, the smell of orange blossom is always suggestive of southern California.* **2** °provocative, °naughty, °risqué, ribald, °off colour, °racy, °bawdy, °earthy, °lusty, °rude, indelicate, °unseemly, °immodest, °improper, °indecent, °prurient, °blue, °offensive, °vulgar, smutty, °dirty, °pornographic, °lewd, salacious, *Colloq* °sexy, °spicy, *Slang* raunchy: *He used to sing his suggestive songs in night clubs.*

suit *v.* **1** °adapt, °accommodate, °fit, °adjust, °tailor, make °appropriate or °suitable: *It will require some reorganization to suit the office space to our needs.* **2** °please, °satisfy, °fill (someone's) needs, °gratify, be °acceptable or °suitable or °convenient to or for, befit; °conform to: *Choose whichever room suits you. The schedule does not suit my personal plans at all.*

—*n.* **3** jacket and trousers or skirt, °outfit, °uniform, °ensemble, °costume, °habit; garb, clothing, °clothes, livery: *He showed up wearing a new silk suit.* **4** lawsuit, °action, °case, °proceeding, °process, °cause, °trial; °litigation: *I do not want to enter into a suit over the damage to my car.* **5** °petition, °plea, °request, entreaty, °prayer, solicitation, °application, °appeal, °supplication; courtship: *The king rejected all suits for his daughter's hand in marriage.*

suitable *adj.* °appropriate, apt, °fit, °fitting, °befitting, °becoming, °right, °proper, °correct, °acceptable, °satisfactory, °applicable, °meet, °seemly; °timely, °opportune: *John has at last found suitable employment. A chandelier is not suitable at all for such a low room. Is this a suitable time for me to ask you a favour?*

suitcase *n.* °bag, valise, overnight °bag, holdall, °grip or *Brit* handgrip, *Brit formerly* portmanteau: *She packed enough for a week's holiday into one small suitcase.*

suite *n.* **1** °set, series, °collection, °number: *They gave us a beautiful suite of rooms at the hotel.* **2** °set: *She bought a new suite of dining-room furniture.* **3** following, °retinue, entourage, °train, cortège, convoy, °escort; followers, attendants, retainers: *Her suite includes advisers, secretaries, hairdressers, and bodyguards.*

suitor *n.* °admirer, beau, wooer; boyfriend, °paramour, °lover, inamorato, cicisbeo, °escort, *Archaic* swain: *Madelaine has more suitors than I can count.*

sulk *v.* mope, °brood, °pout, be °sullen or °moody or ill-humoured: *I wish you'd get a job instead of sulking about the house all day.*

sullen *adj.* sulky, sulking, morose, brooding, pouting, °gloomy, °moody, °temperamental, °dour, lugubrious, °funereal, °dismal, °dreary, °grim, depressing, depressed, churlish, ill-humoured, °glum, grumpy, °sombre, out of humour, antisocial, unsociable, °cross, °petulant, °perverse, crusty, crotchety, choleric, crabby, ill-natured, ill-tempered, bad-tempered, splenetic, °peevish, dyspeptic, out of sorts, *US* °cranky: *He remained quite sullen and refused to associate with anyone.*

sully *v.* besmirch, °stain, smirch, °blemish, °mar, defile, °soil, °disgrace, °dirty, °tarnish, °pollute, °spoil, °ruin, °destroy, °wreck: *Sadly, his reputation was sullied when his company was found to be involved in insider trading.*

sultry *adj.* **1** °hot, °humid, °sticky, °stuffy, stifling, °oppressive, °close, °muggy, °steamy, steaming, °moist, °damp, °sweltering, suffocating: *I was happy to be languishing again in the sultry warmth of St Lucia.* **2** °lusty, °lustful, °passionate, °erotic, °seductive, °voluptuous, °provocative, °sensual, *Colloq* °sexy, °hot: *She continued her sultry, slow, sinuous dance.*

sum *n.* **1** °total, aggregate, grand °total, sum °total, °whole, °totality; °amount, °quantity: *The sum of money found in the satchel was not revealed by the police. He would give the neighbourhood children small sums to spend on sweets.*
—*v.* **2 sum up: a** °recapitulate, summarize, encapsulate, synopsize, °digest, °abridge, condense, consolidate, epitomize, °review: *He summed up by reminding the children not to accept gifts from strangers.* **b** °reckon, °add up, °calculate, °total, °tot up, °measure (up), take the °measure of: *They summed up their chances of*

escaping. **c** °estimate, °evaluate, °size up, assess: *She had summed him up the minute she saw him.*

summarily *adv.* **1** °immediately, at °once, straight away, °directly, °quickly, without °delay, unhesitatingly, without hesitation, forthwith, °promptly, °swiftly, speedily, expeditiously, instantly, *Colloq* p.d.q. (= 'pretty damned quick'): *Any dog caught without a muzzle will be impounded summarily.* **2** °suddenly, without °warning, abruptly, peremptorily, precipitately: *He was summarily dismissed, with no advance notice.*

summary *n.* **1** summarization, recapitulation, encapsulation, compendium, °synopsis, °digest, °abridgement, condensation, shortening, consolidation, °epitome, epitomization, °review, distillate, conspectus, °brief, °outline, °précis, résumé: *I want a summary of the meeting on my desk in the morning.* —*adj.* **2** °abrupt, °peremptory, °short, quick, °brief, laconic, °perfunctory, °curt, °terse: *My simple request for some time off was denied with a summary, 'No!'*

summit *n.* °peak, °top, apex, °acme, °pinnacle, °zenith, °crown; culmination, °climax: *The winds at the summit of Annapurna reached hurricane force. There was no doubt that I had reached the summit of my achievements.*

summon *v.* **1** °call, °assemble, convoke, convene, °send for, invite, °muster, °get together, °arouse, °rouse: *Why would he summon us to the office at midnight?* **2** Often, **summon up**: °call or °draw on or upon, °draw up, °mobilize, °muster (up), °work up, °gather, invoke: *I had to summon up all my courage to ask Eve to go out.*

sumptuous *adj.* °expensive, costly, °extravagant, °exorbitant, °dear, °rich; °lavish, °luxurious, de luxe, °opulent, °palatial, °royal, °majestic, °regal, °magnificent, °dazzling, °splendid, °showy, *Colloq* °posh, °plush, ritzy: *The family treated us to a sumptuous repast to celebrate our 50th wedding anniversary.*

sun *n.* **1** (old) Sol, Helios, Phoebus (Apollo), Ra, Sunna, day-star: *Many early cultures worshipped the sun.* —*v.* **2** tan, suntan, sunbathe, bask, bake, brown, bronze: *They spent their holidays sunning themselves on the beach.*

sundries *n.pl.* knick-knacks, trinkets, °small items, notions, miscellanea, °miscellany, kickshaws, Brummagem, frippery, bric-à-brac or bric-a-brac, °odds and ends: *We might find a button for your shirt in a shop that sells sundries.*

sundry *adj.* °various, °varied, °miscellaneous, assorted, °different, °mixed, diversified, °diverse, divers: *In addition to food, supermarkets stock sundry other items.*

sunken *adj.* **1** °hollow, hollowed-out, °haggard, °drawn: *From her sunken cheeks the child looked as if she hadn't eaten for weeks.* **2** submerged, undersea, underwater, submersed: *The boat hit a sunken wreck and foundered.* **3** buried, °underground, in-ground, below-ground, settled, lowered: *The old term for a sunken fence is 'ha-ha'.*

sunless *adj.* °dark, °grim, cheerless, °unhappy, °joyless, °funereal, depressing, °dreary, drear, °sombre, °gloomy, °grey, Stygian, °black, pitchy, inky, °shadowy, tenebrous, unlit, unlighted, °dusky, subfusc or subfuscous, darkling: *It was an overcast sunless day, with rain in the offing.*

sunny *adj.* **1** sunlit, sunshiny, °brilliant, °bright, °radiant, °fair, °fine, cloudless, °clear, unclouded: *The enchanting scenery and warm sunny climate makes it a perfect place for holidays.* **2** °cheerful, cheery, °happy, joyous, °joyful, light-hearted, smiling, beaming, °buoyant, °blithe, °gay, mirthful, °jolly, °bubbly, °ebullient, °genial, °warm, °friendly, °outgoing: *Being with someone who has a sunny disposition was a pleasant change.*

super *adj.* wonderful: See **superb**, below.

superb *adj.* wonderful, °marvellous, °excellent, °superior, °gorgeous, °glorious, °magnificent, °outstanding, °exquisite, °fine, °splendid, unequalled, °sensational, °noteworthy, °admirable, °peerless, °matchless, unrivalled, °first-rate, °superlative, °perfect, °classic, °exceptional, °extraordinary, °striking, °brilliant, °dazzling, °miraculous, °incredible, °unbelievable, °fantastic, °fabulous, stupendous, staggering, mind-boggling, breathtaking, °divine, *Colloq* °great, °super, smashing, °magic, °terrific, fantabulous, °unreal, out of °this °world, mind-blowing, *Slang* out of °sight, far-out, boss, solid, cool, hot, bad: *The curator said he had never seen such a superb collection. She does a superb Hedda Gabler. We were treated to a superb dinner.*

supercilious *adj.* °haughty, °contemptuous, °superior, °snobbish, °disdainful, °arrogant, °condescending, patronizing, °overbearing, °scornful, lordly, high and mighty, °pompous, °lofty, °stuffy, °pretentious, *Colloq* °hoity-toity, highfalutin or hifalutin, uppity, snooty, stuck-up, *Brit* toffee-nosed, °uppish, la-di-da or lah-di-dah or la-de-da: *She was very supercilious towards her customers.*

superficial *adj.* **1** °surface, °external, °exterior, °shallow, °skin-deep, °slight, °outside: *I suffered a superficial wound to the forehead.* **2** °surface, °slight, °external, °apparent, °skin-deep, °outward, °cursory, °insignificant, °passing, unimportant, trivial, °empty, °insubstantial, paying lip-service, for appearances' sake, cosmetic: *She bears a superficial resemblance to your sister. His interest in your welfare is entirely superficial.* **3** °cursory, slapdash, quick, °hurried, °hasty, °perfunctory, °nominal, °meaningless, °passing: *The machinery is subjected to a superficial inspection before shipping.*

superficies *n.* (outer) °surface, façade, °face, externals, °outside: *The superficies may appeal to children, but adults appreciate the book's profundities.*

superfluity *n.* °excess, superabundance, over-abundance, °surplus, oversupply, °surfeit, °glut, superfluousness, °profusion, plethora, oversupply, supersaturation: *The middle and upper classes wallow in a superfluity of goods.*

superfluous *adj.* °excessive, °excess, superabundant, over-abundant, supererogatory, °surplus, unneeded, uncalled-for, °unnecessary, °redundant, °extra; °needless, dispensable, °gratuitous: *The superfluous grain that remains unsold should be donated to third-world countries. They knew each other so well that words were superfluous between them.*

superhuman *adj.* **1** °heroic, Herculean, °godlike, °legendary, valiant, °courageous, °brave, °daring, °dangerous, death-defying, °extraordinary, °miraculous, °phenomenal,

°incredible, °fabulous, °fantastic, °unbelievable, °amazing: *His superhuman feats would never be duplicated.*
—*n.* **2** superman, °hero, superhero, übermensch, Hercules: *They still believe that one day a superhuman will come along to lead them.*

superintendent *n.* °supervisor, °foreman, °overseer, °manager, administrator, °chief, °head, °boss; governor, controller, °director, conductor: *Alan has been appointed superintendent of the new project.*

superior *adj.* **1** higher, higher-ranking, higher-level, higher-class, higher-calibre, °upper, upper-level, °upper-class, loftier, nobler, °better; of a higher °order *or* °status *or* standing, *Colloq* classier, tonier: *He was reported to his superior officer.* **2** °high-class, °elevated, °first-rate, °distinguished, °exceptional, °excellent, preferred, °choice, °select, élitist, °outstanding, °superlative, °matchless, unequalled, °peerless, °nonpareil, °sterling, °supreme, °fine, °noteworthy, °notable, °worthy, °estimable: *Kenneth has had the benefit of a superior education.* **3** See **supercilious**, above.
—*n.* **4** See **supervisor**, below.

superiority *n.* **1** ascendancy, °pre-eminence, °supremacy, °leadership, °lead, dominance, °predominance, primacy, hegemony: *Her superiority in the field is unchallenged.* **2** °excellence, greatness, peerlessness, matchlessness, inimitability, superlativeness, °prominence, eminence, °importance, °distinction, °prestige, °renown: *All commented on the superiority of Mark's contribution.*

superlative *adj.* unsurpassed, °paramount, °supreme, consummate, °superior, °best, choicest, finest, °matchless, °peerless, unequalled, unrivalled, °singular, °unique, °incomparable, °excellent, °superb, °sterling, °dazzling, °first-rate, °exceptional, °extraordinary, °marvellous, spectacular, °capital, *Colloq* tiptop, °super, smashing, °great, ace, °terrific, °fantastic, *Slang* crack: *Max turned in a superlative performance in the tournament.*

supernatural *adj.* preternatural, °unusual, °extraordinary, °exceptional, °unnatural, °miraculous, °remarkable, °fabulous, preterhuman, °ghostly, °spectral, °abnormal, °inexplicable, unexplainable; metaphysical, other-worldly, °unearthly, ultramundane, supramundane, extramundane, °occult, mystic, paranormal, °psychic, uncanny, °weird, °mysterious, arcane, °unreal, magical, °dark: *Some claim to hear supernatural voices speaking to them. Many characters in children's stories have supernatural powers.*

supersede *v.* °replace, °succeed, °displace, °supplant, oust, take the °place of, °substitute for: *The 286 computers have been superseded by 386 models.*

supervise *v.* °oversee, °overlook, °watch (over), °manage, °run, °control, superintend, °govern, °direct, be in *or* have °charge (of), °handle, keep an °eye on, °administer: *They are moving you up to supervise the production department.*

supervisor *n.* °overseer, °foreman, °manager, controller, °superintendent, °superior, governor, °director, °boss, °chief, °head, administrator: *As supervisor, you are responsible for the work done in your department.*

supervisory *adj.* managerial, administrative, °executive: *Do you think that Len is ready for supervisory responsibilities?*

supine *adj.* **1** °flat (on one's back), °lying (down), °prostrate, °recumbent, *Formal or technical* procumbent, accumbent, decumbent: *When I found him, he was supine, staring up at the stars.* **2** °indolent, °lazy, °lethargic, °idle, °listless, °indifferent, apathetic, unconcerned, uninterested, °torpid, languid, languorous, sluggish, °slothful, °phlegmatic, lymphatic, °lackadaisical, °inert, °inactive, °passive, motionless, °inanimate, spiritless, abject: *During the entire crisis, the town council was completely supine and uncaring.*

supplant *v.* °replace, °displace, oust, °turn out, °eject, °remove, °expel, °dismiss, unseat, °supersede, °substitute, °exchange: *The council should be supplanted by a new group more sympathetic to the needs of the people.*

supple *adj.* **1** °flexible, flexile, pliant, bendable, °elastic, resilient, °pliable, tractile, fictile: *He made a rug-beater out of some supple lengths of bamboo.* **2** °willowy, lithe, limber, °nimble, pliant, lissom *or* lissome, °graceful, athletic: *She has the supple body of a dancer.* **3** °tractable, compliant, °yielding, °accommodating, °obliging, complaisant, acquiescent, °submissive, unresistant, unresisting, °servile, °obsequious, °ingratiating, fawning, toadying: *With supple words the miserable sycophant wormed his way into father's confidence.*

supplement *n.* **1** addendum, °addition, appendix, epilogue, end-piece, postscript, appendage, °extension, continuation, adjunct, annexe, appurtenance, °accessory, codicil, °insert, °sequel; supplementation; *Technical* suppletion: *The later version includes the 1909 supplement.*
—*v.* **2** °add (on *or* to), °extend, augment; °complement: *Various scholars supplemented the earlier work with their own notes and comments. He supplements his income by working at a restaurant.*

supplementary *adj.* **1** additional, added, annexed, adjunct, °new: *The supplementary buildings increased the size of the hospital greatly.* **2** supplemental, °supportive, contributory, ancillary, °secondary, °subordinate, annexed, additional, °attached, added, appended, °subsidiary, adscititious; °extraneous, adventitious, supervenient, °extra, °excess; *Technical* suppletive: *The supplementary material expanded the original work fivefold.*

supplicant *adj.* **1** suppliant, supplicating, entreating, petitioning, supplicatory, beseeching, praying, imploring, °solicitous, importunate, begging, mendicant: *In 1897, he carved a supplicant group in white marble, now in the Fraser Museum.*
—*n.* **2** suppliant, applicant, petitioner, beseecher, °suitor, pleader, aspirant, appellant, plaintiff, °beggar, mendicant: *He came to me as a supplicant, begging forgiveness for what he had done.*

supplication *n.* **1** entreaty, °petition, °prayer, °appeal, pleading, °plea, °suit, solicitation, obsecration, obtestation, impetration: *Heeding the pitiful supplications of the beggars, they gave them some money.* **2** supplicating, begging, pleading, soliciting, petitioning, entreating, beseeching: *All his supplication could not wring a farthing from the old skinflint.*

supply v. 1 °furnish, °provide, °give, endow, °present, purvey, °deliver, come up with, °contribute, °distribute, °sell; stock, °accommodate, °afford, °equip, °outfit, °gear (up), °rig (out), °fit (out), °provision, °cater to, *Chiefly Brit* °kit out *or* up; victual: *Her company supplies radios to the army. Her husband's firm supplies the navy with anti-fouling paint.* 2 °yield, °give, °contribute, come up with, °deliver, °provide, °furnish: *The farm supplies our basic foods.* 3 °satisfy, °fulfil, °replenish, °fill: *Can you supply the demand for clothing?*
—n. 4 °stock, stockpile, °store, inventory, °quantity, reservoir, °reserve, °cache, °hoard, °accumulation, °fund: *Our supply is big enough to serve the entire area.* 5 furnishing, °provision, °providing, purveying, supplying, °distribution, equipping, outfitting, provisioning, °delivery, stocking, stockpiling: *The supply of microchips on a large scale is beyond our capacity.*

support v. 1 back (up), °stand by, °help, °bolster, °uphold, °brace, °strengthen, °fortify, °buttress, °prop (up), shore up, °reinforce, °boost, °champion, °assist, take up the cudgels for, °aid, °promote, °forward, °second, °advance, °advocate, °stand up for, be °supportive (of *or* in), *Colloq* °stick up for: *Peterson agreed to support him in his bid for the presidency.* 2 °brace, °hold up, °carry, °prop (up); °strengthen, shore up, °reinforce, °fortify, °buttress: *You need a column to support this beam.* 3 °tolerate, °bear, °stand (for), °suffer, °submit to, °undergo, °brook, °stomach, °endure, °abide, countenance, °face, *Brit* °stick, *Colloq* °put up with: *He cannot support the notion that she might be guilty.* 4 °pay for, °fund, °maintain, °keep, °finance, °subsidize, °underwrite, °sponsor, *Colloq US* bankroll: *I can no longer support myself or my family.* 5 °sustain, °withstand, °stand, °take, °bear, °tolerate, °hold up under, °weather: *His legs were too weak to support his own weight.* 6 °verify, corroborate, °authenticate, °vouch for, °endorse, °confirm, affirm, °bear out, °attest to, °certify, °substantiate, validate, °ratify: *Can anyone support his alibi?*
—n. 7 °help, °backing, backup, °reinforcement, bolstering, °encouragement, reinforcing, fortifying, °assistance, °aid, succour, °sustenance: *Thank you for your support over the years.* 8 °brace, °prop, °stay, °frame, °foundation, underpinning, substructure, truss, °beam, column, °pillar, °strut, guy, guy wire, °mainstay, °buttress, °bolster, °reinforcement, °supporter: *The supports failed under the grandstand and it fell, injuring a few. Alan was a tremendous support during my illness.* 9 °sustenance, (living) expenses, °keep, °maintenance, °subsistence, °upkeep; finances, funding: *Mona is suing David for the support of their child. He lives mainly on government support.*

supportable adj. 1 °tolerable, °bearable, endurable, °acceptable, sufferable: *Thoughts of death are more supportable when it seems remote.* 2 defensible, confirmable, verifiable, °demonstrable, °tenable, believable: *The argument that we should keep the old tax structure is simply not supportable.*

supporter n. 1 °enthusiast, °champion, promoter, °fan, aficionado, °devotee, °admirer, °backer, °follower, °support, °advocate, exponent, adherent, °aid, °assistant, helper: *I wish to thank my many supporters, who were there when I needed them.* 2 See support, 8, above.

supportive adj. °helpful, sustaining, supporting, encouraging, °sympathetic, °understanding, reassuring: *Among our many friends, Cleo was the most supportive during the recent trouble.*

suppose v. 1 °assume, °presume, °presuppose, °surmise, °take, °take as °given *or* as read, °take for granted; °believe, °think, °fancy, °imagine; *Colloq* °take it: *Don't people usually suppose that civil servants are honest? I supposed her to be his wife. Do you suppose you could return my key today?* 2 hypothesize, °theorize, postulate, °posit, °assume: *Supposing a reduced rate of inflation, will they reduce interest rates? Suppose that you have lost the election—what will you do?*

supposed adj. 1 °alleged, °assumed, putative, °reputed, presumed, °hypothetical, °theoretical, theorized, imagined, suppositious, supposititious: *Her supposed drug addiction turned out to be a myth.* 2 °obliged, expected, required; meant, intended: *You were supposed to return my key. What is that supposed to mean?*

supposedly adv. allegedly, reputedly, theoretically, °hypothetically, °presumably; °rumour has it: *The bridge was blown up, supposedly by terrorists.*

supposing conj. if, °even if, in the °event that, °despite the °fact that, although, °though: *Supposing he says no, what will you do?*

supposition n. assumption, °presumption, °surmise, °belief, °thought, °fancy, theory, °hypothesis, postulate, °proposal, °proposition: *On the supposition that your calculations are correct, we will have made a profit this year.*

suppress v. 1 °end, °discontinue, °cut off, °cease, °stop, °terminate, put an °end to, °halt, °prohibit, °preclude, °prevent, °repress, censor, °forbid, interdict, °block, °obstruct, °withhold, °stifle, °inhibit, °hinder, °arrest: *They have been unable to suppress the publication of the book.* 2 °put down, °quell, °crush, °squelch, °quash, °subdue, °check, °stamp out, snuff out, °smother, °extinguish, °quench, °crack down on: *The uprising was suppressed with the shooting of the students.* 3 °keep down, °control, °keep under °control, °keep *or* °hold in °check, °restrain, °hold in *or* back, °repress, °cover up, °conceal, °hide, °keep °quiet *or* °secret, °mute, °muffle, °quiet(en), °silence: *Objections to the guest speaker were suppressed at the request of the university's chancellor.*

suppression n. suppressing, ending, °end, discontinuation, discontinuing, °cutting off, cut-off, cessation, ceasing, surcease, stopping, °stop, terminating, °termination, °halting, °halt, prohibiting, °prohibition, preclusion, precluding, preventing, °prevention, repressing, °repression, censoring, censorship, °forbidding, forbiddance, interdicting, interdiction, blocking, obstructing, °obstruction, withholding, stifling, hindering; putting down, °put-down, quelling, crushing, squelching, quashing, subduing, checking, °check, stamping out, smothering, snuffing out, extinguishing, extinction, elimination, quenching, cracking down on, crack-down; °control, controlling, restraining, °restraint, concealing, concealment, hiding, muting, muffling, quieting, silencing: *That constitutes suppression of the freedom of speech. The* *suppression of heresy is a perennial church problem. Dictators confuse the suppression of ideas with the oppression of people.*

supremacist *n.* supremist, bigot, racist, racialist, dogmatist, °zealot, °fanatic: *Supremacists' philosophies are based on hatred, not love.*

supremacy *n.* **1** transcendency, °pre-eminence, °superiority, ascendancy, °excellence, primacy, peerlessness, matchlessness, incomparability, inimitability: *Colonialism depends on military supremacy.* **2** °sovereignty, °dominion, °sway, mastery, °control, dominance, (°supreme *or* °absolute) °rule *or* °authority, autarchy, omnipotence, hegemony: *They maintained their supremacy over the Iberian peninsula for centuries.*

supreme *adj.* **1** highest, loftiest, topmost, greatest, °first, °foremost, °principal, unsurpassed, °top, °uppermost, °chief, °paramount, °sovereign: *There is no appeal to a decision of the supreme tribunal.* **2** greatest, °maximum, °extreme, uttermost, utmost, °ultimate: *I fear that your son has made the supreme sacrifice, Mrs Atkins.* **3** °best, greatest, °first, °outstanding, °pre-eminent, °first-rate, °prime, °primary, unexcelled, °leading, crowning, consummate: *Many regard her as the supreme artist of her day.* **4** °superb, °marvellous, °excellent, °outstanding, °superlative, °matchless, °peerless, °incomparable, °unparalleled, °masterful, masterly, °sublime, °brilliant, °transcendent, inimitable, °choice: *There is no doubt that she is a supreme artist.*

supremely *adv.* °very, °extremely, °completely, °perfectly, superlatively, sublimely, transcendently: *I have never been so supremely happy as I was in Capri in '38.*

sure *adj.* **1** °certain, assured, convinced, persuaded, °positive, °definite, unwavering, unswerving, unflinching, °steadfast, °steady, unshakeable *or* unshakable, °confident, satisfied, undeviating, unfaltering: *How can you be so sure in your opinion that Jack did it? I'm sure I've met you before.* **2** established, °firm, °solid, trusty, °stable, °steadfast, °secure, °safe, °trustworthy, °reliable: *I never travel without my sure companions, courage and caution.* **3** °accurate, °reliable, dependable, tried and °true, unfailing, °infallible, °foolproof, °effective, *Colloq* sure-fire: *A high temperature is a sure sign of illness.* **4** °certain, °inevitable, indubitable, °unavoidable, ineluctable, inescapable, guaranteed: *He who enters the Devil's Cave meets sure death.*

surely *adv.* **1** certainly, to be °sure, °positively, °absolutely, °definitely, °undoubtedly, indubitably, unquestionably, beyond the shadow of a °doubt, beyond °question, °doubtless, doubtlessly, assuredly, *Colloq* °sure, *US* absolutely-posolutely: *He is surely one of the finest riders I've ever seen.* **2** °firmly, solidly, confidently, unfalteringly, steadily, unswervingly, unhesitatingly, determinedly, doggedly, securely: *Slowly but surely, the Great Bamboni stepped out onto the tightrope stretched across the Reichenbach Falls.*

surface *n.* **1** °exterior, covering, °outside, °top, °skin, integument, façade, °face, °boundary, interface, °superficies; °side, °plane: *Most of the earth's surface is covered by water. How many surfaces on an icosahedron?* **2 on the surface**: superficially, to all appearances, at first glance,

°outwardly, to the casual observer, extrinsically, °ostensibly: *It looks pretty enough on the surface, but it is rotten underneath.* —*v.* **3** °appear, °show up, °emerge, °materialize, °arise, °rise, °come up, *Colloq* °pop up, crop up: *Guess who surfaced after ten years in Tierra del Fuego! An enormous turtle surfaced near our boat.* **4** °pave, °concrete, tarmac: *They are surfacing the road in front of my house.*

surfeit *n.* over-abundance, superabundance, plethora, °glut, °excess, °surplus, oversupply, overdose, °satiety, overflow, °flood, deluge, °superfluity, nimiety: *There has been a surfeit of those dolls on the market. She is suffering from a surfeit of rich food and alcohol.*

surfeited *adj.* gorged, overfed, satiated, sated, stuffed, glutted, °jaded: *He passed the sleeping surfeited diners and stole into the library unseen.*

surge *v.* **1** °swell, °wave, billow, °bulge, °heave, °roll, undulate, °well forth *or* up, °rise and °fall, °ebb and °flow, °pulsate; °rush, °gush, °pour, °flood, °stream, °flow: *The sea surged through the narrow gorge with a roar. The crowd surged round their hero.* —*n.* **2** °swell, °wave, billow, °roller, whitecap, white horse, breaker, comber, upsurge, °eddy, °rush, °gush, °flood, °stream, °flow: *The raft was caught by a surge and tossed high up on the beach.*

surly *adj.* unpleasant, °rude, crusty, °cantankerous, curmudgeonly, churlish, crabby, crabbed, choleric, splenetic, dyspeptic, °bilious, °temperamental, °cross, crotchety, grouchy, grumpy, bearish, °testy, °touchy, °short-tempered, ill-tempered, bad-tempered, ill-natured, bad-natured, ill-humoured, °peevish, °quarrelsome, °argumentative, °obnoxious, uncivil, °rough, °obstreperous: *I see no reason to shop where the sales staff are surly.*

surmise *v.* **1** °imagine, °guess, conjecture, °speculate, °suppose, hypothesize, °theorize, °assume, °presume, conclude, °gather, °infer, °understand, °fancy, °suspect, °feel, °sense: *I surmised that the treaty terms were arranged by deputies long before the summit.* —*n.* **2** °guess, conjecture, °speculation, °notion, °hypothesis, theory, °supposition, assumption, °presumption, conclusion, °understanding, °fancy, °suspicion, °feeling, °sense: *It was an early surmise of the experts that man could not survive passing through the Van Allen belts.*

surpass *v.* °exceed, °excel, °go *or* °pass beyond, °outdo, °beat, worst, °better, °best, °outstrip, outdistance, outperform, outclass, outshine, °eclipse, °overshadow, °top, °cap, °transcend, °prevail over, leave behind: *He easily surpassed the statesmen of his time.*

surpassing *adj.* °excessive, °extraordinary, °great, °enormous, unrivalled, °matchless, °peerless, unmatched, unequalled, unsurpassed: *I could not believe the surpassing gall of the man.*

surpassingly *adv.* °exceedingly, extraordinarily, incomparably, *Literary* °surpassing: *The girls on the beach were surpassingly beautiful.*

surplus *n.* **1** surplusage, overage, °excess, °leftover(s), °surfeit, over-abundance, oversupply, overdose, °glut: *The price of oil dropped owing to the surplus in the market.* —*adj.* **2** °excess, °leftover, °extra, °spare, over-abundant, °superfluous, °unused, °redundant: *The surplus grain is sold abroad.*

surprise v. **1** °shock, °astound, °astonish, °amaze, disconcert, °nonplus, °dumbfound or dumfound, °stagger, °take aback, °strike, °hit, Colloq °floor, °bowl over, flabbergast, °rock or set (someone) back on his or her or chiefly Brit their heels, Brit knock (someone) for six, US knock (someone) for a loop: What surprised me was her coolness in the face of danger. **2** take or °catch °unawares, °catch °red-handed or in the act or in flagrante delicto, °discover: When Samuel Johnson's wife found him with a maid, she said, 'Dr Johnson! I am surprised!', to which he replied, 'No, madam: you are amazed. I am surprised'.
—n. **3** °shock, °astonishment, °amazement, stupefaction, °wonder, incredulity: Imagine my surprise to learn that I was being arrested. **4** °blow, °jolt, shocker, °bolt from or US also out of the blue, °bombshell, eye-opener: It came as a surprise to me that my sister was pregnant.

surrender v. **1** °give up, °yield, °let go (of), °relinquish, °deliver (up), °hand over, °forgo, °forsake, °turn over, °turn in, °part with, °cede, °concede: We were forced at gunpoint to surrender our valuables. **2** °give up, °yield, °quit, cry quits, °capitulate, throw in the sponge or the towel, raise the white flag, throw up one's hands, °succumb, °submit, °give °way, acquiesce, °comply, °give in, °concede, °crumble: The argument is so overwhelming that I must surrender.
—n. **3** °submission, capitulation, °yielding, renunciation, relinquishment, transferral, °transfer, transference, handing or turning over, conveyancing, ceding, cession, concession: The official surrender of the disputed territory took place in the following year.

surreptitious adj. °furtive, °secret, clandestine, °stealthy, underhand(ed), covert, (on the) °sly, °secretive, °private, concealed, °hidden, °veiled, Colloq °sneaky: She stole surreptitious glances at him.

surround v. **1** encompass, °encircle, °envelop, °enclose, hem in, °ring: She likes being surrounded by flowers. Troops surrounded the building.
—n. **2** environs, °environment, surroundings, °atmosphere, ambience or ambiance, °setting: The formal gardens make a charming surround for the art gallery.

surrounding adj. °nearby, °neighbouring, °local, °adjoining, °neighbourhood, adjacent, bordering, abutting, circumambient, circumjacent: The surrounding countryside was bursting into bloom.

surveillance n. °observation, °watch, °scrutiny, °reconnaissance: The police kept him under constant surveillance.

survey v. **1** °examine, appraise, °evaluate, take the °measure of, °inspect, °study, °scan, °scrutinize, °measure, °size up, assess, °investigate, °look into or over, °review: He surveyed the situation and found nothing wrong. **2** °view, °look at, get a bird's eye view of, °contemplate: From the top of the tower I surveyed the surrounding countryside.
—n. **3** surveying, °examination, appraisal, °evaluation, °measure, °study, °scan, scanning, °scrutiny, °inquiry or enquiry, °measurement, °investigation, inspection: Our survey of the company finances yielded some very interesting information.

survive v. **1** °continue, °last, °live (on), °persist, subsist, °pull through, °endure: The village was destroyed, but its people survived. **2** °outlast, outlive: At the age of 114, MacMurtagh has survived all his children and many of his grandchildren.

susceptible adj. **1** Often, **susceptible of** or **to**: °open (to), °prone (to), °subject (to), °disposed (to), predisposed (to), °receptive (to), °affected by, °responsive (to): Brass is susceptible of a high shine. Are you still susceptible to her blandishments? **2** °impressionable, influenceable, °vulnerable, reachable, °accessible, credulous, °suggestible, °gullible, °naïve: Susceptible youngsters need protection from commercial exploitation.

suspect v. **1** disbelieve, °doubt, °mistrust, °distrust, harbour or have suspicions about or of, be °suspicious of: Do you suspect the butler? **2** °feel, °think, °believe, °sense, have a °feeling, °fancy, °imagine, °theorize, °guess, °surmise, have a sneaking °suspicion, think it likely or probable, Colloq °expect: I suspect that the butler might have done it.
—adj. **3** °suspicious, °questionable, °doubtful, dubious, °shady, °shadowy; suspected: If you ask me, his behaviour since boarding the Orient Express has been highly suspect.

suspend v. **1** °hold up or off (on), °withhold, °put off, put or °hold or keep in or into °abeyance, °shelve, °postpone, °delay, °defer, °interrupt, °stop or °check or °cease or °discontinue temporarily, US °table: We suspended payment pending inspection of the work already done. Train services on this route will be suspended till further notice. Suspend your disbelief for a moment to consider the possible motive for stealing a prune. **2** °hang, °attach, °fasten, °dangle, °swing: She suspended the cameo from a gold chain which she wore as a necklace. **3** debar, °exclude, °eliminate, °reject, °expel, °eject, °evict; °deprive of the rights of, °deny the privileges of; blackball: A member may be suspended if his dues are six months or more in arrears.

suspense n. **1** uncertainty, indefiniteness, insecurity, °doubt, irresolution, expectancy, °indecision, not knowing: May I have the envelope please?—I cannot stand the suspense! **2** °anxiety, °tension, apprehension, nervousness, °agitation, anxiousness, °anticipation, °expectation, °excitement: A story that creates suspense for the reader is often suitable for film treatment.

suspension n. **1** debarring, disbarment, °exclusion, elimination, °rejection, expulsion, °ejection, °eviction, deprivation, °denial: The suspension of privileges cannot last for more than a fortnight. **2** °intermission, °moratorium, deferment, °hold-up, °delay, delaying, °interruption, °postponement, postponing, discontinuing, discontinuation, °stay: Luckily, the suspension of hostilities lasted till the summer.

suspicion n. **1** °doubt, dubiousness, dubiety, °misgiving, °mistrust, °distrust, °scepticism, °qualm, wariness, apprehension, apprehensiveness, cautiousness, hesitation, second thought(s), uncertainty, leeriness, Colloq funny °feeling, bad °vibes: We all had our suspicions about Edward's genuine intentions. My worst suspicions have now been confirmed. **2** °notion, °inkling, °suggestion, °hint, °trace, °flavour, soupçon, °taste, °dash, glimmer, tinge, °touch, °shadow, °shade, scintilla, Colloq chiefly US and

Canadian tad: *If you have even a suspicion of doubt, do not find the defendant guilty. Did I detect a suspicion of a sneer?*

suspicious *adj.* **1** °doubtful, in °doubt, dubious, °questionable, °debatable, °suspect(ed), under °suspicion, °open to °doubt or °question or misconstruction, *Colloq* °shady, °fishy: *There is something very suspicious about his behaviour.* **2** mistrustful, °distrustful, °doubtful, in °doubt, °sceptical, suspecting, disbelieving, °unbelieving, °leery, apprehensive, °wary, °uncertain, uneasy: *I was suspicious of Douglas from the very beginning.*

sustain *v.* **1** °uphold, °support, °keep up, °maintain, °continue, °keep (someone or something) going, °keep °alive, °preserve; °prolong, °persist in: *He has been sustained on a life-support system for weeks. If Georgette can sustain the pretence of loving him, he won't change his will.* **2** °support, °carry, °bear, °bolster, °buoy (up), °reinforce, °keep (someone) going, strengthen, shore up, underpin, °prop up, °buttress: *During those long months as a hostage, only prayer sustained him.* **3** °endure, °stand, °withstand, °bear up under, °put up with, °suffer, °undergo, °experience, °tolerate, °weather, °brave: *It is amazing how much punishment the human body can sustain.* **4** °bear, °carry, °support: *This column is supposed to sustain the weight of half the building.* **5** °uphold, °recognize, °allow, °admit, °approve, °ratify, °sanction, °authorize, °endorse, validate: *The judge sustained the objection by the defence.*

sustained *adj.* continued, °continuous, °continual, prolonged, unremitting, °steady, ceaseless, unceasing, incessant, interminable; °uniform, °even, °level, unchanged, unchanging: *The neighbours keep up that sustained caterwauling every night. The audience was thrilled by her sustained top C.*

sustenance *n.* **1** nutriment, °nourishment, °food (and °drink), daily bread, °rations, victuals, provisions, °provender, groceries, aliment, °edibles, eatables, foodstuff(s), viands, °meat, *Colloq* grub, eats, chow, nosh, *Slang Brit* prog, °scoff: *My first concern is sustenance for my family.* **2** livelihood, °support, °maintenance, °upkeep, °keep, °subsistence, living: *The fur trade provided the sustenance of early Canadian settlers.*

swagger *v.* **1** °strut, °prance, °parade, *Archaic* swash, *Colloq US* sashay, cut a swath: *Look at that Charlie swaggering down the street in his new suit!* **2** °boast, °brag, °show off, vaunt, crow, *Colloq Brit* swank: *He is always swaggering on about his war experiences.*
—*n.* **3** °strut, °prance, strutting, swaggering, °show, °display, showing off, °ostentation, braggadocio, °arrogance, boastfulness: *Paul's outrageous swagger developed only after he was promoted.*

swallow *v.* **1** °eat, °consume, °devour, ingest, °dispatch or despatch; °drink, °gulp, guzzle, down, *Colloq* °put or pack away, swig, °swill: *Snakes swallow their prey whole. The amount that man can swallow at one meal is incredible.* **2** °accept, °allow, °credit, °believe, °take, *Colloq* °buy, °fall for: *She swallowed that tale about an aeroplane hook, line, and sinker.* **3** Often, **swallow up**: absorb, make disappear, engulf, °consume, assimilate:

The fugitive was swallowed up by the crowd. **4** Sometimes, **swallow back**: keep or °choke back or down, °repress, °suppress, °control, °stifle, °smother, °overcome, °conquer: *Harriet swallowed back the tears. Try swallowing your pride just this once.*
—*n.* **5** °bite, nibble, °morsel, °mouthful; °drink, °gulp, guzzle, *Colloq* swig: *Have a swallow of this to warm you up a little.*

swamp *n.* **1** °bog, fen, °marsh, quagmire, °morass, °moor, *Chiefly literary* slough, *Scots and No. Eng. dialect* moss, *So. US* everglade: *The draining of swamps destroys the breeding places of mosquitoes.*
—*v.* **2** °overwhelm, °overcome, °flood, inundate, °submerge, °immerse, deluge, °overload, overtax, overburden, *Colloq* snow under: *I'm so swamped with work I'm sleeping at the office.* **3** scuttle, °sink, °founder: *A huge wave swamped the boat and she sank quickly.*

swanky *adj.* °smart, °stylish, °fashionable, °chic, chichi, °fancy, °luxurious, °grand, °elegant, *Colloq* swank, snazzy, °neat, °nifty, °plush, °posh, ritzy, *Brit* °swish: *Living in a swanky house and wearing swanky clothes—what else would anyone want?*

swarm *n.* **1** °throng, horde, army, °host, multitude, hive, °herd, °mob, °mass, drove, °flood, °stream, cloud, °flock, °pack, shoal, °bunch: *Swarms of people showed up for our garden party.*
—*v.* **2** °throng, °mass, °crowd, congregate, °flock, °gather, °flood, °stream, °flow: *The fans swarmed round the rock group.* **3 swarm with**: Often, **be swarming with**: °crawl with, °abound in or with, °throng with, °teem with, °burst with, °bristle with, be °overrun with: *In two minutes the place was swarming with police.*

swarthy *adj.* swart, °black, ebon, ebony, sable, °pitch-black, jet-black, coal-black, raven, °dark: *His swarthy complexion contrasted with her china-like pallor.*

swashbuckling *adj.* °adventurous, °daring, °daredevil, swaggering, roisterous, °bold, °dashing, °flamboyant: *Those old swashbuckling films with Errol Flynn, Richard Greene, and Douglas Fairbanks, formed a genre all their own.*

swath *n.* °swathe, °path, °belt, °strip: *A flock of birds was feeding along the swath cut by the harvester.*

swathe *v.* °tie, °bind, bandage, °wrap, enwrap, swaddle, °bundle (up), °envelop, °shroud, °muffle (up): *I can't tell who he is as his head is swathed in bandages.*

sway *v.* **1** °wave, waver, °swing, °sweep, °oscillate, undulate, °reel, °totter, °swing or °move to and fro or back and forth or from side to side or backwards and forwards, °rock, °fluctuate; °bend, °lean: *The reeds swayed in the breeze.* **2** °move, °incline, °divert, °tend, veer, °tilt, °lean, °slant, °bias; °influence, °persuade, °impress, °win over, °bring round, °convince, °talk into: *The wind is causing the trees to sway towards the east. We tried to sway him to our way of thinking.*
—*n.* **3** °sweep, °wave, °swing, (period of) oscillation, libration: *There must be a sway of twenty feet in the top of that skyscraper.* **4** °influence, °control, °power, °command, °authority, °dominion, °rule, °sovereignty, °leadership, mastery; °grip, clutches, °grasp: *His ambition was to get the mountain people under his sway.*

swear v. **1** depose, aver, asseverate, °declare, °insist, assert, solemnly affirm or °state, °testify, °promise, take an °oath, °undertake, °vow, avow, °vouchsafe, °warrant, °pledge, give one's °word, °agree: *He swore he had not done any such thing.* **2** °curse, °blaspheme, imprecate, use °profanity, utter profanities, execrate, *Colloq* cuss: *Priscilla stopped her ears at the men's swearing.* **3 swear by**: °trust (in), °believe in, °rely on, have °confidence in, °count on: *The colonel swears by the same old fountain-pen he has used for years and will use no other.* **4 swear off**: forswear, °renounce, abjure, go off, °forgo, °shun, °avoid, °give up, eschew, °forsake, °throw over: *Brian tells me he's sworn off alcohol for a while.*

sweat v. **1** perspire, °glow: *That workout made me sweat.* **2** Often, **sweat out**: °worry, be °anxious, agonize, °anguish, bite (one's) nails, be on pins and needles, °fret, °fuss, °stew, torture or °torment oneself, lose sleep (over), *Colloq* sweat blood, be in a tizzy, *US* sweat bullets: *The professors really like to make students sweat, don't they? Fiona is sweating it out till the results are posted.* **3** °slave (away), °labour, drudge, °grind, toil and moil, slog, °work like a Trojan or a horse, *Slang Brit* swot: *I sweat over a hot stove all day while you're out and about town.* **4** °ooze, exude, °squeeze out, transude: *When a boy, he believed that dew came from flowers sweating water.*
—n. **5** °perspiration, *Technical* diaphoresis, sudor: *In addition to body moisture, salt and other minerals are lost in sweat.* **6** (hard) °work, °labour, laboriousness, °grind, toil, °drudgery, slogging, sweating, *Slang Brit* swotting: *Nothing worthwhile is gained without some sweat.* **7** state of °confusion or °upset or °excitement or °distraction or °agitation or °anxiety or °distress or °worry; pother, *Colloq* dither, tizzy, °lather: *Henry has really worked himself up into a sweat over this problem.* **8 No sweat!**: No problem!, Don't worry!, Everything is taken care of!, All is well!, That presents no difficulty!: *When asked to change a flat tyre, the stranger's response was, 'No sweat!'*

sweep v. **1** °brush, °whisk, °clean, °clear, °tidy up: *This weekend I have to sweep out the basement.* **2** Often, **sweep away**: °carry or °take (away or off), °destroy, °wipe out, °demolish, °remove, °wash (away); °blow (away): *The raging torrent swept away the bridge. The wind swept the debris before it.* **3** °swoop, °flounce, °glide, °sail, °march, °parade, °skim, °tear, °dash, zoom: *Hattie swept into the room majestically.* **4** curve, arc, °arch, °bend, °bow, °circle, °turn: *The long drive to the house sweeps round the pond and gardens.*
—n. **5** °pass, °clearance, °stroke; °purge: *In one clean sweep the police rounded up all the suspects.* **6** curve, arc, °arch, °bow, °bend, curvature, flexure: *Note the sweep of those main arches holding up the dome.* **7** °range, °extent, compass, °reach, °stretch, °scope, °swing, °span: *The Hubbell space telescope has a farther sweep than any on earth.*

sweeping adj. **1** °comprehensive, (all-)°inclusive, °general, °extensive, °universal, all-embracing, °broad, widespread, °wide(-ranging), far-ranging, blanket, °umbrella, °catholic, °exhaustive, °radical, °thorough(-going), °out-and-out, across the °board, wholesale, *Colloq* wall-to-wall: *We must institute sweeping reforms of the party before the*

election. **2** °complete, °total, °overwhelming, decisive: *The first team enjoyed a sweeping victory in track and field events.*

sweet adj. **1** sugary, honey-like, honeyed, sweetened: *Sweet breakfast cereals are bad for your teeth.* **2** °fragrant, perfumed, scented, °aromatic, ambrosial, sweet-smelling, sweet-scented, balmy, °redolent: *The night air was sweet with jasmine.* **3** °harmonious, °melodious, sweet-sounding, euphonious, dulcet, °musical, °tuneful, euphonic, mellifluous, °mellow, °lyric, silvery, bell-like, °golden: *I could hear McCormick's sweet voice singing 'Danny Boy'.* **4** °gentle, °amiable, °agreeable, °genial, °warm, °friendly, °kind, °nice, unassuming, °easygoing; °attractive, appealing, charming, °winning, °pleasant, °pleasing, °lovely; °cute, pretty: *Jane normally has such a sweet disposition. Old Mrs Hughes was always sweet to me when I was little. Amy looks so sweet in her new dress. What a sweet little kitten!* **5** °dear, °beloved, °precious, prized, treasured, wonderful, °marvellous, °splendid, *Colloq* °great: *How sweet life can be!* **6** °considerate, °attentive, °solicitous, °thoughtful, °sympathetic, compassionate, °kind, kind-hearted, °generous, °gracious, °accommodating: *How sweet it was of you to bring flowers!* **7** cloying, °sentimental, syrupy, saccharine, treacly, °precious, honeyed, sickening, *Colloq* gushing, °gushy, °sloppy, soppy, °maudlin, °sticky, *Brit* °twee, *Colloq* icky: *Claire is so sweet that she really overdoes it sometimes.* **8 sweet on**: °fond of, °taken with, °keen on, °devoted to, enamoured of, °infatuated with, (°head over heels) in °love with, *Colloq* °wild or °mad or °crazy about, nuts about or over, *Slang* gone on, stuck on, batty about: *We were teasing Rick about being sweet on Anne.*
—n. **9** Often, **sweets**: bon-bon, chocolate, confection, sweetmeat, *Old-fashioned* comfit, *US* °candy: *Harry always brings a box of sweets for my mother when he comes to see me.* **10** °dessert, *Brit* pudding, *Colloq Brit* pud, afters: *For a sweet we can offer you a choice between chocolate gateau and gooseberry pie.*

sweeten v. **1** sugar, sugar-coat: *Can you think of nothing that would sweeten the bad news?* **2** °dress up, make more °attractive or °agreeable, sugar-coat, °embellish, embroider; make less painful, °mitigate, alleviate, assuage, °lighten, °soften, palliate, mollify, °ease, allay, °moderate, °temper: *Perhaps the shareholders would be more amenable to the take-over were the buyers to sweeten the offer.*

sweetheart n. girlfriend, boyfriend, °friend, °admirer, beau, °darling, °dear, °love, °beloved, °lover, °paramour, inamorato, inamorata, lady-love, betrothed, intended, fiancé(e), *Archaic* swain, *Colloq* heartthrob, °flame, sweetie, °steady: *She married her childhood sweetheart and lived happily ever after.*

swell v. **1** Often, **swell out** or **up**: °grow, °increase, °enlarge, °expand, °blow or °puff up or out, distend, °inflate, dilate, wax; mushroom, belly, balloon, bloat, °bulge, billow, fatten, °rise, tumefy: *After cooking, the mixture swells to twice its original volume.* **2** °grow, °increase, mushroom, snowball, °accumulate, °mount: *Forgotten for years, her savings had swelled to become a small fortune.* **3** °increase, °raise, augment, °enlarge, °boost, °step up: *Something must be done to swell the number of recruits.*

—n. **4** enlargement, broadening, °increase, °extension, °spread, °swelling, inflation, °expansion, °rise, °surge: *Have you noted the swell in popularity of health foods?* **5** °wave, °surge, billow: *As we rose to the top of each swell, we could see the shore.* **6** fop, °dandy, gay °blade, fashion plate, Beau Brummell, *Archaic* coxcomb, *Historical* macaroni, *Colloq* clothes-horse, *US* fancy Dan, *Slang* nob, *Archaic* lounge lizard, *Brit* toff: *He frequented the clubs populated by the other London swells.*
—adj. **7** °smart, °chic, °stylish, °fashionable, modish, °grand, °luxurious, de luxe, °elegant, °first-rate, first-class, top-grade, *Colloq* °posh, swank, °swanky, ritzy: *Charlie always took Diane to the swellest places.* **8** °marvellous, °thrilling, °splendid, spectacular, °first-rate, °fine, *Colloq* °great, °super, °terrific: *I really had a swell time at your party.*

swelling *n.* enlargement, distension, tumescence, protuberance, °bump, °prominence, °bulge, °lump, excrescence, °protrusion, °tumour, node, nodule: *It is a good idea to have any unexplained swelling examined by the doctor.*

sweltering *adj.* °hot, °torrid, steaming, °sultry, °steamy, °muggy, °sticky, °oppressive, stifling, °stuffy, suffocating, °clammy, °humid, °wet, broiling, boiling, °scorching, roasting, baking, wilting, melting, tropical, *Colloq* °close: *I cannot live through another sweltering summer in the Amazon jungle.*

swerve *v.* veer, °career, °swing, °diverge, °deviate, °sheer off, skew, °stray, °turn (aside): *The car swerved wildly off the road and into a ditch.*

swift *adj.* °fleet, °fast, °rapid, °speedy, °hasty, °lively, °nimble, °expeditious; quick, °brisk, °sudden, °abrupt: *The postman was bent on the swift completion of his rounds. What Bill needs is a swift kick to jolt him out of his lethargy.*

swiftly *adv.* °fast, °quickly, speedily, °rapidly, expeditiously; briskly, hurriedly, °hastily, °suddenly, abruptly, in a °flash, in a trice, in the wink of an eye, before you can say 'Jack Robinson', before you can say 'knife', like a shot, in an °instant, in (less than) no time, precipitately, unexpectedly, *Colloq* like greased lightning, *US* lickety-split, in a jiffy, *Slang* pronto, like a bat out of hell: *The assembly is done much more swiftly by machine. Swiftly, I ducked into a doorway to avoid being seen.*

swill *n.* **1** hogwash, pigswill, °refuse, pigwash, slop(s), °garbage, °waste: *If you saw the swill that pigs eat, you might not eat pork.* **2** °nonsense, °rot, rubbish, *Slang* crap: *That novel of hers was the worst swill I've read in a long time.*
—v. **3** °drink, guzzle, quaff, °swallow, *Colloq* swig, toss off or down, throw down, °polish off, °knock back or off, *US* chug-a-lug: *They waste every evening swilling beer.*

swimmingly *adv.* smoothly, °easily, effortlessly, °well, successfully, without a °hitch or a °problem, like a dream, cosily, like clockwork, without °difficulty, °handily, °readily: *The plan has gone swimmingly thus far.*

swindle *v.* **1** °cheat, cozen, bilk, °defraud, °deceive, °hoodwink, °take in, °fleece, °dupe, °fool, mulct, gull, make a °fool or °sucker (out) of, °victimize, °exploit, °trick, *Old-fashioned or literary* euchre, *Archaic* chouse, *Colloq* bamboozle, °chisel, diddle, pull a fast one on, flimflam, pluck, burn, take (someone) for a °ride, *Brit* °fiddle, *US*

buffalo, *Slang* con, °sting, °screw, rook, gyp, °rip (someone) off: *The gang has swindled several elderly people out of their life savings.*
—n. **2** °fraud, confidence game or trick, cheating, swindling, defrauding, °deception, °racket, °trickery, °sharp practice, thimblerigging, °chicanery, knavery, *Colloq Brit* °fiddle, swizzle or swizz, *Slang* °rip-off, scam, con (game), gyp, *US* bunco: *Those old-time swindles are nothing compared with the activities of unscrupulous stock brokers.*

swindler *n.* °cheat, confidence man or woman, hoaxer, mountebank, charlatan, knave, °scoundrel, sharper, °fraud, trickster, thimble-rigger, °villain, *Technical* defalcator, *Colloq* flimflam man or artist, *Slang* con man or woman, *US* bunco-artist, four-flusher: *Swindlers tricked them out of all their cash and traveller's cheques.*

swing *v.* **1** °sway, °move or °go to and fro or back and forth or °backwards and forwards, °come and °go, °wave, °fluctuate, °flap, °oscillate, °vibrate, librate, waver, wobble, waggle, zigzag, wigwag, °flourish: *The branches swung in the wind. They swung their arms in time to the music.* **2** °hang, °dangle; be hanged, be suspended: *They watched the monkeys swinging from tree to tree. He will swing for his crime.*
—n. **3** swinging, °sway, swaying, toing and froing, coming and going, waving, °fluctuation, fluctuating, flapping, °flap, oscillation, oscillating, vibration, vibrating, libration, waver, wavering, wobble, wobbling, waggle, waggling, zigzag, zigzagging, wigwag, wigwagging, °flourish, flourishing, °stroke: *Catch the rope on its next swing. He was caught on the shoulder by a wild swing of the bat.* **4** °sweep, °scope, °range, °trend, °limit(s); °change, °switch, °shift: *The swing of public opinion is unpredictable in these matters. There has been a small percentage swing to the Conservatives.* **5** °pace, °routine, °groove, °pattern: *Don't you find it hard to get into the normal swing of things after a long holiday?* **6 in full swing**: in (full) °operation, under °way, in °business, °animated, °lively, on the °move, °moving, going, *Colloq* on the hop, cooking: *The party was in full swing when we arrived.*

swingeing *adj.* °huge, °immense, °enormous, °considerable, °drastic, °severe, °harsh, stringent, °punishing, °devastating, °painful, °excruciating, °major, daunting, Draconian, °oppressive, °exorbitant, °excessive, °violent, *Colloq* °thumping: *They have instituted a truly swingeing increase in commuter fares. She gives me a swingeing headache.*

swinging *adj.* °fashionable, °chic, up to °date, °modern, *Colloq* à gogo, in the swim, with it, *Chiefly Brit* °trendy, *Slang* °hip, groovy, in the groove: *That's what the swinging '60s were like in London.*

swipe *v.* **1** Usually, **swipe at**: °swing at, °strike at, °hit at, °lash out at: *He swiped away at the golf ball but kept missing it.* **2** °steal, filch, °pilfer, purloin, *Colloq* °pinch, °lift, snitch, *Chiefly Brit* °nick, °whip, snaffle: *They caught Freddie swiping a bag of mints at Woolworth's.*
—n. **3** °swing, °strike, °clip: *Ronald took a swipe at the ball with his racket.*

swirl *v.* **1** whirl, °spin, °eddy, churn, °circulate, °gyrate, °surge, °boil, °seethe: *Faster and faster the water swirled round in the maelstrom.* **2** °twist,

whirl, whorl, curl, °roll, furl, °spin, curve, °spiral, °twirl, °wind (round): *She swirled her hair round her head and fastened it with a large clip.*
—*n.* **3** °twist, whirl, curl, °roll, °twirl, °spiral: *At the fabric exhibition swirls of textiles were decoratively displayed.*

swish *v.* **1** °hiss, °whisk, °rustle, °whisper, susurrate: *I heard Elena swish up behind me in her taffeta dress.*
—*n.* **2** °hiss, hissing sound, whoosh, swoosh, °rustle, whistle: *With a quick swish the machete knifed through the underbrush.*
—*adj.* **3** °elegant, °fashionable, °stylish, *de rigueur*, °smart, *Colloq* °posh, °plush, ritzy, °swell, swank(y): *Liza bought a swish new outfit for the wedding.* **4** °homosexual, °gay, °effeminate: *All the following are offensive and derogatory:* *Colloq chiefly Brit* °bent, *Slang* °queer, °camp, campy, °kinky, *Chiefly US* fruity, limp-wristed, faggy, swishy: *He used to bring his swish friends here, but not lately.*

switch *n.* **1** twitch, °lash, °rod, °whip, birch (°rod), °scourge: *He picked up the switch as if to hit me with it.* **2** °change, °alteration, °exchange, °shift, change-over, °reversal, deflection, °trade, swap *or* swop: *A switch of costume was done swiftly backstage, yielding the expression 'quick-change artist'.*
—*v.* **3** twitch, °lash, °whip, birch, °beat, °strike, thrash, °scourge, °flog: *The headmaster switched the boys for the slightest misdemeanour.* **4** °change, °shift, °exchange, °divert, °deviate: *The colonel switched to another subject. They switched the two stones, leaving the fake emerald.* **5** °divert, °turn, rechannel, redirect, °direct: *They switched the funds to another project.*

swivel *v.* **1** °pivot, °turn, °rotate, °spin, °revolve, °pirouette, °move freely: *This joint allows the arm to swivel in all directions.*
—*n.* **2** °pivot, elbow-joint, gimbal, ball-and-socket °joint: *The stern-chaser is fitted with a swivel, allowing it to be fired at any angle.*

swollen *adj.* enlarged, distended, °inflated, °bloated, bulging, puffed up *or* out, tumid, tumescent, expanded, turgid, puffy, oversized, outsized, *Technical* dropsical, hypertrophied, proud: *My knee was swollen for three days after that knock.*

swoop *v.* **1** °descend, °dive, °sweep down, °pounce, °stoop: *The eagle swooped down across the stream, catching a salmon in its talons.*
—*n.* **2** descent, °dive, °sweep, °pounce, °stoop, °stroke, °blow, °rush: *The police raid caught several drug dealers in one fell swoop.*

sybarite *n.* °epicure, °epicurean, hedonist, voluptuary, °sensualist, °aesthete, gastronome, °gourmet, *bon vivant*, *bon viveur*, pleasure-seeker, °playboy, jet-setter: *These sybarites spend all their time and their parents' money in the fleshpots of the world.*

symbol *n.* °representation, °figure, °metaphor, allegory, insigne (*singular; plural is* insignia), °token, °sign, °emblem, badge, °image, logotype, °mark, °trade °mark, colophon, °brand, °code, °abbreviation, phonogram, initialism, cryptogram, acronym, monogram, °password, °shibboleth, watchword, °code word; arms, °bearing, armorial °bearing, °crest, escutcheon, °coat of arms, °banner, °flag, °pennant, °standard, *Colloq* logo: *This jewel is a mere symbol of my devotion and love for you.*

symbolic *adj.* Often, **symbolic of**: symbolical (of), tokening, betokening, °emblematic (of), figurative, allegoric(al), °typical (of), °representative (of), °symptomatic (of), °characteristic (of), °metaphoric(al), allusive (of), denotative (of), connotative (of), mnemonic (of): *From ancient times the laurel, or bay, has been regarded as symbolic of praiseworthiness.*

symbolize *v.* °represent, °stand for, °denote, connote, °suggest, °express, °imply, °signify, °mean, °typify, °exemplify, betoken, °illustrate, °embody, epitomize: *Green symbolizes envy and jealousy, red anger, blue sadness, white purity, and so on.*

symmetrical *adj.* symmetric, (°well-)balanced, proportionate, °proportional, well-proportioned, °orderly, (well-)ordered, in °proportion, °even, °regular, congruous, congruent, °uniform, °harmonious; °equal, mirror-image, mirror-like: *The temple was exactly symmetrical, with a wing on each side. The two wings are symmetrical.*

symmetry *n.* °balance, °proportion, evenness, °order, orderliness, °regularity, °uniformity, congruity, congruousness, correspondence, °agreement, °harmony, consistency, °equality: *With the crudest of tools, the pyramid builders achieved incredible symmetry.*

sympathetic *adj.* **1** Often, **sympathetic to** *or* **toward(s)**: compassionate (to *or* toward(s)), commiserating (with), commiserative (with), °understanding (of), °supportive (of), caring (to *or* toward(s)), °concerned (about *or* with), °solicitous (of *or* to *or* toward(s)), warm-hearted (to *or* toward(s)), kind-hearted (to *or* toward(s)), °responsive (to *or* toward(s)), well-meaning, well-intentioned, °good-natured (to *or* toward(s)), °considerate (of *or* to *or* toward(s)), empathetic *or* empathic (with *or* to *or* toward(s)); sympathizing, °kindly, comforting, consoling: *The social workers are sympathetic to the people's problems. One should be more sympathetic. Julie takes a sympathetic outlook.* **2** Often, **sympathetic to** *or* **toward(s)**: °agreeable, °pleasant, °friendly, well-disposed, °favourably °disposed, encouraging, like-minded, °responsive, congenial, *en rapport*, simpatico: *You will find a sympathetic ear at the council. The people are not sympathetic to a tax increase.*

sympathize *v.* **1** Often, **sympathize with**: °suffer *or* °grieve *or* °mourn (with), °feel (°sorry) (for), have °pity (for), empathize (with), condole (with), commiserate (with): *I sympathized with you over the loss of your grandfather. Now that mine is gone, it is your turn to sympathize.* **2** Often, **sympathize with**: harmonize (with), °get along (with), °relate (to), °identify (with), °go along (with), see eye to eye (with), °agree (with), °side (with), °understand, be *en rapport* (with), be in °sympathy (with), be simpatico (with), have (a) °rapport (with), *Colloq* be *or* vibrate on the same frequency *or* wavelength (with), *Slang* °dig: *I can sympathize with anyone who despises terrorism.*

sympathizer *n.* condoner, approver, conspirator, co-conspirator, collaborator, °accomplice, °accessory, °supporter, fellow-traveller, °ally: *At one time, they tried to incarcerate all suspected of being Fascist sympathizers.*

sympathy *n.* **1** compassion, commiseration, °pity, °concern, tenderness, empathy,

°understanding, solicitousness, °warmth, tender-heartedness, warm-heartedness, *Archaic* ruth: *We feel great sympathy for any child who loses a pet.* **2** °agreement, °harmony, compatibility, °rapport, concord, °accord, fellow-feeling, congeniality, °affinity, closeness, °unity, communion, °fellowship, camaraderie: *It is amazing that there can be so much sympathy between two such different people.*

symptom *n.* °manifestation, °evidence, syndrome, °mark, °token, °indication, °cue, °clue, (°warning) °sign, °characteristic, °trait, °feature, earmark, marker: *Esmeralda is extremely jealous—I recognize the symptoms.*

symptomatic *adj.* Often, **symptomatic of**: indicative (of), °representative (of), °suggestive (of), °characteristic (of), °emblematic (of), °symbolic (of), °peculiar (to), °specific (to), idiosyncratic (of); indicating, suggesting: *A high fever is symptomatic of many illnesses.*

syndicate *n.* **1** °trust, monopoly, bloc, cartel, syndication: *They were part of a syndicate that controlled the worldwide sale of nickel.* **2** (crime) family, Cosa Nostra, mafia: *Guido used to be an enforcer for the syndicate.*
—*v.* **3** affiliate, °ally, °associate, °amalgamate, consolidate, °league, confederate, synthesize: *Mrs Cartwright was successful in syndicating the milk producers in the entire county.* **4** serialize, °distribute: *His business is syndicating old movies to television stations.*

synonymous *adj.* Often, **synonymous with** *or* **to**: °equal (to), °equivalent (to), tantamount (to), identified (with), corresponding (to *or* with); transposable (with), exchangeable (with), °identical (to *or* with), interchangeable (with),

the °same (as): *A word is almost never truly synonymous with another in all respects. Even terms like 'salt' and 'sodium chloride' are not synonymous.*

synopsis *n.* °summary, condensation, °abridgement, epitomization, °outline, °abstract, °digest, °précis, °epitome, compendium, conspectus, *aperçu,* résumé: *He was assigned to write a ten-page synopsis of a 600-page book.*

synthesis *n.* °blend, °compound, °merge, °union, °amalgamation, coalescence, integration, unification, composite, °composition, °mixture, °combination; compounding, combining, blending, merging, integrating, mixing, fusing, fusion, unifying: *This mixture is a synthesis of many different ingredients. How do they effect the synthesis of coal, water, and air to make nylon?*

synthetic *adj.* °artificial, man-made, manufactured, ersatz; °fake, °false, °counterfeit, °sham, °bogus, °spurious, °mock, °imitation, pseudo, °plastic, *Colloq* °phoney *or US also* phony: *Because of the animal rights activists, many women today wear synthetic fur.*

system *n.* **1** organized °whole, °organization, °set, °group, °combination; °structure, °arrangement, °pattern, °set-up: *Some believe that the universe is a vast ordered system, others that it is chaos in which only man sees order. It took years to establish the banking system in this country.* **2** °scheme, °method, °approach, modus operandi, °way, procedure, methodology, °technique, °plan, °process, °practice, °routine: *There is a proper system for doing the job and you should keep to it.*

systematic *adj.* organized, systematized, planned, °methodical, businesslike, °orderly, well-organized, well-ordered, °regular, °routine, standardized, °standard: *There are several systematic ways for cataloguing books.*

T

tab n. **1** °flap, °tag, °loop, ticket, sticker, °label, °flag, lappet, strap, °handle: *Pull on the red tab and the life jacket inflates automatically.* **2** °charge, °bill, °account, °reckoning, *Chiefly US* °check: *They left me to pick up the tab at the restaurant for everyone.*

table n. **1** °food, victuals, °provender, comestible(s), °edibles, eatables, °fare, °board, °provisions: *One can rely on a fine table at Mrs McGuire's.* **2** °plain, flatland, mesa, tableland, °plateau, steppe: *The area is barren lava table from horizon to horizon.* **3** (tabular *or* columnar) °list *or* listing, °register, °record, tabulation, °chart, catalogue, °index, inventory, itemization, °précis, table of contents: *The figures are easier to understand when arranged in a table.*
—v. **4** °submit, °present, °offer, proffer, °bring forward, °bring up, °propose: *The bill will be tabled for action today.* **5** °shelve, °postpone, °defer, °suspend, °put off, °stay, pigeon-hole, mothball, *Colloq* put on ice: *When the bill came up we tabled it for six months.*

tableau n. °scene, °sight, °spectacle, °picture, °image, °composition, °arrangement, grouping, °effect: *The children raptly listening to their father telling a story—what a charming tableau!*

tablet n. **1** (scribbling *or* writing- *or* note- *or* memo) °pad, (spiral(-bound)) notebook, *US* scratch °pad: *I write all my dreams in a little tablet in case I forget to relate them to my psychiatrist.* **2** °slab, °plaque, °plate, panel, plaquette: *The tablet on the base of the statue says it is of Disraeli.* **3** stone, gravestone, headstone, °tombstone, °memorial: *We each contributed to the tablet that marks Croombender's grave.* **4** °pill, capsule, troche, pellet, pastille, drop, lozenge, bolus: *Take three tablets twice a day.*

taboo adj. **1** tabu, anathema, forbidden, interdicted, off limits, out of bounds, *verboten*, proscribed, banned, prohibited, restricted, °unmentionable, unspeakable; censored, censorable, °unacceptable, °rude, °impolite, indecorous, °dirty, °explicit; outlawed, °illegal, °illicit, °unlawful: *Our holiday in Benidorm is a taboo subject in my house. Many people dislike hearing taboo language used on radio or television.*
—n. **2** tabu, anathema, interdict, interdiction, proscription, °ban, °prohibition, °restriction: *There is still a strict taboo against mentioning bodily functions in public.*
—v. **3** tabu, °forbid, interdict, proscribe, °ban, °prohibit: *The hotel taboos the sharing of a room by unmarried couples.*

tabulate v. systematize, °organize, °order, °group, °list, °arrange, classify, °categorize, °rate, °grade, catalogue, codify, pigeon-hole, °sort, assort, °index, °itemize; °record, note: *We shall report the results of the poll as soon as they have been tabulated.*

tacit adj. unspoken, undeclared, unsaid, unstated, unvoiced, unuttered, °silent, °understood, unexpressed, implied, °implicit: *The sisters have a tacit agreement not to poach each other's boyfriends. He gave me a look of tacit gratitude.*

taciturn adj. °silent, uncommunicative, °mum, °mute, °reticent, °reserved, unforthcoming, °tight-lipped, close-lipped, untalkative, °quiet: *Even when he was small, Chris was quite taciturn, saying little but evidently thinking much.*

tack n. **1** °pin, push-pin, °nail, *Brit* drawing-pin, tin-tack, *US* thumbtack: *Someone keeps stealing the tacks from the bulletin board.* **2** °fastening, stitch, baste: *Could you put some tacks in the hem so I can try on the skirt?* **3** °direction, °bearing, heading, °course, °approach; °way, °path, °procedure, °method, °technique, °attack, °line: *Our new tack was due east. They may have to take a different tack to win the contract.* **4** °tackle, °gear, °equipment, equipage, harness, saddlery, °fittings, fitments, °kit, °outfit, °rig, rigging, accoutrements *or US also* accouterments: *He has ordered all new tack for his horse.*
—v. **5** °pin, °attach, °fasten, °secure, °join, °couple, °unite, °combine, °stick, °fix, affix, °staple, °nail, skewer, °peg, °screw, °bolt, rivet; baste, stitch, °sew, °bind, °tie; paste, °glue, °cement, solder, braze, °weld: *You were only supposed to tack these together lightly, but now I can't pull them apart.* **6** °change direction *or* heading *or* course, *Nautical* °go *or* °come about; zigzag, veer off *or* away, *Nautical* °beat: *We tacked quickly to avoid striking the buoy.* **7 tack on**: °add (on), append, annex, °attach, tag on: *When they tacked on a rider to the contract, we refused to sign it.*

tackle n. **1** °gear, °rig, °fittings, °equipment, equipage, rigging, °paraphernalia, °outfit, °tools, °apparatus, °trappings, accoutrements *or US also* accouterments, *Colloq Brit* clobber: *The steeplejack brought along all his tackle and made ready for his climb.* **2** block (and tackle), fall, hoisting °gear, °pulley, sheave: *You'll need heavier tackle to lift this cargo.*
—v. **3** come to grips with, °grapple with, °approach, °take on, °try to solve, (°try to) °deal *or* °cope with, °stand *or* °face up to, °face, confront, °address oneself to, °attend to, °set about, °pursue, *Colloq* take a crack at, have a °go at: *Perhaps you'd better tackle the parking problem yourself. I'll tackle the boss on the matter as soon as I see him.* **4** °attack, °fall upon, °devour, °consume, °demolish, °destroy: *You've seen nothing till you've seen Graham tackle a roast turkey.*

tacky¹ adj. °sticky, gluey, gummy, adhesive, °ropy, viscous, viscid, *Colloq* °gooey: *The varnish is still tacky and must dry before sanding.*

tacky² adj. °tawdry, °cheap, brummagem, °gaudy, °tasteless, °vulgar, °shabby, tatty, °sleazy, chintzy, °shoddy, °seedy: *Richard consistently buys the tackiest suits on the market.*

tact n. °discretion, °diplomacy, °sensitivity, savoir faire, °judgement, politesse, °delicacy, °finesse, cleverness, °prudence, °care, carefulness, °dexterity, dexterousness, discernment, judiciousness, adroitness, °skill, acumen, acuteness, °perception, °understanding, °consideration, thoughtfulness, politeness: *You can count on Robert to handle such matters with consummate tact.*

tactful adj. °discreet, °diplomatic, °sensitive, °politic, °judicious, °delicate, °clever, °prudent, °careful, °dexterous, discerning, adroit, °skilful, °acute, °perceptive, °considerate,

°understanding, °thoughtful, °polite: *Even the people working in the complaints department are tactful.*

tactic *n.* **1** °move, °manoeuvre, ploy, °caper, °plan, °strategy, °stratagem, °device, °ruse, °plot, °scheme, °design: *Inviting her husband along was a tactic merely to avert suspicion.* **2 tactics**: manoeuvres, °strategy, plans, °campaign, generalship, military science, military °operation(s), orchestration, engineering, masterminding: *Entirely different tactics must be employed in jungle fighting.*

tactical *adj.* °artful, °clever, cunning, °shrewd, adroit, °strategic, °skilful, °adept, °politic, °smart, °tactful: *The general was noted for his dazzling strategies and tactical genius.*

tactician *n.* strategist, campaigner, °mastermind, intriguer, plotter, planner, schemer, manipulator, manoeuvrer, orchestrator, *Colloq* °operator: *Montgomery was regarded by some as a master tactician.*

tactless *adj.* °coarse, °boorish, °uncivilized, °unsophisticated, °rough, °rude, uncouth, °discourteous, ungentlemanly, unladylike, °crude, °gruff, °bluff, °abrupt, °blunt, °brusque, °impertinent, °disrespectful, uncivil, °impolite, insensitive, °awkward, bungling, °clumsy, maladroit, °inept, undiplomatic, °thoughtless, gauche, unskilful, impolitic, °imprudent, °inconsiderate, injudicious, °indiscreet, unwise: *It was pretty tactless of him to ask her out in front of his ex-girlfriend.*

tag *n.* **1** °label, name *or* price tag, °mark, marker, °tab, ticket, sticker, °stub, docket: *The tag was clearly marked with a bar-code.* **2** °name, epithet, °label, designation, °title, appellation, °nickname, *Slang* handle, moniker *or* monicker: *Called 'Eddie the dip', he got his tag 'the dip' because he's a pickpocket.*
—*v.* **3** °label, °mark, ticket, °identify, earmark: *Please tag all these cartons so we'll know what's in them without opening them.* **4** °label, °name, °call, dub, °nickname, °style, °entitle, °christen, baptize: *I have already said that Eddie was tagged 'the dip' because he was a pickpocket.* **5 tag along**: °follow, °trail (along) after, °tail, °shadow, °attend, °accompany, °drag along with *or* after: *Does your little brother have to tag along wherever we go?*

tail *n.* **1** appendage, brush (*of a fox*), scut (*of a hare, rabbit, or deer*), dock, caudal fin (*of a fish*), uropygium (*of a bird*), pope's *or* parson's nose, tailpiece, flag: *I just caught a glimpse of the fox's tail as it leapt the fence.* **2** °rear °end, tail-end, backside, °buttocks, croup, rump, °posterior(s), °bottom, behind, *Colloq Brit* °bum, *US* hinie, *Taboo slang Brit* arse, *US* ass: *When I catch you, I'll kick your tail!* **3** °reverse: *The obverse of a coin is the head, the reverse is the tail.*
—*v.* **4** dog, °follow, °trail, °stalk, °shadow, °track: *We tailed the suspect from Newcastle to New Mexico.*

tailor *n.* **1** couturier, couturière, costumier, °dressmaker, modiste, clothier, garment-maker, outfitter, seamstress: *She has all her clothing made by her tailor.*
—*v.* **2** °fit, °adapt, °suit, °adjust, °alter, °accommodate, °modify, °change, °convert, °cut, °fashion, °mould, °stretch, °accustom: *Your telephone system can be tailored to your most exacting demands.*

tailor-made *adj.* **1** °fitted, custom-made, made to order, bespoke; made to measure: *He would not wear anything but tailor-made clothes.* **2** °ideal, °perfect, customized, made to order, custom-made, suited, °suitable, (just) °right, *Colloq* right up one's *Brit* °street *or US* alley: *The job of lighthouse-keeper was tailor-made for a misanthrope.*

taint *n.* **1** °stain, °blot, °blemish, °slur, tinge, tincture, (°black *or* °bad) °mark, °stigma, °imperfection, °flaw, °scar, °defect; discredit, °dishonour: *His writing suffers from the taint of pedantry.*
—*v.* **2** °sully, °tarnish, °stain, °stigmatize, °smear, °harm, °hurt, °damage, °debase, °vitiate, °blacken, °foul, °contaminate, °pollute, °dirty, °muddy, smirch, besmirch, °blemish, °soil, °corrupt, °spoil, defile, °ruin, °destroy: *It takes very little to taint one's reputation in a small village.*

take *v.* **1** °grip, °seize, °grasp, °clasp, °get, °get *or* take °hold of, °grab, snatch, °clutch, °catch, °capture, °obtain, °lay °hold of, °lay (one's) hands on, °procure, °acquire, °gain (°possession of), take °possession of, °secure, °win, °carry off, °abduct, *Colloq* °nab: *The police took him into custody. He takes what he can get. When it comes to ineptitude, Sue certainly takes the prize.* **2** °pick, °select, °choose, opt for, °settle *or* °decide *or* °fasten on *or* upon: *When you get to the fork, take the road to the left.* **3** °appropriate, arrogate, °extract, °carry off *or* away, °steal, purloin, °pilfer, filch, palm, °rob, shoplift, °pocket, °remove, °walk off *or* away with, °run *or* °make off *or* away with; °embezzle, °misappropriate, peculate; plagiarize, °pirate; *Colloq* °lift, °swipe, snitch, *Chiefly Brit* °pinch, °nick, *Slang* °knock off, °hook, °rip off, °liberate, *US* boost, crook: *They took what didn't belong to them.* **4** °reserve, °book, °engage; °hire, °rent, °lease: *He took a room in a small hotel, where he began to write detective fiction.* **5** °acquire, °get, °adopt; °assume, °derive, °obtain, °draw, °receive, °inherit: *He has taken his bad manners from you. The film takes its title from the book.* **6** °accept, °receive, °bear, °withstand, °stand, °endure, °weather, °tolerate, °abide, °brave, °go through, °undergo, °suffer, °submit to, °swallow, *Colloq* °put up with, °brook, °stomach, *Brit* °stick: *She took the news about Leon's relapse quite well. I have taken quite enough from you already.* **7** °assume, °bear, °undertake, °adopt, arrogate; °acknowledge, °accept: *Kevin took full responsibility for the mistake.* **8** °believe, °think, °judge, deem, °hold, °feel; take for, assess (as), °consider (as), °regard (as), °view (as), °accept (for): *I take people to be honest till proven otherwise. She took him for a fool when they first met.* **9** °carry, convey, °bear, °transport, °bring, °deliver, ferry, °haul, °cart: *Will this train take me to Aylesbury? They took the bicycle to Old Lyme in a van.* **10** take up, °study, be °involved *or* occupied in *or* with, °apply oneself to, °learn; °read, *Colloq* °tackle: *I cannot believe that Doreen is taking home economics. He took a course in car maintenance.* **11** prove *or* be °effective *or* °efficacious *or* °operative *or* °functional, take °effect, take °hold, °operate, °function, °work, °perform, *Colloq* do the °trick: *If the transplant fails to take, the doctors will have to operate again.* **12** °exact, °extract, °get: *She took revenge by denying him certain privileges.* **13** °swallow, °eat, °consume, ingest, °devour,

°gulp down, gobble up *or* down, wolf, °bolt; °drink, imbibe, quaff; °inhale: *Rudolf takes pills of every conceivable colour. The doctor said I could take a wee nip now and then. Sonya stepped out to take a breath of fresh air.* **14** °subtract, °deduct, °remove, take away, take from, take off: *Take three from five. Five, take away two, leaves three. It's cheaper when you've taken off the discount.* **15** °end, °terminate, annihilate, °wipe out; °kill: *The assault on Leningrad took tens of thousands of lives. The Lord giveth and the Lord taketh away.* **16** °require, °demand, °need, necessitate, °call for: *Remember, it takes two to tango. It took him two years to complete the fresco. It takes six to sail his yawl.* **17** °hold, °contain, °accommodate, °accept, °fit in: *This storage bin cannot take anything else, it's completely full.* **18** convey, °lead, °conduct; °escort, convoy, °guide, °accompany: *This road takes you directly to the yacht club. He asked to be taken to the manager's office.* **19** °understand, °gather, °interpret, °perceive, apprehend, °deduce, conclude, °infer, °judge, deem, °assume, °suppose, °imagine, °see: *I take him to be a fool. I take it from your expression that you've had bad news.* **20** °charm, °captivate, °capture, °attract, °lure, allure: *There was something about him that took her fancy.* **21** °use, °employ, make °use of, °establish, put in(to) °place, °adopt, put into effect, °effect, °apply; °resort to, have °recourse to, °turn to: *The police have taken measures to ensure that it doesn't happen again.* **22** °clear, °get *or* °go over *or* past *or* round *or* through: *Browning's Delight took the last jump easily. He must have taken that corner at 90!* **23** °experience, °entertain, °feel: *She seemed to take an instant dislike to me.* **24** °express, °voice, °raise, °put forth: *I hope you will not take objection or exception to what I am about to tell you.* **25** °cause *or* °make *or* °induce *or* °drive *or* °persuade (someone) to go *or* be: *What takes you to Málaga in August?* **26** °act, °assume, °play, °perform: *I'm taking the part of the wicked witch in the local pantomime.* **27** bilk, °cheat, °swindle, °defraud, *Colloq* con, *Brit* °fiddle: *When he examined his wallet he realized he'd been taken.* **28 take aback**: °astound, °astonish, °surprise, °startle, °shock: *She was really taken aback at the news.* **29 take after**: **a** °resemble, °look °like, be the spitting °image *or* the °spit and °image of, °favour, °remind one of, *Colloq* be a chip off the old block: *He takes after his grandfather.* **b** Sometimes, **take off after**: °chase, °follow, °run after, °pursue: *When the man stole the newspaper and ran, the shopkeeper took after him at a gallop.* **30 take back**: °retract, °withdraw, °recant, disavow, °repudiate: *He now wants to take back what he said about you.* **31 take down**: **a** °note, make a °note *or* memo *or* °memorandum of, °write down, °record, °put *or* °set down, °put in °writing, °document, °transcribe, °chronicle: *Please take down what I am about to tell you.* **b** °debase, deflate, °lower, °diminish, °belittle, °depreciate, deprecate, °humble, °humiliate, °shame, °disparage, °degrade, °disgrace: *She certainly took that pompous ass down a peg or two.* **32 take in**: **a** °accommodate, °receive, °let in, °quarter, °board, °lodge: *When her children grew up and left home, she decided to take in lodgers.* **b** °deceive, °fool, °trick, °impose upon, overcharge, °cheat, mulct, °defraud, cozen, bilk, °dupe, gull, °hoodwink, °swindle, *Colloq* bamboozle, con,

pull the wool over (someone's) eyes, *Slang Brit* do: *He was really taken in by that time-share deal.* **c** °include, subsume, °embrace, comprise, °cover, encompass, °contain: *Our sales figures take in all of North America, not just Canada.* **33 take it**: **a** °withstand *or* °tolerate *or* °survive punishment *or* abuse, °survive: *The Marines are extremely tough and can take it.* **b** See **19**, above. **34 take off**: **a** °remove, doff, °strip *or* °peel off, °discard, °divest (oneself) of: *Take off your hat in the house.* **b** °satirize, °lampoon, °caricature, °mock, °parody, travesty, °burlesque, °mimic, °imitate, *Colloq* spoof, *Brit* °send up: *It is not always easy to take off members of the Cabinet.* **c** °depart, °leave, °go (away), decamp, °fly off, °become airborne, °lift off, °blast off; *Colloq* skedaddle, make (oneself) scarce, *Slang* hit the road, scram, °beat it, °split: *You'd better take off before they find you here. The plane is due to take off at 18.35.* **35 take on**: **a** °hire, °engage, °employ, °enrol, °enlist, °retain: *We are so busy that we have taken on ten new people.* **b** °challenge, °rival, °face, contend against, °oppose, °match *or* °pit (oneself) against, °vie with, °fight: *Are you in any condition to take on the champion?* **c** °assume, °accept, °undertake, °tackle: *You might be taking on more than you bargained for.* **36 take out**: °entertain, °escort, invite out; court, woo: *He took her out to dinner at a Chinese restaurant.* **37 take over**: °assume *or* take *or* usurp *or* °gain °control *or* °possession *or* °command of: *A huge conglomerate is trying to take over our company.* **38 take to**: **a** °like, find °pleasant *or* °pleasing, feel °affection *or* °liking *or* °affinity for, find °suitable: *We took to each other the very first time we met. He took to computers as a duck takes to water.* **b** °leave *or* °depart *or* take off for, °run for, °head for, °flee to, °make for: *When the attack came, the villagers took to the hills.* **39 take up**: **a** °pick up, °accept, °agree to, acquiesce to, accede to: *She took up his offer, and they've been married for forty years.* **b** °assume, °resume, °carry on, °continue, °go on with, °follow on with, °pick up: *After a pause, he took up the thread of the story once more.* **c** espouse, °embrace, become °interested *or* °involved in, °support, °sponsor, °advocate: *She took up the cause of women's rights at her age?* **d** °occupy, °cover, °use (up), °fill (up): *Bernard's exercise equipment now takes up half the living-room.* **e** °deal with, °treat, °consider, °bring up, °raise: *Next week our panellists will take up the question, 'Who benefits from education?'* —*n.* **40** °revenue, takings, °yield, °return, receipts, proceeds, °gain, °profit(s); °gate, °box office: *How much was the take from the first day?*

taken *adj.* captivated, entranced, °enchanted, °charmed, bewitched, °infatuated: *I was so taken with Lucinda that I started blushing like a teenager.*

take-off *n.* **1** °flight, flying, taking off, departure, leaving, going; °launch, lift-off: *The take-off was delayed by bad weather.* **2** °satire, °lampoon, °caricature, °mockery, °parody, travesty, °burlesque, °imitation, *Colloq* spoof, *Brit* send-up: *The annual students' entertainment was as usual a take-off of the teachers.*

taking *adj.* °attractive, alluring, °engaging, captivating, °winning, winsome, charming, entrancing, °enchanting, bewitching, °fetching,

tale *n.* **1** °story, °narrative, °report, °account, °record, °chronicle, °history, °narration, °recital, anecdote: *We were brought up on tales of the supernatural. Her tale of what happened does not agree with the facts.* **2** °falsehood, °lie, fiction, °fib, °fabrication, untruth, falsification, °exaggeration, *Colloq* °tall tale *or* °story, (cock-and-bull) °story, *US* fish °story: *He told some tale about having been captured by urban guerrillas.* **3** °rumour, °gossip, °slander, °allegation, tittle-tattle, °libel, °story, *US chiefly naval* scuttlebutt: *I have been hearing tales about wild parties at the neighbours' again.*

talebearer *n.* °gossip, rumour-monger, gossip-monger, taleteller, talemonger, scandal-monger, tell-tale, °troublemaker, quidnunc, tattler, °informer, sieve, *Chiefly US and Canadian* tattle-tale, *Slang* big-mouth, °blabbermouth, squealer, stool-pigeon, stoolie, rat, *Brit* °sneak, nark, *US* fink, ratfink: *The words, spoken in private, were repeated to him by some talebearer.*

talent *n.* **1** °ability, °power, °gift, °faculty, °flair, °genius, °facility, °aptitude, °capacity, °knack, °ingenuity, °forte, °strength; °endowment: *Bill's extraordinary talent for playing the trombone was widely acclaimed.* **2** °tendency, proclivity, propensity, °penchant, predilection, predisposition, °bent, °inclination: *Annabel certainly has a talent for saying the wrong thing.*

talented *adj.* °gifted, °accomplished, °brilliant, skilled, °skilful, °masterful, °expert, °adept, adroit, °dexterous, deft, °clever, °good, °polished, °proficient, °first-rate, top-drawer, °excellent, *Colloq* ace, crack, top-notch, *Brit* wizard, whizzo, *US* crackerjack: *Leslie is the most talented player in the school hockey team.*

talisman *n.* °amulet, °charm, tiki, °fetish *or* fetich, ju-ju, periapt, abraxas; wishbone, rabbit's foot, *Brit* merry thought: *He was given a talisman that was supposed to protect its wearer from bad luck.*

talk *v.* **1** Sometimes, **talk in**: °speak (in), °use, °communicate in, °converse in, °express (oneself) in, discourse in: *If you talk English I might understand.* **2** °confer, °consult, °parley, have a (little) talk, (have a) °chat, confabulate, *Colloq* confab, *Slang US* °rap: *I think we ought to talk before you decide which offer to accept.* **3** °chatter, prate, °prattle, °jabber, blather *or* blether, gibber, jibber-jabber, cackle, °babble, °patter, °rattle on, °go on, *Brit* natter, witter, rabbit on, *Colloq* °gab, *Slang* gas, jaw, *US* run off at the mouth: *They talk continuously, mostly about nothing.* **4** °chat, °gossip, °palaver, *Slang* °chew the fat *or* the °rag, shoot the breeze, *US* chin, schmooze, °rap, have a bull session, bat the breeze, shoot the bull: *We were just sitting around talking when Tom suggested we go for a swim.* **5** °inform, °confess, °give the game away, °blab, *Colloq* come °clean, *Slang* rat, °sing, °spill the beans, *Brit* °grass: *If they give him the third degree, you can be sure he'll talk.* **6** °speak, give *or* deliver a °speech *or* a talk *or* an °address, °lecture: *I believe that Professor Hale is talking at the County Library tonight.* **7** **talk about** *or* **over** *or* **of**: °discuss, °confer about *or* on, °parley about: *I don't want to talk about football all the time. Can't we talk it*

over? *She talks only of you.* **8** **talk big**: °boast, °brag, vaunt, crow, °bluster, °exaggerate, blow *or* toot (one's) own horn: *He was never in the war—he just talks big.* **9** **talk down**: **a** °depreciate, deprecate, denigrate, °disparage, °belittle, °minimize, °diminish, °criticize, *Colloq* °knock, °pan, °put down: *It's the only thing he's ever done, and you shouldn't talk it down.* **b** Usually, **talk down to**: °condescend to, °patronize: *I resent your talking down to me in that way.* **10** **talk into**: °convince, °bring round, °sway, °persuade: *We have been trying to talk him into running in the marathon.* **11** **talk over**: °discuss: *We talked over the best way to prepare the advertising proposal.* **12** **talk to** *or* **with**: °speak to *or* with, °communicate with, °converse with: *Since the episode with the monkey, she refuses to talk to me. I talked with him yesterday.* **13** **talk up**: °promote, °support, °sponsor, advertise, °publicize, °push, *Colloq* °plug, hype, ballyhoo: *She has been talking up the book on her radio show.* —*n.* **14** °oration, °lecture, °address, °presentation, °speech, discourse, °report, disquisition, dissertation; °sermon; °harangue, °tirade, *Colloq* spiel: *Claire delivered a talk on computational linguistics. Every week we have to listen to the same talk about sin.* **15** °conversation, °conference, °discussion, °meeting, consultation, °dialogue, colloquy, °parley, °palaver, °chat, °tête-à-tête, confabulation, *Colloq* confab, powwow, *Slang* chin-wag, head-to-head, *US* one-on-one, °rap session: *We must have a little talk about your school report.* **16** subject *or* topic of °conversation *or* °gossip *or* °rumour: *Her behaviour at the wedding was the talk of the town for weeks.* **17** °gossip, °rumour, hearsay, °information, °news, °report, *Colloq* info, *Slang* °dope: *There is some talk that you might be leaving.* **18** °palaver, °gossip, claptrap, °prattle, prattling, °chatter, verbiage, cackle, bunk, °nonsense, °rubbish, balderdash, poppycock, °hot air, °stuff and °nonsense, twaddle, *Colloq* malarkey, piffle, hooey, hokum, bunkum, bosh, hogwash, horse feathers, *Slang* bilge(-water), crap, bull, tripe, *Brit* tosh, balls, *US* apple-sauce, *Taboo slang* horseshit, bullshit: *That's just a lot of talk.* **19** °dialect, °speech, way *or* manner of speaking, façon de parler, °language, °jargon, argot, °cant, patois, °accent, *Colloq* °lingo: *Can you understand musicians' talk? My parents' talk is peppered with words long obsolete in standard English.*

talkative *adj.* garrulous, loquacious, verbose, long-winded, °voluble, prolix, °wordy, chatty, gossipy, °effusive, talky, logorrhoeic *or* logorrhoeal, *Colloq* gabby, blabby, *Slang* big-mouthed; *US* running off at the mouth: *The children are so talkative I can't get a word in edgeways.*

talker *n.* **1** °speaker, lecturer, orator, speech-maker, keynoter, spellbinder, tub-thumper, °rabble-rouser, demagogue, haranguer, ranter: *You might disagree with what he says, but you must admit he's a great talker.* **2** blusterer, blatherskite, swaggerer, °show-off, *Slang* windbag, gasbag, lot of °hot air, blowhard: *He is a big talker, but he never gets anything done.*

tall *adj.* **1** °high, °towering, °big, soaring, °lofty, °giant, gigantic; multi-storey: *The giant sequoias of California are the tallest trees in the world. There are many tall buildings in most major cities.* **2** °lanky, gangling, rangy, leggy, long-legged, °big, °giant, °huge, °gigantic, °large: *Some of those basketball* *players are unbelievably tall.* **3** exaggerated, overblown, °far-fetched, °improbable, °unbelievable, °incredible, °preposterous, °outrageous, overdone, °absurd, *Colloq Brit* °steep: *He told us some amusing tall tales about his fishing adventures.*

tally *v.* **1** °agree, °coincide, °accord, °correspond, °fit, °compare, °match (up), °square, °conform, concur, harmonize, *Colloq US* jibe: *Nothing I could do would make my figures tally with those of the bank.* **2** Sometimes, **tally up**: °count (up *or* out), °enumerate, °record, °register, °reckon, °add (up), °total (up), °tabulate, °itemize, °list, °calculate, °compute: *Please tally up what I owe you.*
—*n.* **3** °count, enumeration, °record, °register, °reckoning, °addition, °total, tabulation, itemization, listing, °calculation, computation: *According to my tally, you owe £156.72.* **4** ticket, °label, °mark, marker, °tag, °tab: *Each plant can be identified by its own tally.* **5** counterfoil, °stub, counterpart, °duplicate, °mate: *If you lose your tally you cannot get your luggage back.*

tame *adj.* **1** tamed, docile, disciplined, °obedient, domesticated, house-broken, trained, °broken: *He used to keep a tame fox in his back garden.* **2** °mild, °gentle, °fearless, unafraid: *It is amazing how tame animals can be when they do not perceive man as a threat.* **3** °tractable, pliant, compliant, °meek, °submissive, °mild, under (someone's) °control *or* °thumb, °subdued, suppressed; unassertive, °feeble, °ineffectual, °timid, timorous, °cowardly, pusillanimous, chicken-hearted, °faint-hearted, white-livered, lily-livered, yellow, *Colloq* wimpish: *Charles is far too tame to defy Kate.* **4** °boring, °tedious, °tiresome, °dull, insipid, °bland, °lifeless, °flat, °vapid, °prosaic, °humdrum, °bland, unexciting, uninspired, uninspiring, run-of-the-mill, °ordinary, uninteresting, °dead, *Colloq* °wishy-washy: *As a nightclub, the place is much too tame for my tastes.*
—*v.* **5** °break, domesticate, °train, house-train, °gentle, °master, °subdue, °subjugate: *The brown bear is a most difficult animal to tame.* **6** °calm, °subdue, °control, mollify, pacify, °mute, °temper, °soften, °curb, °tone down, °moderate, °mitigate, °tranquillize: *After a week the Lord tamed the violent sea and our tiny craft was allowed to continue.*

tamper *v.* °interfere, °meddle, intermeddle, °intrude, °tinker, °mess (about *or* around), *Colloq* °fiddle *or* °fool (about *or* around), °monkey (about *or* around), °muck (about *or* around): *Anyone caught tampering with the machinery will be prosecuted.*

tang *n.* **1** pungency, piquancy, °bite, °zest, zestiness, sharpness, poignancy, spiciness, °nip, °edge, °spice, °taste, °flavour, °savour, °aroma, °smell, °odour, *Colloq US* zip, °kick: *Ginger root gives the dish just the right tang.* **2** tinge, °flavour, °hint, °suggestion, soupçon, °trace, °dab, smack, °touch, smattering: *The new version has the tang of the original without its obsolete words.* **3** prong, °tab, °projection, °tongue, °strip, tine, shank, °pin, °spike: *The tang of a good knife goes right through to the end of the handle.*

tangential *adj.* °divergent, digressive, off *or* beside the °point, °peripheral, °irrelevant, °extraneous, °unrelated: *The matter of cost is tangential to the main issue.*

tangible *adj.* °material, °real, °physical, corporeal, bodily, somatic, °solid, °concrete, touchable, tactile, °manifest, palpable, °evident, °actual, °substantial, °visible, seeable, °discernible, °perceptible, ponderable, °objective, ostensive: *Leaving aside intangibles like taste, smell, and colour, the important tangible characteristic of food is texture.*

tangle *n.* **1** °confusion, °knot, gnarl, °mesh, °snarl, °twist, °kink, entanglement, °jam, °snag, °jumble, °mess, skein, °web, °coil: *It took hours to straighten out the tangle of ribbons.* **2** °muddle, °complication, °jumble, °puzzle, °medley, °complexity, °complication, °scramble, °mishmash, °mix-up, °hotchpotch *or US and Canadian also* hodgepodge, jungle, °maze, labyrinth: *She was rather bewildered by the vast tangle of information on the subject.*
—*v.* **3** Often, **tangle up**: °confuse, °knot, °mesh, °snarl, gnarl, °twist, °kink, ravel, °entangle, °jam, °snag, intertwist, intertwine, interlace, interweave, °jumble, °mess up, °scramble, °shuffle, °muddle: *Now you've tangled all the ribbons I carefully straightened out earlier.* **4** Often, **tangle with**: wrangle (with), contend (with), °fight (with *or* against), (come into) °conflict (with), come *or* go up against, lock horns (with), °dispute (with), cross swords (with), °disagree (with): *The sheriff is the last person I want to tangle with.*

tantalize *v.* °tease, °taunt, °provoke, °torment, torture, bait, °tempt, °plague, °frustrate: *They tantalized him by hanging the keys to his cell just outside his reach.*

tantamount to *adj.* amounting to, as good as, °virtually the °same as, (pretty) °much the °same as, °equal to, °equivalent to, °like, of a °piece with, comparable to, commensurate with: *His response, for all its politeness, was tantamount to a rejection.*

tantrum *n.* °fit (of °anger *or* of °passion), °outburst, °eruption, blow-up, °explosion, flare-up, °storm, °rage, °fury, *Colloq Brit* °paddy, wax: *He has a tantrum every time he fails to get his own way.*

tap[1] *v.* **1** °rap, °knock, °dab, °strike, peck; drum, °beat: *Must you continually tap on the table with that blasted pencil?*
—*n.* **2** °rap, °knock, °dab, °strike, peck, °pat; tapping, tap-tap, rapping, knocking, pecking, °beat, beating, °patter, pattering: *I felt a tap on my shoulder. The tap, tap, tap of the dripping water was driving me mad.*

tap[2] *n.* **1** cock, stopcock, pet-cock, sillcock, seacock, spigot, °spout, valve, *US* faucet: *Replace the washer in the tap to stop the leak.* **2** bung, °stopper, cork, spile, °plug, stopple, °peg: *Move the tap from the empty barrel to the new one.* **3** wire-tap, °bug, listening °device, electronic eavesdropper: *I think there's a tap on my phone.* **4 on tap**: **a** on draught, out of the barrel *or* keg: *They have real ale on tap.* **b** °ready, °available, on *or* at °hand, waiting, in °reserve, on °call: *He promised to be on tap if I needed him for anything.*
—*v.* **5** °drain, °draw (off), siphon off *or* out, °extract, °withdraw: *We tapped the wine directly from the casks.* **6** °open, °drain, unplug, °sap, bleed, °milk, °broach, °mine, °use, utilize, make °use of, put to °use, °draw on *or* upon,

turn to account: *Whenever she needed money, she tapped her savings.* **7** °bug, °eavesdrop on, wire-tap: *M.I.5 still taps her phone.*

tape *n.* **1** °strip, °band, fillet, °stripe, strap, °belt, ribbon: *She wore a colourful woven tape round her head to hold her hair.* **2** (tape) recording, °reel, spool, cassette, video: *He played us the tape of the whole interview.*
—*v.* **3** strap, °band, °bind; °seal, °stick: *If you tape the packet, customs cannot open it for inspection.* **4** °record; tape-record, video: *Pro-grammes can be taped automatically when we are out.*

taper *v.* **1** °narrow (down), °thin, °diminish, come or go down: *Note how the trousers taper towards the ankles.* **2** Often, **taper off**: °diminish, °reduce, °thin out, °wind down, °decrease, °fade, lessen, peter out, °wane, °subside, °let up, slacken, °die away or down or off or out, °decline, °slow (down or up), °weaken, abate, °ebb, °slump, °drop (off), °fall (off), °plummet: *Sales of ice skates can be expected to taper off during the summer.*

tardy *adj.* **1** °late, unpunctual, behind schedule, °overdue, behindhand: *Yet again you have been somewhat tardy in completing your assignments.* **2** °slow, dilatory, °belated, °slack, retarded, sluggish, °reluctant, °indolent, °lackadaisical, °listless, °phlegmatic, °slothful, °lethargic, languid: *They have been tardy in acknow-ledging the importance of Allen's work.*

target *n.* °goal, °object, °objective, °aim, °end; °butt, °quarry: *The target of the charity drive is to raise £30,000. Why make Peter the target of your ridicule?*

tariff *n.* **1** °tax, assessment, °duty, excise, levy, impost, °toll, *Brit* °rate: *The tariff on imported clothing may be increased.* **2** °schedule (of charges), price-list; bill of fare, menu: *I stopped by the hotel to ask about their tariff.*

tarnish *v.* °sully, °disgrace, °taint, °blacken, °blemish, °stain, °blot, °soil, °spot, °dirty, °contaminate, defame, °injure, °spoil, °ruin, °damage, °harm, °hurt, °stigmatize, °debase, °degrade, denigrate, °dishonour, asperse, calum-niate: *By his behaviour, he has tarnished the repu-tation of his entire family.*

tarry *v.* **1** °delay, °pause, °wait, °linger, loiter, °stall, °procrastinate, °dawdle, bide (one's) time, temporize, °hang back, *Colloq* °hang on or about or (a)round: *They tarried in the pub, and missed their train.* **2** °remain, sojourn, °stay, °stop, °rest, dwell, bide (one's) time, °settle: *She plans to tarry at Eastbourne for a while.*

tart[1] *adj.* **1** °sour, acidic, acidulous, acidulated, lemony, citrusy, vinegary, acetous, acescent; °sharp, tangy, astringent, acerb, acerbic, acrid, °bitter, °pungent, piquant, °harsh: *Those grapes are a bit tart for my taste.* **2** °biting, °bitter, °caustic, acid, corrosive, mordant, astringent, acrimonious, °trenchant, °harsh, °scathing, stinging, acerbic, °incisive, °cutting, °keen, barbed, °nasty, curmudgeonly, °testy, crusty, °abusive, °virulent, °sarcastic, °sardonic, satir-ic(al), °vicious, cynical: *You can rely on Henry for a tart rebuff every time.*

tart[2] *n.* **1** pie, tartlet, pastry, °turnover, flan, quiche, patty, *Brit* pasty: *Three guesses who stole the tarts from the Queen of Hearts.* **2** strumpet, streetwalker, °prostitute, whore, harlot, fallen woman, trollop, °wanton, working girl, *fille de*

joie, call-girl, °loose woman, slut, drab, °jade, demi-mondaine, courtesan, woman of ill repute, hussy, doxy, lady of the evening or the night, woman of easy virtue, *Slang* floozie or floozy or floosie, hooker, *US* chippy, roundheels, bimbo: *The paper claimed that the minister was involved with a woman that it described as 'a tart'.*

task *n.* **1** °duty, °assignment, °business, °job, °charge, °stint, °mission, °work, chore, °undertaking: *It will be your task to keep the others working.* **2** (major) °effort, °test (of strength), piece of °work, °struggle, °strain: *Getting him to do anything at all was quite a task.* **3** **take to task**: °scold, °reprimand, call to °account, °blame, censure, recriminate, reproach, °reprove, °rebuke, °criticize, °lecture, °upbraid, chide, reprehend: *I was taken to task for failing to notify the police of the break-in.*

taste *n.* **1** °drop, soupçon, °dash, °pinch, °touch, °hint, °suggestion, °grain, °trace, °bit; °flavour, °savour, °relish, °tang: *I added just the tiniest taste of coriander to the sauce.* **2** °sample, °morsel, °bite, °mouthful, °bite, °sip, °nip, °swallow: *I had a taste of the sauce and it's superb.* **3** palate, °desire, °inclination, °leaning, °partiality, °disposition, °penchant, °liking, °fancy, °preference, fondness, °appetite, °relish, stom-ach, °tolerance: *She developed a taste for caviare and champagne while working in television.* **4** discernment, °discrimination, °perception, °judgement, cultivation, °refinement, styl-ishness, °grace, °polish, °elegance: *Her unerring taste leads her to select only the best.* **5** °style, °mode, °fashion, °manner, °form, °design, °motif: *The room was decorated in Moorish taste.* **6** °decorum, °discretion, tactfulness, °delicacy, °refinement, politesse, politeness, correctness, °propriety, tastefulness: *Evan's taste would never allow him to say anything rude.*
—*v.* **7** °savour, °sample, °examine, °try, °test: *Taste this and see if it's too salty.* **8** °experience, °sample, °know, have knowledge of, °undergo, °encounter, °meet (with), come up against: *As a young man he had tasted the pleasures of Paris.*

tasteful *adj.* in good °taste, °decorous, °refined, finished, °tactful, °polite, °polished, restrained, °correct, °harmonious, °fitting, °fit, °proper, °discriminating, °aesthetic, discriminative, °fastidious, °cultivated, *comme il faut*, °elegant, °graceful, charming: *Though a bit shabby, her clothes were demure and tasteful.*

tasteless *adj.* **1** in bad or poor °taste, °garish, °gaudy, °loud, °tawdry, meretricious, °cheap, °flashy, °unrefined, inelegant, unaesthetic, °improper, °wrong, indecorous, indelicate, uncultivated, uncouth, uncultured, gauche, °boorish, maladroit, °distasteful, °unsavoury, °coarse, °crude, °gross, °vulgar, °base, °low: *That is the most tasteless dress I have ever seen. He made a tasteless remark about her table manners.* **2** insipid, °bland, °dull, °flat, °watery, °vapid, flavourless, °unsavoury, *Colloq* °wishy-washy: *The tea served there is completely tasteless.*

tasty *adj.* °delicious, delectable, °luscious, fla-vorous, flavoursome, flavourful, °savoury, toothsome, palatable, appetizing, sapid, mouth-watering, ambrosial, *Colloq* °yummy, scrumptious: *They serve a very tasty curry at that Indian restaurant.*

tatter *n.* **1** Often, **tatters**: °scrap(s), °rag(s), °shred(s), °bit(s), °piece(s): *Tatters from the culprit's* clothing were found on a thorn-bush. **2 in tatters**: in °ruins, in °shreds, destroyed, ruined, shattered, in disarray, demolished: *My life has been in tatters ever since she left me.*

tattered adj. °ragged, torn, shredded, °rent, °threadbare: *Above the altar in the chapel hang the tattered standards of the regiment, dating from the Crimean War.*

tattle v. **1** °blab, °tell, °reveal or divulge, °give away secrets, *Slang* squeal: *Though sworn to silence, Davis tattled.* **2** °gossip, °prattle, prate, °babble, °chatter, °jabber, blather or blether, *Brit* natter, witter, *Slang* ya(c)k: *The old crones were tattling away in the kitchen.*

taunt v. **1** °tease, °jeer (at), °flout, °twit, °mock, °torment, °annoy, make °fun or °sport of, °poke °fun at, °deride, °sneer (at), °scoff (at), °insult, °ridicule, °burlesque, °lampoon, *US* °ride, *Colloq* kid, rib, roast, °put down, *Brit* °guy, *Slang* °bug, °rag, hassle, *US* get on (someone's) case: *The boys used to taunt him, calling him 'Shrimpo' because he was so short.*
—n. **2** °jeer, °gibe, brickbat, °insult, °scoff, °derision, °sneer, °slap (in the face), raspberry, *Colloq* °dig, *US* Bronx cheer: *At 17, he was six feet tall and no longer had to tolerate his classmates' taunts.*

taut adj. **1** °tight, °tense, °strained, stretched, °rigid, °stiff: *When his jaw goes taut like that I know he's angry.* **2** *Nautical* neat, °tidy, Bristol fashion, °shipshape, °spruce, (in) °trim, °smart, °orderly, well-organized; well-disciplined: *Captain Scriven runs a taut ship, no doubt about it.*

tautology n. °repetition, redundancy, battology, pleonasm, iteration, tautologism; repetitiousness, repetitiveness, wordiness, prolixity, verbiage, verbosity, long-windedness: *Clichés like 'null and void' and 'cease and desist' are tautologies. Tautology, when called 'repetition', is often used for rhetorical effect.*

tawdry adj. °gaudy, °cheap, °flashy, brummagem, °showy, meretricious, °garish, °loud, tatty, tinsel, tinselly, °plastic, °tinny, °shabby, *US* °tacky, *Colloq* cheapjack: *She was wearing a tawdry outfit picked up at a church jumble sale.*

tax n. **1** levy, impost, °duty, °tariff, assessment, °tribute, °toll, excise, customs, °charge, contribution, *Archaic* scot, tithe, *Brit* octroi, cess, °rate(s), °dues: *Most people try to pay the lowest taxes they can get away with.* **2** onus, °burden, °weight, °load, °encumbrance, °strain, °pressure: *The admission of fifty new children put a heavy tax on the school's resources.*
—v. **3** assess, °exact, °demand, °charge, °impose or levy a tax (on), *Archaic* tithe: *If the government doesn't tax citizens, where will the money come from?* **4** °burden, °strain, put a °strain on, °try; °load, °overload, °stretch, °exhaust; °encumber, °weigh down, saddle, *Brit* pressurize, *US* °pressure: *This misbehaviour is really taxing my patience. Our meagre resources were taxed to the limit. Mother was taxed with the responsibility of caring for us.*

taxi n. **1** taxi-cab, °cab, hackney, *Colloq* hack: *Please hurry, as I have a taxi waiting.*
—v. **2** °drive, °ride (on the ground): *After landing, the plane taxied to the gate.*

teach v. °instruct (in), °inform (about), °communicate (to), °educate, °guide, °train, °tutor, °coach, °enlighten, edify, °indoctrinate, inculcate, °instil, °school in, °demonstrate,

°show, °familiarize or °acquaint with, give lessons (in) (to); °drill, °discipline: *She is qualified to teach chemistry. Captain Ross taught many youngsters to sail. She wants to teach when she completes her training.*

teacher n. °schoolteacher, educator, °instructor, professor, °doctor, °tutor, °fellow, lecturer, °master, °mistress, schoolmaster, schoolmistress, °coach, trainer, °guide, mentor, guru, cicerone, °counsellor, advisor; educationist; *Brit* don, *Scots* dominie, *US* docent, *Colloq* schoolma'm: *One can be counted extremely lucky to have inspiring teachers.*

team n. **1** °side, line-up, °group, °band, °gang, °body, °crew, °party, troupe: *Which team does Lineker play for?* **2** °pair, yoke, °span, duo, °set, °rig, tandem: *They hitched a fresh team of horses to the coach and we were soon back on the road.*
—v. **3** Often, **team up**: °join (up or together), °band or °get or work together, °unite, °combine, °link (up), °cooperate, °collaborate; conspire: *If we team up, we'll get the job done better and in half the time.*

tear v. **1** °rip, °rend, rive, °rupture, °pull °apart, °shred, °mutilate, °mangle, °claw, °split, °divide, °separate, °sever: *The tiger is tearing its quarry to shreds. He tore the contract in half and stormed out.* **2** °pull, °snatch, °wrench: *The force of the blast tore the attaché case from my grasp. The child was torn from her mother's arms by the soldier.* **3** °dash, °fly, °run, gallop, °race, sprint, °rush, scoot, °shoot, °speed, °bolt, dart, °flit, °scurry, scuttle, °career, zoom, °hurry, °hasten, *Colloq* zip: *He is tearing around trying to find the money to cover his loan.*
—n. **4** °rip, °rent, °rupture, °hole, °split, °slash, °gore, °cut, °score, °slit, °gash, fissure, °rift, laceration: *Nobody will see the tear in your trousers if you remain seated.*

tearful adj. weeping, crying, in tears, sobbing, whimpering, dewy-eyed, blubbering, snivelling, lachrymose, *Colloq* weepy: *She was tearful as she told him they could not meet again.*

tease v. **1** bait, °taunt, °torment, °harass, bedevil, °bother, nettle, °plague, °chaff, °pester, °annoy, °irritate, needle, goad, badger, °provoke, vex, °twit, °tantalize, °frustrate, *Non-Standard* °aggravate, *Colloq* °guy, °pick on, rib, drive mad or crazy, drive up the °wall, *Brit* take the mickey out of, *Slang* °rag: *Stop teasing the animals! Frances would tease me by agreeing to go out and then begging off with a headache.* **2** °coax, °worry, winkle, °work, °manipulate: *He was finally able to tease the broken piece of key out of the lock.*

technical adj. **1** complex, °complicated, °detailed, °intricate, specialized: *This is a technical matter, not easily understood by the layman.* **2** °mechanical, applied, industrial, polytechnic, technologic(al): *We thought he would be happier attending a technical school.*

technique n. **1** technic, °method, °approach, °manner, °mode, °fashion, °style, °procedure, °system, °tack, °line, modus operandi, standard operating °procedure, *Colloq* MO (= 'modus operandi'), SOP (= 'standard operating procedure'): *After many years, he has developed his own technique for building hot-air balloons.* **2** technic, °art, craftsmanship, artistry, °craft, °knack, °touch, °skill, skilfulness, adroitness, adeptness, dexterousness, °facility, competence, °faculty,

°ability, °aptitude, °performance, °proficiency, °talent, °gift, °genius, know-how, °knowledge, °expertise: *Jason's technique remains unsurpassed.*

tedious *adj.* over-long, long-drawn-out, prolonged, °endless, unending, °monotonous, unchanging, °changeless, unvarying, °laborious, long-winded, wearing, wearying, wearisome, tiring, °exhausting, fatiguing, °tiresome, °boring, °dreary, °dull, dry-as-dust, °drab, °colourless, °vapid, insipid, °flat, uninteresting, °banal, unexciting, °prosaic, prosy, soporific, °humdrum, °routine, °repetitious, °repetitive, °mechanical, automaton-like, °automatic, *Colloq* ho-hum, *Slang* °dead, *US* blah: *For almost fifty years my father had a tedious job on an assembly line.*

tedium *n.* tediousness, monotony, changelessness, invariability, long-windedness, wearisomeness, tiresomeness, °boredom, ennui, dreariness, dullness, drabness, colourlessness, vapidity, insipidity, insipidness, two-dimensionality, banality, °routine, repetitiousness: *How do you survive the tedium of getting up and going to an office every day?*

teem¹ *v.* Usually **teem with**: °proliferate (with), be °prolific (with), °abound, be °abundant, °swarm (with), be °alive (with), °crawl (with), °bristle (with), overflow (with), °overrun (with), be °full (of), °brim (with): *When the panel was removed, the entire foundation was seen to be teeming with termites.*

teem² *v.* °pour, °rain, °stream (down), *Colloq* come down (in buckets *or* by the bucketful), °bucket down, °rain *or* °pour cats and dogs: *It teemed with rain continuously while we were on holiday.*

teenager *n.* °adolescent, °youth, °boy, °girl, young °man, young lady, °juvenile, °minor, *Colloq* kid: *The town ought to provide a place where teenagers can get together.*

teeter *v.* °balance, wobble, °rock, °sway, °totter, waver, °tremble, °stagger: *She screamed when she saw Bruce teetering on the edge of the precipice.*

telegram *n.* °cable, cablegram, radiogram, radio-telegram, wire, telex, (*In France*) bleu, pneu, *Brit trade mark* Telemessage, *US trade mark* Mailgram: *She received a telegram from him, saying that he would be arriving on Monday.*

telephone *n.* **1** handset, phone, *Colloq* blower, *Chiefly US* horn: *Mr Fraser, the Managing Director is on the telephone for you.*
—*v.* **2** phone, °ring (up), °call (up), give (someone) a °ring *or* a °call, *Colloq* get (someone) on the blower *or chiefly US* the horn, give (someone) a tinkle *or* a °buzz, °buzz: *Telephone when you have a chance.*

telescope *n.* **1** spyglass, *Old-fashioned* °glass; refracting telescope, reflecting telescope, radio telescope: *Through the telescope, he could just discern the American coastline.*
—*v.* **2** °shorten, compress, °abbreviate, °curtail, condense, summarize, °précis, °digest, °tighten (up), °boil down, °abridge, truncate, °abstract: *Telescope the report into two columns for page 2.* **3** concertina, squash, °crush: *The first three carriages of the train were telescoped in the crash.*

television *n.* TV, video (receiver), small °screen, *Colloq* box, idiot box, *Brit* telly, *US* boob tube, *Slang* tube, *Brit* goggle-box: *My television was not working over the weekend.*

tell¹ *v.* **1** °relate, °narrate, °recount, °recite: *Tell me a story.* **2** Sometimes, **tell of**: °say, °mention, °hint at, °refer to, °touch on, utter, °state, °declare, °proclaim, °announce, °publish, °broadcast, °communicate, °make known, °report, °impart, °indicate, °release, °break, let (something) be known, advertise, trumpet, herald, bring to °light, °disclose, divulge, °intimate, °leak, °admit, °betray, °acknowledge, °confess, disbosom oneself, get (something) off (one's) chest, unburden *or* disburden (oneself), °blab, °tattle, *Colloq* °talk, °let the cat out of the bag, °spill the beans, °let out, °let °slip, blow the whistle on, °give away the (whole) show, *US* pull the plug on, *Slang* squeal, squeak, rat, peach, *US* spill (one's) guts: *She told of her fears. He refuses to tell where the money is hidden. She talked a lot but told very little.* **3** apprise, °advise, °inform, let (someone) know, °notify, °acquaint (someone) with (something): *He has told me everything. Tell them that I shall be late. He told them nothing of his illness.* **4** °recount, °describe, delineate, °outline, °portray, depict, °express, °put, °word, °explain: *I am not sure how to tell you this.* **5** °order, °command, °require, °demand (that), °charge, °direct, °dictate (that), °instruct, °bid: *Tell them I want no visitors today. She told him to go.* **6** carry °weight, be °influential, be °effective, have (an) °effect: *What we accomplished here today is bound to tell in our favour.* **7** °determine, °say, °confirm, aver, assert, asseverate, °swear, take an °oath, be °sure *or* °certain *or* °positive, °know (for °sure *or* for °certain): *It just shows you never can tell.* **8** ascertain, °determine, °perceive, °understand, °make out, discern, °identify, °recognize, °distinguish, discriminate, °differentiate: *I cannot tell if that is George or not. I can't tell George from John in this photograph.* **9** °predict, °prophesy, °forecast, foretell, °foresee, °determine, ascertain, °know: *Who can tell what tomorrow will bring?* **10 tell off**: °scold, °reprimand, °berate, chide, °castigate, censure, take to °task, °rebuke, °lecture, reproach, °reprove, *Colloq* give (someone) a °tongue-lashing, rake *or* haul (someone) over the coals, give (someone) a °piece of (one's) mind, tick off, *Slang* tear a strip off, *US* °chew out: *He was told off for being late for dinner again.* **11 tell on**: °tattle on, °blab about, *Brit* °grass on: *Charlotte never forgave Tim for telling on her to Aunt Jane.*

tell² *n.* tumulus, °mound, barrow, hillock: *Excavation of the tell exposed ancient skeletons.*

telling *adj.* **1** °effective, °effectual, °influential, °weighty, °important, °powerful, °forceful, °potent, °significant, °considerable, °striking: *The new colour scheme in the office has had a telling effect on morale.*
—*n.* **2** tattling, (too) revealing, *Colloq* letting the cat out of the bag, giving away the whole show: *I cannot say why her key was found in his pocket—that would be telling.*

temper *n.* **1** °mood, °disposition, temperament, °humour, °state *or* °frame of mind, °character, °personality, °nature, °make-up, constitution: *Practising law did not suit his temper, so he became a social worker.* **2** composure, °self-control, self-possession, calmness, equanimity, °balance, °sang-froid, coolness, *Colloq* °cool: *He would lose his temper if she ever mentioned another man.* **3** °ill °humour, °ill temper, °foul temper,

irascibility, irritability, petulance, volatility, peevishness, huffishness, surliness, churlishness, hotheadedness, hot-bloodedness: *At the first sign of temper, just ignore him.* **4** (temper) °tantrum, °fury, °fit (of pique), °rage, °passion, *Colloq Brit* wax, °paddy: *She went off into a temper at the mere mention of his name.*
—v. **5** °modify, °moderate, assuage, mollify, °soften, °cushion, °tone down, allay, soothe, °mitigate, palliate, °reduce, °relax, slacken, °lighten, appease: *The cold currents from the poles are tempered by the equatorial waters. She used all her wiles to temper his fury.* **6** anneal, toughen, °strengthen, °harden: *Plunge the heated blade into water to temper it.*

temperamental *adj.* **1** °moody, °sensitive, °touchy, hypersensitive, °volatile, irascible, °irritable, °petulant, °testy, °short-tempered, hot-tempered, °hotheaded, hot-blooded, °excitable, °explosive, on a short fuse, °capricious, °impatient, bad-humoured, °curt, °brusque, °short, °gruff, °bluff, curmudgeonly, °waspish, °snappish, °peevish, crabby, crabbed, grumpy, huffish, huffy, crotchety, *US* °cranky, *Colloq* grouchy: *He's not usually temperamental—must be something he ate.* **2** °erratic, uneven, °unreliable, °inconsistent, undependable, unpredictable: *That car of mine is getting temperamental in its old age.*

temperance *n.* **1** (self-)°restraint, moderation, (self-) °control, forbearance, (self-)°discipline, continence: *Temperance is one of the four cardinal virtues, alongside justice, prudence, and fortitude.* **2** abstemiousness, teetotalism, abstinence, °sobriety, Rechabitism; °prohibition: *We have always preached temperance to our children.*

temperate *adj.* **1** °moderate, °reasonable, (self-) restrained, disciplined, controlled, forbearing, °sensible, °sane, °rational, not excessive, composed, °steady, °stable, even-tempered, °equable, °sober, sober-sided, sober-minded, °mild, °dispassionate, unimpassioned, °cool, cool-headed, unexcited, °calm, unruffled, °tranquil, imperturbable, unperturbed, °self-possessed, °quiet, °serene: *Even the most temperate of women would lose her cool when dealing with a man like that.* **2** abstemious, teetotal, abstinent, continent, °moderate, °sober; °chaste, °celibate, austere, ascetic, self-denying, puritanical: *Those who lead temperate lives seem to live no longer than those who yield to dissipation.*

tempest *n.* **1** °storm, wind-storm, hailstorm, rainstorm, °hurricane, typhoon, tornado, cyclone, squall, thunderstorm: *The Red Spot on Jupiter is the centre of a perpetual, violent tempest.* **2** °storm, commotion, °disturbance, °upheaval, disruption, °furore *or US* furor, turbulence, °ferment, °tumult, °agitation, perturbation, hurly-burly, °disorder, outbreak, °unrest, °riot, °chaos, °uproar, brouhaha, *Colloq* hoo-ha: *After the tempest of protest died down, a vote was taken and saner heads prevailed.*

tempestuous *adj.* °stormy, °wild, °uncontrolled, uncontrollable, disrupting, disruptive, turbulent, °tumultuous, °riotous, °chaotic, °uproarious, °boisterous, °frantic, frenzied, frenetic, °furious, wrathful, vehement, °fiery, °impassioned, °fierce: *They had a tempestuous relationship, and did not live together for very long.*

template *n.* templet, °pattern, °mould, °guide, °model, °die: *The work on the lathe is matched to the template.*

temple *n.* place *or* house of °worship, °holy place, house of God, church, synagogue, mosque, pagoda, cathedral, °sanctuary, chapel, shrine, *Yiddish* shul *or* schul: *Temples to gods are found throughout the world.*

tempo *n.* °cadence, °rhythm, °beat, °time, °pulse, metre, °measure; °pace, °speed, °rate: *The melody should be played in waltz tempo. Living in the country, Tom is unaccustomed to the tempo of big-city life.*

temporal *adj.* **1** °earthly, °terrestrial, terrene, mundane, °worldly, non-spiritual, non-clerical, °lay, laic(al), °secular, non-religious, non-ecclesiastic(al), °material, °civil, °profane, fleshly, °mortal: *He believed that his temporal miseries would be compensated for by an eternity in the seventh heaven.* **2** See **temporary**, below.

temporarily *adv.* **1** for the °time being, in the interim, *pro tempore*, pro tem, in *or* for the °meantime *or* the °meanwhile, for °now: *Mr Peters is temporarily out of the office, and will contact you on his return.* **2** °briefly, fleetingly, for a (°short *or* °little) while *or* °time, for the °moment: *Your size is temporarily out of stock, madam.*

temporary *adj.* impermanent, °makeshift, °stopgap, °stand-by, °provisional; *pro tempore,* pro tem, transitory, °transient, °fleeting, °fugitive, °passing, ephemeral, °temporal, evanescent, °short-lived, °momentary: *I suppose it will have to do as a temporary substitute.*

tempt *v.* **1** °attract, °entice, °lure, allure, °draw (in), invite, °lead on, °whet (one's) appetite, °seduce, °captivate, °persuade, °coax, °cajole: *They had a special offer to tempt new customers.* **2** °lead, °induce, °persuade, °prompt, °move, °incline, °dispose: *I would be tempted to resign if they treated me that way.* **3** °provoke, °dare, (put to the) °test: *I shouldn't tempt Providence if I were you.*

temptation *n.* **1** °tempting, enticing, leading on, seducing, captivating, persuading, coaxing, cajoling: *The temptation by advertisers never stops, does it?* **2** °enticement, seduction, captivation, °persuasion, allurement, °invitation, °attraction, °draw, °lure, °inducement, °snare, *Colloq* °pull, °come-on: *I could never resist a temptation like that.*

tempting *adj.* **1** °seductive, enticing, °inviting, alluring, captivating, °attractive, tantalizing, appealing, °irresistible, titillating; °fetching, winsome, °prepossessing, °ravishing, °voluptuous, °sensuous, *Colloq* °sexy, *US* °foxy: *They made her a very tempting offer which she found hard to refuse. He was continually distracted by thoughts of tempting young girls.* **2** appetizing, mouth-watering, °delicious, °savoury, delectable, °succulent, °luscious, toothsome: *Why does food always look most tempting when I am on a diet?*

temptress *n.* °seductress, vamp, °siren, *femme fatale,* coquette, °flirt, enchantress, sorceress, Circe, *Slang* sexpot, man-eater, *US* °foxy lady, fox, mantrap: *You warned me against that temptress because you wanted her for yourself.*

tenable *adj.* defensible, °supportable, justifiable, maintainable, workable, °viable, defendable, °plausible, °reasonable, °rational, arguable, believable, credible, creditable, imaginable, conceivable, °possible: *Copernicus showed that Ptolemaic cosmology was no longer tenable.*

tenacious *adj.* **1** °persistent, dogged, unfaltering, pertinacious, unswerving, °determined, °diligent, °resolute, °staunch, °stalwart, °steadfast, °strong, °sturdy, unwavering, strong-willed, °strong-minded, unshaken, unshakeable *or* unshakable, °obstinate, intransigent, °stubborn, adamant, obdurate, refractory, °immovable, °inflexible, °rigid, °firm, unyielding, uncompromising: *Despite his age, Christopher maintains a tenacious grip on reality.* **2** cohesive, °strong, °tough; adhesive, °sticky, clinging; gummy, gluey, mucilaginous, glutinous, viscous, viscid: *The bricks are then smeared over with a tenacious mud, which dries hard.* **3** Often, **tenacious of**: clinging (to), °grasping, maintaining, keeping (up), staying with, retentive (of), persisting *or* °persistent (in), retaining: *She is tenacious of the old ways of doing things.* **4** retentive, °good: *Aunt Agatha has a very tenacious memory.*

tenacity *n.* **1** tenaciousness, °persistence, doggedness, °perseverance, pertinacity, °determination, °grit, diligence, resoluteness, °resolution, purposefulness, °resolve, staunchness, steadfastness, °stamina, assiduity, sedulousness, °strength, strong-mindedness, unshakeability *or* unshakability, °obstinacy, intransigence, stubbornness, obduracy, inflexibility, rigidity, firmness, uncompromisingness, *Colloq US* sand, stick-to-it-iveness: *He persisted with the tenacity of the English bulldog.* **2** tenaciousness, cohesiveness, °strength, °power, toughness, °resilience; adhesiveness, stickiness, gumminess, glueyness, mucilaginousness, glutinousness, viscousness, viscidity, *US* °cling: *The texture of the surfaces affects the tenacity of the bonding cement.*

tenancy *n.* occupancy, °occupation, °possession, °tenure: *Our tenancy of the house expires next month. The tenancy of this position is a year.*

tenant *n.* °occupant, lessee, renter, leaseholder, occupier, °resident, °inhabitant: *We could not redecorate the premises while the tenants were there.*

tend¹ *v.* be °inclined *or* °disposed, be °liable *or* apt *or* °likely, °incline, °lean, have *or* show *or* exhibit *or* demonstrate a °tendency, °favour, °verge, gravitate, be °biased; be °prone: *The judge might tend towards leniency in your case. I tend to agree. Tree growth here tends towards the horizontal.*

tend² *v.* °care for, take °care of, °look after, °look out for, °watch over, °see to, keep an °eye on, °attend (to), °wait on, °cater to, °minister to, °serve, °nurse, nurture: *Marie tended her father lovingly throughout his long illness.*

tendency *n.* °inclination, °bent, °leaning, °disposition, propensity, predisposition, proclivity, predilection, susceptibility, proneness, °readiness, °partiality, °affinity, °bias, °drift, °direction, °trend, °movement: *Brian has always had a tendency to be overweight. The particles exhibit a tendency to align themselves north and south.*

tender¹ *adj.* **1** °sensitive, °delicate, °fragile, °frail, °infirm, °unstable, °shaky, °weak, °feeble, unwell, °sickly, ailing, °unsound: *His condition is still a bit too tender for him to go outside.* **2** chewable, °edible, eatable, °soft: *The steak will become more tender if it is marinated.* **3** °young, youthful, °immature,

°juvenile, °inexperienced, °impressionable, °vulnerable, °green, °new, °raw, °undeveloped, untrained, uninitiated, °callow: *At his tender age he could not have known about such things.* **4** °sensitive, °touchy, °ticklish, °dangerous, °troublesome, °provocative, °difficult, °tricky: *Please avoid mentioning the wedding, it's a tender subject around here.* **5** °gentle, °soft, °delicate, °light, °sensitive, °soothing: *Oh, how he yearned for her tender touch at his fevered brow.* **6** °kind, kind-hearted, loving, °affectionate, °fond, °gentle, °mild, compassionate, °considerate, humane, °benevolent, °sympathetic, °feeling, °thoughtful, °soft-hearted, °warm, caring, °merciful, °solicitous, tender-hearted, warm-hearted, °good-natured: *Wounded and helpless, he succumbed to the tender care of the nurses.* **7** °touching, °emotional, °moving, °stirring, soul-stirring, °heart-rending, °heartfelt, °passionate, °impassioned, impassionate, °poignant, °sentimental, mawkish, °maudlin: *Who could forget the tender scene as Cedric bade farewell to his mother and went off to war?* **8** °sore, °raw, °painful, °sensitive, °inflamed; smarting, °burning, hurting, aching, °agonizing: *This spot, right here, is so tender that it hurts just to think about it.* **9** loving, °affectionate, amatory, amorous, adoring, °romantic: *They exchanged tender, knowing looks.*

tender² *v.* **1** °offer, proffer, °present, °propose, °put forward, °extend, °hold out, °submit, °advance, °put up, °set before: *Donald tendered his resignation yesterday. She has tendered the committee an excellent proposal.*
—*n.* **2** °offer, °bid, °presentation, °proposal, °proposition: *The city is accepting tenders for the construction of a new bridge.* **3** currency, °money, specie, (bank) °notes, °cash, °bills; °payment, compensation: *Pound notes are no longer legal tender in England and Wales.*

tender³ *n.* **1** dinghy, gig, skiff, °launch, °boat, row-boat *or* rowing-boat, jolly-boat: *The yacht moved easily through the water towing a tender.* **2** wagon *or* *Brit* waggon, °truck, °vehicle: *The tender of Felix's toy train was filled with sweets for his birthday.*

tenet *n.* °belief, credo, °creed, article of °faith, °ideology, °precept, °conviction, °principle, dogma, °idea, °opinion, °position, °view, °viewpoint, °maxim, axiom, canon, teaching, °doctrine: *They accept the Golden Rule as a fundamental tenet of their organization.*

tenor *n.* °drift, °tone, °spirit, °essence, °character, °gist, °bias, °import, °substance, °effect, °significance, °meaning, °sense, connotation, °theme, °thread, °implication, °inference, °intent, °purpose, °tendency, purport, °direction: *The general tenor of Mark's letters was unfriendly.*

tense *adj.* **1** °taut, °strained, °stiff, under °tension, °rigid: *One could see how tense the muscles were under the skin.* **2** °intense, °nervous, °anxious, under (a) °strain, highly-strung, high-strung, °strained, on °edge, wrought up, keyed up, worked up, °taut, on tenterhooks, apprehensive, distressed, °upset, °disturbed, °worried, edgy, on pins and needles, °jumpy, fidgety, °overwrought, *Colloq* wound up, jittery, having a case of the °jitters, *Brit* strung up, *US* strung out, *Slang* uptight, *US* antsy: *Try to relax* *and not be so tense.* **3** °nervous, °anxious, worrying, worrisome, distressing, °disturbing, stressful, °nerve-racking *or* nerve-wracking, °fraught, disquieting: *Those were tense moments while we waited for the winner's name to be posted.* —*v.* **4** °tighten, °stretch, °strain, tauten, °tension: *The mast will be secure once the stays have been tensed.*

tension *n.* **1** °stress, tightness, tautness, °strain, °pull, °traction, °pressure, tenseness, °force: *Can this cable withstand so much tension?* **2** nervousness, °anxiety, anxiousness, °strain, edginess, apprehension, °suspense, tautness, °distress, °upset, °worry, jumpiness, fidgetiness, *Colloq* jitteriness, (a case of) the °jitters: *I could feel the tension building among the audience.*

tentative *adj.* **1** °experimental, °speculative, exploratory, probative, °trial, °provisional: *We have tentative plans for introducing a new work methodology.* **2** unsure, °hesitant, °uncertain, °indecisive, °cautious, °timid, °shy, diffident, uneasy, apprehensive: *The child gave him a tentative smile, not knowing what to expect.*

tenuous *adj.* **1** °thin, °slender, °fine, attenuated, °delicate, gossamer, diaphanous, °fragile: *The spider descended slowly on its tenuous thread.* **2** °flimsy, °insubstantial *or* unsubstantial, °paltry, °weak, °feeble, °frail, °meagre, °vague, °negligible, °insignificant, °trifling, °sketchy, °hazy, °nebulous, dubious, °doubtful, °shaky: *Your case rests on very tenuous evidence.*

tenure *n.* **1** °possession, holding, occupancy, incumbency, tenantry, °tenancy, °occupation, residency, °residence: *The laws on tenure are extremely complicated.* **2** (job) °security, °permanence, permanency: *After five years he was automatically guaranteed tenure.*

tepid *adj.* **1** °lukewarm, warmish: *The gelatine should be tepid before refrigerating it.* **2** °lukewarm, °unenthusiastic, °cool, °indifferent, apathetic, uninterested, unconcerned, °nonchalant, uncaring, °neutral, °blasé: *How can he remain tepid on an issue like apartheid?*

term *n.* **1** °name, °title, designation, appellation; °word, °expression, locution, °phrase: *The term for that is* venturi tube. *Habeas corpus is a term of art in law.* **2** semester; °time, °period (of °time), °interval, °length of °time, °span (of °time), duration, °spell, °stretch, while: *During the summer term we played cricket every Saturday. He was sentenced to a long term of imprisonment.* **3** sitting, °stint, °session, °course; incumbency, °administration: *During their latest term of office, interest rates were raised twice.* **4** Often, **terms:** °condition(s), °provision(s), article(s), clause(s), °proviso(s); °stipulation(s), °qualification(s), assumption(s): *According to the terms of the will, proceeds from the patent go into a trust fund.* **5 come to terms:** °agree, come to *or* reach an °agreement *or* an °arrangement *or* an °understanding, °reconcile, °arrange, °settle, compromise: *Can we come to terms on the price? He will simply have to come to terms with his conscience.* **6 in terms of:** °concerning, °regarding, as regards, with °regard to, in °relation to, °relative to, relating to, in the °matter of: *The psychiatrist offered little in terms of direct solutions to my problems.* **7 terms:** **a** °payment, °schedule, rates: *What terms have they offered to settle the debt?* **b** °standing,

°position, °basis, °relationship, relations, °footing: *I always thought you two were on good terms.* —*v.* **8** °call, °name, °label, °designate, denominate, °entitle, °title, °style, dub; °nickname: *Abraham Lincoln was termed, among other things, 'The Great Emancipator'.*

terminal *adj.* **1** closing, concluding, terminating, ending, °final, °ultimate, °extreme; °maximum, greatest: *Spencer wrote that the human being is at once the terminal problem of biology and the initial factor of sociology.* **2** °deadly, °mortal, °fatal, °lethal, °incurable: *The cancer was diagnosed as terminal.* —*n.* **3** terminus, (terminal) °station, °end of the line, depot: *We arrived at the air terminal with five minutes to catch our plane.* **4** keyboard, °monitor, °position, °station, VDU (= 'visual display unit'), PC (= 'personal computer'), module, CRT (= 'cathode ray tube'), °screen, (control) panel: *The computer system supported a terminal for each member of the team.* **5** °connection, wire, connector, coupler, coupling, conductor: *Do I attach the red cable to the positive or the negative terminal?*

terminate *v.* °stop, °end, come to an °end, °finish; put an °end to, °cease, conclude, °discontinue, °drop, abort, bring to an °end *or* a °close, °wind up *or* down, °sign off, °cut off: *The railway line once terminated at the port. They said they wanted to terminate the contract.*

termination *n.* **1** °end, ending, °stop, stopping, stoppage, ceasing, cessation, discontinuation, abortion, *Colloq* wind-up, winding up, °close, °finish, finishing, conclusion: *The rights revert to us at the termination of the agreement. Because of her condition, termination of the pregnancy was recommended.* **2** °suffix, desinence, ending: *The English termination* -ly *usually denotes an adverb but is occasionally adjectival, as in* sickly.

terminology *n.* nomenclature, vocabulary, °language, words, locutions, °wording, terms, phraseology, phrasing, °jargon, shop-talk, argot, °cant, *Colloq* °lingo: *Medical terminology requires specialized dictionaries.*

terrain *n.* topography, °landscape, °ground, °territory: *These vehicles are specially designed for rough terrain.*

terrestrial *adj.* **1** °earthly, earthbound, °worldly, terrene, tellurian *or* telluric, °global, sublunary, subastral; mundane: *He insists that we tackle our terrestrial problems before spending a fortune on space travel.* —*n.* **2** earth-man, earth-woman, earth-person, earthling, °mortal, °human: *My experiences are beyond the imaginations of you mere terrestrials.*

terrible *adj.* **1** °bad, °serious, °grave, °severe, °acute, distressing, °disagreeable, °nasty, °foul, °unbearable, °dreadful, °loathsome, °hideous, °vile, intolerable, °awful, *Colloq* °rotten, °lousy, °beastly: *I've had a terrible virus.* **2** °bad, °remorseful, °regretful, rueful, °sorry, contrite, °ashamed, conscience-stricken, °guilty, distressed, °dreadful, °awful, *Colloq* °rotten, °lousy, °beastly: *I felt terrible having to tell the neighbours about their cat.* **3** °unhappy, unpleasant, °disagreeable, °awful, °miserable, °joyless, °wretched, °unfortunate, *Colloq* °rotten, °lousy, °beastly: *We spent an absolutely terrible evening at the theatre.* **4** °gruesome, °grisly, °macabre, °gory,

°grotesque, °brutal, °savage, °horrible, horrendous, °terrifying, °terrific, °harrowing, horrid, horrifying, °ghastly, °frightening, °frightful, unspeakable, °monstrous, °dread, appalling, °shocking, alarming, °awful, °foul: *The casualties that were arriving had the most terrible wounds.* **5** °disgusting, °revolting, nauseating, °nauseous, °offensive, vomit-provoking, °obnoxious, stomach-turning, stomach-churning, °abominable, mephitic, noisome, noxious, °loathsome, °horrible, °hideous, °terrific, °awful, °evil, °vile, °rotten: *The compost heap was giving off the most terrible stench.* **6** °terrifying, °frightening, °frightful, °fearsome, °formidable, redoubtable, °awesome, awe-inspiring, °terrific: *The animal gave a terrible roar and charged into the clearing.*

terribly *adv.* °very, °extremely, °exceedingly, °thoroughly, decidedly, unbelievably, incredibly, monumentally, outrageously, °awfully, fabulously, *Colloq* °frightfully: *They were terribly apologetic about being late. I missed him terribly when he left.*

terrific *adj.* **1** See terrible, 4, 5, 6, above. **2** wonderful, °marvellous, °splendid, breathtaking, °extraordinary, °outstanding, °magnificent, °exceptional, °unbelievable, °incredible, mind-boggling, stupendous, °superb, °excellent, first-class, °superior, *Colloq* °great, ace, °fantastic, °fabulous, °sensational, smashing, °super: *They really put on a terrific show.*

terrify *v.* °alarm, °frighten, °scare, terrorize, °shock, make one's flesh crawl *or* creep, °horrify, make one's blood run cold, make one's hair stand on end, °stun, °paralyse, °petrify: *Are you trying to terrify the child with those horror stories?*

terrifying *adj.* alarming, °frightening, °scary, °shocking, horrifying, paralysing, petrifying: *Being chased by a bull is a terrifying experience.*

territory *n.* **1** °area, °region, °district, °neighbourhood, °zone, sector, °tract, °land, °precinct, °quarter, vicinage, °vicinity, purlieu: *Each one of these animals stakes out its own territory and protects it.* **2** °area, bailiwick, °domain, °province, haunts, °patch, *Colloq* stamping-ground, *US* °turf: *Richard would be best advised to stick to his own territory.*

terror *n.* **1** °fright, °dread, °fear, °horror, °panic, °shock, °alarm, °anxiety, °dismay, consternation, intimidation, awe: *They felt a sense of terror when they caught sight of the enemy forces.* **2** °scourge, °demon, °brute, °monster, °fiend, °devil, *US* mad dog: *The gang of teenagers was the terror of the neighbourhood. Her daughter is a little terror.*

terrorist *n.* °subversive, °radical, insurgent, °revolutionary, anarchist, nihilist; bomber, arsonist, incendiary; desperado, gunman, °thug, °felon, °criminal: *The shooting was carried out by a previously unknown gang of terrorists.*

terse *adj.* **1** °concise, °brief, °short, °compact, pithy, °succinct, °summary, laconic, °short and sweet, to the °point, sententious, °crisp, °epigrammatic, aphoristic; distilled, condensed, compendious, °abbreviated, abridged, shortened, concentrated: *He gave a terse account of what had happened.* **2** °abrupt, °curt, °short, °brusque, °blunt, °gruff, bluff, °ungracious, °petulant, °tart, °rude: *His answer was terse and unhelpful.*

test *n.* **1** °trial, °examination, exam, °proof, °evaluation, assay, °check, check-up, °investigation, °study, °analysis: *My physics test is tomorrow. Have you had a blood test lately?* —*v.* **2** °try (out), °check (up) (on), °examine, °evaluate, assess, assay, °prove, °probe: *Someone ought to test the water for purity.*

testify *v.* °state, aver, assert, °attest, °swear, °say, affirm, °declare, give °evidence *or* °testimony, bear °witness, avow, °vouchsafe, °proclaim, °announce: *He testified that he saw you there. Is your mother going to testify at the trial? The fingerprints testify to the fact that she was here.*

testimonial *n.* °endorsement, certification, commendation, (letter of) °recommendation, °reference, *Colloq* blurb: *I am happy to write a testimonial for you.*

testimony *n.* °evidence, attestation, affirmation, confirmation, verification, authentication, corroboration, avowal, deposition, °statement, affidavit, °declaration, °assertion, °claim, averral, asseveration, °information: *We have only his testimony that the woman caused the accident.*

testy *adj.* °irritable, bad-tempered, irascible, °short-tempered, °petulant, °touchy, tetchy, °querulous, °peevish, hot-tempered, crusty, °cross, grumpy, grouchy, bearish, crabby, crabbed, °fretful, captious, °waspish, °snappish, °quarrelsome, fractious, contentious, choleric, splenetic, ill-humoured, °disagreeable, ill-tempered, edgy, on °edge, °quick-tempered, crotchety, °cantankerous, *US* °cranky, *Colloq and US and Canadian dialect* ornery: *The old colonel made a few testy remarks about the boys' haircuts. Why make excuses for his being so testy?*

tête-à-tête *n.* **1** (cosy *or* personal) °chat, °dialogue, causerie, pillow °talk, private °talk *or* °word, °parley, °interview, *Colloq* confab, *US* one-on-one: *Will we have time for a brief tête-à-tête after dinner?* —*adv.* **2** intimately, privately, in °private, °face to face, confidentially, °secretly, *à deux*, in °secret, *Colloq US* one-on-one: *Could we meet tête-à-tête some time?* —*adj.* **3** °intimate, °private, intime, °cosy: *I arranged a little tête-à-tête dinner at my flat.*

tether *n.* **1** °lead, leash, °rope, °cord, fetter, °restraint, halter, °tie, °chain: *The dog had broken loose from its tether and was running around in the yard.* —*v.* **2** °tie (up *or* down), °restraint, fetter, °chain (up *or* down), leash, °manacle, °secure, °shackle, °fasten, °picket, °stake: *Why don't you tether the goat where the grass is more plentiful?*

text *n.* **1** °wording, words, °content, (°subject-)°matter; printed °matter, (main) °body (text), °contents: *The editor had no right to make changes in the text without consulting the author. The text is in 10-point roman type, the footnotes in 8-point.* **2** °extract, °abstract, °section, °quotation, °part, paragraph, °passage, verse, °line: *What text from the Scripture are we discussing next week?* **3** °subject(-matter), °topic, °theme, °motif, °issue, °focus: *For today's talk I have chosen for my text the problem of alcoholism.* **4** textbook, °school-book, reader, °manual, primer, workbook, exercise °book, *Archaic* hornbook: *Today's science texts are much more advanced than those of twenty years ago.*

texture n. °feel, °surface, °character, °grain, features, consistency, °weave; configuration, °nature, °structure, °fabric, constitution, °substance: *The material has a rough texture. The texture of the plot is reinforced by the dialogue.*

thank v. **1** express or show (one's) °gratitude or thanks or °appreciation, say thank you or thanks, give or offer or tender thanks: *Don't forget to thank your uncle for the gift, William.* **2** °blame, hold °responsible, °credit, °acknowledge: *You have your mother to thank for the present state of affairs.* —n. **3** **thanks**: °gratitude, °appreciation, gratefulness, °acknowledgement, °recognition, thanksgiving: *I gave thanks that I was again on dry land.* **4** **thanks to**: owing to, because of, as a °result of, thanks be given to, in consequence of, as a consequence of, by °reason of, °through, *Sometimes non-standard* °due to: *Thanks to you, I have to commute to work by train.*

thankful adj. °grateful, appreciative, °indebted, °pleased, °glad, °obliged, obligated, under °obligation, °beholden to: *I am most thankful that you came, doctor.*

thankless adj. unappreciated, unacknowledged, °useless, unrewarding, °fruitless, °unprofitable, profitless, unrequited, °vain, °futile, °bootless: *She always regarded housekeeping as a thankless task.*

thaw v. **1** *Sometimes,* **thaw out**: °melt, de-ice, liquefy, defrost, °warm (up), °heat (up), unfreeze: *We cannot leave till the river thaws. Why not thaw out the shepherd's pie for dinner?* **2** °soften, °warm, become (more) °cordial or °friendly, °relax, °yield, °relent, °bend, unbend, let (oneself) go: *After he got to know some of us better he began to thaw.*

theatre n. **1** playhouse, (opera) °house, (music-) °hall, auditorium, amphitheatre, theatre-in-the-round, coliseum, hippodrome, arena (theatre): *A long run in a West End or Broadway theatre is every playwright's dream.* **2** °drama, stagecraft, dramaturgy, melodrama, theatrics, histrionics, staginess, acting, performing, °performance: *Even the way Mary serves dinner is pure theatre.* **3** **the theatre**: °drama, the °stage, dramaturgy, °dramatic or °Thespian or histrionic art(s), the boards, show business, *Colloq* showbiz: *The theatre is a risky profession.* **4** °area, arena, °scene, °sphere or °place or °field of action, °setting: *In which theatre of war did you serve?*

theatrical adj. **1** theatric, °dramatic, °stage, histrionic, °Thespian, °repertory: *He joined a theatrical company and his family disowned him.* **2** stagy, overdone, °camp, campy, °melodramatic, °overwrought, exaggerated, °forced, overacted, overacting, °sensational, sensationalistic, °fake, °false, °mannered, °affected, °unnatural, °artificial, °showy, °ostentatious, spectacular, °extravagant, *Colloq* °phoney or *US also* phony, ham or hammy, grandstand: *Does Fergus's theatrical behaviour ever embarrass you?*

theft n. °robbery, °stealing, pilferage, pilfering, filching, shoplifting, thievery, purloining, °embezzlement, hijacking, larceny, *Colloq* lifting, appropriation, pocketing, pinching, swiping, snitching, *Chiefly Brit* nicking, *US* boosting, *Slang* heist, knocking off, °rip-off: *The theft of the jewellery was reported to the police immediately.*

theme n. **1** °subject(-matter), °topic, °idea, °notion, concept, °thesis, °text, °thread, keynote, °gist, °core, °substance, °point, °essence: *What is the central theme of your article?* **2** °essay, °paper, °composition, °review, article, °story, °piece, °exposition, °study, °exercise, °monograph, °tract, °thesis, dissertation, disquisition, treatise: *I have to hand in two themes next week.*

theorem n. **1** °hypothesis, °proposition, assumption, conjecture, °thesis, postulate: *He has set forth a clever proof of the binomial theorem.* **2** °statement, dictum, °rule, °deduction, °formula, axiom, °principle: *After a lifetime of experience, his theorem is that honesty is the best policy.*

theoretical adj. **1** °hypothetical, conjectural, °speculative, untested, unproved, unproven, °moot, putative, °debatable, supposititious, suppositional: *The theoretical trajectory will take it beyond Uranus.* **2** °impractical, °unrealistic, °pure, °ideal, °abstract, °academic: *The suggestion was purely theoretical, since we have no means of carrying it out.*

theorist n. theoretician, speculator, hypothecator, hypothesizer, theorizer, philosopher, °dreamer: *Leave guesswork to the theorists: we need hard facts.*

theorize v. °guess, hypothesize, conjecture, °speculate: *It is logically illogical to theorize about articles of faith.*

therapeutic adj. therapeutical, healing, curative, remedial, restorative, salutary, health-giving, °healthy, °beneficial, corrective, salubrious, medical, °medicinal: *Primitive medicine men knew of the therapeutic powers of these herbs.*

therapist n. psychotherapist, psychologist, analyst, therapeutist, psychiatrist, psychoanalyst, °counsellor, advisor, *Colloq* shrink: *For some problems it is best to seek the advice of a trained counsellor or therapist.*

therapy n. **1** °remedy, °treatment, remedial programme; °cure: *As therapy, he suggested I swim a mile every day.* **2** psychotherapy, psychoanalysis, °analysis, group therapy: *If it weren't for my weekly therapy sessions, I'd never see anyone.*

therefore adv. °consequently, so, °thus, as a °result or consequence, °hence, ergo, for this or that °reason, wherefore, °accordingly, that being so or the °case: *Demand for our products has fallen dramatically, and we cannot therefore expect to make a profit this year.*

thesaurus n. **1** °treasury, °treasure trove, °storehouse, armoury, arsenal, repository, °cache: *It is hoped that this book will be regarded as a thesaurus of linguistic treasures.* **2** synonym °dictionary, synonymy, °dictionary, lexicon: *He checked in his thesaurus for a synonym of 'idea'.*

thesis n. **1** °argument, theory, °proposition, °point, contention, °belief, °idea, °premise or premiss, assumption, °view, °assertion, °precept, °opinion, °notion, °theorem, axiom, postulate: *Think how many centuries it took man to come to grips with the thesis that all men are created equal.* **2** See theme, 2, above.

Thespian adj. **1** °dramatic, °theatrical or theatric, histrionic, acting, performing; *Colloq* ham, hammy: *His Thespian talents went unnoticed until he appeared as an extra in a James Bond movie.*

—*n.* **2** actor, actress, °performer, trouper, °player; supernumerary; matinée °idol, °star; *Colloq* ham: *For many years she was one of the most beloved Thespians who ever trod the boards.*

thick *adj.* **1** °broad, °wide, °solid, thickset, °burly, °ample, °bulky, °substantial, °beamy: *He sank his teeth into the thickest sandwich I have ever seen. She is a bit thicker in the mid-section than I had remembered, but a good ketch none-theless.* **2** Usually, **thick with**: °dense, °solid, °compact, concentrated, condensed, °packed, close-packed, compressed, crowded, choked, filled, °full, °deep, clotted, chock-full *or* choke-full *or* chuck-full, chock-a-block, teeming, swarming, °alive, bristling, crawling, bursting, crammed, jammed, brimming, *Colloq* °lousy with: *The gallery was thick with visitors.* **3** °compact, condensed, compressed, choking, °packed, impenetrable, impassable, °dense; pea-soup, soupy, °murky, °misty, foggy, smoggy, smoky, °opaque, °obscure, obscuring, °hazy: *We plunged deeper into the thick jungle. A thick fog blanketed the valley.* **4** °abundant, °plentiful, bushy, °luxuriant: *Her thick red hair tumbled down over her shoulders.* **5** °dense, viscid, viscous, gelatinous, mucilaginous, gluey, glutinous, °ropy, coagulated, clotted, congealed, jelled, jellied, inspissated, stiffish; °stiff, °firm, °rigid, °solid: *For a thicker sauce, use corn-flour.* **6** thickheaded, thick-witted, thick-skulled, °dense, °stupid, °slow, slow-witted, °dull, dull-witted, °stolid, °obtuse, gormless, bone-headed, fat-headed, pin-headed, wooden-headed, addle-pated, °halfwitted, blockheaded, doltish, Boeotian, cretinous, imbecilic, moronic, *US* thimble-witted; insensitive, °thick-skinned; *Colloq* dim-witted, *Slang* dopey: *How could anyone so thick have become an executive?* **7** guttural, hoarse, throaty, raspy, rasping, °rough, °husky, °grating, gravelly, °indistinct, distorted, °inarticulate; °gruff, °raucous: *'I need you,' he moaned, his voice thick with emotion.* **8** °close, °friendly, like that, inseparable, °devoted, °hand in glove, on good terms, on the best (of) terms, °intimate, *Colloq* °chummy, pally, (as) thick as thieves, *Brit* matey, well in, *US* palsy-walsy: *We were thick in the old days, going everywhere together.* **9** °marked, °pronounced, °strong, °decided, °obvious, °typical: *She speaks English with a thick Polish accent.*
—*n.* **10** °core, °heart, °centre, °middle, °focus, °midst: *If it's a fight, you can be sure that Timothy will be in the thick of it.*

thicken *v.* °coagulate, clot, congeal, °jell, gel, °set, °solidify, °stiffen, °harden, °firm up, °cake, incrassate, inspissate: *Cornflour can be used to thicken sauces.*

thicket *n.* copse, °brake, grove, covert, wood, *Brit* spinney: *We concealed our horses in the thicket and stole ahead on foot.*

thick-skinned *n.* insensitive, insensate, °dull, °obtuse, °stolid, °callous, °numb(ed), steeled, hardened, toughened, °tough, unsusceptible, inured, unfeeling, case-hardened, impervious, pachydermatous, *Colloq* hard-boiled: *You must be very thick-skinned not to realize that they were getting at you.*

thief *n.* **1** °robber, °burglar, cat °burglar, house-breaker, picklock, sneak-thief, safe-cracker, pilferer, shoplifter, purloiner; embezzler, peculator; pickpocket, cutpurse, purse-snatcher, mugger, highwayman, footpad, brigand, bandit, °thug, dacoit, ruffian, °outlaw, desperado, hijacker, gunman, plunderer; poacher; *Technical* kleptomaniac, *Australian* bush-ranger, *US* road-agent, *Colloq* °hold-up man, crook, *US* second-story *or* second-storey man, bandito *or* bandido, *Slang* cracksman, box man, dip, stick-up man: *They caught the thief who took the paintings.* **2** °cheat, °swindler, confidence man, mountebank, charlatan, sharper, trickster, flimflam artist *or* man, thimblerigger, *Colloq* con man, con artist, shell-game artist, *US* highbinder: *That thief cheated them out of their savings.* **3** °pirate, (sea) rover, picaroon *or* pickaroon, corsair, freebooter, buccaneer, marauder, filibuster, privateer: *They might seem romantic in retrospect, but at the time, pirates were no more than common thieves.*

thin *adj.* **1** °slim, °slender, °lean, °spare, °slight, °lanky, spindly, °skinny, thin as a rail *or* reed *or* rake, wispy, twiggy, skeletal, °gaunt, gangling, bony, °emaciated, cadaverous, °meagre, °scrawny, all skin and bones, scraggy, under-nourished, underfed, underweight, °undersized, °puny, °sparse, hollow-cheeked, (half-) °starved, pinched, withered, shrunken, shrivelled (up): *Douglas is quite thin as a result of his illness.* **2** °sparse, unsubstantial, °poor, scant, °insufficient, °inadequate, °slight, °worthless, unimportant, °deficient, skimpy, unplentiful, °paltry, piddling: *This year's harvest has been very thin.* **3** attenuated, threadlike, stringlike, pencil-thin, °fine; °narrow: *Draw a thin line between the columns. Please slice the bread thin.* **4** °flimsy, °weak, °feeble, °slight, unsubstantial, °insubstantial, °fragile, °frail, °poor, °lame; °unbelievable, unconvincing: *Harry gave some thin excuse for being late.* **5** °filmy, diaphanous, gossamer, °sheer, °light, °delicate, chiffon, °silky, silken, gauzy, translucent, °see-through, °transparent: *She had nothing but a thin negligee to protect her from the cold.* **6** °watery, watered down, °dilute(d), °weak, unsatisfying: *My dinner, as usual, consisted of thin gruel and a dry crust.* **7 thin on the ground**: °rare, uncommon, °scarce, °few (and far between), °unusual, °hard to come by *or* find, scant, °scanty: *Good managers are thin on the ground.*
—*v.* **8** Often, **thin down**: °draw out, attenuate, °reduce, °trim, °cut down, °prune; °sharpen: *At one end, thin the dowel to a point.* **9** Often, **thin down** *or* **out**: °dilute, °water (down), °decrease, °reduce, °diminish: *They always thin the wine with some water. The crowd thinned out after a while.*

thing *n.* **1** °item, (inanimate) °object, article, °possession: *They went without leaving a thing behind.* **2** °item, °subject, °matter, °detail, °feature, °aspect, °affair, constituent, °element, °factor, °point: *There's one thing that I forgot to mention. It's a small thing, but I like coffee with my breakfast.* **3** °fad, °trend, °fashion: *Let me show you the latest thing in sports cars.* **4** °feeling, °reaction, °attitude, °sentiment, emotional °attachment, °quirk, °fixation, preoccupation, °obsession; °fetish *or* fetich, *idée fixe*, °affection, °liking, °partiality, predilection, °fancy, °love, °passion, °mania; °phobia, °fear, °terror, °aversion, °loathing, °horror, detestation, °dislike, *Colloq* hang-up: *A chocoholic has a thing about chocolate. Pet snakes are not Patricia's thing.*

Roger has a thing about going out in public.
5 °device, °item, °gadget, °object, °entity, °mechanism, contrivance, °apparatus, °instrument, utensil, *Colloq* dingus, doodah, doodad, whatchamacallit, thingumajig, whosis, whatsis, thingummy, thingumabob, *Chiefly US and Canadian* gismo *or* gizmo: *the thing that is supposed to hold the flywheel in place?* **6** chore, °task, °responsibility, °matter; °act, °action, °deed, °activity, °proceeding: *The first thing I must do is to phone home.* **7** °opportunity, °chance, °possibility: *See me first thing tomorrow.* **8 things**: **a** °affairs, °matters, °business, °concerns: *I have to take care of some things at the office today.* **b** °circumstances, °events, °happenings: *Things are rarely what they seem.* **c** °belongings, °luggage, baggage, impedimenta, °possessions, °paraphernalia, °effects, °clothes, clothing, °goods; °equipment, °tools, utensils, °implements, °apparatus, *Colloq* °gear, °stuff, *Slang Brit* clobber, *US* crap, °junk, *Taboo slang US* shit: *Take your things and leave at once! The plumber left his things at the shop.*

think *v.* **1** °believe, °imagine, °expect, °dream, °fantasize, °suppose: *When do you think that you will retire?* **2** °judge, °reckon, °consider, deem, °regard (as), °characterize (as), °believe, °assume, °mark: *They thought him a fool for making such a fuss.* **3** °contemplate, cogitate (on *or* over *or* about), ruminate (over *or* about), °reflect (on), °meditate (on *or* over *or* about), °muse (on *or* over *or* about), °deliberate (on *or* over *or* about), °think about *or* of *or* over: *He likes to sit in the bath and think. I need time to think over your proposal.* **4** Often, **think of**: °recall, °remember, °recollect, °call *to* °mind: *I simply cannot think of the name of that film we saw last week.* **5 think of** *or* **about**: **a** °consider, °ponder, °weigh, °contemplate, °muse over, have in °mind, °mull over, °entertain the idea *or* °notion of, °intend, °propose: *Do you ever think of retiring?* **b** assess, °evaluate, value, °judge: *What do you think about their latest suggestion?* **6 think up** *or* **of**: °devise, concoct, contrive, come up with, °invent, °conceive (of), °dream up, °create, °make up, °improvise: *Who thinks up the plots for these dreadful TV series?*

thinkable *adj.* conceivable, °possible, imaginable, °feasible, °reasonable, °tenable, not °unlikely, °plausible, believable, credible: *It is hardly thinkable that they can be serious.*

thinker *n.* °sage, °wise man, savant, Nestor, Solomon, pundit, °mastermind, philosopher, °scholar, °learned person, mentor, °expert: *She has been looked on as one of the great thinkers of her time.*

thinking *adj.* **1** °rational, °sensible, ratiocinative, °intelligent, °reasoning, °reasonable; °meditative, contemplative, °reflective, °philosophical, cogitative, °pensive, °thoughtful, °intellectual: *Any thinking person would have done the same as you.* —*n.* **2** °opinion, °judgement, °belief, °thought, °point of °view, °viewpoint, assessment, °evaluation, theory, °reasoning, conclusion, °idea, °philosophy, °outlook: *There is nothing either good or bad, but thinking makes it so. Do you concur with the current thinking on education?*

thirst *n.* **1** craving, °desire, °appetite, °hunger, °eagerness, avidity, ravenousness, voracity, voraciousness, °lust, °passion, °enthusiasm, °fancy, hankering, °longing, yearning, *Colloq* °itch, yen: *It was the thirst for gold that drove them mad. She has an insatiable thirst for knowledge.* —*v.* **2** Often, **thirst for** *or* **after**: crave, °desire, °hunger for *or* after, °lust for *or* after, °fancy, °hanker for *or* after, °long for, °yearn for, °wish for: *These men are thirsting for power.*

thirsty *adj.* **1** parched, °dry, dehydrated; arid: *I need another drink—I'm really thirsty. The thirsty land welcomes the rain.* **2** °desirous, °hungry, avid, °eager, °ravenous, °voracious, °burning, °greedy, °avaricious, hankering, yearning, craving, *Colloq* itching: *The students are thirsty for knowledge and very hard-working.*

thorn *n.* **1** barb, °spine, °spike, °prickle, °bristle, brier *or* briar, bur *or* burr, °point, bramble, cocklebur: *My sleeve caught on the thorn and tore.* **2** Often, **thorn in (one's) side**: °bother, irritation, °annoyance, °nuisance, vexation, °torment, torture, °scourge, °plague, °affliction, irritant, bane, *Colloq* °pain in the neck, *Taboo slang* °pain in the *Brit* arse *or US* ass: *His nagging brother has been a thorn in his side for years.*

thorny *adj.* **1** °prickly, barbed, spiny, spiked, brambly, spinous, *Technical* spinose, acanthoid, spiculose, spiculate, spinulose, aciculate, muricate, barbellate, setigerous, setaceous, setiferous, setose: *The insect's feet have tiny thorny projections.* **2** °difficult, °hard, °tough, °prickly, nettlesome, °painful, °ticklish, °delicate, °intricate, °critical, complex, °complicated, °problematic, vexatious, knotty, tangled, °involved, °troublesome, °controversial, °nasty, worrying, *Colloq* °sticky, *Slang* °hairy: *Many thorny questions have vexed us throughout the ages.*

thorough *adj.* **1** thoroughgoing, °complete, °downright, °perfect, through-and-through, °total, °unmitigated, °undiluted, unmixed, unalloyed, °out-and-out, °unqualified, °sheer, utter, arrant, °absolute, °proper: *I have rarely encountered such thorough stupidity.* **2** °exhaustive, °extensive, °painstaking, °meticulous, assiduous, °careful, °scrupulous, °particular, °conscientious, °methodical: *Police conducted a thorough search but found nothing.* **3** °extensive, °exhaustive, °detailed, in-depth, °comprehensive, °full, °complete, all-inclusive, °total, all-embracing, °encyclopedic *or* encyclopaedic, °universal, A-to-Z, *Colloq* all-out: *We need someone who has a thorough knowledge of the terrain.*

thoroughly *adv.* **1** °completely, °downright, °perfectly, °totally, unqualifiedly, °utterly, °absolutely, °entirely, °extremely, unreservedly, °wholly, fully, °positively, °definitely, °quite: *He is thoroughly stupid, as we all know.* **2** carefully, painstakingly, exhaustively, extensively, assiduously, sedulously, methodically, conscientiously, scrupulously, meticulously, intensively, comprehensively, °completely, °throughout, from top to bottom, from stem to stern, backwards and forwards, in every nook and cranny: *Police searched thoroughly again, but could still find no murder weapon.*

though *conj.* **1** although, °even though, while, in °spite of *or* °despite the fact that, °notwithstanding that, albeit, granted, granting *or* conceding that, allowing *or* admitting that, °even if, °supposing: *Though it is the right size, I hate the colour.*

—*adv.* **2** °however, °nonetheless, °nevertheless, °yet, but, °still, °even so, be that as it may, all the same, °notwithstanding, for all that: *She lost the original; I kept a copy though.*

thought *n.* **1** °thinking, °reflection, reflecting, meditation, meditating, contemplation, contemplating, cogitation, cogitating, °musing, pondering, rumination, ruminating, brooding, °mental activity, mentation, brown study; brainwork, cerebration, deliberation, deliberating, °consideration, °considering: *She was deep in thought. The solution may require considerable thought.* **2** °idea, °notion, brainstorm, °observation: *I have a thought that I'd like to share with you.* **3** °consideration, contemplation, planning, °plan, °scheme, °design, °intention, °expectation, °hope, °prospect, °anticipation, °dream, °vision: *Any thought of taking a few days off had to be abandoned.* **4** thoughtfulness, °consideration, kindliness, kind-heartedness, °concern, compassion, tenderness, °kindness, °sympathy, attentiveness, °regard, °solicitude: *I don't need any help, but I appreciate the thought.* **5** Often, **thoughts**: °recollection(s), °memory or memories, °remembrance(s), °reminiscence(s): *Now and then he comforted himself with thoughts of his happy childhood.* **6** °intellect, °intelligence, °reasoning, rationality, ratiocination, °reason: *Some believe that only humans are capable of thought.* **7** °bit, °trifle, °touch, small amount, °trace, soupçon, °little, tinge: *This champagne is a thought too sweet.*

thoughtful *adj.* **1** °considerate, °kind, °kindly, kind-hearted, compassionate, °tender, °sympathetic, °attentive, °solicitous, °helpful, °charitable: *Wasn't it thoughtful of Simon to offer his help?* **2** contemplative, °pensive, °reflective, musing, in a brown study, pondering, °meditative, engrossed, introspective, °rapt, °wistful, brooding, wool-gathering, day-dreaming: *Every time I mentioned Clarissa, he would become thoughtful.* **3** °prudent, °wary, °cautious, °mindful, heedful, °thinking, °attentive, circumspect, °careful, caring: *The crew are ever thoughtful of the passengers' safety.*

thoughtless *adj.* **1** °inconsiderate, °rude, °impolite, insensitive, °tactless, undiplomatic, untactful, °unthinking: *It was thoughtless of you to mention her son, who is serving time for possession of drugs.* **2** °rash, °imprudent, negligent, °foolish, °stupid, °careless, neglectful, °reckless, °silly, °unthinking, unreflective, °absent-minded, °forgetful, °remiss, ill-considered, °heedless, °inadvertent, °inattentive: *How thoughtless of me to forget your birthday!*

thrashing *n.* **1** beating, drubbing, °whipping, flogging, °assault, caning, belting, mauling, lashing, trouncing, basting, battering, pounding, *Colloq* hiding, tanning, lambasting, hammering, pasting: *Every time he stepped into the ring he got a thrashing.* **2** °punishment, chastisement, disciplining, °discipline, castigation: *He dreaded the thrashing his father administered at any sign of disobedience.*

thread *n.* **1** °fibre, filament, strand, (piece of) °yarn; °string, °line, °cord, °twine: *Threads from his jacket were found clutched in the victim's hand. The glass is spun out into fine threads.* **2** °theme, °plot, story-line, °subject, °motif, °thesis,

°course, °drift, °direction, °tenor, °train (of thought), °sequence or °train or °chain of events: *It is difficult to follow the thread of the story when it has so many digressions.* —*v.* **3** °string: *Carefully thread the beads onto the wire.* **4** °file, °wind, °pass, °squeeze (through), pick or make (one's) way (through), inch, °ease: *He threaded his way through the crowd to reach the dais.*

threadbare *adj.* **1** frayed, °worn (out), °worn to a frazzle, °ragged, moth-eaten, °tattered, tatty, scruffy, °shabby, °seedy, torn, °wretched, °sorry, slovenly: *My old winter coat is looking a bit threadbare.* **2** trite, hackneyed, overused, overworked, reworked, °stale, °tired, stereotyped, commonplace, clichéd, cliché-ridden, °banal, °prosaic, °dull, °monotonous, °tedious, °tiresome, °boring, played out, *Colloq* °old hat: *You'll never make it as a comedian by relying on that threadbare material of yours.*

threat *n.* **1** intimidation, °menace, commination, °warning, °peril, °risk, °danger, Damoclean sword: *It is not honesty but the threat of punishment that deters many from crime.* **2** °omen, presage, portent, °foreboding, forewarning, intimation: *The villagers lived under a constant threat from the smoking volcano.*

threaten *v.* **1** °intimidate, °menace, terrorize, °daunt, cow, °bully, °browbeat, °warn, °caution: *The headmaster threatened those who misbehaved with the most dire punishment.* **2** imperil, put at °risk, °endanger, °jeopardize, put in °jeopardy: *All life is threatened if the environment is not better looked after.* **3** impend, °loom; augur, portend, presage, forebode: *The creatures crawl into their burrows if danger threatens. The gathering clouds threatened rain.*

threatening *adj.* °ominous, °menacing, °portentous, °sinister, looming, °inauspicious, minatory, minacious, comminatory, intimidating, °foreboding, °imminent, °impending: *Threatening storm clouds began to build in the western sky.*

threshold *n.* **1** sill, door-sill, doorstep; doorway, °entrance: *He stood at the threshold and peered into the room.* **2** °brink, °verge, °edge, °beginning, commencement, °outset, °start, °dawn: *The emigrants were at the threshold of a new life.*

thrift *n.* °economy, husbandry, °care, carefulness, °prudence, parsimony, frugality, thriftiness, sparingness, scrimping, skimping; penuriousness, close-fistedness, tight-fistedness, niggardliness, stinginess, miserliness: *Only through our thrift were we able to save enough for a new car.*

thrifty *adj.* °economical, °careful, °prudent, parsimonious, °frugal, °sparing, scrimping, skimping; °penurious, close-fisted, tight-fisted, niggardly, stingy, °miserly, penny-pinching, °cheap: *He talked about the need to save money and be thrifty in every way.*

thrill *n.* **1** °excitement, titillation, frisson, tingle, tingling (°sensation), stimulation, *Colloq* °kick, bang, °charge, °buzz: *Victor feels a tremendous thrill when his daughter wins a tennis match.* **2** tremor, °quiver, quivering, °shudder, shuddering, °tremble, trembling, °flutter, throb, throbbing, pulsation, vibration: *The only warning was a slight thrill in the earth just before the main quake.*

—v. **3** °excite, °stimulate, °animate, °electrify, galvanize, °enliven, °stir, titillate, °touch, °strike, °move, impassion, °arouse, Slang °send, give (someone) a kick: They were thrilled to discover that they had won an award.

thrilling adj. °exciting, °stimulating, animating, electrifying, galvanizing, enlivening, °stirring, titillating, °striking, °moving, arousing, °rousing, gripping, °sensational, °riveting, spine-tingling, soul-stirring: Last year's Cup Final was a thrilling match, with most sides playing their hearts out. I have never had such thrilling rides at the fun fair.

thrive v. °succeed, °prosper, °boom, °advance, °flourish, °grow, bloom, burgeon, °develop, wax, °increase, fructify, °ripen: They thrived in the invigorating mountain air.

throe n. Usually, **throes**: °pang, °anguish, °struggle, °chaos, turmoil, °tumult, °paroxysm, °spasm, °fit, °seizure, convulsion, Technical ictus: She was in the throes of despair at the dreadful news from home.

throng n. **1** horde, °crowd, °host, assemblage, °assembly, °gathering, °mass, °crush, °jam, multitude, congregation, °press, °swarm, °herd, °flock, bevy, drove: Throngs of people packed the shopping mall on Saturday.
—v. **2** °crowd (into), °fill, °pack (into), °cram (into), °crush (into), °jam (into), °press (into), °swarm (into), °herd (into), °flock (into or to); °assemble (in or at), °gather (in or at), °mass (in or at), congregate (in or at): Thousands thronged the stadium to watch the tennis matches.

through prep. **1** because of, on °account of, owing to, as a consequence or °result of, by °virtue of, via, by °means of, by °way of, with the °aid or °help of, under the aegis or °auspices of, Sometimes non-standard °due to: It was through his good graces that I got the appointment. **2** during, °throughout, in the °course or °middle of: The dog barked all through the night. **3** °inclusive of, including: When I say 'the third through the sixth' I mean 'including the sixth'. **4** to; into: I went through a lot of trouble to find this book.
—adj. **5** Often, **through with**: done (with), finished (with); at the end of one's tether (with), washing (one's) hands (of): Let me know when you are through. How many times has she sworn she was through with him forever?
—adv. **6** °by, °past: I am just passing through. **7** °entirely, through and through, °completely, °thoroughly, °totally, °wholly, °utterly, fully, to the core, from head to foot or toe, from top to bottom, from stem to stern, from one end to the other, in every way, in all respects: By the time I got home, I was soaked through.

throughout prep. **1** during, all (the way) °through, from the beginning to the end of: We worked throughout the day and night. Throughout his life he felt the need for constant support. **2** °everywhere in, all over, in every part of, in every nook and cranny of, from one end to the other of: I searched throughout the house for my keys.
—adv. **3** all (the way) °through, °everywhere, from one end to the other, °wholly, °entirely, °completely, fully: They were busy tidying the house throughout before his mother came to stay.

throw v. **1** °toss, °cast, °hurl, °fling, °sling, °pitch, °dash, °propel, °project, °shy, °bowl, °send, °launch, Colloq chuck: He threw the ball to the batter with all his might. **2** °cast, °shed, °project: I was hoping you might throw some light on the subject. Coming events throw their shadow before them. **3** °throw or °bring down, °floor, °fell, °knock down or over, overthrow, °upset, °overturn: He threw the vase on the floor. **4** °dismay, confound, °confuse, °dumbfound or dumfound, baffle, disconcert, °unnerve, throw off or out, unsettle, °put off, °put (someone) off his or her or their stride or pace or stroke, Colloq discombobulate: Her frank questions about my private life really threw me. **5 throw away: a** °discard, °cast off, °dispose of, jettison, get °rid of, °scrap, throw out, °dispense with, Colloq °dump, °trash, chuck out, Slang ditch: He is a hoarder, refusing to throw anything away. **b** °waste, squander, °lose, °forgo, °fritter away, fail to exploit or take advantage of, Slang °blow: He threw away his last chance for a decent life when he left her. **6 throw off: a** °eject, °expel, °emit, throw up or out: The volcano throws off rocks every so often. **b** °shake off, °rid or °free (oneself) of, get °rid of, °reject, °renounce, °repudiate: He finally managed to throw off his mother's pernicious influence. **c** °deceive, °mislead, °decoy, misguide, °misdirect, °distract, °divert, °bewilder, confound, °confuse, Colloq °flummox, bamboozle: He doubled back to throw the dogs off. **d** See 4, above. **7 throw out: a** °radiate, °emit, °send forth, °give out or off, °diffuse, °put out or forth, disseminate: The substance throws out a greenish light. **b** °expel, °eject, °force out, °evict, Colloq Brit °turf out, Slang bounce: Henry was thrown out of the pub for rowdy behaviour. **c** See 5 a, above. **d** See 6 a, above. **8 throw over:** °jilt, °leave, °abandon, °desert, °forsake, °break or °split up with, Colloq °walk out on, chuck, °drop: She was heartbroken when he threw her over and married her sister. **9 throw up: a** °vomit, °spit up, puke, °spew up, be °sick; °regurgitate, disgorge, Colloq °heave (up): He felt as if he was going to throw up. **b** °abandon, °quit, °leave, throw over, °give up, °relinquish, °resign, °renounce, Colloq chuck: He threw up a perfectly good job to go and live on a boat. **c** °reveal, °bring out or up, °bring to the surface or the top, °bring forward or forth, bring to °light or to notice: Their treachery was thrown up in high relief by the events that followed. **d** throw or °slap or °knock together, jerry-build: The house was thrown up overnight—and it looks like it. **e** See 6 a, above.

thrust v. **1** °push, shove, °drive, °force, impel, °ram, °jam, °butt, °propel, °prod, °urge, °press; °shoulder, jostle, elbow: A stranger thrust this note into my hand. She thrust her way through the crowd. **2** °stab, °plunge, °stick, °jab, °poke; °lunge: He thrust the dagger into the man's back. She thrust at me with an ice pick. **3** Usually, **thrust upon:** °press (upon or on), °impose (upon or on), °force (upon or on), °urge (upon or on): They were willing to help, but rather thought the problem had been thrust upon them.
—n. **4** shove, °push, °drive, °lunge, °poke, °prod, °stab: He depended on his agility to avoid the thrusts of the rapier. **5** °propulsion, °force, °power, °energy: The thrust of the photon engines drives the spaceship at nearly the speed of light.

thud n. clunk, thump, whomp, wham, clonk, °bump: His head hit the wall with a thud.

thug n. hooligan, °gangster, desperado, gunman, °terrorist, °hoodlum, °robber, assassin, °murderer, °killer, °cutthroat, ruffian, Mafioso, *In Paris* apache, mugger, *Technical* p'hansigar, *Brit* °rough, *Slang* °tough, hood, crook, °hit man, heavy, *US* goon, larrikin: *Some thugs roughed him up and took his wallet.*

thumb n. **1** *Technical* pollex. **2 all thumbs**: °awkward, °clumsy, maladroit, *Colloq* butter-fingered, ham-fisted, cack-handed: *I am all thumbs when it comes to threading needles.* **3 give (something) the thumbs down** *or* **turn thumbs down (on)**: °disapprove (of), °reject, °rebuff, °turn down: *We turned thumbs down to the idea of a picnic.* **4 turn** *or* **give thumbs up (to)**: °approve (of), °accept, °welcome, *Colloq* °OK *or* okay: *The boss gave thumbs up to our request for a Christmas party.* **5 under (one's) thumb**: under (one's) °control, wrapped (a)round (one's) little °finger, in the palm of (one's) hand, eating out of (one's) hand, at (one's) beck and call: *She has the directors under her thumb.*
—v. **6** hitchhike, *Colloq* °hitch, *US* hook a ride: *They thumbed their way across the country.* **7** Often, **thumb through**: leaf (through), flick *or* °flip (through), riffle (through), °skim (through), °browse (through): *I was thumbing through City Life and came across your picture, Bernard!*
8 thumb (one's) nose at: °scoff at, °deride, °jeer at, °mock, °dismiss, °scorn, °flout, be °contemptuous of, show °contempt for, exhibit defiance for, be °defiant of, contemn, *Brit* cock a snook at: *He has thumbed his nose at authority all his life.*

thumbnail adj. °rough, undetailed, °cursory, °sketchy, °superficial; °brief, °short, quick; °compact, °concise, pithy, °succinct: *His poetry is a chilling, thumbnail sketch of the way we live now.*

thumping adj. **1** °great, °huge, °colossal, stupendous, °gigantic, °enormous, °immense, °monumental, °massive, titanic, elephantine, behemoth, gargantuan, mammoth, °jumbo, *Colloq* °whopping, thundering, walloping: *That is the biggest thumping beach ball I have ever seen! That was a thumping lie.* **2** °complete, utter, °unmitigated, 24-carat *or esp. US* 24-karat, °perfect: *Anyone who would turn down a salary increase must be a thumping idiot.*

thunder n. **1** °roll, reverberation, °boom, booming, °roar, roaring, pealing, rumble, rumbling; °crash, crashing, °crack, cracking, °explosion, °blast: *We were deafened by the thunder of the tanks crossing the bridge above us.*
—v. **2** °roll, reverberate, °boom, °roar, rumble, °resound; °explode, °crash, °crack, °blast: *The noise of the jets thundered through the valley.* **3** °shout, °yell, °scream, °bellow, bark, °roar; °denounce, fulminate against, °swear (at), °rail (at), °curse (at), execrate; °threaten, °intimidate, °menace: *'Fee, fie, foe, fum!' thundered the giant. No secretary will tolerate his thundering at her.*

thunderous adj. roaring, booming, thundering, °tumultuous, °noisy, °loud, ear-splitting, deafening: *They took curtain calls to thunderous applause.*

thunderstruck adj. °dumbfounded *or* dumfounded, astonished, astounded, awestruck, awed, °speechless, struck °dumb, amazed, °taken aback, staggered, stunned, shocked, dazed, °numb, paralysed, aghast,

open-mouthed, nonplussed, *Colloq* flabbergasted, floored, bowled over, *Brit* knocked for six: *We were thunderstruck to learn that our team had been disqualified.*

thus adv. **1** so, in this °manner *or* °way *or* °fashion *or* wise, as follows, *Non-Standard* thusly: *On receipt of the payment, I wrote thus to him.* **2** °therefore, ergo, °consequently, as a consequence, as a °result, °accordingly, (and) so, then, for this *or* that °reason, °hence, in which °case *or* °event, that being the °case, that being so: *He has already decided; thus, your efforts to persuade him are useless.*

thwart v. **1** °frustrate, °impede, °check, °stymie, baffle, °stop, °foil, °stump, °hinder, °obstruct, balk, °block, °oppose, negate, nullify, *Colloq* short-circuit: *They have thwarted all our efforts to become friendly.*
—n. **2** °brace, cross-brace; (rowing-)seat, bench: *These canoes are fitted with two thwarts.*

tickle v. titillate, °delight, °please, °gratify, °amuse, °entertain, °divert, °captivate, °thrill, tickle pink *or* to death: *The show we saw last night really tickled my fancy. She was tickled to receive the flowers.*

ticklish adj. **1** °uncertain, unsteady, unsure, °unstable, °unsettled, °fickle, touch-and-go, °touchy: *Power that relies on the sword has a ticklish basis.* **2** °delicate, °precarious, °risky, °hazardous, °dangerous, °critical, °thorny, °fragile, °awkward: *As the canoe drifted towards the waterfall, we found ourselves in a very ticklish predicament.* **3** °delicate, °sensitive, hypersensitive, °difficult, °touchy, °prickly: *Cornelia is a bit ticklish on the subject of her holiday plans.*

tidy adj. **1** °neat, °orderly, °trim, °shipshape, °spruce, spick and span, °clean, well-kept, °well-groomed: *Change your clothes and come back when you're tidy.* **2** well-organized, organized, well-ordered, °methodical, °systematic, °trim: *They refused to clean his office till he had made it tidy.* **3** °respectable, sizeable, °significant, °considerable, °substantial, °good, °goodly, good-sized, °ample, °large, °big, °fair, °generous, not °insignificant; *Colloq* not to be sneezed at: *They settled a tidy sum on their daughter when she was married.*
—v. **4** Often, **tidy up**: °neaten (up), °straighten (out *or* up), °clean (up), put in °order, *Colloq* °fix (up), °spruce up, °organize, reorganize, °arrange, rearrange: *You can't watch television until you've tidied up your room. Please tidy up the files by the end of the week.*

tie v. **1** °bind, °fasten, make °fast, tie up, °lash, °secure, truss, °attach, °tether, °rope, °chain, °moor, °connect, °join, °knot, °link, °couple, °splice, °unite: *He keeps a vicious dog tied to a stake in his garden. Tie the ends of the rope together.* **2** °bind, truss (up), tie up, °lash, pinion, °restrict, confine, °restrain; °limit, tie down, °curtail, °curb, cramp, °hamper, °hinder: *His hands are tied behind his back. According to the terms of the agreement, my hands are tied and I can do nothing.* **3** °connect, °associate, °unite, °join, °link, °bind (up), affiliate, °ally, °league, °team (up): *Our business interests are tied to those of the major banks.* **4** °equal, °even, be °equal *or* °even (with), °match, be neck and neck (with): *We tied them for first place. Yesterday, we were tied for second.* **5 tie down**: **a** °clinch, °secure, °confirm, *Colloq* °nail down: *I tied down the PBT contract this*

morning. **b** °restrict, °restrain, constrain, confine, °curtail: *He won't marry because he doesn't want to feel tied down.* **6 tie in: a** be °consistent, make °sense, °correspond, °coincide, °fit (in), be °logical, °coordinate: *His alibi ties in with the witness's testimony.* **b** °relate, °connect, °link, °associate, °coordinate: *They cleverly tie in concern for the environment with their product.* **7 tie up: a** °occupy, °engage, (keep) °busy: *This affair will tie me up till Tuesday.* **b** °use, °take up, °encroach on, °impose on: *I won't tie up your time any longer.* **c** °stop, °halt, bring to a °standstill: *The traffic was tied up for hours.* **d** °commit, °oblige, °obligate, °bind: *We have tied up all their output for a year.* **e** See 1, above. **f** See 2, above.
—*n.* **8** °link, °fastening, °bond, °band, °connection, °tie-up, °relationship, affiliation, °liaison, involvement, entanglement: *Isn't there some tie between those two companies?* **9** °string, °cord, °lace, °rope, thong, ribbon, °band, ligature, shoelace, °line, leash, stop: *The tie of her dressing-gown came loose.* **10** °equality, dead heat, °deadlock, °draw, °stalemate: *When there is a tie, the game ought to go into 'sudden death' overtime.* **11** cravat, *US* necktie: *Please put on a tie for dinner.* **12** railway tie, sleeper: *Ties in Europe are now made of concrete.*

tie-in *n.* °tie-up, °relationship, °relation, °association, °connection, °link, linkage: *They say that there is a tie-in between smoking and lung cancer.*

tier *n.* °row, °line, °level, °order, °range, °course, series, °stratum, layer, echelon, °file, °rank, °storey: *The trireme is said to have had three tiers of oarsmen.*

tie-up *n.* **1** *In US and Canada*: slow-down, slow-up, entanglement, stoppage, °jam, log-jam, traffic °jam, °delay, congestion: *The tie-up was caused by fog on the highway.* **2** See tie-in, above.

tiff *n.* (petty) °quarrel, °disagreement, °misunderstanding, °dispute, °argument, °difference (of opinion), squabble, °bicker, °row, wrangle, *US* spat: *Clare and Geoff have had their first tiff.*

tiffin *n.* luncheon, lunch, light repast, °snack: *The new arrivals were to join us for tiffin.*

tight *adj.* **1** °secure, °firm, °fast, °fixed, secured, close-fitting, °snug, sealed, hermetically sealed, leak-proof, °hermetic, impervious, impenetrable, °impermeable, airtight, °watertight, waterproof: *Make sure that the lid is tight.* **2** °taut, stretched, °tense, constricting, (too) °small, ill-fitting: *She was wearing a very tight dress.* **3** °strict, binding, restrictive, stringent, °severe, °tough, uncompromising, unyielding, rigorous, °stern, austere, autocratic, °harsh, °hard and °fast, °inflexible: *You can't get away with anything under such tight regulations. I have a tight schedule next week.* **4** *Chiefly nautical* taut, (well-)disciplined, °orderly, °neat, well-organized, °trim, °tidy, °smart: *He runs a tight ship.* **5** stingy, niggardly, °mean, °penurious, °miserly, parsimonious, penny-pinching, tight-fisted, close-fisted, *Colloq Brit* mingy: *Glenn is much too tight to buy anyone a drink.* **6** °close, (°almost) °even, (highly) competitive, neck and neck, evenly matched: *It is going to be a tight race.* **7** °difficult, °trying, °dangerous, °perilous, °risky, °hazardous, °touchy, °problematic, °sticky, °tricky, °ticklish,

°precarious, touch-and-go: *The strike has created a tight situation at the office.* **8** tipsy, °drunk, intoxicated, *Colloq* °high, woozy, under the °influence, *Brit* tiddly: *When I saw her, she was too tight to drive.* **9** °scarce, °scanty, hard to find or come by, °rare; °dear, °expensive: *Entrepreneurs have found investment money to be pretty tight this year.*
—*adv.* **10** °tightly, securely, °firmly; closely: *Keep this door closed tight. Hold me tight. Her hands were clasped tight in prayer.* **11** compactly, densely, solidly, °firmly, closely: *We were packed so tight in the bus that no one could move.*

tighten *v.* **1** Sometimes, **tighten down** or **up**: °anchor, °fasten, °fix, °tense, °secure: *Tighten those last two screws and you're finished.* **2** make tighter or tenser or stronger, °strengthen: *He tightened his grip on my hand.* **3** Sometimes, **tighten up**: make more rigorous or °strict or stringent or °severe or restrictive, close gaps in: *We ought to tighten security at the warehouse.* **4** Sometimes, **tighten up**: tauten, °stiffen, °tense, °close: *I felt the noose begin to tighten round my neck.*

tight-lipped *adj.* close-mouthed, °silent, °quiet, °mum, °mute, close-lipped, °noncommittal, °reticent, °secretive, °taciturn, unforthcoming, uncommunicative, °reserved: *He remained tight-lipped about his activities during the war.*

tightly *adv.* closely, tensely, °vigorously, rigorously: *It was a tightly fought race.*

tights *n.pl. US and Canadian and New Zealand* panty hose, *Australian and US also* pantihose: *It was much too hot to wear tights.*

till[1] *v.* °plough or *US* also plow, °cultivate, °farm, °work, °dig, hoe, harrow, manure, *Literary* delve: *My family has tilled this land for seven generations.*

till[2] *n.* money or cash-drawer, cash-box or °register: *He insists that the money was in the till when he left last night.*

tilt *v.* **1** °lean, °slant, °incline, °slope, °angle, °tip, °heel over, °pitch, °list, °cant: *She caught the lamp just as the table tilted.* **2 tilt at:** joust with, °compete with, °battle against, contend with, °spar with, cross swords with, °attack: *In tilting at the media, he has chosen some formidable opponents.*
—*n.* **3** °lean, °slant, °incline, °slope, °angle, °tip, °heel, °list, °pitch, °cant, °inclination: *The wall is at a perilous tilt and could easily fall.* **4** joust, tourney, °tournament, °meeting, tilting, °engagement, °encounter, °match, °contest, °test, °trial, °fight, °combat, °dispute, °argument, °difference, °quarrel, altercation, squabble, °tiff, *US* spat, *Colloq* set-to: *I have enjoyed the various tilts I have had with the editor over the years.*

timber *n.* **1** trees, forest, woodland: *The standing timber has been seriously depleted in Brazil.* **2** wood, °beams, °boards, °planks, *US and Canadian* °lumber: *The timber for our new house arrived today.* **3** °material, °potential, °stuff, °character, °quality, °talent, °prospect: *Agatha seems to be good management timber.*

timbre *n.* °tone (°colour or °quality), tonality, °colour, resonance: *Kurt's voice has a rich, full timbre.*

time *n.* **1** °period, °interval, °stretch, °spell, °patch: *I was going through a bad time when we last met.* **2** °period, °interval, °stretch, while,

°span, °space, °term, duration: *It is a long time since I have seen you. In the time I took to write this, she had vanished.* **3** hour; °point, °moment: *What time is it? At what time is our appointment?* **4** °age, °period, epoch, °era, lifetime, heyday, °day(s): *The novel is set in the time of the Caesars.* **5** °opportunity, °chance, °occasion: *You must make time to visit your mother.* **6** °experience: *I had a wonderful time at your party.* **7** °tempo, °beat, °rhythm, metre, °measure: *They are playing 'Teddy Bears' Picnic' in march time.* **8** °ease, °leisure; convenience: *He'll be there in his own time.* **9** Often, **times**: °life, °things, °circumstance, °conditions, °everything, °culture, mores, °habits, values: *How times have changed since we were young!* **10 ahead of time**: (bright and) °early, °prematurely, beforehand, in good time: *He arrived ahead of time and had to wait.* **11 all the time**: °always, °ever, constantly, continuously, continually, perpetually, at all times, without surcease, unceasingly: *Mother is after me all the time to do my homework.* **12 at one time**: **a** °once, °once upon a time, on one °occasion, °previously, in days of yore, °formerly, heretofore, in the (good) °old days: *At one time you thought me beautiful.* **b** simultaneously, (all) at °once, at the same time, together, all together, in °unison: *The car can only carry five people at one time.* **13 at the same time**: **a** all the °same, °nonetheless, °yet, °even so, but, °however, be that as it may, °nevertheless, °notwithstanding, just the °same: *I love her; at the same time, I cannot live with her.* **b** See 12 b, above. **14 at times**: from time to time, °occasionally, (every) °now and then, °once in a while, on °occasion, at intervals, °sometimes, *Colloq* every so °often: *At times, Ingrid would come over and cook dinner for me.* **15 behind the times**: °old-fashioned, out-dated, dated, outmoded, °antiquated, °passé, °obsolescent, °obsolete, *Colloq* °old hat, °dead: *Isn't 'The Lambeth Walk' a bit behind the times?* **16 for the time being**: for °now, for the °present, for the °moment, °meanwhile, °temporarily, *pro tempore*, *Colloq* pro tem, *Archaic* for the nonce: *He has been appointed chairman for the time being.* **17 in no time**: at °once, forthwith, straight away, °immediately, °quickly, speedily, without °delay, °swiftly: *The pizza we ordered was delivered in no time.* **18 in time**: **a** in °timely fashion, °early, in good time, in the nick of time: *The doctor arrived in time to save the baby.* **b** °soon, one of these days, °sometime, someday, one day, °eventually, sooner or later, anon: *In time, people might be living on the moon.* **19 on time**: **a** °punctually, on the °dot, in good time: *He is never on time for his appointments.* **b** in instalments, on terms, on account, on credit, *Colloq Brit* on the never-never, on hire purchase or h.p.: *We bought the car on time.* **20 take (one's) time**: °dawdle, dilly-dally, °shilly-shally, °delay, °linger, loiter: *He's certainly taking his time with his report.* **21 time and again**: again (and again), °repeatedly, (over and) over again, time and time again, time after time, °frequently, °often, °many times, on °many °occasions: *Time and again I warned him he'd get a ticket if he parked there.*
—*v.* **22** °schedule, °set, °regulate, °control: *The trains are timed to arrive five minutes*

apart. **23** °schedule, °set, °organize, °adjust, °fix: *She timed her entrance to coincide exactly with the crash of the cymbals.*

time-honoured *adj.* established, °traditional, °habitual, °customary, °rooted, °conventional, age-old, °set, °fixed; °venerable, venerated, respected, revered, honoured: *We observed the time-honoured custom of kissing the Blarney Stone.*

timeless *adj.* °eternal, °everlasting, °immortal, undying, °endless, unending, ceaseless, °abiding, °deathless, ageless, °changeless, unchanged, immutable, unchanging, °permanent, °indestructible: *He was enraptured by the timeless beauty of the heavens.*

timely *adj.* °punctual, °prompt, °well-timed, °propitious, °opportune, °convenient, °favourable, auspicious: *We welcomed the timely arrival of our rescuers.*

time-serving *adj.* self-seeking, self-serving, °selfish, °self-indulgent, °ambitious, °mercenary, °venal, °greedy, profit-oriented, fortune-hunting, gold-digging, °opportunistic, °hypocritical, °obsequious, sycophantic, toadying, toad-eating, boot-licking, subservient, *Colloq* on the °make, on the take, *Slang US* out for numero uno, *Taboo slang* brown-nosing: *Members of the party were known to be time-serving and untrustworthy.*

timetable *n.* °schedule, °calendar, curriculum, °programme, agenda, *Chiefly Brit* °diary: *My timetable doesn't allow for long lunches.*

time-worn *adj.* ageing, °old, °tired, °worn, time-scarred, °decrepit, °dilapidated, °tumbledown, °ramshackle, °run-down, dog-eared, °ragged, moth-eaten, °threadbare, °seedy, °shabby, archaic, °antique, well-worn, °worn out, °passé, broken-down, °old-fashioned, out-dated, dated, °antiquated, °ancient, °obsolescent, °obsolete, stereotyped, stereotypic(al), hackneyed, °stale, trite, overused, *Colloq* °old hat: *She went into her time-worn routine about two living as cheaply as one.*

timid *adj.* °shy, °retiring, °modest, °coy, °bashful, diffident, timorous, °fearful, apprehensive, °mousy, °scared, frightened, °nervous, °cowardly, pusillanimous, craven, *Colloq* chicken-hearted, yellow, yellow-bellied, chicken, chicken-livered, lily-livered, gutless: *I knew this strapping marine when he was a timid little boy.*

tinker *v.* °trifle, °dabble, °meddle, °mess (around or about), °toy, °fool or °play (around or about), *Brit* °potter or *US* putter (about or around), *Colloq* °fiddle or °monkey or °muck (about or around): *Graham has always enjoyed tinkering with engines.*

tinny *adj.* **1** °shabby, °flimsy, flimsily or °poorly made, °shoddy, °inferior, °cheap, °tawdry: *He bought himself a tinny old rattletrap of a car.* **2** metallic, °harsh, twangy: *She plays that tinny old trumpet day and night.*

tint *n.* **1** tincture, °wash, °hue, °colour, °cast; tinge, °touch, °hint, °trace, °dash, colouring, °shade, °tone, °suggestion: *In the west a tint of pink lingered in the sky. I thought I detected a tint of anger in his voice.* **2** dye, °rinse, wash, °stain, tincture, colourant, colouring, touch-up: *What's the harm in granny's using blue hair tint?*
—*v.* **3** dye, °stain, °colour, °rinse, tinge, °touch up: *Sandra tints her hair to give it a coppery sheen.* **4** tinge, °colour, °influence, °affect, °taint, °stain: *A deep pessimism tints all his writing.*

tiny *adj.* microscopic, infinitesimal, °minute, minuscule, °diminutive, °wee, °small, °little, °miniature, micro, mini, pocket, pocket-sized, bantam, pygmy, midget, Lilliputian, °petite, °delicate, °dainty, °elfin, °slight, °insignificant, °negligible, °trifling, °paltry, °inconsequential, °puny, *Colloq* pint-sized, teeny, teeny-weeny, teensy-weensy, itty-bitty, itsy-bitsy: *She wore the tiniest bikini I had ever seen. When I saw them together I realized how tiny she is. Forgetting my birthday was only a tiny thing.*

tip[1] *n.* **1** °end, °extremity, °peak, apex, °summit, °vertex, °cap, °top, °pinnacle, tiptop, °crown, °head, °terminal, ferrule *or* ferule, finial, nib *or* neb, °point: *The tip of the mountain showed above the clouds. He broke off the tip of the billiard cue.* —*v.* **2** °top, °cap, °crown, surmount: *The foil is tipped with a rubber button to prevent injury.*

tip[2] *v.* **1** Often, **tip over**: °upset, °overthrow, °knock *or* °cast *or* °throw down, up-end, °knock over, °overturn, °topple (over), °capsize: *His elbow tipped the lamp, which fell with a crash.* **2** °slant, °lean, °incline, °tilt, cant: *The statue is tipped a bit off the vertical.* **3** °empty, °unload, °dump, °deposit, *Slang Brit* ditch: *They tipped their load of gravel all over my driveway.* —*n.* **4** (°rubbish *or US* °garbage) °dump, °rubbish *or* °refuse *or* °trash °heap, dumping-ground: *This old chair belongs in the tip.*

tip[3] *n.* **1** gratuity, baksheesh, *pourboire,* douceur, lagniappe *or* lagnappe, °present, °gift, *Colloq* little something: *That waiter didn't deserve a tip.* **2** tip-off, (inside) °information, °warning, °advice, °suggestion, °clue, °hint, °pointer, °forecast, °prediction, *Colloq Brit* gen: *Louie had a tip that the police were coming. Her tip was 'Flap-doodle' to win the fifth race.* —*v.* **3** °reward: *Why did you tip the barmaid?* **4** Usually, **tip off**: °advise, °warn, °caution, °alert, forewarn, °notify, let (someone) °know, *Colloq* let (someone) in on: *The thieves were tipped off and never arrived.*

tirade *n.* declamation, °harangue, diatribe, philippic, °outburst, onslaught, screed, jeremiad, denunciation, °stream *of* °abuse, invective: *He let loose with such a vituperative tirade that I walked out.*

tire *v.* **1** °weary, tire out, °fatigue, °exhaust, °wear out, °drain, °sap, °enervate, debilitate, °weaken, *Colloq* take it out of, °fag (out), *The long climb tired me.* **2** °bore, °exasperate, °weary, °irk, °irritate, °annoy, °bother: *I wish you wouldn't tire me with your accounts of your shopping expeditions.*

tired *adj.* **1** °exhausted, tired out, °worn out, °weary, °fatigued, °spent, drained, *Colloq* all in, (°dead) °beat, knocked out, fagged (out), dog-tired, ready to drop, °dead tired, done in, *Brit* knackered, whacked, *US* bushed, pooped, wiped out: *I was really tired after that ten-hour flight.* **2** Usually, **tired of**: bored with, exasperated by, °weary of, irked *or* irritated *or* annoyed *or* bothered by, °sick (and tired) of, *Colloq* fed up (to here) with: *Perhaps she's tired of your constant nagging.* **3** overworked, overused, clichéd, stereotyped, stereotypic(al), hackneyed, unimaginative, trite, °stale, °worn out, unoriginal, commonplace, *Colloq* bromidic: *The gossip columns are filled with the same old tired rubbish day after day.*

tireless *adj.* °energetic, °vital, °vigorous, °dynamic, °spirited, °lively, indefatigable, hard-working, °industrious, °untiring, unflagging, unfaltering, unfailing, °persistent, dogged, °tenacious, pertinacious, persevering, °staunch, sedulous, unwavering, unswerving, undeviating, °steady, °steadfast, °resolute, °determined: *We all appreciate the honorary secretary's tireless efforts on behalf of our fund-raising this year.*

tiresome *adj.* **1** °boring, °dull, fatiguing, °humdrum, °monotonous, °flat, °tedious, wearisome, tiring, uninteresting, insipid, °bland, dry-as-dust, soporific, hypnotic: *Ibsen wrote plays that actors love and audiences find tiresome.* **2** irritating, °irksome, vexing, vexatious, annoying, bothersome, exasperating, °trying, °disagreeable, °troublesome, unpleasant: *I wish she would take her tiresome problems elsewhere.*

tissue *n.* °fabric, °network, °web, interweaving, °combination, °chain, series, °accumulation, conglomeration, concatenation, °pile, °mass, °pack: *Their entire testimony was a tissue of lies.*

titbit *n.* °delicacy, (°dainty) °morsel, °treat, °choice °item, *bonne bouche, US* tidbit, *Colloq* goody: *Sally likes to steal little titbits off my plate. I heard a juicy titbit of gossip this morning.*

title *n.* **1** °name: *You cannot tell much from a book's title.* **2** designation, appellation, epithet: *Aubrey is now an earl, but he rarely uses his title.* **3** caption, inscription, headline, °head, subtitle, °legend, subhead, rubric: *The title on this picture has nothing to do with its subject.* **4** championship, °crown: *He holds the world heavyweight boxing title.* **5** °right, °interest, °privilege, entitlement, ownership, °possession, °tenure; (°title-)°deed, documentation of ownership: *My aunt has sole title to these lands.* —*v.* **6** °name, °call, °designate, °style, °label, °term, °entitle, °christen, baptize, °nickname, denominate, °tag, dub: *Harold was titled King of the Revels.*

titter *v.* **1** °chuckle, °snicker, chortle, °giggle; snigger: *He told the most awful jokes at which his staff would titter politely.* —*n.* **2** °chuckle, °snicker, °giggle, (suppressed) °laughter, chortle, snigger: *A titter ran through the audience.*

titular *adj.* °nominal, °so-called, so-designated, so-styled, °self-styled, *soi-disant,* °token, putative, °theoretical: *He may be the titular head of the company, but his brother is really the boss.*

toast *n.* **1** °tribute, °pledge, salutation(s), °greeting(s), felicitations, °honour, good wishes, °appreciation, °remembrance(s), °cheers: *The speaker proposed a toast to the editor-in-chief.* **2** °heroine, °hero, °favourite, °darling, °idol: *Jenny was the toast of the town.* —*v.* **3** °pay °tribute to, °salute, °drink to, °honour, °greet, °congratulate, felicitate: *We toasted our fallen comrades.*

toilet *n.* **1** (water) closet, WC, men's (room), ladies' (room), (public) convenience, °facility *or* facilities, washroom, bathroom, °lavatory, °privy, outhouse, urinal, *In France* pissoir, ves-pasienne; *Nautical* head, *Chiefly military* latrine, *Chiefly US* rest room, *New England* °necessary, *Colloq* the Gents, the Ladies('), powder-room, little girls' room, little boys' room, *Brit* loo, smallest room (in the house), *Military* ablutions, *Slang Brit* bog, karzy, *US and Canadian* john, can, crapper: *They excused themselves to go to the* *toilet.* **2** *Formal or literary* grooming, dressing, making up, *Brit* toilette: *She was still at her toilet when we arrived.*

toilsome *adj.* °arduous, °laborious, °tough, °hard, °difficult, °strenuous, °burdensome, onerous, back-breaking, °exhausting, fatiguing, tiring, enervating, wearying, draining: *After a toilsome ascent we finally reached the first camp.*

token *n.* **1** °coin, disc: *You need to buy a token to get through the turnstile.* **2** °symbol, °sign, °mark, marker, badge, °emblem, °indication, °proof, °evidence: *The purple trim on a Roman toga was a token of its wearer's elevated status.* **3** souvenir, °memento, °keepsake, °reminder, °remembrance, *Archaic* remembrancer: *The miniature Statue of Liberty and Eiffel Tower are tokens of our trips abroad.* —*adj.* **4** °symbolic, °emblematic, °representative: *The panel was made up of three men and a token woman.* **5** °superficial, cosmetic, °surface, °perfunctory, °minimal, °slight, °nominal: *We encountered only token resistance when taking over the communications centre.*

tolerable *adj.* **1** °bearable, °supportable, allowable, endurable, °acceptable, sufferable: *The heat and humidity are barely tolerable.* **2** °acceptable, unexceptional, °common, °fair, common-or-garden variety, middling, °ordinary, °average, °so so, °mediocre, °adequate, run-of-the-mill, °passable, °indifferent, *Colloq* °OK or okay, not (too) °bad, pretty or fairly °good: *They serve a tolerable lunch in the hotel bar.*

tolerance *n.* **1** open-mindedness, toleration, forbearance, broad-mindedness, permissiveness, magnanimity, °indulgence, sufferance, °patience, freedom from °bigotry or °prejudice: *You must exercise more tolerance in dealing with people who are poorer than you.* **2** °play, °clearance, °allowance, °variation: *The tolerance between these parts is less than a ten-thousandth of a millimetre.* **3** toleration, °resistance, °endurance, imperviousness; °immunity, insensitivity: *His tolerance of the outrages of stupidity seems limitless. She has a low tolerance for sugar.*

tolerant *adj.* open-minded, °objective, forbearing, °unprejudiced, unbigoted, °dispassionate, broad-minded, °indulgent, magnanimous, °patient, °generous, °charitable, °catholic, latitudinarian, °permissive, °liberal, big-hearted, °fair, even-handed, °considerate: *I am more tolerant of people than of their ideas.*

tolerate *v.* **1** °stand (for), °allow, °permit, °bear, °suffer, °brook, countenance, °abide, °admit, °indulge, °concede, °sanction, °swallow, °stomach, turn a blind eye to, *Colloq* °put up with, *Brit* °stick: *The teacher refused to tolerate any more misbehaviour.* **2** °bear, °stand, °submit to, °endure, °weather, °take, °accept, °undergo: *Tests show that the product can tolerate considerable wear and tear.*

toll¹ *v.* **1** °ring, °peal, °chime, °strike, °sound: *The clock tower bell tolled three.* —*n.* **2** °ring, ringing, °peal, pealing, °chime, chiming, °striking, °sound, sounding, tolling, knell: *Each toll of the bell marked the death of another victim.*

toll² *n.* **1** °charge, °fee, °dues, assessment, °tariff; excise, °duty, impost, levy, °tribute: *New motorways will be funded by means of a toll on traffic*

using them. **2** °loss, °penalty, °cost, °damage(s); exaction: *The death toll from the earthquake reached 50,000.*

tomb *n.* °sepulchre, °crypt, vault, mausoleum, °grave, catacomb, burial-chamber, final or last resting-place: *Every year his tomb is visited by a mysterious woman in black.*

tombstone *n.* gravestone, headstone, marker, °monument, cenotaph: *The tombstones in the military cemetery stood in serried ranks.*

tone *n.* **1** °sound, note: *Odd tones emanated from the electronic music-maker.* **2** °stress, °emphasis, °force, °accent, °intonation, modulation, phrasing, inflection, °pitch, tonality, °timbre, °sound (°colour), tone °colour or °quality, colour or colouring, resonance, sonorousness, sonority, fullness, richness: *The tone of his voice is extraordinarily melodic.* **3** °manner, °style, °attitude, °air, °aspect, °approach, note, °tenor, tone of °voice, °mode of °expression, °temper, °vein, °spirit, °air: *Do not take that imperious tone with me!* **4** °tint, tinge, °shade, °hue, °colour, colouring, °cast: *The fabric has a silvery tone that makes it shimmer.* —*v.* **5 tone down:** °temper, °modify, °reduce, °moderate, °modulate, °soften, °quiet(en), °dampen, °dull, °subdue, °mute, soft-pedal: *Please tone down your voice or the neighbours will hear you.* **6 tone up:** (re)invigorate, °tune (up), °brighten (up), (re)vitalize, °freshen (up), limber up, get into °condition or °shape: *I really have to tone up my body before I put on a swimsuit this summer.*

tongue *n.* **1** °language, °speech; °dialect, patois, Creole, °idiom, °parlance, argot, °talk, °vernacular, *façon de parler: The people in that area speak a strange tongue.* **2** (°verbal) °expression, utterance, °voice, articulation: *Michael is reluctant to give tongue to his real feelings.* **3 hold (one's) tongue:** be or °remain or °keep °silent, °keep °mum, °say °nothing or nought, not breathe a word, °keep (one's) °counsel, not °say a word, *Slang* °shut up: *Hold your tongue till you are spoken to!* **4 slip of the tongue:** °slip, °mistake, gaffe, °blunder, faux pas, Freudian °slip, *Colloq Brit* boob: *Saying 'bald' when I meant 'bold' was a slip of the tongue.* **5 (with (one's)) tongue in (one's) cheek:** facetiously, whimsically, ironically, jocularly, jokingly, not °seriously, in jest, jestingly, in °fun, to be °funny, *Colloq* kiddingly: *As he is my older brother, I call him 'Dad' with tongue in cheek, of course.*

tongue-lashing *n.* scolding, berating, °reproof, °rebuke, °reprimand; (°verbal) °abuse, castigation, chastisement, vituperation, revilement, *Colloq* dressing-down, telling-off, talking-to, *Brit* slating, ticking-off, wigging: *For all his efforts to please, he only got a tongue-lashing for interfering.*

tongue-tied *adj.* °speechless, at a °loss for words, struck °dumb, °dumbfounded or dumfounded, °mute, °inarticulate: *I was so nervous when the Prince of Wales spoke to me that I got tongue-tied.*

tonic *n.* **1** °stimulant, restorative, invigorant, °boost, refresher; *Obsolete or literary* ptisan or tisane, *Technical* roborant, analeptic, *Colloq* bracer, pick-me-up, pick-up, °shot in the arm, *US* picker-upper: *His father made his money selling snake-oil tonic.*

—*adj.* **2** °stimulant, °stimulating, restorative, °invigorating, fortifying, °bracing, strengthening, reviving, enlivening, °refreshing, *Technical* analeptic, roborant: *Seeing Maddie and Max again had a tonic effect.*

tool *n.* **1** utensil, °implement, °instrument, °device, °apparatus, appliance, contrivance, °aid, °machine, °mechanism, °gadget, *Colloq* °contraption, °gimmick, *Chiefly US and Canadian* gismo or gizmo: *The work would go faster if you had the proper tools.* **2** °means, °way, °agency, weapon, °medium, °vehicle, instrumentality, avenue, °road: *Education is the tool you need to get anywhere in life.* **3** °puppet, cat's-paw, °pawn, °dupe, *Slang* stooge, °sucker: *I had been used merely as a tool in her ambitious rise to the top.* —*v.* **4** °work, °carve, °cut, °embellish, °decorate, °ornament, °dress, °shape: *This is the shop where the leather is tooled and gold-stamped.*

top *n.* **1** °summit, apex, °peak, °acme, °crest, °head, °pinnacle, °vertex, °zenith, meridian, °crown, culmination, °high °point, °height, apogee: *They reached the top of the mountain at dawn. For a change, I should like to be at the top looking down. Samantha remains at the top of her profession.* **2** lid, °cover, °cap, covering, °stopper, cork: *Put the top back on the bottle when you're through.* —*v.* **3** °surpass, °better, °best, °outstrip, °exceed, °outdo, °excel, °beat, °transcend: *It would be impossible to top some of his achievements.* **4** surmount, °cover, °cap, °crown, °tip; °finish, °complete, garnish: *The entire concoction was topped by a maraschino cherry.* **5** °trim, crop, °lop or °cut off, °clip, °prune, °nip, °pinch (back): *All the trees in this area have been topped to let in more sunlight.* **6** °scale, °climb, ascend, surmount: *The party topped Annapurna the next day.* **7** **top up** °fill (up), °refresh, refill, °replenish, *US* °freshen (up): *He asked the barman to top up our drinks.* —*adj.* **8** °best, greatest, °foremost, °leading, °pre-eminent, °eminent, °first, °first-rate, °principal, °prime, finest, choicest, topmost; °excellent, °superior, superb, top-drawer, top-grade, top-notch, °supreme, °peerless, unequalled, °incomparable, *Colloq* crack, ace, A-1 or A-one: *Is he the top man in his field? She is a top economics adviser to the government.* **9** °uppermost, topmost, highest: *The top fruit is the best.*

topic *n.* °subject(-matter), °matter, °issue, °question, °point, °thesis, °theme, °text, keynote, °field or °area of °study or of °inquiry: *We need to decide on a topic for tonight's discussion.*

topical *adj.* **1** °contemporary, °current, up to °date, °timely: *Drug addiction is certainly a topical subject.* **2** °local, °superficial: *For a minor injury we give a topical, not a general anaesthetic.*

topple *v.* **1** °upset, up-end, °knock down or over, °bring down, °fell, °capsize, °collapse: *Scores of buildings were toppled by the tornado.* **2** °bring or °throw down, °overthrow, °defeat, vanquish, °overcome, °overturn, unseat, oust: *The leaders of the coup succeeded in toppling the government in a week.* **3** °fall (over or down), °drop, °collapse, keel over, °tumble down: *Seven guardsmen toppled over because of the heat on the parade ground.*

topsy-turvy *adj.* **1** upside down, °wrong side up, °head over heels, inverted, reversed, °backwards, °vice versa: *The children were wearing*

their pyjamas topsy-turvy. **2** °chaotic, muddled, jumbled, °disorderly, disordered, disorganized, °confused, mixed-up, messy, °untidy, in a °muddle, higgledy-piggledy, *Colloq* arsy-versy, every which way: *The room was completely topsy-turvy and it was impossible to find anything.*

torment *v.* **1** torture, °abuse, maltreat, °mistreat, °distress, agonize, excruciate, crucify, harrow, °rack, °pain: *Hunger tormented his weary body.* **2** °worry, °trouble, °plague, °annoy, bedevil, vex, harry, badger, hector, °harass, °pester, °nag, °persecute, needle, nettle, °irk, °irritate, °bother, torture, °afflict, *Brit* chivvy or chivy or chevy: *I was tormented by the suspicion that something was wrong.* —*n.* **3** °agony, wretchedness, °anguish, °distress, °misery, °pain, °woe, painfulness, torture, °suffering, °curse, °hell: *How can parents endure the torment of losing a child?* **4** °worry, vexation, °annoyance, harassment, °ordeal, °persecution, needling, °nuisance, bane, irritation, °bother, °affliction, °scourge, torture: *For yet another day I had to suffer the torment of their company.*

torpid *adj.* sluggish, °slow, slow-moving, slow-paced, tortoise-like, °lethargic, apathetic, °indolent, °passive, °slothful, °dull, stupefied, °sleepy, somnolent, °inactive, °inert, languid, languorous, °phlegmatic, spiritless, °lifeless, °listless, fainéant, °lackadaisical, pococurante, °indifferent, uncaring, unconcerned, insouciant: *Johnson said that it is a man's own fault if his mind grows torpid in old age.*

torpor *n.* °sluggishness, °sloth, °lethargy, apathy, °indolence, passivity, slothfulness, dullness, stupefaction, drowsiness, sleepiness, somnolence, °inactivity, °inertia, inertness, languor, laziness, phlegm, lifelessness, listlessness, °idleness, fainéance, pococurant(e)ism, °indifference, unconcern, insouciance: *The heat produced a certain torpor in all of us.*

torrent *n.* °stream, °rush, °flood, deluge, effusion, gushing, °outburst, °outpouring, °spate, inundation, °flow, overflow, tide, cascade: *In minutes the brook became a rushing torrent. They assailed us with a torrent of abuse.*

torrential *adj.* rushing, streaming, copious, °profuse, teeming, °relentless, °violent; °fierce, vehement, vociferous, °ferocious: *The torrential monsoons inundated the land. I had never heard such a torrential outpouring of oaths.*

torrid *adj.* **1** °hot, °fiery, °sultry, stifling, °sweltering, broiling, sizzling, roasting, blazing, °burning, baking, cooking, boiling, blistering, blistery, °scorching, scorched, parched, parching, arid; °humid, °steamy, steaming, °muggy; tropical: *It seemed impossible that any creature could survive in such a torrid climate.* **2** °fervent, fervid, °passionate, °intense, °ardent, °inflamed, °impassioned, °lustful, amorous, °erotic, *Colloq* °sexy, °hot: *The film was noted for its torrid love scenes.*

tortuous *adj.* **1** twisted, twisting, winding, wandering, °serpentine, turning, °crooked, sinuous, °bent, curled, curling, curved, curvy, curvilinear, flexuous, anfractuous, convoluted, involuted, zigzag, maze-like, °labyrinthine: *They followed a tortuous trail through the jungle.* **2** °roundabout, °indirect, °devious, °intricate, °involved, unstraightforward, °complicated, °ambiguous, ambagious, circuitous, warped, °crooked, °tricky, misleading, °deceptive: *We could not help being intrigued by the tortuous Machiavellianism of the scheme.*

toss v. **1** °throw, °cast, °lob, °pitch, °fling, °hurl, °heave, °shy, °launch, °send, °let °fly, °propel, catapult, °sling, °bowl, *Colloq* chuck: *The goalkeeper tossed the ball into the middle of the field.* **2** °shake, °jerk, °stir up, °agitate, °fling: *Lucy disdainfully tossed her head.* **3** °shake (up), °stir (up), °agitate, °jiggle, °tumble, joggle; °wave, °lash, thrash: *Don't you put the dressing on before you toss the salad? The branches of the huge oak were being tossed about in the storm.* **4** writhe, °wriggle, °squirm, toss and °turn, thrash: *I tossed all night, unable to get a moment's sleep.* **5** °pitch, yaw, °wallow, °roll, °lurch, undulate, °plunge: *Our little boat was tossed this way and that in the heavy seas.*
—n. **6** °throw, °lob, °pitch, °heave, °shy: *His toss went wild and the ball rolled over the cliff.*

tot n. °child, toddler, infant, °baby: *Can you recall when you were a tiny tot?*

total n. **1** °sum (total), °totality, aggregate, °whole, °amount, total °number: *The total of wounded came to only fifteen.*
—adj. **2** °whole, °entire, °complete, °full, °gross, °overall, °comprehensive: *Total rainfall in that area is only three inches per annum.* **3** °complete, unalloyed, °unmitigated, °unqualified, unconditional, utter, °out-and-out, °thorough, thoroughgoing, °perfect, °outright, °downright, all-out, °absolute: *My son is a total failure in everything he attempts.*
—v. **4** °add (up), °tot up, °sum up, °reckon, compute: *Please total my bill.* **5** °amount to, °add up to, °come to, °mount up to: *The bill totals twice the amount I paid yesterday.*

totalitarian adj. °absolute, absolutist, °arbitrary, °authoritarian, autocratic, °dictatorial, Fascist(ic), undemocratic, illiberal, °monolithic, Nazi, °oppressive, °despotic, °tyrannical: *Sooner or later, totalitarian governments get overthrown.*

totality n. °total, aggregate, °sum (total), °whole, °entirety, beginning and end, alpha and omega, be-all and end-all: *The totality of his interests lies in watching soap operas on TV.*

totally adv. °completely, °utterly, °entirely, fully, unqualifiedly, unconditionally, °perfectly, °absolutely, °thoroughly, °wholly, consummately: *We then decided on a totally different approach. The weather was totally awful.*

totter v. waver, °topple, falter, °tremble, °teeter, °sway, °rock, °stagger, °stumble, wobble, °quiver, °shake, °quake, °shiver, dodder: *He seemed to totter a bit as he left the pub.*

touch v. **1** put (one's) hand on, °feel, °handle: *She leant forward and touched my hand.* **2** bring into °contact with, °apply, °put, °set: *He touched a match to the fuse and ran.* **3** Sometimes, **touch (up) against**: be in °contact (with), °border, adjoin, °meet, come up or be (up) against, °push or °press or °lean (up) against, °brush or °rub (up) against, come or be together, abut: *The ladder is touching the freshly painted wall.* **4** °lay a hand or finger on; °meddle with, have to do with, °interfere with, come °near, °approach: *If you touch me, I'll scream.* **5** °drink, °eat, °consume, °partake of, °take, °use, °taste, have to do with: *He swore that he would never touch*

alcohol again. **6** °affect, °impress, °influence, °disturb, °move, °stir, °arouse, °excite, impassion, °stimulate, °strike, *Colloq* °get to: *We were touched by your sympathetic note.* **7** °rival, °match, °equal, °compare with, come up to, be on a °par with, be a °match for, be in the °same league or class as or with, be on an °equal footing with, °reach, come or get °near or °close to, hold a candle to, °measure up to or against, *Colloq US* °stack up to or with or against: *No other car can touch our new model for speed and safety.* **8** Usually, **touch on** or **upon**: °refer to, °have °reference to, °pertain to, °relate to, have a °bearing on, °regard, °mention, allude to, °speak or °write of, °tell of, °bring up or in, °raise, °deal with, °cover: *I must now touch upon a delicate matter.* **9** have access to, access, °use, °employ, make °use of, °put to °use, avail (oneself) of, °take, °get, °take °advantage of: *I do not touch the principal, but try to live off the interest.* **10 touch down**: °land, alight, come to °earth: *We touched down for fuel at Gander, Newfoundland.* **11 touch off**: **a** detonate, °spark (off), °set alight, °set off, ignite, °light, °fire, put a match to: *We touched off the gunpowder and blew up the arsenal.* **b** instigate, °initiate, °begin, °start, set in °motion, ignite, °set off, trigger, °provoke, °foment, °cause, give °rise to: *Her offhand remark touched off a family row that lasted for years.* **12 touch up**: °retouch, °patch up; °beautify, °enhance, titivate, °renovate, °spruce up: *She said that the painting had recently been touched up. Mandy is upstairs touching up her make-up.*
—n. **13** °feeling, °feel, °texture: *She wants nothing but the touch of silk next to her body.* **14** °pat, °tap, °blow, °hit, °stroke, °brush, °caress: *She hated him so much that she cringed at the touch of his hand.* **15** °dash, °hint, intimation, °suggestion, soupçon, °bit, °pinch, °jot, °spot, °trace, tinge, °taste, °suspicion, smattering, colouring, smack, °speck, °drop, whiff, °odour, °scent, °smell: *Cynthia has a touch of hypocrisy about her. The salad dressing could use a touch more garlic.* **16** °ability, deftness, °expertise, °dexterity, adroitness, °facility, °skill, skilfulness, °knack, °capability, °genius, °talent, °gift, °flair: *Richard has a master's touch in everything he does.* **17** °response, °feel, responsiveness, °feeling, °movement, °operation, performance level: *This piano action has an excellent touch.* **18** signature, °trade °mark, characteristic, °influence, °approach, °style, °manner, °technique, °execution, °method: *I thought I recognized your touch in the furniture selection. A woman's touch might have helped.*

touching adj. °moving, °stirring, °emotional, °tender, °poignant, °pathetic, soul-stirring, °heart-rending, heartbreaking, °sad, °pitiful, distressing, distressful: *The most touching scene is the one where the boy meets his father for the first time.*

touchstone n. °standard, °yardstick, criterion, °reference, benchmark, °test, °norm, °measure: *His craftsmanship is the touchstone by which the others are judged.*

touchy adj. **1** (over-)°sensitive, supersensitive, hypersensitive, highly-strung, °tense, thin-skinned, crabby, crabbed, °testy, irascible, °irritable, tetchy, °temperamental, grouchy, °peevish, °querulous, °petulant, pettish, splenetic, captious, bad-tempered, °short-tempered, hot-tempered, °quick-tempered, crusty, °cross, curmudgeonly, °cantankerous, choleric, dyspeptic, °waspish, bearish, snarling, °snappish, °argumentative, disputatious, contentious, US high-strung, °cranky: *She is very touchy on the subject of her family. He's always touchy in the morning.* **2** °critical, touch-and-go, °sensitive, °ticklish, °risky, °precarious, °hazardous, chancy, unsure, °uncertain, °close, hairbreadth, °dangerous, hair-raising, °frightening, °terrifying, °nerve-racking *or* nerve-wracking, *Jocular* °parlous, *Colloq* °hairy: *There was a touchy moment when the fuel leaked into the astronauts' cabin.*

tough *adj.* **1** °hard, °firm, °durable, long-lasting, wear-resistant, °substantial, °strong, °stout, °rugged, °sturdy, °sound, well-built: *Only one kind of material is tough enough to endure such conditions for so long.* **2** °stiff, °hard, leathery, °inflexible, chewy, fibrous, cartilaginous, °sinewy, °ropy, °wiry, °stringy: *That steak was as tough as shoe-leather.* **3** °strong, °stalwart, °brawny, °burly, °muscular, °powerful, virile, °manly, °sturdy, doughty, °intrepid, °stout, °rough, °vigorous, strapping, athletic: *Two tough-looking characters moved towards us, so we left.* **4** °difficult, °demanding, °exacting, °hard, °troublesome; °laborious, taxing, °strenuous: *We deal with tough complaints every day. It's a tough job.* **5** baffling, °thorny, °puzzling, °perplexing, mystifying, knotty, °irksome, °difficult: *The examiners asked us some very tough questions.* **6** °stubborn, hardened, inured, °obstinate, obdurate, °hard, °harsh, °severe, °stern, °inflexible, refractory, intractable, adamant, unyielding, ungiving, °rigid, unbending, unsentimental, unfeeling, °unsympathetic, °callous, hard-boiled, uncaring, °cold, °cool, °icy, °stony, *Colloq* hard-nosed: *He's a tough man to work for, but he's fair.*
—*interj.* **7** *Colloq* Too bad!, Tough luck!, Hard luck!, *Brit* Hard cheese!, *Slang* Tough titty!, *Taboo slang* Tough shit!: *When I told him that my money had been stolen, he said 'Tough!'*
—*n.* **8** °bruiser, hooligan, °bully (boy), °rowdy, °thug, ruffian, *Colloq* roughneck, °bruiser, tough guy, gorilla: *A couple of toughs who had been threatening the cashier disappeared when they saw our uniforms.*

tour *n.* **1** °journey, °trip, °excursion, °outing, °expedition, voyage, trek, peregrination, jaunt, junket: *We went on a guided tour because we were short of time and wanted to see everything.* **2** °stroll, perambulation, walkabout, °ramble, °walk, °drive; °round, °circuit, ambit: *The government representatives are on a tour of all nuclear facilities.* **3** °spell, °shift, °assignment, °turn, *Military* °period of °service *or* enlistment: *His tour of duty is not finished till midnight.*
—*v.* **4** °journey, °travel, voyage, °visit, °trip, trek, sightsee, °cruise; *Colloq* globe-trot: *On retirement we spent a year just touring around Europe.*

tourist *n.* °traveller, voyager, °visitor, °sightseer, *Colloq* °rubberneck(er), out-of-towner, *Brit* tripper, day-tripper, holiday-maker: *During the summer, this place is inundated with tourists.*

tournament *n.* tourney, °competition, °contest, °match, °meeting, °event, °meet: *The tennis tournament was delayed by rain.*

tousle *v.* dishevel, °disorder, °ruffle, disarrange, °tangle (up), °mess (up), °rumple, disarray, *US* muss (up): *Her hair was all tousled by the wind.*

tout *v.* **1** hawk, °peddle, °sell, °promote, °talk up, *Colloq* °push, °plug: *They tout these new headache tablets as miraculous.*
—*n.* **2** tipster: *He is often seen with racetrack touts.*

tow *v.* °pull, °drag, °draw, °haul, °lug, °trail, °tug, trawl: *The boat was towing a long purse seine. I arrived just as the police were towing away my car.*

towards *prep.* **1** toward, in the °direction of, to; °for, so as to °approach *or* °near, on the way *or* road to: *She turned towards me. I'd appreciate a lift if you're going towards Aston Clinton.* **2** toward, to, °for, as a help to, supporting, promoting, assisting: *We welcome any contribution towards the charitable works of our order.* **3** toward, °near, nearing, °close to, approaching, °shortly before: *Towards the close of day, the cattle wander back to the barns.*

tower *n.* **1** bell-tower, campanile, minaret, pagoda, obelisk; belfry, °spire, turret, steeple, flèche: *There was a time when the church tower was the tallest building in the town.* **2** fortress, citadel, °stronghold, °castle, fastness; °keep, °dungeon, °prison: *The princess was imprisoned in the tower for a year and a day.*
—*v.* **3** Often, **tower over** *or* **above**: °loom, °soar, °rise, ascend, °rear: *These ugly high-rise buildings tower over everything, blocking out the sun.*

towering *adj.* **1** °lofty, °tall, °high, soaring, °outstanding, °elevated, sky-scraping, sky-high, °great, °impressive, °imposing, °huge, °gigantic, °supreme, °superior, °paramount, °extraordinary, unmatched, unequal, unrivalled, °unparalleled, unsurpassed: *The towering American economy dominated the world for decades after World War II.* **2** °violent, °fiery, °burning, °passionate, °excessive, vehement, °intense, consuming, °mighty, °overwhelming, unrestrained, °immoderate, °inordinate, intemperate, °extreme, °colossal, °enormous: *Every time she mentioned Valentino, he went into a towering rage.*

town *n.* township, village, hamlet, community; °municipality, °city, °metropolis, borough, burgh: *She was born in Stornoway, a small town in the Outer Hebrides. We have to drive into the town to do our shopping.*

toy *n.* **1** °plaything: *Whenever he visited, Uncle Jed brought toys for the children.* **2** °trifle, trinket, °bauble, °gewgaw, gimcrack, knick-knack, bagatelle, kickshaw, bit of frippery: *After marrying her, he treated her as a rich man's toy.*
—*v.* **3** Usually, **toy with**: °trifle (with), dally (with), °play (with), °sport (with), °fool (with), °fiddle (with), °tinker (with): *He kept toying with his watch chain.* **4** Usually, **toy with**: °flirt (with), dally (with), dilly-dally (with), °play (with), deal with carelessly, °amuse oneself with: *The cad was only toying with her affections.*
—*adj.* **5** °miniature, °tiny, °diminutive, °small, °dwarf: *She breeds toy poodles.* **6** °imitation, °fake, °phoney *or US also* phony, simulated, °artificial: *This is only a toy watch and doesn't work.*

trace *n.* **1** °hint, intimation, °sign, °token, °suggestion, °touch, °vestige, °indication, °mark, °record, °evidence, °clue: *There wasn't any trace of the intruders.* **2** °bit, °spot, °speck, °jot, °drop, °dash, °suspicion, °remnant, tinge, soupçon, iota, whiff, °suggestion, °trifle: *The traces of mud on the suspect's shoes proved he had been there.* **3** Often, **traces**: °track(s), °trail, spoor, footprint(s), °print(s), footmark(s): *They were following the traces of a buffalo.*

—v. **4** dog, °pursue, °follow (in the footsteps of), °stalk, °track (down), °shadow, °trail, Colloq °tail: We traced him to a seedy hotel in Caracas. **5** °investigate, °discover, ascertain, °detect, °determine, °find, °seek, °search for, °hunt down or up, unearth, °track: Have you traced her whereabouts? I am able to trace my ancestry back to the time of the First Crusade. **6** delineate, °outline, °copy, °draw, map, °chart, °mark (out), °record, °reproduce, sketch: We traced Marco Polo's route to China and back.

track n. **1** °line, °rail(s), °way, °railway, US °railroad: New track was laid between London and Manchester. **2** °path, °trail, °route, footpath, °course, °road, °street, alley: A rough track leads over Sty Head Pass. Are you sure you're on the right track? **3** spoor, °trail, footprint(s), °print(s), °trace(s), footmark(s), °scent, °slot, °wake: The last time I saw him he was following the track of a yeti. **4 keep track of**: °trace, track, °keep an °eye on, °follow, °pursue, °monitor, °supervise, °oversee, °keep up with or on, °watch, °keep a °record of or on, °record: Using an electronic tag, we were able to keep track of the animal's movements. **5 lose track of**: °lose, misplace, °mislay, °lose sight of, °forget: She lost track of some important papers. I lost track of what I was saying.
—v. **6** °follow, dog, °pursue, °trace, °stalk, °shadow, °trail, °hunt down, °chase, Colloq °tail: She was tracked to Istanbul, where they lost her. **7** See **4**, above. **8 track down**: °find, °seek out, ferret out, °hunt down, °trace, °catch, apprehend, °capture, smell or sniff out, °run to earth or ground, Colloq °run down: We finally tracked him down at his mother's house in Putney.

trackless adj. °empty, pathless, untrodden, unexplored, °uncharted, virgin, untrod: We found ourselves in the trackless wilderness of central Australia.

tract¹ n. °region, °area, °stretch, °territory, °expanse, °zone, °portion, °section, sector, °quarter, °district, °patch, °plot, °parcel, US °lot: The developers own a tract of land where they plan to build a shopping mall.

tract² n. treatise, °monograph, °essay, article, °paper, dissertation, disquisition, homily, °sermon, critique; °pamphlet, booklet, °brochure, °leaflet: Daphne was distributing tracts to passers-by in front of the church.

tractable adj. **1** docile, amenable, °tame, °manageable, biddable, persuadable or persuasible, compliant, °easygoing, °willing, °submissive, °obedient, governable, °yielding: It was a pleasure to teach a student who was so tractable. **2** °manageable, handleable, workable, °adaptable, malleable, °pliable, °plastic, ductile, fictile: The new materials are quite tractable and can be drawn or moulded with ease.

traction n. °grip, gripping power, °drag, °purchase, °friction, adhesion: Unable to get any traction on the ice, the car skidded off the road.

trade n. **1** °commerce, °business, °traffic, °exchange, barter, dealing(s), buying and selling, merchandising, marketing, mercantilism, °truck: Have we any trade in shoes with South Korea? We are establishing trade with Eastern Europe? **2** °calling, °occupation, °pursuit, °work, °business, °employment, °line (of °work), métier, °job, °vocation, °craft, °career, °profession: Just what trade are you engaged in?

3 swap or swop, °exchange, interchange, barter: Was exchanging your microwave cooker for a hi-fi set a good trade? **4** customers, °clientele, °custom, °patrons, following, °patronage, shoppers: Her shop caters chiefly to the holiday trade.
—v. **5** °transact or do °business, °buy, °sell, °deal, °traffic, °merchandise, have °dealings: There are laws against Sunday trading in some areas. **6** °exchange, swap or swop, interchange, °switch, barter; °return: Having traded his car for the boat, Sam has no way of reaching the marina.

trader n. °dealer, °merchant, businessman, businesswoman, °broker, merchandiser, distributor, °seller, salesman, saleswoman, °salesperson, vendor, °buyer, purchaser, retailer, wholesaler: All sorts of traders can be found in the covered market.

tradesman n. **1** °merchant, °dealer, shopkeeper, retailer, vendor, °seller: A tradesman had been ringing at the door for several minutes. **2** artisan, craftsman, journeyman, handicraftsman: He is a tradesman, a skilled cabinet-maker by profession.

tradition n. °custom, °practice, °habit, °usage, °convention, °ritual, °rite, unwritten °law, °institution, °form, praxis, °lore: Exchanging gifts on Christmas Eve has long been a tradition in our family.

traditional adj. °customary, °usual, °routine, °habitual, °standard, household, stock, °time-honoured, established, °well-known, °conventional, °ritual, unwritten, °accustomed, °historic, °old, ancestral: Mazetta mocha tarts were the traditional birthday cakes at home when I was a child.

traffic n. **1** °movement, conveyance, shipping, °transport, °freight, Chiefly US transportation: Traffic across the border has resumed. **2** See **trade, 1**, above: Drug traffic has increased greatly in recent years.
—v. **3** See **trade, 5**, above: The police think that Baines is trafficking in stolen goods.

tragedy n. °catastrophe, °calamity, °disaster, °misfortune, adversity, °blow: The death of their dog was a terrible tragedy, especially for the children.

tragic adj. °sad, depressing, °lamentable, °unhappy, °funereal, °forlorn, °melancholy, cheerless, °mournful, lachrymose, dolorous, °grievous, morose, lugubrious, °dismal, °piteous, °pitiable, °pitiful, °pathetic(al), appalling, °wretched, °dreadful, °awful, °terrible, °horrible, °deplorable, °miserable, distressing, °disturbing, upsetting, °shocking, unlucky, °unfortunate, hapless, ill-fated, °inauspicious, star-crossed, ill-omened, ill-starred, °calamitous, catastrophic, crushing, °disastrous; tragical: It was really tragic that we couldn't get there in time to say goodbye.

trail n. **1** (beaten) °path, °way, footpath, °route, °track, °course: There is a well-worn trail through the wood. **2** °track, spoor, °scent, smell, °trace, footsteps, footprints, °path, °wake: The trail of the elephant herd was quite easy to follow. **3** See **train, 2**, below: She was always followed by a trail of admirers.
—v. **4** °tow, °draw, °drag (along), °haul, °pull, °tag along, trawl, °bring along (behind), °carry along (behind): We were moving slowly because we were trailing a dinghy. **5** °drag, °pull, °move, be °drawn, °stream, °sweep, °dangle: I heard the whisper of silken gowns trailing across Persian

carpets. **6** °lag (behind), °dawdle, loiter, °linger, °follow, °straggle, bring up the °rear, °hang back, °fall *or* °drop behind: *Our team was trailing three-five in the final.* **7** °follow, °pursue, dog, °trace, °shadow, °stalk, °track, °chase, °hunt, *Colloq* °tail: *We trailed the suspect to Victoria Station, where we lost him.* **8 trail off** *or* **away**: °diminish, °decrease, °fade away *or* out, °disappear, °dwindle, lessen, °die out *or* away, peter out, °subside, °taper off, °weaken, grow °faint *or* °dim: *As they drove away, the noise of their blasting radio trailed off.*

train *n.* **1** °carriage, °coach, *Baby-talk* choo-choo: *Will this train take me to Newcastle?* **2** °retinue, entourage, cortège, °suite, following, °escort, °guard, attendants, retainers, followers, °trail; °staff, court, household: *After the duke's coffin came a train of several hundred hangers-on.* **3** °line, °queue, °procession, °succession, °string, °set, °sequence, °chain, °progression, caravan, cavalcade, °parade, column, °file: *The baggage train of the advancing army stretched for miles.*
—v. **4** °discipline, °exercise, °tutor, °teach, °coach, °drill, °school, °instruct, °prepare, °educate, edify, °guide, °bring up, °indoctrinate, °rear, °raise: *We had been trained to put things away and avoid clutter.* **5** °work out, °exercise, °practise: *Hannah is training for the next Olympics.*

trait *n.* °feature, °characteristic, °attribute, °quality, °peculiarity, idiosyncrasy, °quirk, lineament, °mark, °property: *He has some unpleasant traits, like spitting when he talks.*

traitor *n.* °turncoat, Judas, quisling, betrayer, °renegade, fifth-columnist, *US* Benedict Arnold, *Colloq* double-crosser, °snake in the grass, double-dealer, two-timer: *Some traitor in their midst had revealed their plans to the enemy.*

traitorous *adj.* treacherous, °perfidious, °seditious, °subversive, insurrectionist, °renegade, insurgent, °disloyal, °deceitful, °untrue, unfaithful, °faithless; treasonable, *Colloq* double-crossing, double-dealing, two-timing: *They identified the traitorous wretch and hanged him. Consorting with the enemy is a traitorous act.*

trajectory *n.* flight °path, °course, °track: *The missile has a high trajectory.*

tram *n.* tramcar, trolley bus, *US and Canadian* streetcar, trolley(-car): *Most cities with a traffic problem have replaced trams with buses.*

trammel *n.* **1** Usually, **trammels**: °impediment(s), °hindrance(s), °shackle(s), °handicap(s), °check(s), °restriction(s), °restraint(s), °curb(s), °deterrent(s), constraint(s), °hitch(es), °snag(s), (stumbling) °block(s), °obstacle(s), °bar: *He managed to avoid the trammels of domesticity.*
—v. **2** °impede, °hinder, °handicap, °check, °restrain, °curb, constrain, °block, °deter, °obstruct, fetter, confine: *Do not let the limitations of what's practical and possible trammel your imagination.*

tramp *v.* **1** °march, hike, trudge, °plod, slog, °plough, tread, trek, °walk, *US* mush: *I must have tramped across half of England looking for work.* **2** Usually, **tramp on** *or* **upon**: See trample, 1, below.
—n. **3** °march, trudge, °plod, slog, trek, hike, °walk: *Every day we had to make the five-mile tramp into the village for water.* **4** °derelict, °vagabond, vagrant, °drifter, °rover, gypsy, beachcomber,

Brit dosser, down-and-out, *Australian* swagman, *US* hobo, °bum, down-and-outer: *The police do not allow tramps to sleep in public parks.* **5** °step, tread, footfall, °footstep: *She couldn't get to sleep until she heard her husband's tramp on the stair.*

trample *v.* **1** trample on *or* upon, °tramp (on *or* upon), °stamp (on), tread (on), °step on, °crush, °press, squash, °flatten, *Colloq* stomp (on *or* upon), squish, squash *or* squoosh: *After the harvest, we would take turns trampling the grapes.* **2** Often, **trample on** *or* **upon**: °violate, °damage, °harm, °hurt, °infringe *or* °encroach on, ride roughshod over, set at naught, °scorn, contemn, disdain, °defy, °disregard, °ignore, °fly in the face of, fling *or* cast *or* throw to the winds: *The military regime trampled on the people's civil rights.* **3** Usually, **trample out**: trample down, trample underfoot, °stamp out, °extinguish, °put out, °destroy, °crush, °break down: *The left-wing parties were trampled in a military coup.*

trance *n.* °daze, °stupor, semi-conscious *or* half-conscious *or* hypnotic *or* cataleptic *or* °dream state, state of semi-consciousness *or* half-consciousness *or* catalepsy *or* suspended animation *or* stupefaction *or* abstraction *or* (complete) absorption *or* exaltation *or* °rapture *or* °ecstasy; brown study: *He walked about all day in a trance, oblivious to what was going on around him.*

tranquil *adj.* °calm, °serene, placid, °quiet, °peaceful, °still, °smooth, unagitated, halcyon, °relaxed; unruffled, °sedate, °steady, °regular, °even, °dispassionate, °self-possessed, °cool, self-controlled, cool-headed, unexcited, undisturbed, untroubled, unperturbed: *He often thought back to the tranquil, sultry summer days of his youth. How can Eleanor be so tranquil when everything about her is so chaotic?*

tranquillize *v.* °calm, soothe, pacify, °still, °quiet(en), °relax, °lull, °compose, °sedate: *He soon fell asleep, tranquillized by the medication that had been administered to him.*

tranquillizer *n.* bromide, barbiturate, opiate, °sedative, anti-psychotic, anti-anxiety °drug, *Slang* downer, red: *She had been prescribed tranquillizers, and developed severe side-effects.*

transact *v.* do, °carry on *or* out, °conduct, °manage, °handle, °negotiate, °administer, °discharge, °perform, °enact, °settle, conclude, °complete, °finish: *We are flying to Frankfurt today to transact some business.*

transaction *n.* **1** °deal, dealing, °negotiation, °matter, °affair, °business, °action, °proceeding, °agreement, °arrangement, °bargain: *This transaction must not be revealed to the stock market.* **2 transactions**: °proceedings, °record(s), °acts, °minutes, annals, *Colloq* goings-on, doings: *The Society's transactions are published annually.*

transcend *v.* °surpass, °outstrip, °exceed, go beyond, outdistance, °overstep, °outdo, °excel, °overshadow, °top, outvie, °rise above, outshine, °beat: *Her performance at La Scala transcended that of every other Mimi I have heard.*

transcendent *adj.* °peerless, °incomparable, unequalled, °matchless, unrivalled, °unparalleled, °unique, consummate, °paramount, °superior, °surpassing, °supreme, °pre-eminent, °sublime, °excellent, °superb, °magnificent, °marvellous; transcendental: *Can there be any doubt of Einstein's transcendent genius?*

transcribe v. **1** °copy, °reproduce, replicate, °duplicate: *I am busy transcribing my lecture notes.* **2** °translate, transliterate, °write out, °render, °represent, °show, °interpret: *The Rosetta Stone has the same text transcribed in Egyptian hieroglyphics and in demotic as well as in Greek.*

transcript n. **1** transcription, °translation, transliteration, °rendering, °interpretation, °representation: *Most linguists regarded writing as a mere transcript of language.* **2** (carbon or machine or Xerox or photostatic or xerographic) °copy, carbon, °duplicate, duplication, photocopy, °reproduction, Photostat, *Colloq* dupe; *I have requested a transcript of the court proceedings.*

transfer v. **1** °move, °transport, convey, °remove, °carry, °take, °deliver, °bring, °transmit, °cart, °haul, °shift, °hand (on or over), °turn over, °give, °pass (on or along or over): *The documents will be transferred to you today.* —n. **2** °move, conveyance, transmittal, °transmission, °delivery, °change: *The papers documenting the transfer of the property are here.*

transfix v. **1** °pin, °fix, °impale, skewer, °nail, °pierce, spear, °spike, °spit, °stick: *The shrike, or butcher-bird, transfixes its prey on a thorn, then picks its bones clean.* **2** °enrapture, galvanize, °electrify, °hypnotize, mesmerize, rivet, °fascinate, °bewitch, °enchant, ensorcell, engross, °root to the spot, °stun, °paralyse, *Colloq* °stop °dead (in one's tracks): *The felon stood transfixed with terror as the judge pronounced sentence.*

transform v. °change, °modify, transfigure, °alter, transmute, metamorphose, °turn into, °convert, transmogrify, mutate, permute: *What will it take to transform these students into civilized human beings?*

transformation n. °change, modification, transfiguration, transfigurement, °alteration, transmutation, metamorphosis, conversion, transmogrification, °mutation, permutation: *The transformation in her appearance over a few short months was miraculous.*

transfuse v. **1** °instil, °transmit, °transfer, °inject: *Her greatest success was to transfuse a sense of history into her students.* **2** infuse, °permeate: *An embarrassed blush transfused his face.*

transgress v. **1** °sin, trespass, °offend, °err, °lapse, °fall from grace, °disobey, °misbehave, go °wrong or astray, do °wrong: *She knew she had transgressed and was ready to atone.* **2** °break or °violate or contravene or go beyond or °exceed or °overstep or °infringe or °defy or °disobey (the law): *He had blatantly transgressed the laws of decency.*

transgression n. °sin, trespass, °offence, °error, °lapse, °fall from grace, disobedience, °misbehaviour, °wrong, °violation, °fault, °misdeed, misdemeanour, °crime, wrongdoing, infraction: *How should he be punished for his transgressions?*

transgressor n. °sinner, °offender, °criminal, °felon, °culprit, lawbreaker, trespasser, wrongdoer, evil-doer, °villain, °miscreant, malefactor, °delinquent: *The majority of transgressors are apprehended within 24 hours of the crime.*

transient adj. transitory, °temporary, °brief, °fleeting, °momentary, °passing, ephemeral, fugacious, °fugitive, evanescent, °short-lived, short-term, impermanent, °fly-by-night, °volatile: *The peace was transient, as the outbreak of civil war soon followed. A souvenir shop obviously sells more to the transient trade than to residents.*

transit n. **1** °moving, °movement, °travel, °travelling, °motion, °passing, °progress, °progression, °transition; °passage, °traverse, traversal, traversing: *We were unable to mail any letters while we were in transit. The overland transit of the island took three days.* **2** °transport, transportation, °carriage, haulage, cartage, conveyance, °transfer, transference, transferral, transmittal: *The transit of the merchandise will be handled by our regular shipping company.* —v. **3** °cross, °traverse, °go or °move or °pass or °travel across or over or through: *They were advised to check with authorities of every country visited or transited during their journey.*

transition n. **1** °change, °alteration, metamorphosis, change-over, °transformation, transmutation, °mutation, °development, °evolution, conversion, modification, metastasis: *Tracing the transition from tadpole to frog is exciting for young pupils.* **2** See transit, 1, above.

translate v. **1** °convert, °paraphrase, °change, rewrite, °interpret, °transcribe, °render, decode, °decipher, metaphrase: *Can you translate this German document?* **2** °transform, °convert, °change, mutate, °turn, transmute, metamorphose, transubstantiate, °alter, transmogrify: *Why are people always trying to translate the dross of reality into the gold of dreams?* **3** °interpret, rewrite, °explain, °reword, elucidate, °spell out: *Can you translate this technical legal jargon into plain English?* **4** °transfer, convey, °carry, °move, °transport, °forward, °ship, °send, °dispatch or despatch: *Soon after being made bishop of Worcester, he was translated to Winchester.*

translation n. **1** conversion, °paraphrase, °interpretation, transcription, transliteration, °rendering, °rendition, metaphrase, °gloss, decipherment, decoding: *It was Michael Ventris who was responsible for the translation of Linear B.* **2** metamorphosis, °change, °alteration, transmutation, transfiguration, °transformation, transmogrification, transubstantiation, conversion: *The translation from the caterpillar to the butterfly is miraculous.* **3** °interpretation, rewriting, rewrite, °explanation, rewording, elucidation: *He is well known for his translation of abstract ideas into terms that an intelligent layman could cope with.* **4** °transfer, transference, transferral, conveyance, carrying, °moving, °movement, transportation, °transport, forwarding, shipping, shipment, sending, °transmission, °dispatch or despatch: *His translation to a minor consular post in the south Pacific was expected.*

transmission n. **1** °transfer, transference, transferral, transferring, conveyance, carrying, °moving, °movement, transportation, °transport, transporting, forwarding, shipping, shipment, sending, transmittal, transmitting, °dispatch or despatch, dispatching or despatching: *We were unable to arrange for the transmission of the papers in time for the meeting.* **2** °broadcast, broadcasting, sending, telecasting, dissemination, communication: *Transmission of the new programmes begins next year.*

transmit v. **1** °send, °transfer, convey, °communicate, °pass on, °deliver, °forward, °dispatch or despatch; °post, °ship, °cable,

°radio, telegraph, fax, telex, °telephone, phone, *Chiefly US and Canadian* °mail, *Colloq* wire: *Your message was transmitted last night.* **2** °pass or °go through, °pass on, °send, °put, °direct, °conduct, °channel: *The mirror transmits the light through this filter.*

transparent *adj.* **1** (crystal) °clear, pellucid, diaphanous, °see-through, limpid, crystalline, °sheer, transpicuous: *I want completely transparent glass in this window, instead of that frosted glass.* **2** °plain, °apparent, °obvious, °evident, unambiguous, °patent, °manifest, unmistakable, (crystal) °clear, as °plain as day, as °plain as the nose on (one's) face, °undisguised, recognizable, understandable, transpicuous: *The origin of many English words is transparent because of their spelling.* **3** °candid, °open, °frank, plain-spoken, °direct, unambiguous, unequivocal, straightforward, °ingenuous, °forthright, °above-board, °artless, guileless, °simple, °naïve, undissembling, *Colloq* on the °level, upfront: *His transparent honesty makes Clive unsuited to a career in diplomacy.*

transpire *v.* **1** become known, be rumoured, be revealed, come to °light: *It transpired that she had been seeing him while she was still married.* **2** (*Disputed*): happen, °occur, take °place, °come about, °come to °pass, °materialize, °arise, °turn out: *No improvement has yet transpired in their living conditions.*

transplant *v.* °displace, °move, °remove, relocate, °shift, °uproot, resettle, °transfer: *This is the third time the company has transplanted Harry in a year!*

transport *v.* **1** °carry, °bear, convey, °move, °remove, °transfer, °deliver, °fetch, °bring, °get, °take, °ship, °haul, °transmit, °send, °forward: *The goods were transported by ship.* **2** °exile, °banish, deport, °send away: *Australia was settled mainly by people who had been transported from England.* **3** °carry away, °enrapture, °captivate, °delight, °charm, spellbind, °bewitch, °fascinate, °enchant, °entrance, °hypnotize, mesmerize, °electrify, °ravish: *Flavia's parents were totally transported by her winning the decathlon.* —*n.* **4** transportation, °carrier, conveyance, shipping, °transfer, transferral, shipment, haulage, cartage, °carriage, °moving: *Can't you give me any idea of what the transport costs might come to?* **5** Usually, **transports**: °rapture, °ecstasy, exaltation, exultation, euphoria, °delight, (seventh) °heaven, °happiness, °bliss, elation, exhilaration, °thrill, Elysium, °paradise; Elysian Fields, *Colloq* cloud nine: *Helen succumbed to transports of delight at seeing her son receive such an important award.*

transpose *v.* °exchange, interchange, metathesize, °switch, swap or swop, °trade, commute, °transfer: *The bank transposed two figures on my statement, reducing my balance by £450.*

trap *n.* **1** °snare, °pitfall, gin, springe, deadfall, booby-trap: *After the Pied Piper left, Hamelin had no further need for rat traps.* **2** °trick, °subterfuge, °wile, °ruse, °stratagem, °ambush, °deception, °device, °artifice, ploy: *Oscar was the man for whom Esther set a neat trap.* **3** °mouth, *Slang* °yap, °gob, mush, °face: *Shut your trap or get out.* —*v.* **4** °snare, ensnare, entrap, °catch, °net: *We dug a pit to trap the marauding lion.* **5** °imprison, confine, °lock, °hold, °keep: *The boy was trapped*

in the cave without a means of escape. **6** °trick, °deceive, °fool, °dupe, °beguile, inveigle: *Esther finally trapped Oscar into marrying her.*

trappings *n.pl.* accoutrements or *US* also accouterments, panoply, caparison, equipage, °apparatus, °equipment, °paraphernalia, appointments, furnishings, °furniture, °gear, °rig, habiliments, °decoration(s), °embellishment(s), °accessories, frippery or fripperies, adornment(s), trimmings, raiment, °fittings, °finery: *Many respect the trappings of office more than the office-holder.*

trash *n.* **1** °rubbish, (°stuff and) °nonsense, balderdash, °moonshine, °gibberish, °gobbledegook or gobbledygook, tommy-rot, bunkum, °garbage, twaddle, *Colloq* °rot, flapdoodle, crap, codswallop, bosh, piffle, hooey, bunk, malarkey, poppycock, boloney or baloney, eyewash, hogwash, bilge-water, bull, *Scots* havers, *Brit* tosh, gammon, *US* a crock, hokum, gurry, horse feathers, *Slang Brit* (a load of (old)) cobblers, *Taboo slang* bullshit, horseshit, *Brit* balls, *US* a crock of shit: *Don't believe him—he is talking trash.* **2** *Chiefly in US and Canada*: °junk, brummagem, knick-knacks, gewgaws, °trifles, °bric-à-brac or bric-a-brac, frippery or fripperies, bits and pieces, °odds and ends, trinkets, tinsel, 'Not Wanted on Voyage': *There was mostly trash in the flea market, but there were one or two more valuable items.* **3** *In US and Canada*: °rubbish, °litter, °garbage, °waste, °refuse, °junk, debris, rubble, °dregs, dross, scoria, slag, offscourings, °dirt, sweepings, *Slang* crap: *The service comes to remove the trash once a week.* —*v.* **4** *Slang chiefly in US*: destroy, °ruin, °wreck, vandalize, °deface: *The lodgers trashed the flat before doing a moonlight flit.*

traumatic *adj.* °shocking, upsetting, °disturbing, °painful, °agonizing, distressing, °harmful, °hurtful, °injurious, damaging, wounding, traumatizing: *Few experiences are more traumatic than losing a child.*

travel *n.* **1** °travelling, tourism, touring, globe-trotting: *Travel is an enriching experience. Travel by air is the commonest means of long-distance transport.* **2 travels**: °trips, °expeditions, °journeys, °excursions, °tours, voyages, touring, treks, trekking, °travelling, wanderings, peregrinations, junkets, °pilgrimages: *In all your travels, have you ever encountered an honest man?* —*v.* **3** °journey, °go, °move, °proceed, °roam, rove, °traverse, °tour, take or make a °trip or °tour or °excursion or junket or °journey, trek, voyage: *As one who has travelled far and wide, what is your favourite country?* **4** °go, °move, °socialize, °fraternize, °associate, *Colloq* °hang around or about: *Cordelia and I do not travel in the same circles.*

traveller *n.* °tourist, voyager, °sightseer, globe-trotter, gypsy, wanderer, hiker, °rover, wayfarer, *Jocular* bird of passage, *Colloq* °rubberneck(er), jet-setter, *Chiefly Brit* tripper, day-tripper, holiday-maker: *Travellers have been greatly inconvenienced by the strike of customs officials.*

travelling *adj.* itinerant, wandering, peripatetic, roving, °mobile, nomadic, touring, wayfaring, migratory, °restless: *At fourteen, he joined a travelling circus.*

traverse *v.* **1** °cross, criss-cross, °pass or °move over or through, °walk, °cover, °travel (over or through), °roam, °wander, °range, °tramp,

°tour: *He has traversed the country from end to end innumerable times.* **2** °cross, criss-cross, °go across; °lie *or* °extend across *or* athwart, °bridge, intersect: *The road traverses the river several times at Newtown.* **3** °oppose, °cross, °thwart, go *or* act against, go *or* act in °opposition *or* °counter to, °conflict (with), controvert, contravene, °counter, °obstruct, °contradict, gainsay, °deny: *The policies of today seem to traverse those set forth only last year.* **4** °examine, °look into, °scrutinize, °inspect, °investigate, °review, °study, °look at, °consider, °contemplate, °scan, °look over, °check, °survey, °reconnoitre, °observe: *Certain areas of knowledge are seldom traversed by scholars.*

treasure *n.* **1** °wealth, °riches, °money, °fortune, valuables, °cash, °cache, °hoard: *The existence of the treasure came to light only last week.* **2** °pride (and °joy), °delight, °joy, °darling, °ideal, apple of (one's) eye, *Colloq* °jewel, °gem, °prize, °find, °catch: *Kathy is a treasure and I don't know what we did before we hired her.* —*v.* **3** °hold °dear, °cherish, value, °prize, °esteem, rate *or* value highly: *We treasure the signed letter that Churchill wrote to my father. I treasure every moment we can spend together.*

treasury *n.* exchequer, bank, °cache, resources, funds, °money(s): *There was not enough money in the treasury to pay for the scheme. The Treasury indicated their concern at the current state of the economy.*

treat *v.* **1** °handle, °manage, °behave *or* °act toward(s), °deal with; °use: *Why should we treat female employees any differently?* **2** °handle, °manage, °deal with, °discuss, °touch on *or* upon, °consider, °take up, °study, °examine, °explore, °investigate, °scrutinize, °analyse, °go into, °probe, °survey, expound (on), °criticize, °review, critique: *That subject is treated in Chapter VI.* **3** °nurse, °doctor, °attend, °care for, °look after, °prescribe for, medicate: *He is being treated for gallstones.* **4** °entertain, °take out, °pay for, °regale, play °host to; wine and dine: *Our visitors treated us when we went out to dinner yesterday.* **5 treat (someone) to (something)**: °pay (the bill) for, °buy (something) for: *Edward treated us all to ice-cream.* —*n.* **6** °favour, °gift, °present, °boon, °bonus, °premium, *Colloq US and Canadian* freebie: *Put your money away—this is my treat.*

treatment *n.* **1** Often, **treatment of**: °behaviour (towards), °conduct (towards), °action (towards), handling (of), °care (of), °management (of), dealing(s) (with), manipulation (of), °reception (of); °usage (of): *I am not accustomed to such rude treatment. Your treatment of our customers must be more courteous, Miss Davidson.* **2** °therapy, °care, curing, remedying, healing: *They received extensive medical treatment for the injuries they had sustained.*

treaty *n.* °pact, °agreement, °alliance, concordat, entente, covenant, °deal, °contract, °compact, °accord: *They entered into a treaty not to violate each other's borders.*

tremble *v.* **1** °quiver, °shake, °quake, °shiver, °shudder, °quaver, quail; °vibrate, °rock: *Her first big role and she was trembling like a leaf! The earth trembled as the tanks rolled past.* —*n.* **2** °quiver, °shake, °quake, °shiver, °shudder, °quaver, tremor; vibration: *There was a little tremble, and then the building collapsed.*

tremulous *adj.* **1** trembling, a-tremble, quivering, shaking, quaking, shivering, shuddering, quavering, °hesitant, wavering, unsure, unsteady, faltering, °doubtful, °nervous, °shaky, palpitating, °jumpy, *Colloq* jittery: *His tremulous hands revealed just how apprehensive he was.* **2** °timid, °shy, °bashful, °anxious, °worried, timorous, °fearful, °afraid, frightened, °scared: *I cannot remember when I felt so tremulous before meeting someone.*

trenchant *adj.* °cutting, °keen, °acute, °sharp, °pointed, °poignant, °penetrating, °incisive, °biting, mordant, mordacious, °sarcastic, °bitter, acerbic, acid, vitriolic, °tart, acrid, acrimonious, acidulous, corrosive, °caustic: *The critics dismissed the play with a few trenchant remarks.*

trend *n.* **1** °tendency, °leaning, °bias, °bent, °drift, °course, °inclination, °direction: *The trend seems to be towards shorter skirts.* **2** °fashion, °style, °vogue, °mode, °look, °rage, *Colloq* °fad, °craze, °thing: *Why is she so compulsive about keeping up with the latest trends?* —*v.* **3** °tend, °lean, be °biased, °bend, °drift, °incline, veer, °turn, °swing, °shift, °head: *At the convention, the party leaders trended more to the left of centre.*

trendy *adj.* **1** °fashionable, °stylish, à la °mode, °modern, up to °date, up to the °minute, in °vogue, voguish, all the °rage, *Slang* °hot, °now, with it, groovy, in the °groove, in, °flash: *Sibyl travels with that trendy set from Belgravia.* —*n.* **2** °show-off, clothes-horse, coxcomb, exhibitionist, *Slang Brit* pseud, grandstander: *Don't you just hate those trendies down at Cole's wine bar?*

trial *n.* **1** °test, testing, °experiment, °proof, try-out, °trying out, trial run, °examination, °check, checking, *Colloq* dry run: *The trials of the new life-jackets are to be conducted soon.* **2** hearing, enquiry *or* °inquiry, °examination, inquisition, °litigation, °judicial °proceeding, lawsuit, °contest: *Throughout the trial, the accused protested his innocence.* **3** °try, °attempt, °endeavour, °effort, °venture, °essay, *Colloq* °go, °shot, °stab, °fling, whirl, crack, whack: *This was their first trial at climbing the north face.* **4** °trouble, °affliction, tribulation, °hardship, adversity, °suffering, °grief, °woe, °misery, °distress, bad *or* hard °luck, °misfortune, hard times: *Mona acknowledged the trial of having ten children and no husband.* **5** °nuisance, irritation, °bother, bane, °annoyance, °pest, irritant, °thorn in the flesh *or* side, *US* bur *or* burr under the saddle, *Colloq* °plague, hassle, °pain (in the neck), °headache, *Taboo slang* °pain in the *Brit* arse *or* *US* ass: *William, who is full of mischief, is a constant trial to his mother.* —*adj.* **6** °sample, °experimental, exploratory, °provisional, probationary, °tentative, conditional, °pilot: *Will you consider a trial subscription to* Verbatim, The Language Quarterly?

tribe *n.* °race, °stock, °strain, °nation, °breed, °people, °seed, (ethnic) °group, gens, °clan, blood, °pedigree, °family, sept, °dynasty, °house; °caste, °class: *It was important in that society to marry someone from the same tribe.*

tribunal *n.* court (of °justice), °bar, bench, judiciary, Inquisition, Star Chamber: *Should he be tried before a judicial tribunal or pilloried by the tribunal of public opinion?*

tributary *n.* °branch, °offshoot, streamlet, feeder, °brook, rivulet, °run, rill, runnel, runlet,

Scots and No. Eng. burn, No. Eng. beck, US °creek, NE US kill: The Teviot is one of the tributaries of the Tweed.

tribute n. **1** °honour, °homage, °recognition, °celebration, °respect, °esteem, °testimonial, °compliment, encomium, °acknowledgement, acclaim, acclamation, commendation, °praise, °kudos, laudation, panegyric, °eulogy, glorification, exaltation: No greater tribute could be bestowed than recognition by one's fellows. **2** °tax, exaction, impost, °duty, excise, levy, °dues, assessment, °tariff, °charge, surcharge, °payment, contribution, °offering, °gift; °ransom; tithe, Peter's or Peter pence: In exchange for their freedom, the king demanded an annual tribute of a thousand oxen.

trick n. **1** °ruse, °artifice, °device, °stratagem, °wile, °deception, °manoeuvre, °deceit, °fraud, °hoax, imposture, °intrigue, °machination, °conspiracy, °subterfuge, °dodge, confidence trick, °sham, Slang con: The government's 'dirty tricks squad' perpetrated crimes against their political adversaries. **2** °prank, °frolic, antic, (practical) °joke, °hoax, tomfoolery, °caper, jape; °sport, horseplay, °mischief; Scots cantrip, Colloq leg-pull, °gag, shenanigans, US dido: The boys meant no harm, they're just up to their tricks. **3** °art, °knack, °technique, °skill, °secret, °gift, °ability, Colloq hang: He has an odd trick of persuading people to buy life insurance. **4** Usually, **no mean trick**: °feat, °accomplishment, °deed: It was no mean trick to train a cat to fetch his slippers. **5** sleight of hand, legerdemain, °magic, °stunt: I have taught him all the tricks I know. **6** °trait, °characteristic, °peculiarity, idiosyncrasy, °eccentricity, °quirk, °practice, °habit, °mannerism, crotchet, °weakness, °foible: He has an odd trick of winking while giving a sly smile. **7 do the trick**: °work, °answer, °fulfil the need, °suffice, be °effective, °solve or take °care of the problem, do or °accomplish the necessary, US turn the trick, Colloq fill the bill: Replacing the battery cable did the trick. —v. **8** °fool, °hoodwink, °dupe, °mislead, °outwit, outmanoeuvre, °deceive, misguide, °misinform, gull, bilk, °cheat, °defraud, cozen, °take in, °swindle, humbug, Colloq bamboozle, °take, °put something over on (someone), pull the wool over (someone's) eyes, Brit gammon, Slang rook: I knew I had been tricked when I missed my wallet. For years the couple made a living tricking tourists out of their money. She tricked me into taking her to dinner. —adj. **9** See tricky, 3, below.

trickery n. °chicanery, °deception, °deceit, guile, shrewdness, craftiness, slyness, shiftiness, evasiveness, artfulness, °artifice, °craft, imposture, swindling, knavery, duplicity, double-dealing, °fraud, cheating, Colloq °hanky-panky, skulduggery, funny or monkey business, jiggery-pokery: He separated her from her money by trickery.

trickle v. **1** °drip, °drop, dribble, drizzle, °run, °flow, °spill; °ooze, seep, °leak, exude: The water trickled onto the floor. Blood is trickling from the wound. —n. **2** °drip, seepage, °spill, dribble, runnel, runlet, rivulet: A tiny trickle of saliva appeared at the corner of his mouth.

tricky adj. **1** °deceitful, °shady, °deceptive, °shifty, °dodgy, °artful, guileful, °crafty, duplicitous, °shrewd, cunning, °dishonest, °devious,

°sly, °wily, °slippery, °foxy, double-dealing, cheating: Arthur is a tricky chap and I shouldn't trust him. **2** °ticklish, °risky, °hazardous, °sensitive, °delicate, touch-and-go, °thorny, °difficult, °awkward, complex, °complicated, knotty, °uncertain, °debatable, Colloq iffy, °sticky: It is a tricky decision whether you tell a patient how ill he really is. **3** unfair, unjust, unsportsmanlike, °deceptive, Colloq °trick: There were some tricky questions in today's exam.

trifle n. **1** knick-knack, trinket, °bauble, bagatelle, °toy, °gewgaw, °nothing, °plaything, beotise, Colloq doodah: Oh, it's nothing, just a trifle I picked up in the Seychelles. **2** °little, °bit, °drop, iota, scintilla, °suggestion, °dash, °dab, °pinch, whiff, mite, whit, °jot, tittle, Colloq smidgen or smidgin, US tad: I'd like a trifle more sugar in my coffee, if you don't mind. —v. **3** Usually, **trifle with**: dally (with), °flirt (with), °wanton (with), °mess about or around (with), °toy (with); °play (with), °fiddle (with), dandle, °tinker (with), °fidget (with): I hated to see the way he trifled with my sister's affections. While trifling with this knob, I was able to get Radio Moscow.

trifling adj. trivial, °insignificant, unimportant, °puny, °minor, °paltry, °slight, °petty, °inconsequential, °frivolous, °superficial, °incidental, °negligible, commonplace, inconsiderable, °shallow, valueless, °worthless, US and Canadian picayune, Colloq piddling: Their contribution to musical scholarship has been trifling.

trim adj. **1** °neat, °tidy, °orderly, well-ordered, °well-groomed, well turned out, well-kempt, °smart, °crisp, °dapper, spick and span, °spruce, °shipshape (and Bristol fashion), Archaic or dialectal trig, Colloq natty, US spiffy: Nancy arrived wearing her trim new flight-attendant's uniform. **2** in good or fine fettle, °fit (as a fiddle), athletic, °slim, °slender, clean-cut, °shapely, °streamlined, °compact: Larry looks so trim that I asked him if he had lost weight. The new convertible model is a very trim little motor car. —v. **3** °curtail, °shorten, °prune, °pare, °lop (off), crop, bob, °clip, °cut, °shave, shear, °snip, °dock; barber: They trimmed the article by cutting two paragraphs from the end. He had shaved off his beard and trimmed his moustache. **4** °decorate, °embellish, °dress up, embroider, adorn, °ornament, deck out, caparison, °beautify: When should we trim the Christmas tree? —n. **5** trimming, edging, piping, purfling, ricrac or rickrack, embroidery, °border, hem, °frill, °fringe, °ornament, ornamentation, °decoration, °embellishment, adornment: The skirt was spoilt by a rather cheap trim round the hem. **6** °condition, °state, fettle, °health, °form, °order, °fitness, °repair, Colloq °shape: Sid's car seemed to be in good trim when I saw it yesterday.

trio n. threesome, trilogy, triad, triplex, triple, troika, triptych, triumvirate, triplet, trine, triune, trinity, three: An interesting trio showed up for dinner.

trip n. **1** °stumble, °slip, °blunder, °false °step, °misstep, °fall: He sprained his ankle in that trip on the stair. **2** °stumble, °slip, °blunder, °false °step, °misstep, faux pas, °error, °mistake, °indiscretion, °lapse, °slip of the tongue, lapsus linguae, erratum, °oversight; Freudian °slip; Slang Brit boob: If it hadn't been for that one trip, we would have had a perfect score. **3** °tour,

°journey, °excursion, °outing, °expedition, voyage, trek, peregrination, jaunt, junket, °drive: *We took a short side-trip to visit Khios.*
—*v.* **4** °dance, °caper, °skip, °cavort, gambol, °frisk, °hop, °spring: *Joanne came tripping gaily down the Champs Élysées.* **5** °stumble, °slip, °blunder, °misstep, °fall (down), °tumble, °topple, °dive, °plunge, °sprawl, °lurch, °flounder, °stagger, falter: *I tripped on the doorstep and went head over heels.* **6** Often, **trip up**: °trap, °trick, °catch out, unsettle, °throw off, disconcert: *She has been trying to trip me up and confess to something I didn't do.* **7** °journey, °travel, voyage, °visit, °tour, trek, sightsee, °cruise; *Colloq* globe-trot: *They have been tripping all over Europe this summer.* **8** detonate, °set off, trigger, °operate, °release, °explode, °spark off: *When he touched the wire, he tripped the charge.* **9** Often, **trip out**: hallucinate, *Slang* °freak out, °turn on: *There's no talking to him when he's tripping out on coke.*

triumph *n.* **1** °victory, °conquest, °success, °achievement, °accomplishment, attainment, coup, ascendancy: *The discovery of the drug was perhaps the greatest of his many triumphs.* **2** exultation, rejoicing, exulting, elation, °delight, °rapture, exhilaration, jubilation, °happiness, °joy, °celebration, °glory: *There was great triumph on winning the World Cup.*
—*v.* **3** Often, **triumph over**: °win, °succeed, carry the day, be °victorious, °gain a °victory, take the honours, °thrive, °dominate, °prevail; °defeat, °beat, °rout, vanquish, °best, °conquer, °overcome, °overwhelm, °subdue: *Does justice always triumph? The book is about how man triumphed over pain.*

triumphal *adj.* celebratory, °rapturous, jubilant, °joyful, °glorious, °exultant; commemorative: *A holiday was declared to celebrate her triumphal entry into the city. This triumphal arch commemorates Trajan's victory over the Dacians.*

triumphant *adj.* °victorious, °successful, conquering, °winning; undefeated: *The triumphant hero returns tonight!*

triviality *n.* **1** smallness, unimportance, insignificance, meaninglessness, inconsequentiality or inconsequentialness or inconsequence or inconsequentness, trivialness, pettiness, paltriness: *I have difficulty coping with the triviality of some of my boss's requests.* **2** °trifle, technicality, °non-essential, °small matter, unimportant or °insignificant or °inconsequential or trivial or °petty °detail, beotise: *He tends to get bogged down in trivialities, unable to see what is important.*

trivialize *v.* °belittle, denigrate, lessen, °minimize, undervalue, °depreciate, °underestimate, underrate, make °light of, °laugh off, underplay, °dismiss, °disparage, misprize, °beggar, deprecate, °slight, °scoff at, °scorn, °run down, decry, *Colloq* °put down, °play down, pooh-pooh: *Edward tends to trivialize the work of others.*

trophy *n.* **1** °prize, laurel(s), wreath, cup, °award, °reward, °honour(s), medal, citation, palm, bays; °booty, °spoils, *Colloq* gold, °silver, silverware: *He has won trophies for more boat races than I have participated in.* **2** °memento, souvenir, °token, °record, °reminder, °remembrance, °keepsake: *That scar is a trophy of a hand-to-hand fight near El Alamein.*

trot *v.* **1** °jog, °run; bustle, °hustle, °hurry, °hasten, scamper, scoot, *Colloq* skedaddle: *I trot round the park every morning for exercise. As I need some butter, I'd better trot down to the shop before it closes.* **2** **trot out**: °bring out, °show, °display, °exhibit, °flaunt, °come out with; dredge up, °drag out; °recite, °repeat: *Our neighbour trotted out his new lawnmower for us to admire.*
—*n.* **3** °jog, lope, single-foot, °pace; °run: *It was a delight to watch the young horses in a fast trot round the track.* **4** °translation, °gloss, °interpretation, crib, *Colloq US* pony, horse: *He couldn't read Homer without a trot.*

trouble *v.* **1** °bother, °upset, °anguish, °alarm, °worry, °afflict, °agitate, disquiet, °discomfit, make uncomfortable, °grieve, °perturb, discommode, °inconvenience, discompose, discountenance, °put out, °burden, °encumber, °weigh down: *I don't mean to trouble you with my problems, but I have no one else to turn to.* **2** °annoy, °irritate, °irk, vex, °bother, °plague, °pester, °torment, °harass, hector, harry, °provoke, nettle, °exasperate, °ruffle, *Colloq* get or grate on (someone's) °nerves, give (someone) a hard time, get under (someone's) skin: *Vincent keeps troubling me for advice on starting a new business.* **3** discommode, incommode, °impose on, °inconvenience, °put out, thank: *I'll trouble you to turn off the light when you leave the room.* **4** °care, be °concerned, take the trouble or the time, go to the trouble, °bother, °exert (oneself), °concern (oneself), take °pains: *He never troubled to find out if his family was safe.*
—*n.* **5** °distress, °worry, °concern, °difficulty, °discomfort, unpleasantness, °inconvenience, vexation, °grief, °woe, °affliction, disquiet, °suffering, tribulation, °anxiety, °torment, °anguish, °strife: *Her trouble began when her ex-husband stopped paying for child support. How can someone so insignificant cause so much trouble?* **6** °annoyance, °bother, tormentor or tormenter, irritation, °nuisance, °nag, heckler, °pest, *Slang US* nudnik: *Ever since she lost her job, she's been a trouble to her family.* **7** °disorder, °agitation, °row, °disturbance, turbulence, °tumult, °upset, °dissatisfaction, °unrest, °discord, °dispute, turmoil, °rebellion, °revolt, °uprising, outbreak, fighting, °fight, skirmishing, °skirmish: *The trouble began when workers refused to allow management to hire replacements.* **8** °affliction, °defect, °disability, °disease, °ailment, °illness, sickness, °disorder, °complaint: *With her trouble she ought to see a doctor.* **9 in trouble**: **a** in deep trouble, in a °mess, in a °predicament, in dire °straits, *Colloq* in a pickle, in hot water, on the °spot, in a °scrape, *Slang Brit* in shtook or shtuk or shtuck or schtuck, *Taboo slang* in deep shit, up shit creek (without (the vestige of) a paddle): *They will be in terrible trouble if the bank forecloses on the mortgage.* **b** unmarried or unwed and impregnated or °pregnant or with child or °expecting or in a delicate condition or colloq in a family way: *Most of the girls who are in trouble are teenagers.*

troublemaker *n.* mischief-maker, °rabble-rouser, gadfly, firebrand, *agent provocateur*, stormy petrel, incendiary, gossip-monger, scandalmonger, malcontent, instigator, meddler, °agitator: *As far as the police were concerned, any protester was, by definition, a troublemaker.*

troublesome adj. worrisome, worrying, annoying, °irksome, irritating, vexatious, bothersome, distressing, °difficult, °burdensome, Colloq pestiferous, US and Canadian pesky: We sometimes have to put up with troublesome motor-cycle gangs.

truant n. **1** malingerer, °runaway, absentee, °delinquent, dodger, shirker, °idler, °loafer, layabout, Slang Brit skiver, Brit military scrimshanker: Truants were warned that their parents would be required to visit the school.
—adj. **2** malingering, °runaway, °absent, absentee, °delinquent, shirking, loafing, Slang Brit skiving: The officer brought in three truant boys found fishing at the lake.

truce n. **1** armistice, cease-fire, °suspension of hostilities, °lull, °moratorium, °respite, °let-up, °intermission, °interval, °interlude: It looked as if the truce might last. **2** °pact, °treaty, °compact, °agreement, cease-fire, armistice: If both sides abide by the truce the war might be over.

truck n. **1** °merchandise, commodities, goods, stock, °wares, °stuff, °odds and ends, °sundries, °junk, °rubbish, US °trash: There was no one in the shop and all the truck was stacked in the corner. **2** dealing(s), °traffic, °business, °transaction, °trade, °commerce, communication, °contact, °connection, (business or social) °relations: She refuses to have any truck with the likes of you.

truckle v. °kowtow, be °obsequious, toady, °defer, °bow, °scrape, genuflect, salaam, °drop to the ground or to (one's) knees or down on (one's) knees, °submit, °yield, cower, °cringe, grovel, °crawl, quail, fawn (on or upon), Colloq butter up, fall all over, lick (someone's) boots, boot-lick, US apple-polish, Slang suck up to, Taboo slang brown-nose, kiss (someone's) Brit arse or US ass: Just look how Caroline is always truckling to the boss, hoping for favours.

truculent adj. °surly, °sullen, bad-tempered, ill-tempered, unpleasant, °nasty, °obstreperous, °rude, °ferocious, °fierce, °savage, feral, barbarous, °harsh, °scathing, °virulent, combative, °belligerent, antagonistic, bellicose, °hostile, contentious, °warlike, °violent, °pugnacious, Colloq scrappy: I don't care enough for this job to endure the boss's truculent attitude a moment longer.

true adj. **1** °accurate, °correct, °truthful, °faithful, °literal, °authentic, veracious, °actual, °factual, °realistic, °genuine, °right, valid, unelaborated, °unvarnished, unadulterated, verified, verifiable: Do you swear that this is a true account of what actually took place? **2** °staunch, °faithful, °devoted, dedicated, °loyal, °fast, °firm, unswerving, °steady, °steadfast, °trustworthy, trusty, °dutiful, °upright, °honourable, °constant, unwavering, °stable, dependable, °sincere, °reliable, true-blue: D'Artagnan proved himself to be a true friend. **3** °proper, °exact, °accurate, unerring, °correct, °precise, °right, Slang Brit spot on: It is important that these matters be seen in their true perspective. If this is a true copy of the original, please sign it.
—adv. **4** °truly, truthfully, °honestly, accurately, candidly, frankly, °sincerely, straightforwardly: Tell me true, do you love me? If the report speaks true, then we must find the culprit. **5** °exactly, correctly; geographically: We sail true north to Iceland.
6 come true: come to °pass, °occur, take °place,

°happen, be realized, become a °reality, be fulfilled: Her dreams finally came true when she bought a little house in Kent.

truism n. commonplace, platitude, bromide, axiom, °cliché, °maxim: You can rely on Vera to utter a truism like, 'It's a nice day', on a warm, sunny day.

truly adv. **1** truthfully, °actually, °really, °honestly, in °fact, in °truth, in actuality, in °reality, in all °honesty, °sincerely, genuinely: Are you truly giving up your job to get married? I truly believed her to be guilty. **2** °properly, rightly, rightfully, justly, legitimately, justifiably, °duly, °well and truly, accurately: In the circumstances, can we truly condemn him for behaving as he did? **3** °definitely, °really, °actually, °undoubtedly, indubitably, beyond (the shadow of) a doubt, beyond question, without a doubt, °indeed, unquestionably, °absolutely, °positively, decidedly, certainly, °surely: I believed her to be truly guilty. **4** in °truth, °indeed, °really, °honestly, °sincerely, genuinely, Archaic (yea,) verily, Usually ironic forsooth: I love you, darling, truly I do.

trunk n. **1** main °stem, °stalk, °stock, Technical bole: After the tornado, only the trunks of the trees remained upright. **2** torso, °body: All that was found of the corpse was the trunk. **3** °chest, locker, foot-locker, °box, °case, bin, coffer, °casket: We found a trunk full of old books in the attic. **4** snout, proboscis: The elephant reached for the food with its trunk. **5** US and Canada: luggage compartment, Brit boot: We cannot get all the luggage into the trunk of the car.

trust n. **1** °confidence, °reliance, °faith, °conviction, certitude, °certainty, sureness, positiveness, °assurance, °belief: Place your trust in me. **2** °credit, reliability, dependability, credibility, trustworthiness: The company will sell you the piano on trust. **3** °custody, °care, keeping, °charge, guardianship, °protection, °safe keeping, trusteeship: The money is in trust for Gillian's grandchildren. **4** monopoly, cartel; °group, corporation, conglomerate: An international trust controls the world market in diamonds.
—v. **5** °rely (on or upon), have °faith or °confidence (in), confide (in), °depend or bank or °count (on or upon), pin (one's) °faith or °hopes on or upon: I trust that you will attend the meeting. In God we trust—others must pay cash. Can I trust you to keep a secret? Don't trust to luck. **6** °entrust, °commit, °give, °delegate, °make or turn or °sign or °hand over, depute, °assign, empower, consign: I shouldn't trust my money to her.

trusting adj. trustful, unsuspicious, confiding, °confident, °unsuspecting, °naïve, °innocent, °gullible, incautious, credulous: It is a good thing that her husband has a trusting nature. Samantha might be a little too trusting and could easily be deceived.

trustworthy adj. °reliable, trusty, dependable, °accurate; °responsible, °steady, °steadfast, °loyal, °faithful, (tried and) °true, °honourable, °honest, °ethical, °principled, °moral, incorruptible: Is this thermometer trustworthy? Isaac's former employer said that he is completely trustworthy.

truth n. **1** genuineness, °reality, actuality, correctness, °accuracy, °fact: The truth of the matter is that he's in love with you. **2** °fact(s): To tell the *truth, I came here to kill you.* **3 in truth**: in °fact, °truly, °actually, °really: *In truth, his name is not Jack Armstrong at all but Ebenezer Braithwaite.*

truthful *adj.* °true, °accurate, °factual, veracious, true to life, °honest, °realistic, °reliable, °faithful, °trustworthy, straightforward, °candid, °frank, °sincere, °earnest, °forthright, °unvarnished, unembellished: *He gave a truthful account of his experiences in the jungle.*

try *v.* **1** °attempt, °endeavour, °essay, °seek, °undertake, °venture, °strive, °struggle, make an °effort, try (one's) hand at, *Colloq* have a °stab or °go or whack (at), take a °shot or crack (at): *He tried to help me with my homework.* **2** °test, °try out, °prove, °evaluate, °examine, °inspect, °check out, °sample, appraise, assay, °look over, °analyse, °scrutinize, assess, °judge: *I'll try your way of solving the problem. You won't know if it works till you try it.* **3** °test, °prove, °strain, °tax: *You are trying my patience with your silly questions.* **4** °hear, sit on, adjudicate, °judge, adjudge: *There are three more cases to try this month.* —*n.* **5** °attempt, °endeavour, °essay, °undertaking, °venture, °struggle, °effort, °turn, *Colloq* °go, °stab, whack, °fling, °shot, crack: *You have three tries to pin the tail on the donkey.*

trying *adj.* irritating, exasperating, frustrating, annoying, °irksome, infuriating, maddening, bothersome, °tiresome, vexing, °troublesome, worrying, worrisome, distressing, disquieting, upsetting, dispiriting, taxing, °demanding, °tough, stressful, °difficult, tiring, fatiguing: *This must be a trying time for you, caring for eight small children.*

tug *v.* **1** °pull, °tow, °yank, °jerk, °draw, °drag, °haul, °wrench: *The boy was tugging a little puppy along on a lead.* —*n.* **2** °pull, °tow, °yank, °jerk, °drag, °haul, °wrench: *I gave a tug and the doorknob came away in my hand.*

tuition *n.* °education, teaching, tutelage, training, °schooling, °instruction, °guidance, °preparation: *The course fees cover tuition and accommodation.*

tumble *v.* **1** °fall (down), °pitch, °turn end over end *or* °head over heels, °roll, °drop: *Giggling hysterically, we tumbled in a heap on the lawn.* **2** °drop, °toss, °dump, °jumble: *The waiter tumbled several spoonfuls of berries on to my plate.* **3 tumble to**: °understand, apprehend, °perceive, °comprehend, °see the °light, *Colloq* °get the °signal *or* °message, °catch on, *Brit* °twig to, *Slang* °get °wise, °wise up, dig: *I finally tumbled to what she was trying to tell me.* —*n.* **4** °fall, °slip, °stumble, *Colloq* header, °spill: *Joshua took a bad tumble on the stairs yesterday.*

tumbledown *adj.* °ramshackle, °dilapidated, ruined, in ruins, °decrepit, °rickety, °shaky, falling °apart *or* to °pieces, disintegrating, tottering, broken-down, crumbling, gone to rack and °ruin: *He lived for years in a tumbledown shanty near the railway.*

tumour *n.* neoplasm, cancer, melanoma, sarcoma, malignancy, carcinoma, °growth, °lump, °swelling, protuberance, excrescence: *The doctor found a tumour that he said ought to be removed.*

tumult *n.* commotion, °disturbance, °upset, °uproar, °riot, °disorder, disquiet, insurrection, °agitation, °bedlam, °chaos, brouhaha, °fracas, hubbub, °stir, °pandemonium, hullabaloo, °furore *or US* furor, °brawl, Donnybrook, affray,

°row, meolée *or* melee, turbulence, °ferment, ado, turmoil, °confusion, °rampage, °frenzy, °rage, °excitement, °rumpus, *Colloq US* ruckus: *The tumult caused by the football hooligans spread through the city.*

tumultuous *adj.* clamorous, °noisy, °boisterous, °disorderly, turbulent, °violent, °uproarious, °chaotic, frenzied, °furious, °excited, °agitated, °hectic, °riotous, °rowdy, °unruly, unrestrained, °fierce, °savage, °wild, °hysterical, °frantic, rumbustious, °obstreperous, °tempestuous, °stormy: *The heroes received a tumultuous welcome on their return.*

tune *n.* **1** °melody, °air, °song, °strain, °motif, °theme: *David presents a marvellous half-hour radio programme of show tunes every week.* **2** euphony, °pitch, °harmony, °accord, accordance, consonance, °unison, correspondence, conformity: *She cannot sing in tune. The guitar is out of tune with the piano. Her husband is out of tune with today's fashion.* —*v.* **3** °tune up, °calibrate, °adjust, °regulate, °coordinate, °adapt, attune, align, °set: *That garage charges too much for tuning an engine.* **4 tune in (on)**: °attend (to), pay °attention (to), °listen (to), °understand, be °aware (of), be on the qui vive, be °alert (to), *Slang* be on the same wavelength *or* frequency (with): *I am not sure that Bernard is tuned in to what his sister does for a living.* **5 tune out**: °ignore, °disregard, turn a blind eye to, be °blind to, turn one's back on, turn a deaf ear to: *Sally is able to tune out anything she doesn't like to hear.*

tuneful *adj.* melodic, °musical, sweet-sounding, °melodious, euphonious, dulcet, mellifluent, mellifluous, harmonic, catchy, °mellow, °smooth, °rich, °rhythmic, *Colloq* easy on the ear(s): *Irving Berlin wrote some of the most tuneful music that we have.*

tunnel *n.* **1** °shaft, °subway, (°underground) °passage(way), underpass; °burrow, °hole; Channel Tunnel, *Colloq* Chunnel: *The cat got out through this tunnel.* —*v.* **2** °burrow, °dig, °hole, °excavate, °penetrate, °mine: *The prisoners tunnelled under the wall and escaped.*

turf *n.* **1** sod, sward, °green, °grass, greensward, °lawn: *We bought some turf for the new lawn.* **2** °territory, bailiwick, °area, °neighbourhood, backyard, *Colloq* stamping-ground, °home ground, (personal) °space: *You're on my turf now, so you'll do as I say.* **3 the turf**: horse-racing, racing, the racing world, racecourse, racetrack: *The attractions of the turf keep them from other pursuits.* —*v.* **4 turf out**: °eject, °dismiss, °expel, °throw out, oust, °banish, °exile, *Colloq* °sack, °bounce, give (someone) the boot *or* the °sack *or* the (old) heave-ho, chuck *or* toss *or* kick *or* °boot out, °fire: *The committee said he had brought the sport into disrepute and turfed him out of the team.*

turn *v.* **1** °rotate, °revolve, °spin, °roll, °reel, °circle, °gyrate, whirl, °wheel, °go (a)round *or* about, °pivot, °swivel: *The earth turns on its axis. Turn the crank to raise the bucket.* **2** °move, °shift, °wheel, veer, °swing, °face: *As she turned I noticed a horrible scar.* **3** °reverse, turn (a)round, °alter, °change, °adapt, reorganize, remodel, °modify, refashion, reshape, °reform, °transform, °make over, °convert, bring over: *He has been trying to* turn the business into a profit-making enterprise. He has turned defeat into advance. She managed to turn one of the most loyal members of the government. **4** °go or °pass or °move (a)round, veer, °drive, °walk: Turn left at the corner. **5** go °bad, become °rancid, °spoil, curdle, addle, °sour, °decay, moulder, °rot, °putrefy, Colloq °go off: All the milk in the fridge had turned because of the power cut. **6** °apply, °put, °use, °employ: Is there any way we can turn this situation to our advantage? **7** Sometimes, **turn aside** or **away**: °block, avert, °thwart, °prevent, balk or baulk, parry, °deflect, °fend off, °check: He deftly turned aside the thrust of the dagger. **8** °form, °make up, °fashion, °formulate, °construct, °cast, °create, °coin, concoct, °express: Donald certainly knows how to turn a felicitous phrase. **9** °direct, °aim, °point: He turned the gun on himself and pulled the trigger. **10** °twist, sprain, °wrench: I have turned my ankle and cannot walk. **11** °twist, °wind, °snake, curve, °bend, arc, °coil, °loop, °meander, zigzag: The road turned this way and that, following the river bank. **12 turn against**: °defy, °mutiny, °rebel, °revolt, °rise (up) against: The captain had not expected the first mate to turn against him, too. **13 turn back**: **a** °reverse, °repulse, °repel, °rebuff, °drive back, °beat back: At last we turned back the enemy's advance. **b** °go back, retrace (one's) steps, °return: We must turn back before it is too late. **14 turn down**: **a** °refuse, °reject, °rebuff, °decline, °deny: My request for help was turned down. **b** °decrease or °diminish or lessen or °lower or °soften the sound of: Turn down the radio, I'm on the phone. **15 turn in**: **a** go to bed or °sleep, °retire, °withdraw, call it a day, Slang hit the °sack or the hay: I usually turn in by eleven o'clock. **b** °hand in or over, turn over, °deliver, °give in, °submit, °offer, proffer, °tender, °give back, °return, °surrender, °yield: Please turn in your visitors' badges before you leave. **c** turn over, °deliver (up), °inform on, °betray, Colloq squeal on, rat on, °finger, °tell on: For enough money, he'd turn in his own mother. **16 turn into**: **a** turn to, °become, °change into or to, metamorphose into or to: Right before her, the prince turned into a frog again. **b** °go or °come into, °drive into, °pull into, °walk into: They lost sight of the suspect when he turned into a side-street. **17 turn off**: **a** °stop, °switch off, deactivate, °discontinue; °extinguish: First turn off the water, then the light. **b** °disillusion, °depress, °cool (off), disenchant, disaffect, °alienate, °repel, °repulse, °bore, °offend, °put off, °displease, °sicken, °nauseate, °disgust: People who don't brush their teeth turn me off. **c** °deviate, °diverge: When you come to the fork, turn off to the right. **18 turn on**: **a** °start (up), °switch on, °energize, °activate, set in °motion, cause to °function or °operate: Turn on the light. **b** °depend on or upon, hinge on or upon, be °subject to: The success of the venture turns on our ability to capitalize it. **c** °excite, °thrill, °arouse, °stimulate, titillate, °work up, impassion: He was really turned on by the girl in the bar. **19 turn on** or **upon**: **a** °concern, °revolve about, °relate to: The discussion turned on his ability to write music. **b** be °hostile to, °attack, assail, °set upon, Colloq °tear into: Oliver is so unpopular that his own dog turned on him and bit him. **20 turn out**: **a** °make, °form, °shape, °construct, °build, °fabricate, put together, °assemble, °manufacture, °produce, °put out, °bring out:

The plant turns out a thousand cars a week. **b** °develop, evolve, eventuate, °happen, °result, °prove, °occur, °end up, °arise: As it turned out, he lost anyway. It turns out that he knows my sister. **c** °eject, °evict, °throw out, °expel, oust, °dismiss, °terminate, cashier, Colloq °fire, °sack, kick out, axe, Brit °turf out: When they found I wasn't a member, they turned me out. **d** °dress, °fit out, °equip, °rig out, accoutre or US also accouter: She was well turned out in a beautiful ball gown. **e** °come, °arrive, °appear, °attend, °assemble, °meet, Colloq °show (up), °surface: 55,000 turned out for the rock concert. **21 turn over**: **a** °consider, °muse or ruminate over or about, °revolve, °ponder (over): I needed a while to turn over the job offer in my mind. **b** °reverse, invert, turn upside down: Turn over the clock and read the inscription on the bottom. **c** °overturn, °upset, °knock over: In my haste, I turned over the punch bowl. **d** °sell, °merchandise: A shop in that location ought to turn over a million a year. **e** °rotate, °revolve, °spin, °kick over: The engine turns over, but it won't start. **22 turn tail**: °run away, °flee, °bolt, scoot, show a clean pair of heels, cut and °run, take to (one's) heels, beat a hasty °retreat, Colloq °take off, °beat it, scram, skedaddle: He turned tail when I shouted for help. **23 turn to**: **a** °appeal to, °apply to, °resort to: She turned to me for help. **b** advert to, °refer to, °pick or °take up, have °recourse to: Please turn to your exercise books now. **c** get to °work, °pitch in, buckle or knuckle down: The neighbours turned to in helping clean up the mess after the storm. **d** turn into, °change to, °convert into, °become: Lot's wife was turned to salt. **24 turn turtle**: °capsize, °overturn, keel over, °upset, up-end, Colloq go bottoms up: The overloaded barge turned turtle and sank in the river. **25 turn up**: **a** °surface, °appear, °arrive, Colloq °show (up), show one's face: Guess who turned up at our wedding? **b** °come up, °arise, Colloq crop up, °pop up: Something will turn up soon for you. **c** uncover, °discover, °find, °unearth, °come across, °hit upon, °dig up, °expose, °disclose, °reveal, bring to °light: We turned up a formerly unknown fact about the shipwreck. **d** °increase or °raise or °amplify or °intensify the sound of: Turn up the TV—I can't hear what they're saying.

—n. **26** °revolution, rotation, °cycle, °spin, whirl, °circuit, °round, °roll, °twirl, °pirouette: He gave the top another turn, just to make sure it was on securely. **27** curve, °bend, turning, corner, sinuosity, dog-leg, hairpin °bend or curve, irregularity, °meander, °twist, zigzag, Colloq toing and froing: There are many dangerous turns on that road. **28** °loop, °coil, °spiral, °twist: Take two turns of this rope round your waist, then knot it. **29** deviation, turning, °detour, °shift, °change of direction or course: A turn to the right is not permitted at this corner. **30** °opportunity, °chance, °say, °round, °spell, °time, °watch, °shift, °stint, °tour (of duty), °move, °trick, Colloq whack, crack, °shot, °go: You have had your turn, now let someone else go. **31** °drive, °spin, °ride; airing, constitutional, °ramble, °saunter, °stroll, °walk, °promenade, amble: Let's take a short turn round the park. **32** °trend, °direction, °drift: The conversation took a new turn.

33 °change, °alteration, °switch: The doctor says that Valerie has taken a turn for the better.

34 Usually, **bad turn**: °disservice, °harm,

°injury, °wrong: *If you do someone a bad turn, what can you expect?* **35** Usually, **good turn**: °favour, (°good) °deed, °act (of °kindness), °courtesy, °boon, °mercy: *One good turn deserves another.* **36** °shock, °fright, °surprise, °start, °scare: *You really gave me a turn, jumping out like that!* **37** °form, °style, °manner, °mode: *Each turn of phrase in her writing seems original and refreshing.* **38** °disposition, °inclination, °bent, °bias, °leaning, °tendency: *Alistair is of a rather dour turn of mind tonight.* **39 at every turn**: °everywhere, constantly, °always, all the °time: *In Scotland, we met with kindness and hospitality at every turn.* **40 by turns**: alternately, reciprocally, in rotation, successively, in °succession: *The book is fascinating and frustrating by turns.* **41 in turn**: sequentially, one after the other, in °succession, successively, in (proper) °order: *Each patient will be treated in turn.* **42 out of turn**: **a** out of °sequence, out of °order: *I don't want you answering questions out of proper turn, Jonathan.* **b** imprudently, indiscreetly, improperly, disobediently, inappropriately: *I apologize if I am speaking out of turn on this issue.* **43 take turns**: °alternate, °vary, °rotate, °exchange: *Let's take turns looking through the telescope.*

turn-about *n.* reciprocity, °exchange: *Turn-about is fair play.*

turncoat *n.* °renegade, °traitor, betrayer, °deserter, fifth-columnist, apostate, tergiversator, °defector, backslider, Vicar of Bray, *US* Benedict Arnold, *Colloq* °snake in the grass: *Labour members who voted with the Tories on the issue were branded turncoats.*

turn-off *n.* **1** °exit, side-road, feeder (°road), °auxiliary (°road), °ramp, *Brit* slip-road, *US* (°exit *or* °entrance) °ramp: *Our shop is at the first turn-off after the traffic light.* **2** damper, °killjoy, *Colloq* wet blanket, *Slang US* freeze-out: *It was a real turn-off to discover that his hobby was model railways.*

turnout *n.* **1** assemblage, °muster, °attendance, audience, °crowd, °gate, °throng, °gathering: *The turnout for the first day of the sale was enormous.* **2** °output, °production, out-turn, °volume; gross national °product, GNP, gross domestic °product, GDP: *Turnout has improved since the settlement of the labour dispute.* **3** °gear, °outfit, clothing, °apparel, °apparatus, °equipment, °trappings, °fittings, equipage: *Have you seen Charlie in his mountain-climbing turnout?*

turnover *n.* gross (°revenue), (total) °business, °volume: *Although turnover increased by ten per cent, profits were down by two per cent.*

tutor *n.* **1** °teacher, °instructor, educator, °coach, mentor, guru: *Bernard engaged a tutor to coach him through the examinations.* —*v.* **2** °teach, °instruct, °coach, °educate, °school, °train, °indoctrinate, °drill, °enlighten, °advise, °direct, °guide, °prepare, °ground: *Twitchell needs someone to tutor him in the fine art of going out with girls.*

tweak *v.* **1** °pinch, °nip, twitch, °squeeze, °jerk, °grip: *I do wish that adults would refrain from tweaking my nose, though it is pretty cute.* —*n.* **2** °pinch, °nip, twitch, °squeeze, °jerk, °grip: *He gave her nose an affectionate little tweak.*

twee *adj.* °precious, °sweet, °sentimental, °quaint, °dainty, °cute, mignon(ne), bijou: *The tearoom atmosphere is a bit too twee for my taste.*

twiddle *v.* **1** °play with, °twirl, °fiddle (with), wiggle, °juggle, °toy with, °fidget with, *Colloq* °fool with, °mess with, °monkey with: *Stop twiddling with the dial on that radio!* **2 twiddle (one's) thumbs**: do °nothing, be °idle, °idle *or* while away (the) time, °waste time, bide (one's) time: *I sat there, twiddling my thumbs, while you were being entertained royally.*

twig¹ *n.* sprig, °stem, °shoot, °offshoot, branchlet, °stick, °sucker, °sprout, withe *or* withy, tendril: *Gather up some dry twigs for kindling.*

twig² *v.* °understand, °grasp, °fathom, °get, °comprehend, °see, °know, °sense, °divine, *Colloq* °catch on, be *or* get *or* become °wise to, °tumble to, *Slang* rumble, dig: *She twigged the situation at once but didn't let on she knew.*

twilight *n.* **1** °dusk, sunset, gloaming, sundown, half-light, crepuscule *or* crepuscle: *We enjoyed dinner at twilight on the terrace overlooking the sea.* **2** °decline, °wane, waning, °ebb, downturn, down-swing, °slump, °decay, weakening, declination, diminution: *Even at the twilight of his career, Jonas enjoyed the respect of his colleagues.* **3 Twilight of the Gods**: Götter-dämmerung, Ragnarök *or* Ragnarok: *The world ends at the Twilight of the Gods, only to be born anew.* —*adj.* **4** °evening, crepuscular, dimming, darkening, darkish, darksome, °shadowy, °shady, °dim, °dark, °obscure, °sombre, °gloomy, *Literary* darkling: *The Nymphs in twilight shade of tangled thickets mourn.* **5 twilight zone**: °limbo: *He lives in the twilight zone, unable to distinguish reality from fantasy.*

twin *n.* **1** °double, clone, °duplicate, °look-alike, counterpart, *Slang* ringer: *I cannot distinguish these twins.* —*adj.* **2** °identical, °matching, matched, °duplicate, corresponding, °look-alike: *The bedroom had twin beds with pink covers.* —*v.* **3** °pair, °match, yoke, °join, °link, °couple, °combine, °connect, °associate: *Many towns in Britain are twinned with similar towns on the Continent.*

twine *n.* **1** °cord, °string; °rope, °cable, °yarn: *Have you some twine for tying up this package?* —*v.* **2** °entwine, °braid, °twist, intertwine, curl, wreathe, °spiral, °wind, °weave, interweave, °encircle, °wrap: *Annette's front door has roses twined all round it.*

twinge *n.* **1** °stab, °pang, cramp, °spasm, °pinch, stitch, (sharp) °pain, °prick, °bite, °gripe: *I get a terrible twinge in my back when I lift anything heavy.* **2** °pang, °pain: *I felt a twinge of remorse at leaving.*

twinkle *v.* **1** scintillate, °sparkle, coruscate, °glitter, °shimmer, wink, °flicker, °glisten, glint, °flash, fulgurate, °spark, °dance, °blink, °shine, °gleam: *The stars were twinkling in the icy black sky. Nicole's eyes twinkled as she told me about Max's latest success.* —*n.* **2** °twinkling, scintillation, °scintillating, °sparkle, sparkling, coruscation, coruscating, °glitter, glittering, °shimmer, shimmering, winking, °flicker, flickering, glistening, glint, °flash, flashing, fulguration, °spark, sparking, dancing, blinking, °shine, shining, °gleam, gleaming, °dazzle, °dazzling: *From far off, I caught the twinkle of the sun on car windscreens.*

twinkling *n.* **1** (split) °second, °flash, twinkling *or* wink of an eye, °instant, trice, *Colloq* jiffy, two shakes (of a lamb's tail), tick: *Liza called out, and in a twinkling, Joseph was at her side.* **2** See twinkle, 2, above.

twirl *v.* **1** °spin, whirl, °rotate, °revolve, °wheel, °turn, °gyrate, °twist, °wind (about *or* around): *The windmills twirled in the breeze. Katherine absently twirled a lock of hair round her finger.*
—*n.* **2** twirling, °spin, spinning, whirl, whirling, °turn, turning, °revolution: *He was hypnotized by each twirl of the roulette wheel.* **3** whorl, winding, convolution, °spiral, helix, °coil, volute: *The pattern consists of interlocking twirls of green and brown.*

twist *v.* **1** plait, °braid, °weave, °entwine, intertwine, °twine, interweave, pleach, °splice, wreathe, interlace: *She twisted together some daisies to make a garland for her hair.* **2** °distort, °warp, contort, °pervert, °alter, °change, °slant, °bias, °colour, °falsify, misquote, misstate, °garble, miscite, °misrepresent, °violate; °misinterpret, mistranslate, °misunderstand, misconstrue: *He twisted her words so that she seemed to be saying the opposite of what she intended.* **3** °wriggle, worm, °squirm, writhe, wiggle: *The little beggar twisted out of my grasp and ran for his life.* **4** °wind, °snake, °meander, °turn, zigzag, worm, °bend, curve: *I lost sight of the stream where it twisted through the undergrowth.* **5** °wrench, °turn, sprain, rick *or* wrick: *I twisted my ankle on a faulty step.* **6 twist (one's** *or* **someone's) arm**: °force, coerce, °make, °persuade, °bully, *Brit* pressurize, *US* °pressure: *I didn't want to go, but she twisted my arm.*
—*n.* **7** °coil, °spiral, skew, zigzag, dog-leg, °turn, curve, °angle, °bend, °bow, °meander: *The road is full of twists and turns.* **8** °interpretation, °analysis, °understanding, °slant, °angle, construction, construal; °treatment, °approach, °version, °variation: *This book puts a new twist on the fall of the Roman Empire.* **9** distortion, °interpretation, contortion, °perversion, warping, °alteration, °change, departure, °bias, colouring, falsification, misquotation, °misstatement, garbling, misrepresentation; mistranslation, °misunderstanding, misconstrual, misconstruction: *It was a twist of fate that brought us together again. She gave everything he said such a twist that he scarcely recognized his own ideas.* **10** °quirk, idiosyncrasy, crotchet, °peculiarity, °oddity, °trick, °eccentricity, incongruity, inconsistency, irregularity; °weakness, °flaw, °fault, °foible, °failing: *Owing to a twist in his character, he has developed a hatred of women.* **11 round the twist**: °mad, °crazy, °insane, °eccentric, *Colloq* °daft, *Brit* round the bend, *Slang* nuts, nutty, bonkers, cuckoo, batty, off (one's) rocker, *Brit* barmy *or* balmy: *Kevin's gone round the twist if he thinks I am going out with his sister.*

twister *n.* **1** °cheat, °swindler, confidence man *or* woman, °rogue, °scoundrel, trickster, mountebank, deceiver, °fraud, °impostor *or* imposter, *Colloq* con man *or* woman, crook: *This particular twister preys on the elderly.* **2** tornado, cyclone, typhoon, °hurricane, °whirlwind; waterspout: *The twister picked up my bicycle and dropped it in my neighbour's garden.*

twit[1] *v.* °tease, °cajole, °taunt, °jeer (at), make °fun of, °banter, °tweak, °gibe *or* jibe, °chaff, °ridicule, °mock; °blame, °berate, °deride,

°scorn, contemn, censure, revile, reproach, °upbraid; *Colloq* kid, pull (someone's) °leg: *She never seemed to mind being twitted about her height.*

twit[2] *n.* nitwit, nincompoop, ass, ninny, ninny-hammer, °fool, imbecile, blockhead, °halfwit, idiot, simpleton, *Colloq* chump, moron, *Brit* °silly billy, *Slang* °dope, *US and Canadian* °jerk: *That silly twit told the teacher what we were planning.*

twitter *v.* **1** °peep, cheep, tweet, °chirp, warble, trill, chirrup, °chatter: *The birds twitter so loudly that they wake me every morning.* **2** °chatter, °prattle, °gossip, °giggle, prate, °titter, °snicker, snigger, simper: *I was embarrassed because my classmates always twittered when I did a recitation.*
—*n.* **3** °peep, peeping, cheep, cheeping, twittering, tweet, tweeting, chirrup, chirruping, °chirp, chirping, warble, warbling, trill, trilling: *The twitter of the birds was driving me mad.* **4** ado, bustle, °excitement, °flutter, dither, whirl, °agitation, *Colloq* °stew, tizzy: *The girls were in a twitter of apprehension.*

two-faced *adj.* double-dealing, °hypocritical, duplicitous, dissembling, °deceitful, Janus-faced, treacherous, °dishonest, untrustworthy, °insincere, °scheming, °designing, °crafty, Machiavellian, °sly, °perfidious, °lying, mendacious: *That two-faced liar told you one story and me another!*

tycoon *n.* °mogul, magnate, baron, °financier, (multi)millionaire, billionaire, °merchant prince, potentate, *Colloq* °big shot, (big-time) °operator, wheeler-dealer, big-timer, *US* °big wheel, °big cheese: *What makes you think that Castenado is an oil tycoon?*

type *n.* **1** °class, °category, classification, °kind, °sort, °genre, °order, °variety, °breed, species, °strain, °group, genus, ilk, kidney: *Just what type of person would you say the president is?* **2** typeface, *Brit* fount, *US* font: *The body text ought to be set in Bodoni Book type, the headings in Times bold.* **3** °prototype, paradigm, archetype, °epitome, exemplar, °model, °specimen, °pattern, personification, °standard, °quintessence: *She doesn't consider him to be the usual type of businessman.*
—*v.* **4** typewrite; keyboard; °transcribe: *She types at a speed of about sixty words a minute.*

typical *adj.* **1** °representative, °characteristic, °conventional, °normal, °standard, °ordinary, °regular: *On a typical day I get up at 6.30.* **2** °orthodox, °classic, °conventional, in °character, in keeping, °usual, commonplace, run-of-the-mill, °natural, °customary, °common, to be expected, °ordinary: *His way of looking at life is typical for someone of his educational and social background.*

typify *v.* °exemplify, °instance, epitomize, °personify, °represent, °characterize, °embody, evince, °symbolize, °suggest: *John's views typify the conservative approach.*

tyrannical *adj.* tyrannous, °oppressive, °dictatorial, Fascistic, °despotic, autocratic, °authoritarian, °arbitrary, imperious, °overbearing, unjust, high-handed, °severe, °harsh, iron-handed, °heavy-handed: *The people suffered under one tyrannical form of government after another for generations.*

tyrannize *v.* Often, **tyrannize over**: domineer over, °bully, °subjugate, enthral, °enslave, °dominate, °intimidate, °dictate to, °order

about *or* around, ride roughshod over,
°browbeat, keep under (one's) °thumb, °oppress,
°subdue, °suppress, keep down: *The people have
been tyrannized long enough.*

tyranny *n.* autocracy, Fascism, authoritarianism,
absolutism, °despotism, dictatorship, Stalinism,
Nazism; arbitrariness, °oppression,

°suppression, subjugation, enslavement,
enthralment, °domination: *Tyranny would not survive long were it not expedient for its supporters.*

tyrant *n.* °dictator, °despot, autocrat, martinet,
Hitler, °bully, °oppressor, °authoritarian, hard
taskmaster, slave-driver, Simon Legree, overlord:
*It seems that no people or part of the world is immune
from tyrants.*

U

ugly adj. **1** unattractive, unlovely, unprepossessing, °unsightly, °hideous, °grotesque, °gruesome, °ghastly, °offensive, repulsive-looking, °plain, plain-looking, plain-featured, bad-featured, ill-favoured, dreadful-looking, awful-looking, terrible-looking, horrible-looking, frightful-looking, monstrous-looking, US and Canadian °homely: *The Georgian houses were demolished and replaced by ugly tower-blocks.* **2** objectionable, °disagreeable, unpleasant, °offensive, °nasty, °loathsome, °repellent, °repugnant, °repulsive, noisome, nauseating, °nauseous, °revolting, sickening, °disgusting, °obnoxious, mephitic, °rotten, °corrupt, °filthy, °vile, heinous, °bad, °sordid, °evil, °foul, °perverted, °immoral, depraved, °degenerate, °base, debased, detestable, °hateful, °abominable, execrable, °despicable, odious: *The East End murders were among the ugliest crimes of the century. He sprang from his seat with an ugly curse on his lips.* **3** disquieting, uncomfortable, discomfiting, °troublesome, °awkward, disadvantageous, °ominous, °dangerous, °perilous, °hazardous: *He found himself in a very ugly position, with no apparent means of escape.* **4** unpleasant, °disagreeable, °surly, °hostile, °nasty, °spiteful, bad-tempered, ill-tempered, currish, irascible, curmudgeonly, °cantankerous, crabby, crabbed, crotchety, °cross, °cranky, °mean: *He's in an ugly mood till he's had his coffee.*

ulcer n. **1** °sore, lesion, abscess, ulceration, canker, chancre, °boil, gumboil, °eruption, carbuncle, °inflammation: *That ulcer should be treated before it gets any worse.* **2** cancer, canker, festering spot, °blight, °scourge, °poison, °disease, °pestilence, °curse, bane, °plague: *We must purge this ulcer before it corrupts the entire organization.*

ulcerous adj. ulcerative, cancerous, cankerous, festering, ulcerated, suppurating, suppurative, gangrenous, septic, *Technical* furuncular, furunculous, necrotic, necrosed, sphacelated: *The wound is in an ulcerous condition and requires immediate surgery.*

ulterior adj. **1** °hidden, concealed, covert, °secret, unrevealed, undisclosed, unexpressed, °private, °personal, underlying, °surreptitious, underhand(ed): *She had an ulterior motive for arriving early.* **2** °outside, beyond, °further, °remote, remoter: *What you propose is ulterior to our immediate plan.*

ultimate adj. **1** °final, °last, terminating, °terminal, °end, °eventual, conclusive, concluding, decisive, deciding: *The ultimate outcome will not be known till next week. Who is the ultimate authority in such matters?* **2** °final, °maximum, highest, greatest, °supreme, utmost, °paramount: *Her ultimate goal is to win the gold medal.* **3** °elemental, °basic, °fundamental, underlying, °primary, °essential, °final: *He believes that the ultimate truths were set down in Scripture.* **4** remotest, furthest, farthest, °extreme, uttermost, °last, °final: *The ultimate stage of the experiment will be at a distance of five light-years.*

ultimately adv. °finally, at long °last, in the °final *or* °last analysis, in the °end, at the °end of the day, after all is said and done, at (the) °last, in the long run; fundamentally, essentially, basically, at °bottom: *I thought it might ultimately come to this. He came to understand that ultimately people must depend on each other.*

ultimatum n. °demand(s), °term(s), °condition(s), °stipulation(s), °requirement(s): *If we refuse to comply with his ultimatum, he'll kill the hostage.*

ultra- adj. °extreme, °immoderate, °excessive, °drastic, °radical, °fanatic(al), °unmitigated, °outrageous, °unqualified, °sheer, °blatant, °out-and-out, °complete, °thorough, thoroughgoing, dyed in the wool, die-hard, °rabid, °opinionated, unregenerate, °unrepentant, unreformed, fundamentalist, °prejudiced, °bigoted, *Colloq* hard-nosed: *Ultra-conservativism marked his views till the day he died.*

umbrage n. Usually, **take umbrage**: feel *or* be °offended, take °offence, feel °displeasure *or* °annoyance *or* exasperation *or* °indignation *or* vexation *or* °bitterness *or* °resentment, be piqued *or* displeased *or* annoyed *or* exasperated *or* °indignant *or* vexed *or* °resentful, harbour a °grudge: *She took umbrage at the way he seemed to ignore her.*

umbrella n. **1** parasol; *Colloq chiefly Brit* gamp, *Brit* brolly, *US* bumbershoot: *You will need an umbrella today.* **2** °protection, °cover, coverage, aegis, °shield, °screen, °patronage, °agency: *What benefits are included under the umbrella of this policy?*

umpire n. **1** referee, arbiter, °judge, °moderator, adjudicator, arbitrator; °official; *Colloq* ref, *Australian* umpy, *US* ump: *The sides agree to abide by the decision of the umpire.*
—v. **2** referee, arbitrate, °judge, °moderate, adjudicate; °officiate: *When Peter Jones umpires a game, the players know they will get a fair decision.*

umpteen adj. a °lot of, °many, innumerable, unnumbered, countless, a °huge °number of, very °many, numerous, hundreds of, thousands of, millions of, billions of, trillions of: *You've been told umpteen times, 'Don't go near the water'.*

unabashed adj. unashamed, unblushing, unembarrassed, °brazen, °blatant, °bold, undaunted, unawed, undismayed, unconcerned: *I couldn't put up with his unabashed conceit for another moment.*

unable adj. not °able, °powerless, unfit, °unqualified, °impotent: *The company was unable to give guarantees about continuity of employment.*

unabridged adj. **1** uncut, °whole, full-length, °entire, °complete, °intact, uncondensed, unshortened; unbowdlerized, unexpurgated: *This is the original, unabridged edition, with nothing removed.* **2** °extensive, °thorough, °comprehensive, °exhaustive, all-encompassing, (all-)°inclusive: *That word is too rare to be listed in anything but an unabridged dictionary.*

unaccented adj. unstressed, unemphasized, unaccentuated, °weak, *Technical* lenis: *The first syllable of 'before' is unaccented.*

unacceptable adj. °unsatisfactory, objectionable, °wrong, °bad, °improper, unallowable, °undesirable, not de rigueur, °distasteful, °disagreeable, unsuitable, °inappropriate, unpleasant, °tasteless: Murder is generally regarded as an unacceptable way to relieve oneself of unwanted company.

unaccompanied adj. °alone, °solo, on (one's) own, unescorted, unchaperoned, unattended, Music a cappella, Colloq stag: We went to the dance unaccompanied.

unaccountable adj. **1** unexplained, °inexplicable, unexplainable, °mysterious, inscrutable, °incomprehensible, unintelligible, °strange, °puzzling, baffling, °peculiar, °odd, °bizarre, unfathomable: I found it unaccountable that anyone would arrive for an appointment four hours early. **2** not answerable, not °responsible: How can you have a governmental committee that is unaccountable to anyone? **3** °weird, °unheard-of, °extraordinary, °unusual, °unorthodox, uncanny: Sophie has unaccountable powers of perception.

unaccustomed adj. **1** °unfamiliar, °unusual, °rare, unexpected, uncommon, unprecedented, unanticipated, °curious, °peculiar: They encountered unaccustomed hostility from local people. **2 unaccustomed to:** °unused to, °inexperienced in or at, amateurish at, unpractised in or at, °unfamiliar with, uninitiated in: Unaccustomed as I am to public speaking, I had better be brief.

unadorned adj. °plain, °simple, unembellished, undecorated, unornamented, °stark, °bare, austere: She prefers an unadorned style, without frills.

unaffected[1] adj. °genuine, °real, °sincere, °natural, °simple, °plain, unpretentious, unassuming, °ingenuous, °unsophisticated, unstudied, °honest, guileless, °artless, unartificial, straightforward, unfeigned: He conveyed in simple unaffected language a clear impression of the nightmarish quality of that day.

unaffected[2] adj. Usually, **unaffected by:** impervious (to), °immune (to), untouched (by), °unmoved (by), unresponsive (to), °aloof (to or from), uninfluenced (by), unimpressed (by), °remote (to or from), °cool or °cold (to), unconcerned (by), unstirred (by): The duchess remained totally unaffected by the children's appeals for help.

unapproachable adj. **1** °distant, °remote, °aloof, °reserved, °standoffish, austere, °withdrawn, unfriendly, °forbidding, °chilly, °cool, °cold, °frigid: James seems unapproachable, but in fact he's a very warm person. **2** °inaccessible, °remote, unreachable, °out-of-the-way, out of °reach, beyond °reach: Her house is unapproachable except from the sea.

unarmed adj. unprotected, °defenceless, weaponless: The army began shooting unarmed civilians.

unasked adj. uninvited, unrequested, undemanded, °unsolicited, unsought, unwanted, unprompted, °gratuitous, unbidden, °spontaneous, °unwelcome, °unasked for: I wish he would keep his unasked opinions to himself.

unattached adj. **1** °separate, unconnected, °detached, °independent, unaffiliated, self-governing, self-regulating, self-regulated, autonomous, self-reliant, self-sustaining, self-sustained: The committee was established as an unattached body, not associated with any organization. **2** °single, °unmarried, uncommitted, unengaged, on (one's) own, unspoken for: I joined the club hoping to meet some unattached people.

unauthorized adj. unsanctioned, unapproved, °unofficial, °unlawful, °illegal, °illicit, °illegitimate: Unauthorized use of the company's parking spaces is prohibited.

unavoidable adj. inescapable, ineluctable, °inevitable, °irresistible, inexorable, °sure, °certain, °fated, °destined, predestined, °determined, °predetermined, unchangeable, unalterable, settled, °fixed, °definite: Punishment is an unavoidable consequence of getting caught for something you shouldn't have done.

unaware adj. °ignorant, °oblivious, unknowing, °unsuspecting, °unconscious, °uninformed, unenlightened, incognizant, inobservant, °insensible, °heedless, unmindful: She was totally unaware of the huge spider dangling directly over her.

unawares adv. **1** unexpectedly, abruptly, by °surprise, °suddenly, off (one's) guard: We caught the sentry unawares. **2** inadvertently, unconsciously, unintentionally, unknowingly, unwittingly, by °mistake, mistakenly, by °accident, accidentally, in an °unguarded moment: She had betrayed her closest friend unawares.

unbalanced adj. **1** uneven, asymmetric(al), unsymmetric(al), °lopsided, unequal, overbalanced, °unstable, wobbly, °shaky, unsteady: That stack of chairs is unbalanced and could fall any minute. **2** °mad, demented, certifiable, °crazy, °insane, °eccentric, non compos mentis, touched (in the head), °unstable, unhinged, °deranged, °disturbed, of °unsound mind, out of (one's) head, Colloq daffy, °dizzy, Chiefly Brit °daft, Slang nuts, bats, off (one's) rocker, Chiefly Brit bonkers, US out of one's gourd, loco: The boy is clearly unbalanced, but that doesn't excuse his appalling behaviour.

unbearable adj. intolerable, unsupportable, unendurable, °insufferable, °unacceptable, too much: The pain in her side was almost unbearable.

unbeatable adj. unsurpassable, undefeatable, °excellent, unexcelled, °incomparable, °matchless, unrivalled, °peerless, °unparalleled, °superlative, °supreme: She'll go far with such an unbeatable combination of looks and brains.

unbecoming adj. **1** unsuited, unsuitable, °inappropriate, ill-suited, unfitting, unfit, inapt, unapt, out of °character, out of °place: It is unbecoming to wear your mink coat to the Save the Animals fund-raising dinner. **2** indecorous, °unseemly, °indelicate, °improper, ungentlemanly, unladylike, °offensive, °tasteless: Father said it was unbecoming for her to use such foul language.

unbelievable adj. °incredible, °preposterous, °inconceivable, unimaginable, mind-boggling, °implausible, °unthinkable: The amount of money they spend on clothes is unbelievable. He told an unbelievable tale about having been picked up by a flying saucer.

unbelieving adj. °incredulous, disbelieving, non-believing, doubting, mistrusting, distrusting, mistrustful, °distrustful, °suspicious, °sceptical, unpersuaded, unconvinced: The unbelieving world thinks that the age of miracles is past.

uncertain *adj.* **1** unsure, indeterminate, unpredictable, undeterminable, unforeseeable, unascertainable, °haphazard, °chance, °arbitrary, °random, aleatory, serendipitous, hit-or-miss, °casual: *It is uncertain whether interest rates will rise again next month.* **2** unsure, in *or* of two minds, vacillating, undecided, unclear, ambivalent, °irresolute, °indecisive, °hesitant, hesitating, undetermined, shilly-shallying, *Brit* at a loose °end, *US* at loose °ends: *Julia is uncertain about what to do next.* **3** unsure, indeterminate, up in the air, °indefinite, unpredictable, °unresolved, °unsettled, in the balance, conjectural, °speculative, °debatable, touch-and-go, °unreliable, °doubtful, dubious, °questionable, °vague, °hazy: *The future of the company is now uncertain. The results of the election are still uncertain.* **4** °variable, °changeable, °inconstant, unfixed, °unsettled, °irregular, °fickle, °erratic, °fitful, unsteady, wavering, °unreliable, °sporadic, °occasional; unmethodical, unsystematic: *The pictures in the cave danced in the uncertain light of the torch. How can we make an appointment if your plans are so uncertain?*

uncharted *adj.* unmapped, °unknown, unexplored, undiscovered, °unfamiliar, °strange, virgin, °trackless: *For weeks he wandered lost in the uncharted jungle.*

unchaste *adj.* °impure, °wanton, °immoral, unvirtuous, °promiscuous, °immodest, Cyprian, debased, °lecherous, °lewd, °lascivious: *Her unchaste conduct was a topic of conversation throughout the school.*

uncivilized *adj.* **1** barbarous, °savage, °wild, uncultivated, °barbarian, barbaric, °crude, °primitive, brutish: *He was an uncivilized man living in uncivilized surroundings.* **2** °unrefined, uncultured, uncouth, loutish, °coarse, °uneducated, untutored, unpolished, churlish, °boorish, °philistine, °provincial, °rough, °rude, unlearned, °ill-mannered, incondite, unmannerly, °unsophisticated, inelegant, °gross, gauche: *Anna's father forbade her to go out with the uncivilized boors in the nearby town.*

unconscionable *adj.* **1** conscienceless, °unscrupulous, amoral, unprincipled, °immoral, unethical, °evil, °criminal, unjust, °wicked, arrant: *This unconscionable thief stole from his own mother.* **2** °excessive, extortionate, egregious, °extreme, °unwarranted, °unreasonable, °outrageous, °inordinate, °immoderate, °exorbitant, indefensible, unpardonable, °inexcusable, unforgivable: *When I questioned the unconscionable size of his bill, the plumber explained that he charges extra for house calls.*

unconscious *adj.* **1** °insensible, out (cold), knocked out, °senseless, °numb, stunned, comatose, °dead to the world, *Colloq* blacked-out: *The patient was unconscious for hours.* **2** Often, **unconscious of**: °heedless (of or to), unheeding, unheedful (of), insensitive (to), °mindless, unmindful (of), reflex, °automatic, °involuntary, unintentional, °instinctive, °subliminal, °unthinking, °unpremeditated, °subconscious, unwitting; °blind (to), °unaware (of), °oblivious (to or of), °deaf (to): *For Tim, scratching his head is an unconscious act. Tim is totally unconscious of how irritating his mannerisms are.*

uncontrolled *adj.* unrestrained, ungoverned, unchecked, untrammelled, °undisciplined, °wild, °unruly, °boisterous, °riotous, out of hand or of °control, °rampant, frenzied, °frantic; going °berserk, running amok *or* amuck: *He hit his brother in a moment of uncontrolled anger.*

under *prep.* **1** °beneath, °below, underneath, covered by: *What is under that blanket? The wreck lies a mile under the surface.* **2** °subordinate to, answerable to, °inferior to, °second to, °secondary to, subservient to, °below, °beneath, underneath, °junior to, directed *or* supervised *or* controlled by, under (the) °control of, at the °mercy of, at the beck and call of: *The bashi-bazouks were under the sultan's top officers.* **3** included *or* comprised in *or* under, subsumed under: *This should be under the heading, 'What is the Stupidest Thing you know Today?' Under which category is 'Software'?* **4** under the aegis *or* °protection *or* °eye *or* guardianship *or* °care of: *The prince was trained under the grand vizier.* **5** less than, °lower than: *I paid under £200 for my VCR.* **6 under the influence**: °drunk, tipsy, °high, impaired: *The police charged him with driving while under the influence.* —*adv.* **7** °below, underneath, °beneath: *You looked on top of the bed, but have you looked under?* **8** under-water, beneath the waves, down, out of °sight: *We watched helpless as he went under for the third time.*

underclothes *n.* underclothing, underwear, undergarments, lingerie, *Old-fashioned* °unmentionables, *Colloq* underthings, undies, *Brit* smalls, *Old-fashioned Brit* small-clothes, *US* skivvies: *When a salesman she met on the train said he was in ladies' underclothes, she moved to another carriage.*

undercover *adj.* °secret, °private, clandestine, °confidential: *He doesn't look much like an undercover agent.*

undercurrent *n.* **1** undertow, cross-current, rip tide, rip (°current), underflow: *Caught in the undercurrent, he was carried out to sea.* **2** undertone, subcurrent, °trend, °tendency, °overtone, °tenor, °suggestion, °murmur, °implication, connotation, °sense, °feeling, °aura, tinge, °flavour, °atmosphere, ambience *or* ambiance; vibrations, *Colloq* °vibes: *There is a sinister undercurrent of gloom about this place.*

undercut *v.* **1** °undermine, °excavate, °hollow out, °cut out or away, °gouge out: *If you undercut the roadway it will collapse.* **2** underprice, undercharge, °sacrifice, °sell cheaply or at a loss, undersell: *The supermarkets undercut prices and put the independent grocers out of business.*

underdog *n.* °loser, °scapegoat, °victim; vanquished, °defenceless; *Colloq* fall guy, little fellow *or* guy: *It has always been our policy to fight for the underdog.*

underestimate *v.* undervalue, underrate, °discount, misjudge, °miscalculate, misprize, °minimize, °depreciate, °belittle, not do justice to, fail to appreciate, set (too) little °store by, think (too) little of: *No one should underestimate the physical and mental effort involved.*

undergo *v.* °suffer, °bear, °endure, °experience, °live *or* °go through, be subjected to, °subject oneself to, °sustain, °submit to, °weather, °stand, °withstand: *The hotel has recently undergone extensive refurbishing.*

underground *adj.* **1** subterranean, buried, below-ground, °sunken, covered: *They crept through the underground passage into the treasure*

room. **2** °secret, clandestine, concealed, °hidden, covert, °undercover, °surreptitious, °stealthy, °private: *The secret service has a world-wide underground network of agents.* **3** °alternative, °radical, °experimental, °avant-garde, °nonconformist, °revolutionary: *Some underground newspapers that sprang up in the 1960s are still being published.*
—*n.* **4** tube, metro, underground °railway, *US* °subway: *Two more stops on the underground and we'll be there.* **5** °resistance, partisans *or* partizans, freedom fighters, *in France* Maquis, insurgents, seditionaries *or* seditionists, insurrectionists, guerrillas *or* guerillas, extremists, revolutionaries; fifth columnists, fifth column, saboteurs, subversives: *The underground helped the family to escape to England. The government blames the underground for the bombings.*

undermine *v.* **1** °sap, °drain, disable, °weaken, debilitate, °threaten, °sabotage, °subvert, °damage, °hurt, °harm, °impair, °ruin, °dash, °wreck, °spoil, *Slang* °queer, °bugger (up): *He said that the entire campaign would be undermined if the events of January 17th were ever revealed.* **2** See **undercut, 1**, above.

undersized *adj.* under-size, °little, °short, °small, °petite, °tiny, °elfin, bantam, °slight, mignon(ne); °stunted, underdeveloped, runty, runtish, dwarfish, dwarfed, pygmy, squat; underweight, °undeveloped: *These cattle are a bit undersized for market.*

understand *v.* **1** °grasp, °comprehend, °see, °perceive, discern, °make out, °get the °drift *or* the hang of, °appreciate, °interpret, take °cognizance of, °recognize, be °aware *or* °conscious of, be conversant with, °know, °realize, °conceive of, apprehend, °penetrate, *Colloq* °get (it), °dig, °catch on (to), °tumble to, cotton on (to), *Brit* °twig: *I can understand what you are saying. I didn't think you understood.* **2** °accept, °agree, °arrange, covenant, °take: *I understand the terms of the agreement.* **3** °interpret, °take, °read, °gather from, construe, °surmise from, °assume from, °infer from, °view, °see: *As I understand the regulation, only residents may use the facilities.* **4** °hear (of), °gather, get °wind (of), °take it, be told *or* °informed *or* advised, have found out *or* learnt, *Colloq* °hear tell: *I understand that you've applied for another job.* **5** °sympathize *or* empathize (with), be in °sympathy (with), show compassion (for), commiserate (with); °accept, °tolerate, °allow, °forgive: *Surely your employer will understand your being late because of the funeral.*

understanding *n.* **1** °agreement, °contract, °arrangement, °bargain, covenant, concession, °pact, °compact, °accord, °treaty, concordat, entente, °alliance, °truce, armistice, °reconciliation, °settlement: *They reached an understanding with respect to nuclear weapons.* **2** discernment, °sensitivity, sensitiveness, °sympathy, empathy, °perception, °insight, good °sense, °intuition, enlightenment, percipience, sagacity, sageness, sapience, °wisdom, *Colloq* savvy: *Georgianna brings so much understanding to her treatment of the aged.* **3** Usually, **understanding of**: comprehension *or* awareness *or* °grasp *or* °control *or* °idea *or* °conception *or* °knowledge *or* mastery (of), °acquaintance *or* °familiarity *or* intimacy *or* °dexterity *or* skilfulness *or* deftness *or* adroitness *or* adeptness

(with), competence *or* °skill *or* expertness *or* know-how *or* °proficiency *or* °expertise (in), *Colloq US* fix (on), handle (on): *I know no one with a better understanding of medieval Welsh.* **4** reading, °interpretation, °opinion, °judgement, °estimation, °notion, °view, °perception, apperception, apprehension: *My understanding of what took place is at odds with yours.* **5** °intellect, °intelligence, °mind, °brain, brainpower, °sense, °reason, °reasoning power, °wisdom, *Colloq* brains: *I'm afraid that he lacks the understanding needed to cope with the subtleties of the situation.*

understated *adj.* °subtle, restrained, low-key, °simple, °basic, unembellished, °unadorned: *Alexandra was wearing an understated black dress with a string of pearls.*

understood *adj.* accepted, agreed, arranged, °given, covenanted, settled, conceded: *It was understood that we would be dining together that night. The terms of the agreement are now fully understood.*

understudy *n.* **1** °second, °substitute, °stand-in, °alternate, backup, °double, sub, °reserve, *US* pinch-hitter: *The understudy got her break one night when the star fell ill.*
—*v.* **2** °substitute for, °stand in for, back up, °double for, °second, °replace, *US* pinch-hit for: *He is understudying Hamlet as well as playing the part of Laertes.*

undertake *v.* **1** °assume, °take on *or* upon (oneself), °accept, °take *or* °assume *or* °bear the responsibility for, °enter upon, °begin, °start, °set about, °embark on, °tackle, °try, °attempt: *Gates might be undertaking a bit too much, considering his condition.* **2** °promise, covenant, °agree, °contract, °pledge, °vow, °swear, °warrant, °guarantee, °bargain, °commit (oneself), °stipulate, °engage: *Is it not true that you undertook to complete the work in six months?*

undertaker *n.* mortician, °funeral °director: *The body is available for viewing at the undertaker's tonight.*

undertaking *n.* **1** °enterprise, °affair, °business, °project, °task, °effort, °venture, °work, °feat: *The scope of the undertaking was far beyond her capacity.* **2** doing, performing, °performance, °realization, °achievement: *Giles's undertaking of the work makes me feel more confident.* **3** °promise, °pledge, commitment, °assurance, °contract, °agreement, °vow, °guarantee *or* guaranty, °warranty: *You gave an undertaking to complete the work by Friday.*

underworld *n.* **1** Usually, **the underworld**: organized crime, the °syndicate, the Mafia, the °mob, Cosa Nostra, °criminals, the °criminal element, *Colloq* gangland: *Lorenzo was fast becoming a well-known figure in the underworld.* **2** nether regions, abode of the dead, Hades, Hell, Avernus, Dis, Orcus, *Facetious* Egyptian °underground: *I think I prefer contemplating the Happy Hunting Ground of the American Indian to the underworlds of Christianity and classical Mediterranean culture.*

underwrite *v.* **1** back (up), °finance, °support, °invest in, °subsidize, °sponsor, °uphold, °approve, insure, °guarantee, *US* subvene: *The company has agreed to underwrite the development of your invention.* **2** °subscribe to, °endorse *or* indorse, °sign, countersign, °consent to, °agree to, °confirm, accede to, °sanction, °ratify,

°approve, validate, *Colloq* °OK *or* okay: *The government underwrote the action one day, then denied knowledge of it the next.*

undesirable *n.* **1** *persona non grata,* pariah, °outcast, °exile, °reject, leper: *The police had many requests to run the undesirables out of town.* —*adj.* **2** unwanted, objectionable, °offensive, °unacceptable, °obnoxious, °unsavoury, °unwelcome, disliked, °distasteful, °repugnant, unfit, °unbecoming, unsuitable: *The parks are filled with tramps, drug addicts, and other undesirable elements.*

undeveloped *adj.* embryonic, °premature, °immature, incipient, inchoate, °potential, latent: *His sense of beauty remained undeveloped till he visited Rome.*

undiluted *adj.* °pure, °neat, °straight, unmixed, uncut, unblended, unadulterated, unwatered, unalloyed: *No ice, please—I like my whisky undiluted. How do you like the undiluted gall of the fellow walking in here uninvited!*

undisciplined *adj.* untrained, unschooled, °unprepared, untutored, °uneducated, untaught, unpractised, °uncontrolled, °disobedient, °naughty, °bad, °wilful, wayward, unrestrained, °erratic, unpredictable, °unruly, °wild: *The sergeant has taken quite a few undisciplined recruits and knocked them into shape.*

undisguised *adj.* °open, °out-and-out, unmistakable, °overt, unconcealed, unreserved, unrestrained, unfeigned, unpretended, °obvious, °evident, °patent, °clear, °explicit, °transparent, °sincere, °heartfelt, unalloyed, °unmitigated: *They regarded the traitor with undisguised contempt.*

undisputed *adj.* unquestioned, °unquestionable, beyond °question, accepted, acknowledged, admitted, °indisputable, indubitable, undoubted, °certain, °sure, unmistakable, °definite, °explicit, °clear, (self-)°evident, °obvious, uncontested, unchallenged, incontestable, irrefutable, °incontrovertible, undeniable, conclusive: *He proved once again that he is the undisputed heavyweight champion of the world.*

undistinguished *adj.* °ordinary, commonplace, °common, °everyday, run-of-the-mill, °pedestrian, unexceptional, °plain, °homespun, °simple, °prosaic, unremarkable; °mediocre, middling, °indifferent, unexciting, unimpressive, unpretentious, *Brit* °homely, *Colloq* °so so, no °great shakes, no big deal, °nothing to write home about, °nothing °special *or* °unusual *or* °extraordinary: *It was an undistinguished modern building near the roundabout.*

undivided *adj.* **1** °whole, °entire, unbroken, uncut, °intact, unseparated, °complete, unsplit: *The family lands remained undivided for generations.* **2** undiverted, °whole, °entire, °devoted, concentrated, °full, °complete, °exclusive, undistracted: *You have my undivided attention.*

undo *v.* **1** °loosen, °loose, °open, unfasten, unhook, unlace, unzip, unsnap, unbutton, untie, unpin; unlock, unbolt: *Help me undo my blouse. Don't undo the gate—you'll let the dogs out.* **2** unwrap, uncover, °open, untie, unbind: *Why have you allowed the children to undo their Christmas presents a week early?* **3** °cancel, annul, rescind, nullify, °void, declare null and °void, °reverse, invalidate: *If one could undo things there would be no such thing as regret.*

undoing *n.* **1** °ruin, ruination, °destruction, devastation, °defeat, °downfall, °overthrow, °fall, °collapse, descent, debasement, °degradation, abasement, mortification, °humiliation, °shame, °disgrace: *It is not easy to identify the factors that brought about the demagogue's undoing.* **2** °curse, °misfortune, bane, °affliction, °trouble, °blight: *As the novelists would have it, a beautiful woman was his undoing.*

undone¹ *adj.* **1** ruined, °lost, wrecked, crushed, destroyed, devastated, shattered, brought to °ruin, defeated, prostrated, °overcome: *Brian was completely undone by that gold-digging heart-breaker he met in Caracas. If the headmaster finds out about the glue, we are undone!* **2** °open, °loose, loosened, untied, unfastened, °detached, unhooked, unlaced, unzipped, unsnapped, unbuttoned, unpinned, unstuck: *Your shoelaces are undone. The knot came undone.*

undone² *adj.* unaccomplished, uncompleted, °incomplete, unfinished, omitted, neglected, left (out), skipped, missed, passed over, forgotten, unattended to: *From this list of chores, how many are still undone?*

undoubtedly *adv.* indubitably, without (a) °doubt, indisputably, unquestionably, beyond (a *or* the shadow of a) °doubt, certainly, °definitely, °surely, assuredly, unmistakably, explicitly, °clearly, °obviously, incontestably, irrefutably, incontrovertibly, undeniably: *If they win, they will undoubtedly go to the pub to celebrate.*

unduly *adv.* **1** disproportionately, excessively, °overly, unnecessarily, inordinately, unreasonably, irrationally, unjustifiably, improperly, inappropriately: *He claimed that he was being unduly harassed by the police.* **2** immoderately, lavishly, profusely, extravagantly: *Don't be unduly generous in tipping our waiter—he did spill the soup in your lap.*

unearth *v.* °dig up, disinter, exhume; °excavate, dredge up, °mine, °quarry, °find, °pull *or* °root out, °come across, °discover, °turn up, expose, uncover: *The artefacts were unearthed at Boghazköy, ancient Hattusas. They had unearthed some evidence that would put him away for years.*

unearthly *adj.* **1** °supernatural, °unnatural, preternatural, unworldly, other-worldly, °psychic(al), extramundane, extraterrestrial, extrasensory, supersensory, out-of-(the-)body, asomatous, incorporeal, °sublime, °celestial, astral: *They speculated about what unearthly experiences space travel might lead to.* **2** °weird, °bizarre, °macabre, °nightmarish, uncanny, °eerie, °strange, °ghostly, spectral, °unreal, *Literary* eldritch, *Colloq* spooky, creepy: *An unearthly creature appeared in a mist before her.* **3** °strange, °odd, °peculiar, °unusual, °abnormal, °absurd, out of the °ordinary, °extraordinary, °outrageous; °unheard-of, °unreasonable, *Colloq* °ungodly: *The baby wakes up at the unearthly hour of three o'clock every morning.*

uneducated *adj.* unschooled, untaught, uncultivated, unread, uncultured, °illiterate, unlettered, °ignorant, unenlightened: *It is debatable whether the fault for being uneducated lies with the student, the teacher, or the system.*

unemployed *adj.* out of °work, jobless, °idle, laid off, out of a °job, unoccupied, °inactive, *Brit* °redundant, *Colloq Brit* on the °dole, *Facetious* resting, at °liberty, at °leisure: *He has been unemployed ever since he was made redundant.*

unenthusiastic *adj.* °lukewarm, °cool, °cold, uninterested, °indifferent, °blasé, unresponsive, apathetic, unexcited, unimpressed: *Bentley presented the new design, but the directors were unenthusiastic and turned it down.*

unenviable *adj.* uncoveted, °undesirable, unwished for, unattractive: *He was given the unenviable task of informing the victim's family.*

unfamiliar *adj.* **1** °new, °novel, °unknown, unconventional, °unusual, °different, uncommon, °strange, °odd, °peculiar, °bizarre: *The man spoke in a tongue that was totally unfamiliar to me.* **2** Usually, **unfamiliar with**: unacquainted with, °unaccustomed to, °inexperienced in *or* with, °unused to, unconversant with, °uninformed about, °ignorant of, unpractised in, unskilled in *or* at, uninitiated in, unversed in: *The Americans were as unfamiliar with cricket as the Englishmen were with baseball.*

unflattering *adj.* **1** °harsh, °unsympathetic; °realistic, °stark, °candid: *Her hairstyle was unflattering and made her face look rather heavy.* **2** uncomplimentary, insulting, unfavourable: *Saying that I look just like my grandmother is quite unflattering.*

unfledged *adj.* °undeveloped, °immature, unmatured, °inexperienced, °green, °callow, °young, °raw, ungrown: *Take these unfledged recruits and turn them into men.*

unfold *v.* **1** °open (out *or* up), °spread (out), unfurl, °stretch out, °expand, uncoil, unwind, °straighten out: *Emerging from the pupa, it unfolds its wings and becomes a beautiful butterfly.* **2** °develop, evolve, °happen, take °place, °occur, be divulged, be disclosed *or* revealed: *What will unfold next in our little drama?*

unforeseen *adj.* unexpected, surprising, unanticipated, unpredicted, unlooked-for, unsought, unhoped for, undreamed of *or* undreamt of, unthought of, °startling, °surprise, °chance, fortuitous: *The sales manager's resignation was an unforeseen event.*

unfortunate *adj.* **1** unlucky, luckless; cursed, out of °luck, unblessed, *Colloq* down on (one's) °luck: *She was unfortunate enough to have married early and divorced late.* **2** °poor, °miserable, °wretched, °woebegone, °pathetic, °dismal, °unhappy, °forlorn, °pitiable, °doomed, ill-starred, star-crossed, ill-fated: *These unfortunate refugees have nowhere to go if we refuse them asylum.* **3** °deplorable, °terrible, °awful, catastrophic, °disastrous, °calamitous, °tragic, °lamentable, °regrettable, distressing, upsetting, °disturbing, °inauspicious, °grievous, °ruinous: *It was an unfortunate decision, and led to many problems. The flood was a most unfortunate sequel to the earthquake.*

unfounded *adj.* baseless, °groundless, °unwarranted, unjustified, unsupported, unsupportable, °unsound, unjustifiable, unattested, unproven: *Reports of a typhoid outbreak are completely unfounded.*

ungodly *adj.* **1** °wicked, °sinful, °impious, °blasphemous, °heretical, irreligious, iconoclastic, atheist(ic), anti-religious, °sacrilegious, demonic, demoniac(al), °diabolic(al), °satanic, °fiendish, hellish, °infernal; depraved, °godless, °corrupt, °immoral, °evil, iniquitous, °bad, °villainous, heinous, flagitious, °profane, °vile: *The crusaders believed that they had a duty to deliver Jerusalem from the ungodly heathens.* **2** °awful,

°outrageous, °indecent, °monstrous, °nasty, °dreadful, °terrible, appalling, °frightful, °shocking, *Colloq* God-awful, °unearthly, *Brit* °beastly: *Margot and I were subjected to another ungodly evening at the Dawsons'.*

ungovernable *adj.* °unruly, refractory, intractable, unmanageable, uncontrollable, °rebellious, °wild, °disobedient, unrestrainable, °incorrigible: *The nursemaid was saddled with two ungovernable children whom she had to cosset.*

ungraceful *adj.* **1** °awkward, °clumsy, ungainly, lubberly, *Colloq* all °thumbs, butter-fingered, *Slang US and Canadian* klutzy: *People in the aerobics class are always ungraceful to start off with.* **2** inelegant, graceless, °coarse, °crude, inartistic, °vulgar, °tasteless, unaesthetic, °unrefined, barbarous, unlovely, °ugly, unharmonious, unattractive, ill-proportioned, unsymmetric(al), asymmetric(al): *Some regard the Albert Memorial as a paragon of ungraceful Victorian design.*

ungracious *adj.* °discourteous, °overbearing, churlish, gauche, °rude, uncivil, °impolite, ill-bred, bad-mannered, unmannerly, ungentlemanly, unladylike, °gruff, °bluff, °brusque, °abrupt, °surly, curmudgeonly: *It was ungracious of him not to acknowledge the help of his staff.*

ungrateful *adj.* unthankful, unappreciative, °rude; °selfish, °heedless: *That ungrateful wretch never thanked me for all my help.*

unguarded *adj.* **1** incautious, °unwary, °careless, °inattentive, °heedless, inobservant, °inadvertent, °unthinking, unwatchful, unvigilant: *He let the intruder past him in an unguarded moment.* **2** °defenceless, unprotected, undefended, unfortified, °open, uncovered, exposed, °vulnerable: *The sentry insisted that he had left his post unguarded for only a few minutes.* **3** °indiscreet, °careless, °imprudent, unwise, °hasty, °unthinking, °thoughtless; guileless, incautious: *He was anxious to restore good relations after his unguarded remarks about their associates.*

unhappy *adj.* **1** °sad, depressed, °blue, °dejected, °melancholy, °despondent, downcast, °gloomy, °downhearted, dispirited, heavy-hearted, long-faced, disconsolate, °sorrowful, °miserable, crestfallen, cheerless, °forlorn, low-spirited, °glum, distressed, °tearful, *Formal* lachrymose, *Colloq* down, *Slang US* bummed out: *Mary is very unhappy that John is to be away a whole month.* **2** °unlucky, °unfortunate, unpropitious, °inauspicious, unfavourable, luckless, hapless, cursed, °wretched, ill-omened, ill-fated, ill-starred, star-crossed, jinxed, °disastrous: *Let me tell you how this unhappy state of affairs came about.* **3** infelicitous, unfitting, °inappropriate, unsuitable, unsuited, °wrong, inexpedient, °ill-advised, °poor, °unfortunate: *Vivian was an unhappy choice as his successor.*

unhealthy *adj.* **1** ailing, unwell, °ill, °sickly, °infirm, °feeble, °frail, debilitated, °unsound, °sick, in °poor *or* °delicate health *or* condition, °indisposed, °invalid, valetudinary: *The boys had pasty, unhealthy faces.* **2** °unwholesome, °harmful, noxious, °detrimental, insalubrious, damaging, °injurious, °destructive, malign: *The doctor said that this climate is unhealthy for people with respiratory disorders.* **3** °risky, °dangerous, °perilous, life-threatening, touch-and-go: *You might find it unhealthy to criticize the government here.*

unheard-of *adj.* **1** °unknown, °unfamiliar, °obscure, °unidentified, °nameless, °unsung: *She is busy trying to promote some unheard-of sculptor.* **2** unimaginable, undreamed of *or* undreamt of, unprecedented, unimagined, °unbelievable, °inconceivable, °unusual: *They took the unheard-of step of requiring that refunds be paid. Her starting salary is an unheard-of £100,000.* **3** °shocking, offensive, °outrageous, °disgraceful, °extreme, °unthinkable, °outlandish: *The victims were subjected to unheard-of tortures.*

unheralded *adj.* unannounced, unpublicized, unadvertised; unexpected, °surprise, unanticipated, °unforeseen, unpredicted: *Published by some obscure company, the book turned out to be an unheralded success.*

unhesitating *adj.* **1** °swift, °rapid, quick, °immediate, instantaneous, °prompt, °ready, unhesitant: *The response was an unhesitating 'No!'* **2** unfaltering, unwavering, °wholehearted, °unqualified, unswerving, undeviating, °staunch, °steadfast, °implicit, °resolute: *We appreciate your unhesitating devotion to duty.*

unhurried *adj.* leisurely, unrushed, °easy, °easygoing, °casual, °gradual, °deliberate, °steady, °sedate, °calm: *We proceeded at an unhurried pace, eventually arriving at dusk at the castle gates.*

unidentified *adj.* °nameless, anonymous, °unknown, unmarked, unnamed, °unfamiliar, unrecognized, °mysterious: *The police found the body of an unidentified woman in the park.*

uniform *adj.* **1** °homogeneous, °consistent, unvaried, unchanged, unaltered; unvarying, unchanging; °invariable, unchangeable, unalterable, regimented, °standard; ordered, °orderly, °equal, °even, °like, °identical; °alike: *The mixture is uniform throughout. The rules are uniform for everyone. Line up in ten uniform rows of ten each.* **2** °even, unbroken, °smooth, °regular, °flat: *Not one irregularity marred the uniform surface of the plain.* —*n.* **3** livery, °habit, °regalia, °costume, °outfit; regimentals: *When I next saw him, he was in the uniform of a Gestapo officer.*

uniformity *n.* **1** °regularity, similarity, sameness, homogeneity, consistency, °symmetry, evenness, invariability, unchangeability, similitude, conformity, °agreement, concord, °accord, harmoniousness; °harmony, concordance, accordance, conformance, correspondence: *One can easily see the lack of uniformity even in what is supposed to be a classless society.* **2** dullness, monotony, drabness, sameness, °tedium, featurelessness, flatness, invariability, lack of °variety, changelessness: *After a few days, the uniformity of the routine began to get on my nerves.*

unify *v.* consolidate, °unite, °combine, °amalgamate, coalesce, bring together, °fuse, °join, °weld, °merge, confederate, °integrate: *The separate elements were unified into a coherent whole. Successive Reform Bills unified the nation.*

unimpeded *adj.* unblocked, unchecked, °free, unconstrained, unrestrained, unhindered, unhampered, unencumbered, °open, untrammelled, unrestricted: *They insist on having unimpeded access to the files.*

unimposing *adj.* unimpressive, nugatory, trivial, °trifling, °minor, unimportant, °puny, inconsiderable, °negligible: *It was an unimposing building sandwiched between two office blocks. A more unimposing little cockalorum has seldom assailed my sensibilities.*

uninformed *adj.* °ignorant, nescient, unknowledgeable, unenlightened, °uneducated, unschooled, untutored, untaught, uninstructed, °unaware, incognizant: *The problem is not that they are stupid, merely uninformed and misinformed.*

uninhabited *adj.* °desolate, °empty, °abandoned, °deserted, unoccupied, °vacant, vacated, tenantless, untenanted; °desert, unpopulated, unpeopled, °trackless, depopulated, °waste, °barren: *Tristan da Cunha, in the south Atlantic, is an uninhabited island.*

uninhibited *adj.* °wild, unchecked, unbridled, uncurbed, intemperate, °boisterous, unrepressed, unconstrained, unrestrained, °uncontrolled, unselfconscious, unreserved, °relaxed, °casual, °easygoing, °free (and °easy), °open, °frank, °candid, °outspoken, *Colloq* upfront: *Their behaviour at the party was totally uninhibited. I will tell you what I think only if I can be totally uninhibited about it.*

uninviting *adj.* °repulsive, °repellent, °offensive, unappealing, unattractive, unpleasant, °disagreeable, °distasteful, unappetizing, °unsavoury, sickening, °revolting, °obnoxious, °nasty, °disgusting, *Brit* off-putting: *The food he put on the table was cold and uninviting.*

union *n.* **1** uniting, °unity, combining, °combination, joining, °junction, conjoining, conjunction, allying, °alliance, associating, °association, coalition, amalgamating, °amalgamation, fusing, fusion, marrying, °marriage, confederating, confederation, confederacy, synthesizing, °synthesis, mixing, °mixture, °federation, togetherness: *Monarchies favour the union of Church and State.* **2** °alliance, °association, °organization, °society, °circle, °fraternity, °club, °fellowship, °team, °ring, °gang, °syndicate, coalition, °party, confederation, confederacy, °federation, Bund, °league, consortium, bloc, cartel, °trust: *The countries formed a union to control their joint economies.* **3** °joint, °seam, °splice, °junction, conjunction, °graft, °weld; coupling: *The union between the two pieces may be stronger than the material itself.* **4** °agreement, °accord, °harmony, harmoniousness, congruity, coherence, compatibility, unanimity, °unity: *The union of the various elements in the painting was skilfully effected.*

unique *adj.* **1** °single, lone, (°one and) °only, °solitary, °one of a kind, *sui generis*: *Natural forces conspired to create this unique situation.* **2** unequalled, °unparalleled, unrivalled, °incomparable, inimitable, °peerless, unmatched, unsurpassed, unexcelled, second to none: *Stimble's genius is unique in the annals of cardiology.*

unison *n.* **in unison (with)**: in °harmony, together, corresponding °exactly, in (perfect) °accord, consonant, °harmonious: *Why is his singing never in unison with ours? We all responded in unison with a rousing 'No!'*

unit *n.* °element, component, °entity, °part, °item, constituent, °piece, °portion, °segment, °section, module: *The units fit together almost seamlessly.*

unite v. **1** °combine, °unify, °merge, coalesce, °amalgamate, °mix, °mingle, commingle, intermix, °blend, consolidate, °fuse: *The splinter parties have united to form a coalition.* **2** °join (forces), °unify, °wed, °marry, °link, °connect, °merge: *The two families are united by marriage.* **3** °bond, °fuse *or* °weld *or* solder *or* °glue *or* °stick *or* °tie *or* °bind *or* °fasten *or* °fix *or* °fit (together): *Unite these pieces and the job is done.*

united adj. **1** unified, °common, °mutual, combined, merged, coalesced, pooled, shared, collective, °joint, amalgamated, connected: *The new law will serve our united interests.* **2** °joint, cooperative, °common, communal, collaborative, synergetic *or* synergistic, collective, concerted, coordinated, allied; partnership: *We must make a united effort if we are to survive.* **3** agreed, unanimous, in °agreement, of °one °mind, of °like °mind *or* opinion, like-minded, in °accord, in °harmony, °harmonious: *We are united in our assessment of last night's performance.*

unity n. **1** consistency, unanimity, constancy, °uniformity, sameness, consensus, °agreement, concord, concordance, °accord, °solidarity, compatibility, concurrence, continuity, consentaneousness, °rapport, °sympathy, like-mindedness: *All members of the association enjoy a unity of purpose.* **2** oneness, °singularity, °integrity, singleness, congruity, °uniformity, congruousness, homogeneity, °identity, sameness, °resemblance, °likeness, similarity, similitude: *If there is little unity between your ideas and those of the organization, perhaps you should resign.* **3** unification, uniting, °combination: *In unity is strength.*

universal adj. **1** °prevalent, °prevailing, °general, worldwide, widespread, ubiquitous, omnipresent, °limitless, °unlimited, °common, pandemic, °epidemic: *The end of the 20th century is marked by a universal preoccupation with greed.* **2** cosmic, °infinite, °boundless, °limitless, °unlimited, measureless, °endless, uncircumscribed, all-inclusive, all-embracing, all-encompassing, wide-ranging, °comprehensive: *Renaissance man was regarded as possessing universal knowledge.*

universally adv. in every case *or* instance, in all cases *or* instances, unexceptionally, without exception, uniformly, °always, invariably: *In those days, it was universally accepted that the earth was flat.*

universe n. **1** cosmos, °creation, macrocosm: *What arrogance makes man believe that in all the vast universe God pays him any heed?* **2** °world, bailiwick, °sphere, °province, °domain, °circle, °milieu, °territory, corner, °quarter, microcosm: *Such behaviour may be acceptable in her tiny universe.*

unkempt adj. dishevelled, uncombed, tousled, disarranged, ungroomed, wind-blown, °untidy, disordered, mussed (-up), messy, messed-up, °bedraggled, °shaggy, scruffy, rumpled, slovenly, frowzy *or* frouzy *or* frowsy, blowzy, *Archaic* draggle-tailed, *Colloq* °sloppy: *Mother would refuse to allow us to the table if we were unkempt.*

unkind adj. °inconsiderate, unthoughtful, °thoughtless, unfeeling, unconcerned, insensitive, unkindly, °unsympathetic, uncharitable, unchristian, uncaring, hard-hearted, °heartless, flinty, °hard, °rigid, °callous, °tough, °inflexible, unyielding, unbending, °severe, °harsh, °stern, °cruel, °mean, °inhuman: *It was very unkind of you to refuse the beggar.*

unknown adj. **1** unrecognized, °unfamiliar, °strange, unnamed, anonymous, °nameless, °unidentified; °obscure, °unheard-of, little-known, °humble, °undistinguished, °unsung: *Some unknown person left this package for you. Bill is in some unknown place for the weekend. An unknown poet won the competition.* **2** °unfamiliar, unexplored, uninvestigated, unresearched, unrevealed, °mysterious, °uncharted, °unidentified, °dark: *We were now going into unknown territory.* **3** unbeknownst, °untold, unrevealed: *Unknown to me, the thieves were at that moment breaking in through the kitchen window.*

unlamented adj. unmissed, unmourned, unbemoaned, unbewailed, unloved: *They destroyed a statue of the late, unlamented Joseph Stalin.*

unlawful adj. °illegal, °illicit, against the °law, °illegitimate, under the table, under the counter, °criminal, felonious; outlawed, banned, prohibited, forbidden, interdicted, disallowed, proscribed, *verboten;* °unauthorized, unlicensed, unsanctioned: *Unlawful payments had been made to councillors. Gambling has been declared unlawful in that county.*

unlike adj. **1** °different (from), °dissimilar (to), unalike, °distinct (from), °opposite (from *or* to), contrasting *or* contrastive (with *or* to), °separate (from), °divergent (from), °incompatible (with), distinguishable (from), far apart (from), °far (from), °distant (from), ill-matched (with), unequal (to), unequivalent (to): *His notions of right and wrong are unlike those of other people. Although they're brothers, they look quite unlike each other.* **2** atypical, uncharacteristic, untypical: *It is unlike you to complain.* —*prep.* **3** °different from, differing from, in contradistinction to, in °contrast with *or* to, °dissimilar from, °distinct from, °opposite from *or* to, contrasting with *or* to, °divergent from, °incompatible with, distinguishable from, ill-matched with, unequal to, unequivalent to: *Unlike you, I've been there and know what it's like.*

unlikely adj. **1** °improbable, °doubtful, dubious, °remote, °unthinkable, unimaginable, °inconceivable, °implausible: *His story was unlikely, but she decided to believe him. It is not unlikely that he will come even if we ask him to stay away.* **2** °unseemly, °inappropriate, unfit, unfitting, unsuitable, uncongenial, objectionable, °unbecoming, °unacceptable, unattractive, °distasteful: *Claire had seldom seen a more unlikely prospect for a husband.* **3** unpropitious, °unpromising, °inauspicious: *The tiny shop seemed an unlikely place to find a great treasure.*

unlimited adj. **1** unrestricted, unrestrained, °limitless, unconstrained, °unqualified, °full, °absolute, unconditional, far-reaching, unchecked, °uncontrolled: *He has unlimited authority to issue all the paper money he wishes.* **2** °limitless, °boundless, °endless, °vast, unbounded, °immense, °immeasurable, measureless, °numberless, innumerable, °inexhaustible, interminable, never-ending, °infinite, myriad, °extensive: *As the wealthiest woman in the world, she has unlimited resources to do as she pleases.*

unload v. °empty, °dump, unpack, offload, °discharge; disburden, unburden: *We unloaded the cargo at Sulawesi. The camels must be unloaded every night.*

unmarried adj. °single, unwed(ded), bachelor, spinster, old-maid, °maiden, °unattached, unengaged, unbetrothed, unplighted, unpromised, °free, uncommitted: *He was thirty-five, unmarried, and lived alone in a tiny flat.*

unmentionable adj. **1** unspeakable, unutterable, °ineffable, °taboo, °scandalous, forbidden, interdicted; °inexpressible: *I will not have Karen or her unmentionable boyfriend in this house again!* **2** °disgraceful, °indecent, °immodest, °shameful, °shocking, appalling, °dishonourable, indescribable, °obscene, °filthy: *In carnivals, geeks do unmentionable things with live chickens.*
—n. **3 unmentionables**: °underclothes, underclothing, underwear, undergarments, lingerie, *Archaic* small-clothes, *Colloq* underthings, undies, *Brit* smalls, *US* skivvies: *The woman next door insists on hanging out her unmentionables in full view of the whole street.*

unmerciful adj. °merciless, pitiless, unsparing, °unkind, °relentless, unpitying, °heartless, stony-hearted, hard-hearted, flinty, unfeeling, °unsympathetic, unforgiving, °mean, °cruel, °savage, °brutal, brutish, °vicious, barbarous: *The boys gave him an unmerciful beating for cheating.*

unmitigated adj. °undiluted, unalloyed, unmixed, untempered, unmoderated, unmodified, unabated, unlessened, undiminished, unreduced, unrelieved, °oppressive, unalleviated, unmollified, unsoftened, °relentless, °unqualified, °out-and-out, °thorough, thoroughgoing, °outright, °downright, °categorical, °absolute, °immoderate, °sheer, °complete, consummate, °total, °perfect, °true, °pure, arrant, utter, °plain: *That man is an unmitigated bore. The project was an unmitigated disaster.*

unmoved adj. °cool, aloof, °calm, °collected, °unaffected, untouched, °unsympathetic, unstirred, undisturbed, apathetic, stoical, °impassive, °dispassionate, unemotional, unfeeling, unconcerned, °indifferent, unreactive, unresponsive, °stolid, °stony, adamant, stony-hearted, hard-hearted: *Despite her child's tears, she remained totally unmoved.*

unnatural adj. **1** *Derogatory* abnormal, °perverse, °perverted, °monstrous, °unusual, °peculiar, °strange, aberrant, °improper, °unseemly; *Slang* kinky, *Chiefly Brit* °bent: *There was a scandal when the senator was found to have engaged in some unnatural act.* **2** sodomitic(al), bestial, tribadic, tribadistic: *They still coyly referred to homosexual activities as 'unnatural acts'.* **3** uncharacteristic, out of °character, °odd, °peculiar, °strange, unexpected, °abnormal, °unusual: *Isn't it unnatural for someone who has won the sweepstakes to look so unhappy?* **4** °laboured, °forced, °stilted, °stiff, restrained, °artificial, °false, °insincere, feigned, contrived, °affected, °mannered, self-conscious, °theatrical, stagy: *She has an irritating, unnatural laugh.* **5** °outlandish, °weird, uncanny, °strange, °odd, °unaccountable, °supernatural, preternatural, °queer, °grotesque, °bizarre,

°extraordinary, °eccentric, freakish: *Let me tell you about the unnatural events that took place in that house.*

unnecessary adj. unneeded, °needless, unrequired, °dispensable, °disposable, °expendable, unwanted, °surplus, °superfluous, supererogatory, inessential, unessential, °non-essential: *The children were asleep, so we asked the workmen to avoid making any unnecessary noise.*

unnerve v. °upset, °agitate, °perturb, °ruffle, °fluster, °rattle, °discomfit, unsettle, disconcert, °dismay, °intimidate, °stun, stupefy, *Colloq* °shake (up), faze: *Peter drove home slowly: the accident he had seen had unnerved him.*

unnoticed adj. unnoted, overlooked, unobserved, undiscovered, unremarked, unmarked, unperceived; unseen, unheard: *Fortunately, Martha's nasty aside went unnoticed.*

unobtrusive adj. °inconspicuous, unostentatious, low-key, °retiring, °modest, self-effacing, unpresuming, unpretentious, unassuming, °quiet, °humble, unaggressive, unassertive, non-assertive, °subdued, °reserved, °reticent, suppressed: *Agatha may seem unobtrusive, but she's a tigress when aroused.*

unofficial adj. °informal, °unauthorized, undocumented, off the °record, °private, °secret, unpublicized, unannounced: *The builder acknowledged having had unofficial meetings with the council.*

unopened adj. closed, °shut: *The book lay, unopened, on the bedside table.*

unorthodox adj. °irregular, unconventional, °nonconformist, unconforming, nonconforming, aberrant, aberrational, °deviant, heteroclite, °unusual, °abnormal, uncustomary, uncommon: *Roebuck's unorthodox methods almost lost him his job.*

unpaid adj. **1** °payable, °outstanding, owed, owing, °due, unsettled: *In the end he absconded, leaving a pile of unpaid bills.* **2** unsalaried, °voluntary, volunteer, °honorary, *US* dollar-a-year: *On retirement, she took an unpaid job with Oxfam.*

unpalatable adj. °distasteful, °disagreeable, unpleasant, °unsavoury, unappetizing, unattractive, °repugnant, °nasty, °offensive; °rancid, °sour, °off, turned, °bitter, inedible, uneatable: *Without an education, they are often offered the unpalatable jobs. We found heavy claret totally unpalatable with the sole.*

unparalleled adj. unequalled, °incomparable, °matchless, °peerless, unrivalled, unmatched, inimitable, unexcelled, °superior, °supreme, °superlative, unsurpassed, °unusual, °special, °singular, °rare, °unique, °exceptional, consummate: *In our experience, the food and service aboard the Normandie were unparalleled.*

unperfumed adj. unscented, °plain, °natural: *This deodorant is available in sandalwood, forest pine, mint, or unperfumed.*

unpopular adj. out of °favour, in bad odour, unliked, disliked, shunned, avoided, snubbed, ignored, unsought after, unaccepted, unwanted, rejected, °unwelcome, °undesirable; unloved, friendless: *New taxes are always unpopular. James had always been an unpopular boy at school.*

unprejudiced adj. unbigoted, unbiased, °impartial, unjaundiced, °just, °fair, °objective, °disinterested, fair-minded, °non-partisan,

°liberal, open-minded, undogmatic: *An unprejudiced opinion would be difficult to find, since everyone has an axe to grind.*

unpremeditated *adj.* °unprepared, unplanned,
unarranged, uncontrived, unstudied,
°coincidental, °spontaneous, spur-of-the-
moment, last-minute, impromptu,
°extemporaneous *or* extemporary, extempore,
ad lib, °offhand, °casual, °impulsive, °natural,
°involuntary, °automatic, °unconscious, *Colloq*
off the cuff: *I had no inkling of her plans, so my
running into her was entirely unpremeditated. Her
immediate, unpremeditated reaction was to run away.*

unprepared *adj.* **1** unready, surprised, °taken
aback, (caught) napping *or* off guard,
°dumbfounded *or* dumfounded, at sixes and
sevens, *Colloq* (caught) with (one's) °pants
down, *Brit* caught on the hop, *US* asleep at the
switch: *The sudden squall found us unprepared and
we lost a sail.* **2** unfinished, °incomplete, uncompleted: *Dinner was still unprepared at eight
o'clock.* **3** unwarned, unreadied, not set up, not
forewarned: *I was unprepared for the strange events
that followed.* **4** See **unpremeditated**, above.

unprofessional *adj.* **1** °unbecoming,
°improper, unethical, unprincipled, °unseemly,
undignified, unfitting, unbefitting, °unworthy,
unscholarly, negligent, °lax: *The Medical Association is quick to act against doctors whose conduct
might be judged unprofessional.* **2** amateurish,
°amateur, inexpert, °inexperienced, untrained,
untutored, unschooled, °incompetent, unskilled,
unskilful, °inferior, second-rate, °inefficient,
°poor, °shoddy, low-quality, °sloppy: *It was an
astonishingly unprofessional way to audit
accounts.* **3** non-technical, unspecialized,
non-specialist, °lay, °everyday, °ordinary, °plain
(English), understandable: *What does all that
gobbledegook mean when translated into unprofessional language?*

unprofitable *adj.* **1** profitless, ungainful, unremunerative, unfruitful, non-profit-making;
breaking even; losing, loss-making: *The last
quarter was unprofitable for car manufacturers.*
2 °bootless, °pointless, °purposeless,
unavailing, °futile, °useless, unproductive,
°worthless, °ineffective, °inefficient: *Having
employees sitting about waiting for the telephone to
ring is unprofitable.*

unpromising *adj.* °inauspicious, unpropitious,
unfavourable, °gloomy, °ominous, adverse,
°portentous, baleful, °hopeless: *The forecast for
the economy looked unpromising yesterday but has
suddenly brightened.*

unqualified *adj.* **1** °ineligible, unfit, untrained,
ill-equipped, unsuited, unequipped,
°unprepared: *He was rejected as unqualified for the
job of repairing computers.* **2** unrestricted, unreserved, unconditional, °categorical, °outright,
°unmitigated, °downright, °out-and-out, °pure
(and °simple), °true, °perfect, utter, °absolute,
consummate: *If he told you that he flew jets in the
RAF, he is an unqualified liar. Cato's unqualified
'Delenda est Cartago' was echoed in every speech he
made in the Roman senate.*

unquenchable *adj.* insatiable, unslakeable *or*
unslakable, unsatisfiable, °inextinguishable,
unsuppressible, °irrepressible, °indestructible:
*She had an unquenchable thirst for knowledge. Those
principles have kindled an unquenchable fire in the
hearts of the oppressed.*

unquestionable *adj.* unexceptionable, indubitable, undoubted, °indisputable, incontestable,
unimpeachable, undeniable, °certain, °sure,
°positive, irrefutable, °manifest, °obvious,
°patent, °clear, °definite, °incontrovertible,
unequivocal, unmistakable, conclusive: *Their
integrity is unquestionable, and I have complete confidence in them.*

unreal *adj.* **1** °imaginary, °fantastic, chimerical,
°fanciful, °fancied, °illusory, make-believe,
phantasmagoric(al), phantasmal, °spectral,
figmental, °unrealistic, °non-existent: *Fear made
the whole scene unreal to Martha.* **2** °theoretical,
°hypothetical, °mythical, °imaginary, made-up,
°fictitious, make-believe, °fanciful: *Although the
example is unreal, it will serve its purpose in my
argument.* **3** °artificial, °synthetic, synthesized,
°mock, °false, °fake(d), °counterfeit,
°fraudulent, °dummy, °spurious, falsified,
°pretend(ed), °sham, pseudo, make-believe: *The
countryside looked a little unreal, too luxuriant and
too sculptured.*

unrealistic *adj.* **1** °impractical, illogical,
°unreasonable, unworkable, unrealizable,
°quixotic, °romantic, °fanciful, °visionary, delusional, delusive, delusory: *However exciting it is
to think of travelling faster than light, the notion is
unrealistic.* **2** °unreal, unlifelike, °unnatural,
unauthentic, non-representational, unrep-
resentative, °inaccurate: *The background paintings
are poorly done and unrealistic.*

unreasonable *adj.* **1** irrational, illogical,
°unthinking, °absurd, °foolish, °senseless,
°nonsensical, °mindless, brainless,
°thoughtless, °silly, °mad, °crazy, °insane,
idiotic, moronic, imbecilic, °stupid, fatuous,
°ridiculous, °ludicrous, laughable,
°preposterous, °far-fetched, °short-sighted,
unperceptive, unperceiving, undiscerning,
myopic, °blind: *Some people have an unreasonable
aversion to anything scientific. Is it unreasonable to
expect you to spend a little time with your mother?*
2 °excessive, °outrageous, °exorbitant,
°extravagant, °immoderate, extortionate,
°inordinate, °unconscionable, unjust,
°unwarranted, inequitable, unfair, unequal,
°improper, unjustified, unjustifiable,
uncalled-for: *The new tax puts an unreasonable
demand on those with lower incomes.*
3 °inappropriate, unapt *or* inapt, °unsuitable,
unbefitting, °impractical, °unrealistic: *His conduct was quite unreasonable for a man of the cloth.*

unrefined *adj.* **1** °coarse, °rude, °rough,
°unsophisticated, uncultured, °uncivilized,
uncultivated, unpolished, inelegant, ill-bred,
°impolite, °discourteous, unmannerly,
°ill-mannered, bad-mannered, ignoble,
°plebeian, undignified, unladylike, ungentle-
manlike, ungentlemanly, uncourtly,
°ungracious, °boorish, loutish, °gross, °vulgar,
uncouth, cloddish, bumbling, °awkward,
gauche: *Consider their background before criticizing
them for being unrefined.* **2** °impure, unpurified,
unclarified, °raw, °crude, °coarse, untreated,
unfinished, °natural, unprocessed: *The unrefined
ore is first washed thoroughly.*

unrelated *adj.* °independent, °separate,
°distinct, °different, °dissimilar, °incompatible,
°inappropriate, °foreign, °alien, unassociated,
unaffiliated, unconnected, uncoupled,
unlinked, unallied, uncoordinated: *Why raise a
totally unrelated issue?*

unreliable adj. °irresponsible, °disreputable; untrustworthy, undependable, °uncertain, °unstable, treacherous, °flimsy, °weak: *He is unreliable and unlikely to be there when you need him. The equipment was expensive, slow, and unreliable.*

unrepentant adj. unrepenting, unremorseful, impenitent, unapologetic, unregretful, unashamed, unembarrassed, unselfconscious, °remorseless, unreformed, unrehabilitated, unregenerate, recidivist or recidivistic or recidivous: *They were quite unrepentant, though they had seen for themselves the harm they had done.*

unresolved adj. °unsettled, °open, up in the air, °moot, °pending, °debatable, arguable, °problematic(al), °indefinite, °vague, open to °question, °questionable, unanswered, unsolved; undetermined, undecided, °uncertain, unsure, ambivalent, wavering, vacillating, °irresolute: *The matter of joining the monetary union remained unresolved. I am still unresolved on the issue.*

unrest n. disquiet, uneasiness, °distress, °anxiety, anxiousness, nervousness, °anguish, unease, °worry, °concern, °agitation, turmoil, °disturbance, °trouble, °strife, °agony: *The proximity of the huge army on our borders caused considerable unrest among the populace.*

unruly adj. unmanageable, °ungovernable, uncontrollable, °undisciplined, unregulated, °lawless, °disobedient, °insubordinate, °rebellious, °mutinous, fractious, refractory, contumacious, °obstreperous, °wilful, headstrong, °stubborn, °recalcitrant, intractable, °defiant, uncooperative, wayward, °disorderly, turbulent, °riotous, °tumultuous, °violent, °stormy, °tempestuous: *She had no idea of how to handle a capricious and unruly teenager. The first reading of the bill led to an unruly session of Parliament.*

unsatisfactory adj. °insufficient, °inadequate, °inferior, °poor, °unacceptable, displeasing, °disappointing, °unworthy, °inappropriate, °deficient, °weak, °wanting, lacking, unsuitable, °imperfect, °flawed, °defective, °faulty: *The report was unsatisfactory in that it failed to meet the committee's demands. Why put up with unsatisfactory workmanship?*

unsavoury adj. °distasteful, objectionable, unpleasant, °disagreeable, unappetizing, °unpalatable, °offensive, °repugnant, °obnoxious, °repellent, °nasty, °repulsive, °revolting, °disgusting, nauseating, sickening: *Her ex-husband is a totally unsavoury character. Even the most unsavoury swill tasted like ambrosia to the starving inmates.*

unscathed adj. unharmed, unhurt, uninjured, unmarked, untouched, undamaged, unscarred, unscratched, °safe and °sound, in one piece, as °new, *Archaic* scatheless, *Colloq* like °new: *Miraculously, he came out of the battle unscathed.*

unscrupulous adj. °unconscionable, conscienceless, unprincipled, amoral, unethical, °immoral, °dishonourable, °corrupt, °dishonest, °deceitful, °sly, cunning, °artful, insidious, °shifty, °sneaky, °slippery, roguish, knavish, °disingenuous, treacherous, °perfidious, °faithless, °false, untrustworthy, °wicked, °evil, *Colloq* °crooked: *Some people are totally unscrupulous in the pursuit of their ambitions.*

unseasonable adj. unsuitable, °inopportune, °inappropriate, untimely, ill-timed, inexpedient: *Unseasonable frosts in April caused severe damage to the flower buds.*

unseemly adj. **1** °improper, °unrefined, °unbecoming, indecorous, indelicate, unladylike, ungentlemanly, undignified, in poor or bad °taste, °disreputable, discreditable, °risqué, °naughty, °indecent, °shameful, °offensive, °lewd, °lascivious, °obscene, °rude, °coarse: *Out of desperation, they engaged in some unseemly activities.* **2** impolitic, unwise, °imprudent, inapt, °inappropriate, °inopportune, °inconvenient, uncalled-for, unsuitable, °improper, inadvisable, °ill-advised, unbefitting, unfitting, out of °place or keeping, °awkward, °inauspicious, inexpedient, °unfortunate, ill-timed, untimely: *It would be unseemly for you to become involved with such a notorious individual.*

unselfish adj. °generous, °charitable, open-handed, ungrudging, unstinting, unsparing, giving, magnanimous, °philanthropic, °humanitarian, °free, °liberal, altruistic, °selfless, self-sacrificing: *We were all greatly impressed by her unselfish concern for the well-being of her colleagues.*

unsettled adj. **1** unfixed, °unstable, changing, varying, °variable, °changeable, °inconstant, ever-changing, °protean, unpredictable, °uncertain: *The weather remained unsettled all week. They told me of their unsettled life as gypsies.* **2** °disturbed, turbulent, riled, °agitated, disquieted, °upset, perturbed, ruffled, rattled, flustered, °restive, °restless, unnerved, *US* roiled: *It was being kept in the dark about Father that made us feel unsettled.* **3** disoriented, °confused, °mixed up, unorganized, disorganized, °disorderly, disordered, °tumultuous: *The unsettled situation in the east worried us.* **4** See unresolved, above: *Some questions about Ian remain unsettled.*

unsettling adj. unnerving, upsetting, °disturbing, perturbing, discomfiting, °disconcerting: *Sorry for being a wet blanket, but I have had some unsettling news from home.*

unsightly adj. °ugly, °hideous, awful-looking, °horrible, frightful-looking, unattractive, unprepossessing, unlovely, unpretty, °plain, *US and Canadian* °homely: *The property borders an unsightly junk-yard.*

unsocial adj. unsociable, unfriendly, °cool, °cold, °chilly, °aloof, uncongenial, unamiable, unforthcoming, °standoffish, °inhospitable, °withdrawn, °reserved, °solitary, °retiring, °distant, °detached, °reclusive, hermitic(al), eremitic(al), anchoritic or anchoretic(al); antisocial, °misanthropic, °hostile: *Erwin, who prefers to be alone, is definitely unsocial. Donna, who despises other people, is unsocial for different reasons.*

unsolicited adj. unlooked-for, unsought, unsought after, unrequested, °unasked for, uncalled-for, °gratuitous, uninvited; *Colloq US* over-the-transom: *Tanya is always offering unsolicited advice on every conceivable subject. The publishers receive scores of unsolicited book manuscripts each week.*

unsophisticated adj. **1** °naïve, °inexperienced, °simple, °childlike, unworldly, °innocent, °ingenuous, °artless, guileless: *Is the unsophisticated consumer sufficiently protected against unscrupulous traders?* **2** °simple, °plain, uncomplicated, undetailed, uninvolved, °unrefined: *The computers of twenty years ago were unsophisticated compared with those of today.*

unsound *adj.* **1** °weak, °feeble, °frail, °rickety, °shaky, °ramshackle, °infirm, °unstable, wobbly, tottering, unsteady, broken-down, crumbling, disintegrating, °dilapidated, °defective, °imperfect, °faulty, decayed, °rotten: *The building inspector condemned the structure as unsound and unsafe.* **2** °unhealthy, °diseased, °ill, afflicted, in °poor °health, ailing, °sickly, °sick, unwell, °delicate, injured, wounded: *The attack of flu left him unsound in wind and limb.* **3** °insane, °mad, °psychotic, °unbalanced, °unstable, demented, °deranged: *The doctors said that she was still of unsound mind and ought not be released.* **4** illogical, °faulty, °flawed, fallacious, °untenable, °invalid, °groundless, °unfounded, °erroneous, °defective, °specious: *We thought that his arguments were unsound, so we rejected his recommendations.*

unspoiled *adj.* unspoilt, unsullied, °pristine, virgin, °whole, untainted, unstained, °immaculate, uncorrupted, unpolluted, °spotless, stainless: *The house has been preserved in its original condition, unspoiled by modern additions.*

unstable *adj.* **1** °changeable, °variable, unsteady, °inconstant, °inconsistent, °insecure, °capricious, °fickle, °irregular, unpredictable, °unreliable, °erratic, °volatile, fluctuating, °flighty, mercurial, vacillating, tergiversating, °indecisive, undecided, °irresolute, °indefinite, °unsettled: *He seems too unstable to maintain a long-standing relationship.* **2** See unsound, 1, above.

unsuccessful *adj.* **1** °unfortunate, unavailing, °vain, abortive, °useless, °bootless, °fruitless, unfruitful, unproductive, °ineffective, °ineffectual, °inefficacious, °worthless, °unprofitable, °sterile: *We made an unsuccessful attempt to regain control of the company.* **2** unlucky, hapless, °unfortunate, luckless, defeated, beaten, jinxed, cursed, foiled, frustrated, balked: *Trevor complained that he had been unsuccessful in business all his life.*

unsung *adj.* uncelebrated, unrecognized, unglorified, unexalted, unpraised, unhonoured, °unnoticed, disregarded, °unknown, anonymous, °unidentified, °nameless, °obscure, °insignificant, °inconspicuous: *I have no wish to add to the long list of unsung authors of the twentieth century.*

unsuspecting *adj.* unsuspicious, °unwary, unknowing, °ignorant, °unconscious, °gullible, credulous, °naïve, °ingenuous, °innocent, °trusting; °unaware, off guard: *Martin became an unsuspecting dupe in Lambert's plot to embezzle money from the bank.*

unsympathetic *adj.* uncaring, unconcerned, °callous, unfeeling, °unaffected, untouched, °unmoved, °indifferent, unemotional, °dispassionate, uncompassionate, unreactive, unresponsive, °impassive, °stolid, °cold, °cool, °aloof, unstirred, apathetic, insensitive, stoical, °stony, adamant, stony-hearted, hard-hearted, unpitying, pitiless, °ruthless: *We were unable to understand Taylor's unsympathetic attitude to the suffering around him.*

untamed *adj.* undomesticated, °wild, unbroken, unsubdued, uncontrollable, °savage, °fierce, feral, °ferocious: *In the story, the wolf boy behaves like an untamed beast.*

untarnished *adj.* unsoiled, unsullied, °immaculate, °spotless, unspotted, untainted, °faultless, uncorrupted, unfouled, °chaste, lily-white, undefiled, virginal: *Despite the obloquy heaped on his colleagues, his own reputation remained untarnished.*

untenable *adj.* insupportable *or* unsupportable, indefensible, unsustainable, unmaintainable, unjustified, unjustifiable, baseless, °groundless, °unfounded, °flawed, °faulty, °weak, illogical, °specious, °implausible, °unreasonable, °unsound: *It is beyond me why he holds so tenaciously to such untenable views.*

unthinkable *adj.* **1** °inconceivable, °unbelievable, unimaginable, °incredible, °incomprehensible, beyond °belief, °extraordinary, *Colloq* mind-boggling, *Slang* mind-blowing: *It seemed unthinkable that such a mild-mannered man could have been a mass murderer.* **2** °unacceptable, °absurd, illogical, °impossible, °improbable, °unlikely, out of the °question, °preposterous, °ridiculous, laughable, °ludicrous, *Colloq* not on: *It is simply unthinkable for her to go to the ball unattended.*

unthinking *adj.* **1** °thoughtless, °mindless, undiscriminating, unconsidered, unwitting, unreflecting, unthoughtful, irrational, °unreasonable, illogical, unperceptive, unperceiving, undiscerning, witless, brainless, °foolish, °senseless, °nonsensical, °rash, °stupid, °silly, °mad, °crazy, °insane, idiotic, moronic, imbecilic, °hasty, °short-sighted: *It was unthinking of me to ask her mother to go out to dinner with us.* **2** °inconsiderate, °impolite, °tactless, °rude, °thoughtless, undiplomatic, °discourteous, uncivil, °imprudent, unwise, °indiscreet, neglectful: *On the other hand, it would have been unthinking of me not to ask her mother.*

untidy *adj.* °disorderly, messy, dishevelled, °unkempt, slovenly, slatternly, °bedraggled, rumpled, frowzy *or* frouzy *or* frowsy, °sloppy, °dirty; littered, cluttered, °chaotic, °helter-skelter, jumbled, *Archaic* draggle-tailed, *Colloq US* mussy, mussed-up: *You should never go to the door looking so untidy. Ken's papers are always so untidy.*

untiring *adj.* unflagging, °determined, indefatigable, dogged, persevering, perseverant, °tireless, unwearying, unwearied, dedicated, unfailing, unfaltering, °steady: *Kim has always been an untiring perfectionist.*

untold *adj.* **1** countless, uncounted, uncountable, unnumbered, °numberless, innumerable, myriad, incalculable; °immeasurable, measureless, °unlimited: *Untold millions are lost through tax fraud each year.* **2** unrecounted, unnarrated, undescribed, unpublished, unrevealed, undisclosed, undivulged, unreported, °private, °hidden, °secret: *How many untold stories are there in the naked city?* **3** °inexpressible, unutterable, indescribable, unimaginable, °inconceivable, °unthinkable, unspeakable: *The untold agony that man went through because of his family's illnesses!*

untoward *adj.* **1** adverse, unfavourable, unpropitious, discouraging, °inopportune, °unpromising, °bleak, °inauspicious, °bad, °unfortunate: *The rainstorm created untoward conditions, causing the river to rise dangerously.* **2** °unbecoming, unfitting, °awkward, °inappropriate, unapt, unsuitable,

°improper, °impolite, °rude, °boorish, ungentlemanly, unladylike, indecorous, indelicate,
°unwarranted, uncalled-for, °unrefined,
°unseemly, unwise, °imprudent, undiplomatic,
°tactless, untactful, ill-conceived, °silly, °foolish,
°stupid, ill-timed, vexatious, vexing, irritating,
annoying: *Charles made some untoward remark about
the size of Sandra's feet.*

untried *adj.* untested, unproved *or* unproven,
°new: *He may be good at homes, but he is as yet
untried as the designer of a library.*

untrue *adj.* **1** unfaithful, °faithless, °disloyal,
°fickle, °capricious, undependable, °unreliable,
°dishonourable, untrustworthy, °false,
°hypocritical, °dishonest, °insincere, °two-faced,
duplicitous, °devious, °deceitful, treacherous,
°perfidious: *Only when I saw her with Henry did I
realize that Pauline had been untrue to me.*
2 °wrong, °false, °inaccurate, °incorrect,
°erroneous, misleading, °mistaken, distorted:
*What you said about Pauline was simply
untrue.* **3** °inexact, non-standard, substandard,
°imprecise, °imperfect: *How unfortunate for
legend had William Tell's aim been untrue!*

unused *adj.* **1** (°brand-)°new, untouched,
°pristine, °original, °intact, °fresh, firsthand: *He
sold me his unused computer for half what it
cost.* **2** °disused, °abandoned, °derelict, neglected, given up: *We hid in an old unused factory
building.* **3** unconsumed, °leftover, °remaining,
°left: *If dissatisfied with this product, return the
unused portion for a full refund.* **4 unused to**:
°unaccustomed to, °unfamiliar with,
°inexperienced in *or* at, amateurish at, unpractised in *or* at, uninitiated in: *I am quite unused
to doing that sort of thing.*

unusual *adj.* uncommon, °exceptional, atypical,
untypical, °different, unexpected, °singular,
out of the °ordinary, °extraordinary, °odd,
°peculiar, °curious, °bizarre, °strange, °queer,
°remarkable, °unique, freakish, unprecedented,
unconventional, °unorthodox, *Slang* off-the-wall:
*It takes an unusual person to be as charitable as Jean.
Don't you agree that an egg-laying mammal is a bit
unusual?*

unvarnished *adj.* °plain, °simple, °pure, unembellished, straightforward, °straight, °direct,
°honest, unelaborated, °naked, °stark, °sincere,
°frank, °candid, °outspoken: *My dear, let me tell
you the unvarnished truth about Marnie and Jim.*

unveil *v.* °reveal, °expose, uncover, °lay °bare *or*
°open, °bare, bring to °light: *They will unveil a
rival bid at tomorrow's meeting. Only after William
died did Cynthia unveil the truth about his double life.*

unwarranted *adj.* uncalled-for, °unasked (for),
unjustified, indefensible, unjust, unfair,
°unconscionable, °unworthy, °improper,
°inexcusable, °gratuitous, unmerited,
undeserved, unprovoked, °outrageous,
°excessive, °unreasonable, unrestrained, intemperate, untempered, °immoderate, undue,
°unnecessary: *The police were accused of unwarranted use of force in ejecting the rowdies from the
pub.*

unwary *adj.* °heedless, °careless, °hasty, incautious, °unguarded, °imprudent, °rash,
°foolhardy, °reckless, °thoughtless, °indiscreet,
°unthinking, °mindless, unwise: *Many perils
await the unwary traveller. It was unwary of you not
to lock the doors and windows.*

unwashed *adj.* **1** °dirty, uncleaned, unclean,
uncleansed: *Separate your personal things from
the unwashed laundry in the hamper.*
—*n.* **2 the (great) unwashed**: *Derogatory* the
rabble, the masses, the °mob, the plebs, °people
(at large *or* in general), the °population, the
°populace, the man *or* woman in the street,
Mr (& Mrs) Average, the working class(es), most
°people, the (silent) majority, *US* John Q. Public:
*The effort to sell expensive brandy to the great
unwashed failed miserably.*

unwelcome *adj.* **1** uninvited, unsought for,
unwished for, undesired, °undesirable, displeasing, unpleasing, °distasteful, unpleasant:
*My day was further ruined by the unwelcome arrival
of all those bills.* **2** unwanted, rejected, unaccepted, excluded; *persona non grata*, anathema:
*Following that episode, Curshaw was made to feel
unwelcome at the club.*

unwholesome *adj.* **1** °unhealthy, unhealthful,
°detrimental, deleterious, pernicious, insalubrious, unhygienic, insalutary, °harmful, noxious, toxic, °injurious, °destructive: *Fernthwaite
finally succumbed to the unwholesome climate and
had to be sent home.* **2** °corrupt, °immoral, °bad,
°wicked, °evil, °sinful, °perverted; demoralizing, depraved, °degrading, corrupting, perverting: *The social worker said it was wrong for a
child to be raised in such an unwholesome
atmosphere.* **3** °ill, ailing, °sickly, °sick, °pale,
°wan, anaemic, pallid, °pasty: *Their unwholesome
complexion comes from malnutrition.*

unwieldy *adj.* °awkward, °clumsy, °bulky, oversized, cumbersome, ungainly, unmanageable,
unhandy, unmanoeuvrable: *The huge oil tankers,
though economical, often proved unwieldy in the ports
they visited.*

unwonted *adj.* infrequent, °unusual, uncustomary, uncommon, °unfamiliar, unprecedented, °rare, °singular, atypical, °abnormal,
°peculiar, °odd, °strange, °irregular, unconventional, °unorthodox: *All this unwonted physical
exercise made them exhausted by evening.*

unworthy *adj.* **1** unequal, meritless, unmerited,
substandard, °inferior, second-rate, °menial,
°puny, °petty, °paltry, °unprofessional,
°mediocre, °despicable, °contemptible,
°dishonourable, ignoble, °disreputable, discreditable, °unqualified, °ineligible, unfit,
undeserving: *I consider Patrick an unworthy opponent.* **2 unworthy of**: °unbecoming to,
°inappropriate to, unsuitable for, unfit for, out
of °character for, °inconsistent with *or* for, out
of °place with *or* for, °incongruous with *or* for:
*That sort of petty haggling is unworthy of your
position and of you.*

upbeat *adj.* °positive, °optimistic, °sanguine,
°favourable, °cheerful, encouraging, heartening, °buoyant, light-hearted: *Christopher has a
very upbeat attitude towards life despite his age.*

upbraid *v.* °scold, °rebuke, °reprimand,
reproach, °berate, °castigate, °chastise, °reprove,
chide, censure, take to °task, *Colloq* °tell off,
tick off, °dress down, give a dressing-down,
give (someone) a piece of (one's) °mind, °tell
(someone) a thing or two, rake (someone) over
the coals, °jump on *or* all over, °bawl out, *US*
°chew out: *The boys were soundly upbraided for
going near the railway tracks.*

upbringing *n.* rearing, raising, training, °education, cultivation, nurture, °breeding: *The way one behaves through life is really a matter of upbringing.*

upheaval *n.* °upset, °unrest, commotion, °change, cataclysm, disruption, °disturbance, °disorder, °confusion, °chaos, °furore *or US* furor: *Those were times of drastic political upheaval in Asia.*

uphold *v.* °support, °maintain, °sustain, °preserve, °hold up, °defend, °protect, °advocate, °promote, espouse, °embrace, °endorse, °back, °champion, °stand by: *All demagogues claim to uphold democratic principles.*

upkeep *n.* **1** °maintenance, °repair, °support, °sustenance, °preservation, °conservation, °subsistence, °running, °operation: *The upkeep of the infrastructure came to ten per cent of the annual budget last year.* **2** (operating) °costs, (°running) °expenses, °outlay, °expenditure, *Brit* °overheads, oncosts, *US* °overhead: *Have you included upkeep in the annual expenses?*

upper *adj.* **1** higher (up), loftier, topmost, more °elevated, °uppermost: *Air is less dense in the upper parts of the atmosphere. Our flat is on an upper floor. Her best notes are sung in the upper register.* **2** higher, upland, more °elevated; (more) northerly, northern: *We visited the cataracts on the upper reaches of the Nile. We spent the holiday in upper Canada.* **3** later, more °recent: *These strata were laid down in the Upper Cretaceous period.* **4 upper case**: °capital letter(s), °capital(s), majuscule (letters *or* characters): *The heading ought to be in upper case.* **5 upper crust**: upper °class, °élite, aristocrats, °nobles, blue bloods, °wealthy, *US* Four Hundred: *Gregory thinks of himself as a member of the upper crust and won't associate with us.* **6 upper hand**: °advantage, °control, °authority, °power, °sway, °superiority, °supremacy, °command, dominance, ascendancy, *Colloq* °edge: *Purvis kowtows to whoever has the upper hand.*
—*n.* **7 on (one's) uppers**: °poor, °indigent, °destitute, poverty-stricken, *Colloq* °broke: *Stanley has been on his uppers since losing his job.*

upper-class *adj.* **1** °élite, aristocratic, blue-blooded, well-born, °noble, high-born, patrician, *Colloq* °upper crust: *Eunice comes from an upper-class Irish family.* **2** °high-class, °elegant, °fancy, °luxurious, °first-rate, de luxe, °royal, °regal, °sumptuous, *Colloq* swank(y), ritzy, °posh: *I'll have you know that we stayed only in upper-class hotels on our tour.*

uppermost *adj.* **1** highest, topmost, loftiest, °top: *These curious animals live in the uppermost branches of the trees.* **2** °foremost, °first, most °important *or* °prominent *or* °influential *or* °telling, °principal, °paramount, °pre-eminent, °predominant: *Uppermost in my mind is the safety of the children.*

uppish *adj.* °affected, putting on airs, °snobbish, °conceited, overweening, °self-important, *Colloq* uppity, snooty, °high and mighty, °hoity-toity, highfalutin *or* hifalutin, stuck-up, on (one's) high horse, *Slang* snotty, *Brit* toffee-nosed: *Even if she is in charge she doesn't have to be so uppish.*

upright *adj.* **1** °erect, °perpendicular, vertical, on °end, °straight up and down, °plumb, stand-up, °standing up, *Brit* upstanding: *Few upright columns of the Greek temple remained.*

2 °moral, °principled, high-minded, °ethical, °virtuous, upstanding, °straight, °righteous, straightforward, °honourable, °honest, °just, °trustworthy, unimpeachable, uncorrupt(ed), incorruptible, °decent, °good: *David had long been an upright member of the church council.*
—*n.* **3** °post, °pole, column, vertical, °perpendicular: *We need another upright to support the floor over here.*
—*adv.* **4** perpendicularly, vertically, upward(s), °straight up (and down): *The javelin was sticking upright out of the ground.* **5** °right side up: *Miraculously, the platter with the roast on it landed upright on the floor.*

uprising *n.* °rebellion, °revolt, °mutiny, °revolution, insurrection, rising, putsch, coup, coup d'état: *The government quelled the uprising with water cannons and tear gas.*

uproar *n.* clamour, hubbub, °disturbance, commotion, hullabaloo, brouhaha, °din, °racket, °pandemonium, °tumult, turmoil, pother, °outcry, °outburst, °bedlam, °agitation, °frenzy, °broil, °rumpus, °fuss; affray, °fracas, °brawl; *Colloq* hoo-ha, to-do, *US* hoop-la, *Brit* kerfuffle *or* carfuffle *or* kurfuffle: *The announcement of the new taxes caused a nationwide uproar.*

uproarious *adj.* **1** clamorous, °noisy, deafening, °tumultuous, turbulent, °tempestuous, °excited, frenzied, °rowdy, °riotous, °disorderly, °wild: *We had an uproarious party on New Year's Eve.* **2** °hilarious, °hysterical, (screamingly) °funny, side-splitting, *Colloq* too °funny for words, killing: *Leslie told his uproarious story about Colonel Cholmondley and the tiger.*

uproot *v.* **1** °transfer, °transplant, °move, °displace; °exile, °banish: *Finney has been uprooted five times in his career with the firm.* **2** deracinate, extirpate, °root out, °dig out, °pluck out, °tear out; °destroy, °demolish, °ruin, eradicate, annihilate, °kill, °devastate, °ravage: *Thousands of trees were uprooted by the hurricane.*

upset *v.* **1** °disturb, °agitate, °distress, unsettle, °put off, °put out, °perturb, disquiet, °fluster, °ruffle, °frighten, °scare, disconcert, °dismay, °trouble, °worry, °bother, discompose, make (someone) °nervous: *We once had a nanny who told the children horror stories just to upset them.* **2** °overturn, °capsize, °topple, up-end, °tip over, °knock over *or* down, invert, °turn °topsy-turvy *or* upside down, °spill: *That is the third time this week you have upset the cream jug.* **3** °disturb, derange, °disrupt, disarrange, °mess up, disorganize, °snarl up, °jumble, °muddle, *Colloq Brit* kerfuffle *or* carfuffle *or* kurfuffle: *The boys upset the entire house with their horseplay.* **4** °overthrow, °defeat, °beat, worst, thrash, °rout, °conquer, °overcome, °win out over, get the °better of, get *or* gain the °advantage over, °triumph over, be °victorious over, vanquish: *The question is whether the challenger will upset the champion in the Wimbledon finals.* **5** °defeat, °ruin, °spoil, °thwart, °interfere with, °destroy, °demolish, °mess up, °disturb, *Colloq* throw a *Brit* spanner in(to) *or US* monkey wrench into (the °works), *US* discombobulate, *Slang* °screw up, gum up, put the kibosh on, *Taboo slang* fuck up, *Brit* °bugger up: *Your coming early upset my plan to shampoo my hair.*
—*adj.* **6** capsized, overturned, upside down, bottom side up, inverted, reversed, toppled, tipped

over, °topsy-turvy: *We clung to the bottom of the upset boat till help arrived.* **7** °sick, °queasy: *Eve has an upset stomach and cannot go.* **8** perturbed, °disturbed, disquieted, °disconcerted, °agitated, distressed, °worried, troubled, unnerved, distracted, apprehensive, °nervous, frightened, °scared, °afraid: *We found Vladimir in a terribly upset state at Natasha's disappearance.* **9** disordered, °confused, disorganized, messed-up, jumbled, muddled, °disturbed, disarranged: *The house is never so upset as after a party.* **10** °angry, irate, °furious, beside oneself, °mad, *Colloq* fit to be tied, *Slang* freaked out: *Father was upset because I took the car without his permission.*
—*n.* **11** °defeat, upsetting, °conquest, °overthrow, °rout, °thrashing, °triumph, °victory: *We celebrated the upset of Queen's Park Rangers by Manchester United.* **12** °surprise, unexpected event or occurrence: *The upset of the season was when Carridoff won the Derby.*

upshot *n.* °result, °end (°result), °outcome, ending, conclusion, °termination, °effect, after-effect, fallout, °wake, backwash, °repercussion, after-clap, feedback, °resolution, culmination, denouement or dénouement, °issue, *Colloq* °pay-off, *US* wrap-up: *The upshot of the nasty business was that Bowles was sent to prison for life.*

upstart *n.* °parvenu(e), arriviste, nouveau riche, (social) climber, status-seeker, °pretender, °nobody: *That upstart husband of Dora's tried to get me to invest in some scheme of his.*

uptake *n.* comprehension, °understanding, apprehension, °grasp, °perception, °insight, perspicaciousness, perspicacity, perceptiveness, °sensitivity: *Billie was very quick on the uptake, and knew immediately what the man was after.*

urge *v.* **1** °press, °push, °drive, °force, impel, °speed, accelerate, °hurry, °rush, °hustle, °move, goad, °prod, egg on, °spur: *He urged his steed onward.* **2** °press, goad, °prod, egg on, °spur, °prompt, °induce, °incite, constrain, exhort, °encourage, °demand, °request, °ask, °plead (with), °beseech, °beg, entreat, importune: *We've been urging the police for months to investigate the goings-on at that house.* **3** °coax, °persuade, °induce, °prevail (up)on, °campaign (with), °sway, °influence, °talk into, °advise, °suggest, °counsel: *The agents urged them to sell their house while the market was good.* **4** °argue, °set forth, affirm, °state, °allege, assert, °hold, °advise, °advocate, °demand: *The residents urged that the planning board should deny permission for a supermarket.*
—*n.* **5** °pressure, °impetus, °desire, compulsion, impulse, °itch, °longing, yearning, °drive, °fancy, °hunger, °thirst, craving, *Colloq* yen: *We stopped because Corey felt the urge to have some ice-cream.*

urgency *n.* imperativeness, °pressure, °stress, °extremity, °importance, seriousness, importunity, °necessity, °need, insistence, exigency, °emergency: *She was told to ring back as a matter of some urgency.*

urgent *adj.* **1** °immediate, °instant, °imperative, °pressing, compelling, °vital, life-and-death or life-or-death, °important, °serious, °necessary, exigent, °rush, °emergency, °pressing, high-priority: *There was an urgent need to do something at once, so she screamed.* **2** supplicative, begging, °solicitous, °earnest, importunate,

°insistent, °loud, clamorous, °active, °energetic, pertinacious, °tenacious, °forceful, °firm: *Both parties were urgent in pressing for tax reform.*

urinate *v.* pass or make °water, *Technical* micturate; *Babytalk* (make a) wee, (go) wee-wee, (have a or *US* also take a) pee, (make) pee-pee, do number one, tinkle, piddle; *Euphemistic* go to the men's or ladies' (room), go to the °lavatory, excuse (oneself), wash (one's) hands, go to the bathroom, go to the powder-room; *Mincing* go to the little boys' or girls' room; *Colloq Brit* spend a penny, go to the loo, *Slang* (take or have a) piss, *Brit* have a or go for a slash: *One symptom of cystitis is pain when urinating.*

usage *n.* **1** °use, °custom, °habit, °practice, °routine, °convention, °form, °tradition: *British usage reflects decreasing use of the subjunctive mood.* **2** °treatment, °use, °management, handling, °operation, manipulation: *It would appear that the car has been subjected to some rough usage.*

use *v.* **1** °employ, make use of, put into °practice or °operation, °practise, utilize, °exercise, bring into play, have °recourse to, °resort to, put or press into °service, put to use, avail (oneself) of; °say, utter, °speak: *If you use a hammer you might damage the surface. Why do you have to use bad language?* **2** capitalize on, turn to °account, °profit by or from, °exploit, utilize, make use of, take °advantage of, °manipulate, °manoeuvre, °handle, °abuse, °misuse, °play, °work: *She used her smile to lure men on. Dorothy never forgave Conrad for the way he used her and her contacts to get his job.* **3** °consume, °eat, °drink, smoke, °take, °partake of, ingest, °inject, *Slang* °shoot (up): *He has never used a habit-forming substance.* **4** °consume, °buy, °purchase, °employ, utilize: *Which kind of detergent do you use?* **5 use up**: °consume, °exhaust, °expend, °run through, °run out of, deplete; °waste, squander, °fritter away, pour down the °drain, °throw away: *He used up all the toothpaste. She used up her entire inheritance gambling.*
—*n.* **6** °usage, °application, °employment, utilization; using: *The use of unleaded fuel is recommended.* **7** °function, utility, °application; °advantage, °benefit, °good, °service, °interest, °profit, avail: *What's the use of a radio that doesn't work?* **8** °wear (and tear), utilization, °treatment, °usage, handling: *Long use has worn the workbench smooth.* **9** usability, °usefulness, utility, utilization, °usage, °function, functioning, °service(s), serviceability, °power: *He lost the use of his right arm in an accident at work.* **10** °licence, °permission, °permit, °privilege: *We paid a high fee for the use of this parking space.* **11** consumption, °purchase, buying, °acquisition: *The use of cigarettes has diminished in the last decade.* **12** °advantage, °purpose, °point, °end, °object, °reason, °basis, °ground: *I have tried to help him overcome his habit, but what's the use? Many are the uses of adversity.* **13** °demand, °need, °necessity, °urgency, exigency: *The world has as much use for art as for engineering.* **14** See usage, 1, above. **15 have no use for**: execrate, °detest, °abhor, °hate, °despise, °scorn, contemn, °spurn, °reject, °dislike: *We have no use for cowards in this regiment.*

used *adj.* **1** °second-hand, cast-off, °old, °worn, *Euphemistic* pre-owned, *Colloq* hand-me-down, *Brit* reach-me-down: *You're better off buying a good used car, since new ones depreciate so quickly.* **2** utilized, employed, occupied; in °use: *We slept in a rarely used room.* **3 used to:** °accustomed to, habituated to, acclimatized *or* acclimated to, adapted to, hardened *or* toughened *or* inured to *or* against, tempered to, °tolerant of; °familiar *or* °acquainted with: *After all those years, Amanda was used to Bill's shouting.*

useful *adj.* utilitarian, °functional, °serviceable, °practical, usable, of °use, °beneficial, salutary, °advantageous, °expedient, °profitable, valuable, °gainful, °helpful, °fruitful, °productive, °effective, °worthwhile: *Does this knob serve any useful purpose? We had some very useful conversations with the bank manager.*

usefulness *n.* utility, applicability, practicability, °purpose, purposefulness, °point, practicality, °benefit, °advantage, expediency, °profit, profitability, value, °gain, °help, fruitfulness, effectiveness, °worth: *I never could see the usefulness of all the forms one has to fill in.*

useless *adj.* **1** °ineffective, °ineffectual, unserviceable, °impractical, °impracticable, unpractical, unavailing, °vain, °pointless, °purposeless, °idle, °futile, unproductive, °unsuccessful, °impotent, effete, °sterile, °barren, abortive, unusable, °bootless, °worthless, *Rare* inutile: *The treatment that she tried was quite useless.* **2** °inefficient, °incompetent, unproductive, °ineffectual, °ineffective, °hopeless, °inept: *My dachshund has proved totally useless as a watchdog.*

user *n.* **1** consumer, °buyer, purchaser, °owner; °operator: *Users of the equipment report excellent results.* **2** (alcohol *or* drug *or* narcotic) °addict: *The police have been interviewing users in order to obtain more information about the dealers.*

user-friendly *adj.* °simple, °practicable, usable, °explicit, °accommodating, understandable: *The system is designed to be particularly user-friendly.*

usual *adj.* °same, °customary, °habitual, °accustomed, °familiar, °well-known, °common, °everyday, established, °traditional, °set, °time-honoured, °old, °conventional, workaday, stock, wonted, °regular, °ordinary, °normal, expected, °routine, °typical, run-of-the-mill, stereotypic(al), hackneyed, trite, °prosaic, °worn out, shop-worn, °predictable, unexceptional, unoriginal, unremarkable, unimaginative: *The usual answer I get is 'Why?' I missed my usual train this morning. They still sing the usual drinking songs.*

usually *adv.* customarily, as a °rule, °generally (speaking), most of the time, for the most °part, most °often, mostly, almost °always, inveterately, on the °whole, normally, commonly, regularly, predominantly, °chiefly, all things considered, in the °main, °mainly, by and large, as °usual, *Colloq* as per °usual: *I usually walk home from the office. Johnson usually interviews applicants in the morning.*

Utopia *n.* °paradise, °heaven, seventh °heaven, (Garden of) Eden, °bliss, cloud-cuckoo-land, Nephelococcygia, never-never land, Shangri-La, Cockaigne *or* Cockayne, °heaven on earth, °perfection: *He dreams about a Utopia where everyone is rich and there are no taxes.*

utterly *adv.* °completely, °perfectly, °absolutely, °thoroughly, fully, °entirely, °wholly, unreservedly, °totally, unqualifiedly, °out-and-out, °altogether, overwhelmingly, unequivocally, categorically, °definitely, °properly; °extremely, *Brit dialect* proper; (with) no holds barred, body and soul, °head over heels: *The proposal was utterly defeated in the Commons. That was an utterly foolish act. She gave herself to him utterly.*

vacancy n. **1** °emptiness, °void, °gap, lacuna, hiatus, °blank, deficiency, °opening, °breach, vacuum: *Only after she left did Hubert sense the vacancy in his life.* **2** (°job) °opening, °slot, °position, °post, °situation: *Her promotion created a vacancy in the personnel department.* **3** blankness, °emptiness, vacuity, absent-mindedness, inanity, vacuousness, incomprehension, fatuity, unawareness: *I knew by the vacancy of his look that he hadn't any idea of what I was talking about.*

vacant adj. **1** °empty, °void, °hollow, un-occupied, untenanted, °uninhabited, °abandoned, °deserted: *The house remained vacant all summer.* **2** °blank, expressionless, deadpan, °empty, vacuous, °dull, °absent-minded, °inane, uncomprehending, fat-uous, °unaware: *After the accident, she would just sit, for hours on end, with a vacant look on her face.* **3** unoccupied, °free, °unused, unutilized, °spare, °extra, °idle, unfilled, unengaged, unspoken for: *The doctor has a vacant hour tomor-row at ten and could see you then.*

vacate v. **1** °leave, °depart (from), °withdraw from, °quit, °evacuate, °get or °go out of; °desert, °abandon: *In a fire drill, employees must vacate the building in five minutes.* **2** °give up, °relinquish, °sacrifice, °renounce, let go, °resign, °abdicate, °cede, °give up right or claim to, °abandon: *We vacated all claims to my aunt's prop-erty.* **3** annul, declare null and °void, nullify, °void, °repudiate, override, overrule, rescind, °revoke, °recall, °quash, °set aside, invalidate: *The judge vacated the defendant's plea of diminished capacity.*

vade-mecum n. handbook, °manual, ready °reference, °book, °guide: *She always had with her a vade-mecum on rare poisons.*

vagabond n. **1** gypsy, °tramp, vagrant, wayfarer, °rover, wanderer, itinerant, °migrant, bird of passage, rolling stone, beachcomber, °derelict, *Chiefly US and Canadian* hobo, *Australian* swag-man, *Colloq US* °bum, *Slang US* bindle-stiff: *The police interviewed every vagabond they could find for a clue to the murder.*
—adj. **2** vagrant, wayfaring, roving, wandering, itinerant, °migrant, derelict, nomadic, gypsy, °rambling, roaming, drifting, peripatetic, °transient, peregrinating: *When will he give up his vagabond ways and settle down?*

vague adj. **1** °indefinite, °indistinct, °imprecise, °inexact, unclear, °confused, unspecified or non-specified, °general, generalized, unspecific or non-specific, inexplicit or unexplicit, ill-defined, °hazy, °fuzzy, °ambiguous, °obscure, amorphous; °shapeless, blurred, blurry, °filmy, °dim, °shadowy, °veiled, bleary, foggy, °misty, cloudy, clouded, hardly or barely dis-tinguishable or discernible: *I have only a vague recollection of our having met. She must have had a vague idea of your intentions. Leon could almost make out the vague shape of an approaching figure.* **2** undetermined, indeterminate, unfixed, °indefinite, °inexact, unspecified or non-specified, unspecific or non-specific, °ambiguous, °doubtful, in °doubt, °uncertain,

°equivocal: *For security reasons, her time of arrival was left vague.* **3** °veiled, concealed, °hidden, shrouded, °obscure, ill-defined, unspecific or non-specific, inexplicit or unexplicit, °ambiguous: *There had been a vague threat of kidnapping, which should not have been ignored.* **4** °subliminal, °subconscious, inde-finable, unexplained: *I had a vague sensation of being followed.* **5** °indefinite, °ambiguous, °wishy-washy, undecided, °indecisive, °irresolute, vacillating, wavering, °inconstant, °unsettled, °uncertain, °nebulous, up in the air: *Leonore is vague about her plans to run for re-election.* **6** °vacant, °empty, °blank, expres-sionless, vacuous, °dull; puzzled: *By their vague expressions I could see they hadn't understood a word.*

vaguely adv. **1** distantly, remotely, indefinitely, dimly, subliminally, subconsciously, inex-plicably: *I became vaguely aware of another presence in the room.* **2** ambiguously, imprecisely, inexactly, unclearly, confusedly, confusingly, hazily, fuzz-ily, nebulously, obscurely: *Kenston claims that he expresses his theories vaguely to allow for broad interpretation.* **3** °idly, vacantly, detachedly, absent-mindedly, dreamily, absently, dis-tractedly: *Manton listened only vaguely to the judge's words.*

vain adj. **1** °proud, °conceited, °haughty, °arrogant, °boastful, °egotistical, °cocky, °self-important, vainglorious, narcissistic, *Colloq* big-headed, swell-headed or swelled-headed, stuck-up, swollen-headed: *They are so vain that they have mirrors in every room.* **2** °worthless, profitless, °bootless, °pointless, °unsuccessful, °empty, °futile, °useless, unavailing, unpro-ductive, °fruitless, °ineffective, abortive: *Peter sent Carol flowers every day in a vain attempt to win her back.* **3 in vain: a** vainly, futilely, unsuc-cessfully, fruitlessly, bootlessly: *In vain, we sought the help of the police.* **b** irreverently, blas-phemously, disrespectfully, improperly: *Despite his mother's admonitions, he continues to take the Lord's name in vain.*

valley n. glen, dale, dell, vale, dingle, °hollow, coomb or coombe or combe or comb, *No. Brit and Welsh* cirque or corrie or cwm, *Scots* strath: *Oh, to stroll once again the cool valleys and the heathered hills of home!*

vanity n. **1** °conceit, conceitedness, egotism, narcissism, °arrogance, cockiness, self-importance, vainglory, haughtiness, °pride, self-admiration, self-worship, *Colloq* swell-headedness, big-headedness: *It is disgraceful what some people do to satisfy their vanity.* **2** vainness, °emptiness, hollowness, worth-lessness, futility, unreality, bootlessness, point-lessness, uselessness, °folly, vapidity, silliness, vacuousness, vacuity, foolishness, fatuity, frivo-lousness: *The vanity of trying to complete the book in a year must be obvious by now.*

vapid adj. insipid, flavourless, °tasteless, °bland, °watery, watered down, °wishy-washy, jejune, °colourless, °unpalatable, °flat, °tame, °lifeless, °boring, °tedious, °tiresome, uninteresting, trite, wearisome, wearying, °humdrum, *Colloq* blah, ho-hum: *The minister attacked green politics as vapid romanticism.*

vapour *n.* **1** °mist, °fog, steam, cloud, smoke, smog, °exhalation: *There arose from the bog a suffocating, miasmic vapour.* **2 the vapours:** morbidity, hypochondria, hysteria, nervousness, °depression, rheuminess, *Archaic* distemper, *Colloq* the pip: *Charlotte suffered an attack of the vapours and retired to her room.*

variable *adj.* °changeable, °protean, changing, °inconstant, varying, wavering, mercurial, °fickle, °capricious, unsteady, unfixed, °unstable, °uncertain, undependable, unpredictable, fluctuating, vacillating, mutable, chameleonic, chameleon-like: *The weather can be quite variable depending on the season.*

variance *n.* **1** °variation, °difference, °disparity, °discrepancy, °disagreement, deviation, inconsistency, divergence, incongruity: *The monitor takes account of minute variance in blood pressure.* **2** °disagreement, °misunderstanding, °discord, °difference (of opinion), °dissension, contention, °dispute, dissent, °controversy, °quarrel, °conflict, °argument, °debate, lack of harmony, falling out, °schism, °rift: *There has never been any variance between us about the disciplining of the children.* **3 at variance:** in °dispute, in °disagreement, quarrelling, in contention, in °conflict: *The workforce was at variance with management in the matter of day care.*

variant *n.* **1** °alternative, modification, °variation: *'Labor' is an American spelling variant of 'labour'.*
—adj. **2** varying, °variable, changing, altering, °unstable, °deviant, deviating, °different, differing; °separate, °distinct: *It is claimed that the law is given variant interpretations depending on the social standing of the suspect.*

variation *n.* **1** °change, changing, °alteration, altering, °variety, varying, modification, modifying, °difference, differing, diversification, °diversity, diversifying, modulation, modulating, conversion, converting, permutation, permuting: *We have to allow for variation in the intensity of the light.* **2** °variety, °choice, °novelty, °diversity, departure (from the norm *or* usual), °change of pace, divergence, variegation, deviation (from the norm): *This restaurant offers considerable variation in its menu.*

varied *adj.* **1** °diverse, diversified, °mixed, °miscellaneous, assorted, heterogeneous: *An insufficiently varied diet may lead to malnutrition.* **2** See **various**, below. **3** See **variegated**, below.

variegated *adj.* multicolour(ed), particolour(ed), varicoloured, many-coloured, motley, pied, piebald, brindled, °mottled, polychrome, polychromatic; nacreous, changeant, °opalescent, opaline: *Plants with variegated foliage always add interest to a garden.*

variety *n.* **1** °diversity, diversification, multifariousness, multiplicity, °number, °range, °assortment, °medley, °mixture, °mix, °miscellany, heterogeneity, °choice, °selection, °collection: *Don't you find that the variety of foods in supermarkets today is astonishing? There was certainly a wide variety of people at their party.* **2** °difference, heterogeneity, °discrepancy, °diversity, °disparity, °variation, °contrast: *The flora and fauna of Australia display*

great variety. **3** °sort, °brand, °make, °mark, °kind, °class, °category, °breed, °type, °order, °genre, species, genus, classification, °strain: *Which variety of washing powder do you prefer? Rex cultivated only the rarest varieties of orchid.*

various *adj.* **1** °different, a °number of, a °variety of, diversified, °diverse, °several, °many, numerous, °sundry, heterogeneous, °miscellaneous, *Literary* °divers: *We are considering various offers for the painting. Catherine held various executive positions in the company.* **2** °different, °distinct, °individual: *There are various ways of looking at the problem.*

vary *v.* **1** °change, °alter, °diversify, °transform, reshape, remodel, restyle, °modify, reorganize: *We vary the programme each month to make it more interesting.* **2** °change, °switch, °alternate, °fluctuate, vacillate: *The manager's attitude varies from helpful to downright rude.* **3** °depart, °deviate, °differ, °diverge, °shift, veer: *These results do not vary from the average by more than five per cent.*

vast *adj.* °infinite, °unlimited, °boundless, °limitless, unbounded, interminable, °endless, never-ending, °inexhaustible, indeterminate, °immeasurable, incalculable, measureless; °immense, °enormous, °huge, tremendous, °great, °prodigious, stupendous, °gigantic, °massive, °voluminous, capacious, °colossal, °monumental, mammoth, °jumbo, elephantine, behemoth, Cyclopean, Brobdingnagian, titanic, *Literary* vasty, *Colloq* ginormous, humongous: *It is difficult to comprehend the vast distances of space. There is a vast difference between the climates of California and the Midwest.*

vastly *adv.* immensely, greatly, hugely, enormously, considerably, °substantially, (almost) entirely, infinitely, °exceedingly, °extremely, °very much, *Colloq* worlds: *Their new house was vastly different from the way I had pictured it. Katy looks vastly better since she lost two stone.*

vehicle *n.* **1** conveyance: *The police report that two vehicles were damaged in the crash.* **2** °means, °channel, °mechanism, °carrier, conduit, °agency, °instrument: *Water is the vehicle used in many sprays.*

veil *n.* **1** covering, °cover, °screen, °camouflage, °cloak, curtain, °mask, °shroud: *A veil of silence has been drawn over the meetings. He stole away under the veil of darkness.*
—v. **2** °cover, °conceal, °hide, °camouflage, °cloak, °mask, °disguise, °shroud, °shield, °obscure: *The writer's identity was veiled from us till recently.*

veiled *adj.* concealed, °hidden, masked, °obscure, unrevealed, covert, disguised, °secret, sub rosa, °subtle: *There seemed to be a veiled threat in the way he said goodbye.*

vein *n.* **1** blood-vessel; nervure: *He killed himself by opening a vein in his wrist.* **2** °streak, °seam, °stripe, striation, stria, °thread, °line: *The reddish vein gives this marble a warm feeling.* **3** °seam, lode, °stratum, °course, °deposit, bed: *The prospector discovered a vein of almost pure gold in the old mine.* **4** °thread, °hint, °suggestion, °touch, °trace, °streak, °line, °strain, °mood, °spirit, °tone, note, °tenor, °feeling, °attitude, °disposition, °humour, °temper; °tendency *or* °inclination *or* proclivity toward(s): *Underlying her apparent kindness is a vein of bitter* hatred. **5** °way, °manner, °course, °fashion, °style, °mode, °pattern: *He would have continued in that same vein if the chairman hadn't stopped him.*

velocity *n.* °speed, swiftness, °rapidity, fleetness, quickness, briskness, alacrity, celerity, °pace, °rate of °speed, miles per hour, m.p.h., kilometres per hour, km/hr: *Our velocity slowed as we neared the outer atmosphere.*

venal *adj.* °corrupt, corruptible, bribable, buyable, purchasable, °mercenary, unprincipled, °dishonourable, °rapacious, °avaricious, °greedy, simoniacal, *Colloq* °crooked, *Slang* °bent: *All we had to do was to find a venal official, cross his palm with silver, and they would release our son.*

vendetta *n.* (blood) °feud, °quarrel, °dispute, °conflict, °rivalry, enmity, °bitterness, hatred, °ill will, bad blood: *Fifty years after leaving Palermo, the vendetta between their families still persisted.*

veneer *n.* °gloss, façade, °finish, °pretence, (false) °front, (°outward) °show *or* °display, °appearance, °mask, °guise, °aspect, °superficies: *Beneath that veneer of elegance and refinement lie the heart and soul of a monstrous criminal.*

venerable *adj.* °respectable, °honourable, °estimable, respected, honoured, esteemed, august, °sedate, °impressive, revered, reverenced, worshipped: *Venerable old military men were called on for advice.*

venerate *v.* °respect, °honour, °esteem, °revere, °reverence, °worship, °hallow, °adore, °admire, °look up to: *Schweitzer was widely venerated for his charitable works.*

veneration *n.* °respect, °honour, °esteem, °reverence, °deference, °homage, °devotion, °worship, °admiration, adoration, idolization, awe: *Their veneration for their hero turned to contempt when his past was revealed.*

venereal *adj.* °sexual; genital; °social, sexually transmitted, gonorrhoeal *or* gonorrhoeic, syphilitic: *Syphilis was once the most feared venereal disease.*

vengeance *n.* **1** °revenge, retaliation, °retribution, °requital, °reprisal: *Her vengeance for what he had done was to disinherit him.* **2 with a vengeance: a** violently, °fiercely, ferociously, wildly, vehemently, furiously, forcefully: *The wind blew with a vengeance all night.* **b** energetically, to the fullest extent, to the utmost *or* the fullest *or* the limit, (with) no holds barred, enthusiastically, wholeheartedly: *Give Richard a job to do and he goes at it with a vengeance.*

venial *adj.* forgivable, excusable, pardonable, °tolerable, tolerated, °minor, °petty, °insignificant, unimportant, remittable *or* remissible: *That hypocrite considers even his most heinous crimes to be venial.*

venom *n.* **1** °poison, toxin: *The snakes are 'milked' of their venom, which is collected for research in antitoxins and pharmaceuticals.* **2** malice, maliciousness, malevolence, °ill will, malignity, °animosity, °hate, hatred, °hostility, °antagonism, °spite, spitefulness, spleen, °rancour, °bitterness, embitteredness, °gall, °poison, poisonousness, °virulence: *Vinnie was totally unprepared for the venom of the attack.*

venomous *adj.* **1** °poisonous, °deadly, toxic, °dangerous, life-threatening, °lethal: *There are few venomous snakes in the British Isles.* **2** °poisonous, °virulent, malicious, malevolent, malign, °malignant, °savage, baleful, envenomed, °hostile, antagonistic, °spiteful, splenetic, acerbic, °rancorous, °bitter, °embittered, °mean, °vicious: *That venomous little man caused me to lose my job.*

vent *n.* **1** °opening, °slit, °slot, °hole, °aperture, air-hole, blow-hole, spiracle, orifice, °outlet, inlet, funnel, flue, duct, °passage; fumarole, fissure, °pipe, mofette: *The tepee has a vent at the peak to let the smoke of the fire escape.* **2 give vent to:** See 3, below.
—*v.* **3** give vent to, °express, verbalize, °air, articulate, °enunciate, °declare, °voice, °announce, °communicate, °pronounce, °proclaim, °reveal, °release, let go, let °loose, allow to become known, °make known, °blurt out, make °public, °broadcast: *Has Margie ever vented her true feelings about your work as a bomb disposal expert? Arnold vents his spleen on any unfortunate who will stand for it.* **4** °discharge, °release, °emit, °eject, °issue, °empty, °dump, °expel, °send *or* °pour out *or* forth, °throw out: *It is illegal to vent poisonous fumes into the atmosphere.*

venture *n.* **1** °risk, °chance, °hazardous °undertaking, °experiment, °speculation, °gamble, °plunge, °fling: *Their new publishing venture turned out to be quite a success.*
—*v.* **2** °dare(say), make °bold, °hazard, volunteer, °tender, °offer, °broach, °advance, proffer, °put forward: *Ambrose ventured some nasty remark and was asked to leave.* **3** °jeopardize, °risk, °endanger, °hazard, imperil; °gamble, °bet, wager, °plunge, °put down: *Thomas ventured his last chip on the number four.*

venturesome *adj.* **1** °daring, °bold, °intrepid, °adventurous, °courageous, plucky, adventuresome, °audacious, °fearless, doughty, °brave, °spirited: *Henderson felt that he was being truly venturesome by sailing single-handed round the Isle of Wight.* **2** °risky, °rash, °reckless, sporting, °game, °daredevil: *Taking one's family into the American West was truly a venturesome undertaking—even in the 20th century.*

verbal *adj.* **1** °spoken, °oral, vocal, said, uttered, expressed, enunciated, articulated, colloquial, conversational, viva voce, word-of-mouth, unwritten: *We had a verbal agreement that you would behave yourself.* **2** word-for-word, °verbatim, °literal: *We have an accurate verbal transcript of the proceedings.* **3** °word, lexical, vocabulary: *She did very well on the verbal parts of the examination but poorly on the mathematics.*

verbatim *adj.* **1** word-for-word, verbatim et literatim (= 'word-for-word and letter for letter'), °literal, °exact, °precise, °accurate, °faithful, °strict: *This verbatim translation may be accurate but all the poetic expressiveness is lost.*
—*adv.* **2** word for word, verbatim et literatim, °literally, °exactly, °precisely, accurately, faithfully, to the letter, strictly: *To make certain there would be no misunderstanding, the speech was copied verbatim.*

verge[1] *n.* **1** °edge, °border, °boundary, °margin, °brink, °threshold, °brim: *Frances is jealous of John to the verge of insanity.* **2 on the verge of:** about to, °ready to, on the (very) °point of, preparing to, °soon to: *Many smaller companies are on the verge of bankruptcy.*

—v. **3** Often, **verge on**: °border (on), °approach, come °close or °near (to), *Technical* be asymptotic to: *Cathy's idea of comfort verges on what is more commonly thought of as luxury. Her charitable contributions last year verged on zero.*

verge² v. °incline, °lean, °tend, °extend, °stretch, °turn; °approach, °draw, °move: *The road verges southwards after the bridge.*

verify v. affirm, °confirm, °testify to, °attest (to), bear °witness to, °vouch for, corroborate, °support, °substantiate, °clinch or clench, °prove, °demonstrate, °show, °bear out, °authenticate, validate, °certify, °guarantee, back up, °warrant: *Can you verify the accuracy of his testimony?*

veritable adj. °real, °true, °virtual, °genuine, °actual, °legitimate, °authentic: *Frank becomes a veritable monster if denied his daily doughnut.*

vernacular adj. **1** °native, °local, regional, °indigenous, autochthonous: *Old Hebrew fell out of use, to be replaced by vernacular Aramaic.* **2** °popular, °informal, colloquial, conversational, °ordinary, °familiar, °everyday, °spoken, °vulgar, vulgate; °plain, °simple, straightforward, °easy: *We have both the vernacular and the formal, literary, or clerical levels of language. Can you translate this scientific gobbledegook into vernacular English that we can understand?* —n. **3** °jargon, patois, argot, °cant, °idiom, phraseology, °language, °talk, °speech: *Alf occasionally slips into the vernacular of a Billingsgate fishmonger (his former calling).*

versatile adj. **1** °adaptable, °resourceful, all-round, all-purpose, many-sided, multi-purpose, multifaceted, °flexible, adjustable, °protean, °dexterous, °handy, facile: *Everett is a versatile painter who works in many media and styles.* **2** °variable, °changeable, °protean, changing, °flexible, fluctuating: *Any versatile organization should be able to accommodate staff losses.*

versed adj. Usually, **well-versed in**: well-read or (°well-)°informed in or (well-)°trained or (well-)grounded or (well-)schooled or (well-)°educated or (well-)tutored or °learned or cultured or °lettered or °cultivated or literate or °competent or °accomplished or skilled in, (well) posted on, °knowledgeable in or about, °proficient or °experienced or °practised or °expert or °good in or at, conversant or °familiar or (well-)°acquainted with: *The applicant appears to be sufficiently well-versed in several subjects to be qualified to teach them.*

version n. **1** °form, °variant, °variation, °type, °model, °style, °kind, °variety, °manifestation, portrayal, °adaptation, °rendition, °interpretation, °construct, construction, °conception, °idea: *This is yet another modern designer's version of 1920s' and 1930s' art deco.* **2** °story, °account, °rendering, °rendition, °translation, °interpretation, reading, °understanding, °view, °side: *Simon's version of what happened is completely distorted.*

vertex n. °top, °tip, °extremity, °zenith, meridian, apogee, °peak, apex, °acme, °summit, °pinnacle, °crest, °crown, °cap, °height(s): *The building is surmounted by a pyramidal dome at the vertex of which is a statue of Osiris.*

vertigo n. dizziness, light-headedness, giddiness, instability, *Colloq* wooziness: *Vertigo suddenly overcame me, and I grabbed a rail to steady myself.*

verve n. °spirit, vivacity, vivaciousness, °vitality, °life, liveliness, °animation, °sparkle, °energy, °vigour, °exuberance, briskness, brio, esprit, élan, °dash, °flair, °panache, °flourish, °enthusiasm, zeal, °zest, °gusto, *Colloq* pizazz or pizzazz, zip, vim, get-up-and-go, zing, oomph: *Helen's verve adds much to this production of Carmen.*

very adv. **1** °extremely, °truly, °really, to a °great extent, °exceedingly, greatly, (very) much, °profoundly, °deeply, acutely, unusually, extraordinarily, uncommonly, exceptionally, remarkably, °absolutely, °completely, °entirely, °altogether, °totally, °quite, °rather, hugely, °vastly, *Dialect* right, *Brit* jolly, *Colloq* °damn(ed), °terribly, °awfully, darned, *US dialect* danged, plumb, *Slang Brit* bleeding, *Chiefly Brit* bloody: *The Bell Inn has a very fine wine list. Vicky was very attached to her pony. I shall be there very soon.* **2** most, °extremely, certainly, °surely, °definitely, decidedly, unequivocally, unquestionably, °quite, °entirely, °altogether: *If you ask her out, she is very likely to say no.* —adj. **3** °exact, °precise, °perfect; °same, self-same, °identical, °particular: *Her hopes were the very opposite of his. I arrived the very day she left. He is the very model of a hard-working student.* **4** least, °mere, merest, °bare, barest, °sheer, sheerest; utter, °pure, °simple: *The very thought of war makes me ill. The very mention of her name strikes terror into the hearts of the local residents.*

vessel n. **1** container, °receptacle, utensil, holder; *Food was stored in vessels neatly arrayed around the sarcophagus.* **2** °craft, °boat, °ship, ark, *Literary* barque or *US also* bark: *The vessel docked gently at the airlock of the space station.*

vestige n. °trace, °suggestion, soupçon, °hint, glimmer, °inkling, °suspicion, °sign, °evidence, °mark, °token, °scent, whiff, tinge, °taste; °remnant, °scrap, °fragment, °memorial, °residue, °relic, remains: *Vestiges of an ancient city have been found in the sea off Cyprus.*

vestigial adj. °imperfect, °undeveloped, underdeveloped, °rudimentary, °incomplete: *Anatomists regard the coccyx in man and apes as a vestigial tail.*

vet v. °examine, °review, °investigate, °scrutinize, °inspect, °check (out), °look over, °scan; validate, °authenticate; *Colloq* give (something or someone) the once-over, °size up: *We engaged an expert to vet the definitions of culinary terms for the new dictionary.*

veteran n. **1** °old hand, past °master, old-timer, trouper, *Colloq* warhorse: *Barlow was a veteran of twenty years' experience in the service.* —adj. **2** °experienced, °practised, °seasoned, °mature, long-serving, battle-scarred: *Did it never occur to this veteran politician that there are degrees of misconduct?*

veto v. **1** °stop, °block, °deny, °ban, °turn down, °reject, disallow, °rule out, °quash, °prevent, °prohibit, interdict, °taboo, °outlaw, proscribe, °preclude, *Colloq* put the kibosh on, °kill, nix: *Father vetoed the idea that we go to Brighton for the holiday. Any measure he proposed was summarily vetoed.*

—*n.* **2** °denial, °ban, stoppage, °block, °embargo, turn-down, °rejection, disallowance, quashing, °prevention, °prohibition, interdiction, °taboo, proscription, preclusion, vetoing, *Colloq* °killing, nixing: *The home secretary's veto of the abortion measure greatly angered the women's groups.*

viable *adj.* sustainable, °supportable, °sensible, °reasonable, °practical, °practicable, °applicable, workable, °feasible, °possible: *We have three days to come up with a viable plan for continuing the research project.*

vibes *n.pl.* vibrations, °feelings, °sensations, resonance(s), °rapport, empathy, °sympathy: *I felt the place had really good vibes the minute I walked in.*

vibrate *v.* °quiver, °shiver, °shudder, °fluctuate, °quake, °shake, °tremble, throb, °pulsate, °oscillate, °pulse, reverberate, resonate, *Brit* judder: *The house began to vibrate, the windows rattled, and the dishes danced off their shelves.*

vicarious *adj.* surrogate, delegated, deputed, commissioned, assigned, °indirect, substituted: *He derived vicarious pleasure from seeing his children do the things that he no longer could.*

vice *n.* **1** immorality, corruption, °evil, badness, depravity, °degradation, degeneracy, iniquity, villainy, venality, evil-doing, wickedness, °profligacy, °sin, sinfulness, °transgression: *She described the town as a den of indecency, exhibitionism, and vice.* **2** °flaw, °defect, °fault, °imperfection, °blemish, °shortcoming, °failing, °weakness, °frailty, °foible, °infirmity, deficiency: *Rejection without due consideration is a prejudicial vice of editors.*

vice versa *adv.* conversely, contrariwise, to *or* on the °contrary, reversed, the other °way around: *She made the facts fit her conclusions, instead of vice versa.*

vicinity *n.* °area, °neighbourhood, °locale, vicinage, environs, locality, precincts, purlieus, °territory: *All people living in the vicinity of the nuclear plant were tested for radiation poisoning.*

vicious *adj.* **1** °immoral, unprincipled, amoral, barbarous, °corrupt, °evil, °bad, °base, depraved, °vile, °atrocious, execrable, degraded, °degrading, °degenerate, °venal, iniquitous, heinous, odious, °perverted, nefarious, °wicked, flagitious, °devilish, °diabolic(al), °fiendish, °monstrous, °profligate, °shameful, °shameless, °abominable, °sinful: *The vicious, bloody dictatorship on the island lasted only a dozen years.* **2** malicious, °spiteful, °mean, °nasty, °hateful, malevolent, °malignant, °bitter, acrimonious, °rancorous, °venomous, °vindictive, defamatory, °slanderous, °scandalous, *Slang* °rotten, bitchy: *When they argued, they said terribly vicious things to one another.* **3** °savage, °wild, °untamed, °ferocious, °fearful, °brutal, °fierce, °fiendish, bestial, feral, brutish, ravening, *Literary* fell: *The local children were terrified of his vicious Rottweiler.*

vicissitude *n.* **1** °change, °mutation, °alteration, changeability, changeableness, mutability, °variation, variability, °variety, °alternation, °flux, °fluctuation, unpredictability: *Who seeks stability in life often encounters its vicissitude.* **2 vicissitudes**: °fluctuations, °changes, °variations, °contrasts, °inconstancy, unpredictability, uncertainties, *Colloq* ups and downs, flukiness: *His success is amazing in the light of the vicissitudes he survived.*

victim *n.* **1** sufferer, martyr, °casualty, °scapegoat, °sacrificial lamb, injured °party: *It is a pity that you had to be the victim of her greed.* **2** °dupe, gull, °fool, °butt, fair °game, *Colloq* chump, fall guy, *Slang* °sucker, °sap, *Chiefly US and Canadian* patsy, *US* schnook, schlemiel *or* schlemihl *or* shlemiel: *She was an easy victim for any confidence man.*

victimize *v.* **1** °prey on, °pursue, go after, °pick on, °bully, take °advantage of, °persecute, °exploit, °use: *Increasingly, older people are being victimized by unscrupulous relatives.* **2** °cheat, °swindle, bilk, °defraud, °dupe, °hoodwink, °deceive, gull, °fool, °trick, °outwit, °outsmart, outfox, *Colloq* snooker, flimflam, *Slang* suck *or* °sucker in, °screw, shaft, °take (in), rook: *The confidence team used the old Spanish handkerchief trick to victimize unsuspecting tourists.*

victor *n.* °winner, °champion, conqueror, prize-winner: *They came home unchallenged victors by an overwhelming 11 point margin.*

victorious *adj.* °triumphant, °successful: *Caesar was victorious over the Gauls.*

victory *n.* °triumph, °conquest, °supremacy, °superiority, °success, overcoming, mastery, °winning, quelling, crushing: *Alexander's victory over Darius at Arbela was one of the decisive battles of history.*

vie *v.* °compete, contend, °struggle, °strive: *The brothers constantly vied for their father's affection.*

view *n.* **1** °outlook, °aspect, °prospect, °scene, °perspective, vista, panorama, °spectacle, °picture, °tableau; °landscape, seascape, cityscape: *From the tower we had a view of the devastation below.* **2** °opinion, °point of view, °approach, °position, °judgement, °belief, way of °thinking, °conception, °understanding, °impression, °feeling, °sentiment, °notion: *Denham's view is that the country's defences are inadequate.* **3** °aspect, °angle, °position, °prospect, °perspective, °vision, °representation, °projection: *Here is a termite's-eye view of the timbers in your house.* **4** inspection, °survey, °vision, °sight, °observation, °scrutiny, °examination, contemplation, °study: *The shroud was pulled away, exposing the revolting object to our view.* **5** °aim, °direction, °intent, °intention, °purpose, °objective, °object, °expectation, °prospect, °vision, °hope, °dream: *We cultivated their friendship with a view to being invited aboard their yacht.* **6 in view of**: in (the) °light of, °considering, in °consideration of, because of, on °account of: *In view of your failure to respond to our letters, we must refer the matter to our lawyers.* —*v.* **7** °look at or upon or over, °see, °take in, °watch, °observe, °scrutinize, °examine, °regard, °behold: *From this vantage point one can view the entire valley.* **8** °witness, °see, °watch, °observe, °take in: *We viewed the entire robbery as it took place.* **9** °regard, °consider, °think of, °look on or upon, °judge, deem, °believe, °hold, °estimate, °rate, °gauge, assess: *Control views Craven as a threat.*

viewpoint *n.* °standpoint, (°point of) °view, °attitude, °angle, °slant, °position, °stance, vantage °point, °perspective, °frame of reference, °way of °thinking, °context: *From our viewpoint, widening the road only encourages speeding.*

vigilance *n.* watchfulness, alertness, °observance, guardedness, circumspection, attentiveness, °caution: *While the dog remains loose, we must exercise vigilance.*

vigilant *adj.* watchful, °alert, °sharp, °observant, °guarded, circumspect, °attentive, °wakeful, °cautious, °careful, °wary, chary, on one's °guard, on the °alert, on the °lookout, °eagle-eyed, hawk-eyed, Argus-eyed, on the qui vive, on one's toes, with one's eyes open, *Colloq* with one's eyes skinned *or* peeled: *As long as we remain vigilant, they will never be able to take us by surprise.*

vigorous *adj.* °energetic, °active, °vivacious, °dynamic, °brisk, °lively, °spirited, °robust, °strong, °hardy, °hale, °hearty, °vital, °fit, °lusty, °stalwart, in good *or* fine fettle, spry, °sprightly, resilient, *Colloq* peppy, full of °pep, full of get-up-and-go, full of beans: *At 63, he is just as vigorous as he was at 40.*

vigorously *adv.* energetically, actively, vivaciously, dynamically, briskly, spiritedly, robustly, strongly, hardily, heartily, lustily, stalwartly, eagerly, with °might and °main, with a °vengeance, strenuously, *Colloq* like °mad, like crazy, hammer and tongs: *It may not be good for you to exercise vigorously every day.*

vigour *n.* °vitality, °resilience, °strength, °power, °energy, forcefulness, °force, °stamina, °endurance, mettle, mettlesomeness, °pith, °dynamism, °spirit, liveliness, °animation, °verve, vivacity, °exuberance, brio, briskness, °zest, zealousness, °enthusiasm, °gusto, °eagerness, *Colloq* °spunk, °pep, pizazz *or* pizzazz, vim, oomph, zing, get-up-and-go: *When attacked, they defended themselves with extraordinary vigour.*

vile *adj.* **1** °base, abject, °contemptible, debased, °degenerate, depraved, °bad, iniquitous, execrable, °atrocious, °sordid, °immoral, amoral, °wicked, °evil, °sinful, hellish, °fiendish, ignoble, °revolting, °despicable, horrid, °horrible, °dreadful, °terrible, °corrupt, °mean, °wretched, °miserable, °degrading, ignominious, °disgraceful, °shameful, °shameless: *In every age, the vilest specimens of human nature are to be found among demagogues.* **2** °disgusting, °nasty, sickening, °nauseous, nauseating, °foul, °loathsome, °offensive, noxious, °repulsive, °repellent, °repugnant: *It is, indeed, a vile disease, but at least it is not contagious. She had prepared some vile cocktail that I refused to drink.*

vilify *v.* °depreciate, devalue, deprecate, °debase, °disparage, denigrate, °diminish, traduce, defame, speak °ill of, revile, °slander, °libel, °abuse, defile, °sully, °smear, °tarnish, malign, calumniate, asperse, °run down, decry, *Rare* vilipend, *Colloq US* bad-mouth: *His political and religious views became notorious and were often vilified.*

villain *n.* °wretch, evil-doer, °criminal, °miscreant, blackguard, °rogue, °rascal, cad, scallywag *or* scalawag, malefactor, °scoundrel, dog, cur, viper, reptile, °snake in the grass, rat, *Archaic* rapscallion, *Literary* knave, caitiff, *Colloq Brit* bounder, blighter, *Slang* bastard, son of a bitch, *Brit* rotter, *US* SOB *or* s.o.b. (= 'son of a bitch'): *The villain of the film is a smooth-talking charmer who swindles old ladies out of their savings.*

villainous *adj.* **1** treacherous, °perfidious, °dishonest, °unscrupulous, °traitorous, °corrupt, °faithless, °criminal, felonious, °murderous, *Colloq* °crooked, °bent: *Few activities are more villainous than being a double agent.* **2** See vile, 1, above.

vindicate *v.* **1** °clear, exonerate, absolve, acquit, exculpate, °excuse: *She was vindicated of any complicity in the affair.* **2** °justify, °support, °uphold, °prove: *Subsequent events vindicated his actions.*

vindictive *adj.* avenging, vengeful, vindicatory, revengeful, retaliatory, °spiteful, unforgiving, splenetic, °resentful, °rancorous, °implacable: *She later turned vindictive, attacking everyone for real or imagined slights.*

vintage *n.* **1** year, crop, °harvest, °origin, °generation: *Which vintage is the better for Bordeaux, 1949 or 1954?* —*adj.* **2** °quality, °choice, °superior, °better, °good, °select, °best, °classic; °aged, °seasoned, °mature(d), °mellow(ed): *Mark has become an expert in vintage wines.* **3** °antiquated, °old-fashioned, old-fogyish *or* old-fogeyish, °antique, °bygone, old-time, °collector *or* collector's, *Colloq* over the hill: *Claud used to drive his vintage car to work every day.*

violate *v.* **1** °break, °breach, °disobey, °disregard, contravene, °infringe, °ignore: *He habitually violated the law by carrying a pistol.* **2** °dishonour, °desecrate, °profane, defile, °degrade, °debase, treat irreverently: *Vandals were found to have violated the sacred shrine.* **3** °rape, debauch, °ravish, °ravage, °molest, °attack, °assault, °outrage: *The victim identified the man who had violated her.*

violation *n.* **1** °infringement, °breach, °disregard, disobedience, contravention, °abuse; ignoring, infringing, breaching, disregarding, disobeying, contravening, abusing, violating: *Parking here is a violation of the law. Violation of the rules will be dealt with summarily.* **2** profanation, °sacrilege, desecration, desecrating, defilement, defiling, °degradation, °degrading, °dishonour, dishonouring, debasement, debasing, violating: *The authorities take a serious view of the violation of a place of worship or a cemetery.* **3** °rape, ravishment, molestation, °attack, °outrage, °assault, violating: *The defendant is charged with the violation of three women.*

violence *n.* **1** (brute *or* physical) °force, °might, mightiness, °power, °strength, °severity, °intensity, °energy, vehemence, ferocity, ferociousness, fierceness, °fury, °vigour; destructiveness, °virulence: *The violence of the storm continued unabated throughout the night. The violence of the seizures diminished after she was given the medication.* **2** bestiality, brutality, °barbarity, savagery, cruelty, bloodthirstiness, wildness, ferocity, °frenzy, °fury, °passion, fierceness, vehemence, murderousness: *The marauders attacked with a violence that terrified the villagers.* **3 do violence to: a** °harm, °damage, °injure: *The scandal did violence to her reputation. Humphrey's singing could do violence to any melody.* **b** °warp, °twist, °distort: *In reporting that her views are antifeminist, the newspaper did violence to the import of her speech.*

violent *adj.* **1** °wild, °physical, °destructive, vehement, °brutal, brutish, °beastly, °nasty, °cruel, °mean, barbarous, °inhuman, °savage, °fierce, °ferocious, °furious, frenzied, uncontrollable, °untamed, °ungovernable, raging, °raving, irrational, °insane, crazed, *Colloq* fit to be tied: *Tony turned into a violent maniac when he suspected her of seeing another man.* **2** °harmful, °injurious, damaging, °detrimental,

°destructive, deleterious, catastrophic, cataclysmic, °ruinous, °devastating: *This was the most violent earthquake to hit Mexico in recorded history.* **3** °acute, °serious, °severe, °extreme, °harsh, °trenchant, °virulent, °intense, °energetic, °forceful, vehement, °passionate, °impetuous,°tempestuous: *The proceedings were interrupted by an outburst of violent abuse from the public gallery.*

virtual *adj.* °effective, °essential; °practical, °understood, accepted: *In rush hours, the motorway traffic comes to a virtual standstill.*

virtually *adv.* essentially, effectively, °practically, °almost, to all intents and purposes, for all practical purposes, more or less, °nearly, as good as, °substantially, in °effect, in °essence: *He had virtually won the Brisbane–London sailing race when he passed the Lizard, but then he hit a rock.*

virtue *n.* **1** °morality, high-mindedness, °honour, goodness, justness, righteousness, fairness, °integrity, right-mindedness, °honesty, probity, uprightness, °rectitude, decency, °worth, worthiness, °nobility, °character, respectability: *You will find the Billingses to be people of unassailable virtue.* **2** virginity, °chastity, chasteness, °honour, innocence, °purity: *As Healey had six daughters, he was kept quite busy protecting their virtue.* **3** °quality, °credit, °strength, °good °point, °asset: *Opposing the seven deadly sins are the three theological virtues, faith, hope, and charity, and the four cardinal virtues, fortitude, justice, prudence, and temperance.* **4 by virtue of:** by dint of, owing to, thanks to, by °reason of, because of, on °account of: *Gerry was a part owner by virtue of his investment in the company.*

virtuosity *n.* (technical) °skill, °technique, °ability, °expertise, mastery, °excellence, °brilliance, craftsmanship, °craft, °flair, °dash, élan, éclat, °panache, pyrotechnics, showmanship, °show, staginess, *Colloq* razzle-dazzle: *The concerto was performed with signal virtuosity but little imagination or understanding.*

virtuoso *n.* **1** °master, maestro, °expert, °genius, °talent, °prodigy, °old hand, *Colloq* wizard, whiz *or* whizz *or* wiz, whiz-kid *or* whizz-kid, *Chiefly Brit* °dab hand, *US* maven *or* mavin: *Walter is a veritable virtuoso on the harmonica.*
—*adj.* **2** °masterful, masterly, °expert, °talented, °brilliant, °dazzling, bravura, °prodigious, °excellent, °superb, °extraordinary, °exceptional, °superior, °first-rate, °superlative, °matchless, °peerless, °sterling, °marvellous, °remarkable: *His virtuoso performance of the B minor sonata won him a standing ovation.*

virtuous *adj.* **1** °moral, °honourable, °ethical, °honest, °good, upstanding, high-principled, °upright, °righteous, °pure, uncorrupted, incorruptible, °just, °fair, right-minded, fair-minded, high-minded, °scrupulous, °trustworthy: *Thomas has proved himself a virtuous young man.* **2** °chaste, °innocent, virginal, virgin; °decent, °proper, unsullied, °faithful, °true, uncorrupted: *A virtuous woman makes a virtuous wife.*

virulence *n.* **1** virulency, poisonousness, venomousness, toxicity, noxiousness, deadliness, perniciousness, injuriousness, destructiveness, malignity, malignancy, °violence, balefulness: *The virulence of his affliction was not recognized till it was too late.* **2** virulency, acrimony, acrimoniousness, °bitterness, acerbity, °rancour, spleen, °poison, poisonousness, °venom, venomousness, malignity, malevolence, maliciousness, malice, °spite, °hostility, °resentment, °antagonism, hatred: *We were taken aback by the virulence of the priest's attack on Miss Thompson's morals.*

virulent *adj.* **1** °lethal, life-threatening, °deadly, °fatal, pernicious, septic, °poisonous, toxic, baleful, noxious, °dangerous, °harmful, °injurious, °detrimental, deleterious, °destructive, °unhealthy, °unwholesome: *He died from a virulent form of dysentery that he caught in the tropics.* **2** °vicious, °venomous, °bitter, °spiteful, °malignant, malign, malicious, malevolent, °poisonous, splenetic, acrimonious, acerbic, acid, mordant, °sarcastic, °nasty, °trenchant, °caustic, antagonistic, °hateful, °hostile: *What did I do to the reviewer of* The Herald *to merit such a virulent review?*

visible *adj.* **1** seeable, perceivable, °perceptible, °discernible, detectable, discoverable, °noticeable, unmistakable, °clear, °obvious, °observable; visual: *The visible part of the energy spectrum is relatively small. The entrance holes to their burrows were clearly visible.* **2** °obvious, °conspicuous, °evident, °apparent, °prominent, °manifest, °distinct, °patent, well-defined, identifiable: *The consequences of the Act of Union of 1707 are still visible in Scotland today.*

vision *n.* **1** eyesight, °perception, °sight: *The optician said there is nothing wrong with MacKenzie's vision.* **2** far-sightedness, °understanding, °imagination, °foresight, foresightedness, °insight: *MacKenzie has brought great vision to this scheme for developing the Australian outback.* **3** °view, °perspective, °perception, envisioning, envisaging, °dream, °idea, °plan, °scheme: *MacKenzie's vision of making the desert bloom seemed impossibly remote.* **4** °phantom, apparition, chimera, °delusion, °hallucination, mirage, °spectre, °shade, eidolon, revenant, phantasm, materialization, °illusion, °ghost, wraith: *A vision appeared to MacKenzie as he slept, telling him that her name was Alice Springs.* **5** °sight for sore eyes, (welcome) °sight, °dream, °epitome: *To MacKenzie Alice was a vision of great beauty, and he proposed marriage.*

visionary *adj.* **1** °dreamy, °speculative, unpractical, °impractical, °fanciful, °imaginary, °unrealistic, °unreal, °romantic, °idealistic, unworkable, Utopian: *It is a pity that none of MacKenzie's visionary plans ever came to pass.*
—*n.* **2** °dreamer, idealist, °romantic, fantast, wishful °thinker, Don Quixote: *The world needs more visionaries like MacKenzie.*

visit *v.* **1** (go *or* come to) °see, °call (in *or* on *or* upon), °look in on, °stop in *or* by, *Colloq* °pop in *or* by, °drop in (on), °take in: *I plan to visit Leslie. Did you visit the Smithsonian Institution?* **2** °afflict, °attack, befall, °fall upon, assail, °seize, smite, °scourge, °descend upon, °inflict, °affect: *Horrible diseases and tortures were said to visit those who denied God.*
—*n.* **3** °stay, °call, °sojourn, °stop, stopover: *The minister will be here for only a brief visit.*

visitation *n.* **1** staying, °calling, visiting, sojourning, stopping (over): *The father has visitation rights to his children on weekends.* **2** °affliction, °ordeal, °trial,

°punishment, °disaster, °catastrophe, cataclysm, °calamity, °tragedy, °curse, °scourge, °blight, °plague, °pestilence: *In the story, the tyrant succumbed finally to a visitation from the Almighty.*

visitor *n.* caller, °guest, °company; visitant: *May I phone you back after my visitors have gone?*

vital *adj.* **1** °imperative, °essential, °necessary, needed, requisite, required, °indispensable, °mandatory, compulsory, °cardinal, °fundamental, °basic, °critical, °crucial, °central, °pivotal: *Air and water are vital for the existence of most known organisms.* **2** °important, °key, °central, °critical, °crucial, life-and-death or life-or-death, °pivotal, °paramount, °main: *In an emergency, the captain must make the vital decision whether to abandon ship. This is a matter of vital concern for us all.* **3** °lively, full of °life, °vivacious, °spirited, °vigorous, °dynamic, °alive, °animated, °brisk, °energetic: *We have lost a vital member of the community. She took a vital interest in community affairs.* **4** °invigorating, quickening, life-giving, animating, vitalizing, reviving, vivifying, enlivening, rejuvenating: *I could feel the vital energies returning to my limbs.*

vitality *n.* **1** °energy, °life, life-force, °vigour, °power, °intensity, °force, liveliness, vivacity, vivaciousness, °animation, °sparkle, spiritedness, °exuberance, *Colloq* zing, °pep, pizazz or pizzazz, oomph, get-up-and-go, zip, vim: *My great-grandfather has the vitality of a forty-year-old.* **2** °stamina, hardiness, °endurance, °energy, °strength, robustness: *Does this society have the vitality needed to take it into the next decade?*

vitalize *v.* °stimulate, °activate, °arouse, vivify, °animate, °awaken, inspirit, invigorate, °enliven, °inspire, °revive, °rejuvenate, innervate, °energize, °fortify, reinvigorate, °renew, °refresh, °charge (up): *The tonic vitalized him to the point where he felt young again.*

vitiate *v.* **1** °spoil, °ruin, °harm, °impair, °mar, °sully, °corrupt, °pervert, °contaminate, °adulterate, °weaken, °degrade, °downgrade, °depreciate, °diminish, °depress, vulgarize, °lower, °reduce, °undermine: *Words appropriated from other languages tend to enrich rather than vitiate modern English.* **2** °debase, deprave, °pervert, °corrupt, °demoralize, defile: *Despite other strengths his entire character was vitiated by overriding avarice.* **3** invalidate, °destroy, °delete, °cancel, nullify, annul, °revoke, °void, abrogate, °abolish, °withdraw, °quash, °suppress: *The invoice was effectively vitiated by the plaintiff's failure to deliver the goods.*

vituperate *v.* °berate, °rate, reproach, revile, °vilify, execrate, °abuse, °denounce, decry, deprecate, °disparage, devalue, °diminish, °put down, °run down, devaluate, °depreciate, °blame, inculpate, censure, find °fault with, °attack, assail, °castigate, °scold, °reprimand, °upbraid, °rebuke, chide, °chasten: *From the pulpit he continued to vituperate the vices of the court.*

vituperative *adj.* °abusive, calumniatory, calumnious, °scurrilous, °derogatory, belittling, depreciatory, depreciative, detractory, °contemptuous, damning, denunciatory, denigrating, deprecatory, censorious, aspersive, defamatory, °slanderous, libellous, castigatory, condemnatory, malign, °scornful, °withering,

°harsh, °sardonic, °sarcastic, °biting, acid, contumelious, opprobrious, insulting, *Formal* vilipenditory, *Colloq* down-putting: *Why should he have directed this vituperative speech at the very person whom he loves?*

vivacious *adj.* °lively, °spirited, °sprightly, °energetic, °animated, °brisk, °ebullient, °effervescent, °bubbly, °gay, °cheerful, °happy, °blithe, °jaunty, light-hearted, °sunny, °merry, high-spirited, °buoyant, chipper, *Colloq* up, peppy, full of °pep, full of beans, zippy: *Had he not gone on the cruise, Michael would never have met the vivacious redhead who became his bride.*

vivid *adj.* **1** °intense, °strong, °brilliant, °fresh, °bright, °dazzling, lucid, °rich, °clear, colourful, °glowing: *Michelle looked splendid in a silk dress of vivid yellow.* **2** °clear, °detailed, °sharp, °realistic, °graphic, true to life, °lifelike, °distinct, °powerful, °strong, °memorable, °dramatic, °striking: *It brought back to me vivid memories of our first meeting in 1985.* **3** °prolific, °fruitful, °fertile, fecund, inventive, °creative: *That kiss, which never took place, is a figment of Bagley's vivid imagination.*

vocalist *n.* °singer, soloist, choirboy, choir girl, choir member, chorus-boy, chorus °girl, chorus-member, chorister, caroller; diva, prima donna, *chanteuse*; cantor, crooner; *Colloq* songbird, canary, thrush, nightingale: *It was sung by a female vocalist with a high-pitched girlish voice.*

vocation *n.* °calling, °trade, métier, °business, °profession, °occupation, °career, °employment, °job, °pursuit, life's-work, life-work, °line (of °work), *Slang* °bag, °thing: *I left university with no particular vocation in mind.*

vogue *n.* **1** °fashion, °mode, °style, °look, °taste, °trend, °rage, °craze, °last °word, *dernier cri*, (°latest) °thing, *Colloq* °fad, °the °latest: *Black leather boots were in vogue once again.* **2** °popularity, °favour, °preference, acceptance, currency, °prevalence, fashionableness: *They are capitalizing on the vogue for torn jeans.*

voice *n.* **1** °speech, utterance, articulation, words, °expression: *Keith found it difficult to give voice to his innermost thoughts.* **2** °share, °part, °vote, participation, °say, °decision, °option, °turn, °chance: *As a junior member of the board, Nicholas had no voice in major decisions.* **3** spokesman, spokeswoman, spokesperson, °representative, °agent, °agency, °instrument, °organ, °medium, °vehicle, forum, °publication: *Throughout his time in government, Logan had served as the voice of the miners. The Clarion views itself as the voice of all the people, though it actually represents only a few.*
—*v.* **4** °express, utter, articulate, °enunciate, °present, verbalize, put into °words, give utterance or voice or °expression or °vent to, °communicate, convey, °declare, assert, °make known, °reveal, °disclose, °raise, °bring up, °air: *I must voice my misgivings about the step you are planning to take.*

void *adj.* **1** null and void, °invalid, not (legally) binding, inoperative, unenforceable, °ineffectual, °futile, °ineffective, °vain, unavailing, °idle, °useless, °pointless, °bootless: *Owing to irregularities, the election was declared void. If a card is turned face-up, the deal is void.* **2** °empty, °vacant, unoccupied, °unused, unutilized, unfilled, °blank, °clear; °deserted: *It is up to the council to appoint new members as places become*

void. **3 void of**: devoid of, without, lacking, °destitute of: *The man was utterly void of imagination. In a minute, the room was void of people.*
—*n.* **4** °emptiness, vacantness, vacuum, blankness, nothingness: *Without a word, he leaped off the edge and plunged into the void.* **5** °space, °niche, °slot, °opening, °place, °vacancy, °gap, °emptiness: *Who will fill the void left by Edgar's departure?*
—*v.* **6** nullify, annul, °cancel, °delete, disannul, declare *or* render null and void, invalidate, °quash, °vacate, °discharge, °abandon, disestablish, °neutralize, disenact, °set *or* °put aside, rescind, °reverse, abnegate, abrogate: *They had to void the accusation for lack of evidence.* **7** °evacuate, °discharge, °expel, °emit, °purge, °clear, °empty, °drain, °eject; °pass, excrete, °urinate, °defecate: *The tanker went far out to sea before voiding its tanks. This medication will help in voiding the patient's bowels.*

volatile *adj.* **1** vaporizing, evaporable, evaporative: *A volatile solvent, which evaporates quickly, is the vehicle for thermosetting plastics.* **2** °changeable, °fickle, °flighty, °inconstant, °erratic, °restless, °unstable, °variable, mercurial, °capricious: *She was so volatile that one could never predict what she would do next.* **3** °explosive, hair-trigger, °sensitive, charged, eruptive, °tense, tension-ridden: *Be careful of Christine's volatile temper.*

volition *n.* (free) °will, °choice, °option, choosing, °choice, °discretion, °preference: *She pursued a course of her own volition.*

volley *n.* **1** salvo, bombardment, barrage, cannonade, fusillade, °discharge, °hail, °shower: *A volley of shot struck the tower, which collapsed.* **2** °outpouring, °torrent, °flood, deluge, inundation, °burst, °storm, outbreak: *The cracks of the muleteer's whip were accompanied by a volley of abuse.* **3** °give and take, to-and-fro, interaction, reciprocity, °exchange, volleying, crossfire, badinage, bantering: *Samuel enjoyed the volley of haggling that accompanied every sale.*

voluble *adj.* °talkative, °glib, °fluent, loquacious, garrulous, chatty, °profuse, gossipy, °exuberant, long-winded, °bombastic, °windy, °wordy, *Colloq* blessed with the gift of the °gab: *He is the House of Commons' most voluble advocate of capital punishment.*

volume *n.* **1** °amount, °quantity, °supply, °mass, °bulk, °abundance, °sum °total, aggregate: *The volume of ore from the mine created a pile hundreds of feet high. Her volume of output is greater than yours and mine together.* **2** °capacity, °size, °measure: *The volume of this bottle is not more than a litre.* **3** loudness: *Turn down the volume on that ghetto-blaster.* **4** °book, tome: *I bought a twenty-volume set of Dickens.*

voluminous *adj.* **1** °large, °extensive, °great, °spacious, capacious, °expansive, °roomy, °loose, °ample, °big, °bulky, cavernous, copious, °massive, °huge, °substantial, tremendous, °enormous, °gigantic, mammoth, °vast: *Rose's voluminous skirt was supported by a farthingale.* **2** oversized, outsized, °ample, billowing: *The voluminous spinnaker filled and we wafted down the estuary at hull speed.*

voluntarily *adv.* °freely, °willingly, spontaneously, of (one's) own °free °will, on (one's) own (°initiative *or* recognizance *or* °responsibility), without prompting, without

being prompted *or* asked, gratis, gratuitously; by °choice, intentionally, purposely, on °purpose, °deliberately: *Some of the students spent their summer vacation voluntarily helping the needy.*

voluntary *adj.* **1** °free, elective, °willing, °spontaneous, °unsolicited, unbidden, °unasked, °gratuitous, contributed: *All work done on behalf of the cause is voluntary.* **2** discretionary *or* discretional, unconstrained, °intentional, °wilful, °deliberate, intended, °premeditated, planned, volitional, °optional: *His confession was entirely voluntary, and he was not coerced in any way.*

voluptuous *adj.* **1** °sensual, sensualistic, °sensuous, °luxurious, voluptuary, sybaritic, hedonist(ic), pleasure-seeking, pleasure-loving, luxury-loving, (self-)°indulgent: *He longed to taste once again the voluptuous delights of the Corinthian court.* **2** °seductive, °attractive, °desirable, °beautiful, °tempting, °inviting, appealing, enticing, alluring, °ravishing, °luscious, °delicious, °gorgeous, °shapely, °buxom, well-proportioned, well-endowed, well-built, *Colloq* curvaceous, °sexy, eye-filling, *Slang* (well-)stacked, busty, *US* built: *As he lolled on silken cushions, voluptuous houris danced round him in tightening circles.*

vomit *v.* °spew out *or* up, °spit up, belch forth; °regurgitate, °throw up, °gag, retch, °heave, *US* keck, *Colloq* puke, °return (food), *Brit* °sick up, *Slang chiefly Australian* chunder, *US* barf, upchuck, toss (one's) cookies, spiff (one's) biscuits: *The ancient steam engine vomited smoke and cinders from its huge stack. The very thought of going on a sea voyage almost made me vomit.*

voracious *adj.* **1** insatiable, °gluttonous, °ravenous, ravening, °rapacious, piggish, °hoggish, predacious, edacious, devouring, °greedy, °avaricious, esurient, uncontrollable, °uncontrolled, °unquenchable, °enormous, °prodigious, *US* cormorant: *Is there no satisfying the man's voracious appetite?* **2** °thirsty, °hungry, °desirous, avid, °eager, zealous, °enthusiastic, °fervent, fervid, °ardent, °earnest, °passionate, °devoted: *It was becoming difficult to satisfy the public's voracious demand for gossip.*

vote *n.* **1** ballot, ticket, show of hands; referendum, °plebiscite: *We must have a vote on the issue.* **2** °suffrage, franchise: *Women did not have the vote in those days.* **3** °opinion; voter, elector: *Do you think your platform can win over the liberal vote?*
—*v.* **4** opt, °choose, come out (for *or* against), express *or* signify (one's) °opinion *or* °preference *or* °desire: *Many people vote for a party rather than an individual.*

vouch *v.* Usually, **vouch for**: °support, °guarantee, °back (up), °endorse, °certify; °uphold, °sponsor, bear °witness, °attest to: *My neighbour will vouch for me. Can she vouch for your not leaving the house all evening?*

vouchsafe *v.* **1** °offer, °give (up), °yield, °accord, °supply, °grant, °impart, °bestow, °deign *or* °condescend to give: *The minister vouchsafed no information regarding interest rates.* **2** °permit, °allow, °suffer: *The government vouchsafed the hostages safe passage out of the country.*

vow *v.* **1** °swear, °pledge, °promise, °assure, °state, °declare, give (one's) (solemn) °word (of honour): *I vowed to return after the war to care for those who had helped me escape.*

—*n.* **2** °oath, °pledge, °promise, °agreement; (solemn) °word (of honour): *She will keep her vow, you may be certain.*

vulgar *adj.* **1** indelicate, °boorish, uncultured, uncultivated, °low, °unrefined, °common, °plebeian, inelegant, unladylike, ungentlemanly, gauche, uncouth, °coarse, °tasteless, °ostentatious, ignoble, low-class, *Colloq* °flash: *The boss's wife was known for her vulgar behaviour at the dinner table.* **2** °tasteless, indelicate, °indecent, °rude, °crude, °naughty, °dirty, °improper, °off colour, °risqué, ribald, °blue, indecorous, °nasty, °offensive, °gross, °lustful, °obscene, °lewd, °lascivious, licentious, smutty, salacious, scatological, °filthy, °pornographic, *Slang US* raunchy: *He made a lot of money through publishing vulgar magazines and videos.* **3** °popular, °vernacular, °ordinary, °everyday, °general, °homespun, commonplace, household, °average: *Dictionaries should record the vulgar language as well as the literary.*

vulgarity *n.* **1** coarseness, lack of refinement *or* sophistication, crudeness, rudeness, °indelicacy, tawdriness, baseness, humbleness, unsophistication, gaucherie, gaucheness, ignobility: *When you consider his upbringing you can scarcely blame him for his vulgarity.* **2** °impropriety, lewdness, grossness, foulness, vileness, filthiness, obscenity, *Slang US* raunchiness: *The magazine was refused an import licence because of its vulgarity.*

vulnerable *adj.* exposed, °defenceless, °weak, °sensitive, unprotected, °unguarded, unshielded, °helpless, °powerless: *She felt vulnerable to those who prey on the elderly.*

W

wad *n.* **1** °pad, °mass, °lump, °clod, ball, °plug, chunk, hunk, °block, °pack: *He had a wad of cotton wool in each ear.* **2** °roll, pocketful, °heap, °quantity, °load, *Colloq US* bankroll: *Over coffee James made up a wad of notes.*

waddle *v.* toddle, °shuffle, wobble *or* wabble, °totter, °paddle, °pad, waggle, duck-walk, *Brit dialect* wamble: *He waddled down the road, a shopping-bag on each arm.*

wade *v.* **1** ford, °cross, °traverse, °walk, make one's way: *The water is only knee-deep, and you can wade across.* **2** °paddle, °play, °splash: *There is a shallow pool where the little children can wade.* **3 wade in** *or* **into: a** °enter, °get in (or into), °join (in): *When the fight began, Patrick waded in with arms flailing.* **b** °attack, °approach, get *or* °set to work, °plunge *or* °dive into: *I have to wade into an enormous pile of mail that accumulated while I was away.* **4 wade through**: °plough through, °work (one's) way through, hammer *or* °pound away at, °plod through, °peg away at: *You really have to wade through that entire book to write your report.*

waffle *v.* **1** Often, **waffle on**: °carry on, °jabber (on), °prattle (on), prate, blather (on *or* away), *Colloq* run on, *Brit* witter (on), natter (on), rabbit on, *Slang* run off at the mouth: *He kept waffling on about his new computer and, frankly, I wasn't listening.* **2** °equivocate, hedge, °quibble, °shuffle, tergiversate, hem and haw, prevaricate, *Brit* beat about the bush, *US* beat around the bush, *Colloq* fudge: *I wish he would stop waffling and say what he means.*
—*n.* **3** °talk, °palaver, verbiage, °prattle, twaddle, blather, prolixity, wordiness, °jabber, jibber-jabber, *Colloq* °hot air: *All I got was a lot of waffle when I asked for the best interest rate on a loan.*

waft *v.* **1** °drift, °float, °blow, whiff, be borne *or* carried *or* transported: *The scent of jasmine wafted towards me on the warm breeze.*
—*n.* **2** °breath, °suggestion, °puff, whiff, °hint: *A waft of cool, fresh air momentarily eased the stench of the dungeon.*

wag[1] *v.* **1** °wave, waggle, °oscillate, °fluctuate, °sway, undulate, °flutter, °flap, °flip, °flicker, °shake, °vibrate, °quiver, °nod, °rock, °dance, wobble, bob, bobble, waver, *Rare* vellicate: *Misty's tail wagged as I approached the house.*
—*n.* **2** °wave, waggle, oscillation, °fluctuation, °sway, undulation, °flutter, vellication, °flap, °flip, °flicker, °shake, vibration, °quiver, °nod, wobble, bobble, waver: *The dying animal recognized me and gave a feeble wag of her tail.*

wag[2] *n.* °comedian, comedienne, °wit, punster, pundit, °joker, jester, °comic, jokester, droll, °merry andrew, °clown, *Colloq* °card: *A wag said that tailors were like storks—known for their big bills.*

wage *n.* **1** Often, **wages**: °pay, compensation, emolument, °remuneration, °payment, °fee, °salary, °stipend, recompense, °reward, °earnings; °honorarium: *The strikers wanted a ten per cent increase in their hourly wage.*
—*v.* **2** °carry on, °pursue, °conduct, °engage in, °undertake, °practise, °prosecute, °proceed with: *History shows that wars are often waged over trifling differences.*

wait *v.* **1** °tarry, °linger, °hold on, °stay, bide (one's) time, mark time, °stand by, *Colloq* cool (one's) heels, °stick around, °sit tight, °hang on, *Brit* °hang about, *US* °hang around: *If you wait till I've finished this, I'll join you for dinner.* **2** be delayed *or* postponed *or* deferred *or* shelved *or* °put off, *US* be tabled, *Colloq* be put on ice or on the back burner: *The quarterly sales figures can wait—we haven't yet completed those for this month.* **3 wait on** *or* **upon**: °serve, °attend (to), °minister (to): *Rose made such a fuss that the restaurant staff refused to wait on her.*
—*n.* **4** °delay, °pause, °stay, °hold-up, °interval, °halt, °stop, stoppage, °break, hiatus, lacuna, °gap, °respite, °rest (°period), °intermission, discontinuation, °recess: *There was an extra long wait between trains because of track repairs further up the line.*

waiter *n.* waitress, head waiter, maître d'hôtel, °host, hostess, *sommelier (des vins)*, wine steward, stewardess; cup-bearer, Ganymede, Hebe: *Marie asked the waiter to bring her a clean plate.*

waive *v.* **1** °give up, °relinquish, °renounce, °resign, °forsake, °forgo, °cede, °sign away, °surrender, °abandon, °yield, °dispense with: *I waived my right to the inheritance in favour of my daughters.* **2** °set *or* °put aside, °except, °ignore, °disregard, °overlook, °abandon, °defer, °postpone: *We are happy to waive the rules in your case, madam.*

waiver *n.* renunciation, relinquishment, forgoing, ceding, cession, °resignation, °surrender, abandonment, setting *or* putting aside, deferral, °remission, °postponement: *Her waiver of all rights to the inheritance was duly recorded.*

wake[1] *v.* **1** Often, **wake up**: °awaken, °awake, °rouse, waken, °bring around; °stir, bestir (oneself), °get up, °come to, get going: *Wake me when it is over. She didn't wake up till noon.* **2** °awake, waken, °awaken, °animate, °stimulate, °enliven, galvanize, °fire, °quicken, inspirit, °inspire, °activate, °liven up, vivify, °kindle, °vitalize, °stir, °arouse, get (someone) going, bring to °life: *When I feel this tired, it takes a lot to wake me up. Seeing Margo woke a spark in me I thought had long since died.*
—*n.* **3** vigil, °watch, death-watch, °funeral: *If you have ever been to an Irish wake, you will know what I mean.*

wake[2] *n.* **1** °track, °trail, aftermath, °path, backwash, °wash, bow °wave; °trace, spoor, °scent: *The wake from the passing boats damages the docks. No matter where he went, they followed in his wake.* **2 in the wake of**: following (on *or* upon), after, °subsequent to; as a °result *or* consequence of, on °account of, because of, owing to, by °virtue of: *In the wake of the law's enactment, scores of abortions were performed.*

wakeful *adj.* **1** °awake, °sleepless, waking, unsleeping, °restless, °restive, insomniac: *The children were wakeful the entire night in anticipation of* *a visit from Santa Claus.* **2** watchful, (on the) °alert, on the qui vive, °sharp, °attentive, °vigilant, °wary, °cautious, °observant, heedful, on the °lookout: *We remained wakeful, alert to any footstep.*

walk *v.* **1** °advance, °proceed, °move, °go, wend, °go *or* make (one's) way by foot, tread, °step, perambulate, °stalk, stride, °tramp, °stroll, amble, °ramble, ambulate, shamble, °pad, °shuffle, °saunter, trudge, trek, °plod, slog, hike, °parade, °promenade, °strut, °swagger, °prance, °march, goose-step, °pace, °trip, °sidle, tiptoe, sashay, °flounce, °stagger, °lurch, °limp, °waddle, °stamp, mince, °slink, steal, °prowl, skulk, °sneak, °creep, *Colloq* go by *or* ride by shanks's *or* shanks' mare *or* pony, hoof it, foot it, traipse, °pussyfoot, *Slang US* boogie: *Guthrie certainly has a peculiar way of walking.* **2** °take, convoy, °accompany, °escort, °go with; °conduct, °lead; °empty: *Let me walk you to the station. I have to walk the dog twice a day.* **3** °patrol, °trace out, °stalk, °cover, °haunt, °prowl, °wander, °roam, rove *or* °range about in *or* on, °frequent: *Her mother could not understand why Maizie walked the streets nightly.* **4 walk out**: **a** °leave, °depart, °desert: *She just walked out and no one has seen her since.* **b** °strike, go (out) on °strike, °protest, take industrial action, *Brit* down tools: *Negotiations reached an impasse, so the employees walked out.*
—*n.* **5** °path, lane, pathway, pavement, footpath, °promenade, esplanade, boardwalk, *Brit* footway, *US* °sidewalk: *We strolled along the pleasant walks that lead through the park.* **6** gait, °step, °carriage, °bearing, stride: *He had great fun imitating Groucho Marx's slinky walk.* **7** constitutional, °stroll, amble, °slog, °tramp, hike: *Lettie likes to take a walk in the park after dinner. We had a five-day walk through the jungle before reaching civilization.*

wall *n.* **1** °screen, °partition, divider, °enclosure, separator, bulkhead, °barrier, °obstruction, °obstacle, °impediment, °block, °fence: *Marcie built herself a wall of resentment which no one could penetrate.* **2** barricade, fortification, °protection, °bulwark, breastwork, embankment, °rampart, palisade, stockade: *It was questionable whether the walls would withstand the cannon-balls.* **3 drive up the wall**: drive crazy *or* insane *or* mad, °madden, °exasperate, derange, °try, °irritate, °infuriate, °enrage: *The constant caterwauling from the next flat is driving me up the wall.* **4 go to the wall**: °fail, °collapse, be ruined, face °ruin, go bankrupt, lose everything, *Colloq* go °broke, °go under, °fold (up), *Slang* go bust: *Unicold went to the wall because of increased costs and decreased sales.*
—*v.* **5** Often, **wall up** *or* **off**: °enclose, °partition (off), °close (off), °brick up, immure: *A bricklayer was hired to wall up the openings where the windows had been.*

wallet *n.* °purse, pocketbook, *Brit* notecase, *US* billfold: *An anonymous good Samaritan found my wallet and sent it to me intact, with all the money in it.*

wallow *v.* **1** °roll *or* loll about *or* around, °welter, writhe, °tumble, °splash *or* plash: *He enjoys watching the pigs wallowing in the mud.* **2** Usually, **wallow in**: °luxuriate in, bask in, °revel in, °glory in, °indulge (oneself) in, °give (oneself) up to, °succumb to, °take to, °appreciate, °fancy, enjoy, °like, °love, savour,

Slang get a kick *or* a bang *or* a boot from *or* out of: *Now that Gabriel is a big rock star, he simply wallows in all the attention he is getting.* **3** °stumble, °stagger, °lurch, °flounder, °teeter, °totter, falter, °pitch: *Without its engines, the ship was lifted skyward by a wave one moment only to wallow in a trough the next.*

wan *adj.* **1** °white, °sickly, °pale, pallid, livid, °pasty, ashen, bloodless, waxen, whey-faced, sallow, °colourless, deathly, °ghostly, °ghastly, cadaverous: *I almost wept at seeing the child's wan face against the pillow.* **2** °weary, weak, °hollow, °feeble, °frail, °ineffectual, °sorry, °pitiful: *She offered no more than a wan smile in response to questions about her family.*

wand *n.* baton, °stick, °staff: *The magician pointed with his wand and a bottle of gin appeared.*

wander *v.* **1** °walk, °go, °roam, rove, °range, °stray, °ramble, °stroll, °saunter, °meander, °drift, °cruise, °prowl, *Colloq* mosey: *We wandered about the village square, chatting and window-shopping.* **2** °wind, °meander, zigzag, °turn this way and that: *A trout stream wanders past our house.* **3** digress, go off, become °absent-minded, go wool-gathering, lose concentration *or* focus: *My mind wandered as the speaker droned on.* **4** °deviate, digress, °turn, divagate, °stray, °drift, °depart, go off at a tangent, lose (one's) train of thought, °lapse: *The speaker tended to wander occasionally.*

wane *v.* **1** °decrease, °diminish, grow less, lessen, °decline, °die out, abate, °ebb, °subside, °fade (away), °dim, taper off, peter out, °wind down, °weaken: *The waning moon cast its pale light on the dying knight. As his strength waned he could no longer lift his sword.* **2** draw to a °close, °end, °terminate: *The day waned into a gloomy evening.*
—*n.* **3** °decrease, diminution, lessening, °decline, abatement, °ebb, subsidence, fading, tapering off, petering out, winding down, weakening, deterioration, degeneration: *The 1970s saw the wane in popularity of large, gas-guzzling cars.* **4 on the wane**: on the °decrease *or* °decline *or* °ebb, diminishing, decreasing, declining, abating, subsiding, fading, tapering off, petering out, winding down, weakening, deteriorating, degenerating: *The economy is recovering, and inflation is on the wane. Since that latest illness, my energy has been on the wane.*

wangle *v.* °scheme, °plot, °work out, contrive, °manoeuvre, °engineer, °manage, °manipulate, machinate, *Colloq* °fix, °fiddle, °work, °pull off, finagle, °swing: *I hear that you were able to wangle an audience with the pope.*

want *v.* **1** °desire, crave, °wish (for), °long for, pine for, °hope (for), °fancy, covet, °hanker after, °lust after, °hunger for *or* after, °thirst for *or* after, °yearn for, *Colloq* have a yen for: *I want you near me. Ignore his crying—he just wants some ice-cream. Maybe he's crying because he wants to go.* **2** °need, °lack, °miss, °require, °call for, °demand, be °deficient in, be *or* stand in want *or* in °need of, necessitate; be *or* °fall °short of: *This engine wants proper maintenance. The bottle wants only a few more drops to fill it.*
—*n.* **3** °need, °lack, °shortage, deficiency, °dearth, °scarcity, scarceness, insufficiency, scantiness, inadequacy, paucity: *For want of good writers, the literary quarterly diminished in size and finally disappeared.* **4** °appetite, °hunger, °thirst,

craving, °desire, °fancy, °wish, °longing, yearning, hankering, °demand, °necessity, °requirement, requisite, °prerequisite, *Colloq* yen: *She gave up trying to satisfy his wants.* **5** °poverty, °need, indigence, homelessness, destitution, °privation, pauperism, penury, neediness, impecuniousness: *The civilized nations are trying to solve the problems of want, which seem to increase daily.*

wanting *adj.* **1** °deficient, °inadequate, not up to °par *or* expectations, °insufficient, leaving much to be desired, °unsatisfactory, unsatisfying, °disappointing, second-rate, °inferior, °poor, °shabby, °shoddy, °flawed, °faulty, °imperfect, °incomplete, unfinished, °defective, patchy, impaired, damaged, °broken, °unsound: *These robots were tested at the factory and were found wanting.* **2** °absent, missing, lacking, °short (of), *US and Canadian* °shy (of): *What good is a banjo wanting its strings?*

wanton *adj.* **1** °immoral, °dissolute, °profligate, dissipated, depraved, °loose, °promiscuous, °lustful, licentious, °lecherous, °wild, libidinous, °lewd, °lascivious, °unchaste: *She is a wanton hussy who is no better than she ought to be.* **2** °abandoned, unrestrained, °undisciplined, ungoverned, °ungovernable, unmanageable, °outrageous, °immoderate, intemperate, untempered: *It is not the boy's fault, it is the wanton company he keeps.* **3** °reckless, °rash, uncaring, °lavish, °extravagant, °wilful, °heedless, °irresponsible, °careless: *This situation arises from the parents' wanton disregard for their children's moral training.* **4** °wicked, °evil, malevolent, malicious, °merciless, inhumane, °vicious, °cruel, °violent, unjustified, unprovoked, uncalled-for, °purposeless, motiveless, unjustifiable, °arbitrary, °gratuitous: *We were subject to wanton attacks by the hill people.*
—*n.* **5** vamp, strumpet, whore, harlot, °loose woman, °prostitute, voluptuary, slut, trollop, Jezebel, *Colloq* °tart, *Slang* hooker, working girl, call-girl: *Who invited that wanton, with her tight-fitting, shamelessly low-cut dress?*

war *n.* **1** warfare, °combat, °conflict, fighting, °clash, hostilities, °battle, °struggle, °engagement, °encounter, °strife, contention: *The war, in which several millions died, lasted six years.* **2 at war**: fighting, battling, in °combat, in °conflict; in °disagreement, in °dispute, in contention, struggling, antagonistic, at daggers drawn: *They are at war because an ambassador refused to retract some silly insult.*
—*v.* **3** do °battle *or* °fight *or* °struggle *or* (°engage in) °combat with *or* against, make *or* °wage war with *or* against, take up arms *or* °strive *or* °campaign *or* °tilt against, cross swords *or* contend *or* joust with: *We must continue to war against the forces of evil.*

ward *n.* **1** °district, °division, °precinct, °section, °zone, °quarter: *Perkin was running for re-election as councillor of the Eastgate ward.* **2** °minor, dependant: *The child was made a ward of the court.*
—*v.* **3 ward off**: °fend off, °repel, avert, °avoid, °block, °thwart, keep away or, off or at bay or at arm's length, °check, °repulse, °chase away or off, °forestall: *This brandy should help ward off the night chill.*

wardrobe *n.* **1** (collection *or* stock of) clothing *or* °clothes *or* attire *or* °apparel: *At the time, my entire wardrobe consisted of a pair of jeans, a shirt,*

and a dinner suit. **2** clothes-press, closet, clothes-cupboard: *In her wardrobe they found more than three thousand pairs of shoes.*

warehouse *n.* °storehouse, °store, storeroom, depository, stockroom, depot, go-down: *The books are kept in a warehouse and shipped to customers as needed.*

wares *n.pl.* °merchandise, °goods, commodities, manufactures, °produce, stock-(in-trade), °supplies, °lines: *A blind man peddled his wares on this corner for twenty years.*

warlike *adj.* combative, °belligerent, bellicose, °aggressive, °pugnacious, °hostile, °bloodthirsty; hawkish, militaristic, jingoistic, warmongering: *Violation of the border was a warlike act that must be punished. There are warlike factions in every government.*

warm *adj.* **1** °heated, °tepid, °lukewarm, °cosy, °comfortable, not uncomfortable, balmy: *We chose a beautiful warm day for our picnic.* **2** °passionate, °impassioned, °excited, °animated, °fervent, fervid, °spirited, °lively, °ardent, zealous, °keen, °eager, °emotional, °heated, °intense, irritated, annoyed, vexed, °angry, irate, °furious, °testy, °short-tempered, °touchy, °quick-tempered, irascible, °irritable, °stormy, turbulent, °vigorous, °violent, *Colloq* worked up, °hot under the collar, steamed up: *Charles occasionally became a bit warm on the subject of architecture. The debate grew warm as we joined in.* **3** °amiable, °friendly, °cordial, affable, °pleasant, °genial, °cheerful, °kindly, °hospitable, °hearty, °affectionate, °tender, °mellow, loving, amorous: *After a warm greeting from our host, we went in to meet the other guests. Her generous gifts to charity revealed that she really has a warm heart.* **4** °ardent, °enthusiastic, °earnest, °eager, °sincere: *Our ideas for the new campaign met with warm approval from the client.* **5** uncomfortable, °awkward, unpleasant, °strained, °tense: *The people in this town tend to make things a bit warm for strangers.* **6** Often, **getting warm**: °close *or* °near to making a discovery, about to make a discovery: *From her look as I approached the cabinet, I knew I was getting warm.*
—*v.* **7** °heat (up), warm up *or* over: *I warmed myself by the fire.* **8** Often, **warm to**: become less antagonistic *or* hostile to *or* toward(s), become °enthusiastic *or* °supportive of, become °excited *or* °animated about *or* over, be attracted to *or* toward(s), °like, feel °affection for: *Martin never did warm to my idea of using the village notice-board for his message.* **9** °stir, °move, °please, °delight, make (one *or* someone) feel good: *It warmed me to know that she had at last found someone to love.*

warm-blooded *adj.* **1** *Technical* homoeothermic *or* homoeothermal *or* homoiothermic *or* homoiothermal *or* homeothermic *or* homeothermal: *Birds and mammals are warm-blooded, reptiles and fish are cold-blooded.* **2** °passionate, °ardent, fervid, hot-blooded, °impetuous, *Colloq* °randy: *He tried to excuse his behaviour towards her by saying that he was just a normal, warm-blooded man.*

warmly *adv.* **1** affectionately, tenderly, °fondly, lovingly: *Linda kissed him warmly to thank him for the gift.* **2** cordially, amiably, amicably, solicitously, warm-heartedly: *We were greeted warmly by the manager on our arrival and shown to our rooms.* **3** earnestly, eagerly, fervently, enthusiastically, °well, °kindly: *The directors are warmly disposed to your plan for reorganization.*

4 °vigorously, intensely, °fiercely, intensively, °intently, energetically, doggedly, persistently, zealously, fervently, fervidly, °hotly, ardently, enthusiastically: *We learned that she was being warmly pursued by Interpol.* **5** heatedly, vehemently, vociferously, forcefully, energetically, °vigorously, feverishly, frantically, furiously, angrily, violently: *The sending of a peace-keeping force was being warmly debated in the UN.*

warmth n. **1** °heat: *We basked in the welcome warmth of the sun.* **2** cordiality, heartiness, friendliness, geniality, amiableness, kindliness, tenderness, affability, °love: *Mother thrives on the warmth of a family environment and should not be put in a nursing home.* **3** °ardour, effusiveness, °enthusiasm, zeal, excitement, °fervour, vehemence, °vigour, ebullience, °passion: *I was taken aback by the warmth of the stranger's greeting. The resolution was debated with considerable warmth.* **4** irritation, °annoyance, pique: *The warmth of his reaction to the accusation is understandable.*

warn v. **1** °caution, admonish, °advise, °notify, apprise, °inform, give (fair) °warning, °alert, give (prior) °notice, put (someone) on °notice or on guard or on the °alert, make (someone) °aware (of), forewarn, °tip off, *Rare* premonish: *The entire population has been warned about the imminent hurricane.* **2** °advise, °counsel, °caution: *You did warn me against investing in llama farms.*

warning n. **1** °caution, admonition, °advice, °counsel, caveat, word (to the wise), °tip, notification, °notice, °threat; °lesson, °example: *Cyril never took seriously his doctor's warning about his cholesterol level. Let that be a warning to you not to drink and drive.* **2** °omen, °sign, °signal, °indication, augury, foretoken, portent, foreshadowing, forewarning, °prophecy: *Sailors take that kind of sky and a falling barometer as warning of a hurricane.*

warp v. **1** °twist, contort, °distort, deform, °bend out of shape, °wrench, °pervert, misshape: *Using steam, the timber was warped to fit the hull. You certainly have a warped idea of what Yvette does for a living.*
—n. **2** °twist, contortion, distortion, °bias, deformity, deformation, °bend, °wrench, °perversion, °kink, idiosyncrasy, °quirk, deviation: *There is too much of a warp in this veneer to repair it. Harry has to overcome a serious warp in his attitude towards food.*

warrant n. **1** authorization, °sanction, °reason, justification, °approval, validation, °licence, °right, certification, entitlement, grounds, °cause, °rationale, °basis, °assurance, *carte blanche*, °guarantee, °pledge, °security, °charter, °warranty: *We demand to know what warrant may exist for such an action.* **2** writ, °order, affidavit, °paper, °document, credential, °permit, entitlement, °licence, summons, subpoena, mandate, °decree, fiat, edict, ukase: *Do not let them search the premises without a warrant. A warrant has been issued for her arrest.*
—v. **3** °guarantee, °promise, °assure, °ensure or insure, °answer for, be answerable for, °certify, °vouch for, °underwrite, °back up, °uphold, °stand by or behind: *All these products are warranted by the manufacturer for one year.*
4 °authorize, °sanction, °justify, °explain, °approve, °verify, validate, °permit, °allow, provide or offer grounds or justification or cause or

reason for, °call for, necessitate, °entitle, empower, °excuse, °license: *What is it that warrants such accusations of malfeasance?*

warranty n. °guarantee, °assurance, °promise, commitment, covenant, °undertaking, °agreement, °pledge, °bond: *There is a maker's warranty that repairs any defects will be made at no cost to the buyer.*

wary adj. °cautious, °careful, on (one's) guard, circumspect, °prudent, apprehensive, chary, watchful, °vigilant, on the qui vive, heedful, °observant, on (one's) toes, *Colloq* cagey, *Slang* °leery (of): *Phoebe is wary of going out with someone she doesn't know.*

wash v. **1** °wash up, °clean (up), °cleanse, bathe, °shower, douche, douse, °scrub (up), shampoo, soap up, °lather, °launder, °scour, °soak, °rinse, °flush, °wet, °drench, deterge, sponge (off), *Facetious* perform (one's) ablutions, *Archaic* absterge, *Formal or literary* lave, *Brit* bath: *Please wash the dishes when you have finished eating. I must wash before I do anything else.* **2** Sometimes, **wash away** or **out** or **off**: °remove, °move, °transport, °carry, °bear, convey, °deliver, °deposit, °drive, °sweep: *The silt, with the gold dust, is washed downstream. In this process, the impurities are washed away.* **3** °splash, °spatter, splatter, plash, °dash, °beat, °pound, thrash, °break, °toss, °surge, undulate, °rush, °run, °lap, °ripple, °roll, °flow: *We stood watching the sea washing against the breakwater.* **4** Usually, **wash away** or **off**: °erode, °wear off or away, °remove, °delete, °erase, expunge, °destroy, eradicate, °obliterate, °extinguish, °blot out, °wipe out: *After 5,000 years, the action of the waves had washed away all traces of the Vengorian civilization.* **5** Often, **wash away** or **out**: °erode, °cut or °dig or °wear or °eat or dredge (away or out), °excavate, °channel: *The river eventually washed out a new course, fifteen miles to the west.* **6** °decontaminate, °purify, °sift, °filter, depurate: *The wastes are thoroughly washed in these tanks before being discharged into the ocean.* **7** overlay, °film, °coat, °paint, °glaze; °plate: *What do you think of the colour they washed the wall?* **8** °hold up, °stand up, stand the test of time, carry weight, bear scrutiny, °prove °true, make sense, be believable or credible, *Colloq* hold °water: *I'm afraid that Helen's explanation of her whereabouts at the time of the murder simply won't wash.* **9 wash down**: °swallow: *Here, wash the pill down with this.* **10 wash (one's) hands of**: stay or keep away from, disown, °repudiate, turn (one's) °back on, have nothing more or further to do with, get °rid of, °rid (oneself) of, °desert, °abandon, °leave: *After Neil took the money, Violet washed her hands of him and his problems.*
—n. **11** washing, cleaning, cleansing, scrubbing, °scrub, scouring, shampoo, shampooing, bathing, °shower, sponge bath, tub-bath; laundering; *Facetious* ablutions; *Colloq Brit* tub, tubbing: *He always likes a good wash and shave before breakfast.* **12** °wave, °wake, °surge, backwash: *The wash from passing ships almost swamped our skiff.* **13** °lotion, °rinse, liniment, °salve, embrocation, emulsion, °preparation; mouthwash, gargle; eyewash, collyrium: *Use this wash twice a day till the condition disappears.* **14** °flow, °wave, °swell, welling, °sweep, °sweeping, ebb and flow, °surge, surging, undulation, rise and fall: *Shellfish in the gap cleanse themselves of impurities in the constant tidal wash running through*

there. **15** °coat, coating, °film, overlay, °glaze; plating: *There is a microscopic wash of gold over the tin to lend the bracelet a little cachet.*

washed out *adj*. **1** °wan, °pale, pallid, °colourless, faded, °lacklustre, °flat; blanched, bleached, etiolated: *Gene looks washed out because he never gets out in the sun. She was wearing washed-out jeans and a torn T-shirt.* **2** °exhausted, °spent, °tired, °tired out, °weary, °worn out, °fatigued, drained, *Colloq* dog-tired, bone-tired, done in, all in, fagged out, bushed, *Brit* knocked up, *US* knocked out, *Slang* °beat, *US and Canadian* tuckered out, pooped: *After a hard day in the office, I feel completely washed out.*

washed up *adj*. finished, °through, failed, done for, played out, over (and done with), *Slang* kaput, fini: *After that last fiasco, he's no more than a washed-up has-been.*

washout *n*. °failure, °disaster, débâcle, (total) °loss, °fiasco, °disappointment, *Colloq* °flop, °dud, *Brit* damp squib, *US* lead balloon: *His attempts to revive the hula-hoop craze were a washout.*

waspish *adj*. irascible, bad-tempered, foul-tempered, °temperamental, °testy, grouchy, °sensitive, °volatile, °querulous, edgy, °petulant, °spiteful, °peevish, °cantankerous, curmudgeonly, °cross, crabby, crabbed, crotchety, splenetic, grumpy, captious, °cranky, crusty: *Elaine is feeling very waspish today—no one can do anything right.*

waste *v*. **1** squander, °misuse, °throw away, °fritter away, misspend, °splurge, °dissipate, *Slang* °blow: *Why I wasted so much time on him I'll never know. Don't waste your money on such frivolities.* **2** Often, **waste away**: °diminish, °deteriorate, °dwindle, °decline, °decay, atrophy, wither, °shrink, °weaken, °become debilitated, °fade, °become enervated *or* enfeebled, regress, °ebb, °sink: *She is just wasting away, and I am seriously worried that she may not recover.* **3** °enervate, enfeeble, emaciate, °gnaw, °destroy, °consume, debilitate, °exhaust, disable: *Arkwright contracted a terrible wasting disease while in the tropics.* **4** assassinate, °murder, °kill, *Slang* °put away, °rub out, *US* ice: *Don't worry, Boss, we'll waste Andy and you won't have no more trouble.*
—*n*. **5** °misuse, misapplication, squandering, °dissipation, misemployment, °abuse, °neglect: *What a terrible waste of talent to have such a person doing such lowly work! Do not let that genius go to waste.* **6** wasting, °extravagance, °prodigality, wastefulness, squandering, °indulgence, lavishness, °profligacy, dissoluteness, improvidence, overindulgence: *Government waste is one of our biggest problems.* **7** °refuse, °rubbish, °garbage, °dregs, debris, leavings, °scrap, offscourings, sweepings, °litter, *Archaic* orts, *US and Canadian* °trash: *Techniques are being developed to process the waste in order to avoid using landfills, incineration, or dumping at sea.* **8** wasteland, °desert, wilderness, barrens, °wilds, °emptiness, vastness: *Beyond that system were vast wastes of uninhabited space.*
—*adj*. **9** °extra, °leftover, °unused, °superfluous, °worthless, °useless: *The waste food was usually fed to the animals.* **10** °barren, unproductive, unusable, unsalvageable, °useless, unrecyclable, °unprofitable, °worthless: *The waste products of manufacture are a big problem.* **11 lay waste**:

°devastate, °destroy, °demolish, despoil, °ruin, °wreck, °ravage, °pillage, °sack, °plunder, °loot, °rob, °strip, °spoil, °gut, ransack, °wreak °havoc (up)on, °crush, °raze, annihilate, eradicate, extirpate, °wipe out: *These lands and cities, laid waste by the invaders, have never recovered.*

wasteful *adj*. °extravagant, °spendthrift, °profligate, °prodigal, °lavish, °improvident, unthrifty, uneconomical, overindulgent, open-handed, free-handed, penny wise and pound foolish: *It was very wasteful of you to buy me that expensive jewellery.*

wastrel *n*. **1** °spendthrift, °profligate, waster, °prodigal, big spender, squanderer: *That wastrel went through his inheritance in a year.* **2** °idler, layabout, malingerer, °loafer, shirker, °good-for-nothing, ne'er-do-well, *Chiefly Brit* drone, *Slang Brit* skiver: *The workhouse is the place for wastrels like you!*

watch *v*. **1** °observe, °regard, °look at, °gaze at *or* on, °take in, °contemplate: *Daniel loves to watch the bears at the zoo.* **2** °look after, °tend, °mind, keep an °eye on, watch over, °guard, °care for, take °care of, °safeguard, °protect, °shield, keep safe, °supervise, superintend; chaperon, °accompany, °attend; *Colloq* babysit (for), sit (with): *Could you please watch Suzie while I go shopping?* **3** °observe, note, °notice, make *or* take note of, °see, pay °attention (to), °attend (to), °follow, (take) °heed (of), °examine, °inspect, °scrutinize, °pore over; °spy, °peer at; °ogle, make °eyes at: *Watch the way I bone this fish. Ted enjoys watching the girls going by.* **4** Often, **watch (out) for**: °look for, be on the watch *or* °lookout *or* °alert *or* qui vive (for), °guard (against), keep an °eye open (for), be watchful (for), note, take note *or* °notice of, be °vigilant (for *or* of), keep (one's) °eyes open (for), keep a (sharp) °lookout (for), be prepared *or* °ready for, be °careful of, °anticipate, await, °wait (for), *Colloq* keep (one's) °eyes peeled *or* skinned (for), keep a weather °eye open (for): *We were watching for irregularities in the test results. Watch where you're going! Watch out for that last step!*
—*n*. **5** vigil, °surveillance, °observation, °lookout: *Our six-hour watch was rewarded by the appearance of a yellow-bellied sapsucker.* **6** clock, timepiece, pocket watch, wrist-watch; chronometer: *I always set my watch by the GMT time signal on the radio.* **7** sentry, °sentinel, °guard, °watchman: *The midnight watch just returned from his rounds.* **8 on the watch (for)**: on the °alert (for), on the °lookout (for), on (one's) °guard (for), on the qui vive (for), °alert (for *or* to), °awake (to), °observant (of), watchful (of), °cautious (of), °wary (of), °vigilant, circumspect: *We remained on the watch for the slightest movement in the bushes.*

watchman *n*. (°security) °guard, °sentinel, sentry, °watch, night-watchman, custodian, caretaker; watchdog: *After retiring from the police, he worked as a watchman.*

water *n*. **1** H_2O; distilled water, °tap water, drinking-water, bottled water, spa water, still water, soda (water), effervescent water, mineral water; sea water, salt water; ditch-water, dishwater, bath-water, *US* branch water, *Facetious* Adam's ale, *Technical or Latin* aqua; *Technical* heavy water *or* deuterium oxide *or* D_2O; *Brit* fizzy water: *Pure water is odourless, tasteless, and colourless.* **2 not hold water**: be illogical *or*

°unsound or °invalid, not be sensible, be °inconsistent, not make sense, be °unbelievable or °incredible, be indefensible, be unfeasible or unworkable, not work, not function, not hold up under or bear scrutiny or examination, not ring true, ring false, Colloq not °wash: Her account of her whereabouts that day just doesn't hold water. **3 like water:** lavishly, extravagantly, °freely, wastefully, profligately, open-handedly, liberally, excessively, copiously, unstintingly, unreservedly: They've been spending money like water since they won the football pools. **4 make water:** °urinate, pass water, Colloq pee, piss: When a dog makes water, it marks off a territory bounded by its scent. **5 of the first water:** of °superior or °excellent or °first or top or A-one or the finest or the highest or the °best °quality or °grade; first-grade, top-grade: These were not industrial stones but diamonds of the first water. —v. **6** inundate, °flood, °drench, °saturate, °soak, douse, irrigate, hose, °wet, °shower, °splash, °spray, sprinkle, moisten, °damp, °dampen, bedew: If you don't water the garden, the vegetables will die. **7** Often, **water down:** °dilute, °weaken, °thin out, °adulterate; °cut; mollify, °modify, °soften, °tone down, °qualify: We no longer go there because they water the drinks. They told the children a watered-down version of what had happened.

water-colour n. aquarelle: John's water-colours sell as fast as he paints them.

waterfall n. cascade, cataract, °fall(s), °chute, Niagara, No. Brit force, Scots linn: In front of them, a waterfall tumbled down a rock-face into a deep pool.

watertight adj. **1** sealed, waterproof: The escape hatch has been made watertight. **2** unassailable, °impregnable, °solid, airtight, °flawless, °faultless, °incontrovertible; without °loopholes: Landry has a watertight alibi for the night of the crime.

watery adj. **1** °weak, °dilute(d), watered down, °tasteless, insipid, flavourless, °bland, °flat, °dull, °thin, runny, pallid, anaemic, Colloq °wishy-washy: He asked me in, then gave me some watery tea to drink. **2** weeping, teary, °tearful, °running, weepy, lachrymose, rheumy: The child looked up at him with watery eyes and then collapsed, sobbing. **3** °wet, swampy, boggy, marshy, aqueous, squelchy; soggy, °moist, °damp, °humid; Colloq squushy or squooshy: It took days to make our way across that watery plain to the high ground.

wave n. **1** °swell, undulation, billow, °sea, °heave, °roller, whitecap, white horse; °ripple, wavelet, breaker, comber: A huge wave tossed me up on the beach. **2** °surge, °swell, welling up, ground °swell, °movement, °flood, upsurge, °uprising, °current, tide: The period is marked by a wave of materialism and greed that swamped all morality and integrity. **3** °signal, °sign, gesticulation, °gesture: Was his wave intended for you or for me? —v. **4** undulate, billow, °move to and fro, °flap, °flutter, °quiver, flip-flop, °swing, °sway, °ripple, °oscillate, zigzag, °fluctuate, °shake; °wag, whiffle, wigwag, wiggle, waggle, brandish: The streamer waved slowly in the quickening breeze. Stop waving that knife at me! **5** °signal, °sign, °indicate, °signify; °gesture, gesticulate: Hazel waved goodbye from the train.

way n. **1** °manner, °method, °mode, °fashion, °means, °system, °course (of action), procedure, °approach, °scheme, °technique, °practice, modus operandi, Colloq MO (= 'modus operandi'): That's no way to talk to your mother! We have ways of making you talk. Is that any way to treat a lady?! It's the wrong way to deal with the problem. **2** °manner, °spirit, °feeling, °sense, °character, °approach, °personality, temperament, °disposition, modus vivendi (= 'life-style'), °nature, °technique, °style, °conduct, °habit, °behaviour °pattern, °custom: He has such a pleasant way about him. Lucinda certainly has a way with children and dogs. You city people may not approve of our down-to-earth country ways. **3** °path, °road, °street, avenue, °course, °route, °trail, °direction: Show me the way to go home. The way to the village lies through dark woods. **4** °distance; °route, °trail, °course, °road: You've come a long way since we last met. **5** °progress, °passage, °advance, °headway; °speed, °velocity, °motion, (forward) °movement: We made our way to the front of the crowd. Who has the right of way at the crossing? The tide was too strong for us to get any way on. **6** °aspect, °respect, °particular, °detail, °point, °sense, °feature: In certain ways, you remind me of Attila the Hun. **7** °clearance, pathway, avenue, °scope, °freedom, °opportunity: When you hear a siren, drive to the side and give way. Make way for the Lord High Executioner! **8** °condition, °situation: She prefers the prissy 'in a family way' to the straightforward 'pregnant' and the vulgar 'have a bun in the oven'. I saw Luke yesterday and he was really in a bad way. **9 by the way:** °incidentally, °moreover, by the by, parenthetically: By the way, have I told you how beautiful you look tonight? **10 by way of: a** via, °through, by °means of: We drove from London to Oxford by way of Reading. **b** (functioning) as, in (the) way of, in the capacity of, °equivalent to, more or less, something °like: Richard is by way of being an expert on eccentric behaviour. **11 give way: a** °collapse, °break (down), °fail, °cave in, °fall (down), °crumble, °crumple, °disintegrate, go to °pieces: The cable gave way, causing the bridge to collapse. **b** °yield, °surrender, °retreat, °concede, °withdraw, accede, make concessions, acquiesce, °acknowledge: The trouble is that they both think they are in the right and neither will give way. **12 under way:** proceeding, progressing, on the °move, moving, advancing, going, begun, started, in °progress, operating, functioning, at work, US in °work, Colloq in the works, US in the °pipeline: Once under way, it takes the ship three days to make the crossing. Plans are under way to reclaim the slum area for a park.

waylay v. **1** °ambush, lie in wait for, await, °intercept, °pounce upon or on, °swoop down on or upon, accost: You'll have to waylay him on his way to lunch if you want to speak to him. **2** °attack, °mug, °seize, °assault, accost, °set upon: He was waylaid by a band of thieves and stripped of his belongings.

way-out adj. **1** °bizarre, °mad, °weird, °crazy, °strange, °odd, °peculiar, freakish, freaky, °eccentric, °queer, °abnormal, °offbeat, °outrageous, °wild, °exotic, esoteric, Colloq °kinky, Slang kooky, off-the-wall, far-out, screwy, nutty, US flaky, screwball: The police did not take kindly to the boys' way-out behaviour after the party. **2** °avant-garde, advanced, °original, innovative, °unorthodox, unconventional, °experimental, precedent-setting, °progressive, exploratory, ground-breaking, *Slang* far-out: *Spencer thinks that the way-out art of the 1960s will have great value one day.*

weak *adj.* **1** °feeble, °frail, °fragile, unsubstantial, °flimsy, breakable, frangible, °delicate, °rickety, unsteady, °unsound, °decrepit, °shaky, °infirm: *That chair is too weak for you to stand on.* **2** °frail, °infirm, debilitated, enervated, °delicate, °sickly, anaemic, wasted, °decrepit, °puny, effete, °worn out, °tired, °exhausted: *When I last saw Tindell he was so weak he could hardly lift his brandy glass.* **3** unassertive, °retiring, namby-pamby, °spineless, °irresolute, °impotent, °ineffectual, °ineffective, °incompetent, feckless, °inept, °wishy-washy, °timid, °meek, craven, timorous, °cowardly, pusillanimous, lily-livered, chicken-hearted, *Colloq* chicken, yellow: *We know which is the weaker partner in that marriage, don't we?* **4** °feeble, °lame, half-baked, °poor, °miserable, unconvincing, unpersuasive, °empty, °shallow, °flimsy, °hollow, °pathetic, °pitiful, °unbelievable, °untenable: *Edward made some weak excuse for being late. I found Mona's argument against birth control very weak indeed.* **5** weak-minded, dim-witted, dull-witted, slow-witted, °foolish, °feeble-minded, °simple, simple-minded, soft-headed, °stupid, °dull, moronic, imbecilic, *Colloq* °dumb: *They seek out people of weaker intelligence and make fools of them.* **6** °faint, °dim, °poor, °dull, °pale, faded, °indistinct, °vague, °hazy, °imperceptible, indiscernible, unclear, blurred, blurry, muzzy, wavering, faltering, ill-defined, °feeble, flickering, °subdued: *I could hardly see her face in the weak light of the candle.* **7** °feeble, °subdued, °low, °soft, hushed, muffled, muted, almost °inaudible, stifled, °indistinct: *When the victim finally spoke, his voice was very weak.* **8** See watery, 1, above. **9 weak point**: See weakness, 3, below.

weaken *v.* **1** debilitate, enfeeble, °enervate, emasculate, °mitigate, °moderate, °dilute, deplete, °diminish, lessen, °depress, °lower, °reduce, °sap, °undermine, °exhaust, impoverish: *The continuous torture helped to weaken Errol's resolve.* **2** °fade, °dwindle, °tire, °droop, °sag, fail, give °way, °crumble, °flag: *My determination weakened when I saw what had happened to the children.* **3** °give in, °relent, acquiesce, give °way, °yield, accede, °consent, °agree, assent, °soften, °bend, °ease up, °let up, °ease off, °relax: *If you ask very politely, she might weaken and allow you to go out and play.* **4** °water (down), °dilute, °thin (out): *Adding the water so weakened the soup that it tasted like dishwater.*

weakling *n.* °milksop, °baby, mollycoddle, lightweight, namby-pamby, *US and Canadian* milquetoast, *Colloq* °sissy *or Brit also* cissy, °loser, cream puff, jellyfish, °pushover, softie *or* softy, *Slang* wimp, twerp *or* twirp, *US* weak sister, schnook, schlemiel *or* schlemihl *or* shlemiel: *If you count on a weakling like Geoffrey, nothing will ever get done.*

weakness *n.* **1** feebleness, °frailty, fragility, °delicacy, delicateness, vulnerability, °infirmity, °decrepitude: *They discovered a weakness in the structure of the bridge, so it had to be closed.* **2** incapacity, irresolution, irresoluteness, °impotence, powerlessness, puniness: *He is ashamed of his*

weakness in being unable to stop smoking. **3** °weak point, °foible, °failing, °fault, °shortcoming, °flaw, Achilles' heel, °defect, °imperfection, °liability: *Her one great weakness is her inability to deny her children anything.* **4** soft spot, fondness, °affection, °liking, °preference, °bent, °leaning, °inclination, °fancy, °penchant, predilection, proneness, proclivity, predisposition, °partiality, °appreciation, °appetite, sweet tooth, °taste, °eye: *The two of them share a weakness for good food and wine.*

wealth *n.* **1** affluence, °riches, °money, opulence, °prosperity, °property, holdings, °capital, assets, wherewithal, °cash: *Most of their wealth comes from illicit trade in diamonds.* **2** °profusion, °abundance, °bounty, plenteousness, bounteousness, copiousness, °mine, plenitude, fullness, °store, cornucopia, richness: *Janet has a wealth of ideas for situation-comedy plots.*

wealthy *adj.* °rich, affluent, °well off, °prosperous, well-to-do, °opulent, °comfortable, moneyed, *Colloq* in the °money, on Easy Street, °flush, well-heeled, in clover, *Slang* °loaded, stinking (°rich), filthy °rich, quids in, rolling in it: *Bill has a wealthy aunt who sends him a little something now and then.*

wear *v.* **1** be dressed *or* clothed in, °dress in, °put on, don, be in, step *or* °get into *or* in, °have on, °sport: *I shall wear my new suit tonight.* **2** °display, °show, °exhibit, °have, °adopt, °assume: *I wondered why she wore such a curious expression.* **3** Often, **wear down** *or* **away** *or* **off**: °damage, °impair, °harm, °fray, °erode, abrade, corrode, °rub (off): *The water has worn down the rocks till they are round and shiny. The inscription on the stone is worn away. After years of use, the paint has worn off.* **4** Often, **wear well**: °last, °endure, °survive, °hold up, °bear up, °stand up: *I wrote to the makers telling them the shoes have worn well.* **5** °drag, °pass slowly, °creep by *or* along, °go by gradually *or* tediously: *The hours wore on as I waited for the test results.* **6** Often, **wear out**: °tire, °fatigue, °exhaust, debilitate, °weary, °enervate, °drain, °burden: *You must be worn out from carrying those heavy books.* **7** °bore, °exasperate, °harass, vex, °annoy, °irritate, °tax, °strain: *I find it wearing to listen to that music all day long.* —*n.* **8** wearing, °use, utilization; attire, garb, clothing, °clothes, °apparel, °dress, °gear: *Did you get much wear out of your new hat? Suzanne is modelling a silver lamé dress for evening wear.* **9** wear and tear, attrition, deterioration, °damage, fraying, chafing, abrasion, °erosion, corrosion, °friction: *As the engine ages, heavier oil is needed to offset the normal wear.*

weary *adj.* **1** °tired, °fatigued, °exhausted, °worn out, drained, °spent, *Colloq* all in, ready to drop, fagged (out), done in, °dead (on (one's) feet), frazzled, °dead °beat, dog-tired, *Brit* knocked up, *US* knocked out, *Slang Brit* whacked, knackered, *US* pooped, zonked (out), shot: *He is so weary after work that he can scarcely eat his dinner.* **2** °boring, °irksome, irritating, °tedious, vexing, annoying, exasperating, °burdensome, wearying, tiring, fatiguing, draining, taxing, wearisome: *We walked many a weary mile before reaching the oasis.* **3** bored, °impatient, °jaded, °blasé, *Colloq* fed up, °sick and °tired, *Taboo slang* browned off: *I wish he would wipe that weary expression off his smug face.*

—v. **4** Often, **weary of**: °tire (of), be or become bored (with or by) or °impatient (with) or °jaded (with or by), *Colloq* be or become fed up (with) or °sick and °tired (of): *I soon wearied of her nagging.* **5** °exhaust, °enervate, °fatigue, °tire, debilitate, °drain, °tax, °wear or °tire out: *The long trek across country had wearied us all.*

weather n. **1** (meteorological) condition(s), °climate: *The weather suddenly changed, and we arrived home cold and wet.* **2 under the weather**: ailing, °ill, °sickly, unwell, °indisposed, out of sorts, °sick, *Colloq* °poorly, °seedy: *I didn't go sailing because I was feeling a bit under the weather.* —v. **1** °stand, °survive, °suffer, °bear up against, °endure, °withstand, rise above, ride out, °live through, °brave: *Gemma didn't think she could weather much more sarcasm from the critics.*

weave v. **1** °loom; °braid, plait, °entwine, intertwine, interlace, interweave, °knit (together): *These fabrics were woven by hand. Weave these leather strands together to make a belt.* **2** °blend, °combine, °fuse, °merge, °unite, intermingle, °mesh, °splice, dovetail, °join: *The threads of their lives are inextricably woven together.* **3** °construct, °make, contrive, °build, °create, °fabricate, °compose, °spin, °design: *Oh, what a tangled web we weave When first we practise to deceive!* **4** zigzag, criss-cross, wend or make (one's) way, °dodge, bob and weave, °shift: *Look at that motor cyclist weaving in and out of the traffic!* **5 get weaving**: get started, get a °move on, °hurry (up), °start, *Colloq* shake a °leg, *Brit* get or pull (one's) °finger out, *Chiefly US* get a wiggle on: *If you're going to get to work on time, you'd best get weaving.*

web n. spider's web, cobweb; °net, °network, entanglement, °snare, °trap: *Don't you just hate getting those webs in your hair? She became entangled in a web of deception.*

wed v. **1** °marry, espouse, get married, become husband and wife, say or take (one's) (°marriage) vows, °join or °unite in holy wedlock or matrimony; lead down the aisle, lead to the altar, *Archaic* wive; *Colloq* tie the knot, get hitched, get spliced: *They were wed on the fourth of July, 1921. That was when Harry wed Annabel.* **2** °combine, °unite, °ally, °marry, °blend, °merge, °join, °mingle, intermingle, commingle, coalesce, °mix, intermix, °amalgamate, °compound, °alloy, °fuse, homogenize: *As a chef, he is extremely fortunate to be able to wed business to pleasure.*

wedded adj. Usually, **wedded to**: intimately or obstinately °attached or connected (to), enamoured (of): *He has always been wedded to the notion of living alone on an island.*

wedding n. **1** °marriage (ceremony), wedding ceremony, nuptials; confarreation: *Our son's wedding was attended by members of the royal family.* **2** combining, °combination, uniting, °union, joining, °juncture, blending, °blend, allying, °alliance, associating, °association, marrying, °marriage, merging, °merger, mingling, intermingling, commingling, coalescing, coalescence, mixing, °mixture, intermixing, amalgamating, °amalgamation, compounding, °compound, alloying, °alloy, fusing, fusion, homogenizing, homogenization: *Through her wedding of vision to observation she has produced some truly remarkable paintings.*

wedge n. **1** °block, chock: *A shoe with a wedge heel is called a 'wedgie'. We forced wedges into the cracks in the stone to split it.* **2** °separation, separator, °division, °partition, °split, fissure, cleavage: *That woman tried to drive a wedge between me and my husband.* —v. **3** °ram, °jam, °stuff, °cram, °crowd, °force, °squeeze, °pack, °thrust: *You couldn't have wedged another person into the back seat of that Mini with a shoehorn.*

wee adj. **1** °tiny, °small, °diminutive, °little, minuscule, midget, °minute, °miniature, lilliputian, microscopic, *Colloq* itty-bitty, itsy-bitsy, teeny(-weeny), teensy-weensy: *Johnny caught his wee little finger in the door.* **2** unimportant, °insignificant, trivial, °little, °puny: *It was only a wee thing, of no interest to anyone but me.*

weep v. **1** °cry, °shed tears, °bawl, blubber, °keen, sob, °lament, °mourn, °bemoan, °bewail, °moan, °grieve, whine, whimper, mewl, pule, °snivel, *Colloq* blub, boohoo, *Brit and Australian* whinge: *A small child, sitting by herself, was weeping bitterly.* **2** °ooze, seep, exude, °drip: *The wound had started weeping and needed bandaging.*

weigh v. **1** Sometimes, **weigh in at** or **out at**: *Colloq* tip the scales at: *The sailboard weighed in at 250 pounds. I weigh more than I should.* **2** °consider, °ponder, °contemplate, °think on or over or about, °mull over, °turn over in the or (one's) mind, ruminate over, °chew over, °reflect on or upon, °brood over, °pore over, °study, °examine: *After weighing the qualifications of the candidates, we voted for you. Weigh your words carefully before responding.* **3** °judge, °estimate, assess, °evaluate, value, °determine: *It is not easy to weigh each person's contribution to the effort.* **4** Usually, **weigh on** or **upon**: °lie heavy on, °burden, °depress, °prey on, °oppress, °disturb, °perturb, °upset: *Loneliness weighs heavily on Dave's widow.* **5** °matter, °count, have (an) °effect or °influence, carry °weight, be of value or °account, *Colloq* cut any ice: *Certain factors—like the sizes of the bribes—are likely to weigh heavily with the judges of this particular beauty contest.* **6 weigh down**: °burden, overburden, °load, °overload, °encumber, °tax, overtax, °strain, °trouble, °worry, °depress, °oppress: *He's been weighed down by financial worries since losing his job.*

weight n. **1** heaviness, avoirdupois, °mass, tonnage, *Dialect* heft: *They sell peaches by weight but melons are individually priced. The weight of these books must be enormous.* **2** °burden, °load, millstone, onus, °pressure, °strain, albatross, °cross: *He has to support the weight of the entire family's expenses.* **3** °influence, °authority, °power, °substance, °force, °moment, °importance, consequence, °impact, persuasiveness, value, °worth, *Colloq* clout: *Clyde brought down his full weight in favour of the liberal candidate. Clyde's opinion carries little weight with me. He must stop throwing his weight around.* **4** °mass, °majority, °preponderance or preponderancy, °bulk, °superiority: *The weight of the voters is in favour of reducing taxes. The weight of the evidence is against us.* —v. **5** °load, °charge, ballast: *The policemen's truncheons are weighted with lead.* **6** °arrange, °manipulate, °bias, °incline, °slant, *Colloq* °rig: *The statistics are weighted so as to make the advertiser's product look superior.*

weighty adj. **1** °heavy, °ponderous, °massive, °huge, °bulky, °substantial, °ample, °large, mammoth, °colossal, °immense, °enormous, °gigantic, °prodigious; corpulent, °fat, °obese, adipose, Colloq °hefty: I found myself face to face with a rather weighty gentleman who was blocking the doorway. **2** °important, consequential, °significant, °momentous, °grave, °crucial, °portentous, thought-provoking, °provocative: These are weighty matters and should be handled with circumspection. **3** °influential, convincing, °persuasive, °impressive, °telling, °powerful, °potent, °leading; °forceful: Weighty arguments have been put forward in support of these proposals.

weird adj. °strange, °odd, °peculiar, °bizarre, °unnatural, °eerie, °queer, °grotesque, freakish, °outlandish, uncanny, °unearthly, other-worldly, °supernatural, preternatural, Literary eldritch, Colloq spooky, freaky, °kinky, Slang far-out, °way-out: There was something decidedly weird about the creature at the door.

weirdo n. °eccentric, °madman, madwoman, lunatic, °psychotic, Colloq °crazy, weirdie, nut-case, oddball, queer fish, °crank, Slang °freak, loony, psycho, Brit nutter, US screwball, nut, kook: Why belong to a club whose members are weirdos who refuse to talk to one another?

welcome v. **1** °greet, °hail, °meet, °receive, °accept, offer °hospitality (to): Everywhere she went she was welcomed with open arms.
—adj. **2** accepted, °acceptable, well-received, °desirable, °agreeable, gratifying, appreciated: Norma is always a welcome guest at my house. Ice-cream was a welcome relief from the perennial plum duff. **3** freely permitted or allowed, invited, entitled, suffered: At that hotel, guests are welcome to dine when they please.
—n. **4** °reception, °greeting, salutation: We gave the ambassador a warm welcome.

weld v. **1** °unite, °combine, °merge, °fuse, °connect, °link, °join; solder, braze, °cement, °bond: We felt welded together in a brotherhood that would last forever. The brace must be welded all the way along the edge.
—n. **2** °seam, °joint, °juncture, commissure: The weld must be filed down smooth.

welfare n. °benefit, °good, °advantage, well-being, °prosperity, (good) °fortune, °profit, °interest, (good) °health, °happiness, felicity: It is up to the parents to look after their children's welfare.

well¹ adv. **1** satisfactorily, sufficiently, adequately, agreeably, nicely, (well) enough, Colloq °OK or okay: Alan is doing well these days. **2** successfully, °famously, marvellously, wonderfully, fabulously, incredibly, splendidly, admirably, spectacularly, excellently, superbly: Barbara and David really get along well together. **3** articulately, understandably, expressively, correctly, accurately, °properly, proficiently, effectively, artistically, poetically; grammatically: Henry will make a good announcer because he speaks well. **4** comfortably, luxuriously, prosperously, extravagantly, showily, pretentiously, ostentatiously, sumptuously, grandly, opulently: How can Rita live so well with no visible income? Living well is the best revenge. **5** graciously, °kindly, °highly, °favourably, glowingly, approvingly, °warmly, genially, cordially, amiably, kind-heartedly, warm-heartedly, affectionately, lovingly: Rudolph has always spoken well

of you, Aileen. **6** skilfully, expertly, adeptly, proficiently, ably: Does Anne play well enough to compete professionally? Paul sings well. **7** °far, by a long way, immeasurably, (°very) much; °far and away, °definitely, °positively, °obviously, °clearly, plainly, °manifestly, °evidently, unquestionably, decidedly, beyond (the shadow of a) doubt, Colloq by a long chalk: Keep well away from the fuel tank before lighting that cigarette. She is well beyond the beginner stage. This painting is well worth what you paid. **8** good-naturedly, equably, coolly, serenely, calmly, soberly, unexcitedly, sedately: Burt took the bad news about his car very well. **9** °likely, °probably, in all probability, doubtlessly, without doubt, not unexpectedly, °indeed: He might well say he needs no help. **10** °easily, without difficulty: Though he gave her the money, he could not well spare it. **11** °completely, °entirely, °wholly: Before she could well finish her sentence, he was out of the house. **12** °thoroughly (cooked), (cooked) through and through, °completely (cooked): He likes his roast beef well done. **13** intimately, closely, familiarly, °personally; °thoroughly, °profoundly, soundly, fully: Do you know Boris well? I learnt my lesson well. **14** °fairly, justly, suitably, °properly, adequately, reasonably, fully, generously, °amply: James is well paid for his work. **15** °happily, mercifully, fortunately, luckily: After the divorce, both said they were well rid of each other.
—adj. **16** °healthy, °fit, °hale, °robust, °vigorous, °hearty, in fine or good fettle, Colloq in good shape: Wendy felt really well after her holiday. **17** °satisfactory, °pleasing, °agreeable, °good, °right, all °right, °fine, °proper, °OK or okay: When he phoned the office, they told him all was well.

well² n. **1** well-spring, °spring, °fountain, well-head, fountain-head, fount, °source, reservoir: The well provided a constant supply of cool clear water.
—v. **2** Often, **well up** or **out** or **forth**: °flow, °spring, °surge, °rise, °stream, °trickle, °brim over, °swell, °start; °gush, °spurt, jet, °spout; °ooze, seep, °leak: Tears welled up in the child's eyes when she saw the broken doll.

well-advised adj. °prudent, °wise, °sensible, °intelligent, °smart: You would be well-advised to avoid Chichicastenango at this time of year.

well-balanced adj. **1** °rational, °sane, °sensible, °reasonable, °level-headed, °sober, °sound, well-adjusted, °cool(-headed), Slang together: Ray is as well-balanced as people seem to be these days. **2** °even, symmetrical, °harmonious, well-proportioned, °orderly, well-ordered, well-disposed: Note the well-balanced arrangement of the windows in this Palladian façade.

well-bred adj. °well brought up, well-mannered, °polite, °decorous, mannerly, °refined, °courteous, °cultivated, °polished, cultured, gentlemanly, °ladylike, °elegant, °suave, urbane, °sophisticated, °gracious, courtly, °genteel, °gallant, °chivalrous: Jane prefers bikers to the well-bred gentlemen her mother selects for her.

well-established adj. long-standing, °traditional, °set, °venerable, °well-known, accepted, well-founded: He works for a well-established firm of solicitors. It's a well-established fact that the English discuss the weather a lot.

well-fed adj. °plump, chunky, thickset, °chubby, rounded, °rotund, portly, °stout, fleshy, overweight, adipose, °fat, °obese, °gross, Brit podgy or US pudgy: On the westward crossing we were seated with a well-fed Austrian couple.

well-groomed adj. °neat, °dapper, °fastidious, °tidy, °trim, °smart, clean-cut, °spruce, natty, well-dressed, Colloq °nifty, Slang US and Canadian spiffy: Well-groomed gentleman sought as escort to attractive widow.

well-informed adj. °knowledgeable, °learned, well-read, well-versed, well-educated, literate, °educated, Colloq in the °know, °wise, US vibrating on the right frequency, Slang °hip or hep: With access to all the media, what excuse have you for not being well-informed?

well-known adj. **1** known, °familiar, (°well-) established, acknowledged, °customary, °everyday: Plain salt is a well-known remover of wine stains. **2** °famous, °noted, °notable, °celebrated, °renowned, °illustrious, famed, °prominent, °eminent, °pre-eminent: The scandal linked a former Cabinet Minister with several well-known City names.

well off adj. °comfortable, °wealthy, °rich, affluent, °prosperous, well-to-do, Colloq well-heeled, US well-fixed: They are well off and live in a charming house on the edge of the Cotswolds.

well-thought-of adj. admired, °highly regarded, respected, °reputable, venerated, esteemed, revered, looked-up-to, valued: Timothy is a well-thought-of member of the community.

well-timed adj. °timely, °seasonable, °opportune, auspicious, °favourable, °advantageous, °beneficial: Tax incentives gave a well-timed boost to the economy.

welsher n. non-payer, °cheat, cheater, °swindler, Slang dead-beat, US welcher: That welsher never paid the money he lost to me at poker.

welt n. **1** bead, °ridge, °seam, °edge, wale, °stripe: The cushion has a welt of contrasting colour binding it. **2** °bruise, contusion, °bump, °lump, °scar, weal or wale or wheal: The boy's back was covered with red welts where he had been birched.

welter n. **1** °mass, °mess, °jumble, °tangle, °confusion, °mishmash, °muddle, °clutter, Brit °hotchpotch or US also hodgepodge: Her assignment was to sort out a welter of discarded clothing for the poor. My mind was assailed by a welter of disorganized images.
—v. **2** be sunk or °involved in, °flounder, be bogged down in, be entangled or ensnarled in: Till I found a new secretary, I would have to continue weltering in a sea of correspondence and unfiled papers.

wet adj. **1** °moist, moistened, °damp, dampened, soaked, °soaking, sopping, wringing, dripping, sodden, soppy, saturated, drenched: During the rainy season, the ground is far too wet for planting. **2** rainy, raining, teeming, pouring, drizzling, showery: We have had a very wet spring this year. **3** °feeble, °weak, °irresolute, effete, namby-pamby, °foolish, °ineffectual, °ineffective, °spineless, timorous, °cowardly: She considered some of her colleagues too wet to take the tough action needed.
—n. **4** moisture, °water, wetness, dampness, °damp, humidity, °liquid: The wet stood out on his forehead. **5** °rain, wetness, °mist, dew, °fog, °damp, humidity: Come in out of the wet, and

warm yourself by the fire. **6** °milksop, softie or softy, lightweight, Colloq °drip, °loser, Brit weed, Slang wimp, US weak sister: Why is he such a wet about standing up for his rights?

wheedle v. °coax, °cajole, inveigle, °charm, °beguile, °persuade, °talk; butter up; Colloq con, sweet-talk: Irena always managed to wheedle someone into taking her dancing.

wheel n. **1** disc, °ring, annulus, °circle, hoop: It seems odd that no culture in the western hemisphere ever invented the wheel.
—v. **2** °spin, °turn, veer, °swivel, °pivot, °swing, whirl: Medusa wheeled to face him and he promptly turned to stone.

whereabouts n.pl. or sg. **1** location, position, place, site, situation, locale, neighbourhood, vicinity: Her present whereabouts are unknown to me. The culprit concealed his whereabouts from the police.
—adv. **2** where, in or at or to what °place, whither: Whereabouts are you going to spend your holiday? Whereabouts are you going?

whet v. **1** °sharpen, hone, °grind, °file, put an °edge on, strop: He whetted the knife on an oiled stone till it was razor-sharp. **2** pique, °sharpen, °awaken, °arouse, °stimulate, °kindle, °fire, °increase, °excite, °enhance: The cruise on Bill's yacht whetted my appetite to own a small sailing-boat.

whimsical adj. **1** °quaint, fey, °fanciful, °odd, °curious, °unusual, chimerical, °queer, °singular, °peculiar, °funny, °fantastic(al), pixyish, °playful, puckish, °absurd, °preposterous, Colloq °offbeat: When Andrew's whimsical drawings caught on they were bought by greetings card makers. **2** °capricious, °erratic, °eccentric, wavering, °flighty, °unsettled, °fickle, mercurial, fluctuating, unpredictable, °inconsistent, °volatile, unsteady: The buses in our village run on what could best be termed a whimsical timetable.

whip v. **1** °beat, thrash, °lash, °flog, horsewhip, °scourge, °switch, cane, birch, flagellate, leather, °spank, strap; °castigate, °chastise, °punish, °discipline; Slang tan, US wale: They learnt right from wrong because father whipped them when they were wrong. **2** °trounce, °defeat, °beat, °conquer, °overwhelm, °rout, °overcome, °overpower, °thwart, °check, °best, worst, drub, °stop, °outdo, Colloq lick, wipe the floor with, °batter, Slang °pulverize, clobber, °destroy, °ruin, °murder, °slaughter, °kill, squash, smash, US cream: Karpilova whipped O'Meara 6-0, 6-2 at today's match. **3** °run, scamper, scoot, °race, °scurry, °scramble, °hurry, °flit, °rush, °dash, dart, Colloq zip, zoom, skedaddle: I whipped round the corner and dived behind a tree to hide. **4** °beat, °whisk, °fluff up: Whip the egg-whites till they are stiff. **5** Nautical seize, °bind, °wind, °fasten, °tie: The end of the line is whipped to prevent its unravelling. **6** whip out: °yank out, °jerk out, °pull (out), °whisk out, °present, °exhibit, °flash, °produce: He suddenly whipped out a gun and started shooting. **7** whip up: **a** °stir up, °agitate, °arouse, °rouse, °work up, °excite, °incite: The rabble-rousers whipped the crowd into a frenzy. **b** °improvise, put together or °assemble or °prepare °quickly or hurriedly, Colloq knock together, °knock up, US slap together: Tina whipped up a snack while we were waiting for Ken to arrive.

—n. **8** °scourge, knout, °lash, cat-o'-nine-tails, rawhide, quirt, horsewhip, bull-whip, cane, birch, °switch, thong, (riding-)crop, Colloq cat: We dreaded it when Dr Hazen eyed the whip hung behind the classroom door.

whipping n. **1** beating, °thrashing, lashing, flogging, horsewhipping, scourging, switching, caning, birching, flagellation, °spanking: Once he had had a whipping, the boy would not misbehave again. **2** Nautical seizing, binding, tying, winding, fastening: The whipping will prevent the end of the line from unravelling.

whirlpool n. maelstrom, vortex, °eddy, whirl, °swirl, Heraldry gurges: As we watched in horror, the canoe was drawn down into the whirlpool and disappeared.

whirlwind n. **1** waterspout, dust devil, cyclone, typhoon, anticyclone, °hurricane, extra-tropical cyclone, tropical cyclone, Nontechnical tornado, Nautical white squall, Australian willy-willy, Colloq US whirly: A whole row of houses was destroyed in the whirlwind. —adj. **2** °speedy, °quick, °swift, °sudden, °precipitous, lightning, headlong, °hasty, °rash, °impetuous: It was one of those whirlwind romances that last till the wind dies down.

whisk v. **1** °rush, dart, °sweep, °brush: Agatha whisked about the room, aimlessly moving small objects about on tables and shelves. **2** °speed, °rush, °carry, °whip, °hasten, °hustle, °hurry: The taxi came and whisked Fran off to the airport. **3** See whip, 4, above. —n. **4** °sweep, °wave, °brush, flick: With a whisk of his hand he dismissed the servants. **5** °brush, fly-whisk: The chief flicked his whisk to signal that the audience was ended. **6** beater, °whip: It is quicker to whip cream with a whisk.

whisky n. whiskey, °alcohol, spirits, John Barleycorn, usquebaugh, Scotch, home-brew, mother's ruin (= 'gin'), Scots barley-bree, US rye, bourbon, white lightning, white mule, °moonshine, Colloq °booze, hooch, rot-gut, US corn, fire-water, Slang US Sneaky Pete, smoke: Peter is a welcome guest who always remembers to bring a bottle of whisky.

whisper v. **1** °breathe, °murmur, °mutter, °mumble, °hiss, °speak or °say softly or under (one's) breath, °sigh, susurrate: He whispered sweet nothings in her ear. **2** °gossip, bruit about, °noise abroad, °murmur, °insinuate, °hint, °rumour, °disclose, divulge, °reveal, °breathe a word: We have all heard Corin whispering of your wife's infidelities. —n. **3** °murmur, undertone, hushed tone(s): Why do you always speak in whispers when talking about Nesta? **4** °hint, °suggestion, soupçon, °suspicion: There was never the slightest whisper of gossip about Eleanor.

white adj. **1** snow-white, snowy, chalk-white, chalky, ivory, creamy, milky, milk-white, oyster-white, off-white; °silver, hoary: Many buildings in the tropics are painted white. Do you believe that a person's hair can turn white overnight? **2** °pale, pallid, °pasty, °wan, whey-faced, ashen, bloodless, drained, whitish, waxen, °ghastly, °ghostly, anaemic, °dead white, deathly white, cadaverous, corpse-like: Her black dress contrasted starkly with her white complexion. **3** °innocent, °pure, unsullied, stainless, unblemished, °spotless, °immaculate, virginal, °virtuous, undefiled, °chaste: She came to you with white

hands, which you have sought to dirty with your vicious accusations. **4** Caucasian, Caucasoid, light-skinned, fair-skinned, pale-complexioned: The American Indian was—and still is—treated very unfairly by the White man.

whitewash v. °gloss over, °cover up, sugar-coat, °hide, °camouflage, °conceal, °qualify, °minimize, extenuate, °diminish, °play down, downplay, make °light of, °rationalize, °excuse: We are being accused of whitewashing the dishonest actions of the previous administration.

whittle v. **1** °pare (down or away), °shave, °trim, °cut, °carve, hew, °shape: Remember when Grandpapa used to whittle those tiny figures of elves when we were children? **2** Usually, **whittle away at** or **down**: °pare, °shave, °cut, °trim, °reduce, °diminish, °erode, °eat away at: If he keeps whittling away at his trust fund, he might have to get a job.

whole adj. **1** °entire, °complete, uncut, °full, °intact, unbroken, °total: I can't believe she ate the whole chicken. Were you here the whole time? **2** in °one piece, °intact, unharmed, undamaged, °unscathed, unimpaired, unhurt, uninjured: How could anyone emerge whole from that smash-up? **3** °well, °healthy, °sound, °fit, °strong: The surgeons have made him whole again. —n. **4** °everything, aggregate, (°sum) °total, °totality, °lot, °entirety; °ensemble; Colloq whole kit and caboodle: I look at the whole and don't bother about petty details. **5 on the whole**: °largely, mostly, °usually, more often than not, for the most part, in °general, °generally, by and large, with few exceptions, all things considered, all in all, as a rule, °chiefly, °mainly, in the °main, predominantly: On the whole, our clients collect only originals, not copies or prints.

wholehearted adj. °devoted, dedicated, committed, °earnest, °sincere, unqualified, °unmitigated, unreserved, °complete, °entire, unstinting, °real, °true, °genuine, °hearty, °heartfelt, °serious, °enthusiastic, zealous, °warm, °fervent, °ardent, °spirited, °eager, °energetic: Once I agree to help, you can rely on my wholehearted support.

wholesome adj. **1** healthful, °healthy, health-giving, °nutritious, nourishing, °beneficial, °tonic, salutary, salubrious, strengthening, °bracing, °stimulating: Everyone should regularly engage in wholesome exercise. **2** °moral, °ethical, °righteous, °upright, °honourable, °decent, °principled, °proper, °fit, °meet: I am not sure that the child is being brought up in a wholesome atmosphere.

wholly adv. **1** °altogether, °entirely, °absolutely, °quite, °totally, °thoroughly, °completely, in toto, fully, in all respects, in every way, all in all, °utterly, unqualifiedly, every inch, 100%; lock, stock, and barrel; root and branch; backwards and forwards; from the ground up; Colloq bag and baggage; °hook, line, and sinker; to the nth degree; (the) °whole hog, US up one side and down the other: We are wholly on your side in this matter. The company has been wholly reorganized. **2** °only, exclusively, solely, unexceptionally, categorically, unequivocally, unambiguously, explicitly: The success or failure of the plan depends wholly on you.

whoop n. **1** °shout, °shriek, °yell, °roar, °bellow, hoot, (battle or war) °cry, war-whoop, °outcry,

°scream, screech, squeal, yelp, yowl, °howl, bark; °cheer, hurrah, huzzah; *Colloq* holler: *At his whoop of joy we knew he had passed the exam.*
—*v.* 2 °shout, °shriek, °yell, °roar, °bellow, hoot, °cry (out), °scream, screech, squeal, yelp, yowl, °howl, bark; °cheer, hurrah, huzzah; *Colloq* holler: *He heard the tribesmen whooping as they descended on the fort.*

whopping *adj.* 1 °huge, °great, °enormous, °colossal, °gigantic, °immense, tremendous, °prodigious, °monstrous, °thumping, mammoth, °massive, Brobdingnagian: *With that whopping Great Dane of yours in the kitchen there's no room to move about.* 2 °flagrant, °outrageous, °extravagant, °terrible, °awful: *Jones tells such whopping lies I don't know when to believe him.*

wicked *adj.* 1 °evil, °bad, °immoral, amoral, unprincipled, °sinful, °impious, irreligious, °blasphemous, °profane, °sacrilegious, °ungodly, °godless, °diabolic(al), °satanic, Mephistophelian, demonic, demoniac(al), hellish, °infernal, accursed, °damnable, °fiendish, °ghoulish: *How wicked must one be to murder one's own child? She has done many wicked things, but this was the worst.* 2 depraved, °dissolute, °villainous, black-hearted, iniquitous, °horrible, horrid, °hideous, heinous, °beastly, °base, °low, °vile, debased, °degenerate, °perverse, °perverted, °corrupt, °foul, °offensive, °abominable, °disgraceful, °shameful, °dreadful, °awful, °gross, °gruesome, °grim, appalling, °grisly, °loathsome, °lawless, °unrepentant, unregenerate, °incorrigible, °criminal, felonious, rascally, knavish, °terrible, egregious, execrable: *The Deluge was regarded as divine vengeance on a wicked world. He was a wicked man, in league with the devil himself.* 3 °dirty, °pornographic, °filthy, °erotic, °obscene, °lewd, °offensive, °indecent, °prurient, smutty, °rude, °taboo, °blue, °coarse, °bawdy, °vulgar, salacious, licentious, °nasty, X-rated, *Colloq US* raunchy: *The townspeople took the wicked books and burnt them all.* 4 °vicious, °beastly, °savage, °nasty, °bad, °violent, °mean, °cruel: *Graham has a wicked temper. The boys were subjected to the most wicked treatment.* 5 °naughty, °mischievous, impish, °sly, °devilish, rascally, roguish, scampish, puckish; vexatious, exasperating, annoying, irritating, °irksome, °trying, galling, bothersome: *What trouble have those wicked children got themselves into now? It is wicked of you to make pig noises every time I mention Bertha.* 6 °foul, °offensive, pernicious, baleful, mephitic, °disgusting, °revolting, sickening, °repulsive, °repellent, °nauseous, °repugnant, °rotten, pestilential, noxious: *That liniment the doctor prescribed has a wicked odour.* 7 °expert, °ingenious, °superior, °superb, °superlative, °outstanding, °masterful, masterly, °skilful, deft, °adept: *That chap Gough plays a wicked game of tennis.*

wide *adj.* 1 °spacious, °roomy, °ample, °extensive, °broad: *The road is wide enough for two cars to pass. If the book is set in wider type, it will have more pages.* 2 °broad, °extensive, °comprehensive, °encyclopedic *or* encyclopaedic, °inclusive, far-reaching, wide-ranging, widespread: *He has wide interests, from music to archaeology to sport.* 3 °extreme, °considerable, °substantial, sizeable, °major, °big, °large; widespread: *There have been wide fluctuations in market prices.* **4 wide of the mark**: off the °mark, astray, °deviant, deviating, off

(the) °target, not on °target, °inappropriate: *Forecasts from analysts were based on erroneous assumptions and proved to be very wide of the mark.* —*adv.* 5 astray, afield, wide of the °mark, off the °mark, off (the) °target, to one side: *He took careless aim and the shot went wide.* 6 all the way, as much as °possible, fully, °completely, to the utmost: *The dentist said, 'Open wide'. When I heard the drill, I was suddenly wide awake.*

widely *adv.* 1 extensively, °thoroughly, °universally, °everywhere, °generally, by °many: *In the days when it was widely believed that the earth was flat, perhaps it was.* 2 to a °large or a °great extent, greatly, °largely, °very much, °extremely, considerably, °substantially: *Opinions differ widely regarding the origin of the universe.*

widen *v.* distend, dilate, °spread, °stretch, °enlarge, °increase, °expand, °extend, broaden, °supplement, °add to, augment: *It will be necessary to widen the opening to allow insertion of the device. We are planning to widen the news coverage we provide our readers.*

width *n.* 1 °breadth, wideness, compass, broadness, °span; diameter, °calibre, °bore; °measure; *Nautical* °beam: *What is the standard width of railway track in this country? The width of the cannon-ball is three inches.* 2 °reach, °scope, °range, °breadth, °extent, extensiveness: *There is an impressive width of choice at the restaurant.*

wield *v.* 1 °flourish, °swing, brandish, °wave, °handle, °use, °employ: *He wields that machete as if he means business.* 2 °exercise, °have, °employ, °exert, °use, utilize: *Since Juan is the one who wields the power, he is the one to deal with.*

wife *n.* °mate, helpmeet, helpmate, spouse, bride, °partner, *Colloq* better half, little woman, the missis *or* missus, old lady *or* woman, ball and chain, *Slang* trouble and strife: *Doesn't your wife mind your going out every night?*

wild *adj.* 1 undomesticated, °untamed, unbroken, °savage, feral: *The only four-legged animals inhabiting the island were wild pigs.* 2 uncultivated, °uninhabited, °waste, °desert, °desolate, virgin, unpopulated, °empty, °trackless, °barren, °lifeless, °deserted: *The cottage overlooks an expanse of wild moorland.* 3 °savage, °uncivilized, barbarous, °primitive, °rude, uncultured, uncultivated, brutish, barbaric, °fierce, °ferocious: *Some early explorers studied the wild people they encountered in far-off lands.* 4 °uncontrolled, unrestricted, unrestrained, untrammelled, unbridled, unfettered, unshackled, °free, unchecked, °lively, °impetuous, unconventional, °undisciplined, °disobedient, °insubordinate, self-willed, wayward, °mutinous, °rowdy(ish), °boisterous, °unruly, °tumultuous, turbulent, °tempestuous, °uproarious; uncontrollable, unmanageable, °ungovernable, intractable, unrestrainable: *Peter led quite a wild youth. We cannot cope with their wild behaviour after they have had too much to drink.* 5 °mad, °maniac(al), crazed, °crazy, irrational, distracted, frenzied, °frantic, °distraught, °hysterical, °raving, raging, unhinged, demented, °delirious; °berserk; run amok *or* amuck: *William had a wild look about him. Nellie has been driven wild by the pressures of business.* 6 °exciting, °excited, vehement, °passionate, °romantic, turbulent, °chaotic, °tempestuous, °reckless, madcap: *At the time, Ernest was having a wild love affair with*

Charles's widow. **7** °absurd, irrational, °unreasonable, °extravagant, °fantastic, °imprudent, °foolish, °foolhardy, °impractical, °impracticable, unpractical, unworkable, °ridiculous, °reckless, °silly, °giddy, °flighty, madcap, °outrageous, °preposterous, °bizarre, °strange, °odd, °peculiar, *Colloq* °offbeat: *He lost thousands on some wild scheme for reducing shipping costs by filling bubble packing with helium.* **8** tousled, wind-blown, °unkempt, dishevelled, °untidy, disordered, °disorderly, messed-up, *Colloq* mussed-up: *Her hair was in wild disarray.* **9** °enthusiastic, avid, °eager, °agog, *Colloq* °crazy, °mad, °daft, dotty, *Brit* potty, *Slang* nutty, nuts: *I'm just wild about Harry, And Harry's wild about me.*
—*n.* **10** Usually, **wilds**: wasteland, wilderness, °desert, vastness, °emptiness, *Colloq* °sticks, middle of nowhere, back of beyond: *His idea of adventure was to trek through the wilds of Hyde Park.*

wile *n.* Often, **wiles**: °trick, °stratagem, °ruse, °artifice, °subterfuge, °dodge, °trap, °snare, °manoeuvre, ploy, contrivance, °move, gambit, °plot, °scheme, °machination, *Colloq* (little) °game: *You won't get far trying to work your wiles on me, young lady.*

wilful *adj.* **1** °intentional, °deliberate, °voluntary, °conscious, intended, °purposeful, °premeditated, *US* willful: *The jury decided that such a wilful act of vandalism must be punished. She is accused of wilful neglect of her children.* **2** °stubborn, headstrong, pigheaded, °obstinate, mulish, °inflexible, adamant, obdurate, intransigent, unyielding, °self-willed, °ungovernable, °recalcitrant, °unruly, °immovable, intractable, dogged, °determined, refractory, uncompromising, wayward, °perverse, °contrary: *Jim is far too wilful, and tends to have a tantrum if he fails to get his own way.*

will *n.* **1** °desire, °wish, °longing, °liking, °inclination, °disposition, °drive, purposefulness, °purpose, °intent, °intention, °resolve, commitment, °resolution, °determination; will-power: *Where there's a will there's a way. Some believe that taking medication is against God's will. Marguerite seems to have lost the will to live.* **2** °choice, °wishes, °desire, °inclination: *He was forced to submit against his will.* **3** (last will and) testament, last °wishes: *In accordance with his will, Josiah was buried at sea.* **4 at will**: as or when (one) pleases or wishes or thinks °fit(ting), at (one's) °desire or whim or °pleasure or °discretion: *If he brings his own car, then he can leave at will.*
—*v.* **5** °want, °desire, °wish, °choose, see °fit, °make, compel, °force, °command, °order, ordain, °require: *When she willed him to appear, there was a flash of lightning and he was there.* **6** °leave, °bequeath, °devise, °hand down or on, °pass on, °transfer; settle upon or on: *My great-uncle Philip willed me his collection of 19th-century theatre memorabilia.*

willing *adj.* °agreeable, acquiescent, compliant, amenable, consenting, assenting, °passive, complaisant, docile, °ready, well-disposed, °happy, °content, °pleased, °delighted, °enthusiastic, avid, °eager, zealous, *Colloq* °game: *Albert might not have thought up the pranks, but he was a willing accomplice.*

willingly *adv.* °readily, °happily, contentedly, °gladly, cheerfully, amenably, agreeably, °freely, passively, docilely, of (one's) own °accord or °free °will, on (one's) own, ungrudgingly, by °choice, °voluntarily, unhesitatingly, nothing loath, eagerly, enthusiastically, zealously, avidly, *Colloq* at the drop of a hat: *We did not coerce him in any way—he went along quite willingly. You can rely on Hubert to give willingly and generously to support any good cause.*

willowy *adj.* **1** lissom or lissome, pliant, lithe, °flexible, °supple, limber, loose-limbed: *Everyone enjoys watching the willowy athletes training for the Olympics.* **2** °slim, °slender, °graceful, sylphlike, svelte, °thin, long-limbed, clean-limbed: *How does Jeanne keep her willowy figure without dieting?*

willy-nilly *adv.* **1** whether one likes it or not, inevitably, °necessarily, of °necessity, perforce, whether or no, like it or not, *nolens volens, bon gré, mal gré*: *Having borrowed the money, you must, willy-nilly, repay it.*
—*adj.* **2** °necessary, °unavoidable, °inevitable, °involuntary: *He joked about a willy-nilly choice, meaning one offering no alternatives.*

wilt *v.* **1** °sag, °droop, wither, °shrink, °shrivel (up or away), °diminish: *My house-plants wilted because they weren't watered.* **2** °sag, °droop, °bow, °weaken, °sink, °wane, wither, lose courage or nerve, °flag, °dwindle, languish: *The lad wilted under the stern glare of the headmaster.*

wily *adj.* °shrewd, cunning, °crafty, °sly, °artful, guileful, °clever, °foxy, vulpine, °disingenuous, °shifty, °scheming, plotting, °calculating, °designing, °sharp, canny, °deceitful, deceiving, °deceptive, treacherous, °perfidious, °false, double-dealing, °dishonest, underhand(ed), °tricky, °smooth, °slick, °slippery, °oily, unctuous, *Scots and No. Eng.* pawky, *Colloq* cagey, °crooked, two-timing, *Slang chiefly Brit* fly: *Rats are wily and cunning, and have to be taken seriously.*

win *v.* **1** come (in or out) °first, carry the day, °conquer, °overcome; carry off (the palm), finish °first (in), °achieve °first place (in), °triumph (in), be °victorious (in), be the °victor (in), °gain a °victory (in), °prevail (in), °succeed (in), take °first °prize (in), *Colloq* bring home the bacon: *Which team is more likely to win today? We seem to have won the battle but not the war.* **2** °gain, °carry off or away, attain, °acquire, °get, obtain, °secure, °procure, °receive, °collect, °net, °bag, °earn, °realize, °pick up, glean: *Look at all those trophies Gillian has won playing golf!* **3 win over**: °influence, °sway, °incline, °persuade, °charm, °prevail (up)on, °convert, °induce, °bring °round or around, °convince: *Don't think that Gilbert can be won over without a strong argument.*
—*n.* **4** °victory, °conquest, °triumph, °success: *So far this season we have recorded six wins and one loss for the Surrey Scouts.*

wind[1] *n.* **1** °breeze, zephyr, °puff, °gust, °breath, °draught, light °air, °current (of °air): *A gentle wind wafted our little boat across the bay.* **2** puffery, °bombast, rodomontade, °bluster, boasting, braggadocio, vain speech, blather, (idle or empty) °talk, fustian, °nonsense, twaddle, humbug, °babble, °gibberish, *Colloq* °gab, °hot air, claptrap, hogwash, °rot, hooey, boloney, *Slang Brit* (load of (old)) cobblers: *I went there for advice and all I got was a lot of wind.* **3** gas, flatulence, windiness, flatus, borborygmus (= 'stomach rumbling (as from gas)'), heartburn, *Taboo slang* fart (= 'anal °release of gas'): *I have to take a pill to relieve this wind.* **4 before the wind**: *Nautical* downwind, off the wind: *We were racing before the wind with every scrap of sail flying.* **5 break wind**: *Taboo slang* fart: *It is considered rude to break wind.* **6 get** or **have wind of**: °hear of, °learn of, come to °know, °pick up, be made or become °aware of, °gather, °understand, °hear on the °grapevine, *Colloq* °hear tell of: *We got wind of the company's plans to close this plant.* **7 get** or **have the wind up**: take °fright, become frightened or °afraid or apprehensive: *When I heard a window being raised I got the wind up.* **8 in the wind**: around, °about, rumoured, in the air, detectable, °discernible, discoverable, °imminent, °impending, approaching, °close (at °hand), about to °happen or take °place or °occur, afoot, in the offing, °near, on the way, *Colloq Brit* on the cards, *US* in the cards: *We knew that a change was in the wind, but never expected the chairman to resign.* **9 off the wind**: See 5, above. **10 on the** or **a wind**: *Nautical* upwind, windward, to the wind, into (the teeth or the eye of) the wind: *Because 'Syrena' was a sloop, she could sail closer on the wind than the schooner.* **11 put the wind up**: °scare, °frighten, °alarm: *The leakage at the nuclear plant really put the wind up everyone living in the area.* **12 sail close** or **near to the wind**: take °risks, throw caution to the winds, play with °fire, skate on thin ice, take (one's) life in (one's) hands, *Colloq* stick (one's) neck out, *Slang* go for broke: *One nude scene is highly salacious, and we think the director is sailing very close to the wind by including it.* **13 take the wind out of (someone's) sails**: deflate (someone), disconcert (someone), destroy (someone's) advantage, ruin (someone's) superiority or supremacy or ascendancy: *It rather took the wind out of her sails when he announced that he was leaving anyway.*

wind² v. **1** °turn, °bend °twist, °snake, worm, °twine, zigzag, slew, °swerve, °loop, coil, curve, °meander, °ramble, veer: *The river winds along the valley floor.* **2** °reel, °roll, °spiral, °turn, °twist, curl, °coil, °wrap, °twine, wreathe; °crank (up), wind up: *The streamers are wound around the columns for decoration.* **3 wind down**: **a** °taper off, °slow down, °diminish, °reduce, °close out, slacken or °slack off (on), °ease (up on), °decrease, °cut back or down (on); wind up: *They were going to wind down their sportswear department, but then business suddenly perked up.* **b** °relax, become °calm or °tranquil, °calm down, °cool off or down, regain (one's) equilibrium, °ease up or off, *Colloq* unwind, let (one's) hair down, take it °easy: *It takes me a couple of days to wind down from the hectic activity in the office.* **4 wind up**: **a** °terminate, conclude, come or bring to an °end or a °close or a conclusion, °end (up), °close down or up, °finish (up), °wrap up; liquidate; °settle: *After calmly winding up his affairs, Evan sailed off in his boat and was never seen again.* **b** °end up, °finish (up), °become °ultimately: *I understand that Sally wound up as a bar girl in Tampico.* **c** °excite, innervate, °energize, °stimulate, invigorate, °stir up: *After getting us all wound up about that weekend party in Paris, she called the whole thing off.* **d** °agitate, °fluster, disconcert, °ruffle: *Don't let such trifles get you so wound up.* **e** See 3 a, above.

windfall n. bonanza, °godsend, stroke of (good) °fortune, serendipitous °find, °boon, piece of (good) °luck, jackpot, (°lucky) strike: *The sale of the house provided a windfall that saved them from imminent bankruptcy.*

windy adj. **1** blustery, blowing, blowy, °breezy, gusting, gusty, °wild, squally, °tempestuous; windswept: *It is quite windy today. I waited at that windy corner for you and you never showed up!* **2** °talkative, long-winded, garrulous, °wordy, verbose, prolix, loquacious, °rambling, °voluble, °fluent, °effusive, glib, turgid, °bombastic, °pompous, longiloquent: *Potter does tend to be windy at times.*

winner n. °victor, °champion, prizewinner, title-holder, conqueror, conquering °hero, *Colloq* champ: *The winner will receive a new car.*

winning adj. **1** °engaging, °attractive, alluring, captivating, °endearing, °prepossessing, winsome, bewitching, °fetching, °taking, °enchanting, °pleasing, °delightful, charming, °amiable, °friendly, °pleasant, °sweet: *Maggie's winning ways are a tremendous asset in making friends.* **2** °triumphant, conquering, °victorious, °successful: *The winning team is invited to dine at the Red Lion.*

wintry adj. **1** hiemal, brumal, hibernal; °icy, snowy, °freezing, frozen, frosty, °cold, °frigid, °bitter (°cold), °chilly, chilling, °piercing, °cutting, glacial, Siberian, arctic, hyperborean: *It was cold and the sky was clear and wintry with premonitions of frost.* **2** °cold, °frigid, °chilly, °cool, chilling, glacial: *She got a very wintry reception from Dan's parents, who disliked the idea of their living together.* **3** °forbidding, °bleak, °dismal, cheerless, °dreary, °harsh, unfriendly, °ugly, °menacing, °ominous, °threatening, °dark: *His comment about her age evoked only a wintry look from Margot.*

wipe v. **1** Sometimes, **wipe off** or **out** or **up**: °rub, °clean (off or out or up), °cleanse; °dry (off or out or up), dust (off), mop (up), swab, sponge (off or up): *For God's sake, wipe your nose! Please wipe the crumbs off the table when you've finished eating. Stop crying and wipe up the spilt milk.* **2** Often, **wipe off**: °remove, °erase, °take off or away, get °rid of: *Wipe that grin off your face, stranger.* **3 wipe out**: °kill (off), annihilate, °massacre, °destroy, °finish (off), °dispose of, eradicate, °obliterate, °exterminate, do away with, °stamp out, get °rid of, °remove, wipe off the face of the earth: *Scientists have succeeded in wiping out smallpox.*

wiry adj. °muscular, °sinewy, °lean, lank, °thin and °strong, °tough and °flexible: *He was a stocky and wiry little man, rather like a short-legged terrier.*

wisdom n. **1** sagacity, sageness, °judgement, discernment, °reason, °prudence, judiciousness, (common) °sense, °insight, °penetration, sapience, °understanding, rationality, clear-sightedness, clear-headedness, perspicacity, perspicuity, percipience, °perception, perceptiveness, °intelligence, acuteness, acumen, astuteness, sharpness, shrewdness, long-headedness: *At least she had the wisdom not to shoot the intruder. Allen's wisdom stems from long experience in such matters.* **2** °knowledge, °learning, erudition, °lore, °scholarship, enlightenment: *The wisdom of the ages is locked away in these books.*

wise adj. **1** °sage, sagacious, °judicious, °reasonable, commonsensical, °prudent,

°sensible, insightful, sapient, °understanding, °rational, °sound, clear-sighted, clear-headed, discerning, perspicacious, perspicuous, percipient, °perceptive, °intelligent, °acute, °astute, °sharp, °shrewd, °crafty, °clever, °bright, °quick-witted, °smart, °brilliant, long-headed, *Colloq* brainy: *Among the wisest of men were Solomon, Confucius, Buddha, and, perhaps, Aristotle.* **2** °knowledgeable, °learned, °enlightened, °informed, erudite; (well-)°educated, °knowing, well-read, well-versed, °lettered, °scholarly: *We saw to it that they escaped, and the police were none the wiser. Wise heads prevailed at the college on what constituted worthwhile research.* **3** °well-advised, °advisable, °judicious, °sensible, °expedient, °reasonable, °strategic, °tactful, °tactical, °prudent, °politic, °discreet, °diplomatic, well-thought-out, well-considered, °proper, °fitting, °appropriate, °meet: *Do you think it wise to punish the child so severely?* **4 put wise (to):** °inform *or* °advise *or* °warn (*of or about*): *If you must know how he found out, it was Myrna who put him wise. Did she also put him wise to where the money is hidden?* **5 wise to:** °aware *or* °knowledgeable *or* °informed of *or* about, °sensitive to, on to *or* onto, *Colloq* in the know about: *You are wrong if you think she isn't wise to your little tricks. Get wise to what's going on, man.*
—*v.* **6 wise up (to):** become °informed *or* °aware (*of or about*), °wake up (to), *Colloq* get °wise (to) *or* in the know (about): *If Cooley doesn't wise up, he'll be in deep trouble. Was it you who wised Meg up to the fact that Tom no longer cares?*

wisecrack *n.* **1** °joke, °quip, rejoinder, °witticism, °pun, barb, jest, °gibe *or* jibe, *Colloq* °gag; °dig: *Everything is a potential subject for a wisecrack.*
—*v.* **2** °joke, °quip, °pun, °gibe *or* jibe: *Get serious and stop wisecracking for a change.*

wise guy *n.* wiseacre, °smart alec *or* aleck, *Archaic* witling, *Colloq* know-all *or* know-it-all, *Brit* Clever Dick *or* cleverdick, *Slang* smarty-pants, smarty, *Brit* smart-arse, *US* smart-ass, wisenheimer: *There's always some wise guy waiting to make a clever remark.*

wish *v.* **1** °desire, °want; °yearn, crave, °long, °hope, °hanker, have a °mind, (have a) °fancy, °choose, °care: *I wish you'd go now. If you had Aladdin's lamp, what would you wish for?* **2** °require, °request, °demand, °order, °specify: *Did you wish lemon or milk in your tea?* **3** °foist *or* °force *or* °thrust *or* °impose upon, *Colloq* fob off on *or* upon, palm off on: *The job of treasurer was wished on me when Jock left.*
—*n.* **4** °desire, °request, whim, °want, craving, °longing, hankering: *Your every wish is my command.* **5** °desire, °longing, craving, °need, yearning, hankering, °passion, keenness, °thirst, °appetite, °hunger, whim, °urge, °liking, fondness, °fancy, °preference, predisposition, °disposition, °inclination, *Colloq* yen, *Slang* °itch: *She expressed a wish for nightingale tongues, truffles, and champagne.*

wishy-washy *adj.* **1** neither here nor there, undecided, °indecisive, °irresolute, °half-hearted, shilly-shallying, tergiversating, vacillating, °uncertain, of *or* having °mixed feelings, of two minds: *Make up your mind and stop being so wishy-washy about everything!* **2** °feeble, °weak, °watery, watered down, °thin,

°vapid, °flat, °bland, runny, diluted, °tasteless, insipid, flavourless, °stale: *Isabel served me some wishy-washy tea and sent me on my way.*

wisp *n.* °shred, °scrap, strand, °thread, snippet, tuft, °lock: *The laboratory matched the wisp of hair found in the victim's hand with the hair of the suspect.*

wistful *adj.* **1** °melancholy, °mournful, °sad, morose, °sorrowful, disconsolate, heartsick, °forlorn, woeful, °woebegone, °desirous, °longing, yearning: *She gave a last, wistful look at the aeroplane as it rose into the clouds.* **2** °thoughtful, contemplative, °pensive, absent-minded, °detached, °absorbed, in a brown study, °preoccupied, meditating, °meditative, °reflective, ruminating, ruminative, °dreamy, dreaming, day-dreaming, musing: *Some might have misinterpreted his wistful gaze at her photograph.*

wit *n.* **1** °intelligence, brains, °mind, (common) °sense, °judgement, °understanding, discernment, °wisdom, sagacity, °insight, astuteness, cleverness, *Slang* savvy: *He hasn't the wit to know when he's being insulted.* **2** °humour, drollery, °levity, joking, °repartee, °raillery, facetiousness, waggishness, badinage, jocularity, wordplay, paronomasia; °amusement, °entertainment: *Some say that sarcasm is the lowest form of wit.* **3** °comedian, comedienne, humorist, °comic, °wag, °joker, *farceur, farceuse,* punster, madcap, °zany; °parodist, satirist, caricaturist; *Colloq* pundit, °card, °character: *In the face of such a devastating remark, even the club wit was struck dumb.*

witch *n.* **1** sorceress, enchantress, °magician, sibyl, pythoness; warlock: *The witches prophesied that Macbeth would be king.* **2** °hag, °fury, battle-axe, crone, gorgon, Medusa, ogress, Xanthippe, °shrew, virago, harridan, fishwife, termagant, *Archaic* beldam, *Offensive* old °bag, bitch: *How could you stand living with the old witch for so many years?*

withdraw *v.* **1** °draw back, °retract, °pull back, °recoil, °shrink back: *He would suddenly withdraw into his cocoon whenever she said the name, 'Elsie'.* **2** °retract, °recall, °take back, °cancel, rescind, °recant, disavow, disclaim, abjure, °void, annul, °go back on, °back down (on): *If she doesn't withdraw that remark, I shall sue her for slander.* **3** °pull out, °extract, °remove, *Technical* retrude: *Afterwards, she withdrew the knife, washed it, and replaced it in the rack.* **4** °retire, °retreat, °go, °repair: *After dinner, we withdrew to the drawing-room for brandy and cigars.* **5** °leave, °depart, °go, make (oneself) scarce, °absent (oneself), °retire: *We waited till the servants withdrew before exchanging news about Cora.*

withdrawn *adj.* **1** °reserved, °detached, °distant, °standoffish, °aloof, °shy, diffident, °bashful, °timid, timorous, introverted, °taciturn, °reticent, °silent, °quiet, °retiring, shrinking: *Why is Henry acting so withdrawn tonight?* **2** °remote, °distant, °isolated, °solitary, °hidden, °secluded, °private, °out-of-the-way, °reclusive: *Sarah and Ben have led a withdrawn existence since the children married and moved away.*

withering *adj.* °destructive, °devastating, death-dealing, °murderous, °deadly: *The enemy laid down a withering barrage of machine-gun fire.*

withhold *v.* **1** °hold *or* °keep back, °retain, °reserve, °restrain, °control, °repress, °check, °hide, °conceal: *He could withhold his anger no* longer. **2** °hold *or* °keep back, °deduct, °retain, °reserve: *The company is required to withhold a percentage of wages and salaries for taxes.*

withstand v. °resist, °oppose, °stand (up to), °face, °defy, confront, °combat, °grapple with, °fight (against), °cope with, °hold out against, °weather, °suffer, °survive, °tolerate, °take, °bear, °last through, °endure, °brave, *Colloq Brit* °stick: *Can Brian withstand the pressure of his new job? Our small force withstood the attack for days.*

witness n. **1** °observer, °onlooker, °spectator, viewer, °eyewitness, °bystander, watcher, *Rare* earwitness: *Were you a witness to what took place here?* **2** deponent, testifier, corroborating °witness, corroborator: *The defence will call its witnesses today.* **3 bear witness (to** *or* **of):** °testify (to), °attest (to), be *or* give *or* provide *or* furnish *or* constitute °evidence *or* °proof *or* °testimony (of *or* to), °verify, °confirm, corroborate, °show, °prove: *The bent poker bears witness to the violence of the attack.*
—v. **4** °see, °observe, °watch, °look on *or* at, °view, °behold, °mark, note, °notice, °take in, *Colloq* °spot, °catch: *I did witness the way they looked at each other.* **5** countersign, °sign, °certify, °endorse, °substantiate, °document, certificate: *Would you mind witnessing our signatures, Miss Cabot?* **6** See 3, above.

witticism n. °pun, °quip, play on words, bon mot, jest, °joke, °epigram, °clever °remark, sally, *Archaic or literary* °conceit, *Colloq* °gag, one-liner: *Clive is just as likely to utter a witticism as say something excruciatingly banal.*

witty adj. °ingenious, °subtle, °clever, °humorous, °sarcastic, °sardonic, piquant, °comic(al), °farcical, °ludicrous, facetious, amusing, jocular, waggish, droll, °funny: *Corbett, not ready with his usual witty riposte, shouted an obscenity at the bus driver.*

wizened adj. wrinkled, shrunken, shrivelled (up), withered, °gnarled, dried up, wilted, faded, wasted: *The wizened old crone is his grandmother.*

woe n. °trouble, °hardship, adversity, °misery, °anguish, tribulation, °calamity, °trial, wretchedness, °grief, unhappiness, °desolation, dolour, °melancholy, °gloom, °depression, sadness, disconsolateness, °misfortune, °affliction, °sorrow, °distress: *How much more woe could beset one small family?*

woebegone adj. troubled, °miserable, anguished, °wretched, grief-stricken, °unhappy, °desolate, °doleful, dolorous, °melancholy, melancholic, °gloomy, °mournful, °sorrowful, depressed, °dejected, °sad, °glum, crestfallen, chap-fallen, lugubrious, downcast, disconsolate, °unfortunate, star-crossed, afflicted, distressed, woeful, °forlorn, °downhearted, °broken-hearted, °heartbroken, disheartened, *Slang US* bummed out: *Timmy has been so woebegone since his puppy was stolen!*

woman n. **1** female, lady; °girl: *Elvira was the first woman to be elected to the board.* **2** °wife, spouse, bride, lady-love, °sweetheart, lady, °girl, girlfriend, °mistress, concubine, °mate, helpmeet, helpmate, °partner, *Colloq* sweetie, better half, little woman, the missis *or* missus, old lady *or* woman, ball and chain, *Slang* trouble and strife: *In this scene, Porgy tells Bess that she is his woman, now and forever.* **3** °lass, °maid, °maiden, °miss, lassie, *Slang* gal, dame, bird,

skirt, chick, bit of fluff, °broad, piece (of work), number, baggage, moll, popsy: *The soldiers went into town to try to find some women for an evening's entertainment.* **4** °domestic, housekeeper, °maid, cleaning woman *or* lady, maidservant, chambermaid, handmaiden, abigail, lady-in-waiting, *Brit* charwoman, *Colloq Brit* char, °daily: *They have a woman who comes in every other day.*

wonder n. **1** °marvel, °prodigy, °phenomenon, °spectacle, °rarity, °sight, °curiosity, miracle, *Slang* °knockout, stunner, mind-blower, mind-boggler, °trip: *Surely, the wheel must rank high among the wonders of technology. And still he gazed, and still the wonder grew, That one small head could carry all he knew.* **2** awe, °astonishment, °admiration, °amazement, wonderment, °surprise, stupefaction, °fascination: *Facsimile transmission, which used to excite so much wonder, is now used in offices all over the world.*
—v. **3** °ponder, °muse, °meditate, °think, °theorize, conjecture, °puzzle, °query, °question, °inquire, be °inquisitive, be °curious, °ask oneself, °speculate, cudgel (one's) brains: *I wondered if I would be invited to the dance. Have you ever wondered what makes the world go round?* **4** °marvel (at), goggle, °gawk, °gape, °stare, be awed, be °thunderstruck, be amazed, be astonished: *We wondered at the death-defying skills of the trapeze artistes.* **5 wonder about:** °question *or* °doubt the sanity *or* reason *or* reasonableness of: *I wondered about Tammy after that streaking episode.*

wooded adj. sylvan, forested, bosky, tree-covered, woody, timbered: *We rested and had our lunch in the coolness of a wooded glen.*

wooden adj. **1** wood, woody, ligneous, xyloid: *The wooden cabinet for the kitchen is almost finished.* **2** °stiff, °rigid, °artificial, °clumsy, °stilted, °unnatural, °awkward, ungainly, spiritless, unanimated, °dead, °lifeless, °dry, passionless, unimpassioned, °impassive, °vacant, °empty, °colourless, expressionless, deadpan: *The understudy gave a wooden performance as Uncle Vanya.* **3** unintelligent, blockheaded, °stupid, °dull, insensitive, slow-witted, dull-witted, °obtuse, oafish, doltish, tiny-minded, dim-witted, dunderpated, *Colloq* °thick, wooden-headed, knuckle-headed: *Clancy has some pretty wooden ideas about how to run a business.*

woolly adj. **1** fleecy, woollen, wool-bearing, laniferous, lanate *or* lanose, lanuginose *or* lanuginous, downy, °fuzzy, °shaggy, flocculent *or* floccose, flocky: *He was wearing a woolly hat. After two days one test tube contained a woolly precipitate.* **2** °hazy, °fuzzy, unclear, °obscure(d), foggy, °indistinct, °confused, °vague, cloudy, clouded, °nebulous, ill-defined: *My recollection of the event is a bit woolly after all these years.*

word n. **1** (little) °talk, (brief) °conversation, °chat, °discussion, consultation, °dialogue, °huddle, °parley, °tête-à-tête, chit-chat, confabulation, °conference, °interview, *Colloq* powwow, confab: *Could I have a word with you before you leave for the day?* **2** °news, °intelligence, °information, °facts, °data, °report, °story, tidings, °account, communiqué, °bulletin, °dispatch *or* despatch, °message, *Colloq* °low-down, *Slang* info, °dope, *Brit* gen, *US* poop: *Have you had any word about the situation in the Middle East?* **3** °name, °term, designation, locution, appellation, °expression, °phrase: *What is* the word for 'write' in Greek? **4** °promise, °pledge, °vow, °oath, (solemn) word of honour, °undertaking, °assurance, °warrant, °guarantee *or* guaranty, °warranty: *You have my word that I won't mention this to anyone.* **5** utterance, °expression, °declaration, °statement: *Let me give you a word of warning, my friend.* **6** °suggestion, °hint, scintilla, °bit: *I promise that I won't breathe a word of this to anyone.* **7** °command, °order, °signal, °direction, °instruction, *Colloq US* high °sign: *I shall not press the red button till you give the word.* **8 in a word**: succinctly, °briefly, in °brief, in a °few words, concisely, in °short, in °summary, in °sum, not to mince words, to make a long story short, when all is said and done, in the final analysis, not to beat about the bush, *Colloq* in a nutshell: *His bedside manner was, in a word, menacing.* **9 words: a** °quarrel, °dispute, °argument, unpleasantness: *Paul and Kitty had words and are not on speaking terms.* **b** lyrics, °book, libretto, °text: *Did Irving Berlin write the words as well as the music to his songs?* —*v.* **10** °put (forth), °say, °couch, °express, °phrase, utter, °state, °term, °style, °set forth: *Had you worded your complaint in politer language, you might have spared yourself a punch in the eye.*

wording *n.* phraseology, °language, phrasing, °choice of words, °word °choice: *From the confused wording of this note I cannot tell whether you are coming to my party or not.*

wordy *adj.* verbose, prolix, °rambling, long-winded; pleonastic, °redundant, garrulous, °windy, °talkative, loquacious: *This contract is too wordy and could be cut to two pages. Try to make your replies less wordy.*

work *n.* **1** °labour, toil, °effort, °drudgery, travail, °exertion, °industry: *Few people make it to the top and stay there without hard work.* **2** °employment, °business, °occupation, °vocation, °calling, °profession, °trade, °line, métier, °career, livelihood, °job, °post, °position, °situation: *Does your work as a test pilot interfere much with your home life?* **3** °task, °function, °duty, °assignment, °charge, °responsibility, chore, commission, °undertaking, °stint: *When you are finished with that work, clean out the cellar.* **4** °feat, °achievement, °creation, °accomplishment, °opus, handiwork, *oeuvre*, °production, °composition, °piece, master-work, °masterpiece, *chef-d'œuvre, magnum opus*, °output: *Some of Edwin's recent works have won prizes.* **5 in work**: in °production, under °way, being done, in the works, being planned, in the planning stage(s): *The budget has been approved and the project is already in work.* **6 out of work**: °unemployed, °idle, jobless, at °liberty, between engagements, °available, °free, *Brit* °redundant, *Colloq Brit* on the °dole, *US* on *or* collecting unemployment: *How long have you been out of work?* —*v.* **7** °labour, toil, °exert oneself, °sweat, moil, °slave (away), °peg away, slog (away): *His father worked in the mines from the age of nine till he died of black-lung disease at forty.* **8** °till, °plough, °farm, °cultivate: *Would he have been healthier and longer-lived had he worked the land?* **9** have a °job, °hold (down) a °post *or* °position, °earn a living, be °employed: *His wife works as a designer in a Parisian fashion house.* **10** °control, °manage, °manipulate, °manoeuvre, °wield, °handle, °operate, °use, make °use of, utilize, °exploit, °deal with, bring into play: *Are you sure you*

know how to work all those dials and buttons? **11** °function, °operate, °run, °go, °develop, °turn out, *Colloq* °pan out: *Are you sure that the plan is working to your advantage?* **12** °function, °operate, °run, °go: *The drill works better if you turn on the power.* **13** knead, °mould, °form, °fashion, °shape; °mix, stir, °incorporate: *Work the clay into long, narrow strips. Try to work the colour in with your fingers.* **14** °manoeuvre, °manipulate, °guide: *See if you can work him over into a corner where you can grab him.* **15** °operate, °use, °employ, put to (good *or* effective) °use, °wield, °manipulate, °ply, °apply, °exploit: *Tanya must have worked her magic on Eustace to make him that docile.* **16** °bring about, °effect, °accomplish, °carry out *or* off, °make, °produce, °achieve, engender, beget, °create, do, °put through, °execute, °fulfil, °effectuate, °implement, °realize: *I doubt that the new sports centre will work many changes in the area.* **17 work in**: find °time *or* °space for, °include, °insert, °introduce, °fit in, °squeeze in, °accommodate: *I'll try and work in your comments when I write up my report.* **18 work on**: °wheedle, °coax, importune, °press, *Brit* pressurize, *US* °pressure; °influence, °persuade, °act on, °prevail (up)on, °induce, °dispose, °urge: *Keep working on him to try to change his mind.* **19 work out: a** °exercise, do callisthenics, do aerobics, °warm up, do setting-up exercises, do (one's) daily dozen, °jog, lift weights, °train, °drill: *I try to work out for an hour every day.* **b** Often, **work out at** *or* **to**: °equal, °total (up to), °result in, °amount to, °come to: *Let's see—that works out at one car for every 4.7 people.* **c** °clear up, °resolve, solve, *Slang Brit and New Zealand* suss out: *Thaddeus is old enough to work out his own problems. Can they work out their differences?* **d** evolve, °develop, °succeed, °prosper, °come out all °right, prove satisfactory, °go °well, be °effective, *Colloq* °pan out: *How can you be so sure that everything will work out?* **e** °formulate, work up, contrive, °draw up, °detail, °plan, °develop, °devise, put together, °elaborate, °expand, °enlarge (on): *The captain worked out a way for them to escape.* **20 work up: a** °excite, make °excited, °agitate, °inflame, enkindle, °arouse, °rouse, °stir, °move, °animate, °incite, °spur, *Colloq* °fire (up), get (someone) (all) steamed *or* hopped *or* het up: *Those fire-and-brimstone preachers used to get the people all worked up.* **b** °prepare, (make *or* get) °ready, whip into shape, °develop, come up with, °write up, put together, °produce, °turn out: *Can you work up that proposal in time for Monday's meeting?* **c** °advance, ascend, °rise, °move up *or* ahead *or* on: *In no time at all, Greg worked his way up from assembler to foreman.* **d** See 19 e, above.

worker *n.* °labourer, working man *or* woman, workman, °hand, °employee, artisan, craftsman, °tradesman, white-collar worker, blue-collar worker, proletarian, breadwinner, wage-earner: *It seems unlikely that the workers would strike for longer hours and less pay.*

workmanship *n.* handicraft, °craft, craftsmanship, artistry, °art, °technique, handiwork, °skill, skilfulness, mastery, *US* artisanship: *One cannot help but admire the workmanship in those marquetry tabletops.*

works *n.pl.* **1** °plant, °factory, workshop, °shop, °mill: *We were taken on a tour of the works to see how the marble is carved.* **2** °mechanism, machinery, workings, (moving *or* working) parts; clockwork, *Colloq* innards, insides, *Slang* guts: *We once had a clock with all the works exposed.* **3 the works: a** °everything, the °lot, *Colloq* the whole kit and caboodle, the whole shooting match, °everything but the kitchen sink, *Chiefly US and Canadian* the whole she-bang: *We ordered two hamburgers with the works.* **b** °thrashing, a beating, a drubbing, a battering, a flogging, a lambasting: *When he refused to tell them where the money was hidden, they gave him the works.*

world *n.* **1** °earth, planet, °sphere, °globe, Terra; °universe, cosmos, °existence, °creation, °life: *Do you believe the world is round? Buckland lives in his own, private world.* **2** °humanity, mankind, °people, the human °race, °society, the °public, men, humankind, everybody, °everyone, the world at °large: *We know what he thinks of the world, but what does the world think of him?* **3** °area, °sphere, °domain, community, °clique, °crowd, °circle, °fraternity, °faction, °set, coterie: *What value does the art world place on Longchamps' paintings?* **4** °period, °time(s), °age, °era, epoch: *They have produced an excellent series of programmes on the ancient world.* **5 bring into the world: a** °deliver, °have, give birth to, beget, *Rare or dialect* birth: *Grandmother brought sixteen children into the world.* **b** °deliver, midwife: *The town family doctor brought hundreds of children into the world in his long career.* **6 for all the world**: °precisely, °exactly, in all °respects, in every °respect, in every °way, °just: *He behaved for all the world like a man possessed by the devil.* **7 on top of the world**: °ecstatic, °delighted, °elated, °happy, °exultant, °overjoyed, °rapturous, *Brit* in the seventh °heaven, *US* in seventh °heaven, *Colloq* on cloud nine, *Brit* over the moon: *George has been on top of the world ever since Prudence agreed to marry him.* **8 out of this world**: °marvellous, wonderful, °exceptional, °unbelievable, °incredible, °excellent, °superb, *Colloq* °great, smashing, °fantastic, °fabulous, *Slang* out of °sight, far-out, *Brit* °magic, *US* to the max: *The place we stayed at Ibiza was out of this world!*

worldly *adv.* **1** mundane, °earthly, °terrestrial, °temporal, °physical, °carnal, fleshly, cor-poreal, °human; °lay, non-spiritual, non-religious, civic, °secular, °profane: *Theo indulged in worldly pleasures in the fleshpots of the continent. Veronica put aside worldly things and took the veil.* **2** urbane, °suave, °sophisticated, cos-mopolitan, worldly-wise, *Slang* with it, °hip, °cool: *Behind that worldly manner is the heart of a peasant.*

worn *adj.* **1** °shabby, °threadbare, tatty, °tattered, °ragged, frayed: *Burt wears an old, worn tweed jacket when he's around the house.* **2** °haggard, °drawn: *He looked anxiously at his mother's thin, worn face.* **3 worn out**: °tired, °fatigued, °exhausted, frazzled, °spent, °jaded, played out, °haggard, °drawn, the worse for wear, *Colloq* dog-tired, all in, done in, *Slang* °dead (on one's feet), °beat, *US* pooped: *I was completely worn out from climbing those stairs.*

worried *adj.* °fearful, apprehensive, °anxious, distressed, °nervous, uneasy, anguished, dis-quieted, agonized, °agonizing, °distraught, on °edge, on tenterhooks, °ill at ease, troubled, °fretful, °agitated, perturbed, °upset, °suffering: *The two worried mothers waited at the police station for news of their children.*

worry *v.* **1** be °anxious, be °fearful, be °concerned, °fret, agonize, be distressed, be vexed, *Colloq* °stew, bite *or* chew (one's) nails, go *or* get grey, get grey hair, *Slang* °sweat blood, *US* °sweat bullets: *I worry about you when you stay out so late.* **2** °annoy, °irk, °pester, nettle, harry, °harass, °tease, °bother, °tantalize, °torment, °plague, hector, badger, nettle, °gall, peeve, *Colloq* hassle: *The police have been worrying me the way a dog worries a bone.* —*n.* **3** °concern, °care, °responsibility; °problem, °bother, °trouble, °affliction, irritation, °annoyance, vexation: *I cannot see why that is your worry. I am sorry to hear about your financial worries.* **4** °anguish, °anxiety, uneasiness, unease, nervousness, °distress, apprehension, disquiet, perturbation, °agitation, °upset, °misgiving: *Your association with that crowd has caused your mother and me a great deal of worry.*

worsen *v.* **1** °increase, exacerbate, °heighten, °intensify, °aggravate: *The recent rains have worsened the drainage problem.* **2** °weaken, °deteriorate, °decline, °degenerate, °decay, °slip, °sink, °slide, °fail, °disintegrate, take a turn for the worse, get worse, go from bad to worse, *Colloq* go downhill: *Her condition continues to worsen.*

worship *v.* **1** °venerate, °revere, °reverence, °extol, °honour, °exalt, °praise, °admire, °adore, adulate, °glorify, deify, °idolize, be °devoted to, pay °homage to, °bow down before, kneel before, put on a °pedestal: *When he arrived, he found the people worshipping huge stone idols.* —*n.* **2** °veneration, °reverence, adoration, °devotion, °homage, °honour, °respect, °esteem, exaltation, °praise, °admiration, adulation, glorification, deification, idolatry: *A healthy respect for security should not be confused with the worship of money.*

worth *n.* °quality, °merit, value, °advantage, °benefit, °good, °importance, °significance, °usefulness: *You have underestimated Roberta's worth to the community.*

worthless *adj.* **1** valueless, unimportant, °insignificant, inessential *or* unessential, °dispensable, °disposable, °paltry: *His con-tribution to the work of the committee proved utterly worthless.* **2** °pointless, °bootless, °silly, °inane, °vain, unavailing, °useless, °futile, °fruitless, unproductive, °unprofitable: *It is worthless to try to salvage that wreck.* **3** °cheap, valueless, °tawdry, °poor, trashy, rubbishy, °shabby, °wretched, *Colloq* °tinny, crappy, cheesy, *Slang* chintzy: *The deceased's handbag contained only a few items of worthless jewellery.*

worthwhile *adj.* **1** °profitable, justifiable, °productive, °gainful, °rewarding, °fruitful, cost-effective, remunerative: *Would it be worth-while to buy up that land as a long-term investment?* **2** °useful, valuable, °good, °helpful, °beneficial, °worthy, beneficent, °desirable, °exemplary, °matchless, °honourable, °upright, °sterling, °irreproachable: *Brian Smith is one of the most worthwhile people I met at university.*

worthy *adj.* **1** °worthwhile, °deserving, merit-ing, °meritorious, °praiseworthy, °good,

°estimable, °qualified, creditable: *He is a worthy recipient of the honour.* **2** See **worthwhile, 2,** above.

—*n.* **3** °dignitary, °personage, °notable, eminence, luminary: *The dinner was attended by all the local worthies.*

wound *n.* **1** °damage, °hurt, °injury, trauma, traumatism; laceration, °puncture, °cut, °gash, °slash, lesion, °bruise, contusion: *We dressed and bandaged the wounds of the victims.* **2** °slight, °damage, °injury, °harm, °blow, °distress, mortification, °torment, torture, °anguish, °pain, °insult: *Hugh takes the slightest criticism as a deep wound to his self-esteem.*

—*v.* **3** °damage, °harm, °injure, °hurt, traumatize; °cut, °slash, gash, °lacerate, °slit, °stab, °shoot, *Colloq* wing: *He was wounded in the leg in the war.* **4** °slight, °distress, °damage, °mortify, °insult, °hurt, °pain, °grieve, °offend, aggrieve, °wrong: *I was terribly wounded by the things she said about me.*

wrap *v.* **1** Sometimes, **wrap up**: °swathe, swaddle, °bind, °cover, enwrap, °envelop, °wind, enshroud, °shroud, enfold, °fold, °muffle, °enclose, sheathe, encase; °pack, °package, do up, gift-wrap: *Wrap up well—it's cold outside. I've just finished wrapping some Christmas presents.* **2 wrapped up in**: immersed in, submerged in, buried in, °absorbed in, engrossed in, °bound up in, °involved in, occupied with *or* by *or* in, °engaged in, dedicated to, °devoted to: *While Irma is completely wrapped up in her grandchildren, Henry is wrapped up in his books.* **3 wrap up: a** °complete, conclude, °finish, °end, bring to a °close, °terminate, °wind up, °settle, °tidy up: *We'll be able to wrap things up in an hour and go home.* **b Wrap up!**: Be °silent!, Be °quiet!, Stop talking!, Hold your °tongue!, *Slang* °Shut up!, Shut your face!, Shut your °trap!, Shut your °mouth!, *Brit* Put a sock in it!: *He would have kept on wittering away if she hadn't told him to wrap up.*

—*n.* **4** °stole, shawl, °mantle, poncho, serape, °cloak, °cape: *Sonia adjusted her evening wrap before going out to dinner.*

wrapper *n.* **1** housecoat, °robe, dressing-gown, bathrobe, kimono, negligee, lounging °robe, peignoir, *US* house-dress: *Peggy threw on a wrapper and went to answer the door.* **2** envelope, °package, packing, wrapping, covering, jacket, °case, casing, container: *Throw the wrapper in the dustbin.*

wreak *v.* °inflict, °exercise, °exert, °carry out, °bring (to bear), °visit, °effect, °work, unleash, °execute, °impose, °force, °vent, let go: *The tribesmen wreaked vengeance on the hill people for destroying their farms.*

wreck *v.* **1** °destroy, °ruin, °devastate, °demolish, smash, °shatter, °spoil, °dash (to °pieces), reduce to nothing, turn into °scrap, annihilate: *He drove my motor-bike into a tree and wrecked it.* **2** °sink, scuttle, run aground, °founder, °capsize: *The ship was wrecked on a reef near Rarotonga.*

—*n.* **3** °hulk, shipwreck, °ruins: *The wreck finally rusted away to nothing.* **4** °mess, °disaster, °ruin; °havoc: *That man made a wreck of her life.* **5** °destruction, °loss, °sinking, devastation, foundering, grounding, °capsize, capsizing, disabling, disablement, wrecking; demolition, demolishing, levelling, tearing down, razing,

pulling down, obliteration: *The wreck of the Titanic was a major news event in 1912. The wreck of the old tower block is scheduled for next month.*

wreckage *n.* debris, fragments, remains, rubble, °ruin(s): *The wreckage of the building is being searched for survivors.*

wrench *v.* **1** °yank, °twist, °jerk, °force, °pull, °tug, °tear, wring, °rip, wrest: *The gun was wrenched from my grasp, breaking my finger.* **2** °strain, sprain, °twist, overstrain: *After she wrenched her ankle on the ladder, Mary couldn't walk for a week.* **3** °extract, wrest, wring, °force, °pry, °draw: *The only way they could wrench the information from Michael was by torturing him.*

—*n.* **4** °yank, °twist, °jerk, °pull, °tug, °rip: *One wrench at the doorknob and it came off in my hand.* **5** °pang, °pain, °agony, torture, °blow, °ache, °throe, °anguish, °sadness, °grief, heartbreak: *The severest wrench at my heartstrings came when we had to part.* **6** *Brit* spanner, shifting spanner, adjustable spanner, *US* monkey wrench: *We need metric wrenches to work on your car.*

wrestle *v.* °battle, °fight, °struggle, tussle, °strive: *After thirty years Garth wrestled his way to the top in the company.*

wretch *n.* **1** °scoundrel, blackguard, worm, °villain, cur, °beast, dog, swine, °rogue, °good-for-nothing, knave, varlet, scallywag *or* scalawag, °rascal, rapscallion, *Archaic* caitiff, whoreson, *Colloq* rat, °stinker, louse, creep, *Slang* bastard, *Brit* rotter, bounder, blighter, *US* °bum: *That wretch not only stole my watch but asked me for money to support her!* **2** °unfortunate, °poor °fellow *or* °chap, °miserable °creature, °poor °devil, pilgarlic, *Slang* °poor bastard *or* son of a bitch, *Brit* °poor °bugger *or* sod, *US* °sad sack: *The poor wretch cannot keep a job and lives off others' charity.*

wretched *adj.* **1** °miserable, °awful, °terrible, °atrocious, °deplorable, *Colloq* °lousy, °rotten: *We had the most wretched weather throughout our holiday.* **2** °unhappy, °sad, °miserable, °woebegone, woeful, °dismal, °downhearted, °heartbroken, °broken-hearted, heartsick, °dejected, depressed, melancholic, °melancholy, °mournful, disconsolate, °inconsolable, °doleful, cheerless, crestfallen, °joyless, °desolate: *If you want to see a wretched human being, look at a boy whose dog is lost.* **3** °pitiable, °pathetic, °sorry, °pitiful, hapless, °hopeless, °unfortunate, °miserable: *The poor in these tropical paradises are some of the most wretched people on earth.* **4** °vile, °shameful, °scurvy, underhand(ed), treacherous, °contemptible, °despicable, °base, °low, °mean, °paltry, mean-spirited, detestable: *It was hard to see how the people could support such a wretched little demagogue.*

wriggle *v.* **1** wiggle, wobble, °shake, °tremble, °quiver, °jiggle, waggle, writhe, °twist, °fidget: *She managed to wriggle free of the ropes and run away. The dog was wriggling with excitement at seeing its master.* **2** °twist, °squirm, °snake, worm, writhe, °slither, °crawl: *He wriggled through the narrow opening into the strongroom.*

—*n.* **3** wiggle, zigzag, wavy °line, *Colloq* squiggle, squiggly °line: *The page had no writing on it, only a lot of wriggles.* **4** wriggling, writhing, °squirm, squirming, wiggle, wiggling, shaking, trembling, °quiver, quivering, shimmying, waggle, waggling, twisting, °twist: *Don't confuse that rhythmic wriggle of the hips with dancing.*

wrinkle[1] *n.* **1** crease, °fold, °line, °furrow, crinkle, crow's-foot, corrugation, °pucker, °ridge: *She hasn't a wrinkle on her face—but then she's only nine.*
—*v.* **2** crease, °fold, °line, °furrow, crinkle, corrugate, °pucker, °gather, ruck, crimp, °screw up, °rumple, °crumple: *I love the way you wrinkle your nose when you're perplexed.*

wrinkle[2] *n.* °dodge, °gimmick, °device, ploy, °ruse, °scheme, °trick, °idea, °plan, °plot, °stunt, °way, °approach, °technique, °method, *Slang chiefly Brit* wheeze: *Leave it to Edmund to come up with a new wrinkle for fleecing pensioners.*

write *v.* **1** °pen, scribble, get off, °dash off; indite, inscribe, °make out: *I was writing you a note when you phoned. She wrote out a cheque for £1,000.* **2** °correspond (with), °send a letter *or* a note *or* a postcard *or US also* a postal °card, °communicate (with): *You don't write home often enough. Write and let me know when you get a job.* **3** °compose, °create, °make up, °author: *We saw the house in which Elgar wrote the 'Enigma' Variations.* **4 write down: a** °register, °list, catalogue, note, make a note *or* °notation, °record, °transcribe, °set *or* °jot *or* °take down, note, put in writing, put in black and white: *The teacher was known for Irish bulls like, 'All absent students must write down their names'.* **b** derogate, decry, °disparage, °put down, °minimize, make little of, °play down, °detract, °belittle: *Cumberland's contributions have been written down by his critics.* **5 write off:** °delete, °cancel, °disregard, °ignore, °forgive, °forget (about), annul, eradicate, °erase: *The bad debts have been written off.*

writer *n.* °author, novelist, littérateur, essayist, man of letters, °scribe, scribbler, wordsmith, freelancer, penny-a-liner, °hack, Grub Streeter, °journalist, newsman, °reporter, °correspondent, member of the fourth estate, (gossip) columnist, stringer, *Brit* paragraphist, *US* paragrapher, *Colloq* pen-pusher, pencil-pusher, sob sister, *Brit* journo: *These days all those who know how to write call themselves writers.*

writing *n.* **1** handwriting, longhand, °penmanship, °script, calligraphy *or* chirography, scribble: *I sometimes have trouble reading your writing.* **2** Sometimes, **writings**: °(literary) °work(s), °composition, °theme, °book, article, critique, °criticism, °review, °editorial, column, exposé, °essay, °poetry, °poem, °novel, non-fiction, fiction, °document, letter, correspondence, °publication, *Chiefly Brit journalism* leading article *or* leader, *Chiefly US journalism* op-ed article: *Her writing has been widely published. Poe's writings are collected in this book.* **3** °literature, belles-lettres, letters: *I don't agree that British writing has declined since 1900.*

wrong *adj.* **1** °improper, unjust, unfair, injudicious, unethical, °terrible, °foul, °awful, °bad, °immoral, °sinful, °evil, iniquitous, °villainous, °wicked, °vile, °diabolic(al), °infernal, °fiendish, °corrupt, °dishonest, reprehensible, °abominable, °dreadful, °dishonourable, blameworthy, °naughty, °shameful, °disgraceful, opprobrious, °criminal, felonious, °illegal, °illicit, °unlawful, °illegitimate, *Colloq* °crooked: *They believe that all war is wrong. It was wrong of you to come here while my husband was away.* **2** °mistaken, in °error, °erroneous, °incorrect, °inaccurate, °imprecise, °inexact, fallacious, askew, °false, °wide of the mark; °strange, °odd, °peculiar, °curious; *Colloq* off target *or US also* off the target, *Brit* off beam, *US* off the beam: *The answers to these four questions were all wrong. You certainly have some wrong ideas about me.* **3** °incorrect, °improper, unsuitable: *They must have given us the wrong baby at the hospital.* **4** °inappropriate, inapt, °improper, indecorous, °unseemly, unfitting, °unacceptable, °undesirable, °incongruous, °unbecoming, out of °place, ill-considered, wrong-headed, °imprudent, °misguided, inexpedient, impolitic, infelicitous, *Colloq* out of line: *You saw nothing wrong in inviting girls to stay with you in your rooms? Your mother thinks she's the wrong girl for you.* **5** out of °order, not working, °faulty, awry, °amiss, the °matter, °defective, °imperfect, °unsound, °flawed, °deficient: *Considering the noise my car makes, there must be something wrong.* **6** °opposite, °reverse, °incorrect, °improper: *That is the wrong direction to the post office.*
—*adv.* **7** awry, imperfectly, incorrectly, improperly, inappropriately, °amiss, °badly, wrongly, *Scots and No. Eng. and literary* agley, *Colloq* out of sync: *You've wired up the video all wrong.* **8 go wrong: a** go astray, falter, °fail, °lapse, °err, °fall from grace, go to the °bad, °deteriorate, go downhill, backslide, regress, retrogress, recidivate: *Her father was convinced that she would go wrong if she went into the theatre.* **b** °fail, malfunction, °break down, °miscarry, backfire, °fall through, *Colloq* °flop, come to °grief, go kaput, *Brit* go phut: *The entire plan went wrong when Clara started screaming.*
—*v.* **9** °abuse, °mistreat, °injure, °misuse, maltreat, ill-use, °ill-treat, °discredit, asperse, calumniate, malign, °dishonour, °impose upon, take °advantage of, °harm, °damage, °oppress: *He believes he was wronged by his commanding officer.*

wry *adj.* **1** distorted, contorted, twisted, °lopsided, °deformed, °crooked, aslant, °one-sided, askew, °bent, tilted, off-centre: *He is afflicted by a rheumatic disorder, which gives his neck a wry appearance.* **2** °dry, droll, °witty, °sardonic, °sarcastic, ironic(al), amusing; °perverse, fey; *Scots* pawky: *Bill has a wry sense of humour that does not appeal to everyone.*

yank v. **1** °jerk, °jolt, °tug, °wrench, °snatch, °hitch: *He yanked the chair from beneath me just as I sat down.*
—n. **2** °jerk, °jolt, °tug, °wrench, °snatch, °hitch: *Give two yanks on the rope when you want me to pull you up.*

yap v. **1** bark, yelp: *Their dog was yapping away all night.* **2** gabble, °babble, blither or blather, °chatter, °jabber, °tattle, °prattle, prate, *Colloq chiefly Brit* witter, natter, *Slang* jaw, run on, *US* run off at the mouth: *I wish she'd stop her yapping and give me some peace.*
—n. **3** °mouth, *Slang* °trap, °gob, *US* bazoo: *If only Sam would shut his big yap once in a while!*

yardstick n. °measure, benchmark, criterion, °standard, °gauge, °basis, °touchstone, °scale, exemplar: *We thought she sang beautifully, but then we had no yardstick against which to judge.*

yarn n. **1** °thread, °fibre, strand: *I haven't enough yarn to finish knitting these socks.* **2** °tale, °story, °account, °narrative, anecdote; °tall °tale, fable, °fabrication, fiction, cock-and-bull °story, *Colloq* whopper, *Brit* fishing °story, *US* fish °story, fish °tale: *The old salt had many yarns to spin during the long evenings by the fire.*

yearly adv. **1** annually, perennially, every year, °once a year, year after year, year in (and) year out, regularly: *We watch the Canada geese migrate north yearly.* **2** per year, per annum, by the year, each year: *What is the interest rate yearly?*
—adj. **3** annual, °perennial, once-a-year, °regular: *Those yearly migrations told us when to plant the first crop.*

yearn v. °long, pine, °ache, °hanker, °itch, °hunger, °thirst, crave, have a craving, °desire, °wish, °want, °fancy, °prefer: *I yearn to see the green-clad hills of home once more, Before my vessel bears me from this mortal shore.*

yell v. **1** °shout, °scream, °bellow, °howl, screech, yowl, °roar, °bawl, caterwaul, squall, yelp, *Colloq* holler: *'Stop yelling at your sister!' shouted my father.*
—n. **2** °shout, °scream, °cry, °bellow, °howl, screech, yowl, °roar, caterwaul, squall, yelp, *Colloq* holler: *I think I heard a yell for help.*

yeomanly adj. yeoman, workmanlike, °useful, °staunch, °courageous, °loyal, dedicated, °faithful, °steadfast, unswerving, unwavering, °firm, °sturdy, °reliable, °solid: *Carruthers certainly did a yeomanly job on reorganizing the system.*

yes-man n. toady, sycophant, toad-eater, time-server, °hanger-on, lickspittle, bootlicker, truckler, °flunkey, courtier, jackal, spaniel, lap-dog, *Taboo slang Brit* arse-kisser, arse-licker, *US* ass-kisser, ass-licker, brown-noser: *He surrounds himself with yes-men, then says he refuses to take no for an answer.*

yet adv. **1** as yet, (up) till or until now, so °far, thus far, hitherto, to the °present (time): *She hasn't arrived yet.* **2** °still, up to this °time, up to °now, even now, till or until now, to this day: *She was there earlier and I think she's there yet.* **3** °moreover, furthermore, °besides, °further, °still: *He made yet another excuse.* **4** in the °future, in °time to come, later, °eventually: *Despite the*

life I've led, I might yet get to heaven. **5** °still, °notwithstanding, anyway, anyhow, °nonetheless, °nevertheless, °regardless, in °spite of or °despite everything, just or all the °same, °even so, after all, *US* still and all: *Despite the life I've led, I might get to heaven yet.*
—conj. **6** °notwithstanding, in °spite of or °despite it or that or the fact, °still, °nevertheless, but: *He goes out every night, yet never oversleeps in the mornings.*

yield v. **1** °surrender, °give up (the fight or struggle), °give in, knuckle under, °submit, °cede, cry quits, throw in the towel or the sponge, °capitulate, °succumb, raise the white flag: *The captain of the enemy company asked if we would yield.* **2** °give up, °surrender, °give over, °hand in or over, °abandon, °relinquish, °renounce, °cede: *We agreed to yield our arms to the enemy.* **3** °agree, °consent, °comply, °concede, °relent, assent, give °way, accede, concur: *He did his best to persuade me, and I finally yielded.* **4** °earn, °return, °pay, °bring in, °supply, °generate, °produce, °net: *She has investments that yield more than 15% a year.*
—n. **5** °return, °production, °output, °revenue, takings, °gate, °earnings, °income, °proceeds, °profit, °gain: *The yield from that operation is not even enough to pay the rent.*

yielding adj. **1** pliant, flexile, °flexible, °pliable, °soft, °plastic, fictile, °elastic, resilient, °supple, springy, bouncy, spongy, rubbery: *The frame is of a yielding material that gives way under pressure.* **2** °accommodating, docile, °submissive, amenable, °tractable, compliant, °obedient, °flexible, acquiescent, °agreeable, °obliging, °manageable, manipulable: *He wanted a wife with a yielding temperament who would tolerate his foibles.*

young adj. **1** youthful, teenage(d), °adolescent, prepubescent, pubescent, °juvenile, °minor, °junior, under °age: *Would you believe that she has young children?* **2** °boyish, girlish; °immature, °callow, °green, °inexperienced, °unfledged, uninitiated, °unsophisticated, °childlike, °innocent, °naïve: *This programme may contain material unsuitable for young ears.* **3** °childish, °puerile, °infantile, babyish, *US* sophomoric: *He's too young to invite to the party.*
—n. **4** °offspring, babies, °issue, little ones, °progeny, °litter, °brood; children: *The cat's young should stay with her for a few weeks.*

youth n. **1** °childhood, boyhood, girlhood, °young manhood, °young womanhood, prepubescence, pubescence, adolescence, salad days; immaturity, minority: *In our youth we do many foolish things we might later regret.* **2** °child, youngster, schoolchild, °teenager, teen, °minor, °juvenile, °adolescent; °boy, schoolboy, °stripling, °young °boy or °man, °lad, laddie, whippersnapper; °girl, °lass, lassie, schoolgirl, °maid, °maiden, *Literary* damsel, demoiselle, mademoiselle, *Colloq* kid, (little) shaver, *US and Canadian* tad, *Slang* teeny-bopper, *Brit* sprog: *As*

*youths, they used to spend time at rock con-
certs.* **3** children, youngsters, juveniles, adolescents, °young °people, °young, *Colloq* kids:
The youth of today have little respect for their elders.

yucky *adj.* yukky *or US also* yuchy, °disgusting,
°repugnant, °repellent, unappetizing,
vomit-provoking, sick-making, ill-making,

°nauseous, nauseating, °revolting, °foul,
mucky, °beastly, °awful, *Slang Brit* grotty: *We get
this yucky mess at school that we call 'mystery meat'.*

yummy *adj.* °delicious, mouth-watering,
°luscious, appetizing, °tasty, toothsome,
°savoury, delectable, ambrosial, *Colloq* scrumptious: *At our school tuck shop we get the most
yummy ice-cream.*

Z

zany *adj.* **1** clownish, °mad, °wild, °frolicsome, °sportive, °playful, °gay, °merry, slapstick, °crazy, °funny, °comic(al), amusing, °hilarious, °absurd, °nonsensical, °ludicrous, °silly, °foolish, °inane, *Colloq* wacky, loony, madcap, crackpot, nutty, goofy, *US* kooky: *The buskers put on the zaniest show I have seen for some time.*
—*n.* **2** °clown, °comic, jester, °fool, °joker, buffoon, °wag, °comedian, comedienne, °merry andrew, laughing-stock, *Slang* nut, *US* screwball: *The two zanies kept the crowd in stitches while the pickpockets stole their wallets.*

zap *v.* °destroy, °kill, °slaughter, annihilate, °murder, slay, assassinate, liquidate, °erase; °shoot, electrocute, *Slang* °rub out, °polish off, °knock off, °bump off, snuff (out), °waste, °hit, *US* ice: *The baddies got zapped by the ray gun, one after the other.*

zealot *n.* °fanatic, extremist, °radical, bigot, °maniac, °militant: *We have to deal with ruthless zealots who are willing to die for their cause.*

zealotry *n.* °fanaticism, extremism, radicalism, °bigotry, militantism, terrorism, single-mindedness, monomania, °fervour, °frenzy, hysteria, °obsession, obsessiveness: *Their attacks on innocent civilians show how far their zealotry can take them.*

zenith *n.* meridian, °summit, °acme, apex, °vertex, apogee, °high °point, °top, °peak, °pinnacle: *The dictator reached the zenith of his power very quickly.*

zero *n.* **1** °nil, null, °nothing, nought *or* °naught, aught, cipher, *Cricket* duck, *Colloq* nix, *US* goose-egg, nada, niente, *Slang Brit* (sweet) Fanny Adams *or* F.A., bugger-all, *US* zilch: *Temperatures have remained below zero all day. The visiting team won three games, we won zero.* **2** (rock) °bottom, nadir: *On a scale of one to ten, she is a zero.* **3** °nobody, °nothing, nonentity, *Slang US* nebbish, bupkis: *That fellow she married is a real zero.*
—*v.* **4 zero in on**: °focus on, pinpoint, °fix on, home in on, °concentrate on, bring to bear on: *We zeroed in on the problem and then rapidly found the answer.*

zest *n.* **1** °spice, °relish, °gusto, °tang, °pepper, ginger, piquancy, pungency, °edge, °bite, °flavour, *Colloq* zing, zip, pizazz *or* pizzazz: *Put in a little of my home-made sauce to add some zest.* **2** °eagerness, zestfulness, °exuberance, °appetite, °interest, °enthusiasm, °hunger, °thirst: *Where does Sidney get his zest for life?*

zone *n.* °area, °quarter, °district, °region, sector, °section, °sphere, °belt, °territory, °province, °realm, °domain, °precinct, bailiwick, °department, °terrain, °circle, locality, °locale, *Slang US* °turf: *A duty-free zone will allow for quicker transshipment of goods. The northern and southern hemispheres each have a frigid, temperate, and torrid zone.*

zoo *n.* **1** zoological garden, menagerie, Tiergarten, (safari) °park: *When I was a child, I enjoyed going to the zoo almost as much as I do now.* **2** madhouse, °mess; °chaos, °pandemonium, °bedlam, *Colloq US* three-ring circus, Chinese fire-drill: *When my husband and the three children get ready in the morning the kitchen is like a zoo.*

Reverse Dictionary Supplement

Compiled by
David Edmonds

A

aardvark *alternative term*: ant bear

Aaron's beard *alternative term*: rose of Sharon

abalone *alternative term*: ear shell

abandoned child *alternative term*: foundling

abandonment *abandonment of claim etc.*: waiver

abbreviation *adjectives*: acrologic, acrological

abele *alternative term*: white poplar

abominable snowman *alternative term*: yeti

about *combining forms*: circum-, peri-

about to happen imminent, impending

about-turn volte-face

above *combining forms*: epi-, super-, supra-, sur-, trans-

absence without permission □ French leave □ *child absent without permission from school etc.*: truant

absolute power or dictatorship autocracy, despotism, totalitarianism

absurdity □ *absurd misrepresentation*: travesty □ *seemingly absurd but in fact true statement*: paradox □ *demonstration of a statement's absurdity by developing it to its logical conclusion*: reductio ad absurdum

academic □ *academic conference*: colloquium □ *academic thesis etc.*: dissertation

accent *Irish accent*: brogue

accepted *generally accepted, believed, etc.*: received

accessory fruit *technical term*: pseudocarp

account book ledger

across *combining forms*: dia-, trans-

acting □ *combining form*: pro- □ *person acting for absent etc. doctor*: locum □ *person acting for absent etc. monarch*: regent

actor □ *sardonic term for actor*: Thespian □ *bad actor*: ham □ *actor who has prepared another actor's role, in order to replace him if necessary*: understudy □ *actor who performs in silence*: mime

acupuncture *technical term*: stylostixis

acupressure *Japanese acupressure therapy*: shiatsu

addition □ *addition to will etc.*: codicil □ *addition to a collection etc.*: accession

additional □ *combining form*: epi- □ *additional charge*: surcharge □ *additional clause to a parliamentary bill, jury's verdict, or other document*: rider

address □ *address used as a collecting-point for mail*: accommodation address □ *address for a letter to be left at a post office until called for*: poste restante □ *African polite form of address to a man*:

bwana □ *Indian polite form of address to a man*: sahib □ *Turkish polite form of address to a man*: effendi

adjective □ *technical terms*: modifier, qualifier, determiner, attributive adjective, predicative adjective □ *abusive or disparaging adjective*: epithet

admiration *deserving admiration*: commendable, estimable, laudable, admirable, praiseworthy

admission □ *admission ritual to tribe etc.*: initiation □ *admission ceremony to university etc.*: matriculation □ *right of admission*: entrée, entry

adultery □ *man whose wife has committed adultery*: cuckold □ *person alleged in a divorce case to have committed adultery etc.*: respondent □ *person alleged in a divorce case to have committed adultery with the respondent*: co-respondent

advance *advance payment*: ante

adverb *technical term*: modifier, qualifier

advertisement □ *catchphrase used in an advertisement*: slogan □ *simple tune used in an advertisement*: jingle □ *large board to display advertisements*: hoarding □ *person who writes the text for advertisements*: copywriter □ *stick up unauthorized advertisements*: fly-post

adviser *influential but unofficial adviser(s) to a person in authority*: guru, kitchen cabinet

afraid of *combining form*: -phobe

after *combining forms*: epi-, post-

afterbrain *technical term*: myencephalon

afternoon □ *adjective*: postmeridian □ *afternoon sleep*: siesta □ *afternoon performance*: matinée

again *combining forms*: ana-, re-

against *combining forms*: anti-, contra-, counter-, ob-

agnail *alternative term*: hangnail

agreed □ *agreed by everyone*: unanimous □ *general agreement*: consensus

air □ *combining forms*: aero-, atmo-, pneum(o)- □ *adjective*: pneumatic

airship □ *technical term*: dirigible □ *German military airship used in First World War*: Zeppelin □ *cabin etc. suspended beneath an airship*: gondola

airsock *alternative term*: windsock

airtight *adjective*: hermetic

alcoholism □ *technical term*: dipsomania □ *delusions etc. caused by alcoholism*: delirium tremens

alfalfa *alternative term*: lucerne

all *combining forms*: omni-, pan-, panto-

allergy *medicine used to treat allergies*: antihistamine

alligator pear *alternative term*: avocado

all-in *alternative term*: freestyle

all-knowing *alternative term*: omniscient

all-powerful *alternative term*: omnipotent

all together *alternative terms*: en bloc, en masse

almond □ *adjective*: amygdalate □ *almond paste, used on cakes etc.*: marzipan □ *scald almonds to remove skin*: blanch □ *almond-shaped*: amygdaloid

alone *combining forms*: mon-, mono-, uni- □ *person who lives alone*: recluse

almost *combining form*: quasi-

alpine house chalet

altar □ *altar canopy*: baldacchino, ciborium □ *embroidered etc. hanging in front of altar*: frontal □ *sculpture etc. on wall behind altar*: reredos

altar boy *alternative terms*: acolyte, server

alternative energy *alternative term*: renewable energy

altitude sickness *alternative term*: mountain sickness

amenity bed *alternative term*: pay bed

American eagle *alternative term*: bald eagle

American Indian Amerindian, Native American, Red Indian

among *combining form*: inter-

among other things inter alia

amoretto *alternative term*: cherub, putto

ancient *combining forms*: archaeo-, palaeo-

angle □ *combining form*: -gon □ *instrument to measure or draw angles*: protractor, set square

aniline *technical term*: phenylamine

animal □ *combining forms*: theri-, zoo- □ *animals of a particular region*: fauna □ *animal used to pull carts, ploughs, etc.*: draught animal □ *animal used to carry loads*: beast of burden

ankh *alternative term*: crux ansata

ankle *ankle-covering, worn over shoe etc.*: gaiter, spat

ankle bones *technical terms*: astragalus, talus

annual ring *alternative term*: tree ring

anointing □ *ritual anointing for religious purposes*: unction □ *oil used for ritual anointing*: chrism

answer *witty answer that occurs to one after the opportunity to make it has gone*: esprit de l'escalier

ant □ *adjective*: formic □ *combining form*: myrmec(o)- □ *study of ants*: myrmecology

ant bear *alternative term*: aardvark

antidote *supposed antidote to all poisons*: mithridate

antique *alternative term*: object of virtu

antler □ *flat section of antler*: palm □ *prong of antler*: tine

anus □ *combining form*: proct(o)- □ *surgical construction of an artificial anus*: colostomy □ *muscle closing the anus*: sphincter

anvil *anvil in ear, technical term*: incus

apart *combining form*: dia-

ape *adjective*: simian

Aphrodite *Latin name*: Venus

appeal *litigant who appeals to a higher court*: appellant

appearance *combining form*: -phany

appendix □ *medical term*: vermiform appendix □ *surgical removal of appendix*: appendectomy

appetite *adjective*: orectic

appetizer □ *first course of a meal*: hors d'oeuvre, starter □ *small open sandwich etc. served as appetizer*: canapé □ *alcoholic drink taken before a meal as an appetizer*: aperitif

apple □ *apple brandy*: Calvados □ *apple of one's eye*: cynosure

approved school *official term*: community home

aquilegia columbine

Arab □ *Arab sailing boat*: dhow □ *Arab covered market*: souk □ *Arab quarter in town*: kasbah □ *Arab prince etc.*: emir, sheik □ *Arab cloak*: burnous, djellaba □ *Arab headdress*: keffiyeh

archer *astrological term*: sagittarius

Ares *Latin name*: Mars

argument *adjective*: eristic

arm □ *adjective*: brachial □ *arm of octopus etc.*: tentacle

armed forces *adjective*: military

armpit □ *adjective*: axillary □ *technical term*: axilla

around *combining forms*: amph-, circum-, epi-, peri-

arrogance *arrogance leading to one's downfall*: hubris

arrow □ *arrow for crossbow*: bolt, quarrel □ *case for arrows*: quiver

art *vulgar or sentimental art*: kitsch

Artemis *Latin name*: Diana

artery *hardening of the arteries, technical term*: arteriosclerosis

artist □ *artist's studio*: atelier □ *artist's complete output*: corpus, oeuvre

ash □ *adjectives*: cinerary, cinerous □ *container for cremated ashes*: urn

assumed name alias

Athena *Latin name*: Minerva

athlete's foot *technical term*: tinea pedis

atom smasher *technical term*: accelerator

attack *medical combining form*: -lepsy

autumn crocus meadow saffron

away *combining forms*: ap-, apo-, ec-, ex-

B

baby □ *set of clothes etc for a new-born baby*: layette □ *discourage a baby from breast-feeding*: wean □ *apparatus providing special environment for a premature baby*: incubator □ *abandoned baby of unknown parentage*: foundling □ *baby secretly substituted for another*: changeling

Bacchus □ *Greek name*: Dionysus □ *female follower of Bacchus*: Maenad □ *staff carried by Bacchus' followers*: thyrsus

back □ *combining forms*: dors-, not- □ *adjective*: dorsal □ *lying on one's back*: supine □ *back of a leaf of paper*: verso

back again *combining form*s: ana-, re-, retr(o)-

backbone □ *adjective*s: spinal, myeloid □ *technical term*: spinal column □ *having a backbone*: vertebrate □ *having no backbone*: invertebrate □ *joint of meat containing a backbone*: chine

back country *alternative terms*: hinterland, outback

bacon-and-eggs *alternative term*: bird's-foot trefoil

bad *combining form*s: caco-, dys-, mal-, mis-

bad breath *technical term*: halitosis

badger's burrow sett

bagpipes □ *pipe on bagpipes on which the tune is played*: chanter □ *pipe on bagpipes used to produce a continuous bass note*: drone

balance □ *adjective*: equilibrious □ *noun*: equilibrium □ *astrological term*: libra

ball *adjective*: globular, spherical

ball and socket joint *technical term*: enarthrosis

ballerina *ballerina's short skirt*: tutu

bandage *bandage etc. bound tight to stop the flow of blood*: tourniquet

barber *adjective*: tonsorial

barking deer muntjac

barrel □ *person who makes barrels*: cooper □ *plank from which barrels are made*: stave □ *metal band compressing a barrel's staves*: hoop □ *open a barrel*: broach

basket □ *basket for picnic food or laundry*: hamper □ *basket for strawberries etc.*: punnet □ *basket for garden vegetables*: trug □ *basket on a bicycle or donkey*: pannier

bastardy *heraldic indication of bastardy*: bend sinister

bath □ *adjective*: balneal □ *hot bath with underwater jets*: jacuzzi™ □ *steam bath*: Turkish bath □ *hot-air bath*: sauna

battle *the ultimate battle, or one causing huge destruction*: Armageddon

beach *adjective*: littoral

beach flea *alternative term*: sand-hopper

beads □ *large string of beads used in prayer*: rosary □ *small string of beads used in prayer*: chaplet

beam □ *beam supporting a ceiling etc.*: joist □ *beam supporting joists*: summer □ *beam above a window, door etc.*: lintel □ *horizontal beam dividing a window*: transom □ *vertical beam dividing a window*: mullion

bean *adjective*: leguminous

bean aphid *alternative term*: blackfly

bear *adjective*: ursine

bearer *combining form*s: -fer, -phore, -phorous

bearing *combining form*: -ferous

beast *adjective*: bestial, animal, feral

becoming *combining form*: -escent

bed □ *canvas bed suspended by cords at its ends*: hammock □ *Japanese quilted mattress used on the floor as a bed*: futon □ *canopy over a bed*: tester

bedsore *technical term*: decubitus ulcer

bee □ *adjective*: apian □ *female bee*: queen □ *male bee*: drone □ *group of beehives*: apiary

beekeeper *technical term*: apiarist

beetle □ *adjective*: coleopterous □ *sacred beetle of ancient Egypt*: scarab

before □ *combining form*s: ante-, fore-, pre- □ *feeling, when in a new situation, of having experienced it before*: déjà vu

beggar *adjective*: mendicant

begging the question *technical term*: petitio principii

beginning □ *combining form*: -escent □ *adjective*s: embryonic, incipient, inceptive, inchoate, nascent

behaviour *person's distinctive behaviour*: trait, quirk, mannerism, idiosyncrasy

being *combining form*: onto-

bell □ *bell rung to instruct people to return to their houses*: curfew □ *bell rung for the recitation of Roman Catholic prayers commemorating the Incarnation*: angelus □ *art of bell-ringing*: campanology □ *alarm bell*: tocsin

belladonna *alternative term*: deadly nightshade

bellflower *alternative term*: campanula

bell tower campanile

below □ *combining form*s: hypo-, infra-, sub- □ *below the threshold of consciousness*: subliminal

belt □ *belt worn by some army officers, with a strap over the shoulder*: Sam Browne □ *similar belt, carrying cartridges*: bandoleer □ *ornamental belt, worn with men's evening dress*: cummerbund □ *ornamental belt, won by champion boxer*: Lonsdale Belt

bench □ *long wooden bench with high back*: settle □ *upholstered bench against wall in restaurant etc.*: banquette

bends *technical terms*: caisson disease, decompression sickness

beneath □ *combining form*s: hypo-, infra-, sub- □ *beneath one's dignity*: infra dig

beside *combining form*: para-

best *best of all*: crème de la crème

between *combining form*: inter-

beyond □ *combining form*s: hyper-, meta-, para, super-, supra-, sur-, trans-, ultra- □ *beyond one's authority*: ultra vires □ *beyond what is necessary*: supererogatory, de trop

bicycle □ *bicycle for two riders, one seated behind the other*: tandem □ *bicycle with one wheel*: monocycle, unicycle □ *early bicycle with one very large and one small wheel*: penny-farthing

big toe *technical term*: hallux

big wheel *alternative term*: Ferris wheel

bile *combining form*: chole-

bilharzia *technical term*: schistostomiasis

billionth *combining form*: nano-

bindweed *alternative term*: convolvulus

biological classification *technical term*: taxonomy

bird □ *combining form*: ornith- □ *adjective*s: avian, ornithic □ *study of birds*: ornithology □ *mythical bird, said to burn itself every 500 years and rise again from the ashes*: phoenix

birth □ *combining form*: -genesis □ *adjective*:

natal □ *giving birth by means of eggs*: oviparous □ *giving birth to live offspring*: viviparous □ *giving birth from eggs hatched within the body*: ovoviviparous

bishop □ *adjective*: episcopal □ *bishop's hat*: mitre □ *bishop's staff*: crosier □ *bishop's area of authority*: diocese, see □ *chief bishop*: primate

black □ *combining forms*: melan- □ *black box in an aircraft, technical term*: flight recorder

blackcurrant syrup cassis

blackhead *technical term*: comedo

black hole □ *technical term in astronomy*: collapsar □ *boundary of black hole*: event horizon

black lung *technical terms*: pneumoconiosis, anthracosis

black magic □ diabolism, the occult □ *black magic as practised on Haiti*: voodoo □ *black magic as practised in the West Indies*: obeah

blackthorn *alternative term*: sloe

bladder □ *combining form*: cyst- □ *adjective*: vesical

blame □ *free from blame*: exculpate, exonerate □ *person made to bear the blame for another's wrongdoing*: scapegoat, whipping boy

bleeder *medical technical term*: haemophiliac

blind gut *technical term*: caecum

blind worm *alternative term*: slow-worm

blink *technical term*: nictitate

blood □ *combining forms*: haem-, haemat- □ *adjectives*: haemal, haematic, sanguineous □ *blood transfer*: transfusion □ *artificial purification of the blood*: haemodialysis

blood clot *combining form*: thromb(o)-

blood feud *alternative term*: vendetta

blood poisoning *technical term*: septicaemia, toxaemia

blood pressure □ *high blood pressure*: hypertension □ *low blood pressure*: hypotension □ *instrument for measuring blood pressure*: sphygmomanometer

blunder *social blunder*: gaffe, faux pas

blush *adjective*: erubescent

body □ *combining forms*: somat-, -some □ *adjective*: corporal □ *entertainer who twists his body into abnormal positions*: contortionist

bogbean *alternative term*: buckbean

bog myrtle *alternative term*: sweet gale

bomb □ *hand-thrown bomb*: grenade □ *crude hand-thrown petrol bomb*: Molotov cocktail □ *bomb containing jellied petrol*: napalm bomb

bone □ *combining form*: osteo- □ *adjectives*: osseous, osteal □ *person who manipulates bones to ease pain etc.*: osteopath □ *brittleness of bones in the old*: osteoporosis □ *bone-house in church etc.*: charnel house

book □ *combining form*: biblio- □ *account-book*: ledger □ *list of books*: bibliography

bookplate *alternative term*: ex-libris

borderland *borderland between England and Wales or Scotland*: marches

born □ *born in wedlock*: legitimate □ *born out of wedlock*: illegitimate, natural

both *combining forms*: ambi-, amphi-, bi-

bottle □ *unmarked bottle for serving wine or water*: carafe, decanter □ *large bottle for acids etc.*: carboy

bow □ *traditional Muslim bow of greeting*: salaam □ *former Chinese bow of greeting*: kowtow

bowls □ *large black ball used in bowls*: wood □ *small white ball used in bowls*: jack □ *French bowls*: boules, pétanque

brain □ *combining forms*: encephal-, cerebr(o)- □ *adjective*: cerebral □ *technical term*: encephalon

branch *adjective*: ramose

breast □ *combining form*: mast- □ *adjectives*: mammary, pectoral □ *chemical polymer used in breast implants*: silicone □ *surgical removal of a breast*: mastectomy □ *surgical removal of a breast tumour*: lumpectomy

breastbone *technical term*: sternum

breastwork *alternative term*: parapet

breath *combining form*: spiro-

bridge □ *many-arched bridge carrying road or railway*: viaduct □ *many-arched bridge carrying river or canal*: aqueduct □ *raisable bridge in front of castle etc.*: drawbridge

bring □ *bring back to life*: resuscitate, reanimate, revivify □ *bring up (food etc.)*: regurgitate

bristle *adjective*: setaceous

broadcast *simultaneous broadcast of a programme on radio and television*: simulcast

bronze *combining form*: chalco-

brother □ *combining form*: fratr(i)- □ *adjective*: fraternal □ *murder of one's brother*: fratricide

brown coal *technical term*: lignite

brown lung *technical term*: byssinosis

brown owl *alternative term*: tawny owl

building □ *adjectives*: architectural, tectonic □ *sham building erected as a landscape decoration etc.*: folly

bulge *adjectives*: bulbous, tumescent

bull □ *adjective*: taurine □ *astrological term*: taurus

bundle *adjectives*: fascicular, fasciculate

burden *adjective*: onerous

burial *adjectives*: funerary, sepulchral

busy Lizzie *alternative term*: balsam

butter *clarified butter, used in Indian cuisine*: ghee

butterfly *butterfly expert*: lepidopterist

butterfly bush *alternative term*: buddleia

butterfly nut *alternative term*: wing nut

buttock *technical term*: natis (pl. nates)

buyer *let the buyer beware*: caveat emptor

buzzing *buzzing in the ears*: tinnitus

C

cabbage salad coleslaw

cable □ *cable for securing a ship to a pier*: hawser □ *cable for steadying a mast etc.*: guyrope

caisson disease *alternative terms*: decompression sickness, bends

cake shop *alternative term*: patisserie

calamus *alternative term*: sweet flag
calceolaria *alternative term*: slipperwort
calf love *alternative term*: puppy love
call in or **up** invoke
Cambridge University □ *Cambridge college annual feast*: Commemoration □ *Cambridge college servant*: gyp □ *Cambridge first-degree examination or course*: tripos □ *person gaining first-class honours in the Cambridge mathematical tripos*: wrangler
camel □ *camel with one hump*: dromedary □ *camel with two humps*: Bactrian camel
camellia *alternative term*: japonica
camera □ *crosswise movement of a camera*: pan □ *move a camera towards or away from object*: track □ *bring an object into close or distant camera focus*: zoom
campanula *alternative term*: bellflower
canal □ *path along side of a canal*: towpath □ *boat used on Venetian canals*: gondola □ *bridge to carry a canal over a valley, road, etc.*: aqueduct
cancer □ *combining form*: carcin- □ *technical term*: carcinoma □ *cancer treatment by drugs*: chemotherapy □ *cancer treatment by X-rays*: radiotherapy
cancerous *technical term*: carcinomatous, malignant
candlestick □ *candlestick attached to wall*: sconce □ *suspended multi-light candlestick*: chandelier □ *Jewish liturgical candlestick*: menorah
cane *cane carried by military officers*: swagger stick
cannibal *adjective*: anthropophagous
car □ *old and inefficient car*: banger, jalopy, rattletrap, tin lizzie □ *car that is modified to give high performance*: hot rod
carbohydrate *combining form*: -ose
career *summary of a person's career and education*: curriculum vitae
carnation *alternative term*: clove pink
carrying *combining forms*: -fer, -ferous, -phore, -phorous
cart *cart used in the French Revolution to convey condemned persons to the guillotine*: tumbril
Carthage *adjective*: Punic
cartilage *combining form*: chondr(o)-
case history *technical term*: anamnesis
cassava *alternative term*: manioc
cast off □ *cast off an old skin (of a snake etc.)*: slough □ *the skin so cast off*: slough □ *action of casting off a skin*: ecdysis
castrate □ *castrated man*: eunuch □ *castrated male singer in baroque opera or the papal chapel*: castrato □ *castrated cockerel*: capon □ *castrated stallion*: gelding □ *castrated ram*: wether
cat *adjective*: feline
Catherine wheel *alternative term*: pinwheel
cattle *adjective*: bovine
cauliflower ear *technical term*: aural hematoma
cause *adjective*: aetiological
causing *combining forms*: -genesis, -genous, -facient, -fic, -otic

cave *combining form*: speleo-
cell *combining forms*: -cyt-, cyto-, -cyte, -blast, -plast
cement □ *cement used between bricks*: pointing □ *cement used between tiles*: grout □ *cement used to cover a floor*: screed □ *cement used to cover a wall*: parget
centre *combining form*: mes-
ceremony □ *admission ceremony*: initiation □ *ceremony to make an award*: investiture □ *ceremony to place a person in office*: induction □ *ceremony to denote a turning-point in a person's life*: rite of passage □ *memorial ceremony*: commemoration
Ceres *Greek name*: Demeter
chalk *adjective*: calcareous
chamber *adjective*: cameral
chance *adjective*: fortuitous
change □ *combining forms*: -trop-, -tropic, tropo- □ *radical change*: quantum leap □ *change sides*: apostatize □ *change of the Eucharistic elements*: transubstantiation □ *person who changes his principles to suit the times*: trimmer, time-server
change of life *technical term*: menopause
charity *adjective*: eleemosynary
Charlemagne *adjectives*: Carolingian, Carlovingian
Charles I and II *adjective*: Caroline
cheek *adjectives*: buccal, malar
cheekbone *technical term*: zygomatic bone
cheese □ *adjective*: caseous □ *sprinkled with grated cheese and browned*: au gratin
chemical *combining forms*: chem-, chemi-, chemo-
cherry brandy *alternative term*: kirsch
cherub *technical terms in art*: amoretto, putto
chess □ *winning position in chess*: checkmate □ *draw in chess*: stalemate □ *opening tactic in chess*: gambit
chest □ *adjectives*: pectoral, thoracic □ *technical term*: thorax
chew *chew the cud, technical term*: ruminate
chicken pox *technical term*: varicella
chickpea □ *chickpea paste*: hummus □ *chickpea rissole*: felafel
child □ *combining form*: paedo-, paedi- □ *child under state guardianship*: ward of court □ *nursery for young children*: crèche
childbirth □ *technical terms*: confinement, parturition □ *adjective*: puerperal □ *medical care and study of those giving birth*: obstetrics □ *doctor providing such care, or person making such study*: obstetrician □ *nurse attending at childbirth*: midwife □ *matter discharged after childbirth*: afterbirth
Chinese □ *combining form*: Sino- □ *Chinese frying pan*: wok □ *Chinese game played with small tiles*: mah-jong □ *Chinese therapy by needles*: acupuncture □ *Chinese official*: mandarin □ *study of Chinese culture etc.*: Sinology □ *Chinese gooseberry*: kiwi fruit □ *Chinese ink*: Indian ink
choice □ *difficult choice*: dilemma □ *choice with no real alternatives*: Hobson's choice □ *choice made to allocate scarce resources*: triage
church □ *adjective*: ecclesiastical □ *church*

usher: verger □ *churchwarden's assistant*: sidesman □ *church gravedigger etc.*: sexton □ *forms of church service*: liturgy □ *church assembly*: synod, convocation □ *church court*: consistory □ *church law*: canon □ *expel from a church*: excommunicate □ *grotesque stone figure on the outside of a church*: gargoyle □ *roofed gate in a churchyard, for cover when starting the burial service*: lich gate □ *a tenth of one's income given to the Church*: tithe

cider *strong and rough cider*: scrumpy

circle □ *combining form*: cycl- □ *imagined circle joining the earth's poles*: meridian □ *imagined circle round the earth equidistant from its poles*: equator □ *prehistoric circle of stones etc.*: henge

city □ *adjective*: civic, urban □ *chief city*: metropolis □ *large city made by the fusion of several towns or cities*: megalopolis

classification □ *classification of plants and animals*: taxonomy □ *classification of plants and animals by genus and species*: Linnaean nomenclature, binomial nomenclature □ *classification according to rank*: hierarchy □ *classification according to shared ancestry*: cladistics

clay □ *clay used for pottery*: argil □ *clay used to make reddish pottery*: terracotta □ *thin clay used to decorate pottery*: slip □ *clay used for bricks and walls*: adobe □ *clay used as a filter*: fuller's earth

clerical collar *alternative term*: dog collar

climb *climb down a sheer cliff etc. using ropes*: abseil

clock □ *clock mechanism*: escapement □ *art or study of clock-making*: horology □ *precise clock*: chronometer

cloth □ *cloth-merchant*: mercer, draper □ *roll of cloth in a shop etc.*: bolt □ *cloth to cover a corpse*: shroud, winding sheet

clothes □ *adjective*: sartorial □ *clothes for a new baby*: layette □ *liturgical clothes*: vestments □ *clothes designer*: couturier

cloud *adjective*: nebulous

clove pink *alternative term*: carnation

club □ *adjectives*: clavate, claviform □ *Irish club*: shillelagh □ *Australian aborigine's club*: waddy □ *African club*: knobkerrie □ *veto someone's proposed membership of a club etc.*: blackball

coal miner's lung *technical terms*: pneumoconiosis, anthracosis

coast □ *adjective*: littoral □ *scenic coast road*: corniche

coat □ *coat with flour, sugar, etc.*: dredge □ *coat with plaster or cement*: render □ *coat with planks etc.*: clad

codes □ *study of codes*: cryptography, cryptology □ *deciphering of codes*: cryptanalysis

coffee □ *strong black coffee made under steam pressure*: espresso □ *coffee topped with frothed milk*: cappuccino □ *stimulant in coffee*: caffeine

coffin □ *stone coffin*: sarcophagus □ *stand for a coffin*: bier, catafalque □ *coffin-carrier*: pallbearer

coin □ *adjective*: nummary □ *face of a coin*: obverse □ *back of a coin*: reverse □ *ridges on a coin's edge*: milling □ *study of coins*: numismatics

cold □ *combining forms*: cryo-, psychro- □ *sleepy etc. state brought on by extreme cold*: hypothermia

cold sore *technical term*: herpes labialis

collarbone *technical term*: clavicle

collection □ *collection of writings etc.*: anthology, miscellany, omnibus □ *collection of miscellaneous items*: farrago, job lot

collective farm □ *collective farm in Israel*: kibbutz □ *collective farm in Russia*: kolkhoz

collector □ *collector of bygones*: antiquary □ *collector of beer mats*: tegestologist □ *collector of books*: bibliophile □ *collector of butterflies and moths*: lepidopterist □ *collector of coins and medals*: numismatist □ *collector of matchboxes*: phillumenist □ *collector of stamps*: philatelist

college □ *college dining room*: hall, refectory □ *college doorkeeper*: porter □ *college doorkeeper's room*: lodge □ *college principal's apartments*: lodgings □ *annual college feast*: gaudy, commemoration

colour □ *adjective*: chromatic □ *range of colours*: spectrum

columbine *alternative term*: aquilegia

combat □ *medieval mock-combat between mounted knights*: joust □ *place for such combat*: lists □ *mock sea battle staged in a Roman arena*: naumachia

combatant *person who fought in a Roman arena to entertain*: gladiator

combination *combination of businesses*: conglomerate, consortium, syndicate, cartel

command *adjectives*: mandatory, preceptive

command economy *alternative term*: planned economy

comment *comment made in passing*: obiter dictum

common fraction *alternative term*: simple fraction

Common Market *official name*: European Community

common noun *technical term*: appellative

complaint □ *adjective*: querulous □ *government official investigating complaints*: ombudsman

complete *combining form*: hol(o)-

complex fraction *alternative term*: compound fraction

compliance *minimal compliance with a law etc.*: tokenism

compressed air *adjective*: pneumatic

conclusion □ *conclusion derived by logic*: deduction, inference □ *conclusion inferred from a limited number of instances*: generalization □ *conclusion wrongly inferred*: non sequitur

condition *combining forms*: -osis, -tude

connoisseur □ *connoisseur of food and drink*: gourmet, gastronome □ *connoisseur of antiques etc.*: virtuoso

conqueror *Spanish conqueror of South America*: conquistador

contact *spread by contact*: contagious

contain *combining form*: -fer-

container □ *container for fluids*: reservoir, cistern □ *sealed container for a measured amount of medicine etc.*: ampoule □ *container for molten metal*: crucible □ *container for wine or oil*: ampulla, cruse

□ *container for tea*: caddy □ *container for petrol or water*: jerrycan □ *container for relics*: reliquary

continental quilt *alternative term*: duvet

contradiction *apparent contradiction used for rhetorical effect*: oxymoron

contrast *contrast of light and shade in a picture etc.*: chiaroscuro

cooked *lightly cooked*: al dente

cooking *adjective*: culinary

copper □ *combining forms*: chalc-, cupr- □ *adjectives*: cupric, cuprous

copy □ *copying the work of another and claiming it as one's own*: plagiarism, piracy □ *exact genetic copy*: clone

corn on the cob *alternative term*: maize

corpse □ *combining form*: necr- □ *corpse used for medical research*: cadaver □ *dissection of a corpse*: post-mortem, autopsy □ *building etc. for storing corpses*: mortuary, morgue □ *deep-freezing of corpses*: cryonics □ *preservation of a corpse by injecting chemicals*: embalmment □ *destruction of a corpse by fire*: cremation □ *burial of a corpse*: interment □ *corpse revived by witchcraft*: zombie

correct *combining form*: ortho-

cot death *technical term*: sudden infant death syndrome

cottage pie *alternative term*: shepherd's pie

cough □ *technical term*: tussis □ *cough medicine*: expectorant

counterpoint *adjective*: contrapuntal

country *adjectives*: rural, pastoral

cowboy □ *South American cowboy*: gaucho □ *cowboy's leather overtrousers*: chaps

coyote *alternative term*: prairie wolf

crab *astrological term*: cancer

crane-fly *alternative term*: daddy-long-legs

criminal □ *criminal who betrays his fellows to the police* (Brit): grass □ *criminal intent, technical term*: mens rea

criticism *person etc. thought to be above criticism*: sacred cow

crow *adjective*: corvine

crown □ *crown worn by a nobleman*: coronet □ *crown worn by the pope*: tiara

crux ansata *alternative term*: ankh

cud-chewer *technical term*: ruminant

culture □ *person having no cultural interests*: philistine □ *study of primitive cultures*: ethnology

cup *Eucharistic cup*: chalice □ *cup used by Christ at the Last Supper*: Holy Grail

Cupid *Greek name*: Eros

curve *adjective*: sinuous

cut *combining forms*: -tom-, -tomy

D

daddy-long-legs *alternative term*: crane-fly

dancer *dancer's close-fitting garment covering the torso, and sometimes the arms and legs*: leotard

danger □ *hidden danger*: pitfall □ *danger inherent in a task etc.*: occupational hazard

dalton *alternative term*: atomic mass unit

daughter *adjective*: filial

dawn *adjective*: auroral

day □ *adjective*: diurnal □ *day in which hours of daylight and darkness are equal*: equinox □ *longest or shortest day*: solstice

day blindness *technical term*: hemeralopia

dayfly *alternative term*: mayfly

Day of Atonement *alternative term*: Yom Kippur

dead □ *service for the dead*: requiem □ *medical examination of a dead person*: post-mortem □ *medical examiner of a dead person*: pathologist □ *published history of a dead person*: obituary □ *tomb-inscription*: epitaph □ *summon up the dead by magic*: necromancy

dead end □ *road with no exit at its far end*: cul-de-sac □ *deadlock in argument or discussion*: impasse, stalemate

deadly nightshade *alternative term*: belladonna

dean *adjective*: decanal

death □ *combining form*: mori-, necr-, -thanasia □ *adjectives*: fatal, lethal, mortal □ *causing death*: lethal, fatal, terminal □ *at the point of death*: moribund □ *death inflicted to relieve suffering*: euthanasia □ *death of body tissue*: necrosis, mortification, gangrene □ *stiffness of joints after death*: rigor mortis □ *magistrate investigating cause of person's death*: coroner □ *reminder of death's inevitability*: memento mori □ *after-death*: posthumous

decay □ *combining form*: sapr- □ *decay of teeth or bones*: caries □ *decayed organic matter in the soil*: humus

deceive *easily deceived*: credulous, gullible

decompose *able to be decomposed by bacteria*: biodegradable

decompression sickness *alternative terms*: caisson sickness, the bends

deep *combining form*: bath-

deer □ *adjective*: cervine □ *deer meat*: venison □ *deer's track*: slot

degree □ *degree awarded to a candidate who was ill at the time of the examination*: aegrotat □ *degree conferred when the graduate is elsewhere*: in absentia

delay □ *adjective*: dilatory □ *delay by non-cooperation*: stonewall □ *delay by lengthy speeches*: filibuster

delusion *delusions of being persecuted*: paranoia

Demeter *Latin name*: Ceres

dentist □ *dentist who corrects the position of teeth*: orthodontist □ *dentist's assistant who cleans teeth*: hygienist

descent □ *direct descent*: lineal □ *descent by a parallel line*: collateral □ *of the male line of descent*: patrilineal □ *of the female line of descent*: matrilineal

desire □ *adjective, technical term*: orectic □ *desire another's property*: covet

despair *despair at imagined lack of progress*: accidie

destruction ▢ *destruction from within*: sabotage ▢ *destruction of revered objects or ideas*: iconoclasm ▢ *malicious or purposeless destruction*: vandalism ▢ *total destruction*: holocaust

detail *subtle detail*: nicety, quibble, niggle, technicality, punctilio

devil ▢ *adjectives*: diabolic, diabolical ▢ *worship of the devil*: diabolism

dial ▢ *conventional watch etc. dial with moving hands*: analog ▢ *watch etc. dial with changing numerical display*: digital

Diana *Greek name*: Artemis

diaphragm *medical adjective*: phrenic

dictator ▢ *title of German dictator*: führer ▢ *title of Italian dictator*: duce ▢ *title of Spanish dictator*: caudillo ▢ *small group exercising dictatorial powers*: junta

dictionary ▢ *small dictionary at the back of a textbook etc.*: glossary, vocabulary ▢ *dictionary of places etc.*: gazetteer ▢ *dictionary of synonyms and antonyms*: thesaurus ▢ *dictionary in which the definition precedes the headword (as here)*: reverse dictionary ▢ *person who compiles dictionaries*: lexicographer

difference ▢ *subtle difference*: nuance ▢ *difference in brightness in a picture*: contrast

different ▢ *combining forms*: allo-, aniso-, heter-, vari- ▢ *of many different colours*: motley, pied, variegated ▢ *having a different content*: heterogeneous

difficult *combining form*: dys-

digestion *adjective*: peptic

dinner *adjective*: prandial

Dionysus ▢ *Latin name*: Bacchus ▢ *female follower of Dionysus*: Maenad ▢ *staff carried by Dionysus' followers*: thyrsus

disappointing *disappointing outcome*: anticlimax, bathos

discharge *combining forms*: -rrhoea, -rrhagia

discontinue *discontinue meetings of a parliament etc. without dissolution*: prorogue

discovery ▢ *method of discovery by trial and error*: heuristic ▢ *faculty of making fortunate discoveries*: serendipity

discuss ▢ *discuss publicly*: ventilate, air ▢ *avoid discussion*: fence, prevaricate

disease ▢ *combining forms*: nos(o)-, patho-, -pathy, -osis ▢ *temporary abatement of a disease*: remission ▢ *general outbreak of a disease*: epidemic ▢ *resumption of a disease*: recrudescence ▢ *study of disease*: pathology ▢ *group of symptoms indicating a particular disease*: syndrome ▢ *denoting a disease passed on by physical contact*: contagious ▢ *denoting a disease often or only found in a certain region or race*: endemic

diseased *combining forms*: dys-, -otic

dislike *person or thing particularly disliked*: bête noire

dismiss *dismiss with dishonour (from the armed forces etc.)*: cashier

disseminated sclerosis *alternative term*: multiple sclerosis

dissolution *combining forms*: lyso-, -lys-, -lysis

distance *combining form*: tel(e)-

distant *ultimately distant spot*: ultima Thule

distillation flask retort

distinction ▢ *subtle distinction*: nicety, nuance ▢ *over-subtle distinction*: hair-splitting, quibble

ditch *hidden ditch separating gardens from parkland*: ha-ha

diver ▢ *diver's compressed-air apparatus*: scuba, aqualung ▢ *diver's enclosed vessel for deep-sea observations*: bathyscaphe ▢ *painful condition suffered by diver after sudden reduction of pressure*: the bends, caisson disease, decompression sickness

divide *combining form*: -sect

divine *divine for water*: dowse

division ▢ *combining form*: schiz(o)- ▢ *division into opposing factions etc.*: polarization, schism

divorce ▢ *spouse initiating a divorce action*: applicant ▢ *spouse against whom a divorce action is brought*: respondent ▢ *person cited in a divorce action as having committed adultery with the partner being sued*: co-respondent ▢ *court's provisional divorce ruling*: decree nisi ▢ *court's final divorce ruling*: decree absolute ▢ *financial support to be given by a former spouse after divorce*: maintenance

doctor ▢ *doctor in charge of a particular branch of medicine at a hospital*: consultant ▢ *hospital doctor assisting a consultant*: registrar ▢ *junior hospital doctor*: houseman ▢ *family doctor*: general practitioner ▢ *replacement doctor*: locum

document ▢ *document containing a sworn statement*: affidavit ▢ *document recording a contract*: deed ▢ *document showing ownership of a property*: title deed ▢ *document recording the transfer of ownership of a property*: conveyance ▢ *document written entirely by its author*: holograph ▢ *document signed by its author*: autograph

doer *combining forms*: -tor, -tress, -trix

dog ▢ *adjective*: canine ▢ *female dog*: bitch ▢ *male dog*: dog ▢ *give birth to dogs*: whelp

dog collar *alternative term*: clerical collar

done *something done and unalterable*: fait accompli

doorman ▢ *doorman at an hotel or theatre etc.*: commissionaire ▢ *doorman at a block of flats*: concierge ▢ *doorman at a college etc.*: porter

downwards *combining form*: cata-

drawing ▢ *combining form*: -graphy ▢ *drawing of a machine etc. showing its parts as if separated by an explosion*: exploded view ▢ *drawing of a machine etc. with parts of its casing removed to show inner workings*: cutaway ▢ *drawing of a vertical aspect of a building*: elevation ▢ *drawing of a floor layout of a building*: plan

dream ▢ *combining form*: oneir(o)- ▢ *adjective*: oneiric

drift anchor *alternative term*: sea anchor

dripstone *alternative term*: hood mould

drug ▢ *combining forms*: pharmaco-, narco- ▢ *drug that sharpens the senses*: stimulant ▢ *drug that dulls the senses*: narcotic ▢ *drug producing hallucinations*: psychedelic, hallucinogenic ▢ *hormonal drug used by athletes to improve performance*: steroid ▢ *inject a drug directly into a vein*: mainline ▢ *cure of addiction by complete* *deprivation of drugs*: cold turkey □ *cure of addiction by progressive deprivation of drugs*: withdrawal

drum □ *pitched bowl-shaped drum*: timpano, kettledrum □ *drum with resonating strings along its underside*: snare drum □ *drum in Latin American band*: bongo □ *jazz drum beaten with the hands*: tom-tom □ *Indian drum*: tabla

dry *combining form*: xero-

dummy *jointed dummy used by artists*: lay figure

dung □ *combining form*: copro- □ *dung-eating, technical term*: coprophagous □ *dung of seabirds sold as a fertilizer*: guano

duty □ *adjective*: deontic □ *beyond the call of duty*: supererogatory

duvet *alternative term*: continental quilt

dwarf □ *dwarf bean*: French bean, kidney bean □ *dwarf plant or tree as cultivated in Japan*: bonsai

E

each other *adjectives*: mutual, reciprocal

eagle *adjective*: aquiline

eagle's nest *alternative term*: eyrie

ear □ *adjective*: aural □ *combining forms*: ot-, oto-

earache *technical term*: otalgia

eardrum *technical terms*: tympanic membrane, tympanum

ear, nose, and throat *technical term*: otorhinolaryngology

ear-shaped *adjective*: auriculate

ear shell *alternative term*: abalone

earth *adjectives*: terrestrial, telluric

earth *combining form*: geo-

earthquake *adjective*: seismic

earwax *technical term*: cerumen

east *adjective*: oriental

Easter *adjective*: Paschal

Easter cactus *alternative term*: Christmas cactus

East Germany *official title*: German Democratic Republic

eating □ *combining forms*: -phag-, -phagous, -vorous □ *eating all foods*: omnivorous □ *meat-eating*: carnivorous □ *plant-eating*: herbivorous □ *eating grasses and cereals*: graminivorous □ *fish-eating*: piscivorous □ *eating corpses*: necrophagous □ *eating dung*: coprophagous

ebonite *alternative term*: vulcanite

ecology *technical term*: bionomics

ecstatic speech *technical term*: glossolalia

eel-shaped *adjective*: anguilliform

efficiency *analysis of workplace efficiency*: operational research

egg *combining forms*: -oo-, -ovi-, -ovo-

egg-shaped *adjective*: oval, ovate, ovoid

eglantine *alternative term*: sweetbrier

Egyptian scripts demotic, hieratic

Egyptian tomb mastaba

eight *combining form*: octo-, octa-

eighty-year-old *alternative term*: octogenarian

election □ *election campaign*: hustings □ *study of voting at elections*: psephology

electric eye *alternative term*: photocell

electric □ *electric shock treatment*: electroconvulsive therapy □ *electric supply failure*: outage

electronic music keyboard moog synthesizer

elements *table of the chemical elements arranged by atomic number*: periodic table

elephant □ *elephant driver*: mahout □ *seat on elephant's back*: howdah

eleven *combining form*: hendeca-

elf □ *alternative term*: pixie □ *in Irish folklore*: leprechaun

emotion *adjective*: affective

emotional release *in response to a moving play, novel, etc.*: catharsis

emotional shock *technical term*: trauma

emperor □ *emperor of Germany*: Kaiser □ *emperor of Japan*: Mikado □ *emperor of Russia*: Tsar

end □ *combining forms*: □ *purpose*: tel-, tele- □ *tip*: acro-

end of the world *theological study of the end of the world*: eschatology

enemy *adjective*: inimical

English *combining form*: Anglo-

English-speaking *adjective*: anglophone

engraving *adjective*: glyptic

enlightenment *theological term in Buddhism or Hinduism*: nirvana

enteric fever *alternative term*: typhoid fever

entertain *adjective*: amusing, diverting

entire *combining forms*: pan-, panto-

environment *combining form*: eco-

enzyme *combining form*: -ase

equal *combining form*: equi-, iso-

equal in size *adjective*: coextensive, coterminous

equivalent return quid pro quo

Eros *Latin name*: Cupid

erosion *projecting wall or fence to limit sea's erosion of coast*: groyne

error in logic fallacy

escape *person who entertains audiences by demonstrating skill in escaping*: escapologist

escort □ *female escort for young woman*: chaperone, duenna □ *male escort for older woman*: gigolo

Eskimo □ *Eskimo ice-house*: igloo □ *Eskimo sledge-dog*: husky, malamute □ *Eskimo canoe*: kayak □ *Eskimo inhabitant of the islands off Alaska*: Aleut □ *Eskimo inhabitant of North America or Greenland*: Inuit

essential condition prerequisite, sine qua non

estimator *one who estimates the cost of a proposed building etc.*: quantity surveyor

estragon *alternative term*: tarragon

euphrasy *alternative term*: eyebright

evaporating rapidly *technical term*: volatile

event □ *important event*: milestone, landmark □ *possible sequence of events*: scenario

everyday speech *technical terms*: demotic, vernacular

everything *combining forms*: pan-, panto-

evidence *object shown in court as evidence*: exhibit

evil *averting evil*: apotropaic

evil spirit □ *spirit said to take female form to seduce a sleeping man*: succubus □ *spirit said to take male form to seduce a sleeping woman*: incubus □ *person posssessed by an evil spirit*: demoniac □ *drive out evil spirits*: exorcize

examination □ *combining forms*: -opsy, -scopy □ *examination of financial accounts*: audit □ *verbal examination*: oral, viva □ *supervisor of persons taking a written examination*: invigilator □ *medical examination of a corpse*: autopsy, postmortem □ *medical examination of tissue from a living body*: biopsy □ *theological examination of heretic etc.*: inquisition □ *mental examination of one's thoughts etc.*: introspection

example □ *example to be imitated*: paradigm □ *example cited to justify similar action*: precedent □ *cite as an example*: adduce

exceeding *combining forms*: super-, ultra-

excessive *combining form*: hyper-

excrement □ *combining form*: copro-, scato- □ *eating excrement, technical term*: coprophagous □ *excrement of seabirds sold as a fertilizer*: guano

exempt from blame exonerate

existence *combining form*: onto-

existing situation status quo

expelling *combining form*: -fuge

experience □ *in handling tricky social or business situations etc.*: savoir faire □ *a short but unpleasant interview etc.*: mauvais quart d'heure

experimentation *on living animals*: vivisection

explanation □ *provisional explanation*: hypothesis □ *of a difficult word in a text etc.*: gloss

explosive □ *explosive material in a missile's warhead*: payload □ *explosive charge to propel a rocket etc.*: propellant □ *explosive situation*: powder keg, tinderbox

extermination *extermination of an entire nation or race*: genocide

external *combining form*: exo-

extra *combining form*: super-, ultra-

eye □ *adjectives*: ocular, ophthalmic □ *combining form*: ophthalmo- □ *medical specialist for vision problems*: oculist, optician, optometrist □ *an eye for an eye, legal concept*: lex talionis

eyeblack *alternative term*: mascara

eyebright *alternative term*: euphrasy

eyelash *technical term*: cilium

eyelid *adjective*: palpebral

eyeshadow *alternative term*: kohl

eye socket *technical term*: orbit

eyestrain *technical term*: asthenopia

eye tooth *technical term*: canine

F

face □ *combining form*: -hedron □ *with an unexpressive face*: deadpan, inscrutable, poker-faced

facing □ *combining forms*: -ward, -wards □ *lying facing downwards*: prone □ *lying facing upwards*: supine

fact *an unalterable fact*: fait accompli

false *combining form*: pseud(o)-

false fruit *technical term*: pseudocarp

family *narrowest family unit, consisting of a couple and their children only*: nuclear family

family tree *alternative terms*: genealogy, pedigree

fantasy □ *fantasy world*: Cockaigne, cloud-cuckoo-land, Utopia □ *person living in a fantasy world*: Walter Mitty

Far East *adjective*: oriental

far sight *technical terms*: hyperopia, hypermetropia, presbyopia

farming *adjective*: agr-

fast *combining form*: tach-

fat □ *combining forms*: lipo-, seb(o)-, steat(o)- □ *adjective*: sebaceous

fate □ *fate in Hindu and Buddhist thought*: karma □ *fate in Islamic thought*: kismet

father □ *combining form*: patr(i)- □ *adjective*: paternal □ *murder of one's father*: patricide

fault □ *fault-finding*: captious, carping, niggling □ *minor personal fault*: foible, peccadillo

faulty *combining form*: dys-

Faunus *Greek name*: Pan

favouritism *favouritism towards one's relatives*: nepotism

fear □ *combining form*: -phobia □ *fear of confined spaces*: claustrophobia □ *fear of foreigners*: xenophobia □ *fear of public places*: agoraphobia □ *fear of homosexuals*: homophobia □ *fear of heights*: acrophobia □ *fear of water*: hydrophobia

feast *adjective*: festal

Feast of Lights *alternative term*: Hannukkah

Feast of Tabernacles *alternative term*: Sukkoth

Feast of Weeks *alternative term*: Shavuoth

fee □ *initial fee paid to a barrister*: retainer □ *further fee paid to a barrister*: refresher □ *fee paid to cover expenses etc. of someone doing 'unpaid' work*: honorarium □ *percentage fee on sales made etc.*: commission □ *fee paid to an author etc. for copies sold or performances given*: royalty

feeding *combining forms*: troph-, -trophy

feelings □ *combining form*: -pathy □ *ability to share another's feelings*: empathy

female *combining forms*: gyno-, -gyn-, -ess, -tress, -trix

ferroconcrete *alternative term*: reinforced concrete

fever *technical term*: pyrexia

field *adjective*: campestral

film □ *combining form*: cine- □ *film expert or enthusiast*: cineaste

filtration *filtration process for blood of patient suffering kidney failure*: dialysis

final □ *final part of a speech*: peroration □ *final part of a play*: denouement, epilogue □ *final part of a piece of music*: coda

finger □ *combining form*: dactyl(o)- □ *adjective*: digital

fingerprint *technical term*: dactylogram

fire □ *combining form*: pyro- □ *fire for burning a corpse*: pyre □ *person starting fires for malicious purposes*: arsonist □ *mythical creature living in fire*: salamander

fireplace □ *grid at front of fireplace to keep in burning material*: fender □ *shelf along side of fireplace for kettle etc.*: hob □ *stand for kettle etc. at front of fireplace*: trivet □ *stand to support logs in a fireplace*: andiron, firedog □ *metal plate at the back of a fireplace*: reredos

first □ *combining forms*: proto-, ur- □ *first example*: prototype □ *first appearance of a performer*: debut □ *first performance*: premiere □ *first-year student at a university*: freshman

fish □ *combining forms*: ichthy(o)-, pisc- □ *adjective*: piscine □ *fish eggs*: spawn □ *fish sperm*: milt

fishes *astrological term*: pisces

fishing □ *adjective*: piscatorial □ *catch fish with one's hands*: guddle

five □ *combining forms*: pent-, quin-, quinque- □ *five-sided figure*: pentagon □ *five-pointed star*: pentagram □ *group of five*: pentad

flag *adjective*: vexillary

flat □ *top-floor flat*: penthouse □ *flat on two or more floors, with its own outside door*: maisonette □ *flat kept for occasional use*: pied-à-terre □ *large building divided into flats*: tenement

fleet □ *fleet of warships*: armada □ *fleet of merchant ships*: argosy □ *fleet of small ships*: flotilla

flesh □ *combining forms*: carn-, sarc(o)- □ *adjective*: carnal

float □ *float attached to side of a canoe etc*: outrigger □ *float supporting a bridge*: pontoon □ *float used to raise sunken ships*: caisson

flood □ *adjective*: diluvial □ *sudden flood*: flash flood □ *before the (biblical) Flood*: antediluvian

floor □ *floor of a building having principal reception rooms etc.*: piano nobile □ *floor set in a building between main floors*: mezzanine □ *floor of wood blocks*: parquet

flour *adjective*: farinaceous

flow *combining forms*: rheo-, -rrhoea, -rrhagia

flower □ *combining forms*: antho-, flor-, anthous □ *adjective*: floral □ *sweet liquid collected by bees from flowers*: nectar □ *fine dust collected by bees from flowers*: pollen □ *flower that keeps its colour when dried*: immortelle

fluid □ *body fluid in early medicine*: humour □ *body fluid surrounding embryo*: amniotic fluid □ *body fluid around joints*: sinovia

fodder □ *fodder of fermented grass etc.*: silage □ *tall fodder plant with yellow flowers*: rape

fond *combining forms*: phil(o)-, -phile

food □ *adjective*: alimentary □ *food for the gods*: ambrosia □ *food for pigs*: swill □ *food for horses*: tack □ *seasoning for food*: condiment □ *food additive used in Chinese cuisine*: monosodium glutamate □ *shop selling foreign foods*: delicatessen □ *denoting food prepared in accordance with Jewish law*: kosher □ *denoting food unacceptable to Jewish law*: tref □ *food poisoning*: botulism, salmonellosis

fool's gold *technical term*: iron pyrites

foot □ *combining forms*: pedi-, -pod, -pode □ *wart growing on feet*: verruca □ *specialist treating hands and feet*: chiropodist

forehead *adjectives*: frontal

foreign □ *combining form*: xeno- □ *foreign girl who does domestic work in return for keep and English lessons*: au pair

foreskin □ *technical term*: prepuce □ *removal of the foreskin*: circumcision

forest *adjective*: sylvan

form *combining forms*: morpho-, -morphic

formal logic *alternative term*: symbolic logic

fortification □ *fortification of wooden stakes*: palisade, stockade □ *concrete fortification, with loopholes for guns etc.*: blockhouse □ *underground fortified shelter*: bunker

fortune telling □ *fortune telling from lines on the hand*: palmistry □ *fortune telling from the stars*: astrology □ *fortune telling from playing cards*: cartomancy □ *fortune telling from dreams*: oneiromancy □ *fortune telling by drawing lots*: sortilege

found object *alternative term*: objet trouvé

four □ *combining forms*: quadr-, tetr- □ *four children born at a birth*: quadruplets □ *four-legged animal*: quadruped □ *four-line verse stanza*: quatrain □ *four-track stereophonic sound*: quadraphony

fowl □ *adjective*: gallinaceous □ *castrated fowl*: capon □ *fowl's edible offal*: giblets

fox □ *adjective*: vulpine □ *female fox*: vixen □ *male fox*: dog □ *fox's lair*: earth □ *fox's tail*: brush

fraction □ *number placed above the line in a fraction*: numerator □ *number placed below the line in a fraction*: denominator □ *fraction equal to less than one*: proper fraction □ *fraction equal to more than one*: improper fraction

France *combining forms*: Franco-, Gallo-

freeze *combining form*: cryo-

French bean *alternative terms*: dwarf bean, haricot, kidney bean

friction *combining form*: tribo-

frog *adjective*: batrachian

front □ *front of a building*: façade □ *front of an army*: vanguard □ *front of a leaf of paper*: recto

fruit *combining forms*: fruct-, -carp

fruit fly *alternative term*: drosophila

fruit sugar *technical term*: fructose

fungus □ *combining forms*: myco-, -mycete □ *edible fungus growing underground*: truffle

furnace □ *furnace for steel*: blast furnace □ *furnace for pottery*: kiln □ *furnace for rubbish*: incinerator

fusion bomb *alternative term*: thermonuclear bomb

G

gall *combining form*: chole-

gallery *exterior gallery on an upper floor*: loggia

game *game killed during a day's shoot etc.*: bag

gangrene *technical terms*: necrosis, mortification

garden □ *formal garden with paths between small beds etc.*: knot garden □ *garden pavilion with view*: gazebo □ *garden shelter*: alcove, arbour, bower □ *ornamental hedge-clipping in a garden*: topiary

garlic □ *adjective*: alliaceous □ *garlic mayonnaise*: aioli

gas □ *combining forms*: aero-, pneum(o)- □ *laboratory gas burner*: Bunsen burner □ *gas in the digestive tract*: flatulence □ *foul-smelling gas*: mephitis, effluvium □ *gas formerly thought to fill all space*: ether

gas mask *technical term*: respirator

gate □ *revolving gate*: turnstile □ *fortified gate*: barbican □ *back gate*: postern

gear □ *gear system causing the parts to revolve at the same speed before engagement*: synchromesh □ *system changing cycle gears by moving the chain*: derailleur

general assistant factotum

German shepherd dog *alternative term*: alsatian

germ warfare *alternative term*: biological warfare

gift of tongues *technical term*: glossolalia

glandular fever *technical term*: infectious mononucleosis

glass *adjective*: vitreous

goat *adjectives*: caprine, hircine

goose □ *adjective*: anserine □ *group of geese*: gaggle □ *group of geese flying in formation*: skein

geranium *alternative term*: pelargonium

germ □ *technical term*: pathogen □ *blood protein counteracting germs*: antibody □ *germ provoking the production of antibodies*: antigen

German measles *technical term*: rubella

ghost □ *ghostly double of a living person*: doppelgänger □ *ghost that throws things about*: poltergeist □ *ghostly emanation from a medium during a seance*: ectoplasm

give *person who gives*: donor

glandular fever *technical term*: infectious mononucleosis

Glasgow *adjective*: Glaswegian

glass □ *combining form*: vitr- □ *adjectives*: vitreous

glass fibre *alternative term*: optical fibre

glue-sniffing *technical term*: solvent abuse

gnu *alternative term*: wildebeest

goat □ *adjectives*: caprine, hircine □ *male goat*: billy goat □ *female goat*: nanny goat □ *fabric made from goat hair*: mohair □ *astrological term*: capricorn

god □ *combining form*: the- □ *adjective*: divine □ *belief in a single god*: monotheism □ *belief in many gods*: polytheism □ *belief that God is identical with the created universe*: pantheism □ *drink of the gods*: nectar □ *food of the gods*: ambrosia □ *blood of the gods*: ichor □ *woodland god*: satyr, faun □ *creator-god*: demiurge □ *god's appearance to men*: epiphany, theophany □ *of a god taking animal form*: zoomorphic □ *of a god taking human form*: anthropomorphic □ *belief that there can be no sure evidence of a god's existence*: agnosticism □ *belief that there is no god*: atheism

gold □ *combining forms*: auri-, chryso-, -chrys- □ *gold in bulk*: bullion □ *gold bar*: ingot □ *lump of natural gold*: nugget □ *search for natural gold*: prospect □ *stone said to turn base metals to gold*: philosopher's stone

goose *adjective*: anserine

goose-flesh *technical term*: horripilation

government □ *combining forms*: -archy, -cracy, -nomy □ *moral authority given to a government by its election majority*: mandate □ *transfer of governmental power to regional authorities*: devolution □ *organization that is independent but government-sponsored*: quango

gradual □ *gradual development*: evolution □ *gradual absorption*: osmosis

grain □ *combining form*: grani- □ *grain-eating*: granivorous □ *grain fungus*: ergot □ *funnel for dispensing grain*: hopper □ *gather leftover grain from a harvest field*: glean □ *separate chaff from grain by the wind*: winnow □ *separate chaff from grain by beating*: thresh □ *storage tower or pit for threshed grain*: silo □ *storehouse for threshed grain*: granary

grammar □ *mistake in grammar*: solecism □ *mistake in grammar made by inappropriate application of a rule*: hypercorrection

grape □ *grape harvest*: vintage □ *fermenting grape juice*: must □ *remains of grapes after pressing*: marc

grandfather clock *alternative term*: longcase clock

grass □ *adjectives*: graminaceous, gramineous □ *grass-eating*: graminivorous □ *circle of darker grass in lawn etc.*: fairy ring □ *clump of grass dislodged by horse's hoof etc.*: divot □ *synthetic grass surface used on sports fields*: AstroTurf™

grassland □ *extensive grassland in Russia*: steppe □ *extensive grassland in North America*: prairie □ *extensive grassland in South America*: pampas □ *extensive grassland in warm regions*: savannah □ *extensive grassland in South Africa*: veldt

grave □ *adjective*: sepulchral □ *prehistoric grave mound*: barrow, tumulus

Greek □ *combining form*: Graeco-, Hellen- □ *adjective*: Hellenic □ *Greek restaurant*: taverna □ *Greek resin-flavoured wine*: retsina □ *Greek mandolin*: bouzouki □ *white skirt in Greek men's traditional dress*: fustanella □ *citadel of ancient Greek city*: acropolis

green □ *combining forms*: chlor(o)- □ *adjective*: verdant □ *green pepper*: capsicum □ *green pigment in plants*: chlorophyll □ *green crystallized crust forming on exposed copper, brass, etc.*: verdigris

groin *adjective*: inguinal

groove *adjective*: sulcate

group □ *group of people of equal social status*: peer group □ *group of people living together and sharing all property*: commune □ *group of people pressing a common interest*: lobby □ *group of actors etc.*: troupe □ *group of businesses*: consortium, syndicate, cartel

guard *adjective*: custodial

guardian *adjective*: tutelary

guide □ *moral guide*: mentor, guru □ *tourists' guide*: cicerone

guillotine □ *cart carrying prisoners to the guillotine*: tumbrel □ *woman knitting by the guillotine*: tricoteuse

guilt □ *produce arguments or evidence to lessen someone's guilt*: extenuate, mitigate □ *feeling of guilt*: compunction

guitar *small disc used to pluck a guitar's strings*: plectrum

gullet *technical term*: oesophagus

gum □ *technical term*: gingiva □ *gum disease caused by plaque, with bleeding etc.*: gingivitis

gunfire □ *simultaneous fire from all the guns on one side of a ship*: broadside □ *rapid burst of gunfire*: fusillade, volley

gunman *hidden gunman*: sniper

guru *Hindu guru*: maharishi

gut *adjective*: visceral

gypsy □ *gypsy person, or their language*: Romany □ *Romany word for 'man'*: rom □ *Romany word for a non-gypsy*: gorgio □ *Italian gypsy*: Zingaro □ *Hungarian gypsy*: tzigane □ *itinerant tinker or scrap-metal dealer*: didicoi

H

habit □ *strange habit*: eccentricity, idiosyncrasy, mannerism □ *of a person possessed by compulsive habits*: inveterate, pathological

hair □ *combining forms*: pil-, -trich- □ *adjective*: capillary □ *bristling of the hair in fear etc.*: gooseflesh □ *removal of unwanted hair*: depilation □ *having tightly curled hair*: ulotrichan □ *study of hair and its diseases*: trichology

hairdressing *adjective*: tonsorial

hair oil brilliantine, pomade, Macassar oil

half □ *combining forms*: demi-, hemi-, semi- □ *half-board*: demi-pension □ *half-line of verse*: hemistich

hallucination □ *producing or produced by hallucinations*: psychedelic □ *hallucinations etc. suffered by alcoholics*: delirium tremens

hammer □ *hammer used by auctioneers etc.*: gavel □ *diagnostic hammer used by doctors*: plexor □ *flat part of a hammer head, used for striking*: face □ *rounded or wedge-shaped part of a hammer head, opposite to the face*: peen □ *V-shaped device for removing nails, set opposite to the face*: claw □ *technical term for a bone in the ear*: malleus

hand □ *combining forms*: chiro-, manu- □ *adjective*: manual, palmate □ *able to use both hands equally well*: ambidextrous

hand over *hand over a person to a foreign power for trial etc.*: extradite

handle □ *handle of a sword or knife*: haft, hilt □ *handle of an axe or hammer*: helve □ *handle of a whip or fishing rod*: stock

handwriting *psychological study of handwriting*: graphology

hangnail *alternative term*: agnail

hard *combining form*: scler(o)-

hard coal *alternative term*: anthracite

hardening of the arteries *technical term*: arteriosclerosis

hare □ *adjective*: leporine □ *female hare*: doe □ *male hare*: buck □ *young hare*: leveret □ *hare-hunting*: coursing

haricot *alternative term*: French bean

hat □ *cowboy's hat*: stetson □ *Mexican hat*: sombrero □ *academic hat*: square, mortarboard, bonnet □ *soft cloth hat with brims at front and back, and earflaps that may be tied up*: deerstalker □ *hat of stiffened straw with a low flat crown*: boater □ *sailor's oilskin hat*: sou'wester

hate *combining forms*: mis-, -phobe, -phobia, -phobic

hatred □ *hatred of men*: misandry □ *hatred of women*: misogyny □ *hatred of people*: misanthropy

head *combining forms*: cephalo-, -cephal-, -capit-

headache *severe headache with nausea and impaired vision*: migraine

headband □ *Arab's headband*: agal □ *Jew's liturgical headband*: frontlet

health *person obsessed by his own health*: hypochondriac, valetudinarian

hearing □ *combining form*: audi- □ *adjectives*: acoustic, auditory

heart □ *combining form*: cardi- □ *adjective*: cardiac □ *heart specialist*: cardiologist

heart attack *technical term*: coronary thrombosis, myocardial infarction

heartbeat □ *electrically traced record of a heartbeat*: electrocardiogram □ *irregular heartbeat*: arrhythmia □ *abnormally slow heartbeat*: bradycardia □ *abnormally fast heartbeat*: tachycardia

heat □ *combining forms*: cal(o)-, therm(o)-, -thermy □ *adjectives*: thermal, caloric □ *heat milk etc. to increase shelf-life*: pasteurize □ *heat spiced wine or ale*: mull

heating □ *underfloor heating system in Roman houses*: hypocaust □ *progressive heating of the earth's atmosphere due to breaches in ozone layer*: global warming, greenhouse effect

hedge-trimming *ornamental hedge-trimming*: topiary

hedgehog *adjective*: erinaceous

heel *combining form*: -calc-

heel bone *technical term*: calcaneus

height □ *combining forms*: acro-, alt-, hyps- □ *dizziness caused by heights etc.*: vertigo □ *fear of heights*: acrophobia □ *instrument measuring an aircraft's height*: altimeter

heir *adjective*: hereditary

Hermes □ *Latin name*: Mercury □ *Hermes' snake-twined staff*: caduceus

hermit □ *adjective*: eremitic □ *hermit living on the top of a pillar*: stylite

hiccup *technical term*: singultus

hidden □ *combining form*: crypt(o)- □ *hidden store*: cache, stash

higher *combining form*: super-, supra-

Hindu □ *Hindu teacher*: guru, maharishi, pandit □ *Hindu ascetic*: fakir □ *Hindu state of blessedness*: nirvana □ *Hindu erotic classic*: Karma Sutra □ *Hindu seclusion of women*: purdah □ *Hindu widow's self-cremation*: suttee □ *Hindu meditation technique poupular in the West*: Transcendental Meditation

hip □ *hip bone*: innominate bone, coxa □ *hip joint*: coxa □ *hip socket for thigh bone*: acetabulum

hives *technical term*: urticaria

holy *combining form*: hagi(o)-, hier(o)-

holy war □ *by Christians to recover the Holy Land*: crusade □ *by Muslims against infidels*: jihad

honey □ *alcoholic drink made from honey*: mead □ *sweetmeat made of honey and sesame flour*: halva □ *liquid collected by bees from flowers to make honey*: nectar

hook □ *hooked pole used to land large fish etc.*: gaff □ *hooked device on a rope thrown to gain purchase on the top of a wall etc.*: grappling iron, grapnel

hoop *hoop attached to a skirt to support it*: farthingale

hormone □ *hormone secreted when under stress*: adrenaline □ *hormone regulating blood sugar levels*: insulin □ *hormone used by athletes to inprove performance*: steroid □ *hormone used to treat allergies and arthritis*: cortisone □ *hormone governing female secondary sexual characteristics*: oestrogen □ *hormones governing male secondary sexual characteristics*: androgen, testosterone

horn □ *combining form*: kerat(o)- □ *adjective*: corneous □ *horn of plenty*: cornucopia

horse □ *combining forms*: equi-, hippo- □ *adjective*: equine □ *small prehistoric horse*: eohippus □ *female horse*: mare □ *young female horse*: filly □ *castrated male horse*: gelding □ *uncastrated male horse*: stallion, entire horse □ *young male horse*: colt □ *thoroughbred horses*: bloodstock □ *wild American horse*: mustang, bronco □ *person who rides horses*: equestrian □ *person who shoes horses*: farrier □ *horse-slaughterer*: knacker

hospital *hospital for the terminally ill*: hospice

hot water □ *natural hot spring*: geyser □ *pan of hot water above which food may be cooked or kept warm*: bain-marie

house □ *Eskimo's house made of ice blocks*: igloo □ *Russian summer residence*: dacha □ *traditional wooden house in Switzerland*: chalet □ *traditional conical stone house of southern Italy*: trullo □ *children's play-house*: Wendy house

housemaid's knee *technical term*: prepatellar bursitis

huge *combining forms*: mega-, megalo-, macro-

human □ *combining forms*: -anthrop(o)- □ *attribution of human form or behaviour to gods, animals, or inanimate objects*: anthropomorphism □ *assumption of human form by a god, concept, etc.*: embodiment, incarnation □ *attribution of human emotions etc. to inanimate objects*: pathetic fallacy

hundred *combining forms*: cent-, hecto-

Hungarian □ *Hungarian cavalryman*: hussar □ *Hungarian gypsy*: tzigane □ *Hungarian stew*: goulash □ *Hungarian person or his language*: Magyar

hunting □ *adjective*: venatic □ *animal etc. pursued by hunters*: quarry □ *time of year when hunting etc. is permitted*: open season □ *artificial scent used in sham hunts*: drag

husband □ *monarch's husband*: consort □ *husband of unfaithful wife*: cuckold □ *servility of a husband towards his wife*: uxoriousness □ *custom or state of having only one husband at a time*: monandry □ *custom or state of having several husbands at a time*: polyandry

hymn □ *hymn sung as the clergy etc. enter the church for a service*: introit □ *hymn sung during a procession*: processional □ *hymn sung as the clergy etc. leave the church after a service*: recessional □ *Lutheran hymn or its music*: chorale

I

ice □ *adjective*: glacial □ *river of ice*: glacier □ *floating sheet of ice*: floe □ *large floating block of ice*: iceberg □ *area of water crowded with floating blocks of ice*: pack ice □ *thin transparent layer of ice on road etc.*: black ice □ *drink poured over crushed ice*: frappé □ *water ice made from fruit etc.*: sorbet □ *Italian ice cream of various flavours with glacé fruits etc.*: cassata

identical □ *identical twins, technical term*: monozygotic twins □ *genetically identical organism*: clone

illegal □ *official's illegal use of powers or funds entrusted to him*: malversation □ *alcohol distilled illegally in Ireland*: poteen □ *alcohol distilled illegally in the USA*: moonshine

illegitimacy *heraldic indication of illegitimacy*: bar sinister

illness □ *feign illness to avoid work etc.*: malinger □ *denoting a physical illness that has a psychological cause*: psychosomatic □ *denoting an illness caused by medical intervention*: iatrogenic

illusion □ *illusion seen in a desert*: mirage □ *illusion seen on mountain peaks*: Brocken spectre □ *illusionist technique of mural painting*: trompe l'oeil

illustration □ *illustration at the front of a book*: frontispiece □ *illustration used to fill the page at the end of a chapter etc.*: tailpiece □ *illustration of a machine etc. showing the parts separated for clarity*: exploded view □ *illustration of a machine etc. showing its casing cut away*: cutaway

immature *immature works of an artist etc.*: juvenilia

immigrant *immigrant worker in Germany*: Gastarbeiter

immunity □ *immunity offered to previous offenders*: amnesty □ *immunity from local laws enjoyed by foreign diplomats*: extraterritoriality

imprisonment □ *wartime imprisonment of enemy aliens*: internment □ *imprisonment with forced labour*: penal servitude □ *writ to assess the legality of someone's imprisonment*: habeas corpus

impurities *add impurities to food or drink*: adulterate

in *combining forms*: endo-, entro-, intra-, intro-

incidental *incidental remark in a legal judgement*: obiter dictum

income □ *person's income before taxes are deducted*: gross income □ *person's income after taxes have been deducted*: net income, disposable income □ *adequate income*: competence

inconsistency *statement containing two apparently inconsistent elements*: paradox, oxymoron

Indian □ *Indian ruler*: maharaja, raja, nawab, nizam □ *Indian soldier*: sepoy □ *Indian elephant-driver*: mahout □ *Indian fan*: punkah □ *Indian corn, alternative term*: maize □ *flight of steps leading down to a river in India*: ghat □ *Indian ink, alternative term*: Chinese ink

indigestion □ *technical term*: dyspepsia □ *bloated feeling resulting from indigestion*: flatulence

individual *combining form*: idio-

industrial disputes □ *use of a third party to negotiate a settlement*: conciliation □ *recourse to a third party who adjudicates a settlement*: arbitration

inferior *combining forms*: infra-, sub-

inflammation *medical combining form*: -itis

informer *criminal supplying information to the police*: stool-pigeon, nark, grass

inhabitant *original inhabitant*: aboriginal, autochthon

inscription *study of ancient inscriptions*: epigraphy

insect □ *combining form*: entomo- □ *study of insects*: entomology □ *insect in immature grub-like form*: larva □ *insect in inactive stage between larva and adult*: pupa, chrysalis □ *larva of certain insects which develops directly into the adult stage*: nymph □ *transformation of an insect between these stages*: metamorphosis □ *mature insect*: imago □ *insect's feeding tube*: proboscis □ *insect excrement*: frass □ *insect of greenfly or blackfly type, living on plant juices*: aphid

interest □ *interest paid on capital only*: simple interest □ *interest paid on capital and on accumulated interest of previous periods*: compound interest □ *lowest available rate of interest on a bank loan*: prime rate

interval □ *interval between two successive reigns etc.*: interregnum □ *music etc. performed in a theatre interval*: intermezzo, entr'acte

intestines □ *combining form*: enter(o)- □ *pig's intestines prepared as food*: chitterlings □ *pain in the intestines*: colic

into *combining form*: intro-

introductory *combining form*: fore-

invention *document granting an inventor sole right to the exploitation of his work*: patent

investment □ *list of investments made*: portfolio □ *certificate assuring ownership of investments*: securities □ *company holding a wide and changing share portfolio and inviting clients to invest in the whole*: unit trust □ *person living off dividends from investments etc.*: rentier

inward *combining form*: intro-

ion □ *ion having a negative charge*: anion □ *ion having a positive charge*: cation

Ireland □ *adjective*: Hibernian □ *Celtic language of Ireland*: Erse □ *citizen of Ireland, especially if an Erse-speaker*: Gael □ *area of Ireland where Erse is spoken*: Gaeltacht □ *citizen of Northern Ireland who wishes to retain political links with the UK*: Unionist, Loyalist □ *citizen of Ireland who seeks the political unification of the island*: Nationalist

Irish □ *Irish social gathering*: ceilidh □ *Irish accent*: brogue □ *Irish cudgel*: shillelagh □ *Irish police force*: Garda

iron □ *combining forms*: ferro-, ferri-, sider(o)- □ *adjectives*: ferrous □ *block of crude cast iron*: pig

irrigation □ *irrigation device of a bucket on a pole*: shadouf □ *irrigation device of buckets on a wheel*: Noria

island □ *adjective*: insular □ *island on a lake or river*: ait, holm, eyot □ *group of islands*: archipelago □ *low coral island*: cay, key

Israeli □ *Israeli nationalist*: Zionist □ *Israeli collective farm*: kibbutz □ *Israeli smallholders' co-operative*: moshav

itch □ *technical term*: pruritus □ *itchy feeling as if of ants crawling over the skin*: formication

J

Jamaican *Jamaican religion regarding Haile Selassie as God*: Rastafarianism

Japanese □ *Japanese emperor*: mikado □ *Japanese art of paper-folding*: origami □ *Japanese wrestling*: sumo □ *Japanese warrior*: samurai □ *ritual suicide required of dishonoured Japanese warrior etc.*: hara-kiri □ *Japanese sport of self-defence*: judo, jujitsu, aikido □ *Japanese sport of fencing with wooden swords*: kendo □ *Japanese suicide pilot*: kamikaze □ *Japanese prostitute*: geisha □ *Japanese alcoholic drink made from rice*: sake □ *Japanese dwarf tree*: bonsai □ *Japanese puppet theatre*: bunraku □ *Japanese traditional theatre*: Noh □ *Japanese popular theatre*: kabuki □ *Japanese poem of 17 syllables*: haiku

japonica *alternative term*: camellia

jar *storage jar in classical times*: amphora

jaundice □ *technical term*: icterus □ *liver disease producing jaundice*: hepatitis

Java *Javan percussion orchestra*: gamelan

jaw □ *combining forms*: -gnath-, -gnathic □ *adjective*: gnathic □ *paralysis of the jaws*: lockjaw, trismus

jelly □ *jelly made from meat or fish stock*: aspic □ *dish served in aspic*: galantine

jester □ *jester's cap*: coxcomb □ *jester's baton*: bauble □ *jester's particoloured suit*: motley

Jew □ *combining form*: Judaeo- □ *food etc. that conforms to Jewish dietary regulations*: kosher □ *food etc. that does not conform to Jewish dietary regulations*: tref □ *Jewish unleavened bread*: matzo □ *Jewish seven-branched candlestick*: menorah □ *Orthodox Jew's skullcap*: yarmulke □ *Jewish* *girl's coming of age ceremony*: bat mitzvah □ *Jewish boy's coming of age ceremony*: bar mitzvah □ *language used by Jews of central and eastern Europe*: Yiddish □ *language used by some mediterranean Jews*: Ladino □ *Jewish quarter in a city*: ghetto □ *organized massacre of Jews in 19th-c. Russia etc.*: pogrom □ *Hitler's programme for the extermination of European Jews*: Holocaust □ *Jewish term for non-Jew*: goy

job *job in which no work is required*: sinecure

joint □ *combining forms*: arthr-, -arthr- □ *painful inflammation of the joints*: arthritis

judge □ *adjective*: judicial □ *judge's office for private hearings etc.*: chambers □ *judge's order for enforcement of a law etc.*: injunction □ *expert adviser who sits with a judge in technical cases*: assessor □ *attempt to corrupt a judge*: embracery

judo □ *judo teacher*: judoka □ *judo suit*: judogi □ *judo mat*: dojo

jump □ *sprung stick for making large jumps*: pogo stick □ *sheet stretched taut for jumping on*: trampoline

justice □ *system of justice where the judge or magistrate acts as prosecutor*: inquisitorial system □ *system of justice where the judge or magistrate adjudicates between prosecution and defence*: accusatorial system □ *out-of-court negotiations between prosecution and defence lawyers to secure a reduced charge in return for an admission of guilt*: plea bargaining

K

kidney □ *combining forms*: nephr-, ren-, -ren- □ *adjective*: renal, nephritic

kidney bean *alternative term*: dwarf bean, French bean

kidney machine *technical term*: haemodialyser

kidney stone *technical term*: renal calculus, renal concretion

kill □ *kill by beheading*: decapitate □ *kill by suffocation*: asphyxiate □ *kill selectively, to reduce a herd etc.*: cull □ *killing one's brother*: fratricide □ *killing one's father*: patricide □ *killing one's mother*: matricide □ *killing a parent or other near relative*: parricide □ *killing oneself*: suicide □ *killing a sovereign*: regicide □ *killing a whole race*: genocide □ *mercy killing*: euthanasia

killer *combining form*: -cide

king □ *adjectives*: royal, regal □ *person who governs during a king's illness etc.*: regent □ *disease formerly thought to be cured by the sovereign's touch*: king's evil

kitchen □ *adjective*: culinary □ *kitchen on a ship or aircraft*: galley

kiwi *technical term*: apteryx

kiwi fruit *alternative term*: Chinese gooseberry

kneecap *technical term*: patella

knee-jerk *technical term*: patellar reflex

kidney vetch *alternative terms*: ladies' fingers, okra

knife *knife-maker*: cutler

knotwork *ornamental knotwork made with string*: macramé

knowledge □ *combining forms*: -gnosis, -nomy, -sophy □ *scholarly knowledge*: erudition □ *rote knowledge*: pedantry □ *shallow knowledge*: sciolism □ *instinctive knowledge*: intuition □ *social knowledge*: savoir-faire □ *knowledge before the event*: precognition □ *knowledge after the event*: hindsight □ *knowledge of many subjects*: polymathy □ *knowledge of everything*: omniscience

L

lake □ *adjective*: lacustrine □ *Scottish lake*: loch □ *Irish lake*: lough □ *mountain lake*: tarn □ *lake made by blocked-up loop of river*: oxbow lake □ *study of lakes*: limnology

ladies' fingers *alternative terms*: kidney vetch, okra

Lama □ *chief Lama of Tibet*: Dalai Lama □ *second Lama of Tibet*: Panchen Lama, Tashi Lama

lament □ *Irish lament*: keen □ *Scottish lament*: pibroch

land □ *adjective*: terrestrial □ *right of way over another's land*: easement □ *ownership of land or the land owned*: domain □ *a government's right to take privately owned land into public use*: eminent domain □ *the taking of such land*: expropriation □ *land given for the support of a beneficed clergyman*: glebe □ *land in Holland etc. reclaimed from the sea*: polder □ *narrow strip of land projecting into water*: peninsula □ *narrow strip of land connecting two larger areas*: isthmus □ *narrow strip of land projecting into the holdings of others*: panhandle

language □ *combining forms*: lingu-, -glot □ *adjective*: linguistic □ *everyday language*: vernacular □ *simplified language, often drawn from several sources, used by foreign traders etc.*: pidgin, lingua franca □ *form of a native language that has been corrupted by colonists' speech*: creole □ *basic sound unit in a language*: phoneme □ *basic meaning unit in a language*: semanteme, sememe □ *basic word unit in a language*: morpheme □ *distinctive language of an individual*: idiolect □ *distinctive language of a region*: dialect □ *language as people actually use it*: parole □ *language as described in grammar books*: langue □ *study of language*: linguistics

large *combining forms*: macro-, maxi-, mega-, megalo-

laser *laser-produced three-dimensional image*: hologram

laughing jackass *alternative term*: kookaburra

law □ *adjective*: legal □ *redress of an injustice offered or gained by law*: remedy □ *required by law*: liable □ *academic study of law*: jurisprudence

lead *combining forms*: plumb-

leader □ *combining forms*: -agogue, -arch □ *nominal leader*: figurehead, front man, puppet

leaf □ *combining forms*: foli-, -phyll- □ *adjectives*: foliaceous, foliate □ *leaves in general*: foliage □ *leaf-stalk*: petiole □ *strip of leaves*: defoliate

leap year □ *adjective*: bissextile □ *technical term*: intercalary year

learning □ *learning from a course in a book or computer*: programmed learning □ *learning through tapes played while asleep*: hypnopaedia □ *learning by controlled trial and error*: heuristic

lease □ *person granting a lease*: lessor □ *person taking a lease*: lessee

leather □ *leather formerly used for writing*: parchment □ *leather strap formerly used to punish Scottish schoolchildren*: tawse □ *impressed ornamentation on leather*: tooling

leave □ *leave to be absent from school*: exeat □ *leave taken without asking permission*: French leave

left □ *combining form*: laev(o)- □ *adjective*: sinistral □ *left-hand page in a book*: verso □ *left-handed person*: southpaw □ *left side of a ship as seen by one facing its prow*: port

leg □ *adjective*: crural □ *swollen vein on the leg*: varicose vein □ *metal support strapped to a broken etc. leg*: calliper

lemon *adjectives*: citric, citrous, citrine

lens □ *variable opening for a camera lens*: aperture □ *camera lens allowing rapid changes in magnification*: zoom lens □ *uneven focus of an eye due to a fault in the cornea or lense*: astigmatism

leprosy *technical term*: Hansen's disease

let *let the buyer beware*: caveat emptor

letter □ *adjective*: epistolary, literal □ *letter sent to all bishops by the Pope*: encyclical □ *letter which each recipient is asked to copy out and send to several others*: chain letter □ *letter sent by a woman breaking off a relationship*: Dear John □ *conventional letter of thanks for hospitality etc.*: Collins □ *opening greeting in a letter*: salutation □ *message added to a letter after the writer's signature*: postscript □ *write out in the letters of a different alphabet*: transliterate

level □ *social level*: stratum, echelon □ *set level to each other, making a single flat surface*: flush □ *device with an air-bubble in liquid to show if surfaces are level*: spirit level

lice *infestation with lice*: pediculosis

lie □ *adjective*: mendacious □ *telling lies when under oath to speak the truth*: perjury □ *lie detector*: polygraph

life □ *combining form*: bio-, vit- □ *adjectives*: animate, vital □ *bodily processes that support life*: metabolism □ *study of living organisms*: physiology □ *long life*: longevity

lifeboat *ship's crane for a lifeboat*: davit

lift □ *lift for food in restaurant etc.*: dumb waiter □ *continuously moving lift with doorless compartments*: paternoster

light *combining forms*: lumin-, photo-, -phos-, -phot-

like *combining forms*: -esque, -oid, -ose

liker *combining forms*: phil(o)-, -phile

lilac *alternative term*: syringa

lime *combining form*: calci-

line □ *line of latitude*: parallel □ *line of longitude*: meridian

lion □ *adjective*: leonine □ *astrological term*: leo

lip □ *combining form*: labi(o)- □ *adjective*: labial

live □ *living on land*: terrestrial □ *living in or near water*: aquatic □ *living in the sea*: marine □ *able to live on land and in water*: amphibious

liver □ *combining form*: hepat- □ *adjective*: hepatic □ *inflammation of the liver, causing jaundice*: hepatitis □ *degeneration of the liver due to alcoholism or hepatitis*: cirrhosis

Liverpool *adjective*: Liverpudlian

lizard □ *combining forms*: sauro-, -saur, -saurus □ *adjective*: saurian □ *lizard that can change its colour for camouflage*: chameleon □ *mythical lizard said to live in fire*: salamander

loan translation *alternative term*: calque

locomotive *frame on the top of an electric locomotive that rises to the overhead wires*: pantograph

loin *adjective*: lumbar

logic □ *false step in reasoning*: fallacy, non sequitur, paralogism □ *deliberately misleading step in reasoning*: sophism □ *disproof of a proposition by demonstrating the absurdity of its consequences*: reductio ad absurdum □ *system of logical reasoning that moves from a general rule to a particular instance*: deduction □ *system of logical reasoning that derives a general rule from particular instances*: induction □ *logical proposition that is verified by the meanings of the words that make it*: analytic proposition □ *logical proposition that is verified by experience*: synthetic proposition

lockjaw *technical term*: trismus

long sight *technical terms*: hypermetropia, hyperopia, presbyopia

lorry □ *articulated lorry's skid into a V-shape*: jackknife □ *device recording a lorry driver's speeds and spells of driving*: tachograph □ *lorry's unladen weight*: tare □ *large covered lorry for furniture etc.*: pantechnicon

loudspeaker □ *loudspeaker for low-pitched sounds*: woofer □ *loudspeaker for high-pitched sounds*: tweeter

love □ *combining forms*: philo-, -phil-, -phile □ *adjectives*: amorous, amatory

loyalty *group loyalty*: esprit de corps

lucerne *alternative term*: alfalfa

luggage *rotating luggage delivery system at an airport etc.*: carousel

lung □ *combining form*: pneumo- □ *adjective*: pulmonary

lying □ *lying face-downwards*: prone □ *lying face-upwards*: supine

M

machine □ *adjective*: mechanical □ *person who behaves like a machine*: automaton □ *person opposed to the introduction of machines*: Luddite

mad cow disease *technical term*: bovine spongiform encephalitis

mad dog *disease caused by the bite of a mad dog*: rabies

made to order *technical term*: bespoke

Mafia □ *Neapolitan Mafia*: Camorra □ *US Mafia*: Cosa Nostra □ *leader of US Mafia*: capo, godfather

magic *object thought to have magic powers*: amulet, fetish, juju, talisman

magistrate *professional magistrate*: stipendiary magistrate

magnetism □ *destroy an object's magnetism*: degauss □ *personal magnetism*: charisma

maidenhead *medical term*: hymen

maize *alternative term*: Indian corn

making *combining forms*: -facient, -fic, -poiesis

malaria □ *drug that cures malaria*: quinine □ *type of mosquito that carries malaria*: anopheles

Malayan □ *Malayan village*: kampong □ *Malayan dagger*: kris □ *Malayan garment*: sarong

male □ *combining forms*: andro-, -andr- □ *aggressive maleness*: machismo □ *development of male characteristics is women*: virilism

mammal □ *mammal with incisor teeth*: rodent □ *mammal that chews the cud*: ruminant □ *thick-skinned mammal (e.g. rhinoceros)*: pachyderm

man □ *combining forms*: andro-, anthropo-, -andr-, -anthrop- □ *adjectives*: male, virile

Manchester *adjective*: Mancunian

mania □ *mania for drink*: dipsomania □ *mania for books*: bibliomania □ *mania for starting fires*: pyromania □ *mania for power or self-aggrandizement*: megalomania □ *manic obsession with a single idea*: monomania □ *mania for stealing*: kleptomania

manioc *alternative term*: cassava

manipulation □ *therapeutic manipulation of bones*: osteopathy □ *manipulation of electoral boundaries for party advantage*: gerrymandering

manners *code of good manners*: etiquette

manuscript □ *manuscript written by the author of the text it contains*: autograph □ *manuscript wholly written by the author of the text it contains*: holograph □ *manuscript with a text written over an earlier text*: palimpsest □ *sheepskin or goatskin prepared for use as a manuscript*: parchment □ *calfskin prepared for use as a manuscript*: vellum

Manx *Manx emblem of three legs*: triskelion

many *combining forms*: multi-, poly-, pluri-

marble *adjective*: marmoreal

marriage □ *combining form*: -gam- □ *adjectives*: conjugal, connubial, marital, matrimonial, nuptial □ *unsuccessful marriage*: misalliance □ *marriage with a social inferior*: mésalliance □ *marriage formalized by a legal ceremony only*: civil marriage □ *clothing etc. collected by a bride before her marriage*: trousseau, bottom drawer □ *property etc. brought by a bride to her marriage*: dowry □ *crime of being simultaneously married to several spouses*: bigamy □ *practice of being simultaneously married to several spouses*: polygamy □ *practice of having only one spouse at a time*: monogamy □ *practice of living together without being married*: cohabitation, common-law marriage

Mars *Greek name*: Ares

marsh □ *adjective*: paludal □ *marsh gas*: methane □ *moving light seen over marshes when the methane ignites*: will-o'-the-wisp, ignis fatuus

mask □ *mask to protect the eyes*: visor □ *mask to aid breathing*: respirator □ *mask with attached cloak*: domino

massage *massage treatment using fragrant oils*: aromatherapy

master *adjective*: magisterial

matchbox *collector of matchbox labels*: phillumenist

matter *combining form*: hyl-

mattress □ *mattress stuffed with straw*: pallet, palliasse □ *strong cloth used to cover mattresses, pillows, etc.*: ticking

meadow saffron *alternative term*: autumn crocus

meal □ *meal taken as breakfast and lunch*: brunch □ *self-service meal*: buffet □ *light meal*: tiffin, collation □ *restaurant meal with a fixed global price and offering few alternatives*: table d'hôte □ *restaurant meal chosen from a range of separately priced dishes*: à la carte

meaning □ *adjective*: semantic □ *general meaning of a text etc.*: burden, gist, gravamen □ *word having the same meaning as another*: synonym □ *word having the opposite meaning to another*: antonym

measles *technical term*: morbilli, rubella

measurement □ *combining forms*: -metr-, -metry □ *adjectives*: mensural, metrical

meat □ *cold cooked meats*: charcuterie □ *meat minced for stuffing*: forcemeat □ *seasoned smoked beef*: pastrami □ *German pork sausage*: bratwurst □ *Italian peppered pork and beef sausage*: pepperoni □ *Italian garlic sausage*: salami □ *spiced Italian pork sausage*: mortadella □ *Italian ham*: prosciutto □ *meat cooked very rare*: au bleu □ *meat cooked rare*: saignant □ *medium-cooked meat*: à point □ *well-cooked meat*: bien cuit

medical examination *combining form*: -opsy

medical treatment □ *combining form*: -pathy □ *medical treatment of children*: paediatrics □ *medical treatment of old people*: geriatrics □ *medical treatment of women*: gynaecology □ *medical treatment of the skin*: dermatology □ *medical treatment of bones and muscles*: orthopaedics □ *medical treatment of the blood*: haematology □ *medical treatment of the nervous system*: neurology □ *medical teatment of mental diseases*: psychiatry □ *medical treatment by small doses of drugs that would induce the disease*: homoeopathy □ *medical treatment by drugs that resist the disease*: allopathy

medicine *combining form*: pharm(aco)-

meeting □ *meeting for academic discussion*: colloquium, seminar, symposium □ *meeting for church government*: synod, consistory □ *meeting of cardinals to elect a pope*: conclave □ *meeting of political delegates etc.*: congress, convention □ *mass meeting of supporters etc.*: rally □ *meeting of heads of state*: summit □ *minimum attendance required for a meeting to be valid*: quorum

membrane □ *membrane dividing the thorax from the abdomen*: diaphragm □ *membrane lining the abdomen*: peritoneum □ *membrane blocking a virgin's vagina*: hymen

memory □ *loss of memory*: amnesia, oblivion □ *formula etc. used to aid memorization or recall*: mnemonic

men □ *rule by men*: patriarchy □ *hatred of men*: misandry □ *party for men*: stag party

menstruation □ *first onset of menstruation at puberty*: menarche □ *menstrual blood*: menses □ *painful or difficult menstruation*: dysmenorrhoea □ *abnormal absence of menstruation*: amenorrhoea □ *cessation of menstruation in middle age*: menopause

Mercury □ *Greek name*: Hermes □ *Mercury's snake-twined staff*: caduceus

mercy killing *technical term*: euthanasia

middle □ *combining forms*: medi-, mes- □ *adjectives*: medial, median □ *middle ear*: tympanum

military □ *swift and intense military attack*: blitzkrieg □ *military officer assisting a senior officer*: adjutant, aide-de-camp □ *military officers who plan a campaign*: general staff □ *long-term military plans*: strategy □ *short-term military plans*: tactics □ *provision of military manpower and supplies*: logistics □ *military stores and materials*: ordnance □ *military court*: court martial

milk □ *combining forms*: lact-, galact- □ *adjectives*: lactic, lacteal

million *combining form*: mega-

millionth *combining form*: micro-

mind *adjective*: mental

Minerva *Greek name*: Athena

mirror *adjective*: catoptric

misfortune *delight in the misfortunes of others*: schadenfreude

mix □ *mix to make uniform throughout*: homogenize □ *mix to create something different*: synthesize □ *mix socially with*: fraternize

mock orange *alternative term*: syringa

modification *modification to parliamentary bill or judicial verdict*: rider

moisture □ *combining form*: hygro- □ *full of moisture*: saturated, desiccated □ *void of moisture*: dehydrated

mole *technical term*: naevus

Monaco *adjective*: Monegasque

money □ *adjectives*: pecuniary, monetary, numismatic □ *money paid to ensure secrecy*: hush money □ *money paid as a political bribe*: slush money □ *money paid as consolation to a redundant etc. executive*: golden handshake, golden parachute □ *extra money paid to employees working in a high cost-of-living area*: weighting □ *dispose of money so as to conceal its illegal origins*: launder

mongolism *technical term*: Down's syndrome

monkey *adjective*: simian

moon □ *combining forms*: lun-, selen- □ *adjective*: lunar

mortgage □ *person granting a mortgage*: mortgagee □ *person taking out a mortgage*: mortgager

Moscow *adjective*: Muscovite

mosque □ *mosque tower*: minaret □ *person calling the faithful to prayer from a minaret*: muezzin □ *mosque's pulpit*: mimbar □ *niche in a mosque's wall facing Mecca*: mimbar

moss □ *combining form*: bryo- □ *study of mosses*: bryology

mother □ *combining form*: matri- □ *adjective*: maternal □ *murder of one's mother*: matricide

motion *adjective*: kinetic

mountain sickness *alternative term*: altitude sickness

mouse *adjective*: murine

mouth □ *combining forms*: or-, stomato-, -stom-, -stome □ *adjectives*: oral, buccal

much *combining forms*: multi-, poly-

muscle *muscle-building drug used by athletes etc.*: anabolic steroid

musician *street musician*: busker

Muslim □ *Muslim name for God*: Allah □ *Muslim scriptures*: Koran □ *Muslim month-long fast*: Ramadan □ *Muslim pilgrimage to Mecca*: haj □ *Muslim mystic*: dervish, sufi □ *Muslim who calls the faithful to prayer*: muezzin □ *Muslim religious leader*: ayatollah, imam, mullah □ *Muslim holy war*: jihad □ *Muslim prince*: emir □ *Muslim princess*: begum □ *Muslim judge*: cadi □ *Muslim chronological era*: Hegira □ *Muslim food regulations*: halal □ *Muslim term for forbidden foods*: haram □ *Muslim seclusion of women*: purdah □ *Muslim woman's veil*: yashmak □ *Muslim woman's overgarment*: chador

N

nail □ *adjective*: ungual □ *dead skin at the base of a nail*: cuticle □ *piece of torn skin beside a nail*: agnail □ *inflammation near a nail*: whitlow

name □ *combining forms*: onom-, nomin-, -nym □ *adjective*: onomastic □ *false name*: pseudonym, alias, nom de plume

Naples *adjective*: Neapolitan

Native American *alternative terms*: American Indian, Amerindian, Red Indian

navel □ *technical term*: umbilicus □ *adjective*: umbilical

navigation *navigation based on computation of position from speed and direction of travel*: dead reckoning

Nazi □ *official title*: National Socialist □ *Nazi emblem*: swastika □ *Nazi marching step*: goose step □ *Nazi secret police*: Gestapo □ *Nazi regional governor*: Gauleiter

neck □ *adjective*: jugular □ *fold of skin hanging from a bird's neck*: wattle □ *fold of skin hanging from the necks of cattle*: dewlap

Neptune *Greek name*: Poseidon

nerve □ *combining form*: neur(o)- □ *adjective*: neural

net □ *adjective*: retiform □ *woman's hairnet*: snood □ *Roman gladiator armed with net*: retiarius

nettle-rash *technical term*: urticaria

new □ *combining forms*: ana-, neo- □ *new thing*: innovation □ *new word*: neologism

newspaper □ *newspaper with large pages*: broadsheet □ *newspaper with small pages*: tabloid

night □ *combining forms*: noct-, nyct- □ *adjective*: nocturnal

night blindness *technical term*: nyctalopia

non-interference *government policy of non-interference*: laissez-faire

non-violence □ *Hindu and Buddhist principle of non-violence towards all living things*: ahimsa □ *non-violent resistance as a form of political protest*: civil disobedience □ *non-violent resistance as advocated by Gandhi in India*: satyagraha

north *adjective*: boreal

northern lights *technical term*: aurora borealis

nose □ *combining forms*: nas(o)-, -rhin(o)- □ *adjectives*: nasal, rhinal □ *hooked nose*: Roman nose □ *straight nose*: Grecian nose

nosebleed *technical term*: epistaxis

nostril □ *technical term*: naris (*plural* nares) □ *adjective*: narial

not *combining forms*: a-, an,- dis-, un-

notebook *notebook containing a personal collection of literary quotations etc.*: commonplace book

noun *adjective*: nominal

novel □ *novel depicting real persons or events but with changed names*: roman à clef □ *novel depicting its hero's early life*: Bildungsroman □ *family novel, usually dealing with several generations*: roman-fleuve □ *novel presented as a series of letters*: epistolary novel

nuclear reactor □ *type of nuclear reactor producing more nuclear fuel than it consumes*: breeder □ *overheating and destruction of a nuclear reactor's core*: meltdown

number □ *number indicating quantity*: cardinal number □ *number indicating position in a sequence*: ordinal number □ *whole number*: integer □ *number system based on 10*: decimal system □ *number system based on 0 and 1*: binary system □ *number system based on 12*: duodecimal system

nut *combining forms*: nuci-

nutrition *combining forms*: troph-, -troph-

nymph □ *tree nymph*: hamadryad □ *wood nymph*: dryad □ *mountain nymph*: oread □ *river nymph*: naiad □ *sea nymph*: nereid □

O

oath □ *evidence given under oath*: deposition □ *written statement made under oath*: affidavit □ *solicitor entitled to administer oaths*: Commissioner for Oaths

offal □ *deer's offal*: umbles □ *fowl's offal*: giblets

official *government official investigating complaints against public bodies*: ombudsman

oil □ *combining form*: ole- □ *adjective*: oleaginous □ *sacramental oil*: chrism, unguent

okra *alternative terms*: kidney vetch, ladies' fingers

old *combining forms*: archaeo-, palaeo-

old age □ *combining form*: geront- □ *mental and physical decay characteristic of old age*: senility □ *study of old age*: geriatrics

old woman *adjective*: anile

one *combining forms*: mon(o)-, uni-

one and a half *combining form*: sesqui-

opera □ *word-book of an opera*: libretto □ *running translation of an opera displayed above the stage*: surtitles □ *famous female opera singer*: diva □ *person teaching opera singers in their music*: répétiteur

opposite □ *opposite side of the world*: antipodes □ *word having the opposite sense*: antonym

orbit □ *point in an orbit furthest from the earth, moon, sun*: apogee, apolune, aphelion □ *point in an orbit closest to the earth, moon, sun*: perigee, perilune, perihelion □ *orbit that keeps a satellite fixed over a terrestrial point*: geostationary orbit □ *star etc. round which a satellite orbits*: primary

order □ *order for supplies*: requisition □ *order for work to be undertaken*: commission □ *order sent from a higher to a lower court*: mandamus □ *order for a person to attend a court*: summons, subpoena □ *court order requiring a certain actions to be performed or avoided*: writ, injunction

organization □ *organization sponsored but not controlled by government*: quango □ *detailed practical organization required to implement a plan*: logistics

origin □ *combining forms*: -genesis, -geny □ *geographical origin of a work of art*: provenance □ *study of the origins of words*: etymology □ *study of the origins of names*: onomastics

Orkneys *adjective*: Orcadian

ostrich *adjective*: struthious

other *combining form*: heter(o)-

otter *otter's lair*: holt, lodge

out *combining forms*: e-, ec-, ex-

ovary □ *combining form*: oophor- □ *immature ovum in the ovary*: oocyte □ *ovary cavity for the ovum*: follicle

over *combining forms*: hyper-, super-, supra-, sur-, trans-

overeating *compulsive overeating*: bulimia

Oxford University □ *Oxford University annual feast*: encaenia □ *Oxford University formal dress*: subfusc □ *Oxford college annual feast*: gaudy □ *Oxford college servant*: scout

P

pain □ *combining forms*: alg-, -algia □ *pain that shoots along a nerve*: neuralgia □ *pain felt away from its real source*: referred pain

painting □ *painting on wet plaster*: fresco □ *painting on dry plaster*: secco □ *painting intended to give a deceptive three-dimensional view*: trompe l'oeil □ *painting in shades of grey to imitate sculpture, masonry, etc.*: grisaille □ *painting in shades of a single colour*: monochrome □ *small cracks on an old painting's surface*: craquelure □ *reappearance of traces of earlier painting*: pentimento

pair *combining form*: zyg-

pancake □ *French pancake*: crêpe □ *Russian pancake*: blini

paper □ *front side of a sheet of paper*: recto □ *reverse side of a sheet of paper*: verso □ *maker's emblem etc. in a sheet of paper*: watermark □ *quality of paper used for top copies*: bond □ *quality of paper used for carbon copies etc.*: bank □ *art of folding paper into decorative shapes*: origami

parachute □ *cord pulled by the parachuter to open a parachute*: ripcord □ *cord fixed to the aircraft to open a jumper's parachute*: static line □ *expanding part of a parachute that arrests and directs its movement*: canopy □ *ropes that hold and control a parachute's canopy*: shrouds □ *sort of parachute used to decelerate a landing aircraft*: drogue parachute

paralysis □ *combining form*: -plegia □ *paralysis from the neck down*: quadriplegia, tetraplegia □ *paralysis from the waist down*: paraplegia □ *paralysis of one side of the body*: hemiplegia □ *paralysis of a single limb*: monoplegia

parish *adjective*: parochial

parrot □ *adjective*: psittacine □ *pneumonia-like disease caught by humans from parrots*: psittacosis

part □ *combining forms*: mero-, -merous □ *composed of similar parts*: homogeneous □ *composed of dissimilar parts*: heterogeneous

Passover □ *adjective*: paschal □ *Jews' name for Passover*: Pesach □ *Passover ceremonies and feast*: Seder □ *Passover bread*: matzo

pastry □ *place where pastries are sold*: patisserie □ *soft light pastry for éclairs etc.*: choux pastry □ *light pastry used in sausage rolls etc.*: puff pastry □ *Greek pastry rolled into thin leaves*: filo pastry

patch □ *having black and white patches*: piebald □ *having patches of white and of some other colour (not black)*: skewbald

path □ *raised path used by models in a fashion show*: catwalk □ *raised path over land liable to flooding*: causeway □ *country path for walkers and horseriders*: bridlepath □ *path alongside a canal*: towpath

pause □ *pause for food, sleep, private discussion, etc. in a court or parliamentary session*: adjournment □ *pause for holidays in a parliamentary session*: recess □ *pause for holidays in a court session*: vacation □ *pause in the middle of a line of verse*: caesura

pay bed *technical term*: amenity bed

payment □ *divorced person's payment to former spouse*: maintenance □ *advance payment made for club membership, or for a series of performances, issues of a journal, etc.*: subscription □ *payment made for services not officially charged for*: honorarium □ *payment made in kind*: truck □ *initial payment made to a barrister*: retainer □ *subsequent payment made to a barrister in a long case*: refresher

peacock *adjective*: pavonine

Peking *currently preferred transliteration*: Beijing

permission □ *permission to be absent from school*: exeat □ *ecclesiatical permission to publish a book*: imprimatur □ *absence without permission*: French leave

permit *customs permit for the temporary import of a motor vehicle*: carnet

petrol bomb □ *crude bomb made by filling a bottle with petrol*: Molotov cocktail □ *jellied petrol used in US incendiary bombs in Vietnam etc.*: napalm

picture □ *simplified picture used to represent a word in some ancient writing systems*: pictograph □ *picture puzzle in which a word is represented by pictures of objects whose names make its syllables*: rebus

pig □ *adjective*: porcine □ *pig's offal used as food*: chitterlings, haslet □ *pig's feet used as food*: trotters □ *smallest piglet in a litter*: runt

piles *technical term*: haemorrhoids

pillar □ *combining forms*: styl-, -stylar □ *prehistoric ring of pillars*: henge □ *classical pillar carved to resemble a man*: telamon □ *classical pillar carved to resemble a woman*: caryatid □ *early Christian saint living on the top of a pillar*: stylite □ *Amerindian carved pillar*: totem pole

pilot *Japanese suicide pilot*: kamikaze

pimento *alternative term*: pimiento

pinwheel *alternative term*: Catherine wheel

pipe □ *long-stemmed clay pipe*: churchwarden □ *Amerindian peace pipe*: calumet □ *oriental smoker's pipe in which the smoke is passed through water*: hookah, narghile

pitch *drop in pitch of a sound that passes the hearer and moves away*: Doppler effect

pith helmet *alternative term*: sola topi

pituitary gland *technical term*: hypophysis

pivot □ *pivot on a rudder*: pintle □ *pivot on a large gun*: trunnion

place □ *combining form*: top- □ *list of places*: gazetteer □ *'feel' of a place*: genius loci

plain □ *plain in Russia*: steppe □ *plain in South Africa*: veldt □ *grassy plain in warm countries*: savannah □ *Arctic plain*: tundra

planning □ *planning method that evaluates a complex set of alternatives*: critical path analysis □ *practical planning, especially of transport*: logistics □ *planning schedule*: PERT chart

plant □ *combining forms*: phyto-, -phyte □ *plant living for one year only*: annual □ *plant living for two years only*: biennial □ *plant living for three or more years*: perennial □ *use by green plants of sunlight energy*: photosynthesis

plant louse *technical term*: aphid

planned economy *alternative term*: command economy

plaster □ *decorative plasterwork*: pargeting □ *fine plaster for frescos etc.*: stucco □ *roughen a plaster surface to aid adhesion*: key □ *smooth a plaster surface*: float

plastic □ *sheet plastic used as glazing etc.*: Perspex™ □ *plastic-coated cloth used for tablecloths etc.*: American cloth □ *plastic lamination for kitchen work surfaces etc.*: Formica™ □ *plastic used for gramophone records etc.*: vinyl □ *plastic used in paints*: acrylic, vinyl □ *plastic used for packing*: expanded polystyrene

plastic surgery *technical term*: anaplasty

platform □ *platform for a gibbet etc.*: scaffold □ *platform for election speeches*: hustings

pleasure □ *pleasure-loving*: hedonistic □ *pleasure derived from the suffering of others*: Roman holiday □ *pleasure gained from the contemplation of others' misfortunes*: schadenfreude

plug □ *plug for the vent of a cask*: spigot, spile □ *plug for the muzzle of a large gun*: tampion □ *plug for a cannon's touch-hole*: spike

poem □ *poem celebrating a marriage*: epithalamium, prothalamium □ *poem about rural life*: bucolic, eclogue, georgic □ *poem lamenting a person's death*: elegy, threnody □ *five-line nonsense poem*: limerick □ *Japanese three-line poem of 17 syllables*: haiku □ *poem constructed so that certain letters from each line form a name etc.*: acrostic

poet □ *successful poet at an Eisteddfodd*: bard □ *French medieval poet*: troubadour, trouvère □ *Scandinavian medieval poet*: skald

Poseidon □ *Latin name*: Neptune □ *Poseidon's three-pronged spear*: trident

poison □ *combining forms*: toxi-, toxo- □ *poison produced by a fungus on peanuts*: aflatoxin □ *poison produced by a fungus on cereals*: ergot □ *poison drunk by Socrates*: hemlock □ *cure for a poison*: antitoxin, antivenin

pole *pole used to push a punt etc.*: quant

police □ *police van*: Black Maria □ *police kit for assembling a likeness of a wanted person*: identikit, photofit

policy □ *published policy statement*: manifesto □ *reversal of policy*: about-face, volte-face, U-turn

polio *technical terms*: poliomyelitis, infantile paralysis

politics □ *political agenda driven by practical needs rather than moral principles*: realpolitik □ *persistent dissemination of political propaganda via the media*: agitprop □ *discarded political system*: ancien régime □ *political opposition in a one-party state*: dissidence □ *splinter group within a political party*: faction, caucus □ *political enthusiast*: activist, militant, Young Turk

poll □ *public poll on some issue of current concern*: plebiscite, referendum □ *officer who counts the votes cast in a poll*: scrutineer □ *officer administering a poll and announcing its result*: returning officer

pope □ *adjective*: papal □ *pope's triple crown*: tiara □ *pope's letter to the Church*: bull, brief, encyclical □ *pope's ambassador*: nuncio □ *clergyman acting as a pope's representative*: legate □ *pope's administrative staff*: curia □ *meeting of cardinals to elect a new pope*: conclave

population □ *combining form*: dem(o)- □ *study of population statistics*: demography

possession □ *useless possession*: white elephant □ *possession giving social prestige*: status symbol

post-mortem □ *technical term*: autopsy □ *doctor conducting post-mortem examination*: pathologist □ *magistrate conducting post-mortem judicial inquiry*: coroner

posture *cross-legged position with the legs resting on opposite thighs*: lotus position

pouch □ *kangaroo's pouch*: marsupium □ *Scotsman's pouch*: sporran

power □ *combining form*: dynam(o)- □ *absolute power*: carte blanche □ *transfer of power from central to regional authorities*: devolution

prairie wolf *alternative term*: coyote

pregnancy □ *technical term*: cyesis □ *adjectives*: antenatal, prenatal □ *craving for strange foods during pregnancy*: pica □ *custom in some cultures of the husband's taking to his bed during the latter stages of a pregnancy*: couvade □ *spontaneous expulsion of the foetus early in pregnancy*: miscarriage □ *medically induced expulsion or destruction of an unviable foetus*: abortion □ *diagnostic sampling of amniotic fluid during pregnancy*: amniocentesis □ *toxic condition during pregnancy*: eclampsia □ *false pregnancy*: pseudocyesis

price □ *lowest price at which an auctioned item may be sold*: reserve price □ *raise a previously agreed price*: gazump

prickly heat *technical term*: miliaria

priest □ *adjective*: sacerdotal □ *priest's robes*: vestments □ *Roman Catholic priest's hat*: biretta □ *Anglican priest's house*: rectory, vicarage □ *Roman Catholic priest's house*: presbytery □ *Buddhist priest in China or Japan*: bonze □ *Orthodox priest in Greece*: pope, papas □ *Orthodox priest in Russia*: pope

principle □ *principle that if anything can go wrong it will*: Murphy's law, sod's law □ *principle that employees are always promoted beyond their abilities*: Peter principle □ *principle that work expands to fill the time available*: Parkinson's law

prison □ *Nazi prison camp*: stalag □ *Soviet labour prison*: gulag

prisoner *prisoner who has won privileges by good behaviour*: trusty

prize □ *prize given to near-winner*: consolation prize, proxime accessit □ *prize given to worst contestant*: booby prize, wooden spoon

problem □ *problem-solving by application of logic*: vertical thinking □ *problem-solving by a seemingly illogical thought process*: lateral thinking □ *problem-solving by random trial and error*: heuristic

producing *combining forms*: -facient, -fer, -fic, -gen, -genic, -genous

property □ *legal document transferring ownership of property*: conveyance □ *government's right to seize private property for state use*: eminent domain □ *seize property for the repayment of a debt*: distrain, sequester □ *repossess a mortgaged property upon failure of payments*: foreclose

prophet □ *prophet of doom*: Jeremiah □ *prophet of doom who is ignored*: Cassandra

pulp □ *pulp of pressed grapes*: marc □ *pulp of pressed apples*: pomace

punishment □ *combining form*: pen(o)- □ *adjective*: penal □ *punishment seen as a deterrent to others*: exemplary punishment □ *punishment seen as society's revenge on the criminal*: retributive punishment □ *study of punishment*: penology

puppy love *alternative term*: calf love

purification *purification of the emotions through drama etc.*: catharsis

pus □ *combining form*: pyo- □ *adjective*: purulent

putto *alternative terms*: amoretto, cherub

Q

queen *adjectives*: royal, regal

question □ *set of questions and answers used as a means of instruction*: catechism □ *question returned diplomat etc. about his misson*: debrief

quick □ *quick and efficient*: expeditious □ *quick and careless*: perfunctory

R

rabbit □ *female rabbit*: doe □ *male rabbit*: buck □ *very young rabbit*: kitten □ *disease fatal to rabbits*: myxomatosis

rabies *technical term*: hydrophobia

radioactivity □ *instrument for measuring radioactivity*: Geiger counter □ *atmospheric radioactivity after a nuclear explosion*: fallout □ *radioactive substance whose passage though the body is monitored for diagnostic purposes*: tracer

rain □ *combining form*: pluvi(o)- □ *rain cloud*: nimbus □ *rainy season in India etc.*: monsoon □ *spraying chemicals into a cloud to produce rain*: seeding

rainbow *band of colours seen in the rainbow*: spectrum

rally *rally of Scouts and/or Guides*: jamboree

random *of music allowing for some random elements in its performance*: aleatoric

rapid *combining form*: tach(o)-, tach(y)-

raven *adjective*: corvine

ray *adjective*: radial

read □ *inability to read due to ignorance*: illiteracy □ *inability to read due to brain damage*: alexia □ *difficulty with reading due to brain dysfunction*: dyslexia

reason *adjective*: rational

recent *combining form*: neo-

record *combining form*: -gram □ *set of records, papers, etc. on a particular topic*: dossier □ *record of a person's education and career*: curriculum vitae □ *record of a business meeting*: minutes □ *record of a learned society's meetings*: proceedings, transactions □ *collection of written etc. records*: archive

recorder *combining form*: -graph

recruitment □ *former services' recruitment unit, employing force and trickery*: pressgang □ *entice (esp. senior) employees away from other companies*: headhunt

rectum *combining form*: proct(o)-

red *combining forms*: erythr(o)-, rhod(o)-, rub(i)

Red Indian *alternative terms*: American Indian, Amerindian, Native American

refuse □ *refuse to do business with*: boycott □ *refuse to socialize with*: ostracize

registration plate *specially purchased vehicle registration plates that contain the owner's initials etc.*: vanity plates

reign □ *adjective*: regnal □ *period between two reigns*: interregnum

related □ *related by blood*: consanguineous □ *related through marriage or adoption*: affined □ *related through the paternal line*: agnate □ *related through the maternal line*: cognate □ *(of words) related by having a common source*: cognate □ *related at a distance of* x *generations*: *x* times removed

relative density *apparatus measuring a liquid's relative density*: hydrometer

religion □ *religious belief in the existence of a single god*: monotheism □ *religious belief in the existence of several gods*: polytheism □ *religious belief in counterbalanced forces of good and evil*: dualism □ *religious belief that God created the world but has had no further involvement with it*: deism □ *religious belief that God created the world and continues to be active in it*: theism □ *religious belief that God and the universe are identical*: pantheism

remote *remote area*: ultima Thule

renewable energy *alternative term*: alternative energy

rent □ *nominal rent*: peppercorn rent □ *excessive rent*: rack-rent □ *person living on rental income*: rentier

replacement □ *temporary replacement for doctor etc.*: locum □ *fertile woman replacing a would-be mother unable to bear children*: surrogate

report □ *government report with proposals for public discussion*: green paper □ *government report with proposals for legislation*: white paper

reproduction □ *combining forms*: gon-, -gen-, -genesis □ *reproducing by means of eggs*: oviparous □ *reproducing live offspring*: viviparous □ *reproducing by giving birth from eggs hatched within the body*: ovoviviparous

reptile *combining form*: herpet(o)-

retort *witty retort that comes to mind after the chance to make it has gone*: esprit de l'escalier

rhyme □ *rhyme between final stressed syllables*: masculine rhyme □ *rhyme between words with final unstressed syllables*: feminine rhyme □ *false rhyme between words that look but do not sound the same*: eye-rhyme □ *game of inventing successive lines of rhyming verse*: crambo

rib *adjective*: costal

riches *imaginary land of great riches*: eldorado

rickets *technical term*: rachitis

right □ *combining forms*: □ *hand*: dextro- □ *correct, upright*: ortho- □ *right of way etc. enjoyed over another's property*: easement □ *right of way etc. that one must allow another over one's property*: servitude □ *right side of a ship as seen by one facing its prow*: starboard

ring □ *adjective*: annular □ *ring for the leash on a dog's collar*: terret □ *leather ring for Scout's neckerchief*: woggle □ *finger ring having a seal instead of a stone*: signet ring □ *plain ring worn in a pierced ear to prevent its healing*: sleeper □ *ring inserted in the lip*: labret □ *ring of muscle*: sphincter □ *ring of light round the sun or moon*: aureole, corona

ringing *persistent ringing sound heard in one or both ears*: tinnitus

ringworm *technical term*: tinea pedis

risk *risk inherent in a particular activity*: occupational hazard

ritual □ *admission ritual*: initiation □ *ritual marking a new stage in life*: rite of passage □ *ritual pouring of liquid*: libation

river □ *adjectives*: fluvial, potamic, riverine □ *ice river*: glacier □ *small island in a river*: ait, eyot □ *horseshoe-shaped bend in a river's course*: oxbow □ *triangular area, with many streams, at a river's mouth*: delta □ *wide area of water at a river's mouth*: estuary □ *low dam in a river to regulate its flow*: weir □ *dry river bed*: wadi □ *high wave moving up a river at the spring tide*: bore, eagre

river bank *adjective*: riparian

road □ *scenic coast road*: corniche □ *road on which no stopping is permitted*: clearway □ *road with no exit*: cul-de-sac □ *rise in a road's surface towards the centre, to assist drainage*: camber □ *hump built across a road to limit speeds*: sleeping policeman

rock □ *combining forms*: litho-, petro-, -lith-, -lite □ *loose pieces of rock on a hillside*: scree

rocket □ *rocket's curving course*: trajectory □ *scaffold supporting a space rocket before take-off*: gantry

rod □ *rod said to indicate underground springs etc. by twitching*: dowsing rod □ *bundle of rods with an axe, carried before Roman magistrates*: fasces

root □ *combining forms*: rhiz-, -radic- □ *adjective*: radical

rope □ *adjective*: funicular □ *ship's heavy rope for mooring etc.*: hawser □ *secure a rope*: belay □ *interweave two ropes*: splice □ *bind a rope-end to prevent fraying*: whip □ *descend a rock face using a double rope coiled round the body*: abseil

rot *combining form*: sapr-

row *combining forms*: stich-, -stichous

rowing boat □ *support for rowing boat's oar*: rowlock □ *seat for oarsman*: thwart □ *rowing boat for a single oarsman*: scull □ *steersman in a rowing boat*: cox □ *oarsman next to the cox*: stroke

rule □ *combining forms*: -archy, -cracy □ *rules for social behaviour*: etiquette □ *procedural rules for diplomatic etc. occasions*: protocol □ *rules for the grammatical arangement of words in a language*: syntax □ *rules of boxing*: Queensberry Rules

ruler □ *combining forms*: -arch, -crat □ *former chief magistrate at Genoa and Venice*: doge □ *Nazi ruler of Germany*: führer □ *former rulers in India*: nawab, nizam □ *former ruler of Iran*: shah □ *Islamic rulers*: ayatollah, caliph, emir □ *Fascist ruler of Italy*: duce □ *former Japanese rulers*: mikado, shogun □ *Ottoman rulers*: aga, bey, khedive, pasha, sultan □ *Spanish military dictator*: caudillo □ *former ruler of Tibet*: Dalai Lama □ *former ruler of Russia*: tsar □ *ruling group (often military officers) following a coup d'état*: junta

rumour □ *false, often malicious, rumour*: canard □ *source of rumours*: bush telegraph, grapevine

runic alphabet *technical term*: futhorc

running *combining form*: -dromous

rupture *technical term*: hernia

Russian □ *Russian script*: Cyrillic □ *old Russian woman*: babushka □ *set of Russian babushka dolls*: matrioshka □ *Russian cavalryman*: cossack □ *Russian country cottage*: dacha □ *Russian citadel*: kremlin □ *Russian guitar*: balalaika □ *Russian pancake*: blini □ *Russian beetroot soup*: bortsch □ *Russian beer*: kvass □ *Russian tea urn*: samovar

S

sacred *combining form*: hier(o)-

saddle *second saddle on a horse or motorcycle*: pillion

safety *safety switch in a locomotive cab that cuts the engine unless constantly depressed by the driver*: dead man's handle

sailor □ *ordinary sailor*: rating □ *sailor's canvas bed*: hammock □ *dried bread formerly eaten by sailors*: hard tack, ship's biscuit □ *punish a sailor by dragging him beneath the ship*: keelhaul

saint □ *combining form*: hagi(o)- □ *declare a person to be a saint*: canonize □ *person arguing for a saint's canonization*: postulator □ *person arguing against a saint's canonization*: devil's advocate

Saint Vitus' dance *technical term*: Sydenham's chorea

same □ *combining form*: taut(o)- □ *of the same age or time*: coetaneous, coeval, contemporary □ *of the same size*: commensurate □ *of the same extent or meaning*: coterminous □ *of the same shape*: congruent □ *having the same meaning*: synonymous

satellite *communications etc. satellite orbiting at a fixed position relative to the earth*: geostationary satellite, geosynchronous satellite

sausage □ *seasoned smoked sausage*: saveloy □ *small thin spicy sausage*: chipolata □ *German pork sausage*: bratwurst □ *Italian peppered pork and beef sausage*: pepperoni □ *Italian garlic sausage*: salami □ *spiced Italian pork sausage*: mortadella

saying □ *wise saying*: aphorism, epigram □ *trite saying*: platitude, cliché, chestnut

scale □ *scale for wind velocities*: Beaufort scale □ *scale for earthquake intensities*: Richter scale □ *scale for child intelligence*: Binet–Simon scale □ *relating to a twelve-tone musical scale*: chromatic □ *relating to an eight-tone musical scale*: diatonic

scales *astrological term*: libra

scaly *technical term*: squamose

scarlet fever *technical term*: scarlatina

scent *dried petals used for scent*: pot-pourri

scissors *tailor's serrated scissors*: pinking shears

scorpion *astrological term*: scorpio

screen □ *sliding screen in a Japanese house*: shoji □ *screen in an Indian house concealing women from view*: purdah

screw □ *screw with a cross-shaped slot*: Phillips screw □ *screw with a hexagonal slot*: Allen screw

scriptures □ *Islamic scriptures*: Koran □ *Sikh scriptures*: Granth □ *Hindu scriptures*: Veda □ *Buddhist scriptures*: Tripitaka □ *Zoroastrian scriptures*: Avesta

scurvy *adjective*: scorbutic

sea *adjectives*: marine, maritime

second *combining forms*: deut-, deutero-

secret societies □ *Sicilian secret criminal and political organization*: Mafia □ *Neapolitan branch of the Mafia*: Camorra □ *US branch of the Mafia*: Cosa Nostra □ *Chinese secret criminal gang*: Tong, Triad □ *US secret society promoting White supremacy*: Klu Klux Klan □ *international secret society with allegedly social purposes*: Freemasonry

security *security given for a loan*: collateral

seed *adjective*: seminal

seizure *seizure of a debtor's property*: distraint, sequestration

self □ *combining form*: aut(o)- □ *self-government*: autonomy, autarchy □ *self-sufficiency*: autarky

sell □ *selling by sending out unsolicited items and then demanding payment if they are not returned*: inertia selling □ *selling through a hierarchy of agents*: pyramid selling □ *sell goods by association (e.g. inscribed sweatshirts at a pop concert)*: merchandize □ *sell goods abroad at a giveaway price, to maintain their home price*: dump

seller □ *combining form*: -monger □ *person selling from door to door*: hawker, pedlar □ *person selling fruit etc. in a street market*: costermonger □ *person selling a specified type of goods*: chandler □ *former seller of quack medicines etc. at fairs*: mountebank

sentence □ *sentence containing every letter of the alphabet*: pangram □ *sentence that tails off uncompleted*: aposiopesis □ *prison sentence to be served only upon re-offending*: suspended sentence □ *reduction of a prison sentence for good behaviour*: remission

sentimentality *sentimentality in music or art*: kitsch, schmaltz

servant □ *military officer's servant*: batman □ *junior public-school boy who acts as servant to a senior boy*: fag □ *Cambridge college servant*: gyp □ *Oxford college servant*: scout □ *Indian servant operating a large ceiling fan*: punkah wallah

sesame □ *paste made from sesame seeds*: tahini □ *sweet made from sesame seeds*: halva

seven □ *combining forms*: hept(a)-, sept(i)- □ *adjective*: septenary

sexual activity *adjective*: venereal

shakes *technical term*: Parkinson's disease

shape *combining forms*: morph(o)-, -form, -morphic

share □ *list of an investor's shares*: portfolio □ *share-buying company selling to the public shares in its whole portfolio*: unit trust □ *offer shares for sale*: float □ *periodic payment made by a successful company to its shareholders*: dividend □ *shares offering a guaranteed dividend*: gilts □ *speculator who sells shares because he expects their price to fall*: bear □ *speculator who buys shares because he expects their price to rise*: bull □ *speculator who buys new share issues for a quick resale*: stag

sharp □ *combining form*: oxy- □ *sharpness of a picture*: definition □ *mental sharpness*: acuity

shed □ *shed feathers or fur*: moult □ *shed an outer skin or shell*: slough □ *shedding its leaves annually*: deciduous

sheep □ *adjective*: ovine □ *sheep's brain disease thought to cause BSE*: scrapie □ *castrated male sheep, leader of the flock*: bellwether

sheet *sheet for a corpse*: shroud

shell □ *combining forms*: concho-, -conch- □ *fragments of an exploding artillery shell*: shrapnel

shell-shock *technical term*: combat neurosis

shepherd *adjective*: bucolic

shepherd's pie *alternative term*: cottage pie

shield □ *shield bearing a coat of arms*: escutcheon □ *knob in the centre of a shield*: boss, umbo □ *Roman legionaries' roof of linked shields*: testudo

shin bone *technical term*: tibia

shingles *technical term*: herpes zoster

ship □ *adjective*: marine, maritime □ *line painted on a ship's side to show permitted submersion levels*: Plimsoll line □ *list of a ship's cargo*: bill of lading, manifest □ *dock worker employed to unload a ship*: stevedore □ *recovery of a wrecked or abandoned ship*: salvage □ *cargo thrown overboard from a ship to lighten it in a storm*: jetsam □ *cargo washed overboard from a ship*: flotsam □ *cargo thrown overboard from a ship but marked with buoys etc. for later recovery*: lagan □ *common room for a warship's senior officers*: wardroom □ *common room for a warship's junior officers*: gunroom

shock *shock that may cause lasting psychological harm*: trauma

shock treatment *technical term*: electroconvulsive therapy

shoot □ *shoot growing from a plant's roots etc.*: sucker □ *shoot prepared for planting or grafting*: scion, slip □ *climbing plant's shoot used to gain support*: tendril

shore *adjective*: littoral

short *combining form*: brach-

short-sightedness *technical term*: myopia

shoulder blade *technical term*: scapula

sickle *adjective*: falcate

sickly *sickly person*: valetudinarian

sided *combining forms*: -gon, -gonal

sight □ *combining form*: -scopy □ *adjective*: visual

signal □ *bell rung as an alarm*: tocsin □ *signalling system based on combinations of long and short flashes, marks, or sounds*: Morse □ *signalling system based on flags hand-held in various positions*: semaphore □ *signalling system used by bookmakers' assistants*: tick-tack

silence *Cistercian monk vowed to silence*: Trappist

silver *adjective*: argent-

simple fraction *alternative term*: common fraction

singer □ *range of notes a singer can sing*: compass, register □ *range within which the majority of notes in a song fall*: tessitura

single *combining forms*: mono-, uni-

sister □ *combining form*: soror(i)- □ *murder of a sister*: sororicide

situation *perplexing situation*: dilemma, predicament

six *combining forms*: hexa-, hexi-, sexa-, sexi-

sixth sense *perception by a 'sixth sense'*: extrasensory perception

skin □ *combining forms*: derm(o)-, dermat(o)- □ *technical term*: cutis, dermis □ *adjective*: cutaneous □ *beneath the skin*: hypodermic, subcutaneous □ *blemish on the skin*: naevus, macula, stigma □ *strip off the skin*: flay □ *shed a skin*: slough □ *shedding of a skin*: slough, ecdysis

skirt □ *ballet dancer's stiff short skirt*: tutu □ *short skirt as part of traditional Greek male dress*: fustanella □ *padding formerly worn under the rear of a skirt*: bustle □ *hoops formerly supporting a skirt*: farthingale

skull □ *combining forms*: cephal(o)-, -cephal- □ *technical term*: cranium □ *study of the size and shape of the skull as a supposed indicator of character and mental ability*: phrenology □ *bore a hole in the skull for surgical purposes*: trepan, trephine

skullcap □ *skullcap worn by some Roman Catholic clergymen*: zucchetto □ *skullcap worn by male Orthodox Jews*: yarmulka

slave *adjective*: servile

sleep □ *combining forms*: hypn(o)-, narc(o)-, somni-, somno- □ *learning while asleep*: hypnopaedia □ *sleep with dreaming and eye movements*: paradoxical sleep, REM sleep □ *shallow sleep induced by surgical anaesthesia*: twilight sleep □ *sleep through the winter*: hibernate □ *sleep through the summer*: aestivate

sleeping sickness □ *technical term*: encephalitis lethargica, trypanosomiasis □ *African fly causing sleeping sickness*: tsetse

sleepwalking *technical terms*: somnambulism, noctambulism

slip of the tongue □ *technical term*: lapsus linguae □ *slip of the tongue thought to reveal the speaker's true thoughts*: Freudian slip

sloe *alternative term*: blackthorn

slope □ *combining forms*: clin-, -clin- □ *steep slope at the end of a plateau*: escarpment □ *slope of a stage etc.*: rake □ *slope of a road etc.*: gradient □ *skier's diagonal route across sloping ground*: traverse

slow □ *combining form*: brady- □ *Chinese system of slow exercises*: t'ai chi ch'uan

slum clearance *alternative term*: urban renewal

small □ *combining forms*: micro-, mini-, nano-, -cle, -ule □ *smallest possible*: marginal, minimal, minuscule □ *infinitely small*: infinitesimal □ *small amount*: soupçon, smidgen, vestige

smallpox *technical term*: variola

smell □ *adjectives*: □ *sense of smell*: olfactory □ *stink*: mephitic, hircine

smelling salts *technical term*: sal volatile

snake □ *adjective*: anguine □ *snake's poison*: venom □ *antidote to this*: serum, antivenin

snapdragon *alternative term*: antirrhinum

sneezing *technical term*: sternutation

soccer *technical term*: Association Football

social □ *socially correct*: comme il faut □ *social rules or custom*: etiquette □ *social blunder*: gaffe, faux pas □ *social skills*: savoir-faire □ *social climber*: arriviste, parvenu □ *social prestige*: cachet □ *gaining social status*: upwardly mobile □ *losing social status*: déclassé

society □ *person ostracized by society*: pariah □ *group thought to have a hidden but pervasive control of society*: the Establishment

solar system *mechanical model of the solar system*: orrery

sole of the foot *adjectives*: plantar, volar

solvent □ *universal solvent sought by alchemists*: alkahest □ *strong solvent attacking most substances*: aqua regia

son *adjective*: filial

song □ *improvised West Indian song on topical theme*: calypso □ *sailors' work song*: shanty □ *gondolier's song*: barcarole □ *Renaissance secular part-song*: madrigal □ *German art-song*: lied

soot *adjective*: fuliginous

sound □ *combining forms*: audi-, phon(o)-, -phony □ *adjectives*: acoustic, sonic □ *of sound recorded and reproduced via a single channel*: monophonic □ *of sound recorded and reproduced via several channels*: streophonic □ *of sound recorded and reproduced via two separate channels*: binaural □ *of sound recorded and reproduced via four separate channels*: quadraphonic □ *slow pitch-distortion of recorded sound*: wow □ *fast pitch-distortion of recorded sound*: flutter □ *name for the indefinite sound often made by English vowels*: schwa

south *adjectives*: austral, meridional

South Africa □ *South African barbecue*: braai □ *South African native club*: knobkerrie □ *South African native spear*: assegai □ *South African whip*: sjambok □ *South African cattle pound*: kraal □ *small town in South Africa*: dorp □ *South African wagon encampment*: laager □ *open bush in South Africa*: bundu □ *veranda in South Africa*: stoep □ *former South African policy of racial segregation*: apartheid

South American □ *South American cloak having a hole for the head*: poncho □ *South American cowboy*: gaucho

Soviet □ *Soviet party official*: commissar □ *Soviet secret police*: KGB □ *Soviet forced labour camp*: gulag □ *Soviet collective farm*: kolkhoz □ *Soviet worker who achieves exceptional output*: stakhanovite □ *underground publishing in Soviet Russia*: samizdat □ *Soviet youth organization*: Komsomol

speak *that cannot be spoken*: ineffable

specific gravity □ *technical term*: relative density □ *apparatus measuring a liquid's specific gravity*: hydrometer

spectacles □ *spectacles supported by a nose clip*: pince nez □ *single eyeglass*: monocle □ *pair of eyeglasses on a long handle*: lorgnette □ *spectacles with combined lenses to give near and far vision*: bifocals

speech □ *combining forms*: logo-, phono-, -log-, -phon(o)-, -logue, -phone, -phony □ *adjective*: oral □ *inability to express or understand speech due to brain damage*: aphasia □ *inability to express speech due to loss of voice*: aphonia

speed □ *combining form*: tach- □ *speed at which an object can defy gravity*: escape velocity □ *object's maximum possible air speed*: terminal velocity □ *instrument measuring a vehicle's speed*: speedometer □ *instrument measuring an engine's speed*: rev counter, tachometer □ *automatic regulator of an engine's speed*: governor □ *automatic recorder of a vehicle's speed*: tachograph

spelling *technical term*: orthography

spirit □ *combining forms*: pneumat- □ *spirit of the age*: zeitgeist □ *spirit of a place*: genius loci, numen

spiritualist □ *spiritualist thought to be able to contact the dead*: medium □ *spiritualist meeting for contact with the dead*: seance □ *substance said to exude from a spritualist medium during a trance*: ectoplasm □ *boards used for messages in a spiritualist seance*: ouija board, planchette □ *form of spiritualism practised by some Native Americans, Aleuts, etc.*: shamanism

split *combining form*: schiz(o)-

squint *technical term*: strabismus

squirrel *squirrel's nest*: drey

staff □ *bishop's staff*: crosier □ *monarch's staff*: sceptre □ *beadle's staff*: mace □ *verger's staff*: verge □ *Dionysus' staff*: thyrsus □ *Hermes' staff*: caduceus

stain *brownish stain on the paper of a book or engraving*: foxing

stained glass *lead strip holding pieces of stained glass*: came

stamp collecting *technical term*: philately

standard *standard used for comparison*: benchmark, control, yardstick

star □ *combining forms*: astr-, sider(o)- □ *adjectives*: astral, sidereal, stellar □ *cluster of stars*: asterism □ *exploding star*: nova □ *large cool star*: red giant □ *small cool star*: red dwarf □ *group of stars thought to form a particular figure*: constellation □ *star that is the brightest in its constellation*: alpha □ *measure of a star's brightness*: magnitude □ *building with a domed ceiling for displaying images of the stars*: planetarium

start □ *start a car from another car's battery*: jump-start □ *start a car by pushing it and then engaging the gears*: bump-start

state *combining forms*: -osis, -tude

statement *legal statement made under oath*: affidavit, deposition

steal □ *steal someone's ideas*: plagiarize □ *steal from money entrusted to one*: embezzle, peculate, defalcate □ *steal small items from the workplace*: pilfer □ *person who knowingly buys or stores stolen goods*: receiver □ *person who finds a buyer for stolen goods*: fence □ *compulsive urge to steal, regardless of need*: kleptomania

stirrup bone *technical term*: stapes

stomach □ *combining form*: gastr(o)- □ *adjective*: gastric

stomach-ache *technical term*: gastralgia

stone □ *combining forms*: lapid-, lith(o)-, petr(o)- □ *adjective*: lithic □ *large standing stone in a prehistoric monument*: megalith □ *prehistoric stone chamber tomb*: dolmen □ *stone coffin*: sar-

cophagus □ *person who shapes building stone or builds with it*: mason, stonemason □ *grotesque stone figure serving as rainwater spout*: gargoyle □ *stone believed by alchemists to turn base metals into gold*: philosophers' stone

store □ *secret store*: cache, stash □ *funnel-shaped store for coal, grain, etc.*: hopper

storm *still area at the centre of a storm*: eye

strangle *execute a criminal by strangling*: garrotte

stroke *technical term*: cerebral haemorrhage

study □ *combining form*: -logy □ *study of the universe*: cosmology □ *study of the stars*: astronomy □ *study of mankind*: anthropology □ *study of primitive cultures*: ethnology □ *study of statistics of births, deaths, and disease*: demography □ *study of language*: philology □ *study of living organisms*: physiology □ *study of the skin*: dermatology □ *study of diseases*: pathology □ *study of resistance to infection*: immunology □ *study of tumours*: oncology □ *study of poisons*: toxicology □ *study of voting at elections*: psephology □ *study of crime*: criminology □ *study of punishment*: penology □ *study of family trees*: genealogy □ *study of the soil*: pedology □ *study of mosses*: bryology □ *study of fossils*: palaeontology □ *study of earthquakes*: seismology □ *study of the weather*: meteorology □ *study of unidentified flying objects*: ufology

stuffing □ *stuffing dead animals*: taxidermy □ *stuffing made of chopped meat or vegetables*: forcemeat

substitute *fraudulently substituted*: supposititious

subtraction □ *number from which subtraction is to be made*: minuend □ *number to be subtracted*: subtrahend

sugar □ *combining forms*: glyc(o)-, sacchar- □ *adjective*: saccharine □ *hormone regulating the blood sugar level*: insulin □ *disease characterized by excess sugar in the blood and urine*: diabetes mellitus

sugar pea *alternative term*: mangetout

summer □ *adjective*: aestival □ *resumption of summer weather in the autumn*: Indian summer

summer house *raised summer house with a view*: gazebo, belvedere

sun □ *combining forms*: heli-, sol- □ *adjective*: solar □ *sun's highest point in the sky*: zenith □ *orbiting planet's furthest point from the sun*: aphelion □ *orbiting planet's nearest point to the sun*: perihelion

sunburn *technical term*: erythema solare

supporting *combining form*: pro-

surgical cutting *combining forms*: -tom-, -tome, -tomy

surgical opening *combining form*: -stomy

surgical removal *combining form*: -ectomy

surveyor □ *surveyor's rotating telescope for measuring angles*: theodolite □ *surveyor's incised mark in wall etc.*: benchmark □ *surveyor's striped sight-pole*: ranging pole

survive *capable of surviving independently*: viable

suspicious *pathologically suspicious*: paranoid

sweat □ *technical term*: hidrosis □ *adjective*: hidrotic

sweating sickness *technical term*: miliary fever

sweet □ *excessively sweet*: cloying □ *sweet-voiced*: mellifluous

Swiss □ *Swiss state*: canton □ *Swiss breakfast food of cereals, dried fruit, and nuts*: muesli □ *Swiss mountaineers' style of song*: yodelling

symbol □ *identifying symbol used for a company, product, etc.*: logo, trade mark □ *symbol replacing a word*: logogram □ *system of symbols, each of which represents a syllable in a certain language*: syllabary □ *system of symbols, each of which represents a word in a certain language*: ideograms

symptom *set of symptoms whose joint presence indicates a particular disease*: syndrome

syringa *alternative terms*: lilac, mock orange

T

table □ *table of the elements arranged to group those of similar chemical structure*: periodic table □ *table giving the results of various mathematical calculations*: ready reckoner

tail □ *combining forms*: caud-, -urous □ *adjective*: caudal □ *fox's tail*: brush □ *rabbit or deer's tail*: scut

tailor *adjective*: sartorial

tar □ *tar used to preserve wood*: creosote □ *tar used on roofs and roads*: bitumen □ *tar mixed with gravel etc. for road-making*: asphalt

target □ *disk thrown up as a shooting target*: clay pigeon □ *revolving target in a medieval tilt-yard*: quintain

tawny owl *alternative term*: brown owl

taxation □ *adjective*: fiscal □ *taxation of income*: direct taxation □ *taxation of expenditure*: indirect taxation □ *avoidance of tax liability by legal means*: tax avoidance □ *avoidance of tax liability by dishonest means*: tax evasion □ *former tax of 10% payable to the Church*: tithe □ *former tax levied upon every adult*: poll tax

teacher *teacher engaged to give a few lessons at each of several schools*: peripatetic

tear *adjective*: lachrymal

tear gas *alternative term*: CS gas

telephone □ *telephone link for a computer*: modem □ *direct emergency telephone line between heads of state*: hotline

temper *temper metal or glass by heating and cooling*: anneal

temperament □ *of a gloomy temperament*: saturnine □ *of a changeable temperament*: mercurial, volatile

temperature □ *temperature-controlled switch*: thermostat □ *cooling effect of the wind upon air temperature*: chill factor, wind-chill factor

ten *combining forms*: deca-, deci-

tent □ *Native American tent*: teepee, wigwam □ *large tent for flower shows etc.*: marquee □ *tent shrine used by the ancient Israelites*: tabernacle

territory *national policy of regaining former territories*: revanchism, irredentism

test *test of actors or musicians applying for work*: audition

thermometer □ *thermometer that plots the temperature on a revolving graph*: thermograph □ *thermometer for low temperatures*: cryometer □ *thermometer for high temperatures*: pyrometer □ *pair of thermometers that measure humidity*: psychrometer

thermonuclear bomb *alternative term*: fusion bomb

thigh bone *technical term*: femur

thing □ *thing as perceived by the senses*: phenomenon □ *thing as conceived by the mind*: noumenon

thinking □ *thinking in which problems are solved by logical deduction*: vertical thinking □ *thinking in which problems are solved by apparently illogical association of ideas*: lateral thinking

this side *combining form*: cis-

thoroughbred *thoroughbred horses*: bloodstock

thousand *combining forms*: kilo-, milli-

thousand million *combining form*: giga-

thousand millionth *combining form*: nano-

thousandth *combining form*: milli-

threat □ *threat made by a hostile military build-up*: sabre-rattling □ *constant threat of disaster*: sword of Damocles

three □ *combining forms*: ter-, tri- □ *adjectives*: ternary, treble, triple □ *occurring once in, or lasting for, three years*: triennial □ *Three Wise Men*: Magi □ *three in one*: triune □ *painting etc. covering three panels*: triptych □ *ancient ship with three banks of oars*: trireme □ *three-dimensional picture produced by lasers*: hologram

threshold *adjective*: liminal

ticket *person buying up tickets to resell at inflated prices*: tout

tide □ *tide that rises highest*: spring tide □ *tide that rises least*: neap tide □ *rising tide*: flood tide □ *falling tide*: ebb tide

tile □ *wooden exterior tile for roofs and walls*: shingle □ *curved interlocking roof tile*: pantile

time □ *combining forms*: chron(o)-, temp- □ *adjective*: chronological, temporal □ *ticking device that helps musicians keep time*: metronome □ *law setting a time limit for initiating a prosecution*: statute of limitations

times over *combining form*: -fold

toast □ *thin crisp toast*: Melba toast □ *small piece of toast served on soup or a salad*: crouton

tomb □ *large and elaborate tomb*: mausoleum □ *inscription on a tomb*: epitaph

tongue □ *combining forms*: gloss(o)- □ *adjectives*: glossal, lingual

tooth □ *combining forms*: dent-, odont-, -odont □ *adjective*: dental □ *narrow tooth used to cut*: incisor □ *broad tooth used to grind*: molar □ *pointed tooth at front corner of mouth*: canine □ *tooth emerging at the back of the jaw during adulthood*: wisdom tooth □ *tooth decay*: caries □ *bacterial film on teeth*: plaque □ *hard yellowish deposit forming on teeth*: tartar □ *alloy used to fill* *teeth*: amalgam □ *teeth present in a mouth*: dentition □ *toothed wheel*: cog □ *toothed projection on a wheel or cylinder*: sprocket

toothache *technical term*: odontalgia

touch *adjective*: tactile

tournament *tournament for medieval knights*: joust

tower □ *stepped temple tower in ancient Mesopotamia*: ziggurat □ *ancient Scottish tower*: broch □ *mosque tower*: minaret

trade □ *adjective*: mercantile □ *trade restrictions imposed upon a foreign country until it changes its policies*: sanctions

training *training mock-up of an aircraft's flight deck etc.*: simulator

transplant *drug given to prevent rejection of a transplanted organ*: immunosuppressor

treaty □ *formal acceptance of a treaty*: accession □ *formal rejection of a treaty*: denunciation □ *basic draft of a treaty*: protocol

tree □ *combining forms*: arbor-, dendro-, dendri-, silv(i)- □ *adjective*: arboreal □ *type of tree that sheds its leaves annually*: deciduous □ *type of tree that retains its leaves*: evergreen □ *botanical garden devoted to trees*: arboretum

tree ring *alternative term*: annual ring

trellis □ *trellis along which the branches of fruit trees are trained*: espalier □ *trellis carrying climbing plants over a garden path or arbour*: pergola

trial and error *trial-and-error method of solving problems*: heuristic

triangle □ *triangle with three equal sides*: equilateral triangle □ *triangle with two equal sides*: isosceles triangle □ *triangle with unequal sides*: scalene □ *longest side of a right-angled triangle*: hypotenuse

tumour □ *combining forms*: onco-, -cele, -oma □ *tumour that does not seriously threaten health*: benign □ *tumour that spreads out of control and returns after treatment*: malignant

tunnel *tunnel dug under an enemy's defences*: sap

turn □ *combining forms*: trop-, -trop-, -tropic □ *turn in office etc. assigned by rote*: Buggins' turn □ *turn into stone*: petrify □ *turn into bone*: ossify

turning □ *combining forms*: trop-, -tropism, -tropy □ *turning force*: torque □ *crucial turning point*: Rubicon, watershed

twelve □ *combining form*: dodeca- □ *adjectives*: duodecimal, duodenary □ *twelve-tone musical system*: serialism, dodecaphony

twenty *adjective*: vigesimal

twice □ *combining forms*: bi-, di-, duo-, semi- □ *occurring twice a year*: biannual, semi-annual

twilight *adjective*: crepuscular

twin □ *combining form*: zyg- □ *twin-hulled boat*: catamaran

trust *adjective*: fiduciary

turpentine *adjective*: terebinthine

twins *astrological term*: gemini

two □ *combining forms*: ambi-, bi-, di-, du(o)- □ *adjectives*: binary, double, dual □ *cut in two*: bisect □ *having two parts*: binary, dual □ *two-sided*: bilateral □ *living for, or occurring once every, two years*: biennial □ *having two chambers (of a parliament etc.)*: bicameral □ *painting etc. covering two panels*: diptych □ *two-faced*: duplicitous

U

unanimously *technical term*: nem. con.

unarmed combat *sports giving skill in unarmed combat*: martial arts

uncle *adjective*: avuncular

unconsciousness □ *long period of deep unconsciousness*: coma □ *state of unconsciousness with bodily rigidity*: catalepsy, catatonia

under *combining forms*: hypo-, infra-, sub-

underground □ *underground cemetery*: catacomb □ *underground railway in London*: tube □ *underground railway in Paris*: metro □ *underground railway in Rome*: metropolitana □ *underground railway in New York*: subway

undermine □ *undermine a fortification by tunnelling beneath it*: sap □ *undermine an organization by establishing agents within it*: infiltrate

understanding □ *sympathetic understanding*: empathy □ *informal diplomatic understanding negotiated between two nations*: entente cordiale

underwater □ *sealed underwater chamber for repair workers etc.*: caisson □ *underwater wall reaching to the surface to provide a dry area for repairs etc.*: coffer □ *divers' underwater vessel open at the bottom and filled with air*: diving bell □ *submarine-like vessel for deep underwater exploration*: bathyscaphe

unequal *combining form*: aniso-

unity *pursuit of unity between all Christian churches*: ecumenism

union □ *enforced union of Austria with Germany in 1938*: Anschluss □ *temporary union between political parties to form a government*: coalition □ *temporary union between business companies undertaking a large project*: consortium □ *secret union between firms to prevent competition*: cartel □ *secret union of purchasers at an auction etc. to force down prices*: ring

urinate *technical term*: micturate

urine □ *duct by which urine passes from the kidney to the bladder*: ureter □ *duct by which urine passes from the bladder to the kidney*: urethra □ *substance causing increased production of urine*: diuretic □ *tube inserted into the body for draining off urine*: catheter □ *horse and cattle urine*: stale

uterus □ *combining forms*: hyster(o)-, metr-, uter(o)- □ *surgical scraping of the uterus*: dilatation and curettage □ *vacuuming the uterus as a means of abortion*: vacuum aspiration □ *diagnostic sampling of fluid from a pregnant uterus*: amniocentesis □ *surgical removal of the uterus*: hysterectomy

V

V *V-shaped pattern*: chevron

vaccine *supplementary dose of vaccine*: booster

vagina □ *combining form*: colp- □ *membrane partially blocking the entrance of a virgin's vagina*: hymen □ *surgical cutting of the vagina to ease childbirth*: episiotomy

valley □ *valley in Scotland or Ireland*: glen □ *valley in Wales*: cwm □ *wooded valley*: dene

value *loss of value due to wear and tear*: depreciation

vegetarian *strict vegetarian who avoids all animal products*: vegan

vein □ *combining forms*: phleb(o)-, vene-, veni-, veno- □ *adjective*: venous □ *swollen vein in the legs*: varicose vein □ *in or into a vein*: intravenous □ *surgical opening of a vein*: phlebotomy, venesection

Venice □ *former ruler of Venice*: Doge □ *small Venetian passenger boat*: gondola □ *song of Venetian gondoliers*: barcarole □ *Venetian water bus*: vaporetto

Venus *Greek name*: Aphrodite

verse □ *metrical analysis of verse*: scansion □ *theory and practice of versification*: prosody □ *metrical unit in versification*: foot □ *central pause in a line of verse*: caesura

viceroy *adjective*: viceregal

vine □ *cultivation of vines*: viticulture □ *insect that destroys vines*: phylloxera

vinegar *adjective*: acetic

virgin *astrological term*: virgo

virgin birth *technical term*: parthenogenesis

voice □ *combining forms*: phon(o)-, -phone, -phony □ *adjective*: vocal

vote □ *chairman's vote to decide a tied poll*: casting vote □ *vote given to exclude a candidate*: blackball □ *person empowered to cast another's vote*: proxy □ *parliamentary vote*: division

voting □ *voting strategy aimed at defeating an otherwise strong candidate or party*: tactical voting □ *study of voting patterns etc.*: psephology

W

wagon *wagon for condemned prisoners in the French Revolution*: tumbril

wake *signal for waking in an army camp etc.*: reveille

walking *combining form*: -grade

walking stick □ *walking stick with a handle that makes a seat*: shooting stick □ *walking stick's metal tip*: ferrule

wall □ *adjectives*: □ *of a building*: mural □ *in the body*: parietal □ *building's wall of two layers with a gap between*: cavity wall □ *layer of cement etc. on a wall surface*: rendering □ *row of spikes or broken glass set on a wall's top*: cheval-de-frise □ *rounded bricks etc. at a wall's top*: coping □ *watertight wall dividing the interior of a ship etc.*: bulkhead □ *wall of a body cavity*: paries

wandering □ *wandering in search of trade*: itinerant □ *wandering in search of adventure*: errant

war □ *adjective*: martial □ *of a war waged without nuclear weapons*: conventional □ *person favouring recourse to war*: hawk □ *person avoiding recourse to war*: dove

wasp *adjective*: vespine

water □ *combining forms*: aqua-, aqui-, hydr- □ *adjectives*: aqueous, aquatic □ *operated by water*: hydraulic □ *temporary vertical water pipe with a tap*: standpipe

water-carrier *astrological term*: aquarius

water on the brain *technical term*: hydrocephalus

weakness □ *minor weakness of character etc.*: foible □ *weak spot*: Achilles' heel

wealth □ *wealth or its pursuit seen as a corrupting influence*: Mammon □ *source of wealth*: bonanza □ *fabulous place of great wealth*: eldorado

wear *gradual wearing down*: attrition, erosion

weather □ *low-pressure weather system*: cyclone □ *high-pressure weather system*: anticyclone □ *line on a weather map linking places with the same atmospheric pressure*: isobar □ *line on a weather map linking places with the same temperature*: isotherm □ *balloon-borne radio transmitter sending weather information*: radiosonde

weaving □ *threads running lengthways in weaving*: weft, woof □ *threads running crossways in weaving*: warp □ *cylinder holding a weaver's thread*: bobbin □ *double-ended bobbin used on a mechanical loom*: shuttle

week *adjective*: hebdomadal

well *well in which the water rises by natural pressure through a borehole*: artesian well

Welsh □ *adjectives*: Cambrian, Cymric □ *Welsh Nationalist Party*: Plaid Cymru □ *Welsh competition for poets and musicians*: eisteddfod □ *Welsh poetry sung in counterpoint to a traditional harp melody*: penillion

west *adjective*: occidental

West Indian □ *West Indian song improvised on a topical theme*: calypso □ *West Indian popular music with a strong secondary beat*: reggae □ *West Indian sorcery*: obeah, voodoo

whiplash injury *technical term*: hyperextension-hyperflexion injury

white □ *combining forms*: leuc(o)-, leuk(o)- □ *white-skinned person*: Caucasian □ *person or animal having white skin and hair due to a pigment defect*: albino

white ant *alternative term*: termite

white whale *alternative term*: beluga

whooping cough *technical term*: pertussis

widow □ *widow holding a title from her late husband*: dowager □ *estate etc. left a widow by her late husband's will*: jointure

wife *adjective*: uxorial

will □ *adjectives*: □ *wish*: volitional, voluntary □ *legal document*: testamentary □ *person making a will*: testator □ *person appointed to carry out he terms of a will*: executor □ *gift made in a will*: bequest, legacy □ *person receiving a gift from a will*: beneficiary □ *legal authentication of a will*: probate

wildebeest *alternative term*: gnu

wind □ *combining form*: anemo- □ *instrument for measuring wind speed*: anemometer □ *scale for wind velocities*: Beaufort scale □ *build-up of gas in the digestive tract causing the breaking of wind*: flatulence □ *humid southerly wind in southern Europe*: sirocco □ *cold northerly wind blowing down the Rhone*: mistral □ *warm southerly wind blowing off the Alps*: föhn

window □ *adjective*: fenestral □ *window made of vertically sliding glazed sections*: sash window □ *side-hinged window*: casement □ *small window over a door etc.*: fanlight □ *small diamond-shaped pane of window-glass*: quarry □ *ornamental stonework subdividing a window*: tracery □ *angled wall-opening for a window*: embrasure

windpipe *technical term*: trachea

wine □ *combining form*: vin- □ *adjective*: vinous □ *spice and warm wine*: mull □ *wine expert*: oenologist □ *wine merchant*: vintner □ *wine waiter*: sommelier □ *charge made for serving the customer's own wine at a restaurant*: corkage

wing □ *combining forms*: pter(o)-, -pter- □ *adjective*: alar

winter □ *adjectives*: hibernal, hiemal □ *sleep through the winter*: hibernate

wire *wires used to start a car from the battery of another*: jump leads

wisdom tooth *technical term*: third molar

witch □ *gathering of witches*: coven □ *witch's attendant spirit*: familiar □ *male witch*: warlock

without *combining forms*: a-, an-

witness □ *witness's evidence given in court*: testimony □ *sworn statement made by a witness out of court*: deposition □ *lying by a witness under oath*: perjury

wolf □ *adjective*: lupine □ *person who changes into a wolf*: lycanthrope, werewolf

woman □ *combining forms*: gyn(o)-, gynaeco- □ *adjective*: feminine □ *woman with intellectual or literary pretensions*: bluestocking □ *arrogant and domineering woman*: prima donna □ *woman whose husband is often absent*: grass widow

□ *party for women only*: hen party □ *hatred of women*: mysogyny

wood □ *combining forms*: ligno-, ligni-, xylo-, xyli- □ *wooden plate*: trencher □ *ornamental inlay of wood, ivory, etc.*: marquetry

womb *technical term*: uterus

word □ *combining forms*: lexi-, logo-, logi-, -log-, -nym □ *adjective*: verbal □ *study of the meaning of words*: semantics □ *study of the forms of words*: morphology

word-blindness *technical term*: alexia

work □ *combining form*: erg(o)- □ *belief that work has an intrinsic moral value*: work ethic □ *person addicted to work*: workaholic

works *complete works of an artist etc.*: oeuvre, corpus

worm □ *combining form*: vermi- □ *adjectives*: vermicular, vermiform

worship *combining form*: -latry

wrist □ *technical term*: carpus □ *adjective*: carpal

wrong *combining forms*: caco-, mal-, mis-

X-rays □ *study or use of X-rays*: radiography □ *X-ray of a section through the body*: tomography □ *X-ray of body tissue*: computerized axial tomography □ *treatment of cancer etc. by X-rays*: radiotherapy

youth *artistic creations of one's youth, often later suppressed as immature*: juvenilia

zigzag *zigzag course taken by a vessel sailing into the wind*: tacking, traverse

zinc *coat a metal with zinc*: galvanize